LONDON IN 1890, FROM THE "ILLUSTRATED LONDON NEWS" (bottom)

This royal throne of kings, this scepter'd isle,
This earth of majesty, this seat of Mars,
This other Eden, demi-paradise,
This fortress built by Nature for herself
Against infection and the hand of war,
This happy breed of men, this little world,
This precious stone set in the silver sea,
Which serves it in the office of a wall
Or as a moat defensive to a house
Against the envy of less happier lands,
This blessed plot, this earth, this realm, this
England . . .   SHAKESPEARE, "RICHARD II"

Edited by

B. J. WHITING   *Harvard University*

FRED B. MILLETT   *Wesleyan University*

ALEXANDER M. WITHERSPOON   *Yale University*

ODELL SHEPARD   *Trinity College*

ARTHUR PALMER HUDSON   *The University of North Carolina*

EDWARD WAGENKNECHT   *University of Washington*

LOUIS UNTERMEYER

THE COLLEGE SURVEY
OF
ENGLISH LITERATURE

Volume One

THE EARLY PERIOD

THE SIXTEENTH CENTURY

THE SEVENTEENTH CENTURY

THE EIGHTEENTH CENTURY

1949

HARCOURT, BRACE AND COMPANY, NEW YORK

COPYRIGHT, 1942, BY
HARCOURT, BRACE AND COMPANY, INC.

All rights reserved. No part of this book may be reproduced in any form, by mimeograph or any other means, without permission in writing from the publisher.

[i·9·49]

PRINTED IN THE UNITED STATES OF AMERICA

PUBLISHERS' PREFACE

The College Survey of English Literature was made in much the same way as English literature itself was—caught up and handed on by the men of one period to the men of another.

As the men of each epoch of English literature were connected with their predecessors only in the transfer of a literary heritage, so the editors of this SURVEY, though more closely associated, are specialists for their periods, each as much at home in the age he edits as he is in his present-day world. Just as every person thinks his own period in time the most crucial and important in history, so each of the seven editors believes the period he edits the most fascinating one of all.

Let us see what this specialization does for the reader of the whole SURVEY. The clatter of reality sounds through the open window of each century, lending intensity and significance to what unfolds on the page. Through our guide, who for all his twentieth-century clothes and manner lives in the age he edits, we hear the ashen thump of a spear shaft being grounded in the courtyard as the minstrel chants in the great hall. We are roused by the cries for bread in the far edges of the street rabble as the virgin queen passes in embroidered silks to her royal barge. We see the dark look of the peasant lover, the terrified white face of the country lass whose innocence has attracted the roving eye of one of King Charles's men. The cautious talk of sedan-chair bearers lends undertone to the patterns of the flute tracing the minuet. Revolution's wave breaks, spuming, against the stout sea wall of an England beginning to feel again; nature burgeons; but we hear, too, the clucking shuttle of bobbins tended by children of seven and nine. There is word that the young queen will marry; commerce rumbles, and there is much loose talk about science mingled with the cries of "Well done! Oh, very well done, sir!" coming faintly up to the manor house from the cricket ground. And so Victoria. . . . Lemonade, and the parish fete, and the growing rumor of war. Then the four years of world struggle, followed by the bickering, disillusioned peace, appeasement, and war again. It's all here, and this is exactly how it happened, and our man saw it and will show you just where and how it occurred.

It was for this sense of reality that the publishers carefully sought for and found that scholar-teacher of each period who could best take you there—intimately, with enthusiasm and accuracy.

The content of this book had an especially interesting development: all seven editors read in manuscript, and offered critical advice upon, the period introduction of each of their colleagues, and similarly commented upon the selections proposed for each period. This advisory work not only brought the broad teaching experience of the whole group of editors into focus with the particular understanding of the specialist in each field, but also made for richness of interpretation and unity of development throughout the SURVEY. Professor Whiting assumed the special responsibility for the Early Period, Professor Millett for the Sixteenth Century, Professor Witherspoon for the Seventeenth, Professor Shepard for the Eighteenth, Professor Hudson for the Romantic Period, Professor Wagenknecht for the Victorian, and Mr. Untermeyer for the Contemporary.

The survey course in English literature is rightly regarded as one of the most important courses in college. In spite of the disproportion between the scope of the literature and the shortness of the time allotted to the course, there is no reason why the student should not form satisfying literary acquaintances through the survey and learn his way to the doors of still other writers whom he will meet often in later courses and in future reading. Accordingly, THE COLLEGE SURvey gives emphatic space to the major writers—includes, by virtue of its larger page, a greater representation of more of the major writers than is available in comparable anthologies. For instance, the survey has more of the Romances, Chaucer, Shakespeare, Donne, Johnson, Coleridge, Shelley, Keats, Browning, Ruskin, and Arnold than is currently found in similar collections. Such representation permits both intensive study of the major figures and wide choice among their writings. It makes possible the inclusion of complete long selections (*Rasselas*, for example) and satisfying units of works of great length (as Book One of *Gulliver's Travels*, Book Seven of *The Ring and the Book*, much of *The Prelude* and of *In Memoriam*). But inclusion of the major writers alone would show only partially the grandeur and sweep of English literature. The publishers have therefore chosen a page size that is in concurrence with the wish of the editors to present an adequate consideration of all the important literary and social movements of England and to introduce the student to all groups of intrinsically enjoyable literary selections.

The editors felt it would be entirely inconsistent with the importance of Shakespeare as the greatest English writer not to represent him at all in that literary form upon which his reputation primarily rests. Rather than evade this important responsibility on the ground that each individual teacher would want to select the Shakespearean play his sophomores should read, the publishers systematically checked the experience of numerous college teachers against the three plays the editors most strongly recommended. It was, of course, unwise to consider plays which the student had probably read earlier. Similarly, it seemed inadvisable to include a play like *King Lear* which would be too mature for the sophomore to absorb within a limited number of assignments. *The First Part of Henry the Fourth* was thus the play selected, for in it are action, history, humor (what undergraduate can fail to love the bibulous old braggart, Falstaff!)—and some of Shakespeare's tenderest and most moving passages. Sophomores will not have read the play before; it will be within their range; it should be an immediate delight to them. Nothing, of course, prevents the purchase and use by the class of some other play if the instructor wishes it, for the quantity of other representative Shakespearean material is still ample for the course.

The growth and development of the drama has been represented by the inclusion of six significant plays, from *The Second Play of the Shepherds* to Synge's *The Playboy of the Western World*. The plays included coincide with the wish of the editors that no play be included which was not intrinsically interesting, not representative of its time, and not important enough to demand actual study in class.

Freshness of point of view has been constantly sought in the preparation of this anthology. An outstanding example of this is the treatment of *Paradise Lost*. Instead of including the traditional Books One and Two of *Paradise Lost*, the survey includes Book One, complete, lines 1–520 of Book Two (showing the mock-democratic procedure of Hell), lines 376 to the end of Book Nine (showing the temptation in the Garden, which is what this poem is professedly about), and lines 552 to the end of Book Twelve, and, in addition, the *Arguments* of all twelve books. Similarly, in the treatment of Chaucer, not only are "The Prologue," "The Pardoner's Tale," "The Prioress's Tale," and "The Nun's Priest's Tale" included, but also the complete framework of the *Canterbury Tales* is shown by links and synopses.

An earnest attempt has been made to obtain a better balance between prose and poetry than is ordinarily available, in the belief that such a balance will offer more appeal to students. This purpose is discernible in the selections for each period; it is particularly noticeable in the contemporary selections. Some literature of essentially social significance, like that selected from the work of Mill and Morris, will be found, in addition to the belletristic, historical, and personal literature.

For the first time in such a book, the Contemporary Period has received what the publishers

PUBLISHERS' PREFACE

feel to be appropriate and varied representation. The six previous periods show the range and temper of English literature; they also whet the sophomore's appetite for a satisfying taste of the literature of his own time. More than two hundred double-column pages of contemporary prose, poetry, and drama are included in THE COLLEGE SURVEY.

Some indication of the value to be had from a collaboration of specialists has already been touched upon. It should be added that the seven period introductions have been so co-ordinated that together they constitute an eighty-thousand-word historical interpretation of the development of English literature; furthermore, each period introduction has been synchronized with the introductions to authors and to individual selections within that particular period. Thus, for example, it is possible to see that Romanticism existed in every period from *Beowulf* and *Sir Gawain and the Green Knight* in the Early Period to Yeats's poetry in our own; one can see the ever changing forms of it appear pronouncedly in the Eighteenth-Century introduction, to burst into elaborate view in that of the Romantic Period. Further, one can see references, let us say in the introduction to Wordsworth, that echo the trends of Romanticism elaborated in the period introduction; and this, again, is echoed in the introduction to a single poem: "Ode on Intimations of Immortality."

The texts used in THE COLLEGE SURVEY are uniformly those of standard editions; for example, the Manly and Rickert edition of *The Canterbury Tales*. In Volume Two the capitalization, punctuation, and spelling of each selection are reproduced exactly as they appeared in an edition approved by the author or accepted as authentic by the readers of his time. Since printing practices were extremely varied before 1800, the capitalization, punctuation, and spelling of the selections in Volume One follow the best modern versions consistent with the flavor of the period in which the selections appeared. The arrangement of authors is based on the dates when they "flourished" rather than on strict chronology. It has been the purpose of the editors, in preparing their introductions and notes, to give effective help to the average sophomore reader without cluttering up his thought with esoteric information.

Much thought has been given toward making the format and illustrations of THE COLLEGE SURVEY attractive and instructive. The four pages of half-tone illustrations preceding each period were designed to show, consecutively, something of the country life of the time, the urban life, the topics the people of the period were most concerned about, and, finally, portraits of the leading literary figures. The wash drawing headpieces, drawn especially for the SURVEY by Mr. Herbert Gute of the School of Fine Arts of Yale University—one of which appears at the beginning of each period—symbolize the nature of the respective periods they introduce. The maps in the end papers were chosen more for their effectiveness as visual aids than for decoration. The reading lists at the end of each section were carefully drawn up not for the scholar, but for the student. A chapter on versification prepared by Mr. Untermeyer will be found in the Appendix, and, following it, a chronological list of the English rulers. An essay on the approach to English literature, especially prepared for this anthology by Professor Shepard, has been placed at the beginning of Volume One. It is intended that the student begin with this essay and read with satisfying and growing pleasure the content of THE COLLEGE SURVEY.

English literature is rich, lasting. English cathedrals may crumble into smoking ruin, their cherished windows shattered, their chancels dust; the streets and ghost-haunted lanes of ancient London may become hardly recognizable to recent travelers; the green slopes, the towered lawns, may be scarred with the horror that has marked England's greatest struggle for life. But in English literature all that was England remains, all that was England's endures. No greater hope could be expressed for this book than to have the reader say: Here is England.

CONTENTS

THE APPROACH TO ENGLISH LITERATURE   1

THE EARLY PERIOD

PART I: THE OLD ENGLISH ERA

INTRODUCTION   9

BEOWULF   16

DEOR   51

THE DREAM OF THE ROOD   52

RIDDLES   53
- 2. Storm on Land   54
- 16. Mother Badger   54
- 28. Mead   54
- 35. Rake   54
- 48. Bookworm   54
- 52. Pen and Three Fingers   54
- 58. Swallows   54
- 61. Reed   55
- 77. Oyster   55
- 81. Weathercock   55
- 86. One-Eyed Garlic Seller   55

CHARMS   55
- Against a Dwarf   55
- Against Wens   55
- For Elf-Disease   56
- For the Water-Elf Disease   56
- The Virtues of Jet   56
- For Elf-Shot   56
- The Mandrake   57

THE WANDERER   57

THE BATTLE OF MALDON   58

BEDE   62
- King Edwin's Conversion   62
- Caedmon   63

ALFRED   65
- The Voyages of Ohthere and Wulfstan   66

AELFRIC   68
- Saint Cuthbert   68
- The Colloquy   73

WULFSTAN   77
- Sermon to the English   78

THE OLD ENGLISH CHRONICLES   87
- The Year of the Conquest   81
- King William   82
- The Reign of Stephen   83

PART II: THE LATER MIDDLE AGES

INTRODUCTION   85

The Romances   95

KING HORN   96

GAMELYN   104

SIR GAWAIN AND THE GREEN KNIGHT   114

RALPH THE COLLIER   138

THE LAY OF SIR ORFEO   147

THE TOURNAMENT OF TOTTEN-HAM   152

Middle English Pronunciation   155

Middle English Lyrics — 156

- The Cuckoo Song — 156
- Now Springs the Spray — 156
- Lady, Have Ruth on Me — 157
- Alysoun — 157
- Lenten Is Come with Love to Town — 158
- The Loveliest Lady in the Land — 158
- De Clerico et Puella — 160
- A Love Message — 160
- The Matchless Maiden — 161
- Bless the Time the Apple Was Taken! — 161
- Signs of Death — 161
- Of One That Is So Fair and Bright — 161

THE VISION OF WILLIAM CONCERNING PIERS THE PLOWMAN — 162

- Prologue: The Field of Folk — 163
- Passus V
  - Gloton — 165
  - Sloth — 167

GEOFFREY CHAUCER — 168

From *The Canterbury Tales*
- The General Prologue — 173
- Synopsis of *The Knight's Tale* — 183
- The Miller's Prologue — 183
- Synopsis of *The Miller's Tale* — 184
- The Reeve's Prologue — 184
- Synopsis of *The Reeve's Tale* — 185
- The Cook's Prologue — 185
- Synopsis of *The Cook's Tale* — 185
- The Man of Law's Prologue — 185
- Synopsis of *The Man of Law's Tale* — 186
- The Man of Law's Epilogue — 187
- From *The Wife of Bath's Prologue* — 187
- Synopsis of *The Wife of Bath's Tale* — 189
- The Friar's Prologue — 189
- From *The Friar's Tale* — 190
- From *The Summoner's Prologue* — 190
- From *The Summoner's Tale* — 191
- The Clerk's Prologue — 192
- From *The Clerk's Tale* — 192
- The Merchant's Prologue — 193
- Synopsis of *The Merchant's Tale* — 194
- The Merchant's Epilogue — 194
- The Squire's Prologue — 194
- The Squire's Epilogue — 194
- Synopsis of *The Squire's Tale* — 194
- The Franklin's Prologue — 195
- Synopsis of *The Franklin's Tale* — 195
- Synopsis of *The Physician's Tale* — 195
- The Physician's Epilogue — 195
- The Pardoner's Prologue — 196
- The Pardoner's Tale — 197
- Synopsis of *The Shipman's Tale* — 203
- The Shipman's Epilogue — 203
- The Prioress's Prologue — 203
- The Prioress's Tale — 204
- The Prologue to *Sir Thopas* — 206
- Synopsis of *Sir Thopas* — 206
- The Prologue to *Melibee* — 206
- Synopsis of *Melibee* — 207
- The Monk's Prologue — 207
- Synopsis of *The Monk's Tale* — 208
- The Nun's Priest's Prologue — 208
- The Nun's Priest's Tale — 209
- Synopsis of *The Second Nun's Tale* — 216
- The Canon's Yeoman's Prologue — 216
- Synopsis of *The Canon's Yeoman's Tale* — 218
- The Manciple's Prologue — 218
- Synopsis of *The Manciple's Tale* — 219
- The Parson's Prologue — 220
- Synopsis of *The Parson's Tale* — 220
- Chaucer's Retraction — 220

Popular Ballads — 221

- The Twa Sisters — 224
- Lord Randal — 225
- Edward — 225
- Hind Horn — 226
- The Twa Corbies — 227
- Kemp Owyne — 227
- Thomas Rymer — 228
- The Cherry-Tree Carol — 229

CONTENTS

Sir Patrick Spens	230
Fair Margaret and Sweet William	230
The Unquiet Grave	231
The Wife of Usher's Well	232
Bonny Barbara Allan	232
Robin Hood and Guy of Gisborne	233
Johnie Armstrong	236
Mary Hamilton	237
The Bonny Earl of Murray	238
Get Up and Bar the Door	238

MIDDLE ENGLISH DRAMA

THE SECOND PLAY OF THE SHEPHERDS	239
SIR THOMAS MALORY	250
From *Le Morte Darthur*	252
Caxton's Preface	252
Book XXI	254
Suggestions for Further Reading	266

THE SIXTEENTH CENTURY

INTRODUCTION	269
JOHN SKELTON	282
From *Colin Clout*	282
From *A Garland of Laurel*	
To Mistress Margaret Hussey	284
SIR THOMAS MORE	285
From *Utopia*	285
Of Their Living and Conversation Together	286
Of Warfare	288
SIR THOMAS WYATT	293
The Lover Compareth His State to a Ship in Perilous Storm Tossed on the Sea	294
Description of the Contrarious Passions in a Lover	294
The Lover for Shamefastness Hideth His Desire within His Faithful Heart	294
Whoso List to Hunt	294
The Lover Showeth How He Is Forsaken of Such as He Sometime Enjoyed	294
Forget Not Yet	295
Of the Courtier's Life	295
HENRY HOWARD, EARL OF SURREY	296
Description of Spring, Wherein Each Thing Renews Save Only the Lover	297
The Frailty and Hurtfulness of Beauty	297
Description and Praise of His Love Geraldine	298
A Complaint by Night of the Lover Not Beloved	298
Complaint of a Lover Rebuked	298
Of the Death of Sir T. W. the Elder	298
The Things That Cause a Quiet Life, Written by Martial	299
Prisoned in Windsor, He Recounteth His Pleasure There Passed	299
THOMAS SACKVILLE, EARL OF DORSET	300
From *A Mirror for Magistrates*	
Induction and Complaint of the Duke of Buckingham	301
SIR THOMAS HOBY	305
From *The Courtier*	305
WILLIAM PAINTER	314
From *The Palace of Pleasure*	
Romeo and Julietta	314
ROGER ASCHAM	321
From *The Schoolmaster*	321
RAPHAEL HOLINSHED	329
From *Chronicles*	329

SIR THOMAS NORTH — 335

From *Plutarch's Lives of the Noble Greeks and Romans*
  Julius Caesar — 336

JOHN LYLY — 342

From *Euphues, The Anatomy of Wit* — 343
Cupid and My Campaspe — 349
What Bird So Sings — 349
Song by Fairies — 350

SIR PHILIP SIDNEY — 350

From *Astrophel and Stella* — 351
My True Love Has My Heart — 352
From *Certain Sonnets* — 352
From *The Defence of Poesy* — 353

CHRISTOPHER MARLOWE — 363

The Passionate Shepherd to His Love — 364
From *Hero and Leander* — 364
The Tragical History of Dr. Faustus — 370

RICHARD HAKLUYT — 389

From *Principal Voyages* — 390

EDMUND SPENSER — 394

From *The Shepheardes Calender*
  October — 395
From *Amoretti* — 399
Epithalamion — 400
From *The Faerie Queene* — 405
  Book I
    Canto I — 406
    Canto XI — 412
    Canto XII — 419
  Book II
    Canto XII — 424
  Book III
    Canto VI — 428

SIR WALTER RALEGH — 431

A Vision upon This Conceit of the Faery Queene — 432
The Nymph's Reply to the Shepherd — 432
The Lie — 433
His Pilgrimage — 434
Even Such Is Time — 434
A Report of the Truth of the Fight about the Isles of Azores This Last Summer betwixt the *Revenge*, One of Her Majesty's Ships, and an Armada of the King of Spain — 435

THOMAS DEKKER — 441

From *The Gull's Hornbook*
  Chapter 6: How a Gallant Should Behave Himself in a Play-House — 441
  Chapter 7: How a Gallant Should Behave Himself in a Tavern — 444
  Chapter 8: How a Gallant Is to Behave Himself Passing through the City, at All Hours of the Night, and How to Pass by Any Watch — 445
Art Thou Poor? — 447

SAMUEL DANIEL — 447

From *Delia* — 448
The Complaint of Rosamond — 449
To the Lady Margaret, Countess of Cumberland — 452

MICHAEL DRAYTON — 453

From *Idea's Mirrour* — 454
To the Virginian Voyage — 455
To the Cambro-Britons and Their Harp, His Ballad of Agincourt — 456
To My Most Dearly Loved Friend, Henry Reynolds, Esquire of Poets and Poesy — 457

WILLIAM SHAKESPEARE — 460

From *Sonnets* — 461
  Shall I compare thee to a summer's day — 461
  Weary with toil, I haste me to my bed — 461
  When in disgrace with fortune and men's eyes — 461
  When to the sessions of sweet silent thought — 462
  How heavy do I journey on the way — 462
  Not marble, nor the gilded monuments — 462
  Being your slave, what should I do but tend — 462

CONTENTS

No longer mourn for me when I am dead	462
That time of year thou may'st in me behold	462
Farewell! thou art too dear for my possessing	463
How like a winter hath my absence been	463
When in the chronicle of wasted time	463
Let me not to the marriage of true minds	463
No, Time, thou shalt not boast that I do change	463
The expense of spirit in a waste of shame	464
My mistress' eyes are nothing like the sun	464
When my love swears that she is made of truth	464
Two loves I have of comfort and despair	464
Poor soul, the centre of my sinful earth	464
The First Part of King Henry the Fourth	465

Songs from Shakespeare's Plays

When Daisies Pied	500
When Icicles Hang by the Wall	500
Who Is Silvia?	500
Over Hill, over Dale	501
Tell Me Where Is Fancy Bred	501
Blow, Blow, Thou Winter Wind	501
Under the Greenwood Tree	501
Come Away, Come Away, Death	501
O Mistress Mine	502
Sigh No More	502
Take, Oh, Take Those Lips Away	502
Hark, Hark! the Lark	502
Fear No More the Heat o' the Sun	502
When Daffodils Begin to Peer	503
Full Fathom Five	503

Elizabethan Lyrics 504

A Nymph's Disdain of Love	504
Back and Side Go Bare, Go Bare	504
The Promise of a Constant Lover	505

RICHARD BARNFIELD 505

If Music and Sweet Poetry Agree	505

NICHOLAS BRETON 505

A Pastoral of Phillis and Corydon	505

THOMAS CAMPION 506

Thrice Toss These Oaken Ashes	506
Never Love Unless You Can	506
Jack and Joan	506
To Music Bent Is My Retired Mind	506
The Man of Life Upright	507
When to Her Lute Corinna Sings	507
My Sweetest Lesbia	507
There Is a Garden in Her Face	507

HENRY CONSTABLE 508

The Shepherd's Song of Venus and Adonis	508

JOHN DOWLAND 509

Fine Knacks for Ladies	509

SIR EDWARD DYER 509

My Mind to Me a Kingdom Is	509

JOHN FLETCHER 510

Lay a Garland on My Hearse	510
Melancholy	510
Sleep	510
The Drinking Song	510
Let the Bells Ring	510
Weep No More	511

ORLANDO GIBBONS 511

The Silver Swan	511

GRAY OF READING 511

The King's Hunt Is Up	511

ROBERT GREENE 511

Sephestia's Song to Her Child	511
The Shepherd's Wife's Song	512
Sweet Are the Thoughts	512
Cupid Abroad Was Lated	512

TOBIAS HUME 513

Tobacco, Tobacco	513

THOMAS LODGE	513	ROBERT SOUTHWELL	515
Rosalynde's Madrigal	513	The Burning Babe	515
ANTHONY MUNDAY	513		
To Colin Clout	513	JOHN WEBSTER	515
THOMAS NASHE	514	Dirge	515
Spring, the Sweet Spring	514	Death-Song	515
Litany in Time of Plague	514		
GEORGE PEELE	514	THOMAS WEELKES	516
Paris and Oenone	514	These Things Seem Wondrous	516
His Golden Locks	515	*Suggestions for Further Reading*	516

THE SEVENTEENTH CENTURY

INTRODUCTION	519	Of Love	547
		Of Great Place	548
From *The Authorized or King James Version of the Holy Bible*		Of Travel	549
		Of Studies	550
The Twenty-Third Psalm (Varying translations)		From *New Atlantis*	
The Great Bible, 1540	538	Solomon's House	551
The Geneva Bible, 1560	539		
The Douai Bible, 1609	539	BEN JONSON	556
The Authorized Version, 1611	539	Epigrams	
From *The Book of Job*		To the Reader	557
Chapter 38	540	To My Book	557
Chapter 42	541	To King James	558
From *The Psalter*		On the Union	558
Psalm 91	541	On My First Daughter	558
Psalm 139	541	To John Donne	558
From *The Gospel According to St. Matthew*		On My First Son	558
Chapter 6:19–34	542	Epitaph on S[alathiel] P[avy], a Child of Queen Elizabeth's Chapel	558
From *The Gospel According to St. Luke*		Epitaph on Elizabeth, L. H.	559
Chapter 10:25–37	542	Songs from the Plays and Masques	
From *The First Epistle of St. Paul to the Corinthians*		Slow, Slow, Fresh Fount	559
Chapter 13	543	Queen and Huntress	559
FRANCIS BACON	544	Come, My Celia, Let Us Prove	559
		Still to Be Neat	560
From *Essays or Counsels, Civil and Moral*		Gipsy Songs	560
Of Truth	545	Though I Am Young	560
Of Death	546	Song: To Celia	560
Of Marriage and Single Life	546		

CONTENTS

From *Underwoods*
   A Hymn on the Nativity of My Saviour   560
From *A Celebration of Charis*
   His Excuse for Loving   561
   Her Triumph   561
An Ode to Himself   561
From *A Pindaric Ode*
   To the Immortal Memory and Friendship of That Noble Pair Sir Lucius Cary and Sir H. Morison   562
   To the Memory of My Beloved the Author, Mr. William Shakespeare, and What He Hath Left Us   562

JOHN DONNE   563

From *Songs and Sonnets*
   Song (Go and catch a falling star)   564
   The Indifferent   564
   The Canonization   565
   The Good-Morrow   565
   A Valediction Forbidding Mourning   566
   Song (Sweetest love, I do not go)   566
   The Ecstasy   567
   The Funeral   568
Holy Sonnets   568
A Hymn to God the Father   569

GEORGE WITHER   569

The Author's Resolution in a Sonnet   570
A Christmas Carol   571

The Character-Writers   572

SIR THOMAS OVERBURY   572

From *Sir Thomas Overbury His Wife . . . and Divers More Characters*
   A Good Wife   573
   A Fair and Happy Milkmaid   574
   A Franklin   574

JOHN EARLE   575

From *Microcosmography*
   A Child   575
   A Young Man   576
   A Young Gentleman of the University   576

ROBERT BURTON   577

From *The Anatomy of Melancholy*
   Democritus Junior to the Reader   578
   [The Utopia of Democritus Junior]   582

GEORGE HERBERT   587

Easter Wings   588
The Collar   588
The Quip   589
The Pulley   589
The Elixir   589
Discipline   590
Love   590
The Flower   590
Virtue   591

ROBERT HERRICK   592

From *Hesperides*
   The Argument of His Book   593
   Cherry-Ripe   593
   Delight in Disorder   593
   Corinna's Going a-Maying   593
   To the Virgins, to Make Much of Time   594
   To Anthea, Who May Command Him Anything   594
   To Daffodils   595
   The Mad Maid's Song   595
   Mistress Susanna Southwell, upon Her Feet   595
   Meat without Mirth   595
   His Prayer to Ben Jonson   595
   An Ode for Him   596
   His Content in the Country   596
   The Night-Piece, to Julia   596
   The Hag   596
   His Grange, or Private Wealth   597
   A Ternary of Littles upon a Pipkin of Jelly Sent to a Lady   597
   Upon Julia's Clothes   597
   Upon Prue, His Maid   597
   Ceremonies for Christmas   597
   The Pillar of Fame   598
From *Noble Numbers*
   His Litany to the Holy Spirit   598

A Thanksgiving to God for His House	598
To Death	598
Another Grace for a Child	598
The Bellman	598

TOM O' BEDLAM'S SONG — 600

THOMAS CAREW — 602

Upon a Ribbon	603
A Song (Ask me no more where Jove bestows)	603
Disdain Returned	603

SIR JOHN SUCKLING — 604

Song (Why so pale and wan, fond lover?)	605
Song (Honest lover whatsoever)	605
Constancy	605
A Ballad upon a Wedding	606

RICHARD LOVELACE — 608

To Althea, from Prison	608
To Lucasta, Going to the Wars	609
To Lucasta, Going beyond the Seas	609

EDMUND WALLER — 610

Say, Lovely Dream	611
On a Girdle	611
Go, Lovely Rose	611
Of the Last Verses in the Book	611

RICHARD CRASHAW — 612

Wishes	613
From *The Holy Nativity of Our Lord God* A Hymn Sung as by the Shepherds	614
From *The Flaming Heart*	615

HENRY VAUGHAN — 616

The Retreat	617
Peace	617
The World	617
They Are All Gone into the World of Light	618
The Waterfall	619

SIR THOMAS BROWNE — 619

From *Religio Medici* The Second Part	619
From *Hydriotaphia: Urn Burial* Chapter 5	627

THOMAS FULLER — 631

From *The History of the Worthies of England* Devonshire: Sir Walter Raleigh	632
Westminster: Benjamin Jonson	632
Warwickshire: William Shakespeare	632

IZAAK WALTON — 633

From *The Compleat Angler* Chapter 4	634
[The Milkmaid's Song]	638
[The Milkmaid's Mother's Answer]	638

JOHN MILTON — 639

On the Morning of Christ's Nativity	640
On Shakespeare	644
How Soon Hath Time	644
L'Allegro	644
Il Penseroso	646
On Time	649
At a Solemn Music	649
Lycidas	649
When I Consider How My Light Is Spent	653
On the Late Massacre in Piemont	653
Cyriack, This Three Years' Day	653
From *Paradise Lost*	654
Book I	655
From Book II	665
Arguments for Books III–VIII	671
From Book IX	672
Arguments for Books X–XI	681
From Book XII	682
From *Areopagitica*	683

ANDREW MARVELL — 693

The Garden	694
The Definition of Love	695

CONTENTS

To His Coy Mistress	695
Bermudas	696

ABRAHAM COWLEY — 696

From *Several Discourses by Way of Essays, in Verse and Prose*
- Of Liberty — 697
- Of Myself — 702

JOHN BUNYAN — 705

From *The Pilgrim's Progress*
- From *The First Part* — 705
- From *The Second Part* — 716

SAMUEL PEPYS — 717

From *The Diary* — 718

JOHN DRYDEN — 725

- Ah, Fading Joy — 726
- You Pleasing Dreams — 726
- From *Absalom and Achitophel* — 727
- From *Threnodia Augustalis* — 731
- Lines Printed under the Engraved Portrait of Milton — 731
- Alexander's Feast — 732
- From *An Essay of Dramatic Poesy* — 734
- From Preface to the *Fables* — 735

WILLIAM CONGREVE — 739

The Way of the World — 740

Suggestions for Further Reading — 773

THE EIGHTEENTH CENTURY

INTRODUCTION — 775

DANIEL DEFOE — 788

- From *An Essay on Projects* — 789
- From *Of Academies* — 789
- The Shortest Way with the Dissenters — 792
- A True Relation of the Apparition of One Mrs. Veal — 798

JONATHAN SWIFT — 802

- From *Gulliver's Travels*
  - Part I: A Voyage to Lilliput — 803
- Thoughts on Various Subjects — 828
- From *Journal to Stella*
  - Letter XIX — 830
- An Argument — 834
- A Modest Proposal — 840

JOSEPH ADDISON AND RICHARD STEELE — 844

From *The Tatler* — 845
- No. 25. Tuesday, June 7, 1709 (Steele) — 845
- No. 158. Thursday, April 13, 1710 (Addison) — 846
- No. 181. June 6, 1710 (Steele) — 847

From *The Spectator*
- No. 2. Friday, March 2, 1711 (Steele) — 848
- No. 10. Monday, March 12, 1711 (Addison) — 850
- No. 109. Thursday, July 5, 1711 (Steele) — 851
- No. 112. Monday, July 9, 1711 (Addison) — 853
- No. 122. Friday, July 29, 1711 (Addison) — 854
- No. 159. Saturday, September 1, 1711 (Addison) — 856
- No. 160. Monday, September 3, 1711 (Addison) — 857
- No. 291. Saturday, February 2, 1712 (Addison) — 859
- No. 323. Tuesday, March 11, 1712 (Addison) — 860
- No. 335. Tuesday, March 25, 1712 (Addison) — 862
- No. 454. Monday, August 11, 1712 (Steele) — 864

PHILIP DORMER STANHOPE, EARL OF CHESTERFIELD — 866

From *Letters to His Son*
- Bath, February 22, O. S. 1748 — 867
- London, December 12, O. S. 1749 — 868
- London, January 8, O. S. 1750 — 870

ALEXANDER POPE — 871

From *An Essay on Criticism*
  Part I — 872
  Part II — 874
From *An Essay on Man*
  Epistle I — 878
  Epistle II — 881
The Universal Prayer — 884
The Rape of the Lock — 885
Eloïsa to Abelard — 893

JAMES THOMSON — 897

A Hymn on the Seasons — 898
To the Memory of Sir Isaac Newton — 899
From *The Castle of Indolence* — 902

THOMAS GRAY — 911

Ode on a Distant Prospect of Eton College — 912
Elegy Written in a Country Church-Yard — 913
Sonnet (In vain to me the smiling Mornings shine) — 915
Hymn to Adversity — 915
The Progress of Poesy — 915
The Bard — 917
The Fatal Sisters — 919
Letters
  To Richard West, December, 1736 — 920
  To Horace Walpole — 921
  To Richard West, London, April, Thursday (1742) — 921
  To Horace Walpole, Cambridge, February 11, 1751 — 922

WILLIAM COLLINS — 923

Ode to Simplicity — 923
Ode to Evening — 924
The Passions: An Ode for Music — 925
Ode Written in the Beginning of the Year 1746 — 926
A Song from Shakespear's Cymbeline — 926
Ode on the Death of Mr. Thomson — 927

CHRISTOPHER SMART — 928

A Song to David — 928
From *Rejoice in the Lamb* — 932

JAMES MACPHERSON — 934

Carthon: A Poem — 934

JAMES BOSWELL — 939

From *The Life of Samuel Johnson*
  A. D. 1763: Aetat. 54 — 940
  A. D. 1776: Aetat. 67 — 957

SAMUEL JOHNSON — 961

The History of Rasselas, Prince of Abissinia — 962
From *The Preface to Shakespeare* — 1007

OLIVER GOLDSMITH — 1011

The Deserted Village — 1012
She Stoops to Conquer — 1017

EDMUND BURKE — 1048

From *Reflections on the Revolution in France* — 1049

WILLIAM COWPER — 1061

From *The Task*
  Book IV — 1061
From *Yardley Oak* — 1069
The Poplar-Field — 1071
The Castaway — 1071
Letters
  To the Rev. William Unwin — 1072
  To the Rev. John Newton — 1073
  To Lady Hesketh — 1074
  [To Wm. Cowper, of the Inner Temple, Esq.] — 1075
On the Receipt of My Mother's Picture out of Norfolk — 1076

ROBERT BURNS — 1077

The Cotter's Saturday Night — 1078
To a Mouse — 1080
To a Mountain Daisy — 1081

CONTENTS

Green Grow the Rashes	1082
Willie Brewed a Peck o' Maut	1082
Address to the Unco Guid, or the Rigidly Righteous	1082
Address to the Deil	1083
Holy Willie's Prayer	1085
Tam O' Shanter	1086
Comin' thro' the Rye	1088
Of A' the Airts	1089
John Anderson My Jo	1089
Scots, Wha Hae	1089
Auld Lang Syne	1090
Duncan Gray	1090
Highland Mary	1090
For A' That and A' That	1091
A Red, Red Rose	1091
The Jolly Beggars	1092
Ae Fond Kiss	1096
Afton Water	1096
Mary Morison	1096
Ye Flowery Banks	1097
O, Wert Thou in the Cauld Blast	1097

WILLIAM BLAKE — 1097

From *Poetical Sketches*	
To the Muses	1098
To Spring	1099
To the Evening Star	1099
Song (Fresh from the dewey hill, the merry year)	1099
Song (How sweet I roamed from field to field)	1099
Song (My silks and fine array)	1100
Song (Memory, hither come)	1100
Mad Song	1100
From *Songs of Innocence*	
Introduction	1100
The Ecchoing Green	1101
The Lamb	1101
The Little Black Boy	1101
The Chimney-Sweeper	1102
Laughing Song	1102
A Cradle Song	1102
Nurse's Song	1102
Infant Joy	1103
From *Songs of Experience*	
The Chimney-Sweeper	1103
The Tyger	1103
Ah! Sun-Flower	1104
London	1104
The Human Abstract	1104
Auguries of Innocence	1104
From *Milton*	1106
The Marriage of Heaven and Hell	1106
Suggestions for Further Reading	1111

POETIC FORMS AND PATTERNS — 1113

CHRONOLOGY OF THE ENGLISH RULERS — 1121

GENERAL INDEX — 1123

INDEX OF FIRST LINES — 1137

The Approach to English Literature

Black marks on a white ground—that is all these words would be to a savage who might glance at them for a moment and then away. To you, the present reader, they are something more. With no other guides than these black marks you are following the thought of another mind. For you they are building a bridge across time and space.

Surely it is one of the strangest things we know, that mere printer's ink on wood-pulp can so draw two minds together and enclose them for a moment within a single thought. Illiterate people have good reason for feeling that there is something magical about these messages in black and white that men have been sending one another for several thousand years. Without their help we should be, at the best, barbarians; but with it we have made several civilizations. And they stand ready to help us onward still, binding mankind together in ever enlarging sympathies and understandings, if only we will learn to use their total power. There is no end to the beneficent work that written and printed words can do—that is, when they are the right words in the right order and when they are rightly read.

This qualification is important. Only a small portion of the words that are recorded in black and white are really beneficent, and among the numberless millions who can gather some kind of sense from the printed page there are never enough real readers. To the editors of the present book, in which a large amount of literature has been brought together for college students, it has seemed best not to assume that all those who will use the book already know what literature is, what it can do for them, and how they can most readily get what it has to offer.

Literature is the enduring expression of significant human experience in words well chosen and arranged.

This definition implies that literature is an art. As such, its main concern must be with the creation of beauty. Now beauty is created for the sake of the pure pleasure that normal people find in making and in contemplating beautiful things. Literature exists, then, for pleasure.

To be sure, the creation of beauty is not its only concern. Composed of words, literature cannot ignore the practical uses for which most words were at first invented. Voices of the actual world sound across the borders of this art more clearly than they do into the realms of music, architecture, sculpture, and painting. Literary artists, moreover, often try to inform, persuade, and improve us as other artists do not. And yet it holds true that their main purpose has always been to give pleasure—of a distinct but not easily describable kind.

The pleasures of literature are not those of ordinary entertainment. Rest and relaxation are always to be found in it, but found together with an intense activity. A sense of liberation and enlargement makes a part of this pleasure, and so does the delight of seeing life's apparent disarray subdued to order and form. Often, too, there comes the excitement of discovery, when a novel or poem or play becomes to us a Northwest Passage leading to countries of the mind which, without it, we should never have entered. And always in any reading worthy of the name there is that sober pleasure, often strangely heightened and concentrated, which every whole and gladsome heart must find in life itself.

All those who love to live must love literature also, if only because it so hugely amplifies one's living and provides a store of observation, experience, thought, and feeling enormously greater than any of us can crowd into his three-score years and ten. Literature, as George Eliot said of art in general, is "the nearest thing to life." The illiterate man lives only once, but the citizen of the world of books multiplies his years by hundreds.

Other studies are usually undertaken for the maintenance or the better understanding of life, but the right study of literature provides in itself a deep and full experience. It need not and should not involve a retreat from life into books. It may and should be an advance through books toward a larger and happier living.

Yet even here nothing is sold for nothing. The pleasures and rewards of literature are like those of the mountain-climber. They demand labor, courage, persistence, and a faith that wherever the human mind has been we too can go. To read well is to climb toward the level of one's author—and this, when such minds as Shakespeare, Milton, and Shelley are concerned, is no holiday task. Whatever may be said of poets, good readers are made, not born.

This is not to say that natural gifts are of no importance. The question whether one is to be a good reader may depend in some degree upon the sheer physical, mental, and emotional energy that one can bring to bear on the reading process. It may depend upon the strength, the precision, and the delicacy of one's physical senses. Sight, hearing, touch, taste, and smell are the pathmakers of literature and the scouts of those who follow the trail. Much depends upon the reader's power of visual and auditory imagination. One who cannot make and revive clear mental pictures will of course find many of the finest passages in literature "as is a landscape to a blind man's eye." Yet even this defect would be less serious than inability to hear and delight in the chiming and contrasting of Spenser's syllables, the oceanic roll and clangor of Milton's verse, or the somber harmonies that reverberate in the prose of Sir Thomas Browne.

For literature began as an address to the ear. It was, to begin with, an art of the singing, chanting, or speaking voice, usually sustained by the dance and by musical instruments. And even today, in spite of the deadening effects of print, there is to be heard in all good prose and verse a throb of those immemorial rhythms and a whisper of ancient tunes. Always a main part is played in the skillful choice and arrangement of words by cadence, echo, run and pause, clash and concord. These are not decorations. They are indispensable modes of expression. Without them words may convey clear thought, as algebraic symbols do, but not the effects of literature.

What this means to readers should be clear. A musician who contented himself with the study of musical scores, never caring to hear actual music, would be little more absurd than those who pretend to study literature without knowing or wishing to know how literature sounds.

No better counsel can be given the young student than that he use every opportunity for reading good prose and verse aloud, listening intently for the subtlest niceties of expressive pace and tone, striving steadily to make himself a better instrument for the rendering of literary music. And let him not fear that in this emphasis upon the esthetic qualities of literature he will be neglecting the intellectual. What literature says to the mind is in large part determined by its manner of speaking to the ear. A single brief passage of prose or verse, chosen and memorized for its musical value and repeated over and over, may teach one more about literary essences than the silent reading of a thousand pages.

Let us suppose that the student has chosen those enchanted lines in which John Keats says of the nightingale's song that it is

"Perhaps the self-same song that found a path
Through the sad heart of Ruth, when, sick for home,
She stood in tears amid the alien corn;
The same that oft-times hath
Charmed magic casements, opening on the foam
Of perilous seas, in faery lands forlorn."

Here is a cluster of common workaday words, all but one or two of which might stand unnoticed in the most prosaic context. Yet somehow, taken together, they weave a spell. Their total effect is greater by far than the discernible ingredients promise. What witchcraft is there here? What powder of immortality has been sprinkled over these syllables?

With questions of this sort the student plunges into the problems of style, from which he is not likely to emerge very soon with a set of complete answers. Saying the lines over to himself a score of times, he comes to realize that they have a beauty apart from all that they signify to the mind. They would be lovely still, he feels sure, if he understood not one word that they contain. These syllables make a pattern of sound as delightful for its own sake as any little company of tones to be found in Mozart or Chopin. They are caught in a kind of dance according to which their regular step is one *two*, one *two*, one *two*, one *two*, one *two*. But this iambic dance, the student soon discovers, is thwarted now and then by freer rhythms cutting across it, as the steady scansion of rollers along a seacoast is diversified by smaller waves and wavelets running and rippling back from off the strand. That is, one hears in these lines both law and liberty, interwoven as in one's life. Is this the source of their charm? And is there some echo here of the heart's steady meter, enlivened by the rhythms of the breath?

These are deep waters, not yet fully explored by any diver. One secret of style may lie hid in them, but only one of several. Meter and rhythm and changing pace play their part in all literary effects, but so do the tones of the singing vowels, always surrounded and suffused by consonantal harmonies. In those six wonderful lines of Keats's poem there are delicacies of tonal as well as rhythmical pattern that reveal themselves only to prolonged attention.

But when the student has heard all of these he has made hardly more than a beginning. For literary music is not meant to pause in the porch of the ear. It must penetrate inward, roll onward through the chambers of the mind, and echo along the halls of memory. Its value lies not so much in itself as in its fruitful union with images, moods, and ideas; and the children of this union are numberless.

The fact is that literary style is a mysterious thing, and that more than two thousand years of criticism have done little to reduce its mystery. We simply do not understand how the rhythms of prose and verse enhance, restrain, glorify, and deepen our thoughts and feelings. We cannot retrace the paths of imagination by which John Keats found his way from the song of the nightingale to that strange image, apparently so remote and yet so perfectly fitting, of windows looking out on the sea. And when we come to consider words themselves, the very stuff of style —when, for example, we pause upon such radioactive words as "magic," "perilous," "forlorn," and "faery," or over such a phrase as "alien corn"—then the hardiest critic among us may well throw up his hands.

"What do you read, my lord?" asked old Polonius, expecting a superficial answer. "Words, words, words," Lord Hamlet replied, intending to put him off. Yet Hamlet, just possibly, may have had it in mind that anyone who can really read words has an enormous intellectual advantage over the empty chatterers whom Polonius represents.

There are many complaints in literature against the frailty and evanescence of the materials out of which all literature is made. Many a writer has longed for a medium as lasting as that of the sculptor and architect, as vivid as that of the painter, and as free from taint as that of the musician. For words perish in the moment of utterance. Their very birth is a farewell. They shift and fade and are rebuilded like the clouds. Like the chameleon they change in hue with every altering context. They do a double duty, serving the needs of every day and also those of the mind and spirit. Moreover, they are stubborn and deceitful things, and until they are mastered they make terrible tyrants.

And yet how wonderful they are, these children of our breath called words! They are beautiful in themselves, fascinating in their histories, and magical in their powers of evocation. Fleeting and changeful though they be, some of the basic words of English speech are probably older in their origins than the Pyramids. And difficult though the control and understanding of words has always been found, it is yet possible for a college student to share, by means of them, the burning fancy of Keats, the thought of Shakespeare, and the kindly humor of a man who lived and wrote in London more than five hundred years ago.

Two ways of using words, the "denotative" and the "connotative," may be distinguished. The former is shown in scientific statements where an effort is made to strip off all "peripheral" meanings and thus to confine every term to a single, precise, and limited sense. Such a use of a given word is like the sounding of a pure unqualified tone on a pitch pipe. In literature, on the other hand, peripheral meanings are usually not rejected but welcomed; and here the analogy is that of playing on an intricate instrument so made that echoes and overtones crowd in from all the related keys to enrich every note that is struck.

"A circle," says Euclid, "is a plane figure contained by one line called the circumference, and is such that all straight lines drawn from a certain point within the figure to the circumference are equal to one another."—That sentence is clearly a triumph in the taut, spare use of language which lets no syllable go to waste. It has the precision of a well-aimed rifle-shot. And there is an unmistakable beauty in it, too, which is not in the least dependent upon any adornment. This is "beauty bare."

Over against that of Euclid let us set a statement by St. Augustine which happens to involve the same terms: "God is a circle whose center is everywhere and its circumference nowhere."—This puts language to a different use, of the kind we call "metaphorical." There is beauty here also, and a corresponding delight, but delight and beauty of a different sort.

Euclid confines our thought to a definite subject-matter, with regard to which he gives us a sense of full understanding. St. Augustine, on the other hand, tries only to enlarge and liberate thought, and to launch it forth on flights of conjecture. Euclid does all the necessary work, but St. Augustine calls for collaboration. To the statement of Euclid there is nothing to be added; it means the same thing to all men in all ages; it silences every doubt. The sentence from St. Augustine does not even attempt finality. It is exciting, rather, and stimulating; it leaves room for each individual's private interpretation; it suddenly floods the mind with "thoughts beyond the reaches of our souls."

To one who has been accustomed chiefly to the denotative use of words this connotative or metaphorical mode of expression may be at first perplexing. One does well to assume, however, that most literature has been written not to hide but to reveal meanings, and that the masters of writing have usually been as simple in statement as their purposes and subject matters would allow. If we find that words are often used less precisely in imaginative literature than in scientific statement, one reason may be that literature has at once a more difficult and a less defined territory than that of science to explore. Thus, the nature of the Divine Being is a harder thing to suggest in words than the nature of the geometrical figure called a circle.

In spite of these difficulties literature aspires, no less than science, to a universal validity. In works that are rightly called "classics" there is always an effort, at least, to find and to state a universal law for the human mind and heart. Indeed this is the chief mark of classic literature, in whatever period it may be composed, that it is addressed by one mind to all minds, that it "makes the whole world kin," and that it seems never new and never old but always contemporary with all good readers.

One sees, then, an additional reason that may be urged for the study of literary classics. Apart from the sheer pleasure they give us, their influence tends to make us more normal and more representative human beings. It is for this reason that they stand supreme among the group of studies called "the humanities." They lift us over the boundaries of time and space, they help us to transcend the limitations of race and creed, they unite us with the universal and everlasting society of mankind.

For American students the classics of English literature have this advantage over those of other tongues, ancient or modern, that they present few barriers of language. As compared with American literature that of England, reaching back for more than a thousand years, is, to say the least, more extensive; and there can be no violation of our patriotic pride in the admission that English literature is in other ways superior to our own. We may well remember, too, that English poetry and prose written down to the time of Shakespeare is as much ours as it is England's. Any American of Anglo-Saxon descent may read the popular ballads of England with the assurance that his forefathers made and sang them, just as he may stand before one of England's older cathedrals and say "My ancestors laid those stones." And Americans of all other racial origins may also say, while reading Chaucer and Shakespeare and Milton, that here are some of the foremost shapers of that tradition by which their lives are guided and sustained.

England is the pit whence we Americans were digged. Within her boundaries our language grew and ramified and was enriched until it became, for range and vigor if not for precision or beauty of sound, the most perfect instrument of verbal expression ever known. England gave us the English Bible, which has been the main source of our profound idealism through all our years. She gave us our common law, and such respect for legal customs and restraints as we have shown. From England we brought our basic notions of representative government, of liberty under the law, of town and village communities, and of home life. Our revolt against the homeland, carried out as it was by Englishmen in the spirit of English ideals, was one of the most characteristic things that English people have ever accomplished. And so it would seem to follow that in the study of English literature we study not only the richest body of poetry and prose that any people has ever produced; we study, also, ourselves.

No other nation has ever had such good fortune as ours, to find upon its coming-of-age a great literature ready made, in its own tongue, expressing its own fundamental thoughts and feelings. Ancient Rome, when her time of leisure came, could only attempt the wholesale importation of a culture completely foreign, to be studied in a foreign language. The cultivated American of our day makes himself at home in two intellectual countries, subtly different and yet strongly similar.

To an American England seems a small country. Her territory, about as large as the State of Illinois, is almost entirely surrounded by water. The breath of the sea blows into every nook of the land, bearing mist and fog and fleets of cloud. Considering that she lies in the latitude of Labrador, the climate of England is remarkably mild. The flowers of autumn almost overlap the flowers of spring, the grass is evergreen, and the robin sings throughout the year.

The landscape of England is seldom grand. There is nothing savage about it, and little that an American would call even wild. It is, so to speak, a man-sized landscape, and its loveliness is the product of many centuries in which men and nature have worked together. It has been adorned by its use.

In millions of English lives the love of nature has been a controlling passion. This passion underlies the Englishman's delight in sport, which, for the modern world, he may almost be said to have invented. It may be related also to his eagerness in adventure, exploration, colonization, and empire-building. In English landscape-painting it is clearly apparent, and in English poetry from Chaucer to Masefield it sounds a pervading tone. Neither sentimental nor primarily esthetic, this English love of the land is a patriotism and a kind of religion at once.

American readers should remember that England is an ancient country as well as a modern, and that much of her literature has been written with a subconscious awareness of her antiquity. Historic continuity stretching through thirty centuries is visibly written upon the land. Along the South Downs of Sussex and Berkshire there runs a wide pathway beaten out by the naked feet of peoples who lived so long ago that we scarcely try to name them, and from this path one may look out over a country still studded with Norman towers, rutted by crooking Saxon lanes, deeply scored by straight Roman highways, and strewn with ancient burial mounds. Relics and reminders of the past are everywhere in England, and it is not strange, therefore, that English literature should be steeped in time.

The ancestry of the people called English, like that of most other modern peoples, is confused and complex. The name of this people—"English" is derived from *Anglisc*, pertaining to the small Germanic tribe called Angles—would indicate that the Anglo-Saxon element is fundamental. If it is so, then the strain of those Germanic farmers and villagers who came to the island in the fifth and sixth centuries, settling down there to a life chiefly agricultural, must have undergone great change. This change began in the eleventh century under the dominance of the Normans—a people of swift and keen intelligence, with a gift for government and an insatiable lust for power. Here was a mingling of elements almost antithetical, but this was not all. In the northeast of England many place names remind the traveler that the region was once predominantly Danish, and other names in the northwest show that the Lake District was once overrun by another lot of Scandinavian invaders. These Danes and Norsemen did not "die out," any more than have the Normans to whom they were closely related. They contributed largely to the blood of those "true-born Englishmen" whose contempt for foreigners has been, at various times, among their more amusing traits. In fact we may doubt whether any racial strain once represented in Great Britain has ever died out. As the Normans did not exterminate but only subjugated the Saxons, so these did not destroy but merely displaced the remnants of Roman, Celtic, Iberian, and other peoples which they found on coming to the land. The facial and cranial characteristics of Iberian, Celtic, and Roman peoples are still discernible today in many who bear purely English names; and in English literature the special contribution of the Celt has been precious and pervasive beyond computation.

From a people of such various origins we should not expect a literature clearly stamped with a few racial marks. Certainly we do not find it. A Frenchman, looking above all for clarity, may find the literature of England obscure; a German, looking for a Teutonic obscurity, may think it too clear; but one who listens for the multiple voice of that humanity which outlasts creed and race will find it all things to all men. As Dryden said of Chaucer's poems alone, "Here is God's plenty."

The language of this literature is even more diverse in origin than the people who speak and write it. Those Old English dialects brought to Britain fourteen centuries ago by groups of farmers from the mainland belonged to the Low German branch of the West Germanic languages, and these in turn were of the Teutonic family of the Indo-European race of tongues. Upon these dialects the Norman French of the conquerors exerted a strong and protracted influence, so that even by the time of Chaucer English had become what we call an analytical language—one, that is, which shows the relations between words rather by connectives than by variations in the words themselves. English gained at the same time in precision, it increased its vocabulary and enlarged its range of expressiveness. Before this process was complete there began the influence upon it of Latin, emanating at first from the Church and then from the new learning of the Renaissance. The modern scientific interest, beginning the search for a fresh and yet stable nomenclature, led to many adoptions from ancient Greek, and meanwhile the rapid spread of British power fed the language with importations from the ends of the earth.

English has always been an extremely hospitable language, so that it has today by far the largest vocabulary ever possessed by any civilized tongue. So great have been its powers of assimilation, however, that the general character of the language has not been altered since the time when William Caxton, in 1477, produced the first book printed in England. Now as then, it is a masculine, downright, freely growing and freely moving language, caring less for elegance than for force and less for precision than for large suggestiveness. It offers a wide scope for individual peculiarities, whether good or bad. It will not sustain or conceal a feeble writer so well as French, but it opens a larger field for originality. As compared with Spanish or Latin it is less sonorous, and as compared with Italian or Greek it has less charm of sound, but all that it lacks in pure beauty is atoned for by the bristling strength of its close-packed consonants. The range and expressiveness of its rhythms, whether in prose or verse, is inexhaustible. All speakers, writers, and readers of English are the inheritors and custodians of an incalculable treasure. They enter into a wealth stored up by centuries of the labor of millions of minds.

This fact is the more remarkable because English people have usually been more interested in action than in thought. Since Elizabethan times the conscious cultivation of the graces of speech has not been common in England, and what study of style there has been among the privileged classes has been done chiefly in terms of Latin and Greek. While the French language has been for these three centuries an object of national pride and care, English has been allowed to sprawl and ramble and grow as it would and could.

If it were not for their actual accomplishment one would not think of the English as a people of high artistic gifts. And indeed they have excelled in only one of the arts. In sculpture and in the more creative aspects of the dance they have done little. What has been good in their architecture has been for the most part imported. Although at one time and another England has been deeply interested in music, she has never produced a composer of quite the first rank, and there have been long periods in her history during which even highly cultivated persons were ignorant and almost contemptuous of all musical matters. In painting, to be sure, the national record is highly honorable. In literature it is supreme.

What is meant by this assertion may not be immediately clear. The literatures of China and India have qualities which England cannot approach in their kind. The writing of ancient Greece and Rome, and of several nations of modern Europe, is superior to hers in this and that important respect. England's supremacy in literature has been won not by outdoing each of her rivals in that rival's own peculiar excellence but by an amazing variety and volume of work excellent in many ways at once. In matters of structure, form, and the "feeling for the whole" English writers have usually lagged behind the European. In poise, moderation, and evenness of tone they have often failed. It is in sheer fecundity and in overmastering masculine force that they have won their supremacy.

The poetry of England is even more clearly supreme than its prose. This too is surprising, for without the evidence of what they have written one would not think of the English as a poetic people. Their preoccupation has usually been with facts, with ways and means, and not with visionary or ideal ends. As compared with America England is less dreamy and idealistic. As compared with France she shows more common sense. As compared with Germany she is more steadily aware that "the facts are what they are, and their results will be what they will be." How comes it, then, that the great name of the days when England was founding her empire is not that of Lord Burleigh, chief adviser in business affairs to Queen Elizabeth, but that of the poet Shakespeare? And how did it happen that in those very years when England's empire was haughtiest, when her merchants were most arrogant, and when her treatment of the poor was stupidly brutal, she produced one of the most sensitive, ethereal, and idealistic poets of all time—Percy Shelley?

The fact is that generalizations of the sort in which we have just been indulging are even less applicable to England than they are to most other nations. To understand how so practical a people has made so great a poetry one must consider the number of racial strains and the range of breeding and social rank to be found among them. One must remember, too, that England has usually honored the right of the individual to think his own thoughts, to feel in his own way, and to say what he feels and thinks as he sees fit. A poet of any worth is always and everywhere one in a million, but in England this has seldom discouraged him from bringing in a minority report. That final resort of liberty, often endangered, has never been lost for long, and out of it the English poets have spoken and sung for more than a thousand years.

We are not to suppose that this liberty was easily won, or that it has not needed a stanch defense in every generation. The poetry and the political freedom of England have grown together as though from a single root. In the verse of John Masefield, written today, there is something of Magna Carta. Many years of radical agitation and revolt went to the making of *Piers Plowman*. The splendors of Shakespeare owe much to the political genius of Elizabeth and her ministers. Without Hampden, Pym, and Cromwell *Paradise Lost* would have been a different and a poorer thing. The Romantic Movement, no less than the Neoclassical, was profoundly conditioned if not caused by political changes. Throughout its whole career English poetry has been the privileged voice of that individual freedom, that respect for the dignity and rights of the "single separate person," which we of the English-speaking world owe mainly to the English Houses of Parliament.

It is no wonder, therefore, that England's poets have often served practical ends, or that her men of affairs have often brought the passion of a pure ideal into political life. Edmund Burke speaks many times as a poet, although using "that other harmony of prose," and the John Dryden of the greater satires is as certainly a politician. In the large utterance of Milton at his best no one can fail to hear the hugely magnified echoes of political debate. And often where we should least expect it, as for example in the verses of the mystical shopkeeper William Blake, the worlds of the political reformer and the poetic dreamer are shown to be only one world after all. With a fierce and wholly English audacity Blake welds them together. It is as though an unknown man took the floor for a moment in some representative assembly to speak these burning words:

"I will not cease from mental fight,
   Nor shall my sword sleep in my hand,
Till we have built Jerusalem
   In England's green and pleasant land."

English poetry in its total range and sweep, because it has been made chiefly by free men determined at all hazards to use their freedom, defies every attempt at a compact characterization. With Chaucer it treads the dear brown earth, with Shelley it sings among the clouds, and then with Browning it burrows inward to brood and grope and darkle. Now swift and impetuous and now strongly controlled, it goes richly adorned in one century and sober-suited in another. It can be harsh and raucous as a crow's croak in the gnarled lyrics of John Donne, yet nothing in the world's verbal music surpasses the witchery of Spenser, Swinburne, and Yeats. It can dance in shackles for a hundred years and then suddenly burst into the wind-blown freedom of a fountain.

England's prose is almost as various as her poetry, yet here we can trace the gradual outworking of two traditions found separately in the work of some writers but combined in that of the greatest. In one of these traditions Englishmen have developed a style, well represented by Jonathan Swift, which attains beauty by plain directness. It has the virtue of simplicity, and that of being at all times clear. Some say that this is the only style suited to the English mind and mood. The fact is, however, that from Anglo-Saxon days until this present there has been in English prose a tendency sharply opposed to it, a tradition based on the belief that for the full statement of any thought or feeling a writer should use every device he knows of figurative language, rhythm, and verbal music. Masters of this manner such as Aelfric, Browne, Carlyle, Newman, and Pater do not regard prose as a mere telegraphic mechanism for signaling information from mind to mind. It is to them an ancient and intricate instrument, at least as sensitive as that of verse, for the expression of every thought and mood and guess that can enter the heart or mind.

English literature is by no means simple, and the right reading of it is probably the most difficult task that American college students are set to perform. Fortunately, it is also one of the most rewarding. In good reading one is seldom aware of effort, and one is never wearied. Those are the reader's best hours in which he feels that he himself is bringing forth these phrases with spontaneous ease from some inexhaustible word-hoard of his own. In such a sharing of the creative ecstasy he can almost believe that he has really climbed to his author's level.

Surely it is one of the richest privileges of our lives, and certainly it is a noble companionship—this that is made possible by black marks on white paper.

O.S.

The Early Period

Stonehenge, the most remarkable monument on the isle of Britain. Circles and rows of stone, probably witness to the sacred rites of some of the early inhabitants, rise from the solitude of Salisbury plain, and though partially in ruins today still overpower one with their grandeur, their boldness of construction, their symmetry of design, and the vast labour and mechanical skill requisite to arrange and erect them. (Culver)

The interior of a fourteenth-century hall. This reconstruction of Penshurst, Kent, shows the servants grouped around the fire while the lord and lady dine. Beside the table the jester plays with the dog. (Metropolitan Museum of Art)

Right below. Waterfront of a fourteenth-century continental city. This highly stylized drawing, reproduced from a fourteenth-century manuscript, suggests some of the fancied dangers of sea travel as well as the pomp and circumstance of urban life. (Metropolitan Museum)

Left below. A ship of the middle ages. This miniature painting, out of a manuscript of Froissart's *Chronicles*, represents the Duke of Ireland starting on an expedition. (Bettmann Archive)

Above left. A late scriptorium. The master scribe, Colard Mansion, who became partner in Bruges of William Caxton, later the first English printer, is here dictating to his assistants. (Bettmann Archive)

Above right. A London street scene during the Peasants' Revolt of 1381. Drawn after an illustration in a manuscript of Froissant's *Chronicles*.

Students at a lecture. In the fourteenth century most of the schools were those attached to a religious or charitable institution.

Left. The Tower of London, the grand state prison of England. This engraving from a fifteenth-century manuscript permits a view of the interior showing the heavily guarded French prisoner, the Duke of Orleans, busily writing. Behind the Tower will be seen old London Bridge and beyond that the city itself. This picture is sometimes called the first view of London. (Culver)

Above left. A princely pair hunting with hawks. From long before the days of King Alfred hawking amused the noble and wealthy classes of society. (Bettmann Archive)

Above center. Magdalen (pronounced Maudlen) College, Oxford. In the middle of the thirteenth century regular colleges with living quarters for students were first established. This photograph shows one of the earliest buildings of Magdalen, founded in 1458. (Metropolitan Museum)

Above right. Caxton's workshop in Westminster Abbey. This engraving from a painting by Wenhert suggests the excitement that well may have collected his assistants when Caxton read his first proof sheets in 1477. (Bettmann Archive)

The tournament. The knight when not engaged in defending the lord of the manor spent many hours at tilting-matches and tournaments. (Culver)

Battering castle walls. All the pomp of chivalry was gradually changed by the appearance of cannon and other efficient instruments of war. In the beginning gunpowder was used only as a supplement to long-bows, battering rams, and breaching towers. (Culver)

Above left. A page from Beowulf. (MS in the British Museum)

Above right. A page from Malory's Morte d'Arthur. (Printed in 1529)

Geoffery Chaucer. The Seddon Portrait (fifteenth century). Harvard College Library

Below. Canterbury pilgrims leaving the Tabard. (Bettmann Archive)

THE EARLY PERIOD

PART I: THE OLD ENGLISH ERA

Britain before the English

THE geography of Britain was a determining factor in the spread of its peoples and culture. The island is divided into two clearly demarcated zones: south and midlands, comparatively flat, rich of soil and potentially of great agricultural value; west and north, rude and mountainous. The first (lowland) zone was worth conquest and relatively easy to attack; there the first impacts of peoples and cultures came. To the second (highland) zone they came late and often not at all.

The most striking of the early groups to invade Britain came in Neolithic times; this group moved up the coast from Spain, and is therefore often called Iberian. To it we owe the monuments of various sorts which culminated in such impressive structures as Stonehenge. With the Iron Age the Celts made their first appearance on the island, in the sixth century B.C. There were two waves of invasion, one, the Goidelic (Gaelic), going directly to Ireland, and the other, the Brythonic (British), coming to Britain. A third group of Celtic invaders of Britain were members of the Belgic tribes (partly Germanic in stock) on whom Roman pressure was becoming intolerable in the first century B.C.

British culture followed Continental developments, inevitably with a noticeable time lag. The basic economy was agricultural, but the fact that most of the island was heavily wooded confined early farming to the open upland slopes of the south and west. Soil was originally broken by a light scratch plow; the Belgic Celts seem to have been the first to use a plow of sufficient weight to clear and cultivate the heavier and more fertile soil of the valleys. The usual domestic animals were found; sheep, for example, appeared as early as the Neolithic period. The first account of Britain to be preserved even in part was written by one of Alexander the Great's contemporaries, Pytheas of Marseille, who traded in Cornwall for tin and observed with interest the current methods of curing grain in what is now Kent.

After the family the ordinary human unit was the village or town tribe, sometimes, as in the great fortified hill towns, of considerable size. We have no information concerning the earlier governmental and social institutions, but the Belgic Celts brought the tribal organization of Gaul. The regular presence of funeral goods in the early graves indicates a belief in immortality, running back even to Neanderthal man. Much imaginative nonsense has been, and is being, written about the Celtic priests, the Druids. They had peculiar rites and costumes, they seem to have practiced human sacrifice, they believed in immortality and transmigration, but beyond that it is safe to say only that they were a powerful priestly class with their cult probably originating in, if not centered in, Britain.

With the coming of the Romans, Britain may be said to enter the daylight of history. The Roman invasion was in two parts: first, the raids made by Julius Caesar in 54 and 53 B.C., which were followed by nearly a hundred years of British independence, associated with the name of Cunobelinus (Shakespeare's Cymbeline); and secondly, the final conquest, which began in 43 A.D., under the Emperor Claudius. Caesar was incited by a desire for profit and a wish to prevent the British from aiding their cousins in Gaul; the final Roman invasion arose from the inevitable need of a great predatory military state to extend its frontiers until there are no more. From the middle of the first century until the first quarter of the fifth, Britain was part of the Roman world. Romanization was extensive, appearing especially in the growth of town life, the development of the system of villas (large, often self-sufficient, estates of which the most characteristic feature was the manor house surrounded by slave huts), and the spread of the knowledge of Latin. Indeed, had it not been for the Anglo-Saxon conquest, the present inhabitants would undoubtedly speak a dialect of Latin derivation, akin to French and Spanish.

During this period a considerable number of the Roman Empire's numerous religious cults were introduced by soldiers and merchants. Among these was Christianity, which established itself at least by the third century. The Romano-British Church was small, poor, and largely restricted to the towns. Only the troubles attendant on the English invasions brought Christianity to the countryside, which had hitherto maintained its old paganism. Outstanding among British Christians were their first martyr, St. Alban, their first heretic, Pelagius, and their first missionary, St. Patrick, who carried the faith to Ireland, whence it was to return to North Britain centuries later. With the coming of the English, Christianity fled to Wales, and the strictly British Church was thereafter without significance.

Britain was never among the well-to-do sections of the Roman Empire, but it enjoyed a reasonable prosperity (based on the export of grain and metals) until the fourth century, when a depression hit the towns and had a subsequent unfortunate effect on the villa economy. Added to economic troubles were invasions. The wild tribes north of the walls of Hadrian and Antoninus were constantly ready to break through, and opportunities were given them by governmental disorders, notably the folly of many Roman and Romano-British leaders who took their forces to the Continent in fruitless efforts to seize imperial power. There were raids from Ireland, in one of which the youthful Patrick was carried away to be a slave in the land of his future triumph. Even worse for the Romano-British future were the increasing numbers of Frankish and Saxon pirates who struck from across the Channel and the North Sea. The hard-pressed government in Rome found it increasingly difficult to aid the beleaguered province, and finally in 410 the Emperor Honorius was forced to tell his British subjects that henceforth they were at liberty to defend themselves.

The English Invasions

The Anglo-Saxon *Chronicle* (page 81), drawing from Bede (page 62), tells us that in 449 a British king invited two Germanic chieftains, Hengist and Horsa, to come to Britain as mercenary soldiers against the marauding Picts. The visitors were eminently successful in battle, but shortly, having perceived "the sluggishness of the Britons and the excellence of the land," they sent home for reinforcements. Then "there came men from three German tribes, the Old Saxons, the Angles, and the Jutes. From the Jutes came the men of Kent and the Isle of Wight. . . . From the Old Saxons came the East Saxons, the South Saxons, and the West Saxons. From the Angles . . . came the East Anglians, the Middle Anglians, the Mercians and all the Northumbrians."

Unfortunately we are unable to accept this succinct account at its face value. The English conquest of Britain was very nearly the last of those extensive mass migrations from the North which accompanied and hastened the breakup of the Roman Empire. Despite all that the Romano-Britons could do, by the middle of the fifth century numerous groups of Germans had come to Britain to stay.

These Germanic tribes—and to those listed in the *Chronicle* we must add a few Frisians and fewer Franks—had a number of things in common. They all came from the coastal area on one side or the other of the Danish Peninsula or from the lower part of that peninsula. Linguistically they all spoke the Low German branch of the West Germanic dialect (from the other branch of West Germanic—High German—modern literary German developed). In the main they were a simple farmer and fisher folk. The piratical expeditions which we associate almost exclusively with their way of life were probably no more than the source of incidental luxuries, while the ordinary means of existence were wrested with heavy labor from the soil and the sea.

Thanks to the tenacity of the peat bogs, we have even today the scanty remains of a few of our linguistic ancestors attired in their habit as they lived. We are particularly struck by the trousers, which, belt holes and all, are singularly modern in appearance. They also wore linen tunics, often bolstered with fur against the winter cold. Their armor and arms, many of Roman origin or on Roman models, have survived, proving that they were well equipped in the materials of war.

Many of their gods were only local divinities inseparably attached to local shrines, but they had some deities in common, and by the fourth century Woden (Odin) drove Thunor (Thor) from his place as chief god. Thor was the fighting farmers' god, a simple giant-killer likely to attract the common people, while Woden was a clever god who invented runes, went about in disguise, and appeared as a somewhat gloomy, one-eyed solver of difficulties in mainly aristocratic circles. The tribes had an alphabet of peculiar-looking letters called runes, which were used for inscriptions indicating the ownership of property, for purposes of divination, and for magic healing, but not, so far as we know, for literary composition.

The first social unit was the family, developing inevitably into the clan. The spirit of the comitatus (strong feeling of loyalty to the chieftain) is marked in English literature and history; see the famous passages in *Beowulf* (page 45) and *The Battle of Maldon* (page 61) and compare the action of Harold's house carls in dying around their lord at Hastings. As far as the larger aspects of government go, the Continental Angles had had at least one powerful king, Offa; about the Saxons we are by no means so sure, as there is evidence of their having had many minor local leaders. There was doubtless co-operation and local leeway, but if our ancestors actually conducted their affairs by a series of moots from the small town meeting up to the general folk moot, they were not considerate enough to leave any records of them.

Our knowledge of the course of the English conquest of Britain is inferential and often confused. The invasion was actually in two chapters, in the first of which the invaders swept back and forth across the island, seeking only plunder and leaving behind them a trail of sacked towns and burning villas. Because their sole aim was immediate gain, they could strike lightning blows at the weakest and richest points, while the Britons, bound to their individual localities by tradition and inertia, were able to put up at best only the sterile and limited resistance of self-preservation. The second chapter, however, shows a consolidation of British forces, and in it we seem to find the Britons rather more than holding their own. With this period we associate the names of Ambrosius Aurelianus, whose historicity we have no reason to doubt, and Arthur, who—if he existed at all—was apparently a military leader of less than royal rank, at the head of a mobile fighting force. The course of the invasion, although slowed down, could not be checked, and when in the sixth century we first get a reasonably clear view of the situation, we find the so-called lowland zone occupied by at least ten English kingdoms of varying sizes, of which the most important were, or were to be, Kent, Northumbria, Mercia, and Wessex. Around them on the west and north from Cornwall to the land of the Picts stretched a line of Celtic kingdoms, the gradual assimilation of which by the English was not to be completed until the seventeenth century.

It was formerly believed that those Britons who did not escape to the Celtic kingdoms of the highland zone, or across the Channel to Gaul, were massacred. It is now held that a very considerable number of Britons survived as slaves, or subtenants nearly on the level of slaves, to be ultimately absorbed into the largely Germanic population. The next few centuries of English history saw the steady growth of the larger English kingdoms at the expense of the Celts or their smaller Germanic neighbors, and a shift of political supremacy from Northumbria to Mercia and finally to Wessex.

Heroic Poetry

Most so-called primitive races possess an oral literature which is transmitted by word of mouth from generation to generation. The Anglo-Saxons were no exception to this rule, and they brought with them to Britain the rich traditions of the general Germanic heroic literature, with its stirring tales—already crystallized into poetic form—of gods and heroes. That relatively little of this older story-stuff survives is due in part to the long, troublous period intervening between the invasion and the establishment of a written tradition, in part to Christian expurgation and substitution, and in part to the vicissitudes which befell Old English manuscripts, viscissitudes ranging in time from the Danish invasions to the dissolution of the monasteries under Henry VIII. The amazing thing, actually, is that we have as much as we do.

The poet, scop, or gleeman was a prominent and respected figure in Germanic life. He recited or chanted the traditional poems, and could compose more or less extemporaneously on subjects new as well as old, as is shown in *Beowulf* (page 28). He needed a good memory, a ready wit, and an ability to apply old formulas to new events but, unlike his descendant of today, he did not need trained vocal organs. Delivery was much, no doubt, but matter was more. Old English poetry employed not end rhyme but initial rhyme or alliteration ("apt alliteration's artful aid"), a device known to almost all literatures but employed systematically only by the Germanic peoples. The line ordinarily has four feet, divided in the middle by a marked pause, and ordinarily contains three alliterating syllables. The opening lines of *Beowulf* may be quoted as an example:

"Hwaet, we Gar-Dena   in geardagum
þeodcyninga   þrym gefrunon,
Hu þa æþelingas   ellen fremedon!
Oft Scyld Scefing   sceaþena þreatum
Monegum mægþum   meodosetla ofteah,
Egsode eorlas,   syþþan ærest wearð
Feasceaft funden;   he þæs frofre gebad,
Weox under wolcnum,   weorðmyndum þah,
Oð þæt him æghwylc   þara ymbsittendra
Ofer hronrade   hyran scolde,
Gomban gyldan;   þæt wæs god cyning!"

The possible wealth of Old English poetic themes is illustrated by *Widsith*, a very early poem which, under an obviously fictitious autobiographical guise, is clearly a catalogue, perhaps a reminder, of the heroes about whom a bard could sing. Here we find listed some seventy peoples—a few of them sufficiently Biblical or classical to be the result of interpolation—and nearly as many heroes. When we turn from this imposing list to the remnants of Old English heroic verse we see at once what our loss has been. Apart from a few names scattered here and there in works to which they are merely incidental, we find little enough. *Deor's Lament* (page 51) is almost as much a catalogue as *Widsith* and in some respects more tantalizing. In addition there are two brief fragments, one of which, *The Finnsburg Fragment*, supplements, or is supplemented by, a passage in *Beowulf* (page 30). The second fragment, really two fragments, is *Waldere*, which tells the story of the escape of Walter of Aquitaine and his betrothed Hildegund from the court of Attila. The English fragments would give us no notion of the story, but we have an early tenth-century Latin version, the *Waltharius*. The greatest monument of Old English heroic poetry—indeed, in some respects the greatest monument of Germanic poetry—is *Beowulf*. This poem is discussed more particularly later (pages 16–17), but here we must note that the plot, part folk tale, part heroic legend, and part history, has nothing English about it; the Christian element and the style, however, could not have been found anywhere in the northern Germanic world except England at the time of the composition of the poem.

Often certain other poems, such as *The Wanderer*, *The Seafarer*, *The Ruin*, *The Wife's Complaint*, *The Husband's Message*, are referred to as being in spirit, if not in substance, of the non-Christian period, but Old English poetry is so permeated with Christianity as to make any differentiation between pagan and Christian poetry an almost futile formality.

The Growth of Christianity

In 597 the relatively small kingdom of Kent was, for the only time in its history, the leading English state, mainly because of the wisdom and diplomatic skill of its ruler, Aethelbert,[1] who had married the daughter of the Christian Frankish king of Paris, and had permitted his wife to practice her Christian faith in Canterbury, his capital. When Augustine, sent by Pope Gregory with a band of fellow missionaries, arrived, Kent became Christian speedily and without opposition. The people as a whole took to the new faith with passivity, if not with enthusiasm. During the first century or so the English showed a disconcerting tendency to apostasy, but they did not fight Christianity. One may plausibly explain this on the grounds that Germanic heathenism, bound as it was to sacred places and local shrines, did not lend itself to transportation. The Christian missionaries, in other words, had to contend not with a flourishing rival faith but rather with a somewhat wearied agnosticism (see especially Bede's account of the conversion of King Edwin, page 62).

Augustine established in England the diocesan organization of the Church, which was to prevail in the years to come. The various dioceses were to be strictly controlled by their bishops. The head of the English Church was the Bishop, soon the Archbishop, of Canterbury, who in his turn was directly responsible to Rome.

In the meantime the Irish Church, cut off almost completely from the rest of the Christian world, was winning converts in the north. Differing from the

[1] For the chronology of the English rulers see page 1121.

Roman Church in organization (monastic rather than diocesan), in the form of the tonsure, and in the dating of Easter, it was brought to Iona, an island off the west coast of Scotland, by Columba in 565. The first great Irish missionary to Northumbria, the saintly Aidan—to whom King Oswald gave Lindisfarne (Holy Island) off the east coast— was simple, pious, unaffected, as zealous for the salvation of a peasant as for that of a king. St. Cuthbert (pages 68–73) was a worthy successor of Aidan in spirit and practice.

It was inevitable that there should be rivalry and conflict between the two variants of Christianity, and inevitably this rivalry came to a head. When in 664, Oswy, King of Northumbria and the greatest monarch in England, called a synod at Whitby, the result seemed by no means certain; but Oswy declared in favor of the Roman side. The importance of the complete shift to Rome does not require emphasis; it brought an infant Church and an infant civilization into firm and lasting contact with the wellspring and reservoir of faith and civilization on the Continent.

Aside from pure religion, the greatest value of the Church lay in the field of education. Augustine had established a school at Canterbury, but it was only in 669 with the coming of Theodore of Tarsus (602–690), the great organizer and administrator of the early English Church, and his coadjutor Hadrian that it took genuine stature as an institution of higher ecclesiastical learning. Latin, of course, was the basic language in instruction, but Greek, still used in some of the services, was taught, and Hebrew was not unknown to the more advanced scholars. Naturally enough the chanting of the services demanded that great emphasis be laid on music. Although the remains of Old English architecture are few and disappointing, we know that masons, master builders, and workers in stained glass were imported from the Continent. So too, and far more important for literary development, were manuscripts, which while largely religious in character were not without a valuable admixture of classical literary material. Trips to the Continent, especially to Rome, were frequent, and introduced a wholesome leaven of cosmopolitan culture; the pilgrims included laymen as well as clerics, and apparently a not inconsiderable number of women. Such men as Benedict Biscop (628–690), an inveterate traveler and collector of books, relics, and craftsmen, did much to enrich English culture.

The Church also came to play an important role in strictly governmental affairs. It held itself to be a power apart from, at least equal, and in some respects superior, to secular authority. As such it favored the codification and writing down of laws, the survey and regularization of landholdings, the systematization of taxes and tithes, and, as the Church grew more powerful, the general domination of one national state in the place of several smaller, weaker, poorer kingdoms. Naturally enough, the mere ability to read and write made clerics invaluable to the kings and nobles and gave them rich opportunities to advance their desires, although it must be admitted that the opposition of a stubborn State to a proud Church arose early in England.

Christian Poetry

With the coming of Christianity Old English literature received its first chance of preservation. However much the English loved and however long they remembered their traditional lays, the mechanical aid of an alphabet was necessary for survival through the centuries. The missionaries brought an alphabet; in addition they early established scriptoria in which copying, and even composition, went on incessantly. Most Old English poetry was written or revised by clerics, and it was all copied by them. Naturally, this Christian influence had a profound effect on the substance and coloring of the literature. We could hardly expect that pagan poetry, glorifying the old way of life, presenting heathen customs and emphasizing gods whom the Christian considered at best the Devil's first cousins, should meet with Christian approval and win preservation at Christian hands; but much that is characteristic of the older days escaped expurgation.

The poems of Continental origin whose stories evolved in pagan surroundings are given a Christian coloring in England. *Beowulf* (page 16) is an intrinsically Christian poem, even the brief *Waldere* fragments contain Christian touches, and the charms (pages 55–57), which are in essence folk poetry of a somewhat sophisticated nature, are an almost inextricable mixture of heathen and Christian. The tinting, however, was not all in one direction. Old English verse of Christian or even of classical origin is often surprisingly heroic in spirit. We are naturally impressed when the Germanic demigod Welund (Wayland; page 51) turns up in an English version of Boethius's *De Consolatione Philosophiae*, but elements in the strictly Christian verse, though less spectacular, are really more important.

We know two Old English Christian poets by name. The earlier of these is Caedmon, of whom we know what Bede tells us (pages 63–64), and of whose authentic works we have only the hymn which Bede paraphrases, which also survives in its original Northumbrian form. Of the poems formerly, but no longer, ascribed to Caedmon, but which may well have sprung from the school of Biblical paraphrase which he inaugurated, two deserve mention. *Genesis* is really two poems, one inserted bodily into the other. This interpolation, denominated *Genesis B*, is a translation or adaptation from Old Saxon and could not have been written before the time of Alfred. It deals with the revolt and fall of Satan and contains some of the best passages in Old English Christian poetry. *Genesis A*, while a far less meritorious piece, contains vivid battle scenes which exhibit the Germanic taste evident in much Old English Christian poetry. *Exodus* has been often called a little epic, almost as much Germanic as Christian. The poem deals with the crossing of the Red Sea, and the author describes the fate of the unhappy Egyptians with a zest which still moves the reader.

When we come to Cynewulf, second of the Old English Christian poets, we find a situation quite opposite to that of Caedmon: we know little or nothing of the poet's life and a good deal about his poems. Cynewulf had the convenient habit of signing his name (by the insertion of letters from the old runic alphabet) near the end of his works. Thus we know that he wrote *Juliana*, *The Fates of the Apostles*, *Elene*, and at least the middle portion of *Christ*. Cynewulf's poems afford clear proof that he came later than the author of the Caedmonian pieces (except *Genesis B*). He was a man trained in religious scholarship, primarily interested in non-Biblical Christian literature, and far more subjective than any of his predecessors. War was of little interest to him, but the sea exercised an enormous fascination upon his imagination. Among the poems sometimes ascribed to Cynewulf is *Andreas*, an account of St. Andrew's trip to aid St. Matthew among the Mermedonians. No other Old English poem, not even *The Seafarer*, treats the sea so well, and in addition the feeling of Christ's disciples toward their Master is as purely that of the members of the heroic comitatus as anything we find in *Beowulf* or *The Battle of Maldon*. Also ascribed to Cynewulf, *The Dream of the Rood* (pages 52–53), in many respects the high-water mark of Old English Christian poetic endeavor, glows with genuine and touching spirituality.

Early Old English poetry was all composed in one of the two Anglian dialects, those of Northumbria and Mercia, and was largely Northumbrian. The overwhelming bulk of Old English literature has, however, been transmitted to us in West Saxon, the dialect of Wessex. This situation is due to the fact that the surviving literary prose, invariably later in origin than verse, was of West Saxon composition, and that the older poetry was "translated" for a West Saxon audience.

The Danes and Alfred

We cannot attempt to trace here the tangled course of Anglo-Saxon political history before the accession of Alfred (871). After the short-lived leadership of Kent, the spasmodically united Northumbrian kingdoms of Bernicia and Deira had a long, though fitful, period of political supremacy, until the eighth century saw Northumbria pass into a period of virtual anarchy, from which it never recovered. In the meantime two long-lived and gifted kings brought Mercia to its period of greatness. In the ninth century Mercia stagnated and saw the rise of the hitherto obscure state of Wessex, which under the energetic leadership of King Ecgbert assumed the overlordship of England and much of Wales by 830. But a new wave of invaders—beginning as early as 787—made the leadership of Wessex a painful and almost empty matter. Not long after there were more disastrous raids in the north, during which Lindisfarne, sacred to Aidan and Cuthbert, and Jarrow, where Bede (page 62) had lived his long and fruitful life, were sacked. These new invaders, Norwegians as well as Danes, were the last of the Germanic peoples to strike out from their Northern home. They were a tough, hard, aggressive lot, not without interest in the arts, boasting an unwritten literature as tough as themselves and brilliant to a degree; they were careless of human life, risking their own existences at the drop of a sword or a spear, massacring hundreds, even thousands, of captured foes as a blood sacrifice to Odin, wily in battle, merciless in victory, and blandly treacherous in defeat. Like their cousins the Anglo-Saxons, they came first as piratical plunderers and later became invaders and settlers. Unlike the Anglo-Saxons, they did not devote themselves solely to England; Ireland and West Scotland absorbed most of their energies during the period when Ecgbert was establishing the overlordship of Wessex. But in 886 a Danish army came to England for bad and all. With sensational, remorseless speed the Danes made Northumbria and East Anglia their own, terrified and partly occupied the remnants of Mercia, and forced Wessex to the first of a long series of inglorious and unsuccessful efforts to buy even a temporary peace.

In 871 Alfred ascended a far from stable throne. Alfred was the first king of the English to be acclaimed as truly great by tradition and history, and it is doubtful whether any subsequent monarch fares as well in the people's judgment. From his boyhood Alfred was the bookish—that is, literate—member of his family, but the days of trial found him the only real heir of Ecgbert. Our literary emphasis makes us picture Alfred too much as the king of letters, the pallid scholar rising reluctantly from his manuscripts to kill a book-destroying Dane. Despite a predilection for learning, despite the lifelong ill-health which hounded all his father's sons, Alfred was the greatest strategist, the most canny diplomat, and well-nigh the bravest fighter of all the long line of English rulers in whose veins has flowed—and, however diluted, still flows—the blood of the Wessex kings. Alfred's genuine greatness shines forth nowhere more radiantly than in those horrible months when he was forced to lurk, almost alone, in the misty, dismal swamps of Somersetshire. He had trust in his star, in the integrity of his faith, in the loyalty of his folk, and in the future of his land. In no one of these things was he mistaken, and in seven years he brought about the miracle of excluding the Danes from that part of England which lies south of a line drawn from the mouth of Thames to Chester, where the river Dee runs downward to the Irish Sea. Alfred and Guthrum, temporarily ruler of the unruly Scandinavians, came to terms in 878 in the so-called Peace of Wedmore, which meant one overwhelming thing: English England was to survive.

With a few relatively minor disturbances, Alfred was able to devote the remainder of his reign (for which see also page 65) to the political and intellectual betterment of his realm. He possessed singularly clear foresight in governmental matters. He saw and observed the wisdom of preserving local autonomy in the sections of his kingdom other than his own Wessex. As a practical measure of defense he created a series of boroughs (towns) at strategic points. Here we are probably justified in finding the origin of organized town life in England. The earlier English had not perceived the advantages of Romano-British urban centers, nor did their manner of existence lend itself to closely settled areas. The older English unit was the tun (modern English town); that is, a central hall where communal life was carried out and where the unmarried retainers slept, the hall surrounded by smaller and more private residences, sheds, and barns, the whole shut in by a palisade which sometimes had the added protection of a ditch (moat). The tun might well be the nucleus for the huts of serfs and slaves, who in times of trouble fled to the safety of the stockade. By discreet use of public lands Alfred strengthened patriotic and competent noblemen as focal points of local rule and, what is historically even more important, he made use of foreign craftsmen to create an effective English navy.

Alfred's heirs brought considerable sections of Danish England back under English rule, until Aethelstan—at least after the battle of Brunanburh in 937, where he defeated a miscellaneous but ferocious confederacy of Danes, Scots, and Welsh—was generally recognized at home and on the Continent as "*Rex totius Britanniae.*" Under Aethelstan's successors, however, internal dissension, weakness and cowardice, desire for private privilege and personal immunity, had by 1016 subjected the unhappy English to a renewed and even more fateful series of Scandinavian raids. Then Canute the Dane, lord of an Anglo-Scandinavian empire for the nineteen years of his reign, proved himself a devoted ruler of his adopted land, the last able and successful king of England before the Norman Conquest.

Beowulf

About the year 1000 two scribes copied a manuscript in which were brought together in this order three prose works: a fragmentary *Christophorus*, *The Wonders of the East*, *The Letter of Alexander to Aristotle;* and two poems: *Beowulf* and *Judith*. This manuscript, now in the British Museum under the name of Cotton Vitellius A. XV, is probably the most valuable single treasure of English literary history, and that because it contains the *Beowulf*, which is not only our sole Old English epic but also by many centuries the first great literary work to be preserved in any of the vernacular languages of Europe. For five hundred years and more the manuscript doubtless remained in some ecclesiastical library until the time of the dissolution of the monasteries in the thirties of the sixteenth century. While untold thousands of its fellows suffered immediate destruction or the greater humiliation of wrapping fish or butter, it was preserved, probably not because of anyone's appreciation of its actual value, but because of current theological and antiquarian interests which were leading to a gradual rediscovery of the Old English language and literature.

Lawrence Nowell, the earliest compiler of an Old English dictionary, would appear to have had it in his possession in 1563, and it subsequently passed into the hands of Sir Robert Cotton, who died in 1631. In 1700 one of Sir Robert's descendants presented it, with the rest of the family's priceless collection, to the English Government. Humfrey Wanley, writing in George Hickes's *Thesaurus*, 1705, was the first to notice the *Beowulf*, but he evidently treated it in singularly cursory fashion, with especial reference to beginning and end, since his summary shows that he thought the poem to deal with the wars of Beowulf, a Danish prince of the Scylding stock, against the Swedes. In 1731 the manuscript, then lodged in Ashburnham House, narrowly escaped burning in the fire which consumed so many of its companions; as it was it suffered a scorching, which, for want of proper attention, resulted in the breaking away of a number of the margins with a consequent loss or mutilation of words and letters. An Icelander living in Denmark, Grimur Thorkelin, began in 1786 to prepare an edition which finally appeared in 1815; ironically enough, he had been nearly ready to publish his work when the English bombardment of Copenhagen in 1807 burned his house and destroyed much of his material. The first English edition appeared in 1833, and since that time there have been numerous editions and translations and innumerable studies, many of which, notably the meteorological interpretations and the frenzied pleas for multiple authorships, are as dead as the scholars who wrote them.

The *Beowulf* is an epic, but of "literary" rather than "popular" composition, which relates two widely separated episodes in the life of its hero. Despite the relative lateness of the manuscript and the fact that the language of the poem as we have it is predominantly West Saxon, the original was composed in the first half of the eighth century in an Anglian dialect, almost certainly Northumbrian. The story is simple enough: Beowulf, a youthful prince of the Geats, goes to Denmark and there kills two monsters, one in the king's hall and the other in an underwater lair. Later he becomes king of the Geats, and in his old age is killed while slaying a dragon which is ravaging his land. By means of an expansive treatment, frequent digressions (taking up some seven hundred lines), many speeches (ranging from four to one hundred sixty lines and using over thirteen hundred lines in all), descriptions, reflections, and moralization, the poet has spun his material out to cover nearly thirty-two hundred lines. Obviously this is no direct narrative, and the use of reminiscence and prophecy, coupled with such purely stylistic devices as variation, litotes, and kennings (metaphorical names), will often make the reader feel that the last thing the author is attempting is to advance his story in a lucid and logical fashion. Indeed, the reader who feels this will probably be correct, for it is not merely the story element which makes *Beowulf* a great poem.

A widely spread folk tale, usually called "The Bear's Son Tale," was attached in Northern Europe to a lad called Beowulf, whose very name, "beewolf," is a kenning for "bear." There are numerous analogues to the story, the most striking of which occur in the lively Icelandic saga of *Grettir the Strong* (translated by G. A. Hight, Everyman's Library; see especially pages 86–100, and 170–77). Later Beowulf was made into a prince, the folk tale was lifted bodily to a historical or pseudo-historical setting, and the whole was finally worked into an epic, with the emphasis on the noble character of the hero rather than on bold deeds alone. Character analysis is one of the author's chief preoccupations. As Klaeber remarks: "He is ever ready to analyze the thoughts and feelings of Beowulf and Hrothgar, the Danes and the Geats, Grendel and his kind, even down to the sea-monsters and the birds of prey. Their intentions, resolutions, expectations, hopes, fears, longings, rejoicings, and mental sufferings engage his constant attention. In a moment of intensest action, such as the combat with Grendel, the state of mind of the characters is carefully taken note of."[1]

The mingling of heathen and Christian elements is a matter which has long interested students of the poem. We have here an old pagan story retold by a Christian poet and, almost inevitably, certain heathen traces remain. Among these are the frequent references to Wyrd or Fate; the fashion in which the Danes are said to have tried to ward off the sudden attacks of Grendel: "Sometimes they offered sacrifices at the heathen temples, begged with words that the slayer of demons would aid them against the great calamity. Such was their custom, the hope of the heathen"; and the references to burning the dead, especially the striking and full account of Beowulf's funeral rites. All these things are truly pagan, but there is no possibility, as was formerly held, that the Christian elements are the result of interpolation. Christianity, although not of the profoundly theological kind, is part of the essence of the poem.

In judging the *Beowulf* we must not permit our pleasure at its very existence to inspire extravagant praise, nor should we allow apparent defects to lead us to an attitude of unappreciative scorn. Critics who complain that the *Beowulf* is inferior to the best parts of the *Iliad* and the *Odyssey* are simply ignoring the realities of literary history and literary criticism. The *Beowulf* is a genuine poem; it is no fortuitous aggregation of rough and primitive ballads. It was written by an artist of no mean skill, and we must not quarrel with him because his material is not always to our taste or his methods always our methods. We may not fancy his continual allusions to other stories, but that is because we do not understand the references, and this very allusiveness must have given the greatest associative pleasure to the original hearers or readers of the poem. Again, we are not always pleased with his sententiousness and moralizations, but here one may venture to suggest that great literature, of whatever age or land, has seldom been devoid of ethical significance and expression. He had an almost complete mastery over his verse form and a great talent for powerful statement and vivid description. There are few things to equal Hrothgar's picture of the mere in which Grendel's mother lived, and the subsequent first-hand account of it is almost as good. One has only to read the passage telling of Grendel's visit to Heorot to understand the poet's skill in building up an effect.

Above all the poem is idealistic, and here Christianity has had a profound effect on the pagan reality. Beowulf is no bloodthirsty Viking or mad berserker, but one of the first great Christian heroes. His life is one of bravery and justice, and his death illustrates the conduct of the perfect king, and also that of the perfect retainer, and this is the climax and the lesson of the poem, basically pagan and of the North, but somehow restrained, purified, and ennobled.

An admirable book for the beginner is William W. Lawrence, *Beowulf and Epic Tradition*, Harvard University Press, 1928, while the more advanced student will turn to R. W. Chambers, *Beowulf*, 2d ed., Macmillan, 1932. Some of the most acute and rewarding criticism of the poem is to be found in the introduction of Friedrich Klaeber's edition, already referred to, published by Heath, from the third edition of which the present translation has been made.

---

1. **Beowulf**, ed. by Friedrich Klaeber, 3d ed., Heath, 1936, pages lviii–lix.

Genealogies

Careful study of, and frequent references to, the following genealogies of the principal royal families who appear in the *Beowulf* should be of considerable assistance to the student.

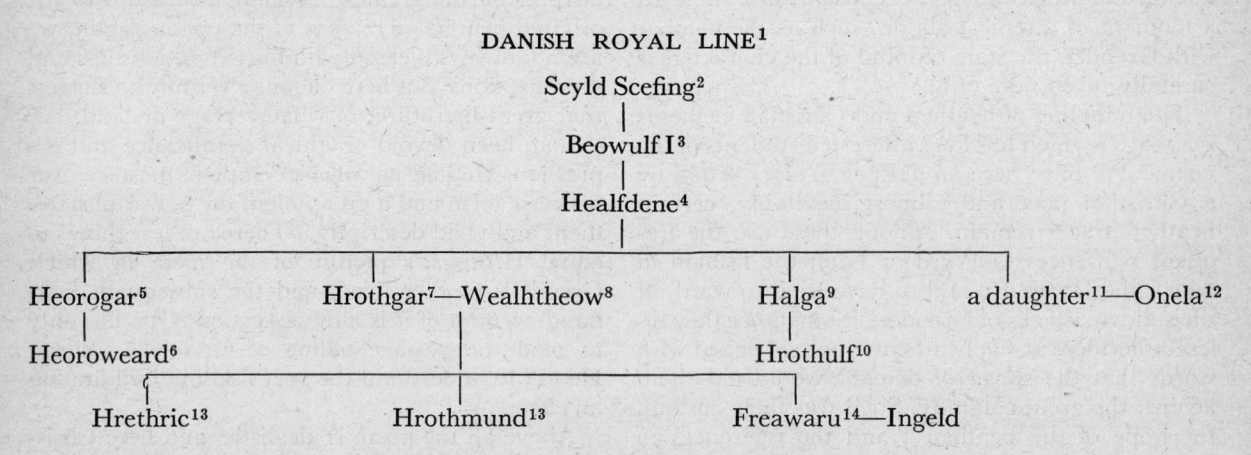

DANISH ROYAL LINE[1]

Scyld Scefing[2]
|
Beowulf I[3]
|
Healfdene[4]

Heorogar[5]	Hrothgar[7]—Wealhtheow[8]	Halga[9]	a daughter[11]—Onela[12]
Heoroweard[6]		Hrothulf[10]	
Hrethric[13]	Hrothmund[13]	Freawaru[14]—Ingeld	

[1] For a more complete account of the members of the Danish royal line, see Klaeber, *op. cit.*, pages xxx ff.

[2] Scyld, that is, Shield, son of Scef ("-ing" is a patronymic suffix), that is, Sheaf, is completely mythical. He is evidently a culture hero symbolizing war or defense, who followed a culture hero symbolizing agriculture.

[3] Not the hero of the poem, but a Beowa or Beaw or the like, whose name has been contaminated by poet or scribe under the influence of the name of Beowulf the Geat.

[4] The first historical or semihistorical king of the Danes.

[5] Heorogar succeeded his father, but had only a short reign.

[6] At his father's death Heoroweard was passed over in favor of his uncle Hrothgar.

[7] King of the Danes during the first part of the poem.

[8] His queen, whose position at court serves to illustrate the high place held by women in the Germanic world.

[9] Nothing is known of Halga, except that he was Healfdene's son and died leaving a young son of his own.

[10] Hrothulf was brought up by his uncle Hrothgar and occupied a position in the Danish court second only to the king. The poet, however, hints darkly at family strife in the future, in the course of which Hrothulf would seem to have taken the throne for himself, despite the greater claims of his two cousins.

[11] A very shadowy figure.

[12] See the genealogy of the Swedish royal line, page 19, note 5.

[13] The sons of Hrothgar, who were, one would judge, fated to be deprived of their royal rights by their older cousin Hrothulf.

[14] Freawaru was married to Ingeld, a prince of the Heathobards, in what was destined to be a vain attempt to end a feud, since the ultimate result was the burning of Heorot.

GEATISH ROYAL LINE[1]

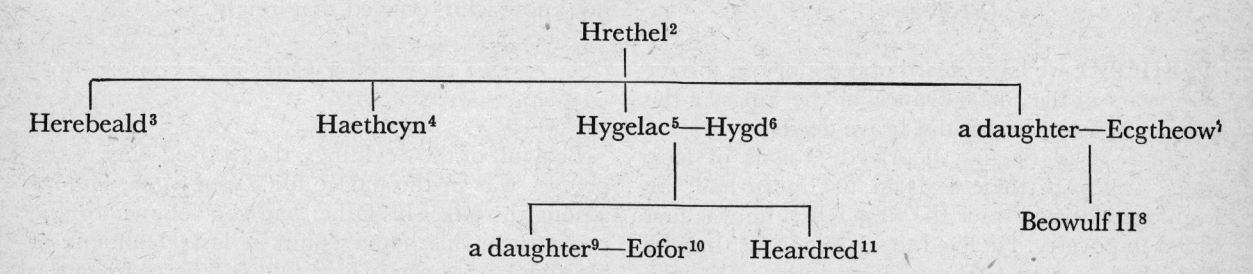

Hrethel[2]

- Herebeald[3]
- Haethcyn[4]
- Hygelac[5]—Hygd[6]
  - a daughter[9]—Eofor[10]
  - Heardred[11]
- a daughter—Ecgtheow[7]
  - Beowulf II[8]

[1] For a more complete account of the Geatish royal line see Klaeber, *op. cit.*, pages xxxviii ff.

[2] No mythological figure appears among the Geats. Hrethel is the first ruler named, and although Swerting, mentioned in line 1203, has been conjectured to be Hrethel's father, this is far from certain.

[3] Herebeald was accidentally killed by an arrow from the bow of his brother Haethcyn.

[4] Haethcyn, who succeeded Hrethel, was killed in a war against the Swedes, but the remnant of his forces was rescued by his brother Hygelac.

[5] Hygelac was king of the Geats during the first part of the poem. He is identified with the historical Chlochilaicus, who was killed in a raid against the Franks and Frisians about 521.

[6] Hygd is sometimes thought to have been Hygelac's second wife, but this is without substantial proof.

[7] Ecgtheow was a Waegmunding who, because of having killed a man, was forced to leave the Geats and take refuge with the Danes. Hrothgar settled the feud, and gratitude for this kindness was one of the factors which moved Beowulf to attempt the cleansing of Heorot. As a matter of fact, it is more than likely that Ecgtheow is unhistorical and was introduced among the Waegmundings, of whom Wiglaf and his father Weohstan were genuine members, to furnish Beowulf with a father.

[8] The hero of the poem, not to be confused with the Beowulf who appears in the Danish royal line.

[9] This nameless daughter has been taken as the offspring of Hygelac's first marriage, but see note 6 above.

[10] Eofor killed Ongentheow in the battle referred to in note 4 above, and was rewarded with the hand of the new king's daughter.

[11] When Hygelac died, the throne was offered to Beowulf, who, however, refused to interfere with the rightful succession of Heardred. The hero served as his cousin's guardian and, when Heardred was killed in a renewed war with the Swedes succeeded him.

SWEDISH ROYAL LINE[1]

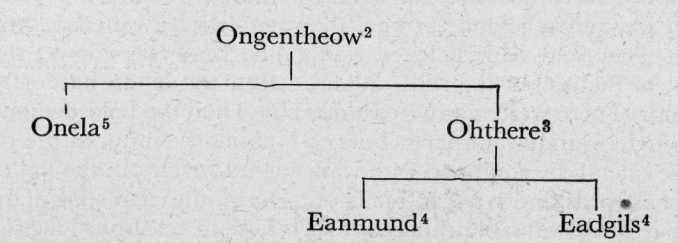

Ongentheow[2]

- Onela[5]
- Ohthere[3]
  - Eanmund[4]
  - Eadgils[4]

[1] See Klaeber, *op. cit.*, pages xxxviii ff.

[2] Ongentheow was king of the Swedes when war broke out between them and the Geats after Haethcyn became king of the latter. Following an initial success of the Geats, Ongentheow attacked and killed Haethcyn, but next day was himself overthrown and slain by Hygelac and his men.

[3] Ohthere apparently succeeded his father, but his reign would appear to have been of short duration.

[4] When their father died, the two princes were driven into exile by their uncle Onela, and sought shelter among the Geats.

[5] Onela, whose wife was Hrothgar's sister, usurped the throne at his brother's death, and pursued his nephews into Geatland, where he and his forces killed Eanmund and his protector Heardred. He did not, however, prevent Beowulf from becoming king of the Geats. Ultimately Eadgils, with Geatish assistance, slew Onela and became king of the Swedes.

BEOWULF

[Prologue]

BEHOLD, we have heard of the glory in former years of the Spear-Danes, of the kings of the people, how the heroes did brave deeds!

Often Scyld Scefing deprived crowds of foes, many tribes, of their seats in the mead-hall; he frightened heroes, after the time when he was first found in poverty. He lived to see solace for that, he flourished on earth, prospered in honors, until each of the neighboring peoples across the whale-road had to obey him and pay tribute—that was a good king. Afterwards a son, youthful in the house, was born to him, whom God sent as a comfort to the people. He beheld the great distress that they had suffered before, when they were earlier without a king for a long time. On that account the Lord of Life, the Ruler of Glory, gave him worldly honor. Beowulf, the son of Scyld, was famous in Scedeland, his renown spread far. Thus a young man ought to bring about good, with splendid gifts from his father's possessions, so that his dear companions in turn will stand by him in his old age, his people serve him when war comes. With praiseworthy deeds a man is sure to prosper among every people. At his fated hour the vigorous Scyld went into the protection of the Lord. His dear companions brought him to the shore of the sea, as the friendly lord of the Scyldings himself had requested while he could still use words. There at the harbor stood a ring-prowed ship which the beloved ruler had had for a long time, covered with ice and ready to set out, the boat of the prince. They laid their beloved lord, their giver of rings, in the hull of the ship, the famous one by the mast. There were many treasures, precious objects brought from distant parts. I never heard of a ship more splendidly equipped with war-weapons and armor, swords and coats of mail; on his breast lay a great many valuable things which were to go with him far into the water's possession. Not at all less did they provide him with gifts, great treasures, than did those who in the beginning sent him out alone, a child over the waves. Then, too, they set a golden banner high over his head, let the sea bear him, gave him to the ocean; theirs was a sad heart, a mournful mind. To tell the truth, the men, counselors in hall, warriors under heaven, did not know who received that freight.

[Part One]

I

Beowulf of the Scyldings, the beloved king of the people, was in the palace for a long time, famous among the folk—his father had gone elsewhere, the prince from his home—until at last Healfdene of high rank was born to him. Old and fierce in battle, he ruled the joyful Scyldings as long as he lived. To the leader of hosts four children all told were born into the world: Heorogar and Hrothgar and the good Halga; I have heard that the fourth was Onela's queen, the dear bedfellow of the Battle-Scylfing.

Then success in war and glory in battle was given to Hrothgar, so that his retainers obeyed him gladly, until the young warriors increased, a great band of youthful followers. It occurred to him that he would order a hall built, a greater mead-hall than the children of men had ever heard of, and within it distribute to young and old all that God gave him, except for the public lands and the lives of his men. Then, as I heard, work was ordered widely to many people throughout the earth, to make a beautiful hall. In time it came to pass, speedily among men, that the greatest of halls was completed; he who had power over his word both far and wide named it Heorot. He did not leave his promise unfulfilled, but gave away rings, precious things, at the feast. The hall stood high and wide-gabled; it awaited the hostile flames, the hateful fire; the time was not yet come when war was to arise from the deadly hate of father-in-law and son-in-law.

Then the bold demon who dwelt in darkness impatiently endured the distress of hearing each day loud revelry in the hall; there was the sound of the harp, the clear song of the poet. He spoke who knew how to tell from long ago the creation of men, related that the Almighty made the earth, the beautiful land, as far as water surrounds it; triumphant

---

Prologue. [Lines 1–52.] **8–9. Scyld Scefing.** For this and other proper names on the following pages, see the genealogical tables, pages 18–19. **deprived . . . mead-hall,** that is, he subjugated them. **13. whale-road,** the sea; the first of the many kennings in the poem. **21. Scedeland,** the lower tip of the Scandinavian peninsula. This Beowulf is not the hero of the poem. **31. Scyldings,** Danes. **35. boat,** probably the very boat in which he had drifted ashore as a child. **4. freight.** This variety of sea burial was not unusual in northern Germanic territory. **I.** [Lines 53–114.] **17. Battle-Scylfing,** the Swede. **25–26. except . . . men.** The limitations of the arbitrary power of a Germanic prince are here admirably suggested. **as I heard.** The poet occasionally alludes to his dependence on authority and information received. **31. Heorot,** so called, no doubt, because of the stag's antlers which surmounted the building. **32–33. gave . . . precious things.** The prescribed generosity of the chieftain is alluded to again and again. **36. father-in-law.** See the genealogy of the Danish royal line, page 18, note 14, above. **40. He spoke,** a poet, author of a poem not unlike Caedmon's; see page 64.

BEOWULF

He fixed the sun and the moon as luminaries for light to earth-dwellers and adorned the corners of the earth with branches and leaves. He also created life for each race of those who move about alive. Thus the warriors lived happily with rejoicing until a hellish fiend began to do evil. The angry spirit was named Grendel, a well-known wanderer in the waste borderland, who ruled the moors, the fen and stronghold; for a time the unhappy creature inhabited the land of monsters, after the Creator had condemned him among the race of Cain. The eternal Lord avenged the murder because he killed Abel; he had no joy in the feud, but God banished him far from mankind because of that crime. From him all the evil brood arose, giants and elves and monsters, also the giants who fought against God for a long time. He gave them their reward for that.

II

When night came, he went to inspect the high house, to see how the Ring-Danes had taken possession of it after the beer-drinking. He found within there the troop of men sleeping after the feast; they did not know sorrow, the misery of men. The creature of evil, grim and greedy, was at once ready; savage and cruel, he seized thirty thanes from their beds. Exulting in his booty, he went from there to his home, sought out his dwelling-place with the carnage. Then at dawn, in the early morning, the war-strength of Grendel was clear to men; after the feasting lamentation was made, a great cry in the morning. The famous lord, the very good prince, sat unhappy; the great one suffered, felt sorrow for his followers, when they saw the track of the hateful creature, the evil spirit. That fight was too severe, too hateful and long-drawn-out! It was after no longer time than a single night that he again committed additional murder; he did not shrink from hostility and crime: he was too confirmed in them. Then the man was easy to find who sought elsewhere a resting-place farther away, a bed in the chambers, when the hate of the hall-thane was pointed out to him, told truthfully with clear evidence. The man who escaped from the fiend kept himself thereafter farther away and more securely.

So he ruled and fought against right, one against all, until the best of houses stood empty. It was a long time: for twelve years the lord of the Scyldings endured trouble, every woe, great sorrows. Thus it became known to the children of men, mournfully through songs, that Grendel fought for a time against Hrothgar, carried on hostilities, crime and feud, continuous fighting for many a half-year. He did not wish peace with any man of the Danish host, to remove the deadly evil or to settle for money; none of the counselors, as things were, had reason to expect bright compensation at the hands of the killer; but the monster, the dark death-shadow, was continually persecuting warriors and youths; he lay in wait and ambushed. In continual night he ruled the misty moors. Men do not know where such demons wander in their courses.

So the enemy of mankind, the terrible solitary one, often did many crimes, severe injuries. In the black nights he inhabited Heorot, the richly decorated hall. He might not approach the throne, precious to the Lord, nor did He take thought of him. This was great distress, sorrow of heart, to the lord of the Scyldings. Many men strong in counsel often sat together. They deliberated what would be best for brave men to do against these sudden attacks. Sometimes they offered sacrifices at the heathen temples, begged with words that the slayer of demons would aid them against the great calamity. Such was their custom, the hope of the heathen; they thought of hell in their hearts, they knew not the Lord, the Judge of deeds, they knew not the Lord God, nor were they at all able to praise the protector of heaven, the Ruler of Glory. Woe to him who through cruel need shall thrust his soul into the embrace of fire, not hope for divine help or change in any way. Well is it for him who after death can seek the Lord and ask for safety in the Father's embrace.

III

The son of Healfdane was constantly agitated by care; the wise man was unable to put aside his woe. The struggle which had come upon the people was too great, too hateful, and too long, the cruel and violent persecution, greatest of evils by night.

A thane of Hygelac, a good man among the

---

7. Grendel, a troll-like creature, whose exact appearance is left to the audience's imagination. **11. Cain,** an important Biblical allusion. **II.** [Lines 115–88.] **32. lord,** Hrothgar. **40. man . . . easy to find,** a good example of litotes, or artistic understatement. These remarks often strike us as humorous, but it is not easy to be sure that they were always so intended by the author. **42. hall-thane,** Grendel. **3. songs,** a highly interesting reference to the composition and circulation of topical ballads. **7–8. settle for money.** Grendel had no intention of paying the conventional and legal wergeld (fine) which a murderer, or his family, was obligated to pay to the family of the victim. **12–13. In continual night,** all night long. **18–19. He . . . of him,** a difficult and obscure passage. Is there, perhaps, a hint that some divinity hedges a throne? **24–26. heathen temples.** The pagan setting of the original story is preserved here in striking fashion. **slayer of demons.** One would like to see in this a reference to Thor, the famous and popular slaughterer of trolls and giants. **III.** [Lines 189–257.] **44. thane of Hygelac,** Beowulf.

Geats, heard at home of Grendel's deeds; he was greatest in strength among the men of his day, noble and mighty. He ordered a good ship to be made ready for him; he said that he would seek out the war-king, over the swan-road, since the famous prince had need of men. Wise men dissuaded him but little from that journey, although he was dear to them; they encouraged the valiant man, they examined the omens. The good man had chosen warriors of the Geatish people, the bravest whom he could find. With fourteen others he went to the ship; the man who had knowledge of the sea led the way to the shore. Time passed and now the ship was in the waves, the boat at the foot of the cliff. Ready men mounted the prow—the currents eddied, the water against the sand. The men bore bright weapons, splendid armor, into the hull of the ship; the men pushed off the joined ship, warriors on a wished-for journey. Then, propelled by the wind, the foamy-necked boat, most like to a bird, went over the sea, until about the same time on the following day the ship with curved prow had gone so far that the seafarers saw land, gleaming sea-cliffs, steep hills, great headlands. Then, at the end of the voyage, the sea was crossed. The Weder folk quickly went on shore and tied up their ship—their shirts of mail, their armor, rattled. They thanked God that their voyage had been easy for them.

Then the watchman of the Scyldings, the man who had to guard the sea-cliff, saw shining shields, ready armor borne over the gangplank. Curiosity pressed upon his thoughts as to who the men were. Hrothgar's thane went then to the shore, riding on a horse; he brandished a great spear mightily with his hands, and asked with formal words: "What warriors are you, armed with coats of mail, who come thus bringing a high ship over the sea-road, here across the waves? I have been coastguard for a long time, have kept watch by the sea, that no foes with a naval force might make a raid on the land of the Danes. No men bearing shields have ever come here more openly, nor did you know surely that you would have permission from the warriors, the consent of my compatriots. I never saw a greater warrior on earth than is one of you, a man in armor; that is no mere retainer, adorned with weapons, unless his appearance belie him, a glorious sight. Now I must know your origin rather than that you go farther from here like spies on the land of the Danes. You seafarers who dwell afar, hear now my plain thought: it is best that you make known at once from where you come."

IV

The chief answered him, the leader of the band opened his store of words: "We are of the race of the people of the Geats and retainers of Hygelac. My father, Ecgtheow by name, was well known among the nations, a noble leader; he lived through a great many winters before he, an old man, went on his way from his home. Every wise man far and wide over the earth remembers him well. With friendly mind we have come to seek your lord, the son of Healfdene, the protector of the people. Be good to us in counsel. We have an important message for the famous king of the Danes, nor do I think that it need be secret. You know if it is, as we have reliably heard say, that among the Scyldings some enemy, I know not what, a mysterious oppressor, in the dark nights shows in a terrible manner strange hostility, injury and slaughter. I may well give Hrothgar advice through magnanimity how he, wise and good, may overcome the fiend—if change and relief from the misery of afflictions shall ever come to him again—and the seethings of sorrow become cooler; else ever after he will suffer distress and tribulation while the best of houses stands there on the high place."

The watchman spoke, a fearless officer, where he sat on his horse: "An acute warrior who has a clear mind must be a judge of both words and deeds. I hear that this is a band friendly to the lord of the Scyldings. Go forward carrying your weapons and armor; I will show you the way. Also I will order my young followers to guard with honor your boat, the newly tarred ship on the sand, against each foe, until once more the vessel with curved prow carries over the sea to Wedermark the beloved man and whichever of the brave ones to whom it will be granted to survive unhurt the storm of battle."

Then they began to go. The boat remained still, the roomy ship rested on its rope, fast at anchor. The figures of boars, adorned with gold, shone above the helmets, decorated and hardened by fire. The warlike man kept guard over the lives of the fierce ones. The men made haste; they marched together until they could see the timbered hall, stately

---

1. Geats, apparently inhabitants of southern Sweden. **5. swan-road,** another kenning for "sea." **25. Weder folk,** the Geats. **35. "What warriors . . . you come"** (*col.* 2, *l.* 3). The watchman's address is a skillful mixture of suspicion and praise. **48. Now . . . Danes** (*col.* 2, *l.* 1). That is, "I don't want you to get into trouble."

IV. [Lines 258–319.] **9. Ecgtheow.** See page 19, note 7. **20. I know not what.** Beowulf puts the matter very delicately. **31–32. clear mind . . . words and deeds,** an example of the poet's beloved sententiousness. **41. survive . . . battle,** the usual gloomy prognostication. **46. warlike man.** If we translate the sentence thus, which is by no means certainly correct, the reference is to the watchman. **48. timbered hall,** Heorot.

BEOWULF

and shining with gold. To men that was the most famous of buildings under heaven, in which the ruler dwelt. Its light shone over many lands. The brave warrior pointed out the bright hall of brave men to them, so that they could go directly to it. That warrior turned his horse and spoke: "It is time for me to go. May the omnipotent Father with His grace hold you safe on your venture. I will go to the sea, to keep guard against any hostile band."

V

The street was paved with stones, it showed the way to the men together. The coat of mail shone, hard and linked by hand, the bright iron rings sang in the armor when they first came, going to the hall in their warlike equipment. The sea-weary men put down their broad shields, the very strong bucklers, by the wall of the house. They sat down on the bench; the coats of mail rang, the armor of the men; the spears, the armor of the seamen, stood all together, ash-spears gray at the top. The armed troop was honorably supplied with weapons.

Then a proud man there asked the warriors about their race: "From where do you bring ornamented shields, gray shirts of mail, vizored helmets, and a heap of spears? I am Hrothgar's messenger and servant. I never saw so many foreign men who were more valiant. I feel sure that you sought Hrothgar because of pride, not in exile, but in greatness of heart."

The brave man answered him, the proud prince of the Weders spoke words, brave beneath his helmet: "We are table-companions of Hygelac; my name is Beowulf. I will tell my errand to your lord, the famous king, the son of Healfdene, if he will permit us to greet so good a man." Wulfgar spoke—he was a man of the Vandals, whose character in valor and wisdom was known to many. "As you request I will ask the friend of the Danes, the lord of the Scyldings, the giver of rings, the famous king, about your journey, and speedily make known to you the answer which the good man sees fit to give me."

He went then quickly where Hrothgar, old and white-haired, sat with his band of warriors. The brave man went until he stood by the shoulder of the prince of the Danes: he knew the correct behavior of a retainer. Wulfgar spoke to his lord: "Men of the Geats, come from far away over the expanse of the sea, have traveled here. The warriors call their leader Beowulf. They desire, my lord, that they may exchange words with you. Do not refuse them your answer, kind Hrothgar. They, in their armor, seem worthy of the esteem of warriors; at any rate the chief who led the men here is strong."

VI

Hrothgar spoke, the protector of the Scyldings: "I knew him when he was a boy; his father was named Ecgtheow, to whom Hrethel of the Geats gave his only daughter in marriage. Now his brave son has come here to seek a true friend. Moreover, sailors who carried gifts there for the satisfaction of the Geats said that the man brave in battle has the strength of thirty men in his grip. Holy God, I think, sent him to us as a help to the Danes against the terror of Grendel. I shall offer the good man gifts for his daring. Make haste and order the band of kinsmen to come in together to see me. Tell them that they are welcome to the Danish people."

The famous hero then went to the door, and spoke words from within: "My victorious lord, the leader of the Danes, orders you to be told that he knows your prince, and that you brave-minded men are welcome to him here from over the waves. Now you may go in your armor under your helmets, to see Hrothgar. Leave your shields and wooden spears here to await the result of your interview."

The great man arose; around him was many a man, a great troop of warriors; some stayed there to guard the equipment, as the brave man ordered. Together they hastened—the man showed them the way—under Hrothgar's roof. The warrior, hardy beneath his helmet, proceeded until he stood by the hearth. Beowulf spoke—his coat of mail shone on him, the corslet linked by the skill of the smith: "Be in good health, Hrothgar! I am the kinsman and retainer of Hygelac. I have undertaken many glorious deeds in my youth. The affair of Grendel became well known to me in my native land. Sailors said that for this reason the hall, best of buildings, stands empty and useless to every man after the setting sun becomes hidden under the clear sky. Then my people, the best and wisest men, advised me, King Hrothgar, that I visit you, because they knew the power of my strength. They themselves had seen me when I came from battle, bloodstained from the foe, where I had bound five, destroyed the kin of the giants, slain the water-mon-

V. [Lines 320–70.] **13. paved with stones**, probably inspired by the paved roads which the Romans had built in Britain.

VI. [Lines 371–455.] **15. strength . . . grip**, an important characteristic of the hero. **17–18. offer . . . gifts**, a perfectly normal statement, however crass it may appear to us. **39–40. glorious deeds**. This naïve boasting is thoroughly in the heroic tradition.

sters in the waves by night—they asked for trouble; I suffered great distress, avenged the persecution of the Weders, crushed the hostile ones. And now I shall go against Grendel, against the monster, settle the dispute alone with the demon. Now, lord of the Danes, prince of the Scyldings, I will ask you one favor, now that I have come thus far, that you, protector of warriors, dear friend of the people, will not refuse that alone with my band of warriors, this brave troop, I may cleanse Heorot. I have also learned that the monster in his recklessness does not care to use weapons; therefore I scorn—as I wish that Hygelac, my lord, may be gracious in mind toward me—that I should bear sword or broad shield, the yellow shield, to the battle, but I shall seize the fiend with my grasp and contend for life, foe against foe. There and then shall he whom death takes resign himself to the judgment of God. I expect that if he can manage it he will eat the people of the Geats, the host of the Hrethmen, without hesitation in the battle-hall, as he has often done. You will never need to shroud my head, but he will have me stained with dripping blood if death takes me. He will carry away a bloody corpse, think to eat it; the solitary one will eat me ruthlessly, mark his moor-retreats with my blood. You will no longer need to care for the sustenance of my body. Send to Hygelac, if battle should carry me off, the best of war-garments, the finest of coats of mail, which protects my breast; that is the heirloom of Hrethel, the work of Welund. Fate goes ever as it must!"

VII

Hrothgar spoke, the protector of the Scyldings: "You visit us, my friend Beowulf, because of deeds done and through kindness. Your father fought the greatest fight; with his hands he killed Heatholaf among the Wylfings; then the Weder people could not keep him because of fear of war. Thence over the rolling waves he sought the Danish people, the Honor-Scyldings. I was then first ruling the Danish folk, and in youth controlled the wide kingdom, the treasure-city of men; Heorogar was then dead, my older brother, the son of Healfdene was not living—he was a better man than I! Afterward I settled the feud with money, I sent old treasures to the Wylfings over the water's back. He swore oaths to me.

"It is sorrow in my heart for me to tell any man what harm Grendel with his thoughts of hate has done to me in Heorot, what hostile attacks he has carried out. My hall-troop, my band of warriors, is diminished; Fate has swept them away into the terror of Grendel. God may easily restrain the desperate foe from his deeds. Often enough men drunk with beer have boasted over the ale-cup that they would wait in the beer-hall for Grendel's attack with the terror of swords. Then in the morning, when day broke, was this mead-hall, this splendid hall, stained with gore, all the benches were wet with blood, the hall covered with battle-blood. I had fewer loyal men, dear band of followers, since death had taken those away. Sit down now to the feast and disclose your thoughts, tell men of the fame you have won, as your heart may urge you."

Then a bench was cleared in the beer-hall for the men of the Geats all together; the brave men, proud with strength, went to sit there. A retainer attended to his office, one who carried in his hand the decorated ale-cup, he poured out the clear sweet drink. The scop sometimes sang clear-voiced in Heorot. There was joy of warriors, a great band of Danes and Weders.

VIII

Unferth spoke; Ecglaf's son, who sat at the feet of the lord of the Scyldings, began a hostile speech. The undertaking of Beowulf, the brave seafarer, was a great vexation to him, because he could not endure that any other man on earth should ever achieve more fame under heaven than he himself: "Are you that Beowulf who contended against Breca, competed in swimming in the broad sea, where you two out of pride explored the waves and for foolish boasting ventured your lives in the deep water? Nor could any man, were he friend or foe, dissuade you from the perilous journey when you swam in the sea. There you covered the sea with your arms, measured the sea-paths, moved quickly with your hands, glided over the ocean; the sea surged with waves and with the floods of winter. You both labored in the water's power for seven days. He overcame you in swimming, he had more strength. Then in the morning the sea carried him to the Heatho-Raemas; from there he, dear to his

---

12. weapons. We learn later that Grendel is impervious to weapons; see pages 27 and 29. **20. Hrethmen,** another name for the Geats. **22. shroud my head,** carry out funeral rites for me. **31. Welund.** See page 51 below. **VII.** [Lines 456–98.] **35–36. deeds done,** a reference to Hrothgar's service to Ecgtheow; see page 19, note 7. **47. He swore.** Ecgtheow, apparently, swore to maintain peace in the future.

23. scop, bard. **VIII.** [Lines 499–558.] **28. Unferth,** who held a very distinguished position at the Danish court, was probably expected to make a flattering speech of welcome to Beowulf; thus his insulting and envious remarks are all the more startling. **35. Breca.** This youthful adventure of Beowulf's, told in one way by Unferth and in another by the hero, illustrates the poet's method of adding to our information by means of "flash-backs." **47. Heatho-Raemas.** They probably lived in what is now Romerike, north of Oslo.

people, sought his beloved home, the land of the Brondings, the fair stronghold, where he had people, a town, and treasure. The son of Beanstan truly fulfilled all his boast with you. Therefore I expect worse result for you, although you have everywhere been strong in the storm of battle, in the fierce fight, if you dare to wait near for Grendel during a night-long space of time."

Beowulf, the son of Ecgtheow, spoke: "Well, my friend Unferth, you have said a good many things about Breca, spoken concerning his journey—drunken as you are with beer! I maintain the truth, that I had more strength in the sea, a harder struggle in the waves, than any other man. When we were boys we agreed and boasted—we were both still in our youth—that we would venture our lives on the ocean, and we carried that out. We had naked swords, hard in hand, when we swam in the sea; we intended to protect ourselves against the whales. He was not at all able to swim far away from me in the waves, more quickly over the sea, nor did I wish to go from him. We were together in the sea for a space of five days, until the flood separated us; the surging water, coldest of storms, the darkening night, and the fierce north wind turned against us—the waves were rough. The temper of the fish was aroused. There my coat of mail, hard and linked by hand, helped me against the foe; the woven wargarment, adorned with gold, lay on my breast. The hostile enemy pulled me to the bottom, had me fast, fierce in his grip; however, it was granted me by fate that I should reach the monster with my point, my battle-sword. Storm of battle destroyed the great sea-beast through my hand.

IX

"So the evil-doers frequently pressed me hard. I served them as was fitting, with my dear sword. By no means did they have their fill of joy, those evil-doers, that they could devour me, sitting about the feast near the bottom of the sea. But in the morning they lay up by the shore, wounded by swords, put to sleep by the weapons, so that never again did they hinder the journey of the sailors over the high sea. Light came from the east, God's bright beacon; the waves subsided so that I could see the headlands, the windy walls. Fate often protects a man not yet fated to die, when his courage is good. Anyhow, it chanced that I killed nine of the water-monsters with the sword. I never heard of a harder fight in the night under the vault of heaven, nor of a man more distressed in the sea. Yet I survived with life the grip of my foes, weary of my journey. Then the sea, the flood along the ocean, surging waters, bore me to the land of the Lapps. I never heard tell of such battles, such terror of swords, concerning you. Breca—nor either of you—never yet in battle accomplished so bold a deed with shining swords—I shall not boast much about it—although you were the murderer of your brothers, your near relatives. For this you must suffer damnation in hell, although your intelligence is good. I tell you truly, son of Ecglaf, that the terrible monster Grendel would never have done so many deeds of horror to your prince, so much harm in Heorot, if your heart, your spirit, were as fierce in battle as you yourself claim. But he has discovered that he need not greatly dread the hostile acts, the fierce fight, of your people, the Victory-Scyldings. He takes his toll, he does not spare any of the Danish people, but he enjoys himself, he kills and feasts, he does not expect opposition from the Spear-Danes. But I shall soon offer him battle, the strength and daring of the Geats. He who is able shall go again in high spirits to the mead, when the morning light, the sun clothed in brightness from the south, shines over the children of men on the second day."

The gray-haired dispenser of treasures, brave in battle, was then joyful; the lord of the Bright-Danes counted on assistance; the guardian of the people perceived a firmly resolved purpose in Beowulf.

There was laughter of warriors, the din made a pleasing sound, words were pleasant. Wealhtheow came forth, Hrothgar's queen, mindful of correct behavior. Adorned with gold she greeted the men in the hall; the noble woman first gave the cup to the king of the Danes, she asked him, dear to the people, to be happy at the beer-drinking. The victorious king joyfully accepted the banquet and the hall-cup. The lady of the Helmings went round to each group of retainers and youths, she passed the precious vessels until the time came when she, the ring-adorned queen, excellent in mind, brought the mead-cup to Beowulf. She greeted the prince of

---

2. Brondings. Breca and his Brondings are mentioned in the Old English poem *Widsith*, line 25. **3. son of Beanstan,** Breca. **IX.** [Lines 559–661.] **47–48. Fate . . . good,** an early example of "Put your trust in God, but keep your powder dry." **5. Lapps,** in northern Norway. **10–11. murderer . . . relatives.** This is indeed a serious accusation, and one wonders how such a criminal could have held a place of honor, but a later passage (page 31) suggests that Beowulf is overemphasizing Unferth's failure to protect his relatives in battle. **35. Wealhtheow.** The first element in Wealhtheow means "foreign," even specifically "Celtic," and the second means "captive," but the original sense of the word need not be applied literally to Hrothgar's queen. **42. Helmings,** the name of Wealhtheow's family.

the Geats and thanked God with wise words that she had experienced the pleasure that she could expect relief from wicked deeds from any man. The warrior, fierce in battle, received the cup from Wealhtheow, and then spoke, ready for fight. Beowulf, the son of Ecgtheow, spoke: "I resolved when I set out on the sea, sat down in the boat with my band of men, that I would certainly fulfill the desire of your people or fall in battle, fast in the clutch of the fiend. I shall accomplish heroic deeds of valor, or live to see my last day in this mead-hall." These words, the boasting speech of the Geat, were very pleasing to the woman. The noble queen, adorned with gold, went to sit by her lord.

Then, as before, brave words were spoken in the hall, the people joyful, the noise of the gallant folk, until presently the son of Healfdene wished to go to his bed. He knew that the monster had intended battle against the high hall from the time that they could see the light of the sun until darkening night over all, shapes of darkness, came gliding black under the heavens. All the company arose. One man greeted the other, Hrothgar Beowulf, wished him good luck and control of the wine-hall, and said these words: "Never before, since I could lift hand and shield, have I entrusted the splendid hall of the Danes to any man, save to you now. Now have and hold the best of houses, think of glory, exhibit mighty valor, keep watch for the foe! You will have no lack of good things if you survive this courageous deed with your life."

X

Then Hrothgar, king of the Scyldings, went out of the hall with his band of warriors; the war-chief wished to seek Wealhtheow, his queen, for bedfellow. God, as men heard, had set against Grendel a hall-guard who attended to a special service for the king of the Danes, he offered watch against the giant. Truly the prince of the Geats trusted firmly in his brave strength and the favor of God. He then took off his iron coat of mail, his helmet from his head, he gave his decorated sword, the best of weapons, to his attendant, and ordered him to keep the war equipment. Beowulf of the Geats then spoke certain boasting words before he mounted his bed: "I do not account myself less in martial vigor of warlike deeds than Grendel does himself. Therefore I do not wish to kill him with the sword, to deprive him of life, although I am completely able to do so. He does not know of the advantages with which he could strike me, cut my shield to pieces, although he may be famous for evil deeds. But we two shall forgo the use of swords tonight, if he dares to seek battle without weapons, and then may wise God, the holy Lord, adjudge glory to whichever side may seem proper to Him." Then the man brave in battle bent down, the pillow received the face of the warrior, and around him many a bold sailor lay down on the hall-bed. None of them thought that he would ever again go to his dear home, his people, or the noble town where he had been brought up, for they had learned that murderous death had taken away all too many of the Danish people in that wine-hall. But the Lord gave the fortunes of victory, comfort and aid to the people of the Weders, so that they all overcame their enemy through the strength of a single man, by his own might. The truth is well known, that Almighty God has ever ruled over mankind.

In the black night the walker in darkness came striding. The warriors who should guard the gabled house were sleeping, all save one. It was known to men that the hostile demon might not, when the Lord did not wish it, draw them down to the shades. But Beowulf, watching in anger against the foe, awaited, enraged, the result of the battle.

XI

Then, under cover of darkness, came Grendel going from the moor; he bore God's anger. The evil-doer thought to ensnare some man or other in the high hall. He went under the clouds to the point where he best knew the wine-hall to be, the gold-hall, shining with plate. This was not the first time that he had visited Hrothgar's home, but never in his life, before or after, did he find worse luck, braver hall-thanes. The joyless man came traveling to the building. The door, fast with fire-forged bands, sprang open when he touched it with his hands. The hostile one, since he was enraged, then swung open the door of the building. Immediately after that the fiend stepped on the fair-paved floor; he went in angry mood. A horrible light, most like to a flame, shone from his eyes. He saw many men, a band of kinsmen, a crowd of young warriors, sleeping together in the hall. Then his spirit laughed

18–22. **He knew . . . heavens,** a puzzling sentence, the exact meaning of which is by no means clear. **X.** [Lines 662–709.] 34–35. **out of the hall.** Even when Heorot was unthreatened, the king would normally sleep in a smaller separate dwelling. 37–38. **hall-guard,** Beowulf.

1–2. **He does not know . . . strike me.** But see page 24, line 12, and pages 29 and 44. It is evident that Grendel's attitude toward weapons is not altogether clear in the author's mind. 15–18. **But the Lord . . . might.** The maintenance of suspense is of little concern to our poet. **XI.** [Lines 710–90.] 39. **man.** Grendel and his mother, however monstrous, are often referred to as human in form.

aloud; the horrid monster thought that before day came he would separate the life of each one of them from his body, for hope of a plentiful meal had come to him. Yet by no means was it destined that he should devour more of mankind after that night. The strong kinsman of Hygelac observed how the evil-doer would proceed with his sudden attacks. The monster did not think to delay, but he quickly seized for his first exploit a sleeping warrior, he tore him eagerly, he bit into his body, drank the blood in streams, swallowed him with one bite after another. Soon he had eaten up all the dead man, feet, hands, and all. He stepped nearer, seized the stronghearted warrior on his bed—the fiend reached toward him with his hand. Beowulf quickly received him with hostile intent, and sat up supporting himself on his arm. The guardian of crimes quickly discovered that he had never in the world come upon a greater hand-grip in another man of any region of the earth. He became frightened in mind and soul, but he could not get away any the sooner. His heart was eager to escape, he wished to flee to his hiding-place, to go to the assembly of devils. His experience there was not as he had found it in the former days of his life. The strong kinsman of Hygelac remembered his evening speech, stood upright, and seized the other firmly. His fingers cracked; the giant was trying to escape; the hero advanced further. The notorious creature intended, if he could do so, to go to a place farther away, to flee from there to his fen-retreats. He realized that the control of his fingers was in the grip of his foe. That was a sad journey which the wicked enemy took to Heorot! The splendid hall was full of noise. Distress came upon the men, the Danish castle-dwellers, upon each of the bold ones. The fierce guardians of the house were both angry. The building resounded. Then it was a great wonder that the wine-hall withstood the battle-brave, that the fair building did not fall to the earth, except that it was firmly and skillfully fastened inside and out with iron bands. There started from the floor, as I have heard say, many a gold-adorned mead-bench, where the hostile ones fought. Never before had the wise men of the Scyldings thought that any man in any way could ever shatter that hall, splendid and adorned with bone,

destroy it with any cunning, unless the fire's embrace were to swallow it in flame. The noise arose, very strange indeed. Horrible fear seized the Danes, each of those who from the wall heard the lamentation, God's enemy sing his terrible song, his song of defeat, hell's captive bewailing his pain. He held him fast who was the strongest in might of men in that day of this life.

XII

Not for anything would the protector of men let the murderous visitor go away alive, nor did he reckon his life-days as useful to any of the people. There many a one of Beowulf's men drew his old sword, wished to defend the life of his lord, his famous leader, if he could do so. The brave-minded warriors did not know when they began to fight, and thought to strike on all sides, to reach his life, that no war-sword nor any one of the best of weapons on earth would hurt the miscreant; but he had bewitched victory weapons, every sword. His death on that day of this life was destined to take place in a miserable way, and the alien spirit to journey far in the power of the fiends. Then he who earlier in mirth of heart had accomplished many crimes against mankind—he was in a state of feud with God—discovered that his body would not accompany him, but that the brave kinsman of Hygelac had him by the hand; each one was hateful to the other while living. The terrible monster suffered bodily pain; a very great wound became visible on his shoulder, the sinews sprang apart, the joints cracked. Glory in battle was granted to Beowulf. Grendel, mortally wounded, had to flee from there under the marshy tracts, seek his joyless dwelling. He knew the more clearly that the end of his life was come, the number of his days.

After the bloody conflict happiness came to all the Danes. The man, wise and brave, who had previously come from afar had cleansed Hrothgar's hall, saved it from persecution. He rejoiced in his night-work, in his heroic deeds. The prince of the Geats had fulfilled his boast to the Danes, also he had remedied all the grief and evil care which they had formerly suffered, and for sad necessity must have continued to endure, a great affliction. That was clearly proved when the brave warrior put up a hand, an arm, and a shoulder—there all together was Grendel's gripping apparatus—under the vaulted roof.

6-7. observed . . . attacks. There is something a little cold-blooded in the way in which Beowulf familiarizes himself with Grendel's procedure. **9. sleeping warrior.** The warrior's name, as we learn later, is Hondscio. **23. devils.** Grendel's lair is either thought of as evil enough to be a fitting home for devils, or else Grendel and his mother are identified with the fiends. **27. His fingers,** Grendel's, or, less probably, Beowulf's. **36. guardians,** Beowulf and Grendel. **46. splendid . . . with bone,** a reference to the antlers which gave the hall its name.

1-2. destroy . . . flame, an anticipation of the fate of Heorot; see page 18, note 14, and page 20. **XII.** [Lines 791-836.] **21. sword.** See page 26.

XIII

Then in the morning, as I have heard say, there was many a warrior around the gift-hall. Leaders came from far and near over the wide ways to see the wonder, the footprints of the foe. His death did not seem sad to any of the men who looked at the tracks of the vanquished one, how he, disheartened, overcome in battle, doomed to die and put to flight, bore his bloody tracks on the way to the water-monster's pool. There the water was surging with blood, the terrible surf of the waves mixed with hot gore, boiled with battle-blood. Doomed to death, he had concealed himself when, devoid of joys, he had given up his life, his heathen soul, in his fen-refuge. Hell received him there.

The old retainers, as well as many a young man, returned again from their joyous journey, brave, riding their steeds from the pool, warriors on their horses. There Beowulf's fame was spoken of; many often said that south or north, between the seas, over the spacious earth, there was not a better warrior, one more worthy of rule, under the expanse of the sky. They did not, however, find fault with their lord, gracious Hrothgar, for he was a good king. At times the men famed in battle let their bay horses gallop, run in contest, where the roads seemed fair to them, known for their excellence. At times one of the king's thanes, covered with glory, mindful of songs, one who remembered many old traditions, found other words fast bound with truth. The man began again to recite skillfully Beowulf's adventure and to utter successfully an apt story, to vary words. He told everything that he had heard said about Sigemund's deeds of valor, many an unknown thing, the fight of the Waelsing, his journeys far and wide, his feud and troubles, of which the children of men did not know at all, save Fitela, who was with him when he wished to speak of such things, the uncle to his nephew, for they were comrades in need in every battle. They had slain with the sword many of the race of giants. Great glory had arisen for Sigemund after his death, since, bold in battle, he had killed the dragon, the guardian of the treasure. The son of the prince engaged in the bold deed under the gray stone alone, nor was Fitela with him. It turned out, however, that the sword went through the wonderfully shining serpent, so that the splendid sword was fixed in the wall. The dragon died in torment. The hero had brought it about with his daring that he could enjoy his own choice of the treasure. The son of Waels loaded his boat, carried the bright treasures into the hull of the ship. The worm, being hot, melted.

He was far and wide the most famous of heroes among the nations, a protector of warriors by his brave deeds—for that at first he prospered—after Heremod's valor, his might and courage, diminished. Among the Jutes Heremod was betrayed into the power of the fiends, quickly put to death. Great sorrows oppressed him too long; to his people, to all the warriors, he became a great care. Likewise in earlier times many a wise man who counted on him for relief from miseries often deplored the brave man's journey, held that the son of a prince should prosper, receive his father's rank, protect the people, treasure, and stronghold, the kingdom of warriors, the native land of the Scyldings. The kinsman of Hygelac became more pleasing in all these things to his friends and to mankind. Sin took possession of Heremod.

At times in competition they measured the yellow road with their horses. Then the morning light had moved forward and hastened. Many a brave man went to the high hall to see the wonderful thing. The king himself, guardian of treasure, well known for his virtues, went glorious from the woman's apartment with a large company, and his queen beside him passed over the path to the mead-hall with a troop of women.

XIV

Hrothgar spoke—he went to the hall, stood on the flight of steps, looked at the high roof shining with gold, and at Grendel's hand: "Thanks quickly be to the Almighty for this sight! I suffered much hostility and afflictions from Grendel, but God, the Guardian of glory, can always do wonder after wonder. It was not long ago that I did not think ever to experience relief from woes, when the best of houses stood stained with blood, gory, a far-reach-

---

XIII. [Lines 837–924.] **25. good king,** an excellent indication of natural and devoted loyalty. **30. one,** the minstrel, who could recite old songs or improvise new and appropriate ones. **35–38. Sigemund.** The story of Sigemund the Volsung (**Waelsing**) is related as analogous to Beowulf's heroic accomplishment. **Fitela,** Sinfjotli in the Norse accounts, was Sigemund's son by his own sister and assisted him in carrying out the family feud against King Siggeir. The fight with the dragon, which may perhaps be considered a curious foreshadowing of the second part of the poem, is nowhere else told of Sigemund, but since this account is much earlier than any other version, it may well be that it was originally among Sigemund's exploits and subsequently transferred to his more famous son, Siegfried.

15. Heremod. For another reference to Heremod, see page 36 below. The present passage is obscure and difficult of interpretation, due in large part to our lack of other information about Heremod. Clearly enough, however, his evil qualities and bad luck make him serve as a foil to Sigemund and Beowulf. **25–26. kinsman of Hygelac,** Beowulf. **30. morning light,** the sun. **32. thing,** Grendel's arm. XIV. [Lines 925–90.]

ing misery to all the counselors, who did not expect that they could ever defend the stronghold of the people against foes, against goblins and demons. Now a warrior through God's might has accomplished the deed which we before were not able to bring to pass with our skill. Whatever woman who has brought forth such a son among men can say, if she still lives, that God was kind to her in her childbearing. Now, Beowulf, best of warriors, I wish to have you for a son, to love in my heart: hold from now on this new relationship. There will be for you no lack of any worldly good which I have in my control. Often enough I have assigned reward for less, an honorable gift to an inferior warrior, one weaker in battle. You by yourself have accomplished deeds by which your fame will live forever and ever. May the Almighty reward you with good, as he has done just now."

Beowulf, the son of Ecgtheow, spoke: "We carried out that deed of bravery very gladly, accomplished the fight, boldly dared the might of the unknown. I wish rather that you yourself might have seen him, the fiend killed in his war-gear. I thought to bind him quickly to his death-bed with my strong grip, so that he should lie struggling for life in my grasp, but his body escaped. Since the Lord did not wish it I could not hinder his departure, nor did I hold the deadly foe firmly enough; the fiend was too powerful in his going. However, to save his life he let his hand remain behind, his arm and shoulder, but the wretched man did not obtain any help there. The evil-doer, pressed down with sins, lives no longer on that account, but pain with evil bonds has seized him closely in its forceful grip. There the creature outlawed for crime must await the great Judgment, how the glorious Lord will judge him."

Then the man, Ecglaf's son, was more silent in his boastful speech about warlike deeds, since the warriors saw the hand, the fingers of the fiend, above the high roof through the hero's strength. In front each of the hard nails was most like to steel, the horrible, frightful claw of the heathen warrior. Each one said that nothing hard, no very good sword, could touch him in such a way that it would harm the bloody battle-hand of the monster.

XV

Then it was quickly ordered that Heorot be adorned within by hands; there were many of those, both men and women, who made ready that wine-hall, that guest-hall. Gold-adorned tapestries shone on the walls, many a wonderful sight for all of the warriors who gaze at such things. The shining building, though fast on the inside with iron bands, was very much broken, and the hinges sprung apart. The roof alone came through entirely uninjured when the monster, guilty of wicked deeds, turned in flight, despairing of life. That is not at all easy to escape—try it who will—but each human being, every one of the children of men, each of the inhabitants of the earth, must seek the ready place forced on him by necessity, where his body fast in the grave shall sleep after the feast.

Then it was time and occasion that the son of Healfdene went to the hall; the king himself wished to take part in the banquet. I never heard of people in a larger group behave themselves better around their treasure-giver. The glorious ones sat down on the benches and rejoiced in the feast; their valiant kinsmen, Hrothgar and Hrothulf, pleasantly drank many a mead-cup in the high hall. Heorot was filled inside with friends; the Scyldings had not then done treachery. Healfdene's son then gave Beowulf a golden standard as the reward of his victory, a decorated battle-banner, a helmet, and a coat of mail. Many saw a famous precious sword brought before the man. Beowulf drank the cup in the hall; he had no need to be ashamed of the costly gift before the warriors—I have never heard of many men who in a more friendly fashion gave four gold-ornamented treasures to another on the ale-bench. Around the crown of the helmet a rim bound with wires held the head-protection on the outside, so that the leavings of files, hard in battle, should not severely harm him when the warrior had to go against his foes. Then the protector of men ordered eight horses with gold-plated headgear to be led into the hall inside the enclosure. On one of them there was a skillfully decorated saddle, adorned with jewels. This was the war-seat of the high king, when Healfdene's son would perform the play of swords. The valor of the famous one never failed at the front when the corpses fell. Then the prince of the Danes gave possession of both, horses and weapons, to Beowulf; he ordered him to make good use of them. Thus nobly the famous king, the treasure-guardian of men, repaid the onslaught with horses and treasures, in such a way that no man would ever find fault with them if he would speak the truth in accordance with right.

10–11. hold . . . relationship, a formal and complimentary, rather than actual adoption. **19. We.** Note the modest way in which Beowulf includes his men in the victory. **37. Ecglaf's son,** Unferth. **40–42. In front . . . warrior.** This passage is by no means clear. **44–45. touch him . . . monster.** See pages 24 and 26. **XV.** [Lines 991–1049.]

9. That, death. **21. Hrothgar and Hrothulf.** See page 18, note 10. **35. leavings of files,** a kenning for "swords."

XVI

Then in addition the lord of men gave treasures, heirlooms, on the mead-bench to each of those who went on the voyage with Beowulf, and he ordered that the man should be paid for with gold whom Grendel before had killed sinfully—as he would have killed more of them had not the wise God and the courage of the man prevented such a fate. God ruled all the race of mankind as He still does. Therefore understanding is everywhere best, forethought of mind. The man who long enjoys life in the world in these days of strife must endure much pleasure and pain.

There was song and music together in the presence of Healfdene's battle-leader. The harp was touched, many a song was recited, when Hrothgar's minstrel had to give entertainment along the mead-bench in the hall about Finn's men, when disaster came upon them, when the hero of the Half-Danes, Hnaef of the Scyldings, had to fall on the Frisian battlefield.

Hildeburg, however, had no need to praise the good faith of the Frisians; without her fault she was deprived of her loved ones, of her sons and brothers, in battle; wounded by the spear, they fell at the appointed time. She was a sad lady! Not without cause did the daughter of Hoc mourn over the decree of fate, after morning came, when she could see under heaven the slaughter of her kinsmen in the place where she had formerly had most of the world's joy. Battle carried off all the followers of Finn save a few only, so that he could not in any way fight against Hengest on the battlefield, nor protect in battle those of the prince's thanes who survived. But they offered them terms, that they would yield to them the whole of another building, hall and high seat, so that they could have control over half with the children of the Jutes, and that the son of Folcwalda would honor the Danes each day at the distribution of treasure, would present rings to the troop of Hengest, just as much as he would encourage the people of the Frisians in the beer-hall with treasures of plated gold. Then they confirmed strong pledges of peace on both sides. Finn strongly and incontestably affirmed with oaths to Hengest that he would rule the survivors honorably, according to the judgment of his advisers, so long as no man should break the treaty by word or deed, or ever complain through malice that, lordless, they followed the killer of their ring-giver, when it was thus forced upon them by necessity. If, on the other hand, any one of the Frisians were to be a reminder with daring speech of the murderous hate, then the edge of the sword must settle it.

A funeral pile was made ready and gold lifted from the hoard. The best of the warriors of the Army-Scyldings was ready to be placed on the pyre. On the funeral pile were easily visible the blood-stained shirt of mail, the golden boar's image, iron-hard, and many a hero destroyed by wounds—not a few had fallen in battle! Then Hildeburg ordered her own son committed to the flames on Hnaef's pyre, to place him on the pile by his uncle's side, and burn the bodies. The lady lamented, mourned with sad songs. The warrior was placed on the pyre. The greatest of funeral fires rose to the clouds, roared before the mound. The heads melted, gashes burst open—then blood flowed out—the wounds of the body. Fire, greediest of elements, swallowed up all of those whom battle had carried away from either side. Their vigor was gone.

XVII

Then the warriors, deprived of friends, went to seek out their dwelling-places, to go to their part of Friesland, their homes and great town. Hengest still lived through the slaughter-stained winter with Finn, and his lot was not a happy one. He thought of home, if only he could drive his ring-prowed ship over the sea. The ocean surged with storm, fought against the wind, winter locked up the waves in its

---

XVI. [Lines 1050–1124] **15. battle-leader**, Hrothgar. **18. Finn's men.** The Finnsburg Episode which follows has been the subject of much scholarship and discussion. With the aid of the Finnsburg Fragment, all that survives of a (probably) short epic poem on the same subject, a consistent plot can be put together. The following brief account follows Klaeber (*op. cit.*, pages 231 ff.). The Danish prince Hnaef, with a band of men, is visiting King Finn of Frisia, whose wife is Hnaef's sister, Hildeburg. The Danes are treacherously attacked at night by their hosts, but they defend themselves valiantly for five days without losing a man. Thus far the Fragment. From the Episode we learn that the fight continues until Hnaef and a number of his men are killed. The Frisian losses are also severe, and so a treaty is made between Finn and Hengest, on whom leadership of the Danes has devolved after Hnaef's death. The Danes spend the winter with the Frisians, but they long to carry out the vengeance which it is their duty to exact for their lord's death, and in the spring they attack Finn, kill him, and carry his wife and treasure off to Denmark. Other reconstructions of the story have been made, but this one seems reasonable and satisfactory, though not, of course, incontrovertible. **24–25. sons and brothers**, actually, one gathers, of her son and brother. **35. But they**, the Frisians. **they**, the Danes.

2–3. control over half, equal power. **Jutes.** "Jutes" and "Frisians" are used interchangeably. **4. son of Folcwalda**, Finn. **15. followed . . . ring-giver.** Here we have recognition of the duty of the followers to die for or with their lord, and of the shame that submission to his slayers brings. **20–21. A funeral . . . hoard.** Neither the reading nor the translation of this sentence is certain. **24. boar's image**, on the helmet. **32–34. The heads . . . body**, a realistic description. XVII. [Lines 1125–91.] **37. warriors**, the Frisians.

icy bond, until another year came to the dwellings of men, as it still does when the gloriously bright weather always observes its season. Then winter was gone and the face of the earth was fair; the exile was eager to go, the guest from the dwelling. He thought more about revenge than of the sea-journey, if he would be able to bring about an hostile meeting, for he kept inwardly in mind the sons of the Jutes. So, then, he did not refuse a combat to the king when Hunlafing laid a sword, the best of weapons, in his lap. Its edges were well known to the Jutes. Likewise, in turn, cruel death by the sword came upon the bold-spirited Finn in his own home, when Guthlaf and Oslaf, after the sea-journey, complained of the fierce attack and their sorrow, blamed him for many misfortunes. The restless spirit could not remain in the breast. Then the hall was reddened with the life-blood of enemies; also Finn was slain, the king among his band, and the queen captured. The warriors of the Scyldings took to the ships all the household goods of the king, whatever in the way of jewels and curious gems they could find in Finn's house. On the voyage they brought the noble wife to the Danes, led her to her people.

The song was sung, the minstrel's tale. Mirth arose again, noise from the benches sounded loudly. Cup-bearers gave wine from wonderful vessels. Then Wealhtheow came forth under her golden crown to where the two good men, nephew and uncle, sat. There was then still peace between them, each true to the other. There also sat Unferth, the orator, at the feet of the prince of the Scyldings. Each of them trusted his spirit, that he had great courage, although he had not been dutiful to his kinsmen at the play of swords. Then the lady of the Scyldings spoke: "My dear lord, dispenser of treasures, receive this cup! Be happy, generous prince of men, and speak to the Geats with kind words, as one ought to do. Be gracious toward the Geats and mindful of the gifts which you now have from near and far. I am told that you wish to have the warrior as a son. Heorot is cleansed, the shining ring-hall; make use of many presents while you are able, and leave people and kingdom to your sons when you must go forth to look upon death. I know that my kind Hrothulf will protect the youths with honor if you, lord of the Scyldings, leave the earth before he does. I think that he will repay our sons well, if he remembers all that we two did earlier in the way of kindness for his pleasure and honor when he was a child." Then she went to the bench where her sons were, where the youths sat together, Hrethric and Hrothmund, and the children of warriors. There the good man sat, Beowulf of the Geats, by the two brothers.

XVIII

The cup was carried to him and friendship offered with words, and gold made into rings presented in kindly fashion, two arm-ornaments, a coat of mail, and rings, the greatest of collars that I ever heard of on earth. I never heard under heaven of a better treasure of heroes, since Hama carried away the necklace of the Brosings, brooch and costly object, to the bright city—he fled the treacherous quarrels of Eormenric and chose eternal counsel. Hygelac of the Geats, nephew of Swerting, had the ring on his last expedition, when he defended the treasure beneath his banner, protected the spoil of battle. Fate carried him off when for pride he sought for trouble, battle among the Frisians. The powerful prince carried the treasures, the precious stones, over the sea. He fell beneath his shield. The king's body came into the power of the Franks, his coat of mail and the necklace as well. Inferior warriors plundered the slain after the slaughter; the people of the Geats covered the place of corpses.

The hall received the noise. Wealhtheow spoke, she said words before the company: "Enjoy this necklace, dear Beowulf, with good fortune, and, youth, make use of this coat of mail, great treasures, and prosper well. Show yourself strong, and be kind in counsel to these boys. I will remember you for it with a gift. You have brought it about that far and wide men shall praise you, just as far as the sea, the home of winds, surrounds the high shores. Be happy, prince, while you live. I wish you many treasures. In your acts be kind to my son, holding him in joy. Here each warrior is true to the other, mild of mind, loyal to his lord; the thanes are

1. **another year**, spring. **8–12. for . . . Jutes**, not a certain rendering. **So . . . lap**, even more difficult than the preceding sentence; the **king** is no doubt Finn. **14–15. sea-journey**. The reference is probably to the original journey of the Danes to Friesland, and does not mean that Guthlaf and Oslaf were reinforcements from Denmark. **30–31. nephew and uncle**, Hrothulf and Hrothgar. **35–36. not been dutiful . . . swords**. See page 25, line 10. **45–47. leave . . . death**. The queen is apprehensive lest Hrothgar take his adoption of Beowulf seriously enough to make him his successor. **3. if he remembers**, a pathetic anticipation of the inevitable strife. **XVIII.** [Lines 1192–1250.] **17. Hama carried away**. We judge from this that Hama stole from **Eormenric** (for whom see *Deor's Lament*, page 51) the famous necklace which had once belonged to the goddess Freyja. **20. chose eternal counsel**, perhaps became a Christian. **21–22. Hygelac . . . expedition**. We learn later (page 40) that Beowulf gave the necklace to Hygd; perhaps she in turn gave it to her husband. **nephew of Swerting**, or grandson; see page 19, note 2. **25. battle . . . Frisians**. See page 19, note 5. **42. son**, Hrethric.

united, the people alert, the drunken warriors do as I command."

She went then to her seat. It was the best of feasts, the men drank wine. They did not know Fate, grim destiny as it was to come to pass for many men after evening had come and Hrothgar had gone to his house, the prince to his bed. A countless number of warriors occupied the hall, just as they often had done before. They cleared away the benches; the space was overspread with beds and cushions. One of the beer-drinkers, ready for death and doomed to die, went to his couch in the hall. They placed their shining shields at their heads; on the bench above a man was clearly visible the helmet towering in battle, the ringed coat of mail, and the mighty spear. It was their habit that they were often ready for battle, both at home and when out with the army, and in either case, at any such time as trouble came to their lord, the people were good.

XIX

Then they fell asleep. One of them paid bitterly for his evening's rest, as had often happened to them before when Grendel haunted the gold-hall and did wrong until his end came, death as a result of his crimes. It became evident and widely known to men that an avenger still lived for a long time after the foe, in consequence of the bitter strife: Grendel's mother, a monstrous female, thought of her sorrow, she who had to inhabit the dreadful water, the cold stream, since Cain became the murderer of his only brother, his father's son. Then he went outlawed and marked by murder, he fled human joys and lived in the wasteland. From him sprang many fated spirits. Grendel was one of these, the hateful and savage outcast, who found in Heorot a wakeful man waiting for battle. There the monster laid hold of him, but nevertheless Beowulf thought of the strength of his might, the liberal gift which God had given to him, and he trusted to the Lord for kindness, for comfort and aid. For that reason he overcame the fiend, subdued the hellish spirit. Then Grendel went away defeated, deprived of joy, the enemy of mankind, to see the place of his death. And his mother, ravenous and gloomy, then still wished to go on a sorrowful journey, to avenge her son's death.

She came then to Heorot where the Danes were sleeping throughout the hall. There at once the men experienced a return to the old way of things after Grendel's mother made her way inside. The force of attack was less to the same extent that the strength of maidens, the warlike power of a woman, is less in comparison with men, when the bound sword, forged with the hammer, the sword stained with blood, strong of edge, cuts opposite the boar above the helmet. Then in the hall was the hard-edged sword drawn above the seats, many a broad shield was raised firmly in hand. No one thought of a helmet, a great coat of mail, when that terror seized him. She was in haste, she wished to go out from there, to save her life, when she was discovered. She had quickly and firmly seized one of the warriors when she was on her way to the swamp. This was Hrothgar's most-beloved retainer, as companions go, between the seas, a powerful warrior, whom she killed on his bed, a glorious man. Beowulf was not there, but another lodging had been assigned to the famous Geat after the treasure-giving. There was an uproar in Heorot. She took the well-known hand covered with blood. Grief was renewed in the dwellings. It was not a good exchange that they must pay on either side with the lives of their friends.

Then the wise king, the gray-haired warrior, was troubled in mind when he knew that his chief thane was lifeless, his dearest retainer dead. Beowulf, the victorious warrior, was speedily fetched from his chamber. At daybreak the prince, the excellent warrior, went with his fellows to the place where the wise man waited to see whether the Almighty would bring about a change for the better after the sorrowful news. The distinguished warrior walked across the floor with his companions—the hall-wood resounded—until he could address the wise lord of the Danes with his words. He asked if the night had been agreeable to his wishes.

XX

Hrothgar, protector of the Scyldings, spoke: "Do not ask about happiness! Trouble is renewed for the Danish people. Aeschere is dead, the older brother of Yrmenlaf, my confidant and counselor, my comrade shoulder to shoulder when we defended our heads in battle, when the troops clashed together and struck the boars on the helmets. Whatever a man should be, a very good warrior, that Aeschere was! A wandering and murderous spirit became his slayer in Heorot. I do not know where the terrible creature exulting in her carrion has returned, rejoicing in her feast. She has avenged the feud in

---

1. **drunken,** not to be taken too literally.   **5. destiny . . . many men,** an exaggeration: only one man was killed. **XIX.** [Lines 1251–1320.]   **17. not there.** Beowulf, like Hrothgar, had sleeping-quarters outside Heorot.   **20. well-known hand,** Grendel's.   **36. night . . . wishes,** a pricelessly inappropriate morning's greeting by an innocent guest.   **XX.** [Lines 1321–82.]

BEOWULF

which you last night killed Grendel in a violent manner with strong grapplings, because he had too long diminished and destroyed my people. He fell in fight having forfeited his life, and then a second mighty evil-doer came who wished to avenge her son and who has carried the feud far, as it may appear to many a thane who weeps in his heart for his treasure-giver—severe distress. Now the hand lies low which treated you well in every desire.

"I have heard inhabitants of the land, my countrymen, hall-counselors, say that they had seen two such great wanderers in the waste borderlands, alien spirits, hold the moors. One of these, as they could most clearly make out, was in the likeness of a woman; the other miserable creature walked the paths of exile in the form of a man, except that he was larger than any other man; men in earlier days named him Grendel. They did not know any father, nor whether any evil spirits had been born before them. They inhabit a secret land, the retreats of wolves, windy headlands, the dangerous fen-path where the mountain brooks go down under the mists of the cliffs, the stream beneath the earth. It is not far from here in miles that the pool stands; above it hang groves covered with frost, a firm-rooted wood overshadows the water. Then on each night one can see a fearful wonder, fire on the water. There is no one so wise among the children of men that he knows the bottom. Although the stag, the hart strong with horns, pressed hard by dogs, may seek the wood, put to flight from far away, he will give up his life on the bank before he will go into the pool to save his head. The place is not safe! Thence black surging water ascends to the clouds when the wind stirs up hateful storms until the sky becomes gloomy, and the heavens weep. Now help depends upon you alone. You do not yet know the region, the dangerous place, where you may find the sinful creature. Seek if you dare! I shall reward you for the battle with riches, ancient treasures, as I did before, with twisted gold, if you come away alive."

XXI

Beowulf spoke, the son of Ecgtheow: "Do not grieve, wise man! It is better for any man that he should avenge his friend rather than that he should mourn too much. Each of us must await the end of life in the world. Let him who is able endeavor to win glory before death; that shall afterwards be best for a dead warrior. Arise, protector of the kingdom, and let us go quickly to examine the track of Grendel's relative. I promise this to you: she shall not escape in any hiding-place, nor in the bosom of the earth, nor in the mountain-wood, nor at the bottom of the sea, go where she will! Be patient this day in each misfortune, as I expect you to be." The old man sprang up and thanked God, the mighty Lord, for what the man had said.

Then a horse was bridled for Hrothgar, a steed with curly mane. The wise prince rode in stately fashion; a band of warriors marched along on foot. The footprints were visible far and wide along the forest paths, the track over the plain, as she had gone forward across the dark moor. She bore lifeless the best of the thanes who watched over the house with Hrothgar. The children of men went over the steep rocky slopes, the narrow paths, cheerless lonely ways, unknown tracts, precipitous cliffs, many a home of water-monsters. Hrothgar with a few wise men went ahead to examine the place, until he suddenly found mountain-trees, a joyless wood, leaning over the gray stone; the water stood below, bloody and stirred up. It was painful in mind to all the Danes, the people of the Scyldings, to many a retainer, grief to every man, when on the cliff they found Aeschere's head. The flood surged with blood—the people looked on—with hot gore. The horn rang forth again and again its ready war-song. The troop all sat down. They saw then on the water many of the race of serpents, strange sea-snakes, exploring the waves, also water-monsters lying on the slopes of the headlands, serpents and wild beasts, such as in the morning often carry out a perilous trip on the sea. They rushed on their way, fierce and enraged; they heard the noise, the war-horn sing. A man of the Geats with an arrow shot from a bow deprived one of them of his life, of the art of swimming, in that a hard war-arrow stood in his vitals. He was the slower in swimming in the sea to the extent to which death took him away. Quickly he was pressed hard in the waves with barbed boar-spears, attacked by force, and pulled up on the cliff, a wonderful sea-creature. The men looked at the horrible stranger.

Beowulf dressed himself in armor; he did not fear at all for his life. His hand-knit coat of mail, spacious and cunningly decorated, which was able to protect his body so that the hostile grasp could not injure his breast, the malicious attack of the angry one harm his life, had to explore the sea. And the shining helmet, which must stir up the depths of the pool, visit the surging water, adorned as it was with jewels, encircled with splendid chains, as the

1. **last night,** night before last (?). 7-8. **thane . . . treasure-giver.** This would suggest that Aeschere was a chief in his own right. **XXI.** [Lines 1383-1472.]

35. **man of the Geats,** Beowulf. 39. **death . . . away,** litotes!

maker of weapons wrought it in days of old, wonderfully made, set about with boar-figures, so that no sword nor battle-weapon could cut him thereafter, this was to protect his head. Nor was that, further, the most insignificant of powerful helps which Hrothgar's orator lent to him in his need: the name of the hilted sword was Hrunting. It was a pre-eminent ancient treasure; the edge was iron, decorated with poison stripes, hardened with blood shed in battle. In fight it never failed any of the men who grasped it with their hands, who dared enter upon perilous expeditions, the battlefield of the hostile ones. This was not the first time that it should do a courageous act. Indeed the kinsman of Ecglaf, powerful of strength, did not remember what he had said earlier, drunken with wine, when he lent the weapon to a better swordsman. He himself did not dare to risk his life under the turmoil of the waves, to perform bravery; there he lost glory and fame for heroic deeds. It was not so with the other after he had made himself ready for battle.

XXII

Beowulf spoke, the son of Ecgtheow: "Remember, glorious kinsman of Healfdene, wise king, generous friend of men, now that I am ready for the adventure, what we two spoke about formerly, in case I should lose my life for your necessity, that you would ever be in the place of a father to me when I was dead. Be a guardian to my young retainers, my companions, if battle takes me away. Also send the treasures which you gave to me, dear Hrothgar, to Hygelac. The lord of the Geats can perceive from the gold, the son of Hrethel understand, when he gazes at that treasure, that I found a giver of rings who was good in manly virtues, one whom I enjoyed while I could. And let Unferth, the famous man, have the old heirloom, the splendid sword with wavy ornamentation, the hard-edged weapon. I shall achieve glory with Hrunting or death shall take me!"

After these words the prince of the Weder-Geats hastened quickly—he did not wish to wait for an answer. The surge of the lake received the warrior. It was a good part of the day before he could see the bottom of the pool. At once she who, fiercely ravenous, had inhabited the region of the waves for a hundred half-years, perceived, angry and greedy, that a man from above was exploring the land of monsters. Then she grasped at him, seized the warrior with terrible grips. None the sooner did she harm his sound body; the ring-mail protected him round about the outside so that she could not penetrate the coat of mail, the intertwined armor, with her hateful fingers. Then the she-wolf of the lake, when she came to the bottom, bore the prince of rings to her dwelling, so that he was not able—no matter how brave he was—to wield weapons, but many strange creatures harassed him in the water, many a sea-beast tried to pierce his coat of mail with battle-tusks, the monsters pursued him. Then the hero saw that he was in some kind of hostile hall, where no water at all harmed him, nor could the sudden attack of the flood reach him because of the roofed hall. He saw fire-light, a brilliant flame, shine brightly.

Then the good man beheld the accursed monster of the deep, the great water-witch. He gave a mighty impetus to his sword—his hand did not withhold the blow—so that the ring-sword sang a fierce battle-song on her head. Then the visitor discovered that the flashing sword would not cut her or harm her life, but the edge failed the prince in his need. It had earlier endured many battles, often cut through a helmet, the war-garment of one doomed to die. This was the first time that glory failed the excellent treasure.

The kinsman of Hygelac was again resolute, not at all slow in courage, but mindful of glorious deeds. The angry warrior threw the sword with curved markings and ornaments so that it lay on the earth, hard and steel-edged. He trusted in his strength, in the grip of his might. So must a man do who thinks to win enduring praise in battle; nor can he care for his life. The prince of the Geats then grasped Grendel's mother by the shoulder—he did not shrink from battle. The man brave in fight, since he was angry, flung his deadly foe so that she fell to the floor. She in turn quickly gave him requital with fierce grippings and grasped against him. Then, weary at heart, the strongest of warriors on foot stumbled so that he fell. Then she sat upon the hall-visitor and drew her knife, broad and bright-edged. She wished to avenge her son, her only offspring. The woven coat of mail lay on his shoulder; that preserved his life, prevented the entrance of point and edge. The son of Ecgtheow, the warrior of the Geats, would have perished under the wide earth had not his coat of mail, his hard armor, been

---

6. **orator,** Unferth. 9. **decorated . . . stripes.** This is usually taken to be a reference to the use of acid in tracing lines on metal, but it can be interpreted in a more literal fashion: poisoned weapons were, by no means uncommon in early days, and putrid blood was, and is, often used for that purpose. 19-20. **lost glory . . . deeds.** The poet finds it hard to forgive Unferth, even after his obvious amendment. **XXII.** [Lines 1473-1556.] 40. **weapon,** presumably Beowulf's own sword, which he is leaving behind.

25-26. **cut her . . . life.** Like Grendel, his mother was impervious to ordinary weapons.

of aid to him—and holy God brought about victory. The wise Lord, the ruler of the heavens, decided easily for right when Beowulf stood up again.

XXIII

He then saw among other weapons a victorious sword, an ancient sword made by giants, firm in edge, the glory of warriors. That was the best of weapons, except that it was larger than any other man could carry to battle, good and adorned, the handiwork of giants. Then the champion of the Scyldings seized the linked hilt, rough and fierce, drew the ring-sword, despairing of life, struck angrily, so that it grasped her strongly on the neck, and broke the vertebrae. The sword went all the way through her doomed body. She fell to the floor; the sword was bloody; the man rejoiced in his work. The flame shone, the light arose inside, just as from heaven brightly shines the candle of the skies. He looked through the building. Hygelac's thane then went to the wall, angry and resolute, he raised the hard weapon by the hilt. The sword was not at all useless to the warrior, for he quickly wished to repay Grendel for the many attacks which he had made on the Danes, much more often than on that one occasion when he had killed Hrothgar's retainers in their sleep, eaten fifteen sleeping men of the Danish people, and carried off an equal number, a hideous booty. He had given him his reward for this, the fierce warrior, so that now he saw Grendel, worn out with fighting, lying lifeless on his resting-place, just as the fight in Heorot had earlier injured him. The corpse sprang far when it suffered a blow after death, a hard sword-stroke, and thus he cut off the head.

Soon the wise men, those who looked at the water with Hrothgar, saw that the tossing waves were stirred up, the water stained with blood. The gray-haired old men spoke together about the brave man, said of the hero that they did not think that he would come again victorious to seek their famous king. Many agreed in thinking that the she-wolf of the lake had killed him. Then the ninth hour of the day came. The valiant Scyldings left the cliff; the generous friend of men went home from there. The strangers sat sick at heart and stared at the pool. They wished but did not expect that they would see again their friendly lord himself.

Then that sword, that battle-weapon, began to waste away in consequence of drops of the blood shed in battle. That was a wonderful thing that it all melted most like ice when the Father, who has power over seasons and times, loosens the bond of frost, unwinds the water-fetters. That is the true God. The prince of the Weder-Geats took no more of the treasures in the dwelling-place, although he saw many there, than the head and with it the jewel-adorned hilt; the sword had melted away before, the ornamented blade had burned up; the blood was hot to that extent, the alien spirit so poisonous who died in there. The man who in battle had lived to see the fall in fight of his foes was swimming at once, he dove up through the water. The tossing waves were all cleansed, the spacious regions, when the alien spirit left her life-days and this transitory world.

Then the stout-hearted lord of the seafarers came swimming to the land. He rejoiced in his sea-booty, in the mighty burden of the things which he had with him. A splendid group of retainers went to meet him then, they were glad of their lord, they thanked God that they were able to see him unharmed. Then the helmet and the coat of mail were quickly taken off the agile man. The lake became quiet, water under the heavens, stained with the blood of slaughter. They went forth from there walking, glad at heart they traversed the path, the familiar street. The brave men carried the head from the cliff by the water-side with difficulty for each of the valiant ones. It took four with labor to carry the head of Grendel to the gold-hall on the shaft of a spear, until presently fourteen Geats, courageous and warlike, came walking to the hall. The leader, brave among the troop, trod the plain near the mead-hall. Then the lord of thanes, the man daring in deeds and exalted for glory, the warrior brave in battle, came walking in to greet Hrothgar. Then Grendel's head, terrible to the men and the lady with them, was carried by the hair into the hall where the men were drinking, a wonderful spectacle. The men looked on.

XXIV

Beowulf spoke, the son of Ecgtheow: "Son of Healfdene, prince of the Scyldings, we have gladly brought to you as a sign of glory this sea-booty which you look on here. With difficulty I came through that fight beneath the water with my life, engaged in the task painfully. The battle was almost

XXIII. [Lines 1557–1650.] **20. candle of the skies,** sun. **35–36. cut off the head.** The head would be a nice thing to take home to Hrothgar; decapitation would prevent Grendel from haunting the Danes, and besides, our ancestors did not make a fetish of the sanctity of a dead foe's body. **44. ninth hour,** 3 P.M. **47. strangers,** the Geats.

1–3. began . . . battle, or perhaps: "began to waste away in battle-icicles because of (the action of the) blood shed in battle." **XXIV.** [Lines 1651–1739.]

brought to an end, save that God protected me. I was unable to accomplish anything with Hrunting in the fight, although that weapon is good. But the ruler of men granted to me that I saw a beautiful and large old sword hang on the wall—most often He directs the friendless—and that I drew the weapon. When I had an opportunity I killed in the fight the guardians of the house. Then that battle-sword, the ornamented weapon, burned up as soon as the blood, hottest of gore shed in battle, sprang forth. I carried the hilt away from the fiends. I avenged the wicked deeds, the slaughter of the Danes, as was fitting. Therefore, I promise you that you can sleep free from care in Heorot with the company of your men and with every retainer among your people, both tried followers and young warriors, since from that side, prince of the Scyldings, you have no need to fear death for your men, as you did before." Then the gilded hilt, the ancient work of the giants, was given into the hand of the old warrior, the gray fighter. After the death of the demons the work of the wonderful smiths passed into the possession of the lord of the Danes; when the hostile-hearted creature, God's adversary, guilty of murder, and his mother, too, had left this world, it came into the control of the best of those kings who distribute treasure in Skåne between the two seas.

Hrothgar spoke—he looked at the hilt, the old heirloom, on which was written the origin of the ancient strife, when the flood, rushing sea, killed the race of giants; they suffered terribly. They were a people estranged from the eternal Lord; the Ruler gave them their final reward for that through the surging of the water. Also on the sword-guards of shining gold was rightly marked by means of runic letters, set down and stated, for whom that sword, the best of weapons, with twisted hilt and serpentine ornamentation, was first made. Then the wise man, the son of Healfdene, spoke—all were silent: "Behold, this may he say who does truth and right among the people, who remembers all far-back time, an old king, that this man was born of superior people. Your glory is established throughout distant regions, my friend Beowulf, over every people. You possess it all steadily, strength and wisdom of mind. I shall carry out my friendship, just as we spoke together a short time ago. You are bound to be a comfort for a long time to your people, a help to the warriors. Heremod was not the same to the men of Ecgwela, the Honor-Scyldings. He did not develop to the pleasure but rather to slaughter and death for the Danish people. Enraged he killed his table-companions, his close comrades, until the famous prince went alone away from the joys of men, despite the fact that omnipotent God had advanced him mightily to the delights of power, brought him forth above all men. For all that a bloodthirsty thought grew in his mind; he gave no rings to the Danes in order to obtain glory. He lived joyless until on that account he suffered the distress of strife, a long-lasting affliction. Do you learn from that, understand manly virtues! Wise from many winters, I recited this speech to you.

"It is a wonderful thing to tell how mighty God through His ample spirit distributes to mankind wisdom or land and nobility; He has control of all things. At times He lets the thoughts of a man of illustrious family turn to love, gives him the joy of earth in his native land, to control the stronghold of men, makes subject to him sections of the world, a spacious realm, so that he himself in his folly cannot conceive of the end of it. He lives in abundance; neither illness nor age hinder him at all, nor does evil care become grievous to his mind, nor does enmity anywhere manifest itself in war, but all the world goes in accordance with his desire. He knows nothing worse,

XXV

until within him great arrogance grows and flourishes. Then the guard sleeps, the keeper of the soul; that sleep is too sound, bound with troubles, for the murderer who shoots wickedly from his bow is very near. Then beneath his helmet he is struck in the breast by the sharp arrow—he cannot protect himself—by the perverse and mysterious commands of the evil spirit. He thinks that which he long held to be too little for him, angry in mind he becomes avaricious, not at all does he proudly give ornamented rings, and he forgets and neglects the future state because God, the ruler of heaven, had earlier given him a share of honors. In the end again, it happens that the perishing body declines, falls doomed to die. Another succeeds who distributes treasures, the hero's ancient riches, recklessly, and does not care for fear. Guard yourself, my dear Beowulf, best of men, against wickedness, and choose the better course, eternal counsels. Shun pride, famous warrior! Now for a little while the power of your might will exist; soon in turn it will

---

8. **guardians**, really, of course, only one.   27. **Skåne**, the southern part of Scandinavia, applied to the land of the Danes.   49. **Heremod.** See page 28.   50. **Ecgwela**, evidently a Danish king, but otherwise unidentified.

15–16. **distributes . . . nobility.** Some men are given wisdom, others prosperity.   **XXV.** [Lines 1740–1816.]   33. **murderer**, the Devil, whose evil suggestions are compared to arrows shot from a bow.

BEOWULF

happen that sickness or the sword will deprive you of your strength, or else the grasp of fire, or the surging of the flood, or the attack of the sword, or the flight of the spear, or terrible old age; or else the brightness of your eyes will fail and become dim. Presently, warrior, death will overcome you.

"So I have ruled the Ring-Danes under the sky for a hundred half-years, protected them with spears and swords in war against many tribes, until I did not consider anyone under the expanse of the heaven an enemy to me. Behold, a change from this came to me in my native land, grief after joy, as soon as Grendel, the old adversary, became my invader. Continually I endured the visitation with great sorrow of soul. Thanks be to God for this, to the eternal Lord, that I have remained in life until I could look with my eyes on the blood-stained head after the old strife. Go now to your seat, a man distinguished in war, and enjoy the delightful feast. For us two there will be many common treasures when it is morning."

The Geat was glad at heart, at once he went to seek out his seat, as the wise man commanded. Then again as before was a feast fittingly prepared a second time for the brave sitters in the hall. The cover of night lowered, dark above the warriors. The retainers all rose; the gray-haired old Scylding wished to go to bed. The Geat, the bold warrior, desired exceedingly to rest. At once a chamberlain, who for courtesy attended to all the needs which sea-fighters in those days ought to have, showed him forth, weary of his journey, from a far country.

Then the large-hearted man rested himself. The hall towered, vaulted and ornamented with gold. The guest slept within until the black raven with a happy heart proclaimed the joy of heaven. Then the bright light came hastening over the shadows. The warriors hurried, the men were eager to go again to their people; the bold visitor wished to seek his ship for a journey far away. Then the brave son of Ecglaf ordered Hrunting to be brought, bade him [Beowulf] to take his sword, the precious weapon. He [Beowulf] said thanks to him for the gift and said that he considered the sword good, strong in battle; with no words did he find fault with the sword's edge. He was a courageous man. And then, eager to depart, the men were ready in their armor; the warrior, honored by the Danes, went to the high seat where the other was; the man brave in battle greeted Hrothgar.

XXVI

Beowulf spoke, the son of Ecgtheow: "Now we seafarers, come from afar, wish to say that we desire to go to Hygelac. We were entertained here fittingly and delightfully. You have treated us well. If, ruler of men, I can at all earn your affection by warlike deeds more than I have already done, I shall be ready at once. If I hear across the expanse of the sea that neighboring peoples are threatening you terribly, as your enemies have done formerly, I will bring to you a thousand retainers, warriors to your aid. I know in the case of Hygelac, king of the Geats, guardian of the people, although he is young, that he will assist me with words and deeds so that I may honor you well, and bear a spear as help for you, the support of strength, in case you have need of men. If, on the other hand, Hrethric, son of the king, determines to go to the courts of the Geats, he can find many friends there. Far countries, when visited, are better for him who is himself good."

Hrothgar spoke in answer to him: "The wise God sent these words into your mind. I never heard a man so young in age speak more knowingly. You are strong in might, prudent in mind, and wise of words. I hold the expectation that if it happens that the spear, fierce battle, disease, or the sword carries away the son of Hrethel, your lord, the guardian of the people, and you have your life, that the Sea-Geats will have no better king to choose, a protector of men, if you will keep the kingdom of your kinsmen. The longer I know you, dear Beowulf, the better your character pleases me. You have brought it about that there shall be a mutual peace between the two people, the Geats and the Spear-Danes, that strife shall rest, the hostile acts which they formerly performed. There shall be treasures in common so long as I rule the wide realm, and many a man shall greet another with gifts across the gannet's bath. The ring-prowed ship shall bring presents and tokens of love over the sea. I know the people firmly disposed towards both foe and friend, blameless in every respect after the old fashion."

Then the protector of men, the kinsman of Healfdene, gave him twelve treasures within the hall; he ordered him to seek his own people in health with the gifts, and to come again soon. Then the king,

---

8. hundred half-years, a favorite period of time: Grendel's mother had inhabited the pool for fifty years, and Beowulf's own reign was to be of that duration. **36. joy of heaven,** the sun. **41-42. Hrunting . . . sword,** an ambiguous passage, which sometimes receives an exactly opposite interpretation, with Beowulf the giver, and Unferth the recipient, of the sword.

XXVI. [Lines 1817-87.] **31. son of Hrethel,** Hygelac. **34. keep the kingdom.** After Hygelac's death the kingdom was offered to Beowulf, but he refused to accept it while Heardred lived. **43. gannet's bath,** a kenning for "sea."

the lord of the Scyldings, good in character, kissed the best of warriors, and took him by the neck. Tears fell from the gray-haired man. To the wise old man there was expectation of two things, but of the alternate more, that they might not see each other again, courageous men in council. The man was dear to him to such an extent that he could not restrain his emotion, but in his breast, fixed by his heart-strings, a secret longing for the dear man burned in his blood. Beowulf, a warrior splendidly adorned with gold, walked from there over the greensward exulting in his treasure. The ship, which was riding at anchor, awaited its owner. Then the gift of Hrothgar was often praised on the way. That was a king blameless in everything until old age, which has often injured many, deprived him of the joys of strength.

XXVII

Then a troop of very brave young men came to the sea; they bore coats of mail, linked armor. The coastguard saw the return of the warriors, as he had done before. He did not greet the visitors with an insult from the promontory, but rode to meet them; he said that the warriors in bright armor went to their ship as welcome persons for the people of Weders. The spacious boat was on the sand, the ring-prowed ship loaded with armor, with horses and treasures; the mast towered above Hrothgar's precious things. Beowulf gave a sword bound with gold to the boat-guard, so that he was thereafter the more honored at the mead-bench for the treasure, the ancient heirloom. The boat went on, stirring up the deep water; it left the land of the Danes. Then a sea-garment was by the mast, a sail fixed with a rope; the ship creaked. The wind over the waves did not hinder the ship in its voyage. The boat went, it sailed with foamy neck over the waves, the ship with bound prow over the ocean streams, until they were able to make out the cliffs of the Geats, the familiar headlands. The ship pressed forward, driven by the wind, and rested on the land. Quickly the harbor-guard, who for a long time before had looked far out at sea longing for the dear men, was ready at the water. He fastened the roomy ship fast by anchor ropes to the sand, lest the force of the waves might drive away the fair wood. Then Beowulf ordered them to carry up the treasure of the warriors, the precious things and plated gold. It was not far from there for him to go to the distributor of treasure, Hygelac, son of Hrethel, where he lived at home with his retainers near the shore.

XXVII. [Lines 1888–1962.]   26–27. welcome ... Weders. "Your countrymen will be glad to see you."

The building was splendid, the king very valiant, exalted in his hall. Hygd was very young, wise and accomplished, although she, the daughter of Haereth, had spent but a small number of years within the castle. However, she was not illiberal nor too niggardly of gifts and of treasures to the people of the Geats. Modthrytho, the distinguished queen of the people, was moved by terrible sin. No brave man among the dear companions except for the great lord, dared venture so far that he gazed on her openly with his eyes; but if he did he considered the hand-woven deadly bonds destined for him. Quickly after being seized the sword was appointed for him, so that the ornamented blade might settle the matter, make known his death. Such is not a womanly custom for a lady to perform, that a peace-weaver should deprive a dear man of his life on account of a pretended insult. However, the kinsman of Hemming checked that: ale-drinkers told another story, namely, that she did less harm to the people, fewer hostile acts, after she was first given, gold-adorned, illustrious for her family, to the young warrior, when she had sought at her father's counsel the hall of Offa by a voyage over the yellowish-green sea. Afterwards there she, famous for goodness, enjoyed life on the throne very much, kept great love for the lord of heroes, who was, as I have heard say, the best of all mankind, of the human race, between the seas. Because Offa was a brave man in gifts and battles, honored far and wide, he guarded his native land with wisdom. From him Eomer was born as a help for warriors, the kinsman of Hemming, grandson of Garmund, powerful in battles.

XXVIII

The brave man himself then went with his troop over the sand, treading the beach, the broad shores. The candle of the world shone, the sun hurrying from the south. They took their way, they went quickly, to the place where, as they had heard, the guardian of men, the killer of Ongentheow, the

7. **Modthrytho.** This lady, presented as a foil for Hygd, is an ambiguous character. Even her name is uncertain: usually given as Thryth, recent scholarship leans, though not very confidently, to the present form. We gather that she was a wild and haughty maiden, taking affront easily and bringing about the death of those who annoyed her; after her marriage, however, her character and behavior changed and she became an admirable queen.   10. **great lord,** her father or her husband.   17. **peace-weaver,** woman.   19. **Hemming.** The relationship of Hemming to Offa is not clear.   24. **Offa,** the husband of Modthrytho, legendary king of the continental Angles, presumably at the end of the fourth century.   33. **Garmund,** Offa's father. XXVIII. [Lines 1963–2038.]   42. **Ongentheow.** See page 19, note 2.

BEOWULF

good young war-king, distributed rings inside the castle. The arrival of Beowulf was quickly announced to Hygelac, that there into the precincts of the palace the protector of warriors, the comrade in battle, was coming alive to the court, unhurt by the fight. The interior of the hall was cleared for those who were coming on foot, as the king ordered.

He who had survived the fighting sat then opposite him, kinsman by kinsman, after he had greeted his friendly lord with ceremonious speech and earnest words. The daughter of Haereth went through the hall with the mead-cups; she loved the people and bore the cup of strong drink to the hands of the warriors. Hygelac began to question his comrade fairly in the high hall, curiosity pressed him as to what the adventures of the Sea-Geats had been: "How did it happen to you on your trip, dear Beowulf, when you suddenly resolved to seek battle afar over the salt water, war in Heorot? Did you in any way remedy the widely known trouble for Hrothgar, the famous prince? I brooded over it with sorrow of soul and surging cares, nor did I have faith in the dear man's venture. For a long time I begged you that you would in no way approach the murderous spirit, but that you should let the Danes themselves settle the war with Grendel. I say thanks to God because I am able to see you uninjured."

Beowulf spoke, the son of Ecgtheow: "To many men, lord Hygelac, the great encounter is clear, what a fight there was between us two, Grendel and myself, in the place where for a long time he had accomplished very many troubles and miserable actions against the Victory-Scyldings. I avenged all that so that none of Grendel's kinsmen on earth, whoever lives longest of that hateful race, enveloped in crime, need exult over that din in the night. First I came there to the ring-hall to greet Hrothgar; as soon as the famous kinsman of Healfdene knew my mind he assigned me a seat beside his own sons. The company was joyful; I never saw in my whole life greater festivity among hall-inhabitants under the arch of heaven. From time to time the glorious queen, the pledge of peace for the people, went throughout the entire hall and urged the young men. Often she gave a ring to a man before she went to her seat. Now and then Hrothgar's daughter, whom I heard the men sitting in hall name Freawaru when she was giving the studded vessel to the warriors, bore the ale-cup to the old retainers, to the men one after another. She is betrothed, young and gold-adorned, to the gracious son of Froda; the lord of the Scyldings, the guardian of the kingdom, has decided upon this and considers it a good counsel that by means of the woman he may settle the strife, a part of the deadly feuds. As a rule it is only in rare cases where, after the fall of a prince, the deadly spear rests for more than a little while, even though the bride be a good one.

"It may then be displeasing to the prince of the Heathobards and to each warrior of the people, when he goes into the hall with the woman, to see the noble children of the Danes, the warriors being entertained; on them gleam the heirlooms of their own ancestors, hard and adorned with rings, the treasure of the Heathobards, while they had been able to wield the weapons,—

XXIX–XXX

until they led their dear companions and their own lives to destruction in the shield-play. Then one man, an old warrior, who sees the treasure, speaks at the beer-drinking, he who remembers everything, the death of men by the spear—his heart is angry within him—begins, sad of mind, to try the heart of a young warrior through the thought of his breast, to stir up war, and speaks as follows: 'Are you able, my friend, to recognize the sword which your father, under his helmet, carried to battle for the last time, the precious weapon, when the Danes killed him, the valiant Scyldings who controlled the battlefield after Withergyld lay dead and after the fall of the warriors? Now the son of some one of their murderers goes, exulting in ornaments, into the hall, he boasts of the murder and carries the treasure which you rightfully should possess.' Thus he urges and reminds on every occasion with bitter words until the time comes when the woman's retainer sleeps in death for his father's acts, stained with blood, after the cut of the sword, having forfeited his life. The other gets away from there alive: he knows the land well. Then the oaths of men are broken on both sides. After that hostility boils up in Ingeld, and his love for his wife becomes cooler in consequence of seething sorrows. On that account I do not consider the friendship of the Heathobards,

9. him, Hygelac. **11. daughter of Haereth,** Hygd. **24–26. begged you . . . Grendel.** But compare page 22 above, where we were told that Beowulf was encouraged rather than dissuaded. **44–45. urged the young men,** to let themselves be served.

1–2. son of Froda, Ingeld. Froda was chief of the Heathobards. **7–8. the deadly spear . . . while.** In other words, the attempt to stop a feud by means of marriage is not likely to succeed. **9–13. It may . . . entertained.** The translation of this sentence is anything but certain, although the sense of the whole passage is reasonably clear. **XXIX–XXX.** [Lines 2039–2143.] **21. treasure,** a sword. **37–38. retainer,** one of Freawaru's Danish attendants, who had had the bad taste to carry into the Heathobard court a sword previously taken from a dead Heathobard warrior, possibly Withergyld, whose son was still alive and persuaded to avenge his father. **40. The other,** the Heathobard avenger.

all of their alliance with the Danes, to be sincere, or their friendship firm.

"I shall go on speaking further about Grendel, so that you, giver of treasure, may know well to what end the hand-to-hand encounter of the warriors came. After the gem of heaven had glided over the plains the angry spirit came, terrible and hostile in the evening, to attack us where we in good health were guarding the hall. There the fatal attack was against Hondscio, a deadly evil to the doomed man. The belted warrior was the first to lie in death; Grendel became the devourer of the glorious young retainer, he completely swallowed up his body. Nor would the bloody-toothed murderer, intent on evil, go away empty-handed from the gold-hall any the sooner for that, but he, strong in might, made trial of me, seized me with ready hand. A pouch in the shape of a glove, spacious and wonderful, was hanging at his side, made firm with cunningly wrought clasps; it was all made with ingenuity, by the devil's skill and from the skins of a dragon. The fierce doer of wicked deeds wanted to put me, guiltless, inside with many others. It could not be so, since I stood upright in anger. It is too long to relate how I gave the people's enemy his reward for each evil act; there, my lord, I honored your people by my deeds. He got away and enjoyed his life for a little while; nevertheless his right hand remained behind in Heorot, and he, going from there humiliated, mournful in spirit, fell to the bottom of the lake. The lord of the Scyldings rewarded me greatly for the bloody conflict, with plated gold, many treasures, when morning had come and we were seated at the feast. There was song and entertainment; a wise old Scylding recounted deeds of long ago. At times the man brave in battle touched the joy of the harp, the wood of mirth, at times he recited a story both true and sad; at times the noble-spirited king told truthfully a wonderful tale. At times again the aged warrior, bound down by age, began to mourn for his youth, his might in battle. His breast surged within him when he, wise with years, remembered many things. Thus we inside there took our pleasure the entire day until another night came to men. Then again quickly Grendel's mother was ready for revenge for her injury, she came full of sorrow; death, the warlike enmity of the Weders, had carried off her son. The frightful woman avenged her child, killed a man boldly; then life departed from Aeschere, the wise old counselor. Nor when morning came could the people of the Danes burn him, the dead man, with fire, nor place the dear man on the funeral pile. She carried that body away under the mountain-stream in a foe's arms. That was the bitterest sorrow for Hrothgar of any which had happened to the prince of the people for a long time. Then the king, troubled in mind, begged me by your life that I should do an heroic deed in the tumult of the waters, should risk my life, perform a glorious act; he promised me a reward. Then, as is known far and wide, I found the fierce and horrible guardian of the deep surging water. There for a time was hand-to-hand combat between us. The water boiled with blood and I cut off the head of Grendel's mother in the battle-hall with the great sword. I carried my life away from there with difficulty; I was then not yet doomed to die, but the protector of men, the kinsman of Healfdene, again gave me many treasures.

XXXI

"Thus the king of the people lived in good customs; not at all had I lost my gifts, the reward of my strength, but he, the son of Healfdene, gave me at my own discretion treasures which I wish to bring to you, my king, to present them to you with good will. All my joys are still dependent on you; I have few near relatives except you, Hygelac."

He then ordered them to bear in the boar-banner, the helmet towering in battle, the gray coat of mail, the adorned war-sword, after which he recited a speech: "Hrothgar gave me this armor, wise prince; in a word he ordered that I should first tell you about his gracious gift. He said that king Heorogar, prince of the Scyldings, had had it for a long while; none the sooner would he give the coats of mail to his son, the valiant Heoroweard, although he was well-disposed to him. Make good use of it all!" I heard that four bay horses, swift and all alike, followed the treasures. He bestowed the gift upon him, both horses and precious things. So ought a kinsman to do, and not at all weave a net of malice for the other with secret craft, or prepare death for his companion. His nephew was very loyal to Hygelac, brave in battles, and each was mindful of the other's pleasures. I heard that he gave to Hygd the collar, splendid with its wondrous jewel, which Wealhtheow, the king's daughter, had given him, and together with it three supple and saddle-bright horses. After receiving the jewel her breast was adorned with it.

So the son of Ecgtheow, a man known for his good deeds in battles, showed himself to be brave, acted in accordance with honor. He did not kill his hearth-companions when they had been drinking;

6–7. After the gem ... plains, after sunset.

XXXI. [Lines 2144–2220.]   **32. Heorogar.** See page 18, note 5.

his heart was not savage, but he, brave in battle, kept with the greatest self-control of mankind the ample gift which God had given to him. He was humiliated for a long time, as the sons of the Geats did not consider him good, nor would the lord of the Weders make him worth a great deal at the mead-bench; they thought that he was slow, a man without energy. A reversal of each of his troubles came to the famous man.

Then the protector of men, the king bold in fight, ordered them to bring in the heirloom of Hrethel, adorned with gold. There was not then among the Geats a better treasure in the form of a sword. He placed that in Beowulf's lap, and gave him seven thousand hides of land, a hall, and a principality. The land in the country was inherited by them both together, the country and the ancestral domain, but, more especially great rule for the other, because he was higher in rank.

[Part Two]

Again it came about in later days through the crashes of battle after Hygelac lay dead, and battle-swords became the death of Heardred under the shield when the Heatho-Scylfings sought him out among the glorious people, the fierce warriors assailed the nephew of Hereric in battle, that then the broad kingdom passed into Beowulf's hand.

He held it well for fifty years—the king was then advanced in age, the old guardian of the land—until on dark nights one began to act violently, a dragon who on the high heath watched over a hoard, a towering stone-barrow; a path unknown to men ran underneath. Some man or other went inside, made his way near to the heathen hoard, and took a cup, large and decorated with jewels, in his hand. Nor did he conceal it afterwards, although he had been tricked while sleeping by the thief's craft. The nation, the neighboring people of men, discovered the fact that he was angry.

8–9. **A reversal . . . man.** In his youth Beowulf was evidently a "male Cinderella," the name given to a hero who at first appears sluggish and so is scorned and neglected by his companion, but who inevitably comes forward at some time of stress to prove himself a paragon of bravery and strength. 15. **hides.** A hide was originally thought of as the amount of land necessary for the support of a single family; the exact area was uncertain and probably variable from period to period, perhaps with a maximum of 120 acres. 18. **the other,** Hygelac. 26. **Heatho-Scylfings,** the Swedes. 28. **Hereric,** Hygd's brother. 29. **Beowulf's hand.** The folio which begins at this point is in very bad shape and both readings and translation are often highly conjectural. 34. **stone-barrow,** a prehistoric burial mound, of the type often found in northern Europe, whose stone sides and top were covered with earth. 38. **he,** the dragon.

XXXII

Not at all of his own accord or of his own desire did he break into the dragon's hoard, the man who harmed him sorely, but for bitter necessity the servant of some one of the children of men fled from hostile blows, and in need of a house made his way inside there, a guilty man. At once it came about that horror arose in him from the strange creature; nevertheless when the miserable fugitive escaped from the terrible serpent—strife was made for him—hastening in his going when danger came upon him, he had the precious cup.

There were many similar ancient treasures in the earth-house just as a certain thoughtful man in former days hid them there, the immense legacy of a noble race, precious treasures. Death had taken them all away in earlier times, and the one man from the host of the people who still moved about there longest, the guardian who was mourning for his friends, expected the same outcome, namely, that he would be able to enjoy the old treasures for but a little space of time. The barrow, quite ready, was situated on a plain near the waves of the sea, new by the headland, firm in its prisoning powers. The guardian of rings carried inside there the part of the treasure worthy of being hoarded, ornamented gold. He spoke a few words: "Hold now, earth, since the warriors no longer are able, the property of men. Indeed, good men formerly got it from you. Death in battle, fearful deadly evil, carried off each of the men of my people who left this life, who had seen the last of joy in the hall. I do not have anyone who might wear a sword or polish the gold-plated cup, the excellent drinking-vessel; the retainers have gone elsewhere. The hard helmet with its fairly wrought gold is fated to be deprived of its plate; the polishers sleep in death whose duty it was to prepare the helmet; and also the armor, which in battle withstood the cut of swords across the crashing of shields, falls to pieces after the hero. Nor may the coat of mail made of rings go far with the war-chief, by the side of the heroes. There is no joy of the harp, no mirth of the glee-wood, nor does

XXXII. [Lines 2221–2311.] 3–13. **Not at all . . . cup.** This passage is hopelessly corrupt in the manuscript. 17. **precious treasures.** With the aid of a subsequent passage (page 49 below) the story of the hoard may be given as follows: In ancient days the treasure had been hidden and a curse placed upon it. Certain warriors found it, but the curse would appear to have fallen upon them and their number gradually diminished, until their last survivor put the hoard in the barrow with an elegiac accompaniment. The dragon then came upon it and guarded it for three hundred years, at the end of which time a cup was stolen from the hoard and the dragon's anger was directed against the Geats. 44. **glee-wood,** a kenning for "harp."

the good hawk fly through the hall, nor the swift horse tramp in the court. Death and destruction have sent away many of the race of men." So, sad in mind, the one left after all the others complained of his care, went about sadly day and night until the hot touch of death reached at his heart. The old robber in the night, he who goes burning to the barrows, the smooth, hostile dragon who flies by night encircled with fire, found the pleasant treasure standing open. Men fear him very much. He has to seek treasure in the earth, where, old in years, he guards the heathen gold; nor is it at all the better for him on that account.

Thus the foe of the people guarded a huge treasure-house in the earth for three hundred years, until a man angered him in his mind; he carried to his liege lord an ornamented cup, asked his lord for a compact of peace. When the treasure was explored, the hoard of rings diminished, the poor man's prayer was granted. The lord looked at the ancient work of men for the first time.

When the serpent awoke a quarrel was brought to life; then he sniffed along the stone, the stouthearted one found the footprints of his foe; he had stepped in his advance with secret cunning near the head of the dragon. Thus may one not fated to die easily endure misery and exile, he whom the favor of the Lord guards. The keeper of the treasure sought earnestly along the ground, he wished to find the man who had dealt with him grievously in his sleep; hot and fierce in mind, he often went all about the outside of the mound. There was not any man in the wilderness, yet he rejoiced in battle, in the work of fighting. Now and again he went into the mound and looked for the precious cup; he at once discovered this, that some man had tampered with the gold, the splendid treasures. The guardian of the treasure waited with difficulty until evening had come; the keeper of the barrow was angry then, the hostile one wished to repay with fire for the excellent drinking-vessel. When the day was gone, to the delight of the serpent, he did not wish to remain longer on the wall, but he went with fire, impelled by flame. The beginning was terrible to the people of the land, just as it was ended quickly and sorrowfully for their giver of treasure.

XXXIII

Then the demon began to vomit flames, to burn the splendid houses—the gleam of fire arose to the horror of men; the hostile air-flier did not wish to leave anything alive there. The warfare of the serpent was widely visible, the persecution of the cruelly hostile creature both near and far, how the destroyer hated and harmed the people of the Geats. He shot back again to the treasure, to his secret dwelling before daytime. He had enveloped the people of the land with flame, with fire and burning. He trusted in the barrow, in his fighting force and the wall, but the expectation deceived him.

Then in truth the terror was quickly announced to Beowulf, that his own home, the best of houses, the throne of the Geats, had melted in the surge of fire. That was distress in the breast, the greatest sorrow of the heart, for the good man. The wise man thought that contrary to the old law he had bitterly offended the Lord, the eternal God; his breast within him boiled with gloomy thoughts, as was not usual for him. The fire-dragon had destroyed with flames the fort of the people, the waterland from without, the stronghold; for this the war-king, prince of the Weders, devised a punishment for him. The protector of warriors, the lord of men, ordered them to make a splendid battle-shield all of iron; he knew surely that a wooden shield could not help him, a linden shield against fire. The very good prince was fated to see the end of transitory days, of his life in the world, and the serpent with him, though the latter had guarded the hoarded wealth for a long time. The prince of rings scorned then that he should seek out the far-flier with a band of men, a large army; he did not dread that contest, nor consider in any way the serpent's fighting ability, its strength and courage, because he had earlier passed safely through many a fight, braving distress, crashes of battle, when he, a victorious man, had purged Hrothgar's dwelling, and crushed to death in battle the family of Grendel belonging to a hateful race.

That was not the least of battles where they killed Hygelac, when the king of the Geats, the friendly lord of the people, the son of Hrethel, died by the drinks of the sword, struck down by the weapon, in the battle charges in the land of the West Frisians. Beowulf came away from there by means of his own strength, he engaged in swimming. He had on his arm, he alone, thirty suits of armor, when he went to the sea. Not at all did the Hetware who

18. compact of peace. The man who stole the cup was evidently a fugitive from justice who used his booty to buy back his position in the community. **XXXIII.** [Lines 2312–2390.]

21. from without, "outside the sea-board," or "around the island." **43. drinks of the sword,** blood flowing from his wounds. **45–48. Beowulf . . . the sea.** Observe that in this, the only fairly certain historical event in the poem, Beowulf's share is a feat which belongs to folk tale rather than to history. **Hetware,** a Frankish people on the lower Rhine; here to be equated with the Frisians.

bore their linden shields against him in front have reason to be exulting in their fight on foot; few of the warriors came again to seek out their homes! The son of Ecgtheow swam across the expanse of the sea, a wretched solitary man, to his people again. There Hygd offered him treasure and the kingdom, rings and the throne; she did not put trust in her son, that he could hold the ancestral seats against foreigners when Hygelac was dead. None the sooner could the poor people prevail upon the prince that on any consideration he would be lord over Heardred or would take the royal power; yet he guarded him among the people with friendly counsels, with good-will and help, until he became older, and had power over the Weder-Geats.

Banished men, the sons of Ohthere, came to him across the sea; they had rebelled against the protector of the Scylfings, the best of those sea-kings who dealt out treasure in Sweden, a famous lord. That became his life's end for him; for his hospitality he, the son of Hygelac, obtained a mortal wound there with blows of the sword. And after Heardred lay dead the son of Ongentheow went again to visit his home, and he let Beowulf keep the principality, have power over the Geats: that was a good king.

XXXIV

He thought of a reward in later days for the fall of his prince: he became a friend to the wretched Eadgils. He aided the son of Ohthere with his people across the broad sea, with men and weapons. He avenged it afterwards with cold and sorrowful expeditions, he deprived the king of his life.

Thus the son of Ecgtheow had survived each of his contests, of his dangerous battles, of his courageous deeds, until that one day when he had to fight against the serpent. The lord of the Geats enraged with anger went with eleven others to see the dragon. He had by then heard whence the feud arose, the evil affliction of men. The famous and precious vessel had come into his possession from the hand of the informer. He who had brought about the beginning of the trouble was the thirteenth man in the troop; a captive, sad in mind and wretched, he had to guide them thence to the place. He went against his will until he recognized an earth-hall, a barrow under the ground, near the surge of the sea, the tossing water; inside it was full of works of art and ornaments. The monstrous guardian, the ready fighter, old under the earth, kept the gold treasures; it was not an easy bargain for any man to win it. The king brave in battle sat down on the headland; then the generous prince of the Geats saluted his retainers. His heart was sad, restless and ready for death, the fate was exceedingly near which was to greet the old man, try to reach his soul's treasure, part asunder his life from his body. Not long after that was the life of the prince enclosed by flesh.

Beowulf spoke, the son of Ecgtheow: "In my youth I survived storms of battle, many times of war; I remember all of that. I was seven years old when my lord of treasures, the friendly prince of the people, took me away from my father. King Hrethel protected me and had me, gave me precious things and banquets, remembered kinship. During his life I, a boy in the castle, was not at all more hateful to him than any one of his sons, Herebeald and Haethcyn, or even my Hygelac. A bed of death was unfittingly spread for the eldest by the acts of his kinsman, when Haethcyn struck down his friendly lord with an arrow from his horn-bow: he missed his mark and shot his kinsman, one brother the other with a bloody missile. That was an inexpiable fight, wrong done exceedingly, wearying the mind in the breast. The prince, however, had to lose his life unavenged.

"Thus it is sad for an old man to live to see his son ride young on the gallows. Then he would recite a lay, a mournful song, when his son hangs as a joy to the raven, and he, old and wise with years, cannot bring him any aid. Always on each morning will he call to mind the death of his son. He does not care to wait for any other heir in the castle, since the one has experienced unhappy deeds through the necessity of death. He sees, sorrowfully, in his son's dwelling the deserted wine-hall, the windy resting-place deprived of joy. The horsemen sleep, the warriors in the grave. There is no sound of the harp there, or mirth in the dwelling there as had been before.

XXXV

"He goes then to his couch, sings a song of sorrow, he alone for his only son. The fields and the dwelling-place now seemed to him all too large.

"So the protector of the Weders had boiling sorrow in his heart for Herebeald; in no way could

---

17. Ohthere. See page 19, notes 3–4. **21. him,** Heardred. **24. son of Ongentheow,** Onela. **XXXIV.** [Lines 2391–2459.] **32. Eadgils.** See page 19, notes 4–5. **35. the king,** Onela. **46. a captive.** He was in custody because of his ultimate responsibility for the devastation.

22. the eldest, Herebeald; see page 19, note 3. **29. unavenged.** Hrethel could hardly take revenge for one son from another, especially since the killing had been accidental, and yet the duty of vengeance is stressed. **XXXV.** [Lines 2460–2601.]

he settle the feud by punishment to the slayer; none the more could he persecute the warrior with hateful acts, although he was not dear to him. He then gave up the joys of men because of the sorrow which had happened to him too sorely: he chose God's light. To his sons, as a prosperous man does, he left land and towns when he departed from life.

"Then there was wrong-doing and fighting, mutual strife over the broad water, between the Swedes and the Geats, severe hostility, after Hrethel died and the sons of Ongentheow were brave and warlike. They did not wish to preserve peace across the sea, but often did terrible and malicious slaughter around Hreosnabeorh. My relatives avenged that, the feud and crime, as it was learned, although one of them paid with his life for the hard bargain: the fight was fatal for Haethcyn, prince of the Geats. Then on a morning, as I heard, one relative with the edges of the sword avenged the other on the murderer, when Ongentheow attacks Eofor. The old Scylfing fell mortally wounded, his war-helmet split in two; his hand remembered battles enough, it did not withhold the deadly blow.

"I paid him with the gleaming sword in battle, as it was granted me, for the precious things which he had given to me; he gave me land, an estate and a delightful home. There was no need for him that he should seek among the Gifthas or the Spear-Danes or in Sweden to buy a poorer warrior for a price. I always wished to be before him in the troop, alone in front, and so I shall always carry out battle while this sword endures, this sword which early and late has often served me since for glory's sake I became the slayer of Daeghrefn, champion of the Hugas. In no way could he bring the decorated armor and breast-ornament to the king of the Frisians, but the guardian of the banner fell in the battle, the hero in his strength. The sword was not his slayer, but a hostile grasp destroyed the beatings of his heart and his body. Now the sword's edge, the hand and the hard sword, fight for the treasure."

Beowulf spoke and said his words of boasting for the last time: "I engaged in many battles in my youth. Again, as wise guardian of the people, I will seek battle, accomplish a glorious deed, if the evil-doer will come to me from the cave." Then he greeted each of his men, the bold warriors, his dear comrades, for the last time. "I would not carry a sword, a weapon against the serpent, if I knew how otherwise I could fulfill my boast against the monster, as I did formerly against Grendel; but I expect hot battle-fire, breath and venom; on that account I have shield and coat of mail on me. I do not wish to flee a footstep from the guardian of the mount, but it shall be with us at the wall as Fate, the ruler of each man, allots. I am bold in mind, so that I shall dispense with any boast against the war-flier. Do you remain on the barrow, protected by your coats of mail, warriors in armor, to see which of us two may be better able to survive his wound after the bloody conflict. This is not your undertaking nor the measure of any man save of me alone, that he should fight against the monster and achieve heroic deeds. I shall win the gold with valor, or battle, the fearful and deadly evil, shall take away your king!"

Then the brave warrior rose beside his shield, strong under his helmet; he bore his coat of mail under the rocky cliffs; he trusted in the might of one man. Such is not the undertaking of a coward! He who, good with manly virtues, had passed safely through a great many battles, crash of onslaughts, when men on foot clash together, then saw by the wall a stone arch stand, a stream burst forth thence from the barrow. The flood of the stream was hot with deadly flames, nor could anyone at any time pass safely through the hollow passage near the treasure because of the dragon's fire. The prince of the Weder-Geats, since he was enraged, let words go forth from his breast, the stout-hearted man shouted. His voice, clear in battle, came in to roar under the gray stone. Hate was aroused, the guardian of the treasure recognized the speech of man; there was no more time to ask for friendship. First the breath of the monster came from out of the stone, the hot and hostile vapor. The ground resounded. The man under the barrow, the prince of the Geats, swung his shield against the dreadful stranger. Then the heart of the coiled creature was incited to seek battle. The good battle-king had already drawn his sword, the ancient heirloom, sharp of edges; to each of the hostile ones there was terror from the other. The prince of friends stood firm against his high shield when the serpent quickly coiled itself together; he waited in his armor. Then the burn-

2. the warrior, Haethcyn. **12. sons of Ongentheow.** See the genealogy of the Swedish royal line, page 19. **15. Hreosnabeorh,** a hill in Geatland; the reference is to the Swedish raids which led to Haethcyn's invasion of Sweden. **20. relative,** Hygelac. **21. the other,** Haethcyn. It is to be noted that Hygelac carried out his vengeance by proxy. See page 49, below. **22. old Scylfing,** Ongentheow. **29. him,** Hygelac. **30. Gifthas,** an East Germanic tribe. **36. Daeghrefn,** a Frankish warrior, possibly the killer of Hygelac. **37. Hugas,** Franks.

ing coiled thing went gliding, hastened to its fate. The shield protected the famous king well in life and body for a less time than his mind wished, if he might have managed the allotted period for the first time, but fate did not decree him triumph in battle. The ruler of the Geats raised his hand and struck the terribly colored monster with his sword so that the edge failed, the bright sword on the bone; it cut less strongly than the king of the people, oppressed with afflictions, had need. Then the guardian of the barrow was in a fierce temper after the battle-stroke: he threw out his deadly fire. The flames sprang far and wide. The generous prince of the Geats did not boast of glorious victories; his war-sword failed, insufficient in the battle, as it should not have been, that very good sword. That was not an easy course of action that the glorious kinsman of Ecgtheow should be willing to leave the earth; he was fated against his will to inhabit a dwelling-place elsewhere, as every man must abandon his transitory days.

It was not long until the opponents met each other again. The keeper of the treasure took heart, his breast surged anew with his breathing. He who before had ruled the people suffered distress, encircled with fire. Not at all did his comrades, sons of nobles, stand around him with valor in a troop, but they turned to the wood, saved their lives. In one of them only the mind boiled with sorrows. Nothing can ever put aside kinship for him who thinks well.

XXXVI

His name was Wiglaf, the son of Weohstan, an admirable shield-warrior, prince of the Scylfings, a relative of Aelfhere. He saw his lord suffer heat beneath his helmet. He remembered then the property which he had given to him before, the prosperous dwelling-place of the Waegmundings, every folk-right which his father had had. He could not restrain himself then, his hand seized his shield, the yellow linden wood, and he drew his ancient sword, which was the heirloom among men of Eanmund, the son of Ohthere, a friendless exile, whose slayer Weohstan became in battle with the edge of the sword, and carried away from his kinsmen the brown-colored helmet, the ringed coat of mail, the old sword made by giants. Onela gave him that, the armor of his kinsman, the ready battle-equipment—he did not speak about the feud, although he had killed his brother's son. He kept the weapons for many half-years, the sword and coat of mail, until his son could do heroic deeds as his old father had done. He gave him then among the Geats war-equipment, a countless number of each sort, when he went from life, old and wise on his way forth.

This was the first time that the young warrior should accomplish the onslaught of battle with his dear lord. His spirit did not melt, nor the heirloom of his kinsman give way in the fight: the serpent discovered that after they had come together.

Wiglaf spoke, he said many a censorious word to his companions—his heart was sad: "I remember the time, where we were taking the mead, when we promised our lord in the beer-hall. he who gave us these rings, that we would repay him for the war-equipment, the helmets and the hard swords, if such need should ever happen to him. On this account of his own will he chose us among the troop, considered us worthy of glorious deeds, and gave me and the rest of us these treasures, because he accounted us good spear-fighters, brave warriors—although our lord, the guardian of the people, thought to carry through this deed of valor alone, because he most among men had accomplished glorious acts, daring feats. Now the day has come when our lord has need of might, of good warriors. Let us go forward, help our chieftain, while heat is there, the fierce fire-terror. God knows, for my part, that it is greatly preferable to me that the flame should embrace my body with my gold-giver. It does not seem fitting to me that we should carry our shields back to our home, unless we first are able to fell the foe, protect the life of the prince of the Weders. I know surely that this would not be the desert for his former deeds that he alone of the troop of the Geats should suffer sorrow, fall in fight. Sword and helmet, coat of mail and war-garment, shall be common to

---

3-5. if he ... first time, a puzzling passage, but the meaning probably is "If he had been able to determine how long his shield would protect him." **XXXVI.** [Lines 2602–93.] **34. Wiglaf.** Wiglaf's family connections are not clear, but the following account may be hazarded. Weohstan, by birth a Geat, had, for some reason, been in the service of Onela, king of the Swedes, and had killed Eanmund, son of Onela's brother, Ohthere, when Onela pursued his two nephews to Geatland. When Eadgils, Eanmund's brother, with Geatish aid, overthrew his uncle, and became himself king of the Swedes, Weohstan was forced to flee, and, rather oddly, had no difficulty in establishing himself among his own people, the Geats, although he had been on the Swedish side in the campaign which resulted in Heardred's death, and had been himself the slayer of Eanmund, Heardred's protégé. There is much here that requires elucidation, and perhaps this is not the right explanation; certainly, other suggestions have been made. **39. Waegmundings,** the family to which Beowulf and his father belonged.

1. folk-right, his share in the common property of the tribe. **11–12. speak about ... son,** naturally not, since Weohstan had killed Eanmund on Onela's behalf.

us both." He advanced then through the deadly fumes, bore his helmet to the aid of his lord, and said a few words: "Dear Beowulf, perform all things properly, as you said long ago in your youth, that during your life you would not let your reputation decline. Now, resolute hero, renowned for your deeds, you must defend your life with all your strength: I will stand by you."

After these words the angry serpent, the horrid and malicious foe, came a second time, shining in the surge of fire, to attack his enemies, the hostile men. The wave of flame burned the shield clear to the edge, the coat of mail was not able to give aid to the young spearman, but the youth went quickly under his relative's shield, since his own was destroyed by the flames. Then once more the war-king set his mind on glorious deeds; with great strength he struck with his battle-sword, so that it stood fast in the head, forced by violence. Naegling burst asunder; Beowulf's sword, old and gray-colored, failed in the fight. It was not granted to him that the edge of his sword should be able to help him in battle; the hand was too strong, which, as I have heard, sought too much from each sword with its blow, when it carried the wonderfully hard weapon into battle. He was in no way the better for it.

Then for a third time the people's foe, the terrible fire-dragon, was intent on hostile acts; he rushed upon the brave man, hot and fierce in battle, when an opportunity was given to him; he enclosed his neck completely with his sharp teeth. He became bloodied with his life-blood; the blood welled out in waves.

XXXVII

Then I heard that in the need of the people's king the hero, rising to his full height, showed courage, strength and boldness, as was natural to him. He paid no attention to the head, but the hand of the brave man was burned when he aided his relative in that he, the man in armor, struck the malicious foe a little lower down, so that the sword, decorated and ornamented, sank in to the extent that that fire began afterwards to subside. Then the king himself once more controlled his senses, and drew the battle-knife, keen and sharp in fight, which he carried on his coat of mail. The protector of the Weders cut the serpent through in the middle. They killed the fiend—strength drove out life—and then they both had destroyed him, the noble kinsmen. Such ought a man to be, a warrior in time of need! For the king that was his latest time of victory by his own deeds, of his work in the world.

Then the wound which the earth-dragon had given him before began to burn and swell. He at once discovered that the poison within him was working with fierce rage in his breast. Then the hero went until he, wise in thought, sat on a seat by the wall. He looked at the work of the giants and saw how the eternal earth-house had within stone arches fastened with posts. Then the exceedingly good warrior bathed with his hand his blood-stained famous prince, his friendly lord wearied by battle, with water, and unclasped his helmet.

Beowulf spoke—he spoke over his wound, his deadly wound. He knew clearly that he had passed through his allotted days, his joy on earth. Then the number of his days was gone, death was exceedingly near: "Now I could wish to give this armor to my son, in case any heir belonging to my body had been granted to remain after me. I held this people for fifty years; there was no folk-king nor any of the neighboring peoples who dared to attack me with warriors, to threaten me with terror. I waited for my destiny on earth, held to my own in proper fashion, did not seek treacherous quarrels, nor swore many oaths wrongfully. Sick with mortal wounds, I may now have joy in all that; since the ruler of men will not need to charge me with the murder of kinsmen, when my life goes from the body. Go quickly now, dear Wiglaf, to look at the treasure under the gray stone, now that the serpent lies dead, sleeps in death, grievously wounded, deprived of the treasure. Be in haste now, that I may see the ancient wealth, the treasure of gold, that I may examine completely the brilliant precious jewels, so that in consequence of the wealth of treasure I may the more easily give up my life and the nation which I held so long."

XXXVIII

Then I heard that the son of Weohstan after these words quickly obeyed his wounded and battle-sick prince; he wore his coat of mail, his woven battle-shirt, under the roof of the mound. The triumphant man, the courageous young retainer, when he went by the seat, saw many precious jewels, gold lying on the ground and shining, wonderful things on the wall, and the lair of the serpent, the old night-flier; cups standing, vessels of the men of old, without anyone to polish

20. Naegling, the name of Beowulf's sword. 33. He, Beowulf. XXXVII. [Lines 2694–2751.] 38. the hero, Wiglaf.

XXXVIII. [Lines 2752–2820.]

them, deprived of their ornaments. There were many helmets, old and rusty, many bracelets twisted with skill.—Treasure, gold on the ground, can easily overcome each member of mankind, let him hide it who will!—Also he saw a gold-wrought banner, greatest of wonderful things made by hand, woven by manual skill, hang above the treasure. From it a light arose, so that he could see the floor, look over the precious things. There was no sight of the serpent there, for the edge of the sword had carried him away. Then, as I was told, a certain man plundered the treasure in the mound, the ancient work of the giants, heaped up in his bosom cups and plates at his own discretion. He also took the banner, most splendid of standards. The sword, its edge of iron, of his old lord had earlier injured him who had been guardian of the treasures for a long time, who carried the fire-terror, hot in front of the treasure, welling fiercely at midnight, until he died a violent death. The messenger was in haste, eager to journey back, impelled by the treasures. Curiosity tormented him as to whether he, excited as he was, would find the prince of the Weders alive in the place where he had left him before, deprived of strength. Then, carrying the treasure, he found the famous king, his lord, bloody and at the end of his life. He began again to throw water on him until a first word broke through his breast.

The king spoke, the old man in his sorrow—he looked upon the gold: "I say thanks with words to God, to the king of glory, the eternal Lord, for all of the treasures which I gaze on here, because before the day of my death I was able to gain the like for my people. Now that I have sold my old life for the hoard of treasures, do you attend to the need of the people: I am not able to be here longer. Order the men renowned in battle to make a mound, glorious after the funeral fire, on a cape of the sea. It shall stand high on Hronesness as a memorial for my people, so that seafarers, those who drive their ships from afar over the mists of the waves, shall hereafter call it Beowulf's cliff."

The bold-minded prince took from his neck a golden ring and gave it to his retainer, the young spearman, with it his gold-adorned helmet, his bracelet and coat of mail; he told him to make good use of them. "You are the last remnant of our race, of the Waegmundings; Fate has swept away all my kinsmen by death, the heroes in their strength. I must go after them."

That was the last word for the old man from the thoughts of his heart, before he tried the funeral fire, the hot and hostile flames. His soul went from his breast to seek the judgment of the righteous.

XXXIX

Then it went sorrowfully with the young man when he saw his dearest one fare wretchedly on the earth at his life's end. The slayer also lay dead, the horrible earth-dragon deprived of life, oppressed by evil. The coiled serpent could no longer guard the hoard of rings, but the edges of the sword, the hard, battle-sharp remnants of hammers, had taken him off, so that the far-flier, quiet from his wounds, fell to the earth near the treasure-house. No more did he move about flying through the air at midnight, nor, proud of his possessions, show his form, but he fell to the earth on account of the deed of strength of the warrior. Indeed few men, even mighty men, were so successful in the land, although they might be daring in every deed, that they should rush against the breath of a poisonous foe, or disturb a ring-hall with their hands, if they should find the guardian dwelling in the mound awake. Beowulf had paid with his death for a part of the noble treasures; each had reached the end of his transitory life.

Then it was not long until the cowards left the wood, ten weak traitors together, who before had not dared to fight with javelins in their lord's great need; but now ashamed they carried their shields and armor to where the old man lay. They looked at Wiglaf. The foot-warrior sat wearied by his lord's shoulder, and tried to rouse him with water. He succeeded in no way. Although he wished it well he could not keep life on earth in the chieftain, nor change anything pertaining to the Lord. The judgment of God would control the deeds of every man, as it still does. Then it was easy to obtain a stern answer from the youth to those who formerly had lost their courage. Wiglaf spoke, the son of Weohstan, a man sad at heart—he looked at the unloved men: "This, indeed, may he say who wishes to speak the truth, that the prince who gave you treasures, the warlike equipments which you stand in there—when at the ale-bench he often gave helmet and coat of mail, the prince to his retainers, the most splendid he could find anywhere far or near—that he had completely thrown away the armor, when once war came upon him. The people's king had no need to boast of his war-comrades; however, God,

---

12. **certain man,** Wiglaf.　40. **Hronesness,** Whale's Headland.　43. **cliff,"** or "mound."　　XXXIX. [Lines 2821–91.]　13. **hammers,** a kenning for "swords."　23. **ring-hall,** barrow.

the ruler of victories, granted to him that he alone avenged himself with the sword's edge, when he had need of might. I was able to give him a little protection for his life in the fight, and undertook, although it was beyond my power, to help my relative. He was ever the worse for it when I struck the deadly foe with my sword, the fire came less strongly from his head. Too few defenders pressed forward around the prince when distress befell him. Now the receiving of treasure and giving of swords must cease, all joy of country and comfort to your kin. Each man of the clan shall go deprived of his land-right, when warriors from afar shall hear of your flight, that inglorious act. To every man death is better than a life of disgrace."

XL

He ordered then that the battle be announced in the enclosure up over the steep cliff, where that band of warriors had sat the whole forenoon sad at heart, the shield-bearers, in expectation of both, either the last day or the return of the dear man. The man who rode up the cliff was not silent concerning the unheard-of tale, but spoke truly before them all: "The lord of the people of the Weders, the ruler of the Geats, is now fast on his deathbed, he remains on the bed of slaughter from the deeds of the serpent. Beside him lies the deadly enemy sick with dagger-wounds; with the sword he could not in any way make a wound on the monster. Wiglaf, the son of Weohstan, is sitting over Beowulf, one man over the other lifeless one; in distress of soul he holds the death-watch over friend and foe.

"Now there is an expectation of a time of war for the people when the death of the king becomes widely known to the Franks and the Frisians. The severe enmity with the Hugas was brought about when Hygelac came with a naval force to the land of the Frisians, where the Hetware assailed him in battle, valiantly brought it to pass with their superior force that the mailed warrior had to fall, sink among the troop. The prince gave no precious things at all to his body of retainers. Ever since then the kindness of the Merovingian king has been denied us.

"Nor do I at all expect peace or truth from the Swedes, for it was known far and wide that Ongentheow deprived Haethcyn, the son of Hrethel, of his life at Ravenswood when the people of the Geats in their presumption first attacked the Battle-Scylfings. Immediately the wise father of Ohthere, old and terrible, gave him back a counterblow; he killed the sea-king, the old man rescued the woman, the old wife deprived of her gold, the mother of Onela and Ohthere. Then he followed his deadly foes until they escaped with difficulty to Ravenswood, without a chief. He besieged those who survived the sword, exhausted by their wounds, with a huge army. Often throughout the whole night he threatened misery to the wretched company; he said that in the morning he would kill them with the edges of the sword, some on the gallows-tree would be a sport to the birds. Relief came to the sad-hearted at daybreak when they heard the sound, Hygelac's horn and trumpet, as the good man came along the trail with a band of people.

XLI

"The bloody track of the Swedes and the Geats, the murderous conflict of men, was widely visible, how the peoples had stirred up battle between them. Then the good man, wise and very sad, went with his companions to seek his fastness, King Ongentheow moved farther up. He had learned of Hygelac's valor, the prowess in battle of the bold man. He did not trust in his ability to resist, that he could fight against the seamen, defend his treasure, his children and women, against the sea-warriors. The old man went from there again inside the earth-wall. Then was chase given to the people of the Swedes; Hygelac's standards passed forth over the field of refuge, when the Hrethlings pressed forward to the entrenchment. There Ongentheow the gray-haired was brought to bay, and the people's king had to submit to the sole judgment of Eofor. Wulf, son of Wonred, hit him angrily with a weapon, so that from the blow blood in streams burst forth from under his hair. However, the old Scylfing was not afraid, but speedily paid back the deadly stroke with a worse exchange, as soon as the people's king had turned in that direction. Nor could the brave son of Wonred give a counterblow to the old man, for he had previously cut through the helmet on his head, so that he was fated to sink down stained with blood, fall to the ground. He was not yet doomed to die, but he recovered, although the

---

6. He, the dragon. XL. [Lines 2892–2945.] 38. Hugas, Franks. 40. Hetware, Frisians. 45. Merovingian, Frankish.

2. father of Ohthere, Ongentheow; see the genealogy of the Swedish royal line, page 19. 5–6. mother . . . Ohthere. In his initial attack Haethcyn had captured Ongentheow's wife. 8. without a chief. Haethcyn was killed. XLI. [Lines 2946–3057.] 33. Hrethlings, Geats. 36. Wonred, father of Eofor and Wulf. 44. he, Ongentheow. 45. so that he, Wulf.

wound hurt him. The strong retainer of Hygelac, when his brother lay low, allowed his broad sword, the old sword made by giants, to break the giant helmet across the shield-wall. Then the king, the guardian of the people, fell; he was struck in a mortal spot. There were many then who bound up his kinsman, raised him up at once, when an opportunity was given to them that they might have possession of the battlefield. Meanwhile one warrior plundered the other, took from Ongentheow the iron coat of mail, the hard, hilted sword, and his helmet too. He took the armor of the gray old man to Hygelac. He received the precious things and promised him fairly a reward among the people, and he carried it out as he had made it. The lord of the Geats, the son of Hrethel, when he had come home repaid Eofor and Wulf for the attack with great treasures. He gave to each of them a hundred thousand of land and linked rings—nor did any man on earth have need to reproach him for the reward, after they performed such famous deeds. And then he gave his only daughter to Eofor as an ornament to the home and as a pledge of favor.

"This is the feud and the hostility, the deadly hate of men, as I have expectation, which the people of the Swedes will seek out upon us, after they learn our lord to be lifeless, he who formerly guarded treasure and kingdom, the valiant shield-warriors, against our enemies, after the death of heroes; he carried out what was for the people's benefit and further still did heroic deeds. Now is haste best, that we go there to see the king of the people and bring the one who gave us rings on the way to the funeral pile. Nor shall one part only melt with the brave man, but there is a hoard of treasures, countless gold purchased grimly, and rings now finally paid for with his own life. The flame shall eat up these, the fire cover them—no warrior shall carry the treasure as a memorial, nor fair maiden have the ring-adornment on her neck, but she, sad of mind, deprived of gold, shall walk, not once but often, in a foreign land, now that the army leader has laid down laughter, joy, and mirth. So must many a spear, cold in the morning, be grasped in the fingers, lifted by the hands. The music of the harp will not rouse the warriors, but the dark raven, hastening above the dead, shall speak much, shall say to the eagle how he throve at the meal, when with the wolf he despoiled those slain in battle."

So the brave man told his grievous message; he did not lie much about either events or words. The band all rose and went sorrowful, with gushing tears, to see the wonder under Earnaness. They found him then on the sand lifeless, keeping his bed of rest, who had given them rings at earlier times. Then had the last day come to the good man, so that the war-king, prince of the Weders, died a wonderful death. Already they had seen there the strange creature, the hateful serpent, lying opposite on the plain. The fire-dragon, fierce and terrible in its coloring, was scorched with flames. It was fifty foot-marks long in the place where it lay. It had ruled the joyous air in the night-time, and afterwards had come down to visit its den. Now it was fast in death, it had made its last use of earth-caves. By it stood drinking-vessels and cups, dishes lay there and excellent swords, rusty and eaten through, just as they had remained there in the bosom of the earth for a thousand years. Further, that huge heritage, the gold of men of old, was bound with a spell, so that no man could reach the ring-hall, unless God himself, the true king of victories—He is the protection of men—granted it to whom He would to open the hoard, even to such a man as seemed to Him proper.

XLII

Then it was clear that the course of action did not turn to profit for him who wrongfully hid the ornaments beneath the wall within. The guardian had slain one and a few others; then the hostile act was cruelly avenged. It is a mystery when a strong man shall reach the end of his life, when the man is no longer able to inhabit the mead-house with his relatives. So it was with Beowulf, when he sought out the guardian of the barrow and the battle; he himself did not know by what means his separation from the world should come to pass. The famous lords who put that treasure there solemnly laid a curse on it until the day of doom so that the man who plundered the place should be guilty of sins, restrained in heathen shrines, fast in bonds of hell, tormented grievously, all this unless earlier the grace of God had more surely favored the person wishing the gold.

Wiglaf spoke, the son of Weohstan: "Often must

---

1. retainer of Hygelac, Eofor. **7. kinsman,** Eofor's brother, Wulf. **9. one warrior,** Eofor. **18–19. hundred thousand.** The unit of value is, perhaps, the *sceatt*, a coin of relatively small, but varying, value. **38–44. The flame . . . mirth,** a prophecy that the Geats will be attacked and conquered.

6. Earnaness, Eagle's Headland. **XLII.** [Lines 3058–3136.] **32. him who . . . hid,** the dragon. **34. one and a few others.** Possibly only Beowulf is meant, but the dragon's earlier incendiary attacks may well have killed other Geats. **45. heathen shrines,** a Christian way of describing hell.

many a man for the sake of one endure misery, as is happened to us. Nor were we able to persuade our dear lord, the guardian of the kingdom, by means of any advice that he should not approach the keeper of the gold, but let him lie where he had been so long, inhabit his abode until the end of the world. He held to his high destiny; the treasure is shown, obtained terribly; that fate was too harsh which incited the people's king here. I was inside there and looked over all that, the precious objects of the building, when I was given an opportunity to do so; not at all in friendly manner was the journey granted in under the earth-wall. I seized in haste a great burden of stored-up possessions with my hands and carried it out here to my king. He was then still alive, sound in mind and conscious; the old man in his sorrow said a great many things, ordered you to be greeted and commanded that you should build, in memory of the deeds of your friend, at the place of the pyre, a high barrow, great and famous, just as he was of all men the most illustrious warrior, far and wide throughout the earth, as long as he was able to enjoy his castle's wealth. Let us now hasten on a second occasion to see and seek out the heap of curious gems, the wonderful things under the wall; I will guide you, so that you may look from near by at the abundant rings and the broad gold. Let the bier be ready, quickly prepared, when we come out, and then let us carry our lord, the dear man, there where he shall long abide in the protection of the Lord."

Then the son of Weohstan, the hero brave in battle, ordered them to command many warriors, house-owners, chiefs, that they should bring wood from afar towards the good man for the funeral pile: "Now must the flame devour—the dark fire shall increase—the ruler of warriors, the man who often lived through the iron shower when the storm of arrows, urged on by strength, came hastening over the shield-wall, when the shaft did its duty, ready in its feather-gear it kept up with the arrowhead."

However, the wise son of Weohstan summoned from the troop the seven best of the king's retainers, and went himself as the eighth warrior under the evil roof. One who went in front carried a torch in his hand. It was not then decided by lot who should plunder the treasure, when the men saw any part remain in the hall without a guardian, lie perishing. Not at all did anyone scruple that they should quickly carry out the excellent treasures.

Also they pushed forward the dragon, the serpent, over the cliff, let the wave take it, the flood embrace the guardian of the precious things. Then the twisted gold was loaded on a wagon, a countless amount of every kind, and the hero, the gray warrior, was carried to Hronesness.

XLIII

Then the people of the Geats made ready for him a splendid funeral pile on the earth, hung about with helmets, shields, and shining coats of mail, as he had requested. In the midst of it then the lamenting heroes laid the famous chief, their dear lord. The warriors then began to kindle the greatest of funeral fires on the barrow; the wood-smoke ascended black over the fire, the resounding fire surrounded by weeping—the tumult of winds subsided—until, hot in his breast, it had destroyed his body. Sad of soul they complained of their sorrow, the death of their lord; also the old woman with bound-up hair sang, sorrowful, a mournful song about Beowulf, said earnestly that she dreaded sorely the evil days, the great slaughter, the fear of the warrior, the humiliation and captivity. Heaven swallowed up the smoke.

Then the people of the Weders made on the cliff a mound which was high and broad, widely visible to seafarers, and they finished in ten days the beacon of the man bold in battle, built a wall around what the flames had left, as clever men could devise it most splendidly. Into the barrow they put the rings and jewels, all such ornaments as hostile men had taken from the hoard before; they permitted the earth to hold the wealth of heroes, gold in the ground, where it now still lives as useless to men as it was before. Then men brave in battle, sons of princes, twelve in all, rode around the mound; they wished to bewail their sorrow and lament their king, recite an elegy and speak about the man. They praised his heroic deeds and appraised highly his works of valor—as it is fitting that one should honor his friendly lord with words, love him from the heart, when he must be brought forth from the body. Thus the people of the Geats, his retainers, lamented the fall of their lord; they said that he was among earthly kings the mildest of men and the most gracious, kindest to his people and most eager for praise.

---

12. not . . . in friendly manner. This may mean only that Wiglaf was in great haste and anxiety because of Beowulf's condition. **47. not . . . lot,** that is, they did not stand on ceremony.

XLIII. [Lines 3137–82.] **22. the old woman,** often identified as Beowulf's widow, but completely without proof. **37–38. gold . . . as useless . . . as . . . before.** Beowulf's death, then, had not brought wealth to his people.

Deor

The song of *Deor*, one of the many lyric treasures in the Exeter Book, cannot be dated with any certainty, but we may follow Malone in suggesting very tentatively that it was perhaps composed in an Anglian dialect about the year 900. The purpose of the poem is to suggest to a troubled reader or hearer that since so many worldly tribulations have proved to be transitory, his own cares may all pass away. The poet achieves this by citing a number of specific examples from heroic story and an autobiographical instance (probably fictitious). The first two episodes are taken from the story of Welund (Wayland), the well-known smith who in Germanic tradition occupies the place of Hephaestus-Vulcan in classical lore. Welund's adventures are recounted in the *Völundarkvitha*, a poem in the *Elder Edda*, and in a portion of the Old Norwegian *Thithrekssaga*. Briefly, Welund is captured by King Nithhad (Nithuthr), who hamstrings him and forces him to labor in captivity. By a series of ruses he kills the king's two sons, from whose skulls, eyes, and teeth he makes ornaments for their family, rapes the king's daughter Beadohild (Böthvildr), and flies away by means of a pair of wings which he has made. The passing of Welund's sorrow is evident, and we are probably to believe that Beadohild's troubles were lightened when the son she bore grew up to be the hero Widia.

The love affair of Maethhild and Geat, in itself obscure, is otherwise apparently unknown. The Theodoric of the poem has usually been taken to be Theodoric of Verona, known in heroic legend as Dietrich of Bern, but Malone presents evidence that probably Theodoric the Frank, the Wolfdietrich of Germanic story, son of Clovis and king at Rheims from 511 to 534, is meant, and that the reference is to his exile. Eormanric (Ermanric), a historical king of the Ostrogoths in the third quarter of the fourth century, who is reputed to have killed himself in expectation of defeat by the Huns, became in heroic legend a prodigy of cruelty and tyranny, and so his death might well bring relief to his suffering subjects.

Next to the interesting and often tantalizing references to general Germanic tradition, the reader's attention is most strongly drawn to the systematic use of what, as Malone says, "for want of a term more fitting" we may call a refrain; the only other example of the use of this device in Old English literature is in the fragmentary and puzzling *Wulf and Eadwacer*, which follows *Deor* in the Exeter Book. The present translation is from the edition by Kemp Malone, London, 1933.

WELUND experienced persecution by means of swords, the resolute warrior endured troubles; he had sorrow and longing as traveling companions, severe misfortune; he often met with misery after Nithhad laid fetters on him, supple sinew-bonds on a better man.
It is all over with that; so it can be with this.

The death of her brothers was not so grievous to Beadohild in her mind as was her own difficulty, when she had clearly realized that she was pregnant; she could never think boldly how it was fated to be about that.
It is all over with that; so it can be with this.

We learned this, that the love affair of Maethhild, the passion of Geat, became boundless, so that sorrowful love deprived them of all sleep.
It is all over with that; so it can be with this.

Theodoric possessed the stronghold of the Maerings for thirty years; that was known to many.
It is all over with that; so it can be with this.

We learned of the wolfish mind of Eormanric; he ruled far and wide the people of the kingdom of the Ostrogoths; he was a grim king. Many a man sat bound with sorrows, expecting woe, and wished constantly that that royal power were subdued.
It is all over with that; so it can be with this.

If a sorrowful man sits, deprived of joys, becomes gloomy in his mind, if it seems to him that the number of his troubles is endless, he can then think that the wise Lord goes constantly throughout this world, shows honor, certain prosperity, to many men, but to some others a multitude of woes.

I will say this about myself, that I was for a time the minstrel of the Heodenings, dear to my lord; my name was Deor. For many years I had a good office, a kind lord, until now Heorrenda, a man skilled in song, has received the estate which the protector of men formerly gave to me.
It is all over with that; so it can be with this.

The Dream of the Rood

The Dream of the Rood has been generally considered the most exquisite, poignant, and moving of Old English religious lyrics, and there is no reason to quarrel with that opinion. It is often attributed to Cynewulf, but the appearance of a slightly altered portion of the poem in a runic inscription on the Ruthwell Cross in Dumfriesshire, which is almost certainly from before Cynewulf's time, suggests that if the poem in its present form is by Cynewulf, he was adapting an older work. At all events, in this earliest dream-vision in the English language, we have a remarkably effective treatment of the great Christian tragedy, rendered all the more appealing by the device of having the Cross itself tell the story. The final paragraph alludes to the Harrowing of Hell. The present translation is from the edition by A. S. Cook, Oxford Press, 1905.

LISTEN! I wish to tell the best of dreams, what I dreamt at midnight after human beings were at rest. It seemed to me that I saw a marvelous tree surrounded with light move on high, the brightest of crosses. All that sign was covered with gold; lovely gems stood on it by the surface of the earth, and so, too, there were five more up on the shoulder-beam. All the angels of the Lord, fair through all time, gazed upon it there: truly that was no cross for the wicked, but holy spirits looked at it, men upon the earth, and all this glorious universe.

The cross of victory was wonderful, and I, stained with sins, was sorely wounded with evil deeds. I saw the tree of glory, decorated with streamers, shine joyfully, adorned with gold; gems had worthily covered the tree of the Lord. Nevertheless through that gold I could perceive the ancient strife of miserable men, that it formerly had bled on the right side. I was completely troubled with sorrows; I was afraid because of the beautiful vision. I saw the hastening sign vary in hangings and colors: at times it was wet with moisture, stained with the flow of blood, and at times adorned with treasure.

So, lying there for a long time, I looked, sorrowful, at the cross of the Saviour, until I heard that it uttered a sound; then the best of trees began to speak words:

"It was long ago—I still remember that—that I was cut down at the verge of the wood, taken from my stem. Strong foes seized me there, made me into a spectacle for them, ordered me to lift up their criminals. There men carried me on their shoulders, until they placed me on a hill; enemies enough fastened me there.

"Then I saw the Master of mankind hasten with great courage to mount me there. I did not dare to bend or break contrary to the Lord's command, when I saw the surfaces of the earth tremble. I could have killed all the foes, yet I stood fast.

"The young Hero—that was God almighty—stripped Himself, strong and resolute; He ascended the high cross, bold in the sight of many, when He wished to redeem mankind. I trembled when the Hero embraced me, yet I did not dare to bend to the earth, fall to the surface of the ground, but I had to stand fast. I was set up as a cross; I lifted up the powerful King, the Lord of heaven. I did not dare to bow down.

"They pierced me with black nails; the scars are visible on me, the open, malicious wounds. I did not dare to harm any of them. They mocked us both together. I was all wet with blood, shed from the Man's side, after He had given up His spirit.

"I endured many cruel experiences on the hill: I saw the God of hosts violently extended. Darkness with clouds had covered the dead body of the Lord, that bright splendor. A shadow came forth, black under the clouds. All creation wept, mourned the fall of the King: Christ was on the cross.

"Still eager ones came to the Lord from far away; I saw all that. I was deeply troubled with sorrows, but still I bowed humbly to men's hands with great zeal. They took God almighty there, raised Him from heavy torture. The warriors left me then to stand covered over with blood. I was all wounded with darts. They put Him down, weary of limb; they stood at the head of His body, there they beheld the Lord of heaven, and He rested for a time, tired after the great struggle. Then men began to make Him a tomb in the sight of the murderers; they cut it out of shining stone; in it they put the Lord of victories. They then began, wretched in the evening, to sing a dirge, when they were to go exhausted from the noble Lord. He rested there with no companions.

"So we crosses stood dripping there in the place for a long time after the cry of the warriors went up. The dead body grew cold, the lovely abode of the soul. Then people began to cut us down completely to the earth—that was a fearful experience! They buried us in a deep hole. Still the disciples

44. **dirge.** Compare the dirge sung by Beowulf's men around his burial mound.

of the Lord, friends, found me; they lifted me then from the earth, and adorned me with gold and silver.

"Now, my dear man, you can hear that I have endured evil pain, grievous troubles. The time is now come when men on earth and all this noble creation do me honor far and wide; they pray to this sign. The Son of God suffered on me for a time, and therefore I now tower glorious under heaven, and I can save every one who is fearful of me.

"I long ago became the most severe of tortures, most hateful to the people, before I opened the true way of life to men. Then the Prince of glory, the Lord of heaven, honored me above the other trees of the forest, just as God almighty for the sake of mankind also honored His mother Mary above all the race of women.

"Now, my dear man, I order you to tell this vision to men: make clear with words that this is the tree of glory on which God almighty suffered for the many sins of mankind and for Adam's deeds of old.

"He tasted death there; yet again the Lord arose with His great strength as a help to men. He then ascended into the heavens. The Lord Himself will come here to this earth again to visit mankind on the day of doom, God almighty with His angels with Him, and He who has the power of judgment will then judge everyone as he has already deserved in this transitory life. No one there can be fearless because of the word which the Lord will say: He will ask in the presence of the throng where the man is who is willing to taste bitter death for the Lord's name, as He Himself did earlier on the cross; but then they will be fearful and think little about what they should begin to say to Christ. No one needs to be timid there who already carries in his breast the best of signs, but every soul who proposes to dwell with the Lord must seek the kingdom away from earth through the cross."

Then I prayed to the cross with great zeal, happy in mind, there where I was alone with no company. The heart was ready for departure; it had often endured all kinds of longings. Now there is hope of life for me that I alone can seek the cross of victory more often than all men, and honor it well; the desire for that is great in my soul, and my life is directed to the cross. I do not have many powerful friends on earth, but they have gone away from the pleasures of the world, have sought for themselves the King of glory, live now with God the Father in heaven, and on each day I look for the time when the cross of the Lord, which I formerly saw here on earth, will fetch me from this transitory life, and then bring me where there is great joy, happiness in heaven, where the Lord's people are placed at the feast, where there is continual bliss; and will set me then where I can afterwards live in glory, enjoy pleasure fully with the saints. May the Lord be a friend to me, He who suffered here on earth on the cross for the sins of men. He redeemed us, and gave us life, a heavenly dwelling.

Hope was renewed with blessedness and with joy to those who had earlier suffered from fire. The Son was victorious on the journey, powerful and successful, when He came with a multitude, with a company of spirits, into the kingdom of God; to the joy of the angels and of all the saints who had earlier lived in glory, He, the almighty Ruler, their King, God almighty, came where His native land was.

Riddles

As is the case with many other Old English poems the *Riddles* were once ascribed to Cynewulf, but that opinion has been abandoned, and it is generally held that the *Riddles*, like the Exeter Book itself, in which they are found, really constitute an anthology and as a group can be given to no one author, although most of them were probably composed during the eighth century. Certain of these poems are derived from Latin riddles, especially from the collections credited to Symphosius, Aldhelm, Eusebius, and Tatwine, but the similarities are often slight and disputed. The English riddles are largely original. The modern reader will find these usually not riddles of the sort to which he is accustomed, but rather enigmas "in which something is described by intentionally obscure metaphors, in order to afford an exercise for the ingenuity of the reader or hearer in guessing what is meant" (*New English Dictionary*). The *Riddles* vary greatly in difficulty of solution, and while those given below are all reasonably clear, others have taxed the ingenuity of scholars, sometimes with astonishingly different results, as when one has been taken to be a flail or a bell; another interpreted as ten chickens, the fingers and thumbs, or the letters of the alphabet; another variously as wood or rain water; another a beaker or a flute; another a cuttle fish, the sun, water, or a siren; and yet another the Lamb of God or Cynewulf. Apart from their interest, admittedly rather slight, as intellectual problems, the riddles often contain poetry of great merit, and many of them give clear and fascinating vignettes of ordinary life among our ancestors. The following translations are based on Frederick Tupper's edition of *The Riddles of the Exeter Book*, Ginn, 1910, but use has been made of A. J. Wyatt, ed., *Old English Riddles*, Boston, 1912, and of the admirable translations in W. S. Mackie's *The Exeter Book, Part II*, Early English Text Society, Original Series No. 194, London, 1934. The numbering follows the order in which the riddles appear in the Exeter Book.

2. STORM ON LAND

Who among men is so wise and so keen of wit that he can declare who drives me on my journey, when I arise in violence, very fierce, thunder greatly? At times I go with hostility over the ground, burn the people's buildings, waste the halls; the smoke mounts gray above the roofs; there is noise on earth and violent death of men. When I stir the wood, the groves rich with fruits, when, covered with water, I throw down the trees, sent far and wide by the exalted powers to drive forth on my journey, then I have on my back that which earlier covered the persons of men, bodies and spirits together in the sand. Say what covers me, or how I who bear those burdens am named.

16. MOTHER BADGER

My neck is white, my head yellowish, and my sides as well; I am swift in walking and I carry war-weapons; hairs stand on my back just as on my cheeks; two ears stick out above my eyes; I go on my toes in the green grass. Grief is fated for me if someone, a cruel warrior, finds me hidden where I live in my house, my building with my children; if I remain there with my young family until the enemy comes to my doors, then death is decreed for them. Therefore, afraid, I must carry my children out of our home, save them by flight, if he follows me very close: he crawls on his breast. I do not dare to wait for the fierce one in my room— good counsel would not wish that—but I must swiftly make a path through the high hill with my forefeet. I can easily save the lives of my free ones if I may lead my family, dear and related, on a secret way through a hole of the hill; then I need not at all fear battle with the murderous dog. If the malignant enemy follows on my track to the narrow path, he will not lack battle on the hostile way after I reach the top of the hill, and with war-darts I shall strike violently the hated foe whom I had long fled.

28. MEAD

I am dear to men, found far and wide, brought from groves and from city heights, from valleys and from hills. By day wings carried me in the air, bore me with skill under the cover of a roof. Men afterwards bathed me in a tub. Now I am a binder and whipper; at once I throw a young man to the ground, sometimes an old churl. He who receives me and contends against my force immediately finds out this, that he must seek the earth with his back, if he has not already left off his evil course; deprived of strength, violent in speech, his might taken away, he has no power over his mind, feet, or hands. Ask what I am named who thus bind young men on the earth, foolish from my blows in the light of day.

35. RAKE

I saw a creature which feeds the cattle in the cities of men; it has many teeth; its beak is useful to it, it goes downward, plunders gently, and returns home, hunts along walls and seeks plants. It always finds those which are not fixed; it allows the beautiful ones which are firm to stand quietly in their place, to shine brightly, to bloom and grow.

48. BOOKWORM

A moth ate words; that seemed to me a wonderful event when I heard about that marvel, that the worm, a thief in the darkness, had swallowed up the song of a certain man, his glorious speech, and the strong man's firm support. The thievish guest was not at all the wiser because he swallowed the words.

52. PEN AND THREE FINGERS

I saw four curious creatures travel together; their tracks were black, their footprints very dark. The support of the swift ones was rapid on his journey, it flew in the air, dived under the wave. The laboring warrior who shows to all four their paths over the rich gold worked restlessly.

58. SWALLOWS

The air bears over the mountain slopes little creatures which are very black, swarthy, dark-

RIDDLES

coated. Strong in song, they go in flocks and cry loudly; they tread upon the woody shores, at times in the city houses of the children of men. Name them yourselves.

61. REED*

I was by the sand, near the cliff by the sea, at the ocean wave; I dwelt firm in my original place. There were few of mankind who could see my dwelling there in the desert, but each day before dawn the brown wave took me in its watery embrace. I little thought that I, before or after, should ever, mouthless, speak above the mead-bench, should interchange words. That is a great wonder, marvellous to the mind of him who does not know such a thing, how the point of the knife and the right hand, the thought of a man and the blade together, purposely fashioned me so that I should boldly utter a message to you before us two alone, in such a way that other men could not tell our words more widely.

77. OYSTER

The sea fed me, the covering sea enveloped me, and the waves were over me, without feet, close to the shore. I often opened my mouth to the sea. Now some man wishes to eat my flesh; he does not care for my covering after he tears off the skin from my side with the point of a knife and then quickly eats me uncooked also. . . .

81. WEATHERCOCK

I am puff-breasted, swollen-necked, I have a head and an elevated tail, eyes and ear and one foot, a back and a hard beak, a neck standing up and two sides, a rod in the middle, and a place above men. I suffer misery when he who shakes the wood moves me, and when floods beat upon me standing there, the hard hail and hoarfrost cover me and frost and snow fall on me, the one with the pierced stomach. . . .

86. ONE-EYED GARLIC SELLER

A creature came walking in where many men, wise in mind, sat in assembly. It had one eye and two ears and two feet, twelve hundred heads, back and belly and two hands, arms and shoulders, one neck and two sides. Say what I am called.

* It has been suggested that this poem is not a riddle at all, but rather the opening of *The Husband's Message* which follows it in the Exeter Book.

Charms

The Old English *Charms*, some in verse, some in prose, and others in a combination of the two, admirably illustrate the survival of old beliefs and methods in a Christian community. Here we find mixed, or side by side, heathen and Christian formulas, the latter often as superstitious in nature as the former. The English accepted Christianity with singularly little protest, but they long clung, not without the tacit consent of the Church, to what evidently struck them as particularly beneficent and effective aspects of paganism. Not unnaturally the interpretation and translation of the charms is often difficult and uncertain. The following selections are taken from Felix Grendon's "Anglo-Saxon Charms," *Journal of American Folk-Lore*, Vol. XXII (1909), pp. 167–209 passim, with the exception of the last, which is from T. Oswald Cockayne, ed., *Leechdoms, Wortcunning, and Starcraft of Early England*, 3 vols., London, 1864–66, Vol. I, pp. 244 ff. Grendon's introduction and notes contain much useful and interesting information.

AGAINST A DWARF

You must take seven little wafers, such as are used in worship, and write these names on each wafer: Maximianus, Malchus, Johannes, Martinianus, Dionisius, Constantinus, Serafion. Then again, you must sing the charm which is stated below, first into the left ear, then into the right ear, then over the man's head. And let a virgin go to him, and hang it on his neck, and do this for three days. He will soon be well.

Here came a spider wight a-walking in,
He had his harness in his hand.
Quoth that thou his blood-horse wert.
He puts his traces on thy neck.
They from the strand began to sail.
As soon as from the land they came,
They then began to cool.
The sister of the beast then came a-walking in.
Then she ceased and swore these oaths:
That this should never scathe the sick,
Nor him who might this charm acquire,
Nor him who could this charm intone.
Amen, *fiat*.

AGAINST WENS

Wen, wen, little wen,
Here you shall not build, nor any dwelling have,

But forth you must, even to the near-by hill,
Where a poor wretch, a brother you have;
He shall lay you a leaf at your head.
Under the wolf's foot, under the eagle's wing,
Under the eagle's claw—ever may you wither!
Shrivel as the coal upon the hearth!
Shrink as the muck in the stream,
And dwindle even as water in a pail!
May you become as little as a linseed grain,
And much smaller, likewise, than a hand-worm's hip-bone!
And even so small may you become, that you become as nought.

FOR ELF-DISEASE[1]

On Wednesday night when the sun is set, go where you know that elecampane stands; then sing the *Benedicite* and a *Paternoster* and a litany, and stick your knife into the herb; let it stick fast therein and go away. Go again thither, just as day and night divide. During this same daybreak go first to church and cross yourself and commend yourself to God. Then go in silence, and, though something of a fearful kind or a man should come upon you, say not a single word to it until you reach the herb you marked the night before. Then sing the *Benedicite* and a *Paternoster* and a litany, delve up the herb, letting the knife stick fast in it. As quickly as you can, go to church and place it with the knife under the altar; let it lie until the sun has risen. Afterwards wash it and make it and bishop's-wort and lichen off a crucifix into a drink; boil the drink three times in milk, pour holy water into it three times, sing over it a *Paternoster* and a *Credo* and a *Gloria in excelsis Deo*, and sing a litany over it; and also, with a sword, inscribe a cross round it on four sides, and after that let the patient drink the draught. He will soon be well.

FOR THE WATER-ELF DISEASE

If a person has the water-elf disease, his finger nails will be livid and his eyes tearful and he will look downwards. Do this for him by way of medical treatment: take carline, hassock, the netherward part of iris, yew-berry, lupine, elecampane, a head of marshmallow, water-mint, dill, lily, betony, pennyroyal, horehound, dock, elder-wood, earth-gall, wormwood, strawberry leaves, comfrey; steep them in ale, add holy water, sing this charm over them three times:—

[1]. Some disease, often nightmare, caused by the maleficient action of an elf.

"Round the wounds I have wreathed the best of healing amulets,
That the wounds may neither burn nor burst,
Nor grow worse nor putrefy,
Nor throb, nor be filthy wounds,
Nor cut in deeply; but let him keep the sacred water for himself,
Then it will pain you no more than it pains the land by the sea."

Sing this many times: "May Earth remove you with all her might and main." This charm may be sung on the wound.

THE VIRTUES OF JET

Of the stone called jet it is said that it has eight virtues. One is: when the thunder crashes, it will not harm the man who carries this stone with him. Another virtue is: in whatsoever house it may be, no demon can stay therein. The third virtue is: that no poison can injure the person who carries this stone with him. The fourth virtue is: that if the man who is secretly possessed with the hateful fiend, take, in liquid, any portion of the shavings of the stone—then that which before was profoundly concealed, will soon be visibly manifested in him. The fifth virtue is: if the person who is afflicted with any disease take the stone in liquid, he will soon be well. The sixth virtue is: that sorcery will not injure the man who carries the stone with him. The seventh virtue is: that he who takes the stone in a potion, will have so much the smoother body. The eighth virtue of the stone is: that no bite of any kind of snake can injure him who takes the stone in liquid.

FOR ELF-SHOT[2]

If a horse is elf-struck, take a knife of which the handle is horn from a tawny ox and on which are three brass nails. Then inscribe a cross on the horse's forehead until it bleed; next mark a cross on the animal's back and on each of the limbs that you can hold on to. Then grasp the left ear, pierce it in silence. This you must do: take a stick, strike the horse on its back, then it will be well. And on the horn of the knife inscribe these words:—

"Benedicite omnia opera domini dominum."

Be the elf who he may, this will suffice as a cure for him.

[2]. If an animal in the early morning ate an elf along with the grass in which it was concealed, the elf was thought to express its displeasure by shooting arrows into the lining of its host's stomach.

THE MANDRAKE

This herb which is called the mandrake is large and noble in appearance, and it is useful. You must take it in this manner: when you come to it, then you will recognize it because it shines in the night like a lantern. When you first see its head, then cut around it instantly with iron, lest it escape you. Its power is so great and so noble that it will immediately flee from an impure man when he comes to it. Therefore cut around it, as we said before, with iron. And you must dig about it in such a fashion that you do not touch it with the iron; but you must earnestly dig the earth with an ivory staff, and when you see its hands and its feet, then tie them up. Then take the other end of the string and fasten it to the neck of a dog, and let it be a hungry dog; after that throw meat before the dog so that he can not reach it unless he pulls the herb up with him. Of this herb it is said that it has so great power that whatever pulls it up will soon be deceived in the same manner. Therefore as soon as you see that it is pulled up, and you have possession of it, take it at once in your hand and wring the juice from its leaves into a glass phial, and when the need arises that you should help some man with it, then help him in this way: For head ache and in case a man can not sleep, take the juice and smear the forehead; and the herb in the same manner cures the head ache, and also you will wonder how quickly sleep comes.

The Wanderer

In *The Wanderer* we find a rather characteristic Old English mixture of personal elegy—here the lament of an exiled retainer for the good old days under his dead lord—and more general moralization, of, however, an equally gloomy nature. Notable in the poem are the almost purely pagan sense of an inescapable and crushing Fate, the utter dependence of the man on his lord, the description of stormy weather at sea, to be compared with *The Seafarer*, and the striking *ubi sunt* passage toward the end of the poem, which carries us ahead to François Villon's "*Où sont les neiges d'antan?*"—"Where are the snows of yesteryear?" The present translation is from the text as printed by M. H. Turk, ed., *An Anglo-Saxon Reader*, New York, Scribner, pp. 189–92.

19–20. **whatever pulls . . . manner.** This, of course, is the reason for using the dog, who will suffer the evil consequences which follow upon the disturbance of the herb.

The solitary man often asks for mercy, for the favor of the Creator, although he, sad at heart, for a long time must stir with his hands the ice-cold sea over the ocean way, must travel the paths of exile: fate is relentless. Thus spoke the Wanderer, mindful of hardships, of angry slaughter, of the death of his dear kinsmen:

"Alone I must often bewail my sorrow at every dawn; there is no one alive to whom I dare clearly say my mind. I know truly that it is a noble virtue in a man that he should close his bosom, preserve the treasury of his thoughts, let him think as he will. The weary mind cannot withstand fate, nor the troubled man bring about help. On that account those eager for glory often fasten sad thoughts tight within their hearts. So I, miserable and sad, deprived of my native land, far from my kindred, often had to bind my heart with fetters, when in years gone by the darkness of earth covered my lord, and I, abject, depressed by winter, went from there over the band of waves. Downcast, I sought the hall of some giver of treasure, wherever I could find him far or near, who would show me favor in the mead-hall, or comfort me, friendless, and treat me kindly. He who has tried it knows how cruel sorrow is to the man who has few dear protectors: his is the path of exile and not the twisted gold, the frozen body and not the riches of earth; he remembers his fellow retainers and the receiving of treasure, how in his youth his lord entertained him at the feast. The joy had all passed away! Therefore, he knows that who must for long be deprived of the counsels of his dear lord, when sorrow and sleep together often bind the wretched wanderer; he imagines that he embraces and kisses his lord and lays hand and head on his knee, as when sometimes in former days he enjoyed gifts. Then the friendless man awakes again and sees before him the dark waves, sea-fowls bathing, spreading their wings, frost and snow falling mixed with hail. Then the wounds of his heart are heavier, sorrow for his loved one; grief is renewed when memory of his relatives passes through his mind; he greets them joyfully, looks eagerly at the companions of warriors. They vanish again; the heart of the sailor does not bring many known songs; care is renewed for him who must often send his weary soul over the band of waves.

"I cannot think why in the world my mind does not grow sad when I consider all the lives of warriors, how they suddenly desert the mansion and the bold retainers. So this world perishes and falls each day; for no man can become wise until he has had his share of years in the kingdom of earth. A wise man must be patient, he must not be too wrathful nor too hasty of speech, neither too weak nor too rash in war, neither too timid nor too glad, nor too avaricious, nor ever too quick in boasting before he clearly understands. A man ought to wait, when he makes his boast, until he, bold in spirit, knows readily which way the purpose of hearts will turn. The wise man must perceive how terrible it is when all the happiness of this world is desolate, as now in many places throughout the earth walls stand, covered with frost, the dwellings storm-beaten. The wine-halls crumble, the rulers lie deprived of joy; the proud warriors all fell by the wall; war took some and bore them away; a bird carried one over the high sea; the gray wolf gave one to death; a sad-faced man hid another in the tomb. So the Creator of men laid waste this world, until the old work of the giants stood empty, deprived of the mirth of its citizens. Then he who thought wisely of this place where the walls stand and considers this gloomy life profoundly, often remembers, wise in mind, the multitude of far-away slaughters, and speaks these words:

" 'What has become of the horse? What has become of the man? What has become of the prince? Where are the joys in the hall? Alas for the bright cup! Alas for the mail-clad warriors! Alas for the glory of the chieftain! How that time has passed away, grown dark under the shadows of night, as though it never had been! Now there stands on the pathway of the beloved men a wonderfully high wall, covered with the shapes of serpents. A multitude of ashwood spears, weapons eager for slaughter, have destroyed the men, a glorious fate; and the storms beat against the cliffs, the falling tempests bind the earth, the noise of winter. Then the darkness comes, the shadow of night grows black and sends from the north the rough hailstorm in anger against men. All is full of hardship in the kingdom of earth, the decree of fate changes the world beneath the heavens: here property is transitory, a friend transitory, man transitory, kinsman transitory; all the structure of earth becomes vain!' "

Thus the wise man spoke in his mind, and sat apart in secret. He is good who holds his faith; a man ought never too quickly to reveal his sorrow from his breast, unless the warrior knows already how to bring about relief courageously. It is well with him who seeks mercy, comfort from the Father in heaven, where all safety stands for us.

18–19. **old work . . . empty.** As in the Old English poem *The Ruin*, this passage was doubtless inspired by the sight of some of the many dilapidated Roman structures in England.

The Battle of Maldon

The most notable late Old English poem, and one of the finest of all martial poems, is *The Battle of Maldon*, which was composed, no doubt, not long after August 11, 991, the date of the battle itself. Laborde has recently made it clear that the fight took place on the mainland opposite the end of the causeway which makes it possible even today to cross to the mainland from Northey Island in the estuary of the Blackwater (Panta) in Essex. The Scandinavians had their base on the island, and it was the generous but, as it proved, foolhardy gesture of the English leader which allowed them to gain the mainland. The author of the poem may well have been an eyewitness of the fight, and certainly he received firsthand information, as we find him mentioning numerous English warriors otherwise known slightly or not at all to history. The Scandinavians are unnamed, even to their leader, and while he was long thought to have been the great Olaf Tryggvason, that opinion is no longer universally held. The hero of the poem, Byrhtnoth of Essex, was one of the leading figures of his day, and took an active part in the politico-ecclesiastical controversies centering around the Benedictine reform. Since Byrhtnoth sided vigorously with the reformers, he was highly praised in the monkish annals, especially as he adorned his support with liberal benefactions. Indeed, the author of the *Vita Oswaldi* describes the end of the battle with truly classic simplicity: "*Byrihtnothus cecidit et reliqui fugerunt*"—"Byrhtnoth was killed and the rest fled." This statement, by the way, does scant justice to many of the English warriors if the poetic version is to be believed, for the poet makes much of the contrast between those who fought and those who ran away. The duty of the individual member of the *comitatus* to protect his lord or to die with him is strongly emphasized, and when we make the inevitable comparison with the dragon fight in *Beowulf* we are not likely to feel that *Maldon* suffers in realism or nobility.

The style of the poem is more simple than that of much of the earlier poetry, but it has a strength in substance which more than compensates for lack of ornamentation. As Sedgfield says on pages vii–viii of the book noted below: "When we reach the end of the poem we are out of breath; there remains with us a vision of flying darts, of brandished swords, sounds as of breastplates hacked, of cries and groans, while over all wheel the raven and the eagle. There remains too a feeling of pride in the old patriot and of admiration for the doomed bands of devoted men. And our pride and admiration are not wasted; for all we have read really happened." If the creative spirit of Old English poetry died with *The Battle of Maldon*, it may be said to have died like Byrhtnoth, worthily.

A full and comprehensive account of the poem and its historical background is to be found in E. D. Laborde, *Byrhtnoth and Maldon*, London, 1936, and one should also consult E. V. Gordon's edition of *The Battle of Maldon*, London, 1937. The present translation is from the edition by W. J. Sedgfield, Heath, 1904, with assistance from Laborde's notes.

. . . it was broken. He ordered one of the warriors to abandon the horses, to drive them far away and go forward, to trust to hands and good heart. When the kinsman of Offa first discovered that the chieftain was unwilling to suffer slackness, he then let his beloved hawk fly from his hands to the wood, and advanced to the battle; then one could recognize that the retainer would not weaken in the fight when he seized weapons. Eadric too wished to help his prince, his lord in battle; he started then to bear forth his spear to the conflict; his purpose was good, while he could hold in his hands shield and broad sword; he carried out his boast, when he had to fight before his prince.

Byrhtnoth then began to exhort his men. He rode and gave instructions, he taught the warriors how they ought to stand, and maintain their station, and ordered them to hold their shields firmly upright with their hands, and not to be afraid. When he had encouraged the troop well, he dismounted with the people there where it was most agreeable to him, where he knew his retainers most loyal.

Then a messenger of the pirates stood on the shore; he called out sternly, he uttered words, and boastfully announced the message of the pirates to the warrior, who was standing on the riverbank: "The bold seamen sent me to you; they ordered me to tell you that you must quickly send rings in return for safety; and it will be better for you to buy off this battle with tribute than that we share so severe a conflict. We need not kill each other if you can manage this: we are willing to establish peace with gold. If you, who are the greatest here, decide that you wish to save your people, give to the sailors, at their own discretion, money with good will, and receive peace from us; we are willing to go to the ships, to travel over the sea, and maintain peace with you."

Byrhtnoth spoke, he raised his shield, brandished his pliant ash-spear, he uttered words, angry and resolute, he gave him his answer: "Will you hear, pirate, what this people say? For tribute they will give you spears, the poisoned point and the ancient sword, war-gear which will not help you in battle. Messenger of the pirates, announce in return, say to your people a more hostile message, that here stands a brave leader with his troop, who will defend this land, the country of my lord Aethelred, the people and the earth; the heathen shall fall in the battle. It seems to me too shameful that you should go to the ships with our tribute without a fight, now that you have come thus far here into our land. You shall not conquer the treasure so easily: point and edge must reconcile us first, fierce battle, before we give tribute."

He ordered the men to go forward, to carry their shields, so that they all stood on the riverbank. Because of the water neither troop could come at the other: the flood tide came flowing in there after the ebb, the streams intertwined; it seemed too long for them before they carried their spears together. The battle-front of the East Saxons and the ship-army in array surrounded the stream of Panta; no one of them was able to molest the other, except for the one who received death from the flight of an arrow. The flood went out; the pirates stood ready, many Vikings, eager for battle. The lord of warriors ordered a hard-fighting soldier to hold the bridge; he was named Wulfstan, bold among his kindred, the son of Ceola, who shot down with his spear the first man who most boldly stepped there upon the bridge. There stood with Wulfstan two fearless men, Aelfere and Maccus, a daring pair; they would not flee at the ford, but firmly guarded themselves against the enemy as

---

19. . . . it was. The beginning and end of the poem, which we have only in a printed copy of a manuscript destroyed in the same fire which scorched the *Beowulf*, are lost, but it is unlikely that very many lines are missing. **He,** Byrhtnoth. **20. abandon the horses,** to prepare to fight on foot. **33. Byrhtnoth . . . men.** The warriors had come in sight of their foes on the opposite shore.

18. Aethelred. He ruled from 979 to 1016, coming to the throne in consequence of the cowardly murder of his stepbrother, Edward. His reign was a disastrous one for England, and his ineptitude and folly led to national disgrace and to the subsequent years of Danish rule. His nickname, "the Unready" or "Redeless" (that is, lacking in *rede*, "counsel"), was all too well deserved. **24. point and edge,** spear and sword. **30. streams intertwined.** "The tide flows in from two directions around Northey and meets at the causeway."—Laborde, *op. cit.* page 120. **44. the ford.** The causeway was still submerged, and so could be called "ford" as well as "bridge."

long as they were able to use weapons. When the hostile visitors perceived that, and saw clearly that they found the bridge-guards fierce, then they began to act cunningly: they asked for leave to land, to go over the ford, to lead the troop across. Then through his overconfidence the chief granted too much ground to the hostile people. The son of Byrhthelm called over the cold water—the men listened: "Now room has been made for you, come to us at once, men to battle. God alone knows who may have control of the battlefield."

The wolves of slaughter waded west across the Panta, the band of Vikings did not worry about the water; they carried their shields across the bright water, the pirates bore their shields to land. Byrhtnoth and his warriors stood ready to meet the fierce men: he ordered the war-hedge to be made with shields, and commanded the troop to hold fast against the foe. Then the fight was near, glory in battle; the time had come when doomed men must fall. An outcry rose; the ravens flew, the eagles eager for carrion; there was uproar on earth. They let go from their hands spears hard as files, let sharp-ground lances fly; the bows were busy, the shield received the point, the onslaught was fierce; men fell on every hand, warriors lay dead. Wulfmaer was wounded, the kinsman of Byrhtnoth, his sister's son, chose the grave: he was cut down with swords. Repayment was given to the Vikings there: I heard that Edward struck one severely with his sword, he did not hold back his blow, so that the doomed warrior fell at his feet; for this his lord gave thanks to the chamberlain when he had an opportunity. So the resolute warriors stood firm in battle; they considered earnestly who with the spear could first take the lives of fated men, warriors with weapons; the slain fell to the earth. They stood steadfast. Byrhtnoth urged them on: he ordered each warrior who wished to win glory from the Danes by fighting to think of battle. He who was bold in conflict went forward, he lifted his weapon, his shield in defense, and stepped toward the man. The leader went on resolutely against the man, each one planned harm for the other. Then the pirate sent a spear from the south, so that the lord of warriors was wounded; he struck then with his shield and the shaft broke, and that spear was loosened and sprang back. The warrior became angry; with his spear he stabbed the proud Viking who had given him the wound.

The experienced fighter let his spear pierce the neck of the warrior; his hand directed it so that it reached the life of the foe. Then he threw a second quickly, so that the coat of mail broke apart; he was wounded in the breast through the armor; the poisoned point stood in his heart. The chief was happier, the proud man laughed, gave thanks to the Lord for the day's work which God had granted to him.

One of the warriors then let a dart go from his hands, it flew from his fingers and went through Aethelred's noble retainer. There stood by his side a half-grown youth, a boy in the battle; young Wulfmaer, the son of Wulfstan, boldly pulled the bloody spear from the man. He let the very hard dart go back again: the point went in, so that he who had grievously hit his lord before lay now on the earth. Now an armed warrior went to the chief; he wanted to take the man's rings, his armor and ornaments, and his adorned sword. Then Byrhtnoth drew his broad, brown-edged sword from its scabbard, and struck at the coat of mail; too quickly one of the pirates stopped him by checking the warrior's arm. The golden-hilted sword fell to the ground, nor might he hold the dagger or direct a weapon. Still the gray-haired fighter spoke a word, encouraged the warriors, he told the good men to go forward; no longer could he stand firmly on his feet. He looked up to heaven: "I give thanks to You, Ruler of the peoples, for all the pleasures which I enjoyed in the world. Now, gentle Lord, I have the greatest need, that You will grant good to my spirit, that my soul may go to You, may travel, Ruler of angels, with peace into Your power. I entreat You that the devils may not do it harm."

The heathen rascals cut him down and both the men who stood by him, Aelfnoth and Wulmaer both lay dead: they gave their lives alongside of their lord. Now those went from the battle who no longer wished to be there. The sons of Odda were first in retreat; Godric went from the fight and deserted the good man who had often given him many a horse. He mounted the horse which had belonged to his lord, on the trappings to which he had no right, and both his brothers ran with him; Godwine and Godwig did not care for fighting, but went from the battle and sought the wood, they fled to the place of safety and saved their lives; and many more did so than would have been right if they had remembered all the favors which the warrior had done as an honor to them. It was just

---

7–8. **son of Byrhthelm,** Byrhtnoth.   33. **chamberlain,** Edward.   41. **He who was bold,** a Viking.   43. **the man. The leader,** Byrhtnoth.   45–46. **from the south,** presumably a weapon from the south of Europe.

12. **retainer,** Byrhtnoth.   41–42. **deserted the good man.** The mere fact that Byrhtnoth was dead did not lessen the responsibility of his men.

THE BATTLE OF MALDON

as Offa had said one day earlier, when he had had an assembly at the meeting-place, that many spoke boldly there who would not hold out in time of need.

Now the leader of the people, Aethelred's noble, had fallen; his close retainers all saw that their lord lay dead. The proud thanes advanced there then, the brave men hastened eagerly: they all wished one of two things, to avenge their dear lord or lose their lives. Aelfwine, son of Aelfric, a man young in years, urged them forward, he said words and spoke boldly: "Remember the times when we often spoke over the mead, when we, warriors in the hall, made boasts on the benches about the severe battle; now one may prove who is brave. I wish to make known to all my noble birth, that I was of a great family in Mercia. My father's name was Ealhelm, a wise and prosperous chief. None of the thanes of this people shall reproach me because I wished to desert the expedition, to seek my native land, now that my lord lies cut down in battle. No grief could be greater for me: he was both my kinsman and my lord." Then he went forward, mindful of the feud, and hit one of the pirates in the band with his spear, so that he lay on the ground, killed by his weapon. He then began to urge his friends and companions to go forward.

Offa spoke and brandished his spear. "Aelfwine, you have incited all the thanes to their duty. Now that our lord lies dead, the leader on the earth, it is necessary for each of us to encourage the other warrior to battle, while he may have and hold a weapon, hard knife, spear, and good sword. Godric, the cowardly son of Odda, has betrayed us all. When he rode on the horse, on the proud steed, many a man thought that it was our lord; on that account the people became dispersed on the field, the wall of shields broken. May his effort perish who put so many men to flight here!"

Leofsunu spoke and lifted his linden-wood, his shield as a protection; he spoke to the man: "I promise this, that I will not flee a step from here, but will go on to avenge my friendly lord in battle. There will be no need for the steadfast warriors around Sturmere to reproach me with words, that when my friend fell I would come home lordless, turn from the battle; but rather the weapon shall take me, spear and iron sword." He went very angry, he fought stoutly, he despised flight.

Dunhere then spoke, shook his dart, the simple peasant cried out above all the battle, demanded that every man avenge Byrhtnoth: "No man who thinks to avenge his lord among the people can hesitate or care for life."

Then they went forward, they took no thought of life; the retainers began to fight resolutely, the fierce spearmen, and they prayed to God that they might avenge their friendly lord, and bring destruction to their foes. The hostage began to aid them eagerly; his name was Aescferth, the son of Ecglaf, and he was of a bold race among the Northumbrians. He did not hesitate in battle, but sent forth arrows in abundance; sometimes he shot at a shield, sometimes he pierced a man. Every now and again he gave someone a wound as long as he was able to bear weapons.

Edward the tall, ready and eager, stood in the battle-front; he spoke boastful words, that he would not flee a foot's length when his lord lay dead. He broke through the wall of shields, and fought against the men until he had fittingly avenged his lord on the pirates, before he lay among the slain. Aethelric, the brother of Sigbyrht, a noble comrade, did the same, eager and alert, he fought fiercely, and very many others split the hollow shields; they defended themselves bravely: the edge of the shield broke, and the coat of mail sang a song of fear. Then in the fight Offa struck a pirate so that he fell to the earth, and there the kinsman of Gadd sought the ground: Offa was quickly cut down in the battle. None the less he had accomplished what he had promised his lord, when he boasted earlier with his patron, that they should both ride to the walled town, home unharmed, or fall in the army, die of wounds on the battlefield. He lay as a thane ought, near to his lord.

Then there was breaking of shields; the pirates advanced, maddened with battle; the spear often went through the body of the doomed man. Wigstan, the son of Thurstan, went forward and fought against the men; he was the slayer of three of them before the son of Wighelm lay among the dead. The encounter was severe; the warriors stood firm in the battle, the fighters, weary from wounds; the slain fell to the earth. The two brothers, Oswold and Eadwold, encouraged the men all the while, with words they commanded their dear kinsmen that they must hold out there at the time of need, handle their weapons without wavering.

Byrhtwold spoke and raised his shield; he was an

---

45. **Sturmere.** "Undoubtedly Sturmer in Essex."—Laborde, *op. cit.*, page 132. 51. **peasant.** Heroic poetry does not ordinarily single out a man of humble origin. 15. **bear weapons.** One could have excused a hostage for retreating. 29. **kinsman of Gadd,** Offa. 35–36. **He lay . . . lord,** a concise statement of a thane's ultimate duty. 42. **Wighelm,** another name for Thurstan.

old retainer; he shook his spear and very boldly exhorted the men: "The mind must be the harder, the heart bolder, the courage greater, now that our strength grows less. Our lord lies here cut all to pieces, the good man in the dust; he will ever grieve who now thinks to turn away from this battle. I am old in life; I will not go from here, but I plan to lie beside my lord, by the man so dear." So, too, Godric, the son of Aethelgar, encouraged them all to the fight; often he let fly his dart, his fatal spear, among the Vikings, as he went foremost among the people; he hewed and cut down until he fell in the battle. This was not that Godric who escaped from the fight.

Bede

Bede, first and in many respects one of the greatest in the long line of English historians, led, by his own account, a simple and uneventful life. From the age of seven until his death in 735, he was a member of the joint monastic foundation dedicated to Peter and Paul at Wearmouth and Jarrow, and there "amidst the observance of regular discipline, and the daily care of singing in the church, [he] always took delight in learning, teaching, and writing." The range and the amount of his writings are surprising, and his scientific treatises, especially those on the calendar and chronology in general, were of vast importance; indeed, by argument and example, he did more than almost anyone else to popularize our present method of dating from before and after the birth of Jesus. His numerous theological works, mainly Biblical commentaries, show learning and were undoubtedly valuable as disseminators of knowledge, but he will always be remembered as the author of the *Ecclesiastical History of the English Nation*, which he completed in 731. As a historian Bede shows industry and skill in gathering information, discretion and fairness in marshaling it, and clarity and precision in setting it forth. Of course he does not have a modern historian's prejudice in favor of unvarnished fact, but while he believed in the miracles which add so much to the attraction of his book for us, he was actually chary in the use of them and almost scrupulous in avoiding the more highly embellished forms of supernaturalism.

The two extracts given here are both well known. In "King Edwin's Conversion" the crass materialism of Coifi serves as an admirable foil to the melancholy, but superbly poetic, conception of human life expressed by his nameless companion. The reference in the story of Caedmon to extemporaneous public composition and recitation of songs at feasts and the like is perhaps of greater value than is the story of divine poetic inspiration, since that had been, and was to be, told of other poets than Caedmon. Despite subsequent ascription of a number of Biblical paraphrases to Caedmon, the only poem which can be safely accredited to him is the little hymn on the creation imbedded in Bede's account. The present translations are not from Bede's original Latin, but from the Alfredian translation, *The Old English Version of Bede's Ecclesiastical History of the English People*, ed. by T. Miller, Early English Text Society, Original Series, Nos. 95–96, 1890–91, pp. 132 ff. and 342 ff.

KING EDWIN'S CONVERSION

THEN Bishop Paulinus preached and taught the word of God, but the king still hesitated to believe, and during a certain time, just as we have said before, he customarily sat alone and earnestly considered with himself, and thought what was best for him to do, and what religion he should observe; then on a particular day the man of God came in to him where he sat alone, and placed his right hand on his head, and asked him if he could recognize that sign. Then at once he recognized it clearly, and became very much afraid and fell at his feet; and the man of God lifted him up and spoke to him pleasantly and said: "Well now, through God's grace you have escaped the hand of your enemies, those whom you feared, and through His gift and favor you have received the kingdom which you desired. But remember now that you carry out the third thing which you promised, that you would accept His faith and keep His commandments, who saved you from temporal hardships and raised you into the honor

1. **Paulinus,** who was sent by Gregory in 601 to join Augustine in England; in 625 he went to Northumbria, where King Edwin accepted Christianity in 627 and gave Paulinus a see in York. 2. **the king,** Edwin of Northumbria (585–633), who came to the throne after many years of exile. 7–8. **man of God,** Paulinus. 10. **that sign.** While Edwin was in exile in East Anglia he had had a vision in which a mysterious stranger foretold his ultimate victory over his foes, and urged him to obey the advice of a man who would come to him and place his hand on his head.

of a temporal kingdom. And if you will hereafter be obedient to His will, which He preaches and teaches through me, He will also rescue you from the torments of eternal evil, and make you a sharer with Him of the eternal kingdom in heaven."

When the king heard these words, then he answered him and said, that he both wished and ought to receive the belief which he taught. He said, however, that he desired to have discussion and counsel with his friends and wise men, so that if they would consent to that with him, they too would be consecrated to Christ in the fountain of life. Then the king did just as he said and the bishop permitted it. Then he had speech and deliberation with his wise men, and asked them all separately how this new learning and worship of the Deity which was taught to them there seemed and appeared to them.

His chief priest whose name was Coifi answered him then, "Observe, king, what this teaching is which is now preached to us. I truly confess that I have clearly learned that the faith which we have had and followed up to now has absolutely not a bit of power or usefulness. For none of your followers has subjected himself more dutifully or more joyfully to the worship of our gods than have I; and none the less there are many who have received more presents and benefits from you than I, and have had more prosperity in all things. Now I know, if our gods had any strength, then they would have aided me more, because I served and obeyed them more eagerly. Therefore it seems to me wise, if you consider the things which are newly preached to be better and stronger, that you should accept them."

Another king's councilor and ealdorman gave assent to this man's words, and began to speak, and said thus: "Such appears to me, king, this present life of man on earth in comparison with the time which is unknown to us, as though you were sitting at the banquet with your leaders and thanes in winter and the fire was lighted and your hall warmed, and it rained and snowed and stormed outside; and there should come a sparrow and quickly fly through the house, come in through one door and go out through the other. Now in the time that he is inside he is not touched by the storm of winter; but that is only the twinkling of an eye and the least interval, and at once he comes from winter back to winter again. So this life of men appears save for but a little while; what goes before or what follows after we do not know. Therefore, if this teaching should bring anything more certain and more proper, it is fitting that we follow it." Other ealdormen and king's councilors spoke words similar to these.

CAEDMON

IN the monastery of this abbess was a certain brother particularly glorified and honored by divine grace. Therefore he was accustomed fittingly to make songs which concerned faith and piety, so that whatever he learned of sacred writings from scholars, he brought forth after a short time well composed in the English language in poetry, adorned with the greatest sweetness and inspiration. And by his songs the minds of many men were often inspired to a disregard of the world and to association with the heavenly life. And also many others after him among the English people began to compose religious songs, but none, however, could do that like to him. For he had not been taught by men or through men that he should learn poetic art, but he was divinely aided and received skill in song through the grace of God. And for that reason he could not compose any false or frivolous poetry, but only that which concerned religion, and which it was proper for his pious tongue to sing.

He was a man situated in secular life until the time that he was advanced in years, and he had never learned any poetry. And often on that account at the beer-drinking, when it was decided there for the sake of enjoyment that they should all, one after the other, sing to the harp, when he saw the harp come near him, then he got up from the feast for shame, and went home to his house. Then he did this at a certain time, that he left the house of the drinking party and was going out to the cattle-shed, the care of which had been entrusted to him for the night. When he laid his limbs to rest there at a fitting time and slept, then in a dream a man stood beside him and saluted and greeted him and called him by his name: "Caedmon, sing me something." Then he answered and said: "I am not able to sing; on that account I went away from this drinking party and came here, because I do not know how to sing anything." Again he who was speaking to him said: "Nevertheless you *are* able to sing." Then he said: "What shall I sing?" He said:

---

7. **abbess.** Hilda (614–680), was abbess of Whitby from 657. The important role played by women in the early English church is nowhere better illustrated than by the fact that Hilda presided for many years over this famous monastery, which included men as well as women among its members.

"Sing me of the Creation." When he received that answer he began at once to sing in praise of God the Creator verses and words which he had never heard before, the order of which is this:

"Now let us praise the Guardian of the kingdom of heaven, the might of the Creator and His purpose, the work of the Father of Glory, as He, the eternal Lord, established the beginning of every wonder. He first, the holy Creator, created heaven as a roof for the children of men; then the Guardian of mankind, the eternal Lord, the Almighty Lord, afterwards made the earth, the land for men."

Then he arose from sleep and he had fast in his memory all that he had sung sleeping. And to those words he at once added many other words in the same style of song worthy of God. In the morning he came to the steward, who was his overseer, and told him what a gift he had received; and he at once led him to the abbess and made known and said it to her. She commanded all the most learned men and scholars to come together, and in their presence ordered him to tell the dream and to sing the song, that it might be decided by the judgment of them all, what this was or from where it had come. Then it was seen by all of them, just as it was, that the heavenly gift had been given to him by the Lord Himself. They then narrated and told him a certain holy story and words of religious learning and instructed him then, if he were able, that he should turn that into the melody of song.

6–13. "Now let us . . . men." Bede gives a Latin paraphrase of the hymn, with the comment, "This is the sense, but not the words in order as he sang them in his sleep: for verses, though never so well composed, cannot be literally translated out of one language into another, without losing much of their beauty and loftiness." However, four manuscripts of the Latin text contain what is apparently Caedmon's hymn in its original Northumbrian dialect, and it was this, not Bede's paraphrase, which the Alfredian translator turned into West Saxon.

When he had received the matter, he went home to his house, and came again in the morning, and sang and returned to them what had been entrusted to him, adorned in the best poetry.

Then the abbess began to prize and love God's gift in the man; and she exhorted and advised him that he should leave secular life and accept monastic; and he consented to that. She received him into that monastery with his goods, and joined him to the congregation of God's servants, and commanded them to teach him the series of the holy story and narrative. And he remembered all that he could learn by hearing, and, as it were a pure animal ruminating, changed it into the sweetest song. And his song and his poetry were so pleasant to hear that his teachers themselves wrote down and learned from his mouth. He sang first about the Creation of the earth and the beginning of mankind and all the story of Genesis, which is the first book of Moses; and afterwards about the exodus of the people of Israel from the land of Egypt and their entrance into the promised land; and about many other stories in the books of the canon of holy writ; and about the incarnation of Christ, and about His passion, and about His ascension into heaven; and about the coming of the Holy Ghost, and the teaching of the apostles, and again about the day of the approaching judgment, and about the terror of infernal torture; and about the sweetness of the heavenly kingdom, he made many a song. And he likewise made many others about divine benefits and judgments. In all these he took care eagerly that he should draw men from the love of sins and wicked deeds, and to arouse them to love and zeal for good deeds. For he was a very pious man and humbly subjected himself to regular discipline, and he was inspired with a flame of great fervor against those who wished to do otherwise. And he therefore closed and ended his life with a fair conclusion.

Alfred
849–901

When Alfred, the fourth son of Aethelwulf to rule Wessex after the latter's death in 858, came to the throne in 871, most of England outside Wessex was in Danish hands or under Danish domination. Wessex had watched her sister kingdoms raided and devoured with a curious mixture of smugness and fear, varied only occasionally by the dispatch of an expeditionary force. On the whole the attitude of the West Saxons had been one of passive appeasement, if we may use the word without too modern a connotation. The behavior of Aethelwulf in 855–856 is suggestive. He gave away a tenth of his landholdings for the good of the Church, thus removing so much income from the national defense; he went to Rome and stayed there a long time, making lavish offerings; and on his way home he stopped at the court of Charles the Bald to marry the thirteen-year-old princess Judith. That such far from heroic conduct aroused an unsuccessful rebellion is not surprising, but perhaps we may feel that this trip to the Continent which Alfred, then six or seven, made with his father helped to develop his interest in scholarship and literature, subjects of small concern, it would seem, to the other members of his family.

Alfred had little time for literary pursuits in the first years of his reign. Wessex was in grave peril and, indeed, early in 878 it looked very much as though Wessex must go the sorry way of the other English kingdoms. The Danes, however, had never before been confronted with an English leader as intrepid, resourceful, and inspiring as Alfred, and before the end of the year their hold on Wessex was broken by the battle of Ethandun (Eddington). The Peace of Wedmore excluded the Danes from the area below a line drawn roughly from London to Chester, and Alfred and Wessex had a breathing-space which lasted, with but few interruptions, until 892.

Alfred, with great good sense, reorganized the internal affairs of his kingdom; he codified and improved the legal system, but, above all, he devoted himself to the education of his people. In the preface to the *Pastoral Care* he tells us that when he came to the throne there were "very few on this side of the Humber who could understand their services in English or even translate an epistle from Latin into English"; and then he adds, with a grim humor rare in his writings, "and I imagine that there were not many on the other side of the Humber." It is unlikely that Alfred himself translated all the works associated with his name, and we know that his method of translation was a communal one, with ample help from his attendant scholars. Nevertheless, without his enthusiasm, energy, and intellectual curiosity the books would never have been written, and we must not let niggling scholarship deprive him of due gratitude. He tried to give his people—not all his people, of course, but those whose circumstances made them eligible for education—a compendious library of information and admonition. In addition to the translation of Orosius and the *Old English Chronicles*, to both of which we shall come presently, Alfred's "library" contained at least four books. Pope Gregory's *Cura Pastoralis*, turned into English as the *Hirdeboc*, or *Shepherd's Book*, was apparently his first translation, and was to serve as a guidebook for the clergy, especially those of higher rank. We have already noticed Bede's *Ecclesiastical History* (page 62) and have read two sections from the Alfredian translation. The *Consolations of Philosophy* by Boethius (c. 480–524) was Alfred's effort to furnish his countrymen with a philosophic code of, as it happens, Neo-Platonic content. This book received more independent treatment than the earlier translations, and contains many original passages, some philosophical in character and others expanding or explaining allusions in the original. Among Alfred's successors as translators of Boethius were Chaucer and Queen Elizabeth. Finally, we have a version of the *Soliloquies* of St. Augustine of Hippo (354–430), which, like the foregoing work, is philosophical and Neo-Platonic; Alfred in his Preface says, "Augustine, bishop of Carthage, made two books about his own mind." Here again Alfred shows great independence, the third book being almost completely new, although the substance was not original with Alfred.

When we take everything into consideration, Alfred's intellectual gifts to England almost, though of course only to a degree, equal his achievements as military leader and statesman.

THE VOYAGES OF OHTHERE AND WULFSTAN

When Alfred wished to furnish his people with domestic history, he found Bede at hand; he could not have done better and, what is more, we can hardly ask for better. When, however, he sought for a "universal" history, he chose something which we cannot commend very highly. The *Historiae adversum Paganos* of Paulus Orosius was inspired by St. Augustine early in the fifth century. Few historians are completely without bias, but Orosius's was particularly calculated to distort truth. He wrote at a time when many people, especially among the intellectuals and the aristocrats, were seriously considering whether or not Christianity had been a benefit to the civilized (that is, the Roman) world. This heresy was naturally repugnant to the Fathers of the Church, and Orosius's history was part of the campaign against it. His thesis was that bad as times are now, they were worse in the wicked old pagan days; a beautiful list of ancient calamities is produced, and the amours of Jupiter are brought in with sour relish. The book, of course, is wretched history, but it was the best that Alfred could find. We must give him credit for free treatment of his original; he abridges severely and leaves out much of the propaganda. Anti-Olympianism was, after all, a fairly dead issue in the late ninth century. He adds a considerable section dealing with the geography of northern Europe, to which he appends, as if for documentation, the voyages of two of his contemporaries, Ohthere, who sailed around the North Cape, and Wulfstan, who traveled in the Baltic. As we read we can almost hear the sailors as they tell their stories in response to questions from the King, while a secretary takes down the narrations. The accounts were first printed by Hakluyt (see Everyman's Library edition, Vol. I, pp. 56 ff.), and frequently thereafter. Ohthere's first voyage inspired Longfellow's "The Discoverer of the North Cape" (Oxford edition, London, 1917, pp. 313 ff.).

A map will be of assistance to the student, and an admirable one, with the voyages indicated, is in Kemp Malone's "King Alfred's North," *Speculum*, Vol. V. (1930), pp. 139 ff., especially pp. 157 ff. The following translation is from the text as printed by M. H. Turk, *An Anglo-Saxon Reader*, Scribner, rev. ed., 1930, pp. 57 ff.

OHTHERE told his lord, King Alfred, that he dwelt farthest to the north of all the Norwegians. He said that he lived northward in the land by the North Sea. He said, however, that that land stretched far to the north from there, but that it was all waste, save that in a few places here and there Lapps camped, engaged in hunting by winter and by summer in fishing in the sea.

He said that at a certain time he wanted to find out how far the land ran northward, whether anyone lived north of the waste. Then he went northward along the coast for three days; and he always had the wasteland on the starboard and open sea on the larboard. By that time he was as far north as the whalers ever go. After that he went north again as far as he was able to sail in a second three days. Then the land turned to the east, or the sea into the land, he did not know which, but he did know that he waited there for a wind from the west and a little from the north; now he sailed east along the coast as far as he could in four days. At this point he had to wait for a due north wind, because the land curved to the south there, or the sea into the land, he did not know which. He sailed from there south along the coast as far as he could in five days. There a great river ran up into the land. They turned up the river, because they did not dare to sail beyond it for fear of hostility, since the land was all inhabited on the other side of the river. Before that he had not found any cultivated land since he left his home, but there had been wasteland on the starboard all the way, except for fishermen and fowlers and hunters, and they were all Lapps; and the open sea was always on the larboard. The Permians had cultivated their land very well, but they did not dare come onto it. The land of the Terfinns was all waste, except where hunters or fishermen or fowlers camped.

The Permians told him many stories, both of their own country and of the lands which were round about them, but he didn't know what the truth was, because he did not see it himself. It seemed to him that the Lapps and the Permians spoke very nearly the same language. In addition to seeing the country, he went there most of all for the walruses, for they have very good bone in their teeth—they brought some of the teeth to the king—and their hide is apt to be very good for cables. This kind of whale is much smaller than other whales: it is never longer than seven ells. The best whale-hunting is in his own country; these are forty-eight ells long, and the biggest fifty ells long. He said that he and five others killed sixty of them in one day.

He was a very well-to-do man in the possessions in which their wealth consists, that is, in wild animals. At the time when he visited the king he still

---

44. his lord. Ohthere was evidently in Alfred's service; he was perhaps one of the foreigners whom Alfred called in to help him build up a naval force.

5. starboard, right.   **9–10. Then the land . . . the land.** He was rounding the North Cape, but he thought that it might be a bay.   **17. along the coast,** in the White Sea.   **18. river,** the Varsuga.   **29. Terfinns,** Lapps.

ALFRED

had six hundred unsold tame animals. These animals they call reindeer. Six of them were decoys, and these are very valuable among the Lapps, because they capture the wild reindeer with them. He was one of the leading men in the country, nevertheless he had no more than twenty cattle, twenty sheep, and twenty swine, and what he plowed he plowed with horses. But their wealth is mostly in the tribute which the Lapps pay to them. This tribute is paid in the skins of wild animals, the feathers of birds, whalebone, and cables made of whale's hide or seal's hide. Each Lapp pays according to his rank. Those of highest rank have to pay fifteen martin skins, five reindeer, a bearskin, ten measures of feathers, a cloak of bearskin or otter skin, and two cables; each of the cables must be sixty ells long, one made of whale's hide and the other of seal's hide.

He said that the land of the Norwegians was very long and very narrow. All of it which one can either graze or plow lies along the sea, and even that is very rocky in some places; to the east, along the cultivated land, stretch wild moors. Lapps dwell in these moors. The cultivated land is broadest to the east, and the farther north it goes the more narrow it becomes. To the east it may be sixty miles broad, or a little broader, in the middle thirty miles or broader, and in the north, where it was narrowest, he said that it might be three miles broad to the moor. The moor beyond is so broad in some places that it takes a man two weeks to cross it, and in other places no broader than a man can cross in six days.

Alongside the land to the south on the other side of the moor, is Sweden, stretching up to the north, and in the north the land is bordered by the country of the Cwenas. The Cwenas sometimes make war on the Norwegians across the moor, and sometimes the Norwegians make war on them. There are many lakes in the moors, and the Cwenas carry their boats over land to the lakes, and thence make war on the Norwegians; they have very little and very light boats.

Ohthere said that the district he lived in is called Halgoland. He said that no one lived north of him. There is a harbor in the southern part of the country, which is called Sciringesheal. He said that it would take a man a month to sail there, if he camped at night and had a favorable wind each day; and all the time he would sail along the coast. On the starboard he would have first Ireland and then the islands which are between Ireland and this country. Then this country would be on the starboard until he comes to Sciringesheal, and Norway is on the larboard all the way. South of Sciringesheal there runs up into the land a great bay, which is broader than any man can see over. Jutland is opposite it on the other side, and then Zeeland. This bay runs up into the land many hundred miles.

From Sciringesheal he said that he sailed in five days to the harbor which is called Haddeby; it stands between the Wends, the Saxons, and the Angles, and belongs to the Danes. When he was sailing there from Sciringesheal, Denmark was on the larboard, and, for three days, open sea was on the starboard; and then, two days before he came to Haddeby, Jutland, Zeeland, and many islands were on the starboard. The Angles lived in these lands before they came to this country. And on his larboard for these two days were the islands which belong to Denmark.

Wulfstan said that he set out from Haddeby, that he was in Truso in seven days and nights and that the ship was running under sail all the way. Wendland was on his starboard and on his larboard was Langeland, Laaland, Falster, and Skaane—these lands all belong to Denmark. After that on the larboard was the land of the Burgundians, and they have a king of their own. After the land of the Burgundians we had on the larboard the lands which are called, first, Blekinge, Möre, Oeland and Gothland; and these lands belong to Sweden. Wendland was on our starboard all the way to the mouth of the Vistula. The Vistula is a very large river, and it separates Witland and Wendland; and Witland belongs to the Ests. The Vistula runs out of Wendland and into the Frisches Haff, which is about fifteen miles broad. Then the Elbing comes from the east into the Frisches Haff from the lake on the shore of which Truso stands. The two rivers come out together into the Frisches Haff, the Elbing from Estland on the east, and the Vistula from Wendland on the south. And then the Vistula deprives the Elbing of its name and runs out of the

---

8. with horses. The English plowed with oxen. **9. tribute . . . to them.** An interesting account of the collection of this tribute is in the Icelandic saga of Egil, the son of Skallagrim (chaps. 10, 14, 17, tr. by W. C. Green, London, 1893, or by E. R. Eddison, Macmillan, 1930). **37. Cwenas,** Finns. **45. Halgoland,** modern Norwegian Helgeland. **47. Sciringesheal,** Skiringssalr, well up in the Oslo Fiord.

3. Ireland. "Iceland" has been suggested as the correct reading, but see Malone, *op. cit.*, page 143. **8–9. great bay,** Oslo Fiord. **32. land of the Burgundians,** the island of Bornholm. **40. Ests,** probably not the ancestors of the Estonians. **43. lake,** the Drausensee. **47–48. Vistula . . . name.** Two rivers, the Elbing and the Vistula, run into the Frisches Haff, but only one, the Vistula, runs out.

Frisches Haff west and north into the sea; for that reason it is called the mouth of the Vistula.

Estland is very large, and there are very many towns, and in each town there is a king. There is a great deal of honey and fishing. The king and the most powerful men drink mare's milk, and the poor and servants drink mead. There is much fighting among them. There is no ale brewed by the Ests, but there is mead enough.

There is a custom among the Ests, that when a man dies there he lies in his house unburned with his relatives and friends for a month, or sometimes two; and the kings and the other men of high rank as much longer as they have more property, sometimes remaining unburned a half-year, lying above-ground, in their houses. All the time that the body lies within, there is drinking and games, until the day he is burned. Then on the same day that they are going to carry him to the pyre, they divide all of his property, that which is left after the drinking and the games, into five or six portions, sometimes more, according to the amount of the possessions. They lay it down in the space of about a mile, the largest portion farthest from the town, then the second, then the third, until it is all laid down in the one mile, and the least portion is nearest to the town in which the dead man is lying. Then are gathered all the men who have the swiftest horses in the country, about five or six miles from the goods. Now they all race toward the goods; then the man who has the fastest horse comes to the first and largest portion, and so each after the other, until it is all taken; and he gets the least part who reaches the portion nearest the town. Then they all ride their ways with the goods, and they can have them all; for that reason swift horses are extremely valuable there. When the dead man's belongings are thus all spent, then they carry him out and burn him, with his weapons and clothes; and they squander almost all his possessions what with the long lying in of the dead man, and with what they lay down by the way, which strangers race for and take.

It is a custom among the Ests to burn men of every tribe; and if anyone there finds a bone unburned, he must make amends for it greatly. There is one tribe among the Ests who are able to make cold; and because of that the dead men are able to lie so long and not decay, since they work this cold on them. If a man were to set two vessels full of ale or water, they would bring it about that both were frozen over, whether it were summer or winter.

Aelfric

c.955—c.1020

Aelfric of Eynsham, preacher, teacher, scholar, and abbot, was the outstanding English man of letters between Alfred and the Norman Conquest. He had been a student of Aethelwold, Bishop of Winchester, himself a student of Dunstan, and was thus an inheritor of the zeal and learning of the Benedictine reformation, which did so much to raise the level of English religious life and literature. The range of Aelfric's intellectual interests is extensive indeed, and we find him writing sermons, saints' lives, a grammar, translations of various books of the Old Testament, a life of his teacher St. Aethelwold, a Latin colloquy, an abridgment of the Benedictine Rule, a treatise on astronomy, and arguments in favor of celibacy and ecclesiastical chastity. Despite the fact that Aelfric's writings were of a decidedly utilitarian nature, he developed the most striking and individual prose style of any author before, or for long after, the Norman Conquest. This style is characterized by balance, rhythm, and a free use of alliteration, often carried so far as to tempt editors, especially of the *Lives of the Saints*, to arrange the texts in metrical form; it seems likely, however, that Aelfric was consciously writing an elaborate, resonant prose, making use, or overuse, of the devices of the preacher and orator, rather than a debased, degenerate, and halting verse.

Of the selections which are given here the account of St. Cuthbert illustrates Aelfric's work as a preacher, and the *Colloquy* his work as a teacher.

SAINT CUTHBERT

Cuthbert was one of the most popular of English saints, and Aelfric's homily, which is for March 20, the day of Cuthbert's death in 687, in the second series of the *Ser-*

---

6. **mare's milk**, probably similar to the fermented drink called koummis.

mones Catholici, gives an admirable explanation. We have here a very appealing picture of a simple, pious man in whom the evangelical spirit of the Irish Church was still strong, with its emphasis on bringing the Word of Life to the humblest folk in the most remote villages. Indeed Bede (*Ecclesiastical History*, Book IV, Chapter 27) says of Cuthbert that "he was wont chiefly to resort to those places, and preach in villages, as being seated high up amid craggy uncouth mountains, were frightful to others to behold, and whose poverty and barbarity rendered them inaccessible to other teachers." Among Cuthbert's miracles the number in which birds and animals play a part is noteworthy, and these add much to the charm which the modern reader finds in the account of his life. The following translation is made from Henry Sweet's *Selected Homilies of Aelfric*, Oxford, 1922. Both series of the *Sermones Catholici* were edited and translated by Benjamin Thorpe in two volumes, London, 1844–1846.

CUTHBERT, the holy bishop, shining with many merits and high dignities, reigning in the kingdom of heaven in eternal bliss with the almighty Creator, lives in glory.

Bede, the wise teacher of the English people, wrote the life of this saint from beginning to end with wonderful praises, both in simple narration and in versified tale. Bede told us truly that the blessed Cuthbert when he was a child of eight years ran, as his ignorant youth encouraged him, playing with children of his own age; but Almighty God wished to rouse the ignorance of His chosen Cuthbert through the warnings of a suitable teacher, and sent to him a three-year-old child, that it might wisely rebuke his foolish play with serious words. Truly the aforesaid three-year-old child asked the frolicking Cuthbert, "Why do you make yourself subject to this useless play, you who are consecrated by God with heavenly honor? It is not fitting for a bishop to be like men of the people in his actions. Desist, my dear, from such unseemly sport, and attach yourself to God, who chose you as a bishop for His people, to whom you must open the entrance to the kingdom of heaven." But Cuthbert still continued with his playing, until his teacher, weeping sadly with bitter tears, suddenly put a stop to the games of all the children. In truth the crowd of children wished to comfort the sorrow of the one child, but all of them with their consolation could not remove his unhappiness until Cuthbert gladdened it with gracious kisses. And he himself afterwards always persisted in lofty seriousness in accordance with the child's warning.

After this the knee of the blessed Cuthbert was injured with a hard swelling so that he had to assist his walking with crutches. When he was sitting one day by himself in the sun and warming his leg, there came riding to him a venerable horseman seated on a snow-white horse and himself clothed in white garments; and he greeted the saint pleasantly with friendly words, asking that he would give him a suitable meal. Cuthbert then said eagerly to the angel: "I would prepare your meal now myself if I were able to go on foot, but my diseased knee is badly afflicted so that no drug can cure it, though it be applied to it frequently." Then the stranger alighted and laid hold of his knee with his health-giving hands, and ordered him to take wheaten flour, and boil it in milk, and so to bind up the swollen limb with the heat; and after these words he mounted his horse, going away along the road on which he had come there. Then Cuthbert warmed his knee in accordance with the angel's counsel, and he at once enjoyed the ability to walk in health, and he understood that God had cured him by means of his angel, God who had of old miraculously given sight to the blind Tobias through His archangel Raphael.

Again the holy Cuthbert, when he was watching with shepherds in the field in his youth, saw the heavens open and angels lead the soul of Bishop Aidan with great glory into the joy of heaven. Once also Cuthbert was going through the country preaching faith in God when, because of stormy weather, he turned aside to the cottage of a shepherd which stood empty in the wilderness which he was crossing, and tied his horse inside it. Then, while he was singing his prayers, the horse tore the thatch from the roof of the cottage and there fell down, as if from the roof, a warm loaf and food to go with it. He then thanked God for the meal and fed himself with it.

After this the blessed Cuthbert forsook all worldly things and with holy habits subjected himself to the monastic life; and immediately after he became a monk he was made attendant for guests, so that he took care of the guesthouse and was helpful to those who came to the monastery. Then at a certain time on a winter's day there came to him an angel of God in the form of a guest, and Cuthbert received him with all hospitality. Then he went out about food for the stranger, but when he came in he found no guest but there lay there three heavenly loaves, shining with the brightness of lilies, giving off the odor of roses, and sweeter in taste than the honey of bees. The holy Cuthbert

26. **Aidan,** Bishop of Lindisfarne in Northumbria (d. 651). At King Oswald's request he had been sent from the Irish monastic settlement at Iona to bring back the Northumbrians to Christianity.

looked everywhere in the snow to see where the visitor had gone on his way, but when he saw no footprints in the snow, then he understood that the stranger was an angel and not a man, who had brought him heavenly food and did not care for that of earth.

This holy man was accustomed to go at night to the sea, and stand in the salt ocean up to his neck, singing his prayers. Then on a certain night another monk was on the watch for his going and with stealthy tread followed his footsteps until they both came to the sea. Cuthbert did as was his custom, he sang his prayers, standing in the waves of the sea up to his neck, and then bent his knees on the sand, with palms upstretched to heaven. Just then two seals came from the bottom of the sea, and they dried his feet with their fur, and warmed his limbs with their breath, and then with a sign asked for his blessing, lying at his feet on the yellow sand. Then Cuthbert sent the sea-animals back into the water with a true blessing, and in the morning returned to the monastery. The other monk became very much frightened and sick; at daybreak he humbled himself at the saint's knees, praying that he would completely put his illness to flight and pity his curiosity in a fatherly way. The saint then answered at once: "I will secretly pity your error, if you will conceal that sight with silence until my soul has gone from here, summoned from the present life to heaven." Cuthbert then healed the sickness of his beholder with prayer, and forgave the offense of his curious journey.

Many miracles were done by the holy Cuthbert, but for brevity we will suppress some, lest this account seem too long to you. Truly Cuthbert was going, as was his custom, preaching concerning the faith, so that he might teach the way of life to uneducated people. Then an eagle flew before him on his path, and he began to ask his companion who should give them food on that day. His companion said that he had been considering for some time where they should ask for food, since they went on the trip without provisions. Cuthbert then said to him, "Almighty God can easily provide for us through this eagle, He who of old fed Elijah by means of the black raven, before he went to heaven." They went on their way, and just then the eagle lighted on the bank, having flown there with a fish which it had just caught. Then the saint said to his companion: "Run to the eagle and take from him part of the fish which he has caught as food for us. Praise be to the Almighty who wishes to feed us by means of this bird. However, give some part of it to the eagle as a reward for his labor."

After the meal they went on their way, and Cuthbert preached to the people well, that they should be wary of the Devil's tricks, lest with lying he should injure their belief, and draw their minds away from the preaching. The people then suddenly began to rush away in the middle of this admonition, greatly deceived, so that they paid too little attention to the instruction. The guileful fiend deceived them very much, making it appear as though a house was really burning there, roaring with flames; it was, however, by illusion. Then the people wanted to put out the fire, if any water could lessen it; but the presence of the saint easily quenched the delusion of the Devil, which they had followed foolishly, and heeded the Word of Life too little. The people then returned ashamed to the instruction which they had abandoned before, begging gentle mercy from the teacher because formerly they had paid too little attention to his lesson, when he had told them in advance of the peril.

Cuthbert, however, on another occasion with holy prayers alone saved a completely burning house from the damage of fire, and put to flight the blast of wind, Cuthbert, who had very often before put out the poisonous arrows of devilish temptation in himself with the protection of the true Lord. Often he would preach without fear to people in a far-off land. Almighty God had given him a fair eloquence for teaching the people, and men could not hide their minds from him, but they humbly confessed their secrets to him, daring not to do otherwise, and made atonement secretly by his command.

A certain religious man also had great familiarity with the holy Cuthbert, and frequently enjoyed his preaching. Then it happened worse for his wife than was good for him, in that she was greatly afflicted with madness. The pious man came to the blessed Cuthbert, who was at that time appointed as provost in the monastery which is called Lindisfarne. Then for shame he was not able to say openly that his pious wife was lying in madness, but asked that he would send a brother who could give her the last rites before she was brought from life. Cuthbert then knew all about the wife and wished to come to her at once himself, because she had lived piously before, although this misfortune had happened to her so. Then the man began to weep sadly, being fearful of the misfortune. Cuthbert comforted him with his words, said that the devil who wished to harm her should leave her on his visit, and flee away with great fear, and the woman speaking sensibly in her right mind should come to meet him and take his bridle. It happened in accordance with the teacher's words that the woman, now sane, greeted him with words, asked that she might prepare food for him, and told how the devil left her secretly, and had taken to flight very much afraid, when the saint was coming there.

The holy Cuthbert afterwards, dwelling in the monastery, did miracles in a wonderful way. He began greatly to consider in his mind how he could escape the praise of the people, lest he become too famous in the world and be alien to the glory of heaven. He wished then to practice a solitary life as a hermit and to live completely in secrecy: he went, then, to Farne in the flowing wave. That island is altogether beat upon by the salt ocean, in the middle of the sea, and before that time was within very much filled with black spirits, so that men could not inhabit the earth for the threats of the dark devils; but they fled all together and opened up the island wholly to the noble warrior, and he lived there alone, safe from their malice through the aid of God Almighty. The island was then completely deprived of the pleasantness of water in the waste rocks, but the holy man at once ordered the hardness to hollow out in the middle of the floor of his fair house; and a pleasant spring then sprang up, sweet in taste, for the use of the man who once had miraculously turned water to a winelike taste, when God wished it so.

The saint then ordered them to bring him seed, for he wished to cultivate fruit in the wilderness, if Almighty God granted it to him, so that he could feed himself with footwork. He sowed wheat on the plowed land, but it could not grow up to fruit, nor was the land even growing with grass. Then he ordered them to bring him barley for seed, and sowed the earth again past any usual time for planting. It grew with pleasure and ripened well. Then ravens wished to rob him of his labors, if they dared. The saint said to the hard-beaked ones, "If the Almighty grants you this, enjoy the fruits and do not ask me; but if He has not granted it to you, go away, cruel birds, from this island to your own home." Then the ravens at once flew all together over the salt sea, and the saint enjoyed the fruit of his toil.

After that two other black ravens came traveling again and tore at his house with hard bills and took some of it as a shelter for their nestlings. These also the blessed man drove from his country with a

16. **Farne,** an island near Lindisfarne (Holy Island).
35. **footwork,** use of the spade.

single word; but one of these birds came flying back after three days, very sad, and flew to his feet, begging for peace, that he might live ever harmless in that land and his mate with him. Then the saint granted him this and they came joyfully to that land, and brought the teacher a present as a reward, hog's fat for the care of his shoes, and they afterwards lived there innocently.

Then the saint wanted to build a house for his needs, with the aid of his brothers; he asked them for a sill with which to support the house on the side next the sea. The brothers promised him they would bring the timber to him when they came again. They came, just as they had said, but nevertheless they were forgetful of the tree; but God Almighty was mindful of it, and sent him the sill Himself on the sea-tide, and the wave cast it up just where he himself had planned to erect the house on the salt shore. The saint lived very strictly for many years in the solitary life, and pious men visited him often, and directed their lives by his teaching.

Then there came to him an abbess whose name was Aelflaed, the sister of king Egfrith; she wished to strengthen her mind by means of his admonitions. In the midst of their conversation she began to beg the holy man that he should tell her how long her brother Egfrith was to possess his kingdom. Then the saint answered her with equivocal speech and said, "The pleasure of a year is estimated as nothing, where black death is approaching." She understood then that her brother could not enjoy his life above that one year and at once she asked him, weeping sadly, "My dear, tell me who is to ascend his throne, since he has no brother, nor does he leave a child." Then the holy man said again to the maiden, "The Almighty Creator has preserved a fit man as a king for this people, and he will be as dear to you as the other is now." The maiden dared to speak to him yet again, and said, "The hearts of men think in unlike ways: some desire the dignity of this world, some fulfill their wicked lusts, and they all afterwards become miserably destitute. You scorn exalted glory and it is more agreeable to you that you should sit in this mean hovel than in a hall as a glorious bishop." Then the wise man said that he was not worthy of so great an office nor of the throne, but, nevertheless, that no man could escape the power of God in any retreats of heaven, or of earth, or, third, of the sea. "I believe, however, if the Almighty ordered me to be of that station, that I could again come to this island after the lapse of two years, and possess this land. I ask you, Aelflaed, that you do not betray our conversation to anyone during my life."

After these words an assembly was held, and Egfrith sat in it, and Theodore, the archbishop of this island, with many other excellent counselors, and they all unanimously chose the blessed Cuthbert as a bishop. Then they at once sent writings with that message to the blessed man, but they could not bring him from his hermitage. King Egfrith himself then rowed to the island, and Bishop Trumwine with other pious men, and they implored the saint very much, bent their knees, and begged them with tears, until they drew him weeping from the wasteland to the council with them; and he undertook the rank at their bidding, just as it had been said long before by the mouth of the child, and by that of the famous Bishop Boisil, who had told him with true prophecy the course of his life.

In that same year also Egfrith, the noble king, was killed on his unfortunate journey, when he began to fight against the Picts too rashly against the Lord's will, and his illegitimate brother ruled after him, who had gone to the Irish for wisdom, so that he, a foreigner, might excel in learning. Then the aforesaid conversation was fulfilled, just as the holy man had said to the maiden about her brother before he was a bishop. After that the holy Cuthbert, suffragan bishop of the congregation of Lindisfarne, cared for his people with all diligence, in imitation of the blessed apostles, and guarded them from the Devil with continual prayers, and invited them to heaven with health-giving admonition; and he lived just as he himself taught, and always fortified his preachings with examples, and also adorned them well with miracles, and ever sweetened them with true love, and moderated them with great patience, and was very gracious in every speech. He would not change his customary food nor his dress, which he had had in the wilderness, but kept the rigor of his hard diet in his life among laymen. He was very rich for paupers and beggars and always very poor for himself.

He then did many miracles during the time that he was a bishop. With holy water he healed a certain woman, the wife of an ealdorman, from a miserable disease, and she, immediately well, waited upon him. Again at the same time he anointed with oil a maiden lying in long suffering from a troublesome headache, and she was at once better. A certain pious man was also diseased and lay near death, despaired of by his friends. One of them had a holy loaf, which the happy man had formerly blessed, and he immediately dipped it in water and poured it into the mouth of his sick relative, and at once quieted the disease. Also at another time a sick boy was suddenly carried before the wise man, when he was going through the land with instruction; then the bearers eagerly begged for his blessing, and he at once aroused the boy, so that he who had been brought there on a litter went away well on his feet. A wretched mother, very sad, with difficulty carried her half-dead child on the same road on which the wise man was going; then he felt pity for the sorrowful mother, and kissed her son lovingly; he said that her child should be whole, and all her household enjoy health; and the words of the prophet were fulfilled.

Afterwards Aelflaed, the noble maiden, invited the teacher to her; when he was sitting at table greatly excited, he looked up to heaven and threw away his knife. The blessed woman then asked him why he left his food so quickly. The bishop said with inspired heart, "Just now I saw angels bear a blessed soul from your freehold to high heaven with holy song, and his name will be quickly revealed at dawn, when I am offering the living gift to God in the pious church." The report was then spread abroad, just as the prophet had said, that her herdsman, who had climbed an oak tree in discharge of his duty, and was feeding his herd with the top leaves of the tree, fell heavily, and went with glory from the world to God because of his loyalty to his charge. Who can ever relate all the great miracles of this holy man, how often he easily healed the sick, and always put the black spirits to flight, and how he, foreseeing, told the death of doomed men, wise through the prophecy of the spirit of wisdom?

A very pious priest named Herbert lived in a hermitage in accordance with his instructions and visited him each year, thoughtful in mind. Cuthbert then spoke with him at once alone, and said that he must then most fully inquire about his need before his last day; he said that he could not see him again in human life after that present day. Herbert then became very thoughtful, and

---

4. Theodore. Theodore of Tarsus (602–690), Archbishop of Canterbury, arrived in England in 669 and immediately set about the reform and reorganization of the English Church. **17. Boisil,** St. Boswell, who had preceded Cuthbert as abbot of Lindisfarne. **22–23. against the Lord's will.** Cuthbert had warned Egfrith against his invasion of the land of the Picts, which resulted in an overwhelming defeat for the English at the battle of Nechtansmere on May 20, 685. Egfrith and most of his followers were killed, and Northumbria never recovered from the disaster. **brother,** Aldfrid.

fell at his feet, and prayed with flowing tears that he might go with him from this strife into the heavenly glory, just as he had obeyed his teaching in life. The bishop bowed his knees in this prayer with happy heart, and immediately afterward comforted the priest; he told him that the Almighty Ruler granted them that they could go together from these afflictions to eternal joy. Herbert then went home, and lying on his sickbed, awaited with sick limbs the other's death.

The holy Cuthbert then hastened quickly to the hermitage which he had formerly occupied through the holy admonitions of the mighty Lord; he wished to end his life in the land where he earlier long dwelt living. And in that land he was bedridden, very ready for death in his departure to God, in the third year of his episcopate, and on this day he went to the Lord, and Herbert, the holy priest, with him, just as they had earlier in life learned through the spirit of God, with good will. His body was buried in the church of Lindisfarne, and there very many miracles were done through the merits of his blessed life. It was then pleasing to the suffragan bishop, Edbert himself, his successor, that he should have his body put up in the church, in the eleventh year after his end. Then that holy body was found sound in the earth, lying whole, just as if he were sleeping, as flexible in limbs as when he was laid there.

Glory and praise be to the rich Lord, who honors his chosen ones so graciously after mortal life, living with him forever in the eternity of all worlds. Amen.

THE COLLOQUY

Aelfric's Latin *Colloquy*, which belongs with his Latin grammar and his Latin-English glossary, was intended to teach English boys in a monastic school to speak Latin. The highly practical nature of the vocabulary involved, with its emphasis on everyday life, should be noted, as should the often surprisingly good dramatic value of the dialogue. There is nothing cut and dried or professionally pedagogic about this piece in which the students are brought forward to play verbally the roles which their elders were taking in real life. One manuscript of the *Colloquy* contains an almost complete interlinear rendering into Old English, and it is that version which, with occasional assistance from the Latin, and the addition of the names of the characters in the margin, is translated below. We cannot say whether or not Aelfric is the author of the English version, though, while most authorities are inclined to deny the possibility, we may be tempted to think that Aelfric would have recognized the value of such an interlinear translation, not only to teachers less learned than himself, but also to the students. We must never forget that the alphabetically arranged glossary which waits comfortably at the end of a modern school edition was not among the tools of the medieval classroom. The following translation is taken from the edition by G. N. Garmonsway, London, 1939.

Monk. We children ask, teacher, that you will teach us to speak Latin correctly, for we are illiterate and speak ungrammatically.

Teacher. What do you wish to speak?

Monk. What should we care what we say, so long as it is correct and useful and not foolish or wicked?

Teacher. Do you want to be flogged as you learn?

Monk. It is preferable to us to be flogged for the sake of learning than not to know it. But we know that you are kind and unwilling to inflict blows upon us, unless we compel you to it.

Teacher. I ask you, what do you say to me? What kind of work do you have?

Monk. I am a professed monk, and each day I sing the seven canonical hours with the brothers, and am busy with reading and singing, but nevertheless I wish between times to learn to speak in the Latin tongue.

Teacher. What do these companions of yours know?

Monk. Some are plowmen, some shepherds, some oxherds, some also are hunters, some fishermen, some fowlers, some traders, some shoemakers, salters, and bakers.

Teacher. What do you say, plowman? How do you go about your work?

Plowman. O dear master, I work hard. I go out at daybreak, driving the oxen to the field, and I yoke them to the plow; never is the winter weather so sharp that I dare hide at home for fear of my master, but once I have yoked the oxen and fastened the share and colter to the plow I have to plow a whole acre or more every day.

Teacher. Do you have any companion?

Plowman. I have a boy who drives the oxen with a goad, who now also is hoarse from the cold and shouting.

Teacher. What more do you do during a day?

Plowman. Certainly I do still more. I have to fill the mangers of the oxen with hay, and water them, and carry out their dung.

8. **Monk.** The child taking the part of a monk acts as spokesman for the others.   23. **canonical hours,** the principal services of the day.

Teacher. Oh! Oh! That is a great deal of work.
Plowman. Yes, sir, it is a great deal of work, because I am not a free man.

Teacher. What do you say, shepherd, have you any work?
Shepherd. Yes, sir, I have: in the early morning I drive my sheep to their pasture and stand guard over them with dogs in heat and in cold lest wolves devour them, and I lead them back to their folds and I milk them twice a day and I move their folds, and in addition I make cheese and butter and am faithful to my master.

Teacher. O oxherd, what work do you do?
Oxherd. O master, I work a lot. When the plowman unyokes the oxen I lead them to pasture, and all night I stand guard over them on account of thieves, and then in the early morning I turn them over to the plowman well fed and watered.

Teacher. Is this one of your companions?
Monk. Yes, he is.
Teacher. Do you know anything?
Hunter. I know one calling.
Teacher. What?
Hunter. I am a hunter.
Teacher. Whose?
Hunter. The king's.
Teacher. How do you go about your business?
Hunter. I knit myself nets and put them in a likely place, and urge on my dogs so that they chase wild animals until the beasts come unexpectedly to the nets and so are snared, and I kill them in the nets.
Teacher. Don't you know how to hunt except with nets?
Hunter. Yes, indeed, I am able to hunt without nets.
Teacher. How?
Hunter. With swift dogs I pursue wild animals.
Teacher. What creatures do you catch most often?
Hunter. I catch harts, boars, roe deer, both buck and doe, and sometimes hares.
Teacher. Were you hunting today?
Hunter. I was not, because today is Sunday, but I was hunting yesterday.
Teacher. What did you get?
Hunter. Two harts and a boar.
Teacher. How did you catch them?
Hunter. I caught the harts in nets, but I killed the boar.

Teacher. How were you brave enough to stab a boar?
Hunter. The dogs drove him to me and, standing before him, I stabbed him suddenly.
Teacher. You were very daring then.
Hunter. A hunter mustn't be timid, because all sorts of wild animals live in the woods.
Teacher. What do you do with your bag?
Hunter. I give the king whatever I catch, because I am his hunter.
Teacher. What does he give you?
Hunter. He clothes me well and feeds me, and sometimes gives me a horse or a bracelet that I may go about my business more willingly.

Teacher. What occupation do you know?
Fisherman. I am a fisherman.
Teacher. What do you get from your trade?
Fisherman. Food, clothing, and money.
Teacher. How do you catch fish?
Fisherman. I go on board my boat and throw my nets into the water, and cast out hook and bait and fish traps of wickerwork, and whatever they catch I take.
Teacher. What if they are unclean fish?
Fisherman. I throw away the unclean ones and take the clean for food.
Teacher. Where do you sell your fish?
Fisherman. In the city.
Teacher. Who buys them?
Fisherman. The citizens. I am unable to catch as many as I can sell.
Teacher. What kinds of fish do you catch?
Fisherman. Eels, pike, minnows, burbot, trout, lampreys, and whatever swims in the water.
Teacher. Why don't you fish in the sea?
Fisherman. Sometimes I do, but seldom, because there is much rowing for me out to sea.
Teacher. What do you catch in the sea?
Fisherman. Herring and salmon, porpoise and sturgeon, oysters and crabs, mussels, periwinkles, cockles, plaice and flounder, lobsters, and many such.
Teacher. Do you want to catch a whale?
Fisherman. Not I!
Teacher. Why not?
Fisherman. Because it is a dangerous thing to catch a whale. It is safer for me to go on the river with my boat than to go with many boats hunting whales.

24. unclean fish. See the Mosaic Law, Deuteronomy, 14:10: "and whatsoever hath not fins and scales ye shall not eat."

Teacher. Why so?

Fisherman. Because I would rather catch fish which I am able to kill than a fish which with one blow could sink or kill not myself alone, but also my companions.

Teacher. And yet many do catch whales and escape danger and gain great profit from it.

Fisherman. You speak the truth, but I do not dare because of the cowardice of my heart.

Teacher. What do you have to say, fowler? How do you ensnare birds?

Fowler. I ensnare birds in many ways, with nets, with snares, with birdlime, with whistling, with a hawk, or with traps.

Teacher. Have you a hawk?

Fowler. I have.

Teacher. Do you know how to tame them?

Fowler. Yes, I do. What good would they be to me unless I knew how to tame them?

Hunter. Give me a hawk.

Fowler. I will give you one gladly, if you will give me a swift dog. Which hawk will you have, the larger or the smaller?

Hunter. Give me the larger.

Teacher. How do you feed your hawks?

Fowler. They feed themselves and me in winter, and in the spring I let them escape to the woods and catch myself young birds in the autumn and tame them.

Teacher. And why do you let the tame ones escape from you?

Fowler. Because I do not wish to feed them through the summer, since they eat a great deal.

Teacher. And yet many feed the tame ones through the summer, so that they may have them ready.

Fowler. Yes, so they do, but I do not wish to work so much over them, for I can catch others, not one alone but very many.

Teacher. What do you say, trader?

Trader. I say that I am useful to the king, to the noblemen, to the rich, and to all people.

Teacher. And how?

Trader. I board my ship with my cargo and row over the high seas, and sell my goods and buy valuable things which are not produced in this country, and I bring them here to you with great danger over the sea, and sometimes I suffer shipwreck with loss of all my goods, hardly escaping alive.

Teacher. What things do you bring us?

Trader. Purple garments and silk, precious gems and gold, rare garments and spices, wine and oil, ivory and brass, bronze and tin, sulphur, glass and many such.

Teacher. Are you willing to sell your goods here for the same price that you bought them there?

Trader. I am not. What, then, would my labor gain me? But I am willing to sell them here more dearly than I bought them there, so that I may get myself some profit with which to feed myself, my wife, and my son.

Teacher. You, shoemaker, what do you do that is useful for us?

Shoemaker. My craft is certainly very useful and necessary to you.

Teacher. How?

Shoemaker. I buy hides and skins and prepare them with my art and make of them shoes of different kinds, slippers and shoes, gaiters and leather bottles, reins and trappings, flasks and leather cups, spur-straps and halters, bags and vessels. None of you would care to go through the winter without my calling.

Teacher. Salter, how does your occupation benefit us?

Salter. My calling helps you all greatly. None of you would enjoy satisfaction in meal or food unless my work is hospitable to him.

Teacher. How?

Salter. What man really enjoys very sweet foods without the flavor of salt? Who replenishes his cellar or storeroom without my craft? All butter-curd and cheese-curd would spoil unless I am present as preserver for you, nor could you even use your vegetables without me.

Teacher. What have you to say, baker; whom does your calling benefit? Can we endure life without you?

Baker. You can endure life for a time without my calling, but not long nor too well: truly without my art every table seems empty, and without bread every food is turned to loathing. I strengthen the heart of man, I am the strength of men, and even children do not wish to shun me.

Teacher. What shall we say about the cook—do we need his craft in any way?

Cook. If you drive me out of your fellowship, you will eat your vegetables raw and your meat uncooked, and you cannot even have rich broth without my art.

Teacher. We do not care for your calling, nor is it necessary to us, since we ourselves are able to boil the things that are to be boiled, and roast the things that are to be roasted.

Cook. If you get rid of me on that account, so that you may do so, then you will all be servants, and none of you will be master, and, nonetheless, without my craft you will not eat.

Teacher. Monk, you who speak to me, I have proved that you have good and very necessary companions, and now I ask if you have others in addition to these?

Monk. Indeed I do have others both necessary and excellent.

Teacher. Who are they?

Monk. I have smiths, an ironsmith, a goldsmith, a silversmith, a coppersmith, carpenters, and other workers in many different occupations.

Teacher. Have you a wise counselor?

Monk. Certainly I have. How can our community be guided without an adviser?

Teacher. What do you say, wise man? What calling among these seems to you to be the most important?

Counselor. I tell you that it seems to me that the service of God holds supremacy among these occupations, just as it reads in the Gospel: "First seek the kingdom of God and his righteousness and all these things shall be added to you."

Teacher. And which among secular occupations seems to you to have pre-eminence?

Counselor. Agriculture, because the plowman feeds us all.

Smith. Whence would the plowman have plowshare or colter, or even a goad, without my trade? Whence would the fisherman have a hook, or the shoemaker an awl, or the tailor a needle? Is it not all from my labor?

Counselor. Certainly you speak the truth, but we would rather dwell with you, plowman, than with you, smith, since the plowman gives us bread and drink. What do you, smith, give us in your smithy except iron fire-sparks and the clang of beating blows and blowing bellows?

Carpenter. Which of you does not make use of my trade, when I make houses, various utensils, and ships for all of you?

Smith. Carpenter, why do you speak thus, when you cannot make even a hole without my art?

Counselor. Comrades and good workers, let us stop these disputes at once, and let there be peace and agreement between us, and let each help the other in his trade and always agree with the plowman, whence we have foods for ourselves and fodder for our horses. And I give this advice to all workers, that each shall practice his calling diligently, since he who neglects his calling is neglected by his calling. Whatsoever you may be, priest or monk, peasant or soldier, practice or exercise yourself in this, and be what you are, for it is a great humiliation and shame to a man not to be willing to be what he is and what he ought to be.

Teacher. Children, how do you like this conversation?

Pupils. It pleases us well, but you talk very profoundly, and you speak beyond our comprehension: but we talk to you in accordance with our understanding, that we may understand the things which you say.

Teacher. I ask you, why you learn so eagerly?

Pupils. Because we are unwilling to be like foolish animals, which know nothing except grass and water.

Teacher. And what do you desire?

Pupils. We wish to be wise.

Teacher. In what kind of wisdom? Do you wish to be sly or shifty in lies, crafty in speech, artful, deceitful, speaking well and thinking evil, given to bland words, cherishing deceit within you, like a tomb painted on the outside, but full of stench within?

Pupils. We do not wish to be wise in that way, for he is not wise who deceives himself with delusion.

Teacher. But how do you wish to be wise?

Pupils. We wish to be sincere without deceit, and wise that we may turn from evil and do good. Still you are speaking to us more deeply than our age can grasp. Speak to us after our manner, not so profoundly.

Teacher. I will do as you ask. You, boy, what did you do today?

Monk. I did many things. In the night, when I heard the sound of the bell, I got up from my bed

---

35–37. "First . . . you. See Matthew 6:33.

and went to the church and sang matins with the brothers; after that we sang of All Saints and the morning lauds; after this prime and seven psalms with the litany and the chapter mass; then tierce, and the daily mass; after this we sang sext, and ate and drank and slept, and arose again and sang nones. And now we are here before you, ready to hear what you have to say to us.

Teacher. When will you sing vespers or compline?

Monk. When it is time.

Teacher. Were you flogged today?

Monk. I was not, because I behaved warily.

Teacher. And how about your comrades?

Monk. Why do you ask me about that? I dare not reveal our secrets to you. Every one knows if he was flogged or not.

Teacher. What did you eat today?

Monk. I still partake of flesh, because I am a child living under the rod.

Teacher. What else do you eat?

Monk. Vegetables and eggs, fish and cheese, butter and beans, and all clean things I eat with great thanks.

Teacher. You are very greedy when you eat everything which is set before you.

Monk. I am not so great a glutton that I can eat all kinds of food at a single meal.

Teacher. But how?

Monk. I eat now that food and now this with moderation, as is fitting to a monk, not with voracity, for I am not a glutton.

Teacher. And what do you drink?

Monk. Ale, if I have it, or water if I have no ale.

Teacher. Don't you drink wine?

10 *Monk.* I am not so rich that I can buy myself wine, and wine is not a drink for children and fools, but for grown-ups and wise men.

Teacher. Where do you sleep?

Monk. In the dormitory with the brothers.

Teacher. Who wakes you for matins?

Monk. Sometimes I hear the bell and get up; sometimes my teacher wakes me forcibly with a stick.

Teacher. O children and happy students, your
20 teacher urges you to obey sacred precepts and to behave yourselves decorously in every place. Go obediently when you hear the church bell and enter the church and bow humbly to the holy altars and stand in orderly fashion, and sing with one accord and pray for your sins, and go out without jesting to the cloister or to study.

Wulfstan

Wulfstan, next to Aelfric, is the most important single figure in the last period of Old English literary history. Like Aelfric, he was a churchman, but, unlike him, he rose to high position; like Aelfric, he was a preacher, but we have few sermons which can be confidently called his. Here, however, any real similarity ends, for Wulfstan was a man of action and emotion, while Aelfric was a man of scholarship and reflection. Of Wulfstan's early life we know little, and the remainder may be sketched briefly. He became Bishop of London in 996, and in 1002 he was made Bishop of Worcester and at the same time Archbishop of York. The first of these offices he held until 1016, the second until his death in 1023. He took an active part in public affairs, was among King Aethelred's councilors, and had a large share in preparing Aethelred's legal codes of 1008 and 1014. His best-known and best work is his *Sermo Lupi ad Anglos* (*Wolf's Sermon to the English*), which is given here. Its tone and substance reflect the gloomy period through which England was passing. We have seen from the *Battle of Maldon* (see page 58) how, by 991, the Scandinavian's incursions had become serious once more. In 994 the Danish leader Sweyn, and the Norwegian Olaf Tryggvason, besieged London unsuccessfully, but Aethelred was compelled to buy a peace. Olaf returned to Norway and kept his word not to invade England again. Sweyn, on the other hand, was back in 997, and late in 1013, after sixteen years of hardly interrupted warfare, he was recognized as king of England, while the wretched Aethelred fled to Normandy. When Sweyn died early in the next year England turned back to Aethelred, but Sweyn's son Cnut (Canute) kept up the fight. Aethelred himself died, unlamented, in 1016; his brave and competent son, Edmund Ironside, did not live long enough to free England, and after his death in November of the same year Cnut was chosen king of England.

We must read Wulfstan's sermon against this

1–10. matins . . . compline. The canonical hours are: **matins,** followed by **lauds,** originally said or sung at midnight, later before daybreak; **prime** at 6 A.M.; **tierce** at 9 A.M.; **sext** at 12 noon; **nones** at 3 P.M.; **vespers,** originally before nightfall, later in the late afternoon or evening; **compline,** at 9 P.M., or just before retiring.

background of misery and humiliation, made even worse by the unspeakable ineptitude of Aethelred and the selfishness, cowardice, and treachery of many of the English. Wulfstan, incidentally, survived Sweyn's brief rule, and seems to have accepted Cnut and to have been accepted by him.

Wulfstan's style is highly effective for pulpit oratory. He makes use of assonance, alliteration, and rhyming phrases, and is a master of balance and antithesis. His long, loosely constructed sentences, bound together by an almost too liberal employment of "and," often need to be broken up in translation, but in the original they have a pulsing, beating force which must have had a profound effect on an audience. The present translation is from the *Sermo Lupi ad Anglos*, ed. by Dorothy Whitelock, London, 1939.

SERMON TO THE ENGLISH

WULFSTAN'S sermon to the English when the Danes persecuted them greatly, which was in the year 1014 after the incarnation of our Lord Jesus Christ.

Dear men, know the truth: this world is in haste, and it approaches the end, and the later it is in the world, the worse things become. So it must be of necessity, for the sins of the people grow very much worse before the coming of Antichrist and then, indeed, things will become terrible and cruel throughout the world. Consider carefully, too, that the Devil has led this people greatly astray for many years now, and that there was little loyalty among men, even though they spoke well, and too many wrongs have prevailed in the land. There were not many men who thought about atonement as carefully as one ought to do, but daily men added one offense to another and set up wrongs and injustices all too widely throughout the whole people. Therefore, we have suffered many losses and insults, and if we are to obtain any improvement, we must merit it better from God than we have done before this time. For great cause we earned the miseries which weigh upon us, and with equally great cause we must obtain amendment from God, if things are destined to improve in the future.

Lo, now, we know that great offense must needs have great atonement, and a great fire much water, if one is to put the fire out at all. Great, then, is the requirement on every man that he should obey God's law from now on and pay God's dues justly. No man among the heathen dares to hold back anything, little or great, which is appointed by law for the worship of the false gods, and yet everywhere we hold back God's dues all too often. Nor, among the heathen people, does a man dare, within or without, to decrease any of the things which are brought to the false gods and given over as offerings, yet we have rifled God's house completely, both inside and out. God's servants are stripped of honor and protection nearly everywhere, but no one among the heathen people dares ill-use the servants of the false gods in any such way as people do God's servants too widely, there where Christian men ought to hold God's law and protect his servants.

But it is the truth which I tell you, there is need of amendment, for God's dues have diminished for too long a time in every district among the people, public laws have grown worse altogether too much, sanctuaries are violated too generally, and God's houses are completely deprived of their old privileges and stripped of everything proper within. Widows are wrongfully forced to remarry, and too many are reduced to poverty and greatly humiliated. Poor men are grievously betrayed and cruelly defrauded and, innocent, are widely sold out of this land into the possession of foreigners. Throughout the people children in the cradle are enslaved by cruel injustice for a little theft. The rights of free men are taken away, the rights of slaves restricted, and charitable obligations diminished. To say it most quickly, God's laws are hateful and His teachings despised. For this we all frequently have shame because of God's wrath; he who is able may perceive this, and the injury will become common to all this people, though one may not think so, unless God protect us.

It is clear and evident to us all that formerly we offended more often than we atoned, and for that reason there are many attacks upon our people. Nothing has prospered for a long time now, either within or without, but in every district frequently and often there have been devastation and famine, burning and bloodshed, theft and murder, plague and pestilence, epidemic of cattle and disease; malice and hate and the ravishing of robbers have injured us greatly. Excessive taxes have oppressed us and bad seasons have often brought about failure of crops. All this, it would seem, because there have been in this land for many years now many wrongs and unstable faith among men everywhere. Now kinsman has not spared kinsman any more than strangers, nor the father his son, nor sometimes the son his own father, nor one brother the other. None of us conducted his life as he ought, those in holy orders according to their rule or laymen lawfully. All too often we made lust our law and obeyed the teachings and law of neither God nor man as we ought to do. Nor has anyone thought about another as justly as he should, but almost all deceived and harmed others with word and deed. Indeed, almost everyone cuts down another with shameful attack, and does worse, if he is able. Thus, there is in the land much treachery toward both God and man, and also there are in the country many acts of treason in various ways. The greatest treason of all in the world is that a man should betray his lord's soul, and there is another great treason in the world, namely, that a man should kill his lord treacherously or drive him living from the land—and both have happened in this country. Men plotted against Edward and killed him and then burned him, and they drove Aethelred from his native land. Too many sponsors and godchildren have been killed throughout the nation and all too many holy places have perished because certain men were placed there earlier, as they ought not to have been, if one wished to show respect to God's sanctuary. Too many Christian people have been sold out of this country at all times. All this is hateful to God, as one may well believe. It is shameful to mention what has happened too commonly, and horrible to know what too many who commit the crime often do, that men club together and buy a woman as a joint purchase and practice foul sin with her, one by one, each after the other, most like to dogs who do not trouble about sin; and afterward for a price they sell out of the land, into the power of the enemy, God's creature and own purchase, whom He redeemed at great cost. Also we know well where the crime has occurred that a father has sold his son for profit, and a son his mother, and one brother has sold the other into the hands of foreigners. He who will may understand that all these are great and awful deeds, and yet there are other and more various things which injure this nation. Many are perjured and ruined, and oaths are frequently broken, and it is seen in this people that the anger of God weighs violently upon us. Let him recognize this who is able to do so.

How can greater shame happen to men through God's anger than often does to us for our own deeds? If some slave escape from his master and turn from the Christians to the Vikings, and it later happens that there is a fight between the master and the slave, if the slave kill the master altogether, the latter lies unpaid-for so far as his family are concerned. If, however, the master kill the slave whom he formerly owned, he must pay the wergild as for a thane. Very degrading laws and shameful exactions are common with us because of God's anger, as he who is able may understand, and many misfortunes happen to this people frequently and often. Nothing has prospered for a long time now, either in or out, but devastation and hatred often and again in every section, and the English have been long defeated and disheartened because of the anger of God. The pirates, with God's consent, are so strong that often in battle one drives away ten, sometimes fewer, sometimes more, and all for our sins. Oftentimes ten or twelve, one after the other, will outrage the wife of a thane, or sometimes his daughter or near kinswoman, while he looks on who had considered himself important and powerful and good enough before that happened. Alas for the misery and for the great disgrace which the English now have, and all through God's anger! Often two pirates, or sometimes three, will drive a band of Christian men, huddled together, out through the people from sea to sea, to the public shame of all of us, if we were able to understand anything seriously. But all the disgrace which we often suffer we repay with honor to those who shame us: we pay them continually, and they humiliate us daily; they raid and burn, they rob and plunder and carry all to the ships. Is there anything else clear and visible in all these events save the wrath of God?

It is also no wonder if things go amiss with us, because we know very well that for many years now men have often failed to care what they did in words or deeds. This nation was, as it may appear, very corrupt through manifold sins and many misdeeds, through murder and crime, through avarice and greed, through theft and robbery, through slave dealing and heathen vices, through deceits and frauds, through breaches of the law and deceptions, through attacks on kinsmen and manslaughter, through assaults on people in holy orders and adulteries, through incest and various fornications. In addition, as we said before, more than should be are perjured and utterly lost through violations of oaths and pledges and numerous other lies. Failures to observe festivals and fasts frequently take place. Also there are in the land apostates fallen away from their faith, violent persecutors of the Church, and all too many fierce tyrants, and despisers of divine laws and Christian virtues, and everywhere in the nation foolish deriders, most often of the things

18. **Edward,** Aethelred's predecessor and half-brother.
19. **drove Aethelred,** in 1013; see the head note.

which God's messengers command, and especially in the matters which ever rightfully pertain to God's law. Therefore it has become an evil custom far and wide that men now are more often ashamed of good deeds than of evil, because too often men abuse good deeds with scorn and revile the God-fearing far too much, and men all too often reproach and attack with contempt those who love the right and have to any degree the fear of God. And because men do thus, that they abuse what they ought to praise and hate too much what they ought to love, through that all too many are brought into evil thoughts and to wicked deeds, so that they are not at all ashamed even though they sin completely against God Himself; but for vain attacks they are ashamed to amend their crimes as the books teach, like fools who through the weakness of pride are unwilling to save themselves before the time when they cannot, even though then they may wish it completely.

Here there are many sorely injured, as it may appear, through the blemishes of sin. Here there are homicides, slayers of kinsmen, priest-killers and oppressors of monasteries, here are perjurers and murderers, here are harlots, infanticides, and many foul, adulterous fornicators, here are witches and sorcerers, here are robbers, plunderers, and pillagers, and, to put it briefly, a countless number of all kinds of sinners. Of this we are not at all ashamed, but we are ashamed to begin atonement, as the books teach us, and that is evident in this poor, corrupt people. A great many can easily remember that which one man could not quickly investigate, that is, how miserably things have gone for a long while among the people. Indeed, let each one think about himself and not hesitate altogether too long. But, in God's name, let us act as is necessary for us, protect ourselves as best we may, lest we perish entirely.

27. **sorcerers.** Wulfstan's word is *waelcyrian*, "Valkyries."

There was a historian named Gildas in the time of the Britons, who wrote about their misdeeds, how they angered God so very often with their sins that He finally let the English army conquer their land and destroy the British power. That happened, as he said, because of robbery by the powerful and avarice of ill-gotten gains, because of injustice of the people and unjust verdicts, because of laziness of the bishops and the wicked cowardice of God's messengers, who kept silent all too often about truth and mumbled with their jaws when they should have called out. Because of the foul pride of the people, and because of gluttony and various sins, they forfeited their land and perished themselves. Let us, then, do as is necessary for us: take warning by such as this. This is true which I say, that we know of worse deeds among the English than we heard anywhere among the Britons; therefore there is great need that we reflect and intercede eagerly with God Himself. Let us act as is necessary for us, turn to right and to some degree leave wrong, and atone very eagerly where we formerly transgressed. Let us love God and obey God's laws and perform gladly what we promised when we received baptism, or what those promised who were our sponsors at baptism. Let us correctly order words and works, cleanse our consciences zealously, keep oath and pledge carefully, and have between us a certain amount of loyalty without deceit. Let us frequently consider the great judgment to which we must all come and guard ourselves with care against the boiling fire of the pit of hell, and let us earn the glory and joy which God has prepared for those who do His will on earth.

May God help us. Amen.

1. **Gildas**, the "hysterical historian" of the Anglo-Saxon conquest of Britain, who wrote his *De excidio Britanniae* in the first half of the sixth century. Like Wulfstan, he sought some ulterior cause for the miseries of his countrymen and, like him, he found it in the wickedness and impiety by means of which they had angered God.

The Old English Chronicles

The history of the *Old English Chronicles*, a better name for what is often called the *Anglo-Saxon Chronicle*, is complex and need not be detailed here. Briefly, we may assume, in the absence of proof, that Alfred made or inspired a revision of an older chronicle, copies of which were then sent to various ecclesiastical centers to be continued. This "chronicle" now became "chronicles," since the continuations naturally differed in accordance with local events and local emphasis. Possibly "news releases" were occasionally sent out from a central source, and certainly localities which had lost their chronicles by fire or other disaster borrowed and copied others. The copy of the chronicles which was continued at Peterborough until 1154, the year in which Henry II came to the throne, is an invaluable linguistic link between Old and Middle English. The following selections, the first from the Worcester version and the others from the Peterborough, give a "native" account of the Norman Conquest, an Englishman's just, if unflattering, portrait of William, and a graphic picture of the social and cultural advantages which nearly a century of Norman rule had brought to England. The standard edition of the *Old English Chronicles* is by Charles Plummer, *Two of the Saxon Chronicles*, 2 vols., Oxford, 1892–99.

I

THE YEAR OF THE CONQUEST

1066 In this year King Harold came from York to Westminster on the Easter after the midwinter when the king died, and that Easter fell on April 16. Then was seen all over England such a sign in the heavens as no man had ever seen before. Men said that it was a comet, which some men call the hairy star; it appeared on the eve of the major litany, that is, the evening of April 24, and was shining for an entire week.

Soon after that Earl Tostig came from across the sea to the Isle of Wight with as large a fleet as he could get, and he was given both money and provisions there. King Harold, his brother, gathered a larger navy and army than any king in the country had done before, because he was told that William the Bastard intended to come here and conquer this country, just as it afterwards turned out. In the meantime Tostig came into the Humber with sixty ships, and Earl Edwin came with an army and drove him out. He went to Scotland with twelve small vessels and King Harald of Norway met him there with three hundred ships, and Tostig yielded to him and became his man. They both came up the Humber until they reached York; there Earl Edwin and his brother, Earl Morkere, fought against them, but the Norsemen had the victory.

Harold, king of the English, was told that things had gone thus, and this battle was on the vigil of St. Matthew. Then our King Harold came unawares upon the Norsemen, and met them beyond York at Stamford Bridge with a great army of English, and that day there was very severe fighting on both sides. Harald the fair-haired was killed and Earl Tostig, and such Norsemen as were left were put to flight, and the English attacked them fiercely from behind, until some came to the ships, some were drowned, some burned, and others perished in such various ways that few were left. The English had possession of the battlefield. The king made a truce with Olaf, son of the Norse king, with their bishop, and with the Earl of Orkney and all the others who were left in the ships. They came to our king and swore oaths that they desired to maintain peace and friendship with this country. The king let them go home with twenty-four ships. These two major engagements took place within five days.

Then William, Earl of Normandy, came to Pevensey on the eve of Michaelmas, and as soon as they were able, they built a castle at the port of Hastings. This was reported to our King Harold, and he gathered a great army, and came to meet

---

33. Harold, son of Earl Godwine, who was elected king by the Witan on January 6, 1066, the day after the death of Edward the Confessor. **34. York.** He had gone there, no doubt, as part of his effort to unite the kingdom about himself. **38. comet,** Halley's comet, which last appeared in 1910 and should be back in the latter part of 1985. **42. Earl Tostig,** Harold's brother, who had been exiled for good cause in 1065. He now returned from Flanders, anxious to do anything to harm his brother, who apparently had acquiesced in his banishment.

9. Earl Edwin, Earl of Mercia, whose brother, Morkere, had supplanted Tostig as Earl of Northumbria. **11. Harald.** It is likely that Harald had been in touch with Tostig at an earlier time. **18–19. vigil of St. Matthew,** eve of St. Matthew, September 20. **23. Harald the fair-haired.** Most accounts have this error, but the Norwegian king was Harald Hardrada, not Harald Haarfager, who had been dead since 933. **38. eve of Michaelmas,** September 28. **40. Hastings,** about fourteen miles from Pevensey. **reported to . . . Harold.** He was still in York. **41. a great army,** but not as great, one would think, as a less impetuous strategy might have brought him.

William at the hoar apple tree, and William came on him unawares before his people were drawn up. The king fought against him stoutly with the men who would stand by him, and there was a great slaughter on either side. There King Harold was killed, his brothers Leofwine and Gyrth and many other good men, and the French had possession of the battlefield, as God granted to them for the sins of the people.

Archbishop Ealdred and the Londoners wanted to have Child Edgar as king, as was his natural right, and Edwin and Morkere promised that they would fight with them. But just as things ought ever to have got forward, so they became from day to day later and worse, just as it all turned out in the end.

Earl William went back to Hastings, and waited there to see whether people would yield to him. When he saw that no one wanted to come to him, he went inland with all that was left of his army, and those who since had come to him from across the sea, and he harried all the land that he went through, until he came to Berkhamstead. There Archbishop Ealdred, Child Edgar, Earl Edwin, and Earl Morkere, and all the leading men of London, came to him, and yielded for necessity, when the greatest harm had been done. It was very bad counsel that it had not been done before, since God would not amend the situation because of our sins. They gave him hostages and swore oaths to him, and he promised them that he would be a loyal lord to them, and yet all this time they were ravaging all that they conquered. On midwinter day Archbishop Ealdred consecrated him king at Westminster, and he gave him possession of England on the Bible, and also he swore, before he put the crown on his head, that he would preserve this people as well as any king before him had done at his best, if they would be loyal to him. Nevertheless he levied a very severe tax on the people, and then after Lent he went across the sea to Normandy, and took with him Archbishop Stigand, Aegelnath, Abbot of Glastonbury, Child Edgar, Earl Edwin, Earl Morkere, Earl Waltheof, and many other good Englishmen. And Bishop Odo and Earl William remained here after that, and they built castles throughout the land, and distressed the poor people very much, and ever since then things have become bad. May the end be good when God wills!

1. **hoar apple tree,** Appledore. 11. **Child Edgar,** the grandson of Edmund Ironside. "Child" is a title of dignity, usually applied to a young nobleman. 31. **they were ravaging,** the Normans. 41. **Stigand,** Archbishop of Canterbury. He was no great loss to England. 43. **Earl Waltheof,** the son of Earl Siward; after passing in and out of William's favor, he was finally executed in 1076. 44. **Bishop Odo,** William's brother on the mother's side.

II

KING WILLIAM

IF anyone wishes to know what sort of man he was, or what dignity he had, or of how many lands he was lord, then we will write about him as we perceived him who looked at him and lived for a while in his household. King William, whom we speak about, was a very wise man and very powerful, and more honorable and stronger than any of his predecessors had been. He was mild to those good men who loved God, and beyond all measure severe to those who contradicted his will. In the very place where God granted to him that he might conquer England he built a famous monastery, established monks there and subsidized it well. In his day the famous cathedral in Canterbury was built and also very many others throughout all England. Then, too, this land was very full of monks, who lived their lives in accordance with the rule of St. Benedict; and Christendom was such in his day that every man, whatever his rank, followed it as he would.

He was very stately: three times each year he wore his diadem, as often as he was in England. At Easter he wore it at Winchester, at Pentecost at Westminster, at midwinter at Gloucester; and then were with him all the great men from all over England, archbishops and suffragan bishops, abbots and earls, thanes and knights. Likewise he was a very severe man and violent, so that no one dared to do anything against his will. He had earls in his chains who did against his will. Bishops he removed from their bishoprics and abbots from their abbeys, thanes he put in prison, and finally he did not even spare his own brother, named Odo. Odo was a very powerful bishop in Normandy, with his see at Bayeux, and he was the most prominent man next to the king. When the king was in Normandy, then Odo was master in this country, and yet he put him in prison.

Among other things one should not forget the good peace which he made in this land, so that a man who was of any account could go across his kingdom unmolested with his bosom full of gold; and no man dared to kill another man, even though the other had done ever so much harm to him.

8–10. **as we perceived him . . . household.** This frank account was evidently written by a native Englishman who had managed to gain Norman favor. 17. **monastery,** Battle Abbey. 19. **cathedral,** not the building as it stands today. 20–24. **Then, too . . . he would,** a difficult sentence. 46. **unmolested.** In pre-Conquest days a good peace had been expressed by saying that a woman with a child in her arms could go across the kingdom unmolested.

He ruled over England, and searched it out so with his cunning, that there was not a hide of land in England that he didn't know who had it, or what it was worth, and afterward he put it down in his writing. Wales was in his power and he built castles there, and controlled that people entirely; also he subjected Scotland by his great strength. The land of Normandy was his inheritance and he ruled over the country which is called Maine; and if he could have lived two years more, he would have won Ireland with his cunning, and without any weapons.

Truly in his time men had great toil and very many wrongs. He had castles built, and distressed poor men greatly. The king was very severe and took from his subjects many marks of gold and more hundred pounds of silver. This he took from his countrymen by weight, with great injustice, and for little need; he had fallen into covetousness, and he loved greed completely. He established a great deer-protection and he added laws thereto, that whatever man killed hart or hind should be blinded. He laid a prohibition upon harts and also upon boars. He loved the stags as though he were their father. Also he decreed about the hares that they might travel free. Powerful men lamented it and poor men complained of it. But he was so hard that he did not care for all their enmity; but they had to follow the king's will completely if they wished to live or to hold land, land or possessions or even his favor. Alas, that any man should grow so proud as to exalt himself, and account himself over all men! May Almighty God show mercy to his soul and grant him forgiveness of his sins!

We have written these things about him, both good and evil, so that good men may follow after the good and flee the evil completely, and go on the way which leads us to the kingdom of heaven.

III

THE REIGN OF STEPHEN

1137. ... When the traitors understand that he was a mild man and soft and good, then they did all sorts of horrible things. They had done homage to him and sworn oaths, but they did not hold their word: they all perjured themselves and their troth was broken, because every powerful man made castles for himself and held them against the king, and they filled the land full of castles. Then they took the people who they thought had any property, men or women, day and night, and they put them in prison for their gold and silver, and tortured them with indescribable torments. The very martyrs were not tortured as they were: they were hanged up by the feet and smoked with foul smoke; they hanged them up by the thumbs or by the head and fastened suits of armor to their feet; they put knotted strings about their heads and twisted them so that they went through to their brains. They put them in prisons where there were adders and snakes and toads and killed them so. Some they put into "torture-house," that is, a chest that was short and narrow and shallow and full of sharp stones, and they forced people into that so that all their limbs were broken. In many of the castles were "lof and grin;" those were chains so heavy that it would take two or three men to carry one of them; they were so arranged that a collar was fastened to a beam, and a man's neck put into it, and the sharp iron about the man's neck kept him from moving in any direction, sitting, or lying, or sleeping: he just stood and bore the weight of the great iron chain. Many thousands were killed by hunger.

I am not able to tell—nor might I tell—all the horrors nor all the outrages that they did to poor men in this country; and that lasted the nineteen years that Stephen was king, and it always got worse and worse. They exacted tribute from the towns from time to time and called it "tenserie." When the poor men had no more to give they robbed them and burned all the towns, so that you could travel a whole day's journey and never find people living in towns or land cultivated. Then grain was expensive and meat and cheese and butter—for there were none of them in the land. Poor men died of hunger; some begged for alms who had formerly been rich men; some fled the country. There had never been more misery in the land, nor had the heathen ever done as badly as they did; for

---

5. **writing,** the Doomsday Book. **10–11. he would ... without any weapons,** a highly optimistic statement. **15–17. took ... by weight,** refused to accept coins at their face value. **44. he,** Stephen of Blois (1097?–1154), son of the Conqueror's daughter Adela. He succeeded his uncle Henry I, despite the fact that he and the other barons had sworn to accept Henry's daughter Matilda as queen. The circumstances of his elevation, the bitter opposition of Matilda and her partisans, and the natural depravity of the second and third generation of Norman lords, added to the inherent weakness of his own character, made Stephen's reign one of the blackest pages in English history.

4. **castles for himself.** Castles should be licensed by the king. Many of these so-called "adulterine" castles were dismantled by order of Henry II. **17–18. killed them so.** The dungeon full of adders and snakes was common in literature, but in real life it must have been difficult to maintain: no self-respecting snake would long tolerate a medieval dungeon. **22. "lof and grin,"** probably "headband and noose." **35. tenserie,** considered, ironically enough, a payment in return for protection and defense. **44–45. There had never ... as they did.** The chronicler is looking back to the days of King Aethelred or before. The entire entry should be compared with Wulfstan's *Sermon to the English* (page 78).

they spared neither church nor churchyard, but they took all the property that was in them and afterwards they burned the church and everything else. They did not exempt the land of bishops or abbots or priests, but they plundered monks and clerks and everyone else who had anything. If two or three men were seen riding up to a town all the people fled because they thought that they were robbers. Bishops and other ecclesiastics were always excommunicating them, but they paid no attention to that, for they were all damned and excommunicated to start with. Wherever men worked the soil the earth did not bring forth grain, for the land was completely ruined with such deeds and people said commonly that Christ slept—and His saints with Him. Such and even more than we can express we suffered nineteen years for our sins.

THE EARLY PERIOD

PART II: THE LATER MIDDLE AGES

The Norman Invasion

THE only contemporary English account of the Norman Conquest (page 81) gives little to show how it was possible for the Duke of Normandy to conquer with ease a land many times larger and more thickly populated than his own. England was disunited, disillusioned, and weary. Edward the Confessor was too much a cleric and too foreign in his sympathies to bring together a stubbornly, even selfishly, individualistic people, and there is little reason to doubt that he had encouraged his cousin William of Normandy to consider himself as his favored heir. In 1066 William, at thirty-nine, was firmly established as ruler of Normandy, influential in the neighboring provinces and regarded with respectful distaste by his feudal lord, the King of France. Nevertheless, when Edward died childless in 1066, those of the Witan (Council of State), who could be brought hastily together did not hesitate to elect Harold Godwinson King of England. Harold's genuine abilities might well have won him the confidence of all England—which held many who remembered all too well his unscrupulous father—had he been free from foreign interference.

While confronted with the threat of Norman invasion in the south, Harold was suddenly called to York to repel a Norwegian attack. His success there was complete, but an unkind sky chose this very moment to give William of Normandy the winds he needed to carry his fleet across the Channel. Without a moment of delay or rest for himself and his men, Harold dashed south to meet this new threat, and at the first possible opportunity staked his life and his throne on a single battle at Hastings—and lost. With apparently no more than five thousand men, perhaps two thousand of them mounted knights, of whom many were non-Norman volunteers, William conquered the English people in one pitched battle. In the years after Hastings England was forced to adjust itself to the most thorough exploitation which it had ever known, most thorough because carried out systematically, legalistically, and by a very few.

Some hundred and fifty years before William came to England a band of Scandinavians had forced the King of France to recognize their ownership of the territory which, because they were Northmen, came to be called Normandy. They mingled freely with the native population, speedily abandoned their own language, and soon became all but indistinguishable from the inhabitants of the neighboring provinces. They retained, however, a fierce, driving energy, and a willingness to take desperate chances. They also kept, or acquired, a passion for order, always provided, however, that the order be of their own choosing. They were, at least nominally, feudal subjects of the French king, but the Norman dukes regarded the feudal bonds between themselves and their subjects with far more veneration than they did that which bound them in allegiance to the king. When William conquered England he took it, literally, as his own. Naturally he could not keep it all in his own hands. He had committed himself to reward his followers and he did so generously, but he had no intention of permitting any of his nobles to acquire the independent local authority which he himself possessed in Normandy at the expense of the French king.

The immediate result of the Conquest was to wipe out the English ruling class economically, but for some 90 per cent of the population there was merely a change of masters. The overwhelming majority of Englishmen had been serfs, in fact if not in name, in 1065, and they remained so in 1067. There was more exploitation, more resentment, and perhaps less hope, but the basic difference was only in degree.

So far as English literature is concerned, the Conquest was decidedly detrimental in its immediate effects. The change in masters put secular and spiritual rule into the hands of men who, having Norman French as a native and Latin as an acquired tongue, could have no use for English. The vernacular English educational system was destroyed. The bulk of the people continued to speak English, many of the newcomers acquired a working knowledge of their subjects' tongue, but it was well nigh a century and a half before English was again taken seriously as a vehicle for literary expression.

The Conquest brought about notable and, for the most part, advantageous changes in the English Church, which was in need of a strong and righteous hand. This William found in Lanfranc, Italian by birth, whom he named Archbishop of Canterbury. Lanfranc, a man of learning, integrity, and wisdom, was able to adhere firmly to the principles of the Church Universal and still work hand in glove with William, who was strongly of the belief that he and not the Pope must have practical control of the English Church. The sees of numerous bishops were moved to more populated centers, thus bringing clerical and secular administrators into closer touch. Bishops were excluded from the lay courts, a step which served to strengthen and even extend the authority of the ecclesiastical courts. A comprehensive, if not completely realistic, picture of the duties and functioning of these latter is given by Chaucer in his descriptions of the Summoner on the pilgrimage and the other summoner who is lampooned by the Friar (pages 180 and 190).

The monasteries were purged and purified; there was a new emphasis on a knowledge of Latin, and inevitably, of French; and promising Anglo-Norman and English youths were sent to study in Continental schools. The monasteries were enriched, and new monkish orders appeared in England. Notable among these last were the Cistercians, who must be praised for their practical encouragement of sheep-breeding, soon to become the cornerstone of England's economic structure, and their artistic taste in erecting such abbeys as Tintern, Fountains, and Rievaulx. Strong steps were taken to remove married priests and to prevent those not yet wed from entering the bonds of matrimony. We must not forget that sacerdotal celibacy was unheard of before the third century, that long thereafter it was considered an impractical ideal. William's contemporary Gregory VII was the first to apply it rigorously to those ecclesiastics who were not members of an order. It is probable that in 1066 most English parish priests were married men, and that there was a marked tendency to treat benefices as hereditary.

In architecture, at least, the Norman Conquest brought an unqualified artistic improvement over what had gone before. We have already seen what the Old English residence was like: its rambling nature prevented unity and its wooden materials prevented permanence. Ecclesiastical architecture was little better. The Normans were able workers in stone in the Romanesque style. In addition to improved churches, they gave England an architectural novelty, the castle. One of William's first steps was to frighten the conquered populace by means of strategically placed and impregnable fortresses, built and maintained either by himself or by his trusted lieutenants. The Anglo-Saxons had learned nothing from the walled Romano-British towns, and their first lessons in artificial defense seem to have been slowly and painfully imparted by the marauding Danes, who had a disconcerting trick of throwing up earthworks to which they could retire in case of temporary defeat. Old English fortifications were singularly shoddy affairs at best, never equaling the great hill forts of the Celtic Iron Age. The typical rectangular Norman keep, built on or around a natural or artificial eminence, with towers at the four corners and one small and well-defended entrance, was something both to surprise the English and to discourage revolt. The earlier Norman castles were simple affairs; it was only gradually that they came to be elaborated by the addition of complicated systems of outworks calculated to permit those within to endure long sieges. Defense kept ahead of offense, and prolonged siege and starvation remained the only effective way to reduce a well-arranged fortress until the use of gunpowder rendered both castles and armor obsolete. Even so, more than one medieval castle in Royalist hands caused trouble to the Parliamentarian forces in the mid-seventeenth century.

The Church

The Church was, without exception, the greatest single factor in the medieval world. Every medieval Englishman was a Roman Catholic, since heresy was practically unknown on the island from the time of Pelagius to that of John Wyclif. The parish system was by no means perfect, even a century after the Conquest, but the monasteries, usually rural in location, served many souls otherwise unreached, and for a time after their arrival in the twelfth century the friars made every effort to minister to the spiritually underprivileged of both city slum and country moor. The basis of the Church's authority was spiritual in that it and it alone could make clear the path to Heaven, and the Pope was the head of Western Christendom.

But the Church had more than spiritual power; from the time of Constantine on it had been given great temporal possessions, until the Middle Ages saw the corporate Church infinitely richer and potentially more powerful than any single king or emperor. Under the feudal system all land belonged to the king and was leased by him to individuals who paid for its use in various ways, usually in terms of military service. Since church land was no exception to this rule, we find secular authority vested in the persons who administered the lands which the Church held of the king. Consequently, the king felt that he had a right, even a duty, to dictate appointments to high religious offices, and the lay lords under the king felt an equal interest in the holders of the lesser ecclesiastical posts. Moreover, because it was first necessary and later customary for the king to appoint churchmen to fill those high administrative posts in which education, or at least literacy, was required, many men without true spiritual vocation were made bishops or even archbishops because of their practical usefulness to the state.

William I (1066–87) and Lanfranc worked together without apparent friction, whereas Lanfranc's successor, Anselm, was unable in conscience to endure the tyranny of William Rufus (1087–1100). Henry I (1100–35) restored Anselm to his position, disagreed with him over the lay investiture of clerics, and technically relinquished all but purely feudal authority, but in practice controlled most elections and customarily received the oath of feudal loyalty before the actual consecration. Despite the political activities of many of the higher ecclesiastics, Stephen's reign (1135–54) saw the Church make notable gains, especially in the establishment of scores of monastic houses. Men, and women too, in a troubled world sought security and a place to exercise their talents in the peace and useful activity which the cloisters alone could offer. The guiding principle of Henry II (1154–89) was a desire for order in his land. He intended to curtail the powers which the Church had wrung from Stephen; when in 1162 he had a chance to fill the see of Canterbury, he doubtless felt that by promoting his able, congenial, and worldly Chancellor, Thomas à Becket, he was giving himself a willing ally. Nothing could have been farther from the truth: Becket acted with the single purpose of defending the rights of the Church and, wherever possible, extending them. The result was the drawn-out and undignified feud which ended with Becket's murder by some of Henry's knights in 1170. Henry was forced to do penance, but he lost few of the royal powers. The real test of strength between State and Church came in John's day (1199–1216), when the Papacy won. Between John and the appearance of Wyclif, this general rule holds true: a strong king controlled the Church, the Church checked or controlled a weak king.

The State

In affairs of state William the Conqueror consulted his lords at appropriate times and followed their counsel, especially when it coincided with his own judgment. For a century after the Conquest, local justice was administered by means of the traditional hundred (a subdivision of a shire) and shire moots, of which all freemen were theoretically members. The feudal system brought with it the lord's (seignorial) courts, which were to be found on every manor, and these gradually took into their own jurisdiction matters previously dealt with by the moots.

William Rufus, son of the Conqueror, suppressed every attempted revolt against his authority. His brother, Henry I, was defied by the great lords, still more attached to their Norman estates than to their English ones; but the dogged support of the English and those lesser lords of Norman blood whose holdings were solely English enabled him to maintain his prerogative in both England and Normandy. He made use of able clerics to strengthen his administration and widened the base of his government by consulting not only his official household and the greater lords, but also the lesser lords; indeed, he advanced men of purely English blood and included them among his councilors.

The anarchy of Stephen's reign (page 83) prepared the English people to accept the absolutism of Henry II, but Henry brought England territorial problems which were to distress the country for centuries, since he was lord of all Western France except Brittany. Yet he contrived to give England an efficient and lasting system for the administration of government. He vastly extended the authority and activity of his own court of justice at Westminister, and developed a series of assizes, presided over by justices in eyre (traveling justices), who at regular intervals brought royal decisions and royal authority to every part of England. The result was one of almost incalculable benefit for the social underdog, since it overthrew in large measure the petty tyranny of the manor courts. While Richard I was king (1189-99) the executive machinery set in motion by his father operated smoothly, and there was a steady growth in the principle of election of the men who weighed evidence at the assizes, the forerunners of the jury, and the no less important group whose duty it was to assess, and often to collect, taxes.

During John's reign the loss of Normandy and the struggle with the Papacy pale into insignificance beside the signing of Magna Carta (1215), although the Great Charter is more of a symbol than anything else. Most of its provisions merely put down in due form and brought together "customs" which had been long observed, but either not cast into permanent shape or not considered in relation to one another. Its intention was not so much to decrease the king's power as to prevent the king's misuse of that power. The best wills in the later world have had difficulty in perceiving the slightest taint of democracy in Magna Carta.

The Towns

The winning of the Great Charter shows us the emergence of the free townsmen, the middle class, as an influential group. The two most important factors in the growth of an English town were the freeing of the municipality from any feudal obligation save to the central government and the close organization of the merchants and craftsmen into the fraternities called guilds. The first step toward feudal freedom lay in an ability to anticipate a demand for services by means of coins. The growth of trade brought money to the traders. Commerce drew together those who benefited from it and taught them first the use and then the power of common action. The towns soon found that they could buy privileges from their lords by taking advantage of inertia, inability, or financial weakness.

The sense of unity in the urban middle class found practical expression in three types of guilds. There was the merchants' guild, in which all the important merchants of a town pooled their resources in order to further their interests as citizens and men of business. Then there were the craft or trade guilds, in which the followers of various occupations—brewers, bakers, hatmakers, water-carriers, goldsmiths—joined to maintain standards of income and good workmanship. Finally, there were those guilds which cut across craft and even class lines to improve the religious and social lives of their members. Every layman of importance in a town was an active member of a guild, with the result that municipal government was guild government.

By all modern standards medieval London was a small city indeed. At the end of Edward III's reign (1377) it is estimated to have held some forty-five thousand out of the country's total population of two and one half millions. The next largest city, York, had less than eight thousand. Norman London was a walled city, but most of the houses were small, mean, and inflammable. The fourteenth century erected buildings of as many as three stories, but seldom more. The streets were narrow, often crooked, and the houses themselves were not always in regular order. Residential sections being unknown, the ground floor of almost every dwelling was a shop or a small manufactory. The noise and the confusion in the crowded shopping sections were overwhelming. Sidewalks were nonexistent, there was no paving, and the open gutters, which also served as sewers, did little more than to make mud and mire general.

On holidays, boys and young men, apprentices and all, raced horses, matched cocks, and played football. Songs were sung and stories were told by professional minstrels and amateurs; there was dancing in the open places of the city and in the fields. There were wrestling matches and bouts with quarter-staves, and bears and bulls were baited with dogs. There was practically no night life, and what there was caused the authorities and all proper people to be extremely anxious to eliminate it. Lack of lighting made the streets, bad enough by day, totally unsafe at night, and indeed it was the general custom of our ancestors, great and small, to rise before dawn and retire shortly after sunset.

Education

There had been formal education in England ever since the conversion of the island to Christianity. Aelfric's *Colloquy* (page 73) pictures daily life in a monastic school. Similar schools were attached to the cathedrals, and parish and chantry priests gave elementary instruction in song schools such as that in Chaucer's *Prioress's Tale* (page 204). Grammar schools emphasized reading, writing, and speaking Latin. Higher education was scantily represented in England before the close of the twelfth century, but English scholars went freely to

Continental schools, such as those at Paris and Bologna, since the universality of Latin made education completely international.

Oxford University emerged suddenly about 1170 as the result of a mass migration of English masters and students from Paris. At first the organization of the university was extremely loose. Gradually, however, the students came to live together in halls, each with a principal, usually a Master of Arts, and with expenses paid out of a common fund to which all contributed. Although there was nothing which resembled any kind of uniformity, students would seem to have started their university career at fourteen or fifteen. The Bachelor of Arts degree followed upon four years' devotion to the seven liberal arts, divided into the elementary trivium (grammar, rhetoric, and logic), partly anticipated in the grammar schools, and the more advanced quadrivium (arithmetic, geometry, music, and astronomy). The Master of Arts degree required three or four more years and the degree of Doctor of Divinity perhaps another twelve. As early as 1250 every student was obliged to be under one special master from whom he was to receive daily instruction, but discipline was difficult to maintain. The students, lacking the restraint of today, were an unruly lot; their quarrels among themselves and the townsmen often resulted in riots and even murder.

Discipline and order came with the regularly endowed colleges, of which the first was Merton, established after 1263, with a warden and twenty students who received all their expenses and some pocket money. The elaborate rules included silence at meals, save for one student who read edifying works aloud. The first attempt to co-ordinate school and university education was the establishment of a secondary school at Winchester (the first English "public" school), from which students proceeded after the age of fifteen to New College, which had been founded to receive seventy of them at Oxford. Some were to study civil or canon law, a few medicine or astronomy, and the rest arts or divinity. At its height Oxford had perhaps three thousand students, the majority preparing for a place in the Church. They came, for the most part, from the middle class, since the sons of the very poor rarely received even elementary schooling and the sons of the nobility were trained for other things in other ways and were usually no more than barely literate. Chaucer makes clear the difference between the Squire, who was educated in the hall, in the bower, and on the jousting field, and the Clerk of Oxford (page 176).

Few medieval studies have the horrifying fascination for modern times that medicine does. Popular medicine was partly superstition and partly a practical utilization of common herbs, mainly of a purgative effect, an admirable example of which is afforded by Pertelote's advice to her husband (page 210). The surgeon was only an ill-esteemed blood-letter, bonesetter, tooth-puller, and barber. The educated physician was almost too well read in classical, Arabic, and contemporary authorities. Chaucer's Doctor of Physic (page 178) is a prime specimen. Medieval physicians often meant well; some of them showed great heroism in time of pestilence, even though their most portentous utterances have the odor of quackery. But the Middle Ages saw the beginning of experimental science in such figures as the misunderstood, persecuted, and silenced scholar, Roger Bacon (c. 1214-1294), who denounced authority and insisted on the validity of observation. And modern chemistry owes its start to the alchemists, who experimented tirelessly in search of the unattainable; see Chaucer's alchemist Canon (page 216).

Middle English Literature to 1300

Literary activity in English after the Norman Conquest fell for a time to almost nothing. At first there is little evidence of composition in Anglo-French, but gradually we find an increasing number of works in that dialect, none really distinguished. Englishmen who wrote in Latin produced the outstanding work of the twelfth century; among these authors were Geoffrey of Monmouth, the first comprehensive "historian" of Britain and of King Arthur (page 113), and Nigellus Wireker, a poet and humorous satirist (page 215).

The second half of the twelfth century, however, saw the shy emergence of original compositions in English, two of which proved not only that English was a fit medium for extensive works of genuine genius, but that the Old English literary tradition had, in some measure, continued to live underground. The *Brut* of Lawman (sometimes called Layamon), who took his material from Wace, a Norman poet, who in his turn had put Geoffrey of Monmouth's *Histories of the Kings of Britain* into Norman French verse, is a poem of high literary quality almost throughout, and contains many exalted and moving passages. The verse is principally in a modified version of the Old English alliterative line, but rhyme and assonance are also found. The language is almost purely English, with few traces of French influence. The *Ancrene Wisse*

(*Ancrene Riwle*), *The Rule for Anchoresses*, is a prose manual (rule) for the guidance of ladies who have retired from the world. The unknown author wrote in simple, direct, vigorous English almost free of French words. The best pieces of literature in English in the thirteenth century are the secular and religious lyrics (page 156), which show metrical skill and virtuosity, combined with amorous and religious emotion. Romances dealing with most of the themes to be popular later (page 95) were developed, among which *King Horn* (page 96) is outstanding.

Fourteenth-Century England

England in the fourteenth century was profoundly affected by three related series of events: the Hundred Years' War, the Black Death, and the Peasants' Revolt. In 1337 war began between England and France, a war destined to last longer than the hundred years from which it gets its name. We are likely to ascribe its beginning to the claims of Edward III that through his mother, daughter of Philip IV, he was the rightful king of France. The real cause, however, is to be found in the fact that English kings were vassals of the French Crown forced to do homage to the French kings for their lands in France. The French cast covetous eyes on the English possessions, made the homage as annoying as possible, and pursued a systematic policy of interfering, legally and otherwise, between the King of England and his French vassals. It was as much to keep what he had, and to regain what he and his predecessors had lost, as to acquire something new that Edward made war.

It was not until 1346 that a decisive engagement was fought at Crécy, where the overwhelming English victory was due to simple and brilliant strategy. This tactics was to give to a heavy center of well-equipped men at arms two long wings of archers, and when the enemy charged the center, to throw him into confusion with arrows. There was incredible French slaughter at Crécy, and almost incredibly little English loss of life. Ten years later the invincible conservatism of the French permitted the same tactics to work again at Poitiers, and this time Philip's son and successor, King John, was one of the spoils of war. Between the two great victories, however, England had made little progress.

The inability of the English to take advantage of Crécy was due to the widespread pestilence which swept Europe in 1348 and 1349. The Black Death, a particularly virulent variety of bubonic plague carried by rats, appeared in Constantinople in 1347 after a leisurely trip across Asia. Mediterranean traffic picked it up promptly, and by midsummer of 1348 it was raging throughout Western Europe and had broken out in England, where it remained in all its deadly liveliness throughout 1349. It is impossible to estimate just how many died, but certainly from one-third to one-half of the population, with, naturally enough, the heaviest losses among the poorest classes who lived in particularly crowded and dirty quarters.

A labor problem immediately arose. One of the most important phenomena of the late thirteenth century and the fourteenth in England had been the gradual and irregular reduction of land-bound serfs and the emergence of a group of landless laborers who worked for wages. With a growing population, as was the case up to 1348, employers were able to get workmen at what seemed to them reasonable rates. In and after 1349 the laborers who survived suddenly found themselves in a position to demand higher wages. Such subversive action called for remedial steps on the part of the employers (not all nobles by any means), and the Statute of Laborers of 1349 declared it illegal to give and accept wages above the general level of 1346. Valiant efforts were made to enforce the law, but individual employers with work which had to be done did not hesitate to violate it by paying higher wages and even by taking fugitive serfs into their employ as free laborers. Those who were still serfs, and they were many, had their unhappy lot brought even more clearly home to them by the increased prosperity of the free and of their more energetic fellows who dared to emancipate themselves by means of an agile pair of heels. Then too, despite pious hopes, sometimes expressed in laws, that prices would not rise, a planned economy was by no means feasible, and the standard of living became lower even for those whose wages were increased. By 1381 a very considerable proportion of the lower classes was ripe for mischief, in a state of hopeless misery which made them willing to risk the dangerous and, for England, unprecedented step of a revolt against their betters. The majority of the revolters, however, had no thought of changing the form of government. They considered themselves loyal to the king, though exasperated by his agents, especially those engaged in collecting the highly unpopular poll tax, and, as it seemed to them, they were merely trying to gain what they saw others possess under the current order. Nor were they engaged in an antireligious or heretical movement. They hated and attacked certain ecclesiastics, to be sure, but only as landowners and government officials. Above all, there is no good reason to put responsibility for the Peasants' Revolt at Wyclif's door; indeed, there is some evidence that the spirit of revolt prevailed least in the regions where his influence was strongest.

The Peasants' Revolt was one of those rare revolutions born of the desperation of the abjectly poor rather than of the dissatisfaction of a considerable group of the well-to-do. This very flouting of tradition, which made the initial attitude of the gentry one of pained incredulity, was probably largely responsible for the early success of the insurrection, whose short, violent, but rather aimless life was ended by a masterly stroke of royal treachery (when the young king promised to be the rebels' leader, but did not specify the direction in which he would lead them), and was buried under the corpses of a few hundreds of its participants. The uprising had little genuine effect on the gradual process of the freeing of the serfs; if anything, it retarded the movement when it implemented by fear the natural suspicion which the ruling classes felt for innovation.

English Literature in the Fourteenth Century

A brief sketch of the literary scene in Chaucer's day, with no more at the moment than passing reference to Chaucer himself, reveals first that the majority of the extant Middle English romances (page 95) were composed between 1300 and 1400. Among these, perhaps the most noteworthy are a group composed after 1350 in alliterative verse. The meter is considerably less regular than that employed by the Old English poets, and there is a large proportion of words of French origin; still, we have here undeniable evidence that the pre-Conquest poetic tradition had not died, but was preserved by the people in their orally transmitted compositions until a group of gifted literary artists saw fit to adopt it. By far the best is *Sir Gawain and the Green Knight* (page 114). All the alliterative romances (by unknown authors) are united by a vigorous style, acute observation of nature, realistic description of action, and occasional passages of quiet but genuine humor.

The tribulation, disorder, and inequalities of the fourteenth century produced a literature of social complaint and satire. There are many documents of the kind in the century, but the greatest of these is *Piers Plowman* (page 162), which contains more than satire. John Gower began his literary career with a French poem of nearly thirty thousand lines, the *Mirour de l'Omme* (*Mirror of Man*), written before 1377. Gower describes the genealogy and nature of the Seven Deadly Sins (Pride, Envy, Wrath, Sloth, Avarice, Gluttony, and Lust) and the corresponding Virtues. He then enumerates the various categories and classes of mankind, from the Pope to the peasant, and takes them to task for their wickedness. This last section contains good satire and a vivid, if depressing, picture of contemporary life. The same can be said for portions of his ten-thousand-line Latin poem, *Vox Clamantis* (*The Voice of One Crying*—in the wilderness), although the major interest of that work lies in its revelation of the impression the Peasants' Revolt made on an observant and somewhat judicious man of property and position. He allegorizes the rebels as monstrous and ferocious beasts, can say no good of them or their motives, and ends by counseling repressive measures.

The greatest religious figure of the period was John Wyclif (*c.* 1330–1384). At first he was an eminently successful Scholastic philosopher and theologian, an accepted member of the Church and rewarded by it. Gradually, however, he came to doubt and attack certain features of the ecclesiastical system of his day, from administrative matters to those purely theological. He was then repudiated by the Church and owed his sustenance and safety to secular support. At no time did he consider himself outside the Church; rather he conceived it to be his duty to purge the Church of those elements which were not validated by a fairly literal interpretation of the Bible. He began about 1374 by asserting that the lay power, as represented by the king, had authority over the Church, as represented by the Pope. He also declared that the Church was made corrupt by too many possessions, and that it was wrong for the clergy to meddle in worldly affairs. He attacked the ignorance and laziness of the higher and lower clergy and of the far too wealthy monks. These views (not expressed at one time or in one book) made Wyclif a marked man. They aroused both anger and fear in bishops and monks, but they brought him the favor of John of Gaunt, a son of Edward III, in 1376 the most powerful lord in England. The friendship of Gaunt and the court freed him from several attempted ecclesiastical trials, and permitted him to die personally unmolested at a time when his followers were being brought to book. It is certain that Wyclif inspired and probably supervised the first complete rendering into English of the Bible, but there is no evidence that any of the actual translations are his. The so-called Wyclif or Lollard Bible has come down to us in two versions. The first is a fairly literal translation of the Vulgate (St. Jerome's Latinization of the Hebrew Old and the Greek New Testament); the second contains glosses and interpretations, some of which can be interpreted as heretical.

A literary form which may be said to have reached its highest level in English in the fourteenth century is the short story in verse. Its foremost practitioner was Geoffrey Chaucer (page 168), but we must not fail to pay tribute to John Gower, who finally found, in the *Confessio Amantis* (*The Lover's Confession*), his true place as a man of letters, that of a neat and accomplished storyteller. Like the *Canterbury Tales* (page 171), the *Confessio Amantis* is a frame story, but unlike the *Canterbury Tales* it was completed; it runs to over thirty-three thousand lines of octosyllabic couplets of an almost excessive regularity. Many of the tales are the equal of anything of the sort in Middle English outside of Chaucer. Gower emphasizes the plots of his stories and, generally speaking, omits those details of description and characterization which make Chaucer's narratives particularly alive and real. Gower at times gives evidence of a slight sense of humor, but the adjective applied to him at the end of Chaucer's *Troilus and Criseyde*, "moral Gower," is too fitting to allow him to view any situation other than seriously. And, finally, although Gower draws his stories from numerous ancient and medieval stories, none of them deal with contemporary England.

We can make the same contrast between Chaucer's *Canterbury Tales* and the anonymous romances, with the exception of *Gamelyn* (page 104). However good their stories, the romances almost never give an identifying touch of ordinary contemporary life. Medieval narratives in general, if we except some of the chivalric elements—and medieval chivalry would seem often to have sprung from literature rather than to have inspired it—are almost purely a literature of escape. They are stories of other times and other lands; the characters are almost without exception kings and nobles; little attention is paid to the middle class and none, save for an occasional abusive reference, to the lower class; supernatural creatures and events abound; the way of life, the buildings, the food, and the attire are usually so splendid as to have no relation to reality. There is little or nothing in the bulk of medieval fiction to remind a reader or a listener of that time of the world in which he lived. If his existence was hard, if his surroundings were sordid, if his future was dark, the romances opened the door to a world in which he could find temporary relief from his cares and fears.

In Chaucer, to be sure, we find gods and goddesses, kings and queens, lords and ladies, scenes in Troy and Athens and Tartary, palaces, feasts, magic, and the lure of the unknown. But we find more than that; we find side by side with the customary paraphernalia of romance carefully drawn pictures of the commonplace England about him. We must not expect the exact, often depressing, realism of some present-day writers, although it sometimes appears. Chaucer was an artist—a painter, not a photographer. He realized and exploited the emotional appeal of recognizable details. Chaucer makes us say not "I wish that *I* could see, or do, something like that," but "Why, of course, that's exactly what must have happened." Chaucer was a middle-class man who spent most of his life in close association with the nobility. He wrote for the upper and middle classes, and it would almost seem that he was the first to understand that the English nobles, unlike their Continental counterparts, were becoming essentially middle-class in thought and reaction. Chaucer won the favor of all Englishmen to whom circumstances gave a right to an opinion by presenting them, among other things, with a series of pictures from the middle- (often the lower-middle) class England of their day. Chaucer was a consummate storyteller, but when we think back on his tales after an interval the passages which are most vivid are likely to be those in which the plot does not progress so much as receive substance from characterization and setting.

The religious drama of the Middle Ages played an important role in bringing about what we may term a sense of national literary unity. Developed by the Church, the mystery plays, which altogether gave a roughly consecutive picture of Biblical history from the Fall of Lucifer to the Last Judgment, were taken over by the guilds. Each had its wagon (pageant) which could be moved from place to place. A "pageant" was a box-shaped structure on wheels in the interior of which the actors could remain when not playing. The flat, railed-in roof, which afforded an upper stage, was reached by a trap door; there was another door in one of the sides of the pageant. A number of low platforms were erected in the roomier streets or squares of the town; these were the stations at which the plays were performed. At dawn of the appointed day the first pageant, that of the Fall of Lucifer, would lumber up to the first station, perhaps just inside the west gate. There, using the platform for a lower stage and the roof for an upper one, the play was put on for the benefit of the crowd which packed the street and filled the windows of the surrounding houses. When the performance was over the pageant moved on to the next station and a new audience; the second pageant, that of the Creation, took its place. Soon there was a pageant at each station all the way across the city; by staying in one place all day long a person could see the entire cycle, sometimes consisting of nearly fifty plays.

The actors were at first ordinary members of the guilds, and though in time it was recognized that a certain amount of histrionic ability was advisable for the leading roles, nothing like a caste of professional actors was ever developed. It was a cross-section of England which saw the plays; king and nobles, churchmen of all ranks, citizens and countrymen, rich men and poor men, beggarmen and thieves—all were there, and all were on that common level which is an audience.

Just as the mystery plays dramatized the Bible, so the moralities dramatized allegorical literature. The morality, it is often said, seeks to answer the question "What must I do to be saved?" In the typical morality there is a neutral figure, who represents Man, for whom Vices and Virtues contend with word and action. At the beginning of the play the hero is good, surrounded by and obeying the Virtues. After a few years, however, the Vices appear and make him their all too willing captive while the Virtues look on in helpless sorrow. Often there is a temporary return to proper behavior, but the Vices prevail once more, and it is only when Death approaches that Man finally turns back to good. Sometimes, as a matter of fact, he does not turn back at all, and is carried to Hell. *Everyman*, the best and best known of the genre, gives only the last portion of the typical plot.

Fifteenth-Century England

With Chaucer's death in 1400 English literature entered a period of decline from which it was not to emerge for more than a century. Men like Hoccleve and Lydgate wrote voluminously, praised Chaucer and considered themselves, however unworthy, his disciples; but their works, although often interesting and even significant in subject matter, exhibit no trace of literary taste or skill. While the Scottish followers of Chaucer, such as Henryson, Dunbar, and Gavin Douglas, show much greater ability, their use of the Northern dialect kept them out of the direct stream of English literature; except for Henryson, their best work was done in the sixteenth century.

This literary eclipse was only one phase of a larger and more momentous event. The medieval period was coming to a close, and the fifteenth century saw the prolonged death struggle of it. At the beginning of the century Henry V gave England a brief period of renewed military glory, but his French conquests were wiped out during the long reign of his son, while at home England underwent the dynastic feud between the Houses of York and Lancaster which goes under the name of the Wars of the Roses. Once more there was a period of virtual anarchy. Chivalry, where it survived at all, was mere playacting and literary reminiscence; see the introduction to the selections from Malory (page 251). The Church, suffering from the devastating effects of schism, was not sufficiently alarmed by the ominous outbursts of heresy in England and Bohemia to amend its ways, and, in the main, it continued in corrupt and contented indolence, ripe for Reformation and Counter-Reformation. The impulse which had led to the erection of the Gothic cathedrals and splendid abbeys was gone, and whatever artistic genius survived expressed itself in relatively little things.

But we must not paint too dark a picture of fifteenth-century England. The machinery of government and justice continued to function. Parliaments were called and continued to control the public purse strings, no matter who was king. Although trade fell off and the Hanseatic League enjoyed favors denied English merchants, the burgess class, as a whole, increased in wealth and authority. Throughout the shires, too, many of the country families, well-to-do nonnoble landholders like Chaucer's Franklin (page 177) of the previous century, prospered and somehow managed to keep aloof from the bloody wars. Such a family is the Pastons, whose habit of hoarding every scrap of paper with writing on it has left us an invaluable picture of fifteenth-century England. Their sons went to the university, their womenfolk were literate, and members of the family owned books and employed scribes.

Even more significant is the gradual appearance in England of the Renaissance and Humanism. The first generations of English Humanists, down to perhaps 1485, were collectors of manuscripts and men who had studied in Italy and been associated with Italian scholars, but they were few in number and their influence was slight, because they made no systematic effort to pass their learning on to others. In 1487 Thomas Linacre went to Italy, where he stayed twelve years, and with his return English Humanism passed from sterile acquisition to active transmission when it entered the teaching phase.

The influence of Humanism as a factor in the birth of Elizabethan literature is incalculable, but without William Caxton (page 252) it could never have attained its full growth. Just as the Christian introduction of writing into England made possible the preservation of what had hitherto been an oral, and thus ultimately an ephemeral, literature, so the invention of printing made books—previously few in number, uncertain in quality, and hard to obtain—available to the general run of men. The printing press was to become the most important single factor in the making of the modern world, although unfortunately with gunpowder, the use of which first became general in the fifteenth century, claiming a close second place.

Summary

The thousand years that lay between the Anglo-Saxon invasion of England and the accession of Henry VII in 1485 had seen the inhabitants of the island welded into one nation. The scattered and unorganized warrior bands of the mid-fifth century had united to form a people cohesive and rugged enough to absorb many Britons and to assimilate successive waves of Danish and Norman invaders. Under the stimulus of the Norman sense of order, loose and largely personal codes of law and government had been systematized and centralized until there was a firm machinery capable of ruling the land and administering justice. The feudal system had come and gone; slavery had vanished and there was little more serfdom than there is today. For the old folk moot and witenagemot (council of the wise men) a Parliament had been substituted which represented the burgesses and the country gentry as well as the nobles and the churchmen. The people, acting as a whole, had known how to curb bad rulers, but it had also learned by sad experience that despotism was preferable to anarchy. England had lost all its Continental holdings and its pride lay now in those things which were distinctively English. The old distaste for town life had vanished, commerce and manufacture had steadily increased, and these things, coupled with the growing feeling that the sea, especially the "narrow sea," was peculiarly an English possession were starting England along the road which was to make it for a time the richest nation on earth. Despite the continued existence of local dialects, there was now one standard language for all England, a position attained in the late fourteenth century by the dialect of London and the Thames Valley, the dialect in which Chaucer wrote. The English language had also rid itself of most of its inflectional endings, and by extensive borrowings from Latin, Scandinavian, and French had become a worthy vehicle for the most elevated literary expression.

England now had one people, one law, and one language; even more than that, it had a strength not yet fully tested, an exuberance almost of youth, a vigor and an ambition that were to carry the people and the language to the four quarters of the globe. Seven years after Henry VII came to the throne a New World was discovered across the ocean, and that discovery was destined to influence and direct English action, thought, and literature until the present day.

Romances

In the later Middle Ages there was far more intelligent interest in literature than we are always accustomed to realize. Like most periods, it was a time in which the principal appeal, even to the literate, as opposed to the scholarly, was in narrative, in stories and storytelling. If these stories had the semblance of history, they were all the more appreciated. The stories which interested our ancestors are grouped under the general heading of "Romances." The word "romance" originally meant something written in French, or some other vernacular dialect of Latin descent, rather than in Latin; something, in other words, written for the entertainment of the laity. A romance, as we understand it, is a fictitious narrative, at first always in verse, but later also in prose, dealing with the adventures, often wild and incredible, of a hero or a group of heroes. With such a definition it may seem difficult to differentiate a romance from such heroic poems as the *Beowulf* and the *Song of Roland*. The difference lies in the fact that whereas in heroic poetry the emphasis is on feats of bravery, in the romances the central point is ordinarily love. We do not suggest by this that the romances contain no accounts of brave heroes overcoming enormous odds, human or even superhuman, because the contrary is true. In *Guy of Warwick*, for example, Guy goes throughout Christendom and beyond, fighting Saracens and all other comers up to dragons; in the number and nature of his exploits he puts Beowulf to shame; but we must never forget that Guy left Warwick on his proud career because Felice, the Earl's daughter, declared that she could give him her love only when he had proved himself the first knight in all the world. We shall find the matter summed up neatly in certain remarks made to Sir Gawain by the Green Knight's wife (see page 129).

The introduction of the love element was partly due to the fact that, from the twelfth century on, women took an increasingly active interest in literature and, naturally enough, they wished to read or hear or write about love. A literary influence has been found in the passionate love lyrics of the troubadours of Provence. Then, too, the rise of the romance was contemporaneous with the establishment of the Courts of Love, and, at a less complete extreme than one might think, the intense devotion lavished on the Virgin Mary.

We group medieval romances in accordance with their subject matter. Jean Bodel, who died about 1210, said that the stories which people generally read deal with three matters: the matter of France, the matter of Britain, and the matter of Rome the Great. The matter of France contains the stories of Charlemagne and his peers, that of Britain those of Arthur and his knights, and that of Rome the Great the whole mass of stories inherited from classical antiquity, whether the subject be Thebes, Troy, Alexander, or Julius Caesar. Modern literary scholarship has, of course, added other categories to those of Jean Bodel, notably the matter of England, but his classification is still serviceable.

We must never forget that, by and large, every English romance is derived from a French original. Middle English literature was largely imitative of French models, but the English were not slavish copyists. During the earliest period romances in English were intended for the lower classes, who did not understand French, and certain rather fundamental changes were made. The English were obviously little interested in fine points of courtly love or in artistic details of motivation and description. The author of *Ywain and Gawain*, which is drawn from Chrétien de Troyes's *Yvain, ou Le Chevalier au Lion*, gets along with over four thousand fewer lines than his original, and, while he does not ignore the subject, it is in the sometimes painfully minute dissections of amorous psychology that he makes his most effective condensation. Though the English did not relish the wails and self-analyses of (at least temporarily) frustrated or unfulfilled love, they did want more and better deeds of daring. Where the hero of a French romance may kill four or five hundred of his foes on a single occasion, the carefree exuberance of the English adapter will often take the figure up to ten thousand or even more. Despite this occasional happy lack of realism the English versions gain as stories by the excision of extraneous matter, and are likely to be far more lively, racy, and to a certain extent even more wholesome than their French originals.

MATTER OF ENGLAND

The matter of England contains those romances which have English, or at least Germanic, heroes. In addition to the two stories given here, the group includes *Havelock the Dane, Guy of Warwick, Beves of Hamtoun,* and *Athelston.* Most of the plots, it is worth noting, look back to the period before the Norman Conquest, and the prevalence of Scandinavian raids is particularly stressed.

KING HORN

King Horn is the earliest of the Middle English romances and, in many respects, one of the best. The plot, like those of several other romances in this same group, belongs to the type called "exile and return"; that is, the hero, usually in early youth, is driven from his native land, but, after many adventures, returns to claim his own, and more. In *King Horn* we find the motif doubled: Horn is driven from his own country and later from the land in which he had taken refuge. The story is full of elements that were to become part of the stock in trade of the romance-writer: the pagan invaders, the princess who loves, apparently, beneath her, magic rings, prophetic dreams, the treacherous friend, the credulous king, the giant to be killed, the forced marriage, the disguised hero, the ring in the cup—all these things became common enough, but are somehow spontaneous in *Horn*. There is an earlier French version of the story, but the relationship between it and the English poem is by no means clear. Later English tellings of the stories are found, one of which, the ballad "Hind Horn," is printed in this volume (page 226).

King Horn is a lively and direct narrative, the plot at times being handled in an almost telegraphic style. There can be no doubt as to the audience for which it was intended. The appeal is obviously to the common people, whose preference is for deeds of bravery rather than pangs of love. There is love in the poem, to be sure, but it is Rimenhild who personifies it, while Horn himself is a fighting man. The present translation is from *The Geste of Kyng Horn*, ed. by Joseph Hall, London, 1901.

MAY all who listen to my song be happy: I shall sing you a song of King Murry; he was king in the west as long as his life lasted. His queen was called Godhild, one fairer than she could not be. He had a son named Horn, than whom none fairer could be born, nor the rain fall upon, nor the sun shine on. There was none fairer than he was; he was as bright as glass, he was as white as the lily-flower, and his complexion was rose-red. There was not his like in any country. He had twelve companions whom he led about with him. They were all sons of noble men and were all handsome fellows to sport with him. And he loved two most, one was called Child Athulf and the other Fikenhild; Athulf was the best and Fikenhild the worst.

It was on a summer day, as I can tell you, that good King Murry rode for his recreation by the seaside, as he was used to do. Only two rode with him, they were all too few; he found by the shore fifteen ships full of bold Saracens who had arrived in his land. He asked them what they were seeking, or what they had brought to the country. A heathen heard this and answered him very soon: "We shall kill the people of this land and all who believe in Christ, and you yourself at once. You shall not go from here today." The king dismounted from his horse, for he then had need, and his two good knights—he had all too few. They gripped their swords and dashed together. They struck below their shields so that some felt it. The king had all too few against so many rascals: so many could easily bring those three to death.

The heathen came to the land and took possession of it. They killed the people and threw down the churches; neither strangers nor kinsmen could live there unless they gave up their faith and took that of the heathen. Godhild was then the most miserable of all women; she wept bitterly for Murry and still more for Horn. She went out of the hall, away from all her maidens, under a crag of stone, where she lived by herself. There she worshiped God contrary to the prohibition of the heathen; there she worshiped Christ so that no heathen knew it. She ever prayed for Child Horn that Christ might be gracious to him. Horn with his companions of the country was in the hands of the heathen. Great was his beauty, for Jesus Christ had created him. The heathen would have killed him or flayed him alive, if it had not been for his fairness. The children would all have been slain, when an admiral spoke—he was bold in his words: "Horn, you are very brave, and that is evident. You are great and strong, handsome and tall. You will grow more for seven full years. If you and your companions also continue to live, if it should happen so, you would kill us all. Therefore, you and your fellows must go to ship; you must hasten on board a boat and sink to the bottom. The sea will drown you, and that will not make us sorry, for if you were alive we should all die by sword or knife to pay for your father's death." They brought the children, wringing their hands, to the shore, and put them aboard ship without delay. Horn had often had trouble, but things were never worse for him than then. The sea began to rise and Child Horn to row; the sea drove the ship so fast that the children were afraid of it. All day and all night until day dawned they certainly expected to lose their lives;

2. **Saracens,** a term used indiscriminately for heathen invaders; here, of course, Scandinavian pirates. 22. **under . . . stone,** into a cave. 32–33. **admiral,** an emir, any Saracen commander.

then Horn saw men on the shore going about the land. "My young companions," he said, "I tell you news: I hear birds sing and see grass grow. Be glad that we are alive; our ship is at the shore." They went from the ship and set foot on the earth; they let their ship ride at anchor by the seaside. Then Child Horn, who had been born in Suddene, spoke: "Ship by the seaside, may your days be good; may no water sink you by the edge of the sea. If you should come to Suddene, greet well my kinfolk, greet well my mother, the good Queen Godhild, and tell the heathen king, Jesus Christ's enemy, that I am arrived whole and sound here in this land, and say that he shall experience a blow from my hand."

The children made their way by valleys and hills. They met King Ailmar—Christ give him his blessing!—king of Westernesse—Christ give him much joy! He spoke mild words to Child Horn: "From where do you come, handsome lads, all thirteen, very bold in body, who have landed here? By God who made me, I never saw at any time a fairer company in the western land. Tell me what you are seeking." Horn acted as their spokesman, he spoke for them all, for so it had to happen: he was the fairest and the best in intelligence.

"We are from Suddene, come of good family, from Christian people and from very good kings. Heathen men came there and killed them. They slew and tore into pieces all too many Christian men. As Christ may help me, it is now two days ago that they brought us into a galley to amuse ourselves on the sea without sail or rudder. Our ship swam to the border of this land. Now you may kill us or bind our hands behind us; but, if it is your will, help us so that we do not perish."

Then spoke the good king—indeed he was no villain: "Tell me, child, what your name is. You shall have nothing but pleasure." The child answered him as soon as he heard what he said: "I am called Horn, come out of the boat from the seaside." Then the good king spoke to him: "Live up to your name. A horn goes clearly over valley and hill, and through every town the noise of a horn sounds: so shall your name spread from king to king, and your beauty throughout Westernesse, the strength of your hand into every country. Horn, you are so sweet that I cannot part from you." King Ailmar rode home and with him Horn, his foundling, and all his companions, who were so dear to him.

The king came into the hall among all his knights. He called forward Athelbrus, who was the steward of his house. "Steward, now take my foundling here and teach him your craft, about hunting and hawking, and teach him to play the harp with his sharp nails, how to carve before me and to attend with the cup. Instruct him in all the accomplishments that you ever knew, and direct his companions to other employment. Do you take Horn in charge and teach him harping and singing."

Athelbrus instructed Horn and his companions. Horn grasped in his mind all that was taught him. In the court and outside, and elsewhere all about, men loved Child Horn. And most of all Rimenhild, the king's own daughter, loved him, he was more in her mind than any other. She loved Child Horn so much that she nearly fell in passion, for she could not speak a word to him at table, nor in the hall among all the knights, nor in any other place. She was afraid of people, by day or night she could not speak with him; her sorrow and pain could never end. She sent her messenger to Athelbrus, that he should come to her and also bring Horn to her chamber, for she began to be depressed. The messenger said that the maiden lay sick, and ordered him to come at once, as she was not at all happy. The steward had sorrow in his heart, for he did not know what to do. What Rimenhild wanted, to bring young Horn to her chamber, seemed to him a bad thing. He thought in his mind that it was for no good. He took instead another, Horn's sworn brother, Athulf.

"Athulf," he said, "you shall go with me at once to the lady's chamber to speak secretly with Rimenhild and learn her desire. You shall deceive her in Horn's likeness. I am very much afraid that she would give Horn bad advice." Athelbrus led Athulf and went with him into the lady's chamber. Rimenhild showed strong affection for Child Athulf: she thought that it was Horn whom she had there. She had him sit on the bed, and exhibited passion for him; she took Athulf in her two arms. "Horn," she said, "I have loved you greatly for a long time. You must plight your troth in my hand right now to have me as wife and I will have you as my husband." Athulf said as quietly as possible in her ear: "Stop your story now, for Horn is not in here. We are not alike: Horn is highborn and more handsome, more handsome by a rib

---

7. Suddene, the Isle of Man. **17. Westernesse**, not certainly identified; the place names in *King Horn* are the subject of much dispute. **41–42. Live . . . name.** Ailmar evidently likes even a poor pun. **4–5. teach him . . . carve.** Compare the Squire in the Prologue to the *Canterbury Tales*, page 174. **39. she thought that it was Horn**, a quaint lack of realism. **48. by a rib.** Hall explains this as meaning "that Horn's beauty exceeds that of any other man as woman's beauty generally exceeds that of man," since woman was made of Adam's rib and man made of earth.

than any man alive. Though Horn were underground or anywhere else he might choose to be, or a thousand miles from here, I would not deceive him or you."

Rimenhild turned around and abused Athelbrus foully. "Go away, you dirty scoundrel, you will never more be dear to me. Go out of my chamber with great misfortune! May you get shame and hang on a high cross! I am not speaking to Horn, he is not so ugly. Horn is more handsome than this man is. May you die in great shame!"

Athelbrus then fell to the ground. "My own lady, listen to me for a little while. Hear why I hesitated to bring Horn into your presence. Because Horn is fair and noble—his equal is nowhere—Ailmar, the good king, put him in my care. I am very much afraid that if Horn were in this neighborhood you and he would have sorrowful play between your two selves. Then assuredly the king would make us unhappy. Lady Rimenhild, my queen, forgive me your anger, and I shall bring Horn to you, whomsoever it may trouble."

Rimenhild stopped speaking as well as she could. She became very happy, and had pleasure at that time. "Go now," she said, "at once, and after midday send him in the dress of a squire, when the king rises from table to amuse himself in the wood: there is no one who will betray him. He shall remain with me until it is nearly night, for me to have my will of him. After that I do not care what men may say."

Athelbrus left her; he found Horn in the hall pouring wine before the king at table. "Horn," he said, "so courteous, now go secretly after the meal to the lady's chamber, to stay with Rimenhild. Keep any presumptious words in your heart. Be true to me, Horn, you shall never regret it." Horn stored up all that he said in his heart. He went in at once to the fair Rimenhild, put himself on his knees, and greeted her sweetly. All the chamber grew bright from his fair appearance. He spoke proper words—no man needed to instruct him. "May you live well and comfortably, fair Rimenhild, with your six maidens who are sitting beside you. Our king's steward sent me to your chamber, that I should speak to you. Tell me what you wish; speak, and I shall hear what your desire may be."

Rimenhild stood up and took him by the hand; she seated him on a rich coverlet to drink his full of wine. She acted pleasantly and put her arms about his neck. She often kissed him as it pleased her so well to do. "Horn," she said, "without a doubt, you shall have me as your wife. Horn, have pity on me, and pledge me your faith."

Horn then considered what he could say. "Christ guide you," said he, "and give you heavenly joy in your husband, wherever in the world he may be. I am born too low to know such a woman. I am come from a serf and have become a foundling. It would not be naturally fitting for you to be bound to me as wife. It would not be a fair wedding between a serf's son and a king's daughter."

Then this was unpleasing to Rimenhild, and she began to sigh bitterly; she dropped her arms and fell down in a swoon. Horn was sorry in his heart and took her in his two arms. He certainly kissed her very often. "Dear sweetheart," he said, "control your heart. Help me to knighthood with all your power; ask my lord the king to make me a knight; then my serfdom will be changed into knighthood, and I shall grow of more worth, sweetheart, and follow your counsel."

Rimenhild, the sweet creature, awoke from her swoon. "Horn," she said, "that shall be done at once. You shall be made a knight before a week has passed. Take this cup here, and this ring in addition, to the steward Athelbrus, and see that he keeps the agreement. Say that I beg him, with loving speech, that he fall down before the king in the hall and ask the king to make you a knight right away. He will be well repaid with silver and gold. Christ give him success to present your mission!"

Horn took his leave, for it was nearly evening. He sought out Athelbrus and gave him what he brought, and told him very quickly how he had made out, and told him what he wanted, and promised him his reward.

Athelbrus went to the hall as quickly as possible. "King," he said, "listen to a very good speech. You will wear your crown in this town tomorrow; tomorrow is your feast, and acts of celebration are fitting. It would not be a wasted effort to knight Child Horn to bear arms for you. He will repay you by being a good knight."

The king said at once: "That is a good thing to do. Horn pleases me very much; he seems likely to be a good knight. He shall be knighted by me, and afterward be my favorite. And he himself shall knight all his twelve companions, he shall knight all of them in my presence tonight."

It seemed long to Ailmar before day dawned. Day broke and Horn came before the king with his twelve fellows—some of them were wicked. He made Horn a knight with sword and gleaming spurs; he set him on a white horse: there was no

39. feast, perhaps his birthday.

knight like him. He struck him gently and bade him be a good knight.

Athulf fell on his knees there before King Ailmar. "Brave king," he said, "grant me a request. Now Sir Horn, who was born in Suddene, is a knight. He is rightful lord over us who stand by him; he has your arms and shield with which to fight on the field of battle. Let him knight all of us, for that is our right."

Ailmar said at once, "Do whatever your will is." Horn dismounted and made them all knights. The feast, with all its handsome ceremonies, was merry, but Rimenhild was not there, and it seemed to her to last seven years. She sent for Horn and he went to her chamber. He did not wish to go alone; Athulf was his companion. Rimenhild stood on the floor—Horn's coming pleased her—and said: "Welcome, Sir Horn, and Athulf who comes before you. Now is your time, knight, to sit beside me. Do what you spoke of earlier: take me as your wife. If you are true in deeds, do now as you said before. Now that you have your desire, release me from my torment."

"Rimenhild," he said, "be quiet. I will carry out all your desire, as it may befall. I shall first ride with spear and prove my knighthood, before I begin to woo you. We are young knights, all promoted on one day, and this is the manner of our trade: a man must fight well with another knight for his sweetheart before he may take a wife; on that account the more haste is necessary for me. Today, may Christ bless me, I will do deeds of bravery in the field with shield and spear for your love. If I survive I shall take you to wife."

"True knight," said she, "I think that I may believe you. Now take here this gold ring, whose decoration is good; Rimenhild the Young is engraved on the ring; there is none better under the sun that any man could tell of. Do you wear it for my love, and carry it on your finger. The stones are of such power that you need not be afraid of any blows in any place, or be dismayed in battle, if you look at it and think about your sweetheart. And your brother, Sir Athulf, shall have another. Horn, I pray for you with loving words, that Christ grant you a successful mission, and bring you back again."

The knight kissed her, and she wished him happiness. He took his leave of her, and came into the hall. The knights went to dinner and Horn went to the stable; there he took his good horse, which was as black as coal. The horse shook its covering of chain mail, so that the courtyard resounded. The steed began to leap, and Horn to sing merrily. Horn rode more than a mile in a short time. He found a ship full of heathen dogs at anchor; he asked them what they were seeking or what brought them to the land.

A dog who spoke bold words answered him: "We will conquer this land and kill those who are in it." Horn gripped his sword and wiped it on his sleeve. He struck the Saracens until his blood grew hot; at every blow a head went off. Then the dogs came about Horn alone; he looked at the ring and thought of Rimenhild; he promptly killed at least a hundred there, no man could count the people whom he put to death. None of those who were left alive could succeed in their purpose. Horn took the leader's head, of which he had deprived him, and set it on his sword, aloft at the point. He went home to the hall among all the knights. "King," he said, "may you keep your place well, and all your knights with you! Today, after my knighting, as I rode for my enjoyment, I found a ship sailing when the sea began to rise, completely full of Saracen folk, not men of this land, to trouble you and all your people today. They assailed me, but my sword did not fail me. I struck them all to the ground, or gave them mortal wounds. I bring you the head of the chief king. Now, king, your willingness to knight me is rewarded."

When the day dawned in the morning the king rode hunting. He left at home Fikenhild, who was the worst man alive. Horn went to the lady's chamber to find adventure. He saw Rimenhild sitting as though she were out of her senses. She sat in the sunshine, all wet with tears. Horn said: "Darling, grant me your favor. Why do you weep so bitterly?" She said: "I weep only for this: as I lay asleep I threw my net into the sea, and it would not remain whole; a great fish promptly broke my net. I think that I shall lose the fish which I wish to have."

"May Christ and St. Stephen," said Horn "turn your dream to good. I shall not deceive you or do anything which may displease you. I shall make myself your own to hold and to acknowledge before every other person, and to that I pledge you my faith."

The sorrow was great which was at that pledging, for Rimenhild cried bitterly, and Horn let the tears fall in drops. "Dear sweetheart," he said, "you shall hear more: your dream will either turn to good or some man will injure us. The fish which

---

44. brother. Horn and Athulf were evidently sworn brothers.

41–42. the fish . . . have. See page 102.

broke the line will certainly cause us sorrow; that will give us suffering, and will soon become evident."

Ailmar rode along the Sture, and Horn lay in the bower. Fikenild was envious and said this foolish thing: "Ailmar, I warn you that Horn will burn you. I heard where he spoke, and unsheathed his sword, that he would kill you and take Rimenhild as wife. He lies in the chamber under the bed cover beside your daughter Rimenhild, and so he does very often. If you were to go there at once, you might find him. Put him out of the land or he will do you harm."

Ailmar turned back, very angry and sorrowful; he found Horn embraced on Rimenhild's bosom. "Go away," he said, "foul thief, you will never again be dear to me. Go out of my chamber and great misfortune go with you. Unless you go at once I shall strike you with my sword. Go out of my land or you shall have disgrace."

Horn saddled his horse, and spread on it its covering of chain mail. He fastened his coat of mail as if he were going to fight. He seized his sword, and did not stay too long. He went forth quickly to his wife Rimenhild. He said: "Darling sweetheart, now you have your dream fulfilled. The fish which tore your net has sent me from you. Good-by, Rimenhild, I can stay no longer. I will go to a strange land to experience more adventures: I shall remain there seven whole years. If I neither come nor send at the end of seven years, take yourself a husband: do not hesitate on my account. Take me in your arms and kiss me for a long while." He kissed her for a time, and Rimenhild fell to the ground. Horn took his leave, he could not remain longer. He seized his companion Athulf about the neck, and said: "True knight, guard my new love well. You never failed me: keep and protect Rimenhild."

He mounted his horse; he rode forth. Athulf wept with his eye, and all who saw him. He went to the haven and hired a good ship which would put him ashore in the western country. There he went on shore and set foot in the stirrup. He found two king's sons along the road, the one named Athyld and the other Berild. Berild begged him that he would tell him what his name was, and what he wished there. "I am called Cutberd," he said, "come out of the boat, from very far in the west country, to seek profit for myself." Berild rode nearer to him and took him by the bridle: "Well met with, knight; stay with me a while. As sure as I must die, you shall serve the king. I never in my life saw so fair a knight arrive." He led Cutberd into the hall, and they fell on their knees; they knelt and greeted the good king well. Then Berild said at once: "Sir King, you have business with this man: take him to guard your land. No man shall harm it, for he is the fairest man who ever yet came into your country." Then the dear king said: "Be welcome here. Go now, Berild, at once, and make him very happy, and when you go to woo, give him your glove: when you have proposed to marry, he will drive you away. You will never do well because of Cutberd's beauty."

It was at Christmas, neither earlier nor later: there came in very promptly at noon an armed giant from heathendom, who said this speech: "Sit still, Sir King, and hear this news: pagans have arrived here, many more than five are on the shore, King, in your land. One of them will fight against three knights; if the other three kill our man, all the land is yours, but if our one overcomes your three, all this land shall be ours. Let the fighting be tomorrow when the light of day appears."

Then said King Thurston: "Cutberd shall be the one, Berild shall be the second, and the third his brother Athyld, for they are the strongest and the best in arms. But what is our best course? I think that we are all as good as dead."

Cutberd sat at the table and said these words: "Sir King, it is no fair play for one to fight against three, to try three Christian men against one dog. Sir, I alone, without more company, shall very easily bring three of them to death."

The king, who had much sorrow, arose in the morning, and Cutberd rose from his bed, and clothed himself with arms; Horn threw on his coat of mail, laced it fast, and came to the king at his rising from bed. "King," he said, "come to the field to see how we shall fight and go together." They rode out at just six o'clock, and found a very bold giant on a green, with his companions beside him awaiting their death.

Cutberd began to attack this same band of enemies, he gave plenty of blows, the knights fell in a swoon. He withheld his blow, for they were nearly slain, and said, "Knights, rest now for a while, if it pleases you." They said that they had never had

---

4. **Sture,** Stour? Mersey? 5. **Fikenild.** Evidently he had gone to join the king. 7. **burn you,** kill you. 8. **his sword,** to swear on it. 25. **wife.** Betrothal and marriage were often confused. 43. **western country,** Ireland. 48. **Cutberd,** Cuthbert.

11–15. **Go now . . . never do well,** a difficult passage. The meaning may be: "See to it that Cutberd is not your rival in love." 48. **the knights,** the pagans.

such hard blows from a knight, except from King Murry, who was very strong: he was of Horn's family, and born in Suddene.

Horn began to shudder and his blood rose; he saw stand before him those who had driven him from his country, and had killed his father. He drew his sword; he looked at his ring and thought of Rimenhild. He struck them through the heart, so that it pained them greatly. The pagans, who were so fierce before, began to run away. Horn and his company hastened after them very fast, and killed all the dogs before they found their ships. He brought them all to death: they paid dearly for his father's death. Of all the king's knights no man was injured, except that he saw his two sons dead before him. The king began to lament and to let the tears fall. Men placed them on a bier and buried them very quickly.

The king came into the hall among all his knights. "Horn," he said, "I tell you, do as I shall advise you. My heirs are slain, and you are a knight of much worth, of great strength, and fair in length of body. You shall rule my kingdom, and have as wife my daughter Reynild, who sits in an upper room."

"O Sir King, I should accept it wrongfully, your daughter, whom you offer to me, and the rule of your kingdom. I shall serve you more, Sir King, before you die. Your sorrow shall depart before the end of seven years. When it is gone, Sir King, give me my reward: when I wish for your daughter, you shall not refuse her to me." Cutberd remained there for seven whole years, during which he did not send to Rimenhild or go to her himself. Rimenhild was in Westernesse in very great sorrow.

A king arrived there who wished to have her as wife; he was in accord with the king about that wedding. The days were short, so that Rimenhild did not dare to delay in any way. She composed a letter; Athulf, whom Horn loved not a little, wrote it. She sent her messenger to every land to seek out Horn the knight where one might find him. Horn heard nothing of that until one day when he went to the wood to shoot arrows. He met a young man. Horn said, "Dear fellow, what do you seek here?" "Knight, if it is your pleasure, I can tell you at once. From the west country I am seeking Horn of Westernesse for the maiden Rimenhild, who is going mad on his account. A king wishes to marry her and bring her to his bed, King Mody of Reynes, one of Horn's enemies. I have traveled far by the seaside: he is nowhere to be found. Alas for the evil hour! Alas for the evil time! Now Rimenhild will be betrayed." Horn heard with his ears, and spoke with bitter weeping. "Boy, good luck come to you; Horn stands beside you. Go to her again and tell her not to mourn, for I shall be there in good time, on Sunday by six o'clock." The lad was very happy, and hastened back quickly. The sea became stormy beneath her castle wall. The youth was drowned there; it might well make Rimenhild sad. Rimenhild pulled out the bar of the door of the house in which she was, to look with her eyes, if she could see anything of Horn. Then she found drowned the lad whom she had sent for Horn and who should bring Horn to her. She wrung her hands.

Horn came to King Thurston and told him this news. Then he admitted that Rimenhild was his own, and told of his good kinsman, the king of Suddene, and how he had slain in battle the man who killed his father, and said: "Wise king, pay me for my service: help me to win Rimenhiid, so that you do not fail me, and I shall cause your daughter to be married well: she shall have as husband my good companion Athulf, one of the best and truest among good knights." The king said quietly, "Horn, have your wish now." He had letters sent into Ireland after nimble knights, Irish men ready to fight. To Horn came plenty of men who drew to the ship.

Horn got under way on a good galley. In a little while the wind began to blow him; the sea drove him straight into Westernesse. They struck both sail and mast and threw out the anchor before day had dawned or bell rung. Word began to spread of Rimenhild's wedding. Horn was on the water: he could have come no later. He let his ship ride at anchor and went to the land. He had his people remain by the edge of the wood. Horn went as alone as though he just then had sprung from a rock. He met a palmer there and saluted him pleasantly: "Palmer, you must tell me all your news." In the course of his tale he said: "I come from a wedding feast. I was at the marriage of the maiden Rimenhild. She could not help from crying with her eyes. She said that she did not wish to be married with a gold ring, but that she already had a husband, even if he was out of the country. And in the strong hall, within the castle's walls, where I was at the gate, they would not let me in.

38. **the king,** Ailmar. 41–42. **Athulf . . . wrote it.** The princess, it would appear, could not write.

37. **no later,** without being too late. 42–43. **Palmer . . . news.** Palmers (wandering religious votaries), like shipmen and merchants, were considered general purveyors of news.

Mody had ordered that they lead her to the chamber. I went away, for I did not wish to endure that sorrow; the bride weeps bitterly, and that is a painful sight." Said Horn: "As Christ counsels me, we shall change our garments. Have here my clothes and let me take your pilgrim's robe. Today I shall drink there so that some may regret it." He laid off his robe and Horn put it on his back. The palmer took Horn's clothes, which were not displeasing to him. Horn took the staff and wallet and distorted his face. He made a dirty countenance for himself and blackened his neck. He made himself ugly, as he had never been before.

He came to the porter, who answered him roughly. Horn many times and often gently asked him to unbar the gate, but he could not bring it about that he should come inside. Horn turned to the gate and kicked open the wicket. The varlet had to pay for his conduct: Horn threw him over the drawbridge so that his ribs were broken, and then came in at the gate. He sat down in lowly fashion in the beggar's row. With his face grimy he looked about him, and saw Rimenhild sitting, weeping bitterly and steadily, as though she were out of her mind; no one could stop her. He looked into each corner, but, so far as he could make out, he did not see his comrade Athulf walking anywhere.

Athulf was in the tower, looking eagerly for Horn's coming, if any ship would bring him. He saw the sea swell and Horn rowing nowhere there. He said in his words: "Horn, you are very long in coming. You entrusted Rimenhild to me so that I should protect her. Until now I have always guarded her: come now or never. I am no longer able to keep her, and now I weep for sorrow."

Rimenhild rose from the bench to pour the wine, both wine and ale after the meal. She bore a horn in her hand, as was the custom in the country. Knights and squires all drank the beer, save that Horn alone had no share of it. Horn sat on the floor; it seemed to him that he was ill-used. He said: "Courteous queen, come to me. Serve us among the first; the beggars are thirsty."

She put down her horn and filled for him a brown bowl, one holding a gallon, for she thought he was a glutton. She said, "Take this cup, and this thing in addition: I never saw, so I think, a beggar who was so forward." Horn gave it to his fellow and said: "Dear queen, I do not wish much or little wine, except from a white cup. You think that I am a beggar, but I am a fisherman, come very far to the westward to fish at your feast. My net is lying here at hand by a fair shore. It has lain there seven full years. I have come to see if it has taken any fish. I am come to fish; drink to me from the dish, drink to Horn from the horn. I have traveled far." Rimenhild looked at him, and her heart began to grow cold. She did not recognize his fishing nor anything about Horn himself, but it seemed a wonder to her why he bade drink to Horn. She filled her horn with wine and drank to the pilgrim. She said, "Drink your fill, and then tell me if you ever saw Horn in a forest glade." Horn drank from the horn for a time and threw the ring to the bottom. The queen went to her chamber with her four maidens. Then she found what she wished: a ring engraved of gold which Horn had had from her. She was sorely afraid that Horn was dead, for the ring was there. Then she sent a maiden after the palmer. "Loyal palmer," she said, "tell me where you got the ring which you threw, and why you have come here." He said: "By St. Gilles, I have gone many a mile far in the west, to seek gain for myself. I found Child Horn on his way to a ship in a certain land. He said that he would try to arrive in Westernesse. The ship took to the water with me and Horn the good. Horn was sick and died, and he begged me fairly: 'Go with the ring to young Rimenhild.' He kissed it often, may God give his soul rest!"

Rimenhild said at once, "Now break, my heart, for you no longer have Horn, who has pained you so bitterly." She fell on her bed, where she had hidden a knife with which to kill both the hateful king and herself on that same night, if Horn could not come. She set the knife to her heart, but Horn caught her up at once. He wiped the black from his neck and said: "Queen, so sweet and dear, I am your own Horn. Can't you recognize me? I am Horn of Westernesse, kiss me in your arms." They kissed each other truly and made much joy.

"Rimenhild," he said, "I am going down to the end of the wood, where my knights are ready to fight, armed beneath their clothing. They shall make the king and the guests who come to the feast angry: today I shall teach them a lesson and strike them painfully."

Horn sprang out of the hall and let his palmer's cloak fall off. The queen went to her chamber and found Athulf in the tower. "Athulf," she said, "be

---

15. roughly. The unmannerly porter is a common figure in medieval stories. **50. white cup.** He refuses to drink from the bowl which Rimenhild had thought good enough for a palmer.

5. taken any fish. The net represents Rimenhild, and Horn is inquiring if she has taken another lover. **37–38. black . . . neck.** Such a simple disguise has seldom been so effective!

happy, and go to Horn at once. He is under the forest boughs and with him plenty of knights."

Athulf began to leap because of the news. He ran at once after Horn, as fast as his horse could go. He certainly overtook him and they had great joy. Horn took his band and set them on the road. He came in very soon, for the gates were open. Armed completely from foot to neck, he brought them all to sorrow who were at the feast, all who were in there except his twelve companions and King Ailmar. The others left their lives there. Horn did no terrible act for Fikenhild's false tongue. They swore loyal oaths that they never would betray Horn, though they lay at death's door. They rang the bell to celebrate that wedding. Horn went with his men to the king's palace, where there was a pleasant wedding feast, since powerful men ate there. No tongue could tell the songs that were sung there.

Horn sat on a chair and ordered them all to listen. "King," he said, "listen to one of the best of stories: I do not say it to incur blame. My name is Horn, you elevated me to be a knight, and I have proved my knighthood. Men told you, King, that I betrayed you; you made me an exile and caused me to leave your land. You believed that I did what I never thought to do, namely, lie with Rimenhild. That I deny, nor shall I do so until I win Suddene. Do you keep her for a time while I hasten to my heritage and to my body of retainers. I shall obtain that land and do vengeance for my father. I shall be king of a city and bear a king's crown; then Rimenhild shall lie by the king."

Horn went to the ship with his Irish companions and with him his brother Athulf; he wanted no one else. The ship began to hasten, and the wind blew loudly. Within five days at about midnight the ship arrived. Horn went directly; he took Athulf by the hand and went up on the shore. He found under his shield a knight skilled in battle; the knight lay asleep beside the road. Horn took hold of him and said: "Awake, knight. Say what it is you guard, and why you are sleeping here? It seems to me by your shining cross you serve your Lord. Unless you will disclose yourself to me, I shall cut you to pieces." The good knight rose up; he was afraid of the words. He said: "Against my will I serve very evil heathen. I was a Christian at one time, but then there came to this island black Saracens who made me deny that I believe in Christ. They made me prefect to guard this pass against Horn, who is of age, and who lives in the west, one of the best of knights. He killed with his own hand the king of this country, and many hundreds with him, and therefore it is a wonder that he does not come to fight. May God give him the right side, and a wind to drive him here to bring them out of life. They killed King Murry, Horn's father, a courteous king. They sent Horn out of the land; twelve companions went with him, among them Athulf the good, my own child, my dear son. If Child Horn is whole and healthy, then Athulf is without a wound, he loves him so dearly and is such a guardian to him. If I could see those two, I should die for joy."

"Be happy then, knight, more than ever before: Horn and his fellow Athulf are both here." He went to Horn and greeted him at once. They made much joy there while they were together. "Children," he said, "how have things gone with you? It is a long time since I saw you. Do you wish to conquer this country and kill whoever is in it?" He said: "Dear Child Horn, your mother Godhild still lives. She would not fail to be joyful if she knew that you were alive."

Horn said in his speech: "Blessed be the time that I came to Suddene with my Irishmen. We shall teach the dogs to speak our language. We shall kill them all and skin them all alive." Horn blew his horn. His people recognized it at once, and they came out of the boat, away from Horn's banner. They struck and fought through the night and to the time just before dawn. At the end none of the Saracen race were left alive. Horn had chapels and a church built; he caused the bells to ring and had masses sung. He came to his mother's hall in a crag side. He had grain brought and made a merry feast; he led a joyful life, and Rimenhild paid dearly for it.

Fikenhild was arrogant at heart, and that caused him to suffer pain. He gave presents to young and old to stick by him. He had stone carted, where he hoped for success; he had a strong castle built surrounded by the sea, where nothing could land save a bird in flight; but when the sea retreated plenty of men could come. Fikenhild planned to injure Rimenhild. He began to woo her eagerly; the king did not dare refuse him. Rimenhild was greatly wrought up: she wept bloody tears. That night Horn began to sweat and to dream oppressively of his mate Rimenhild, that she was taken onto a ship. The ship began to lurch; his sweetheart was going to drown. Rimenhild tried to pull herself to the land with her hands, but Fikenhild pushed her back with the hilt of his sword.

Horn woke from sleep as a man who had need of

43. **cross,** on his shield.

8–10. **If . . . to him.** The original is not clear. 24. **teach . . . language,** make trouble for them.

haste. "Athulf," he said, "my companion, we must take to the ship. Fikenhild has brought me down and put Rimenhild in distress. May Christ, for his five wounds, carry me there tonight!" Horn rode to the ship, and his fellows with him.

Before day had dawned Fikenhild went at once to the king, after the fair Rimenhild, to marry her by night. He led her in the nighttime into his new fortification. They began the feast before the sun rose. Before Horn knew about this and before the rising of the sun, his ship stood under the tower by Rimenhild's chamber. Rimenhild then little thought that Horn should be alive. They did not recognize the castle, because it was so new. Horn found sitting Arnoldin, Athulf's cousin, who was there at that time to wait for Horn. "Knight Horn," he said, "king's son, you have come well to the land. Today Fikenhild has married your sweetheart Rimenhild. I shall not lie to you, he has deceived you twice. He had this tower made entirely on your account. No man can get in with any device. Horn, now may Christ direct you so that you do not lose Rimenhild!"

Horn knew all the cunning that any man could know. He brought out a harp and took a few companions, very active knights, who clothed themselves as they chose. They went along the beach toward the castle. They began to sing merrily and to do their harping.

Rimenhild heard it, and asked what they were. They said that they were harpers, and some of them were fiddlers. She had Horn admitted right at the hall gate. He seated himself on the bench to pluck his harp. He made a song for Rimenhild, and she lamented. Rimenhild fell in a faint; there was no one there who laughed. It struck Horn to the heart, so bitterly did it pain him. He looked at the ring and thought of Rimenhild. He went up to the table with his good sword's edge: he laid Fikenhild's head low and he threw down all his men one after another. When his men were slain they had Fikenhild torn to pieces. There Horn made Arnoldin for his meekness king of all Westernesse, after King Ailmar. The king and his vassals gave tribute to Arnoldin.

Horn took Rimenhild by the hand and led her to the shore, and took with him Athelbrus, the good steward of his household. The sea began to rise and Horn to row. They arrived where King Mody had been lord. He made Athelbrus king there, for his good training. He showed favor to all the knights because of their counsel. Horn began to sail again, and the wind blew amply for him. He arrived in Ireland, where he had experienced sorrow, and there he caused Child Athulf to marry the maiden Reynild. Horn then came to Suddene, among all his kinfolk. He made Rimenhild his queen, as it might well be. All people might have compassion for them, who had loved so truly. Now they are both dead—may Christ lead them to Heaven!

Here ends the story of Horn, who was fair and not ugly. Let us make merry continually, because Horn's song ends thus. May Jesus, who is king of Heaven, give us all His sweet blessing!

Amen

GAMELYN

Because of its subject matter, the place it was supposed to fill, and its subsequent literary history, *Gamelyn* is among the most interesting of the romances. The poem is found in twenty-five manuscripts of Chaucer's *Canterbury Tales*, always in the gap after the unfinished "Cook's Tale." Although printed in early editions of Chaucer's works, it has long since been dropped from the canon of the poet's original writings. The chances are that the poet had intended to rework it for one of the pilgrims, probably the Knight's Yeoman, and that some early scribe transferred it from Chaucer's "library" to his "works." Thomas Lodge used the story in his *Rosalynde, Euphues' Golden Legacie*, from which Shakespeare took the plot of *As You Like It*. A comparison of the three versions is a rewarding exercise in the history of literary taste.

Stirring, realistic, extraordinarily well told, the romance is like a cross section, brutal but real, of the seamier side of fourteenth-century life. The connection between *Gamelyn* and the outlaw ballads, such as those in the Robin Hood cycle, is obvious. The present translation is from the text of W. W. Skeat, *The Complete Works of Geoffrey Chaucer*, Oxford, 1900, Vol. IV, pp. 645 ff.

PAY attention, and listen and harken correctly, and you shall hear a tale of a brave knight. His right name was Sir John of Boundys; he knew plenty about good breeding and much about sport. The knight had three sons which he had begotten with his body; the eldest was a great rascal and he began to show that early. His brothers loved their father well and stood in awe of him, but the oldest deserved his father's curse and had it at last.

The good knight his father lived such a long time that death came to him and handled him very sorely. The good knight was bitterly anxious, when he lay sick, as to how his children should live after his day. He had been in many lands, but had not been a very good householder: all the land that he had was held in fee simple. He was desirous that it

---

51–52. **He showed . . . counsel,** an uncertain translation.

53. **held in fee simple.** He could dispose of it as he chose.

GAMELYN

should be divided evenly among them all, so that each of them should have his part as it might happen. Then he sent throughout the country for wise knights to help him deal out his lands and divide them rightly. He sent them word by letters that they should come quickly if they wanted to speak with him while he was alive.

When the knights heard that he lay sick, they had no rest by night or day until they came to him where he lay quiet on his deathbed awaiting the will of God. Then the good knight said, as he lay sick, "Lords, I warn you truly, without hope of denial, that I may live no longer, here at this time, for through God's will death is pulling me to the ground." There were none of all who heard him rightly who did not have pity on that same knight, and they said, "Sir, for the love of God, do not be dismayed. God may make a remedy for the evil that is now brought about."

Then the good knight spoke where he lay sick: "God can send remedy for evil, I know that there is no denying it, but, knights, for my love, go and divide my lands among my three sons, and sirs, for the love of God, do not divide it wrongly, and don't forget my young son Gamelyn. Pay attention to the one as well as to the other; you seldom see any heir help his brother."

Then they left the knight, who was not in good health, to lie there, and went into counsel to divide his lands; it was their thought to bestow them all on one, and that Gamelyn should have nothing because he was youngest. They divided all the land that there was into two parts, and let young Gamelyn go without land; and each of them said loudly to the other that his brothers could give him land when he became competent. When they had divided the land at their will, they came again to the knight where he lay very quiet, and told him at once how they had done. Then said the knight, "By St. Martin, despite all that you have done the land is still mine. For the love of God, neighbors, let everything remain as it is, and I will divide my land after my own desire. John, my eldest son, shall have five plowlands, that was my father's heritage while he was alive; and my second son shall have five plowlands which I helped to get with my right hand; and all my other purchases of lands and serfs I bequeath to Gamelyn, and also all my good horses. And I beg you, good men, who know the law of the land, for Gamelyn's love, that my bequest stand." Thus the knight divided his land while still alive, just as he lay sick on his deathbed.

And right afterwards he lay stone-still and died when the time came as was the will of Christ.

And at once when he was dead and buried under the grass, the elder brother immediately deceived the young boy: he took into his own hands his land and his serfs and Gamelyn himself to clothe and to feed. He clothed and fed him evilly and poorly, and let his lands, his houses, his parks, and his woods go to ruin, and did nothing well; and afterwards he paid for it with his fair skin.

Gamelyn was in his brother's hall so long that they all of their own accord feared him because he was the strongest: no one was there, young or old, who would anger Gamelyn, no matter how bold he was. Gamelyn stood in his brother's yard one day, and began to touch his beard with his hand. He thought about his lands which lay unsown, and about his fair oaks which were pulled down, his parks which were broken into and his deer stolen. None of his good horses were left to him, his houses were unroofed and in bad order. Then Gamelyn thought that things were not going as they should.

Afterward his brother came walking there, and said to Gamelyn, "Is our food ready?" Then Gamelyn became angry and swore by God's book, "You shall go bake for yourself, I will not be your cook!" "What, brother Gamelyn, how are you answering now? You never spoke such a word before as you are doing now." "By my faith," said Gamelyn, "it seems to me there's need for it. I never paid any attention before to all the injuries I have. My parks are broken into and my deer stolen. Nothing is left to me of my armor and horses. All that my father bequeathed to me is going to shameful ruin, and therefore, brother, by your name, have the curse of God!" Then his brother, who was quick in his anger, spoke: "Stand still, fellow, and hold your peace. You shall be glad to have your food and your clothing. What do you have to say, Gamelyn, about land or serfs?" Then Gamelyn, the young child, said, "May he have Christ's curse who calls me a fellow! I am no worse fellow and no worse person than you, but born of a lady and begotten by a knight."

He didn't dare to go nearer Gamelyn on foot, but called his men to him and said to them then, "Go and beat this boy and take his wits from him, and let him learn to answer me better another time." Then said the child, young Gamelyn: "May you have Christ's curse, my brother! And if I must be beaten right now anyway, may you have Christ's

---

44. **plowlands.** A plowland, like a hide, is usually reckoned at 120 acres.

12. **they all,** the members of his brother's household.
16. **touch his beard.** He realized that he was growing up.
25. **by God's book.** The oaths in the poem are worth observing.

curse again unless you are the one to do it!" And then his brother in his great anger made his men fetch clubs to beat Gamelyn. And when every one of them had taken a club, Gamelyn was aware at once when he saw them coming. When Gamelyn saw them come, he looked all around and perceived a pestle which stood under a wall. Gamelyn was light of foot and leaped there, and drove all his brother's men into a heap. He looked like a wild lion and laid on plentifully. When his brother saw that, he began to go away; he fled up into a loft and shut the door tight.

Thus Gamelyn with the pestle made them all afraid. Some for love of Gamelyn, and some for fear of him, they all drew away on different sides when he began to play. "What! How now?" said Gamelyn. "May you have bad luck! Will you begin a fight and run away so soon?" Gamelyn sought where his brother had fled and saw him looking out of a window. "Brother," said Gamelyn, "come a little nearer, and I will teach you a game with the buckler." His brother answered him, and swore by St. Richard: "While the pestle is in your hand I shall come no nearer. Brother, I swear by the mercy of Christ, I will make peace with you. Throw away the pestle and don't be angry any more." "I was forced," said Gamelyn, "to get angry at once, for you would have made your men break my bones. If I hadn't had might and main in my arms so as to put them away from me, they would have done me harm." "Gamelyn," said his brother, "don't be angry, it would have been very displeasing to me to see you have any injury; I only did it, brother, for a test, just to see if you were strong while still so young." "Come down to me then and grant me my request for a thing which I will ask you, and we shall be reconciled at once."

Then his brother who was false and cruel came down, and was very much afraid of the pestle. He said, "Brother Gamelyn, ask me your request, and take care that you blame me unless I grant it at once." Then said Gamelyn, "Certainly, brother, if we are to be reconciled you must grant me this: if we are not to quarrel, you must let me have all that my father bequeathed to me while he was alive." "That shall you have, Gamelyn, I swear by Christ's mercy! all that your father bequeathed to you, and even more if you wanted it. Your land, which lies fallow, shall be very well sown, and your houses, that are laid so low, shall be raised up." Thus the knight spoke to Gamelyn with his mouth, and thought, nevertheless, falseness, as he well knew how to do. The knight thought of treason and Gamelyn of none, and he went and kissed his brother, and when they were at peace young Gamelyn, alas! did not know at all with what a false treason his brother kissed him.

Pay attention, and listen and hold your tongue, and you shall hear a tale of young Gamelyn.

A wrestling match was announced near there, and as prize a ram and a ring were put up, and Gamelyn was anxious to go there to prove what he could do with his strength. "Brother," said Gamelyn, "by St. Richard, tonight you must lend me a little courser which is brisk to the spur to ride on. I must go on an errand not far from here." "By God," said his brother, "go and choose for yourself the best of the horses in my stall, and don't pass by any of the steeds or the coursers that stand beside them. And tell me, good brother, where do you want to ride?"

"Near here, brother, a wrestling match is proclaimed, and a ram and a ring are to be put up as prizes. It would be a great honor, brother, to all of us, if I were able to bring the ram and the ring home to this hall." A horse was saddled quickly and swiftly. Gamelyn put a pair of spurs securely on his feet. He put his foot into the stirrup, and he mounted the horse, and the young child rode away toward the wrestling match. When young Gamelyn had ridden out at the gate, the false knight, his brother, locked it after him, and begged Jesus Christ, who is king of Heaven, that he might break his neck at that wrestling.

As soon as Gamelyn came to the place he jumped down from his horse and stood on the grass, and there he heard a franklin complain woefully and saw him begin to wring his hands bitterly. "Good man," said Gamelyn, "why do you carry on so? Is there no man who is able to help you out of this trouble?" "Alas!" said the franklin, "that I was ever born! For I believe that I have lost two stalwart sons. There is a champion here who has caused me sorrow, for he has slain my two sons, unless God preserve them. I would give ten pounds, by Jesus Christ! and more, provided I could find a man to handle him roughly." "Good man," said Gamelyn, "if you want to do well, hold my horse while my man pulls off my shoes, and help my man to watch my clothes and my horse, and I will go to the place to see if I can have success." "By God," the franklin said, "it shall be done at once. I will be your man myself and pull off your shoes, and do you go into the place, and may Jesus Christ give you success,

---

23. **St. Richard,** bishop of Chichester (d. 1253), who typified fraternal love.

9. **ram.** See the Miller in the General Prologue to the *Canterbury Tales*, page 179.

GAMELYN

and don't be afraid about your clothes or your good horse."

Barefoot and ungirt Gamelyn came in, and all that were in the place paid attention to him and wondered how he dared adventure himself to prove his strength on one who was so brave a champion in wrestling and fighting. The champion jumped up quickly and at once, and began to go toward young Gamelyn, and said: "Who is your father and who is your master? In truth you are a great fool to come here!" Gamelyn answered the champion then: "You knew my father well while he was able to go about and while he was alive, by St. Martin! His name was Sir John of Boundys, and I am Gamelyn." "Fellow," said the champion, "as I hope to prosper, I knew your father well while he was alive. And as for yourself, Gamelyn, I want you to hear this: while you were a young boy you were a great rascal." Then said Gamelyn, and swore by Christ's mercy, "Now that I am grown older you shall find me a greater!" "By God!" said the champion, "you'll be welcome! If you come once into my hands you'll never prosper."

It was well into the night and the moon was shining when Gamelyn and the champion came together. The champion tried his tricks on Gamelyn, who was ready for them, and Gamelyn stood still and told him to do his best. Then Gamelyn said to the champion: "You are doing your best to bring me down. Now that I have experienced many of your tricks, you must," he said, "try one or two of mine." Then Gamelyn at once went briskly to the champion, and of all the tricks that he knew he showed him only one, and threw him on the left side so that three ribs broke, and also one of his arms gave a great crack. Then Gamelyn said smartly, "Shall that be counted a throw or shall it be called none?" "By God!" said the champion, "whichever you count it, the man who once comes into your hands shall never thrive!" Then said the franklin who had his sons there, "Blessed be you, Gamelyn, that you were ever born!" The franklin said to the champion, of whom he stood in no awe, "This is young Gamelyn who taught you this trick!" Then the champion, who liked nothing about the whole business, answered: "He is an evil master and his play is very cruel. It is a very long time ago since I first wrestled, but I was never handled so sorely in my life." Gamelyn stood in the place alone and without his shirt, and said: "If there are any others, let them come to work. The champion who put himself out to deal so sorely, it seems by his appearance that he doesn't want any more." Gamelyn stood as still as stone in the place to wait for more wrestling, but none came; there was no one who wished to wrestle further with Gamelyn, because he had handled the champion so very sorely. There were two gentlemen who took care of the place and who came to Gamelyn—God give him good favor!—and said to him, "Put on your hose and shoes, for truly the fair is done at this time."

And then said Gamelyn, "As I hope to do well, I have not yet sold half of my wares." Then said the champion, "As I hope to have the continued use of my neck, he is a fool who buys your ware, you sell it so dearly." Then said the franklin, who was in great sorrow: "Fellow," he said, "why are you blaming his ware? By St. James in Galicia, whom many a man has visited, it is still too good a bargain that you have bought." Those who were wardens of that wrestling match came and brought Gamelyn the ram and the ring, and said, "Gamelyn, take the ring and the ram as the best wrestler who ever came here." Thus Gamelyn won the ram and the ring, and in the morning went home with great joy. His brother saw where he was coming with a large company and ordered them to shut the door and to keep him outside. The porter was very much afraid of his master and went at once to the gate and locked it fast.

Now listen and harken, both young and old, and you shall hear something amusing about Gamelyn the brave.

Gamelyn came up in order to enter, and then the gate was shut fast with a bolt. Then said Gamelyn, "Porter, open the gate, for many a good man's son is standing outside it." Then the porter answered and swore by God's beard, "You shall not come into this yard, Gamelyn." "You lie," said Gamelyn, "as I hope to have the use of my chin!" He struck the wicket with his foot and broke off the bolt. When the porter saw that it could not be any better, he set foot to earth and began to run away. "By my faith," said Gamelyn, "that effort is wasted, for I am as light of foot as you, even though you had sworn the contrary." Gamelyn overtook the porter and avenged the injury done him, and hit him in the neck so that the bone broke, and took him by one arm and threw him in a well, which was seven fathoms deep, as I have heard.

When young Gamelyn had played his game thus, all those who were in the yard drew away from him. They were very much afraid of him for the deeds he had done and for the fair company which he had

---

7. the fair is done, the show is over.   **23–24. large company.** He had evidently invited the spectators to come home with him.

brought there with him. Gamelyn went to the gate and opened it wide. He admitted all the men who wanted either to walk or to ride in, and said, "You are welcome without any trouble, for we will be masters here and ask no man for permission. Yesterday," said young Gamelyn, "I left five tuns of wine in my brother's cellar. I do not want this company to break up—if you will act according to my advice—while there is a drop to drink left, and if my brother complains or puts on a displeased look for the cost of either food or drink which we spend here, I am our caterer and carry our common purse; he shall have St. Mary's curse for his faultfinding. I swear by God's mercy that my brother is a niggard, and we will spend generously what he has formerly saved. And whoever makes any complaint because we remain here, he shall go to the porter in the draw-well."

For seven days and nights Gamelyn held his feast with much mirth and pleasure and no quarreling there. His brother lay fastened up in a little turret and saw them waste his property, but he did not dare say anything. Early in the morning on the eighth day the guests came to Gamelyn and wanted to leave. "Lords," said Gamelyn, "will you hurry off so? All the wine isn't drunk yet, as I hope to have the use of my eye." Gamelyn was very sorrowful in his heart when his guests took their leave to go away from him. He wished that they would stay longer, but they said "No" and commended Gamelyn to God and wished him good day. Thus Gamelyn made his feast and brought it well to an end, and afterward his guests took their leave to depart.

Listen, and give heed and hold your tongue, and you shall hear something amusing about young Gamelyn. Harken, lords, and listen carefully, how Gamelyn was treated after the guests were gone.

All the time that Gamelyn was holding his feast his brother thought to be revenged on him with treachery. When Gamelyn's guests had ridden or walked away, Gamelyn stood quite alone, for he had no friends. Very soon after that, within a little while, Gamelyn was captured and bound. The false knight came forth out of the upper room; he went much nearer to his brother Gamelyn, and said to him, "Who made you so bold as to waste the store of my household?" "Brother," said Gamelyn, "don't be angry about that, for it is many a day now since it was bought. For, by St. Richard, brother, you have had for sixteen years all the produce of fifteen plowlands, and you have bred for yourself all the animals that my father left to me on his deathbed. I will give you the profit of all these sixteen years for the food and drink that we have used just now." Then said the false knight—may he have bad luck!—"Listen, brother Gamelyn, what I will give you: since I have begotten no heir, brother, of my body, I will make you my heir, I swear it by St. John." "By my faith," said Gamelyn, "if it be so and if you think the same as you say, may God reward you for it!"

Gamelyn knew nothing of his brother's fraud and therefore he tricked him in a little while. "Gamelyn," said he, "one thing I must tell you: when you threw my porter into the draw-well, I swore in my wrath, and in that great company, that you should be bound both hand and foot. Therefore I beg you, brother Gamelyn, that you will not let me be forsworn, since you are my brother. Let me bind you now both hand and foot to keep my vow as I promised." "Brother," said Gamelyn, "as I hope to get ahead, you shall not be forsworn because of love of me."

Then they made Gamelyn sit down—he could not stand—until they had tied him hand and foot. The false knight, his brother, was afraid of Gamelyn and sent for fetters to fasten him securely. His brother told lies about him as he stood there and told the people who came in that Gamelyn was crazy. Gamelyn stood bound to a post in the hall and those who came in there all looked at him. Ever Gamelyn stood there straight upright, but he had no food nor drink either by day or night. Then Gamelyn said: "By my neck, brother, I have now discovered that you are somewhat false. If I had known the treason which you had thought up, I would have given you blows before I had been bound!" Gamelyn stood tied as still as any stone; for two days and two nights he had no food. Then said Gamelyn, who stood fastened securely, "Adam Spencer, it seems to me that I fast too long. Adam Spencer, now I beg you for the great love my father had for you, if you can get at the keys, let me out of captivity, and I will share my free land with you." Then said Adam, who was the butler, "I have served your brother for sixteen years, and if I were to let you go out of his house he would say afterwards that I was a traitor." "Adam," said Gamelyn, "as I hope to enjoy the use of my neck, you will find my brother false in the end; therefore, brother Adam, free me from my bonds and I will share my free land with you." "Upon such an agreement," said Adam, "certainly I will do all that I am able to that effect." "Adam," said Gamelyn, "as I hope to prosper, I will hold my bargain with you if you will hold yours with me." As soon as Adam's master had gone to bed, Adam took the keys and let Gamelyn out at once. He unlocked

GAMELYN

both Gamelyn's hands and feet, in hope of the advancement which he had promised him. Then Gamelyn said: "May God's grace be thanked! Now I am freed both hand and foot. If I had eaten and drunk properly, now there is no one in this house who would bind me tonight." Adam took Gamelyn as still as any stone and led him into the pantry quickly and without delay, and set him down to supper in a secret place; he told him to do gladly what he would, and Gamelyn did so. As soon as Gamelyn had eaten well and excellently and also drunk enough of the red wine, "Adam," said Gamelyn, "what is your advice now? Shall I go to my brother and strike off his head, or not?" "Gamelyn," said Adam, "it shall not be so. I can teach you a trick that is worth two of that. I know indeed for a truth that this fact cannot be denied: we shall have a feast right here on Sunday. There will be many abbots and priors here and other men of Holy Church, as I am telling you. You shall stand up by the post as though you were fastened by the hands, but I shall leave the fetters unlocked so that you may throw them off. When they have eaten and washed their hands, you shall beg them all to get you out of the bonds. If they will go bail for you, that would be a good thing, because then you would be out of prison and I would be out of blame. But if each of them should say 'No' to us, I shall try another course, I swear by this day! You shall have a good staff and I will have another, and may he who fails the other have Christ's curse!" "Yes, for God's sake," said Gamelyn, "I say this for myself, if I fail on my side, may I prosper poorly! If we must in any case absolve them of their sin, warn me, brother Adam, when I ought to start." "Gamelyn," said Adam, "by St. Charity, I will warn you in advance when it shall be. When I wink at you, get ready to go, and throw off the fetters, and come to me at once." "Adam," said Gamelyn, "may your bones be blessed! That is good advice given for the occasion. If they refuse then to bring me out of my fetters, I will apply good blows right to their loins."

When Sunday had come, and the people to the feast, both greatest and least were welcomed pleasantly, and always as they came in at the hall door they looked at young Gamelyn. The false knight, his brother, full of treachery, told all the guests who were at the banquet all the harm and shame about his brother Gamelyn that he could tell with his mouth. When they had been served with two or three courses, then Gamelyn said: "How are you serving me? By God who made all things, it is not well served that I should sit fasting while other men make merry." The false knight, his brother, who stood there told all his guests that Gamelyn was crazy. And Gamelyn stood still and answered nothing, but he kept Adam's words in mind. Then Gamelyn spoke very sadly to the great lords who were sitting in the hall. "Lords," he said, "for Christ's Passion, help to bring Gamelyn out of prison." Then said an abbot—sorrow fall on his cheek!—"He shall have Christ's curse and also St. Mary's who would beg for you to get out of prison or go your bail, but may it ever go well with those who cause you great sorrow!" After that abbot another spoke: "I would wish that your head were off, even though you were my brother! May evil befall all those who go your bail!" Thus they all spoke who were in the hall. Then a prior said—evilly may he prosper!—"It is a great pity, boy, that you are alive." "Oh," said Gamelyn, "as I hope to make use of my bones, I have now discovered that I have no friends. May he be accursed, both blood and flesh, whoever does any good to a prior or an abbot!"

Adam the butler took off the cloth, and looked at Gamelyn and saw that he was angry. Adam thought little in the pantry, but brought two good staves to the hall door. Adam looked toward Gamelyn, who was soon aware of him and threw off the fetters and began to move. When he came to Adam he took one of the staves, and went to work and gave good blows. Gamelyn and the butler both came into the hall, and looked about them as though they were angry. Gamelyn sprinkled holy water with an oaken club so that some who had been standing upright fell into the fire. There was no layman who was in the hall that wished to do anything but good to Gamelyn, but stood aside and let them both work, for they had no pity on the men of Holy Church. Abbot or prior, monk or canon, whom Gamelyn overtook went down at once. There was no one of them all who met with his stave that he did not overthrow him and pay him his debt. "Gamelyn," said Adam, "for St. Charity, pay a liberal allowance for love of me, and I will keep the door as sure as ever I hear mass! There shall none pass before they are absolved." "Don't be afraid," said Gamelyn, "while we are together. Keep the door well, and I will work here; hurry up, good Adam, and let none flee there, and we shall count fully how many there are." "Gamelyn," said Adam, "do them nothing save good. These are men of Holy Church, draw no blood from them, protect the crown well and do them no in-

24. **thought little**, about anything but fighting. 34–35. **layman . . . good to Gamelyn.** The men of the household were on Gamelyn's side.

juries, but break both their legs and afterwards their arms." Thus Gamelyn and Adam worked very rapidly and played with the monks and made them afraid. They had come there riding in a jolly manner with servants, and they were carried home again in carts and wagons. When they were all done, a gray friar said: "Alas, Sir Abbot, what were we doing here now? It was unprofitable counsel that we should come here: we would have been better off at home with bread and water."

While Gamelyn was making new orders of the monks and friars, his brother stood and had a displeased look all the time. Gamelyn lifted up his stave, which he well knew how to use, and hit him in the neck so that he knocked him over—the backbone broke a little above the girdle—and put him in the fetters which he himself had sat in recently. "Sit there, brother," said Gamelyn, "in order to cool your blood as I did mine,"

As soon as they had avenged themselves on their foes, they asked for water and washed at once; some for love of them and some for fear of them, all the servants waited on them in the best possible order. The sheriff was only five miles from there, and in a short time everything was told to him, how Gamelyn and Adam had made a grievous attack, had bound and wounded men against the king's peace. Then at once strife began to arise, and the sheriff set about to capture Gamelyn.

Now harken and listen, as you hope to have God give you a good end, and you shall hear good sport about young Gamelyn.

Twenty-four young men who considered themselves very brave came to the sheriff and said, by their faith, that they would fetch Gamelyn and Adam. The sheriff gave them permission—I am telling you the truth—they hurried fast, they would not tarry until they came to the gate inside which Gamelyn was. They knocked on the gate; the porter was near by and looked out through a hole like a sly man. The porter looked at them for a little while; he loved Gamelyn very much and was afraid of trickery, so he let the wicket stand fastened tight, and asked those without what they wanted. Then one spoke for all the large company, "Open the gate, porter, and let us enter." Then the porter said, "As I hope to have the use of my chin, you must tell your errand before you come in." "Tell Gamelyn and Adam that if they are willing we would like to speak two or three words with them." "Fellow," said the porter, "stand still there and I will go to Gamelyn to find out his wishes." The porter went in to Gamelyn at once and said: "Sir, I warn you that your foes have come here. The sheriff's men are at the gate to capture you both if you don't escape." "Porter," said Gamelyn, "as I hope to prosper well, I shall pay you for your words when I see my chance. Go to the gate again and stay with them a while, and very soon, porter, you shall see a trick." "Adam," said Gamelyn, "get ready to go; we have foes at the gate and not one friend. They are the sheriff's men who have come here, and they are sworn together that we shall be taken." "Gamelyn," said Adam, "hurry up quickly, and if I fail you today, may I have ill luck. We will welcome the sheriff's men in such a fashion that some of them shall make their beds in the mud." Gamelyn went out of the postern gate and he took a good cart pole in his hand. Adam took another great stave with which to help Gamelyn and he gave good blows. Adam felled two, and Gamelyn felled three, the others put their feet to the earth and began to run away.

"What?" said Adam, "as surely as I expect to hear mass, I have a drink of good wine—have some before you go!" "No, by God," they said, "your drink is not good, it would make a man's brain come out in his cap."

Gamelyn stood still and looked about him, and saw the sheriff coming with a great company. "Adam," said Gamelyn, "what is your advice now? Here comes the sheriff and wants to have our heads." Adam said: "Gamelyn, my counsel now is this, let us stay here no longer for fear things go badly with us. I suggest that we go to the woods before we are found: it is better for us to be at liberty there than tied up in town." Adam took young Gamelyn by the hand and each of the two drank a cup of wine, and afterward they took their course and went their way. Then the sheriff found the nest, but no eggs. The sheriff dismounted and went into the hall and found the lord fettered quite securely. The sheriff unfastened him at once and without delay, and sent for a doctor to heal his backbone.

Now let us leave this false knight to lie in his trouble and talk of Gamelyn and see how he is getting along.

Gamelyn marched quietly into the forest, and Adam the butler liked that very little. Adam swore to Gamelyn by St. Richard, "I see now that it is pleasant to be a butler, and that it would be preferable for me to carry the keys than to walk in this wild wood and tear my clothes." "Adam," said Gamelyn, "don't distress yourself: many a good man's child is brought into sorrow." And as they both stood talking together Adam heard the voices of men, and it seemed to him that they were near by. Then Gamelyn looked through the woods and saw sevenscore well-equipped young men, all of whom sat in a circle at their food. "Adam," said Gamelyn, "let us have no fear now, after misfortune comes improvement through the mercy of Almighty God; it seems to me that I catch sight of food and drink." Then Adam looked under the boughs of the trees, and he was glad enough when he saw food, for he hoped to God that he would have his share and he was filled with great longing for a good meal.

As he said that word the chief of the outlaws saw Gamelyn and Adam in the thicket. "Young men," said the chief, "by the good cross, I am aware of guests—may God send us none but good! Over there are two very well-equipped young men, and it may be that there are more if one were to look carefully. Get up, young men, and bring them to me. It is good that we should know what kind of men they are." Up jumped seven from the dinner and went to meet Gamelyn and Adam the butler. When they were near them then one of them said, "Young men, give up your bows and your arrows." Then said Gamelyn, who was young of age: "May he have great sorrow who gives them to you! I am putting this curse on myself only. Though you were to add five to your number, there would still be only twelve of you!" When they judged by his words that there was strength in his arm, there was no one of them all who wished to harm him, but rather said to Gamelyn mildly and quietly, "Come before our chief and tell him your desire." "Young men," said Gamelyn, "by your faith, what sort of man is your chief with whom you are?" They all answered without lying, "Our chief is crowned king of the outlaws." "Adam," said Gamelyn, "let us go in the name of Christ. He cannot refuse us food or drink for shame. If he is courteous and comes of gentle family, he will give us food and drink and do us some good." "By St. James," said Adam, "whatever harm I might get I will venture as far as the door if I might have food."

Gamelyn and Adam went forth together and they greeted the chief whom they found there. Then said the chief king of the outlaws, "What are you seeking, young men, in the thickets?" Gamelyn replied to the crowned king, "He has to walk in the wood who may not walk in the town. Sir, we do not come here to do any harm, unless we were to meet a deer to shoot at, as men who are hungry and can find no food, and are in hard circumstances beneath the linden trees." The chief had pity for Gamelyn's words and said, "You shall have enough. God have my pledge for that." He told them to sit down to rest themselves, and to eat and drink, and that of the best. As they sat and ate and drank well and finely then, one man said to another, "This is Gamelyn." Then the chief outlaw was taken into council and told that it was Gamelyn who had come there. As soon as he heard how things had happened he made him chief under him over them all. Within three weeks news came to them, to the chief outlaw who was then their king, that he should come home, for his peace was made, and he was very glad because of that good news. Then he said to his young men: "To tell the truth, news has come to me that I may no longer remain here." Then at once and without delay Gamelyn was made chief outlaw and crowned their king.

Then Gamelyn was crowned king of the outlaws, and lived for a time in the forest thickets. The false knight, his brother, was sheriff and lord and had his brother indicted out of hate and anger. Then his serfs were sorry and not a bit glad when their lord Gamelyn was made and proclaimed a wolf's head, and they sent out some of his men to where they could find him, to visit Gamelyn under the linden trees, to tell him the news as to how the wind had turned, and how all his property was stolen away and his men put to shame.

When they found him, they put themselves on their knees and lowered their hoods and greeted their lord: "Sir, for the good cross, do not get angry: we have brought you news, but it is not good. Your brother is sheriff now and has control of the bailiwick, and he has indicted you and caused you to be proclaimed wolf's head."

"Alas," said Gamelyn, "that I was ever so negligent that I did not break his neck when I broke his back! Go and greet well my servants and their wives. I will be at the next shire court, God protect my life!"

Gamelyn came to the next shire court ready enough, and there his brother was both lord and sire. Gamelyn came boldly into the moot hall and put down his hood among all the lords. "God save you all, lords who are here now. But ill may you prosper, broken-backed sheriff! Why have you done such shame and villainy to me as to have me indicted and proclaimed wolf's head?" Then the false knight thought to be avenged and he had Gamelyn seized so that he might speak no more. There could be no mercy finally but that Gamelyn was cast into prison and fettered firmly.

Gamelyn had a brother who was named Sir Ote, as good and courteous a knight as ever walked on foot. At once a messenger went to that good knight and told him completely how Gamelyn was treated.

19. **a wolf's head,** an outlaw.   39. **moot hall,** council hall.   49. **Ote,** the second brother.

As soon as Sir Ote heard how Gamelyn was served he was very sorry and not at all joyful, and he had a horse saddled and took to the road and came immediately to his two brothers. "Sir," said Sir Ote to the sheriff then, "we are only three brothers and we shall never be more, and you have put the best of us in prison. May evil come to such another brother as you are!" "Sir Ote," said the false knight, "leave your curse alone. By God, it shall go the worse with him because of your words. He has just been taken to the king's prison and there he shall remain until the judge comes." "By God," said Sir Ote, "it shall be better! I demand that you give him to me on bail until the next assize for general jail delivery, and then let Gamelyn stand to his chance." "Brother, on such an agreement I turn him over to you, and, by the soul of your father, who begot both you and me, unless he is ready when the judge sits you shall bear the judgment for all your great intelligence." "I agree indeed," said Sir Ote, "that it shall be so. Have him freed at once and hand him over to me."

Then Gamelyn was delivered to his brother Sir Ote, and that night the two of them remained together. In the morning Gamelyn said to the courteous Sir Ote: "Brother," he said, "in truth I must leave you, to see how my young men are leading their lives, whether they live in joy or in quarreling." "By God," said Sir Ote, "that is bad news: now I see that all the charge must fall on my head; for when the judge sits, if you are not found I shall be taken at once and tied up in your place." "Brother," said Gamelyn, "do not be dismayed, for by St. James in Galicia, whom many men have visited, if Almighty God preserves my life and reason, I will be there ready when the judge sits." Then Sir Ote said to Gamelyn: "May God protect you from dishonor! Come when you see that it is time and bring us out of blame."

Listen, and harken and keep still, and you shall hear how Gamelyn had his way completely.

Gamelyn went again under the forest branches, and found young men of valor playing there. Then young Gamelyn was happy and glad enough when he found his merry men under the boughs of the trees. Gamelyn and his men talked together, and they had good fun in hearing their master. They told him about the adventures which they had come upon, and Gamelyn told them again how he was tightly bound. While Gamelyn was outlawed he had no man's curse; there was no one who was the worse off on his account, except abbots and priors, monks and canons: he left nothing on them which he could take from them.

While Gamelyn and his men were having much amusement, his brother, the false knight—evil may he thrive!—was busily employed from one day to the other to bribe the jury to hang his brother. One day Gamelyn stood, and as he looked at the woods and the thickets in the uncultivated field, he thought about his brother and how he had promised him that he would be ready when the judge should sit. He decided that he would come before the judge without delay to keep his appointed day, and he said to his young men, "Get yourselves ready quickly, for when the judge sits we must be there, for I am under bail until I come, and my brother will be taken to prison in my place." "By St. James," said his young men, "if you advise that, command how it shall be and so it shall be done." While Gamelyn was coming where the judge sat, the false knight, his brother, did not forget to hire the men on his jury to hang his brother—if he didn't have one of them, he would have the other. Then Gamelyn came from under the forest branches and brought his brave young men with him.

"I see clearly," said Gamelyn, "that the judge is sitting. Go ahead, Adam, and see how things are going." Adam went into the hall and looked about; he saw great and strong lords standing there, and Sir Ote fettered very securely. Then Adam went out of the hall as though he were afraid. Adam said to Gamelyn and to all his companions, "Sir Ote stands fettered in the moot hall." "Young men," said Gamelyn, "you all hear this: Sir Ote stands fettered in the moot hall. If God gives us the grace to do well, he who brought him there shall pay for it." Then said Adam, who had gray hair: "May he have Christ's curse who bound him so painfully! If you, Gamelyn, will follow my advice, there is no one in the hall who shall come away with his head." "Adam," said Gamelyn, "we shall not do so, but we will kill the guilty and let the others go free. I will go into the hall and speak to the judge. I shall be avenged on those who are guilty. Take care, young men, to let none escape at the door, for I shall be judge this day to give judgments. God aid me in my new work today! Come with me, Adam, for you shall be my clerk." His men answered him and told him to do his best: "And if you have need of us, you shall find us ready. We will stand by you while we can hold out, and if we don't work in manly fashion, pay us no wages!" "Young men," said Gamelyn, "as I hope to prosper well, you shall find just as trusty a master in me."

Right where the judge was sitting in the hall Gamelyn went in among them. Gamelyn had his brother unfettered from his bonds. Then said his courteous brother, Sir Ote, "Gamelyn, you had almost stayed away too long, for the verdict has been brought in for me that I must hang." "Brother," said Gamelyn, "as God may give me good rest, they shall be hanged this day who are on your jury, and the justice too, who is the judge, and also the sheriff through whom it began." Then Gamelyn said to the judge, "Your power is over now, and you must rise. You have given judgments that are in bad order; I will sit in your seat and rearrange them correctly." The judge sat still and did not rise at once, and Gamelyn split his cheekbone. Gamelyn took him in his arms and said no more, but threw him over the bar and broke his arm. No one dared say anything but good to Gamelyn, for fear of the band who stood outside.

Gamelyn sat himself down in the judge's seat and Sir Ote, his brother, with him, and at his feet, Adam. Listen now to the joke that Gamelyn made when he was in the judge's place. He had the judge and his false brother fettered, and made them both come to the bar. When Gamelyn had done this, he did not rest until he had inquired who had been on the jury to judge his brother, Sir Ote, to hang. It seemed a long time to him before he knew who they were, but as soon as he did know he had them all fettered together, and brought to the bar and set in a row.

"By my faith," said the judge, "the sheriff is a rogue!" Then Gamelyn said to the judge, "You have given judgments of the worst assize, and the twelve jurors who were on the jury shall be hanged this day, as I hope to rest well." Then the sheriff said to young Gamelyn, "Lord, I ask you for mercy: you are my brother!" "Therefore," said Gamelyn, "have the curse of Christ, for if you were master, I should have the worst of it."

To make a short story and not to delay long, he ordered for himself a jury of his own strong men. The judge and the sheriff both were hanged high, to swing about with the ropes and to dry in the wind. And the twelve jurors—may he have sorrow who cares for that!—were all hanged securely by the neck. Thus the false knight, who had always led his life in falseness and folly, ended with his treachery. He was hanged by the neck and not by the purse. That was the reward which he got for his father's malediction.

Sir Ote the elder and young Gamelyn went with their friends to the king himself, and they made peace with the king in the best manner. The king loved Sir Ote greatly and made him judge, and after that the king made Gamelyn chief justice of all his free forest in both east and west. The king forgave all his strong young men their guilt, and afterward placed them in good offices.

Thus Gamelyn won his land and his people, and avenged him on his foes and paid them their reward. Sir Ote, his brother, made him his heir, and then Gamelyn married a wife who was both good and handsome. They lived together while it was Christ's will, and then Gamelyn was buried under the earth. And so shall we all be, no man can escape it. May God bring us to the joy that shall last forever!

MATTER OF BRITAIN

Arthur of Britain, his origin shrouded in mystery, caught and held the imagination of the world of story. We need not debate here whether or not there actually was a late fifth-century British or Romano-British leader who had some success against the invading Germans. If Arthur did not exist in life, it was necessary to invent him for literature. After a hint in the writing of the sixth-century historian Gildas, and a reference in the ninth-century work of Nennius, the first full-length biography was given in Geoffrey of Monmouth's *Historia Regum Britanniæ*, c. 1137. Geoffrey's sources are still a matter for furious controversy, but it is probably safe to say that he molded popular Celtic —that is, Welsh and Breton—traditions into historical or pseudo-historical form. Geoffrey's Arthur was a great king, an invincible conqueror, who was finally brought low by treachery in his own household. French writers of romance, notably Chrétien de Troyes, adopted him at once, and almost immediately we find a change in his character and position. The great king remains great in name and royal rank, but in the individual romances the emphasis shifts from him to some one of his knights. Gradually, almost imperceptibly, we see the operation of what is known as "epic degeneration," or the tendency to debase a hero. Instead of majestic, we find him petty and ridiculous, though often pathetic; no longer the great king-conqueror, but a deceived husband, more or less complacent in his shame. Except for the "historical" framework Arthur is in the background, a subsidiary figure from whose court knights set forth on adventures and to which they return, in triumph or disgrace, at the end.

Nowadays we think of Lancelot as Arthur's chief knight, but he is actually a newcomer, an upstart invented by the French writers of romance. Arthur's closest companion in the earliest forms of the cycle had been Gawain, the king's sister's son. This close uncle-nephew relationship is thought to be a survival from the ancient matriarchal system, and there are other significant examples: Hygelac and Beowulf, Charlemagne and Roland, Conchobar and Cu Chulainn, even Robin Hood and Will Scathlok (Scarlet). Gawain was the darling of the Middle English romancers, and his fame is celebrated in a dozen poems, the greatest of which by far is *Sir Gawain and the Green Knight*.

SIR GAWAIN AND THE GREEN KNIGHT

Sir Gawain and the Green Knight is found in a manuscript of the late fourteenth or early fifteenth century which also contains *The Pearl, Patience*, and *Purity*. The four poems are often held to be by one author, called for convenience' sake the Pearl Poet, a theory which, although impossible of absolute demonstration, is attractive. *Sir Gawain*, one of the finest of medieval romances, combines two stories, both of which had been told independently about Gawain and other heroes before they were brought together here. The Challenge or Beheading Game is found in the Old Irish *Bricriu's Feast* (see T. P. Cross and C. H. Slover, eds., *Ancient Irish Tales*, Holt, 1936, pp. 277 ff.), from which it made its way into French and ultimately into English. The story of the Temptation is also common, but it was the author of the lost French poem which lies directly behind our romance who first united the two. We must not, however, think of the Temptation as something put into the story in a haphazard way; it is an integral part of the romance, and every detail of it is woven into the mesh of the whole story.

The poet was an idealist who utilized his material in such a way as to stress the best virtues of knighthood as exemplified in the person of Gawain: bravery, honor, faith, and chastity. We must also admire his minute attention to detail in such passages as the description of the Green Knight and his steed, the arming of Gawain, and, above all, the accounts of the Green Knight's three hunting expeditions, which are as full as most medieval manuals of the chase and certainly far more picturesque. One of the most striking things about the poem is the attention given to external nature, which the poet handles in a way quite different from most medieval writers. Here is no conventional May-morning mood, no picture of a man-made, carefully tended landscape, but a realistic and varied portrayal of actuality.

Readers for whom Malory, or perhaps Tennyson, has been the authorized version of the Arthurian story will hardly recognize the principal character. This is the old Gawain before he was supplanted by Lancelot and deliberately debased by the writers who advanced the new hero. This Gawain is the one referred to by Chaucer:

"This straunge knyght, that cam thus sodeynly,
Al armed, save his heed, ful richely,
Salueth kyng and queene and lordes alle,
By ordre, as they seten in the halle,
With so heigh reverence and obeisaunce,
As wel in speche as in contenaunce,
That Gawayn, with his olde curteisye,
Thogh he were come agayn out of fairye,
Ne koude hym nat amende with a word."

He is the antithesis of Tennyson's Gawain, who came in a dream to Arthur before "that last weird battle in the west":

"the ghost of Gawain blown
Along a wandering wind, and past his ear
Went shrilling: 'Hollow, hollow all delight!
Hail, King! to-morrow thou shall pass away.
Farewell! there is an isle of rest for thee.
And I am blown along a wandering wind,
And hollow, hollow, hollow all delight!'"

And Bedivere says:

"'Light was Gawain in life, and light in death
Is Gawain, for the ghost is as the man.'"

It was a long unhappy road which ran from *Sir Gawain and the Green Knight* and "The Squire's Tale" to "The Passing of Arthur."

The poem is written in strophes of varying lengths, a number of long alliterative lines being followed by five short rhyming lines which mark the end of the stanza. The language is very difficult; love of detail, the requirements of alliteration, and an apparent fondness for unusual expressions led the poet to make use of a vocabulary far different from that found in the ordinary run of fourteenth-century verse.

The most comprehensive account of the poem is G. L. Kittredge's *A Study of Gawain and the Green Knight*, Harvard University Press, 1916. The present translation is from the edition of J. R. R. Tolkien and E. V. Gordon, Oxford, 1936; after the translation was already in proof, it was possible to take advantage of some of the suggestions in the edition by Sir Israel Gollancz, with introductory essays by Mabel Day and M. S. Serjeantson, Early English Text Society, No. 210, London, 1940.

I

AFTER the siege and the assault had come to an end at Troy, the city destroyed and burned to brands and ashes, then the man who had made the plots of treason there was well-known for his treachery, the greatest example on earth. It was Aeneas the glorious, and his noble kindred, who afterward subjugated kingdoms and became lords of

3. **the man**, probably Antenor, although Aeneas was also held guilty of treason in medieval accounts of the Trojan War.

SIR GAWAIN AND THE GREEN KNIGHT

very nearly all the wealth in the Western Isles. When noble Romulus went quickly to Rome, first of all he built that city with great pomp, and named it with his own name, as it is now called. Ticius went to Tuscany and began to build, Langobard to Lombardy and erected dwellings, and far across the English Channel with joy Felix Brutus founded Britain on many a wide slope, wherein fighting and distress and disaster have been at times, and both happiness and trouble have often alternated there since then.

And when Britain was founded by this powerful warrior, bold men who loved fighting multiplied there, and caused trouble which came to pass at many a time. More marvels have often occurred in this land since that very time than in any other of which I know. But of all the kings of Britain who dwelt here Arthur, as I have heard say, was ever the noblest. Therefore, I intend to relate a strange event on the earth, which some men consider a wonder to see, and a very curious adventure from among the marvelous tales concerning Arthur. If you will listen to this poem for a little while, I shall tell it with tongue as quickly as I heard it among men, as it is put down and set out in a brave and strong story, linked with true letters as has long been the custom in the land.

The king was lodged at Camelot on Christmas, with many fair lords, the best of knights, all the noble brothers of the Round Table in courteous fashion, with splendid revelry and carefree pleasures. Men took part in many tournaments there; these noble knights jousted very gallantly, and then rode to the court to sing and dance. The feast was the same there for fully fifteen days, with all the food and pleasure which men could devise; such noise of merrymaking and joy was glorious to hear, pleasant din in the daytime, dancing at night; all was happiness to the utmost degree in halls and chambers among the lords and ladies, as seemed most delightful to them. They remained there together in all the pleasure in the world, the most famous knights beneath Christ himself, and the loveliest ladies who ever lived, and he who ruled the court was the fairest of kings. All these comely people in the hall were in the prime of life, the most fortunate under heaven, and the king the greatest in spirit. It would be hard to name as bold a company on any castle mound.

When New Year was so fresh that it was but just come, on that day the company on the dais was served with twice the usual amount, after the king had come into the hall with his knights, when singing of mass in the chapel had been finished. Loud shouting was the speech of clerks and others, who celebrated Christmas once more, named it very often. Then the nobles ran forward to give presents, cried on high gifts of the New Year, gave them with their own hands, and argued earnestly concerning them. Ladies laughed very loudly, although they had lost, and he who won was not angry, as you may well believe. They made merry in this way until mealtime. After they had washed with due dignity, they went to their seats, the noblest knight always in a higher seat, as seemed best. Queen Guenever, very fair, was placed in the middle, arranged on the costly dais, adorned all about, fine rich silk at the sides, a canopy of excellent fabric of Toulouse over her, and carpets enough of cloth of gold, which were embroidered and set with the finest gems that could ever be proved of value, bought with money. The fairest to behold looked on there with gray eyes; no man could say truthfully that he ever saw one more beautiful.

But Arthur would not eat until all were served, he was so gay in his youth, and somewhat boyish: he liked his life to be an active one, and he loved little either to lie or to sit too long, his young blood and his restless brain stirred him so. Also another custom, which he had adopted in his magnificence, influenced him so that he would never eat on such a festal day before he had been related a strange story of some perilous matter, of some great marvel in which he could believe, of kings, of arms, or of other adventures, or unless a man implored him for some trusty knight to join with him in jousting, to hazard his existence, to set life against life, each to allow the other to have the advantage, as Fortune would help them. This was the king's custom wherever he was in court, at every splendid feast among his noble company in the hall. Therefore, proud of face, he stood up very bold on that New Year's day; he made merry with everyone.

Thus the bold king himself stood there, talking of courtly trifles in front of the high table. Gawain the good was set beside Guenever, and Agravain of the hard hand on the other side, both of them sons of the king's sister and very trusty knights. Bishop Baldwin sat at the head of the table, and Iwain, the son of Urien, dined beside him. These were set

---

5. **Ticius,** not mentioned elsewhere, but probably thought of as a descendent of Aeneas. 7. **Felix Brutus,** the eponymous founder of Britain, great-grandson of Aeneas— nowhere else called Felix. 26. **linked with true letters,** alliterative. 11. **had lost,** not clear; perhaps they had failed to receive particularly good gifts. 45. **high table,** on the dais. 46–48. **of the hard hand,** "à la dure mayn." **sons of . . . sister,** and King Loth of Orkney.

on the dais and sumptuously served, and afterwards many true men at the side tables. Then the first course came with the blaring of trumpets, which had many very bright banners hanging from them. There was a new noise of kettledrums along with the noble pipes, wild warblings and loudly awakened sounds, so that many a heart was uplifted at their bursts of music. Dainties of very costly foods came in addition, an abundance of fresh meats, and so many dishes that it was difficult to find a place before the people to set the silver plates which held the various stews on the table. Each knight took gladly what he desired. Each couple had twelve dishes and both good beer and bright wine.

Now I shall tell you no more of how they were served, for every man may know well that there was no lack there. A second new noise came near quickly, so that the prince could have permission to take his food, for scarcely had the sound ceased for a moment, and the first course been duly served in the court, when there came in at the hall door a terrible knight, one of the tallest on earth in stature. From the neck to the waist he was so squarely built and so thick, and his loins and his limbs so long and so great, that I believe he may have been half a giant on earth, or at all events I declare him to be the biggest of men, and also the most pleasant in size who could ride. His body was grim in back and breast, and his stomach and waist becomingly small, and all the parts of his body were in like manner very fair. Men wondered at the color which was seen in his appearance: he went as a hostile knight, and was entirely bright green.

This man and his clothes were all arrayed in green: a close-fitting and very straight coat which clung to his flanks, a fair robe over that, adorned on the inside with visible trimmed fur, the lining very elegant, the white fur shining, and his hood the same, which was caught back from his locks and laid on his shoulders; hose neat and pulled up of the same green, which clung to his calf, and below were fair spurs of bright gold, upon embroidered strips of silk richly marked with parallel stripes, and supports under his arches as the man rode; and all his clothing truly was bright green, both the stripes on his belt and the other gay stones which were profusely arranged on his fair dress, about him and his saddle, upon silk embroidery, so that it would be too hard to tell of half the details which were worked upon it, with birds and flies, in gay hue of green, with gold always in the middle. The pendants on the breast trapping of his horse, the splendid crupper, the ornamented studs on its bit, and all the rest of the metal, were enameled; the stirrups in which he stood were colored in the same way, and his saddlebow entirely after a similar fashion, and also the noble saddle-skirts, which always gleamed and glinted with green jewels. The horse which he rode on was certainly gay with that same green, a green horse, great and stout, a steed very hard to manage, restive in its linked bridle—it was completely suited to the man.

This man was very brightly clothed in green, and the hair of his head matched his horse. Fair waving hair covered his shoulders: a big beard like a bush hung over his breast, and it, with the noble hair that extended from his head, was clipped round in a circle above his elbows, so that half his arms under it were enclosed in the fashion of a royal cape that encloses the neck. The mane of that great horse was much like to it, well curled and combed with very many knots plaited in with gold thread about the beautiful green, with always one strand of hair and the next of gold. The tail and the forelock were plaited to match, and both fastened with a band of bright green adorned with very precious stones as far as the trimmed hair reached, then bound tight by a thong with an intricate knot at the top, where many a bright bell of refined gold rang. Such a horse on earth, nor such a man as rode him, was never before seen in that hall by sight of eye. He looked as bright as lightning, as all who saw him said. It seemed as though no man could survive his blows.

All the same he had neither helmet nor hauberk, nor armor for his upper body nor any plate armor that had to do with warfare, nor any spear nor shield with which to thrust or strike, but in one hand he had a branch of holly, which is most green when the groves are bare, and in the other hand a huge and monstrous axe, a cruel battle-axe to describe, if one could do so. The head was as great as an ell-long stick in length, the spike was all of green steel and hammered gold, the blade polished bright with a broad edge made to cut as well as sharp razors. The grim knight gripped it by a strong staff of steel which was bound with iron to the end, and all carved with beautiful designs in green. A thong was folded about it and fastened at the head, and so looped very often about the handle, with fine tassels enough fastened to it on buttons of bright green embroidered very richly. This knight came in and entered the hall, making his way to the high dais; he feared no danger,

---

2. **side tables,** the tables which were placed along the sides of the hall. 13–14. **Each couple.** The diners were served in pairs.

greeted no one, but he looked high above everyone. The first word that he uttered was: "Where," he said, "is the ruler of this company? I would gladly see that man and have speech with him." He looked at the knights and rolled his eyes back and forth. He ceased and looked carefully to determine who had the most renown there.

For a long time there was staring to behold the man, for everyone wondered what it could mean that a knight and a horse could get such a color, grown as green as grass and even greener it seemed, glowing brighter than green enamel on gold. Everyone who stood there watched intently and walked cautiously nearer to him, with all the wonder in the world as to what he would do. They had seen many marvels, but never such as this before, and therefore the people there considered it to be an illusion and magic. And so many a noble knight was afraid to answer, and they were all astonished at his voice, and sat stone-still in a dead silence through the splendid hall. It was as if they were all fallen asleep, their voices were so stilled—I think it was not all for fear, but somewhat for politeness—but they let him whom all should reverence speak to that knight.

Then Arthur beheld that marvelous happening before the high dais and courteously saluted him, for he was never afraid, and said: "Knight, welcome indeed to this place. I am the ruler of this dwelling and my name is Arthur. Alight graciously and remain, I pray you, and after that we will know what your desire is." "No," said the knight, "as He who dwells on high may help me, it was not my errand to remain any time in this dwelling; but because your glory, prince, is lifted up so high, and your city and your men are held the best, the boldest to ride in armor on horses, the most valiant and the worthiest among men, brave to amuse oneself with in other noble games; and here you have shown courtesy, as I have heard say, and that surely has brought me here at this time. You may be certain from this branch which I carry that I come in peace and seek no danger; for if I had journeyed martially in warlike fashion, I have a hauberk at home and a helmet too, a shield and a sharp spear, shining bright, and also, I think surely, other weapons to wield, but since I wish no battle, my apparel is less warlike. But if you are as brave as all men say, you will grant me cheerfully the game which I claim by right." Arthur answered and said, "Sir courteous knight, if you wish for actual battle, here you will lack no opportunity to fight."

"No, I seek no battle, I tell you faithfully; there are only beardless children about this bench. If I were arrayed in arms on a tall steed, there are no men here to match me, because their power is so weak. On that account I desire a Christmas game in this court, for it is Yule and New Year, and here are many brave men: if any in this house considers himself so hardy, so bold in blood, so mad in his head, that he valiantly dare to strike one blow for another, I shall give him as my gift this fine battle-axe—this axe, which is heavy enough—to handle as he pleases, and I shall take the first blow as unprotected as I sit here. If any man is so fierce as to try what I speak of, let him come swiftly to me and take this weapon—I relinquish it forever, let him keep it as his own—and I shall stand unflinching on this floor and take a blow from him. On the other hand, you will adjudge me the right to give him another without his offering resistance, and all the same I shall give him a respite of a twelvemonth and a day. Now hasten and let us see at once if anyone in here dares say anything."

If he had amazed them at first, now all the courtiers in the hall, both high and low, were even more silent. The knight on his horse turned in his saddle and rolled his red eyes about horribly, bent his bristling brows, shining green, swept his beard from side to side watching to see who would rise. When no one would speak to him, he coughed loudly and cleared his throat in lordly fashion and proceeded to speak to them. "What, is this Arthur's house," said the knight then, "all the fame of which runs through so many kingdoms? Where now are your pride and your conquests, your fierceness and your wrath and your boasts? Now the revelry and the renown of the Round Table is overthrown with a word of one man's speech, for all cower for fear without a blow offered!" With that he laughed so loudly that the king took offense; for shame the blood shot into his fair face and cheek. He became angry as wind, as did all who were there. The king, bold by nature, stood near that strong man, and said: "Knight, by heaven, your request is foolish, and as you have asked folly, it is right that you should find it. I know no man who is afraid of your big words. Now, for God's sake, give me your battle-axe and I shall grant you the request which you have asked." He jumped quickly to him and caught at his hand. Then the other warrior alighted proudly on his feet. Now Arthur had his axe and gripped the handle, sternly brandished it about, and thought to strike with it. The stout man before him stood upright, higher by a head and more than anyone in the house. There where he stood he stroked his beard with a fierce expression, and with an un-

17. **without . . . resistance,** not a certain translation.

moved countenance he drew down his coat, no more daunted or dismayed at his great blows than if any man at the bench had brought him wine to drink. Gawain, who was seated by the queen, bowed to the king: "I beg you now in plain words that this contest may be mine.

"If you would, honored lord," said Gawain to the king, "tell me to go from this bench and stand there by you, so that I might leave this table without discourtesy, and if my lady were not displeased, I would come to advise you before your noble court. For it does not seem proper, as is well known, when such a request is raised so loudly in your hall, that you should be desirous to take it upon yourself, while so many bold men sit about you at the bench, than whom there are none under heaven readier in temper, nor better bodies where fighting comes up on the field of battle. I am the weakest, I know, and feeblest in sense, and if one wished to know the truth, there would be the least loss in my life, for I am only praiseworthy inasmuch as you are my uncle, nor do I know any virtue in my body save your blood. And since this business is so foolish that it is not fitting for you, and since I have asked it from you first, grant it to me, and if I am not speaking fittingly let all this noble court decide freely." The nobles whispered together and then they all advised to relieve the crowned king and give the game to Gawain.

The king then commanded the knight to rise, and he arose very promptly and proceeded courteously, knelt down before the king, and seized that weapon, and he gave it to him amiably, and lifted up his hand and gave him God's blessing, and gladly bade him that his heart and hand should both be hardy. "Take care, cousin," said the king, "how you set about your cutting, and if you manage him correctly, I certainly believe that you will withstand the blow that he will offer you later." Gawain went to the man with the battle-axe in his hand, and he boldly awaited him: he was not the more dismayed for that. Then the knight in green spoke to Sir Gawain: "Let us restate our agreement, before we go further. First I entreat you, knight, that you tell me truly, so that I can believe it, how you are named." "In good faith," said the good knight, "I am called Gawain who offers you this blow, whatever may happen afterwards, and at twelvemonth from this time will take another from you, with whatever weapon you choose, and from no other living person." The other answered again, "Sir Gawain, as I hope to prosper, I am exceedingly anxious that you shall strike this blow.

"By God," said the green knight, "Sir Gawain, it pleases me that I shall receive from your hand what I have asked for here. And you have readily rehearsed, with very true reason and without omission, all the agreement for which I asked the king, except that you must give me your word, knight, that you will seek for me yourself, wherever you think that I may be found upon earth, and take such payment as you give me today before this noble company." "Where should I find you?" said Gawain. "Where is your place? By Him who created me, I don't know where you dwell, nor do I know you, knight, either your court or your name. But direct me there truly and tell me what you are named and I will employ all my intelligence to get there, and that I swear to you as truth, and by my faithful plighted word." "That is enough at New Year, no more is needed," said the knight in green to the courteous Gawain, "if I tell you truly—when I have the blow and you have struck me properly—and instruct you promptly about my house and my home and my own name, then you can ask how I am getting on and keep the compact. And if I utter no speech, then you will be better off, for you can stay in your own country and seek no further—but enough! Take your grim weapon and let us see how you can deal a blow." "Gladly, sir, in truth," said Gawain; he stroked his axe.

The green knight took his stand at once, he bent his head a little and uncovered the flesh, he laid his long lovely locks over the crown of his head, and let the naked neck appear in readiness. Gawain gripped his axe and lifted it on high, he put his left foot on the ground before him, and let the axe come down swiftly on the bare flesh, so that the sharp edge cleaved the bones of the man, and penetrated through the white flesh, and severed it in two, so that the blade of the brown steel bit into the ground. The fair head fell from the neck to the earth, so that many kicked it with their feet where it rolled away. The blood spurted from the body and gleamed on the green, and yet the man did not falter or fall any the more, but undismayed he sprang forward upon unweakened legs, and he reached out roughly to where the knights stood, seized his fair head, and lifted it at once. And then he went to his horse and caught the bridle, stepped into the stirrup irons, and leaped into the saddle, and he held his head in his hand by the hair. And the man sat down in the saddle as firmly as if no mishap troubled him, although he was headless there. He twisted his headless trunk about, that ugly body which was bleeding. Many were afraid of him by the time that he had made his speech.

For he held the head in his hand straight up, he

turned the face toward the noblest on the dais, and it lifted up its eyelids and looked with wide-open eyes, and spoke much with its mouth, as you may now hear: "See to it, Gawain that you prepare yourself to go as you promised, and seek faithfully, knight, until you find me, as you have promised in this hall, in the hearing of these warriors. Go to the Green Chapel, I charge you, to get such a blow as you have dealt—you have deserved it—which will be promptly given on New Year's morn. Many men know me as the Knight of the Green Chapel: on that account you will never fail if you seek to find me. Come, therefore, or you must be called recreant." With a violent roar he turned the reins and went out at the hall door with his head in his hands, so that fire flew from the flint beneath the hoofs of the horse. No one there knew to what land he went, any more than they knew from where he had come. What then? The king and Gawain laughed and grinned at that green man, yet without qualification it was declared among the men there to be a miracle.

Although Arthur, the courteous king, had wonder in his heart, he allowed no appearance of that to be seen, but spoke very loudly to the lovely queen with courteous speech: "Dear lady, do not be at all dismayed today. Such affairs are very fitting at Christmas, the playing of interludes, laughing and singing, along with the courtly carols of knights and ladies. Nevertheless, I may well turn to my food, for I have seen a marvel, I cannot deny that." He looked at Sir Gawain, and said courteously, "Now, sir, hang up your axe, which has cut enough." And it was put above the dais to hang on the wall tapestry, where all men could look upon it as a marvelous thing, and by a faithful description of it tell the wonder. Then these men together went to the table, the king and the good knight, and bold men served them with a double supply of all delicacies, the most excellent which could be; with all kinds of food and with minstrelsy too; with joy they spent that day until it came to an end in the land. Now take care, Sir Gawain, that because of danger you do not neglect to make trial of this adventure which you have undertaken.

II

This gift of adventure Arthur had first of all in the young year, for he desired to hear boasting. Although such words had been wanting for him when they went to their seats, now they were fully provided with serious work, their hands cram-full. Gawain was happy to begin these games in the hall, but have no surprise even if the outcome should be grievous; for though men are merry in their minds when they have strong drink, still a year passes very swiftly and never brings the same events: the beginning very seldom matches the end. Therefore this Yule went by, and the year after, and each season in turn followed the other. After Christmas came crabbed Lent, which makes trial of human flesh with fish and plainer food; but then the weather of the world contends with winter; cold shrinks into the earth, clouds rise; the rain descends in bright, warm showers, it falls upon the fair meadowland; and flowers appear there, the raiment of both grounds and groves are green; birds get ready to build, and sing gloriously for delight in the soft summer which afterward comes on the slopes; blossoms swell to bloom in the splendid and luxuriant hedgerows, and glorious enough music is heard in the lovely wood.

After that, the summer season comes with soft breezes, when the west wind blows gently on seeds and herbs. The plant which grows out of doors is very lovely when the moistening dew drops from the leaves, waiting for a delightful gleam from the bright sun. But then the autumn hurries and at once becomes severe, warns the plant to grow ripe for winter. With drought autumn makes the dust to rise, to fly very high above the face of the earth. Angry winds from the heavens struggle with the sun, leaves fall from the tree and light on the ground, and the grass which was formerly green now turns all gray; then everything which grew in the beginning becomes ripe and rots, and so the year passes through many yesterdays, and winter returns again, as in truth the world requires, until the harvest moon was come with the pledge of winter. Then Gawain at once thought of his troublesome journey.

Still he remained with Arthur until All Saints Day, and the king made a feast on that holiday for the knight's sake, with great and rich revelry of the Round Table. Very courteous knights and lovely ladies were in grief for love of that man, but nevertheless they spoke only of mirth: many a joyless man made jests there for the sake of that gentle knight. For after the meal he addressed his uncle with sorrow, and spoke of his journey and said plainly: "Now, sovereign lord of my life, I ask you for leave. You know the nature of this affair, and I am not anxious to tell you its troubles, not a bit; but I am setting out for the onslaught tomorrow without fail to seek the man in green, as God will guide me." Then the best men in the castle came together, Iwain, and Erec, and very many others, Sir Dodi-

38–39. All Saints Day, November 1.

nel le Savage, the Duke of Clarence, Lancelot, Lionel, and Lucan the good, Sir Bors and Sir Bedivere, both large men, and many other noble knights with Mador de la Port. All this company of the court came nearer to the king with sorrow in their hearts in order to advise the knight. There was much bitter grief felt in the hall, that anyone as noble as Gawain should go on that errand, to endure a grievous blow, and give no more blows with his own sword. The knight remained cheerful all the time, and said: "What should I fear? What can a man do except try severe and noble fates?"

He remained there all day and prepared himself in the morning; he asked early for his arms and they were all brought. First a carpet of rich silk stuff was spread on the floor, and much was the gilded armor that glinted on it. The bold man stepped upon it and handled the steel weapons, arrayed in a jacket of costly silk of Tharsia, and then fastened closely around his neck a cunningly made tunic of Cappadocian leather, which was trimmed on the inside with a pure white fur. Then they put the broad-toed steel shoes on the man's feet; his legs were wrapped in steel by means of fair greaves, with knee armor fastened on them, polished very clean, attached about his knees with knots of gold. Then excellent thigh-pieces, which fully covered his thick muscular thighs, tied to them with laces; and then the linked coat of mail of shining steel rings on fine material enveloped the man, and a well-burnished pair of arm pieces upon both his arms, with good and bright elbow guards, and gauntlets of steel plate, and all the fine equipment which should be of use to him at that time, with a vest of rich stuff; his gold spurs fastened proudly, girt with a very trusty sword on a silk girdle about his flank.

When he was clasped in arms, his armor was splendid: the smallest latchet or loop shone with gold. Armed as he was, he listened to mass, which was offered and honored at the high altar. Then he came to the king and to his companions at court, courteously took his leave of the lords and ladies; and they kissed him and conveyed him on his way, commending him to Christ. By that time Gringolet was ready and girt with a saddle which gleamed very gaily with many gold fringes, newly studded everywhere with nails prepared for that purpose. The bridle was marked around with stripes and trimmed with bright gold. The adornment of the breast-trappings and of the superb skirts, the crupper and the horsecloth, matched the saddlebow; and all was arrayed on a background of rich red-gold nails, which glittered and gleamed like a sunbeam. He then took his helmet, which was strengthened with staples and padded on the inside, and quickly kissed it. It was high on his head and fastened behind, with a fine covering over the visor, embroidered and adorned with the best gems on a wide silk strip, and on the seams birds, such as parrots, painted preening here and there, turtle-doves, and truelove knots depicted as thickly as though many a maiden in town had been engaged upon it for seven years. The circlet which surrounded the crown of his head was more precious: it had as many diamonds, both bright and shining, as one could desire.

Then they showed him the shield, which was of bright red with the pentangle painted in pure gold color. He seized it by the baldric and threw it around his neck—that became the man very well indeed. And I am determined to tell you why the pentangle belongs to that noble prince, even though it should delay me. It is a sign which Solomon once upon a time set as a token of fidelity by the symbolism which it has, for it is a figure which contains five points, and each line overlaps and is fastened to the other, and it is always endless and the English, as I hear, everywhere call it "the endless knot." On that account it is fitting for this knight and for his fair arms, because Gawain was known as a good knight, ever faithful in five ways and five times in each way, and as refined gold, free from every discourtesy, and graced with virtues among men. Therefore he bore the new pentangle on his shield and vest, as a man most true in words and the most gentle knight in speech.

First he was found faultless in his five senses, and secondly his five fingers never failed the knight, and all his trust on earth was in the five wounds which Christ received on the cross, as the creed tells us. And wherever this man was present in battle his steadfast thought was fixed on this, beyond all other things, that he derived all his high courage from the five joys that the gracious queen of heaven had from her child; for this reason the knight had her image suitably painted on the upper part of his shield, so that when he looked at it his courage never failed. The fifth five which I find that the man used consisted of his generosity, and his love of his fellow men more than all other things, his purity and his chivalry, which never failed, and last piety, which surpasses all qualities; these fault-

---

12. **severe and noble,** bad and good.   19. **Tharsia,** Turkestan.   44. **Gringolet,** Gawain's horse.   16. **pentangle** (pentacle), a five-pointed star. It was used by the Pythagoreans, and symbolizes perfection.   21. **Solomon.** Solomon's seal is a circle with a pentangle inside it.   42. **five joys,** the Annunciation, the Nativity, the Resurrection, the Ascension, and the Assumption.

less five were more firmly fixed in this knight than in any other. Now all these five virtues, truly, were arrayed in this knight, and each was joined to the other so that it had no end, and fixed upon five points, which were nowhere incomplete, nor came together in any direction, nor separated either, and, I find, it was without end at any angle anywhere, wherever the process began or came to an end. Therefore the knot was splendidly fashioned on his bright shield with red gold upon a red background: that is called by learned people the pure pentangle. Now the fair Gawain was prepared, and he caught his lance right there and bade them all good day, as he thought, forevermore.

He pricked his horse with the spurs and sprang on his way, so vigorously that sparks were struck out of the stones behind him. All who saw that fair knight sighed in their hearts, and all the knights together spoke quietly to each other, grieving for the handsome man: "By Christ, it is a pity that you, knight, who are so noble in life, must be lost. It is not easy, in truth, to find his match upon earth. It would have been more sense to have acted more carefully, and to have made that dear man a duke; it would suit him well to be a brilliant leader of the people of the land, and so it would have been better than to be destroyed completely, beheaded by an elvish man, for the vanity of pride. Whoever knew any king to take such counsel, like knights in trifles at Christmas games?" There was much warm water which poured from the eyes when that fair lord went from the house that day. He made no stop, but went swiftly on his way. He went on many a bewildering road, as I heard the book say.

Now this knight, Sir Gawain, rode through the kingdom of Logres for God's sake, although it seemed no jest to him. He often spent the night without companion in places where he did not find before him fare which he liked. He had no company but his horse in woods and on hills, nor any person save God to speak with along the way, until he had come nearly into North Wales. He kept all the islands of Anglesey on his left, and crossed over the fords by the promontories, over at the Holy Head, until he reached land again in the wilderness of Wirral; in that place lived but few who loved either God or man with a good heart. And ever as he went he asked the men whom he met if they had heard any talk of a green knight, or of the Green Chapel, in any region thereabout; and all said "No" to him, that never in their lives had they seen any man who was of such a green color. The knight went along strange roads on many a dreary slope. His countenance changed very often before he saw that chapel.

He climbed over many a cliff in strange countries; he rode as a stranger, having wandered far from his friends. At each riverside or stream where the knight passed he found a foe before him, except on unusual occasions, and that so foul and so dangerous that it was necessary for him to fight. The man found so many wonderful things among the hills that it would be too difficult to tell about the tenth part. Sometimes he fought with dragons, and also with wolves, sometimes with trolls which lived in the crags, with bulls and bears and at other times with boars, and with giants which pursued him from the high fell. Had he not been brave and enduring, and had the Lord not aided him, without doubt he would have been killed and dead on more than one occasion. But battle did not afflict him so much but that winter was worse, when the clear cold water was shed from the clouds, and froze before it could fall to the pale earth. He slept in his armor, nearly slain by the sleet, more nights than enough among the bare rocks, where the cold stream ran splashing from the mountain top and hung high above his head in hard icicles. Thus in peril and pain and very severe hardships this knight rode alone over the land until Christmas Eve. The knight at that time made his complaint to Mary, that she would direct him how to go and guide him to some habitation.

In the morning he rode gaily over a mountain into a deep forest, which was exceedingly wild; high hills were on every side, and at their feet woods of a hundred very great gray oak trees together. The hazel and the hawthorn were tangled one to the other, arrayed everywhere with rough shaggy moss, with many unhappy birds upon the bare twigs, which cheeped there piteously for pain of the cold. The knight hastened under them on Gringolet, all alone through many a mist and swamp, concerned for his religious observances, lest he should not manage to see the service of that Lord who on that very night was born of a maid to end our sorrow. And therefore he said, sighing: "I beg you, Lord, and Mary, who is the mildest mother so dear, for some lodging where I might devoutly hear mass and Your matins tomorrow; I ask it meekly and in addition, I pray promptly my pater and ave and creed." He rode along praying and cried out for his misdeeds; he crossed himself many times, and said, "Christ's cross bless me!"

The knight had only blessed himself three times when he became aware of a dwelling inside a moat

---

36. **Logres,** England, or at all events, Arthur's land. He was starting from Camelot.   46. **Wirral,** in the palatinate of Chester.

in the wood, above a lawn on a knoll, shut in under the boughs of many massive tree trunks about the ditches; the fairest castle that a knight ever owned, erected in a meadow with a park all around it, enclosed closely with a spiked palisade, which surrounded many trees for more than two miles. The knight beheld the castle from one side as it shimmered and shone through the fair oaks. Then he took his helmet off courteously and devoutly thanked Jesus and St. Julian, who are both kindly, that they had shown him courtesy and listened to his cry. "Now a good lodging," said the knight, "I beg from you still!" He then struck spurs into Gringolet with his gilt heels, and he went by chance to the main road, which speedily brought the knight in haste to the end of the bridge. The bridge was pulled up stoutly, the gates were shut fast, the walls were well constructed; it feared no blast of wind.

The knight who sat on his horse waited on the bank of the deep, double-channeled ditch which enclosed the place. The wall stood very deep in the water, and again it rose a huge height aloft, of hard hewn stone up to the cornice moldings, with projecting horizontal courses in the best style under the battlements; and then very fair watch-towers fashioned at intervals, with many pleasing windows that were fastened very neatly: that knight had never looked at a better outwork. And further he saw that very high hall, towers set up here and there, profusely provided with ornamental pinnacles, handsome and wonderfully high turrets which matched, with carved tops made with cunning art. He perceived many chalk-white chimneys on the tower roofs, which gleamed very white. So many painted pinnacles were scattered everywhere, clustered so thickly among the embrasures of the castle, that it certainly seemed as though it were cut out of paper. The noble knight on the horse thought it would be good enough if he might manage to come inside the enclosure, pleasant to lodge in that dwelling while the holy day lasted. He called out, and at once there came a very civil porter, who went to the wall on his business, and greeted the knight errant.

"Good sir," said Gawain, "will you take my message to the noble lord of this house, to beg for shelter?" "Yes, by Peter," said the porter, "and I certainly believe, knight, that you are welcome to remain while you like." Then that man went again quickly, and people courteously with him, to receive the knight. They let down the great drawbridge and went out politely, and knelt down on their knees upon the cold earth to welcome this same knight as seemed to them fitting. They allowed him to pass the broad gate, set open wide, and he raised them promptly, and rode over the bridge. Many men took him by the saddle while he alighted, and after that men bold enough stabled his horse. Knights and esquires came down then to bring this man into the hall with joy. When he lifted up his helmet, plenty of them hastened to take it from his hand, in order to serve the gracious man. They took both his sword and his shield. He then greeted each of the men very courteously, and many proud men pressed forward to honor that prince. They brought him all dressed in his armor to the hall, where a fine fire burned fiercely on the floor. Then the lord of the people came from his chamber to meet the man in the hall with honor. He said: "You are welcome to remain as you like. All that is here is your own to have and use at your will." "Many thanks," said Gawain. "May Christ repay you for it!" Each embraced the other in his arms as men who were glad.

Gawain looked at the man who was greeting him graciously, and thought that he was a bold warrior who owned the castle, a big man, indeed, and in the prime of life. His beard was broad, bright, and beaver-colored; he was stern, standing firm on stalwart legs, with a face fierce as fire, and noble in his speech. And it became him well, truly, as the man thought, to hold a lordship over good retainers in tranquillity. The lord went to a chamber and quickly commanded that a man be assigned to Gawain, to serve him humbly; and there were men enough ready at his command, who brought him to a fair bedroom, where the bedding was splendid, curtains of pure silk with bright-gold borders, and coverlets of very elaborate design with beautiful panels, of white fur embroidered above at the sides, curtains running on ropes, red-gold rings, tapestries of red silk of Toulouse and also silk of Tharsia hung on the walls, and on the floor underfoot of similar sort. There, with mirthful talk, the man was relieved of his coat of mail and of his clothes. Men promptly brought him fine robes, to take possession of, and to change and to choose the best. As soon as he took one with flowing skirts which fitted him well and was clothed in it, to nearly every man it seemed that spring was in his appearance, all his limbs under it brilliant and delightful in colors, so that it appeared to them that Christ never made a fairer knight. From wherever in the world he came it seemed that he must be a matchless prince where fierce men fought in the field.

10. **St. Julian,** the saint of hospitality; see *The Canterbury Tales*, "The General Prologue," l. 340, page 177.

27. **beaver-colored,** reddish brown.

Before the fireplace, where charcoal burned, a chair was agreeably prepared for Gawain with coverings, cushions upon quilted counterpanes, both of which were beautiful; and then a gay mantle of rich brown stuff was thrown on the man, embroidered very finely, and inside well lined with fur of the best skins, all adorned with ermine, and his hood of the same material. And he sat on that seat very nobly, and warmed himself quickly, and then his state of mind improved. Soon a table was set upon very fair trestles, covered with a clean cloth that appeared pure white, an overcloth, and salt cellar, and silver spoons. The knight washed to his pleasure and went to his food. Men served him properly with various and excellent broths, seasoned in the best fashion, with twice the usual amount, as was right, and many kinds of fish, some baked in bread, some grilled on the flames, some boiled, some flavored with spices in a stew, and always such cunningly made sauces as were pleasing to the man. The warrior readily and often courteously called it a feast, when all the knights together spoke to him in friendly fashion as to a well-bred man: "You now take this fast fare, but later it shall be improved." That man made merry because of the wine that went to his head.

Then it was inquired and asked tactfully by discreet questions put to him by that prince, until he acknowledged that he was of the court which the noble and courteous Arthur rules alone, he who is the powerful royal king of the Round Table, and that it was Gawain himself who was sitting in that dwelling, come for that Christmas feast, as chance had befallen him. When the lord learned that he had that man with him, he laughed loudly at it, so pleasant it seemed to him, and all the men in the castle were very joyful to appear promptly at that time in his presence, to whose person belongs all excellence and bravery and refined manners, and who is ever praised: his fame is the greatest above all men on earth. Each man said quietly to his companion: "Now we shall properly see acts of practiced skill in manners and spotless expressions of noble conversation; we may learn without asking what profit there is in speech, since we have received that fine father of good breeding. Truly God has graciously given us His mercy, in that He permits us to have such a guest as Gawain at a time when men shall sit and sing joyfully of His birth. This man will now bring us to an understanding of noble manners; I expect that those who listen to him will learn about the way lovers ought to talk."

When the dinner was over and the nobles risen, the time had nearly reached night. Chaplains took the path to the chapels, and rang the bells with festive peals, just as they ought, for the devout evensong of the festival. The lord went there, and also the lady, who entered gracefully into a beautiful closed pew. Gawain hastened gaily and went there at once. The lord seized him by the fold of his garment and led him to sit down, and recognized him familiarly and called him by his name, and said that he was the most welcome man in the world. And he thanked him heartily, and each saluted the other, and they sat soberly together during the service. Then the lady wished to look at the knight, and she came out of her pew with many beautiful women. She was fairest of all others in skin, flesh, and face, and in proportion and color and qualities, and, as the knight thought, more lovely than Guenever. He went through the chancel to salute the gracious one. Another lady, who was older than she, led her by the left hand; she seemed to be an aged lady, and greatly honored by the knights round about. But those ladies were unlike to look at, for if the young one was fresh, the other was withered; rich red appeared everywhere on the one, but rough wrinkled cheeks hung in loose folds on the other; the kerchiefs of the one, with many fine pearls, exposed her breast and her bright naked throat, which shone whiter than snow that falls on the hills; that other was attired with a gorget over the throat, wrapped over her black chin with chalk-white veils, her forehead enfolded in silk, muffled up everywhere, turreted and tricked out with ornamental details, so that no part of that lady was exposed except the black eyebrows, the two eyes, the nose, and the naked lips, and those were unpleasant to look at and extremely bleared. Men might call her a worshipful lady on earth, in God's name! Her body was short and thickset, her buttocks swelling and broad—sweeter to taste was the one whom she was leading!

When Gawain glanced at that gay lady, who was looking at him graciously, he took leave of the lord and went to meet them. He greeted the elder, bowing very low, but the lovelier he embraced a little in his arms, he kissed her sweetly, and spoke in knightly fashion. They asked him for his acquaintance, and he quickly requested to be their true servant, if it were pleasing to them. They took him between them, with conversation they led him to the chamber and to the fireplace, and they asked at once for spices, which men hastened to bring to them unsparingly, and each time pleasant wine with them. The lord jumped up joyfully very often, thought to have mirth made at many times, took his hood off gaily, hung it on a spear, and offered it for them to win as an honor to see who could make the greatest mirth that Christmas time: "And I shall try, by my faith, to contend with the best, before I lose my garment with the help of my friends." Thus the lord made merry with laughing words, to please Sir Gawain with games in the hall that night, until it was time that the lord ordered lights. Sir Gawain took his leave and went to his bed.

On the morning as each man remembered the time when Our Lord was born to die for our fate, joy grew in every place in the world for His sake; and so it did there on that day by means of many delights, at both meat and mealtime brave men arranged carefully made dishes of food upon the dais. The old, ancient woman sat in the highest seat; the lord, as I believe, took his place beside her politely. Gawain and the gay lady sat together, right in the middle, where the food properly came first, and then was fairly served through all the hall to each man according to his rank, as seemed best fitting for them. There was food, there was mirth, there was much joy, so that to tell of it would be difficult for me, even if, by chance, I took pains to trouble myself to describe it in detail. But yet I know that Gawain and the fair lady got such comfort from their companionship together, because of the pleasant conversation in their private words, with pure and courteous talk free of all indelicacy, that their amusement was superior in truth to any princely play. Trumpets and kettledrums, much music of pipes was present there. Every man minded his own business, and those two minded theirs.

Great joy was made there on that day and on the next, and the third came on afterwards as merrily. The joy on St. John's Day[35] was excellent to hear, and it was the last day of the entertainment, as the people there thought. There were guests to leave in the gray morning, and so they stayed awake marvelously, drank wine, and danced unceasingly with pleasant carols. At last, when it was late, they took their leave, each strong man to go on his way. Gawain said good day to the lord, but the good man seized him, led him to his own chamber, beside the fireplace, and there he held him back, and courteously thanked him for the delightful favor which he had shown him, in honoring his house at that festival and gracing his castle with his fair company: "Certainly, sir, while I live, I will be the better because Gawain has been my guest at God's own feast." "Many thanks, sir," said Gawain. "In good faith it is yours, all the honor is your own—may the High King reward you! And I am a man to do your command at your will in high and low, as I am bound thereto with right." The lord earnestly tried to keep the knight longer; Gawain answered him that in no way could he do that.

Then the warrior asked him courteously what grievous deed had driven him from the king's court, so daringly at that precious time to ride by himself, before the holy days had completely passed from the dwellings of man. "Truly, sir," said the man, "you are telling the truth, a great and pressing mission forced me from home, for I myself am summoned to such a place that I do not know where in the world to go to find it. I would not fail to reach it on New Year's morn for all the land in Logres, as Our Lord may help me! On that account, sir, I make this enquiry of you here, namely, that you will tell me truly if you have ever heard any story about the Green Chapel, where it stands on the ground, and of the knight, green in color, who guards it. An appointment was established between us by solemn agreement for me to meet that man at that fixed place, if I could live to do it. And but a little time now remains before that same New Year, and I would rather see that man, if God will permit me, by God's Son, than have power over any good thing! Therefore, certainly, by your leave, it is necessary for me to go; I have barely three days to get about, and I would as soon fall dead as fail in my business." Then the lord said, laughing: "Now it is necessary for you to stay, for I shall direct you to that place by the time's end; let the place on earth where the Green Chapel is trouble you no more. For you shall be at ease in your bed, man, until late in the day, and ride on the first of the year, and come to that place in mid-morning, to do what you like there. Remain here until New Year's Day, and then get up and depart. Someone will put you on the right road; it is not two miles from here."

Then Gawain was very glad and he laughed merrily: "Now I thank you heartily for this beyond everything else; now that my adventure is accomplished I shall remain at your desire, and do whatever else you decide." Then the lord took hold of him and set him beside him, and let the ladies be fetched to please them the better. There was pleasant delight for them among themselves. The lord out of love uttered such merry words, as if he were a man who was likely to take leave of his senses and did not know what he was about. Then he spoke to the knight, crying loudly: "You have determined to do the thing which I command; will you keep that promise here at this very moment?" "Yes, sir, truly," said the faithful knight, "while I remain in your castle, I will be obedient to your command." "Because you have traveled," said the man, "jour-

---

35. St. John's Day, December 27.

neyed from far away, and then kept awake with me, you are not well recovered in either sustenance or sleep, as I know truly. Tomorrow you shall remain in your upper room and be at your ease until time for mass, and go to meals when you wish with my wife, who shall sit with you and amuse you with her company until I come to court. You stay here, and I shall get up early, for I wish to go hunting." Gawain agreed to all this, bowing like a courteous man.

"Still further," said the man, "let us make an agreement: whatever I get in the woods shall become yours, and whatever gain you acquire, exchange it with me. Good sir, let us strike a bargain thus, to answer with truth, whether, man, something worthless or better fall to our lot." "By God," said Gawain the good, "I agree to it, and whatever you wish to play, it seems pleasant to me." "Bring us the drink; this bargain is made," so said the lord of that people. They each laughed, these lords and ladies drank and trifled and reveled as long as they liked; and then with elaborately polite behavior and many fair words they stood up and halted and spoke softly, kissed very sweetly, and took their leave. With many active servants and shining torches each man was brought at the last very quietly to his bed. Yet before they went to bed they often recalled the terms of the compact. The old lord of that people knew well how to keep sport going.

III

The people arose very early before day, the guests who wished to go called their servants, and they made haste to saddle the horses quickly, prepare equipments, pack their bags; those of the highest rank dressed themselves, all prepared to ride, they leaped up lightly, seized their bridles, each man on the way which pleased him well. The dear lord of the land, with very many men, was not the last clothed for riding. When he had heard mass he ate a light meal hurriedly, and made haste quickly with his bugle to the hunting-field. By the time that any daylight shone upon the earth he and his men were on their tall horses. Then the dog-grooms who could leash their dogs together opened the kennel door and called them out, blew mightily three single notes on the bugles. The hounds barked for that reason and made a loud noise. And they punished and turned back those dogs that strayed away—there were, as I have heard, a hundred of the best hunters. The keepers went to the hunting stations, huntsmen cast off the leashes. Then a great noise rose in the forest from the good blasts.

At the first utterance of the quest the wild creatures trembled. Deer ran in the valley, foolish with fear; they hastened for the heights, but they were suddenly turned back by the ring of beaters, who shouted vigorously. They let the harts with high heads have the path, the fierce bucks, too, with their spreading horns, for the generous lord had forbidden that any man should interfere with the male deer in the close season. The hinds were restrained with "Hey!" and "Ware!" The does were driven to the deep valleys with great noise. There one could see the rushing flight of arrows as they were loosed—at each turn in the wood an arrow flew—which mightily bit into the brown hide with their broad heads. Behold! they cried out, and bled, and died on the slopes, and hounds in a rush always followed them swiftly. Hunters with loud horns hastened after them with such an echoing cry as though the cliffs had broken. Whatever animal escaped the men who were shooting was pulled down and torn apart at the receiving-stations, by the time they were driven from the heights and pursued to the waters. The men at the lower stations were so skillful, and the greyhounds so large, that they seized them at once and tore them down right there, as fast as men could look. The lord, carried away with joy, often galloped and dismounted and thus passed the day with pleasure until dark night.

Thus the lord sported by the borders of the woods, and the good man Gawain lay in his fair bed, rested snug until the daylight shone on the walls, under the fair coverlet, curtained about. And as he was slipping into slumber, he heard a little noise made quietly at his door and heard it quickly open. He lifted his head up out of the bed clothes, and threw up a corner of the curtain a little, and looked warily in that direction to see what it might be. It was the lady, most lovely to behold, who drew the door to after her very stealthily and still, and came toward the bed; and the man was embarrassed and laid himself down cunningly and acted as though he were asleep. And she stepped quietly and stole to his bed, threw up the curtain and crept inside, and sat down gently on the side of the bed, stayed there a very long time to see when he would awake. The man lay lurking for a long while, and pondered in his mind what that occurrence might result in or amount to—it seemed to him a strange thing, but still he said to himself, "It would be more proper for me to discover at once with conversation what she wishes." Then he awoke, and stretched himself and turned toward her, and opened his eyelids, and made out as if

1. **quest,** baying of the hounds.   5. **high,** antlered.

surprised, and blessed himself with his hand, as if to be the safer from temptation by his prayer. She appeared very lovely, with chin and sweet cheek in which red and white were mingled, and with small laughing lips.

"Good morning, Sir Gawain," said that gay lady. "You are an unwary sleeper, since one can steal in here. Now you are caught in a moment! Unless we can make a truce, I shall bind you in your bed, be sure of that." All laughing, the lady uttered these jests. "Good morning, fair lady," said Gawain the joyful. "I shall be at your desire, and that pleases me very well, for I surrender promptly and cry for mercy, and that is the best course, by my judgment, as I am compelled to it by necessity." And so he jested in return with many a happy laugh. "But, lovely lady, if you would grant me leave, and release your prisoner, and ask him to rise, I would go from this bed and dress myself better; then I should obtain more comfort in talking with you." "Certainly not, fair sir," said that sweet thing. "You shall not rise from your bed, I have a better plan for you: I shall wrap up the other half of you too, and then talk with my knight whom I have taken. For I know well, truly, that you are Sir Gawain, whom all the world honors wherever you ride. Your honor, your courtliness, is courteously praised by lords, by ladies, by all who have life. And now you are here, indeed, and we are but alone. My lord and his people are gone far away, the other men are in their beds and also my women, the door is closed and locked with a stout door-pin. And since I have in this house the man whom everyone likes, I shall in speech make good use of my time while it lasts. You are welcome to my body, to take your own pleasure; it is fitting of sheer necessity for me to be your servant, and I must be."

"In good faith," said Gawain, "it seems to me fortunate, although I am not the man of whom you spoke. I am a creature unworthy to merit such honor as you describe here, I know myself too well. By God, I would be glad, if it seemed good to you, to do what I could in word or deed for your pleasure—it would be a great joy." "In good faith, Sir Gawain," said the gay lady, "if I were to find fault with or count as little the excellence and prowess which pleases everyone else, it would show little courtesy. But there are enough ladies who would now rather have you, gracious one, in their possession, as I have you here, to play pleasantly with your charming words, to obtain comfort for themselves and to assuage their troubles, than to have much of the treasure and gold which they own. But I praise that very Lord who rules the sky that I have through His grace wholly in my hand that which all desire." She who was so fair of face behaved graciously to him, and the knight replied to everything she chanced to say with proper remarks.

"Madam," said the merry man, "may Mary reward you, for, in good faith, I have found your generosity to be noble; and people very often receive praise from others because of their deeds, but the honor that they give me is not at all for my deserts. The honor is really yours, who know only good." "By Mary," said the noble lady, "I think quite otherwise, for if I were worth all the multitude of women alive, and all the wealth of the world were in my hand, and if I were to bargain and choose to get myself a husband, because of the qualities of beauty, courtesy, and happy manner which I have known here, knight, in you, and which I had heard of before and hold now to be true, there would be no man on earth chosen before you." "Certainly, noble lady," said the man, "you have chosen much better, but I am proud of the value which you put on me, and as your sincere servant, I hold you my sovereign, and I become your knight, and Christ repay you!" Thus they spoke many things until past mid-morning, and the lady always behaved as if she loved him very much. The knight acted with discretion and behaved very courteously. "Though I were the fairest of women," the lady thought, "the less love would he have for me"—by reason of the harm that he sought without delay, the blow which must strike him down, and which must necessarily be done. The lady then spoke of leave-taking, and he granted it to her at once.

Then she said good day to him, and laughed with a glance, and, as she was standing there, she amazed him with strong words: "Now may He who blesses each speech reward you for this entertainment, but I am debating in my mind if you are Gawain." "Why is that?" said the knight, and he asked quickly, afraid lest he had done amiss in the manner of his speech. But the lady reassured him and said as follows: "As good a man as Gawain is properly held to be—and good manners are enclosed in him so completely—could not easily have stayed so long with a lady without having asked a kiss, out of his courtliness, by the hint of some trifle at the end of some story or another." Then said Gawain, "Let it be done as you wish. I shall kiss at your command, as a knight ought to do, and, further, lest he displease you; so plead the case no more."

7–10. **and people . . . deserts**, a difficult passage.
47–48. **hint . . . another.** He would have found some way to lead up to it.

With that she came nearer, and took him in her arms, bent down lovingly and kissed the man. Each entrusted the other fittingly to Christ. She went out of the door without more noise, and he prepared to rise and at once made haste, called to his chamberlain, chose his clothes, came forth, when he was ready, gladly to mass. And then he went to his meal, which duly occupied him, and made merry with play all day until the moon rose. Never was a man entertained better by two such noble ladies, the older and the younger. They had much pleasure together.

And all this time the lord of the land had gone about his sports, to hunt in the woods and heath for barren hinds. He slew such a number of does and other deer by the time that the sun sank in the west, that it would be a wonderful thing to tell of. Then they impetuously assembled in a throng at the end, and quickly made a quarry of the slain deer. Those of highest rank went with plenty of men, brought together the fattest animals that were there, and had them cut open as the task demanded. Some who were there examined them at the assay, and they found two fingers' breadth of fat in the poorest of them all. Then they slit the hollow above the breastbone, and took out the first stomach, cut it away with a sharp knife and sewed up the flesh. After that they cut at the four legs and tore off the hide, then cut open the belly and took out the bowels, throwing them out swiftly, and also took out the flesh of the knot. They laid hold of the throat, and promptly separated the gullet from the windpipe, and tossed out the guts. Then they cut out the shoulders with their sharp knives, drew them through a little hole, so that they had whole sides. Afterwards they cut up the breast and pulled it in two, and once more they began at the throat, cut it up swiftly as far as the fork of the legs, cleared out the avanters, and truly after that quickly cut all the membranes along the ribs. So they cleared away correctly along the backbone, straight down to the haunch, which hung all together, and heaved it up whole and cut it off there, and that they took to be the numbles, as I believe it is naturally called by name. They cut the folds of skin behind by the fork of the thighs. They hurried to cut it in two, and to separate it by the backbone.

Then they cut off both the head and the neck, and afterwards swiftly separated the flanks from the backbone, and they threw the raven's fee up in a thicket. Now they pierced either thick side through by the rib, and hung each of them by the hocks of the legs, as it was fitting for each man to have for his fee. Upon the skins of a fair beast they fed their hounds with the liver and the lungs, the tripe, and with bread soaked in blood mixed in with them. They blew the capture-blast vigorously, and bayed their hounds, then they took their flesh, turned toward home, blowing loudly many resounding notes. By the time that daylight was over, the company had all come into the pleasing castle, where the knight remained quietly. The lord came where there was joy and a bright fire kindled; when Gawain met him there was only delight to their desire.

Then the lord commanded to gather all the household in the hall, both the ladies to come down with their maidens before all the people on the floor. He ordered men truly to bring his venison before him, and pleasantly in sport he called Gawain, exhibited to him the tally of nimble beasts, and showed him the white grease cut from the ribs. "How does this game please you? Have I won esteem? Have I deserved hearty thanks for my skill?" "Yes, certainly," said the other man, "here is the fairest bag that I have seen in winter this seven years." "And I give it all to you," said the man then, "for you claim it as your own by the agreement of the covenant." "This is true," said the knight, "and I say the same to you: that which I have won with honor in this dwelling, certainly it belongs to you with as good will." He embraced his fair neck in his arms and kissed him as fittingly as he could devise. "Take there my winnings, I gained nothing else. I would freely grant it, even if it were more." "It is good," said the good man, "many thanks for it. It may be of such a nature that it is the better of the two, if you will declare to me where you won this same wealth by your own wit." "That was not the bargain," said he; "you can ask me no more—for you have taken what is due to you, be certain that you may have nothing else." They laughed and made merry with words that were praiseworthy. They went to supper at once, with dainties fresh enough.

And then they sat in the chamber by the fireplace, men often brought excellent wine to them, and once more they agreed in their boasting to carry out in the morning the same compact that they had made before: that whatever happened they would exchange their winnings, whatever new they got, when they met at night. They agreed to the compact before all the court; the drink was brought forth joyfully at that time, and then at the

---

19. quarry, the pile of the animals killed during the day. **23. assay,** to see how fat they were. **31. knot,** probably a knot of flesh in the neck. **39. avanters,** part of the **numbles** (entrails used for food). **50. raven's fee,** a regular offering.

last they lovingly took their leave, each man quickly made haste to his bed. By the time that the cock had crowed and cackled no more than thrice, the lord had jumped from his bed, and each one of his followers, so that before day broke the food and the mass had been duly dispatched, and the company gone to the wood to the hunt. Loud with hunting array and horns they soon passed through plains, and uncoupled the dogs that ran a headlong course among the thorns.

Soon they called for a quest on the side of a marsh, the huntsman encouraged the hounds which first drew attention to it; he uttered wild words with a loud noise. The hounds which heard it hurried there quickly, and forty at once fell swiftly on the trail. Then there rose such a babel and din of the assembled dogs that the rocks round about rang. The hunters encouraged them with horn and mouth. Then they rushed all together in a throng between a pool in that wood and a forbidding crag. On a rocky hill by a cliff, at the edge of the marsh, where the rough rock was fallen in confusion, the dogs came to the dislodgment, and the men after them. The men cast about both the crag and the rocky hill until they knew that the beast which the bloodhounds were announcing there was within them. They then beat on the bushes and ordered him to arise, and he disastrously made out at the men across his path. The most marvelous of swine rushed out there, a wild boar which had long since grown to great age away from the herd. For he was fierce, the greatest of all boars, very grim when he grunted, which dismayed many, for he thrust three to the ground at the first rush, and sprang forth at great speed without more harm. The others shouted "Hi!" very loudly, and cried "Hay! Hay!" They had horns to their mouths, they called the recheat vigorously. Many were the merry voices of men and hounds that made haste after this boar with clamor and noise to kill him. He very often stood at bay, and injured the hunting-pack on all sides. He hurt some of the hounds, and they howled and yelled piteously.

The men pressed ahead to shoot at him then, loosed their arrows at him, hit him often; but the points that struck in the skin and flesh at his shoulders failed at the toughness, and the barbs would not bite on his brow, though the smooth shaft burst asunder in pieces. The head rebounded wherever it hit. But when the blows of their severe strokes hurt him, then, frenzied from fighting, he rushed at the men, hurt them fiercely where he hastened forth, and many became terrified at that and drew back.

37. **recheat**, a call to bring the hounds together.

But the lord galloped after him on a light horse, he blew his bugle like a man bold in battle. He blew the recall, and rode through thick bushes, following this wild swine until the sun came down. In this way they carried on the day with such deeds, while our lovely man, Gawain, lay pleasantly at home in his bed, in clothes rich in color. The lady did not forget, but came to greet him. She attacked him very early in order to alter his attitude.

She came to the curtain and peeped at the knight. Sir Gawain welcomed her fittingly first of all, and she replied to him again very eagerly with her words, seated herself gently by his side, laughed very much, and with a loving look said these words to him: "Sir, if you are Gawain, it seems a wonder to me that a man who is always disposed to good behavior should not know how to perceive the manners of polite society, and if someone teaches you to understand them, you put them out of your mind. You have promptly forgotten what I taught you yesterday in the truest kind of talk I knew." "What is that?" said the knight. "Certainly I don't know. If what you say is true, the blame is my own." "Yet I taught you about kissing," said the fair lady then, "that wherever a favorable look is evident one should claim it at once. This is fitting for every knight who uses courtesy." "My dear lady," said the bold man, "stop such talk, because I dared not do so, lest I be refused. If I were denied, I should certainly have been wrong when I offered." "My faith," said the noble woman, "you cannot be refused, for you are stout enough to compel with strength, if you wish, in case anyone were so ill-bred as to deny you." "Yes, by God," said Gawain, "your speech is good, but compulsion is considered unlucky in the country where I dwell, and so too is every gift that is not given with good will. I am at your command, to kiss when you like, you may begin when you wish, and leave off soon after when it pleases you." The lady bent down and kissed his face sweetly. They had much discussion about the grief and happiness that there is in love-making.

"I should like to know from you, knight," the noble lady said there, "if you will not be angry about it, what the reason is that, so young and brisk as you are at this time, so courteous, so knightly, as you are known to be, and reputed to be the fairest warrior of your time, with your words and your honor spread abroad everywhere, I, who

35. **your speech is good**, what you say is true. 48. **to be**. At this point the translator departs from the original order, so that a long parenthesis may be removed from the middle of a sentence.

have sat here by you on two occasions, have never yet heard from your mouth any words, few or many, which deal with love. For conspicuous in all knighthood, and the chief thing praised, is the faithful game of love, and the science of arms. To tell of the deeds of true knights is the inscribed title and text of their works, how men for their true love have risked their lives, endured grievous times for their love, and afterwards avenged themselves with their valor and dispelled their care, and brought joy to bower by their own virtues. And you, who are so courteous and gracious in your vows, ought eagerly to show and teach a young thing some signs of the ways of true love. Why! are you ignorant, who have all this renown? Or do you consider me too stupid to hear your courtly conversation? For shame! I came here all alone, and sit here to learn some sport from you. Do teach me some of your knowledge while my husband is away from home."

"In good faith," said Gawain, "God reward you! The joy is great and the sport huge to me, that one as noble as you should wish to come here, and trouble yourself with so poor a man, as to sport with your knight with favor of any kind; it gives me pleasure. But to take upon myself the hard task of expounding true love, of touching on the themes of that text and tales of arms to you who, I well know, have more skill by half in that art than a hundred such as I am have, or ever shall have while I live on earth, that, my noble lady, would be a manifold folly, by my faith. I want to do your will as far as I can, as I am in duty bound, and evermore will be your servant, may the Lord save me!" Thus the noble lady tempted him, and tested him often, to have brought him to sin, whatever she thought besides; but he defended himself so well that no fault was to be seen, nor any evil on either side; they knew nothing but joy. They laughed and played for a long time. At the last she kissed him, took her leave politely indeed, and went her way.

Then the knight bestirred himself and rose to mass, and then their dinner was prepared and splendidly served. The knight sported all day with the ladies, but the lord galloped over the countryside very often, followed his ill-fated swine, which rushed over the slopes and bit in two the backs of the best of his hounds where it stood at bay, till bowmen broke it, and made him move into the open in spite of himself, so many arrows flew there when the people gathered. But still at times he made the boldest to start aside, till at last he was so tired that he could run no longer, but in what haste he could he reached a hole in the smooth bank by a rock where the stream ran. He got the bank at his back and began to paw the ground. The froth foamed at the corners of his ugly mouth and he sharpened his white tusks. The men so bold who stood about him were tired of him and of annoying him from a distance, but none dared come near him because of the danger. He had hurt so many before that all were then loath to be any more torn with the tusks of that fierce and frenzied creature.

Then the knight himself came, urging on his horse, and saw him standing at bay alongside his men. He alighted easily and left his horse, pulled forth a shining sword, and walked forward boldly, hastened quickly through the ford where the wild beast was waiting. The animal was aware of the man with a weapon in his hand, and made his hair bristle; he snorted so fiercely that many were afraid for the man, lest the worst befall him. The swine rushed directly at the warrior, so that both man and boar were in a heap in the most turbulent part of the water. The other had the worst of it, for the man aimed a good blow at him when they first met, set his spear firmly right in the hollow above the breastbone, pierced him up to the hilt, so that the heart burst asunder, and he gave up snarling, and went quickly down the stream. A hundred hounds seized him and bit him fiercely; men drove him to open ground and the dogs killed him.

There was blowing of capture on many a loud horn, noisy shouting on high by the men who could. The dogs barked at the beast as the masters ordered, those who had been the chief hunters of that toilsome chase. Then a man who was skilled in woodcraft began to cut up the boar carefully. First he cut off his head and placed it on high, and then cut him roughly all along the back, pulled out the bowels, broiled them on the red-hot coals, and rewarded his dogs with bread mixed with them. Then he cut up the flesh in bright broad slabs, and had out the numbles, as was proper. And now they fastened the halves together all whole, and then hung them securely on a stiff pole. Then they went home with this swine. The boar's head was carried before the very man who killed him at the ford with the might of his strong hand. It seemed to him a long time before he saw Gawain in the hall. He called out, and Gawain came promptly to receive his payments there.

The lord spoke loud and joyously, and laughed merrily when he saw Sir Gawain. The good ladies were brought and the company gathered. He showed them the slabs of flesh and told them the story of the great size and length of the wild ani-

49. **broke it,** the boar's stand.

mal, also of the ferocity of his fight where he had fled in the wood. The other knight commended his deeds courteously, and praised it as great excellence which he had shown, for the bold man said that he had never before seen such flesh of a boar nor such flanks of a swine. Then they handled the head; the courteous man praised it and expressed horror at it to honor the lord. "Now, Gawain," said the good man, "this game is yours by fully ratified and fast agreement, as you know well." "That is true," said the knight, "and as truly I shall give you, by my faith, all that I got." He took the warrior about the neck and kissed him courteously, and again he served him there in the same way. "Now we are even," said the warrior, "this evening, of all the agreements which we made fast by law since I came here." The lord said, "By St. Giles, you are the best man whom I know! You will be rich presently if you carry on such a trade."

Then they set up tables on trestles, and threw cloths on them. The clear light from wax torches was kindled along the walls, and men sat and were served all about in the hall. Much noise and merriment sprang up in there around the fire in the hall, and in various ways at supper and after, they sang many noble songs, such as Christmas carols and dance songs, with all the seemly mirth that one could tell of. And the lovely knight always sat beside the lady. She sweetly showed such a demeanor toward that knight with looks of love secretly bestowed to please the stalwart man that he was completely astonished, and angry with himself, but out of his good breeding he would not refuse her, but behaved to her with courtesy, however amiss the affair went. When they had sported in the hall as long as their desire lasted, the lord called him to his bedroom, and they went to the room with a fireplace.

And there they drank and contended in sport, and decided once more to propose the same terms on New Year's Eve. But the knight asked permission to ride in the morning, for it was near the appointment to which he had to go. The lord restrained him in that, bade him remain and linger, and said: "As I am a true man, I give my word that you shall make your way to the Green Chapel to carry out your business, sir, on New Year's dawn, long before prime. Therefore lie in your upper room and take your ease, and I shall hunt in this wood, and keep the agreements, exchange winnings with you when I return here; for I have tried you twice, and I find you trustworthy. Now 'third time, turn out best,' let us remember in the morning.

52-53. 'third . . . best,' a proverb.

Let us make merry while we can, and think upon joy; for a man may seize disaster whenever he likes." This was granted at once and Gawain stayed. Drink was gaily brought to them, and then they went to bed with lights. Gawain lay and slept quietly and softly all night. The lord, who attended to his pursuits, was dressed very early.

After mass he and his men took a small meal. The morning was pleasant and he asked for his mount. All the men who were to go after him on horseback were prepared and ready on their steeds before the hall gates. The earth was very fair, for the frost clung to it. In fiery red the sun rose above the drifting clouds, and passed clearly by the side of the clouds in the sky. The hunters unleashed their hounds alongside a wood. The rocks in the forest rang with the noise of their horns. Some hit on the track where the fox waited, followed it often back and forth in practice of their wiles. A small dog gave tongue at it, and the huntsman called to him. His companions, sniffing close together, followed after him, ran forth in a rabble on the fox's very track, and he scampered before them. They dislodged him at once, and when they saw him with sight they pursued him fast, denouncing him very clearly with an angry noise. And he dodged and doubled through many a rough thicket, turned back and listened often by the hedges. Finally he leaped over a thorn hedge by a little ditch, stole very quietly by the border of a patch of tall herbage, thought to have escaped the hounds from the wood by means of his tricks. Then he came, before he knew it, to an excellent hunting-station, where three fierce men all in gray at once attacked him with a rush. He swerved again quickly and started undaunted in a new direction. With all the woe on earth he went away to the wood.

Then it was brave sport to hear the hounds when all the hunting-pack, mingled together, had met him: such an imprecation they called down on his head at that sight, that it was as if all the clustering cliffs had fallen clattering down in heaps. Here he was shouted at, when the men met him, he was greeted loudly with chiding speech; there he was threatened and often called thief and always the dogs were at his tail, so that he could not delay. He was often run at when he made for the open, and he often turned suddenly in again, so wily was Reynard. And indeed by devious ways he led the lord and his troop in this manner along the mountains until midday, while the courteous knight slept healthfully at home within the fair curtains on the cold morning. But the lady for love did not allow herself to sleep, nor let the purpose fail that was fixed in her heart, but got up promptly and went there in a pretty mantle, reaching to the ground, which was finely furred with well-trimmed skins. There was no good covering on her head except the well-wrought jewels which were twined in clusters of twenty about the fret enclosing her hair. Her face was fair, her throat laid all naked, and her breast bare, both in front and behind. She came inside the chamber door and closed it after her, swung open a window, and called to the man, and thus swiftly and merrily rebuked him with her pleasant words: "Ah! man, how can you sleep? This morning is so bright!" He was deep in the gloom of sleep, but then he heard her.

In the heavy gloom of dreams that noble knight was muttering like a man who was troubled with many grievous thoughts of how destiny that next day must deal him his fate at the Green Chapel, when he met the man and had to await his blow without more resistance. But he recovered his wits when that fair one came, hastened out of dreams, and answered quickly. The lovely lady came laughing sweetly, bent low over his fair face, and kissed him gracefully. He welcomed her courteously with an excellent demeanor. He saw her to be so glorious and so gaily clothed, so faultless in her features, and in such fine colors, that welling joy ardently warmed his heart. With well-bred and gentle smiles they fell at once to merry speech, so that all that was uttered between them was bliss and pleasure and joy. They spoke fair words and there was then much happiness in there. There would have been great danger between them if Mary had not had thought of her knight.

For that precious princess importuned him so continually, pressed him so near to the limit, that it was necessary for him either to accept her love there or refuse it offensively. He was concerned for his courtesy, lest he appear a coward, and even more for the disaster to him if he should commit sin and be a traitor to the knight who owned that dwelling. "God defend me!" said the man. "That must not happen!" With a little loving laugh he parried all the fond speeches which sprang from her mouth. That lady said to the knight: "You deserve blame, if you do not love the person who lies beside you, she who is wounded in heart more than all the creatures in the world, but if you have a sweetheart, a dearer one, who pleases you better, and if you have plighted faith to that noble lady, bound so firmly that you do not desire to break troth—and that I now believe—then I pray you that you now tell me that truly; for all the loves there are, do not conceal the truth with guile."

"By St. John," said the knight and smiled pleasantly, "I possess none, nor do I wish to possess one at present."

"That is a word," said the lady, "which is the worst of all, but I am answered in truth, and that seems painful to me. Kiss me nicely now, and I shall go from here. I can only mourn in life, as a maid who loves greatly." She stooped down sighing and kissed him pleasantly, and then she departed from him and said as she stood there: "Now, dear, at this parting, do me this consolation: give me something as your gift, your glove perhaps, that I may think of you, man, to lessen my sorrow." "Now, certainly," said that knight, "for your sake I wish that I had here the dearest thing which I own in the world, for you very often have truly deserved more reward by rights than I could give. But to give you something for love would avail but little. It is not to your honor to have at this time a glove as a keepsake of Gawain's gift; and I am here on a mission in strange regions, and I have no attendants with bags full of things of value. That displeases me at this time, lady, because of your sake. Each man must do as his circumstances permit; take it not amiss nor in grief." "No, good sir, full of high honors," said that lovely lady, "though I have nothing of yours, yet shall you have something of mine."

She gave him a precious ring of red goldwork, with a clear-cut blazing gem which had gleaming beams like the bright sun; know well that it was worth great wealth. But the knight refused it, and said promptly: "At this time, my noble lady, I wish no gifts for myself. I have none to offer you, nor will I take any." She offered it to him earnestly, and he refused her offer, and swore quickly on his word that he would not accept it, and she was grieved that he refused, and afterwards said: "If you reject my ring, because it appears too precious, and you would not be so greatly indebted to me, I shall give you my girdle, which will be of less profit to you." She swiftly took hold of a thong that was fastened around her flanks, knotted to her kirtle beneath the bright mantle. It was fashioned of green silk and hemmed with gold, embroidered only at the edges, ornamented with fingerwork; and that she offered to the man, and gaily implored him that he would take it, though it was unworthy. And he denied that he would in any way accept either gold or treasure, before God had sent him the favor to reach the adventure which he had undertaken there. "And, therefore, I beg you, that you be not displeased, and cease your importunity, for I shall never consent to grant it to you. I am greatly indebted to you for your kindly demeanor, and I shall always be your true servant through thick and thin."

"Now do you refuse this silk," said the lady then, "because it is simple in itself? And it certainly seems so. Lo! it is indeed little, and less valuable; but whoever knew the qualities that are bound within it would perhaps esteem it at more value. For whatever man is girt with this green thong, while he has it neatly fastened about him, there is no knight on earth who could kill him, for he may not be slain by any means." Then the knight pondered, and it came into his heart that this would be a precious thing for the peril that was assigned to him when he reached the chapel to obtain his fate. Could he escape unslain, it would be a noble device. Then he became patient with her importunity and allowed her to speak, and she pressed the belt on him and offered it to him earnestly— and he accepted—and she gave it to him with good will, and begged him, for her sake, never to reveal it, but to conceal it faithfully from her husband. The knight agreed that no man should ever know of it on any account certainly, except they two. He thanked her often and very heartily, sincerely in heart and thought. By that time she had kissed the firm knight three times.

Then she took her departure and left him there, for she could get no more pleasure from that man. When she was gone Sir Gawain clothed himself at once, rose and dressed himself in noble array, put away the love-lace which the lady had given him, hid it very faithfully where he could find it again. Then he made his way quickly to the chapel, privately approached a priest and begged him there that he would elevate his life and teach him better how his soul should be saved when he had to go hence. There he confessed himself and laid bare his misdeeds, both the greater and the smaller, and asked for mercy, and called on the man for absolution. And the priest absolved him surely and made him as pure as if Doomsday should have been appointed for the morrow. And after that he made merry among the noble ladies, with pleasing carols and joy of all kinds delightfully until the dark night, as he had never done before save on that day. Each man there took pleasure in him, and said, "Certainly he was never so merry before this since he came here."

Now let him stay in that place where love may befall him! The lord was still in the field, having his sport. He had killed this fox which he followed so long. As he leaped over a thorn hedge to get a sight of the villain where he heard the hounds which pressed him closely, Reynard came making his way through a rough thicket, and all the pack in a rush right at his heels. The man was aware of the beast and waited warily, and drew out his bright sword and cast at the animal. And he swerved from the sharp blade and would have turned, but before he could a dog hastened to him, and right under the horse's feet they all fell upon him, and worried the wily creature with a fierce noise. The lord dismounted quickly and took hold of him at once, lifted him speedily out of the dogs' mouths, held him high over his head, shouted loudly, and there many fierce dogs bayed him. Huntsman with many horns hurried there, always blowing the recall correctly until they saw the man. When his noble company had come, all those who carried bugles blew at once, and all the others who had no horns shouted. It was the merriest baying of hounds that one ever heard, the echoing noise that was raised with sound for Reynard's soul. They rewarded their dogs there, they stroked and rubbed their heads; and then they took Reynard and stripped off his coat.

And then they went home, for it was near night, sounding calls vigorously on their mighty horns. The lord finally alighted at his dear home, found a fire in the hall, and the knight there beside it, Sir Gawain the good, who was glad moreover, since he had had much joy for love among the ladies. He wore a blue mantle which reached to the earth, his softly furred surcoat became him well, and his hood of the same material hung on his shoulders, both adorned all about with white fur. He met this good man in the middle of the floor, and he greeted him all merrily, and said graciously, "I shall now first fulfill our covenant which, where no drink was spared, we agreed on with good results." He then embraced the knight and kissed him three times, with as much relish and as vigorously as he could do. "By Christ," said that other knight, "you get much happiness in obtaining this merchandise, if you have good bargains." "Yes, the price does not matter," said the other quickly, "so long as the goods that I owed for are openly paid." "Mary," said the other man, "mine is inferior, for I have hunted all this day, and have obtained nothing except this vile fox skin—the fiend take the goods!— and that is very poor with which to pay for such precious things as you have pressed heartily on me here, three such good kisses." "Say no more," said Sir Gawain. "I thank you, by the Cross." And as they stood there he told him how the fox was slain.

With mirth and music, with food to their desire, they made as merry as any men might. What with the laughing of ladies and jesting words Gawain and the good man were both as glad as though the company had been foolish or else drunk. Both the man and the household made many jokes until the time had come when they must part; at last it was necessary for men to go to their beds. Then this noble man first humbly took his leave of the lord, and thanked him fairly: "May the high king repay you for such an excellent stay as I have had here, and for your hospitality at this great feast. I will give you myself to be one of your men; for tomorrow, as you know, I must of necessity move on, if you, as you promised, will assign me some man to direct me the way to the Green Chapel, where God will suffer me to perform on New Year's Day the judgment of my fates." "In good faith," said the good man, "I shall keep readily and with good will all that I ever promised you." There he assigned him a servant to set him on the road, and to conduct him along the hills, so that he would have no trouble in riding through the wood and going most directly through the thicket. Gawain thanked the lord, such honor would he give him. Then the knight took his leave of the noble ladies.

He spoke to them with grief and with kissing, and he pressed them to have many hearty thanks, and they promptly returned the same to him. They commended him to Christ with very grievous sighs. Afterwards he departed courteously from the household. He gave thanks to every man whom he met for his service and kindness and the various troubles that they had undertaken to serve him with solicitude; and each man was as sorry to part from him there as if they had always lived honorably with that hero. Then with men and lights he was led to his chamber and brought happily to his bed to be at his rest. Whether or not he slept soundly I dare not say, for he had much to remember in thought on the morrow, if he would. Let him lie there still, he nearly has what he sought. If you will be quiet for a time, I shall tell you how they acted.

IV

Now the New Year grew near and the night passed; the daylight came upon the darkness, as the Lord ordered. But wild storms arose out of doors in the world, clouds bitterly threw the cold to the earth, with sharpness enough from the north to torment the flesh. The snow, which nipped the wild beasts cruelly, came shivering down bitterly. The shrill-blowing wind rushed from the high ground, and drove each valley full of very great drifts. The man who was lying in his bed listened well; although he closed his lids, he slept but little; by each cock that crew he was reminded of the appointed hour. He got up quickly before day broke, for there was the light of a lamp which shone in his chamber. He called to his chamberlain, who promptly answered him, and ordered him to bring his coat of mail and to saddle his horse. The other got up and brought him his raiment, and dressed Sir Gawain in magnificent fashion. First he clad him in his clothes to ward off the cold, and afterwards his other armor, which had been kept carefully, both his stomach armor and his steel plate, polished very bright, the rings of his rich coat of mail cleansed from rust. And everything was as fresh as at first, and he was then anxious to give thanks for it. He had polished each piece well and nobly. The fairest knight from here to Greece ordered the man to bring his horse.

In the meantime he put the loveliest clothes on himself, his coat with the badge of fine embroidery set as an adornment upon velvet, precious stones set about and trimmed, embroidered seams, and fairly furred inside with beautiful skins. Yet he did not leave the belt, the lady's gift—that Gawain did not forget for his own good. When he had belted his sword about his smooth haunches, then he fastened his love-token double about him; about his waist the knight wrapped with pleasure the girdle of green silk that seemed very gay upon that splendid red cloth which was rich to look at. But this same man did not wear the girdle for its costliness, or for pride in the pendants, though they were polished, and even if the glittering gold glinted at the ends, but rather to save himself when it was necessary for him to suffer, to await death without resistance of sword or knife to defend himself. When the bold man was dressed he went out quickly, and he abundantly thanked all the noble household.

Then Gringolet, who was great and huge, was made ready, and he had been stabled to his liking and in a safe fashion; it pleased that proud horse then to gallop in good condition. The knight went to him and looked at his coat, and spoke to himself without exaggeration and swore by his faith: "Here in this castle is a company who think about courtesy; may the man who maintains them have joy, and may love come to the dear lady during her life! If they entertain a guest for charity's sake and dispense honor, may the Lord who rules heaven on high repay them, and also all of you! And if I may have my life on earth for any time I shall readily give you some reward if I am able." Then he stepped into the stirrup, strode into the saddle. His man produced his shield, and he put it on his shoulder. He spurred Gringolet with his gilded heels, and the horse sprang forward on the pavement; he waited no longer to prance. His man, who bore his spear and lance, was then on horseback. "I commend this castle to Christ, may He always give it good fortune!"

The bridge was pulled down, and the broad gates unbarred and laid open on both sides. The man blessed himself speedily and crossed the planks—he praised the porter, who was kneeling before the prince, and the porter commended him to God that He save Gawain, and wished him good day—and he went on his way with only his man, who should direct him to go to that dismal place where he must receive the sorrowful attack. They turned by slopes where the boughs were bare, and they climbed along cliffs where the cold clung. The clouds were high, but it was ugly under them. Mist drizzled on the moor and melted on the mountains; each hill had a hat, a huge cloak of mist. Brooks boiled and foamed along the banks, dashing and breaking in white on the shores where they made their way down. The road was very wandering where they had to go by the wood until it was the season that the sun rose at that time. They were on a very high hill, the white snow lay round about them. The man who rode with him commanded his master to stop.

"I have brought you here, knight, at this time, and now you are not far from that noted place which you have looked for and asked after so particularly. But I shall tell you in truth, since I know you, and you are a man in life whom I love well, that if you would work in accordance with my intelligence you would be the better for it. The place which you hasten to is considered very dangerous. A creature dwells in that waste who is the worst on earth, for he is strong and stern and loves to strike, and he is greater than any man in the world, and his body is bigger than the four best men who are in Arthur's house, or Hector, or anyone else. He brings it to pass at the Green Chapel that no one so proud in his arms goes by that place that he does not strike him to death with a blow of his hand; for he is a violent man and uses no mercy, for if it be a peasant or a chaplain who rides by the chapel, a monk or a priest, or any other man, it seems to him as pleasant to kill him as to go alive himself. Therefore, I tell you that, as truly as you are sitting in your saddle, if you come there you will be killed, if the knight may have his will—believe me truly in that—although you had twenty lives to spend. He has lived here a very long time, and has brought about much strife on the field of battle; you cannot defend yourself against his heavy blows.

"Therefore, good Sir Gawain, let the man alone, and go away some other road, for God's sake! Ride over some other land, where Christ may give you success, and I shall hurry home again, and I promise you further that I shall swear by God and all his good saints—so help me God and holy relics and oaths enough!—that I shall keep your secret loyally, and never tell the story that you ever tried to flee because of any man that I knew of." "Thank you," said Gawain, and he spoke in annoyance. "May good fortune befall you, who wish my good, and I well believe that you would keep my secret loyally, but though you held it never so faithfully, and I passed by here, tried to flee because of fear in the manner that you tell of, then I would be a coward knight and could not be excused. But I will go to the Chapel in spite of anything that may happen, and talk with that same man the speech that pleases me, whether it be joy or woe, as fate likes to have it. Though he be a grim fellow to deal with, and stands there with a club, the Lord can well bring it about to save His servants."

"Mary!" said that other man. "Now you say so much that you will take your own harm on yourself, and if you choose to lose your life I will neither hinder nor keep you. Have here your helmet on your head, your spear in your hand, and ride down this same path beside that rock until you come to the bottom of the wild valley. Then look a little in the glade on your left hand, and you shall see in that valley the very Chapel, and the strong man who keeps it there. Now farewell, for God's sake, noble Gawain! I would not go with you or bear you company through this wood one foot further for all the gold on earth." At that the man turned his bridle in the wood, struck his horse as hard as he could with his heels, galloped over the countryside, and left the knight there alone. "By God's self," said Gawain, "I will neither weep nor groan. I am quite obedient to God's will, and I have committed myself to Him."

Then he spurred Gringolet, and picked up the path, made his way in by a steep rock at the side of a wood, rode along the rough slope straight to the valley. And then he looked about and it seemed wild to him, and he saw no sign of shelter anywhere beside him, but high and steep banks on both sides, and rugged, knobbed crags with gnarled stones; it seemed to him that the clouds were grazed by the jutting rocks. Then he halted and held back his horse at that time, and often turned this way and that to find the Chapel: he saw nothing of the sort in any direction, and it seemed strange to him, but soon, a little way off, he saw something like a mound, a bare hill on a bank beside the water's edge, by a waterfall of the stream which went by there; the water bubbled in it as if it were boiling. The knight urged on his horse and came to the mound, alighted gracefully, and fastened the rein and his noble steed to a tree by a rough branch. Then he went to the mound and walked about it, debating with himself as to what it might be. It had a hole in the end and on either side, and was everywhere overgrown with grass in patches, and was all hollow inside; only an old cave or a fissure in an old crag, he could not say which. "Alas! Lord," said the gentle knight, "is this the Green Chapel? The Devil might say his matins here about midnight!

"Now certainly," said Gawain, "it is desolate here; this chapel is ugly and overgrown with plants. It is very fitting for the creature clad in green to perform his devotions here in the Devil's fashion. Now I feel in my five senses that it is the fiend who has imposed this appointment on me to destroy me here. This is a chapel of disaster, may ill luck befall it! It is the most cursed church in which I ever came!" With his tall helmet on his head and his lance in his hand, he made his way up to the roof of the rough dwelling. Then he heard from that high hill, in a hard rock on a slope beyond the brook, a wonderfully loud noise. Listen! It clattered on the cliff, as if it would split it, as though someone were grinding a scythe on a grindstone. Listen! It whirred and made a grinding noise, like water at a mill. Listen! It made a rushing sound and rang, grievous to hear. Then said Gawain: "By God, I believe that contrivance is prepared as a salutation on the way to mark out the field of combat for me. Let God work his will! 'Ah well!' helps me not a bit. Though I lose my life, no noise makes me afraid."

Then the knight called loudly: "Who is master in this place to keep appointment with me? For now good Gawain is walking right here. If any man wishes anything, let him come here at once, now or never, to accomplish his need." "Wait," said someone on the bank above his head, "and you shall have in haste all that I once promised you." Yet he went on with that noise quickly for a time, and turned away towards his whetting, before he would come down. And then he made his way by a crag and came from a hole, whirling out of a nook with a dangerous weapon with which to give the blow, a new-made Danish axe, with a massive blade curved back in line to the handle, sharpened on a whetstone and four feet wide—it was no less measured by the lace which gleamed very bright—and the man in green was attired as at first, both the face and the legs, hair and beard, save that he hastened fairly over the ground on his feet, placed the haft of the axe on the stone and stalked beside it. When he came to the water he would not wade there, but he hopped over on his axe, and strode actively, very fierce, over the broad ground which was covered about with snow. Sir Gawain met the knight and did not bow at all low to him. That other said, "Now, sweet sir, one may trust you in the matter of an appointment.

"Gawain," said that green man, "may God guard you! Certainly you are welcome, knight, to my place, and you have timed your journey as a true man should, and you know the agreement made between us: at this time a year ago you took what fell to your lot, and on this New Year's I was to repay you promptly. And truly we are entirely alone in this valley. Here there are no men to separate us, however it may please us to sway in combat. Take your helmet off your head, and have your pay here. Make no more resistance than I offered you then when you slashed off my head at a single blow." "No," said Sir Gawain, "by God who gave me a soul, I shall not at all bear you ill will for any hurt that occurs. But limit yourself to one stroke, and I shall stand still and utter no refusal anywhere to keep you from doing as you wish." He inclined his neck bowed and showed the flesh all bare, and acted as if he feared nothing; he would not cower for dread.

Then the man in green got ready at once, and lifted up his grim weapon to hit Gawain. He bore it on high with all the strength in his body, swung as powerfully as if he would destroy him; had it hurtled down as forcibly as he intended, the man who had ever been brave would have been dead from his blow. But Gawain glanced sideways at that axe as it came gliding down to destroy him on the ground, and flinched a little from the sharp iron with his shoulders. The other man with a swerve withheld the bright blade and then reproved the prince with many arrogant words. "You are not Gawain," said the man, "who is accounted so good, who never quailed for any host by hill or vale, and now you flinch for fear before you feel any harm. I never heard such cowardice of that knight. I neither dodged nor ducked, man, when you swung, nor did I make any objecting in King Arthur's house. My head flew to my foot, and still I never flinched. And you, before any hurt received, are terrified in your heart, wherefore I ought to be called the better man." Said Gawain, "I flinched

13. **Green Chapel.** This was a fairy mound; actually, from the description, a prehistoric tumulus. **33–35. I believe . . . me,** a difficult passage. **50. Danish axe,** with a long blade.

once, and I will do so no more, but if my head falls on the stones I cannot replace it.

"But make haste, man, by my faith, and come to the point with me. Give me my fate, and do it straight away, for I shall stand and take a stroke from you and start aside no more until your axe has hit me: have here my pledge." "Have at you then!" said the other, and lifted it aloft, and looked as angrily as if he were mad. He struck powerfully at him, but did not cut the man open, withheld his hand suddenly before it could hurt. Gawain awaited it duly and swerved with no limb, but stood still as a stone or a stump that is entwined in rocky ground with a hundred roots. Then the man in green spoke again merrily: "So now that you have your heart whole, it is time for me to hit. Hold up the noble hood which Arthur gave you, and keep your windpipe from this stroke, if it can survive." Gawain then said wrathfully and angrily: "Why! Smite on, you fierce man, you threaten too long. I think that your heart is afraid of your own self." "Truly," said the other man, "you speak so fiercely that I will no longer leave your errand in delay right now." Then he took stance to strike, and puckered both lip and brow. No wonder though it displeased the man who hoped for no rescue.

He lifted his weapon lightly and let it down deftly with the cutting edge of the blade over the bare neck; although he struck fiercely, it hurt him none the more for that, but cut him lightly on one side, which broke the skin. The sharp blade penetrated through the white fat to the flesh, so that the bright blood sprang over his shoulders to the earth. And when the knight saw the blood gleam on the snow, he sprang forth, striking out with his feet, more than a spear length, seized his helmet vigorously and put it on his head, jerked his shield to the front with a movement of his shoulders, pulled out a shining sword, and spoke fiercely—never since he was a man born of his mother had he been half so happy in this world: "Cease from your violence, man, offer me no more! I have received a blow in this place without resistance, but if you give me any more I shall repay you quickly, and return promptly again and fiercely—you may believe that! Only one stroke is coming to me here—the agreement made in Arthur's halls appointed it just so—and therefore, good sir, now stop!"

The man turned away and rested on his axe, set the haft on the ground and leaned on the blade, and looked at the knight who was in the clearing, saw that fearless brave man boldly stand there armed, without fear. It pleased him in his heart. Then he spoke merrily in a loud voice, and in ringing tones said to the knight: "Bold warrior, do not be so fierce. No man here has ill-used you or treated you discourteously, but only as the covenant was arranged at the king's court. I promised you a blow and you have had it: consider yourself well paid. I release you from the remainder of all other obligations. If I had been nimble, perhaps I could have dealt you a buffet more harshly, which would have done you harm. First I threatened you merrily with a feint only, and did not cut you with a painful wound—which with justice I offered you because of the agreement we made fast the first night, and you held your compact with me faithfully and truly, and gave me all that you obtained, as a good man ought. The second feint I gave you for the next day you kissed my fair wife—you gave me the kisses. For both of these I gave you here only two mere feints without harm. A true man restores faithfully, and then a man need dread no danger. But you failed there the third time, and therefore you got that tap.

"For it is my garment that you are wearing, that same woven girdle; my own wife gave it, I know that for the truth. Now I well know your kisses, and your manners too, and the wooing of my wife: I brought it about myself. I sent her to test you, and truly you seem to me the most faultless man who ever went on foot. As a pearl is of more value beside white peas, so is Gawain, in good faith, beside other gay knights. But here you were a little at fault, sir, and were lacking in fidelity; but that was not for intrigue nor wooing, but because you loved your life—I blame you the less." The other stout man stood in thought for a great while, so overcome with mortification that he cried in anguish internally; all the blood in his breast streamed together in his face, so that he winced for shame at all the man said. The first word that the knight said there was: "Cursed be both cowardice and covetousness! In you are the villainy and vice which destroy virtue." Then he caught at the knot and loosed the fastening and fiercely flung the belt at the warrior himself: "See! There is the breaking of faith, evilly may it fare! For fear of your blow, cowardice taught me to associate with covetousness, to forsake my nature, which is the generosity and loyalty which belong to knights. Now I am faulty and false, and have always been afraid of treachery and perfidy: may both have sorrow and care! Here, knight, I confess to you between ourselves that my behavior is all faulty. Let me win your good will, and I shall be on my guard another time."

12. **the first night.** Gawain now learns for the first time the identity of the Green Knight.

SIR GAWAIN AND THE GREEN KNIGHT

Then that other man laughed and said lovingly: "I certainly consider the injury I had amended. You have confessed so completely, acknowledged your faults, and have had the plain penance from the point of my blade, that I hold you cleansed of that offense and purified as completely as if you had never transgressed since you were first born. And, sir, I give you the gold-hemmed girdle, for it is green like my gown. Sir Gawain, you may think about this same contest, where you make your way among noble princes, and this will be an excellent token among chivalrous knights of the adventure of the Green Chapel. And you shall come again to my dwelling this New Year and we shall celebrate the remainder of this noble feast very pleasantly." Then the lord invited him earnestly and said: "I think that we shall reconcile you with my wife, who was your bitter enemy."

"No, truly," said the knight, and caught hold of his helmet, took it off politely, and thanked the man, "I have stayed long enough. May you have good fortune, and may He who ordains all honors give it to you fully. And commend me to that courteous lady, your beautiful wife, to her and to the other, both my honored ladies, who have thus adroitly deceived their knight with their trick. But it is no wonder that a fool should act madly and be brought to grief by the wiles of women, for so Adam was actually deceived by one, and Solomon by very many, and Samson in his turn—Delilah gave him his fate—and David after that was deluded by Bathsheba and suffered much woe. Since those men were brought to disaster by their wiles, it would be a great gain to love them well and believe them not at all, if a man could do that. For these men were of old the noblest; to all of them prosperity came excellently above all others who meditated under heaven; and they were all deceived by women with whom they had dealings. Although I were now tricked, it seems to me I ought to be excused.

"But," said Gawain, "God reward you for your girdle! That I will own gladly, not for the lovely gold, nor the material, nor the silk, nor the pendants at the side, neither for costliness nor honor, nor for the beautiful workmanship, but as a sign of my transgression I shall look at it often, when I ride in glory, and call to mind with remorse the faultiness and frailty of perverse flesh, how liable it is to catch spots of defilement; and so, when pride shall stir me for prowess in arms, a glance at this love-lace shall make my heart humble. But one thing I would beg of you, take no offense at it: since you are lord of the land in which I have stayed with you honorably—may He who upholds the heaven and sits on high reward you for it!—how do you call your right name, and then no more?" "I shall tell you that truly," said the other then, "In this land I am called Bertilak de Hautdesert. Through the power of Morgan le Fay, who stays in my house, and is cunning in magical lore, by well-learned crafts—she has taken many of the arts of Merlin; for she sometimes had pleasant love-dealings with that excellent sage, who knows all your knights at home. Therefore her name is Morgan the Goddess: no one has such great pride that she cannot make him tame.

"She sent me in this fashion to your delightful hall, to test its pride and to find out if the great fame that is current of the Round Table were true. She sent this marvel to take away your senses, to dismay Guenever and to make her die with fear of that same man who spoke like a phantom with his head in his hand before the high table. That is the ancient lady who is at home. She is actually your aunt, Arthur's half-sister, the daughter of the Duchess of Tintagel, by whom the noble Uther afterwards had Arthur who is now so glorious. Therefore I entreat you, knight, to come to your aunt and make merry in my house. My people love you and by my faith, man, I will love you as well as any man under God for your great loyalty." And he said "No" to him, he would by no means do it. They embraced and kissed and commended each other to the Prince of Paradise, and parted right there on the cold ground. Gawain went boldly on his fair horse to the king's court, and the knight in bright green went wherever he wished.

Gawain, who had received the gift of his life, now rode over wild ways in the world on Gringolet. He often lodged in a house and often outside, and had many adventures by the way, and often won, but I do not intend to recount them at this time in the story. The wound which he had received on his neck was healed, and he wore the gleaming belt about him slantwise like a baldric bound to his side, the lace fastened under his left arm with a knot, in token that he had been taken in the stain of a fault. And thus the knight came to the court in safety. Joy arose in that dwelling when the king knew that good Gawain had come; it seemed a fine thing to him. The king kissed the knight, and so did the queen, and then many a true knight who tried to

4. **Through the power . . .** The sentence is incomplete; perhaps a line is lost which stated that the Green Knight owed his ability as a shape-shifter to Morgan's power. 16–17. **to dismay Guenever,** who had interfered in one of Morgan's love-affairs. 22. **Duchess of Tintagel,** Ygern, on whom Uther Pendragon begot Arthur after Merlin had given him her husband's shape.

embrace him. They asked him about his journey, and he told it wonderfully, confessing all the hardships he had had: the adventure of the Chapel, the behavior of the knight, the love of the lady, and finally the belt. He showed them naked the slight cut on his neck which he had received from the lord's hands as a rebuke for his disloyalty. He suffered torment when he had to tell it and groaned for sorrow and mortification. The blood ran to his face for shame when he had to reveal it.

"Ah! lord," said the knight, and handled the belt, "this which I wear on my neck is the band of shame, this is the injury and the damage which I have taken from the cowardice and covetousness which I caught there, this is a sign of the untruth in which I was taken, and I must needs wear it while I live. For no one can hide his misfortune without ill luck ensuing, for where it is once fastened it will never depart." The king comforted the knight, and all the court also laughed loudly at it, and lovingly agreed that the lords and ladies who belong to the Table, each man of the brotherhood, should have a baldric, a slantwise band of bright green about him, and, following suit, wear it for the sake of that knight. For that sign was accorded the glory of the Round Table, and he who had it was honored evermore, as is written down in the best book of romance. Thus this adventure took place in Arthur's day, and the books of Brutus bear witness of it. After the bold hero Brutus first came here, when, certainly, the siege and the assault had come to an end at Troy, many adventures such as this had happened before now. Now may He who wore the crown of thorns bring us to His bliss! Amen.

HONY SOYT QUI MAL PENCE.

MATTER OF FRANCE

Just as the individual romances in the matter of Britain deal less with Arthur than with his knights, so in the matter of France we find Roland, Oliver, Firumbras, and Otuel more prominent than Charlemagne. These heroes were popular in Great Britain; indeed, Barbour tells us that King Robert Bruce read to his men "romanys off worthi Ferumbras," but the English poems are usually markedly inferior to the French originals, and in many cases are not taken from the best French versions.

RALPH THE COLLIER

Some apology must be made for presenting *Ralph the Collier*, late fifteenth-century and Scottish in origin, as a specimen of the matter of France. The poem is not an organic part of the group, although some of the regular characteristics, such as the discomfiture and conversion of a Saracen, do appear; the basic plot, that of the king in disguise, is common and widespread, but not told elsewhere of Charlemagne; and, finally, we know no French original, nor is it particularly likely that one existed. Despite these considerations, the little romance is so good in plot and characterization, so instinct with typically pawky Scottish humor, that it justifies a claim to the reader's attention which many of the longer romances can hardly show.

The first part of the poem, retelling the familiar story of the disguised king who visits an unsuspecting subject, finds its most familiar parallel, perhaps, in the story of King Alfred and the cakes. But there are many other analogues, the closest to *Ralph the Collier* being the early fifteenth-century poem *John the Reeve*. Ralph's trip to court and his discovery of the true identity of his host is common to most of the allied stories; the fight with the Saracen, however, is peculiar to *Ralph the Collier* and is unquestionably modeled on similar scenes in the serious chansons de geste. It has sometimes been suggested that the second part is an addition by another and inferior author, but this theory seems hardly likely. The poem is a unit, the second part follows naturally upon the first, and the character of Ralph is consistent throughout. The author takes liberties with chivalric conventions, but he is writing broadly humorous burlesque, rather than in a vein of satire or travesty.

A study of the poem is to be found in H. M. Smyser's "The Taill of Rauf Collyear and Its Sources," *Harvard Studies and Notes in Philology and Literature*, Vol. XIV (1932), pp. 135 ff. The present translation is from the edition by W. H. Browne, *The Taill of Rauf Collyear*, Johns Hopkins University Press, 1903, with use of the notes to F. J. Amour's edition, Scottish Text Society, Nos. 27, 38, Edinburgh, 1892–97.

HERE begins the story of how Ralph the Collier lodged King Charles.

In the reign of Charles, that eminent ruler, there took place a terrible storm in those wild moors where emperors and earls and many others were returning from the shrine of St. Thomas before Yuletide. The proudest in attire were going to Paris, with many prelates and princes who were

---

25–26. **that sign . . . Round Table.** This passage is sometimes taken to be a connection between *Sir Gawain and the Green Knight* and the founding of the order of the Garter, but even the presence of the motto of the Garter at the end of the poem does not make this a very attractive theory.
29–30. **books of Brutus bear witness.** The term "Brut" came to be applied to any chronicle of Britain; we know of no chronicle which mentions this story.

41–42. **from the shrine . . . Yuletide**, or, after St. Thomas' Day, December 21; the passage is almost certainly corrupt.

full of great pride. They were all going with the king to his splendid dwelling; by his side they went across the fair fields. All the most noble went in the morning, both dukes and the Douzepers, barons and knights, many a bold man went from town with the king.

And as that royal man rode over the rough moor, I heard that a tempest overtook him at that time. The wind blew strongly and violently out of the east: the snow drove steadily into many a deep valley, it came so fiercely and bitterly from the sky that no one could keep his footing on the high moor. The proudest and the noblest were on the point of perishing, none knew where to stay in those bad storms. They wandered so at random among the dark mountains that by mid-forenoon they had traveled so very painfully that each one had taken a separate way and had scattered far and wide.

A constant storm drove so hard from the east that it buffeted and blew about whatever remained out in it. By the time that they had parted in various directions mid-morning was passed and no knight of the court knew which way the king was riding. He finally saw there was nothing better than God to help him, and his horse walked stoutly against the storm. His luck was such that he went away from the court to a point where there was no one about him for a distance of five miles. Truly he became completely lost in those mountains, in the fierce and violent storm, among those high hills. By nightfall the king liked the situation very little. It greatly displeased the king that night overtook him so late and that he had no suitable lodging. Just then a strong peasant came along the road with a horse, and two baskets fastened onto it. The king spoke to the peasant without delay: "For love of the Cross, sir, tell me your right name." He replied, "People call me Ralph Collier, as I know well. I live in this region with great trouble, in hard work I spend both tide and time. I dwell more than seven miles from here and carry coals to sell. Since you inquire, I tell you all the whole truth."

"As I hope to prosper," said the king, "I ask for no harm. You seem to be a fine fellow, your answer is so good." "In truth," said the collier, "trust as you wish, for I believe if your question isn't honest, you will shift for yourself." "Mary, God forbid!" said the king. "That would make but little sense. Both myself and my horse are ready to perish. I pray you, bring me to some place of rest, the weather is so cold; for I forbid that we should fall into any altercation. I have much more need to find friendship, and if you know more than I, in the name of St. Julian, bring me to some lodging, and do not leave me behind."

"I know of no lodging near at hand here worthy to serve such a man as you seem to me, none except my own house, the largest in this part of the country, far off in the forest, among the high moors. If you will be content with such as you find, you certainly will be welcome to come home with me, you or any other good fellow whom I find here going astray, as you seem to be; for the storms which fall on the plain are so fierce." The king, as he rode, was happy because of the promise which the collier had made, and said, with a glad heart, "Sir, may God repay you."

"Nay, don't thank me too soon, lest we quarrel, for so far my service to you has been little to boast about; you have had of me neither fire, drink, nor food, nor any other comforts for the traveler's use. But if we can make this lodging tonight, then we could thus both excuse ourselves rightly. When you mount your horse tomorrow in the morning, then give praise at the parting according as you have made out, for first to praise and then to blame, that is a shame, by St. Peter!" The king said, "In good faith, sir, what you say is true." They fell into such talk until they were near home.

They both came to the collier's house before they stopped; the peasant knew very well where the road ran. "Open the door at once! Wife, are you in? Why the devil don't you take some trouble on account of this bad day? The chins of both my guest and me are trembling. By my good faith, I never felt so fierce a storm!" The good wife hurried to begin the hospitality, for she never dared disobey any orders which she heard him give; the peasant was rude in speech, and grew very angry. All abashed by the rebuke, the mistress of the house went to the door. She said, "Sir, you are welcome home, and your guest, too."

"Wife, I have bought all today's profits dearly, walking much out of my way in fierce, wet storms. Wife, make it known that I have come home, and kindle a fire; I believe that our guest has fared as badly on the road. It would be my desire to have a fine, strong, hot fire, to do better for his sake, if we could do so. Pull down some of the best capons outside in the stable—here we have only homely fare—go quickly, Gill." He hastily ordered two of his strong servants: "The one of you take my horse, the other his courser too, and go at once to the stable." Then the king was glad.

The collier, polite in company, took him by the

---

4. **Douzepers,** the body of twelve peers who appear often in French romances.   24. **He,** the king.   23. **give . . . parting,** a common proverb.

hand and made him go ahead of him, as was right. When they came to the door, the king started to stand still and made an effort to let the collier in first. The collier said, "You are ill-bred, that I'll warrant." He seized the king by the neck, two-thirds in anger; "You should be prompt and obedient at an order, and if you ever knew anything about good manners, you have clean forgotten it. This is one time when breeding ought to show itself, since otherwise you are ignorant enough to make me master of my own. As I hope to prosper, I am angry: we are beginning to quarrel."

Then they went to the inner room where burning logs were bright, to a brightly burning fire, as the peasant had ordered. He called to Gillian, his wife, to prepare their supper. "Help us to have the best that there is, [since it is proper] to have a merry night after a bad day, for I was never so hard-pressed and bothered with storms; it blew so terribly from each point of the east. I was in still worse plight when I met this man." They told such stories until supper was ready.

Soon supper was prepared and the fire kindled, and when they had washed, truly, the best of everything was there. "Take my wife by the hand; the two of you, go without delay and sit in the best place," said the collier. "Surely that would be improper with yourself unseated." The king invited him to go and made unfamiliar gestures. "This makes twice," said the collier, "that I think you have forgotten." He let go at the king without more ado, and hit him below the ear with his right hand, so that he staggered there half the breadth of the hall. He did not stop falling until he hit the ground.

He started up stoutly again, although he could hardly stand for pain from the outrage which he had received there. The collier called to Gillian, his wife: "Go, take him by the hand, and go back to the table, where you should have gone before. Sir, you are ignorant, and that I'll maintain. You ought to have plenty of breeding and you have none. You have traveled, surely, in many strange lands; you should have from that the more sense to keep yourself out of blame. You ought by nature to be courteous and an accomplished courtier. Although I am a simple man, do as I tell you: the house is mine, by God, and everything that is here."

The king said to himself: "This is an evil life, I was never before in my life taught in this fashion, and I have often been where there has been an abundance of good men who knew most about courtesy of anyone in this Christian land. There is nothing so good as to leave off and make no more strife, for I am stunned by this blow which has shaken me so." Courteously he went together with the good wife where the collier ordered, so violently had he stormed. When he had done his bidding, as seemed good to him, the collier sat down near the king and made good and happy cheer and said: "By Him who redeemed me, you are welcome here."

When they were served and set down to supper, Gill and the gentle king, Charles the Great, then the collier sat on the other side; without more company they were arranged and paired that night. They brought bread to the table and boar's flesh, and the best wine went round about. These people, as I think, had enough there, within that handsome house, lighted up very brightly. Then dainties came in on the handsomely arranged dais. Truly they lacked nothing in that splendid dwelling. Gillian said with happy countenance, "Sir, enjoy yourself."

The peasant spoke well and loudly to the king: "Sir, the foresters of this wood, truly, all have spite against me for fear of the deer. They charge that I strike down some of the fattest. They say that I'll have to go to Paris, to appear there before our handsome king, and to be treated badly. Every year, indeed, they make such threats against me, and still I have enough for myself and one guest. Therefore feast on and spare not such as you see." The noble Charlemagne thus spoke to the collier in return: "There are times when the king himself would have been glad of such fare."

They had plenty of capons and rabbits, with wine to their desire and also venison; birds baked in pastry, the best that could be. Thus they gaily fared in abundance. The peasant spoke loudly in a clear voice and said: "Gill, let the cup go round for my blessing. Let our guest begin, and then you drink to me. That seems right to me, since he is a stranger." They drank around regularly, they washed, and they rose from the table. With happy countenance the king thanked the collier, and then all three went together to the fire.

When they had made themselves comfortable, the collier told many different stories after supper. A bright fire was burning briskly. The king behaved well and companionably, and always gave an answer to the collier's question, until finally he began to inquire still further. "Truly, friend, I'd like to know, if you wish to tell, where is your principal dwelling-place?" said the collier. "Beyond a doubt," said the king, "I have never hesitated to

---

11. **make me . . . own**, act as host. 17. **[since . . . proper]**. Two lines are missing from the text at this point. 29. **unfamiliar gestures**. The king's elegant manners were strange to the collier.

tell: these fifteen years I have lived at the court in the highest office with my lady the queen."

"What kind of office are you in when you are at home, if you dwell with the queen, finest in dress?" "A servant of her chamber, sir, by St. James, and, though I say it myself, the most intimate of all. I am afraid that I shall be blamed for staying away tonight." "What shall I call you," said the collier, "when you are gone from here?" "Wymond of the Wardrobe is my right name. Wherever you find me before you, your lodging is ready for you. If you come to the court, I promise that on my account you shall have the better sale for your fuel, and profit for your work worth a load or two."

He said, "I have no notion as to where the court is, and I am very loath to come where I am unknown." "And I shall indeed tell you the truth in every detail, so that you will know well enough before I leave you. Both the king and the queen meet in Paris to keep their Yule together, for she has been sent after. There you may sell, by right, as dearly as you will price; and I shall assist you further if I can help in anything, for I am known to the officers in case you come there. Keep my name well in mind, and ask if I am at home, for I think, by St. James, that you will do the better for it."

"It seems to me reasonable, by the Cross, that I follow your advice in case I come to the court and know no one except you. Now there is nothing so good as to drink and go to our beds, for, as far as I know, the night is advanced." They led him quickly to a private room, where a handsome bed had been set up in that dwelling, enclosed with curtains and finely covered. They lacked none of the best wine. The collier and his wife both went with him to serve him in all that they could until he was brought to bed. The king said nothing more except to thank them for what they had done.

Early in the morning, when it was day, the king got ready at once, with few squires to help him. The guards and chamberlains who were accustomed to awaken many a noble man were all absent. A servant had quietly brought him his horse; the king had grown tired of this kind of life, and mounted quickly. Then he called to the peasant, where he lay close by, to take his leave, and he spoke in a friendly fashion. Then they both woke up and heard that he was there. The peasant started up at once and begged him to wait until noon. "I advise you not to go until this fierce storm is over."

"As I hope to prosper," said the king, "I am loath to remain. Isn't tomorrow Christmas, principal day of the year? A man who at this season is supposed to perform his duties will no doubt be found out in his fault if he is absent. I see the sky clear on every side; I want to return to the court while the weather is fair. Call forth the good wife, let us pay her for the fine lodging which I have found here before we ride away." "Stop! God forbid," the collier said, "that you, one of the retinue of Charles, chief king of chivalry, should be charged for a night's lodging."

"Well, since it is so that you will take no pay, come tomorrow to the court and follow my advice. Hurry and bring a load and make no delay. You must not be ashamed of your trade, if you are to prosper. If I can help you to sell anything, truly I shall try, and I myself will have some of your fuel." "By St. Peter," he said, "I shall try in the morning, if I can, to bring coals to the court, to see if they will sell." "See to it that you don't delay, I beg you," said the king. "In truth," said the collier, "trust well that I shall be there, for you will never again undertake to tell a lie."

"But tell me now, honestly, what is your right name? I shall forget you tomorrow, if anyone molests me." "Wymond of the Wardrobe. I ask you not to conceal it; take good heed of my name if you will try to come to court." "I shall hold to what I have said, that I tell you plainly. I count on succeeding where any collier can do business." When he had agreed to come the king was happy, and he took his leave without further delay. The collier then took great thought of the knowledge he had acquired and went to the charcoal in haste to get his merchandise ready. He prepared himself a load against early morning.

The sky lightened up quickly, and the day was bright. The king had a close knowledge of the country. Sir Roland and Oliver came riding along the road and with them a thousand and more able-bodied men who had been wandering all night long, and many more than they, ten times as many, who had been appointed to go out in each direction, to see if they could hear of the king or come upon the place where he was. They prayed to Jesus Christ that he would grant them grace. As soon as Sir Roland saw it was the king he knelt down on the spot, thanking God for a long time. There was a thankful meeting at that encounter.

The gentle knight, Sir Roland, fell to his knees, thanking Almighty God whose power was great. Sir Oliver was beside him and three bishops, not counting the common people who had come, and many another knight. Then all that chivalrous company came to Paris between noon and night on

Christmas Eve. They saw the noble Bishop Turpin coming with thirty dozen priests, arranged in like vestments, preaching of prophecy in a procession. After them, both far and near, people were following in a group, thanking God with good cheer that their lord had returned.

When these princes appeared in Paris, each street decked itself out in royal splendor. A fitting service was conducted at St. Denis, with many proud prelates, as the book says. Afterwards they went to supper in the palace; minstrels played before that mirthful man. Many a strong mother's son, both worthy and wise, was seen at that assembly for twenty-one days; with all kinds of princely plenty for his pleasure. They called it the best Christmas and the most nobly celebrated since King Charles was ever a man, or ever was in France.

Then early in the morning, when the day dawned, the collier took great thought of what he had undertaken. He threw two baskets with plenty of coals on a horse, and bound them with ropes to go to that dwelling. "Mary, it is not my advice," said Gillian, "unless you knew that man, to trust yourself to his mercy. You gave him an outrageous blow and blew a great brag. In faith you would have paid dearly for it if he had been alone. Therefore keep away from the court on all accounts. That man whom you outraged is not of as low degree as he said. I dare stake my life that you will hear and see that."

"Now, wife, have no fear for my life today; let me do as I choose, the fate is my own. I did not speak unreasonably, to tell the truth, to Wymond of the Wardrobe, if the truth were known. I shall hold to what I have promised, turn out as it may, whether it leads to sorrow or gain." He put two baskets on a horse and by the time day had dawned went on his way across the difficult valleys, traveling briskly along the highway to Paris as fast as he could; with a whip in his hand he sought the court to fulfill his covenant.

The good king readily thought about the agreement and called Sir Roland—a man whom he trusted most above all other people, one who would never undertake anything without his assent—to him and gave a command: "In the morning take your horse and armor; I should like you to go and watch the roads well. If you meet any man traveling on the moor, have him come to this city—I tell you my will. Or if you see any man coming along the way, whatsoever he may be, bring him quickly to me, that I may see him in this hall before noon today."

26. **alone**, that is, if I, a woman, had not been present.

Sir Roland wondered greatly and reflected in his heart what that which the king had said might mean, that he should be obliged to keep watch in the open country on the solemn Christmas Day when every man ought to rest and when he ought to have prepared himself to serve his God; and then with a happy countenance that brave man made ready. Fully armed, he rode proudly and rapidly out of Paris to keep his promise. He surveyed the country outside the town, but he saw nothing stirring, either far or near, only the fields there, both valleys and hills.

He waited and lingered until mid-morning and later, looking at the high hills and the level road, until he saw where the collier was coming with all his load, with two baskets on a horse; he was glad of this. He went to him quickly among the gray woodlands, ready at his bidding to bring him promptly to the king. The collier knelt politely to the knight, and Sir Roland himself saluted him in return, and then ordered him to cease his courtesy and prepare to go. He said, "You must go to Paris to the king without delay. Hurry fast straightway, since I find no more than you."

"In truth," said the collier, "I was never as foolish as that. Sir Knight, it is not polite to make fun of common people. There's many a man better than I who often comes to Paris, of whom the king knows nothing, neither night nor morning. As for mauling me or laying hold of me, even though my clothes are dirty, I'll lose my life before I'll be intimidated in that way." "Stop," said Sir Roland, "you do not seem wise to me. I advise you, by all that we have sworn, to be obedient, and don't call it mocking, but do as I direct you, since you have heard my pleasure. It is the king's order; you should go at this time even if I had met ten such as you are."

"I am but one, madman, whom you have met here, and I have no need to match myself against overbearing men, traveling over the plains to fetch fuel, and often fouling my feet in many a dirty swamp, going with loads to get my living. There are many peasants in the country whom you cannot order around: unless I be hard beset I shall keep what I have promised to Wymond of the Wardrobe, I know very well when." "As I hope to prosper," said Roland, "it is my intention that you shall keep no promise to Wymond or to Will until I have brought you to fulfill the king's command."

The peasant looked at the knight, as he was standing there. He bore, engraved in gold and red in color, glittering very gaily when the gleams began, a tiger tied to a tree, a symbol of anger; truly

RALPH THE COLLIER

that angry creature was trembling there, well made and adorned on that bright shield. He had won worthily great honor in war before, which had been seen in combat with many a valiant man. His steel cap was bordered and burnished bright with stone of costly beryl, diamonds, and sapphires, rich rubies also, most fittingly arranged.

His plate armor was set all over with precious stones, and his knee-pieces equally fine; his leg-armor consisted of great plates of gold then, and his fine thigh-pieces were shining very brightly. There were gleaming arm-protectors of steel about his arms, studded with beryls and clear crystals, set about with both topaz and truelove knots. It would be very tedious to tell the tenth part of his jewels. His saddle was adorned and ornamented perfectly on all sides; his bridle handsome and fine, and his horse stout on the road. He was the most royal in apparel of any who could ride on a horse.

Ralph in his heart praised the fine appearance of the regal array in which Roland rode. "He is the finest in equipment who ever went over the earth; may he be blessed with success in every day's undertaking! If he were as manly a man as he is well built, it would be a very mighty man who dared to endure a hostile meeting with him." In wrath he ordered the collier without delay to throw the baskets off the horse and go to the king. "In truth, that would be a great shame," said the collier. "I guaranteed that they should be brought today, despite whatever might happen. Sir Knight, you are wasting your words here. You're hanging around in these woods and also keeping me here until half the whole day has reached its height." "By Christ, who was baptized, and his noble Mother, you must go to court, there will be no begging you about that. It might be counted an insult unless you should appear to see what favor the king will grant you." "As Christ may save me, I would not be found false to the king for any gold on earth." "I must make you come and be recognized, as I am commanded. I do not know what his will is, nor did he any more name you to me than any other man, just whomsoever I should find."

"You found me bringing nothing which would lead to a feud. I should be a fool if I had fled, and had found no cause for alarm, but I was bringing my loads like a law-abiding man who lives, in faith, with great loyalty and labor. By the Mother and Maiden who redeemed us, if you trouble me any more, come what may afterwards, you and I shall exchange blows until one of us is dead, for the deeds you have done to me on this blessed day." Sir Roland had great wonder at this speech. He saw no weapons which the collier bore there except an old shield and a rusty sword.

"It is likely," said Sir Roland and laughed lightly, "that such a sturdy countryman would hit stoutly; there are many townsmen who are tough in a tussle, even though their swords are black and ugly. Fine birds are often found cowardly and unreliable, moreover. I forbid that we fight or fall into such folly. Let us rather see how we can part with suitable dignity, and put ill-temper away—I advise it in Christ's name! Where does that Wymond dwell whom you promised to meet today?" "With the queen, he told me, and there I promised to be, in Paris, by God, without delay."

"And I am known to the queen," said Sir Roland, "and to many ladies in her chamber, by books and bells. The king is in Paris, that I'll guarantee, and all the retinue who live at his court. I need have no trouble about my mission, for I think from what you say that you will be there. But since I have found you, go ahead now and keep my covenant." "Sir Knight," said the collier, "trust me to do nothing else, unless some sudden obstacle delay it, for what I promise of free will, if no man threatens me to it, that I am bound to carry out, and I shall do so while I am able."

"Very well, since you will be there to make your promises good, I do not need to complete my mission until noon today." "You may trust, man," said the collier, "as I am true, I shall not hurry myself one foot faster along the road; but unless you get out of my way, you will soon regret it, or, by the Cross, I shall spoil your royal array. Though your body is armed in that bright color, you will be held weak in your good faith." Sir Roland said to himself, "To quarrel any more with him is only folly; I see plainly that he will be there." He took his leave of the collier amicably.

"By Christ," said the collier, "that would be a dirty shame, that you, who are so shining, should get away without my knowing you just because you see that my clothes are old and all worn out. You believe nothing of the stories which I am telling. Let us bring no men with us, but alone as we were born, and these horses which carry us, and I make an agreement to this, that if I keep my health, I will meet you here on the moor tomorrow, and have my hand on it, since you have no leisure to take at this time." At a crossroads they took different paths, both, in truth, to Paris; thus the two parted.

The noble knight, Sir Roland, rode off quickly and left the collier to come along as he had agreed; and when he came to Paris, High Mass was over, and the king and many handsome people had gone out of the church. Without delay he pulled off his armor hastily and dressed himself in one of the richest robes. In that handsome garment he went in at noon, as he was accustomed, with the man who owned the dwelling, on foot, courteously with the other, and first of all. The king was well pleased with Sir Roland's arrival; then he had him summoned to ask for his news.

The king spoke to him in private: "Come here, sir knight, have you done my bidding, as I commanded you?" "In faith," said Sir Roland, "I rode straight on to watch the roads carefully, and that I'll maintain. Today no warrior seemed to be prepared for combat; I found very few traveling there over the plains; except for just one man who came into my sight there was no living person abroad in this land." "What kind of a fellow was that one, sir, I beg of you?" "A man in peasant's dress, who went forth boldly; he was taking the road to Paris, bringing coals."

"Why have you not brought the peasant, as I ordered you? I fear that he frightened you so that you did not dare to deal with him." "In faith," said Sir Roland, "if he had done so it would have been a hard blow to my heart, and I a man in good health." He saw that the king was annoyed and gladly went out to see if the collier's loyalty held good. "I should have pressed him hard in combat if I had known that the fellow would steal away, but I didn't believe that he would trick me today." As he went straight out he met a porter's boy coming hastily toward him right from the gate.

"Where are you going, fellow, that you are walking so fast?" "By God," the lad said, "I have something special to announce here: I see that there is a lone man at the gate who does not want to leave unless he is let in quickly. With a horse and two baskets cast on the ground, he insists on trying to come into this palace." "I am indeed happy if you have found that man. Let him in gladly, it will do no harm. But does he ask earnestly after any man?" Then the servant said, "Yes, certainly, at this moment he is asking after one Wymond as urgently as he can."

"Go back, porter, and let him in at once among the proudest in the crowd, handsome in dress. Say that you are not worthy to go to Wymond, but tell him to seek him out himself, if there is such a one." Sir Roland went back where mirth should begin, and the brisk yeoman went to the gate, where he fastened the bars quickly before he would pause, and then let the man wander about the building at his will. "Go seek him yourself," he said loudly. "I myself have no leisure to leave these gates." "By Christ," said the collier, "I care but little about that. If you will not seek him, I'll do it myself, for I have often sweated very painfully in work. Take care of my horse, so that no one may call him away until I come from the court," said the collier. "I should be sorry to lose my load, all of which I leave here. See that you do not lose them, but guard them carefully." With that the bold man went hastily into the hall, to find out if Wymond's dwelling was there. He argued with the usher more than once: "Sir, can you tell at all where Wymond is today? I beg you, bring him out of this building, if you can do so."

He believed that the man would have known of Wymond, whom he was expecting, but the former paid no attention to his noisy words. There were no men there who recognized Wymond's name, and they reckoned the collier as scarcely worth notice. When he saw that neither meekness or moderation could help him, he hastened inside speedily and spared none of them. There were no five of the men who could keep him from going on; he went in so resolutely that he hurt some of them. He pushed in through them violently and with threats. When he came among them all, the king was still in the hall, and many good men with him, not yet gone to the meal.

Though he had looked for such a sight these seven years, he would not have seen such an imposing assembly. The hall was fittingly decked and painted without equal, with diamonds beautifully set at intervals. It was attractively ornamented on every side, red glittering very handsomely, shining on green; flowers, with the fleur-de-lis foremost of all, with more than fifteen marvelous devices blazing. The roof above was bordered with circular red ornaments; roses, columbines, and lilies were arranged to perfection; this was a pleasant lodging in a splendid place.

With hangings arranged by the doors, whoever would judge them, with all kinds of ornaments finely prepared, bordered with silver beautiful in appearance, the hall was cunningly adorned in wonderful variety. On the hangings there were merry birds above and beautiful animals, handsome birds in groves and fish with their young. The floor was carpeted and clad and covered entirely. Coming down from the corners and joining perfectly there were bright tapestries embroidered all over. Large coats of arms on high, painted and well made, were arranged exactly right along the hall.

"Here is regal splendor enough for the time being," said Ralph, "adorned with all splendor, and

RALPH THE COLLIER

there is no denying it. If I had one word of Wymond, I would go out of this building, to go on my way, certainly, from these men, but I must yet hear more as to what in short has become of him, and ever have my eye after him attentively." He pushed in through thirty all at once, where many men brave in deeds were assembled that day. They pulled him backward because he was rough. He received many a great shove as he got in through, but he was strong, I believe, and unwilling to give up.

He thrust in through them and pushed violently and made his way to the front rank. Soon he got a glimpse of the noble king beside him. "There is Wymond, I know, there is no doubt about it. I recognize him well, although he is clad in other attire, in clothes of pure gold, showing clearly who he is. When he lodged with me he was not as imposing by half as he is here. In truth, he is of higher station than he ever told me. Alas that I was enticed here! I sorely fear that I am tricked." The king smiled to himself when he saw that bold man.

Handsome men were served there in that hall, many noble lords on every side. The collier, with an anxious face, cast his eye on the lovely queen, who was courteous and fair: "Lady, by the gracious God who redeemed us so dearly, I take no pleasure in your glittering attire. The Devil came to me to teach me a king's courtesy, and so I think I may say before I get away from here. If I could escape from this adventure, which makes my face change, there would be no man so wise as to make me come to Paris to see where the king lives any time in the next seven years!"

When the nobles had washed and gone from the tables, they were amazed, certainly, at their wise lord. The king fell into conversation and spoke his mind, he told his story to many gracious men, how the rough fellow met him on the heath, and how the frost was so bitter, and from then straight on. Then the collier trembled as though he had been put to shame when he heard the truth told how he had threatened the king. "Great God! If only I and yourself together were now suddenly set on the moor where we met—or any good knight whom you could get in your hall!"

The lords laughed aloud and listened to the king, how he had been guided and lodged and so lightly regarded; then the courageous knights asked to have him hanged. "For, in our opinion," they said, "he has deserved that." "God forbid," said the king, "that my thanks should be such a thing to the man who protected my life on so bad a night! He seems to be a stalwart man and strong in striking:

16. who he is. A line is missing from the text at this point.

for his courtesy that peasant shall be made a knight. I consider that advice very bad which kills Christian men, for I have need of more and not to destroy those who might be worthy to go and fight against God's foes."

In the presence of many noble men, dukes and worthy lords, in that fine hall, he made him a knight: "Sir, look out for yourself, you appear to be strong; take care of this order, I call you a knight; to make you a manly man I make you one of power. Each year I shall allot you three hundred pounds, and also the next vacancy, by reasonable right, which occurs in France, wherever it may happen, forfeiture or free ward, which first comes to hand, I give you here heritably, on condition that I hear, when I am pressed, that you are found ready with coat of mail and sword.

"It would be my will, worthy man, that you won your shoes, and went with these warriors who are strongest in battle. Here are courageous knights, even if they do not know you because of the simple rank which you are in here. I beg God of His mercy to make you a good man, and I shall give you gleaming equipment to begin with." The king then and there had a chamber of armor assigned to a squire and made him its keeper, with close-fitting armor of steel for that strong knight, and sixty squires in his service to be his retinue. It was a fine company which Sir Ralph got that night.

In the morning early Sir Ralph would not delay, but made ready to ride in regal array: "I think that it is best to keep what I have promised to that violent man who bullied me into staying. I am only a joke among these gallant men. I will go the readiest way to that fine fellow: while my life lasts there shall no lord laugh aloud, that I should live in cowardice; and, besides, should I live thus it would be a wicked good fortune that I had come into, if the king were to hear said openly that he had made a peasant knight among these bold warriors, and that he dared not do anything."

He rushed out of town on a rugged horse and rode straight ahead in his regal attire. He took his way directly to the mountain where he had engaged to meet the knight Sir Roland. He boldly surveyed the hill across the valleys to see if any brave man was prepared for combat that day. He tied his horse to a bush on the brown heath, and then waited by the open road to keep what he had promised, until it was near the time of day that he had been there before. He looked a little distance away from him, and saw the largest man he had ever seen coming along in haste.

A knight on a camel came up briskly, with a

countenance courageous and cruel to behold. He appeared to be waiting boldly with coat of mail and sword, his mount was ungainly, broad, and too tall. Sir Ralph made ready at once and came riding, and at the right distance for a charge he put his spear in the brace. The other seemed much more ferocious than when he first met him; he tried in his courage to find out who he was; he struck the horse with the spurs and galloped forward over the heath. They ran so hard a course that both their steeds lay dead. Their spears flew away above their heads in splinters.

Thus because of their strength they were both left on foot, those stout mounts lay struck dead at that blow. These noble eager warriors rushed out quickly, drew out two swords and ran together, planned with good will to do each other harm; these men struck on each other's helmets before they paused. They quickly cut at each other, were loath to leave off, to lose the glory in war that they had won before; they did not go away for any fear of being conquered. Thus each attacked the other with metal swords, and for an hour of the day they had a long fight.

These bold armed men hewed on hastily, they became sluggish from the heat and also angry until they had so exhausted themselves that they almost fainted, so unwilling was either to diminish his reputation. The active noble men went out from the lists, exhausted by their weapons and badly wounded, too. There was no truce there until one gave up the ghost. "Ask for quarter!" they cried from either side. Sir Ralph proceeded to cool himself and to get more light: with a chivalrous countenance he cast up his visor and saw coming near at hand another bold knight.

"Now, by the Cross," said Sir Ralph, "I reprove you! You have broken the condition, you have not done right. You promised to bring no supporter here, but only ourselves. I took your hand to that, as you were a true knight." The Saracen said aloud: "Now I hear you lie! I never saw you before this very day. Now, if Mahomet and Termagant will maintain my strength, you will think it too soon that you have met with me." Sir Ralph was happy at that remark and his face beamed: "You say you are a Saracen: now the Lord be thanked, one of us shall never go from this place alive."

Then the Saracen spoke arrogantly to Sir Ralph: "I have no such desire to live as to leave you with kindly feelings." He gave the man beside him a blow with his sword, so that the blood spurted out above his brow. The bold knight staggered heavily there, the Saracen made him give way the length of a broad rod. Sir Ralph rushed up again and hit him quickly: they pressed forward boldly to test their strength. Each one quickly whipped out a short knife. With two knives in hand they stood firmly in battle, and at that moment Sir Roland came when they were nearly done.

The noble knight Sir Roland rode straight up, jumped from his horse, and ran between them. He said: "I see that you are a Saracen, who is attacking so boldly to defeat our Christian men. Tell me your name at once, you vagabond knight! Confound your fighting! You have been fierce. You are stout and strong and stalwart in battle; so, truly, is your fellow, and that is very apparent. If you will believe in Christ you will receive no outrage." "In truth," said the Saracen, "you yourself have never so frightened me that I would have asked for indulgence, nor shall I today. Don't speak to me with your boast, but both of you get ready. Lay on boldly the best you can, I beg you."

"No," said Sir Roland, "that would not be reasonable. I believe, by the mighty God who can do the greatest of all things, that since one of us is able to make you a prisoner, some men would say that it was no knightly deed for two of us to do so. I advise you sincerely to forsake your Mahomet—out on that foul fiend!—for your religion is false. Become a Christian, sir knight, and call upon Christ. It is my desire to convert you—this wicked world is but a moment—and do you have Him who is the Maker of all things wholly in your heart."

"Sir Roland, I care nothing for your ravings, you do but reverence to those who regard it not. You yourself have often slain my kinsmen, sultans and relatives, who tried to put you to shame. Now you try to gain favor with your cajolery. Now I should marvel were I to favor you at all. We shall ravage you pitilessly in the springs to come, and make your dwellings bare—I have brought a message to that effect—chase Charles your king far out of France. I wish to bear these tidings to him from the Khan of Tartary, to tell him them without any courtesy, as I have told you."

"It is of no use, tell me your name at once. You Saracens are always arrogant and self-willed: a bright fire could never be brought from so evil a burning log; the Fiend is so wicked as far as he has power." "As I hope to thrive," said the Saracen, "my intention is to fight. My relatives are the ones who lie in wait for the Christians with hostility. My

---

43. **Termagant**, an imaginary deity worshiped, according to medieval Christian nations, by the Mohamedans.

24–27. **I believe . . . to do so**, a free translation of a difficult sentence.

name is Magog, and my desire, if I might do so, is to strike down violently those whosoever are in my path: therefore my reward is very good back home where I live." "In truth," said Sir Roland, "that is a very bad bargain, to have pleasant land while you are living and then hell at your death. If you would be converted at once and reform yourself from sin, you would have more profit and much pardon: several rich duchies to be invested with until the day dawns which will never end; to wed a noble lady as wife and possess her with happiness in this way, one of the rich ones of our kingdom, the noble duchess, Lady Jane, who claims by descent Anjou and other lands, with many a rich town. Thus you may, if you desire, act in the best way. I'll relieve you of doubt: there is none as fair in all France as she, heir apparent to two duchies."

"I care nothing for your riches, Sir Roland," said the rude Saracen in regal array, "I set no store either by your gold or your treasure, but if your God is as good as I hear you say, I will forsake Mahomet and commit myself to His power perpetually forevermore, as to one who is of greater strength. With heart and good will I pledge you my faith here that I shall always believe faithfully in your Lord, and I beseech Him for grace and ask Him for mercy, and also Christ His very glorious Son. For I have seen Christian men who have been in many afflictions cry out to Him often."

"That speech pleases me," said Roland, "I thank God and his sweet Son Christ who has sent you this grace." All three quickly swore on their swords and held themselves friends until the end of their lives, ever ready to live and die in any trouble. Those knights returned to the court, as Christ had directed them. The king made game and sport on their arrival, with many happy men to increase their joys. Venerable bishops had that bold man brought that day, gave him the various sacraments, and named him Sir Gawteir. Afterwards with a ring he married the fair duchess.

Then Sir Ralph received a donation to maintain his knighthood. Tidings came to the king within nine days that the marshal of France had just died, and then and there, with the advice of many bold knights, he considered Ralph worthy to be placed in his stead, fitting and bold to hold that honor. He would not forget his wife, for fear of God's anger, but he sent for that courteous lady, to live together, as was right. He then founded in St. Julian's name a fair house in the place where he met the king so that all who needed lodging should evermore have hospitality.

Finis

OTHER ROMANCES

THE LAY OF SIR ORFEO

The group of short romantic poems which are called lays, or more specifically Breton lays, contains some of the most attractive medieval narratives. A majority of these poems, which are found in both French and English, state specifically that they were first composed by Breton harpers. Nothing survives in the Breton tongue which in any way resembles a lay, but we have clear evidence that Breton harpers plied their trade in France, and since many of the stories themselves are of undisputedly Celtic origin, there can be little reason to doubt that the plots, in one form or another, were carried from Brittany to France and thence to England. The most distinguished writer of lays was Marie de France, a talented authoress of the second half of the twelfth century, who probably spent at least part of her life at the court of Henry II of England. We have twelve of her lays, two of which, *Sir Launfal* and *Lai le Freine*—the latter being so called because the heroine was named for the ash tree (*fraisne*) in which she was found as a baby—were turned into Middle English. The modern reader who feels, quite often with justification, that a besetting sin of medieval literature is length out of all proportion to interest, will be well advised to read the poems of Marie and of the authors of what may be fairly termed her school.

Sir Orfeo, written at the beginning of the fourteenth century, is one of the most appealing of the English lays. The French original is lost, and the story itself is neither Celtic nor even medieval in origin. Behind Sir Orfeo we have the classical myth of Orpheus and Eurydice, but changed almost beyond recognition. The story is given a medieval setting which in charm and beauty compares favorably with anything classical; and, whatever its ultimate source, the Celtic elements in the poem are unmistakable. There is no comparison between the grim ruler of Hades and this fairy king from the Celtic otherworld, hunting gaily, though not always successfully, through the forests of the human world. The story is given a happy ending, so that Orfeo and his queen may rule over their kingdom in felicity and prosperity once more. It is not hard to see why the classical harper appealed to the Bretons, or to French imitators, nor why they altered the tale to suit their world and their conventions, but we must marvel at the genuine skill with which the alterations were made. The first lines of the poem, which, curiously enough, also occur at the beginning of *Lai le Freine*, give an admirable definition of a lay, and are perhaps worth quoting in the original:

> We redyn ofte and fynde ywryte,
> As clerkes don us to wyte,
> Þe layes þat ben of harpyng
> Ben yfounde of frely þing.
> Sum ben of wele and sum of wo;
> And sum of ioy and merþe also;

Sum of trechery and sum of gyle,
And sum of happes þat fallen by whyle,
Sum of bourdys and sum of rybaudry,
And sum þer ben of þe feyré.
Off alle þing þat men may se,
Moost to lowe forsoþe þey be.
In Brytayn þis layes arne ywryte,
Furst yfounde and forþe ygete—
Of aventures þat fillen by dayes,
Wher of Brytouns maden her layes;
When þey myght owher heryn
Of aventures þat þer weryn,
Þey toke her harpys wiþ game,
Maden layes and 3af it name.

The present translation is from the text printed in *Middle English Metrical Romances*, edited by W. H. French and C. B. Hale, Prentice-Hall, 1930, pp. 323 ff.

WE often read and find written, as learned writers cause us to know, that the lays which are for harping are composed about wonderful things: some are of prosperity and some of sorrow, and some of joy and mirth too, some of treachery and some of guile, and some of events that happen now and then, some of jokes and some of ribaldry, and there are some of fairyland. They are certainly the most to praise of all the things which men can see. In Brittany these lays are written, first composed and brought forth, of adventures which happened in other times, about which the Bretons made their lays; when they could hear anywhere of adventures which had occurred there, they took their harps with joy, composed lays and gave them names. Of adventures which have happened, I can tell some, but not all.

Listen, lords who are true, and I will tell you about Sir Orfeo. Orfeo was a king, a great lord in England, a stalwart man and brave as well, generous, and also courteous. His father was descended from King Pluto, and his mother from King Juno, who at one time were considered as gods because of adventures which they did and told about.

Orfeo loved the sport of harping most of anything; every good harper was sure to have much honor from him. He himself loved to harp and devoted his keen wits to it. He learned so well that there was not a better harper anywhere. There was never a man born in the world who ever sat before Orfeo, and could hear his harping, that he did not think he was in Paradise, there was so much joy and melody in his playing.

This king lived in Thrace, which was a splendidly defensible city; for Winchester, without a doubt, was then called Thrace. The king had an excellent queen who was called Lady Herodis, the fairest lady at the time who could go in flesh and bones; she was full of love and goodness, and no man can describe her fairness.

It happened at the beginning of May when the day is pleasant and hot, and the winter showers are gone, and every field is full of flowers, and fresh blossoms grow merrily enough all about on every bough, that this same queen, Lady Herodis, took two noble maidens and went on a certain morning to amuse herself by the side of an orchard, to see the flowers spread and grow and to hear the birds sing.

All three of them sat down under a fair young tree, and very soon this beautiful queen fell asleep on the green grass. Her maidens did not dare to wake her, but let her lie and take her rest. So she slept until the morning was all gone and afternoon came. But as soon as she awoke, she cried out and made a hideous noise, she twisted her hands and feet and scratched her face, so that it was wet with blood. She tore all her rich robe and took leave of her senses. The two maidens beside her did not dare to remain with her any longer, but ran to the palace at once, and told both squires and knights that their queen would go mad, and ordered them to go and seize her. Knights ran and also ladies, sixty damsels and more. They came to the queen in the orchard and took her up in their arms and brought her finally to her bed and held her there very firmly. But she kept on crying in the same fashion and wished to be up and away.

Nothing had ever made Orfeo feel worse than he did when he heard this news. He came with ten knights to the chamber right before the queen and looked at her and said with great pity: "My dear life, what is wrong with you, who have ever before been so quiet, and who now cry so wonderfully loud? Your body, which was of such perfect whiteness, is all torn by your nails! Your complexion, alas, which was so red, is as colorless as though you were dead! And your small fingers, also, are all bloody and all pale! Alas! your two lovely eyes look as a man looks at his enemy! O lady, I beg you, mercy! Stop this piteous crying, and tell me what is wrong with you and how it happened, and what thing can help you now!"

Then she lay still at last and began to weep

---

38. England. Orpheus was the son of Calliope and Oeagrus, king of Thrace. **41. King Juno.** To counterbalance the resexing of Juno, we find in the early fifteenth-century *Batayl or Seege of Troy*, a curious version of the Judgment of Paris, in which there are four contestants, Venus, Jupiter, Saturn and Mercury, referred to as "four ladies from elfen land."

THE LAY OF SIR ORFEO

steadily and spoke thus to the king: "Alas! Sir Orfeo, my lord, we were never once angry since we were first together, but I have always loved you as my life, and so have you loved me. But now we must part; do your best for yourself, for I must go." "Alas," he said, "I am desolate! Where will you go, and to whom? Where you go, I will go with you, and where I go, you shall go with me." "No, no, sir, that is of no avail. I will tell you how it all is: as I lay this morning and slept by the side of our orchard, there came to me two handsome knights, well and properly armed, who ordered me to come in haste and speak with the king their lord. And I answered with bold words that I neither dared nor would do so. They rode back as fast as they could go, and then their king came at once with a hundred or more knights and also a hundred maidens, all on snow-white horses; their clothes were as white as milk. I never before saw such beautiful and distinguished creatures. The king had a crown on his head: it was not of silver or of red gold, but of a precious stone; it shone as bright as the sun. And as soon as he came to me, whether I would or not, he took me and made me ride with him on a palfrey by his side and brought me to his palace, which was well ordered in every way, and showed me castles and towers, rivers, forests, fields full of flowers, and each of his noble steeds, and then he brought me home again into our own orchard and said afterward to me as follows: 'See to it, lady, that you be under this same young tree tomorrow, and then you must go with us and live with us forevermore. And if you cause us any delay, wherever you are, you will be fetched, and all your limbs torn, so that nothing will help you; and even though you are thus torn to pieces, still you will be carried away with us.'"

When King Orfeo heard of this event, "Oh woe," he said, "alas! alas! I would rather leave my life than thus to lose the queen, my wife!" He asked advice from each man, but no one could help him.

Next day when morning came, Orfeo took his arms, and with him at least ten hundred knights, each armed stoutly and grimly, and they went with the queen straight to the young tree. They made a close troop on every side and said that they would remain there and die there every one, before the queen should go from them. But yet from their very midst the queen was snatched away, carried off by magic: men never knew where she had gone.

The king went into his chamber; he often fainted on the stone floor, and made such complaint and such lament that his life was nearly exhausted. Since there was no chance for amendment, he called together his barons, earls, and famous lords, and when they were all come, "Lords," he said, "here before you I appoint my high steward to guard my kingdom hereafter. He shall be in my place to keep my lands everywhere. For now that I have lost my queen, the fairest lady who was ever born, I never again wish to look upon a woman. I shall hurry into the wilderness and live there forevermore with wild animals in the gray woods. And when you believe that I am dead, then hold a parliament and choose yourselves a new king. Now do what seems best to you with all my property."

Then there was weeping in the hall and a great outcry among all of them. Old and young could scarcely say a word with their tongues because of weeping. They all knelt down together and begged him, if it was his desire, that he should not go from them. "Say no more," he said. "It must be so." He left behind all his kingdom; he took only a pilgrim's robe on him, he had neither tunic nor hood, shirt nor any other property. But nonetheless he took his harp and went barefoot out at the gate. No man could go with him. Oh woe, but there was weeping and sorrow when he who had been a crowned king went so poorly from the town!

He went through the wood and over the heath into the wilderness. He found nothing which gave him ease, but always lived in great discomfort. He who had worn ermine and gray fur, and had had purple linen on his bed, now lay on the hard heath, and covered himself with leaves and grass. He who had had castle and towers, rivers, forests, fields full of flowers, now, although it began to snow and freeze, this king had to make his bed in the moss. He who had had noble knights and ladies kneeling before him, now saw nothing which pleased him, only wild serpents gliding by him. He who had had plenty of food and drink, of every delicacy, now had to dig and grub all day before he found his fill of roots. In summer he lived on wild fruit and berries which were good for little; in winter he found nothing but roots, grass, and bark. His whole body dwindled away from distress, and was all chapped.

Lord, who can tell the pain this king suffered for ten years and more! The hair of his beard, black and rough, had grown down to his waist. His harp, in which was all his pleasure, he hid in a hollow tree, and when the weather was clear and bright, he took his harp to him at once and played at his own desire. The noise resounded through all the wood, so that the wild animals which are there hurried about him for joy. And all the birds there were came and sat on every brier to hear his harping to the end, there was so much melody in it. And when he would leave off his harping, no animal would stay with him.

In the hot mornings he could often see near him the king of fairyland with his company come to hunt all about with faint cries, and blowing, and also dogs barking with them. But they took no animal, nor did he ever know where they went. And at another time he could see them hasten by him like a great host ten hundred well-dressed knights, each suitably armed, strong and fierce in appearance, with many banners displayed, and each holding his sword drawn; but he never knew where they wanted to go. And again he saw another thing: knights and ladies in unusual attire come dancing skillfully and softly an intricate step. Drums and trumpets went beside them, and all sorts of minstrelsy. And one day he saw sixty ladies, gentle and gay as bird on bough, ride on horseback beside him, and there was not one man among them there. And each carried a falcon on her hand and rode hawking along a river. They found a very good resort of game, mallards, herons, and cormorants. The birds rose from the water, the falcons separated them well: each falcon killed his prey.

Orfeo saw that and laughed. "By my faith," said he, "there is fair sport. I will go there, in God's name: I was accustomed to see such deeds." He arose and hurried there. He came to a lady, looked at her, and clearly understood and saw by everything that it was his own queen, Lady Herodis. He beheld her eagerly and she him also, but neither spoke a word to the other. Because of the distress which she saw in him, who had been so powerful and so noble, tears fell from her eyes. The other ladies saw this and made her ride away; she could stay with him no longer. "Alas," he said, "now I am sorrowful! Why will death not kill me now? Alas, wretch, that I cannot die now after this vision! Alas! My life lasts too long, when I dare not speak one word to my wife, nor she to me. Alas! Why will my heart not break! By my faith," he said, "happen what may, wherever these ladies ride, I will go the same way: I care for neither life nor death!"

He quickly put on his pilgrim's robe and hung his harp on his back and had very good will to proceed—he did not stop for either stump or stone. The ladies rode into a cave; he went after them and did not remain behind. When he had gone into the cave a good three miles or more, he came into a fair land, as bright as the sun on a summer's day, smooth and flat and all green; there was neither hill nor valley visible. In the middle of the country he saw a castle, rich and royal and wonderfully high; all the outer wall was clear and shone like crystal. A hundred towers were about it, strangely and strongly battlemented; the buttress rose from the ditch, richly arched of red gold; the vaulting was ornamented with all kinds of different animals. Within these were spacious chambers all of precious stones. The worst pillar to look at was entirely of polished gold. The whole land was always light, for when it should be night and dark, the rich stones shone as brightly as does the sun at noon. No man can tell or think in his mind the rich work that had been made there. It seemed to him from everything that it was the noble court of Paradise. The ladies alighted in this castle and he desired to go in after them if he could. Orfeo knocked at the gate; the porter was ready at that, and asked him what he would have. "In truth," he said, "I am a minstrel, to entertain your lord with my music, if it be his sweet will." The porter opened the gate at once and let him go into the castle. Then he looked all about and saw lying inside the wall people who were brought there and seemed dead and were not: some stood without heads, and some had no arms, and some had wounds through the body, and some lay mad and tied up; some sat armed on horseback, and some had been strangled as they ate; some were drowned in water, and some were all shriveled by fire; wives lay there in childbed, some dead and some crazed; and very many lay there besides just as they sleep here mornings; each had been taken thus in the world, and come here by means of magic. There he saw his own wife, Lady Herodis, his dear love, sleeping under a young tree; he recognized her by her clothes.

And when he had beheld all these marvels he went into the king's hall. There he saw a handsome sight: a pleasing and bright canopy under which their head king sat and their fair, sweet queen. Their crowns and their clothes shone so brightly that he could hardly look at them. When he had beheld all that, he knelt down before the king. "O lord," he said, "if it were your will, you should hear my music." The king answered: "What man are you, who have come here now? Neither I nor any who is with me ever sent after you. Since I began to reign here I never found a man so foolhardy that he dared to come to us unless I wished to send for him." "Lord," he said, "believe well, I am only a poor minstrel, and, sir, it is a custom among us to seek many a lord's house; although we may not be welcome, still we can offer our music."

He sat down before the king and took his harp of so merry a sound, and tuned it, as he could well

THE LAY OF SIR ORFEO

do, and began such pleasant notes that all who were in the palace came to hear him, and to lie down at his feet, his melody seemed so sweet to them. The king listened and sat very quietly; he had good will to hear the music and took great pleasure from it, and so, too, did the noble queen. When he had ceased his harping, the king said to him: "Minstrel, your music pleases me well. Now ask me for whatever it may be, I will pay you generously. Now speak, if you are able."

"Sir," he said, "I beg you that you will give me that lady, bright of face, who is sleeping under the young tree." "No," said the king, "that would be unfitting. You would make a sorry couple, for you are lean, rough, and black, and she is lovely without blemish. It would, therefore, be a foul thing to see her in your company." "O sir," he said, "gentle king, yet it would be a much fouler thing to hear a falsehood from your mouth. So, sir, you said now that what I would ask for, I should have, and you must needs keep your word." The king said, "Since it is so, take her by the hand and go. I wish that you may be happy with her." He knelt down and thanked him greatly.

He took his wife by the hand and went at once out of that country, and departed out of that land; he went the same way that he had come.

He followed the road so long that he came to Winchester, which was his own city, but no man knew that it was he. For fear of recognition he dared go no further than the outskirts of the town, but there in narrow quarters he took lodging for himself and his own wife with a beggar, as though he were a minstrel in poor circumstances, and asked news of that country, and who had control of the kingdom. The poor beggar in his cottage told him every bit: how their queen had been stolen away by magic ten years before, and how their king had gone into exile, but no one knew into what country, and how the steward held the land, and he told him many other things. Next day toward noontime he made his wife remain there, and then borrowed the beggar's clothes, hung his harp on his back, and went into that city where men could behold and see him. Earls and bold barons, citizens and ladies, looked at him.

"Look," they said, "what a man! How long the hair hangs on him! See how his beard hangs to his knees! He is withered like a tree!" As he went in the street he met his steward, and loudly set up a cry to him: "Sir steward," he said, "help! I am a harper from the heathen land. Help me now in this distress!" The steward said, "Come home with me. You shall have some of what I have. For love of my lord, Sir Orfeo, every good harper is welcome to me." In the castle the steward sat at his food, and many lords were seated beside him. There were trumpeters and drummers, many harpers and fiddlers. They all made much melody, and Orfeo sat still in the hall and listened. When they were all quiet, he took his harp and tuned it musically. He played the most pleasant notes there that any man ever heard with his ear. Every man liked his music well. The steward looked, and saw and recognized the harp at once. "Minstrel," he said, "as you hope to prosper, where and how did you get this harp? I beg you that you tell me now." "Lord," he said, "in a strange land, as I was going through a wilderness, there I found in a valley a man torn to small pieces by lions, and wolves were eating him with sharp teeth. Beside him I found this very harp. That is ten good years ago." "Oh," said the steward, "now is sorrow for me! That was my lord, Sir Orfeo. Alas, wretch, what shall I do, who have lost such a master! It is a pity that I was born! That such hard luck was prepared for him and doomed to so vile a death!"

He fell down fainting to the ground. His barons took him up at that time and told him how things are: there is no remedy for a man's death! King Orfeo knew well by that that his steward was a faithful man, and loved him as he ought to do, and he stood up and spoke as follows: "Look, steward, listen now to this thing: If I were King Orfeo, and had suffered much pain for a long time in the wilderness, and had won back my own queen out of fairyland, had brought the courteous lady right here to the edge of the town, and taken lodgings for her with a beggar, and had come here to you myself in poor appearance, thus quietly, to test your good will; and if I found you thus loyal, you would never repent it: truly for love or fear, you shall be king after my time. And if you had been happy for my death, you would have been dismissed at once." Then those who were sitting there understood that it was King Orfeo, and the steward recognized him clearly; he threw the table over and fell down at the king's feet; so did every lord who sat there, and all said with one shout: "You are our lord, sir, and our king!"

They were glad because he was alive. They led him to his chamber at once, bathed him and shaved his beard, and dressed him as a king ought to be; then with a great procession they brought the queen into the town, with all kinds of minstrelsy. Lord, but there was great melody! Those who saw them come in such good health wept for joy with their eyes. Now Sir Orfeo was crowned anew and also his queen, Lady Herodis, and lived long afterwards, and then the steward was king.

Harpers in Brittany after this heard how this marvelous event began, and made of it a lay of good appeal and named it for the king. That lay is called "Orfeo." The lay is good, the music sweet. Thus Sir Orfeo came out of his sorrow. God grant us all to do well!

THE TOURNAMENT OF TOTTENHAM

Writers of medieval romances, however ludicrous their excesses may sometimes seem to us, ordinarily took themselves, their plots, and their characters very seriously indeed. Convention reigned long, but the very gravity with which the less-gifted authors retailed their long-winded farragos of bombast and fancy led inevitably to burlesque or parody. Chaucer's *Tale of Sir Thopas* is the earliest and, thanks to Chaucer's genius, the best, of the mock romances which were to flourish into the Elizabethan period. The satire in *Sir Thopas*, to be sure, is not directed against such a poem as *Sir Gawain and the Green Knight*, but rather against a host of poorer products which made their appeal to vulgar and insensitive taste. Chaucer's approach is so subtle, advanced so deftly by the marshaling of innumerable details (many of them innocent in themselves) borrowed from the metrical romances that the reader who has not saturated himself in the earlier poems may often miss the point of the attack. *The Tournament of Tottenham*, written in the middle of the fifteenth century is less sophisticated and intricate than *Sir Thopas*, and on that account, perhaps, more likely to be enjoyed by the reader who is not a professed medievalist. Its author concentrates his satire on a few common features of chivalric romance: the tournament with a lady for its prize, the making of ceremonial boasts to do deeds of daring, and the detailed description of heraldic devices. The first of these is so recurrent that the hero who has not jousted his way to the hand and heart of at least one fair lady is poor indeed. Then, too, the romances are sprinkled with boastful vows, made often over a peacock, a heron, or a pheasant. Chaucer ridicules these when he has Sir Thopas swear "by ale and bread," and perhaps we are to find the equivalent of the peacock in Tyb's brood-hen, Copple.

The poem is a lively one, and we enjoy the boldness with which the author has brought the fanfare and pomp of chivalry down to the level of barnyard and village green. The present translation is from the text printed in *Middle English Metrical Romances*, edited by W. H. French and C. B. Hale, Prentice-Hall, 1930, pp. 989 ff.

IT would be natural to speak of all these bold conquerors: we find marvelous things about many warlike people. We have the Tournament of Tottenham in mind: it would be too bad if such bravery were concealed, as we read in history of Hawkyn, of Herry, of Tomkyn, of Terry, of those who were brave and stalwart in deeds.

It happened in Tottenham, on a famous day, that a festival was made by the high road. There came all the men of the countryside, from Islington, from Highgate, and from Hackney, and all the sweet workers. There Hawkyn hopped, there Dawkyn danced, there Tomkyn blew the trumpet—and all were true drinkers—till day was done and evensong passed, and they had to reckon their bill and figure their accounts. Perkyn the potter moved into the crowd, and said: "Bailiff Randal, you have a daughter, dear Tyb: therefore I should like to know which of all these young men is best worthy to marry her as his wife."

These rogues with their long staves started up, and said: "Bailiff Randal, see! this lad is raving! He asks boldly for your daughter among us, and we are richer men than he, and have more property in cattle and grain." Then Perkyn said: "I have promised Tyb that I shall always be ready to defend my rights, if that should have to be a week from today or even tomorrow."

Then said Bailiff Randal: "May he be ever cursed who would waste any more time on this talking! I don't wish my daughter to make a poor match, but rather I want her to be married to her best advantage. Therefore a tournament shall begin a week from today, to fight with a flail, and he who is of most strength shall enjoy her pleasantly. Whoever conducts himself best in the tournament, wins my daughter with strength of blow, to him shall be given the prize by common agreement, and also Copple, my brood-hen, who was brought out of Kent, and my brown cow. I shall spare no expense; I shall care for no cattle: he shall have my gray mare and my spotted sow!"

There were many bold lads there to offer their bodies. They then took their leave and went home, and all the week after they prepared their attire, until the day came that they should do their deed. They armed themselves with mats, to guard their crowns they put good black bowls on their heads as a protection against the blows of bats. They sewed themselves up in sheepskins, so that they should not be injured; each took a black hat in place of a crest; higher up on their breasts an arrow as broad as a fan, and a flail in their hands, ready to fight. Forth they go! There was great strength shown as to who

1. Tottenham, at this time a village quite distinct from London.

THE TOURNAMENT OF TOTTENHAM

should best defend his body. The man who had no good horse got himself a mare.

I have not often seen such another gathering! When all the great company came riding to the field, Tyb was set on high on a gray mare, on a sack full of seeds so that she should sit soft, and she was led to the gap in the hedge. Despite the crying of all the men Tyb would then go no further until she had her good setting hen placed in her lap. Tyb had on a gay girdle, borrowed for the occasion, and a garland on her head, full of round bones, and a brooch on her breast, full of sapphire stones, ornamented with the sign of the holy cross: no expense was spared there! When jolly Gyb saw her he struck his gray mare so that she let off a cannonade at the rear.

"I vow to God," said Herry, "that I shall not remain behind! If I may meet with Bernard, on blind Bayard, each man should keep himself out of my course, for whatsoever he may be whom I find before me, I know that I shall grieve him!" "Well spoken!" said Hawkyn. "And I declare," said Dawkyn, "if I can meet with Tomkyn, I shall take his flail from him."

"I vow to God," said Hud, "Tyb, you shall soon see to which of all these young men the prize is granted! I shall discomfort them all, for love of you. In whatever place I come, they shall have fear of me, my arms are so shining: I bear a cart rail and a rake, decorated with a burning dragon, and three sections of a cake in each corner."

"I vow to God," said Hawkyn, "although I have the gout, once I have ridden two or three times through the crowd, all whom I find charging about here in the field will have fear of me wherever they see me when I begin to play. I make a vow that I shall not come away once, unless Tyb call me, until I have fallen down three times."

Then said Terry, and swore by his creed: "You never saw a young boy offer his body on that account, for when they fight hardest and are most in dread, I shall take Tyb by the hand and lead her away. I am armed completely: on my coat of arms I bear a dough trough and baker's shovel, a saddle without a cloth, with a fleece of wool."

"I vow to God," said Dudman, "and swear by the straw, while I have my mare left you will not get her thus, for she is well shaped and light as the roe deer: there is no horse who will go before her in this mile; she will not betray me. She will carry me, I dare say, in a long summer's day from Islington to Hackney, and not another half-mile!"

"I vow to God," said Perkyn, "you speak of a cold roast! I shall do more wisely, without any boasting: I know that I shall win, and bring to my side, five of the best horses that are in this host, and here and now I give them to Tyb. Well, boys, here is the man who will fight and not run away, for I am in good spirits, with 'Come on Gib!'"

When they had made their vows, they hurried forth, with flails and horns and trumpets made of wood. All the young men of the countryside were there; they were dressed in such array as they themselves desired. Their banners made of an old rotten hide were very bright: the chevron in the shape of a plow mallet, the silhouette of a bell, with moonlight shed on the field.

I know it was no child's play when they met together! When each man in the field beat on his fellow, and laid on stoutly—they would stop for nothing! And they fought wonderfully hard until their horses sweated, and that with few words spoken. There were flails all split, there were shields all smashed, bowls and dishes all shattered, and many heads broken. There was the clinking of cart saddles and the clattering of cans; the shovels of men in the field were smashed; the heads of some were broken, and the skulls of others; and it was ill with some before they went from there, what with swipes from the flail leathers. The boys were fought out so thoroughly that they could no more fight on horseback, but crept about on the field, as though they were crooked cripples.

Perkyn was so weary that he began to sink: "Help, Hud, I am dead in this same crowd! Forty pence for a horse, a good one and strong, that I may easily come out of my distress! I will spare no cost." He started up like a snail, grabbed a horse by the tail, took Dawkyn's flail from him, and won a mare there. Perkyn won five and Hud won two, and they were glad and happy that they had done so: they wished to bring them to Tyb and present them to her. The horses were so weary that they could not go, but stood still. "Alas!" said Hud, "I lose my joy! I had rather than fourteen pounds of cheese that dear Tyb had all these and knew they were of my sending."

Perkyn turned about in that same crowd; he twisted and jerked among these weary boys; he was throwing them down to the earth and poking

---

19. Bayard, originally the magic horse given by Charlemagne to Aimon's son Renaud; it became the proverbial name for a horse, especially a blind one. **29. arms,** armorial bearings.

4. cold roast! nonsense. **6. horses.** The horses of the vanquished were the prizes for the victors. **12. wood.** See "The Nun's Priest's Tale," l. 578, page 216. **15. chevron,** a ∧-shaped device on the escutcheon.

among them, when he saw Terry start away with Tyb, and ran after him. He pulled him from his horse, gave him plenty of his flail. "Whee, tee-hee!" said Tyb, and laughed. "You're a doughty man!"

Thus they tugged and scuffled until it was nearly dark. All the women of Tottenham came to see that sight, with wisps of straw and flax and rushes lighted there, to fetch home their plighted husbands. And some brought great sledges to carry home their men; some on doors and some on gratings, some on hurdles and some on lattices, and some on wheelbarrows.

They gathered about Perkyn on every hand and granted him the victory: the more was his pride. Tyb and he rode homeward with great joy, and were together all night, until the morning. And they agree with one another: so well has he succeeded in his needs that he has married dear Tyb. The excellent people who conducted her were from the tournament.

Many came to the feast on that occasion: some came limping, and some tripping on the stones, some with a staff in their hand, and some with two at once; of some the heads were broken, and of some the shoulder bones: they came there with sorrow! Woe was Hawkyn, woe was Herry, woe was Tomkyn, woe was Terry, and so were all the young men when they met together.

They were served at that feast with a rich fare: each five and five had a cook, and so they sat in jollity all the long day, and at last they went to bed with very great unsteadiness. There was much mirth among them; in every corner of the house was delicious melody, pleasant to hear, of six men's singing.

Explicit

Middle English: Pronunciation

The student who wishes to get the most satisfaction out of Middle English literature, especially the lyrics and Chaucer, must be willing to take the trouble to learn to pronounce the language in an approximately correct fashion. Study of the following table and practice in reading aloud should soon give a reasonable facility. The beginner will doubtless be forgiven if, unlike Chaucer, he does not make a careful distinction between open and close ē and ō.

VOWELS AND DIPHTHONGS

SOUND	PRONUNCIATION	SPELLING	EXAMPLES
ā	like *a* in *father*	a, aa	ale, caas
a	like *a* in German *Mann*	a	that, pace (vb.)
ē (close)	like *a* in *date*	e, ee	slepen, sweete
ę̄ (open)	like *e* in *there*	e, ee	ever, heeth
e	like *e* in *set*	e	tendre
e (final unstressed)	like *a* in *China*	e	soote, roote
ī, ȳ	like *i* in *machine*	i, y	shires, tyme
i, y	like *i* in *pit*	i, y	priketh, nyght
ō (close)	like *o* in *note*	o, oo	bote, roote
ǭ (open)	like *oa* in *broad*	o, oo	cold, rood (vb.)
o	like *o* in *lot*	o	holt
ū	like *oo* in *boot*	ou, ow	hous, fowles
u	like *u* in *full*	u, o	but, sonne
iū	like *u* in *mute*	u, ew	vertu, Pruce, trewe
ēi	like ę̄ (open) + i	ai, ay, ei, ey	batailles, sayle, feith, wey
au	like *ou* in *mouse*	au, aw	draughte, sawe
ēu	like ē (close) + u	eu, ew	reule, knew
ę̄u	like ę̄ (open) + u	eu, ew	lewed
oi	like *oy* in *boy*	oi, oy	poison, joye
ōu	like *ow* in *know*	ou, ow	soule, growe

CONSONANTS

The pronunciation of Middle English consonants is much the same as in modern English. Certain points, however, must be kept in mind. Consonants were sounded which have become "silent" in modern English, such as the *k* in *knyght* and *knowe*, the *g* in *gnawe*, the *w* in *wrighte*, the *l* in *folk* and *palmeres* and the like. Double consonants were given their full value; thus *son-ne* (sun) is quite distinct from *so-ne* (son).

SOUND	PRONUNCIATION	EXAMPLES
c before back vowels (a, o, u)	like *k*	caas, corages, curs
c before front vowels (e, i, y)	like *s*	certes, citole
ch	like *tch*	chapman, charge
gg (except in words like "frogges" and "legges")	like *dg* in *bridge*	juggen, brigge
h (medial and final, written gh, after back vowels)	like *ch* in German *doch*	foghtren, though
h (medial and final, written gh, after front vowels)	like *ch* in German *ich*	knyght
ng	like *ng* in *finger*	thing
r	strongly trilled	
s (except as below)	like *s* in *sand*	
s (between two vowels)	like *s* in *those*	
th (except as below)	like *th* in *thin*	
th (between two vowels)	like *th* in *those*	

Middle English Lyrics

The Middle English lyric, as illustrated in the following pages, did not spring directly from anything to be found in Old English literature. Certain Old English poems are often called lyrics, but the reference is not to the form, but rather to the elegiac tone, to the prevailingly subjective melancholy of content. Even here we miss the outstanding theme of lyric poetry—romantic love, the love of courtship. Lyrics readily recognizable to us did not appear in England until after the Norman Conquest, and an analysis of style, metrics, and subject matter shows the strong influence of compositions in Latin, Provençal, and French. Although we know that English lyrics, secular as well as religious, were being sung in the twelfth century, only fragments survive from the period before 1200. The great majority of the extant Middle English lyrics are religious, but while many of these are extremely good, the fewer secular, usually amorous, lyrics are of higher artistic quality.

The lyrics make a more immediate appeal to us than do most medieval poems, and that despite the frequent difficulty of the language. Translations spoil the meter or the sense, and frequently both, as witness the critic who translated the first line of the sixth lyric given here as "I shot a bird in bower bright." We respond readily to the lilting melody, the images and figures taken from nature, the prevailing atmosphere of spring and youth. We may feel, perhaps, that too many of the lovers are unsuccessful, and that they celebrate their misfortunes rather too freely in histrionic lovesick wailing, but here we have part of the conventions of courtly love. One wonders just how effective this approach has ever been to the female heart, and perhaps we can afford to conclude that it is a literary, rather than a practical, device.

Of the twelve lyrics given here the ninth and tenth are reprinted from Carleton Brown's *Religious Lyrics of the XVth Century*, Oxford Press, 1939, and the remainder from the same author's *English Lyrics of the XIIIth Century*, Oxford Press, 1932.

THE CUCKOO SONG

"The Cuckoo Song" is the best-known Middle English lyric, and probably familiarity has given it a fame beyond its intrinsic merit. We must admit, however, that it has the freshness of youth, as well as spring, and a realism not always appreciated by its readers. Modern versifiers have frequently given it the supreme accolade of parody, the most striking example of which appeared in Ezra Pound's *Lustra*.

Sumer is icumen in,
Lhude sing cuccu!
Groweth sed and bloweth med
And springth the wode nu.
Sing cuccu!   5

Awe bleteth after lomb,
Lhouth after calve cu,
Bulluc sterteth, bucke verteth.
Murie sing cuccu!
Cuccu, cuccu,   10
Wel singes thu, cuccu.
Ne swik thu naver nu!

Sing cuccu nu, Sing cuccu!
Sing cuccu, Sing cuccu nu!

NOW SPRINGS THE SPRAY

In this lyric we find a dramatic setting not unlike that commonly given to the *chanson d'aventure*. The poet overhears and repeats the lament of the forsaken maiden. In many respects this is one of the loveliest and most skillful of the lyrics; the way in which the poor girl's threat collapses in the pathos of the refrain is beautiful, and beautifully done.

Als i me rode this endre dai
  O mi pleyinge,
Seih i hwar a litel mai
  Bigan to singge:
   "The clot him clingge!
Wai es him i louve-longinge
  Sal libben ai,
    Nou sprinkes the sprai,
  Al for love icche am so seeke
  That slepen i ne mai."   10

Son icche herde that mirie note,
  Thider i drogh;

The Cuckoo Song. **2. Lhude,** loudly.   **3. bloweth med,** blooms (the) meadow.   **4. nu,** now.   **6. Awe,** ewe. **7. Lhouth,** lows.   **8. sterteth,** leaps. **verteth,** breaks wind. **12. swik,** cease.   *Now Springs the Spray.* **1. Als,** as. **endre,** recent.   **2. O,** on, about.   **3. Seih,** saw. **mai,** maid. **5. "The clot ... clingge!** May the clod cling to him! **6. Wai,** woe.   **7. Sal libben,** shall live.   **9. icche,** I. **11. Son,** soon.   **12. drogh,** drew.

I fonde hire in an herber swot
   Under a bogh
   With joie inogh.
Son i asked, "thou mirie mai
   Hwi sinkes-tou ai
      'Nou sprinkes the sprai,
      Al for love icche am so seeke
      That slepen i ne mai?' "   20

Than answerde that maiden swote
   Midde wordes fewe:
"Mi lemman me haves bi-hot
   Of louve trewe;
   He chaunges a newe.
Yiif i mai, it shal him rewe
   Bi this dai,
      Nou sprinkes the sprai,
      Al for love icche am so seeke
      That slepen i ne mai."   30

LADY, HAVE RUTH ON ME

"Lady, Have Ruth on Me" is a typical example of the self-abasement of the unsuccessful lover and lyricist.

With longyng y am lad,
On molde y waxe mad,
A maide marreth me;
Y grede, y grone un-glad,
For selden y am sad
That semly forte se.
Leuedi, thou rewe me!
To routhe thou havest me rad,
Be bote of that y bad,
My lyf is long on the.   10

Leudy of alle londe,
Les me out of bonde,
Broht icham in wo;
Have resting on honde,
And sent thou me thi sonde
Sone, er thou me slo.
My reste is with the ro.
Thah men to me han onde,
To love nuly noht wonde,
Ne lete for non of tho.   20

Leuedi, with al my miht
My love is on the liht,
To menske when y may,
Thou rew and red me ryht;
To dethe thou havest me diht,
Y deye longe er my day,
Thou leve upon mi lay,
Treuthe ichave the plyht,
To don that ich have hyht
Whil mi lif leste may.   30

Lylie-whyt hue is,
Hire rode so rose on rys,
That reveth me mi rest.
Wymmon war and wys,
Of prude hue bereth the pris,
Burde on of the best.
This wommon woneth by west,
Brihtest under bys;
Hevene y tolde al his,
That o nyht were hire gest.   40

ALYSOUN

Even if the author of "Alysoun" had not been sleeping well, he wrote a poem whose lilt and swing has seldom been equaled. The refrain displays a happy optimism by no means common in the lyrics.

Bytuene Mersh and Averil
When spray beginneth to springe,
The lutel foul hath hire wyl
On hyre lud to synge.
Ich libbe in lovelonginge
For semlokest of alle thynge;
He may me blisse bringe,
Icham in hire baundoun.
   An hendy hap ichabbe yhent,
   Ichot from hevene it is me sent—   10
   From alle wymmen mi love is lent,
   And lyht on Alysoun.

On heu hire her is fayr ynoh,
Hire browe broune, hire eye blake,
With lossum chere he on me loh;
With middel smal and wel ymake.

Now Springs the Spray. **13. herber swot,** sweet arbor. **14. bogh,** bough. **22. Midde,** with. **23. lemman,** sweetheart. **bi-hot,** promised. **26. Yiif,** if. *Lady Have Ruth on Me.* **1. lad,** lead. **2. molde,** earth. **3. marreth,** injures. **4. grede,** cry. **5. sad,** satisfied. **6. semly forte,** fair one for to. **7. Leuedi,** lady. **rewe,** have pity on. **8. routhe,** compassion. **rad,** advised. **9. bote,** remedy. **bad,** prayed. **10. is long on,** depends on. **12. Les,** release. **13. icham,** I am. **15. sonde,** message. **16. slo,** slay. **17. ro,** roe. **18. Thah,** though. **onde,** envy. **19. nuly,** I will not. **wonde,** cease. **20. lete,** stop. **tho,** those. **22. on the liht,** alighted on you. **23. menske,** worship. **24. red,** advise. **25. diht,** ordained. **27. lay,** faith. **28. ichave,** I have. **29. hyht,** promised. **31. hue,** she. **32. rode,** complexion. **rys,** branch. **34. war,** wary. **36. Burde on,** lady one. **37. woneth by west,** dwells in the west. **38. bys,** a fine cloth. **39. tolde,** considered. **40. o,** one. **4. lud,** song. **5. libbe,** live. **6. semlokest,** fairest. **7. He,** she. **8. baundoun,** power. **9. hendy hap,** pleasant fortune. **yhent,** received. **10. Ichot,** I know. **11. lent,** gone. **15. lossum chere,** lovely complexion. **loh,** laughed. **16. ymake,** made.

Bote he me wolle to hire take
Forte buen hire owen make,
Longe to lyven ichulle forsake
And feye fallen adoun.   20
   An hendy hap &c.

Nihtes when y wende and wake—
For-thi myn wonges waxeth won—
Leuedi, al for thine sake,
Longinge is ylent me on.
In world nis non so wyter mon
That al hire bounte telle con;
Hire swyre is whittore then the swon,
And feyrest may in toune.
   An hendy hap &c.   30

Icham for wowyng al forwake,
Wery so water in wore;
Lest eny reve me my make
Ychabbe y-yyrned yore.
Betere is tholien whyle sore
Then mournen evermore;
Geynest under gore,
Herkne to my roun.
   An hendy hap &c.

LENTEN IS COME WITH LOVE TO TOWN

This song shows how effective a contrast can be made between the almost automatic happiness which spring brings to Nature, and the sorrows and fears of the human lover.

Lenten ys come with love to toune,
With blosmen and with briddes roune,
That al this blisse bryngeth;
Dayes-eyes in this dales,
Notes suete of nyhtegales,
Uch foul song singeth;
The threstelcoc him threteth oo;
Away is huere wynter woo,
When woderove springeth.
This foules singeth ferly fele,   10
Ant wryteth on huere wunne wele,
That al the wode ryngeth.

17. **wolle**, will. 18. **buen**, be. **make**, mate. 19. **ichulle**, I will. 20. **feye**, fated to die. 22. **wende**, turn. 23. **For-thi**, therefore. **wonges**, cheeks. **won**, pallid. 25. **ylent**, arrived. 26. **nis**, is not. **wyter**, wise. 27. **bounte**, goodness. 28. **swyre**, neck. 31. **Icham**, I am. **forwake**, wearied with waking. 32. **wore**, sea beach. 33. **reve me**, take from me. 34. **Ychabbe y-yyrned yore**. I have yearned for a long time. 35. **tholien whyle sore**, suffer sorrow for a time. 37. **Geynest under gore**, handsomest under (any) garment. 38. **roun**, song. 1. **Lenten**, spring. 4. **this**, these. 5. **suete**, sweet. 6. **Uch**, each. 7. **threstelcoc**, thrush. **oo**, only. 8. **huere**, their. 9. **woderove**, woodruff. 10. **ferly fele**, wonderfully much. 11. **Ant wryteth**, and warbles. **wunne wele**, pleasant prosperity.

The rose rayleth hire rode,
The leves on the lyhte wode
Waxen al with wille.
The mone mandeth hire bleo,
The lilie is lossom to seo,
The fenyl and the fille;
Wowes this wilde drakes,
Miles murgeth huere makes,   20
Ase strem that striketh stille;
Mody meneth so doh mo,
Ichot ycham on of tho,
For love that liketh ille.

The mone mandeth hire lyht,
So doth the semly sonne bryht,
When briddes singeth breme;
Deawes donketh the dounes,
Deores with huere derne rounes,
Domes forte deme;
Wormes woweth under cloude,   30
Wymmen waxeth wounder proude,
So wel hit wol hem seme.
Yef me shal wonte wille of on,
This wunne weole y wole forgon,
Ant wyht in wode be fleme.

THE LOVELIEST LADY IN THE LAND

This poem contains more than most to illustrate the manner and content of the school of the Court and Code of Love. The poet begins with the familiar praise of his mistress, proceeds to a detailed description of her bodily perfection, speaks well of her disposition and demeanor—she is even attractive when she wakes up!—and proceeds to characterize her by means of comparisons from the herbals and lapidaries. He goes on with three stanzas in which he compresses a very pretty bit of amorous allegory of the conventional type, and ends with an almost gloating account of his carking, caring, drooping, fearing, paling, waking, mourning, and moaning despair.

The refrain, lovely as it is, would appear to have been borrowed, since it properly belongs in the mouth of a woman sighing for her lover at, or beyond, the sea.

Ichot a burde in boure bryht
That fully semly is on syht,

13. **rayleth**, arrays. **rode**, complexion. 16. **mone mandeth**, moon sends forth. **bleo**, color. 17. **lossom**, lovable. 18. **fenyl**, fennel. **fille**, chevril. 19. **Wowes**, woos. 20. **Miles . . . makes**, animals make their mates merry. 21. **striketh**, flows. 22. **Mody meneth**, a proud person complains. **doh**, do. 23. **tho**, those. 24. **liketh**, pleases. 27. **breme**, clearly. 28. **Deawes donketh**, dews wet. 29. **Deores**, deer. **derne rounes**, hidden secrets. 30. **Domes . . . deme**, make their judgments. 31. **cloude**, clod. 32. **wounder**, wonderfully. 36. **wyht**, creature. **fleme**, banished. 1. **Ichot**, I know. **burde**, lady. **boure**, bower.

MIDDLE ENGLISH LYRICS

Menskful maiden of myht,
Feir ant fre to fonde;
In al this wurhliche won,
A burde of blod ant of bon
Never yete y nuste non
Lussomore in londe.
   Blow, northerne wynd,
   Sent thou me my suetyng!   10
   Blow, northerne wynd,
   Blou! blou! blou!

With lokkes lefliche ant longe,
With frount ant face feir to fonde,
With murthes monie mote heo monge,
That brid so breme in boure,
With lossom eye grete ant gode,
With browen blysfol under hode.
He that reste him on the rode
That leflich lyf honoure!   20
   Blow &c.

Hire lure lumes liht
Ase a launterne a-nyht,
Hire bleo blykyeth so bryht,
So feyr heo is ant fyn.
A suetly suyre heo hath to holde,
With armes, shuldre ase mon wolde
Ant fyngres feyre forte folde.
God wolde hue were myn!

Middel heo hath menskful, smal,   30
Hire loveliche chere as cristal;
Theyes, legges, fet, ant al
Ywraht wes of the beste.
A lussum ledy lasteles
That sweting is ant ever wes;
A betere burde never nes,
Yheryed with the beste.

Heo is dereworther in day,
Graciouse, stout, ant gay,
Gentil, jolyf so the Jay,   40
Worhliche when heo waketh.
Maiden murgest of mouth;
Bi est, bi west, by north ant south,
Ther nis fiele ne crouth
That such murthes maketh.

Heo is coral of godnesse,
Heo is rubie of ryhtfulnesse,
Heo is cristal of clannesse,
Ant baner of bealte,
Heo is lilie of largesse,   50
Heo is parvenke of prouesse,
Heo is solsecle of suetnesse
Ant ledy of lealte.

To Love, that loflich is in londe,
Y tolde him as ych understonde
Hou this hende hath hent in honde
On huerte that myn wes;
Ant hire knyhtes me han so soht,
Sykyng, Sorewyng, ant Thoht,
Tho thre me han in bale broht   60
Ageyn the poer of Pees.

To love y putte pleyntes mo,
Hou Sykyng me hath siwed so,
Ant eke Thoht me thrat to slo
With maistry yef he myhte,
Ant Serewe swore, in balful bende
That he wolde, for this hende,
Me lede to my lyves ende,
Unlahfulliche in lyhte.

Hire Love me lustnede uch word   70
Ant beh him to me over bord,
Ant bed me hente that hord
Of myne huerte hele
Ant bisecheth that swete ant swote,
"Er then thou falle ase fen of fote,
That heo with the wolle of bote
Dereworthliche dele."

For hire love y carke ant care,
For hire love y droupne ant dare,
For hire love my blisse is bare,   80
And al ich waxe won;
For hire love in slep y slake,
For hire love al nyht ich wake,
For hire love mournyng y make
More then eny mon.

3. **Menskful**, graceful. 4. **fre**, noble. **fonde**, test. 5. **wurhliche won**, estimable world. 7. **nuste**, did not know. 8. **Lussomore**, lovelier. 13. **lefliche**, lovely. 14. **frount**, forehead. 15. **heo**, she. **monge**, mingle (with). 16. **brid**, lady. **breme**, bright. 19. **rode**, cross (rood). 22. **lure lumes**, face shines. 24. **bleo blykyeth**, complexion shines. 26. **suyre**, neck. 27. **wolde**, would wish. 29. **hue**, she. 31. **chere**, countenance. 32. **Theyes**, thighs. 33. **Ywraht**, made. 34. **lasteles**, blameless. 37. **Yheryed**, praised. 38. **derewortheh**, dearly esteemed. 39. **stout**, stately. 41. **Worhliche**, estimable. 42. **murgest**, merriest. 44. **fiele**, fiddle. **crouth**, crowd (a stringed musical instrument). 48. **clannesse**, purity. 49. **bealte**, beauty. 50. **largesse**, generosity. 51. **parvenke**, periwinkle. 52. **solsecle**, marigold. 53. **lealte**, loyalty. 56. **hende**, courteous (lady). **hent**, seized. 57. **On huerte**, a heart. 58. **soht**, sought out. 59. **Thoht**. It is worth observing that thought is always a discomfort to a lover. 60. **Tho**, those. **bale**, trouble. 61. **Ageyn . . . Pees**, against the power of Peace. 63. **siwed**, pursued. 64. **thrat to slo**, threatened to slay. 66. **bende**, bonds. 69. **lyhte**, delay. 70. **lustnede**, listened. 71. **beh**, bowed. **bord**, table. 72. **bed**, ordered. **hente**, take. **hord**, hoard. 73. **huerte hele**, heart's health. 74. **swote**, sweet. 75. **fen of fote**, mud from a foot. 76. **bote**, remedy. 78. **carke**, fret. 79. **droupne**, droop. **dare**, am afraid. 82. **slake**, slacken, that is, lose sleep.

DE CLERICO ET PUELLA

"De Clerico et Puella" has a far greater narrative element than do most lyrics. We are able to put together the story of two lovers whose affair resulted in their separation and the man's outlawry. When he returns, disguise, or a convention common to ballads and romances, keeps her from recognizing him until he alludes to a specific incident of former years. She at once leaves off her dire threats and warnings and promises to let no family opposition stand in the way of their happiness. We apparently have here a ballad theme, perhaps a specific ballad, reworked, not with complete consistency, into an *estrif* or debate; if this is the case, we must recognize the poem as a significantly early adaptation, or at the very least an adumbration, of a romantic ballad theme. The poem is composed in a variation of the old septenary (seven-stress) line, but already medial rimes and sense pauses are pointing the way to the breakup of the septenary couplet into the standard four-three, four-three ballad stanza.

My deth y love, my lyf ich hate, for a leuedy shene,
Heo is briht so daies-liht, that is on me wel sene;
Al y falewe so doth the lef in somer when hit is grene.
Yef mi thoht helpeth me noht, to wham shal y me mene?

Sorewe and syke and drery mod byndeth me so faste
That y wene to walke wod yef hit me lengore laste;
My serewe, my care, al with a word he myhte awey caste.
"Whet helpeth the, my suete lemmon, my lyf thus forte gaste?"

"Do wey, thou clerc, thou art a fol, with the bydde y noht chyde;
Shalt thou never lyve that day mi love that thou shalt byde, 10
Yef thou in my boure art take, shame the may bityde.
The is bettere on fote gon, then wycked hors to ryde."

"Weylawei! whi seist thou so? Thou rewe on me, thy man!
Thou art ever in my thoht in londe wher ich am.
Yef y deye for thi love, hit is the mykel sham;
Thou lete me lyve and be thi luef, and thou my suete lemman."

Be stille, thou fol, y calle the riht; cost thou never blynne?
Thou art wayted day and nyht with fader and al my kynne.
Be thou in mi bour ytake, lete they for no synne
Me to holde, and the to slon; the deth so thou maht wynne." 20

"Suete ledy, thou wend thi mod, sorewe thou wolt me kythe;
Ich am al so sory mon so ich was whylen blythe.
In a wyndou ther we stod we custe us fyfty sythe—
Feir biheste maketh mony mon al is serewes mythe."

"Weylawey! whi seist thou so? mi serewe thou makest newe.
Y lovede a clerk al par amours, of love he wes ful trewe,
He nes nout blythe never a day bote he me sone seye;
Ich lovede him betere then my lyf—whet bote is hit to leye?"

"Whil y wes a clerc in scole, wel muchel y couthe of lore;
Ych have tholed for thy love woundes fele sore, 30
Fer from bour and eke from men, under the wode-gore.
Suete ledy, thou rewe of me—nou may y no more."

"Thou semest wel to ben a clerc, for thou spekest so scille;
Shalt thou never for mi love woundes thole grylle.
Fader, moder, and al my kun ne shal me holde so stille
That y nam thyn, and thou art myn, to don al thi wille."

A LOVE MESSAGE

When the nyhtegale singes the wodes waxen grene,
Lef ant gras ant blosme springes in Averyl, y wene,
Ant love is to myn herte gon with one spere so kene,
Nyht ant day my blod hit drynkes, myn herte deth me tene.

Ich have loved al this yer, that y may love namore,
Ich have siked moni syk, lemmon, for thin ore;

17. **calle the riht . . . blynne?** I name you correctly; can you never cease? 18. **wayted**, watched for. 19. **lete**, desist. 21. **wend**, change. **kythe**, manifest. 22. **whylen**, formerly. 23. **custe**, kissed. **sythe**, times. 24. **biheste**, promise. **mythe**, conceal. 27. **nes**, was not. **seye**, saw. 28. **leye**, lie. 29. **couthe**, knew. 30. **tholed**, suffered. 31. **wode-gore**, forest plot. 33. **scille**, cleverly. 34. **thole grylle**, suffer painful. 35. **kun**, kin. 36. **nam**, am not. 3. **one**, a 4. **deth me tene**, causes me grief. 6. **siked**, sighed. **ore**, favor.

---

1. **shene**, beautiful. 3. **falewe**, fade. 4. **Yef**, if. **mene?** complain. 5. **syke**, sigh. **mod**, mood, feeling. 6. **wene to walke wod**, expect to go mad. 7. **he**, she. 8. **forte gaste**, to ruin. 9. **Do wey**, stop. **bydde**, ask. 10. **byde**, wait for, expect. 12. **The is . . . ryde**, a proverb. 13. **Weylawei! alas! rewe**, have pity. 16. **luef**, dear.

Me nis love never the ner, ant that me reweth sore.
Suete lemmon, thench on me, ich have loved the yore.

Suete lemmon, y preye the of love one speche;
Whil y lyve in world so wyde other nulle y seche. 10
With thy love, my suete leof, mi blis thou mihtes eche;
A suete cos of thyn mouth mihte be my leche.

Suete lemmon, y preye the of a love bene;
Yef thou me lovest ase men says, lemmon as y wene,
Ant yef hit thi wille be, thou loke that hit be sene.
So muchel y thenke upon the, that al y waxe grene.

Bituene Lyncolne ant Lyndeseye, Norhamptoun ant Lounde,
Ne wot y non so fayr a may as y go fore ybounde.
Suete lemon, y preye the thou lovie me a stounde.
Y wole mone my song on wham that hit ys on ylong. 20

THE MATCHLESS MAIDEN

I syng of a myden   that is makeles,
Kyng of alle kynges   to here sone che ches.

He cam also stylle   ther his moder was
As dew in Aprylle,   that fallyt on the gras.

He cam also stylle   to his moderes bowr   5
As dew in Aprille,   that fallyt on the flour.

He cam also stylle   ther his moder lay
As dew in Aprille,   that fallyt on the spray.

Moder and mayden   was never non but che—
Wel may swych a lady   Godes moder be.   10

BLESS THE TIME THE APPLE WAS TAKEN!

Adam lay y-bowndyn, bowndyn in a bond,
Fowre thowsand wynter thowt he not to long;
And al was for an appil, an appil that he tok,
As clerkis fyndyn wretyn in here book.

Ne hadde the appil take ben, the appil taken ben, 5
Ne hadde never our Lady a ben hevene Qwen;
Blyssid be the tyme that appil take was,
Ther-fore we mown syngyn, "Deo gracias!"

SIGNS OF DEATH

This poem is an excellent specimen of the specific, lively, and almost jovial way in which the Middle Ages could appreciate human mortality and its painful fore-runners.

Wanne mine eyhnen misten,
And mine heren sissen,
And mi nose koldet,
And mi tunge ffoldet,
And mi rude slaket,
And mine lippes blaken,
And mi muth grennet,
And mi spotel rennet,
And min her riset,
And min herte griset,   10
And mine honden bivien,
And mine ffet stivien,
Al to late, al to late,
Wanne the bere ys ate gate.

Thanne y schel fflutte
Ffrom bedde to fflore,
Ffrom fflore to here,
Ffrom here to bere,
Ffrom bere to putte,
And te putt ffor-dut.   20
Thanne lyd min hus uppe min nose,
Off al this world ne gyffe ihic a pese.

OF ONE THAT IS SO FAIR AND BRIGHT

Macaronic poetry—the name given loosely to verse in which two or more languages are used somewhat systematically—is suited rather to burlesque than to anything of a serious nature. "Of One That Is so Fair and Bright" proves conclusively, however, that in the hands of a master this hybrid form can add charm and melody to an elevated theme. In poems of this type the Latin lines are often no more than senseless rhyme tags, but here we find that they play their part in the regular sentence structure.

De Clerico. **7. nis**, is not. **ner**, nearer. **me reweth**, makes me feel sorry. **8. the yore**, for a long time. **10. nulle y seche**, I will not seek. **11. eche**, increase. **12. cos**, kiss. **leche**, physician. **13. bene**, prayer. **14. wene**, expect. **16. grene**, a not uncommon color for the pining lover. **17. Lounde**, London. **18. fore ybounde**, fettered for. **19. stounde**, time, while. **20. on ylong**, dependent. *The Matchless Maiden.* **1. myden**, maiden. **makeles**, matchless. **2. che ches**, she choose. *Bless the Time.* **1. y-bowndyn**, bound. **4. here**, their.

Bless the Time. **6. a**, have. **8. mown**, may. **Deo gracias!** thanks be to God! *Signs of Death.* **1. Wanne**, when. **eyhnen misten**, eyes become dim. **2. heren sissen**, ears stop. **3. koldet**, grows cold. **4. ffoldet**, folds. **5. rude slaket**, complexion falls off. **6. blaken**, grow pale. **7. grennet**, grimaces. **8. spotel rennet**, spittle runs. **10. griset**, trembles. **11. bivien**, trembles. **12. stivien**, becomes rigid. **14. bere**, bier. **ate**, at the. **15. fflutte**, go. **17. here**, shroud (haircloth). **19. putte**, pit, grave. **20. ffor-dut**, shut up. **21. lyd**, lies. **uppe**, upon. **22. ihic a pese**, I a pea.

Of on that is so fayr and bright
velud maris stella,
Brighter than the day-is light,
parens et puella,
Ic crie to the, thou se to me,
Leuedy, preye thi sone for me
tam pia,
That ic mote come to the,
Maria.

Of kare conseil thou ert best,   10
felix fecundata;
Of alle wery thou ert rest,
mater honorata.
Bi-sek him wit milde mod
That for ous alle sad is blood
in cruce,
That we moten komen to him
in luce.

Al this world was for-lore
Eva peccatrice   20
Tyl our lord was y-bore
de te genitrice;

With *ave* it went a-wey,
Thuster nyth and comet the day
salutis,
The welle springet hut of the
virtutis.

Leuedi, flour of alle thing
rosa sine spina,
Thu bere Jhesu, hevene-king,   30
gratia divina.
Of alle thu berst the pris,
Leuedi, quene of parays
electa,
Mayde milde Moder ec
effecta.

Wel he wot he is thi sone
ventre quem portasti;
He wyl nout werne the thi bone
parvum quem lactasti.   40
So hende and so god he his,
He havet brout ous to blis
superni;
That havet hi-dut the foule put
inferni.

The Vision of William Concerning Piers the Plowman

Piers Plowman, customarily ranked next to the poems of Chaucer in literary merit, is, in many respects, one of the most puzzling of fourteenth-century writings. The poem, which survives in some fifty manuscripts, has come down to us in three versions, conveniently designated A, B, and C, which vary greatly in length and material. Version A is by far the shortest and clearest; its some twenty-five hundred lines are divided into a prologue and twelve passus (books or cantos) and contain the visions of the Field of Folk, Holy Church, and Lady Mead, of Piers the Plowman, and of Dowell, Dobet, and Dobest, the last of which has sometimes been considered an addition or afterthought on the author's part. Version B is greatly amplified, running to over seven thousand lines, and adds many new visions. Version C is a much less drastic revision of B than B was of A; despite the fact that there are a number of important and significant original passages, the length is hardly altered, but there are a multitude of minor changes in language and phrasing. It was long believed that all three versions were the work of one man, William Langland, whose life was put together from scattered passages (some of them requiring a good deal of teasing to fit into the pattern) out of all three versions. He was

2. **velud . . . stella,** like the star of the sea.   4. **parens et puella,** parent (mother) and child.   5. **se to me,** attend to me, provide for me.   7. **tam pia,** so devout.   8. **mote,** may.   11. **felix fecundata,** happy fruitful one.   13. **mater honorata,** revered mother.   14. **Bi-sek,** beseech. **wit,** with.   15. **sad is,** shed his.   16. **in cruce,** on the Cross.   18. **in luce,** in the light (of Heaven).   19. **for-lore,** ruined.   20. **Eva peccatrice,** by Eve the sinner.   21. **y-bore,** born.   22. **de te genitrice,** of thee his mother.   23. **ave,** the angelic salutation to Mary.   24. **Thuster,** dark.   25. **salutis,** of salvation.   26. **hut,** out.   27. **virtutis,** (of) virtue.   29. **rosa sine spina,** rose without a thorn.   30. **bere,** gave birth to.   31. **gratia divina,** by divine favor.   33. **parays,** Paradise.   34. **electa,** the chosen one.   35. **ec,** also.   36. **effecta,** complete.   38. **ventre quem portasti,** whom thou carried in thy womb.   39. **werne,** refuse. **bone,** prayer.   40. **parvum quem lactasti,** whom thou suckled when he was little.   41. **hende,** gracious. **god,** good.   42. **ous,** us.   43. **superni,** supernal.   44–45. **hi-dut,** shut up. **put inferni,** pit of hell.

held to have been born about 1330, to have written the A text in 1362 or thereabouts, to have revised it, thus giving the B text, in 1377, and to have gone over that in turn sometime between 1392 and 1399, probably near the latter date. This older opinion has been vigorously attacked, and many valid objections to it having been pointed out, so that today many scholars hold that there was a separate author for each of the three versions, the B and C poets each enlarging and revising the work of his immediate predecessor. A careful reading of the three texts is likely to confirm this latter view, even if we make due allowance for the changes in style and outlook which advancing years inevitably bring to any author. Nevertheless the problem is amazingly complex; there are distinguished scholars who maintain the theory of unity of authorship, and we are probably well advised to consider the question still open.

Whether written by one author or three, the poem—to speak of it, at least, as a unit—is extraordinarily powerful. In the later versions it is often rambling, incoherent, badly arranged, the allegory sometimes ill-considered and unfulfilled, but out of the whole emerges a detailed picture of England in the second half of the fourteenth century. Parts of the picture remind us of what we gather about contemporary life from Chaucer's *Canterbury Tales*, but the differences between the two impressions are greater than the similarities. Chaucer's own feelings may have been deep enough, and there are subtle hints that they were, but he wrote for an audience which did not care to be reminded too directly of painful, shameful events and trends. Many of Chaucer's audience, indeed, must have been uneasily aware of their own complicity in the sorry state of the nation. *Piers Plowman*, on the other hand, shows none of Chaucer's compunction or restraint. Here, only occasionally obscured by the allegory, we see how, as the century dragged out its weary years, England suffered from the effects of a series of catastrophes: the Black Death of 1348–49, with the consequent disruption of the balance and distribution of man power; the Hundred Years' War, at first so glorious and so rich in booty, but always expensive and debilitating, and later conducted in a shamefully inept fashion; the uncertain, uneven, unequal, but inevitable breaking-down of the feudal system; the Peasants' Revolt of 1381; the unblushing rapacity of the various cliques which controlled or sought to control the Government; the corruption, ignorance, and greed of many of the clergy; the conflict within the Church itself, symbolized, perhaps, by the Schism; the bitter dynastic feud which culminated in the overthrow and death of Richard II. All these things and more combined to keep the land from being a "Merry England," and it is no "Merry England" which emerges from the pages of *Piers Plowman*.

The poem reveals an intense awareness of the interrelation of events, of the connection between corruption at the top and misery at the bottom of the social scale, but it is in no way class-conscious. Rather it is a dissection, too passionate to be aloof, of all the classes. *Piers Plowman* has sometimes been considered a Lollard or Wycliffite document; that, however, is not the case. Its basic doctrine is orthodox, conservative Catholicism, however painfully aware it is of abuses in the Church. There is no opposition to the tenets of the Church, but there is a pitiless exposure of the misuse of its forms, and an indignant outcry against the rascals who utilize Holy Church as a screen for their misdeeds.

Piers Plowman belongs to a common medieval literary type, the dream-vision, but it is very different from the typical dream-visions of the French poets whom Chaucer followed. The spiritual kinship of *Piers Plowman* is not with the limpid and conventional allegories of love which sprang from the first part of the *Roman de la Rose*, but rather with the *Divine Comedy*.

The meter of the poem is the long alliterative line which was revived with such successful results in the middle of the fourteenth century. The present text is taken from the edition of W. W. Skeat, 2 vols., Oxford Press, 1896.

from THE VISION OF WILLIAM CONCERNING PIERS THE PLOWMAN

PROLOGUE

The Field of Folk

In a somer sesun, whon softe was the sonne,
I schop me in-to a schroud, a scheep as I were;
In habite of an hermite unholy of werkes,
Wende I wydene in this world wondres to here.
Bote in a Mayes morwnynge on Malverne hulles
Me bi-fel a ferly, a feyrie me thouhte;
I was weori of wandringe and wente me to reste

Version A, ll. 1–109. **2. schop . . . schroud,** got myself into a garment. **scheep,** shepherd. **4. wydene,** wide. **5. Bote in,** but on. **Malverne hulles,** hills on the border of Worcestershire and Herefordshire. **6. ferly,** wonder. **feyrie me thouhte,** enchantment, it seemed to me.

Under a brod banke bi a bourne syde,
And as I lay and leonede and lokede on the watres,
I slumberde in a slepyng, hit sownede so murie.   10
    Thenne gon I meeten a mervelous swevene,
That I was in a wildernesse, wuste I never where,
And as I beo-heold in-to the est, an-heigh to the sonne,
I sauh a tour on a toft, triyely i-maket;
A deop dale bi-neothe, a dungun ther-inne,
With deop dich and derk and dredful of siht.
    A feir feld ful of folk fond I ther bi-twene,
Of alle maner of men, the mene and the riche,
Worchinge and wondringe, as the world asketh.
    Summe putten hem to the plough and pleiden hem ful seldene,   20
In eringe and in sowynge swonken ful harde,
That monie of theos wasturs in glotonye distruen.
    And summe putten hem to pruide, apparaylden hem ther-after,
In cuntinaunce of clothinge, queinteliche de-gyset;
To preyere and to penaunce putten heom monye,
For love of ur lord liveden ful harde,
In hope for to have hevene-riche blisse;
As ancres and hermytes that holdeth hem in heore celles,
Coveyte not in cuntre to carien a-boute,
For non likerous lyflode heore licam to plese.   30
    And summe chosen chaffare to cheeven the bettre,
As hit semeth to ure siht that suche men scholden;
And summe murthhes to maken, as munstrals cunne,
And gete gold with here gle, giltles, I trowe.
    Bote japers and jangelers, Judas children,
Founden hem fantasyes and fooles hem maaden,
And habbeth wit at heor wille to worchen yif hem luste.
That Poul precheth of hem I dar not preoven heere;
Qui loquitur turpiloquium, hee is Luciferes hyne.

    Bidders and beggers faste a-boute eoden,   40
Til heor bagges and heore balies weren bratful i-crommet;
Feyneden hem for heore foode, foughten atte alle;
In glotonye, God wot, gon heo to bedde,
And ryseth up with ribaudye, this Roberdes knaves;
Sleep and sleughthe suweth hem evere.
    Pilgrimes and palmers plihten hem to-gederes
For to seche seint Jeme and seintes at Roome;
Wenten forth in heore wey with mony wyse tales,
And hedden leve to lyyen al heore lyf aftir.
Ermytes on an hep with hokide staves,   50
Wenten to Walsyngham, and here wenchis aftir.
    Grete lobres and longe, that loth weore to swynke,
Clotheden hem in copes to beo knowen for bretheren;
And summe schopen hem to hermytes, heore ese to have.
    I font there freres, all the foure ordres,
Prechinge the peple for profyt of heore wombes,
Glosynge the gospel, as hem good liketh,
For covetyse of copes construeth hit ille;
For monye of this maistres mowen clothen hem at lyking,
For moneye and heore marchaundie meeten ofte to-gedere.   60
Seththe charite hath be chapmon, and cheef to schriven lordes,
Mony ferlyes han bi-falle in a fewe yeres.
But holychirche bi-ginne holde bet to-gedere,
The moste mischeef on molde mounteth up faste.
    Ther prechede a pardoner, as he a prest were,
And brought up a bulle with bisschopes seles,
And seide that him-self mihte a-soylen hem alle
Of falsnesse and fastinge and of vouwes i-broken.
The lewede men likede him wel and leeveth his speche,

40. **Bidders**, beggars. **eoden**, went.   41. **heor... balies weren bratful i-crommet**, their bellies were crammed brimful.   42. **Feyneden**, pretended. **atte alle**, at the alehouse.   44. **ribaudye**, ribaldry. **Roberdes knaves**, rogues; the significance of the proper name Robert is not explained.   45. **sleughthe suweth**, sloth attends.   46. **plihten**, agreed.   47. **seint Jeme**, the shrine of St. James at Compostella in Galicia.   49. **And ... lyyen**, and had permission to lie.   50. **Ermytes**, hermits. **hep**, crowd.   51. **Walsyngham**, the shrine of Our Lady at Walsingham in Norfolk.   52. **lobres**, lubbers. **longe**, tall. **swynke**, work.   54. **schopen hem**, made themselves.   55. **font**, found. **foure ordres**, Carmelites, Augustinians, Dominicans (Jacobins), and Minorites.   56. **wombes**, stomachs.   57. **Glosynge**, interpreting. **as hem good liketh**, as they like.   60. **For ... to-gedere**, an allusion to the willingness of the friars to take money in place of giving a stiff penance.   61. **Seththe charite**, since Christian love. **chapmon**, merchant. **cheef**, chiefly. **schriven**, hear confession and administer absolution.   63. **But**, unless.   64. **molde**, earth.   65. **pardoner**. Compare Chaucer's Pardoner, pages 181 and 196.   66. **bulle**, episcopal (or papal) edict.   67. **a-soylen**, absolve.   69. **lewede**, unlearned, lay. **leeveth**, believes.

8. **bourne**, brook.   9. **leonede**, reclined.   10. **sownede**, sounded.   11. **gon I meeten ... swevene**, did I dream a dream.   12. **wuste**, knew.   13. **an-heigh**, on high.   14. **tour**, tower. **toft**, hillock. **triyely**, excellently.   17. **A feir feld**, the world.   18. **mene**, common people.   19. **Worchinge and wondringe**, working and wandering.   20. **pleiden hem**, amused themselves.   21. **eringe**, plowing. **swonken**, worked.   22. **That**, (for) that which.   24. **cuntinaunce**, outward appearance. **queinteliche de-gyset**, elegantly appareled.   26. **ful harde**, very severely.   27. **hevene-riche**, of the kingdom of heaven.   28. **ancres**, anchorites.   29. **carien**, wander.   30. **likerously flode**, luxurious livelihood. **licam**, body.   31. **chaffare**, merchandise. **cheeven**, succeed.   33. **cunne**, know how to do.   34. **gle**, singing.   35. **japers and jangelers**, jesters and storytellers.   36. **Founden ... maaden**, invent fictions for themselves.   37. **wit**, intelligence. **yif hem luste**, if it pleased them.   38. **preoven**, declare plainly.   39. **Qui ... turpiloquium**, who speaks base words. **hyne**, servant.

PIERS THE PLOWMAN

And comen up knelynge, and cusseden his bulle; 70
He bonchede hem with his brevet and blered heore eiyen,
And rauhte with his ragemon ringes and broches.
Thus ye giveth oure gold glotonye to helpen,
And leveth hit to losels that lecherie haunten.
Weore the bisschop i-blesset and worth bothe his eres,
Heo scholde not beo so hardi to deceyve so the peple.
Save hit nis not bi the bisschop that the boye precheth;
Bote the parisch prest and he de-parte the selver,
That have schulde the pore parisschens, yif that heo ne weore.
 Persones and parisch prestes playneth to heore bisschops, 80
That heore parisch hath ben pore seththe the pestilence tyme,
And asketh leve and lycence at Londun to dwelle,
To singe ther for simonye, for selver is swete.
 Ther hoveth an hundret in houves of selk,
Serjauns hit semeth, to serven atte barre;
Pleden for pons and poundes the lawe,
Not for love of ur lord un-loseth heore lippes ones.
Thow mihtest beter meten the myst on Malverne hulles,
Then geten a mom of heore mouth til moneye weore schewed.
 I sauh ther bisschops bolde and bachilers of divyn 90
Bi-coome clerkes of a-counte, the kyng for to serven;
Erchedekenes and deknes that dignite haven
To preche the peple, and pore men to feede,
Beon lopen to Londun bi leve of heore bisschopes,
To ben clerkes of the kynges benche, the cuntre to schende.
 Barouns and burgeis and bonde-men also
I saugh in that semble, as ye schul heren her-aftur.
 Bakers, bochers, and breusters monye,
Wollene websteris, and weveris of lynen,
Taillours, tanneris, and tokkeris bothe, 100
Masons, minours, and mony other craftes,
Dykers, and delvers, that don heore dedes ille,
And driveth forth the longe day with "Deu vous save, dam Emme!"
 Cookes and heore knaves cryen "Hote pies, hote!
Goode gees and grys! Gowe dyne, gowe!"
Taverners to hem tolde the same tale,
With good wyn of Gaskoyne, and wyn of Oseye,
Of Ruyn, and of Rochel, the rost to defye.
Al this I saugh slepynge and seve sithes more. 109

PASSUS V

Glutton

Nou ginneth the Gloton for to go to schrifte,
And carieth him to chircheward, his schrift forte telle.
Thenne Betun the breustere bad him gode morwe,
And seththen heo asked of him, "Whoder that he wolde?" 149
"To holi chirche," quod he, "for to here masse,
And seththen I-chule ben i-schriven and sunge no more."
"Ic have good ale, gossip," quod heo, "Gloten, woltou asaye?"
"Hastou ought i thi pors," quod he, "eny hote spices?"
"Ye, Glotun, gossip," quod heo, "God wot, ful goode;
I have peper and piane, and a pound of garlek,
A ferthing-worth of fenel-seed, for this fastyng dayes."
 Thene geth Gloton in and grete othus after;
Sesse the souters wyf sat on the benche,
Watte the warinar, and his wyf bothe,
Tomkyn the tinkere, and tweyne of his knaves, 160
Hikke the hakeney mon, and Hogge the neldere,

70. **cusseden**, kissed. 71. **bonchede**, banged. **brevet**, letter of indulgence. **blered heore eiyen**, bleared their eyes, that is, hoodwinked them. 72. **rauhte**, got. **ragemon**, bull. 74. **losels**, vagabonds. **haunten**, practice. 75. **i-blesset**, a holy man. 76. **Heo**, the pardoner. 77. **bi**, concerning, against. **boye**, fellow. 78. **de-parte**, divide. 79. **yif that heo ne weore**, if it were not for them. 80. **playneth**, complain. 81. **pestilence tyme**, no doubt 1348–49, the years of the Black Death. 82–83. **And asketh . . . swete.** Compare Chaucer's Parson, page 178. 84. **hoveth**, dwell. **houves**, hoods. 85. **Serjauns**, serjeants (of the law). 86. **pons**, pence. 88. **meten**, measure. 89. **mom**, sound. 90–95. **I sauh . . . schende.** There were frequent protests against the number of clerics in public service, protests which came as much from hopeful laymen as from indignant ecclesiastical purists. **divyn**, divinity. **lopen**, run away. **kynges benche**, the supreme court of the common law. **schende**, ruin. 96. **bonde-men**, laborers. 97. **semble**, assembly. 98. **breusters**, female brewers. 99. **websteris**, female weavers. 100. **tokkeris**, tuckers, that is, fullers of cloth. 102. **Dykers**, ditchers. 103. **driveth forth**, pass away. "**Deu vous save, dam Emme!**" evidently a quotation from an otherwise lost popular song. 105. **grys!** pigs. **Gowe**, let's go. 107. **Oseye**, Alsace. 108. **Ruyn**, the Rhine. **Rochel**, La Rochelle. **defye**, digest. 109. **seve sithes**, seven times. Version A, Passus V, ll. 146–221. 146. **schrifte**, confession. 147. **carieth him**, betakes himself. 149. **seththen**, then. **wolde**, would (go). 151. **I-chule**, I will. **sunge**, sin. 152. **gossip**, neighbor. **asaye**, try. 153. **pors**, purse. **spices**, eaten as a thirst-provoker. 155. **piane**, peony seeds. 156. **this**, these; l. 211 indicates that Gloton's mishap occurred on Friday. 157. **othus after**, oaths along with him. 158. **Sesse**, Cis, short for Cicely. **souters**, cobbler's. 159. **Watte**, short for Walter. **warinar**, one employed to watch over the game in a preserve. 160. **Tomkyn**, diminutive of Tom. 161. **hakeney mon**, man who kept horses for hire. **Hogge**, a nickname for Roger. **neldere**, needle-seller.

Clarisse of Cokkes lone, and the clerk of the churche,
Sire Pers of Pridye, and Pernel of Flaundres,
Dauwe the dykere, and a doseyn othere.
A ribibor, a ratoner, a rakere of Chepe,
A ropere, a redyng-kyng, and Rose the disschere,
Godfrei of Garlesschire, and Griffin the Walsche,
And of up-holders an hep, erly bi the morwe,
Give the Gloton, with good wille, good ale to honsel.
    Thenne Clement the cobelere cast of his cloke,
And atte newe feire he leyde hire to sulle;   171
And Hikke the ostiler hutte his hod aftur,
And bad Bette the bocher ben on his bi-syde.
Ther weore chapmen i-chose the chaffare to preise;
Hose hedde the hod schulde have amendes.
Thei risen up raply and rouneden to-gedere,
And preiseden the peniworthus, and parteden bi hemselven;
Ther weoren othes an hep, hose that hit herde.
Thei couthe not bi heore concience a-corde to-gedere,
Til Robyn the ropere weore rad forte a-ryse,   180
And nempned for a noumpere, that no de-bat neore,
For he schulde preise the penyworthes as hym good thought.
    Thenne Hikke the ostiler hedde the cloke,
In covenaunt that Clement schulde the cuppe fulle,
And habbe Hikkes hod the ostiler, and hold him wel iservet;
And he that repenteth rathest schulde arysen aftur,
And greten sir Gloten with a galun of ale.
    Ther was laughyng and lotering, and "Let go the cuppe!"

Bargeyns and beverages bi-gonne to aryse,   189
And seeten so til evensong and songen sum while,
Til Gloten hedde i-gloupet a galoun and a gille. . . .

He hedde no strengthe to stonde til he his staf hedde;   196
Thenne gon he for to go lyk a gleo-monnes bicche,
Sum tyme asyde, and sum tyme arere,
As hose leith lynes to lacche with foules.
    Whon he drouh to the dore, then dimmede his eiyen,   200
He thrompelde atte threxwolde and threuh to the grounde.
Clement the coblere caughte Glotoun by the mydle,
And for to lyfte hym aloft, leide hym on his knees;
And Glotoun was a gret cherl and grym in the lyftynge,
And cowhede up a cawdel in Clementis lappe,
That the hungriest hound of Hertforde schire
Ne durst lape of that laveyne, so unloveli it smakith.
That with al the wo of this world his wyf and his wenche
Beeren him hom to his bed, and brouhten him ther-inne.
And after al this surfet an accesse he hedde,   210
That he slepte Saturday and Sonenday til sonne wente to reste.
    Thenne he wakede of his wynk, and wypede his eiyen;
The furste word that he spac was, "Wher is the cuppe?"
His wyf warnede him tho of wikkednesse and of sinne.
Thenne was he a-schomed, that schrewe, and schraped his eren,
And gon to grede grimliche, and gret deol to make
For his wikkede lyf that he i-lived hedde.
"For hungur other for furst I make myn a-vou,
Schal never fysch on Frydai defyen in my mawe,
Er Abstinence myn aunte have i-give me leve—   220
And yit ichave i-hated hire al my lyf-tyme."

    162. Cokkes lone, Cock Lane, an area set aside for prostitutes.   **163. Sire Pers,** Sir Piers, a priest. **Pernel,** Peronelle, a name commonly given to a woman of suspect reputation.   **164. Dauwe,** Davie, from David.   **165. ribibor,** player on the rebibe, a kind of fiddle. **ratoner,** rat-catcher. **rakere,** scavenger. **Chepe,** Cheapside.   **166. ropere,** ropemaker. **redyng-kyng,** a term of uncertain meaning. **disschere,** dish-seller.   **167. Garlesschire.** Version B reads "Garlekehithe," a landing near Vintry Ward, and C, "garlek-mongere." **Walsche,** Welshman.   **168. up-holders,** dealers in small wares and secondhand goods.   **169. to honsel,** as a treat.   **170–87. Thenne . . . ale,** a game of barter in which the two traders, Clement and Hick, were represented by deputies, only one of whom, Bet, is named here. In this case, being unable to agree, they were forced to call in Robin as an umpire.   **171. atte newe feire,** at the new fair, the name of the game. **sulle,** sell.   **172. ostiler,** ostler; Hick had been called a hackney man earlier. **hutte,** threw. **hod,** hood.   **173. bi-syde,** side.   **174. chaffare to preise,** goods to value.   **175. Hose,** whosoever.   **176. raply,** quickly. **rouneden,** whispered.   **180. rad,** bidden.   **181. nempned,** named. **noumpere,** umpire; the modern form is from the shift of "a noumpere" to "an umpire," just as "a nadder" became "an adder." The process is known as false division, and can work the other way, as when "an eke-name" became "a nickname."   **185. Hikkes hod the ostiler,** the hood of Hick the ostler.   **186. rathest,** soonest.   **188. lotering,** of uncertain meaning, perhaps "cunning," but Version B has "louryng," frowning.

    191. i-gloupet, gulped down.   **197. gleo-monnes bicche,** minstrel's bitch; perhaps the reference is to a blind minstrel led by his dog.   **198. asyde,** sidewise. **arere,** backward.   **199. As . . . foules,** like one who sets snares to catch birds with.   **200. drouh,** drew near. **eiyen,** eyes.   **201. thrompelde,** stumbled. **threxwolde,** threshold. **threuh,** fell.   **204. grym,** heavy.   **205. cowhede,** coughed. **cawdel.** The *New English Dictionary* defines caudle as "a warm drink consisting of thin gruel, mixed with wine or ale, sweetened and spiced, given chiefly to sick people." Here the word is used in a slightly transferred sense.   **207. laveyne,** slop. **smakith,** tastes.   **208. wenche,** servant girl.   **210. accesse,** sickness.   **212. wynk,** sleep.   **214. tho,** then.   **215. schrewe,** sinner. **schraped,** scratched.   **216. grede,** lament.   **218. other,** or. **furst,** thirst.   **219. defyen,** digest. **mawe,** stomach.   **221. ichave,** I have.

III

Sloth

Thanne come Sleuthe al bislabered, with two slymy eiyen: 392
"I most sitte," seyde the segge, "or elles schulde I nappe;
I may noughte stonde ne stoupe, ne with-oute a stole knele.
Were I broughte abedde, but if my taille-ende it made,
Sholde no ryngynge do me ryse ar I were rype to dyne."
He bygan *benedicite* with a bolke and his brest knocked,
And roxed and rored, and rutte atte laste.
"What! awake, renke!" quod Repentance, "and rape the to shrifte."
"If I shulde deye bi this day, me liste noughte to loke; 400
I can noughte perfitly my *pater-noster* as the prest it syngeth,
But I can rymes of Robyn Hood and Randolf erle of Chestre,
Ac neither of owre Lorde ne of owre Lady, the leste that evere was made.
I have made vowes fourty and for-gete hem on the morne;
I parfourned nevre penaunce as the prest me highte,
Ne ryghte sori for my synnes yet was I nevere.
And yif I bidde any bedes, but if it be in wrath,
That I telle with my tonge is two myle fro myne herte.
I am occupied eche day, haliday and other, 409
With ydel tales atte ale, and otherwhile in cherches;
Goddes peyne and his passioun ful selde thynke I there-on.
I visited nevere fieble men, ne fettered folke in puttes;
I have levere here an harlotrie, or a somer-game of souteres,
Or lesynges to laughe at, and belye my neighbore,
Than al that evere Marke made, Mathew, John, and Lucas.
And vigilies and fastyng-dayes, alle thise late I passe,
And ligge abedde in lenten, an my lemman in myn armes,
Tyl matynes and masse be do, and thanne go to the freres;
Come I to *ite, missa est*, I holde me yserved.
I nam noughte shryven some tyme, but if sekenesse it make, 420
Nought tweies in two yere, and thanne up gesse I schryve me.
I have be prest and parsoun passynge thretti wynter,
Yete can I neither solfe, ne synge, ne seyntes lyves rede,
But I can fynde in a felde, or in a fourlonge, an hare;
Better than in *beatus vir* or in *beati omnes*
Construe oon clause wel, and kenne it to my parochienes.
I can holde lovedayes and here a reves rekenynge,
Ac in canoun ne in the decretales I can noughte rede a lyne.
Yif I bigge and borwe it, but yif it be ytailled,
I forgete it as yerne, and yif men me it axe 430
Sixe sithes or sevene I forsake it with othes,
And thus tene I trewe men ten hundreth tymes.
And my servauntz some tyme, her salarye is bihynde,

413. levere, rather. harlotrie, a dirty story. somer-game. It was customary to have a festival on Midsummer's Day, or St. John Baptist's Day, June 24. The reference here is presumably to a celebration put on by the cobblers' (souteres) guild. 414. belye, lie about. 415. made, wrote. 416. late, let. 417. ligge, lie. an, and. lemman, sweetheart. 418. do, done. 419. ite, missa est, the end of the service of the mass. 420. if sekenesse it make, unless illness frightens me. 421. up gesse, by guess. 423. solfe, sol-fa, sing the scale. 424. fourlonge, a furrow. 425. beatus vir, Psalm 1 or 112. beati omnes, Psalm 138. 426. kenne, teach. 427. lovedayes, fixed days on which common people sought to settle their disputes by arbitration rather than by recourse to the lawcourts. Men of consequence and reputed learning, such as Sloth and Chaucer's Friar (see page 175) would serve as master. reves rekenynge. The reeve, as his lord's immediate representative on an estate, made regular financial reports which the lord, not without reason, would have examined by someone with a knowledge of local conditions; see Chaucer's Reeve, page 180. 428. canoun, canon, the laws of the Church or, less probably, a part of the mass. decretales, a collection of papal decrees which were part of the canon law. 429. bigge and borwe it, buy and give a pledge for it. ytailled, marked on a tally stick. 430. yerne, soon. 431. forsake, deny. 432. tene, annoy.

Version B, Passus V, ll. 392–464. 393. segge, man. 395. it made, caused it. 396. ryngynge, of church bells. rype, ready. 397. bolke, belch. 398. roxed, not certain, perhaps "stretched." rutte, snored. 399. renke, man. rape, hurry. 400. bi, for. me liste, it pleases me. 401. can, know. 402. Robyn Hood, the earliest allusion to the famous outlaw, but it indicates clearly that ballads, which is what rymes doubtless means here, about him were thoroughly familiar by the last quarter of the fourteenth century. Randolf. A case can be, and has been, made for either the Randolph who was Earl of Chester between 1128 and 1153 or his grandson, the earl from 1181 to 1232. Whichever may have been the hero, we have evidence here of a lost cycle of ballads dealing with an indisputably historical character. 405. highte, ordered. 407. bidde any bedes, pray any prayers. in wrath, as an oath. 408. That, which. 410. atte ale, at the alehouse. cherches. Foolish chatter in the church was considered then, as now, especially reprehensible. 412. fieble, helpless. puttes, dungeons.

Reuthe is to here the rekenynge whan we shal rede acomptes;
So with wikked wille and wraththe my werkmen I paye.
   Yif any man doth me a benfait or helpeth me at nede,
I am unkynde agein his curteisye and can noughte understonde it;
For I have and have hadde some dele haukes maneres,
I nam noughte lured with love but there ligge aughte under the thombe.
   The kyndenesse that myne evene-cristene kidde me fernyere,   440
Sixty sythes I, Sleuthe, haue forgete it sith,
In speche and in sparynge of speche yspilte many a tyme
Bothe flesche and fissche, and many other vitailles;
Bothe bred and ale, butter, melke, and chese
Forsleuthed in my servyse, til it myghte serve no-man.
   I ran aboute in youthe and gaf me noughte to lerne,
And evere sith have be beggere for my foule sleuthe;
Heu michi, quod sterilem vitam duxi juvenilem."
   "Repentestow the naughte?" quod Repentance, and righte with that he swowned,
Til *Vigilate* the veille fette water at his eyyen,   450
And flatte it on his face and faste on hym criede,
And seide, "Ware the fram wanhope, wolde the bitraye.
'I am sori for my synnes,' sey so to thi-selve,
And bete thi-selve on the breste and bidde hym of grace;
For is no gult here so grete that his goodnesse nys more."
   Thanne sat Sleuthe up and seyned hym swithe,
And made avowe to-fore God for his foule sleuthe,
"Shal no Sondaye be this sevene yere, but sykenesse it lette,
That I ne shal do me er day to the dere cherche,   459
And heren matines and masse, as I a monke were.
Shal none ale after mete holde me thennes,
Tyl I have evensonge herde, I behote to the rode.
And yete wil I yelde agein, if I so moche have,
Al that I wikkedly wan, sithen I wytte hadde."

Geoffrey Chaucer
c. 1340–1400

About 1340 Geoffrey Chaucer was born into a turbulent century, one which saw change and decay in almost every institution, whether secular or spiritual, in Western Europe. Chaucer lived through the rest of the fourteenth century and in many of its ceaseless, tragic activities he took a part. For Chaucer, we must not forget, was no stooped, retiring scholar, living in the ageless universe of books and unaware of what was going on about him. Nor, on the other literary extreme, was he the pure poet, aloof, usually a little petulantly so, feeding on his appreciation of his own genius. Chaucer had his way to make in the world, and he made it, for the most part, in the public service. He knew as well as anyone what was going on, although he was doubtless that happy mixture of conservative and optimist who believes unpleasant innovations are a passing phase and that the good old days will come back when people get their feet on the ground once more. It is hard not to find a paradox in the fact that the great social, political, and economic events of Chaucer's life time are hardly reflected in his writings.[1]

Chaucer's family were reasonably well-to-do mercantile folk; both his father and grandfather were in the wine business, which may or may not account for the appreciative description of the fraudulent dilution of wine which Chaucer put into "The Pardoner's Tale." His father held a few positions in the royal service at one time or another and evidently had influence enough to get Geoffrey a berth in the royal household, for when we first

---

434. **Reuthe,** pity.   437. **agein,** to.   438. **some dele,** partly.   439. **ligge aughte,** something lie; compare the proverb "With empty hands men may lure no hawks."   440. **evene-cristene kidde me fernyere,** fellow Christian showed me years ago.   441. **sith,** since.   442. **yspilte,** wasted. **many a tyme,** on many occasions.   445. **Forsleuthed,** wasted by carelessness.   446. **gaf me noughte,** did not set myself.

448. **Heu . . . juvenilem."** Woe is me, what a fruitless life I led when I was young.   449. **he,** Sloth.   450. **Vigilate.** See Mark, 13:37. **veille fette,** watcher fetched.   451. **flatte,** dashed.   452. "**Ware the fram wanhope,** beware of despair. **wolde,** (which) will.   454. **hym,** God.   455. **gult,** guilt. **nys,** is not.   456. **seyned hym,** crossed himself.   458. **lette,** prevent.   459. **do me,** go.   462. **behote,** promise. **rode,** Cross.   463. **yelde agein,** pay back.

[1] See the introduction to *Piers Plowman* (page 162) for a brief and gloomy picture of Chaucer's world.

GEOFFREY CHAUCER

hear of him in 1357 he was in the service of Lionel, one of the royal princes. We next find him a prisoner in France, then released by an opportune payment of £16 by the King in 1360. Then follows a gap of seven years at the end of which he emerges with a pension given him as the king's "dilectus vallectus noster"—"our dearly beloved attendant." It has been suggested that he spent much of this seven years in Ireland with Prince Lionel, or, better still, at school.

What do we know about Chaucer's formal schooling? Precisely nothing. We can always remember the delightful picture of the little scholar and his school in "The Prioress's Tale," but we have no real right to take that as a transcript from personal experience. Chaucer may have gone to one of the universities, and he certainly knew university men. There is the learned, bookish, half-starved Clerk among the pilgrims, to say nothing of his fellow Jankin who was the fifth husband of the wife of Bath, and with them goes the reprehensible Nicholas of the Miller's sorry tale—men of Oxford, one and all. But balancing them we have the Reeve's tale of two Cambridge scamps to pull us up short. Then, too, there is the story that somebody told somebody in the sixteenth century that Chaucer as a member of the Inner Temple was once fined two shillings for beating a Franciscan friar in Fleet Street. Whether or not he had a formal education, one thing is certain: he managed to become very well read indeed.

With 1368 begins a ten-year period during which Chaucer was frequently employed as a diplomatic agent of the Government, making frequent trips to the Continent, but usually on errands the nature of which we do not know.

Literary historians have a way of dividing Chaucer's literary life into three periods, French, Italian, and English. This arrangement is convenient and will do very well so long as we bear in mind that the process was progressive—namely, that in the Italian period he had added Italian and Latin books to his library and their contents to his brain, and that in the so-called English period all his reading is fused and reinforced by the fine sensibility with which he observed human action and human character.[1]

In 1369 Blanche, Duchess of Lancaster, and wife of King Edward's son John of Gaunt, died of the plague, and Chaucer wrote *The Book of the Duchess* to memorialize her death and to console the bereaved husband. This poem may be considered typical of Chaucer's work when he was largely under French influence, but even here we find unmistakable signs of genius and literary innovation. He had already translated all or part of the *Roman de la Rose*, the fountain and source of the current French poetic style, and he was on borrowing terms with two living French authors, Machaut and Froissart. Of these two Froissart was the younger; indeed he was but a few years older than Chaucer and had spent several of the years between 1360 and 1369 at the English court. One can hardly doubt that Chaucer had known him and that the acquaintance had influenced the younger man's reading and style. The popular French poetic form, which Froissart had learned from Machaut, was the dream-vision, in which the author goes to sleep and undergoes a series of dismally allegorical adventures of a discretely amorous nature. Poems of this sort are naturally much alike, and soon become tedious. What Chaucer did was to alter the purpose and purport of the type while retaining the form, and give us a genuinely moving personal elegy, through which we are made to feel the grief of the knight in black. John of Gaunt, as a matter of fact, was not quite inconsolable; he married again, and later still yet again, and his third wife had been his mistress and the mother of several of his children before he married her. The fact that this third wife was the sister of Chaucer's own wife need hardly make us find prophetic irony in *The Book of the Duchess*.

Late in 1372 and early in 1373 Chaucer was in Italy on the King's business in Genoa and Florence. From this trip we ordinarily date the beginning of his interest in Italian literature, especially Dante, Petrarch, and Boccaccio His reading in Latin, too, was increased, and he added Virgil to Ovid, the latter his first and longest love among the Roman poets. These additions to his literary tools make themselves felt in *The House of Fame*. Here we have the dream-vision once more, but divided into books, adorned with a summary of the *Aeneid*, the emphasis cunningly thrown on Dido's faux pas, embellished with prologues which owe much to Dante, and scintillating with even more miscellaneous learning. All this sounds formidable enough, but Chaucer's self is strikingly present, for the poem is one of the most hilarious things that he ever wrote. The dismal scholarship which would make it a deliberate parody of the *Divine Comedy*, or, even worse, Chaucer's measured views on worldly reputation, vanish before the fresh humor of passage after passage. Chaucer's forced flight with the eagle is a high spot indeed. After the eagle's long lecture

---

[1] In the following account Chaucer's lesser poems have been deliberately stressed at the expense of his two masterpieces, *Troilus and Criseyde* and the *Canterbury Tales*.

on the nature of sound, he asks Chaucer a question —"And y answered and seyde 'yis.'" Could the fear and discomfort of the amateur and unwilling flier be expressed more simply, more pathetically, or more comically? *The House of Fame* is unfinished, but that is a matter of little moment. More would have been better, but what there is is good enough.

In 1374 Chaucer was appointed Controller of Customs for the Port of London, a position in which he was reconfirmed by Richard when he became king in 1377. This was a good and remunerative position, but one which required regular attendance and personal clerical work. He kept the job twelve years, living for the most part in a house above Aldgate, and seems to have lost it thanks to the change in administration when the Duke of Gloucester, posing as a strict constitutionalist, seized political control, liquidated the young King's party, and put his own followers in office. Chaucer was lucky, perhaps, to lose no more than his position in the purge, as some of the King's friends were exiled and others executed. During the time that he was in the customs Chaucer had engaged in intermittent diplomatic activity, including at least one more trip to Italy in 1378.

Chaucer's most important literary work before *The Canterbury Tales* was done during his later years in the customhouse and the first year of his release. Thus we may reasonably date between 1380 and 1387 *The Parliament of Fowls*, the story of "Palamon and Arcite," later to appear as *The Knight's Tale*, *Troilus and Criseyde*, and the *Legend of Good Women*.

The Parliament of Fowls is another dream-vision in which Scipio Africanus takes the poet to see the birds assemble on Valentine's Day to choose their mates for the coming year. The assembly is marked by the conflicting suits of three noble male eagles for the fair female eagle's claw. The poem is extraordinarily vivacious, and some of the birds are very well characterized, especially the lower-class birds who have little patience with the doctrines of courtly love which their betters utter. The turtle-dove arouses the duck's scorn when she declares that a lover should never let his adoration slacken even though his lady be ever cold and regard him not:

> "Well bourded," quod the duke, "by myn hat!
> That men shulde loven alwey causeles,
> Who can a resoun fynde or wit in that?
> Daunseth he murye that is myrtheless?
> Who shulde recche of that is recheles?
> Ye quek!" yit seyde the duke, ful wel and fayre,
> "There been mo sterres, God wot, than a payre!"

The Parliament of Fowls is an occasional poem, and scholars have busied themselves to find the occasion, that is, to identify the eagles with European royalty a-wooing gone. There have been many identifications made, but all in vain, since scholars have seldom succeeded in convincing others than themselves.

In "Palamon and Arcite" and *Troilus and Criseyde* we find Chaucer dealing with themes taken from classical antiquity, the first connected with Thebes and Athens and the second with Troy. Chaucer's immediate source in each case is a contemporary Italian author, Giovanni Boccaccio. Let it be understood that there is here no conscientious attempt to recreate the classical setting, none of the laudable desire for historical and sociological accuracy which haunts, or may haunt, the modern historical novelist. Here Chaucer rather follows common medieval usage, and the Middle Ages remade the ancient world in their own image and let anachronisms go hang. Chaucer himself puts it very well when, after describing a warrior in the Athens of Theseus bearing a Prussian shield, he blandly comments, "Ther nis no newe gyse that it nas old." If Bohemia has no seacoast, let us give it one!

Both "The Knight's Tale" and *Troilus and Criseyde* came from Boccaccio, and the way Chaucer treats his sources in the two poems is in the sharpest contrast. "The Knight's Tale" is only one-fourth the length of its original, but Chaucer's independent genius is less evident here than elsewhere. Although he adds humor, the characters remain as distressingly vague as they were in Boccaccio. It is not easy to distinguish between Palamon and Arcite, and the fair Emily is little better than a dummy. In *Troilus and Criseyde* all is different. Chaucer's poem is nearly three thousand lines longer than Boccaccio's. He transforms the principal actors. Troilus is given more character and a genuinely deep philosophical attitude toward his problems of love and life, but he is far less changed than are Cressida and Pandarus. From an attractive, rather elemental, and decidedly fleshly young woman, Cressida in the English poem becomes a singularly subtle enigma, about whom critics still argue in a mood composed in varying proportions of love and suspicion. Pandarus, a very ordinary and somewhat lewd young man-about-town in Boccaccio, now is made a figure not unworthy to take a place along with the Wife of Bath, Falstaff, and Parson Adams.

The most interesting thing about *The Legend of Good Women* is its Prologue, which has come down to us in two versions, one a fairly thoroughgoing revision of the other. Here Chaucer returns to the dream-vision and to his French sources, but now a new French poet, Eustache Deschamps, is added to Machaut and Froissart. In the Prologue the poet begins by telling of his devotion to the daisy, and then how he goes forth into the fields and worships his favorite flower until, night falling, he returns to his home and his bed. In a dream he soon finds himself in the meadow again and there sees the God of Love leading a beautiful queen by the hand. She is Alceste, and the god, seeing the poet, warns him away because he has written against love and womanhood such horrid things as *The Romaunt of the Rose* and *Troilus and Criseyde*. The lady defends the poet, pointing out that he has also written *The House of Fame*, *The Book of the Duchess*, "Palamon and Arcite," and other works in praise of love. With the god's consent she orders Chaucer to redeem himself fully by writing the lives of the saints of Cupid, women who, faithful, died for love's sweet sake. The poet awakes, and begins with the life of Cleopatra, a saint surely in no calendar but Cupid's. The lives themselves differ in quality, and are not particularly to our taste. Chaucer tired of them and did not complete his scheme.

From 1387 until his death Chaucer was engaged with *The Canterbury Tales*, but he had other duties as well. When Richard became of age in 1389 and took the government into his own hands once more, Chaucer was made Clerk of the King's Works, a position which he held for nearly two years. It was his duty to direct and oversee the care, maintenance, and repair of ten scattered royal residences, including the Tower and the palace at Westminster. Then, too, for a time he was a member of the Thames Commission, and had to inspect its bridges and banks and, figuratively at least, to look into the sewers and ditches that ran into the stream between Greenwich and Woolwich. He must have traveled extensively, controlled numerous groups of men, and expended much public money. In September, 1390, he managed to be robbed twice within two or three days, once of £10 and again of £9 and a horse. The money was the King's, but the horse was his. The following year he gave up his office, or was removed. He still enjoyed the royal favor—gifts, an annuity, and a butt of wine a year. Even an evident association with Henry, Earl of Derby, son of his old patron John of Gaunt, and now Richard's rival, did not lose the poet Richard's friendship. When Henry came to the throne in October, 1399, he renewed Chaucer's annuity and the annual butt of wine. Full of optimism, on December 4, 1399, Chaucer took a fifty-three year lease of a house in Westminster, but he occupied it less than one year. We place Chaucer's death in 1400, not because we have any contemporary record, but simply because his pension was collected in June of that year and not thereafter. Surely, however, one could ask for no better proof!

The Canterbury Tales is a frame story; that is, a device is used to make it appear natural that a number of quite unrelated stories should appear together in the pages of one book. Chaucer's device is to have a group of pilgrims take part in a storytelling competition on their journey from London to the shrine of St. Thomas à Becket in Canterbury. There was nothing new about a frame story. It had originated centuries before, and we have the Sanscrit *Panchatantra* and *Hitopadesha* and *The Arabian Nights* to illustrate its popularity in India and the Near East. The European Middle Ages had their frame stories, too, *The Seven Sages of Rome*, Boccaccio's *Decameron*, Sercambi's *Novelle*, itself a pilgrimage frame, and John Gower's *Confessio Amantis*. Nor did it die out with the Middle Ages, for we have yesterday's *Tales of a Wayside Inn* and William Morris's *Earthly Paradise*, and today's *Salzburg Tales* of Christina Stead. There was no innovation, then, and some of the other practitioners of the genre were storytellers of rare merit, notably the authors of *The Arabian Nights* and Boccaccio. Yet nowhere is Chaucer's mastery more evident than in the handling of his frame. In almost all the others the stories alone matter, but the tellers of Chaucer's tales are more real than the tales they tell. Most of them stand out in our minds as clearly not only as the characters in the best of literature, but as the people in our own world. They are distinct individuals one and all, and among them is one of the two greatest and richest comic creations in English literature. That is the Wife of Bath, and her fitting mate in fame is Sir John Falstaff. However real the portraits are in "The General Prologue," Chaucer does not leave them there. They continue to live along the way, and in link, prologue, and epilogue, in interpolations in the tales themselves, we grow to know them better and better as we observe their actions and reactions. We see their friendships and their feuds, their quarrels and rivalries, their foibles and weaknesses. Their very stories sometimes grow out of their conduct. The Miller and the Reeve, the Friar and the Summoner, the Host and the Cook, the Cook again and the Manciple, all fight and tell tales out of school. Gallant and irrepressible Alice of Bath manages to outrage the sensibilities of all the other pilgrims. Her attack on celibacy is an affront to the ecclesiastics, to whom that state is dear, at least in theory, and when she insists that the wife should rule the husband in marriage she annoys and probably frightens the laymen, male to a man. As Dryden, paraphrasing Chaucer himself, wrote, "Here is God's plenty." The vast sprawling drama, even in its unfinished and disjointed state, is one of the glories of English literature.

Now, finally, let us return to the problem which perplexed us at the start—Chaucer's failure to reflect the really critical events of his time. Some critics have found this reprehensible, yet herein lies his greatest strength, and perhaps his greatest good for us. Chaucer lived in a wicked world, and through that world he walked, not aloof but reserved, conscious enough, but deliberately choosing to focus his talent on the individual, not the mass. He saw and portrayed, with a vividness and truth which makes his scenes as clear today as when he penned them, those little virtues and little vices, those smaller joys and smaller tragedies, that are the very essence and being of humanity's daily life. And, above all, he exemplified that friendly curiosity and healthy interest in others which can let the normal and alert man find a joy in living, somehow, somewhere, every day. Now, we too live in a wicked world. We too can see, feel in the air around us, much of the poverty and misery and despair, the ambition and greed and terrorism, that Chaucer must have seen and felt. And it cannot be called cowardice or escape or evasion if we turn back to Chaucer and let his genius show us that there are other things to see and feel sometimes, things, too, which may well last their six hundred years.

The selections which follow bring out clearly the fundamentally dramatic nature of *The Canterbury Tales*. All of the prologues and links are given, and with them brief accounts of the omitted tales. It should be remembered that not only did Chaucer fail to complete the scheme which is outlined in "The General Prologue," but that he apparently did not make any provisional arrangement of those tales which he had written. The beginning and the end are indicated plainly enough, but the internal arrangement must rest on the varying and inconsistent order of the manuscripts or the more or less arbitrary judgment of modern editors. Certain tales or groups of tales are unmistakably united, and these fragments of the unfinished whole are commonly designated by the letters A to I. By means of chronological, geographical, and other indications one can arrange these groups in a sequence that will satisfy some of the demands of probability and possibility. Such an ordering was made in the famous Six-Text Edition of the Chaucer Society and has been adopted, often with varying degrees of reluctance, by most subsequent editors. We must emphasize that this arrangement is neither Chaucer's nor that of any manuscript, nor is it clearly consistent by the very standards adopted. Indeed, we may doubt if any genuinely satisfactory effort can be made to recreate what Chaucer had in mind when he last worked on *The Canterbury Tales*. Recent editors—notably J. M. Manly, *Canterbury Tales*, Henry Holt and Company, 1928; F. N. Robinson, *The Complete Works of Geoffrey Chaucer*, Houghton Mifflin, 1933, and J. M. Manly and Edith Rickert, *The Text of the Canterbury Tales*, University of Chicago Press, 1940—have reverted to the order, however inconsistent it may be, of the best manuscripts. For the sake of convenience, especially of reference to W. W. Skeat's *The Complete Works of Geoffrey Chaucer*, 7 vols., Oxford Press, 1894-97, recent editions have indicated the groups and line references of the standard modern arrangement.

The present text is taken, by the kind permission of the copyright owner, from Manly and Rickert's monumental *Text of the Canterbury Tales*. The present editor has supplied punctuation and standard capitalization, and has followed modern typographical usage in the matter of "i," "j," "u," "v," and the like. The standard groupings are given, but the individual units have been renumbered independently to make immediate reference to line numbers simpler and more convenient. The notes, which are intended to explain words and idioms obsolete, strange, or altered in sense, have been kept at a minimum. Certain more or less conventional expurgations are indicated in the line numbering. For a more complete exegesis of the text the student is advised to turn to the notes of the editions already mentioned.

Of the almost innumerable writings on Chaucer and his works the following are listed for their general factual and critical usefulness: G. G. Coulton, *Chaucer and His England*, Putnam, 1908; R. D. French, *A Chaucer Handbook*, Crofts, 1927; G. L. Kittredge, *Chaucer and His Poetry*, Harvard University Press, 1915; Emile Legouis, *Geoffrey Chaucer*, translated by Lailavoix, Dutton, 1912; J. L. Lowes, *Geoffrey Chaucer*, Houghton Mifflin, 1934; H. R. Patch, *On Rereading Chaucer*, Harvard University Press, 1939; R. K. Root, *The Poetry of Chaucer*, Houghton Mifflin, 1922.

from THE CANTERBURY TALES

THE GENERAL PROLOGUE

Whan that Aprill with his shoures soote
The droghte of March hath perced to the roote,
And bathed every veyne in swich licour
Of which vertu engendred is the flour;
Whan Zephirus eek with his sweete breeth
Inspired hath in every holt and heeth
The tendre croppes, and the yonge sonne
Hath in the Ram his half cours yronne,
And smale foweles maken melodye,
That slepen al the nyght with open eye   10
(So priketh hem nature in hir corages):
Than longen folk to goon on pilgrymages,
And palmeres for to seken straunge strondes,
To ferne halwes, kouthe in sondry londes;
And specially from every shires ende
Of Engelond to Caunterbury they wende,
The holy blisful martir for to seke,
That hem hath holpen whan that they were seeke.

Bifel that, in that sesoun on a day,
In Southwerk at the Tabard as I lay   20
Redy to wenden on my pilgrymage
To Caunterbury with ful devout corage,
At nyght was come into that hostelrye
Wel nyne and twenty in a compaignye,
Of sondry folk, by aventure yfalle
In felaweshipe, and pilgrymes were they alle,
That toward Caunterbury wolden ryde.
The chambres and the stables weren wyde,
And wel we weren esed atte beste.
And shortly, whan the sonne was to reste,   30
So hadde I spoken with hem everichon,
That I was of hir felaweshipe anon,
And made forward erly for to ryse,
To take oure wey ther as I yow devyse.

But nathelees, whil I have tyme and space,
Er that I ferther in this tale pace,
Me thynketh it acordant to resoun
To telle yow al the condicioun

Of ech of hem, so as it semed me,
And whiche they weren, and of what degree,   40
And eek in what array that they were inne:
And at a Knyght than wol I first bigynne.

A Knyght ther was, and that a worthy man,
That fro the tyme that he first bigan
To riden out, he loved chivalrye,
Trouthe and honour, fredom and curteisye.
Ful worthy was he in his lordes werre,
And ther-to hadde he riden, no man ferre,
As wel in Cristendom as in hethenesse,
And evere honoured for his worthynesse.   50
   At Alisaundre he was whan it was wonne.
Ful ofte tyme he hadde the bord bigonne
Aboven alle nacions in Pruce.
In Lettow hadde he reysed and in Ruce,
No Cristen man so ofte of his degree.
In Gernade at the seege eek hadde he be
Of Algezir, and riden in Belmarye.
At Lyeys was he and at Satalye,
Whan they were wonne; and in the Grete See
At many a noble armee hadde he be.   60
At mortal batailles hadde he been fiftene,
And foghten for oure feith at Tramyssene
In lystes thries, and ay slayn his foo.
This ilke worthy knyght hadde been also
Som-tyme with the lord of Palatye,
Agayn another hethen in Turkye.
   And evere-moore he hadde a sovereyn prys;
And though that he were worthy, he was wys,
And of his port as meke as is a mayde.
He nevere yet no vileynye ne sayde   70
In al his lyf un-to no maner wight.
He was a verray, parfit gentil knyght.
   But for to tellen yow of his array,
Hise hors were goode, but he was nat gay.
Of fustian he wered a gypoun

---

45. riden out, go on expeditions. **46. fredom**, generosity. **47. his lordes werre**, his king's war, the Hundred Years' War in France. **48. ferre**, farther. **51–66. At Alisaundre . . . Turkye.** The Knight campaigned in three crusades against the enemies of Christian Europe: (1) the Moors in Spain and North Africa, (2) the Turks and other Mohammedans in Asia Minor and Egypt, (3) the pagan Prussians, Lithuanians, and Russians on the shores of the Baltic. It is unlikely that any one actual knight could have taken part in wars so widely separated in time. **52. the bord bigonne**, taken the head of the table. **54. reysed**, campaigned. **59. Grete See**, Mediterranean. **60. armee**, armed expedition. **63. lystes**, lists, enclosed places for a tournament. **64. ilke**, same. **67. prys**, reputation. **68. wys**, prudent. **70. vileynye**, discourtesy. **72. verray, parfit**, true, perfect. **74. hors**, horses. **75. fustian**, thick cotton cloth **gypoun**, short blouse.

Group A. 1. soote, sweet. **3. swich**, such. **4. vertu**, power. **5. Zephirus**, the west wind. **7. croppes**, new shoots. **sonne**, sun. **8. Ram**, Aries, a sign of the zodiac. **11. priketh**, incites. **corages**, hearts. **13. palmeres**, pilgrims, especially those who had been to the Holy Land. **strondes**, shores. **14. ferne**, distant. **halwes**, shrines. **kouthe**, known. **17. martir**, St. Thomas à Becket. **18. holpen**, cured. **seeke**, sick. **25. aventure**, chance. **yfalle**, fallen. **28. wyde**, spacious. **29. esed atte beste**, entertained in the best manner. **31. everichon**, everyone. **33. forward**, agreement. **37. Me thynketh it**, it seems to me.

Al bismotered with his habergeoun,
For he was late ycome from his viage,
And wente for to doon his pilgrymage.

    With hym ther was his sone, a yong SQUYER,
A lovere and a lusty bacheler,   80
With lokkes crulle, as they were leyd in presse.
Of twenty yeer of age he was, I gesse.
    Of his stature he was of evene lengthe,
And wonderly delyvere, and of greet strengthe
And he hadde been som-tyme in chivachye
In Flaundres, in Artoys, and Picardye,
And born hym wel, as of so litel space,
In hope to stonden in his lady grace.
    Embrouded was he, as it were a meede
Al ful of fresshe floures, white and reede.   90
Syngynge he was, or floytynge, al the day;
He was as fressh as is the monthe of May.
Short was his gowne, with sleves longe and wyde.
Wel koude he sitte on hors and faire ryde.
He koude songes make and wel endite,
Juste and eek daunce, and wel purtreye and write.
So hoote he lovede, that by nyghtertale
He slepte namoore than dooth a nyghtyngale.
    Curteys he was, lowely, and servysable,
And carf biforn his fader at the table.   100

    A YEMAN hadde he and servantz namo
At that tyme, for hym liste ryde so;
And he was clad in coote and hood of grene.
A sheef of pecok arwes bright and kene
Under his belt he bar ful thriftily,
(Wel koude he dresse his takel yemanly:
His arwes drouped noght with fetheres lowe),
And in his hand he bar a myghty bowe.
A not heed hadde he, with a broun visage.
Of wodecraft wel koude he al the usage.   110
Upon his arm he bar a gay bracer,
And by his syde a swerd and a bokeler,
And on that oother syde a gay daggere,
Harneysed wel and sharp as poynt of spere,
A Cristofre on his brest of silver shene.
An horn he bar, the bawdryk was of grene;
A forster was he, soothly, as I gesse.

    Ther was also a nonne, a PRIORESSE,
That of hir smylyng was ful symple and coy;
Hir gretteste ooth was but by Seint Loy;   120
And she was cleped Madame Eglentyne.
    Ful wel she soong the servyce dyvyne,
Entuned in hir nose ful semely,
And Frenssh she spak ful faire and fetisly,
After the scole of Stratford-atte-Bowe,
For Frenssh of Parys was to hire unknowe.
    At mete wel ytaught was she with alle:
She let no morsel from hir lippes falle,
No wette hir fyngres in hir sauce depe.
Wel koude she carie a morsel and wel kepe   130
That no drope ne fille up-on hir brest.
In curteisie was set ful muchel hir lest.
Hir over lippe wyped she so clene
That in hir coppe ther was no ferthyng sene
Of grece, whan she dronken hadde hir draughte.
Ful semely after hir mete she raughte.
And sikerly she was of greet desport,
And ful plesaunt, and amyable of port,
And peyned hire to countrefete cheere
Of court, and to been estatlich of manere,   140
And to been holden digne of reverence.
    But, for to speken of hir conscience,
She was so charitable and so pitous
She wolde wepe, if that she sawe a mous
Caught in a trappe, if it were deed or bledde.
Of smale houndes hadde she, that she fedde
With rosted flessh, or mylk and wastel breed.
But soore wepte she if oon of hem were deed,
Of if men smoot it with a yerde smerte;
And al was conscience and tendre herte.   150
    Ful semely hir wympel pynched was;
Hir nose tretys, hir eyen greye as glas,
Hir mouth ful smal, and ther-to softe and reed;
But sikerly she hadde a fair forheed:
It was almoost a spanne brood, I trowe;
For, hardily, she was nat undergrowe.

---

76. bismotered, stained. **habergeoun,** coat of mail. **79. Squyer,** candidate for knighthood. **81. crulle,** curly. **83. evene lengthe,** medium height. **84. delyvere,** agile. **85. chivachye,** cavalry expedition. **88. lady,** lady's. **89. Embrouded,** embroidered; the reference is either to his costume or to his complexion. **91. floytynge,** flute-playing. **95. songes . . . endite,** compose both music and words. **96. Juste,** joust, fight in a tournament. **97. nyghtertale,** nighttime. **99. Curteys,** courteous. **100. carf biforn,** carved the meat for. **101. Yeman,** yeoman. **he,** the Knight. **102. hym liste ryde,** it pleased him to ride. **104. arwes,** arrows. **106. dresse his takel,** prepare his weapons. **109. not heed,** closely clipped head, or one shaped like a nut. **111. bracer,** archer's arm-protector. **112. bokeler,** buckler. **114. Harneysed,** mounted. **115. Cristofre,** image of St. Christopher. **shene,** bright. **116. bawdryk,** belt to hold the horn. **117. forster,** gamekeeper. **soothly,** truly. **118. nonne,** nun. **Prioresse,** head of a nunnery. **119. symple and coy,** unaffected and quiet. **120. Seint Loy,** a French saint who was artist and courtier. **121. cleped,** called. **123. semely,** properly. **124. fetisly,** elegantly. **132. ful muchel hir lest,** very much her delight. **134. ferthyng,** particle. **135. grece,** grease. **136. raughte,** reached. **137. sikerly,** certainly. **desport,** mirth. **138. port,** bearing. **139. peyned . . . cheere,** took pains to imitate the manners. **140. estatlich,** stately. **141. digne,** worthy. **142. conscience,** sensitivity of feeling. **143. pitous,** merciful. **147. wastel breed,** fine white bread. **149. yerde smerte,** stick sharply. **151. wympel pynched,** covering for head, neck, and chin; pleated. **152. tretys,** well formed. **155. trowe,** believe. **156. hardily,** certainly.

Ful fetys was hir cloke, as I was war.
Of smal coral aboute hir arm she bar
A peyre of bedes, gauded al with grene,
And there-on heng a brooch of gold ful shene,   160
On which ther was first writen a crowned A,
And after *Amor vincit omnia.*

   Another NONNE with hire hadde she,
That was hir chapeleyne, and preestes thre.

   A MONK ther was, a fair for the maistrye,
An outridere, that lovede venerye,
A manly man, to been an abbot able.
Ful many a deyntee hors hadde he in stable,
And whanne he rood, men myghte his brydel heere
Gynglen in a whistlynge wynd as cleere,   170
And eek as loude, as dooth the chapel belle,
Ther-as this lord was kepere of the celle.
   The reule of Seint Maure or of Seint Beneit,
By cause that it was old and somdel streit,—
This ilke Monk leet olde thynges pace,
And heeld after the newe world the space.
He yaf nat of that text a pulled hen,
That seith that hunters been nat holy men,
Ne that a monk whan he is recchelees,
Is likned til a fissh that is waterlees—   180
This is to seyn, a monk out of his cloystre;
But thilke text heeld he nat worth an oystre,
And I seyde his opinioun was good.
What sholde he studie and make hym-selven wood,
Upon a book in cloistre alwey to poure,
Or swynken with his handes, and laboure,
As Austyn bit? How shal the world be served?
Lat Austyn have his swynk to hym reserved!
Therfore he was a prikasour aright;
Grehoundes he hadde, as swift as fowel in flight;   190
Of prikyng and of huntyng for the hare
Was al his lust, for no cost wolde he spare.
   I seigh his sleves ypurfiled at the hond
With grys, and that the fyneste of a lond;
And, for to festne his hood under his chyn,
He hadde of gold wroght a ful curious pyn;
A love knotte in the gretter ende ther was.
His heed was balled, that shoon as any glas,
And eek his face, as he hadde been enoynt.
He was a lord ful fat and in good poynt;   200
Hise eyen stepe, and rollynge in his heed,
That stemed as a forneys of a leed;
His bootes souple, his hors in greet estat.
   Now certeynly he was a fair prelat;
He was nat pale as a forpyned goost.
A fat swan loved he best of any roost.
His palfrey was as broun as is a berye.

   A FRERE ther was, a wantowne and a merye,
A lymytour, a ful solempne man.
In alle the ordres foure is noon that kan   210
So muche of daliaunce and fair langage.
He hadde maad ful many a mariage
Of yonge wommen at his owene cost.
Un-to his ordre he was a noble post.
Ful wel biloved and famulier was he
With frankeleyns over al in his contree,
And with worthy wommen of the toun;
For he hadde power of confessioun,
As seyde hym-self, moore than a curat,
For of his ordre he was licenciat.   220
Ful swetely herde he confessioun,
And plesaunt was his absolucioun;
He was an esy man to yeve penaunce,
Ther-as he wiste to have a good pitaunce.
For un-to a poure ordre for to yive
Is signe that a man is wel yshryve;
For if he yaf, he dorste make avaunt,
He wiste that a man was repentaunt;
For many a man so hard is of his herte,
He may not wepe, al-thogh hym soore smerte.   230
Ther-fore in stede of wepynge and preyeres,
Men moote yeve silver to the poure freres.
   His typet was ay farsed ful of knyves
And pynnes, for to yeven faire wyves.
And certeynly he hadde a murye note;
Wel koude he synge and pleyen on a rote;
Of yeddynges he bar outrely the prys.
His nekke whit was as the flour de lys;

   159. **peyre . . . grene,** string with large green beads at intervals.   162. **Amor . . . omnia.** Love conquers all things.   164. **chapeleyne,** secretary. **preestes thre,** probably a slip of some kind, since we hear of but one later, and three would have made the pilgrims' number thirty-one instead of the twenty-nine of l. 24.   165. **a fair . . . maistrye,** an extremely good one.   166. **outridere,** inspector of monastic estates. **venerye,** hunting.   172. **celle,** subordinate monastery.   173. **reule . . . Beneit,** rule of the Benedictine order. **Seint Maure,** St. Maurus.   174. **somdel streit,** somewhat strict.   176. **the space,** in the meantime.   177. **pulled,** plucked.   179. **recchelees,** careless, negligent.   180. **til,** to.   184. **hym-selven wood,** himself mad.   186. **swynken,** work.   187. **Austyn bit,** St. Augustine of Hippo commands.   189. **prikasour,** hard-riding hunter.   192. **lust,** pleasure.   193. **seigh,** saw. **ypurfiled,** trimmed.   194. **grys,** gray fur.

199. **eek,** also. **enoynt,** anointed.   200. **poynt,** condition.   201. **stepe,** protruding or shining.   202. **stemed,** shone. **forneys . . . leed,** furnace under a caldron.   205. **forpyned,** wasted away.   208. **Frere,** begging friar. **wantowne,** gay.   209. **lymytour,** licensed to beg within a limited territory. **solempne,** splendid.   210. See *Piers Plowman,* I, l. 55 (page 164). **kan,** knows.   211. **daliaunce,** playfulness.   216. **frankeleyns,** prosperous country squires.   223. **yeve,** give.   224. **wiste,** knew. **pitaunce,** gift.   226. **yshryve,** shriven.   227. **dorste make avaunt,** dared boast.   230. **hym . . . smerte,** it pains him sorely.   232. **moote,** may.   233. **typet,** cape. **farsed,** stuffed.   236. **rote,** stringed instrument.   237. **yeddynges,** ballads.

Ther-to he strong was as a champioun.
    He knew the tavernes wel in every toun,   240
And every hostiler and tappestere
Bet than a lazar or a beggestere;
For un-to swich a worthy man as he
Accorded nat, as by his facultee,
To have with sike lazars aqueyntaunce.
It is nat honeste, it may nat avaunce
For to deelen with no swich poraille,
But al with riche and selleres of vitaille.
And over-al, ther as profit sholde arise,
Curteys he was and lowely of servyse.   250
Ther was no man no wher so vertuous.
He was the beste beggere in his hous,
For thogh a wydwe hadde noght a sho,
So plesaunt was his *In principio*,
Yet wolde he have a ferthyng, er he wente.
His purchas was wel bettre than his rente.
And rage he koude, as it were right a whelpe.
    In lovedayes ther koude he muchel helpe:
For ther he was nat lyk a cloystrer
With a thredbare cope, as is a poure scoler,   260
But he was lyk a maister or a pope.
Of double worstede was his semycope,
That rounded as a belle out of the presse.
Somwhat he lipsed, for his wantownesse,
To make his Englissh sweete up-on his tonge;
And in his harpyng, whan that he hadde songe,
Hise eyen twynkled in his heed aright,
As doon the sterres in the frosty nyght.
This worthy lymytour was cleped Huberd.

    A Marchant was ther with a forked berd,   270
In motlee, and hye on hors he sat,
Up-on his heed a Flaundryssh bevere hat,
His bootes clasped faire and fetisly.
    Hise resons he spak ful solempnely,
Sownynge alwey th' encrees of his wynnyng.
He wolde the see were kept for any thyng
Bitwixe Middelburgh and Orewelle.
Wel koude he in eschaunge sheeldes selle.
    This worthy man ful wel his wit bisette:
Ther wiste no wight that he was in dette,   280
So estatly was he of his governaunce,
With his bargaynes and with his chevysaunce.
    For sothe he was a worthy man with alle,
But, sooth to seyn, I noot how men hym calle.

    A Clerk ther was of Oxenford also,
That un-to logyk hadde longe ygo.
    As leene was his hors as is a rake,
And he was nat right fat, I undertake,
But looked holwe, and ther-to sobrely.
Ful thredbare was his overeste courtepy;   290
For he hadde geten hym yet no benefice,
Ne was so worldly for to have office.
For hym was levere have at his beddes heed
Twenty bookes, clad in blak or reed,
Of Aristotle and his philosophie,
Than robes riche, or fithele, or gay sautrie.
    But al be that he was a philosophre,
Yet hadde he but litel gold in cofre;
But al that he myghte of his frendes hente,
On bookes and on lernynge he it spente,   300
And bisily gan for the soules preye
Of hem that yaf hym wher-with to scoleye.
    Of studie took he moost cure and moost heede.
Noght oo word spak he moore than was neede,
And that was seid in forme and reverence,
And short and quyk and ful of heigh sentence.
Sownynge in moral vertu was his speche,
And gladly wolde he lerne and gladly teche.

    A Sergeant of the Lawe, war and wys,
That often hadde been at the Parvys,   310
Ther was also, ful riche of excellence.
Discreet he was and of greet reverence—
He semed swich, hise wordes weren so wyse.
    Justice he was ful often in assise,
By patente and by pleyn commissioun.
For his science and for his heigh renoun,
Of fees and robes hadde he many oon.
So greet a purchasour was nowher noon;
Al was fee symple to hym in effect,
His purchasyng myghte nat been infect.   320

---

241. **tappestere**, barmaid. 242. **lazar**, leper. **beggestere**, female beggar. 244. **facultee**, position. 246. **honeste**, respectable. **avaunce**, be profitable. 247. **poraille**, poor folk. 248. **vitaille**, provisions. 253. **sho**, shoe. 254. **In principio**, "In the beginning," opening of the Gospel of John, held by the ignorant to be a magic formula, and consequently used by friars as a prelude to begging. 256. **purchas**, (illegal) gains. **rente**, (legal) income. 257. **rage**, behave wantonly. 258. **lovedayes**, days for settling disputes by arbitration. 262. **semycope**, short cape. 264. **lipsed**, lisped. 270. **Marchant**, merchant. 271. **motlee**, figured cloth. 273. **fetisly**, neatly. 274. **resons**, opinions. **solempnely**, pompously. 275. **Sownynge**, proclaiming. 278. **sheeldes**, French coins. 279. **bisette**, employed. 280. **wight**, person.

282. **chevysaunce**, business dealing, often with a hint of illegality. 284. **noot**, know not. 285. **Clerk**, ecclesiastical student. 286. **ygo**, begun. 289. **holwe**, hollow. 290. **overeste courtepy**, upper short coat. 292. **office**, secular employment. 293. **hym was levere**, he had rather. 296. **fithele**, fiddle. **sautrie**, stringed instrument. 299. **hente**, obtain. 302. **scoleye**, study. 303. **cure**, care. 306. **heigh sentence**, elevated meaning. 307. **Sownynge in**, tending toward. 309. **Sergeant of the Lawe**, legal servant of the king; one of the twenty or so leading lawyers in the land. **war**, prudent. 310. **Parvys**, gathering-place of lawyers. 316. **science**, knowledge. 318. **purchasour**, buyer of land. 319. **fee symple**, absolute possession. 320. **infect**, defective in title.

Nowher so bisy a man as he ther nas,
And yet he semed bisier than he was.

   In termes hadde he caas and doomes alle,
That from the tyme of Kyng William were falle.
Ther-to he koude endite, and make a thyng,
Ther koude no wight pynchen at his writyng;
And every statut koude he pleyn by roote.

   He rood but hoomly in a medlee coote,
Girt with a ceynt of silk, with barres smale;
Of his array telle I no lenger tale.   330

   A Frankeleyn was in his compaignye;
Whit was his berd as is the dayesye;
Of his complexioun he was sangwyn.
Wel loved he by the morwe a sop in wyn.
To lyven in delyt was evere his wone,
For he was Epicurus owene sone,
That heeld opynyoun that pleyn delit
Was verray felicitee parfit.

   An housholdere, and that a greet, was he;
Seint Julyan he was in his contree.   340
His breed, his ale, was alweys after oon;
A bettre envyned man was nevere noon.
Withoute bake mete was nevere his hous,
Of fissh and flessh, and that so plentevous,
It snewed in his hous of mete and drynke.
Of alle deyntees that men koude thynke
After the sondry sesons of the yeer,
So chaunged he his mete and his soper.
Ful many a fat partrich hadde he in muwe,
And many a breem and many a luce in stuwe.   350
Wo was his cook, but if his sauce were
Poynaunt and sharp, and redy al his geere.
His table dormaunt in his halle alway
Stood redy-covered al the longe day.

   At sessions ther he was lord and sire;
Ful ofte tyme he was knyght of the shire.
An anlaas and a gipser al of silk
Heeng at his girdel, whit as morne mylk.
A shirreve hadde he been, and a countour;
Was nowher swich a worthy vavasour.   360

   An Haberdasshere and a Carpenter,
A Webbe, a Dyere, and a Tapycer—
And they were clothed alle in oo lyveree
Of a solempne and a greet fraternytee.
Ful fressh and newe hir geere apiked was;
Hir knyves were chaped noght with bras,
But al with silver; wroght ful clene and wel
Hir girdles and hir pouches everydel.
Wel semed ech of hem a fair burgeys
To sitten in a yeldehalle on a deys.   370
Everych for the wisdom that he kan,
Was shaply for to been an alderman.
For catel hadde they ynogh and rente,
And eek hir wyves wolde it wel assente;
And elles certeyn they were to blame:
It is ful fair to been ycleped madame,
And goon to vigilies al bifore,
And have a mantel roialliche ybore.

   A Cook they hadde with hem for the nones,
To boille the chiknes with the marybones,   380
And poudre marchaunt tart, and galyngale.
Wel koude he knowe a draughte of Londoun ale.
He koude rooste, and sethe, and broille, and frye,
Maken mortreux, and wel bake a pye.
But greet harm was it, as it thoughte me,
That on his shyne a mormal hadde he,
For blankmanger that made he with the beste.

   A Shipman was ther, wonyng fer by weste:
For aught I woot, he was of Dertemouthe.
He rood upon a rouncy, as he kouthe,   390
In a gowne of faldyng to the knee.
A daggere hangynge on a laas hadde he
Aboute his nekke, under his arm adoun.
The hoote somer had maad his hewe al broun.

   And certeynly he was a good felawe;
Ful many a draughte of wyn hadde he drawe
Fro Burdeuxward, whil that the chapman sleep.
Of nyce conscience took he no keep.
If that he faught, and had the hyer hond,
By water he sente hem hoom to every lond.   400

---

   323. **caas and doomes,** law cases and judgments.   325. **endite . . . thyng,** draw up a legal document.   326. **pynchen at,** find fault with.   327. **koude,** knew.   328. **hoomly,** informally. **medlee,** of mixed color.   329. **ceynt,** girdle.   334. **sop,** piece of bread.   335. **wone,** custom.   340. **Seint Julyan.** See note 10 on page 122. **contree,** district.   341. **after oon,** of uniform quality.   342. **envyned,** stocked with wine.   345. **snewed,** snowed.   348. **soper,** supper.   349. **muwe,** pen.   350. **breem . . . luce,** fish. **stuwe,** fishpond.   352. **geere,** utensils.   353. **dormaunt,** fixed.   355. **sessions,** local court sessions.   356. **knyght of the shire,** member of Parliament.   357. **anlaas,** dagger. **gipser,** purse.   359. **shirreve,** sheriff. **countour,** auditor.   360. **vavasour,** country squire.   362. **Webbe,** weaver. **Tapycer,** tapestry-maker.   365. **apiked,** adorned.   366. **chaped,** mounted.   369. **burgeys,** burgess.   370. **yeldehalle,** gildhall. **deys,** dais, platform.   371. **kan,** knows.   373. **catel,** property.   377. **vigilies,** religious services on the eves of feasts.   379. **for the nones,** for the occasion.   380. **chiknes,** chickens. **marybones,** marrowbones.   381. **poudre marchaunt,** a sour flavoring powder. **galyngale,** an aromatic East Indian spice.   383. **sethe,** boil.   384. **mortreux,** stew.   385. **it thoughte me,** it seemed to me.   386. **mormal,** sore.   387. **blankmanger,** creamed fowl sweetened and spiced.   388. **Shipman,** ship's captain. **wonyng . . . weste,** living far to the west.   389. **woot,** know.   390. **rouncy . . . kouthe,** nag as well as he knew how to.   391. **faldyng,** coarse wool.   392. **laas,** cord.   395. **felawe,** rascal.   397. **chapman sleep,** merchant slept.   398. **nyce conscience,** tenderheartedness. **keep,** heed.

But of his craft to rekene wel his tydes,
His stremes and his daungers hym bisydes,
His herberwe, and his moone, his lodemenage,
Ther nas noon swich from Hulle to Cartage.
Hardy he was, and wys to undertake;
With many a tempest hadde his berd been shake.
He knew alle the havenes, as they were,
Fro Gootland to the cape of Fynystere,
And every cryke in Britaigne and in Spayne.
His barge ycleped was the Mawdelayne. 410

With us ther was a DOCTOUR OF PHISIK,
In al this world ne was ther noon hym lyk,
To speke of phisik and of surgerye,
For he was grounded in astronomye.
He kepte his pacient a ful greet deel
In houres by his magik natureel.
Wel koude he fortunen the ascendent
Of hise ymages for his pacient.
He knew the cause of every maladye,
Were it of hoot, or coold, or moyste, or drye, 420
And where engendred, and of what humour.
He was a verray, parfit practisour.
  The cause yknowe, and of his harm the roote,
Anon he yaf the sike man his boote.
Ful redy hadde he hise apothecaries,
To sende hym drogges and his letuaries,
For ech of hem made oother for to wynne:
Hir frendshipe nas nat newe to begynne.
  Wel knew he the olde Esculapius,
And Deïscorides, and eek Rusus, 430
Old Ypocras, Haly, and Galyen,
Serapion, Razis, and Avycen,
Averrois, Damascien, and Constantyn,
Bernard, and Gatesden, and Gilbertyn.
  Of his diete mesurable was he,
For it was of no superfluitee,
But of greet norissynge and digestible.
His studie was but litel on the Bible.
  In sangwyn and in pers he clad was al,
Lyned with taffata and with sendal; 440
And yet he was but esy of dispence;
He kepte that he wan in pestilence.

403. **herberwe**, harbor. **lodemenage**, pilot's craft. 411. **Doctour of Phisik**, physician and surgeon. 413. **phisik**, medicine. 414. **astronomye**, astrology. 415–16. **kepte . . . houres**, watched for favorable hours for his patient. **magik natureel**, astrology and the like, not witchcraft. 417. **fortunen . . . ascendent**, cast the horoscope. 418. **ymages**, representations either of the patient or of signs of the zodiac, probably the latter. 424. **boote**, help. 426. **letuaries**, remedies. 429–34. **Esculapius . . . Gilbertyn**, the authors, classical, Arabian, and medieval, of the standard works on medicine consulted in Chaucer's day. 435. **mesurable**, temperate. 437. **norissynge**, nourishment. 439. **sangwyn**, red. **pers**, blue-gray. 440. **sendal**, thin silk.

For gold in phisik is a cordial,
Therfore he loved gold in special.

  A good WYF was ther of biside BATHE,
But she was som del deef, and that was scathe.
Of clooth makyng she hadde swich an haunt,
She passed hem of Ypres and of Gaunt.
In al the parisshe wyf ne was ther noon
That to the offrynge bifore hire sholde goon; 450
And if ther dide, certeyn so wrooth was she,
That she was out of alle charitee.
Hir coverchiefs ful fyne were of ground;
I dorste swere they weyeden ten pound
That on a Sonday weren up-on hir heed.
Hir hosen weren of fyn scarlet reed,
Ful streite yteyd, and shoes ful moyste and newe.
Boold was hir face, and fair, and reed of hewe.
  She was a worthy womman al hir lyve;
Housbondes at chirche dore she hadde fyve, 460
With-outen oother compaignye in youthe,—
But ther-of nedeth nat to speke as nouthe.
  And thries hadde she been at Jerusalem;
She hadde passed many a straunge strem;
At Rome she hadde been, and at Boloyne,
In Galice at Seint Jame, and at Coloyne.
She koude muche of wandrynge by the weye.
Gat tothed was she, soothly for to seye.
  Upon an amblere esily she sat,
Ywympled wel, and on hir heed an hat 470
As brood as is a bokeler or a targe;
A foot mantel aboute hir hipes large,
And on hir feet a peyre of spores sharpe.
In felawshipe wel koude she laughe and carpe.
Of remedies of love she knew par chaunce,
For she koude of that art the olde daunce.

  A good man was ther of religioun,
And was a poure PERSOUN of a toun,
But riche he was of holy thoght and werk.
He was also a lerned man, a clerk, 480
That Cristes gospel trewely wolde preche;
His parisshens devoutly wolde he teche.
Benygne he was, and wonder diligent,
And in adversitee ful pacient,
And swich he was preved ofte sithes.

443. **cordial**, stimulant for the heart. 445. **Wyf**, matron. **biside**, just outside. 446. **scathe**, a pity. 447. **haunt**, skill. 450. **offrynge**, the offering of something as an act of worship. 452. **charitee**, Christian love. 453. **coverchiefs**, head-coverings. **ground**, texture. 454. **dorste**, might venture to. 457. **streite yteyd**, tightly tied. 462. **as nouthe**, now. 463. **thries**, thrice. 464. **straunge**, foreign. 468. **Gat tothed**, with widely spaced teeth. 471. **targe**, shield. 472. **foot mantel**, riding-skirt. 474. **carpe**, talk. 478. **Persoun**, parson. 485. **preved ofte sithes**, proved many times.

Ful looth were hym to cursen for his tithes,
But rather wolde he yeven, out of doute,
Un-to his poure parisshens aboute
Of his offrynge and eek of his substaunce.
He koude in litel thyng have suffisaunce.   490
Wyd was his parisshe, and houses fer asonder,
But he ne lafte nat, for reyn ne thonder,
In siknesse nor in meschief, to visite
The ferreste in his parisshe, muche and lite,
Up-on his feet, and in his hond a staf.
This noble ensample to his sheep he yaf,
That first he wroghte, and afterward he taughte.
Out of the gospel he tho wordes caughte,
And this figure he added eek ther-to,
That if gold ruste, what sholde iren do?   500
For if a preest be foule, on whom we truste,
No wonder is a lewed man to ruste;
And shame it is, if a preest take keep,
A shiten shepherde and a clene sheep.
Wel oghte a preest ensample for to yive,
By his clennesse, how that his sheep sholde lyve.

He sette nat his benefice to hyre,
And leet his sheep encombred in the myre,
And ran to Londoun, un-to Seint Poules,
To seken hym a chauntrye for soules,   510
Or with a bretherhede to been withholde;
But dwelte at hoom, and kepte wel his folde,
So that the wolf ne made it nat myscarye;
He was a shepherde and noght a mercenarye.

And thogh he hooly were and vertuous,
He was noght to synful men despitous,
Ne of his speche daungerous ne digne,
But in his techyng discreet and benigne.
To drawen folk to hevene by fairnesse,
By good ensample, this was his bisynesse,   520
But it were any persone obstinat,
What so he were, of heigh or lowe estat,
Hym wolde he snybben sharply for the nonys.

A bettre preest I trowe that nowher noon ys.
He wayted after no pompe and reverence,
Ne maked hym a spiced conscience,
But Cristes loore, and his apostles twelve,
He taughte, but first he folwed it hym-selve.

With hym ther was a PLOWMAN, was his brother,
That hadde ylad of donge ful many a fother;   530
A trewe swynkere and a good was he,
Lyvynge in pees and parfit charitee.
God loved he best with al his hoole herte
At alle tymes, thogh hym gamed or smerte,
And thanne his neighebore right as hym-selve.
He wolde thresshe, and ther-to dyke and delve,
For Cristes sake, for every poure wight,
With-outen hire, if it lay in his myght.
His tithes payde he ful faire and wel,
Bothe of his propre swynk and his catel.   540
In a tabard he rood upon a mere.

Ther was also a REVE, and a MILLERE,
A SOMNOUR, and a PARDONER also,
A MAUNCIPLE, and my-self: ther were namo.

The MILLER was a stout carl for the nones,
Ful big he was of brawn, and eek of bones;
That proved wel, for over-al ther he cam,
At wrastlynge he wolde have alwey the ram.
He was short sholdred, brood, a thikke knarre;
Ther was no dore that he nolde heve of harre,   550
Or breke it at a rennyng, with his heed.
His berd as any sowe or fox was reed,
And ther-to brood as though it were a spade.
Upon the cop right of his nose he hade
A werte, and ther-on stood a tuft of herys,
Reed as the bristles of a sowes erys;
His nosethirles blake were and wyde.
A swerd and a bokeler bar he by his syde.

His mouth as greet was as a greet fourneys.
He was a jangler and a goliardeys,   560
And that was moost of synne and harlotries.
Wel koude he stelen corn and tollen thries;
And yet he hadde a thombe of gold, pardee.
A whit cote and a blew hood wered hee.
A baggepipe wel koude he blowe and sowne,
And therwithal he broghte us out of towne.

A gentil MAUNCIPLE was ther of a temple,
Of which achatours myghte take exemple
For to be wys in byynge of vitaille;

531. **swynkere,** worker.   534. **thogh . . . smerte,** though things pleased him or pained him.   536. **dyke,** dig ditches.   541. **tabard,** laborer's loose coat.   542. **Reve,** an administrative officer of a country estate.   543. **Somnour,** (summoner) a process-server for an ecclesiastical court. **Pardoner,** seller of papal indulgences (remission of temporal or purgatorial punishments).   544. **Maunciple,** purchasing agent for a college or similar organization.   545. **carl for the nones,** fellow, exceptionally.   549. **knarre,** knotted, thickset churl.   550. **nolde . . . harre,** would not heave off its hinges.   551. **rennyng,** running.   554. **cop,** top.   555. **werte,** wart. **herys,** hairs.   556. **erys,** ears.   557. **nosethirles,** nostrils.   560. **jangler,** babbler. **goliardeys,** coarse jester.   562. **stelen corn and tollen thries,** steal corn and take triple toll for grinding.   563. **he . . . gold,** proverbial: "He was honest for a miller."   564. **wered,** wore.   565. **sowne,** play upon.   567. **of a temple,** law school, perhaps the Inner or Middle Temple.   568. **achatours,** buyers.

---

486. **looth were hym to cursen,** he was loath to excommunicate.   487. **yeven,** give.   492. **lafte,** neglected.   494. **muche and lite,** great and small.   496. **yaf,** gave.   498–500. **gospel . . . do?** See Matthew 5:19.   502. **lewed,** ignorant.   506. **clennesse,** purity.   508. **leet,** left.   510. **chauntrye for soules,** endowment for singing masses for the dead.   511. **bretherhede,** guild. **withholde,** engaged as chaplain.   516. **despitous,** spiteful.   517. **daungerous ne digne,** disdainful nor scornful.   523. **snybben,** rebuke.   525. **wayted after,** demanded.   526. **spiced,** overscrupulous.   530. **ylad . . . fother,** drawn very many loads of manure.

For wheither that he payde or took by taille,   570
Algate he wayted so in his achaat,
That he was ay biform and in good staat.
Now is nat that of God a ful fair grace
That swich a lewed mannes wit shal pace
The wisdom of an heep of lerned men?
Of maistres hadde he mo than thries ten,
That weren of lawe expert and curious,
Of whiche ther were a dozeyne in that hous
Worthy to been stywardes of rente and lond
Of any lord that is in Engelond,   580
To make hym lyve by his propre good,
In honour dettles, but if he were wood,
Or lyve as scarsly as hym list desire;
And able for to helpen al a shire
In any caas that myghte falle or happe;
And yet this Maunciple sette hir aller cappe.

    The Reve was a sclendre, colerik man.
His berd was shave as neigh as ever he kan;
His heer was by his erys ful round yshorn;
His top was dokked lyk a preest byforn.   590
Ful longe were his legges and ful lene,
Ylik a staf ther was no calf ysene.

    Wel koude he kepe a gerner and a bynne;
Ther was noon auditour koude on hym wynne.
Wel wiste he by the droghte and by the reyn
The yeldynge of his seed and of his greyn.
His lordes sheep, his neet, his dayerye
His swyn, his hors, his stoor, and his pultrye,
Was hoolly in this Reves governynge,
And by his covenant yaf the rekenynge,   600
Syn that his lord was twenty yeer of age.
Ther koude no man brynge hym in arrerage.
Ther nas baillif, ne hierde, ne oother hyne,
That he ne knew his sleighte and his covyne:
They were adrad of hym as of the deeth.

    His wonyng was ful faire upon an heeth,
With grene trees shadwed was his place.
He koude bettre than his lord purchace.
Ful riche he was astored pryvely,
His lord wel koude he plesen subtilly,   610
To yeve and lene hym of his owene good,
And have a thank, and yet a coote and hood.

    In youthe he hadde lerned a good myster:
He was a wel good wrighte, a carpenter.

    This Reve sat up-on a ful good stot,
That was al pomely grey and highte Scot.
A long surcote of pers up-on he hade,
And by his syde he baar a rusty blade.
Of Northfolk was this Reve of which I telle,
Biside a toun men clepen Baldeswelle.   620
Tukked he was as is a frere aboute,
And evere he rood the hyndreste of oure route.

    A Somnour was ther with us in that place,
That hadde a fyr-reed cherubynnes face,
For saucefleem he was, with eyen narwe.
As hoot he was and lecherous as a sparwe;
With scaled browes blake, and piled berd;
Of his visage children were aferd.
Ther nas quyk silver, lytarge, ne brymstoon,
Boras, ceruce, ne oille of tartre noon,   630
Ne oynement that wolde clense and byte,
That hym myghte helpen of his whelkes white,
Nor of the knobbes sittynge on his chekes.
    Wel loved he garlek, oynons, and eek lekes,
And for to drynke strong wyn, reed as blood.
Thanne wolde he speke and crye as he were wood;
And whan that he wel dronken hadde the wyn,
Thanne wolde he speke no word but Latyn.
A fewe termes hadde he, two or thre,
That he had lerned out of som decre—   640
No wonder is: he herde it al the day—
And eek ye knowen wel how that a jay
Kan clepen "Watte" as wel as kan the pope.
But who so koude in oother thyng hym grope,
Thanne hadde he spent al his philosophie;
Ay "*Questio quid juris*" wolde he crie.

    He was a gentil harlot and a kynde;
A bettre felawe sholde men noght fynde.
He wolde suffre for a quart of wyn
A good felawe to have his concubyn   650
A twelf monthe, and excuse hym atte fulle.
Ful pryvely a fynch eek koude he pulle.
And if he foond owher a good felawe,
He wolde techen hym to have noon awe,
In swich caas, of the ercedekenes curs,
But if a mannes soule were in his purs;
For in his purs he sholde ypunysshed be.
"Purs is the ercedekenes helle," seyde he.

---

570. **by taille**, on credit.   571. **Algate . . . achaat**, in every way he watched so in his buying.   577. **curious**, skillful.   579. **stywardes**, stewards.   582. **wood**, mad.   583. **scarsly as hym list**, economically as it pleases him to.   586. **sette . . . cappe**, made fools of all of them.   593. **gerner**, granary.   597. **neet**, cattle.   598. **stoor**, stock.   601. **Syn**, since.   602. **brynge hym in arrerage**, catch him arrears.   603. **baillif**, bailiff, overseer subordinate to the Reeve. **hierde**, herdsman. **hyne**, farm laborer.   604. **sleighte**, trickery. **covyne**, deceitfulness.   606. **wonyng**, dwelling.   611. **lene**, lend.   613. **myster**, craft.   615. **stot**, stallion.   616. **pomely**, dappled. **highte**, was called.   624. **fyr . . . face**, fire-red face of a cherub.   625. **saucefleem**, afflicted with a disease not unlike leprosy.   627. **scaled**, scabby. **piled berd**, thin beard.   629–30. **quyk silver . . . tartre**, the regular remedies for the Summoner's disease.   632. **whelkes**, pimples.   636. **wood**, mad.   643. **clepen "Watte,"** call "Wat," short for Walter; jays were trained to say "Watte" as parrots are to say "Polly."   644. **grope**, test.   646. "**Questio . . . juris.**" "The question is what part of the law is involved."   647. **harlot**, rascal.   652. **fynch . . . pulle**, practice seduction.   653. **owher**, anywhere.   655. **ercedekenes**, archdeacon's.

But wel I woot he lyed right in dede;
Of cursyng oghte ech gilty man hym drede, 660
For curs wol slee right as assoillyng savith,
And also war hym of a *Significavit!*
   In daunger hadde he at his owene gyse
The yonge gerles of the diocise,
And knew hir counseil, and was al hir reed
   A gerland hadde he set up-on his heed
As greet as it were for an ale stake;
A bokeler hadde he maad hym of a cake.

   With hym ther rood a gentil PARDONER
Of Rouncival, his freend and his comper, 670
That streight was comen fro the court of Rome.
Ful loude he soong, "Com hider, love, to me!"
This Somnour bar to hym a stif burdoun,
Was nevere trompe of half so greet a soun.
   This Pardoner hadde heer as yelow as wex,
But smothe it heeng as dooth a strike of flex;
By ounces henge his lokkes that he hadde,
And ther-with he his shuldres overspradde;
But thynne it lay, by colpons oon and oon;
But hood, for jolitee, wered he noon, 680
For it was trussed up in his walet.
Hym thoughte he rood al of the newe jet;
Dischevelee, save his cappe, he rood al bare.
Swiche glarynge eyen hadde he as an hare.
   A vernycle hadde he sowed up-on his cappe.
His walet biforn hym in his lappe,
Bret-ful of pardoun, comen from Rome al hoot.
   A voys he hadde as smal as hath a goot.
No berd hadde he, ne nevere sholde have,
As smothe it was as it were late yshave: 690
I trowe he were a geldyng or a mare.
   But of his craft, fro Berwyk into Ware,
Ne was ther swich another pardoner.
For in his male he hadde a pilwe beer,
Which that he seyde was Oure Lady veyl;
He seyde he hadde a gobet of the seyl
That Seint Peter hadde, whan that he wente
Up-on the see, til Jesu Crist hym hente.

He hadde a croys of latoun ful of stones,
And in a glas he hadde pigges bones. 700
But with thise relikes, whan that he fond
A poure persoun dwellyng up-on lond,
Up-on a day he gat hym moore moneye
Than that the persoun gat in monthes tweye.
And thus, with feyned flaterye and japes,
He made the persoun and the peple his apes.
   But trewely to tellen, atte laste,
He was in chirche a noble ecclesiaste.
Wel koude he rede a lessoun or a storie,
But alderbest he song an offertorie; 710
For wel he wiste, whan that song was songe,
He moste preche and wel affile his tonge
To wynne silver, as he ful wel koude;
Ther-fore he song the murierly and loude.

   Now have I told yow soothly, in a clause,
Th' estaat, th' array, the nombre, and eek the cause
Why that assembled was this compaignye
In Southwerk, at this gentil hostelrye
That highte the Tabard, faste by the Belle.
But now is tyme to yow for to telle 720
How that we baren us that ilke nyght,
Whan we were in that hostelrie alyght;
And after wol I telle of oure viage,
And al the remenant of oure pilgrymage.
   But first I pray yow, of youre curteisye,
That ye n'arette it nat my vileynye,
Thogh that I pleynly speke in this matere,
To telle yow hir wordes and hir cheere,
Ne thogh I speke hir wordes proprely.
For this ye knowen also wel as I, 730
Who-so shal telle a tale after a man,
He moot reherce as neigh as evere he kan
Everich a word, if it be in his charge,
Al speke he nevere so rudeliche and large,
Or ellis he moot telle his tale untrewe,
Or feyne thyng, or fynde wordes newe.
He may nat spare, al-thogh he were his brother,
He moot as wel seye o word as another.
Crist spak hym-self ful brode in holy writ,
And wel ye woot, no vileynye is it. 740
Eek Plato seith, who-so kan hym rede,
The wordes mote be cosyn to the dede.

660. drede, dread. **661. slee**, slay. **assoillyng savith**, absolution saves. **662. war . . . Significavit!** Let him beware of a writ of arrest, so called from its first word. **663. daunger**, control. **gyse**, way. **664. yonge gerles**, young of both sexes. **665. reed**, adviser. **666. gerland**, wreath. **667. ale stake**, sign of an alehouse. **670. comper**, comrade. **672. hider**, hither. **673. bar . . . burdoun**, accompanied him with a strong bass. **674. trompe**, trumpet. **soun**, sound. **675. wex**, wax. **676. strike . . . flex**, bunch of flax. **677. ounces**, thin strands. **679. colpons**, shreds. **682. Hym thoughte**, it seemed to him. **jet**, fashion. **683. Dischevelee**, with hair hanging loosely. **684. eyen**, eyes. **685. vernycle**, reproduction of St. Veronica's handkerchief bearing the likeness of Christ's face. **687. Bret-ful of pardoun**, brimful of pardons. **694. male**, bag. **pilwe beer**, pillowcase. **695. Oure Lady veyl**, The Virgin's veil. **696. gobet**, piece. **698. hente**, caught.

699. croys of latoun, cross of latten, a mixed metal much like brass. **702. up-on lond**, in the country. **705. japes**, tricks. **706. made . . . his apes**, made fools of the parson and the people. **710. alderbest**, best of all. **711. wiste**, knew. **712. affile**, smooth. **719. faste by**, close to. **722. alyght**, alighted. **723. viage**, journey. **726. n'arette . . . vileynye**, blame it not on my lack of good breeding. **727. pleynly**, plainly. **728. hir cheere**, their behavior. **729. proprely**, exactly as they spoke. **733. Everich a**, every single. **734. Al**, although. **rudeliche and large**, rudely and broadly. **736. feyne thyng**, make something up. **739. brode**, plainly. **742. cosyn**, cousin.

Also I pray yow to foryeve it me,
Al have I nat set folk in hir degree
Here in this tale, as that they sholde stonde:
My wit is short, ye may wel understonde.

    Greet cheere made oure Hoost us everichon,
And to the soper sette he us anon.
He served us with vitaille at the beste;
Strong was the wyn, and wel to drynke us leste.   750

    A semely man oure Hoost was with-alle
For to been a marchal in an halle.
A large man he was with eyen stepe,
A fairer burgeys was ther noon in Chepe,
Boold of his speche, and wys, and wel ytaught,
And of manhode hym lakked right naught.

    Eke ther-to he was right a murye man,
And after soper pleyen he bigan,
And spak of myrthe amonges othere thynges,
Whan that we hadde maad oure rekenynges,   760
And seyde thus, "Now, lordynges, trewely,
Ye been to me right welcome, hertely;
For by my trouthe, if that I shal not lye,
I saugh nat this yeer so murye a compaignye
At ones in this herberwe as is now.
Fayn wolde I doon yow myrthe, wiste I how.
And of a myrthe I am right now bythoght,
To doon yow ese, and it shal coste noght.

    "Ye goon to Caunterbury—God yow spede,
The blisful martir quyte yow youre mede!   770
And wel I woot, as ye goon by the weye,
Ye shapen yow to talen and to pleye;
For trewely, confort ne myrthe is noon
To ryde by the weye domb as a stoon;
And ther-fore wol I maken yow disport,
As I seyde erst, and doon yow som confort.
And if yow liketh alle, by oon assent,
For to stonden at my juggement,
And for to werken as I shal yow seye,
Tomorwe, whan ye riden by the weye,   780
Now, by my fader soule that is deed,
But ye be murye, I wol yeve yow myn heed!
Hoold up youre hondes, with-outen moore speche."

    Oure conseil was nat longe for to seche;
Us thoughte it was nat worth to make it wys,
And graunted hym with-outen moore avys,
And bad hym seye his voirdit as hym leste.

    "Lordynges," quod he, "now herkneth for the beste;
But taketh it not, I pray yow, in desdeyn;
This is the poynt, to speken short and pleyn,   790
That ech of yow, to shorte with oure weye,
In this viage shal telle tales tweye
To Caunteruryward, I mene it so,
And homward he shal tellen othere two,
Of aventures that whilom have bifalle.
And which of yow that bereth hym best of alle,
That is to seyn, that telleth in this caas
Tales of best sentence and moost solaas,
Shal have a soper at oure aller cost
Here in this place, sittyng by this post,   800
Whan that we come agayn fro Caunterbury.
And for to make yow the moore mury,
I wol my-self goodly with yow ryde,
Right at myn owene cost, and be your gyde.
And who-so wole my juggement withseye
Shal paye al that we spende by the weye.
And if ye vouche sauf that it be so,
Tel me anoon, with-outen wordes mo,
And I wol erly shape me ther-fore."

    This thyng was graunted, and oure othes swore   810
With ful glad herte, and preyden hym also
That he wolde vouche sauf for to do so,
And that he wolde been oure governour,
And of oure tales juge and reportour,
And sette a soper at a certeyn prys,
And we wol reuled been at his devys
In heigh and lough; and thus by oon assent
We been acorded to his juggement.
And ther-upon the wyn was fet anoon;
We dronken, and to reste wente echon,   820
With-outen any lenger taryynge.

    Amorwe, whan that day bigan to sprynge,
Up roos oure Hoost, and was oure aller cok,
And gadred us togidre in a flok,
And forth we riden, a litel moore than pas,
Unto the wateryng of Seint Thomas;
And there oure Hoost bigan his hors areste,
And seyde, "Lordynges, herkneth, if yow leste:

744. Al have . . . degree, although I have not arranged the tales in the order of the tellers' social ranks. **747. Hoost,** Harry Bailly, the innkeeper. **everichon,** every one. **748. anon,** at once. **750. us leste,** it pleased us. **753. eyen stepe,** protruding, or sparkling, eyes. **754. Chepe,** Cheapside, the business district of London. **762. hertely,** heartily. **764. saugh,** saw. **765. herberwe,** lodging. **770. quyte . . . mede,** repay you your reward. **771. goon,** go. **772. shapen yow to talen,** intend to tell tales. **776. erst,** before. **777. yow . . . alle,** it pleases you all. **778. stonden . . . juggement,** submit to my judgment. **781. by . . . deed,** by the soul of my dead father. **783. Hoold . . . hondes,** vote by show of your hands. **784. seche,** seek. **785. Us . . . wys.** It seemed to us not worth making any difficulty about.

786. graunted hym, we granted his wish. **avys,** deliberation. **787. voirdit,** decision. **788. quod,** said. **791. to shorte . . . weye,** to shorten our way with. **795. whilom,** formerly. **798. sentence,** instruction. **solaas,** entertainment. **799. oure aller cost,** the cost of us all. **805. withseye,** oppose. **807. vouche sauf,** grant. **810. swore,** were sworn. **811. preyden,** we asked. **816. devys,** direction. **817. In . . . lough,** in all respects. **819. fet,** fetched. **823. roos . . . cok,** our Host awakened us all, as by a rooster's crowing. **825. litel moore . . . pas,** a little more than a footpace.

Ye woot youre forward, and I it yow recorde.
If evensong and morwesong acorde, 830
Lat se now who shal telle the firste tale.
As evere moot I drynke wyn or ale,
Who so be rebel to my juggement
Shal paye for al that by the wey is spent.
Now draweth cut, er that we ferrer twynne;
He which that hath the shorteste shal bigynne.
Sire Knyght," quod he, "my mayster and my lord,
Now draweth cut, for that is myn acord.
Cometh neer," quod he, "my lady Prioresse,
And ye, sire Clerk, lat be youre shamefastnesse, 840
Ne studieth noght; ley hond to, every man!"

Anoon to drawen every wight bigan,
And shortly for to tellen as it was,
Were it by aventure, or sort, or cas,
The sothe is this, the cut fil to the Knyght,
Of which ful blithe and glad was every wight,
And telle he moste his tale, as was resoun,
By forward and by composicioun,
As ye han herd; what nedeth wordes mo?

And whan this goode man saugh that it was so,
As he that wys was and obedient 851
To kepe his forward by his free assent,
He seyde, "Syn I shal bigynne the game,
What, welcome be the cut, a Goddes name!
Now lat us ryde, and herkneth what I seye."
And with that word we ryden forth oure weye,
And he bigan with right a murye cheere
His tale anoon, and seyde as ye may heere.

["The Knight's Tale," freely adapted from Boccaccio's "Teseide," is an elaborate romance of courtly love set in ancient Athens. Palamon and Arcite suffer and fight for the love of Emelye. Arcite wins the fight but loses his life; Palamon wins the lady.]

THE MILLER'S PROLOGUE

Whan that the Knyght had thus his tale ytold,
In al the compaignye nas ther yong ne old
That he ne seyde it was a noble storie,
And worthy for to drawen to memorie;
And namely the gentils everichon.

Oure Hoost lough and swoor, "So moot I gon,
This gooth aright: unbokeled is the male.
Lat se now who shal telle another tale;
For trewely the game is wel bigonne.
Now telleth ye, sire Monk, if that ye konne 10
Somwhat to quyte with the Knyghtes tale."
The Miller that for dronken was al pale,
So that unnethe upon his hors he sat,
He nolde avalen neither hood ne hat,
Ne abyden no man for his curteisye,
But in Pilates voys he gan to crye,
And swoor, "By armes, and by blood and bones,
I kan a noble tale for the nones,
With which I wol now quyte the Knyghtes tale."
Oure Hoost saugh that he was dronke of ale, 20
And seyde, "Abyde, Robyn, leeve brother,
Som bettre man shal telle us first another.
Abyde, and lat us werken thriftily."
"By Goddes soule," quod he, "that wol nat I;
For I wol speke, or elles go my wey."
Oure Hoost answerde, "Tel on, a devel wey!
Thow art a fool, thy wit is overcome."

"Now herkneth," quod the Millere, "alle and some!
But first I make a protestacioun:
That I am dronke, I knowe it by my soun; 30
And therfore, if that I mysspeke or seye,
Wite it the ale of Southwerk, I yow preye,
For I wol telle a legende and a lyf
Both of a carpenter and of his wyf,
How that a clerk hath set the wrightes cappe."

The Reve answerde and seyde, "Stynt thy clappe!
Lat be thy lewed dronken harlotrye.
It is a synne and eek a greet folye
To apeyren any man, or hym defame,
And eek to bryngen wyves in swich fame. 40
Thow mayst ynow of othere thynges seyn."

This dronken Millere spak ful sone ageyn,
And seyde, "Leve brother Osewold,
Who hath no wyf, he is no cokewold,
But I seye nat therfore that thow art oon;
Ther been ful goode wyves many oon,
And evere a thousand goode ayeyns oon badde;

829. **forward**, agreement. **recorde**, recall. 830. **acorde**, agree ("if you feel this morning as you felt last night"). 832. **As . . . moot**, as surely as I hope to. 835. **draweth cut**, draw lots. **ferrer twynne**, set out farther. 838. **acord**, agreement. 840. **shamefastnesse**, shyness. 841. **studieth**, meditate. 844. **aventure, or sort, or cas**, chance. 845. **sothe**, truth. **fil**, fell. 848. **composicioun**, agreement. 854. **a . . . name**, in God's name. 5. **namely the gentils**, especially the gentlefolk. 6. **So . . . gon**, a mild oath: "As surely as I hope to continue to be able to walk." 7. **unbokeled . . . male**, unbuckled is the bag, that is, now things are starting.

11. **quyte with**, requite. 12. **for dronken**, because of being drunk. 13. **unnethe**, with difficulty. 14. **nolde avalen**, would not take off (in sign of politeness). 15. **abyden**, wait for. **for his**, out of. 16. **Pilates voys**, a bellow like that of Pilate in the mystery plays. 17. "**By . . . bones**, strong oaths by parts of Christ's body. 18. **kan**, know. 21. **leeve**, dear. 23. **thriftily**, properly. 26. **Tel . . . a devel wey!** Tell away in the devil's name! 28. **alle and some!** one and all. 30. **by my soun**, by the sound of my voice. 31. **seye**, missay. 32. **Wite it**, blame it on. 33. **legende**, story. 35. **set . . . cappe**, made a fool of the carpenter. 36. **Reve**, who was a carpenter by trade. "**Stynt . . . clappe!** Stop your chattering! 37. **lewed**, ignorant. **harlotrye**, ribaldry. 39. **apeyren**, injure. 41. **ynow**, enough. **seyn**, say. 44. **cokewold**, cuckold. 47. **ayeyns**, against.

That knowestow wel thyself but if thow madde.
Why artow angry with my tale now?
I have a wyf, pardee, as wel as thow,   50
Yet nolde I, for the oxen in my plough,
Take upon me moore than ynough,
As demen of my-self that I were oon;
I wol bileve wel that I am noon.
An housbonde shal noght been inquisityf
Of Goddes pryvetee, nor of his wyf.
So he may fynde Goddes foyson there,
Of the remenant nedeth noght enquere."

   What sholde I moore seyn, but this Millere
He nolde his wordes for no man forbere,   60
But tolde his cherles tale in his manere.
M'athynketh that I shal reherce it here.
And therfore every gentil wight I preye,
Demeth noght, for Goddes love, that I seye
Of yvel entente, but for I moot reherce
Hir tales alle, be they bet or werse,
Or elles falsen som of my matere.
And therfore, whoso list it noght yhere,
Turne over the leef, and chese another tale;
For he shal fynde ynowe, grete and smale,   70
Of storial thyng that toucheth gentillesse,
And eek moralitee and holynesse;
Blameth noght me if that ye chese amys.
The Millere is a cherl, ye knowe wel this;
So was the Reve eek, and othere mo,
And harlotrye they tolden bothe two.
Avyseth yow and put me out of blame;
And eek men shal noght make ernest of game.

["The Miller's Tale" is a fabliau, a broadly humorous satirical story. An ingenious young clerk, to cloak his intrigue with an old carpenter's young wife, persuades the husband that the world is about to be destroyed by flood, but becomes himself the butt of the joke in the end.]

THE REEVE'S PROLOGUE

   Whan folk had laughen at this nyce cas
Of Absolon and hende Nicholas,
Diverse folk diversely they seyde,
But for the moore part they loughe and pleyde,
Ne at this tale I saugh no man hym greve,
But it were oonly Osewold the Reve;
Bycause he was of carpenteres craft,
A litel ire is in his herte ylaft;
He gan to grucche and blamed it a lite.
"So the ik," quod he, "ful wel koude I thee quyte   10
With bleryng of a proud milleres eye,
If that me liste speke of rybaudye.
But ik am oold, me list not pleye for age;
Gras tyme is doon, my fodder is now forage;
This white top writeth myne olde yerys;
Myn herte is also mowled as myne herys,
But if I fare as dooth an openers:
That ilke fruyt is ever lenger the wers,
Til it be roten in mullok or in stree.
We olde men, I drede, so fare we;   20
Til we be roten, kan we noght be rype;
We hoppen alwey whil that the world wol pipe.
For in oure wyl ther stiketh evere a nayl,
To have an hoor heed and a grene tayl,
As hath a leek; for thogh oure myght be goon,
Oure wil desireth folie evere in oon.
For whan we may noght doon, than wol we speke;
Yet in oure asshen olde is fyr yreke.

   "Foure gleedes have we, whiche I shal devyse:
Avauntyng, lyyng, anger, coveitise;   30
Thise foure sparkles longen unto eelde.
Oure olde lymes mowe wel been unweelde,
But wil ne shal noght faillen, that is sooth.
And yet ik have alwey a coltes tooth,
As many a yeer as it is passed henne
Syn that my tappe of lyf bigan to renne.
For sikerlik, whan I was bore, anon
Deeth drough the tappe of lyf and leet it goon;
And evere sith hath so the tappe yronne,
Til that almoost al empty is the tonne.   40
The streem of lyf now droppeth on the chymbe.
The sely tonge may wel rynge and chymbe
Of wrecchednesse that passed is ful yoore;
With olde folk, save dotage, is namoore."

---

48. **madde**, art crazy.   50. **pardee**, certainly.   53. **demen**, judge.   56. **pryvetee**, secret counsel.   57. **foyson**, plenty.   58. **enquere**, inquire.   61. **cherles**, churl's.   62. **M'athynketh**, it grieves me. **reherce**, repeat.   68. **list . . . yhere**, wishes not to hear it.   69. **chese**, choose.   71. **gentillesse**, good breeding.   73. **amys**, amiss.   77. **Avyseth yow**, deliberate.   78. **make . . . game**, take a jest seriously.   1. **nyce cas**, foolish mischance.   2. **Absolon . . . Nicholas**. Absolom and "gentle" Nicholas are characters in "The Miller's Tale."   4. **loughe and pleyde**, laughed and were amused.

8. **ylaft**, left.   9. **grucche**, grumble. **lite**, little.   10. **"So the ik,"** so prosper I, as I hope to prosper.   11. **bleryng . . . eye**, deluding.   12. **rybaudye**, ribaldry.   13. **me list . . . age**, on account of age, it pleases me not to jest.   14. **Gras tyme**, grass time, youth. **forage**, winter food, age.   15. **yerys**, years.   16. **herte**, heart. **mowled**, moldy. **herys**, hairs.   17. **openers**, medlar, edible only when partly decayed.   18. **is ever . . . wers**, the longer it is kept, the worse it is.   19. **roten . . . stree**, rotten in refuse or in straw.   20. **drede**, fear.   26. **evere in oon**, ever the same.   28. **asshen**, ashes. **yreke**, covered.   29. **gleedes**, live coals. **devyse**, enumerate.   30. **Avauntyng**, boasting. **coveitise**, greed.   31. **longen . . . eelde**, belong to age.   32. **lymes mowe**, limbs may. **unweelde**, unwieldy.   34. **coltes tooth**, colt's tooth, youthful appetite.   35. **henne**, hence.   36. **renne**, run.   37. **sikerlik**, certainly. **bore**, born.   39. **sith**, since.   40. **tonne**, cask.   41. **chymbe**, rim of a cask.   42. **sely**, poor. **chymbe**, chime.   43 **ful yoore**, long ago.

Whan that oure Hoost had herd this sermonyng,
He gan to speke as lordly as a kyng;
He seyde, "What amounteth al this wit?
What shal we speke al day of holy writ?
The devel made a reve for to preche,
Or of a soutere a shipman or a leche. 50
Sey forth thy tale, and tarie noght the tyme.
Lo Depeford! and it is half wey pryme.
Lo Grenewych! ther many a shrewe is inne;
It were al tyme thy tale to bigynne."

"Now, sires," quod this Osewold the Reve,
"I pray yow alle that ye noght yow greve,
Thogh I answere and somdel sette his howve;
For leveful is with force force of-showve.
This dronken Millere hath ytold us heer,
How that bigiled was a carpenter, 60
Paraventure in scorn, for I am oon.
And, by youre leve, I shal hym quyte anoon;
Right in his cherles termes wol I speke.
I pray to God his nekke mote to-breke!
He kan wel in myn eye seen a stalke,
But in his owene he kan noght seen a balke."

[In "The Reeve's Tale," also a fabliau, a miller cheats two young clerks. They not only recover their loss but, thanks to a series of chances, avenge themselves to their complete satisfaction.]

THE COOK'S PROLOGUE

The Cook of Londoun, whil the Reve spak,
For joye, hym thoughte, he clawed hym on the bak.
"Ha! ha!" quod he, "for Cristes passioun,
This millere hadde a sharp conclusioun
Upon his argument of herbergage!
Wel seyde Salomon in his langage,
'Ne bryng nat every man into thyn hous':
For herberwyng by nyghte is perilous.
Wel oghte a man avysed for to be
Whom that he broghte into his pryvetee. 10
I pray to God, so yeve me sorwe and care,
If ever, sith I highte Hogge of Ware,
Herde I a millere bettre yset a werk.
He hadde a jape of malice in the derk.
But God forbede that we stynten heere;
And therfore, if ye vouche sauf to heere
A tale of me, that am a poure man,
I wol yow telle as wel as evere I kan
A litel jape that fil in oure citee."

Oure Hoost answerde and seyde, "I graunte it thee. 20
Now tel on, Roger, look that it be good;
For many a pastee hastow laten blood,
And many a Jakke of Dover hastow soold
That hath been twies hoot and twies coold.
Of many a pilgrym hastow Cristes curs,
For of thy persely yet they fare the wors,
That they han eten with thy stubbul goos,
For in thy shoppe is many a flye loos.
Now telle on, gentil Roger by thy name,
But yet I praye thee, be nat wrooth for game: 30
A man may seye ful sooth in game and pley."

"Thow seist ful sooth," quod Roger, "by my fey!
But 'sooth pley, quade pley,' as the Flemyng seith.
And ther-fore, Herry Bailly, by thy feith,
Be thou nat wrooth, er we departen heer,
Thogh that my tale be of an hostileer.
But nathelees I wol nat telle it yit,
But er we parte, ywis, thow shalt be quyt."
And therwithal he lough and made cheere,
And seyde his tale, as ye shal after heere. 40

[Chaucer wrote only a few lines of "The Cook's Tale," enough to indicate that it was to be a fabliau resembling the two just told, but not enough to give an idea of the plot.]

THE MAN OF LAW'S PROLOGUE

Oure Hoost saugh wel that the brighte sonne
The ark of his artificial day hath ronne
The ferthe part, and half an houre and moore,
And thogh he were nat depe ystert in loore,
He wiste it was the xviij^the day
Of Aprill, that is messager to May;
And saw wel that the shadwe of every tree
Was as in lengthe the same quantitee
That was the body erect that caused it.
And therfore by the shadwe he took his wit 10
That Phebus, which that shoon so clere and brighte,
Degrees was fyve and fourty clombe on highte;
And for that day, as in that latitude,

---

47. **"What,** to what. 48. **What,** why. 50. **soutere,** cobbler. **leche,** physician. 52. **half wey pryme,** 7:30 A.M. 53. **shrewe,** scoundrel. 57. **somdel,** somewhat. **sette . . . howve,** make a fool of him. 58. **leveful . . . of-showve.** It is lawful to repulse force with force. 61. **Paraventure,** peradventure. 64. **mote to-breke,** may break in two. 65–66. **stalke,** bit of straw (mote). **balke,** beam. See Matthew 7:3; Luke 6:41. 5. **herbergage,** harboring. The Miller had allowed the clerks to pass a night in his house. 12. **sith I highte,** since I have been called. **Hogge,** a nickname for Roger. 14. **jape of malice,** malicious trick.

22. **pastee . . . blood,** you have drained the gravy from many a meat pie. 23. **Jakke of Dover,** warmed-over food. **hastow,** hast thou. 26. **persely,** parsley. 27. **stubbul goos,** goose fattened on stubble. 28. **flye loos,** fly loose. 30. **wrooth for game,** angry at a jest. 32. **fey!** faith. 33. **'sooth . . . pley,'** a true jest is a bad jest. 34. **Herry Bailly.** There seems to be no question that the Host was an actual person. 36. **hostileer,** innkeeper. 38. **ywis,** assuredly. Group B. 2. **ark of his artificial day,** arc of the time between sunrise and sunset. 4. **depe . . . loore,** far advanced in learning. 11. **Phebus,** the sun (Apollo).

It was ten at the clokke, he gan conclude,
And sodeynly he plighte his hors aboute.
    "Lordynges," quod he, "I warne yow, al this route,
The ferthe party of this day is goon.
Now, for the love of God and of Seint John,
Leseth no tyme, as ferforth as ye may.
Lordynges, the tyme wasteth nyght and day,   20
And steleth from us, what pryvely slepynge,
And what thurgh necligence in oure wakynge,
As dooth the streem, that turneth nevere agayn,
Descendynge fro the montaigne into playn.
    "Wel kan Senec and many a philosophre
Biwaillen tyme moore than gold in cofre.
For 'los of catel may recovered be,
But los of tyme shendeth us,' quod he.
It wol nat come agayn, with-outen drede,
Namoore than wol Malkyns maydenhede,   30
Whan she hath lost it in hir wantownesse,
Lat us nat mowlen thus in ydelnesse.
Sire Man of Lawe," quod he, "so have ye blis,
Tel us a tale anon, as forward is;
Ye been submytted, thurgh youre free assent,
To stonden in this cas at my juggement.
Acquiteth yow nowe of youre biheste;
Thanne have ye doon youre devoir atte leste."
    "Hoost," quod he, "*depardieux*, ich assente;
To breke forward is nat myn entente.   40
Biheste is dette, and I wol holde fayn
Al my biheste, I kan no bettre sayn.
For swich lawe as a man yeveth another wight,
He sholde hym-self usen it by right;
Thus wol oure text. But nathelees, certeyn,
I kan right now no thrifty tale seyn,
That Chaucer, thogh he kan but lewedly
On metres and on rymyng craftily,
Hath seyd hem in swich Englissh as he kan
Of olde tyme, as knoweth many a man.   50
And if he have nat seyd hem, leeve brother,
In o book, he hath seyd hem in another.
For he hath told of lovers up and doun
Mo than Ovide made of mencioun
In his Epistles, that been ful olde,
What sholde I tellen hem, syn they been tolde?
    "In youthe he made of Ceys and Alcione,

And sithen hath he spoke of everychone,
Thise noble wyves and thise loveres eke.
Who-so that wol his large volume seke,   60
Cleped the Seintes Legende of Cupide,
Ther may he seen the large woundes wyde
Of Lucresse, and of Babilan Tesbee;
The swerd of Dido for the false Enee;
The tree of Phillis for hir Demophon;
The pleinte of Dianire and of Hermyon,
Of Adriane, and of Isiphilee;
The bareyne ile stondynge in the see;
The dreynte Leandre for his Erro;
The teeris of Eleyne, and eke the wo   70
Of Brixseyde, and of the, Ladomya;
The crueltee of the, queene Medea,
The litel children hangyng by the hals,
For thy Jason, that was of love so fals!
O Ypermystra, Penolopee, Alceste,
Youre wifhode he comendeth with the beste!
    "But certeinly no word ne writeth he
Of thilke wikke ensample of Canacee,
That loved hir owene brother synfully;
Of swiche cursed stories I sey 'fy!'   80
Or ellis of Tyro Appollonius,
How that the cursed kyng Antiochus
Birafte his doghter of hir maydenhede,
That is so horrible a tale for to rede,
Whan he hir threw up-on the pavement.
And ther-fore he, of ful avysement,
Nolde nevere write in noon of his sermons
Of swiche unkynde abhominacions,
Ne I wol noon reherce, if that I may.
    "But of my tale how shal I doon this day?   90
Me were looth be likned, doutelees,
To Muses that men clepe Pierides—
Methamorphosios woot what I mene—
But nathelees, I recche noght a bene
Thogh I come after hym with hawe-bake.
I speke in prose and lat hym rymes make."
    And with that word he, with a sobre cheere,
Bigan his tale as ye shal after heere.

["The Man of Law's Tale" is a "moral romance" inculcating the virtue of constancy by the example of the

---

15. plighte, pulled. **17. party,** part. **19. Leseth,** lose. **ferforth,** far. **25. Senec,** Seneca. **28. shendeth,** injures. **32. mowlen,** mold. **37. Acquiteth . . . biheste.** Acquit yourself now of your promise. **38. devoir atte leste,** duty at the least. **39. depardieux, ich,** in God's name, I. **41. fayn,** gladly. **46. thrifty,** profitable. **seyn,** tell. **47. That.** The sense seems to require "But that." **kan . . . lewedly,** knows only in an unlearned fashion. **48. On . . . on,** about. **craftily,** skillfully. **52. o,** one. **54. Mo,** more. **Ovide made of mencioun.** Ovid made mention of. **56. What,** why. **syn,** since. **57. made,** wrote (in *The Book of the Duchess*).

58. sithen, since. **61. Cleped . . . Cupide,** called the Legend of Cupid's Saints (*The Legend of Good Women*). Chaucer, however, did not tell the stories of all these ladies. **68. bareyne ile,** barren isle. **69. dreynte,** drowned. **70. teeris,** tears. **73. hals,** neck. **78. wikke ensample,** wicked example, illustrative story. **86. avysement,** deliberation. **87. sermons,** writings. **88. unkynde,** unnatural. **91. Me . . . likned,** I should be loath to be likened. **93. Methamorphosios woot.** Ovid's *Metamorphoses* knows. **94. nathelees . . . bene,** nevertheless I care not a bean. **95. hawe-bake,** baked haws (plain food). **96. prose.** Without changing this line, Chaucer wrote "The Man of Law's Tale" in verse.

GEOFFREY CHAUCER

heroine, Constance. Brutally mistreated by two wicked mothers-in-law in turn, she miraculously survives every hardship, and has the satisfaction of knowing that her son will be the next Roman emperor. Chaucer's primary source is the Anglo-Norman Chronicle of Nicholas Trivet, probably with incidental use of the version told in the *Confessio Amantis* by his contemporary and acquaintance, John Gower, to whose telling, in the same work, of two incestuous stories the Man of Law seems to have referred in lines 77–89 above.]

THE MAN OF LAW'S EPILOGUE

Oure Hoost up-on his stiropes stood anoon,
And seyde, "Gode men, herkneth everichoon:
This was a thrifty tale for the nones!
Sire Parisshe Prest," quod he, "for Goddes bones,
Tel us a tale, as was thy forward yore.
I se wel that ye lerned men in lore
Kan muche good, by Goddes dignytee!"
   The Persoun hym answerde, "Benedicite!
What eyleth the man, so synfully to swere?"
   Our Hoost answerde, "O Jankyn, be ye there?   10
I smelle a Loller in the wynd," quod he.
"Now, gode men," quod our Hoost, "herkneth me:
Abydeth, for Goddes digne passioun,
For we shal han a predicacioun;
This Loller heer wil prechen us som-what."
   "Nay, by my fader soule, that shal he nat!"
Seyde the Somnour, "heer shal he nat preche,
He shal no gospel glosen heer ne teche.
We leve alle in the grete God," quod he,
"He wolde sowen som difficultee,   20
Or spryngen cokkel in oure clene corn;
And, therfor, Hoost, I warne thee biforn,
My joly body shal a tale telle,
And I shal clynken yow so mery a belle,
That I shal waken al this compaignye.
But it shal nat ben of philosophye,
Ne phislyas, ne termes queynte of lawe:
Ther is but litel Latyn in my mawe."

1. **stiropes,** stirrups.   3. **for the nones!** extremely.   8. **Benedicite!** Bless ye (the Lord).   9. **eyleth,** aileth.   10. **Jankyn,** "Johnnykin," rudely familiar diminutive of "Sir John," slang term for a priest.   11. **Loller,** Lollard, follower of John Wyclif.   13. **Goddes . . . passioun,** Christ's noble Passion.   14. **predicacioun,** sermon.   16. **fader,** father's.   17. **Somnour,** a decided crux. The best manuscripts do not contain the Epilogue at all, thus indicating that Chaucer had decided to cancel it; of those which do, a majority read "squire," a few "sommoner," and one, of little authority but followed by most editors, "shipman." This is one of the most glaring cases of the confusion brought about by Chaucer's gradual and unsystematic revision of his plan. 18. **glosen,** interpret.   19. **leve,** believe.   21. **spryngen cokkel,** sow weeds.   23. **My joly body,** my jolly self. 27. **phislyas,** meaning uncertain; possibly an error intentionally put in the ignorant speaker's mouth. **termes . . . lawe,** curious legal diction.   28. **mawe,** stomach.

from THE WIFE OF BATH'S PROLOGUE

"Experience, thogh noon auctoritee
Were in this world, is right ynogh for me
To speke of wo that is in mariage;
For, lordynges, sith I twelve yeer was of age,
Thonked be God that is eterne on lyve,
Housbondes at chirche dore I have had fyve—
If I so ofte myghte han wedded be—
And alle were worthy men in hir degree.
But me was told, certeyn, noght longe agon is,
That sith that Crist ne wente nevere but onys   10
To weddyng, in the Cane of Galilee,
That by the same ensample taughte he me,
That I ne sholde wedded be but ones.
Herke eek, lo, which a sharp word for the nones
Bisyde a welle, Jesus, God and man,
Spak in repreeve of the Samaritan:
'Thow hast yhad fyve housbondes,' quod he,
'And that ilke man that now hath thee
Is nat thyn housbonde,' thus he seyde, certeyn;
What that he mente ther-by, I kan nat seyn;   20
But that I axe, why that the fifthe man
Was noon housbonde to the Samaritan?
How manye myghte she have in mariage?
Yet herde I nevere tellen in myn age
Upon this nombre diffinicioun.
Men may dyvyne and glosen up and doun,
But wel I woot, expres, with-outen lye,
God bad us for to wexe and multiplye;
That gentil text kan I wel understonde.
Eek wel I woot, he seyde myn housbonde   30
Sholde lete fader and moder, and take to me.
But of no nombre mencioun made he,
Of bigamye or of octogamye;
Why sholde men thanne speke of it vileynye?
   "Lo, here the wise kyng, Daun Salomon:
I trowe he hadde wyves mo than oon. . . .

Welcome the sixte, whan that evere he shal.   45
For sith I wol nat kepe me chaast in al,
Whan myn housbonde is fro the world ygon,
Som Cristen man shal wedde me anon;
For thanne, th' apostle seith that I am free
To wedde, a Goddes half, wher it liketh me.   50

Group D. 1. **auctoritee,** authoritative book to be cited in proof.   5. **that . . . lyve,** who lives eternally.   9. **was told,** by one of the ecclesiastics among the pilgrims, no doubt. 11. **the Cane,** Cana.   14. **for the nones,** extremely.   18. **ilke,** very, same.   21. **axe,** ask.   26. **dyvyne and glosen,** guess and explain.   27. **expres,** expressly.   28. **wexe,** increase.   32. **nombre mencioun,** number mention.   33. **bigamye . . . octogamye,** being married twice or eight times, respectively, in succession.   34. **vileynye,** reproach. 35. **Daun,** Lord.   36. **trowe,** believe. **mo,** more.   45. **shal** shall appear.   50. **a Goddes half,** in God's name.

He seith that to be wedded is no synne;
Bet is to be wedded than to brynne.
What rekketh me, theigh folk seye vileynye
Of shrewed Lameth and his bigamye?
I woot wel Abraham was an holy man,
And Jacob eek, as fer as evere I kan,
And ech of hem hadde wyves mo than two,
And many another holy man also.
Where kan ye seye, in any maner age,
That heighe God defended mariage   60
By expres word? I pray yow, telleth me.
Or where comanded he virginitee?
I woot as wel as ye, it is no drede,
Th' apostle whan he speketh of maydenhede,
He seyde that precept ther-of hadde he noon.
Men may conseille a womman to be oon,
But conseillyng is no comandement.
He put it in oure owene juggement;
For hadde God comanded maydenhede,
Thanne hadde he dampned weddyng with the dede.
And certes, if ther were no seed ysowe,   71
Virginitee, thanne wher-of sholde it growe?
Poul dorste nat comanden, at the leeste,
A thyng of which his maister yaf noon heeste.
The dart is set up for virginitee:
Cacche who so may, who renneth best lat se!

"But this word is noght take of every wight,
But ther as God list yeve it of his myght.
I woot wel that th' apostle was a mayde,
But nathelees, thogh that he wroot and sayde   80
He wolde that every wight were swich as he,
Al nys but conseil to virginitee.
And for to been a wyf, he yaf me leve
Of indulgence; so is it no repreve
To wedde me, if that my make dye,
With-oute excepcioun of bigamye.
Al were it good no womman for to touche—
He mente as in his bed or in his couche—
For peril is bothe fyr and tow t'assemble;
Ye knowe what this ensample may resemble.   90
This al and som, he heeld virginitee
Moore parfit than weddyng in freletee.

Freletee clepe I, but if that he and she
Wolde leden al hir lyf in chastitee.
  "I graunte it wel, I have noon envye,
Thogh maydenhede preferre bigamye.
It liketh hem to be clene in body and goost;
Of myn estat ne wol I make no boost.
For wel ye knowe, a lord in his houshold,
Ne hath nat every vessel al of gold;   100
Somme been of tree, and doon hir lord servyse.
God clepeth folk to hym in sondry wyse,
And everich hath of God a propre yifte,
Som this, som that, as hym liketh shifte.

  "Virginitee is greet perfeccioun,
And continence eek with devocioun,
But Crist, that of perfeccioun is welle,
Bad nat every wight he sholde go selle
Al that he hadde, and yeve it to the poore,
And in swich wise folwe hym and his foore.   110
He spak to hem that wolde lyve parfitly;
And lordynges, by youre leve, that am nat I.
I wol bistowe the flour of al myn age
In th'actes and in fruyt of mariage. . . .

Crist was a mayde, and shapen as a man,
And many a seynt, sith that the world bigan,   140
Yet lyved they evere in parfit chastitee.
I nyl envye no virginitee.
Lat hem be breed of pured whete seed,
And lat us wyves hote barly breed;
And yet with barly breed, Mark telle kan,
Oure Lord Jesu refresshed many a man.
In swich estat as God hath cleped us
I wol persevere, I nam nat precius. . . .

An housbonde wol I have, I wol nat lette,   154
Which shal be bothe my dettour and my thral,
And have his tribulacioun with-al
Upon his flessh, while that I am his wyf.
I have the power duryng al my lyf
Upon his propre body, and nat he.
Right thus th' apostle tolde it unto me;   160
And bad oure housbondes for to love us wel.
Al this sentence me liketh every del—"
  Up stirte the Pardoner, and that anon;
"Now dame," quod he, "by God and by Seint
  John!

52. **Bet**, better. **brynne**, burn. See I Corinthians 7:9. 53. **theigh**, though. 54. **shrewed**, cursed. 56. **as . . . kan**, as far as ever I know. 59. **seye**, say. 60. **heighe**, high. **defended**, forbade. 63. **drede**, fear. 64. **Th' apostle**, St. Paul. **maydenhede**, maidenhood, virginity. 66. **to be oon**, to be (remain) a virgin. 70. **dampned**, condemned. **dede**, deed. 71. **ysowe**, sown. 73. **Poul**, St. Paul. 74. **yaf noon heeste**, gave no command. 75. **dart**, prize (for a race). 76. **Cacche**, catch. **renneth best lat se!** let us see who runs best! 77. **take . . . wight**, applied to every person. 79. **was a mayde**, was a virgin. 82. **Al nys but**, all is only. 84. **repreve**, reproach. 85. **make**, mate. 89. **fyr**, fire. 91. **This al and som**, this is the whole truth and every part of it. 92. **parfit**, perfect. **freletee**, frailty.

93. **clepe**, call. 96. **preferre**, be preferable to. 97. **It liketh hem**, it pleases them. **goost**, spirit. 101. **tree**, wood. 102. **in . . . wyse**, in various ways. 103. **propre yifte**, personal endowment. 104. **as . . . shifte**, as it pleases Him to assign it. 107. **welle**, the spring or source. 110. **foore**, path. See Matthew 19:21. 112. **leve**, leave. 140. **sith that**, since. 143. **breed of pured whete**, bread of very fine wheat. 144. **hote**, be called. 148. **precius**, fastidious. 154. **lette**, desist. 155. **dettour**, debtor. **thral**, slave. 162. **sentence**, instruction. **del**, bit. 163. **stirte**, started.

Ye been a noble prechour in this cas!
I was aboute to wedde a wyf; allas!
What sholde I bye it on my flessh so deere?
Yet hadde I levere wedde no wyf to-yeere!"

"Abyde!" quod she, "my tale is nat bigonne!
Nay, thow shalt drynken on another tonne,   170
Er that I go, shal savoure wors than ale.
And whan that I have toold forth my tale
Of tribulacioun in mariage,
Of which I am expert in al myn age,
This is to seye, my-self hath been the whippe—
Thanne maystow chese whether thow wolt sippe
Of thilke tonne that I shal abroche.
Be war of it, er thow to neigh approche;
For I shal telle ensamples mo than ten.
'Who so that nyl be war by othere men,   180
By hym shal othere men corrected be.'
Thise same wordes writeth Ptholome;
Rede in his Almageste, and take it there."

"Dame, I wolde praye yow, if youre wil were,"
Seyde this Pardoner, "as ye bigan,
Telle forth youre tale, spareth for no man,
And teche us yonge men of youre praktyke."

"Gladly," quod she, "sith it may yow lyke.
But that I praye to al this compaignye,
If that I speke after my fantasye,   190
As taketh nat agrief of that I seye;
For myn entente nys but for to pleye.

"Now, sire, thanne wol I telle yow forth my tale:
As evere moot I drynke wyn and ale,
I shal seye sooth, tho housbondes that I hadde,
As three of hem were goode and two were badde. . . .

But at the laste with muchel care and wo,   811
We fille acorded by us selven two.
He yaf me al the brydel in myn hond,
To han the governaunce of hous and lond,
And of his tonge and of his hond also,
And made hym brenne his book anon right tho.
And whan that I hadde geten unto me,
By maistrye, al the soveraynetee
And that he seyde, 'Myn owene trewe wyf,
Do as thee lust the terme of al thy lyf,   820
Keep thyn honour, and keep eek myn estaat'—

After that day we hadden nevere debaat.
God help me so, I was to hym as kynde
As any wyf from Denmark unto Inde,
And also trewe, and so was he to me.
I pray to God, that sit in magestee,
So blesse his soule for his mercy deere!
Now wol I seye my tale, if ye wol here."

The Frere logh, whan he hadde herd al this.
"Now, dame," quod he, "so haue I joye or blis,   830
This is a long preamble of a tale!"
And whan the Somnour herde the Frere gale,
"Lo!" quod the Somnour, "Goddes armes two!
A frere wol entremette hym evere mo.
Loo, goode men, a flye and eek a frere
Wol falle in every dyssh and matere.
What spekestow of preambulacioun?
What! amble, or trotte, or pees, or go sit doun!
Thow lettest oure disport in this manere."

"Ye, woltow so, sir Somnour?" quod the Frere,   840
"Now, by my feith, I shal, er that I go,
Telle of a Somnour swich a tale or two,
That al the folk shal laughen in this place."

"Now, elles, Frere, I wol bishrewe thy face,"
Quod this Somnour, "and I bishrewe me,
But if I telle tales two or three
Of freres, er I come to Sydyngborne,
That I shal make thyn herte for to morne,
For wel I woot thy pacience is gon."

Oure Hoost cride "Pees! and that anon!"   850
And seyde, "Lat the womman telle hir tale.
Ye fare as folk that dronken ben of ale.
Do, dame, tel forth youre tale, and that is best."

"Al redy, sire," quod she, "right as yow lest,
If I have licence of this worthy Frere."

"Yis, dame," quod he, "tel forth, and I wol here."

["The Wife of Bath's Tale," a romance of courtly love in the realm of King Arthur, is the "exemplum" of that racy "sermon" on the sovereignty of women, her Prologue. A young knight's loathsome and unwanted old wife is transformed into a beautiful maiden when he grants her the control of their life together.]

THE FRIAR'S PROLOGUE

This worthy lymytour, this noble Frere,
He made alwey a maner louryng cheere
Upon the Somnour, but for honestee
No vileyns word as yet to hym spak he.

165. **prechour . . . cas**, preacher on this topic. 167. **What**, why. **bye**, pay for. **deere**, dearly. 168. **to-yeere**, this year. 170. **on . . . tonne**, from another cask. 171. **savoure**, taste. 176. **chese**, choose. 177. **thilke**, the same. **abroche**, broach. 182. **Ptholome**, Ptolemy, author of the Ptolemaic system. 183. **Almageste**, Ptolemy's great treatise. 187. **praktyke**, practice. 191. **taketh nat agrief of**, take not amiss. 195. **tho**, those. 812. **us . . . two**, our two selves. She is speaking of her fifth husband. 813. **brydel**, bridle. 816. **made**, I made. **book**. This book had contained many stories not to the credit of women. 820. **thee lust**, it pleases you.

829. **logh**, laughed. 832. **gale**, cry out. 834. **entremette hym**, interfere. 839. **lettest**, hinder. 844. **bishrewe**, curse. 1. **lymytour**. See "The General Prologue," l. 209, page 175. 2. **maner . . . cheere**, rather frowning expression. 3. **honestee**, good manners. 4. **vileyns**, rude.

But atte laste he seyde unto the Wyf,
"Dame," quod he, "God yeve yow right good lyf!
Ye han heer touched, also mote I thee,
In scole matere greet difficultee.
Ye han seyd muche thyng right wel, I seye;
But, dame, here as we ryden by the weye,   10
Us nedeth nat to speken but of game,
And lete auctoritees, on Goddes name,
To prechyng and to scole of clergye.
But if it like to this compaignye,
I wol yow of a somnour telle a game.
Pardee, ye may wel knowe by the name,
That of a somnour may no good be sayd—
I praye that noon of yow be yvel apayd.
A somnour is a rennere up and doun
With mandementz for fornicacioun,   20
And is ybet at every tounes ende."

 Oure Hoost tho spak, "A! sire, ye sholde be hende
And curteys, as a man of youre estaat;
In compaignye we wol no debaat.
Telleth youre tale, and lat the Somnour be."

 "Nay," quod the Somnour, "lat hym seye to me
What so hym list; whan it comth to my lot,
By God! I shal hym quyten every grot.
I shal hym telle which a gret honour
It is to be a flaterynge lymytour;   30
And of many another manere cryme
Which nedeth nat rehercen at this tyme;
And his office I shal hym telle, ywys."

 Oure Hoost answerde, "Pees! namoore of this!"
And after this he seyde unto the Frere,
"Tel forth youre tale, leeve maister deere."

from THE FRIAR'S TALE

"Whilom ther was dwellynge in my contree
An erchedekene, a man of heigh degree,
That boldely dide execucioun
In punysshynge of fornicacioun,
Of wicchecraft, and eek of bawderye,
Of diffamacioun, and avoutrye,
Of chirche reves, and of testamentz,
Of contractes, and of lakke of sacramentz,
Of usure, and of symonye also.
But certes, lecchours dide he grettest wo;   10
They sholde syngen if that they were hent;
And smale tytheres were foule yshent,
If any persone wolde upon hem pleyne;
Ther myghte asterte hym no pecunyal peyne.
For smale tithes and smal offrynge,
He made the peple pitously to synge.
For er the bisshop caughte hem with his hook,
They weren in the erchedekenes book;
And thanne hadde he thurgh his jurisdiccioun,
Power to doon on hem correccioun.   20
He hadde a somnour redy to his hond,
A slyer boy was noon in Engelond;
For subtilly he hadde his espiaille,
That taughte hym wher hym myghte availle.
He koude spare of lecchours oon or two,
To techen hym to foure and twenty mo.
For theigh this somnour wood were as an hare,
To telle his harlotrye I wol nat spare;
For we been out of his correccioun.
They han of us no jurisdiccioun,   30
Ne nevere shullen terme of alle hir lyves,—"
"Peter! so been wommen of the styves,"
Quod the Somnour, "yput out of my cure!"
"Pees! with myschaunce and with mysaventure!"
Thus seyde oure Hoost, "and lat hym telle his tale.
Now telleth forth, thogh that the Somnour gale,
Ne spareth nat, myn owene maister deere."

 "This false theef, this somnour," quod the Frere— . . .

[The Friar's fabliau continues to expose the rascalities of its summoner, who is finally carried off to hell by his traveling companion, the Devil in disguise, at the heartfelt prayer of a desperate widow.]

from THE SUMMONER'S PROLOGUE

This Somnour in his stiropes hye stood;
Upon this Frere his herte was so wood,
That lyk an aspen leef he quook for ire.
"Lordynges," quod he, "but o thyng I desire;
I yow biseke that, of youre curteisye,
Syn ye han herd this false Frere lye,
As suffreth me I may my tale telle.

The Friar's Prologue. **7.** also . . . thee, as I hope to prosper.   **18.** be . . . apayd, be ill-pleased.   **19.** rennere, runner.   **20.** mandementz, summonses to appear in court.   **21.** ybet, beaten.   **22.** hende, pleasant.   **28.** grot, bit.   **36.** leeve . . . deere, dearly beloved master.   *The Friar's Tale.* **1.** "Whilom, once upon a time.   **6.** diffamacioun, libel. avoutrye, adultery.   **7.** chirche reves, church stewards. testamentz, wills.   **8.** lakke of sacramentz, failure to take the required sacraments.   **9.** usure, loaning on interest. symonye, selling church offices.   **10.** lecchours, lewd people.   **11. syngen,** cry. **hent,** caught.   **12. smale tytheres,** those who failed to pay the full tithe (church tax). **foule yshent,** foully injured.   **13. persone,** parson. **pleyne,** complain.   **16. He made . . . synge.** The archdeacon never omitted a pecuniary punishment.   **17. hook,** an allusion to the bishop's crosier.   **20. doon . . . correccioun,** punish them.   **22. boy,** knave.   **23. espiaille,** crew of spies.   **24. hym . . . availle,** he might catch someone.   **26. techen hym to,** show him how to find.   **27. theigh,** though. **wood,** mad.   **28. harlotrye,** rascality.   **29. For . . . correccioun,** for we friars are out of his power to punish.   **31. terme of,** during.   **32. Peter!** oath by St. Peter. **styves,"** brothels.   **33. cure!"** care, custody.   **36. gale,** cry out.   *The Summoner's Prologue.* **2. wood,** angry.   **3. quook,** quaked.   **5. biseke,** beseech.

This Frere bosteth that he knoweth helle,
And God it woot, that it is litel wonder;
Freres and feendes been but lyte a-sonder.　　10
For, pardee, ye han ofte tyme herd telle
How that a frere ravysshed was to helle
In spirit ones by a visioun;
And as an aungel ladde hym up and doun,
To shewen hym the peynes that ther were,
In al the place saugh he nat a frere;
Of oother folk he saugh ynowe in wo.
Unto this aungel spak the frere tho:
'Now, sire,' quod he, 'han freres swich a grace
That noon of hem shal come to this place?'　　20
"'Yis,' quod this aungel, 'many a milioun!'
And unto Sathanas he ladde hym doun. . . .

God save yow alle, save this cursed Frere!　　43
My prologe wol I ende in this manere."

from THE SUMMONER'S TALE

Lordynges, ther is in Yorkshire, as I gesse,
A mersshy contree called Holdernesse,
In which ther wente a lymytour aboute,
To preche, and eek to begge, it is no doute.
And so bifel that on a day this frere
Hadde preched at a chirche in his manere,
And specially, aboven every thyng,
Excited he the peple in his prechyng
To trentals, and to yeve, for Goddes sake,
Wher-with men myghten holy houses make,　　10
Ther as dyvyne service is honoured,
Nat ther as it is wasted and devoured,
Ne ther it nedeth nat for to be yeve,
As to possessioners, that mowen lyve,
Thanked be God, in wele and habundaunce.
"Trentals," seyde he, "delyvereth from penaunce
Hir freendes soules, as wel olde as yonge,
Ye, whan that they been hastily ysonge;
Nat for to holde a preest joly and gay,
He syngeth nat but o masse in a day.　　20
Delyvereth out," quod he, "anon the soules!
Ful hard it is with flessh hook or with oules
To been yclawed, or to brenne or bake.
Now spede yow hastily, for Cristes sake!"

And whan this frere hadde seyd al his entente,
With *qui cum patre* forth his wey he wente.
　Whan folk in chirche hadde yeve hym what hem leste,
He wente his wey, no lenger wolde he reste.
With scrippe and tipped staf, ytukked hye,
In every hous he gan to poure and prye,　　30
And beggeth mele, and chese, or ellis corn.
His felawe hadde a staf tipped with horn,
A peyre of tables al of yvory,
And a poyntel polysshed fetisly,
And wroot the names alwey, as he stood,
Of alle folk that yaf hem any good,
Ascaunces that he wolde for hem preye.
"Yif us a busshel whete, malt, or reye,
A Goddes kechyl, or a tryp of chese,
Or ellis what yow list, we may nat chese;　　40
A Goddes hal-peny, or a masse peny,
Or yif us of youre brawn, if ye have any,
A dagoun of youre blanket, leeve dame—
Oure suster deere, lo heere! I write youre name—
Bacoun or beef, or swich thyng as ye fynde."
　A sturdy harlot wente hem ay bihynde,
That was hir hostes man, and baar a sak,
And what men yaf hem, leyde it on his bak.
And whan that he was out atte dore anon,
He planed awey the names everichon　　50
That he biforn hadde writen in his tables;
He served hem with nyfles and with fables."
　"Nay, ther thow lixt, thow Somnour!" quod the Frere.
　"Pees!" quod oure Hoost, "for Cristes moder deere!
Tel forth thy tale, and spare it nat at al."
　"So thryve I," quod this Somnour, "so I shal!" . . .

[The Summoner's fabliau follows its blackguard of a friar into the cottage of a sick man whose credulity has in the past made him an easy victim. Enlightened at last, he gives the friar a contribution which should stop his begging for all time.]

26. *qui cum patre,* who with the Father, a phrase from the benediction.　29. **scrippe**, bag. **ytukked hye,** with his robe tucked up high to give freedom for walking.　30. **poure,** peer.　32. **felawe,** companion; friars went in pairs. 33. **tables,** writing tablets. **yvory,** ivory coated with wax. 34. **poyntel,** pointed instrument for writing in wax. **fetisly,** handsomely.　37. **Ascaunces,** as if to say.　39. **A Goddes kechyl,** a little cake of (sent from) God. **tryp,** small piece.　40. **chese,** choose.　41. **hal-peny,** halfpenny. **masse peny,** offering for a mass.　42. **brawn,** flesh, often specifically of a boar.　43. **dagoun,** piece.　46. **harlot,** rascal.　47. **hir hostes man,** the man who served the guests, or recipients of charity, at their friary.　49. **he,** the "felawe" of l. 32. He smoothed the wax with his horn-tipped staff. 52. **nyfles,** mockeries. **fables,** lies.　53. **lixt,** liest.

The Summoner's Prologue.　10. **been . . . a-sonder,** differ but slightly.　12. **ravysshed,** carried.　17. **ynowe,** enough. 19. **han,** have.　22. **Sathanas,** Satan.　*The Summoner's Tale.*　2. **mersshy,** marshy.　9. **trentals,** thirty successive masses for the dead.　10. **holy houses,** establishments of friars.　11–13. **Ther . . . ther,** where . . . where.　14. **possessioners,** monks of endowed monasteries and salaried clergymen.　16. **penaunce,** pains of purgatory described in ll. 22–23.　17. **freendes,** friends'.　18. **ysonge,** sung. 19–20. **a preest . . . day,** a priest is not criticized for being jolly and gay when he sings but one mass daily.　22. **oules,** awls.

THE CLERK'S PROLOGUE

"Sire Clerk of Oxenford," oure Hoost sayde
"Ye ride as coy and stille as dooth a mayde
Were newe spoused, sittyng at the bord;
This day ne herde I of youre tonge a word.
I trowe ye studie aboute som sophyme,
But Salomon seith, 'every thyng hath tyme.'

"For Goddes sake, as beth of bettre cheere,
It is no tyme for to studien heere.
Tel us som murie tale, by youre fey!
For what man that is entred in a pley,   10
He nedes moot unto the pley assente.
But precheth nat, as freres doon in Lente,
To make us for oure olde synnes wepe,
Ne that thy tale make us nat to slepe.

"Tel us som murye thyng of aventures,
Youre termes, youre colours, and youre figures—
Kepe hem in stoor til so be ye endite
Heigh stile, as whan that men to kynges write.
Speketh so pleyn at this tyme, we yow preye,
That we may understonde what ye seye."   20

This worthy clerk benygnely answerde:
"Hoost," quod he, "I am under youre yerde;
Ye han of us as now the governaunce,
And therfore wol I do yow obeisaunce,
As fer as reson asketh, hardily.
I wol yow telle a tale which that I
Lerned at Padwe of a worthy clerk,
As preved by his wordes and his werk.
He is now deed and nayled in his cheste,
I pray to God so yeve his soule reste!   30

"Frauceys Petrak, the laureat poete,
Highte this clerk, whos rethoryk swete
Enlumyned al Ytaille of poetrie,
As Lynyan dide of philosophie,
Or lawe, or oother art particuler;
But deeth, that wol nat suffre us dwellen heer,
But as it were a twynklyng of an eye,
Hem bothe hath slayn, and alle shul we dye.

"But forth to tellen of this worthy man
That taughte me this tale, as I bigan,   40
I seye that first with heigh stile he enditeth,
Er he the body of his tale writeth,
A prohemye, in the which discryveth he
Pemond, and of Saluces the contree,
And speketh of Appenyn, the hilles hye,
That been the boundes of Westlumbardye,
And of mount Vesulus in special,
Wher as the Poo, out of a welle smal,
Taketh his firste spryngyng and his sours,
That estward ay encresseth in his cours   50
To Emeleward, to Ferare, and Venyse;
The which a long thyng were to devyse.
And trewely, as to my juggement,
Me thynketh it a thyng inpartinent,
Save that he wole conveyen his matere;
But this his tale, which that ye shal heere."

["The Clerk's Tale," derived from Petrarch's Latin version of the last story in Boccaccio's *Decameron*, is, like "The Man of Law's Tale," a "moral romance." By the example of Griselda, lowborn wife of a nobleman who "tries" her by pretending to kill their children and to divorce her, the Clerk teaches patience. Griselda, of course, is happily reinstated and reunited with her children. He also doubly answers the Wife of Bath, who had said that clerks never spoke well of women, by praising Griselda's patience and asserting the necessity of the husband's sovereignty for happiness in marriage.

Of the concluding stanzas of the tale, which follow, the first three give Petrarch's serious application of the tale, the rest, the Clerk's ironic one.]

from THE CLERK'S TALE

This storie is seyd, nat for that wyves sholde
Folwen Grisilde as in humylitee,
For it were inportable, thogh they wolde;
But for that every wight in his degree,
Sholde be constant in adversitee
As was Grisilde; therfore Petrak writeth
This storie, which with heigh stile he enditeth.

For, sith a womman was so pacient
Unto a mortal man, wel moore us oghte   1150
Receyven al in gree that God us sent;
For greete skile is, he preve that he wroghte.
But he ne tempteth no man that he boghte,
As seith Seint Jame, if ye his pistel rede;
He preveth folk al day, it is no drede,

And suffreth us, as for oure excercise,
With sharpe scourges of adversitee
Ful ofte to be bete in sondry wise;

Group E.   **2. coy,** quiet.   **3. spoused,** wed. **bord,** table.   **5. sophyme,** subtle argument in logic.   **9. fey!** faith.   **16. termes . . . colours . . . figures,** rhetorical devices.   **18. Heigh stile,** high, formal style.   **22. yerde,** rod for beating.   **24. obeisaunce,** obedience.   **25. hardily,** certainly.   **27. Padwe,** Padua.   **29. cheste,** coffin.   **31. Petrak,** Petrarch (1304–1374). **laureat,** laurel-crowned.   **32. Highte,** was called.   **33. Enlumyned al Ytaille,** illumined all Italy.   **34. Lynyan,** Giovanni di Lignano (1310–1383), professor at the University of Bologna.   **43. prohemye,** prologue. **discryveth,** describes.

44–51. Pemond . . . Venyse. Capitals indicate place names of northern Italy.   **54. inpartinent,** irrelevant.   **55. conveyen . . . matere,** introduce his material.   **56. this his,** this is his.   **1144. inportable,** intolerable. **wolde,** wished to.   **1151. Receyven . . . gree,** take in good spirit.   **1152. skile,** reason. **he preve,** that he should test.   **1153. boghte,** redeemed.   **1154. Jame,** James. **pistel,** epistle.   **1155. it . . . drede,** there is no doubt.   **1158. bete in sondry wise,** beaten in various ways.

Nat for to knowe oure wyl, for certes he,
Er we were born, knew al oure freletee; 1160
And for oure beste is al his governance.
Lat us thanne lyve in vertuous suffrance.

But o word, lordynges, herkneth er I go:
It were ful hard to fynde now a dayes
In al a toun Grisildis thre or two;
For, if that they were put to swiche assayes,
The gold of hem hath now so badde alayes
With bras, that thogh the coyne be fair at eye,
It wolde rather breste atwo than plye.

For which heere, for the Wyves love of Bathe, 1170
Whos lyf and al hir secte God mayntene
In heigh maistrie, and elles were it scathe,
I wol with lusty herte, fressh and grene,
Seye yow a song to glade yow, I wene,
And lat us stynte of ernestful matere.
Herkneth my song, that seith in this manere:

L'ENVOY

Grisilde is deed, and eek hir pacience,
And bothe atones buryed in Ytaille;
For which I crie in open audience,
No wedded man so hardy be t'assaille 1180
His wyves pacience, in trust to fynde
Grisildis, for in certein he shal faille.

O noble wyves, ful of heigh prudence,
Lat noon humilitee youre tonge nayle,
Ne lat no clerk have cause or diligence
To write of yow a storie of swich mervaille
As of Grisildis pacient and kynde,
Lest Chichivache yow swelwe in hir entraille!

Folweth Ekko, that holdeth no silence,
But evere answereth at the countretaille. 1190
Beth nat bidaffed for youre innocence,
But sharply tak on yow the governaille.
Emprenteth wel this lessoun in youre mynde
For commune profit, sith it may availle.

Ye archewyves, stondeth at defense,
Syn ye be strong as is a greet camaille;
Ne suffreth nat that men yow doon offense.
And sklendre wyves, fieble as in bataille,
Beth egre as a tigre yond in Ynde;
Ay clappeth as a mille, I yow consaille. 1200

Ne dreed hem nat, dooth hem no reverence;
For thogh thyn housbond armed be in maille,
The arwes of thy crabbed eloquence
Shal perce his brest, and eek his aventaille.
In jalousie I rede eek thow hym bynde,
And thow shalt make hym couche as dooth a
    quaille.

If thow be fair, ther folk ben in presence
Shewe thow thy visage and thyn apparaille;
If thow be foul, be fre of thy dispence,
To gete thee freendes ay do thy travaille; 1210
Be ay of cheere as light as leef on lynde,
And lat hym care, and wepe, and wrynge, and
    waille!

THE MERCHANT'S PROLOGUE

"Wepyng and waylyng, care, and oother
    sorwe
I knowe ynogh, on even and amorwe,"
Quod the Marchant, "and so doon othere mo
That wedded been. I trowe that it be so,
For wel I woot it fareth so with me.
I have a wyf, the worste that may be;
For thogh the feend to hire ycoupled were,
She wolde hym overmacche, I dar wel swere.
What sholde I yow reherce in special
Hir hye malice? She is a shrewe at al. 10
Ther is a long and a large difference
Bitwix Grisildis grete pacience
And of my wyf the passyng crueltee.
Were I unbounden, also moot I thee!
I wolde nevere eft come in the snare.
We wedded men lyve in sorwe and care;
Assaye who so wol, and he shal fynde
That I seye sooth, by Seint Thomas of Ynde,

1159. **certes,** certainly. 1160. **freletee,** frailty. 1162. **suffrance,** endurance. 1163. **o,** one. **herkneth,** listen to. 1166. **swiche assayes,** such tests. 1167. **alayes,** alloys. 1168. **coyne,** coin. 1169. **It . . . plye.** It would break in two rather than bend. 1170. **for . . . Bathe,** for the love of the Wife of Bath. 1171. **secte,** sex. **mayntene,** maintain. 1172. **scathe,** shame. 1174. **glade . . . wene,** make you glad, I think. 1175. **stynte . . . matere,** discontinue serious matter. 1178. **atones,** at once. 1184. **youre . . . nayle,** nail down your tongues. 1186. **swich mervaille,** such marvels. 1188. **Chichivache . . . entraille!** "Lest 'Thin-Cow' swallow you in her entrails." "Thin Cow" ate patient wives (hence her thinness); Bicorne ("Two-Horns") ate patient husbands: he was very fat. 1189. **Ekko,** Echo. 1190. **at the countretaille,** in reply. 1191. **bidaffed,** made a fool of. 1192. **governaille,** governance.

1195. **archewyves,** physically strong wives. 1196. **Syn,** since. **camaille,** camel. 1198. **sklendre,** physically weak. **fieble . . . bataille,** feeble in fight. 1199. **Beth egre,** be fierce. 1200. **Ay . . . mille,** always clatter as a mill does. **consaille,** counsel. 1204. **aventaille,** front of a helmet. 1205. **rede,** advise. 1206. **couche,** cower. 1207. **fair,** beautiful. 1209. **foul,** ill-favored. **dispence,** spending. 1210. **do . . . travaille,** exert yourself. 1211. **cheere,** behavior. **leef on lynde,** leaf on a linden tree. 1212. **care,** worry. **wrynge,** wring his hands. 2. **on . . . amorwe,** by night and day. 9. **special,** detail. 10. **shrewe . . . al,** shrew in all respects. 14. **also . . . thee!** as I hope to prosper. 15. **eft,** again.

As for the moore part, I sey nat alle.
God shilde that it sholde so bifalle! 20
　"A! goode sire Hoost, I have ywedded be
Thise monthes two, and moore nat, pardee;
And yet, I trowe, he that al his lyve
Wyflees hath been, though that men wolde hym ryve
Unto the herte, ne koude in no manere
Tellen so muchel sorwe, as I now heere
Koude tellen of my wyves cursednesse!"
　"Now," quod oure Hoost, "Marchant, so God yow blesse,
Syn ye so muchel knowen of that art,
Ful hertely I pray yow telle us part." 30
　"Gladly," quod he, "but of myn owene soore,
For sory herte, I telle may namoore."

["The Merchant's Tale," a cynical denial of any possibility of happiness in marriage, is the reply to both the Wife of Bath and the Clerk of a man so embittered by his wife in less than two months that he cannot bear to go into details. Instead he tells the story of old January, who, after a long debate concerning marriage, weds young May and is deceived by her despite his jailerlike precautions.]

THE MERCHANT'S EPILOGUE

"Ey! Goddes mercy!" seyde oure Hoost tho,
"Now swich a wyf I prey God kepe me fro!
Lo, whiche sleightes and subtiltees
In wommen ben! For ay as bisy as bees
Ben they, us sely men for to deceyve,
And from a sooth evere wol they weyve;
By this Marchantes tale it preveth weel.
But doutelees, as trewe as any steel
I have a wyf, thogh that she poore be,
But of hir tonge a labbyng shrewe is she, 10
And yit she hath an heep of vices mo;
Ther of no fors, lat alle swiche thynges go.
But wite ye what? In conseil be it seyd,
Me reweth soore I am unto hire teyd.
For, and I sholde rekenen every vice
Which that she hath, ywis, I were to nyce,
And cause why, it sholde reported be
And toold to hire of somme of this meynee;
Of whom, it nedeth nat for to declare,
Syn wommen konnen oute swich chaffare; 20
And eek my wit suffiseth nat ther-to,
To tellen al, wherfore my tale is do."

THE SQUIRE'S PROLOGUE

"Squyer, com neer, if it youre wille be,
And sey som-what of love; for, certes, ye
Konnen ther-on as muche as any man."
"Nay, sire," quod he, "but I wol seye as I kan
With hertly wyl; for I wol nat rebelle
Agayn youre lust; a tale wol I telle.
Have me excused if I speke amys,
My wyl is good, and lo, my tale is this."

["The Squire's Tale" was left unfinished (a fact lamented by Milton in "Il Penseroso"), but enough was written to show that it was to have been a romance of Oriental wonders, set in the court of Genghis Khan or of his grandson Kublai Khan, host of Marco Polo and subject of Coleridge's poem.]

THE SQUIRE'S EPILOGUE

"In feith, Squyer, thow hast thee wel yquyt
And gentilly; I preise wel thy wit,"
Quod the Frankeleyn, "consideryinge thy youthe,
So feelyngly thow spekest, sire, I allow the!
As to my doom, ther is noon that is heere
Of eloquence that shal be thy peere,
If that thow lyve; God yeve thee good chaunce,
And in vertu sende thee continuance!
For of thy speche I have gret deyntee.
I have a sone, and by the Trinitee, 10
I hadde levere than twenty pound worth lond,
Thogh it right now were fallen in myn hond,
He were a man of swich discrecioun
As that ye ben! Fy on possessioun,
But if a man be vertuous with-al!
I have my sone snybbed, and yit shal,
For he to vertu listeth nat entende;
But for to pleye at dees, and to despende
And lese al that he hath, is his usage.
He hath levere talken with a page 20
Than to commune with any gentil wight
Wher he myghte lerne gentillesse aright."
"Straw for youre gentillesse!" quod oure Hoost;
"What, Frankeleyn! pardee, sire, wel thow woost

The Merchant's Prologue. **20. shilde,** forbid. **so,** that *all married men* "live in sorrow and care." **24. ryve,** pierce. *The Merchant's Epilogue.* **5. sely,** innocent. **6. sooth,** truth. **weyve,** turn aside. **10. labbyng,** blabbing. **12. Ther . . . fors,** never mind about that. **13. wite,** know. **In conseil,** confidentially. **14. Me . . . soore,** I regret sorely. **teyd,** tied. **16. to nyce,** too foolish. **18. meynee,** company. **20. konnen . . . chaffare,** know how to let out such matter.

The Merchant's Epilogue. **22. do,** done. *The Squire's Prologue.* Group F. **5. hertly,** hearty. *The Squire's Epilogue.* **4. allow the!** commend thee. **5. As . . . doom,** in my judgment. **9. deyntee,** delight. **11. I hadde . . . lond,** I had rather than have land bringing an income of £20 a year. **16. snybbed,** reproved. **17. listeth . . . entende,** is not pleased to apply himself. **18. dees,** dice. **19. lese,** lose. **usage,** custom. **22. gentillesse,** a combination of all the virtues which formed a **gentil wight**; far broader and deeper in meaning than the modern "gentility." **24. woost,** know.

That ech of yow moot tellen atte leste
A tale or two, or breken his biheste.''
"That knowe I wel, sire," quod the Franke-
  leyn,
"I prey yow, haveth me nat in desdeyn,
Thogh to this man I speke a word or two."
"Telle on thy tale with-outen wordes mo!" 30
"Gladly, sire Hoost," quod he, "I wol obeye
Unto youre wyl; now herkneth what I seye.
I wol yow nat contrarien in no wise
As fer as that my wittes wol suffise.
I prey to God that it may plesen yow,
Thanne woot I wel that it is good ynow."

THE FRANKLIN'S PROLOGUE

"Thise olde gentil Britons in hir dayes
Of diverse aventures maden layes,
Rymeyed in hir firste Briton tonge;
Whiche layes with hir instrumentz they songe,
Or elles redden hem for hir pleasaunce;
And oon of hem have I in remembraunce,
Which I shal seyn with good wyl as I kan.
  "But, sires, by cause I am a burel man,
At my bigynnyng first I yow biseche,
Have me excused of my rude speche.   10
I lerned nevere rethorik, certeyn;
Thyng that I speke, it moot be bare and pleyn.
I sleep nevere on the mount of Parnaso,
Ne lerned Marcus Tullius Scithero.
Colours ne knowe I none, with-outen drede,
But swich colours as growen in the mede,
Or ellis swiche as men dye or peynte.
Colours of rethoryk ben to queynte;
My spirit feeleth nat of swich matere.
But if yow list, my tale shul ye heere."   20

["The Franklin's Tale" proposes *gentillesse* as the solution to the problem of marital relations. Mutual deference and forbearance replace a struggle for dominance between husband and wife and happily solve a threatening "triangle plot." Incidentally, *gentillesse* is shown to be independent of social position and wealth: a wealthy knight, a moderately well-to-do squire, and a poor clerk all exhibit it. Despite the Franklin's claim to be telling a Breton lay, it is more than likely that the source of the story is to be found in the "Filocolo" of Boccaccio.]

25. moot, must. **atte leste**, at the least. **28. desdeyn**, disdain. *The Franklin's Prologue.* **1. Britons**, Bretons, Celts of Brittany in France; see the introduction to "Sir Orfeo" (page 147). **2. layes**, short metrical romances. **3. Rymeyed**, rhymed. **8. burel**, unlearned. **13. Parnaso**, Mt. Parnassus, haunt of the Greek Muses. **14. Scithero**, Cicero. **15. Colours**, rhetorical figures of speech. **16. mede**, meadow. **18. queynte**, strange.

["The Physician's Tale" (Group C), lacks a prologue. It is a short moral story derived from Livy's history of Rome by way of the *Roman de la Rose*. A false judge and a false churl conspire to ravish a maiden (Virginia) who prefers decapitation by her father to dishonor. A popular uprising avenges her death.]

THE PHYSICIAN'S EPILOGUE

Oure Hoost gan to swere as he were wood,
"Harrow!" quod he, "by nayles and by blood!
This was a fals cherl and a fals justice!
As shameful deeth as herte kan devyse
Come to thise juges and hir advocatz!
Algate this sely mayde is slayn, allas!
Allas, to deere boghte she beautee!
Wherfore I seye alday that men may se
That yiftes of fortune and of nature
Been cause of deeth to many a creature.   10
Hir beaute was hir deth, I dar wel sayn;
Allas, so pitously as she was slayn!
Of bothe yiftes that I speke of now
Men han ful ofte moore for harm than prow.
  "But trewely, myn owene maister deere,
This is a pitous tale for to heere.
But nathelees, passe over, is no fors.
I pray to God, so save thy gentil cors,
And eek thyne urinals and thy jurdones,
Thyn Ypocras, and eek thy Galiones,   20
And every boyste ful of thy letuarie;
God blesse hem, and oure lady Seinte Marie!
So mote I then, thow art a propre man,
And lyk a prelat, by Seint Ronyan!
Seyde I nat wel? I kan nat speke in terme;
But wel I woot thow doost myn herte to erme,
That I almoost have caught a cardynacle.
By corpus bones! but I have triacle,
Or elles a draghte of moyste and corny ale,
Or but I heere anon a myrie tale,   30
Myn herte is lost for pitee of this mayde.
Thow beel amy, thow Pardoner," he sayde,
"Tel us som myrthe or japes right anon."

2. Harrow! Help! **6. Algate**, nevertheless. **7. deere**, dearly. **14. prow**, advantage. **18. cors**, body. **19. jurdones**, vessels used by alchemists and physicians, but destined, perhaps as early as this, to play a more humble role. **20. Ypocras**, sweetened and spiced wine, but the Host, who has a genius for malapropisms, is doubtless thinking of Hippocrates and Galen. **21. boyste**, box. **letuarie**, remedy. **23. So . . . then**, as I hope to prosper. **24. Ronyan**, probably a saint of the Host's invention. **25. in terme**, formally; here, in medical terms. **26. thow . . . erme**, you make my heart ache. **27. That**, so that. **cardynacle**, pain about the heart. **28. corpus bones!** In this macaronic hybrid the Host telescopes two oaths, "by the body" and "by the bones" (of Christ). Compare l. 2 above. **triacle**, remedy. **29. moyste and corny**, new and tasting strongly of malt. **30. myrie**, merry. **32. beel amy**, fair friend.

"It shal be doon," quod he, "by Seint Ronyon!
But first," quod he, "heere at this ale stake
I wol bothe drynke, and eten of a cake."
But right anon thise gentils gonne to crye,
"Nay, lat hym telle us of no ribaudye!
Tel us som moral thyng, that we may leere
Som wit, and thanne wol we gladly heere."   40

"I graunte, ywis," quod he, "but I moot thynke
Up-on som honeste thyng whil that I drynke."

THE PARDONER'S PROLOGUE

Radix malorum est Cupiditas. Ad Thimotheum sexto

"Lordynges," quod he, "in chirches whan I preche,
I peyne me to han an hauteyn speche,
And rynge it out as round as gooth a belle,
For I kan al by rote that I telle.
My theme is alwey oon and evere was:
Radix malorum est cupiditas.

"First I pronounce whennes that I come,
And thanne my bulles shewe I, alle and some.
Oure lige lordes seel on my patente,
That shewe I first, my body to warente,   10
That no man be so boold, ne preest ne clerk,
Me to destourbe of Cristes holy werk.
And after that thanne telle I forth my tales,
Bulles of popes and of cardynales,
Of patriarkes and bisshopes I shewe,
And in Latyn I speke a wordes fewe,
To saffron with my predicacioun,
And for to stire hem to devocioun.
Thanne shewe I forth my longe cristal stones,
Ycrammed ful of cloutes and of bones,   20
Relikes been they, as wenen they echon.
Thanne have I in latoun a shulder-bon
Which that was of an holy Jewes sheep.
'Goode men,' I seye, 'tak of my wordes keep:
If that this boon be wasshe in any welle,
If cow, or calf, or sheep, or oxe swelle
That any worm hath ete, or worm ystonge,
Taak water of that welle and wassh his tonge,
And it is hool anoon; and forther-moor,

Of pokkes and of scabbe, and every soor   30
Shal every sheep be hool, that of this welle
Drynketh a draughte; taak kepe eek what I telle.
" 'If that the goode man, that the bestes oweth,
Wol every wyke, er that the cok hym croweth,
Fastynge, drynken of this welle a draughte,
As thilke holy Jew oure eldres taughte,
Hise bestes and his stoor shal multiplie.
" 'And, sire, also it heeleth jalousie;
For, thogh a man be falle in jalous rage,
Lat maken with this water his potage,   40
And nevere shal he moore his wyf mystriste,
Thogh he the soothe of hir defaute wiste,
Al hadde she taken preestes two or thre.
" 'Heere is a miteyn eek, that ye may se.
He that his hand wol putte in this mitayn,
He shal have multiplyyng of his grayn,
Whan he hath sowen, be it whete or otes,
So that he offre pens, or ellis grotes.
" 'Goode men and wommen, o thyng warne I yow:
If any wight be in this chirche now   50
That hath doon synne horrible, that he
Dar nat, for shame, of it yshryven be,
Or any womman, be she yong or old,
That hath ymaked hir housbond cokewold,
Swich folk shal have no power ne no grace
To offren to my relikes in this place.
And who-so fyndeth hym out of swich blame,
They wol come up and offre a Goddes name,
And I assoille hym by the auctoritee
Which that by bulle ygraunted was to me.'   60

"By this gaude have I wonne, yeer by yeer,
An hundred mark sith I was pardoner.
I stonde lyk a clerk in my pulpet,
And whan the lewed peple is doun yset,
I preche so as ye han herd bifore,
And telle an hundred false japes more.
Thanne peyne I me to strecche forth the nekke,
And est and west up-on the peple I bekke,
As dooth a dowve sittyng on a berne.
Myne handes and my tonge goon so yerne,   70
That it is joye to se my bisynesse.
Of avarice and of swich cursednesse
Is al my prechyng, for to make hem free
To yeven hir pens, and namely un-to me.
For myn entente is nat but for to wynne,
And no-thyng for correccioun of synne.

---

35. **ale stake**, sign of an alehouse, here used for the house itself.   36. **cake**, loaf of bread.   37. **gonne**, began.   39. **leere**, learn.   41. **ywis**, certainly.   2. **hauteyn**, arrogant.   3. **round**, melodiously.   4. **kan**, know.   6. **Radix . . . cupiditas.** The Authorized version of the Bible translates the Vulgate here: "For the love of money is the root of all evil."—I Timothy 6:10.   8. **bulles.** See *Piers Plowman*, ll. 65 ff. and notes, page 164.   9. **Oure . . . seel**, the seal of a bishop. **patente**, license.   10. **warente**, protect.   12. **destourbe of**, disturb in.   17. **saffron**, spice or color (my preaching).   19. **cristal stones**, glass cases.   20. **cloutes**, rags.   21. **wenen they**, his audience thinks.   22. **latoun**, a brasslike mixed metal.   24. **keep**, heed.   27. **That . . . ystonge**, that has eaten any worm, or any worm has stung.   30. **pokkes**, the pustules of any eruptive disease.   31. **hool**, cured.   33. **oweth**, owneth.   34. **wyke**, week.   37. **stoor**, stock.   38. **heeleth**, heals.   40. **potage**, broth.   41. **mystriste**, mistrust.   42. **defaute**, fault.   44. **miteyn eek**, mitten also.   48. **pens**, pennies. **grotes**, small coins.   51. **that he**, so that he.   61. **gaude**, trick.   64. **lewed**, uneducated.   68. **bekke**, nod.   69. **dowve . . . berne**, dove on a barn.   70. **yerne**, briskly.   73. **free**, generous.

I rekke nevere, whan that they been beryed,
Thogh that hir soules goon a blakeberyed!
For certes, many a predicacioun
Comth ofte tyme of yvel entencioun; 80
Som for plesance of folk and flaterye,
To been avanced by ypocrisye,
And som for veyne glorie, and som for hate.
For whan I dar noon oother weyes debate,
Thanne wol I stynge hym with my tonge smerte
In prechyng, so that he shal nat asterte
To been defamed falsly, if that he
Hath trespased to my bretheren or to me.
For thogh I telle noght his propre name,
Men shal wel knowe that it is the same 90
By signes and by othere circumstances.
Thus quyte I folk that doon us displesances;
Thus spitte I out my venym under hewe
Of holynesse, to seme holy and trewe.

"But shortly myn entente I wol devyse:
I preche of no thyng but for coveityse.
Ther-fore my theme is yet, and evere was,
Radix malorum est cupiditas.
Thus kan I preche agayn that same vice
Which that I use, and that is avarice. 100
But though my-self be gilty in that synne,
Yet kan I maken oother folk to twynne
From avarice, and soore to repente.
But that is nat my principal entente;
I preche no-thyng but for coveitise;
Of this matere it oghte ynow suffise.

"Thanne telle I hem ensamples many oon
Of olde stories, longe tyme agoon.
For lewed peple loven tales olde;
Swiche thynges kan they wel reporte and
   holde. 110
What, trowe ye, that whiles I may preche,
And wynne gold and silver for I teche,
That I wol lyve in poverte wilfully?
Nay, nay, I thoghte it nevere, trewely!
For I wol preche and begge in sondry landes;
I wol nat do no labour with myne handes,
Ne make baskettes, and lyve ther-by,
By cause I wol nat beggen ydelly.
I wol noon of the apostles countrefete;
I wol have moneye, wolle, chese, and whete, 120
Al were it yeven of the pouereste page,

Or of the pouereste widwe in a village,
Al sholde hir children sterve for famyne.
Nay, I wol drynke licour of the vyne,
And have a joly wenche in every toun.

"But herkneth, lordynges, in conclusioun,
Your likyng is that I shal telle a tale.
Now have I dronke a draghte of corny ale,
By God, I hope I shal yow telle a thyng
That shal, by resoun, been at youre likyng. 130
For thogh my-self be a ful vicious man,
A moral tale yet I yow telle kan,
Which I am wont to preche, for to wynne.
Now holde youre pees, my tale I wol bigynne."

THE PARDONER'S TALE

In Flaundres whilom was a compaignye
Of yonge folk that haunteden folye,
As riot, hasard, stewes, and tavernes,
Where-as, with harpes, lutes, and gyternes,
They daunce and pleyen at dees bothe day and
   nyght,
And ete also and drynke over hir myght,
Thurgh which they doon the devel sacrifise
With-inne that develes temple, in cursed wise,
By superfluytee abhomynable.
Hir othes been so grete and so dampnable, 10
That it is grisly for to heere hem swere;
Oure blissed Lordes body they to-tere—
Hem thoughte that Jewes rente hym noght
   ynough—
And ech of hem at otheres synne lough.
And right anon thanne comen tombesteres
Fetys and smale, and yonge frutesteres,
Syngeres with harpes, baudes, wafereres,
Whiche been the verray develes officeres
To kyndle and blowe the fyr of lecherye,
That is annexed un-to glotonye. 20
The holy writ take I to my witnesse,
That luxurie is in wyn and dronkenesse.

Lo, how that dronken Loth, unkyndely,
Lay by his doghtres two, unwityngly;
So dronke he was, he nyste what he wroghte.
Herodes, who-so wel the stories soghte,
Whan he of wyn was replet at his feste,

---

133. **wynne**, gain money. 1. **whilom**, once upon a time. 3. **riot . . . stewes**, riotous conduct, gambling (specifically a game at dice), brothels. 4. **gyternes**, guitars. 5. **dees**, dice. 11. **grisly**, horrible. 12. **blissed**, blessed. **to-tere**, tear in pieces. 13. **Hem thoughte**, it seemed to them. 14. **lough**, laughed. 15. **tombesteres**, female dancers. 16. **Fetys**, graceful. **frutesteres**, female fruit-sellers. 17. **baudes**, **wafereres**, bawds, pastry-sellers. 22. **luxurie**, lust. 23. **Loth**, **unkyndely**, Lot, unnaturally. 24. **unwityngly**, unknowingly. 25. **nyste . . . wroghte**, knew not what he did. 26. **Herodes . . . soghte**, Herod, as whoever searched the accounts well would know.

77. **rekke**, care. **beryed**, buried. 78. **goon . . . blakeberyed!** go blackberrying, that is, any old place. 80. **Comth**, comes. **yvel entencioun**, evil intention. 85. **hym**, some man in the congregation. 86. **asterte**, avoid. 88. **bretheren**, other pardoners. 92. **quyte**, requite. 95. **entente**, purpose. **devyse**, explain. 99. **agayn**, against. 102. **twynne**, turn. 103. **soore**, sorely. 106. **ynow**, enough. 107. **ensamples**, examples, illustrative anecdotes. 113. **wilfully**, willingly. 119. **countrefete**, imitate. 120. **wol**, will. **wolle**, wool. 121. **Al**, although.

Right at his owene table he yaf his heste
To sleen the Baptist John ful giltelees.
Senec seith a good word doutelees: 30
He seith he kan no difference fynde
Bitwix a man that is out of his mynde
And a man which that is dronkelewe,
But that woodnesse, yfallen in a shrewe,
Persevereth lenger than dooth dronkenesse.
O glotonye, ful of cursednesse!
O cause first of oure confusioun!
O original of oure dampnacioun,
Til Crist hadde boght us with his blood agayn!
Lo, how deere, shortly for to sayn, 40
Aboght was thilke cursed vileynye!
Corrupt was al this world for glotonye!
   Adam oure fader, and his wyf also,
Fro Paradys to labour and to wo
Were dryven for that vice, it is no drede;
For whil that Adam fasted, as I rede,
He was in Paradys; and whan that he
Eet of the fruyt defended on the tree,
Anon he was out cast to wo and peyne.
O glotonye, on thee wel oghte us pleyne! 50
O, wiste a man how manye maladies
Folwen of excesse and of glotonyes,
He wolde been the moore mesurable
Of his diete, sittyng at his table.
Allas! the shorte throte, the tendre mouth,
Maketh that est and west, and north and south,
In erthe, in eyr, in water, men to swynke
To gete a glotoun deyntee mete and drynke!
Of this matere, O Paul, wel kanstow trete:
"Mete un-to wombe, and wombe eek un-to mete, 60
Shal God destroyen bothe," as Paulus seith.
Allas! a foul thyng is it, by my feith,
To seye this word, and fouler is the dede,
Whan man so drynketh of the white and rede
That of his throte he maketh his pryvee,
Thurgh thilke cursed superfluitee.
   The apostle wepyng seith ful pitously,
"Ther walken manye of whiche yow toold have I,
I seye it now wepyng with pitous voys,
Ther been enemys of Cristes croys, 70
Of whiche the ende is deth, wombe is hir god!"
O wombe! O bely! O stynkyng cod,
Fulfilled of donge and of corrupcioun!
At either ende of thee foul is the soun.
How greet labour and cost is thee to fynde!
Thise cokes, how they stampe, and streyne, and grynde,
And turnen substaunce in to accident,
To fulfillen al thy likerous talent!
Out of the harde bones knokke they
The mary, for they caste noght awey 80
That may go thurgh the golet softe and soote.
Of spicerie, of leef, bark, and roote
Shal been his sauce ymaked by delit,
To make hym yet a newer appetit.
But, certes, he that haunteth swiche delices
Is deed, whil that he lyveth in tho vices.
   A lecherous thyng is wyn, and dronkenesse
Is ful of stryvyng and of wrecchednesse.
O dronke man, disfigured is thy face,
Sour is thy breeth, foul artow to embrace, 90
And thurgh thy dronke nose semeth the soun
As thogh thou seydest ay "Sampsoun, Sampsoun!"
And yet, God woot, Sampsoun drank nevere no wyn.
Thou fallest as it were a stiked swyn;
Thy tonge is lost, and al thyn honeste cure;
For dronkenesse is verray sepulture
Of mannes wit and his discrecioun.
In whom that drynke hath dominacioun,
He kan no conseil kepe, it is no drede.
Now kepe yow fro the white and fro the rede, 100
And namely fro the white wyn of Lepe,
That is to selle in Fisshstrete or in Chepe.
This wyn of Spaigne crepeth subtilly
In othere wynes, growynge faste by,
Of which ther riseth swich fumositee,
That whan a man hath dronken draghtes thre,
And weneth that he be at hoom in Chepe,
He is in Spaigne, right at the toune of Lepe,
Nat at the Rochel, ne at Burdeux toun; 109
And thanne wol he seyn "Sampsoun, Sampsoun!"

28. **yaf . . . heste,** gave his command. 29. **sleen,** slay. 33. **dronkelewe,** drunken. 34. **woodnesse . . . shrewe,** madness having come upon an ill-tempered person. 37. **confusioun,** ruin. 39. **boght . . . agayn,** redeemed by with his blood. 40–41. **deere . . . Aboght,** dearly atoned for. **vileynye,** evil deed. 48. **defended,** forbidden. 50. **pleyne!** complain. 51. **wiste a man,** if a man knew. 52. **Folwen of,** follow on. 53. **mesurable,** temperate. 57. **swynke,** labor. 59. **kanstow trete,** can you treat. 60–61. "**Mete . . . bothe.**" "Meats for the belly . . ." See I Corinthians 6:13. 64. **white and rede,** white wine and red. 65. **That . . . pryvee,** that is, so that he vomits. 68–71. "**Ther . . . god.**" See Philippians 3:18–19. **croys,** cross.

72. **cod,** stomach. 75. **fynde,** provide for. 77. **substaunce,** essence. **accident,** externals. 78. **likerous talent,** greedy appetite. 80. **mary,** marrow. 81. **golet,** gullet. 83. **by delit,** delightfully. 85. **delices,** delights. 91. **semeth the soun,** seems the sound. 92. "**Sampsoun,** the sound a drunkard makes in snoring. 94. **stiked swyn,** stuck pig. 95. **thyn . . . cure,** care for your reputation. 101. **Lepe,** a Spanish wine center. 102. **Fisshstrete . . . Chepe,** in London's market section. 105. **fumositee,** vapors which were supposed to be able to rise from the stomach into the head. 107. **weneth,** thinks. 109. **Rochel . . . Burdeux toun,** La Rochelle, Bordeaux (French wine centers); a reference, apparently, to the practice of adulterating French wines with the cheaper Spanish varieties.

GEOFFREY CHAUCER

But herkneth, lordynges, o word, I yow preye,
That alle the sovereyn actes, dar I seye,
Of victories in the Olde Testament,
Thurgh verray God, that is omnipotent,
Were doon in abstinence and in prayere;
Looketh the Bible, and ther ye may it leere.

Looke, Attila, the grete conquerour,
Deyde in his sleep, with shame and dishonour,
Bledyng at his nose in dronkenesse.
A capitayn sholde lyve in sobrenesse. 120
And over al this, avyseth yow right wel,
What was comaunded un-to Lamwel—
Nat Samuel, but Lamwel, seye I—
Redeth the Bible, and fynd it expresly
Of wyn-yevyng to hem that han justise.
Namoore of this, for it may wel suffise.

And now that I have spoken of glotonye,
Now wol I yow defenden hasardrye.
Hasard is verray moder of lesynges,
And of deceite, and cursed forsweryinges, 130
Blaspheme of Crist, manslaughtre, and wast also
Of catel and of tyme; and forther-mo,
It is repreve and contrarie of honour
For to ben holde a commune hasardour.
And evere the hyer he is of estaat,
The moore is he holden desolat.
If that a prynce useth hasardrye,
In alle governaunce and policye
He is, as by commune opynyoun,
Yholde the lasse in reputacioun. 140

Stilbon, that was a wys embassadour,
Was sent to Corynthe, in ful gret honour,
Fro Lacedomye, to make hire alliaunce.
And whan he cam, hym happed, par chaunce,
That alle the gretteste that were of that lond,
Pleiynge atte hasard he hem fond.
For which, as soone as it myghte be,
He stal hym hoom agayn to his contree,
And seyde, "Ther wol I nat lese my name,
N'y wol nat take on me so greet defame, 150
Yow for to allie un-to none hasardours.
Sendeth othere wise embassadours;
For, by my trouthe, me were levere dye
Than I yow sholde to hasardours allye.
For ye that been so glorious in honours
Shal nat allye yow with hasardours.
As by my wyl, ne as by my tretee."
This wise philosophre, thus seyde he.

Looke eek that, to the kyng Demetrius,
The kyng of Parthes, as the book seith us, 160
Sente hym a paire of dees of gold in scorn,
For he hadde used hasard ther-biforn;
For which he heeld his glorie or his renoun
At no value or reputacioun.
Lordes may fynden oother manere pley
Honeste ynow to dryve the day awey.

Now wol I speke of oothes false and grete
A word or two, as olde bokes trete.
Greet sweryng is a thyng abhomynable,
And fals sweryng is yet moore reprevable. 170
The heighe God forbad sweryng at al,
Witnesse on Mathew; but in special
Of sweryng seith the holy Jeremye,
"Thow shalt swere sooth thyne othes, and nat lye,
And swere in doom, and eek in rightwisnesse;"
But ydel sweryng is a cursednesse.
Bihoold and se, that in the firste table
Of heighe Goddes hestes honurable,
How that the seconde heste of hym is this:
"Take nat my name in ydel or amys." 180
Lo, rather he forbedeth swich sweryng
Than homycide or many a cursed thyng;
I seye that, as by ordre, thus it standeth;
This knowen, that hise hestes understandeth,
How that the seconde heste of God is that.
And forther-over, I wol thee telle al plat,
That vengeance shal nat parten from his hous
That of hise othes is to outrageous
"By Goddes precious herte! and by his nayles!
And by the blood of Crist that is in Hayles! 190
Sevene is my chaunce, and thyn is *cynk* and *treye*!"
"By Goddes armes, if thow falsly pleye,
This daggere shal thurgh-out thyn herte go!"
This fruyt cometh of the bicched bones two,
Forsweryng, ire, falsnesse, homycide.
Now, for the love of Crist, that for us dyde,
Lete youre othes, bothe grete and smale.
But, sires, now wol I telle forth my tale.

Thise riotours thre of whiche I telle,
Longe erst er pryme rong of any belle, 200
Were set hem in a taverne to drynke,
And as they sat, they herde a belle clynke
Biforn a cors was caried to his grave.

116. Looketh, look in. **leere,** learn. **117. Attila,** Hunnish conqueror of much of Europe; died A.D. 453. **120. capitayn,** military leader. **122. Lamwel,** Lemuel. See Proverbs 31:4 ff. **128. defenden hasardrye,** forbid gambling. **129. lesynges,** lies. **131. wast,** waste. **132. catel,** property. **133. repreve,** shame. **136. desolat,** abandoned, evil. **141. Stilbon,** really Chilon. **148. stal hym,** hurried secretly. **149. lese,** lose. **150. N'y wol nat,** nor will I. **160. Parthes,** Parthians. **175. doom,** judgment. **rightwisnesse,** righteousness. **177–78. firste . . . hestes,** first half of the table (of the Ten Commandments). **181. rather,** earlier. **184. This . . . understandeth,** those who understand his commandments know this. **186. plat,** plainly. **188. to,** too. **189–193.** "**By . . . go,**" dicers' profane talk. **in Hayles,** at the abbey of Hayles, near Wichcomb in Gloucestershire. **cynk and treye!** five and three! **194. bicched,** cursed. **197. Lete,** leave off. **200. Longe . . . pryme,** long before 6 A.M. Sometimes prime was the period between 6 and 9, and even the latter hour.

That oon of hem gan callen to his knave,
"Go bet," quod he, "and axe redily,
What cors is this that passeth heer forby;
And looke that thow reporte his name wel."
　"Sire," quod this boy, "it nedeth never-a-del.
It was me told er ye cam heer two houres;
He was, pardee, an old felawe of youres; 210
And sodeynly he was yslayn to-nyght,
Fordronke, as he sat on his bench up-right.
Ther cam a pryvee theef, men clepeth Deeth,
That in this contree al the peple sleeth,
And with his spere he smoot his herte atwo,
And wente his wey with-outen wordes mo.
He hath a thousand slayn this pestilence;
And, maister, er ye come in his presence,
Me thynketh that it were necessarie
For to be war of swich an adversarie. 220
Beth redy for to meete hym evere-moore;
Thus taughte me my dame; I sey namoore."
　"By Seinte Marie," seyde this taverner,
"The child seith sooth, for he hath slayn this yer,
Henne over a myle, with-inne a greet village
Bothe man and womman, child, and hyne, and page.
I trowe his habitacioun be there.
To been avysed greet wisdom it were,
Er that he dide a man a dishonour."
　"Ye, Goddes armes!" quod this riotour, 230
"Is it swich peril with hym for to meete?
I shal hym seke by wey and eek by strete,
I make avow to Goddes digne bones!
Herkneth, felawes, we thre been al ones;
Lat ech of us holde up his hand til oother,
And ech of us bicome otheres brother,
And we wol sleen this false traytour Deeth;
He shal be slayn, he that so manye sleeth,
By Goddes dignytee, er it be nyght!"
　Togidres han thise thre hir trouthes plight, 240
To lyve and dyen ech of hem for oother,
As thogh he were his owene ybore brother.
And up they stirte al dronken, in this rage,
And forth they goon towardes that village
Of which the taverner hadde spoke biforn;
And many a grisly ooth thanne han they sworn,
And Cristes blessed body they to-rente;
Deeth shal be deed if that they may hym hente!

Whan they han goon nat fully half a myle,
Right as they wolde han treden over a stile, 250
An old man and a poure with hem mette.
This olde man ful mekely hem grette,
And seyde thus, "Now, lordes, God yow se!"
　The proudeste of thise riotours thre
Answerde agayn, "What! carl, with sory grace!
Why artow al forwrapped save thy face?
Why lyvestow so longe in so greet age?"
　This olde man gan looke in his visage,
And seyde thus, "For I ne kan nat fynde
A man, thogh that I walked in-to Inde, 260
Neither in citee ne in no village,
That wolde chaunge his youthe for myn age;
And therfore moot I han myn age stille,
As longe tyme as it is Goddes wille.
　"Ne Deeth, allas! ne wol nat han my lyf.
Thus walke I, lyk a restelees caytyf,
And on the ground, which is my modres gate,
I knokke with my staf, bothe erly and late,
And seye, 'Leeve moder, leet me in!
Lo, how I vanysshe, flessh, and blood, and skyn! 270
Allas! whan shul my bones been at reste?
Moder, with yow wolde I chaunge my cheste,
That in my chambre longe tyme hath be,
Ye, for an heyre clowt to wrappe me!'
But yet to me she wol nat do that grace,
For which ful pale and welked is my face.
　"But, sires, to yow it is no curteisye
To speken to an old man vileynye,
But he trespase in word, or elles in dede.
In holy writ ye may your self wel rede: 280
'Agayns an old man, hoor up-on his heed,
Ye sholde arise'; wherfore I yeve yow reed,
Ne dooth un-to an old man noon harm now,
Namoore than that ye wolde men dide to yow
In age, if that ye so longe abyde.
And God be with yow, wher ye go or ryde.
I moot go thider as I have to go."
　"Nay, olde cherl, by God, thow shalt nat so!"
Seyde this oother hasardour anon,
"Thow partest nat so lightly, by Seint John! 290
Thow spak right now of thilke traytour Deeth,
That in this contree alle oure freendes sleeth.
Have here my trouthe, as thow art his espye,

---

250. **wolde . . . stile,** would have climbed over a stile. 252. **grette,** greeted. 253. **se!"** see (with favor), protect. 255. **carl . . . grace!** fellow, ill luck to you! 256. **forwrapped,** wrapped about. 266. **caytyf,** wretch. 267. **modres,** mother's. 273. **be,** been. 274. **heyre clowt,** piece of haircloth. 276. **welked,** withered. 278. **vileynye,** rudeness. 279. **But,** unless. 281. **Agayns,** in the presence of. **hoor,** white-haired. 282. **yeve . . . reed,** give you counsel. 286. **wher . . . ryde,** whether you walk or ride; that is, under all circumstances. 287. **thider,** thither. 293. **espye,** spy.

205. **Go bet,** go quickly. 206. **heer forby,** past here. 208. **it . . . never-a-del,** it is not a bit necessary. 211. **to-nyght,** last night. 212. **Fordronke,** very drunken. 213. **pryvee theef,** secret criminal. 214. **sleeth,** slays. 222. **my dame,** my mother. 225. **Henne . . . myle,** over a mile hence. 226. **hyne,** hind, farm laborer. 240. **Togidres,** together. **plight,** plighted. 242. **ybore,** born. 243. **stirte,** jump. 247. **to-rente,** rent in pieces. 248. **hente,** catch.

GEOFFREY CHAUCER

Telle wher he is, or thow shalt it abye,
By God, and by the holy sacrament!
For soothly thow art oon of his assent,
To sleen us yonge folk, thow false theef!"
    "Now sires," quod he, "if that yow be so leef
To fynde Deeth, turn up this croked wey,
For in that grove I lafte hym, by my fey,   300
Under a tree, and ther he wol abyde;
Nat for youre boost he wol hym no thyng hyde.
Se ye that ook? Right ther ye shal hym fynde.
God save yow, that boghte agayn man-kynde,
And yow amende!" Thus seyde this olde man.
And everich of thise riotours ran
Til they came to that tree, and ther they founde
Of floryns fyne of gold ycoyned rounde,
Wel ny an eighte busshels, as hem thoughte.
No lenger thanne after Deeth they soughte,   310
But ech of hem so glad was of the sighte,
For that the floryns been so faire and brighte,
That doun they sette hem by this precious hoord.
The worste of hem he spak the firste word.
    "Bretheren," quod he, "taak kepe what I seye;
My wit is greet, thogh that I bourde and pleye.
This tresor hath fortune un-to us yeven,
In myrthe and jolitee oure lyf to lyven,
And lightly as it cometh, so wol we spende.
By Goddes precious dignytee, who wende   320
To-day that we sholde han so fair a grace?
But myghte this gold be caried fro this place
Hoom to myn hous, or ellis un-to youres—
For wel ye woot that al this gold is oures—
Thanne were we in heigh felicitee.
But trewely, by daye it may nat be;
Men wolde seyn that we were theves stronge,
And for oure owene tresor doon us honge.
This tresor moste ycaried be by nyghte
As wisly and as slyly as it myghte.   330
Wher-fore I rede that cut among us alle
Be drawe, and lat se wher the cut wol falle;
And he that hath the cut with herte blithe
Shal renne to toune, and that ful swithe,
And brynge us breed and wyn ful pryvely.
And two of us shul kepen subtilly
This tresor wel; and, if he wol nat tarie,
Whan it is nyght, we wol this tresor carie,
By oon assent, wher as us thynketh best."
That oon of hem the cut broghte in his fest,   340
And bad hem drawe, and looke wher it wol falle;
And it fil on the yongeste of hem alle,
And forth toward the toun he wente anon.
And also soone as that he was agon,
That oon of hem spak thus un-to that oother:
"Thow knowest wel thow art my sworn brother,
Thy profit wol I telle thee anon.
Thow woost wel that oure felawe is agon,
And heere is gold, and that ful greet plentee,
That shal departed been among us thre.   350
But nathelees, if I kan shape it so
That it departed were among us two,
Hadde I nat doon a freendes torn to thee?"
    That oother answerde, "I noot how that may be.
He woot that the gold is with us tweye;
What shal we doon? What shal we to hym seye?"
    "Shal it be conseil?" seyde the firste shrewe,
"And I shal tellen in a wordes fewe
What we shul doon, and brynge it wel aboute."
    "I graunte," quod that oother, "out of doute,   360
That, by my trouthe, I wol thee nat biwreye."
    "Now," quod the firste, "thow woost wel we be tweye,
And two of us shul strenger be than oon.
Looke whan that he is set, that right anoon
Arys, as though thow woldest with hym pleye,
And I shal ryve hym thurgh the sydes tweye
Whil that thow strogelest with hym as in game,
And with thy daggere looke thow do the same;
And thanne shal al this gold departed be,
My deere freend, bitwixe me and thee.   370
Thanne may we bothe oure lustes al fulfille,
And pleye at dees right at oure owene wille."
And thus acorded been thise shrewes tweye
To sleen the thridde, as ye han herd me seye.
    This yongeste, which that wente to the toun,
Ful ofte in herte he rolleth up and doun
The beautee of thise floryns newe and brighte.
"O Lord!" quod he, "if so were that I myghte
Have al this tresor to my-self allone,
Ther is no man that lyveth under the trone   380
Of God, that sholde lyve so myrie as I!"
And atte laste the feend, oure enemy,
Putte in his thoght that he sholde poyson beye,
With which he myghte sleen his felawes tweye;
For-why the feend foond hym in swich lyvynge
That he hadde leve hym to sorwe brynge.
For this was outrely his ful entente
To sleen hem bothe, and nevere to repente.
And forth he goth, no lenger wolde he tarie,
In to the toun, un-to a pothecarie,   390

---

294. **it abye,** suffer for it.   296. **assent,** opinion.   298. **yow . . . leef,** you desire so.   300. **fey,** faith.   308. **floryns,** coins.   316. **bourde,** jest.   317. **tresor,** treasure.   320. **wende,** would have thought.   328. **doon us honge,** cause us to be hanged.   331. **rede,** advise.   334. **swithe,** quickly.   340. **fest,** fist.

357. **conseil,** in confidence. **shrewe,** scoundrel.   361. **biwreye,** reveal, betray.   362. **tweye,** two.   366. **ryve,** thrust.   380. **trone,** throne.   382. **feend,** devil.   383. **beye,** buy.   385. **For-why . . . lyvynge,** because the fiend found him in such a manner of life.   386. **leve,** permission.   387. **outrely his,** utterly the youngest rioter's.

And preyed hym that he hym wolde selle
Som poysoun, that he myghte his rattes quelle;
And eek ther was a polcat in his hawe,
That, as he seyde, his capouns hadde yslawe,
And fayn he wolde wreke hym, if he myghte,
On vermyn that destroyed hym by nyghte.

    The pothecarie answerde, "And thow shalt have
A thyng that, also God my soule save,
In al this world ther is no creature,
That ete or dronke hath of this confiture   400
Nat but the montaunce of a corn of whete,
That he ne shal his lyf anoon forlete;
Ye, sterve he shal, and that in lasse while
Than thow wolt goon a paas nat but a myle,
The poysoun is so strong and violent."

    This cursed man hath in his hond yhent
This poysoun in a box, and sith he ran
In-to the nexte strete un-to a man,
And borwed hym large botels thre;
And in the two his poyson poured he;   410
The thridde he kepte clene for his drynke.
For al the nyght he shoop hym for to swynke
In cariyng of the gold out of that place.
And whan this riotour, with sory grace,
Hadde filled with wyn hise grete botels thre,
To hise felawes agayn repaireth he.

    What nedeth it to sermone of it moore?
For right as they hadde cast his deeth bifore,
Right so they han hym slayn, and that anon.
And whan that this was doon, thus spak that oon: 420
"Now lat us sitte and drynke, and make us merye,
And afterward we wol his body berye."
And with that word it happed hym, par cas,
To take the botel ther the poysoun was,
And drank, and yaf his felawe drynke also,
For which anon they storven bothe two.

    But, certes, I suppose that Avycen
Wroot nevere in no canon, ne in no fen,
Mo wonder signes of empoysonyng
Than hadde thise wrecches two, er hir endyng.   430
Thus ended been thise homicides two,
And eek the false empoysonere also.

    O cursed synne of alle cursednesse!
O traytours homicide, o wikkednesse!
O glotonye, luxurie, and hasardrye!
Thou blasphemour of Crist with vileynye
And othes grete, of usage and of pryde!
Allas! mankynde, how may it bityde,
That to thy Creatour, which that thee wroghte,
And with his precious herte blood the boghte,   440
Thow art so fals and so unkynde, allas!

    Now, goode men, God foryeve yow youre trespas,
And ware yow fro the synne of avarice!
Myn holy pardoun may yow alle warice,
So that ye offre nobles or sterlynges,
Or elles silver broches, spones, rynges.
Boweth youre heed under this holy bulle!
Cometh up, ye wyves, offreth of youre wolle!
Youre name I entre here in my rolle anon;
In-to the blisse of hevene shul ye gon;   450
I yow assoille, by myn heigh power,
Yow that wol offre, as clene and eek as cler
As ye were born.—And lo, sires, thus I preche.
And Jesu Crist, that is oure soules leche,
So graunte yow his pardoun to receyve,
For that is best; I wol yow nat deceyve.

    But, sires, o word forgat I in my tale:
I have relikes and pardon in my male,
As faire as any man in Engelond,
Whiche were me yeven by the Popes hond.   460
If any of yow wol, of devocioun,
Offren, and han myn absolucioun,
Com forth anon, and kneleth here adoun,
And mekely receyveth my pardoun;
Or ellis, taketh pardoun as ye wende,
Al newe and fressh, at every myles ende,
So that ye offren alwey newe and newe
Nobles or pens, whiche that been goode and trewe.
It is an honour to everich that is heer
That ye mowe have a suffisant pardoner   470
T'assoille yow, in contree as ye ryde,
For aventures whiche that may bityde.
Peraventure ther may falle oon or two
Doun of his hors, and breke his nekke atwo.
Looke which a seuretee is it to yow alle
That I am in youre felaweship yfalle,
That may assoille yow, bothe moore and lasse,
Whan that the soule shal fro the body passe.

392. **quelle**, kill. 393. **hawe**, yard. 394. **capouns**, capons. **yslawe**, been killed. 395. **fayn . . . hym**, he would be glad to avenge himself. 396. **destroyed**, disturbed. 398. **also**, as may. 400. **confiture**, concoction. 401. **montaunce**, amount. **corn**, grain. 402. **forlete**, give up. 403. **sterve**, die. **lasse while**, less time. 404. **goon a paas**, walk at a footpace. 409. **borwed**, borrowed. 412. **shoop hym**, planned. 417. **sermone**, speak. 418. **cast**, planned. 423. **par cas**, by chance. 426. **storven**, died. 427. **Avycen**, Avicenna (980–1037), Arabian authority on medicine. 428. **canon**, rule. **fen**, division of his book. 429. **Mo . . . signes**, more wonderful symptoms. 441. **unkynde**, unnatural. 443. **ware**, guard. 444. **warice**, cure. 445. **nobles . . . sterlynges**, coins of considerable value. 446. **spones**, spoons. 452. **cler**, clear of sin. 453. [What follows is the Pardoner's Epilogue. In it he speaks to his fellow pilgrims directly instead of addressing an imaginary congregation.] 454. **leche**, physician. 458. **male**, bag. 460. **Whiche . . . hond**, a lie, of course. 465. **wende**, travel. 470. **mowe**, may. **suffisant**, able. 471. **in . . . ryde**, as you ride in the country. 472. **aventures**, accidents. **bityde**, happen. 473. **Peraventure**, perhaps. 474. **of**, off. **atwo**, in two. 475. **seuretee**, insurance. 477. **moore . . . lasse**, more and less important—everyone. 478. **fro**, from.

GEOFFREY CHAUCER

I rede that oure Hoost shal bigynne,
For he is moost envoluped in synne.   480
Com forth, sire Hoost, and offre first anon,
And thow shalt kisse the relikes everychon,
Ye, for a grote! Unbokele anon thy purs."
    "Nay, nay!" quod he, "thanne have I Cristes
        curs!
Lat be," quod he, "it shal nat be, so theech!
Thow woldest make me kisse thyn olde breech,
And swere it were a relyk of a seint!" . . .

    This Pardoner answerde nat a word;
So wrooth he was, no word ne wolde he seye.
    "Now," quod oure Hoost, "I wol no lenger pleye
With thee, ne with noon oother angry man."
But right anon the worthy Knyght bigan,
Whan that he saugh that al the peple lough,
"Namoore of this, for it is right ynough.   500
Sire Pardoner, be glad and murye of cheere;
And ye, sire Hoost, that been to me so deere,
I pray yow that ye kisse the Pardoner.
And Pardoner, I pray thee, drawe thee neer,
And, as we diden, lat us laughe and pleye."
Anon they kiste, and ryden forth hir weye.

["The Shipman's Tale" (Group B continued) has no prologue, although many editions give "The Man of Law's Epilogue" (page 187) as "The Shipman's Prologue" and follow it with "The Shipman's Tale." The tale is a fabliau concerning a worldly monk, an unfaithful wife, and an unsuspecting husband. Because the lady yields only for money, she is made the victim of a neat trick.]

THE SHIPMAN'S EPILOGUE

"Wel seyd, by *corpus dominus*," quod oure Hoost,
"Now longe moote thow saille by the coost,
Sire gentil maister, gentil maryner!
God yeve the monk a thousand last quade yeer!
A ha! felawes, beth war of swich a jape!
The monk putte in the mannes hood an ape,
And in his wyves eek, by Seint Austyn!
Draweth no monkes moore in-to youre in.
    "But now passe over, and lat us seke aboute,
Who shal now telle first of al this route   10
Another tale." And with that word he sayde,
As curteisly as it hadde been a mayde,
"My lady Prioresse, by youre leve,
So that I wiste I sholde yow nat greve,
I wolde demen that ye tellen sholde
A tale next, if so were that ye wolde.
Now wol ye vouche sauf, my lady deere?"
    "Gladly," quod she, and seyde as ye shal heere.

THE PRIORESS'S PROLOGUE

Domine dominus noster
"O Lord, oure Lord, thy name how merveillous
Is in this large worlde ysprad," quod she;
"For nat oonly thy laude precious
Parfourned is by men of dignytee,
But by the mouth of children thy bountee
Parfourned is, for on the brest soukynge
Som tyme shewen they thyn heriynge.

Wher-fore in laude, as I best kan or may,
Of thee and of the white lilye flour
Which that the bar, and is a mayde alway,   10
To telle a storie I wol do my labour;
Nat that I may encressen hir honour,
For she hir-self is honour and the roote
Of bountee, next hir Sone, and soules boote.

O moder Mayde! o mayde Moder free!
O bussh unbrent, brennyng in Moyses sighte,
That ravysedest doun fro the Deitee,
Thurgh thyn humblesse, the Goost that in th' alighte,
Of whos vertu, whan he thyn herte lighte,
Conceyved was the Fadres sapience,   20
Help me to telle it in thy reverence!

Lady, thy bountee, thy magnificence,
Thy vertu, and thy grete humylitee,
Ther may no tonge expresse in no science;
For som tyme, Lady, er men praye to thee,
Thow goost biforn of thy benygnytee,
And getest us the light of thy prayere
To gyden us un-to thy Sone so deere.

My konnyng is so wayk, O blisful Queene,
For to declare thy grete worthynesse,   30
That I ne may the weighte nat sustene,
But as a child of twelf month old, or lesse,

---

479. **rede**, advise. 480. **envoluped**, enveloped. 485. **so theech!** as I hope to prosper! 499. **saugh**, saw. 506. **ryden . . . weye**, rode forth on their way. 1. **corpus dominus**, the Host's blundering Latin for "body of the Lord." 4. **thousand . . . yeer!** thousand loads of bad years. 5. **beth war**, beware. 6. **putte . . . ape**, made a fool of the man. 8. **in**, dwelling. 12. **as it**, as though he.

The Shipman's Epilogue. 15. **demen**, judge. 17. **vouche sauf**, consent. *The Prioress's Prologue.* 1. **merveillous**, marvelous. 2. **ysprad**, spread. 3. **laude**, honor. 4. **Parfourned**, completed. 5. **bountee**, kindness. 6. **on . . . soukynge**, nursing. 7. **heriynge**, praise. 10. **the**, thee. 14. **soules boote**, soul's salvation. 16. **unbrent**, unburnt. **Moyses**, Moses'. 17. **ravysedest**, drew. 18. **Goost . . . alighte**, (Holy) Ghost that alighted in you. 19. **lighte**, illuminated. 20. **sapience**, wisdom. 24. **science**, learned book. 29. **konnyng is so wayk**, ability is so weak. 31. **sustene**, sustain.

That kan unnethe any word expresse,
Right so fare I, and ther-fore I yow preye,
Gydeth my song that I shal of yow seye."

Explicit.

THE PRIORESS'S TALE

Ther was in Asye, in a greet citee,
Amonges Cristen folk, a Jewerye,
Sustened by a lord of that contree
For foul usure and lucre of vileynye,
Hateful to Crist and to his compaignye;
And thurgh this strete men myghte ryde and wende,
For it was free, and open at eyther ende.

A litel scole of Cristen folk ther stood
Doun at the ferther ende, in which ther were
Children an heep, ycomen of Cristen blood, 10
That lerned in that scole yeer by yere
Swich manere doctrine as men used there,
This is to seyn, to syngen and to rede,
As smale children doon in hir childhede.

Among thise children was a wydwes sone,
A litel clergeoun, seven yeer of age,
That day by day to scole was his wone,
And eek also, wher as he say th'ymage
Of Cristes moder, hadde he in usage,
As hym was taught, to knele adoun and seye   20
His *Ave Marie*, as he goth by the weye.

Thus hath this wydwe hir litel sone ytaught
Oure blisful Lady, Cristes moder deere,
To worshipe ay, and he forgat it naught,
For sely child wol alwey soone lere.
But ay, whan I remembre on this matere,
Seint Nicholas stant evere in my presence,
For he so yong to Crist dide reverence.

This litel child, his litel book lernynge,
As he sat in the scole at his prymer,   30
He *Alma redemptoris* herde synge,
As children lerned hir Antiphoner;
And, as he dorste, he drow hym ner and ner,
And herkned ay the wordes and the note,
Til he the firste vers koude al by rote.

Noght wiste he what this Latyn was to seye,
For he so yong and tendre was of age.
But on a day his felawe gan he preye
T'expounden hym this song in his langage,
Or telle hym why this song was in usage;   40
This preyde he hym to construen and declare
Ful ofte tyme up-on his knowes bare.

His felawe, which that elder was than he,
Answerde hym thus: "This song, I have herd seye,
Was maked of oure blisful Lady free,
Hire to salue, and eek hire for to preye
To been oure help and socour whan we deye.
I kan namoore expounde in this matere:
I lerne song, I kan but smal gramere."

"And is this song maked in reverence   50
Of Cristes moder?" seyde this innocent.
"Now, certes, I wol do my diligence
To konne it al er Cristemasse be went;
Thogh that I for my prymer shal be shent,
And shal be beten thries in an houre,
I wol it konne oure Lady for to honoure."

His felawe taughte hym homward pryvely
Fro day to day, til he koude it by rote,
And thanne he song it wel and boldely
Fro word to word, acordyng with the note.   60
Twyes a day it passed thurgh his throte,
To scoleward and homward whan he wente;
On Cristes moder set was his entente.

As I have seyd, thurgh out the Juerye,
This litel child, as he cam to and fro,
Ful murily wolde he synge, and crye
O alma Redemptoris evere mo.
The swetnesse his herte perced so
Of Cristes moder, that, to hire to preye,
He kan nat stynte of syngyng by the weye.   70

Oure firste foo, the serpent Sathanas,
That hath in Jewes herte his waspes nest,
Up swal, and seyde, "O Hebrayk peple, allas!
Is this to yow a thyng that is honest,
That swich a boy shal walken as hym lest
In youre despit, and synge of swich sentence
Which is agayns oure lawes reverence?"

The Prioress's Prologue. **33. unnethe,** scarcely. *The Prioress's Tale.* **1. Asye,** Asia. **2. Jewerye,** ghetto. **3. Sustened,** maintained. **4. usure,** lending on interest, forbidden by the medieval Church. **lucre of vileynye,** filthy lucre. **6. wende,** walk. **15. wydwes sone,** widow's son. **16. clergeoun,** pupil. **17. That . . . wone,** whose habit was to go to school day by day. **18. say,** saw. **25. sely,** innocent. **lere,** learn. **27. stant,** stands. **31. Alma redemptoris** (mater), "Dear mother of the Redeemer," opening of a hymn to the Virgin. **32. Antiphoner,** anthem book. **33. as he dorste,** as much as he dared. **ner,** nearer. **34. note,** tune. **35. koude,** knew.

36. was to seye, meant. **42. knowes,** knees. **46. salue,** salute. **47. socour,** succor. **49. kan,** know. **53. konne,** learn. **er,** before. **went,** gone. **54. shent,** reproached. **57. homward pryvely,** secretly on the way home. **68–69. The swetnesse . . . moder,** the sweetness of Christ's mother so pierced his heart. **73. swal,** swelled. **Hebrayk,** Hebrew. **74. honest,** honorable. **75. as . . . lest,** as it pleases him. **76. In youre despit,** in scorn of you. **sentence,** matter.

GEOFFREY CHAUCER

Fro thennes forth the Jewes han conspired
This innocent out of the world to chace.
An homycide ther-to han they hired, 80
That in an aleye hadde a pryvee place;
And as the child gan for-by for to pace,
This cursed Jew hym hente and heeld hym faste,
And kitte his throte, and in a pit hym caste.

I seye that in a wardrobe they hym threwe
Wher as thise Jewes purgen hir entraille.
O cursed folk of Herodes al newe,
What may youre yvel entente yow availle?
Mordre wol out, certeyn, it wol nat faille,
And namely ther as th'onour of God shal sprede, 90
The blood out crieth on youre cursed dede.

O martir, souded to virginitee,
Now maystow syngen, folwyng evere in oon
The white Lamb celestial—quod she—
Of which the grete evangelist, Seint John,
In Pathmos wroot, which seith that they that gon
Biforn this Lamb, and synge a song al newe,
That nevere, flesshly, wommen they ne knewe.

This poure wydwe awaiteth al that nyght
After hir litel child, but he cam noght; 100
For which, as soone as it was dayes lyght,
With face pale of drede and bisy thoght,
She hath at scole and elles-where hym soght,
Til fynally she gan so fer espie
That he last seyn was in the Jewerie.

With modres pitee in hir brest enclosed,
She goth, as she were half out of hir mynde,
To every place wher she hath supposed
By liklyhede hir litel child to fynde;
And evere on Cristes moder meke and kynde 110
She cryde, and at the laste thus she wroghte,
Among the cursed Jewes she hym soghte.

She frayneth and she preyeth pitously
To every Jew that dwelte in thilke place,
To telle hire if hir child wente oght forby.
They seyde, "Nay"; but Jesu, of his grace,
Yaf in hir thought, in-with a litel space,
That in that place after hir sone she cryde,
Wher he was casten in a pit bisyde.

O grete God that parfournest thy laude 120
By mouth of innocentz, lo, here thy myght!
This gemme of chastitee, this emeraude,
And eek of martirdom the ruby bright,
Ther he with throte ykorven lay upright,
He *Alma Redemptoris* gan to synge
So loude, that al the place gan to rynge.

The Cristen folk, that thurgh the strete wente,
In coomen for to wondre up-on this thyng,
And hastily they for the provost sente;
He cam anon with-outen tariyng, 130
And herieth Crist that is of hevene kyng,
And eek his moder, honour of mankynde,
And after that the Jewes leet he bynde.

This child with pitous lamentacioun
Up-taken was, syngynge his song alway,
And with honour of greet processioun
They carien hym un-to the nexte abbay.
His moder swownyng by his beere lay;
Unnethe myghte the peple that was there
This newe Rachel bryngen fro his beere. 140

With torment and with shameful deth echon
This provost dooth thise Jewes for to sterve
That of this mordre wiste, and that anon;
He nolde no swich cursednesse observe.
Yvel shal have, that yvel wol deserve;
Ther-fore with wilde hors he dide hem drawe,
And after that he heng hem by the lawe.

Up-on this beere ay lith this innocent
Biforn the chief auter, whil the masse laste,
And after that, the abbot with his covent 150
Han sped hem for to burien hym ful faste;
And whan they holy water on hym caste,
Yet spak this child, whan spreynd was holy water,
And song *O alma Redemptoris mater!*

This abbot, which that was an holy man
As monkes ben, or elles oghten be,
This yonge child to conjure he bigan,
And seyde, "O deere child, I halsen thee,
In vertu of the holy Trinitee,

83. **hente**, seized. 84. **kitte**, cut. 85. **wardrobe**, privy. 87. **of Herodes al newe**, (composed) of new Herods. 89. **Mordre wol out**, a proverb. 90. **And . . . sprede**, and especially where the honor of God will be spread by its discovery. 92. **souded to**, confirmed in. 93. **evere in oon**, always the same. 96. **Pathmos**, Patmos, where St. John wrote Revelation. 98. **flesshly**, carnally. 104. **espie**, discover. 109. **liklyhede**, likelihood. 113. **frayneth**, asks. 117. **Yaf . . . thought**, put it into her thought. 124. **ykorven**, cut. **upright**, face up. 128. **coomen**, came. 129. **provost**, magistrate. 131. **herieth**, praises. 133. **leet he bynde**, caused to be bound. 137. **nexte**, nearest. 138. **swownyng**, swooning. **beere**, bier. 141. **torment**, torture. **echon**, each one. 142. **dooth . . . sterve**, causes to die. 144. **observe**, favor. 146. **with . . . drawe**, he had each one tied to the tail of a wild horse and dragged (to the gallows). 147. **heng . . . by**, hanged them according to. 148. **ay lith**, still lies. 149. **auter**, altar. 150. **covent**, monastery; "convent" was not synonymous with "nunnery" in the Middle Ages. 153. **spreynd**, sprinkled. 157. **conjure**, beseech. 158. **halsen**, implore.

Tel me what is thy cause for to synge,   160
Sith that thy throte is kit, to my semynge?"

"My throte is kit un-to my nekke boon,"
Seyde this child, "and, as by wey of kynde,
I sholde have dyed, ye, longe tyme agoon,
But Jesu Crist, as ye in bokes fynde,
Wol that his glorie laste and be in mynde,
And for the worship of his moder deere
Yet may I synge *O alma* loude and clere.

"This welle of mercy, Cristes moder swete,
I loved alwey, as after my konnynge;   170
And whan that I my lyf sholde forlete,
To me she cam, and bad me for to synge
This anteme verraily in my deiynge,
As ye han herd, and whan that I had songe,
Me thoughte she leyde a greyn up-on my tonge.

"Wher-fore I synge, and synge moot certeyn,
In honour of that blisful Mayden free,
Til fro my tonge of-taken is the greyn;
And after that thus seyde she to me:
'My litel child, now wol I fecche thee,   180
Whan that the greyn is fro thy tonge ytake;
Be nat agast, I wol thee nat forsake.' "

This holy monk, this abbot, hym mene I,
His tonge out-caughte, and took awey the greyn,
And he yaf up the goost ful softely.
And whan this abbot hadde this wonder seyn,
His salte teerys trikled doun as reyn,
And gruf he fil al plat up-on the grounde,
And stille he lay as he hadde been ybounde.

The covent eek lay on the pavement   190
Wepynge, and heryinge Cristes moder deere,
And after that they ryse, and forth been went,
And toke awey this martir from his beere,
And in a tombe of marbilstones cleere
Enclosen they this litel body swete.
Ther he is now, God leve us for to meete!

O yonge Hugh of Lyncoln, slayn also,
With cursed Jewes, as it is notable,
For it is but a litel while ago,
Preye eek for us, we synful folk unstable,   200

That, of his mercy, God so merciable
On us his grete mercy multiplie,
For reverence of his moder Marie. *Amen.*

THE PROLOGUE TO SIR THOPAS

Whan seyd was al this myracle, every man
As sobre was that wonder was to se,
Til that oure Hoost japen to bigan,
And thanne at erst he looked up-on me,
And seyde thus, "What man artow?" quod he;
"Thow lookest as thow woldest fynde an hare,
For evere up-on the ground I se thee stare.

"Approche neer, and looke up myrily.
Now war yow, sires, and lat this man have place!
He in the wast is shape as wel as I;   10
This were a popet in an arm t'enbrace
For any womman, smal and fair of face!
He semeth elvyssh by his contenaunce,
For un-to no wight dooth he daliaunce.

"Sey now som-what, syn oother folk han sayd;
Telle us a tale of myrthe, and that anon."
"Hoost," quod I, "ne beth nat yvele apayd,
For oother tale certes kan I noon,
But of a rym I lerned longe agoon."
"Ye, that is good," quod he, "now shul we heere   20
Som deyntee thyng, me thynketh by his cheere."

["Sir Thopas" is certainly a burlesque of the absurdities of inferior metrical romances, and has been represented as being also a satire on the aristocratic aspirations of Flemish burghers. The hero does all the correct things incorrectly, but scarcely gets started on his adventures when the Host rudely interrupts.]

THE PROLOGUE TO MELIBEE

"Namoore of this, for Goddes dignytee,"
Quod oure Hoost, "for thow makest me
So wery of thy verray lewednesse
That, also wisly God my soule blesse,
Myne erys aken of thy drasty speche.
Now swich a rym the devel I biteche!
This may wel be rym dogerel," quod he.

201. **merciable,** merciful.   *The Prologue to Sir Thopas.* 1. **myracle,** the technical name for "The Prioress's Tale," a miracle of Our Lady. 8. **myrily,** merrily. 9. **war yow,** take heed. 10. **He in . . . I,** he is as well shaped in the waist (girth) as I. Chaucer and the Host were both stout. 11. **popet,** doll (ironic). **t'enbrace,** to embrace. 13. **elvyssh,** elflike, aloof. 14. **For . . . daliaunce,** for he chats with no one. 15. **syn,** since. 17. **ne . . . apayd,** do not be displeased. 19. **rym,** rhyme. 21. **deyntee,** especially good.   *The Prologue to Melibee.* 3. **wery,** weary. **lewednesse,** ignorance. 4. **also . . . blesse,** as surely as I trust that God will bless my soul. 5. **Myne . . . speche,** my ears ache with your worthless talk. 6. **the devel I biteche!** I commit to the devil.

163. **as . . . kynde,** according to the law of nature. 170. **as . . . konnynge,** according to my knowledge. 171. **forlete,** give up. 172. **cam,** came. 173. **anteme,** anthem. 175. **greyn,** perhaps a pearl, symbol of the Virgin. 182. **agast,** frightened. 188. **gruf . . . plat,** face down he fell all flat. 192. **been went,** have gone. 196. **leve,** permit. 197. **Hugh,** victim of a similar crime said to have been perpetrated in Lincoln, England, in 1255.

GEOFFREY CHAUCER

"Why so?" quod I, "why wiltow lette me
Moore of my tale than another man,
Syn that it is the beste rym I kan?"　　　　10
"By God," quod he, "for pleynly, at o word,
Thy drasty rymyng is nat worth a tord!
Thow doost noght ellis but despendest tyme;
Sire, at o word, thow shalt no lenger ryme.
Lat se wher thow kanst tellen aught in geste,
Or telle in prose somwhat at the leeste,
In which ther be som myrthe or som doctryne."
"Gladly," quod I, "by Goddes swete pyne,
I wol yow telle a litel thyng in prose
That oghte liken yow, as I suppose,　　　　20
Or elles, certes, ye be to daungerous.
It is a moral tale vertuous,
Al be it toold som tyme in sondry wise
Of sondry folk, as I shal yow devyse.

"As thus, ye woot that euery evaungelist,
That telleth us the peyne of Jesu Crist,
Ne seith nat alle thyng as his felawe dooth,
But nathelees hir sentence is al sooth,
And alle acorden as in hir sentence,
Al be ther in hir tellyng difference.　　　　30
For somme of hem seyn moore, and somme seyn lesse,
Whan they his pitous passioun expresse—
I mene of Mark, Mathew, Luk, and John—
But doutelees hir sentence is al oon.

"Ther-fore, lordynges alle, I yow biseche,
If that ye thynke I varie as in my speche,
As thus, thogh that I telle somwhat moore
Of proverbes, than ye han herd bifore
Comprehended in this litel tretys heere,
To enforcen with th'effect of my matere,　　　　40
And thogh I nat the same wordes seye
As ye han herd, yet to yow alle I preye
Blameth me nat; for as in my sentence
Shul ye nowher fynden difference
Fro the sentence of this tretys lite
After the which this myrie tale I write.
And ther-fore herkneth what that I shal seye,
And lat me tellen al my tale, I preye."

["Melibee" is a long moral tale in prose inculcating the virtue of prudence. The grievously wronged husband is dissuaded from hasty vengeance by his wife, whose counsels bring about a conclusion satisfactory to all the characters.]

8. **wiltow lette,** will you hinder. 13. **despendest,** waste. 15. **wher,** whether. **geste,** unrhymed alliterative verse. 18. **swete pyne,** sweet (in its results for humanity) Passion. 20. **liken,** please. 21. **daungerous,** hard to please. 28. **sentence,** meaning. **sooth,** truth. 29. **acorden,** agree. 39. **tretys,** treatise. 45. **lite,** little.

THE MONK'S PROLOGUE

Whan ended was my tale of Melibee,
And of Prudence and hire benygnytee,
Oure Hoost seyde, "As I am feithful man,
And by that precious *corpus* Madrian,
I hadde levere than a barel ale
That Goodelief, my wyf, hadde herd this tale!
For she nys no thyng of swich pacience
As was this Melibeus wyf Prudence.
By Goddes bones! whan I bete my knaves,
She bryngeth me the grete clobbed staves,　　　　10
And crieth, 'Slee the dogges everichon,
And breke hem, bothe bak and every bon!'

"And if that any neighebore of myne
Wol nat in chirche to my wyf enclyne,
Or be so hardy to hire to trespace,
Whan she cometh hoom, she raumpeth in my face,
And crieth, 'False coward, wrek thy wyf!
By *corpus* bones, I wol have thy knyf,
And thow shalt have my distaf and go spynne!'
Fro day to nyght right thus she wol bigynne:　　　　20
'Allas!' she seith, 'that evere I was shape
To wedden a milksop, or a coward ape,
That wol been overlad with every wight!
Thow darst nat stonden by thy wyves right!'

"This is my lif, but if that I wol fighte;
And out at dore anon I moot me dighte,
Or elles I am but lost, but if that I
Be lyk a wilde leoun, fool hardy.
I woot wel she wol do me sle som day
Som neighebore, and thanne go my way;　　　　30
For I am perilous with knyf in honde,
Al be it that I dar nat hire withstonde,
For she is big in armes, by my feith,
That shal he fynde that hire mysdooth or seith.
But lat us passe awey fro this matere.

"My lord the Monk," quod he, "be myrie of cheere,
For ye shul telle a tale trewely.
Lo, Rouchestre stant heer faste by!
Ryd forth, myn owene lord, brek nat oure game;
But, by my trouthe, I knowe nat youre name.　　　　40
Wher shal I calle yow, my lord Daun John,

2. **benygnytee,** magnanimity. 3. **feithful man,** a Christian. 4. **corpus Madrian,** body of Madrian, an unknown saint; probably an invention of the Host. 5. **I . . . ale,** I had rather than have a barrel of ale. 9. **bete my knaves,** beat my menservants. 10. **grete . . . staves,** great club-shaped cudgels. 14. **enclyne,** bow. 15. **to . . . trespace,** to do her a (real or fancied) wrong. 16. **raumpeth . . . face,** flies in my face. 17. **wrek,** avenge. 21. **shape,** created. 23. **overlad,** put upon. 26. **dighte,** hasten. 29. **do me sle,** cause me to slay. 30. **go my way,** flee. 34. **hire . . . seith,** acts or speaks contrary to her wishes. 38. **Rouchestre . . . by!** Rochester stands here just beside us.

Or Daun Thomas, or elles Daun Albon?
Of what hous be ye, by youre fader kyn?
I vow to God, thow hast a ful fair skyn;
It is a gentil pasture ther thow goost;
Thow art nat lyk a penaunt or a goost,
Up-on my feith, thow art som officer,
Som worthy sexteyn, or som celerer,
For by my fader soule, as to my doom,
Thow art a maister whan thou art at hom;   50
No poure cloistrer, ne no novys,
But a governour, wily and wys.
And ther-with-al of brawnes and of bones,
A wel farynge persone for the nones.
I prey to God yeve hym confusioun
That first thee broghte un-to religioun! . . .

Allas, why werestow so wyd a cope?   61
God yeue me sorwe, but, and I were a pope,
Nat oonly thow, but every myghty man,
Thogh he were shore ful hye up-on his pan,
Sholde have a wyf; for al the world is lorn!   65
Religioun hath take up al the corn. . . .

But be nat wrooth, my lord, thogh that I pleye,   75
Ful ofte in game a sooth I have herd seye!"
    This worthy monk took al in pacience,
And seyde, "I wol doon al my diligence,
As fer as sowneth in to honestee,
To telle yow a tale, or two, or three.   80
And if yow list to herkne hiderward,
I wol yow seyn the lyf of Seint Edward;
Or ellis, first, tragedies wol I telle,
Of which I have an hundred in my celle.
    Tragedie is to seyn a certeyn storie,
As olde bokes maken us memorie,
Of hym that stood in greet prosperitee,
And is yfallen out of heigh degree
In-to myserie, and endeth wrecchedly.
And they been versified comunly   90
Of sixe feet, whiche men clepen *exametron*.
In prose eek been endited many oon,
And eek in metre, in many a sondry wise.
Lo, this declaryng oghte ynogh suffise.

"Now herkneth, if yow liketh for to heere.
But first I yow biseke in this matere,
Though I by ordre telle nat thise thynges,
Be it of popes, emperours, or kynges,
After hir ages, as men writen fynde,
But telle hem som bifore and som bihynde;   100
As it now cometh to my remembraunce,
Have me excused of myn ignoraunce."

["The Monk's Tale," derived primarily from Boccaccio's Latin work, *Concerning the Falls of Illustrious Men and Women*, is a collection of short "tragedies" as defined by the Monk in his Prologue. The seventeen unhappy subjects range from Lucifer and Adam to Alexander the Great and Julius Caesar, and from them to Ugolino of Pisa (died 1289), whose story is taken from Dante's *Inferno*, and three contemporaries of Chaucer.]

THE NUN'S PRIEST'S PROLOGUE

    "Ho!" quod the Knyght, "good sire, namoore of this!
That ye han seyd is right ynow, ywis,
And muchel moore; for litel hevynesse
Is right ynow to muche folk, I gesse.
I seye for me, it is a greet disese,
Wher-as men han been in greet welthe and ese,
To heeren of hir sodeyn fal, allas!
And the contrarie is joye and greet solas,
As whan a man hath been in poure estaat,
And clymbeth up, and wexeth fortunat,   10
And ther abideth in prosperitee;
Swich thyng is gladsom, as it thynketh me,
And of swich thyng were goodly for to telle."
    "Ye," quod oure Hoost, "by Seint Poules belle!
Ye seye right sooth; this Monk, he clappeth loude.
He spak how Fortune covered with a cloude—
I noot nevere what; and also of a tragedie
Right now ye herde, and, pardee, no remedie
It is for to biwaille ne compleyne
That that is doon, and als it is a peyne,   20
As ye han seyd, to heere of hevynesse.
    "Sir Monk, namoore of this, so God yow blesse!
Youre tale anoyeth al this compaignye.
Swich talkyng is nat worth a boterflye,
For ther-inne is ther no desport ne game.
    "Wher-fore, sire Monk, Daun Piers by youre name,
I prey yow hertely telle us som-what elles,

---

43. **hous**, monastery. 44. **ful**, very. 45. **It is . . . goost**, you feed well where you live. 46. **penaunt**, fasting penitent. **goost**, ghost. 48. **sexteyn**, sacristan, superintendent of buildings and equipment. **celerer**, superintendent of kitchen and cellar, and their provisioning. 49. **as to my doom**, in my judgment. 51. **poure cloistrer**, poor dweller in a cloister. **novys**, novice, probationer in a monastery. 52. **wys**, wise. 53. **brawnes**, muscles. 54. **wel . . . nones**, well-conditioned person; especially. 56. **religioun**, the monastic life. 61. **werestow**, do you wear. **cope**, cloak. 64. **shore . . . pan**, shorn very high on his skull—tonsured. 65. **lorn!** wasted. 79. **sowneth . . . honestee**, tends toward honor. 91. **exametron**, hexameter.

96. **biseke**, beseech. 2. **right ynow**, true enough. 3. **muchel moore**, much more than enough. **hevynesse**, sorrow. 4. **right ynow**, certainly enough. 5. **disese**, unpleasantness. 7. **sodeyn**, sudden. 8. **solas**, comfort. 10. **wexeth**, becomes. 12. **thynketh me**, seems to me. 14. **Seint Poules**, St. Paul's Cathedral, London. 17. **noot**, know not. 20. **als**, also. 23. **anoyeth**, bores.

For sikerly, nere clynkyng of youre belles,
That on youre bridel hange on every syde,
By hevene Kyng, that for us alle dyde, 30
I sholde er this have fallen doun for sleep,
Al-thogh the slough hadde nevere ben so deep;
Thanne hadde youre tale al be toold in veyn:
For certeynly, as that thise clerkes seyn,
Where-as a man may have noon audience,
Noght helpeth it to tellen his sentence.
And wel I woot the substaunce is in me,
If any thyng shal wel reported be.
Sire, sey som-what of huntyng, I yow preye." 39
"Nay," quod this Monk, "I have no lust to pleye.
Now lat another telle, as I have toold."
   Thanne spak oure Hoost with rude speche and boold,
And seyde un-to the Nonnes Preest anon,
"Com neer, thow preest, com hider, thow sire John,
Telle us swich thyng as may oure hertes glade.
Be blithe, though thow ryde up-on a jade.
What though thyn hors be bothe foul and lene,
If he wol serve thee, rekke nat a bene!
Looke that thyn herte be murye evere-mo."
   "Yis, sire," quod he, "yis, Hoost, so mote I go, 50
But I be murye, ywis, I wol be blamed."
And right anon his tale he hath attamed,
And thus he seyde un-to us everichon,
This sweete preest, this goodly man, sire John.

THE NUN'S PRIEST'S TALE

   A poure widwe, somdel stape in age,
Was whilom dwellynge in a narwe cotage,
Biside a grove, stondyng in a dale.
This widwe, of which I telle yow my tale,
Syn thilke day that she was last a wyf,
In pacience ladde a ful symple lyf,
For litel was hire catel and hire rente.
By housbondrye of swich as God hire sente
She foond hire-self, and eek hire doghtren two.
Thre large sowes hadde she, and namo, 10
Thre kyn, and eek a sheep that highte Malle.
Ful sooty was hire bour, and eek hire halle,
In which she eet ful many a sklendre meel.

Of poynaunt sauce hir neded never a deel.
No deyntee morsel passed thurgh hir throte;
Hir diete was acordant to hir cote.
Repleccioun ne made hire nevere syk;
Attempree diete was al hir phisyk,
And excercise, and hertes suffisaunce.
The goute lette hire no-thyng for to daunce, 20
N'apoplexie shente nat hir heed
No wyn ne drank she, neither whit ne reed;
Hir bord was served moost with whit and blak,
Milk and broun breed, in which she foond no lak,
Seynd bacoun, and som-tyme an ey or tweye,
For she was, as it were, a maner deye.
   A yeerd she hadde, enclosed al aboute
With stikkes, and a drye dych with-oute,
In which she hadde a cok, heet Chauntecleer;
In al the land of crowyng nas his peer. 30
His voys was murier than the myrie orgon
On massedayes that in the chirche gon.
Wel sikerer was his crowyng in his logge
Than is a clokke or any abbey orlogge.
By nature he knew ech ascensioun
Of the equinoxial in thilke toun;
For whan degrees fiftene were ascended,
Thanne krew he, that it myghte nat ben **amended**.
His comb was redder than the fyn coral,
And batailled as it were a castel wal. 40
His byle was blak, and as the jeet it shoon;
Lyk asure were hise legges and his toon;
Hise nayles whitter than the lylye flour,
And lyk the burned gold was his colour.
This gentil cok hadde in his governaunce
Sevene hennes for to doon al his plesaunce,
Whiche were hise sustres and his paramours,
And wonder lyke to hym as of colours;
Of whiche the faireste hewed on hire throte
Was cleped faire damoysele Pertelote. 50
Curteys she was, discreet, and debonaire,
And compaignable, and bar hir-self so faire,
Syn thilke day that she was seven nyght oold,
That trewely she hath the herte in hoold

---

28. **nere**, were it not for. 30. **hevene Kyng**, the king of heaven. **dyde**, died. 32. **slough**, mud, mire. 36. **sentence**, matter. 37. **substaunce**, basis, foundation; that is, only by the Host can any tale be reported and judged. 46. **jade**, poor nag. 47. **foul and lene**, ugly and lean. 48. **rekke . . . bene!** care less than the worth of a bean. 50. **so . . . go**, as I hope to continue to be able to walk. 52. **attamed**, commenced. 1. **stape**, advanced. 2. **narwe**, small. 3. **dale**, valley. 7. **catel**, property. **rente**, income. 9. **foond**, provided for. **doghtren**, daughters. 11. **kyn**, cows. 12. **bour**, bower, women's apartments. **halle**, great hall (ironic, since the widow lived in a one-room cottage). 13. **sklendre meel**, skimpy meal.
14. **poynaunt**, sharp. **hir . . . deel**, she never needed a bit. 16. **acordant . . . cote**, suitable to her cottage. 17. **Repleccioun**, overeating. 18. **Attempree**, temperate. **phisyk**, medicine. 19. **hertes suffisaunce**, a satisfied heart. 20. **goute lette**, gout hindered. 21. **shente**, harmed. 25. **Seynd**, broiled. **ey**, egg. 26. **maner deye**, kind of dairywoman. 27. **yeerd**, yard. 28. **stikkes**, paling fence. **with-oute**, surrounding the fence. 29. **cok, heet**, rooster, called. 30. **peer**, equal. 31–32. **orgon . . . gon**, organs . . . that are played. 33. **sikerer**, more accurate. 34. **orlogge**, clock. 35. **By nature.** The Middle Ages believed that roosters could tell time by instinct as well as men did by the heavenly bodies. 38. **that . . . amended**, so that it might not be improved. 40. **batailled . . . wal**, notched like the battlements on a castle wall. 41. **byle**, bill. **jeet**, jet. 42. **toon**, toes. 47. **paramours**, sweethearts. 52. **compaignable**, companionable. 54. **in hoold**, in her hold.

Of Chauntecleer, loken in every lith;
He loved hire so that wel was hym ther-with.
But swich a joye was it to here hem synge,
Whan that the brighte sonne gan to sprynge,
In swete acord, "My leef is faren in londe!"
For thilke tyme, as I have understonde,   60
Beestes and briddes koude speke and synge.

    And so bifel, that in a dawenynge,
As Chauntecleer among hise wyves alle
Sat on his perche, that was in the halle,
And next hym sat this faire Pertelote,
This Chauntecleer gan gronen in his throte,
As man that in his dreem is drecched soore.

    And whan that Pertelote thus herde hym rore,
She was agast, and seyde, "Herte deere,
What eyleth yow, to grone in this manere?   70
Ye ben a verray slepere, fy, for shame!"

    And he answerde, and seyde thus, "Madame,
I prey yow that ye take it nat agrief.
By God, me mette I was in swich meschief
Right now, that yet myn herte is soore afright.
Now God," quod he, "my swevene recche aright,
And kepe my body out of foul prisoun!
Me mette how that I romed up and doun
With-inne oure yeerd, where-as I say a beest
Was lyk an hound, and wolde han maad areest   80
Up-on my body, and han had me deed.
His colour was bitwixe yelow and reed,
And tipped was his tayl and bothe hise erys
With blak, unlik the remenaunt of hise herys,
His snowte smal, with glowyng eyen tweye.
Yet of his look for fere almoost I deye;
This caused me my gronyng, doutelees."

    "Avoy!" quod she, "fy on yow, hertelees!
Allas!" quod she, "for by that God above,
Now han ye lost myn herte and al my love!   90
I kan nat love a coward, by my feith!
For, certes, what so any womman seith,
We alle desiren, if it myghte be,
To han housbondes hardy, wise, and fre,
And secree, and no nygard, ne no fool,
Ne hym that is agast of every tool,
Ne noon avauntour, by that God above!
How dorste ye seyn, for shame, un-to youre love
That any thyng myghte make yow aferd?
Have ye no mannes herte, and han a berd?   100

    "Allas! and konne ye ben agast of swevenys?
No thyng, God woot, but vanytee in swevene is.
Swevenes engendren of replexions,
And ofte of fume, and of complexions,
Whan humours ben to habundant in a wight.

    "Certes this dreem which ye han met to-nyght,
Comth of the grete superfluytee
Of youre rede colera, pardee,
Which causeth folk to dreden in hir dremes
Of arwes, and of fyr with rede lemes,   110
Of rede bestes, that they wol hem byte,
Of contek, and of whelpes grete and lyte;
Right as the humour of malencolie
Causeth ful many a man in sleep to crie
For fere of blake beres, or boles blake,
Or elles blake develes wol hem take.

    "Of othere humours koude I telle also,
That werken many a man in sleep ful wo;
But I wol passe as lightly as I kan.

    "Lo Catoun, which that was so wys a man,   120
Seyde he nat, thus, 'Ne do no fors of dremes?'

    "Now sire," quod she, "whan we fle fro the bemes,
For Goddes love, as taak some laxatif;
Up peril of my soule and of my lif,
I conseille yow the beste, I wol nat lye,
That bothe of colere and of malencolye
Ye purge yow; and for ye shal nat tarye,
Thogh in this toun is noon apothecarye,
I shal my-self to herbes techen yow,   129
That shul ben for youre heele and for youre prow;
And in oure yerd tho herbes shal I fynde
The whiche han of hire propretee, by kynde,
To purge yow bynethe and eek above.
Foryet nat this, for Goddes owene love!
Ye ben ful colerik of complexioun.
Ware the sonne in his ascensioun
Ne fynde yow nat replet of humours hote;
And if it do, I dar wel leye a grote,

    55. loken . . . lith, locked in every limb.   **58. sprynge,** rise.   **59. "My . . . londe!"** "My beloved has gone to the country."   **64. halle.** The chicken roost was inside the widow's cottage.   **67. drecched soore,** sorely troubled.   **71. verray,** out-and-out.   **74. me mette,** I dreamed.   **76. swevene . . . aright,** interpret my dream fortunately.   **79. say,** saw.   **80–81. maad . . . deed,** seized my body and killed me.   **83. erys,** ears.   **84. remenaunt,** rest.   **88. "Avoy!"** "Fie!"   **hertelees!** faint-hearted.   **94. fre,** generous.   **95. secree,** opposite of **avauntour,** boaster, l. 97.   **nygard,** stingy person.   **96. agast . . . tool,** afraid of every weapon.

    99. aferd, afraid.   **103. replexions,** overeating.   **104. fume.** See note on "fumositee," page 198.   **105. humours.** According to classical and later medical theory, the four humours were four fluids (blood, phlegm, bile, black bile), the relative proportions of which in a person's body determined his "complexion" or temperament as sanguine, phlegmatic, choleric, or melancholy.   **to habundant,** too plentiful.   **106. Certes,** certainly.   **met to-nyght,** dreamed last night.   **108. rede colera,** red bile, as opposed to black.   **110. lemes,** flames.   **111. bestes,** beasts.   **112. contek,** strife.   **113. malencolie,** black bile.   **115. beres,** bears.   **boles,** bulls.   **120. Lo Catoun,** the so-called Dionysius Cato, supposed author of a collection of wise sayings popular in the Middle Ages and the Renaissance.   **121. Ne . . . of,** pay no attention to.   **122. fle fro,** fly from.   **124. Up,** upon.   **126. colere,** bile.   **127. for,** in order that.   **129. to . . . yow,** to teach you concerning herbs.   **132. propretee, by kynde,** function, naturally.   **136. Ware,** beware lest.

That ye shul have a fevere terciane,
Or an agu, that may be youre bane.   140
A day or two ye shul have digestyves
Of wormes, er ye take youre laxatyves
Of lauriol, centaure, and fumetere,
Or elles of ellebor, that groweth there,
Of katapuce, or of gaitrys beryis,
Of herbe yve, growyng in oure yerd, ther merye is;
Pekke hem up right as they growe and ete hem in.
Be myrie, housbonde, for youre fader kyn!
Dredeth no dreem, I kan sey yow namoore."

"Madame," quod he, "graunt mercy of youre
 loore.   150
But nathelees, as touchyng Daun Catoun,
That hath of wisdom swich a gret renoun,
Thogh that he bad no dremes for to drede,
By God, men may in olde bokes rede
Of many a man, moore of auctoritee
Than evere Catoun was, so mote I thee,
That al the revers seyn of his sentence,
And han wel founden by experience
That dremes ben significaciouns
As wel of joye as of tribulaciouns   160
That folk enduren in this lyf present.
Ther nedeth make of this noon argument:
The verray preeve sheweth it in dede.

"Oon of the gretteste auctor that man rede
Seith thus, that whilom two felawes wente
On pilgrymage, in a ful good entente;
And happed so, they coomen in a toun,
Where as ther was swich congregacioun
Of peple, and eek so streit of herbergage,
That they ne founde as muche as a cotage   170
In which they bothe myghte ylogged be.
Wherfore they mosten of necessitee,
As for that nyght, departen compaignye;
And ech of hem gooth to his hostelrye,
And took his loggyng as it wolde falle.
That oon of hem was logged in a stalle,
Fer in a yeerd, with oxen of the plough,
That oother man was logged wel ynough,
As was his aventure or his fortune,
That us governeth alle as in commune.   180

"And so bifel that, longe er it were day,
This man mette in his bed, ther as he lay,
How that his felawe gan up-on hym calle,
And seyde, 'Allas! for in an oxes stalle
This nyght I shal be mordred ther I lye.
Now help me, deere brother or I dye!
In alle haste com to me!' he sayde.

"This man out of his sleep for feere abrayde;
But whan that he was wakned of his sleep,
He turned hym, and took of this no keep.   190
Hym thoughte his dreem nas but a vanytee.
Thus twies in his slepyng dremed he.
And atte thridde tyme yet his felawe
Cam, as hym thoughte, and seyde, 'I am now
 slawe!
Bihoold my blody woundes, depe and wyde!
Arys up erly in the morwe tyde,
And at the west gate of the toun,' quod he,
'A carte ful of donge ther shaltow se,
In which my body is hid ful pryvely;
Do thilke carte aresten boldely.   200
My gold caused my mordre, sooth to seyn.'
And tolde hym every poynt how he was slayn,
With a ful pitous face, pale of hewe.
And truste wel, his dreem he fond ful trewe,
For on the morwe, as soone as it was day,
To his felawes in he took the way;
And whan that he cam to this oxes stalle,
After his felawe he bigan to calle.

"The hostiler answerde hym anon,
And seyde, 'Sire, youre felawe is agon;   210
As soone as day he wente out of the toun.'

"This man gan fallen in suspecioun,
Remembrynge on hise dremes that he mette,
And forth he gooth, no lenger wolde he lette,
Unto the west gate of the toun, and fond
A dong-carte, wente as it were to donge lond,
That was arrayed in the same wise
As ye han herd the dede man devyse.
And with an hardy herte he gan to crye
Vengeaunce and justice of this felonye: 220
'My felawe mordred is this same nyght,
And in this carte heere he lyth gapyng upright.
I crye out on the mynystres,' quod he,
'That sholden kepe and reulen this citee.
Harrow! allas! heere lith my felawe slayn!'
What sholde I moore un-to this tale sayn?
The peple out sterte, and caste the cart to
 grounde,

---

139. fevere terciane, fever striking every third (alternate) day. **140. agu**, ague. **bane**, death. **142. wormes**, not henyard lore: earthworms mashed up with wine or oil were prescribed for tertian fever from ancient Greek times to Chaucer's day. **144-46. ellebor . . . yve**, common medieval medicinal herbs with purging properties. **150. graunt . . . loore**, thank you very much for your learning. **151. nathelees**, nonetheless. **156. so . . . thee**, as I hope to prosper. **157. revers seyn**, opposites say. **sentence**, opinion. **169. streit**, inadequate. **173. departen**, part. **179. aventure**, chance. **182. mette**, dreamed.

186. or, before. **188. abrayde**, started up. **190. took . . . keep**, paid no attention to this. **194. slawe!** slain. **196. Arys**, arise. **morwe tyde**, morning. **198. donge**, manure. **200. Do . . . boldely**, boldly cause this cart to be stopped. **206. in**, lodging. **214. lette**, tarry. **215. fond**, found. **216. wente . . . lond**, that was going, as it seemed, to spread manure on a field. **218. devyse**, describe. **222. upright**, face up. **223. mynystres**, administrators of justice.

And in the myddel of the dong they founde
The dede man, that mordred was al newe.

   "O blisful God, that art so just and trewe,   230
Lo, how that thow biwreyest mordre alway!
Mordre wol out, that se we day by day.
Mordre is so wlatsom and abhomynable
To God, that is so just and resonable,
That he ne wol nat suffre it heled be;
Though it abyde a yeer, or two, or thre,
Mordre wol out, this is my conclusioun.
And right anon ministres of that toun
Han hent the cartere, and so soore hym pyned,
And eek the hostiler so soore engyned,   240
That they biknewe hir wikkednesse anon,
And were an-hanged by the nekke bon.

   "Heere may men seen that dremes ben to drede.
And, certes, in the same book I rede,
Right in the nexte chapitre after this—
I gabbe nat so have I joye or blys—
"Two men that wolde han passed over see,
For certeyn cause, in-to a fer contree,
If that the wynd ne hadde ben contrarie,
That made hem in a citee for to tarie,   250
That stood ful myrie up-on an haven syde.
But on a day, agayn the even-tyde.
The wynd gan chaunge, and blew right as hem leste.
Jolif and glad they wente un-to reste,
And casten hem ful erly for to saille.

   "But herkneth, to that o man fil a greet mervaille:
That oon of hem, in slepyng as he lay,
Hym mette a wonder dreem, agayn the day;
Hym thoughte a man stood by his beddes syde,
And hym comanded that he sholde abyde,   260
And seyde hym thus, 'If thow tomorwe wende,
Thow shalt be dreynt; my tale is at an ende.'

   "He wook, and tolde his felawe what he mette,
And preyde hym his viage to lette;
As for that day, he preyde hym to abyde.

   "His felawe, that lay by his beddes syde,
Gan for to laughe, and scorned hym ful faste.
'No dreem,' quod he, 'may so myn herte agaste
That I wol lette for to do my thynges,
I sette nat a straw by thy dremynges,   270
For swevenes ben but vanytees and japes.

Men dreme alday of owles and of apes,
And of many a maze ther-with-al;
Men dreme of thyng that nevere was ne shal.
But sith I see that thow wolt here abyde,
And thus forslewthen wilfully thy tyde,
God woot, it reweth me; and have good day.'
And thus he took his leve, and wente his way.
But er that he hadde half his cours yseyled,
Noot I nat why, ne what meschaunce it eyled,   280
But casuelly the shippes botme rente,
And ship and man under the water wente
In sighte of othere shippes it bisyde,
That with hem seyled at the same tyde.
And therfore, faire Pertelote so deere,
By swiche ensamples olde maystow leere
That no man sholde been to recchelees
Of dremes, for I sey thee, doutelees,
That many a dreem ful soore is for to drede.

   "Lo, in the lyf of Seint Kenelm I rede,   290
That was Kenulphus sone, the noble kyng
Of Mercenrike, how Kenelm mette a thyng.
A lite er he was mordred, on a day,
His mordre in his avysioun he say.
His norice hym expowned every del
His swevene, and bad hym for to kepe hym wel
For traisoun, but he nas but sevene yeer old,
And therfore litel tale hath he told
Of any dreem, so holy was his herte.
By God! I hadde levere than my sherte   300
That ye hadde rad his legende, as have I.
Dame Pertelote, I sey yow trewely,
Macrobeus that writ the avysioun
In Affrike of the worthy Cipioun,
Affermeth dremes, and seith that they ben
Warnynge of thynges that men after sen.

   "And forther-moore, I pray yow, looketh wel
In the Olde Testament, of Danyel,
If he heeld dremes any vanytee.

   "Rede eek of Joseph, and there shul ye see   310
Wher dremes be som-tyme—I sey nat alle—
Warnynge of thynges that shul after falle.

   "Looke of Egipte the kyng, Daun Pharao,
His bakere and his butiller also,

---

229. **al newe**, recently. 231. **biwreyest**, expose. 233. **wlatsom**, disgusting. 235. **heled**, hidden. 239. **Han hent**, have seized. **soore hym pyned**, tortured him sorely. 240. **engyned**, tortured on the rack. 241. **biknewe**, made known. 242. **an-hanged . . . bon**, hanged by the neck bone. 246. **gabbe**, speak idly. 252. **agayn . . . even-tyde**, toward the time of evening. 254. **Jolif**, jolly. 255. **casten**, planned. 258. **wonder**, wonderful. 259. **Hym thoughte**, it seemed to him that. 261. **wende**, set forth. 262. **dreynt**, drowned. 264. **viage to lette**, to delay his voyage. 268. **agaste**, frighten. 273. **maze**, bewilderment. 276. **forslewthen**, waste in sloth. **tyde**, time. 277. **it . . . me**, it makes me sorry. 280. **it eyled**, ailed it. 281. **casuelly**, by chance. **rente**, burst. 287. **recchelees**, unheedful. 289. **ful . . . drede**, is very sorely to be dreaded. 291–92. **Kenulphus**, king of Mercia (**Mercenrike**), d. 821. 293. **lite er**, little before. 294. **avysioun**, vision. **say**, saw. 295. **norice**, nurse. **expowned**, explained. 296–97. **kepe . . . traisoun**, guard himself well against treason. 298. **litel . . . told**, he took little heed. 301. **legende**. The *Somnium Scipionis* was part of Cicero's *De Republica;* it was edited by Macrobius about A.D. 400, and the latter's commentary became the leading medieval handbook on dreams.

Wher they ne felte noon effect in dremes.
Who-so wol seke actes of sondry remes
May rede of dremes many a wonder thyng.
  "Lo Cresus, which that was of Lyde kyng,
Mette he nat that he sat up-on a tree, 320
Which signified he sholde an-hanged be?
  "Lo heere Andromacha, Ectores wyf,
That day that Ector sholde lese his lyf,
She dremed on the same nyght biforn,
How that the lyf of Ector sholde be lorn,
If thilke day he wente in-to bataille;
She warned hym, but it myghte nat availle;
He wente for to fighte nathelees,
But he was slayn anon of Achilles.
But thilke tale is al to long to telle,
And eek it is ny day, I may nat dwelle. 330
Shortly I seye, as for conclusioun,
That I shal han of this avysioun
Adversitee; and I seye forther-moor,
That I ne telle of laxatyves no stoor,
For they ben venymes, I woot it wel;
I hem deffye, I love hem never a del!
  "Now lat us speke of myrthe, and stynte al this.
Madame Pertelote, so have I blis,
Of o thyng God hath sent me large grace:
For whan I se the beautee of youre face, 340
Ye ben so scarlet reed aboute youre eyen,
It maketh al my drede for to dyen;
For also siker as *In principio,
Mulier est hominis confusio*—
  "Madame, the sentence of this Latyn is,
'Woman is mannes joye and al his blis.'
For whan I feele a nyght youre softe syde,
Al be it that I may nat on you ryde,
For that oure perche is maad so narwe, allas!
I am so ful of joye and of solas, 350
That I deffye bothe swevene and dreem!"
And with that word he fley doun fro the beem,
For it was day, and eke hise hennes alle,
And with a chuk he gan hem for to calle,
For he hadde founde a corn lay in the yerd.
Real he was, he was namoore aferd;
He fethered Pertelote twenty tyme,
And trad as ofte, er it was pryme.
He looketh as it were a grym leoun,
And on hise toos he rometh up and doun, 360
Hym deyned nat to sette his foot to grounde.

He chukketh, whan he hath a corn yfounde,
And to hym rennen thanne hise wyves alle.
Thus real, as a prince is in his halle,
Leve I this Chauntecleer in his pasture,
And after wol I telle his aventure.
  Whan that the monthe in which the world bigan,
That highte March, whan God first maked man,
Was complet, and passed were also,
Syn March bigan, thritty dayes and two, 370
Bifel that Chauntecler in al his pryde,
Hise sevene wyves walkyng hym bisyde,
Caste up hise eyen to the brighte sonne,
That in the signe of Taurus hadde yronne
Twenty degrees and oon, and som-what moore,
And knew by kynde, and by noon oother loore,
That it was pryme, and krew with blisful stevene.
"The sonne," he seyde, "is clomben up on hevene
Fourty degrees and oon, and moore ywis.
Madame Pertelote, my worldes blis, 380
Herkneth thise blisful briddes how they synge,
And se the fresshe floures how they sprynge,
Ful is myn herte of revel and solas!"
But sodeynly him fil a sorweful cas;
For evere the latter ende of joye is wo.
God woot that worldly joye is soone ago;
And if a rethor koude faire endite,
He in a cronycle saufly myghte it write,
As for a sovereyn notabilitee.
Now every wys man, lat hym herkne me: 390
This storie is also trewe, I undertake,
As is the book of Launcelot de Lake,
That wommen holde in ful gret reverence.
Now wol I torne agayn to my sentence.
  A colfox, ful of sly iniquitee,
That in the grove hadde woned yeres three,
By heigh ymaginacioun forncast,
The same nyght thurgh-out the hegges brast
In-to the yerd, ther Chauntecleer the faire
Was wont, and eek hise wyves, to repaire; 400
And in a bed of wortes stille he lay,

362. **corn**, grain.   367–68. **Whan . . . man**. The Creation was believed to have taken place at the spring equinox (now March 21).   374. **Taurus**, sign of the zodiac (the Bull).   376. **kynde**, natural ability.   377. **pryme**, 6 A.M.; sometimes the period from 6 to 9, and even the latter hour. **stevene**, voice.   378. **is clomben**, has climbed.   381. **briddes**, birds.   383. **revel**, revelry.   384. **him fil . . . cas**, a sorry chance befell him.   386. **ago**, gone.   387. **rethor**, rhetorician.   388. **cronycle saufly**, chronicle safely.   389. **sovereyn notabilitee**, exceptionally notable event.   391. **also**, as. **undertake**, guarantee.   392–93. **As . . . reverence**, probably as much a sly dig at female literary taste as an attack on the veracity of the romance of Lancelot.   394. **torne**, turn. **sentence**, matter.   395. **colfox**, fox with considerable black in its fur.   396. **woned**, lived.   397. **By . . . forncast**, predestined by divine foreknowledge.   398. **thurgh-out . . . brast**, broke through.   400. **repaire**, resort.   401. **wortes**, herbs.

315. **Wher . . . dremes**, whether they experienced no reality in dreams.   316. **remes**, realms.   321. **Ectores**, Hector's.   322. **lese**, lose.   324. **lorn**, lost.   330. **ny**, near. **dwelle**, tarry.   334. **telle . . . stoor**, take no stock in. 335. **venymes**, poisons.   343. **siker**, certain. **In principio**. See note to line 254 on page 176.   344. **Mulier . . . confusio**. Woman is man's ruin.   345. **sentence**, meaning. 352. **fley**, flew.   356. **Real**, regal.   359. **leoun**, lion. 361. **Hym . . . nat**, he did not deign.

Til it was passed undren of the day,
Waitynge his tyme on Chauntecleer to falle,
As gladly doon thise homycides alle,
That in awayt liggen to mordre men.
O false mordrour, lurkynge in thy den!
O newe Scariot, newe Genyloun!
False dissimilour, O Greek Synoun,
That broghtest Troye al outrely to sorwe!
O Chauntecleer, acursed be that morwe   410
That thow in-to the yerd flaugh fro the bemes!
Thow were ful wel ywarned by thy dremes,
That thilke day was perilous to thee.
But what that God forwoot moot nedes be,
After the opynyoun of certeyn clerkis.
Witnesse on hym that any parfit clerk is,
That in scole is greet altercacioun
In this matere, and greet disputisoun,
And hath ben of an hundred thousand men.
But I ne kan nat bulte it to the bren,   420
As kan the holy doctour Augustyn,
Or Boece, or the bisshop Bradwardyn,
Wheither that Goddes worthy forewityng
Streyneth me nedely for to doon a thyng—
"Nedely" clepe I symple necessitee—
Or ellis, if fre choys be grauntted me
To do that same thyng, or do it noght,
Though God forwoot it, er that it was wroght;
Or if his wityng streyneth never a del
But by necessitee condicionel.   430
I wol nat han to do of swich matere;
My tale is of a cok, as ye may heere,
That took his conseil of his wyf, with sorwe,
To walken in the yerd up-on that morwe
That he hadde met the dreem that I yow tolde.
Wommens conseils ben ful ofte colde;
Wommanes conseil broghte us first to wo,
And made Adam fro Paradys to go,
Ther as he was ful myrie and wel at ese.
But for I noot to whom it myghte displese,   440
If I conseil of wommen wolde blame,
Passe over, for I seyde it in my game.
Rede auctours, where they trete of swich matere,
And what they seyn of wommen ye may heere.
Thise ben the cokkes wordes, and nat myne;
I kan noon harm of no womman devyne.
    Faire in the sond, to bathe hire myrily,
Lith Pertelote, and alle hir sustres by,
Agayn the sonne, and Chauntecleer so free
Song myrier than the mermayde in the see;   450
For Phisiologus seith sikerly,
How that they syngen wel and myrily.
    And so bifel that, as he caste his eye
Among the wortes, on a boterflye,
He was war of this fox that lay ful lowe.
No-thyng ne liste hym thanne for to crowe,
But cryde anon, "Cok! cok!" and up he sterte,
As man that was affrayed in his herte.
For naturelly a beest desireth flee
Fro his contrarie, if he may it see,   460
Though he nevere erst hadde seyn it with his eye.
    This Chauntecleer, whan he gan hym espye,
He wolde han fled, but that the fox anon
Seyde, "Gentil sire, allas! wher wol ye gon?
Be ye affrayed of me that am youre freend?
Now, certes, I were worse than a feend,
If I to yow wolde harm or vileynye!
I am nat come youre conseil for t'espye,
But trewely, the cause of my comynge
Was oonly for to herkne how that ye synge.   470
For trewely, ye han as myrie a stevene
As any aungel hath, that is in hevene.
Ther-with ye han in musyk moore feelynge
Than hadde Boece, or any that kan synge.
My lord youre fader—God his soule blesse!—
And eek youre moder, of hire gentillesse,
Han in myn hous yben, to my greet ese;
And, certes, sire, ful fayn wolde I yow plese.
    "But for men speke of syngynge, I wol seye,
So mote I brouke wel myne eyen tweye,   480
Save ye, I herde nevere man so synge
As dide youre fader in the morwenynge.
Certes, it was of herte, al that he song.
And for to make his voys the moore strong,
He wolde so peyne hym, that with bothe hise eyen
He moste wynke, so loude he wolde cryen,
And stonden on his tiptoon ther-with-al,
And strecche forth his nekke long and smal.
And eek he was of swich discrecioun,
That ther nas no man in no regioun   490
That hym in song or wisdom myghte passe.

---

402. **undren,** the time indicated by "undren" varies; here, apparently, it is early forenoon. 404. **gladly,** habitually. 405. **liggen,** lie. 407. **Scariot,** Judas Iscariot. **Genyloun,** Ganelon, traitor in *The Song of Roland*. 408. **dissimilour,** dissembler. **Synoun,** Sinon, who secured the entry of the Trojan Horse into the city. 409. **outrely,** utterly. 411. **flaugh,** flew. 415. **clerkis,** learned authorities. 420. **bulte . . . bren,** sift it to the bran. 421. **Augustyn,** St. Augustine of Hippo. 422. **Boece,** Boethius (d. 524), whose *Consolations of Philosophy* Chaucer translated and drew upon constantly, and who also wrote on music (see l. 474). **Bradwardyn,** Thomas Bradwardyn, Archbishop of Canterbury (d. 1349). 423. **forewityng,** foreknowing. 424. **Streyneth,** constrains. 425. **clepe,** call. 433. **with sorwe,** a mild oath. 436. **colde,** fatal; the line is proverbial.

447. **sond,** sand. 448. **Lith,** lies. **sustres,** sisters. 449. **Agayn,** exposed to. 451. **Phisiologus,** the Latin bestiary, a medieval treatise on animals, real and imaginary. 459. **naturelly,** by instinct. 460. **contrarie,** a creature instinctively his enemy. 461. **erst,** before. 471. **stevene,** voice. 477. **Han . . . yben,** have been in my house. 480. **brouke,** have the use of. 485-86. **with . . . wynke,** he had to shut both eyes. 487. **tiptoon,** tiptoes.

GEOFFREY CHAUCER

I have wel rad in Daun Burnel the Asse,
Among his vers, how that ther was a cok,
For a preestes sone yaf hym a knok
Up-on his leg, whil he was yong and nyce,
He made hym for to lese his benefice.
But certeyn, ther nys no comparisoun
Bitwix the wisdom and discrecionn
Of youre fader and of his subtiltee.
Now syngeth, sire, for seinte Charitee! 500
Lat se, konne ye youre fader countrefete?"

   This Chauntecleer hise wynges gan to bete,
As man that koude his traysoun nat espie,
So was he ravysshed with his flaterie.
   Allas! ye lordes, many a fals flatour
Is in youre court, and many a losengeour,
That plesen yow wel moore, by my feith,
Than he that soothfastnesse un-to yow seith.
Redeth Ecclesiaste of flaterye;
Beth war, ye lordes, of hir trecherye. 510
This Chauntecler stood hye up-on his toos,
Strecchynge his nekke, and heeld hise eyen cloos,
And gan to crowe loude for the nones.
And Daun Russell the fox stirte up atones,
And by the gargat hente Chauntecleer,
And on his bak toward the wode hym beer,
For yet ne was ther no man that hym sewed.
   O destynee, that mayst nat ben eschewed!
Allas, that Chauntecler fleigh fro the bemes!
Allas, his wif ne roghte nat of dremes! 520
And on a Friday fil al this meschaunce.
   O Venus, that art goddesse of plesaunce,
Syn that thy servant was this Chauntecleer,
And in thy servyce dide al his power,
Moore for delit, than world to multiplie,
Why woldestow suffre hym on thy day to dye?
   O Gaufred, deere maister soverayn,
That, whan thy worthy kyng, Richard, was slayn
With shot, compleynedest his deth so soore,
Why ne hadde I now thy sentence and thy loore, 530
The Friday for to chide, as diden ye?
For on a Friday, soothly, slayn was he.
Thanne wolde I shewe yow how that I koude pleyne
For Chauntecleres drede and for his peyne.
   Certes, swich cry ne lamentacioun
Was nevere of ladyes maad whan Ylioun
Was wonne, and Pirrus with his streite swerd,
Whanne he hadde hent Kyng Priam by the berd,
And slayn hym, as seith us *Eneydos,*
As maden alle the hennes in the cloos, 540
Whan they hadde seyn of Chauntecleer the sighte.
But sovereynly Dame Pertelote shrighte,
Ful louder than dide Hasdrubales wyf,
Whan that hire housbonde hadde lost his lyf,
And that the Romayns hadden brend Cartage:
She was so ful of torment and of rage,
That wilfully in-to the fyr she sterte,
And brende hir-selven with a stedefast herte.
   O woful hennes, right so cryden ye,
As whan that Nero brende the citee 550
Of Rome, cryden senatours wyves,
For that hir housbondes losten alle hire lyves;
With-outen gilt this Nero hath hem slayn.
Now wol I turne to my tale agayn.
   The sely widwe, and eek hire doghtres two,
Herden thise hennes crye and maken wo,
And out atte dores stirten they anon,
And syen the fox toward the grove gon,
And bar up-on his bak the cok away,
And criden, "Out! harrow! and weilaway! 560
Ha! ha! the fox!" and after hym they ran,
And eek with staves many another man.
Ran Colle oure dogge, and Talbot, and Gerland,
And Malkyn, with a distaf in hire hand;
Ran cow and calf, and eek the verray hogges,
So fered for berkyng of the dogges
And showtynge of the men and wommen eek,
They ronne so, hem thoughte hir herte breek.
They yelléden as fendes doon in helle;
The dokes cryden as men wolde hem quelle; 570
The gees for feere flowen over the trees;
Out of the hyve cam the swarm of bees.
So hydous was the noyse, a! *benedicitee!*
Certes, he Jakke Straw, and his meynee,

---

492. Daun Burnel, the hero of a twelfth-century satire by Nigellus Wireker. **495. nyce,** foolish. **496. lese his benefice,** lose his benefice, salaried church office. The cock crowed so late that the young man overslept on the crucial day of his ordination. **499. his,** that of the vengeful cock. **500. seinte,** blessed. **501. countrefete,** imitate. **503. his,** that of the fox. **505. flatour,** flatterer. **506. losengeour,** flatterer. **508. soothfastnesse,** truthfulness. **509. Ecclesiaste,** Ecclesiasticus, in the Apocrypha. **510. Beth war,** beware. **513. for the nones,** especially. **515. by . . . hente,** seized by the throat. **516. wode,** wood. **beer,** bore. **517. sewed,** pursued. **518. eschewed,** avoided. **519. fleigh,** flew. **520. ne . . . of,** cared nothing for. **526. thy day.** Friday is "the day of the goddess Frigg," a translation of *dies Veneris,* the day of Venus—French *vendredi.* **527. Gaufred,** Geoffrey de Vinsauf, twelfth-century poet. **528. Richard,** Richard I, the Lion-hearted. **530. sentence,** sententiousness. **loore,** poetic skill.

534. drede, dread. **peyne,** suffering. **536. Ylioun,** Troy. **537. Pirrus,** Pyrrhus, son of Achilles. **streite,** drawn. **539. as . . . Eneydos,** as the *Aeneid* tells us. **540. cloos,** enclosure. **542. sovereynly,** above the rest. **shrighte,** shrieked. **543. Hasdrubales,** of Hasdrubal, Carthaginian ruler. **545. brend,** burned. **555. sely,** poor. **558. syen,** saw. **563. oure,** "our" from the point of view of the widow; two more dogs are named in the line. **566. fered for,** frightened by. **568. ronne,** ran. **hem . . . breek,** it seemed to them that their hearts broke. **570. dokes,** ducks. **quelle,** kill. **573. hydous,** hideous. **574. Jakke Straw,** Jack Straw, one of the leaders of the Peasants' Revolt of 1381. **meynee,** followers.

Ne made nevere shoutes half so shrille,
Whan that they wolden any Flemyng kille,
As thilke day was maad up-on the fox.
Of bras they broghten bemes, and of box,
Of horn, of boon, in whiche they blewe and powped, 579
And ther-with-al they skryked and they howped:
It semed as that heuene sholde falle!
Now, goode men, I prey yow herkneth alle:
 Lo, how Fortune turneth sodeynly
The hope and pryde eek of hire enemy!
This cok, that lay up-on the foxes bak,
In al his drede un-to the fox he spak,
And seyde, "Sire, if that I were as ye,
Yit sholde I seyn, as wys God helpe me,
'Turneth agayn, ye proude cherles alle!
A verray pestilence up-on yow falle!' 590
Now I am come un-to this wodes syde,
Maugree youre heed, the cok shal here abyde.
I wol hym ete, in feith, and that anon!'"
 The fox answerde, "In feith, it shal be done."
And as he spak that word, al sodeynly
This cok brak from his mouth delyverly,
And hye up-on a tree he fley anon.
And whan the fox say that he was gon,
 "Allas!" quod he, "O Chauntecleer, allas!
I have to yow," quod he, "ydoon trespas, 600
In as muche as I maked yow aferd,
Whan I yow hente, and broghte out of the yerd.
But, sire, I dide it in no wikke entente.
Com doun, and I shal telle yow what I mente.
I shal seye sooth to yow, God help me so!"
 "Nay thanne," quod he, "I shrewe us bothe two!
And first I shrewe my-self, bothe blood and bones,
If thow bigile me any ofter than ones.
Thow shalt namoore, thurgh thy flaterye,
Do me to synge and wynke with myn eye. 610
For he that wynketh, whan he sholde see,
Al wilfully, God lat hym nevere thee!"
 "Nay," quod the fox, "but God yeve hym meschaunce,
That is so undiscreet of governaunce,
That jangleth whan he sholde holde his pees."

 Lo, swich it is for to be recchelees
And necligent, and truste on flaterye.
 But ye that holden this tale a folye,
As of a fox, or of a cok and hen,
Taketh the moralitee, goode men. 620
For Seint Poul seith, that al that writen is,
To oure doctryne it is ywrite, ywis:
Taketh the fruyt, and lat the chaf be stille.
 Now, goode God, if that it be thy wille,
As seith my lord, so make us alle goode men,
And brynge us to his heye blisse! Amen.

["The Second Nun's Tale," (Group G) follows her "Prologue" of seventeen devotional stanzas, but lacks a link to a preceding tale. It is a "legend" in the technical meaning the Middle Ages gave the term, recounting the martyrdom of St. Cecelia. In Chaucer's day she was regarded not as the patron saint of music but as an example of miraculous power to endure torture.]

THE CANON'S YEOMEN'S PROLOGUE

Whan ended was the lyf of Seinte Cecile,
Er we hadde riden fully fyve mile,
At Boghtoun under Blee us gan atake
A man that clothed was in clothes blake,
And under that he hadde a whit surplys.
His hakeney, that was al pomely grys,
So swatte, that it wonder was to see;
It semed he hadde priked myles three.
The hors eek that his Yeman rood up-on
So swatte that unnethe myghte he gon. 10
Aboute the peitrel stood the foom ful hye;
He was of foom al flekked as a pye.
A male tweyfolde on his croper lay,
It semed that he caried lite array;
Al light for somer rood this worthy man.
And in myn herte wondren I bigan
What that he was, til that I understood
How that his cloke was sowed to his hood;
For which, whan I longe hadde avysed me,
I demed hym som chanoun for to be. 20
His hat heeng at his bak doun by a laas,
For he hadde riden moore than trot or paas;
He hadde ay priked lik as he were wood.

576. **Flemyng.** The Flemish had annoyed the native English laboring class, not particularly the peasants, by furnishing cheap, but good, foreign labor. Chaucer's only clear reference to the Peasants' Revolt is thus curiously limited. 578. **bemes,** trumpets. **box,** boxwood. 579. **powped,** puffed. 580. **skryked . . . howped,** shrieked . . . whooped. 592. **Maugree,** in spite of. 596. **brak,** broke away. **delyverly,** agilely. 597. **fley,** flew. 598. **say,** saw. 603. **in . . . entente,** with no wicked intention. 606. **shrewe,** curse. 610. **Do me to,** cause me to. 612. **thee,** thrive. 613. **meschaunce,** misfortune. 614. **governaunce,** behavior. 615. **jangleth,** chatters. **pees,** peace.

616. **recchelees,** careless. 617. **necligent,** negligent. 621–22. **Seint Poul . . . ywrite,** St. Paul. See II Timothy 3:16. 623. **fruyt,** grain. **lat . . . stille,** leave the chaff alone. 626. **heye,** high. 3. **atake,** overtake. 5. **surplys,** loose robe. 6. **hakeney,** riding horse. **pomely grys,** dapple-gray. 7. **swatte,** sweated. 8. **priked,** ridden fast. 9. **Yeman,** yeoman, servant. 10. **unnethe,** scarcely. **gon,** walk. 11. **peitrel,** horse collar. 12. **pye,** magpie. 13. **male tweyfolde,** bag folded double. **croper,** crupper. 14. **lite array,** few clothes. 20. **chanoun,** canon, ecclesiastic ordinarily attached to a cathedral. 21. **heeng,** hung. **laas,** cord. 22. **moore . . . paas,** faster than a trot or a footpace. 23. **ay,** continually.

GEOFFREY CHAUCER

A clote leef he hadde under his hood
For swoot, and for to kepe his heed from hete.
But it was joye for to seen hym swete!
His forheed dropped as a stillatorie,
Were ful of plantayne and of paritorie.
And whan that he was come, he gan to crye,
"God save," quod he, "this joly compaignye! 30
Faste have I priked," quod he, "for youre sake,
By cause that I wolde yow atake,
To ryden in this myrie compaignye."
His Yeman eek was ful of curteisye,
And seyde, "Sires, now in the morwe tyde
Out of youre hostelrie I saugh yow ryde,
And warned here my lord and my soverayn,
Which that to riden with yow is ful fayn,
For his desport; he loveth daliaunce."
    "Freend, for thy warnyng God yeve thee good
       chaunce!" 40
Thanne seyde oure Hoost, "For certeyn it wolde
   seme
Thy lord were wys, and so I may wel deme.
He is ful jocunde, also dar I leye.
Kan he oght telle a myrie tale or tweye,
With which he glade may this compaignye?"
    "Who, sire? my lord? ye, ye, with-outen lye,
He kan of myrthe and eek of jolitee
Nat but ynogh; also, sire, trusteth me,
And ye hym knewe as wel as do I,
Ye wolde wondre how wel and craftily 50
He koude werke, and that in sondry wise.
He hath take on hym many a greet emprise,
Which were ful hard for any that is heere
To brynge aboute, but they of hym it leere.
As hoomly as he rit amonges yow,
If ye hym knewe, it wolde be for youre prow;
Ye wolde nat forgoon his aqueyntaunce
For muchel good, I dar leye in balaunce
Al that I have in my possessioun.
He is a man of heigh discrecioun; 60
I warne yow wel, he is a passyng man."
    "Wel," quod oure Hoost, "I pray thee, telle me
       than,
Is he a clerk, or noon? Telle what he is."
    "Nay, he is gretter than a clerk, ywis,"
Seyde this Yeman, "and in wordes fewe,
Hoost, of his craft som-what I wol yow shewe.
    "I seye my lord kan swich subtiltee—
But al his craft ye may nat wite at me,
And som-what helpe I yet to his werkyng—
That al this ground on which we been ridyng, 70
Til that we come to Caunterbury toun,
He koude al clene turnen up-so-doun,
And pave it al of silver and of gold."
    And whan this Yeman hadde thus ytold
Un-to oure Hoost, he seyde, "*Benedicitee!*
This thyng is wonder merveillous to me,
Syn that thy lord is of so heigh prudence
By cause of which men sholde hym reverence,
That of his worship rekketh he so lite;
His oversloppe nys nat worth a myte, 80
As in effect to hym, so moot I go!
It is al baudy and to-tore also.
Why is thy lord so sluttissh, I thee preye,
And is of power bettre cloth to beye,
If that his dede acorde with thy speche?
Telle me that, and that I thee biseche."
    "Why?" quod this Yeman, "wher-to axe ye me?
God help me so, for he shal nevere thee!
(But I wol nat avowe that I seye,
And ther-fore kepe it secree, I yow preye.) 90
He is to wys, in feith, as I bileve;
That that is overdoon, it wol nat preve
Aright, as clerkes seyn; it is a vice.
Wherfore in that I holde hym lewed and nyce.
For whan a man hath over-greet a wit,
Ful ofte hym happeth to mysusen it;
So dooth my lord, and that me greveth soore;
God it amende, I kan seye yow namoore."
    "Ther of no fors, good Yeman," quod oure Hoost,
"Syn of the konnyng of thy lord thow woost, 100
Telle how he dooth, I pray thee hertely,
Syn that he is so crafty and so sly.
Where dwellen ye, if it to telle be?"
    "In the suburbes of a toun," quod he,
"Lurkynge in hernes and in lanes blynde,
Where-as thise robbours and thise theves by kynde
Holden hir pryvee fereful residence,
As they that dar nat shewen hir presence;
So faren we, if I shal seye the sothe."
    "Now," quod oure Hoost, "yet lat me talke to
       the: 110
Why artow so discoloured of thy face?"

   24. **clote leef**, burdock leaf.   25. **For swoot**, to protect from sweat. 27. **stillatorie**, still. 28. **paritorie**, the herb pellitory. 37. **warned**, informed. **soverayn**, master. 38. **Which that**, who. **ful fayn**, very eager. 39. **daliaunce**, social companionship. 43. **jocunde**, gay. **leye**, bet, as in l. 58. 52. **emprise**, undertaking. 54. **leere**, learn. 55. **rit**, rides. 56. **prow**, advantage. 61. **passyng**, surpassing. 68. **wite at**, learn from.

   72. **up-so-doun**, upside down. 79. **worship rekketh**, dignity cares. 80. **oversloppe**, outer garment. 81. **As . . . hym**, for a man like him actually. 82. **baudy and to-tore**, dirty and badly torn. 83. **sluttissh**, slovenly. 84. **beye**, buy. 87. **wher-to axe**, why ask. 88. **thee**, prosper. 89. **avowe**, acknowledge. 90. **secree**, secret. 91. **to**, too. 92. **preve**, prove. 94. **lewed and nyce**, ignorant and foolish. 102. **crafty**, skillful. **sly**, clever. 104. **suburbes**, usually not a place of residence to boast of in the Middle Ages. 105. **hernes . . . blynde**, corners and "dead-end" side streets. 106. **robbours**, robbers. **by kynde**, by nature. 107. **pryvee fereful**, secret (and) full of fear (of being discovered).

"Peter!" quod he, "God yeve it harde grace
I am so used in the fyr to blowe
That it hath chaunged my colour, I trowe.
I am nat wont in no myrour to prie,
But swynke soore and lerne multiplie.
We blondren evere and pouren in the fir,
And for al that we faille of oure desir,
For evere we lakken oure conclusioun.
To muchel folk we doon illusioun,   120
And borwe gold, be it a pound or two,
Or ten, or twelve, or manye sommes mo,
And make hem wenen, at the leeste weye,
That of a pound we koude make tweye.
Yet is it fals, and ay we han good hope
It for to doon, and after it we grope.
But that science is so fer us biforn,
We mowen nat, al-thogh we hadde it sworn,
It overtake, it slit awey so faste.
It wol us maken beggers atte laste."   130
   Whil this Yeman was thus in his talkyng,
This Chanoun drough hym neer, and herde al thyng
Which this Yeman spak, for suspecioun
Of mennes speche evere hadde this Chanoun.
For Catoun seith that he that gilty is
Demeth al thyng be spoke of hym, ywis.
That was the cause he gan so ny hym drawe
To his Yeman, to herknen al his sawe.
And thus he seyde un-to his Yeman tho:
"Hoold thow thy pees, and speke no wordes mo,   140
For if thow do thow shalt it deere abye!
Thow sclaundrest me heere in this compaignye,
And eek discoverest that thow sholdest hyde."
   "Ye," quod oure Hoost, "telle on, what so bityde.
Of al this thretyng, rekke nat a myte!"
   "In feith," quod he, "namoore I do but lyte."
   And whan this Chanoun saw it wolde nat bee,
But his Yeman wolde telle his pryvetee,
He fledde awey for verray sorwe and shame.
   "A!" quod the Yeman, "heere shal arise game; 150
Al that I kan anon now wol I telle.
Syn he is goon, the foule feend him quelle!
For nevere heer-after wol I with hym mete
For peny ne for pound, I yow bihete.
He that me broghte first un-to that game,

Er that he dye, sorwe have he and shame!
For it is ernest to me, by my feith;
That feele I wel, what so any man seith.
And yet for al my smerte and al my grief,
For al my sorwe, labour, and meschief,   160
I koude nevere leve it in no wise.
Now wolde God my wit myghte suffise
To tellen al that longeth to that art!
But nathelees yow wol I tellen part.
Syn that my lord is gon, I wol nat spare;
Swich thyng as I knowe, I wol declare."

["The Canon's Yeoman's Tale" recounts the seven years of hard work and disappointment which have disgusted the Yeoman with alchemy, then narrates in detail the tricks by which an alchemist cheated a gullible priest.]

THE MANCIPLE'S PROLOGUE

   Woot ye nat where ther stant a litel toun
Which that ycleped is Bobbe-up-and-doun,
Under the Blee, in Caunterbury weye?
Ther gan oure Hoost for to jape and pleye,
And seyde, "Sires, what! Don is in the myre!
Is ther no man, for preyere ne for hyre,
That wol awake oure felawe al bihynde?
A theef myght hym ful lightly robbe and bynde.
Se how he nappeth! Se how, for cokkes bones,
That he wol falle from his hors atones!   10
Is that a cook of Londoun, with meschaunce?
Do hym com forth, he knoweth his penaunce,
For he shal telle a tale, by my fey,
Al thogh it be nat worth a botel hey.
Awake thow Cook," quod he, "God yeve thee sorwe,
What eyleth thee to slepe by the morwe?
Hastow had fleen al nyght or artow dronke,
Or hastow with som quene al nyght yswonke
So that thow mayst nat holden up thyn heed?"
   This Cook, that was ful pale and no thyng reed, 20
Seyde to oure Hoost, "So God my soule blesse,
As ther is falle on me swich hevynesse,
Noot I nat why, that me were levere slepe
Than the beste galoun wyn in Chepe."

---

112. **Peter**, oath, "by St. Peter." **harde grace**, misfortune. 116. **swynke soore**, work hard. **multiplie**, change base metals into silver or gold by alchemy. 117. **blondren**, act blindly. **pouren**, peer. 119. **lakken . . . conclusioun**, fail of the desired results. 120. **doon illusioun**, deceive. 123. **wenen . . . weye**, believe at least. 127. **is . . . biforn**, is so far ahead of us. 128. **mowen**, may. 129. **slit**, slides. 132. **drough**, drew. 138. **sawe**, speech. 141. **deere abye!** dearly pay for. 142. **sclaundrest**, slander. 143. **discoverest**, reveal. 145. **thretyng**, threatening. **rekke**, care. 148. **pryvetee**, secrets. 152. **quelle**, kill. 154. **bihete**, promise. 155. **that game**, alchemy.

157. **ernest**, no game. 159. **smerte**, pain. 160. **meschief**, harm. 161. **leve**, leave. 163. **longeth**, belongs. Group H. 1. **stant**, stands. 2. **ycleped**, called. 3. **Blee**, Blean Forest. 5. **Don . . . myre!** Dun (common name for a horse) is in the mud (name of a rural game). 9. **cokkes bones**, corruption of "God's bones." 10. **atones**, at once. 11. **with meschaunce?** a mild oath. 12. **Do . . . forth**, make him come forward. 14. **botel**, small bundle of. 16. **by the morwe?** in the daytime. 17. **fleen**, fleas. 18. **yswonke**, toiled. 22. **hevynesse**, torpor. 23. **Noot I nat**, I know not. 24. **Than**, than have. **galoun wyn**, gallon of wine.

GEOFFREY CHAUCER

"Wel," quod the Manciple, "if it may doon ese
To thee, sire Cook, and to no wight displese
Which that here rideth in this compaignye,
And that oure Hoost wol, of his curteisye,
I wol as now excuse thee of thy tale.
For, in good feith, thy visage is ful pale, 30
Thyne eyen daswen eek, as that me thynketh,
And wel I woot, thy breeth ful soure stynketh,
That sheweth wel thow art nat wel disposed.
Of me, certeyn, thow shalt nat been yglosed.
Se how he ganeth, lo, this dronken wight,
As thogh he wolde swolwe us anon-right!
Hoold cloos thy mouth, man, by thy fader kyn!
The devel of helle sette his foot ther-yn!
Thy cursed breeth infecte wol us alle.
Fy, stynkynge swyn, fy, foule moot thee falle! 40
A! taketh hede, sires, of this lusty man,
Now, swete sire, wol ye justen atte fan?
Ther-to me thynketh ye been wel yshape!
I trowe that ye dronken han wyn ape,
And that is whan men pleyen with a straw."
And with his speche the Cook wax wrooth and wraw,
And on the Manciple he gan nodde faste
For lakke of speche, and doun the hors hym caste,
Wher as he lay, til that men hym up took.
This was a fair chyvachee of a cook! 50
Allas! he nadde yholde hym by his ladel!
And er that he agayn were in his sadel,
Ther was gret showvyng bothe to and fro
To lifte hym up, and muchel care and wo,
So unweldy was this sory palled goost.
And to the Manciple thanne spak oure Hoost:
"By cause drynke hath domynacioun
Up-on this man, by my savacioun,
I trowe he lewedly telle wolde his tale.
For, were it wyn, or old or moisty ale, 60
That he hath dronke, he speketh in his nose,
And fneseth faste, and eek he hath the pose.
"He hath also to do moore than ynow
To kepen hym and his capul out of the slow;
And if he falle from his capul eft-soone,
Than shal we alle have ynow to doone,
In liftynge up his hevy dronken cors.
Telle on thy tale, of hym make I no fors.
"But yet, Manciple, in feith thow art to nyce,
Thus openly repreve hym of his vice. 70
Another day he wole, par aventure,
Reclayme thee, and brynge thee to lure;
I mene, he speke wole of smale thynges,
As for to pynchen at thy rekenynges.
That were nat honeste, if it cam to preef."
"No," quod the Manciple, "that were a gret mescheef!
So myghte he lightly brynge me in the snare.
Yet hadde I levere payen for the mare
Which he rit on, than he sholde with me stryve;
I wol nat wrathe hym, also mote I thryve! 80
That that I spak, I seyde it in my bourde.
And wite ye what? I have here in a gourde
A draghte of wyn, ye, of a ripe grape,
And right anon ye shul seen a good jape.
This Cook shal drynke ther-of, if I may.
Up peyne of deeth, he wol nat seye me nay."
And certeynly, to tellen as it was,
Of this vessel the Cook drank faste, allas!
What neded it? He drank ynow biforn.
And whan he hadde pouped in this horn, 90
To the Manciple he took the gourde agayn,
And of that drynke the Cook was wonder fayn,
And thanked hym in swich wise as he koude.
Thanne gan oure Hoost to laughen wonder loude,
And seyde, "I se wel it is necessarie,
Where that we goon, good drynke with us carie;
For that wol turne rancour and disese
T'acord and love, and many a wrong appese.
"O Bacus, yblessed be thy name,
That so kanst turnen ernest in-to game! 100
Worship and thank be to thy deitee!
Of that matere ye gete namoore of me.
Telle on thy tale, Manciple, I the preye."
"Wel, sire," quod he, "now herkneth what I seye."

["The Manciple's Tale" tells how the crow, once white and able to converse with mortals and immortals, was reduced to a dingy croaker in punishment for talebearing.]

---

31. **daswen**, are dazed. 34. **yglosed**, flattered. 35. **ganeth**, yawns. 36. **anon-right!** right away. 37. **fader kyn**, father's relatives. 39. **wol**, will. 40. **foule . . . falle!** foul luck to you! 42. **justen . . . fan?** joust at a vane, the game of quintain. 44. **dronken . . . ape**, have drunk so much that you act like an ape. 46. **wrooth and wraw**, angry. 47. **on . . . nodde**, shake his head at the Manciple. 50. **chyvachee**, feat of horsemanship. 51. **nadde . . . ladel!** had not stuck to his ladle. 53. **showvyng**, shoving. 55. **unweldy**, unwieldy. **palled**, pale. 58. **savacioun**, salvation. 59. **lewedly**, badly. 60. **moisty**, new. 62. **fneseth**, snort. **pose**, head cold. 64. **capul**, nag. **slow**, mud. 65. **eft-soone**, again soon.

68. **of . . . fors**, I completely disregard him. 70. **repreve**, reprove. 72. **Reclayme . . . lure.** an expression from hawking, meaning "He will take vengeance on you." 74. **pynchen at**, find fault with. 75. **honeste**, creditable. **preef**, test, that is, "if your books were ordered to be audited." 76. **mescheef**, misfortune. 77. **lightly**, easily. 79. **rit**, rides. 80. **wrathe**, anger. **also . . . thryve!** as I hope to thrive. 81. **bourde**, jest. 82. **wite**, know. 85. **if I may**, if I can bring it about. 86. **Up**, upon. 90. **pouped**, blown (a pun on the drinking-horn and the musical instrument). 91. **took**, handed. 92. **wonder fayn**, wonderfully glad.

THE PARSON'S PROLOGUE

By that the Maunciple hadde his tale ended,
The sonne fro the south lyne was descended
So lowe, that he nas nat, to my sighte,
Degrees nyne and twenty as of highte.
Ten of the clokke it was, so as I gesse,
For ellevene foot, or litel moore or lesse,
My shadwe was at thilke tyme, as there,
Of swiche feet as my lengthe parted were
In sixe feet equal of proporcioun.
Ther-with the mones exaltacioun,   10
I mene Libra, alwey gan ascende,
As we were entryng at a thropes ende.

For which oure Hoost, as he was wont to gye,
As in this cas, oure joly compaignye,
Seyde in this wise, "Lordynges everichon,
Now lakketh us no tales mo than oon.
Fulfild is my sentence and my decree;
I trowe that we han herd of ech degree.
Almoost fulfild is al myn ordinaunce.
I pray to God, so yeve hym right good chaunce,   20
That telleth this tale to us lustily.

"Sire Preest," quod he, "artow a vicary?
Or artow a person? sey sooth, by thy fey!
Be what thow be, ne breke thow nat oure pley;
For every man, save thow, hath toold his tale.
Unbokele, and shewe us what is in thy male;
For trewely, me thynketh by thy cheere
Thow sholdest knytte up wel a greet matere.
Telle us a fable anon, for cokkes bones!"

This Person answerde, al atones,   30
"Thow getest fable noon ytoold for me;
For Poul, that writeth un-to Thymothe,
Repreveth hem that weyven soothfastnesse,
And tellen fables and swich wrecchednesse.
Why sholde I sowen draf out of my fest,
Whan I may sowen whete, if that me lest?
For which I seye, if that yow list to heere
Moralitee and vertuous matere,
And thanne that ye wol yeve me audience,
I wole ful fayn, at Cristes reverence,   40
Do yow plesaunce leveful, as I kan.

But trusteth wel, I am a Southren man,
I kan nat geste 'rom, ram, ruf' by lettre,
Ne, God woot, rym holde I but litel bettre;
And therfore, if yow lest, I wol nat glose,
I wol yow telle a myrie tale in prose
To knytte up al this feste, and make an ende.
And Jesu, for his grace, wit me sende
To shewe yow the wey, in this viage,
Of thilke parfit glorious pilgrymage   50
That highte Jerusalem celestial.
And if ye vouche sauf, anon I shal
Bigynne up-on my tale, for which I preye
Telle youre avys, I kan no bettre seye.

"But natheless, this meditacioun
I putte it ay under correccioun
Of clerkes, for I am nat textuel;
I take but the sentence, trusteth wel.
Therfore I make protestacioun
That I wol stonde to correccioun."   60

Up-on this word we han assented soone,
For, as it semed, it was for to doone,
To enden in som vertuous sentence,
And for to yeve hym space and audience;
And bede oure Hoost he sholde to hym seye
That alle we to telle his tale hym preye.
Oure Hoost hadde the wordes for us alle:
"Sire Preest," quod he, "now faire yow bifalle!
Telleth," quod he, "youre meditacioun
But hasteth yow, the sonne wole adoun;   70
Beth fructuous, and that in litel space,
And to do wel God sende yow his grace!
Sey what yow list, and we wol gladly heere."
And with that word he seyde in this manere.

["The Parson's Tale," which Chaucer had optimistically described as "a myrie tale in prose," is a long treatise on penitence, in the midst of which has been inserted a comprehensive account of the Seven Deadly Sins. There has been much scholarly discussion as to whether we have "The Parson's Tale" in the form in which it left Chaucer's hands, or indeed if it was ever in Chaucer's hands at all.]

Chaucer's Retraction

The authenticity of the "Retraction" has also been challenged, and each reader, no doubt, must determine

Group I.   **12. at . . . ende,** at the edge of a village. **13. gye,** guide.   **14. As . . . cas,** on this pilgrimage. **16. Now lakketh . . . oon.** Excluding that of the Canon's Yeoman, not planned for in "The General Prologue," only 23 of the intended 116 tales have come down to us in whole or in part. But whatever reduction in scope Chaucer may have decided on, he obviously intended "The Parson's Tale" to conclude the series.   **18. ech degree,** each step in the social ladder.   **22. vicary,** vicar, subordinate to a parson.   **23. person,** parson, priest of a parish.   **26. Unbokele,** unbuckle. **male,** bag (of stories).   **29. fable,** story. **cokkes, bones.** With the Host's oath here, compare l. 28 (col. 2) on page 195 and l. 1 (col. 1) on page 203.   **35. draf,** chaff. **fest,** fist.   **41. leveful,** permissible.

43–44. rom . . . rym, a reference to, and burlesque of, the alliterative verse found in such poems as *Sir Gawain* and *Piers Plowman*, and especially used in the poets of the northwest Midlands and the North.   **45. glose,** speak speciously, conceal one's real intention.   **47. knytte,** gather together. **54. avys,** opinion.   **57. I . . . textuel,** I do not pretend to textual exactness.   **58. sentence,** substance.   **65. bede,** commanded.   **67. hadde . . . alle,** spoke for all of us. **71. fructuous,** profitable.

for himself as to the likelihood of such a profound spiritual revulsion on Chaucer's part.

Heere taketh the makere of this book his leve:

Now preye I to hem alle that herkne this litel tretys or rede, that if ther be any thyng in it that liketh hem, that ther-of they thanken oure Lord Jesu Crist, of whom procedeth al wit and al goodnesse, And if ther be any thyng that displese hem, I preye hem also that they arrette it to the defaute of myn unkonnynge, and nat to my wyl, that wolde fayn have seyd bettre if I hadde had konnynge. For oure book seith, "Al that is writen is writen for oure doctrine," and that is myn entente.

Wherfore I biseke yow mekely, for the mercy of God, that ye preye for me that Crist have mercy on me and foryeve me my giltes, and namely, of my translacions and enditynges of worldly vanitees, the whiche I revoke in my retracciouns: As is the book of Troilus; The book also of Fame; The book of the xxv Ladies; The book of the Duchesse; The book of Seint Valentynes day of the parlement of briddes; The Tales of Caunterbury, thilke that sownen in-to synne; The book of the Leoun; and many another book, if they were in my remembrance, and many a song and many a leccherous lay; that Crist for his grete mercy foryeve me the synne.

But of the translacioun of Boece *de consolacione*, and othere bookes of legendes of seintes, and omelies, and moralitee, and devocioun, that thanke I oure Lord Jesu Crist and his blisful Moder, and alle the seintes of hevene, bisekynge hem that they from hennes forth un-to my lyves ende, sende me grace to biwayle my giltes, and to studie to the savacioun of my soule, and graunte me grace of verray penitence, confessioun and satisfaccioun to doon in this present lyf; thurgh the benigne grace of hym that is Kyng of kynges and Preest of alle preestes, that boughte us with the precious blood of his herte; so that I may ben oon of hem at the day of doome that shulle be saved. *Qui cum patre &cetera*

Heere is ended the book of the tales of Caunterbury, compiled by Geffrey Chaucer, of whos soule Jesu Crist have mercy. Amen.

The Popular Ballad

Although the present brief discussion must necessarily deal exclusively with English and Scottish popular ballads, it must not be forgotten that the ballad, despite various and natural differences from country to country, is a distinct and recognizable literary form found all over Europe and wherever European settlers have gone.

The man can hardly be accused of overstatement who says that the popular, or traditional, ballads have had a universality of appeal granted to almost no other literary type. Created by, or close to, the common people—the folk, as students of their lore find it convenient to term them—ballads have been loved and remembered, sung or recited, from the often dateless time of their origin until the present day. But they have not been limited to the cottage fireside or the village green. At least since the sixteenth century critics and creative men of letters have picked them out, often after having borne them in mind from childhood, for praise and for the sincere, if frequently misguided, flattery of imitation. The charm of the ballad is re-proved from day to day: student after student who has professed himself—complacently, sadly, or stoically—to be unable to "get anything out of poetry," finds that "Chevy Chase" or "Sir Patrick Spens" or "Barbara Allen" can quicken a hitherto dormant sense of the beauty of measured syllables and chiming sounds.

What is a popular ballad? A ballad is a narrative poem, usually but not invariably short, originally and ordinarily intended to be sung. The importance of the musical accompaniment, largely unrecognized or ignored by the eighteenth- and nineteenth-century collectors, whose primary interest was in the words, is now clearly recognized. Indeed, some students believe that the association of the words with a short and recurrent melody had much to do with fixing the traditional form and texture of the ballad as a literary type.

A ballad, then, as the late George Lyman Kittredge put it years ago, is "a song that tells a story"; but the story is presented in terms of a relatively fixed formula and method. A ballad is

---

6. **rede,** read it. 10–11. **arrette,** ascribe. **defaute of myn unkonnynge,** fault of my ignorance. 18. **enditynges,** literary compositions. 20–21. **The book of the xxv Ladies,** *The Legend of Good Women.*

1. **sownen,** tend toward. **The book of the Leoun,** lost, but probably a translation of Machaut's *Dit du Lyon.* 4. **lay,** poem. 7. **omelies,** homilies. 10. **bisekynge,** beseeching. 14. **satisfaccioun,** performance of penance.

severely concentrated on a single theme, indeed on a single episode—the climactic one—of that theme. We find ourselves plunged into the situation in the middle of things; whatever background we are to receive is given to us incidentally as we go along, sometimes given obscurely and often not given at all. Why, for instance, did Sir Patrick Spens put to sea? The version which we print will never tell us, although there are others which say that he was sent to Norway to bring back—or take home—a princess, who is sometimes Scottish, sometimes Norse. Motivation, then, is reduced to a minimum or may even be wanting altogether. Once the situation is before us, the plot develops rapidly and naturally by means of action, simply stated, and dialogue, tersely expressed. The amount of dialogue in the ballads and the effect of drama which it arouses is worthy of notice. Above all else, perhaps, the narrative advances impersonally; at no time are we aware of the individuality of the author. The ballad, indeed, is often said to sing itself. In style we notice a simplicity of language which never lapses into vulgarity; use of only the most transparent figures of speech—"milk-white steed" and "berry-brown sword"; the repetition of set phrases to describe identical or almost identical situations; and a complete lack of differentiation between the speech of king and commoner. All these things are the hallmarks of the ballad and serve to distinguish it sharply from more conscious and formal literary compositions.

Two other and highly important ballad characteristics must be noted, for they lead us directly to the troublesome problem of ballad origins. The first is the appearance in many, though by no means all, of our ballad texts of a refrain, which suggests choral singing by what is often called in this connection a "dancing throng." Dancing to the accompaniment of the dancers' own singing of songs, lyric or narrative, has been an established custom from the earliest times to the present. Second, we find in certain ballads what Gummere designated "incremental repetition," a term which indicates a method of carrying on a story by means of significant variations within an otherwise repeated pattern. This device is found in "Lord Randal" (Child 12), and another excellent example is "The Maid Freed from the Gallows" (Child 95), the first three stanzas of which are:

"O good Lord Judge, and sweet Lord Judge,
    Peace for a little while!
Methinks I see my own father,
    Come riding by the stile.

"Oh father, oh father, a little of your gold,
    And likewise of your fee!
To keep my body from yonder grave,
    And my neck from the gallows-tree."

"None of my gold now you shall have,
    Nor likewise of my fee;
For I am come to see you hanged,
    And hanged you shall be."

The fourth and fifth stanzas are identical with the first and second, except that "mother" is substituted for father, and the sixth repeats the third. Then follow "brother" and "sister," each as heartless as the unnatural parents. But in the thirteenth and fourteenth stanzas we have the "true-love," so that the ballad ends triumphantly;

"Some of my gold now you shall have,
    And likewise of my fee;
For I am come to see you saved,
    And saved you shall be."

The English version, we must confess, does not depict a very comprehensible situation, but it was certainly easy to compose and is equally easy to remember, a point demonstrated by the fact that despite its relative lack of interest it is still sung in England, the West Indies, and the United States.

The problem of ballad origins has been made one of the most perplexing problems in literary history and is almost too complex and disputed for brief discussion, but we must glance in its direction. The earliest commentators ascribed the ballads to medieval minstrels, without being too specific about the matter. With the Romantic period, however, a new theory appeared; namely, that the popular ballad somehow bubbled out, full-fledged and lilting, from the massed voices of a homogeneous folk. This "communal theory," as it is called, is usually fathered on the great Jacob Grimm, but not with complete justice, since his utterances on the subject have been well called Delphic. The theory has been attacked and defended, varied and modified, until the surveyor of this wordy war, which has lasted now nearly one hundred and fifty years, may well feel that it is better to read ballads than to read about their origin. Two things must be kept clearly in mind: first, that no sane critic ever seriously contended that a group of people, no matter how small or how large, suddenly with one accord and, as it were, with one voice sang a hitherto unknown song; and second, that the origin of the ballad as a literary type, which occurred, we may hazard a venture, not too long after the year 1000, must not be confused with the origin of any one of the ballads which we possess today. We may believe that groups of men and women, all with essentially the same background and outlook, got in the habit of accompanying their simple dances with simple melodies to which, as they danced, they extemporized simple narrative songs, with more than one of the dancers taking part in the composition of the words. That is one thing and, though not capable of scientific demonstration, it is by no means improbable; but to maintain that "Sir Patrick Spens" or "Edward" came into existence in any such way is something quite different and manifestly absurd. Nevertheless, the theory that postulates a dancing, singing, extemporizing, homogeneous group, although in the very nature of the case documents are lacking to prove it to the satisfaction of the determined skeptic, will account for most of the characteristics which we associate with the popular ballad.

The folk, then, supplied the mold in which individual authors made the ballads we have. The term "individual authors," must perhaps be defined in connection with the ballads. These individuals were scarcely separated from their fellows to whom, and with whom, as the use of the refrain shows, they sang. They composed orally, or even if, late in the period, they put their words first into writing, they delivered them orally and transmitted them orally. That neither the author nor the hearers of a ballad had, or have, any sense of personal ownership is evidenced by the impersonality of the ballad itself. Nor was there anything sacred in the exact words of the text. If we today read a poem and like it well enough to memorize it, and have the fortune to find others with patience to hear our rendition, we feel bound to name the author and not to deviate from his phrasing. If, on the other hand, we hear a good story, we seldom think it necessary to give credit to the person who told it to us, and we certainly alter the phraseology in retelling, either unconsciously or in hope of improvement. So it was with a ballad; once it was sung it became the property of all who heard it, and, as has been said, it may well be affirmed that a ballad is recomposed with every rendition. Although in a volume such as *The College Survey* only one version of a ballad can be given, we must not forget that most of the eighteen ballads which are printed here have been collected more than once (sometimes, as in the case of "Barbara Allen," literally hundreds of times) and that no two versions are likely to be identical. Every singer makes changes of his own, changes as often due to poetic taste, however unconscious, as to forgetfulness or carelessness. This process of variation plays so marked a part in ballad development, it has operated so clearly from generation to generation and from century to century, it has involved so many individuals without names or literary personalities, that even if we reject original communal authorship for a given ballad, we accept, tacitly or otherwise, what amounts to communal re-creation of the ballad between its author's day and our own.

There is one last consideration of particular interest to American students. Despite the gloomy prognostications of each new generation of ballad collectors and critics from the late eighteenth century on, the traditional ballad is quite alive today, not only in Great Britain but in many parts of the United States and Canada. The seventeenth- and eighteenth-century settlers of the English-speaking sections of the Western Hemisphere brought their songs with them and, less miraculously than we are at first inclined to think, the songs survived, especially in the more isolated communities. During the past thirty years collectors have done notable work in recording variants of popular ballads, including approximately one-third of the three hundred and five brought together in Child's collection. Nor is the field worked out. There is scarcely a person who reads these words, especially if he has access to rural communities along the Atlantic seaboard, and in the hills behind it, from Maine to Florida, who cannot with a little patience and ingenuity come upon individuals able to sing or recite the old ballads. In many cases they scarcely know that they know them, but they do know them just the same. Few greater thrills of a literary kind can be experienced than to find for oneself a ballad, say "Lord Randal," treated as a real story in a living song and not as one of the dry bones which clatter dully in anthologies.

Our standard collection of traditional ballads is Francis J. Child's *English and Scottish Popular Ballads* (5 vols., Boston, 1882–1898). An abridged, but in itself complete, edition of this great work was made by H. C. Sargent and G. L. Kittredge (Houghton Mifflin, 1904), and from this the following ballads are taken by permission of the copyright owner. In addition to Kittredge's brief but invaluable introduction to the volume in question, the following studies are commended to the student: Francis B. Gummere, *The Popular Ballad*, Houghton Mifflin, 1907; Louise Pound, *Poetic Origins and the Ballad*, Macmillan, 1921; G. H. Gerould, *The Ballad of Tradition*, Oxford University Press, 1932; and William J. Entwistle, *European Balladry*, Oxford University Press, 1939. Among the many collections from America are the following: Phillips Barry, F. H. Eckstrom, and M. W. Smyth, *British Ballads from Maine*, Yale University Press, 1929; C. J. Sharp and O. D. Campbell, *English Folk-Songs from the Southern Appalachians*, Oxford University Press, 1929; A. K. Davis, Jr., *Traditional Ballads of Virginia*, Harvard University Press, 1929; W. R. Mackenzie, *Ballads and Sea Songs from Nova Scotia*, Harvard University Press, 1928; Reed Smith, *South Carolina Ballads*, Harvard University Press, 1928.

THE TWA SISTERS

This ballad is found in Scandinavia as well as Great Britain, and was brought to the United States. By means of repetition of the first line and use of the refrain (which, like most, has no connection with the plot) a single couplet is built up to a seven-line stanza. There is a recording of an American version by Andrew R. Summers in Columbia, Old World Ballads in America (M–408).

There was twa sisters in a bowr,
   Edinburgh, Edinburgh
There was twa sisters in a bowr,
   Stirling for ay
There was twa sisters in a bowr,
There came a knight to be their wooer.
   Bonny Saint Johnston stands upon Tay.

He courted the eldest wi glove an ring,
But he lovd the youngest above a' thing.

He courted the eldest wi brotch an knife,   10
But lovd the youngest as his life.

The eldest she was vexed sair,
An much envied her sister fair.

Into her bowr she could not rest,
Wi grief an spite she almos brast.

Upon a morning fair an clear,
She cried upon her sister dear:

"O sister, come to yon sea stran,
An see our father's ships come to lan."

She's taen her by the milk-white han   20
An led her down to yon sea stran.

The youngest stood upon a stane,
The eldest came an threw her in.

She tooke her by the middle sma,
An dashd her bonny back to the jaw.

"O sister, sister, tak my han,
An Ise mack you heir to a' my lan.

"O sister, sister, tak my middle,
An yes get my goud and my gouden girdle.

"O sister, sister, save my life,   30
An I swear Ise never be nae man's wife."

"Foul fa the han that I should tacke,
It twined me an my wardles make.

"Your cherry cheeks an yallow hair
Gars me gae maiden for evermair."

Sometimes she sank, an sometimes she swam,
Till she came down yon bonny mill-dam.

O out it came the miller's son,
An saw the fair maid swimmin in.

"O father, father, draw your dam,   40
Here's either a mermaid or a swan."

The miller quickly drew the dam,
An there he found a drownd woman.

You coudna see her yallow hair
For gold and pearle that were so rare.

You coudna see her middle sma
For gouden girdle that was sae braw.

You coudna see her fingers white,
For gouden rings that was sae gryte.

An by there came a harper fine,   50
That harped to the king at dine.

When he did look that lady upon,
He sighd and made a heavy moan.

He's taen three locks o her yallow hair,
And wi them strung his harp sae fair.

The first tune he did play and sing,
Was, "Farewell to my father the king."

The Twa Sisters (Child 10). **10. brotch**, brooch. **12. sair**, sorely. **15. brast**, burst. **20. taen**, taken. **24. sma**, small. **25. jaw**, billow. **27. Ise**, I shall. **29. yes**, ye shall. **goud**, gold. **32. fa**, fall. **33. twined**, separated. **wardles make**, world's mate. **35. Gars**, causes. **47. braw**, handsome. **49. gryte**, great. **51. dine**, dinner.

THE POPULAR BALLAD

The nextin tune that he playd syne,
Was, "Farewell to my mother the queen."

The lasten tune that he playd then,   60
Was, "Wae to my sister, fair Ellen."

LORD RANDAL

Incremental repetition is a significant feature of this ballad as well as of one which follows it. So, too, as in "Edward," we find the common device of the "legacy" of a dying or departing hero, "Lord Randal" was, and is, popular in the United States and has been collected in New England as well as in the South.

"O where ha you been, Lord Randal, my son?
And where ha you been, my handsome young man?"
"I ha been at the greenwood; mother, mak my bed soon,
For I'm wearied wi hunting, and fain wad lie down."

"An wha met ye there, Lord Randal, my son?
An wha met you there, my handsome young man?"
"O I met wi my true-love; mother, mak my bed soon,
For I'm wearied wi huntin, an fain wad lie down."

"And what did she give you, Lord Randal, my son?
And what did she give you, my handsome young man?"   10
"Eels fried in a pan; mother, mak my bed soon,
For I'm wearied wi huntin, and fain wad lie down."

"And wha gat your leavins, Lord Randal, my son?
And wha gat your leavins, my handsom young man?"
"My hawks and my hounds; mother, mak my bed soon,
For I'm wearied wi hunting, and fain wad lie down."

"And what becam of them, Lord Randal, my son?
And what becam of them, my handsome young man?"
"They stretched their legs out an died; mother, mak my bed soon,
For I'm wearied wi huntin, and fain wad lie down."   20

"O I fear you are poisoned, Lord Randal, my son!
I fear you are poisoned, my handsome young man!"

58. **syne,** afterward.   *Lord Randal* (Child 12).

"O yes, I am poisoned; mother, mak my bed soon,
For I'm sick at the heart, and I fain wad lie down."

"What d' ye leave to your mother, Lord Randal, my son?
What d' ye leave to your mother, my handsome young man?"
"Four and twenty milk kye; mother, mak my bed soon,
For I'm sick at the heart, and I fain wad lie down."

"What d' ye leave to your sister, Lord Randal, my son?
What d' ye leave to your sister, my handsome young man?"   30
"My gold and my silver; mother, mak my bed soon,
For I'm sick at the heart, an I fain wad lie down."

"What d' ye leave to your brother, Lord Randal, my son?
What d' ye leave to your brother, my handsome young man?"
"My houses and my lands; mother, mak my bed soon,
For I'm sick at the heart, and I fain wad lie down."

"What d' ye leave to your true-love, Lord Randal, my son?
What d' ye leave to your true-love, my handsome young man?"
"I leave her hell and fire; mother, mak my bed soon,
For I'm sick at the heart, and I fain wad lie down."   40

EDWARD

The "surprise ending," though by no means uncommon, is not altogether typical of the popular ballads, but in "Edward" it is used with superb effect. The mother's persistent questioning is given a grim underscoring by the last stanza, which makes clear that she had in some way caused her son to kill his own father. "Edward" is an excellent example of how few details the ballad authors need to give in order to make us feel a complete and even haunting impression of a situation.

"Why dois your brand sae drap wi bluid,
                      Edward, Edward,
Why dois your brand sae drap wi bluid,
    And why sae sad gang yee O?"
"O I hae killed my hauke sae guid,
                      Mither, mither,

27. **kye,** cows.   *Edward* (Child 13).   4. **gang,** go.

O I hae killed my hauke sae guid,
  And I had nae mair bot hee O."

"Your haukis bluid was nevir sae reid,
              Edward, Edward,   10
Your haukis bluid was nevir sae reid,
  My deir son I tell thee O."
"O I hae killed my reid-roan steid,
              Mither, mither,
O I hae killed my reid-roan steid,
  That erst was sae fair and frie O."

"Your steid was auld, and ye hae gat mair,
              Edward, Edward,
Your steid was auld, and ye hae gat mair,
  Sum other dule ye drie O."   20
"O I hae killed my fadir deir,
              Mither, mither,
O I hae killed my fadir deir,
  Alas, and wae is mee O!"

"And whatten penance wul ye drie for that,
              Edward, Edward?
And whatten penance will ye drie for that?
  My deir son, now tell me O."
"Ile set my feit in yonder boat,
              Mither, mither,   30
Ile set my feit in yonder boat,
  And Ile fare ovir the sea O."

"And what wul ye doe wi your towirs and your ha,
              Edward, Edward?
And what wul ye doe wi your towirs and your ha,
  That were sae fair to see O?"
"Ile let thame stand tul they doun fa,
              Mither, mither,
Ile let thame stand tul they doun fa,
  For here nevir mair maun I bee O."   40

"And what wul ye leive to your bairns and your wife,
              Edward, Edward?
And what wul ye leive to your bairns and your wife,
  Whan ye gang ovir the sea O?"
"The warldis room, late them beg thrae life,
              Mither, mither,
The warldis room, late them beg thrae life,
  For thame nevir mair wul I see O."

"And what wul ye leive to your ain mither deir,
              Edward, Edward?   50

And what wul ye leive to your ain mither deir?
  My deir son, now tell me O."
"The curse of hell frae me sall ye beir,
              Mither, mither,
The curse of hell frae me sall ye beir,
  Sic counseils ye gave to me O."

HIND HORN

We are able to compare this ballad with its original, the romance of *King Horn* (see page 96). It will be observed that details of action and motivation have disappeared, and that the ballad really deals with only one episode, though that perhaps the most striking, of the romance. At the end we get more than a hint of the popular ballad scene in which the hero tests the heroine's love by making it appear that he is reduced to poverty. The refrain is merely a series of meaningless syllables to carry the tune.

In Scotland there was a babie born,
  Lill lal, etc.
And his name it was called young Hind Horn.
  With a fal lal, etc.

He sent a letter to our king
That he was in love with his daughter Jean.

He's gien to her a silver wand,
With seven living lavrocks sitting thereon.

She's gien to him a diamond ring,
With seven bright diamonds set therein.   10

"When this ring grows pale and wan,
You may know by it my love is gane."

One day as he looked his ring upon,
He saw the diamonds pale and wan.

He left the sea and came to land,
And the first that he met was an old beggar man.

"What news, what news?" said young Hind Horn;
"No news, no news," said the old beggar man.

"No news," said the beggar, "no news at a',
But there is a wedding in the king's ha.   20

"But there is a wedding in the king's ha,
That has halden these forty days and twa."

13. **reid-roan**, of a prevailingly red color mixed thickly with some other. 16. **erst**, once. **frie**, spirited. 20. **dule**, grief. **drie**, suffer. 25. **whatten**, what kind of. 33. **ha**, hall. 37. **tul**, till. **fa**, fall. 40. **maun**, must. 41. **bairns**, children. 45. **late**, let. **thrae**, through.

56. **Sic**, such. *Hind Horn* (Child 17). 3. **Hind**, Youth. 7. **gien**, given. 8. **lavrocks**, larks.

"Will ye lend me your begging coat?
And I'll lend you my scarlet cloak.

"Will you lend me your beggar's rung?
And I'll gie you my steed to ride upon.

"Will you lend me your wig o hair,
To cover mine, because it is fair?"

The auld beggar man was bound for the mill,
But young Hind Horn for the king's hall.   30

The auld beggar man was bound for to ride,
But young Hind Horn was bound for the bride.

When he came to the king's gate,
He sought a drink for Hind Horn's sake.

The bride came down with a glass of wine,
When he drank out the glass, and dropt in the ring.

"O got ye this by sea or land?
Or got ye it off a dead man's hand?"

"I got not it by sea, I got it by land,
And I got it, madam, out of your own hand."   40

"O I'll cast off my gowns of brown,
And beg wi you frae town to town.

"O I'll cast off my gowns of red,
And I'll beg wi you to win my bread."

"Ye needna cast off your gowns of brown,
For I'll make you lady o many a town.

"Ye needna cast off your gowns of red,
It's only a sham, the begging o my bread."

The bridegroom he had wedded the bride,
But young Hind Horn he took her to bed.   50

THE TWA CORBIES

The ballad's power of suggestion is made unusually striking here, when we contrast the blandly sinister fashion in which the ravens detail their future conduct with the little they tell us about the way in which the unfortunate knight came to his death. The hawk and the hound show too little concern, and the wife too much, but her reaction is hardly elegiac in nature.

  As I was walking all alane,
   I heard twa corbies making a mane;

25. **rung**, staff. *The Twa Corbies* (Child 26). 2. **corbies,** ravens. **mane,** lament.

  The tane unto the t'other say,
  "Where sall we gang and dine to-day?"

"In behint yon auld fail dyke,
I wot there lies a new slain knight;
And naebody kens that he lies there,
But his hawk, his hound, and lady fair.

"His hound is to the hunting gane,
His hawk to fetch the wild-fowl hame,   10
His lady's ta'en another mate,
So we may mak our dinner sweet.

"Ye'll sit on his white hause-bane,
And I'll pike out his bonny blue een;
Wi ae lock o his gowden hair
We'll theek our nest when it grows bare.

"Mony a one for him makes mane,
But nane sall ken where he is gane;
Oer his white banes, when they are bare,
The wind sall blaw for evermair."   20

KEMP OWYNE

There are many stories similar to this ballad of transformation and disenchantment; we are reminded of Chaucer's "Wife of Bath's Tale" in which the "loathly lady" can be restored only by gaining sovereignty over a husband. In one of the analogues to the "Wife's Tale," John Gower's "Tale of Florent," the heroine has been changed by a wicked stepmother; indeed, the stepmothers of story are much given to such practices. In most such tales one act is sufficient for disenchantment, but here the ballad's fondness for doing things in threes is brought into play.

  Her mother died when she was young,
   Which gave her cause to make great moan;
  Her father married the warst woman
   That ever lived in Christendom.

  She served her with foot and hand,
   In every thing that she could dee,
  Till once, in an unlucky time,
   She threw her in ower Craigy's sea.

  Says, "Lie you there, dove Isabel,
   And all my sorrows lie with thee;   10
  Till Kemp Owyne come ower the sea,
   And borrow you with kisses three,

The Twa Corbies. 3. **tane,** t(he) one. 4. **sall,** shall. 5. **fail dyke,** turf wall. 7. **kens,** knows. 13. **hause-bane,** neck bone. 14. **een,** eyes. 15. **gowden,** golden. 16. **theek,** thatch. *Kemp Owyne* (Child 34). 6. **dee,** do. 11. **Kemp,** Champion. 12. **borrow,** ransom.

Let all the warld do what they will,
    Oh borrowed shall you never be!"

Her breath grew strang, her hair grew lang,
    And twisted thrice about the tree,
And all the people, far and near,
    Thought that a savage beast was she.

These news did come to Kemp Owyne,
    Where he lived, far beyond the sea;   20
He hasted him to Craigy's sea,
    And on the savage beast lookd he.

Her breath was strang, her hair was lang,
    And twisted was about the tree,
And with a swing she came about:
    "Come to Craigy's sea, and kiss with me.

"Here is a royal belt," she cried,
    "That I have found in the green sea;
And while your body it is on,
    Drawn shall your blood never be;   30
But if you touch me, tail or fin,
    I vow my belt your death shall be."

He stepped in, gave her a kiss,
    The royal belt he brought him wi;
Her breath was strang, her hair was lang,
    And twisted twice about the tree,
And with a swing she came about:
    "Come to Craigy's sea, and kiss with me.

"Here is a royal ring," she said,
    "That I have found in the green sea;   40
And while your finger it is on,
    Drawn shall your blood never be;
But if you touch me, tail or fin,
    I swear my ring your death shall be."

He stepped in, gave her a kiss,
    The royal ring he brought him wi;
Her breath was strang, her hair was lang,
    And twisted ance about the tree,
And with a swing she came about:
    "Come to Craigy's sea, and kiss with me.   50

"Here is a royal brand," she said,
    "That I have found in the green sea;
And while your body it is on,
    Drawn shall your blood never be;
But if you touch me, tail or fin,
    I swear my brand your death shall be."

He stepped in, gave her a kiss,
    The royal brand he brought him wi;
Her breath was sweet, her hair grew short,
    And twisted nane about the tree,   60
And smilingly she came about,
    As fair a woman as fair could be.

THOMAS RYMER

Thomas the Rymer, that is, Thomas of Ercildoune, would appear to have been a historical personage of the thirteenth century who had, or gained soon after his death, a great reputation as poet and prophet. In the former capacity a version of the romance of Tristram was ascribed to him as early as 1330, and in the latter he is probably still remembered in Scotland. According to a late fourteenth-century poem which bears his name (see J. E. Wells, *A Manual of the Writings in Middle English*, Yale University Press, 1916, pp. 224 ff.) his prophecies were given to him by the queen of the elves or fairies. Some progenitor of this poem which did not contain, or at least, stress, the prophecies, is doubtless the ultimate source of the ballad.

One of the best of the numerous tales which deal with the union of a mortal to a fairy—the "otherworld bride" motif—is Marie de France's lay of "Lanval," which was turned into Middle English by Thomas Chester.

True Thomas lay oer yond grassy bank,
    And he beheld a ladie gay,
A ladie that was brisk and bold,
    Come riding oer the fernie brae.

Her skirt was of the grass-green silk,
    Her mantel of the velvet fine,
At ilka tett of her horse's mane
    Hung fifty silver bells and nine.

True Thomas he took off his hat,
    And bowed him low down till his knee: 10
"All hail, thou mighty Queen of Heaven!
    For your peer on earth I never did see."

"O no, O no, True Thomas," she says,
    "That name does not belong to me;
I am but the queen of fair Elfland,
    And I'm come here for to visit thee.

"But ye maun go wi me now, Thomas,
    True Thomas, ye maun go wi me,
For ye maun serve me seven years,
    Thro weel or wae as may chance to be."   20

27–30. belt . . . be. Compare the girdle which the Green Knight's wife gave to Gawain (page 131). **34. him wi,** with him. **51. brand,** sword.

Thomas Rymer (Child 37). **4. brae,** hillside. **7. ilka tett,** each lock. **16. thee.** There is something missing after this line. **17. maun,** must.

She turned about her milk-white steed,
    And took True Thomas up behind,
And aye wheneer her bridle rang,
    The steed flew swifter than the wind.

For forty days and forty nights
    He wade thro red blude to the knee,
And he saw neither sun nor moon,
    But heard the roaring of the sea.

O they rade on, and further on,
    Until they came to a garden green: 30
"Light down, light down, ye ladie free,
    Some of that fruit let me pull to thee."

"O no, O no, True Thomas," she says,
    "That fruit maun not be touched by thee,
For a' the plagues that are in hell
    Light on the fruit of this countrie.

"But I have a loaf here in my lap,
    Likewise a bottle of claret wine,
And now ere we go farther on,
    We'll rest a while, and ye may dine."   40

When he had eaten and drunk his fill,
    "Lay down your head upon my knee,"
The lady sayd, "ere we climb yon hill,
    And I will show you fairlies three.

"O see not ye yon narrow road,
    So thick beset wi thorns and briers?
That is the path of righteousness,
    Tho after it but few enquires.

"And see not ye that braid braid road,
    That lies across yon lillie leven?   50
That is the path of wickedness,
    Tho some call it the road to heaven.

"And see not ye that bonny road,
    Which winds about the fernie brae?
That is the road to fair Elfland,
    Where you and I this night maun gae.

"But Thomas, ye maun hold your tongue,
    Whatever you may hear or see,
For gin ae word you should chance to speak,
    You will neer get back to your ain countrie."   60

He has gotten a coat of the even cloth,
    And a pair of shoes of velvet green,
And till seven years were past and gone
    True Thomas on earth was never seen.

44. fairlies, wonders.   49. braid, broad.   50. lillie leven, charming glade.   59. gin ae, if one.   61. even, uniform in quality.

THE CHERRY-TREE CAROL

This delightful bit of New Testament apocrypha has been popular among American ballad-singers, and a version was recorded by Andrew R. Summers for Columbia, Old World Ballads in America (M–408).

    Joseph was an old man,
        And an old man was he,
    When he wedded Mary,
        In the land of Galilee.

    Joseph and Mary walked
        Through an orchard good,
    Where was cherries and berries,
        So red as any blood.

    Joseph and Mary walked
        Through an orchard green,   10
    Where was berries and cherries,
        As thick as might be seen.

    O then bespoke Mary,
        So meek and so mild:
    "Pluck me one cherry, Joseph,
        For I am with child."

    O then bespoke Joseph,
        With words most unkind:
    "Let him pluck thee a cherry
        That brought thee with child."   20

    O then bespoke the babe,
        Within his mother's womb:
    "Bow down then the tallest tree,
        For my mother to have some."

    Then bowed down the highest tree
        Unto his mother's hand;
    Then she cried, "See, Joseph,
        I have cherries at command."

    O then bespake Joseph:
        "I have done Mary wrong;   30
    But cheer up, my dearest,
        And be nōt cast down."

    Then Mary plucked a cherry,
        As red as the blood,
    Then Mary went home
        With her heavy load.

    Then Mary took her babe,
        And sat him on her knee

The Cherry-Tree Carol (Child 54).

Saying, "My dear son, tell me
    What this world will be."   40

"O I shall be as dead, mother,
    As the stones in the wall;
O the stones in the streets, mother,
    Shall mourn for me all.

"Upon Easter-day, mother,
    My uprising shall be;
O the sun and the moon, mother,
    Shall both rise with me."   48

SIR PATRICK SPENS

It really matters very little whether it is possible to identify Sir Patrick Spens with some Scottish sea dog or other, or whether his death is to be connected in any way with the marriage in 1281 of Margaret, daughter of Alexander III of Scotland, to King Eric of Norway. The ballad, whatever its source, celebrates the acts of men who, without too much regard to their own immediate judgment, carry out the orders of their king. Even with a tear in his eye Sir Patrick is of the breed that lived, lives, and must live.

The king sits in Dumferling toune,
    Drinking the blude-reid wine:
"O whar will I get guid sailor,
    To sail this schip of mine?"

Up and spak an eldern knicht,
    Sat at the kings richt kne:
"Sir Patrick Spence is the best sailor
    That sails upon the se."

The king has written a braid letter,
    And signd it wi his hand,   10
And sent it to Sir Patrick Spence,
    Was walking on the sand.

The first line that Sir Patrick red,
    A loud lauch lauched he;
The next line that Sir Patrick red,
    The teir blinded his ee.

"O wha is this has don this deid,
    This ill deid don to me,
To send me out this time o' the yeir,
    To sail upon the se!   20

"Mak hast, mak haste, my mirry men all,
    Our guid schip sails the morne":
"O say na sae, my master deir,
    For I feir a deadlie storme.

Sir Patrick Spens (Child 58). **16. ee,** eye.

"Late late yestreen I saw the new moone,
    Wi the auld moone in hir arme,
And I feir, I feir, my deir master,
    That we will cum to harme."

O our Scots nobles wer richt laith
    To weet their cork-heild schoone;   30
Bot lang owre a' the play wer playd,
    Thair hats they swam aboone.

O lang, lang may their ladies sit,
    Wi thair fans into their hand,
Or eir they se Sir Patrick Spence
    Cum sailing to the land.

O lang, lang may the ladies stand,
    Wi thair gold kems in their hair,
Waiting for thair ain deir lords,
    For they'll se thame na mair.   40

Haf owre, haf owre to Aberdour,
    It's fiftie fadom deip,
And thair lies guid Sir Patrick Spence,
    Wi the Scots lords at his feit.

FAIR MARGARET AND SWEET WILLIAM

"Fair Margaret and Sweet William" is an attractive specimen of a large group of ballads in which the hero, either for gold and lands, or, as here, for no very prominent reason, marries a "brown bride," and then speedily follows his own truelove to the grave.

Sweet William would a wooing ride,
    His steed was lovely brown;
A fairer creature than Lady Margaret
    Sweet William could find none.

Sweet William came to Lady Margaret's bower,
    And knocked at the ring,
And who so ready as Lady Margaret
    To rise and to let him in.

Down then came her father dear,
    Clothed all in blue: 10
"I pray, Sweet William, tell to me
    What love's between my daughter and you?"

29. laith, loath. **31. owre,** before. **32. aboone,** above. **35. Or eir,** before. **38. kems,** combs. **41. haf owre,** half (the way) over. *Fair Margaret and Sweet William* (Child 74). **6. ring,** the door knocker.

"I know none by her," he said,
    "And she knows none by me;
Before tomorrow at this time
    Another bride you shall see."

Lady Margaret at her bower-window,
    Combing of her hair,
She saw Sweet William and his brown bride
    Unto the church repair.   20

Down she cast her iv'ry comb,
    And up she tossed her hair,
She went out from her bowr alive,
    But never so more came there.

When day was gone, and night was come,
    All people were asleep,
In glided Margaret's grimly ghost,
    And stood at William's feet.

"How d' ye like your bed, Sweet William?
    How d' ye like your sheet?   30
And how d' ye like that brown lady,
    That lies in your arms asleep?"

"Well I like my bed, Lady Margaret,
    And well I like my sheet;
But better I like that fair lady
    That stands at my bed's feet."

When night was gone, and day was come,
    All people were awake,
The lady waket out of her sleep,
    And thus to her lord she spake.   40

"I dreamd a dream, my wedded lord,
    That seldom comes to good;
I dreamd that our bowr was lined with white swine,
    And our brid-chamber full of blood."

He called up his merry men all,
    By one, by two, by three,
"We will go to Lady Margaret's bower,
    With the leave of my wedded lady."

When he came to Lady Margaret's bower,
    He knocked at the ring,   50
And who were so ready as her brethren
    To rise and let him in.

"Oh is she in the parlour," he said,
    "Or is she in the hall?
Or is she in the long chamber,
    Amongst her merry maids all?"

    27. grimly, terrible.   **43. lined,** filled.

"She's not in the parlour," they said
    "Nor is she in the hall;
But she is in the long chamber,
    Laid out against the wall."   60

"Open the winding sheet," he cryed,
    "That I may kiss the dead;
That I may kiss her pale and wan
    Whose lips used to look so red."

Lady Margaret died on the over night,
    Sweet William died on the morrow;
Lady Margaret died for pure, pure love,
    Sweet William died for sorrow.

On Margaret's grave there grew a rose,
    On Sweet William's grew a briar;   70
They grew till they joined in a true lover's knot,
    And then they died both together.

THE UNQUIET GRAVE

Seldom has a melancholy mood been fixed so firmly or so well as in the first two lines of this ballad.

"The wind doth blow today, my love,
    And a few small drops of rain;
I never had but one true-love,
    In cold grave she was lain.

"I'll do as much for my true-love
    As any young man may;
I'll sit and mourn all at her grave
    For a twelvemonth and a day."

The twelvemonth and a day being up,
    The dead began to speak: 10
"Oh who sits weeping on my grave,
    And will not let me sleep?"

"'Tis I, my love, sits on your grave,
    And will not let you sleep;
For I crave one kiss of your clay-cold lips,
    And that is all I seek."

"You crave one kiss of my clay-cold lips;
    But my breath smells earthy strong;
If you have one kiss of my clay-cold lips,
    Your time will not be long.   20

"'Tis down in yonder garden green,
    Love, where we used to walk,
The finest flower that ere was seen
    Is withered to a stalk.

    65. over night, night before.   *The Unquiet Grave* (Child 78).

"The stalk is withered dry, my love,
   So will our hearts decay;
So make yourself content, my love,
   Till God calls you away."

THE WIFE OF USHER'S WELL

In many ballads and tales the dead return, but almost never in the casual fashion of the sons in this version of "The Wife of Usher's Well." Here the revenants seem anxious only to give momentary consolation to their sorrowing mother. The simplicity of the poem is profoundly moving, and we are especially touched by the quiet enumeration of domestic details in the final stanza. An American version called "Lady Gay" was recorded by Andrew R. Summers for Columbia, Old World Ballads in America (M–408).

There lived a wife at Usher's Well,
   And a wealthy wife was she;
She had three stout and stalwart sons,
   And sent them oer the sea.

They hadna been a week from her,
   A week but barely ane,
Whan word came to the carline wife
   That her three sons were gane.

They hadna been a week from her,
   A week but barely three,   10
Whan word came to the carlin wife
   That her sons she'd never see.

"I wish the wind may never cease,
   Nor fashes in the flood,
Till my three sons come hame to me,
   In earthly flesh and blood."

It fell about the Martinmass,
   When nights are lang and mirk,
The carlin wife's three sons came hame,
   And their hats were o the birk.   20

It neither grew in syke nor ditch,
   Nor yet in ony sheugh;
But at the gates o Paradise,
   That birk grew fair eneugh.

"Blow up the fire, my maidens,
   Bring water from the well;
For a' my house shall feast this night,
   Since my three sons are well."

And she has made to them a bed,
   She's made it large and wide,   30
And she's taen her mantle her about,
   Sat down at the bed-side.

Up then crew the red, red cock,
   And up and crew the gray;
The eldest to the youngest said,
   " 'T is time we were away."

The cock he hadna crawd but once,
   And clappd his wings at a',
When the youngest to the eldest said,
   "Brother, we must awa."   40

"The cock doth craw, the day doth daw,
   The channerin worm doth chide;
Gin we be mist out o our place,
   A sair pain we maun bide.

"Fare ye weel, my mother dear!
   Fareweel to barn and byre!
And fare ye weel, the bonny lass
   That kindles my mother's fire!"

BONNY BARBARA ALLAN

It is probably safe to say that no one of the Child ballads has been collected in America more often than "Barbara Allan." Samuel Pepys heard his favorite Mrs. Knipp sing it in 1666 and we can still hear it today. Of the many American recordings the best is that of John J. Niles for Victor, Early American Ballads (M–604).

It was in and about the Martinmas time,
   When the green leaves were a falling,
That Sir John Graeme, in the West Country,
   Fell in love with Barbara Allan.

He sent his man down through the town,
   To the place where she was dwelling:
"O haste and come to my master dear,
   Gin ye be Barbara Allan."

O hooly, hooly rose she up,
   To the place where he was lying,   10
And when she drew the curtain by,
   "Young man, I think you 're dying."

"O it's I'm sick, and very, very sick,
   And 't is a' for Barbara Allan:"

The Wife of Usher's Well (Child 79). **7. carline,** woman, old woman. **14. fashes,** troubles. **17. Martinmass,** November 11. **18. mirk,** dark. **20. birk,** birch. **21. syke,** trench. **22. sheugh,** furrow.

36. 'T is time. At cockcrow the dead must return to their graves. **38. And,** and (had not). **41. daw,** dawn. **42. channerin,** fretting. **46. byre,** cow house. *Bonny Barbara Allan* (Child 84). **8. Gin,** if. **9. hooly,** softly.

"O the better for me ye's never be,
  Tho your heart's blood were a spilling.

"O dinna ye mind, young man," said she,
  "When ye was in the tavern a drinking,
That ye made the healths gae round and round,
  And slighted Barbara Allan?"   20

He turnd his face unto the wall,
  And death was with him dealing:
"Adieu, adieu, my dear friends all,
  And be kind to Barbara Allan."

And slowly, slowly raise she up,
  And slowly, slowly left him,
And sighing said, she coud not stay,
  Since death of life had reft him.

She had not gane a mile but twa,
  When she heard the dead-bell ringing, 30
And every jow that the dead-bell geid,
  It cry'd, Woe to Barbara Allan!

"O mother, mother, make my bed!
  O make it saft and narrow!
Since my love died for me to-day,
  I'll die for him to-morrow."

ROBIN HOOD AND GUY OF GISBORNE

We have already seen (page 114) that poems about Robin Hood were current during the last quarter of the fourteenth century, and *Gamelyn* proves that other greenwood heroes were not unknown. The present ballad, one of the oldest in which Robin figures, shows him still able to win his battles unaided. In many of the later ballads we find him conquered with surprising ease by men who subsequently join his band and become his loyal followers. Robin, as a matter of fact, suffered from the same epic degeneration which affected Arthur and Charlemagne. Indeed, it is not too inexact to refer to Robin as the hero of an epic which never quite crystallized. Efforts to identify the hero as a historical figure, or as the god Odin fallen on relatively evil days, are not to be taken seriously.

When shawes beene sheene, and shradds full fayre,
  And leeves both large and longe,
Itt is merry, walking in the fayre fforrest,
  To heare the small birds songe.

The woodweele sang, and wold not cease,
  Amongst the leaves a lyne:
And it is by two wight yeomen,
  By deare God, that I meane.

"Me thought they did mee beate and binde,
  And tooke my bow mee froe;   10
If I bee Robin a-live in this lande,
  I'le be wrocken on both them towe."

"Sweavens are swift, master," quoth John,
  "As the wind that blowes ore a hill;
Ffor if itt be never soe lowde this night,
  To-morrow it may be still."

"Buske yee, bowne yee, my merry men all,
  Ffor John shall goe with mee;
For I'le goe seeke yond wight yeomen
  In greenwood where the bee."   20

The cast on their gowne of greene,
  A shooting gone are they,
Untill they came to the merry greenwood,
  Where they had gladdest bee;
There were the ware of a wight yeoman,
  His body leaned to a tree.

A sword and a dagger he wore by his side,
  Had beene many a mans bane,
And he was cladd in his capull-hyde,
  Topp, and tayle, and mayne.   30

"Stand you still, master," quoth Litle John,
  "Under this trusty tree,
And I will goe to yond wight yeoman,
  To know his meaning trulye."

"A, John, by me thou setts noe store,
  And that's a ffarley thinge;
How offt send I my men beffore,
  And tarry my-selfe behinde?

"It is noe cunning a knave to ken,
  And a man but heare him speake;   40
And itt were not for bursting of my bowe,
  John, I wold thy head breake."

But often words they breeden bale,
  That parted Robin and John;

15. **ye's**, you shall.   17. **dinna ye mind**, do you not remember.   31. **jow**, stroke. **geid**, gave. *Robin Hood and Guy of Gisborne* (Child 118). 1. **shawes**, woods. **sheene**, beautiful. **shradds**, twigs.   5. **woodweele**, perhaps the golden oriole.   6. **leaves a lyne**, linden leaves.   7. **wight**, strong.   8. **meane**. There is a gap after this line—in which Robin dreams of having been beaten, presumably by two yeomen.   10. **froe**, from.   12. **wrocken**, avenged.   13. **Sweavens**, dreams.   17. **Buske**, prepare. **bowne**, make ready.   21. **The**, they.   25. **ware**, aware.   28. **bane**, death.   29. **capull-hyde**, horse hide.   36. **ffarley**, strange.   39. **ken**, know.   41. **And**, if.   43. **bale**, trouble.

John is gone to Barnesdale,
    The gates he knowes eche one.

And when hee came to Barnesdale,
    Great heavinesse there hee hadd;
He ffound two of his fellowes
    Were slaine both in a slade,   50

And Scarlett a ffoote flyinge was,
    Over stockes and stone,
For the sheriffe with seven score men
    Fast after him is gone.

"Yett one shoote I'le shoote," sayes Litle John,
    "With Crist his might and mayne;
I'le make yond fellow that flyes soe fast
    To be both glad and ffaine."

John bent up a good veiwe bow,
    And ffetteled him to shoote;   60
The bow was made of a tender boughe,
    And fell downe to his foote.

"Woe worth thee, wicked wood," sayd Litle John,
    "That ere thou grew on a tree!
Ffor this day thou art my bale,
    My boote when thou shold bee!"

This shoote it was but looselye shott,
    The arrowe flew in vaine,
And it mett one of the sheriffes men;
    Good William a Trent was slaine.   70

It had beene better for William a Trent
    To hange upon a gallowe
Then for to lye in the greenwoode,
    There slaine with an arrowe.

And it is sayd, when men be mett,
    Six can doe more then three:
And they have tane Litle John,
    And bound him ffast to a tree.

"Thou shalt be drawen by dale and downe," quoth
    the sheriffe,
    "And hanged hye on a hill:"   80
"But thou may ffayle," quoth Litle John,
    "If itt be Christs owne will."

Let us leave talking of Litle John,
    For hee is bound fast to a tree,
And talke of Guy and Robin Hood,
    In the green woode where they bee.

How these two yeomen together they mett,
    Under the leaves of lyne,
To see what marchandise they made
    Euen at that same time.   90

"Good morrow, good fellow," quoth Sir Guy;
    "Good morrow, good ffellow," quoth hee;
"Methinkes by this bow thou beares in thy hand,
    A good archer thou seems to bee."

"I am wilfull of my way," quoth Sir Guye,
    "And of my morning tyde:"
"I'le lead thee through the wood," quoth Robin
    "Good ffellow, I'le be thy guide."

"I seeke an outlaw," quoth Sir Guye,
    "Men call him Robin Hood;   100
I had rather meet with him upon a day
    Then forty pound of golde."

"If you tow mett, itt wold be seene whether were
    better
    Afore yee did part awaye;
Let us some other pastime find,
    Good ffellow, I thee pray.

"Let us some other masteryes make,
    And wee will walke in the woods even;
Wee may chance meet with Robin Hoode
    Att some unsett steven."   110

They cutt them downe the summer shroggs
    Which grew both under a bryar,
And sett them three score rood in twinn,
    To shoote the prickes full neare.

"Leade on, good ffellow," sayd Sir Guye,
    "Lead on, I doe bidd thee:"
"Nay, by my faith," quoth Robin Hood,
    "The leader thou shalt bee."

The first good shoot that Robin ledd
    Did not shoote an inch the pricke ffroe;   120
Guy was an archer good enoughe,
    But he cold neere shoote soe.

The second shoote Sir Guy shott,
    He shott within the garlande;

46. gates, ways. **48. heavinesse**, sorrow. **50. slade**, valley. **59. veiwe**, yew. **60. ffetteled**, made ready. **63. Woe . . . thee**, woe come to you. **66. boote**, help. **77. tane**, taken. **89. marchandise**, dealing. **95. wilfull . . . way**, lost. **96. tyde**, time. **103. tow**, two. **whether**, which. **107. masteryes**, feats of skill. **110. Att . . . steven**, at some unappointed time. **111. shroggs**, rods. **113. in twinn**, apart. **114. prickes**, butts, marks. **124. garlande**, a wreath on the rod.

But Robin Hoode shott it better then hee,
    For he clove the good pricke-wande.

"Gods blessing on thy heart!" sayes Guye,
    "Goode ffellow, thy shooting is goode;
For an thy hart be as good as thy hands,
    Thou were better then Robin Hood.   130

"Tell me thy name, good ffellow," quoth Guy
    "Under the leaves of lyne:"
"Nay, by my faith," quoth good Robin,
    "Till thou have told me thine."

"I dwelle by dale and downe," quoth Guye,
    "And I have done many a curst turne;
And he that calles me by my right name
    Calles me Guye of good Gysborne."

"My dwelling is in the wood," sayes Robin;
    "By thee I set right nought;   140
My name is Robin Hood of Barnesdale,
    A ffellow thou has long sought."

He that had neither beene a kithe nor kin
    Might have seene a full fayre sight,
To see how together these yeomen went,
    With blades both browne and bright.

To have seene how these yeomen together fought,
    Two howers of a summers day;
Itt was neither Guy nor Robin Hood
    That ffettled them to flye away.   150

Robin was reacheles on a roote,
    And stumbled at that tyde,
And Guy was quicke and nimble with-all,
    And hitt him ore the left side.

"Ah, deere Lady!" sayd Robin Hoode,
    "Thou art both mother and may!
I thinke it was never mans destinye
    To dye before his day."

Robin thought on Our Lady deere,
    And soone leapt up againe,   160
And thus he came with an awkwarde stroke;
    Good Sir Guy hee has slayne.

He tooke Sir Guys head by the hayre,
    And sticked itt on his bowes end:
"Thou hast beene traytor all thy liffe,
    Which thing must have an ende."

Robin pulled forth an Irish kniffe,
    And nicked Sir Guy in the fface,
That hee was never on a woman borne
    Cold tell who Sir Guye was.   170

Saies, "Lye there, lye there, good Sir Guye,
    And with me be not wrothe;
If thou have had the worse stroakes at my hand,
    Thou shalt have the better cloathe."

Robin did off his gowne of greene,
    Sir Guye hee did it throwe;
And hee put on that capull-hyde,
    That cladd him topp to toe.

"The bowe, the arrowes, and litle horne,
    And with me now I'le beare;   180
Ffor now I will goe to Barnesdale,
    To see how my men doe ffare."

Robin sett Guyes horne to his mouth,
    A lowd blast in it he did blow;
That beheard the sheriffe of Nottingham,
    As he leaned under a lowe.

"Hearken! hearken!" sayd the sheriffe,
    "I heard noe tydings but good;
For yonder I heare Sir Guyes horne blowe,
    For he hath slaine Robin Hoode.   190

"For yonder I heare Sir Guyes horne blow,
    Itt blowes soe well in tyde,
For yonder comes that wighty yeoman,
    Cladd in his capull-hyde.

"Come hither, thou good Sir Guy,
    Aske of mee what thou wilt have:"
"I'le none of thy gold," sayes Robin Hood,
    "Nor I'le none of itt have.

"But now I have slaine the master," he sayd,
    "Let me goe strike the knave;   200
This is all the reward I aske,
    Nor noe other will I have."

"Thou art a madman," said the shiriffe,
    "Thou sholdest have had a knights ffee;
Seeing thy asking hath beene soe badd,
    Well granted it shall be."

But Litle John heard his master speake,
    Well he knew that was his steven;

136. curst turne, mean trick.   **143.** kithe nor kin, friend nor relative.   **151.** reacheles on, careless about.   **161.** awkwarde, backhanded.   **169.** on, of.   **185.** beheard, heard.   **186.** lowe, hill.   **208.** steven, voice.

"Now shall I be loset," quoth Litle John,
    "With Christs might in heaven." 210

But Robin hee hyed him towards Litle John,
    Hee thought hee wold loose him belive;
The sheriffe and all his companye
    Fast after him did drive.

"Stand abacke! stand abacke!" sayd Robin;
    "Why draw you mee soe neere?
Itt was never the use in our countrye
    One's shrift another shold heere."

But Robin pulled forth an Irysh kniffe,
    And losed John hand and ffoote, 220
And gave him Sir Guyes bow in his hand,
    And bade it be his boote.

But John tooke Guyes bow in his hand—
    His arrowes were rawstye by the roote—;
The sheriffe saw Litle John draw a bow
    And ffettle him to shoote.

Towards his house in Nottingham
    He ffled full fast away,
And soe did all his companye,
    Not one behind did stay. 230

But he cold neither soe fast goe,
    Nor away soe fast runn,
But Litle John, with an arrow broade,
    Did cleave his heart in twinn.

JOHNIE ARMSTRONG

Centuries of warfare between England and Scotland inevitably led to the creation of a disputed borderland between the two countries; as inevitably the inhabitants of the border became so inured to strife and its convenient confusion between "mine and thine" that they felt free to overlook an occasional truce or peace. The borderers, however, were not only fighters and thieves; they were also composers and singers of ballads, and some of our most stirring poems sprang from their irregular way of life. John Armstrong, like most of his peers, was no respecter of nationality, and, himself a Scot, was executed during James V's efforts to pacify his borders in 1530. Despite the tenor of the ballad, doubtless composed and cherished in the Armstrong clan, we need not feel that John's death was necessarily an act of treachery and murder.

209. **loset,** freed. 212. **belive,** at once. 218. **shrift,** confession. 222. **boote,** help. 224. **rawstye . . . roote,** rusty at the end. 234. **in twinn,** in two. *Johnie Armstrong* (Child 169).

There dwelt a man in faire Westmerland,
    Jonne Armstrong men did him call,
He had nither lands nor rents coming in,
    Yet he kept eight score men in his hall.

He had horse and harness for them all,
    Goodly steeds were all milke-white;
O the golden bands an about their necks,
    And their weapons, they were all alike.

Newes then was brought unto the king
    That there was sicke a won as hee, 10
That lived lyke a bold out-law,
    And robbed all the north country.

The king he writt an a letter then,
    A letter which was large and long;
He signed it with his owne hand,
    And promised to doe him no wrong.

When this letter came Jonne untill,
    His heart it was as blythe as birds on the tree:
"Never was I sent for before any king,
    My father, my grandfather, nor none but mee. 20

"And if wee goe the king before,
    I would we went most orderly;
Every man of you shall have his scarlet cloak,
    Laced with silver laces three.

"Every won of you shall have his velvett coat,
    Laced with sillver lace so white;
O the golden bands an about your necks,
    Black hatts, white feathers, all alyke."

By the morrow morninge at ten of the clock,
    Towards Edenburough gon was hee, 30
And with him all his eight score men;
    Good lord, it was a goodly sight for to see!

When Jonne came befower the king,
    He fell downe on his knee;
"O pardon, my soveraine leige," he said,
    "O pardon my eight score men and mee!"

"Thou shalt have no pardon, thou traytor strong,
    For thy eight score men nor thee;
For to-morrow morning by ten of the clock,
    Both thou and them shall hang on the gallow-tree." 40

But Jonne looke'd over his left shoulder,
    Good Lord, what a grevious look looked hee!

10. **sicke a won,** such a one.

THE POPULAR BALLAD

Saying, "Asking grace of a graceles face—
    Why there is none for you nor me."

But Jonne had a bright sword by his side,
    And it was made of the mettle so free,
That had not the king stept his foot aside,
    He had smitten his head from his faire bodde.

Saying, "Fight on, my merry men all,
    And see that none of you be taine;   50
For rather then men shall say we were hanged,
    Let them report how we were slaine."

Then, God wott, faire Eddenburrough rose,
    And so besett poore Jonne rounde,
That fowerscore and tenn of Jonnes best men
    Lay gasping all upon the ground.

Then like a mad man Jonne laide about,
    And like a mad man then fought hee,
Untill a falce Scot came Jonne behinde,
    And runn him through the faire boddee.   60

Saying, "Fight on, my merry men all,
    And see that none of you be taine;
And I will stand by and bleed but awhile,
    And then will I come and fight againe."

Newes then was brought to young Jonne Armestrong,
    As he stood by his nurses knee,
Who vowed if ere he lived for to be a man,
    O the treacherous Scots revengd hee'd be.

MARY HAMILTON

The tragic and moving story of Mary Hamilton has been connected with an incident at the Scottish court and with another, involving a Scots girl named Hamilton, at the court of Peter the Great of Russia. In the ballad itself the "hichest Stewart of a'" is Darnley and the "auld queen," who would have taken little pleasure in the adjective, since she was only twenty-five when Darnley was murdered, is Mary Queen of Scots. An American version, which omits the reason for the execution, was recorded by Andrew R. Summers for Columbia, Old World Ballads in America (M—408).

    Word's gane to the kitchen,
        And word's gane to the ha,
    That Marie Hamilton gangs wi bairn
        To the hichest Stewart of a'.

He's courted her in the kitchen,
    He's courted her in the ha,
He's courted her in the laigh cellar,
    And that was warst of a'.

She's tyed it in her apron
    And she's thrown it in the sea;   10
Says, "Sink ye, swim ye, bonny wee babe!
    You'l neer get mair o me."

Down then cam the auld queen,
    Goud tassels tying her hair:
"O Marie, where's the bonny wee babe
    That I heard greet sae sair?"

"There was never a babe intill my room,
    As little designs to be;
It was but a touch o my sair side,
    Come oer my fair bodie."   20

"O Marie, put on your robes o black,
    Or else your robes o brown,
For ye maun gang wi me the night,
    To see fair Edinbro town."

"I winna put on my robes o black,
    Nor yet my robes o brown;
But I'll put on my robes o white,
    To shine through Edinbro town."

When she gaed up the Cannogate,
    She laughed loud laughters three;   30
But whan she cam down the Cannogate
    The tear blinded her ee.

When she gaed up the Parliament stair,
    The heel cam aff her shee;
And lang or she cam down again
    She was condemnd to dee.

When she cam down the Cannogate,
    The Cannogate sae free,
Many a ladie lookd oer her window,
    Weeping for this ladie.   40

"Ye need nae weep for me," she says,
    "Ye need nae weep for me;
For had I not slain mine own sweet babe,
    This death I wadna dee.

"Bring me a bottle of wine," she says,
    "The best that eer ye hae,

---

46. **mettle so free**, metal so fine.   50. **taine**, taken.   68. **O**, on.   *Mary Hamilton* (Child 173). 2. **ha**, hall.   4. **hichest**, highest.   7. **laigh**, low.   14. **Goud**, gold.   16. **greet**, cry, weep.   23. **maun**, must.   34. **shee**, shoe.   46. **eer ye hae**, ever you have.

That I may drink to my weil-wishers,
    And they may drink to me.

"Here's a health to the jolly sailors,
    That sail upon the main;   50
Let them never let on to my father and mother
    But what I'm coming hame.

"Here's a health to the jolly sailors,
    That sail upon the sea;
Let them never let on to my father and mother
    That I cam here to dee.

"Oh little did my mother think,
    The day she cradled me,
What lands I was to travel through,
    What death I was to dee.   60

"Oh little did my father think,
    The day he held up me,
What lands I was to travel through,
    What death I was to dee.

"Last night I washd the queen's feet,
    And gently laid her down;
And a' the thanks I've gotten the nicht
    To be hangd in Edinbro town!

"Last nicht there was four Maries,
    The nicht there'l be but three;   70
There was Marie Seton, and Marie Beton,
    And Marie Carmichael, and me."

THE BONNY EARL OF MURRAY

James Stewart, Earl of Murray, was killed in 1592 by his bitter enemy George Gordon, first Marquess of Huntly.

Ye Highlands, and ye Lawlands,
    Oh where have you been?
They have slain the Earl of Murray,
    And they layd him on the green.

"Now wae be to thee, Huntly!
    And wherefore did you sae?
I bade you bring him wi you,
    But forbade you him to slay."

He was a braw gallant,
    And he rid at the ring;   10
And the bonny Earl of Murray,
    Oh he might have been a king!

The Bonny Earl of Murray (Child 181). **9. braw**, fine. **10. rid . . . ring**, a riding game, the point of which was to catch on one's spear a ring hanging from a pole.

He was a braw gallant,
    And he playd at the ba;
And the bonny Earl of Murray
    Was the flower amang them a'.

He was a braw gallant,
    And he playd at the glove;
And the bonny Earl of Murray,
    Oh he was the Queen's love!   20

Oh lang will his lady
    Look oer the castle Down,
Eer she see the Earl of Murray
    Come sounding thro the town!

GET UP AND BAR THE DOOR

"Get Up and Bar the Door" is one of the very few humorous popular ballads. Another, "Our Goodman," is still current in many American versions, most of which are none too seemly.

It fell about the Martinmas time,
    And a gay time it was then,
When our good wife got puddings to make,
    And she's boild them in the pan.

The wind sae cauld blew south and north,
    And blew into the floor;
Quoth our goodman to our goodwife,
    "Gae out and bar the door."

"My hand is in my hussyfskap,
    Goodman, as ye may see;   10
An it shoud nae be barrd this hundred year,
    It's no be barrd for me."

They made a paction tween them twa,
    They made it firm and sure,
That the first word whaeer shoud speak,
    Shoud rise and bar the door.

Then by there came two gentlemen,
    At twelve oclock at night,
And they could neither see house nor hall,
    Nor coal nor candle-light.   20

"Now whether is this a rich man's house,
    Or whether is it a poor?"
But neer a word wad ane o them speak,
    For barring of the door.

14. ba, ball. **22. Down**, Doune in Perthshire. **24. sounding**, blowing a trumpet or bugle. *Get Up and Bar the Door* (Child 275). **1. Martinmas**, November 11. **3. puddings**, sausages. **9. hussyfskap**, housewifery. **15. whaeer**, whoever.

And first they ate the white puddings,
    And then they ate the black;
Tho muckle thought the goodwife to hersel,
    Yet neer a word she spake.

Then said the one unto the other,
    "Here, man, tak ye my knife;   30
Do ye tak aff the auld man's beard,
    And I'll kiss the goodwife."

"But there's nae water in the house,
    And what shall we do than?"

"What ails ye at the pudding-broo,
    That boils into the pan?"

O up then started our goodman,
    An angry man was he:
"Will ye kiss my wife before my een,
    And scad me wi pudding-bree?"   40

Then up and started our goodwife,
    Gied three skips on the floor:
"Goodman, you've spoken the foremost word,
    Get up and bar the door."

Middle English Drama

THE SECOND PLAY OF THE SHEPHERDS

One of the most fascinating chapters in medieval literary history is that which deals with the development of the vernacular drama. These new plays came into being without the conscious use of models taken from classical sources, but it is a striking fact that their origin was closely parallel to what we postulate for the birth of Greek drama. Just as Greek tragedy grew out of the ceremonial worship of Dionysus, so medieval drama was called into being by the exigencies of the Christian Church. The earliest traces of medieval dramatic representation grew from an effort to make clear to a non-Latin-speaking congregation the significance of the principal events in the life of Christ. This is not the place to outline the growth of medieval drama from the simple Easter trope to the completed cycles of Biblical plays, and, beside or beyond them, to the miracles and moralities. One thing, however, we must not fail to note: If the plays were to increase in scope and dramatic significance, it was necessary for them to escape the hampering bonds of strict adherence to Biblical narrative. This freedom from static sterility was gained by the introduction, somehow or other, of an essentially nonreligious and thoroughly contemporary note which, however crude and elementary as it often is, we may call humor. Certain characters, non-Biblical or Biblical, but seldom carrying any profound religious connotation, were early shown in a ludicrous light. Satan, Cain, Cain's servant, Noah's wife, the shepherds, Herod, and Pilate were either burlesqued or allowed to do amusing things and speak in a salty way. The humorous scenes were always mere incidents in the religious plays and no doubt served as leaven for a mass of rather heavy dramatic dough.

Among the cycles, or collections of Biblical plays arranged for presentation in chronological order from the fall of Lucifer to the Day of Doom, by far the best is the Towneley, which receives its name from the family which once owned it. It seems reasonably clear that the cycle, which has affiliations with that of York, is to be associated with the town of Wakefield in Yorkshire. This cycle owes its literary fame to the fact that some of its plays were written, and others revised, by a man whom it is customary to call the first comic genius of the English stage, and to name, for want of anything better, "the Wakefield Master." All of the plays in which he had a hand are far above the average, but *The Second Play of the Shepherds*, so called because he had previously written another *Shepherds' Play* of more conventional sort, is his greatest accomplishment. Here for the first time we get an original plot treated in such a fashion as to divorce it completely from the ordinary Biblical drama. Although we may enjoy the humor of Cain, Noah's wife, or the shepherds of earlier plays, we are always aware that they are part of a dramatic exercise which, however conventional, was basically devotional. We can read or see the *Second Shepherds' Play* through six hundred and twenty-eight of its seven hundred and fifty-four lines without having any reason to believe it other than a purely secular comedy. Indeed, we may even call the story of Mak a long farcical curtain-raiser for a short religious play. It is but a slight step from a production of this kind to such an interlude as John Heywood's *Johan Johan the Husband*.

27. **Tho muckle,** then much.   35. **broo,** broth.   40. **scad,** scald.

The present text is based on the edition of the *Towneley Cycle* made by George England and A. W. Pollard for the Early English Text Society, Vol. LXXI, London, 1897.

Dramatis Personae

FIRST SHEPHERD (COLL)   MAK   ANGEL
SECOND SHEPHERD (GIB)   GYLL, his wife JESUS
THIRD SHEPHERD (DAW)   MARY

First Shep. Lord, what these weders ar cold!
  and I am yll happyd;
I am nere-hande dold so long have I nappyd;
My legys thay fold, my fyngers ar chappyd,
It is not as I wold, for I am al lappyd
  In sorow.
In stormes and tempest,
Now in the eest, now in the west,
Wo is hym has never rest
  Myd-day nor morow!

Bot we sely shepardes that walkys on the moore, 10
In fayth we are nere-handys outt of the doore;
No wonder as it standys, if we be poore,
Ffor the tylthe of oure landys lyys falow as the floore,
  As ye ken.
We ar so hamyd,
Ffor-taxed and ramyd,
We ar mayde hand-tamyd,
  With thyse gentlery-men.

Thus thay refe us oure rest, Oure Lady theym
  wary!
These men that ar lord-fest, thay cause the ploghe
  tary. 20
That men say is for the best, we fynde it contrary;
Thus ar husbandys opprest, in pointe to myscary,
  On lyfe,
Thus hold thay us hunder,
Thus thay bryng us in blonder;
It were greatte wonder,
  And ever shuld we thryfe.

Ther shall com a swane as prowde as a po,
He must borow my wane, my ploghe also,
Then I am full fane to graunt or he go. 30
Thus lyf we in payne, anger, and wo,
  By nyght and day;
He must have if he langyd,
If I shuld forgang it,
I were better be hangyd
  Then oones say hym nay.

Ffor may he gett a paynt slefe or a broche now-on-
  dayes,
Wo is hym sat hym grefe or onys agane says!
Dar noman hym reprefe, what mastry he mays,
And yit may noman lefe oone word that he says, 40
  No letter.
He can make purveance,
With boste and bragance,
And all is thrugh mantenance
  Of men that are gretter.

It dos me good, as I walk thus by myn oone,
Of this warld for to talk in maner of mone.
To my shepe wyll I stalk and herkyn anone,
Ther abyde on a balk or sytt on a stone
  Ffull soyne. 50
Ffor I trowe, perde,
Trew men if thay be,
We gett more compane
  Or it be noyne.

Second Shep. Benste and Dominus! What may this
  bemeyne?
Why, fares this warld thus oft have we not sene?
Lord, thyse weders ar spytus and the weders full
  kene.
And the frostys so hydus thay water myn eeyne,
  No ly.
Now in dry, now in wete, 60
Now in snaw, now in slete,
When my shone freys to my fete,
  It is not all esy.

Bot as far as I ken or yit as I go,
We sely wedmen dre mekyll wo;
We have sorow then and then, it fallys oft so;
Sely Capyle, oure hen, both to and fro
  She kakyls;
Bot begyn she to crok,
To groyne, or to clok, 70

1. **weders**, weather. **happyd**, wrapped. 2. **nere-hande dold**, almost dulled. 4. **lappyd**, surrounded. 10. **sely**, innocent. 11. **doore**, that is, house and home. 13. **tylthe**, condition. 15. **hamyd**, crippled. 16. **Ffor-taxed**, excessively taxed. **ramyd**, beaten down. 17. **hand-tamyd**, subdued. 19. **refe**, rob. **wary!** curse. 20. **lord-fest**, attached to a lord, that is, his agents. 22. **husbandys**, farmers. 28–36. **Ther shall . . . nay.** These lines follow ll. 37–45 in the manuscript, but the sense is improved by reversing the order. **swane**, servingman. **po**, peacock. **wane**, wagon. **langyd**, longed.

37. **paynt**, painted, ornamented with a badge. 38. **agane**, against. 40. **lefe**, believe. 42. **purveance**, the requisition of provisions and the like at an arbitrarily fixed price. 49. **balk**, ridge. 50. **soyne**, soon. 51. **perde**, *par dieu*, by God. 55. **Benste**, Benedicite. **bemeyne**, mean. 57. **spytus**, spiteful. 62. **shone**, shoes. 65. **wedmen**, married men. **dre**, suffer. 69. **crok**, croak. 70. **groyne**, grumble. **clok**, cluck.

MIDDLE ENGLISH DRAMA

Wo is hym is of oure cok,
   Ffor he is in the shekyls.

These men that ar wed haue not all thare wyll,
When they ar full hard sted thay sygh full styll;
God wayte thay ar led full hard and full yll;
In bower nor in bed thay say noght ther-tyll,
   This tyde.
My parte have I fun,
I know my lesson.
Wo is hym that is bun,   80
   Ffor he must abyde.

Bot now late in oure lyfys, a mervell to me,
That I thynk my hart ryfys sich wonders to see.
What that destany dryfys it shuld so be;
Som men wyll have two wyfys and som men thre,
   In store;
Som ar wo that has any,
Bot so far can I,
Wo is hym that has many,
   Ffor he felys sore.   90

Bot yong men of wowyng, for God that you boght,
Be well war of wedyng, and thynk in youre thoght,
"Had I wyst" is a thyng it servys of noght;
Mekyll styll mowrnyng has wedyng home broght,
   And grefys;
With many a sharp showre,
Ffor thou may cach in an owre
That shall savour fulle sowre
   As long as thou lyffys.

Ffor, as ever red I pystyll, I have oone to my
   fere,   100
As sharp as a thystyll, as rugh as a brere;
She is browyd lyke a brystyll, with a sowre-loten
   chere;
Had she oones wett hyr whystyll she couth syng
   full clere
   Hyr pater-noster.
She is as greatt as a whall,
She has a galon of gall:
By hym that dyed for us all,
   I wald I had ryn to I had lost hir.

   First Shep. God looke over the raw, ffull defly ye
   stand.

   Second Shep. Yee, the dewill in thi maw, so tari-
   and.   110
Sagh thou awro of Daw?
   First Shep.   Yee, on a ley land
Hard I hym blaw; he commys here at hand,
   Not far;
Stand styll.
   Second Shep. Qwhy?
   First Shep. Ffor he commys, hope I.
   Second Shep. He wyll make us both a ly
   Bot if we be war.

   Third Shep. Crystys crosse me spede, and Sant
   Nycholas!
Ther of had I nede, it is wars then it was.
Whoso couthe take hede and lett the warld pas,   120
It is ever in drede and brekyll as glas,
   And slythys.
This warld fowre never so,
With mervels mo and mo,
Now in weyll, now in wo,
   And all thyng wrythys.

Was never syn Noe floode sich floodys seyn;
Wyndys and ranys so rude, and stormes so keyn;
Som stamerd, som stod in dowte, as I weyn;
Now God turne all to good, I say as I mene,   130
   Ffor ponder.
These floodys so thay drowne,
Both in feyldys and in towne,
And berys all downe,
   And that is a wonder.

We that walk on the nyghtys oure catell to kepe,
We se sodan syghtys when othere men slepe.
Yit me thynk my hart lyghtys, I se shrewys pepe;
Ye ar two all wyghtys, I wyll gyf my shepe
   A turne.   140
Bot full yll have I ment:
As I walk on this bent,
I may lyghtly repent,
   My toes if I spurne.

A, sir, God you save and master myne!
A drynk fayn wold I have and somwhat to dyne.
   First Shep. Crystys curs, my knave, thou art a
   ledyr hyne!
   Second Shep. What! the boy lyst rave; abyde unto
   syne

71. **Wo . . . cok**, woe is our cock. 74. **sted**, placed. 75. **wayte**, knows. 78. **fun**, found. 80. **bun**, bound. 83. **ryfys**, splits. 88. **can**, know. 91. **boght**, redeemed. 93. **"Had I wyst,"** "if I had but known," a proverbial expression. 100. **pystyll**, epistle. **fere**, companion. 101. **rugh**, rough. **brere**, briar. 102. **sowre-loten chere**, sour-looking countenance. 108. **to**, until. 109. **raw**, row. **defly**, lonely. 111. **awro**, anywhere, anything. **ley**, fallow. 115. **hope**, suppose. 117. **war**, wary. 121. **brekyll**, brittle. 122. **slythys**, slides. 123. **fowre**, fared. 127. **Noe**, Noah's. 131. **ponder**, to weigh the matter. 138. **shrewys**, rascals. 139. **all**, perhaps for "tall." 142. **bent**, field. 147. **ledyr hyne**, bad servant. 148. **lyst**, wants to. **unto syne**, until after.

We have mayde it.
Yll thryft on thy pate!
Though the shrew cam late,
Yit is he in state
    To dyne, if he had it.

Third Shep. Sich servandys as I that swettys and swynkys,
Etys oure brede full dry, and that me forthynkys;
We ar oft weytt and wery, when master-men wynkys,
Yit commys full lately both dyners and drynkys,
    Bot nately.
Both oure dame and oure syre,
When we have ryn in the myre,
Thay can nyp at oure hyre,
    And pay us full lately.

Bot here my trouth, master, for the fayr that ye make,
I shall do therafter wyrk as I take;
I shall do a lytyll, sir, and emang ever lake,
Ffor yit lay my soper never on my stomake
    In feyldys.
Wherto shuld I threpe?
With my staf can I lepe,
And men say "lyght chepe
    Letherly for-yeldys."

First Shep. Thou were an yll lad to ryde on wowyng
With a man that had bot lytyll of spendyng.
Second Shep. Peasse, boy, I bad, no more jangling,
Or I shall make the full rad, by the heven's kyng!
    With thy gawdys;
Wher ar oure shepe, boy, we skorne?
Third Shep. Sir, this same day at morne
I thaym left in the corne,
    When thay rang lawdys;
Thay have pasture good, thay can not go wrong.
First Shep. That is right, by the roode! thyse nyghtys ar long,
Yit I wold, or we yode, oone gaf us a song.
Second Shep. So I thoght as I stode to myrth us emong.
Third Shep. I grauntt.

First Shep. Lett me syng the tenory.
Second Shep. And I the tryble so hye.
Third Shep. Then the meyne fallys to me;
Lett se how ye chauntt.

[*Tunc intrat* MAK, *in clamide se super togam vestitus.*]

Mak. Now Lord, for Thy naymes sevyn, that made both moyn and starnes,
Well mo then I can neven, Thi will, Lorde, of me tharnys;
I am all uneven, that moves oft my harnes,
Now wold God I were in heven, for there wepe no barnes
    So styll.
First Shep. Who is that pypys so poore?
Mak. Wold God ye wyst how I foore!
Lo, a man that walkys on the moore,
    And has not all his wyll!

Second Shep. Mak, where has thou gon? Tell us tythyng.
Third Shep. Is he commen? Then ylkon take hede to his thyng.
    [*Et accipit clamidem ab ipso.*]
Mak. What! Ich be a yoman, I tell you, of the king;
The self and the same sond from a greatt lordyng,
And sich.
Ffy on you! goyth hence
Out of my presence!
I must have reverence;
    Why, who be ich?

First Shep. Why make ye it so qwaynt? Mak, ye do wrang.
Second Shep. Bot, Mak, lyst ye saynt? I trow that ye lang.
Third Shep. I trow the shrew can paynt, the dewyll myght hym hang!
Mak. Ich shall make complaynt and make you all to thwang

154. **swynkys**, labor. 155. **me forthynkys**, makes me sorry. 156. **wynkys**, sleep. 158. **nately**, thoroughly. 163. **fayr**, fuss. 165. **lake**, play. 168. **threpe**, argue. 170–71. **lyght . . . for-yeldys**, a proverb: "A cheap bargain pays badly." 172. **on wowyng**, a-wooing. 175. **rad**, afraid. 176. **gawdys**, tricks. 177. **we skorne**, perhaps, whom we scorn. 180. **lawdys**, lauds, the service between midnight and 6 A.M. 182. **roode**, cross. 183. **yode**, went.

186. **tenory**, tenor. 187. **tryble**, soprano. 188. **meyne**, middle part, especially between alto and tenor. *Stage dir.* [**Tunc . . . vestitus.**] Then MAK enters, clad in a cloak over his shirt. 190. **naymes sevyn**, the lists vary: the following is quoted from the *Jewish Encyclopaedia* by the *New English Dictionary*: El, Elohim, Adonai, YHWH (Yahweh), Ehyeh-Asher-Ehyeh, Shaddai, and Zeba'ot. 191. **neven**, name. **tharnys**, is lacking. 192. **harnes**, brains. 196. **foore**, fare. 199. **tythyng**, news. 200. **ylkon**, each one. *Stage dir.* [**Et . . . ipso.**] And takes his cloak from him. 202. **sond**, messenger. 203. **sich**, such. 208. **make . . . qwaynt**, act affectedly. Mak is imitating a more southern English pronunciation than is natural to him; see ll. 215–16. 209. **saynt**, act like a saint; here, perhaps, show off. **lang**, desire something. 210. **paynt**, talk falsely, deceive. 211. **thwang**, be flogged.

At a worde,
And tell evyn how ye doth.
  First Shep. Bot, Mak, is that sothe?
Now take outt that sothren tothe,
  And sett in a torde!

  Second Shep. Mak, the dewill in youre ee, a stroke
    wold I leyne you.
  Third Shep. Mak, know ye not me? By God, I
    couthe teyn you.
  Mak. God looke you all thre! Me thoght I had
    sene you,
Ye ar a fare compane.
  First Shep.   Can ye now mene you? 220
  Second Shep. Shrew, jape!
Thus late as thou goys,
What wyll men suppos?
And thou has an yll noys
  Of stelyng of shepe.

  Mak. And I am trew as steyll, all men waytt,
Bot a sekenes I feyll that haldys me full haytt,
My belly farys not weyll, it is out of astate.
  Third Shep. Seldom lyys the dewyll dede by the
    gate.
  Mak. Therfor   230
Full sore am I and yll,
If I stande stone-styll;
I ete not an nedyll
  Thys moneth and more.

  First Shep. How farys thi wyff? By my hoode, how
    farys sho?
  Mak. Lyys walteryng, by the roode, by the fyere,
    lo!
And a howse full of brude; she drynkys well to;
Yll spede othere good that she wyll do!
  Bot so
Etys as fast as she can,   240
And ilk yere that commys to man
She bryngys furth a lakan,
  And som yeres two.

Bot were I not more gracyus and rychere be far,
I were eten outt of howse and of harbar;
Yit is she a fowll dowse, if ye com nar:
Ther is none that trowse nor knowys a war,
  Then ken I.

Now wyll ye se what I profer,
To gyf all in my cofer   250
To morne at next to offer
  Hyr hed mas-penny.

  Second Shep. I wote so forwakyd is none in this
    shyre:
I wold slepe if I takyd les to my hyere.
  Third Shep. I am cold and nakyd and wold have
    a fyere.
  First Shep. I am wery, for-rakyd and run in the
    myre.
  Wake thou!
  Second Shep. Nay, I wyll lyg downe by,
Ffor I must slepe truly.
  Third Shep. As good a man's son was I   260
  As any of you.

Bot, Mak, com heder! Betwene shall thou lyg
    downe.
  Mak. Then myght I lett you bedene of that ye
    wold rowne,
  No drede.
Ffro my top to my too,
Manus tuas commendo,
Poncio Pilato,
  Cryst crosse me spede!
    [*Tunc surgit, pastoribus dormientibus, et dicit;*]

Now were tyme for a man that lakkys what he wold,
To stalk prevely than unto a fold,   270
And neemly to wyrk than and be not to bold,
Ffor he might aby the bargan if it were told
  At the endyng.
Now were tyme for to reyll;
Bot he nedys good counsell
That fayn wold fare weyll,
  And has bot lytyll spendyng.

Bot abowte you a serkyll as rownde as a moyn,
To I have done that I wyll, tyll that it be noyn,
That ye lyg stone-styll to that I have doyne, 280
And I shall say thertyll of good wordys a foyne.
  On hight
Over youre heydys my hand I lyft,
Outt go youre een, fordo your syght,

  252. hed mas-penny, payment for masses for the dead.
253. forwakyd, tired with watching. **256. for-rakyd,** tired
with walking. **258. lyg,** lie. **263. lett you bedene,** hinder
you occasionally. **rowne,** whisper. **266–67.** a sufficiently
odd prayer: "Into Thy hands I commend (my spirit):
by Pontius Pilate." *Stage dir.* [**Tunc . . . dicit.**] Then, the
shepherds being asleep, he gets up and says. **271. neemly,**
nimbly. **272. aby,** pay for. **274. reyll,** set things in order.
280. to that, until. **doyne,** done. **281. thertyll,** thereto.
foyne, few. **282. hight,** high. **284. fordo,** ruin.

---

217. ee, eye. **leyne,** lend. **218. teyn,** injure. **220. mene
you,** complain. **224. noys,** reputation. **226. waytt,** know.
227. haytt, hot. **229. gate,** road; the phrase is a proverb.
233. nedyll, needle. **236. walteryng,** rolling about.
237. brude, children. **242. lakan,** plaything, that is,
child. **246. dowse,** sweetheart, but here ironical. **nar,**
near.

Bot yit I must make better shyft,
 And it be right.

Lord! What thay slepe hard! That may ye all here;
Was I never a shepard, bot now wyll I lere.
If the flok be skard, yit shall I nyp nere,
How! Drawes hederward! Now mendys oure chere 290
 Ffrom sorow:
A fatt shepe I dar say,
A good flese dar I lay,
Eft-whyte when I may,
 Bot this will I borow.   [MAK *goes home.*

How, Gyll, art thou in? Gett us som lyght.
 His Wife. Who makys sich dyn this tyme of the nyght?
I am sett for to spyn; I hope not I myght
Ryse a penny to wyn. I shrew them on hight!
 So farys 300
A huswyff that has bene
To be rasyd thus betwene:
Here may no note be sene
 Ffor sich small charys.

 Mak. Good wyff, open the hek! Seys thou not what I bryng?
 Wife. I may thole the dray the snek. A! com in, my swetyng!
 Mak. Yee, thou thar not rek of my long standyng.
 Wife. By the nakyd nek art thou lyke for to hyng.
 Mak. Do way:
I am worthy my mete, 310
For in a strate can I gett
More then thay that swynke and swette
 All the long day.

Thus it fell to my lott, Gyll, I had sich grace.
 Wife. It were a fowll blott to be hanged for the case.
 Mak. I have skapyd, Jelott, oft as hard a glase.
 Wife. Bot so long goys the pott to the water, men says,
 At last
Comys it home broken.
 Mak. Well knowe I the token, 320
Bot let it never be spoken;
 Bot com and help fast.

287. **here**, hear. 288. **lere**, learn. 289. **skard**, scared. **nyp**, come (?). 293. **lay**, wager. 294. **Eft-whyte**, repay. 299. **shrew**, curse. **on hight**, aloud. 302. **To . . . betwene**, forced to rise. 303. **note**, business. 304. **charys**, odd jobs. 305. **hek**, hatch. 306. **thole . . . snek**, permit you to draw the latch. 307. **thar . . . rek**, need not care. 309. **Do way**. Don't say that! 311. **strate**, pinch. 316. **Jelott**, diminutive of Gyll. **glase**, swift blow, difficult position. 317–19. **so long . . . broken**, a proverb.

I wold he were slayn, I lyst well ete:
This twelmothe was I not so fayn of oone shepe mete.
 Wife. Com thay or he be slayn and here the shepe blete!
 Mak. Then myght I be tane, that were a cold swette!
 Go spar
The gaytt-doore.
 Wife.   Yis, Mak,
Ffor and thay com at thy bak,—
 Mak. Then myght I by, for all the pak, 330
 The dewill of the war.
 Wife. A good bowrde have I spied, syn thou can none.
Here shall we hym hyde to thay be gone:
In my credyll abyde; lett me alone,
And I shall lyg besyde in chylbed, and grone.
 Mak. Thou red;
And I shall say thou was lyght
Of a knave-childe this nyght.
 Wife. Now well is me day bright,
 That ever was I bred. 340

This is a good gyse and a far cast;
Yit a woman avyse helpys at the last.
I wote never who spyse, agane go thou fast.
 Mak. Bot I com or thay ryse, els blawes a cold blast!
 I wyll go slepe.

[MAK *returns to the shepherds, and resumes his place.*]

Yit slepys all this meneye,
And I shall go stalk prevely,
As it had never bene I
 That caryed thare shepe.

 First Shep. Resurrex a mortruis! Have hald my hand. 350
Judas carnas dominus! I may not well stand:
My foytt slepys, by Jhesus, and I water fastand.
I thoght that we layd us full nere Yngland.
 Second Shep. A ye!
Lord! What I have slept weyll!
As fresh as an eyll,
 As lyght I me feyll
 As leyfe on a tre.

324. **oone**, any. 326. **tane**, taken. 327. **spar**, shut. 330. **by**, pay for. 331. **the war**, the worse. 332. **bowrde**, jest. 333. **to**, until. 334. **abyde**, let him remain. 336. **red**, advise (well). 341. **gyse**, plan. **far cast**, fair trick. 346. **meneye**, company. 352. **I water fastand**, I am fasting except for water. 353. **thoght . . . nere Yngland**, perhaps in a dream. 356. **eyll**, eel.

MIDDLE ENGLISH DRAMA 245

Third Shep. Benste be here-in! So my hart qwakys,
My hart is outt of skyn, what so it makys. 360
Who makys all this dyn? So my browes blakys,
To the dowore wyll I wyn! Harke felows, wakys!
 We were fowre:
Se ye awre of Mak now?
 First Shep. We were up or thou.
 Second Shep. Man, I gyf God a vowe,
Yit yede he nawre.

Third Shep. Me thoght he was lapt in a wolfe-skyn.
First Shep. So are many hapt, now namely within.
Second Shep. When we had long napt me thoght
 with a gyn 370
A fatt shepe he trapt, bot he mayde no dyn.
Third Shep. Be styll:
Thi dreme makys the woode?
It is bot fantom, by the roode.
 First Shep. Now God turne all to good,
If it be his wyll.

Second Shep. Ryse, Mak, for shame! Thou lygys
 right lang.
Mak. Now Crystys holy name be us emang!
What is this? For Sant Jame I may not well gang!
I trow I be the same! A! My nek has lygen
 wrang 380
 Enoghe;
Mekill thank, syn yister-even,
Now, by Sant Strevyn,
I was flayd with a swevyn,
 My hart out of sloghe.

I thoght Gyll began to crok and travell full sad,
Welner at the fyrst cok, of a yong lad,
Ffor to mend oure flok; then be I never glad.
I have tow on my rok more then ever I had.
 A, my heede! 390
A house full of yong tharmes,
The dewill knok outt thare harnes!
Wo is hym has many barnes,
 And therto lytyll brede!

I must go home, by youre lefe, to Gyll, as I thoght.
I pray you looke my slefe that I steyll noght:
I am loth you to grefe or from you take oght.
 Third Shep. Go furth, yll myght thou chefe! Now
 wold I we soght,

This morne,
That we had all oure store. 400
 First Shep. Bot I will go before;
Let us mete.
 Second Shep. Whore?
 Third Shep. At the crokyd thorne.

Mak. Undo this doore! Who is here? How long
 shall I stand?
Wife. Who makys sich a bere? Now walk in the
 wenyand.
Mak. A, Gyll, what chere? It is I, Mak, youre
 husbande,
Wife. Then may we be here the dewill in a bande,
 Syr Gyle;
Lo, he commys with a lote
As he were holden in the throte. 410
I may not syt at my note,
 A hand-lang while.

Mak. Wyll ye here what fare she makys to gett hir
 a glose,
And dos noght bot lakys and clowse hir toose.
 Wife. Why, who wanders, who wakys, who
 commys, who gose?
Who brewys, who bakys? What makys me thus hose?
 And than,
It is rewthe to beholde,
Now in hote, now in colde,
Ffull wofull is the householde 420
 That wantys a woman.

Bot what ende has thou mayde with the hyrdys,
 Mak?
 Mak. The last worde that thay sayde when I
 turnyd my bak,
Thay wold looke that thay hade thare shepe all
 the pak.
I hope thay wyll nott be well payde when thay
 thare shepe lak,
 Perde.
Bot how so the gam gose,
To me thay wyll suppose,
And make a fowll noyse,
 And cry outt apon me. 430
Bot thou must do as thou hyght
 Wife. I accorde me thertyll.
I shall swedyll hym right in my credyll;

359. **Benste,** Benedicite. 361. **blakys,** grow pale. 364. **awre,** anything. 365. **or,** before. 367. **yede,** went. 369. **hapt,** wrapped. 370. **gyn,** trap. 373. **woode,** crazy. 383. **Strevyn,** Stephen. 385. **sloghe,** slough, here despondency or degradation. 387. **Welner,** almost. 389. **rok,** distaff. 391. **tharmes,** intestines, that is, children. 392. **harnes,** brains. 393. **barnes,** children. 398. **chefe,** succeed.

405. **bere,** noise. **wenyand,** waning moon—a curse. 407. **in a bande,** on a string. 409. **lote,** noise. 413. **glose,** falsehood. 414. **lakys,** plays. **clowse,** claws. 416. **What . . . hose?** Why do I thus make hose? 418. **rewthe,** a pity. 422. **hyrdys,** shepherds. 425. **hope,** expect. **well payde,** pleased. 427. **gam,** game. 428. **To me . . . suppose.** They will attribute it to me. 431. **hyght,** promised. 432. **swedyll,** swaddle.

If it were a gretter slyght, yit couthe I help tyll.
I wyll lyg downe stright; com hap me;
   Mak.   I wyll.
   Wife. Behynde.
Com Coll and his maroo,
Thay will nyp us full naroo.
   Mak. Bot I may cry out "haroo,"
     The shepe if thay fynde.

   Wife. Harken ay when thay call; thay will com
     onone.   440
Com and make redy all, and syng by thyn oone;
Syng "lullay" thou shall, for I must grone,
And cry outt by the wall on Mary and John,
     Ffor sore.
Syng "lullay" on fast
When thou heris at the last;
And bot I play a fals cast,
     Trust me no more.

             [*The scene shifts to the shepherds.*]
   Third Shep. A, Coll, goode morne; why slepys
     thou nott?
   First Shep. Alas, that ever was I borne! We have a
     fowll blott.   450
A fat wedir have we lorne.
   Third Shep.   Mary! Godys forbott!
   Second Shep. Who shuld do us that skorne? That
     were a fowll spott.
   First Shep. Som shrewe.
I have soght with my dogys
All Horbery Shrogys,
And of fefteyn hogys
     Ffond I bot oone ewe.

   Third Shep. Now trow me, if ye will, by Sant
     Thomas of Kent,
Ayther Mak or Gyll was at that assent.
   First Shep. Peasse, man, be still! I sagh when he
     went;   460
Thou sklanders hym yll; thou aght to repent,
     Goode spede.
   Second Shep. Now as ever myght I the,
If I shuld evyn here de,
I wold say it were he
     That dyd that same dede.

   Third Shep. Go we theder, I rede, and ryn on oure
     feete.
Shall I never ete brede the sothe to I wytt.

   First Shep. Nor drynk in my heede, with hym tyll
     I mete.
   Second Shep. I wyll rest in no stede tyll that I hym
     grete,   470
     My brothere.
Oone I will hight:
Tyll I se hym in sight
Shall I never slepe one nyght
     Ther I do anothere.

     [*As they come near they hear* MAK *sing and* GYLL *groan.*]
   Third Shep. Will ye here how thay hak? Oure
     Syre, lyst, croyne!
   First Shep. Hard I never none crak so clere out of
     toyne;
Call on hym.
   Second Shep. Mak! Undo youre doore soyne.
   Mak. Who is that spak, as it were noyne,
     On loft?   480
Who is that, I say?
   Third Shep. Goode felowse, were it day.
   Mak. As far as ye may,
Good, spekys soft,
Over a seke woman's heede that is at mayll-easse;
I had lever be dede or she had any dyseasse.
   Wife. Go to an othere stede! I may not well
     qweasse.
Ich fote that ye trede goys thorow my nese.
So hee!
   First Shep. Tell us, Mak, if ye may,   490
How fare ye, I say?
   Mak. Bot ar ye in this towne to day?
Now how fare ye?

Ye have ryn in the myre and ar weytt yit:
I shall make you a fyre, if ye will syt.
A nores wold I hyre, thynk ye on yit,
Well qwytt is my hyre, my dreme this is itt,
     A seson.
I have barnes, if ye knew,
Well mo then enewe,   500
Bot we must drynk as we brew,
     And that is bot reson.

I wold ye dynyd or ye yode, me thynk that ye
     swette.
   Second Shep. Nay, nawther mendys oure mode
     drynke nor mette.
   Mak. Why, sir, alys you oght bot goode?

---

    434. **hap**, wrap.   436. **maroo**, companion.   438. **haroo**, alas!   444. **sore**, pain.   447. **cast**, trick.   451. **wedir**, weather. **lorne**, lost. **forbott**, forbidding, that is, God forbid!   455. **Shrogys**, shrubs.   456. **hogys**, young sheep.   463. **the**, prosper.   464. **de**, die.   467. **ryn**, run.   468. **to**, until.   472. **Oone**, one thing.   476. **hak**, break a note. **lyst, croyne**, hear (how they) croon!   477. **toyne**, tune.   480. **On loft**, loudly.   485. **at mayll-easse**, in sickness.   487. **qweasse**, wheeze.   488. **nese**, nose.   496. **nores**, nurse. **thynk . . . yit**, think the thing over.   503. **yode**, went.   504. **mode**, mood.

MIDDLE ENGLISH DRAMA

Third Shep. Yee, oure shepe that we gett,
Ar stollyn as thay yode; oure los is grette.
Mak. Syrs, drynkys!
Had I bene thore,
Som shuld have boght it full sore.
First Shep. Mary, som men trowes that ye wore, 510
And that us forthynkys.

Second Shep. Mak, som men trowys that it shuld be ye.
Third Shep. Ayther ye or youre spouse, so say we.
Mak. Now if ye have suspowse to Gill or to me,
Com and rype oure howse, and then may ye se
Who had hir,
If I any shepe fott,
Aythor cow or stott;
And Gyll, my wyfe, rose nott
Here syn she lade hir. 520

As I am true and lele, to God here I pray,
That this be the fyrst mele that I shall ete this day.
First Shep. Mak, as have I ceyll, avyse the, I say;
He lernyd tymely to steyll that couth not say nay.
Wife. I swelt!
Outt, thefys, fro my wonys!
Ye com to rob us for the nonys.
Mak. Here ye not how she gronys?
Youre hartys shuld melt.

Wife. Outt, thefys, fro my barne! negh hym not thor. 530
Mak. Wyst ye how she had farne, youre hartys wold be sore.
Ye do wrang, I you warne, that thus commys before
To a woman that has farne—bot I say no more.
Wife. A, my medyll!
I pray to God so mylde,
If ever I you begyld,
That I ete this chylde
That lygys in this credyll.

Mak. Peasse, woman, for Godys payn, and cry not so;
Thou spyllys thy brane and makys me full wo. 540
Second Shep. I trow oure shepe be slayn, what finde ye two?

Third Shep. All wyrk we in vayn, as well may we go.
Bot hatters,
I can fynde no flesh,
Hard nor nesh,
Salt nor fresh,
Bot two tome platers.
Whik catell bot this, tame nor wylde,
None, as have I blys, as lowde as he smylde.
Wife. No, so God me blys and gyf me joy of my chylde! 550
First Shep. We have merkyd amys, I hold us begyld.
Second Shep. Syr don,
Syr, Oure Lady hym save!
Is youre chyld a knave?
Mak. Any lord myght hym have
This chyld to his son.
When he wakyns he kyppys that joy is to se.
Third Shep. In good tyme to hys hyppys and in cele.
Bot who was his gossyppys so sone rede?
Mak. So fare fall thare lyppys!
First Shep. Hark now, a le!
Mak. So God thaym thank, 561
Parkyn, and Gybon Waller, I say,
And gentill John Horne, in good fay,
He made all the garray,
With the greatt shank.

Second Shep. Mak, freyndys will we be, ffor we ar all oone.
Mak. We! Now I hald for me, for mendys gett I none.
Ffare-well all thre, all glad were ye gone.
[*The Shepherds leave.*
Third Shep. Ffare wordys may ther be, bot luf is ther none
This yere. 570
First Shep. Gaf ye the chyld any thyng?
Second Shep. I trow not oone farthyng.
Third Shep. Ffast agane will I flyng,
Abyde ye me there. (*Goes back to the house.*)
Mak, take it to no grefe, if I com to thi barne.
Mak. Nay, thou dos me greatt reprefe and fowll has thou farne.

508. **thore,** there.   510. **wore,** were.   511. **us forthynkys,** makes us sorry.   514. **suspowse,** suspicion.   515. **rype,** examine.   517. **fott,** fetched.   518. **stott,** steer.   521. **lele,** loyal.   523. **ceyll,** bliss.   525. **swelt,** grow faint.   526. **wonys,** dwellings.   527. **for the nonys,** now.   530. **barne,** child. **negh,** approach.   531. **farne,** fared.   540. **spyllys,** destroy.   543. **hatters,** confound it! (?)   545. **nesh,** soft.   547. **tome,** empty.   548. **Whik,** living.   549. **he,** Mak.   552. **don,** lord.   554. **knave,** boy.   557. **kyppys,** snatches.   558. **cele,** happiness.   559. **gossyppys,** godparents. **rede,** ready.   560. **fare,** fair. **le,** lie.   564. **garray,** noisy celebration.   567. **I hald for me,** I hold off, so far as I am concerned. **mendys,** amends.   573. **flyng,** go quickly.   576. **farne,** behaved.

Third Shep. The child will it not grefe, that lytyll
    day-starne.
Mak, with youre leyfe let me gyf youre barne
    Bot sex-pence.
Mak. Nay, do way: he slepys.   580
Third Shep. Me thynk he pepys.
Mak. When he wakyns he wepys.
    I pray you go hence.
            [*The other Shepherds come back.*]

Third Shep. Gyf me lefe hym to kys and lyft up
    the clowtt.
What the dewill is this? He has a long snowte.
    First Shep. He is merkyd amys. We wate ill
        abowte.
Second Shep. Ill spon weft, iwys, ay commys foull
    owte.
Ay, so !
He is lyke to oure shepe !
    Third Shep. How, Gyb ! May I pepe?   590
    First Shep. I trow, kynde will crepe
    Where it may not go.

Second Shep. This was a qwantt gawde and a far
    cast.
It was a hee frawde.
    Third Shep.   Yee, syrs, wast?
Lett bren this bawde and bynd hir fast.
A fals skawde hang at the last;
    So shall thou.
Wyll ye se how thay swedyll
His foure feytt in the medyll?
Sagh I never in a credyll   600
    A hornyd lad or now.

Mak. Peasse byd I: What ! Lett be youre fare;
I am he that hym gatt and yond woman hym bare.
    First Shep. What dewill shall he hatt, Mak? Lo
        God ! Makys ayre !
    Second Shep. Lett be all that. Now God gyf hym
        care,
    I sagh.
Wife. A pratty child is he
As syttys on a waman's kne;
A dyllydowne, perde,
    To gar a man laghe.   610

    Third Shep. I know hym by the eere-marke, that
        is a good tokyn.

Mak. I tell you, syrs, hark ! Hys noyse was
    brokyn.
Sythen told me a clerk that he was forspokyn.
    First Shep. This is a fals wark, I wold fayn be
        wrokyn:
    Gett wepyn.
    Wife. He was takyn with an elfe,
I saw it myself.
When the clok stroke twelf
    Was he forshapyn.
    Second Shep. Ye two ar well feft sam in a stede.   620
    Third Shep. Syn thay manteyn thare theft let do
        thaym to dede.
Mak. If I trespas eft gyrd of my heede.
With you will I be left.
    First Shep.   Syrs, do my reede.
Ffor this trespas,
We will nawther ban ne flyte,
Ffyght nor chyte,
Bot have done as tyte,
    And cast hym in canvas.
        [*They toss* MAK *in a sheet and then go away.*]

Lord ! What I am sore in poynt for to bryst.
In fayth I may no more, therfor wyll I ryst.   630
    Second Shep. As a shepe of sevyn skore he weyd in
        my fyst.
Ffor to slepe ay-whore me thynk that I lyst.
    Third Shep. Now I pray you,
Lyg downe on this grene.
    First Shep. On these thefys yit I mene.
    Third Shep. Wherto shuld ye tene
    So, as I say you?
        [Angelus cantat "*Gloria in excelsis*": *postea dicat:*]

Angel. Ryse, hyrd-men heynd ! For now is He
    borne
That shall take fro the feynd that Adam had lorne:
That warloo to sheynd this nyght is He borne.   640
God is made youre freynd now at this morne.
    He behestys,
At Bedlem go se,
Ther lygys that fre
In a cryb full poorely,
    Betwyx two bestys.

612. noyse, nose. 613. forspokyn, bewitched. 614. wrokyn, avenged. 619. forshapyn, transformed. 620. feft sam, joined together. stede, place. 621. dede, death. 622. eft gyrd, again strike. 625. ban ne flyte, curse nor quarrel. 626. chyte, chide. 627. tyte, quickly. 629. bryst, burst. 630. ryst, rest. 632. ay-whore, anywhere. 635. mene, think. 636. tene, be vexed. *Stage dir.* [Angelus . . . dicat]. The Angel sings "Glory in the highest," afterward says. 638. heynd, gentle. 639. that, that which. 640. warloo, sorcerer, that is, the devil. sheynd, destroy. 642. behestys, orders. 643. Bedlem, Bethlehem. 644. fre, noble one.

577. day-starne, day star. 584. clowtt, swaddling clothes. 586. We . . . abowte, we're wasting our time. 587. weft, woven stuff. 591. kynde, nature. 592. go, walk. 593. gawde, trick. 594. hee, high. wast, was it not? 595. bren, burn. 596. skawde hang, scold hangs. 602. fare, goings-on. 603. gatt, begot. 604. hatt, be called. ayre, heir. 606. sagh, say. 610. gar, make. laghe, laugh.

MIDDLE ENGLISH DRAMA

First Shep. This was a qwant stevyn that ever yit I hard.
It is a mervell to nevyn thus to be skard.
Second Shep. Of Godys son of hevyn he spak upward.
All the wod on a levyn me thoght that he gard 650
  Appere.
Third Shep. He spake of a barne
In Bedlem, I you warne.
First Shep. That betokyns yond starne.
  Let us seke hym there,

Second Shep. Say, what was his song? Hard ye not how he crakyd it?
Thre brefes to a long.
Third Shep. Yee, Mary, he hakt it.
Was no crochett wrong, nor no thyng that lakt it.
First Shep. Ffor to syng us emong right as he knakt it,
  I can. 660
Second Shep. Let se how ye croyne.
Can ye bark at the mone?
Third Shep. Hold youre tonges, have done!
First Shep. Hark after, than.

Second Shep. To Bedlem he bad that we shuld gang:
I am full fard that we tary to lang.
Third Shep. Be mery and not sad, of myrth is oure sang,
Ever-lastyng glad to mede may we fang,
  Withoutt noyse.
First Shep. Hy we theder for-thy; 670
If we be wete and wery,
To that chyld and that lady
  We have it not to lose.

Second Shep. We fynde by the prophecy—let be youre dyn—
Of David and Isay and mo then I myn,
Thay prophecyed by clergy that in a vyrgyn
Shuld He lyght and ly to slokyn oure syn
  And slake it,
Oure kynde from wo;
Ffor Isay sayd so, 680
Citè virgo
  Concipiet a chylde that is nakyd.

Third Shep. Ffull glad may we be and abyde that day
That lufly to se that all myghtys may.
Lord, well were me for ones and for ay,
Myght I knele on my kne som word for to say
  To that chylde.
Bot the angell sayd,
In a cryb wos he layde;
He was poorly arayd 690
  Both mener and mylde.

First Shep. Patryarkes that has bene and prophetys beforne,
Thay desyryd to have sene this chylde that is borne.
Thay ar gone full clene, that have thay lorne.
We shall se Hym, I weyn, or it be morne,
  To tokyn.
When I se Hym and fele,
Then wote I full weyll
It is true as steyll 700
  That prophetys have spokyn:

To so poore as we ar that he wold appere,
Ffyrst fynd, and declare by his messyngere.
Second Shep. Go we now, let us fare, the place is us nere.
Third Shep. I am redy and yare; go we in fere
  To that bright.
Lord, if Thi wylles be,
We ar lewde all thre,
Thou grauntt us somkyns gle
  To comfort Thi wight.
  [*They enter the stable.*]

First Shep. Hayll, comly and clene! Hayll, yong child! 710
Hayll, Maker, as I meyne, of a madyn so mylde!
Thou has waryd, I weyne, the warlo so wylde;
The fals gyler, of teyn now goys he begylde.
  Lo, He merys;
Lo, He laghys, my swetyng,
A welfare metyng,
I have holden my hetyng;
  Have a bob of cherys.

Second Shep. Hayll, sufferan Savyoure! Ffor Thou has us soght;
Hayll, frely foyde and floure that all thyng has wroght! 720

647. stevyn, voice. 648. nevyn, relate. skard, scared. 649. upward, from above. 650. on a levyn, in a lightning flash. gard, made. 652. barne, child. 657. brefes, short notes. 658. crochett, quarter-note. 659. knakt, sang with trills. 666. fard, afraid. 668. glad, gladness. mede, reward. fang, take. 669. noyse, annoyances. 670. Hy, hurry. for-thy, therefore. 675. Isay, Isaiah. myn, remember. 676. clergy, learning. 677. slokyn, quench. 679. kynde, kindred. 681–82. Citè . . . Concipiet. Behold, a virgin shall conceive. See Matthew 1:23.

691. mener, handsome(?). 695. weyn, believe. 704. yare, ready. in fere, together. 707. lewde, ignorant. 708. somkyns gle, some kind of joy. 710. clene, pure. 711. Maker, Creator. of, from. 712. waryd, cursed. 713. gyler, beguiler. teyn, sorrow. 714. merys, grows merry. 717. hetyng, promise. 718. bob, bunch. 720. frely foyde, noble child.

Hayll, full of favoure that made all of noght!
Hayll! I kneyll and I cowre. A byrd have I broght
  To my barne.
Hayll, lytyll tyné mop!
Of oure crede thou art crop:
I wold drynk on thy cop,
  Lytyll day-starne.

Third Shep. Hayll, derlyng dere, full of Godhede!
I pray The be nere when that I have nede.
Hayll! Swete is Thy chere! My hart wold blede   730
To se The sytt here in so poore wede,
  With no pennys.
Hayll! Put furth thy dall!
I bryng thee bot a ball:
Have and play the with-all,
  And go to the tenys.

Mary. The Fader of Heven, God omnypotent,
That sett all on seven, His Son has He sent.

My name couth He neven and lyght or He went.
I conceyvyd Hym full even thrugh myght as He
    ment,   740
  And now is He borne.
He kepe you fro wo!
I shall pray Hym so;
Tell furth as ye go,
  And myn on this morne.

First Shep. Ffarewell, lady so fare to beholde,
With thy childe on thi kne!
Second Shep.   Bot He lygys full cold.
Lord, well is me; now we go, Thou behold.
Third Shep. Ffor sothe all redy; it semys to be told
Full oft.   750
First Shep. What grace we have fun.
Second Shep. Com furth, now ar we won.
Third Shep. To syng ar we bun:
  Let take on loft.
        Explicit pagina Pastorum.

Sir Thomas Malory
c. 1408–1471

Sir Thomas Malory, Ben Jonson, John Bunyan, Leigh Hunt, Oscar Wilde, and "O. Henry" are an oddly assorted group of English and American writers, but if brought together they would have a ready subject for a ghostly symposium: Should Men of Letters Be Thrown into Jail? Sir Thomas's court record is rather more extensive than those of his brother authors: between 1451 and 1468 he was arrested at least four times and variously charged with "hurt," extortion, breaking prison, robbing the Abbey of Blessed Mary of Coombe, ambushing the Duke of Buckingham, breaking into the Abbey again, this time adding insult to the abbot to robbery, extortion a second time, but now from several people, cattle-stealing, twice raping the goods, chattels, and wife of one Hugh Smyth, and finally sedition. One might almost hesitate to introduce the writings of such an active desperado to an innocent audience were it not for the fact that there is a fair chance that Malory's various crimes were legal rather than real. It was not hard to bring charges against an enemy; medieval authorities seemed to consider the violence of the indictment more than half the court battle, and the crimes which could be laid at the door of a relatively innocent person often beggar description. In any case, all save one of these offenses were allegedly committed in 1451 and 1452, and Malory seems to have escaped with but brief periods of incarceration. The charge of sedition, however, had him in prison at least by 1468 and, for all we know, kept him there until his death in 1471.

All this is based on the assumption, which, though short of actual proof, seems fairly well assured, that the author of the *Morte Darthur* was Sir Thomas Malory of Newbold Revel in Warwickshire. His family was good and his early career distinguished. In his youth he had served under Richard Beauchamp, Earl of Warwick, whose early career resembles that of Chaucer's Knight and whom the Emperor Sigismund gratefully called "Father of Courtesy." In 1445, some years after he had succeeded his father, he sat in Parliament. His difficulties in 1451 seem to have centered about a dispute,

---

724. **mop,** young creature. 725. **crop,** top. 731. **wede,** attire. 733. **dall,** hand. 734. **bot,** but. 736. **tenys,** tennis. 738. **That . . . seven,** who made all in seven days. 739. **couth,** could. **neven,** name. 740. **full even,** completely. 745. **myn on,** remember. 749. **semys,** is fitting. 751. **fun,** found. 753. **bun,** bound. 754. **Let . . . loft.** Sing out loudly. **Explicit . . . Pastorum.** Here ends the play of the Shepherds.

probably over lands, with a monastery, while his later trouble may well have been because he was a Lancastrian partisan; if that is the case, it is ironical enough that Caxton, the printer of his book, enjoyed extensive Yorkist patronage. Malory tells us that he ended his book in the ninth year (1469–70) of King Edward's reign, and we may safely assume that it had served to while away his dreary days in prison.

The *Morte Darthur* has certainly received its due meed of praise. A general reading public which had been first introduced to a knowledge of Arthur and his knights in juvenile paraphrases, had then gone on to Tennyson's perverted if sonorous versions, was bound to find in Malory a miraculous combination of sense and style. The relatively few who were familiar with the older English poetic accounts from Lawman (Layamon, c. 1205) on to *Le Morte Arthur*, written in Malory's own day, whispered wistful protests, but their complaints were nothing to the genteel uproar which welcomed Mark Twain's "vulgarization" of Tennyson and Malory in *A Connecticut Yankee at King Arthur's Court*. A useful corrective of Maloriolatry is to be found in the detailed criticisms of Eugène Vinaver's *Malory* (Oxford Press, 1929), by far the best comprehensive study of Malory and the *Morte Darthur*.

With the exception of one English poem, the fourteenth-century alliterative *Morte Arthure*, Malory's known sources were the French prose Arthurian romances. Vinaver suggests that he possessed them in a single manuscript, probably of such great length as to be split into three or four volumes. Malory's major task was one of selection and condensation, by means of which he sought, not always very successfully, to bring some order out of the chaos of conflicting and overlapping plots which marked and marred the French episodic romances. In his own additions and alterations he shows himself a practical realist, but his realism, as in his disapproval of adulterous love, his distaste for the supernatural, and his occasional emphasis on the financial and economic motives for chivalric action, are in conflict with the "romantic" nature of his sources. Vinaver well says: "And if there are readers who are ignorant of this antagonism between the author and his book, readers to whom the *Morte Darthur* still remains the apotheosis of chivalrous romance, it is because the work has preserved some remnants of the old and powerful stories which, stronger than Malory, have survived and conquered his prosaic realism." (*Op. cit.*, p. 54.)

However much he may have disliked or misunderstood many of the trappings of chivalry there can be no doubt as to his enthusiasm for knighthood and the ideal knight. He unquestionably felt that here his book would furnish an inspiration and a corrective for his own age. Sir Ector's eulogy of the dead Lancelot (see page 264) sums up, if not without a certain confusion, Malory's conception of the perfect knight. With it we may compare Chaucer's Knight (see page 173), and Froissart's remarks on Guichard d'Angle, Earl of Huntington: "And truly this gentyll knyght was well worthy to have honoure, for in his tyme he had all noble vertues that a knyght ought to have; he was mery, true, amorous, sage, secrete, large, prewe, hardy, adventurous and chyvalrous." If Malory could have known that Roger Ascham was to write of his book that its whole pleasure "stands in two special points, in open manslaughter and bold bawdry," he would have been deeply hurt, for he attempted valiantly to guide his somewhat intransigent material from both adultery and wanton slaughter. His lack of humor (see Vinaver, *op. cit.*, pp. 64 ff.) would have made him equally distressed by such modern treatments of his imaginary world as *A Connecticut Yankee*, John Erskine's *Galahad*, or T. H. White's thoroughly delightful novels, the best of which are *The Sword in the Stone* (Putnam, 1939) and *The Ill-Made Knight* (Putnam, 1940).

Malory tried to revivify a way of life which, always more literary than real, was thoroughly dead by his day. There was no place for chivalry in the wholesale proscriptions and abrupt executions of the Wars of the Roses, and his introduction of practical realism served to cloud rather than to clarify the knightly ideal. To quote Vinaver once more: "Ever since Malory's time poets and critics have regarded the *Morte Darthur* as a means of moral and spiritual perfection. . . . With less faith in the moral elevation and educational value of Malory's romance, we can only accept his modest effort as an expression of his simple and narrow ideal. His was not a crusading chivalry raised to its highest energy by the reunion of the knightly and monastic ideals of service, love, and sacrifice. What he advocated were the comfortable virtues of a righteous gentleman who 'does after the good and leaves the evil,' but whose spiritual attainments are limited to social discipline and gentle manners." (*Op. cit.*, pp. 68–69.)

If we may appear to have been somewhat nonconformist, or even severe, in our approach to Malory, we can end on a note of unqualified praise. Malory's simple, flexible, and lucid style made the *Morte Darthur* the first extensive piece of English prose which has been read with pleasure and comprehension by succeeding generations. More than any other factor, Malory's presentation has been responsible for the continued popularity of the Arthurian story in the English-speaking world, and especially for its amazing literary vitality in the nineteenth and twentieth centuries.

LE MORTE DARTHUR

CAXTON'S PREFACE

William Caxton (*c.* 1424–*c.* 1491), even apart from his own writings unquestionably one of the greatest practical benefactors English literature ever had, was born in Kent. We know little specific about his family, but his parents were well connected enough to be able to apprentice him in 1438 to Robert Large, a prominent member of the wealthy Mercer's Company. When Large died in 1441 Caxton's apprenticeship was still unfinished, and it would appear that he went to complete it at Bruges, one of the great Flemish textile cities. For more than thirty years Bruges was his home, and there he rose to a position of affluence and influence, being at one time governor of the English Nation. We may assume that he had long had an interest in literature and that he gladly agreed to the request of Margaret, Duchess of Burgundy, sister to Edward IV of England, that he should carry to completion a translation of Raoul le Fèvre's *Le recueil des histoires de Troyes*. Caxton was in Cologne in 1471–72 and there, no doubt, he learned the printer's trade. Returning to Bruges, he took a partner and established a printing office, from which in 1474 came Caxton's *Recuyell of the Historyes of Troye*, the first English book to appear in print.

In 1476 he came back to England, set up a shop in the precincts of Westminster Abbey and, probably after a number of undated pamphlets and books, brought forth Lord Rivers's translation, *The Dictes or Sayengis of the Philosophres*, in 1477. There is romance and high adventure in what Caxton had done. When nearly fifty, an age proportionally far more advanced then than now, he had turned from the mercantile routine of a lifetime to literature and, what is more amazing, to the practice of a new mechanical craft. By the time that he was fifty-three he had printed the first books in English and in England.

From then until his death, probably in 1491, he labored at a prodigious rate as author, translator, editor, and printer. The list of his works testifies amply to his literary taste, piety, patriotism, and, what is sometimes overlooked, sound sense of that which would, as well as should, sell. There is no space here to list the hundred books which are known to have issued from Caxton's shop. Among the English "classics" he printed much of Chaucer, Gower's *Confessio Amantis*, some of John Lydgate, and the *Morte Darthur* of his contemporary, Sir Thomas Malory. His own translations were many and often extensive, ranging from the *Distichs* of Cato to the *Golden Legend*, from the *Game and Playe of the Chesse* to the *Mirrour of the World*, from the *History of Jason* to *Charles the Grete*, and from the *Eneydos* to *Reynard the Fox*. We do not expect great originality or stylistic excellence in translations, especially when the sources are often themselves undistinguished, but Caxton's style was adequate, and on occasion he did not hesitate to amplify his originals. The Prologues and Epilogues to his various books afford the best clue to a sound, stimulating, and often whimsical personality. The debt which the English Renaissance owes to William Caxton can never be adequately expressed.

Two useful and informative books on Caxton are Henry R. Plomer's *William Caxton*, Small, Maynard, 1925, and Nellie S. Aurner, *Caxton, Mirrour of Fifteenth Century Letters*, Houghton Mifflin, 1926.

AFTER that I had accomplished and finished divers histories, as well of contemplation as of other historical and worldly acts of great conquerors and princes, and also certain books of ensamples and doctrine, many noble and divers gentlemen of this realm of England came and demanded me many and oft times, wherefore that I have not had made and imprint the noble history of the Saint Grail, and of the most renowned Christian king, first and chief of the three best Christian, and worthy, King Arthur, which ought most to be remembered among us Englishmen tofore all other Christian kings; for it is notoriously known through the universal world, that there be nine worthy and the best that ever were, that is to wit, three Paynims, three Jews, and three Christian men. As for the Paynims, they were tofore the Incarnation of Christ, which were named, the first Hector of Troy, of whom the history is common both in ballad and in prose, the second Alexander the Great, and the third Julius Caesar, Emperor of Rome, of whom the histories be well known and had. And as for the three Jews, which also were tofore the incarnation of our Lord, of whom the first was duke Joshua which brought the children of Israel into the land of behest, the second David king of Jerusalem, and the third Judas Maccabeus, of these three the Bible rehearseth all their noble histories and acts. And since the said Incarnation have been three noble Christian men, stalled and admitted through the universal world into the number of the nine best and worthy. Of whom was first the noble Arthur,

4. **ensamples**, illustrative instances. 8. **Saint**, holy. 10. **worthy**, one of the nine worthies. 12. **tofore**, before. 13. **notoriously**, admittedly. 26. **behest**, promise. 30. **stalled**, placed.

whose noble acts I purpose to write in this present book here following. The second was Charlemagne, or Charles the Great, of whom the history is had in many places, both in French and in English. And the third and last was Godfrey of Bouillon, of whose acts and life I made a book unto the excellent prince and king of noble memory, King Edward the Fourth.

The said noble gentlemen instantly required me to imprint the history of the said noble king and conqueror King Arthur, and of his knights, with the history of the Saint Grail, and of the death and ending of the said Arthur; affirming that I ought rather to imprint his acts and noble feats, than of Godfrey of Bouillon, or any of the other eight, considering that he was a man born within this realm, and king and emperor of the same: and that there be in French divers and many noble volumes of his acts, and also of his knights. To whom I answered that divers men hold opinion that there was no such Arthur, and that all such books as been made of him be feigned and fables, because that some chronicles make of him no mention, nor remember him nothing, nor of his knights. Whereto they answered, and one in special said, that in him that should say or think that there was never such a king called Arthur might well be aretted great folly and blindness. For he said that there were many evidences of the contrary. First ye may see his sepulchre in the monastery of Glastonbury. And also in *Polychronicon*, in the fifth book the sixth chapter, and in the seventh book the twenty-third chapter, where his body was buried, and after found, and translated into the said monastery. Ye shall see also in the history of Boccaccio, in his book *De Casu Principum*, part of his noble acts, and also of his fall. Also Geoffrey in his British book recounteth his life: and in divers places of England many remembrances be yet of him, and shall remain perpetually, and also of his knights. First in the Abbey of Westminster, at St. Edward's shrine, remaineth the print of his seal in red wax closed in beryl, in which is written, *Patricius Arthurus Britannie, Gallie, Germanie, Dacie, Imperator.* Item, in the castle of Dover ye may see Gawaine's skull, and Cradok's mantle; at Winchester the Round Table; in other places Launcelot's sword and many other things. Then all these things considered, there can no man reasonably gainsay but there was a king of this land named Arthur. For in all places, Christian and heathen, he is reputed and taken for one of the nine worthy, and the first of the three Christian men. And also, he is more spoken of beyond the sea, more books made of his noble acts than there be in England, as well in Dutch, Italian, Spanish, and Greekish, as in French. And yet of record remain in witness of him in Wales, in the town of Camelot, the great stones and the marvellous works of iron lying under the ground, and royal vaults, which divers now living have seen. Wherefore it is a marvel why he is no more renowned in his own country, save only it accordeth to the Word of God, which saith that no man is accepted for a prophet in his own country.

Then all these things aforesaid alleged, I could not well deny but that there was such a noble king named Arthur, and reputed one of the nine worthy, and first and chief of the Christian men. And many noble volumes be made of him and of his noble knights in French, which I have seen and read beyond the sea, which be not had in our maternal tongue. But in Welsh be many and also in French, and some in English but nowhere near all. Wherefore, such as have late been drawn out briefly into English I have after the simple cunning that God hath sent to me, under the favour and correction of all noble lords and gentlemen, emprised to imprint a book of the noble histories of the said King Arthur, and of certain of his knights, after a copy unto me delivered, which copy Sir Thomas Malory did take out of certain books of French, and reduced it into English. And I, according to my copy, have done set it in imprint, to the intent that noble men may see and learn the noble acts of chivalry, the gentle and virtuous deeds that some knights used in those days, by which they came to honour, and how they that were vicious were punished and oft put to

5. **Godfrey of Bouillon** (*c.* 1060–1100), one of the leaders of the First Crusade. After the capture of Jerusalem in 1099 he was made the first head of the new kingdom. 7–8. **Edward the Fourth** (1442–1483), became king of England in 1461. His sons Edward (briefly king) and Richard were murdered in the Tower at the order of their father's brother Richard; see Shakespeare's *Richard the Third*. 27. **aretted,** charged with. 30. **Polychronicon,** a highly popular universal history by Ranulph, or Ralph, Higden (*c.* 1299–1363), was translated from Latin into English by John of Trevisa (d. 1412), in 1387. Trevisa's translation, in "modernized" form, was printed by Caxton in 1482. 33. **translated,** moved. 35. **De . . . Principum,** Boccaccio's *De Casibus Virorum Illustrium* inspired Chaucer's "Monk's Tale" and was translated into English by Lydgate from a French version. 37. **British book.** Geoffrey of Monmouth's *Historia Regum Britanniae,* drawn, doubtless, from oral and written sources, contains the first full-length picture of Arthur. 40. **St. Edward's,** of Edward the Confessor.

2. **beryl,** a transparent precious stone. 5. **Cradok's mantle,** a reference to an amusing by-product of Arthurian romance. In the ballad of "The Boy and the Mantle" (Child 29) a boy brings to Arthur's Court a mantle which will not fit a wife who has "done amisse." The wife of Cradok (Caradoc) is the only lady who can wear it, and other proof is given that Cradok is no cuckold. 17. **Camelot,** not safely identified with any modern locality. 36. **emprised,** undertaken. 40. **reduced,** translated.

shame and rebuke; humbly beseeching all noble lords and ladies, with all other estates of what estate or degree they been of, that shall see and read in this said book and work, that they take the good and honest acts in their remembrance, and follow the same. Wherein they shall find many joyous and pleasant histories, and noble and renowned acts of humanity, gentleness, and chivalry. For herein may be seen noble chivalry, courtesy, humanity, friendliness, hardiness, love, friendship, cowardice, murder, hate, virtue, and sin. Do after the good and leave the evil, and it shall bring you to good fame and renown. And for to pass the time this book shall be pleasant to read in, but for to give faith and belief that all is true that is contained herein, ye be at your liberty: but all is written for our doctrine, and for to beware that we fall not to vice nor sin, but to exercise and follow virtue, by which we may come and attain to good fame and renown in this life, and after this short and transitory life to come unto everlasting bliss in heaven; the which He grant us that reigneth in heaven, the blessed Trinity. Amen.

Then to proceed forth in this said book, which I direct unto all noble princes, lords and ladies, gentlemen or gentlewomen, that desire to read or hear read of the noble and joyous history of the great conqueror and excellent king, King Arthur, sometime king of this noble realm, then called Britain; I, William Caxton, simple person, present this book following, which I have emprised to imprint: and treateth of the noble acts, feats of arms of chivalry, prowess, hardiness, humanity, love, courtesy, and very gentleness, with many wonderful histories and adventures. And for to understand briefly the content of this volume, I have divided it into twenty-one books, and every book chaptered, as hereafter shall by God's grace follow. The first book shall treat how Uther Pendragon begot the noble conqueror King Arthur, and containeth twenty-eight chapters. The second book treateth of Balin the noble knight, and containeth nineteen chapters. The third book treated of the marriage of King Arthur to Queen Guenever, with other matters, and containeth fifteen chapters. The fourth book, how Merlin was assotted, and of war made to King Arthur, and containeth twenty-nine chapters. The fifth book treateth of the conquest of Lucius the emperor, and containeth twelve chapters. The sixth book treateth of Sir Launcelot and Sir Lionel and marvellous adventures, and containeth eighteen chapters. The seventh book treateth of a noble knight called Sir Gareth, and named by Sir Kay, Beaumains, and containeth thirty-six chapters. The eighth book treateth of the birth of Sir Tristram the noble knight, and of his acts, and containeth forty-one chapters. The ninth book treateth of a knight named by Sir Kay, Le Cote Male Taille, and also of Sir Tristram, and containeth forty-four chapters. The tenth book treateth of Sir Tristram and other marvellous adventures, and containeth eighty-eight chapters. The eleventh book treateth of Sir Launcelot and Sir Galahad, and containeth fourteen chapters. The twelfth book treateth of Sir Launcelot and his madness, and containeth fourteen chapters. The thirteenth book treateth how Galahad came first to King Arthur's court, and the quest how the Saint Grail was begun, and containeth twenty chapters. The fourteenth book treateth of the quest of the Saint Grail, and containeth ten chapters. The fifteenth book treateth of Sir Launcelot, and containeth six chapters. The sixteenth book treateth of Sir Bors and Sir Lionel his brother, and containeth seventeen chapters. The seventeenth book treateth of the Saint Grail, and containeth twenty-three chapters. The eighteenth book treateth of Sir Launcelot and the queen, and containeth twenty-five chapters. The nineteenth book treateth of Queen Guenever and Launcelot, and containeth thirteen chapters. The twentieth book treateth of the piteous death of Arthur, and containeth twenty-two chapters. The twenty-first book treateth of his last departing, and how Sir Launcelot came to revenge his death, and containeth thirteen chapters. The sum is twenty-one books, which contain the sum of five hundred and seven chapters, as more plainly shall follow hereafter.

BOOK XXI

Chapter 1: *How Sir Mordred presumed and took on him to be King of England, and would have married the queen, his father's wife.*

AS Sir Mordred was ruler of all England, he did do make letters as though that they came from beyond the sea, and the letters specified that King Arthur was slain in battle with Sir Launcelot.

---

16. **all ... doctrine.** See Romans 15:4, and Chaucer's "Nun's Priest's Tale," ll. 621–22, page 216.   47. **assotted**, infatuated, with the lady Nimue (Nimiane, Vivian), who shut him up in a rock.

5. **Beaumains**, Fair-hands.   9–10. **Le Cote ... Taille**, that is as much to say, the evil-shapen coat.   47. **do make**, have made.   49. **King Arthur ... Launcelot.** Arthur had invaded Launcelot's country of Benwick in France, for "Sir Launcelot and his nephews were lords of **all** France."

SIR THOMAS MALORY

Wherefore Sir Mordred made a parliament, and called the lords together, and there he made them to choose him king; and so was he crowned at Canterbury, and held a feast there fifteen days; and afterward he drew him unto Winchester, and there he took the Queen Guenever, and said plainly that he would wed her which was his uncle's wife and his father's wife. And so he made ready for the feast, and a day prefixed that they should be wedded; wherefore Queen Guenever was passing heavy. But she durst not discover her heart, but spake fair and agreed to Sir Mordred's will. Then she desired of Sir Mordred for to go to London, to buy all manner of things that longed unto the wedding. And because of her fair speech Sir Mordred trusted her well enough and gave her leave to go. And so when she came to London she took the Tower of London, and suddenly in all haste possible she stuffed it with all manner of victual, and well garnished it with men, and so kept it.

Then when Sir Mordred wist and understood how he was beguiled he was passing wroth out of measure. And a short tale for to make, he went and laid a mighty siege about the Tower of London, and made many great assaults thereat, and threw many great engines unto them, and shot great guns. But all might not prevail Sir Mordred, for Queen Guenever would never for fair speech nor for foul trust to come in his hands again.

Then came the Bishop of Canterbury, the which was a noble clerk and an holy man, and thus he said to Sir Mordred: "Sir, what will ye do? Will ye first displease God and sithen shame yourself, and all knighthood? Is not King Arthur your uncle, no farther but your mother's brother, and on her himself King Arthur begat you upon his own sister, therefore how may you wed your father's wife? Sir," said the noble clerk, "leave this opinion or I shall curse you with book and bell and candle." "Do thou thy worst," said Sir Mordred, "wit thou well I shall defy thee." "Sir," said the Bishop, "and wit you well I shall not fear me to do that me ought to do. Also where ye noise where my lord Arthur is slain, and that is not so, and therefore ye will make a foul work in this land." "Peace, thou false priest," said Sir Mordred, "for an thou chafe me any more I shall make strike off thy head." So the Bishop departed and did the cursing in the most orgulist wise that might be done. And then Sir Mordred sought the Bishop of Canterbury, for to have slain him. Then the Bishop fled, and took part of his goods with him, and went nigh unto Glastonbury; and there he was as priest-hermit in a chapel, and lived in poverty and in holy prayers, for well he understood that mischievous war was at hand.

Then Sir Mordred sought on Queen Guenever by letters and sonds, and by fair means and foul means, for to have her to come out of the Tower of London; but all this availed not, for she answered him shortly, openly and privily, that she had liefer slay herself than to be married with him. Then came word to Sir Mordred that King Arthur had araised the siege for Sir Launcelot, and he was coming homeward with a great host to be avenged upon Sir Mordred; wherefore Sir Mordred made write writs to all the barony of this land, and much people drew to him. For then was the common voice among them that with Arthur was none other life but war and strife, and with Sir Mordred was great joy and bliss. Thus was Sir Arthur depraved, and evil said of. And many there were that King Arthur had made up of nought, and given them lands, might not then say him a good word. Lo ye, all Englishmen, see ye not what a mischief here was! For he that was the most king and knight of the world, and most loved the fellowship of noble knights, and by him they were all upholden, now might not these Englishmen hold them content with him. Lo, thus was the old custom and usage of this land; and also men say that we of this land have not yet lost nor forgotten that custom and usage. Alas, this is a great default of us Englishmen, for there may no thing please us no term. And so fared the people at that time, they were better pleased with Sir Mordred than they were with King Arthur; and much people drew unto Sir Mordred, and said they would abide with him for better and for worse. And so Sir Mordred drew with a great host to Dover, for there he heard say that Sir Arthur would arrive, and so he thought to beat his own father from his lands; and the most part of all England held with Sir Mordred, the people were so new-fangle.

8. **uncle's ... wife.** Mordred was the offspring of an incestuous, though casual, union between Arthur and his own sister. 9. **prefixed,** appointed. 10–11. **wherefore ... heavy.** In some of the earlier versions Guenever was Mordred's willing mistress. 15. **longed unto,** concerned. 20. **garnished,** supplied. 27. **engines,** catapults and the like. 28. **guns,** an obvious anachronism. 35. **sithen,** afterwards. 41. **curse,** excommunicate. 45. **noise,** report.

1. **an,** if. 4. **orgulist,** proudest, most ceremonious. 13. **sonds,** messages. 19. **araised,** lifted. 26. **depraved,** defamed. 38–39. **Alas ... term.** The Wars of the Roses had given sufficient examples of this. 49–50. **new-fangle,** fond of novelty.

Chapter 2: *How after that King Arthur had tidings, he returned and came to Dover, where Sir Mordred met him to let his landing; and of the death of Sir Gawaine.*

AND so as Sir Mordred was at Dover with his host, there came King Arthur with a great navy of ships and galleys and carracks. And there was Sir Mordred ready awaiting upon his landing, to let his own father to land upon the land that he was king over. Then there was launching of great boats and small, and full of noble men of arms, and there was much slaughter of gentle knights, and many a full bold baron was laid full low on both parties. But King Arthur was so courageous that there might no manner of knights let him to land, and his knights fiercely followed him; and so they landed maugre Sir Mordred and all his power, and put Sir Mordred aback, that he fled and all his people.

So when this battle was done, King Arthur let bury his people that were dead. And then was noble Sir Gawaine found in a great boat, lying more than half dead. When Sir Arthur wist that Sir Gawaine was laid so low, he went unto him; and there the king made sorrow out of measure, and took Sir Gawaine in his arms, and thrice he there swooned. And then when he awaked, he said: "Alas, Sir Gawaine, my sister's son, here now thou liest, the man in the world that I loved most; and now is my joy gone, for now, my nephew Sir Gawaine, I will discover me unto your person: in Sir Launcelot and you I most had my joy and mine affiance, and now have I lost my joy of you both; wherefore all mine earthly joy is gone from me." "Mine uncle, King Arthur," said Sir Gawaine, "wit you well my death-day is come, and all is through mine own hastiness and wilfulness; for I am smitten upon the old wound the which Sir Launcelot gave me, on the which I feel well I must die; and had Sir Launcelot been with you as he was, this unhappy war had never begun; and of all this am I causer, for Sir Launcelot and his blood, through their prowess, held all your cankered enemies in subjection and daunger. And now," said Sir Gawaine, "ye shall miss Sir Launcelot. But alas, I would not accord with him, and therefore," said Sir Gawaine, "I pray you, fair uncle, that I may have paper, pen, and ink, that I may write to Sir Launcelot a cedle with mine own hands."

And then when paper and ink was brought, then Gawaine was set up weakly by King Arthur, for he was shriven a little tofore; and then he wrote thus, as the French book maketh mention: "Unto Sir Launcelot, flower of all noble knights that ever I heard of or saw by my days, I, Sir Gawaine, King Lot's son of Orkney, sister's son unto the noble King Arthur, send thee greeting, and let thee have knowledge that the tenth day of May I was smitten upon the old wound that thou gavest me afore the city of Benwick, and through the same wound that thou gavest me I am come to my death-day. And I will that all the world wit, that I, Sir Gawaine, knight of the Table Round, sought my death, and not through thy deserving, but it was mine own seeking; wherefore I beseech thee, Sir Launcelot, to return again unto this realm, and see my tomb, and pray some prayer more or less for my soul. And this same day that I wrote this cedle, I was hurt to the death in the same wound, the which I had of thy hand, Sir Launcelot; for of a more nobler man might I not be slain. Also Sir Launcelot, for all the love that ever was betwixt us, make no tarrying, but come over the sea in all haste, that thou mayst with thy noble knights rescue that noble king that made thee knight, that is my lord Arthur; for he is full straitly bestead with a false traitor, that is my half-brother, Sir Mordred; and he hath let crown him king, and would have wedded my lady Queen Guenever, and so had he done had she not put herself in the Tower of London. And so the tenth day of May last past, my lord Arthur and we all landed upon them at Dover; and there we put that false traitor, Sir Mordred, to flight, and there it misfortuned me to be stricken upon thy stroke. And at the date of this letter was written, but two hours and a half afore my death, written with mine own hand, and so subscribed with part of my heart's blood. And I require thee, most famous knight of the world, that thou wilt see my tomb." And then Sir Gawaine wept, and King Arthur wept; and then they swooned both. And when they awaked both, the king made Sir Gawaine to receive his Saviour. And then Sir Gawaine prayed the king for to send for Sir Launcelot, and to cherish him above all other knights.

And so at the hour of noon Sir Gawaine yielded up the spirit; and then the king let inter him in a chapel within Dover Castle; and there yet all men may see the skull of him, and the same wound is seen that Sir Launcelot gave him in battle. Then

---

8. **carracks,** large ships.   10. **let,** prevent.   18. **maugre,** despite.   32. **discover me,** make known, speak candidly.   34. **affiance,** trust.   43. **blood,** relatives.   44. **cankered,** malignant.   50. **cedle,** schedule, short note.

2. **weakly,** in weak condition.   27. **straitly bestead,** closely harassed.   44. **his Saviour,** the bread of the Sacrament.

was it told the king that Sir Mordred had pight a new field upon Barham Down. And upon the morn the king rode thither to him, and there was a great battle betwixt them, and much people was slain on both parties; but at the last Sir Arthur's party stood best, and Sir Mordred and his party fled unto Canterbury.

Chapter 3: *How after, Sir Gawaine's ghost appeared to King Arthur, and warned him that he should not fight that day.*

AND then the king let search all the towns for his knights that were slain, and interred them; and salved them with soft salves that so sore were wounded. Then much people drew unto King Arthur. And then they said that Sir Mordred warred upon King Arthur with wrong. And then King Arthur drew him with his host down by the seaside, westward toward Salisbury; and there was a day assigned betwixt King Arthur and Sir Mordred, that they should meet upon a down beside Salisbury, and not far from the seaside; and this day was assigned on a Monday after Trinity Sunday, whereof King Arthur was passing glad, that he might be avenged upon Sir Mordred. Then Sir Mordred araised much people about London, for they of Kent, Southsex, and Surrey, Essex, and of Suffolk, and of Norfolk, held the most part with Sir Mordred; and many a full noble knight drew unto Sir Mordred and to the king: but they that loved Sir Launcelot drew unto Sir Mordred.

So upon Trinity Sunday at night, King Arthur dreamed a wonderful dream, and that was this: that him seemed he sat upon a chaflet in a chair, and the chair was fast to a wheel, and thereupon sat King Arthur in the richest cloth of gold that might be made; and the king thought there was under him, far from him, an hideous deep black water, and therein were all manner of serpents, and worms, and wild beasts, foul and horrible; and suddenly the king thought the wheel turned up-so-down, and he fell among the serpents, and every beast took him by a limb; and then the king cried as he lay in his bed and slept, "Help!" And then knights, squires, and yeomen awaked the king; and then he was so amazed that he wist not where he was; and then he fell a-slumbering again, not sleeping nor thoroughly waking. So the king seemed verily that there came Sir Gawaine unto him with a number of fair ladies with him. And when King Arthur saw him, then he said: "Welcome, my sister's son; I weened thou hadst been dead, and now I see thee alive, much am I beholden unto Almighty Jesu. O fair nephew and my sister's son, what be these ladies that hither be come with you?" "Sir," said Sir Gawaine, "all these be ladies for whom I have foughten when I was man living, and all these are those that I did battle for in righteous quarrel; and God hath given them that grace at their great prayer, because I did battle for them, that they should bring me hither unto you: thus much hath God given me leave, for to warn you of your death; for an ye fight as tomorn with Sir Mordred, as ye both have assigned, doubt ye not ye must be slain, and the most part of your people on both parties. And for the great grace and goodness that almighty Jesu hath unto you, and for pity of you, and many more other good men there shall be slain, God hath sent me to you of his special grace, to give you warning that in no wise ye do battle as tomorn, but that ye take a treaty for a month day; and proffer you largely, so as tomorn to be put in a delay. For within a month shall come Sir Launcelot with all his noble knights, and rescue you worshipfully, and slay Sir Mordred, and all that ever will hold with him." Then Sir Gawaine and all the ladies vanished.

And anon the king called upon his knights, squires, and yeomen, and charged them wightly to fetch his noble lords and wise bishops unto him. And when they were come, the king told them his avision, what Sir Gawaine had told him, and warned him that if he fought on the morn he should be slain. Then the king commanded Sir Lucan the Butler, and his brother Sir Bedivere, with two bishops with them, and charged them in any wise, an they might, "Take a treaty for a month day with Sir Mordred, and spare not, proffer him lands and goods as much as ye think best." So then they departed, and came to Sir Mordred, where he had a grim host of an hundred thousand men. And there they entreated Sir Mordred long time; and at the last Sir Mordred was agreed for to have Cornwall and Kent, by Arthur's days: after, all England, after the days of King Arthur.

Chapter 4: *How by misadventure of an adder the battle began, where Mordred was slain, and Arthur hurt to the death.*

THEN were they condescended that King Arthur and Sir Mordred should meet betwixt both their hosts, and each of them should bring

---

1–2. **pight . . . Down,** prepared for battle (in Kent). 23. **Trinity Sunday,** the Sunday after Whitsunday. 34. **chaflet,** platform (?). 48. **seemed,** thought. 21. **month day,** the space of a month. **largely,** generously. 28. **wightly,** quickly. 43. **by,** during. 49. **condescended,** agreed.

fourteen persons; and they came with this word unto Arthur. Then said he: "I am glad that this is done"; and so he went into the field. And when Arthur should depart, he warned all his host that an they see any sword drawn: "Look ye come on fiercely, and slay that traitor, Sir Mordred, for I in no wise trust him." In like wise Sir Mordred warned his host that: "An ye see any sword drawn, look that ye come on fiercely, and so slay all that ever before you standeth; for in no wise I will not trust for this treaty, for I know well my father will be avenged on me." And so they met as their appointment was, and so they were agreed and accorded thoroughly; and wine was fetched, and they drank. Right soon came an adder out of a little heath bush, and it stung a knight on the foot. And when the knight felt him stung, he looked down and saw the adder, and then he drew his sword to slay the adder, and thought of none other harm. And when the host on both parties saw that sword drawn, then they blew bemes, trumpets, and horns, and shouted grimly. And so both hosts dressed them together. And King Arthur took his horse, and said: "Alas this unhappy day!" and so rode to his party. And Sir Mordred in like wise. And never was there seen a more dolefuller battle in no Christian land; for there was but rushing and riding, foining and striking, and many a deadly stroke. But ever King Arthur rode throughout the battle of Sir Mordred many times, and did full nobly as a noble king should, and at all times he fainted never; and Sir Mordred that day put him in devoir, and in great peril. And thus they fought all the long day, and never stinted till the noble knights were laid to the cold earth; and ever they fought still till it was near night, and by that time was there an hundred thousand laid dead upon the down. Then was Arthur wood wroth out of measure, when he saw his people so slain from him.

Then the king looked about him, and then was he ware, of all his host and of all his good knights, were left no more alive but two knights; that one was Sir Lucan the Butler, and his brother Sir Bedivere, and they were full sore wounded. "Jesu mercy," said the king, "where are all my noble knights become? Alas that ever I should see this doleful day, for now," said Arthur, "I am come to mine end. But would to God that I wist where were that traitor Sir Mordred, that hath caused all this mischief." Then was King Arthur ware where Sir Mordred leaned upon his sword among a great heap of dead men. "Now give me my spear," said Arthur unto Sir Lucan, "for yonder I have espied the traitor that all this woe hath wrought." "Sir, let him be," said Sir Lucan, "for he is unhappy; and if ye pass this unhappy day ye shall be right well revenged upon him. Good lord, remember ye of your night's dream, and what the spirit of Sir Gawaine told you this night, yet God of his great goodness hath preserved you hitherto. Therefore, for God's sake, my lord, leave off by this, for blessed be God ye have won the field, for here we be three alive, and with Sir Mordred is none alive; and if ye leave off now this wicked day of destiny is past." "Tide me death, betide me life," saith the king, "now I see him yonder alone he shall never escape mine hands, for at a better avail shall I never have him." "God speed you well," said Sir Bedivere.

Then the king got his spear in both his hands, and ran toward Sir Mordred, crying: "Traitor, now is thy death-day come." And when Sir Mordred heard Sir Arthur, he ran until him with his sword drawn in his hand. And there King Arthur smote Sir Mordred under the shield, with a foin of his spear, throughout the body, more than a fathom. And when Sir Mordred felt that he had his death wound he thrust himself with the might that he had up to the burr of King Arthur's spear. And right so he smote his father Arthur, with his sword held in both his hands, on the side of the head, that the sword pierced the helmet and the brain-pan, and therewithal Sir Mordred fell stark dead to the earth; and the noble Arthur fell in a swoon to the earth, and there he swooned ofttimes. And Sir Lucan the Butler and Sir Bedivere ofttimes heaved him up. And so weakly they led him betwixt them both, to a little chapel not far from the seaside. And when the king was there he thought him well eased.

Then heard they people cry in the field. "Now go thou, Sir Lucan," said the king, "and do me to wit what betokens that noise in the field." So Sir Lucan departed, for he was grievously wounded in many places. And so as he yede, he saw and hearkened by the moonlight, how that pillers and robbers were come into the field, to pill and to rob many a full noble knight of brooches and beads, of many a good ring, and of many a rich jewel; and who that were not dead all out, there they slew them for their harness and their riches. When Sir Lucan understood this work, he came to the king

21. **bemes,** trumpets. 22. **dressed them,** went. 28. **foining,** thrusting. 29. **battle,** army. 32. **put ... devoir,** did what he could. 38. **wood,** mad. 4. **unhappy,** troublesome. 16. **avail,** advantage. 23. **foin,** thrust. 27. **burr,** the ring on a spear just behind the place for the hand. 43. **yede,** went. 44. **pillers,** thieves. 48. **all out,** completely.

as soon as he might, and told him all what he had heard and seen. "Therefore by my rede," said Sir Lucan, "it is best that we bring you to some town." "I would it were so," said the king.

Chapter 5: *How King Arthur commanded to cast his sword Excalibur into the water, and how he was delivered to ladies in a barge.*

BUT I may not stand, mine head works so. Ah Sir Launcelot," said King Arthur, "this day have I sore missed thee: alas, that ever I was against thee, for now have I my death, whereof Sir Gawaine me warned in my dream." Then Sir Lucan took up the king the one part, and Sir Bedivere the other part, and in the lifting the king swooned; and Sir Lucan fell in a swoon with the lift, that the part of his guts fell out of his body, and therewith the noble knight's heart brast. And when the king awoke, he beheld Sir Lucan, how he lay foaming at the mouth, and part of his guts lay at his feet. "Alas," said the king, "this is to me a full heavy sight, to see this noble duke so die for my sake, for he would have helped me, that had more need of help than I. Alas, he would not complain him, his heart was so set to help me: now Jesu have mercy upon his soul!" Then Sir Bedivere wept for the death of his brother. "Leave this mourning and weeping," said the king, "for all this will not avail me, for wit thou well an I might live myself, the death of Sir Lucan would grieve me evermore; but my time hieth fast," said the king. "Therefore," said Arthur unto Sir Bedivere, "take thou Excalibur, my good sword, and go with it to yonder water-side, and when thou comest there I charge thee throw my sword in that water, and come again and tell me what thou there seest." "My lord, said Bedivere, "your commandment shall be done, and lightly bring you word again."

So Sir Bedivere departed, and by the way he beheld that noble sword, that the pommel and the haft was all of precious stones; and then he said to himself: "If I throw this rich sword in the water, thereof shall never come good, but harm and loss." And then Sir Bedivere hid Excalibur under a tree. And so, as soon as he might, he came again unto the king, and said he had been at the water, and had thrown the sword in the water. "What saw thou there?" said the king. "Sir," he said, "I saw nothing but waves and winds." "That is untruly said of thee," said the king, "therefore go thou lightly again, and do my commandment; as thou art to me lief and dear, spare not, but throw it in." Then Sir Bedivere returned again, and took the sword in his hand; and then him thought sin and shame to throw away that noble sword, and so eft he hid the sword, and returned again, and told to the king that he had been at the water, and done his commandment. "What saw thou there?" said the king. "Sir," he said, "I saw nothing but the waters wap and waves wane." "Ah, traitor untrue," said King Arthur, "now hast thou betrayed me twice. Who would have weened that, thou that has been to me so lief and dear? And thou art named a noble knight, and would betray me for the richness of the sword. But now go again lightly, for thy long tarrying putteth me in great jeopardy of my life, for I have taken cold. And but if thou do now as I bid thee, if ever I may see thee, I shall slay thee with mine own hands; for thou wouldst for my rich sword see me dead."

Then Sir Bedivere departed, and went to the sword, and lightly took it up, and went to the water-side; and there he bound the girdle about the hilts, and then he threw the sword as far into the water as he might; and there came an arm and an hand above the water and met it, and caught it, and so shook it thrice and brandished, and then vanished away the hand with the sword in the water. So Sir Bedivere came again to the king, and told him what he saw. "Alas," said the king, "help me hence, for I dread me I have tarried over long." Then Sir Bedivere took the king upon his back, and so went with him to that water-side. And when they were at the water-side, even fast by the bank hoved a little barge with many fair ladies in it, and among them all was a queen, and all they had black hoods, and all they wept and shrieked when they saw King Arthur. "Now put me into the barge," said the king. And so he did softly; and there received him three queens with great mourning; and so they set them down, and in one of their laps King Arthur laid his head. And then that queen said: "Ah, dear brother, why have ye tarried so long from me? Alas, this wound on your head hath caught over-much cold." And so then they rowed from the land, and Sir Bedivere beheld all those ladies go from him. Then Sir Bedivere cried, "Ah my lord Arthur, what shall become of me, now ye go from me and leave me here alone among mine enemies?" "Comfort thyself," said the king, "and do as well as thou mayst, for in me is no trust for to trust in; for I will into the vale of Avalon to heal me of my grievous wound: and if

---

2. **rede**, advice.   10. **works**, hurts.   19. **brast**, burst.   5. **eft**, again.   9. **wap**, beat (?), **wane**, ebb.   34. **hoved**, waited.
39. **lightly**, quickly.

thou hear never more of me, pray for my soul." But ever the queens and ladies wept and shrieked, that it was pity to hear. And as soon as Sir Bedivere had lost the sight of the barge, he wept and wailed, and so took the forest; and so he went all that night, and in the morning he was ware betwixt two holts hoar, of a chapel and an hermitage.

Chapter 6: *How Sir Bedivere found him on the morrow dead in an hermitage, and how he abode there with the hermit.*

THEN was Sir Bedivere glad, and thither he went; and when he came into the chapel, he saw where lay an hermit grovelling on all four, there fast by a tomb was new graven. When the hermit saw Sir Bedivere he knew him well, for he was but little tofore Bishop of Canterbury, that Sir Mordred flemed. "Sir," said Bedivere, "what man is there interred that ye pray so fast for?" "Fair son," said the hermit, "I wot not verily, but by deeming. But this night, at midnight, here came a number of ladies, and brought hither a dead corpse, and prayed me to bury him; and here they offered an hundred tapers, and they gave me an hundred bezants." "Alas," said Sir Bedivere, "that was my lord King Arthur, that here lieth buried in this chapel." Then Sir Bedivere swooned; and when he awoke he prayed the hermit he might abide with him still there, to live with fasting and prayers. "For from hence will I never go," said Sir Bedivere, "by my will, but all the days of my life here to pray for my lord Arthur." "Ye are welcome to me," said the hermit, "for I know ye better than ye ween that I do. Ye are the bold Bedivere, and the full noble duke, Sir Lucan the Butler, was your brother." Then Sir Bedivere told the hermit all as ye have heard tofore. So there bode Sir Bedivere with the hermit that was tofore Bishop of Canterbury, and there Sir Bedivere put upon him poor clothes, and served the hermit full lowly in fasting and in prayers.

Thus of Arthur I find never more written in books that be authorised, nor more of the very certainty of his death heard I never read, but thus was he led away in a ship wherein were three queens; that one was King Arthur's sister, Queen Morgan le Fay, the other was the Queen of Northgalis, the third was the Queen of the Waste Lands. Also there was Nimue, the chief lady of the lake, that had wedded Pelleas the good knight; and this lady had done much for King Arthur, for she would never suffer Sir Pelleas to be in no place where he should be in danger of his life; and so he lived to the uttermost of his days with her in great rest. More of the death of King Arthur could I never find, but that ladies brought him to his burials; and such one was buried there, that the hermit bare witness that sometime was Bishop of Canterbury, but yet the hermit knew not in certain that he was verily the body of King Arthur; for this tale Sir Bedivere, knight of the Table Round, made it to be written.

Chapter 7: *Of the opinion of some men of the death of King Arthur; and how Queen Guenever made her a nun in Amesbury.*

YET some men say in many parts of England that King Arthur is not dead, but had by the will of our Lord Jesu into another place; and men say that he shall come again, and he shall win the holy cross. I will not say it shall be so, but rather I will say: here in this world he changed his life. But many men say that there is written upon his tomb this verse: *Hic jacet Arthurus, Rex quondam, Rexque futurus.* Thus leave I here Sir Bedivere with the hermit, that dwelled that time in a chapel beside Glastonbury, and there was his hermitage. And so they lived in their prayers, and fastings, and great abstinence. And when Queen Guenever understood that King Arthur was slain, and all the noble knights, Sir Mordred and all the remnant, then the queen stole away, and five ladies with her, and so she went to Amesbury; and there she let make herself a nun, and wore white clothes and black, and great penance she took, as ever did sinful lady in this land, and never creature could make her merry; but lived in fasting, prayers, and almsdeeds, that all manner of people marvelled how virtuously she was changed. Now leave we Queen Guenever in Amesbury, a nun in white clothes and black, and there she was abbess and ruler as reason would; and turn we from her; and speak we of Sir Launcelot du Lake.

Chapter 8: *How when Sir Launcelot heard of the death of King Arthur, and of Sir Gawaine, and other matters, he came into England.*

AND when he heard in his country that Sir Mordred was crowned king in England, and made war against King Arthur, his own father, and

---

5. **took,** went into. 6–7. **holts hoar,** gray woods. 18. **flemed,** put to flight. 21. **deeming,** surmise. 25. **bezants,** gold coins worth a sovereign or less. 37. **bode,** remained. 48. **Nimue,** the lady who had betrayed Merlin.

17. **had,** was taken. 23–24. **Hic jacet . . . futurus.** Here lies Arthur, King that was, and King that is to be. 32. **Amesbury,** in Wiltshire.

would let him to land in his own land; also it was told Sir Launcelot how that Sir Mordred had laid siege about the Tower of London, because the queen would not wed him; then was Sir Launcelot wroth out of measure, and said to his kinsmen: "Alas, that double traitor Sir Mordred, now me repenteth that ever he escaped my hands, for much shame hath he done unto my lord Arthur; for all I feel by the doleful letter that my lord Sir Gawaine sent me, on whose soul Jesu have mercy, that my lord Arthur is full hard bestead. Alas," said Sir Launcelot, "that ever I should live to hear that most noble king that made me knight thus to be overset with his subject in his own realm. And this doleful letter that my lord, Sir Gawaine, hath sent me afore his death, praying me to see his tomb, wit you well his doleful words shall never go from mine heart, for he was a full noble knight as ever was born; and in an unhappy hour was I born that ever I should have that unhap to slay first Sir Gawaine, Sir Gaheris the good knight, and mine own friend Sir Gareth, that full noble knight. Alas, I may say I am unhappy," said Sir Launcelot, "that ever I should do thus unhappily, and, alas, yet might I never have hap to slay that traitor, Sir Mordred."

"Leave your complaints," said Sir Bors, "and first revenge you of the death of Sir Gawaine; and it will be well done that ye see Sir Gawaine's tomb, and secondly that ye revenge my lord Arthur, and my lady Queen Guenever." "I thank you," said Sir Launcelot, "for ever ye will my worship."

Then they made them ready in all the haste that might be, with ships and galleys, with Sir Launcelot and his host to pass into England. And so he passed over the sea till he came to Dover, and there he landed with seven kings, and the number was hideous to behold. Then Sir Launcelot speered of men of Dover where was King Arthur become. Then the people told him how that he was slain, and Sir Mordred and an hundred thousand died on a day; and how Sir Mordred gave King Arthur there the first battle at his landing, and there was good Sir Gawaine slain; and on the morn Sir Mordred fought with the king upon Barham Down, and there the king put Sir Mordred to the worse. "Alas," said Sir Launcelot, "this is the heaviest tidings that ever came to me. Now, fair sirs," said Sir Launcelot, "shew me the tomb of Sir Gawaine." And then certain people of the town brought him into the castle of Dover, and shewed him the tomb. Then Sir Launcelot kneeled down and wept, and prayed heartily for his soul. And that night he made a dole, and all they that would come had as much flesh, fish, wine, and ale, and every man and woman had twelve pence, come who would. Thus with his own hand dealt he this money, in a mourning gown; and ever he wept, and prayed them to pray for the soul of Sir Gawaine. And on the morn all the priests and clerks that might be gotten in the country were there, and sang mass of requiem; and there offered first Sir Launcelot, and he offered an hundred pound; and then the seven kings offered forty pound apiece; and also there was a thousand knights, and each of them offered a pound; and the offering dured from morn till night, and Sir Launcelot lay two nights on his tomb in prayers and weeping.

Then on the third day Sir Launcelot called the kings, dukes, earls, barons, and knights, and said thus: "My fair lords, I thank you all of your coming into this country with me, but we came too late, and that shall repent me while I live, but against death may no man rebel. But sithen it is so," said Sir Launcelot, "I will myself ride and seek my lady, Queen Guenever, for as I hear say she hath had great pain and much disease; and I heard say that she is fled into the west. Therefore ye all shall abide me here, and but if I come again within fifteen days, then take your ships and your fellowship, and depart into your country, for I will do as I say to you."

Chapter 9: *How Sir Launcelot departed to seek the Queen Guenever, and how he found her at Amesbury.*

THEN came Sir Bors de Ganis, and said: "My lord Sir Launcelot, what think ye for to do, now to ride in this realm? Wit ye well ye shall find few friends." "Be as be may," said Sir Launcelot, "keep you still here, for I will forth on my journey, and no man nor child shall go with me." So it was no boot to strive, but he departed and rode westerly, and there he sought a seven or eight days; and at the last he came to a nunnery, and then was Queen Guenever ware of Sir Launcelot as he walked in the cloister. And when she saw him there she swooned thrice, that all the ladies and gentlewomen had work enough to hold the queen up. So when she might speak, she called ladies and

---

20. **unhap,** misfortune.   32–33. **will . . . worship,** desire my honor.   40. **speered,** asked.

11. **requiem,** for the repose of the souls of the dead.   16. **dured,** lasted.   27. **disease,** discomfort.   44. **boot,** use.

gentlewomen to her, and said: "Ye marvel, fair ladies, why I make this fare. Truly," she said, "it is for the sight of yonder knight that yonder standeth; wherefore I pray you all call him to me."

When Sir Launcelot was brought to her, then she said to all the ladies: "Through this man and me hath all this war been wrought; for through our love that we have loved together is my most noble lord slain. Therefore, Sir Launcelot, wit thou well I am set in such a plight to get my soul-heal; and yet I trust through God's grace that after my death to have a sight of the blessed face of Christ, and at doomsday to sit on his right side, for as sinful as ever I was are saints in heaven. Therefore, Sir Launcelot, I require thee and beseech thee heartily, for all the love that ever was betwixt us, that thou never see me more in the visage; and I command thee, on God's behalf, that thou forsake my company, and to thy kingdom thou turn again, and keep well thy realm from war and wrack; for as well as I have loved thee, mine heart will not serve me to see thee, for through thee and me is the flower of kings and knights destroyed; therefore, Sir Launcelot, go to thy realm, and there take thee a wife, and live with her with joy and bliss; and I pray thee heartily, pray for me to our Lord that I may amend my misliving." "Now, sweet madam," said Sir Launcelot, "would ye that I should now return again unto my country, and there to wed a lady? Nay, madam, wit you well that shall I never do, for I shall never be so false to you of that I have promised; but the same destiny that ye have taken you to, I will take me unto, for to please Jesu, and ever for you I cast me specially to pray." "If thou wilt do so," said the queen, "hold thy promise, but I may never believe but that thou wilt turn to the world again." "Well, madam," said he, "ye say as pleaseth you, yet wist you me never false of my promise, and God defend but I should forsake the world as ye have done. For in the quest of the Saint Grail I had forsaken the vanities of the world had not your lord been. And if I had done so at that time, with my heart, will, and thought, I had passed all the knights that were in the Saint Grail except Sir Galahad, my son. And therefore, lady, sithen ye have taken you to perfection, I must needs take me to perfection, of right. For I take record of God, in you I have had mine earthly joy; and if I had found you now so disposed, I had cast me to have had you into mine own realm."

Chapter 10: *How Sir Launcelot came to the hermitage where the Archbishop of Canterbury was, and how he took the habit on him.*

BUT sithen I find you thus disposed, I ensure you faithfully, I will ever take me to penance, and pray while my life lasteth, if I may find any hermit, either gray or white, that will receive me. Wherefore, madam, I pray you kiss me and never no more." "Nay," said the queen, "that shall I never do, but abstain you from such works"; and they departed. But there was never so hard an hearted man but he would have wept to see the dolour that they made; for there was lamentation as they had been stung with spears; and many times they swooned, and the ladies bare the queen to her chamber.

And Sir Launcelot awoke, and went and took his horse, and rode all that day and all night in a forest, weeping. And at the last he was ware of an hermitage and a chapel stood betwixt two cliffs; and then he heard a little bell ring to mass, and thither he rode and alighted, and tied his horse to the gate, and heard mass. And he that sang mass was the Bishop of Canterbury. Both the Bishop and Sir Bedivere knew Sir Launcelot, and they spake together after mass. But when Sir Bedivere had told his tale all whole, Sir Launcelot's heart almost brast for sorrow, and Sir Launcelot threw his arms abroad, and said: "Alas, who may trust this world?" And then he kneeled down on his knee, and prayed the Bishop to shrive him and assoil him. And then he besought the Bishop that he might be his brother. Then the Bishop said: "I will gladly"; and there he put an habit upon Sir Launcelot, and there he served God day and night with prayers and fastings.

Thus the great host abode at Dover. And then Sir Lionel took fifteen lords with him, and rode to London to seek Sir Launcelot; and there Sir Lionel was slain and many of his lords. Then Sir Bors de Ganis made the great host for to go home again; and Sir Bors, Sir Ector de Maris, Sir Blamore, Sir Bleoberis, with more other of Sir Launcelot's kin, took on them to ride all England overthwart and endlong, to seek Sir Launcelot. So Sir Bors by fortune rode so long till he came to the same chapel where Sir Launcelot was; and so Sir Bors heard a little bell knell, that rang to mass; and there he alighted and heard mass. And when

2. **fare**, display. 18. **in the visage**, to my face. 21. **wrack**, harm. 35. **cast me**, intend. 47. **sithen**, since.

6. **ensure**, assure. 13. **departed**, separated. 15. **dolour**, sorrow. 34. **assoil**, absolve. 46–47. **overthwart and endlong**, throughout.

mass was done, the Bishop, Sir Launcelot, and Sir Bedivere came to Sir Bors. And when Sir Bors saw Sir Launcelot in that manner clothing, then he prayed the Bishop that he might be in the same suit. And so there was an habit put upon him, and there he lived in prayers and fasting. And within half a year, there was come Sir Galihud, Sir Galihodin, Sir Blamore, Sir Bleoberis, Sir Villiars, Sir Clarras, and Sir Gahalantine. So all these seven noble knights there abode still. And when they saw Sir Launcelot had taken him to such perfection, they had no lust to depart, but took such an habit as he had.

Thus they endured in great penance six year; and then Sir Launcelot took the habit of priesthood of the Bishop, and a twelvemonth he sang mass. And there was none of these other knights but they read in books, and helped for to sing mass, and rang bells, and did bodily all manner of service. And so their horses went where they would, for they took no regard of no worldly riches. For when they saw Sir Launcelot endure such penance, in prayers and fastings, they took no force what pain they endured, for to see the noblest knight of the world take such abstinence that he waxed full lean. And thus upon a night, there came a vision to Sir Launcelot, and charged him, in remission of his sins, to haste him unto Amesbury: "And by then thou come there, thou shalt find Queen Guenever dead. And therefore take thy fellows with thee, and purvey them of an horse-bier, and fetch thou the corpse of her, and bury her by her husband, the noble King Arthur." So this avision came to Sir Launcelot thrice in one night.

Chapter 11: *How Sir Launcelot went with his eight fellows to Amesbury, and found there Queen Guenever dead, whom they brought to Glastonbury.*

THEN Sir Launcelot rose up or day, and told the hermit. "It were well done," said the hermit, "that ye made you ready, and that you disobey not the avision." Then Sir Launcelot took his eight fellows with him, and on foot they yede from Glastonbury to Amesbury, the which is little more than thirty mile. And thither they came within two days, for they were weak and feeble to go. And when Sir Launcelot was come to Amesbury within the nunnery, Queen Guenever died but half an hour afore. And the ladies told Sir Launcelot that Queen Guenever told them all or she passed, that Sir Launcelot had been priest near a twelvemonth, "And hither he cometh as fast as he may to fetch my corpse, and beside my lord, King Arthur, he shall bury me." Wherefore the queen said in hearing of them all: "I beseech Almighty God that I may never have power to see Sir Launcelot with my worldly eyes." And thus, said all the ladies, was ever her prayer these two days, till she was dead. Then Sir Launcelot saw her visage, but he wept not greatly, but sighed. And so he did all the observance of the service himself, both the dirge, and on the morn he sang mass. And there was ordained an horse-bier; and so with an hundred torches ever brenning about the corpse of the queen, and ever Sir Launcelot with his eight fellows went about the horse-bier, singing and reading many an holy orison, and frankincense upon the corpse incensed. Thus Sir Launcelot and his eight fellows went on foot from Amesbury unto Glastonbury.

And when they were come to the chapel and the hermitage, there she had a dirge, with great devotion. And on the morn the hermit that sometime was Bishop of Canterbury sang the mass of requiem with great devotion. And Sir Launcelot was the first that offered, and then also his eight fellows. And then she was wrapped in cered cloth of Raines, from the top to the toe, in thirtyfold; and after she was put in a web of lead, and then in a coffin of marble. And when she was put in the earth Sir Launcelot swooned, and lay long still, while the hermit came and awaked him, and said: "Ye be to blame, for ye displease God with such manner of sorrow-making." "Truly," said Sir Launcelot, "I trust I do not displease God, for He knoweth mine intent. For my sorrow was not, nor is not, for any rejoicing of sin, but my sorrow may never have end. For when I remember of her beauty, and of her nobility, that was both with her king and with her, so when I saw his corpse and her corpse so lie together, truly mine heart would not serve to sustain my careful body. Also when I remember me how by my default, mine orgule and my pride, that they were both laid full low, that were peerless that ever was living of Christian people, wit you well," said Sir Launcelot, "this remembered, of their kindness and mine unkindness, sank so to mine heart, that I might not sustain myself." So the French book maketh mention.

---

12. **lust,** desire. 23. **took no force,** paid no heed to. 31. **purvey them of,** provide them with. 41. **or,** before. 45. **yede,** went. 15. **brenning,** burning. 18. **orison,** prayer. 28. **cered cloth,** cerecloth, a waxed winding-sheet. 30. **web,** sheet. 43. **careful,** sorrowful. 44. **orgule,** pride.

Chapter 12: *How Sir Launcelot began to sicken, and after died, whose body was borne to Joyous Gard for to be buried.*

THEN Sir Launcelot never after ate but little meat, nor drank, till he was dead. For then he sickened more and more, and dried, and dwined away. For the Bishop nor none of his fellows might not make him to eat, and little he drank, that he was waxen by a cubit shorter than he was, that the people could not know him. For evermore, day and night, he prayed, but sometime he slumbered a broken sleep; ever he was lying grovelling on the tomb of King Arthur and Queen Guenever. And there was no comfort that the Bishop, nor Sir Bors, nor none of his fellows, could make him, it availed not. So within six weeks after, Sir Launcelot fell sick, and lay in his bed; and then he sent for the Bishop that there was hermit, and all his true fellows. Then Sir Launcelot said with dreary steven: "Sir Bishop, I pray you give to me all my rites that longeth to a Christian man." "It shall not need you," said the hermit and all his fellows, "it is but heaviness of your blood, ye shall be well mended by the grace of God tomorn." "My fair lords," said Sir Launcelot, "wit you well my careful body will into the earth, I have warning more than now I will say; therefore give me my rites." So when he was houseled and aneled, and had all that a Christian man ought to have, he prayed the Bishop that his fellows might bear his body to Joyous Gard. Some men say it was Alnwick, and some men say it was Bamborough. "Howbeit," said Sir Launcelot, "me repenteth sore, but I made mine avow sometime, that in Joyous Gard I would be buried. And because of breaking of mine avow, I pray you all, lead me thither." Then there was weeping and wringing of hands among his fellows.

So at a season of the night they all went to their beds, for they all lay in one chamber. And so after midnight, against day, the Bishop that was hermit, as he lay in his bed asleep, he fell upon a great laughter. And therewith all the fellowship awoke, and came to the Bishop, and asked him what he ailed. "Ah Jesu mercy," said the Bishop, "why did ye awake me? I was never in all my life so merry and so well at ease." "Wherefore?" said Sir Bors. "Truly," said the Bishop, "here was Sir Launcelot with me with more angels than ever I saw men in one day. And I saw the angels heave up Sir Launcelot unto heaven, and the gates of heaven opened against him." "It is but dretching of swevens," said Sir Bors, "for I doubt not Sir Launcelot aileth nothing but good." "It may well be," said the Bishop, "go ye to his bed, and then shall ye prove the sooth." So when Sir Bors and his fellows came to his bed they found him stark dead, and he lay as he had smiled, and the sweetest savour about him that ever they felt.

Then was there weeping and wringing of hands, and the greatest dole they made that ever made men. And on the morn the Bishop did his mass of requiem; and after, the Bishop and all the nine knights put Sir Launcelot in the same horse-bier that Queen Guenever was laid in tofore that she was buried. And so the Bishop and they all together went with the body of Sir Launcelot daily, till they came to Joyous Gard; and ever they had an hundred torches brenning about him. And so within fifteen days they came to Joyous Gard. And there they laid his corpse in the body of the choir, and sang and read many psalters and prayers over him and about him. And ever his visage was laid open and naked, that all folks might behold him. For such was the custom in those days, that all men of worship should so lie with open visage till that they were buried. And right thus as they were at their service, there came Sir Ector de Maris, that had seven years sought all England, Scotland, and Wales, seeking his brother, Sir Launcelot.

Chapter 13: *How Sir Ector found Sir Launcelot his brother dead, and how Constantine reigned next after Arthur; and of the end of this book.*

AND when Sir Ector heard such noise and light in the choir of Joyous Gard, he alighted and put his horse from him, and came into the choir, and there he saw men sing and weep. And all they knew Sir Ector, but he knew not them. Then went Sir Bors unto Sir Ector, and told him how there lay his brother, Sir Launcelot, dead; and then Sir Ector threw his shield, sword, and helm from him. And when he beheld Sir Launcelot's visage, he fell down in a swoon. And when he waked it were hard any tongue to tell the doleful complaints that he made for his brother. "Ah Launcelot," he said, "thou were head of all Christian knights, and now I dare say," said Sir Ector, "thou Sir Launcelot, there thou liest, that thou were never matched of earthly knight's hand. And thou were the courteoust knight that ever bore shield. And thou were the truest friend to thy lover that ever bestrode horse. And

---

7. **dwined,** wasted.   10. **cubit,** a unit of length varying from 18 to 22 inches.   21. **steven,** voice.   29. **houseled and aneled,** given the sacrament and extreme unction.   32–33. **Alnwick . . . Bamborough,** in Northumberland.   50. **heave,** lift.

2. **dretching of swevens,** torment of dreams.

thou were the truest lover of a sinful man that ever loved woman. And thou were the kindest man that ever struck with sword. And thou were the goodliest person that ever came among press of knights. And thou were the meekest man and the gentlest that ever ate in hall among ladies. And thou were the sternest knight to thy mortal foe that ever put spear in the rest." Then there was weeping and dolour out of measure.

Thus they kept Sir Launcelot's corpse aloft fifteen days, and then they buried it with great devotion. And then at leisure they went all with the Bishop of Canterbury to his hermitage, and there they were together more than a month. Then Sir Constantine, that was Sir Cador's son of Cornwall, was chosen king of England. And he was a full noble knight, and worshipfully he ruled this realm. And then this King Constantine sent for the Bishop of Canterbury, for he heard say where he was. And so he was restored unto his Bishopric, and left that hermitage. And Sir Bedivere was there ever still hermit to his life's end. Then Sir Bors de Ganis, Sir Ector de Maris, Sir Gahalantine, Sir Galihud, Sir Galihodin, Sir Blamore, Sir Bleoberis, Sir Villiars le Valiant, Sir Clarrus of Clermont, all these knights drew them to their countries. Howbeit King Constantine would have had them with him, but they would not abide in this realm. And there they all lived in their countries as holy men. And some English books make mention that they went never out of England after the death of Sir Launcelot, but that was but favour of makers. For the French book maketh mention, and is authorised, that Sir Bors, Sir Ector, Sir Blamore, and Sir Bleoberis, went into the Holy Land there as Jesu Christ was quick and dead, and anon as they had stablished their lands. For the book saith, so Sir Launcelot commanded them for to do, or ever he passed out of this world. And these four knights did many battles upon the miscreants or Turks. And there they died upon a Good Friday for God's sake.

Here is the end of the book of King Arthur, and of his noble knights of the Round Table, that when they were whole together there was ever an hundred and forty. And here is the end of the death of Arthur. I pray you all, gentlemen and gentlewomen that readeth this book of Arthur and his knights, from the beginning to the ending, pray for me while I am alive, that God send me good deliverance, and when I am dead, I pray you all pray for my soul. For this book was ended the ninth year of the reign of King Edward the Fourth, by Sir Thomas Malory, knight, as Jesu help him for his great might, as he is the servant of Jesu both day and night.

Thus endeth this noble and joyous book entitled Le Morte Darthur. Notwithstanding it treateth of the birth, life, and acts of the said King Arthur, of his noble knights of the Round Table, their marvellous enquests and adventures, the achieving of the Saint Grail, and in the end the dolorous death and departing out of this world of them all. Which book was reduced into English by Sir Thomas Malory, knight, as afore is said, and by me divided into twenty-one books, chaptered and enprinted, and finished in the abbey, Westminster, the last day of July the year of our Lord MCCCCLXXXV.

Caxton me fieri fecit.

10. **aloft,** unburied. 32. **makers,** authors. 4. **miscreants,** infidels. 26. **enquests,** quests. 35. **Caxton . . . fecit.** Caxton had me made.

SUGGESTIONS FOR FURTHER READING

This list is to be supplemented by the brief lists of books given at the ends of the various introductions to specific works and authors.

GENERAL BIBLIOGRAPHICAL AIDS

Heusinkveld, A. H., and Bashe, E. J., *A Bibliographical Guide to Old English*, University of Iowa Press, 1931

Tucker, L. L., and Benham, A. R., *A Bibliography of Fifteenth Century Literature*, University of Washington Press, 1928

Wells, J. E., *A Manual of the Writings in Middle English, 1050–1400*, Yale University Press, 1916, and supplements, 1923–38. Invaluable for summaries and criticism, as well as bibliographies.

HISTORICAL BACKGROUND

Cambridge Medieval History, 8 vols., Macmillan, 1911–36; Vols. I, Chap. 13; II, 15–17; IV, 13–15, 19, 20; V, 15–17; VI, 7, 8, 17, 24, 25; VII, 12, 14–19; VIII, 7, 12–14, 23, 25. Concise and scholarly chapters which integrate English and Continental events; valuable bibliographies.

Collingwood, R. S., and Myres, J. N. L., *Roman Britain and the English Settlements*, new ed., Oxford University Press, 1937. The most up-to-date account of the period.

Davis, H. W. C., *England under the Normans and Angevins, 1066–1272*, Putnam, 1926. A standard history.

Gummere, F. B., *Founders of England*, rev. by F. P. Magoun, Jr., Stechert, 1930. A rich account of the public and private life of the Germanic people, both before and after their coming to England.

Hodgkin, R. H., *A History of the Anglo-Saxons*, 2 vols., Oxford University Press, 1939. A sumptuously printed, richly illustrated, and highly readable work but extending only through Alfred.

Oman, Sir Charles, *England before the Norman Conquest*, Putnam, 1910. The standard work for the entire Anglo-Saxon period.

Vickers, Kenneth, *England in the Later Middle Ages*, Putnam, 1919. Standard.

SOCIAL AND INTELLECTUAL LIFE

Bennett, H. S., *Life on the English Manor; A Study of Peasant Conditions, 1150–1400*, Macmillan, 1938. By far the best account of the shift from serfdom to freedom.

———, *The Pastons and Their England*, Macmillan, 1922; see page 93. An admirable digest of the famous letters.

Calthrop, D. C., *English Costume from William I to George IV, 1066–1830*, Macmillan, 1937. Illustrated in colors and easy to read.

Chadwick, Dorothy, *Social Life in the Days of Piers Plowman*, Macmillan, 1922

Coulton, G. G., *Medieval Panorama: The English Scene from Conquest to Reformation*, Macmillan, 1938. Informative and readable on almost every phase of medieval life.

Furnivall, F. J., *The Babees Book, etc.*, Early English Text Society, Vol. XXXII, 1868; "Manners and Meals in olden time." The Emily Posts of the later Middle Ages; it is difficult to imagine more amusing reading.

Hartley, Dorothy, and Elliot, M. M., *Life and Work of the People of England: A Pictorial Record from Contemporary Sources: the Fourteenth and Fifteenth Centuries*, 2 vols., Putnam, 1926

Jusserand, J. J., *English Wayfaring Life in the Middle Ages*, rev. ed., Putnam, 1921. A book of irresistible charm and interest.

Mead, W. E., *The English Medieval Feast*, Houghton Mifflin, 1931. A survey of medieval food which in part takes away the breath, and in part, the appetite.

Oman, C. W. C., *A History of the Art of War in the Middle Ages*, Houghton Mifflin, 1924. Sad proof that we have not improved.

Power, Eileen E., *Medieval People*, Houghton Mifflin, 1924

Rashdall, Hastings, *The Universities of Europe in the Middle Ages*, 3 vols., Oxford University Press, 1936. Standard and encyclopedic.

Riesman, David, *The Story of Medicine in the Middle Ages*, Hoeber, 1935. Grimly fascinating.

Taylor, H. O., *The Medieval Mind*, 2 vols., Macmillan, 1927. "A history of the development of thought and emotion in the Middle Ages."

THE ENGLISH LANGUAGE

Baugh, A. C., *A History of the English Language*, Appleton-Century, 1935. The most up-to-date, systematic, clear and usable book on the subject.

Greenough, J. B., and Kittredge, G. L., *Words and Their Ways in English Speech*, Macmillan, 1923. A fascinating volume full of striking and unusual information about the English vocabulary.

Krapp, G. P., *The English Language in America*, 2 vols., Century, 1925. Learned and entertaining; the first volume is of particular interest to the general student of English.

Mencken, H. L., *The American Language*, Knopf, 1936. Certain to charm and instruct any student of English.

Weekley, Ernest, *Concise Etymological Dictionary of Modern English*, Dutton, 1924. Invaluable for those who are interested in the origins and changes in meaning of the words they use and read.

LITERATURE

General Histories

Brooke, S. A., *English Literature from the Beginning to the Norman Conquest*, Macmillan, 1926. Now somewhat out of date in scholarship, but useful for background, summaries, and excerpts.

THE EARLY PERIOD

Cambridge History of English Literature, 15 vols., Macmillan, 1933. Standard accounts, but not always well integrated.

Chambers, E. K., *The Mediaeval Stage*, 2 vols., Oxford University Press, 1903. The standard, encyclopedic work.

Ker, W. P., *Epic and Romance*, Macmillan, 1926. One of the best possible introductions to medieval narrative poetry.

Renwick, W. L., and Orton, Harold, *Beginnings of English Literature to Skelton*, Cresset Press, 1939. A spirited introduction, followed by extensive and explanatory bibliographies.

Schofield, W. H., *English Literature from the Norman Conquest to Chaucer*, Macmillan, 1925. The standard work, with valuable sections on Anglo-Latin, Anglo-Norman, and Anglo-French writings.

Thomas, P. G., *English Literature before Chaucer*, Longmans, Green, 1924. Brief, but admirable for arrangement and clarity.

Wilson, R. M., *Early Middle English Literature*, Methuen, 1939. Up-to-date in scholarship.

Anthologies and Collections

Cook, A. S., and Tinker, C. B., *Select Translations from Old English Poetry*, Harvard University Press, 1926. Renderings in both verse and prose.

——— *Select Translations from Old English Prose*, Harvard University Press, 1908

French, W. H., and Hale, C. B., *Middle English Metrical Romances*, Prentice-Hall, 1930. The most comprehensive collection of its kind; well-glossed originals.

Gordon, R. K., *Anglo-Saxon Poetry*, Dutton, 1937 (Everyman's Library). Prose translation of nearly the whole body of Old English poetry.

Neilson, W. A., and Webster, K. G. T., *Chief British Poets of the Fourteenth and Fifteenth Centuries*, Houghton Mifflin, 1916. Translations and originals, including the *Pearl*, tales from Gower, selections from Lydgate, Hoccleve, and the Scottish Chaucerians.

Reinhard, J. R., *Medieval Pageant*, Harcourt Brace, 1939. Translations or adaptations of many medieval short stories in both prose and verse; very lively reading.

Schlauch, Margaret, *Medieval Narrative; A Book of Translations*, Prentice-Hall, 1928. None of the works, which include sagas, chansons de geste, saints' lives, fabliaux, and material on Troy and Alexander, was originally English, but all are of the greatest interest and value to students of medieval English fiction.

Thoms, W. J., *Early English Prose Romances*, Dutton, 1906. Accounts, some Elizabethan, of such figures as Reynard the Fox, Hamlet, Friar Bacon, Guy of Warwick, Robin Hood, and Dr. Faustus.

Weston, J. L., *Chief Middle English Poets*, Houghton Mifflin, 1914. Especially valuable for the number of romances it contains; the translations, unfortunately, are in somewhat indifferent verse.

Everyman, with Other Interludes, including Eight Miracle Plays, Dutton, 1926 (Everyman's Library)

Individual Authors

Ancren Riwle (Ancrene Wisse), trans. by J. Morton, ed. by Abbot Gasquet, Oxford University Press, 1924 (Medieval Library). See pages 89–90.

Bartholomew Anglicus, *On the Properties of Things*, as ed. by Robert Steele in *Medieval Lore*, Oxford University Press, 1924 (Medieval Library). Selections from a thirteenth-century encyclopedia of science, geography, and natural history; revealing and amusing.

Geoffrey of Monmouth, *Histories of the Kings of Britain*, Dutton, 1928 (Everyman's Library). See page 113.

Lawman (Layamon), *The Brut*, in Eugene Mason, *Arthurian Chronicles Represented by Wace and Layamon*, Dutton, 1921 (Everyman's Library). See page 89.

Marie de France, in Eugene Mason, *French Medieval Romances from the Lays of Marie de France*, Dutton, 1924 (Everyman's Library). Prose translations of some of the best poetic short stories ever written. For Marie, see page 147.

Rolle, Richard, in F. M. M. Comper's *The Life of Richard Rolle, together with an Edition of His English Lyrics*, Dutton, 1929. An admirable account of a great fourteenth-century religious mystic, with specimens of his work.

The Voiage and Travayle of Syr John Maundeville, Knight, Dutton, 1928 (Everyman's Library). A travel book the appeal of which is doubled by the fact that much in it is not true.

ART

Braun, Hugh, *The English Castle*, Scribner, 1936

Brown, G. B., *The Arts in Early England*, new ed., 6 vols., London, 1903–37. A monumental study which is also clear.

Clapham, A. W., *English Romanesque Architecture after the Conquest*, Oxford University Press, 1930

James, M. R., *Abbeys*, Doubleday, Page, 1926. A stimulating combination of historical description and modern direction.

Saunders, O. E., *History of English Art in the Middle Ages*, Oxford University Press, 1932

PHONOGRAPHIC RECORDINGS

Gregorian Chants, 2 vols.—Sung by the choir of monks of the Abbey of Saint-Pierre de Solesmes. RCA Victor, Album—M. 87

L'Anthologie Sonore, Vols. I, No. 8, II, No. 16, IV, Nos. 34, 35, and VI, No. 59, the Gramophone Shop, Inc., New York City. Contain French, Italian, and English religious and secular music of the thirteenth and fourteenth centuries.

Old English: Selections from *Beowulf* and from Aelfric read by H. C. Wyld, Linguaphone, Nos. N. C. S and 1–2 respectively.

Middle English: Selections from Chaucer and the "Debate of the Body and the Soul" read by F. N. Robinson, Harvard Film Service; selections from Chaucer read by H. C. Wyld, Linguaphone, Nos. 3–4

HISTORICAL AND "LITERARY" FICTION

Frankland, Edward, *Huge as Sin*, Jonathan Cape, 1932. A brutal and compelling account of Scandinavian raids and settlement in ninth-century England; continued in *The Path of Glory*, London, 1935.

Gaye, Phoebe F., *Good Sir John*, Liveright, 1930. Sir John Falstaff in late fourteenth-century England.

Lindsay, Philip, *The Little Wench*, London, 1935. The lady of the title is Guinevere, and the characters are very human indeed.

———— *London Bridge is Falling*, Little, Brown, 1934. "A 'Street Scene' of the mid-fifteenth century."

Paget, Guy, *The Rose of London*, London, 1934. England in the late fifteenth century; the principal characters are Edward IV, Jane Shore, and Richard III.

Sheppard, Alfred T., *Here Comes an Old Sailor*, Doubleday, Doran, 1930. England in the thirteenth century; a vivid narrative with supernatural overtones.

White, T. H., *The Sword in the Stone*, Putnam, 1939. A delightfully humorous fantasy of the boyhood of Arthur; the author's later *Witch in the Wood*, Putnam, 1939, and *The Ill-Made Knight*, Putnam, 1940, are also recommended.

Williams, Patry, *I am Canute*, Ryerson Press, 1938. A romantically realistic account of England's great Danish king.

of the human form in magnificent canvases and statues. Such masterpieces as Titian's "Venus and the Lute Player" and Michelangelo's "David" would have been unthinkable in the Middle Ages. More clearly than any literary tradition whatever, they make intelligible such sensuous Italianate narratives as Marlowe's *Hero and Leander* and Shakespeare's *Venus and Adonis*. Marlowe and Shakespeare were attempting to achieve in poetry what Titian and Michelangelo had attained in painting and sculpture.

Modern capitalism began in the greatest economic crisis Europe had seen since the fall of Rome. Profound changes were taking place in both the external and the internal economies of European politics. The economic decline of Venice and the cities of Southern Germany, the economic expansion of Spain and Portugal, and the rise to pre-eminence of Antwerp as the center of international finance were paralleled by equally important changes in the internal economy: the substitution of the livery company for the craft guild, the organization of trade on national rather than on local lines, and the application of capital to the mining and textile industries. The importation of great quantities of gold that resulted from the Spanish ravages of Mexico and Central America intensified the monetary problems inherited from the Middle Ages.[3]

From the point of view of science, the Renaissance was definitely not a rebirth. For although the intellectual curiosity of the Humanists was wide-ranging, their acceptance of Greek and Latin writers as supreme authorities tended to inhibit rather than to promote advances in scientific studies during the period when Humanism was dominant. It was only when Humanism began to deteriorate into linguistic study that scientific research became important.

To science, sixteenth-century England made no important contributions. It was not until the work of Bacon and Harvey in the early seventeenth century that England's activity in science became significant. For really memorable scientific advances we have to turn to such Continental works of the first half of the sixteenth century as Copernicus' *Concerning the Revolutions of the Heavenly Bodies*, 1543, which put the earth in its right place in the solar system, and Vesalius' *Concerning the Structure of the Human Body*, 1543, which overthrew the medieval authority of Galen and prepared the way for anatomical studies based on observation and dissection.

The classical revival, however, was an indirect cause of important developments in physics and anatomy. Artists under the sway of their passionate admiration for Greek sculpture found themselves forced to study the human figure scientifically before they could represent it with anatomical accuracy, and the sketches and studies of such artists as Pollaiuolo and Leonardo da Vinci have as great scientific as esthetic interest. Furthermore, the quickened interest in the world around the artist, and the incentive to represent its buildings, furniture, and tiled floors precisely rather than symbolically, encouraged studies in mechanics and perspective which resulted in scientific as well as artistic progress.[4]

But neither on the Continent nor in England was the sixteenth century prolific in epoch-making scientific studies; it remained for the seventeenth century to establish modern science and the scientific view of the world which we take for granted.

The Reformation

For England at least, the influence of the movement generally known as the Reformation had results, in the sixteenth century, though more particularly in the seventeenth century, comparable in depth and range to the secular movements of the Renaissance. In England, the Renaissance and the Reformation developed simultaneously. This simultaneity, the vigor of the medieval inheritance in England, and the strongly moralistic bent in the English character gave the Reformation a significance and a weight in England beyond that found in any other European country except Germany. It is the equal strength of the two forces—the Renaissance and the Reformation—that gives Spenser and Milton, for instance, a markedly English character, and that accounts for the relatively slight reaction in England away from otherworldliness to worldliness. Michelet's famous definition of the Renaissance as "the discovery of the world and of man" is broadly applicable to England, but Englishmen in their discovery of man never lost sight of the fact that his most important element was his soul, and that its salvation was of greater moment than anything the world could give.

Of the origins and the causes of the Reformation

---

[3] For a fuller treatment of this aspect of the Renaissance, see Richard H. Tawney, *Religion and the Rise of Capitalism*, Harcourt, Brace, 1926, pp. 66–79.

[4] For a fuller discussion of this general topic, see George Sarton, "Science in the Renaissance" in *The Civilization of the Renaissance*, pp. 75–95.

as a European movement we can do no more here than recall the rise of Lutheranism in Germany after Luther posted his ninety-five theses on the doors of the cathedral at Wittenberg in 1517, the development of Calvinism with its theological headquarters in Geneva, and the rise of Presbyterianism (Scottish Calvinism) under John Knox. Unquestionably, the Reformation would have had its effect on English religious thought and practice through gradual infiltration, but Henry VIII's severance of England's relationship to the Pope, and his assumption of the title of Supreme Head of the Church, hastened immeasurably the progress of Protestantism in England. To the theological and political consequences of his action, Henry was almost completely blind. The King himself had already won from the Pope the title of Defender of the Faith as a doughty champion against Lutheranism, and, strict Catholic that he was, he would have been horrified if he had been able to foresee the consequences of his act.

Of the major religious events of Henry's reign, the most consequential was the severing of relations with Rome. However dubious its motivation, that severance led immediately, not to a reformation of the Church (such a reformation was the least of Henry's intentions) but to a revolution in the relations between Church and State. Henceforth the heads of Church and State were to be not two, the Pope and the King, but one, the English sovereign; and numerous powers and privileges hitherto appertaining to the Pope now fell into the eager hands of Henry. The dissolution or spoliation of the monasteries, however justified on grounds of religious and moral decadence, had its primary motivation in the greed of Henry and his nobles, but that motive could hardly have resulted in violent action under the previously existing relations between Church and State. Although on the theological and doctrinal side Henry remained resolutely conservative, he could not prevent an increase in the discussion of doctrinal issues or the raising of questions already argued among Protestants abroad.

Of these questions one of the most potentially revolutionary was that of the translation of the Bible into English. The major argument against such a procedure was that if the Bible were accessible in the only language known to the unlettered among the laity, it might encourage novel and dangerous interpretations of the Scriptures. But although many of Henry's counselors, lay and clerical, regarded the procedure with apprehension, Archbishop Cranmer in 1544 gave his sanction to an English translation of the Bible. This act—far more than Henry's break with Rome—prepared the way for the development of the Reformation and ultimately the rise of Puritanism in England. For with the Scriptures accessible, men soon came to feel that the private individual had the right and the duty to decide for himself problems involved in his relation to the Deity. This right of private judgment was the ultimate source not only of the modern liberal-democratic doctrine of freedom of thought and expression but also of all the extravagant heresies possible under Protestantism.

By the Act of Succession (1536), the King secured the throne for his puny son, Edward VI, but on Henry's death in 1547 the real power passed into the hands of the Duke of Somerset, who through the medium of the Privy Council ruled England, and strenuously furthered the cause of the Reformation. England opened her doors to a horde of Protestant teachers exiled from the Continent, and, despite the opposition of such conservative members of the clergy as Bishops Gardiner and Bonner, the Protector encouraged practices and doctrines far more extreme than those permitted under Henry. Orders in Council were issued for the destruction of "abused images," that is to say, statues, stained-glass windows, paintings, and carvings that might be regarded as objects of idolatry; the marriage of the clergy was permitted; church services could be conducted in English; the communion in both kinds was authorized.[5]

Edward VI died in 1553 at the age of sixteen, and was succeeded by his older sister Mary, the Catholic daughter of Queen Catherine of Aragon, whom Henry had put away. Upon Mary's accession, the changes brought about under Henry and his son were promptly wiped out, and the Anglican Church was once more united with the Roman. Church and State were purged of Protestant heretics, college and university were cleansed of unbelievers, and the clerical leaders of the Reformation, Cranmer and Latimer, were burned at the stake. In the main, the bulk of the clergy accepted the reversion to Catholicism without compunction, and popular tradition has probably been unfair in burdening Mary with the epithet "Bloody."

When Mary died in 1558 and Elizabeth came to the throne at the age of twenty-five, England was faced with the necessity of plotting its course between Catholicism and the Protestantisms stem-

---

[5] Communion in both kinds permits the laity to partake of both bread and wine; wine is not given the laity in the Roman Catholic rite.

ming from the Continent and Scotland. Within England itself there were not only Romanist and Anglican elements but even indications of the beginnings of Puritanism and Separatism. The problem that confronted Elizabeth and her counselors was weighty and difficult, since it had not merely theological but also national and international political implications. Elizabeth herself was personally sympathetic with the conservative doctrinal views of her father, but her most influential advisers favored the reformed doctrines on theological and political grounds, and Elizabeth saw the wisdom of following the middle course. The Act of Supremacy and the Act of Uniformity indicated that course by defining the doctrine of the Church narrowly enough to eliminate both determined Romanists and determined Calvinists, but broadly enough to include both conservative and advanced Protestants. During most of the Queen's long reign, the Elizabethan compromise worked admirably. Toward the end of it, as her personal prestige waned, there arose from the Puritan elements within the Church louder and louder protests against various points of Anglican doctrine, in particular, the system of the government of the Church by bishops. With this Puritan movement, Elizabeth's closest counselors, Lord Burghley, Sir Francis Bacon, the Earl of Leicester, and Sir Francis Walsingham, were openly or secretly in sympathy. But Elizabeth's shrewdness and skill were sufficient to keep the Puritan movement in hand and to transmit the knotty problem to her less adroit successor, James I, son of her rival, Mary Queen of Scots, her Catholic cousin whose death warrant Elizabeth had been brought reluctantly to sign in 1587.

The Influence of the Classics

The revival of interest in classical literature and life was not, as one might think, primarily esthetic but rather moral in its motivation. Renaissance students of the classics were only remotely concerned with the esthetic excellence of the literature of classical antiquity; they were more profoundly stirred by the conviction that the classics would open up to them another way to the good life than that laid down by the Church and the Scriptures. But before the new way could be explored, and certainly before it could be imitated, various practical problems had to be solved. Since Latin had for centuries been the language for learned and international communication, its renewed study did not present the acute problem that faced men who wished to penetrate the enchanted world of Greek literature. Even in Italy in the fifteenth century, the number of people able to teach Greek was almost negligible. Thus the Italian Humanist Leonardo Bruni wrote: "For seven hundred years, no one in Italy has possessed Greek letters; and yet we confess that all knowledge is derived from them. How great advantage to your knowledge, enhancement of your fame, increase of your pleasure, will come from an understanding of this tongue? There are doctors of civil law everywhere; and the chance of learning will not fail thee. But if this one and only doctor of Greek letters disappears, no one can be found to teach thee. Overcome at length by these reasons, I gave myself to Chrysoloras, with such zeal to learn, that what through the wakeful day I gathered, I followed after in the night, even when asleep."[6] As the fifteenth century passed, young Englishmen in increasing numbers made their way to Italy as the only place where a knowledge of Greek could be satisfactorily acquired. But not all eager students could travel so far afield, and it soon seemed desirable and became practicable to bring to English universities men capable of teaching Greek.

A further problem that faced the early Humanists was that of acquiring adequate texts. This involved the collating of manuscripts, the establishment and annotation of texts, and the printing and publishing of editions of the classics that could be easily diffused through western Europe. In this particular service, the printing and publishing house of Aldus in Venice played the primary role. The various members of that distinguished family who successively headed this press displayed extraordinary energy and intelligence in their selection of the most capable editors available for the preparation of classical texts, and in their persistence in printing, as the decades passed, most of the important Greek and Latin classics in beautifully designed editions.

Of the eager and enthusiastic study of the classics, the major results were perhaps four: the translating of the classics for readers inexpert in the tongues; the application of classical critical standards to the existent vernacular literatures; the attempt by imitation to create a new literature worthy of comparison with classical literature; and the attempt to evolve out of the ethical elements in classical literature a new conception of the good life. Of the first three of these results, more will be said below; to the fourth—the movement commonly known as Humanism—some consideration must be given here.

[6] Henry O. Taylor, *Thought and Expression in the Sixteenth Century*, Macmillan, 1920, Vol. I, pp. 36–37.

Humanism was not primarily an esthetic or literary or antitheological movement, but an ethical and moral one. It was an attempt to sketch in the outlines of the good life and to point the way toward it. It has all too frequently been said that Humanism was one of the Renaissance manifestations of a general reaction from medieval otherworldliness, that it found its values in this world and not in another. Such an interpretation falsifies the position of such major English Humanists as Colet, Linacre, Fisher, and More. These men were all devout and also enlightened Catholics. What these English Humanists aimed at was a redefinition of the good life in the light of the reformed religion and the teachings of the classical philosophers and moralists. Their aim was the synthesis of the best in religion and the best in classical secular thought.

The Humanists strove for a fresh conception of the life of the individual and of his relation to society, and for the consequent reform of the state itself. No one of the early Humanists defined his purpose more clearly than did John Milton, over a century later, when, writing his *Tractate on Education* in the full Humanistic spirit, he defined the ideal education as that which fitted "a man to perform justly, skilfully, and magnanimously all the duties, public and private, of peace and war." The Humanists believed in the freedom of the will and in man's perfectibility. They believed man capable of developing public and private virtues through the proper sort of education. They were concerned with the nature of true as distinguished from conventional nobility, and believed that the former was to be found only in association with character, virtue, learning, and the ability to serve the commonweal. They were concerned with the reform, not the destruction, of the Church, and while some of them attacked satirically its current weaknesses, others attempted to purify the concepts of religion much as the Puritans attempted to do a century later. The Humanists were concerned with the ethical aspects of government. Their ideal was Plato's philosopher-king, surrounded by officials similarly trained in virtue and wisdom, and dedicated to the service of the state.

To the great generation of English Humanists belong John Colet (1467?-1519), Thomas Linacre (1460?-1524), John Fisher, Bishop of Rochester (1459-1535), and Sir Thomas (now St. Thomas) More (1478-1535). John Colet, Dean of St. Paul's, is best known as the founder of St. Paul's School, a private school with a secular board of control. The Latin-English grammar devised for this school by Colet, and by its first headmaster William Lyly, was later revised by Erasmus, the great Dutch Humanist and close friend of Colet and More, and was still in use two hundred years later. But equally important was Colet's devotion to the reform of the Church. Like many another devout Catholic, he opposed relics and pilgrimages, and believed that the Bible should be translated for the use of the unlettered laity. More significantly, he insisted in his sermons on the historical interpretation of the Bible as against the medieval allegorical and mystical interpretations, and pleaded for a thoroughgoing reform of the spiritual life of the Church. For these advanced views, he was summoned before Archbishop Warham on charges of heresy, which the broad-minded prelate dismissed. Thomas Linacre's services to Humanism were more secular. After studying Greek at Oxford under Cornelio Vitelli, he continued his classical studies in Italy under the tutors of Lorenzo de' Medici's sons, read Plato in the Vatican library, assisted the printing-house of Aldus in its edition of Aristotle, and studied medicine at Padua and Vicenza. After his return to England, he taught Greek to Colet, More, and Erasmus, became Henry VIII's personal physician, founded the Royal College of Physicians, and acted as tutor to the Princess Mary. He translated classical works on medicine, restored the Hippocratic method of treating diseases on the basis of careful observation, and gave a valuable medical library to All Souls College, Oxford. Bishop Fisher's services to Humanism were primarily administrative. As Chancellor of the University of Cambridge, he encouraged preaching in English and was instrumental in persuading Erasmus to teach Greek there between 1511 and 1514. In religion and theology, he was stanchly conservative, and his writings were intensely anti-Protestant. He refused to acknowledge Henry VIII's claim to be head of the Church, and was, in consequence, executed on June 22, 1535. In his heroic devotion to the old faith, he had a close companion in the greatest of the English Humanists, Sir Thomas More.[7]

The Course of Education

The program the Humanists laid down was to be carried out by means of education, and it is natural therefore that their work should have played a considerable part in the rise of Humanistic education in Renaissance England. Public education during the sixteenth century suffered from a number of profoundly disturbing influences, of

[7] For More's relation to Humanism, see page 285.

which the two most important were the dissolution of the monasteries and the conflict between Catholicism and Protestantism. The dissolution of the monasteries had certain immediate unfortunate results: the destruction of precious books and manuscripts; the breaking up of those colleges at Oxford and Cambridge that were sponsored and controlled by the monastic orders and the consequent decline in the number of university students; the cessation of elementary schools maintained by the monasteries; and the severance of cultural intercourse between English monastic houses and the Continental orders. Educationally, the dissolution of the monasteries may be taken as a violent symbol of the process of secularization which is one of the major distinguishing characteristics of the Renaissance. Unhappy as the immediate results were, the dissolution meant, for better or worse, the ultimate secularization of education, the substitution of a Humanistic for a Scholastic educational ideal, and the rapid increase in educational institutions of all ranks as the laity and the state became increasingly aware of their responsibilities in the field of education.

Educational progress in the sixteenth century may be measured in two ways: the founding of new institutions, and the definition and discussion of the ideals and methods of education. The institutions founded in this century ranged from grammar schools to universities. On the whole, the number of foundations increased rapidly under Edward VI, declined under Mary Tudor, and multiplied under Elizabeth.

The ideals and methods of the new education were derived not only from the general reawakening enthusiasm for the study of Greek and Latin, but specifically from three classical works on education: Cicero's *Concerning Invention*, Quintilian's *Oratorical Education*, and Plutarch's *On the Education of Children*. Cicero's youthful and incomplete treatise maintained its prestige from the twelfth century to the seventeenth century because of its author's pre-eminence as an orator. His prose style came to be regarded by many educators of the Renaissance as the ideal to be aimed at, and an important school of writers in both Latin and English attempted to write with the precise rhythms of Cicero. Quintilian's treatise, known imperfectly during the Middle Ages, achieved a wider fame after a complete manuscript of it was discovered at St. Gall in 1416. The book was a guide not only to success in oratory but to life as well, for, according to Quintilian, "No man unless he be good can be an orator." "We are educating," he wrote, "a man who will bring to human affairs a mind eminent in natural endowments and, in particular, embracing the fairest qualities within its folds, a man such as no previous age has known, and perfect on every side, thinking the best thoughts and expressing them in the best language."[8] It was from the particular point of view of the orator that Quintilian considered the utility of various forms of knowledge, but it was his ideas on more general educational topics that achieved the widest currency in the Renaissance. To him may be traced the unfortunate emphasis on the training of the child's memory, the importance of play as a mode of educating little children, and the significance of rivalry and rewards in attaining the desired results. On the subject of the imitation of Cicero, Quintilian displayed a balance that the sixteenth-century rhetoricians might well have imitated. For although he said, "Let a man know that he has made progress when he takes great pleasure in Cicero," he also said, "What is the harm in assuming in certain passages the force of Caesar, the roughness of Caelius, the earnestness of Pollio, the discernment of Calvus?" Plutarch's little treatise *On the Education of Children* had a long and complex history of translation and adaptation during the Renaissance.[9] The aim of education, according to Plutarch, is the moral life, since virtue is the best of all earthly goods. To the attainment of this end, education and especially philosophical studies are the major means. But the Renaissance was most attentive to Plutarch's specific observations with regard to the nursing of children by their mothers rather than by hired nurses, the habitual carelessness of parents in the selection of their children's tutors, and the importance of the example set their children by parents. His distribution of emphasis over morals, manners, effective speech, and bodily exercise had a potent influence, especially in England.

Sixteenth-century England produced no first-rate original thinkers on educational theory, but there were a number of men who did valiant service in making the classical doctrines available to English readers. Probably the most important was Roger Ascham, whose *The Schoolmaster*[10] greatly influenced the teaching of the time.

The Ideal Courtier

A special branch of Renaissance educational doctrine was concerned not so much with education

[8] John W. Adamson, *A Short History of Education*, Macmillan, 1919, pp. 93–94. [9] For the details of its vogue in the Renaissance, see the introductory note on John Lyly, page 342. [10] For fuller comment on Ascham and a selection from his major work, see page 321.

generally as with the education of the gentleman, the courtier, or the prince. The source of this special interest was the Humanists' belief that if the right goal for education could be envisioned and the right methods discovered, there could be trained a philosopher-king, who, with similarly trained courtly advisers, might bring about the reformation of the state and of the relations of all classes to the state. To the education of the courtier, or more generally to the doctrine of courtesy, almost a thousand treatises of one or another kind were devoted during the Renaissance.[11] Of these, by all odds the most influential was Count Baldassare Castiglione's *Il Cortegiano* (*The Courtier*), published by Aldus in 1528, and translated by Sir Thomas Hoby in 1561.[12]

The courtly ideal was the many-sided but harmonious development of all the gentleman's potentialities; the elaborateness and the complexity of the ideal would make it seem impossible of attainment if the Renaissance had not furnished us numerous examples of men like Sir Philip Sidney, the Earl of Essex, and Sir Walter Ralegh who came close to embodying it. The ideal involved the development of the courtier as a physical, political, religious, social, and esthetic being. The physical program laid down for the neophyte was an arduous one. Its results were to be grace in society, skill in sports, and valor in battle. No military exercise or game of physical skill was denied him except those which might impair his social standing in a rigidly stratified society. Thus, Sir Thomas Elyot in his *Book Named the Governour*, 1531, writes: "Wrestling is a very good exercise . . . so that it be with one that is equal in strength or somewhat under, and that the place be soft so that in falling their bodies be not bruised." But of bowling and quoits, he says: "Verily as for two the last, [they] be to be utterly abjected of all noble men, in like wise football, wherein is nothing but beastly fury and extreme violence, whereof proceedeth hurt, and consequently rancour and malice do remain with them that be wounded; wherefore it is to be put into perpetual silence." In his relation to the philosopher-king, the ideal courtier should be trained to serve as adviser and diplomat in times of peace and as a soldier in times of war.

But it was perhaps to the courtier as a social being and as an amateur artist that the Renaissance gave the freshest and most attractive turn to the chivalric ideal. The doctrine of courtesy assumed an equality between the sexes in social relations that implied for both gentlemen and ladies a high degree of skill in discourse, both light and learned. In Boccaccio's *Decameron*, for example, we have an early Renaissance illustration of the conversational resources of a group of seven ladies and three gentlemen who have fled from the plague to a country refuge at Fiesole, and Castiglione in the *Courtier* thought it appropriate to impart his doctrine through the discussions of a similar courtly group.

The courtier's more specific social graces lay in the field of the arts. Not only must he be able to sing and to play an instrument to accompany his singing, but also he must be able to write verses in honor of his lady. In all these activities, however, he must preserve his amateur standing, and allow no financial consideration to enter into his poetic or musical productions. Thence derives the custom persistent in the Renaissance, and illustrated strikingly in the case of Sir Philip Sidney, of circulating one's works in manuscript and persistently refraining from the publication of them.

Not the least important aspect of courtly education was the training of the courtier as a lover, and probably no facet of the complex ideal had so great an influence on Renaissance literature as the code of love developed during the Renaissance. This code was a synthesis of the medieval code of courtly love, the elaboration of this tradition by Dante and Petrarch, and the revival of the Neo-Platonic conception of love that derived ultimately from Plato's *Symposium*. Plato had conceived of love as one of the major modes of experience by means of which man could attain an awareness of ideal and perfect Beauty, as important an element in the Platonic triad as Truth and Goodness. So considered, love became a highly idealized and moral experience, and however short of the ideal men and women of the Renaissance may have fallen, the poets at any rate welcomed this intense ennobling of the universal human experience.

The Program for Literature

Before turning to a discussion of the imaginative literature of the Renaissance, we must give some attention to the critical and esthetic background of that literature, since most of it was produced in a conscious attempt to carry out a well-considered program. Renaissance critical theorists and estheticians faced two major problems, which they at-

---

[11] Most of these are listed, and their doctrines analyzed and systematized, in Ruth Kelso's *The Doctrine of the English Gentleman in the Sixteenth Century*, University of Illinois, 1930.
[12] For further comment on *The Courtier* and on Hoby's translation, and for a selection from it, see page 305.

tempted to solve with all the intelligence and ingenuity at their disposal. Their first task was the justification of literature, the defense of its value, and the determination of its purpose. The second major task was the laying down of a program which writers should follow in order to create a native literature worthy of comparison with Greek and Latin literature and of evaluation in terms of it.

The defense of literature followed several fairly distinct lines: historical, esthetic, and moral. The historical argument called attention to the exceeding antiquity of poetry, its universality, and its approval by the learned and great. The chief esthetic defense was grounded on Aristotle's theory of imitation as expressive of a fundamental human instinct and as giving what we should nowadays call the pleasure of recognition, even though the object imitated be itself unpleasant. With this esthetic delight in imitation, the Renaissance critics generally linked a didactic or moral value. Horace himself had written:

> "*Aut prodesse volunt, aut delectare poetae*
> *Aut simul et jucunda, et idonea dicere vitae*";

or as Ben Jonson had translated it:

> "Poets would either profit or delight
> Or mixing sweet and fit, teach life the right."

The authority of either poet was enough for most budding classicists of the late sixteenth century. This combination of delight and profit is repeated again and again in the critical theory of the period. Thus, Webbe in his *Discourse of English Poetrie*, 1586, wrote, "The perfect perfection of poetry is this, to mingle delight with profit in such wise that a reader might by his reading be partaker of both," although Puttenham was liberal enough to say in his *Arte of English Poetry*, 1589, that poetry, "being used for recreation only, may allowably bear matter not always of the gravest or of any great commodity of profit, but rather in some sort, vain, dissolute, or wanton if it be not very scandalous or of evil purpose." [13]

But the defense of literature against its assailants was only one of the tasks of the critical theorists of the Renaissance. Once literature had been justified, it became necessary for them to lay down a program to the carrying out of which serious-minded writers should devote themselves. The need for such a program was felt because to the critical temper, heightened by close contact with the Greek and Latin classics, the existing vernacular literature seemed faulty in almost every respect. Furthermore, the newborn nationalism of the Renaissance aroused in writers the desire to produce works in their native language that should be comparable with the masterpieces of antiquity. It seemed to most of the Renaissance theorists that the surest means of achieving the desired results was to use the classics as models and to follow them as closely as possible. They were encouraged in this conception of esthetic imitation not only by their misunderstanding of Aristotle's use of the term and Horace's more narrow interpretation of it, but by their own abysmal humility before the masterpieces of classical literature. As a result, therefore, the literary types exhibited by ancient literature—epic, drama, lyric, elegy, epistle, epigram, and pastoral—became the sanctioned forms for Renaissance writing, and the stylistic and technical features of these types were carefully worked out and systematized, although it remained for the Frenchman Boileau in the seventeenth century and Pope in the eighteenth century to give them their final Neoclassical delineation.

Broadly speaking, then, the program of Renaissance writers was the classicizing of native literature. This program met with varying success in various countries. During the sixteenth century in England it met with only modified success, since it had to combat the profoundly romantic and undisciplined spirit of most of the major writers of the century. As the period neared its end, the theory and practice of Ben Jonson pointed the way to a complete assimilation of the classical spirit.

Different Types of Prose

In considering the development of sixteenth-century prose, we should do well to distinguish between utilitarian and imaginative prose, that is, between prose the purpose of which is primarily information or didacticism and the prose the purpose of which is primarily "delight" or esthetic pleasure. In both utilitarian and imaginative prose the sixteenth century is rich indeed, but it is possible to maintain that Tudor writers solved the problems of utilitarian prose more satisfactorily than they did those of artistic prose, if general effectiveness and cogency of communication are the criteria of success.

The rise of nationalism during the Tudor period was accompanied and perhaps to a degree reenforced by a widespread curiosity concerning

---

[13] For Sir Philip Sidney's treatment of the arguments for and against literature, see the selections from his *Defence of Poesy* on page 353.

England's past. This appetite was fed not merely by an astonishing amount of poetry and drama utilizing historical material, but by less widely read works of a more strictly historical sort. Such was the impressive series of chronicles which stud the sixteenth century, from Robert Fabyan's *New Chronicles of England and of France*, 1516, and Edward Hall's *Union of the Noble and Illustrate Families of Lancaster & York*, 1542, to Raphael Holinshed's *Chronicles*, of which the first edition appeared in 1578 and a revised edition in 1587. Holinshed's is the best and most famous of the chronicles. Shakespeare made much use of the second edition of it in writing some of his plays. [14]

The sixteenth century was also richly productive in accounts of voyages, either historical or contemporary. The most avid collector of accounts of discovery and exploration in all the languages of western Europe was Richard Hakluyt, the crown of whose life work was *The Principall Voyages, Traffiques, and Discoveries of the English Nation*, which appeared in three huge volumes between 1598 and 1600. [15] The most interesting examples of travel literature were, of course, produced by the voyagers themselves. In this category fall such memorable accounts as Sir John Hawkins's *True Declaration of the Troublesome Voyage of M. John Hawkins to the Parts of Guiana and the West Indies*, 1569; Sir Humphrey Gilbert's *Discourse of a Discovery for a New Passage to Cataia* (China), 1576; and Sir Walter Ralegh's *Discoverie of the Large, Rich, and Beautiful Empire of Guiana*, 1596.

On a wavering line between fact and fiction lies the vast body of Tudor pamphleteering literature, of which the avowed purpose was reformatory, but of which the initial incentive was frequently purely commercial. Perhaps the best-known pamphleteer of the period is Robert Greene, who during the 1590's launched upon a sensation-eager audience his accounts, avowedly autobiographical, of his adventures in the criminal world of London and in the countryside. These "cony-catching" pamphlets —so called, because the criminal's victim was, in the underworld slang of the period, called a cony, that is, a rabbit, and so easily befuddled—give us vivid if not perfectly reliable glimpses into the Tudor underworld.[16] Thomas Dekker was another poverty-stricken hack writer who turned out pamphlets to every taste. Of these the most famous is *The Gull's Hornbook*, 1609, a satirical handbook for the would-be man-about-town. [17] A special type of pamphlet emanated from Puritan sources. Some of these, like Stephen Gosson's *School of Abuse* and Philip Stubbes's *Anatomy of Abuses*, attacked the vices and foibles of the time from a severely moralistic point of view. Others, like the "Martin Marprelate" pamphlets, which were printed surreptitiously in the last few years of the century, were virulent attacks on episcopacy by Puritan extremists.

The character of sixteenth-century prose was, in large measure, the result of confused theories as to the border line between prose and verse and the role of the imagination in literature. Writers of prose fiction, that is, of prose dealing with imaginative subjects with the aim primarily of delight, felt it incumbent upon them to create a prose which should be comparable in quality with the poetry which was being produced under the impetus of the classical revival. The means by which they solved their problem were conditioned by their conviction that if prose were to be comparable to poetry, it ought to have as many of the characteristics of poetry as possible, with the exception of verse and rhyme. This conviction explains the excessively ornamental character of the two types of imaginative prose (euphuistic and Arcadian) which had a marked influence on minor and imitative writers. The first—euphuistic prose—took its name from the novel of John Lyly, *Euphues, the Anatomy of Wit*, 1578. [18] Lyly used to be regarded as the inventor of euphuistic prose, but English writers before Lyly had used all or most of the devices found in *Euphues*, and it has now been shown that prose of this type originated in the attempt to carry over into English stylistic devices that appear in late Latin writers and that flourish in medieval Latin, particularly in sermons. Aside from the numerous figures of speech from what has been called "unnatural natural history," the basic feature of euphuistic prose is the excessive use of "word schemes," various complicated patterns of sound that take the form of balanced words, phrases, clauses, or sentences, or of simple or complex forms of alliteration. By using these devices more lavishly than any of his English predecessors had done, Lyly initiated a vogue that for a decade had a good deal of intensity. The second major type of imaginative prose—Arcadian—takes its name from the long pastoral romance which Sir Philip Sidney

---

[14] For Holinshed's account of Macbeth's career, on which Shakespeare based his tragedy of the same name, see page 329. [15] For an example of the literature of discovery, see pages 390–94. [16] A number of Greene's "cony-catching" pamphlets have been reprinted by John Lane in the Bodley Head Quartos series. A convenient collection of Tudor rogue literature is Arthur V. Judges, ed., *The Elizabethan Underworld*, Dutton, 1930.

[17] For a selection from *The Gull's Hornbook*, see page 441.
[18] For the text of an appendix to *Euphues*, see page 343.

wrote for the amusement of his learned sister, the Countess of Pembroke. Here there is less emphasis on patterns of sound and more on figures of speech. Sidney seems to be aiming to come just as close to the tone, language, and figures of poetry as he could come without writing verse. The result has a complex poetic charm, but the style, like Lyly's, is so weighted with poetic devices that it quite loses the movement essential to narrative. Sidney, like Lyly, had a host of imitators no one of whom, with the possible exception of Thomas Lodge in his *Rosalynde* (the source of Shakespeare's *As You Like It*), caught the overelaborate charm of their master. [19]

Different Types of Poetry

Sixteenth-century poets writing under the influence of the critical theories of the period were well schooled in the types and styles appropriate for poetry that aimed at qualities in English comparable to those of classical poetry. The major classical categories—epic, drama, and lyric—challenged their powers and imaginations, and the minor types—epistle, elegy, epigram, and satire—found fairly frequent adherents.

Two problems of very different degrees of importance the Tudor poets had some difficulty in solving, and some of their answers seem to us to have been exceedingly unfortunate. One problem was that of metrics. The question was raised as to whether English poets could produce a poetry really comparable to classical poetry unless they abandoned the traditional accentual metrical system and adopted the classical quantitative system. A part of the controversy involved rhyme, which some writers regarded askance because they did not find it in classical Greek and Latin. Not until the end of the century were both these questions emphatically decided in favor of accentual meter, with or without rhyme, although as late as Dryden's *Essay of Dramatic Poesie*, 1668, the question of rhyme *vs.* no-rhyme was being discussed animatedly.

The other problem which Tudor poets were less successful in solving was that of the subject matter appropriate to poetry. Both dramatic and nondramatic poets utilized a great deal of subject matter—historical or even geographical—which seems to us poetically refractory. Their incentive was the ambition to produce epic poetry as fine as that of Homer and Virgil. This ambition necessitated their utilizing material from English history, and although not all the historical poems of the period are cast in the true epic mold, they all aim at something like epic grandeur and national significance. [20]

In the minor classical forms—satire and epistle—the sixteenth century is not very rich. In the vein of the classical satires of Horace are such early poems as Sir Thomas Wyatt's "Of the Mean and Sure Estate" and "Of the Courtier's Life." [21] Toward the end of the century several books of satires appeared in the more virulent veins of Juvenal and Martial; such books are Joseph Hall's *Virgidemiarum*, 1597, and John Marston's *The Scourge of Villainy*, 1598. These were so violent in tone that the Archbishop of Canterbury ordered them burned. In this period, the epistle is a more important form than the satire. It was used frequently by such major poets as Samuel Daniel and Michael Drayton, not to mention Ben Jonson and John Donne, whose work is usually associated with the seventeenth century. The type of epistle most popular was that addressed to some noble and cultivated lady or patroness of poets, and devoted to the meditative presentation of a philosophical or moral subject. [22] Other types of epistles are illustrated in John Donne's "The Calm" and "To Sir Henry Wotton" and Ben Jonson's "To Penshurst." Michael Drayton's "To Henry Reynolds" is a particularly attractive epistle, sketching in his poetic education and giving his opinions of other contemporary poets. [23]

The finest poetical product of the sixteenth century—aside, of course, from the drama—was the lyric. An astonishing number of writers—from Henry VIII to hack writers like Robert Greene and Thomas Dekker—wrote lyrics of great beauty and charm. It is in the lyric that the sunny golden spirit of the Elizabethan period expresses itself most directly, most economically, and most beguilingly. Lyrics were omnipresent and inescapable. They reached the public in diversified ways: in miscellanies or anthologies, in songbooks where they were

---

[19] Certain writers of prose fiction who for one or another reason worked outside the euphuistic and Arcadian modes produced prose that is nowadays decidedly more readable. Thomas Nashe, although he parodied Sidney in certain passages in his picaresque novel *The Unfortunate Traveller*, 1594, was too willing to use any type of prose that seemed momentarily effective, to create a consistent prose style. Thomas Deloney, who wrote tales of bourgeois life for a middle-class audience, produced in his collection of stories, *The Gentle Craft*, 1597(?), a type of prose much closer to that of later English prose fiction. Its diction and sentence-structure are colloquial and earthy.

[20] For examples of literary works utilizing historical materials, see pages 449–51, 456–57. [21] For the text of the latter poem, see page 295. [22] For the text of Daniel's "To the Lady Margaret, Countess of Cumberland," see page 452. [23] For the text of this poem, see page 457.

accompanied by music, in the drama from the lips of sweet singers, and in the form of broadside ballads sold at street corners and at the annual fairs in town and country. The lyric attempted many moods, tragic and humorous, impassioned and gallant, decorous and indecorous, and many subjects—amatory, philosophical, didactic, and elegiac. In no other literary form cultivated in this century was perfection so frequently achieved. [24]

A special and intensive manifestation of the lyrical impulse was the writing of sonnets, a vogue which reached its peak in the early 1590's. To a very large extent, the subjects, attitudes, forms, and style of the Elizabethan sonnet were determined by Petrarch and his innumerable imitators in every modern European language, particularly Italian and French. By the time the craze of sonneteering reached England, the poetic game had developed an almost incredible number of rules and conventions. The wonder is that even minor sonneteers occasionally achieved an effect of freshness and sincerity. And even though many of the sonnets of such writers as Spenser, Sidney, Shakespeare, Daniel, and Drayton are little more than literary exercises, all these writers occasionally, and some of them very frequently, stamp the form with what seems to be personal emotion and intensity. [25]

The Drama

The Elizabethan playhouse was modeled on the inn courtyards in which strolling bands of actors presented plays for the delectation of audiences assembled from the neighborhood. The typical theater was a structure, circular or polygonal in shape, built around an open court or "pit" into which projected a rectangular raised platform. In the pit and on three sides of the platform stood the "groundlings." The more well-to-do members of the audiences paid a higher admission fee and sat in the tiers of galleries that surrounded the pit and that were partitioned off into "boxes." Thus, the theaters accommodated audiences with a very wide social and intellectual range, from noblemen to pickpockets, from scholars to fishwives.

The play was acted on the raised platform, which was closed in at the back by a curtained alcove or "inner stage," to be used for scenes that took place indoors. Above this alcove was a balcony, also curtained off, which could serve for scenes on city walls or in bedchambers. At either side of the inner stage were entrances from the actors' "tiring" rooms. On the front or "apron" of the platform, adequately equipped with trapdoors, occurred most of the action, especially of those scenes for which the text indicated no specific location. Over a large portion of this outer stage a slanting roof extended, from above the balcony to two supporting pillars. This covering protected the actors and their splendid costumes from disagreeable weather, and housed mechanisms used for lowering gods and spirits to the level of the stage.

Each theatrical company was required by law to secure a nobleman as its patron. Most of the companies adopted the name of their patron and used it for purposes of identification, not only during their London seasons but also on the frequent tours occasioned by the closing of the city theaters on account of epidemics or disagreements with the Puritanical city fathers. The companies were usually organized on a profit-sharing plan by which the leading actors were joint owners of equipment, repertory, and playhouse. Full membership in the troupe was granted on the basis of ability and years of service. The underlings served as apprentices until they became eligible for promotion. Women's parts were acted by young men or boys. Plays were supplied or revised by dramatists who were likely to keep in mind the talents or the capacities of a particular company.

It is in the drama, particularly in the plays of Shakespeare, that the age achieved transcendent expression, and it is by its drama and by its lyrics—most frequently those from plays—that the literature of the period is now most widely known. The drama of the English Renaissance was the result of the fusion of certain medieval and classical elements. From the medieval drama came the conception of drama as a succession of scenes occurring in a series of places and times, the habit of mingling tragedy and comedy, the use of verse, and the fundamentally moral interpretation of human experience. From the classical tradition came conventions as to subject matter and form. In tragedy, for instance, there was almost universal acceptance of the convention of noble personages as the characters required by tragedy, and of the Aristotelian theory as to the nature of the tragic hero, namely, a person of unusual position or powers who falls to disaster as a result of a flaw of character or an error of judgment. Elizabethan playwrights ransacked the Latin tragedies of Seneca rather than the more subtle and civilized Greek tragedies, not

---

[24] For a collection of lyrics from various sources, see pages 503–16. [25] For further comment on the sonnet conventions, see the introductory note on Sir Philip Sidney's sonnets, page 350.

only for elaborate stylistic effects and sententious utterances but also for an imposing array of devices of terror and horror—ghosts, dreams, prophecies, and appallingly gruesome details of bloodshed, suicide, and murder. From the Graeco-Roman comedy came conventions as to the plot structure and tone, and a handy collection of easily adaptable comic character types. The more devout among the Renaissance classicists attempted to impose the three unities on English drama, but it was only in the comedies and tragedies of Ben Jonson that these restrictive conventions played any very important part.

The conventional classification of Shakespeare's plays as tragedies, comedies, or histories is serviceable for the drama as a whole. It reminds us that in the history or chronicle play the age was conscious of creating a type of drama that does not fit easily into either of the conventional classical dramatic categories. But this threefold classification fails to indicate the rich variety of the drama of the English Renaissance. On the whole, the age found the somewhat dry and satirical vein of classical comedy inadequate for the expression of its comic spirit, and it somewhat fumblingly created a type of romantic comedy difficult to characterize but easy to identify. In romantic comedy the plot, though sometimes intricate, is of little consequence; there is frequent use of mistaken identities; there is a tendency to use exotic settings—the Forest of Arden, Illyria, Venice; the characters are less definitely types than are those of classical comedy, and are more genially contemplated; the happy ending, though frequently huddled, is inevitable, and even villains and knaves usually escape with light punishment. Atmosphere and mood are all-important; the dramatists lure their audience into a world where the characters "fleet the time carelessly as they did in the golden world," where every shepherd has his pipe and plays it "as though he should never be old."

In addition to tragedies and comedies, classical or romantic, and history plays, we can also see the beginnings of a comedy and a tragedy that might be called realistic. Dekker's *The Shoemaker's Holiday*, 1599, is touched with the gaiety and glamour of the period, but, though sentimental, it recreates realistically the lives of the London streets, of prosperous craftsmen and lusty apprentices. In the anonymous *Arden of Feversham*, 1592, and Thomas Heywood's *A Woman Killed with Kindness*, 1603, there are premonitions of modern domestic or bourgeois tragedy.

The drama of the English Renaissance was very slow of fruition, and despite serious though unsuccessful efforts, in such plays as *Gorboduc*, 1561, and *The Misfortunes of Arthur*, 1588, to apply the classical technique to English subject matter, it is not until 1590 that we reach any dramatic work approaching the first-rate in quality. Then Marlowe and Shakespeare, Kyd, Greene, Lyly, and Lodge, appear almost simultaneously on the stage. Of these the greatest, of course, are Marlowe[26] and Shakespeare,[27] but each of the others contributed some important element to the development of the Elizabethan drama. At the very end of the sixteenth century, Ben Jonson began to devote his great talent to a series of valiant attempts to subdue English drama to the classical spirit. But despite a considerable influence on the comedies of Thomas Middleton, Philip Massinger, and James Shirley, Jonson failed to overcome the indomitable romanticism of the Elizabethan drama. To the first decade and the very beginning of the second decade of the seventeenth century belong Shakespeare's great tragedies and his late dramatic romances. In the early seventeenth century appear the most notable plays of John Webster, a poet of macabre powers and sinister imagination. With the second decade of the century begins the career of the prolific John Fletcher, who in the course of fifteen years, with a series of collaborators from Francis Beaumont to Philip Massinger, produced a quantity of drama immensely rich in comic verve and tragic variety, if somewhat poetically and morally lax. After Fletcher's death in 1625, Massinger dominated the scene with a series of notable satirical comedies in the Jonsonian tradition and a number of tragedies loftier in tone and style than those written by his less scrupulous contemporaries.

It is a commonplace of literary history to describe the drama of the third and fourth decades of the seventeenth century as decadent. In a sense, this charge is unfounded. On the whole, the decadence of the early seventeenth-century drama is esthetic rather than moral. That is to say, decadence is apparent in an absence of originality and in the skillful repetition of time-worn situations, characters, and devices, such as one finds in the tragedies of James Shirley. Decadence of a moral sort was unquestionably a preoccupation of John Ford, the best of the later dramatists. But when the Puritans closed the theaters in 1642, numerous gifted playwrights were still active, and in Shirley's comedies of manners and in the Cavalier dramas of love and honor, one can see types and tastes that were to persist surreptitiously until the Restoration.

[26] For an account of Marlowe's contribution to the drama, see pages 363 ff. [27] For an account of Shakespeare's contribution to the drama, see pages 460 ff.

John Skelton
1460?–1529

There is some question as to whether John Skelton is the last of the medieval poets or the first poet of the English Renaissance. Probably the truth of the matter is that he represents more satisfactorily than any of his contemporaries the transition from one poetic mode to another. His fondness for allegory in both poetry and drama, his formlessness and voluminousness, his sense of indebtedness to Chaucer, all suggest the fifteenth century rather than the sixteenth. His energy and vigor, his satirical audacity and metrical individuality, are symptomatic of the new spirit.

The facts of Skelton's life are rather meager. He seems to have been born about 1460, and by 1493 he had achieved a sufficient reputation as a poet to receive, on recommendation of Henry VII, the academic distinction of "poet laureate" from the universities of Oxford and Cambridge, and possibly Louvain. Before 1500, he had served as tutor to Prince Henry, taken holy orders, and been appointed to the living of Diss in Norfolk. Shortly after the accession of Henry VIII, he probably returned to London and engaged in Humanistic activities at court. His latest biographer, William Nelson, believes that his morality play *Magnificence* (1515–16), an attack on the evil counselors of a king, was directed at Cardinal Wolsey, and that his obscure but virulent satires on Wolsey—*Speak, Parrot*, 1521; *Colin Clout*, 1522; and *Why Come Ye Not to Court*, 1522—were written in the early twenties. But Skelton was apparently reconciled with his powerful adversary, because *A Garland of Laurel*, 1523, is dedicated to both the King and the Cardinal, and in 1528 he wrote at Wolsey's request an attack on heresy, *Replication against Certain Young Scholars*. The tradition that Wolsey drove Skelton from court into sanctuary at Westminster now seems to be disproved, though he resided in Westminster after 1512, and died there in 1529.

Skelton is noteworthy not merely for the audacity of his satire and the uncontrolled vigor of his utterance, but for the invention of the type of verse called Skeltonics. The form may be described as very freely handled trimeters, with the rhymes running sometimes in couplets but frequently in a much longer unbroken series. The effect is of breathless, onrushing motion. Aside from the works already mentioned and the poems from which selections are given below, Skelton was the author not only of a great deal of Latin and English verse dealing with contemporary historical events and royal personages, but also of *The Bowge of Court*, an allegorical satire on self-seeking and intrigue in courtly circles, *Philip Sparrow*, an interminable mock elegy, and *The Tunning of Eleanour Rumming*, a broad coarse picture of an alewife and her disreputable customers.

from COLIN CLOUT

Colin Clout is a poem of about twelve hundred lines in which an honest man of the people attacks the social evils of the time, especially the greed and tyranny of great prelates. It is noteworthy that Edmund Spenser adopted the name to represent himself in his pastoral poems *The Shepheardes' Calender* and *Colin Clout's Come Home Again*. The selection given here is introductory in function. The first forty-six lines discuss the futility of trying to utter social truths; lines 53–58 give Skelton's own view of the verse form he is using; and the rest of the selection depicts the shortcomings of both laity and clergy, but particularly the latter.

<blockquote>

What can it avail
To drive forth a snail,
Or to make a sail
Of an herring's tail?
To rhyme or to rail,
To write or to indite,
Either for delight
Or else for despite?
Or books to compile
Of divers manner style,   10
Vice to revile
And sin to exile?
To teach or to preach
As reason will reach?
Say this, and say that:
His head is so fat
He wotteth never what
Nor whereof he speaketh;
He crieth and he creaketh,
He prieth and he peeketh,   20

</blockquote>

2–4. drive . . . tail? fantastic examples of futile actions.

JOHN SKELTON

He chides and he chatters,
He prates and he patters,
He clitters and he clatters,
He meddles and he smatters,
He glozes and he flatters!
Or if he speak plain,
Then he lacketh brain,
He is but a fool;
Let him go to school.
A three-footed stool!   30
That he may down sit,
For he lacketh wit!
And if that he hit
The nail on the head,
It standeth in no stead;
The devil, they say, is dead,
The devil is dead.
   It may well so be,
Or else they would see
Otherwise, and flee   40
From worldly vanity,
And foul covetousness
And other wretchedness,
Fickle falseness,
Variableness
With unstableness.
   And if ye stand in doubt
Who brought this rhyme about,
My name is Colin Clout.
I purpose to shake out   50
All my cunning bag
Like a clerkly hag;
For though my rhyme be **ragged**,
Tattered and jagged,
Rudely rain-beaten,
Rusty and moth-eaten,
If ye take well therewith
It hath in it some pith.
For, as far as I can see,
It is wrong with each degree: 60
For the temporalty
Accuseth the spiritualty;
The spiritual again
Doth grudge and complain
Upon temporal men;
Thus each of other blother,
The t'one against the t'other,—
Alas, they make me shudder!
For in hudder-mudder
The church is put in faute;   70
The prelates been so haut,
They say, and look so high

As though they would fly
Above the starry sky.
   Laymen say indeed
How they take no heed
Their seely sheep to feed,
But pluck away and pull
The fleeces of their wool;
Unnethes they leave a lock   80
Of wool amongst their flock;
And as for their cunning,
A glomming and a mumming,
And make thereof a jape;
They gasp and they gape
All to have promotion,
There is their whole devotion,
With money, if it will hap,
To catch the forkèd cap;
Forsooth, they are too lewd   90
   To say so,—all beshrewed! . . .

   Thus I, Colin Clout,
As I go about,
And wand'ring as I walk,
I hear the people talk.
Men say, for silver and gold
Mitres are bought and sold;
There shall no clergy appose
A mitre nor a crose,
But a full purse;   100
A straw for Goddès curse!
What are they the worse?
For a simoniac
Is but a harmoniac;
And no more ye make
Of simony, men say,
But a child's play.
   Over this, the foresaid lay
Report how the Pope may
A holy anker call   110
Out of the stony wall
And him a bishop make,
If he on him dare take
To keep so hard a rule—
To ride upon a mule
With gold all betrapped,
In purple and pall belapped;
Some hatted and some capped,
Richèly bewrapped,

66. blother, gabble.   **69. in hudder-mudder**, in disorder.   **71. haut**, exalted.

77. seely, simple.   **80. Unnethes**, scarcely.   **83. glomming**, looking stern. **mumming**, keeping mum or mumbling. **89. forkèd cap**, bishop's mitre.   **91. all beshrewed!** altogether accursed.   **98. appose**, approach.   **99. crose**, crozier.   **103. simoniac**, one who buys and sells ecclesiastical offices.   **104. harmoniac**, probably a made word, meaning harmonizer.   **108. lay**, laity.   **110. anker**, anchorite.

God wot to their great pains,
In rotchets of fine Raynes,   120
White as morrow's milk;
Their tabards of fine silk,
Their stirrups of mixed gold begarred;
There may no cost be spared;
Their mulès gold doth eat,
Their neighbours die for meat.
    What care they though Gil sweat,
Or Jack of the Noke?
The poor people they yoke   130
With summons and citations
And excommunications,
About churches and market;
The bishop on his carpet
At home full soft doth sit.
This is a fearful fit,
To hear the people jangle,
How warily they wrangle,—
Alas, why do ye not handle
And them all mangle?   140
Full falsely on you they lie,
And shamefully you ascry,
And say as untruly
As the butterfly
A man might say in mock
Were the weathercock
Of the steeple of Poules;
And thus they hurt their souls
In slandering you, for truth:
Alas, it is great ruth! . . .   150

from A GARLAND OF LAUREL

A Garland of Laurel is a poem of sixteen hundred lines, in which Skelton presents his claims for poetic distinction. Summoned before Pallas to plead his case, he gives a list of his own works, meets Gower, Chaucer, and Lydgate, and is at last crowned by the Countess of Surrey. The poem includes a series of tributes to the ladies who are represented as weaving a crown of laurel for the poet. The following lyrical passage is one of these tributes. The feeling seems spontaneous, and the figures are quaint and unhackneyed.

TO MISTRESS MARGARET HUSSEY

Merry Margaret,
As midsummer flower,
Gentil as falcon
Or hawk of the tower;
    With solace and gladness,
Much mirth and no madness,
All good and no badness,
So joyously,
So maidenly,
So womanly   10
Her demeaning
In every thing,—
Far, far passing
That I can endite
Or suffice to write
Of merry Margaret,
As midsummer flower,
Gentil as falcon
Or hawk of the tower.
    As patient and as still   20
And as full of good will
As fair Isiphill,
Coliander,
Sweet pomander,
Good Cassaunder;
Steadfast of thought,
Well made, well wrought;
Far may be sought
Erst that ye can find
So curteise, so kind   30
As merry Margaret,
This midsummer flower,
Gentil as falcon
Or hawk of the tower.

121. **rotchets**, surplices of a special type. **Raynes**, linen from Rennes. 123. **tabards**, coats or cloaks. 124. **begarred**, trimmed. 136. **fit**, experience. 142. **ascry**, denounce. 147. **Poules**, St. Paul's Cathedral, London.

3. **Gentil**, carefully bred. 4. **hawk of the tower**, one trained to fly high. 22. **Isiphill**, Hypsipyle, a beautiful woman from Lemnos. 23. **Coliander**, an aromatic herb. 24. **pomander**, a perfumed or scented ornament of dress. 25. **Cassaunder**, Cassandra, the Trojan prophetess. 30. **curteise**, courteous.

Sir Thomas More
1478-1535

Thomas More was born in 1478, the son of Sir John More, a judge. He received his elementary education at St. Anthony's School, London, and then became a page in the household of John Morton, Archbishop of Canterbury, Lord Chancellor, and later Cardinal. In this brilliant Humanistic household, he may have witnessed the beginnings of the English secular drama in the performances of Henry Medwall's *Fulgens and Lucrece*, and, according to tradition, showed his own wit in dramatic improvisations. Later, at Canterbury Hall, Oxford, he began the study of Greek under Linacre and Grocyn, who became his lifelong mentors and friends. He read for the law in London, made friends with the great Dutch Humanist Erasmus, and for a time contemplated becoming a monk. He decided, however, on marriage and a career in the world. His rise to a position of great power and responsibility was rapid. He became a Privy Councillor in 1518, was knighted and made Treasurer of the Exchequer in 1521, became Speaker of the House of Commons in 1523, and was made Chancellor of the Duchy of Lancaster in 1525. When Wolsey fell, Henry VIII appointed him Lord Chancellor against his own wishes. He discharged his duties wisely and well, but a conflict between More's principles and the King's lack of principle was bound to come, and when More, though willing to swear to obey the Act of Succession, refused to affirm that Henry's marriage to Catherine of Aragon had been void *ab initio*, he was sent to the Tower, charged with high treason, tried, and condemned. He was beheaded on July 7, 1535. He was sanctified by the Roman Catholic Church in 1886, and was canonized in 1935.

Sir Thomas More combined the sternest principles with great intelligence and wit and a compelling personal charm. His friendships with the early Humanists were warm and devoted. Erasmus, who described More's "kind and friendly cheerfulness, with a little air of raillery," wrote at his suggestion *The Praise of Folly*, the Latin title of which, *Encomium Moriae*, contains a pun on his host's name. Though privately devoted to ascetic practices, More was the witty and genial center of a household famous for affection and culture, and through his relationships with the Rastells and the Heywoods was the fountainhead of a strong Catholic tradition which manifested its religious devotion through the persecutions of the sixteenth century. It is not too fanciful, perhaps, to believe that something of John Donne's genius depended on descent from this talented group.

Aside from the *Utopia*, 1516, More's writings in both verse and prose are infinitely less attractive than the man. Of them, one of the most significant is his translation from the Latin in 1510 of a life of Pico della Mirandola, who attracted More by a curious blend of philosophical ideas not unlike his own. Perhaps the most brilliant of the prose works ascribed to him is the *History of Richard the Third*, written probably in 1513. Some scholars believe this to be the work of Cardinal Morton himself; others, that it is a translation by More of a Latin work of Morton's. Certainly, much of the material came from the Cardinal's reminiscences of the royal tyrant. The artful vivid characterization makes it an important contribution to the pre-Shakespearian Richard III saga. Most of More's other works belong to the literature of anti-Protestant controversy, and although attempts have been made, especially by R. W. Chambers, to establish More as the first modern prose stylist, most readers find his prose formless and undisciplined and his controversial manners the equal of Milton's worst.

from UTOPIA

More's most famous work, the *Utopia*, gave its name to the literary type to which it belongs. It is only one of many works, from Plato's *Republic* to Aldous Huxley's *Brave New World*, which attempt to depict an ideal society. The *Utopia* is divided into two books. In the first, More represents himself as meeting in Antwerp his friend Peter Giles in company with an old sailor, Raphael Hythloday (Teller-of-Idle-Tales). They retire to More's garden, where they listen to the sailor's tales of his adventures in the New World, and discuss the shocking social wrongs of the Old World. In the second book, Hythloday explains to them the ideal society on the island Utopia, in sharp contrast to the defective society of Europe. In Utopia (Nowhere), social and economic life is elaborately planned and supervised. The work, play, home life, and education of every man, woman, and child are exactly and monotonously prescribed. Every form of religion, including Christianity, is tolerated; atheism alone is prohibited. War and the use of gold as coinage are severely condemned. Ethics is completely rationalistic.

There has been much discussion in recent years as to the agreement of the theories set forth in the *Utopia* with More's personality and beliefs. Views of the question range from that which regards it as a serious expression of More's ideas to that which considers it only a sally of wit. In coming to a conclusion on this subject, one should remember that the work is in the form of a dialogue, and that Utopian society is described not by More but by Hythloday. But there is certainly no psychological incongruity between the regimented society of Utopia and More's severe, ascetic practices.

More wrote the *Utopia* in Latin, and it was published in Louvain in 1516. The first English translation, by Ralph Robinson, was published in 1551. The selections given below are from Robinson's translation.

OF THEIR LIVING AND CONVERSATION TOGETHER

BUT now will I declare how the citizens use themselves one towards another: what familiar occupying and entertainment there is among the people, and what fashion they use in the distribution of every thing. First the city consisteth of families; the families most commonly be made of kindreds. For the women, when they be married at a lawful age, they go into their husbands' houses. But the male children with all the whole male offspring continue still in their own family and be governed of the eldest and ancientest father, unless he dote for age: for then the next to him in age is placed in his room. But to the intent the prescript number of the citizens should neither decrease, nor above measure increase, it is ordained that no family which in every city be six thousand in the whole, besides them of the country, shall at once have fewer children of the age of fourteen years or thereabout than ten or more than sixteen, for of children under this age no number can be prescribed or appointed. This measure or number is easily observed and kept, by putting them that in fuller families be above the number into families of smaller increase. But if chance be that in the whole city the store increase above the just number, therewith they fill up the lack of other cities. But if so be that the multitude throughout the whole island pass and exceed the due number, then they choose out of every city certain citizens, and build up a town under their own laws in the next land where the inhabitants have much waste and unoccupied ground, receiving also of the same country people to them, if they will join and dwell with them. They thus joining and dwelling together do easily agree in one fashion of living, and that to the great wealth of both the peoples. For they so bring the matter about by their laws, that the ground which before was neither good nor profitable for the one nor for the other, is now sufficient and fruitful enough for them both. But if the inhabitants of that land will not dwell with them to be ordered by their laws, then they drive them out of those bounds which they have limited and appointed out for themselves. And if they resist and rebel, then they make war against them. For they count this the most just cause of war, when any people holdeth a piece of ground void and vacant to no good nor profitable use, keeping others from the use and possession of it, which notwithstanding by the law of nature ought thereof to be nourished and relieved. If any chance do so much diminish the number of any of their cities that it cannot be filled up again, without the diminishing of the just number of the other cities (which they say chanced but twice since the beginning of the land through a great pestilent plague), then they fulfil and make up the number of citizens fetched out of their own foreign towns, for they had rather suffer their foreign towns to decay and perish than any city of their own island to be diminished. But now again to the conversation of the citizens among themselves. The eldest (as I said) ruleth the family. The wives be ministers to their husbands, the children to their parents, and, to be short, the younger to their elders. Every city is divided into four equal parts or quarters. In the midst of every quarter there is a market-place of all manner of things. Thither the works of every family be brought into certain houses. And every kind of thing is laid up several in barns or storehouses. From hence the father of every family or every householder fetcheth whatsoever he and his have need of, and carrieth it away with him without money, without exchange, without any gage, pawn, or pledge. For why should anything be denied unto him, seeing there is abundance of all things, and that it is not to be feared lest any man will ask more than he needeth? For why should it be thought that that man would ask more than enough, which is sure never to lack? Certainly in all kinds of living creatures either fear of lack doth cause covetousness and ravin, or, in

---

26. **occupying and entertainment,** business and intercourse. 37. **prescript,** prescribed.

2. **next land,** the nearest portion of the continent. 41. **several,** separately. 52. **ravin,** plunder.

man only, pride, which counteth it a glorious thing to pass and excel other in the superfluous and vain ostentation of things. The which kind of vice among the Utopians can have no place. Next to the market-places that I spoke of, stand meat markets: whither be brought not only all sorts of herbs, and the fruits of trees, with bread, but also fish, and all manner of four-footed beasts, and wild fowl that be man's meat. But first the filthiness and ordure thereof is clean washed away in the running river without the city in places appointed meet for the same purpose. From thence the beasts be brought in killed and clean washed by the hands of their bondmen. For they permit not their free citizens to accustom themselves to the killing of beasts, through the use whereof they think clemency, the gentlest affection of our nature, by little and little to decay and perish. Neither they suffer anything that is filthy, loathsome, or uncleanly to be brought into the city, lest the air, by the stench thereof infected and corrupt, should cause pestilent diseases.

Moreover every street hath certain great large halls set in equal distance one from another, every one known by a several name. In these halls dwell the Syphogrants. And to every one of the same halls be appointed thirty families, on either side fifteen. The stewards of every hall at a certain hour come into the meat markets, where they receive meat according to the number of their halls. But first and chiefly of all, respect is had to the sick that be cured in the hospitals. For in the circuit of the city, a little without the walls, they have four hospitals, so big and so wide, so ample, and so large, that they may seem four little towns, which were devised of that bigness partly to the intent the sick, be they never so many in number, should not lie too throng or strait, and therefore uneasily and incommodiously: and partly that they which were taken and holden with contagious diseases, such as be wont by infection to creep from one to another, might be laid apart far from the company of the residue. These hospitals be so well appointed, and with all things necessary to health so furnished, and moreover so diligent attendance through the continual presence of cunning physicians is given, that though no man be sent thither against his will, yet notwithstanding there is no sick person in all the city that had not rather lie there than at home in his own house. When the steward of the sick hath received such meats as the physicians have prescribed, then the best is equally divided among the halls, according to the company of every one, saving that there is had a respect to the prince, the bishop, the tranibors, and to ambassadors and all strangers, if there be any, which be very few and seldom. But they also when they be there have certain several houses appointed and prepared for them.

To these halls at the set hours of dinner and supper come all the whole syphogranty or ward, warned by the noise of a brass trumpet, except such as be sick in the hospitals, or else in their own houses. Howbeit no man is prohibited or forbid, after the halls be served, to fetch home meat out of the market to his own house, for they know that no man will do it without a cause reasonable. For though no man be prohibited to dine at home, yet no man doth it willingly, because it is counted a point of small honesty. And also it were a folly to take the pain to dress a bad dinner at home when they may be welcome to good and fine fare so nigh hand at the hall. In this hall all vile service, all slavery and drudgery, with all laboursome toil and base business is done by bondmen. But the women of every family by course have the office and charge of cookery for seething and dressing the meat, and ordering all things thereto belonging. They sit at three tables or more, according to the number of their company. The men sit upon the bench next the wall, and the women against them on the other side of the table, that if any sudden evil should chance to them, as many times happeneth to women with child, they may rise without trouble or disturbance of anybody and go thence into the nursery. The nurses sit several alone with their young sucklings in a certain parlour appointed and deputed to the same purpose, never without fire and clean water, nor yet without cradles, that when they will they may lay down the young infants, and at their pleasure take them out of their swaddling clothes, and hold them to the fire, and refresh them with play. Every mother is nurse to her own child, unless either death or sickness be the let. When that chanceth, the wives of the Syphogrants quickly provide a nurse. And that is not hard to be done, for they that can do it proffer themselves to no service so gladly as to that, because that there this kind of pity is much praised,

5. **meat,** formerly, any kind of food.   25. **Syphogrants,** a word apparently made from the Greek word for "sty," and possibly punning on "steward," styward.   29. **number of their halls,** number of persons in the thirty families eating in their respective halls.   31. **cured in the hospitals,** cared for in the hospitals.   37. **throng or strait,** crowded or confined.

6. **tranibors,** a word made from Greek roots meaning "bench-eaters" and probably intended to suggest the Benchers of an Inn of Court.   27. **by course,** in turn.   28. **seething,** boiling.   32. **against,** opposite.   46. **let,** hindrance.

and the child that is nourished ever after taketh his nurse for his own natural mother. Also among the nurses sit all the children that be under the age of five years. All the other children of both kinds, as well boys as girls, that be under the age of marriage, do either serve at the tables, or else if they be too young thereto, yet they stand by with marvellous silence. That which is given to them from the table they eat, and other several dinner time they have none. The syphogrant and his wife sit in the midst of the high table, forasmuch as that is counted the honourablest place, and because from thence all the whole company is in their sight, for that table stands overthwart the over end of the hall. To them be joined two of the ancientest and eldest, for at every table they sit four at a mess. But if there be a church standing in that syphogranty or ward, then the priest and his wife sit with the syphogrant, as chief in the company. On both sides of them sit young men, and next unto them again old men. And thus throughout all the house equal of age be set together, and yet be mixed and matched with unequal ages. This, they say, was ordained to the intent that the sage gravity and reverence of the elders should keep the youngers from wanton licence of words and behaviour. Forasmuch as nothing can be so secretly spoken or done at the table, but either they that sit on the one side or on the other must needs perceive it. The dishes be not set down in order from the first place, but all the old men (whose places be marked with some special token to be known) be first served of their meat, and then the residue equally. The old men divide their dainties as they think best to the younger on each side of them.

Thus the elders be not defrauded of their due honour, and nevertheless equal commodity cometh to everyone. They begin every dinner and supper of reading something that pertaineth to good manners and virtue. But it is short, because no man shall be grieved therewith. Hereof the elders take occasion of honest communication, but neither sad nor unpleasant. Howbeit they do not spend all the whole dinnertime themselves with long and tedious talks, but they gladly hear also the young men; yea, and purposely provoke them to talk, to the intent that they may have a proof of every man's wit and towardness or disposition to virtue, which commonly in the liberty of feasting doth show and utter itself. Their dinners be very short, but their suppers be somewhat longer, because that after dinner follows labour, after supper sleep and natural rest, which they think to be of more strength and efficacy to wholesome and healthful digestion. No supper is passed without music. Nor their banquets lack no conceits nor junkets. They burn sweet gums and spices or perfumes, and pleasant smells, and sprinkle about sweet ointments and waters; yea, they leave nothing undone that makes for the cheering of the company. For they be much inclined to this opinion: to think no kind of pleasure forbidden, whereof cometh no harm. Thus therefore and after this sort they live together in the city, but in the country they that dwell alone far from any neighbours do dine and sup at home in their own houses. For no family there lacketh any kind of victuals, as from whom cometh all that the citizens eat and live by.

OF WARFARE

WAR or battle as a thing very beastly, and yet to no kind of beasts in so much use as to man, they do detest and abhor. And contrary to the custom almost of all other nations, they count nothing so much against glory as glory gotten in war. And therefore though they do daily practise and exercise themselves in the discipline of war, and not only the men but also the women upon certain appointed days, lest they should be to seek in the feat of arms, if need should require, yet they never go to battle, but either in the defence of their own country, or to drive out of their friends' land the enemies that have invaded it, or by their power to deliver from the yoke and bondage of tyranny some people that be therewith oppressed. Which thing they do of mere pity and compassion. Howbeit they send help to their friends, not ever in their defence, but sometimes also to requite and revenge injuries before to them done. But this they do not unless their counsel and advice in the matter be asked while it is yet new and fresh. For if they find the cause probable, and if the contrary part will not restore again such things as be of them justly demanded, then they be the chief authors and makers of the war. Which they do not only as often as by inroads and invasions of soldiers preys and

---

14. **overthwart the over end,** across the upper end. 34. **dainties.** After this word Robinson omitted a clause which Burnet translated "if there be not such an abundance of them that the whole company may be served alike."

5–6. **banquets,** desserts. **conceits nor junkets,** fancy confectionery and cakes. 17. **as from whom,** as they are those from whom. 27. **against glory,** contrary to true glory. 31–32. **be to seek in the feat of arms,** be found lacking in the knowledge of the use of weapons. 39. **not ever,** not always. 44. **probable,** that may be supported, a just cause. **the contrary part,** the opposing side.

SIR THOMAS MORE

booties be driven away, but then also much more mortally, when their friends' merchants in any land, either under the pretence of unjust laws, or else by the wresting and wrong understanding of good laws, do sustain an unjust accusation under the colour of justice. Neither the battle which the Utopians fought for the Nephelogetes against the Alaopolitanes a little before our time was made for any other cause, but that the Nephelogete merchant men, as the Utopians thought, suffered wrong of the Alaopolitanes, under the pretence of right. But whether it were right or wrong, it was with so cruel and mortal war revenged, the countries round about joining their help and power to the puissance and malice of both parties, that most flourishing and wealthy peoples, being some of them shrewdly shaken, and some of them sharply beaten, the mischiefs were not finished nor ended until the Alaopolitanes at the last were yielded up as bondmen into the jurisdiction of the Nephelogetes. For the Utopians fought not this war for themselves. And yet the Nephelogetes before the war, when the Alaopolitanes flourished in wealth, were nothing to be compared with them. So eagerly the Utopians prosecute the injuries done to their friends; yea, in money matters, and not their own likewise. For if they by covin or guile be wiped beside of their goods, so that no violence be done to their bodies, they wreak their anger by abstaining from occupying with that nation until they have made satisfaction. Not forbecause they set less store by their own citizens than by their friends, but that they take the loss of their friends' money more heavily than the loss of their own. Because that their friends' merchant men, forasmuch as that they lose is their own private goods, sustain great damage by the loss. But their own citizens lose nothing but of the common goods, and of that which was at home plentiful and almost superfluous; else had it not been sent forth. Therefore no man feeleth the loss. And for this cause they think it too cruel an act to revenge that loss with the death of many, the incommodity of the which loss no man feeleth neither in his life, nor yet in his living. But if it chance that any of their men in any other country be maimed or killed, whether it be done by a common or a private counsel, knowing and trying out the truth of the matter by their ambassadors, unless the offenders be rendered unto them in recompense of the injury they will not be appeased; but incontinent they proclaim war against them. The offenders yielded, they punish either with death or with bondage. They be not only sorry, but also ashamed, to achieve the victory with bloodshed, counting it great folly to buy precious wares too dear. They rejoice and avaunt themselves, if they vanquish and oppress their enemies by craft and deceit. And for that act they make a general triumph, and as if the matter were manfully handled, they set up a pillar of stone in the place where they so vanquished their enemies, in token of the victory. For then they glory, then they boast and crack that they have played the men indeed, when they have so overcome, as no other living creature but only man could; that is to say, by the might and puissance of wit. For with bodily strength (say they) bears, lions, boars, wolves, dogs and other wild beasts do fight. And as the most part of them do pass us in strength and fierce courage, so in wit and reason we be much stronger than they all. Their chief and principal purpose in war is to obtain that thing which, if they had before obtained, they would not have moved battle. But if that be not possible, they take so cruel vengeance of them which be in the fault that ever after they be afraid to do the like. This is their chief and principal intent, which they immediately and first of all prosecute and set forward. But yet so, that they be more circumspect in avoiding and eschewing jeopardies than they be desirous of praise and renown. Therefore immediately after that war is once solemnly denounced, they procure many proclamations signed with their own common seal to be set up privily at one time in their enemy's land, in places most frequented. In these proclamations they promise great rewards to him that will kill their enemy's prince, and somewhat less gifts, but them very great also, for every head of them whose names be in the said proclamations contained. They be those whom they count their chief adversaries, next unto the prince. Whatsoever is prescribed unto him that kills any of the proclaimed persons, that is doubled to him that brings any of the same to them alive; yea, and to the proclaimed persons themselves, if they will change their minds and come in to them, taking their parts, they proffer the same great rewards with pardon and surety of their lives. Therefore it quickly cometh to pass that their enemies have all other men in suspicion, and be unfaithful and mistrusting among themselves one to another, living in great fear and in no less jeopardy. For it

---

1–2. **much more mortally,** with much greater fierceness.
7. **Nephelogetes,** dwellers in cloudland.   8. **Alaopolitanes,** dwellers in the city of the blind.   27–28. **covin,** treachery.   **wiped . . . goods,** deprived of their goods.   30. **occupying,** business.
24. **moved battle,** made war.   28. **set forward,** promote.
32. **denounced,** declared.

is well known that divers times the most part of them (and specially the prince himself) hath been betrayed of them in whom they put their most hope and trust. So that there is no manner of act nor deed that gifts and rewards do not enforce men unto. And in rewards they keep no measure. But remembering and considering into how great hazard and jeopardy they call them, endeavour themselves to recompense the greatness of the danger with like great benefits. And therefore they promise not only wonderful great abundance of gold, but also lands of great revenues lying in most safe places among their friends. And their promises they perform faithfully without any fraud or covin. This custom of buying and selling adversaries among other people is disallowed as a cruel act of a base and a cowardish mind. But they in this behalf think themselves much praiseworthy, as who, like wise men, by this means dispatch great wars without any battle or skirmish. Yea, they count it also a deed of pity and mercy, because that by the death of a few offenders the lives of a great number of innocents, as well of their own men as also of their enemies, be ransomed and saved, which in fighting should have been slain. For they do no less pity the base and common sort of their enemies' people than they do their own, knowing that they be driven and enforced to war against their wills by the furious madness of their princes and heads. If by none of these means the matter go forward as they would have it, then they procure occasions of debate and dissension to be spread among their enemies, as by bringing the prince's brother or some of the noble men in hope to obtain the kingdom. If this way prevail not, then they raise up the people that be next neighbours and borderers to their enemies, and them they set in their necks under the colour of some old title of right, such as kings do never lack. To them they promise their help and aid in their war. And as for money, they give them abundance. But of their own citizens they send to them few or none. Whom they make so much of and love so entirely that they would not be willing to change any of them for their adversaries' prince. But their gold and silver, because they keep it all for this only purpose, they lay it out frankly and freely, as who should live even as wealthy if they had bestowed it every penny. Yea, and besides their riches, which they keep at home, they have also an infinite treasure abroad, by reason that (as I said before) many nations be in their debt. Therefore they hire soldiers out of all countries and send them to battle, but chiefly of the Zapoletes. This people is five hundred miles from Utopia eastward. They be hideous, savage and fierce, dwelling in wild woods and high mountains, where they were bred and brought up. They be of an hard nature, able to abide and sustain heat, cold and labour, abhorring from all delicate dainties, occupying no husbandry nor tillage of the ground, homely and rude both in building of their houses and in their apparel, given unto no goodness, but only to the breeding and bringing up of cattle. The most part of their living is by hunting and stealing. They be born only to war, which they diligently and earnestly seek for. And when they have gotten it, they be wonders glad thereof. They go forth of their own country in great companies together, and whosoever lacketh soldiers, there they proffer their service for small wages. This is only the craft they have to get their living by. They maintain their life by seeking their death. For them whomwith they be in wages they fight hardily, fiercely, and faithfully. But they bind themselves for no certain time. But upon this condition they enter into bonds, that the next day they will take part with the other side for greater wages, and the next day after that, they will be ready to come back again for a little more money. There be few wars there away wherein is not a great number of them in both parties. Therefore it daily chanceth that nigh kinsfolk, which were hired together on one part, and there very friendly and familiarly used themselves one with another, shortly after being separate in contrary parts, run one against another enviously and fiercely, and forgetting both kindred and friendship, thrust their swords one in another. And that for none other cause, but that they be hired of contrary princes for a little money. Which they do so highly regard and esteem that they will easily be provoked to change parts for a halfpenny more wages by the day. So quickly they have taken a smack in covetousness. Which for all that is to them no profit. For that they get by fighting, immediately they spend unthriftily and wretchedly in riot. This people fighteth for the Utopians against all nations, because they give them greater wages than any other nation will. For the Utopians, like as they seek good men to use well, so they seek these evil and vicious men to abuse. Whom, when need requireth, with promises of great rewards they put forth into great jeopardies. From whence the most part of them never come

6. **keep no measure,** set no bounds. 1. **Zapoletes,** a word made from Greek roots meaning "easily bought."   6. **abhorring from,** turning in disgust from.   14. **wonders,** wondrous(ly).   20. **whomwith they be in wages,** from whom they receive their wages.   39–40. **taken a smack in,** acquired a taste for.

again to ask their rewards. But to them that remain alive they pay that which they promised faithfully, that they may be the more willing to put themselves in like danger another time. Nor the Utopians pass not how many of them they bring to destruction. For they believe that they should do a very good deed for all mankind, if they could rid out of the world all that foul stinking den of that most wicked and cursed people. Next unto this they use the soldiers of them for whom they fight. And then the help of their other friends. And last of all, they join to their own citizens. Among whom they give to one of tried virtue and prowess the rule, governance, and conduction of the whole army. Under him they appoint two other, which, while he is safe, be both private and out of office. But if he be taken or slain, the one of the other two succeedeth him, as it were by inheritance. And if the second miscarry, then the third taketh his room, lest that (as the chance of battle is uncertain and doubtful) the jeopardy or death of the captain should bring the whole army in hazard. They choose soldiers, out of every city those which put forth themselves willingly. For they thrust no man forth into war against his will, because they believe, if any man be fearful and faint hearted of nature, he will not only do no manful and hardy act himself, but also be occasion of cowardness to his fellows. But if any battle be made against their own country, then they put these cowards (so that they be strong bodied) in ships among other bold hearted men. Or else they dispose them upon the walls, from whence they may not fly. Thus what for shame that their enemies be at hand, and what for because they be without hope of running away, they forget all fear. And many times extreme necessity turns cowardness into prowess and manliness. But as none of them is thrust forth of his country into war against his will, so women that be willing to accompany their husbands in times of war be not prohibited or letted. Yea, they provoke and exhort them to it with praises. And in set field the wives do stand every one by their own husbands' side. Also every man is compassed next about with his own children, kinsfolk and alliance. That they whom nature chiefly moves to mutual succour, thus standing together, may help one another. It is a great reproach and dishonesty for the husband to come home without his wife, or the wife without her husband, or the son without his father. And therefore if the other part stick so hard by it that the battle come to their hands, it is fought with great slaughter and bloodshed, even to the utter destruction of both parts. For as they make all the means and shifts that may be to keep themselves from the necessity of fighting, or that they may dispatch the battle by their hired soldiers; so when there is no remedy but that they must needs fight themselves, they do as courageously fall to it, as before, while they might, they did wisely avoid and refuse it. Nor they be not most fierce at the first brunt. But in continuance by little and little their fierce courage increaseth, with so stubborn and obstinate minds that they will rather die than give back an inch. For that surety of living which every man hath at home being joined with no careful anxiety or remembrance how their posterity shall live after them (for this pensiveness oftentimes breaketh and abateth courageous stomachs) makes them stout and hardy, and disdainful to be conquered. Moreover, their knowledge in chivalry and feats of arms putteth them in a good hope. Finally the wholesome and virtuous opinions, wherein they were brought up even from their childhood, partly through learning, and partly through the good ordinances and laws of their weal public, augment and increase their manful courage. By reason whereof they neither set so little store by their lives that they will rashly and unadvisedly cast them away, nor they be not so far in lewd and fond love therewith that they will shamefully covet to keep them when honesty bids leave them. When the battle is hottest and in all places most fierce and fervent, a band of chosen and picked young men, which be sworn to live and die together, take upon them to destroy their adversary's captain. Whom they invade, now with privy wiles, now by open strength. At him they strike both near and far off. He is assailed with a long and a continual assault, fresh men still coming in the wearied men's places. And seldom it chanceth (unless he save himself by flying) that he is not either slain or else taken prisoner and yielded to his enemies alive. If they win the field, they persecute not their enemies with the violent rage of slaughter. For they had rather take them alive than kill them. Neither they do so follow the chase and pursuit of their enemies but they leave behind them one part of their host in battle array under their standards. In so much that if all their whole army be discomfited and overcome, saving the rearward, and that they therewith achieve the victory, then they had rather let all their enemies escape than to follow them out of array. For they remember, it has chanced unto

  4. pass, care. **12. join to,** add. **18–19. miscarry,** come to grief. **30. so that they be,** provided they be.
  41. letted, prevented. **42. in set field,** in battle array.
  25–26. weal public, commonwealth.

themselves more than once, the whole power and strength of their host being vanquished and put to flight, while their enemies rejoicing in the victory have persecuted them, flying some one way and some another; a small company of their men lying in an ambush, there ready at all occasions, have suddenly risen upon them thus dispersed and scattered out of array, and through presumption of safety unadvisedly pursuing the chase, and have incontinent changed the fortune of the whole battle, and spite of their teeth wresting out of their hands the sure and undoubted victory, being a little before conquered, have for their part conquered the conquerors. It is hard to say whether they be craftier in laying an ambush or wittier in avoiding the same. You would think they intend to fly, when they mean nothing less. And contrary wise when they go about that purpose, you would believe it were the least part of their thought. For if they perceive themselves either overmatched in number or closed in too narrow a place, then they remove their camp either in the night season with silence, or by some policy they deceive their enemies, or in the day time they retire back so softly that it is no less jeopardy to meddle with them when they give back than when they press on. They fence and fortify their camp surely with a deep and a broad trench. The earth thereof is cast inward. Nor they do not set drudges and slaves awork about it. It is done by the hands of the soldiers themselves. All the whole army worketh upon it, except them that keep watch and ward in harness before the trench for sudden adventures. Therefore by the labour of so many, a large trench closing in a great compass of ground is made in less time than any man would believe. Their armour or harness, which they wear, is sure and strong to receive strokes, and handsome for all movings and gestures of the body, insomuch that it is not unwieldy to swim in. For in the discipline of their warfare among other feats they learn to swim in harness. Their weapons be arrows aloof, which they shoot both strongly and surely, not only footmen, but also horsemen. At hand strokes they use not swords but poleaxes, which be mortal, as well in sharpness as in weight, both for foins and down strokes. Engines for war they devise and invent wonders wittily. Which when they be made they keep very secret, lest if they should be known before need require, they should be but laughed at and serve to no purpose. But in making them, hereunto they have chief respect, that they be both easy to be carried, and handsome to be moved and turned about. Truce taken with their enemies for a short time they do so firmly and faithfully keep that they will not break it; no, not though they be thereunto provoked. They do not waste nor destroy their enemies' land with foragings, nor they burn not up their corn. Yea, they save it as much as may be from being overrun and trodden down either with men or horses, thinking that it groweth for their own use and profit. They hurt no man that is unarmed, unless he be a spy. All cities that be yielded unto them they defend. And such as they win by force of assault, they neither despoil nor sack, but them that withstood and dissuaded the yielding up of the same, they put to death; the other soldiers they punish with bondage. All the weak multitude they leave untouched. If they know that any citizens counselled to yield and render up the city, to them they give part of the condemned men's goods. The residue they distribute and give freely among them whose help they had in the same war. For none of themselves take any portion of the prey. But when the battle is finished and ended, they put their friends to never a penny cost of all the charges that they were at, but lay it upon their necks that be conquered. Them they burden with the whole charge of their expenses, which they demand of them partly in money to be kept for like use of battle, and partly in lands of great revenues to be paid unto them yearly for ever. Such revenues they have now in many countries. Which by little and little rising of divers and sundry causes be increased above seven hundred thousand ducats by the year. Thither they send forth some of their citizens as lieutenants, to live there sumptuously like men of honour and renown. And yet, this notwithstanding, much money is saved, which comes to the common treasury; unless it so chance that they had rather trust the country with the money. Which many times they do so long until they have need to occupy it. And it seldom happeneth that they demand all. Of these lands they assign part unto them which, at their request and exhortation, put themselves in such jeopardies as I spake of before. If any prince stir up war against them, intending to invade their land, they meet him incontinent out of their own borders with great power and strength. For they never lightly make war in their own country. Nor they be never brought into so extreme necessity as to take help out of foreign lands into their own island.

10. incontinent, speedily. **11. spite of their teeth,** despite all opposition. **33. sudden adventures,** unexpected attacks. **42. aloof,** shot from a distance **46. foins,** thrusts. **26-27. lay it . . . conquered,** make the conquered pay for it.

Sir Thomas Wyatt
c. 1503–1542

Sir Thomas Wyatt comes as close as any of the pre-Elizabethan poets to the courtly ideal of the Renaissance. His life, though brief, was many-sided; his manifold gifts, political and esthetic, were utilized to the full. He was born in Kent in the castle of his father, who while Wyatt was a child was joint constable of Norwich Castle along with Sir Thomas, the father of Anne Boleyn. Wyatt served as a page at court, and entered St. John's College, Cambridge, in 1516, the year of its founding. He took his M.A. degree about 1520, and in the following year married Elizabeth, the daughter of Lord Cobham. An extant letter to his son Thomas suggests that his married life was not very happy; at any rate, Wyatt sought consolation elsewhere.

In the service of the King, he made an important journey to Italy in 1526–27, visiting Rome, Venice, and other cities, and from 1528 to 1532 he served as Marshal of Calais. He was knighted in 1536, but was imprisoned in the same year, ostensibly because of a quarrel with the Duke of Suffolk but presumably on the suspicion that he was a lover of Queen Anne. He regained the King's favor, however, became a member of the Privy Council, and served as Ambassador to Spain from 1537 to 1539. In 1541, he was imprisoned on the charge of traitorous behavior during his residence in Spain, but defended himself eloquently and was unconditionally pardoned. In 1542, he was a member of Parliament, and was appointed Commander of the Fleet. In the autumn, on a hurried trip to Falmouth to meet the Spanish Ambassador, he fell ill of a fever, and died at Sherborne, Dorsetshire, on October 11, 1542.

Wyatt's visit to Italy was all-important for his poetic activities. There he became deeply interested in Petrarch and other Italian lyricists, and he later drew heavily on them for themes and verse forms. One of his first works, however, was a translation of a Latin version of Plutarch's περὶ εὐθυμίας which he presented under the title of *Quiet of Mind* as a New Year's gift to Queen Catherine in 1528. His *Seven Penitential Psalms* was a very free rendering of a work by Pietro Aretino, the sensualist and satirist. Aside from the sonnets and lyrics, most of Wyatt's work was in the newly revived forms: satires, influenced by Horace and the contemporary Italian Luigi Alamanni, and epigrams, inspired by the *Strambotti* of Serafino dell' Aquila. The sonnets, numbering about thirty, are important, not only as the first to be written in English, but also as evidence of the strong appeal of the Petrarchan love conventions. Many of these Wyatt accepted humbly, but occasionally he rebelled manfully against the traditionally subservient role of the lover. Wyatt's renderings frequently seem rough and awkward, but it has been argued that some of the crudities are due to Tottell's highhanded editing of Wyatt's manuscripts, and others to our failure to understand Wyatt's personal system of stresses and accents. Probably his lyrics—obviously intended for singing with a lute accompaniment—represent the height of his technical skill. But Wyatt was as important as an influence, on Surrey and other courtly makers, as he was as a poet.

A few of Wyatt's poems were first printed about 1542 in a miscellany entitled *The Court of Venus*, of which only a few fragments are extant. Ninety-seven of his poems were included by Tottell in his famous miscellany *Songs and Sonnets*, 1557. Other poems have been recovered in modern times from contemporary manuscripts.

SONNETS

Wyatt and Surrey introduced the sonnet into English on the pattern derived from Petrarch and Sannazaro through Saint-Gelais and other French poets. Wyatt retains the conventional Petrarchan love themes embellished by conceits, but he often departs from the rhyme scheme of his Italian models by ending his sonnets with a final couplet; thus the rhyme scheme of a majority of his sonnets is $abba, abba, cddc, ee$.

With the adoption of this form, Wyatt revived lyrical beauty in English poetry. Imitation of Petrarch introduced bold and new images, variety in metaphor, and subtleties of phrasing. The individual quality of Wyatt's verse, however, is its strong, rapid flow combined with simplicity and directness of speech. Since the sonnets describe a lover's emotional state under the trials of court romance, imaginative feeling prevails throughout. Wyatt sang his love tale in spontaneous, virile notes modulated by strains of melancholy and sweetness, but always maintaining its tone of deep earnestness.

THE LOVER COMPARETH HIS STATE TO A SHIP IN PERILOUS STORM TOSSED ON THE SEA

My galley chargèd with forgetfulness
Through sharp seas, in winter nights, doth pass
'Tween rock and rock; and eke my foe, alas,
That is my lord, steereth with cruelness;
And every oar a thought in readiness,
As though that death were light in such a case.
An endless wind doth tear the sail apace,
Of forcèd sighs and trusty fearfulness;
A rain of tears, a cloud of dark disdain,
Have done the wearied cords great hinderance;   10
Wreathèd with error and with ignorance,
The stars be hid that led me to this pain;
Drowned is reason, that should be my comfort,
And I remain despairing of the port.

DESCRIPTION OF THE CONTRARIOUS PASSIONS IN A LOVER

I find no peace, and all my war is done;
I fear and hope; I burn, and freeze like ice;
I fly aloft, yet can I not arise;
And nought I have, and all the world I season.
That locks nor looseth holdeth me in prison,
And holds me not, yet can I 'scape no wise;
Nor lets me live, nor die, at my devise,
And yet of death it giveth me occasion.
Without eye, I see; without tongue, I plain;
I wish to perish, yet I ask for health;   10
I love another, and thus I hate myself;
I feed me in sorrow, and laugh in all my pain.
Lo, thus displeaseth me both death and life,
And my delight is causer of this strife.

THE LOVER FOR SHAMEFASTNESS HIDETH HIS DESIRE WITHIN HIS FAITHFUL HEART

The long love that in my thought I harbour,
And in my heart doth keep his residence,
Into my face presseth with bold pretence
And there campeth, displaying his banner.
She that me learns to love and to suffer
And wills that my trust and lust's negligence
Be reined by reason, shame, and reverence,
With his hardiness takes displeàsure.
Wherewith love to the heart's forest he fleeth,
Leaving his enterprise with pain and cry,   10
And there him hideth, and not appeareth:
What may I do when my master feareth
But in the field with him to live and die?
For good is the life ending faithfully.

WHOSO LIST TO HUNT

Whoso list to hunt, I know where is an hind,
　But as for me—alas, I may no more.
　The vain travail hath wearied me so sore,
　I am of them that farthest come behind.
Yet may I, by no means, my wearied mind
　Draw from the deer; but as she fleeth afore
　Fainting I follow. I leave off therefore,
　Since in a net I seek to hold the wind.
Who list her hunt, I put him out of doubt,
　As well as I, may spend his time in vain.   10
　And graven with diamonds in letters plain
There is written, her fair neck round about:
　Noli me tangere, for Caesar's I am,
　And wild for to hold, though I seem tame.

THE LOVER SHOWETH HOW HE IS FORSAKEN OF SUCH AS HE SOMETIME ENJOYED

They flee from me, that sometime did me seek,
With naked foot stalking within my chamber.
Once have I seen them gentle, tame, and meek,
That now are wild, and do not once remember
That sometime they have put themselves in danger
To take bread at my hand; and now they range,
Busily seeking in continual change.
　Thanked be fortune it hath been otherwise,
Twenty times better; but once especial,
In thin array, after a pleasant guise,   10
When her loose gown did from her shoulders fall,
And she me caught in her arms long and small,
And therewithal so sweetly did me kiss
And softly said, Dear heart, how like you this?
　It was no dream, for I lay broad awaking.
But all is turned now, through my gentleness,
Into a bitter fashion of forsaking;
And I have leave to go, of her goodness,
And she also to use newfangleness.
But since that I unkindly so am served,   20
How like you this? what hath she now deserved?

The Lover Compareth. **3. my foe,** my love, as is also **my lord** in the next line.   *Description.* **4. season,** seize. **9. plain,** complain.
　The Lover for Shamefastness. The student should compare this translation of Petrarch's Sonnet 109 with Surrey's translation of it under the title "Complaint of a Lover Rebuked."

Whoso list. **13. Noli me tangere.** Touch me not. This line has led some scholars to believe that this sonnet refers to Anne Boleyn.

SIR THOMAS WYATT

FORGET NOT YET

Forget not yet the tried intent
Of such a truth as I have meant,
My great travail, so gladly spent,
    Forget not yet.

Forget not yet when first began
The weary life ye know, since whan
The suit, the service none tell can,
    Forget not yet.

Forget not yet the great assays,
The cruel wrong, the scornful ways;   10
The painful patience in denays,
    Forget not yet.

Forget not yet, forget not this,
How long ago hath been, and is,
The mind that never meant amiss,—
    Forget not yet.

Forget not, then, thine own approved,
The which so long hath thee so loved,
Whose steadfast faith yet never moved,
    Forget not this.   20

OF THE COURTIER'S LIFE

WRITTEN TO JOHN POINS

This satire sets forth Wyatt's aversion to life at court in a verse epistle to John Poins, explaining the author's reasons for leaving the court to return home. He is unable to tolerate the hypocrisy and dissipation characteristic of the court. Pomp, avarice, deceit, servility, cruelty, and lechery, he ironically observes, are the traits requisite for a courtier. In preference to these, Wyatt chooses to live in liberty within the bounds of his father's estate, where he is free to walk and rhyme as he pleases. He contrasts the life at court with the life in the country, and ends with an invitation to John Poins to join him.

Mine own John Poins, since ye delight to know
The causes why that homeward I me draw,
And flee the press of courts, whereso they go,
Rather than to live thrall under the awe
Of lordly looks, wrappèd within my cloak,
To will and lust learning to set a law;
It is not because I scorn or mock
The power of them, whom fortune here hath lent
Charge over us, of right to strike the stroke.
But true it is that I have always meant   10
Less to esteem them than the common sort,
Of outward things that judge in their intent
Without regard what inward doth resort.
I grant sometime of glory that the fire
Doth touch my heart. Me list not to report
Blame by honour, and honour to desire.
But how may I this honour now attain,
That cannot dye the colour black a liar?
My Poins, I cannot frame my tune to feign,
To cloak the truth, for praise without desert,   20
Of them that list all vice for to retain.
I cannot honour them that set their part
With Venus and Bacchus all their life long;
Nor hold my peace of them, although I smart.
I cannot crouch nor kneel to such a wrong,
To worship them like God on earth alone,
That are as wolves these seely lambs among.
I cannot with my words complain and moan
And suffer nought, nor smart without complaint,
Nor turn the word that from my mouth is gone;   30
I cannot speak and look like as a saint,
Use wiles for wit, and make deceit a pleasure;
Call craft counsel, for lucre still to paint;
I cannot wrest the law to fill the coffer;
With innocent blood to feed myself fat;
And do most hurt where that most help I offer.
I am not he that can allow the state
Of high Caesar, and damn Cato to die;
That with his death did scape out of the gate
From Caesar's hands, if Livy doth not lie,   40
And would not live where liberty was lost,
So did his heart the commonwealth apply.
I am not he, such eloquence to boast,
To make the crow in singing as the swan,
Nor call the lion of coward beasts the most,
That cannot take a mouse as the cat can;
And he that dieth for hunger of the gold,
Call him Alexander, and say that Pan
Passeth Apollo in music manifold;
Praise Sir Thopas for a noble tale,   50
And scorn the story that the Knight told;
Praise him for counsel that is drunk of ale;
Grin when he laughs that beareth all the sway,
Frown when he frowns, and groan when he is pale;
On others' lust to hang both night and day.
None of these points would ever frame in me;
My wit is nought, I cannot learn the way.
And much the less of things that greater be,
That asken help of colours to devise
To join the mean with each extremity;   60
With nearest virtue aye to cloak the vice.
And as to purpose likewise it shall fall,
To press the virtue that it may not rise;

Forget Not Yet. **6. whan,** when. **11. denays,** denials.   **27. seely,** foolish. **56. frame in,** serve, profit.

As drunkenness good fellowship to call;
The friendly foe, with his fair double face,
Say he is gentle and courteous therewithal;
Affirm that favel hath a goodly grace
In eloquence; and cruelty to name
Zeal of justice, and change in time and place;
And he that suff'reth offence without blame,   70
Call him pitiful, and him true and plain
That raileth reckless unto each man's shame;
Say he is rude that cannot lie and feign;
The lecher a lover, and tyranny
To be the right of a prince's reign.
I cannot, I; no, no, it will not be.
This is the cause that I could never yet
Hang on their sleeves, that weigh, as thou mayst see,
A chip of chance more than a pound of wit.
This maketh me at home to hunt and hawk,   80
And in foul weather at my book to sit,
In frost and snow then with my bow to stalk.
No man doth mark whereso I ride or go.

In lusty leas at liberty I walk,
And of these news I feel nor weal nor woe,
Save that a clog doth hang yet at my heel.
No force for that, for it is ordered so
That I may leap both hedge and dike full well;
I am not now in France, to judge the wine,
With sav'ry sauce those delicates to feel.   90
Nor yet in Spain where one must him incline
Rather than to be, outwardly to seem.
I meddle not with wits that be so fine,
Nor Flanders' cheer lets not my sight to deem.
Of black and white, nor takes my wits away
With beastliness; such do those beasts esteem.
Nor I am not where truth is given in prey
For money, poison, and treason; of some
A common practice, usèd night and day.
But I am here in Kent and Christendom,   100
Among the Muses, where I read and rhyme;
Where if thou list, mine own John Poins, to come,
Thou shalt be judge how I do spend my time.

Henry Howard, Earl of Surrey
c. 1517 –1547

Surrey, Wyatt's most brilliant disciple, had a life that was briefer and more turbulent than his poetic master's, but which, like his, was in many ways a very close approximation of the ideal of Castiglione's *Courtier*. Born about 1517, he was of royal blood, since his father, the Earl of Surrey (afterwards Duke of Norfolk), was descended from Edward the Confessor, and his mother, Elinor Percy, from Edward III. His mother was apparently a patroness of letters. Skelton composed *A Garland of Laurel* under her roof, and represents her as crowning him at the end of the poem.

Surrey was tutored by the learned John Clerk, and was well trained in Latin, Spanish, Italian, and French. At the age of thirteen, he was appointed companion to the Duke of Richmond, the illegitimate son of Henry VIII, and enjoyed princely privileges at Windsor and in 1532 in France, whither the young friends went in the train of the King to the ceremonies at the Field of the Cloth of Gold and where they remained as guests of the young sons of King Francis I. They were recalled to England for the marriage of Richmond to Surrey's sister Mary. Surrey had already been married to Lady Frances Vere in 1532, but because of their youth, the couple did not set up a household until 1535, when he built Mount Surrey, a classical mansion on St. Leonard's Hill, near Norwich.

Surrey is described in a contemporary record as "the most foolish proud boy that is in England," and he seems to have been guilty of an unusual number of violent misdemeanors. In 1537, he struck a courtier who cast aspersions on his devotion to the King, and since the offense occurred in the royal park at Hampton Court, Surrey ran the risk of losing his right hand; but this gruesome penalty was commuted to punishment, and Surrey was imprisoned for a season at Windsor. In 1542 he was imprisoned again as the result of another quarrel, and in 1543 he was consigned to Fleet Prison for rioting in the streets and eating meat in Lent.

But in the service of the King he performed a

---

67. **favel**, cunning, deception by flattery; from the favel, or fallow-colored horse, used as a type of cunning, as in the proverbial expression "to curry favel (favor)." 69. **change . . . place.** Cruelty is often excused by the plea that in some times and places custom makes or has made it justifiable. 79. **chip of chance . . . wit.** Wyatt's several imprisonments were due to a sudden change in the temper or policy of the King.

86. **clog.** Wyatt was not at perfect liberty, but was confined to his father's estate on parole. 94–95. **Flanders' cheer . . . Of,** the strong liquor of Flanders does not prevent my sight's distinguishing between.

HENRY HOWARD, EARL OF SURREY

number of official and martial services. He assisted his father in suppressing a rebellion in Yorkshire, in bringing about the overthrow of Thomas Cromwell, and in repressing the Scots. In 1540 he was a leader of a tournament in honor of the marriage of Henry and Anne of Cleves, and in 1541 served as steward of Cambridge University. Between 1544 and 1546 he engaged in various campaigns against France, and in 1545-46 he was commander at Boulogne. In December, 1546, he was arrested and charged with high treason, possibly through the influence of a brother of Queen Jane Seymour. At the time, Henry VIII was seriously ill, and the problem of the succession was in the minds of all. Surrey was charged with putting forth his father's claim to the throne by quartering his arms with those of Edward the Confessor. He was condemned to death, and was beheaded on January 21, 1547, a week before the death of Henry himself.

Surrey's poems give little evidence of his haughty and violent nature. In them he submitted himself with greater ease than Wyatt to the Petrarchan love conventions, and the dominant tone of his lyrics is rather sweetly melancholy. He is, moreover, a much more smooth and skillful versifier than his poetic master. Surrey made two important contributions to English poetic forms. The first is the English or Shakespearean sonnet, consisting of three quatrains, rhyming alternately, and a concluding couplet. The second, and more important contribution, was what is loosely called blank verse, namely, unrhymed iambic pentameters.

Probably Surrey's first printed work was his elegy on Sir Thomas Wyatt, which appeared under the title *An Excellent Epitaph* about 1542; his next publication was the translation of Martial's epigram which William Baldwin incorporated in his *Treatise of Moral Philosophy* in 1547. Surrey's blank-verse translation of the fourth book of Virgil's *Aeneid* was probably first printed about 1554. A slightly different version of this and of the second book was printed by Tottell in 1557, about two weeks after he had published forty of Surrey's poems in his *Songs and Sonnets*. Surrey's use of blank verse was probably encouraged by various Italian unrhymed translations of Virgil.

SONNETS

In addition to the new English rhyme scheme, Surrey's sonnets anticipated Elizabethan poetry in their fine musical quality and dramatic strength. They show the influence of a sensitive ear and a mind that sees life vividly in terms of action.

This verse has an easy motion and slow and stately harmonies. Concordant vowel sounds echo through the sonnets and assume the quality of overtones: *flowering, to-morrow, soote, bloom, bright, hight*, and the alliteration has a similar effect in accentuating the rhythm. Ordinarily the impression is distinctly pleasing, but occasionally Surrey overemploys this device, as in "The soote season that bud and bloom forth brings," where this self-conscious attention to sound has the effect of surfeit. For the most part, fortunately, the melody of these sonnets has a cumulative, sonorous effect.

Surrey's diction is direct and firm, but flexible and euphonious. He employs just enough words of Latin and French origin to give richness and dignity to the homely native element without appearing highly artificial. There is an archaic flavor in his use of certain characteristically Chaucerian words, phrases, and constructions; and quaintness in his tendency to use nouns and adjectives as verbs, or adjectives and verbs as nouns: "With *green* hath clad the hill and eke the vale."

His subject matter is almost exclusively Petrarchan love themes or nature descriptions, which he treats with a gentle, sentimental melancholy. In general the slight trace of insincerity of feeling found in Surrey's sonnets is lost in the beauty of his lyrical expression.

DESCRIPTION OF SPRING, WHEREIN EACH THING RENEWS SAVE ONLY THE LOVER

The soote season that bud and bloom forth brings
With green hath clad the hill and eke the vale,
The nightingale with feathers new she sings,
The turtle to her make hath told her tale.
Summer is come, for every spray now springs,
The hart hath hung his old head on the pale,
The buck in brake his winter coat he flings,
The fishes float with new repairèd scale,
The adder all her slough away she slings,
The swift swallow pursueth the flyès smale,　　10
The busy bee her honey now she mings,—
Winter is worn, that was the flowers' bale:
And thus I see, among these pleasant things
Each care decays—and yet my sorrow springs.

THE FRAILTY AND HURTFULNESS OF BEAUTY

Brittle beauty that nature made so frail,
Whereof the gift is small, and short the season,
Flow'ring to-day, to-morrow apt to fail,
Tickle treasure, abhorred of reason,
Dangerous to deal with, vain, of none avail,

Description of Spring. **1. soote,** sweet, as used by Chaucer. **4. make,** mate. **6. pale,** paling, fence; Surrey has in mind the deer kept in enclosures. **10. smale,** small. **11. mings,** mingles, produces by mixing, though "remembers" is a possible meaning. **12. bale,** funeral pyre. *The Frailty.* **4. Tickle,** delicate.

Costly in keeping, passed not worth two peason,
Slipper in sliding as is an eelè's tail,
Hard to attain, once gotten not geason,
Jewel of jeopardy that peril doth assail,
False and untrue, enticèd oft to treason,   10
En'my to youth (that most may I bewail!),
Ah, bitter sweet! infecting as the poison,
Thou farest as fruit that with the frost is taken:
To-day ready ripe, to-morrow all to-shaken.

DESCRIPTION AND PRAISE OF HIS LOVE GERALDINE

This sonnet gave rise to the persistent legend that Surrey was the lover of Elizabeth Fitzgerald, daughter of the Irish Earl of Kildare, and that he addressed all his love poetry to her. Modern scholars consider this poem the only reference to a passing fancy for this young girl.

From Tuscan came my lady's worthy race,
Fair Florence was sometime her ancient seat,
The western isle whose pleasant shore doth face
Wild Camber's cliffs did give her lively heat;
Fostered she was with milk of Irish breast,
Her sire an earl, her dame of princes' blood;
From tender years in Britain she doth rest
With king's child, where she tasteth costly food.
Hunsdon did first present her to mine eyne;
Bright is her hue, and Geraldine she hight;   10
Hampton me taught to wish her first for mine,
And Windsor, alas, doth chase me from her sight.
Her beauty, of kind; her virtues, from above;
Happy is he that can obtain her love.

A COMPLAINT BY NIGHT OF THE LOVER NOT BELOVED

Alas, so all things now do hold their peace,
Heaven and earth disturbèd in nothing;
The beasts, the air, the birds their song do cease,
The nightè's chair the stars about doth bring;
Calm is the sea, the waves work less and less.
So am not I, whom love, alas, doth wring,
Bringing before my face the great increase
Of my desires, whereat I weep and sing
In joy and woe, as in a doubtful ease.   9
For my sweet thoughts sometime do pleasure bring,
But by and by the cause of my disease
Gives me a pang that inwardly doth sting,
When that I think what grief it is again
To live and lack the thing should rid my pain.

COMPLAINT OF A LOVER REBUKED

Love that liveth and reigneth in my thought,
That built his seat within my captive breast,
Clad in the arms wherein with me he fought,
Oft in my face he doth his banner rest.
She that me taught to love and suffer pain,
My doubtful hope and eke my hot desire
With shamefast cloak to shadow and refrain,
Her smiling grace converteth straight to ire;
And coward love then to the heart apace
Taketh his flight, whereas he lurks and plains   10
His purpose lost, and dare not show his face.
For my lord's guilt thus faultless bide I pains;
Yet from my lord shall not my foot remove,—
Sweet is his death that takes his end by love.

OF THE DEATH OF SIR T. W. THE ELDER

Wyatt resteth here, that quick could never rest;
Whose heavenly gifts increasèd by disdain,
And virtue sank the deeper in his breast,
Such profit he by envy could obtain.
  A head where wisdom mysteries did frame,
Whose hammers beat still in that lively brain
As on a stithy, where that some work of fame
Was daily wrought, to turn to Britain's gain.
  A visage stern and mild, where both did grow
Vice to contemn, in virtue to rejoice;   10
Amid great storms whom grace assurèd so
To live upright and smile at fortune's choice.
  A hand that taught what might be said in rhyme,
That reft Chaucer the glory of his wit,
A mark the which (unparfited, for time)
Some may approach, but never none shall hit.
  A tongue that served in foreign realms his king;
Whose courteous talk to virtue did inflame
Each noble heart; a worthy guide to bring
Our English youth by travail unto fame.   20
  An eye whose judgment none affect could blind,
Friends to allure and foes to reconcile;
Whose piercing look did represent a mind
With virtue fraught, reposèd, void of guile.

The Frailty. **6. peason,** peas. **8. geason,** rare. *Description and Praise*. **1. Tuscan.** The Fitzgeralds were supposed to be descended from the Geraldis of Florence. **3–4. western isle . . . cliffs.** Elizabeth grew up in a part of Ireland that faces the cliffs of Wales. **6. princes' blood.** Elizabeth's mother was the granddaughter of Edward IV's queen. **8. With king's child,** in the household of the Princess Mary. **9. Hunsdon.** The meeting of Surrey and Elizabeth probably took place at Hunsdon in March, 1537. **11. Hampton.** Princess Mary, and presumably Elizabeth, were at Hampton Court in July, 1537. *Complaint*. **4. chair,** chariot.

Of the Death. **15. unparfited,** unfinished. **21. none affect,** no passion.

A heart where dread was never so impressed,
To hide the thought that might the truth advance;
In neither fortune lost nor yet repressed,
To swell in wealth or yield unto mischance.

A valiant corps where force and beauty met,
Happy—alas, too happy, but for foes! 30
Lived, and ran the race that nature set,
Of manhood's shape where she the mould did lose.

But to the heavens that simple soul is fled,
Which left with such as covet Christ to know
Witness of faith that never shall be dead;
Sent for our health, but not receivèd so.
Thus for our guilt this jewel have we lost:
The earth, his bones; the heavens possess his ghost.

THE THINGS THAT CAUSE A QUIET LIFE

WRITTEN BY MARTIAL

My friend, the things that do attain
The happy life be these, I find:
The riches left, not got with pain,
The fruitful ground, the quiet mind.

The equal friend—no grudge, no strife;
No charge of rule, nor governance;
Without disease, the healthy life,
The household of continuance;

The mean diet, no dainty fare;
Wisdom joined with simpleness; 10
The night dischargèd of all care,
Where wine the wit may not oppress.

The faithful wife, without debate;
Such sleeps as may beguile the night:
Content thyself with thine estate,
Neither wish death, nor fear his might.

PRISONED IN WINDSOR, HE RECOUNTETH HIS PLEASURE THERE PASSED

So cruel prison how could betide, alas,
As proud Windsor? Where I in lust and joy
With a king's son my childish years did pass
In greater feast than Priam's sons of Troy;
Where each sweet place returns a taste full sour:
The large green courts where we were wont to hove
With eyes cast up into the maidens' tower,
And easy sighs, such as folk draw in love;
The stately seats, the ladies bright of hue,
The dances short, long tales of great delight; 10
With words and looks that tigers could but rue,
Where each of us did plead the other's right;
The palm play where, despoilèd for the game,
With dazèd eyes oft we by gleams of love
Have missed the ball and got sight of our dame,
To bait her eyes, which kept the leads above;
The gravel ground, with sleeves tied on the helm,
On foaming horse, with swords and friendly hearts,
With cheer, as though one should another whelm,
Where we have fought, and chasèd oft with darts; 20
With silver drops the mead yet spread for ruth,
In active games of nimbleness and strength,
Where we did strain, trainèd with swarms of youth,
Our tender limbs that yet shot up in length;
The secret groves which oft we made resound
Of pleasant plaint and of our ladies' praise,
Recording oft what grace each one had found,
What hope of speed, what dread of long delays;
The wild forest, the clothèd holts with green,
With reins avaled, and swift ybreathèd horse, 30
With cry of hounds and merry blasts between,
Where we did chase the fearful hart of force;
The wide vales eke that harboured us each night,
Wherewith, alas, reviveth in my breast
The sweet accord; such sleeps as yet delight,
The pleasant dreams, the quiet bed of rest;
The secret thoughts imparted with such trust,
The wanton talk, the divers change of play,
The friendship sworn, each promise kept so just,
Wherewith we passed the winter night away. 40
And with this thought the blood forsakes the face,
The tears berain my cheeks of deadly hue,
The which as soon as sobbing sighs, alas,
Upsuppèd have, thus I my plaint renew:
O place of bliss, renewer of my woes,
Give me account—where is my noble fere?
Whom in thy walls thou dost each night enclose,
To other lief, but unto me most dear!
Echo, alas, that doth my sorrow rue,
Returns thereto a hollow sound of plaint. 50
Thus I alone, where all my freedom grew,
In prison pine with bondage and restraint;
And with remembrance of the greater grief
To banish the less, I find my chief relief.

11. **rue,** melt, awaken pity in. 13. **palm play,** old form of tennis, resembling modern handball. **despoilèd,** with impeding garments stripped off. 16. **leads,** either the leaden window-strips of the maiden's tower or small flat roofs whence the ladies watched the game. 17. **sleeves... helm,** a lady's favor on the helmet. 21. **silver drops,** probably dew, in which case **for ruth** later in the line is figurative. 30. **avaled,** slackened, lowered. 46. **fere?** companion. 48. **lief,** pleasing, acceptable.

38. **ghost,** spirit. *The Things That Cause.* 8. **continuance,** permanence, stability. *Prisoned.* 6. **hove,** linger.

Thomas Sackville, Earl of Dorset
1536-1608

Thomas Sackville, later Earl of Dorset, was born in 1536, and as a young member of the Inner Temple showed the interest in the arts expected of a Renaissance courtier. Before 1561, he had contributed the last two acts to the blank-verse tragedy *Gorboduc, or Ferrex and Porrex*, the first serious attempt to write a tragedy on English material in the classical form. After his contribution to *A Mirror for Magistrates* (see below), Sackville entered public life, became a member of Parliament in 1558, was knighted in 1567, was employed by Elizabeth on various important missions, became a member of the Privy Council, and served as Lord Treasurer. Elizabeth rewarded him with the titles of Baron Buckhurst and Earl of Dorset. He died in 1608.

The precise intention of Sackville's contribution to the *Mirror* is still in dispute. Certain of his collaborators, according to Baldwin, seem to have been surprised at his composing what we know as the *Induction*. " 'Hath he made a preface?' said one. 'What meaneth he thereby, seeing none other hath used the like order?' 'I will tell you the case thereof,' said I, 'which is this: after that he understood that some of the Council would not suffer the book to be printed in such order as we had agreed and determined, he purposed to have gotten at my hands all the tragedies that were before the Duke of Buckingham's, which he would have preserved in one volume. . . . And therefore to make a meet induction into the matter, he devised this poesy, which, in my judgment, is so well penned that I would not have any verse thereof left out of our volume.' " The implication of this discourse would seem to be that the *Induction* was planned as an introduction to the whole work, and that Sackville intended to frame all the complaints in a journey to the underworld.

A manuscript of Sackville's poem was discovered in 1931 in the library of St. John's College, Cambridge, of which Sackville had been a student almost four hundred years before. The manuscript contained about a hundred hitherto unknown lines and a number of unfinished stanzas. Not the least interesting of the new lines express Sackville's critical appreciation of Virgil "with his metre's majesty," of "old Ovid in his unkind exile," of Chaucer "chief that wrote in English verse," and of his contemporaries Wyatt and Surrey.

A Mirror for Magistrates was probably the most widely read collection of secular verse published during the reign of Elizabeth. It commended itself strongly to the average taste of the period. Even Puritans did not need to feel uncomfortable while reading this encyclopedia of historical poetry, since its intention was unwaveringly moralistic, it was completely lacking in humor, and its procession of great personages who had come to tragic ends furnished repeated opportunities for self-gratulation. Its popularity is also evidence of the persistence of medieval tastes throughout the sixteenth century, since, except for Sackville's contribution, there was little to differentiate the collection in either substance or style from such a fifteenth-century creation as Lydgate's *Fall of Princes*.

The original conceiver of the scheme seems to have been William Baldwin, an Oxford man, assistant to the printer Edward Whitchurch, and a friend of the Heywoods who inherited the Humanistic tradition of Sir Thomas More. The first version of the poems was apparently ready for publication in 1554, and Whitchurch began the printing of it under the title *A Memorial of Such Princes as Since the Time of King Richard the Second Have Been Unfortunate in the Realm of England*. He was prevented from going on with his work by a royal proclamation of June 13, 1555, suppressing undesirable books, including Hall's *Chronicle*. Since much of the material in the *Mirror* was derived from Hall, its publication was prevented by the Lord Chancellor, and it was only in 1559 that the *Mirror* appeared. Even then, certain "falls" had to be omitted.

The first part of the *Mirror*, 1559, contained nineteen tragedies; the second part, 1563, contained eight more, including what is commonly known as Sackville's *Induction and Complaint of the Duke of Buckingham*. Additions to the canon of lives before Richard II and long after appeared in 1574, 1578, 1587, and 1610. In the last and largest of these collections, the editor omitted the prose links of the earlier edition, and used Sackville's *Induction* as the introduction to the second of three groups of lives. In all, the *Mirror* treated a hundred tragedies, each of which ran to from fifty to four hundred lines. Some thirty historical plays written during the fifty years of the evolution of the collection drew material from the *Mirror*.

INDUCTION

The *Induction* is in the form of a medieval allegorical vision. On a gloomy winter night, as the poet is reflecting on the miserable fates of many great personages in England's history, he encounters Sorrow, who offers to conduct him to the realm of the dead, where he may hear from the victims' own lips their tragedies. On the way, they encounter the vividly visualized figures of Remorse, Dread, Revenge, Misery, Care, Sleep, Age, Malady, Famine, and War. The poet crosses the Acheron and enters Pluto's kingdom, where the first of the fallen heroes, the Duke of Buckingham, appears to relate his woes.

If the poem deserves its reputation as the finest long poem between Chaucer and Spenser, the grounds for its distinction are the sustained unity of its mood and tone, the powerful imagination with which an atmosphere is created and allegorical figures are realized, and its high metrical and technical competence and assurance.

The wrathful winter, 'proaching on apace,
With blustering blasts had all ybared the treen,
And old Saturnus, with his frosty face,
With chilling cold had pierced the tender green;
The mantles rent, wherein enwrappèd been
    The gladsome groves that now lay overthrown,
    The tapets torn, and every bloom down blown.

The soil, that erst so seemly was to seen,
Was all despoilèd of her beauty's hue;
And soote fresh flowers, wherewith the summer's queen
Had clad the earth, now Boreas' blasts down blew;   10
And small fowls flocking, in their song did rue
    The winter's wrath, wherewith each thing defaced
    In woeful wise bewailed the summer past.

Hawthorn had lost his motley livery,
The naked twigs were shivering all for cold,
And dropping down the tears abundantly;
Each thing, methought, with weeping eye me told
The cruel season, bidding me withhold
    Myself within; for I was gotten out   20
    Into the fields, whereas I walked about.

When lo, the night with misty mantles spread,
Gan dark the day and dim the azure skies;

2. **ybared**, bared. The "y" is a vaguely intensive archaic prefix to verbs, adverbs, adjectives, and nouns.   7. **tapets**, figured cloths, tapestries; here used figuratively for foliage. 10. **soote**, sweet.

And Venus in her message Hermes sped
To bloody Mars, to will him not to rise,
Which she herself approached in speedy wise;
    And Virgo, hiding her disdainful breast,
    With Thetis now had laid her down to rest.

Whiles Scorpio, dreading Sagittarius' dart,
Whose bow prest bent in fight, the string had slipped,   30
Down slid into the ocean flood apart;
The Bear, that in the Irish seas had dipped
His grisly feet, with speed from thence he whipped;
    For Thetis, hasting from the Virgin's bed,
    Pursued the Bear, that ere she came was fled.

And Phaëthon now, near reaching to his race
With glist'ring beams, gold streaming where they bent,
Was prest to enter in his resting place;
Erythius, that in the cart first went,
Had even now attained his journey's stent;   40
    And, fast declining, hid away his head,
    While Titan couched him in his purple bed.

And pale Cynthia, with her borrowed light,
Beginning to supply her brother's place,
Was past the noonstead six degrees in sight,
When sparkling stars amid the heaven's face
With twinkling light shone on the earth apace,
    That, while they brought about the nightè's chair,
    The dark had dimmed the day ere I was ware.

And sorrowing I to see the summer flowers,   50
The lively green, the lusty leas forlorn,
The sturdy trees so shattered with the showers,
The fields so fade that flourished so beforn,
It taught me well all earthly things be born
    To die the death, for nought long time may last;
    The summer's beauty yields to winter's blast.

Then looking upward to the heaven's leams,
With nightè's stars thick powdered everywhere,
Which erst so glistened with the golden streams
That cheerful Phoebus spread down from his sphere,   60
Beholding dark oppressing day so near;
    The sudden sight reducèd to my mind
    The sundry changes that in earth we find.

28. **Thetis**, an asteroid.   30. **prest**, ready.   39. **Erythius**, related to the island Erythia, one of the "happy isles" in the west; perhaps a western star.   40. **stent**, end. 42. **Titan**, the sun.   43. **Cynthia**, the moon.   48. **chair**, chariot, car.   57. **leams**, gleams, lights.   60. **Phoebus**, another name for the sun.

That musing on this worldly wealth in thought,
Which comes and goes more faster than we see
The flickering flame that with the fire is wrought,
My busy mind presented unto me
Such fall of peers as in this realm had be,
   That oft I wished some would their woes descrive,
   To warn the rest whom fortune left alive.   70

And straight forth stalking with redoubled pace,
For that I saw the night drew on so fast,
In black all clad there fell before my face
A piteous wight, whom woe had all forwaste;
Forth from her eyne the crystal tears out brast,
   And sighing sore, her hands she wrung and fold,
   Tare all her hair, that ruth was to behold.

Her body small, forwithered and forspent,
As is the stalk that summer's drought oppressed;
Her welkèd face with woeful tears besprent,   80
Her colour pale, and, as it seemed her best,
In woe and plaint reposèd was her rest;
   And as the stone that drops of water wears,
   So dented were her cheeks with fall of tears.

Her eyes swollen with flowing streams afloat;
Wherewith, her looks thrown up full piteously,
Her forceless hands together oft she smote,
With doleful shrieks that echoed in the sky;
Whose plaint such sighs did straight accompany,
   That, in my doom, was never man did see   90
   A wight but half so woebegone as she.

I stood aghast, beholding all her plight,
'Tween dread and dolor, so distrained in heart
That, while my hairs upstarted with the sight,
The tears outstreamed for sorrow of her smart;
But when I saw no end that could apart
   The deadly deule which she so sore did make,
   With doleful voice then thus to her I spake:

Unwrap thy woes, whatever wight thou be,
And stint betime to spill thyself with plaint;   100
Tell what thou art, and whence, for well I see
Thou canst not dure, with sorrow thus attaint.
And with that word of sorrow, all forfaint
   She lookèd up, and prostrate as she lay,
   With piteous sound, lo, thus she gan to say:

Alas, I, wretch whom thus thou seest distrained
With wasting woes that never shall aslake,
Sorrow I am, in endless torments pained
Among the Furies in the infernal lake
Where Pluto, god of Hell, so grisly black,   110
   Doth hold his throne, and Lethe's deadly taste
   Doth reave remembrance of each thing forepast.

Whence come I am, the dreary destiny
And luckless lot for to bemoan of those
Whom fortune, in this maze of misery,
Of wretched chance, most woeful mirrors chose;
That when thou seest how lightly they did lose
   Their pomp, their power, and that they thought most sure,
   Thou mayst soon deem no earthly joy may dure.

Whose rueful voice no sooner had out brayed   120
Those woeful words wherewith she sorrowed so,
But out, alas, she shright and never stayed,
Fell down, and all-to dashed herself for woe;
The cold pale dread my limbs gan overgo,
   And I so sorrowed at her sorrows eft
   That, what with grief and fear, my wits were reft.

*   *   *

Lastly, stood War, in glittering arms yclad,
With visage grim, stern looks, and blackly hued;
In his right hand a naked sword he had,
That to the hilts was all with blood imbrued;   130
And in his left, that kings and kingdoms rued,
   Famine and fire he held, and therewithal
   He razèd towns and threw down towers and all.

Cities he sacked and realms that whilom flowered
In honour, glory, and rule above the best,
He overwhelmed and all their fame devoured,
Consumed, destroyed, wasted, and never ceased
Till he their wealth, their name, and all oppressed;
   His face forhewed with wounds, and by his side
   There hung his targe, with gashes deep and wide.   140

In midst of which, depainted there, we found
Deadly Debate, all full of snaky hair,
That with a bloody fillet was ybound,
Out-breathing nought but discord everywhere,
And round about were portrayed, here and there,
   The hugy hosts, Darius and his power,
   His kings, princes, his peers, and all his flower.

---

74. **wight**, creature. **forwaste**. The "for" is an intensive—"very," "all."   75. **brast**, burst.   77. **ruth**, pitiful. 80. **welkèd**, faded, withered.   97. **deule**, dole, lamentation. 102. **dure**, endure.

112. **reave**, take away.   122. **shright**, shrieked. 123. **all-to**, entirely.   125. **eft**, in turn.   140–217. **targe . . . town** (page 303). This elaborate description of the shield of War should be compared with the description of Achilles' shield in the *Iliad*, Book XVIII. Such descriptions, under the influence of Homer's great example, became an important epic convention. Compare the building of Pandemonium in *Paradise Lost*, Book I.

Whom great Macedo vanquished there in sight
With deep slaughter, despoiling all his pride,
Pierced through his realms and daunted all his
    might;   150
Duke Hannibal beheld I there beside,
In Canna's field victor how he did ride,
    And woeful Romans that in vain withstood,
    And consul Paulus covered all in blood.

Yet saw I more: the fight at Thrasimene,
And Treby field, and eke when Hannibal
And worthy Scipio last in arms were seen
Before Carthago gate, to try for all
The world's empire, to whom it should befall;
    There saw I Pompey and Caesar clad in arms,
    Their hosts allied and all their civil harms. 161

With conquerors' hands, forbathed in their own
    blood.
And Caesar weeping over Pompey's head;
Yet saw I Sulla and Marius where they stood,
Their great cruelty and the deep bloodshed
Of friends; Cyrus I saw and his host dead,
    And how the queen with great despite hath flung
    His head in blood of them she overcome.

Xerxes, the Persian king, yet saw I there
With his huge host that drank the rivers dry,   170
Dismounted hills, and made the vales uprear,
His host and all yet saw I plain, perdy;
Thebes I saw, all razed how it did lie
    In heaps of stones, and Tyrus put to spoil,
    With walls and towers flat evened with the soil.

But Troy, alas, methought above them all,
It made mine eyes in very tears consume,
When I beheld the woeful word befall,
That by the wrathful will of gods was come;
And Jove's unmovèd sentence and foredoom   180
    On Priam king, and on his town so bent,
    I could not lin, but I must there lament.

And that the more, sith destiny was so stern
As, force perforce, there mought no force avail,
But she must fall, and by her fall we learn
That cities, towers, wealth, world, and all shall
    quail;
No manhood, might, nor nothing mought prevail;
    All were there prest, full many a prince and peer,
    And many a knight that sold his death full dear.

Not worthy Hector, worthiest of them all,   190
Her hope, her joy, his force is now for nought;
O Troy, Troy, Troy, there is no boot but bale,
The hugy horse within thy walls is brought;
Thy turrets fall, thy knights, that whilom fought
    In arms amid the field, are slain in bed,
    Thy gods defiled and all thy honour dead.

The flames upspring and cruelly they creep
From wall to roof till all to cinders waste;
Some fire the houses where the wretches sleep,
Some rush in here, some run in there as fast;   200
In everywhere or sword or fire they taste;
    The walls are torn, the towers whirled to the
        ground;
    There is no mischief but may there be found.

Cassandra yet there saw I how they haled
From Pallas' house, with spercled tress undone,
Her wrists fast bound and with Greeks' rout em-
    paled;
And Priam eke, in vain how did he run
To arms, whom Pyrrhus with despite hath done
    To cruel death, and bathed him in the baign
    Of his son's blood, before the altar slain.   210

But how can I descrive the doleful sight
That in the shield so livelike fair did shine?
Sith in this world I think was never wight
Could have set forth the half, not half so fine;
I can no more but tell how there is seen
    Fair Ilium fall in burning red gledes down,
    And from the soil great Troy, Neptunus' town.

Herefrom when scarce I could mine eyes withdraw,
That filled with tears as doth the springing well,
We passèd on so far forth till we saw   220
Rude Acheron, a loathsome lake to tell,
That boils and bubs up swelth as black as hell;
    Where grisly Charon, at their fixèd tide,
    Still ferries ghosts unto the farther side.

The aged god no sooner Sorrow spied,
But hasting straight unto the bank apace,
With hollow call unto the rout he cried
To swerve apart and give the goddess place;
Straight it was done, when to the shore we pace,
    Where, hand in hand as we then linkèd fast,   230
    Within the boat we are together placed.

And forth we launch full fraughted to the brink,
When with the unwonted weight, the rusty keel

---

148. **Macedo,** Alexander the Great.   156. **Treby,** Trebia, a river in northern Italy, the scene of Hannibal's victory over the Romans.   171. **Dismounted,** leveled.
172. **perdy,** verily, corruption of the French "by God."
182. **lin,** cease.   183. **sith,** since.   184. **mought,** might.
205. **spercled,** sparkled.   209. **baign,** bath.
216. **gledes,** burning pieces.   222. **swelth,** whirlpool.

Began to crack as if the same should sink;
We hoise up mast and sail, that in a while
We fetched the shore, where scarcely we had while
   For to arrive, but that we heard anon
   A three-sound bark confounded all in one.

We had not long forth passed but that we saw
Black Cerberus, the hideous hound of hell,   240
With bristles reared and with a three-mouthed jaw
Fordinning the air with his horrible yell,
Out of the deep dark cave where he did dwell;
   The goddess straight he knew, and by and by,
   He peased and couched while that we passèd by.

Thence come we to the horror and the hell,
The large great kingdoms and the dreadful reign
Of Pluto in his throne where he did dwell,
The wide waste places and the hugy plain,
The wailings, shrieks, and sundry sorts of pain,   250
   The sighs, the sobs, the deep and deadly groan,
   Earth, air, and all, resounding plaint and moan.

Here puled the babes, and here the maids unwed
With folded hands their sorry chance bewailed,
Here wept the guiltless slain, and lovers dead,
That slew themselves when nothing else availed;
A thousand sorts of sorrows here, that wailed
   With sighs and tears, sobs, shrieks, and all yfear,
   That oh, alas, it was a hell to hear.

We stayed us straight, and with a rueful fear,   260
Beheld this heavy sight, while from mine eyes
The vapoured tears down stillèd here and there,
And Sorrow eke, in far more woeful wise,
Took on with plaint, upheaving to the skies

Her wretched hands, that with her cry the rout
Gan all in heaps to swarm us round about.

Lo here, quoth Sorrow, princes of renown,
That whilom sat on top of fortune's wheel,
Now laid full low, like wretches whirlèd down,
Even with one frown, that stayed but with a smile;   270
And now behold the thing that thou, erewhile,
   Saw only in thought, and what thou now shalt hear,
   Recount the same to kesar, king, and peer.

Then first came Henry, Duke of Buckingham,
His cloak of black all pilled and quite forworn,
Wringing his hands, and fortune oft doth blame,
Which of a duke hath made him now her scorn;
With ghastly looks, as one in manner lorn,
   Oft spread his arms, stretched hands he joins as fast
   With rueful cheer and vapoured eyes upcast.   280

His cloak he rent, his manly breast he beat,
His hair all torn, about the place it lay;
My heart so molt to see his grief so great,
As feelingly methought it dropped away;
His eyes they whirled about withouten stay,
   With stormy sighs the place did so complain,
   As if his heart at each had burst in twain.

Thrice he began to tell his doleful tale,
And thrice with sighs did swallow up his voice,
At each of which he shriekèd so withal,   290
As though the heavens rivèd with the noise;
Till at the last, recovering his voice,
   Supping the tears that all his breast berained,
   On cruel fortune, weeping, thus he plained.

245. **peased**, became still.   253. **puled**, whined.
262. **stillèd**, dropped.

273. **kesar**, kaiser, Roman emperor (Caesar).   275. **pilled**, bald, the fur worn off.   283. **molt**, melted.

Sir Thomas Hoby
1530–1566

Sir Thomas Hoby, the English translator, was reasonably well equipped for his task. Born in 1530, he attended St. John's College, Cambridge, when it was at the peak of its Humanistic brilliance under Sir John Cheke, and completed his education by traveling widely on the Continent, keeping a lively journal of his observations. In the autumn of 1552, he translated at the request of the Marchioness of Northampton the part of *Il Cortegiano* of Count Baldassare Castiglione dealing with the courtly ideal of womanhood. In 1558, he married Elizabeth Cooke, a sister of Sir Thomas Bacon's mother and, like her sister, one of the most learned young women of the time. The complete translation, *The Courtier*, was published in 1561. Hoby was knighted by Queen Elizabeth in 1566, and died on July 13 of the same year.

Hoby's motives in translating *The Courtier* were distinctly patriotic. He says that whereas foreigners "set their delight and bend themselves with an honest strife of matching others to turn into their mother tongue not only the witty writings of other languages but also of all the philosophers and all sciences both Greek and Latin, our men ween it sufficient to have a perfect knowledge to no other end but to profit themselves." He also had a distinct theory about translation. "I have endeavoured," he writes, "myself to follow the very meaning and words of the author without being misled by fancy or leaving out any parcel one or other, whereof I know not how some of the interpreters of this book into other languages can excuse themselves, and the more they be conferred, the more it will perchance appear." As a matter of fact, Hoby carried out his theory of translation almost too faithfully. On some occasions his translation is awkwardly literal. He fails to capture the grace and elegance of the original; but he enlivens his translation with vivid colloquial phrases which give the work a distinctly Elizabethan quality.

from THE COURTIER

Il Cortegiano (*The Courtier*) of Count Baldassare Castiglione is the greatest of the Renaissance books of courtesy. Published in Venice by the house of Aldus in 1528, it was translated into Spanish in 1534, into French in 1538, and into English in 1561. Before 1603, it had run through one hundred and five editions on the Continent and in England. *The Courtier* expounds in a series of dialogues among various distinguished guests at the court of the Duke of Urbino—where Castiglione had been in service from 1504 to 1508—the Renaissance ideal of courtly training and accomplishments for both men and women. Its superiority to the hundreds of other similar discussions of the period is to be found in the comprehensiveness and detail of the ideal painted, and the elegance and eloquence with which it is described.

The Courtier was one translation from the Italian of which even the sternest English moralists could approve. Of it, the pedagogue Ascham wrote before 1570: "To join learning with comely exercises, Count Baldassare Castiglione, in his book *Cortegiano*, doth trimly teach, which book, advisedly read, and diligently followed but one year in England would do a young man more good, I wis, than three years' travel abroad spent in Italy. And I marvel this book is no more read in the Court than it is, seeing it is so well translated into English by a worthy gentleman, Sir Thomas Hoby, who was many ways well furnished with learning and very expert in knowledge of divers tongues." Sidney is said never to have gone abroad without a copy of *The Courtier* in his pocket.

The passage given below is Bembo's discourse on Platonic love. This interpretation of the Platonic doctrine was one of the major avenues by which it reached and influenced profoundly a whole generation of Renaissance poets. The ultimate source of this passage is Socrates' report of his conversation with Diotima, in Plato's *Symposium*.

HERE Bembo paused a while as though he would breathe him, and when all things were whist Messer Morello, of Ortona, said: "And in case there were some old man more fresh and lusty and of a better complexion than many young men, why would you not have it lawful for him to love with the love that young men love?"

The Duchess laughed, and said: "If the love of young men be so unlucky, why would you, Messer
10 Morello, that old men should also love with this unluckiness? But in case you were old, as these men say you be, you would not thus procure the hurt of old men."

Messer Morello answered: "The hurt of old men, meseemeth, Messer Pietro Bembo procureth, who will have them to love after a sort that I for my

3. **whist,** silent.

part understand not; and, methink, the possessing of this beauty which he praiseth so much, without the body, is a dream."

"Do you believe, Messer Morello," quoth then Count Lodovico, "that beauty is always so good a thing as Messer Pietro Bembo speaketh of?"

"Not I, in good sooth," answered Messer Morello. "But I remember rather that I have seen many beautiful women of a most ill inclination, cruel and spiteful, and it seemeth that, in a manner, it happeneth always so, for beauty maketh them proud, and pride, cruel."

Count Lodovico said, smiling: "To you perhaps they seem cruel, because they content you not with that which you would have. But cause Messer Pietro Bembo to teach you in what sort old men ought to covet beauty, and what to seek at their ladies' hands, and what to content themselves withal; and in not passing out of these bounds you shall see that they shall be neither proud nor cruel, and will satisfy you with what you shall require."

Messer Morello seemed then somewhat out of patience, and said: "I will not know the thing that toucheth me not. But cause you to be taught how the young men ought to covet this beauty that are not so fresh and lusty as old men be."

Here Sir Federico, to pacify Messer Morello and to break their talk, would not suffer Count Lodovico to make answer, but interrupting him said: "Perhaps Messer Morello is not altogether out of the way in saying that beauty is not always good, for the beauty of women is many times cause of infinite evils in the world—hatred, war, mortality, and destruction, whereof the razing of Troy can be a good witness; and beautiful women for the most part be either proud and cruel, as is said, or unchaste; but Messer Morello would find no fault with that. There be also many wicked men that have the comeliness of a beautiful countenance, and it seemeth that Nature hath so shaped them because they may be the readier to deceive, and that this amiable look were like a bait that covereth the hook."

Then Messer Pietro Bembo: "Believe not," quoth he, "but beauty is always good."

Here Count Lodovico, because he would return again to his former purpose, interrupted him and said: "Since Messer Morello passeth not to understand that which is so necessary for him, teach it me, and show me how old men may come by this happiness of love, for I will not care to be counted old, so it may profit me."

Messer Pietro Bembo laughed, and said: "First will I take the error out of these gentlemen's mind, and afterward will I satisfy you also." So beginning afresh: "My Lords," quoth he, "I would not that with speaking ill of beauty, which is a holy thing, any of us as profane and wicked should purchase him the wrath of God. Therefore, to give Messer Morello and Sir Federico warning, that they lose not their sight, as Stesichorus did—a pain most meet for whoso dispraiseth beauty—I say that beauty cometh of God and is like a circle, the goodness whereof is the center. And therefore, as there can be no circle without a center, no more can beauty be without goodness. Whereupon doth very seldom an ill soul dwell in a beautiful body. And therefore is the outward beauty a true sign of the inward goodness, and in bodies this comeliness is imprinted more or less, as it were, for a mark of the soul, whereby she is outwardly known; as in trees, in which the beauty of the buds giveth a testimony of the goodness of the fruit. And the very same happeneth in bodies, as it is seen that palmisters by the visage know many times the conditions and otherwhile the thoughts of men. And, which is more, in beasts also a man may discern by the face the quality of the courage, which in the body declareth itself as much as it can. Judge you how plainly in the face of a lion, a horse, and an eagle, a man shall discern anger, fierceness, and stoutness; in lambs and doves, simpleness and very innocency; the crafty subtlety in foxes and wolves; and the like, in a manner, in all other living creatures. The foul therefore for the most part be also evil, and the beautiful good. Therefore it may be said that beauty is a face pleasant, merry, comely, and to be desired for goodness; and foulness a face dark, uglesome, unpleasant, and to be shunned for ill. And in case you will consider all things, you shall find that whatsoever is good and profitable hath also evermore the comeliness of beauty. Behold the state of this great engine of the world, which God created for the health and preservation of everything that was made: the heaven round beset with so many heavenly lights; and in the middle the earth environed with the elements and upheld with the very weight of itself; the sun, that compassing about giveth light to the whole, and in winter season draweth to the lowermost sign, afterward by little and little climbeth again to the other part; the moon, that of him taketh her light, according as she draweth nigh or goeth farther from him; and the other five stars that diversely keep the

7. **Stesichorus,** Greek lyric poet (c. 640–555 B.C.), said to have been struck blind for slandering Helen of Troy in a poem. 31. **foul,** ugly, ill-favored. 50. **five stars,** the planets then known. Uranus, Neptune, and Pluto have since been added.

very same course. These things among themselves have such force by the knitting together of an order so necessarily framed that, with altering them any one jot, they should all be loosed and the world would decay. They have also such beauty and comeliness that all the wits men have cannot imagine a more beautiful matter.

"Think now of the shape of man, which may be called a little world, in whom every parcel of his body is seen to be necessarily framed by art and not by hap, and then the form altogether most beautiful, so that it were a hard matter to judge whether the members (as the eyes, the nose, the mouth, the ears, the arms, the breast, and in like manner the other parts) give either more profit to the countenance and the rest of the body or comeliness. The like may be said of all other living creatures. Behold the feathers of fowls; the leaves and boughs of trees, which be given them of Nature to keep them in their being, and yet have they withal a very great sightliness. Leave Nature, and come to art. What thing is so necessary in sailing vessels as the forepart, the sides, the mainyards, the mast, the sails, the stern, oars, anchors, and tacklings? All these things notwithstanding are so well-favoured in the eye that unto whoso beholdeth them they seem to have been found out as well for pleasure as for profit. Pillars and great beams uphold high buildings and palaces, and yet are they no less pleasureful unto the eyes of the beholders than profitable to the buildings. When men began first to build, in the middle of temples and houses they reared the ridge of the roof, not to make the works to have a better show, but because the water might the more commodiously avoid on both sides; yet unto profit there was forthwith adjoined a fair sightliness, so that if, under the sky where falleth neither hail nor rain, a man should build a temple without a reared ridge, it is to be thought that it could have neither a sightly show nor any beauty. Besides other things, therefore, it giveth a great praise to the world in saying that it is beautiful. It is praised in saying the beautiful heaven, beautiful earth, beautiful sea, beautiful rivers, beautiful woods, trees, gardens, beautiful cities, beautiful churches, houses, armies. In conclusion, this comely and holy beauty is a wondrous setting out of everything. And it may be said that good and beautiful be after a sort one self thing, especially in the bodies of men; of the beauty whereof the nighest cause, I suppose, is the beauty of the soul; the which, as a partner of the right and heavenly beauty, maketh sightly and beautiful whatever she

35. avoid, leave (drain off).

toucheth, and most of all, if the body, where she dwelleth, be not of so vile a matter that she cannot imprint in it her property. Therefore beauty is the true monument and spoil of the victory of the soul, when she with heavenly influence beareth rule over material and gross nature, and with her light overcometh the darkness of the body. It is not, then, to be spoken that beauty maketh women proud or cruel, although it seem so to Messer Morello. Neither yet ought beautiful women to bear the blame of that hatred, mortality, and destruction which the unbridled appetites of men are the cause of. I will not now deny that it is possible also to find in the world beautiful women unchaste; yet not because beauty inclineth them to unchaste living, for it rather plucketh them from it, and leadeth them into the way of virtuous conditions, through the affinity that beauty hath with goodness; but otherwhile ill bringing up, the continual provocations of lovers' tokens, poverty, hope, deceits, fear, and a thousand other matters, overcome the steadfastness, yea, of beautiful and good women; and for these and like causes may also beautiful men become wicked."

Then said the Lord Cesare: "In case the Lord Gaspar's saying be true of yesternight, there is no doubt but the fair women be more chaste than the foul."

"And what was my saying?" quoth the Lord Gaspar.

The Lord Cesare answered: "If I do well bear in mind, your saying was that the women that are sued to always refuse to satisfy him that sueth to them, but those that are not sued to sue to others. There is no doubt but the beautiful women have always more suitors, and be more instantly laid at in love, than the foul. Therefore the beautiful always deny, and consequently be more chaste than the foul, which, not being sued to, sue unto others."

Messer Pietro Bembo laughed, and said: "This argument cannot be answered to."

Afterward he proceeded: "It chanceth also, oftentimes, that as the other senses, so the sight is deceived and judgeth a face beautiful which indeed is not beautiful. And because in the eyes and in the whole countenance of some woman a man beholdeth otherwhile a certain lavish wantonness painted, with dishonest flickerings, many, whom that manner delighteth because it promiseth them an easiness to come by the thing that they covet, call it beauty; but indeed it is a cloaked unshamefastness, unworthy of so honourable and holy a name."

Messer Pietro Bembo held his peace, but those

lords still were earnest upon him to speak somewhat more of this love and of the way to enjoy beauty aright, and at the last: "Methink," quoth he, "I have showed plainly enough that old men may love more happily than young, which was my drift; therefore it belongeth not to me to enter any farther."

Count Lodovico answered: "You have better declared the unluckiness of young men than the happiness of old men, whom you have not as yet taught what way they must follow in this love of theirs; only you have said that they must suffer themselves to be guided by reason, and the opinion of many is that it is unpossible for love to stand with reason."

Bembo notwithstanding sought to make an end of reasoning, but the Duchess desired him to say on, and he began thus afresh: "Too unlucky were the nature of man, if our soul, in which this so fervent coveting may lightly arise, should be driven to nourish it with that only which is common to her with beasts, and could not turn it to the other noble part, which is proper to her. Therefore, since it is so your pleasure, I will not refuse to reason upon this noble matter. And because I know myself unworthy to talk of the most holy mysteries of Love, I beseech him to lead my thought and my tongue so that I may show this excellent Courtier how to love contrary to the wonted manner of the common ignorant sort. And even as from my childhood I have dedicated all my whole life unto him, so also now that my words may be answerable to the same intent, and to the praise of him: I say, therefore, that since the nature of man in youthful age is so much inclined to sense, it may be granted the Courtier, while he is young, to love sensually; but in case afterward also, in his riper years, he chance to be set on fire with this coveting of love, he ought to be good and circumspect, and heedful that he beguile not himself to be led wilfully into the wretchedness that in young men deserveth more to be pitied than blamed and contrariwise in old men, more to be blamed than pitied. Therefore when an amiable countenance of a beautiful woman cometh in his sight, that is accompanied with noble conditions and honest behaviours, so that, as one practised in love, he wotteth well that his hue hath an agreement with hers, as soon as he is aware that his eyes snatch that image and carry it to the heart, and that the soul beginneth to behold it with pleasure, and feeleth within herself the influence that stirreth her and by little and little setteth her in heat, and that those lively little spirits that twinkle out through the eyes put continually fresh nourishment to the fire, he ought in this beginning to seek a speedy remedy and to raise up reason, and with her to fence the fortress of his heart, and to shut in such wise the passages against sense and appetites that they may enter neither with force nor subtle practice. Thus, if the flame be quenched, the jeopardy is also quenched. But in case it continue or increase, then must the Courtier determine, when he perceiveth he is taken, to shun thoroughly all filthiness of common love, and so enter into the holy way of love with the guide of reason, and first consider that the body where that beauty shineth is not the fountain whence beauty springeth, but rather because beauty is bodiless and, as we have said, an heavenly shining beam, she loseth much of her honour when she is coupled with that vile subject and full of corruption, because the less she is partner thereof, the more perfect she is, and, clean sundered from it, is most perfect. And as a man heareth not with his mouth, nor smelleth with his ears, no more can he also in any manner wise enjoy beauty, nor satisfy the desire that she stirreth up in our minds, with feeling, but with the sense unto whom beauty is the very butt to level at, namely, the virtue of seeing. Let him lay aside, therefore, the blind judgment of the sense, and enjoy with his eyes the brightness, the comeliness, the loving sparkles, laughters, gestures, and all the other pleasant furnitures of beauty, especially with hearing the sweetness of her voice, the tunableness of her words, the melody of her singing and playing on instruments (in case the woman beloved be a musician), and so shall he with the most dainty food feed the soul through the means of these two senses which have little bodily substance in them and be the ministers of reason, without entering farther toward the body with coveting unto any longing otherwise than honest. Afterward let him obey, please, and honour with all reverence his woman, and reckon her more dear to him than his own life, and prefer all her commodities and pleasures before his own, and love no less in her the beauty of the mind than of the body. Therefore let him have a care not to suffer her to run into any error, but with lessons and good exhortations seek always to frame her to modesty, to temperance, to true honesty, and so to work that there may never take place in her other than pure thoughts and far wide from all filthiness of vices. And thus in sowing of virtue in the garden of that mind, he shall also gather the fruits of most beautiful conditions, and savour them with a marvellous good relish. And this shall be the right engendering and imprinting of beauty in beauty, the which some hold opinion to be the end of love. In this manner shall our Courtier be most acceptable to his lady, and she will always show herself toward him tractable, lowly, and sweet in language, and as willing to please him as to be beloved of him; and the wills of them both shall be most honest and agreeable, and they consequently shall be most happy."

Here Messer Morello: "The engendering," quoth he, "of beauty in beauty aright were the engendering of a beautiful child in a beautiful woman; and I would think it a more manifest token a great deal that she loved her lover, if she pleased him with this than with the sweetness of language that you speak of."

Messer Pietro Bembo laughed, and said: "You must not, Messer Morello, pass your bounds. I may tell you it is not a small token that a woman loveth when she giveth unto her lover her beauty, which is so precious a matter; and by the ways that be a passage to the soul (that is to say, the sight and the hearing) sendeth the looks of her eyes, the image of her countenance, and the voice of her words, that pierce into the lover's heart and give a witness of her love."

Messer Morello said: "Looks and words may be, and oftentimes are, false witnesses. Therefore whoso hath not a better pledge of love, in my judgment he is in an ill assurance. And surely I looked still that you would have made this woman of yours somewhat more courteous and free toward the Courtier than my Lord Giuliano hath made his; but meseemeth you be both of the property of those judges that, to appear wise, give sentence against their own."

Bembo said: "I am well pleased to have this woman much more courteous toward my Courtier not young than Lord Giuliano's is to the young; and that with good reason, because mine coveteth but honest matters, and therefore may the woman grant him them all without blame. But my Lord Giuliano's woman, that is not so assured of the modesty of the young man, ought to grant him the honest matters only, and deny him the dishonest. Therefore more happy is mine, that hath granted him whatsoever he requireth, than the other, that hath part granted and part denied. And because you may moreover the better understand that reasonable love is more happy than sensual, I say unto you that self-same things in sensual ought to be denied otherwhile, and in reasonable granted; because in the one they be honest, and in the other dishonest. Therefore the woman, to please her good lover, besides the granting him merry countenances, familiar and secret talk, jesting, dallying, hand-in-hand, may also lawfully and without blame come to kissing, which in sensual love, according to Lord Giuliano's rule, is not lawful. For since a kiss is a knitting together both of body and soul, it is to be feared lest the sensual lover will be more inclined to the part of the body than of the soul; but the reasonable lover wotteth well that although the mouth be a parcel of the body, yet is it an issue for the words that be the interpreters of the soul, and for the inward breath, which is also called the soul; and therefore hath a delight to join his mouth with the woman's beloved with a kiss— not to stir him to any unhonest desire, but because he feeleth that that bond is the opening of an entry to the souls, which, drawn with a coveting the one of the other, pour themselves by turn the one into the other's body, and be so mingled together that each of them hath two souls, and one alone so framed of them both ruleth, in a manner, two bodies. Whereupon a kiss may be said to be rather a coupling together of the soul than of the body, because it hath such force in her that it draweth her unto it, and, as it were, separateth her from the body. For this do all chaste lovers covet a kiss as a coupling of souls together. And therefore Plato, the divine lover, saith that in kissing his soul came as far as his lips to depart out of the body. And because the separating of the soul from the matters of the sense, and the thorough coupling of her with matters of understanding, may be betokened by a kiss, Solomon saith in his heavenly book of ballads, 'Oh that he would kiss me with a kiss of his mouth,' to express the desire he had that his soul might be ravished through heavenly love to the beholding of heavenly beauty in such manner that, coupling herself inwardly with it, she might forsake the body."

They stood all hearkening heedfully to Bembo's reasoning, and after he had stayed a while and saw that none spake, he said: "Since you have made me to begin to show our not young Courtier this happy love, I will lead him yet somewhat farther forward, because to stand still at this stay were somewhat perilous for him, considering, as we have oftentimes said, the soul is most inclined to the senses, and for all reason with discourse chooseth well, and knoweth that beauty not to spring of the body, and therefore setteth a bridle to the unhonest desires, yet to behold it always in that body doth oftentimes corrupt the right judgment. And where no other inconvenience ensueth upon it, one's absence from the wight beloved carrieth a great passion with it; because the influence of that beauty when it is present giveth a wondrous delight to the lover, and, setting his heart on fire, quickeneth and melteth certain virtues in a trance and congealed in the soul, the which, nourished with the heat of love, flow about and go bubbling nigh the heart, and thrust out through the eyes those spirits which be most fine vapours made of the purest and clearest part of the blood, which receive the image of beauty and deck it with a thousand sundry furnitures. Whereupon the soul taketh a delight, and with a certain wonder is aghast, and yet enjoyeth she it, and, as it were, astonied together with the pleasure, feeleth the fear and reverence that men accustomably have toward holy matters, and thinketh herself to be in paradise. The lover, therefore, that considereth only the beauty in the body, loseth this treasure and happiness as soon as the woman beloved with her departure leaveth the eyes without their brightness, and consequently the soul as a widow without her joy. For since beauty is far off, that influence of love setteth not the heart on fire, as it did in presence. Whereupon the pores be dried up and withered, and yet doth the remembrance of beauty somewhat stir those virtues of the soul in such wise that they seek to scatter abroad the spirits, and they, finding the ways closed up, have no issue, and still they seek to get out, and so with those shootings enclosed prick the soul and torment her bitterly, as young children when in their tender gums they begin to breed teeth. And hence come the tears, sighs, vexations, and torments of lovers; because the soul is always in affliction and travail and, in a manner, waxeth wood, until the beloved beauty cometh before her once again, and then she is immediately pacified and taketh breath, and, throughly bent to it, is nourished with most dainty food, and by her will would never depart from so sweet a sight. To avoid, therefore, the torment of this absence, and to enjoy beauty without passion, the Courtier by the help of reason must full and wholly call back again the coveting of the body to beauty alone, and, in what he can, behold it in itself simple and pure, and frame it within his imagination sundered from all matter, and so make it friendly and loving to his soul, and there enjoy it, and have it with him day and night, in every time and place, without mistrust ever to lose it; keeping always fast in mind that the body is a most diverse thing from beauty, and not only not increaseth but diminisheth the perfection of it. In this wise shall our not young Courtier be out of all bitterness and wretchedness that young men feel, in a manner continually, as jealousies, suspicions, disdains, angers, desperations, and certain rages full of madness, whereby many times they be led into so great error that some do not only beat the women whom they love, but rid themselves out of their life. He shall do no wrong to the husband, father, brethren, or kinsfolk of the woman beloved. He shall not bring her in slander. He shall not be in case with much ado otherwhile to refrain his eyes and tongue from discovering his desires to others. He shall not take thought at departure or in absence, because he shall evermore carry his precious treasure about with him shut fast within his heart. And besides, through the virtue of imagination, he shall fashion within himself that beauty much more fair than it is indeed. But among commodities the lover shall find another yet far greater, in case he will take this love for a stair, as it were, to climb up to another far higher than it. The which he shall bring to pass, if he will go and consider with himself what a strict bond it is to be always in the trouble to behold the beauty of one body alone. And therefore, to come out of this so narrow a room, he shall gather in his thought by little and little so many ornaments that mingling all beauties together he shall make a universal concept, and bring the multitude of them to the unity of one alone, that is generally spread over all the nature of man. And thus shall he behold no more the particular beauty of one woman, but a universal, that decketh out all bodies. Whereupon, being made dim with this greater light, he shall not pass upon the lesser, and, burning in a more excellent flame, he shall little esteem it that he set great store by at the first. This stair of love, though it be very noble and such as few arrive at it, yet is it not in this sort to be called perfect, forsomuch as where the imagination is of force to make conveyance and hath no knowledge but through those beginnings that the senses help her withal, she is not clean purged from gross darkness; and therefore, though she do consider that universal beauty in sunder and in itself alone, yet doth she not well and clearly discern it, nor without some doubtfulness, by reason of the agreement that the fancies have with the body. Wherefore such as come to this love are like young birds almost flush, which for all they flutter a little their tender wings, yet dare they not stray far from the nest, nor commit themselves to the wind and open weather. When our Courtier, therefore, shall be come to this point, although he may be called a good and happy lover, in respect of them that be drowned in the misery of sensual love, yet will I not have him to set his heart at rest, but boldly proceed farther, following the highway after his guide, that leadeth him to the point of true happiness. And

13. **commodities,** profits.

thus, instead of going out of his wit with thought, as he must do that will consider the bodily beauty, he may come into his wit to behold the beauty that is seen with the eyes of the mind, which then begin to be sharp and thorough-seeing, when the eyes of the body lose the flower of their sightliness.

"Therefore the soul, rid of vices, purged with the studies of true philosophy, occupied in spiritual, and exercised in matters of understanding, turning her to the beholding of her own substance, as it were raised out of a most deep sleep, openeth the eyes that all men have and few occupy, and seeth in herself a shining beam of that light which is the true image of the angel-like beauty partened with her, whereof she also partneth with the body a feeble shadow; therefore, waxed blind about earthly matters, is made most quick of sight about heavenly. And otherwhile when the stirring virtues of the body are withdrawn alone through earnest beholding, either fast bound through sleep, when she is not hindered by them, she feeleth a certain privy smell of the right angel-like beauty, and, ravished with the shining of that light, beginneth to be inflamed, and so greedily followeth after that in a manner she waxeth drunken and beside herself, for coveting to couple herself with it, having found, to her weening, the footsteps of God, in the beholding of whom, as in her happy end, she seeketh to settle herself. And therefore, burning in this most happy flame, she ariseth to the noblest part of her, which is the understanding, and there, no more shadowed with the dark night of earthly matters, seeth the heavenly beauty; but yet doth she not for all that enjoy it altogether perfectly, because she beholdeth it only in her particular understanding, which cannot conceive the passing great universal beauty; whereupon, not thoroughly satisfied with this benefit, love giveth unto the soul a greater happiness. For like as through the particular beauty of one body he guideth her to the universal beauty of all bodies, even so in the last degree of perfection through particular understanding he guideth her to the universal understanding. Thus the soul kindled in the most holy fire of true heavenly love fleeth to couple herself with the nature of angels, and not only clean forsaketh sense, but hath no more need of the discourse of reason, for, being changed into an angel, she understandeth all things that may be understood; and without any veil or cloud she seeth the main sea of the pure heavenly beauty, and receiveth it into her, and enjoyeth that sovereign happiness that cannot be comprehended of the senses. Since, therefore, the beauties which we daily see with these our dim eyes in bodies subject to corruption, that nevertheless be nothing else but dreams and most thin shadows of beauty, seem unto us so well-favoured and comely that oftentimes they kindle in us a most burning fire, and with such delight that we reckon no happiness may be compared to it that we feel otherwhile through the only look which the beloved countenance of a woman casteth at us; what happy wonder, what blessed abashment, may we reckon that to be that taketh the souls which come to have a sight of the heavenly beauty? What sweet flame, what sweet incense, may a man believe that to be which ariseth of the fountain of the sovereign and right beauty? Which is the origin of all other beauty, which never increaseth nor diminisheth, always beautiful, and of itself, as well on the one part as on the other, most simple, only like itself, and partner of none other, but in such wise beautiful that all other beautiful things be beautiful because they be partners of the beauty of it.

"This is the beauty unseparable from the high bounty which with her voice calleth and draweth to her all things; and not only to the endowed with understanding giveth understanding, to the reasonable reason, to the sensual sense and appetite to live, but also partaketh with plants and stones, as a print of herself, stirring, and the natural provocation of their properties. So much, therefore, is this love greater and happier than others as the cause that stirreth it is more excellent. And therefore, as common fire trieth gold and maketh it fine, so this most holy fire in souls destroyeth and consumeth whatsoever is mortal in them, and relieveth and maketh beautiful the heavenly part, which at the first by reason of the sense was dead and buried in them. This is the great fire in the which, the poets write, that Hercules was burned on the top of the mountain Oeta, and, through that consuming with fire, after his death was holy and immortal. This is the fiery bush of Moses; the divided tongues of fire; the inflamed chariot of Elias; which doubleth grace and happiness in their souls that be worthy to see it, when they forsake this earthly baseness and flee up into heaven. Let us, therefore, bend all our force and thoughts of soul to this most holy light, which showeth us the way that leadeth to heaven; and after it, putting off the affections we were clad withal at our coming down, let us climb up the

---

12. **occupy,** make use of. 14. **partened with,** communicated to. 18. **stirring virtues,** motive forces. 27. **weening,** expectation.

30–31. **provocation,** instinct. 43–44. **Moses.** See Exodus 3:2. **tongues of fire.** See Acts 2:3. **Elias.** See 2 Kings 2:11.

stairs which at the lowermost step have the shadow of sensual beauty, to the high mansion place where the heavenly, amiable, and right beauty dwelleth, which lieth hid in the innermost secrets of God, lest unhallowed eyes should come to the sight of it; and there shall we find a most happy end for our desires, true rest for our travails, certain remedy for miseries, a most healthful medicine for sickness, a most sure haven in the troublesome storms of the tempestuous sea of this life.

"What tongue mortal is there then, O most holy love, that can sufficiently praise thy worthiness? Thou most beautiful, most good, most wise, art derived of the unity of heavenly beauty, goodness, and wisdom, and therein dost thou abide, and unto it through it, as in a circle, turnest about. Thou the most sweet bond of the world, a mean betwixt heavenly and earthly things, with a bountiful temper bendest the high virtues to the government of the lower, and turning back the minds of mortal men to their beginning, couplest them with it. Thou with agreement bringest the elements in one, and stirrest nature to bring forth that which ariseth and is born for the succession of the life. Thou bringest severed matters into one, to the unperfect givest perfection, to the unlike likeness, to enmity amity, to the earth fruits, to the sea calmness, to the heaven lively light. Thou art the father of true pleasures, of grace, peace, lowliness, and good will, enemy to rude wildness and sluggishness—to be short, the beginning and end of all goodness. And forsomuch as thou delightest to dwell in the flower of beautiful bodies and beautiful souls, I suppose that thy abiding-place is now here among us, and from above otherwhile showest thyself a little to the eyes and minds of them that be worthy to see thee. Therefore vouchsafe, Lord, to hearken to our prayers, pour thyself into our hearts, and with the brightness of thy most holy fire lighten our darkness, and, like a trusty guide in this blind maze, show us the right way; reform the falsehood of the senses, and after long wandering in vanity give us the right and sound joy. Make us to smell those spiritual savours that relieve the virtues of the understanding, and to hear the heavenly harmonies so tunable that no discord of passion take place any more in us. Make us drunken with the bottomless fountain of contentation that always doth delight and never giveth fill, and that giveth a smack of the right bliss unto whoso drinketh of the running and clear water thereof. Purge with the shining beams of thy light our eyes from misty ignorance, that they may no more set by mortal beauty, and well perceive that the things which at the first they thought themselves to see be not indeed, and those that they saw not to be in effect. Accept our souls that be offered unto thee for a sacrifice. Burn them in the lively flame that wasteth all gross filthiness, that after they be clean sundered from the body they may be coupled with an everlasting and most sweet bond to the heavenly beauty. And we, severed from ourselves, may be changed like right lovers into the beloved, and, after we be drawn from the earth, admitted to the feast of the angels, where, fed with immortal ambrosia and nectar, in the end we may die a most happy and lively death, as in times past died the fathers of old time, whose souls with most fervent zeal of beholding thou didst hale from the body and coupledst them with God."

When Bembo had hitherto spoken with such vehemency that a man would have thought him, as it were, ravished and beside himself, he stood still without once moving, holding his eyes toward heaven as astonied, when the Lady Emilia, which together with the rest gave most diligent ear to this talk, took him by the plait of his garment and plucking him a little, said: "Take heed, Messer Pietro, that these thoughts make not your soul also to forsake the body."

"Madam," answered Messer Pietro, "it should not be by any mean the first miracle that love hath wrought in me."

Then the Duchess and all the rest began afresh to be instant upon Messer Bembo that he would proceed once more in his talk, and every one thought he felt in his mind, as it were, a certain sparkle of that godly love that pricked him, and they all coveted to hear farther; but Messer Bembo: "My Lords," quoth he, "I have spoken what the holy fury of love hath, unsought for, indited to me; now that, it seemeth, he inspireth me no more, I wot not what to say. And I think verily that love will not have his secrets discovered any farther, nor that the Courtier should pass the degree that his pleasure is I should show him, and therefore it is not perhaps lawful to speak any more in this matter."

"Surely," quoth the Duchess, "if the not young Courtier be such a one that he can follow this way which you have showed him, of right he ought to be satisfied with so great a happiness, and not to envy the younger."

Then the Lord Cesare Gonzaga: "The way," quoth he, "that leadeth to this happiness is so steep,

---

24. **for the succession of the life,** to the perpetuation of life. 48. **contentation,** content. 49. **smack,** taste.

1. **set by,** value. 14. **lively,** living. 16. **beholding,** contemplation.

in my mind, that I believe it will be much ado to get to it."

The Lord Gaspar said: "I believe it be hard to get up for men, but unpossible for women."

The Lady Emilia laughed, and said: "If you fall so often to offend us, I promise you you shall be no more forgiven."

The Lord Gaspar answered: "It is no offence to you in saying that women's souls be not so purged from passions as men's be, nor accustomed in beholdings, as Messer Pietro hath said is necessary for them to be that will taste of the heavenly love. Therefore it is not read that ever woman hath had this grace; but many men have had it, as Plato, Socrates, Plotinus, and many other, and a number of our holy fathers, as Saint Francis, in whom a fervent spirit of love imprinted the most holy seal of the five wounds. And nothing but the virtue of love could hale up Saint Paul the Apostle to the sight of those secrets which is not lawful for man to speak of; nor show Saint Stephen the heavens open."

Here answered the Lord Giuliano: "In this point men shall nothing pass women, for Socrates himself doth confess that all the mysteries of love which he knew were oped unto him by a woman, which was Diotima. And the angel that with the fire of love imprinted the five wounds in Saint Francis hath also made some women worthy of the same print in our age. You must remember, moreover, that Saint Mary Magdalen had many faults forgiven her, because she loved much; and perhaps with no less grace than Saint Paul was she many times through angelic love haled up to the third heaven. And many other, as I showed you yesterday more at large, that for love of the name of Christ have not passed upon life, nor feared torments, nor any other kind of death how terrible and cruel ever it were. And they were not, as Messer Pietro will have his Courtier to be, aged, but soft and tender maidens, and in the age when he saith that sensual love ought to be borne withal in men."

The Lord Gaspar began to prepare himself to speak, but the Duchess: "Of this," quoth she, "let Messer Pietro be judge, and the matter shall stand to his verdict, whether women be not as meet for heavenly love as men. But because the plea between you may happen be too long, it shall not be amiss to defer it until to-morrow."

"Nay, to-night," quoth the Lord Cesare Gonzaga.

"And how can it be to-night?" quoth the Duchess.

The Lord Cesare answered: "Because it is day already," and showed her the light that began to enter in at the clefts of the windows. Then every man arose upon his feet with much wonder, because they had not thought that the reasonings had lasted longer than the accustomed wont, saving only that they were begun much later, and with their pleasantness had deceived so the lords' minds that they wist not of the going away of the hours. And not one of them felt any heaviness of sleep in his eyes, the which often happeneth when a man is up after his accustomed hour to go to bed. When the windows then were opened on the side of the palace that hath his prospect toward the high top of Mount Catri, they saw already risen in the east a fair morning like unto the colour of roses, and all stars voided, saving only the sweet governess of the heaven, Venus, which keepeth the bound of the night and the day, from which appeared to blow a sweet blast that, filling the air with a biting cold, began to quicken the tunable notes of the pretty birds among the hushing woods of the hills at hand. Whereupon they all, taking their leave with reverence of the Duchess, departed toward their lodgings without torch, the light of the day sufficing.

And as they were now passing out at the great chamber door, the Lord General turned him to the Duchess and said: "Madam, to take up the variance between the Lord Gaspar and the Lord Giuliano, we will assemble this night with the judge sooner than we did yesterday."

The Lady Emilia answered: "Upon condition that in case my Lord Gaspar will accuse women, and give them, as his wont is, some false report, he will also put us in surety to stand to trial, for I reckon him a wavering starter."

10–11. **accustomed in beholdings,** given to contemplation. 16. **Saint Francis,** of Assisi (1181?–1226). 19. **Saint Paul.** See 2 Cor. 12:1–4. 21. **Saint Stephen.** See Acts 7:55–56. 30. **Saint Mary Magdalen.** See Luke 7:47.

3. **plea,** controversy, dispute. 45. **wavering starter,"** shifty disputant.

William Painter

c. 1540-1594

Little is known of the early life of William Painter. He was born somewhere in Kent about 1540. In 1554 he entered St. John's College, Cambridge, and later was master of a school. In 1561 he became clerk of the ordnance in the Tower of London, and apparently became rich out of the public funds. In 1587 he was charged with embezzlement, and later confessed that he had been untrue to his trust; but despite that fact he retained his office until his death in 1594.

Painter's chief claim to fame is that his was the first important translation of the novella into English. The novella was one of the most important points of contact between the Italian and the English Renaissance. Either in the original or in translation it furnished material for a large number of Elizabethan and Stuart dramas. The novella was more like a condensed novel than it was like the modern short story, for although it did not exceed in length most modern short stories, it frequently contained a more complex and elaborate plot than is nowadays customary. The writers of novelle usually summarized a considerable portion of their story, and then developed the major scenes with details of dialogue and action. The archetype among writers of novelle was Giovanni Boccaccio, whose *Decameron*, written between 1358 and 1369, represented a company of Florentines, seven young women and three young men, taking refuge in Fiesole from the plague, and beguiling their ten days' stay by telling in order ten stories each day. The *Decameron* was the direct inspiration of the *Heptameron* by Queen Marguerite of Navarre, in which the narrators are represented as detained in an inn by a flood.

Painter's first collection of sixty stories was printed in 1566; a second volume containing thirty-four additional stories appeared in 1567. An enlarged edition of the first volume was published in 1569, and the whole collection, now numbering a hundred stories, in 1575. His sources were not only French and Italian novelle, but various classical writers. In his collection, twenty-six stories were translated from Matteo Bandello, sixteen each from Boccaccio and Queen Marguerite, and thirteen from Aulus Gellius, a Latin writer of the second century A.D. whose *Noctes Atticae* in twenty books was a storehouse of miscellaneous classical lore.

In the year in which Painter's second volume appeared, there was published Geoffrey Fenton's *Certain Tragical Discourses Written out of French and Latin*, a collection of thirteen stories based on Belleforest's French translation of tales by Matteo Bandello. It is to such stories as these that Roger Ascham objected when he wrote in the *Schoolmaster*, 1570: "Suffer these books to be read, and they shall soon displace all books of godly learning. For they, carrying the will to vanity, and marring good manners, shall easily corrupt the mind with ill opinions and false judgment in doctrine: first to think ill of all true religion, and at last to think nothing of God himself, one special point that is to be learned in Italy and Italian books." Despite or because of such strictures as Ascham's, translations in this field multiplied.

The novelle, whether translated or untranslated, furnished plots for some of the most famous of Renaissance plays. Shakespeare found the plots of *Romeo and Juliet* and *All's Well That Ends Well* in Painter. John Webster based *The Duchess of Malfi* on a story in Painter.

Painter's version of the Romeo and Juliet story was translated from Boisteau's French version of a story which had been treated in succession by three Italian writers: Masuccio, Luigi da Porto, and Bandello.

from THE PALACE OF PLEASURE

ROMEO AND JULIETTA

According to Painter's narrative, there lived in Verona two families, the Montesches and the Capellets, who bitterly hated each other. But at a ball Romeo Montesche and Julietta Capellet met and fell deeply in love, and although they discovered each other's identity, they refused to permit the family feud to stand in the way of their love. They were secretly married by Friar Lawrence, and for a month or more were blissfully happy.

But on a day when a street fight began between the rival families, Romeo attempted to stop the quarreling. Julietta's cousin, Thibault, however, attacked him, and in defending himself Romeo killed Thibault. For this crime he was banished. Julietta's grief was misconstrued by her parents as sorrow for her unmarried state. Accordingly, her father arranged her marriage to Count Paris. Julietta's vehement opposition to this proposal angered her father greatly. Here the story continues.

WILLIAM PAINTER

AND the next morning, feigning to go hear service, she went forth with the woman of her chamber to the Friar's, where she caused Father Lawrence to be called unto her, and prayed him to hear her confession; and when she was upon her knees before him, she began her confession with tears, telling him the great mischief that was prepared for her by the marriage accorded between her father and the Count Paris; and for conclusion said unto him: "Sir, forasmuch as you know I cannot by God's law be married twice, and that I have but one God, one husband, and one faith, I am determined when I am from hence, with these two hands which you see joined before you, this day to end my sorrowful life, that my soul may bear witness in the heavens, and my blood upon the earth of my faith and loyalty preserved." Then having ended her talk, she looked about her, and seemed by her wild countenance as though she had devised some sinister purpose; wherefore Friar Lawrence, astonished beyond measure, fearing lest she would have executed that which she was determined, said unto her: "Mistress Julietta, I pray you in the name of God by little and little to moderate your conceived grief, and to content yourself whilst you be here, until I have provided what is best for you to do, for before you part from hence, I will give you such consolation and remedy for your afflictions, as you shall remain satisfied and contented." And resolved upon this good mind, he speedily went out of the church unto his chamber, where he began to consider of many things, his conscience being moved to hinder the marriage between the Count Paris and her, knowing by his means she had espoused another, and calling to remembrance what a dangerous enterprise he had begun by committing himself to the mercy of a simple damsel, and that if she failed to be wise and secret, all their doings should be descried, he defamed, and Romeo her spouse punished. He then after he had well debated upon infinite number of devices, was in the end overcome with pity, and determined rather to hazard his honour than to suffer the adultery of the Count Paris with Julietta; and being determined hereupon, opened his closet and taking a vial in his hand, returned again to Julietta, whom he found like one that was in a trance, waiting for news either of life or death, of whom the good old father demanded upon what day her marriage was appointed. "The first day of that appointment," quoth she, "is upon Wednesday, which is the day ordained for my consent of marriage accorded between my father and Count Paris, but the nuptial solemnity is not before the tenth day of September."

"Well then," quoth the religious father, "be of good cheer, daughter, for our Lord God hath opened a way unto me both to deliver you and Romeo from the prepared thraldom. I have known your husband from his cradle, and he hath daily committed unto me the greatest secrets of his conscience, and I have so dearly loved him in turn, as if he had been my own son; wherefore my heart cannot abide that any man should do him wrong in that specially wherein my counsel may stand him in stead. And forasmuch as you are his wife, I ought likewise to love you, and seek means to deliver you from the martyrdom and anguish wherewith I see your heart besieged; understand then, good daughter, of a secret which I purpose to manifest unto you, and take heed above all things that you declare it to no living creature, for therein consisteth your life and death. Ye be not ignorant by the common report of the citizens of this city, and by the same published of me, that I have travelled through all the provinces of the habitable earth, whereby during the continual time of twenty years I have sought no rest for my wearied body, but rather have many times protruded the same to the mercy of brute beasts in the wilderness, and many times also to the merciless waves of the seas, and to the pity of common pirates together with a thousand other dangers and shipwrecks upon sea and land. So it is, good daughter, that all my wandering voyages have not been altogether unprofitable. For besides the incredible contentation received ordinarily in mind, I have gathered some particular fruit, whereof by the grace of God you shall shortly feel some experience. I have proved the secret properties of stones, of plants, metals, and other things hidden within the bowels of the earth, wherewith I am able to help myself against the common law of men, when necessity doth serve, specially in things wherein I know mine eternal God to be least offended. For as thou knowest, I being approached as it were, even to the brim of my grave, and that the time draweth near for yielding of mine account before the Auditor of all Auditors, I ought therefore to have some deep knowledge and apprehension of God's judgment more than I had when the heat of inconsiderate youth did boil within my lusty body. Know you, therefore, good daughter, that with those graces and favours which the heavens prodigally have bestowed upon me, I have learned and proved of long time the composition of a certain paste, which I make of divers soporiferous simples,

14. **understand,** learn.   24. **protruded,** thrust forward, offered.   31. **contentation,** content.   51. **simples,** medicinal plants.

which beaten afterwards to powder and drunk with a quantity of water, within a quarter of an hour after, bringeth the receiver into such a sleep, and burieth so deeply the senses and other spirits of life, that the cunningest physician will judge the party dead; and besides that, it hath a more marvellous effect, for the person which useth the same feeleth no kind of grief, and according to the quantity of the dough, the patient remaineth in a sweet sleep, but when the operation is wrought and done, he returneth into his first estate. Now then, Julietta, receive mine instruction, put off all feminine affection by taking upon you a manly stomach, for by the only courage of your mind consisteth the hap or mishap of your affairs. Behold, here I give you a vial which you shall keep as your own proper heart, and the night before your marriage, or in the morning before day, you shall fill the same up with water, and drink so much as is contained therein. And then you shall feel a certain kind of pleasant sleep which encroaching by little and little all the parts of your body, will constrain them in such wise, as immovable they shall remain, and by not doing their accustomed duties, shall lose their natural feelings, and you abide in such ecstasy the space of forty hours at the least, without any beating of pulse or other perceptible motion, which shall so astonie them that come to see you, as they will judge you to be dead, and according to the custom of our city, you shall be carried to the churchyard hard by our church, where you shall be entombed in the common monument of the Capellets, your ancestors, and in the meantime we will send word to Lord Romeo by a special messenger of the effect of our device, who now abideth at Mantua. And the night following I am sure he will not fail to be here; then he and I together will open the grave, and lift up your body, and after the operation of the powder is past, he shall convey you secretly to Mantua, unknown to all your parents and friends. Afterwards (it may be), Time, the mother of Truth, shall cause concord between the offended city of Verona and Romeo. At which time your common cause may be made open to the general contentation of all your friends."

The words of the good father ended, new joy surprised the heart of Julietta, who was so attentive to his talk as she forgot no one point of her lesson. Then she said unto him: "Father, doubt not at all that my heart shall fail in performance of your commandment, for were it the strongest poison or most pestiferous venom, rather would I thrust it into my body than to consent to fall in the hands of him whom I utterly mislike; with a right strong reason then may I fortify myself, and offer my body to any kind of mortal danger to approach and draw near to him upon whom wholly dependeth my life and all the solace I have in this world." "Go your ways then, my daughter," quoth the Friar, "the mighty hand of God keep you, and His surpassing power defend you and confirm that will and good mind of yours, for the accomplishment of this work."

Julietta departed from Friar Lawrence and returned home to her father's palace about two of the clock, where she found her mother at the gate attending for her, and in good devotion demanded if she continued still in her former follies. But Julietta with more gladsome cheer than she was wont to use, not suffering her mother to ask again, said unto her: "Madam, I come from St. Francis' Church, where I have tarried longer peradventure than my duty requireth, howbeit not without fruit and great rest to my afflicted conscience, by reason of the godly persuasions of our ghostly father Friar Lawrence, unto whom I have made a large declaration of my life. And chiefly have communicated unto him in confession, that which hath passed between my lord my father and you, upon the marriage of Count Paris and me. But the good man hath reconciled me by his holy words and commendable exhortations, that where I had mind never to marry, now I am well disposed to obey your pleasure and commandment. Wherefore, madam, I beseech you, to recover the favour and good will of my father, ask pardon in my behalf, and say unto him (if it please you) that by obeying his fatherly request, I am ready to meet the Count Paris at Villafranco, and there in your presence to accept him for my lord and husband; in assurance whereof, by your patience, I mean to repair into my closet, to make choice of my most precious jewels, that I being richly adorned and decked, may appear before him more agreeable to his mind and pleasure." The good mother, rapt with exceeding great joy, was not able to answer a word, but rather made speed to seek out her husband the Lord Antonio, unto whom she reported the good will of her daughter, and how by means of Friar Lawrence her mind was changed. Whereof the good old man, marvellous joyful, praised God in heart, saying: "Wife, this is not the first good turn which we have received of that holy man, unto whom every citizen of this commonwealth is dearly bound. I would to God that I had redeemed twenty of his years with the third part of my goods, so grievous is to me his extreme old age."

9. **dough,** paste.   28. **astonie,** astonish, daze.

The self-same hour the Lord Antonio went to seek the Count Paris, whom he thought to persuade to go to Villafranco. But the Count told him again that the charge would be too great, and that better it were to reserve that cost to the marriage day, for the better celebration of the same. Notwithstanding, if it were his pleasure, he would himself go visit Julietta, and so they went together. The mother, advertised of his coming, caused her daughter to make herself ready, and to spare no costly jewels for adorning of her beauty against the Count's coming, which she bestowed so well for garnishing of her personage that before the Count parted from the house, she had so stolen away his heart as he lived not from that time forth but upon meditation of her beauty, and slacked no time for acceleration of the marriage day, ceasing not to be importunate upon father and mother for the end and consummation thereof.

And thus with joy enough passed forth this day and many others until the day before the marriage, against which time the mother of Julietta did so well provide that there wanted nothing to set forth the magnificence and nobility of their house. Villafranco whereof we have made mention was a place of pleasure, where the Lord Antonio was wont many times to recreate himself a mile or two from Verona; there the dinner was prepared, forasmuch as the ordinary solemnity of necessity must be done at Verona.

Julietta, perceiving her time to approach, dissembled the matter so well as she could; and when time forced her to retire to her chamber, her woman would have waited upon her, and have lain in her chamber, as her custom was; but Julietta said unto her: "Good and faithful mother, you know that to-morrow is my marriage day, and for that I would spend the most part of the night in prayer, I pray you for this time to let me alone, and to-morrow in the morning about six of the clock come to me again to help make me ready." The good old woman, willing to follow her mind, suffered her alone, and doubted nothing of that which she did mean to do.

Julietta, being within her chamber, having an ewer full of water standing upon the table, filled the vial which the friar gave her, and after she had made the mixture, she set it by her bedside, and went to bed. And being laid, new thoughts began to assail her, with a conceit of grievous death, which brought her into such case as she could not tell what to do, but plaining incessantly, said: "Am not I the most unhappy and desperate creature that ever was born of woman? For me there is nothing left in this wretched world but mishap, misery, and mortal woe; my distress hath brought me to such extremity, as to save mine honour and conscience, I am forced to devour the drink whereof I know not the virtue; but what know I," said she, "whether the operation of this powder will be too soon or too late, or not correspondent to the due time, and that my fault being discovered, I shall remain a fable to the people? What know I, moreover, if the serpents and other venomous and crawling worms which commonly frequent the graves and pits of the earth will hurt me, thinking that I am dead? But how shall I endure the stench of so many carrions and bones of my ancestors which rest in the grave, if by fortune I do awake before Romeo and Friar Lawrence do come to help me?" And as she was thus plunged in the deep contemplation of things, she thought that she saw a certain vision or fancy of her cousin Thibault, in the very same sort as she saw him wounded and imbrued with blood, and musing how that she must be buried quick amongst so many dead carcasses and deadly naked bones, her tender and delicate body began to shake and tremble, and her yellow locks to stare for fear, in such wise as, frightened with terror, a cold sweat began to pierce her heart and bedew the rest of all her members, in such wise as she thought an hundred thousand deaths did stand about her, haling her on every side, and plucking her in pieces, and feeling that her forces diminished by little and little, fearing that through too great debility she was not able to do her enterprise, like a furious and insensate woman, without further care gulped up the water within the vial; then crossing her arms upon her stomach, she lost at that instant all the powers of her body, resting in a trance.

And when the morning light began to thrust his head out of his orient, her chamber woman which had locked her in with the key, did open the door, and thinking to awake her, called her many times, and said unto her: "Mistress, you sleep too long; the Count Paris will come to raise you." The poor old woman spake unto the wall and sang a song unto the deaf. For if all the horrible and tempestuous sounds of the world had been cannoned forth out of the greatest bombards and sounded through her delicate ears, her spirits of life were so fast bound and stopped as she by no means could awake; wherewith the poor old woman, amazed, began to shake her by the arms and hands, which

---

9. **advertised,** informed.   16. **slacked no time,** missed no opportunity.   52. **plaining,** complaining.

22. **imbrued,** stained, drenched.   23. **quick,** alive.
30. **haling her,** pulling at her.   48. **bombards,** cannon.

she found so cold as marble stone. Then putting hand unto her mouth, suddenly perceived that she was dead, for she perceived no breath in her. Wherefore like a woman out of her wits, she ran to tell her mother, who so mad as a tiger bereft of her fawns, hied herself into her daughter's chamber, and in that pitiful state beholding her daughter, thinking her to be dead, cried out: "Ah, cruel death, which hast ended all my joy and bliss, use the last scourge of thy wrathful ire against me, lest by suffering me to live the rest of my woeful days, my torment do increase." Then she began to fetch such straining sighs as her heart did seem to cleave in pieces. And as her cries began to increase, behold the father, the Count Paris, and a great troop of gentlemen and ladies which were come to honour the feast, hearing no sooner tell of that which chanced, were struck into such sorrowful dumps, as he which had beheld their faces would easily have judged that the same had been a day of ire and pity, specially the Lord Antonio's, whose heart was frapped with such surpassing woe as neither tear nor word could issue forth, and knowing not what to do, straightway sent to seek the most expert physicians of the town, who after they had enquired of the life passed of Julietta, deemed by common report that melancholy was the cause of that sudden death, and then their sorrows began to renew afresh. And if ever day was lamentable, piteous, unhappy, and fatal, truly it was that wherein Julietta her death was published in Verona; for she was so bewailed of great and small that by the common plaints the commonwealth seemed to be in danger, and not without cause; for besides her natural beauty (accompanied with many virtues wherewith nature had enriched her) she was else so humble, wise and debonair, as for that humility and courtesy she had stolen away the hearts of every wight, and there was none but did lament her misfortune.

And whilst these things were in this lamented state, Friar Lawrence with diligence dispatched a friar of his convent, named Friar Anselm, whom he trusted as himself, and delivered him a letter written with his own hand, commanding him expressly not to give the same to any other but to Romeo, wherein was contained the chance which had passed between him and Julietta, specially the virtue of the powder, and commanded him the next ensuing night to speed himself to Verona, for that the operation of the powder that time would take end, and that he should carry with him back again to Mantua his beloved Julietta in dissembled apparel, until Fortune had otherwise provided for them. The friar made such haste as too late he arrived at Mantua, within a while after. And because the manner of Italy is, that the friar travelling abroad ought to take a companion of his convent to do his affairs within the city, the friar went into his convent, and for that he was within, it was not lawful for him to come out again that day, because that certain days before, one religious of that convent as it was said did die of the plague; wherefore the magistrates appointed for the health and visitation of the sick commanded the warden of the house that no friars should wander abroad the city, or talk with any citizen, until they were licensed by the officers in that behalf appointed, which was the cause of the great mishap which you shall hear hereafter. The friar being in this perplexity, not able to go forth and not knowing what was contained in the letter, deferred his journey for that day.

Whilst things were in this plight, preparation was made at Verona to do the obsequies of Julietta. There is a custom also (which is common in Italy) to lay all the best of one lineage and family in one tomb; whereupon Julietta was entombed in the ordinary grave of the Capellets, in a churchyard hard by the church of the friars, where also the Lord Thibault was interred, whose obsequies honourably done, every man returned: whereunto Pietro, the servant of Romeo, gave his assistance: for as we have before declared, his master sent him back again from Mantua to Verona, to do his father service, and to advertise him of that which should chance in his absence there: who seeing the body of Julietta enclosed in tomb, thinking with the rest that she had been dead indeed, incontinently took post-horse, and with diligence rode to Mantua, where he found his master in his wonted house, to whom he said with his eyes full of tears: "Sir, there is chanced unto you so strange a matter, as if so be you do not arm yourself with constancy, I am afraid that I shall be the cruel minister of your death: be it known unto you, sir, that yesterday morning my mistress Julietta left her life in this world to seek rest in another: and with these eyes I saw her buried in the churchyard of St. Francis'." At the sound of which heavy message, Romeo began woefully to lament, as though his spirits, grieved with the torment of his passion, at that instant would have abandoned his body. But strong love, which would not permit him to faint until the extremity, framed a thought in his fantasy, that if it were possible for him to die beside her, his death should be more glorious, and she (as he thought) better contented; by reason whereof, after he had

---

22. **frapped**, struck, seized.

washed his face for fear to discover his sorrow, he went out of his chamber, and commanded his man to tarry behind him, that he might walk throughout all the corners of the city, to find proper remedy (if it were possible) for his grief. And amongst others, beholding an apothecary's shop of little furniture and less store of boxes and other things requisite for that science, thought that the very poverty of the master apothecary would make him willingly yield to that which he pretended to demand; and after he had taken him aside, secretly said unto him: "Sir, if you be the master of the house, as I think you be, behold here fifty ducats, which I give you to the intent you deliver me some strong and violent poison, that within a quarter of an hour is able to procure death unto him that shall use it." The covetous apothecary, enticed by gain, agreed to his request, and feigning to give him some other medicine before the people's face, he speedily made ready a strong and cruel poison; afterwards he said unto him softly: "Sir, I give you more than is needful, for the one half is able to destroy the strongest man of the world," who after he had received the poison, returned home, where he commanded his man to depart with diligence to Verona, and that he should make provision of candles, a tinder box, and other instruments meet for the opening of the grave of Julietta, and that above all things, he should not fail to attend his coming beside the churchyard of St. Francis', and upon pain of life to keep his intent in silence. Which Pietro obeyed in order as his master had required, and made therein such expedition as he arrived in good time to Verona, taking order for all things that were commanded him. Romeo in the meanwhile being solicited with mortal thoughts caused ink and paper to be brought unto him, and in few words put in writing all the discourse of his love, the marriage of him and Julietta, the mean observed for the consummation of the same, the help that he had of Friar Lawrence, the buying of his poison, and last of all his death. Afterwards, having finished his heavy tragedy, he closed the letters and sealed the same with his seal, and directed the superscription thereof to his father; and putting the letters into his purse, he mounted on horseback, and used such diligence as he arrived upon dark night at the city of Verona, before the gates were shut, where he found his servant tarrying for him with a lantern and instruments, as is before said, meet for the opening of the grave, unto whom he said: "Pietro, help me to open this tomb, and so soon as it is open, I command thee upon pain of thy life not to come near me, nor to stay me from the thing I purpose to do. Behold, there is a letter which thou shalt present to-morrow in the morning to my father at his uprising, which peradventure shall please him better than thou thinkest." Pietro, not able to imagine what was his master's intent, stood somewhat aloof to behold his master's gests and countenance. And when they had opened the vault, Romeo descended down two steps, holding the candle in his hand, and began to behold with pitiful eye, the body of her, which was the organ of his eyes, and kissed it tenderly, holding it hard between his arms, and not able to satisfy himself with her sight, put his fearful hands upon the cold stomach of Julietta. And after he had touched her in many places, and not able to feel any certain judgment of life, he drew the poison out of his box, and swallowing down a great quantity of the same, cried out: "O Julietta, of whom the world was unworthy, what death is it possible my heart could choose out more agreeable than that which it suffereth hard by thee? What grave more glorious than to be buried in thy tomb? What more worthy or excellent epitaph can be vowed for memory than the mutual and pitiful sacrifice of our lives?" And thinking to renew his sorrow, his heart began to fret through the violence of the poison, which by little and little assailed the same, and looking about him, espied the body of the Lord Thibault lying next unto Julietta, which as yet was not altogether putrefied, and speaking to the body as though it had been alive, said: "In what place so ever thou art, O cousin Thibault, I most heartily do cry thee mercy for the offence which I have done by depriving of thy life; and if thy ghost do wish and cry out for vengeance upon me, what greater or more cruel satisfaction canst thou desire to have, or henceforth hope for, than to see him which murdered thee, to be empoisoned with his own hands and buried by thy side?" Then ending his talk, feeling by little and little that his life began to fail, falling prostrate upon his knees, with feeble voice he softly said: "O my Lord God, which to redeem me didst descend from the bosom of Thy Father, and tookest human flesh in the womb of the Virgin, I acknowledge and confess that this body of mine is nothing else but earth and dust." Then seized upon with desperate sorrow, he fell down upon the body of Julietta with such vehemence as the heart, faint and attenuated with too great torments, not able to bear so hard a violence, was abandoned of all his sense and natural powers, in such sort as the siege of his soul failed him at that instant, and his members stretched forth remained stiff and cold.

6. gests, gestures, deportment. **51. siege,** seat.

Friar Lawrence, which knew the certain time of the powder's operation, marvelled that he had no answer of the letter which he sent to Romeo by his fellow Friar Anselm, departed from St. Francis' and with instruments for the purpose, determined to open the grave to let in air to Julietta which was ready to wake; and approaching the place, he espied a light within, which made him afraid until that Pietro, which was hard by, had certified him that Romeo was within, and had not ceased there to lament and complain the space of half an hour; and when they two were entered into the grave and finding Romeo without life, made such sorrow as they can well conceive which love their dear friend with like perfection. And as they were making their complaints, Julietta, rising out of her trance and beholding light within the tomb, uncertain whether it were a dream or fantasy that appeared before her eyes, coming again to herself, knew Friar Lawrence, unto whom she said: "Father, I pray thee in the name of God to perform thy promise, for I am almost dead." And then Friar Lawrence, concealing nothing from her (because he feared to be taken through his too long abode in that place), faithfully rehearsed unto her how he had sent Friar Anselm to Romeo at Mantua, from whom as yet he had received no answer. Notwithstanding, he found Romeo dead in the grave, whose body he pointed unto, lying hard by her, praying her sith it was so, patiently to bear that sudden misfortune, and that if it pleased her, he would convey her into some monastery of women where she might in time moderate her sorrow and give rest unto her mind. Julietta had no sooner cast eye upon the dead corpse of Romeo, but began to break the fountain pipes of gushing tears, which ran forth in such abundance, as not able to support the furore of her grief, she breathed without ceasing upon his mouth, and then throwing herself upon his body and embracing it very hard, seemed that by force of sighs and sobs, she would have revived and brought him again to life, and after she had kissed and rekissed him a million of times, she cried out: "Ah, the sweet rest of my cares and the only port of all my pleasures and pastimes, hadst thou so sure a heart to choose thy churchyard in this place between the arms of thy perfect lover, and to end the course of thy life for my sake in the flower of thy youth when life to thee should have been most dear and delectable? How had this tender body power to resist the furious combat of death, very death itself here present? How could thy tender and delicate youth willingly permit that thou shouldest approach into this filthy and infected place, where from henceforth thou shalt be the pasture of worms unworthy of thee? Alas, alas, by what means shall I now renew my plaints, which time and long patience ought to have buried and clearly quenched? Ah, I, miserable and caitiff wretch, thinking to find remedy for my griefs, have sharpened the knife that hath given me this cruel blow, whereof I receive the cause of mortal wound. Ah, happy and fortunate grave which shalt serve in world to come for witness of the most perfect alliance that ever was between two most unfortunate lovers, receive now the last sobbing sighs and entertainment of the most cruel of all the cruel subjects of ire and death." And as she thought to continue her complaints, Pietro advertised Friar Lawrence that he heard a noise beside the citadel, wherewith being afraid, they speedily departed, fearing to be taken; and then Julietta, seeing herself alone and in full liberty, took again Romeo between her arms, kissing him with such affection as she seemed to be more attainted with love than death, and drawing out the dagger which Romeo wore by his side, she pricked herself with many blows against the heart, saying with feeble and pitiful voice: "Ah death, the end of sorrow and beginning of felicity, thou art most heartily welcome: fear not at this time to sharpen thy dart: give no longer delay of life, for fear that my spirit travail not to find Romeo's ghost amongst such number of carrion corpses; and thou, my dear lord and loyal husband Romeo, if there rest in thee any knowledge, receive her whom thou hast so faithfully loved, the only cause of thy violent death, which frankly offereth up her soul that none but thou shalt joy the love whereof thou hast made so lawful conquest, and that our souls passing from this light, may eternally live together in the place of everlasting joy." And when she had ended those words she yielded up her ghost. . . .

Upon the discovery of the bodies of the two lovers, Friar Lawrence and Pietro were accused of murder. Both, however, were proved innocent by the Friar's confession and by the evidence furnished by the Nurse and the letters left by Romeo. The hostile families, moved by their common sorrow, became reconciled and erected a monument over the grave of the star-crossed lovers.

8. **caitiff**, mean, despicable.

Roger Ascham
1515-1568

Roger Ascham was the best-known English writer of sixteenth-century treatises on education. His life and experience were an admirable preparation for the composition of his distinguished book, *The Schoolmaster*. Born in 1515 in Yorkshire, he entered St. John's College, Cambridge, about 1530,—shortly after his teacher and master, Sir John Cheke—and became one of the brightest ornaments of this period in the university's Humanistic ascendancy. He became a distinguished classicist, and is said to have been the first lecturer on the Platonic dialogues at Cambridge. In 1545, he published *Toxophilus*, a dialogue modeled on Plato on the benefits of archery, as a pastime, a means of defense—for which he prefers it to cannon—and a form of physical training. In this discourse he strongly reprobated gambling, although, as Andrew Lang pointed out, he displayed "a rather unholy knowledge of all the tricks of the dice-board." On many aspects of archery, Ascham is still regarded as authoritative. The *Toxophilus* introduces a charming reminiscence at second hand of Erasmus at Cambridge, to illustrate the point that most scholars do not take enough exercise: "This pastime for the mind only be nothing fit for students, because the body which is the most hurt by study should take away no profit at all thereat. This knew Erasmus very well when he was at Cambridge; which, when he had been sore at his book (as Garret our bookbinder hath oft told me) for lack of better exercise would take his horse and ride about the market hill and come again."

From 1548 to 1550, Ascham and his protégé William Grindal acted as tutors to the Princess Elizabeth, and under their direction she acquired a thorough knowledge of Greek and Latin literature, and the faculty of expressing herself with vigor in Latin, Italian, and French. His admiration for her intellectual parts is expressed enthusiastically in the selection which follows. That she was not unaware of her accomplishments may be gleaned from one of her speeches to Parliament: "I thank God that if I were turned out of the realm in my petticoat, I were able to live in any place in Christendom." Between 1550 and 1553, Ascham served as secretary to Sir Thomas Morison, Ambassador at the court of Emperor Charles V. In 1553, Ascham wrote up his impressions of his experience, which were printed in 1570 under the title *The Report and Discourse of the Affairs and State of Germany*. Ascham, like his friend Sir John Cheke, was an ardent Protestant, but when on Mary's accession to the throne Cheke fled into exile, Ascham, by some gift of tact, became Mary's Latin Secretary. Ascham died in 1568, and in the year of his death, Camden, the antiquarian, in his *Annales* records that he lived and died a poor man because of his addiction to dicing and to cockfighting; on the latter subject, at least, he had promised in *The Schoolmaster* to write a treatise.

That Ascham left his family in poor circumstances is apparent from the dedication to *The Schoolmaster* which his wife Margaret addressed to Lord Burghley. In the course of it, she wrote "how much my said husband was many ways bound into you, and how gladly and comfortably he used in his life to recognize and report your goodness toward him, leaving with me then his poor widow and a great sort of orphans a good comfort in the hope of your good continuance, which I have truly found to me and mine." In the preface to the work, Ascham, explaining the occasion for writing it, gives us a vivid impression of an Elizabethan dinner-table conversation. At dinner at Sir William Cecil's, there was talk of some boys who had run away from Eton to escape whipping. In the discussion of educational methods that followed, Sir Richard Sackville asked Ascham to write out his views for the sake of his little grandson Robert. Despite Sir Richard's death, Ascham carried out his request.

from THE SCHOOLMASTER

The Schoolmaster is in two books, and although it is marked by many digressions, it covers rather thoroughly Ascham's views on the reasons for the decay of learning in England, his general theories on education, and his methods for teaching Latin prose. On the latter point, he particularly recommends translating from Latin into English, and then, after an interval, translating the English back into Latin, and comparing the results. In his conception of Latin prose, Ascham was a fairly stanch Ciceronian, but the fact that he decided to write his treatise in English suggests his awareness of the trend of the times. He realizes that writing in Latin would be "more honest" for his name, but writing in English will further "the pleasure or commodity of the gentlemen and yeomen of England," and will also set the example of a good style, since most English prose is composed "in a manner so meanly, both for matter and handling, that no man can do worse." Most interesting to modern readers are Ascham's extended digressions—on the glories of Cambridge during his student days, on his brilliant pupils, from the unfortunate Lady Jane Grey to Queen Elizabeth, and on his pious Puritan hostility to medieval literature and to contemporary Italian life and literature.

In the passage given below, Ascham sets forth some of the reasons for the deplorable behavior of the younger generation of his day.

THERE is another discommodity, besides cruelty in schoolmasters in beating away the love of learning from children, which hindereth learning and virtue and good bringing up of youth, and namely young gentlemen, very much in England. This fault is clean contrary to the first. I wished before to have love of learning bred up in children; I wish as much now to have young men brought up in good order of living, and in some more severe discipline than commonly they be. We have lack in England of such good order as the old noble Persians so carefully used; whose children, to the age of twenty-one years, were brought up in learning and exercises of labour; and that in such place where they should neither see that was uncomely nor hear that was unhonest. Yea, a young gentleman was never free to go where he would and do what he list himself; but under the keep and by the counsel of some grave governor, until he was either married or called to bear some office in the commonwealth.

And see the great obedience that was used in old time to fathers and governors. No son, were he never so old of years, never so great of birth, though he were a king's son, might not marry but by his father's and mother's also consent. Cyrus the Great, after he had conquered Babylon and subdued rich king Croesus, with whole Asia Minor, coming triumphantly home, his uncle Cyaxeres offered him his daughter to wife. Cyrus thanked his uncle, and praised the maid; but for marriage, he answered him with these wise and sweet words, as they be uttered by Xenophon: ὦ Κυαξάρη, τό τε γένος ἐπαινῶ, καὶ τὴν παῖδα, καὶ δῶρα. Βούλομαι δέ, ἔφη, σὺν τῇ τοῦ πατρὸς γνώμῃ καὶ τῇ τῆς μητρὸς ταῦτά σοι συναινέσαι. That is to say, "Uncle Cyaxeres, I commend the stock, I like the maid, and I allow well the dowry; but"—saith he—"by the counsel and consent of my father and mother, I will determine farther of these matters."

Strong Samson also in Scripture saw a maid that liked him; but he spake not to her, but went home to his father and his mother and desired both father and mother to make the marriage for him. Doth this modesty, doth this obedience, that was in great King Cyrus and stout Samson, remain in our young men at this day? No surely; for we live not longer after them by time than we live far different from them by good order. Our time is so far from that old discipline and obedience as now not only young gentlemen but even very girls dare, without all fear, though not without open shame, where they list, and how they list, marry themselves in spite of father, mother, God, good order, and all. The cause of this evil is that youth is least looked unto when they stand in most need of good keep and regard. It availeth not to see them well taught in young years, and after when they come to lust and youthful days to give them licence to live as they lust themselves. For if ye suffer the eye of a young gentleman once to be entangled with vain sights, and the ear to be corrupted with fond or filthy talk, the mind shall quickly fall sick, and soon vomit and cast up all the wholesome doctrine that he received in childhood, though he were never so well brought up before. And being once inglutted with vanity, he will straightway loathe all learning, and all good counsel to the same; and the parents, for all their great cost and charge, reap only in the end the fruit of grief and care.

This evil is not common to poor men, as God will have it, but proper to rich and great men's children, as they deserve it. Indeed from seven to seventeen, young gentlemen commonly be carefully enough brought up; but from seventeen to seven-and-twenty (the most dangerous time of all a man's life, and most slippery to stay well in) they have commonly the rein of all licence in their own hand, and specially such as do live in the court. And that which is most to be marvelled at, commonly the wisest and also best men be found the fondest fathers in this behalf. And if some good father would seek some remedy herein, yet the mother (if the house hold of our lady) had rather, yea, and will too, have her son cunning and bold, in making him to live trimly when he is young, than by learning and travel to be able to serve his prince and his country, both wisely in peace and stoutly in war, when he is old.

The fault is in yourselves, ye noble men's sons, and therefore ye deserve the greater blame, that

---

3-6. **Samson . . . for him.** See Judges 14.

commonly the meaner men's children come to be the wisest counsellors and greatest doers, in the weighty affairs of this realm. And why? For God will have it so of his providence, because ye will have it no otherwise by your negligence.

And God is a good God, and wisest in all his doings, that will place virtue and displace vice in those kingdoms where he doth govern. For he knoweth that nobility without virtue and wisdom is blood indeed, but blood truly without bones and sinews; and so of itself, without the other, very weak to bear the burden of weighty affairs.

The greatest ship indeed commonly carrieth the greatest burden, but yet always with the greatest jeopardy, not only for the persons and goods committed unto it but even for the ship itself, except it be governed with the greatest wisdom.

But nobility, governed by learning and wisdom, is indeed most like a fair ship, having tide and wind at will, under the rule of a skilful master: when contrariwise, a ship carried, yea, with the highest tide and greatest wind, lacking a skilful master, most commonly doth either sink itself upon sands or break itself upon rocks. And even so, how many have been either drowned in vain pleasure or overwhelmed by stout wilfulness, the histories of England be able to afford over-many examples unto us. Therefore, ye great and noble men's children, if ye will have rightfully that praise and enjoy surely that place which your fathers have and elders had and left unto you, ye must keep it as they gat it; and that is by the only way of virtue, wisdom, and worthiness.

For wisdom and virtue, there be many fair examples in this court for young gentlemen to follow; but they be like fair marks in the field, out of a man's reach, too far off to shoot at well. The best and worthiest men indeed be sometimes seen, but seldom talked withal. A young gentleman may sometime kneel to their person, but smally use their company for their better instruction.

But young gentlemen are fain commonly to do in the court as young archers do in the field; that is, take such marks as be nigh them, although they be never so foul to shoot at: I mean, they be driven to keep company with the worst; and what force ill company hath to corrupt good wits, the wisest men know best.

And not ill company only, but the ill opinion also of the most part, doth much harm; and namely of those which should be wise in the true deciphering of the good disposition of nature, of comeliness in courtly manners, and all right doings of men.

But error and fantasy do commonly occupy the place of truth and judgment. For if a young gentleman be demure and still of nature they say he is simple and lacketh wit; if he be bashful, and will soon blush, they call him a babish and ill brought up thing; when Xenophon doth precisely note in Cyrus, that his bashfulness in youth was the very true sign of his virtue and stoutness after. If he be innocent and ignorant of ill, they say he is rude and hath no grace: so ungraciously do some graceless men misuse the fair and godly word "grace."

But if ye would know what grace they mean, go and look, and learn amongst them, and ye shall see that it is:

First, to blush at nothing; and "blushing in youth," saith Aristotle, "is nothing else but fear to do ill"; which fear being once lustily frayed away from youth, then followeth to dare do any mischief, to contemn stoutly any goodness, to be busy in every matter, to be skilful in everything, to acknowledge no ignorance at all. To do thus in court is counted of some the chief and greatest grace of all; and termed by the name of a virtue, called courage and boldness; when Crassus in Cicero teacheth the clean contrary, and that most wittily, saying thus, "Audere, cum bonis etiam rebus conjunctum, per seipsum est magnopere fugiendum:" which is to say, "To be bold, yea in a good matter, is for itself greatly to be eschewed."

Moreover, where the swing goeth, there to follow, fawn, flatter, laugh, and lie lustily at other men's liking; to face, stand foremost, shove back; and to the meaner man, or unknown in the court, to seem somewhat solemn, coy, big, and dangerous of look, talk, and answer; to think well of himself, to be lusty in contemning of others, to have some trim grace in a privy mock; and in greater presence to bear a brave look, to be warlike; though he never looked enemy in the face in war, yet some warlike sign must be used, either a slovenly buskin, or an overstaring frounced head, as though out of every hair's top should suddenly start out a good big oath when need requireth. Yet, praised be God, England hath at this time many worthy captains and good soldiers, which be indeed so honest of behaviour, so comely of conditions, so mild of manners, as they may be examples of good order to a good sort of others, which never came in war.— But to return where I left: in place also to be able to raise talk, and make discourse of every rishe;

---

40. smally, in small degree.   **45. foul,** poor.   **6. babish,** babyish.   **18. frayed,** frightened.
50. namely, especially.   **30. eschewed,"** avoided.   **31. where the swing goeth,** wherever one's inclination leads.   **51. rishe,** rush, that is, a trifle.

to have a very good will to hear himself speak; to be seen in palmistry, whereby to convey to chaste ears some fond and filthy talk.

And if some Smithfield ruffian take up some strange going, some new mowing with the mouth, some wrinching with the shoulder, some brave proverb, some fresh new oath that is not stale, but will run round in the mouth; some new disguised garment, or desperate hat, fond in fashion, or garish in colour, whatsoever it cost, how small soever his living be, by what shift soever it be gotten, gotten must it be, and used with the first, or else the grace of it is stale and gone. Some part of this graceless grace was described by me in a little rude verse long ago.

> To laugh, to lie, to flatter, to face,
> Four ways in court to win men grace.
> If thou be thrall to none of these,
> Away good Peckgoose, hence John Cheese.
> Mark well my word, and mark their deed,
> And think this verse part of thy creed.

Would to God this talk were not true, and that some men's doings were not thus. I write not to hurt any, but to profit some; to accuse none, but to monish such who, allured by ill counsel and following ill example contrary to their good bringing up, and against their own good nature, yield overmuch to these follies and faults. I know many serving-men of good order, and well staid; and again, I hear say there be some serving-men do but ill service to their young masters. Yea, read Terence and Plautus advisedly over, and ye shall find in those two wise writers, almost in every comedy, no unthrifty young man that is not brought thereunto by the subtle enticement of some lewd servant. And even now in our days, Getae, and Davi, Gnathos, and many bold bawdy Phormios too, be pressing in to prattle on every stage, to meddle in every matter; when honest Parmenos shall not be heard, but bear small swing with their masters. Their company, their talk, their over-great experience in mischief, doth easily corrupt the best natures and best brought up wits.

But I marvel the less that these misorders be amongst some in the court; for commonly in the country also every where, innocency is gone, bashfulness is banished; much presumption in youth, small authority in age; reverence is neglected, duties be confounded; and, to be short, disobedience doth overflow the banks of good order almost in every place, almost in every degree of man.

Mean men have eyes to see, and cause to lament, and occasion to complain of these miseries; but other have authority to remedy them, and will do so too, when God shall think time fit. For all these misorders be God's just plagues, by his sufferance brought justly upon us for our sins, which be infinite in number and horrible in deed; but namely for the great abominable sin of unkindness; but what unkindness? Even such unkindness as was in the Jews, in contemning God's voice, in shrinking from his word, in wishing back again for Egypt, in committing adultery and whoredom, not with the women, but with the doctrine of Babylon, and did bring all the plagues, destructions, and captivities that fell so oft and horrible upon Israel.

We have cause also in England to beware of unkindness, who have had in so few years the candle of God's word so oft lightened, so oft put out; and yet will venture by our unthankfulness in doctrine and sinful life to leese again light, candle, candlestick and all.

God keep us in his fear; God graft in us the true knowledge of his word, with a forward will to follow it, and so to bring forth the sweet fruits of it; and then shall he preserve us by his grace from all manner of terrible days.

The remedy of this doth not stand only in making good common laws for the whole realm, but also (and perchance chiefly) in observing private discipline, every man carefully in his own house; and namely, if special regard be had to youth; and that not so much in teaching them what is good as in keeping them from that that is ill.

Therefore, if wise fathers be not as well ware in weeding from their children ill things and ill company, as they were before in grafting in them learning and providing for them good schoolmasters, what fruit they shall reap of all their cost and care, common experience doth tell.

Here is the place, in youth is the time when some ignorance is as necessary as much knowledge; and not in matters of our duty towards God, as some wilful wits willingly against their own knowledge, perniciously against their own conscience, have of late openly taught. Indeed St. Chrysostom, that noble and eloquent doctor, in a sermon *contra fatum*, and the curious searching of nativities, doth wisely say that ignorance therein is better than knowledge. But to wring this sentence, to wrest thereby out

---

4. **Smithfield**, a low section in London. 26. **monish**, admonish. 37–40. **Getae**, . . . **Parmenos**, characters in the comedies of Plautus and Terence.

2. **Mean**, humble, common. 21. **leese**, lose. 35. **ware**, careful. 46. **St. Chrysostom**, St. John Chrysostom (345?–407). 47. **contra fatum**, against fate. 48. **curious searching of nativities**, overinquisitive casting of horoscopes.

of men's hands the knowledge of God's doctrine, is without all reason, against common sense, contrary to the judgment also of them which be the discreetest men and best learned on their own side. I know Julianus Apostata did so: but I never heard or read that any ancient Father of the primitive church either thought or wrote so.

But this ignorance in youth which I speak on, or rather this simplicity, or most truly this innocency, is that which the noble Persians, as wise Xenophon doth testify, were so careful to breed up their youth in. But Christian fathers commonly do not so. And I will tell you a tale, as much to be misliked as the Persians' example is to be followed.

This last summer I was in a gentleman's house, where a young child, somewhat past four year old, could in no wise frame his tongue to say a little short grace; and yet he could roundly rap out so many ugly oaths, and those of the newest fashion, as some good man of fourscore year old hath never heard named before. And that which was most detestable of all, his father and mother would laugh at it. I much doubt what comfort another day this child shall bring unto them. This child, using much the company of serving-men and giving good ear to their talk, did easily learn which he shall hardly forget all the days of his life hereafter. So likewise in the court, if a young gentleman will venture himself into the company of ruffians, it is over-great a jeopardy lest their fashions, manners, thoughts, talk, and deeds, will very soon be ever like. The confounding of companies breedeth confusion of good manners, both in the court and everywhere else.

And it may be a great wonder, but a greater shame to us Christian men, to understand what a heathen writer, Isocrates, doth leave in memory of writing, concerning the care that the noble city of Athens had to bring up their youth in honest company and virtuous discipline; whose talk in Greek is to this effect in English:

"The city was not more careful to see their children well taught than to see their young men well governed; which they brought to pass not so much by common law as by private discipline. For they had more regard that their youth by good order should not offend than how by law they might be punished; and if offence were committed, there was neither way to hide it, nor hope of pardon for it. Good natures were not so much openly praised as they were secretly marked and watchfully regarded, lest they should leese the goodness they had. Therefore in schools of singing and dancing, and other honest exercises, governors were appointed more diligent to oversee their good manners than their masters were to teach them any learning. It was some shame to a young man to be seen in the open market; and if for business he passed through it, he did it with a marvellous modesty and bashful fashion. To eat or drink in a tavern was not only a shame, but also punishable, in a young man. To contrary, or to stand in terms with an old man, was more heinous than in some place to rebuke and scold with his own father." With many other more good orders and fair disciplines, which I refer to their reading that have lust to look upon the description of such a worthy commonwealth.

And to know what worthy fruit did spring of such worthy seed, I will tell you the most marvel of all, and yet such a truth as no man shall deny it except such as be ignorant in knowledge of the best stories.

Athens, by this discipline and good ordering of youth, did breed up, within the circuit of that one city, within the compass of one hundred year, within the memory of one man's life, so many notable captains in war, for worthiness, wisdom, and learning, as be scarce matchable, no, not in the state of Rome, in the compass of those seven hundred years when it flourished most.

And because I will not only say it, but also prove it, the names of them be these: Miltiades, Themistocles, Xantippus, Pericles, Cimon, Alcibiades, Thrasybulus, Conon, Iphicrates, Xenophon, Timotheus, Theopompus, Demetrius, and divers other more; of which every one may justly be spoken that worthy praise which was given to Scipio Africanus, who Cicero doubteth, whether he were more noble captain in war, or more eloquent and wise counsellor in peace. And if ye believe not me, read diligently Aemilius Probus in Latin, and Plutarch in Greek; which two had no cause either to flatter or lie upon any of those which I have recited.

And beside nobility in war, for excellent and matchless masters in all manner of learning, in that one city, in memory of one age, were more learned men, and that in a manner altogether, than all time doth remember, than all place doth afford, than all other tongues do contain. And I do not mean of those authors which by injury of time, by negligence of men, by cruelty of fire and sword, be lost; but even of those which by God's grace are left yet unto us; of which, I thank God, even my poor study lacketh not one. As, in philosophy, Plato, Aristotle, Xenophon, Euclid, and Theophrast;

---

5. Julianus Apostata, Julian the Apostate (331–363), Roman emperor 361–63. **37. Isocrates,** Athenian orator and teacher (436–338 B.C.).

in eloquence and civil law, Demosthenes, Aeschines, Lycurgus, Dinarchus, Demades, Isocrates, Isaeus, Lysias, Antisthenes, Andocides; in histories, Herodotus, Thucydides, Xenophon, and, which we lack to our great loss, Theopompus and Ephorus; in poetry, Aeschylus, Sophocles, Euripides, Aristophanes, and somewhat of Menander, Demosthenes' sister son.

Now let Italian, and Latin itself, Spanish, French, Dutch, and English bring forth their learning and recite their authorities; Cicero only excepted, and one or two more in Latin, they be all patched clouts and rags, in comparison of fair woven broadcloths; and truly, if there be any good in them it is either learned, borrowed, or stolen from some of those worthy wits of Athens.

The remembrance of such a commonwealth, using such discipline and order for youth, and thereby bringing forth to their praise, and leaving to us for our example, such captains for war, such counsellors for peace, and matchless masters for all kind of learning, is pleasant for me to recite, and not irksome, I trust, for other to hear, except it be such as make neither account of virtue nor learning.

And whether there be any such or no, I cannot well tell; yet I hear say, some young gentlemen of ours count it their shame to be counted learned; and perchance they count it their shame to be counted honest also; for I hear say they meddle as little with the one as with the other. A marvellous case, that gentlemen should so be ashamed of good learning, and never a whit ashamed of ill manners! Such do say for them that the gentlemen of France do so; which is a lie, as God will have it. Langaeus and Bellaeus, that be dead, and the noble Vidam of Chartres, that is alive, and infinite more in France, which I hear tell of, prove this to be most false. And though some in France, which will needs be gentlemen, whether men will or no, and have more gentleship in their hat than in their head, be at deadly feud with both learning and honesty; yet I believe if that noble prince, King Francis the First, were alive they should have neither place in his court nor pension in his wars, if he had knowledge of them. This opinion is not French, but plain Turkish, from whence some French fetch more faults than this; which I pray God keep out of England, and send also those of ours better minds, which bend themselves against virtue and learning, to the contempt of God, dishonour of their country, to the hurt of many others, and at length to the greatest harm and utter destruction of themselves.

Some other, having better nature but less wit (for ill commonly have over-much wit), do not utterly dispraise learning, but they say that without learning, common experience, knowledge of all fashions, and haunting all companies shall work in youth both wisdom and ability to execute any weighty affair. Surely long experience doth profit much, but most, and almost only, to him (if we mean honest affairs) that is diligently before instructed with precepts of well doing. For good precepts of learning be the eyes of the mind, to look wisely before a man, which way to go right and which not.

Learning teacheth more in one year than experience in twenty; and learning teacheth safely, when experience maketh more miserable than wise. He hazardeth sore that waxeth wise by experience. An unhappy master he is that is made cunning by many shipwrecks; a miserable merchant, that is neither rich nor wise but after some bankrouts. It is costly wisdom that is bought by experience. We know by experience itself that it is a marvellous pain to find out but a short way by long wandering. And, surely, he that would prove wise by experience, he may be witty indeed, but even like a swift runner, that runneth fast out of his way, and upon the night, he knoweth not whither. And verily they be fewest of number that be happy or wise by unlearned experience. And look well upon the former life of those few, whether your example be old or young, who without learning have gathered by long experience a little wisdom and some happiness; and when you do consider what mischief they have committed, what dangers they have escaped (and yet twenty for one do perish in the adventure), then think well with yourself whether you would that your own son should come to wisdom and happiness by the way of such experience or no.

It is a notable tale, that old Sir Roger Chamloe, sometime chief justice, would tell of himself. When he was ancient in Inn of Court, certain young gentlemen were brought before him to be corrected for certain misorders: and one of the lustiest said, "Sir, we be young gentlemen; and wise men before us have proved all fashions, and yet those have done full well." This they said because it was well known that Sir Roger had been a good fellow in his youth. But he answered them very wisely: "Indeed," saith he, "in youth I was as you are now; and I had twelve fellows like unto myself, but not one of them came to a good end. And therefore follow not my example in youth, but follow my

---

19. bankrouts, bankruptcies.   **41. ancient,** the designation of the oldest barristers.

counsel in age, if ever ye think to come to this place, or to these years that I am come unto; lest ye meet either with poverty or Tyburn in the way."

This experience of all fashions in youth, being in proof always dangerous, in issue seldom lucky, is a way indeed to over-much knowledge, yet used commonly of such men which be either carried by some curious affection of mind, or driven by some hard necessity of life, to hazard the trial of over-many perilous adventures.

Erasmus, the honour of learning of all our time, said wisely that experience is the common schoolhouse of fools and ill men. Men of wit and honesty be otherwise instructed. For there be, that keep them out of fire, and yet was never burned; that be ware of water, and yet was never nigh drowning; that hate harlots, and was never at the stews; that abhor falsehood, and never brake promise themselves.

But will ye see a fit similitude of this adventured experience? A father that doth let loose his son to all experiences is most like a fond hunter that letteth slip a whelp to the whole herd; twenty to one he shall fall upon a rascal, and let go the fair game. Men that hunt so be either ignorant persons, privy stealers, or night-walkers.

Learning therefore, ye wise fathers, and good bringing up, and not blind and dangerous experience, is the next and readiest way that must lead your children, first to wisdom, and then to worthiness, if ever ye purpose they shall come there.

And to say all in short, though I lack authority to give counsel, yet I lack not good will to wish, that the youth in England, especially gentlemen, and namely nobility, should be by good bringing up so grounded in judgment of learning, so founded in love of honesty, as, when they should be called forth to the execution of great affairs, in service of their prince and country, they might be able to use and to order all experiences, were they good, were they bad, and that according to the square, rule, and line of wisdom, learning, and virtue.

And do I not mean, by all this my talk, that young gentlemen should always be poring on a book, and by using good studies should leese honest pleasure and haunt no good pastime; I mean nothing less. For it is well known that I both like and love, and have always, and do yet still use, all exercises and pastimes that be fit for my nature and ability; and beside natural disposition, in judgment also I was never either stoic in doctrine or anabaptist in religion, to mislike a merry, pleasant, and playful nature, if no outrage be committed against law, measure, and good order.

Therefore I would wish that beside some good time fitly appointed and constantly kept, to increase by reading the knowledge of the tongues and learning, young gentlemen should use and delight in all courtly exercises and gentlemanlike pastimes. And good cause why; for the self-same noble city of Athens, justly commended of me before, did wisely, and upon great consideration, appoint the Muses, Apollo, and Pallas, to be patrons of learning to their youth. For the Muses, besides learning, were also ladies of dancing, mirth, and minstrelsy; Apollo was god of shooting, and author of cunning playing upon instruments; Pallas also was lady mistress in wars. Whereby was nothing else meant but that learning should be always mingled with honest mirth and comely exercises; and that war also should be governed by learning and moderated by wisdom; as did well appear in those captains of Athens named by me before, and also in Scipio and Caesar, the two diamonds of Rome. And Pallas was no more feared in wearing *aegida* than she was praised for choosing *oliva;* whereby shineth the glory of learning, which thus was governor and mistress in the noble city of Athens, both of war and peace.

Therefore to ride comely, to run fair at the tilt or ring; to play at all weapons, to shoot fair in bow, or surely in gun; to vault lustily, to run, to leap, to wrestle, to swim; to dance comely, to sing, and play of instruments cunningly; to hawk, to hunt; to play at tennis, and all pastimes generally, which be joined with labour, used in open place, and on the day-light, containing either some fit exercise for war, or some pleasant pastime for peace, be not only comely and decent, but also very necessary for a courtly gentlemen to use.

But of all kind of pastimes fit for a gentleman, I will, God willing, in fitter place more at large declare fully, in my book of the cockpit; which I do write to satisfy some, I trust with some reason, that be more curious in marking other men's doings than careful in mending their own faults. And some also will needs busy themselves in marvelling, and adding thereunto unfriendly talk, why I, a man of good years, and of no ill place, I thank God and my prince, do make choice to spend such time in writing of trifles, as the School of Shooting, the Cockpit, and this book of the First Principles of Grammar, rather than to take some weighty matter in hand, either of religion or civil discipline.

3. **Tyburn,** the gallows on Tyburn Hill. 22. **fond,** foolish. 24. **rascal,** an inferior deer. 43. **do I not,** I do not.

23-24. **aegida . . . oliva,** shields (for war), olive branches (for peace).

Wise men, I know, will well allow of my choice herein; and as for such who have not wit of themselves but must learn of others to judge right of men's doings, let them read that wise poet Horace in his *Arte Poetica*, who willeth wise men to beware of high and lofty titles. For great ships require costly tackling, and also afterward dangerous government: small boats be neither very chargeable in making, nor very oft in great jeopardy; and yet they carry many times as good and costly ware as greater vessels do. A mean argument may easily bear the light burden of a small fault, and have always at hand a ready excuse for ill handling; and some praise it is, if it so chance to be better indeed than a man dare venture to seem. A high title doth charge a man with the heavy burden of too great a promise; and therefore saith Horace, very wittily, that that poet was a very fool that began his book with a goodly verse indeed but overproud a promise:

"Fortunam Priami cantabo, et nobile bellum."

And after as wisely:

"Quanto rectius hic, qui nil molitur inepte!" etc.;

meaning Homer; who, within the compass of a small argument of one harlot and of one good wife, did utter so much learning in all kind of sciences as, by the judgment of Quintilian, he deserveth so high a praise that no man yet deserved to sit in the second degree beneath him. And thus much out of my way, concerning my purpose in spending pen and paper and time upon trifles; and namely, to answer some that have neither wit nor learning to do anything themselves, neither will nor honesty to say well of other.

To join learning with comely exercises, Conto Baldesar Castiglione, in his book *Cortegiano*, doth trimly teach; which book advisedly read and diligently followed but one year at home in England would do a young gentleman more good, I wiss, than three years' travel abroad spent in Italy. And I marvel this book is no more read in the court than it is, seeing it is so well translated into English by a worthy gentleman, Sir Thomas Hoby, who was many ways well furnished with learning, and very expert in knowledge of divers tongues.

And beside good precepts in books, in all kind of tongues, this court also never lacked many fair examples for young gentlemen to follow; and surely one example is more valuable, both to good and ill, than twenty precepts written in books; and so Plato, not in one or two, but divers places, doth plainly teach.

If King Edward had lived a little longer, his only example had bred such a race of worthy learned gentlemen as this realm never yet did afford.

And in the second degree, two noble primroses of nobility, the young Duke of Suffolk and Lord Henry Matrevers, were two such examples to the court for learning as our time may rather wish than look for again. At Cambridge, also, in St. John's College, in my time, I do know that not so much the good statutes as two gentlemen of worthy memory, Sir John Cheke and Dr. Redman, by their only example of excellency in learning, of godliness in living, of diligency in studying, of counsel in exhorting, of good order in all things, did breed up so many learned men in that one college of St. John's at one time as I believe the whole university of Louvain in many years was never able to afford.

Present examples of this present time I list not to touch; yet there is one example for all the gentlemen of this court to follow, that may well satisfy them, or nothing will serve them, nor no example move them to goodness and learning.

It is your shame (I speak to you all, you young gentlemen of England) that one maid should go beyond you all in excellency of learning and knowledge of divers tongues. Point forth six of the best given gentlemen of this court, and all they together show not so much good will, spend not so much time, bestow not so many hours daily, orderly, and constantly, for the increase of learning and knowledge, as doth the Queen's Majesty herself. Yea, I believe that beside her perfect readiness in Latin, Italian, French, and Spanish, she readeth here now at Windsor more Greek every day than some prebendary of this church doth read Latin in a whole week. And that which is most praiseworthy of all, within the walls of her privy chamber she hath obtained that excellency of learning to understand, speak, and write both wittily with head and fair with hand, as scarce one or two rare wits in both the universities have in many years reached unto. Amongst all the benefits that God hath blessed me withal, next the knowledge of Christ's true religion, I count this the greatest, that it pleased God to call me to be one poor minister in setting forward these excellent gifts of learning in this most excellent prince; whose only example if the rest of our nobility would follow, then might England be for learning and wisdom in nobility a spectacle to all the world beside. . . .

---

8. **chargeable**, costly.   20. "**Fortunam . . . bellum.**" "The fortune of Priam I shall sing, and the famous war."   23. "**Quanto . . . inepte!**" "How much better this other, who attempted nothing foolishly."   40. **wiss**, know.   43–44. **translated . . . by . . . Hoby.** For a selection from this see page 305.

Raphael Holinshed
d. 1580?

Raphael Holinshed was born in Cheshire at an uncertain date. After graduation from Cambridge he is said to have become a clergyman. Early in the reign of Queen Elizabeth he moved to London and worked as a translator for Reginald Wolfe, the printer. While employed by Wolfe, Holinshed undertook the responsibility for the British section of an ambitious project, a proposed universal history. Wolfe died before the project was completed, and three other publishers united to sponsor the great project. The completed work included descriptions and histories of England, Scotland, and Ireland. Holinshed himself was mainly responsible for the history of England, which he drew judiciously from early chronicles, bringing his account up to the year 1575. He also compiled the history of Scotland from the Latin chronicle of Hector Boece and other Scottish historians. The Reverend William Harrison, rector of Radwinter and Canon of Windsor, anglicized Bellenden's Scottish version of Boece's description of Scotland, and composed the description of England, a remarkably vivid and detailed depiction of contemporary England, drawn from his own observations and from personal inquiry and correspondence. Richard Stanyhurst, who a few years later was to publish a translation of the first four books of the *Aeneid* into hexameters, based his description of Ireland on the notes left by Edmund Campion, the Jesuit, and Richard Hooker translated Giraldus Cambrensis' history of Ireland.

The first edition of the *Chronicles* was published in 1578 in two large folio volumes, of which the first volume bears the date 1577. A few passages offended Elizabeth and her Privy Council, and they were expunged. The expurgated passages exist in one copy, now in the possession of the British Museum. Holinshed seems to have died about 1580. A second edition of the *Chronicles*, with many additions and a continuation up to 1586, was brought out by John Hooker in 1587. Elizabeth's Privy Council again took exception to many passages dealing with recent events, and again the work was expurgated. In general, the second editor gave his account of the history of the preceding generation an anti-Catholic bias not apparent in Holinshed.

from the CHRONICLES

The second edition of Holinshed was one of Shakespeare's favorite sources. On it, he drew heavily for the material of the chronicle plays—*King John*, *Richard III*, *Richard II*, the two parts of *Henry IV*, and *Henry V*—as well as *Macbeth*, *King Lear*, and *Cymbeline*. The three passages given below contain the account of the murder of King Duff, the great-grandfather of Lady Macbeth, and an account of Macbeth's bloody career. It is of interest to note that Shakespeare transferred to the murder of Duncan many details that belonged to the earlier murder.

DONWALD, thus being the more kindled in wrath by the words of his wife, determined to follow her advice in the execution of so heinous an act. Whereupon devising with himself for a while, which way he might best accomplish his cursed intent, at length he got opportunity, and sped his purpose as followeth. It chanced that the king upon the day before he purposed to depart forth of the castle, was long in his oratory at his prayers, and there continued till it was late in the night. At the last, coming forth, he called such before him as had faithfully served him in pursuit and apprehension of the rebels, and, giving them hearty thanks, he bestowed sundry honourable gifts amongst them, of the which number Donwald was one, as he that had been ever accounted a most faithful servant to the king.

At length, having talked with them a long time, he got him into his privy chamber, only with two of his chamberlains, who having brought him to bed, came forth again, and then fell to banqueting with Donwald and his wife, who had prepared diverse delicate dishes and sundry sorts of drinks for their rear-supper or collation, whereat they sat up so long, till they had charged their stomachs with such full gorges that their heads were no sooner got to the pillow but asleep they were so fast that a man might have removed the chamber over them sooner than to have awaked them out of their drunken sleep.

Then Donwald, though he abhorred the act greatly in his heart, yet through instigation of his wife, he called four of his servants unto him (whom he had made privy to his wicked intent before, and framed to his purpose with large gifts) and now declaring unto them after what sort they should work the feat, they gladly obeyed his instructions, and speedily going about the murder, they entered the chamber (in which the king lay) a little before cock's crow, where they secretly cut his throat as he lay sleeping, without any buskling at all: and immediately by a postern gate they carried forth the dead body into the fields, and throwing it upon an horse there provided ready for that purpose, they convey it unto a place, about two miles distant from the castle, where they stayed, and got certain labourers to help them to turn the course of a little river running through the fields there, and digging a deep hole in the channel, they bury the body in the same, ramming it up with stones and gravel so closely, that setting the water in the right course again, no man could perceive that anything had been newly digged there. This they did by order appointed them by Donwald as is reported, for that the body should not be found, and by bleeding (when Donwald should be present) declare him to be guilty of the murder. For such an opinion men have, that the dead corpse of any man being slain, will bleed abundantly if the murderer be present. But for what consideration soever they buried him there, they had no sooner finished the work but that they slew them whose help they used herein, and straightway thereupon fled into Orkney.

Donwald, about the time that the murder was in doing, got him amongst them that kept the watch, and so continued in company with them all the residue of the night. But in the morning when the noise was raised in the king's chamber how the king was slain, his body conveyed away, and the bed all buried with blood, he with the watch ran thither, as though he had known nothing of the matter, and breaking into the chamber, and finding cakes of blood in the bed and on the floor about the sides of it, he forthwith slew the chamberlains, as guilty of that heinous murder, and then like a mad man running to and fro, he ransacked every corner within the castle, as though it had been to have seen if he might have found either the body or any of the murderers hid in any privy place: but at length coming to the postern gate and finding it open, he burdened the chamberlains, whom he had slain, with all the fault, they having the keys of the gates committed to their keeping all the night, and therefore it could not be otherwise (said he) but that they were of counsel in the committing of that most detestable murder.

Finally, such was his over earnest diligence in the severe inquisition and trial of the offenders herein, that some of the lords began to mislike the matter and to smell forth shrewd tokens that he should not be altogether clear himself. But for so much as they were in that country, where he had the whole rule, what by reason of his friends and authority together, they doubted to utter what they thought, till time and place should better serve thereunto, and hereupon got them away every man to his home. For the space of six months together, after this heinous murder thus committed, there appeared no sun by day nor moon by night in any part of the realm, but still was the sky covered with continual clouds, and sometimes such outrageous winds arose, with lightnings and tempests, that the people were in great fear of present destruction. . . .

Shortly after happened a strange and uncouth wonder, which afterward was the cause of much trouble in the realm of Scotland, as you shall after hear. It fortuned as Makbeth and Banquho journeyed towards Fores, where the king then lay, they went sporting by the way together without other company, save only themselves, passing through the woods and fields, when suddenly in the midst of a land, there met them three women in strange and wild apparel, resembling creatures of elder world, whom when they attentively beheld, wondering much at the sight, the first of them spake and said, "All hail Makbeth, thane of Glammis" (for he had lately entered into that dignity and office by the death of his father Sinell). The second of them said, "Hail Makbeth, thane of Cawder." But the third said, "All hail Makbeth that hereafter shalt be king of Scotland."

Then Banquho: "What manner of women," saith he, "are you, that seem so little favourable unto me, whereas to my fellow here, besides high offices, you assign also the kingdom, appointing forth nothing for me at all?" "Yes," saith the first of them, "we promise greater benefits unto thee than unto him, for he shall reign indeed, but with an unlucky end: neither shall he leave any issue behind him to succeed in his place, where contrarily you indeed shall not reign at all, but of you those shall be born which shall govern the Scottish kingdom by long order of continual descent." Herewith the aforesaid women vanished immediately out of their sight. This was reputed at the first but some vain fantastical illusion by Makbeth and Banquho, insomuch that Banquho would call Makbeth in jest, king of Scotland; and Makbeth again would call him in sport likewise, the father of many kings. But afterwards the common opinion

6. **buskling,** agitation, disturbance.

was, that these women were either the **weird sisters**, that is (as you would say) the goddesses of destiny, or else some nymphs or fairies, indued with knowledge of prophecy by their necromantical science, because every thing came to pass as they had spoken. For shortly after, the thane of Cawder being condemned at Fores of treason against the king committed, his lands, livings, and offices were given of the king's liberality to Makbeth.

The same night after, at supper, Banquho jested with him and said, "Now, Makbeth, you have obtained those things which the two former sisters prophesied; there remaineth only for you to purchase that which the third said should come to pass." Whereupon Makbeth, revolving the thing in his mind, began even then to devise how he might attain to the kingdom: but yet he thought with himself that he must tarry a time, which should advance him thereto (by the divine providence) as it had come to pass in his former preferment. But shortly after, it chanced that king Duncane, having two sons by his wife which was the daughter of Siward earl of Northumberland, he made the elder of them called Malcolme prince of Cumberland, as it were thereby to appoint him his successor in the kingdom, immediately after his decease. Makbeth, sore troubled herewith, for that he saw by this means his hope sore hindered (where, by the old laws of the realm, the ordinance was, that if he that should succeed were not of able age to take the charge upon himself, he that was next of blood unto him should be admitted) he began to take counsel how he might usurp the kingdom by force, having a just quarrel so to do (as he took the matter) for that Duncane did what in him lay to defraud him of all manner of title and claim, which he might, in time to come, pretend unto the crown.

The words of the three weird sisters also (of whom before you have heard) greatly encouraged him hereunto, but specially his wife lay sore upon him to attempt the thing, as she that was very ambitious, burning in unquenchable desire to bear the name of a queen. At length therefore, communicating his purposed intent with his trusty friends, amongst whom Banquho was the chiefest, upon confidence of their promised aid, he slew the king at Enverns, or (as some say) at Botgosuane, in the sixth year of his reign. Then having a company about him of such as he had made privy to his enterprise, he caused himself to be proclaimed king, and forthwith went unto Scone, where (by common consent) he received the investiture of the kingdom according to the accustomed manner. The body of Duncane was first conveyed unto Elgine, and there buried in kingly wise; but afterwards it was removed and conveyed unto Colmekill, and there laid in a sepulchre amongst his predecessors, in the year after the birth of our Saviour, 1046.

Malcolme Cammore and Donald Bane, the sons of king Duncane, for fear of their lives (which they might well know that Makbeth would seek to bring to end for his more sure confirmation in the estate) fled into Cumberland, where Malcolme remained, till time that Saint Edward the son of Ethelred recovered the dominion of England from the Danish power, the which Edward received Malcolme by way of most friendly entertainment: but Donald passed over into Ireland, where he was tenderly cherished by the king of that land. Makbeth, after the departure thus of Duncane's sons, used great liberality towards the nobles of the realm, thereby to win their favour, and when he saw that no man went about to trouble him, he set his whole intention to maintain justice, and to punish all enormities and abuses which had chanced through the feeble and slothful administration of Duncane. . . .

These and the like commendable laws Makbeth caused to be put as then in use, governing the realm for the space of ten years in equal justice. But this was but a counterfeit zeal of equity shown by him, partly against his natural inclination to purchase thereby the favour of the people. Shortly after, he began to show what he was, instead of equity practising cruelty. For the prick of conscience (as it chanceth ever in tyrants and such as attain to any estate by unrighteous means) caused him ever to fear lest he should be served of the same cup as he had ministered to his predecessor. The words also of the three weird sisters would not out of his mind, which as they promised him the kingdom, so likewise did they promise it at the same time unto the posterity of Banquho. He willed therefore the same Banquho, with his son named Fleance, to come to a supper that he had prepared for them, which was indeed, as he had devised, present death at the hands of certain murderers, whom he hired to execute that deed, appointing them to meet with the same Banquho and his son without the palace, as they returned to their lodgings, and there to slay them, so that he would not have his house slandered, but that in time to come he might clear himself, if anything were laid to his charge upon any suspicion that might arise.

34. **quarrel**, cause, reason.

It chanced yet by the benefit of the dark night, that though the father were slain, the son yet by the help of almighty God reserving him to better fortune, escaped that danger: and afterwards having some inkling (by the admonition of some friends which he had in the court) how his life was sought no less than his father's, who was slain not by chance meddling (as by the handling of the matter Makbeth would have had it to appear) but even upon a prepensed device: whereupon to avoid further peril he fled into Wales. . . .

But to return unto Makbeth, in continuing the history, and to begin where I left, you shall understand that after the contrived slaughter of Banquho, nothing prospered with the foresaid Makbeth: for in manner every man began to doubt his own life, and dared not appear in the king's presence; and even as there were many that stood in fear of him, so likewise stood he in fear of many, in such sort that he began to make those away by one surmised cavillation or other, whom he thought most able to work him any displeasure.

At length he found such sweetness by putting his nobles to death that his earnest thirst after blood in this behalf might in no wise be satisfied: for you must consider he won double profit (as he thought) hereby: for first they were rid out of the way whom he feared, and then again his coffers were enriched by their goods which were forfeited to his use, whereby he might better maintain a guard of armed men about him to defend his person from injury of them whom he had in any suspicion. Further, to the end he might the more cruelly oppress his subjects with all tyrant-like wrongs, he builded a strong castle on the top of a high hill called Dunsinane, situated in Gowrie, ten miles from Perth, on such a proud height that standing there aloft, a man might behold well near all the countries of Angus, Fife, Stermond, and Ernedale, as it were lying underneath him. This castle then being founded on the top of that high hill, put the realm to great charges before it was finished, for all the stuff necessary to the building could not be brought up without much toil and business. But Makbeth being once determined to have the work go forward, caused the thanes of each shire within the realm to come and help towards that building, each man his course about.

At the last, when the turn fell unto Makduffe thane of Fife to build his part, he sent workmen with all needful provision, and commanded them to show such diligence in every behalf that no occasion might be given for the king to find fault with him, in that he came not himself as other had done, which he refused to do, for doubt lest the king, bearing him (as he partly understood) no great good will, would lay violent hands upon him, as he had done upon diverse others. Shortly after, Makbeth coming to behold how the work went forward, and because he found not Makduffe there, he was sore offended, and said, "I perceive this man will never obey my commandments, till he be ridden with a snaffle; but I shall provide well enough for him." Neither could he afterwards abide to look upon the said Makduffe, either for that he thought his puissance over-great; either else for that he had learned of certain wizards, in whose words he put great confidence (for that the prophecy had happened so right, which the three fairies or weird sisters had declared unto him) how that he ought to take heed of Makduffe, who in time to come should seek to destroy him.

And surely hereupon had he put Makduffe to death but that a certain witch, whom he had in great trust, had told that he should never be slain with man born of any woman, nor vanquished till the wood of Bernane came to the castle of Dunsinane. By this prophecy Makbeth put all fear out of his heart, supposing he might do what he would, without any fear to be punished for the same, for by the one prophecy he believed it was impossible for any man to vanquish him, and by the other impossible to slay him. This vain hope caused him to do many outrageous things, to the grievous oppression of his subjects. At length Makduffe, to avoid peril of life, purposed with himself to pass into England, to procure Malcolme Cammore to claim the crown of Scotland. But this was not so secretly devised by Makduffe but that Makbeth had knowledge given him thereof: for kings (as is said) have sharp sight like unto lynx, and long ears like unto Midas. For Makbeth had in every noble man's house one sly fellow or other in fee with him, to reveal all that was said or done within the same, by which slight he oppressed the most part of the nobles of his realm.

Immediately then, being advertised whereabout Makduffe went, he came hastily with a great power into Fife, and forthwith besieged the castle where Makduffe dwelled, trusting to have found him therein. They that kept the house, without any resistance opened the gates, and suffered him to enter, mistrusting none evil. But nevertheless Makbeth most cruelly caused the wife and children

---

10. **prepensed,** premeditated.   22. **cavillation,** captious objection.   15. **puissance,** power.   46. **advertised,** advised.

of Makduffe, with all other whom he found in that castle, to be slain. Also he confiscated the goods of Makduffe, proclaimed him traitor, and confined him out of all the parts of his realm; but Makduffe was already escaped out of danger, and gotten into England unto Malcolme Cammore, to try what purchase he might make by means of his support to revenge the slaughter so cruelly executed on his wife, his children, and other friends. At his coming unto Malcolme, he declared into what great misery the estate of Scotland was brought, by the detestable cruelties exercised by the tyrant Makbeth, having committed many horrible slaughters and murders, both as well of the nobles as commons, for the which he was hated right mortally of all his liege people, desiring nothing more than to be delivered of that intolerable and most heavy yoke of thraldom which they sustained at such a caitiff's hands.

Malcolme hearing Makduffe's words, which he uttered in very lamentable sort, for mere compassion and very ruth that pierced his sorrowful heart, bewailing the miserable state of his country, he fetched a deep sigh; which Makduffe perceiving, began to fall most earnestly in hand with him, to enterprise the delivering of the Scottish people out of the hands of so cruel and bloody a tyrant as Makbeth by too many plain experiments did show himself to be: which was an easy matter for him to bring to pass, considering not only the good title he had, but also the earnest desire of the people to have some occasion ministered, whereby they might be revenged of those notable injuries which they daily sustained by the outrageous cruelty of Makbeth's misgovernance. Though Malcolme was very sorrowful for the oppression of his countrymen the Scots, in manner as Makduffe had declared; yet doubting whether he were come as one that meant unfeignedly as he spake, or else as sent from Makbeth to betray him, he thought to have some further trial, and thereupon dissembling his mind at the first, he answered as followeth,

"I am truly very sorry for the misery chanced to my country of Scotland, but though I have never so great affection to relieve the same, yet by reason of certain incurable vices, which reign in me, I am nothing meet thereto. First, such immoderate lust and voluptuous sensuality (the abominable fountain of all vices) followeth me, that if I were made king of Scots, I should seek to deflower your maids and matrons, in such wise that my intemperance should be more importable unto you than the bloody tyranny of Makbeth now is." Hereunto Makduffe answered, "This surely is a very evil fault, for many noble princes and kings have lost both lives and kingdoms for the same; nevertheless there are women enough in Scotland, and therefore follow my counsel. Make thyself king, and I shall convey the matter so wisely that you shall be so satisfied at your pleasure in such secret wise that no man shall be aware thereof."

Then said Malcolme, "I am also the most avaricious creature on the earth, so that if I were king, I should seek so many ways to get lands and goods that I would slay the most part of all the nobles of Scotland by surmised accusations, to the end I might enjoy their lands, goods, and possessions; and therefore to show you what mischief may ensue on you through my insatiable covetousness, I will rehearse unto you a fable. There was a fox having a sore place on him overset with a swarm of flies that continually sucked out her blood: and when one that came by and saw this manner, demanded whether she would have the flies driven beside her, she answered: "No: for if these flies that are already full, and by reason thereof suck not very eagerly, should be chased away, other that are empty and feeling hungered should light in their places, and suck out the residue of my blood far more to my grievance than these which now being satisfied do not much annoy me." Therefore said Malcolme, "Suffer me to remain where I am, lest if I attain to the regiment of your realm, my unquenchable avarice may prove such that you would think the displeasures which now grieve you should seem easy in respect of the unmeasurable outrage which might ensue through my coming amongst you."

Makduffe to this made answer how it was a far worse fault than the other; for avarice is the root of all mischief, and for that crime the most part of our kings have been slain and brought to their final end. "Yet notwithstanding follow my counsel, and take upon you the crown. There is gold and riches enough in Scotland to satisfy your greedy desire." Then said Malcolme again, "I am furthermore inclined to dissimulation, telling of leasings, and all other kinds of deceit, so that I naturally rejoice in nothing so much as to betray and deceive such as put any trust or confidence in my words. Then since there is nothing that more becometh a prince than constancy, verity, truth, and justice, with the other laudable fellowship of those fair and noble virtues which are comprehended only in soothfastness, and that lying utterly overthroweth the same; you see how unable I am to govern any province or region: and therefore since you have

---

22. **ruth**, pity.　52. **importable**, unendurable.　　50–51. **soothfastness**, truthfulness, honesty.

remedies to cloak and hide all the rest of my other vices, I pray you find shift to cloak this vice amongst the residue."

Then said Makduffe, "This yet is the worst of all, and there I leave thee, and therefore say, Oh ye unhappy and miserable Scotchmen, which are thus scourged with so many and sundry calamities, each one above other! Ye have one cursed and wicked tyrant that now reigneth over you, without any right or title, oppressing you with his most bloody cruelty. This other that hath the right to the crown, is so replete with the inconstant behaviour and manifest vices of Englishmen that he is nothing worthy to enjoy it: for by his own confession he is not only avaricious, and given to insatiable lust, but so false a traitor withal that no trust is to be had unto any word he speaketh. Adieu Scotland, for now I account myself a banished man forever, without comfort or consolation," and with those words the brackish tears trickled down his cheeks very abundantly.

At the last, when he was ready to depart, Malcolme took him by the sleeve, and said, "Be of good comfort, Makduffe, for I have none of these vices before remembered, but have jested with thee in this manner, only to prove your mind: for diverse times heretofore hath Makbeth sought by this manner of means to bring me into his hands, but the more slow I have shown myself to condescend to your motion and request, the more diligence shall I use in accomplishing the same." Incontinently hereupon they embraced each other, and promising to be faithful the one to the other, they fell in consultation how they might best provide for all their business, to bring the same to good effect. Soon after, Makduffe repairing to the borders of Scotland, addressed his letters with secret dispatch unto the nobles of the realm, declaring how Malcolme was confederate with him, to come hastily into Scotland to claim the crown, and therefore he required them, since he was right inheritor thereto, to assist him with their powers to recover the same out of the hands of the wrongful usurper.

In the meantime, Malcolme purchased such favour at king Edward's hands that old Siward, Earl of Northumberland, was appointed with ten thousand men to go with him into Scotland, to support him in this enterprise, for recovery of his right. After these news were spread abroad in Scotland, the nobles drew into two several factions, the one taking part with Makbeth, and the other with Malcolme. Hereupon ensued oftentimes sundry bickerings and diverse light skirmishes: for those that were of Malcolme's side would not jeopard to join with their enemies in a pight field till his coming out of England to their support. But after that Makbeth perceived his enemies' power to increase, by such aid as came to them forth of England with his adversary Malcolme, he recoiled back into Fife, there purposing to abide in camp fortified, at the castle of Dunsinane, and to fight with his enemies, if they meant to pursue him; howbeit some of his friends advised him that it should be best for him, either to make some agreement with Malcolme, or else to flee with all speed into the Isles, and to take his treasure with him, to the end he might wage sundry great princes of the realm to take his part, and retain strangers, in whom he might better trust than in his own subjects, which stole daily from him; but he had such confidence in his prophecies that he believed he should never be vanquished till Birnane wood were brought to Dunsinane; nor yet to be slain with any man that should be or was born of any woman.

Malcolme, following hastily after Makbeth, came the night before the battle unto Birnane wood, and when his army had rested a while there to refresh them, he commanded every man to get a bough of some tree or other of that wood in his hand, as big as he might bear, and to march forth therewith in such wise that on the next morrow they might come closely and without sight in this manner within view of his enemies. On the morrow when Makbeth beheld them coming in this sort, he first marvelled what the matter meant, but in the end remembered himself that the prophecy which he had heard long before that time, of the coming of Birnane wood to Dunsinane castle, was likely to be now fulfilled. Nevertheless, he brought his men in order of battle, and exhorted them to do valiantly; howbeit his enemies had scarcely cast from them their boughs when Makbeth, perceiving their numbers, betook him straight to flight, whom Makduffe pursued with great hatred even till he came unto Lunfannaine, where Makbeth, perceiving that Makduffe was hard at his back, leapt beside his horse, saying, "You traitor, what meaneth it that you should thus in vain follow me that am not appointed to be slain by any creature that is born of a woman? Come on, therefore, and receive your reward which you have deserved for your pains," and therewithal he lifted up his sword, thinking to have slain him.

But Makduffe, quickly avoiding from his horse, ere he came at him, answered (with his naked sword

2. **pight**, small.   14. **wage**, hire, employ.

in his hand) saying, "It is true, Makbeth, and now shall thine insatiable cruelty have an end, for I am even he that your wizards have told you of, who was never born of my mother, but ripped out of her womb." Therewithal he stepped unto him, and slew him in the place. Then cutting his head from his shoulders, he set it upon a pole, and brought it unto Malcolme. This was the end of Makbeth, after he had reigned 17 years over the Scotchmen. In the beginning of his reign he accomplished many worthy acts, very profitable to the commonwealth (as you have heard), but afterward by illusion of the devil, he defamed the same with most terrible cruelty. He was slain in the year of the Incarnation, 1057, and in the 16th year of King Edward's reign over the Englishmen.

Sir Thomas North
c. 1535–1601

So far as we know, Sir Thomas North, best known as the English translator of Plutarch, had an uneventful life. He was born about 1535, the younger son of Edward, first Baron North. He seems to have been educated at Cambridge, and to have read for the law at Lincoln's Inn. In 1557, he translated from the Spanish Guevara's *The Dial of Princes*, a briefer version of which, translated by Lord Berners under the title *The Golden Book of Marcus Aurelius*, was already in its seventh edition. *The Dial* is a treatise on education, like Erasmus's *Education of a Christian Prince* and Ascham's *The Schoolmaster*. Its precepts are illustrated by numerous anecdotes from the classical historians. By 1568, North had settled at Cambridge, for the freedom of the city was conferred upon him in that year. In 1570 he published his second translation, this time from the Italian, *The Moral Philosophy of Doni*. This is a book of beast fables in the manner of Aesop. It has been called "one of the most charming books of beast fables ever written." The ultimate original was in Sanskrit, but before it reached the hands of Doni, the Italian translator, it had passed through the sieve of Arabic, Hebrew, Latin, and Spanish translations. In 1574, North made a journey to France in the train of his older brother Roger, who had succeeded to the family title. Despite the fact that this brother gave him "a lease of a house and household stuff" in 1576, North seems to have been in constant financial difficulties. The publication of the translation of Plutarch in 1579 does not seem to have relieved his distress, for in the following year the Earl of Leicester, writing to Lord Burghley, described him as "a very honest gentleman, and hath many good things in him, which are drowned only by poverty." His grandnephew Dudley, the fourth Baron North, described his granduncle as a man of courage who at the time of the Armada was in command of three hundred men from Ely. Elizabeth knighted him in 1591; he received a pension from Cambridge in 1598, and a royal pension in 1601. He probably died before the appearance of the third edition of the Plutarch in 1603.

Sir Thomas North is one of the great English translators. Despite his linguistic equipment, he did not feel equal to translating Plutarch from the Greek. Instead, he turned to the distinguished French translation which Bishop James Amyot had made in 1559. North followed Amyot closely, although he seems at times to have referred to the original Greek. But North gave his translation a rich and vigorous Elizabethan flavor by substituting specific colloquial and sensory words for Amyot's abstract terms. He used freely the language of the street and the stores of proverbial wisdom. For the elegance of Amyot he substituted the hearty realism of a man of affairs. It is no wonder that Shakespeare found North's Plutarch not only a storehouse of information about the Roman history on which he drew repeatedly in the Roman plays—*Julius Caesar*, *Antony and Cleopatra*, and *Coriolanus*—but also the raw material for brilliant poetic paraphrases. To gauge the service North rendered Shakespeare, the student can do no better than to compare North's description of Cleopatra in her barge with Shakespeare's poetic version of it.

Plutarch's *Lives* attracted the attention and the admiration of the Renaissance for a number of reasons: the fullness of their accounts of the worthies of Greece and Rome, the brilliance of their historical portraiture, and the supposed didactic value of the examples offered by heroes' lives. Of Plutarch the great French essayist Montaigne wrote, in the words of Florio's translation, "Plutarch of all authors I know hath best commixed art with nature, and coupled judgment with learning." And again, Plutarch "is so universal and so full that upon all occasions, and whatsoever extravagant subject you have undertaken, he intrudeth himself into your work and gently reacheth you a help-affording hand, fraught with rare embellishment and inexhaustible of precious riches. . . . He can no sooner come in my sight, or if I cast but a glance upon him, but I pull some leg or wing from him." Shakespeare was not the least of the Elizabethans who found it convenient to pull at least some leg or wing from Plutarch.

from PLUTARCH'S LIVES

JULIUS CAESAR

In his life of Julius Caesar, from which the selection given below is taken, Plutarch tells how Caesar, after an unpromising beginning, advanced rapidly in public life. From being quaestor and then praetor in Spain, he returned to Rome to be named high priest. His lavish expenditures won him a wide popular support, and he was given the province of Spain to govern; there he extended the area of Roman rule. After his return to Italy, his reconciliation with Pompey and Crassus, and his election as consul, he was assigned to the governorship of the province of Gaul. There he campaigned successfully against the Helvetii, the Germanni, and the Belgae, and even crossed the channel to England.

Then Caesar and his experienced army marched on Rome, bent on the overthrow of Pompey. The latter fled, and Caesar, after defeating Pompey's lieutenants in Spain, pursued him and defeated him at Pharsalia. Pompey fled to Egypt, where he was murdered. After Caesar's campaign in Egypt and his adventure with Cleopatra, he drove Mithridates' son out of Asia Minor, and defeated Pompey's followers in Africa. He returned to celebrate these triumphs in Rome, and was named consul for the fourth time. He then defeated Pompey's sons in Spain.

BUT the triumph he made into Rome for the same did as much offend the Romans, and more, than anything that ever he had done before: because he had not overcome captains that were strangers, nor barbarous kings, but had destroyed the sons of the noblest man in Rome, whom fortune had overthrown. And because he had plucked up his race by the roots, men did not think it meet for him to triumph so for the calamities of his country, rejoicing at a thing for the which he had but one excuse to allege in his defence unto the gods and men, that he was compelled to do that he did. And the rather they thought it not meet, because he had never before sent letters nor messengers unto the commonwealth at Rome for any victory that he had ever won in all the civil wars but did always for shame refuse the glory of it. This notwithstanding, the Romans inclining to Caesar's prosperity and taking the bit in the mouth, supposing that, to be ruled by one man alone, it would be a good mean for them to take breath a little, after so many troubles and miseries as they had abidden in these civil wars: they chose him perpetual Dictator. This was a plain tyranny: for to this absolute power of Dictator they added this, never to be afraid to be deposed. Cicero propounded before the Senate that they should give him such honours as were meet for a man; howbeit others afterwards added-to honours beyond all reason. For, men striving who should most honour him, they made him hateful and troublesome to themselves that most favoured him by reason of the unmeasurable greatness and honours which they gave him. Thereupon, it is reported that even they that most hated him were no less favourers and furtherers of his honours than they that most flattered him: because they might have greater occasions to rise, and that it might appear they had just cause and colour to attempt that they did against him. And now for himself, after he had ended his civil wars, he did so honourably behave himself that there was no fault to be found in him; and therefore methinks, amongst other honours they gave him, he rightly deserved this, that they should build him a temple of clemency, to thank him for his courtesy he had used unto them in his victory. For he pardoned many of them that had borne arms against him, and furthermore, did prefer some of them to honour and office in the commonwealth: as, amongst others, Cassius and Brutus, both the which were made Praetors. And where Pompey's images had been thrown down, he caused them to be set up again; whereupon Cicero said then, that Caesar setting up Pompey's images again, he made his own stand the surer. And when some of his friends did counsel him to have a guard for the safety of his person, and some also did offer themselves to serve him, he would never consent to it, but said, it was better to die once than always to be afraid of death. But to win himself the love and good will of the people, as the honourablest guard and best safety he could have, he made common feasts again and general distributions of corn. Furthermore, to gratify the soldiers also, he replenished many cities again with inhabitants, which before had been destroyed, and placed them there that had no place to repair unto: of the which the

---

40–41. **the same,** Caesar's victory over Pompey's sons at Munda.

9. **abidden,** endured.

noblest and chiefest cities were these two, Carthage and Corinth, and it chanced also that, like as aforetime they had been both taken and destroyed together, even so were they both set afoot again and replenished with people at one self time. And as for great personages, he wan them also, promising some of them to make them Praetors and Consuls in time to come, and unto others honours and preferments, but to all men generally good hope, seeking all the ways he could to make every man contented with his reign. Insomuch as one of the Consuls called Maximus chancing to die a day before his Consulship ended, he declared Caninius Rebilius Consul only for the day that remained. So, divers going to his house (as the manner was) to salute him, and to congratulate with him of his calling and preferment, being newly chosen officer, Cicero pleasantly said, "Come, let us make haste, and be gone thither before his Consulship come out." Furthermore, Caesar being born to attempt all great enterprises, and having an ambitious desire to covet great honours, the prosperous good success he had of his former conquests bred no desire in him quietly to enjoy the fruits of his labours, but rather gave him hope of things to come, still kindling more and more in him thoughts of greater enterprises, and desire of new glory, as if that which he had present were stale and nothing worth. This humour of his was no other but an emulation with himself as with another man, and a certain contention to overcome the things he prepared to attempt. For he was determined and made preparation also to make war with the Persians. Then, when he had overcome them, to pass through Hyrcania (compassing in the sea Caspium and Mount Caucasus) into the realm of Pontus, and so to invade Scythia: and over-running all the countries and people adjoining unto high Germany, and Germany itself, at length to return by Gaul into Italy, and so to enlarge the Roman Empire round that it might be every way compassed in with the great sea Oceanus. But whilst he was preparing for this voyage, he attempted to cut the bar of the strait of Peloponnesus, in the place where the city of Corinth standeth. Then he was minded to bring the rivers of Anien and Tiber straight from Rome unto the city of Circeii with a deep channel and high banks cast up on either side, and so to fall into the sea at Terracina, for the better safety and commodity of the merchants that came to Rome to traffic there. Furthermore, he determined to drain and seaw all the water of the marishes betwixt the cities of Nomentum and Setium, to make it firm land for the benefit of many thousands of people: and on the seacoast next unto Rome to cast great high banks, and to cleanse all the haven about Ostia of rocks and stones hidden under the water, and to take away all other impediments that made the harbourough dangerous for ships, and to make new havens and arsenals meet to harbour such ships as did continually traffic thither. All these things were purposed to be done, but took no effect. But the ordinance of the calendar and reformation of the year, to take away all confusion of time, being exactly calculated by the mathematicians and brought to perfection, was a great commodity unto all men. For the Romans, using then the ancient computation of the year, had not only such incertainty and alteration of the month and times that the sacrifices and yearly feasts came by little and little to seasons contrary for the purpose they were ordained but also in the revolution of the sun (which is called *Annus Solaris*) no other nation agreed with them in account and, of the Romans themselves, only the priests understood it. And therefore, when they listed, they suddenly (no man being able to control them) did thrust in a month above their ordinary number, which they called in old time *Mercedonius*. Some say that Numa Pompilius was the first that devised this way, to put a month between, but it was a weak remedy, and did little help the correction of the errors that were made in the account of the year, to frame them to perfection. But Caesar, committing this matter unto the philosophers and best expert mathematicians at that time, did set forth an excellent and perfect calendar, more exactly calculated than any other that was before, the which the Romans do use until this present day, and do nothing err as others in the difference of time. But his enemies notwithstanding that envied his greatness did not stick to find fault withal. As Cicero the orator, when one said, "To-morrow the star Lyra will rise": "Yea," said he, "at the commandment of Caesar," as if men were compelled so to say and think by Caesar's edict. But the chiefest cause that made him mortally hated was the covetous desire he had to be called king: which first gave the people just cause, and next his secret enemies honest colour, to bear him ill will. This notwithstanding, they that procured him this honour and dignity gave it out among the people that it was written in the Sibylline prophecies how the Romans might overcome the Parthians, if they

---

6. **wan**, won.   47. **Circeii**, near the modern Monte Circello.   51. **seaw**, drain.   52. **marishes**, marshes.

1. **Nomentum and Setium**, cities near Rome.   4. **Ostia**, at the mouth of the Tiber.   27. **Numa Pompilius**, second legendary emperor of Rome (715–672 B.C.).

made war with them and were led by a king, but otherwise that they were unconquerable. And furthermore they were so bold besides, that, Caesar returning to Rome from the city of Alba, when they came to salute him, they called him king. But the people being offended and Caesar also angry, he said he was not called king, but Caesar. Then, every man keeping silence, he went his way heavy and sorrowful. When they had decreed divers honours for him in the Senate, the Consuls and Praetors accompanied with the whole assembly of the Senate went unto him in the market-place, where he was set by the pulpit for orations, to tell him what honours they had decreed for him in his absence. But he, sitting still in his majesty, disdaining to rise up unto them when they came in, as if they had been private men, answered them that his honours had more need to be cut off than enlarged. This did not only offend the Senate, but the common people also, to see that he should so lightly esteem of the Magistrates of the commonwealth, insomuch as every man that might lawfully go his way departed thence very sorrowfully. Thereupon also Caesar rising departed home to his house, and tearing open his doublet collar, making his neck bare, he cried out aloud to his friends that his throat was ready to offer to any man that would come and cut it. Notwithstanding, it is reported that afterwards, to excuse this folly, he imputed it to his disease, saying that their wits are not perfect which have his disease of the falling evil, when standing of their feet they speak to the common people, but are soon troubled with a trembling of their body and a sudden dimness and giddiness. But that was not true. For he would have risen up to the Senate, but Cornelius Balbus, one of his friends but rather a flatterer, would not let him, saying: "What, do you not remember that you are Caesar, and will you not let them reverence you, and do their duties?" Besides these occasions and offences, there followed also his shame and reproach, abusing the Tribunes of the people in this sort. At that time the feast Lupercalia was celebrated, the which in old time men say was the feast of shepherds, or herdmen, and is much like unto the feast of the Lycaeans in Arcadia. But howsoever it is, that day there are divers noblemen's sons, young men, (and some of them Magistrates themselves that govern then) which run naked through the city, striking in sport them they meet in their way with leather thongs, hair and all on, to make them give place. And many noblewomen and gentlewomen also go of purpose to stand in their way, and do put forth their hands to be stricken, as scholars hold them out to their schoolmaster to be stricken with the ferula: persuading themselves that, being with child, they shall have good delivery, and also, being barren, that it will make them to conceive with child. Caesar sat to behold that sport upon the pulpit for orations, in a chair of gold, apparelled in triumphing manner. Antonius, who was Consul at that time, was one of them that ran this holy course. So, when he came into the market-place, the people made a lane for him to run at liberty, and he came to Caesar, and presented him a diadem wreathed about with laurel. Whereupon there rose a certain cry of rejoicing, not very great, done only by a few appointed for the purpose. But when Caesar refused the diadem, then all the people together made an outcry of joy. Then, Antonius offering it him again, there was a second shout of joy, but yet of a few. But when Caesar refused it again the second time, then all the whole people shouted. Caesar having made this proof found that the people did not like of it, and thereupon rose out of his chair, and commanded the crown to be carried unto Jupiter in the Capitol. After that, there were set up images of Caesar in the city with diadems upon their heads, like kings. Those the two Tribunes, Flavius and Marullus, went and pulled down: and furthermore, meeting with them that first saluted Caesar as king, they committed them to prison. The people followed them rejoicing at it, and called them Brutes, because of Brutus, who had in old time driven the kings out of Rome, and that brought the kingdom of one person unto the government of the Senate and people. Caesar was so offended withal that he deprived Marullus and Flavius of their Tribuneships, and, accusing them, he spake also against the people, and called them *Bruti* and *Cumani*, to wit, beasts and fools. Hereupon the people went straight unto Marcus Brutus, who from his father came of the first Brutus and by his mother of the house of the Servilians, a noble house as any was in Rome, and was also nephew and son-in-law of Marcus Cato. Notwithstanding, the great honours and favour Caesar shewed unto him kept him back, that of himself alone he did not conspire nor consent to depose him of his kingdom. For Caesar did not only save his life after the battle of Pharsalia when Pompey fled, and did at his request also save many more of his friends besides; but, furthermore, he put a marvellous confidence in him. For he had already preferred him to the Praetorship for that year, and furthermore was appointed to be Consul the fourth year after that, having through Caesar's

31. **falling evil,** epilepsy.

friendship obtained it before Cassius, who likewise made suit for the same; and Caesar also, as it is reported, said in this contention, "Indeed Cassius hath alleged best reason, but yet shall he not be chosen before Brutus." Some one day accusing Brutus while he practised this conspiracy, Caesar would not hear of it, but clapping his hand on his body told them, "Brutus will look for this skin," meaning thereby that Brutus for his virtue deserved to rule after him, but yet that for ambition's sake he would not shew himself unthankful nor dishonourable. Now they that desired change and wished Brutus only their prince and governor above all other, they durst not come to him themselves to tell him what they would have him to do, but in the night did cast sundry papers into the Praetor's seat where he gave audience, and the most of them to this effect: "Thou sleepest, Brutus, and art not Brutus indeed." Cassius, finding Brutus' ambition stirred up the more by these seditious bills, did prick him forward and egg him on the more for a private quarrel he had conceived against Caesar, the circumstance whereof we have set down more at large in Brutus' life. Caesar also had Cassius in great jealousy and suspected him much; whereupon he said on a time to his friends, "What will Cassius do, think ye? I like not his pale looks." Another time, when Caesar's friends complained unto him of Antonius and Dolabella that they pretended some mischief towards him, he answered them again, "As for those fat men and smooth-combed heads," quoth he, "I never reckon of them, but these pale-visaged and carrion lean people, I fear them most," meaning Brutus and Cassius. Certainly, destiny may easier be foreseen than avoided, considering the strange and wonderful signs that were said to be seen before Caesar's death. For, touching the fires in the element and spirits running up and down in the night, and also the solitary birds to be seen at noon-days sitting in the great market-place: are not all these signs perhaps worth the noting in such a wonderful chance as happened? But Strabo the philosopher writeth that divers men were seen going up and down in fire; and furthermore, that there was a slave of the soldiers, that did cast a marvellous burning flame out of his hand, insomuch as they that saw it thought he had been burnt, but when the fire was out, it was found he had no hurt. Caesar self also, doing sacrifice unto the gods, found that one of the beasts which was sacrificed had no heart; and that was a strange thing in nature, how a beast could live without a heart. Furthermore, there was a certain Soothsayer that had given Caesar warning long time afore, to take heed of the day of the Ides of March (which is the fifteenth of the month), for on that day he should be in great danger. That day being come, Caesar going unto the Senate-house, and speaking merrily to the Soothsayer, told him, "The Ides of March be come." "So be they," softly answered the Soothsayer, "but yet are they not past." And the very day before, Caesar, supping with Marcus Lepidus, sealed certain letters, as he was wont to do, at the board; so, talk falling out amongst them, reasoning what death was best, he preventing their opinions cried out aloud, "Death unlooked for." Then going to bed the same night as his manner was, and lying with his wife Calpurnia, all the windows and doors of his chamber flying open, the noise awoke him, and made him afraid when he saw such light, but more, when he heard his wife Calpurnia, being fast asleep, weep and sigh, and put forth many fumbling lamentable speeches. For she dreamed that Caesar was slain, and that she had him in her arms. Others also do deny that she had any such dream, as amongst other Titus Livius writeth that it was in this sort. The Senate having set upon the top of Caesar's house, for an ornament and setting forth of the same, a certain pinnacle, Calpurnia dreamed that she saw it broken down, and that she thought she lamented and wept for it. Insomuch that, Caesar rising in the morning, she prayed him if it were possible not to go out of the doors that day, but to adjourn the session of the Senate until another day. And if that he made no reckoning of her dream, yet that he would search further of the Soothsayers by their sacrifices, to know what should happen him that day. Thereby it seemed that Caesar likewise did fear and suspect somewhat, because his wife Calpurnia until that time was never given to any fear or superstition and then, for that he saw her so troubled in mind with this dream she had. But much more afterwards, when the Soothsayers, having sacrificed many beasts one after another, told him that none did like them; then he determined to send Antonius to adjourn the session of the Senate. But in the meantime came Decius Brutus, surnamed Albinus, in whom Caesar put such confidence that in his last will and testament he had appointed him to be his next heir, and yet was of the conspiracy with Cassius and Brutus; he, fearing that if Caesar did adjourn the session that day the conspiracy would out, laughed the Soothsayers to scorn, and reproved Caesar, saying that he gave the Senate occasion to mislike with him, and that they might think he mocked them, considering that by his command-

11. **preventing,** anticipating.

ment they were assembled, and that they were ready willingly to grant him all things, and to proclaim him king of all the provinces of the Empire of Rome out of Italy, and that he should wear his diadem in all other places both by sea and land. And furthermore, that if any man should tell them from him they should depart for that present time, and return again when Calpurnia should have better dreams, what would his enemies and ill-willers say and how could they like of his friends' words? And who could persuade them otherwise, but that they would think his dominion a slavery unto them, and tyrannical in himself? "And yet, if it be so," said he, "that you utterly mislike of this day, it is better that you go yourself in person, and saluting the Senate to dismiss them till another time." Therewithal he took Caesar by the hand, and brought him out of his house. Caesar was not gone far from his house, but a bondman, a stranger, did what he could to speak with him; and, when he saw he was put back by the great press and multitude of people that followed him, he went straight unto his house, and put himself into Calpurnia's hands to be kept till Caesar came back again, telling her that he had great matters to impart unto him. And one Artemidorus also, born in the Isle of Gnidos, a Doctor of Rhetoric in the Greek tongue, who by means of his profession was very familiar with certain of Brutus' confederates, and therefore knew the most part of all their practices against Caesar, came and brought him a little bill written with his own hand, of all that he meant to tell him. He, marking how Caesar received all the supplications that were offered him, and that he gave them straight to his men that were about him, pressed nearer to him, and said: "Caesar, read this memorial to yourself, and that quickly, for they be matters of great weight, and touch you nearly." Caesar took it of him, but could never read it, though he many times attempted it, for the number of people that did salute him; but holding it still in his hand, keeping it to himself, went on withal into the Senate-house. Howbeit other are of opinion that it was some man else that gave him that memorial, and not Artemidorus, who did what he could all the way as he went to give it Caesar, but he was always repulsed by the people. For these things they may seem to come by chance; but the place where the murder was prepared, and where the Senate were assembled, and where also there stood up an image of Pompey dedicated by himself amongst other ornaments which he gave unto the Theatre: all these were manifest proofs that it was the ordinance of some god that made this treason to be executed specially in that very place. It is also reported that Cassius (though otherwise he did favour the doctrine of Epicurus) beholding the image of Pompey, before they entered into the action of their traitorous enterprise, he did softly call upon it to aid him. But the instant danger of the present time, taking away his former reason, did suddenly put him into a furious passion, and made him like a man half beside himself. Now Antonius, that was a faithful friend to Caesar, and a valiant man besides of his hands, him Decius Brutus Albinus entertained out of the Senate-house, having begun a long tale of set purpose. So, Caesar coming into the house, all the Senate stood up on their feet to do him honour. Then part of Brutus' company and confederates stood round about Caesar's chair, and part of them also came towards him, as though they made suit with Metellus Cimber, to call home his brother again from banishment; and thus, prosecuting still their suit, they followed Caesar till he was set in his chair. Who denying their petitions, and being offended with them one after another, because the more they were denied, the more they pressed upon him, and were the earnester with him, Metellus at length, taking his gown with both his hands, pulled it over his neck, which was the sign given the confederates to set upon him. Then Casca behind him strake him in the neck with his sword; howbeit the wound was not great nor mortal, because, it seemed, the fear of such a devilish attempt did amaze him, and take his strength from him, that he killed him not at the first blow. But Caesar, turning straight unto him, caught hold of his sword, and held it hard: and they both cried out, Caesar in Latin: "O vile traitor Casca, what doest thou?" And Casca in Greek to his brother, "Brother, help me." At the beginning of this stir, they that were present, not knowing of the conspiracy, were so amazed with the horrible sight they saw that they had no power to fly, neither to help him, not so much as once to make any outcry. They on the other side that had conspired his death compassed him in on every side with their swords drawn in their hands, that Caesar turned him nowhere but he was stricken at by some, and still had naked swords in his face, and was hacked and mangled among them, as a wild beast taken of hunters. For it was agreed among them that every man should give him a wound, because all their parts should be in this murder; and then Brutus himself gave him one wound about his

---

3. **Epicurus,** Greek philosopher (342–270 B.C.). He did not believe in divine interference with earthly matters.
31. **amaze,** bewilder.

privities. Men report also that Caesar did still defend himself against the rest, running every way with his body: but when he saw Brutus with his sword drawn in his hand, then he pulled his gown over his head, and made no more resistance, and was driven either casually or purposedly by the counsel of the conspirators against the base whereupon Pompey's image stood, which ran all of a gore-blood till he was slain. Thus it seemed that the image took just revenge of Pompey's enemy, being thrown down on the ground at his feet, and yielding up his ghost there for the number of wounds he had upon him. For it is reported that he had three-and-twenty wounds upon his body; and divers of the conspirators did hurt themselves, striking one body with so many blows. When Caesar was slain, the Senate (though Brutus stood in the midst amongst them, as though he would have said somewhat touching this fact) presently ran out of the house, and flying filled all the city with marvellous fear and tumult. Insomuch as some did shut-to their doors, others forsook their shops and warehouses, and others ran to the place to see what the matter was; and others also that had seen it ran home to their houses again. But Antonius and Lepidus, which were two of Caesar's chiefest friends, secretly conveying themselves away, fled into other men's houses, and forsook their own. Brutus and his confederates on the other side, being yet hot with this murder they had committed, having their swords drawn in their hands, came all in a troop together out of the Senate, and went into the market-place, not as men that made countenance to fly, but otherwise boldly holding up their heads like men of courage, and called to the people to defend their liberty, and stayed to speak with every great personage whom they met in their way. Of them some followed this troop and went amongst them as if they had been of the conspiracy, and falsely challenged part of the honour with them: among them was Caius Octavius, and Lentulus Spinther. But both of them were afterwards put to death, for their vain covetousness of honour, by Antonius and Octavius Caesar the younger: and yet had no part of that honour for the which they were put to death, neither did any man believe that they were any of the confederates, or of counsel with them. For they that did put them to death took revenge rather of the will they had to offend than of any fact they had committed. The next morning Brutus and his confederates came into the market-place to speak unto the people, who gave them such audience that it seemed they neither greatly reproved nor allowed the fact: for by their great silence they showed that they were sorry for Caesar's death, and also that they did reverence Brutus. Now the Senate granted general pardon for all that was past, and to pacify every man, ordained besides that Caesar's funerals should be honoured as a god, and established all things that he had done, and gave certain provinces also and convenient honours unto Brutus and his confederates, whereby every man thought all things were brought to good peace and quietness again. But when they had opened Caesar's testament, and found a liberal legacy of money bequeathed unto every citizen of Rome, and that they saw his body (which was brought into the market-place) all bemangled with gashes of swords, then there was no order to keep the multitude and common people quiet, but they plucked up forms, tables, and stools, and laid them all about the body, and setting them afire burnt the corse. Then, when the fire was well kindled, they took the firebrands, and went unto their houses that had slain Caesar, to set them afire. Other also ran up and down the city to see if they could meet with any of them, to cut them in pieces; howbeit they could meet with never a man of them, because they had locked themselves up safely in their houses. There was one of Caesar's friends called Cinna that had a marvellous strange and terrible dream the night before. He dreamed that Caesar bade him to supper, and that he refused, and would not go, then, that Caesar took him by the hand, and led him against his will. Now Cinna hearing at that time that they burnt Caesar's body in the market-place, notwithstanding that he feared his dream and had an ague on him besides, he went into the market-place to honour his funerals. When he came thither, one of mean sort asked him what his name was. He was straight called by his name. The first man told it to another, and that other unto another, so that it ran straight through them all, that he was one of them that murdered Caesar (for indeed one of the traitors to Caesar was also called Cinna as himself); wherefore, taking him for Cinna the murderer, they fell upon him with such fury that they presently dispatched him in the market-place. This stir and fury made Brutus and Cassius more afraid than of all that was past, and therefore, within few days after, they departed out of Rome; and touching their doings afterwards, and what calamity they suffered till their deaths, we have written it at large in the life of Brutus. Caesar died at six-and-fifty years of age, and Pompey also lived not passing four years more than he. So he reaped no other fruit of all his reign and dominion, which he had so vehemently desired all his life, and pursued with such extreme danger, but a vain name only, and a superficial glory that procured him the envy and hatred of his country. But his great prosperity and good fortune, that favoured him all his lifetime, did continue afterwards in the revenge of his death, pursuing the murderers both by sea and land, till they had not left a man more to be executed, of all them that were actors or counsellors in the conspiracy of his death. Furthermore, of all the chances that happen unto men upon the earth, that which came to Cassius above all other is most to be wondered at. For he, being overcome in battle at the journey of Philippi, slew himself with the same sword with the which he strake Caesar. Again, of signs in the element, the great comet, which seven nights together was seen very bright after Caesar's death, the eighth night after was never seen more. Also the brightness of the sun was darkened, the which all that year through rose very pale, and shined not out, whereby it gave but small heat; therefore the air being very cloudy and dark, by the weakness of the heat that could not come forth, did cause the earth to bring forth but raw and unripe fruit, which rotted before it could ripe. But, above all, the ghost that appeared unto Brutus shewed plainly that the gods were offended with the murder of Caesar. The vision was thus. Brutus, being ready to pass over his army from the city of Abydos to the other coast lying directly against it, slept every night (as his manner was) in his tent, and being yet awake thinking of his affairs, (for by report he was as careful a captain, and lived with as little sleep, as ever man did) he thought he heard a noise at his tent door, and, looking towards the light of the lamp that waxed very dim, he saw a horrible vision of a man, of a wonderful greatness and dreadful look, which at the first made him marvellously afraid. But when he saw that it did him no hurt, but stood by his bedside and said nothing, at length he asked him what he was. The image answered him: "I am thy ill angel, Brutus, and thou shalt see me by the city of Philippi." Then Brutus replied again, and said: "Well, I shall see thee then." Therewithal the spirit presently vanished from him. After that time Brutus being in battle near unto the city of Philippi against Antonius and Octavius Caesar, at the first battle he won the victory, and, overthrowing all them that withstood him, he drave them into young Caesar's camp, which he took. The second battle being at hand, this spirit appeared again unto him, but spake never a word. Thereupon Brutus, knowing he should die, did put himself to all hazard in battle, but yet fighting could not be slain. So, seeing his men put to flight and overthrown, he ran unto a little rock not far off, and there setting his sword's point to his breast fell upon it, and slew himself, but yet, as it is reported, with the help of his friend that dispatched him.

John Lyly
c. 1553–1606

John Lyly is commonly known as the author of "the first English novel" and as an influential predecessor of Shakespeare in the writing of comedy. Of the young men who turned from their university studies to engage in literature, he had perhaps the most fortunate career. Born, probably in Kent, in 1553 or 1554, he entered Magdalen College, Oxford, in 1569, and received his bachelor's degree in 1573 and his master's degree in 1575. He was an unsuccessful competitor for a fellowship. In 1579, he achieved literary fame on the publication of his prose narrative *Euphues: The Anatomy of Wit*, and attempted to capitalize on its success by writing and publishing a sequel, *Euphues and His England*, in 1580. His connection with the theater began in 1583, when, after serving as secretary to the Earl of Oxford, he was given the lease of the private theater Blackfriars, and undertook to furnish plays for the company of child-actors assembled from the choirboys of the Chapel Royal and St. Paul's Cathedral. It was for this company and this playhouse that Lyly wrote his first two plays in 1584, *Alexander and Campaspe* and *Sappho and Phao*. In that year the company was forced to vacate Blackfriars, and in 1585 Lyly was made assistant master of St. Paul's Cathedral School, with the duty of providing the choirboys with plays. Between 1585 and 1590, the rest of Lyly's plays were written and performed by this company, among them *Endymion*, 1591; *Midas*, 1592; and *Mother Bombie*, 1594.

Lyly's comedies retell freely some familiar classical legend, the main features of which the dramatist was bent on utilizing. But he felt free to invent subsidiary and comic figures, and his witty page boys engage in charming verbal banter. In certain of his plays, there was for a courtly audience the additional curiosity of an alleged allegorical significance. Thus, *Sappho and Phao* is supposed to allude to the courtship of Queen Elizabeth by the Duke of Alençon, *Endymion* refers to the rivalry between Elizabeth and her cousin Mary Queen of Scots, and *Midas* satirizes the overweening ambition of Philip II of Spain.

Lyly's contribution to the development of English comedy lay in his unity of tone and mood, his elegant and pointed prose dialogue, his deft grouping of characters, and his romanticizing of ancient classical stories. The exquisite lyrics, which appeared for the first time in a collected edition of his plays printed in 1632, may or may not be from his hand.

Lyly's later life is of little literary significance. Toward the end of his connection with St. Paul's School, he may have got into difficulties through the publication of his anti-Puritan pamphlet, *Pap with a Hatchet*, 1589. He did, however, obtain a minor post in the Revels Office in 1588, and he kept it until 1604. His attempts to become Master of the Revels were unsuccessful. He was a Member of Parliament on four occasions between 1589 and 1601. He died in 1606.

from EUPHUES: THE ANATOMY OF WIT

The plot of Lyly's *Euphues* is an extremely simple one. Euphues, a gifted young gentleman from Athens, goes to Naples, and, although warned by an old man, Eubulus, of its dangers, gives himself over to the dissipations of the city. He makes friends with Philautus, and is introduced to the latter's fiancée, Lucilla. Forgetful of his friendship, he tries to win Lucilla for himself, but in the end the fickle heroine leaves both young men in the lurch. They are reconciled, and Euphues retires into seclusion to devote himself to philosophy.

The slight story is augmented with a series of appendices, consisting of Euphues' letters and essays on the fickleness of women and on the theory of education. The selection given below is from the essay entitled "Euphues and his Ephoebus," that is, Euphues and his disciple. It draws its subject matter from Plutarch's classical tractate *On the Education of Children*, which had been ransacked for ideas by various Renaissance writers (including Erasmus) before Lyly undertook to amplify it. The attack on the state of learning at Athens is a thinly disguised satire on Lyly's own university, Oxford.

I WOULD have them first of all to follow philosophy, as most ancient, yea most excellent, for as it is pleasant to pass through many fair cities, but most pleasant to dwell in the fairest, even so to read many histories and arts it is pleasant, but as it were to lodge with philosophy most profitable.

It was prettily said of Bion the philosopher: even as when the wooers could not have the company of Penelope they run to her handmaids; so they that cannot attain to the knowledge of philosophy, apply their minds to things most vile and contemptible. Wherefore we must prefer philosophy, as the only princess of all sciences, and other arts as waiting maids. For the curing and keeping in temper of the body, man by his industry has found two things, physic and exercise, the one cureth sickness, the other preserveth the body in temper, but there is nothing that may heal diseases or cure the wounds of the mind but only philosophy. By this shall we learn what is honest, what dishonest, what is right, what is wrong, and that I may in one word say what may be said, what is to be known, what is to be avoided, what to be embraced, how we ought to obey our parents, reverence our elders, entertain strangers, honour the magistrates, love our friends, live with our wives, use our servants, how we should worship God, be dutiful to our fathers, stand in awe of our superiors, obey laws, give place to officers, how we may choose friends, nurture our children, and that which is most noble, how we should neither be too proud in prosperity, neither pensive in adversity, neither like beasts overcome with anger. And here I cannot but lament Athens, which having been always the nurse of philosophers, doth now nourish only the name of philosophy. For to speak plainly of the disorder of Athens, who doth not see it, and sorrow at it? Such playing at dice, such quaffing of drink, such dalliance with women, such dancing, that in my opinion there is no quaffer in Flanders so given to tippling, no courtier in Italy so given to riot, no creature in the world so misled as a student in Athens. Such a confusion of degrees, that the Scholar knoweth not his duty to the Bachelor, nor the Bachelor to the Master, nor the Master to the Doctor. Such corruption of manners, contempt of magistrates, such open sins, such privy villainy, such quarrelling in the streets, such subtile practices in chambers, as maketh my heart to melt with sorrow to think of it, and should cause your minds, gentlemen, to be penitent to remember it.

Moreover, who doth know a scholar by his habit? Is there any hat of so unseemly a fashion, any doublet of so long a waist, any hose so short, any attire either so costly or so courtly, either so strange in making or so monstrous in wearing that is not worn of a scholar? Have they not now instead of black cloth black velvet, instead of coarse sackcloth fine silk? Be they not more like courtiers than scholars, more like stage-players than students, more like ruffians of Naples than disputers in Athens? I would to God they did not imitate all other nations in the vice of the mind as they do in the attire of their body, for certainly as there is no nation whose fashion in apparel they do not use, so is there no wickedness published in any place, that they do not practise. I think that in Sodom and Gomorrah there was never more filthiness, never more pride in Rome, more poisoning in Italy, more lying in Crete, more privy spoiling in Spain, more idolatry in Egypt, than is at this day in Athens, never such sects among the heathens, such schisms among the Turks, such misbelief among the infidels, as is now among scholars. Be there not many in Athens which think there is no God? no redemption? no resurrection?

What shame is this, gentlemen, that a place so renowned for good learning should be so shamed for ill lying? that where grace doth abound, sin should so superabound? that where the greatest profession of knowledge is, there should also be the least practising of honesty? I have read of many universities, as of Padua in Italy, Paris in France, Wittenberg in Germany, in England of Oxford and Cambridge, which if they were half so ill as Athens they were too too bad, and as I have heard as they be, they be stark nought.

But I can speak the less against them, for that I was never in them; yet can I not choose but be aggrieved, that by report I am enforced rather to accuse them of vanity than excuse them any way. Ah, gentlemen, what is to be looked for, nay, what is not to be feared, when the temple of Vesta where virgins should live is like the stews, fraught with strumpets, when the altar where nothing but sanctity and holiness should be used is polluted with uncleanness, when the universities of Christendom which should be the eyes, the lights, the leaven, the salt, the seasoning of the world are dimmed with blind concupiscence, put out with pride, and have lost their savour with impiety?

Is it not become a byword amongst the common people that they had rather send their children to the cart than to the university, being induced so to say for the abuse that reigneth in the universities, who, sending their sons to attain knowledge, find them little better learned, but a great deal worse

50. **the cart,** the wagon taking prisoners to the gallows.

lived than when they went, and not only unthrifty of their money, but also bankrupt of good manners: was not this the cause that caused a simple woman in Greece to exclaim against Athens, saying:

"The master and the scholar, the tutor and the pupil be both agreed, for the one careth not how little pain he taketh for his money, the other how little learning."

I perceive that in Athens there be no changelings: When of old it was said to a Lacedemonian, that all the Grecians knew honesty, but not one practised it. When Panathaenea were celebrated at Athens, an old man going to take a place was mockingly rejected, at the last, coming among the Lacedemonians, all the youth gave him place, which the Athenians liked well of; then one of the Spartans cried out: "Verily the Athenians know what should be done, but they never do it." When one of the Lacedemonians had been for a certain time in Athens seeing nothing but dancing, dicing, banqueting, surfeiting, and licentious behaviour, returning home he was asked how all things stood in Athens, to whom he answered, "All things are honest there," meaning that the Athenians accounted all things good, and nothing bad. How such abuses should or might be redressed in all universities, especially in Athens, if I were of authority to command, it should be seen, or of credit to persuade those that have the dealings with them, it should soon be shown.

And until I see better reformation in Athens, my young Ephoebus shall not be nurtured in Athens. I have spoken all this that you gentlemen might see how the philosophers in Athens practise nothing less than philosophy. What scholar is he that is so zealous at his book as Chrisippus, who, had not his maid Melissa thrust meat into his mouth had perished with famine, being always studying? Who so watchful as Aristotle, who going to bed would have a ball of brass in his hand, that if he should be taken in a slumber it might fall and awaken him? No, no, the times are changed, as Ovid saith, and we are changed in the times; let us endeavour every one to amend one, and we shall all soon be amended; let us give no occasion of reproach, and we shall more easily bear the burden of false reports, and as we see by learning what we should do, so let us do as we learn; then shall Athens flourish, then shall the students be had in great reputation, then shall learning have his hire, and every good scholar his hope. But return we once again to philosophy.

There is among men a threefold kind of life: active, which is about civil function and administration of the common weal; speculative, which is in continual meditation and study; the third, a life led, most commonly a lewd life, an idle and vain life, the life that the Epicures account their whole felicity, a voluptuous life replenished with all kinds of vanity. If this active life be without philosophy, it is an idle life, or at the least a life evil employed, which is worse. If the contemplative life be separated from the active, it is most unprofitable. I would therefore have my youth so to bestow his study as he may both be exercised in the common weal, to common profit, and well employed privately for his own perfection, so as by his study the rule he shall bear may be directed, and by his government his study may be increased: in this manner did Pericles deal in civil affairs, after this sort did Architas the Tarentine, Dion the Syracusian, the Theban Epaminondas govern their cities.

For the exercise of the body it is necessary also somewhat be added, that is, that the child should be at such times permitted to recreate himself, when his mind is overcome with study, lest dulling himself with overmuch industry he become unfit afterward to conceive readily; besides this, it will cause an apt composition and that natural strength that it before retained. A good composition of the body layeth a good foundation of old age, for as in the fair summer we prepare all things necessary for the cold winter, so good manners in youth and lawful exercises be as it were victuals and nourishments for age; yet are their labours and pastimes so to be tempered that they weaken not their bodies more by play than otherwise they should have done by study, and so to be used that they addict not themselves more to the exercise of the limbs than the following of learning; the greatest enemies to discipline, as Plato recounteth, are labours and sleep. It is also requisite that he be expert in martial affairs, in shooting, in darting, that he hawk and hunt, for his honest pastime and recreation, and if after these pastimes he shall seem secure, nothing regarding his books, I would not have him scourged with stripes, but threatened with words, not dulled with blows, like servants the which the more they are beaten the better they bear it, and the less they care for it; for children of good disposition are either incited by praise to go forward, or shamed by dispraise to commit the like offence; those of obstinate and blockish behaviour are neither with words to be persuaded, neither with stripes to be corrected. They must now be taunted with sharp rebukes, straightways admonished with fair words, now threatened a payment, by and by promised a reward, and dealt withal as nurses do with the babes, whom after they have made to cry, they proffer the teat. But diligent heed must be taken that he be not praised above measure, lest standing too much in his own conceit, he become also obstinate in his own opinions. I have known many fathers whose great love towards their sons hath been the cause in time that they loved them not, for when they see a sharp wit in their son to conceive, for the desire they have that he should outrun his fellows, they load him with continual exercise, which is the only cause that he sinketh under his burden, and giveth over in the plain field. Plants are nourished with little rain, yet drowned with much; even so the mind with indifferent labour waxeth more perfect; with much study it is made fruitless. We must consider that all our life is divided into remission and study.

As there is watching, so is there sleep; as there is war, so is there peace; as there is winter, so is there summer; as there be many working days, so is there also many holidays; and if I may speak all in one word, ease is the sauce of labour, which is plainly to be seen not only in living things, but also in things without life. We unbend the bow that we may the better bend him; we unloose the harp that we may the sooner tune him; the body is kept in health as well with fasting as eating, the mind healed with ease as well as with labour. Those parents are in mind to be misliked which commit the whole care of their child to the custody of a hireling, neither asking, neither knowing, how their children profit in learning. For if the father were desirous to examine his son in that which he hath learned, the master would be more careful what he did teach. But seeing the father careless what they learn, he is also secure what he teacheth. That notable saying of the horse-keeper may here be applied, which said, nothing did so fatten the horse as the eye of the king. Moreover, I would have the memory of children continually to be exercised, which is the greatest furtherance to learning that can be. For this cause they fained in their old fables memory to be the mother of perfection.

Children are to be chastised if they shall use any filthy or unseemly talk, for, as Democrates saith, the word is the shadow of the work: they must be courteous in their behaviour, lowly in their speech, not disdaining their cockmates or refraining their company; they must not live wantonly, neither speak impudently, neither be angry without cause,

50. blockish, stupid. **44. fained,** liked (to make). **50. cockmates,** friends, intimates.

neither quarrelsome without colour. A young man being perverse in nature and proud in words and manners gave Socrates a spurn, who, being moved by his fellows to give him another: "If," said Socrates, "an ass had kicked me, would you also have me to kick him again?" The great wisdom in Socrates in compressing his anger is worthy great commendation. Architas the Tarentine, returning from war and finding his ground overgrown with weeds and turned up with moles, sent for his farmer, unto whom he said: "If I were not angry I would make thee repent thy ill husbandry." Plato, having a servant whose bliss was in filling of his belly, seeing him on a time idle and unhonest in behaviour, said, "Out of my sight, for I am incensed with anger."

Although these examples be hard to imitate, yet should every man do his endeavour to repress that hot and heady humour which he is by nature subject unto. To be silent and discreet in company, though many think it a thing of no great weight or importance, yet is it most requisite for a young man and most necessary for my Ephoebus. It never hath been hurtful to any to hold his peace; to speak, damage to many; what so is kept in silence is hushed, but whatsoever is babbled out cannot again be recalled. We may see the cunning and curious work of Nature, which hath barred and hedged nothing in so strongly as the tongue, with two rows of teeth, therewith two lips; besides she hath placed it far from the heart that it should not utter that which the heart had conceived; this also should cause us to be silent, seeing those that use much talk though they speak truly are never believed. Wine, therefore, is to be refrained which is termed to be the glass of the mind, and it is an old proverb: Whatsoever is in the heart of the sober man, is in the mouth of the drunkard. Bias, holding his tongue at a feast, was termed there of a tattler to be a fool, who said, "Is there any wise man that can hold his tongue amidst the wine?" unto whom Bias answered, "There is no fool that can."

A certain gentleman here in Athens invited the King's Legates to a costly and sumptuous feast, where also he assembled many philosophers, and talking of diverse matters both of the common weal and learning, only Zeno said nothing. Then the ambassadors said, "What shall we show of thee, O Zeno, to the king?" "Nothing," answered he, "but that there is an old man in Athens that amidst the pots could hold his peace." Anacharsis, supping with Solon, was found asleep, having his right hand before his mouth, his left upon his privities; whereby was noted that the tongue should be reined with the strongest bridle. Zeno because he would not be enforced to reveal anything against his will by torments, bit off his tongue and spit it in the face of the Tyrant.

Now when children shall by wisdom and use refrain from overmuch tattling, let them also be admonished that when they shall speak, they speak nothing but truth: to lie is a vice most detestable, not to be suffered in a slave, much less in a son. But the greatest thing is yet behind, whether that those are to be admitted as cockmates with children which love them entirely, or whether they be to be banished from them.

When as I see many fathers more cruel to their children than careful of them, which think it not necessary to have those about them that most tender them, then I am half, as it were, in a doubt to give counsel. But when I call to my remembrance Socrates, Plato, Xenophon, Eschines, Saebetes, and all those that so much commend the love of men, which have also brought up many to great rule, reason, and piety, then I am encouraged to imitate those whose excellency doth warrant my precepts to be perfect. If any shall love the child for his comely countenance, him would I have to be banished as a most dangerous and infectious beast; if he shall love him for his father's sake, or for his own good qualities, him would I have to be with him always as supervisor of his manners: such hath it been in times past, the love of one Athenian to the other, and of one Lacedemonian to the other.

But having said almost sufficient for the education of a child, I will speak two words how he should be trained when he groweth in years. I cannot but mislike the nature of divers parents which appoint overseers and tutors for their children in their tender age, and suffer them when they come to be young men to have the bridle in their own hand, knowing not that age requireth rather a hard snaffle than a pleasant bit, and is sooner allured to wickedness than childhood. Who knoweth not the escapes of children, as they are small, so they are soon amended? Either with threats they are to be remedied or with fair promises to be rewarded. But the sins and faults of young men are almost or altogether intolerable, which give themselves to be delicate in their diet, prodigal in their expense, using dicing, dancing, drunkenness, deflowering of virgins, abusing wives, committing adulteries, and accounting all things honest that are most detestable. Here therefore must be used a due regard that their lust may be repressed, their riot abated, their courage cooled, for hard it is to

17. **tender them,** treat them with tenderness.

see a young man to be master of himself which yieldeth himself as it were a bond slave, to fond and overlashing affections. Wise parents ought to take good heed, especially at this time, that they frame their sons to modesty, either by threats or by rewards, either by fair promises or severe practices, either showing the miseries of those that have been overcome with wildness, or the happiness of them that have contained themselves within the bands of reason: these two are, as it were, the ensigns of virtue, the hope of honour, the fear of punishment. But chiefly parents must cause their youths to abandon the society of those which are noted of evil living and lewd behaviour, which Pythagoras seemed somewhat obscurely to note in these his sayings.

First, that one should abstain from the taste of those things that have black tails. That is, we must not use the company of those whose corrupt manners do, as it were, make their life black. Not to go above the balance, that is, to reverence justice, neither for fear of flattery to lean to any one partially. Not to lie in idleness, that is, that sloth should be abhorred. That we should not shake every man by the hand, that is, we should not contract friendship with all. Not to wear a straight ring, that is, that we should lead our life so as we need not to fetter it with chains. Not to bring fire to a slaughter, that is, we must not provoke any that is furious with words. Not to eat our hearts, that is, that we should not vex ourselves with thoughts, consume our bodies with sighs, with sobs, or with care to pine our carcasses. To abstain from beans, that is, not to meddle in civil affairs or business of the common weal, for in the old times the election of magistrates was made by the pulling of beans. Not to put our meat in Scapio, that is, we should not speak of manners or virtue to those whose minds are infected with vice. Not to retire when we are come to the end of our race, that is, when we are at the point of death, we should not be oppressed with grief, but willingly yield to nature. But I will return to my former precepts, that is, that young men should be kept from the company of those that are wicked, especially from the sight of the flatterer. For I say now as I have oftentimes before said, that there is no kind of beast so noisome as the flatterer, nothing that will sooner consume both the son and the father and all honest friends. When the father exhorteth the son to sobriety, the flatterer provoketh him to wine; when the father weaneth them to continence, the flatterer allureth them to lust; when the father admonisheth them to thrift, the flatterer haleth them to prodigality; when the father encourageth them to labour, the flatterer layeth a cushion under his elbow to sleep, bidding them to eat, drink, and be merry, for that the life of man is soon gone, and but as a short shadow, and seeing that we have but a while to live, who would live like a servant? They say that now their fathers be old and dote through age like Saturnus.

Hereof it comes that young men, giving not only attentive ear but ready coin to flatterers, fall into such misfortune; hereof it proceeds that they haunt the stews, marry before they be wise, and die before they thrive. These be the beasts which live by the trenchers of young gentlemen, and consume the treasures of their revenues; these be they that soothe young youths in their own sayings, that uphold them in all their doings with a yea, or nay; these be they that are at every beck, at every nod, freemen by fortune, slaves by free will. Wherefore, if there be any father that would have his children nurtured and brought up in honesty, let him expel these panthers, which have a sweet smell but a devouring mind: yet would I not have parents altogether precise, or too severe in correction, but let them with mildness forgive light offences, and remember that they themselves have been young; as the physician by mingling bitter poisons with sweet liquor bringeth health to the body, so the father with sharp rebukes seasoned with loving looks causeth a redress and amendment in his child. But if the father be thoroughly angry upon good occasion, let him not continue his rage, for I had rather he should be soon angry than hard to be pleased, for when the son shall perceive that the father hath conceived rather a hate than a heat against him, he becometh desperate, neither regarding his father's ire, neither his own duty.

Some light faults let them dissemble as though they knew them not, and, seeing them, let them not seem to see them, and, hearing them, let them not seem to hear. We can easily forget the offences of our friends, be they never so great, and shall we not forgive the escapes of our children, be they never so small? We bear oftentimes with our servants, and shall we not sometimes with our sons? The fairest jennet is ruled as well with the wand as with the spur; the wildest child is as soon corrected with a word as with a weapon. If thy son be so stubborn obstinately to rebel against thee, or so wilful to persevere in his wickedness, that neither for fear of punishment, neither for hope of reward,

3. overlashing, extravagant.   **33. pine,** wear out.   **44. escapes,** mistakes, transgressions.   **47. jennet,** small Spanish horse.

he is any way to be reclaimed, then seek out some marriage fit for his degree, which is the surest bond of youth, and the strongest chain to fetter affections that can be found. Yet let his wife be such a one as is neither much more noble in birth, or far more richer in goods, but according to the wise saying: choose one every way, as near as may be equal in both: for they that do desire great dowries do rather marry themselves to the wealth than to their wife. But, to return to the matter, it is most requisite that fathers both by their discreet counsel and also their honest conversation, be an example of imitation to their children, that they seeing in their parents, as it were in a glass, the perfection of manners, they may be encouraged by their upright living, to practise the like piety: for if a father rebuke his child of swearing, and he himself a blasphemer, doth he not see, that in detecting his son's vice, he also noteth his own? If the father counsel the son to refrain wine, as most unwholesome, and drink himself immoderately, doth he not as well reprove his own folly as rebuke his son's? Age always ought to be a mirror for youth, for where old age is impudent, there certainly youth must needs be shameless; where the aged have no respect of their honourable and grey hairs, there the young gallants have little regard of their honest behaviour, and in one word to conclude all, where age is past gravity, there youth is past grace.

The sum of all wherewith I would have my Ephoebus endued, and how I would have him instructed, shall briefly appear in this following. First, that he be of honest parents, nursed of his mother, brought up in such a place as is incorrupt both for the air and manners, with such a person as is undefiled, of great zeal, of profound knowledge, of absolute perfection, that he be instructed in philosophy, whereby he may attain learning, and have in all sciences a smack, whereby he may readily dispute of anything. That his body be kept in his pure strength by honest exercise, his wit and memory, by diligent study.

That he abandon all allurements of vice, and continually incline to virtue, which if it shall, as it may, come to pass, then do I hope that if ever Plato's commonweal shall flourish, that my Ephoebus shall be a citizen, that if Aristotle find any happy man it will be my child, if Tully confess any to be an absolute orator, it will be my young youth. I am here therefore, gentlemen, to exhort you, that with all industry you apply your minds to the study of philosophy, that as you profess yourselves students, so you may be students; that as you disdain not the name of a scholar, so you will not be found void of the duty of scholars. Let not your minds be carried away with vain delights, as with travelling into far and strange countries where you shall see more wickedness than learn virtue and wit. Neither with costly attire of the new cut, the Dutch hat, the French hose, the Spanish rapier, the Italian hilt, and I know not what.

Cast not your eyes on the beauty of women, lest ye cast away your hearts with folly; let not that fond love, wherewith youth fatteth himself as fat as a fool, infect you, for as a sinew being cut, though it be healed, there will always remain a scar, or as fine linen stained with black ink, though it be washed never so often, will have an iron mole, so the mind once mangled or maimed with love, though it be never so well cured with reason or cooled by wisdom, yet there will appear a scar by the which one may guess the mind hath been pierced, and a blemish whereby one may judge the heart hath been stained.

Refrain from dicing, which was the only cause that Pyrrhus was stricken to the heart, and from dancing, which was the means that lost John Baptist's head. I am not he that will disallow honest recreation, although I detest the abuses. I speak boldly unto you because I myself know you; what Athens hath been, what Athens is, what Athens shall be, I can guess. Let not every inn and alehouse in Athens be as it were your chamber; frequent not those ordinary tables where either for the desire of delicate cates or the meeting of youthful companions, you both spend your money vainly and your time idly. Imitate him in life whom you honour for his learning, Aristotle, who was never seen in the company of those that idly bestowed their time.

There is nothing more swifter than time, nothing more sweeter: we have not, as Seneca saith, little time to live, but we lose much; neither have we a short life by Nature, but we make it shorter by naughtiness; our life is long if we know how to use it. Follow Apelles, that cunning and wise painter, which would let no day pass over his head without a line, without some labour. It was prettily said of Hesiodas, let us endeavour by reason to excel beasts, seeing beasts by nature excel men, although strictly taken it be not so, for that man is endowed with a soul, yet taken touching their perfection of senses in their kind it is most certain. Doth not the lion for strength, the turtle for love, the ant for labour excel man? Doth not the eagle see clearer, the vulture smell better, the mole hear lightlier? Let us, therefore, endeavour to excel in

48. Tully, Cicero.

virtue, seeing in qualities of the body we are inferior to beasts. And here I am most earnestly to exhort you to modesty in your behaviour, to duty to your elders, to diligence in your studies. I was of late in Italy, where mine ears glowed and my heart was galled to hear the abuses that reign in Athens. I can not tell whether those things sprang by the lewd and lying lips of the ignorant, which are always enemies to learning, or by the reports of such as saw them and sorrowed at them. It was openly reported of an old man in Naples that there was more lightness in Athens than in all Italy, more wanton youths of scholars than in all Europe besides, more papists, more atheists, more sects, more schisms, than in all the monarchies of the world, which things, although I think they be not true, yet can I not but lament that they should be deemed to be true, and I fear me they be not altogether false; there can no great smoke arise but there must be some fire, no great report without great suspicion. Frame, therefore, your lives to such integrity, your studies to the attaining of such perfection, that neither the might of the strong, neither the malice of the weak, neither the swift reports of the ignorant be able to spot you with dishonesty or note you of ungodliness. The greatest harm that you can do unto the envious, is to do well; the greatest corasive that you can give unto the ignorant is to prosper in knowledge; the greatest comfort that you can bestow on your parents is to live well, and learn well; the greatest commodity that you can yield unto your country is with wisdom to bestow that talent that by grace was given you.

And here I cannot choose but give you that counsel, that an old man in Naples gave me most wisely, although I had then neither grace to follow it, neither will to give ear to it, desiring you not to reject it because I did once despise it. It is this as I can remember word for word.

Descend into your own consciences; consider with your selves the great difference between staring and stark blind, wit and wisdom, love and lust; be merry but with modesty; be sober but not too sullen; be valiant but not too venturous; let your attire be comely but not too costly; your diet wholesome but not excessive; use pastime, as the word importeth, to pass the time in honest recreation. Mistrust no man without cause; neither be you credulous without proof; be not light to follow every man's opinion, neither obstinate to stand in your own conceits; serve God, fear God, love God, and God will bless you, as either your hearts can wish, or your friends desire. This was his grave and godly advice whose counsel I would have you all to follow: frequent lectures, use disputations openly, neglect not your private studies, let not degrees be given for love but for learning, not for money but for knowledge, and because you shall be the better encouraged to follow my counsel, I will be as it were an example myself, desiring you all to imitate me. . . .

SONGS

These songs from plays, and others attributed to Lyly, were printed for the first time in 1632 in a posthumous edition of his plays. Modern scholars have disagreed as to their authorship. But whether or not they come from the hand of Lyly, they exhibit the charm and grace of the songs frequently introduced into the plays of this period. The second and third songs illustrate the happy use of motifs from English country life and folklore. The first two are from *Alexander and Campaspe*, the third from *Endymion*.

CUPID AND MY CAMPASPE

Cupid and my Campaspe played
At cards for kisses; Cupid paid.
He stakes his quiver, bow, and arrows,
His mother's doves and team of sparrows,
Loses them too; then down he throws
The coral of his lip, the rose
Growing on's cheek (but none knows how),
With these the crystal of his brow,
And then the dimple of his chin:
All these did my Campaspe win.   10
At last he set her both his eyes;
She won, and Cupid blind did rise.
  O Love! has she done this to thee?
  What shall, alas, become of me?

WHAT BIRD SO SINGS

What bird so sings, yet so does wail?
Oh, 'tis the ravished nightingale.
Jug, jug, jug, jug, tereu, she cries,
And still her woes at midnight rise.
Brave prick-song! who is't now we hear?
None but the lark so shrill and clear;
How at heaven's gates she claps her wings,
The morn not waking till she sings.
Hark, hark, with what a pretty throat
Poor robin redbreast tunes his note;   10
Hark how the jolly cuckoos sing
Cuckoo, to welcome in the spring,
Cuckoo, to welcome in the spring.

---

28. **corasive**, corrosive.

What Bird So Sings? 5. **prick-song**, written music.

SONG BY FAIRIES

Omnes. Pinch him, pinch him, black and blue,
Saucy mortals must not view
What the queen of stars is doing,
Nor pry into our fairy wooing.
1 Fairy. Pinch him blue.
2 Fairy. And pinch him black.
3 Fairy. Let him not lack
Sharp nails to pinch him blue and red,
Till sleep has rocked his addlehead.
4 Fairy. For the trespass he hath done, 10
Spots o'er all his flesh shall run.
Kiss Endymion, kiss his eyes,
Then to our midnight haydegyes.

Sir Philip Sidney
1554–1586

In character and attainments, Sidney was a closer approximation to the ideal of the Renaissance courtier than any other person of his time. He was born on November 30, 1554, at the fine country place of his father, Penshurst, Kent. His father was Sir Henry Sidney, who served three times as Lord Deputy of Ireland; his mother was Lady Mary Dudley, a sister of Elizabeth's favorite, Robert Dudley, first Earl of Leicester. His sister Mary, after her marriage to the second Earl of Pembroke, became the greatest patroness of letters of her time.

Sidney entered Shrewsbury School on the same day as Fulke Greville, who became his lifelong friend and his first biographer. From 1567 to 1571, he was a student at Christ Church, Oxford, and later for a brief time at Cambridge, but he took no degree from either university. In May, 1572, he embarked on a grand tour of Europe which was to last until 1575. First, he went to Paris in the train of the English Ambassador and there he witnessed the Massacre of St. Bartholomew, an experience which deepened his attachment to the Protestant cause. He spent a considerable period at Frankfort in the company of the Humanist Hubert Languet, and traveled with him to Vienna. He penetrated to Hungary, and in Italy visited Venice, Genoa, and Padua. In the first of these cities, he met the great painters Tintoretto and Veronese. He passed the winter of 1574–75 in Vienna, but returned through the Low Countries to England in time to be present at the extravagant series of entertainments which Leicester staged in honor of Elizabeth's visit to Kenilworth, July 9–27, 1575. He followed the court to Chartley Castle, the home seat of the Earl of Essex, and there may be supposed to have met Penelope Devereux, Essex's daughter, then a girl of thirteen. By 1576, he was a serious suitor for her hand, and Essex before his death in 1576 expressed a wish that the marriage should take place. But though Sidney's uncle, Leicester, married Penelope's mother, Lady Essex, in 1577, the young people's marriage did not take place.

In 1577 Sidney was sent abroad by the Queen to serve as Ambassador to the Emperor of Germany and the Elector Palatine. In the following year, he wrote a masque, *The Lady of May*, which was presented before the Queen at Leicester's castle at Wanstead. During the next few years Sidney was a member of an informal group called the Areopagus, interested in literature generally, but more particularly in the movement to adapt classical meters to English usage. He was further inspired to composition by the publication in 1579 of Stephen Gosson's Puritanical attack on poetry and the drama in *The School of Abuse*, dedicated to Sidney without the latter's permission. Sidney's reply, *The Defence of Poesy*, was probably begun shortly after this event.

In 1580, Sidney was afforded a further opportunity for composition when as a result of his open letter to Elizabeth, protesting against her projected marriage to the Duke of Anjou, he was forced into temporary retirement. At the Pembrokes' beautiful country seat, Wilton House, Wiltshire, he began his long pastoral romance, *Arcadia*, for the amusement of his sister, the Countess of Pembroke. In 1581, the marriage of Penelope Devereux to the elderly Lord Rich seems to have rekindled his interest in the young girl, and most of his amatory sonnets were probably written during this period.

Restored to court favor in 1581, Sidney was knighted by Elizabeth in 1583, and in the same

---

13. **haydegyes,** popular dances. This song occurs in a scene where Corsites is prevented by the fairies from carrying off the sleeping Endymion.

SIR PHILIP SIDNEY

year married Frances, the daughter of Sir Francis Walsingham, one of the Queen's intensely Protestant counselors. In the winter of 1584-85 he sat in Parliament, and was considering an expedition to America with Sir Francis Drake when he was appointed Governor of Flushing, Holland, as a part of the Queen's plans for aiding the Protestants in the Low Countries against her archenemy, Philip II. In September, 1586, he was mortally wounded in an unimportant engagement between the English and the Spanish at Zutphen. Fulke Greville tells how, as Sidney was about to slake his thirst after being wounded, he saw a dying soldier, and took the drink "from his head before he drank, and delivered it to the poor man with these words, 'Thy necessity is greater than mine.'" He lingered for twenty-six days, during which he composed a song about his wound, "*La Cuisse Rompue*," and had it sung to him. He died on October 17, 1586, and was given a magnificent funeral and burial in St. Paul's Cathedral. Elegies upon his death were written by Spenser, James I, Drayton, and other poets.

Sidney complied with the Renaissance courtly code by not allowing his writing to be published. But two of his poems were set to music by William Byrd and printed in songbooks of 1588 and 1589. An incompletely revised version of the *Arcadia* was published in 1590, and a version revised by his sister in 1593. Two printed editions of *Astrophel and Stella* appeared in 1591. His critical treatise was published twice in 1593, first under the title *The Defence of Poesy* and then under the title *An Apology for Poetry*. An authorized edition of his principal works, prepared by the Countess of Pembroke, was published in 1598. By 1724, his works had reached a fourteenth edition.

Sidney served English literature in a number of important ways, as poet, as fictionist, and as critic. Aside from a great deal of interesting though unimpressive poetic experimentation in the lyrical interludes of *Arcadia*, his most notable poetic achievement was *Astrophel and Stella*, the first real sonnet sequence in English and the stimulus to an extraordinary amount of emulation in the decade after its publication. In the *Arcadia*, he wrote the first very extended piece of Renaissance prose fiction, blended the pastoral and the heroic modes, and demonstrated the poetic potentialities of a highly decorated prose style. Probably *The Defence of Poesy* is his most noteworthy contribution, since this critical work is the most important in its kind produced in England during the Renaissance.

from ASTROPHEL AND STELLA

The publication of *Astrophel and Stella* in 1591 was the signal for the production of a large number of sequences of sonnets in the Petrarchan vein. Wyatt and Surrey had introduced Petrarchan themes and stylistic devices into English poetry, but Sidney was the first English poet to tell an orderly story in this exacting form.

Although Sidney asserts his independence of Petrarch and other sonneteers, both his subject and his style are highly conventional. Like the other Petrarchans, he represents his lady as unattainable, and his love as unrequited. Like them, also, he treats the inevitable topics: the lover's instability of emotion, his sleeplessness, his invocation to the moon, his ecstatic hopes and abysmal fears. But Sidney's chaste and modest spirit makes itself felt despite the basic conventionality of the poetic type.

1

Loving in truth, and fain in verse my love to show,
  That she, dear she, might take some pleasure of my pain,
  Pleasure might cause her read, reading might make her know,
  Knowledge might pity win, and pity grace obtain,—
I sought fit words to paint the blackest face of woe;
  Studying inventions fine, her wits to entertain,
  Oft turning others' leaves to see if thence would flow
  Some fresh and fruitful showers upon my sunburned brain.
But words came halting forth, wanting invention's stay;
  Invention, nature's child, fled step-dame Study's blows,   10
  And others' feet still seemed but strangers in my way.
Thus, great with child to speak, and helpless in my throes,
  Biting my truant pen, beating myself for spite,
  Fool, said my muse to me, look in thy heart and write.

5

It is most true that eyes are formed to serve
  The inward light, and that the heavenly part
  Ought to be king, from whose rules who do swerve,
  Rebels to nature, strive for their own smart.
It is most true what we call Cupid's dart
  An image is which for ourselves we carve,
  And, fools, adore in temple of our heart
  Till that good god make church and churchman starve.

True, that true beauty virtue is indeed,
  Whereof this beauty can be but a shade,
  Which elements with mortal mixture breed.
True, that on earth we are but pilgrims made,
  And should in soul up to our country move;
  True, and yet true that I must Stella love.

14

Alas, have I not pain enough, my friend,
  Upon whose breast a fiercer gripe doth tire
  Than did on him who first stole down the fire,
  While Love on me doth all his quiver spend,—
But with your rhubarb words ye must contend,
  To grieve me worse, in saying that desire
  Doth plunge my well-formed soul even in the mire
  Of sinful thoughts which do in ruin end?
If that be sin which doth the manners frame,
  Well stayed with truth in word and faith of deed,
  Ready of wit and fearing nought but shame;
If that be sin which in fixed hearts doth breed
  A loathing of all loose unchastity,
  Then love is sin, and let me sinful be.

31

With how sad steps, O moon, thou climb'st the skies!
  How silently, and with how wan a face!
  What! may it be that even in heavenly place
  That busy archer his sharp arrows tries?
Sure, if that long-with-love-acquainted eyes
  Can judge of love, thou feel'st a lover's case;
  I read it in thy looks,—thy languished grace
  To me, that feel the like, thy state descries.
Then, ev'n of fellowship, O moon, tell me,
  Is constant love deemed there but want of wit?
  Are beauties there as proud as here they be?
Do they above love to be loved, and yet
  Those lovers scorn whom that love doth possess?
  Do they call virtue there ungratefulness?

39

Come sleep! O sleep, the certain knot of peace,
  The baiting place of wit, the balm of woe,
  The poor man's wealth, the prisoner's release,
  Th' indifferent judge between the high and low;
With shield of proof shield me from out the prease
  Of those fierce darts despair at me doth throw;
  O make in me those civil wars to cease;
  I will good tribute pay, if thou do so.

Sec. 14. **5. rhubarb**, bitter, tart, with the suggestion also of medicinal. *Sec. 39.* **5. prease**, press.

Take thou of me smooth pillows, sweetest bed,
  A chamber deaf to noise and blind to light,
  A rosy garland and a weary head;
And if these things, as being thine by right,
  Move not thy heavy grace, thou shalt in me,
  Livelier than elsewhere, Stella's image see.

54

Because I breathe not love to every one,
  Nor do not use set colours for to wear,
  Nor nourish special locks of vowèd hair,
  Nor give each speech a full point of a groan,
The courtly nymphs, acquainted with the moan
  Of them who in their lips Love's standard bear,
  What, he! say they of me, Now I dare swear
  He cannot love; no, no, let him alone.
And think so still, so Stella know my mind;
  Profess indeed I do not Cupid's art;
  But you, fair maids, at length this true shall find,
That his right badge is but worn in the heart;
  Dumb swans, not chattering pies, do lovers prove;
  They love indeed who quake to say they love.

MY TRUE-LOVE HATH MY HEART

My true-love hath my heart, and I have his,
  By just exchange one for another given:
I hold his dear, and mine he cannot miss,
  There never was a better bargain driven:
    My true-love hath my heart, and I have his.

His heart in me keeps him and me in one,
  My heart in him his thoughts and senses guides:
He loves my heart, for once it was his own,
  I cherish his because in me it bides:
    My true-love hath my heart, and I have his.

from CERTAIN SONNETS

This sonnet is eloquently expressive of the deeply religious side of Sidney's nature.

Leave me, O love which reachest but to dust;
And thou, my mind, aspire to higher things;
Grow rich in that which never taketh rust,
Whatever fades but fading pleasure brings.
Draw in thy beams, and humble all thy might
To that sweet yoke where lasting freedoms be;
Which breaks the clouds and opens forth the light,
That doth both shine and give us sight to see.
O take fast hold; let that light be thy guide
In this small course which birth draws out to death,

And think how evil becometh him to slide,
Who seeketh heaven, and comes of heavenly breath.
   Then farewell, world; thy uttermost I see;
   Eternal Love, maintain thy life in me.

from THE DEFENCE OF POESY

Sidney's *Defence of Poesy* is a skillful synthesis of Classical and Renaissance literary-critical theory. It represents wide reading in the Renaissance interpreters of the doctrines of Plato, Aristotle, and Horace, and a willing acceptance of their theories. The essay is carefully organized. The first part is devoted to an affirmative statement of the case for poetry. The second part is an attempt at a rebuttal of the attack on poetry. The final section evaluates the English literature of Sidney's time in accordance with the Neoclassical principles in which he believes. The author's amiability and good humor are apparent throughout the essay. The selection given below consists of the summary of the first part and all the remainder of *The Defence*.

SINCE, then, poetry is of all human learnings the most ancient, and of most fatherly antiquity, as from whence other learnings have taken their beginnings; since it is so universal that no learned nation doth despise it, nor barbarous nation is without it; since both Roman and Greek gave such divine names unto it, the one of prophesying, the other of making, and that indeed that name of making is fit for him, considering that where all other arts retain themselves within their subject, and receive, as it were, their being from it, the poet only, only bringeth his own stuff, and doth not learn a conceit out of a matter, but maketh matter for a conceit; since neither his description nor end containeth any evil, the thing described cannot be evil; since his effects be so good as to teach goodness, and delight the learners of it; since therein (namely in moral doctrine, the chief of all knowledges) he doth not only far pass the historian, but, for instructing, is well nigh comparable to the philosopher, for moving, leaveth him behind him; since the Holy Scripture (wherein there is no uncleanness) hath whole parts in it poetical, and that even our Saviour Christ vouchsafed to use the flowers of it; since all his kinds are not only in their united forms but in their severed dissections fully commendable; I think, and think I think rightly, the laurel crown appointed for triumphant captains doth worthily, of all other learnings, honour the poet's triumph.

But because we have ears as well as tongues, and that the lightest reasons that may be will seem to weigh greatly if nothing be put in the counter-balance, let us hear, and, as well as we can, ponder, what objections be made against this art, which may be worthy either of yielding or answering.

First, truly, I note, not only in these μισομούσοι, poet-haters, but in all that kind of people who seek a praise by dispraising others, that they do prodigally spend a great many wandering words in quips and scoffs, carping and taunting at each thing which, by stirring the spleen, may stay the brain from a thorough beholding the worthiness of the subject. Those kind of objections, as they are full of a very idle easiness (since there is nothing of so sacred a majesty but that an itching tongue may rub itself upon it), so deserve they no other answer but, instead of laughing at the jest, to laugh at the jester. We know a playing wit can praise the discretion of an ass, the comfortableness of being in debt, and the jolly commodities of being sick of the plague; so, of the contrary side, if we will turn Ovid's verse,

"Ut lateat virtus, proximitate mali."

"That good lie hid in nearness of the evil," Agrippa will be as merry in showing the vanity of science, as Erasmus was in the commending of folly; neither shall any man or matter escape some touch of these smiling railers. But for Erasmus and Agrippa, they had another foundation than the superficial part would promise. Marry, these other pleasant fault-finders, who will correct the verb before they understand the noun, and confute others' knowledge before they confirm their own; I would have them only remember, that scoffing cometh not of wisdom; so as the best title in true English they get with their merriments is to be called good fools; for so have our grave forefathers ever termed that humorous kind of jesters.

But that which giveth greatest scope to their scorning humour is rhyming and versing. It is already said, and, as I think, truly said, it is not rhyming and versing that maketh poesy; one may be a poet without versing, and a versifier without poetry. But yet, presuppose it were inseparable, as indeed it seemeth Scaliger judgeth, truly it were an inseparable commendation; for if *oratio* next to *ratio*, speech next to reason, be the greatest gift bestowed upon mortality, that can not be praiseless which doth most polish that blessing of speech; which considereth each word, not only as a man may say by his forcible quality, but by his best measured quantity; carrying even in themselves a harmony; without, perchance, number, measure, order, proportion be in our time grown odious.

But lay aside the just praise it hath, by being the only fit speech for music—music, I say, the most divine striker of the senses—thus much is undoubtedly true, that if reading be foolish without remembering, memory being the only treasure of knowledge, those words which are fittest for memory are likewise most convenient for knowledge. Now, that verse far exceedeth prose in the knitting up of the memory, the reason is manifest; the words, besides their delight, which hath a great affinity to memory, being so set as one cannot be lost but the whole work fails; which accusing itself calleth the remembrance back to itself, and so most strongly confirmeth it. Besides, one word so, as it were, begetting another as, be it in rhyme or measured verse, by the former a man shall have a near guess to the follower. Lastly, even they that have taught the art of memory have showed nothing so apt for it as a certain room divided into many places, well and thoroughly known; now that hath the verse in effect perfectly, every word having his natural seat, which seat must needs make the word remembered. But what needs more in a thing so known to all men? Who is it that ever was scholar that doth not carry away some verses of Virgil, Horace, or Cato, which in his youth he learned, and even to his old age serve him for hourly lessons? as,

> "*Percontatorem fugito: nam garrulus idem est.*
> *Dum sibi quisque placet credula turba sumus.*"

But the fitness it hath for memory is notably proved by all delivery of arts, wherein, for the most part, from grammar to logic, mathematics, physic, and the rest, the rules chiefly necessary to be borne away are compiled in verses. So that verse being in itself sweet and orderly, and being best for memory, the only handle of knowledge, it must be in jest that any man can speak against it.

Now then go we to the most important imputations laid to the poor poets; for aught I can yet learn, they are these:

First, that there being many other more fruitful knowledges, a man might better spend his time in them than in this.

Secondly, that it is the mother of lies.

Thirdly, that it is the nurse of abuse, infecting us with many pestilent desires, with a siren's sweetness drawing the mind to the serpent's tail of sinful fancies; and herein, especially, comedies give the largest field to ear, as Chaucer saith; how, both in other nations and ours, before poets did soften us, we were full of courage, given to martial exercises, the pillars of manlike liberty, and not lulled asleep in shady idleness with poets' pastimes.

And lastly and chiefly, they cry out with open mouth, as if they had overshot Robin Hood, that Plato banished them out of his commonwealth. Truly this is much, if there be much truth in it.

First, to the first, that a man might better spend his time is a reason indeed; but it doth, as they say, but *petere principium.* For if it be, as I affirm, that no learning is so good as that which teacheth and moveth to virtue, and that none can both teach and move thereto so much as poesy, then is the conclusion manifest, that ink and paper cannot be to a more profitable purpose employed. And certainly, though a man should grant their first assumption, it should follow, methinks, very unwillingly, that good is not good because better is better. But I still and utterly deny that there is sprung out of earth a more fruitful knowledge.

To the second, therefore, that they should be the principal liars, I answer paradoxically, but truly, I think truly, that of all writers under the sun, the poet is the least liar; and though he would, as a poet can scarcely be a liar. The astronomer, with his cousin the geometrician, can hardly escape when they take upon them to measure the height of the stars. How often, think you, do the physicians lie, when they aver things good for sicknesses which afterwards send Charon a great number of souls drowned in a potion before they come to his ferry? And no less of the rest which take upon them to affirm. Now for the poet, he nothing affirmeth, and therefore never lieth; for, as I take it, to lie is to affirm that to be true which is false; so as the other artists, and especially the historian, affirming many things, can, in the cloudy knowledge of mankind, hardly escape from many lies. But the poet, as I said before, never affirmeth; the poet never maketh any circles about your imagination, to conjure you to believe for true what he writeth; he citeth not authorities of other histories, but even for his entry calleth the sweet Muses to inspire into him a good invention; in truth, not labouring to tell you what is or is not, but what should or should not be. And, therefore, though he recount things not true, yet because he telleth them not for true he lieth not; without we will say that Nathan lied in his speech, before alleged, to David; which, as a wicked man durst scarce say, so think I none so simple would say that Aesop lied in the tales of his beasts; for who

---

29–30. "**Percontatorem . . . sumus.**" "Fly from the inquisitive man, for he is likewise garrulous. While each one pleases himself we are a credulous crowd." 51. **ear**, plow.

11. **petere principium,** beg the question. 49. **Nathan.** See II Samuel 12:1–14. Sidney had referred to this earlier.

thinketh that Aesop wrote it for actually true were well worthy to have his name chronicled among the beasts he writeth of. What child is there that cometh to a play, and seeing Thebes written in great letters upon an old door, doth believe that it is Thebes? If then a man can arrive to the child's age, to know that the poet's persons and doings are but pictures what should be, and not stories what have been, they will never give the lie to things not affirmatively, but allegorically and figuratively written; and therefore, as in history, looking for truth, they may go away full fraught with falsehood, so in poesy, looking but for fiction, they shall use the narration but as an imaginative groundplot of a profitable invention.

But hereto is replied, that the poets give names to men they write of, which argueth a conceit of an actual truth, and so, not being true, proveth a falsehood. And doth the lawyer lie then, when, under the names of John of the Stile, and John of the Nokes, he putteth his case? But that is easily answered. Their naming of men is but to make their picture the more lively, and not to build any history. Painting men, they cannot leave men nameless; we see we cannot play at chess but that we must give names to our chessmen; and yet, methinks, he were a very partial champion of truth that would say we lied for giving a piece of wood the reverend title of a bishop. The poet nameth Cyrus and Aeneas no other way than to show what men of their fames, fortunes, and estates should do.

Their third is, how much it abuseth men's wit, training it to wanton sinfulness and lustful love. For, indeed, that is the principal if not only abuse I can hear alleged. They say the comedies rather teach than reprehend amorous conceits; they say the lyric is larded with passionate sonnets; the elegiac weeps the want of his mistress; and that even to the heroical Cupid hath ambitiously climbed. Alas! Love, I would thou couldst as well defend thyself as thou canst offend others! I would those on whom thou dost attend could either put thee away or yield good reason why they keep thee! But grant love of beauty to be a beastly fault, although it be very hard, since only man, and no beast, hath that gift to discern beauty; grant that lovely name of love to deserve all hateful reproaches, although even some of my masters the philosophers spent a good deal of their lamp-oil in setting forth the excellency of it; grant, I say, what they will have granted, that not only love, but lust, but vanity, but, if they list, scurrility, possess many leaves of the poets' books; yet, think I, when this is granted, they will find their sentence may, with good manners, put the last words foremost; and not say that poetry abuseth man's wit, but that man's wit abuseth poetry. For I will not deny but that man's wit may make poesy, which should be φραστική, which some learned have defined, figuring forth good things, to be φανταστική, which doth contrariwise infect the fancy with unworthy objects; as the painter that should give to the eye either some excellent perspective, or some fine picture fit for building or fortification, or containing in it some notable example, as Abraham sacrificing his son Isaac, Judith killing Holofernes, David fighting with Goliath, may leave those, and please an ill-pleased eye with wanton shows of better-hidden matters.

But, what! Shall the abuse of a thing make the right use odious? Nay, truly, though I yield that poesy may not only be abused, but that being abused, by the reason of his sweet charming force it can do more hurt than any other army of words, yet shall it be so far from concluding that the abuse shall give reproach to the abused, that, contrariwise, it is a good reason that whatsoever being abused doth most harm, being rightly used (and upon the right use each thing receives his title) doth most good. Do we not see skill of physic, the best rampire to our often-assaulted bodies, being abused, teach poison, the most violent destroyer? Doth not knowledge of law, whose end is to even and right all things, being abused, grow the crooked fosterer of horrible injuries? Doth not (to go to the highest) God's word abused breed heresy, and his name abused become blasphemy? Truly, a needle cannot do much hurt, and as truly (with leave of ladies be it spoken) it cannot do much good. With a sword thou mayst kill thy father, and with a sword thou mayst defend thy prince and country; so that, as in their calling poets fathers of lies they said nothing, so in this their argument of abuse, they prove the commendation.

They allege herewith, that before poets began to be in price, our nation had set their heart's delight upon action, and not imagination; rather doing things worthy to be written than writing things fit to be done. What that before-time was, I think scarcely Sphinx can tell; since no memory is so ancient that gives not the precedence to poetry. And certain it is that, in our plainest homeliness, yet never was the Albion nation without poetry. Marry, this argument, though it be levelled

5-6. φραστική . . . φανταστική. In the two adjectives Sidney contrasts poetry that is soundly creative and poetry that is morbidly creative. **19. his,** its—as always at this time. **27. rampire,** rampart.

against poetry, yet it is indeed a chain-shot against all learning—or bookishness, as they commonly term it. Of such mind were certain Goths, of whom it is written that having in the spoil of a famous city taken a fair library, one hangman, belike fit to execute the fruits of their wits, who had murthered a great number of bodies, would have set fire in it. "No," said another, very gravely, "take heed what you do, for while they are busy about those toys we shall with more leisure conquer their countries." This, indeed, is the ordinary doctrine of ignorance, and many words sometimes I have heard spent in it; but because this reason is generally against all learning, as well as poetry, or rather all learning but poetry; because it were too large a digression to handle it, or at least too superfluous, since it is manifest that all government of action is to be gotten by knowledge, and knowledge best by gathering many knowledges, which is reading; I only say with Horace, to him that is of that opinion,

"*Iubeo stultum esse libenter——*"

for as for poetry itself, it is the freest from this objection, for poetry is the companion of camps. I dare undertake, Orlando Furioso or honest King Arthur will never displease a soldier: but the quiddity of *ens* and *prima materia* will hardly agree with a corselet. And, therefore, as I said in the beginning, even Turks and Tartars are delighted with poets. Homer, a Greek, flourished before Greece flourished; and if to a slight conjecture a conjecture may be opposed, truly it may seem, that as by him their learned men took almost their first light of knowledge, so their active men received their first motions of courage. Only Alexander's example may serve, who by Plutarch is accounted of such virtue that fortune was not his guide but his footstool; whose acts speak for him, though Plutarch did not; indeed, the phoenix of warlike princes. This Alexander left his schoolmaster, living Aristotle, behind him, but took dead Homer with him. He put the philosopher Callisthenes to death, for his seeming philosophical, indeed mutinous, stubbornness; but the chief thing he was ever heard to wish for was that Homer had been alive. He well found he received more bravery of mind by the pattern of Achilles than by hearing the definition of fortitude. And, therefore, if Cato misliked Fulvius for carrying Ennius with him to the field, it may be answered that if Cato misliked it the noble Fulvius liked it, or else he had not done it; for it was not the excellent Cato Uticensis, whose authority I would much more have reverenced, but it was the former, in truth a bitter punisher of faults, but else a man that had never sacrificed to the Graces. He misliked and cried out against all Greek learning, and yet, being fourscore years old, began to learn it, belike fearing that Pluto understood not Latin. Indeed, the Roman laws allowed no person to be carried to the wars but he that was in the soldiers' roll. And, therefore, though Cato misliked his unmustered person, he misliked not his work. And if he had, Scipio Nasica (judged by common consent the best Roman) loved him; both the other Scipio brothers, who had by their virtues no less surnames than of Asia and Afric, so loved him that they caused his body to be buried in their sepulture. So as Cato's authority being but against his person, and that answered with so far greater than himself, is herein of no validity.

But now, indeed, my burthen is great, that Plato his name is laid upon me, whom, I must confess, of all philosophers I have ever esteemed most worthy of reverence; and with good reason, since of all philosophers he is the most poetical; yet if he will defile the fountain out of which his flowing streams have proceeded, let us boldly examine with what reasons he did it.

First, truly, a man might maliciously object that Plato, being a philosopher, was a natural enemy of poets. For, indeed, after the philosophers had picked out of the sweet mysteries of poetry the right discerning true points of knowledge, they forthwith, putting it in method, and making a school-art of that which the poets did only teach by a divine delightfulness, beginning to spurn at their guides, like ungrateful apprentices, were not content to set up shop for themselves, but sought by all means to discredit their masters; which, by the force of delight being barred them, the less they could overthrow them, the more they hated them. For, indeed, they found for Homer seven cities strove who should have him for their citizen, where many cities banished philosophers as not fit members to live among them. For only repeating certain of Euripides' verses many Athenians had their lives saved of the Syracusans, where the Athenians themselves thought many philosophers unworthy to live. Certain poets, as Simonides and Pindarus, had so prevailed with Hiero the First, that of a tyrant they made him a just king; where Plato could do so little with Dionysius that he himself of a philosopher was made a slave. But who should do

---

22. "*Iubeo . . . libenter——.*" "I bid him enjoy his own foolishness."   28. **quiddity**, essence; also, fine distinction. **ens . . . prima materia**, being, primary matter—terms of philosophy.

thus, I confess, should requite the objections made against poets with like cavillations against philosophers; as likewise one should do that should bid one read *Phaedrus* or *Symposium* in Plato, or the discourse of Love in Plutarch, and see whether any poet do authorize abominable filthiness as they do.

Again, a man might ask, out of what commonwealth Plato doth banish them. In sooth, thence where he himself alloweth community of women. So as belike this banishment grew not for effeminate wantonness, since little should poetical sonnets be hurtful when a man might have what woman he listed. But I honour philosophical instructions, and bless the wits which bred them, so as they be not abused, which is likewise stretched to poetry. St. Paul himself sets a watchword upon philosophy, indeed upon the abuse. So doth Plato upon the abuse, not upon poetry. Plato found fault that the poets of his time filled the world with wrong opinions of the gods, making light tales of that unspotted essence, and therefore would not have the youth depraved with such opinions. Herein may much be said; let this suffice: the poets did not induce such opinions, but did imitate those opinions already induced. For all the Greek stories can well testify that the very religion of that time stood upon many and many-fashioned gods; not taught so by poets, but followed according to their nature of imitation. Who list may read in Plutarch the discourses of Isis and Osiris, of the cause why oracles ceased, of the divine providence, and see whether the theology of that nation stood not upon such dreams, which the poets indeed superstitiously observed; and truly, since they had not the light of Christ, did much better in it than the philosophers, who, shaking off superstition, brought in atheism.

Plato, therefore, whose authority I had much rather justly construe than unjustly resist, meant not in general of poets, in those words of which Julius Scaliger saith, "*Qua authoritate barbari quidam atque hispidi abuti velint ad poetas e republica exigendos*": but only meant to drive out those wrong opinions of the Deity, whereof now, without farther law, Christianity hath taken away all the hurtful belief, perchance, as he thought, nourished by the then esteemed poets. And a man need go no further than to Plato himself to know his meaning; who, in his dialogue called *Ion*, giveth high and rightly divine commendation unto poetry. So as Plato, banishing the abuse not the thing, not banishing it, but giving due honour to it, shall be our patron and not our adversary. For, indeed, I had much rather, since truly I may do it, show their mistaking of Plato, under whose lion's skin they would make an ass-like braying against poesy, than go about to overthrow his authority; whom, the wiser a man is, the more just cause he shall find to have in admiration; especially since he attributeth unto poesy more than myself do, namely, to be a very inspiring of a divine force, far above man's wit, as in the forenamed dialogue is apparent.

Of the other side, who would show the honours have been by the best sort of judgments granted them, a whole sea of examples would present themselves; Alexanders, Caesars, Scipios, all favourers of poets; Laelius, called the Roman Socrates, himself a poet; so as part of *Heautontimoeroumenos*, in Terence, was supposed to be made by him. And even the Greek Socrates, whom Apollo confirmed to be the only wise man, is said to have spent part of his old time in putting Aesop's fables into verse; and, therefore, full evil should it become his scholar Plato to put such words in his master's mouth against poets. But what needs more? Aristotle writes the *Art of Poesy;* and why, if it should not be written? Plutarch teacheth the use to be gathered of them; and how, if they should not be read? And who reads Plutarch's either history or philosophy, shall find he trimmeth both their garments with guards of poesy.

But I list not to defend poesy with the help of his underling historiography. Let it suffice to have showed it is a fit soil for praise to dwell upon; and what dispraise may be set upon it is either easily overcome, or transformed into just commendation. So that since the excellences of it may be so easily and so justly confirmed, and the low creeping objections so soon trodden down; it not being an art of lies, but of true doctrine; not of effeminateness, but of notable stirring of courage; not of abusing man's wit, but of strengthening man's wit; not banished, but honoured by Plato; let us rather plant more laurels for to ingarland the poets' heads (which honour of being laureate, as besides them only triumphant captains were, is a sufficient authority to show the price they ought to be held in) than suffer the ill-savoured breath of such wrong speakers once to blow upon the clear springs of poesy.

But since I have run so long a career in this matter, methinks, before I give my pen a full stop, it shall be but a little more lost time to inquire why England, the mother of excellent minds, should be

---

40–41. "Qua . . . exigendos." "Which authority certain barbarous and rude writers would wrest into meaning that poets were to be thrust out of a state."

16. **Heautontimoeroumenos,** *The Self-Tormentor*, a comedy adapted from Menander.

grown so hard a step-mother to poets, who certainly in wit ought to pass all others, since all only proceeds from their wit, being, indeed, makers of themselves, not takers of others. How can I but exclaim,

"*Musa, mihi causas memora, quo numine laeso?*"

Sweet poesy! that hath anciently had kings, emperors, senators, great captains, such as, besides a thousand others, David, Adrian, Sophocles, Germanicus, not only to favour poets, but to be poets; and of our nearer times can present for her patrons, a Robert, King of Sicily; the great King Francis of France; King James of Scotland; such cardinals as Bembus and Bibiena; such famous preachers and teachers as Beza and Melancthon; so learned philosophers as Fracastorius and Scaliger; so great orators as Pontanus and Muretus; so piercing wits as George Buchanan; so grave counsellors as, besides many, but before all, that Hospital of France, than whom, I think, that realm never brought forth a more accomplished judgment more firmly builded upon virtue; I say these, with numbers of others, not only to read others' poesies, but to poetize for others' reading; that poesy, thus embraced in all other places, should only find in our time a hard welcome in England, I think the very earth laments it, and therefore decks our soil with fewer laurels than it was accustomed. For heretofore poets have in England also flourished; and, which is to be noted, even in those times when the trumpet of Mars did sound loudest. And now that an over-faint quietness should seem to strew the house for poets, they are almost in as good reputation as the mountebanks at Venice. Truly, even that, as of the one side it giveth great praise to poesy, which, like Venus (but to better purpose), had rather be troubled in the net with Mars than enjoy the homely quiet of Vulcan; so serveth it for a piece of a reason why they are less grateful to idle England, which now can scarce endure the pain of a pen. Upon this necessarily followeth that base men with servile wits undertake it, who think it enough if they can be rewarded of the printer; and so as Epaminondas is said with the honour of his virtue to have made an office, by his exercising it, which before was contemptible, to become highly respected; so these men, no more but setting their names to it, by their own disgracefulness disgrace the most graceful poesy. For now, as if all the Muses were got with child to bring forth bastard poets, without any commission they do post over the banks of Helicon, until they make their readers more weary than post-horses; while, in the meantime, they,

"*Queis meliore luto finxit praecordia Titan,*"

are better content to suppress the outflowings of their wit than by publishing them to be accounted knights of the same order.

But I, that before ever I durst aspire unto the dignity am admitted into the company of the paper-blurrers, do find the very true cause of our wanting estimation is want of desert, taking upon us to be poets in despite of Pallas. Now, wherein we want desert were a thankworthy labour to express. But if I knew, I should have mended myself; but as I never desired the title, so have I neglected the means to come by it; only, overmastered by some thoughts, I yielded an inky tribute unto them. Marry, they that delight in poesy itself should seek to know what they do, and how they do; and especially look themselves in an unflattering glass of reason, if they be inclinable unto it.

For poesy must not be drawn by the ears, it must be gently led, or rather it must lead; which was partly the cause that made the ancient learned affirm it was a divine gift, and no human skill, since all other knowledges lie ready for any that have strength of wit, a poet no industry can make, if his own genius be not carried into it. And therefore is an old proverb, *Orator fit, poeta nascitur*. Yet confess I always, that as the fertilest ground must be manured, so must the highest flying wit have a Daedalus to guide him. That Daedalus, they say, both in this and in other, hath three wings to bear itself up into the air of due commendation; that is art, imitation, and exercise. But these neither artificial rules nor imitative patterns we much cumber ourselves withal. Exercise, indeed, we do, but that very forebackwardly; for where we should exercise to know, we exercise as having known; and so is our brain delivered of much matter which never was begotten by knowledge. For there being two principal parts, matter to be expressed by words, and words to express the matter, in neither we use art or imitation rightly. Our matter is *quodlibet*, indeed, though wrongly performing Ovid's verse,

"*Quicquid conabor dicere, versus erit;*"

never marshalling it into any assured rank, that almost the readers cannot tell where to find themselves.

6. "Musa . . . laeso?" "Muse, bring to my mind the causes of these things: what divinity was injured?"

3. "Queis . . . Titan." "Whose hearts the Titan formed with a better clay." 29. Orator . . . nascitur. The orator is made, the poet born. 44. quodlibet, what you will. 46. "Quicquid . . . erit." "Whatever I shall try to write will be verse."

SIR PHILIP SIDNEY

Chaucer undoubtedly did excellently in his *Troilus and Criseyde;* of whom, truly, I know not whether to marvel more, either that he in that misty time could see so clearly, or that we in this clear age go so stumblingly after him. Yet had he great wants, fit to be forgiven in so reverent an antiquity. I account the *Mirror of Magistrates* meetly furnished of beautiful parts. And in the Earl of Surrey's lyrics, many things tasting of a noble birth, and worthy of a noble mind. The *Shepherds' Calendar* hath much poesy in his eclogues, indeed, worthy the reading, if I be not deceived. That same framing of his style to an old rustic language, I dare not allow; since neither Theocritus in Greek, Virgil in Latin, nor Sannazaro in Italian, did affect it. Besides these, I do not remember to have seen but few (to speak boldly) printed that have poetical sinews in them. For proof whereof, let but most of the verses be put in prose, and then ask the meaning, and it will be found that one verse did but beget another, without ordering at the first what should be at the last; which becomes a confused mass of words, with a tinkling sound of rhyme, barely accompanied with reason.

Our tragedies and comedies, not without cause cried out against, observing rules neither of honest civility nor skilful poetry. Excepting *Gorboduc* (again I say of those that I have seen), which notwithstanding as it is full of stately speeches and well-sounding phrases, climbing to the height of Seneca his style, and as full of notable morality, which it doth most delightfully teach, and so obtain the very end of poesy; yet, in truth, it is very defective in the circumstances, which grieves me, because it might not remain as an exact model of all tragedies. For it is faulty both in place and time, the two necessary companions of all corporal actions. For where the stage should always represent but one place, and the uttermost time presupposed in it should be, both by Aristotle's precept and common reason, but one day; there is both many days and many places inartificially imagined.

But if it be so in *Gorboduc,* how much more in all the rest? Where you shall have Asia of the one side, and Afric of the other, and so many other underkingdoms, that the player, when he comes in, must ever begin with telling where he is, or else the tale will not be conceived. Now shall you have three ladies walk to gather flowers, and then we must believe the stage to be a garden. By and by, we hear news of shipwreck in the same place, then we are to blame if we accept it not for a rock. Upon the back of that comes out a hideous monster with fire and smoke, and then the miserable beholders are bound to take it for a cave; while, in the meantime, two armies fly in, represented with four swords and bucklers, and then what hard heart will not receive it for a pitched field?

Now of time they are much more liberal; for ordinary it is, that two young princes fall in love; after many traverses she is got with child, delivered of a fair boy, he is lost, groweth a man, falleth in love, and is ready to get another child; and all this in two hours' space; which, how absurd it is in sense, even sense may imagine, and art hath taught, and all ancient examples justified, and at this day the ordinary players in Italy will not err in. Yet will some bring in an example of the *Eunuch,* in Terence, that containeth matter of two days, yet far short of twenty years. True it is, and so was it to be played in two days, and so fitted to the time it set forth. And though Plautus have in one place done amiss, let us hit it with him, and not miss with him. But they will say, how then shall we set forth a story which contains both many places and many times? And do they not know that a tragedy is tied to the laws of poesy, and not of history; not bound to follow the story, but having liberty either to feign a quite new matter or to frame the history to the most tragical conveniency? Again, many things may be told, which cannot be showed—if they know the difference betwixt reporting and representing. As for example, I may speak, though I am here, of Peru, and in speech digress from that to the description of Calicut; but in action I cannot represent it without Pacolet's horse. And so was the manner the ancients took, by some *Nuntius* to recount things done in former time, or other place.

Lastly, if they will represent an history they must not, as Horace saith, begin *ab ovo,* but they must come to the principal point of that one action which they will represent. By example this will be best expressed; I have a story of young Polydorus, delivered, for safety's sake, with great riches, by his father Priamus to Polymnestor, King of Thrace, in the Trojan war time. He, after some years, hearing of the overthrow of Priamus, for to make the treasure his own, murthereth the child; the body of the child is taken up; Hecuba, she, the same day, findeth a sleight to be revenged most cruelly of the tyrant. Where, now, would one of our tragedy-writers begin, but with the delivery of the child? Then should he sail over into Thrace, and so spend I know not how many years, and travel numbers of places. But where doth Euripides? Even with the finding of the body; leaving the rest to be told

33. Nuntius, messenger. **37. ab ovo,** from the egg.

by the spirit of Polydorus. This needs no further to be enlarged; the dullest wit may conceive it.

But, besides these gross absurdities, how all their plays be neither right tragedies nor right comedies, mingling kings and clowns, not because the matter so carrieth it, but thrust in the clown by head and shoulders to play a part in majestical matters, with neither decency nor discretion; so as neither the admiration and commiseration, nor the right sportfulness, is by their mongrel tragi-comedy obtained. I know Apuleius did somewhat so, but that is a thing recounted with space of time, not represented in one moment; and I know the ancients have one or two examples of tragi-comedies as Plautus hath *Amphytrio*. But, if we mark them well, we shall find that they never, or very daintily, match hornpipes and funerals. So falleth it out that, having indeed no right comedy in that comical part of our tragedy, we have nothing but scurrility, unworthy of any chaste ears; or some extreme show of doltishness, indeed fit to lift up a loud laughter, and nothing else; where the whole tract of a comedy should be full of delight; as the tragedy should be still maintained in a well-raised admiration.

But our comedians think there is no delight without laughter, which is very wrong; for though laughter may come with delight, yet cometh it not of delight, as though delight should be the cause of laughter; but well may one thing breed both together. Nay, rather in themselves they have, as it were, a kind of contrariety. For delight we scarcely do, but in things that have a conveniency to ourselves, or to the general nature; laughter almost ever cometh of things most disproportioned to ourselves and nature. Delight hath a joy in it either permanent or present; laughter hath only a scornful tickling. For example, we are ravished with delight to see a fair woman, and yet are far from being moved to laughter; we laugh at deformed creatures, wherein certainly we cannot delight. We delight in good chances; we laugh at mischances. We delight to hear the happiness of our friends and country, at which he were worthy to be laughed at that would laugh; we shall, contrarily, sometimes laugh to find a matter quite mistaken, and go down the hill against the bias, in the mouth of some such men as for the respect of them one shall be heartily sorry he cannot choose but laugh, and so is rather pained than delighted with laughter. Yet deny I not but that they may go well together; for as in Alexander's picture well set out we delight without laughter, and in twenty mad antics we laugh without delight: so in Hercules, painted, with his great beard and furious countenance, in a woman's attire, spinning at Omphale's commandment, it breeds both delight and laughter; for the representing of so strange a power in love procures delight, and the scornfulness of the action stirreth laughter.

But I speak to this purpose, that all the end of the comical part be not upon such scornful matters as stir laughter only, but mix with it that delightful teaching which is the end of poesy. And the great fault, even in that point of laughter, and forbidden plainly by Aristotle, is, that they stir laughter in sinful things, which are rather execrable than ridiculous; or in miserable, which are rather to be pitied than scorned. For what is it to make folks gape at a wretched beggar, and a beggarly clown; or against law of hospitality, to jest at strangers because they speak not English so well as we do? What do we learn? Since it is certain,

"*Nil habet infelix paupertas durius in se,
Quam quod ridiculos homines facit.*"

But rather a busy loving courtier, and a heartless threatening Thraso; a self-wise-seeming schoolmaster; a wry-transformed traveller: these, if we saw walk in stage names, which we play naturally, therein were delightful laughter, and teaching delightfulness; as in the other, the tragedies of Buchanan do justly bring forth a divine admiration.

But I have lavished out too many words of this play matter; I do it because, as they are excelling parts of poesy, so is there none so much used in England, and none can be more pitifully abused; which, like an unmannerly daughter, showing a bad education, causeth her mother Poesy's honesty to be called in question.

Other sorts of poetry almost have we none, but that lyrical kind of songs and sonnets, which, Lord if he gave us so good minds, how well it might be employed, and with how heavenly fruits, both private and public, in singing the praises of the immortal beauty, the immortal goodness of that God who giveth us hands to write and wits to conceive! of which we might well want words, but never matter; of which we could turn our eyes to nothing but we should ever have new-budding occasions.

But, truly, many of such writings as come under the banner of unresistible love, if I were a mistress, would never persuade me they were in love; so coldly they apply fiery speeches, as men that had rather read lovers' writings, and so caught up certain swelling phrases—which hang together like a

19–20. "Nil habet . . . facit." "Unhappy poverty has nothing in it harder than this, that it makes men ridiculous."

man that once told me the wind was at northwest and by south, because he would be sure to name winds enough—than that in truth they feel those passions, which easily, as I think, may be bewrayed by that same forcibleness, or *energia* (as the Greeks call it) of the writer. But let this be a sufficient, though short note, that we miss the right use of the material point of poesy.

Now for the outside of it, which is words, or (as I may term it) diction, it is even well worse; so is it that honey-flowing matron Eloquence, apparelled, or rather disguised, in a courtezan-like painted affectation; one time with so far-fet words that many seem monsters, but must seem strangers, to any poor Englishman; another time with coursing of a letter, as if they were bound to follow the method of a dictionary; another time with figures and flowers, extremely winter-starved.

But I would this fault were only peculiar to versifiers, and had not as large possession among prose-printers; and, which is to be marvelled, among many scholars, and, which is to be pitied, among some preachers. Truly, I could wish (if at least I might be so bold to wish, in a thing beyond the reach of my capacity) the diligent imitators of Tully and Demosthenes (most worthy to be imitated) did not so much keep Nizolian paperbooks of their figures and phrases, as by attentive translation, as it were, devour them whole, and make them wholly theirs. For now they cast sugar and spice upon every dish that is served at the table; like those Indians, not content to wear ear-rings at the fit and natural place of the ears, but they will thrust jewels through their nose and lips, because they will be sure to be fine. Tully, when he was to drive out Catiline, as it were with a thunderbolt of eloquence, often useth the figure of repetition, as "*Vivit et vincit, imo in senatum venit, imo in senatum venit,*" &c. Indeed, inflamed with a well-grounded rage, he would have his words, as it were, double out of his mouth; and so do that artificially which we see men in choler do naturally. And we, having noted the grace of those words, hale them in sometimes to a familiar epistle, when it were too much choler to be choleric.

How well store of *similiter* cadences doth sound with the gravity of the pulpit, I would but invoke Demosthenes' soul to tell, who with a rare daintiness useth them. Truly, they have made me think of the sophister, that with too much subtilty would prove two eggs three, and though he may be counted a sophister, had none for his labour. So these men bringing in such a kind of eloquence, well may they obtain an opinion of a seeming fineness, but persuade few, which should be the end of their fineness.

Now for similitudes in certain printed discourses, I think all herbarists, all stories of beasts, fowls, and fishes, are rifled up, that they may come in multitudes to wait upon any of our conceits, which certainly is as absurd a surfeit to the ears as is possible. For the force of a similitude not being to prove anything to a contrary disputer, but only to explain to a willing hearer: when that is done, the rest is a most tedious prattling, rather overswaying the memory from the purpose whereto they were applied, than any whit informing the judgment, already either satisfied, or by similitudes not to be satisfied.

For my part, I do not doubt, when Antonius and Crassus, the great forefathers of Cicero in eloquence, the one (as Cicero testifieth of them) pretended not to know art, the other not to set by it, because with a plain sensibleness they might win credit of popular ears, which credit is the nearest step to persuasion (which persuasion is the chief mark of oratory); I do not doubt, I say, but that they used these knacks very sparingly; which who doth generally use, any man may see doth dance to his own music; and so to be noted by the audience, more carefully to speak curiously than truly. Undoubtedly (at least to my opinion undoubtedly) I have found in divers small-learned courtiers a more sound style than in some professors of learning; of which I can guess no other cause, but that the courtier following that which by practice he findeth fittest to nature, therein (though he know it not) doth according to art, though not by art: where the other, using art to show art, and not hide art (as in these cases he should do), flieth from nature, and indeed abuseth art.

But what! Methinks I deserve to be pounded for straying from poetry to oratory; but both have such an affinity in the wordish consideration, that I think this digression will make my meaning receive the fuller understanding: which is not to take upon me to teach poets how they should do, but only finding myself sick among the rest, to show some one or two spots of the common infection grown among the most part of writers; that, acknowledging ourselves somewhat awry, we may bend to the right use both of matter and manner; whereto our language giveth us great occasion, being, indeed, capable of any excellent exercising of it. I know some will say, it is a mingled language: and why

---

4. bewrayed, revealed, disclosed. **13. far-fet,** far-fetched. **38–39. "Vivit . . . venit."** "He lives and conquers, nay, comes to the Senate, nay, comes to the Senate." **46. similiter cadences,** cadences produced by groups of words with similar endings.

8. rifled up, ransacked.

not so much the better, taking of the best of both the other? Another will say, it wanteth grammar. Nay, truly, it hath that praise, that it wants not grammar; for grammar it might have, but it needs it not; being so easy in itself, and so void of those cumbersome differences of cases, genders, moods, and tenses; which, I think, was a piece of the tower of Babylon's curse, that a man should be put to school to learn his mother tongue. But for the uttering sweetly and properly the conceit of the mind, which is the end of speech, that hath it equally with any other tongue in the world; and is particularly happy in compositions of two or three words together, near the Greek, far beyond the Latin; which is one of the greatest beauties can be in a language.

Now, of versifying there are two sorts, the one ancient, the other modern. The ancient marked the quantity of each syllable, and according to that framed his verse; the modern, observing only number, with some regard of the accent, the chief life of it standeth in that like sounding of the words, which we call rhyme. Whether of these be the more excellent would bear many speeches; the ancient no doubt more fit for music, both words and tune observing quantity; and more fit lively to express divers passions, by the low or lofty sound of the well-weighed syllable. The latter, likewise, with his rhyme striketh a certain music to the ear; and, in fine, since it doth delight, though by another way, it obtaineth the same purpose; there being in either, sweetness, and wanting in neither, majesty. Truly the English, before any vulgar language I know, is fit for both sorts; for, for the ancient, the Italian is so full of vowels that it must ever be cumbered with elisions; the Dutch so, of the other side, with consonants that they cannot yield the sweet sliding fit for a verse. The French, in his whole language, hath not one word that hath his accent in the last syllable saving two, called antepenultima; and little more hath the Spanish; and therefore very gracelessly may they use dactyls. The English is subject to none of these defects.

Now for rhyme, though we do not observe quantity, we observe the accent very precisely, which other languages either cannot do, or will not do so absolutely. That *caesura*, or breathing-place in the midst of the verse, neither Italian nor Spanish have; the French and we never almost fail of. Lastly, even the very rhyme itself the Italian cannot put in the last syllable, by the French named the masculine rhyme, but still in the next to the last, which the French call the female; or the next before that, which the Italians term "sdrucciola." The example of the former is, "buono," "suono"; of the sdrucciola is, "femina," "semina." The French, of the other side, hath both the male, as "bon," "son," and the female, as "plaise," "taise"; but the "sdrucciola" he hath not. Where the English hath all three, as "due," "true," "father," "rather," "motïon," "potïon"; with much more which might be said, but that already I find the trifling of this discourse is much too much enlarged.

So that since the ever praiseworthy poesy is full of virtue, breeding delightfulness, and void of no gift that ought to be in the noble name of learning; since the blames laid against it are either false or feeble; since the cause why it is not esteemed in England is the fault of poet-apes, not poets; since, lastly, our tongue is most fit to honour poesy, and to be honoured by poesy; I conjure you all that have had the evil luck to read this ink-wasting toy of mine, even in the name of the Nine Muses, no more to scorn the sacred mysteries of poesy; no more to laugh at the name of poets, as though they were next inheritors to fools; no more to jest at the reverend title of "a rhymer"; but to believe, with Aristotle, that they were the ancient treasurers of the Grecians' divinity; to believe, with Bembus, that they were the first bringers in of all civility; to believe, with Scaliger, that no philosopher's precepts can sooner make you an honest man than the reading of Virgil; to believe, with Clauserus, the translator of Cornutus, that it pleased the heavenly deity by Hesiod and Homer, under the veil of fables, to give us all knowledge, logic, rhetoric, philosophy natural and moral, and *quid non;* to believe, with me, that there are many mysteries contained in poetry, which of purpose were written darkly, lest by profane wits it should be abused; to believe, with Landin, that they are so beloved of the gods that whatsoever they write proceeds of a divine fury. Lastly, to believe themselves, when they tell you they will make you immortal by their verses.

Thus doing, your name shall flourish in the printers' shops. Thus doing, you shall be of kin to many a poetical preface. Thus doing, you shall be most fair, most rich, most wise, most all; you shall dwell upon superlatives. Thus doing, though you be "*Libertino patre natus,*" you shall suddenly grow "*Herculea proles,*"

"*Si quid mea Carmina possunt.*"

Thus doing, your soul shall be placed with Dante's Beatrix, or Virgil's Anchises.

32. **quid non,** what not.   45. "**Libertino . . . natus.**" "Born of a freedman."   46. "**Herculea proles.**" "The offspring of Hercules."   47. "**Si quid . . . possunt.**" "If my verses are able to accomplish anything."

But if (fie of such a but!) you be born so near the dull-making cataract of Nilus that you cannot hear the planet-like music of poetry; if you have so earth-creeping a mind that it cannot lift itself up to look to the sky of poetry, or rather, by a certain rustical disdain, will become such a mome as to be a Momus of poetry; then, though I will not wish unto you the ass's ears of Midas, nor to be driven by a poet's verses, as Bubonax was, to hang himself, nor to be rhymed to death, as is said to be done in Ireland; yet thus much curse I must send you in the behalf of all poets: that while you live, you live in love, and never get favour for lacking skill of a sonnet; and when you die, your memory die from the earth for want of an epitaph.

Christopher Marlowe
1564-1593

Marlowe was born at Canterbury in February, 1564, about two months before the birth of Shakespeare at Stratford. His father was a prosperous shoe-manufacturer, and a citizen of good repute. The boy attended the King's School at Canterbury from 1579 to 1581, and then entered Corpus Christi College, Cambridge, on a scholarship created by the will of the late Archbishop Parker. He received his B.A. in 1584, but the award of his M.A. was delayed by repeated absences and by rumors about his conduct displeasing to the academic authorities. Apparently he was engaged in secret government service, for an entry in the Privy Council Register recommends that the "orderly and discreet" young man "be furthered in the degree he was to take this next Commencement, because it was not Her Majesty's pleasure that any one employed in matters touching the benefit of his country should be defamed by those ignorant in the affairs he went about." His master's degree was awarded in July, 1587, shortly after this recommendation. Before he left the university, Marlowe must have abandoned the plan to take religious orders, possibly because of his growing heterodoxy.

Before the end of 1587, Marlowe made a sensational reputation as a playwright by the production of *Tamburlaine*. This and most of his remaining plays were written for the actor Edward Alleyn, whose towering physical stature and great powers of elocution must have been needed to meet the terrific demands of Marlowe's title roles. His last play, *Edward the Second*, 1593, was probably acted by a company—either Lord Strange's or the Earl of Pembroke's—with which Shakespeare was associated near the beginning of his career, and the two young poets may have collaborated on the plays now known as the second and third parts of *Henry VI*.

There are a number of contemporary indications of Marlowe's quarrelsome temperament, and his death was correspondingly violent. According to the depositions discovered by Leslie Hotson in 1925, Marlowe and three companions had spent most of May 30, 1593, in a tavern at Deptford. In the evening, one of them, Ingram Frizer, and Marlowe quarreled about the payment of the reckoning; Marlowe attacked Frizer, and the latter killed Marlowe in self-defense. These records have been interpreted variously. It has been suggested that since Marlowe and Frizer had both been secret political agents, the quarrel may have been due to some obscure factional rivalry. In any case, the records give only the survivors' story, and they were naturally anxious to clear themselves of blame.

The sudden death of the brilliant young poet and playwright at the age of twenty-nine was followed by a number of attacks upon his character. Puritans regarded his murder as an appropriate judgment on a writer of stage plays. Thomas Kyd, the author of *The Spanish Tragedy*, accused Marlowe of having been an atheist, and certainly there is evidence of his wild and ribald talk about the holy mysteries. Marlowe, it is known, belonged to what was erroneously called "Ralegh's School of Atheism," but what was actually a group of freethinkers interested in the new science and philosophy. Both intellectually and imaginatively, Marlowe was closer to the Italian than to the English Renaissance.

Marlowe's audacious dramas are likely to overshadow his nondramatic writing. Most of the latter was a normal result of the influence of a classical university training on a poetic temperament.

---

6. **mome,** buffoon, used as a pun on Momus, a mocking god.

During either his university or his London days, he translated the *Amores* of Ovid, the classical poet to whom he was most devoted, and rendered the first book of Lucan's *Pharsalia* into blank verse. His most substantial poetic achievement, *Hero and Leander*, is an uncompleted elaboration of a Greek poem by Musaeus. The early and feeble drama *Dido, Queen of Carthage*, in which he may have collaborated with Thomas Nashe, was a direct reflection of his intensive classical training.

Marlowe caught the imagination of London theatergoers with his first major play, *Tamburlaine*, which with its sequel was probably performed in 1587. This pair of plays is epic rather than dramatic in conception; they narrate the world-shaking conquests of the fourteenth-century Tatar chief Timur, in monologues and dialogues of untiring imaginative exuberance. More sophisticated audiences soon came to ridicule the extravagant poetic vein of this play, but they could never forget such spectacular scenes as Tamburlaine's victim, Bajazet, beating out his brains on the bars of his cage, or the world hero entering in a chariot drawn by captive kings, whom he hailed as "pampered jades of Asia." In 1589, Marlowe matched the overweening political ambition of Tamburlaine with the unscrupulous intellectual audacity of Dr. Faustus, and soon after exhibited the insatiable hungers for wealth and revenge in *The Jew of Malta*, a most successful play for that time, which may have encouraged Shakespeare in the creation of Shylock a few years later. Marlowe's most subtle and satisfactory drama, *Edward the Second*, a history play, studied the tragedy of a royal weakling with surprising insight, and achieved an impressive dramatic unity and coherence by telescoping the events of many years. Only in the villain, Mortimer, are there echoes of the early exuberance. Shakespeare's *Richard II* seems to be an attempt to invest similar material with an even greater beauty and power.

Marlowe was unquestionably the most gifted of the "university wits" who began to bring their gifts to the English drama in the 1580's. From him Shakespeare and his fellows learned many important lessons in play construction, the focusing of interest on a single overpowering character, and, most significantly, the handling of blank verse. Ben Jonson's commendation of Marlowe's "mighty line" is proverbial, but the poet was capable of other effects than the orotund and the inflated. To him, primarily, is due the demonstration of the extraordinarily various effects of which dramatic blank verse is capable.

THE PASSIONATE SHEPHERD TO HIS LOVE

This delightful pastoral lyric was deservedly popular in the seventeenth century, and inspired a number of imitations or replies. Of these, the best known are Ralegh's "Nymph's Reply," printed below, John Donne's "The Bait," and Robert Herrick's "To Phyllis, to Love and Live with Him."

    Come live with me and be my love,
    And we will all the pleasures prove
    That valleys, groves, hills, and fields,
    Woods, or steepy mountain yields.

    And we will sit upon the rocks,
    Seeing the shepherds feed their flocks,
    By shallow rivers to whose falls
    Melodious birds sing madrigals.

    And I will make thee beds of roses
    And a thousand fragrant posies,   10
    A cap of flowers, and a kirtle
    Embroidered all with leaves of myrtle;

    A gown made of the finest wool
    Which from our pretty lambs we pull;
    Fair linèd slippers for the cold,
    With buckles of the purest gold;

    A belt of straw and ivy buds,
    With coral clasps and amber studs:
    And if these pleasures may thee move,
    Come live with me, and be my love.   20

    The shepherds' swains shall dance and sing
    For thy delight each May morning:
    If these delights thy mind may move,
    Then live with me and be my love.

HERO AND LEANDER

First Sestiad

Hero and Leander, although left uncompleted by Marlowe, is a very much elaborated version of a poem in three hundred and forty lines by Musaeus, a Greek grammarian of the fifth century A.D. The poem is in the mode of the Ovidian erotic narrative, popularized by numerous Italian Renaissance imitations. The story is sluggishly told; the interest of the poem resides in the ardent descriptions of physical beauty and in the orientally exotic background. Despite the strained conceits and the tendency to prettiness and preciosity, the poem has a sensuous warmth and a richness of coloring comparable only to paintings on similar classical subjects by Titian and Tintoretto. The poem had many imitators in the 1590's. The most famous imitations are Shakespeare's *Venus and Adonis* and *The Rape of Lucrece*. Toward the end of the decade, Marlowe's poem and others of the sort were ordered burned by the London authorities.

On Hellespont, guilty of true love's blood,
In view, and opposite, two cities stood,
Sea-borderers, disjoined by Neptune's might;
The one Abydos, the other Sestos hight.
At Sestos, Hero dwelt; Hero the fair,
Whom young Apollo courted for her hair,
And offered as a dower his burning throne,
Where she should sit for men to gaze upon.
The outside of her garments were of lawn,
The lining purple silk, with gilt stars drawn;   10
Her wide sleeves green, and bordered with a grove
Where Venus in her naked glory strove
To please the careless and disdainful eyes
Of proud Adonis, that before her lies;
Her kirtle blue, whereon was many a stain,
Made with the blood of wretched lovers slain.
Upon her head she ware a myrtle wreath,
From whence her veil reached to the ground beneath.
Her veil was artificial flowers and leaves,
Whose workmanship both man and beast deceives;   20
Many would praise the sweet smell as she passed,
When 'twas the odour which her breath forth cast;
And there for honey bees have sought in vain,
And, beat from thence, have lighted there again.
About her neck hung chains of pebble-stone,
Which, lightened by her neck, like diamonds shone.
She ware no gloves, for neither sun nor wind
Would burn or parch her hands, but to her mind,
Or warm or cool them, for they took delight
To play upon those hands, they were so white.   30
Buskins of shells all silvered, usèd she,
And branched with blushing coral to the knee,
Where sparrows perched, of hollow pearl and gold,
Such as the world would wonder to behold;
Those with sweet water oft her handmaid fills,
Which, as she went, would chirrup through the bills.
Some say, for her the fairest Cupid pined,
And, looking in her face, was strooken blind.
But this is true: so like was one the other,
As he imagined Hero was his mother;   40
And oftentimes into her bosom flew,
About her naked neck his bare arms threw,
And laid his childish head upon her breast,
And with still panting rocked, there took his rest.

So lovely fair was Hero, Venus' nun,
As Nature wept, thinking she was undone,
Because she took more from her than she left
And of such wondrous beauty her bereft;
Therefore, in sign her treasure suffered wrack,
Since Hero's time hath half the world been black.   50
Amorous Leander, beautiful and young,
(Whose tragedy divine Musaeus sung)
Dwelt at Abydos; since him dwelt there none
For whom succeeding times make greater moan.
His dangling tresses that were never shorn,
Had they been cut and unto Colchis borne,
Would have allured the venturous youth of Greece
To hazard more than for the Golden Fleece.
Fair Cynthia wished his arms might be her sphere;
Grief makes her pale, because she moves not there.   60
His body was as straight as Circe's wand;
Jove might have sipped out nectar from his hand.
Even as delicious meat is to the taste,
So was his neck in touching, and surpassed
The white of Pelops' shoulder. I could tell ye
How smooth his breast was, and how white his belly,
And whose immortal fingers did imprint
That heavenly path, with many a curious dint,
That runs along his back; but my rude pen
Can hardly blazon forth the loves of men,   70
Much less of powerful gods; let it suffice
That my slack muse sings of Leander's eyes,
Those orient cheeks and lips, exceeding his
That leapt into the water for a kiss
Of his own shadow, and despising many,
Died ere he could enjoy the love of any.
Had wild Hippolytus Leander seen,
Enamoured of his beauty had he been;
His presence made the rudest peasant melt,
That in the vast uplandish country dwelt;   80
The barbarous Thracian soldier, moved with nought,
Was moved with him, and for his favour sought.
Some swore he was a maid in man's attire,
For in his looks were all that men desire:
A pleasant smiling cheek, a speaking eye,
A brow for love to banquet royally;
And such as knew he was a man, would say,
Leander, thou art made for amorous play;

56. **Colchis,** the country east of the Black Sea, legendary location of the Golden Fleece.   65. **Pelops' shoulder,** supplied by Demeter after he had been served as food to the gods, and then restored to life.   73-74. **his That leapt . . . kiss.** The reference is to Narcissus.   77. **Hippolytus,** son of Theseus and Hippolyta, the Amazon; he rejected the advances of his stepmother Phaedra.

Why art thou not in love, and loved of all?
Though thou be fair, yet be not thine own thrall.   90
  The men of wealthy Sestos every year,
For his sake whom their goddess held so dear,
Rose-cheeked Adonis, kept a solemn feast.
Thither resorted many a wandering guest
To meet their loves; such as had none at all,
Came lovers home from this great festival.
For every street, like to a firmament,
Glistered with breathing stars, who, where they went,
Frighted the melancholy earth, which deemed
Eternal heaven to burn, for so it seemed   100
As if another Phaëton had got
The guidance of the sun's rich chariot.
But, far above the loveliest, Hero shined,
And stole away th' enchanted gazer's mind;
For like sea-nymphs' inveigling harmony,
So was her beauty to the standers by.
Nor that night-wandering pale and watery star
(When yawning dragons draw her thirling car
From Latmos' mount up to the gloomy sky,
Where, crowned with blazing light and majesty,   110
She proudly sits) more over-rules the flood,
Than she the hearts of those that near her stood.
Even as when gaudy nymphs pursue the chase,
Wretched Ixion's shaggy-footed race,
Incensed with savage heat, gallop amain
From steep pine-bearing mountains to the plain,
So ran the people forth to gaze upon her,
And all that viewed her were enamoured on her.
And as in fury of a dreadful fight,
Their fellows being slain or put to flight,   120
Poor soldiers stand with fear of death dead-strooken,
So at her presence all, surprised and tooken,
Await the sentence of her scornful eyes;
He whom she favours lives, the other dies.
There might you see one sigh, another rage,
And some, their violent passions to assuage,
Compile sharp satires; but alas, too late,
For faithful love will never turn to hate.
And many, seeing great princes were denied,
Pined as they went, and thinking on her, died.   130
On this feast day, oh, cursèd day and hour!
Went Hero thorough Sestos, from her tower
To Venus' temple, where unhappily,
As after chanced, they did each other spy.
So fair a church as this had Venus none;
The walls were of discoloured jasper stone,
Wherein was Proteus carvèd, and o'erhead
A lively vine of green sea-agate spread,
Where by one hand light-headed Bacchus hung,
And with the other wine from grapes outwrung.   140
Of crystal shining fair the pavement was;
The town of Sestos called it Venus' glass;
There might you see the gods in sundry shapes,
Committing heady riots, incest, rapes;
For know that underneath this radiant floor
Was Danaë's statue in a brazen tower;
Jove slyly stealing from his sister's bed
To dally with Idalian Ganymed,
And for his love Europa bellowing loud,
And tumbling with the rainbow in a cloud;   150
Blood-quaffing Mars heaving the iron net
Which limping Vulcan and his Cyclops set;
Love kindling fire to burn such towns as Troy;
Silvanus weeping for the lovely boy
That now is turned into a cypress tree,
Under whose shade the wood-gods love to be.
And in the midst a silver altar stood;
There Hero sacrificing turtles' blood,
Veiled to the ground, veiling her eyelids close,
And modestly they opened as she rose;   160
Thence flew love's arrow with the golden head,
And thus Leander was enamourèd.
Stone-still he stood, and evermore he gazed,
Till with the fire that from his countenance blazed,
Relenting Hero's gentle heart was strook;
Such force and virtue hath an amorous look.
  It lies not in our power to love or hate,
For will in us is over-ruled by fate.
When two are stripped, long ere the course begin
We wish that one should lose, the other win;   170
And one especially do we affect
Of two gold ingots, like in each respect.
The reason no man knows, let it suffice,
What we behold is censured by our eyes.
Where both deliberate, the love is slight;
Who ever loved, that loved not at first sight?
  He kneeled, but unto her devoutly prayed;
Chaste Hero to herself thus softly said:
"Were I the saint he worships, I would hear him";
And as she spake these words, came somewhat near him.   180
He started up; she blushed as one ashamed;
Wherewith Leander much more was inflamed.
He touched her hand; in touching it she trembled;
Love deeply grounded hardly is dissembled.
These lovers parled by the touch of hands;
True love is mute, and oft amazèd stands.

---

107. **pale and watery star,** the moon; Diana. 114. **Ixion's shaggy-footed race,** the Centaurs.

154. **lovely boy,** Cyparissus in Ovid's *Metamorphoses*. 158. **turtles' blood,** the blood of turtledoves, Venus's birds. 169. **course,** race. 185. **parlèd,** talked.

Thus while dumb signs their yielding hearts entangled,
The air with sparks of living fire was spangled,
And night, deep drenched in misty Acheron,
Heaved up her head, and half the world upon   190
Breathed darkness forth (dark night is Cupid's day).
And now begins Leander to display
Love's holy fire with words, with sighs, and tears,
Which like sweet music entered Hero's ears;
And yet at every word she turned aside,
And always cut him off as he replied.
At last, like to a bold sharp sophister,
With cheerful hope thus he accosted her:
"Fair creature, let me speak without offence;
I would my rude words had the influence   200
To lead thy thoughts as thy fair looks do mine!
Then shouldst thou be his prisoner who is thine.
Be not unkind and fair; misshapen stuff
Are of behaviour boisterous and rough.
Oh, shun me not, but hear me ere you go,
God knows I cannot force love, as you do.
My words shall be as spotless as my youth,
Full of simplicity and naked truth.
This sacrifice, whose sweet perfume descending
From Venus' altar to your footsteps bending,   210
Doth testify that you exceed her far,
To whom you offer, and whose nun you are.
Why should you worship her? her you surpass
As much as sparkling diamonds flaring glass.
A diamond set in lead his worth retains;
A heavenly nymph, beloved of human swains,
Receives no blemish, but ofttimes more grace;
Which makes me hope, although I am but base,
Base in respect of thee, divine and pure,
Dutiful service may thy love procure,   220
And I in duty will excel all other,
As thou in beauty dost exceed Love's mother.
Nor heaven, nor thou, were made to gaze upon;
As heaven preserves all things, so save thou one.
A stately builded ship, well rigged and tall,
The ocean maketh more majestical;
Why vowest thou then to live in Sestos here,
Who on love's seas more glorious would appear?
Like untuned golden strings all women are,
Which long time lie untouched, will harshly jar.   230
Vessels of brass, oft handled, brightly shine;
What difference betwixt the richest mine
And basest mould, but use? for both, not used,
Are of like worth. Then treasure is abused,
When misers keep it; being put to loan,
In time it will return us two for one.
Rich robes themselves and others do adorn;
Neither themselves nor others, if not worn.
Who builds a palace, and rams up the gate,
Shall see it ruinous and desolate.   240
Ah, simple Hero, learn thyself to cherish!
Lone women, like to empty houses, perish.
Less sins the poor rich man that starves himself
In heaping up a mass of drossy pelf,
Than such as you; his golden earth remains,
Which after his decease some other gains;
But this fair gem, sweet in the loss alone,
When you fleet hence, can be bequeathed to none.
Or if it could, down from th' enamelled sky
All heaven would come to claim this legacy,   250
And with intestine broils the world destroy,
And quite confound Nature's sweet harmony.
Well therefore by the gods decreed it is
We human creatures should enjoy that bliss.
One is no number; maids are nothing, then,
Without the sweet society of men.
Wilt thou live single still? one shalt thou be
Though never-singling Hymen couple thee.
Wild savages, that drink of running springs,
Think water far excels all earthly things,   260
But they that daily taste neat wine, despise it;
Virginity, albeit some highly prize it,
Compared with marriage, had you tried them both,
Differs as much as wine and water doth.
Base bullion for the stamp's sake we allow;
Even so for men's impression do we you,
By which alone, our reverend fathers say,
Women receive perfection every way.
This idol which you term virginity
Is neither essence subject to the eye,   270
No, nor to any one exterior sense,
Nor hath it any place of residence,
Nor is 't of earth or mould celestial,
Or capable of any form at all.
Of that which hath no being, do not boast;
Things that are not at all, are never lost.
Men foolishly do call it virtuous;
What virtue is it, that is born with us?
Much less can honour be ascribed thereto;
Honour is purchased by the deeds we do.   280
Believe me, Hero, honour is not won
Until some honourable deed be done.
Seek you, for chastity, immortal fame,
And know that some have wronged Diana's name?
Whose name is it, if she be false or not,
So she be fair, but some vile tongues will blot?
But you are fair, ay me, so wondrous fair,
So young, so gentle, and so debonair,
As Greece will think, if thus you live alone,
Some one or other keeps you as his own.   290

Then, Hero, hate me not, nor from me fly
To follow swiftly blasting infamy.
Perhaps thy sacred priesthood makes thee loath;
Tell me, to whom mad'st thou that heedless oath?"
    "To Venus," answered she, and as she spake,
Forth from those two tralucent cisterns brake
A stream of liquid pearl, which down her face
Made milk-white paths, whereon the gods might trace
To Jove's high court. He thus replied: "The rites
In which love's beauteous empress most delights   300
Are banquets, Doric music, midnight revel,
Plays, masks, and all that stern age counteth evil.
Thee as a holy idiot doth she scorn,
For thou, in vowing chastity, hast sworn
To rob her name and honour, and thereby
Commit'st a sin far worse than perjury,
Even sacrilege against her deity,
Through regular and formal purity.
To expiate which sin, kiss and shake hands;
Such sacrifice as this Venus demands."   310
    Thereat she smiled, and did deny him so
As, put thereby, yet might he hope for mo.
Which makes him quickly reinforce his speech,
And her in humble manner thus beseech:
    "Though neither gods nor men may thee deserve,
Yet for her sake whom you have vowed to serve,
Abandon fruitless cold virginity,
The gentle queen of love's sole enemy.
Then shall you most resemble Venus' nun,
When Venus' sweet rites are performed and done.   320
Flint-breasted Pallas joys in single life,
But Pallas and your mistress are at strife.
Love, Hero, then, and be not tyrannous,
But heal the heart that thou hast wounded thus;
Nor stain thy youthful years with avarice;
Fair fools delight to be accounted nice.
The richest corn dies if it be not reaped;
Beauty alone is lost, too warily kept."
These arguments he used, and many more,
Wherewith she yielded, that was won before.   330
Hero's looks yielded, but her words made war;
Women are won when they begin to jar.
Thus having swallowed Cupid's golden hook,
The more she strived, the deeper was she strook;
Yet, evilly feigning anger, strove she still,
And would be thought to grant against her will.
So having paused a while, at last she said:
"Who taught thee rhetoric to deceive a maid?
Ay me! such words as these should I abhor,
And yet I like them for the orator."   340
    296. **tralucent**, clear, luminous.

With that Leander stooped to have embraced her,
But from his spreading arms away she cast her,
And thus bespake him: "Gentle youth, forbear
To touch the sacred garments which I wear.
Upon a rock, and underneath a hill,
Far from the town, where all is whist and still
Save that the sea playing on yellow sand
Sends forth a rattling murmur to the land,
Whose sound allures the golden Morpheus
In silence of the night to visit us,   350
My turret stands; and there, God knows, I play
With Venus' swans and sparrows all the day.
A dwarfish beldame bears me company,
That hops about the chamber where I lie,
And spends the night, that might be better spent,
In vain discourse and apish merriment.—
Come thither." As she spake this, her tongue tripped,
For unawares, "Come thither," from her slipped;
And suddenly her former colour changed,
And here and there her eyes through anger ranged.   360
And like a planet moving several ways
At one self instant, she, poor soul, assays,
Loving, not to love at all, and every part
Strove to resist the motions of her heart;
And hands so pure, so innocent, nay such
As might have made heaven stoop to have a touch,
Did she uphold to Venus, and again
Vowed spotless chastity, but all in vain.
Cupid beats down her prayers with his wings;
Her vows above the empty air he flings;   370
All deep enraged, his sinewy bow he bent,
And shot a shaft that burning from him went;
Wherewith she, strooken, looked so dolefully,
As made Love sigh to see his tyranny.
And as she wept, her tears to pearl he turned,
And wound them on his arm, and for her mourned.
Then towards the palace of the Destinies,
Laden with languishment and grief, he flies,
And to those stern nymphs humbly made request,
Both might enjoy each other, and be blest.   380
But with a ghastly dreadful countenance,
Threat'ning a thousand deaths at every glance,
They answered Love, nor would vouchsafe so much
As one poor word, their hate to him was such.
Hearken awhile, and I will tell you why:
Heaven's wingèd herald, Jove-born Mercury,
The self-same day that he asleep had laid
Enchanted Argus, spied a country maid,
Whose careless hair, instead of pearl t' adorn it,
Glistered with dew, as one that seemed to scorn it;

349. **Morpheus**, god of sleep.   388. **Argus**, the hundred-eyed monster set to watch Mercury.

CHRISTOPHER MARLOWE

Her breath as fragrant as the morning rose, 391
Her mind pure, and her tongue untaught to gloze;
Yet proud she was, for lofty pride that dwells
In towered courts is oft in shepherds' cells,
And too too well the fair vermilion knew,
And silver tincture of her cheeks, that drew
The love of every swain. On her this god
Enamoured was, and with his snaky rod
Did charm her nimble feet, and made her stay,
The while upon a hillock down he lay, 400
And sweetly on his pipe began to play,
And with smooth speech her fancy to assay;
Till in his twining arms he locked her fast,
And then he wooed with kisses, and at last,
As shepherds do, her on the ground he laid,
And tumbling in the grass, he often strayed
Beyond the bounds of shame, in being bold
To eye those parts which no eye should behold.
And like an insolent commanding lover,
Boasting his parentage, would needs discover 410
The way to new Elysium; but she,
Whose only dower was her chastity,
Having striv'n in vain, was now about to cry,
And crave the help of shepherds that were nigh.
Herewith he stayed his fury, and began
To give her leave to rise; away she ran;
After went Mercury, who used such cunning,
As she, to hear his tale, left off her running;
Maids are not won by brutish force and might,
But speeches full of pleasure and delight; 420
And knowing Hermes courted her, was glad
That she such loveliness and beauty had
As could provoke his liking, yet was mute,
And neither would deny nor grant his suit.
Still vowed he love, she wanting no excuse
To feed him with delays, as women use,
Or thirsting after immortality—
All women are ambitious naturally—
Imposed upon her lover such a task
As he ought not perform, nor yet she ask. 430
A draught of flowing nectar she requested,
Wherewith the king of gods and men is feasted.
He, ready to accomplish what she willed,
Stole some from Hebe (Hebe Jove's cup filled)
And gave it to his simple rustic love;
Which being known (as what is hid from Jove?)
He inly stormed, and waxed more furious
Than for the fire filched by Prometheus,
And thrusts him down from heaven; he wand'ring here
In mournful terms, with sad and heavy cheer, 440
Complained to Cupid. Cupid, for his sake,
To be revenged on Jove did undertake;
And those on whom heaven, earth, and hell relies,
I mean the adamantine Destinies,
He wounds with love, and forced them equally
To dote upon deceitful Mercury.
They offered him the deadly fatal knife
That shears the slender threads of human life;
At his fair-feathered feet the engines laid
Which th' earth from ugly Chaos' den upweighed;
These he regarded not, but did entreat 451
That Jove, usurper of his father's seat,
Might presently be banished into hell,
And aged Saturn in Olympus dwell.
They granted what he craved, and once again
Saturn and Ops began their golden reign.
Murder, rape, war, lust, and treachery
Were with Jove closed in Stygian empery.
But long this blessed time continued not;
As soon as he his wishèd purpose got, 460
He, reckless of his promise, did despise
The love of th' everlasting Destinies.
They seeing it, both Love and him abhorred,
And Jupiter unto his place restored.
And but that Learning, in despite of Fate,
Will mount aloft, and enter heaven-gate,
And to the seat of Jove itself advance,
Hermes had slept in hell with Ignorance;
Yet as a punishment they added this,
That he and Poverty should always kiss. 470
And to this day is every scholar poor;
Gross gold from them runs headlong to the boor.
Likewise, the angry sisters thus deluded,
To venge themselves on Hermes, have concluded
That Midas' brood shall sit in Honour's chair,
To which the Muses' sons are only heir;
And fruitful wits that inaspiring are,
Shall, discontent, run into regions far;
And few great lords in virtuous deeds shall joy,
But be surprised with every garish toy; 480
And still enrich the lofty servile clown,
Who with encroaching guile keeps learning down.
Then muse not Cupid's suit no better sped,
Seeing in their loves the Fates were injurèd.

392. **gloze**, deceive by flattery. 421. **Hermes**, the Greek name for Mercury. He was god of science and invention (see ll. 468–71).

456. **Saturn**, god of seed-sowing. **Ops**, his wife, goddess of the harvest. 475. **Midas' brood.** The phrase suggests not only the wealthy but those without good taste, since Midas gave the palm in singing to Pan and not to Apollo.

THE TRAGICAL HISTORY OF DR. FAUSTUS

Although *Faustus* is not Marlowe's most completely satisfying play, it is highly characteristic of his energetic and influential contributions to the drama. Like Marlowe's other heroes, Tamburlaine and the Jew of Malta, Faustus is dominated by a ruling passion. In his case, it is the yearning for forbidden knowledge and power that brings him to destruction. Despite the anachronistic elements from the morality plays—the Good and Evil Angels, and the pageant of the Seven Deadly Sins—the play depicts with vigor the essential steps in Faustus's tragic downfall: temptation, fall, power, and penalty. Marlowe's dramatic genius is clearly shown in the imaginative handling of these elements.

The weaknesses of the play are obvious. Whether or not the text has been corrupted by the admixture of scenes by other hands, the humor of the low comedy is almost completely ineffective. But, what is worse, Faustus is shown devoting his superhuman powers to insignificant uses. But the intellectual sweep of the serious scenes and the swelling melody of the verse go far to offset the trivialities of the middle of the play.

The text given below is based on that of the First Quarto, published in 1604. Like the Quarto, it does not divide the play into scenes and acts, and it leaves to the lines themselves the necessary indications of the locale of each successive scene. Such a text may assist students in catching the rapid, fluid rhythms of action on an Elizabethan stage. The text has been sparingly emended.

DRAMATIS PERSONAE

THE POPE
CARDINAL OF LORRAIN
EMPEROR OF GERMANY
DUKE OF VANHOLT
FAUSTUS
VALDES and CORNELIUS, friends to FAUSTUS
WAGNER, servant to FAUSTUS
CLOWN
ROBIN
RALPH
VINTNER
HORSE-COURSER
KNIGHT
OLD MAN
SCHOLARS, FRIARS, and ATTENDANTS
DUCHESS OF VANHOLT
LUCIFER
BELZEBUB
MEPHISTOPHILIS
GOOD ANGEL
EVIL ANGEL
THE SEVEN DEADLY SINS
DEVILS
SPIRITS in the shape of ALEXANDER THE GREAT, of his Paramour, and of HELEN OF TROY
CHORUS

[*Enter* CHORUS.]

Chorus. Not marching now in fields of Thrasimene,
Where Mars did mate the Carthaginians;
Nor sporting in the dalliance of love,
In courts of kings where state is overturned;
Nor in the pomp of proud audacious deeds,
Intends our Muse to vaunt his heavenly verse:
Only this, gentlemen,—we must perform
The form of Faustus' fortunes, good or bad.
To patient judgments we appeal our plaud,
And speak for Faustus in his infancy.   10
Now is he born, his parents base of stock,
In Germany, within a town called Rhodes;
Of riper years to Wittenberg he went,
Whereas his kinsmen chiefly brought him up.
So soon he profits in divinity,
The fruitful plot of scholarism graced,
That shortly he was graced with doctor's name,
Excelling all whose sweet delight disputes
In heavenly matters of theology;
Till swollen with cunning, of a self-conceit,   20
His waxen wings did mount above his reach,
And, melting, Heavens conspired his overthrow;
For, falling to a devilish exercise,
And glutted now with learning's golden gifts,
He surfeits upon cursed necromancy.
Nothing so sweet as magic is to him,
Which he prefers before his chiefest bliss.
And this the man that in his study sits!   [*Exit.*

[*Enter* FAUSTUS *in his Study.*]

Faust. Settle my studies, Faustus, and begin
To sound the depth of that thou wilt profess;   30
Having commenced, be a divine in show.
Yet level at the end of every art,
And live and die in Aristotle's works.
Sweet Analytics, 'tis thou hast ravished me,
Bene disserere est finis logices.
Is to dispute well logic's chiefest end?

1. Thrasimene, Lake Trasimenus in northern Italy, where in 217 B.C. Hannibal gained a decisive victory over the Roman army led by the consul Flaminius.   **2. mate,** appears to mean "enter into alliance with," or possibly "defeat."   **7-8. perform The form,** offer a representation.   **9. appeal our plaud,** appeal to the audience for applause.   **12. Rhodes,** Roda, in Saxe-Altenburg.   **13. Wittenberg,** on the Elbe. Its university was founded in 1502.   **20. cunning,** knowledge.   **21. waxen wings,** a reference to Icarus, whose wings were attached by wax.   **31. commenced,** proceeded to a degree, here the doctorate in theology.   **34. Analytics,** Aristotle's treatise on logic.   **35. Bene . . . logices.** The end of logic is to argue well.

Affords this art no greater miracle?
Then read no more, thou hast attained the end;
A greater subject fitteth Faustus' wit.
Bid ὂν καὶ μὴ ὂν farewell; Galen come, 40
Seeing *Ubi desinit Philosophus, ibi incipit Medicus;*
Be a physician, Faustus, heap up gold,
And be eternised for some wondrous cure.
Summum bonum medicinae sanitas,
"The end of physic is our body's health."
Why, Faustus, hast thou not attained that end?
Is not thy common talk sound Aphorisms?
Are not thy bills hung up as monuments,
Whereby whole cities have escaped the plague,
And thousand desperate maladies been eased? 50
Yet art thou still but Faustus and a man.
Wouldst thou make men to live eternally,
Or, being dead, raise them to life again?
Then this profession were to be esteemed.
Physic, farewell.—Where is Justinian?
*Si una eademque res legatur duobus, alter rem, alter
 valorem rei, &c.*
A pretty case of paltry legacies!
Exhaereditare filium non potest pater nisi, &c.
Such is the subject of the Institute 60
And universal Body of the Law.
His study fits a mercenary drudge,
Who aims at nothing but external trash;
Too servile and illiberal for me.
When all is done, divinity is best;
Jerome's Bible, Faustus, view it well.
Stipendium peccati mors est. Ha! *Stipendium, &c.*
"*The reward of sin is death.*" That's hard.
Si peccasse negamus, fallimur, et nulla est in nobis veritas.
"If we say that we have no sin we deceive our- [70
selves and there's no truth in us." Why then, belike
we must sin and so consequently die.
Ay, we must die an everlasting death.
What doctrine call you this, *Che sera sera,*
"What will be shall be"? Divinity, adieu!
These metaphysics of magicians
And necromantic books are heavenly;
Lines, circles, scenes, letters, and characters,
Ay, these are those that Faustus most desires.
O what a world of profit and delight, 80
Of power, of honour, of omnipotence

Is promised to the studious artisan!
All things that move between the quiet poles
Shall be at my command. Emperors and kings
Are but obeyed in their several provinces,
Nor can they raise the wind or rend the clouds;
But his dominion that exceeds in this
Stretcheth as far as doth the mind of man.
A sound magician is a mighty god:
Here, Faustus, try thy brains to gain a deity. 90
Wagner!

[*Enter* WAGNER.]

    Commend me to my dearest friends,
The German Valdes and Cornelius;
Request them earnestly to visit me.
    Wag. I will, sir. [*Exit.*
    Faust. Their conference will be a greater help to me
Than all my labours, plod I ne'er so fast.

[*Enter* GOOD ANGEL *and* EVIL ANGEL.]

    G. Ang. O Faustus! lay that damnèd book aside,
And gaze not upon it lest it tempt thy soul,
And heap God's heavy wrath upon thy head.
Read, read the Scriptures: that is blasphemy. 100
    E. Ang. Go forward, Faustus, in that famous art,
Wherein all Nature's treasure is contained:
Be thou on earth as Jove is in the sky,
Lord and commander of these elements.

[*Exeunt* ANGELS.

    Faust. How am I glutted with conceit of this!
Shall I make spirits fetch me what I please,
Resolve me of all ambiguities,
Perform what desperate enterprise I will?
I'll have them fly to India for gold,
Ransack the ocean for orient pearl, 110
And search all corners of the new-found world
For pleasant fruits and princely delicates;
I'll have them read me strange philosophy
And tell the secrets of all foreign kings;
I'll have them wall all Germany with brass,
And make swift Rhine circle fair Wittenberg;
I'll have them fill the public schools with silk,
Wherewith the students shall be bravely clad;
I'll levy soldiers with the coin they bring,
And chase the Prince of Parma from our land, 120
And reign sole king of all the provinces;

---

40. ὂν . . . ὂν, the Aristotelian "being and not being." **41. Ubi . . . Medicus.** The doctor begins where the philosopher leaves off. **47. Aphorisms?** here, medical memoranda, so called from the aphorisms of Hippocrates. **48. bills,** prescriptions. **56–57. Si . . . rei.** If one and the same thing is left as a legacy to two persons, the one [is to take] the article, the other the value of the article—an incorrect quotation from Justinian's *Institutes.* **59. Exhaereditare . . . nisi.** A father cannot disinherit his son unless. **66. Jerome's Bible,** the Vulgate, mainly translated by St. Jerome. **76. metaphysics,** here, supernatural arts.

82. artisan! here used as a master of the higher arts. **83. quiet,** unmoving. **92. Valdes and Cornelius.** Valdes is unidentified; Cornelius is perhaps Cornelius Agrippa (1486–1535), a famous German philosopher and student of magic. **103. Jove.** The use of "Jove" for "God" was common at the time. **105. glutted with conceit,** filled with idea of gaining power. **110. orient.** From meaning "eastern" the word came to mean "brilliant." **111. new-found world.** Columbus had discovered the West Indies in 1492, and wealth was pouring in from Mexico and Peru. **120. Prince of Parma.** The Prince, afterwards Duke, of Parma was the Spanish Governor-General of the Netherlands from 1579 to 1592.

Yea, stranger engines for the brunt of war
Than was the fiery keel at Antwerp's bridge,
I'll make my servile spirits to invent.
Come, German Valdes and Cornelius,
And make me blest with your sage conference.

[*Enter* VALDES *and* CORNELIUS.]

Valdes, sweet Valdes, and Cornelius,
Know that your words have won me at the last
To practise magic and concealèd arts:
Yet not your words only, but mine own fantasy, 130
That will receive no object, for my head
But ruminates on necromantic skill.
Philosophy is odious and obscure,
Both law and physic are for petty wits;
Divinity is basest of the three,
Unpleasant, harsh, contemptible, and vile:
'Tis magic, magic, that hath ravished me.
Then, gentle friends, aid me in this attempt;
And I that have with concise syllogisms
Gravelled the pastors of the German church, 140
And made the flowering pride of Wittenberg
Swarm to my problems, as the infernal spirits
On sweet Musaeus, when he came to hell,
Will be as cunning as Agrippa was,
Whose shadows made all Europe honour him.
 Vald. Faustus, these books, thy wit, and our experience
Shall make all nations to canònise us.
As Indian Moors obey their Spanish lords,
So shall the subjects of every element
Be always serviceable to us three; 150
Like lions shall they guard us when we please;
Like Almain rutters with their horsemen's staves,
Or Lapland giants, trotting by our sides;
Sometimes like women or unwedded maids,
Shadowing more beauty in their airy brows
Than have the white breasts of the queen of love:
From Venice shall they drag huge argosies,
And from America the golden fleece
That yearly stuffs old Philip's treasury;
If learned Faustus will be resolute. 160
 Faust. Valdes, as resolute am I in this
As thou to live; therefore object it not.
 Corn. The miracles that magic will perform
Will make thee vow to study nothing else.

He that is grounded in astrology,
Enriched with tongues, well seen in minerals,
Hath all the principles magic doth require.
Then doubt not, Faustus, but to be renowned,
And more frequented for this mystery
Than heretofore the Delphian Oracle. 170
The spirits tell me they can dry the sea,
And fetch the treasure of all foreign wracks,
Ay, all the wealth that our forefathers hid
Within the massy entrails of the earth;
Then tell me, Faustus, what shall we three want?
 Faust. Nothing, Cornelius! O this cheers my soul!
Come show me some demonstrations magical,
That I may conjure in some lusty grove,
And have these joys in full possession.
 Vald. Then haste thee to some solitary grove, 180
And bear wise Bacon's and Albanus's works,
The Hebrew Psalter and New Testament;
And whatsoever else is requisite
We will inform thee ere our conference cease.
 Corn. Valdes, first let him know the words of art;
And then, all other ceremonies learned,
Faustus may try his cunning by himself.
 Vald. First I'll instruct thee in the rudiments,
And then wilt thou be perfecter than I.
 Faust. Then come and dine with me, and after meat, 190
We'll canvass every quiddity thereof;
For ere I sleep I'll try what I can do:
This night I'll conjure though I die therefore. [*Exeunt.*

[*Enter two* SCHOLARS.]

 1 *Schol.* I wonder what's become of Faustus that was wont to make our schools ring with *sic probo?*
 2 *Schol.* That shall we know, for see here comes his boy.

[*Enter* WAGNER.]

 1 *Schol.* How now, sirrah! Where's thy master?
 Wag. God in heaven knows!
 2 *Schol.* Why, dost not thou know? 200
 Wag. Yes, I know. But that follows not.
 1 *Schol.* Go to, sirrah! Leave your jesting, and tell us where he is.
 Wag. That follows not necessary by force of argument, that you, being licentiate, should stand upon 't: therefore, acknowledge your error and be attentive.

---

 123. the fiery keel . . . bridge, the fire ship with which the Netherlanders in 1585 made a breach in the bridge which Parma had built across the Scheldt to complete the blockade of Antwerp. **140. Gravelled,** nonplussed. **143. Musaeus,** a semimythical Greek poet, said to have been the son of Orpheus. **148. Moors,** here used of the dark-skinned natives of the New World. **152. Almain rutters,** German horsemen. **159. old Philip's treasury.** Philip II of Spain (reigned 1527–98) received enormous sums each year in treasure ships from his American dominions. **166. well seen,** well versed. **178. lusty,** pleasant. **181. Bacon's and Albanus's works,** Roger Bacon (1214–1294), a student and philosopher some three centuries ahead of his time, and naturally suspected of magic; Albanus, possibly Pietro d'Albano, an Italian physician and chemist who narrowly escaped burning by the Inquisition. **191. quiddity,** essential element. **195. sic probo?** thus I prove. **205. licentiate,** one who has taken a degree at some university and so received a license to practice his calling.

2 Schol. Why, didst thou not say thou knew'st?

Wag. Have you any witness on 't?

1 Schol. Yes, sirrah, I heard you. 210

Wag. Ask my fellow if I be a thief.

2 Schol. Well, you will not tell us?

Wag. Yes, sir, I will tell you; yet if you were not dunces, you would never ask me such a question; for is not he *corpus naturale*? and is not that *mobile*? Then wherefore should you ask me such a question? But that I am by nature phlegmatic, slow to wrath, and prone to lechery (to love, I would say), it were not for you to come within forty foot of the place of execution, although I do not doubt to see you [220 both hanged the next sessions. Thus having triumphed over you, I will set my countenance like a precisian, and begin to speak thus:—Truly, my dear brethren, my master is within at dinner, with Valdes and Cornelius, as this wine, if it could speak, would inform your worships; and so the Lord bless you, preserve you, and keep you, my dear brethren, my dear brethren. [*Exit.*

1 Schol. Nay, then, I fear he has fallen into that damned Art, for which they two are infamous [230 through the world.

2 Schol. Were he a stranger, and not allied to me, yet should I grieve for him. But come, let us go and inform the Rector, and see if he by his grave counsel can reclaim him.

1 Schol. O, I fear me nothing can reclaim him.

2 Schol. Yet let us try what we can do. [*Exeunt.*

[*Enter* FAUSTUS *to conjure.*]

Faust. Now that the gloomy shadow of the earth
Longing to view Orion's drizzling look,
Leaps from th' antarctic world unto the sky, 240
And dims the welkin with her pitchy breath,
Faustus, begin thine incantations,
And try if devils will obey thy hest,
Seeing thou hast prayed and sacrificed to them.
Within this circle is Jehovah's name,
Forward and backward anagrammatised,
The breviated names of holy saints,
Figures of every adjunct to the Heavens,
And characters of signs and erring stars,
By which the spirits are enforced to rise: 250
Then fear not, Faustus, but be resolute,
And try the uttermost magic can perform.

Sint mihi Dei Acherontis propitii! Valeat numen triplex Jehovae! Ignei, aerii, aquatani spiritus, salvete! Orientis princeps Belzebub, inferni ardentis monarcha, et Demogorgon, propitiamus vos, ut appareat et surgat Mephistophilis. Quid tu moraris? Per Jehovam, Gehennam, et consecratum aquam quam nunc spargo, signumque crucis quod nunc facio, et per vota nostra, ipse nunc surgat nobis dicatus Mephistophilis! 260

[*Enter a* DEVIL.]

I charge thee to return and change thy shape;
Thou art too ugly to attend on me.
Go, and return an old Franciscan friar;
That holy shape becomes a devil best. [*Exit* DEVIL.
I see there's virtue in my heavenly words;
Who would not be proficient in this art?
How pliant is this Mephistophilis,
Full of obedience and humility!
Such is the force of magic and my spells.
Now, Faustus, thou art conjuror laureate, 270
Thou canst command great Mephistophilis:
Quin regis Mephistophilis fratris imagine.

[*Re-enter* MEPHISTOPHILIS *like a Franciscan* Friar.]

Meph. Now, Faustus, what would'st thou have me do?

Faust. I charge thee wait upon me whilst I live,
To do whatever Faustus shall command,
Be it to make the moon drop from her sphere,
Or the ocean to overwhelm the world.

Meph. I am a servant to great Lucifer,
And may not follow thee without his leave;
No more than he commands must we perform. 280

Faust. Did he not charge thee to appear to me?

Meph. No, I came hither of mine own accord.

Faust. Did not my conjuring speeches raise thee? Speak.

Meph. That was the cause, but yet *per accidens;*
For when we hear one rack the name of God,
Abjure the Scriptures and his Saviour Christ,
We fly in hope to get his glorious soul;
Nor will we come, unless he use such means
Whereby he is in danger to be damned:
Therefore the shortest cut for conjuring 290
Is stoutly to abjure the Trinity,

215. **corpus naturale ... mobile,** a natural body and therefore movable. 219–20. **place of execution,** dining-room. 223. **precisian,** Puritan. 234. **Rector,** title of the head of a German university. 238–41. **Now ... breath.** Now that darkness comes from the southern to the northern hemisphere. 248. **adjunct to the Heavens,** the heavenly bodies, "joined to" the solid firmament of the sky. 249. **erring stars,** planets. 253–60. **Sint ... Mephistophilis!** May the gods of Acheron be favorable to me! May the threefold might of Jehovah prevail! Hail, ye spirits of fire, air, and water! Beelzebub, prince of the East, monarch of the burning world below, and Demogorgon, we pray your grace that Mephistophilis may appear and arise.—Why dost thou linger?—By Jehovah, Gehenna, the holy water which I now sprinkle, the sign of the cross which I now make, and by my prayers, let Mephistophilis himself arise to do me service. 272. **Quin ... imagine.** Indeed thou rulest in the likeness of the friar Mephistophilis. 284. **per accidens,** through an additional circumstance, that is, his own willingness to come. 285. **rack,** torture, by using it for unholy ends.

And pray devoutly to the prince of hell.
　Faust. So Faustus hath
Already done; and holds this principle,
There is no chief but only Belzebub,
To whom Faustus doth dedicate himself.
This word "damnation" terrifies not him,
For he confounds hell in Elysium;
His ghost be with the old philosophers!
But, leaving these vain trifles of men's souls,　　300
Tell me what is that Lucifer thy lord?
　Meph. Arch-regent and commander of all spirits.
　Faust. Was not that Lucifer an angel once?
　Meph. Yes, Faustus, and most dearly loved of God.
　Faust. How comes it then that he is Prince of devils?
　Meph. O, by aspiring pride and insolence;
For which God threw him from the face of heaven.
　Faust. And what are you that you live with Lucifer?
　Meph. Unhappy spirits that fell with Lucifer,
Conspired against our God with Lucifer,　　310
And are for ever damned with Lucifer.
　Faust. Where are you damned?
　Meph. In hell.
　Faust. How comes it then that thou art out of hell?
　Meph. Why this is hell, nor am I out of it.
Think'st thou that I who saw the face of God,
And tasted the eternal joys of heaven,
Am not tormented with ten thousand hells,
In being deprived of everlasting bliss?
O Faustus! leave these frivolous demands,　　320
Which strike a terror to my fainting soul.
　Faust. What, is great Mephistophilis so passionate
For being deprivèd of the joys of heaven?
Learn thou of Faustus manly fortitude,
And scorn those joys thou never shalt possess.
Go bear these tidings to great Lucifer:
Seeing Faustus hath incurred eternal death
By desperate thoughts against Jove's deity,
Say he surrenders up to him his soul,
So he will spare him four and twenty years,　　330
Letting him live in all voluptuousness;
Having thee ever to attend on me;
To give me whatsoever I shall ask,
To tell me whatsoever I demand,
To slay mine enemies, and aid my friends,
And always be obedient to my will.
Go and return to mighty Lucifer,
And meet me in my study at midnight,
And then resolve me of thy master's mind.　　339
　Meph. I will, Faustus.　　　　　　　　　　[*Exit.*

298. **confounds . . . Elysium,** makes no distinction between Hell and Paradise.　　322. **passionate,** stirred by emotion.　　339. **resolve me of,** inform me of.

　Faust. Had I as many souls as there be stars,
I'd give them all for Mephistophilis.
By him I'll be great Emperor of the world,
And make a bridge through the moving air,
To pass the ocean with a band of men;
I'll join the hills that bind the Afric shore,
And make that country continent to Spain,
And both contributory to my crown.
The Emperor shall not live but by my leave,
Nor any potentate of Germany.　　350
Now that I have obtained what I desire,
I'll live in speculation of this art
Till Mephistophilis return again.　　　　　[*Exit.*

[*Enter* WAGNER *and the* CLOWN.]

　Wag. Sirrah, boy, come hither.
　Clown. How, boy! Swowns, boy! I hope you have seen many boys with such pickadevaunts as I have. Boy, quotha!
　Wag. Tell me, sirrah, hast thou any comings in?
　Clown. Ay, and goings out too. You may see else.
　Wag. Alas, poor slave! See how poverty [360 jesteth in his nakedness! The villain is bare and out of service, and so hungry that I know he would give his soul to the devil for a shoulder of mutton, though it were blood-raw.
　Clown. How? My soul to the Devil for a shoulder of mutton, though 'twere blood-raw! Not so, good friend. By 'r Lady, I had need have it well roasted and good sauce to it, if I pay so dear.
　Wag. Well, wilt thou serve me, and I'll make thee go like *Qui mihi discipulus?*　　370
　Clown. How, in verse?
　Wag. No, sirrah; in beaten silk and stavesacre.
　Clown. How, how, Knave's acre! Ay, I thought that was all the land his father left him. Do you hear? I would be sorry to rob you of your living.
　Wag. Sirrah, I say in stavesacre.
　Clown. Oho! Oho! Stavesacre! Why, then, belike if I were your man I should be full of vermin.
　Wag. So thou shalt, whether thou beest with me or no. But, sirrah, leave your jesting, and bind [380 yourself presently unto me for seven years, or I'll turn all the lice about thee into familiars, and they shall tear thee in pieces.
　Clown. Do you hear, sir? You may save that la-

349. **Emperor,** head of the Holy Roman Empire.　　352. **speculation,** contemplative study.　　355. **Swowns,** God's wounds, an oath.　　356. **pickadevaunts,** short beard, trimmed to a point.　　358. **comings in,** income.　　359. **goings out,** referring to his out-at-elbows and tattered appearance. 370. **Qui mihi discipulus?** You who are my pupil.　　372. **beaten silk and stavesacre,** silk overlaid with some metal stamped or hammered into it and a species of larkspur used for killing vermin.　　373. **Knave's acre!** a strip of ground. 382. **familiars,** attendant demons.

bour; they are too familiar with me already. Swowns! they are as bold with my flesh as if they had paid for their meat and drink.

Wag. Well, do you hear, sirrah? Hold, take these guilders.

Clown. Gridirons! what be they? 390

Wag. Why, French crowns.

Clown. Mass, but for the name of French crowns, a man were as good have as many English counters. And what should I do with these?

Wag. Why, now, sirrah, thou art at an hour's warning, whensoever and wheresoever the Devil shall fetch thee.

Clown. No, no. Here, take your gridirons again.

Wag. Truly I'll none of them.

Clown. Truly but you shall. 400

Wag. Bear witness I gave them him.

Clown. Bear witness I give them you again.

Wag. Well, I will cause two devils presently to fetch thee away—Baliol and Belcher.

Clown. Let your Baliol and your Belcher come here, and I'll knock them, they were never so knockt since they were devils. Say I should kill one of them, what would folks say? "Do you see yonder tall fellow in the round slop?—he has killed the devil." So I should be called Kill-devil all the [410 parish over.

[*Enter two* DEVILS: *the* CLOWN *runs up and down crying.*]

Wag. Baliol and Belcher! Spirits, away!

[*Exeunt* DEVILS.

Clown. What, are they gone? A vengeance on them, they have vile long nails! There was a he-devil, and a she-devil! I'll tell you how you shall know them: all he-devils has horns, and all she-devils has clifts and cloven feet.

Wag. Well, sirrah, follow me.

Clown. But, do you hear—if I should serve you, would you teach me to raise up Banios and [420 Belcheos?

Wag. I will teach thee to turn thyself to anything; to a dog, or a cat, or a mouse, or a rat, or anything.

Clown. How! a Christian fellow to a dog or a cat, a mouse or a rat! No, no, sir. If you turn me into anything, let it be in the likeness of a little pretty frisky flea, that I may be here and there and everywhere. Oh, I'll tickle the pretty wenches' plackets; I'll be amongst them, i' faith.

Wag. Well, sirrah, come. 430

Clown. But, do you hear, Wagner?

Wag. How!—Baliol and Belcher!

Clown. O Lord! I pray, sir, let Banio and Belcher go sleep.

Wag. Villain—call me Master Wagner, and let thy left eye be dimetarily fixt upon my right heel, with *quasi vestigias nostras insistere.* [*Exit.*

Clown. God forgive me, he speaks Dutch fustian. Well, I'll follow him, I'll serve him, that's flat. [*Exit.*

[*Enter* FAUSTUS *in his study.*]

Faust. Now, Faustus, must 440
Thou needs be damned, and canst thou not be saved:
What boots it then to think of God or heaven?
Away with such vain fancies, and despair:
Despair in God, and trust in Belzebub.
Now go not backward: no, Faustus, be resolute.
Why waverest thou? O, something soundeth in mine ears
"Abjure this magic, turn to God again!"
Ay, and Faustus will turn to God again.
To God?—He loves thee not—
The God thou serv'st is thine own appetite, 450
Wherein is fixed the love of Belzebub;
To him I'll build an altar and a church,
And offer lukewarm blood of new-born babes.

[*Enter* GOOD ANGEL *and* EVIL ANGEL.]

G. Ang. Sweet Faustus, leave that execrable art.

Faust. Contrition, prayer, repentance! What of them?

G. Ang. O, they are means to bring thee unto heaven.

E. Ang. Rather illusions, fruits of lunacy,
That makes men foolish that do trust them most.

G. Ang. Sweet Faustus, think of heaven, and heavenly things. 459

E. Ang. No, Faustus, think of honour and of wealth. [*Exeunt.*

Faust. Of wealth!
Why, the signiory of Emden shall be mine.
When Mephistophilis shall stand by me,
What God can hurt thee, Faustus? Thou art safe;
Cast no more doubts. Come, Mephistophilis,
And bring glad tidings from great Lucifer;—
Is 't not midnight? Come, Mephistophilis;
Veni, veni, Mephistophile!

[*Enter* MEPHISTOPHILIS.]

Now tell me, what says Lucifer thy lord?

Meph. That I shall wait on Faustus whilst he lives, 470

---

404. **Baliol and Belcher,** Baliol, probably a corruption of Belial; Belcher, a fire-vomiting demon.   409. **slop,** either baggy breeches or loose jacket.   428. **plackets,** petticoats.   436. **dimetarily,** in a straight line.   437. **quasi . . . insistere,** as though to tread upon my footsteps.   438. **fustian,** jargon, properly a coarse material.   462. **signiory of Emden,** Emden, a town at the mouth of the river Ems in East Friesland, a rich port in the sixteenth century.

So he will buy my service with his soul.
   Faust. Already Faustus hath hazarded that for thee.
   Meph. But, Faustus, thou must bequeath it solemnly,
And write a deed of gift with thine own blood,
For that security craves great Lucifer.
If thou deny it, I will back to hell.
   Faust. Stay, Mephistophilis! and tell me what good
Will my soul do thy lord.
   Meph.   Enlarge his kingdom.
   Faust. Is that the reason why he tempts us thus?
   Meph. Solamen miseris socios habuisse doloris.   480
   Faust. Why, have you any pain that torture others?
   Meph. As great as have the human souls of men.
But tell me, Faustus, shall I have thy soul?
And I will be thy slave, and wait on thee,
And give thee more than thou hast wit to ask.
   Faust. Ay, Mephistophilis, I give it thee.
   Meph. Then, Faustus, stab thine arm courageously.
And bind thy soul that at some certain day
Great Lucifer may claim it as his own;
And then be thou as great as Lucifer.   490
   Faust (*stabbing his arm*). Lo, Mephistophilis, for love of thee,
I cut mine arm, and with my proper blood
Assure my soul to be great Lucifer's,
Chief lord and regent of perpetual night!
View here the blood that trickles from mine arm,
And let it be propitious for my wish.
   Meph. But, Faustus, thou must
Write it in manner of a deed of gift.
   Faust. Ay, so I will. But, Mephistophilis,
My blood congeals, and I can write no more.   500
   Meph. I'll fetch thee fire to dissolve it straight.
                                        [*Exit.*
   Faust. What might the staying of my blood portend?
Is it unwilling I should write this bill?
Why streams it not that I may write afresh?
Faustus gives to thee his soul. Ah, there it stayed.
Why should'st thou not? Is not thy soul thine own?
Then write again, *Faustus gives to thee his soul.*

[*Re-enter* MEPHISTOPHILIS *with a chafer of coals.*]

   Meph. Here's fire. Come, Faustus, set it on.
   Faust. So now the blood begins to clear again;
Now will I make an end immediately.   510

  471. **So,** provided that.   480. **Solamen . . . doloris.** It is a comfort to the wretched to have partakers of their grief. 508. **set it on,** the chafer, a portable grate, upon which Faust is told to set the saucer of blood.

   Meph. O what will not I do to obtain his soul.
   Faust. Consummatum est: this bill is ended,
And Faustus hath bequeathed his soul to Lucifer—
But what is this inscription on mine arm?
Homo, fuge! Whither should I fly?
If unto God, he'll throw me down to hell.
My senses are deceived; here's nothing writ:—
I see it plain; here in this place is writ
Homo, fuge! Yet shall not Faustus fly.   519
   Meph. I'll fetch him somewhat to delight his mind.   [*Exit.*

[*Re-enter* MEPHISTOPHILIS *with* Devils, *giving crowns and rich apparel to* FAUSTUS, *and they dance, and then depart.*]

   Faust. Speak, Mephistophilis, what means this show?
   Meph. Nothing, Faustus, but to delight thy mind withal,
And to show thee what magic can perform.
   Faust. But may I raise up spirits when I please?
   Meph. Ay, Faustus, and do greater things than these.
   Faust. Then there's enough for a thousand souls.
Here, Mephistophilis, receive this scroll,
A deed of gift of body and of soul:
But yet conditionally that thou perform
All articles prescribed between us both.   530
   Meph. Faustus, I swear by hell and Lucifer
To effect all promises between us made.
   Faust. Then hear me read them: *On these conditions following. First, that Faustus may be a spirit in form and substance. Secondly, that Mephistophilis shall be his servant, and at his command. Thirdly, that Mephistophilis shall do for him and bring him whatsoever he desires. Fourthly, that he shall be in his chamber or house invisible. Lastly, that he shall appear to the said John Faustus, at all times, in what form or shape soever he* [540 *pleases. I, John Faustus, of Wittenberg, Doctor, by these presents do give both body and soul to Lucifer, Prince of the East, and his minister, Mephistophilis; and furthermore grant unto them, that twenty-four years being expired, the articles above written inviolate, full power to fetch or carry the said John Faustus, body and soul, flesh, blood, or goods, into their habitation wheresoever. By me, John Faustus.*
   Meph. Speak, Faustus, do you deliver this as your deed?
   Faust. Ay, take it, and the Devil give thee good on't.   550
   Meph. Now, Faustus, ask what thou wilt.

  512. **Consummatum est.** It is finished.   515. **Homo, fuge!** O man, flee!   542–43. **Lucifer,** light-bringer, therefore **Prince of the East.**

Faust. First will I question with thee about hell.
Tell me where is the place that men call hell?
   Meph. Under the heavens.
   Faust. Ay, but whereabout?
   Meph. Within the bowels of these elements,
Where we are tortured and remain for ever;
Hell hath no limits, nor is circumscribed
In one self place; for where we are is hell,
And where hell is there must we ever be: 560
And, to conclude, when all the world dissolves,
And every creature shall be purified,
All places shall be hell that is not heaven.
   Faust. Come, I think hell's a fable.
   Meph. Ay, think so still, till experience change thy mind.
   Faust. Why, think'st thou then that Faustus shall be damned?
   Meph. Ay, of necessity, for here's the scroll
Wherein thou hast given thy soul to Lucifer.
   Faust. Ay, and body too; but what of that?
Think'st thou that Faustus is so fond to imagine 570
That, after this life, there is any pain?
Tush; these are trifles, and mere old wives' tales.
   Meph. But, Faustus, I am an instance to prove the contrary,
For I am damnèd, and am now in hell.
   Faust. How! now in hell!
Nay, an this be hell, I'll willingly be damned here;
What? walking, disputing, &c.?
But, leaving off this, let me have a wife,
The fairest maid in Germany;
For I am wanton and lascivious,   580
And cannot live without a wife.
   Meph. How—a wife?
I prithee, Faustus, talk not of a wife.
   Faust. Nay, sweet Mephistophilis, fetch me one, for I will have one.
   Meph. Well—thou wilt have one. Sit there till I come:
I'll fetch thee a wife in the Devil's name.   [*Exit.*

[*Re-enter* MEPHISTOPHILIS *with a* Devil *dressed like a woman, with fireworks.*]

   Meph. Tell me, Faustus, how dost thou like thy wife?
   Faust. A plague on her for a hot whore!
   Meph. Tut, Faustus,
Marriage is but a ceremonial toy;   590
And if thou lovest me, think no more of it.
I'll cull thee out the fairest courtesans,
And bring them every morning to thy bed;
She whom thine eye shall like, thy heart shall have,

570. so fond to, so foolish as to.

Be she as chaste as was Penelope,
As wise as Saba, or as beautiful
As was bright Lucifer before his fall.
Here, take this book, peruse it thoroughly:
The iterating of these lines brings gold;
The framing of this circle on the ground   600
Brings whirlwinds, tempests, thunder and lightning;
Pronounce this thrice devoutly to thyself,
And men in armour shall appear to thee,
Ready to execute what thou desir'st.
   Faust. Thanks, Mephistophilis; yet fain would I have a book wherein I might behold all spells and incantations, that I might raise up spirits when I please.
   Meph. Here they are, in this book. (*Turns to them.*)
   Faust. Now would I have a book where I [610
might see all characters and planets of the heavens,
that I might know their motions and dispositions.
   Meph. Here they are too. (*Turns to them.*)
   Faust. Nay, let me have one book more,—and then I have done,—wherein I might see all plants, herbs, and trees that grow upon the earth.
   Meph. Here they be.
   Faust. O, thou art deceived.
   Meph. Tut, I warrant thee. (*Turns to them.*)
                                                [*Exeunt.*

[*Enter* FAUSTUS *and* MEPHISTOPHILIS.]

   Faust. When I behold the heavens, then I repent,
And curse thee, wicked Mephistophilis,   621
Because thou hast deprived me of those joys.
   Meph. Why, Faustus,
Thinkest thou Heaven is such a glorious thing?
I tell thee 'tis not half so fair as thou,
Or any man that breathes on earth.
   Faust. How provest thou that?
   Meph. 'T was made for man, therefore is man more excellent.
   Faust. If it were made for man, 'twas made for me;
I will renounce this magic and repent.   630

[*Enter* GOOD ANGEL *and* EVIL ANGEL.]

   G. Ang. Faustus, repent; yet God will pity thee.
   E. Ang. Thou art a spirit; God cannot pity thee.
   Faust. Who buzzeth in mine ears I am a spirit?
Be I a devil, yet God may pity me;
Ay, God will pity me if I repent.
   E. Ang. Ay, but Faustus never shall repent.
                                                [*Exeunt.*

595. Penelope, wife of Odysseus (Ulysses), who faithfully waited for her husband's return from the siege of Troy, though her hand was sought by many suitors.   **596. Saba,** the Queen of Sheba, who visited Solomon (see I Kings 10). **599. iterating,** repeating.   **618. thou art deceived.** Faust cannot believe that Mephistophilis is telling the truth.

Faust. My heart's so hardened I cannot repent.
Scarce can I name salvation, faith, or heaven,
But fearful echoes thunder in mine ears
"Faustus, thou art damned!" Then swords and knives, 640
Poison, gun, halters, and envenomed steel
Are laid before me to despatch myself,
And long ere this I should have slain myself,
Had not sweet pleasure conquered deep despair.
Have I not made blind Homer sing to me
Of Alexander's love and Oenon's death?
And hath not he that built the walls of Thebes
With ravishing sound of his melodious harp,
Made music with my Mephistophilis?
Why should I die then, or basely despair? 650
I am resolved: Faustus shall ne'er repent.
Come, Mephistophilis, let us dispute again,
And argue of divine astrology.
Tell me, are there many heavens above the moon?
Are all celestial bodies but one globe,
As is the substance of this centric earth?
  Meph. As are the elements, such are the spheres
Mutually folded in each other's orb,
And, Faustus,
All jointly move upon one axletree 660
Whose terminine is termed the world's wide pole;
Nor are the names of Saturn, Mars, or Jupiter
Feigned, but are erring stars.
  Faust. But tell me, have they all one motion, both *situ et tempore?*
  Meph. All jointly move from east to west in twenty-four hours upon the poles of the world; but differ in their motion upon the poles of the zodiac.
  Faust. Tush!
These slender trifles Wagner can decide; 670
Hath Mephistophilis no greater skill?
Who knows not the double motion of the planets?
The first is finished in a natural day;
The second thus: as Saturn in thirty years; Jupiter in twelve; Mars in four; the Sun, Venus, and Mercury in a year; the moon in twenty-eight days. Tush, these are freshmen's suppositions. But tell me, hath every sphere a dominion or *intelligentia?*
  Meph. Ay.
  Faust. How many heavens, or spheres, are [680 there?
  Meph. Nine: the seven planets, the firmament, and the empyreal heaven.
  Faust. Well, resolve me in this question: Why have we not conjunctions, oppositions, aspects, eclipses, all at one time, but in some years we have more, in some less?
  Meph. Per inaequalem motum respecta totius.
  Faust. Well, I am answered. Tell me who made the world. 690
  Meph. I will not.
  Faust. Sweet Mephistophilis, tell me.
  Meph. Move me not, for I will not tell thee.
  Faust. Villain, have I not bound thee to tell me anything?
  Meph. Ay, that is not against our kingdom; but this is.
Think thou on hell, Faustus, for thou art damned.
  Faust. Think, Faustus, upon God that made the world.
  Meph. Remember this.
  Faust. Ay, go, accursèd spirit, to ugly hell. 700
'Tis thou hast damned distressèd Faustus' soul.
Is't not too late?

[*Re-enter* GOOD ANGEL *and* EVIL ANGEL.]

  E. Ang. Too late.
  G. Ang. Never too late, if Faustus can repent.
  E. Ang. If thou repent, devils shall tear thee in pieces.
  G. Ang. Repent, and they shall never raze thy skin. [*Exeunt.*
  Faust. Ah, Christ, my Saviour,
Seek to save distressèd Faustus' soul.

[*Enter* LUCIFER, BELZEBUB, *and* MEPHISTOPHILIS.]

  Luc. Christ cannot save thy soul, for he is just;
There's none but I have interest in the same. 710
  Faust. O, who art thou that look'st so terrible?
  Luc. I am Lucifer,
And this is my companion prince in hell.
  Faust. O Faustus! they are come to fetch away thy soul!
  Luc. We come to tell thee thou dost injure us;

---

646. Alexander's love and Oenon's death? Alexander, or Paris, was the son of Priam, king of Troy. He married Oenone, but he fell in love with Helen, wife of Menelaus, king of Sparta, and carried her to Troy. After he was wounded, in the capture of Troy, Paris returned to Oenone, who alone had the power to cure him. She refused, but when he died, she in remorse slew herself on her husband's funeral pyre. **647. he that . . . Thebes.** Amphion's lute-playing was so sweet that stones arranged themselves in their proper places, to form a wall. **654. heavens above the moon?** According to the Ptolemaic system the earth was the central sphere of several concentric ones, with the sphere of the moon next to that of the earth, the others being beyond. **661. terminine,** used here as "extremity." **665. situ et tempore?** in position and in time. **667–68. poles of the world . . . of the zodiac.** These are situated on the same common axis, on which all the spheres revolve. **673–74. The first . . . The second,** the apparent motion caused by the earth's revolution on its axis and that of the seven planetary spheres, which moved at different rates. **677. freshmen's suppositions,** theories current among first-year students at the universities. **678. dominion or intelligentia?** a ruling spirit or angel. **688. Per . . . totius,** owing to their unequal motion with regard to the whole. **706. raze,** touch the surface of, graze.

Thou talk'st of Christ contrary to thy promise;
Thou should'st not think of God: think of the Devil,
And of his dam, too.

Faust. Nor will I henceforth: pardon me in this,
And Faustus vows never to look to Heaven, 720
Never to name God, or to pray to him,
To burn his Scriptures, slay his ministers,
And make my spirits pull his churches down.

Luc. Do so, and we will highly gratify thee. Faustus, we are come from hell to show thee some pastime. Sit down, and thou shalt see all the Seven Deadly Sins appear in their proper shapes.

Faust. That sight will be pleasing unto me,
As Paradise was to Adam the first day
Of his creation. 730

Luc. Talk not of Paradise nor creation, but mark this show: talk of the Devil, and nothing else.—Come away!

[*Enter the* Seven Deadly Sins.]

Now, Faustus, examine them of their several names and dispositions.

Faust. What art thou—the first?

Pride. I am Pride. I disdain to have any parents. I am like to Ovid's flea: I can creep into every corner of a wench; sometimes, like a periwig, I sit upon her brow; or like a fan of feathers, I kiss her [740 lips; indeed I do—what do I not? But, fie, what a scent is here! I'll not speak another word, except the ground were perfumed, and covered with cloth of arras.

Faust. What are thou—the second?

Covet. I am Covetousness, begotten of an old churl in an old leathern bag; and might I have my wish I would desire that this house and all the people in it were turned to gold, that I might lock you up in my good chest. O, my sweet gold! 750

Faust. What art thou—the third?

Wrath. I am Wrath. I had neither father nor mother: I leapt out of a lion's mouth when I was scarce half an hour old; and ever since I have run up and down the world with this case of rapiers wounding myself when I had nobody to fight withal. I was born in hell; and look to it, for some of you shall be my father.

Faust. What are thou—the fourth?

Envy. I am Envy, begotten of a chimney [760 sweeper and an oyster-wife. I cannot read, and therefore wish all books were burnt. I am lean with seeing others eat. O that there would come a famine through all the world, that all might die, and I live alone! then thou should'st see how fat I would be. But must thou sit and I stand! Come down with a vengeance!

Faust. Away, envious rascal! What art thou—the fifth?

Glut. Who, I, sir? I am Gluttony. My parents [770 are all dead, and the devil a penny they have left me, but a bare pension, and that is thirty meals a day and ten bevers—a small trifle to suffice nature. O, I come of a royal parentage! My grandfather was a Gammon of Bacon, my grandmother a Hogshead of Claret-wine; my godfathers were these, Peter Pickleherring, and Martin Martlemas-beef. O, but my godmother, she was a jolly gentlewoman, and well beloved in every good town and city; her name was Mistress Margery Marchbeer. Now, [780 Faustus, thou hast heard all my progeny, wilt thou bid me to supper?

Faust. No, I'll see thee hanged: thou wilt eat up all my victuals.

Glut. Then the Devil choke thee!

Faust. Choke thyself, glutton! Who art thou—the sixth?

Sloth. I am Sloth. I was begotten on a sunny bank, where I have lain ever since; and you have done me great injury to bring me from thence: let [790 me be carried thither again by Gluttony and Lechery. I'll not speak another word for a king's ransom.

Faust. What are you, Mistress Minx, the seventh and last?

Lech. Who, I, sir? I am one that loves an inch of raw mutton better than an ell of fried stockfish; and the first letter of my name begins with Lechery.

Luc. Away to hell, to hell! (*Exeunt the* Sins.) Now, Faustus, how dost thou like this?

Faust. O, this feeds my soul! 800

Luc. Tut, Faustus, in hell is all manner of delight.

Faust. O might I see hell, and return again. How happy were I then!

Luc. Thou shalt; I will send for thee at midnight.

---

718. And of his dam, too. These words may have been added by one of the actors. **726-27. Seven Deadly Sins.** The seven sins enumerated below are entitled "mortal," "capital," or "deadly" because they lead to spiritual death; they are also the sins from which all others (venial sins) are supposed to arise. They frequently appeared in the early moralities and miracle plays. **738. Ovid's flea.** The "Carmen de Pulice" was falsely attributed to Ovid. **743-44. cloth of arras,** cloth woven in Arras in Flanders, used for tapestry hangings, but which Pride would have as a carpet beneath her feet. **755. case of rapiers,** pair of rapiers worn in a single sheath, and used one in each hand. **760-61. begotten . . . oyster-wife,** and therefore black and malodorous. **773. bevers,** light repasts between breakfast and dinner. **776-77. Peter Pickleherring,** a merry-andrew, buffoon. **Martlemas-beef.** Martinmas, November 11, was the customary time for hanging up meat which had been salted for the winter. **780. Marchbeer,** a choice strong ale, made generally in March and not fit to drink until two years old. **781. progeny,** in the obsolete sense of lineage, parentage. **796. raw mutton,** play on the slang term for a loose woman.

In meantime take this book; peruse it thoroughly,
And thou shalt turn thyself into what shape thou
   wilt.
   Faust. Great thanks, mighty Lucifer!
This will I keep as chary as my life.
   Luc. Farewell, Faustus, and think on the Devil. 810
   Faust. Farewell, great Lucifer! Come, Mephis-
tophilis.   [*Exeunt omnes.*

[*Enter* WAGNER.]

   Wagner. Learnèd Faustus,
To know the secrets of astronomy,
Graven in the book of Jove's high firmament,
Did mount himself to scale Olympus' top,
Being seated in a chariot burning bright,
Drawn by the strength of yoky dragons' necks.
He now is gone to prove cosmography,
And, as I guess, will first arrive at Rome,   820
To see the Pope and manner of his court,
And take some part of holy Peter's feast,
That to this day is highly solemnised.   [*Exit.*

[*Enter* FAUSTUS *and* MEPHISTOPHILIS.]

   Faust. Having now, my good Mephistophilis,
Past with delight the stately town of Trier,
Environed round with airy mountain-tops,
With walls of flint, and deep entrenchèd lakes,
Not to be won by any conquering prince;
From Paris next, coasting the realm of France,
We saw the river Maine fall into Rhine,   830
Whose banks are set with groves of fruitful vines;
Then up to Naples, rich Campania,
Whose buildings fair and gorgeous to the eye,
The streets straight forth, and paved with finest
   brick,
Quarter the town in four equivalents.
There saw we learnèd Maro's golden tomb,
The way he cut, an English mile in length,
Thorough a rock of stone in one night's space;
From thence to Venice, Padua, and the rest,
In one of which a sumptuous temple stands,   840
That threats the stars with her aspiring top,
Thus hitherto has Faustus spent his time:
But tell me, now, what resting-place is this?
Hast thou, as erst I did command,
Conducted me within the walls of Rome?
   Meph. Faustus, I have; and because we will not
be unprovided, I have taken up his Holiness'
privy-chamber for our use.

   Faust. I hope his Holiness will bid us welcome.
   Meph. Tut, 't is no matter, man, we'll be [850
bold with his good cheer.
And now, my Faustus, that thou may'st perceive
What Rome containeth to delight thee with,
Know that this city stands upon seven hills
That underprop the groundwork of the same.
Just through the midst runs flowing Tiber's stream,
With winding banks that cut it in two parts:
Over the which four stately bridges lean,
That make safe passage to each part of Rome:
Upon the bridge called Ponto Angelo   860
Erected is a castle passing strong,
Within whose walls such store of ordnance are,
And double cannons, framed of carvèd brass,
As match the days within one còmplete year;
Besides the gates and high pyramides,
Which Julius Caesar brought from Africa.
   Faust. Now by the kingdoms of infernal rule,
Of Styx, of Acheron, and the fiery lake
Of ever-burning Phlegethon, I swear
That I do long to see the monuments   870
And situation of bright-splendent Rome:
Come therefore, let's away.
   Meph. Nay, Faustus, stay; I know you'd fain see
   the Pope,
And take some part of holy Peter's feast,
Where thou shalt see a troop of bald-pate friars,
Whose *summum bonum* is in belly-cheer.
   Faust. Well, I'm content to compass then some
   sport,
And by their folly make us merriment.
Then charm me, Mephistophilis, that I
May be invisible, to do what I please   880
Unseen of any whilst I stay in Rome.

[MEPHISTOPHILIS *charms him.*]

   Meph. So, Faustus, now
Do what thou wilt, thou shalt not be discerned.

[*Sound a sennet. Enter the* POPE *and the* CARDINAL *of* LORRAIN *to the banquet, with* Friars *attending.*]

   Pope. My Lord of Lorrain, wilt please you draw
near?
   Faust. Fall to, and the Devil choke you an you
spare!
   Pope. How now! Who's that which spake?—
Friars, look about.   [889

---

822. **holy Peter's feast.** St. Peter's day is June 29.   823. **to this day,** on this day.   825. **Trier,** the ancient city on the Mosel, now familiar as Treves.   827. **entrenchèd lakes,** the moat.   836. **Maro's golden tomb.** Virgil, whose full name was Publius Vergilius Maro, was buried at Naples, 19 B.C. He bore the reputation of being a great magician.

860. **the bridge . . . Angelo,** Ponte Angelo, formerly the Pons Aelius, built 135 A.D. by Hadrian to connect his mausoleum with the Campus Martius.   863. **double cannons,** perhaps with double bore.   865. **pyramides,** spires, obelisks. Pronounce pĭr-ăm'ĭ-dēz.   876. **summum bonum,** highest good.   *Stage dir.* **sennet,** a set of notes on the trumpet played as a signal.   886. **an,** if.

1 *Friar.* Here's nobody, if it like your Holiness.

Pope. My lord, here is a dainty dish was sent me from the Bishop of Milan.

Faust. I thank you, sir. (*Snatches it.*)

Pope. How now! Who's that which snatched the meat from me? Will no man look? My lord, this dish was sent me from the Cardinal of Florence.

Faust. You say true; I'll ha 't. (*Snatches it.*)

Pope. What, again! My lord, I'll drink to your Grace.

Faust. I'll pledge your Grace. (*Snatches the cup.*) [900

C. of Lor. My lord, it may be some ghost newly crept out of Purgatory, come to beg a pardon of your Holiness.

Pope. It may be so. Friars, prepare a dirge to lay the fury of this ghost. Once again, my lord, fall to. (*The* POPE *crosseth himself.*)

Faust. What, are you crossing of yourself? Well, use that trick no more I would advise you.

[*The* POPE *crosses himself again.*]

Well, there's the second time. Aware the third, I give you fair warning.

[*The* POPE *crosses himself again, and* FAUSTUS *hits him a box of the ear; and they all run away.*]

Come on, Mephistophilis, what shall we do? [910

Meph. Nay, I know not. We shall be cursed with bell, book, and candle.

Faust. How! bell, book, and candle,—candle, book, and bell,
Forward and backward to curse Faustus to hell!
Anon you shall hear a hog grunt, a calf bleat, and an ass bray,
Because it is Saint Peter's holiday.

[*Re-enter all the* Friars *to sing the Dirge.*]

1 *Friar.* Come, brethren, let's about our business with good devotion.

[*They sing:*]

Cursed be he that stole away his Holiness' meat from the table! *Maledicat Dominus!*
Cursed be he that struck his Holiness a blow on the face! *Maledicat Dominus!* 920
Cursed be he that took Friar Sandelo a blow on the pate! *Maledicat Dominus!*
Cursed be he that disturbeth our holy dirge! *Maledicat Dominus!*
Cursed be he that took away his Holiness' wine! *Maledicat Dominus! Et omnes sancti! Amen!*

904. **dirge,** a funeral service, or service of repose for the dead.   912. **with bell, book, and candle,** with all due forms of excommunication.   919. **Maledicat Dominus!** May the Lord curse him.   923. **Et omnes sancti.** And all the saints.

[MEPHISTOPHILIS *and* FAUSTUS *beat the* Friars, *and fling fireworks among them: and so exeunt.*]

[*Enter* CHORUS.]

Chorus. When Faustus had with pleasure ta'en the view
Of rarest things, and royal courts of kings,
He stayed his course, and so returnèd home;
Where such as bear his absence but with grief,
I mean his friends, and near'st companions,
Did gratulate his safety with kind words,
And in their conference of what befell, 930
Touching his journey through the world and air,
They put forth questions of Astrology,
Which Faustus answered with such learnèd skill,
As they admired and wondered at his wit.
Now is his fame spread forth in every land;
Amongst the rest the Emperor is one,
Carolus the Fifth, at whose palace now
Faustus is feasted 'mongst his noblemen.
What there he did in trial of his art, 939
I leave untold—your eyes shall see performed. [*Exit.*

[*Enter* ROBIN *the Ostler with a book in his hand.*]

Robin. O, this is admirable! here I ha' stolen one of Dr. Faustus' conjuring books, and i' faith I mean to search some circles for my own use. Now will I make all the maidens in our parish dance at my pleasure, stark naked before me; and so by that means I shall see more than e'er I felt or saw yet.

[*Enter* RALPH *calling* ROBIN.]

Ralph. Robin, prithee come away; there's a gentleman tarries to have his horse, and he would have his things rubbed and made clean. He keeps such a chafing with my mistress about it; and she [950 has sent me to look thee out. Prithee come away.

Robin. Keep out, keep out, or else you are blown up; you are dismembered, Ralph, keep out, for I am about a roaring piece of work.

Ralph. Come, what dost thou with that same book? Thou canst not read.

Robin. Yes, my master and mistress shall find that I can read, he for his forehead, she for her private study; she's born to bear with me, or else my art fails. [960

Ralph. Why, Robin, what book is that?

Robin. What book! Why, the most intolerable book for conjuring that e'er was invented by any brimstone devil.

937. **Carolus the Fifth.** Charles, king of Spain, was elected Emperor in 1519.   950. **a chafing.** To chafe is to make, or to get, warm, either in body or mind.   954. **roaring,** a slang term which still survives in the phrase "to drive a roaring trade."

Ralph. Canst thou conjure with it?

Robin. I can do all these things easily with it: first, I can make thee drunk with ippocras at any tavern in Europe for nothing; that's one of my conjuring works. [969

Ralph. Our Master Parson says that's nothing.

Robin. True, Ralph; and more, Ralph, if thou hast any mind to Nan Spit, our kitchenmaid, then turn her and wind her to thy own use as often as thou wilt, and at midnight.

Ralph. O brave Robin, shall I have Nan Spit, and to mine own use? On that condition I'll feed thy devil with horse-bread as long as he lives, of free cost.

Robin. No more, sweet Ralph: let's go and make clean our boots, which lie foul upon our hands, [980 and then to our conjuring in the Devil's name.

[*Exeunt.*

[*Enter* ROBIN *and* RALPH *with a silver goblet.*]

Robin. Come, Ralph, did not I tell thee we were for ever made by this Doctor Faustus' book? *Ecce signum*, here's a simple purchase for horse-keepers; our horses shall eat no hay as long as this lasts.

[*Enter the* VINTNER.]

Ralph. But, Robin, here comes the vintner.

Robin. Hush! I'll gull him supernaturally. Drawer, I hope all is paid: God be with you.—Come, Ralph.

Vint. Soft, sir; a word with you. I must yet [990 have a goblet paid from you, ere you go.

Robin. I, a goblet, Ralph; I, a goblet! I scorn you, and you are but a &c. I, a goblet! search me.

Vint. I mean so, sir, with your favour.

Robin. How say you now?

Vint. I must say somewhat to your fellow. You, sir!

Ralph. Me, sir! me, sir! search your fill. Now, sir, you may be ashamed to burden honest men with a matter of truth. [1000

Vint. Well, t' one of you hath this goblet about you.

Robin. You lie, drawer, 't is afore me.—Sirrah you, I'll teach ye to impeach honest men; stand by;—I'll scour you for a goblet!—stand aside you had best, I charge you in the name of Belzebub. Look to the goblet, Ralph.

Vint. What mean you, sirrah?

Robin. I'll tell you what I mean. *Sanctobulorum, Periphrasticon*—Nay, I'll tickle you, vintner. [1010 Look to the goblet, Ralph. *Polypragmos Belseborams framanto pacostiphos tostu, Mephistophilis,* &c.

[*Enter* MEPHISTOPHILIS, *sets squibs at their backs, and then exit. They run about.*]

Vint. O *nomine Domini!* what meanest thou, Robin? Thou hast no goblet.

Ralph. Peccatum peccatorum! Here's thy goblet, good vintner.

Robin. Misericordia pro nobis! What shall I do? Good Devil, forgive me now, and I'll never rob thy library more. [1019

[*Re-enter to them* MEPHISTOPHILIS.]

Meph. Monarch of hell, under whose black survey
Great potentates do kneel with awful fear,
Upon whose altars thousand souls do lie,
How am I vexèd with these villains' charms?
From Constantinople am I hither come
Only for pleasure of these damnèd slaves.

Robin. How from Constantinople? You have had a great journey. Will you take sixpence in your purse to pay for your supper, and begone?

Meph. Well, villains, for your presumption, I transform thee into an ape, and thee into a [1030 dog; and so begone. [*Exit.*

Robin. How, into an ape? That's brave! I'll have fine sport with the boys. I'll get nuts and apples enow.

Ralph. And I must be a dog.

Robin. I' faith thy head will never be out of the pottage pot. [*Exeunt.*

[*Enter* EMPEROR, FAUSTUS, *and a* KNIGHT *with attendants.*]

Emp. Master Doctor Faustus, I have heard strange report of thy knowledge in the black art, how that none in my empire nor in the whole world [1040 can compare with thee for the rare effects of magic; they say thou hast a familiar spirit, by whom thou canst accomplish what thou list. This, therefore, is my request, that thou let me see some proof of thy skill, that mine eyes may be witnesses to confirm what mine ears have heard reported; and here I swear to thee by the honour of mine imperial crown,

967. **ippocras.** Hippocras was spiced wine. 977. **horse-bread,** bread made of beans, bran, and so on for the use of horses. 983–84. **Ecce signum.** Here's proof. **a simple purchase,** a good bargain, without buying. 988. **Drawer.** Robin purposely calls the vintner the servant, a tapster. 993. **you are but a &c.** It was apparently left to the actor to ad-lib. here. 1000. **a matter of truth,** a charge affecting their honesty. 1005. **scour you,** polish you off.

1009. **Sanctobulorum,** mere gibberish, but it succeeds in rousing Mephistophilis. The following remarks are burlesque Latin invocations in language Mephistophilis is supposed to understand. 1013. **nomine Domini,** in the name of the Lord. 1015. **Peccatum peccatorum!** Sin of sins! 1017. **Misericordia pro nobis!** Mercy on us!

that, whatever thou doest, thou shalt be no ways prejudiced or endamaged.

Knight (aside). I' faith he looks much like a [1050] conjuror.

Faust. My gracious Sovereign, though I must confess myself far inferior to the report men have published, and nothing answerable to the honour of your imperial Majesty, yet for that love and duty binds me thereunto, I am content to do whatsoever your Majesty shall command me.

Emp. Then, Doctor Faustus, mark what I shall say. As I was sometime solitary set
Within my closet, sundry thoughts arose   1060
About the honour of mine ancestors,
How they had won by prowess such exploits,
Got such riches, subdued so many kingdoms,
As we that do succeed, or they that shall
Hereafter possess our throne, shall
(I fear me) ne'er attain to that degree
Of high renown and great authority;
Amongst which kings is Alexander the Great,
Chief spectacle of the world's pre-eminence,
The bright shining of whose glorious acts   1070
Lightens the world with his reflecting beams,
As, when I heard but motion made of him,
It grieves my soul I never saw the man.
If, therefore, thou by cunning of thine art
Canst raise this man from hollow vaults below,
Where lies entombed this famous conqueror,
And bring with him his beauteous paramour,
Both in their right shapes, gesture, and attire
They used to wear during their time of life,
Thou shalt both satisfy my just desire,   1080
And give me cause to praise thee whilst I live.

Faust. My gracious lord, I am ready to accomplish your request so far forth as by art, and power of my spirit, I am able to perform.

Knight (aside). I' faith that's just nothing at all.

Faust. But, if it like your Grace, it is not in my ability to present before your eyes the true substantial bodies of those two deceased princes, which long since are consumed to dust.

Knight (aside). Ay, marry, Master Doctor, [1090] now there's a sign of grace in you, when you will confess the truth.

Faust. But such spirits as can lively resemble Alexander and his paramour shall appear before your Grace in that manner that they best lived in, in their most flourishing estate; which I doubt not shall sufficiently content your imperial Majesty.

Emp. Go to, Master Doctor, let me see them presently.

Knight. Do you hear, Master Doctor? You [1100] bring Alexander and his paramour before the Emperor!

Faust. How then, sir?

Knight. I' faith that's as true as Diana turned me to a stag!

Faust. No, sir, but when Actaeon died, he left the horns for you. Mephistophilis, begone.
[*Exit* MEPHISTOPHILIS.

Knight. Nay, an you go to conjuring, I'll begone.
[*Exit.*

Faust. I'll meet with you anon for interrupting me so. Here they are, my gracious lord.   [1110

[*Re-enter* MEPHISTOPHILIS *with* ALEXANDER *and his* Paramour.]

Emp. Master Doctor, I heard this lady while she lived had a wart or mole in her neck: how shall I know whether it be so or no?

Faust. Your Highness may boldly go and see.
[*Exeunt.*

Emp. Sure these are no spirits, but the true substantial bodies of those two deceased princes.

Faust. Will 't please your Highness now to send for the knight that was so pleasant with me here of late?

Emp. One of you call him forth.   1120
[*Exit* Attendant.

[*Re-enter the* KNIGHT *with a pair of horns on his head.*]

How now, sir knight! why I had thought thou had'st been a bachelor, but now I see thou hast a wife, that not only gives thee horns, but makes thee wear them. Feel on, thy head.

Knight. Thou damned wretch and execrable dog, Bred in the concave of some monstrous rock, How darest thou thus abuse a gentleman? Villain, I say, undo what thou hast done!

Faust. O, not so fast, sir; there's no haste; but, good, are you remembered how you [1130 crossed me in my conference with the Emperor? I think I have met with you for it.

Emp. Good Master Doctor, at my entreaty release him; he hath done penance sufficient.

Faust. My gracious lord, not so much for the injury he offered me here in your presence, as to delight you with some mirth, hath Faustus worthily requited this injurious knight; which, being all I

1054. answerable, suitable.   **1071. his,** its.   **1072. motion,** mention.   **1077. paramour,** not Thais, but more probably Roxana.   **1088. two deceased princes,** Alexander and (probably) Roxana.   **1093. lively,** in a lifelike manner.

1099. presently, at once.   **1104. Diana.** Diana, being surprised while bathing by Actaeon, turned him into a stag and set on her dogs to hunt him down.   **1109. meet with you,** get even with you.

desire, I am content to release him of his horns: and, sir knight, hereafter speak [1140] well of scholars. Mephistophilis, transform him straight. Now, my good lord, having done my duty I humbly take my leave.

Emp. Farewell, Master Doctor; yet, ere you go, Expect from me a bounteous reward. [*Exeunt.*

[*Enter* FAUSTUS *and* MEPHISTOPHILIS.]

Faust. Now, Mephistophilis, the restless course
That Time doth run with calm and silent foot,
Shortening my days and thread of vital life,
Calls for the payment of my latest years;
Therefore, sweet Mephistophilis, let us 1150
Make haste to Wittenberg.

Meph. What, will you go on horseback or on foot?

Faust. Nay, till I'm past this fair and pleasant green,
I'll walk on foot.

[*Enter a* HORSE-COURSER.]

Horse-C. I have been all this day seeking one Master Fustian: mass, see where he is! God save you, Master Doctor!

Faust. What, horse-courser! You are well met.

Horse-C. Do you hear, sir? I have brought you forty dollars for your horse. [1160

Faust. I cannot sell him so: if thou likest him for fifty, take him.

Horse-C. Alas, sir, I have no more.—I pray you speak for me.

Meph. I pray you let him have him: he is an honest fellow, and he has a great charge, neither wife nor child.

Faust. Well, come, give me your money. My boy will deliver him to you. But I must tell you one thing before you have him; ride him [1170] not into the water at any hand.

Horse-C. Why, sir, will he not drink of all waters?

Faust. O yes, he will drink of all waters, but ride him not into the water: ride him over hedge or ditch, or where you wilt, but not into the water.

Horse-C. Well, sir.—Now I am made man for ever. I'll not leave my horse for forty. If he had but the quality of hey-ding-ding, hey-ding-ding, I'd make a brave living on him: he has a buttock as slick as an eel. Well, God b' wi' ye, sir, your [1180] boy will deliver him me: but hark ye, sir; if my horse be sick or ill at ease, if I bring his water to you, you'll tell me what it is? [*Exit* HORSE-COURSER.

Faust. Away, you villain; what, dost think I am a horse-doctor?
What art thou, Faustus, but a man condemned to die?
Thy fatal time doth draw to final end;
Despair doth drive distrust unto my thoughts:
Confound these passions with a quiet sleep:
Tush, Christ did call the thief upon the cross; 1190
Then rest thee, Faustus, quiet in conceit.

(*Sleeps in his chair.*)

[*Re-enter* HORSE-COURSER, *all wet, crying.*]

Horse-C. Alas, alas! Doctor Fustian, quotha? Mass, Doctor Lopus was never such a doctor. Has given me a purgation has purged me of forty dollars; I shall never see them more. But yet, like an ass as I was, I would not be ruled by him, for he bade me I should ride him into no water. Now I, thinking my horse had had some rare quality that he would not have had me known of, I, like a venturous youth, rid him into the deep pond at [1200] the town's end. I was no sooner in the middle of the pond, but my horse vanished away, and I sat upon a bottle of hay, never so near drowning in my life. But I'll seek out my Doctor, and have my forty dollars again, or I'll make it the dearest horse!—O, yonder is his snipper-snapper.—Do you hear? You hey-pass, where's your master?

Meph. Why, sir, what would you? You cannot speak with him.

Horse-C. But I will speak with him. [1210

Meph. Why, he's fast asleep. Come some other time.

Horse-C. I'll speak with him now, or I'll break his glass windows about his ears.

Meph. I tell thee he has not slept this eight nights.

Horse-C. An he have not slept this eight weeks, I'll speak with him.

Meph. See where he is, fast asleep.

Horse-C. Ay, this is he. God save you, Master Doctor! Master Doctor, Master Doctor [1220] Fustian!—Forty dollars, forty dollars for a bottle of hay!

Stage dir. **Horse-Courser,** a dealer in horses. "To corse," or "course," an obsolete word of unknown origin, means "to exchange." **1156. Fustian,** a weak jest for Faustus. **1166–67. a great charge . . . child.** Perhaps, since "charge" was a current term for a "thick adhesive plaster applied to the body of a horse," Mephistophilis may intend a poor jest—"He has a big charge, which is neither his wife nor his child." **1177. for forty,** for forty other horses. **1178. quality of hey-ding-ding,** possibly, quality of dancing, "hey-ding-ding" being the one-two-three of dance measure.

1189. Confound these passions. Drive away your agitation. **1191. in conceit,** in your thoughts. **1193. Doctor Lopus,** Dr. Roderigo Lopez, a Spanish Jew, Elizabeth's private physician. **1203. bottle,** bundle. **1206. snipper-snapper,** a conceited young fellow. **1207. hey-pass,** a juggler's exclamation, commanding an object to move; used here as a name for the magician's assistant.

Meph. Why, thou seest he hears thee not.

Horse-C. So ho, ho!—so ho, ho! (*Hollas in his ear.*) No, will you not wake? I'll make you wake ere I go. (*Pulls* FAUSTUS *by the leg, and pulls it away.*) Alas, I am undone! What shall I do?

Faust. O my leg, my leg! Help, Mephistophilis! call the officers. My leg, my leg!

Meph. Come, villain, to the constable. [1230

Horse-C. O lord, sir, let me go, and I'll give you forty dollars more.

Meph. Where be they?

Horse-C. I have none about me. Come to my ostry and I'll give them you.

Meph. Begone quickly. [HORSE-COURSER *runs away.*

Faust. What, is he gone? Farewell he! Faustus has his leg again, and the horse-courser, I take it, a bottle of hay for his labour. Well, this trick shall cost him forty dollars more. [1240

[*Enter* WAGNER.]

How now, Wagner, what's the news with thee?

Wag. Sir, the Duke of Vanholt doth earnestly entreat your company.

Faust. The Duke of Vanholt! an honourable gentleman, to whom I must be no niggard of my cunning. Come, Mephistophilis, let's away to him.

[*Exeunt.*

[*Enter the* DUKE, *the* DUCHESS, FAUSTUS, *and* MEPHISTOPHILIS.]

Duke. Believe me, Master Doctor, this merriment hath much pleased me.

Faust. My gracious lord, I am glad it contents you so well.—But it may be, madam, you [1250 take no delight in this. I have heard that great-bellied-women do long for some dainties or other. What is it, madam? Tell me, and you shall have it.

Duchess. Thanks, good Master Doctor; and for I see your courteous intent to pleasure me, I will not hide from you the thing my heart desires; and were it now summer, as it is January and the dead time of the winter, I would desire no better meat than a dish of ripe grapes.

Faust. Alas, madam, that's nothing! Meph- [1260 istophilis, begone. [*Exit* MEPHISTOPHILIS. Were it a greater thing than this, so it would content you, you should have it.

[*Re-enter* MEPHISTOPHILIS *with the grapes.*]

Here they be, madam; wilt please you taste on them?

Duke. Believe me, Master Doctor, this makes me wonder above the rest, that being in the dead time of winter, and in the month of January, how you should come by these grapes.

Faust. If it like your Grace, the year is [1270 divided into two circles over the whole world, that, when it is here winter with us, in the contrary circle it is summer with them, as in India, Saba, and farther countries in the East; and by means of a swift spirit that I have, I had them brought hither, as ye see.— How do you like them, madam; be they good?

Duchess. Believe me, Master Doctor, they be the best grapes that I e'er tasted in my life before.

Faust. I am glad they content you so, madam.

Duke. Come, madam, let us in, where you [1280 must well reward this learned man for the great kindness he hath showed to you.

Duchess. And so I will, my lord; and whilst I live, rest beholding for this courtesy.

Faust. I humbly thank your Grace.

Duke. Come, Master Doctor, follow us and receive your reward. [*Exeunt.*

[*Enter* WAGNER, *solus.*]

Wag. I think my master means to die shortly,
For he hath given to me all his goods;
And yet, methinks, if that death were near,   1290
He would not banquet and carouse and swill
Amongst the students, as even now he doth,
Who are at supper with such belly-cheer
As Wagner ne'er beheld in all his life.
See where they come! Belike the feast is ended.

[*Enter* FAUSTUS, *with two or three* SCHOLARS *and* MEPHISTOPHILIS.]

1 *Schol.* Master Doctor Faustus, since our conference about fair ladies, which was the beautifullest in all the world, we have determined with ourselves that Helen of Greece was the admirablest lady that ever lived: therefore, Master Doctor, if [1300 you will do us that favour, as to let us see that peerless dame of Greece, whom all the world admires for majesty, we should think ourselves much beholding unto you.

Faust. Gentlemen,
For that I know your friendship is unfeigned,
And Faustus' custom is not to deny
The just requests of those that wish him well,
You shall behold that peerless dame of Greece,
No otherways for pomp and majesty   1310
Than when Sir Paris crossed the seas with her,
And brought the spoils to rich Dardania.
Be silent, then, for danger is in words.

1235. **ostry**, or hostry, an obsolete form of "hostelry," an inn.   1242. **Vanholt**, the Duchy of Anhalt, a small territory in Prussia.   1273. **Saba**, Sheba.

[*Music sounds, and* HELEN *passeth over the stage.*]

  2 Schol. Too simple is my wit to tell her praise,
Whom all the world admires for majesty.
  3 Schol. No marvel though the angry Greeks pursued
With ten years' war the rape of such a queen,
Whose heavenly beauty passeth all compare.
  1 Schol. Since we have seen the pride of Nature's works,
And only paragon of excellence,   1320

[*Enter an* OLD MAN.]

Let us depart; and for this glorious deed
Happy and blest be Faustus evermore.
  Faustus. Gentlemen, farewell—the same I wish to you.   [*Exeunt* SCHOLARS *and* WAGNER.
  Old Man. Ah, Doctor Faustus, that I might prevail
To guide thy steps unto the way of life,
By which sweet path thou may'st attain the goal
That shall conduct thee to celestial rest!
Break heart, drop blood, and mingle it with tears,
Tears falling from repentant heaviness
Of thy most vile and loathsome filthiness,   1330
The stench whereof corrupts the inward soul
With such flagitious crimes of heinous sins
As no commiseration may expel,
But mercy, Faustus, of thy Saviour sweet,
Whose blood alone must wash away thy guilt.
  Faust. Where art thou, Faustus? Wretch, what hast thou done?
Damned art thou, Faustus, damned; despair and die!
Hell calls for right, and with a roaring voice
Says "Faustus! come! thine hour is almost come!"
And Faustus now will come to do thee right.   1340

[MEPHISTOPHILIS *gives him a dagger.*]

  Old Man. Ah stay, good Faustus, stay thy desperate steps!
I see an angel hovers o'er thy head,
And, with a vial full of precious grace,
Offers to pour the same into thy soul:
Then call for mercy, and avoid despair.
  Faust. Ah, my sweet friend, I feel
Thy words do comfort my distressèd soul.
Leave me a while to ponder on my sins.
  Old Man. I go, sweet Faustus, but with heavy cheer,   1349
Fearing the ruin of thy hopeless soul.   [*Exit.*

  Faust. Accursèd Faustus, where is mercy now?
I do repent; and yet I do despair;
Hell strives with grace for conquest in my breast:
What shall I do to shun the snares of death?
  Meph. Thou traitor, Faustus, I arrest thy soul
For disobedience to my sovereign lord;
Revolt, or I'll in piecemeal tear thy flesh.
  Faust. Sweet Mephistophilis, entreat thy lord
To pardon my unjust presumption,
And with my blood again I will confirm   1360
My former vow I made to Lucifer.
  Meph. Do it now then quickly, with unfeigned heart,
Lest danger do attend thy drift.
  Faust. Torment, sweet friend, that base and crooked age,
That durst dissuade me from my Lucifer,
With greatest torments that our hell affords.
  Meph. His faith is great, I cannot touch his soul;
But what I may afflict his body with
I will attempt, which is but little worth.
  Faust. One thing, good servant, let me crave of thee,   1370
To glut the longing of my heart's desire,—
That I might have unto my paramour
That heavenly Helen, which I saw of late,
Whose sweet embracings may extinguish clean
These thoughts that do dissuade me from my vow,
And keep mine oath I made to Lucifer.
  Meph. Faustus, this or what else thou shalt desire
Shall be performed in twinkling of an eye.

[*Re-enter* HELEN.]

  Faust. Was this the face that launched a thousand ships,
And burnt the topless towers of Ilium?   1380
Sweet Helen, make me immortal with a kiss.
Her lips suck forth my soul; see where it flies!—
Come, Helen, come, give me my soul again.
Here will I dwell, for Heaven be in these lips,
And all is dross that is not Helena.

[*Enter* OLD MAN.]

I will be Paris, and for love of thee,
Instead of Troy, shall Wittenberg be sacked;
And I will combat with weak Menelaus,
And wear thy colours on my plumèd crest;
Yea, I will wound Achilles in the heel,   1390
And then return to Helen for a kiss.
Oh, thou art fairer than the evening air
Clad in the beauty of a thousand stars;

1326–27. **goal That shall conduct thee,** that is, a happy death. 1329. **repentant heaviness,** heavy repentance. 1340. **to do thee right,** to pay what he owes.   1363. **drift,** purpose. 1364. **age,** old man. 1380. **topless,** unsurpassed in height. 1390. **wound Achilles,** as Paris did, his arrow being guided by Apollo.

Brighter art thou than flaming Jupiter
When he appeared to hapless Semele;
More lovely than the monarch of the sky
In wanton Arethusa's azured arms:
And none but thou shalt be my paramour. [*Exeunt.*

Old Man. Accursèd Faustus, miserable man,
That from thy soul exclud'st the grace of Heaven,
And fly'st the throne of his tribunal seat! 1401

[*Enter* Devils.]

Satan begins to sift me with his pride:
As in this furnace God shall try my faith,
My faith, vile hell, shall triumph over thee.
Ambitious fiends! see how the heavens smiles
At your repulse, and laughs your state to scorn!
Hence, hell! for hence I fly unto my God. [*Exeunt.*

[*Enter* FAUSTUS *with the* SCHOLARS.]

Faust. Ah, gentlemen!
1 *Schol.* What ails Faustus?
Faust. Ah, my sweet chamber-fellow, had I [1410 lived with thee, then had I lived still! but now I die eternally. Look, comes he not, comes he not?
2 *Schol.* What means Faustus?
3 *Schol.* Belike he is grown into some sickness by being over solitary.
1 *Schol.* If it be so, we'll have physicians to cure him. 'T is but a surfeit. Never fear, man.
Faust. A surfeit of deadly sin that hath damned both body and soul.
2 *Schol.* Yet, Faustus, look up to Heaven; [1420 remember God's mercies are infinite.
Faust. But Faustus' offences can never be pardoned: the serpent that tempted Eve may be saved, but not Faustus. Ah, gentlemen, hear me with patience, and tremble not at my speeches! Though my heart pants and quivers to remember that I have been a student here these thirty years, oh, would I had never seen Wittenberg, never read book! And what wonders I have done, all Germany can witness, yea, the world; for which Faustus [1430 hath lost both Germany and the world, yea Heaven itself, Heaven, the seat of God, the throne of the blessed, the kingdom of joy; and must remain in hell for ever, hell, ah, hell, for ever! Sweet friends! what shall become of Faustus being in hell for ever?
3 *Schol.* Yet, Faustus, call on God.

Faust. On God, whom Faustus hath abjured! on God, whom Faustus hath blasphemed! Ah, my God, I would weep, but the Devil draws in [1440 my tears. Gush forth blood instead of tears! Yea, life and soul! Oh, he stays my tongue! I would lift up my hands, but see, they hold them, they hold them!
All. Who, Faustus?
Faust. Lucifer and Mephistophilis. Ah, gentlemen, I gave them my soul for my cunning!
All. God forbid!
Faust. God forbade it indeed; but Faustus hath done it. For vain pleasure of twenty-four years [1450 hath Faustus lost eternal joy and felicity. I writ them a bill with mine own blood: the date is expired; the time will come, and he will fetch me.
1 *Schol.* Why did not Faustus tell us of this before, that divines might have prayed for thee?
Faust. Oft have I thought to have done so; but the Devil threatened to tear me in pieces if I named God; to fetch both body and soul if I once gave ear to divinity: and now 't is too late. Gentlemen, away! lest you perish with me. [1460
2 *Schol.* Oh, what shall we do to save Faustus?
Faust. Talk not of me, but save yourselves, and depart.
3 *Schol.* God will strengthen me. I will stay with Faustus.
1 *Schol.* Tempt not God, sweet friend; but let us into the next room, and there pray for him.
Faust. Ay, pray for me, pray for me! and what noise soever ye hear, come not unto me, for nothing can rescue me. [1470
2 *School.* Pray thou, and we will pray that God may have mercy upon thee.
Faust. Gentlemen, farewell! If I live till morning I'll visit you: if not—Faustus is gone to hell.
All. Faustus, farewell!
[*Exeunt* SCHOLARS. *The clock strikes eleven.*
Faust. Ah, Faustus,
Now hast thou but one bare hour to live,
And then thou must be damned perpetually!
Stand still, you ever-moving spheres of Heaven,
That time may cease, and midnight never come;
Fair Nature's eye, rise, rise again and make 1481
Perpetual day; or let this hour be but
A year, a month, a week, a natural day,
That Faustus may repent and save his soul!
O lente, lente, currite noctis equi!
The stars move still, time runs, the clock will strike,
The Devil will come, and Faustus must be damned.

1395. **hapless Semele**, who asked Zeus to appear before her in the splendor which he showed Juno but who, when he so appeared, was consumed by lightning. 1396–97. **monarch of the sky . . . Arethusa's azured arms.** If this is Apollo, the sun god, there is no record of his connection with the nymph Arethusa. **wanton,** playful. 1402. **sift me.** See Luke 22:31—"Satan hath desired to have you, that he may sift you as wheat." **pride,** powerful array.

1485. **O lente . . . equi!** Run slowly, slowly, ye steeds of the night!—from Ovid's *Amores*, Book I, sec. 13, ll. 39–40. 1486. **move still,** move without ceasing.

O, I'll leap up to my God! Who pulls me down?
See, see where Christ's blood streams in the firmament!
One drop would save my soul—half a drop: ah, my Christ! 1490
Ah, rend not my heart for naming of my Christ!
Yet will I call on him: O spare me, Lucifer!—
Where is it now? 'Tis gone; and see where God
Stretcheth out his arm, and bends his ireful brows!
Mountain and hills come, come and fall on me,
And hide me from the heavy wrath of God!
No! no!
Then will I headlong run into the earth;
Earth gape! O no, it will not harbour me!
You stars that reigned at my nativity, 1500
Whose influence hath allotted death and hell,
Now draw up Faustus like a foggy mist
Into the entrails of yon labouring clouds,
That when they vomit forth into the air,
My limbs may issue from their smoky mouths,
So that my soul may but ascend to Heaven.

[*The watch strikes.*]

Ah, half the hour is past! 'T will all be past anon!
O God!
If thou wilt not have mercy on my soul,
Yet for Christ's sake whose blood hath ransomed me, 1510
Impose some end to my incessant pain;
Let Faustus live in hell a thousand years—
A hundred thousand, and at last be saved!
O, no end is limited to damned souls!
Why wert thou not a creature wanting soul?
Or why is this immortal that thou hast?
Ah, Pythagoras' metempsychosis! were that true,

This soul should fly from me, and I be changed
Unto some brutish beast! All beasts are happy,
For, when they die, 1520
Their souls are soon dissolved in elements;
But mine must live, still to be plagued in hell.
Curst be the parents that engendred me!
No, Faustus: curse thyself: curse Lucifer
That hath deprived thee of the joys of Heaven.

[*The clock striketh twelve.*]

O, it strikes, it strikes! Now, body, turn to air,
Or Lucifer will bear thee quick to hell.

[*Thunder and lightning.*]

O soul, be changed into little water-drops,
And fall into the ocean—ne'er be found.
My God! my God! look not so fierce on me! 1530

[*Enter* Devils.]

Adders and serpents, let me breathe awhile!
Ugly hell, gape not! come not, Lucifer!
I'll burn my books!—Ah Mephistophilis!

[*Exeunt* Devils *with* FAUSTUS.

[*Enter* CHORUS.]

Cho. Cut is the branch that might have grown full straight,
And burnèd is Apollo's laurel bough,
That sometimes grew within this learned man.
Faustus is gone; regard his hellish fall,
Whose fiendful fortune may exhort the wise
Only to wonder at unlawful things,
Whose deepness doth entice such forward wits 1540
To practise more than heavenly power permits.

[*Exit.*

1493. **it,** the vision of Lucifer.   1517. **Pythagoras' metempsychosis!** Pythagoras, Greek philosopher (born c. 570 B.C.), taught the doctrine of metempsychosis or transmigration of souls.

1535. **Apollo's laurel bough.** Here Apollo is apparently regarded as the patron of learning, an office more commonly assigned to Minerva.

Richard Hakluyt
c. 1553–1616

Richard Hakluyt was born about 1553 of a Herefordshire family. After being educated at Westminster School and at Christ Church, Oxford, he took holy orders, and served as chaplain to Sir Edward Stafford, Ambassador at Paris, from 1583 to 1588. He was rector of Wetheringsett in 1590, and archdeacon of Westminster in 1603. Upon his death in 1616 he was buried in Westminster Abbey.

Hakluyt was an indefatigable agent in collecting and editing all the accounts of English voyages on which he could lay his hands. His motives, like those of the voyagers themselves, were mixed. He was far more conscious than most men of his time of the practical economic significance of the discoveries that were being made, and he saw himself rendering an invaluable service to English enterprise by making available in a systematic and coherent form all the information he could discover concerning the strange lands and seas that were being traversed. Another major motive of Hakluyt's was national pride. He had learned that the French regarded the English as sunk in "slothful security." He made up his mind that he would demonstrate the activity of the English by collecting records of their adventurous voyages. When the great work was completed, he felt a legitimate pride in England's accomplishments, a pride that swells the sails of his prose in such a passage as the following: "Which of the kings of this land before Her Majesty had their banners ever seen on the Caspian Sea? Which of them hath ever dealt with the Emperor of Persia, as Her Majesty hath done, and attained for her merchants large and loving privileges? Who ever saw an English Ligier in the stately porch of the Grand Signor of Constantinople? Who ever found English consuls and agents at Tripolis in Syria, at Aleppo, at Babylon, at Balsana, and which is more, who ever heard of Englishmen at Goa before now? What English ships did heretofore ever anchor in the mighty River of Plate?"

Hakluyt's *Principal Voyages, Traffics, and Discoveries of the English Nation* (commonly called the *Voyages*), was published in three large volumes between 1598 and 1600, and was the crowning work of his life. A briefer version had appeared in one folio volume under a slightly different title in 1589. But he had already published a number of minor works that led up to his masterpiece: *Divers Voyages Touching the Discovery of America*, 1582; *A Particular Discourse Covering Western Discoveries*, written in 1584, but not published until 1887; a translation of René de Laudonnière's *Journal* under the title, *A Notable History Concerning Four Voyages Made by Certain French Captains unto Florida*, 1587; and a revised edition of the Spaniard Peter Martyr's history of the discovery of the New World, *De Orbe Novo*, 1587.

Hakluyt's *Voyages* are an immense encyclopedia of English discovery, exploration, and adventure during the Renaissance. They contain over five hundred accounts, some of them bald and dull, and others vivid and heroic, of the major and minor efforts made by Englishmen to extend the limits of geographical and anthropological knowledge, to take possession of more and more strange lands in the name of the Virgin Queen, to bring home booty, treasure, exotic souvenirs, and terrified natives, to prepare the way for an extension of English trade, and to lay the foundation for the British Empire. The *Voyages* include accounts of the early voyages of the Cabots, Sir John Hawkins's voyage to Guinea and the West Indies, Sir Francis Drake's circumnavigation of the globe, Sir Humphrey Gilbert's last voyage, Martin Frobisher's search for the Northwest passage, and Sir Walter Ralegh's description of Guiana.

Hakluyt's relationship to English literature is mainly indirect. Certain writers borrowed directly from him, but he rendered a greater service to English literature by helping create an exciting atmosphere of patriotism and exoticism to which the imaginations of the poets could react.

from PRINCIPAL VOYAGES, TRAFFICS, AND DISCOVERIES OF THE ENGLISH NATION

The following passages are taken from Edward Hare's account of Sir Humphrey Gilbert's last voyage. Gilbert had obtained a grant of land in North America. After one expedition had met with disaster, he sailed on June 11, 1583, with five ships, the *Delight*, the *Ralegh*, the *Golden Hind*, the *Swallow*, and the *Squirrel*. Because of sickness aboard, the *Ralegh* had to put back to England. The other ships, after a foggy voyage, sighted land on July 30. They dropped anchor in the harbor of St. John, Newfoundland, and on August 5, Gilbert took possession of the land in the name of the Queen. He then sent out men to collect information concerning the nature and resources of the country.

THAT which we do call the Newfoundland, and the Frenchmen Bacalaos, is an island, or rather (after the opinion of some) it consisteth of sundry islands and broken lands, situate in the north regions of America, upon the gulf and entrance of the great river called St. Lawrence in Canada. Into the which, navigation may be made both on the south and north side of this island. The land lieth south and north, containing in length between 300 and 400 miles, accounting from Cape Race (which is in forty-six degrees twenty-five minutes) unto the Grand Bay in fifty-two degrees of septentrional latitude. The island round about hath very many goodly bays and harbours, safe roads for ships, the like not to be found in any part of the known world.

The common opinion that is had of intemperature and extreme cold that should be in this country, as of some part it may be verified, namely the north, where I grant it is more cold than in countries of Europe, which are under the same elevation: even so it cannot stand with reason and nature of the clime that the south parts should be so intemperate as the bruit hath gone. For as the same do lie under the climes of Breton, Anjou, Poictou in France, between forty-six and forty-nine degrees, so can they not so much differ from the temperature of those countries: unless upon the out-coast lying open unto the ocean and sharp winds, it must indeed be subject to more cold than further within the land, where the mountains are interposed, as walls and bulwarks, to defend and to resist the asperity and rigour of the sea and weather. Some hold opinion that the Newfoundland might be the more subject to cold by how much it lieth high and near unto the middle region. I grant that not in Newfoundland alone, but in Germany, Italy and Africa, even under the equinoctial line, the mountains are extreme cold and seldom uncovered of snow in their culm and highest tops, which cometh to pass by the same reason that they are extended towards the middle region; yet in the countries lying beneath them, it is found quite contrary. Even so all hills having their descents, the valleys also and low grounds must be likewise hot or temperate, as the clime doth give in Newfoundland: though I am of opinion that the sun's reflection is much cooled, and cannot be so forcible in Newfoundland, nor generally throughout America, as in Europe or Africa: by how much the sun in his diurnal course from east to west, passeth over (for the most part) dry land and sandy countries, before he arriveth at the west of Europe or Africa, whereby his motion increaseth heat, with little or no qualification by moist vapours. Where, on the contrary, he passeth from Europe and Africa unto America over the ocean, from whence it draweth and carrieth with him abundance of moist vapours, which do qualify and enfeeble greatly the sun's reverberation upon this country chiefly of Newfoundland, being so much to the northward. Nevertheless (as I said before) the cold cannot be so intolerable under the latitude of forty-six, forty-seven, and forty-eight (especially within land) that it should be unhabitable, as some do suppose, seeing also there are very many people more to the north by a great deal. And in these south parts there be certain beasts, ounces or leopards, and birds in like manner which in the summer we have seen, not heard of in countries of extreme and vehement coldness. Besides, as in the months of June, July, August and September, the heat is somewhat more than in England at those seasons: so men remaining upon the south parts near unto Cape Race, until after Hollandtide, have not found the cold so extreme, nor much differing from the temperature of England. Those which have arrived there after November and December have found the snow exceeding deep, whereat no marvel, considering the ground upon the coast is rough and uneven, and the snow is driven into the places most declining, as the like is to be seen with us. The like depth of snow happily shall not be found within land upon the plainer countries, which also are defended by the mountains, breaking off the violence of winds and

---

26. **septentrional**, North.   37. **bruit**, report.

4. **culm**, summit.

weather. But admitting extraordinary cold in those south parts, above that with us here, it cannot be so great as in Swedland, much less in Moscovia or Russia; yet are the same countries very populous, and the rigour of cold is dispensed with by the commodity of stoves, warm clothing, meats and drinks: all which need not to be wanting in the Newfoundland, if we had intent there to inhabit.

In the south parts we found no inhabitants, which by all likelihood have abandoned those coasts, the same being so much frequented by Christians. But in the north are savages altogether harmless. Touching the commodities of this country, serving either for sustentation of inhabitants or for maintenance of traffic, there are and may be made divers; so that it seemeth nature hath recompensed that only defect and incommodity of some sharp cold, by many benefits; viz., with incredible quantity and no less variety of kinds of fish in the sea and fresh waters, as trout, salmon, and other fish to us unknown; also cod, which alone draweth many nations thither, and is become the most famous fishing of the world. Abundance of whales, for which also is a very great trade in the bays of Placentia and the Grand Bay, where is made train oil of the whale; herring, the largest that have been heard of, and exceeding the Malstrond herring of Norway; but hitherto was never benefit taken of the herring fishing. There are sundry other fish very delicate, namely the bonitos, lobsters, turbot, with others infinite not sought after; oysters having pearl but not orient in colour, I took it, by reason they were not gathered in season.

Concerning the inland commodities, as well to be drawn from this land, as from the exceeding large countries adjoining, there is nothing which our east and northerly countries of Europe do yield, but the like also may be made in them as plentifully by time and industry: namely, rosin, pitch, tar, soap-ashes, deal-board, masts for ships, hides, furs, flax, hemp, corn, cables, cordage, linen cloth, metals, and many more. All which the countries will afford, and the soil is apt to yield. The trees for the most in those south parts are fir-trees, pine, and cypress, all yielding gum and turpentine. Cherry-trees bearing fruit no bigger than a small pea. Also pear-trees, but fruitless. Other trees of some sorts to us unknown. The soil along the coast is not deep of earth, bringing forth abundantly peason, small, yet good feeding for cattle. Roses passing sweet, like unto our musk roses in form, raspases, a berry which we call hurts, good and wholesome to eat. The grass and herb doth fat sheep in very short space, proved by English merchants which have carried sheep thither for fresh victual and had them raised exceeding fat in less than three weeks. Peason which our countrymen have sown in the time of May, have come up fair, and been gathered in the beginning of August, of which our General had a present acceptable for the rareness, being the first fruits coming up by art and industry in that desolate and dishabited land. Lakes or pools of fresh water, both on the tops of mountains and in the valleys, in which are said to be mussels not unlike to have pearl, which I had put in trial, if by mischance falling unto me I had not been let from that and other good experiments I was minded to make. Fowl both of water and land in great plenty and diversity. All kinds of green fowl; others as big as bustards, yet not the same. A great white fowl called of some a gaunt. Upon the land divers sorts of hawks, as falcons, and others by report. Partridges most plentiful, larger than ours, grey and white of colour, and rough-footed like doves, which our men after one flight did kill with cudgels, they were so fat and unable to fly. Birds, some like blackbirds, linnets, canary birds, and other very small. Beasts of sundry kinds, red deer, buffaloes, or a beast as it seemeth by the tract and foot very large, in manner of an ox. Bears, ounces or leopards, some greater and some lesser, wolves, foxes, which to the northward a little further are black, whose fur is esteemed in some countries of Europe very rich. Otters, beavers, martins. And in the opinion of most men that saw it, the General had brought unto him a sable alive, which he sent unto his brother, Sir John Gilbert, Knight, of Devonshire, but it was never delivered, as after I understood. We could not observe the hundredth part of creatures in those unhabited lands; but these mentioned may induce us to glorify the magnificent God, who hath superabundantly replenished the earth with creatures serving for the use of man, though man hath not used a fifth part of the same, which the more doth aggravate the fault and foolish sloth in many of our nation, choosing rather to live indirectly, and very miserably to live and die within this realm pestered with inhabitants, than to adventure as becometh men, to obtain an habitation in those remote lands, in which nature very prodigally doth minister unto men's endeavours, and for art to work upon. For besides these already recounted and infinite more, the mountains generally make shew of mineral substance; iron very common, lead, and somewhere

---

15. **sustentation,** maintenance.   44. **apt,** fitted, ready.
50. **peason,** peas.   52. **raspases,** raspberries.

1. **hurts,** whortleberries, huckleberries.   15. **let,** prevented.

copper. I will not aver of richer metals, albeit by the circumstances following, more than hope may be conceived thereof.

For amongst other charges given to inquire out the singularities of this country, the General was most curious in the search of metals, commanding the mineral-man and refiner especially to be diligent. The same was a Saxon born, honest, and religious, named Daniel, who after search brought at first some sort of ore, seeming rather to be iron than other metal. The next time he found ore, which with no small show of contentment he delivered unto the General, using protestation that if silver were the thing which might satisfy the General and his followers, there it was, advising him to seek no further; the peril whereof he undertook upon his life (as dear unto him as the crown of England unto Her Majesty, that I may use his own words) if it fell not out accordingly.

Myself at this instant likelier to die than to live, by a mischance, could not follow this confident opinion of our refiner to my own satisfaction; but afterward demanding our General's opinion therein, and to have some part of the ore, he replied, "Content yourself, I have seen enough, and were it but to satisfy my private humour, I would proceed no further. The promise unto my friends, and necessity to bring also the south countries within compass of my patent near expired, as we have already done these north parts, do only persuade me further. And touching the ore, I have sent it aboard, whereof I would have no speech to be made so long as we remain within harbour; here being both Portugals, Biscayans, and Frenchmen, not far off, from whom must be kept any bruit or muttering of such matter. When we are at sea proof shall be made; if it be our desire, we may return the sooner hither again." Whose answer I judged reasonable, and contenting me well, wherewith I will conclude this narration and description of the Newfoundland, and proceed to the rest of our voyage, which ended tragically. . . .

So upon Saturday in the afternoon of the 31st of August, we changed our course, and returned back for England, at which very instant, even in winding about, there passed along between us and towards the land which we now forsook a very lion to our seeming, in shape, hair, and colour, not swimming after the manner of a beast by moving of his feet, but rather sliding upon the water with his whole body (excepting the legs) in sight, neither yet diving under, and again rising above the water, as the manner is of whales, dolphins, tunnies, porpoises, and all other fish: but confidently showing himself above water without hiding: notwithstanding, we presented ourselves in open view and gesture to amaze him, as all creatures will be commonly at a sudden gaze and sight of men. Thus he passed along turning his head to and fro, yawning and gaping wide, with ugly demonstration of long teeth, and glaring eyes, and to bid us a farewell (coming right against the *Hind*) he sent forth a horrible voice, roaring or bellowing as doth a lion, which spectacle we all beheld so far as we were able to discern the same, as men prone to wonder at every strange thing, as this doubtless was, to see a lion in the ocean sea, or fish in shape of a lion. What opinion others had thereof, and chiefly the General himself, I forbear to deliver. But he took it for *Bonum Omen*, rejoicing that he was to war against such an enemy, if it were the devil. The wind was large for England at our return, but very high, and the sea rough, insomuch as the frigate wherein the General went was almost swallowed up.

Monday in the afternoon we passed in the sight of Cape Race, having made as much way in little more than two days and nights back again, as before we had done in eight days from Cape Race unto the place where our ship perished. Which hindrance thitherward, and speed back again, is to be imputed unto the swift current, as well as to the winds, which we had more large in our return. This Monday the General came aboard the *Hind*, to have the surgeon of the *Hind* to dress his foot, which he hurt by treading upon a nail; at what time we comforted each other with hope of hard success to be all past, and of the good to come. So agreeing to carry out lights always by night, that we might keep together, he departed into his frigate, being by no means to be entreated to tarry in the *Hind*, which had been more for his security. Immediately after followed a sharp storm, which we overpassed for that time, praised be God.

The weather fair, the General came aboard the *Hind* again, to make merry together with the captain, master, and company, which was the last meeting, and continued there from morning until night. During which time there passed sundry discourses, touching affairs past, and to come, lamenting greatly the loss of his great ship, more of the men, but most of all of his books and notes, and what else I know not, for which he was out of measure grieved, the same doubtless being some matter of more importance than his books, which I could not draw from him: yet by circumstance I gathered the same to be the ore which Daniel the

4. amaze, perplex.   **16. Bonum Omen,** a good omen.

Saxon had brought unto him in the Newfoundland. Whatsoever it was, the remembrance touched him so deep as, not able to contain himself, he beat his boy in great rage, even at the same time, so long after the miscarrying of the great ship, because upon a fair day, when we were becalmed upon the coast of the Newfoundland, near unto Cape Race, he sent his boy aboard the *Admiral*, to fetch certain things: amongst which, this being chief, was yet forgotten and left behind. After which time he could never conveniently send again aboard the great ship, much less he doubted her ruin so near at hand.

Herein my opinion was better confirmed diversely, and by sundry conjectures, which maketh me have the greater hope of this rich mine. For whereas the General had never before good conceit of these north parts of the world, now his mind was wholly fixed upon the Newfoundland. And as before he refused not to grant assignments liberally to them that required the same into these north parts, now he became contrarily affected, refusing to make any so large grants, especially of St. John's, which certain English merchants made suit for, offering to employ their money and travel upon the same: yet neither by their own suit, nor of others of his own company, whom he seemed willing to pleasure, it could be obtained. Also laying down his determination in the spring following for disposing of his voyage then to be re-attempted: he assigned the captain and master of the *Golden Hind* unto the south discovery, and reserved unto himself the north, affirming that this voyage had won his heart from the south, and that he was now become a northern man altogether.

Last, being demanded what means he had at his arrival in England to compass the charges of so great preparation as he intended to make the next spring, having determined upon two fleets, one for the south, another for the north, "Leave that to me," he replied, "I will ask a penny of no man. I will bring good tidings unto Her Majesty, who will be so gracious to lend me 10,000 pounds," willing us therefore to be of good cheer; for he did thank God, he said, with all his heart for that he had seen, the same being enough for us all, and that we needed not to seek any further. And these last words he would often repeat, with demonstration of great fervency of mind, being himself very confident and settled in belief of inestimable good by this voyage, which the greater number of his followers nevertheless mistrusted altogether, not being made partakers of those secrets which the General kept unto himself. Yet all of them that are living may be witnesses of his words and protestations, which sparingly I have delivered.

Leaving the issue of this good hope unto God, who knoweth the truth only, and can at His good pleasure bring the same to light, I will hasten to the end of this tragedy, which must be knit up in the person of our General. And as it was God's ordinance upon him, even so the vehement persuasion and entreaty of his friends could nothing avail to divert him from a wilful resolution of going through in his frigate, which was overcharged upon their decks with fights, nettings, and small artillery, too cumbersome for so small a boat, that was to pass through the ocean sea at that season of the year, when by course we might expect much storm of foul weather, whereof, indeed, we had enough.

But when he was entreated by the captain, master, and other his well-willers of the *Hind* not to venture in the frigate, this was his answer, "I will not forsake my little company going homeward, with whom I have passed so many storms and perils." And in very truth he was urged to be so over hard by hard reports given of him that he was afraid of the sea, albeit this was rather rashness than advised resolution, to prefer the wind of a vain report to the weight of his own life. Seeing he would not bend to reason, he had provision out of the *Hind*, such as was wanting aboard his frigate. And so we committed him to God's protection, and set him aboard his pinnace, we being more than 300 leagues onward of our way home.

By that time we had brought the Islands of Azores south of us; yet we then keeping much to the north, until we had got into the height and elevation of England, we met with very foul weather and terrible seas, breaking short and high, pyramid-wise. The reason whereof seemed to proceed either of hilly grounds high and low within the sea (as we see hills and dales upon the land), upon which the seas do mount and fall, or else the cause proceedeth of diversity of winds, shifting often in sundry points, all which having power to move the great ocean, which again is not presently settled, so many seas do encounter together, as there had been diversity of winds. Howsoever it cometh to pass, men which all their lifetime had occupied the sea never saw more outrageous seas. We had also upon our mainyard an apparition of a little fire by night, which seamen do call Castor and Pollux. But we had only one, which they take an evil sign of more tempest. The same is usual in storms.

Monday, the 9th of September, in the afternoon, the frigate was near cast away, oppressed by waves,

12. **fights,** screens to protect the combatants while fighting.

yet at that time recovered; and giving forth signs of joy, the General sitting abaft with a book in his hand, cried out to us in the *Hind* (so oft as we did approach within hearing), "We are as near to heaven by sea as by land," reiterating the same speech, well beseeming a soldier resolute in Jesus Christ, as I can testify he was.

On the same Monday night, about twelve o'clock, or not long after, the frigate being ahead of us in the *Golden Hind*, suddenly her lights were out, whereof as it were in a moment we lost the sight, and withal our watch cried the General was cast away, which was too true; for in that moment the frigate was devoured and swallowed up of the sea.

Yet still we looked out all that night and ever after, until we arrived upon the coast of England, omitting no small sail at sea, unto which we gave not the tokens between us agreed upon to have perfect knowledge of each other, if we should at any time be separated.

In great torment of weather and peril of drowning it pleased God to send safe home the *Golden Hind*, which arrived in Falmouth the 22nd day of September, being Sunday, not without as great danger escaped in a flaw, coming from the southeast, with such thick mist that we could not discern land to put in right with the haven. . . .

Edmund Spenser
c. 1552–1599

The date of Spenser's birth is uncertain, although from the internal evidence of one of his sonnets he seems to have been born about 1552. Although he claimed kinship with a distinguished family in Northamptonshire, his father was a journeyman clothmaker in London, and the circumstances of his education suggest the family's financial status. He attended the Merchant Taylors' School on a scholarship intended for a poor man's son, but what is more important is that the master of the school was Richard Mulcaster, a distinguished educator with a patriotic enthusiasm for the teaching of English as distinct from the classical languages. In 1569, some rough translations young Spenser had made of poems by Du Bellay and Marot were published in a miscellaneous collection, entitled *A Theatre for Voluptuous Worldlings;* twenty years later he took the trouble to polish them up and to include them in the volume entitled *Complaints.* Spenser entered Pembroke Hall, Cambridge, in 1569, and as a sizar was expected to work his way through college. At Pembroke, he came under the influence of a group of enthusiastic Puritans, and found a lasting friend in Gabriel Harvey, one of its Fellows.

Spenser took his B.A. in 1573 and his M.A. in 1576. In 1578 he acted as secretary to John Young, who had been Master of Pembroke while Spenser was an undergraduate, and was now Bishop of Rochester. In 1579, Spenser was a member of the household of the first Earl of Leicester, and in these circumstances he may have become acquainted with Sidney, Leicester's nephew. In any case, Sidney, Fulke Greville, Harvey, and Spenser were the leading spirits in a loosely organized group calling itself the Areopagus, and devoted to introducing classical meters into English poetry. In 1579, Spenser seems to have married Machabyas Childe, of whose subsequent life and death nothing is known. In this year also Spenser by publishing *The Shepheardes Calender* announced the arrival of the first great poet of the English Renaissance. For the next decade, although he continued writing, he seems to have published nothing. During that time, he was occupied with his duties as secretary to Lord Grey, Lord Deputy of Ireland. He lived in Dublin, and in addition to his duties as secretary, he served as Commissioner of Musters in 1583 and 1584, occupying a variety of minor offices. In or about 1586, he leased Kilcolman Castle in the County of Cork, and undertook the management of a huge estate on which he was supposed to plant English farmers. Here he was visited by Ralegh in 1589, to whom he read portions of the earlier books of *The Faerie Queene.*

He returned to London in the autumn of that year, to superintend the publication of the first three books of his great poem in 1590, and to attempt to gain favor at Court. Although Elizabeth granted him a pension of fifty pounds, he seems to have been disappointed by his experiences at court. In 1591 he published a miscellaneous collection of poems called *Complaints,* apparently in order to follow up the success of *The Faerie Queene.* The most

11. **flaw,** squall.

important poems in this volume were two satires, "Mother Hubbard's Tale" and "Muiopotmos, or, The Fate of the Butterfly." There were besides translations from Petrarch and Du Bellay. During the early nineties, he was probably writing the sonnet sequence *Amoretti*, which was published along with his *Epithalamion* in 1595. Both of these poems are generally supposed to refer to his courtship and marriage in 1594 of his second wife, Elizabeth Boyle, who at the time was probably the widow of one Tristram Pease. In 1595 he also published two elegies on Sidney, "Astrophel" and "The Doleful Lay of Clorinda," and "Colin Clout's Come Home Again," poetic reminiscences of Ralegh's visit to Kilcolman and of Spenser's impressions of London from 1589 to 1591. In this year also, he returned to London to see to the publication of a new edition of *The Faerie Queene*, with three more books, and also his *Four Hymns*, the most explicit statement of Spenser's Christian Platonism.

In 1597, he purchased lands in the County Cork for the benefit of his infant son, Peregrine. Before 1598 he wrote *A View of the Present State of Ireland*, which was not, however, published until 1633. In it he supported enthusiastically the stern repressive policy of his chief, Lord Grey. In 1598 Kilcolman Castle was sacked and burned during Tyrone's rebellion, one of Spenser's infant children lost his life, and Spenser, his wife, and the three other children took refuge in Cork. In December, he was sent to London with important dispatches, and died there, according to tradition, in poverty, on January 16, 1599. The expenses of interment in Westminster Abbey were borne by the Earl of Essex.

Spenser was the most successful of the Renaissance poets in achieving a satisfactory synthesis of the complex and seemingly contradictory creeds of his age. For he was not only a great poet, in the narrowly technical sense, but a poet in whose work were blended the elements of Platonism, Puritanism, and patriotism. His Platonism ennobles his love sonnets and exalts his hymns to Heavenly Love, and to Heavenly Beauty. His Puritanism furnishes the most significant moral basis for the sensory mazes of his verse. His patriotism appears in his sense of England's great destiny and his hostility to those forces within and without that seemed to him to threaten her integrity. Spenser has been called the poet's poet, because from him so many have taken lessons in superb artistry. It is easy and tempting to read Spenser on the purely poetic level, but he will not be well read until one weights, as he did, the philosophical, moral, and political elements in his greatest works.

from
THE SHEPHEARDES CALENDER

The Shepheardes Calender is a series of pastoral eclogues, one of which is assigned to each month of the year. The poem is the first important English work in the pastoral tradition. The nucleus of this popular poetic mode is the representation of the poet and his friends in the guise of shepherds and shepherdesses. Eclogues on the Theocritan model concern themselves with the activities and pastimes of real shepherds. Many Renaissance eclogues, however, contain elements of political, religious, or social satire that can be explained only in terms of the allegorical nature of the form.

Certain of Spenser's eclogues reflect the stages in Colin Clout's (that is, the poet's) unrequited love for an unidentified Rosalind. Others discuss such moral matters as youth vs. age, pride vs. humility, ambition vs. contentment. In the October eclogue, Spenser sets forth the rewards and the penalties of being a poet. His Platonized view of poetry should be compared with that of Sidney in his *Defence of Poesy* (page 353). The gloss[1] for this and the other eclogues of Spenser was supplied by a friend of the poet's, who signed himself E. K.

The Shepheardes Calender is a landmark in the history of English poetry, because of its architectonic complexity, metrical and technical virtuosity, and poetic assurance.

OCTOBER

ARGUMENT

*I*N Cuddie is set out the perfecte paterne of a Poete, whiche finding no maintenaunce of his state and studies, complayneth of the contempte of Poetrie, and the causes thereof: Specially having bene in all ages, and even amongst the most barbarous always of singular accounpt and honour, and being indede so worthy and commendable an arte: or rather no arte, but a divine gift and heavenly instinct not to bee gotten by laboure and learning, but adorned with both: and poured into the witte by a certaine ἐνθουσιασμὸς and celestiall inspiration, as the Author hereof els where at large discourseth, in his booke called the English Poete, which booke being lately come to my hands, I mynde also by Gods grace upon further advisement to publish.

PIERS.

Cuddie, for shame hold up thy heavye head,
And let us cast with what delight to chace,
And weary thys long lingring *Phoebus* race.
Whilome thou wont the shepheards laddes to leade,
In rymes, in ridles, and in bydding base:
Now they in thee, and thou in sleepe art dead.

[1] For explanation of the archaic words used, see the "Glosse" at the end of the selection.

CUDDIE.

Piers, I have pypèd erst so long with payne,
That all mine Oten reedes bene rent and wore:
And my poore Muse hath spent her sparèd store,
Yet little good hath got, and much lesse gayne.   10
Such pleasaunce makes the Grashopper so poore,
And ligge so layd, when Winter doth her straine:

The dapper ditties, that I wont devise,
To feede youthes fancie, and the flocking fry,
Delighten much: what I the bett for thy?
They han the pleasure, I a sclender prise.
I beate the bush, the byrds to them doe flye:
What good there of to Cuddie can arise?

PIERS.

Cuddie, the prayse is better, then the price,
The glory eke much greater then the gayne: 20
O what an honour is it, to restraine
The lust of lawlesse youth with good advice:
Or pricke them forth with pleasaunce of thy vaine,
Whereto thou list their traynèd willes entice.

Soone as thou gynst to sette thy notes in frame,
O how the rurall routes to thee doe cleave:
Seemeth thou dost their soule of sence bereave,
All as the shepheard, that did fetch his dame
From *Plutoes* balefull bowre withouten leave:
His musicks might the hellish hound did tame.   30

CUDDIE.

So praysen babes the Peacoks spotted traine,
And wondren at bright *Argus* blazing eye:
But who rewards him ere the more for thy?
Or feedes him once the fuller by a graine?
Sike prayse is smoke, that sheddeth in the skye,
Sike words bene wynd, and wasten soone in vayne.

PIERS.

Abandon then the base and viler clowne,
Lyft up thy selfe out of the lowly dust:
And sing of bloody Mars, of wars, of giusts,
Turne thee to those, that weld the awful crowne,   40
To doubted Knights, whose woundlesse armour rusts,
And helmes unbruzèd wexen dayly browne.

There may thy Muse display her fluttryng wing,
And stretch herselfe at large from East to West:
Whither thou list in fayre *Elisa* rest,
Or if thee please in bigger notes to sing,
Advaunce the worthy whome shee loveth best,
That first the white beare to the stake did bring.

And when the stubborne stroke of stronger stounds,
Has somewhat slackt the tenour of thy string: 50
Of love and lustihead tho mayst thou sing,
And carrol lowde, and leade the Myllers rownde,
All were *Elisa* one of thilke same ring.
So mought our *Cuddies* name to Heaven sownde.

CUDDIE.

Indeede the Romish *Tityrus*, I heare,
Through his *Mecaenas* left his Oaten reede,
Whereon he earst had taught his flocks to feede,
And laboured lands to yield the timely eare,
And eft did sing of warres and deadly drede,
So as the Heavens did quake his verse to here.   60

But ah *Mecaenas* is yclad in claye,
And great *Augustus* long ygoe is dead:
And all the worthies liggen wrapt in leade,
That matter made for Poets on to play:
For ever, who in derring doe were dreade,
The loftie verse of hem was lovèd aye.

But after vertue gan for age to stoupe,
And mighty manhode brought a bedde of ease:
The vaunting Poets found nought worth a pease,
To put in preace emong the learnèd troupe.   70
Tho gan the streames of flowing wittes to cease,
And sonnebright honour pend in shamefull coupe.

And if that any buddes of Poesie,
Yet of the old stocke gan to shoote agayne:
Or it mens follies mote be forst to fayne,
And rolle with rest in rymes of rybaudrye:
Or as it sprong, it wither must agayne:
Tom Piper makes us better melodie.

PIERS.

O pierlesse Poesye, where is then thy place?
If nor in Princes pallace thou doe sitt: 80
(And yet is Princes pallace the most fitt)
Ne brest of baser birth doth thee embrace.
Then make thee winges of thine aspyring wit,
And, whence thou camst, flye backe to heaven apace.

CUDDIE.

Ah *Percy* it is all to weake and wanne,
So high to sore, and make so large a flight:
Her peecèd pyneons bene not so in plight,
For *Colin* fittes such famous flight to scanne:
He, were he not with love so ill bedight,   89
Would mount as high, and sing as soote as Swanne.

PIERS.

Ah fon, for love does teach him climbe so hie,
And lyftes him up out of the loathsome myre:
Such immortall mirrhour, as he doth admire,

Would rayse ones mynd above the starry skie.
And cause a caytive corage to aspire,
For lofty love doth loath a lowly eye.

CUDDIE.

All otherwise the state of Poet stands,
For lordly love is such a Tyranne fell:
That where he rules, all power he doth expell.
The vaunted verse a vacant head demaundes, 100
Ne wont with crabbèd care the Muses dwell.
Unwisely weaves, that takes two webbes in hand.

Who ever casts to compasse weightye prise,
And thinks to throwe out thondring words of threate:
Let powre in lavish cups and thriftie bitts of meate,
For *Bacchus* fruite is frend to *Phoebus* wise.
And when with Wine the braine begins to sweate,
The nombers flowe as fast as spring doth ryse.

Thou kenst not *Percie* howe the ryme should rage.
O if my temples were distaind with wine, 110
And girt in girlonds of wild Ivie twine,
How I could reare the Muse on stately stage,
And teache her tread aloft in buskin fine,
With queint *Bellona* in her aequipage.

But ah my corage cooles ere it be warme,
For thy, content us in thys humble shade,
Where no such troublous tydes han us assayde,
Here we our slender pipes may safely charme.

PIERS.

And when my Gates shall han their bellies layd:
Cuddie shall have a Kidde to store his farme. 120

GLOSSE.

This Aeglogue is made in imitation of Theocritus his xvi. Idilion, wherein hee reproved the Tyranne Hiero of Syracuse for his nigardise towarde Poetes, in whome is the power to make men immortal for theyr good dedes, or shameful for their naughty lyfe. And the lyke also is in Mantuane. The style hereof as also that in Theocritus, is more loftye then the rest, and applyed to the heighte of Poeticall witte.

Cuddie) I doubte whether by Cuddie be specified the authour selfe, or some other. For in the eyght Aeglogue the same person was brought in, singing a Cantion of Colins making, as he sayth. So that some doubt, that the persons be different.

Whilome) sometime. **Oaten reedes**) Avena.
Ligge so layde) lye so faynt and unlustye.
Dapper) pretye.
Frye) is a bold Metaphore, forced from the spawning fishes. For the multitude of young fish be called the frye.

To restraine.) This place seemeth to conspyre with Plato, who in his first booke de Legibus sayth, that the first invention of Poetry was of very vertuous intent. For at what time an infinite number of youth usually came to theyr great solemne feastes called Panegyrica, which they used every five yeere to hold, some learned man being more hable then the rest, for speciall gyftes of wytte and Musicke, would take upon him to sing fine verses to the people, in praysse eyther of vertue or of victory or of immortality or such like. At whose wonderful gyft al men being astonied and as it were ravished, with delight, thinking (as it was indeed) that he was inspired from above, called him vatem: which kinde of men afterwarde framing their verses to lighter musick (as of musick be many kinds, some sadder, some lighter, some martiall, some heroical: and so diversely eke affect the mynds of men) found out lighter matter of Poesie also, some playing wyth love, some scorning at mens fashions, some powred out in pleasures, and so were called Poetes or makers.

Sence bereave) what the secrete working of Musick is in the myndes of men, aswell appeareth, hereby, that some of the auncient Philosophers, and those the moste wise, as Plato and Pythagoras held for opinion, that the mynd was made of a certaine harmonie and musicall nombers, for the great compassion and likeness of affection in thone and in the other as also by that memorable history of Alexander: to whom when as Timotheus the great Musitian playd the Phrygian melodie, it is said, that he was distraught with such unwonted fury, that streight way rysing from the table in great rage, he caused himselfe to be armed, as ready to goe to warre (for that musick is very war like:) And immediatly whenas the Musitian chaunged his stroke into the Lydian and Ionique harmony, he was so furr from warring, that he sat as styl, as if he had bene in matters of counsell. Such might is in musick. Wherefore Plato and Aristotle forbid the Arabian Melodie from children and youth. For that being altogither on the fyft and vii, tone, it is of great force to molifie and quench the kindly courage, which useth to burne in yong brests. So that it is not incredible which the Poete here sayth, that Musick can bereave the soule of sence.

The shepheard that) Orpheus: of whom is sayd, that by his excellent skil in Musick and Poetry, he recovered his wife Eurydice from hell.

Argus eyes) of Argus is before said, that Juno to him committed hir husband Jupiter his Paragon Iô, bicause he had an hundred eyes: but afterwarde Mercury wyth hys Musick lulling Argus aslepe, slew him and brought Iô away, whose eyes it is sayd that Juno for his eternall memory placed in her byrd the Peacocks tayle. For those coloured spots indeede resemble eyes.

Woundlesse armour) unwounded in warre, doe rust through long peace.

Display) A poeticall metaphore: whereof the meaning is, that if the Poet list showe his skill in matter of more dignitie, then is the homely Aeglogue, good occasion is him offered of higher veyne and more Heroicall argument, in the person of our most gratious soveraign, whom (as before) he calleth Elisa. Or if mater of knighthoode and chevalrie please him better, that there be many Noble and valiaunt men, that are both worthy of his payne in theyr deserved prayses, and also favourers of hys skil and faculty.

The worthy) he meaneth (as I guesse) the most honourable and renowmed the Erle of Leycester, whom by his cognisance (although the same be also proper to other) rather then by his name he bewrayeth, being not likely, that the names of noble princes be known to country clowne.

Slack) that is when thou chaungest thy verse from stately discourse, to matter of more pleasaunce and delight.

The Myllers) a kind of daunce.

Ring) company of daunsers.

The Romish Tityrus) wel knowen to be Virgile, who by Mecaenas means was brought into the favour of the Emperor Augustus, and by him moved to write in loftier kinde, then he erst had doen.

Whereon) in these three verses are the three severall workes of Virgile intended. For in teaching his flocks to feede, is meant his Aeglogues. In labouring of lands, is hys Bucoliques. In singing of wars and deadly dreade, is his divine Aeneis figured.

In derring doe) In manhoode and chevalrie.

For ever) He sheweth the cause, why Poetes were wont be had in such honour of noble men; that is, that by them their worthines and valour shold through theyr famous Posies be commended to al posterities. Wherfore it is sayd, that Achilles had never bene so famous, as he is, but for Homeres immortal verses. Which is the only advantage, which he had of Hector. And also that Alexander the great comming to his tombe in Sigeus, with naturall teares blessed him, that ever was his hap to be honoured with so excellent a Poets work: as so renowmed and ennobled onely by hys meanes. Which being declared in a most eloquent Oration of Tullies, is of Petrarch no lesse worthely sette forth in a sonet

> Giunto Alexandro a la famosa tomba
> Del fero Achille sospirando disse
> O fortunato che si chiara tromba. Trovasti &c.

And that such account hath bene alwayes made of Poetes, aswell sheweth this that the worthy Scipio in all his warres against Carthage and Numantia had evermore in his company, and that in a most familiar sort the good olde Poet Ennius: as also that Alexander destroying Thebes, when he was enformed that the famous Lyrick Poet Pindarus was borne in that citie, not onely commaunded streightly, that no man should upon payne of death do any violence to that house by fire or otherwise: but also specially spared most, and some highly rewarded, that were of hys kinne. So favoured he the only name of a Poete. Whych prayse otherwise was in the same man no lesse famous, that when he came to ransacking of king Darius coffers, whom he lately had overthrowen, he founde in a little coffer of silver the two bookes of Homers works, as layd up there for speciall jewells and richesse, which he taking thence, put one of them dayly in his bosome, and thother every night layde under his pillowe. Such honour have Poetes always found in the sight of princes and noble men. Which this author here very well sheweth, as els where more notably.

But after) he sheweth the cause of contempt of Poetry to be idlenesse and basenesse of mynd.

Pent) shut up in slouth, as in a coope or cage.

Tom Piper) An Ironicall Sarcasmus, spoken in derision of these rude wits, whych make more account of a ryming rybaud, then of skill grounded upon learning and judgment.

Ne brest) the meaner sort of men.

Her peecèd pineons) unperfect skil. Spoken wyth humble modestie.

As soote as Swanne) The comparison seemeth to be strange: for the swanne hath ever wonne small commendation for her swete singing: but it is sayd of the learned that the swan a little before hir death, singeth most pleasantly, as prophecying by a secrete instinct her neere destinie. As wel sayth the Poete elswhere in one of his sonetts.

The silver swanne doth sing before her dying day.
As shee that feeles the deepe delight that is in death &c.

Immortall mirrhour) Beauty, which is an excellent object of Poeticall spirites, as appeareth by the worthy Petrachs saying.

> Fiorir faceva il mio debile ingegno
> A la sua ombra, et crescer ne gli affanni.

A caytive corage) a base and abject minde.

For lofty love) I think this playing with the letter to be rather a fault then a figure, aswel in our English tongue, as it hath bene alwayes in the Latine, called Cacozelon.

A vacant) imitateth Mantuanes saying. vacuum curis divina cerebrum Poscit.

Lavish cups) Resembleth that comen verse Faecundi calices quem non fecere disertum.

O if my) He seemeth here to be ravished with a Poetical furie. For (if one rightly mark) the numbers rise so ful, and the verse groweth so big, that it seemeth he hath forgot the meanenesse of shepheards state and stile.

Wild Ivie) for it is dedicated to Bacchus and therefore it is sayd that the Maenades (that is Bacchus franticke priestes) used in theyr sacrifice to carry Thyrsos, which were pointed staves or Javelins, wrapped about with ivie.

In buskin) it was the maner of Poetes and plaiers in tragedies to were buskins, as also in Comedies to use stockes and light shoes. So that the buskin in Poetry is used for tragical matter, as is said in Virgile. Sola sophocleo tua carmina digna cothurno. And the like in Horace, Magnum loqui, nitique cothurno.

Queint) strange Bellona; the goddesse of battaile, that is Pallas, which may therefore wel be called queint for that (as Lucian saith) when Jupiter hir father was in traveile of her, he caused his sonne Vulcane with his axe to hew his head. Out of which leaped forth lustely a valiant damsell armed at all poyntes, whom seeing Vulcane so faire and comely, lightly leaping to her, proferred her some cortesie, which the Lady disdeigning, shaked her speare at him, and threatened his saucinesse. Therefore such straungenesse is well applyed to her.

Aequipage) order.   **Tydes**) seasons.

Charme) temper and order. For Charmes were wont to be made by verses as Ovid sayth.

Aut si carminibus.

from AMORETTI

Spenser's *Amoretti*, which according to tradition were written during his courtship of Elizabeth Boyle, who became his second wife, constitute one of the finer sonnet sequences of the Elizabethan age. They not only show an adroit use of many familiar Petrarchan conventions but are distinguished by a moral beauty and dignity arising from the poet's view of his beloved as a manifestation of the Platonic Idea of Beauty and Goodness.

1

Happy ye leaves when as those lilly hands,
Which hold my life in their dead doing might,
Shall handle you and hold in loves soft bands,
Lyke captives trembling at the victors sight.
And happy lines, on which with starry light,
Those lamping eyes will deigne sometimes to look
And reade the sorrowes of my dying spright,
Written with teares in harts close bleeding book.
And happy rymes bathed in the sacred brooke,
Of *Helicon* whence she derivèd is,   10
When ye behold that Angels blessèd looke,
My soules long lackèd foode, my heavens blis.
Leaves, lines, and rymes, seeke her to please alone,
Whom if ye please, I care for other none.

6

Be nought dismayd that her unmovèd mind
Doth still persist in her rebellious pride:
Such love not lyke to lusts of baser kynd,
The harder wonne, the firmer will abide.
The durefull Oake, whose sap is not yet dride,
Is long ere it conceive the kindling fyre:
But when it once doth burne, it doth divide
Great heat, and makes his flames to heaven aspire.
So hard it is to kindle new desire
In gentle brest that shall endure for ever: 10
Deepe is the wound, that dints the parts entire
With chast affects, that naught but death can sever.
Then thinke not long in taking litle paine,
To knit the knot, that ever shall remaine.

34

Lyke as a ship that through the Ocean wyde,
By conduct of some star doth make her way,
Whenas a storme hath dimd her trusty guyde
Out of her course doth wander far astray;
So I whose star, that wont with her bright ray
Me to direct, with cloudes is overcast,
Doe wander now in darkness and dismay,
Through hidden perils round about me plast.
Yet hope I well that when this storme is past
My Helice the lodestar of my lyfe   10
Will shine again, and looke on me at last,
With lovely light to cleare my cloudy grief,
Till then I wander carefull comfortlesse
In secret sorrow and sad pensivenesse.

37

What guyle is this, that those her golden tresses,
She doth attyre under a net of gold:
And with sly skill so cunningly them dresses,
That which is gold or heare, may scarse be told?
Is it that mens frayle eyes, which gaze too bold,
She may entangle in that golden snare:
And being caught may craftily enfold
Theyr weaker harts, which are not wel aware?
Take heed therefore, myne eyes, how ye doe stare
Henceforth too rashly on that guilefull net,   10
In which if ever ye entrappèd are,
Out of her bands ye by no meanes shall get.
Fondnesse it were for any being free,
To covet fetters, though they golden bee.

67

Lyke as a huntsman after weary chace,
Seeing the game from him escapt away,
Sits downe to rest him in some shady place,
With panting hounds beguilèd of their pray:
So after long pursuit and vaine assay,
When I all weary had the chace forsooke,
The gentle deare returnd the selfe-same way,
Thinking to quench her thirst at the next brooke.
There she beholding me with mylder looke,
Sought not to fly, but fearelesse still did bide: 10
Till I in hand her yet halfe trembling tooke,
And with her owne goodwill hir fyrmely tyde.
Strange thing me seemd to see a beast so wyld,
So goodly wonne with her owne will beguyld.

69

Men call you fayre, and you doe credit it,
For that your selfe ye dayly such doe see:
But the trew fayre, that is the gentle wit
And vertuous mind, is much more praysd of me
For all the rest, how ever fayre it be.

Shall turne to nought and loose that glorious hew:
But onely that is permanent and free
From frayle corruption, that doth flesh ensew.
That is true beautie: that doth argue you
To be divine and borne of heavenly seed: 10
Derived from that fayre Spirit, from whom al true
And perfect beauty did at first proceed.
He onely fayre, and what he fayre hath made,
All other fayre lyke flowres untymely fade.

EPITHALAMION

The *Epithalamion* is generally regarded as the most beautiful nuptial poem in the English language. Spenser not only uses brilliantly the conventions of the classical epithalamia, but achieves a highly individual quality through his remarkable fusion of passionate ardor and moral elevation. In this respect, the poem offers an illuminating contrast with Marlowe's *Hero and Leander*.

Ye learnèd sisters, which have oftentimes
Beene to me ayding, others to adorne:
Whom ye thought worthy of your gracefull rymes,
That even the greatest did not greatly scorne
To heare theyr names sung in your simple layes,
But joyèd in theyr prayse.
And when ye list your owne mishaps to mourne,
Which death, or love, or fortunes wreck did rayse,
Your string could soone to sadder tenour turne,
And teach the woods and waters to lament 10
Your dolefull dreriment.
Now lay those sorrowfull complaints aside,
And having all your heads with girland crownd,
Helpe me mine owne loves prayses to resound,
Ne let the same of any be envide:
So Orpheus did for his owne bride,
Sc I unto my selfe alone will sing,
The woods shall to me answer and my Eccho ring.

Early, before the worlds light giving lampe
His golden beame upon the hils doth spred, 20
Having disperst the nights unchearefull dampe,
Doe ye awake, and with fresh lusty hed,
Go to the bowre of my beloved love,
My truest turtle dove,
Bid her awake; for Hymen is awake,
And long since ready forth his maske to move,
With his bright Tead that flames with many a flake,
And many a bachelor to waite on him,
In theyr fresh garments trim.
Bid her awake therefore and soone her dight, 30
For lo the wishèd day is come at last,
That shall for al the paynes and sorrowes past,

Epithalamion. 11. **dreriment**, affliction. 27. **Tead**, a torch of whitethorn used in Roman bridal processions. 30. **dight**, adorn.

Pay to her usury of long delight:
And whylest she doth her dight,
Doe ye to her of joy and solace sing,
That all the woods may answer and your eccho ring.

Bring with you all the Nymphes that you can heare
Both of the rivers and the forrests greene:
And of the sea that neighbours to her neare,
Al with gay girlands goodly wel beseene. 40
And let them also with them bring in hand,
Another gay girland
For my fayre love of lillyes and of roses,
Bound truelove wize with a blew silke riband.
And let them make great store of bridale poses,
And let them eeke bring store of other flowers
To deck the bridale bowers.
And let the ground whereas her foot shall tread,
For feare the stones her tender foot should wrong
Be strewed with fragrant flowers all along, 50
And diapred lyke the discoloured mead.
Which done, doe at her chamber dore awayt,
For she will waken strayt,
The whiles doe ye this song unto her sing,
The woods shall to you answer and your Eccho ring.

Ye Nymphes of Mulla which with carefull heed,
The silver scaly trouts doe tend full well,
And greedy pikes which use therein to feed,
(Those trouts and pikes all others doo excell)
And ye likewise which keepe the rushy lake, 60
Where none doo fishes take,
Bynd up the locks the which hang scatterd light,
And in his waters which your mirrour make,
Behold your faces as the christall bright,
That when you come whereas my love doth lie,
No blemish she may spie.
And eke ye lightfoot mayds which keepe the deere,
That on the hoary mountayne use to towre,
And the wylde wolves which seeke them to devoure,
With your steele darts doo chace from comming neer, 70
Be also present heere,
To helpe to decke her and to help to sing,
That all the woods may answer and your eccho ring.

Wake, now my love, awake; for it is time,
The Rosy Morne long since left Tithones bed,
All ready to her silver coche to clyme,
And Phoebus gins to shew his glorious hed.
Hark how the cheerefull birds do chaunt theyr laies
And carroll of loves praise.
The merry Larke hir mattins sings aloft, 80
The thrush replyes, the Mavis descant playes,

51. **diapred**, diversified.

The Ouzell shrills, the Ruddock warbles soft,
So goodly all agree with sweet consent,
To this dayes merriment.
Ah my deere love why doe ye sleepe thus long,
When meeter were that ye should now awake,
T'awayt the comming of your joyous make,
And hearken to the birds lovelearnèd song,
The deawy leaves among.
For they of joy and pleasance to you sing,   90
That all the woods them answer and theyr eccho ring.

My love is now awake out of her dreame,
And her fayre eyes like stars that dimmèd were
With darksome cloud, now shew theyr goodly beams
More bright then Hesperus his head doth rere.
Come now ye damzels, daughters of delight,
Helpe quickly her to dight,
But first come ye fayre houres which were begot
In Joves sweet paradice, of Day and Night,
Which doe the seasons of the yeare allot,   100
And al that ever in this world is fayre
Doe make and still repayre.
And ye three handmayds of the Cyprian Queene,
The which doe still adorne her beauties pride,
Helpe to addorne my beautifullest bride:
And as ye her array, still throw betweene
Some graces to be seene,
And as ye use to Venus, to her sing,
The whiles the woods shal answer and your eccho ring.

Now is my love all ready forth to come,   110
Let all the virgins therefore well awayt,
And ye fresh boyes that tend upon her groome
Prepare your selves; for he is comming strayt.
Set all your things in seemely good aray
Fit for so joyfull day,
The joyfulst day that ever sunne did see.
Faire Sun, shew forth thy favourable ray,
And let thy lifull heat not fervent be
For feare of burning her sunshyny face,
Her beauty to disgrace.   120
O fayrest Phoebus, father of the Muse,
If ever I did honour thee aright,
Or sing the thing, that mote thy mind delight,
Doe not thy servants simple boone refuse,
But let this day, let this one day be myne,
Let all the rest be thine.
Then I thy soverayne prayses loud wil sing,
That all the woods shal answer and theyr eccho ring.

Harke how the Minstrels gin to shrill aloud
Their merry Musick that resounds from far,   130
The pipe, the tabor, and the trembling Croud,
That well agree withouten breach or jar.
But most of all the Damzels doe delite,
When they their tymbrels smyte,
And thereunto doe daunce and carrol sweet,
That all the sences they doe ravish quite,
The whyles the boyes run up and downe the street,
Crying aloud with strong confusèd noyce,
As if it were one voyce.
Hymen io Hymen, Hymen they do shout,   140
That even to the heavens theyr shouting shrill
Doth reach, and all the firmament doth fill,
To which the people standing all about,
As in approvance doe thereto applaud
And loud advaunce her laud,
And evermore they Hymen Hymen sing,
That al the woods them answer and theyr eccho ring.

Loe where she comes along with portly pace
Lyke Phoebe from her chamber of the East,
Arysing forth to run her mighty race,   150
Clad all in white, that seemes a virgin best.
So well it her beseemes that ye would weene
Some angell she had beene.
Her long loose yellow locks lyke golden wyre,
Sprinckled with perle, and perling flowres a tweene,
Doe lyke a golden mantle her attyre,
And being crownèd with a girland greene,
Seeme lyke some mayden Queene.
Her modest eyes abashèd to behold
So many gazers, as on her do stare,   160
Upon the lowly ground affixèd are.
Ne dare lift up her countenance too bold,
But blush to heare her prayses sung so loud,
So farre from being proud.
Nathlesse doe ye still loud her prayses sing.
That all the woods may answer and your eccho ring.

Tell me ye merchants daughters did ye see
So fayre a creature in your towne before,
So sweet, so lovely, and so mild as she,
Adornd with beautyes grace and vertues store,   170
Her goodly eyes lyke Saphyres shining bright,
Her forehead yvory white,
Her cheekes lyke apples which the sun hath rudded,
Her lips lyke cherryes charming men to byte,
Her brest like to a bowle of creame uncrudded,
Her paps lyke lyllies budded,
Her snowie necke lyke to a marble towre,

82. **Ruddock,** robin redbreast.   87. **make,** mate.
118. **lifull,** lifeful.
131. **Croud,** violin.   175. **uncrudded,** uncurdled

And all her body like a pallace fayre,
Ascending uppe with many a stately stayre,
To honours seat and chastities sweet bowre.   180
Why stand ye still ye virgins in amaze,
Upon her so to gaze,
Whiles ye forget your former lay to sing,
To which the woods did answer and your eccho ring.

But if ye saw that which no eyes can see,
The inward beauty of her lively spright,
Garnisht with heavenly guifts of high degree,
Much more then would ye wonder at that sight,
And stand astonisht lyke to those which red
Medusaes mazeful hed.   190
There dwels sweet love and constant chastity,
Unspotted fayth and comely womanhood,
Regard of honour and mild modesty,
There vertue raynes as Queene in royal throne,
And giveth lawes alone.
The which the base affections doe obay,
And yeeld theyr services unto her will,
Ne thought of thing uncomely ever may
Thereto approch to tempt her mind to ill.
Had ye once seene these her celestial threasures,   200
And unrevealèd pleasures,
Then would ye wonder and her prayses sing,
That all the woods should answer and your eccho ring.

Open the temple gates unto my love,
Open them wide that she may enter in,
And all the postes adorne as doth behove,
And all the pillours deck with girlands trim,
For to recyve this Saynt with honour dew,
That commeth in to you.
With trembling steps and humble reverence,   210
She commeth in, before th'almighties vew,
Of her ye virgins learne obedience,
When so ye come into those holy places,
To humble your proud faces:
Bring her up to th'high altar, that she may
The sacred ceremonies there partake,
The which do endlesse matrimony make,
And let the roring Organs loudly play
The praises of the Lord in lively notes,
The whiles with hollow throates   220
The Choristers the joyous Antheme sing,
That al the woods may answer and their eccho ring.

Behold whiles she before the altar stands
Hearing the holy priest that to her speakes
And blesseth her with his two happy hands,

   189. **red**, saw.

How the red roses flush up in her cheekes,
And the pure snow with goodly vermill stayne,
Like crimsin dyde in grayne,
That even th'Angels which continually,
About the sacred Altare doe remaine,   230
Forget their service and about her fly,
Ofte peeping in her face that seemes more fayre,
The more they on it stare.
But her sad eyes still fastened on the ground,
Are governèd with goodly modesty,
That suffers not one looke to glaunce awry,
Which may let in a little thought unsownd.
Why blush ye love to give to me your hand,
The pledge of all our band?
Sing ye sweet Angels, Alleluya sing,   240
That all the woods may answer and your eccho ring.

Now al is done; bring home the bride againe,
Bring home the triumph of our victory,
Bring home with you the glory of her gaine,
With joyance bring her and with jollity.
Never had man more joyfull day then this,
Whom heaven would heape with blis.
Make feast therefore now all this live long day,
This day for ever to me holy is,
Poure out the wine without restraint or stay,   250
Poure not by cups, but by the belly full,
Poure out to all that wull,
And sprinkle all the postes and wals with wine,
That they may sweat, and drunken be withall.
Crowne ye God Bacchus with a coronall,
And Hymen also crowne with wreathes of vine,
And let the Graces daunce untò the rest;
For they can doo it best:
The whiles the maydens doe theyr carroll sing,
To which the woods shall answer and theyr eccho ring.   260

Ring ye the bels, ye yong men of the towne,
And leave your wonted labours for this day:
This day is holy; doe ye write it downe,
That ye for ever it remember may.
This day the sunne is in his chiefest hight,
With Barnaby the bright,
From whence declining daily by degrees,
He somewhat loseth of his heat and light,
When once the Crab behind his back he sees.
But for this time it ill ordainèd was,   270
To chose the longest day in all the yeare,
And shortest night, when longest fitter weare:

   252. **wull**, will, wish.   266. **Barnaby the bright**, St. Barnabas' Day, the eleventh of June.   269. **Crab**, Cancer, sign of the zodiac.

Yet never day so long, but late would passe.
Ring ye the bels, to make it weare away,
And bonefiers make all day,
And daunce about them, and about them sing:
That all the woods may answer, and your eccho ring.

Ah when will this long weary day have end,
And lende me leave to come unto my love?
How slowly do the houres theyr numbers spend? 280
How slowly does sad Time his feathers move?
Hast thee O fayrest Planet to thy home
Within the Westerne fome:
Thy tyred steedes long since have need of rest.
Long though it be, at last I see it gloome,
And the bright evening star with golden creast
Appeare out of the East.
Fayre childe of beauty, glorious lampe of love
That all the host of heaven in rankes doost lead,
And guydest lovers through the nightès dread, 290
How chearefully thou lookest from above,
And seemst to laugh atweene thy twinkling light
As joying in the sight
Of these glad many which for joy doe sing,
That all the woods them answer and theyr eccho ring.

Now ceasse ye damsels your delights forepast;
Enough is it, that all the day was youres:
Now day is doen, and night is nighing fast:
Now bring the Bryde into the brydall boures.
Now night is come, now soone her disaray, 300
And in her bed her lay;
Lay her in lillies and in violets,
And silken courteins over her display,
And odourd sheetes, and Arras coverlets.
Behold how goodly my faire love does ly
In proud humility;
Like unto Maia, when as Jove her tooke,
In Tempe, lying on the flowry gras,
Twixt sleepe and wake, after she weary was,
With bathing in the Acidalian brooke. 310
Now it is night, ye damsels may be gon,
And leave my love alone,
And leave likewise your former lay to sing:
The woods no more shal answer, nor your eccho ring.

Now welcome night, thou night so long expected,
That long daies labour doest at last defray,
And all my cares, which cruell love collected,
Hast sumd in one, and cancellèd for aye:
Spread thy broad wing over my love and me,
That no man may us see, 320
And in thy sable mantle us enwrap,
From feare of perrill and foule horror free.
Let no false treason seeke us to entrap,
Nor any dread disquiet once annoy
The safety of our joy:
But let the night be calme and quietsome,
Without tempestuous storms or sad afray:
Lyke as when Jove with fayre Alcmena lay,
When he begot the great Tirynthian groome:
Or lyke as when he with thy selfe did lie, 330
And begot Majesty.
And let the mayds and yongmen cease to sing:
Ne let the woods them answer, nor theyr eccho ring.

Let no lamenting cryes, nor dolefull teares,
Be heard all night within nor yet without:
Ne let false whispers, breeding hidden feares,
Breake gentle sleepe with misconceivèd dout.
Let no deluding dreames, nor dreadful sights
Make sudden sad affrights;
Ne let housefyres, nor lightnings helpelesse harmes, 340
Ne let the Pouke, nor other evill sprights,
Ne let mischivous witches with theyr charmes,
Ne let hob Goblins, names whose sence we see not,
Fray us with things that be not.
Let not the shriech Oule, nor the Storke be heard:
Nor the night Raven that still deadly yels,
Nor damnèd ghosts cald up with mighty spels,
Nor griesly vultures make us once affeard:
Ne let th'unpleasant Quyre of Frogs still croking
Make us to wish theyr choking. 350
Let none of these theyr drery accents sing;
Ne let the woods them answer, nor theyr eccho ring.

But let stil Silence trew night watches keepe,
That sacred peace may in assurance rayne,
And tymely sleep, when it is tyme to sleepe,
May poure his limbs forth on your pleasant playne,
The whiles an hundred little wingèd loves,
Like divers fethered doves,
Shall fly and flutter round about your bed,
And in the secret darke, that none reproves, 360
Their prety stealthes shal worke, and snares shal spread
To filch away sweet snatches of delight,
Conceald through covert night.
Ye sonnes of Venus, play your sports at will,
For greedy pleasure, carelesse of your toyes,
Thinks more upon her paradise of joyes,

341. **the Pouke,** the fairy Robin Goodfellow, known also as Puck.

Then what ye do, al be it good or ill.
All night therefore attend your merry play,
For it will soone be day:
Now none doth hinder you, that say or sing, 370
Ne will the woods now answer, nor your Eccho ring.

Who is the same, which at my window peepes?
Or whose is that faire face, that shines so bright,
Is it not Cinthia, she that never sleepes,
But walkes about high heaven al the night?
O fayrest goddesse, do thou not envy
My love with me to spy:
For thou likewise didst love, though now unthought,
And for a fleece of woll, which privily,
The Latmian shephard once unto thee brought, 380
His pleasures with thee wrought.
Therefore to us be favourable now;
And sith of wemens labours thou hast charge,
And generation goodly dost enlarge,
Encline thy will t'effect our wishfull vow,
And the chast wombe informe with timely seed,
That may our comfort breed:
Till which we cease our hopefull hap to sing,
Ne let the woods us answere, nor our Eccho ring.

And thou great Juno, which with awful might 390
The lawes of wedlock still dost patronize,
And the religion of the faith first plight
With sacred rites hast taught to solemnize:
And eeke for comfort often callèd art
Of women in their smart,
Eternally bind thou this lovely band,
And all thy blessings unto us impart.
And thou glad Genius, in whose gentle hand,
The bridale bowre and geniall bed remaine,
Without blemish or staine, 400

380. **The Latmian shephard**, Endymion.

And the sweet pleasures of theyr loves delight
With secret ayde doest succour and supply,
Till they bring forth the fruitfull progeny,
Send us the timely fruit of this same night.
And thou fayre Hebe, and thou Hymen free,
Grant that it may so be.
Til which we cease your further prayse to sing,
Ne any woods shal answer, nor your Eccho ring.

And ye high heavens, the temple of the gods,
In which a thousand torches flaming bright 410
Doe burne, that to us wretched earthly clods,
In dreadful darknesse lend desirèd light;
And all ye powers which in the same remayne,
More then we men can fayne,
Poure out your blessing on us plentiously,
And happy influence upon us raine,
That we may raise a large posterity,
Which from the earth, which they may long possesse,
With lasting happinesse,
Up to your haughty pallaces may mount, 420
And for the guerdon of theyr glorious merit
May heavenly tabernacles there inherit,
Of blessed Saints for to increase the count.
So let us rest, sweet love, in hope of this,
And cease till then our tymely joyes to sing,
The woods no more us answer, nor our eccho ring.

Song made in lieu of many ornaments,
With which my love should duly have bene dect,
Which cutting off through hasty accidents,
Ye would not stay your dew time to expect, 430
But promist both to recompens,
Be unto her a goodly ornament,
And for short time an endlesse moniment.

from THE FAERIE QUEENE

Spenser planned *The Faerie Queene* both as a great tribute to his own monarch and as a philosophical and moral allegory setting forth, in Prince Arthur's quest for Gloriana, the ordeals and pitfalls that bestrew the path of a noble-minded character. The purpose of the poem, as Spenser himself expressed it, was "to fashion a gentleman or noble person in vertuous and gentle discipline."

Upon that conception, Spenser built his plot. In his original plan, *The Faerie Queene* was to contain twelve books, corresponding to what he called "the twelve moral virtues as Aristotle hath devised," and each book was to illustrate in allegorical fashion the exercise of a separate virtue. To prevent the poem from falling into twelve disconnected stories, however, Spenser conceived as his main plot and connecting links the adventures that befall Prince Arthur on his quest for the Faerie Queen. Thus, before the opening of the poem, Prince Arthur has seen Gloriana in a vision and, stricken by her beauty, has resolved to seek her in Faeryland. As it happens, each year the Faerie Queen holds in her court a great feast lasting twelve days; and on each day she sends forth a knight embodying a different virtue to aid some suppliant in distress. A separate book was to be devoted chiefly to the adventures of each knight, but in all of them, Prince Arthur, still searching for Gloriana, was to play some part so that in the end he would have gained experience in all that befitted a perfect character. Partly because of classical precedent, and partly because of his desire to make his description of Gloriana's court the climax of his poem, Spenser plunged immediately into the midst of his story, beginning with the adventures of his first knight.

Besides its general moral allegory (wherein the Red Cross Knight signifies Holiness; Una, Truth; Duessa, Falsehood; Archimago, Hypocrisy; and so on), *The Faerie Queene* often has a topical significance in that certain characters and situations suggest parallels in the actual world in which Spenser lived. Thus, Queen Elizabeth is portrayed not only in Gloriana, but also in Belphoebe, Una, and Britomart; Arthur is now Sidney, now Leicester; and Sir Calidore, at one time Sidney, at another Essex. By giving life to abstractions and idealizing real persons, Spenser achieves in *The Faerie Queene* a fusion of the real world and the mythological world of faery.

Book I, the Legend of Holiness, is the most carefully organized narrative in *The Faerie Queene*. As Spenser explained in his prefatory letter to Ralegh, the story began with the appearance at the court of Gloriana of a tall, clownish young man who obtained from the astonished Queen the granting of his request to achieve whatever adventure should befall during her annual feast. Shortly thereafter, when Una appeared with her dwarf—who kept charge of a warlike steed and full knightly regalia—and begged aid of the Queen in the liberation of her parents from a great dragon, the young rustic sprang up demanding this assignment. Notwithstanding doubts cast upon his abilities by both Una and the Queen, the youth gained his point, put on the armor, and after assuming the role of Christian knighthood, set off with Una to achieve his quest.

The actual narrative begins at this point and follows a logical pattern through climax and resolution to its denouement at the end. Upon the separation of hero and heroine in the second canto, two lines of action develop; but these are kept closely related, both through Una's search for the knight and through the evil contrivances practiced in common upon the two by their several enemies, as well as through the close relations maintained between those enemies. Moreover, as the following summary of the omitted cantos will show, Spenser tightens his plot still further by means of various repeated motifs. The theme of pride, for example, symbolized by Lucifera in the fourth canto, reappears climactically and in a more dangerous form in Orgoglio; while sorrow, portrayed by Sansjoy, deepens into the sinister embodiment of Despair.

In Canto II, the knight abandons Una because of a trick played upon him by Archimago and falls in with Duessa, who promptly leads him astray after he has despatched Sansfoy, the first of three evil brothers. Una pursues her way alone in Canto III, charms a ferocious lion, and then sets off with him in search of the knight, the lion performing occasional services in her defense. Presently Archimago, disguised as the knight, reappears on the scene intending to mislead Una; before fully accomplishing his purpose, however, he is mistakenly attacked by the vengeful Sansloy, who also slays the lion and makes Una his prisoner. Cantos IV and V take up again the story of the knight, whom Duessa leads to Lucifera's House of Pride. After seeing there the procession of the Seven Deadly Sins, the knight is challenged to a duel by the third brother, Sansjoy, who, though defeated in a fair field, is saved and resuscitated by the faithless Duessa. Sorely beset meanwhile by lecherous Sansloy, Una finds refuge in Canto VI with Satyrane and his creatures of the forest but there receives—again from Archimago—sad though false tidings of the death of her knight. Canto VII approaches the climax as the knight, on the one hand, falls into the power of the giant Orgoglio, whom Duessa now favors; while Una, on the other, meets Prince Arthur, learns of his quest for Gloriana, and enlists his aid in behalf of the knight. With all principals now massed together, the climax occurs in Canto VIII, when Arthur, at Una's instigation, rescues the knight from Orgoglio and strips the false habiliments from Duessa. Thereafter the resolution of the story proceeds, though delayed complications further stimulate the suspense: first, in Despair's tempting of the knight to suicide in Canto IX, and again in Duessa's letter in Canto XII. Having saved the knight from destroying himself, Una brings him in Canto X to the House of Holiness, where through repentance and self-discipline he gains enough courage and moral strength to defeat the dragon of evil. This task he finally accomplishes, after a prolonged battle, in Canto XI.

The stanzaic form in which *The Faerie Queene* is written, the form commonly called the Spenserian stanza, consists of eight lines of iambic pentameter and a final Alexandrine, rhyming *ababbcbcc*. Some critics have felt that the final Alexandrine produces so definite a pause at the end of each stanza that the form is inappropriate to a narrative poem. But Spenser's narrative is intentionally slow-paced, and the definite break between stanzas gives him ample opportunity for static pictorial and descriptive effects. On many occasions, moreover, he bridges the gap between stanzas by repeating the final line, by using the *c*-rhyme of one stanza as the *a*-rhyme of the next, and by other forms of linkage. The revival of this stanza in the eighteenth century and its superb use by Keats in "The Eve of St. Agnes" (see Volume Two, pages 326–30) illustrate the interest the Romantics took in great Renaissance writers whom the Neoclassicists had neglected.

BOOK I

Canto I

The Patron of true Holinesse,
Foule Errour doth defeate:
Hypocrisie him to entrappe,
Doth to his home entreate.

1

A Gentle Knight was pricking on the plaine,
  Y-cladd in mightie armes and silver shielde,
  Wherein old dints of deepe wounds did remaine,
  The cruell markes of many a bloudy fielde;
  Yet armes till that time did he never wield:
  His angry steede did chide his foming bitt,
  As much disdayning to the curbe to yield:
  Full jolly knight he seemd, and faire did sitt,
As one for knightly giusts and fierce encounters fitt.

2

But on his brest a bloudie Crosse he bore,   10
  The deare remembrance of his dying Lord,
  For whose sweete sake that glorious badge he wore,
  And dead as living ever him adored:
  Upon his shield the like was also scored,
  For soveraine hope, which in his helpe he had:
  Right faithfull true he was in deede and word,
  But of his cheere did seeme too solemne sad;
Yet nothing did he dread, but ever was ydrad.

3

Upon a great adventure he was bond,
  That greatest *Gloriana* to him gave,   20
  That greatest Glorious Queene of *Faerie* lond,
  To winne him worship, and her grace to have,
  Which of all earthly things he most did crave;
  And ever as he rode, his hart did earne
  To prove his puissance in battell brave
  Upon his foe, and his new force to learne;
Upon his foe, a Dragon horrible and stearne.

4

A lovely Ladie rode him faire beside,
  Upon a lowly Asse more white then snow,
  Yet she much whiter, but the same did hide   30
  Under a vele, that wimpled was full low,
  And over all a blacke stole she did throw,
  As one that inly mournd: so was she sad,
  And heavie sat upon her palfrey slow:
  Seemèd in heart some hidden care she had,
And by her in a line a milke white lambe she lad.

5

So pure and innocent, as that same lambe,
  She was in life and every vertuous lore,
  And by descent from Royall lynage came
  Of ancient Kings and Queenes, that had of yore   40
  Their sceptres stretcht from East to Westerne shore,
  And all the world in their subjection held;
  Till that infernall feend with foule uprore
  Forwasted all their land, and them expeld:
Whom to avenge, she had this Knight from far compeld.

6

Behind her farre away a Dwarfe did lag,
  That lasie seemd in being ever last,
  Or wearièd with bearing of her bag
  Of needments at his backe. Thus as they past,
  The day with cloudes was suddeine overcast,   50
  And angry Jove an hideous storme of raine
  Did poure into his Lemans lap so fast,
  That every wight to shrowd it did constrain,
And this faire couple eke to shroud themselves were fain.

1. **pricking**, riding, using spurs. 8. **jolly**, handsome. 9. **giusts**, jousts, tournaments. 15. **soveraine hope**, indicating his great hope. 17. **cheere**, countenance. 18. **ydrad**, dreaded, the past participle. 20. **Gloriana**, Queen Elizabeth. 24. **earne**, yearn. 27. **Dragon**, Sin. 28. **Ladie**, Una or Truth. 31. **wimpled**, folded, pleated. 44. **Forwasted**, ravished; the prefix "for-" is intensive. 45. **compeld**, summoned. 46. **Dwarfe**, Prudence. 52. **Lemans lap**, beloved's lap; that is, the earth. 53. **shrowd**, take cover.

7

Enforst to seeke some covert nigh at hand,
   A shadie grove not far away they spide,
   That promist ayde the tempest to withstand:
   Whose loftie trees yclad with sommers pride,
   Did spred so broad, that heavens light did hide,
   Not perceable with power of any starre: 60
   And all within were pathes and alleies wide,
   With footing worne, and leading inward farre:
Faire harbour that them seemes; so in they entred arre.

8

And foorth they passe, with pleasure forward led,
   Joying to heare the birdes sweete harmony,
   Which therein shrouded from the tempest dred,
   Seemd in their song to scorne the cruell sky.
   Much can they prayse the trees so straight and hy,
   The sayling Pine, the Cedar proud and tall,
   The vine-prop Elme, the Poplar never dry,   70
   The builder Oake, sole king of forests all,
The Aspine good for staves, the Cypresse funerall.

9

The Laurell, meed of mightie Conquerours
   And Poets sage, the Firre that weepeth still,
   The Willow worne of forlorne Paramours,
   The Eugh obedient to the benders will,
   The Birch for shaftes, the Sallow for the mill,
   The Mirrhe sweete bleeding in the bitter wound,
   The warlike Beech, the Ash for nothing ill,
   The fruitfull Olive, and the Platane round,   80
The carver Holme, the Maple seeldom inward sound.

10

Led with delight, they thus beguile the way,
   Untill the blustring storme is overblowne;
   When weening to returne, whence they did stray,
   They cannot finde that path, which first was showne,
   But wander too and fro in wayes unknowne,
   Furthest from end then, when they neerest weene,
   That makes them doubt, their wits be not their owne:
   So many pathes, so many turnings seene,
That which of them to take, in diverse doubt they been.   90

11

At last resolving forward still to fare,
   Till that some end they finde or in or out,
   That path they take, that beaten seemd most bare,
   And like to lead the labyrinth about;
   Which when by tract they hunted had through-out,
   At length it brought them to a hollow cave,
   Amid the thickest woods. The Champion stout
   Eftsoones dismounted from his courser brave,
And to the Dwarfe a while his needlesse spere he gave.

12

Be well aware, quoth then that Ladie milde,   100
   Least suddaine mischiefe ye too rash provoke:
   The danger hid, the place unknowne and wilde,
   Breedes dreadfull doubts: Oft fire is without smoke,
   And perill without show: therefore your stroke
   Sir knight with-hold, till further triall made.
   Ah Ladie (said he) shame were to revoke
   The forward footing for an hidden shade:
Vertue gives her selfe light, through darkenesse for to wade.

13

Yea but (quoth she) the perill of this place
   I better wot then you, though now too late   110
   To wish you backe returne with foule disgrace,
   Yet wisedome warnes, whilest foot is in the gate,
   To stay the steppe, ere forcèd to retrate.
   This is the wandring wood, this *Errours den*,
   A monster vile, whom God and man does hate:
   Therefore I read beware. Fly fly (quoth then
The fearefull Dwarfe:) this is no place for living men.

14

But full of fire and greedy hardiment,
   The youthfull knight could not for ought be staide,
   But forth unto the darksome hole he went,   120
   And lookèd in: his glistring armour made
   A litle glooming light, much like a shade,
   By which he saw the ugly monster plaine,
   Halfe like a serpent horribly displaide,
   But th'other halfe did womans shape retaine,
Most lothsom, filthie, foule, and full of vile disdaine.

---

76. **Eugh,** yew.   77. **Sallow,** broad-leaved willow.
80. **Platane,** plane tree.   81. **Holme,** evergreen oak.
84. **weening,** thinking.   88. **doubt,** fear.
94. **about,** out of.   98. **Eftsoones,** promptly, immediately.
112. **gate,** path.   116. **read,** advise.

15

And as she lay upon the durtie ground,
    Her huge long taile her den all overspred,
    Yet was in knots and many boughtes upwound,
    Pointed with mortall sting. Of her there bred   130
    A thousand yong ones, which she dayly fed,
    Sucking upon her poisonous dugs eachone
    Of sundry shapes, yet all ill favourèd:
    Soone as that uncouth light upon them shone,
Into her mouth they crept, and suddain all were gone.

16

Their dam upstart, out of her den effraide,
    And rushèd forth, hurling her hideous taile
    About her cursèd head, whose folds displaid
    Were stretcht now forth at length without entraile.
    She lookt about, and seeing one in mayle   140
    Armèd to point, sought backe to turne againe;
    For light she hated as the deadly bale,
    Ay wont in desert darknesse to remaine,
Where plaine none might see her, nor she see any plaine.

17

Which when the valiant Elfe perceived, he lept
    As Lyon fierce upon the flying pray,
    And with his trenchard blade her boldly kept
    From turning backe, and forcèd her to stay:
    Therewith enraged she loudly gan to bray,   149
    And turning fierce, her speckled taile advaunst,
    Threatning her angry sting, him to dismay:
    Who nought aghast, his mightie hand enhaunst:
The stroke down from her head unto her shoulder glaunst.

18

Much daunted with that dint, her sence was dazd,
    Yet kindling rage, her selfe she gathered round,
    And all attonce her beastly body raizd
    With doubled forces high above the ground:
    Tho wrapping up her wrethèd sterne arownd,
    Lept fierce upon his shield, and her huge traine
    All suddenly about his body wound,   160
    That hand or foot to stirre he strove in vaine:
God helpe the man so wrapt in *Errours* endlesse traine.

19

His Lady sad to see his sore constraint,
    Cride out, Now now Sir knight, shew what ye bee,
    Add faith unto your force, and be not faint:
    Strangle her, else she sure will strangle thee.
    That when he heard, in great perplexitie,
    His gall did grate for griefe and high disdaine,
    And knitting all his force got one hand free,
    Wherewith he grypt her gorge with so great paine,   170
That soone to loose her wicked bands did her constraine.

20

Therewith she spewd out of her filthy maw
    A floud of poyson horrible and blacke,
    Full of great lumpes of flesh and gobbets raw,
    Which stunck so vildly, that it forst him slacke
    His grasping hold, and from her turne him backe:
    Her vomit full of bookes and papers was,
    With loathly frogs and toades, which eyes did lacke,
    And creeping sought way in the weedy gras:
Her filthy parbreake all the place defilèd has.   180

21

As when old father *Nilus* gins to swell
    With timely pride above the *Aegyptian* vale,
    His fattie waves do fertile slime outwell,
    And overflow each plaine and lowly dale:
    But when his later spring gins to avale,
    Huge heapes of mudd he leaves, wherein there breed
    Ten thousand kindes of creatures, partly male
    And partly female of his fruitfull seed;
Such ugly monstrous shapes elswhere may no man reed.

22

The same so sore annoyèd has the knight,   190
    That welnigh chokèd with the deadly stinke,
    His forces faile, ne can no longer fight.
    Whose corage when the feend perceived to shrinke,
    She pourèd forth out of her hellish sinke
    Her fruitfull cursèd spawne of serpents small,
    Deformèd monsters, fowle, and blacke as inke,
    Which swarming all about his legs did crall,
And him encombred sore, but could not hurt at all.

---

129. **boughtes,** coils, folds.   133. **ill favourèd,** of ugly face.   139. **entraile,** coiling.   142. **bale,** destruction. 143. **Ay wont,** always accustomed.   145. **Elfe.** The Red Cross Knight was son of an elf.   152. **enhaunst,** raised, lifted up.

168. **gall did grate for griefe,** anger was stirred through pain.   177. **vomit full of bookes and papers,** anti-Protestant writings attacking Queen Elizabeth and the Church of England.   180. **parbreake,** vomit.   185. **avale,** moderate, abate.   189. **reed,** see.

23

As gentle Shepheard in sweete even-tide,
   When ruddy *Phoebus* gins to welke in west,   200
   High on an hill, his flocke to vewen wide,
   Markes which do byte their hasty supper best;
   A cloud of combrous gnattes do him molest,
   All striving to infixe their feeble stings,
   That from their noyance he no where can rest,
   But with his clownish hands their tender wings
He brusheth oft, and oft doth mar their murmurings.

24

Thus ill bestedd, and fearefull more of shame,
   Then of the certaine perill he stood in,
   Halfe furious unto his foe he came,   210
   Resolved in minde all suddenly to win,
   Or soone to lose, before he once would lin;
   And strooke at her with more then manly force,
   That from her body full of filthie sin
   He raft her hatefull head without remorse;
A streame of cole black bloud forth gushèd from her corse.

25

Her scattred brood, soone as their Parent deare
   They saw so rudely falling to the ground,
   Groning full deadly, all with troublous feare,
   Gathred themselves about her body round,   220
   Weening their wonted entrance to have found
   At her wide mouth: but being there withstood
   They flockèd all about her bleeding wound,
   And suckèd up their dying mothers blood,
Making her death their life, and eke her hurt their good.

26

That detestable sight him much amazde,
   To see th'unkindly Impes of heaven accurst,
   Devoure their dam; on whom while so he gazd,
   Having all satisfide their bloudy thurst,   229
   Their bellies swolne he saw with fulnesse burst,
   And bowels gushing forth: well worthy end
   Of such as drunke her life, the which them nurst;
   Now needeth him no lenger labour spend,
His foes have slaine themselves, with whom he should contend.

27

His Ladie seeing all, that chaunst, from farre
   Approcht in hast to greet his victorie,
   And said, Faire knight, borne under happy starre,
   Who see your vanquisht foes before you lye:
   Well worthy be you of that Armorie,
   Wherein ye have great glory wonne this day,   240
   And prooved your strength on a strong enimie,
   Your first adventure: many such I pray,
And henceforth ever wish, that like succeed it may.

28

Then mounted he upon his Steede againe,
   And with the Lady backward sought to wend;
   That path he kept, which beaten was most plaine,
   Ne ever would to any by-way bend,
   But still did follow one unto the end,
   The which at last out of the wood them brought.
   So forward on his way (with God to frend)   250
   He passèd forth, and new adventure sought;
Long way he travellèd, before he heard of ought.

29

At length they chaunst to meet upon the way
   An agèd Sire, in long blacke weedes yclad,
   His feete all bare, his beard all hoarie gray,
   And by his belt his booke he hanging had;
   Sober he seemde, and very sagely sad,
   And to the ground his eyes were lowly bent,
   Simple in shew, and voyde of malice bad,
   And all the way he prayèd, as he went,   260
And often knockt his brest, as one that did repent.

30

He faire the knight saluted, louting low,
   Who faire him quited, as that courteous was:
   And after askèd him, if he did know
   Of straunge adventures, which abroad did pas.
   Ah my deare Sonne (quoth he) how should, alas,
   Silly old man, that lives in hidden cell,
   Bidding his beades all day for his trespas,
   Tydings of warre and worldly trouble tell?   269
With holy father sits not with such things to mell.

31

But if of daunger which hereby doth dwell,
   And homebred evill ye desire to heare,
   Of a straunge man I can you tidings tell,
   That wasteth all this countrey farre and neare.
   Of such (said he) I chiefly do inquere,
   And shall you well reward to shew the place,
   In which that wicked wight his dayes doth weare:

---

200. **welke**, wane.   208. **bestedd**, placed.   212. **lin**, cease, stop.   215. **raft**, took away.   227. **unkindly**, unnatural.

239. **Armorie**, a Christian's armor.   254. **Sire**, Archimago, playing the part of Hypocrisy.   262. **louting**, bending.   267. **Silly**, simple.   268. **Bidding**, telling.   270. **sits not**, is not fitting. **mell**, meddle.

  For to all knighthood it is foule disgrace,
  That such a cursèd creature lives so long a space.

32

Far hence (quoth he) in wastfull wildernesse 280
 His dwelling is, by which no living wight
 May ever passe, but thorough great distresse.
 Now (sayd the Lady) draweth toward night,
 And well I wote, that of your later fight
 Ye all forwearied be: for what so strong,
 But wanting rest will also want of might?
 The Sunne that measures heaven all day long,
At night doth baite his steedes the *Ocean* waves emong.

33

Then with the Sunne take Sir, your timely rest,
 And with new day new worke at once begin: 290
 Untroubled night they say gives counsell best.
 Right well Sir knight ye have advisèd bin,
 (Quoth then that agèd man;) the way to win
 Is wisely to advise: now day is spent;
 Therefore with me ye may take up your In
 For this same night. The knight was well content:
So with that godly father to his home they went.

34

A little lowly Hermitage it was,
 Downe in a dale, hard by a forests side,
 Far from resort of people, that did pas 300
 In travell to and froe: a little wyde
 There was an holy Chappell edifyde,
 Wherein the Hermite dewly wont to say
 His holy things each morne and eventyde:
 Thereby a Christall streame did gently play,
Which from a sacred fountaine wellèd forth alway.

35

Arrivèd there, the little house they fill,
 Ne looke for entertainement, where none was:
 Rest is their feast, and all things at their will;
 The noblest mind the best contentment has. 310
 With faire discourse the evening so they pas:
 For that old man of pleasing wordes had store,
 And well could file his tongue as smooth as glas;
 He told of Saintes and Popes, and evermore
He strowd an *Ave-Mary* after and before.

36

The drouping Night thus creepeth on them fast,
 And the sad humour loading their eye liddes,
 As messenger of *Morpheus* on them cast
 Sweet slombring deaw, the which to sleepe them biddes.
 Unto their lodgings then his guestes he riddes: 320
 Where when all drownd in deadly sleepe he findes,
 He to his study goes, and there amiddes
 His Magick bookes and artes of sundry kindes,
He seekes out mighty charmes, to trouble sleepy mindes.

37

Then choosing out few wordes most horrible,
 (Let none them read) thereof did verses frame,
 With which and other spelles like terrible,
 He bad awake blacke *Plutoes* griesly Dame,
 And cursèd heaven, and spake reprochfull shame
 Of highest God, the Lord of life and light; 330
 A bold bad man, that dared to call by name
 Great *Gorgon*, Prince of darknesse and dead night,
At which *Cocytus* quakes, and *Styx* is put to flight.

38

And forth he cald out of deepe darknesse dred
 Legions of Sprights, the which like little flyes
 Fluttring about his ever damnèd hed,
 A-waite whereto their service he applyes,
 To aide his friends, or fray his enimies:
 Of those he chose out two, the falsest twoo,
 And fittest for to forge true-seeming lyes; 340
 The one of them he gave a message too,
The other by him selfe staide other worke to doo.

39

He making speedy way through spersèd ayre,
 And through the world of waters wide and deepe,
 To *Morpheus* house doth hastily repaire.
 Amid the bowels of the earth full steepe,
 And low, where dawning day doth never peepe,
 His dwelling is; there *Tethys* his wet bed
 Doth ever wash, and *Cynthia* still doth steepe
 In silver deaw his ever-drouping hed, 350
Whiles sad Night over him her mantle black doth spred.

40

Whose double gates he findeth lockèd fast,
 The one faire framed of burnisht Yvory,

---

288. baite, refresh.   **295. In,** lodging.   **301. wyde,** apart, a short distance away.   **302. edifyde,** built.
317. sad humour, heavy dampness.
320. riddes, dismisses.   **328. Dame,** Proserpine.
332. Gorgon, Demogorgon, the demon magician of the underworld, whose name alone was terrifying to all.   **333. Cocytus . . . Styx,** rivers in Hades.   **338. fray,** frighten.
343. spersèd, dispersed.   **348. Tethys,** the ocean.
349. Cynthia, the moon.

The other all with silver overcast;
And wakefull dogges before them farre do lye,
Watching to banish Care their enimy,
Who oft is wont to trouble gentle Sleepe.
By them the Sprite doth passe in quietly,
And unto *Morpheus* comes, whom drownèd deepe
In drowsie fit he findes: of nothing he takes keepe.

41

And more, to lulle him in his slumber soft,   361
   A trickling streame from high rocke tumbling downe
   And ever-drizling raine upon the loft,
   Mixt with a murmuring winde, much like the sowne
   Of swarming Bees, did cast him in a swowne:
   No other noyse, nor peoples troublous cryes,
   As still are wont t' annoy the wallèd towne,
   Might there be heard: but carelesse Quiet lyes,
Wrapt in eternall silence farre from enemyes.

42

The messenger approching to him spake,   370
   But his wast wordes returnd to him in vaine:
   So sound he slept, that nought mought him awake.
   Then rudely he him thrust, and pusht with paine,
   Whereat he gan to stretch: but he againe
   Shooke him so hard, that forcèd him to speake.
   As one then in a dreame, whose dryer braine
   Is tost with troubled sights and fancies weake,
He mumbled soft, but would not all his silence breake.

43

The Sprite then gan more boldly him to wake,
   And threatned unto him the dreaded name   380
   Of *Hecate:* whereat he gan to quake,
   And lifting up his lumpish head, with blame
   Halfe angry askèd him, for what he came.
   Hither (quoth he) me *Archimago* sent,
   He that the stubborne Sprites can wisely tame,
   He bids thee to him send for his intent
A fit false dreame, that can delude the sleepers sent.

44

The God obayde, and calling forth straight way
   A diverse dreame out of his prison darke,
   Delivered it to him, and downe did lay   390
   His heavie head, devoide of carefull carke,

Whose sences all were straight benumbd and starke.
He backe returning by the Yvorie dore,
Remounted up as light as chearefull Larke,
And on his litle winges the dreame he bore
In hast unto his Lord, where he him left afore.

45

Who all this while with charmes and hidden artes,
   Had made a Lady of that other Spright,
   And framed of liquid ayre her tender partes
   So lively, and so like in all mens sight,   400
   That weaker sence it could have ravisht quight:
   The maker selfe for all his wondrous witt,
   Was nigh beguilèd with so goodly sight:
   Her all in white he clad, and over it
Cast a blacke stole, most like to seeme for *Una* fit.

46

Now when that ydle dreame was to him brought,
   Unto that Elfin knight he bad him fly,
   Where he slept soundly void of evill thought,
   And with false shewes abuse his fantasy,
   In sort as he him schoolèd privily: 410
   And that new creature borne without her dew,
   Full of the makers guile, with usage sly
   He taught to imitate that Lady trew,
Whose semblance she did carrie under feignèd hew.

47

Thus well instructed, to their worke they hast,
   And comming where the knight in slomber lay,
   The one upon his hardy head him plast,
   And made him dreame of loves and lustfull play,
   That nigh his manly hart did melt away,
   Bathèd in wanton blis and wicked joy: 420
   Then seemèd him his Lady by him lay,
   And to him playnd, how that false wingèd boy
Her chast hart had subdewd, to learne Dame pleasures toy.

48

And she her selfe of beautie soveraigne Queene,
   Faire *Venus* seemde unto his bed to bring
   Her, whom he waking evermore did weene
   To be the chastest flowre, that ay did spring
   On earthly braunch, the daughter of a king,
   Now a loose Leman to vile service bound:
   And eke the *Graces* seemèd all to sing,   430
   Hymen Iö Hymen, dauncing all around,
Whilst freshest *Flora* her with Ivie girlond crownd.

360. **keepe,** heed.   363. **loft,** upper floor.   376. **dryer braine.** A dry brain was thought to be more active and stronger than a moist one.   381. **Hecate,** underworld goddess of witchcraft.   382. **lumpish,** heavy.   387. **sent,** sense.   389. **diverse,** misleading.   391. **carke,** worry.

410. **In sort as,** in the way that.   411. **dew,** due, that is, unnaturally.   422. **wingèd boy,** Cupid.

49

In this great passion of unwonted lust,
   Or wonted feare of doing ought amis,
   He started up, as seeming to mistrust
   Some secret ill, or hidden foe of his:
   Lo there before his face his Lady is,
   Under blake stole hyding her bayted hooke,
   And as halfe blushing offred him to kis,
   With gentle blandishment and lovely looke,   440
Most like that virgin true, which for her knight him took.

50

All cleane dismayd to see so uncouth sight,
   And halfe enragèd at her shamelesse guise,
   He thought have slaine her in his fierce despight:
   But hasty heat tempring with sufferance wise,
   He stayde his hand, and gan himselfe advise
   To prove his sense, and tempt her faignèd truth.
   Wringing her hands in wemens pitteous wise,
   Tho can she weepe, to stirre up gentle ruth,   449
Both for her noble bloud, and for her tender youth.

51

And said, Ah Sir, my liege Lord and my love,
   Shall I accuse the hidden cruell fate,
   And mightie causes wrought in heaven above,
   Or the blind God, that doth me thus amate,
   For hopèd love to winne me certaine hate?
   Yet thus perforce he bids me do, or die.
   Die is my dew: yet rew my wretched state
   You, whom my hard avenging destinie
Hath made judge of my life or death indifferently.

52

Your owne deare sake forst me at first to leave   460
   My Fathers kingdome, There she stopt with teares;
   Her swollen hart her speach seemd to bereave,
   And then againe begun, My weaker yeares
   Captived to fortune and frayle worldly feares,
   Fly to your faith for succour and sure ayde:
   Let me not dye in languor and long teares.
   Why Dame (quoth he) what hath ye thus dismayd?
What frayes ye, that were wont to comfort me affrayd?

53

Love of your selfe, she said, and deare constraint
   Lets me not sleepe, but wast the wearie night   470
   In secret anguish and unpittied plaint,
   Whiles you in carelesse sleepe are drownèd quight.
   Her doubtfull words made that redoubted knight
   Suspect her truth: yet since no untruth he knew,
   Her fawning love with foule disdainefull spight
   He would not shend, but said, Deare dame I rew,
That for my sake unknowne such griefe unto you grew.

54

Assure your selfe, it fell not all to ground;
   For all so deare as life is to my hart,   479
   I deeme your love, and hold me to you bound;
   Ne let vaine feares procure your needlesse smart,
   Where cause is none, but to your rest depart.
   Not all content, yet seemd she to appease
   Her mournefull plaintes, beguilèd of her art,
   And fed with words, that could not chuse but please,
So slyding softly forth, she turnd as to her ease.

55

Long after lay he musing at her mood,
   Much grieved to thinke that gentle Dame so light,
   For whose defence he was to shed his blood.
   At last dull wearinesse of former fight   490
   Having yrockt a sleepe his irkesome spright,
   That troublous dreame gan freshly tosse his braine,
   With bowres, and beds, and Ladies deare delight:
   But when he saw his labour all was vaine,
With that misformèd spright he backe returnd againe.

Canto XI

The knight with that old Dragon fights
two dayes incessantly:
The third him overthrowes, and gayns
most glorious victory.

1

High time now gan it wex for *Una* faire,
   To thinke of those her captive Parents deare,
   And their forwasted kingdome to repaire:
   Whereto whenas they now approchèd neare,
   With hartie words her knight she gan to cheare,
   And in her modest manner thus bespake;
   Deare knight, as deare, as ever knight was deare,

---

449. **Tho can**, then did. **ruth**, pity.   454. **amate**, discourage.   469. **constraint**, necessity.   476. **shend**, reproach, reject.   483. **appease**, cease.
1. **wex**, waxed, grew.

1

That all these sorrowes suffer for my sake,
High heaven behold the tedious toyle, ye for me take.

2

Now are we come unto my native soyle,   10
   And to the place, where all our perils dwell;
   Here haunts that feend, and does his dayly spoyle,
   Therefore henceforth be at your keeping well,
   And ever ready for your foeman fell.
   The sparke of noble courage now awake,
   And strive your excellent selfe to excell;
   That shall ye evermore renowmèd make,
Above all knights on earth, that batteill undertake.

3

And pointing forth, lo yonder is (said she)
   The brasen towre in which my parents deare   20
   For dread of that huge feend emprisond be,
   Whom I from far see on the walles appeare,
   Whose sight my feeble soule doth greatly cheare:
   And on the top of all I do espye
   The watchman wayting tydings glad to heare,
   That O my parents might I happily
Unto you bring, to ease you of your misery.

4

With that they heard a roaring hideous sound,
   That all the ayre with terrour fillèd wide,   29
   And seemd uneath to shake the stedfast ground.
   Eftsoones that dreadfull Dragon they espide,
   Where stretcht he lay upon the sunny side
   Of a great hill, himselfe like a great hill.
   But all so soone, as he from far descride
   Those glistring armes, that heaven with light did fill,
He rousd himselfe full blith, and hastned them untill.

5

Then bad the knight his Lady yede aloofe,
   And to an hill her selfe withdraw aside,
   From whence she might behold that battailles proof
   And eke be safe from daunger far descryde: 40
   She him obayd, and turnd a little wyde.
   Now O thou sacred Muse, most learnèd Dame,
   Faire ympe of *Phoebus*, and his agèd bride,
   The Nourse of time, and everlasting fame,
That warlike hands ennoblest with immortall name;

6

O gently come into my feeble brest,
   Come gently, but not with that mighty rage,
   Wherewith the martiall troupes thou doest infest,
   And harts of great Heroès doest enrage,   49
   That nought their kindled courage may aswage,
   Soone as thy dreadfull trompe begins to sownd;
   The God of warre with his fiers equipage
   Thou doest awake, sleepe never he so sownd,
And scarèd nations doest with horrour sterne astownd.

7

Faire Goddesse lay that furious fit aside,
   Till I of warres and bloudy *Mars* do sing,
   And Briton fields with Sarazin bloud bedyde,
   Twixt that great faery Queene and Paynim king,
   That with their horrour heaven and earth did ring,
   A worke of labour long, and endlesse prayse: 60
   But now a while let downe that haughtie string,
   And to my tunes thy second tenor rayse,
That I this man of God his godly armes may blaze.

8

By this the dreadfull Beast drew nigh to hand,
   Halfe flying, and halfe footing in his hast,
   That with his largenesse measurèd much land,
   And made wide shadow under his huge wast;
   As mountaine doth the valley overcast.
   Approching nigh, he rearèd high afore
   His body monstrous, horrible, and vast,   70
   Which to increase his wondrous greatnesse more,
Was swolne with wrath, and poyson, and with bloudy gore.

9

And over, all with brasen scales was armd,
   Like plated coate of steele, so couchèd neare,
   That nought mote perce, ne might his corse be harmd
   With dint of sword, nor push of pointed speare;
   Which as an Eagle, seeing pray appeare,
   His aëry plumes doth rouze, full rudely dight,
   So shakèd he, that horrour was to heare,
   For as the clashing of an Armour bright,   80
Such noyse his rouzèd scales did send unto the knight.

---

13. be . . . keeping well, be well on your guard. **30. uneath**, almost. **37. yede**, go. **42. Muse**, Clio, the Muse of history. **43. agèd bride**, Mnemosyne, or Memory. **52. God of warre**, Mars. **55. fit**, strain of music. **58. Twixt . . . king**, a reference to an incident supposed to take place in one of the later (unwritten) books. **63. blaze**, praise. **74. so couchèd neare**, so closely interlocked. **78. rouze**, ruffle.

10

His flaggy wings when forth he did display,
   Were like two sayles, in which the hollow wynd
   Is gathered full, and worketh speedy way:
   And eke the pennes, that did his pineons bynd,
   Were like mayne-yards, with flying canvas lynd,
   With which whenas him list the ayre to beat,
   And there by force unwonted passage find,
   The cloudes before him fled for terrour great,
And all the heavens stood still amazèd with his threat.   90

11

His huge long tayle wound up in hundred foldes,
   Does overspred his long bras-scaly backe,
   Whose wreathèd boughts when ever he unfoldes,
   And thicke entangled knots adown does slacke,
   Bespotted as with shields of red and blacke,
   It sweepeth all the land behind him farre,
   And of three furlongs does but litle lacke;
   And at the point two stings in-fixèd arre,
Both deadly sharpe, that sharpest steele exceeden farre.

12

But stings and sharpest steele did far exceed   100
   The sharpnesse of his cruell rending clawes;
   Dead was it sure, as sure as death in deed,
   What ever thing does touch his ravenous pawes,
   Or what within his reach he ever drawes.
   But his most hideous head my toung to tell
   Does tremble: for his deepe devouring jawes
   Wide gapèd, like the griesly mouth of hell,
Through which into his darke abisse all ravin fell.

13

And that more wondrous was, in either jaw
   Threeranckes of yron teeth enraungèd were,   110
   In which yet trickling bloud and gobbets raw
   Of late devourèd bodies did appeare,
   That sight thereof bred cold congealèd feare:
   Which to increase, and all atonce to kill,
   A cloud of smoothering smoke and sulphur seare
   Out of his stinking gorge forth steemèd still,
That all the ayre about with smoke and stench did fill.

14

His blazing eyes, like two bright shining shields,
   Did burne with wrath, and sparkled living fyre;
   As two broad Beacons, set in open fields,   120
   Send forth their flames farre off to every shyre,
   And warning give, that enemies conspyre,
   With fire and sword the region to invade;
   So flamed his eyne with rage and rancorous yre:
   But farre within, as in a hollow glade,
Those glaring lampes were set, that made a dreadfull shade.

15

So dreadfully he towards him did pas,
   Forelifting up aloft his speckled brest,
   And often bounding on the brusèd gras,
   As for great joyance of his newcome guest.   130
   Eftsoones he gan advance his haughtie crest,
   As chauffèd Bore his bristles doth upreare,
   And shoke his scales to battell readie drest;
   That made the *Redcrosse* knight nigh quake for feare,
As bidding bold defiance to his foeman neare.

16

The knight gan fairely couch his steadie speare,
   And fiercely ran at him with rigorous might:
   The pointed steele arriving rudely theare,
   His harder hide would neither perce, nor bight,
   But glauncing by forth passèd forward right;   140
   Yet sore amovèd with so puissant push,
   The wrathfull beast about him turnèd light,
   And him so rudely passing by, did brush
With his long tayle, that horse and man to ground did rush.

17

Both horse and man up lightly rose againe,
   And fresh encounter towards him addrest:
   But th' idle stroke yet backe recoyld in vaine,
   And found no place his deadly point to rest.
   Exceeding rage enflamed the furious beast,
   To be avengèd of so great despight;   150
   For never felt his imperceable brest
   So wondrous force, from hand of living wight;
Yet had he proved the powre of many a puissant knight.

18

Then with his waving wings displayèd wyde,
   Himselfe up high he lifted from the ground,
   And with strong flight did forcibly divide
   The yielding aire, which nigh too feeble found
   Her flitting partes, and element unsound,
   To beare so great a weight: he cutting way   159
   With his broad sayles, about him soarèd round:
   At last low stouping with unweldie sway,
Snatcht up both horse and man, to beare them quite away.

85. **pennes,** feathers.   93. **boughts,** coils.

132. **chauffèd,** irritated.

19

Long he them bore above the subject plaine,
  So farre as Ewghen bow a shaft may send,
  Till struggling strong did him at last constraine,
  To let them downe before his flightès end:
  As hagard hauke presuming to contend
  With hardie fowle, above his hable might,
  His wearie pounces all in vaine doth spend,
  To trusse the pray too heavie for his flight;   170
Which comming downe to ground, does free it selfe
  by fight.

20

He so disseizèd of his gryping grosse,
  The knight his thrillant speare againe assayd
  In his bras-plated body to embosse,
  And three mens strength unto the stroke he layd;
  Wherewith the stiffe beame quakèd, as affrayd,
  And glauncing from his scaly necke, did glyde
  Close under his left wing, then broad displayd.
  The percing steele there wrought a wound full
    wyde,
That with the uncouth smart the Monster lowdly
  cryde.   180

21

He cryde, as raging seas are wont to rore,
  When wintry storme his wrathfull wreck does
    threat,
  The rolling billowes beat the ragged shore,
  As they the earth would shoulder from her seat,
  And greedie gulfe does gape, as he would eat
  His neighbour element in his revenge:
  Then gin the blustring brethren boldly threat,
  To move the world from off his stedfast henge,
And boystrous battell make, each other to avenge.

22

The steely head stucke fast still in his flesh,   190
  Till with his cruell clawes he snatcht the wood,
  And quite a sunder broke. Forth flowèd fresh
  A gushing river of blacke goarie blood,
  That drownèd all the land, whereon he stood;
  The streame thereof would drive a water-mill.
  Trebly augmented was his furious mood
  With bitter sense of his deepe rooted ill,
That flames of fire he threw forth from his large
  nosethrill.

23

His hideous tayle then hurlèd he about,
  And therewith all enwrapt the nimble thyes   200
  Of his froth-fomy steed, whose courage stout
  Striving to loose the knot, that fast him tyes,
  Himselfe in streighter bandes too rash implyes,
  That to the ground he is perforce constraynd
  To throw his rider: who can quickly ryse
  From off the earth, with durty bloud distaynd,
For that reprochfull fall right fowly he disdaynd.

24

And fiercely tooke his trenchand blade in hand,
  With which he stroke so furious and so fell,
  That nothing seemd the puissance could with-
    stand: 210
  Upon his crest the hardned yron fell,
  But his more hardned crest was armd so well,
  That deeper dint therein it would not make;
  Yet so extremely did the buffe him quell,
  That from thenceforth he shund the like to take,
But when he saw them come, he did them still for-
  sake.

25

The knight was wrath to see his stroke beguyld,
  And smote againe with more outrageous might;
  But backe againe the sparckling steele recoyld,
  And left not any marke, where it did light;   220
  As if in Adamant rocke it had bene pight.
  The beast impatient of his smarting wound,
  And of so fierce and forcible despight,
  Thought with his wings to stye above the ground;
But his late wounded wing unserviceable found.

26

Then full of griefe and anguish vehement,
  He lowdly brayd, that like was never heard,
  And from his wide devouring oven sent
  A flake of fire, that flashing in his beard,
  Him all amazd, and almost made affeard: 230
  The scorching flame sore swingèd all his face,
  And through his armour all his bodie seard,
  That he could not endure so cruell cace,
But thought his armes to leave, and helmet to
  unlace.

27

Not that great Champion of the antique world,
  Whom famous Poetes verse so much doth vaunt,

---

163. **subject plaine**, ground lying below.   164. **Ewghen**, yew: pronounce "yewen."   167. **hagard**, wild.   168. **hable might**, beyond his power.   169. **pounces**, claws.   170. **trusse**, pierce so as to hold a thing or grip it.   172. **disseizèd**, deprived.   **gryping grosse**, rough, heavy, or awkward grasp.   173. **thrillant**, piercing.   180. **uncouth**, unusual.   187. **brethren**, the winds.

203. **implyes**, enfolds.   205. **can**, "gan," did.   206. **distaynd**, stained.   214. **buffe**, blow.   216. **still**, ever.   217. **beguyld**, foiled.   221. **pight**, pitched.   224. **stye**, ascend.   231. **swingèd**, singed.   235. **Champion**, Hercules.

And hath for twelve huge labours high extold,
  So many furies and sharpe fits did haunt,
  When him the poysoned garment did enchaunt
  With *Centaures* bloud, and bloudie verses charmed,   240
  As did this knight twelve thousand dolours daunt,
  Whom fyrie steele now burnt, that earst him armed,
That erst him goodly armed, now most of all him harmed.

28

Faint, wearie, sore, emboylèd, grievèd, brent
  With heat, toyle, wounds, armes, smart, and inward fire
  That never man such mischiefes did torment;
  Death better were, death did he oft desire,
  But death will never come, when needes require.
  Whom so dismayd when that his foe beheld,
  He cast to suffer him no more respire,   250
  But gan his sturdie sterne about to weld,
And him so strongly stroke, that to the ground him feld.

29

It fortunèd (as faire it then befell)
  Behind his backe unweeting, where he stood,
  Of auncient time there was a springing well,
  From which fast trickled forth a silver flood,
  Full of great vertues, and for med'cine good.
  Whylome, before that cursèd Dragon got
  That happie land, and all with innocent blood
  Defyld those sacred waves, it rightly hot   260
The well of life, ne yet his vertues had forgot.

30

For unto life the dead it could restore,
  And guilt of sinfull crimes cleane wash away,
  Those that with sicknesse were infected sore,
  It could recure, and agèd long decay
  Renew, as one were borne that very day.
  Both *Silo* this, and *Jordan* did excell,
  And th' English *Bath*, and eke the german *Spau*,
  Ne can *Cephise*, nor *Hebrus* match this well:
Into the same the knight backe overthrowen, fell.   270

31

Now gan the golden *Phoebus* for to steepe
  His fierie face in billowes of the west,
  And his faint steedes watred in Ocean deepe,
  Whiles from their journall labours they did rest,
  When that infernall Monster, having kest
  His wearie foe into that living well,
  Can high advance his broad discoloured brest,
  Above his wonted pitch, with countenance fell,
And clapt his yron wings, as victor he did dwell.

32

Which when his pensive Ladie saw from farre,   280
  Great woe and sorrow did her soule assay,
  As weening that the sad end of the warre,
  And gan to highest God entirely pray,
  That fearèd chance from her to turne away;
  With folded hands and knees full lowly bent
  All night she watcht, ne once adowne would lay
  Her daintie limbs in her sad dreriment,
But praying still did wake, and waking did lament.

33

The morrow next gan early to appeare,
  That *Titan* rose to runne his daily race;   290
  But early ere the morrow next gan reare
  Out of the sea faire *Titans* deawy face,
  Up rose the gentle virgin from her place,
  And lookèd all about, if she might spy
  Her lovèd knight to move his manly pace:
  For she had great doubt of his safety,
Since late she saw him fall before his enemy.

34

At last she saw, where he upstarted brave
  Out of the well, wherein he drenchèd lay;
  As Eagle fresh out of the Ocean wave,   300
  Where he hath left his plumes all hoary gray,
  And deckt himselfe with feathers youthly gay,
  Like Eyas hauke up mounts unto the skies,
  His newly budded pineons to assay,
  And marveiles at himselfe, still as he flies:
So new this new-borne knight to battell new did rise.

35

Whom when the damnèd feend so fresh did spy,
  No wonder if he wondred at the sight,
  And doubted, whether his late enemy
  It were, or other new supplièd knight.   310
  He, now to prove his late renewèd might,
  High brandishing his bright deaw-burning blade,
  Upon his crested scalpe so sore did smite,
  That to the scull a yawning wound it made:
The deadly dint his dullèd senses all dismaid.

---

250. **respire**, respite.   251. **sterne**, tail.   260. **hot**, was named.   261. **well of life**. The well symbolizes divine grace.   267. **Silo**, Siloam, a healing pool mentioned in the Bible; the others are well-known streams or watering-places.

274. **journall**, daily.   303. **Eyas**, young.   312. **deaw-burning**, glistening with dew.

36

I wote not, whether the revenging steele
  Were hardned with that holy water dew,
  Wherein he fell, or sharper edge did feele,
  Or his baptizèd hands now greater grew;
  Or other secret vertue did ensew;   320
  Else never could the force of fleshly arme,
  Ne molten mettall in his bloud embrew:
  For till that stownd could never wight him harme,
By subtilty, nor slight, nor might, nor mighty charme.

37

The cruell wound enragèd him so sore,
  That loud he yellèd for exceeding paine;
  As hundred ramping Lyons seemed to rore,
  Whom ravenous hunger did there to constraine:
  Then gan he tosse aloft his stretchèd traine,
  And therewith scourge the buxome aire so sore,   330
  That to his force to yeelden it was faine;
  Ne ought his sturdie strokes might stand afore,
That high trees overthrew, and rocks in peeces tore.

38

The same advauncing high above his head,
  With sharpe intended sting so rude him smot,
  That to the earth him drove, as stricken dead,
  Ne living wight would have him life behot:
  The mortall sting his angry needle shot
  Quite through his shield, and in his shoulder seasd,
  Where fast it stucke, ne would there out be got: 340
  The griefe thereof him wondrous sore diseasd,
Ne might his ranckling paine with patience be appeasd.

39

But yet more mindfull of his honour deare,
  Then of the grievous smart, which him did wring,
  From loathèd soile he can him lightly reare,
  And strove to loose the farre infixèd sting:
  Which when in vaine he tryde with struggeling,
  Inflamed with wrath, his raging blade he heft,
  And strooke so strongly, that the knotty string
  Of his huge taile he quite a sunder cleft,   350
Five joynts thereof he hewd, and but the stump him left.

40

Hart cannot thinke, what outrage, and what cryes,
  With foule enfouldred smoake and flashing fire,
  The hell-bred beast threw forth unto the skyes,
  That all was coverèd with darknesse dire:
  Then fraught with rancour, and engorgèd ire,
  He cast at once him to avenge for all,
  And gathering up himselfe out of the mire,
  With his uneven wings did fiercely fall
Upon his sunne-bright shield, and gript it fast withall.   360

41

Much was the man encombred with his hold,
  In feare to lose his weapon in his paw,
  Ne wist yet, how his talants to unfold;
  Nor harder was from *Cerberus* greedie jaw
  To plucke a bone, then from his cruell claw
  To reave by strength the gripèd gage away:
  Thrise he assayd it from his foot to draw,
  And thrise in vaine to draw it did assay,
It booted nought to thinke, to robbe him of his pray.

42

Tho when he saw no power might prevaile,   370
  His trustie sword he cald to his last aid,
  Wherewith he fiercely did his foe assaile,
  And double blowes about him stoutly laid,
  That glauncing fire out of the yron plaid;
  As sparkles from the Andvile use to fly,
  When heavie hammers on the wedge are swaid;
  Therewith at last he forst him to unty
One of his grasping feete, him to defend thereby.

43

The other foot, fast fixèd on his shield,
  Whenas no strength, nor stroks mote him constraine   380
  To loose, ne yet the warlike pledge to yield,
  He smot thereat with all his might and maine,
  That nought so wondrous puissance might sustaine;
  Upon the joynt the lucky steele did light,
  And made such way, that hewd it quite in twaine;
  The paw yet missèd not his minisht might,
But hong still on the shield, as it at first was pight.

44

For griefe thereof, and divelish despight,
  From his infernall fournace forth he threw   389
  Huge flames, that dimmèd all the heavens light,

---

322. molten mettall, metal that had been forged. **embrew**, plunge.   **330. buxome**, bending, unresisting. **335. intended**, outstretched.   **337. behot**, held out hope for.   **345. can**, "gan."

353. enfouldred, like a thunderstorm.   **363. talants**, claws.   **366. reave**, take.

Enrold in duskish smoke and brimstone blew;
  As burning *Aetna* from his boyling stew
  Doth belch out flames, and rockes in peeces broke,
  And ragged ribs of mountaines molten new,
  Enwrapt in coleblacke clouds and filthy smoke,
That all the land with stench, and heaven with horrour choke.

45

The heate whereof, and harmefull pestilence
  So sore him noyd, that forst him to retire
  A little backward for his best defence,
  To save his bodie from the scorching fire,   400
  Which he from hellish entrailes did expire.
  It chaunst (eternall God that chaunce did guide)
  As he recoylèd backward, in the mire
  His nigh forwearied feeble feet did slide,
And downe he fell, with dread of shame sore terrifide.

46

There grew a goodly tree him faire beside,
  Loaden with fruit and apples rosie red,
  As they in pure vermilion had beene dide,
  Whereof great vertues over all were red:
  For happie life to all, which thereon fed,   410
  And life eke everlasting did befall:
  Great God it planted in that blessèd sted
  With his almightie hand, and did it call
The tree of life, the crime of our first fathers fall.

47

In all the world like was not to be found,
  Save in that soile, where all good things did grow,
  And freely sprong out of the fruitfull ground,
  As incorrupted Nature did them sow,
  Till that dread Dragon all did overthrow.
  Another like faire tree eke grew thereby,   420
  Whereof who so did eat, eftsoones did know
  Both good and ill: O mournefull memory:
That tree through one mans fault hath doen us all to dy.

48

From that first tree forth flowd, as from a well,
  A trickling streame of Balme, most soveraine
  And daintie deare, which on the ground still fell,
  And overflowèd all the fertill plaine,
  As it had deawèd bene with timely raine:
  Life and long health that gratious ointment gave,

409. red, perceived.   412. sted, place.   426. deare, rare, very costly.

  And deadly woundes could heale, and reare againe   430
  The senselesse corse appointed for the grave.
Into that same he fell: which did from death him save.

49

For nigh thereto the ever damnèd beast
  Durst not approch, for he was deadly made,
  And all that life preservèd, did detest:
  Yet he it oft adventured to invade.
  By this the drouping day-light gan to fade,
  And yeeld his roome to sad succeeding night,
  Who with her sable mantle gan to shade
  The face of earth, and wayes of living wight;   440
And high her burning torch set up in heaven bright.

50

When gentle *Una* saw the second fall
  Of her deare knight, who wearie of long fight,
  And faint through losse of bloud, moved not at all,
  But lay as in a dreame of deepe delight,
  Besmeard with pretious Balme, whose vertuous might
  Did heale his wounds, and scorching heat alay,
  Againe she stricken was with sore affright,
  And for his safetie gan devoutly pray;
And watch the noyous night, and wait for joyous day.   450

51

The joyous day gan early to appeare,
  And faire *Aurora* from the deawy bed
  Of aged *Tithone* gan her selfe to reare,
  With rosie cheekes, for shame as blushing red;
  Her golden lockes for haste were loosely shed
  About her eares, when *Una* her did marke
  Clymbe to her charet, all with flowers spred,
  From heaven high to chase the chearelesse darke;
With merry note her loud salutes the mounting larke.

52

Then freshly up arose the doughtie knight,   460
  All healèd of his hurts and woundès wide,
  And did himselfe to battell readie dight;
  Whose early foe awaiting him beside
  To have devourd, so soone as day he spyde,
  When now he saw himselfe so freshly reare,
  As if late fight had nought him damnifyde,
  He woxe dismayd, and gan his fate to feare;
Nathlesse with wonted rage he him advauncèd neare.

441. torch, the moon.   467. woxe, waxed, grew.

53

And in his first encounter, gaping wide,
    He thought attonce him to have swallowd quight,   470
    And rusht upon him with outragious pride;
    Who him r'encountring fierce, as hauke in flight,
    Perforce rebutted backe. The weapon bright
    Taking advantage of his open jaw,
    Ran through his mouth with so importune might,
    That deepe emperst his darksome hollow maw,
And back retyrd, his life bloud forth with all did draw.

54

So downe he fell, and forth his life did breath,
    That vanisht into smoke and cloudès swift;
    So downe he fell, that th' earth him underneath   480
    Did grone, as feeble so great load to lift;
    So downe he fell, as an huge rockie clift,
    Whose false foundation waves have washt away,
    With dreadfull poyse is from the mayneland rift,
    And rolling downe, great *Neptune* doth dismay;
So downe he fell, and like an heapèd mountaine lay.

55

The knight himselfe even trembled at his fall,
    So huge and horrible a masse it seemed;
    And his deare Ladie, that beheld it all,
    Durst not approch for dred, which she misdeemed,   490
    But yet at last, when as the direfull feend
    She saw not stirre, off-shaking vaine affright,
    She nigher drew, and saw that joyous end:
    Then God she praysd, and thankt her faithfull knight,
That had atchieved so great a conquest by his might.

Canto XII

*Faire Una to the Redcrosse knight
betrouthèd is with joy:
Though false Duessa it to barre
her false sleights doe imploy.*

1

Behold I see the haven nigh at hand,
    To which I meane my wearie course to bend;
    Vere the maine shete, and beare up with the land,
    The which afore is fairely to be kend,
    And seemeth safe from stormes, that may offend;
    There this faire virgin wearie of her way
Must landed be, now at her journeyes end:
    There eke my feeble barke a while may stay,
Till merry wind and weather call her thence away.

2

Scarsely had *Phoebus* in the glooming East   10
    Yet harnessèd his firie-footed teeme,
    Ne reard above the earth his flaming creast,
    When the last deadly smoke aloft did steeme,
    That signe of last outbreathèd life did seeme
    Unto the watchman on the castle wall;
    Who thereby dead that balefull Beast did deeme,
    And to his Lord and Ladie lowd gan call,
To tell, how he had seene the Dragons fatall fall.

3

Uprose with hastie joy, and feeble speed
    That agèd Sire, the Lord of all that land,   20
    And lookèd forth, to weet, if true indeede
    Those tydings were, as he did understand,
    Which whenas true by tryall he out fond,
    He bad to open wyde his brazen gate,
    Which long time had bene shut, and out of hond
    Proclaymèd joy and peace through all his state;
For dead now was their foe, which them forrayèd late.

4

Then gan triumphant Trompets sound on hie,
    That sent to heaven the ecchoèd report
    Of their new joy, and happie victorie   30
    Gainst him, that had them long opprest with tort,
    And fast imprisonèd in siegèd fort.
    Then all the people, as in solemne feast,
    To him assembled with one full consort,
    Rejoycing at the fall of that great beast,
From whose eternall bondage now they were releast.

5

Forth came that auncient Lord and agèd Queene,
    Arayd in antique robes downe to the ground,
    And sad habiliments right well beseene;
    A noble crew about them waited round   40
    Of sage and sober Peres, all gravely gownd;
    Whom farre before did march a goodly band
    Of tall young men, all hable armes to sownd,
    But now they laurell braunches bore in hand;
Glad signe of victorie and peace in all their land.

6

Unto that doughtie Conquerour they came,
    And him before themselves prostrating low,

---

477. **retyrd,** withdrawn.   484. **poyse,** crash.   490. **misdeemed,** was mistaken about.   31. **tort,** wrong.   39. **sad habiliments right well beseene,** sober clothing, appropriate to their condition.   43. **armes to sownd,** to clash arms, hence to wage battle.

Their Lord and Patrone loud did him proclame,
  And at his feet their laurell boughes did throw.
  Soone after them all dauncing on a row   50
  The comely virgins came, with girlands dight,
  As fresh as flowres in medow greene do grow,
  When morning deaw upon their leaves doth light:
And in their hands sweet Timbrels all upheld on hight.

7

And them before, the fry of children young
  Their wanton sports and childish mirth did play,
  And to the Maydens sounding tymbrels sung
  In well attunèd notes, a joyous lay,
  And made delightfull musicke all the way,
  Untill they came, where that faire virgin stood;   60
  As faire *Diana* in fresh sommers day
  Beholds her Nymphes, enraunged in shadie wood,
Some wrestle, some do run, some bathe in christall flood.

8

So she beheld those maydens meriment
  With chearefull vew; who when to her they came,
  Themselves to ground with gratious humblesse bent,
  And her adored by honourable name,
  Lifting to heaven her everlasting fame:
  Then on her head they set a girland greene,
  And crownèd her twixt earnest and twixt game;
  Who in her selfe-resemblance well beseene,   71
Did seeme such, as she was, a goodly maiden Queene.

9

And after, all the raskall many ran,
  Heapèd together in rude rablement,
  To see the face of that victorious man:
  Whom all admirèd, as from heaven sent,
  And gazd upon with gaping wonderment.
  But when they came, where that dead Dragon lay,
  Stretcht on the ground in monstrous large extent,
  The sight with idle feare did them dismay,   80
Ne durst approch him nigh, to touch, or once assay.

10

Some feard, and fled; some feard and well it faynd;
  One that would wiser seeme, then all the rest,
  Warnd him not touch, for yet perhaps remaynd
  Some lingring life within his hollow brest,
  Or in his wombe might lurke some hidden nest
  Of many Dragonets, his fruitfull seed;
  Another said, that in his eyes did rest
  Yet sparckling fire, and bad thereof take heed;
Another said, he saw him move his eyes indeed.   90

11

One mother, when as her foolehardie chyld
  Did come too neare, and with his talants play,
  Halfe dead through feare, her litle babe revyld;
  And to her gossips gan in counsell say;
  How can I tell, but that his talants may
  Yet scratch my sonne, or rend his tender hand?
  So diversly themselves in vaine they fray;
  Whiles some more bold, to measure him nigh stand,
To prove how many acres he did spread of land.

12

Thus flockèd all the folke him round about,   100
  The whiles that hoarie king, with all his traine,
  Being arrivèd, where that champion stout
  After his foes defeasance did remaine,
  Him goodly greetes, and faire does entertaine,
  With princely gifts of yvorie and gold,
  And thousand thankes him yeelds for all his paine.
  Then when his daughter deare he does behold,
Her dearely doth imbrace, and kisseth manifold.

13

And after to his Pallace he them brings,
  With shaumes, and trumpets, and with Clarions sweet;   110
  And all the way the joyous people sings,
  And with their garments strowes the pavèd street:
  Whence mounting up, they find purveyance meet
  Of all, that royall Princes court became,
  And all the floore was underneath their feet
  Bespred with costly scarlot of great name,
On which they lowly sit, and fitting purpose frame.

14

What needs me tell their feast and goodly guize,
  In which was nothing riotous nor vaine?
  What needs of daintie dishes to devize,   120
  Of comely services, or courtly trayne?
  My narrow leaves cannot in them containe
  The large discourse of royall Princes state.

---

71. selfe-resemblance well beseene, that is, being crowned, she now resembled her real self. **73. raskall many,** the common crowd. **92. talants,** claws. **110. shaumes,** wind instruments made of a double reed pipe set in a round mouthpiece. **116. scarlot of great name,** noted or costly scarlet cloth.

EDMUND SPENSER

Yet was their manner then but bare and plaine:
  For th' antique world excesse and pride did hate;
Such proud luxurious pompe is swollen up but late.

15

Then when with meates and drinkes of every kinde
  Their fervent appetites they quenchèd had,
  That aunciont Lord gan fit occasion finde,
  Of straunge adventures, and of perils sad,   130
  Which in his travell him befallen had,
  For to demaund of his renowmèd guest:
  Who then with utt'rance grave, and count'nance sad,
  From point to point, as is before exprest,
Discourst his voyage long, according his request.

16

Great pleasure mixt with pittifull regard,
  That godly King and Queene did passionate,
  Whiles they his pittifull adventures heard,
  That oft they did lament his lucklesse state,
  And often blame the too importune fate,   140
  That heapd on him so many wrathfull wreakes:
  For never gentle knight, as he of late,
  So tossèd was in fortunes cruell freakes;
And all the while salt teares bedeawd the hearers cheaks.

17

Then said that royall Pere in sober wise;
  Deare Sonne, great beene the evils, which ye bore
  From first to last in your late enterprise,
  That I note, whether prayse, or pitty more:
  For never living man, I weene, so sore
  In sea of deadly daungers was distrest;   150
  But since now safe ye seisèd have the shore,
  And well arrivèd are, (high God be blest)
Let us devize of ease and everlasting rest.

18

Ah dearest Lord, said then that doughty knight,
  Of ease or rest I may not yet devize;
  For by the faith, which I to armes have plight,
  I bounden am streight after this emprize,
  As that your daughter can ye well advize,
  Backe to returne to that great Faerie Queene,
  And her to serve six yeares in warlike wize,   160
  Gainst that proud Paynim king, that workes her teene:
Therefore I ought crave pardon, till I there have beene.

19

Unhappie falles that hard necessitie,
  (Quoth he) the troubler of my happie peace,
  And vowèd foe of my felicitie;
  Ne I against the same can justly preace:
  But since that band ye cannot now release,
  Nor doen undo; (for vowes may not be vaine)
  Soone as the terme of those six yeares shall cease,
  Ye then shall hither backe returne againe,   170
The marriage to accomplish vowd betwixt you twain.

20

Which for my part I covet to performe,
  In sort as through the world I did proclame,
  That who so kild that monster most deforme,
  And him in hardy battaile overcame,
  Should have mine onely daughter to his Dame,
  And of my kingdome heire apparaunt bee:
  Therefore since now to thee perteines the same,
  By dew desert of noble chevalree,
Both daughter and eke kingdome, lo I yield to thee.   180

21

Then forth he callèd that his daughter faire,
  The fairest *Un*' his onely daughter deare,
  His onely daughter, and his onely heyre;
  Who forth proceeding with sad sober cheare,
  As bright as doth the morning starre appeare
  Out of the East, with flaming lockes bedight,
  To tell that dawning day is drawing neare,
  And to the world does bring long wishèd light;
So faire and fresh that Lady shewd her selfe in sight.

22

So faire and fresh, as freshest flowre in May;   190
  For she had layd her mournefull stole aside,
  And widow-like sad wimple throwne away,
  Wherewith her heavenly beautie she did hide,
  Whiles on her wearie journey she did ride;
  And on her now a garment she did weare,
  All lilly white, withoutten spot, or pride,
  That seemd like silke and silver woven neare,
But neither silke nor silver therein did appeare.

23

The blazing brightnesse of her beauties beame,
  And glorious light of her sunshyny face   200
  To tell, were as to strive against the streame.
  My ragged rimes are all too rude and bace,

---

137. passionate, express sympathetically.   **148. note,** do not know.   **151. seisèd,** reached, got possession of.   **161. teene,** sorrow.   **173. In sort as,** according as.   **192. wimple,** the pleated veil (see Canto I, l. 31).   **196. pride,** decoration.   **197. woven neare,** close-woven.

    Her heavenly lineaments for to enchace.
    Ne wonder; for her owne deare lovèd knight,
    All were she dayly with himselfe in place,
    Did wonder much at her celestiall sight:
Oft had he seene her faire, but never so faire dight.

24

So fairely dight, when she in presence came,
    She to her Sire made humble reverence,
    And bowèd low, that her right well became,   210
    And added grace unto her excellence:
    Who with great wisedome, and grave eloquence
    Thus gan to say. But eare he thus had said,
    With flying speede, and seeming great pretence,
    Came running in, much like a man dismaid,
A Messenger with letters, which his message said.

25

All in the open hall amazèd stood,
    At suddeinnesse of that unwarie sight,
    And wondred at his breathlesse hastie mood.
    But he for nought would stay his passage right 220
    Till fast before the king he did alight;
    Where falling flat, great humblesse he did make,
    And kist the ground, whereon his foot was pight;
    Then to his hands that writ he did betake,
Which he disclosing, red thus, as the paper spake.

26

To thee, most mighty king of *Eden* faire,
    Her greeting sends in these sad lines addrest,
    The wofull daughter, and forsaken heire
    Of that great Emperour of all the West;
    And bids thee be advizèd for the best,   230
    Ere thou thy daughter linck in holy band
    Of wedlocke to that new unknowen guest:
    For he already plighted his right hand
Unto another love, and to another land.

27

To me sad mayd, or rather widow sad,
    He was affiauncèd long time before,
    And sacred pledges he both gave, and had,
    False erraunt knight, infamous, and forswore:
    Witnesse the burning Altars, which he swore,
    And guiltie heavens of his bold perjury,   240
    Which though he hath polluted oft of yore,
    Yet I to them for judgement just do fly,
And them conjure t' avenge this shamefull injury.

28

Therefore since mine he is, or free or bond,
    Or false or trew, or living or else dead,
    Withhold, O soveraine Prince, your hasty hond
    From knitting league with him, I you aread;
    Ne weene my right with strength adowne to tread,
    Through weakenesse of my widowhed, or woe:
    For truth is strong, her rightfull cause to plead,
    And shall find friends, if need requireth soe,   251
So bids thee well to fare, Thy neither friend, nor foe, *Fidessa*.

29

When he these bitter byting words had red,
    The tydings straunge did him abashèd make,
    That still he sate long time astonishèd
    As in great muse, ne word to creature spake.
    At last his solemne silence thus he brake,
    With doubtfull eyes fast fixèd on his guest;
    Redoubted knight, that for mine onely sake
    Thy life and honour late adventurest,   260
Let nought be hid from me, that ought to be exprest.

30

What meane these bloudy vowes, and idle threats,
    Throwne out from womanish impatient mind?
    What heavens? what altars? what enragèd heates
    Here heapèd up with termes of love unkind,
    My conscience cleare with guilty bands would bind?
    High God be witnesse, that I guiltlesse ame.
    But if your selfe, Sir knight, ye faultie find,
    Or wrappèd be in loves of former Dame,   269
With crime do not it cover, but disclose the same.

31

To whom the *Redcrosse* knight this answere sent,
    My Lord, my King, be nought hereat dismayd,
    Till well ye wote by grave intendiment,
    What woman, and wherefore doth me upbrayd
    With breach of love, and loyalty betrayd.
    It was in my mishaps, as hitherward
    I lately traveild, that unwares I strayd
    Out of my way, through perils straunge and hard;
That day should faile me, ere I had them all declard.

32

There did I find, or rather I was found   280
    Of this false woman, that *Fidessa* hight,

---

203. **enchace**, serve as setting to.   214. **pretence**, importance.   218. **unwarie**, unexpected.   220. **passage right**, going straight on.   221. **fast**, close.   225. **disclosing**, unfolding.   229. **Emperour of all the West**, the Pope.   240. **guiltie heavens of**, heavens polluted by.

252. **well to fare**, farewell. **Fidessa**, Duessa, the false enchantress.

Fidessa hight the falsest Dame on ground,
  Most false *Duessa*, royall richly dight,
  That easie was t' invegle weaker sight:
  Who by her wicked arts, and wylie skill,
  Too false and strong for earthly skill or might,
  Unwares me wrought unto her wicked will,
And to my foe betrayd, when least I fearèd ill.

33
Then steppèd forth the goodly royall Mayd,
  And on the ground her selfe prostrating low, 290
  With sober countenaunce thus to him sayd;
  O pardon me, my soveraigne Lord, to show
  The secret treasons, which of late I know
  To have bene wroght by that false sorceresse.
  She onely she it is, that earst did throw
  This gentle knight into so great distresse,
That death him did awaite in dayly wretchednesse.

34
And now it seemes, that she subornèd hath
  This craftie messenger with letters vaine,
  To worke new woe and improvided scath, 300
  By breaking of the band betwixt us twaine;
  Wherein she usèd hath the practicke paine
  Of this false footman, clokt with simplenesse,
  Whom if ye please for to discover plaine,
  Ye shall him *Archimago* find, I ghesse,
The falsest man alive; who tries shall find no lesse.

35
The king was greatly movèd at her speach,
  And all with suddein indignation fraight,
  Bad on that Messenger rude hands to reach. 309
  Eftsoones the Gard, which on his state did wait,
  Attacht that faitor false, and bound him strait:
  Who seeming sorely chauffèd at his band,
  As chainèd Beare, whom cruell dogs do bait,
  With idle force did faine them to withstand,
And often semblaunce made to scape out of their hand.

36
But they him layd full low in dungeon deepe,
  And bound him hand and foote with yron chains.
  And with continuall watch did warely keepe;
  Who then would thinke, that by his subtile trains
  He could escape fowle death or deadly paines?
  Thus when that Princes wrath was pacifide, 321
  He gan renew the late forbidden banes,
  And to the knight his daughter deare he tyde,
With sacred rites and vowes for ever to abyde.

292. pardon me, give me leave.   **300. improvided scath**, unexpected harm.   **302. practicke paine**, artful pains or clever trick.   **311. faitor**, impostor.   **322. banes**, banns.

37
His owne two hands the holy knots did knit,
  That none but death for ever can devide;
  His owne two hands, for such a turne most fit,
  The housling fire did kindle and provide,
  And holy water thereon sprinckled wide;
  At which the bushy Teade a groome did light, 330
  And sacred lampe in secret chamber hide,
  Where it should not be quenchèd day nor night,
For feare of evill fates, but burnen ever bright.

38
Then gan they sprinckle all the posts with wine,
  And made great feast to solemnize that day;
  They all perfumde with frankencense divine,
  And precious odours fetcht from far away,
  That all the house did sweat with great aray:
  And all the while sweete Musicke did apply
  Her curious skill, the warbling notes to play, 340
  To drive away the dull Melancholy;
The whiles one sung a song of love and jollity.

39
During the which there was an heavenly noise
  Heard sound through all the Pallace pleasantly,
  Like as it had bene many an Angels voice,
  Singing before th' eternall majesty,
  In their trinall triplicities on hye;
  Yet wist no creature, whence that heavenly sweet
  Proceeded, yet each one felt secretly
  Himselfe thereby reft of his sences meet, 350
And ravishèd with rare impression in his sprite.

40
Great joy was made that day of young and old,
  And solemne feast proclaimd throughout the land,
  That their exceeding merth may not be told:
  Suffice it heare by signes to understand
  The usuall joyes at knitting of loves band.
  Thrise happy man the knight himselfe did hold,
  Possessèd of his Ladies hart and hand,
  And ever, when his eye did her behold, 359
His heart did seeme to melt in pleasures manifold.

41
Her joyous presence and sweet company
  In full content he there did long enjoy,
  Ne wicked envie, ne vile gealosy
  His deare delights were able to annoy:

328. housling, purifying.   **330. Teade.** See note 27, page 400.   **347. trinall triplicities,** the thrice threefold hierarchy of Angels, first systematized by Dionysius the Areopagite.

Yet swimming in that sea of blisfull joy,
He nought forgot, how he whilome had sworne,
In case he could that monstrous beast destroy,
Unto his Farie Queene backe to returne:
The which he shortly did, and *Una* left to mourne.

42

Now strike your sailes ye jolly Mariners,   370
For we be come unto a quiet rode,
Where we must land some of our passengers,
And light this wearie vessell of her lode.
Here she a while may make her safe abode,
Till she repairèd have her tackles spent,
And wants supplide. And then againe abroad
On the long voyage whereto she is bent:
Well may she speede and fairely finish her intent.

BOOK II
Canto XII
The Bower of Bliss

In Book II, Spenser leads his hero, Sir Guyon, along the highroad of intellectual and moral virtue toward the goal of Temperance. But it too is a highroad with many a tempting intersection similar to those which beckoned the Red Cross Knight; and the last and most famous of them is Acrasia's Bower of Bliss. An apt testing-ground for the stoutest of moral characters, the Bower of Bliss, as Spenser describes it, is one of the most colorful dens of iniquity in literature, peopled with damsels so alluring that even the resolute Guyon, catching a glimpse of them, begins to "relent his earnest pace." Its original source was, of course, the story of Circe, but in this episode there is far more of the allegorical tradition that interpreted the Greek myth as the war of flesh and spirit than ever Homer intended in his version. Spenser adapted the theme, as Milton did later in *Comus*, to show the supreme conquest of sensual appetite by the virtuous will; for when Guyon has bound Acrasia and destroyed the Bower of Bliss, he has won in this last and hardest victory full claim to the title, the Knight of Temperance.

42

Thence passing forth, they shortly do arrive,   370
Whereas the Bowre of *Blisse* was situate;
A place pickt out by choice of best alive,
That natures worke by art can imitate:
In which what ever in this worldly state
Is sweet, and pleasing unto living sense,
Or that may dayntiest fantasie aggrate,
Was pourèd forth with plentifull dispence,
And made there to abound with lavish affluence.

Sec. 42, Bk. I. **371. rode**, roadway, harbor. **375. spent**, worn out. *Sec. 42. Bk. II.* **376. aggrate**, please.

43

Goodly it was enclosèd round about,
Aswell their entred guestes to keepe within,   380
As those unruly beasts to hold without;
Yet was the fence thereof but weake and thin;
Nought feard their force, that fortilage to win,
But wisedomes powre, and temperaunces might,
By which the mightiest things efforcèd bin:
And eke the gate was wrought of substaunce light,
Rather for pleasure, then for battery or fight.

44

Yt framèd was of precious yvory,
That seemd a worke of admirable wit;
And therein all the famous history   390
Of *Jason* and *Medaea* was ywrit;
Her mighty charmes, her furious loving fit,
His goodly conquest of the golden fleece,
His falsèd faith, and love too lightly flit,
The wondred *Argo*, which in venturous peece
First through the *Euxine* seas bore all the flowr of Greece.

45

Ye might have seene the frothy billowes fry
Under the ship, as thorough them she went,
That seemd the waves were into yvory,
Or yvory into the waves were sent;   400
And other where the snowy substaunce sprent
With vermell, like the boyes bloud therein shed,
A piteous spectacle did represent,
And otherwhiles with gold besprinkelèd;
Yt seemd th' enchaunted flame, which did *Creüsa* wed.

46

All this, and more might in that goodly gate
Be red; that ever open stood to all,
Which thither came: but in the Porch there sate
A comely personage of stature tall,   409
And semblaunce pleasing, more then naturall,
That travellers to him seemd to entize;
His looser garment to the ground did fall,
And flew about his heeles in wanton wize,
Not fit for speedy pace, or manly exercize.

47

They in that place him *Genius* did call:
Not that celestiall powre, to whom the care

383–85. Nought feard . . . bin. The physical force of the knight and his guide roused no fear among the inmates that they could capture the fortress. **395. wondred**, wonderful.

Of life, and generation of all
   That lives, pertaines in charge particulare,
   Who wondrous things concerning our welfare,
   And straunge phantomes doth let us oft forsee,
   And oft of secret ill bids us beware: 421
   That is our Selfe, whom though we do not see,
Yet each doth in him selfe it well perceive to bee.

48

Therefore a God him sage Antiquity
   Did wisely make, and good *Agdistes* call:
   But this same was to that quite contrary,
   The foe of life, that good envyes to all,
   That secretly doth us procure to fall,
   Through guilefull semblaunts, which he makes us see.
   He of this Gardin had the governall,   430
   And Pleasures porter was devizd to bee,
Holding a staffe in hand for more formalitee.

49

With diverse flowres he daintily was deckt,
   And strowèd round about, and by his side
   A mighty Mazer bowle of wine was set,
   As if it had to him bene sacrifide;
   Wherewith all new-come guests he gratifide:
   So did he eke Sir *Guyon* passing by:
   But he his idle curtesie defide,
   And overthrew his bowle disdainfully;   440
And broke his staffe, with which he charmèd semblants sly.

50

Thus being entred, they behold around
   A large and spacious plaine, on every side
   Strowèd with pleasauns, whose faire grassy ground
   Mantled with greene, and goodly beautifide
   With all the ornaments of *Floraes* pride,
   Wherewith her mother Art, as halfe in scorne
   Of niggard Nature, like a pompous bride
   Did decke her, and too lavishly adorne,
When forth from virgin bowre she comes in th' early morne.   450

51

Thereto the Heavens alwayes Joviall,
   Lookt on them lovely, still in stedfast state,
   Ne suffred storme nor frost on them to fall,
   Their tender buds or leaves to violate,
   Nor scorching heat, nor cold intemperate
   T' afflict the creatures, which therein did dwell,
   But the milde aire with season moderate
   Gently attemprèd, and disposd so well,
That still it breathèd forth sweet spirit and holesome smell.   459

52

More sweet and holesome, then the pleasaunt hill
   Of *Rhodope*, on which the Nimphe, that bore
   A gyaunt babe, her selfe for griefe did kill;
   Or the Thessalian *Tempe*, where of yore
   Faire *Daphne Phoebus* hart with love did gore;
   Or *Ida*, where the Gods loved to repaire,
   When ever they their heavenly bowres forlore;
   Or sweet *Parnasse*, the haunt of Muses faire;
Or *Eden* selfe, if ought with *Eden* mote compaire.

53

Much wondrèd *Guyon* at the faire aspect
   Of that sweet place, yet suffrèd no delight   470
   To sincke into his sence, nor mind affect,
   But passèd forth, and lookt still forward right,
   Bridling his will, and maistering his might:
   Till that he came unto another gate;
   No gate, but like one, being goodly dight
   With boughes and braunches, which did broad dilate
Their clasping armes, in wanton wreathings intricate.

54

So fashionèd a Porch with rare device,
   Archt over head with an embracing vine,   479
   Whose bounches hanging downe, seemed to entice
   All passers by, to tast their lushious wine,
   And did themselves into their hands incline,
   As freely offering to be gatherèd:
   Some deepe empurpled as the *Hyacint*,
   Some as the Rubine, laughing sweetly red,
Some like faire Emeraudes, not yet well ripenèd.

55

And them amongst, some were of burnisht gold,
   So made by art, to beautifie the rest,
   Which did themselves emongst the leaves enfold,
   As lurking from the vew of covetous guest,   490
   That the weake bowes, with so rich load opprest,
   Did bow adowne, as over-burdenèd.
   Under that Porch a comely dame did rest,
   Clad in faire weedes, but fowle disorderèd
And garments loose, that seemd unmeet for womanhed.

---

435. **Mazer**, large wooden bowl.   441. **charmèd semblants sly**, raised by magic immaterial phantasms.
445. **and goodly.** Possibly "and" is a slip for "was."
451. **Thereto**, besides, in addition to. **Joviall**, propitious.
459. **spirit**, breath.   472. **forward right**, straight ahead.
484. **Hyacint**, probably the sapphire.

56

In her left hand a Cup of gold she held,
    And with her right the riper fruit did reach,
    Whose sappy liquor, that with fulnesse sweld,
    Into her cup she scruzd, with daintie breach
    Of her fine fingers, without fowle empeach,   500
    That so faire wine-presse made the wine more sweet:
    Thereof she usd to give to drinke to each,
Whom passing by she happenèd to meet:
It was her guise, all Straungers goodly so to greet.

57

So she to *Guyon* offred it to tast;
    Who taking it out of her tender hond,
    The cup to ground did violently cast,
    That all in peeces it was broken fond,
    And with the liquor stainèd all the lond:
    Whereat *Excesse* exceedingly was wroth,   510
    Yet no'te the same amend, ne yet withstond,
    But suffered him to passe, all were she loth;
Who nought regarding her displeasure forward goth.

58

There the most daintie Paradise on ground,
    It selfe doth offer to his sober eye,
    In which all pleasures plenteously abound,
    And none does others happinesse envye:
    The painted flowres, the trees upshooting hye,
    The dales for shade, the hilles for breathing space,
    The trembling groves, the Christall running by;
    And that, which all faire workes doth most aggrace,   521
The art, which all that wrought, appearèd in no place.

59

One would have thought, (so cunningly, the rude,
    And scornèd parts were mingled with the fine,)
    That nature had for wantonesse ensude
    Art, and that Art at nature did repine;
    So striving each th' other to undermine,
    Each did the others worke more beautifie;
    So diff'ring both in willes, agreed in fine:
    So all agreed through sweete diversitie,   530
This Gardin to adorne with all varietie.

60

And in the midst of all, a fountaine stood,
    Of richest substaunce, that on earth might bee,
    So pure and shiny, that the silver flood
    Through every channell running one might see;
    Most goodly it with curious imageree
    Was over-wrought, and shapes of naked boyes,
    Of which some seemd with lively jollitee,
    To fly about, playing their wanton toyes,
Whilest others did them selves embay in liquid joyes.   540

61

And over all, of purest gold was spred,
    A trayle of yvie in his native hew:
    For the rich mettall was so colourèd,
    That wight, who did not well avised it vew,
    Would surely deeme it to be yvie trew:
    Low his lascivious armes adown did creepe,
    That themselves dipping in the silver dew,
    Their fleecy flowres they tenderly did steepe,
Which drops of Christall seemd for wantones to weepe.

62

Infinit streames continually did well   550
    Out of this fountaine, sweet and faire to see,
    The which into an ample laver fell,
    And shortly grew to so great quantitie,
    That like a little lake it seemd to bee;
    Whose depth exceeded not three cubits hight,
    That through the waves one might the bottom see,
    All paved beneath with Jaspar shining bright,
That seemd the fountaine in that sea did sayle upright.

63

And all the margent round about was set,
    With shady Laurell trees, thence to defend   560
    The sunny beames, which on the billowes bet,
    And those which therein bathèd, mote offend.
    As *Guyon* hapned by the same to wend,
    Two naked Damzelles he therein espyde,
    Which therein bathing, seemèd to contend,
    And wrestle wantonly, ne cared to hyde,
Their dainty parts from vew of any, which them eyde.

64

Sometimes the one would lift the other quight
    Above the waters, and then downe againe
    Her plong, as over maisterèd by might,   570
    Where both awhile would coverèd remaine,
    And each the other from to rise restraine;
    The whiles their snowy limbes, as through a vele,
So through the Christall waves appearèd plaine:

   499–500. **with daintie breach Of,** crushing them daintily with.

Then suddeinly both would themselves unhele,
And th' amarous sweet spoiles to greedy eyes revele.

65

As that faire Starre, the messenger of morne,
    His deawy face out of the sea doth reare:
    Or as the *Cyprian* goddesse, newly borne
    Of th' Oceans fruitfull froth, did first appeare: 580
    Such seemèd they, and so their yellow heare
    Christalline humour droppèd downe apace.
    Whom such when *Guyon* saw, he drew him neare,
    And somewhat gan relent his earnest pace,
His stubborne brest gan secret pleasaunce to embrace.

66

The wanton Maidens him espying, stood
    Gazing a while at his unwonted guise;
    Then th' one her selfe low duckèd in the flood,
    Abasht, that her a straunger did a vise:
    But th' other rather higher did arise, 590
    And her two lilly paps aloft displayd,
    And all, that might his melting hart entise
    To her delights, she unto him bewrayd:
The rest hid underneath, him more desirous made.

67

With that, the other likewise up arose,
    And her faire lockes, which formerly were bownd
    Up in one knot, she low adowne did lose:
    Which flowing long and thick, her clothed arownd,
    And th' yvorie in golden mantle gownd:
    So that faire spectacle from him was reft, 600
    Yet that, which reft it, no lesse faire was fownd:
    So hid in lockes and waves from lookers theft,
Nought but her lovely face she for his looking left.

68

Withall she laughèd, and she blusht withall,
    That blushing to her laughter gave more grace,
    And laughter to her blushing, as did fall:
    Now when they spide the knight to slacke his pace,
    Them to behold, and in his sparkling face
    The secret signes of kindled lust appeare,
    Their wanton meriments they did encreace, 610
    And to him beckned, to approch more neare,
And shewd him many sights, that courage cold could reare.

69

On which when gazing him the Palmer saw,
    He much rebukt those wandring eyes of his,
    And counseld well, him forward thence did draw.
    Now are they come nigh to the *Bowre of blis*
    Of her fond favourites so named amis:
    When thus the Palmer; Now Sir, well avise;
    For here the end of all our travell is:
    Here wonnes *Acrasia*, whom we must surprise, 620
Else she will slip away, and all our drift despise.

70

Eftsoones they heard a most melodious sound,
    Of all that mote delight a daintie eare,
    Such as attonce might not on living ground,
    Save in this Paradise, be heard elswhere:
    Right hard it was, for wight, which did it heare,
    To read, what manner musicke that mote bee:
    For all that pleasing is to living eare,
    Was there consorted in one harmonee,
Birdes, voyces, instruments, windes, waters, all agree. 630

71

The joyous birdes shrouded in chearefull shade,
    Their notes unto the voyce attempred sweet;
    Th' Angelicall soft trembling voyces made
    To th' instruments divine respondence meet:
    The silver sounding instruments did meet
    With the base murmure of the waters fall:
    The waters fall with difference discreet,
    Now soft, now loud, unto the wind did call:
The gentle warbling wind low answerèd to all.

72

There, whence that Musick seemèd heard to bee,
    Was the faire Witch her selfe now solacing, 641
    With a new Lover, whom through sorceree
    And witchcraft, she from farre did thither bring:
    There she had him now layd a slombering,
    In secret shade, after long wanton joyes:
    Whilst round about them pleasauntly did sing
    Many faire Ladies, and lascivious boyes,
That ever mixt their song with light licentious toyes.

73

And all that while, right over him she hong,
    With her false eyes fast fixèd in his sight, 650
    As seeking medicine, whence she was stong,
    Or greedily depasturing delight:
    And oft inclining downe with kisses light,
    For feare of waking him, his lips bedewd,
    And through his humid eyes did sucke his spright,

575. **unhele**, uncover.   612. **reare**, arouse.   621. **drift**, design.   637. **discreet**, distinct.   648. **toyes**, games, flirtations.

Quite molten into lust and pleasure lewd;
Wherewith she sighèd soft, as if his case she rewd.

74

The whiles some one did chaunt this lovely lay;
    Ah see, who so faire thing doest faine to see,
    In springing flowre the image of thy day;   660
    Ah see the Virgin Rose, how sweetly shee
    Doth first peepe forth with bashfull modestee,
    That fairer seemes, the lesse ye see her may;
    Lo see soone after, how more bold and free
    Her barèd bosome she doth broad display;
Loe see soone after, how she fades, and falles away.

75

So passeth, in the passing of a day,
    Of mortall life the leafe, the bud, the flowre,
    Ne more doth flourish after first decay,
    That earst was sought to decke both bed and bowre,   670
    Of many a Ladie, and many a Paramowre:
    Gather therefore the Rose, whilest yet is prime,
    For soone comes age, that will her pride deflowre:
    Gather the Rose of love, whilest yet is time,
Whilest loving thou mayst lovèd be with equall crime.

BOOK III
Canto VI
The Garden of Adonis

Spenser's description of the "Garden of Adonis" is a striking example of his characteristic method of transforming classic myth into Renaissance symbolism. Although based largely on Ovid's *Metamorphoses*, these passages have little of the simplicity found in their original sources, but are instead a highly ornate and complex pictorial presentation of a mass of traditional ideas concerning otherworld paradises, chaos, creation, mutability, and the like. After telling of Venus' encounter with Diana and of her search for Cupid, another favorite theme among Renaissance poets, Spenser takes us to the Garden of Adonis where Venus lives. Here we find "a thousand thousand naked babes," some of whom are clothed in flesh and sent to live in the world. When their span of life is over, they return to the garden to be replanted and, forgetting their former earthly state, they grow again during "some thousand years" in the same way that animals and plants grow, under the care of nature and "Old Genius." The garden would be a veritable paradise if only Time, the pitiless enemy of this continual renewing of life, did not destroy all "goodly things" with his scythe and "flaggy wings." But even Time cannot wipe out the spot where Venus and Adonis dwell in perpetual bliss, for Adonis, "the Father of all formes," is eternal in mutability. Thus Spenser employs classic myth to set forth the idea of permanence underlying eternal flux. Through the poet's creative imagination, a simple story from Ovid becomes a pseudo-philosophical treatment of the problem of mutability and the relation between form and matter.

29

She brought her to her joyous Paradize,
    Where most she wonnes, when she on earth does dwel.
    So faire a place, as Nature can devize:
    Whether in *Paphos*, or *Cytheron* hill,
    Or it in *Gnidus* be, I wote not well;
    But well I wote by tryall, that this same
    All other pleasant places doth excell,
    And callèd is by her lost lovers name,   260
The *Gardin* of *Adonis*, farre renowmd by fame.

30

In that same Gardin all the goodly flowres,
    Wherewith dame Nature doth her beautifie,
    And decks the girlonds of her paramoures,
    Are fetcht: there is the first seminarie
    Of all things, that are borne to live and die,
    According to their kindes. Long worke it were,
    Here to account the endlesse progenie
    Of all the weedes, that bud and blossome there;
But so much as doth need, must needs be counted here.   270

31

It sited was in fruitfull soyle of old,
    And girt in with two walles on either side;
    The one of yron, the other of bright gold,
    That none might thorough breake, nor overstride:
    And double gates it had, which opened wide,
    By which both in and out men moten pas;
    Th' one faire and fresh, the other old and dride:
    Old *Genius* the porter of them was,
Old *Genius*, the which a double nature has.

32

He letteth in, he letteth out to wend,   280
    All that to come into the world desire;
    A thousand thousand naked babes attend
    About him day and night, which doe require,
    That he with fleshly weedes would them attire:
    Such as him list, such as eternall fate
    Ordainèd hath, he clothes with sinfull mire,
    And sendeth forth to live in mortall state,
Till they againe returne backe by the hinder gate.

675. **crime**, reproach.

268. **account**, enumerate or recount.   269. **weedes**, plants.   270. **counted**, recounted.

33

After that they againe returnèd beene,
   They in that Gardin planted be againe;   290
   And grow afresh, as they had never seene
   Fleshly corruption, nor mortall paine.
   Some thousand yeares so doen they there remaine;
   And then of him are clad with other hew,
   Or sent into the chaungefull world againe,
   Till thither they returne, where first they grew:
So like a wheele around they runne from old to new.

34

Ne needs there Gardiner to set, or sow,
   To plant or prune: for of their owne accord
   All things, as they created were, doe grow,   300
   And yet remember well the mightie word,
   Which first was spoken by th' Almightie lord,
   That bad them to increase and multiply:
   Ne doe they need with water of the ford,
   Or of the clouds to moysten their roots dry;
For in themselves eternall moisture they imply.

35

Infinite shapes of creatures there are bred,
   And uncouth formes, which none yet ever knew,
   And every sort is in a sundry bed
   Set by it selfe, and ranckt in comely rew: 310
   Some fit for reasonable soules t' indew,
   Some made for beasts, some made for birds to weare,
   And all the fruitfull spawne of fishes hew
   In endlesse rancks along enraungèd were,
That seemed the *Ocean* could not containe them there.

36

Daily they grow, and daily forth are sent
   Into the world, it to replenish more;
   Yet is the stocke not lessenèd, nor spent,
   But still remaines in everlasting store,
   As it at first created was of yore.   320
   For in the wide wombe of the world there lyes,
   In hatefull darkenesse and in deepe horrore,
   An huge eternall *Chaos*, which supplyes
The substances of natures fruitfull progenyes.

37

All things from thence doe their first being fetch,
   And borrow matter, whereof they are made,
   Which when as forme and feature it does ketch,
   Becomes a bodie, and doth then invade
   The state of life, out of the griesly shade.
   That substance is eterne, and bideth so,   330
   Ne when the life decayes, and forme does fade,
   Doth it consume, and into nothing go,
But chaungèd is, and often altred to and fro.

38

The substance is not chaungèd, nor alterèd,
   But th' only forme and outward fashion;
   For every substance is conditionèd
   To change her hew, and sundry formes to don,
   Meet for her temper and complexion:
   For formes are variable and decay,
   By course of kind, and by occasion;   340
   And that faire flowre of beautie fades away,
As doth the lilly fresh before the sunny ray.

39

Great enimy to it, and to all the rest,
   That in the *Gardin* of *Adonis* springs,
   Is wicked *Time*, who with his scyth addrest,
   Does mow the flowring herbes and goodly things,
   And all their glory to the ground downe flings,
   Where they doe wither, and are fowly mard:
   He flyes about, and with his flaggy wings
   Beates downe both leaves and buds without regard,   350
Ne ever pittie may relent his malice hard.

40

Yet pittie often did the gods relent,
   To see so faire things mard, and spoylèd quight:
   And their great mother *Venus* did lament
   The losse of her deare brood, her deare delight:
   Her hart was pierst with pittie at the sight,
   When walking through the Gardin, them she spyde,
   Yet no'te she find redresse for such despight.
   For all that lives, is subject to that law:
All things decay in time, and to their end do draw.   360

41

But were it not, that *Time* their troubler is,
   All that in this delightfull Gardin growes,
   Should happie be, and have immortall blis:
   For here all plentie, and all pleasure flowes,
   And sweet love gentle fits emongst them throwes,
   Without fell rancour, or fond gealosie;
   Franckly each paramour his leman knowes,
   Each bird his mate, ne any does envie
Their goodly meriment, and gay felicitie.

306. imply, infold.   **309. sundry**, separate.   **336. conditionèd**, bound as by a contract.

42

There is continuall spring, and harvest there 370
   Continuall, both meeting at one time:
      For both the boughes doe laughing blossomes beare,
      And with fresh colours decke the wanton Prime,
      And eke attonce the heavy trees they clime,
      Which seeme to labour under their fruits lode:
      The whiles the joyous birdes make their pastime
      Emongst the shadie leaves, their sweet abode,
And their true loves without suspition tell abrode.

43

Right in the middest of that Paradise,
   There stood a stately Mount, on whose round top 380
      A gloomy grove of mirtle trees did rise,
      Whose shadie boughes sharpe steele did never lop,
      Nor wicked beasts their tender buds did crop,
      But like a girlond compassèd the hight,
      And from their fruitfull sides sweet gum did drop,
      That all the ground with precious deaw bedight,
Threw forth most dainty odours, and most sweet delight.

44

And in the thickest covert of that shade,
   There was a pleasant arbour, not by art,
      But of the trees owne inclination made, 390
      Which knitting their rancke braunches part to part,
      With wanton yvie twyne entrayld athwart,
      And Eglantine, and Caprifole emong,
      Fashiond above within their inmost part,
      That nether *Phoebus* beams could through them throng,
Nor *Aeolus* sharp blast could worke them any wrong.

45

And all about grew every sort of flowre,
   To which sad lovers were transformd of yore;
      Fresh *Hyacinthus*, *Phoebus* paramoure,
      And dearest love, 400
      Foolish *Narcisse*, that likes the watry shore,
      Sad *Amaranthus*, made a flowre but late,
      Sad *Amaranthus*, in whose purple gore
      Me seemes I see *Amintas* wretched fate,
To whom sweet Poets verse hath given endlesse date.

370. **harvest,** autumn.   374. **they clime.** There is no antecedent for "they."   393. **Caprifole,** honeysuckle or woodbine.   404. **Amintas,** probably Sir Philip Sidney.

46

There wont faire *Venus* often to enjoy
   Her deare *Adonis* joyous company,
      And reape sweet pleasure of the wanton boy;
      There yet, some say, in secret he does ly,
      Lappèd in flowres and pretious spycery, 410
      By her hid from the world, and from the skill
      Of *Stygian* Gods, which doe her love envy;
      But she her selfe, when ever that she will,
Possesseth him, and of his sweetnesse takes her fill.

47

And sooth it seemes they say: for he may not
   For ever die, and ever buried bee
      In balefull night, where all things are forgot;
      All be he subject to mortalitie,
      Yet is eterne in mutabilitie,
      And by succession made perpetuall, 420
      Transformèd oft, and chaungèd diverslie:
      For him the Father of all formes they call;
Therefore needs mote he live, that living gives to all.

48

There now he liveth in eternall blis,
   Joying his goddesse, and of her enjoyd:
      Ne feareth he henceforth that foe of his,
      Which with his cruell tuske him deadly cloyd:
      For that wilde Bore, the which him once annoyd,
      She firmely hath emprisonèd for ay,
      That her sweet love his malice mote avoyd, 430
      In a strong rocky Cave, which is they say,
Hewen underneath that Mount, that none him losen may.

49

There now he lives in everlasting joy,
   With many of the Gods in company,
      Which thither haunt, and with the wingèd boy
      Sporting himselfe in safe felicity:
      Who when he hath with spoiles and cruelty
      Ransackt the world, and in the wofull harts
      Of many wretches set his triumphes hye,
      Thither resorts, and laying his sad darts 440
Aside, with faire *Adonis* playes his wanton parts.

50

And his true love faire *Psyche* with him playes,
   Faire *Psyche* to him lately reconcyld,
      After long troubles and unmeet upbrayes,
      With which his mother *Venus* her revyld,
      And eke himselfe her cruelly exyld:
      But now in stedfast love and happy state

She with him lives, and hath him borne a
    chyld,
Pleasure, that doth both gods and men aggrate,
Pleasure, the daughter of *Cupid* and *Psyche* late.   450

51

Hither great *Venus* brought this infant faire,
    The younger daughter of *Chrysogonee*,
    And unto *Psyche* with great trust and care
    Committed her, yfosterèd to bee,
    And trainèd up in true feminitee:
    Who no lesse carefully her tenderèd,
    Then her owne daughter *Pleasure*, to whom
    shee
Made her companion, and her lessonèd
In all the lore of love, and goodly womanhead.

52

In which when she to perfect ripenesse grew,   460
    Of grace and beautie noble Paragone,
    She brought her forth into the worldès vew,
    To be th' ensample of true love alone,
    And Lodestarre of all chaste affectione,
    To all faire Ladies, that doe live on ground.
    To Faery court she came, where many one
    Admyrd her goodly haveour, and found
His feeble hart wide launched with lovès cruell
    wound.

Sir Walter Ralegh
c. 1552–1618

Sir Walter Ralegh, though not so attractive a character as Sir Philip Sidney, is an even more typical Renaissance courtier and adventurer. His life was longer than Sidney's, and it was marked by greater extremities of good and ill fortune. "Most lofty, insolent, and passionate" are the epithets applied to his verse by Puttenham in the *Art of English Poetry*, 1589, and the adjectives fit his personality even better than they describe his poetry. Unscrupulously ambitious, violent of temper, intellectually audacious, Ralegh is perhaps best remembered as the first Englishman to be stirred imaginatively by the New World and by the possibility of colonizing it.

Ralegh was born in Devonshire about 1552 of a well-connected family that was rising in the world. He seems to have attended Oriel College, Oxford, for a brief period. He served as a volunteer with the Huguenot armies in 1569, and in 1578, with Sir Humphrey Gilbert, his half-brother, he fitted out a fleet ostensibly for purposes of discovery but actually for preying on Spanish shipping. His ship's motto was, characteristically, "*Nec mortem peto, nec finem fugio*"—"I neither seek death nor flee the end." In 1580, he took part in a military expedition to Ireland, and put to death six hundred Spaniards who fell into his hands. He owed his introduction to court to the influence of the Earl of Leicester, an early favorite of Elizabeth's and the uncle of Sir Philip Sidney. Ralegh's person—tall, dark, handsome, vigorous—made a deep impression on the Queen,

156. tenderèd, cared for.

and she lavished so many honors on him that he rapidly became one of the wealthiest of her courtiers. Although the Queen refused to give him permission to lead voyages of discovery in person, he sent out an expedition which took possession of an immense tract on the Atlantic seaboard, to which the Queen, with some self-flattery, gave the name Virginia. Ralegh was knighted in 1585 and was made warden of the mines of Cornwall and Devon and Lord Lieutenant of Cornwall. In 1586, he was made captain of the Queen's guard, and given an estate of forty thousand acres in Ireland. In the late eighties, he invested £40,000 in three expeditions to colonize Virginia. The efforts failed completely; possibly the most important results were the introduction of potatoes and tobacco in England; of tobacco, Ralegh became one of the first enthusiastic smokers.

In the youthful Earl of Essex, Ralegh found an unscrupulous rival for royal favors, and although the Queen was pleased when an expedition he launched captured a Spanish carrack with a cargo of gold worth £500,000 sterling, she was infuriated when she discovered that Ralegh, while addressing poems of adulation to her, had been intriguing with a maid of honor named Elizabeth Throgmorton, and imprisoned them both. She released Ralegh only after she had taken unto herself the larger share of the carrack's spoils. After Ralegh's marriage to his mistress and their settlement at his estate at Sherborne, he seems to have entered into a close association with some of the most advanced thinkers of the day, including Thomas Hariot the deist and Christopher Marlowe, who was suspected of atheism. Although Ralegh's religious views were probably orthodox, the heretical reputation of "Ralegh's School of Atheism" led to an official investigation. Ralegh believed that untold wealth was to be gained if he could find the legendary city of Eldorado, and in 1595 he sailed with an expedition which made its way for about four hundred miles up the Orinoco, but brought back only a cargo of rumors and of "false-gold." He wrote and published in 1596 an account of his venture under the title *Discovery of the Empire of Guiana*. For a time he was reconciled with both the Queen and Essex, and took part in a naval foray that ended with the capture of Fayal, in the Azores. In 1600, he was made governor of the island of Jersey.

Rumors of Ralegh's opposition to James's claim to the throne had reached the King before the death of Elizabeth, and upon James's accession Ralegh was deprived of most of his offices, and in 1603 was sent to the Tower on suspicion of his complicity in a plot against the King's life. He received a most unfair trial, and was sentenced to death. The sentence was commuted to imprisonment, and most of the rest of Ralegh's life was spent with his family in the Tower. There, befriended by the brilliant young Prince Henry, he was encouraged to undertake his *History of the World*, the first part of which was published in 1614. Ralegh had not yet given up hopes of finding Eldorado, and he obtained his release from prison on condition that he should lead an expedition and bring back gold to England. The venture failed miserably, and, under the influence of the Spanish Ambassador, furious at the destruction of San Tomas, Trinidad, by one of Ralegh's captains, the King revived the old charge of conspiracy and had Ralegh executed on October 28, 1618.

Ralegh's reputation as a poet has long been obscured because, aside from a number of commendatory verses like "A Vision upon This Conceit of the Faerie Queene," his poems were published anonymously during his lifetime. The process of accumulating and identifying them has been slow and hazardous, and the results are by no means certain. The longest of Ralegh's poems is the fragment of "The Ocean to Cynthia," a long poem of adulation addressed to the Queen. The extant version is probably later than the one read in 1589 by Ralegh to Spenser, who had already bestowed on him the epithet Shepherd of the Ocean. Ralegh appears most attractively in his lyrics. They are not in the conventional style and mood of most Elizabethan lyrics; instead, they are free in form and show a sardonic and embittered spirit which may have resulted from the author's own experience of human capriciousness and ingratitude.

Ralegh's major prose works are his brief narrative (here reprinted) of the last fight of the *Revenge*, 1591; his *Discovery of Guiana*, 1596; and his *History of the World*, 1614. Ralegh shows little skill in organizing his material, and his digressions are likely to be more interesting than the sweep of his narrative. But his style, although frequently syntactically obscure, is spontaneous and free from the conceits cultivated by Sidney and Lyly, and the apostrophe to Death from the *History* is justly famous:

"O eloquent, just and mighty death, whom none could advise, thou hast persuaded; what none hath presumed, thou hast done; and whom all the world hath flattered, thou hast cast out of the world and despised: thou hast drawn together all the extravagant greatness, all the pride, cruelty and ambition of man, and covered all over with two narrow words: *Hic jacet*."[1]

A VISION UPON THIS CONCEIT OF THE FAERIE QUEENE

This complimentary sonnet was written in honor of Spenser's *Faerie Queene* and first published with it.

Methought I saw the grave where Laura lay,
Within that temple where the vestal flame
Was wont to burn; and passing by that way
To see that buried dust of living fame,
Whose tomb fair Love and fairer Virtue kept,
All suddenly I saw the Fairy Queen;
At whose approach the soul of Petrarch wept,
And from thenceforth those graces were not seen,
For they this Queen attended; in whose stead
Oblivion laid him down on Laura's hearse.   10
Hereat the hardest stones were seen to bleed,
And groans of buried ghosts the heavens did pierce;
   Where Homer's sprite did tremble all for grief,
   And cursed th' access of that celestial thief.

THE NYMPH'S REPLY TO THE SHEPHERD

This is one of the many poetic answers to Marlowe's "The Passionate Shepherd."

   If all the world and love were young,
   And truth in every shepherd's tongue,
   These pretty pleasures might me move
   To live with thee and be thy love.

[1] *Hic jacet*." "Here lies"—usual first words on a tombstone.

Time drives the flocks from field to fold
When rivers rage and rocks grow cold,
And Philomel becometh dumb;
The rest complains of cares to come.

The flowers do fade, and wanton fields
To wayward winter reckoning yields;   10
A honey tongue, a heart of gall,
Is fancy's spring, but sorrow's fall.

Thy gowns, thy shoes, thy beds of roses,
Thy cap, thy kirtle, and thy posies
Soon break, soon wither, soon forgotten,—
In folly ripe, in reason rotten.

Thy belt of straw and ivy buds,
Thy coral clasps and amber studs,
All these in me no means can move
To come to thee and be thy love.   20

But could youth last and love still breed,
Had joys no date nor age no need,
Then these delights my mind might move
To live with thee and be thy love.

THE LIE

    Go, soul, the body's guest,
    Upon a thankless arrant.
    Fear not to touch the best;
    The truth shall be thy warrant.
        Go, since I needs must die,
        And give the world the lie.

    Say to the court, it glows
    And shines like rotten wood;
    Say to the church, it shows
    What's good, and doth no good: 10
        If church and court reply,
        Then give them both the lie.

    Tell potentates, they live
    Acting by others' action,
    Not loved unless they give,
    Not strong but by affection:
        If potentates reply,
        Give potentates the lie.

    Tell men of high condition
    That manage the estate,   20
    Their purpose is ambition,
    Their practice only hate:

        And if they once reply,
        Then give them all the lie.

    Tell them that brave it most,
    They beg for more by spending,
    Who, in their greatest cost,
    Like nothing but commending:
        And if they make reply,
        Then give them all the lie.   30

    Tell zeal it wants devotion;
    Tell love it is but lust;
    Tell time it meets but motion;
    Tell flesh it is but dust:
        And wish them not reply,
        For thou must give the lie.

    Tell age it daily wasteth;
    Tell honour how it alters;
    Tell beauty how she blasteth;
    Tell favour how it falters: 40
        And as they shall reply,
        Give every one the lie.

    Tell wit how much it wrangles
    In tickle points of niceness;
    Tell wisdom she entangles
    Herself in over-wiseness:
        And when they do reply,
        Straight give them both the lie.

    Tell physic of her boldness;
    Tell skill it is prevention;   50
    Tell charity of coldness;
    Tell law it is contention:
        And as they do reply,
        So give them still the lie.

    Tell fortune of her blindness;
    Tell nature of decay;
    Tell friendship of unkindness;
    Tell justice of delay:
        And if they will reply,
        Then give them all the lie.   60

    Tell arts they have no soundness,
    But vary by esteeming;
    Tell schools they want profoundness,
    And stand too much on seeming:
        If arts and schools reply,
        Give arts and schools the lie.

    Tell faith it's fled the city;
    Tell how the country erreth;

The Lie. 2. **arrant,** errand.   16. **affection,** in some MSS. "a faction."

Tell, manhood shakes off pity,
Tell, virtue least preferrèd: 70
   And if they do reply,
   Spare not to give the lie.

So when thou hast, as I
Commanded thee, done blabbing,
Because to give the lie
Deserves no less than stabbing,
   Stab at thee he that will—
   No stab thy soul can kill.

HIS PILGRIMAGE

Give me my scallop-shell of quiet,
My staff of faith to walk upon,
My scrip of joy, immortal diet,
My bottle of salvation,
My gown of glory, hope's true gage,
And thus I'll take my pilgrimage.

Blood must be my body's balmer,
No other balm will there be given,
Whilst my soul like a white palmer
Travels to the land of heaven, 10
Over the silver mountains,
Where spring the nectar fountains;
   And there I'll kiss
   The bowl of bliss,
And drink my eternal fill
On every milken hill.
My soul will be a-dry before,
But after it will ne'er thirst more;
And by the happy blissful way
More peaceful pilgrims I shall see, 20
That have shook off their gowns of clay
And go appareled fresh like me.

I'll bring them first
To slake their thirst,
And then to taste those nectar suckets,
   At the clear wells
   Where sweetness dwells,
Drawn up by saints in crystal buckets.

And when our bottles and all we
Are filled with immortality, 30
Then the holy paths we'll travel,
Strewed with rubies thick as gravel,
Ceilings of diamonds, sapphire floors,
High walls of coral, and pearl bowers.

1. **scallop-shell,** worn by pilgrims as a badge. 3. **scrip,** wallet. 7. **balmer,** embalmer. 25. **suckets,** candied fruits.

From thence to heaven's bribeless hall
Where no corrupted voices brawl,
No conscience molten into gold,
Nor forged accusers bought and sold,
No cause deferred, nor vain-spent journey,
For there Christ is the king's attorney, 40
Who pleads for all without degrees,
And he hath angels, but no fees.
When the grand twelve million jury
Of our sins and sinful fury,
'Gainst our souls black verdicts give,
Christ pleads his death, and then we live.
Be thou my speaker, taintless pleader,
Unblotted lawyer, true proceeder,
Thou movest salvation even for alms,
Not with a bribèd lawyer's palms. 50

And this is my eternal plea
To him that made heaven, earth, and sea,
Seeing my flesh must die so soon,
And want a head to dine next noon,
Just at the stroke when my veins start and spread,
Set on my soul an everlasting head.
Then am I ready, like a palmer fit,
To tread those blest paths which before I writ.

EVEN SUCH IS TIME

According to legend, this stanza was written by Ralegh on the night before his execution. As a matter of fact, a slightly different version had appeared as the final stanza of an earlier poem of thirty-six lines, describing the creation by Nature of a beautiful but heartless woman and the destruction by Time of her beauty, wit, and wantonness. The first stanza of the poem follows:

"Nature, that washed her hands in milk,
   And had forgot to dry them,
Instead of earth took snow and silk,
   At love's request to try them,
if she a mistress could compose
To please love's fancy out of those."

Even such is time, that takes in trust
   Our youth, our joys, our all we have,
And pays us but with earth and dust;
   Who, in the dark and silent grave,
When we have wandered all our ways,
Shuts up the story of our days.
But from this earth, this grave, this dust,
My God shall raise me up, I trust!

35–50. **From thence . . . lawyer's palms,** reference to the unjust trial of Ralegh in 1603 and the bitter denunciations of him by Sir Edward Coke, Attorney-General. **angels,** a pun on the gold coin, the angel.

A REPORT OF THE TRUTH OF THE FIGHT ABOUT THE ISLES OF AÇORES THIS LAST SUMMER BETWIXT THE *REVENGE*, ONE OF HER MAJESTY'S SHIPS, AND AN ARMADA OF THE KING OF SPAIN

BECAUSE the rumours are diversely spread, as well in England as in the Low Countries and elsewhere, of this late encounter between Her Majesty's ships and the Armada of Spain; and that the Spaniards according to their usual manner fill the world with their vainglorious vaunts, making great appearance of victories, when on the contrary themselves are most commonly and shamefully beaten and dishonoured; thereby hoping to possess the ignorant multitude by anticipating and forerunning false reports; it is agreeable with all good reason, for manifestation of the truth, to overcome falsehood and untruth, that the beginning, continuance, and success of this late honourable encounter of Sir Richard Grenville and other Her Majesty's captains, with the Armada of Spain, should be truly set down and published without partiality or false imaginations. And it is no marvel that the Spaniard should seek by false and slanderous pamphlets, advisoes, and letters, to cover their own loss and to derogate from others their due honours, especially in this fight being performed far off; seeing they were not ashamed in the year 1588, when they purposed the invasion of this land, to publish in sundry languages, in print, great victories in words, which they pleaded to have obtained against this realm; and spread the same in a most false sort over all parts of France, Italy, and elsewhere. When shortly after it was happily manifested in very deed to all nations how their navy, which they termed invincible, consisting of 240 sail of ships, not only of their own kingdom but strengthened with the greatest argosies, Portugal carracks, Florentines, and huge hulks of other countries, were by thirty of Her Majesty's own ships of war, and a few of our own merchants, by the wise, valiant, and most advantageous conduction of the Lord Charles Howard, high admiral of England, beaten and shuffled together; even from the Lizard in Cornwall, first to Portland, where they shamefully left Don Pedro de Valdes with his mighty ship; from Portland to Cales, where they lost Hugo de Moncado, with the galliass of which he was captain; and from Cales driven with squibs from their anchors, were chased out of the sight of England, round about Scotland and Ireland. Where for the sympathy of their barbarous religion hoping to find succour and assistance, a great part of them were crushed against the rocks, and those other that landed, being very many in number, were notwithstanding broken, slain, and taken, and so sent from village to village, coupled in halters, to be shipped into England. Where Her Majesty of her princely and invincible disposition disdaining to put them to death, and scorning either to retain or entertain them, they were all sent back again to their countries, to witness and recount the worthy achievements of their invincible and dreadful navy. Of which the number of soldiers, the fearful burthen of their ships, the commanders' names of every squadron, with all other their magazines of provisions, were put in print, as an army and navy unresistible and disdaining prevention. With all which so great and terrible an ostentation they did not in all their sailing round about England so much as sink or take one ship, bark, pinnace, or cockboat of ours, or ever burned so much as one sheepcote of this land. Whenas on the contrary Sir Francis Drake, with only eight hundred soldiers, not long before landed in their Indies and forced Santiago, Santo Domingo, Cartagena, and the forts of Florida. And after that Sir John Norris marched from Peniche in Portugal, with a handful of soldiers, to the gates of Lisbon, being above forty English miles. Where the Earl of Essex himself and other valiant gentlemen braved the city of Lisbon, encamped at the very gates; from whence after many days' abode, finding neither promised party nor provision to batter, they made retreat by land in despite of all their garrisons both of horse and foot.

In this sort I have a little digressed from my first purpose, only by the necessary comparison of theirs and our actions; the one covetous of honour without vaunt or ostentation; the other so greedy to purchase the opinion of their own affairs and by false rumours to resist the blasts of their own dishonours as they will not only not blush to spread all manner of untruths, but even for the least advantage, be it but for the taking of one poor adventurer of the English, will celebrate the victory with bonfires in every town, always spending more in faggots than the purchase was worth they obtained. Whenas we never yet thought it worth the consumption of two billets when we have taken eight or ten of their Indian ships at one time and twenty of the Brazil fleet. Such is the difference between true

---

53. **galliass,** a large galley mounting heavy guns.　　1. **squibs,** charges of powder.　　35. **batter,** bombard.

valour and ostentation, and between honourable actions and frivolous vainglorious vaunts. But now to return to my first purpose.

The Lord Thomas Howard, with six of Her Majesty's ships, six victualers of London, the bark *Ralegh*, and two or three pinnaces, riding at anchor near unto Flores, one of the westerly islands of the Azores, the last of August in the afternoon, had intelligence by one Captain Middleton of the approach of the Spanish Armada. Which Middleton being in a very good sailer had kept them company three days before, of good purpose, both to discover their forces the more, as also to give advice to my Lord Thomas of their approach. He had no sooner delivered the news but the fleet was in sight.

Many of our ships' companies were on shore in the island, some providing ballast for their ships, others filling of water and refreshing themselves from the land with such things as they could either for money or by force recover. By reason whereof our ships being all pestered and roomaging every thing out of order, very light for want of ballast, and that which was most to our disadvantage, the one-half part of the men of every ship sick and utterly unserviceable. For in the *Revenge* there were ninety diseased; in the *Bonaventure* not so many in health as could handle her mainsail. For had not twenty men been taken out of a bark of Sir George Cary's, his being commanded to be sunk, and those appointed to her, she had hardly ever recovered England. The rest for the most part were in little better state. The names of Her Majesty's ships were these as followeth: the *Defiance*, which was admiral, the *Revenge*, vice-admiral, the *Bonaventure* commanded by Captain Cross, the *Lion* by George Fenner, the *Foresight* by Mr. Thomas Vavasour, and the *Crane* by Duffild. The *Foresight* and the *Crane* being but small ships; only the other were of the middle size; the rest, besides the bark *Ralegh* commanded by Captain Thin, were victualers and of small force or none.

The Spanish fleet having shrouded their approach by reason of the island, were now so soon at hand as our ships had scarce time to weigh their anchors, but some of them were driven to let slip their cables and set sail. Sir Richard Grenville was the last weighed, to recover the men that were upon the island, which otherwise had been lost. The Lord Thomas with the rest very hardly recovered the wind, which Sir Richard Grenville not being able to do was persuaded by the master and others to cut his mainsail and cast about, and to trust to the sailing of his ship; for the squadron of Sivil were on his weather bow. But Sir Richard utterly refused to turn from the enemy, alleging that he would rather choose to die than to dishonour himself, his country, and Her Majesty's ship, persuading his company that he would pass through the two squadrons in despite of them, and enforce those of Sivil to give him way. Which he performed upon divers of the foremost, who, as the mariners term it, sprang their luff, and fell under the lee of the *Revenge*. But the other course had been the better, and might right well have been answered in so great an impossibility of prevailing. Notwithstanding, out of the greatness of his mind he could not be persuaded.

In the meanwhile as he attended those which were nearest him, the great *San Philip* being in the wind of him and coming towards him becalmed his sails in such sort as the ship could neither make way nor feel the helm, so huge and high cargoed was the Spanish ship, being of a thousand and five hundred tons. Who after laid the *Revenge* aboard. When he was thus bereft of his sails, the ships that were under his lee, luffing up, also laid him aboard; of which the next was the admiral of the Biscaines, a very mighty and puissant ship commanded by Brittandona. The said *Philip* carried three tier of ordnance on a side, and eleven pieces in every tier. She shot eight forthright out of her chase, besides those of her stern ports.

After the *Revenge* was entangled with this *Philip*, four other boarded her; two on her larboard and two on her starboard. The fight thus beginning at three of the clock in the afternoon continued very terrible all that evening. But the great *San Philip* having received the lower tier of the *Revenge*, discharged with crossbar-shot, shifted herself with all diligence from her sides, utterly misliking her first entertainment. Some say that the ship foundered, but we cannot report it for truth unless we were assured.

The Spanish ships were filled with companies of soldiers, in some two hundred besides the mariners, in some five, in others eight hundred. In ours there were none at all, beside the mariners, but the servants of the commanders and some few voluntary gentlemen only. After many interchanged volleys of great ordnance and small shot, the Spaniards deliberated to enter the *Revenge*, and made divers attempts, hoping to force her by the multitudes of their armed soldiers and musketeers, but were still repulsed again and again, and at all times beaten back into their own ships or into the seas.

21. **roomaging**, knocking about, disarranging. 52. **Sivil**, Seville.

8–9. **sprang their luff**, brought their ship's bow closer to the wind. 20. **laid . . . aboard**, came up alongside. 22. **luffing up**, putting the heads of their ships closer to the wind. 27. **chase**, the part of the ship where "chase" guns are fired from portholes.

In the beginning of the fight the *George Noble* of London, having received some shot through her by the armadas, fell under the lee of the *Revenge* and asked Sir Richard what he would command him, being but one of the victualers and of small force. Sir Richard bid him save himself and leave him to his fortune.

After the fight had thus without intermission continued while the day lasted and some hours of the night, many of our men were slain and hurt, and one of the great galleons of the Armada and the admiral of the hulks both sunk, and in many other of the Spanish ships great slaughter was made. Some write that Sir Richard was very dangerously hurt almost in the beginning of the fight and lay speechless for a time ere he recovered. But two of the *Revenge's* own company, brought home in a ship of line from the islands, examined by some of the lords and others, affirmed that he was never so wounded as that he forsook the upper deck, till an hour before midnight; and then being shot into the body with a musket, as he was a-dressing was again shot into the head, and withal his chirurgeon wounded to death. This agreeth also with an examination taken by Sir Francis Godolphin of four other mariners of the same ship being returned, which examination the said Sir Francis sent unto Master William Killigrue of Her Majesty's Privy Chamber.

But to return to the fight, the Spanish ships which attempted to board the *Revenge*, as they were wounded and beaten off, so always others came in their places, she having never less than two mighty galleons by her sides and aboard her. So that ere the morning, from three of the clock the day before, there had fifteen several armadas assailed her; and all so ill approved their entertainment as they were by the break of day far more willing to hearken to a composition than hastily to make any more assaults or entries. But as the day increased, so our men decreased; and as the light grew more and more, by so much more grew our discomforts. For none appeared in sight but enemies, saving one small ship called the *Pilgrim*, commanded by Jacob Whiddon, who hovered all night to see the success, but in the morning bearing with the *Revenge*, was hunted like a hare amongst many ravenous hounds, but escaped.

All the powder of the *Revenge* to the last barrel was now spent, all her pikes broken, forty of her best men slain, and the most part of the rest hurt. In the beginning of the fight she had but one hundred free from sickness, and fourscore and ten sick, laid in hold upon the ballast. A small troop to man such a ship, and a weak garrison to resist so mighty an army. By those hundred all was sustained, the volleys, boardings, and enterings of fifteen ships of war, besides those which beat her at large. On the contrary, the Spanish were always supplied with soldiers brought from every squadron; all manner of arms and powder at will. Unto ours there remained no comfort at all, no hope, no supply either of ships, men, or weapons; the masts all beaten overboard, all her tackle cut asunder, her upper work altogether rased, and in effect evened she was with the water, but the very foundation or bottom of a ship, nothing being left overhead either for flight or defence.

Sir Richard, finding himself in this distress and unable any longer to make resistance, having endured in this fifteen hours' fight the assault of fifteen several armadas all by turns aboard him, and by estimation eight hundred shot of great artillery, besides many assaults and entries; and that himself and the ship must needs be possessed by the enemy, who were now all cast in a ring round about him, the *Revenge* not able to move one way or other but as she was moved with the waves and billow of the sea; commanded the master gunner, whom he knew to be a most resolute man, to split and sink the ship; that thereby nothing might remain of glory or victory to the Spaniards, seeing in so many hours' fight and with so great a navy they were not able to take her, having had fifteen hours' time, fifteen thousand men, and fifty and three sail of men-of-war to perform it withal; and persuaded the company, or as many as he could induce, to yield themselves unto God and to the mercy of none else, but as they had like valiant resolute men repulsed so many enemies they should not now shorten the honour of their nation by prolonging their own lives for a few hours or a few days.

The master gunner readily condescended, and divers others; but the captain and the master were of another opinion, and besought Sir Richard to have care of them; alleging that the Spaniard would be as ready to entertain a composition as they were willing to offer the same; and that there being divers sufficient and valiant men yet living, and whose wounds were not mortal, they might do their country and prince acceptable service hereafter. And that whereas Sir Richard had alleged that the Spaniards should never glory to have taken one ship of Her Majesty, seeing that they had so long and so notably defended themselves, they answered that the ship had six foot water in hold, three shot under water which were so weakly stopped as with the first working of the sea she must needs sink, and

23. **chirurgeon,** surgeon.

was besides so crushed and bruised as she could never be removed out of the place.

And as the matter was thus in dispute, and Sir Richard refusing to hearken to any of those reasons, the master of the *Revenge* (while the captain wan unto him the greater party) was convoyed aboard the general, Don Alfonso Baçan. Who finding none over-hasty to enter the *Revenge* again, doubting lest Sir Richard would have blown them up and himself, and perceiving by the report of the master of the *Revenge* his dangerous disposition, yielded that all their lives should be saved, the company sent for England, and the better sort to pay such reasonable ransom as their estate would bear, and in the mean season to be free from galley or imprisonment. To this he so much the rather condescended as well, as I have said, for fear of further loss and mischief to themselves, as also for the desire he had to recover Sir Richard Grenville; whom for his notable valour he seemed greatly to honour and admire.

When this answer was returned, and that safety of life was promised, the common sort being now at the end of their peril, the most drew back from Sir Richard and the master gunner, being no hard matter to dissuade men from death to life. The master gunner, finding himself and Sir Richard thus prevented and mastered by the greater number, would have slain himself with a sword, had he not been by force withheld and locked into his cabin. Then the general sent many boats aboard the *Revenge*, and divers of our men fearing Sir Richard's disposition stole away aboard the general and other ships. Sir Richard, thus overmatched, was sent unto by Alfonso Baçan to remove out of the *Revenge*, the ship being marvelous unsavoury, filled with blood and bodies of dead and wounded men like a slaughterhouse. Sir Richard answered that he might do with his body what he list, for he esteemed it not, and as he was carried out of the ship he swounded, and reviving again desired the company to pray for him. The general used Sir Richard with all humanity, and left nothing unattempted that tended to his recovery, highly commending his valour and worthiness, and greatly bewailing the danger wherein he was, being unto them a rare spectacle and a resolution seldom approved, to see one ship turn toward so many enemies, to endure the charge and boarding of so many huge armadas, and to resist and repel the assaults and entries of so many soldiers. All which and more is confirmed by a Spanish captain of the same Armada, and a present actor in the fight, who being severed from the rest

5. **wan,** won.

in a storm was by the *Lion* of London, a small ship, taken, and is now prisoner in London.

The general commander of the Armada was Don Alfonso Baçan, brother to the Marques of Santa Cruz. The admiral of the Biscaine squadron was Brittandona. Of the squadron of Sivil, the Marques of Arumburch. The hulks and fly-boats were commanded by Luis Coutinho. There were slain and drowned in this fight well near two thousand of the enemies, and two special commanders, Don Luis de Sant John, and Don George de Prunaria de Mallaga, as the Spanish captain confesseth, besides divers others of special account whereof as yet report is not made.

The admiral of the hulks and the *Ascension* of Sivil were both sunk by the side of the *Revenge;* one other recovered the road of St. Michael and sunk also there; a fourth ran herself with the shore to save her men. Sir Richard died, as it is said, the second or third day aboard the general, and was by them greatly bewailed. What became of his body, whether it were buried in the sea or on the land, we know not; the comfort that remaineth to his friends is that he hath ended his life honourably in respect of the reputation won to his nation and country, and of the same to his posterity, and that being dead he hath not outlived his own honour.

For the rest of Her Majesty's ships that entered not so far into the fight as the *Revenge*, the reasons and causes were these. There were of them but six in all, whereof two but small ships; the *Revenge* engaged past recovery; the island of Flores was on the one side, fifty-three sail of the Spanish, divided into squadrons, on the other, all as full filled with soldiers as they could contain; almost the one half of our men sick and not able to serve; the ships grown foul, unroomaged, and scarcely able to bear any sail for want of ballast, having been six months at the sea before. If all the rest had entered, all had been lost. For the very hugeness of the Spanish fleet, if no other violence had been offered, would have crushed them between them into shivers. Of which the dishonour and loss to the Queen had been far greater than the spoil or harm that the enemy could any way have received. Notwithstanding, it is very true that the Lord Thomas would have entered between the squadrons, but the rest would not condescend; and the master of his own ship offered to leap into the sea rather than to conduct that Her Majesty's ship and the rest to be a prey to the enemy, where there was no hope nor possibility either of defence or victory. Which also in my

37. **unroomaged,** with the cargo below decks in disorder.

opinion had ill sorted or answered the discretion and trust of a general, to commit himself and his charge to an assured destruction, without hope or any likelihood of prevailing; thereby to diminish the strength of Her Majesty's navy, and to enrich the pride and glory of the enemy. The *Foresight* of the Queen's, commanded by Master Thomas Vavisor, performed a very great fight, and stayed two hours as near the *Revenge* as the weather would permit him, not forsaking the fight till he was like to be encompassed by the squadrons and with great difficulty cleared himself. The rest gave divers volleys of shot and entered as far as the place permitted, and their own necessities to keep the weather gage of the enemy, until they were parted by night.

A few days after the fight was ended and the English prisoners dispersed into the Spanish and Indy ships there arose so great a storm from the west and northwest that all the fleet was dispersed, as well the Indian fleet which were then come unto them as the rest of the Armada that attended their arrival, of which fourteen sail, together with the *Revenge*, and in her two hundred Spaniards, were cast away upon the isle of St. Michael. So it pleased them to honour the burial of that renowned ship the *Revenge*, not suffering her to perish alone, for the great honour she achieved in her life-time. On the rest of the islands there were cast away in this storm fifteen or sixteen more of the ships of war; and of a hundred and odd sail of the Indie fleet, expected this year in Spain, what in this tempest, and what before in the bay of Mexico, and about the Bermudas, there were seventy and odd consumed and lost, with those taken by our ships of London, besides one very rich Indian ship which set herself on fire, being boarded by the *Pilgrim*, and five other taken by Master Wats his ships of London, between the Havana and Cape S. Antonio. The fourth of this month of November we received letters from the Tercera affirming that there are three thousand bodies of men remaining in that island, saved out of the perished ships; and that by the Spaniards' own confession there are ten thousand cast away in this storm, besides those that are perished between the islands and the main. Thus it hath pleased God to fight for us and to defend the justice of our cause against the ambitious and bloody pretences of the Spaniard, who seeking to devour all nations are themselves devoured. A manifest testimony how injust and displeasing their attempts are in the sight of God, who hath pleased to witness by the success of their affairs his mislike of their bloody and injurious designs purposed and practised against all Christian princes, over whom they seek unlawful and ungodly rule and empery.

One day or two before this wrack happened to the Spanish fleet, whenas some of our prisoners desired to be set on shore upon the islands, hoping to be from thence transported into England, which liberty was formerly by the general promised, one Morice Fitz-John, son of old John of Desmond, a notable traitor, cousin german to the late Earl of Desmond, was sent to the English from ship to ship to persuade them to serve the King of Spain. The arguments he used to induce them were these: the increase of pay, which he promised to be trebled; advancement to the better sort; and the exercise of the true Catholic religion and safety of their souls to all. For the first, even the beggarly and unnatural behaviour of those English and Irish rebels that served the King in that present action was sufficient to answer that first argument of rich pay. For so poor and beggarly they were as for want of apparel they stripped their poor countrymen prisoners out of their ragged garments worn to nothing by six months' service, and spared not to despoil them even of their bloody shirts from their wounded bodies, and the very shoes from their feet; a notable testimony of their rich entertainment and great wages. The second reason was hope of advancement if they served well and would continue faithful to the King. But what man can be so blockishly ignorant ever to expect place or honour from a foreign king, having no argument or persuasion than his own disloyalty; to be unnatural to his own country that bred him, to his parents that begat him, and rebellious to his true prince to whose obedience he is bound by oath, by nature, and by religion? No, they are only assured to be employed in all desperate enterprises, to be held in scorn and disdain ever among those whom they serve. And that ever traitor was either trusted or advanced I could never yet read, neither can I at this time remember any example. And no man could have less becomed the place of an orator for such a purpose than this Morice of Desmond. For the earl his cousin being one of the greatest subjects in that kingdom of Ireland, having almost whole countries in his possession, so many goodly manors, castles, and lordships, the Count Palatine of Kerry, five hundred gentlemen of his own name and family to follow him, besides others—all which he possessed in peace for three or four hundred years—was in less than three years after his adhering to the Spaniards and rebellion beaten from all his holds, not so

2. **empery**, imperial sovereignty. 3. **wrack**, wreck, ruin.
9. **cousin german**, first cousin.

many as ten gentlemen of his name left living, himself taken and beheaded by a soldier of his own nation, and his land given by a parliament to Her Majesty and possessed by the English; his other cousin, Sir John of Desmond, taken by Master John Zouch and his body hanged over the gates of his native city to be devoured by ravens; the third brother of Sir James hanged, drawn, and quartered in the same place. If he had withal vaunted of this success of his own house, no doubt the argument would have moved much and wrought great effect; which because he for that present forgot, I thought it good to remember in his behalf. For matter of religion, it would require a particular volume if I should set down how irreligiously they cover their greedy and ambitious pretences with that veil of piety. But sure I am that there is no kingdom or commonwealth in all Europe but, if they be reformed, they then invade it for religion sake; if it be, as they term, Catholic, they pretend title; as if the kings of Castile were the natural heirs of all the world; and so between both no kingdom is unsought. Where they dare not with their own forces to invade, they basely entertain the traitors and vagabonds of all nations; seeking by those and by their runagate Jesuits to win parts, and have by that mean ruined many noble houses and others in this land, and have extinguished both their lives and families. What good, honour, or fortune ever man yet by them achieved is yet unheard of or unwritten. And if our English papists do but look into Portugal, against which they have no pretence of religion, how the nobility are put to death, imprisoned, their rich men made a prey, and all sorts of people captived, they shall find that the obedience even of the Turk is easy and a liberty in respect of the slavery and tyranny of Spain. What they have done in Sicil, in Naples, Millaine, and in the Low Countries; who hath there been spared for religion at all? And it cometh to my remembrance of a certain burger of Antwerp, whose house being entered by a company of Spanish soldiers, when they first sacked the city, he besought them to spare him and his goods, being a good Catholic, and one of their own party and faction. The Spaniards answered that they knew him to be of a good conscience for himself, but his money, plate, jewels, and goods were all heretical and therefore good prize. So they abused and tormented the foolish Fleming, who hoped that an Agnus Dei had been a sufficient target against all force of that holy and charitable nation. Neither have they at any time, as they protest, invaded the kingdoms of the Indies and Peru and elsewhere but only led thereunto rather to reduce the people to Christianity than for either gold or empery. Whenas in one only island, called Hispaniola, they have wasted thirty hundred thousand of the natural people, besides many millions else in other places of the Indies; a poor and harmless people, created of God, and might have been won to His knowledge, as many of them were, and almost as many as ever were persuaded thereunto. The story whereof is at large written by a bishop of their own nation called Bartholomew de las Casas, and translated into English and many other languages, entitled *The Spanish Cruelties*. Who would therefore repose trust in such a nation of ravenous strangers, and especially in those Spaniards which more greedily thirst after English blood than after the lives of any other people of Europe, for the many overthrows and dishonours they have received at our hands, whose weakness we have discovered to the world, and whose forces at home, abroad, in Europe, in India, by sea and land, we have even with handfuls of men and ships overthrown and dishonoured. Let not therefore any English man, of what religion soever, have other opinion of the Spaniards but that those whom he seeketh to win of our nation he esteemeth base and traitorous, unworthy persons, or unconstant fools; and that he useth his pretence of religion for no other purpose but to bewitch us from the obedience of our natural Prince, thereby hoping in time to bring us to slavery and subjection, and then none shall be unto them so odious and disdained as the traitors themselves, who have sold their country to a stranger, and forsaken their faith and obedience contrary to nature or religion; and contrary to that human and general honour, not only of Christians, but of heathen and irreligious nations, who have always sustained what labour soever, and embraced even death itself, for their country, prince, or commonwealth.

To conclude, it hath ever to this day pleased God to prosper and defend Her Majesty, to break the purposes of malicious enemies, of foresworn traitors, and of unjust practises and invasions. She hath ever been honoured of the worthiest kings, served by faithful subjects, and shall by the favour of God resist, repel, and confound all whatsoever attempts against her sacred person or kingdom. In the meantime let the Spaniard and traitor vaunt of their success; and we, her true and obedient vassals guided by the shining light of her virtues, shall always love her, serve her, and obey her to the end of our lives.

---

50. **Agnus Dei,** Lamb of God—either the image or the prayer.

14. **The Spanish Cruelties,** a tendentious title supplied by the Protestant translator.

Thomas Dekker
c. 1570–1632

Though the facts of Thomas Dekker's life are unusually meager, his personality makes itself felt even in his hurried and frequently tasteless collaborations, his pamphleteering and hack writing, and no author of the period excels him in sweetness and fineness of spirit. The dates of both his birth and death are uncertain; 1570 is frequently given as the first, and 1632 or 1641 as the second. He may have been of Dutch stock, but his education was certainly scant, and his life not too fortunate. Like many another hack writer of his time, he seems to have spent various periods of his life in a debtor's prison. One of the earliest records concerning him reveals the shrewd illiterate theatrical manager, Philip Henslow, paying forty shillings to get Dekker out of the "Counter in the Poultry."

Dekker earned his uncertain living by writing plays, by collaborating with other playwrights, good and bad, and by producing miscellaneous prose pamphlets on whatever subject seemed at the moment likely to interest the purchasing public. He is best known as a playwright. Of the plays due to his hand alone, the most important are *Old Fortunatus*, acted in 1599, a dramatization of a German folk tale with many vestigial remains of the medieval drama; *The Shoemaker's Holiday*, acted in 1600, a most genial and sunny comic representation of the London life of citizens and apprentices; and *The Honest Whore*, of which the first part was acted in 1604, and the sequel in 1605. This pair of plays treats with insight and compassion the reformation of a prostitute, although contemporary audiences may have preferred the elementary farce of the subplots which disfigure the plays. Dekker's tenderness and compassion can be discerned in his collaboration with Philip Massinger in *The Virgin Martyr*, and with John Ford in *The Witch of Edmonton*. Dekker's plays are rather carelessly constructed, and his sense of humor is not impeccable, but the plays show a very winning combination of manly robustness and lyrical sweetness. Not the least of their attractions are the singularly pure and lucid and serene lyrics.

Dekker produced most of his prose pamphlets in the first decade of the seventeenth century. *The Wonderful Year*, 1603, is a painfully vivid description of London stricken by an epidemic. To the rogue literature, which Robert Greene had popularized in the nineties, Dekker contributed *The Seven Deadly Sins of London*, 1606; *The Belman of London*, 1608; and *News from Hell Brought by the Devil's Carrier*, 1606. His most famous prose work is *The Gull's Hornbook*, 1609.

from THE GULL'S HORNBOOK

The Gull's Hornbook is a very free adaptation of a sixteenth-century Latin poem by the German poet Frederick Dedekind. But the original Grobianus, a coarse, gross lout, is a very different figure from Dekker's affected pretentious man about town. The type and the milieu are completely domesticated, and Dekker's little book gives us a vivid though ironical series of pictures of some of the absurder follies of his time.

The "gull" is a numskull, an ignorant, boorish person trying to acquire the manners and habits of a gentleman. A "hornbook" was a printed page containing the alphabet and simple words and protected by a thin sheet of horn. Dekker uses it to mean "primer."

In the portions of *The Gull's Hornbook* not printed here, Dekker dedicates the manual of courtesy to unmannerliness, and recommends it for the study of would-be gallants. He urges the gull not to rise before noon, to dispossess those around the fireplace, and, having toasted himself, to don his extravagant attire. He should then go to St. Paul's, where he can hide from his creditors, show off his clothes, and air his acquaintance with knights and squires. For the midday meal, he should choose the restaurant most frequented by gallants and, attaching himself to a company of them, he should talk loudly of his exploits as soldier, courtier, or poet. After gambling away his money, he may go to the latest play.

Chapter 6: HOW A GALLANT SHOULD BEHAVE HIMSELF IN A PLAY-HOUSE

THE theatre is your poets' Royal Exchange, upon which their muses (that are now turned to merchants) meeting, barter away that light commodity of words for a lighter ware than words, plaudities,[5] and the breath of the great beast; which, like the threatenings of two cowards, vanish all into air. Players are their factors, who put away the stuff, and make the best of it they possibly can (as indeed 'tis their parts so to do). Your gallant, your courtier,

---

5. **plaudities,** applause.

and your captain had wont to be the soundest paymasters; and I think are still the surest chapmen; and these, by means that their heads are well stocked, deal upon this comical freight by the gross; when your groundling and gallery-commoner buys his sport by the penny and, like a haggler, is glad to utter it again by retailing.

Sithence then the place is so free in entertainment, allowing a stool as well to the farmer's son as to your templar; that your stinkard has the selfsame liberty to be there in his tobacco fumes, which your sweet courtier hath; and that your carman and tinker claim as strong a voice in their suffrage, and sit to give judgment on the play's life and death, as well as the proudest momus among the tribe of critic; it is fit that he, whom the most tailors' bills do make room for, when he comes, should not be basely (like a viol) cased up in a corner.

Whether therefore the gatherers of the public or private play-house stand to receive the afternoon's rent, let our gallant (having paid it) presently advance himself up to the throne of the stage. I mean not into the lord's room, which is now but the stage's suburbs; no, those boxes, by the iniquity of custom, conspiracy of waiting women and gentlemen ushers, that there sweat together, and the covetousness of sharers, are contemptibly thrust into the rear, and much new satin is there damned by being smothered to death in darkness. But on the very rushes where the comedy is to dance, yea, and under the state of Cambises himself, must our feathered estridge, like a piece of ordnance, be planted, valiantly (because impudently) beating down the mews and hisses of the opposed rascality.

For do but cast up a reckoning, what large comings-in are pursed up by sitting on the stage. First a conspicuous eminence is gotten; by which means the best and most essential parts of a gallant (good clothes, a proportionable leg, white hand, the Persian lock, and a tolerable beard) are perfectly revealed.

By sitting on the stage you have a signed patent to engross the whole commodity of censure; may lawfully presume to be a girder; and stand at the helm to steer the passage of scenes; yet no man shall once offer to hinder you from obtaining the title of an insolent, overweening coxcomb.

By sitting on the stage, you may, without travelling for it, at the very next door ask whose play it is; and, by that quest of inquiry, the law warrants you to avoid much mistaking; if you know not the author, you may rail against him; and peradventure so behave yourself that you may enforce the author to know you.

By sitting on the stage, if you be a knight you may happily get you a mistress; if a mere Fleet-street gentleman, a wife; but assure yourself, by continual residence, you are the first and principal man in election to begin the number of We Three.

By spreading your body on the stage, and by being a justice in examining of plays, you shall put yourself into such true scenical authority that some poet shall not dare to present his muse rudely upon your eyes, without having first unmasked her, rifled her, and discovered all her bare and most mystical parts before you at a tavern, when you most knightly shall, for his pains, pay for both their suppers.

By sitting on the stage, you may (with small cost) purchase the dear acquaintance of the boys; have a good stool for sixpence; at any time know what particular part any of the infants present; get your match lighted, examine the play-suits' lace, and perhaps win wagers upon laying 'tis copper, etc. And to conclude, whether you be a fool or a justice of peace, a cuckold or a captain, a lord-mayor's son or a dawcock, a knave or an under-sheriff; of what stamp soever you be, current or counterfeit, the stage, like time, will bring you to most perfect light and lay you open; neither are you to be hunted from thence, though the scarecrows in the yard hoot at you, hiss at you, spit at you, yea, throw dirt even in your teeth; 'tis most gentlemanlike patience to endure all this and to laugh at the silly animals; but if the rabble, with a full throat, cry, "Away with the fool," you were worse than a madman to tarry by it; for the gentleman and the fool should never sit on the stage together.

Marry, let this observation go hand in hand with the rest; or rather, like a country serving-man, some five yards before them. Present not yourself on the stage (especially at a new play) until the quaking Prologue hath (by rubbing) got colour into his cheeks, and is ready to give the trumpets their cue that he's upon point to enter; for then it is time, as though you were one of the properties or that you dropped out of the hangings, to creep from behind the arras, with your tripos or three-footed stool in one hand and a teston mounted between a forefinger and a thumb in the other; for if you should bestow your person upon the vulgar when the belly of the house is but half full, your apparel is quite

---

7. **utter it,** put it into circulation.   10. **templar,** a member of one of the Inns of Court.   15. **momus,** a carping critic.   31. **estridge,** ostrich.   44. **girder,** sneerer.   8. **We Three,** an allusion to the picture of two boobies with the inscription, "We three, loggerheads be." The spectator supplies the third!   25. **dawcock,** silly fellow.   47. **teston,** a coin worth sixpence.

eaten up, the fashion lost, and the proportion of your body in more danger to be devoured than if it were served up in the Counter amongst the poultry; avoid that as you would the bastone. It shall crown you with rich commendation to laugh aloud in the midst of the most serious and saddest scene of the terriblest tragedy; and to let that clapper, your tongue, be tossed so high that all the house may ring of it. Your lords use it; your knights are apes to the lords, and do so too; your Inn-a-Court-man is zany to the knights, and (many, very scurvily) comes likewise limping after it; be thou a beagle to them all, and never lin snuffing, till you have scented them; for by talking and laughing (like a ploughman in a morris) you heap Pelion upon Ossa, glory upon glory; as first, all the eyes in the galleries will leave walking after the players and only follow you; the simplest dolt in the house snatches up your name, and when he meets you in the streets, or that you fall into his hands in the middle of a watch, his word shall be taken for you; he'll cry "He's such a gallant," and you pass. Secondly, you publish your temperance to the world, in that you seem not to resort thither to taste vain pleasures with a hungry appetite; but only as a gentleman to spend a foolish hour or two, because you can do nothing else; thirdly, you mightily disrelish the audience and disgrace the author; marry, you take up (though it be at the worst hand) a strong opinion of your own judgment, and enforce the poet to take pity of your weakness and, by some dedicated sonnet, to bring you into a better paradise only to stop your mouth.

If you can, either for love or money, provide yourself a lodging by the water side; for, above the convenience it brings to shun shoulder-clapping and to ship away your cockatrice betimes in the morning, it adds a kind of state unto you to be carried from thence to the stairs of your play-house; hate a sculler (remember that) worse than to be acquainted with one o' the scullery. No, your oars are your only sea-crabs, board them, and take heed you never go twice together with one pair; often shifting is a great credit to gentlemen; and that dividing of your fare will make the poor watersnakes be ready to pull you in pieces to enjoy your custom; no matter whether upon landing you have money or no; you may swim in twenty of their boats over the river upon ticket; marry, when silver comes in, remember to pay treble their fare, and it will make your flounder-catchers to send more thanks after you when you do not draw than when you do; for they know it will be their own another day.

Before the play begins, fall to cards; you may win or lose (as fencers do in a prize) and beat one another by confederacy, yet share the money when you meet at supper; notwithstanding, to gull the ragamuffins that stand aloof gaping at you, throw the cards (having first torn four or five of them) round about the stage, just upon the third sound, as though you had lost; it skills not if the four knaves lie on their backs, and outface the audience; there's none such fools as dare take exceptions at them, because, ere the play go off, better knaves than they will fall into the company.

Now, sir, if the writer be a fellow that hath either epigrammed you, or hath had a flirt at your mistress, or hath brought either your feather, or your red beard, or your little legs, etc., on the stage, you shall disgrace him worse than by tossing him in a blanket or giving him the bastinado in a tavern, if, in the middle of his play (be it pastoral or comedy, moral or tragedy) you rise with a screwed and discontented face from your stool to be gone; no matter whether the scenes be good or no; the better they are, the worse do you distaste them; and, being on your feet, sneak not away like a coward, but salute all your gentle acquaintance that are spread either on the rushes or on stools about you, and draw what troop you can from the stage after you. The mimics are beholden to you for allowing them elbow-room; their poet cries, perhaps, "A pox go with you," but care not you for that, there's no music without frets.

Marry, if either the company or indisposition of the weather bind you to sit it out, my counsel is then that you turn plain ape, take up a rush, and tickle the earnest ears of your fellow gallants, to make other fools fall a-laughing; mew at passionate speeches, blare at merry, find fault with the music, whew at the children's action, whistle at the songs; and above all, curse the sharers, that whereas the same day you had bestowed forty shillings on an embroidered felt and feather (Scotch-fashion) for your mistress in the court or your punk in the city, within two hours after you encounter with the very same block on the stage, when the haberdasher swore to you the impression was extant but that morning.

To conclude, hoard up the finest play-scraps you can get, upon which your lean wit may most savourly feed, for want of other stuff, when the Ar-

---

3. **Counter,** a debtors' prison, where Dekker had been confined.   4. **bastone,** a blow with a stick or cudgel.   10. **zany,** buffoon.   13. **lin,** stop.   36. **cockatrice,** mistress.   44. **watersnakes,** river boatmen.

6. **gull,** trick, cheat.   10. **skills,** matters.   41. **sharers,** the members of a theatrical company who shared in the risks and profits of the undertaking.   44. **punk,** whore.

cadian and Euphuized gentlewomen have their tongues sharpened to set upon you; that quality (next to your shuttlecock) is the only furniture to a courtier that's but a new beginner, and is but in his A B C of compliment. The next places that are filled, after the play-houses be emptied, are (or ought to be) taverns. Into a tavern then let us next march, where the brains of one hogshead must be beaten out to make up another.

Chapter 7: HOW A GALLANT SHOULD BEHAVE HIMSELF IN A TAVERN

Whosoever desires to be a man of good reckoning in the city, and (like your French lord) to have as many tables furnished as lackeys (who, when they keep least, keep none), whether he be a young quat of the first year's revenue or some austere and sullen-faced steward who (in despite of a great beard, a satin suit, and a chain of gold wrapped in cypress) proclaims himself to any (but to those to whom his lord owes money) for a rank coxcomb, or whether he be a country gentleman that brings his wife up to learn the fashion, see the tombs at Westminster, the lions in the Tower, or to take physic; or else is some young farmer, who many times makes his wife in the country believe he hath suits in law, because he will come up to his lechery; be he of what stamp he will that hath money in his purse, and a good conscience to spend it, my counsel is that he take his continual diet at a tavern, which (out of question) is the only *rendezvous* of boon company; and the drawers the most nimble, the most bold, and most sudden proclaimers of your largest bounty.

Having therefore thrust yourself into a case most in fashion (how coarse soever the stuff be, 'tis no matter so it hold fashion), your office is (if you mean to do your judgment right) to inquire out those taverns which are best customed, whose masters are oftenest drunk (for that confirms their taste, and that they choose wholesome wines), and such as stand furthest from the counters; where, landing yourself and your followers, your first compliment shall be to grow most inwardly acquainted with the drawers, to learn their names, as Jack, and Will, and Tom, to dive into their inclinations, as whether this fellow useth to the fencing school, this to the dancing school . . . and protest yourself to be extremely in love, and that you spend much money in a year, upon any one of those exercises which you perceive is followed by them. The use which you shall make of this familiarity is this: if you want money five or six days together, you may still pay the reckoning with this most gentleman-like language, "Boy, fetch me money from the bar," and keep yourself most providently from a hungry melancholy in your chamber. Besides, you shall be sure, if there be but one faucet that can betray neat wine to the bar, to have that arraigned before you sooner than a better and worthier person.

The first question you are to make (after the discharging of your pocket of tobacco and pipes, and the household stuff thereto belonging) shall be for an inventory of the kitchen; for it were more than most tailor-like, and to be suspected you were in league with some kitchen-wench, to descend yourself, to offend your stomach with the sight of the larder, and happily to grease your accoutrements. Having therefore received this bill, you shall (like a captain putting up dead pays) have many salads stand on your table, as it were for blanks to the other more serviceable dishes; and according to the time of the year, vary your fare, as capon is a stirring meat sometime, oysters are a swelling meat sometimes, trout a tickling meat sometimes, green goose and woodcock a delicate meat sometimes, especially in a tavern, where you shall sit in as great state as a church-warden amongst his poor parishioners at Pentecost or Christmas.

For your drink, let not your physician confine you to any one particular liquor; for as it is requisite that a gentleman should not always be plodding in one art, but rather be a general scholar (that is, to have a lick at all sorts of learning, and away), so 'tis not fitting a man should trouble his head with sucking at one grape, but that he may be able (now there is a general peace) to drink any stranger drunk in his own element of drink, or more properly in his own mist language.

Your discourse at the table must be such as that which you utter at your ordinary; your behaviour the same, but somewhat more careless; for where your expense is great, let your modesty be less; and though you should be mad in a tavern, the largeness of the items will bear with your incivility; you may, without prick to your conscience, set the want of your wit against the superfluity and sauciness of their reckonings.

If you desire not to be haunted with fiddlers (who by the statute have as much liberty as rogues to travel into any place, having the passport of the house about them) bring then no women along with you; but if you love the company of all the drawers, never sup without your cockatrice; for, having her there, you shall be sure of most officious attendance.

17. **quat**, a young man. 20. **cypress**, a light, transparent material.

37. **mist language**, possibly wine, which clouds the senses.

Inquire what gallants sup in the next room, and if they be any of your acquaintance do not you (after the city fashion) send them in a pottle of wine, and your name, sweetened in two pitiful papers of sugar, with some filthy apology crammed into the mouth of a drawer; but rather keep a boy in fee, who underhand shall proclaim you in every room, what a gallant fellow you are, how much you spend yearly in taverns, what a great gamester, what custom you bring to the house, in what witty discourse you maintain a table, what gentlewomen or citizens' wives you can with a wet finger have at any time to sup with you, and such like. By which encomiastics of his, they that know you not shall admire you and think themselves to be brought into a paradise but to be meanly in your acquaintance; and if any of your endeared friends be in the house, and beat the same ivy bush that yourself does, you may join companies and be drunk together most publicly.

But in such a deluge of drink, take heed that no man counterfeit himself drunk, to free his purse from the danger of the shot; 'tis a usual thing now among gentlemen; it had wont be the quality of cockneys. I would advise you to leave so much brains in your head as to prevent this. When the terrible reckoning (like an indictment) bids you hold up your hand, and that you must answer it at the bar, you must not abate one penny in any particular, no, though they reckon cheese to you when you have neither eaten any, nor could ever abide it, raw or toasted; but cast your eye only upon the *totalis*, and no further; for to traverse the bill would betray you to be acquainted with the rates of the market, nay more, it would make the vintners believe you were *pater-familias*, and kept a house; which, I assure you, is not now in fashion.

If you fall to dice after supper, let the drawers be as familiar with you as your barber, and venture their silver amongst you; no matter where they had it; you are to cherish the unthriftiness of such young tame pigeons, if you be a right gentleman; for when two are yolked together by the purse strings, and draw the chariot of Madam Prodigality, when one faints in the way and slips his horns let the other rejoice and laugh at him.

At your departure forth the house, to kiss mine hostess over the bar, or to accept of the courtesy of the cellar when 'tis offered you by the drawers (and you must know that kindness never creeps upon them but when they see you almost cleft to the shoulders), or to bid any of the vintners good night, is as commendable as for a barber after trimming to lave your face with sweet water.

To conclude, count it an honour either to invite or be invited to any rifling; for commonly, though you find much satin there, yet you shall likewise find many citizens' sons, and heirs, and younger brothers there, who smell out such feasts more greedily than tailors hunt upon Sundays after weddings. And let any hook draw you either to a fencer's supper or to a player's that acts such a part for a wager; for by this means you shall get experience, by being guilty to their abominable shaving.

Chapter 8: HOW A GALLANT IS TO BEHAVE HIMSELF PASSING THROUGH THE CITY, AT ALL HOURS OF THE NIGHT, AND HOW TO PASS BY ANY WATCH

After the sound of pottle-pots is out of your ears, and that the spirit of wine and tobacco walks in your brain, the tavern door being shut upon your back, cast about to pass through the widest and goodliest streets in the city. And if your means cannot reach to the keeping of a boy, hire one of the drawers, to be as a lanthorn unto your feet, and to light you home; and still as you approach near any night-walker that is up as late as yourself, curse and swear (like one that speaks High Dutch) in a lofty voice, because your men have used you so like a rascal in not waiting upon you, and vow the next morning to pull their blue cases over their ears, though, if your chamber were well searched, you give only sixpence a week to some old woman to make your bed, and that she is all the serving-creatures you give wages to. If you smell a watch (and that you may easily do, for commonly they eat onions to keep them in sleeping, which they account a medicine against cold) or if you come within danger of their brown bills, let him that is your candlestick and holds up your torch from dropping (for to march after a link is shoemaker-like), let *ignis fatuus*, I say, being within the reach of the constable's staff, ask aloud, "Sir Giles," or "Sir Abram, will you turn this way, or down that street?" It skills not though there be none dubbed in your bunch; the watch will wink at you, only for the love they bear to arms and knighthood; marry, if the sentinel and his court of guard stand strictly upon his martial law and cry "Stand,"

---

12. **with a wet finger,** easily, at a call or sign. 13. **encomiastics,** praises. 17–18. **beat the same ivy bush,** frequent the same tavern. 23. **shot,** tavern reckoning. 32. **totalis,** total. 1–2. **cleft to the shoulders,** drunk. 6. **rifling,** raffling; dicing party. 14. **shaving,** roguery, cheating. 21. **pottle-pots,** tankards. 27. **lanthorn,** lantern. 41. **bills,** a type of halberd, weapons of the watchmen. 43. **ignis fatuus,** deceptive fire; will-o'-the-wisp.

commanding you to give the word, and to show reason why your ghost walks so late, do it in some jest (for that will show you have a desperate wit, and perhaps make him and his halberdiers afraid to lay foul hands upon you) or, if you read a *mittimus* in the constable's book, counterfeit to be a Frenchman, a Dutchman, or any other nation whose country is in peace with your own; and you may pass the pikes; for being not able to understand you, they cannot by the customs of the city take your examination, and so by consequence they have nothing to say to you.

If the night be old, and that your lodging be in some place into which no artillery of words can make a breach, retire, and rather assault the doors of your punk, or (not to speak broken English) your sweet mistress, upon whose white bosom you may languishingly consume the rest of darkness that is left, in ravishing (though not restorative) pleasures, without expenses, only by virtue of four or five oaths (when the siege breaks up, and at your marching away with bag and baggage) that the last night you were at dice, and lost so much in gold, so much in silver; and seem to vex most that two such Elizabeth twenty-shilling pieces, or four such spur-royals, sent you with a cheese and a baked meat from your mother, rid away amongst the rest. By which tragical yet politic speech you may not only have your night work done gratis, but also you may take diet there the next day and depart with credit, only upon the bare word of a gentleman to make her restitution.

All the way as you pass (especially being approached near some of the gates) talk of none but lords, and such ladies with whom you have played at primero, or danced in the presence the very same day. It is a chance to lock up the lips of an inquisitive bell-man; and being arrived at your lodging door, which I would counsel you to choose in some rich citizen's house, salute at parting no man but by the name of Sir (as though you had supped with knights). . . .

Happily it will be blown abroad that you and your shoal of gallants swam through such an ocean of wine, that you danced so much money out at heels, and that in wild fowl there flew away thus much; and I assure you, to have the bill of your reckoning lost of purpose, so that it may be published, will make you to be held in dear estimation; only the danger is, if you owe money, and that your revealing gets your creditors by the ears; for then look to have a peal of ordnance thundering at your chamber door the next morning. But if either your tailor, mercer, haberdasher, silkman, cutter, linen draper, or sempster stand like a guard of Switzers about your lodging, watching your up-rising, or, if they miss of that, your down-lying in one of the Counters, you have no means to avoid the galling of their small shot than by sending out a light-horseman to call your apothecary to your aid, who, encountering this desperate band of your creditors, only with two or three glasses in his hand, as though that day you purged, is able to drive them all to their holes like so many foxes; for the name of taking physic is a sufficient *quietus est* to any endangered gentleman, and gives an acquittance (for the time) to them all, though the twelve companies stand with their hoods to attend your coming forth and their officers with them.

I could now fetch you about noon (the hour which I prescribed you before to rise at) out of your chamber, and carry you with me into Paul's Churchyard; where planting yourself in a stationer's shop, many instructions are to be given you, what books to call for, how to censure of new books, how to mew at the old, how to look in your tables and inquire for such and such Greek, French, Italian, or Spanish authors, whose names you have there, but whom your mother for pity would not give you so much wit as to understand. From thence you should blow yourself into the tobacco-ordinary, where you are likewise to spend your judgment (like a quacksalver) upon that mystical wonder, to be able to discourse whether your cane or your pudding be sweetest, and which pipe has the best bore, and which burns black, which breaks in the burning, etc. Or, if you itch to step into the barber's, a whole dictionary cannot afford more words to set down notes what dialogues you are to maintain whilst you are doctor of the chair there. After your shaving, I could breathe you in a fence-school, and out of that cudgel you into a dancing school, in both which I could weary you, by showing you more tricks than are in five galleries or fifteen prizes. And, to close up the stomach of this feast, I could make cockneys, whose fathers have left them well, acknowledge themselves infinitely beholden to me, for teaching them by familiar demonstration how to spend their patrimony and to get themselves names, when their fathers are dead and rotten. But lest too many dishes should cast into a surfeit, I will now take away; yet so that, if I perceive you relish this well, the rest shall be (in time) prepared for you. Farewell.

---

5. **mittimus,** a warrant for arrest. 25. **spur-royals,** gold coins worth about 16 s. 27. **rid away,** were lost.

3. **sempster,** seamstress. 13. **quietus est,** acquittance, release.

ART THOU POOR?

This song, from Dekker's play, *Patient Grissill*, illustrates the playwright's skill in investing even poverty with a romantic aura. The theme was a favorite with poets of the period, but the lightly running music and warmth of tone are Dekker's.

    Art thou poor, yet hast thou golden slumbers?
        Oh, sweet content!
    Art thou rich, yet is thy mind perplexed?
        Oh, punishment!
    Dost thou laugh to see how fools are vexed
    To add to golden numbers golden numbers?
        Oh, sweet content, oh, sweet content.
        Work apace, apace, apace, apace;
        Honest labour bears a lovely face,
        Then hey noney, noney, hey noney, noney.   10

Canst drink the waters of the crispèd spring?
    Oh, sweet content!
Swim'st thou in wealth, yet sink'st in thine own
      tears?
    Oh, punishment!
Then he that patiently want's burden bears,
No burden bears, but is a king, a king.
    Oh, sweet content, &c.

Work apace, apace, &c.

Samuel Daniel
1562–1619

Samuel Daniel's career was that of an eminently successful professional poet who was not a man of noble birth and wealth, and who therefore had to depend for his livelihood on patronage. He was born in Somersetshire, the son of a music master. He entered Magdalen Hall, Oxford, in 1579, but is said to have been "more prone to easier and smoother studies than in pecking and hewing at logic." At any rate, after three years' residence, he left the university without taking a degree. His first published work was a preface and translation of an Italian book on impresas by Paulus Jovius, 1585. After traveling on the Continent, he became the tutor of William Herbert, the son of Sidney's sister Mary, the wife of the second Earl of Pembroke, and thus gained access to the cultivated circle around the most famous Elizabethan patroness of letters. She was probably the model for the heroine of Daniel's sonnet sequence "Delia," of which twenty-eight first appeared in the unauthorized edition of Sidney's *Astrophel and Stella* in 1591. In 1592, Daniel published it in a volume containing "The Complaint of Rosamond," a poem of the genre of the "tragedies" in the *Mirror for Magistrates* but of much higher poetic quality. Under the influence of the French Senecan tastes of the Pembroke group, Daniel brought out in 1594 a version of Garnier's *Cleopatra*, which depicts in strict Neoclassical form the events from the death of Antony to the suicide of the Queen. The first four books of the *Civil Wars between the Two Houses of York and Lancaster* appeared in 1595. A few years later, he became the tutor of Lady Anne Clifford, daughter of the Countess of Cumberland, although he complained that he was "constrained to live with children" when he wished to write of "the actions of men." The most important works of this period were his philosophic epistles addressed to his noble patronesses, and *Musophilus, or, Defence of All Learning*, 1599, dedicated to Sidney's friend Sir Fulke Greville, who had been attempting to secure Daniel a living in the Isle of Wight. The poem, which runs to almost a thousand lines, is a dialogue between Philocosmus, a man of the world, and Musophilus (Daniel), a man of letters. It is an eloquent defense of culture against materialism. Its most famous lines contain the prophetic speculations:

"And who, in time, knows whither we may vent
The treasure of our tongue, to what strange shores
The gain of our best glory shall be sent
T' enrich unknowing nations with our stores?
What world in th' yet unformèd Occident
May come refined with th' accents that are ours?"

Daniel's *Defence of Rhyme*, 1602, written in answer to Thomas Campion's attack on rhyme and accentual metre, is probably the only piece of Elizabethan critical writing comparable with Sidney's *Defence of Poesy*.

Daniel had won the favor of the Countess of Bedford, only slightly less influential a patroness of literature than the Countess of Pembroke, and he was recommended by her to the attention of James's Queen, Anne of Denmark. By Her Majesty he was made Master of the Children of the Queen's Revels, and was commissioned to write the first masque for the new court, *The Vision of Twelve Goddesses*, 1604. He composed three other masques for the delectation of the extravagant Stuart court. In 1605, he published another Neoclassical tragedy, *Philotas*, which showed a favorite general of Alexander's accused of conspiracy, tortured, and stoned to death. In it, Daniel was accused of defending the cause of Elizabeth's turbulent favorite, Essex, but he was able to prove that the play had been written before the fate of Essex was in question. In 1609, he brought his historical poem on the Civil Wars to completion in eight books. When he lost the Queen's favor in 1618, he retired to his farm at Beckington in Somersetshire, where he died in 1619. His brother John edited *The Whole Works* in 1623.

Ben Jonson said in private conversation that Daniel was "an honest man but no poet. He wrote *Civil Wars* and yet not one battle in all his book," and his rival Drayton regarded him as "too much historian in verse," and maintained that "his manner better befitted prose." Even Edmund Spenser seems to have been hinting at Daniel's limitations in the line "Then rouse thy feathers quickly, Daniel." But Daniel's reply would have been, "I versify the truth, not poetize." Despite the strictures, Daniel found admirers in his own age and after. William Browne described him as "well-languaged," and Sylvester, the translator of Du Bartas, characterized him sympathetically:

"Deep, moral, grave, invention's oracle,
My dear sweet Daniel, sharp, conceited, brief,
Civil, sententious, for pure accents chief."

Daniel returned to considerable critical favor in the Romantic period. Wordsworth read him carefully and admired him, and Coleridge regarded his poetry as an excellent example of "that style which, as the neutral ground of prose and verse, is common to both," and described his language as "just such as any very pure and manly writer of the present day—Wordsworth, for example—would use."

from DELIA

Daniel's sonnets make free use of the psychological and thematic conventions established by Petrarch. Although the sequence is lacking in emotional warmth, it is noteworthy for purity of diction, tranquillity of rhythm, and the perfection of single lines. The form is that of the English or Shakespearean sonnet.

36

Look, Delia, how w' esteem the half-blown rose,
    The image of thy blush and summer's honour,
    Whilst yet her tender bud doth undisclose
    That full of beauty time bestows upon her.
No sooner spreads her glory in the air
    But straight her wide-blown pomp comes to decline;
    She then is scorned that late adorned the fair;
    So fade the roses of those cheeks of thine.
No April can revive thy withered flowers,
    Whose springing grace adorns the glory now;   10
    Swift speedy time, feathered with flying hours,
    Dissolves the beauty of the fairest brow.
Then do not thou such treasure waste in vain,
But love now whilst thou mayst be loved again.

39

When winter snows upon thy sable hairs,
    And frost of age hath nipped thy beauties near,
    When dark shall seem thy day that never clears,
    And all lies withered that was held so dear,
Then take this picture which I here present thee,
    Limned with a pencil not all unworthy;
    Here see the gifts that God and nature lent thee,
    Here read thyself and what I suffered for thee.
This may remain thy lasting monument,
    Which happily posterity may cherish;   10
    These colours with thy fading are not spent,
    These may remain when thou and I shall perish.
If they remain, then thou shalt live thereby;
They will remain, and so thou canst not die.

51

Care-charmer sleep, son of the sable night,
    Brother to death, in silent darkness born,
    Relieve my languish and restore the light;
    With dark forgetting of my care, return.
And let the day be time enough to mourn
    The shipwreck of my ill-adventured youth;
    Let waking eyes suffice to wail their scorn
    Without the torment of the night's untruth.
Cease, dreams, th' images of day-desires,
    To model forth the passions of the morrow;   10
    Never let rising sun approve you liars,
    To add more grief to aggravate my sorrow.
Still let me sleep, embracing clouds in vain,
And never wake to feel the day's disdain.

52

Let others sing of knights and paladins
    In agèd accents and untimely words,
    Paint shadows in imaginary lines
    Which well the reach of their high wits records;

But I must sing of thee and those fair eyes.
    Authentic shall my verse in time to come,
    When yet th' unborn shall say, Lo where she lies,
    Whose beauty made him speak that else was dumb.
These are the arks, the trophies I erect,
    That fortify thy name against old age;   10
    And these thy sacred virtues must protect
    Against the dark and time's consuming rage.
Though th' error of my youth in them appear,
Suffice, they show I lived and loved thee dear.

THE COMPLAINT OF ROSAMOND

The Complaint of Rosamond belongs to the literary genre exemplified in the English Renaissance by the enormously popular *Mirror for Magistrates*. Daniel has taken as the basis of his poem the nucleus of the genre, the recounting by a hero or heroine who has fallen from prosperity and power of the circumstances and causes of the tragic disaster. But he has enhanced the convention by his sustained and elevated poetic style and by his imaginative appreciation of the dramatic and emotional potentialities of his theme. Although the poem is far too long, it has dignity and pathos, emotional intensity and dramatic force. The following selections are representative of the poem as a whole.

Out from the horror of infernal deeps
My poor afflicted ghost comes here to plain it,
Attended with my shame that never sleeps,
The spot wherewith my kind and youth did stain it;
My body found a grave where to contain it,
    A sheet could hide my face, but not my sin,
    For fame finds never tomb t' inclose it in.

And which is worse, my soul is now denied
Her transport to the sweet Elysian rest,
The joyful bliss for ghosts repurified,   10
The ever-springing gardens of the blest;
Charon denies me waftage with the rest,
    And says my soul can never pass the river,
    Till lovers' sighs on earth shall it deliver.

So shall I never pass, for how should I
Procure this sacrifice amongst the living?
Time hath long since worn out the memory
Both of my life and life's unjust depriving;
Sorrow for me is dead for aye reviving.
    Rosamond hath little left her but her name,   20
    And that disgraced, for time hath wronged the same.

No muse suggests the pity of my case;
Each pen doth overpass my just complaint,

The Complaint of Rosamond. **4. kind,** sex.

Whilst others are preferred, though far more base;
Shore's wife is graced, and passes for a saint;
Her legend justifies her foul attaint.
    Her well-told tale did such compassion find
    That she is passed, and I am left behind.

Which seen with grief, my miserable ghost
(Whilom invested in so fair a veil,   30
Which whilst it lived was honoured of the most,
And being dead, gives matter to bewail)
Comes to solicit thee, whilst others fail,
    To take this task and in thy woeful song
    To form my case and register my wrong.

Although I know thy just lamenting muse,
Toiled in th' affection of thine own distress,
In others' cares hath little time to use,
And therefore mayst esteem of mine the less;
Yet as thy hopes attend happy redress,   40
    The joys depending on a woman's grace,
    So move thy mind a woeful woman's case.

Delia may hap to deign to read our story,
And offer up her sighs among the rest,
Whose merit would suffice for both our glory,
Whereby thou mightst be graced and I be blest;
That indulgence would profit me the best.
    Such power she hath by whom thy youth is led,
    To joy the living and to bless the dead.

So I, through beauty made the woeful'st wight,   50
By beauty might have comfort after death;
That dying fairest, by the fairest might
Find life above on earth, and rest beneath.
She that can bless us with one happy breath,
    Give comfort to thy muse to do her best,
    That thereby thou mayst joy and I might rest.

Thus said, forthwith moved with a tender care
And pity, which myself could never find,
What she desired my muse deigned to declare,
And therefore willed her boldly tell her mind;   60
And I, more willing, took this charge assigned
    Because her griefs were worthy to be known,
    And telling hers, might hap forget mine own.

Then write, quoth she, the ruin of my youth,
Report the downfall of my slipp'ry state;
Of all my life reveal the simple truth,
To teach to others what I learnt too late.

25. Shore's wife. The reference is probably to Churchyard's "Shore's Wife," which appeared in the 1563 edition of the *Mirror for Magistrates*. Jane Shore was the mistress of Edward IV.   **43. Delia,** probably the Countess of Pembroke, Daniel's patroness.

Exemplify my frailty, tell how fate
   Keeps in eternal dark our fortunes hidden,
   And ere they come, to know them 'tis forbidden.   70

For whilst the sunshine of my fortune lasted,
I joyed the happiest warmth, the sweetest heat
That ever yet imperious beauty tasted;
I had what glory ever flesh could get,
But this fair morning had a shameful set.
   Disgrace darked honour, sin did cloud my brow,
   As note the sequel, and I'll tell thee how.

The blood I stained was good and of the best,
My birth had honour and my beauty fame;
Nature and fortune joined to make me blest,   80
Had I had grace t' have known to use the same.
My education showed from whence I came,
   And all concurred to make me happy first,
   That so great hope might make me more accursed.

Happy lived I whilst parents' eye did guide
The indiscretion of my feeble ways,
And country home kept me from being eyed,
Where best unknown I spent my sweetest days;
Till that my friends mine honour sought to raise
   To higher place, which greater credit yields,   90
   Deeming such beauty was unfit for fields.

From country then to court I was preferred,
From calm to storms, from shore into the deeps;
There where I perished, where my youth first erred;
There where I lost the flower which honour keeps;
There where the worser thrives, the better weeps.
   Ah me, poor wench, on this unhappy shelf
   I grounded me and cast away myself. . . .

Thus wrought to sin, soon was I trained from court
T' a solitary grange, there to attend
The time the king should thither make resort,
Where he love's long-desirèd work should end.
Thither he daily messages doth send,
   With costly jewels, orators of love,   370
   Which (ah, too well men know) do women move.

The day before the night of my defeature
He greets me with a casket richly wrought,
So rare that art did seem to strive with nature

373–406. **casket . . . spies.** The description of the casket is an example of the epic convention of the elaborate description of a technical product, like the shield of Achilles in Homer's *Iliad* and the erection of Pandemonium and the manufacture of the heavenly cannon in Milton's *Paradise Lost*.

T' express the cunning workman's curious thought;
The mystery whereof I prying sought,
   And found engraven on the lid above
   Amymone, how she with Neptune strove.

Amymone, old Danaus' fairest daughter,
As she was fetching water all alone   380
At Lerna, whereas Neptune came and caught her,
From whom she strived and struggled to be gone,
Bathing the air with cries and piteous moan;
   But all in vain, with him she's forced to go.
   'Tis shame that men should use poor maidens so.

There might I see describèd how she lay,
At those proud feet not satisfied with prayer;
Wailing her heavy hap, cursing the day,
In act so piteous to express despair.
And by how much more grieved, so much more fair;
   Her tears upon her cheeks, poor careful girl,   391
   Did seem, against the sun, crystal and pearl;

Whose pure clear streams, which lo, so fair appears,
Wrought hotter flames (oh, miracle of love,
That kindles fire in water, heat in tears,
And makes neglected beauty mightier prove,
Teaching afflicted eyes affects to move);
   To show that nothing ill becomes the fair,
   But cruelty, which yields unto no prayer.

This having viewed, and therewith something moved,   400
Figured I find within the other squares
Transformèd Io, Jovè's dearly loved;
In her affliction how she strangely fares,
Strangely distressed (oh beauty, born to cares),
   Turned to a heifer, kept with jealous eyes,
   Always in danger of her hateful spies.

These precedents presented to my view,
Wherein the presage of my fall was shown,
Might have forewarned me well what would ensue,
And others' harms have made me shun mine own;
But fate is not prevented, though foreknown,   411
   For that must hap, decreed by heavenly powers
   Who work our fall yet make the fault still ours. . . .

Shame follows sin, disgrace is duly given,
Impiety will out, never so closely done;
No walls can hide us from the eye of heaven,
For shame must end what wickedness begun;
Forth breaks reproach when we least think thereon,
   And this is ever proper unto courts,
   That nothing can be done but fame reports.   560

Fame doth explore what lies most secret hidden,
Ent'ring the closet of the palace dweller,
Abroad revealing what is most forbidden;
Of truth and falsehood both an equal teller,
'Tis not a guard can serve for to expel her.
    The sword of justice cannot cut her wings,
    Nor stop her mouth from utt'ring secret things.

And this our stealth she could not long conceal
From her whom such a forfeit most concerned,
The wrongèd queen, who could so closely deal   570
That she the whole of all our practice learned,
And watched a time when least it was discerned,
    In absence of the king, to wreak her wrong
    With such revenge as she desirèd long.

The labyrinth she entered by that thread
That served a conduct to my absent lord,
Left there by chance, reserved for such a deed,
Where she surprised me whom she so abhorred.
Enraged with madness, scarce she speaks a word,
    But flies with eager fury to my face,   580
    Off'ring me most unwomanly disgrace.

Look how a tigress that hath lost her whelp
Runs fiercely ranging through the woods astray,
And seeing herself deprived of hope or help,
Furiously assaults what's in her way,
To satisfy her wrath, not for a prey;
    So fell she on me in outrageous wise,
    As could disdain and jealousy devise.

And after all her vile reproaches used,
She forced me take the poison she had brought   590
To end the life that had her so abused,
And free her fears and ease her jealous thought.
No cruelty her wrath could leave unwrought,
    No spiteful act that to revenge is common,
    No beast being fiercer than a jealous woman.

Here take, saith she, thou impudent, unclean,
Base, graceless strumpet, take this next your heart;
Your love-sick heart, that overcharged hath been
With pleasure's surfeit, must be purged with art.
This potion hath a power that will convert   600
    To nought those humours that oppress you so;
    And, girl, I'll see you take it ere I go.

What, stand you now amazed, retire you back?
Tremble you, minion? Come, dispatch with speed;
There is no help, your champion now you lack,
And all these tears you shed will nothing stead;
Those dainty fingers needs must do the deed.
    Take it, or I will drench you else by force,
    And trifle not, lest that I use you worse.

Having this bloody doom from hellish breath,   610
My woeful eyes on every side I cast,
Rigour about me, in my hand my death,
Presenting me the horror of my last,
All hope of pity and of comfort past.
    No means, no power, no forces to contend,
    My trembling hands must give myself my end.

Those hands that beauty's ministers had been,
They must give death, that me adorned of late;
That mouth that newly gave consent to sin,
Must now receive destruction in threat;   620
That body which my lust did violate,
    Must sacrifice itself t' appease the wrong:
    So short is pleasure, glory lasts not long.

And she no sooner saw I had it taken,
But forth she rushes, proud with victory;
And leaves m' alone, of all the world forsaken,
Except of death, which she had left with me;
Death and myself alone together be,
    To whom she did her full revenge refer;   629
    Oh, poor weak conquest, both for him and her.

Then straight my conscience summons up my sin
T' appear before me in a hideous face;
Now doth the terror of my soul begin,
When ev'ry corner of that hateful place
Dictates mine error and reveals disgrace;
    Whilst I remain oppressed in every part,
    Death in my body, horror at my heart.

Down on my bed my loathsome self I cast,
The bed that likewise gives in evidence
Against my soul, and tells I was unchaste,   640
Tells I was wanton, tells I followed sense;
And therefore cast by guilt of mine offence,
    Must here the right of heaven needs satisfy,
    And where I wanton lay, must wretched die.

Here I began to wail my hard mishap,
My sudden, strange, unlooked-for misery;
Accusing them that did my youth entrap,
To give me such a fall of infamy.
And, Poor distressèd Rosamond, said I,
    Is this thy glory got, to die forlorn   650
    In deserts where no ear can hear thee mourn?

Nor any eye of pity to behold
The woeful end of my sad tragedy?
But that thy wrongs unseen, thy tale untold,
Must here in secret silence buried lie,
And with thee thine excuse together die.
    Thy sin revealed, but thy repentance hid,
    Thy shame alive, but dead what thy death did. . . .

TO THE LADY MARGARET, COUNTESS OF CUMBERLAND

Daniel's finest poetic epistle, in celebrating the nobility of the cultivated and disciplined mind, mingles Christian and Stoic ideas adroitly. Both Stoical and Christian are the escape from worldliness and sin, and the cultivation of inner sufficiency and quietude for its own sake. There is confidence that the individual thus ennobled has a place in the universe and that the world was made for noble man. For Daniel, his patroness is obviously an embodiment of the ideal he is analyzing and praising.

He that of such a height hath built his mind,
And reared the dwelling of his thoughts so strong
As neither fear nor hope can shake the frame
Of his resolvèd powers, nor all the wind
Of vanity or malice pierce to wrong
His settled peace, or to disturb the same,
What a fair seat hath he, from whence he may
The boundless wastes and wilds of man survey.

And with how free an eye doth he look down
Upon these lower regions of turmoil   10
Where all the storms of passions mainly beat
On flesh and blood; where honour, power, renown,
Are only gay afflictions, golden toil,
Where greatness stands upon as feeble feet
As frailty doth, and only great doth seem
To little minds, who do it so esteem.

He looks upon the mightiest monarchs' wars
But only as on stately robberies,
Where evermore the fortune that prevails
Must be the right, the ill-succeeding mars   20
The fairest and the best-faced enterprise;
The great pirate, Pompey, lesser pirates quails.
Justice, he sees, as if seducèd, still
Conspires with power, whose cause must not be ill.

He sees the face of right t' appear as manifold
As are the passions of uncertain man,
Who puts it in all colours, all attires,
To serve his ends and make his courses hold;
He sees that let deceit work what it can,
Plot and contrive base ways to high desires,   30
That the all-guiding Providence doth yet
All disappoint, and mocks this smoke of wit.

Nor is he moved with all the thunder-cracks
Of tyrants' threats, or with the surly brow
Of power, that proudly sits on others' crimes,
Charged with more crying sins than those he checks;
The storms of sad confusion that may grow
Up in the present, for the coming times

Appal not him, that hath no side at all
But of himself, and knows the worst can fall.   40

Although his heart, so near allied to earth,
Cannot but pity the perplexèd state
Of troublous and distressed mortality,
That thus make way unto the ugly birth
Of their own sorrows, and do still beget
Affliction upon imbecility;
Yet seeing thus the course of things must run,
He looks thereon, not strange, but as foredone.

And whilst distraught ambition compasses
And is encompassed, whilst as craft deceives   50
And is deceived, whilst man doth ransack man,
And builds on blood, and rises by distress,
And th' inheritance of desolation leaves
To great-expecting hopes, he looks thereon
As from the shore of peace with unwet eye,
And bears no venture in impiety.

Thus, madam, fares that man that hath prepared
A rest for his desires, and sees all things
Beneath him, and hath learned this book of man,
Full of the notes of frailty, and compared   60
The best of glory with her sufferings,
By whom I see you labour all you can
To plant your heart, and set your thoughts as near
His glorious mansion as your powers can bear;

Which, madam, are so soundly fashionèd
By that clear judgment that hath carried you
Beyond the feeble limits of your kind,
As they can stand against the strongest head
Passion can make, inured to any hue
The world can cast, that cannot cast that mind   70
Out of her form of goodness, that doth see
Both what the best and worst of earth can be.

Which makes that, whatsoever here befalls,
You in the region of yourself remain,
Where no vain breath of th' impudent molests;
That hath secured within the brazen walls
Of a clear conscience that without all stain
Rises in peace, in innocency rests,
Whilst all what malice from without procures
Shows her own ugly heart, but hurts not yours.   80

And whereas none rejoice more in revenge
Than women use to do, yet you well know
That wrong is better checked by being contemned
Than being pursued, leaving to him t' avenge
To whom it appertains; wherein you show
How worthily your clearness hath condemned

Base malediction, living in the dark,
That at the rays of goodness still doth bark.

Knowing the heart of man is set to be
The centre of this world, about the which   90
These revolutions of disturbances
Still roll, where all th' aspects of misery
Predominate, whose strong effects are such
As he must bear, being powerless to redress;
And that unless above himself he can
Erect himself, how poor a thing is man!

And how turmoiled they are that level lie
With earth, and cannot lift themselves from thence;
That never are at peace with their desires,
But work beyond their years, and even deny   100
Dotage her rest, and hardly will dispense
With death; that when ability expires,
Desire lives still, so much delight they have
To carry toil and travail to the grave.

Whose ends you see, and what can be the best
They reach unto, when they have cast the sum
And reckonings of their glory, and you know
This floating life hath but this port of rest—
A heart prepared, that fears no ill to come.
And that man's greatness rests but in his show, 110
The best of all whose days consumèd are
Either in war, or peace conceiving war.

This concord, madam, of a well-tuned mind
Hath been so set by that all-working hand
Of heaven, that though the world hath done his
    worst
To put it out by discords most unkind,
Yet doth it still in perfect union stand
With God and man, nor ever will be forced
From that most sweet accord, but still agree,
Equal in fortunes in equality.   120

And this note, madam, of your worthiness
Remains recorded in so many hearts,
As time nor malice cannot wrong your right
In th' inheritance of fame you must possess;
You that have built you by your great deserts,
Out of small means, a far more exquisite
And glorious dwelling for your honoured name
Than all the gold that leaden minds can frame.

Michael Drayton
1563–1631

Michael Drayton was born in Warwickshire in 1563, and was brought up as a page in the household of Sir Henry Goodere at Polesworth Castle on the river Anker on the borders of the Forest of Arden. He seems to have received his education from tutors in the courtly household, and probably did not go on to a university. He developed an early desire to be a poet, and during most of his long life he devoted himself to writing the kinds of poetry most popular at the time, while he subsisted on the favors of a series of noble patrons.

His first published work, *The Harmony of the Church*, 1591, was an unpromising series of Biblical paraphrases in primitive fourteeners. For some reason it attracted the displeasure of the Archbishop of Canterbury, and it was ordered burned. A happier reception awaited his *Idea: The Shepherd's Garland*, 1593, nine eclogues inspired by the *Shepheardes Calender* of Spenser, who was to be the most important and persistent of poetical influences upon Drayton. In 1594, he contributed *Idea's Mirrour* to the sonnet sequences in vogue at the moment. The *Idea* of the title is derived from a French sequence by Claude de Pontoux; although it suggests the Platonic Idea of Beauty, it also represents Drayton's sublimated feelings for Anne, the younger daughter of his patron, with whom he remained on terms of warm friendship for years after her marriage. Probably under the influence of Daniel's *The Complaint of Rosamond*, Drayton wrote a series of short historical poems: *Piers Gaveston*, 1593, which also showed the influence of Shakespeare's *Venus and Adonis*; *Matilda*, 1594; *Robert, Duke of Normandy*, 1596; and in the latter year, he brought out a long historical poem, *Mortimeriades*, on the subject of Edward II's struggles with his nobles, and under the influence of Daniel's *Civil Wars* and the erotic Italianate narratives of Marlowe and Shakespeare. His greatest success in the utilization of historical material was the *Heroical Epistles*, 1597, interchanges of verse letters between nine—later, twelve—pairs of lovers.

In the late nineties, his relations with his patrons seem to have become strained, and he was forced to the distasteful task of hack writing for the stage. Before 1602, he had collaborated on at least thirty plays. He failed to find favor with King James, and expressed his disappointment in two indifferent satires, but under the patronage of Sir Walter Aston he returned to the writing of poetry. In 1603, he published a revised version of *Mortimeriades* under the title *The Barons' Wars;* the rime royal of the original was expanded into ottava rima. His *Poems Lyrical and Pastoral*, 1606, contained some of his most spirited odes. Drayton had long been meditating a major historical work, and in 1612 the first eighteen "songs" of his *Poly-Olbion* (Having Many Blessings) appeared, to be followed by twelve more in 1622. This laborious and uncompleted enterprise undertook a typographical survey of the British Isles, treated allegorically with elaborate historical and legendary interludes. The poem runs to fifteen thousand Alexandrines, and is frequently slavishly dependent on Drayton's reading in the chroniclers and antiquarians. Some of his finest work was done in his old age, when he helped establish the fluent lucid Spenserianism of the period in *The Shepherd's Sirena*, 1627, and *The Muses' Elisium*, 1630. He died in 1631 and was buried in Westminster Abbey.

Francis Meres described Drayton as "a man of virtues of well-governed carriage, which is almost miraculous among good wits of this declining and corrupt time." He seems to have looked for his audience not in the sophisticated court, but among the more solid and serious elements of the minor nobility. His popularity is attested by the large number of editions in which his poems appeared during his lifetime. He was a scrupulous workman, and although on occasions—as in the *Poly-Olbion*—he seems to have been unfortunate in his choice of meter, in general he showed a great sensitivity to metrical forms, and he devoted a great deal of time to reworking his own poems, not always to their advantage. But Drayton was much more than a competent poet; he can be depended on to treat almost any form or type of poem with clarity, elegance, sweetness, and freshness. His poetic powers did not wane with the advance of age, and his latest poems, though diffuse, are more melodious than those of his youth. To the Spenserians of the early seventeenth century, he was a kind of mentor and exemplar. His fondness for the rhymed couplet sustained his reputation into the Restoration. For us, he is perhaps most significant as a representative poet of the period, a writer who reflects with clarity and grace the changing poetic modes of several literary generations.

from IDEA'S MIRROUR

Drayton's sonnets, published under the title *Idea's Mirrour*, differ from most of the sonnet sequences of the time in that they treat of a number of subjects that are not strictly amatory, and do not tell a very coherent story. Despite some Petrarchan elements, Drayton's sonnets are cool rather than impassioned. As the title suggests, they celebrate his beloved, not so much as a woman but as a manifestation of ideal beauty. The most colloquial and dramatic of his sonnets, beginning "Since there's no help, come let us kiss and part," was written long after the earliest of his sonnets was published.

1

Like an adventurous seafarer am I,
Who hath some long and dang'rous voyage been,
And called to tell of his discovery,
How far he sailed, what countries he had seen;
Proceeding from the port whence he put forth,
Shows by his compass how his course he steered,
When east, when west, when south, and when by north,
As how the pole to ev'ry place was reared,
What capes he doubled, of what continent,   9
The gulfs and straits that strangely he had passed,
Where most becalmed, where with foul weather spent,
And on what rocks in peril to be cast:
   Thus in my love, time calls me to relate
   My tedious travels and oft-varying fate.

6

How many paltry, foolish, painted things,
That now in coaches trouble ev'ry street,
Shall be forgotten, whom no poet sings,
Ere they be well wrapped in their winding sheet!
Where I to thee eternity shall give,
When nothing else remaineth of these days,
And queens hereafter shall be glad to live
Upon the alms of thy superfluous praise;
Virgins and matrons reading these my rhymes
Shall be so much delighted with thy story   10
That they shall grieve they lived not in these times,
To have seen thee, their sex's only glory.
   So shalt thou fly above the vulgar throng,
   Still to survive in my immortal song.

47

In pride of wit, when high desire of fame
Gave life and courage to my lab'ring pen,
And first the sound and virtue of my name
Won grace and credit in the ears of men;
With those the throngèd theatres that press

I in the circuit for the laurel strove,
Where the full praise, I freely must confess,
In heat of blood, a modest mind might move.
With shouts and claps at ev'ry little pause,
When the proud round on ev'ry side hath rung, 10
Sadly I sit, unmoved with the applause,
As though to me it nothing did belong.
   No public glory vainly I pursue,
   All that I seek is to eternize you.

53

Clear Anker, on whose silver-sanded shore
My soul-shrined saint, my fair Idea lies,
O blessed brook, whose milk-white swans adore
Thy crystal stream, refinèd by her eyes,
Where sweet myrrh-breathing Zephyr in the spring
Gently distils his nectar-dropping showers,
Where nightingales in Arden sit and sing
Amongst the dainty dew-empearlèd flowers;
Say thus, fair brook, when thou shalt see thy queen;
Lo, here thy shepherd spent his wand'ring years, 10
And in these shades, dear nymph, he oft hath been,
And here to thee he sacrificed his tears.
   Fair Arden, thou my Tempe art alone,
   And thou, sweet Anker, art my Helicon.

61

Since there's no help, come let us kiss and part;
Nay, I have done, you get no more of me,
And I am glad, yea glad with all my heart
That thus so cleanly I myself can free;
Shake hands for ever, cancel all our vows,
And when we meet at any time again,
Be it not seen in either of our brows
That we one jot of former love retain.
Now at the last gasp of love's latest breath,
When, his pulse failing, passion speechless lies, 10
When faith is kneeling by his bed of death,
And innocence is closing up his eyes,
   Now if thou wouldst, when all have given him over,
   From death to life thou mightst him yet recover.

TO THE VIRGINIAN VOYAGE

This poem is a skillful and animated piece of poetical publicity. A number of Drayton's noble friends, and Drayton himself perhaps, had invested heavily in the colonizing venture recommended in the poem. The lush romantic description, suggestive of the jargon of modern advertising, is evidence not only of the meagerness of Drayton's information about Virginia, but also of the romantic aura with which the exotic land was invested in the minds of Elizabethans who had never crossed the Atlantic.

You brave heroic minds
Worthy your country's name,
   That honour still pursue,
   Go, and subdue,
Whilst loit'ring hinds
Lurk here at home, with shame.

Britons, you stay too long;
Quickly aboard bestow you,
   And with a merry gale
   Swell your stretched sail, 10
With vows as strong
As the winds that blow you.

Your course securely steer,
West and by south forth keep,
   Rocks, lee-shores, nor shoals,
   When Aeolus scowls,
You need not fear,
So absolute the deep.

And cheerfully at sea,
Success you still entice, 20
   To get the pearl and gold,
   And ours to hold,
Virginia,
Earth's only paradise,

Where nature hath in store
Fowl, venison, and fish,
   And the fruitful'st soil
   Without your toil
Three harvests more,
All greater than your wish, 30

And the ambitious vine
Crowns with his purple mass
   The cedar reaching high
   To kiss the sky,
The cypress, pine,
And useful sassafras.

To whose the golden age
Still nature's laws doth give,
   No other cares that tend,
   But them to defend 40
From winter's age,
That long there doth not live.

Whenas the luscious smell
Of that delicious land,
   Above the seas that flows,
   The clear wind throws,
Your hearts to swell
Approaching the dear strand,

In kenning of the shore,
　　Thanks to God first given, 50
　　　　O you, the happi'st men,
　　　　Be frolic then,
　　Let cannons roar,
　　Frighting the wide heaven.

　　And in regions far
　　Such heroes bring ye forth
　　　　As those from whom we came,
　　　　And plant our name
　　Under that star
　　Not known unto our north. 60

　　And as there plenty grows
　　Of laurel everywhere,
　　　　Apollo's sacred tree,
　　　　You it may see
　　A poet's brows
　　To crown, that may sing there.

　　Thy voyages attend,
　　Industrious Hakluyt,
　　　　Whose reading shall enflame
　　　　Men to seek fame, 70
　　And much commend
　　To after times thy wit.

TO THE CAMBRO-BRITONS AND THEIR HARP, HIS BALLAD OF AGINCOURT

In this poem Drayton sounds a poetic trumpet in honor of the victory won by King Henry V at Agincourt over the French. In this vigorous and colorful literary ballad the clash of swords and the cries of battle ring out, and the spirited rhythm of the quick iambic and trochaic accents suggests the resistless march of tramping feet.

　　Fair stood the wind for France,
　　When we our sails advance,
　　Nor now to prove our chance,
　　　　Longer will tarry;
　　But putting to the main
　　At Kaux, the mouth of Seine,
　　With all his martial train,
　　　　Landed King Harry.

　　And taking many a fort,
　　Furnished in warlike sort, 10
　　Marcheth towards Agincourt,
　　　　In happy hour;

8. King Harry, Henry V.

　　Skirmishing day by day
　　With those that stopped his way,
　　Where the French gen'ral lay
　　　　With all his power.

　　Which in his height of pride,
　　King Henry to deride,
　　His ransom to provide
　　　　To the King sending; 20
　　Which he neglects the while
　　As from a nation vile,
　　Yet with an angry smile
　　　　Their fall portending.

　　And turning to his men,
　　Quoth our brave Henry then:
　　Though they to one be ten,
　　　　Be not amazèd.
　　Yet have we well begun,
　　Battles so bravely won 30
　　Have ever to the sun
　　　　By fame been raisèd.

　　And for myself, quoth he,
　　This my full rest shall be,
　　England ne'er mourn for me,
　　　　Nor more esteem me;
　　Victor I will remain,
　　Or on this earth lie slain,
　　Never shall she sustain
　　　　Loss to redeem me. 40

　　Poitiers and Crécy tell,
　　When most their pride did swell,
　　Under our swords they fell;
　　　　No less our skill is
　　Than when our grandsire great,
　　Claiming the regal seat
　　By many a warlike feat,
　　　　Lopped the French lilies.

　　The Duke of York so dread
　　The eager vaward led; 50
　　With the main Henry sped
　　　　Amongst his henchmen.
　　Excester had the rear,
　　A braver man not there,
　　O Lord, how hot they were
　　　　On the false Frenchmen!

　　They now to fight are gone,
　　Armour on armour shone,

50. vaward, van.　　**51. main,** main body of troops.
53. Excester, Exeter.

Drum now to drum did groan,
  To hear was wonder,   60
That with cries they make
The very earth did shake,
Trumpet to trumpet spake,
  Thunder to thunder.

Well it thine age became,
O noble Erpingham,
Which didst the signal aim
  To our hid forces;
When from a meadow by,
Like a storm suddenly,   70
The English archery
  Stuck the French horses.

With Spanish yew so strong,
Arrows a cloth-yard long,
That like to serpents stung,
  Piercing the weather;
None from his fellow starts,
But playing manly parts,
And like true English hearts,
  Stuck close together.   80

When down their bows they threw,
And forth their bilboes drew,
And on the French they flew,
  Not one was tardy;
Arms were from shoulders sent,
Scalps to the teeth were rent,
Down the French peasants went;
  Our men were hardy.

This while our noble King,
His broad sword brandishing,   90
Down the French host did ding,
  As to o'erwhelm it;
And many a deep wound lent,
His arms with blood besprent,
And many a cruel dent
  Bruisèd his helmet.

Gloster, that Duke so good,
Next of the royal blood,
For famous England stood
  With his brave brother;   100
Clarence, in steel so bright,
Though but a maiden knight,
Yet in that furious fight,
  Scarce such another.

76. weather, atmosphere, air.   **97. Gloster,** Humphrey, Duke of Gloucester, brother to Henry V, but not senior to the Duke of Clarence, as Drayton's lines indicate.

Warwick in blood did wade,
Oxford the foe invade,
And cruel slaughter made,
  Still as they ran up;
Suffolk his axe did ply,
Beaumont and Willoughby   110
Bare them right doughtily,
  Ferrers and Fanhope.

Upon Saint Crispin's day
Fought was this noble fray,
Which fame did not delay
  To England to carry;
Oh, when shall English men
With such acts fill a pen,
Or England breed again
  Such a King Harry?   120

TO MY MOST DEARLY LOVED FRIEND, HENRY REYNOLDS, ESQUIRE OF POETS AND POESY

The first forty lines of this epistle sketch in Drayton's poetic education during the first quarter of his life. The body of the poem gives us the poet's critical judgments of the poets of the past and of his own time. Its closing verses are devoted to the writer's personal friends among contemporary poets.

The impression left by the poem is that of the informal talk of a man who, refusing to burden us with critical argumentation, speaks his mind in careful phrases and skillful rhymes. Like other Elizabethan critics, he praises Chaucer, though he regards the language as rude and imperfect. The excellence of his critical judgment is clear in his characterization of "grave moral" Spenser and Lyly, "playing with words and idle similes." His admiration of Sandys's "unusual grace" and "neatness" shows his delight in the qualities in which he himself excelled. Though he is hostile to Donne, he pays particular tribute to his personal associates, Sir Francis and John Beaumont and William Browne.

My dearly lovèd friend, how oft have we
In winter evenings, meaning to be free,
To some well-chosen place used to retire,
And there with moderate meat, and wine, and fire,
Have passed the hours contentedly with chat;
Now talked of this, and then discoursed of that,
Spoke our own verses 'twixt ourselves; if not,
Other men's lines which we by chance had got,
Or some stage pieces famous long before,
Of which your happy memory had store;   10
And I remember you much pleasèd were
Of those who livèd long ago to hear,

113. Saint Crispin's day, October 25, 1415.

As well as of those of these latter times
Who have enriched our language with their rhymes,
And in succession how still up they grew,
Which is the subject that I now pursue.
For from my cradle you must know that I
Was still inclined to noble poesy,
And when that once *Pueriles* I had read,
And newly had my Cato construèd,   20
In my small self I greatly marvelled then,
Amongst all other, what strange kind of men
These poets were; and pleasèd with the name,
To my mild tutor merrily I came,
(For I was then a proper goodly page,
Much like a pigmy, scarce ten years of age)
Clasping my slender arms about his thigh,
O my dear master! cannot you, quoth I,
Make me a poet? Do it if you can,
And you shall see I'll quickly be a man.   30
Who me thus answered smiling: Boy, quoth he,
If you'll not play the wag, but I may see
You ply your learning, I will shortly read
Some poets to you. Phoebus be my speed,
To 't hard went I, when shortly he began
And first read to me honest Mantuan,
Then Virgil's *Eclogues;* being entered thus,
Methought I straight had mounted Pegasus,
And in his full career could make him stop
And bound upon Parnassus' bi-clift top.   40
I scorned your ballad then, though it were done
And had for finis, William Elderton.
But soft, in sporting with this childish jest
I from my subject have too long digressed;
Then to the matter that we took in hand,
Jove and Apollo for the Muses stand.

  Then noble Chaucer, in those former times
The first enriched our English with his rhymes,
And was the first of ours that ever brake
Into the Muses' treasure, and first spake   50
In weighty numbers, delving in the mine
Of perfect knowledge, which he could refine
And coin for current; and as much as then
The English language could express to men,
He made it do, and by his wondrous skill,
Gave us much light from his abundant quill.

  And honest Gower, who in respect of him
Had only sipped at Aganippe's brim,
And though in years this last was him before,
Yet fell he far short of the other's store.   60

When after those, four ages very near,
They with the Muses which conversèd were:
That princely Surrey, early in the time
Of the eight Henry, who was then the prime
Of England's noble youth; with him there came
Wyatt, with reverence whom we still do name
Amongst our poets; Bryan had a share
With the two former, which accompted are
That time's best makers, and the authors were
Of those small poems which the title bear   70
Of *Songs and Sonnets*, wherein oft they hit
On many dainty passages of wit.

  Gascoigne and Churchyard after them again
In the beginning of Eliza's reign,
Accompted were great meterers many a day,
But not inspirèd with brave fire; had they
Lived but a little longer they had seen
Their works before them to have buried been.

  Grave moral Spenser after these came on,
Than whom I am persuaded there was none   80
Since the blind bard his *Iliads* up did make
Fitter a task like that to undertake,
To set down boldly, bravely to invent,
In all high knowledge surely excellent.

  The noble Sidney with this last arose,
That heroè for numbers and for prose,
That throughly paced our language as to show
The plenteous English hand in hand might go
With Greek or Latin; and did first reduce
Our tongue from Lyly's writing, then in use: 90
Talking of stones, stars, plants, of fishes, flies,
Playing with words and idle similes;
As th' English apes and very zanies be,
Of everything that they do hear and see,
So imitating his ridiculous tricks,
They spake and writ all like mere lunatics.

  Then Warner, though his lines were not so trimmed,
Nor yet his poem so exactly limned
And neatly jointed, but the critic may
Easily reprove him, yet thus let me say   100
For my old friend: some passages there be
In him which I protest have taken me
With almost wonder, so fine, clear, and new
As yet they have been equallèd by few.

  Neat Marlowe, bathèd in the Thespian springs,
Had in him those brave translunary things
That the first poets had; his raptures were
All air and fire, which made his verses clear,
For that fine madness still he did retain
Which rightly should possess a poet's brain.   110

20. Cato. Dionysius Cato's *Disticha de Moribus*, which had been edited by Erasmus, was almost always used in training Elizabethan students to translate Latin. **36. Mantuan,** Baptista Spagnuoli Mantuanus, whose pastoral *Eclogues* were widely used as a text in Elizabethan schools. **40. bi-clift,** double-peaked. **42. Elderton,** the best-known ballad-writer of the 1570's and 1580's.

67. Bryan, one of the anonymous contributors to *Tottell's Miscellany.*

And surely Nashe, though he a proser were,
A branch of laurel yet deserves to bear;
Sharply satiric was he, and that way
He went, since that his being to this day
Few have attempted, and I surely think
Those words shall hardly be set down with ink,
Shall scorch and blast so as his could, where he
Would inflict vengeance. And be it said of thee,
Shakespeare, thou hadst as smooth a comic vein,
Fitting the sock, and in thy natural brain   120
As strong conception and as clear a rage
As anyone that trafficked with the stage.

    Amongst these, Samuel Daniel, whom if I
May speak of, but to censure do deny,
Only have heard some wise men him rehearse
To be too much historian in verse;
His rhymes were smooth, his metres well did close,
But yet his manner better fitted prose.
Next these, learn'd Jonson in this list I bring,
Who had drunk deep of the Pierian spring,   130
Whose knowledge did him worthily prefer,
And long was lord here of the theatre;
Who in opinion made our learn'st to stick,
Whether in poems rightly dramatic,
Strong Seneca or Plautus, he or they
Should bear the buskin or the sock away.
Others again here lived in my days
That have of us deservèd no less praise
For their translations than the daintiest wit
That on Parnassus thinks he high'st doth sit,   140
And for a chair may 'mongst the muses call
As the most curious maker of them all;
As reverent Chapman, who hath brought to us
Musaeus, Homer, and Hesiodus
Out of the Greek, and by his skill hath reared
Them to that height, and to our tongues endeared,
That were those poets at this day alive
To see their books thus with us to survive,
They would think, having neglected them so long,
They had been written in the English tongue.   150

    And Sylvester, who from the French more weak
Made Bartas of his six days' labour speak
In natural English; who, had he there stayed
He had done well, and never had bewrayed
His own invention to have been so poor,
Who still wrote less in striving to write more.

    Then dainty Sandys, that hath to English done
Smooth sliding Ovid, and hath made him run
With so much sweetness and unusual grace,
As though the neatness of the English pace   160
Should tell the jetting Latin that it came
But slowly after, as though stiff and lame.

    So Scotland sent us hither, for our own,
That man whose name I ever would have known
To stand by mine, that most ingenious knight,
My Alexander, to whom in his right
I want extremely, yet in speaking thus
I do but show the love that was 'twixt us,
And not his numbers which were brave and high,
So like his mind was his clear poesy;   170
And my dear Drummond, to whom much I owe
For his much love, and proud I was to know
His poesy; for which two worthy men,
I Menstry still shall love, and Hawthornden.
Then the two Beaumonts and my Browne arose,
My dear companions whom I freely chose
My bosom friends, and in their several ways
Rightly born poets, and in these last days
Men of much note and no less nobler parts,
Such as have freely told to me their hearts,   180
As I have mine to them; but if you shall
Say in your knowledge that these be not all
Have writ in numbers, be informed that I
Only myself to these few men do tie,
Whose works oft printed, set on every post,
To public censure subject have been most;
For such whose poems, be they ne'er so rare,
In private chambers that encloistered are,
And by transcription daintily must go,
As though the world unworthy were to know   190
Their rich composures, let those men that keep
These wonderous relics in their judgment deep,
And cry them up so, let such pieces be
Spoke of by those that shall come after me;
I pass not for them, nor do mean to run
In quest of these that them applause have won
Upon our stages in these latter days,
That are so many—let them have their bays
That do deserve it; let those wits that haunt
Those public circuits, let them freely chant   200
Their fine composures, and their praise pursue;
And so, my dear friend, for this time, adieu.

151. **Sylvester**, translator of Du Bartas' *Semaines*, a popular poem on the Creation.   174. **Menstry,** Sir William Alexander of Menstry. **Hawthornden,** Drummond of Hawthornden.   175. **two Beaumonts,** Sir John and Francis.   185. **set on every post,** advertised by the posting up of title pages.   189. **transcription.** Drayton was irked by the competition of poems circulated in manuscript by men of birth who were unwilling to turn professional and print their poetry. This passage is probably aimed at John Donne.   200. **circuits,** playhouses.

William Shakespeare
1564–1616

Shakespeare was born on or about the twenty-third of April, 1564, at Stratford-on-Avon. His father was John Shakespeare, a fairly prosperous glover and a citizen of prominence in the little community; his mother, Mary Arden, was the daughter of a well-to-do landowner of Wilmcote. By 1577, however, his father's economic status was seriously impaired, and his civic prestige deteriorated. In all probability, the boy attended the grammar school in the village. So far as is known, he had no further formal education, although there is a tradition that he was for a time a schoolmaster in the country.

On November 28, 1582, he was married hurriedly to Anne Hathaway, eight years his senior. Their first child, Susanna, was born in May, 1583, and they became the parents of twins, Judith and Hamnet, in February, 1585. At about this time Shakespeare seems to have left Stratford in search of opportunities larger than the town offered for maintaining his family and restoring its social status. Before 1593, he had apparently attached himself to a London theatrical company, as an actor-apprentice, and then as a refurbisher of old plays. It is in the latter role that he was attacked by Robert Greene in his *Groatsworth of Wit* as "an upstart crow, beautified with our feathers, that with his Tiger's heart wrapt in a player's hide, supposes he is as well able to bombast out a blank verse as the best of you; and being an absolute Johannes Factotum, is in his own conceit the only Shake-scene in a country." Shakespeare's character was defended by Henry Chettle, and his fortunes mended rapidly. He began to compose plays of his own, and as a result of his earnings as actor, playwright, and a sharer in the company and later in the ownership of the Globe and Blackfriars theaters he encouraged his father to apply for the permission to bear a coat of arms in 1596, bought the second largest house in Stratford in 1597, and in the years to follow added considerably to his real-estate holdings in and around Stratford and in London. For almost twenty years, he produced an average of two plays a year for the brilliant company of which he was a part. But he seems to have been eager to live the part of a country gentleman, for which his restored fortunes had prepared him. He withdrew from dramatic activities early in the second decade of the century, and after a few years spent in retirement, died on April 23, 1616, and was buried in the Stratford church in which he had been baptized.

The incongruity between Shakespeare's hard-working existence and his conventional life ideal on the one hand, and the poetic force and imaginative range of his plays on the other, has encouraged some to believe that he was not the author of the plays ascribed to him. The incongruity can be resolved only by the hypothesis of a genius relatively unconscious of his powers, and certainly careless of the fate of his productions beyond their immediate success or failure.

Persons disappointed by the normality of Shakespeare's life have been unanimous as to the uniqueness of his genius. Shakespeare's dramatic poetry is incomparable; the variety and persuasiveness of his characterization are unparalleled in literature. Shakespeare was not an innovator in the sense that he struck out new forms or new ideas. He did what other playwrights were doing, wrote what the public of the time seemed to want. His distinction lies in the extent to which he outdistanced his rivals and exceeded the expectations of audiences of any period.

It is customary to divide Shakespeare's career as a writer into four periods. These were once regarded as reflecting his own emotional and intellectual history, but a wider study of the Elizabethan drama has made it clear that changes in the type and tone of his plays are the results of external conditions rather than inner promptings. The first period, extending from 1590 to 1596, is that during which he experimented with a number of kinds of comedy: classical in *The Comedy of Errors*, romantic in *The Two Gentlemen of Verona*, euphuistic in *Love's Labour's Lost* and with the history play in *Richard III*, and tragedy in *Romeo and Juliet*. This is also the period in which he wrote and published his erotic narratives, *Venus and Adonis*, 1593, and *The Rape of Lucrece*, 1594, and wrote a considerable number of the sonnets, which were not, however, published until 1609. The second period, running from 1596 to 1601, is that of the great history plays, *King Henry IV* (two parts) and *The Life of King Henry V*, and of the matchless trio of comedies, *Much Ado about Nothing*, *As You Like It*, and *Twelfth-Night*.

WILLIAM SHAKESPEARE

The third period, from 1601 to 1608, is that of the great tragedies, *Hamlet*, *King Lear*, and *Antony and Cleopatra*, and the "bitter" comedies, *All's Well That Ends Well* and *Measure for Measure*. The final period (1608 to 1610) is that of the romances, *Cymbeline*, *The Winter's Tale*, and *The Tempest*, but as late as 1613 he seems to have collaborated with his successor John Fletcher in *Henry VIII* and *The Two Noble Kinsmen*.

It is impossible to do more than suggest some of the reasons for Shakespeare's pre-eminence. The essential conventionality of his ideas and his unerring grasp of moral values have made his work palatable to even the censorious. The fullness and liveliness of his plots have ensured the effectiveness of his plays when produced before even uncultivated audiences. To more perceptive readers and auditors, he is first among playwrights in richness and range of characterization. Shakespeare's interpretations of the English kings, for example, make a far deeper impression upon the imagination than a dozen histories. His equal facility in the creation of both male and female characters has given enduring life to such manifold creatures of the imagination as Juliet and Cleopatra, Falstaff and Hamlet. Although, to judge by his titles, he seems to have taken the writing of comedy more casually than the creation of tragedy, he is unique among playwrights as equally gifted in both the dramatic kinds. His depths are psychological rather than philosophical. His reading of the significance of human destiny is, and should be considered, an incidental and not a primary element in his great works.

from SONNETS

Shakespeare's *Sonnets* were first published in 1609, apparently without authorization by the poet. They were probably written at irregular intervals between the early 1590's and the opening years of the seventeenth century. Although they tell a more complicated story than that of any of the other sequences, that story is neither very clear nor conclusive. The characters involved are a poet, a young male friend, a dark lady, with whom the friend falls in love, and a rival poet. Scholars have naturally been interested in the possible autobiographical significance of the sequence, and countless attempts have been made to identify the characters. No identification has been established without question. One is on safe ground if he reads the *Sonnets* as a poetic narrative which, like other works of Shakespeare, may have borne a relationship, now obscure, to events in his own experience.

The *Sonnets* show a wide range of values. Many of the earlier ones seem little more than poetic finger exercises, rather monotonous variations on a single theme. Some of them, like Sonnet 130 given below, are satires on some aspect of the Petrarchan convention. The finer sonnets are superb expressions of the exaltations and agonies of romantic devotion. The greatest of them, like Sonnets 129 and 146, have a psychological realism, honesty, and depth unequaled in English poetry.

18

Shall I compare thee to a summer's day?
Thou art more lovely and more temperate:
Rough winds do shake the darling buds of May,
And summer's lease hath all too short a date:
Sometime too hot the eye of heaven shines,
And often is his gold complexion dimmed;
And every fair from fair sometime declines,
By chance, or nature's changing course untrimmed;
But thy eternal summer shall not fade,
Nor lose possession of that fair thou ow'st,   10
Nor shall death brag thou wander'st in his shade,
When in eternal lines to time thou grow'st;
  So long as men can breathe, or eyes can see,
  So long lives this, and this gives life to thee.

27

Weary with toil, I haste me to my bed,
The dear repose for limbs with travel tired;
But then begins a journey in my head
To work my mind, when body's work's expired:
For then my thoughts—from far where I abide—
Intend a zealous pilgrimage to thee,
And keep my drooping eyelids open wide,
Looking on darkness which the blind do see:
Save that my soul's imaginary sight
Presents thy shadow to my sightless view,   10
Which, like a jewel hung in ghastly night,
Makes black night beauteous and her old face new.
  Lo! thus, by day my limbs, by night my mind,
  For thee, and for myself no quiet find.

29

When in disgrace with fortune and men's eyes
I all alone beweep my outcast state,
And trouble deaf heaven with my bootless cries,
And look upon myself, and curse my fate,
Wishing me like to one more rich in hope,
Featured like him, like him with friends possessed,
Desiring this man's art, and that man's scope,
With what I most enjoy contented least;
Yet in these thoughts myself almost despising,

No. 18. **7. every fair from fair,** every beauty from its beauty.   **8. untrimmed,** despoiled of its charm.   **12. to time thou grow'st.** Thy fame will grow with the lapse of time.   *No. 27.* **6. Intend,** bend or direct.   **10. shadow,** image.   *No. 29.* **6. like him, like him,** like a second man, like a third.

Haply I think on thee,—and then my state,   10
Like to the lark at break of day arising
From sullen earth, sings hymns at heaven's gate;
   For thy sweet love remembered such wealth brings
   That then I scorn to change my state with kings.

30

When to the sessions of sweet silent thought
I summon up remembrance of things past,
I sigh the lack of many a thing I sought,
And with old woes new wail my dear times' waste:
Then can I drown an eye, unused to flow,
For precious friends hid in death's dateless night,
And weep afresh love's long since cancelled woe,
And moan the expense of many a vanished sight:
Then can I grieve at grievances foregone,
And heavily from woe to woe tell o'er   10
The sad account of fore-bemoanèd moan,
Which I new pay as if not paid before.
   But if the while I think on thee, dear friend,
   All losses are restored and sorrows end.

50

How heavy do I journey on the way,
When what I seek, my weary travel's end,
Doth teach that ease and that repose to say,
"Thus far the miles are measured from thy friend!"
The beast that bears me, tired with my woe,
Plods dully on, to bear that weight in me,
As if by some instinct the wretch did know
His rider loved not speed, being made from thee:
The bloody spur cannot provoke him on
That sometimes anger thrusts into his hide,   10
Which heavily he answers with a groan
More sharp to me than spurring to his side;
   For that same groan doth put this in my mind:
   My grief lies onward, and my joy behind.

55

Not marble, nor the gilded monuments
Of princes, shall outlive this powerful rime;
But you shall shine more bright in these contents
Than unswept stone, besmeared with sluttish time.
When wasteful war shall statues overturn,
And broils root out the work of masonry,
Nor Mars his sword nor war's quick fire shall burn
The living record of your memory.

No. 30. **1–2. sessions . . . summon,** a legal metaphor. **4. new,** anew. **6. dateless,** used in the legal sense of no fixed termination. **8. expense,** the passing away. **vanished sight,** former scene. **9. grievances foregone,** past distresses. *No. 50.* **1. journey.** When a theatrical company was on tour, the leading actors traveled on horseback. *No. 55.* **3. these contents,** what is contained in these verses of mine.

'Gainst death and all-oblivious enmity
Shall you pace forth; your praise shall still **find** room   10
Even in the eyes of all posterity
That wear this world out to the ending doom.
   So, till the judgment that yourself arise,
   You live in this, and dwell in lovers' eyes.

57

Being your slave, what should I do but tend
Upon the hours and times of your desire?
I have no precious time at all to spend,
Nor services to do, till you require.
Nor dare I chide the world-without-end hour
Whilst I, my sovereign, watch the clock for you,
Nor think the bitterness of absence sour
When you have bid your servant once adieu;
Nor dare I question with my jealous thought
Where you may be, or your affairs suppose,   10
But, like a sad slave, stay and think of nought,
Save, where you are how happy you make those.
   So true a fool is love that in your will,
   Though you do anything, he thinks no ill.

71

No longer mourn for me when I am dead
Than you shall hear the surly sullen bell
Give warning to the world that I am fled
From this vile world, with vilest worms to dwell:
Nay, if you read this line, remember not
The hand that writ it; for I love you so,
That I in your sweet thoughts would be forgot,
If thinking on me then should make you woe.
O! if, I say, you look upon this verse,
When I perhaps compounded am with clay,   10
Do not so much as my poor name rehearse,
But let your love even with my life decay;
   Lest the wise world should look into your moan,
   And mock you with me after I am gone.

73

That time of year thou may'st in me behold
When yellow leaves, or none, or few, do hang
Upon those boughs which shake against the cold,
Bare ruined choirs, where late the sweet birds sang.
In me thou see'st the twilight of such day
As after sunset fadeth in the west;
Which by and by black night doth take away,
Death's second self, that seals up all in rest.
In me thou see'st the glowing of such fire,
That on the ashes of his youth doth lie,   10

No. 55. **13. till the judgment that,** till the Judgment Day when. *No. 57.* **13. will,** possibly a pun, as elsewhere in the *Sonnets*, on Shakespeare's name. *No. 71.* **13. wise,** used ironically as equivalent to "worldly-wise."

As the death-bed whereon it must expire
Consumed with that which it was nourished by.
 This thou perceiv'st, which makes thy love more strong,
 To love that well which thou must leave ere long.

87

Farewell! thou art too dear for my possessing,
And like enough thou know'st thy estimate:
The charter of thy worth gives thee releasing;
My bonds in thee are all determinate.
For how do I hold thee but by thy granting?
And for that riches where is my deserving?
The cause of this fair gift in me is wanting,
And so my patent back again is swerving.
Thyself thou gav'st, thy own worth then not knowing,
Or me, to whom thou gav'st it, else mistaking; 10
So thy great gift, upon misprision growing,
Comes home again, on better judgment making.
 Thus have I had thee, as a dream doth flatter,
 In sleep a king, but, waking, no such matter.

97

How like a winter hath my absence been
From thee, the pleasure of the fleeting year!
What freezings have I felt, what dark days seen!
What old December's bareness every where!
And yet this time removed was summer's time;
The teeming autumn, big with rich increase,
Bearing the wanton burden of the prime,
Like widowed wombs after their lords' decease:
Yet this abundant issue seemed to me
But hope of orphans and unfathered fruit; 10
For summer and his pleasures wait on thee,
And, thou away, the very birds are mute:
 Or, if they sing, 'tis with so dull a cheer,
 That leaves look pale, dreading the winter's near.

106

When in the chronicle of wasted time
I see descriptions of the fairest wights,
And beauty making beautiful old rime,
In praise of ladies dead and lovely knights,
Then, in the blazon of sweet beauty's best,
Of hand, of foot, of lip, of eye, of brow,
I see their antique pen would have expressed
Even such a beauty as you master now.
So all their praises are but prophecies
Of this our time, all you prefiguring; 10
And, for they looked but with divining eyes,
They had not skill enough your worth to sing:
 For we, which now behold these present days,
 Have eyes to wonder, but lack tongues to praise.

116

Let me not to the marriage of true minds
Admit impediments. Love is not love
Which alters when it alteration finds,
Or bends with the remover to remove:
O, no! it is an ever-fixèd mark,
That looks on tempests and is never shaken;
It is the star to every wandering bark,
Whose worth's unknown, although his height be taken.
Love's not Time's fool, though rosy lips and cheeks
Within his bending sickle's compass come; 10
Love alters not with his brief hours and weeks,
But bears it out even to the edge of doom.
 If this be error, and upon me proved,
 I never writ, nor no man ever loved.

123

No, Time, thou shalt not boast that I do change:
Thy pyramids built up with newer might
To me are nothing novel, nothing strange;
They are but dressings of a former sight.
Our dates are brief, and therefore we admire
What thou dost foist upon us that is old;
And rather make them born to our desire
Than think that we before have heard them told.
Thy registers and thee I both defy,
Not wondering at the present nor the past, 10
For thy records and what we see doth lie,
Made more or less by thy continual haste.
 This I do vow, and this shall ever be;
 I will be true, despite thy scythe and thee.

No. 73. **12. Consumed . . . by,** choked by the ashes of the wood that sustained the flame. **14. leave,** renounce. *No. 87.* In this sonnet Shakespeare seems to be attempting the effect of the incessant feminine endings in sonnets written in Italian. **2. estimate,** worth. **3. The charter of thy worth,** the privilege your dignity gave you. **4. determinate,** outdated, one of the many legal terms in this sonnet. **8. my patent . . . swerving.** The love granted to me is now reverting to its original possessor. The phrase suggests a royal patent for a monopoly. **11. upon misprision growing,** arising out of an erroneous estimate. **12. on better judgment making,** as a result of a review of the case in a higher court. *No. 97.* **5. this time removed,** this time in which I was remote from thee. **7. the wanton burden of the prime,** the children of the wanton springtime.

No. 106. **5. blazon,** description, with the connotation of encomium. **8. master,** are master of. *No. 116.* **2. impediments,** a reference to the marriage service of the Church of England. The impediments not admitted by Shakespeare are change of circumstance and inconstancy. **4. bends . . . remove,** changes as the beloved changes, in situation or devotion. **8. Whose worth's unknown,** whose occult influence is not calculable. **height,** elevation. *No. 123.* **2. Thy pyramids,** any man-made creation that seems to defy change.

129

The expense of spirit in a waste of shame
Is lust in action; and till action, lust
Is perjured, murderous, bloody, full of blame,
Savage, extreme, rude, cruel, not to trust;
Enjoyed no sooner but despisèd straight;
Past reason hunted; and no sooner had,
Past reason hated, as a swallowed bait,
On purpose laid to make the taker mad:
Mad in pursuit, and in possession so;
Had, having, and in quest to have, extreme;　10
A bliss in proof,—and proved, a very woe;
Before, a joy proposed; behind, a dream.
　　All this the world well knows; yet none knows well
　　To shun the heaven that leads men to this hell.

130

My mistress' eyes are nothing like the sun;
Coral is far more red than her lips' red:
If snow be white, why then her breasts are dun;
If hairs be wires, black wires grow on her head.
I have seen roses damasked, red and white,
But no such roses see I in her cheeks;
And in some perfumes is there more delight
Than in the breath that from my mistress reeks.
I love to hear her speak, yet well I know
That music hath a far more pleasing sound:　10
I grant I never saw a goddess go,—
My mistress, when she walks, treads on the ground:
　　And yet, by heaven, I think my love as rare
　　As any she belied with false compare.

138

When my love swears that she is made of truth,
I do believe her, though I know she lies,
That she might think me some untutored youth,
Unlearnèd in the world's false subtleties.
Thus vainly thinking that she thinks me young,
Although she knows my days are past the best,
Simply I credit her false-speaking tongue:
On both sides thus is simple truth supprest.
But wherefore says she not she is unjust?
And wherefore say not I that I am old?　10
O! love's best habit is in seeming trust,
And age in love loves not to have years told:
　　Therefore I lie with her, and she with me,
　　And in our faults by lies we flattered be.

144

Two loves I have of comfort and despair,
Which like two spirits do suggest me still:
The better angel is a man right fair,
The worser spirit a woman, coloured ill.
To win me soon to hell, my female evil
Tempteth my better angel from my side,
And would corrupt my saint to be a devil,
Wooing his purity with her foul pride.
And whether that my angel be turned fiend
Suspect I may, but not directly tell;　10
But being both from me, both to each friend,
I guess one angel in another's hell:
　　Yet this shall I ne'er know, but live in doubt,
　　Till my bad angel fire my good one out.

146

Poor soul, the centre of my sinful earth,
Fooled by these rebel powers that thee array,
Why dost thou pine within and suffer dearth,
Painting thy outward walls so costly gay?
Why so large cost, having so short a lease,
Dost thou upon thy fading mansion spend?
Shall worms, inheritors of this excess,
Eat up thy charge? Is this thy body's end?
Then, soul, live thou upon thy servant's loss,
And let that pine to aggravate thy store;　10
Buy terms divine in selling hours of dross;
Within be fed, without be rich no more:
　　So shalt thou feed on Death, that feeds on men,
　　And Death once dead, there's no more dying then.

No. 129. **1. expense,** expenditure. **4. not to trust,** treacherous. **9. Mad . . . so,** irrational in anticipation and after fulfillment. **11. in proof,** in the process of its being experienced. **proved,** experienced. **12. proposed,** in theory. *No. 130.* This sonnet satirizes the conventional blond beauty of the Petrarchan heroine. The deliberately unpleasant realism is an element in the satire. **4. If hairs be wires,** a reference to the trite comparison of golden hair to golden wires. *No. 138.* **7. Simply,** like a simpleton. *No. 138.* **9. unjust,** faithless. **11. habit,** deportment. **in seeming trust,** in pretending to be trusting. *No. 144.* The sonnet is built upon the metaphor of man's good and evil angels, represented as dramatis personae in Marlowe's *Faustus*. **2. suggest,** tempt. **11. both from me, both to each friend,** both away from me, each friendly to the other. *No. 146.* **2. these rebel powers,** the rebellious element in the flesh that is the garment of the soul. **10. aggravate,** increase. **11. terms divine,** eternity. **13. feed on Death,** consume the mortal elements in yourself. **14. Death . . . then,** because the mortal has put on immortality.

THE FIRST PART OF KING HENRY THE FOURTH

The First Part of King Henry IV is neither a tragedy nor a comedy, but a history play, an indigenous type of drama extraordinarily popular in the last decade of the sixteenth century. The purpose of such a play was the movingly dramatic representation of striking characters and events in English history. Its tone might be completely serious, as in Marlowe's *Edward the Second* and Shakespeare's *Tragedy of King Richard II;* tragic, as in the latter's *Tragedy of King Richard III*, or, as in *King Henry IV*, predominantly serious with a strong undercurrent of the richest comedy.

The problem of imposing a dramatic form upon the events of recorded history Shakespeare has solved brilliantly in this play. The serious historical plot is focused sharply on the rebellion led by the Percys against Henry IV, and it has the conventional phases of exposition, development, climax, and denouement. The series of comic scenes in which Falstaff figures constitutes as much of a subplot as Elizabethan practice required. Prince Hal is the major device of coherence between the two plots, just as the evolution of his character is the link that connects this play with *The Second Part of King Henry IV* and *The Life of Henry V*.

Henry IV is richer than any other historical play of Shakespeare's in varied and subtle characterizations, from the cold, calculating, lonely, and inexpressive King and Hotspur, the headstrong and exuberant man of action, to the gay-spirited and frolicsome but basically serious Prince Hal and Falstaff, the greatest of the dramatist's comic characterizations. Falstaff is a vitalized amalgam of several ancient comic traditions: the parasite, the braggart soldier, and the alehouse jester or Elizabethan bar-fly. But he is much more than a skillful synthesis of these types; he is a three-dimensional living being, and one of the wittiest talkers in all drama. In this play, the more delightful aspects of his character are presented. In *The Second Part*, the more sordid and seamy side of his behavior is revealed, and in the scene of his rejection, both the King and Shakespeare pass the inevitable moral judgment on this infinitely engaging reprobate.

DRAMATIS PERSONAE

KING HENRY THE FOURTH.
HENRY, Prince of Wales, } Sons to the King.
JOHN OF LANCASTER,
EARL OF WESTMORELAND.
SIR WALTER BLUNT.
THOMAS PERCY, Earl of Worcester.
HENRY PERCY, Earl of Northumberland.
HENRY PERCY, surnamed Hotspur, his son.
EDMUND MORTIMER, Earl of March.
RICHARD SCROOP, Archbishop of York.
ARCHIBALD, Earl of Douglas.
OWEN GLENDOWER.
SIR RICHARD VERNON.
SIR JOHN FALSTAFF.
SIR MICHAEL, a Friend to the Archbishop of York.

POINS.
GADSHILL.
PETO.
BARDOLPH.

LADY PERCY, Wife to Hotspur, and Sister to Mortimer.
LADY MORTIMER, Daughter to Glendower, and Wife to Mortimer.
MISTRESS QUICKLY, Hostess of the Boar's Head Tavern in Eastcheap.

Lords, Officers, Sheriff, Vintner, Chamberlain, Drawers, two Carriers, Travellers, and Attendants.

SCENE.—*England.*

ACT I

SCENE I.—*London. The Palace.*

Enter KING HENRY, WESTMORELAND, *and Others.*

K. Hen. So shaken as we are, so wan with care,
Find we a time for frighted peace to pant,
And breathe short-winded accents of new broils
To be commenced in stronds afar remote.
No more the thirsty entrance of this soil
Shall daub her lips with her own children's blood;
No more shall trenching war channel her fields,
Nor bruise her flowerets with the armèd hoofs
Of hostile paces: those opposèd eyes,
Which, like the meteors of a troubled heaven,   10
All of one nature, of one substance bred,
Did lately meet in the intestine shock
And furious close of civil butchery,
Shall now, in mutual well-beseeming ranks,
March all one way, and be no more opposed
Against acquaintance, kindred, and allies:
The edge of war, like an ill-sheathèd knife,

4. **stronds . . . remote,** strands, shores, of the Holy Land.

11. **All of one nature . . . bred.** The combatants were all Englishmen.

No more shall cut his master. Therefore, friends,
As far as to the sepulchre of Christ,—
Whose soldier now, under whose blessèd cross 20
We are impressèd and engaged to fight,—
Forthwith a power of English shall we levy,
Whose arms were moulded in their mother's womb
To chase these pagans in those holy fields
Over whose acres walked those blessèd feet
Which fourteen hundred years ago were nailed
For our advantage on the bitter cross.
But this our purpose is a twelvemonth old,
And bootless 'tis to tell you we will go:
Therefore we meet not now. Then let me hear 30
Of you, my gentle cousin Westmoreland,
What yesternight our council did decree
In forwarding this dear expedience.
   West. My liege, this haste was hot in question,
And many limits of the charge set down
But yesternight; when all athwart there came
A post from Wales loaden with heavy news;
Whose worst was, that the noble Mortimer,
Leading the men of Herefordshire to fight
Against the irregular and wild Glendower, 40
Was by the rude hands of that Welshman taken,
And a thousand of his people butcherèd;
Upon whose dead corpse there was such misuse,
Such beastly shameless transformation
By those Welshwomen done, as may not be
Without much shame re-told or spoken of.
   K. Hen. It seems then that the tidings of this broil
Brake off our business for the Holy Land.
   West. This matched with other like, my gracious
     lord;
For more uneven and unwelcome news 50
Came from the north and thus it did import:
On Holy-rood day, the gallant Hotspur there,
Young Harry Percy and brave Archibald,
That ever-valiant and approvèd Scot,
At Holmedon met,
Where they did spend a sad and bloody hour;
As by discharge of their artillery,
And shape of likelihood, the news was told;
For he that brought them, in the very heat
And pride of their contention did take horse, 60
Uncertain of the issue any way.
   K. Hen. Here is a dear and true industrious friend,
Sir Walter Blunt, new lighted from his horse,
Stained with the variation of each soil
Betwixt that Holmedon and this seat of ours;
And he hath brought us smooth and welcome
    news.
The Earl of Douglas is discomfited;
Ten thousand bold Scots, two and twenty knights,
Balked in their own blood did Sir Walter see
On Holmedon's plains: of prisoners Hotspur took 70
Mordake the Earl of Fife, and eldest son
To beaten Douglas, and the Earls of Athol,
Of Murray, Angus, and Menteith.
And is not this an honourable spoil?
A gallant prize? ha, cousin, is it not?
   West. In faith,
It is a conquest for a prince to boast of.
   K. Hen. Yea, there thou mak'st me sad and mak'st
    me sin
In envy that my Lord Northumberland
Should be the father to so blest a son, 80
A son who is the theme of honour's tongue;
Amongst a grove the very straightest plant;
Who is sweet Fortune's minion and her pride:
Whilst I, by looking on the praise of him,
See riot and dishonour stain the brow
Of my young Harry. O! that it could be proved
That some night-tripping fairy had exchanged
In cradle-clothes our children where they lay,
And called mine Percy, his Plantagenet.
Then would I have his Harry, and he mine. 90
But let him from my thoughts. What think you,
    coz,
Of this young Percy's pride? the prisoners,
Which he in this adventure hath surprised,
To his own use he keeps, and sends me word,
I shall have none but Mordake Earl of Fife.
   West. This is his uncle's teaching, this is Worces-
    ter,
Malevolent to you in all aspects;
Which makes him prune himself, and bristle up
The crest of youth against your dignity.
   K. Hen. But I have sent for him to answer this; 100
And for this cause a while we must neglect
Our holy purpose to Jerusalem.
Cousin, on Wednesday next our council we
Will hold at Windsor; so inform the lords:
But come yourself with speed to us again;
For more is to be said and to be done
Than out of anger can be uttered.
   West. I will, my liege. [*Exeunt.*

---

22. **power of English . . . levy,** raise and conduct a force of Englishmen. 31. **cousin.** It was the royal custom to use the term "cousin" in addressing the nobility. 33. **expedience,** expedition. 38. **Mortimer,** Earl of March, rightful heir to the throne of England. 52. **Holy-rood day,** Holy Cross day, September 14. 55. **Holmedon,** the modern Humbleton in Northumberland. 69. **Balked,** piled up to form a balk or ridge. 83. **minion,** darling. 87. **some night-tripping fairy.** Shakespeare makes the Prince of Wales and Hotspur equal in years, although Hotspur was really three years older than the King. 95. **I shall have none . . . Fife.** King Henry by law of arms could claim only the Earl of Fife; all of less rank belonged to Hotspur.

SCENE 2.—*The Same. An Apartment of the* PRINCE'S.

Enter the PRINCE *and* FALSTAFF.

Fal. Now, Hal, what time of day is it, lad?

Prince. Thou art so fat-witted, with drinking of old sack, and unbuttoning thee after supper, and sleeping upon benches after noon, that thou hast forgotten to demand that truly which thou wouldst truly know. What a devil hast thou to do with the time of the day? unless hours were cups of sack, and minutes capons, and clocks the tongues of bawds, and dials the signs of leaping-houses, and the blessed sun himself a fair hot wench in flame- [10 coloured taffeta, I see no reason why thou shouldst be so superfluous to demand the time of the day.

Fal. Indeed, you come near me now, Hal; for we that take purses go by the moon and the seven stars, and not by Phoebus, he, "that wandering knight so fair." And, I prithee, sweet wag, when thou art king,—as, God save thy Grace,—Majesty, I should say, for grace thou wilt have none,—

Prince. What! none?

Fal. No, by my troth; not so much as will [20 serve to be prologue to an egg and butter.

Prince. Well, how then? come, roundly, roundly.

Fal. Marry, then, sweet wag, when thou art king, let not us that are squires of the night's body be called thieves of the day's beauty: let us be Diana's foresters, gentlemen of the shade, minions of the moon; and let men say, we be men of good government, being governed as the sea is, by our noble and chaste mistress the moon, under whose countenance we steal. [30

Prince. Thou sayest well, and it holds well too; for the fortune of us that are the moon's men doth ebb and flow like the sea, being governed as the sea is, by the moon. As for proof now: a purse of gold most resolutely snatched on Monday night and most dissolutely spent on Tuesday morning; got with swearing "Lay by"; and spent with crying "Bring in": now in as low an ebb as the foot of the ladder, and by and by in as high a flow as the ridge of the gallows. [40

Fal. By the Lord, thou sayest true, lad. And is not my hostess of the tavern a most sweet wench?

Prince. As the honey of Hybla, my old lad of the castle. And is not a buff jerkin a most sweet robe of durance?

Fal. How now, how now, mad wag! what, in thy quips and thy quiddities? what a plague have I to do with a buff jerkin?

Prince. Why, what a pox have I to do with my hostess of the tavern? [50

Fal. Well, thou hast called her to a reckoning many a time and oft.

Prince. Did I ever call for thee to pay thy part?

Fal. No; I'll give thee thy due, thou hast paid all there.

Prince. Yea, and elsewhere, so far as my coin would stretch; and where it would not, I have used my credit.

Fal. Yea, and so used it that, were it not here apparent that thou art heir apparent—But, I [60 prithee, sweet wag, shall there be gallows standing in England when thou art king, and resolution thus fobbed as it is with the rusty curb of old father antick the law? Do not thou, when thou art king, hang a thief.

Prince. No; thou shalt.

Fal. Shall I? O rare! By the Lord, I'll be a brave judge.

Prince. Thou judgest false already; I mean, thou shalt have the hanging of the thieves and so be- [70 come a rare hangman.

Fal. Well, Hal, well; and in some sort it jumps with my humour as well as waiting in the court, I can tell you.

Prince. For obtaining of suits?

Fal. Yea, for obtaining of suits, whereof the hangman hath no lean wardrobe. 'Sblood, I am as melancholy as a gib cat, or a lugged bear.

Prince. Or an old lion, or a lover's lute.

Fal. Yea, or the drone of a Lincolnshire bag- [80 pipe.

Prince. What sayest thou to a hare, or the melancholy of Moor-ditch?

Fal. Thou hast the most unsavoury similes, and art, indeed, the most comparative, rascalliest, sweet young prince; but, Hal, I prithee, trouble me no more with vanity. I would to God thou and I knew where a commodity of good names were to be bought. An old lord of the council rated me the other day in the street about you, sir, but I [90 marked him not; and yet he talked very wisely, but I regarded him not; and yet he talked wisely, and in the street too.

Prince. Thou didst well; for wisdom cries out in the streets, and no man regards it.

---

3. **sack,** a kind of Spanish wine.   17. **Grace.** The word is punningly used.   38. **ladder,** of the gallows.   43. **Hybla.** There are three towns of this name in Sicily; one was famous for its honey.   44–45. **a buff jerkin,** a leather jacket worn by the officer who took a man to prison. **robe of durance?** pun on durable cloth and imprisonment.

78. **gib cat . . . lugged bear,** tomcat, baited bear, or performing bear.   82. **hare.** Eating the flesh of a hare was supposed to cause melancholy.   83. **Moor-ditch?** a foul and stagnant ditch in Moorfields on the outskirts of London.

Fal. O! thou hast damnable iteration, and art indeed able to corrupt a saint. Thou hast done much harm upon me, Hal; God forgive thee for it! Before I knew thee, Hal, I knew nothing; and now am I, if a man should speak truly, little better [100 than one of the wicked. I must give over this life, and I will give it over; by the Lord, an I do not, I am a villain: I'll be damned for never a king's son in Christendom.

Prince. Where shall we take a purse to-morrow, Jack?

Fal. Zounds! where thou wilt, lad, I'll make one; an I do not, call me a villain and baffle me.

Prince. I see a good amendment of life in thee; from praying to purse-taking. [110

[*Enter* POINS, *at a distance.*]

Fal. Why, Hal, 'tis my vocation, Hal; 'tis no sin for a man to labour in his vocation. Poins! Now shall we know if Gadshill have set a match. O! if men were to be saved by merit, what hole in hell were hot enough for him? This is the most omnipotent villain that ever cried "Stand!" to a true man.

Prince. Good morrow, Ned.

Poins. Good morrow, sweet Hal. What says Monsieur Remorse? What says Sir John Sack- [120 and-Sugar? Jack! how agrees the devil and thee about thy soul, that thou soldest him on Good-Friday last for a cup of Madeira and a cold capon's leg?

Prince. Sir John stands to his word, the devil shall have his bargain; for he was never yet a breaker of proverbs: he will give the devil his due.

Poins. Then art thou damned for keeping thy word with the devil.

Prince. Else he had been damned for cozen- [130 ing the devil.

Poins. But my lads, my lads, to-morrow morning, by four o'clock, early at Gadshill! There are pilgrims going to Canterbury with rich offerings, and traders riding to London with fat purses: I have vizards for you all; you have horses for yourselves. Gadshill lies to-night in Rochester; I have bespoke supper to-morrow night in Eastcheap: we may do it as secure as sleep. If you will go I will stuff your purses full of crowns; if you will not, tarry at [140 home and be hanged.

Fal. Hear ye, Yedward: if I tarry at home and go not, I'll hang you for going.

Poins. You will, chops?

Fal. Hal, wilt thou make one?

Prince. Who, I rob? I a thief? not I, by my faith.

Fal. There's neither honesty, manhood, nor good fellowship in thee, nor thou camest not of the blood royal, if thou darest not stand for ten shillings.

Prince. Well, then, once in my days I'll be a [150 madcap.

Fal. Why, that's well said.

Prince. Well, come what will, I'll tarry at home.

Fal. By the Lord, I'll be a traitor then, when thou art king.

Prince. I care not.

Poins. Sir John, I prithee, leave the prince and me alone: I will lay him down such reasons for this adventure that he shall go.

Fal. Well, God give thee the spirit of per- [160 suasion and him the ears of profiting, that what thou speakest may move, and what he hears may be believed, that the true prince may, for recreation sake, prove a false thief; for the poor abuses of the time want countenance. Farewell: you shall find me in Eastcheap.

Prince. Farewell, thou latter spring! Farewell, All-hallown summer! [*Exit* FALSTAFF.

Poins. Now, my good sweet honey lord, ride with us to-morrow: I have a jest to execute that I [170 cannot manage alone. Falstaff, Bardolph, Peto, and Gadshill shall rob those men that we have already waylaid; yourself and I will not be there; and when they have the booty, if you and I do not rob them, cut this head from my shoulders.

Prince. But how shall we part with them in setting forth?

Poins. Why, we will set forth before or after them, and appoint them a place of meeting, wherein it is at our pleasure to fail; and then will they ad- [180 venture upon the exploit themselves, which they shall have no sooner achieved but we'll set upon them.

Prince. Yea, but 'tis like that they will know us by our horses, by our habits, and by every other appointment, to be ourselves.

Poins. Tut! our horses they shall not see, I'll tie them in the wood; our vizards we will change after we leave them; and, sirrah, I have cases of buckram for the nonce, to inmask our noted outward garments. [190

102. **an,** if. 108. **baffle me,** subject me to disgrace. 113. **Gadshill,** name of a character in the play, also the name of a hill near Rochester on the road to Canterbury, a notorious spot for robberies. 130–31. **cozening,** cheating. 136. **vizards,** masks. 142. **Yedward,** Edward, Poins's Christian name.

148–49. **blood royal . . . shillings,** one pun on "royal," which signified a coin of the value of 10*s.*, and another on "stand for," which could be taken in the two senses of "be worth" and "make a fight for." 167–68. **thou latter spring! . . . summer!** reference to Falstaff's youthful spirit in his old age. All Hallows (All Saints' Day) is November 1, when warm weather (Indian summer) is usual. 188. **sirrah,** a form of address to children and servants, here a sign of Poins's undue familiarity with the Prince.

Prince. Yea, but I doubt they will be too hard for us.

Poins. Well, for two of them, I know them to be as true-bred cowards as ever turned back; and for the third, if he fight longer than he sees reason, I'll forswear arms. The virtue of this jest will be, the incomprehensible lies that this same fat rogue will tell us when we meet at supper: how thirty, at least, he fought with; what wards, what blows, what extremities he endured; and in the reproof of this [200 lies the jest.

Prince. Well, I'll go with thee: provide us all things necessary and meet me to-morrow night in Eastcheap; there I'll sup. Farewell.

Poins. Farewell, my lord. [*Exit.*

Prince. I know you all, and will awhile uphold
The unyoked humour of your idleness:
Yet herein will I imitate the sun,
Who doth permit the base contagious clouds
To smother up his beauty from the world, 210
That when he please again to be himself,
Being wanted, he may be more wondered at,
By breaking through the foul and ugly mists
Of vapours that did seem to strangle him.
If all the year were playing holidays,
To sport would be as tedious as to work;
But when they seldom come, they wished for come,
And nothing pleaseth but rare accidents.
So, when this loose behaviour I throw off,
And pay the debt I never promisèd, 220
By how much better than my word I am
By so much shall I falsify men's hopes;
And like bright metal on a sullen ground,
My reformation, glittering o'er my fault,
Shall show more goodly and attract more eyes
Than that which hath no foil to set it off.
I'll so offend to make offence a skill;
Redeeming time when men think least I will. [*Exit.*

SCENE 3.—*The Same. The Palace.*

Enter KING HENRY, NORTHUMBERLAND, WORCESTER, HOTSPUR, SIR WALTER BLUNT, *and Others.*

K. Hen. My blood hath been too cold and temperate,
Unapt to stir at these indignities,
And you have found me; for accordingly
You tread upon my patience: but, be sure,
I will from henceforth rather be myself,
Mighty, and to be feared, than my condition,
Which hath been smooth as oil, soft as young down,
And therefore lost that title of respect
Which the proud soul ne'er pays but to the proud.

Wor. Our house, my sovereign liege, little deserves 10
The scourge of greatness to be used on it;
And that same greatness too which our own hands
Have holp to make so portly.

North. My lord,—

K. Hen. Worcester, get thee gone; for I do see
Danger and disobedience in thine eye.
O, sir, your presence is too bold and peremptory,
And majesty might never yet endure
The moody frontier of a servant brow.
You have good leave to leave us; when we need 20
Your use and counsel we shall send for you.

[*Exit* WORCESTER.

(*To* NORTHUMBERLAND.) You were about to speak.

North. Yea, my good lord.
Those prisoners in your highness' name demanded,
Which Harry Percy here at Holmedon took,
Were, as he says, not with such strength denied
As is delivered to your majesty:
Either envy, therefore, or misprision
Is guilty of this fault and not my son.

Hot. My liege, I did deny no prisoners:
But I remember, when the fight was done, 30
When I was dry with rage and extreme toil,
Breathless and faint, leaning upon my sword,
Came there a certain lord, neat, and trimly dressed,
Fresh as a bridegroom; and his chin, new reaped,
Showed like a stubble-land at harvest-home:
He was perfumèd like a milliner,
And 'twixt his finger and his thumb he held
A pouncet-box, which ever and anon
He gave his nose and took 't away again;
Who therewith angry, when it next came there, 40
Took it in snuff: and still he smiled and talked;
And as the soldiers bore dead bodies by,
He called them untaught knaves, unmannerly,
To bring a slovenly unhandsome corpse
Betwixt the wind and his nobility.
With many holiday and lady terms
He questioned me; among the rest, demanded
My prisoners in your majesty's behalf.
I then all smarting with my wounds being cold,
To be so pestered with a popinjay, 50
Out of my grief and my impatience
Answered neglectingly, I know not what,
He should, or he should not; for he made me mad
To see him shine so brisk and smell so sweet
And talk so like a waiting-gentlewoman

10–13. Our house, my . . . liege . . . so portly. Worcester's speech is intended to anger the King. **36. milliner.** In Shakespeare's time, milliners (dealers in women's clothes from Milan), were, for the most part, men. **38. pouncet-box,** a small box containing an aromatic powder.

Of guns, and drums, and wounds,—God save the mark!—
And telling me the sovereign'st thing on earth
Was parmaceti for an inward bruise;
And that it was great pity, so it was,
This villanous saltpetre should be digged 60
Out of the bowels of the harmless earth,
Which many a good tall fellow had destroyed
So cowardly; and but for these vile guns,
He would himself have been a soldier.
This bald unjointed chat of his, my lord,
I answered indirectly, as I said;
And I beseech you, let not his report
Come current for an accusation
Betwixt my love and your high majesty.
  Blunt. The circumstance considered, good my lord, 70
Whatever Harry Percy then had said
To such a person and in such a place,
At such a time, with all the rest re-told,
May reasonably die and never rise
To do him wrong, or any way impeach
What then he said, so he unsay it now.
  K. Hen. Why, yet he doth deny his prisoners,
But with proviso and exception,
That we at our own charge shall ransom straight
His brother-in-law, the foolish Mortimer; 80
Who, on my soul, hath wilfully betrayed
The lives of those that he did lead to fight
Against the great magician, damned Glendower,
Whose daughter, as we hear, the Earl of March
Hath lately married. Shall our coffers then
Be emptied to redeem a traitor home?
Shall we buy treason, and indent with fears,
When they have lost and forfeited themselves?
No, on the barren mountains let him starve;
For I shall never hold that man my friend 90
Whose tongue shall ask me for one penny cost
To ransom home revolted Mortimer.
  Hot. Revolted Mortimer!
He never did fall off, my sovereign liege,
But by the chance of war: to prove that true
Needs no more but one tongue for all those wounds,
Those mouthèd wounds, which valiantly he took,
When on the gentle Severn's sedgy bank,
In single opposition, hand to hand,
He did confound the best part of an hour 100
In changing hardiment with great Glendower.
Three times they breathed and three times did they drink,
Upon agreement, of swift Severn's flood,
Who then, affrighted with their bloody looks,
Ran fearfully among the trembling reeds,
And hid his crisp head in the hollow bank
Blood-stainèd with these valiant combatants.
Never did base and rotten policy
Colour her working with such deadly wounds;
Nor never could the noble Mortimer 110
Receive so many, and all willingly:
Then let him not be slandered with revolt.
  K. Hen. Thou dost belie him, Percy, thou dost belie him:
He never did encounter with Glendower:
I tell thee,
He durst as well have met the devil alone
As Owen Glendower for an enemy.
Art thou not ashamed? But, sirrah, henceforth
Let me not hear you speak of Mortimer: 119
Send me your prisoners with the speediest means,
Or you shall hear in such a kind from me
As will displease you. My Lord Northumberland,
We license your departure with your son.
Send us your prisoners, or you'll hear of it.
  [*Exeunt* KING HENRY, BLUNT, *and* Train.
  Hot. An if the devil come and roar for them,
I will not send them: I will after straight
And tell him so; for I will ease my heart,
Albeit I make a hazard of my head.
  North. What! drunk with choler? stay, and pause awhile:
Here comes your uncle.
  [*Re-enter* WORCESTER.]
  Hot.   Speak of Mortimer! 130
'Zounds! I will speak of him; and let my soul
Want mercy if I do not join with him:
In his behalf I'll empty all these veins,
And shed my dear blood drop by drop i' the dust,
But I will lift the down-trod Mortimer
As high i' the air as this unthankful king,
As this ingrate and cankered Bolingbroke.
  North. Brother, the king hath made your nephew mad.
  Wor. Who struck this heat up after I was gone?
  Hot. He will, forsooth, have all my prisoners; 140
And when I urged the ransom once again
Of my wife's brother, then his cheek looked pale,
And on my face he turned an eye of death,
Trembling even at the name of Mortimer.

---

56. **God save the mark!** literally, a prayer that physical blemishes may be averted.   58. **parmaceti,** spermaceti.   80. **His brother-in-law . . . Mortimer.** Shakespeare here confuses Edmund, Earl of March, nephew to Lady Percy, with Sir Edmund Mortimer, who was Lady Percy's brother and brother-in-law to Hotspur.

106. **crisp head,** rippling surface.   143. **an eye of death,** a look that threatened death to Hotspur.

Wor. I cannot blame him: was he not proclaimed
By Richard that dead is the next of blood?
   North. He was; I heard the proclamation:
And then it was when the unhappy king,—
Whose wrongs in us God pardon!—did set forth
Upon his Irish expedition;   150
From whence he, intercepted, did return
To be deposed, and shortly murderèd.
   Wor. And for whose death we in the world's wide
      mouth
Live scandalized and foully spoken of.
   Hot. But, soft! I pray you, did King Richard then
Proclaim my brother Edmund Mortimer
Heir to the crown?
   North.   He did; myself did hear it.
   Hot. Nay, then I cannot blame his cousin king,
That wished him on the barren mountains starve.
But shall it be that you, that set the crown   160
Upon the head of this forgetful man,
And for his sake wear the detested blot
Of murd'rous subornation, shall it be,
That you a world of curses undergo,
Being the agents, or base second means,
The cords, the ladder, or the hangman rather?
O! pardon me that I descend so low,
To show the line and the predicament
Wherein you range under this subtle king.
Shall it for shame be spoken in these days,   170
Or fill up chronicles in time to come,
That men of your nobility and power,
Did gage them both in an unjust behalf,
As both of you—God pardon it!—have done,
To put down Richard, that sweet lovely rose,
And plant this thorn, this canker, Bolingbroke?
And shall it in more shame be further spoken,
That you are fooled, discarded, and shook off
By him for whom these shames ye underwent?
No; yet time serves wherein you may redeem   180
Your banished honours, and restore yourselves
Into the good thoughts of the world again;
Revenge the jeering and disdained contempt
Of this proud king, who studies day and night
To answer all the debt he owes to you,
Even with the bloody payment of your deaths.
Therefore, I say,—
   Wor.   Peace, cousin! say no more:
And now I will unclasp a secret book,
And to your quick-conceiving discontents
I'll read you matter deep and dangerous,   190
As full of peril and adventurous spirit
As to o'er-walk a current roaring loud,
On the unsteadfast footing of a spear.
   Hot. If he fall in, good night! or sink or swim:
Send danger from the east unto the west,
So honour cross it from the north to south,
And let them grapple: O! the blood more stirs
To rouse a lion than to start a hare.
   North. Imagination of some great exploit
Drives him beyond the bounds of patience.   200
   Hot. By heaven methinks it were an easy leap
To pluck bright honour from the pale-faced moon,
Or dive into the bottom of the deep,
Where fathom-line could never touch the ground,
And pluck up drownèd honour by the locks;
So he that doth redeem her thence might wear
Without corrival all her dignities:
But out upon this half-faced fellowship!
   Wor. He apprehends a world of figures here,
But not the form of what he should attend.   210
Good cousin, give me audience for a while.
   Hot. I cry you mercy.
   Wor.   Those same noble Scots
That are your prisoners,—
   Hot.   I'll keep them all;
By God, he shall not have a Scot of them:
No, if a Scot would save his soul, he shall not:
I'll keep them, by this hand.
   Wor.   You start away,
And lend no ear unto my purposes.
Those prisoners you shall keep.
   Hot.   Nay, I will; that's flat:
He said he would not ransom Mortimer;
Forbade my tongue to speak of Mortimer;   220
But I will find him when he lies asleep,
And in his ear I'll holla "Mortimer!"
Nay,
I'll have a starling shall be taught to speak
Nothing but "Mortimer," and give it him,
To keep his anger still in motion.
   Wor. Hear you, cousin; a word.
   Hot. All studies here I solemnly defy,
Save how to gall and pinch this Bolingbroke: 229
And that same sword-and-buckler Prince of Wales,
But that I think his father loves him not,
And would be glad he met with some mischance,
I would have him poisoned with a pot of ale.
   Wor. Farewell, kinsman: I will talk to you
When you are better tempered to attend.
   North. Why, what a wasp-stung and impatient
      fool
Art thou to break into this woman's mood,

145–46. was he not proclaimed ... blood? This was not true of the Edmund Mortimer who was defeated by Owen Glendower, but of his nephew Edmund. Shakespeare's confusion is due to Holinshed.   **149. in us,** caused by us. The Percy family had assisted Henry against Richard.   **176. canker,** dog rose, which has stout hooked prickles.   **208. half-faced,** miserable, venturing to present only half a face to danger.   **228. defy,** renounce.

Tying thine ear to no tongue but thine own!
   Hot. Why, look you, I am whipped and scourged
      with rods,
Nettled, and stung with pismires, when I hear   240
Of this vile politician, Bolingbroke.
In Richard's time,—what do ye call the place?—
A plague upon 't—it is in Gloucestershire;—
'Twas where the madcap duke his uncle kept,
His uncle York; where I first bowed my knee
Unto this king of smiles, this Bolingbroke,
'Sblood!
When you and he came back from Ravenspurgh.
   North. At Berkeley Castle.
   Hot. You say true.   250
Why, what a candy deal of courtesy
This fawning greyhound then did proffer me!
Look, "when his infant fortune came to age,"
And "gentle Harry Percy," and "kind cousin."
O! the devil take such cozeners. God forgive me!
Good uncle, tell your tale, for I have done.
   Wor. Nay, if you have not, to 't again;
We'll stay your leisure.
   Hot.   I have done, i' faith.
   Wor. Then once more to your Scottish prisoners.
Deliver them up without their ransom straight,   260
And make the Douglas' son your only mean
For powers in Scotland; which, for divers reasons
Which I shall send you written, be assured,
Will easily be granted. (*To* NORTHUMBERLAND.)
    You, my lord,
Your son in Scotland being thus employed,
Shall secretly into the bosom creep
Of that same noble prelate well beloved,
The Archbishop.
   Hot. Of York, is it not?
   Wor. True; who bears hard   270
His brother's death at Bristol, the Lord Scroop.
I speak not this in estimation,
As what I think might be, but what I know
Is ruminated, plotted and set down;
And only stays but to behold the face
Of that occasion that shall bring it on.
   Hot. I smell it.
Upon my life it will do wondrous well.
   North. Before the game's afoot thou still lett'st slip.
   Hot. Why, it cannot choose but be a noble plot:
And then the power of Scotland and of York,   281
To join with Mortimer, ha?
   Wor.   And so they shall.

   Hot. In faith, it is exceedingly well aimed.
   Wor. And 'tis no little reason bids us speed,
To save our heads by raising of a head;
For, bear ourselves as even as we can,
The king will always think him in our debt,
And think we think ourselves unsatisfied,
Till he hath found a time to pay us home.
And see already how he doth begin   290
To make us strangers to his looks of love.
   Hot. He does, he does: we'll be revenged on him.
   Wor. Cousin, farewell: no further go in this,
Than I by letters shall direct your course.
When time is ripe,—which will be suddenly,—
I'll steal to Glendower and Lord Mortimer;
Where you and Douglas and our powers at once,—
As I will fashion it,—shall happily meet,
To bear our fortunes in our own strong arms,
Which now we hold at much uncertainty.   300
   North. Farewell, good brother: we shall thrive, I
      trust.
   Hot. Uncle, adieu: O! let the hours be short,
Till fields and blows and groans applaud our sport!
                                          [*Exeunt.*

ACT II

SCENE I.—*Rochester. An Inn-Yard.*

Enter a Carrier, *with a lanthorn in his hand.*

   First Car. Heigh-ho! An 't be not four by the day I'll be hanged: Charles' Wain is over the new chimney, and yet our horse not packed. What, ostler!
   Ost. (*within*). Anon, anon.
   First Car. I prithee, Tom, beat Cut's saddle, put a few flocks in the point; the poor jade is wrung in the withers out of all cess.

[*Enter another* Carrier.]

   Sec. Car. Peas and beans are as dank here as a dog, and that is the next way to give poor jades the bots; this house is turned upside down since Robin [10 Ostler died.
   First Car. Poor fellow! never joyed since the price of oats rose; it was the death of him.
   Sec. Car. I think this be the most villanous house in all London road for fleas: I am stung like a tench.
   First Car. Like a tench! by the mass, there is ne'er

---

240. **pismires,** ants.   241. **politician,** cunning plotter. This word already had a bad sense in Elizabethan times. 244. **kept,** lived.   248. **Ravenspurgh,** the seaport at which Henry IV, then Bolingbroke, landed on his return to England. 279. **Before the game's . . . slip.** You always loose the hounds before the game is started.

285. **head,** armed force.   289. **pay us home,** pay us back. 2. **Charles' Wain,** the Great Bear.   5–7. **beat Cut's saddle,** beat the saddle to soften it. **put a few . . . point,** put some tufts of wool at the pommel of the saddle to prevent it from galling the horse's **withers wrung . . . cess,** galled beyond measure.   15–16. **like a tench,** from an old superstition that fishes are infested with fleas.

a king christen could be better bit than I have been since the first cock.

Sec. Car. Why, they will allow us ne'er a jor- [20 dan, and then we leak in the chimney; and your chamber-lie breeds fleas like a loach.

First Car. What, ostler! come away and be hanged, come away.

Sec. Car. I have a gammon of bacon and two razes of ginger, to be delivered as far as Charing Cross.

First Car. Godsbody! the turkeys in my pannier are quite starved. What, ostler! A plague on thee! hast thou never an eye in thy head? canst not [30 hear? An 'twere not as good a deed as drink to break the pate on thee, I am a very villain. Come, and be hanged! hast no faith in thee?

[*Enter* GADSHILL.]

Gads. Good morrow, carriers. What's o'clock?
First Car. I think it be two o'clock.
Gads. I prithee, lend me thy lanthorn, to see my gelding in the stable.
First Car. Nay, by God, soft: I know a trick worth two of that, i' faith.
Gads. I prithee, lend me thine. [40
Sec. Car. Ay, when? canst tell? Lend me thy lanthorn, quoth a'? marry, I'll see thee hanged first.
Gads. Sirrah carrier, what time do you mean to come to London?
Sec. Car. Time enough to go to bed with a candle, I warrant thee. Come, neighbour Mugs, we'll call up the gentlemen: they will along with company, for they have great charge. [*Exeunt* Carriers.
Gads. What, ho! chamberlain!
Cham. (*within*). "At hand, quoth pick-purse." [50
Gads. That's even as fair as, "at hand, quoth the chamberlain"; for thou variest no more from picking of purses than giving direction doth from labouring; thou layest the plot how.

[*Enter* CHAMBERLAIN.]

Cham. Good morrow, Master Gadshill. It holds current that I told you yesternight: there's a franklin in the wild of Kent hath brought three hundred marks with him in gold: I heard him tell it to one of his company last night at supper; a kind of auditor; one that hath abundance of charge too, God [60 knows what. They are up already and call for eggs and butter: they will away presently.

Gads. Sirrah, if they meet not with Saint Nicholas' clerks, I'll give thee this neck.

Cham. No, I'll none of it: I prithee, keep that for the hangman; for I know thou worship'st Saint Nicholas as truly as a man of falsehood may.

Gads. What talkest thou to me of the hangman? If I hang I'll make a fat pair of gallows; for if I hang, old Sir John hangs with me, and thou know- [70 est he's no starveling. Tut! there are other Troyans that thou dreamest not of, the which for sport sake are content to do the profession some grace; that would, if matters should be looked into, for their own credit sake make all whole. I am joined with no foot-land-rakers, no long-staff sixpenny strikers, none of these mad mustachio-purple-hued malt worms; but with nobility and tranquillity, burgomasters and great oneyers such as can hold in, such as will strike sooner than speak, and speak [80 sooner than drink, and drink sooner than pray: and yet I lie; for they pray continually to their saint, the commonwealth; or, rather, not pray to her, but prey on her, for they ride up and down on her and make her their boots.

Cham. What! the commonwealth their boots? will she hold out water in foul way?

Gads. She will, she will; justice hath liquored her. We steal as in a castle, cock-sure; we have the receipt of fern-seed, we walk invisible. [90

Cham. Nay, by my faith, I think you are more beholding to the night than to fern-seed for your walking invisible.

Gads. Give me thy hand: thou shalt have a share in our purchase, as I am a true man.

Cham. Nay, rather let me have it, as you are a false thief.

Gads. Go to; *homo* is a common name to all men. Bid the ostler bring my gelding out of the stable. [99 Farewell, you muddy knave. [*Exeunt.*

SCENE 2.—*The Road by Gadshill.*

Enter the PRINCE *and* POINS.

Poins. Come, shelter, shelter: I have removed Falstaff's horse, and he frets like a gummed velvet.
Prince. Stand close.

---

18. christen, Christian. **20–21. jordan,** chamber pot. **22. loach,** a fish that breeds several times a year. **25. gammon,** flitch. **26. razes,** roots tied in a bundle. **26–27. Charing Cross,** in Shakespeare's time a village on the road from London to Westminster, now in the heart of London. **56. franklin,** a small freeholder. **63–64. Saint Nicholas' clerks,** highwaymen—not from "Santa Claus," but from "Old Nick." **76–78. foot-land-rakers . . . strikers . . . malt worms,** footpads; cutpurses; drunkards. **79. oneyers.** The meaning is uncertain, perhaps "great ones." **88. liquored,** greased with tallow. **89–90. receipt of fern-seed.** Fern seed was supposed to have the power to make human beings invisible. **98. "homo" is a common . . . men,** quotation from a Latin grammar. "Thief" is not an antithesis to "man," as "false" is to "true." **2. frets like a gummed velvet.** Velvet stiffened with gum very soon chafed.

[*Enter* FALSTAFF.]

Fal. Poins! Poins, and be hanged! Poins!

Prince. Peace, ye fat-kidneyed rascal! What a brawling dost thou keep!

Fal. Where's Poins, Hal?

Prince. He is walked up to the top of the hill: I'll go seek him. (*Pretends to seek* POINS, *and retires.*)

Fal. I am accursed to rob in that thief's com- [10 pany; the rascal hath removed my horse and tied him I know not where. If I travel but four foot by the squire further afoot I shall break my wind. Well, I doubt not but to die a fair death for all this, if I 'scape hanging for killing that rogue. I have forsworn his company hourly any time this two-and-twenty years, and yet I am bewitched with the rogue's company. If the rascal have not given me medicines to make me love him, I'll be hanged: it could not be else: I have drunk medicines. [20 Poins! Hal! a plague upon you both! Bardolph! Peto! I'll starve ere I'll rob a foot further. An 'twere not as good a deed as drink to turn true man and leave these rogues, I am the veriest varlet that ever chewed with a tooth. Eight yards of uneven ground is threescore and ten miles afoot with me, and the stony-hearted villains know it well enough. A plague upon 't when thieves cannot be true one to another! (*They whistle.*) Whew! A plague upon you all! Give me my horse, you rogues; give me [30 my horse and be hanged.

Prince (*coming forward*). Peace, ye fatguts! lie down: lay thine ear close to the ground, and list if thou canst hear the tread of travellers.

Fal. Have you any levers to lift me up again, being down? 'Sblood! I'll not bear mine own flesh so far afoot again for all the coin in thy father's exchequer. What a plague mean ye to colt me thus?

Prince. Thou liest: thou art not colted; thou art uncolted. [40

Fal. I prithee, good Prince Hal, help me to my horse, good king's son.

Prince. Out, you rogue! shall I be your ostler?

Fal. Go, hang thyself in thine own heir apparent garters! If I be ta'en I'll peach for this. An I have not ballads made on you all, and sung to filthy tunes, let a cup of sack be my poison: when a jest is so forward, and afoot too! I hate it.

[*Enter* GADSHILL.]

Gads. Stand.

Fal. So I do, against my will. [50

Poins. O! 'tis our setter: I know his voice.

[*Enter* BARDOLPH *and* PETO.]

Bard. What news?

Gads. Case ye, case ye; on with your vizards: there's money of the king's coming down the hill; 'tis going to the king's exchequer.

Fal. You lie, you rogue; 'tis going to the king's tavern.

Gads. There's enough to make us all.

Fal. To be hanged.

Prince. Sirs, you four shall front them in the [60 narrow lane; Ned Poins and I will walk lower: if they 'scape from your encounter then they light on us.

Peto. How many be there of them?

Gads. Some eight or ten.

Fal. 'Zounds! will they not rob us?

Prince. What! a coward, Sir John Paunch?

Fal. Indeed, I am not John of Gaunt, your grandfather; but yet no coward, Hal.

Prince. Well, we leave that to the proof. [70

Poins. Sirrah Jack, thy horse stands behind the hedge: when thou needst him there thou shalt find him. Farewell, and stand fast.

Fal. Now cannot I strike him if I should be hanged.

Prince (*aside to* POINS). Ned, where are our disguises?

Poins. Here, hard by; stand close.

[*Exeunt* PRINCE *and* POINS.

Fal. Now my masters, happy man be his dole, say I: every man to his business. [80

[*Enter* Travellers.]

First Trav. Come, neighbour; the boy shall lead our horses down the hill; we'll walk afoot awhile, and ease our legs.

Thieves. Stand!

Travellers. Jesu bless us!

Fal. Strike; down with them; cut the villains' throats: ah! whoreson caterpillars! bacon-fed knaves! they hate us youth: down with them; fleece them.

Travellers. O! we are undone, both we and [90 ours for ever.

Fal. Hang ye, gorbellied knaves, are ye undone? No, ye fat chuffs; I would your store were here! On, bacons, on! What! ye knaves, young men must live. You are grand-jurors are ye? We'll jure ye, i' faith.

[*Here they rob and bind them. Exeunt.*

12–13. **by the squire,** measured by the foot rule (square). 38. **colt,** horse. 44–45. **Go, hang thyself . . . garters!** a popular slang phrase. 51. **setter,** decoy. 53. **Case ye,** put on your masks. 87. **caterpillars!** devourers of substance. 92. **gorbellied,** fat-paunched. 93. **chuffs,** clowns, boors.

[*Re-enter the* PRINCE *and* POINS.]

Prince. The thieves have bound the true men. Now could thou and I rob the thieves and go merrily to London, it would be argument for a week, laughter for a month, and a good jest for ever.

Poins. Stand close; I hear them coming. [100

[*Re-enter* Thieves.]

Fal. Come, my masters; let us share, and then to horse before day. An the Prince and Poins be not two arrant cowards, there's no equity stirring: there's no more valour in that Poins than in a wild duck.

Prince. Your money!

Poins. Villains!

[*As they are sharing, the* PRINCE *and* POINS *set upon them. They all run away; and* FALSTAFF, *after a blow or two, runs away too, leaving the booty behind.*]

Prince. Got with much ease. Now merrily to horse: The thieves are scattered and possessed with fear So strongly that they dare not meet each other; [110 Each takes his fellow for an officer. Away, good Ned. Falstaff sweats to death And lards the lean earth as he walks along: Were't not for laugging I should pity him.

Poins. How the rogue roared! [*Exeunt.*

SCENE 3.—*Warkworth. A Room in the Castle.*

Enter HOTSPUR, *reading a letter.*

"But for mine own part, my lord, I could be well contented to be there, in respect of the love I bear your house."

He could be contented; why is he not then? In respect of the love he bears our house: he shows in this he loves his own barn better than he loves our house. Let me see some more.

"The purpose you undertake is dangerous";—

Why, that's certain: 'tis dangerous to take a cold, to sleep, to drink; but I tell you, my lord fool, out [10 of this nettle, danger, we pluck this flower, safety.

"The purpose you undertake is dangerous; the friends you have named uncertain; the time itself unsorted; and your whole plot too light for the counterpoise of so great an opposition."

Say you so, say you so? I say unto you again, you are a shallow cowardly hind, and you lie. What a lack-brain is this! By the Lord, our plot is a good plot as ever was laid; our friends true and constant: a good plot, good friends, and full of expecta- [20 tion; an excellent plot, very good friends. What a frosty-spirited rogue is this! Why, my Lord of York commends the plot and the general course of the action. 'Zounds! an I were now by this rascal, I could brain him with his lady's fan. Is there not my father, my uncle, and myself? Lord Edmund Mortimer, my Lord of York, and Owen Glendower? Is there not besides the Douglas? Have I not all their letters to meet me in arms by the ninth of the next month, and are they not some of them set for- [30 ward already? What a pagan rascal is this! an infidel! Ha! you shall see now in very sincerity of fear and cold heart, will he to the king and lay open all our proceedings. O! I could divide myself and go to buffets, for moving such a dish of skim milk with so honourable an action. Hang him! let him tell the king; we are prepared. I will set forward to-night.

[*Enter* LADY PERCY.]

How now, Kate! I must leave you within these two
    hours.

Lady P. O, my good lord! why are you thus
    alone?
For what offence have I this fortnight been   40
A banished woman from my Harry's bed?
Tell me, sweet lord, what is 't that takes from
    thee
Thy stomach, pleasure, and thy golden sleep?
Why dost thou bend thine eyes upon the earth,
And start so often when thou sitt'st alone?
Why hast thou lost the fresh blood in thy cheeks,
And given my treasures and my rights of thee
To thick-eyed musing and curst melancholy?
In thy faint slumbers I by thee have watched,
And heard thee murmur tales of iron wars,   50
Speak terms of manage to thy bounding steed,
Cry, "Courage! to the field!" And thou hast talked
Of sallies and retires, of trenches, tents,
Of palisadoes, frontiers, parapets,
Of basilisks, of cannon, culverin,
Of prisoners' ransom, and of soldiers slain,
And all the currents of a heady fight.
Thy spirit within thee hath been so at war,
And thus hath so bestirred thee in thy sleep,
That beads of sweat have stood upon thy brow,   60
Like bubbles in a late-disturbèd stream;
And in thy face strange motions have appeared,
Such as we see when men restrain their breath
On some great sudden hest. O! what portents are
    these?

34–35. **I could divide . . . buffets.** I could cut myself in half and let the two parts fight against each other. 51. **manage,** handling a horse (ménage).   55. **basilisks . . . culverin,** cannon.

Some heavy business hath my lord in hand,
And I must know it, else he loves me not.
  Hot. What, ho!

[*Enter* Servant.]

              Is Gilliams with the packet gone?
  Serv. He is, my lord, an hour ago.
  Hot. Hath Butler brought those horses from the sheriff?
  Serv. One horse, my lord, he brought even now. 70
  Hot. What horse? a roan, a crop-ear, is it not?
  Serv. It is, my lord.
  Hot.   That roan shall be my throne.
Well, I will back him straight: O, *Esperance!*
Bid Butler lead him forth into the park.
                      [*Exit* Servant.
  Lady P. But hear you, my lord.
  Hot. What sayst thou, my lady?
  Lady P. What is it carries you away?
  Hot. Why, my horse, my love, my horse.
  Lady P. Out, you mad-headed ape!
A weasel hath not such a deal of spleen 80
As you are tossed with. In faith,
I'll know your business, Harry, that I will.
I fear my brother Mortimer doth stir
About his title, and hath sent for you
To line his enterprise. But if you go—
  Hot. So far afoot, I shall be weary, love.
  Lady P. Come, come, you paraquito, answer me
Directly unto this question that I ask.
In faith, I'll break thy little finger, Harry,
An if thou wilt not tell me all things true. 90
  Hot. Away,
Away, you trifler! Love! I love thee not,
I care not for thee, Kate: this is no world
To play with mammets and to tilt with lips:
We must have bloody noses and cracked crowns,
And pass them current too. God's me, my horse!
What sayst thou, Kate? what wouldst thou have
    with me?
  Lady P. Do you not love me? do you not, indeed?
Well, do not, then; for since you love me not,
I will not love myself. Do you not love me? 100
Nay, tell me if you speak in jest or no.
  Hot. Come, wilt thou see me ride?
And when I am o' horseback, I will swear
I love thee infinitely. But hark you, Kate;
I must not have you henceforth question me

Whither I go, nor reason whereabout.
Whither I must, I must; and, to conclude,
This evening must I leave you, gentle Kate.
I know you wise; but yet no further wise
Than Harry Percy's wife: constant you are, 110
But yet a woman: and for secrecy,
No lady closer; for I well believe
Thou wilt not utter what thou dost not know;
And so far will I trust thee, gentle Kate.
  Lady P. How! so far?
  Hot. Not an inch further. But, hark you, Kate;
Whither I go, thither shall you go too;
To-day will I set forth, to-morrow you.
Will this content you, Kate?
  Lady P.   It must, of force. [*Exeunt.*

SCENE 4.—*Eastcheap. A Room in the Boar's Head Tavern.*

Enter the PRINCE *and* POINS.

  Prince. Ned, prithee, come out of that fat room, and lend me thy hand to laugh a little.
  Poins. Where hast been, Hal?
  Prince. With three or four loggerheads amongst three or four score hogsheads. I have sounded the very base string of humility. Sirrah, I am sworn brother to a leash of drawers, and can call them all by their christen names, as Tom, Dick, and Francis. They take it already upon their salvation, that though I be but Prince of Wales, yet I am the [10 king of courtesy; and tell me flatly I am no proud Jack, like Falstaff, but a Corinthian, a lad of mettle, a good boy,—by the Lord, so they call me,—and when I am king of England, I shall command all the good lads in Eastcheap. They call drinking deep, dyeing scarlet; and when you breathe in your watering, they cry "hem!" and bid you play it off. To conclude, I am so good a proficient in one quarter of an hour, that I can drink with any tinker in his own language during my life. I tell thee, Ned, [20 thou hast lost much honour that thou wert not with me in this action. But, sweet Ned,—to sweeten which name of Ned, I give thee this pennyworth of sugar, clapped even now into my hand by an underskinker, one that never spake other English in his life than—"Eight shillings and sixpence," and—"You are welcome," with this shrill addition,—"Anon, anon, sir! Score a pint of bastard in the Half-moon," or so. But, Ned, to drive away the time till Falstaff come, I prithee do thou stand in [30

---

73. **Esperance!** the motto of the Percy family. Hotspur makes it his battle-cry. 81. **tossed with,** agitated by. 85. **line,** examine. 87. **paraquito,** small parrot, here a term of endearment, but with allusion to chatter. 94. **mammets,** puppets, used contemptuously for women. 96. **pass them current,** pass them on (play on the word "crowns" as currency). **God's me,** a corruption of some such phrase as "God save me" or "God see me."

7. **leash of drawers,** set (as of hounds) of three tapsters. 12. **Corinthian,** prince of topers. 24–25. **underskinker,** underdrawer or tapster. 28–29. **bastard,** a sweet Spanish wine. **Half-moon,** name given to a room in the inn, as is also **Pomgarnet** (Pomegranate) (ll. 39–40).

some by-room, while I question my puny drawer to what end he gave me the sugar; and do thou never leave calling "Francis!" that his tale to me may be nothing but "Anon." Step aside, and I'll show thee a precedent.

Poins. Francis!
Prince. Thou art perfect.
Poins. Francis! [*Exit* POINS.

[*Enter* FRANCIS.]

Fran. Anon, anon, sir. Look down into the Pomgarnet, Ralph. [40
Prince. Come hither, Francis.
Fran. My lord.
Prince. How long hast thou to serve, Francis?
Fran. Forsooth, five years, and as much as to—
Poins (*within*). Francis!
Fran. Anon, anon, sir.
Prince. Five years! by'r lady a long lease for the clinking of pewter. But, Francis, darest thou be so valiant as to play the coward with thy indenture and show it a fair pair of heels and run from it?
Fran. O Lord, sir! I'll be sworn upon all the [50 books in England, I could find in my heart—
Poins (*within*). Francis!
Fran. Anon, sir.
Prince. How old art thou, Francis?
Fran. Let me see—about Michaelmas next I shall be—
Poins (*within*). Francis!
Fran. Anon, sir. Pray you, stay a little, my lord.
Prince. Nay, but hark you, Francis. For the sugar thou gavest me, 'twas a pennyworth, was't not? [60
Fran. O Lord, sir! I would it had been two.
Prince. I will give thee for it a thousand pound: ask me when thou wilt and thou shalt have it.
Poins (*within*). Francis!
Fran. Anon, anon.
Prince. Anon, Francis? No, Francis; but to-morrow, Francis; or, Francis, o' Thursday; or, indeed, Francis, when thou wilt. But, Francis!
Fran. My Lord? [69
Prince. Wilt thou rob this leathern-jerkin, crystal-button, knot-pated, agate-ring, puke-stocking, caddis-garter, smooth-tongue, Spanish-pouch,—
Fran. O Lord, sir, who do you mean?
Prince. Why then, your brown bastard is your only drink; for, look you, Francis, your white canvas doublet will sully. In Barbary, sir, it cannot come to so much.
Fran. What, sir?

Poins (*within*). Francis!
Prince. Away, you rogue! Dost thou not hear [80 them call?
[*Here they both call him; the* Drawer *stands amazed, not knowing which way to go.*]

[*Enter* Vintner.]

Vint. What! standest thou still, and hearest such a calling? Look to the guests within. (*Exit* FRANCIS.) My lord, old Sir John, with half a dozen more, are at the door: shall I let them in?
Prince. Let them alone awhile, and then open the door. (*Exit* Vintner.) Poins!

[*Re-enter* POINS.]

Poins. Anon, anon, sir.
Prince. Sirrah, Falstaff and the rest of the thieves are at the door: shall we be merry? [90
Poins. As merry as crickets, my lad. But hark ye; what cunning match have you made with this jest of the drawer? come, what's the issue?
Prince. I am now of all humours that have showed themselves humours since the old days of goodman Adam to the pupil age of this present twelve o'clock at midnight. (FRANCIS *crosses the stage, with wine.*) What's o'clock, Francis?
Fran. Anon, anon, sir. [*Exit.*
Prince. That ever this fellow should have [100 fewer words than a parrot, and yet the son of a woman! His industry is up-stairs and down-stairs; his eloquence the parcel of a reckoning. I am not yet of Percy's mind, the Hotspur of the North; he that kills me some six or seven dozen of Scots at a breakfast, washes his hands, and says to his wife, "Fie upon this quiet life! I want work." "O my sweet Harry," says she, "how many hast thou killed to-day?" "Give my roan horse a drench," says he, and answers, "Some fourteen," an hour after, "a [110 trifle, a trifle." I prithee call in Falstaff: I'll play Percy, and that damned brawn shall play Dame Mortimer his wife. "Rivo!" says the drunkard. Call in ribs, call in tallow.

[*Enter* FALSTAFF, GADSHILL, BARDOLPH, PETO, *and* FRANCIS.]

Poins. Welcome, Jack: where hast thou been?
Fal. A plague of all cowards, I say, and a vengeance too! marry, and amen! Give me a cup of sack, boy. Ere I lead this life long, I'll sew netherstocks and mend them and foot them too. A plague

---

55. Michaelmas, the Feast of St. Michael, September 29. **71. puke-stocking,** gray-stockinged. **72. caddis-garter,** lace-gartered. **96–97. the pupil age . . . midnight,** the youthfulness of this midnight hour. **112. brawn,** a reference to Falstaff's "mass of flesh." **113. "Rivo!"** an exclamation used in drinking bouts. **118–19. nether-stocks,** stockings.

of all cowards! Give me a cup of sack, [120
rogue.—Is there no virtue extant? (*He drinks.*)

Prince. Didst thou never see Titan kiss a dish of butter—pitiful-hearted Titan, that melted at the sweet tale of the sun? if thou didst then behold that compound.

Fal. You rogue, here's lime in this sack too: there is nothing but roguery to be found in villainous man: yet a coward is worse than a cup of sack with lime in it, a villainous coward! Go thy ways, old Jack; die when thou wilt. If manhood, good [130 manhood, be not forgot upon the face of the earth, then am I a shotten herring. There live not three good men unhanged in England, and one of them is fat and grows old: God help the while! a bad world, I say. I would I were a weaver; I could sing psalms or anything. A plague of all cowards, I say still.

Prince. How now, wool-sack! what mutter you?

Fal. A king's son! If I do not beat thee out of thy kingdom with a dagger of lath, and drive all thy subjects afore thee like a flock of wild geese, I'll [140 never wear hair on my face more. You Prince of Wales!

Prince. Why, you whoreson round man, what's the matter?

Fal. Are you not a coward? answer me to that; and Poins there?

Poins. 'Zounds! ye fat paunch, an ye call me coward, I'll stab thee.

Fal. I call thee coward! I'll see thee damned ere I call thee coward; but I would give a thousand [150 pound I could run as fast as thou canst. You are straight enough in the shoulders; you care not who sees your back: call you that backing of your friends? A plague upon such backing! give me them that will face me. Give me a cup of sack: I am a rogue if I drunk today.

Prince. O villain! thy lips are scarce wiped since thou drunkest last.

Fal. All's one for that. (*He drinks.*) A plague of all cowards, still say I. [160

Prince. What's the matter?

Fal. What's the matter? there be four of us here have ta'en a thousand pound this day morning.

Prince. Where is it, Jack? where is it?

Fal. Where is it! taken from us it is: a hundred upon poor four of us.

Prince. What, a hundred, man?

Fal. I am a rogue, if I were not at half-sword with a dozen of them two hours together. I have 'scaped by miracle. I am eight times thrust through [170 the doublet, four through the hose; my buckler cut through and through; my sword hacked like a hand-saw: *ecce signum!* I never dealt better since I was a man: all would not do. A plague of all cowards! Let them speak: if they speak more or less than truth, they are villains and the sons of darkness.

Prince. Speak, sirs; how was it?

Gads. We four set upon some dozen,—

Fal. Sixteen, at least, my lord.

Gads. And bound them. [180

Peto. No, no, they were not bound.

Fal. You rogue, they were bound, every man of them; or I am a Jew else, an Ebrew Jew.

Gads. As we were sharing, some six or seven fresh men set upon us,—

Fal. And unbound the rest, and then come in the other.

Prince. What, fought ye with them all?

Fal. All! I know not what ye call all; but if I fought not with fifty of them, I am a bunch of [190 radish: if there were not two or three and fifty upon poor old Jack, then am I no two-legged creature.

Prince. Pray God you have not murdered some of them.

Fal. Nay, that's past praying for: I have peppered two of them: two I am sure I have paid, two rogues in buckram suits. I tell thee what, Hal, if I tell thee a lie, spit in my face, call me horse. Thou knowest my old ward; here I lay, and thus I bore my point. Four rogues in buckram let drive at [200 me,—

Prince. What, four? thou saidst but two even now.

Fal. Four, Hal; I told thee four.

Poins. Ay, ay, he said four.

Fal. These four came all a-front, and mainly thrust at me. I made me no more ado but took all their seven points in my target, thus.

Prince. Seven? why, there were but four even now.

Fal. In buckram.

Poins. Ay, four, in buckram suits. [210

Fal. Seven, by these hilts, or I am a villain else.

Prince. Prithee, let him alone; we shall have more anon.

Fal. Dost thou hear me, Hal?

Prince. Ay, and mark thee too, Jack.

Fal. Do so, for it is worth the listening to. These nine in buckram that I told thee of,—

Prince. So, two more already.

Fal. Their points being broken,—

---

122. Titan, the sun.   **124–25. behold that compound,** see Falstaff, who, like butter, shows the effects of heat and exertion.   **126. here's lime in this sack.** It was common to adulterate wine with lime.   **132. shotten herring,** a herring that has cast its roe.

173. ecce signum! behold the proof—words spoken by the Catholic priest when raising the cross. Falstaff shows his sword, with its cross-shaped hilt.   **197. buckram,** a coarse cloth stiffened with glue.   **207. points,** also strings used to fasten parts of clothing together. (See l. 219.)

WILLIAM SHAKESPEARE

Poins. Down fell their hose. [220

Fal. Began to give me ground; but I followed me close, came in foot and hand and with a thought seven of the eleven I paid.

Prince. O monstrous! eleven buckram men grown out of two.

Fal. But, as the devil would have it, three misbegotten knaves in Kendal-green came at my back and let drive at me; for it was so dark, Hal, that thou couldst not see thy hand.

Prince. These lies are like the father that be- [230 gets them; gross as a mountain, open, palpable. Why, thou clay-brained guts, thou knotty-pated fool, thou whoreson, obscene, greasy tallow-ketch,—

Fal. What, art thou mad? art thou mad? is not the truth the truth?

Prince. Why, how couldst thou know these men in Kendal-green, when it was so dark thou couldst not see thy hand? come, tell us your reason: what sayest thou to this?

Poins. Come, your reason, Jack, your reason. [240

Fal. What, upon compulsion? 'Zounds! an I were at the strappado, or all the racks in the world, I would not tell you on compulsion. Give you a reason on compulsion! if reasons were as plenty as blackberries I would give no man a reason upon compulsion, I.

Prince. I'll be no longer guilty of this sin: this sanguine coward, this bed-presser, this horsebackbreaker, this huge hill of flesh;—

Fal. 'Sblood, you starveling, you elf-skin, you [250 dried neat's-tongue, you bull's pizzle, you stockfish! O! for breath to utter what is like thee; you tailor's yard, you sheath, you bow-case, you vile standing-tuck;—

Prince. Well, breathe awhile, and then to it again; and when thou hast tired thyself in base comparisons, hear me speak but this.

Poins. Mark, Jack.

Prince. We two saw you four set on four and you bound them, and were masters of their wealth. [260 Mark now, how a plain tale shall put you down. Then did we two set on you four, and, with a word, out-faced you from your prize, and have it; yea, and can show it you here in the house. And, Falstaff, you carried your guts away as nimbly, with as quick dexterity, and roared for mercy, and still ran and roared, as ever I heard bull-calf. What a slave art thou, to hack thy sword as thou hast done, and then say it was in fight! What trick, what device, what starting-hole canst thou now find out to [270 hide thee from this open and apparent shame?

Poins. Come, let's hear, Jack; what trick hast thou now?

Fal. By the Lord, I knew ye as well as he that made ye. Why, hear you, my masters: was it for me to kill the heir apparent? Should I turn upon the true prince? Why, thou knowest I am as valiant as Hercules; but beware instinct; the lion will not touch the true prince. Instinct is a great matter, I was a coward on instinct. I shall think the [280 better of myself and thee during my life; I for a valiant lion, and thou for a true prince. But, by the Lord, lads, I am glad you have the money. Hostess, clap to the doors: watch to-night, pray to-morrow. Gallants, lads, boys, hearts of gold, all the titles of good fellowship come to you! What! shall we be merry? shall we have a play extempore?

Prince. Content; and the argument shall be thy running away. [289

Fal. Ah! no more of that, Hal, an thou lovest me!

[*Enter* MISTRESS QUICKLY.]

Quick. O Jesu! my lord the prince!

Prince. How now, my lady the hostess! what sayest thou to me?

Quick. Marry, my lord, there is a nobleman of the court at door would speak with you: he says he comes from your father.

Prince. Give him as much as will make him a royal man, and send him back again to my mother.

Fal. What manner of man is he?

Quick. An old man. [300

Fal. What doth gravity out of his bed at midnight? Shall I give him his answer?

Prince. Prithee, do, Jack.

Fal. Faith, and I'll send him packing. [*Exit.*

Prince. Now, sirs: by'r lady, you fought fair; so did you, Peto; so did you, Bardolph: you are lions too, you ran away upon instinct, you will not touch the true prince; no, fie!

Bard. Faith, I ran when I saw others run.

Prince. Faith, tell me now in earnest, how [310 came Falstaff's sword so hacked?

Peto. Why he hacked it with his dagger, and said he would swear truth out of England but he would make you believe it was done in fight, and persuaded us to do the like.

Bard. Yea, and to tickle our noses with spear-grass

---

227. Kendal-green, a dark-green woolen cloth made at Kendal in Westmorland—the traditional costume of Robin Hood.   **233. tallow-ketch,** barrel of fat.   **242. strappado,** Spanish form of torture in which a person's hands were tied behind him, and he was drawn up to a height and let fall, to be brought up with a jerk.   **251–52. stock-fish!** dried cod.   **254. standing-tuck,** small rapier standing on end.

270. starting-hole, hiding-place.   **278–79. the lion . . . prince.** It was a common belief that a lion would not harm a true prince.

to make them bleed, and then to beslubber our garments with it and swear it was the blood of true men. I did that I did not this seven year before; I blushed to hear his monstrous devices. [320

Prince. O villain! thou stolest a cup of sack eighteen years ago, and wert taken with the manner, and ever since thou hast blushed extempore. Thou hadst fire and sword on thy side, and yet thou rannest away. What instinct hadst thou for it?

Bard. (*pointing to his face*). My lord, do you see these meteors? do you behold these exhalations?

Prince. I do.

Bard. What think you they portend?

Prince. Hot livers and cold purses. [330

Bard. Choler, my lord, if rightly taken.

Prince. No, if rightly taken, halter.—

[*Re-enter* FALSTAFF.]

Here comes lean Jack, here comes bare-bone.— How now, my sweet creature of bombast! How long is 't ago, Jack, since thou sawest thine own knee?

Fal. My own knee! when I was about thy years, Hal, I was not an eagle's talon in the waist; I could have crept into any alderman's thumb-ring. A plague of sighing and grief! it blows a man up like a bladder. There's villainous news abroad: [340 here was Sir John Bracy from your father: you must to the court in the morning. That same mad fellow of the north, Percy, and he of Wales, that gave Amaimon the bastinado and made Lucifer cuckold, and swore the devil his true liegeman upon the cross of a Welsh hook—what a plague call you him?

Poins. Owen Glendower.

Fal. Owen, Owen, the same; and his son-in-law Mortimer and old Northumberland; and that sprightly Scot of Scots, Douglas, that runs o' [350 horseback up a hill perpendicular.

Prince. He that rides at high speed and with his pistol kills a sparrow flying.

Fal. You have hit it.

Prince. So did he never the sparrow.

Fal. Well, that rascal hath good mettle in him; he will not run.

Prince. Why, what a rascal art thou then to praise him so for running!

Fal. O' horseback, ye cuckoo! but, afoot he [360 will not budge a foot.

Prince. Yes, Jack, upon instinct.

Fal. I grant ye, upon instinct. Well, he is there too, and one Mordake, and a thousand blue-caps more. Worcester is stolen away to-night; thy father's beard is turned white with the news; you may buy land now as cheap as stinking mackerel.

Prince. Why then, it is like, if there come a hot June and this civil buffeting hold, we shall buy maidenheads as they buy hob-nails, by the [370 hundreds.

Fal. By the mass, lad, thou sayest true; it is like we shall have good trading that way. But tell me, Hal, art thou not horribly afeard? thou being heir apparent, could the world pick thee out three such enemies again as that fiend Douglas, that spirit Percy, and that devil Glendower? Art thou not horribly afraid? doth not thy blood thrill at it?

Prince. Not a whit, i' faith; I lack some of thy instinct. [380

Fal. Well, thou wilt be horribly chid to-morrow when thou comest to thy father: if thou love me, practise an answer.

Prince. Do thou stand for my father, and examine me upon the particulars of my life.

Fal. Shall I? content: this chair shall be my state, this dagger my sceptre, and this cushion my crown.

Prince. Thy state is taken for a joint-stool, thy golden sceptre for a leaden dagger, and thy precious rich crown for a pitiful bald crown! [390

Fal. Well, an the fire of grace be not quite out of thee, now shalt thou be moved. Give me a cup of sack to make mine eyes look red, that it may be thought I have wept; for I must speak in passion, and I will do it in King Cambyses' vein. (*Drinks.*)

Prince. Well, here is my leg. (*Makes a bow.*)

Fal. And here is my speech. Stand aside, nobility.

Quick. O Jesu! This is excellent sport, i' faith!

Fal. Weep not, sweet queen, for trickling tears are vain.

Quick. O, the father! how he holds his [400 countenance.

Fal. For God's sake, lords, convey my tristful queen,

For tears do stop the flood-gates of her eyes.

Quick. O Jesu! he doth it as like one of these harlotry players as ever I see!

Fal. Peace, good pint-pot! peace, good tickle-brain! Harry, I do not only marvel where thou spendest thy time, but also how thou art accompanied: for though the camomile, the more it is trodden on the faster it grows, yet youth, the more it [410 is wasted the sooner it wears. That thou art my son, I have partly thy mother's word, partly my own opinion; but chiefly, a villainous trick of thine eye and a foolish hanging of thy nether lip, that doth

---

330. **Hot livers and cold purses,** drunkenness and poverty. 344. **Amaimon,** a devil. 353. **pistol,** an anachronism: pistols were not used in Hotspur's time. 364. **blue-caps,** blue bonnets of the Scotsmen.

395. **King Cambyses' vein,** an allusion to a ranting character in a play. 406–07. **tickle-brain!** a strong liquor.

warrant me. If then thou be son to me, here lies the point; why, being son to me, art thou so pointed at? Shall the blessed sun of heaven prove a micher and eat blackberries? a question not to be asked. Shall the son of England prove a thief and take purses? a question to be asked. There is a thing, [420 Harry, which thou hast often heard of, and it is known to many in our land by the name of pitch: this pitch, as ancient writers do report, doth defile; so doth the company thou keepest; for, Harry, now I do not speak to thee in drink, but in tears, not in pleasure but in passion, not in words only, but in woes also. And yet there is a virtuous man whom I have often noted in thy company, but I know not his name.

Prince. What manner of man, an it like your [430 majesty?

Fal. A goodly portly man, i' faith, and a corpulent; of a cheerful look, a pleasing eye, and a most noble carriage; and, as I think, his age some fifty, or by'r lady, inclining to threescore; and now I remember me, his name is Falstaff: if that man should be lewdly given, he deceiveth me; for, Harry, I see virtue in his looks. If then the tree may be known by the fruit, as the fruit by the tree, then, peremptorily I speak it, there is virtue in that [440 Falstaff: him keep with, the rest banish. And tell me now, thou naughty varlet, tell me, where hast thou been this month?

Prince. Dost thou speak like a king? Do thou stand for me, and I'll play my father.

Fal. Depose me? if thou dost it half so gravely, so majestically, both in word and matter, hang me up by the heels for a rabbit-sucker or a poulter's hare.

Prince. Well, here I am set. [450
Fal. And here I stand. Judge, my masters.
Prince. Now, Harry! whence come you?
Fal. My noble lord, from Eastcheap.
Prince. The complaints I hear of thee are grievous.
Fal. 'Sblood, my lord, they are false: nay, I'll tickle ye for a young prince, i' faith.
Prince. Swearest thou, ungracious boy? henceforth ne'er look on me. Thou art violently carried away from grace: there is a devil haunts thee in the likeness of a fat old man; a tun of man is thy [460 companion. Why dost thou converse with that trunk of humours, that bolting-hutch of beastliness, that swoln parcel of dropsies, that huge bombard of sack, that stuffed cloak-bag of guts, that roasted Manningtree ox with the pudding in his belly, that reverend vice, that grey iniquity, that father ruffian, that vanity in years? Wherein is he good but to taste sack and drink it? wherein neat and cleanly but to carve a capon and eat it? wherein cunning but in craft? wherein crafty but in villainy? wherein [470 villainous but in all things? wherein worthy but in nothing?

Fal. I would your Grace would take me with you: whom means your Grace?
Prince. That villainous abominable misleader of youth, Falstaff, that old white-bearded Satan.
Fal. My lord, the man I know.
Prince. I know thou dost.
Fal. But to say I know more harm in him than in myself were to say more than I know. That he is [480 old, the more the pity, his white hairs do witness it; but that he is, saving your reverence, a whoremaster, that I utterly deny. If sack and sugar be a fault, God help the wicked! If to be old and merry be a sin, then many an old host that I know is damned: if to be fat be to be hated, then Pharaoh's lean kine are to be loved. No, my good lord; banish Peto, banish Bardolph, banish Poins; but for sweet Jack Falstaff, kind Jack Falstaff, true Jack Falstaff, valiant Jack Falstaff, and therefore more [490 valiant, being, as he is, old Jack Falstaff, banish not him thy Harry's company: banish not him thy Harry's company: banish plump Jack, and banish all the world.

Prince. I do, I will.
[*A knocking heard.*]
[*Exeunt* MISTRESS QUICKLY, FRANCIS, *and* BARDOLPH.]

[*Re-enter* BARDOLPH, *running.*]

Bard. O! my lord, my lord, the sheriff with a most monstrous watch is at the door.
Fal. Out, ye rogue! Play out the play: I have much to say in the behalf of that Falstaff.

[*Re-enter* MISTRESS QUICKLY.]

Quick. O Jesu! my lord, my lord! [500
Prince. Heigh, heigh! the devil rides upon a fiddle-stick: what's the matter?
Quick. The sheriff and all the watch are at the door: they are come to search the house. Shall I let them in?
Fal. Dost thou hear, Hal? never call a true piece of gold a counterfeit: thou art essentially mad without seeming so.
Prince. And thou a natural coward without instinct. [510
Fal. I deny your major. If you will deny the

---
417. **micher,** truant. 462. **bolting-hutch,** bin for sifting meal. 463. **bombard,** a large leather drinking-vessel. 464–65. **Manningtree ox.** The oxen fed on the rich pastureland at Manningtree, in Essex, were famous for their size.
511. **major,** premise.

sheriff, so; if not, let him enter: if I become not a cart as well as another man, a plague on my bringing up! I hope I shall as soon be strangled with a halter as another.

Prince. Go, hide thee behind the arras: the rest walk up above. Now, my masters, for a true face and good conscience.

Fal. Both which I have had; but their date is out, and therefore I'll hide me. [520

[*Exeunt all but the* PRINCE *and* PETO.

Prince. Call in the sheriff.

[*Enter* Sheriff *and* Carrier.]

Now, master sheriff, what's your will with me?

Sher. First, pardon me, my lord. A hue and cry Hath followed certain men unto this house.

Prince. What men?

Sher. One of them is well known, my gracious lord,
A gross fat man.

Car. As fat as butter.

Prince. The man, I do assure you, is not here, For I myself at this time have employed him. And, sheriff, I will engage my word to thee, [530 That I will, by to-morrow dinner-time, Send him to answer thee, or any man, For anything he shall be charged withal: And so let me entreat you leave the house.

Sher. I will, my lord. There are two gentlemen Have in this robbery lost three hundred marks.

Prince. It may be so: if he have robbed these men, He shall be answerable; and so farewell.

Sher. Good night, my noble lord.

Prince. I think it is good morrow, is it not? [540

Sher. Indeed, my lord, I think it be two o'clock.

[*Exeunt* Sheriff *and* Carrier.

Prince. This oily rascal is known as well as Paul's. Go, call him forth.

Peto. Falstaff! fast asleep behind the arras, and snorting like a horse.

Prince. Hark, how hard he fetches breath. Search his pockets. (*He searcheth his pockets, and findeth certain papers.*) What hast thou found?

Peto. Nothing but papers, my lord.

Prince. Let's see what they be: read them. [550

Peto. Item, A capon . . . . . 2s. 2d.
Item, Sauce . . . . . . 4d.
Item, Sack, two gallons . . . 5s. 8d.
Item, Anchovies and sack after
 supper . . . . 2s. 6d.
Item, Bread . . . . . ob.

Prince. O monstrous! but one half-penny-worth of bread to this intolerable deal of sack! What there is else, keep close; we'll read it at more advantage. There let him sleep till day. I'll to the court in [560 the morning. We must all to the wars, and thy place shall be honourable. I'll procure this fat rogue a charge of foot; and, I know, his death will be a march of twelve-score. The money shall be paid back again with advantage. Be with me betimes in the morning; and so good morrow, Peto.

Peto. Good morrow, good my lord. [*Exeunt.*

ACT III

SCENE I.—*Bangor. A Room in the* Archdeacon's *House.*

Enter HOTSPUR, WORCESTER, MORTIMER, *and* GLENDOWER.

Mort. These promises are fair, the parties sure, And our induction full of prosperous hope.

Hot. Lord Mortimer, and cousin Glendower, Will you sit down?
And uncle Worcester: a plague upon it!
I have forgot the map.

Glend. No, here it is.
Sit, cousin Percy; sit, good cousin Hotspur; For by that name as oft as Lancaster Doth speak of you, his cheek looks pale and with A rising sigh he wishes you in heaven. 10

Hot. And you in hell, as often as he hears Owen Glendower spoke of.

Glend. I cannot blame him: at my nativity The front of heaven was full of fiery shapes, Of burning cressets; and at my birth The frame and huge foundation of the earth Shaked like a coward.

Hot. Why, so it would have done at the same season, if your mother's cat had but kittened, though yourself had never been born. 20

Glend. I say the earth did shake when I was born.

Hot. And I say the earth was not of my mind, If you suppose as fearing you it shook.

Glend. The heavens were all on fire, the earth did tremble.

Hot. O! then the earth shook to see the heavens on fire,
And not in fear of your nativity.
Diseasèd nature oftentimes breaks forth In strange eruptions; oft the teeming earth Is with a kind of colic pinched and vexed By the imprisoning of unruly wind 30 Within her womb; which, for enlargement striving,

---

512–13. **become not a cart,** adorn not a hangman's cart. 516. **arras,** tapestry, originally made in Arras, France. 536. **three hundred marks,** £200. 542. **Paul's,** St. Paul's cathedral. 556. **ob,** obolus, or halfpenny.

563. **charge of foot,** command of infantry. 8. **Lancaster,** the King. 15. **cressets,** beacons.

Shakes the old beldam earth, and topples down
Steeples and moss-grown towers. At your birth
Our grandam earth, having this distemperature,
In passion shook.
   Glend.   Cousin, of many men
I do not bear these crossings. Give me leave
To tell you once again that at my birth
The front of heaven was full of fiery shapes,
The goats ran from the mountains, and the herds
Were strangely clamorous to the frighted fields.   40
These signs have marked me extraordinary;
And all the courses of my life do show
I am not in the roll of common men.
Where is he living, clipped in with the sea
That chides the banks of England, Scotland, Wales,
Which calls me pupil, or hath read to me?
And bring him out that is but woman's son
Can trace me in the tedious ways of art
And hold me pace in deep experiments.   49
   Hot. I think there's no man speaks better Welsh.
I'll to dinner.
   Mort. Peace, cousin Percy! you will make him mad.
   Glend. I can call spirits from the vasty deep.
   Hot. Why, so can I, or so can any man;
But will they come when you do call for them?
   Glend. Why, I can teach thee, cousin, to command
The devil.
   Hot. And I can teach thee, coz, to shame the devil
By telling truth: tell truth and shame the devil.
If thou have power to raise him, bring him hither, 60
And I'll be sworn I have power to shame him hence.
O! while you live, tell truth and shame the devil!
   Mort. Come, come;
No more of this unprofitable chat.
   Glend. Three times hath Henry Bolingbroke made head
Against my power; thrice from the banks of Wye
And sandy-bottomed Severn have I sent him
Bootless home and weather-beaten back.
   Hot. Home without boots, and in foul weather too!
How 'scapes he agues, in the devil's name?   70
   Glend. Come, here's the map: shall we divide our right
According to our threefold order ta'en?
   Mort. The archdeacon hath divided it
Into three limits very equally.
England, from Trent and Severn hitherto,
By south and east, is to my part assigned:
All westward, Wales beyond the Severn shore,

And all the fertile land within that bound,
To Owen Glendower: and, dear coz, to you
The remnant northward, lying off from Trent.   80
And our indentures tripartite are drawn,
Which being sealèd interchangeably,
A business that this night may execute,
To-morrow, cousin Percy, you and I
And my good Lord Worcester will set forth
To meet your father and the Scottish power,
As is appointed us, at Shrewsbury.
My father Glendower is not ready yet,
Nor shall we need his help these fourteen days.
(*To* GLENDOWER.) Within that space you may have drawn together   90
Your tenants, friends, and neighbouring gentlemen.
   Glend. A shorter time shall send me to you, lords;
And in my conduct shall your ladies come,
From whom you now must steal and take no leave;
For there will be a world of water shed
Upon the parting of your wives and you.
   Hot. Methinks my moiety, north from **Burton** here,
In quantity equals not one of yours:
See how this river comes me cranking in,
And cuts me from the best of all my land   100
A huge half-moon, a monstrous cantle out.
I'll have the current in this place dammed up,
And here the smug and silver Trent shall run
In a new channel, fair and evenly:
It shall not wind with such a deep indent,
To rob me of so rich a bottom here.
   Glend. Not wind! it shall, it must; you see it doth.
   Mort. Yea, but
Mark how he bears his course, and runs me up
With like advantage on the other side;   110
Gelding the opposèd continent as much,
As on the other side it takes from you.
   Wor. Yea, but a little charge will trench him here,
And on this north side win this cape of land;
And then he runs straight and even.
   Hot. I'll have it so; a little charge will do it.
   Glend. I will not have it altered.
   Hot.   Will not you?
   Glend. No, nor you shall not.
   Hot.   Who shall say me nay?
   Glend. Why, that will I.
   Hot.   Let me not understand you then:
Speak it in Welsh.   120
   Glend. I can speak English, lord, as well as you,
For I was trained up in the English court;
Where, being but young, I framèd to the harp

32. **beldam,** grandmother.

82. **interchangeably,** each party signing each copy.
97. **moiety,** share.   101. **cantle,** piece.   111. **Gelding the opposèd continent,** depriving the opposite bank of.

Many an English ditty lovely well,
And gave the tongue an helpful ornament;
A virtue that was never seen in you.
   Hot. Marry, and I'm glad of it with all my heart.
I had rather be a kitten, and cry mew
Than one of these same metre ballad-mongers;
I had rather hear a brazen canstick turned,   130
Or a dry wheel grate on the axle-tree;
And that would set my teeth nothing on edge,
Nothing so much as mincing poetry:
'Tis like the forced gait of a shuffling nag.
   Glend. Come, you shall have Trent turned.
   Hot. I do not care: I'll give thrice so much land
To any well-deserving friend;
But in the way of bargain, mark you me,
I'll cavil on the ninth part of a hair.
Are the indentures drawn? shall we be gone?   140
   Glend. The moon shines fair, you may away by
     night:
I'll haste the writer and withal
Break with your wives of your departure hence:
I am afraid my daughter will run mad,
So much she doteth on her Mortimer.   [*Exit*.
   Mort. Fie, cousin Percy! how you cross my father!
   Hot. I cannot choose: sometimes he angers me
With telling me of the moldwarp and the ant,
Of the dreamer Merlin and his prophecies,
And of a dragon, and a finless fish,   150
A clip-winged griffin, and a moulten raven,
A couching lion, and a ramping cat,
And such a deal of skimble-skamble stuff
As puts me from my faith. I'll tell thee what;
He held me last night at least nine hours
In reckoning up the several devils' names
That were his lackeys: I cried "hum!" and "well,
     go to."
But marked him not a word. O! he's as tedious
As a tired horse, a railing wife;
Worse than a smoky house. I had rather live   160
With cheese and garlick in a windmill, far,
Than feed on cates and have him talk to me
In any summer-house in Christendom.
   Mort. In faith, he is a worthy gentleman,
Exceedingly well read, and profited
In strange concealments, valiant as a lion
And wondrous affable, and as bountiful
As mines of India. Shall I tell you, cousin?
He holds your temper in a high respect,
And curbs himself even of his natural scope   170
When you do cross his humour; faith, he does.
I warrant you, that man is not alive
Might so have tempted him as you have done,
Without the taste of danger and reproof:
But do not use it oft, let me entreat you.
   Wor. In faith, my lord, you are too wilful-blame;
And since your coming hither have done enough
To put him quite beside his patience.
You must needs learn, lord, to amend this fault:
Though sometimes it show greatness, courage,
     blood,—   180
And that's the dearest grace it renders you,—
Yet oftentimes it doth present harsh rage,
Defect of manners, want of government,
Pride, haughtiness, opinion, and disdain:
The least of which haunting a nobleman
Loseth men's hearts and leaves behind a stain
Upon the beauty of all parts besides,
Beguiling them of commendation.
   Hot. Well, I am schooled; good manners be your
     speed!
Here come our wives, and let us take our leave.   190

[*Re-enter* GLENDOWER, *with the* Ladies.]

   Mort. This is the deadly spite that angers me,
My wife can speak no English, I no Welsh.
   Glend. My daughter weeps; she will not part with
     you:
She'll be a soldier too: she'll to the wars.
   Mort. Good father, tell her that she and my aunt
     Percy,
Shall follow in your conduct speedily.
[GLENDOWER *speaks to* LADY MORTIMER *in Welsh, and
     she answers him in the same.*]
   Glend. She's desperate here; a peevish self-willed
harlotry, one that no persuasion can do good
upon. (*She speaks to* MORTIMER *in Welsh*.)
   Mort. I understand thy looks: that pretty Welsh
Which thou pour'st down from these swelling
     heavens   201
I am too perfect in; and, but for shame,
In such a parley would I answer thee.

        (*She speaks again*.)

I understand thy kisses and thou mine,
And that's a feeling disputation:
But I will never be a truant, love,
Till I have learned thy language; for thy tongue
Makes Welsh as sweet as ditties highly penned,
Sung by a fair queen in a summer's bower,
With ravishing division, to her lute.   210
   Glend. Nay, if you melt, then will she run mad.

---

130. **canstick**, candlestick.   148. **moldwarp**, mole.
163. **summer-house**, country house.
176. **too wilful-blame**, to be blamed for too great wilfulness.   184. **opinion**, obstinacy. This meaning is preserved in the modern "opinionated."   198. **harlotry**, silly girl.

(*She speaks again.*)

Mort. O! I am ignorance itself in this.
Glend. She bids you
Upon the wanton rushes lay you down
And rest your gentle head upon her lap,
And she will sing the song that pleaseth you,
And on your eye-lids crown the god of sleep,
Charming your blood with pleasing heaviness,
Making such difference 'twixt wake and sleep
As is the difference between day and night   220
The hour before the heavenly-harnessed team
Begins his golden progress in the east.
Mort. With all my heart I'll sit and hear her sing:
By that time will our book, I think, be drawn.
Glend. Do so;
And those musicians that shall play to you
Hang in the air a thousand leagues from hence,
And straight they shall be here: sit, and attend.
Hot. Come, Kate, thou art perfect in lying down:
come, quick, quick, that I may lay my head in thy
lap.   230
Lady P. Go, ye giddy goose.

[GLENDOWER *speaks some Welsh words, and music is heard.*]

Hot. Now I perceive the devil understands Welsh;
And 'tis no marvel he is so humorous.
By'r lady, he's a good musician.
Lady P. Then should you be nothing but musical,
for you are altogether governed by humours. Lie
still, ye thief, and hear the lady sing in Welsh.
Hot. I had rather hear Lady, my brach, howl in
  Irish.
Lady P. Wouldst thou have thy head broken?
Hot. No.   240
Lady P. Then be still.
Hot. Neither; 'tis a woman's fault.
Lady P. Now, God help thee!
Hot. To the Welsh lady's bed.
Lady P. What's that?
Hot. Peace! she sings.

[*A Welsh song sung by* LADY MORTIMER.]

Hot. Come, Kate, I'll have your song too.
Lady P. Not mine, in good sooth.
Hot. Not yours, "in good sooth!" Heart! you
swear like a comfit-maker's wife! Not you, "in [250
good sooth"; and, "as true as I live"; and, "as God
shall mend me"; and, "as sure as day":
And giv'st such sarcenet surety for thy oaths,
As if thou never walk'dst further than Finsbury.
Swear me, Kate, like a lady as thou art,
A good mouth-filling oath; and leave "in sooth,"
And such protest of pepper-gingerbread,
To velvet-guards and Sunday-citizens.
Come, sing.
Lady P. I will not sing.   260
Hot. 'Tis the next way to turn tailor or be red-
breast teacher. An the indentures be drawn, I'll
away within these two hours; and so, come in when
ye will.   [*Exit.*
Glend. Come, come, Lord Mortimer; you are as
  slow
As hot Lord Percy is on fire to go.
By this our book is drawn; we will but seal,
And then to horse immediately.
Mort. With all my heart.   [*Exeunt.*

SCENE 2.—*London. A Room in the Palace.*

Enter KING HENRY, *the* PRINCE, *and* Lords.

K. Hen. Lords, give us leave; the Prince of Wales
  and I
Must have some private conference: but be near at
  hand,
For we shall presently have need of you.
                                        [*Exeunt* Lords.
I know not whether God will have it so,
For some displeasing service I have done,
That, in his secret doom, out of my blood
He'll breed revengement and a scourge for me;
But thou dost in thy passages of life
Make me believe that thou art only marked
For the hot vengeance and the rod of heaven   10
To punish my mistreadings. Tell me else,
Could such inordinate and low desires,
Such poor, such bare, such lewd, such mean
  attempts,
Such barren pleasures, rude society,
As thou art matched withal and grafted to,
Accompany the greatness of thy blood
And hold their level with thy princely heart?
Prince. So please your majesty, I would I could
Quit all offences with as clear excuse
As well as I am doubtless I can purge   20
Myself of many I am charged withal:
Yet such extenuation let me beg,
As, in reproof of many tales devised,
Which oft the ear of greatness needs must hear,
By smiling pick-thanks and base newsmongers,

---

224. **book**, schedule of indentures.   238. **brach**, bitch hound.   250. **comfit-maker's**, confectioner's.   253. **sarcenet**, cotton cloth.

258. **velvet-guards and Sunday-citizens**, women wearing dresses trimmed ("guarded") with velvet, and citizens in their Sunday clothes.   261–62. **red-breast teacher**, trainer of singing birds.   25. **pick-thanks**, flatterers.

I may, for some things true, wherein my youth
Hath faulty wandered and irregular,
Find pardon on my true submission.
   K. Hen. God pardon thee! yet let me wonder, Harry,
At thy affections, which do hold a wing   30
Quite from the flight of all thy ancestors.
Thy place in council thou hast rudely lost,
Which by thy younger brother is supplied
And art almost an alien to the hearts
Of all the court and princes of my blood.
The hope and expectation of thy time
Is ruined, and the soul of every man
Prophetically do forethink thy fall.
Had I so lavish of my presence been,
So common-hackneyed in the eyes of men   40
So stale and cheap to vulgar company,
Opinion, that did help me to the crown,
Had still kept loyal to possession
And left me in reputeless banishment,
A fellow of no mark nor likelihood.
By being seldom seen, I could not stir,
But like a comet I was wondered at;
That men would tell their children, "This is he";
Others would say, "Where? which is Bolingbroke?"
And then I stole all courtesy from heaven,   50
And dressed myself in such humility
That I did pluck allegiance from men's hearts,
Loud shouts and salutations from their mouths,
Even in the presence of the crownèd king.
Thus did I keep my person fresh and new;
My presence, like a robe pontifical,
Ne'er seen but wondered at: and so my state,
Seldom but sumptuous, showed like a feast,
And won by rareness such solemnity.
The skipping king, he ambled up and down   60
With shallow jesters and rash bavin wits,
Soon kindled and soon burnt; carded his state,
Mingled his royalty with capering fools,
Had his great name profanèd with their scorns,
And gave his countenance, against his name,
To laugh at gibing boys and stand the push
Of every beardless vain comparative;
Grew a companion to the common streets,
Enfeoffed himself to popularity;
That, being daily swallowed by men's eyes,   70
They surfeited with honey and began
To loathe the taste of sweetness, whereof a little
More than a little is by much too much.
So, when he had occasion to be seen,
He was but as the cuckoo is in June,
Heard, not regarded; seen, but with such eyes
As, sick and blunted with community,
Afford no extraordinary gaze,
Such as is bent on sun-like majesty
When it shines seldom in admiring eyes;   80
But rather drowsed and hung their eyelids down,
Slept in his face, and rendered such aspect
As cloudy men use to their adversaries,
Being with his presence glutted, gorged, and full.
And in that very line, Harry, stand'st thou;
For thou hast lost thy princely privilege
With vile participation: not an eye
But is aweary of thy common sight,
Save mine, which hath desired to see thee more;
Which now doth that I would not have it do,   90
Make blind itself with foolish tenderness.
   Prince. I shall hereafter, my thrice gracious lord,
Be more myself.
   K. Hen.   For all the world,
As thou art to this hour was Richard then
When I from France set foot at Ravenspurgh;
And even as I was then is Percy now.
Now, by my sceptre and my soul to boot,
He hath more worthy interest to the state
Than thou the shadow of succession;
For of no right, nor colour like to right,   100
He doth fill fields with harness in the realm,
Turns head against the lion's armèd jaws,
And, being no more in debt to years than thou,
Leads ancient lords and reverend bishops on
To bloody battles and to bruising arms.
What never-dying honour hath he got
Against renownèd Douglas! whose high deeds,
Whose hot incursions and great name in arms,
Holds from all soldiers chief majority,
And military title capital,   110
Through all the kingdoms that acknowledge Christ.
Thrice hath this Hotspur, Mars in swathling clothes,
This infant warrior, in his enterprises
Discomfited great Douglas; ta'en him once,
Enlargèd him and made a friend of him,
To fill the mouth of deep defiance up
And shake the peace and safety of our throne.
And what say you to this? Percy, Northumberland,
The Archbishop's Grace of York, Douglas, Mortimer,
Capitulate against us and are up.   120
But wherefore do I tell these news to thee?
Why, Harry, do I tell thee of my foes,
Which art my near'st and dearest enemy?
Thou that art like enough, through vassal fear,

---

61. **bavin,** brushwood, which is easily kindled and soon goes out.   62. **carded his state,** debased his high position by associating with unworthy people.   67. **comparative,** one who affects wit.

101. **harness,** armor.   102. **the lion's,** the King's.

Base inclination, and the start of spleen,
To fight against me under Percy's pay,
To dog his heels, and curtsy at his frowns,
To show how much thou art degenerate.

Prince. Do not think so; you shall not find it so:
And God forgive them, that so much have swayed
Your majesty's good thoughts away from me! 131
I will redeem all this on Percy's head,
And in the closing of some glorious day
Be bold to tell you that I am your son;
When I will wear a garment all of blood
And stain my favours in a bloody mask,
Which, washed away, shall scour my shame with it:
And that shall be the day, when'er it lights,
That this same child of honour and renown,
This gallant Hotspur, this all-praisèd knight, 140
And your unthought-of Harry chance to meet.
For every honour sitting on his helm,—
Would they were multitudes, and on my head
My shames redoubled!—for the time will come
That I shall make this northern youth exchange
His glorious deeds for my indignities.
Percy is but my factor, good my lord,
To engross up glorious deeds on my behalf;
And I will call him to so strict account
That he shall render every glory up, 150
Yea, even the slightest worship of his time,
Or I will tear the reckoning from his heart.
This, in the name of God, I promise here:
The which, if he be pleased I shall perform,
I do beseech your majesty may salve
The long-grown wounds of my intemperance:
If not, the end of life cancels all bands,
And I will die a hundred thousand deaths
Ere break the smallest parcel of this vow. 159

K. Hen. A hundred thousand rebels die in this:
Thou shalt have charge and sovereign trust herein.

[*Enter* SIR WALTER BLUNT.]

How now, good Blunt! thy looks are full of speed.

Blunt. So hath the business that I come to speak of.
Lord Mortimer of Scotland hath sent word
That Douglas and the English rebels met,
The eleventh of this month at Shrewsbury.
A mighty and a fearful head they are,—
If promises be kept on every hand,—
As ever offered foul play in a state.

K. Hen. The Earl of Westmoreland set forth to-day, 170
With him my son, Lord John of Lancaster;
For this advertisement is five days old.

On Wednesday next, Harry, you shall set forward;
On Thursday we ourselves will march: our meeting
Is Bridgenorth; and Harry, you shall march
Through Gloucestershire; by which account,
Our business valued, some twelve days hence
Our general forces at Bridgenorth shall meet.
Our hands are full of business: let's away; 179
Advantage feeds him fat while men delay. [*Exeunt.*

SCENE 3.—*Eastcheap. A Room in the Boar's Head Tavern.*

Enter FALSTAFF *and* BARDOLPH.

Fal. Bardolph, am I not fallen away vilely since this last action? do I not bate? do I not dwindle? Why, my skin hangs about me like an old lady's loose gown; I am withered like an old apple-john. Well, I'll repent, and that suddenly, while I am in some liking; I shall be out of heart shortly, and then I shall have no strength to repent. An I have not forgotten what the inside of a church is made of, I am a peppercorn, a brewer's horse: the inside of a church! Company, villainous company, hath [10 been the spoil of me.

Bard. Sir John, you are so fretful, you cannot live long.

Fal. Why, there is it: come, sing me a bawdy song; make me merry. I was as virtuously given as a gentleman need to be; virtuous enough: swore little; diced not above seven times a week; went to a bawdy-house not above once in a quarter—of an hour; paid money that I borrowed three or four times; lived well and in good compass; and now [20 I live out of all order, out of all compass.

Bard. Why, you are so fat, Sir John, that you must needs be out of all compass, out of all reasonable compass, Sir John.

Fal. Do thou amend thy face, and I'll amend my life: thou art our admiral, thou bearest the lanthorn in the poop, but 'tis in the nose of thee: thou art the Knight of the Burning Lamp.

Bard. Why, Sir John, my face does you no harm.

Fal. No, I'll be sworn; I make as good use of [30 it as many a man doth of a Death's head, or a *memento mori:* I never see thy face but I think upon hell-fire and Dives that lived in purple; for there he is in his robes, burning, burning. If thou wert any way given to virtue, I would swear by thy face; my oath should be, "By this fire, that's God's angel": but thou art altogether given over, and wert indeed, but for the light in thy face, the son of utter dark-

---

125. **start of spleen,** malicious impulses.   136. **favours,** features.   147. **factor,** agent.   4. **apple-john,** a kind of apple gathered about St. John's Day; when it is kept long, its skin shrivels.   32. **memento mori,** reminder of death; different objects were used.

ness. When thou rannest up Gadshill in the night to catch my horse, if I did not think thou hadst [40 been an *ignis fatuus* or a ball of wildfire, there's no purchase in money. O! thou art a perpetual triumph, an everlasting bonfire-light. Thou hast saved me a thousand marks in links and torches, walking with thee in the night betwixt tavern and tavern: but the sack that thou hast drunk me would have bought me lights as good cheap at the dearest chandler's in Europe. I have maintained that salamander of yours with fire any time this two-and-thirty years; God reward me for it! 50

Bard. 'Blood, I would my face were in your belly.

Fal. God-a-mercy! so should I be sure to be heart-burned.

[*Enter* MISTRESS QUICKLY.]

How now, Dame Partlet the hen! have you inquired yet who picked my pocket?

Quick. Why, Sir John, what do you think, Sir John? Do you think I keep thieves in my house? I have searched, I have inquired, so has my husband, man by man, boy by boy, servant by servant: the tithe of a hair was never lost in my house before. [60

Fal. You lie, hostess: Bardolph was shaved and lost many a hair; and I'll be sworn my pocket was picked. Go to, you are a woman; go.

Quick. Who, I? No; I defy thee: God's light! I was never called so in my own house before.

Fal. Go to, I know you well enough.

Quick. No, Sir John; you do not know me, Sir John: I know you, Sir John: you owe me money, Sir John, and now you pick a quarrel to beguile me of it: I bought you a dozen of shirts to your back. [70

Fal. Dowlas, filthy dowlas: I have given them away to bakers' wives, and they have made bolters of them.

Quick. Now, as I am true woman, holland of eight shillings an ell. You owe money here besides, Sir John, for your diet and by-drinkings, and money lent you, four-and-twenty pound.

Fal. He had his part of it; let him pay.

Quick. He! alas! he is poor; he hath nothing. 79

Fal. How! poor? look upon his face; what call you rich? let them coin his nose, let them coin his cheeks. I'll not pay a denier. What! will you make a younker of me? shall I not take mine ease in mine inn but I shall have my pocket picked? I have lost a seal-ring of my grandfather's worth forty mark.

Quick. O Jesu! I have heard the prince tell him, I know not how oft, that that ring was copper.

Fal. How! the prince is a Jack, a sneak-cup; 'sblood! an he were here, I would cudgel him like a dog, if he would say so. [90

[*Enter the* PRINCE *and* POINS *marching.* FALSTAFF *meets them, playing on his truncheon like a fife.*]

Fal. How now, lad! is the wind in that door, i' faith? must we all march?

Bard. Yea, two and two, Newgate fashion.

Quick. My lord, I pray you, hear me.

Prince. What sayest thou, Mistress Quickly? How does thy husband? I love him well, he is an honest man.

Quick. Good my lord, hear me.

Fal. Prithee, let her alone, and list to me.

Prince. What sayest thou, Jack? [100

Fal. The other night I fell asleep here behind the arras and had my pocket picked: this house is turned bawdy-house; they pick pockets.

Prince. What didst thou lose, Jack?

Fal. Wilt thou believe me, Hal? three or four bonds of forty pound a-piece, and a seal-ring of my grandfather's.

Prince. A trifle; some eight-penny matter.

Quick. So I told him, my lord; and I said I heard your Grace say so: and, my lord, he speaks most vilely of you, like a foul-mouthed man as he is, [111 and said he would cudgel you.

Prince. What! he did not?

Quick. There's neither faith, truth, nor womanhood in me else.

Fal. There's no more faith in thee than in a stewed prune; nor no more truth in thee than in a drawn fox; and for womanhood, Maid Marian may be the deputy's wife of the ward to thee. Go, you thing, go. [120

Quick. Say, what thing? what thing?

Fal. What thing! why, a thing to thank God on.

Quick. I am no thing to thank God on, I would thou shouldst know it; I am an honest man's wife; and, setting thy knighthood aside, thou art a knave to call me so.

Fal. Setting thy womanhood aside, thou art a beast to say otherwise.

Quick. Say, what beast, thou knave thou?

Fal. What beast! why, an otter. [130

Prince. An otter, Sir John! why, an otter?

Fal. Why? she's neither fish nor flesh; a man knows not where to have her.

---

41. **ignis fatuus**, will-o'-the-wisp. 54. **Dame Partlet**, name of the hen in *Reynard the Fox* and in Chaucer's "Nun's Priest's Tale." 71. **dowlas**, a coarse linen made in Brittany. 72. **bolters**, sieves. 74. **holland**, fine linen. 82. **denier**, a French copper coin worth a tenth of a penny. 83. **younker**, greenhorn.

88. **sneak-cup**, a coward in his potations. 93. **Newgate fashion**, as in the famous London prison. 118. **drawn**, hunted. **Maid Marian**, the sweetheart of Robin Hood.

Quick. Thou art an unjust man in saying so: thou or any man knows where to have me, thou knave thou!

Prince. Thou sayest true, hostess; and he slanders thee most grossly.

Quick. So he doth you, my lord; and said this other day you ought him a thousand pound. [140

Prince. Sirrah! do I owe you a thousand pound?

Fal. A thousand pound, Hal! a million: thy love is worth a million; thou owest me thy love.

Quick. Nay, my lord, he called you Jack, and said he would cudgel you.

Fal. Did I, Bardolph?

Bard. Indeed, Sir John, you said so.

Fal. Yea; if he said my ring was copper.

Prince. I say 'tis copper: darest thou be as good as thy word now? [150

Fal. Why, Hal, thou knowest, as thou art but man, I dare; but as thou art prince, I fear thee as I fear the roaring of the lion's whelp.

Prince. And why not as the lion?

Fal. The king himself is to be feared as the lion: dost thou think I'll fear thee as I fear thy father? nay, an I do, I pray God my girdle break!

Prince. O! if it should, how would thy guts fall about thy knees! But, sirrah, there's no room for faith, truth, or honesty in this bosom of thine; [160 it is all filled up with guts and midriff. Charge an honest woman with picking thy pocket! Why, thou whoreson, impudent, embossed rascal, if there were any thing in thy pocket but tavern reckonings, memorandums of bawdy-houses, and one poor pennyworth of sugar-candy to make thee long-winded; if thy pocket were enriched with any other injuries but these, I am a villain. And yet you will stand to it, you will not pocket up wrong. Art thou not ashamed? [170

Fal. Dost thou hear, Hal? thou knowest in the state of innocency Adam fell; and what should poor Jack Falstaff do in the days of villainy? Thou seest I have more flesh than another man, and therefore more frailty. You confess then, you picked my pocket?

Prince. It appears so by the story.

Fal. Hostess, I forgive thee. Go make ready breakfast; love thy husband, look to thy servants, cherish thy guests: thou shalt find me tractable to [180 any honest reason: thou seest I am pacified. Still! Nay prithee, be gone. (*Exit* MISTRESS QUICKLY.) Now, Hal, to the news at court: for the robbery, lad, how is that answered?

Prince. O! my sweet beef, I must still be good angel to thee: the money is paid back again.

163. **embossed,** inflated.

Fal. O! I do not like that paying back; 'tis a double labour.

Prince. I am good friends with my father and may do anything. [190

Fal. Rob me the exchequer the first thing thou dost, and do it with unwashed hands too.

Bard. Do, my lord.

Prince. I have procured thee, Jack, a charge of foot.

Fal. I would it had been of horse. Where shall I find one that can steal well? O! for a fine thief, of the age of two-and-twenty, or thereabouts; I am heinously unprovided. Well, God be thanked for these rebels; they offend none but the virtuous: I laud them, I praise them. [201

Prince. Bardolph!

Bard. My lord?

Prince. Go bear this letter to Lord John of Lancaster,
To my brother John; this to my Lord of Westmoreland.
Go, Poins, to horse, to horse! for thou and I
Have thirty miles to ride ere dinner-time.
Jack, meet me to-morrow in the Temple-hall
At two o'clock in the afternoon:
There shalt thou know thy charge, and there receive   210
Money and order for their furniture.
The land is burning; Percy stands on high;
And either we or they must lower lie.
  [*Exeunt the* PRINCE, POINS, *and* BARDOLPH.

Fal. Rare words! brave world! Hostess, my breakfast; come!
O! I could wish this tavern were my drum.   [*Exit.*

ACT IV

SCENE I.—*The Rebel Camp near Shrewsbury.*

Enter HOTSPUR, WORCESTER, *and* DOUGLAS.

Hot. Well said, my noble Scot: if speaking truth
In this fine age were not thought flattery,
Such attribution should the Douglas have,
As not a soldier of this season's stamp
Should go so general current through the world.
By God, I cannot flatter; do defy
The tongues of soothers; but a braver place
In my heart's love hath no man than yourself.
Nay, task me to my word; approve me, lord.

Doug. Thou art the king of honour: 10

192. **unwashed hands,** immediately.   208. **Temple-hall,** probably a hall in the Temple, one of the Inns of Court.   215. **drum,** recruiting-station.   7. **soothers,** flatterers.

No man so potent breathes upon the ground
But I will beard him.
    Hot.   Do so, and 'tis well.

    [*Enter a* Messenger, *with letters.*]

What letters hast thou there? (*To* DOUGLAS.) I can
    but thank you.
    Mess. These letters come from your father.
    Hot. Letters from him! why comes he not himself?
    Mess. He cannot come, my lord: he's grievous
    sick.
    Hot. 'Zounds! how has he the leisure to be sick
In such a justling time? Who leads his power?
Under whose government come they along?
    Mess. His letters bear his mind, not I, my lord.   20
    Wor. I prithee, tell me, doth he keep his bed?
    Mess. He did, my lord, four days ere I set forth;
And at the time of my departure thence
He was much feared by his physicians.
    Wor. I would the state of time had first been
    whole
Ere he by sickness had been visited:
His health was never better worth than now.
    Hot. Sick now! droop now! this sickness doth
    infect
The very life-blood of our enterprise;
'Tis catching hither, even to our camp.   30
He writes me here, that inward sickness—
And that his friends by deputation could not
So soon be drawn; nor did he think it meet
To lay so dangerous and dear a trust
On any soul removed but on his own.
Yet doth he give us bold advertisement,
That with our small conjunction we should on,
To see how fortune is disposed to us;
For, as he writes, there is no quailing now,
Because the king is certainly possessed   40
Of all our purposes. What say you to it?
    Wor. Your father's sickness is a maim to us.
    Hot. A perilous gash, a very limb lopped off:
And yet, in faith, 'tis not; his present want
Seems more than we shall find it. Were it good
To set the exact wealth of all our states
All at one cast? to set so rich a main
On the nice hazard of one doubtful hour?
It were not good; for therein should we read
The very bottom and the soul of hope,   50
The very list, the very utmost bound
Of all our fortunes.
    Doug.   Faith, and so we should;
Where now remains a sweet reversion:
We may boldly spend upon the hope of what

Is to come in:
A comfort of retirement lives in this.
    Hot. A rendezvous, a home to fly unto,
If that the devil and mischance look big
Upon the maidenhead of our affairs.   59
    Wor. But yet, I would your father had been here.
The quality and hair of our attempt
Brooks no division. It will be thought
By some, that know not why he is away,
That wisdom, loyalty, and mere dislike
Of our proceedings, kept the earl from hence.
And think how such an apprehension
May turn the tide of fearful faction
And breed a kind of question in our cause;
For well you know we of the offering side
Must keep aloof from strict arbitrament,   70
And stop all sight-holes, every loop from whence
The eye of reason may pry in upon us:
This absence of your father's draws a curtain,
That shows the ignorant a kind of fear
Before not dreamt of.
    Hot.   You strain too far.
I rather of his absence make this use:
It lends a lustre and more great opinion,
A larger dare to our great enterprise,
Than if the earl were here; for men must think,
If we without his help, can make a head   80
To push against the kingdom, with his help
We shall o'erturn it topsy-turvy down.
Yet all goes well, yet all our joints are whole.
    Doug. As heart can think: there is not such a word
Spoke of in Scotland as this term of fear.

    [*Enter* SIR RICHARD VERNON.]

    Hot. My cousin Vernon! welcome, by my soul.
    Ver. Pray God my news be worth a welcome,
    lord.
The Earl of Westmoreland, seven thousand strong,
Is marching hitherwards; with him Prince John.
    Hot. No harm: what more?
    Ver.   And further, I have learned,   90
The king himself in person is set forth,
Or hitherwards intended speedily,
With strong and mighty preparation.
    Hot. He shall be welcome too. Where is his son,
The nimble-footed madcap Prince of Wales,
And his comrades, that daffed the world aside,
And bid it pass?
    Ver.   All furnished, all in arms,
All plumed like estridges that wing the wind,

---

    35. soul removed, stranger.   **47. main,** hand at the card game of **hazard** (l. 48).   **51. list,** limit.

    96. daffed the world aside, thrust on one side all serious concerns.   **98–99. All plumed like estridges . . . bathed,** a double comparison, of men with ostriches and ostriches with eagles. **Baited,** having beaten the wings impatiently and fluttered from a perch.

Baited like eagles having lately bathed,
Glittering in golden coats, like images, 100
As full of spirit as the month of May,
And gorgeous as the sun at midsummer,
Wanton as youthful goats, wild as young bulls.
I saw young Harry, with his beaver on,
His cushes on his thighs, gallantly armed,
Rise from the ground like feathered Mercury,
And vaulted with such ease into his seat,
As if an angel dropped down from the clouds,
To turn and wind a fiery Pegasus
And witch the world with noble horsemanship. 110
   Hot. No more, no more: worse than the sun in March
This praise doth nourish agues. Let them come;
They come like sacrifices in their trim,
And to the fire-eyed maid of smoky war
All hot and bleeding will we offer them:
The mailèd Mars shall on his altar sit
Up to the ears in blood. I am on fire
To hear this rich reprisal is so nigh
And yet not ours. Come, let me taste my horse,
Who is to bear me like a thunderbolt 120
Against the bosom of the Prince of Wales:
Harry to Harry shall, hot horse to horse,
Meet and ne'er part till one drop down a corse.
O! that Glendower were come.
   Ver.   There is more news:
I learned in Worcester, as I rode along,
He cannot draw his power these fourteen days.
   Doug. That's the worst tidings that I hear of yet.
   Wor. Ay, by my faith, that bears a frosty sound.
   Hot. What may the king's whole battle reach unto?
   Ver. To thirty thousand.
   Hot.   Forty let it be: 130
My father and Glendower being both away,
The powers of us may serve so great a day.
Come, let us take a muster speedily:
Doomsday is near; die all, die merrily.
   Doug. Talk not of dying: I am out of fear
Of death or death's hand for this one half year.
                                                      [*Exeunt.*

SCENE 2.—*A public Road near Coventry.*

   Enter FALSTAFF *and* BARDOLPH.

   Fal. Bardolph, get thee before to Coventry; fill me a bottle of sack: our soldiers shall march through: we'll to Sutton-Co'fil' to-night.
   Bard. Will you give me money, captain?

   Fal. Lay out, lay out.
   Bard. This bottle makes an angel.
   Fal. An if it do, take it for thy labour; and if it make twenty, take them all, I'll answer the coinage. Bid my Lieutenant Peto meet me at the town's end.
   Bard. I will, captain: farewell.   [*Exit.*
   Fal. If I be not ashamed of my soldiers, I am [11 a soused gurnet. I have misused the king's press damnably. I have got, in exchange of a hundred and fifty soldiers, three hundred and odd pounds. I press me none but good householders, yeomen's sons; inquire me out contracted bachelors, such as had been asked twice on the banns; such a commodity of warm slaves, as had as lief hear the devil as a drum; such as fear the report of a caliver worse than a struck fowl or a hurt wild-duck. I [20 pressed me none but such toasts-and-butter, with hearts in their bellies no bigger than pins' heads, and they have bought out their services; and now my whole charge consists of ancients, corporals, lieutenants, gentlemen of companies, slaves as ragged as Lazarus in the painted cloth, where the glutton's dogs licked his sores; and such as indeed were never soldiers, but discarded unjust servingmen, younger sons to younger brothers, revolted tapsters and ostlers trade-fallen, the cankers of a [30 calm world and a long peace; ten times more dishonourable ragged than an old faced ancient: and such have I, to fill up the rooms of them that have bought out their services, that you would think that I had a hundred and fifty tattered prodigals, lately come from swine-keeping, from eating draff and husks. A mad fellow met me on the way and told me I had unloaded all the gibbets and pressed the dead bodies. No eye hath seen such scarecrows. I'll not march through Coventry with them, [40 that's flat: nay, and the villains march wide betwixt the legs, as if they had gyves on; for, indeed I had the most of them out of prison. There's but a shirt and a half in all my company; and the half shirt is two napkins tacked together and thrown over the shoulders like a herald's coat without sleeves; and the shirt, to say the truth, stolen from my host at Saint Alban's, or the red-nose inn-keeper of Daventry. But that's all one; they'll find linen enough on every hedge.   50

[*Enter the* PRINCE *and* WESTMORELAND.]

   Prince. How now, blown Jack! how now, quilt!
   Fal. What, Hal! How now, mad wag! what a

---

100. images, of the Virgin Mary and of saints, decked in splendid apparel.   **105. cushes,** guards.   **114. fire-eyed maid of smoky war,** Bellona.   **6. makes an angel,** brings the sum spent to an angel, a coin worth about 10*s*.   **12. soused gurnet,** pickled fish. **19. caliver,** musket.   **21. toasts-and-butter,** eaters of buttered toast, pampered persons.   **36. draff,** hogwash. **38. pressed,** drafted.   **42. gyves,** fetters.

devil dost thou in Warwickshire? My good Lord of Westmoreland, I cry you mercy: I thought your honour had already been at Shrewsbury.

West. Faith, Sir John, 'tis more than time that I were there, and you too; but my powers are there already. The king, I can tell you, looks for us all: we must away all night.

Fal. Tut, never fear me: I am as vigilant as a [60 cat to steal cream.

Prince. I think to steal cream indeed, for thy theft hath already made thee butter. But tell me, Jack, whose fellows are these that come after?

Fal. Mine, Hal, mine.

Prince. I did never see such pitiful rascals.

Fal. Tut, tut; good enough to toss; food for powder, food for powder; they'll fill a pit as well as better: tush, man, mortal men, mortal men.

West. Ay, but, Sir John, methinks they are ex- [70 ceeding poor and bare; too beggarly.

Fal. Faith, for their poverty, I know not where they had that; and for their bareness, I am sure they never learned that of me.

Prince. No, I'll be sworn; unless you call three fingers on the ribs bare. But sirrah, make haste: Percy is already in the field.

Fal. What, is the king encamped?

West. He is, Sir John: I fear we shall stay too long.   80

Fal. Well,
To the latter end of a fray and the beginning of a feast
Fits a dull fighter and a keen guest.   [*Exeunt.*

SCENE 3.—*The Rebel Camp near Shrewsbury.*

Enter HOTSPUR, WORCESTER, DOUGLAS, *and* VERNON.

Hot. We'll fight with him to-night.
Wor.   It may not be.
Doug. You give him then advantage.
Ver.   Not a whit.
Hot. Why say you so? looks he not for supply?
Ver. So do we.
Hot.   His is certain, ours is doubtful.
Wor. Good cousin, be advised: stir not to-night.
Ver. Do not, my lord.
Doug.   You do not counsel well:
You speak it out of fear and cold heart.
Ver. Do me no slander, Douglas: by my life,—
And I dare well maintain it with my life,—
If well-respected honour bid me on,   10
I hold as little counsel with weak fear
As you, my lord, or any Scot that this day lives:

67. **good enough to toss**, good enough to be impaled on the enemy's pikes.

Let it be seen to-morrow in the battle
Which of us fears.
Doug.   Yea, or to-night.
Ver.   Content.
Hot. To-night, say I.
Ver. Come, come, it may not be. I wonder much,
Being men of such great leading as you are,
That you foresee not what impediments
Drag back our expedition: certain horse
Of my cousin Vernon's are not yet come up: 20
Your uncle Worcester's horse came but to-day;
And now their pride and mettle is asleep,
Their courage with hard labour tame and dull,
That not a horse is half the half of himself.
Hot. So are the horses of the enemy
In general, journey-bated and brought low:
The better part of ours are full of rest.
Wor. The number of the king exceedeth ours:
For God's sake, cousin, stay till all come in.

[*The trumpet sounds a parley. Enter* SIR WALTER BLUNT.]

Blunt. I come with gracious offers from the king,
If you vouchsafe me hearing and respect.   31
Hot. Welcome, Sir Walter Blunt; and would to God
You were of our determination!
Some of us love you well; and even those some
Envy your great deservings and good name,
Because you are not of our quality,
But stand against us like an enemy.
Blunt. And God defend but still I should stand so,
So long as out of limit and true rule
You stand against anointed majesty.   40
But, to my charge. The king hath sent to know
The nature of your griefs, and whereupon
You conjure from the breast of civil peace
Such bold hostility, teaching his duteous land
Audacious cruelty. If that the king
Have any way your good deserts forgot,—
Which he confesseth to be manifold,—
He bids you name your griefs; and with all speed
You shall have your desires with interest,
And pardon absolute for yourself and these   50
Herein misled by your suggestion.
Hot. The king is kind; and well we know the king
Knows at what time to promise, when to pay.
My father and my uncle and myself
Did give him that same royalty he wears;
And when he was not six-and-twenty strong,
Sick in the world's regard, wretched and low,
A poor unminded outlaw sneaking home,
My father gave him welcome to the shore;

36. **quality**, fellowship, party.

And when he heard him swear and vow to God 60
He came but to be Duke of Lancaster,
To sue his livery and beg his peace,
With tears of innocency and terms of zeal,
My father, in kind heart and pity moved,
Swore him assistance and performed it too.
Now when the lords and barons of the realm
Perceived Northumberland did lean to him,
The more and less came in with cap and knee;
Met him in boroughs, cities, villages,
Attended him on bridges, stood in lanes, 70
Laid gifts before him, proffered him their oaths,
Gave him their heirs as pages, followed him
Even at the heels in golden multitudes.
He presently, as greatness knows itself,
Steps me a little higher than his vow
Made to my father, while his blood was poor,
Upon the naked shore at Ravenspurgh;
And now, forsooth, takes on him to reform
Some certain edicts and some strait decrees
That lie too heavy on the commonwealth, 80
Cries out upon abuses, seems to weep
Over his country's wrongs; and by this face,
This seeming brow of justice, did he win
The hearts of all that he did angle for;
Proceeded further; cut me off the heads
Of all the favourites that the absent king
In deputation left behind him here,
When he was personal in the Irish war.
  Blunt. Tut, I came not to hear this.
  Hot.   Then to the point.
In short time after, he deposed the king; 90
Soon after that, deprived him of his life;
And, in the neck of that, tasked the whole state;
To make that worse, suffered his kinsman March—
Who is, if every owner were well placed,
Indeed his king—to be engaged in Wales,
There without ransom to lie forfeited;
Disgraced me in my happy victories;
Sought to entrap me by intelligence;
Rated my uncle from the council-board;
In rage dismissed my father from the court; 100
Broke oath on oath, committed wrong on wrong;
And in conclusion drove us to seek out
This head of safety; and withal to pry
Into his title, the which we find
Too indirect for long continuance.
  Blunt. Shall I return this answer to the king?
  Hot. Not so, Sir Walter: we'll withdraw awhile.
Go to the king; and let there be impawned
Some surety for a safe return again,
And in the morning early shall my uncle 110
Bring him our purposes; and so farewell.
  Blunt. I would you would accept of grace and love.
  Hot. And may be so we shall.
  Blunt.   Pray God, you do! [*Exeunt.*

SCENE 4.—*York. A Room in the* ARCHBISHOP'S *Palace.*

Enter the ARCHBISHOP OF YORK *and* SIR MICHAEL.

  Arch. Hie, good Sir Michael; bear this sealèd brief
With wingèd haste to the lord marshal;
This to my cousin Scroop, and all the rest
To whom they are directed. If you knew
How much they do import, you would make haste.
  Sir M. My good lord,
I guess their tenour.
  Arch.   Like enough you do.
To-morrow, good Sir Michael, is a day
Wherein the fortune of ten thousand men
Must bide the touch; for, sir, at Shrewsbury, 10
As I am truly given to understand,
The king with mighty and quick-raisèd power
Meets with Lord Harry: and, I fear, Sir Michael,
What with the sickness of Northumberland,—
Whose power was in the first proportion,—
And what with Owen Glendower's absence thence,
Who with them was a rated sinew too,
And comes not in, o'er-ruled by prophecies,—
I fear the power of Percy is too weak
To wage an instant trial with the king. 20
  Sir M. Why, my good lord, you need not fear:
There is the Douglas and Lord Mortimer.
  Arch. No, Mortimer is not there.
  Sir M. But there is Mordake, Vernon, Lord Harry Percy,
And there's my Lord of Worcester, and a head
Of gallant warriors, noble gentlemen.
  Arch. And so there is; but yet the king hath drawn
The special head of all the land together:
The Prince of Wales, Lord John of Lancaster,
The noble Westmoreland, and war-like Blunt; 30
And many moe corrivals and dear men
Of estimation and command in arms.
  Sir M. Doubt not, my lord, they shall be well opposed.
  Arch. I hope no less, yet needful 'tis to fear;
And, to prevent the worse, Sir Michael, speed:
For if Lord Percy thrive not, ere the king

---

62. **sue his livery,** seek the handing over of his inheritance.
82. **by this face,** by this appearance of sympathy.
92. **tasked,** oppressed.

1. **Sir Michael,** probably the Archbishop's chaplain, to whom "Sir" is used as a title of courtesy. 10. **bide the touch,** be put to the test (as gold is tried by the touchstone). 31. **moe corrivals,** more comrades.

Dismiss his power, he means to visit us,
For he hath heard of our confederacy,
And 'tis but wisdom to make strong against him:
Therefore make haste. I must go write again   40
To other friends; and so farewell, Sir Michael.
                      [*Exeunt.*

ACT V

SCENE I.—*The* KING'S *Camp near Shrewsbury.*

Enter KING HENRY, *the* PRINCE, JOHN OF LANCASTER, SIR WALTER BLUNT, *and* SIR JOHN FALSTAFF.

  K. Hen. How bloodily the sun begins to peer
Above yon busky hill! the day looks pale
At his distemperature.
  Prince.   The southern wind
Doth play the trumpet to his purposes,
And by his hollow whistling in the leaves
Foretells a tempest and a blustering day.
  K. Hen. Then with the losers let it sympathize,
For nothing can seem foul to those that win.

[*Trumpet sounds. Enter* WORCESTER *and* VERNON.]

How now, my Lord of Worcester! 'tis not well
That you and I should meet upon such terms   10
As now we meet. You have deceived our trust,
And made us doff our easy robes of peace,
To crush our old limbs in ungentle steel:
This is not well, my lord; this is not well.
What say you to it? will you again unknit
This churlish knot of all-abhorrèd war,
And move in that obedient orb again
Where you did give a fair and natural light,
And be no more an exhaled meteor,
A prodigy of fear and a portent   20
Of broachèd mischief to the unborn times?
  Wor. Hear me, my liege.
For mine own part, I could be well content
To entertain the lag-end of my life
With quiet hours; for I do protest
I have not sought the day of this dislike.
  K. Hen. You have not sought it! how comes it then?
  Fal. Rebellion lay in his way, and he found it.
  Prince. Peace, chewet, peace!
  Wor. It pleased your majesty to turn your looks   30
Of favour from myself and all our house;
And yet I must remember you, my lord,
We were the first and dearest of your friends.
For you my staff of office did I break
In Richard's time; and posted day and night
To meet you on the way, and kiss your hand,
When yet you were in place and in account
Nothing so strong and fortunate as I.
It was myself, my brother, and his son,
That brought you home and boldly did outdare   40
The dangers of the time. You swore to us,
And you did swear that oath at Doncaster,
That you did nothing purpose 'gainst the state,
Nor claim no further than your new-fall'n right,
The seat of Gaunt, dukedom of Lancaster.
To this we swore our aid: but, in short space
It rained down fortune showering on your head,
And such a flood of greatness fell on you,
What with our help, what with the absent king,
What with the injuries of a wanton time,   50
The seeming sufferances that you had borne,
And the contrarious winds that held the king
So long in his unlucky Irish wars,
That all in England did repute him dead:
And from this swarm of fair advantages
You took occasion to be quickly wooed
To gripe the general sway into your hand;
Forgot your oath to us at Doncaster;
And being fed by us you used us so
As that ungentle gull, the cuckoo's bird,   60
Useth the sparrow: did oppress our nest,
Grew by our feeding to so great a bulk
That even our love durst not come near your sight
For fear of swallowing; but with nimble wing
We were enforced, for safety's sake, to fly
Out of your sight and raise this present head;
Whereby we stand opposèd by such means
As you yourself have forged against yourself
By unkind usage, dangerous countenance,
And violation of all faith and troth   70
Sworn to us in your younger enterprise.
  K. Hen. These things indeed, you have articulate,
Proclaimed at market-crosses, read in churches,
To face the garment of rebellion
With some fine colour that may please the eye
Of fickle changelings and poor discontents,
Which gape and rub the elbow at the news
Of hurlyburly innovation:
And never yet did insurrection want
Such water-colours to impaint his cause;   80
Nor moody beggars, starving for a time
Of pell-mell havoc and confusion.
  Prince. In both our armies there is many a soul
Shall pay full dearly for this encounter,
If once they join in trial. Tell your nephew,
The Prince of Wales doth join with all the world

---

2. **busky,** bushy.   3. **distemperature,** inclemency.
13. **our old limbs.** King Henry was in reality only thirty-seven at the time.   29. **chewet,** jackdaw, chatterer.

44. **new-fall'n right,** the claim to the Duchy of Lancaster.
52. **held the king,** Richard.

WILLIAM SHAKESPEARE

In praise of Henry Percy: by my hopes,
This present enterprise set off his head,
I do not think a braver gentleman,
More active-valiant or more valiant-young, 90
More daring or more bold, is now alive
To grace this latter age with noble deeds.
For my part, I may speak it to my shame,
I have a truant been to chivalry;
And so I hear he doth account me too;
Yet this before my father's majesty—
I am content that he shall take the odds
Of his great name and estimation,
And will, to save the blood on either side,
Try fortune with him in a single fight. 100
   K. Hen. And, Prince of Wales, so dare we venture thee,
Albeit considerations infinite
Do make against it. No, good Worcester, no,
We love our people well; even those we love
That are misled upon your cousin's part;
And, will they take the offer of our grace,
Both he and they and you, yea, every man
Shall be my friend again, and I'll be his.
So tell your cousin, and bring me word
What he will do; but if he will not yield, 110
Rebuke and dread correction wait on us,
And they shall do their office. So, be gone:
We will not now be troubled with reply;
We offer fair, take it advisedly.
               [*Exeunt* WORCESTER *and* VERNON.
   Prince. It will not be accepted, on my life.
The Douglas and the Hotspur both together
Are confident against the world in arms.
   K. Hen. Hence, therefore, every leader to his charge;
For, on their answer, will we set on them;
And God befriend us, as our cause is just! 120
[*Exeunt* KING HENRY, BLUNT, *and* JOHN OF LANCASTER.
   Fal. Hal, if thou see me down in the battle, and bestride me, so; 'tis a point of friendship.
   Prince. Nothing but a colossus can do thee that friendship. Say thy prayers, and farewell.
   Fal. I would it were bed-time, Hal, and all well.
   Prince. Why, thou owest God a death. [*Exit.*
   Fal. 'Tis not due yet: I would be loath to pay him before his day. What need I be so forward with him that calls not on me? Well, 'tis no matter; honour pricks me on. Yea, but how if honour prick me [130 off when I come on? how then? Can honour set to a leg? No. Or an arm? No. Or take away the grief of a wound? No. Honour hath no skill in surgery then? No. What is honour? a word. What is that word, honour? Air. A trim reckoning! Who hath it? he that died o' Wednesday. Doth he feel it? No. Doth he hear it? No. It is insensible then? Yea, to the dead. But will it not live with the living? No. Why? Detraction will not suffer it. Therefore I'll none of it: honour is a mere scutcheon; and so ends my [140 catechism. [*Exit.*

SCENE 2.—*The Rebel Camp near Shrewsbury.*

Enter WORCESTER *and* VERNON.

   Wor. O, no! my nephew must not know, Sir Richard,
The liberal kind offer of the king.
   Ver. 'Twere best he did.
   Wor.   Then are we all undone.
It is not possible, it cannot be,
The king should keep his word in loving us;
He will suspect us still, and find a time
To punish this offence in other faults:
Suspicion all our lives shall be stuck full of eyes;
For treason is but trusted like the fox,
Who, ne'er so tame, so cherished, and locked up, 10
Will have a wild trick of his ancestors.
Look how we can, or sad or merrily,
Interpretation will misquote our looks,
And we shall feed like oxen at a stall,
The better cherished, still the nearer death.
My nephew's trespass may be well forgot,
It hath the excuse of youth and heat of blood;
And an adopted name of privilege,
A hare-brained Hotspur, governed by a spleen.
All his offences live upon my head 20
And on his father's: we did train him on;
And, his corruption being ta'en from us,
We, as the spring of all, shall pay for all.
Therefore, good cousin, let not Harry know
In any case the offer of the king.
   Ver. Deliver what you will, I'll say 'tis so.
Here comes your cousin.

[*Enter* HOTSPUR *and* DOUGLAS; Officers *and* Soldiers *behind.*]

   Hot. My uncle is returned: deliver up
My Lord of Westmoreland. Uncle, what news?
   Wor. The king will bid you battle presently. 30
   Doug. Defy him by the Lord of Westmoreland.

140. mere scutcheon, only an escutcheon, a shield blazoned with a coat of arms and hung up in a church after the owner was dead.   **18. adopted name of privilege,** nickname which carries certain privileges with it.   **28–29. deliver up . . . Westmoreland.** Westmoreland had been in Percy's hands as hostage during the negotiations.

100. Try fortune . . . single fight. This offer is Shakespeare's own addition to the story.   **123. colossus.** The Colossus of Rhodes was a giant statue said to stand astride the harbor.

Hot. Lord Douglas, go you and tell him so.
Doug. Marry, and shall, and very willingly. [*Exit.*
Wor. There is no seeming mercy in the king.
Hot. Did you beg any? God forbid!
Wor. I told him gently of our grievances,
Of his oath-breaking; which he mended thus,
By now forswearing that he is forsworn:
He calls us rebels, traitors; and will scourge
With haughty arms this hateful name in us.   40

[*Re-enter* DOUGLAS.]

Doug. Arm, gentlemen! to arms! for I have thrown
A brave defiance in King Henry's teeth,
And Westmoreland, that was engaged, did bear it;
Which cannot choose but bring him quickly on.
Wor. The Prince of Wales stepped forth before the king,
And, nephew, challenged you to single fight.
Hot. O! would the quarrel lay upon our heads,
And that no man might draw short breath to-day
But I and Harry Monmouth. Tell me, tell me,
How showed his tasking? seemed it in contempt? 50
Ver. No, by my soul; I never in my life
Did hear a challenge urged more modestly,
Unless a brother should a brother dare
To gentle exercise and proof of arms.
He gave you all the duties of a man,
Trimmed up your praises with a princely tongue,
Spoke your deservings like a chronicle,
Making you ever better than his praise,
By still dispraising praise valued with you;
And, which became him like a prince indeed,   60
He made a blushing cital of himself,
And chid his truant youth with such a grace
As if he mastered there a double spirit
Of teaching and of learning instantly.
There did he pause. But let me tell the world,
If he outlive the envy of this day,
England did never owe so sweet a hope,
So much misconstrued in his wantonness.
Hot. Cousin, I think thou art enamoured
On his follies: never did I hear   70
Of any prince so wild a libertine.
But be he as he will, yet once ere night
I will embrace him with a soldier's arm,
That he shall shrink under my courtesy.
Arm, arm, with speed! And, fellows, soldiers, friends,
Better consider what you have to do,
Than I, that have not well the gift of tongue,
Can lift your blood up with persuasion.

43. **engaged,** held as hostage.   50. **tasking?** putting to the proof.

[*Enter a* Messenger.]

Mess. My lord, here are letters for you.
Hot. I cannot read them now.   80
O gentlemen! the time of life is short;
To spend that shortness basely were too long,
If life did ride upon a dial's point,
Still ending at the arrival of an hour.
An if we live, we live to tread on kings;
If die, brave death, when princes die with us!
Now, for our consciences, the arms are fair,
When the intent of bearing them is just.

[*Enter another* Messenger.]

Mess. My lord, prepare; the king comes on apace.
Hot. I thank him that he cuts me from my tale, 90
For I profess not talking. Only this,—
Let each man do his best: and here draw I
A sword, whose temper I intend to stain
With the best blood that I can meet withal
In the adventure of this perilous day.
Now, *Esperance!* Percy! and set on.
Sound all the lofty instruments of war,
And by that music let us all embrace;
For, heaven to earth, some of us never shall
A second time do such a courtesy.   100

[*The trumpets sound. They embrace, and exeunt.*

SCENE 3.—*Between the Camps.*

*Excursions and Parties fighting. Alarum to the Battle.
Then enter* DOUGLAS *and* SIR WALTER BLUNT, *meeting.*

Blunt. What is thy name, that in the battle thus
Thou crossest me? what honour dost thou seek
Upon my head?
Doug.   Know then, my name is Douglas;
And I do haunt thee in the battle thus
Because some tell me that thou art a king.
Blunt. They tell thee true.
Doug. The Lord of Stafford dear to-day hath bought
Thy likeness; for, instead of thee, King Harry,
This sword hath ended him: so shall it thee,
Unless thou yield thee as my prisoner.   10
Blunt. I was not born a yielder, thou proud Scot;
And thou shalt find a king that will revenge
Lord Stafford's death.

[*They fight, and* BLUNT *is slain. Enter* HOTSPUR.]

Hot. O, Douglas! hadst thou fought at Holmedon thus,
I never had triumphed upon a Scot.
Doug. All's done, all's won: here breathless lies the king.

83. **dial's point,** hand of a clock.

Hot. Where?
Doug. Here.
Hot. This, Douglas! no; I know this face full well;
A gallant knight he was, his name was Blunt; 20
Semblably furnished like the king himself.
Doug. A fool go with thy soul, whither it goes!
A borrowed title hast thou bought too dear:
Why didst thou tell me that thou wert a king?
Hot. The king hath many marching in his coats.
Doug. Now, by my sword, I will kill all his coats;
I'll murder all his wardrobe, piece by piece,
Until I meet the king.
Hot.   Up, and away!
Our soldiers stand full fairly for the day. [*Exeunt.*

[*Alarums. Enter* FALSTAFF.]

Fal. Though I could 'scape shot-free at Lon- [30
don, I fear the shot here; here's no scoring but upon the pate. Soft! who art thou? Sir Walter Blunt: there's honour for you! here's no vanity! I am as hot as molten lead, and as heavy too: God keep lead out of me! I need no more weight than mine own bowels. I have led my ragamuffins where they are peppered: there's not three of my hundred and fifty left alive, and they are for the town's end, to beg during life. But who comes here?

[*Enter the* PRINCE.]

Prince. What! stand'st thou idle here? lend me
    thy sword: 40
Many a nobleman lies stark and stiff
Under the hoofs of vaunting enemies,
Whose deaths are unrevenged: prithee, lend me thy
    sword.
Fal. O Hal! I prithee, give me leave to breathe awhile. Turk Gregory never did such deeds in arms as I have done this day. I have paid Percy, I have made him sure.
Prince. He is, indeed; and living to kill thee. I prithee, lend me thy sword. [49
Fal. Nay, before God, Hal, if Percy be alive, thou gett'st not my sword; but take my pistol, if thou wilt.
Prince. Give it me. What! is it in the case?
Fal. Ay, Hal; 'tis hot, 'tis hot: there's that will sack a city.

[*The* PRINCE *draws out a bottle of sack.*]

Prince. What! is't a time to jest and dally now?
    [*Throws it at him, and exit.*
Fal. Well, if Percy be alive, I'll pierce him. If he do come in my way, so: if he do not, if I come in his, willingly, let him make a carbonado of me. I like not such grinning honour as Sir Walter hath: give me life; which if I can save, so; if not, honour [60 comes unlooked for, and there's an end.   [*Exit.*

SCENE 4.—*Another Part of the Field.*

Alarums. Excursions. Enter KING HENRY, *the* PRINCE, JOHN OF LANCASTER, *and* WESTMORELAND.

K. Hen. I prithee,
Harry, withdraw thyself; thou bleed'st too much.
Lord John of Lancaster, go you with him.
Lanc. Not I, my lord, unless I did bleed too.
Prince. I beseech your majesty, make up,
Lest your retirement do amaze your friends.
K. Hen. I will do so.
My Lord of Westmoreland, lead him to his tent.
West. Come, my lord, I'll lead you to your tent.
Prince. Lead me, my lord? I do not need your
    help: 10
And God forbid a shallow scratch should drive
The Prince of Wales from such a field as this,
Where stained nobility lies trodden on,
And rebels' arms triumph in massacres!
Lanc. We breathe too long: come, cousin West-
    moreland,
Our duty this way lies: for God's sake, come.

[*Exeunt* JOHN OF LANCASTER *and* WESTMORELAND.

Prince. By God, thou hast deceived me, Lancaster;
I did not think thee lord of such a spirit:
Before, I loved thee as a brother, John;
But now, I do respect thee as my soul. 20
K. Hen. I saw him hold Lord Percy at the point
With lustier maintenance than I did look for
Of such an ungrown warrior.
Prince.   O! this boy
Lends mettle to us all.   [*Exit.*

[*Alarums. Enter* DOUGLAS.]

Doug. Another king! they grow like Hydra's
    heads:
I am the Douglas, fatal to all those
That wear those colours on them: what art thou,
That counterfeit'st the person of a king?
K. Hen. The king himself; who, Douglas, grieves
    at heart

---

30. shot-free, scot-free, without paying tavern reckoning. **33. here's no vanity!** The expression is ironical—"here's nothing but vanity." **45. Turk Gregory,** Hildebrand, who took the papal name of Gregory VII, and who, while friar, astonished Europe with his military exploits. **58. carbonado,** a piece of meat slashed for broiling. **2-3. Harry . . . thou . . . Lord John of Lancaster . . . you.** Note that the King addresses his eldest son simply as "Harry," and then uses the familiar "thou"; the younger son is given his full title and addressed as "you." **21. at the point,** at spear's or sword's distance. **25. Hydra's,** that of a fabled monster having nine heads; when one was cut off, two new ones grew in its place. Hercules killed it.

So many of his shadows thou hast met 30
And not the very king. I have two boys
Seek Percy and thyself about the field:
But, seeing thou fall'st on me so luckily,
I will assay thee; so defend thyself.

Doug. I fear thou art another counterfeit;
And yet, in faith, thou bear'st thee like a king:
But mine I am sure thou art, whoe'er thou be,
And thus I win thee.

[*They fight.* KING HENRY *being in danger, re-enter the* PRINCE.]

Prince. Hold up thy head, vile Scot, or thou art like
Never to hold it up again! the spirits 40
Of valiant Shirley, Stafford, Blunt, are in my arms:
It is the Prince of Wales that threatens thee,
Who never promiseth but he means to pay.

[*They fight:* DOUGLAS *flies.*]

Cheerly, my lord: how fares your Grace?
Sir Nicholas Gawsey hath for succour sent,
And so hath Clifton: I'll to Clifton straight.

K. Hen. Stay, and breathe awhile.
Thou hast redeemed thy lost opinion,
And showed thou mak'st some tender of my life,
In this fair rescue thou hast brought to me. 50

Prince. O God! they did me too much injury
That ever said I hearkened for your death.
If it were so, I might have let alone
The insulting hand of Douglas over you;
Which would have been as speedy in your end
As all the poisonous potions in the world,
And saved the treacherous labour of your son.

K. Hen. Make up to Clifton: I'll to Sir Nicholas Gawsey. [*Exit.*

[*Enter* HOTSPUR.]

Hot. If I mistake not, thou art Harry Monmouth.
Prince. Thou speak'st as if I would deny my name.
Hot. My name is Harry Percy.
Prince. Why, then, I see 61
A very valiant rebel of that name.
I am the Prince of Wales; and think not, Percy,
To share with me in glory any more:
Two stars keep not their motion in one sphere;
Nor can one England brook a double reign,
Of Harry Percy and the Prince of Wales.

Hot. Nor shall it, Harry; for the hour is come
To end the one of us; and would to God
Thy name in arms were now as great as mine! 70

Prince. I'll make it greater ere I part from thee;
And all the budding honours on thy crest

48. opinion, reputation.

I'll crop, to make a garland for my head.
Hot. I can no longer brook thy vanities.

[*They fight. Enter* FALSTAFF.]

Fal. Well said, Hal! to it, Hal! Nay, you shall find no boy's play here, I can tell you.

[*Re-enter* DOUGLAS; *he fights with* FALSTAFF, *who falls down as if he were dead, and exit* DOUGLAS. HOTSPUR *is wounded, and falls.*]

Hot. O, Harry! thou hast robbed me of my youth.
I better brook the loss of brittle life
Than those proud titles thou hast won of me;
They wound my thoughts worse than thy sword my flesh: 80
But thought's the slave of life, and life time's fool;
And time, that takes survey of all the world,
Must have a stop. O! I could prophesy,
But that the earthy and cold hand of death
Lies on my tongue. No, Percy, thou art dust,
And food for— [*Dies.*

Prince. For worms, brave Percy. Fare thee well, great heart!
Ill-weaved ambition, how much art thou shrunk!
When that this body did contain a spirit,
A kingdom for it was too small a bound; 90
But now, two paces of the vilest earth
Is room enough: this earth, that bears thee dead,
Bears not alive so stout a gentleman.
If thou wert sensible of courtesy,
I should not make so dear a show of zeal:
But let my favours hide thy mangled face,
And, even in thy behalf, I'll thank myself
For doing these fair rites of tenderness.
Adieu, and take thy praise with thee to heaven!
Thy ignomy sleep with thee in the grave, 100
But not remembered in thy epitaph!

(*He spies* FALSTAFF *on the ground.*)

What! old acquaintance! could not all this flesh
Keep in a little life? Poor Jack, farewell!
I could have better spared a better man.
O! I should have a heavy miss of thee
If I were much in love with vanity.
Death hath not struck so fat a deer to-day,
Though many dearer, in this bloody fray.
Embowelled will I see thee by and by:
Till then in blood by noble Percy lie. [*Exit.* 110

Fal. (*rising*). Embowelled! if thou embowel me to-day, I'll give you leave to powder me and eat me too, to-morrow. 'Sblood! 'twas time to counterfeit,

83. I could prophesy, in reference to the belief that men at the point of death are gifted with the power of prophecy.
100. ignomy, ignominy.   **112. powder,** salt.

or that hot termagant Scot had paid me scot and lot too. Counterfeit? I lie, I am no counterfeit: to die, is to be a counterfeit; for he is but the counterfeit of a man, who hath not the life of a man; but to counterfeit dying, when a man thereby liveth, is to be no counterfeit, but the true and perfect image of life indeed. The better part of valour is discre- [120 tion; in the which better part, I have saved my life. 'Zounds! I am afraid of this gunpowder Percy though he be dead: how, if he should counterfeit too and rise? By my faith I am afraid he would prove the better counterfeit. Therefore I'll make him sure; yea, and I'll swear I killed him. Why may not he rise as well as I? Nothing confutes me but eyes, and nobody sees me: therefore, sirrah, (*Stabbing him.*) with a new wound in your thigh come you along with me. 130

(*He takes* HOTSPUR *on his back.*)

[*Re-enter the* PRINCE *and* JOHN OF LANCASTER.]

Prince. Come, brother John; full bravely hast
   thou fleshed
Thy maiden sword.
  Lanc.   But, soft! whom have we here?
Did you not tell me this fat man was dead?
  Prince. I did; I saw him dead,
Breathless and bleeding on the ground.
Art thou alive? or is it fantasy
That plays upon our eyesight? I prithee, speak;
We will not trust our eyes without our ears:
Thou art not what thou seem'st.
  Fal. No, that's certain; I am not a double [140 man: but if I be not Jack Falstaff, then am I a Jack. There is Percy (*Throwing the body down.*): if your father will do me any honour, so; if not, let him kill the next Percy himself. I look to be either earl or duke, I can assure you.
  Prince. Why, Percy I killed myself, and saw thee dead.
  Fal. Didst thou? Lord, Lord! how this world is given to lying. I grant you I was down and out of breath, and so was he; but we rose both at an instant, and fought a long hour by Shrewsbury [150 clock. If I may be believed, so; if not, let them that should reward valour bear the sin upon their own heads. I'll take it upon my death, I gave him this wound in the thigh: if the man were alive and would deny it, 'zounds, I would make him eat a piece of my sword.
  Lanc. This is the strangest tale that e'er I heard.
  Prince. This is the strangest fellow, brother
   John.
Come, bring your luggage nobly on your back:

114–15. termagant, violent. **scot and lot,** in full.

For my part, if a lie may do thee grace, 160
I'll gild it with the happiest terms I have.

[*A retreat is sounded.*]

The trumpet sounds retreat; the day is ours.
Come, brother, let us to the highest of the field,
To see what friends are living, who are dead.

[*Exeunt the* PRINCE *and* JOHN OF LANCASTER.

  Fal. I'll follow, as they say, for reward. He that rewards me, God reward him! If I do grow great, I'll grow less; for I'll purge, and leave sack, and live cleanly, as a nobleman should do. [*Exit.*

SCENE 5.—*Another Part of the Field.*

The trumpets sound. Enter KING HENRY, *the* PRINCE, JOHN OF LANCASTER, WESTMORELAND, *and Others, with* WORCESTER *and* VERNON *prisoners.*

  K. Hen. Thus ever did rebellion find rebuke.
Ill-spirited Worcester! did we not send grace,
Pardon, and terms of love to all of you?
And wouldst thou turn our offers contrary?
Misuse the tenour of thy kinsman's trust?
Three knights upon our party slain to-day,
A noble earl and many a creature else
Had been alive this hour,
If like a Christian, thou hadst truly borne
Betwixt our armies true intelligence. 10
  Wor. What I have done my safety urged me to;
And I embrace this fortune patiently,
Since not to be avoided it falls on me.
  K. Hen. Bear Worcester to the death and Vernon
   too:
Other offenders we will pause upon.

[*Exeunt* WORCESTER *and* VERNON, *guarded.*

How goes the field?
  Prince. The noble Scot, Lord Douglas, when he
   saw
The fortune of the day quite turned from him,
The noble Percy slain, and all his men
Upon the foot of fear, fled with the rest; 20
And falling from a hill he was so bruised
That the pursuers took him. At my tent
The Douglas is, and I beseech your Grace
I may dispose of him.
  K. Hen.   With all my heart.
  Prince. Then, brother John of Lancaster, to you
This honourable bounty shall belong.
Go to the Douglas, and deliver him
Up to his pleasure, ransomless, and free:
His valour shown upon our crests to-day
Hath taught us how to cherish such high deeds, 30

160. do thee grace, help you win the King's favor.

Even in the bosom of our adversaries.
  Lanc. I thank your Grace for this high courtesy,
Which I shall give away immediately.
  K. Hen. Then this remains, that we divide our power.
You, son John, and my cousin Westmoreland
Towards York shall bend you, with your dearest speed,
To meet Northumberland and the prelate Scroop,
Who, as we hear, are busily in arms:
Myself and you, son Harry, will towards Wales,
To fight with Glendower and the Earl of March.   40
Rebellion in this land shall lose his sway,
Meeting the check of such another day:
And since this business so fair is done,
Let us not leave till all our own be won.   [*Exeunt.*

SONGS FROM SHAKESPEARE'S PLAYS

Shakespeare's songs, which are the equal of any to be found in the Elizabethan drama, serve various purposes in his plays. By combining with lyrical utterance the additional charms of the singing voice and instrumental accompaniment, they usually point up the tone of a scene or emphasize the mood of a character, as in the case of the two songs from *Twelfth-Night*, or suggest a view of life akin to that of the play, as in *As You Like It*. More rarely, a song like "Tell Me Where Is Fancy Bred," from *The Merchant of Venice*, or "Full Fathom Five" from *The Tempest*, seems to have a direct bearing on the course of action. But each of Shakespeare's songs, apart from its dramatic context, is an expert evocation of theme, atmosphere, and mood.

WHEN DAISIES PIED

When daisies pied and violets blue
  And lady-smocks all silver-white
And cuckoo-buds of yellow hue
  Do paint the meadows with delight,
The cuckoo then, on every tree,
Mocks married men; for thus sings he,
    "Cuckoo!
Cuckoo, cuckoo!" Oh word of fear,
Unpleasing to a married ear!

When shepherds pipe on oaten straws,   10
  And merry larks are ploughmen's clocks,
When turtles tread, and rooks, and daws,
  And maidens bleach their summer smocks,
The cuckoo then, on every tree,
Mocks married men; for thus sings he,
    "Cuckoo!
Cuckoo, cuckoo!" Oh word of fear,
Unpleasing to a married ear!

WHEN ICICLES HANG BY THE WALL

When icicles hang by the wall,
  And Dick the shepherd blows his nail,
And Tom bears logs into the hall,
  And milk comes frozen home in pail,
When blood is nipped and ways be foul,
Then nightly sings the staring owl,
"Tu-whit, tu-who!" A merry note,
While greasy Joan doth keel the pot.

When all aloud the wind doth blow,
  And coughing drowns the parson's saw,   10
And birds sit brooding in the snow,
  And Marian's nose looks red and raw,
When roasted crabs hiss in the bowl,
Then nightly sings the staring owl,
"Tu-whit, tu-who!" A merry note,
While greasy Joan doth keel the pot.

WHO IS SILVIA?

Who is Silvia? What is she,
  That all our swains commend her?
Holy, fair, and wise is she;
  The heaven such grace did lend her,
That she might admirèd be.

Is she kind as she is fair?
  For beauty lives with kindness.
Love doth to her eyes repair,
  To help him of his blindness;
And, being helped, inhabits there.   10

Then to Silvia let us sing,
  That Silvia is excelling;
She excels each mortal thing
  Upon the dull earth dwelling.
To her let us garlands bring.

When Daisies Pied. This and the following song conclude Shakespeare's early comedy *Love's Labour's Lost.* They are both built on the same pattern, and in each song the mood is given piquancy by the introduction of an alien element, in one, the cuckoo, and in the other, the owl. **2. lady-smocks,** spring flowers of the cress family, sometimes called cuckoo flowers.

When Icicles Hang by the Wall. The accurate Dutch realism of this song is unusual with Shakespeare, most of whose songs are deliberately romantic in tone.   **8. keel,** cool by stirring. **13. roasted crabs,** roasted crab apples, dropped into a bowl of spiced and sweetened ale.   *Who Is Silvia?* This song from *Two Gentlemen of Verona* has been frequently set to music. Schubert's setting is probably the best known in modern times.

WILLIAM SHAKESPEARE

OVER HILL, OVER DALE

Over hill, over dale,
   Thorough bush, thorough brier,
Over park, over pale,
   Thorough flood, thorough fire,
I do wander every where,
Swifter than the moon's sphere;
And I serve the fairy queen,
To dew her orbs upon the green.
The cowslips tall her pensioners be;
In their gold coats spots you see,   10
   Those be rubies, fairy favours,
   In those freckles live their savours.
I must go seek some dewdrops here,
And hang a pearl in every cowslip's ear.

TELL ME WHERE IS FANCY BRED

Tell me where is fancy bred,
Or in the heart, or in the head?
How begot, how nourishèd?
   Reply, reply.
It is engendr'èd in the eyes,
With gazing fed; and fancy dies
In the cradle where it lies.
Let us all ring fancy's knell;
I'll begin it—Ding, dong, bell.
   Ding, dong, bell.

BLOW, BLOW, THOU WINTER WIND

Blow, blow, thou winter wind!
Thou art not so unkind
   As man's ingratitude;
Thy tooth is not so keen,
Because thou art not seen,
   Although thy breath be rude.

Heigh ho! sing, heigh ho! unto the green holly;
Most friendship is feigning, most loving mere folly.
   Then, heigh ho, the holly!
   This life is most jolly.   10

Freeze, freeze, thou bitter sky!
That dost not bite so nigh
   As benefits forgot;
Though thou the waters warp,
Thy sting is not so sharp
   As friend remembered not.

Heigh ho! sing, heigh ho! etc.

UNDER THE GREENWOOD TREE

Under the greenwood tree
Who loves to lie with me,
And turn his merry note
Unto the sweet bird's throat,
Come hither, come hither, come hither!
   Here shall he see
   No enemy
But winter and rough weather.

   Who doth ambition shun,
   And loves to live i' the sun,   10
   Seeking the food he eats,
   And pleased with what he gets,
Come hither, come hither, come hither!
   Here shall he see
   No enemy
But winter and rough weather.

COME AWAY, COME AWAY, DEATH

Come away, come away, death,
   And in sad cypress let me be laid;
Fly away, fly away, breath;
   I am slain by a fair cruel maid.
My shroud of white, stuck all with yew,
   Oh, prepare it!
My part of death, no one so true
   Did share it.

Not a flower, not a flower sweet,
   On my black coffin let there be strown;   10
Not a friend, not a friend greet
   My poor corpse, where my bones shall be thrown.

Over Hill, Over Dale. This song, from *A Midsummer Night's Dream,* is sung to Puck by one of the attendants of Titania, the queen of the fairies. **3. pale,** enclosed ground. **8. orbs,** rings in the greensward made by the dancing fairies. **9. pensioners,** probably a reference to Elizabeth's bodyguard of handsome young nobles. *Tell Me Where Is Fancy Bred.* Sung while Bassanio is making his choice in *The Merchant of Venice,* this song is probably intended to give him a hint as to the lucky casket. The number of words rhyming with lead is significant. **1. fancy,** love aroused by the senses rather than the heart. *Blow, Blow, Thou Winter Wind.* Sung at the request of the exiled Duke in *As You Like It,* this song contrasts the unkindness of man with the less biting unkindness of wintry nature.

Blow, Blow, Thou Winter Wind. **16. As friend remembered not,** as what an unremembered friend feels. *Under the Greenwood Tree.* In contrast to the cynicism of the preceding lyric, this second song from *As You Like It* stresses the carefree and idyllic life of the greenwood where they "fleet the time carelessly as they did in the golden world." The first line is an old ballad refrain. *Come Away, Come Away, Death.* Feste, the clown in *Twelfth-Night,* repeats this song at the request of the love-melancholy Duke, who says it is "old and plain . . . And dallies with the innocence of love, Like the old age." **2. cypress,** a coffin of cypress wood.

A thousand thousand sighs to save,
  Lay me, oh, where
Sad true lover never find my grave,
  To weep there!

O MISTRESS MINE

O mistress mine, where are you roaming?
O, stay and hear; your true love's coming,
  That can sing both high and low.
Trip no further, pretty sweeting,
Journeys end in lovers meeting,
  Every wise man's son doth know.

What is love? 'Tis not hereafter;
Present mirth hath present laughter;
  What's to come is still unsure.
In delay there lies no plenty;
Then come kiss me, sweet and twenty,
  Youth's a stuff will not endure.

SIGH NO MORE

Sigh no more, ladies, sigh no more;
  Men were deceivers ever;
One foot in sea, and one on shore,
  To one thing constant never.
Then sigh not so, but let them go,
  And be you blithe and bonny,
Converting all your sounds of woe
  Into "Hey nonny, nonny!"

Sing no more ditties, sing no moe
  Of dumps so dull and heavy;   10
The fraud of men was ever so,
  Since summer first was leavy.
Then sigh not so, but let them go,
  And be you blithe and bonny,
Converting all your sounds of woe
  Into "Hey nonny, nonny!"

TAKE, OH, TAKE THOSE LIPS AWAY

Take, oh, take those lips away,
  That so sweetly were forsworn;
And those eyes, the break of day,
  Lights that do mislead the morn.
But my kisses bring again,
  Bring again;
Seals of love, but sealed in vain,
  Sealed in vain.

HARK, HARK! THE LARK

Hark, hark! The lark at heaven's gate sings,
  And Phoebus 'gins arise,
His steeds to water at those springs
  On chaliced flowers that lies;
And winking Mary-buds begin
  To ope their golden eyes.
With every thing that pretty is,
  My lady sweet, arise!
    Arise, arise!

FEAR NO MORE THE HEAT O' THE SUN

Fear no more the heat o' the sun,
  Nor the furious winter's rages;
Thou thy worldly task hast done,
  Home art gone, and ta'en thy wages.
Golden lads and girls all must,
As chimney-sweepers, come to dust.

Fear no more the frown o' the great;
  Thou art past the tyrant's stroke;
Care no more to clothe and eat;
  To thee the reed is as the oak.   10
The sceptre, learning, physic, must
All follow this, and come to dust.

Fear no more the lightning-flash,
  Nor the all-dreaded thunder-stone;
Fear not slander, censure rash;
  Thou hast finished joy and moan.
All lovers young, all lovers must
Consign to thee, and come to dust.

No exorciser harm thee!
  Nor no witchcraft charm thee!   20
Ghost unlaid forbear thee!
  Nothing ill come near thee!
Quiet consummation have;
And renownèd be thy grave!

O Mistress Mine. This song is sung by Feste in *Twelfth-Night* at the request of the revelers Sir Toby Belch and Sir Andrew Aguecheek, both of whom pride themselves on their own singing. *Sigh No More.* This is from *Much Ado About Nothing.* **9. moe,** more. **10. dumps,** mournful tunes. **12. leavy,** leafy. *Take, Oh, Take Those Lips Away.* Sung by Mariana's page in *Measure for Measure* and accompanied by her, this song expresses her unhappiness at being jilted by her lover, Angelo. *Take, Oh, Take Those Lips Away.* **7. Seals of love,** written instruments under seal, a legal figure. *Hark, Hark! The Lark.* This song from *Cymbeline* is sung to Imogen, grieved at the exile of her husband, by a musician attendant on Cloten, who is attempting to woo her. **4. chaliced,** cup-shaped. **5. Mary-buds,** marigolds that open at sunrise and close at sunset. *Fear No More the Heat o' the Sun.* This pathetic rather than tragic song from *Cymbeline* is sung over Fidele (Imogen, disguised as a page) by her half-brothers, who have failed to identify her. **14. thunder-stone,** thunderbolt.

WILLIAM SHAKESPEARE

WHEN DAFFODILS BEGIN TO PEER

When daffodils begin to peer,
  With hey! the doxy over the dale,
Why, then comes in the sweet o' the year;
  For the red blood reigns in the winter's pale.

The white sheet bleaching on the hedge,
  With hey! the sweet birds, oh, how they sing!
Doth set my pugging tooth on edge;
  For a quart of ale is a dish for a king.

The lark, that tirra-lirra chants,
  With hey! with hey! the thrush and the jay,
Are summer songs for me and my aunts,
  While we lie tumbling in the hay.

FULL FATHOM FIVE

Full fathom five thy father lies.
  Of his bones are coral made;
Those are pearls that were his eyes;
  Nothing of him that doth fade
But doth suffer a sea-change
Into something rich and strange.
Sea-nymphs hourly ring his knell:
          Ding-dong!
Hark! now I hear them—Ding-dong, bell!

Elizabethan Lyrics

The sixteenth century was pre-eminently a singing era. In no other period in English history was the practice so universal or so esteemed. The incomparable distinction of the lyrics of the time is intimately dependent on the vogue of vocal music. To be able to carry a part was as indispensable a skill of the educated man or woman as the ability to read Latin or to compose verses. An anecdote from Henry Morley's *Plain and Easy Introduction to Practical Music*, 1597, illustrates the universality of this custom. "Supper being ended," he writes, "and music-books (according to the custom) being brought to the tables, the mistress of the house presented me with a part, earnestly requesting me to sing. But when, after many excuses I protested unfainedly that I could not, every one began to wonder. Yea, some whispered to others, demanding how I was brought up." Even the journeyman shoemaker, according to Thomas Deloney's *Gentle Craft*, 1598, had to be able "to sound the trumpet, or play upon the flute, and bear his part in a three man's song, and readily reckon up his tools in rhyme." And as late as 1622 Henry Peacham in *The Compleat Gentleman* could assert that one of the essential accomplishments of the educated man was the ability "to sing your part sure, at first sight, withal to play the same upon your viol or the exercise of your lute."

The Elizabethan lyric is omnipresent—in miscellanies or anthologies, in songbooks that contain both words and music, in works of fiction and plays.

The first and most famous of the miscellanies is that edited by Tottell, published in 1557, under the title *Songs and Sonnets*, but commonly known as *Tottell's Miscellany*. This collection is invaluable for its first printings of ninety-seven poems by Sir Thomas Wyatt and forty poems by Surrey. It ran into eight editions in thirty years, and was obviously a favorite of Shakespeare's Slender, who lamented, "I had rather than forty shillings I had my book of *Songs and Sonnets* here." Other famous miscellanies were Richard Edwards's *Paradise of Dainty Devices*, 1577; Thomas Proctor's *Gorgeous Gallery of Gallant Inventions*, 1578; *The Phoenix Nest*, 1593, which contained lyrics by Spenser, Sidney, Lodge, and Breton; and *England's Helicon*, 1600, the greatest of them all, since it not only drew on the earlier miscellanies but included some exquisite songs from plays, works of fiction, and the songbooks.

The lyrics which appear in the songbooks are treated in two distinct ways. The words may be adapted for singing as an air or as a madrigal. In the air, a solo voice sang the words, to the accompaniment of a lute, a lute and a viola da gamba, or a larger group of instruments, or on occasion by accompanying but subordinate voices. The madrigal, as described by John Hebel and H. H. Hudson in their collection *Poetry of the English Renaissance*, Crofts, 1936, was "an unaccompanied song of from three to six voice parts, to be sung by a small group

---

When Daffodils Begin to Peer. Sung by the rogue Autolycus in *The Winter's Tale*, this song is a fresh and earthy mixture of sensitivity and sensuality. **2. doxy,** thieves' slang for mistress. **4. pale,** a pun on "pallor" and "enclosure." **7. pugging,** thieving.

11. aunts, slang for mistresses. *Full Fathom Five.* This song, sung by Ariel to Ferdinand in the *Tempest*, suggests the supposed fate of Ferdinand's father in the storm with which the play begins. The lyric is a supreme illustration of the power of great poetry to make the unpleasant and abhorrent, in this case, death by drowning, beautiful and consoling.

of friends sitting around a table in a home or in the tavern. It differed from our part-song, for it was polyphonic. No one voice carried the melody with the others subordinated as an accompaniment, but all parts were of equal interest, often of the same melodic material, and the voices entered successively rather than simultaneously. The poem was treated in phrases, each several times repeated, and commonly overlapping in the different voices. With this repetition the true madrigal seldom used more than one stanza of six to ten lines." The finest musicians of England's most brilliant musical period—William Byrd, Thomas Campion, Orlando Gibbons, John Dowland—lavished their talents on song-writing.

Lyrics occur with considerable frequency in works of fiction in the pastoral mode, for the reason that the Continental pastoral literature most influential in England—Sannazaro's *Arcadia* and Montemayor's *Diana*—though in prose, was studded with pastoral lyrics. But it is in the plays of the period that many of the supreme lyrics first found their setting. The prominence of the lyric in the Elizabethan drama is due in very large part not only to the popularity of singing with all classes but also to the facts that the children's companies were made up of boys highly trained in vocal performance, and that the adult companies used for feminine roles and for pages' parts boys who had had identical or similar training. It is not always possible to be certain that the author of a given play is also the author of the songs introduced into that play, but there is a great probability that most of the exquisite songs in Shakespeare's plays are from his hand, and that such playwrights as Fletcher and Dekker wrote almost no lyrics except those incidental to their plays.

A NYMPH'S DISDAIN OF LOVE

Hey down, a down, did Dian sing,
   Amongst her virgins sitting,
Than love there is no vainer thing,
   For maidens most unfitting.
And so think I, with a down, down, derry.

When women knew no woe,
   But lived themselves to please,
Men's feigning guiles they did not know,
   The ground of their disease.
Unborn was false suspect,   10
   No thought of jealousy;

A Nymph's Disdain. This song, taken from the finest of the Elizabethan anthologies, *England's Helicon*, is there signed "Ignoto," that is, "Anonymous."

From wanton toys and fond affect
   The virgin's life was free.
      Hey down, a down, did Dian sing, &c.

At length men usèd charms;
   To which what maids gave ear,
Embracing gladly endless harms,
   Anon enthrallèd were.
Thus women welcomed woe
   Disguised in name of love;   20
A jealous hell, a painted show,
   So shall they find that prove.

Hey down, a down, did Dian sing,
   Amongst her virgins sitting,
Than love there is no vainer thing,
   For virgins most unfitting.
And so think I, with a down, down, derry.

BACK AND SIDE GO BARE, GO BARE

Back and side go bare, go bare,
   Both foot and hand go cold;
But, belly, God send thee good ale enough,
   Whether it be new or old.

I cannot eat but little meat,
   My stomach is not good;
But sure I think that I can drink
   With him that wears a hood.
Though I go bare, take ye no care,
   I am nothing a-cold;   10
I stuff my skin so full within
   Of jolly good ale and old.

Back and side go bare, go bare,
   Both foot and hand go cold;
But, belly, God send thee good ale enough,
   Whether it be new or old.

I love no roast but a nutbrown toast,
   And a crab laid in the fire;
A little bread shall do me stead,
   Much bread I not desire.   20
No frost nor snow, no wind, I trow,
   Can hurt me if I would,
I am so wrapped, and throughly lapped
   Of jolly good ale and old.

Back and side go bare, &c.

Back and Side Go Bare. This lusty drinking song is from the vigorous farce *Gammer Gurton's Needle*, usually ascribed to William Stevenson. The song, however, is probably much older than the play, and is therefore preferably called anonymous. **17. nutbrown toast,** toasted bread, dipped or floated in the beverage. **18. crab,** crab apple.

And Tib my wife, that as her life
    Loveth well good ale to seek,
Full oft drinks she, till ye may see
    The tears run down her cheek.
Then doth she troll to me the bowl,   30
    Even as a maltworm should,
And saith, Sweetheart, I took my part
    Of this jolly good ale and old.

    Back and side go bare, &c.

Now let them drink, till they nod and wink,
    Even as good fellows should do;
They shall not miss to have the bliss
    Good ale doth bring men to;
And all poor souls that have scoured bowls
    Or have them lustily trolled,   40
God save the lives of them and their wives,
    Whether they be young or old.

    Back and side go bare, &c.

THE PROMISE OF A CONSTANT LOVER

As laurel leaves that cease not to be green,
From parching sun, nor yet from winter's threat,
As hardened oak that fear'th no sword so keen,
As flint for tool in twain that will not fret,
As fast as rock or pillar surely set,—
Assurèdly whom I cannot forget,
For joy, for pain, for torment, nor for tene,
For loss, for gain, for frowning, nor for threat:
But ever one,—yea, both in calm and blast,
Your faithful friend, and will be to my last.

Richard Barnfield
1574–1627

IF MUSIC AND SWEET POETRY AGREE

If music and sweet poetry agree,
As they must needs (the sister and the brother),
    Then must the love be great 'twixt thee and me,
    Because thou lov'st the one, and I the other.
    Dowland to thee is dear, whose heavenly touch
Upon the lute doth ravish human sense;
Spenser to me, whose deep conceit is such
    As, passing all conceit, needs no defence.

Thou lov'st to hear the sweet melodious sound
That Phoebus' lute (the queen of music) makes;   10
And I in deep delight am chiefly drowned
    Whenas himself to singing he betakes.
    One god is god of both (as poets feign),
    One knight loves both, and both in thee remain.

Nicholas Breton
1545?–1626?

A PASTORAL OF PHILLIS AND CORYDON

On a hill there grows a flower,
    Fair befall the dainty sweet!
By that flower there is a bower
    Where the heavenly Muses meet.

In that bower there is a chair
    Fringèd all about with gold,
Where doth sit the fairest fair
    That did ever eye behold.

It is Phillis fair and bright,
    She that is the shepherds' joy,   10
She that Venus did despite
    And did blind her little boy.

This is she, the wise, the rich,
    And the world desires to see;
This is *ipsa quae* the which
    There is none but only she.

Who would not this face admire?
    Who would not this saint adore?
Who would not this sight desire,
    Though he thought to see no more?   20

O fair eyes, yet let me see!
    One good look, and I am gone,
Look on me, for I am he—
    Thy poor silly Corydon.

Thou that art the shepherds' queen,
    Look upon thy silly swain;
By thy comfort have been seen
    Dead men brought to life again.

---

30. troll, circulate, pass around.   **31. maltworm**, toper. *The Promise of a Constant Lover*. This anonymous poem is taken from Tottell's *Songs and Sonnets*, 1557. *If Music and Sweet Poetry Agree*. This sonnet by the minor poet Richard Barnfield first appeared in his *Poems in Divers Humours*, 1598.

A Pastoral of Phillis and Corydon. This charming lyric, which has in its first two stanzas the tone and manner of the folk song, was first published in *The Arbour of Amorous Devices* in 1597.   **15. ipsa quae**, the very she, she herself.

Thomas Campion
1567–1620

THRICE TOSS THESE OAKEN ASHES

Thrice toss these oaken ashes in the air,
Thrice sit thou mute in this enchanted chair,
Then thrice three times tie up this true love's knot,
And murmur soft, She will, or she will not.

Go burn these pois'nous weeds in yon blue fire,
These screech-owl's feathers and this prickling brier,
This cypress gathered at a dead man's grave,
That all thy fears and cares an end may have.

Then come, you fairies, dance with me a round;
Melt her hard heart with your melodious sound.   10
In vain are all the charms I can devise:
She hath an art to break them with her eyes.

NEVER LOVE UNLESS YOU CAN

Never love unless you can
Bear with all the faults of man;
Men sometimes will jealous be,
Though but little cause they see,
    And hang the head, as discontent,
    And speak what straight they will repent.

Men that but one saint adore
Make a show of love to more;
Beauty must be scorned in none,
Though but truly served in one;   10
    For what is courtship but disguise?
    True hearts may have dissembling eyes.

Men when their affairs require
Must a while themselves retire,
Sometimes hunt, and sometimes hawk,
And not ever sit and talk.
    If these and such like you can bear,
    Then like, and love, and never fear.

Thrice Toss These Oaken Ashes. This song, which puts to effective use some of the most ancient devices of witchcraft, first appeared in Campion's *Third and Fourth Book of Airs*, 1617. This and the seven following songs illustrate the range and perfection of the lyrical production of the finest of the poet-musicians of the period.   *Never Love Unless You Can.* This serene but worldly wise lyric first appeared in the *Third and Fourth Book of Airs.*   **16. ever,** always.

JACK AND JOAN

Jack and Joan they think no ill,
But loving live, and merry still;
Do their week-days' work and pray
Devoutly on the holy day;
Skip and trip it on the green,
And help to choose the summer queen;
Lash out, at a country feast,
Their silver penny with the best.
Well can they judge of nappy ale,
And tell at large a winter tale;   10
Climb up to the apple loft,
And turn the crabs till they be soft.
Tib is all the father's joy,
And little Tom the mother's boy.
All their pleasure is content,
And care, to pay their yearly rent.
Joan can call by name her cows,
And deck her windows with green boughs;
She can wreaths and tutties make,
And trim with plums a bridal cake.   20
Jack knows what brings gain or loss,
And his long flail can stoutly toss;
Make the hedge, which others break,
And ever thinks what he doth speak.
Now, you courtly dames and knights,
That study only strange delights,
Though you scorn the home-spun gray,
And revel in your rich array;
Though your tongues dissemble deep,
And can your heads from danger keep;   30
Yet for all your pomp and train,
Securer lives the silly swain.

TO MUSIC BENT IS MY RETIRÈD MIND

To music bent is my retirèd mind,
    And fain would I some song of pleasure sing,
But in vain joys no comfort now I find;
    From heavenly thoughts all true delight doth spring.
Thy power, O God, thy mercies, to record,
Will sweeten every note and every word.

All earthly pomp or beauty to express,
    Is but to carve in snow, on waves to write.

Jack and Joan. This song treats the conventional theme of the joys of the simple life in the manner of a folk song. It first appeared in Campion's *Two Books of Airs*, 1613?.   **7. Lash out,** lavish, squander.   **9. nappy,** strong, heady.   **19. tutties,** nosegays, bouquets.   *To Music Bent.* This song, which suggests the more spiritual side of Campion's lyricism, first appeared in his *Two Books of Airs.*

ELIZABETHAN LYRICS

Celestial things, though men conceive them less,
   Yet fullest are they in themselves of light;   10
Such beams they yield as know no means to die,
Such heat they cast as lifts the spirit high.

THE MAN OF LIFE UPRIGHT

   The man of life upright,
     Whose guiltless heart is free
   From all dishonest deeds,
     Or thought of vanity;

   The man whose silent days
     In harmless joys are spent,
   Whom hopes cannot delude,
     Nor sorrow discontent;

   That man needs neither towers
     Nor armour for defence,   10
   Nor secret vaults to fly
     From thunder's violence.

   He only can behold
     With unaffrighted eyes
   The horrors of the deep
     And terrors of the skies.

   Thus, scorning all the cares
     That fate or fortune brings,
   He makes the heaven his book,
     His wisdom heavenly things,   20

   Good thoughts his only friends,
     His wealth a well-spent age,
   The earth his sober inn
     And quiet pilgrimage.

WHEN TO HER LUTE CORINNA SINGS

When to her lute Corinna sings,
Her voice revives the leaden strings,
And doth in highest notes appear
As any challenged echo clear;
But when she doth of mourning speak,
Ev'n with her sighs the strings do break.

And as her lute doth live or die,
Led by her passion, so must I:
For when of pleasure she doth sing,
My thoughts enjoy a sudden spring,   10
But if she doth of sorrow speak,
Ev'n from my heart the strings do break.

MY SWEETEST LESBIA

My sweetest Lesbia, let us live and love,
And though the sager sort our deeds reprove,
Let us not weigh them. Heaven's great lamps do dive
Into their west, and straight again revive,
But soon as once set is our little light,
Then must we sleep one ever-during night.

If all would lead their lives in love like me,
Then bloody swords and armour should not be;
No drum nor trumpet peaceful sleeps should move,
Unless alarm came from the camp of love.   10
But fools do live, and waste their little light,
And seek with pain their ever-during night.

When timely death my life and fortune ends,
Let not my hearse be vexed with mourning friends,
But let all lovers, rich in triumph, come
And with sweet pastimes grace my happy tomb;
And Lesbia, close up thou my little light,
And crown with love my ever-during night.

THERE IS A GARDEN IN HER FACE

   There is a garden in her face,
Where roses and white lilies grow;
   A heavenly paradise is that place,
Wherein all pleasant fruits do flow.
     There cherries grow which none may buy
     Till cherry-ripe themselves do cry.

   Those cherries fairly do enclose
Of orient pearl a double row,
   Which when her lovely laughter shows,
They look like rosebuds filled with snow.   10
     Yet them nor peer nor prince can buy,
     Till cherry-ripe themselves do cry.

   Her eyes like angels watch them still;
Her brows like bended bows do stand,
   Threat'ning with piercing frowns to kill
All that attempt with eye or hand
     Those sacred cherries to come nigh,
     Till cherry-ripe themselves do cry.

The Man of Life Upright. This song, which is one of the finest of the innumerable English adaptations of Horace's *"Integer Vitae"* ode, appeared in Campion's first *Book of Airs*, 1601. The following song is from the same collection.

My Sweetest Lesbia. This song is one of many adaptations English poets have made of Catullus' famous lyric. *There Is a Garden.* This song first appeared in the *Third and Fourth Book of Airs*. **6. cherry-ripe**, the cry of the London street venders.

Henry Constable
1562–1613

THE SHEPHERD'S SONG OF VENUS AND ADONIS

Venus fair did ride,
   Silver doves they drew her
By the pleasant lawns,
   Ere the sun did rise;
Vesta's beauty rich
   Opened wide to view her,
Philomel records
   Pleasing harmonies;
     Every bird of spring
     Cheerfully did sing,   10
       Paphos' goddess they salute.
Now love's queen so fair
   Had of mirth no care,
For her son had made her mute.
In her breast so tender
   He a shaft did enter,
When her eyes beheld a boy,
Adonis was he named,
By his mother shamed,
   Yet he now is Venus' joy.   20

Him alone she met,
   Ready bound for hunting;
Him she kindly greets,
   And his journey stays;
Him she seeks to kiss,
   No devices wanting,
Him her eyes still woo,
   Him her tongue still prays.
He with blushing red
Hangeth down the head,   30
   Not a kiss can he afford;
His face is turned away,
Silence said her nay,
   Still she wooed him for a word.
Speak, she said, thou fairest,
Beauty thou impairest;
   See me, I am pale and wan;
Lovers all adore me,
I for love implore thee.
   Crystal tears with that ran down.   40

Him herewith she forced
   To come sit down by her;
She his neck embraced,
   Gazing in his face;
He, like one transformed,
   Stirred no look to eye her.
Every herb did woo him,
   Growing in that place;
     Each bird with a ditty
     Prayèd him for pity   50
       In behalf of beauty's queen;
Waters' gentle murmur
   Cravèd him to love her,
   Yet no liking could be seen.
Boy, she said, look on me,
Still I gaze upon thee,
   Speak, I pray thee, my delight.
Coldly he replied,
And, in brief, denied
   To bestow on her a sight.   60

I am now too young
   To be won by beauty;
Tender are my years,
   I am yet a bud.
Fair thou art, she said,
Then it is thy duty,
Wert thou but a blossom,
   To effect my good.
     Every beauteous flower
     Boasteth in my power,   70
       Birds and beasts my laws effect.
Myrrha, thy fair mother,
   Most of any other
   Did my lovely hests respect.
Be with me delighted,
Thou shalt be requited,
   Every nymph on thee shall tend;
All the gods shall love thee,
Man shall not reprove thee,
   Love himself shall be thy friend.   80

Wend thee from me, Venus,
   I am not disposed;
Thou wring'st me too hard,
   Prithee, let me go;
Fie, what a pain it is
   Thus to be enclosed;
If love begin with labour,
   It will end in woe.
     Kiss me, I will leave.
     Here a kiss receive.   90
       A short kiss I do it find,

The Shepherd's Song. This pastoral version of the classical myth which Shakespeare had treated in the Italianate fashion in his *Venus and Adonis*, 1593, is taken from *England's Helicon*, 1600.   5. **Vesta**, sometimes identified with Terra, the earth.

72. **Myrrha.** Adonis was the incestuous offspring of Myrrha and her father Cinyras, king of Assyria and Cyprus.

  Wilt thou leave me so?
   Yet thou shalt not go;
    Breathe once more thy balmy wind,
It smelleth of the myrrh tree
That to the world did bring thee,
    Never was perfume so sweet.
When she had thus spoken,
She gave him a token,
    And their naked bosoms meet. 100

Now, he said, let's go,
 Hark, the hounds are crying,
Grisly boar is up,
 Huntsmen follow fast.
At the name of boar
Venus seemèd dying,
Deadly-coloured pale,
 Roses overcast.
   Speak, said she, no more
    Of following the boar; 110
    Thou, unfit for such a chase,
   Course the fearful hare,
    Venison do not spare,
     If thou wilt yield Venus grace.
Shun the boar, I pray thee,
Else I still will stay thee.
    Herein he vowed to please her mind;
Then her arms enlarged,
Loath she him discharged,
    Forth he went as swift as wind. 120

Thetis Phoebus' steeds
 In the west retained;
Hunting sport was past,
 Love her love did seek;
Sight of him too soon,
 Gentle queen she gained.
On the ground he lay;
 Blood had left his cheek,
  For an orpèd swine
   Smit him in the groin, 130
    Deadly wound his death did bring.
Which when Venus found
 She fell in a swound,
    And awaked, her hands did wring.
Nymphs and satyrs skipping
Came together tripping,
   Echo every cry expressed.
Venus by her power
Turned him to a flower,
    Which she weareth in her crest. 140

129. orpèd swine, fierce boar. **139. flower,** the anemone, formerly called the adonium.

John Dowland
1563–1626
FINE KNACKS FOR LADIES

Fine knacks for ladies, cheap, choice, brave, and new!
 Good pennyworths! but money cannot move.
I keep a fair but for the fair to view;
 A beggar may be liberal of love.
Though all my wares be trash, the heart is true.

Great gifts are guiles and look for gifts again;
 My trifles come as treasures from my mind.
It is a precious jewel to be plain;
 Sometimes in shell th' orient'st pearls we find.
Of others take a sheaf, of me a grain. 10

Within this pack, pins, points, laces, and gloves,
 And divers toys fitting a country fair;
But my heart lives where duty serves and loves,
 Turtles and twins, court's brood, a heavenly pair.
Happy the heart that thinks of no removes!

Sir Edward Dyer
1543–1607
MY MIND TO ME A KINGDOM IS

My mind to me a kingdom is;
 Such perfect joy therein I find
That it excels all other bliss
 Which God or Nature hath assigned.
Though much I want that most would have,
Yet still my mind forbids to crave.

No princely port, nor wealthy store,
 No force to win a victory,
No wily wit to salve a sore,
 No shape to win a loving eye; 10
To none of these I yield as thrall,—
For why? my mind despise them all.

I see that plenty surfeit oft,
 And hasty climbers soonest fall;
I see that such as are aloft
 Mishap doth threaten most of all.

Fine Knacks. This song by one of the finest of Elizabethan composers of airs for the lute first appeared in his *Second Book of Songs and Airs,* 1600. *My Mind to Me a Kingdom Is.* This succinct and telling expression of the stoicism popular in the period is the work of one of the minor courtly poets. It was set to music by perhaps the greatest composer of the time, William Byrd, and appeared in his *Psalms, Sonnets, and Songs,* 1588.

These get with toil and keep with fear;
Such cares my mind can never bear.

I press to bear no haughty sway,
    I wish no more than may suffice,   20
I do no more than well I may,
    Look, what I want my mind supplies.
Lo! thus I triumph like a king,
My mind content with anything.

I laugh not at another's loss,
    Nor grudge not at another's gain;
No worldly waves my mind can toss;
    I brook that is another's bane.
I fear no foe, nor fawn on friend,
I loathe not life, nor dread mine end.   30

My wealth is health and perfect ease,
    And conscience clear my chief defence;
I never seek by bribes to please,
    Nor by desert to give offence.
Thus do I live, thus will I die,—
Would all did so as well as I!

John Fletcher
1579–1625

LAY A GARLAND ON MY HEARSE

Lay a garland on my hearse of the dismal yew,
Maidens, willow branches bear, say I dièd true.
My love was false, but I was firm from my hour of birth;
Upon my buried body lay lightly, gently, earth.

MELANCHOLY

Hence, all you vain delights,
    As short as are the nights
        Wherein you spend your folly,
There's nought in this life sweet,
    If man were wise to see't,
        But only melancholy,
        Oh, sweetest melancholy.
Welcome, folded arms and fixèd eyes,
    A sigh that piercing mortifies,
    A look that's fastened to the ground,   10
    A tongue chained up without a sound.
Fountain-heads, and pathless groves,
Places which pale passion loves,
Moonlight walks, when all the fowls
Are warmly housed, save bats and owls,
    A midnight bell, a parting groan,
    These are the sounds we feed upon;
Then stretch our bones in a still gloomy valley,
Nothing's so dainty sweet as lovely melancholy.

SLEEP

Care-charming Sleep, thou easer of all woes,
Brother to Death, sweetly thyself dispose
On this afflicted prince; fall like a cloud
In gentle showers; give nothing that is loud
Or painful to his slumbers; easy, sweet,
And as a purling stream, thou son of Night,
Pass by his troubled senses; sing his pain,
Like hollow murmuring wind or silver rain;
Into this prince gently, oh, gently slide,
And kiss him into slumbers like a bride.   10

THE DRINKING SONG

Drink to-day, and drown all sorrow,
You shall perhaps not do it to-morrow.
Best, while you have it, use your breath;
There is no drinking after death.

Wine works the heart up, wakes the wit;
There is no cure 'gainst age but it.
It helps the headache, cough, and tisic,
And is for all diseases physic.

Then let us swill, boys, for our health;
Who drinks well, loves the commonwealth.   10
And he that will to bed go sober,
Falls with the leaf still in October.

LET THE BELLS RING

Let the bells ring, and let the boys sing,
    The young lasses skip and play,
Let the cups go round, till round goes the ground,
    Our learnèd old vicar will stay.

Let the pig turn merrily, merrily, ah,
    And let the fat goose swim;
For verily, verily, verily, ah,
    Our vicar this day shall be trim.

Lay a Garland. This exquisite dirge is from the play *The Maid's Tragedy,* written by Fletcher in collaboration with Francis Beaumont.   *Melancholy.* This song is from Fletcher's play *Nice Valour.* It is one of the sources of the opening lines of Milton's "Il Penseroso."

Sleep. This song is from Fletcher's tragedy *Valentinian.* *The Drinking Song.* This philosophical defense of potations is from Fletcher's tragedy *The Bloody Brother.*   **7. tisic,** phthisic, consumption.   *Let the Bells Ring.* This homely, lusty lyric is from Fletcher's comedy of intrigue *The Spanish Curate.*

The stewed cock shall crow, cock-a-loodle-loo,
   A loud cock-a-loodle shall he crow;   10
The duck and the drake shall swim in a lake
   Of onions and claret below.

Our wives shall be neat, to bring in our meat
   To thee, our most noble adviser;
Our pains shall be great, and bottles shall sweat,
   And we ourselves will be wiser.

We'll labour and swink, we'll kiss and we'll drink,
   And tithes shall come thicker and thicker;
We'll fall to our plough, and get children enow,
   And thou shalt be learnèd old vicar.   20

WEEP NO MORE

Weep no more, nor sigh, nor groan,
Sorrow calls no time that's gone;
Violets plucked, the sweetest rain
Makes not fresh nor grow again;
Trim thy locks, look cheerfully;
Fate's hid ends eyes cannot see.
Joys as wingèd dreams fly fast,
Why should sadness longer last?
Grief is but a wound to woe;
Gentlest fair, mourn, mourn no mo.   10

Orlando Gibbons
1583–1625
THE SILVER SWAN

The silver swan, who living had no note,
When death approached, unlocked her silent throat;
Leaning her breast against the reedy shore,
Thus sung her first and last, and sung no more.
Farewell, all joys; O death, come close mine eyes;
More geese than swans now live, more fools than wise.

Gray of Reading
THE KING'S HUNT IS UP

The hunt is up, the hunt is up,
And it is well nigh day;

And Harry our king is gone hunting,
To bring his deer to bay.

The east is bright with morning light,
And darkness it is fled;
And the merry horn wakes up the morn
To leave his idle bed.

Behold the skies with golden dyes
Are glowing all around;   10
The grass is green, and so are the treen,
All laughing with the sound.

The horses snort to be at the sport,
The dogs are running free;
The woods rejoice at the merry noise
Of hey tantara tee ree!

The sun is glad to see us clad
All in our lusty green,
And smiles in the sky as he riseth high
To see and to be seen.   20

Awake all men, I say again,
Be merry as you may;
For Harry our king is gone hunting
To bring his deer to bay.

Robert Greene
1558?–1592
SEPHESTIA'S SONG TO HER CHILD

Weep not, my wanton, smile upon my knee,
When thou art old there's grief enough for thee.
   Mother's wag, pretty boy,
   Father's sorrow, father's joy,
   When thy father first did see
   Such a boy by him and me,
   He was glad, I was woe;
   Fortune changed made him so,
   When he left his pretty boy,
   Last his sorrow, first his joy.   10

Weep not, my wanton, smile upon my knee,
When thou art old there's grief enough for thee.
   Streaming tears that never stint,
   Like pearl-drops from a flint,
   Fell by course from his eyes,
   That one another's place supplies.

Let the Bells Ring. **17. swink,** slave. *Weep No More.* This touching consolatory lyric is from Fletcher's *Queen of Corinth.* *The Silver Swan.* This perfect but brief lyric, set to one of the most beautiful of Gibbons's madrigals, becomes more impressive if one recalls the manifold repetitions inevitable in that musical form. It first appeared in his *First Set of Madrigals and Motets,* 1612. *The King's Hunt Is Up.* This lively ballad, although written during the reign of Henry the Eighth, was not printed until some time after 1565. The term "hunt's up" referred originally to the tune played on the hunting horns, to arouse sportsmen in the morning.

Sephestia's Song. This lyric is from Robert Greene's prose romance *Menaphon,* 1589. **1. wanton,** pet.

Thus he grieved in every part;
Tears of blood fell from his heart,
When he left his pretty boy,
Father's sorrow, father's joy.   20

Weep not, my wanton, smile upon my knee,
When thou art old there's grief enough for thee.
The wanton smiled, father wept,
Mother cried, baby leapt;
More he crowed, more we cried,
Nature could not sorrow hide.
He must go, he must kiss
Child and mother, baby bliss,
For he left his pretty boy,
Father's sorrow, father's joy.   30
Weep not, my wanton, smile upon my knee,
When thou art old there's grief enough for thee.

THE SHEPHERD'S WIFE'S SONG

Ah, what is love? It is a pretty thing,
As sweet unto a shepherd as a king—
　　And sweeter too,
For kings have cares that wait upon a crown,
And cares can make the sweetest love to frown.
　　Ah then, ah then,
If country loves such sweet desires do gain,
What lady would not love a shepherd swain?

His flocks once folded, he comes home at night
As merry as a king in his delight—   10
　　And merrier too,
For kings bethink them what the state require,
Where shepherds careless carol by the fire.
　　Ah then, ah then,
If country loves such sweet desires gain,
What lady would not love a shepherd swain?

He kisseth first, then sits as blithe to eat
His cream and curds as doth the king his meat—
　　And blither too,
For kings have often fears when they do sup,   20
Where shepherds dread no poison in their cup.
　　Ah then, ah then,
If country loves such sweet desires gain,
What lady would not love a shepherd swain?

To bed he goes, as wanton then, I ween,
As is a king in dalliance with a queen—
　　More wanton too,
For kings have many griefs, affects to move,
Where shepherds have no greater grief than love.
　　Ah then, ah then,   30
If country loves such sweet desires gain,
What lady would not love a shepherd swain?

Upon his couch of straw he sleeps as sound
As doth the king upon his beds of down—
　　More sounder too,
For cares cause kings full oft their sleep to spill,
Where weary shepherds lie and snort their fill.
　　Ah then, ah then,
If country loves such sweet desires gain,
What lady would not love a shepherd swain?   40

Thus with his wife he spends the year, as blithe
As doth the king, at every tide or sithe—
　　And blither too,
For kings have wars and broils to take in hand,
Where shepherds laugh and love upon the land.
　　Ah then, ah then,
If country loves such sweet desires gain,
What lady would not love a shepherd swain?

SWEET ARE THE THOUGHTS

Sweet are the thoughts that savour of content,
　　The quiet mind is richer than a crown;
Sweet are the nights in careless slumber spent,
　　The poor estate scorns fortune's angry frown:
Such sweet content, such minds, such sleep, such bliss,
Beggars enjoy, when princes oft do miss.

The homely house that harbours quiet rest,
　　The cottage that affords no pride nor care,
The mean that grees with country music best,
　　The sweet consort of mirth and music's fare,   10
Obscurèd life sets down a type of bliss;
A mind content both crown and kingdom is.

CUPID ABROAD WAS LATED

Cupid abroad was lated in the night,
　　His wings were wet with ranging in the rain;
Harbour he sought, to me he took his flight
　　To dry his plumes. I heard the boy complain;
　　I oped the door and granted his desire,
　　I rose myself, and made the wag a fire.

Looking more narrow by the fire's flame,
　　I spied his quiver hanging by his back.
Doubting the boy might my misfortune frame,
　　I would have gone, for fear of further wrack;   10

The Shepherd's Wife's Song. This song is one of the most charming of the Elizabethan poetic treatments of the contrast between the simple and the sophisticated life. It is taken from Greene's prose fiction *Greene's Mourning Garment,* 1590.

The Shepherd's Wife's Song. **42. sithe,** time. *Sweet Are the Thoughts.* This song from *Greene's Farewell to Folly,* 1591, should be compared with the lyrics by Dekker (page 441) and Dyer (page 509), which treat the same stoical theme. *Cupid Abroad.* This song in the Anacreontic vein frequently employed later by Robert Herrick is from Greene's prose tale *Orpharion,* 1599.

But what I drad did me, poor wretch, betide,
For forth he drew an arrow from his side.

He pierced the quick, and I began to start,
 A pleasing wound but that it was too high;
His shaft procured a sharp yet sugared smart.
 Away he flew, for why his wings were dry;
  But left the arrow sticking in my breast,
  That sore I grieved I welcomed such a guest.

Tobias Hume
d. 1645

TOBACCO, TOBACCO

Tobacco, tobacco, sing sweetly for tobacco!
 Tobacco is like love, oh love it;
 For you see, I will prove it.
Love maketh lean the fat men's tumour,
 So doth tobacco.
Love still dries up the wanton humour,
 So doth tobacco.
Love makes men sail from shore to shore,
 So doth tobacco.
'Tis fond love often makes men poor,   10
 So doth tobacco.
Love makes men scorn all coward fears,
 So doth tobacco.
Love often sets men by the ears,
 So doth tobacco.
  Tobacco, tobacco,
  Sing sweetly for tobacco.
  Tobacco is like love, oh love it;
  For you see I have proved it.

Thomas Lodge
1558?–1625

ROSALYNDE'S MADRIGAL

Love in my bosom like a bee
 Doth suck his sweet;
Now with his wings he plays with me,
 Now with his feet.
Within mine eyes he makes his nest,
His bed amidst my tender breast,
My kisses are his daily feast,

And yet he robs me of my rest—
 Ah, wanton, will ye?

And if I sleep, then percheth he   10
 With pretty flight,
And makes his pillow of my knee
 The livelong night.
Strike I my lute, he tunes the string.
He music plays if so I sing,
He lends me every lovely thing,
Yet cruel he my heart doth sting—
 Whist, wanton, still ye!

Else I with roses every day
 Will whip you hence,   20
And bind you, when you long to play,
 For your offence.
I'll shut mine eyes to keep you in,
I'll make you fast it for your sin,
I'll count your power not worth a pin;
Alas! what hereby shall I win
 If he gainsay me?

What if I beat the wanton boy
 With many a rod?
He will repay me with annoy,   30
 Because a god.
Then sit thou safely on my knee,
And let thy bower my bosom be,
Lurk in mine eyes, I like of thee.
O Cupid, so thou pity me,
 Spare not, but play thee!

Anthony Munday
1553–1633

TO COLIN CLOUT

Beauty sat bathing by a spring
 Where fairest shades did hide her;
The winds blew calm, the birds did sing,
 The cool streams ran beside her.
My wanton thoughts enticed mine eye
 To see what was forbidden,
But better memory said fie!
 So vain desire was chidden.
  Hey nonny, nonny, &c.

Into a slumber then I fell,   10
 When fond imagination
Seemed to see, but could not tell
 Her feature or her fashion.
But even as babes in dreams do smile
 And sometime fall a-weeping,

Cupid Abroad. **16. for why,** because. *Tobacco.* This song from Hume's *Musical Humours, the First Part of Airs,* 1605, may suggest the rapidity with which smoking became popular after its introduction by Sir Walter Ralegh. *Rosalynde's Madrigal.* This Anacreontic lyric is taken from Lodge's pastoral romance *Rosalynde,* from which Shakespeare took the plot of *As You Like It.*

To Colin Clout. This song is taken from *England's Helicon.*

So I awaked, as wise this while
As when I fell a-sleeping.
Hey nonny, nonny, &c.

Thomas Nashe
1567–1601

SPRING, THE SWEET SPRING

Spring, the sweet spring, is the year's pleasant king;
Then blooms each thing, then maids dance in a ring,
Cold doth not sting, the pretty birds do sing:
 Cuckoo, jug-jug, pu-we, to-witta-woo!

The palm and may make country houses gay,
Lambs frisk and play, the shepherds pipe all day,
And we hear aye birds tune this merry lay:
 Cuckoo, jug-jug, pu-we, to-witta-woo!

The fields breathe sweet, the daisies kiss our feet,
Young lovers meet, old wives a-sunning sit, 10
In every street these tunes our ears do greet:
 Cuckoo, jug-jug, pu-we, to-witta-woo!
  Spring, the sweet spring!

LITANY IN TIME OF PLAGUE

Adieu, farewell earth's bliss,
This world uncertain is;
Fond are life's lustful joys,
Death proves them all but toys,
None from his darts can fly.
 I am sick, I must die.
  Lord, have mercy on us!

Rich men, trust not in wealth,
Gold cannot buy you health;
Physic himself must fade, 10
All things to end are made.
The plague full swift goes by;
 I am sick, I must die.
  Lord, have mercy on us!

Beauty is but a flower
Which wrinkles will devour:
Brightness falls from the air,
Queens have died young and fair,
Dust hath closed Helen's eye.
 I am sick, I must die. 20
  Lord, have mercy on us!

Strength stoops unto the grave,
Worms feed on Hector brave,
Swords may not fight with fate.

Earth still holds ope her gate;
Come! come! the bells do cry.
 I am sick, I must die.
  Lord, have mercy on us!

Wit with his wantonness
Tasteth death's bitterness; 30
Hell's executioner
Hath no ears for to hear
What vain art can reply.
 I am sick, I must die.
  Lord, have mercy on us!

Haste, therefore, each degree,
To welcome destiny.
Heaven is our heritage,
Earth but a player's stage;
Mount we unto the sky. 40
 I am sick, I must die.
  Lord, have mercy on us!

George Peele
1558?–1597?

PARIS AND OENONE

Oenone. Fair and fair and twice so fair,
 As fair as any may be;
The fairest shepherd on our green,
 A love for any lady.

Paris. Fair and fair and twice so fair,
 As fair as any may be;
Thy love is fair for thee alone,
 And for no other lady.

Oenone. My love is fair, my love is gay,
 As fresh as been the flowers in May, 10
And of my love my roundelay,
My merry, merry, merry roundelay
Concludes with Cupid's curse:
They that do change old love for new,
Pray gods they change for worse.

Ambo simul. They that do change, &c.
Oenone. Fair and fair, &c.
Paris. Fair and fair, &c. Thy love is fair, &c.

Oenone. My love can pipe, my love can sing,
 My love can many a pretty thing, 20
 And of his lovely praises ring

Spring, the Sweet Spring. This song and the next, expressing two very different moods, are from Nashe's play *Summer's Last Will and Testament.*

Paris and Oenone. This song is from Peele's play *The Arraignment of Paris,* which was acted before Her Majesty by the company of Children of the Chapel Royal.

My merry, merry roundelays.
                        Amen to Cupid's curse:
They that do change, &c.

Paris. They that do change, &c.
Ambo. Fair and fair, &c.

HIS GOLDEN LOCKS

His golden locks time hath to silver turned;
  Oh, time too swift, oh, swiftness never ceasing!
His youth 'gainst time and age hath ever spurned,
  But spurned in vain; youth waneth by increasing.
Beauty, strength, youth, are flowers but fading seen;
Duty, faith, love, are roots, and ever green.

His helmet now shall make a hive for bees,
  And lover's sonnets turned to holy psalms,
A man-at-arms must now serve on his knees,
  And feed on prayers, which are age his alms;   10
But though from court to cottage he depart,
His saint is sure of his unspotted heart.

And when he saddest sits in homely cell,
  He'll teach his swains this carol for a song:
Blest be the hearts that wish my sovereign well,
  Cursed be the souls that think her any wrong!
Goddess, allow this agèd man his right,
To be your beadsman now, that was your knight.

Robert Southwell
1561?–1595

THE BURNING BABE

As I in hoary winter's night stood shivering in the snow,
Surprised I was with sudden heat which made my heart to glow;
And lifting up a fearful eye to view what fire was near,
A pretty babe all burning bright did in the air appear;
Who, scorchèd with excessive heat, such floods of tears did shed
As though his floods should quench his flames which with his tears were fed.
Alas, quoth he, but newly born in fiery heats I fry,
Yet none approach to warm their hearts or feel my fire but I!

My faultless breast the furnace is, the fuel wounding thorns,
Love is the fire, and sighs the smoke, the ashes shame and scorns;   10
The fuel justice layeth on, and mercy blows the coals,
The metal in this furnace wrought are men's defilèd souls,
For which, as now on fire I am to work them to their good,
So will I melt into a bath to wash them in my blood.
With this he vanished out of sight and swiftly shrunk away,
And straight I callèd unto mind that it was Christmas day.

John Webster
1580?–1625

DIRGE

Call for the robin redbreast and the wren,
Since o'er shady groves they hover,
And with leaves and flowers do cover
The friendless bodies of unburied men.
Call unto his funeral dole
The ant, the field-mouse, and the mole,
To rear him hillocks that shall keep him warm,
And, when gay tombs are robbed, sustain no harm;
But keep the wolf far thence, that's foe to men,
For with his nails he'll dig them up again.

DEATH–SONG

Hark, now everything is still;
The screech-owl and the whistler shrill
Call upon our dame aloud,
And bid her quickly don her shroud;
Much you had of land and rent,
Your length in clay's now competent.
A long war disturbed your mind;
Here your perfect peace is signed.
Of what is 't fools make such vain keeping?
Sin their conception, their birth weeping,   10
Their life a general mist of error,
Their death a hideous storm of terror.
Strew your hair with powders sweet,
Don clean linen, bathe your feet,
And, the foul fiend more to check,

His Golden Locks. This song was written by Peele at the request of Sir Henry Lee, who, finding himself too old to engage in a tournament in honor of Queen Elizabeth, had this poetic apology rendered instead.   *The Burning Babe.* This impassioned lyric, written in old-fashioned "fourteeners," is the best-known poem of the Catholic poet Southwell.

Dirge. This macabre dirge is from Webster's tragedy *The White Devil.* *Death-Song.* This song from Webster's tragedy *The Duchess of Malfi* suggests admirably his preoccupation with dissolution and death. **6. competent,** qualified, fit.

A crucifix let bless your neck;
'Tis now full tide, 'tween night and day,
End your groan and come away.

Thomas Weelkes
1577?–1623

THESE THINGS SEEM WONDROUS

Thule, the period of cosmography,
Doth vaunt of Hecla, whose sulphureous fire

These Things Seem Wondrous. This lyric first appeared in Weelkes's *Madrigals of Six Parts,* 1600. **1. Thule,** the name given by the ancients to the northernmost country in the world; in this case, Iceland. **2. Hecla,** a volcano.

Doth melt the frozen clime and thaw the sky;
Trinacrian Etna's flames ascend not higher:
These things seem wondrous, yet more wondrous I,
Whose heart with fear doth freeze, with love doth fry.

The Andalusian merchant, that returns
Laden with cochineal and china dishes,
Reports in Spain how strangely Fogo burns
Amidst an ocean full of flying fishes: 10
These things seem wondrous, yet more wondrous I,
Whose heart with fear doth freeze, with love doth fry.

4. Trinacrian, Sicilian. **8. cochineal,** dyestuff. **9. Fogo,** a volcano in the Cape Verde Islands.

SUGGESTIONS FOR FURTHER READING

HISTORICAL BACKGROUND

Black, J. B., *The Reign of Elizabeth, 1558–1603,* Oxford Press, 1936. A recent history embodying the latest results of research

Innes, A. D., *England under the Tudors,* Putnam, 1905. An older and more inclusive history in a standard series

Neale, J. E., *Queen Elizabeth,* Harcourt, Brace, 1937. Probably the best recent historical study of that enigmatical queen

Payne, E. J., ed., *Voyages of the Elizabethan Seamen to America,* Oxford Press, 1893. Lively contemporary accounts of adventure and exploration

Read, Conyers, *The Tudors: Personalities and Practical Politics in Sixteenth Century England,* Holt, 1936. Brief but meaty studies of the Tudor sovereigns

Strachey, Lytton, *Elizabeth and Essex: A Tragic History,* Harcourt, Brace, 1928. A brilliant study of the relations of the two

SOCIAL AND INTELLECTUAL LIFE

Burckhardt, J. C., *The Civilization of the Renaissance in Italy,* Boni, 1935. Containing "The Civilization of the Renaissance in Pictures" selected and arranged by Ludwig Goldscheider

Byrne, M. S. C., ed., *The Elizabethan Home, Discovered in Two Dialogues,* Cobden-Sanderson, 1930. Amusing impressions of Elizabethan life set down by two Huguenots teaching the foreign languages in London

——— *Elizabethan Life in Town and Country,* Houghton Mifflin, 1926. Attractively illustrated

Castiglione, Baldassare, *The Book of the Courtier,* Dutton, 1928 (Everyman's Library). The most famous analysis of the ideals of the Renaissance lady and gentleman

Craig, Hardin, *The Enchanted Glass: The Elizabethan Mind in Literature,* Oxford Press, 1936. A difficult but rewarding book

Clements, Arthur F., ed., *Tudor Translations: An Anthology,* Oxford Press, 1940

Davis, W. S., *Life in Elizabethan Days: A Picture of a Typical English Community at the End of the Sixteenth Century,* Harper, 1930

Dunham, W. H., and Pargellis, S. M., eds., *Complaint and Reform in England, 1436–1714,* Oxford Press, 1938. Fifty writings of the time on politics, religion, society, economics, architecture, science, and education

Einstein, Lewis D., *Tudor Ideals,* Harcourt, Brace, 1921

Eliot, John, *The Parlement of Pratlers,* Fanfrolico Press, 1929. A series of Elizabethan dialogues illustrating daily life and the conduct of a gentleman on the grand tour

Harrison, G. B., *Elizabethan Journals, Being a Record of Those Things Mostly Talked of during the Years 1591–1603,* Macmillan, 1939. A fictitious diary, but one based on historical sources

Harrison, William, *Elizabethan England,* Simmons, 1904. The most famous and full contemporary description of the England of that time

Judges, A. V., ed., *The Elizabethan Underworld,* Routledge, 1930. Tudor and early Stuart tracts and ballads

Montaigne, Michel de, *The Essays of Montaigne,* tr. by John Florio, with introd. by J. I. M. Stewart, Modern Library, 1933

Onions, C. T., ed., *Shakespeare's England, an Account of the Life and Manners of His Age,* Oxford Press, 1916. The standard co-operative scholarly review of the background of the age

Wilson, J. D., *Life in Shakespeare's England: A Book of Elizabethan Prose,* Cambridge University Press, 1911

Wright, L. B., *Middle-Class Culture in Elizabethan England,* University of North Carolina Press, 1935. What the solid citizen was reading and thinking

LITERATURE

Dunn, Esther C., *The Literature of Shakespeare's England,* Scribner, 1936. Perhaps the most readable of the more recent surveys

THE SIXTEENTH CENTURY

PROSE

Ascham, Roger, *The Schoolmaster*, ed. by J. E. B. Mayer, London, 1895

Dekker, Thomas, *The Gull's Handbook*, ed. by R. B. McKerrow, Dutton, 1905. An admirably printed edition of this racy satire on young men about town

Hakluyt, Richard, *Heroes from Hakluyt*, ed. by Charles J. Finger, Holt, 1928

Lodge, Thomas, *Rosalynde, or, Euphues' Golden Legacy*, Ginn, 1910

More, Sir Thomas, *Utopia*, Dutton, 1910 (Everyman's Library)

Nash, Thomas, *The Unfortunate Traveler, or, The Life of Jack Wilton*, Greenberg, 1926. The misadventures of a young scapegrace in his travels over Europe

Sidney, Sir Philip, *Apologie for Poetry*, ed. by J. C. Collins, Oxford Press, 1907

—— *The Countess of Pembroke's Arcadia*, Bell, 1934

POETRY

Ault, Norman, ed., *Elizabethan Lyrics, from the Original Texts*, Longmans, Green, 1925. A distinguished collection of the less familiar lyrics

The Oxford Book of Sixteenth Century Verse, ed. by E. K. Chambers, Oxford Press, 1932

Spenser, Edmund, *Amoretti and Epithalamium*, Payson & Clarke (English Replicas). An interesting photographic facsimile of the first edition of this book

—— *The Faerie Queene*, Dutton, 1909 (Everyman's Library)

Jones, H. S. V., *A Spenser Handbook*, Crofts, 1930

DRAMA

Adams, J. Q., *Shakespearean Playhouses: A History of English Theatres from the Beginning to the Restoration*, Houghton Mifflin, 1917

Schelling, F. E., *Elizabethan Playwrights: A Short History of the English Drama from Mediaeval Times to the Closing of the Theaters in 1642*, Harper, 1925

—— and Black, W. W., *Typical Elizabethan Plays by Contemporaries and Immediate Successors of Shakespeare*, Harper, 1931

SHAKESPEARE

Shakespeare, William, *The Complete Works*, ed. by G. L. Kittredge, Ginn, 1936. A convenient one-volume edition with brief introductions by America's most famous teacher of Shakespeare

Bennett, John, *Master Skylark, a Story of Shakespeare's Time*, Century, 1898

Brooke, C. F. T., *Shakespeare of Stratford: A Handbook for Students*, Yale University Press, 1926. A convenient collection of the documents that concern the poet's life

Spencer, Hazelton, *The Art and Life of William Shakespeare*, Harcourt, Brace, 1940

ART

Baker, C. H. C., and Constable, W. G., *English Painting of the Sixteenth and Seventeenth Centuries*, Harcourt, Brace, 1930

Boston Museum of Fine Arts, *Elizabethan England*, Museum Extension Publications, Illustrative Set. No. 1. A splendid collection of forty plates illustrating various features of Elizabethan life

Hartley, Dorothy, and Elliot, M. M., *Life and Work of the People of England: A Pictorial Record from Contemporary Sources: the Sixteenth Century*, Putnam, 1926

Morse, H. K., *Elizabethan Pageantry, a Pictorial Survey of Costume and Its Commentators from c.1560–1620*, Studio Publications, 1934

DRAMATIC AND MUSICAL RECORDINGS

Byrd, William, *Pavane and Galliard*, RCA-Victor 7873

Music by Byrd, Dowland, Morley, Weelkes, and so on, Columbia 15712–17 (Columbia History of Music through the Ear and Eye)

Shakespeare, William, soliloquies from *Hamlet* and *Henry VI*, John Barrymore, RCA-Victor 6827; letter scene and murder scene from *Macbeth*, Sybil Thorndike and Lewis Casson, G–C 1991; *The Merchant of Venice*, complete with narrations, Orson Welles and Mercury Theater Co., Mercury Text Records, Columbia; Readings by John Gielgud, Linguaphone Album; *Richard II*, Maurice Evans and company, C–M 303; *Songs*, by Marie Houston, RCA-Victor P39

The Seventeenth Century

Above. A village scene. When the theater was revived during the Restoration many innovations — such as the employment of actresses for feminine roles — were borrowed from the continent. This company of players is on its way to a tavern; on the village green a play is already in progress. (Bettmann Archive)

Right above. Bleak Hall, the "honest alehouse, where might be found a cleanly room, lavender in the windows, and twenty ballads stuck about the wall." The hostess serving Piscator and Venator was "both cleanly, and handsome, and civil." (Culver)

Center. Bemerton Church. Because George Herbert spent the last three years of his life in devoted service to this small parish and because many of his poems were written here, this is one of the churches that England cherishes.

Milton's cottage at Chalfont St. Giles. When the plague broke out in London in 1665, Milton retired to this cottage in the village of Chalfont St. Giles, and here finished his manuscript of *Paradise Lost*. (Culver)

King Charles II and his cousin, Elizabeth, Princess Palatine. This painting by Janssens of the royal cousins dancing at The Hague suggests the elaborate costumes and the ornate display of the royalists. (Culver)

Old St. Paul's. Gothic in design, with a spire of 534 feet, the old church, covering three and a half acres, was an impressive building. More familiar and more famous is the present domed cathedral erected by Sir Christopher Wren after the great fire. (Culver)

Whitehall Palace. Here Milton resided when he served as Latin Secretary to the Council of State during the Protectorate. This rendering of the building is by the prolific contemporary engraver, Wenceslaus Hollar, a gifted craftsman brought to England from Holland. (Metropolitan Museum)

Cheapside in 1638. The procession glimpsed here is that of Marie de' Medici on her visit to Charles I and his Queen. Later the Puritans pulled down the cross from this square. (Bettmann Archive)

The title page of the First Edition of *Paradise Lost*, published in 1667. (From the original in the Pierpont Morgan Library)

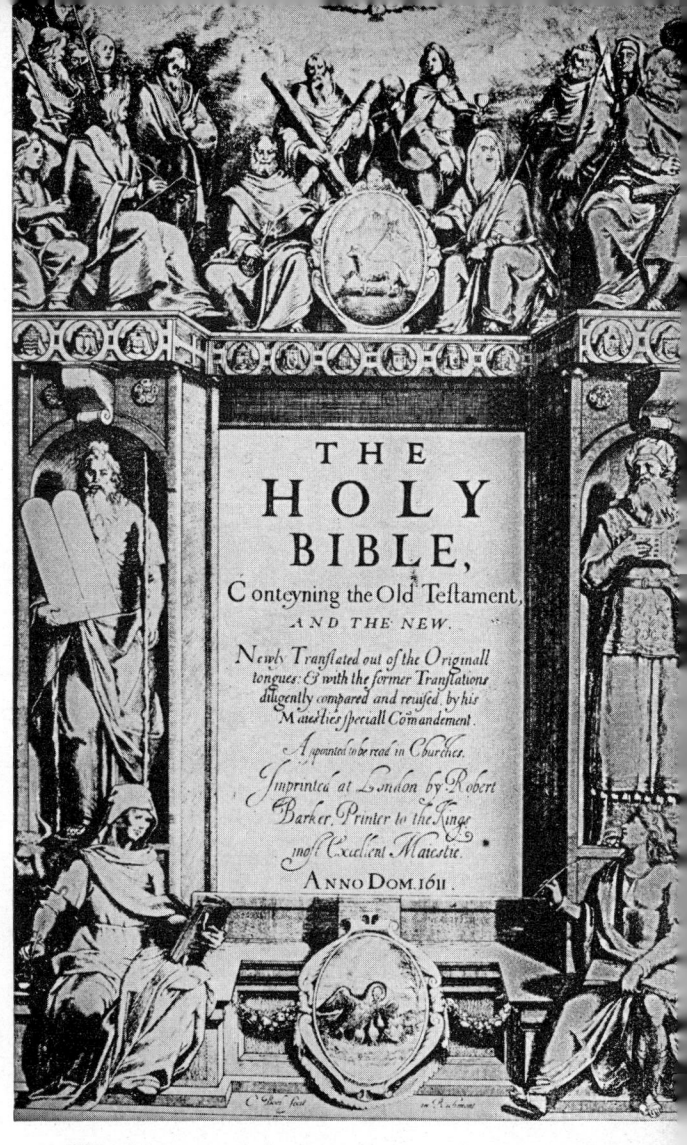

The title page of the King James or Authorized Version of the Bible, 1611. (Museum of Fine Arts, Boston)

Cromwell expelling members from the House of Commons. "I'll put an end to your prating.... Get ye gone! Give way to honest men." This significant event in the Civil War Benjamin West's painting has vigorously commemorated. (Culver)

The *Mayflower* in Plymouth Harbor [Massachusetts]. The Pilgrims, flying from religious persecution, set out from Plymouth, England, to make new homes in America. Trade from England's colonial empire offset somewhat the wastes of the Civil War. (Culver)

JOHN MILTON
From an engraving by Cipriani (Culver)

SAMUEL PEPYS
From a painting by Sir Godfrey Kneller

CHARLES I
After the painting by Van Dyck

SIR JOHN SUCKLING
After the painting by Van Dyck
(The Frick Collection)

THE SEVENTEENTH CENTURY

The Background of the Century

"THE ancients did not know they were ancients," said Voltaire, and by the same token we may say that the people who lived and wrote in the past never thought of themselves as belonging to such periods as the "Age of Chaucer" or the "Age of Elizabeth." It is only through the perspective of centuries and to the eyes of posterity that "ages," "schools," and "spheres of influence" become apparent, and such terms must be used with the consciousness that they are relative and not absolute. The "Age of Elizabeth," for instance, did not end with the passing of the great Queen. Indeed, some of the greatest "Elizabethans" were as much a part of the England of James I and Charles I as of that of Elizabeth. Sir Walter Raleigh, who is commonly regarded as the very embodiment of Elizabethanism, did his greatest work as both man and writer in the seventeenth century. Shakespeare lived on to write all his greatest plays after 1600. By far the most important part of Ben Jonson's work appeared after the turn of the century. On the other hand, John Donne, who is usually thought of as peculiarly of the seventeenth century, probably wrote most of his better-known poetry before the death of Elizabeth. Again, such definitely seventeenth-century figures as Herrick, Milton, and Marvell exhibit here and there so much spiritual kinship with the great writers of the generations preceding them that each has been by someone or other styled "the last of the Elizabethans."

It is clear that the year 1600 marked no special turning-point in English thought or expression, and was neither the end nor the beginning of an "age." Human nature does not step, at a given date, from one condition to another, ticket in hand like a tourist, or brand on flank like a sheep. For the sake of convenience, however, we may take 1603, the year in which Queen Elizabeth died, as a vantage point from which to view the scene that she left, and to survey the stirring acts which were to come.

The hundred years which elapsed between the death of Elizabeth (1603) and the death of William of Orange (1702) saw the coming into being of the England and the British Empire and, indeed, the America that we know. During this period the English language as we know it, English prose as we write it, and a large number of the greatest classics of English literature came into existence. It may be questioned whether any single century in British history added so many strands to the fabric into which are woven the fundamental ideals, faiths, philosophies, habits of mind, and principles of action of the English-speaking peoples. Physically, intellectually, politically, and socially, the England of Elizabeth was transformed almost beyond recognition, and in many ways of which Elizabeth perhaps would not have approved. The old Queen would probably have felt more at home in the London of Chaucer than in that of Dryden and Mr. Pope.

The seventeenth century constitutes one of the major periods of transition in European history. The most fervent Elizabethan imagination could hardly have dreamed of the expansion that was to take place in both the physical boundaries and the intellectual horizons of the English people. At the beginning of the century, England was only a part of a small island in the North Sea. Great Britain itself had not yet come into being as a political unit, as Scotland was still a separate kingdom. In 1601 England did not own a single possession outside Europe. Under the Stuarts the exodus and the great expansion began, prompted by various causes—love of adventure, desire for power, the influence of commerce, and the seeking of freedom from religious persecutions. Whatever the cause, the result was that within the century Englishmen scattered themselves over the world as settlers, traders, and seekers of liberty of worship—in the Americas from Nova Scotia to Florida, in the West Indies and the East Indies, in the Near East and the Far East, and in the Southern Seas. The insularity of England began to pass away; the household gods of little England were carried over the seas to other countries, and there evolved gradually a New England, a new Thames, a new Boston, and a New York. Sir Walter Raleigh, the first of the great empire-builders, had a vision of such an empire as had not been seen on earth for over a thousand years, embracing a vast region in South America, governed by just laws, and developed honorably by the riches of the soil.

While men were extending their boundaries and acquainting themselves with the planet on which they lived, they were also beginning to increase their knowledge of the universe which lies beyond it. Galileo's telescope in 1609 brought within their ken the satellites of Jupiter, and disclosed to their eyes worlds which had not been dreamed of before. It would be hard to overestimate the effect on the human mind and imagination of the "Tuscan artist's optic glass." It was not until Galileo had thus demonstrated Jupiter's system of satellites that the world began to accept the Copernican hypothesis of the solar system, which had been given to the world in 1543. As the man of the twentieth century looks back at the seventeenth, one of the things which impress him most is the sense of space and spaciousness which developed in the European mind during that period. This enlarged universe is reflected in both the prose and the poetry of seventeenth-century writers. The vast cosmic distances of Milton's *Paradise Lost*, as Miss Marjorie Nicolson has pointed out,[1] would have been unthinkable fifty years before. Meanwhile, man was discovering still another world through the microscope, and acquiring an entirely new realm for observation and research. The telescope and the microscope in a single century added perhaps as much to man's accurate knowledge of physical phenomena as all the previous centuries had made possible.

The seventeenth century was not a peaceful, easy, or happy period. Politically, the first half of the century was overshadowed by the progress of the Thirty Years' War. It was, throughout, an age of strife and conflict, of both minds and armies. There were conflicting ideals of liberty and despotism, of reason and authority, of skepticism and superstition, of the laboratory and the library. And yet, defaced as it was by wars, persecutions, intolerance, superstition, and prejudice, the historians of the age find it on the whole a period of progress and development. Preserved Smith in his survey[2] sees no decisive victory on either side in the warfare between many conflicting ideas and ideals, but as the century wore on the progressives and the liberals got the advantage of their opponents, and, for better or worse, "made the world safer for the Republican, the Protestant, the heretic, the scientist, and the modern."

The great men of the century were builders rather than destroyers. And the history of the seventeenth century in Europe is not so much a record of things and events as of men. Few equal periods of time can show such a gallery of great characters. The essence of Renaissance thought was its humanism, its belief in man and in the creative power of man's mind. The individual came into his own, and "rugged individualism" triumphed as it had seldom triumphed before. Whatever department of endeavor one surveys presents men of heroic qualities to the eye. Philosophy flourished with Bacon, Descartes, Spinoza, Hobbes, Leibnitz, and Locke. Galileo and Kepler helped usher in the century, and Newton, Boyle, and Napier illumined its progress and charted its course. Shakespeare's genius reached its maturity during the first two decades, and Milton raised English poetry to new heights during its span. English music flourished as never before with Henry Purcell. The oratorio and the opera came of age with Monteverde and Alessandro Scarlatti. A single year, 1685, saw the birth of Bach, Handel, and Domenico Scarlatti. To paint its canvases the

---

[1] "Milton and the Telescope," *Journal of English Literary History*, Vol. II, pp. 1–32.   [2] *A History of Modern Culture*, Holt, 1930, Vol. 1.

century had, among many others, El Greco, Rembrandt, Rubens, Vermeer, Velasquez, Van Dyck, and Murillo. The captains and the kings included Louis XIV, Richelieu, Cromwell, and Peter the Great. In Britain alone, and among men of lesser stature, the names that come to mind call up stirring memories: Raleigh, Eliot, Hampden, Pym, Donne, Burton, Bunyan, Penn, Pepys, and Dryden. The century mothered such men as Defoe, Swift, Addison, and Pope. "The imaginative drama had died out," says Thorold Rogers, "since living men were more characteristic than the subtlest pictures of the past. There has been and there will be no period in English history which commands and deserves such attention . . . for memory sees gods ascending out of the earth."[3]

Something of the intellectual and social ferment of the time has already been indicated. Many old systems of thought and practice were crumbling, and new systems and ideas were slowly and uncertainly, but none the less surely, taking their places. The discoveries were not always pleasant—they included the spots on the sun as well as the moons of Jupiter. The line of progress was not a straight or a steady one. Bacon, through the inductive method of reasoning that he developed in his *Novum Organum* and the great inspiration which he gave to all inquiring minds by his advocacy of experimental research, proved his right to the title Macaulay gave him—"the man that moved the minds that moved the world." And yet Bacon refused to accept Kepler's theories of the density and solidity of the earth, and steadfastly denied its revolution about the sun. If Galileo felt the effects of the bigotry of the Inquisition, he displayed even worse bigotry in his treatment of Kepler, whose completion of the work of Copernicus he rejected. King Charles II was sufficiently interested in scientific experiments to become in 1662 the patron of the "Royal Society of London for Promoting Natural Knowledge," but Pepys tells us that "he mightily laughed at" the members of the society "for spending time only in weighing of air, and doing nothing else since they sat."[4]

The seventeenth century may be truly said to have laid the foundations of modern astronomy, but astrology continued active long after 1700, and has indeed its ardent adherents in the twentieth century. Kepler, who perfected the Copernican hypothesis and discovered and charted the motions of the planets, was not above casting horoscopes for noble families. It has been wittily remarked that Superstition brought up Science until the ungrateful youngster left home. The first Astronomer Royal of England, the Reverend John Flamsteed, believed in and practiced astrology, and it is a significant fact that the foundation stone of the Royal Observatory at Greenwich was laid on August 10, 1675, at the hour and minute determined as most favorable by Flamsteed's astrological reckonings.

The literature of the day affords numerous illustrations of the intellectual interest in the new astronomy mingled with sentimental attachments to older notions, as in John Donne's sonnet beginning

"At the round earth's imagined corners, blow
Your trumpets, angels. . . ."

Milton seems to have been intellectually convinced of the truth of the Copernican hypothesis, and in Book VIII of *Paradise Lost* the Archangel Raphael speculates interestingly upon "celestial motions." For theological and artistic reasons, however, Milton employs, with adaptations, the Ptolemaic theory for the cosmology of his great poem. Intellectually curious as he was, and as he wished his Adam to be, he represents Raphael as less interested in Adam's acquiring a thorough knowledge of all the heavenly motions than in his pupil's understanding the priority and excellence of spiritual integrity and moral obedience:

"This to attain, whether heaven move or earth,
Imports not, if thou reckon right. . . ."

The seventeenth century gave chemistry to the world, and yet it produced its full quota of treatises on alchemy. Ben Jonson in his play *The Alchemist* was not describing or satirizing an imaginary situation. Alchemy was the great love of Sir Isaac Newton's life, as his notes testify. Robert Boyle, "the father of chemistry," a believer in the transmutability of metals, confided to Newton and Locke his recipe for "multiplying gold," and a company was formed in London to put the process into operation. "I am half of opinion," Sir Thomas Browne has a habit of saying, and the century as a whole was of a mind with Sir Thomas. Samuel Pepys, though a president of the Royal Society, and keenly interested in

---

[3] J. E. Thorold Rogers, *Six Centuries of Work and Wages*, Scribner, 1884, chap. XVI. [4] *Diary*, Feb. 1, 1663/4. "What they were doing," says G. N. Clark, *The Later Stuarts, 1660–1714*, Oxford Press, 1929, p. 42, "was to investigate atmospheric pressure, and it was a short step to the pressure of steam. The experimenters themselves did not foresee that the motive power which came into practical use as a result of their work, and which before the death of Queen Anne was raising water from a mine in Staffordshire, was to become after two more generations one of the governing forces of the world."

every new scientific discovery, nevertheless preserved old charms and spells, and kept his hare's foot in his pocket to be on the safe side. There was no clear distinction between the realms and functions of religion and theology and those of natural science. The Bible was considered the final authority on all matters of which it treats, and sooner or later it treats of most matters in the heavens above and the earth beneath. The Bible declares, "Thou shalt not suffer a witch to live," and in the face of such a categorical statement it was a bold man who would undertake to doubt the existence of witches. Furthermore, to deny the existence of evil spirits, such as witches, seemed to many to imply the denial of the existence of beneficent spiritual forces, and such a denial would have been unthinkable in the seventeenth century. So Sir Thomas Browne, although he undertook in his *Pseudodoxia Epidemica, or Vulgar Errors* to disprove many erroneous opinions "commonly presumed truths," never questioned the existence of witches. Among his learned contemporaries who likewise believed in them were Henry More, Sir Isaac Newton, and Joseph Glanvill.[5] Sir Thomas saw clearly that "the mortallest enemy unto knowledge, and that which hath done the greatest execution upon truth, hath been a peremptory adhesion unto authority, and, more especially, the establishing of our belief upon the dictates of antiquity."[6] In this he agrees with Bacon, but, in characteristic fashion, he calls up one authority to lay low another, and too often blasts one dictate of antiquity with another of the same vintage. Sir Thomas was an experimentalist, and produced some results of lasting value by his use of the laboratory method. But there were occasions when he had to regret that there was no time to conduct "those infallible experiments and those assured determinations which the subject sometimes requireth."

The age of specialization had, of course, not yet arrived. Bacon, it will be remembered, took all knowledge for his province. The seventeenth century was the golden age of the amateur, and the world has perhaps never seen such a group of versatile, accomplished, and well-rounded men. Clergymen were authorities on all matters, bishops designed flying boats, lawyers knew the fine points of theology, physicians wrote exquisite lyrics and impassioned prose. The Warden of the Mint, Sir Isaac Newton, discovered the laws of motion and gravity, and also found time for a treatise on the Book of Revelation which he considered the crowning achievement of his life. If such restless and insatiable curiosity about all things, and such wholesale and universal interest in all departments of human life and thought, were bound to lead often to shallowness and irrelevancy, the men of the seventeenth century at any rate avoided the pitfalls of too great specialization of interest and research, which the men of the twentieth century do not always escape.

There was not yet a sufficient recognition of the fact that there are different categories of knowledge and phenomena. In the desire to solve the great puzzle of the world and to discover relations between groups of phenomena, the love of tracing analogy and the temptation to press an analogy once discerned ever farther and farther led many men of the Middle Ages to false conclusions in many matters.[7] The bulk of medieval science has been briefly characterized as a misuse of analogy, and such misuse has continued to be one of the greatest sources of human error. The importance of the proper use of analogy and its indispensable service as a handmaid of scientific thought are, of course, not to be questioned. But by the extensive misuse of analogy, and by often reasoning logically from false premises, men had managed to construct a scheme of the universe that was fairly coherent, but which, when tested by observation and experiment, was bound to crumble. The seventeenth century inherited such schemes, and much of the ancient and medieval misinformation about natural phenomena remained part of the "mental climate" of Europe until well on in the century, and continued to be part of the impedimenta of enlightened writers as well as of the people at large. The important fact, however, that emerges from a study of the scientific thought and opinion of the century is not that such and such persons believed such and such things, but that a good many persons were beginning to question old beliefs, and to discover that much which had been accepted on the authority of the ancients is not true. A new spirit of inquiry and criticism was making itself felt. At about this time, says Owen Barfield, "the words *curious, curiosity,* and *inquisitive* seem to have lost the air of pious disapproval which they had previously carried with them when used to express the love of inquiry."[8] The very words "skep-

---

[5] For all its belief in witchcraft, the seventeenth century was also the first in which there was expressed an official disbelief of it, and Sir Matthew Hale, the Lord Chief Justice, has the honor of being the first judge in England to refuse a conviction for witchcraft. [6] *Pseudodoxia Epidemica,* Book I, chap. VI.

[7] One of the most interesting of all analogies, and perhaps the most popular in the seventeenth century, is that between the body and life of man, the "microcosm," on the one hand, and the matter and forces of the universe, the "macrocosm," on the other. For a discussion of the ramifications of this analogy and of many other related matters, see John Read, *Prelude to Chemistry,* Macmillan, 1937. [8] *History in English Words,* Doran, 1926, chap. VIII.

tic," "skepticism," "dubious," "dubitable," which we use to express such a spirit, first came into use, as Barfield points out, in the first half of the seventeenth century.

An indication of the progress which was being made in the method of scientific research as early as the 1640's is to be found in the minutes of the proceedings of the "Philosophical or Invisible College," which was later to be incorporated as the Royal Society. The members, says the record,

"will not own any hypothesis, system, or doctrine of the principles of natural philosophy, proposed or maintained by any philosopher ancient or modern . . . nor dogmatically define nor fix axioms of scientifical things; but will question and canvass all opinions, adopting nor adhering to none, till by mature debate and clear arguments, chiefly such as are deduced from legitimate experiments, the truth of such positions be demonstrated invincibly."

The foundations laid three hundred years ago are those upon which the scientists, scholars, and philosophers of the past two centuries have built. Dr. William Harvey, the discoverer of the circulation of the blood, formed his hypotheses only after careful and unfettered observation, and then tested them by experiments, thus providing the essential basis of the contributions of all his distinguished successors in physiology and medicine. The cell theory of modern biology was first announced by Robert Hooke in 1667 in his *Micrographia*, in which he described the little chambers or cells which he had observed through his simple microscope in sections of cork. Rudolf Glauber, alchemist and chemist, while looking for the philosopher's stone discovered hydrochloric acid; and the results of his researches in breaking down inorganic matter into its component parts are among the greatest contributions to modern pharmacy. The development of modern mathematics, physics, and astronomy had to wait until Descartes and the devising of an adequate system of symbolic representations of quantities and operations. The century provided the mathematician with such important new tools as logarithms, analytical geometry, the slide rule, and the calculus. As the century advanced, the results of this intellectual curiosity and scientific experimentation began to be apparent in many ways. New standards of measurement were needed for the new sciences, new names were required for them, and the nomenclature of modern science began to form. It is an interesting coincidence that the words "gas" and "electricity" were both coined about 1645. The Belgian chemist Van Helmont, needing a word to describe all forms of "elastic fluid," invented the word "gas" (it was the Greek word "chaos" which suggested it to him), and Sir Thomas Browne enriched the language by the word "electricity." [9]

Not only was pure science stimulated by all this activity, but applications of scientific principles in various ways were beginning to change and ameliorate social and industrial conditions. Inventions and discoveries increased in spite of opposition, intolerance, and the civil strife. In his *New Atlantis* Bacon gave a mighty impetus to the inventive imagination by his description of the projects of Solomon's House. Experiments with steam engines were made, and in 1680 Newton predicted steam-propelled carriages. There seemed, to the more imaginative at least, no limit to man's capabilities and ingenuity. Of the members of the Royal Society and their work, Joseph Glanvill exclaimed:

"Should those heroes go on, as they have happily begun, they'll fill the world with wonders. And I doubt not but posterity will find many things, that are now but rumours, verified into practical realities. It may be some ages hence, a voyage to the southern unknown tracts, yea possibly the moon, will not be more strange than one to America. To them that come after us it may be as ordinary to buy a pair of wings to fly into remotest regions as now a pair of boots to ride a journey. And to confer at the distance of the Indies by sympathetic conveyances may be as usual to future times as to us in a literary correspondence. The restoration of gray hairs to juvenility, and renewing the exhausted marrow, may at length be effected without a miracle; and the turning of the now comparative desert world into a paradise may not improbably be expected from late agriculture." [10]

Philosophy tended more and more during the century to concern itself with "reason" and with matters capable of scientific experimentation and mathematical demonstration. The "laws of nature" occupied an increasingly larger share of man's thought, and began to take their place by the side of the "revealed truth" of the Bible. To the more devout scientists these studies in natural philosophy

---

[9] "Crystal will calify unto electricity, that is, a power to attract straws or light bodies, and convert the needle freely placed."—*Pseudodoxia Epidemica*, Book II, chap. I. [10] *Scepsis Scientifica*, 1665. Glanvill's book, edited by John Owen, was reprinted in London in 1885. It was from a story in this book that Matthew Arnold drew his inspiration for "The Scholar-Gypsy."

seemed to supplement and re-enforce rather than to supersede the truths of the Bible. Sir Thomas Browne, an ardent believer in the Bible, commended those who magnify God by "judicious inquiry into His acts and deliberate research into His creatures." By the end of the century, thanks to the work of the scientists and the philosophers, a state of mind had been induced in which such phenomena as conflagrations, plagues, and death came to be viewed less as evidences of Divine displeasure than as natural effects and circumstances, and natural methods were undertaken to deal with them. Before the century was over, both fire insurance and life insurance had arrived in England.

The development of education and scholarship, though retarded somewhat by civil unrest, proceeded apace. The opening years of the century found both Oxford and Cambridge largely medieval in methods, aims, and outlook. The medieval shells had not been entirely discarded by 1700, but in no comparable period, perhaps, did more new ideas penetrate the ancient institutions, and seldom have they ever been subject to more severe criticism than they received from their bright young men during that time. Milton, though he would still have found much to disapprove of at Cambridge, would not have had so much justification in 1700 as he had in 1644 for contemptuously dismissing the entire curriculum as "an asinine feast of sow-thistles and brambles." The beginnings of modern English scholarship may be traced to the period of the Stuarts. The study of the Old English language and grammar, of old customs, laws, and precedents, was revived, both to re-enforce the arguments against the prevailing theory of the divine right of kings and out of "remembrance of things past." Interest in medieval scholarship flourished in England as never before. Scholars played an active part in the life of the time, and exercised in their writings a lasting influence on national character.

The intellectual resurgence at Cambridge was due chiefly to the group of scholars and philosophers known as the Cambridge Platonists. Most of their leaders, including Benjamin Whichcote, Ralph Cudworth, and John Smith, were trained at Emmanuel College, which was their physical home and the center from which their spiritual influence radiated. Another leader, Henry More, came from Christ's College, which he had entered half a year before Milton left. Their aim was to bring the Christian Church back to "her old loving nurse, the Platonic philosophy." Their Platonism has been described in the Wordsworthian phrase, "Reason in her most exalted mood," and the best summary of their attitude is the dictum of John Smith: "To follow reason is to follow God." They believed, as did Sir Thomas Browne, that there is no conflict between "reason" and "revelation," and that Divine revelation is not confined to the Bible or to the period of history with which it is concerned. More than any other men of their day they reconciled and brought to a focus in their own system of thought the religious, philosophic, and scientific thinking of the day. They were Puritan in origin, but they steered a middle course between Puritan and Royalist controversy as they did between Protestant and Catholic dogmatism. In their lives they united the vision and spiritual sensitiveness of the mystics with a belief in practical and positive goodness. In their desire to reconcile the historic beliefs of the Christian religion with the philosophy of their time, they were as a group drawn to the principles of Descartes, who had shown sufficiently clearly that faith and reason were not antagonists but mutual supports. Dr. Whichcote went so far as to advocate the use of the inductive method of reasoning in the solution of theological problems as well as those of natural science. They were hostile to the materialistic philosophy of Hobbes, and tried valiantly to check its influence. Since they were moderate men and advocates of "sweet reasonableness," the extremists of the day in religion and politics would have none of them. Their influence, if it could have been more widespread, might have helped to avoid the crisis of civil war. In their quiet way they began the renewal of the intellectual life of Cambridge, and from Emmanuel College their influence spread to other sections of the university. It was from Emmanuel College that John Harvard came to Massachusetts to save the little college that was later to bear his name, and thus the intellectual leaven of the Cambridge Platonists was brought across the Atlantic.[11]

The attempts to improve the educational methods of the secondary schools on the Continent and in England were even more numerous and effective. The modern world is indebted to the theories of Comenius, Milton, Cowley, Locke, and their contemporaries for some of its most cherished ideas relating to the education of children. Learning for learning's sake came to be less and less esteemed; the knowledge of foreign languages was beginning to be regarded as a means rather than as an end in itself. The teaching of things rather than words was

[11] For a discussion of the Cambridge Platonists and their significance, see F. J. Powicke, *The Cambridge Platonists*, Harvard University Press, 1926, and W. R. Inge, *The Platonic Tradition in English Religious Thought*, Longmans, Green, 1926.

advocated. The ideal of education came more and more to be the preparation of a man for service in a world of men and affairs, rather than the production of a cloistered polyglot. For comprehensiveness Milton's definition of education in 1644 can hardly be improved upon: "I call, therefore, a complete and generous education, that which fits a man to perform justly, skilfully, and magnanimously, all the offices, both private and public, of peace and war." John Locke, one of the first great champions of the rights of children as rational individuals, announced in his little book *Some Thoughts Concerning Education*, 1693, what has become the essential formula for all modern education: "A sound mind in a sound body is a short but full description of a happy state in this world. He that has these two has little more to wish for; and he that wants either of them will be but little better for anything else." Before the century had run its course, Mary Astell and others were turning their attention to the education of girls and young women.[12] These educational advantages were, of course, open only to young gentlemen and ladies. The children of the poor had still to wait two centuries before they began to receive similar consideration.

The social changes brought about by some of the circumstances we have mentioned are an important part of the history of the time. Habits, customs, manners, diet—all were affected significantly. Tea, coffee, cocoa, champagne, and ices made their appearance in England. Oranges, lemons, coconuts, and sugar cane came into use. Most Englishmen, however, still looked with suspicion upon fruits and vegetables, and stuck to their old diet. Potatoes had been known since Elizabeth's days, but medical opinion was against them, and the seal of official approval was not put upon them until the eighteenth century. Elegance and convenience were both served when forks made their appearance at table, and by the end of the century gentlemen were beginning to remove their hats when they dined. The ancient and noble sport of falconry was losing to the more democratic diversion of horse racing. Fine new French coaches with glass windows were ordered by the gentry.[13] The first horse-drawn hackney coach began to solicit fares in the streets of London, and the Thames watermen complained that their means of livelihood would be taken from them as people began to use the new vehicles instead of the river boats. Of all the changes brought about by new inventions, the most far-reaching, perhaps, were those attendant upon the introduction of the pendulum clock and the hairspring watch. As Professor G. N. Clark points out,[14] in the seventeenth century clocks became common possessions, and ceased to be articles of luxury. The minute hand was added to the clock, and the seconds began to be numbered for the first time. "The clock is the modern idol," says Professor Clark. "Punctuality, exactness, system, as we understand them, were becoming necessary in daily life."

The ameliorating and civilizing influences of scientific thought, or of invention and discovery, did not during the century penetrate below the upper strata of society. The great mass of the people continued to live as they had lived for generations. The "social consciousness" of the present day had hardly begun to develop. The prevailing temper of the age was aristocratic, and the great figures of the time were too concerned with their particular interests in Church and State, in poetry or philosophy or science—or simply in getting and spending—to be interested in social welfare. Here and there a lone voice called attention to the condition of the poorer classes, and made a suggestion for improving their lot. Robert Burton, the wise and whimsical scholar of Oxford, in his role of Democritus, Junior, in the *Anatomy of Melancholy*, pleads the cause of the "plebeians," the common people who do the world's work, and the "proletaries," who fight the battles. From this strange old book comes one of the most interesting, and radical, recommendations of the time:

"If one half-day in the week were allowed to our household servants for their merry meetings by their hard masters, or in a year some feasts, like those Roman Saturnalia, I think they would labour harder all the rest of their time, and both parties be better pleased."[15]

In Bunyan's *Pilgrim's Progress*, although the author is concerned only with the spiritual and religious significance of Christian's journey, he unwittingly gives us many pictures of the England he lived in and glimpses of the everyday life and conditions of ordinary folk. The plot of the book, reduced to essentials, is the story of a poor man who leaves home, with a bundle on his back, to better his condition. On the way he meets his overlord, Apollyon, who orders him to return to his service. Christian replies:

---

[12] See Mary Astell, *A Serious Proposal to the Ladies for the Advancement of Their True and Greatest Interest*, 1694. [13] For an interesting account of conditions among the upper classes of the time, see Gladys S. Thompson, *Life in a Noble Household, 1641–1700*, Knopf, 1937.

[14] *The Seventeenth Century*, Oxford Press, 1929, chap. II.
[15] *Anatomy of Melancholy*, Partition II, Sec. 2, Member 4.

"I was born, indeed, in your dominions, but your service was hard, and your wages such as a man could not live on . . . therefore, when I was come to years, I did as other considerate persons do, look out, if perhaps I might mend myself. . . . I have let myself to another . . . I like his service, his wages, his servants, his government, his company and country, better than thine; and therefore leave off to persuade me further."

Such a statement, quite apart from its allegorical significance, is evidence of a changing attitude on the part of the working classes, although many years were to elapse before their economic and social conditions were to be materially altered. In general, and by all classes, it was taken for granted that there was a state of life to which it pleased God to call each man, and it was for him to do his duty in it. Those who had been called to the higher ranks did not consider it any business of theirs to interfere with or question the Divine disposal of men and duties.

In spite of social and intellectual cleavages and distinctions, the various classes of society were, nevertheless, in a very real sense members of one another, and all were alike subject to the alarums and excursions of the time. The birth rate and the death rate were high among rich and poor—infant mortality appallingly high. The absence of anything like effective sanitation, and the equally serious deficiency of medical knowledge, were responsible for disease and pestilence among all classes. Famines exacted their toll, and conflagrations, of which the Great Fire of London (1666) was the most terrible, wiped out cathedrals and palaces as well as hovels and tenements. And yet population increased in the midst of wars and plagues and poverty and fire. The England of William III had, it is estimated, five and a half million souls, an increase of a million over that of Elizabeth, and London had by 1700 become a metropolis of more than a quarter of a million inhabitants. The city that was dominated by Sir Christopher Wren's new St. Paul's had more and finer churches than ever, and, in addition, libraries, museums, banks, coffeehouses, and many other institutions which Elizabethan London had never known.

English History in the Seventeenth Century

If we turn from this "general map of man" in the century to a consideration of the more immediate historical background of English literature, we notice that the pattern of events is, even more than in Europe as a whole, one of revolution and change. The most important factor in the political as in the literary history of the time was the religious revolution which came to a focus in the Puritan revolt. In this matter, as in most others, the era of the Stuarts cannot be dissociated from that of Elizabeth. Puritanism as a religious force had already assumed such proportions before Elizabeth died as to cause alarm or thanksgiving, according to the respective principles of those who viewed its growth. Thomas Fuller gives the following account of the origin of the Puritans:

"The English bishops . . . began to show their authority in urging the clergy of their diocese to subscribe to the liturgy, ceremonies, and discipline of the Church, and such as refused the same were branded with the odious name of Puritans; a name which in this notion first began in this year [1563-64]."[16]

The Queen expressed by word and deed her displeasure at the motives and methods of the Puritans, and increasingly severe measures were taken to force them to conform. By 1593 Puritanism had been made an offense against the statute law, and as a result many of the more conspicuous Puritans crossed the sea to Holland. The comparatively peaceful period which closed Elizabeth's reign was abruptly ended when her successor, James I, full of a sense of importance as head of Church and State, and obsessed with the idea of the divine right of both kings and bishops, added to the burdens of the Puritans as well as to those of most of his subjects. James's troubles with Parliament began soon after his accession. Elizabeth, thanks to her sex, her age, and her prestige, had taken many liberties and done many things which her successor, a man and a Stuart, was not permitted by Parliament to do with impunity. But the King had his way in the Church. Hundreds of ministers who could not subscribe to the articles of the Church were deprived of their livings, many of them were imprisoned, and the number of exiles constantly increased. By the end of his reign in 1625, James had, through his bigotry, his worldliness, and his general disregard for the convictions of his more sober and decent subjects, as well as for the opinions of the House of Commons, brought the country to almost open insurrection. The breach between the Puritans on one hand, and Church and State on the other had become irrepa-

[16] *Church History of Britain*, 1655.

rable. The condition in which his son, Charles I, found England is described by one of his subjects, James Howell:

"He is left engaged in a war with a potent prince, the people by long desuetude unapt for arms, the fleet royal in quarter repair, himself without a queen, his sister without a country, the crown pitifully laden with debts, and the purse of the state lightly ballasted, though it never had better opportunity to be rich than it had these last twenty years."[17]

Of all men in England the new king was the least likely to undo the damage and restore national unity. He was more sincerely devoted to the Church than was his father, and, if not so strongly addicted to the doctrine of the divine right of the king, he nevertheless pressed it farther. His absolutist theories, which were encouraged by the bishops, increased the hostility of Parliament to both King and bishops. His marriage to the Roman Catholic princess, Henrietta Maria of France, seriously disturbed the country, which was becoming increasingly fearful of the growth of Catholicism. Financial difficulties increased, the Crown jewels were pawned, and forced loans were instituted. Two Parliaments were dissolved by the imperious sovereign when they failed to comply with his demands for money. But the King could not get along without funds, and he could not get funds without Parliament. He called a third Parliament in 1628, and in this assembly he met his match. He was forced to sign the Petition of Right, which, among other things, declared illegal such measures as forced loans, martial law in time of peace, and invasions of the rights of subjects such as the billeting of soldiers in private houses.[18]

The King's character and methods had not changed, however. This Parliament, too, was dissolved, and for eleven years, from 1629 until 1640, the King ruled without Parliament. Conditions grew steadily more intolerable. The King's activities included both petty exactions and restrictions and major offenses against the law of the land. Obsolete laws and customs were revived. Charles felt it necessary to strengthen the fleet against the French and the Dutch, and as there was no Parliament to grant him the necessary funds, he resorted in 1634 to an ancient custom and issued writs to the port towns requiring them to furnish ships. In the following year he included inland counties in the demand. With the money thus obtained the King built up a navy entirely under his own control, and continued the levy of ship money to maintain the fleet. The principle involved, that of raising taxes without parliamentary grant, was so important, and so capable of abuse, that John Hampden, a gentleman of Buckinghamshire, determined to bring the question of the legality of ship money before the courts by refusing to pay his tax. The courts were under the power of the King, and decided the case in the royal favor.

The decision in the ship-money case opened the eyes of the nation as nothing previously had done, and events moved on to a crisis. The Puritans were meanwhile being further alienated and oppressed by Archbishop Laud. The Earl of Strafford and his policy of "Thorough," by which the country was to be made subject to a standing army, embittered and made hostile a still larger group of civilians. The normal rights and privileges of citizens were abrogated by the courts of Star Chamber and High Commission. As if intoxicated by arbitrary power, and increasingly oblivious or careless of the feelings and temper of his people in both England and Scotland, Charles attempted to force a Book of Common Prayer on Scotland. The opposition to the new liturgy gradually grew into open rebellion, and the long-expected crisis came in 1639 when war between the King and the Scottish Covenanters broke out. Without funds, and with a united and determined Scotland opposing him, Charles was reluctantly forced to summon Parliament after its intermission of eleven years. The "Long Parliament," which sat for thirteen years, and the King were soon at open war. The revenge of the Parliament on the King, the bishops, the heads of the King's army, the inquisitorial courts, and the whole system which the King had established and fostered, was swift and sure.

The principles at issue in the conflict between King and Parliament in the seventeenth century concern themselves so much with such terms as despotism, tyranny, freedom, rights, and liberties, that the struggle has come, in the minds of many in later generations of British and Americans, to be regarded as the pattern conflict between a despot and a people striving to gain its freedom. It is true that Hampden, Pym, Cromwell, Milton, and others of their side with sword or pen fought some of our battles for us, and their names have ever since been an inspiration to men who cherish religious and political freedom, and who have fought or who may have to fight for such freedom. But from a historical point

---

[17] *Familiar Letters*, Sec. 4, Letter 7.   [18] The principles, and some of the provisions, of the Petition of Right are suggestive of those in the Bill of Rights, set forth in the first ten amendments to the Constitution of the United States.

of view it is a mistake to think of the English Civil War in terms of modern political and religious ideas. The members of the Long Parliament were no more democrats than Charles. Politically they were fighting to replace the authority of the King with their own authority, to substitute the rule of a capitalistic oligarchy for that of monarchy, and they succeeded in doing so. In religious matters the Puritans, although they differed from Archbishop Laud on certain details of faith and practice, were as convinced as he of the necessity and wholesomeness of uniformity in religion "according to the Word of God." They disagreed with him violently in the interpretation of that Word. Religious freedom in the modern sense of the word did not exist, and by most God-fearing persons was not desired. Toleration of the religious beliefs, or lack of them, of others was not part of the program of most seventeenth-century Christians. "Toleration," declared a seventeenth-century president of Harvard College, "is the first-born of abominations." Roger Williams was almost the sole advocate of absolute liberty of conscience. He opposed a national church and all state interference with religion, but his real hope was in America rather than in England, and his difficulties even in America make an interesting page of our history. A few souls here and there, among them Sir Thomas Browne, Bishop Jeremy Taylor, Milton, and the Cambridge Platonists, were prepared to tolerate a certain divergence from what was considered the norm, and to recognize a limited variety of religious faiths and practices. But Taylor considered indispensable a belief in the Apostles' Creed, and Milton, in his *Areopagitica*, after an eloquent plea for toleration and freedom of thought and speech, adds "I mean not tolerated popery." The leaders of both sides in the great conflict were sincere in their convictions, religious and political, and proved their sincerity by fighting—but they fought to preserve or to establish the religion and the government which they were convinced were right and good and necessary for all men.

The twentieth century has reversed many of the verdicts of previous generations on both Charles I and the Puritans. Charles and Cromwell and their respective adherents seem to modern students of history to be less villains than victims of the times and circumstances in which they lived and acted. It is conceivable that in happier times Charles might have been a successful and popular monarch; it is doubtful if England has ever produced an essentially greater Englishman than Oliver Cromwell. Though Charles was politically and doctrinally opposed to the Puritans, his own personal character contained many elements which are now commonly called Puritanical. Charles inherited a government of Church and State the corruption of which was patent to most thoughtful Englishmen. The crown which he inherited was barely self-supporting. Taxes were necessary, and the King had to depend on Parliament to levy them. It has been said of Charles that he was a more law-abiding king than most of his predecessors had been, and that it was not altogether his fault if Parliament put upon him so many restrictions that to obey them meant that he would no longer be a king according to the traditional concept of kingship. He had the misfortune to believe in pure monarchy at a time when men like the great lawyer John Selden and the great writer John Milton could think in terms of an impersonal government. He failed partly because he could not see that law, as Dean Pound of Harvard has said, though stable cannot be static.

The momentum of the Puritans carried them farther than in the beginning they had thought of going. Even Milton in 1641 did not dream of any better system than monarchy. He and his fellows were merely bent on improving the existing system. To effect the desired reforms, and particularly to get rid of some of the evils of prelacy, Parliament had to get some of the King's power into its own hands. In return for the financial assistance which it gave the King, the latter was made to sign over some of his authority to Parliament. The zeal of Parliament gradually gathered such impetus that the result was the reformation of the monarchical system out of existence!

The Civil War was marked by gallantry and brave deeds on both sides, and, as always, by the shedding of some of the country's best blood. In the circumstances it could have had only one outcome —the victory of Cromwell's Ironsides. Stronger kings than Charles, and greater armies than those of his Cavaliers, have failed to win against such deadly earnestness and soldierly discipline as that of the Roundheads. In bringing Charles to the block on January 30, 1649, his enemies seemed to have scored a triumph, but though they won the day and the decade, they lost in the century. For the dead King became a martyr, and as a martyr he triumphed as he could never have triumphed in life. By a strange irony he who while still living had come to be more and more the embodiment of royal tyranny came to represent more and more after his death "the sole and sacred repository of the laws and liberties of his people." In the light of history it seems to many an irreparable injury that Cromwell did his cause in 1649, when, as G. M. Young says, "in a volcanic hour of anger, disappointment, ambition, impatience, and perhaps despair, he flung himself against the English tradition at the point where it has always been strongest and most sensitive, its respect for law."[19] As for tyranny, the Puritans in the saddle were to show themselves at times as stern taskmasters as any king or royal court of Star Chamber or High Commission. Those who had themselves suffered from the tyranny of the Church made the adherents of the Church and all others who differed with them feel the weight of their displeasure. The Presbyterians were as ruthless in forbidding the use of the Book of Common Prayer as the King and the bishops had been in enforcing its use. Milton, who had at one time upheld them, had sorrowfully to admit that "New Presbyter is but old Priest writ large," and even to many an ardent Parliamentarian the second tyranny seemed worse than the first.

The republic which came into existence after the execution of Charles brought several years of vigorous and able government. The army and navy of Cromwell were in effect the beginning of the modern British army and navy, and under Cromwell England was more feared and respected in Europe than she had been since the fourteenth century. The republic lasted four years, and Cromwell was installed as Lord Protector at Westminster Abbey in December, 1653. It has been said that the tragedy of Cromwell's career was that men united to support him when he destroyed, but when he tried to build he had to work alone in the midst of squabbling factions. With his army he kept control until his death in 1658, but with his passing all the pent-up forces were released, and a complete disintegration of the Commonwealth followed. The anarchy and military despotism that succeeded the Commonwealth oppressed trade by its foreign policy and by the heavy taxation necessary for a standing army. Cromwell's weak son and successor, Richard, abdicated in 1659, and the exiled son of Charles I came into his own again as Charles II in May, 1660. The cause of the Puritans seemed for the time to have failed, but it was to win its real triumphs later, and the principles that found their best expression in the writings of Milton and Bunyan have over the years contributed effectively to the shaping of the Britain and the America of the present day.

With Charles II on the throne, the forces against which Cromwell had fought regained control. The lords temporal and spiritual began again to exercise their former powers. An Act of Amnesty was passed, but it did not benefit most of the dead King's judges. Some of them escaped to America; thirteen of them were put to death. The bodies of such chief offenders as Cromwell and Ireton were disinterred and hanged in chains. Milton, who had been Cromwell's Latin Secretary and the most eloquent defender of the Commonwealth and the regicides, was heavily fined and had to remain in hiding until after the Act of Oblivion was passed. His anti-Royalist books were burned by the common hangman, and he seems to have escaped being put to death only through the influence of Andrew Marvell and other friends. It was now the turn of the Nonconformist ministers to be deprived of their livings and privileges, and many like John Bunyan found themselves in jail. Royalist clergymen, among them Robert Herrick, who had been ejected from their livings by the Puritans, now returned to them.

To Milton and those who shared his feelings, the country had "fallen on evil days," and the "sons of Belial" were abroad in the land. Public morality sank to its lowest ebb. The scandalousness of Charles's court is proverbial, and the King himself was a pensioner of Louis XIV, a master of intrigue, and a shameless appropriator of public funds. Conditions at home and abroad became more and more unsettled. The plague of 1665, the great fire of 1666, and the burning of English shipping in the Thames by the Dutch in 1667, struck terror into the heart of London. The religious disturbances reached a climax with the famous imposture known as the Popish Plot, invented by certain anti-Catholic fanatics, who accused the Roman Catholics of plotting to murder the King and to restore Roman Catholicism. The ready belief that was accorded the alleged design, and the cruel punishment which was inflicted on innocent people, were symptomatic of the uneasy state of mind which prevailed in the country.

In Parliament the fears and excitement resulted in the proposal of the Exclusion Bill, by which the King's brother, the Duke of York, a Roman Catholic, would have been barred from succeeding him. In the country at large the first Earl of Shaftesbury fomented interest in the bill and headed a plot to depose Charles in favor of his illegitimate son, the Duke of Monmouth, who had in his favor both charming manners and a reputation for loyalty to the established faith.[20] The plot and the Exclusion Bill failed, and Charles died King of England. His reign, for all its disturbances, was marked by real constitutional progress. The great Habeas Corpus Act, which prevented illegal imprisonment by se-

---

[19] *Charles I and Cromwell*, London, 1935, pp. 144-45.

[20] For Dryden's satire on the plot, *Absalom and Achitophel*, see p. 727.

curing the imprisoned citizen's right to be tried or to be liberated, was passed by Parliament in 1679. The two political factions called "Petitioners" and "Abhorrers" with respect to their attitude toward the Exclusion Bill were the beginnings of the two great political parties, the Whigs and the Tories, and their establishment was the greatest single step toward parliamentary rule.

The Duke of York, as James II, succeeded his brother on the throne in 1685. In spite of his oath to preserve the established religion, he set to work to restore the Roman Catholic faith to England. The reign began with a rebellion in Scotland and another in England, the latter headed by the Duke of Monmouth, and both rebellions were inspired by Protestant interests. The necessity of suppressing Monmouth's Rebellion gave the King the excuse for increasing his army, and among the officers added were many Roman Catholics. The rebellion brought into prominence, as the chief prosecutor of the cases of treason arising out of it, the infamous Judge Jeffreys, who took such cruel revenge on Monmouth's followers in the western counties that his sessions of court received the name of the "Bloody Assizes." James's troubled reign of three years was brought to an end by a circumstance which in normal times, and to most kings and subjects, would seem the most favorable event possible—the birth of a son and heir. But the knowledge that the heir to the throne would be a Roman Catholic caused the leaders of both parties to invite Prince William of Orange, the husband of James's daughter Mary, to come to the rescue of England, her laws, and her religion. William landed in November, 1688, and James, deserted by his army, fled to France. The crown was offered in joint sovereignty the following year to William and Mary.

The Revolution of 1688–89, however considered, is one of the most monumental events in English history. It accomplished far more than the securing of a Protestant succession to the throne and the establishment of the Protestant religion in England. For one thing, it transformed the bitter feuds of the two political parties into what was at least an armed truce, to the great benefit of the state. It transferred definitely and finally the ultimate power of the king to the Parliament, and in the Parliament to the House of Commons. The Bill of Rights, which the House of Commons proceeded to pass, limited the powers of the Crown, and expressly provided for the maintenance of the people's liberties. And Parliament has sat every year since 1689.

During the remaining decade of the century, the powers and prerogatives of the Crown were still further curtailed. The first cabinet government was instituted in England when William, acting on advice, selected as his ministers the leading members of the two Houses who had the confidence of the House of Commons. In the year before the King died he gave his assent to the Act of Settlement, which secured the succession of the Crown to the House of Hanover, to the exclusion of Roman Catholic claimants—the act which has determined the occupancy of the throne to the present day.

Within the century England had undergone both a religious and a political revolution. Two other revolutions, the industrial and the social, were forced to wait until the political and religious forces had worked out their destinies. The political events did not, however, leave social conditions entirely unchanged. The civil wars did away with the semi-feudal conditions which governed class relations under Elizabeth and the first two Stuarts. The nobleman at the end of the century had much more in common with the modern English gentleman than with the medieval baron. The country squire and the country parson continued to preside at the top of the hierarchy which had as its broad base the yeomen, the laborers, and the artisans. The progress of these humbler constituents of rural society, the growth and increasing importance of London in the British scheme of things, the rise to wealth and power of the commercial class, the development of agriculture and industry, belong to the history of the century that follows.

"It is one of the chief attractions of seventeenth-century history and literature," wrote Professor Walter Raleigh, "that there is hardly a live question today which was unknown to the men of that time."[21] As one looks over the panorama of events which have been outlined in the foregoing pages, and through the selections from seventeenth-century literature in the following pages, it becomes apparent that the seventeenth and the twentieth centuries have more than the usual elements and qualities in common, and it is evident that both centuries must be classed among the major periods of transition of the human race. The conflict between old and new, between tradition and modernity, between systems that are passing and others that are struggling to take their place, is being waged today after a fashion strikingly suggestive of the conflict of three hundred years ago. There is

[21] Introduction to *The Complete Works of George Savile, First Marquess of Halifax*, Oxford Press, 1912.

something of the same ebb and flow, action and reaction, as the battle goes on.

The spiritual kinship between modern America and seventeenth-century England was pointed out by James Russell Lowell in the preface to the English edition of his *Biglow Papers* in 1859:

"After all, thin speculative Jonathan is more like the Englishman of two centuries ago than John Bull himself is. He has lost somewhat in solidity, has become fluent and adaptable, but more of the original groundwork of character remains. He feels more at home with Fulke Greville, Herbert of Cherbury, Quarles, George Herbert, and Browne, than with his modern English cousins. He is nearer than John, by at least a hundred years, to Naseby, Marston Moor, Worcester, and the time when, if ever, there were true Englishmen."

It is not strange that this should be so, for it was then that English-speaking America came into existence, and then were forged the bonds that still link us in a very special way with the English-speaking nations. The impact of America on the England of the seventeenth century is to be seen throughout its literature. One of the favorite themes and sources of imagery for both poets and prose-writers was the new-found land across the Atlantic. Elizabethan and Jacobean poets and freebooters alike played with it as a novel toy, using it as material for Utopian interludes and dreams like *The Tempest*. Bacon's *New Atlantis* is the precursor of a whole literature of island fiction inspired by the Platonic tradition of the submerged island-continent of Atlantis, of which Hakluyt and many others thought America was the wreck. John Donne in his younger years contemplated the possibility of seeking his fortune in the New World, and constantly exploited it in his poetry. As Dean of St. Paul's, he preached what has been called the first American missionary sermon to the Honourable Company of the Virginia Plantation in 1622. George Herbert saluted the American Church that was to be in the prophetic lines of his poem "The Church Militant":

"Religion now stands on tiptoe in our land,
Ready to pass to the American strand."

The "American strand" was being settled by people whose ideas on religious and political issues had made them unwelcome in their home towns in England, and the character and temper of American civilization have been determined to no small extent by the spirit of such men. Others, like Cromwell and Milton, who stayed at home to wrestle with the problems, shared with them and with us sentiments and principles which have gone into the making of American history. Familiar to American ears is the ring of such words as these of Milton, written over a hundred years before the American Revolution:

"No man who knows aught can be so stupid as to deny that all men are naturally born free . . . the power of kings and magistrates is nothing else but what is only derivative, transferred, and committed to them in trust from the people to the common good of them all." [22]

The historian of today rightly sees in the momentous events of the seventeenth century the first stages of the great social and political movements of the succeeding generations. The liberalism of the eighteenth century grew naturally out of the theories that overthrew Charles I and James II. The English civil wars helped to prepare the way for the French Revolution and the other upheavals of Europe in the centuries following. It is not strange that Voltaire's *Letters Concerning the English Nation* should have been publicly burned in Paris, or that Mirabeau should have translated and used portions of Milton's *Areopagitica* as propaganda.[23] And as for England, out of the welter of civil war, religious intolerance and persecution, and political mismanagement, there emerged gradually the formulation of the democratic principles of the twentieth century. It was of such struggles as these, and of such precedents as the Petition of Right of 1628 and the Bill of Rights of 1689, that Tennyson was thinking when he pictured the England of these latter days—

"A land of settled government,
A land of just and old renown,
Where freedom broadens slowly down
From precedent to precedent."

English Literature in the Seventeenth Century

The literature of seventeenth-century England was not a thing apart from the social, political, religious, and intellectual movements that have been

---

[22] *The Tenure of Kings and Magistrates*, 1649. [23] Of the influence of John Locke on Voltaire, and of the effect of the visits made to England by Montesquieu and Rousseau, see the discussion by Edouard Herriot, former president of the French Assembly, in his book *The Wellsprings of Liberty*, Funk & Wagnalls, 1940.

mentioned in the foregoing pages. The poetry and prose of the period constitute, indeed, the best mirror of the events and forces of the age. The men who wrote the century's literature also helped to fight the century's battles, administer its government, preach its sermons, heal its sick, fish its streams, and carry on the work of the day. Milton, the greatest poet of the century, giving the years of his prime to the service of the state, is symbolic of the close connection between the world of letters and the world of action. Both the poetry and the prose of the time came largely from men who wrote because they had something to say which but for them would go unsaid, not because it was fashionable to write, or to satisfy external demands and requirements. In 1646, when civil strife and pamphlet warfare filled the land, Henry Vaughan, in the preface to his *Poems*, confesses "to all ingenious lovers of poesy": "I know the years, and what coarse entertainment they afford poetry. . . . It is for you only that I have adventured thus far, and invaded the press with verse." Few if any of the writers of the day could be called professional poets or men of letters, and none of them claimed as the privilege of genius the right to retire to an ivory tower. The literature, both religious and secular, was much given to introspection and self-analysis, and the lyrics of the century have been called fragments of autobiographies.

"Complete" was a word much in use in the titles of the day, and the formula of completeness was applied in the investigation of any subject, whether it was Henry Peacham's *Compleat Gentleman*, or Izaak Walton's *Compleat Angler*, or Robert Burton's *Anatomy of Melancholy*, which undertook to examine the eighty-eight varieties of that malady. The subject matter of the literature represents the same sense of completeness and variety. No object was too trivial to inspire a poem, as witness Donne's flea, Marvell's drop of dew, and the ephemeral and pretty things which furnish the argument of Robert Herrick's book. Nor was any subject too large for such a man as Bacon, who had claimed all knowledge for his province, or for Milton, who undertook to sing of "things unattempted yet in prose or rhyme"—of God and man and the cosmos. The complex temperament of the age includes all moods —grave and gay, tender and cynical, religious, convivial, heroic, and satirical. The lyric verse embraces some of the greatest religious poems of the language and the amorous songs of the Cavaliers and the Restoration court poets. Ballads and sonnets, pastorals and epics, essays and allegories, sermons, memoirs, letters, history, and biography are the vehicles which at one time or another the century pressed into service to convey its thought. Comedy and tragedy, first in the hands of Shakespeare and Jonson, and later in those of Congreve and Dryden, reflected in one form or another the moods of the age and mirrored its passions.

One of the most striking facts about the seventeenth century is its preoccupation in both the world of action and the world of thought with religion. We have already seen how inextricably politics and religion were intermingled, and how the nation's energies were concentrated in political and religious channels. The history of the development of natural science is likewise linked at every stage with that of the religious thought of the time. The chief problem of Bacon, as of other philosophers and scientists, was the separation of religious truth and scientific truth. Bacon was pleading, says Basil Willey, for science in an age dominated by religion.[24] In English literature the effect of the century's deep concern with religion is to be seen, in one way or another, in almost every author and in every form of expression. The fact that the most potent influence on the literature of the century was the King James Version of the Bible is the best proof of the dominance of religious and theological thought. J. R. Green's statement in his *Short History of the English People* is as true as it is famous: "England became the people of a book, and that book was the Bible." Of the effect on almost all phases of English life and thought of the King James or Authorized Version of 1611 no proper account can be given here. There is truth as well as wit in the remark that it was King James's Bible that cost his son his head. The substance of the Bible informed most of the literature of the century; its phraseology helped to determine the rhythms and form the style of prose-writers as different as Jeremy Taylor and John Bunyan, and of poets as unlike as Herbert and Milton. It furnished themes for lyric poems, epics, allegories, and satires.

The very conflict between science and religion, and the confusion of mind that resulted from their pitched battles, were responsible for some of the most beautiful poetry and prose of the day. It is not an accident that any anthology of English mystical verse draws more heavily on the poets of the seventeenth century than of any other. Many like Donne, Herbert, Vaughan, and Crashaw, wearied with the conflicting philosophies of the day and with the hoarse noises of dispute, turned from the uncertainties of the world of physical sense and perception to what seemed to them the unchanging truths

[24] *The Seventeenth Century Background*, London, 1934, pp. 29 ff.

of the spiritual mysteries that lay beyond the ken of the intellect. In the realm of prose the contemplation of "this great mystery of our religion" raises such writers as Sir Thomas Browne and Jeremy Taylor to heights of eloquence and a magnificence of phrase which have never been surpassed.

In sermons, as well as in lyrics, epics, and allegories, the exposition of religious and theological truths produced literature of beauty and power. The seventeenth century has been called the golden age of the sermon, and it may be said that no literary form is more characteristic of the age.[25] The richly furnished mind of Donne makes of his sermons prose counterparts of his poems, and a study of the eloquent compositions designed for the congregation of St. Paul's will help greatly in the understanding of his verse. The development of English prose across the century can be fairly and interestingly traced in the sermon literature of the time, from Donne and Andrewes to Baxter, Taylor, Barrow, and Tillotson. Dryden has testified to the influence on the style of his own prose of some of the seventeenth-century divines.

It is the chief glory of the first two decades of the century that they gave to English literature the King James Version of the Bible and all the greater plays of Shakespeare. These alone would serve to make the period the golden age of the literature. They are such a large part of the common heritage, and have entered so much into the language and life of English-speaking people during the past three hundred years, that they cannot be properly represented in any single category or period. In every sense they are not of an age but for all time.

The Drama

During the time of a generation between the death of Elizabeth and the official closing of the theaters in 1642, English drama underwent a general disintegration. The elements which were so mixed in Shakespeare were separated and exploited by lesser persons. What had been a pastime that the public as a whole had enjoyed, an afternoon's entertainment in which both tragedy and comedy had their parts, gave way to a series of plays and entertainments for separate and diverse groups. The masque, a private entertainment in which dance and spectacle were all-important; the "comedy of humors," in which a particular type of man animated by some one predominant trait or "humor" was portrayed; the drama in which poetry gave way to rhetoric, and a perverse passion was exploited beyond measure—these appealed to and were supported by their respective adherents. There are, to be sure, moving scenes and memorable passages of poetry in many of these plays; and even so ephemeral a form as the masque, with its primary appeal to the senses and its dependence on machinery and setting, was made the vehicle for beautiful and enduring poetry by Ben Jonson in a dozen pieces and by Milton in his *Comus*. But there is no better way of demonstrating Shakespeare's superiority as poet or dramatist than by comparing his dramas with the best of those that were written in the quarter of a century following his death. No great loss, perhaps, was suffered by either the English theater or English literature when the Puritans decided in 1642 that "stage plays do not suit with times of humiliation," and decreed that public performances of them should cease.

The official ban on the theaters did not prevent entirely either the writing or the public performance of plays, but civil strife and Puritan domination were not helpful to the already moribund drama. Alfred Harbage, in his study of the drama of the middle years of the century, is of the opinion that if Charles I had stayed on the throne and the playhouses had remained open, the drama would have continued to disintegrate, becoming less and less popular and getting more and more under the control of the court and into the hands of the courtly amateurs.[26] The drama acted in such theaters as might have continued to exist would probably have been very much what was in fashion after the Restoration—heroic tragedy and the comedy of manners. The continuity of the dramatic tradition, such as it was, is illustrated in the work of Sir William Davenant, whose earliest plays came nearly a decade before the official closing of the theaters, and whose drama *The Siege of Rhodes*, 1656, replete with music and elaborate scenery to justify its pretense to being an "opera" and not a play, foreshadowed the heroic drama of the Restoration. Students of the Restoration drama see in Davenant's *Siege of Rhodes* almost all the elements of earlier dramatic compositions—the music and scenery of the masque, the heroic themes of Marlowe and Beaumont and Fletcher, and, as Mr. Harbage has shown, the Cavalier's conception of valor, and even the rhymed heroic couplet. In addition to native elements there were also ingredients of Italian opera

---

[25] For an interesting and thorough discussion of the popularity and importance of the sermon in seventeenth-century life and letters, see C. F. Richardson, *English Preachers and Preaching, 1640–1670*, Macmillan, 1928.

[26] See *Cavalier Drama*, Modern Language Association, 1936.

and French drama. French influence, "after his Majesty's being so long abroad," is to be noted in much of Restoration drama, especially in the rhymed heroic drama of Dryden and Sir Robert Howard, but the result of the combination of French theories and English practices was not such as would have won the approval of the critics or playwrights of Paris.

The dramatic repertory of the Restoration was diversified also by revivals and adaptations of Shakespeare, Jonson, and Beaumont and Fletcher. Dryden, though most of his plays were written in the fashionable heroic couplet, achieved his greatest dramatic success in blank verse in his *All for Love*, 1678, which took its theme from Shakespeare's *Antony and Cleopatra*. In prose the comedy of manners in the hands of Etherege, Wycherley, and Congreve brought to the English stage and to English literature brilliance if not greatness. In the plays of Congreve, especially, English comedy reached a height which it was not to attain again for nearly a hundred years.[27]

Poetry

When we turn our eyes to nondramatic verse, we find that the fabric of seventeenth-century poetry is of a piece with that of the Elizabethan period. The predominating patterns and colors at its beginning are those of three great artists who began their work before the sixteenth century was over—Spenser, Jonson, and Donne. Spenser did not live to see the new century, but the pastoral and allegorical figures of his poetry were the inspiration and the models of much of the work of William Drummond, George Wither, Giles and Phineas Fletcher, and of many other minor poets of the generation following him, and his influence is to be detected in the early work of his great admirer, Milton. The incomparable lyric felicity and melody of Spenser's verse, best described in Milton's phrase, "linkèd sweetness long drawn out," are echoed and imitated in scores of poems which mourn departed shepherds, sing of faithful loves and ideal beauty, and celebrate the fresh woods and green pastures of an England which had not yet ceased altogether to be a land of faerie.

In sharp contrast to the romantic formlessness and long-drawn-out sweetness, as well as to the moralizing songs, of Spenser and his followers, are the neatness, the precision, and the classic grace and restraint of Ben Jonson's lyrics. No single influence in the poetry of the century is so strongly marked as that of Jonson. It informs more or less the society verse of Carew, the songs of the Cavaliers, and the lyrics of Herrick. It was felt by Milton, as may be seen from his early songs, by the court poets of the Restoration, by Marvell, and by Dryden. With Jonson and the "Sons of Ben" the lyric poem could talk as well as sing, and, whether talking or singing, approached more nearly the sureness of the Latin line than English verse had ever done before.

The most vigorous, and certainly the most unconventional, of the poets of Elizabethan and Jacobean England was John Donne. The poetry of Donne and of those who followed more or less his original and fantastic style has, since Dryden's criticism of it in his *Discourse Concerning Satire* and Dr. Johnson's discussion of it in his *Life of Cowley*, been called "metaphysical," although this term does not adequately or properly describe it.[28] No single word could accurately express the extraordinary figurativeness, the intellectual ingenuity and resourcefulness, of John Donne. He is commonly thought of as a rebel against the conventional sweetness and melody, the overworked themes of spring and larks at heaven's gate, the imaginary shepherds and shepherdesses, and the often meaningless but prettily phrased sentiments of Petrarchan and Spenserian poetry, and such in effect he was. But his work, in both verse and prose, was probably not so much the result of a conscious revolt as of an effort to be himself, and to express himself in his own way, without consideration first of all for artistic beauty or appropriateness. His language is essentially the language of prose, and by his use of homely and colloquial diction he brought back the virtues of prose to English poetry at a time when it needed to be revivified and purged of too poetic and artificial phrases. The harshness and ruggedness of Donne's verse, which are perhaps the first qualities to strike a reader, are due both to impatience with conventional patterns and rhythms and to a desire to shock the reader into attention. The richness of his verse, as of the sermons of his later years, he attains not by the archaic effect of Spenser's pseudo-Chaucerian language, or by languorous conceits made up of learned and philosophic terms, but by remote and striking analogies, daring metaphors, bizarre sim-

---

[27] For the best discussion of the literary aspects of Restoration drama see G. H. Nettleton, *English Drama of the Restoration and Eighteenth Century, 1642–1780*, Macmillan, 1923.

[28] The ablest discussion of metaphysical poetry and of the significance of Donne is that of Professor H. J. C. Grierson in the introduction to his *Metaphysical Lyrics and Poems of the Seventeenth Century*, Oxford Press, 1925.

iles, and an amazing fecundity of figurativeness in general. To his subjects he brought candor, a fierce emotional intensity, and an unprecedented intellectual passion and curiosity. The subjects themselves are as varied as the thoughts and experiences of the age in which he lived.

Such an original genius could not fail to attract attention and imitation. Donne's influence upon his contemporaries was peculiar in that it was an influence exerted by poems still in manuscript circulation. Herbert was the first to follow in his steps. He shows Donne's influence in his curiosity, the luxuriance of his figures, and his habit of going into strange places for his metaphors. Vaughan, Crashaw, Carew, Cowley, Marvell, all of them artists in their own right, were affected for better or for worse by Donne's habit of thought and mannerisms, and adapted and modified them, each in his own way. The Cavaliers, Lovelace and Suckling, after their fashion, likewise give evidence that they have studied Donne. Even Dryden, who was to be in his maturer years the chief opponent of the theory and practice of "metaphysical" poetry, began his poetical career under the spell of Donne, and spun his conceits with the best, and the worst, of the "Metaphysicals." For the greater part of the century, English poetry was different because of Donne, and it is this "metaphysical" quality, more easily discerned and felt than defined, that sets so much of the poetry of the seventeenth century apart from that of other periods.[29]

Of all the poets of the far side of the Restoration, Milton alone escaped the influence of Donne's peculiar style and turn of thought. Milton belongs to no one school, although he acknowledged Spenser as his master. But he transcended Spenser, as he transcended all the poets who came after him. Milton embodied in himself and synthesized in his poetry all the wealth of ancient literature and learning, all the richness of myth and legend and fable, all the spiritual harvest of Hebraic morals and classical art and philosophy. Only such a man and such a poet, nourished by all the poets and all the schools, could have given to English literature the body of poetry which unites in itself the moral earnestness of the Hebrew prophets, the classical sense of form, the intellectual vigor of the Renaissance, and the richness and exuberance of the great Elizabethans.

The influence of "metaphysical" poetry waned after the middle of the century, and the inevitable reaction set in against it. The excessive figurativeness and the roughness and angularity of the verse of Donne and of those who followed in his wake came to seem quaintly old-fashioned or downright barbarous and "Gothic" to a younger generation of poets who preferred the smoothness and precision of French verse and the rules and restraints of Latin poets and critics. Waller, Denham, and Dryden developed the closed couplet, and polished it into the perfect medium for commenting brilliantly, sarcastically, and satirically upon public and private topics of the moment, or for generalizations on man's place in the great scheme of things. The labor and the frenzy, the passionate mysticism, of the first half of the century disappeared. It is as if poetry had tired itself out with wonderment and speculation and analysis of the great mysteries of life, and had settled down to a reasoning consideration and a reasonable explanation of the more ordinary phenomena of existence. "Perspicacity, propriety, decency," according to Dryden, are the essential qualities of good poetry, and Dryden dictated to the second half of the century as Donne and Jonson had dictated to the first.[30] The lyric poetry of the Restoration is, therefore, not equal to that of the preceding generations. The sensibility and artistic energy of the period found its best expression in satire, in the comedy of manners, and in heroic tragedy, and, outside literature, in architecture, painting, and scientific experiment. Poetry, especially in the work of Samuel Butler and Dryden, was clever and often brilliant talk, and such it was to remain for half a century more until Gray and Collins and others revived the antiquarian, the archaic, and the picturesque, to be the bases of a new kind of written, not spoken, discourse.

Prose

The history of English prose in the seventeenth century discloses tendencies and developments not unlike those that marked the progress of

[29] The powerful appeal which Donne, more than any other of the older poets, has had for young poets of all political faiths in the present century is interesting to students of contemporary literature. Many poets of the last quarter of a century, both in Britain and in America, have seen in Donne the reflection of an age of instability and confusion, of mental revolt and reorientation, very like our own. Twentieth-century ears, also, have become weary with the more conventional patterns and rhythms of nineteenth-century verse, and the poetry of Donne is refreshing because it is different. For a discussion of some aspects of this present-day interest in Donne and the "metaphysical" poets, see Elisabeth Tomlinson, "The Metaphysical Tradition in Three Modern Poets," *College English*, December, 1939, pp. 208–22.

[30] Milton, like Donne, though in a very different manner, greatly influenced the substance and technique of later poetry. For a thorough discussion of the subject, see R. D. Havens, *The Influence of Milton on English Poetry*, Harvard University Press, 1922.

poetry. There was not during the first half of the century any carefully marked distinction between the style and function of poetry and those of prose, and Bacon is one of the few writers of the time who did not use both mediums. Bacon's prose is, however, rich in imagery, and few poets have been more sensitive than he to felicities of cadence and rhythm. Donne's sermons are at times more truly poetic than many of his poems, and even in such works as Raleigh's *History of the World* and Milton's *Areopagitica*, where one might least expect to find poetry, the thought often takes fire, and chronology and statistics give way to genuinely poetic meditations on the deeper meanings of history and human life, the blessings of freedom, and the excellency of truth. The prose of the period, like the poetry, was much given to introspection and intellectual subtlety. Paradoxes and problems, anatomies, discoveries upon men and matter—these furnished the titles, the methods, and the substance of both poetry and prose. And the artist in prose—for prose was in the early seventeenth century more of an art and less of a handicraft than it has ever been since—brought to the discussion of his subject the same well-furnished mind and the same teeming vocabulary that the poet employed in his art.

Of the types of prose, the essay, which has been called a prose lyric, is the most distinctive contribution of the period to the literature. As the years passed the essay took on the duties of a prose maid-of-all-work. From a collection of apothegms and aphoristic conceits, as usually with Bacon, it developed into such extended, well-knit, and carefully arranged pieces of exposition as the chapters in Hobbes's *Leviathan* and Locke's *Essay Concerning Human Understanding*, or the dialogues of Dryden's *Essay of Dramatic Poesy*. In the interval between Bacon and Locke it served a multitude of men and purposes, and appeared in various forms as "characters," "resolves," meditations, sermons, prefaces, and pamphlets. One of the most interesting uses to which it was put is that of biography, as with Thomas Fuller and Izaak Walton, and it is worth noting that the words "biographer" and "biography" stem from this period of our literature. With the arrival of magazines, such as the *Athenian Gazette* and the *Gentleman's Journal*, came the periodical essay, and before the century had closed the "editorial" of modern journalism had begun to help form the nation's opinions.

The history of the newspaper is not properly part of the story of English literature, but no account of the development of modern literature could fail to mention the genesis in the seventeenth century of this most important institution. The beginnings of the English press are intimately bound up with the events of the time, for it was chiefly out of the desire for news of current happenings, battles and political activities, of the period of the Civil War that the newspaper was born. As early as 1622 there was a *Weekly News*, but it was not until 1642 that the first real English newspaper, a weekly, began under the name, *The Head of Several Proceedings in the Present Parliament, or Diurnal Occurrences*. The honor of being the first daily English newspaper belongs to the *Postbag*, of which four numbers appeared in 1693. It remained for the eighteenth century to produce the first regular daily paper, the *Daily Courant*, but the seventeenth century saw the Fourth Estate through its birth throes, and through the first rounds of the inevitable and unending struggle for the freedom of the press.

To the eighteenth century it was left also to bring English fiction to its maturity in the novel. The seventeenth century's propensity for exposition, as seen in the popularity of the essay, the "anatomy," and the sermon, did not foster the art of narration. Most of the writers of the time were constitutionally unable to get on with the story, and could not resist the temptation to dig in for a bit of analysis. When the author had played with his subject as a cat plays with a mouse, or, as in the words of Burton, when it had been "philosophically, medicinally, historically, opened and cut up," he would move on to the next point, but not till then. To Mrs. Aphra Behn belongs the credit of being the one real novelist of the time, as well as the first professional English authoress. Her most celebrated novel, *Oroonoko, or The Royal Slave*, 1688, presents a picture of the "noble savage" almost a century before Rousseau discoursed upon the virtues of the natural man, and, however one may discount the loftiness of her intentions in writing the romance, or the profundity of her humanitarian sentiments, she contrived, almost two hundred years before *Uncle Tom's Cabin*, to create a sympathetic interest in the victims of human slavery. In other less well-known stories she shows her ability to handle the picaresque, and, what is more remarkable for one who was a successful Restoration dramatist, a knowledge and appreciation of English country life and scenes.

In a work of a very different nature, Bunyan's allegory, *The Pilgrim's Progress*, there is evidence of a genuine gift for storytelling and realistic description, which has made it the most famous prose narrative of the century. The autobiographical and didactic elements of the book prevent its technical classification as fiction, but in the history of the English novel Bunyan's place is assured and unique. The close connection between other forms of biography and autobiography, genuine or fictitious, and the novel is illustrated in the rogue stories of the later seventeenth century. Historians of the novel see in the elements and methods of some of these the germs of the style of Daniel Defoe, "the first great English novelist," who was born the year before the Restoration, and who represents the culmination of the tendencies in fiction during the last decades of the century.

The general trend in prose was toward informality, simplicity, and realism. The progress of scientific thought assisted the process of simplification. Dr. Thomas Sprat in his *History of the Royal Society*, 1667, informs us that that society required of its members reports of the results of their researches in "a close, naked, natural way of speaking; positive expressions; clear senses; a native easiness; bringing all things as near the mathematical plainness as they can: and preferring the language of artisans, countrymen, and merchants before that of wits or scholars." The "poetic prose" of the first half of the century, with its magisterial manner, its purple passages, and its gargantuan sentences, inevitably gave way gradually to the more agile and colloquial style of the memoir, the pamphlet, and the newspaper. The monumental perorations of Donne and Sir Thomas Browne with their sesquipedalian terms and sonorous Latinisms were succeeded by such brief summaries as that which ends Dryden's discussion of Chaucer—"Here is God's plenty"—and the conclusion of *The Pilgrim's Progress*—"So I awoke, and behold it was a dream."

By 1660 the composition of the language with respect to the relative proportions of native and foreign elements had become largely what it is today. English had shaken itself loose from the excessive Latinism of the earlier days, and had proved itself capable of expressing well and sufficiently all the thoughts that might arise in English minds and hearts. English books had become "citizens of the world," which, according to Bacon, they were not at the beginning of the century. English literature, which could hardly be said to have existed for the learned men of the days before the Civil War, achieved sufficient prestige to merit the critical appraisal of Dryden and his contemporaries. The evolution of a critical temper and the development of literary criticism in England are undoubtedly related to the growth of the scientific spirit and habit of thought which took place during the century. In Dryden's *Essay of Dramatic Poesy* and the prefaces to his various works, English literary criticism may be said to have come of age.

Summing Up

It has been well said that before the seventeenth century ended the eighteenth century had begun. The essential truth of the statement may be illustrated in almost every department of thought and activity. To the political historian the realm of the eighteenth century begins with the Revolution of 1688. In the field of science and philosophy we have noticed that the materialistic view of the universe which was to shape the thought of the next hundred years was the culmination of the philosophies of Hobbes, Newton, and Locke. In literature also what may be called peculiarly seventeenth-century characteristics began to disappear after the Restoration. The passion for introspection, the spiritual and intellectual unrest of the early and middle years, are less in evidence in both the poetry and the prose of the closing years. It is as if there were a general and genuine desire to settle down after the disturbances, to get back to normal—a tendency, indeed, to wonder if all the fighting had been worth while. Even a gentleman of Puritan persuasion like Andrew Marvell could go so far as to say that he thought the cause too good to have been fought for.

If the seventeenth century was the first period in history to number the minutes and seconds of the day, it was also the first to reckon the years in "centuries," and it is appropriate that this first century which was conscious of itself as such should have an epitaph composed for it by its last great poet, John Dryden:

> "All, all of a piece throughout:
>   Thy chase had a beast in view;
> Thy wars brought nothing about,
>   Thy lovers were all untrue.
> 'Tis well an old age is out,
>   And time to begin a new."

Like those of most epitaphs, Dryden's lines are more felicitous in phrasing than accurate in their summary of the life and works of the departed. Something of what the century's chase had in view, of what its wars brought about, and of the fidelity or infidelity of its lovers, the preceding pages have tried to indicate, and the succeeding pages will help to illustrate. A more fitting epitaph for the seventeenth century would be that of its famous architect, Sir Christopher Wren, in St. Paul's Cathedral: "*Si monumentum requiris, circumspice*"—*If you seek his monument, look about you.*

from The Authorized or King James Version of the Holy Bible

The Authorized Version of the English Bible was not, as many devout persons have thought, handed down from heaven in its present form. Nor is it entirely or exclusively the work of King James's committee of learned men. It was a revised edition, not a thoroughly new translation, and into it went much of the genius and the labor of earlier translators, both Protestant and Catholic. The revisers generously acknowledged their indebtedness in their Preface: "Truly, good Christian reader, we never thought from the beginning that we should need to make a new translation, nor yet to make of a bad one a good one . . . but to make a good one better, or out of many good ones, one principal good one, not justly to be excepted against; that hath been our endeavour, that our mark."

The man who more than any other laid the foundation of the English Bible as we have it was William Tyndale, whose translation of the New Testament was published at Worms in Germany in 1525—the first printed edition of the New Testament in English. Tyndale subsequently translated about half of the Old Testament, from Genesis through II Chronicles, and would undoubtedly have translated the whole Bible had he lived. But his enemies triumphed, and he was burned at the stake near Brussels in 1536. The sturdy simplicity of Tyndale's diction and the rhythm of his phrases provided the pattern and much of the substance of the 1611 Bible. The task of completing the English Bible fell to Miles Coverdale, who brought out the first printed English Bible in 1535.

Other revisions and editions followed over the years. The Great Bible of 1540 was prepared by Coverdale to meet Henry VIII's injunctions of 1538, that a copy "of the whole Bible of the largest volume in English be set up in churches," and that every person be "expressly provoked, stirred, and exhorted" to read the same. The Geneva Bible, which Shakespeare used and which came to America in the Mayflower, appeared in 1560. The Bishops' Bible, a revision by the Anglican Bishops of the Great Bible, was brought out in 1568, and later served as the working text of the revision of 1611. One other important translation preceded that of the Authorized Version. The Roman Catholic English version of the New Testament, prepared by members of the English College at Douai, was printed at Rheims in 1582, and their version of the Old Testament was published at Douai in 1609. The Authorized Version of 1611, "translated out of the original tongues, and with the former translations diligently compared and revised," was thus the culmination of the efforts of many men, of different faiths and orders, but all devoted to the task of making accessible to English readers the Word of God.

The masterpiece of 1611 has been called "the only classic ever created by a committee," although its compilers never thought of it in such terms, and its translators would have considered irreverent and derogatory to the sacred Scriptures the modern notion that they may be read as literature. From a purely literary point of view, it is something of a miracle that the committee of scholars should have produced such a consistently beautiful book, of which the extracts given below are but the merest sample. Some of the circumstances in their favor may be mentioned. There were the simple, pastoral beauty, the spiritual fervor, and the childlike piety of the original Hebrew Scriptures, and the vigorous Greek which carried the Christian message of the New Testament. The translators lived in an age of faith, and had a conviction that they were handling, as Tyndale put it, "the deep things of God." They had the advantage of all the English versions that had come before them. They wrote at a time when the English language was at the highest point of strength and beauty it had yet reached. Poetry was in the air, and English speech had a natural stateliness which it has since lost. However one may account for the excellence of the work, and after all its indebtedness to other sources and versions has been admitted, the King James Bible remains a classic in its own right, a piece of English literature, different from the original Hebrew or Greek, and unlike the Bible in any other language.

All art, it has been said, relies on the existence of a tradition, on a body of knowledge and ideas taken for granted. Thus the Greek tragedians built on Homer, and English-speaking writers of the last three centuries have built largely on the Authorized Version of the Bible and Shakespeare. The effect of the continual reading of the Bible on the character, imagination, and thought of the British and American peoples is greater, as all historians agree, than that of any other book or of any literary movement in English or European history. The great writers have been under the constant impact of its matchless poetry and prose, and its phrases have enriched the everyday speech of ordinary men and women. It cannot be replaced, though it should be supplemented, by modern versions. To be ignorant of it is to be out of touch with the greatest single influence in both the literature and the life of England and America.

THE TWENTY-THIRD PSALM

(Varying Translations)

THE GREAT BIBLE, 1540

Coverdale's version of the Psalms in the Great Bible was later used in the Bishops' Bible. It is still retained in the Book of Common Prayer of the Church of England, and, with a few alterations, in that of the Protestant Episcopal Church in the United States, both because it has endeared itself to the people and because its melody and felicity of phrase make it especially appropriate to liturgical use.

The Lord is my shepherd; therefore can I lack nothing.

He shall feed me in a green pasture, and lead me forth beside the waters of comfort.

He shall convert my soul, and bring me forth in the paths of righteousness for his Name's sake.

Yea, though I walk through the valley of the shadow of death, I will fear no evil; for thou art with me; thy rod and thy staff comfort me.

Thou shalt prepare a table before me against them that trouble me; thou hast anointed my head with oil, and my cup shall be full.

But thy loving-kindness and mercy shall follow me all the days of my life; and I will dwell in the house of the Lord for ever.

THE GENEVA BIBLE, 1560

The Geneva Bible was the most popular and widely used Bible of the sixteenth and early seventeenth centuries, and it was not until about 1640 that the King James Version finally supplanted it in popular favor. By then some two hundred editions of it had been brought out. It was pre-eminently the Puritan Bible, and its notes largely contributed to the Puritan spirit of the time. It is now popularly known as the "Breeches Bible," because of the translation of Genesis 3:7: "They sewed figtree leaves together, and made themselves breeches."

The Lord is my shepherd; I shall not want.

He maketh me to rest in green pasture, and leadeth me by the still waters.

He restoreth my soul, and leadeth me in the paths of righteousness for his Name's sake.

Yea, though I should walk through the valley of the shadow of death, I will fear no evil; for thou art with me; thy rod and thy staff, they comfort me.

Thou dost prepare a table before me in the sight of mine adversaries; thou dost anoint my head with oil, and my cup runneth over.

Doubtless kindness and mercy shall follow me all the days of my life, and I shall remain a long season in the house of the Lord.

THE DOUAI BIBLE, 1609

The Douai version of the Bible was made from the text of the Latin Vulgate, and being a translation of a translation is not so close to the original Hebrew as the other versions here represented. The chief concern of the English translators was fidelity to the text of the Vulgate, hence the unusual number of Latinisms. This psalm appears as Psalm 22 in the Douai Bible.

Our Lord ruleth me, and nothing shall be wanting to me; in place of pasture there he hath placed me.

Upon the water of refection he hath brought me up; he hath converted my soul.

He hath conducted me upon the paths of justice, for his name.

For although I shall walk in the midst of the shadow of death, I will not fear evils; because thou art with me.

Thy rod and thy staff, they have comforted me.

Thou hast prepared in my sight a table against them that trouble me.

Thou hast fatted my head with oil, and my chalice inebriating, how goodly is it!

And thy mercy shall follow me all the days of my life.

And that I may dwell in the house of our Lord in longitude of days.

THE AUTHORIZED VERSION, 1611

The Lord is my shepherd; I shall not want.

He maketh me to lie down in green pastures: he leadeth me beside the still waters.

He restoreth my soul: he leadeth me in the paths of righteousness for his name's sake.

Yea, though I walk through the valley of the shadow of death, I will fear no evil: for thou art with me; thy rod and thy staff they comfort me.

Thou preparest a table before me in the presence of mine enemies: thou anointest my head with oil; my cup runneth over.

Surely goodness and mercy shall follow me all the days of my life: and I will dwell in the house of the Lord for ever.

from THE BOOK OF JOB

The Book of Job is one of the great philosophical books of the world. Carlyle called it "our first, oldest statement of the never-ending Problem,—man's destiny, and God's ways with him here in this earth." The extracts here given are from the latter part of the poetical portion of the book, and follow the heated discussion between Job and his friends. Job's friends have argued that his troubles are the punishments for his wrongdoing. Against them

Job has indignantly maintained his innocence, and has accused God of being arbitrary in his dealings with men. The Voice from the Whirlwind, as Professor R. G. Moulton says, is to lift the discussion into a wider sphere. "For the hopeless suffering in which there is nothing of guilt, what treatment can be better than to lose the individual pain in sympathetic wonder over nature in her inexhaustible variety? . . . Job and his friends had fastened their attention upon suffering and evil, and had broken down under the weight of the mystery; but the individual experience now seems a small thing in the range of all nature's ways. Hence we have a Fourth Solution of the Mystery of Suffering: That the whole universe is an unfathomed mystery, and the Evil in it is not more mysterious than the Good and the Great."—"The Book of Job" in *The Modern Reader's Bible*, ed. by R. G. Moulton, Macmillan, 1930, pp. 1492-93. The text here and in the following selections is that of the Authorized Version.

Chapter 38

Then the Lord answered Job out of the whirlwind, and said,

Who is this that darkeneth counsel by words without knowledge?

Gird up now thy loins like a man; for I will demand of thee, and answer thou me.

Where wast thou when I laid the foundations of the earth? declare, if thou hast understanding.

Who hath laid the measures thereof, if thou knowest? or who hath stretched the line upon it?

Whereupon are the foundations thereof fastened? or who laid the corner stone thereof;

When the morning stars sang together, and all the sons of God shouted for joy?

Or who shut up the sea with doors, when it brake forth, as if it had issued out of the womb?

When I made the cloud the garment thereof, and thick darkness a swaddling band for it,

And brake up for it my decreed place, and set bars and doors,

And said, Hitherto shalt thou come, but no further: and here shall thy proud waves be stayed?

Hast thou commanded the morning since thy days, and caused the dayspring to know his place;

That it might take hold of the ends of the earth, that the wicked might be shaken out of it?

It is turned as clay to the seal; and they stand as a garment.

And from the wicked their light is withholden, and the high arm shall be broken.

Hast thou entered into the springs of the sea? or hast thou walked in the search of the depth?

Have the gates of death been opened unto thee? or hast thou seen the doors of the shadow of death?

Hast thou perceived the breadth of the earth? declare if thou knowest it all.

Where is the way where light dwelleth? and as for darkness, where is the place thereof,

That thou shouldest take it to the bound thereof, and that thou shouldest know the paths to the house thereof?

Knowest thou it, because thou wast then born? or because the number of thy days is great?

Hast thou entered into the treasures of the snow? or hast thou seen the treasures of the hail,

Which I have reserved against the time of trouble, against the day of battle and war?

By what way is the light parted, which scattereth the east wind upon the earth?

Who hath divided a water-course for the overflowing of waters, or a way for the lightning of thunder;

To cause it to rain on the earth, where no man is; on the wilderness, wherein there is no man;

To satisfy the desolate and waste ground; and to cause the bud of the tender herb to spring forth?

Hath the rain a father? or who hath begotten the drops of dew?

Out of whose womb came the ice? and the hoary frost of heaven, who hath gendered it?

The waters are hid as with a stone, and the face of the deep is frozen.

Canst thou bind the sweet influences of Pleiades, or loose the bands of Orion?

Canst thou bring forth Mazzaroth in his season? or canst thou guide Arcturus with his sons?

Knowest thou the ordinances of heaven? canst thou set the dominion thereof in the earth?

Canst thou lift up thy voice to the clouds, that abundance of waters may cover thee?

Canst thou send lightnings, that they may go, and say unto thee, Here we are?

Who hath put wisdom in the inward parts? or who hath given understanding to the heart?

Who can number the clouds in wisdom? or who can stay the bottles of heaven,

21. the Lord answered Job. God challenges him to the contest which he has been demanding. **44. dayspring,** dawn. **47-48. they stand as a garment.** Professor James Moffatt translates this verse as follows: "earth stands out clear like clay stamped by a seal, in all its colours like a robe."—*The Holy Bible: A New Translation* by James Moffatt, Richard R. Smith, New York, 1926.

35-38. Canst thou bind . . . Arcturus with his sons? Moffatt's translation is:
"Can you bind up the Pleiades in a cluster,
   or loose the chains of Orion:
Can you direct the signs of the Zodiac,
   or guide the constellations of the Bear?"
48. stay the bottles of heaven, Moffatt: "tilt the pitchers of the sky."

When the dust groweth into hardness, and the clods cleave fast together?

Wilt thou hunt the prey for the lion? or fill the appetite of the young lions,

When they couch in their dens, and abide in the covert to lie in wait?

Who provideth for the raven his food? when his young ones cry unto God, they wander for lack of meat.

Chapter 42

Then Job answered the Lord, and said,

I know that thou canst do every thing, and that no thought can be withholden from thee.

Who is he that hideth counsel without knowledge? therefore have I uttered that I understood not; things too wonderful for me, which I knew not.

Hear, I beseech thee, and I will speak: I will demand of thee, and declare thou unto me.

I have heard of thee by the hearing of the ear: but now mine eye seeth thee:

Wherefore I abhor myself, and repent in dust and ashes. . . .

from THE PSALTER

The Book of Psalms, called the Psalter, is a collection of religious and devotional lyrics, and constituted both the hymnbook and the prayer book of the ancient Hebrews. All moods of the religious mind find their perfect expression in the book, and the Psalter early became an essential part of the Christian liturgy and of Christian devotions.

PSALM 91

[Of the Security of Him who Trusts in God]

He that dwelleth in the secret place of the Most High shall abide under the shadow of the Almighty.

I will say of the Lord, He is my refuge and my fortress: my God; in him will I trust.

Surely he shall deliver thee from the snare of the fowler, and from the noisome pestilence.

He shall cover thee with his feathers, and under his wings shalt thou trust: his truth shall be thy shield and buckler.

Thou shalt not be afraid for the terror by night; nor for the arrow that flieth by day;

Nor for the pestilence that walketh in darkness; nor for the destruction that wasteth at noonday.

A thousand shall fall at thy side, and ten thousand at thy right hand; but it shall not come nigh thee.

Only with thine eyes shalt thou behold and see the reward of the wicked.

Because thou hast made the Lord, which is my refuge, even the most High, thy habitation,

There shall no evil befall thee, neither shall any plague come nigh thy dwelling.

For he shall give his angels charge over thee, to keep thee in all thy ways.

They shall bear thee up in their hands, lest thou dash thy foot against a stone.

Thou shalt tread upon the lion and adder: the young lion and the dragon shalt thou trample under feet.

Because he hath set his love upon me, therefore will I deliver him: I will set him on high, because he hath known my name.

He shall call upon me, and I will answer him: I will be with him in trouble; I will deliver him, and honour him.

With long life will I satisfy him, and shew him my salvation.

PSALM 139

[Of God's Omnipotence and Omniscience]

O Lord, thou hast searched me, and known me.

Thou knowest my downsitting and mine uprising, thou understandest my thought afar off.

Thou compassest my path and my lying down, and art acquainted with all my ways.

For there is not a word in my tongue, but, lo, O Lord, thou knowest it altogether.

Thou hast beset me behind and before, and laid thine hand upon me.

Such knowledge is too wonderful for me; it is high, I cannot attain unto it.

Whither shall I go from thy spirit? or whither shall I flee from thy presence?

If I ascend up into heaven, thou art there: if I make my bed in hell, behold, thou art there.

If I take the wings of the morning, and dwell in the uttermost parts of the sea;

Even there shall thy hand lead me, and thy right hand shall hold me.

If I say, Surely the darkness shall cover me; even the night shall be light about me.

Yea, the darkness hideth not from thee; but the

---

17. **Because he hath set his love upon me.** Notice the change of speaker.

night shineth as the day: the darkness and the light are both alike to thee.

For thou hast possessed my reins: thou hast covered me in my mother's womb.

I will praise thee; for I am fearfully and wonderfully made: marvellous are thy works; and that my soul knoweth right well.

My substance was not hid from thee, when I was made in secret, and curiously wrought in the lowest parts of the earth.

Thine eyes did see my substance, yet being unperfect; and in thy book all my members were written, which in continuance were fashioned, when as yet there was none of them.

How precious also are thy thoughts unto me, O God! how great is the sum of them!

If I should count them, they are more in number than the sand: when I awake, I am still with thee.

Surely thou wilt slay the wicked, O God: depart from me therefore, ye bloody men.

For they speak against thee wickedly, and thine enemies take thy name in vain.

Do not I hate them, O Lord, that hate thee? and am not I grieved with those that rise up against thee?

I hate them with perfect hatred: I count them mine enemies.

Search me, O God, and know my heart: try me, and know my thoughts:

And see if there be any wicked way in me, and lead me in the way everlasting.

from THE GOSPEL ACCORDING TO ST. MATTHEW

This extract is taken from the words of Jesus in the passage familiarly called the Sermon on the Mount.

Chapter 6:19-34

Lay not up for yourselves treasures upon earth, where moth and rust doth corrupt, and where thieves break through and steal:

But lay up for yourselves treasures in heaven, where neither moth nor rust doth corrupt, and where thieves do not break through nor steal:

For where your treasure is, there will your heart be also.

The light of the body is the eye: if therefore thine eye be single, thy whole body shall be full of light.

49. single, that is, liberal.

But if thine eye be evil, thy whole body shall be full of darkness. If therefore the light that is in thee be darkness, how great is that darkness!

No man can serve two masters: for either he will hate the one, and love the other; or else he will hold to the one, and despise the other. Ye cannot serve God and mammon.

Therefore I say unto you, Take no thought for your life, what ye shall eat, or what ye shall drink; nor yet for your body, what ye shall put on. Is not the life more than meat, and the body than raiment?

Behold the fowls of the air: for they sow not, neither do they reap, nor gather into barns; yet your heavenly Father feedeth them. Are ye not much better than they?

Which of you by taking thought can add one cubit unto his stature?

And why take ye thought for raiment? Consider the lilies of the field, how they grow; they toil not, neither do they spin:

And yet I say unto you, That even Solomon in all his glory was not arrayed like one of these.

Wherefore, if God so clothe the grass of the field, which to day is, and to morrow is cast into the oven, shall he not much more clothe you, O ye of little faith?

Therefore take no thought, saying, What shall we eat? or, What shall we drink? or, Wherewithal shall we be clothed?

(For after all these things do the Gentiles seek:) for your heavenly Father knoweth that ye have need of all these things.

But seek ye first the kingdom of God, and his righteousness; and all these things shall be added unto you.

Take therefore no thought for the morrow: for the morrow shall take thought for the things of itself. Sufficient unto the day is the evil thereof.

from THE GOSPEL ACCORDING TO ST. LUKE

Chapter 10:25-37

And, behold, a certain lawyer stood up, and tempted him, saying, Master, what shall I do to inherit eternal life?

1. evil, in the sense of grudging, niggardly. The whole passage is a warning against covetousness. **7. mammon,** from the Aramaic, meaning riches. **8. Take no thought,** that is, be not troubled or anxious. **46. tempted him,** "made trial of him."—Revised Version

He said unto him, What is written in the law? how readest thou?

And he answering said, Thou shalt love the Lord thy God with all thy heart, and with all thy soul, and with all thy strength, and with all thy mind; and thy neighbour as thyself.

And he said unto him, Thou hast answered right: this do, and thou shalt live.

But he, willing to justify himself, said unto Jesus, And who is my neighbour?

And Jesus answering said, A certain man went down from Jerusalem to Jericho, and fell among thieves, which stripped him of his raiment, and wounded him, and departed, leaving him half dead.

And by chance there came down a certain priest that way; and when he saw him, he passed by on the other side.

And likewise a Levite, when he was at the place, came and looked on him, and passed by on the other side.

But a certain Samaritan, as he journeyed, came where he was: and when he saw him, he had compassion on him,

And went to him, and bound up his wounds, pouring in oil and wine, and set him on his own beast, and brought him to an inn, and took care of him.

And on the morrow when he departed, he took out two pence, and gave them to the host, and said unto him, Take care of him; and whatsoever thou spendest more, when I come again, I will repay thee.

Which now of these three, thinkest thou, was neighbour to him that fell among the thieves?

And he said, He that shewed mercy on him. Then said Jesus unto him, Go, and do thou likewise.

9. willing to justify himself, wishing to make an excuse for his question. **11. A certain man.** The story that follows is the familiar Parable of the Good Samaritan. **22. Samaritan.** The Samaritans, inhabitants of Samaria, the region north of Judaea, were half-breeds, and were despised by the Jews.

from THE FIRST EPISTLE OF ST. PAUL TO THE CORINTHIANS

Chapter 13

Though I speak with the tongues of men and of angels, and have not charity, I am become as sounding brass, or a tinkling cymbal.

And though I have the gift of prophecy, and understand all mysteries, and all knowledge; and though I have all faith, so that I could remove mountains, and have not charity, I am nothing.

And though I bestow all my goods to feed the poor, and though I give my body to be burned, and have not charity, it profiteth me nothing.

Charity suffereth long, and is kind; charity envieth not; charity vaunteth not itself, is not puffed up,

Doth not behave itself unseemly, seeketh not her own, is not easily provoked, thinketh no evil;

Rejoiceth not in iniquity, but rejoiceth in the truth;

Beareth all things, believeth all things, hopeth all things, endureth all things.

Charity never faileth: but whether there be prophecies, they shall fail; whether there be tongues, they shall cease; whether there be knowledge, it shall vanish away.

For we know in part, and we prophesy in part.

But when that which is perfect is come, then that which is in part shall be done away.

When I was a child, I spake as a child, I understood as a child, I thought as a child: but when I became a man, I put away childish things.

For now we see through a glass, darkly; but then face to face: now I know in part; but then shall I know even as also I am known.

And now abideth faith, hope, charity, these three; but the greatest of these is charity.

8. sounding brass, or a tinkling cymbal. Moffatt: "a noisy gong or a clanging cymbal." **17. vaunteth not itself,** Moffatt: "makes no parade." **35. through a glass, darkly,** as in a mirror, imperfectly. The mirrors of St. Paul's day were polished metal, and the reflections were at best imperfect.

Francis Bacon
1561–1626

The story of the first sixty years of Bacon's life is largely that of his rise to offices and dignities in the world of politics and in the realm of philosophic thought. His last five years were spent "in disgrace with fortune and men's eyes." He was the younger son of Sir Nicholas Bacon, Lord Keeper of the Seals, and Ann Cook, sister-in-law of the Lord Treasurer, Burghley. At twelve he went to Trinity College, Cambridge, but left in disgust two years later. He was admitted to the study of law at Gray's Inn in 1576, and for the next three years he was in France. By 1582 he had begun his advancement in the legal profession. He was in Parliament at the age of twenty-two, and soon won the patronage of the Earl of Essex. In 1596 he was made Queen's Counsel. In 1601 he was appointed to investigate the causes of the Earl of Essex's revolt, and was instrumental in convicting the Earl. Bacon has been accused of downright disloyalty to his friend and patron, but there are reasons for believing that he did what he could to save him. The Earl's own foolishness, the state of mind of the Queen, and the calculating hatred of Burghley would have been enough to condemn him.

Bacon, at any rate, continued to advance. He was knighted by James I in 1603, and he had for patron the Duke of Buckingham. He was married in 1606 to Alice Barnham, the daughter of a wealthy alderman. Within a dozen years he became successively Solicitor-General, Privy Councillor, Lord Keeper, and Lord Chancellor. When King James was making his royal progress in Scotland, Bacon ruled England. He was as much a philosopher as a statesman, however, and he found time during these years to write some of his *Essays*, and to produce *The Advancement of Learning*, 1605, in which he affirmed the dignity of knowledge, reviewed the present state of learning, and suggested methods by which it could be further advanced. The *Novum Organum*, 1620, was his *New Instrument* for inquiring into truth, and a description of the methods by which a renovation of knowledge was to be achieved.

For all his abilities and advancements, however, Bacon was chronically in need of funds. His father's death left him at nineteen an impecunious young man, and he had early to resort to moneylenders. He was always extravagant, living beyond his means, and was pursued by creditors most of his life. In 1621 he was arraigned before the House of Lords on the charge of bribery and judicial corruption. He pleaded guilty to "corruption and neglect," but denied that he had allowed the bribes to influence the decisions of his court. In his confession he pleaded that he had acted no worse than other officials, but acknowledged the justice of the verdict, and expressed the hope that his own disgrace would help to bring about a higher standard of morality in the courts of law. He was deprived of his offices, fined £40,000, and condemned to imprisonment during the King's pleasure. The fine was remitted; Bacon was in the Tower only two days, and was then allowed to retire to his own house. A yearly pension was granted him, and the five remaining years of his life were devoted to his literary and philosophical interests.

In his retirement he enlarged and revised his *Essays*, 1625, wrote the *History of Henry VII*, 1622, and composed the fragment of the *New Atlantis*, which was published posthumously in 1627. In this his last work he describes some aspects of his program of scientific investigation under the control of the Government. He found time for experiments of his own, and it was while collecting snow to test its preservative qualities that he caught the chill from which he died.

No figure in English history has been so variously estimated as Bacon, and none has been the subject of more extravagant praise or vituperation. Pope called him "the wisest, brightest, meanest of mankind." Blake described his *Essays* as "good advice for Satan's kingdom." His contemporary, Ben Jonson, said of him, "He seemed to me ever, by his work, one of the greatest men, and most worthy of admiration that had been in many ages." His character was such a curious mixture of the great and the base that such different evaluations are inevitable. He was a public-spirited man who seems to have lacked a private conscience, and who preferred economic to moral values. It has been said that in his *Essays* he shows us man as he is; in his writings on science, man as he ought to be. Bacon at least had knowledge of both states of man. If there was one thing to which he was genuinely devoted, apart from his own success, it was the welfare of humanity, and especially the good and the security of the State. He is often likened to Bunyan's Mr. Worldly Wiseman. It is only fair to remember that he also had many of the qualities of Valiant-for-truth.

ESSAYS OR COUNSELS, CIVIL AND MORAL

Ten of Bacon's essays, beginning with "Of Studies," were published in 1597. A second edition containing thirty-eight, and including "Of Marriage and Single Life," "Of Great Place," "Of Death," and "Of Love," appeared in 1612. The essay "Of Travel" was published for the first time in the third edition of 1625. In this, the last edition prepared by Bacon, there were fifty-eight essays, of which the earlier ones had been extensively revised and amplified.

OF TRUTH

WHAT is truth? said jesting Pilate; and would not stay for an answer. Certainly there be that delight in giddiness, and count it a bondage to fix a belief; affecting free-will in thinking, as well as in acting. And though the sects of philosophers of that kind be gone, yet there remain certain discoursing wits, which are of the same veins, though there be not so much blood in them as was in those of the ancients. But it is not only the difficulty and labour which men take in finding out of truth; nor again, that when it is found, it imposeth upon men's thoughts, that doth bring lies in favour; but a natural though corrupt love of the lie itself. One of the later schools of the Grecians examineth the matter, and is at a stand to think what should be in it, that men should love lies; where neither they make for pleasure, as with poets; nor for advantage, as with the merchant, but for the lie's sake. But I cannot tell: this same truth is a naked and open daylight, that doth not show the masks and mummeries and triumphs of the world, half so stately and daintily as candle-lights. Truth may perhaps come to the price of a pearl, that showeth best by day, but it will not rise to the price of a diamond or carbuncle, that showeth best in varied lights. A mixture of a lie doth ever add pleasure. Doth any man doubt, that if there were taken out of men's minds vain opinions, flattering hopes, false valuations, imaginations as one would, and the like, but it would leave the minds of a number of men poor shrunken things, full of melancholy and indisposition, and unpleasing to themselves? One of the fathers, in great severity, called poesy *vinum daemonum*, because it filleth the imagination, and yet it is but with the shadow of a lie. But it is not the lie that passeth through the mind, but the lie that sinketh in, and settleth in it, that doth the hurt, such as we spake of before. But howsoever these things are thus in men's depraved judgments and affections, yet truth, which only doth judge itself, teacheth that the inquiry of truth, which is the love-making, or wooing of it, the knowledge of truth, which is the presence of it, and the belief of truth, which is the enjoying of it, is the sovereign good of human nature. The first creature of God, in the works of the days, was the light of the sense: the last was the light of reason: and his sabbath work ever since, is the illumination of his Spirit. First, he breathed light upon the face of the matter, or chaos; then he breathed light into the face of man; and still he breatheth and inspireth light into the face of his chosen. The poet that beautified the sect that was otherwise inferior to the rest saith yet excellently well: "It is a pleasure to stand upon the shore, and to see ships tossed upon the sea: a pleasure to stand in the window of a castle, and to see a battle, and the adventures thereof below: but no pleasure is comparable to the standing upon the vantage ground of truth" (a hill not to be commanded, and where the air is always clear and serene) "and to see the errors, and wanderings, and mists, and tempests, in the vale below": so always that this prospect be with pity, and not with swelling or pride. Certainly, it is heaven upon earth, to have a man's mind move in charity, rest in providence, and turn upon the poles of truth.

To pass from theological and philosophical truth to the truth of civil business; it will be acknowledged even by those that practise it not, that clear and round dealing is the honour of man's nature, and that mixture of falsehood is like alloy in coin of gold and silver, which may make the metal work the better, but it embaseth it. For these winding and crooked courses are the goings of the serpent; which goeth basely upon the belly, and not upon

---

24. **Pilate.** See John 18:38.   26. **giddiness,** that is, "a whirl of thoughts."   28–29. **philosophers of that kind,** the Greek Skeptics, who taught that absolute certainty in knowledge is impossible.   29–30. **discoursing wits,** rambling and talkative minds.   34. **imposeth upon,** restrains.   40. **as with poets.** Here as elsewhere Bacon's derogatory comments on poets and poetry are to be noted.   45. **daintily,** elegantly.

7–8. **One of the fathers,** perhaps St. Augustine, in his *Confessions.*   8–9. **vinum daemonum,** the wine of devils.   27. **poet,** the Epicurean Lucretius, of the first century B.C.   34. **commanded,** subject to attack.   45. **round dealing.** We should say "square dealing."

the feet. There is no vice that doth so cover a man with shame as to be found false and perfidious; and therefore Montaigne saith prettily, when he inquired the reason why the word of the lie should be such a disgrace, and such an odious charge, saith he, "If it be well weighed, to say that a man lieth, is as much as to say that he is brave towards God and a coward towards men. For a lie faces God, and shrinks from man." Surely the wickedness of falsehood and breach of faith cannot possibly be so highly expressed, as in that it shall be the last peal to call the judgments of God upon the generations of men, it being foretold that when "Christ cometh," he shall not "find faith upon the earth."

OF DEATH

MEN fear death as children fear to go in the dark; and as that natural fear in children is increased with tales, so is the other. Certainly, the contemplation of death as the wages of sin, and passage to another world, is holy and religious; but the fear of it, as a tribute due unto nature, is weak. Yet in religious meditations there is sometimes mixture of vanity and of superstition. You shall read in some of the friars' books of mortification that a man should think with himself what the pain is if he have but his finger's end pressed or tortured; and thereby imagine what the pains of death are, when the whole body is corrupted and dissolved; when many times death passeth with less pain than the torture of a limb; for the most vital parts are not the quickest of sense. And by him that spake only as a philosopher, and natural man, it was well said, *Pompa mortis magis terret, quam mors ipsa.* Groans and convulsions, and a discoloured face, and friends weeping, and blacks and obsequies, and the like, show death terrible. It is worthy the observing that there is no passion in the mind of man so weak, but it mates and masters the fear of death; and therefore death is no such terrible enemy when a man hath so many attendants about him that can win the combat of him. Revenge triumphs over death; love slights it; honour aspireth to it; grief flieth to it; fear preoccupateth it; nay, we read, after Otho the emperor had slain himself, pity, which is the tenderest of affections, provoked many to die out of mere compassion to their sovereign, and as the truest sort of followers. Nay, Seneca adds, niceness and satiety: *Cogita quamdiu eadem feceris; mori velle, non tantum fortis, aut miser, sed etiam fastidiosus potest.* A man would die, though he were neither valiant nor miserable, only upon a weariness to do the same thing so oft over and over. It is no less worthy to observe, how little alteration in good spirits the approaches of death make: for they appear to be the same men till the last instant. Augustus Caesar died in a compliment, *Livia, conjugii nostri memor, vive et vale.* Tiberius in dissimulation, as Tacitus saith of him, *Jam Tiberium vires et corpus, non dissimulatio, deserebant;* Vespasian in a jest, sitting upon the stool, *Ut puto Deus fio:* Galba with a sentence, *Feri, si ex re sit populi Romani,* holding forth his neck; Septimus Severus in dispatch, *Adeste, si quid mihi restat agendum,* and the like. Certainly the Stoics bestowed too much cost upon death, and by their great preparations made it appear more fearful. Better, saith he, *qui finem vitae extremum inter munera ponit naturae.* It is as natural to die as to be born; and to a little infant, perhaps, the one is as painful as the other. He that dies in an earnest pursuit, is like one that is wounded in hot blood; who for the time scarce feels the hurt; and therefore a mind fixed and bent upon somewhat that is good, doth avert the dolours of death. But, above all, believe it, the sweetest canticle is *Nunc dimittis,* when a man hath obtained worthy ends and expectations. Death hath this also, that it openeth the gate to good fame, and extinguisheth envy. *Extinctus amabitur idem.*

OF MARRIAGE AND SINGLE LIFE

HE that hath wife and children hath given hostages to fortune; for they are impediments to great enterprises, either of virtue or mischief. Certainly the best works, and of greatest merit for the public, have proceeded from the unmarried or

---

3. **Montaigne,** in his *Essays,* Book II, chap. 18. It was from Montaigne (1533–1592) that Bacon took the name, and doubtless some of the ideas, of his essays.　14. **"find faith upon the earth."** See Luke 18:8.　34. **by him,** Seneca, in his *Epistles,* Book III, Ep. 3, l. 14.　36. **Pompa . . . ipsa.** The circumstances connected with death terrify more than death itself.　38. **blacks,** black draperies.

2. **niceness,** fastidiousness.　3–4. **Cogita . . . potest.** Consider how long you have done the same things; a man may wish to die not only because he is brave, or miserable, but also because he is simply tired of life.　11–12. **Livia . . . vale.** Livia, mindful of our marriage, live on, and fare thee well.　13–14. **Jam . . . deserebant.** His physical powers and vitality were deserting Tiberius, but not his duplicity.　15. **Ut puto Deus fio.** As I think, I am becoming a God.　16. **Feri . . . Romani.** Strike, if it be for the good of the Roman people.　17–18. **Adeste . . . agendum.** Make haste, if anything remains for me to do.　21–22. **qui . . . naturae,** who considers the close of life one of the blessings of nature.—Juvenal, *Satires,* X, l. 358　29. **Nunc dimittis.** Now lettest thou thy servant depart in peace. See Luke 2:29.　32. **Extinctus amabitur idem.** The same man (who was envied while alive) shall be loved when dead.

childless men, which both in affection and means have married and endowed the public. Yet it were great reason that those that have children should have greatest care of future times, unto which they know they must transmit their dearest pledges. Some there are who, though they lead a single life, yet their thoughts do end with themselves, and account future times impertinences. Nay, there are some other that account wife and children but as bills of charges. Nay more, there are some foolish rich covetous men, that take a pride in having no children, because they may be thought so much the richer. For perhaps they have heard some talk, "Such an one is a great rich man," and another except to it, "Yea, but he hath a great charge of children"; as if it were an abatement to his riches. But the most ordinary cause of a single life is liberty, especially in certain self-pleasing and humorous minds, which are so sensible of every restraint, as they will go near to think their girdles and garters to be bonds and shackles. Unmarried men are best friends, best masters, best servants, but not always best subjects, for they are light to run away, and almost all fugitives are of that condition. A single life doth well with churchmen, for charity will hardly water the ground where it must first fill a pool. It is indifferent for judges and magistrates, for if they be facile and corrupt, you shall have a servant five times worse than a wife. For soldiers, I find the generals commonly in their hortatives put men in mind of their wives and children; and I think the despising of marriage amongst the Turks maketh the vulgar soldier more base. Certainly wife and children are a kind of discipline of humanity; and single men, though they be many times more charitable, because their means are less exhaust, yet, on the other side, they are more cruel and hard-hearted (good to make severe inquisitors), because their tenderness is not so oft called upon. Grave natures, led by custom, and therefore constant, are commonly loving husbands, as was said of Ulysses, *Vetulam suam praetulit immortalitati.* Chaste women are often proud and froward, as presuming upon the merit of their chastity. It is one of the best bonds, both of chastity and obedience, in the wife if she think her husband wise, which she will never do if she find him jealous. Wives are young men's mistresses, companions for middle age, and old men's nurses, so as a man may have a quarrel to marry when he will. But yet he was reputed one of the wise men that made answer to the question when a man should marry: "A young man not yet, an elder man not at all." It is often seen that bad husbands have very good wives; whether it be that it raiseth the price of their husbands' kindness when it comes, or that the wives take a pride in their patience. But this never fails, if the bad husbands were of their own choosing, against their friends' consent; for then they will be sure to make good their own folly.

OF LOVE

THE stage is more beholding to love than the life of man. For as to the stage, love is ever matter of comedies, and now and then of tragedies; but in life it doth much mischief, sometimes like a siren, sometimes like a fury. You may observe, that amongst all the great and worthy persons whereof the memory remaineth, either ancient or recent, there is not one that hath been transported to the mad degree of love; which shows that great spirits and great business do keep out this weak passion. You must except, nevertheless, Marcus Antonius, the half partner of the empire of Rome, and Appius Claudius, the Decemvir and lawgiver; whereof the former was indeed a voluptuous man, and inordinate; but the latter was an austere and wise man. And therefore it seems (though rarely) that love can find entrance, not only into an open heart, but also into a heart well fortified, if watch be not well kept. It is a poor saying of Epicurus, *Satis magnum alter alteri theatrum sumus:* as if man, made for the contemplation of heaven and all noble objects, should do nothing but kneel before a little idol, and make himself subject, though not of the mouth, as beasts are, yet of the eye, which was given him for higher purposes. It is a strange thing to note the excess of this passion, and how it braves the nature and value of things by this, that the speaking in a perpetual hyperbole is comely in nothing but in love. Neither is it merely in the phrase. For whereas it hath been well said, "That the arch flatterer, with whom all the petty flatterers have intelligence, is a man's self," certainly the lover is more. For there was never proud man thought so absurdly well of himself as the lover doth of the person loved; and therefore it was well said, "That it is impossible

---

18. **humorous,** eccentric. 42. **Vetulam . . . immortalitati.** He preferred his aged wife (Penelope) to immortality. 50. **quarrel,** pretext. 14. **beholding to,** beholden to, attached to. 24. **Marcus Antonius,** in love with Cleopatra, queen of Egypt. 26. **Claudius.** Appius Claudius tried basely to get possession of Virginia, daughter of a plebeian, Virginius. The father slew his daughter to prevent her falling into the hands of Appius. 32–33. **Satis . . . sumus.** Each of us is to the other a sufficiently large theater. 39. **braves,** insults.

to love and to be wise." Neither doth this weakness appear to others only, and not to the party loved, but to the loved most of all, except the love be reciprocal. For it is a true rule, that love is ever rewarded, either with the reciprocal, or with an inward and secret contempt; by how much the more men ought to beware of this passion, which loseth not only other things, but itself. As for the other losses, the poet's relation doth well figure them, "That he that preferred Helena, quitted the gifts of Juno and Pallas." For whosoever esteemeth too much of amorous affection, quitteth both riches and wisdom. This passion hath his floods in the very times of weakness, which are great prosperity and great adversity, though this latter hath been less observed. Both which times kindle love, and make it more fervent, and therefore show it to be the child of folly. They do best who, if they cannot but admit love, yet make it keep quarter, and sever it wholly from their serious affairs and actions of life. For if it check once with business, it troubleth men's fortunes, and maketh men that they can nowise be true to their own ends. I know not how, but martial men are given to love. I think it is but as they are given to wine, for perils commonly ask to be paid in pleasures. There is in man's nature a secret inclination and motion towards love of others, which if it be not spent upon some one or a few, doth naturally spread itself towards many, and maketh men become humane and charitable, as it is seen sometimes in friars. Nuptial love maketh mankind, friendly love perfecteth it, but wanton love corrupteth and embaseth it.

OF GREAT PLACE

MEN in great place are thrice servants—servants of the sovereign or state, servants of fame, and servants of business. So as they have no freedom, neither in their persons, nor in their actions, nor in their times. It is a strange desire to seek power and to lose liberty; or to seek power over others, and to lose power over a man's self. The rising unto place is laborious, and by pains men come to greater pains; and it is sometimes base, and by indignities men come to dignities. The standing is slippery, and the regress is either a downfall, or at least an eclipse, which is a melancholy thing: *Cum non sis qui fueris, non esse cur velis vivere.* Nay, retire men cannot when they would, neither will they when it were reason; but are impatient of privateness even in age and sickness, which require the shadow; like old townsmen, that will be still sitting at their street-door, though thereby they offer age to scorn. Certainly great persons had need to borrow other men's opinions to think themselves happy; for if they judge by their own feeling, they cannot find it; but if they think with themselves what other men think of them, and that other men would fain be as they are, then they are happy as it were by report, when, perhaps, they find the contrary within. For they are the first that find their own griefs, though they be the last that find their own faults. Certainly men in great fortunes are strangers to themselves, and while they are in the puzzle of business they have no time to tend their health either of body or mind. *Illi mors gravis incubat, qui notus nimis omnibus, ignotus moritur sibi.* In place there is licence to do good and evil; whereof the latter is a curse: for in evil the best condition is not to will, the second not to can. But power to do good is the true and lawful end of aspiring; for good thoughts, though God accept them, yet towards men are little better than good dreams, except they be put in act; and that cannot be without power and place, as the vantage and commanding ground. Merit and good works is the end of man's motion, and conscience of the same is the accomplishment of man's rest: for if a man can be partaker of God's theatre, he shall likewise be partaker of God's rest. *Et conversus Deus, ut aspiceret opera, quae fecerunt manus suae, vidit quod omnia essent bona nimis;* and then the Sabbath.

In the discharge of thy place set before thee the best examples; for imitation is a globe of precepts. And after a time set before thee thine own example; and examine thyself strictly whether thou didst not best at first. Neglect not also the examples of those that have carried themselves ill in the same place; not to set off thyself by taxing their memory, but to direct thyself what to avoid. Reform, therefore, without bravery or scandal of former times and persons; but yet set it down to thyself, as well to create good precedents as to follow them. Reduce things to the first institution, and observe wherein and how they have degenerated; but yet ask counsel of both times—of the ancient time what is best, and

---

10. he that preferred, Paris, son of Priam, king of Troy. His abduction of Helen led to the Trojan War. **21. check,** interfere. **50. Cum . . . vivere.** Since you are not what you were, there is no reason why you should wish to live. **18–20. Illi . . . sibi.** Death lies heavily upon him who, well known to all others, dies unknown to himself. **22. to can,** to know. **29. conscience,** consciousness. **31. theatre,** spectacle; that is, can see what God saw. **32–34. Et conversus . . . nimis.** Genesis 1:31, quoted from the Vulgate: "And God, having looked upon all the works which his hands had made, saw that all were very good." **41. taxing,** censuring. **43. bravery,** boastfulness, ostentation.

of the latter time what is fittest. Seek to make thy course regular, that men may know beforehand what they may expect; but be not too positive and peremptory; and express thyself well when thou digressest from thy rule. Preserve the right of thy place, but stir not questions of jurisdiction; and rather assume thy right in silence, and *de facto*, than voice it with claims and challenges. Preserve likewise the rights of inferior places; and think it more honour to direct in chief than to be busy in all. Embrace and invite helps and advices touching the execution of thy place; and do not drive away such as bring thee information as meddlers, but accept of them in good part. The vices of authority are chiefly four: delays, corruption, roughness, and facility. For delays give easy access, keep times appointed, go through with that which is in hand, and interlace not business but of necessity. For corruption, do not only bind thine own hands or thy servant's hands from taking, but bind the hands of suitors also from offering. For integrity used doth the one, but integrity professed, and with a manifest detestation of bribery, doth the other. And avoid not only the fault, but the suspicion. Whosoever is found variable, and changeth manifestly without manifest cause, giveth suspicion of corruption. Therefore, always when thou changest thine opinion or course, profess it plainly, and declare it, together with the reasons that move thee to change, and do not think to steal it. A servant or a favourite, if he be inward, and no other apparent cause of esteem, is commonly thought but a by-way to close corruption. For roughness, it is a needless cause of discontent: severity breedeth fear, but roughness breedeth hate. Even reproofs from authority ought to be grave, and not taunting. As for facility, it is worse than bribery; for bribes come but now and then; but if importunity or idle respects lead a man, he shall never be without. As Solomon saith, "To respect persons is not good; for such a man will transgress for a piece of bread."

It is most true that was anciently spoken: "A place showeth the man; and it showeth some to the better and some to the worse." *Omnium consensu capax imperii, nisi imperasset*, saith Tacitus of Galba; but of Vespasian he saith, *Solus imperantium Vespasianus mutatus in melius:* though the one was meant of sufficiency, the other of manners and affection. It is an assured sign of a worthy and generous spirit, whom honour amends; for honour is, or should be, the place of virtue; and as in nature things move violently to their place, and calmly in their place, so virtue in ambition is violent, in authority settled and calm. All rising to great place is by a winding stair; and if there be factions, it is good to side a man's self whilst he is in the rising, and to balance himself when he is placed. Use the memory of thy predecessor fairly and tenderly; for if thou dost not, it is a debt will sure be paid when thou art gone. If thou have colleagues, respect them; and rather call them when they look not for it, than exclude them when they have reason to look to be called. Be not too sensible or too remembering of thy place in conversation and private answers to suitors; but let it rather be said, "When he sits in place he is another man."

OF TRAVEL

TRAVEL, in the younger sort, is a part of education; in the elder, a part of experience. He that travelleth into a country before he hath some entrance into the language, goeth to school, and not to travel. That young men travel under some tutor or grave servant, I allow well; so that he be such a one that hath the language, and hath been in the country before; whereby he may be able to tell them what things are worthy to be seen in the country where they go, what acquaintances they are to seek, what exercises or discipline the place yieldeth; for else young men shall go hooded, and look abroad little. It is a strange thing that in sea voyages, where there is nothing to be seen but sky and sea, men should make diaries; but in land travel, wherein so much is to be observed, for the most part they omit it; as if chance were fitter to be registered than observation. Let diaries, therefore, be brought in use. The things to be seen and observed are: the courts of princes, especially when they give audience to ambassadors; the courts of justice, while they sit and hear causes; and so of consistories ecclesiastic; the churches and monasteries, with the monuments which are therein extant; the walls and fortifications of cities and towns; and so the havens and harbours, antiquities and ruins, libraries, colleges, disputations, and lectures, where any are; shipping and navies; houses and gardens of state and pleasure,

---

7. **de facto,** as a matter of course.   15–16. **facility,** easiness to be led.   30. **steal it,** do it by stealth.   31. **inward,** confidential.   39. **Solomon.** See Proverbs 28:21.   44–45. **Omnium . . . imperasset.** Everyone would have thought him capable of ruling—if he had not ruled.   46–47. **Solus . . . melius.** Of the emperors, Vespasian alone changed for the better (when in power).   47–48. **sufficiency,** ability.   48. **affection,** disposition.

7. **side,** stand or be on the side of.   28. **allow,** approve.   33. **discipline,** learning.   48–49. **disputations,** formal philosophical debates, which were a regular part of the academic curriculum in Renaissance Europe.

near great cities; armories, arsenals, magazines, exchanges, burses, warehouses, exercises of horsemanship, fencing, training of soldiers, and the like; comedies, such whereunto the better sort of persons do resort; treasuries of jewels and robes; cabinets and rarities; and, to conclude, whatsoever is memorable in the places where they go; after all which the tutors or servants ought to make diligent inquiry. As for triumphs, masks, feasts, weddings, funerals, capital executions, and such shows, men need not to be put in mind of them; yet are they not to be neglected. If you will have a young man to put his travel into a little room, and in short time to gather much, this you must do: first, as was said, he must have some entrance into the language before he goeth; then he must have such a servant, or tutor, as knoweth the country, as was likewise said; let him carry with him also some card, or book, describing the country where he travelleth, which will be a good key to his inquiry; let him keep also a diary; let him not stay long in one city or town, more or less as the place deserveth, but not long; nay, when he stayeth in one city or town, let him change his lodging from one end and part of the town to another, which is a great adamant of acquaintance; let him sequester himself from the company of his countrymen, and diet in such places where there is good company of the nation where he travelleth. Let him, upon his removes from one place to another, procure recommendation to some person of quality residing in the place whither he removeth, that he may use his favour in those things he desireth to see or know. Thus he may abridge his travel with much profit. As for the acquaintance which is to be sought in travel, that which is most of all profitable is acquaintance with the secretaries and employed men of ambassadors; for so in travelling in one country he shall suck the experience of many. Let him also see and visit eminent persons in all kinds, which are of great name abroad, that he may be able to tell how the life agreeth with the fame. For quarrels, they are with care and discretion to be avoided. They are commonly for mistresses, healths, place, and words. And let a man beware how he keepeth company with choleric and quarrelsome persons, for they will engage him into their own quarrels. When a traveller returneth home, let him not leave the countries where he hath travelled altogether behind him, but maintain a correspondence by letters with those of his acquaintance which are of most worth. And let his travel appear rather in his discourse than in his apparel or gesture; and in his discourse let him be rather advised in his answers, than forward to tell stories. And let it appear that he doth not change his country manners for those of foreign parts, but only prick in some flowers of that he hath learned abroad into the customs of his own country.

OF STUDIES

STUDIES serve for delight, for ornament, and for ability. Their chief use for delight is in privateness and retiring; for ornament, is in discourse; and for ability, is in the judgment and disposition of business. For expert men can execute, and perhaps judge of particulars, one by one; but the general counsels, and the plots and marshalling of affairs come best from those that are learned. To spend too much time in studies is sloth; to use them too much for ornament is affectation; to make judgment wholly by their rules is the humour of a scholar. They perfect nature, and are perfected by experience; for natural abilities are like natural plants, that need pruning by study; and studies themselves do give forth directions too much at large, except they be bounded in by experience. Crafty men contemn studies, simple men admire them, and wise men use them; for they teach not their own use; but that is a wisdom without them and above them, won by observation. Read not to contradict and confute, nor to believe and take for granted, nor to find talk and discourse, but to weigh and consider. Some books are to be tasted, others to be swallowed, and some few to be chewed and digested; that is, some books are to be read only in parts; others to be read, but not curiously; and some few to be read wholly, and with diligence and attention. Some books also may be read by deputy, and extracts made of them by others; but that would be only in the less important arguments and the meaner sort of books; else distilled books are, like common distilled waters, flashy things. Reading maketh a full man; conference a ready man; and writing an exact man. And, therefore, if a man write little, he had need have a great memory; if he confer little, he had need have a present wit; and if he read little, he had need have much cunning, to seem to know that he doth not. Histories make men wise; poets, witty; the mathematics, subtile; natural philosophy, deep; moral, grave; logic and rhetoric,

3. country manners, those of his own country. **12–13. privateness and retiring,** privacy and retirement. **36. curiously,** carefully. **42. flashy,** flat or showy. **49. poets, witty,** another interesting bit of evidence as to Bacon's view of the function of poets and poetry.

2. burses, stock exchanges. **18. card,** chart, map. **25. adamant,** loadstone, magnet.

able to contend. *Abeunt studia in mores.* Nay, there is no stond or impediment in the wit but may be wrought out by fit studies, like as diseases of the body may have appropriate exercises. Bowling is good for the stone and reins, shooting for the lungs and breast, gentle walking for the stomach, riding for the head and the like. So if a man's wit be wandering, let him study the mathematics; for in demonstrations, if his wit be called away never so little, he must begin again. If his wit be not apt to distinguish or find difference, let him study the school men; for they are *Cymini sectores.* If he be not apt to beat over matters, and to call up one thing to prove and illustrate another, let him study the lawyers' cases. So every defect of the mind may have a special receipt.

from NEW ATLANTIS

Bacon's *New Atlantis* furnishes an interesting counterpart to Shakespeare's *The Tempest.* One is the supreme presentation of the scientist's idea of an imaginary island, as the other is of the poet's, and consequently the essential differences between the scientist's mind and methods and those of the poet could hardly be better illustrated than in these two pieces. Bacon's island is not the creation of a poet. It has no such delightful creatures of the imagination as Ariel, or such monsters as Caliban. Instead of magical voices we have telephones (means "to convey sounds in trunks and pipes, in strange lines and distances") and loud-speakers ("to represent small sounds as great and deep"). Solomon's House is no palace of magic, but a matter-of-fact laboratory of scientific research. It is the product not of a magician's wand but of hard work and much cerebration. It may be taken as the prototype of the great Royal Society and of all the other institutions and associations which by co-operation and experimentation are engaged in discovering "the knowledge of causes, and secret motions of things; and the enlarging of the bounds of human empire, to the effecting of all things possible."

[SOLOMON'S HOUSE]

AND as we were thus in conference, there came one that seemed to be a messenger, in a rich huke, that spake with the Jew; whereupon he turned to me, and said, "You will pardon me, for I am commanded away in haste." The next morning he came to me again, joyful as it seemed, and said, "There is word come to the Governor of the city, that one of the fathers of Solomon's House will be here this day seven-night; we have seen none of them this dozen years. His coming is in state; but the cause of his coming is secret. I will provide you and your fellows of a good standing to see his entry." I thanked him, and told him I was most glad of the news.

The day being come he made his entry. He was a man of middle stature and age, comely of person, and had an aspect as if he pitied men. He was clothed in a robe of fine black cloth, with wide sleeves, and a cape: his under garment was of excellent white linen down to the foot, girt with a girdle of the same; and a sindon or tippet of the same about his neck. He had gloves that were curious, and set with stone; and shoes of peach-coloured velvet. His neck was bare to the shoulders. His hat was like a helmet, or Spanish montero; and his locks curled below it decently: they were of colour brown. His beard was cut round and of the same colour with his hair, somewhat lighter. He was carried in a rich chariot, without wheels, litter-wise, with two horses at either end, richly trapped in blue velvet embroidered; and two footmen on each side in the like attire. The chariot was all of cedar, gilt, and adorned with crystal; save that the fore-end had panels of sapphires, set in borders of gold, and the hinder-end the like of emeralds of the Peru colour. There was also a sun of gold, radiant upon the top, in the midst; and on the top before, a small cherub of gold, with wings displayed. The chariot was covered with cloth of gold tissued upon blue. He had before him fifty attendants, young men all, in white satin loose coats to the mid-leg; and stockings of white silk, and shoes of blue velvet; and hats of blue velvet, with fine plumes of divers colours, set round like hat-bands. Next before the chariot went two men, bare-headed, in linen garments down to the foot, girt, and shoes of blue velvet, who carried the one a crosier, the other a pastoral staff like a sheep-hook: neither of them of metal, but the crosier of balm-wood, the pastoral staff of cedar. Horsemen he had none, neither before nor behind his chariot: as it seemeth, to avoid all tumult and trouble. Behind his chariot went all the officers and principals of the companies of the city. He sat alone, upon cushions, of a kind of excellent plush, blue; and under his foot curious carpets of silk of divers colours, like the Persian, but far finer. He held up his bare hand, as he went, as blessing the people, but in silence. The street was wonderfully well kept; so that

---

1. **Abeunt studia in mores.** Studies pass into (that is, form) manners.   2. **stond,** stand, difficulty.   5. **stone,** of the bladder or **reins** (kidneys).   12. **Cymini sectores,** dividers of cuminseed; that is, hairsplitters. See Matthew 23:23.   46. **huke,** a kind of cape with a hood.

15. **curious,** of rare workmanship.   18. **montero,** hunting cap.   31. **displayed,** outspread.   32. **tissued,** worked in threads.

there was never any army had their men stand in better battle-array than the people stood. The windows likewise were not crowded, but every one stood in them, as if they had been placed.

When the show was passed, the Jew said to me, "I shall not be able to attend you as I would, in regard of some charge the city hath laid upon me for the entertaining of this great person." Three days after the Jew came to me again, and said, "Ye are happy men; for the father of Solomon's House taketh knowledge of your being here, and commanded me to tell you, that he will admit all your company to his presence, and have private conference with one of you, that ye shall choose; and for this hath appointed the next day after to-morrow. And because he meaneth to give you his blessing, he hath appointed it in the forenoon."

We came at our day and hour, and I was chosen by my fellows for the private access. We found him in a fair chamber, richly hanged, and carpeted under foot, without any degrees to the state. He was set upon a low throne richly adorned, and a rich cloth of state over his head, of blue satin embroidered. He was alone, save that he had two pages of honour, on either hand one, finely attired in white. His under garments were the like that we saw him wear in the chariot; but instead of his gown, he had on him a mantle with a cape, of the same fine black, fastened about him. When we came in, as we were taught, we bowed low at our first entrance; and when we were come near his chair, he stood up, holding forth his hand ungloved, and in posture of blessing; and we every one of us stooped down, and kissed the hem of his tippet. That done, the rest departed, and I remained. Then he warned the pages forth of the room, and caused me to sit down beside him, and spake to me thus in the Spanish tongue:

"God bless thee, my son; I will give thee the greatest jewel I have. For I will impart unto thee, for the love of God and men, a relation of the true state of Solomon's House. Son, to make you know the true state of Solomon's House, I will keep this order. First, I will set forth unto you the end of our foundation. Secondly, the preparations and instruments we have for our works. Thirdly, the several employments and functions whereto our fellows are assigned. And fourthly, the ordinances and rites which we observe.

"The end of our foundation is the knowledge of causes, and secret motions of things; and the enlarging of the bounds of human empire, to the effecting of all things possible.

"The preparations and instruments are these. We have large and deep caves of several depths: the deepest are sunk six hundred fathoms; and some of them are digged and made under great hills and mountains; so that if you reckon together the depth of the hill, and the depth of the cave, they are, some of them, above three miles deep. For we find that the depth of a hill, and the depth of a cave from the flat, is the same thing; both remote alike from the sun and heaven's beams, and from the open air. These caves we call the lower region, and we use them for all coagulations, indurations, refrigerations, and conservations of bodies. We use them likewise for the imitation of natural mines, and the producing also of new artificial metals, by compositions and materials which we use, and lay there for many years. We use them also sometimes (which may seem strange) for curing of some diseases, and for prolongation of life, in some hermits that choose to live there, well accommodated of all things necessary, and indeed live very long; by whom also we learn many things.

"We have burials in several earths, where we put divers cements, as the Chinese do their porcelain. But we have them in greater variety, and some of them more fine. We also have great variety of composts and soils, for the making of the earth fruitful.

"We have high towers, the highest about half a mile in height, and some of them likewise set upon high mountains, so that the vantage of the hill, with the tower, is in the highest of them three miles at least. And these places we call the upper region, accounting the air between the high places and the low as a middle region. We use these towers, according to their several heights and situations, for insolation, refrigeration, conservation, and for the view of divers meteors—as winds, rain, snow, hail; and some of the fiery meteors also. And upon them, in some places, are dwellings of hermits, whom we visit sometimes, and instruct what to observe.

"We have great lakes, both salt and fresh, whereof we have use for the fish and fowl. We use them also for burials of some natural bodies, for we find a difference in things buried in earth, or in air below the earth, and things buried in water. We have also pools, of which some do strain fresh water out of salt, and others by art do turn fresh water into salt. We have also some rocks in the midst of the sea, and some bays upon the shore for some works, wherein is

---

20. **richly hanged**, with rich hangings. 21. **without any degrees to the state**, without any steps leading to the canopy. 35. **warned**, ordered.

14. **indurations**, experiments of hardening. 28–29. **composts**, fertilizers. 38. **insolation**, exposure to the action of the sun. 39. **meteors**, meterological phenomena.

required the air and vapour of the sea. We have likewise violent streams and cataracts, which serve us for many motions; and likewise engines for multiplying and enforcing of winds to set also on divers motions.

"We have also a number of artificial wells and fountains, made in imitation of the natural sources and baths, as tincted upon vitriol, sulphur, steel, brass, lead, nitre, and other minerals; and again, we have little wells for infusions of many things, where the waters take the virtue quicker and better than in vessels or basins. And amongst them we have a water, which we call Water of Paradise, being by that we do to it made very sovereign for health and prolongation of life.

"We have also great and spacious houses, where we imitate and demonstrate meteors—as snow, hail, rain, some artificial rains of bodies, and not of water, thunders, lightnings; also generations of bodies in air—as frogs, flies, and divers others.

"We have also certain chambers, which we call chambers of health, where we qualify the air as we think good and proper for the cure of divers diseases, and preservation of health.

"We have also fair and large baths, of several mixtures, for the cure of diseases, and the restoring of man's body from arefaction; and others for the confirming of it in strength of sinews, vital parts, and the very juice and substance of the body.

"We have also large and various orchards and gardens, wherein we do not so much respect beauty as variety of ground and soil, proper for divers trees and herbs, and some very spacious, where trees and berries are set, whereof we make divers kinds of drinks, besides the vineyards. In these we practise likewise all conclusions of grafting and inoculating, as well of wild-trees as fruit-trees, which produceth many effects. And we make by art, in the same orchards and gardens, trees and flowers, to come earlier or later than their seasons, and to come up and bear more speedily than by their natural course they do. We make them also by art greater much than their nature; and their fruit greater and sweeter, and of differing taste, smell, colour, and figure, from their nature. And many of them we so order as they become of medicinal use.

"We have also means to make divers plants rise by mixtures of earths without seeds, and likewise to make divers new plants, differing from the vulgar, and to make one tree or plant turn into another.

"We have also parks, and enclosures of all sorts, of beasts and birds; which we use not only for view or rareness, but likewise for dissections and trials, that thereby we may take light what may be wrought upon the body of man. Wherein we find many strange effects: as continuing life in them, though divers parts, which you account vital, be perished and taken forth; resuscitating of some that seem dead in appearance, and the like. We try also all poisons, and other medicines upon them, as well of chirurgery as physic. By art likewise we make them greater or taller than their kind is, and contrariwise dwarf them and stay their growth; we make them more fruitful and bearing than their kind is, and contrariwise barren and not generative. Also we make them differ in colour, shape, activity, many ways. We find means to make commixtures and copulations of divers kinds, which have produced many new kinds, and them not barren, as the general opinion is. We make a number of kinds, of serpents, worms, flies, fishes, of putrefaction, whereof some are advanced (in effect) to be perfect creatures, like beasts or birds, and have sexes, and do propagate. Neither do we this by chance, but we know beforehand of what matter and commixture, what kind of those creatures will arise.

"We have also particular pools where we make trials upon fishes, as we have said before of beasts and birds.

"We have also places for breed and generation of those kinds of worms and flies which are of special use; such as are with you your silkworms and bees.

"I will not hold you long with recounting of our brew-houses, bake-houses, and kitchens, where are made divers drinks, breads, and meats, rare and of special effects. Wines we have of grapes, and drinks of other juice, of fruits, of grains, and of roots, and of mixtures with honey, sugar, manna, and fruits dried and decocted; also of the tears or woundings of trees, and of the pulp of canes. And these drinks are of several ages, some to the age or last of forty years. We have drinks also brewed with several herbs, and roots and spices; yea, with several fleshes and white-meats; whereof some of the drinks are such as they are in effect meat and drink both, so that divers, especially in age, do desire to live with them with little or no meat or bread. And above all we strive to have drinks of extreme thin parts, to insinuate into the body, and yet without all biting, sharpness, or fretting; insomuch as some of them, put upon the back of your hand, will with a little stay pass through to the palm, and taste yet mild to the mouth. We have also waters, which we ripen in that

---

4. **enforcing**, increasing the force. 8. **tincted upon**, tinctured with. 11. **virtue**, the specific property of the substances. 27. **arefaction**, drying up. 36. **conclusions**, theories. 49. **vulgar**, ordinary.

11. **chirurgery**, surgery. 41. **last**, duration.

fashion, as they become nourishing, so that they are indeed excellent drinks, and many will use no other. Bread we have of several grains, roots, and kernels; yea, and some of flesh, and fish, dried; with divers kinds of leavenings and seasonings; so that some do extremely move appetites, some do nourish so, as divers do live of them, without any other meat, who live very long. So for meats, we have some of them so beaten, and made tender, and mortified, yet without all corrupting, as a weak heat of the stomach will turn them into good chylus, as well as a strong heat would meat otherwise prepared. We have some meats also, and breads, and drinks, which taken by men, enable them to fast long after; and some other, that used make the very flesh of men's bodies sensibly more hard and tough, and their strength far greater than otherwise it would be.

"We have dispensatories or shops of medicines; wherein you may easily think, if we have such variety of plants, and living creatures, more than you have in Europe (for we know what you have), the simples, drugs and ingredients of medicines, must likewise be in so much the greater variety. We have them likewise of divers ages, and long fermentations. And for their preparations, we have not only all manner of exquisite distillations and separations, and especially by gentle heats, and percolations through divers strainers, yea, and substances; but also exact forms of composition, whereby they incorporate almost as they were natural simples.

"We have also divers mechanical arts, which you have not; and stuffs made by them, as papers, linen, silks, tissues, dainty works of feathers of wonderful lustre, excellent dyes, and many others: and shops likewise, as well for such as are not brought into vulgar use amongst us, as for those that are. For you must know, that of the things before recited, many of them are grown into use throughout the kingdom, but yet, if they did flow from our invention, we have of them also for patterns and principals.

"We have also furnaces of great diversities, and that keep great diversity of heats: fierce and quick, strong and constant, soft and mild; blown, quiet, dry, moist, and the like. But above all we have heats, in imitation of the sun's and heavenly bodies' heats, that pass divers inequalities, and (as it were) orbs, progresses, and returns, whereby we produce admirable effects. Besides, we have heats of dungs, and of bellies and maws of living creatures and of their bloods and bodies, and of hays and herbs laid up moist, of lime unquenched, and such like. Instruments also which generate heat only by motion. And farther, places for strong insolations; and again, places under the earth, which by nature or art yield heat. These divers heats we use as the nature of the operation which we intend requireth.

"We have also perspective houses, where we make demonstrations of all lights and radiations, and of all colours; and out of things uncoloured and transparent we can represent unto you all several colours, not in rainbows (as it is in gems and prisms), but of themselves single. We represent also all multiplications of light, which we carry to great distance, and make so sharp, as to discern small points and lines. Also all colourations of light; all delusions and deceits of the sight, in figures, magnitudes, motions, colours; all demonstrations of shadows. We find also divers means yet unknown to you, of producing of light, originally from divers bodies. We procure means of seeing objects afar off, as in the heaven and remote places; and represent things near as afar off, and things afar off as near; making feigned distances. We have also helps for the sight, far above spectacles and glasses in use. We have also glasses and means to see small and minute bodies, perfectly and distinctly; as the shapes and colours of small flies and worms, grains, and flaws in gems which cannot otherwise be seen, observations in urine and blood not otherwise to be seen. We make artificial rainbows, halos, and circles about light. We represent also all manner of reflections, refractions, and multiplications of visual beams of objects.

"We have also precious stones of all kinds, many of them of great beauty and to you unknown; crystals likewise, and glasses of divers kinds; and amongst them some of metals vitrificated, and other materials, besides those of which you make glass. Also a number of fossils and imperfect minerals, which you have not. Likewise loadstones of prodigious virtue: and other rare stones, both natural and artificial.

"We have also sound-houses, where we practise and demonstrate all sounds and their generation. We have harmonies which you have not, of quarter sounds and lesser slides of sounds. Divers instruments of music likewise to you unknown, some sweeter than any you have; together with bells and rings that are dainty and sweet. We represent small sounds as great and deep; likewise great sounds, extenuate and sharp; we make divers tremblings and warblings of sounds, which in their original are en-

---

11. **chylus,** chyle.   18. **dispensatories,** dispensaries.
22. **simples,** herbs.   26. **separations,** methods of separating the elements of substances.   29. **forms of composition,** compounds.   40. **principals,** patterns, models.

37. **vitrificated,** turned into glass.   50–51. **extenuate,** made thin.

tire. We represent and imitate all articulate sounds and letters, and the voices and notes of beasts and birds. We have certain helps, which set to the ear do further the hearing greatly. We have also divers strange and artificial echoes, reflecting the voice many times, and as it were tossing it; and some that give back the voice louder than it came, some shriller and some deeper; yea, some rendering the voice, differing in the letters or articulate sound from that they receive. We have also means to convey sounds in trunks and pipes, in strange lines and distances.

"We have also perfume-houses, wherewith we join also practices of taste. We multiply smells, which may seem strange: we imitate smells, making all smells to breathe out of other mixtures than those that give them. We make divers imitations of taste likewise, so that they will deceive any man's taste. And in this house we contain also a confiture-house, where we make all sweatmeats, dry and moist, and divers pleasant wines, milks, broths, and salads, far in greater variety than you have.

"We have also engine-houses, where are prepared engines and instruments for all sorts of motions. There we imitate and practise to make swifter motions than any you have, either out of your muskets or any engine that you have; and to make them and multiply them more easily and with small force, by wheels and other means, and to make them stronger and more violent than yours are, exceeding your greatest cannons and basilisks. We represent also ordnance and instruments of war and engines of all kinds; and likewise new mixtures and compositions of gunpowder, wild-fires burning in water and unquenchable, also fire-works of all variety, both for pleasure and use. We imitate also flights of birds; we have some degrees of flying in the air. We have ships and boats for going under water and brooking of seas, also swimming-girdles and supporters. We have divers curious clocks, and other like motions of return, and some perpetual motions. We imitate also motions of living creatures by images of men, beasts, birds, fishes, and serpents; we have also a great number of other various motions, strange for equality, fineness, and subtlety.

"We have also a mathematical-house, where are represented all instruments, as well of geometry as astronomy, exquisitely made.

"We have also houses of deceits of the senses, where we represent all manner of feats of juggling, false apparitions, impostures and illusions, and their fallacies. And surely you will easily believe that we, that have so many things truly natural which induce admiration, could in a world of particulars deceive the senses if we would disguise those things, and labour to make them seem more miraculous. But we do hate all impostures and lies, insomuch as we have severely forbidden it to all our fellows, under pain of ignomiy and fines, that they do not show any natural work or thing adorned or swelling, but only pure as it is, and without all affectation of strangeness.

"These are, my son, the riches of Solomon's House.

"For the several employments and offices of our fellows, we have twelve that sail into foreign countries under the names of other nations (for our own we conceal), who bring us the books and abstracts, and patterns of experiments of all other parts. These we call Merchants of Light.

"We have three that collect the experiments which are in all books. These we call Depredators.

"We have three that collect the experiments of all mechanical arts, and also of liberal sciences, and also of practices which are not brought into arts. These we call Mystery-men.

"We have three that try new experiments, such as themselves think good. These we call Pioneers or Miners.

"We have three that draw the experiments of the former four into titles and tables, to give the better light for the drawing of observations and axioms out of them. These we call Compilers.

"We have three that bend themselves, looking into the experiments of their fellows, and cast about how to draw out of them things of use and practice for man's life and knowledge, as well for works as for plain demonstration of causes, means of natural divinations, and the easy and clear discovery of the virtues and parts of bodies. These we call dowry-men or Benefactors.

"Then after divers meetings and consults of our whole number, to consider of the former labours and collections, we have three that take care out of them to direct new experiments, of a higher light, more penetrating into Nature than the former. These we call Lamps.

"We have three others that do execute the experiments so directed, and report them. These we call Inoculators.

"Lastly, we have three that raise the former discoveries by experiments into greater observations,

---

11. trunks, tubes. **31. basilisks,** a particular kind of cannon, named after the legendary basilisk serpent, which killed by a glance of the eye. **37. we have some degrees of flying,** that is, we have made some progress in flying. **39. brooking,** enduring, withstanding. **41. motions of return,** oscillation.

axioms, and aphorisms. These we call Interpreters of Nature.

"We have also, as you must think, novices and apprentices, that the succession of the former employed men do not fail; besides a great number of servants and attendants, men and women. And this we do also: we have consultations, which of the inventions and experiences which we have discovered shall be published, and which not; and take all an oath of secrecy for the concealing of those which we think fit to keep secret; though some of those we do reveal sometimes to the State, and some not.

"For our ordinances and rites, we have two very long and fair galleries: in one of these we place patterns and samples of all manner of the more rare and excellent inventions; in the other we place the statues of all principal inventors. There we have the statue of your Columbus, that discovered the West Indies; also the inventor of ships; your monk that was the inventor of ordnance and of gunpowder; the inventor of music; the inventor of letters; the inventor of printing; the inventor of observations of astronomy; the inventor of works in metal; the inventor of glass; the inventor of silk of the worm; the inventor of wine; the inventor of corn and bread; the inventor of sugars; and all these by more certain tradition than you have. Then we have divers inventors of our own, of excellent works, which since you have not seen, it were too long to make descriptions of them; and besides, in the right understanding of those descriptions you might easily err. For upon every invention of value we erect a statue to the inventor, and give him a liberal and honourable reward. These statues are some of brass, some of marble and touchstone, some of cedar and other special woods gilt and adorned; some of iron, some of silver, some of gold.

"We have certain hymns and services, which we say daily, of laud and thanks to God for His marvellous works. And forms of prayer, imploring His aid and blessing for the illumination of our labours, and the turning of them into good and holy uses.

"Lastly, we have circuits or visits, of divers principal cities of the kingdom; where, as it cometh to pass, we do publish such new profitable inventions as we think good. And we do also declare natural divinations of diseases, plagues, swarms of hurtful creatures, scarcity, tempests, earthquakes, great inundations, comets, temperature of the year, and divers other things; and we give counsel thereupon, what the people shall do for the prevention and remedy of them."

And when he had said this he stood up; and I, as I had been taught, knelt down; and he laid his right hand upon my head, and said, "God bless thee, my son, and God bless this relation which I have made. I give thee leave to publish it, for the good of other nations; for we here are in God's bosom, a land unknown." And so he left me; having assigned a value of about two thousand ducats for a bounty to me and my fellows. For they give great largesses, where they come, upon all occasions.

The rest was not perfected

Ben Jonson
1572–1637

Although of Scottish Border descent, Jonson was born at London, and it is as a Londoner that he is known and remembered. His only formal education was at Westminster School, but he amassed enough erudition to supply a university, and he was, indeed, given a degree by both Oxford and Cambridge. After leaving school he began work at his stepfather's trade of bricklaying, from which he ran away to join the English troops in Flanders. When he had had his fill of adventures there, he returned to London and gave up the army for the stage. By 1597 he was connected as player and playwright with Philip Henslowe's company of actors. The thirty years which followed Jonson's entry into the world of the theater were full of excitement for him and his fellows. His incorrigible obstreperousness was continually getting him into quarrels and into prison. He killed a fellow actor, Gabriel Spenser, in a duel, and escaped hanging by claiming the

---

19. **your monk,** Roger Bacon (1214?–1294?), one of the most ingenious English philosophers and men of science. The fame of Friar Bacon in popular estimation rests on his mechanical discoveries. He is reputed to have invented a telescope, and to have discovered gunpowder in his experiments on pure niter. His recipe for gunpowder is, at any rate, the earliest extant.

3. **touchstone,** a fine-grained, dark-colored variety of jasper, used in testing the quality of alloys. 16. **divinations,** forecasts or prognostications based on natural facts.

ancient "benefit of clergy," which exempted from the penalty a person who could read. While in prison he became a Roman Catholic, but after twelve years reverted to the Protestant faith.

To a large extent he found his characters and the materials of his plots in the life about him, and the zest with which he portrayed and emphasized the eccentricities of his colleagues and acquaintances led to further quarrels and further plays. In the history of the English drama, Jonson is famous for his development of the "comedy of humors," in which the development of character consists chiefly in presenting in an exaggerated fashion the outstanding trait or "humor" of a person or a class. The first and most sensational of these comedies was his *Every Man in His Humour*, which was performed, with Shakespeare in the cast, in 1589. At about this time and in such circumstances began the "War of the Theaters," one of the most famous of literary quarrels, which involved some of the foremost dramatists of the day, including Shakespeare, whose company, the Lord Chamberlain's Men, Jonson had slandered in *The Poetaster*, 1601. Of the comedies of "humors," in which he conveyed brilliant criticism of contemporary conditions, the two greatest are *Volpone, or the Fox*, 1606, and *The Alchemist*, 1610. His first extant tragedy, *Sejanus*, was produced by Shakespeare's company at the Globe in Southwark in 1603. In 1604 he was again in prison, this time voluntarily, through sympathy with his collaborators in a comedy *Eastward Ho*, which ridiculed the Scots and King James himself.

In 1605 Jonson began to interest himself in the production of masques, beloved of the Elizabethan and Stuart courts for their music and dancing and ornate settings. For many of the plots and lyrics which Jonson devised, Inigo Jones contrived the spectacle. Out of this collaboration grew in 1631 a final quarrel between the two. Jonson upheld the poet's pre-eminence in the production of the masque over the designer of the external trappings of the piece. The architect won the battle, and Jonson lost the patronage of the court, but the exquisite poetry of his *Oberon*, 1610-11, and *The Gipsies Metamorphosed*, 1621, has long outlived the machinery of even an Inigo Jones.

Jonson's high opinion of his compositions is illustrated by his publication in 1616 of a collection of his plays and poems in a folio volume which he called his *Works*, to the amusement of everybody. About this time he was granted a pension by the King, and became in fact, though not in name, poet laureate. In 1618 he went on foot to Scotland, where he visited William Drummond, "the Scottish Petrarch," whom he shocked with the characteristically racy comments on books and authors which Drummond has recorded in the *Conversations*. In Drummond's notes and in Jonson's own compilation of critical observations entitled *Timber, or Discoveries Made upon Men and Matters*, 1641, we have some of the sagest literary criticism in the language, and invaluable comments on some of Jonson's contemporaries.

The overbearing, satirical Jonson is more spectacular, but not more the essential Jonson, than the man who was the center of a group of friends that included Shakespeare, Marlowe, Raleigh, Bacon, and Donne. Younger poets, among them Herrick, Carew, and Suckling, who worshiped him and delighted to call themselves "Sons of Ben," have written lyric accounts of the meetings over which he presided at the Mermaid and the Devil. No poet in English literature has received more testimonies of affection during his life, or such an outpouring of tributes as when he was buried in the Poet's Corner of the Abbey. The diversity of his gifts, the abounding energy and vitality of his character, the flexibility of his genius, ranging from the severely classical to the gently lyrical, and from robust criticism to creations of the most dainty imagination, cannot be properly illustrated in a few selections. His influence on his "sons" and on those who come after him may be traced through the rest of the century.

EPIGRAMS

TO THE READER

Pray thee, take care, that tak'st my book in hand,
   To read it well: that is, to understand.

TO MY BOOK

It will be looked for, Book, when some but see
   Thy title, Epigrams, and named of me,
Thou shouldst be bold, licentious, full of gall,
   Wormwood, and sulphur, sharp, and toothed withal;
Become a petulant thing, hurl ink and wit
   As madmen stones, not caring whom they hit.
Deceive their malice, who could wish it so,
   And by thy wiser temper, let men know
Thou art not covetous of least self-fame
   Made from the hazard of another's shame.   10
Much less, with lewd, profane, and beastly phrase,
   To catch the world's loose laughter, or vain gaze.
He that departs with his own honesty
   For vulgar praise, doth it too dearly buy.

TO KING JAMES

How, best of kings, dost thou a sceptre bear!
   How, best of poets, dost thou laurel wear!
But two things rare the Fates had in their store,
   And gave thee both, to show they could no more.
For such a poet, while thy days were green,
   Thou wert, as chief of them are said to have been.
And such a prince thou art we daily see,
   As chief of those still promise they will be.
Whom should my Muse then fly to but the best
   Of kings for grace; of poets, for my test?   10

ON THE UNION

England and Scotland were united under James VI of Scotland, who became James I of England in 1603.

When was there contract better driven by Fate?
   Or celebrated with more truth of state?
The world the temple was, the priest a king,
   The spousèd pair two realms, the sea the ring.

ON MY FIRST DAUGHTER

Here lies, to each her parents' ruth,
   Mary, the daughter of their youth;
Yet all heaven's gifts being heaven's due,
   It makes the father less to rue.
At six months' end she parted hence
   With safety of her innocence;
Whose soul heaven's queen, whose name she bears,
   In comfort of her mother's tears,
Hath placed amongst her virgin-train:
   Where while that severed doth remain,   10
This grave partakes the fleshly birth,
   Which cover lightly, gentle earth!

TO JOHN DONNE

Donne, the delight of Phoebus and each Muse,
   Who, to thy one, all other brains refuse;
Whose every work of thy most early wit
   Came forth example, and remains so yet;
Longer a knowing than most wits do live,
   And which no affection praise enough can give!

To King James. **2. best of poets.** James was a poet and a critic of poets and poetry, and was as proud of being an author and scholar as of being king. *On My First Daughter.* **2. Mary, the daughter.** From an entry in the parish register of St. Martin's in the Fields in London, it is supposed that Jonson's daughter died of the plague in November, 1593.

To it, thy language, letters, arts, best life,
   Which might with half mankind maintain a strife;
All which I mean to praise, and yet I would,
   But leave, because I cannot as I should.   10

ON MY FIRST SON

Jonson's son was born in 1596 and died of the plague in 1603. Jonson, who was absent at the time of the boy's death, had a vision of his son in which, as he described it to William Drummond, the lad appeared "of a manly shape," and of that growth "he shall be at the resurrection."

Farewell, thou child of my right hand, and joy;
   My sin was too much hope of thee, loved boy:
Seven years thou wert lent to me, and I thee pay,
   Exacted by thy fate, on the just day.
O could I lose all father now! for why
   Will man lament the state he should envy—
To have so soon 'scaped world's and flesh's rage,
   And if no other misery, yet age?
Rest in soft peace, and asked, say, "Here doth lie
   Ben Jonson his best piece of poetry;   10
For whose sake henceforth all his vows be such
   As what he loves may never like too much."

EPITAPH ON S[ALATHIEL] P[AVY], A Child of Queen Elizabeth's Chapel

Weep with me, all you that read
   This little story;
And know, for whom a tear you shed
   Death's self is sorry.
'Twas a child that so did thrive
   In grace and feature,
As heaven and nature seemed to strive
   Which owned the creature.
Years he numbered scarce thirteen
   When fates turned cruel,   10
Yet three filled zodiacs had he been
   The stage's jewel;
And did act, what now we moan,
   Old men so duly,
As, sooth, the Parcae thought him one,
   He played so truly.

Salathiel Pavy. One of the child actors who had taken part in two of Jonson's plays. **11. three filled zodiacs.** The boy had acted for three full years. **15. the Parcae,** the three Fates, who determined the duration of human life.

BEN JONSON

So, by error, to his fate
    They all consented;
But viewing him since, alas, too late!
    They have repented,   20
And have sought, to give new birth,
    In baths to steep him;
But being so much too good for earth,
    Heaven vows to keep him.

EPITAPH ON ELIZABETH, L. H.

Elizabeth, L. H. has not been identified. It has been suggested that she may have been Elizabeth, Lady Hatton, wife of Sir Edward Coke.

Wouldst thou hear what man can say
In a little? Reader, stay.
Underneath this stone doth lie
As much beauty as could die;
Which in life did harbour give
To more virtue than doth live.
If at all she had a fault,
Leave it buried in this vault.
One name was Elizabeth;
The other, let it sleep with death: 10
Fitter, where it died, to tell,
Than that it lived at all. Farewell!

SONGS FROM THE PLAYS AND MASQUES

SLOW, SLOW, FRESH FOUNT

Slow, slow, fresh fount, keep time with my salt tears;
    Yet slower, yet; oh, faintly, gentle springs;
List to the heavy part the music bears,
    Woe weeps out her division when she sings.
        Droop herbs and flowers;
        Fall grief in showers,
        Our beauties are not ours;
          Oh, I could still,
Like melting snow upon some craggy hill,
    Drop, drop, drop, drop,   10
Since nature's pride is now a withered daffodil.
                —*Cynthia's Revels*

22. In baths to steep him, a reference to the story of Aeson, the aged father of Jason, hero of the expedition for the Golden Fleece, who was made young again by a magic bath administered by Medea.   *Slow, Slow, Fresh Fount.* **4. division,** part of a musical composition.

QUEEN AND HUNTRESS

Queen and huntress, chaste and fair,
Now the sun is laid to sleep,
Seated in thy silver chair,
State in wonted manner keep:
    Hesperus entreats thy light,
    Goddess excellently bright.

Earth, let not thy envious shade
Dare itself to interpose;
Cynthia's shining orb was made
Heaven to clear when day did close: 10
    Bless us, then, with wishèd sight,
    Goddess excellently bright.

Lay thy bow of pearl apart,
And thy crystal-shining quiver;
Give unto the flying hart
Space to breathe, how short soever;
    Thou that mak'st a day of night,
    Goddess excellently bright.
                —*Cynthia's Revels*

COME, MY CELIA, LET US PROVE

This song is, in part, a paraphrase of the fifth ode of Catullus, the Latin lyric poet.

Come, my Celia, let us prove,
While we can, the sports of love;
Time will not be ours for ever,
He, at length, our goods will sever.
Spend not then his gifts in vain:
Suns that set may rise again;
But if once we lose this light,
'Tis with us perpetual night.
Why should we defer our joys?
Fame and rumour are but toys.   10
Cannot we delude the eyes
Of a few poor household spies?
Or his easier ears beguile,
Thus removèd by our wile?
'Tis no sin love's fruits to steal,
But the sweet thefts to reveal;
To be taken, to be seen,
These have crimes accounted been.
                   —*Volpone*

Queen and Huntress. **1. Queen and huntress,** Cynthia, or Diana. A tribute to Queen Elizabeth, who, in the masques that conclude the play, was represented by Cynthia. **5. Hesperus,** the evening star. **10. clear,** make bright.

STILL TO BE NEAT

This poem is based on an anonymous late Latin poem.

    Still to be neat, still to be dressed,
    As you were going to a feast;
    Still to be powdered, still perfumed:
    Lady, it is to be presumed,
    Though art's hid causes are not found,
    All is not sweet, all is not sound.

    Give me a look, give me a face,
    That makes simplicity a grace;
    Robes loosely flowing, hair as free:
    Such sweet neglect more taketh me   10
    Than all the adulteries of art;
    They strike mine eyes, but not my heart.
                            —*Epicoene*

GIPSY SONGS

1

    The faery beam upon you,
    The stars to glister on you;
      A moon of light
      In the noon of night,
    Till the fire-drake hath o'ergone you!
    The wheel of fortune guide you,
    The boy with the bow beside you;
      Run aye in the way
      Till the bird of day,
    And the luckier lot betide you!   10

2

    To the old, long life and treasure,
    To the young, all health and pleasure;
      To the fair, their face
      With eternal grace,
    And the foul to be loved at leisure!
    To the witty, all clear mirrors,
    To the foolish, their dark errors;
      To the loving sprite,
      A secure delight;
    To the jealous, his own false terrors!   10
                     —*Gipsies Metamorphosed*

THOUGH I AM YOUNG

    Though I am young, and cannot tell
      Either that Death or Love is well,
    Yet I have heard they both bear darts,
      And both do aim at human hearts.

    And then again, I have been told
      Love wounds with heat, as Death with cold;
    So that I fear they do but bring
      Extremes to touch, and mean one thing.

    As in a ruin we it call
      One thing to be blown up, or fall;   10
    Or to our end like way may have
      By a flash of lightning, or a wave;
    So Love's inflamèd shaft or brand
      May kill as soon as Death's cold hand;
    Except Love's fires the virtue have
      To fright the frost out of the grave.
                        —*The Sad Shepherd*

SONG: TO CELIA

This, the best known of Jonson's songs, is, like others of his lyrics, based on Latin originals. It is a series of paraphrases of passages in four letters of Philostratus, a Greek rhetorician of the second and third centuries A.D. It has been conjectured that this and the other songs to Celia were written about the same time, and were addressed to some lady of Jonson's acquaintance.

    Drink to me only with thine eyes,
      And I will pledge with mine;
    Or leave a kiss but in the cup,
      And I'll not look for wine.
    The thirst that from the soul doth rise
      Doth ask a drink divine;
    But might I of Jove's nectar sup,
      I would not change for thine.

    I sent thee late a rosy wreath,
      Not so much honouring thee   10
    As giving it a hope, that there
      It could not withered be.
    But thou thereon didst only breathe,
      And sent'st it back to me;
    Since when it grows, and smells, I swear,
      Not of itself but thee.

from UNDERWOODS

A HYMN
ON THE NATIVITY OF MY SAVIOUR

    I sing the birth was born to-night,
    The Author both of life and light,
      The angels so did sound it;
    And like the ravished shepherds said,

Who saw the light, and were afraid,
    Yet searched, and true they found it.

The Son of God, the eternal King,
That did us all salvation bring,
    And freed the soul from danger;
He whom the whole world could not take,   10
The Word which heaven and earth did make,
    Was now laid in a manger.

The Father's wisdom willed it so,
The Son's obedience knew no No,
    Both wills were in one stature;
And as that wisdom had decreed,
The Word was now made Flesh indeed,
    And took on Him our nature.

What comfort by Him do we win,
Who made Himself the price of sin,   20
    To make us heirs of glory!
To see this Babe, all innocence,
A Martyr born in our defence,
    Can man forget this story?

from A CELEBRATION OF CHARIS

HIS EXCUSE FOR LOVING

Let it not your wonder move,
Less your laughter, that I love.
Though I now write fifty years,
I have had, and have, my peers;
Poets though divine are men,
Some have loved as old again.
And it is not always face,
Clothes, or fortune, gives the grace,
Or the feature, or the youth;
But the language and the truth,   10
With the ardour and the passion,
Gives the lover weight and fashion.
If you then will read the story,
First prepare you to be sorry
That you never knew till now
Either whom to love, or how;
But be glad, as soon with me,
When you know that this is she
Of whose beauty it was sung:
She shall make the old man young,   20
Keep the middle age at stay,
And let nothing high decay;
Till she be the reason why
All the world for love may die.

HER TRIUMPH

See the chariot at hand here of Love,
    Wherein my lady rideth!
Each that draws is a swan or a dove,
    And well the car Love guideth.
As she goes, all hearts do duty
        Unto her beauty;
And, enamoured, do wish, so they might
        But enjoy such a sight,
That they still were to run by her side,
Through swords, through seas, whither she would ride.   10

Do but look on her eyes; they do light
    All that Love's world compriseth!
Do but look on her hair; it is bright
    As Love's star when it riseth!
Do but mark, her forehead's smoother
        Than words that soothe her!
And from her arched brows, such a grace
        Sheds itself through the face,
As alone there triumphs to the life
All the gain, all the good, of the elements' strife.   20

Have you seen but a bright lily grow,
    Before rude hands have touched it?
Ha' you marked but the fall of the snow
    Before the soil hath smutched it?
Ha' you felt the wool of beaver
        Or swan's down ever?
Or have smelt o' the bud o' the brier?
        Or the nard in the fire?
Or have tasted the bag of the bee?
O so white, O so soft, O so sweet is she!   30

AN ODE TO HIMSELF

Where dost thou careless lie,
    Buried in ease and sloth?
Knowledge that sleeps doth die;
    And this security,
        It is the common moth
That eats on wits and arts, and destroys them both.

Are all the Aonian springs
    Dried up? Lies Thespia waste?
Doth Clarius' harp want strings,

---

28. **nard**, an aromatic balsam.   *An Ode to Himself*. 4. **security**, carelessness.   7. **Aonian springs**, the springs on the Aonian mount, Helicon, the haunt of the Muses.   8. **Thespia**, a city near Helicon.   9. **Clarius' harp**, the harp of Apollo (called *Clarius* after his oracle at Clarus), the god of song and music, and leader of the Muses.

That not a nymph now sings? 10
    Or droop they as disgraced,
To see their seats and bowers by chattering pies defaced?

If hence thy silence be,
    As 'tis too just a cause,
Let this thought quicken thee:
Minds that are great and free
    Should not on fortune pause;
'Tis crown enough to virtue still, her own applause.

What though the greedy fry
    Be taken with false baits 20
Of worded balladry,
    And think it poesy?
They die with their conceits,
And only piteous scorn upon their folly waits.

Then take in hand thy lyre;
    Strike in thy proper strain;
With Japhet's line aspire
Sol's chariot for new fire
    To give the world again; 29
Who aided him will thee, the issue of Jove's brain.

And, since our dainty age
    Cannot endure reproof,
Make not thyself a page
To that strumpet the stage;
    But sing high and aloof,
Safe from the wolf's black jaw, and the dull ass's hoof.

from A PINDARIC ODE

TO THE IMMORTAL MEMORY AND FRIENDSHIP OF THAT NOBLE PAIR SIR LUCIUS CARY AND SIR H. MORISON

    It is not growing like a tree
    In bulk, doth make man better be;
Or standing long an oak, three hundred year,
To fall a log at last, dry, bald, and sear:
        A lily of a day
        Is fairer far, in May,
    Although it fall and die that night;
    It was the plant and flower of light.
In small proportions we just beauties see,
And in short measures life may perfect be. 10

12. pies, magpies. **27–28. With Japhet's line aspire Sol's chariot.** Prometheus, the son of Japetus, aided by Minerva ("the issue of Jove's brain"), stole fire from the sun and gave it to man.

To the Memory of My Beloved the Author,

MR. WILLIAM SHAKESPEARE,

And What He Hath Left Us

These lines were written for the First Folio of Shakespeare, published in 1623.

To draw no envy, Shakespeare, on thy name,
Am I thus ample to thy book and fame,
While I confess thy writings to be such
As neither man nor Muse can praise too much.
'Tis true, and all men's suffrage. But these ways
Were not the paths I meant unto thy praise:
For seeliest ignorance on these may light,
Which, when it sounds at best, but echoes right;
Or blind affection, which does ne'er advance
The truth, but gropes, and urgeth all by chance; 10
Or crafty malice might pretend this praise,
And think to ruin where it seemed to raise.
These are as some infamous bawd or whore
Should praise a matron—what could hurt her more?
But thou are proof against them, and, indeed,
Above the ill fortune of them, or the need.
I therefore will begin. Soul of the age,
The applause, delight, the wonder of our stage,
My Shakespeare, rise! I will not lodge thee by
Chaucer or Spenser, or bid Beaumont lie 20
A little further to make thee a room:
Thou art a monument without a tomb,
And art alive still while thy book doth live,
And we have wits to read and praise to give.
That I not mix thee so, my brain excuses,
I mean with great, but disproportioned Muses;
For, if I thought my judgment were of years,
I should commit thee surely with thy peers,
And tell how far thou didst our Lyly outshine,
Or sporting Kyd, or Marlowe's mighty line. 30
And though thou hadst small Latin and less Greek,
From thence to honour thee, I would not seek

5. suffrage, vote, consensus of opinion. **7. seeliest,** most foolish. **9. affection,** feeling. **20. Chaucer . . . Spenser . . . Beaumont.** These three poets were buried in Westminster Abbey. Jonson disagrees with those who would have had Shakespeare buried in the Abbey beside them, instead of at Stratford-on-Avon. **26. disproportioned Muses,** poets of less merit. **28. commit,** join. **31. small Latin and less Greek.** Jonson's famous line has caused Shakespeare's knowledge of Latin and Greek to be unduly disparaged. By comparison with the great classical learning of Jonson, Shakespeare's knowledge would seem small, but from what we know of the curriculum of the grammar schools of his day, Shakespeare must have been master of enough Latin, at least, to put the modern college student to shame.

BEN JONSON

For names, but call forth thundering Aeschylus,
Euripides, and Sophocles to us,
Pacuvius, Accius, him of Cordova dead,
To life again, to hear thy buskin tread
And shake a stage; or when thy socks were on,
Leave thee alone for the comparison
Of all that insolent Greece or haughty Rome
Sent forth, or since did from their ashes come. 40
Triumph, my Britain; thou hast one to show
To whom all scenes of Europe homage owe.
He was not of an age, but for all time!
And all the Muses still were in their prime
When like Apollo he came forth to warm
Our ears, or like a Mercury to charm.
Nature herself was proud of his designs,
And joyed to wear the dressing of his lines,
Which were so richly spun, and woven so fit,
As, since, she will vouchsafe no other wit: 50
The merry Greek, tart Aristophanes,
Neat Terence, witty Plautus, now not please,
But antiquated and deserted lie,
As they were not of Nature's family.
Yet must I not give nature all; thy art,
My gentle Shakespeare, must enjoy a part:
For though the poet's matter nature be,
His art doth give the fashion; and that he
Who casts to write a living line must sweat
(Such as thine are) and strike the second heat 60
Upon the Muses' anvil, turn the same,
And himself with it, that he thinks to frame,
Or for the laurel he may gain a scorn;
For a good poet's made as well as born.
And such wert thou! Look how the father's face
Lives in his issue; even so the race
Of Shakespeare's mind and manners brightly shines
In his well-turnèd and true-filèd lines,
In each of which he seems to shake a lance,
As brandished at the eyes of ignorance. 70
Sweet swan of Avon, what a sight it were
To see thee in our waters yet appear,
And make those flights upon the banks of Thames
That so did take Eliza and our James!
But stay; I see thee in the hemisphere
Advanced and made a constellation there!
Shine forth, thou star of poets, and with rage
Or influence chide or cheer the drooping stage,
Which, since thy flight from hence, hath mourned like night
And despairs day, but for thy volume's light. 80

35. Pacuvius, Accius, Martius Pacuvius and Lucius Accius, early Roman tragic poets. **36–37. buskin . . . socks.** The buskin, a high-heeled boot, worn by Greek tragic actors, is used symbolically for Shakespeare's tragedies; the sock, the low-heeled slipper worn by comic actors, for his comedies. **51. tart Aristophanes,** as famous for the satire as for the humor of his comedies. **52. Terence . . . Plautus,** the two best-known writers of Latin comedy.

74. Eliza, Queen Elizabeth. **77. rage,** poetic enthusiasm or rapture. **78. influence,** of the stars. Astrological terms, despite the diminishing belief in astrology, continued to be used in poetry throughout the greater part of the century.

John Donne
1572?–1631

Donne's life spans the last third of the sixteenth and the first third of the seventeenth century, and provides a good index to the intellectual, religious, social, and literary movements of the time. He was born and brought up a Roman Catholic, in a distinguished family of which several members had suffered for their faith. He studied at both Oxford and Cambridge, but left the universities without a degree because, on account of his religion, he could not take the required oaths. Later he studied law at Lincoln's Inn, and found time to dip into the Church Fathers and theology, medicine, and the other sciences old and new. As a gay, handsome, wealthy young gentleman of Elizabethan London, Donne could not give himself wholly to the bar or the university or the Church. Nor, as the possessor of one of the most active, curious, and versatile minds of his age, could he give all his time or energy to his pleasures. By the time he was of age he had argued himself out of the Church of Rome, but had not reached any stable or satisfying religious convictions.

There probably never lived a man more eager for knowledge and experience of all sorts and on all the levels of existence, from the lowest and fleshliest to the highest and most spiritual. The devious paths along which Donne's unsatisfied yearnings led him in his young manhood are not exactly known. He ran through his fortune early. He probably traveled on the Continent in his early twenties. He went with the Earl of Essex on his expedition to Cadiz in 1596, and to the Azores with Essex in 1597.

The poems which came out of the emotions and experiences of these years are unlike any that had appeared before, and may still be called unique. Donne took none of his predecessors or contemporaries as models. For the conventional rhythms and subjects of Spenser and the other Elizabethans he showed the most scornful indifference. In his early poems his attitude toward women and love is almost entirely cynical. In terms now harsh, now playful, at times coarsely bitter, at others amusingly disparaging, he records or reflects upon his experiences, attacks inconstancy in women, or defends the variety of his own experiments and experiences.

A new and very different chapter in his life began upon his return to England when he became secretary to Sir Thomas Egerton, Lord Keeper of the Great Seal. The door to worldly success seemed to have opened to him. But the position was lost and the door was very firmly closed when, in 1601, he fell in love with and secretly married Anne More, Sir Thomas's sixteen-year-old niece. If from the worldly point of view it was the worst thing he could have done, it was, from all others, the best thing that could have happened to him. His love for Anne was as spiritual as it was lasting, and it transformed his life and his poems. Their mutual love was the one ray of light in the dark and poverty-stricken years that followed his dismissal by Egerton.

In 1615, after a dozen unhappy years of religious and intellectual uncertainty, and unsuccessful searching for worldly preferment, Donne was persuaded to enter the priesthood of the Church of England. His brilliant sermons brought him to the notice of King James, and his destiny finally led him to the deanship of St. Paul's Cathedral, and to fame as one of the most eloquent and devout preachers of the English Church.

Donne's poems furnish a curious record of his emotional, intellectual, and spiritual progress through life. He brings all the resources of a mind rich in learning to a focus in his poetry. His mind has been likened to that of a chess-player; he tests mentally all moves, and writes them down as he does so. Into the religious verse and prose of his later years he puts the same fierce energy, the same unconventional figures and expressions, that had distinguished the love poems of his youth. He is the first and greatest of the "Metaphysical Poets." His influence on those who came after him in his own century, as well as the fascination he has held for poets in the twentieth century, will be in evidence in the pages that follow.

from SONGS AND SONNETS

SONG

Go and catch a falling star,
   Get with child a mandrake root,
Tell me where all past years are,
   Or who cleft the Devil's foot,
Teach me to hear mermaids singing,
   Or to keep off envy's stinging,
      And find
      What wind
Serves to advance an honest mind.

If thou be'st born to strange sights,   10
   Things invisible to see,
Ride ten thousand days and nights,
   Till age snow white hairs on thee,
Thou, when thou return'st, wilt tell me
   All strange wonders that befell thee,
      And swear
      Nowhere
Lives a woman true, and fair.

If thou find'st one, let me know;
   Such a pilgrimage were sweet.   20
Yet do not; I would not go,
   Though at next door we might meet.
Though she were true when you met her,
   And last till you write your letter,
      Yet she
      Will be
False, ere I come, to two or three.

THE INDIFFERENT

I can love both fair and brown;
Her whom abundance melts, and her whom want betrays;
Her who loves loneness best, and her who masks and plays;
Her whom the country formed, and whom the town;
Her who believes, and her who tries;
Her who still weeps with spongy eyes,
And her who is dry cork and never cries.

Song. **2. mandrake root.** The forked root of the mandrake (mandragora) suggested the human body. An elaborate discussion of the legends concerning the mandrake is to be found in Sir Thomas Browne's *Pseudoxia Epidemica*, Book II, chap. 6. **5. mermaids,** here identified, as in Spenser and other contemporary authors, with the sirens. *The Indifferent.* **5. tries,** tests, examines.

I can love her, and her, and you, and you;
I can love any, so she be not true.

Will no other vice content you? 10
Will it not serve your turn to do as did your mothers?
Or have you all old vices spent, and now would find out others?
Or doth a fear that men are true torment you?
Oh, we are not; be not you so;
Let me, and do you, twenty know.
Rob me, but bind me not, and let me go.
Must I, who came to travail thorough you,
Grow your fixed subject because you are true?

Venus heard me sigh this song,
And by love's sweetest part, variety, she swore 20
She heard not this till now, and that it should be so no more.
She went, examined, and returned ere long,
And said, "Alas! some two or three
Poor heretics in love there be,
Which think to 'stablish dangerous constancy.
But I have told them, 'Since you will be true,
You shall be true to them who are false to you.'"

THE CANONIZATION

For God's sake hold your tongue, and let me love;
    Or chide my palsy, or my gout,
My five grey hairs, or ruined fortune flout;
    With wealth your state, your mind with arts improve,
        Take you a course, get you a place,
        Observe his Honour, or his Grace,
Or the king's real, or his stamped face
    Contemplate; what you will, approve,
    So you will let me love.

Alas, alas, who's injured by my love? 10
    What merchant's ships have my sighs drowned?
Who says my tears have overflowed his ground?
    When did my colds a forward spring remove?
        When did the heats which my veins fill
        Add one more to the plaguy bill?
Soldiers find wars, and lawyers find out still
    Litigious men, which quarrels move,
    Though she and I do love.

The Indifferent. **10. other,** other than constancy. **17. thorough,** through. *The Canonization.* **7. stamped face,** on coins. **15. plaguy bill,** the list, published weekly, of the victims of the plague.

Call us what you will, we are made such by love;
    Call her one, me another fly, 20
We're tapers too, and at our own cost die,
    And we in us find the Eagle and the Dove.
        The Phoenix riddle hath more wit
        By us; we two being one, are it.
So, to one neutral thing both sexes fit.
    We die and rise the same, and prove
    Mysterious by this love.

We can die by it, if not live by love,
    And if unfit for tombs and hearse
Our legend be, it will be fit for verse; 30
    And if no piece of chronicle we prove,
        We'll build in sonnets pretty rooms;
        As well a well-wrought urn becomes
The greatest ashes, as half-acre tombs,
    And by these hymns all shall approve
    Us canonized for Love;

And thus invoke us: You whom reverend love
    Made one another's hermitage;
You, to whom love was peace, that now is rage;
    Who did the whole world's soul contract, and drove 40
        Into the glasses of your eyes
        (So made such mirrors, and such spies,
That they did all to you epitomize)
    Countries, towns, courts: beg from above
    A pattern of your love!

THE GOOD-MORROW

I wonder, by my troth, what thou and I
Did till we loved? were we not weaned till then?
But sucked on country pleasures, childishly?
Or snorted we in the seven sleepers' den?
'Twas so; but this, all pleasures fancies be.
If ever any beauty I did see,
Which I desired, and got, 'twas but a dream of thee.

And now good-morrow to our waking souls,
Which watch not one another out of fear;
For love all love of other sights controls, 10
And makes one little room an everywhere.
Let sea-discoverers to new worlds have gone;
Let maps to other, worlds on worlds have shown;
Let us possess one world; each hath one, and is one.

4. seven sleepers' den, the cave in which, according to legend, seven Christian youths hid during the persecutions of Decius, and slept on for over two centuries. **5. but this,** except this love of ours

My face in thine eye, thine in mine appears,
And true plain hearts do in the faces rest;
Where can we find two better hemispheres
Without sharp north, without declining west?
Whatever dies, was not mixed equally;
If our two loves be one, or thou and I   20
Love so alike that none do slacken, none can die.

A VALEDICTION FORBIDDING MOURNING

Izaak Walton, in his *Life of Donne*, says that Donne wrote this poem to his wife on the occasion of his going to the Continent in 1612 with his patron, Sir Robert Drury, and Lady Drury. Walton explains that Donne was unwilling to go because his wife's "divining soul boded her some ill in his absence." Mrs. Donne's forebodings were justified, for during her husband's absence she gave birth to a dead child.

As virtuous men pass mildly away,
    And whisper to their souls to go,
Whilst some of their sad friends do say,
    "The breath goes now," and some say, "No";

So let us melt, and make no noise,
    No tear-floods nor sigh-tempests move;
'Twere profanation of our joys
    To tell the laity our love.

Moving of the earth brings harms and fears;
    Men reckon what it did and meant;   10
But trepidation of the spheres,
    Though greater far, is innocent.

Dull sublunary lovers' love
    (Whose soul is sense) cannot admit
Absence, because it doth remove
    Those things which elemented it.

But we, by a love so much refined
    That ourselves know not what it is,
Inter-assurèd of the mind,
    Care less eyes, lips, and hands to miss.   20

Our two souls, therefore, which are one,
    Though I must go, endure not yet
A breach, but an expansion,
    Like gold to airy thinness beat.

If they be two, they are two so
    As stiff twin compasses are two;
Thy soul, the fixed foot, makes no show
    To move, but doth if the other do.

And though it in the centre sit,
    Yet, when the other far doth roam,   30
It leans, and hearkens after it,
    And grows erect as that comes home.

Such wilt thou be to me, who must
    Like the other foot obliquely run:
Thy firmness draws my circle just,
    And makes me end where I begun.

SONG

This song was probably composed on the same occasion as the foregoing "Valediction."

Sweetest love, I do not go
    For weariness of thee,
Nor in hope the world can show
    A fitter love for me;
        But since that I
Must die at last, 'tis best,
To use myself in jest
        Thus by feigned deaths to die.

Yesternight the sun went hence,
    And yet is here to-day;   10
He hath no desire nor sense,
    Nor half so short a way:
        Then fear not me,
But believe that I shall make
Speedier journeys, since I take
        More wings and spurs than he.

O how feeble is man's power,
    That if good fortune fall,
Cannot add another hour,
    Nor a lost hour recall!   20
        But come bad chance,

The Good-Morrow. **15–17. thine in mine . . . hemispheres.** The two lovers find their respective worlds, or hemispheres, in each others' eyes. For a similar expression of the idea, see "The Canonization," ll. 39–44. **20–21. If our two loves . . . die.** Professor Grierson's interpretation of the passage is as follows: "If our two loves are *one*, dissolution is impossible; and the same is true if, though *two*, they are always alike. What is simple—as God or the soul—cannot be dissolved; nor compounds, e.g. the Heavenly bodies, between whose elements there is no contrariety." *A Valediction Forbidding Mourning.* **11. trepidation of the spheres**, a term from the Ptolemaic astronomy, denoting the motion of the eighth (or ninth) sphere, which was thought to cause the "innocent," or harmless, variation in the date of the equinox. **16. elemented**, constituted.

26. stiff twin compasses, a pair of dividers. **35. just**, perfect. **7. use**, practice. **21. come bad chance**, if bad chance come.

And we join it to our strength,
   And we teach it art and length,
      Itself o'er us to advance.

When thou sigh'st thou sigh'st not wind,
   But sigh'st my soul away,
When thou weep'st, unkindly kind,
   My life's blood doth decay.
      It cannot be
That thou lov'st me, as thou say'st,   30
   If in thine my life thou waste,
      That art the best of me.

Let not thy divining heart
   Forethink me any ill;
Destiny may take thy part,
   And may thy tears fulfil;
      But think that we
Are but turned aside to sleep;
   They who one another keep
      Alive, ne'er parted be.   40

THE ECSTASY

Where, like a pillow on a bed,
   A pregnant bank swelled up to rest
The violet's reclining head,
   Sat we two, one another's best.
Our hands were firmly cemented
   With a fast balm, which thence did spring;
Our eye-beams twisted, and did thread
   Our eyes upon one double string.
So to intergraft our hands, as yet
   Was all the means to make us one;   10
And pictures in our eyes to get
   Was all our propagation.
As, 'twixt two equal armies, fate
   Suspends uncertain victory,
Our souls, which, to advance their state,
   Were gone out, hung 'twixt her and me.
And whilst our souls negotiate there,
   We like sepulchral statues lay;
All day, the same our postures were,
   And we said nothing, all the day.   20
If any, so by love refined
   That he soul's language understood,
And by good love were grown all mind,
   Within convenient distance stood,
He, though he knew not which soul spake,
   Because both meant, both spake, the same,
Might thence a new concoction take,
   And part far purer than he came.

The Ecstasy. **27. concoction,** purification or sublimation.

This ecstasy doth unperplex
   (We said) and tell us what we love;   30
We see by this it was not sex;
   We see, we saw not what did move;
But as all several souls contain
   Mixture of things, they know not what,
Love these mixed souls doth mix again
   And makes both one, each this and that.
A single violet transplant,
   The strength, the colour, and the size,
All which before was poor and scant,
   Redoubles still and multiplies.   40
When love with one another so
   Interinanimates two souls,
That abler soul, which thence doth flow,
   Defects of loneliness controls.
We then, who are this new soul, know
   Of what we are composed and made,
For the atomies of which we grow
   Are souls, whom no change can invade.
But O alas! so long, so far,
   Our bodies why do we forbear?   50
They are ours, though they are not we; we are
   The intelligences, they the spheres.
We owe them thanks, because they thus
   Did us, to us, at first convey,
Yielded their forces, sense, to us,
   Nor are dross to us, but allay.
On man heaven's influence works not so,
   But that it first imprints the air;
For soul into the soul may flow,
   Though it to body first repair.   60
As our blood labours to beget
   Spirits, as like souls as it can,
Because such fingers need to knit
   That subtle knot which makes us man,
So must pure lovers' souls descend
   To affections, and to faculties,
Which sense may reach and apprehend;
   Else a great prince in prison lies.
To our bodies turn we then, that so
   Weak men on love revealed may look;   70
Love's mysteries in souls do grow,
   But yet the body is his book.

31–36. We see . . . we saw not . . . this and that. Grierson explains the passage thus: "We see now, that we did not see before the true source of our love. What we thought was due to bodily beauty, we perceive now to have its source in the soul." **47. atomies,** atoms. **52. intelligences . . . spheres.** The heavenly bodies (spheres) were, according to the medieval Schoolmen, moved and controlled by angels, or "intelligences." **56. allay,** alloy. **58. first imprints the air.** The influence of the stars, according to astrology, was transmitted to man through the air. Donne thinks of the body as providing a similar medium between two souls.

And if some lover, such as we,
    Have heard this dialogue of one,
Let him still mark us; he shall see
    Small change when we're to bodies gone.

THE FUNERAL

Professor Grierson thinks that this poem and "The Relique" may have been addressed to Mrs. Magdalen Herbert, the mother of George Herbert.

Whoever comes to shroud me, do not harm
    Nor question much
That subtle wreath of hair which crowns my arm;
The mystery, the sign you must not touch,
    For 'tis my outward soul,
Viceroy to that, which, then to heaven being gone,
    Will leave this to control,
And keep these limbs, her provinces, from dissolution.

For if the sinewy thread my brain lets fall
    Through every part   10
Can tie those parts, and make me one of all,
These hairs which upward grew, and strength and art
    Have from a better brain,
Can better do it; except she meant that I
    By this should know my pain,
As prisoners then are manacled, when they're condemned to die.

Whate'er she meant by it, bury it with me,
    For since I am
Love's martyr, it might breed idolatry
If into other hands these relics came;   20
    As 'twas humility
To afford to it all that a soul can do,
    So, 'tis some bravery,
That since you would have none of me, I bury some of you.

HOLY SONNETS

5

I am a little world made cunningly
Of elements, and an angelic sprite;
But black sin hath betrayed to endless night
My world's both parts, and, oh, both parts must die.
You which beyond that heaven which was most high
Have found new spheres, and of new lands can write,
Pour new seas in mine eyes, that so I might
Drown my world with my weeping earnestly,
Or wash it if it must be drowned no more:
But oh it must be burnt! alas the fire   10
Of lust and envy have burnt it heretofore,
And made it fouler; let their flames retire,
And burn me, O Lord, with a fiery zeal
Of Thee and Thy house, which doth in eating heal.

7

At the round earth's imagined corners, blow
Your trumpets, angels, and arise, arise
From death, you numberless infinities
Of souls, and to your scattered bodies go;
All whom the flood did, and fire shall o'erthrow;
All whom war, dearth, age, agues, tyrannies,
Despair, law, chance, hath slain, and you whose eyes
Shall behold God, and never taste death's woe.
But let them sleep, Lord, and me mourn a space,
For, if above all these, my sins abound,   10
'Tis late to ask abundance of Thy grace,
When we are there; here on this lowly ground,
Teach me how to repent; for that's as good
As if Thou hadst sealed my pardon, with Thy blood.

10

Death be not proud, though some have called thee
Mighty and dreadful, for thou art not so;
For those whom thou think'st thou dost overthrow
Die not, poor Death, nor yet canst thou kill me.
From rest and sleep, which but thy pictures be,
Much pleasure, then from thee much more must flow,
And soonest our best men with thee do go,
Rest of their bones and souls' delivery.
Thou art slave to fate, chance, kings, and desperate men,
And dost with poison, war, and sickness dwell,   10
And poppy, or charms can make us sleep as well,
And better than thy stroke; why swell'st thou then?
One short sleep past, we wake eternally,
And Death shall be no more; Death, thou shalt die.

---

9. **sinewy thread**, the spinal cord.   23. **bravery**, bravado, boldness.   *Holy Sonnets*. 2. **sprite**, spirit.

9. **it must be drowned no more**, a reference to the Divine promise (Genesis 9:11) that the earth will not again be destroyed with a flood.   10. **it must be burnt!** that is, at the Day of Judgment. Compare II Peter 3:5-7.   13. **a fiery zeal**. Compare Psalm 69:9: "For the zeal of thine house hath eaten me up."   *Son.* 7. 1. **imagined corners**. Compare Revelation 7:1: "And after these things, I saw four angels standing on the four corners of the earth, holding the four winds of the earth."   8. **never taste death's woe**. Compare Luke 9:27: "I tell you of a truth, there be some standing here which shall not taste of death till they see the kingdom of God."   *Son.* 10. 9-14. **Thou art slave to fate . . . die.** See Bacon's essay, "Of Death," page 546, for his treatment of this theme.

14

Batter my heart, three-personed God; for You
As yet but knock, breathe, shine, and seek to mend;
That I may rise, and stand, o'erthrow me, and bend
Your force, to break, blow, burn, and make me
  new.
I, like an usurped town to another due,
Labour to admit You, but oh! to no end;
Reason, Your viceroy in me, me should defend,
But is captived and proves weak or untrue.
Yet dearly I love You, and would be lovèd fain,
But am betrothed unto Your enemy.   10
Divorce me, untie, or break that knot again,
Take me to You, imprison me, for I
Except You enthrall me, never shall be free;
Nor ever chaste, except You ravish me.

A HYMN TO GOD THE FATHER

This hymn was written during a serious illness when Donne was about fifty. It was, so Walton tells us, set to music and sung in Donne's hearing in St. Paul's. The score is given in Grierson's edition of Donne, Oxford Press, 1912, Vol. II, pp. 252–54.

Wilt Thou forgive that sin where I begun,
  Which is my sin, though it were done before?
Wilt Thou forgive that sin through which I run,
  And do run still, though still I do deplore?
    When Thou hast done, Thou hast not done,
      For I have more.

Wilt Thou forgive that sin by which I have won
  Others to sin? and made my sin their door?
Wilt Thou forgive that sin which I did shun
  A year, or two, but wallowed in a score?   10
    When Thou hast done, Thou hast not done,
      For I have more.

I have a sin of fear, that when I have spun
  My last thread, I shall perish on the shore;
Swear by Thyself, that at my death Thy Son
  Shall shine as He shines now, and heretofore;
    And, having done that, Thou hast done,
      I fear no more.

George Wither
1588–1667

Of Wither, more often perhaps than of any other poet in the language, it has been said that if he had published much less, he would have been read much more. He was responsible for more than a hundred different works in verse or prose. Of all this mass the twentieth century really knows only one poem, the incomparable "Shall I, Wasting in Despair," but not one of a hundred who sing it can name its author.

Wither was born into a wealthy family, and after his early education was for two years at Magdalen College, Oxford. Later he studied law at Lincoln's Inn in London, and made the acquaintance of young poets there and in the Inns of Court. In 1613, when he was twenty-five, he was thrown into the Marshalsea prison for writing a book of satires on the vices, with the title *Abuses Stript and Whipt*, which was interpreted as criticism of some of the rulers in Church and State. In reality it is a series of general satires on such passions as love, lust, hate, envy, and revenge, and deals with types rather than individuals; but his strictures seem to have hit home. He was finally released after pleas had been made on his behalf by influential persons, including a member of the royal family, and an appeal in verse which he addressed to the King. The copies of his satire were suppressed.

Wither is one of the many for whom a prison became a literary nursery. While he was in the Marshalsea he translated Greek poems and composed the charming pastoral verses of *The Shepherd's Hunting*, 1615. In this poem he represents the shepherd, Philarete, relating "the true occasion of his present state," how with ten couples of dogs (the satires of his *Abuses Stript and Whipt*) he had hunted the beasts of prey "that spoil our folds, and bear our lambs away." The poem is of interest because of its idealization of the scenes of the English countryside from which he was cut off, and its happy combination of Spenserian strains and Jonsonian measures. His prison notes, said Charles Lamb, were finer than the wood-notes of most of his poetical brethren. Only two other works besides this piece have contrived to

5. **When Thou hast done.** Here and elsewhere in the poem a pun is undoubtedly intended on the poet's name, which was pronounced as "done."

retain any readers. His *Fidelia*, in heroic couplets, dating from about 1615, closed with the first version of the lyric "Shall I, Wasting in Despair." In his thirty-fifth year, 1622, he published his *Faire-Virtue, or The Mistress of Philarete*, a pastoral poem of didactic nature in various meters. The poem begins with a description of the scenery about his father's country place, and a modern reader will find in the verses on the mountains, meadows, groves, and streams, and their beneficent influence on those who live among them, many an anticipation of Wordsworth. In 1641 he published one of the earliest English hymnals, entitled *Hallelujah, or Britain's Second Remembrancer*, with hymns for every occasion and of every variety. His verse, both secular and sacred, has probably a larger proportion of simple native words than any other of his day.

The Civil War brought about the great change in Wither's life, for it changed him from a composer of delightful pastoral verse into a soldier, first on the side of the King and later on that of the Parliamentarians. For the latter cause he sold his estate and raised a troop of horse, and in the Parliamentary army he rose to the rank of major. The reasons for Wither's change of sides are not known. He has been accused of fickleness, and there is good reason to believe that the systematic defamation of his character and abilities as a poet by Royalist and other writers of the latter part of the century was due to his about-face. Wither's name became a synonym for any inferior poetaster. There is an amusing anecdote of how he was taken prisoner and escaped execution. Sir John Denham, author of the topographical poem *Cooper's Hill*, is said to have begged the Royalists to spare Wither's life, on the ground that, so long as he remained alive, Denham was not the worst poet in England. Wither indeed lived on to produce some of the worst poetry in the language, and some of the dullest prose, most of it religious in nature, combatant and argumentative. He tried his hand at satire again, and again got thrown into prison.

No other poet in English has had his best work so eclipsed by the great amount of his mediocre work. None of the poets in the early part of the century wrote with more ease and sweetness, or achieved more often and more happily the best qualities of the Elizabethans and the Jacobeans. "If any one could do for Wither what he ought to have done for himself," wrote Henry Morley, "an edition of his works would give him a lasting place among the poets whom we choose for our companions." The poems given here will indicate what this "worst of poets" could do in his happier moments.

THE AUTHOR'S RESOLUTION IN A SONNET

This earliest version of Wither's famous song was printed at the end of his *Fidelia* in 1615. "Sonnet" here means "song," as often in the sixteenth and early seventeenth centuries.

Shall I, wasting in despair,
Die because a woman's fair?
Or make pale my cheeks with care
'Cause another's rosy are?
Be she fairer than the day,
Or the flowery meads in May,
  If she think not well of me,
  What care I how fair she be?

Shall my silly heart be pined
'Cause I see a woman kind?   10
Or a well-disposèd nature
Joinèd with a lovely feature?
Be she meeker, kinder than
Turtle-dove or pelican,
  If she be not so to me,
  What care I how kind she be?

Shall a woman's virtues move
Me to perish for her love?
Or her well-deservings known
Make me quite forget mine own?   20
Be she with that goodness blest
Which may merit name of best,
  If she be not such to me,
  What care I how good she be?

'Cause her fortune seems too high,
Shall I play the fool and die?
She that bears a noble mind,
If not outward helps she find,
Thinks what with them he would do
That without them dares her woo;   30
  And unless that mind I see,
  What care I how great she be?

Great, or good, or kind, or fair,
I will ne'er the more despair;
If she love me, this believe,
I will die, ere she shall grieve:

12. **feature**, form. 14. **pelican**, believed to feed her young with blood from her own breast. 25. **fortune**, birth, position. 28. **she find**, that is, in her suitor.

If she slight me when I woo,
I can scorn and let her go;
  For if she be not for me,
  What care I for whom she be?   40

A CHRISTMAS CAROL

So now is come our joyful'st feast,
  Let every man be jolly;
Each room with ivy leaves is drest,
  And every post with holly.
     Though some churls at our mirth repine,
     Round your foreheads garlands twine,
     Drown sorrow in a cup of wine,
And let us all be merry.

Now all our neighbours' chimneys smoke,
  And Christmas blocks are burning;   10
Their ovens they with baked meats choke,
  And all their spits are turning.
     Without the door let sorrow lie,
     And if for cold it hap to die,
     We'll bury it in a Christmas pie,
And evermore be merry.

Now every lad is wondrous trim,
  And no man minds his labour;
Our lasses have provided them
  A bagpipe and a tabor.   20
     Young men and maids, and girls and boys
     Give life to one another's joys;
     And you anon shall by their noise
Perceive that they are merry.

Rank misers now do sparing shun,
  Their hall of music soundeth;
And dogs thence with whole shoulders run,
  So all things there aboundeth.
     The country-folk themselves advance,
     For Crowdy-Mutton's come out of France,   30
     And Jack shall pipe and Jill shall dance,
And all the town be merry.

Ned Swatch hath fetched his bands from pawn,
  And all his best apparel;
Brisk Nell hath bought a ruff of lawn
  With droppings of the barrel.
And those that hardly all the year
  Had bread to eat or rags to wear,
  Will have both clothes and dainty fare,
And all the day be merry.   40

Now poor men to the justices
  With capons make their arrants,
And if they hap to fail of these,
  They plague them with their warrants.
     But now they feed them with good cheer,
     And what they want they take in beer,
     For Christmas comes but once a year,
And then they shall be merry.

Good farmers in the country nurse
  The poor, that else were undone;   50
Some landlords spend their money worse,
  On lust and pride at London.
     There the roisters they do play,
     Drab and dice their land away,
     Which may be ours another day;
And therefore let's be merry.

The client now his suit forbears,
  The prisoner's heart is easèd;
The debtor drinks away his cares,
  And for the time is pleasèd.   60
     Though others' purses be more fat,
     Why should we pine or grieve at that?
     Hang sorrow, care will kill a cat,
And therefore let's be merry.

Hark how the wags abroad do call
  Each other forth to rambling
Anon you'll see them in the hall,
  For nuts and apples scrambling.
     Hark how the roofs with laughters sound!
     Anon they'll think the house goes round;   70
     For they the cellar's depths have found,
And there they will be merry.

The wenches with their wassail-bowls
  About the streets are singing;
The boys are come to catch the owls,
  The wild mare in is bringing.

10. **blocks**, logs.   20. **tabor**, a small drum.   30. **Crowdy-Mutton**, "a fiddler."—Halliwell   33. **bands**, ruffs.
36. **droppings of the barrel.** Compare Donne, *Satire 2*:
  "as a thrifty wench scrapes kitchen-stuff,
  And barrelling the droppings, and the snuff
  Of wasting candles, which in thirty year
  (Relic-like kept) perchance buys wedding gear."

42. **make their arrants** (errands), that is, seek out excuses for going. 53. **roisters**, roisterers. 73. **wassail-bowls.** Joseph Strutt in his *Sports and Pastimes*, 1801, says: "the wassail bowl . . . was a bowl of spiced ale, formerly carried about by young women on New Year's Eve, who went from door to door in their several parishes singing a few couplets of homely verses composed for the purpose, and presented the liquor to the inhabitants of the house where they called, expecting a small gratuity in return." 75. **catch the owls**, a game. 76. **The wild mare**, the seesaw. **is bringing**, is being brought.

Our kitchen boy hath broke his box,
　And to the dealing of the ox
Our honest neighbours come by flocks,
　And here they will be merry.　　　　　80

Now kings and queens poor sheep-cotes
　　have,
　And mate with everybody;
The honest now may play the knave,
　And wise men play at noddy.
　　Some youths will now a-mumming
　　　　go,
Some others play at rowland-hoe,
　And twenty other gameboys moe;
Because they will be merry.

Then wherefore in these merry days
　Should we, I pray, be duller?　　　　90
No, let us sing some roundelays
　To make our mirth the fuller.
　　And while we thus inspirèd sing,
　　Let all the streets with echoes ring;
　　Woods and hills and everything
Bear witness we are merry.

The Character-Writers

The "character" is one of the most popular and ubiquitous literary forms of the seventeenth century. Almost everyone who wrote anything tried his hand at the character sketch in one form or another, and the character book, with its collection of short and "witty" descriptions of various types of personality, is one of the most distinctive contributions of the century to English literature. The impulse to dissect the character of a fellow human being, whether through admiration or malice, for simple amusement or for information, is doubtless as old as the race itself. Character sketches of one sort or another are to be found scattered through all kinds of literature in all times and countries. In English literature from Chaucer's Prologue to his *Canterbury Tales* on through sermon, allegory, drama, essay, satire, and epigram, one meets with descriptions and characterizations of individuals or types. The student of the literature of the late sixteenth and seventeenth centuries is aware of an increasing tendency toward introspection and analysis of characters and motives of action.

The "character" proper is not a portrait or a description of the character of a particular person, but the analysis, more or less accurate, of a type of person. Fortunately seventeenth-century writers did not adhere to such a strict limitation of the term, and during the century the method of the character was applied to things and institutions as well as to persons, and to particular individuals of the day as well as to perennial types of human beings. Seventeenth-century England was profoundly class-conscious, and the character books throw much light on the social order of the time by their analyses and descriptions of the habits, prejudices, and functions of the various members of the social organism.

It is its enthusiasm for character-writing, and for compiling books of characters, rather than for its invention of the form, that has made the seventeenth century the great age of the character in English literature. The oldest known character book is that of Theophrastus, the pupil of Aristotle, and greatest of ancient botanists. His *Characters* represent a sort of botany of human nature, with various types of human beings analyzed like so many specimens in a herbarium. The author of the first character book published in England was Joseph Hall, whose *Characters of Virtues and Vices*, 1608, professedly followed the method of "that ancient master of morality." The two most popular character books in English are those of Sir Thomas Overbury and John Earle, from which the selections given here are taken.

Sir Thomas Overbury
1581–1613

The events of the short life of Overbury, and the conjectures to which they have given rise, require a volume to relate, and volumes have been written about them. He is more widely known as a central figure in one of the most unsavory and sensational episodes in English history than as the reputed author of the most popular character book of the seventeenth century. The popularity of the book was, however, due in no small measure to the interest of the public in the circumstances of his death, and of

---

77. **broke his box,** opened his Christmas collection box. 78. **dealing,** dividing. 82. **mate,** associate. 84. **play at noddy,** a pun on the word. "Noddy" is a card game, and also a simpleton. 85. **a-mumming,** masquerading.

86. **rowland-hoe,** a game. 87. **gameboys,** gambols. **moe,** more.

the trial of important personages which followed it. The story of his life is largely that of a courtier who climbed to a position of intimacy with the great, and fell, a victim of his own officiousness and of court scandal and intrigue.

Overbury was born in Warwickshire, was graduated B.A. at Queen's College, Oxford, in 1598, and then studied law at the Middle Temple. He began his career at the court of James I under the auspices of Robert Carr, the King's favorite, later Viscount Rochester and Earl of Somerset. Overbury was knighted by King James in 1608. Shortly afterwards he traveled in France and the Low Countries. He had qualities which would have made him a good newspaper reporter, and out of the notes he made on what he saw he wrote his *Observations upon the State of the Seventeen Provinces*, 1609. He returned to court, where, unfortunately for him, he continued to keep his eyes and ears open, and learned much about certain noble persons, among whom was Frances Howard, the Countess of Essex, whose marriage to the young Earl of Essex was annulled in 1613 after a trial which developed into a major scandal. Plans, favored by the King, were made for her marriage to Overbury's friend and patron Carr, now Earl of Somerset. Overbury, who had disapproved of the divorce, now opposed the marriage, and it became expedient for all concerned to get so determined and well-informed a person out of the way. The King offered him the post of ambassador to Russia, which Overbury explicitly refused, and he was committed to the Tower in April, 1613, by his offended sovereign. The account of the intrigues which make up the story of Overbury for the next few months is too involved and uncertain to be detailed here. The circumstances of "the Overbury mystery" have, indeed, never been entirely discovered. The Countess was determined to remove Overbury from the scene, and by the aid of poisons administered regularly and in increasing amounts she finally succeeded. Overbury died in September, 1613, and was buried in the Tower. Such proceedings could not be hushed up, and one of the most sensational trials in English history resulted three years later. Suspicion attached itself even to members of the royal family as the evidence transpired. Both the Earl and the Countess of Essex were found guilty, and the former was imprisoned. A few relatively insignificant persons were hanged.

In 1614, the year after Sir Thomas's death, appeared his poem *The Wife*, a character in verse, which he had written while he was trying to dissuade Somerset from marrying the Countess. The poem, published with the title, *A Wife, Now a Widow*, attracted so much attention that it went through several editions in the same year. In the later editions there were added more than twenty prose characters, "written by himself and other learned gentlemen his friends." After the trial in 1616, the popularity of the book was increased still further. Eleven editions had been called for by 1622, and the characters had increased to eighty-two. There were seventeen editions of the book, now commonly referred to as Overbury's *Characters*, before the century ended.

Of the Overbury collection probably few of the characters were the work of Overbury himself. The authorship of most of them is still undetermined. Such a collection, made up of pieces from various hands, indicates how popular and widespread was the practice of character-writing. Thirty-two of the pieces, among them some of the finest, have within the present century been proved to be the compositions of John Webster, the dramatist, author of *The White Devil* and *The Duchess of Malfi*. Of Webster's life painstaking research has revealed almost nothing. In his characters we see evidence of his ability to portray types less tragically moving but more varied than the figures of his dramas, and we are given a fair cross section of the Elizabethan and Jacobean society from which the dramatist's audiences were recruited.

The characters of the Overbury miscellany follow the literary model of Theophrastus, but the ancient Greek's careful and objective analysis has given way to personal likes and dislikes, and the English authors are more interested in clever conceits and epigrams, and "witty" observations on men and manners, than in careful diagnosis. The Overburian characters are all the more readable, of course, for this variety and human interest, and they set the general style of character-writing for the rest of the century.

from SIR THOMAS OVERBURY HIS WIFE . . . AND DIVERS MORE CHARACTERS

A GOOD WIFE

Is a man's best movable, a scion incorporate with the stock, bringing forth sweet fruit; one that to her husband is more than a friend, less than a trouble; an equal with him in the yoke. Calamities and troubles she shares alike, nothing pleases her that doth not him. She is relative in all; and he without her, but half himself. She is his absent hands, eyes, ears, and mouth; his present and absent all. She frames her nature unto his howsoever: the hyacinth follows not the sun more willingly. Stubbornness and obstinacy are herbs that grow not in her garden. She leaves tattling to the gossips of the town, and is more seen than heard. Her household is her charge; her care to that makes her seldom non-resident. Her pride is but to be cleanly, and her thrift not to be prodigal. By her discretion she hath children, not wantons; a husband without her is a misery in man's apparel; none but she hath an aged husband, to whom she is both a staff and a chair. To conclude, she is both wise and religious, which makes her all this.

A FAIR AND HAPPY MILKMAID [1]

Is a country wench, that is so far from making herself beautiful by art that one look of hers is able to put all face-physic out of countenance. She knows a fair look is but a dumb orator to commend virtue, therefore minds it not. All her excellencies stand in her so silently as if they had stolen upon her without her knowledge. The lining of her apparel (which is herself) is far better than the outside of tissue: for though she be not arrayed in the spoil of the silkworm, she is decked in innocency, a far better wearing. She doth not, with lying long abed, spoil both her complexion and conditions; nature hath taught her too immoderate sleep is rust to the soul: she rises therefore with chanticleer, her dame's cock, and at night makes the lamb her curfew. In milking a cow, and straining the teats through her fingers, it seems that so sweet a milk-press makes the milk the whiter or sweeter; for never came almond glove or aromatic ointment on her palm to taint it. The golden ears of corn fall and kiss her feet when she reaps them, as if they wished to be bound and led prisoners by the same hand that felled them. Her breath is her own, which scents all the year long of June, like a new made hay-cock. She makes her hands hard with labour, and her heart soft with pity; and when winter evenings fall early (sitting at her merry wheel), she sings a defiance to the giddy wheel of fortune. She doth all things with so sweet a grace it seems ignorance will not suffer her to do ill, being her mind is to do well. She bestows her year's wages at next fair; and in choosing her garments, counts no bravery in the world like decency. The garden and bee-hive are all her physic and chirurgery, and she lives the longer for it. She dares go alone, and unfold sheep in the night, and fears no manner of ill, because she means none; yet to say truth, she is never alone, for she is still accompanied with old songs, honest thoughts, and prayers, but short ones; yet they have their efficacy, in that they are not palled with ensuing idle cogitations. Lastly, her dreams are so chaste that she dare tell them; only a Friday's dream is all her superstition; that she conceals for fear of anger. Thus lives she, and all her care is that she may die in the springtime, to have store of flowers stuck upon her winding-sheet.

A FRANKLIN [1]

His outside is an ancient yeoman of England, though his inside may give arms (with the best gentlemen) and ne'er see the herald. There is no truer servant in the house than himself. Though he be master, he says not to his servants, Go to field, but, Let us go; and with his own eye doth both fatten his flock and set forward all manner of husbandry. He is taught by nature to be contented with a little; his own fold yields him both food and raiment; he is pleased with any nourishment God sends, whilst curious gluttony ransacks, as it were, Noah's ark for food, only to feed the riot of one meal. He is ne'er known to go to law; understanding to be law-bound among men is like to be hide-bound among beasts; they thrive not under it; in that such men sleep as unquietly as if their pillows were stuffed with lawyer's pen knives. When he builds, no poor tenant's cottage hinders his prospect; they are indeed his alms-houses, though there be painted on them no such superscription; he never sits up late but when he hunts the badger, the vowed foe of his lambs; nor uses he any cruelty but when he hunts the hare, nor subtlety, but when he sets snares for the snite, or pitfalls for the blackbird; nor oppression, but when in the month of July, he goes to the next river, and shears his sheep. He allows of honest pastime, and thinks not the bones of the dead anything bruised, or the worse for it, though the lasses dance in the churchyard after evensong. Rock Monday, and the wake in summer, shrovings, the watchful catches on

---

[1] This sketch was apparently written by John Webster. **25. tissue,** rich cloth. **49. bravery,** fine dress.

7. palled, weakened.
[1] This is also by John Webster.
33. hinders his prospect. He does not pull down any cottage on this ground. **38. snite,** snipe. **44. Rock Monday,** the Monday following Twelfth-night. Rock Day, or St. Distaff's Day, was the day after Twelfth-night ("rock" means "distaff"). Spinning was resumed on this day, after the Christmas holidays. **45. shrovings,** the festivities attendant on Shrove Tuesday.

Christmas Eve, hoky, or seed cake, these he yearly keeps, yet holds them no relics of popery. He is not so inquisitive after news derived from the privy closet, when the finding an eyrie of hawks in his own ground, or the foaling of a colt come of a good strain, are tidings more pleasant, more profitable. He is lord paramount within himself, though he hold by never so mean a tenure; and dies the more contentedly (though he leave his heir young) in regard he leaves him not liable to a covetous guardian. Lastly, to end him, he cares not when his end comes, he needs not fear his audit, for his *quietus* is in heaven.

John Earle
1601?–1665

Earle, whose little book the *Microcosmography* is, next to the Overbury collection, the best known of seventeenth-century character books, provides at every point a contrast with Overbury. He is one of the best-loved men and authors of his century. In a time of civil war and dissension he kept his temper and his friendships without sacrificing his principles, and drew commendation from men of all parties. He was as much a man of the university and the Church as Overbury and his associates were men of the court and the town. He was born in the city of York, and matriculated at Christ Church, Oxford, at the age of eighteen. For the next twenty years he was connected with Oxford, as undergraduate, fellow of Merton College, and proctor of the university. His book of characters was begun probably during his undergraduate days and was completed at the university. It has consequently a generous number of "campus characters." The *Microcosmography* was first published anonymously in 1628 after it had become known in manuscript. There was a steady succession of editions of the book, new characters being added from time to time. By the time of the author's death the number of characters had reached seventy-eight and the number of editions ten.

About two years after the book first appeared Earle was made chaplain to the Earl of Pembroke, son of Sir Philip Sidney's sister, who was Chancellor of Oxford and Lord Chamberlain. From the Earl he received also the living of Bishopston in Wiltshire. The young clergyman was shortly after made chaplain to Charles I and tutor to the Prince of Wales, later Charles II. During the struggle between the King and the Parliament, the Roundheads had sufficient regard for Earle's character and abilities to nominate him, despite his attachment to the royal cause, as one of the Westminster Assembly of Divines, but he declined the honor. He was deprived of his church livings, and after the execution of Charles I he lived abroad as chaplain to Charles II. At Charles's request he translated into Latin the *Eikon Basilike*, the *King's Book* of Charles I. After the Restoration Earle fared much better than most of the other loyalists. He was made Dean of Westminster, Bishop of Worcester, and, two years before his death, Bishop of Salisbury. He was one of the revisers of the Book of Common Prayer in 1662. It is characteristic of Earle that as a bishop he made vigorous efforts to ameliorate the condition of the Nonconformists during the persecutions of the Restoration days. He succumbed to the plague of 1665 while with the King and his court at Oxford, and was buried in Merton College Church.

Earle's *Microcosmography* is as much a mirror of his own kindly and sympathetic nature as its characters are of the types they describe. He is of all the character-writers of the time the most interested in the springs and processes of character and action, and more than any other he adopts what we should call the psychological approach. Like a good novelist, he finds some of his most interesting human materials in types that are commonly unregarded. He is never clever at the expense of his subjects, and is rather the counsel for the defense than the prosecuting attorney. We may apply to Earle Ben Jonson's description of the ideal critic in his character of Crites in *Cynthia's Revels:* "He strives rather to be that which men call judicious than to be thought so; and is so truly learned that he affects not to show it. . . . In sum, he hath a most ingenious and sweet spirit, a sharp and seasoned wit, a straight judgment, and a strong mind. Fortune could never break him, nor make him less."

from MICROCOSMOGRAPHY,

OR A PIECE OF THE WORLD DISCOVERED

A CHILD

Is a man in a small letter, yet the best copy of Adam before he tasted of Eve or the apple; and he is happy whose small practice in the world can only write his character. He is nature's fresh picture

---

1. **hoky,** or hockey; the festival of harvest home. **seed cake,** a feast in late October, following wheat-sowing.
12. **quietus,** the settling of his accounts.

newly drawn in oil, which time, and much handling, dims and defaces. His soul is yet a white paper unscribbled with observations of the world, wherewith, at length, it becomes a blurred notebook. He is purely happy, because he knows no evil, nor hath made means by sin to be acquainted with misery. He arrives not at the misery of being wise, nor endures evils to come, by foreseeing them. He kisses and loves all, and, when the smart of the rod is past, smiles on his beater. Nature and his parents alike dandle him, and tice him on with a bait of sugar to a draught of wormwood. He plays yet, like a young 'prentice the first day, and is not come to his task of melancholy. All the language he speaks yet is tears, and they serve him well enough to express his necessity. His hardest labour is his tongue, as if he were loth to use so deceitful an organ; and he is best company with it when he can but prattle. We laugh at his foolish sports, but his game is our earnest; and his drums, rattles, and hobby-horses, but the emblems and mocking of man's business. His father hath writ him as his own little story, wherein he reads those days that he cannot remember, and sighs to see what innocence he has out-lived. The older he grows, he is a stair lower from God; and, like his first father, much worse in his breeches. He is the Christian's example, and the old man's relapse; the one imitates his pureness, and the other falls into his simplicity. Could he put off his body with his little coat, he had got eternity without a burden, and exchanged but one heaven for another.

A YOUNG MAN

He is now out of nature's protection, though not yet able to guide himself; but left loose to the world and fortune, from which the weakness of his childhood preserved him; and now his strength exposes him. He is, indeed, just of age to be miserable, yet in his own conceit first begins to be happy; and he is happier in this imagination, and his misery not felt is less. He sees yet but the outside of the world and man, and conceives them, according to their appearing, glister, and out of this ignorance believes them. He pursues all vanities for happiness, and enjoys them best in this fancy. His reason serves not to curb but understand his appetite, and prosecute the motions thereof with a more eager earnestness. Himself is his own temptation, and needs not Satan, and the world will come hereafter. He leaves repentance for grey hairs, and performs it in being covetous. He is mingled with the vices of the age as the fashion and custom, with which he longs to be acquainted, and sins to better his understanding. He conceives his youth as the season of his lust, and the hour wherein he ought to be bad; and because he would not lose his time, spends it. He distastes religion as a sad thing, and is six years elder for a thought of heaven. He scorns and fears, and yet hopes for old age, but dare not imagine it with wrinkles. He loves and hates with the same inflammation, and when the heat is over is cool alike to friends and enemies. His friendship is seldom so steadfast but that lust, drink, or anger may overturn it. He offers you his blood to-day in kindness, and is ready to take yours to-morrow. He does seldom anything which he wishes not to do again, and is only wise after a misfortune. He suffers much for his knowledge, and a great deal of folly it is that makes him a wise man. He is free from many vices, by being not grown to the performance, and is only more virtuous out of weakness. Every action is his danger, and every man his ambush. He is a ship without pilot or tackling, and only good fortune may steer him. If he scape this age, he has scaped a tempest, and may live to be a man.

A YOUNG GENTLEMAN OF THE UNIVERSITY

Is one that comes there to wear a gown, and to say hereafter, he has been at the university. His father sent him thither because he heard there were the best fencing and dancing schools; from these he has his education, from his tutor the oversight. The first element of his knowledge is to be shown the colleges, and initiated in a tavern by the way, which hereafter he will learn of himself. The two marks of his seniority is the bare velvet of his gown, and his proficiency at tennis, where when he can once play a set, he is a freshman no more. His study has commonly handsome shelves, his books neat silk strings, which he shows to his father's man, and is loth to untie or take down for fear of misplacing. Upon foul days for recreation he retires thither, and looks over the pretty book his tutor reads to him, which is commonly some short history, or a piece of Euphormio; for which his tutor gives him money to spend next

---

2. **white paper,** an interesting anticipation of John Locke's theory of the infant's mind as a tabula rasa, or blank paper. See Locke's *Essay Concerning Human Understanding*, 1690, Book I, sec. 1, par. 15. 11. **tice,** old form of "entice." 26. **breeches,** a pun on Genesis 3:7, which in the Geneva Bible states that Adam and Eve, after their first disobedience, "made themselves breeches."

49. **Euphormio,** Euphormio Lusinius, pen name of John Barclay (1582–1621), author of the *Argenis*.

day. His main loitering is at the library, where he studies arms and books of honour, and turns a gentleman critic in pedigrees. Of all things he endures not to be mistaken for a scholar, and hates a black suit though it be made of satin. His companion is ordinarily some stale fellow, that has been notorious for an ingle to gold hatbands,[7] whom he admires at first, afterwards scorns. If he have spirit or wit he may light of better company, and may learn some flashes of wit, which may do him knight's service in the country hereafter. But he is now gone to the inns-a-court, where he studies to forget what he learned before, his acquaintances and the fashion.

Robert Burton
1577–1640

Burton and his book *The Anatomy of Melancholy*, which first appeared in 1621, have long since had exhausted upon them all the words the dictionary can supply to express the ideas of curious, quaint, amazing, paradoxical, unique, and so on. It is difficult to be restrained in speaking of the man or the book, for neither is marked by restraint. As for Burton's own vocabulary, there is not in English literature, nor in the world outside Rabelais, such another torrent of words as flows from the old man's quill pen. For his subject, although he professes only to treat of the eighty-eight kinds of melancholy, "what it is, with all the kinds, causes, symptoms, prognostics, and several cures of it," the reader will find, long before he has got through the *Anatomy*, that there are few things in heaven or earth, or in the little world of man, that Burton does not touch upon, and he touches nothing that he does not adorn and make alive.

This most widely ranging of books was the lifework of a man who was never more than fifty miles from his birthplace at Lindley in Leicestershire. At the age of sixteen he entered Brasenose College, Oxford, and six years later, in 1599, he removed to the neighboring college of Christ Church, where he received the degree of Bachelor of Divinity in 1614, and where he lived for the remaining forty years of his life. He received two church livings, one of them at St. Thomas in Oxford. For nearly half a century he was never out of Oxford, except for a visit on rare occasions into the near-by countryside. His sole recreation, so the legend goes, was to walk down to Folly Bridge in the evening to hear the bargemen swear. Another legend has it that, having forecast the day of his death by a horoscope, he hanged himself to make good his prediction.

The Bodleian Library was his center and source, and though there are evidences in his book of his discontent with the limitations imposed upon him, and of his consciousness of ability to do great things in the world, he seems on the whole to have felt with Prospero that his library was dukedom large enough. It is a never-ceasing wonder how Burton, living his hermit's existence and seeing life only, as Doctor Johnson would say, through the spectacle of books, could have acquired so much knowledge of the world of men and affairs, so much insight into the hidden springs of men's actions, so much of the joy of living, and so much of the pain. But the paradoxes which the man and the book present are endless. It was written by one of the sanest of men on some of the causes of insanity, in order, as the author tells us, to ward off the disease in himself. It is at once the most bookish volume in the world, and the least bookish. Half of it is compounded of learned words and interspersed with Latin, and the other half is as racy and idiomatic as if it had come directly from the lips of a countryman who had never gone to college. It is the least English of books and the most English; one of the least original, for at least one-third of it is taken from other authors, and the most truly original book in the language, for it is like no other. It contains, as do many other books of the time, a mixture of old and new, of superstition and science, of nostalgic longings for the days of which he had read in his folios and remarkable prevision of better days than had ever been, if men would be sensible enough to bring them to pass.

The *Anatomy* has been variously estimated by different groups and generations. It has been called by a distinguished modern physician the greatest medical book ever written by a layman, and by modern psychologists it has been considered as an important treatise on psychopathology. During the nineteenth century, largely as a result of the Romantic enthusiasm of the generation of Keats and Charles Lamb,

---

7. **an ingle to gold hatbands,** that is, a crony of noblemen at the university, who wore gold tassels on their caps.

it came to be known and used more as the world's greatest cabinet of curios and oddments. Keats found the inspiration for his "Lamia" in it, and of one of its racier passages wrote, in a letter to George and Georgiana Keats, September 18, 1819, "I would give my favourite leg to have written this as a speech in a play." It has sometimes even been thought of as a gigantic joke, the elaborate apparatus and intricate details of which were perpetrated by a whimsical old man with his tongue in his cheek. But it is not a joke, although Burton's droll humor enlivens every page of it. It was born out of the disillusionment, the skepticism, the uncertainty, of the age which called forth Hamlet's soliloquies and the agonized soul-searchings of John Donne. Burton was, as he tells us, by his profession a divine, by his inclination a physician. The *Anatomy* is his book of household remedies requisite and necessary as well for the body as the soul.

from THE ANATOMY OF MELAN-CHOLY

DEMOCRITUS JUNIOR TO THE READER

GENTLE Reader, I presume thou wilt be very inquisitive to know what antic or personate actor this is, that so insolently intrudes upon this common theatre to the world's view, arrogating another man's name; whence he is, why he doth it, and what he hath to say. Although, as he said, *Primum si noluero, non respondebo, quis coacturus est?* I am a free man born, and may choose whether I will tell; who can compel me? if I be urged, I will as readily reply as that Egyptian in Plutarch, when a curious fellow would needs know what he had in his basket, *Quam vides velatam, quid inquiris in rem absconditam?* It was therefore covered, because he should not know what was in it. Seek not after that which is hid; if the contents please thee, "and be for thy use, suppose the Man in the Moon, or whom thou wilt, to be the author"; I would not willingly be known. Yet in some sort to give thee satisfaction, which is more than I need, I will show a reason,

both of this usurped name, title, and subject. And first of the name of Democritus; lest any man by reason of it should be deceived, expecting a pasquil, a satire, some ridiculous treatise (as I myself should have done), some prodigious tenent, or paradox of the earth's motion, of infinite worlds, *in infinito vacuo, ex fortuita atomorum collisione,* in an infinite waste, so caused by an accidental collision of motes in the sun, all which Democritus held, Epicurus and their master Leucippus of old maintained, and are lately revived by Copernicus, Brunus, and some others. Besides, it hath been always an ordinary custom, as Gellius observes, "for later writers and impostors to broach many absurd and insolent fictions under the name of so noble a philosopher as Democritus, to get themselves credit, and by that means the more to be respected," as artificers usually do, *Novo qui marmori ascribunt Praxitelen suo.* 'Tis not so with me.

*Non hic Centauros, non Gorgonas, Harpyasque
Invenies, hominem pagina nostra sapit.*

No Centaurs here, or Gorgons look to find,
My subject is of man and humankind.

Thou thyself art the subject of my discourse.

*Quicquid agunt homines, votum, timor, ira, voluptas,
Gaudia, discursus, nostri farrago libelli.*

Whate'er men do, vows, fears, in ire, in sport,
Joys, wand'rings, are the sum of my report.

My intent is no otherwise to use his name, than Mercurius Gallobelgicus, Mercurius Britannicus, use the name of Mercury, Democritus Christianus, etc.; although there be some other circumstances for which I have masked myself under this vizard, and some peculiar respects which I cannot so well express, until I have set down a brief character of this our Democritus, what he was, with an epitome of his life.

Democritus, as he is described by Hippocrates and Laertius, was a little wearish old man, very melancholy by nature, averse from company in his latter days, and much given to solitariness, a famous philosopher in his age, *coaevus* with Socrates, wholly addicted to his studies at the last, and to a private life: writ many excellent works, a great divine, according to the divinity of those times, an expert

---

29. as he said, the philosopher Seneca, in his burlesque on the death of the emperor Claudius Caesar. **30. Primum . . . coacturus est?** It has been thought unnecessary, here and elsewhere in the selections from Burton, to translate a passage of which Burton immediately gives the full sense in his own racy and inimitable English. It has likewise seemed best not to interrupt the torrential flow of Burton's thought by constant mention of the innumerable authors from whom he quotes or to whom he refers. Burton's own learned references and the comments of his editors may be found in any complete edition of *The Anatomy of Melancholy*.

5. tenent, tenet. **18. Novo . . . Praxitelen suo,** who sign Praxiteles' name on their own new marble statue. **42. wearish,** sickly-looking.

physician, a politician, an excellent mathematician, as *Diacosmus* and the rest of his works do witness. He was much delighted with the studies of husbandry, saith Columella, and often I find him cited by Constantinus and others treating of that subject. He knew the natures, differences of all beasts, plants, fishes, birds; and, as some say, could understand the tunes and voices of them. In a word, he was *omnifariam doctus*, a general scholar, a great student; and to the intent he might better contemplate, I find it related by some, that he put out his eyes, and was in his old age voluntarily blind, yet saw more than all Greece besides, and writ of every subject, *Nihil in toto opificio naturae, de quo non scripsit*. A man of an excellent wit, profound conceit; and to attain knowledge the better in his younger years he travelled to Egypt and Athens, to confer with learned men, "admired of some, despised of others." After a wandering life, he settled at Abdera, a town in Thrace, and was sent for thither to be their lawmaker, recorder, or town clerk as some will; or as others, he was there bred and born. Howsoever it was, there he lived at last in a garden in the suburbs, wholly betaking himself to his studies and a private life, "saving that sometimes he would walk down to the haven, and laugh heartily at such variety of ridiculous objects, which there he saw." Such a one was Democritus.

But in the meantime, how doth this concern me, or upon what reference do I usurp his habit? I confess, indeed, that to compare myself unto him for aught I have yet said, were both impudency and arrogancy. I do not presume to make any parallel, *antistat mihi millibus trecentis, parvus sum, nullus sum, altum nec spiro, nec spero*. Yet thus much I will say of myself, and that I hope without all suspicion of pride, or self-conceit, I have lived a silent, sedentary, solitary, private life, *mihi et musis* in the university, as long almost as Xenocrates in Athens, *ad senectam fere* to learn wisdom as he did, penned up most part in my study. For I have been brought up a student in the most flourishing college of Europe, *augustissimo collegio*, and can brag with Jovius, almost, *in ea luce domicilii Vaticani, totius orbis celeberrimi, per 37 annos multa opportunaque didici;* for

thirty years I have continued (having the use of as good libraries as ever he had) a scholar, and would be therefore loth, either by living as a drone to be an unprofitable or unworthy member of so learned and noble a society, or to write that which should be anyway dishonourable to such a royal and ample foundation. Something I have done, though by my profession a divine, yet *turbine raptus ingenii*, as he said, out of a running wit, an unconstant, unsettled mind, I had a great desire (not able to attain to a superficial skill in any) to have some smattering in all, to be *aliquis in omnibus, nullus in singulis*, which Plato commends, out of him Lipsius approves and furthers, "as fit to be imprinted in all curious wits, not to be a slave of one science, or dwell altogether in one subject, as most do, but to rove abroad, *centum puer artium*, to have an oar in every man's boat, to taste of every dish, and sip of every cup," which, saith Montaigne, was well performed by Aristotle and his learned countryman Adrian Turnebus. This roving humour (though not with like success) I have ever had, and like a ranging spaniel, that barks at every bird he sees, leaving his game, I have followed all, saving that which I should, and may justly complain, and truly, *qui ubique est, nusquam est*, which Gesner did in modesty, that I have read many books, but to little purpose, for want of good method; I have confusedly tumbled over divers authors in our libraries, with small profit for want of art, order, memory, judgment. I never travelled but in map or card, in which my unconfined thoughts have freely expatiated, as having ever been especially delighted with the study of cosmography. Saturn was lord of my geniture, culminating, etc., and Mars principal significator of manners, in partile conjunction with mine ascendant; both fortunate in their houses, etc. I am not poor, I am not rich; *nihil est, nihil deest*, I have little, I want nothing: all my treasure is in Minerva's tower. Greater preferment as I could never get, so am I not in debt for it, I have a competency (*laus Deo*) from my noble and munificent patrons, though I live still a collegiate student, as Democritus in his

14. **Nihil . . . scripsit.** There was nothing in the whole range of nature about which he did not write. 34–35. **antistat . . . spero**, he excels me immeasurably, I am a poor thing, a nobody, I have no lofty ambitions or hopes. 38. **mihi et musis**, to myself and the Muses. 39–40. **ad senectam fere**, almost to old age. 43. **augustissimo collegio**, Christ Church, Oxford, which Cardinal Wolsey had designed expressly to be "the most magnificent college in Christendom." 44–45. **in ea luce . . . didici**, in that light of the Vatican, the most renowned library in the world, during thirty-seven years I made good use of my opportunities for study.

12. **aliquis . . . singulis,** a somebody in everything, a nobody in any particular subject. 17. **centum puer artium**, a lad of a hundred different arts. 25–26. **qui ubique . . . est**, he who is everywhere is nowhere. 31. **card**, chart. 37. **fortunate in their houses, etc.** The signs of the zodiac are in astrology distributed among the planets as "houses" or "mansions." When a planet was situated in its house, it was supposed to exert a particularly strong influence. For a discussion of some of the astrological and astronomical data of Burton's horoscope, which was drawn up in his own handwriting, see *The Anatomy of Melancholy*, ed. by Floyd Dell and Paul Jordan-Smith, Farrar and Rinehart, 1927, Appendix II, pp. 978–80.

garden, and lead a monastic life, *ipse mihi theatrum*, sequestered from those tumults and troubles of the world, *et tanquam in specula positus* (as he said), in some high place above you all, like *Stoicus sapiens, omnia saecula, praeterita praesentiaque videns, uno velut intuitu*, I hear and see what is done abroad, how others run, ride, turmoil, and macerate themselves in court and country, far from those wrangling lawsuits, *aulae vanitatem, fori ambitionem, ridere mecum soleo*, I laugh at all; "only secure lest my suit go amiss, my ships perish," corn and cattle miscarry, trade decay, "I have no wife nor children good or bad to provide for." A mere spectator of other men's fortunes and adventures, and how they act their parts, which methinks are diversely presented unto me, as from a common theatre or scene. I hear new news every day, and those ordinary rumours of war, plagues, fires, inundations, thefts, murders, massacres, meteors, comets, spectrums, prodigies, apparitions, of towns taken, cities besieged in France, Germany, Turkey, Persia, Poland, etc., daily musters and preparations, and such-like, which these tempestuous times afford, battles fought, so many men slain, monomachies, shipwrecks, piracies, and sea-fights, peace, leagues, stratagems, and fresh alarums. A vast confusion of vows, wishes, actions, edicts, petitions, lawsuits, pleas, laws, proclamations, complaints, grievances are daily brought to our ears. New books every day, pamphlets, currantoes, stories, whole catalogues of volumes of all sorts, new paradoxes, opinions, schisms, heresies, controversies in philosophy, religion, etc. Now come tidings of weddings, maskings, mummeries, entertainments, jubilees, embassies, tilts and tournaments, trophies, triumphs, revels, sports, plays: then again, as in a new shifted scene, treasons, cheating tricks, robberies, enormous villainies in all kinds, funerals, burials, deaths of princes, new discoveries, expeditions: now comical, then tragical matters. To-day we hear of new lords and officers created, tomorrow of some great men deposed, and then again of fresh honours conferred; one is let loose, another imprisoned; one purchaseth, another breaketh; he thrives, his neighbour turns bankrupt; now plenty, then again dearth and famine; one runs, another rides, wrangles, laughs, weeps, etc. Thus I daily hear, and such-like, both private and public news; amidst the gallantry and misery of the world—jollity, pride, perplexities and cares, simplicity and villainy; subtlety, knavery, candour and integrity, mutually mixed and offering themselves—I rub on *privus privatus;* as I have still lived, so I now continue, *statu quo prius*, left to a solitary life and mine own domestic discontents: saving that sometimes, *ne quid mentiar*, as Diogenes went into the city and Democritus to the haven to see fashions, I did for my recreation now and then walk abroad, look into the world, and could not choose but make some little observation, *non tam sagax observator, ac simplex recitator*, not as they did, to scoff or laugh at all, but with a mixed passion.

Bilem saepe, jocum vestri movere tumultus. . . .

If Democritus were alive now, and should but see the superstition of our age, our religious madness, as Meteran calls it, *religiosam insaniam*, so many professed Christians, yet so few imitators of Christ; so much talk of religion, so much science, so little conscience; so much knowledge, so many preachers, so little practice; such variety of sects, such have and hold of all sides, *obvia signis signa*, . . . etc. What would he say? . . .

What would he have said to see, hear, and read so many bloody battles, so many thousands slain at once, such streams of blood able to turn mills, *unius ob noxam furiasque*, or to make sport for princes, without any just cause, "for vain titles" (saith Austin), "precedency, some wench, or such-like toy, or out of desire of domineering, vainglory, malice, revenge, folly, madness," (goodly causes all, *ob quas universus orbis bellis et caedibus misceatur*), whilst statesmen themselves in the meantime are secure at home, pampered with all delights and pleasures, take their ease, and follow their lusts, not considering what intolerable misery poor soldiers endure, their often wounds, hunger, thirst, etc., the lamentable cares, torments, calamities, and oppressions that accompany such proceedings, they feel not, take no notice of it. "So wars are begun, by the persuasion of a few deboshed, hair-brain, poor, dissolute, hungry captains, parasitical fawners, unquiet Hotspurs, restless innovators, green heads, to satisfy one man's private spleen, lust, ambition, avarice, etc."; *tales rapiunt scelerata in proelia causae. Flos hominum*, proper men,

---

1. **ipse mihi theatrum**, a theater to myself. 3. **et . . . positus**, as if placed among mirrors. 4–6. **Stoicus . . . intuitu**, the wise Stoic, surveying all ages, past and present, at one glance. 9. **aulae . . . soleo**, I am given to laughing to myself at the vanity of the court and the ambition of the forum. 29–30. **currantoes**, gazettes. 2–3. **privus privatus**, in complete privacy. 3–4. **statu quo prius**, in the same condition as before. 5. **ne quid mentiar**, not to tell a lie. 9–10. **non . . . recitator**, not so much a sage observer as a simple narrator. 12. **Bilem . . . tumultus.** Your passions have often moved me to both anger and mirth. 21. **obvia signis signa**, standards raised against standards. 26–27. **unius . . . furiasque**, through the guilt and madness of one person. 31–32. **ob . . . misceatur**, for plunging the whole world into an orgy of war and slaughter. 44–45. **tales . . . causae**, such are the causes that bring about war with its crimes.

well proportioned, carefully brought up, able both in body and mind, sound, led like so many beasts to the slaughter in the flower of their years, pride, and full strength, without all remorse and pity, sacrificed to Pluto, killed up as so many sheep, for devils' food, 40,000 at once. At once, said I, that were tolerable, but these wars last always, and for ages; nothing so familiar as this hacking and hewing, massacres, murders, desolations; *ignoto coelum clangore remugit*, they care not what mischief they procure, so that they may enrich themselves for the present; they will so long blow the coals of contention, till all the world be consumed with fire. . . .

"Who" (saith mine author) "can be sufficiently amazed at their flinty hearts, obstinacy, fury, blindness, who, without any likelihood of good success, hazard poor soldiers, and lead them without pity to the slaughter, which may justly be called the rage of furious beasts, that run without reason upon their own deaths?" *quis malus genius, quae furia, quae pestis*, etc., what plague, what fury brought so devilish, so brutish a thing as war first into men's minds? Who made so soft and peaceable a creature, born to love, mercy, meekness, so to rave, rage like beasts, and run on to their own destruction? How may Nature expostulate with mankind, *Ego te divinum animal finxi*, etc., I made thee an harmless, quiet, a divine creature! how may God expostulate, and all good men! yet, *horum facta* (as one condoles) *tantum admirantur, et heroum numero habent:* these are the brave spirits, the gallants of the world, these admired alone, triumph alone, have statues, crowns, pyramids, obelisks to their eternal fame, that immortal genius attends on them, *hac itur ad astra*. . . .

Generally they prey one upon another as so many ravenous birds, brute beasts, devouring fishes, no medium, *omnes hic aut captantur aut captant; aut cadavera quae lacerantur, aut corvi qui lacerant*, either deceive or be deceived; tear others or be torn in pieces themselves; like so many buckets in a well, as one riseth another falleth, one's empty, another's full; his ruin is a ladder to the third; such are our ordinary proceedings. What's the market? A place, according to Anacharsis, wherein they cozen one another, a trap; nay, what's the world itself? A vast chaos, a confusion of manners, as fickle as the air, *domicilium insanorum*, a turbulent troop full of impurities, a mart of walking spirits, goblins, the theatre of hypocrisy, a shop of knavery, flattery, a nursery of villainy, the scene of babbling, the school of giddiness, the academy of vice; a warfare, *ubi velis nolis pugnandum, aut vincas aut succumbas*, in which kill or be killed; wherein every man is for himself, his private ends, and stands upon his own guard. No charity, love, friendship, fear of God, alliance, affinity, consanguinity, Christianity, can contain them, but if they be anyways offended, or that string of commodity be touched, they fall foul. Old friends become bitter enemies on a sudden for toys and small offences, and they that erst were willing to do all mutual offices of love and kindness, now revile and persecute one another to death, with more than Vatinian hatred, and will not be reconciled. So long as they are behoveful, they love, or may bestead each other, but when there is no more good to be expected, as they do by an old dog, hang him up or cashier him: which Cato counts a great indecorum, to use men like old shoes or broken glasses, which are flung to the dunghill; he could not find in his heart to sell an old ox, much less to turn away an old servant: but they, instead of recompense, revile him, and when they have made him an instrument of their villainy, as Bajazet the Second, Emperor of the Turks, did by Acomethes Bassa, make him away, or instead of reward, hate him to death, as Silius was served by Tiberius. In a word, every man for his own ends. Our *summum bonum* is commodity, and the goddess we adore *Dea Moneta*, Queen Money, to whom we daily offer sacrifice, which steers our hearts, hands, affections, all: that most powerful goddess, by whom we are reared, depressed, elevated, esteemed the sole commandress of our actions, for which we pray, run, ride, go, come, labour, and contend as fishes do for a crumb that falleth into the water. It is not worth, virtue (that's *bonum theatrale*), wisdom, valour, learning, honesty, religion, or any sufficiency for which we are respected, but money, greatness, office, honour, authority; honesty is accounted folly; knavery, policy; men admired out of opinion, not as they are, but as they seem to be: such shifting, lying, cogging, plotting, counterplotting, temporizing, flattering, cozening, dissembling, "that of necessity one must highly offend God if he be conformable to the world," *Cretizare cum Crete*, "or else live in contempt, disgrace, and misery." One takes upon him temper-

---

9–10. ignoto . . . remugit, the sky re-echoes the unwonted noise. **36–37. hac . . . astra,** this is the path to the stars. **51. domicilium insanorum,** a madhouse. **4–5. ubi . . . succumbas,** where you must fight whether you wish to or not, and either conquer or go under. **16. Vatinian hatred,** a reference to Catullus' expression of hatred for Publius Vatinius, Roman consul. **39. bonum theatrale,** a theatrical good. **48. Cretizare cum Crete,** to do in Crete as the Cretans do.

ance, holiness, another austerity, a third an affected kind of simplicity, whenas indeed he, and he, and he, and the rest are hypocrites, ambidexters, outsides, so many turning pictures, a lion on the one side, a lamb on the other. How would Democritus have been affected to see these things! . . .

[THE UTOPIA OF DEMOCRITUS JUNIOR]

I WILL yet, to satisfy and please myself, make an Utopia of mine own, a New Atlantis, a poetical commonwealth of mine own, in which I will freely domineer, build cities, make laws, statutes, as I list myself. And why may I not? *Pictoribus atque poetis*, etc.—you know what liberty poets ever had, and besides, my predecessor Democritus was a politician, a recorder of Abdera, a law-maker, as some say; and why may not I presume so much as he did? Howsoever I will adventure. For the site, if you will needs urge me to it, I am not fully resolved, it may be in *Terra Australis Incognita*, there is room enough (for of my knowledge neither that hungry Spaniard, nor Mercurius Britannicus, have yet discovered half of it), or else one of these floating islands in Mare del Zur, which, like the Cyanean Isles in the Euxine Sea, alter their place, and are accessible only at set times, and to some few persons; or one of the Fortunate Isles, for who knows yet where, or which they are? There is room enough in the inner parts of America and northern coasts of Asia. But I will choose a site, whose latitude shall be forty-five degrees (I respect not minutes) in the midst of the temperate zone, or perhaps under the Equator, that paradise of the world, *ubi semper virens laurus*, etc., where is a perpetual spring: the longitude for some reasons I will conceal. Yet "be it known to all men by these presents," that if any honest gentleman will send in so much money as Cardan allows an astrologer for casting a nativity, he shall be a sharer, I will acquaint him with my project; or if any worthy man will stand for any temporal or spiritual office or dignity (for, as he said of his archbishopric of Utopia, 'tis *sanctus ambitus*, and not amiss to be sought after), it shall be freely given without all intercessions, bribes, letters, etc., his own worth shall be the best spokesman; and because we shall admit of no deputies or advowsons, if he be sufficiently qualified, and as able as willing to execute the place himself, he shall have present possession. It shall be divided into twelve or thirteen provinces, and those by hills, rivers, roadways, or some more eminent limits exactly bounded. Each province shall have a metropolis, which shall be so placed as a centre almost in a circumference, and the rest at equal distances, some twelve Italian miles asunder, or thereabout, and in them shall be sold all things necessary for the use of man, *statis horis et diebus* no market towns, markets or fairs, for they do but beggar cities (no village shall stand above six, seven, or eight miles from a city); except those emporiums which are by the seaside, general staples, marts, as Antwerp, Venice, Bergen of old, London, etc. Cities most part shall be situated upon navigable rivers or lakes, creeks, havens; and for their form, regular, round, square, or long square, with fair, broad, and straight streets, houses uniform, built of brick and stone, like Bruges, Brussels, Rhegium Lepidi, Berne in Switzerland, Milan, Mantua, Crema, Cambalu in Tartary, described by M. Polus, or that Venetian Palma. I will admit very few or no suburbs, and those of baser building, walls only to keep out man and horse, except it be in some frontier towns, or by the seaside, and those to be fortified after the latest manner of fortification, and situated upon convenient havens, or opportune places. In every so built city, I will have convenient churches, and separate places to bury the dead in, not in churchyards; a *citadella* (in some, not all) to command it, prisons for offenders, opportune market-places of all sorts, for corn, meat, cattle, fuel, fish, commodious courts of justice, public halls for all societies, bourses, meeting-places, armouries, in which shall be kept engines for quenching of fire, artillery gardens, public walks, theatres, and spacious fields allotted for all gymnics, sports, and honest recreations, hospitals of all kinds, for children, orphans, old folks, sick men, madmen, soldiers, pest-houses, etc., not built *precario*, or by gouty benefactors, who, when by fraud and rapine they have extorted all their lives, oppressed whole provinces, societies, give something to pious uses, build a satisfactory almshouse, school, or bridge, etc., at their last end, or before perhaps, which is no otherwise than to steal a goose and stick down a feather, rob a thousand to relieve ten; and those hospitals so built and maintained, not by collections, benevolences, donaries, for a set number (as in ours), just so many and no more at such a rate, but for all those who stand in need, be they more or less, and that *ex publico aerario*,

---

22. Terra . . . Incognita, the Unknown Southern Land, that is, Australia. 23–24. that hungry Spaniard, "Ferdinando de Quiros, 1612." (Burton) 26. Mare del Zur, the South Sea, Pacific Ocean. 35. ubi . . . laurus, where the laurel is ever green. 44. sanctus ambitus, a holy ambition; quoted from the prefatory letter of Sir Thomas More's *Utopia*.

10. statis . . . diebus, at stated hours and on stated days. 17–18. long square, oblong. 40. precario, as a favor. 51. ex publico aerario, from the public treasury.

and so still maintained; *non nobis solum nati sumus*, etc. I will have conduits of sweet and good water aptly disposed in each town, common granaries, as at Dresden in Misnia, Stettin in Pomerland, Nuremberg, etc.; colleges of mathematicians, musicians, and actors, as of old at Lebedus in Ionia, alchemists, physicians, artists, and philosophers, that all arts and sciences may sooner be perfected and better learned; and public historiographers, as amongst those ancient Persians, *qui in commentarios referebant quae memoratu digna gerebantur*, informed and appointed by the State to register all famous acts, and not by each insufficient scribbler, partial or parasitical pedant, as in our times. I will provide public schools of all kinds, singing, dancing, fencing, etc., especially of grammar and languages, not to be taught by those tedious precepts ordinarily used, but by use, example, conversation, as travellers learn abroad, and nurses teach their children: as I will have all such places, so will I ordain public governors, fit officers to each place, treasurers, aediles, quaestors, overseers of pupils, widows' goods, and all public houses, etc., and those once a year to make strict accounts of all receipts, expenses, to avoid confusion, *et sic fiet ut non absumant* (as Pliny to Trajan), *quod pudeat dicere*. They shall be subordinate to those higher officers and governors of each city, which shall not be poor tradesmen and mean artificers, but noblemen and gentlemen, which shall be tied to residence in those towns they dwell next, at such set times and seasons: for I see no reason (which Hippolytus complains of) "that it should be more dishonourable" for noblemen to govern the city than the country, or unseemly to dwell there now than of old. I will have no bogs, fens, marshes, vast woods, deserts, heaths, commons, but all enclosed (yet not depopulated, and therefore take heed you mistake me not); for that which is common, and every man's, is no man's; the richest countries are still enclosed, as Essex, Kent, with us, etc., Spain, Italy; and where enclosures are least in quantity, they are best husbanded, as about Florence in Italy, Damascus in Syria, etc., which are liker gardens than fields. I will not have a barren acre in all my territories, not so much as the tops of mountains: where nature fails, it shall be supplied by art: lakes and rivers shall not be left desolate. All common highways, bridges, banks, corrivations of waters, aqueducts, channels, public works, building, etc., out of a common stock, curiously maintained and kept in repair; no depopulations, engrossings, alterations of wood, arable, but by the consent of some supervisors that shall be appointed for that purpose, to see what reformation ought to be had in all places, what is amiss, how to help it, *Et quid quaeque ferat regio, et quid quaeque recuset*, what ground is aptest for wood, what for corn, what for cattle, gardens, orchards, fishponds, etc., with a charitable division in every village (not one domineering house greedily to swallow up all, which is too common with us), what for lords, what for tenants; and because they shall be better encouraged to improve such lands they hold, manure, plant trees, drain, fence, etc., they shall have long leases, a known rent, and known fine, to free them from those intolerable exactions of tyrannizing landlords. These supervisors shall likewise appoint what quantity of land in each manor is fit for the lord's demesnes, what for holding of tenants, how it ought to be husbanded—*Ut Magnetes equis, Minyae gens cognita remis*—how to be manured, tilled, rectified,

"*Hic segetes veniunt, illic felicius uvae,
Arborei foetus alibi, atque injussa virescunt
Gramina,*"

and what proportion is fit for all callings, because private possessors are many times idiots, ill husbands, oppressors, covetous, and know not how to improve their own, or else wholly respect their own, and not public good.

Utopian parity is a kind of government to be wished for rather than effected, *Respub. Christianopolitana*, Campanella's City of the Sun, and that New Atlantis, witty fictions, but mere chimeras, and Plato's community in many things is impious, absurd, and ridiculous, it takes away all splendour and magnificence. I will have several orders, degrees of nobility, and those hereditary, not rejecting younger brothers in the meantime, for they shall be sufficiently provided for by pensions, or so qualified, brought up in some honest calling, they shall be

---

1. **curiously**, studiously, neatly. 2–3. **engrossings**, monopolies. 6–7. **Et quid . . . recuset.** And what each region will bear, and what it refuses to bear. 21–22. **Ut Magnetes . . . remis.** Famed as the Magnesians for horses, the Argonauts for oarsmanship. 24–26. "**Hic . . . Gramina.**" From Virgil's *Georgics*, I, ll. 54–56, translated by Dryden as follows:
"This ground with Bacchus, that with Ceres suits,
The other loads the trees with happy fruits,
A fourth, with grass unbidden, decks the ground."
34–35. **Respub. Christianopolitana**, the "Christianopolitan Republic" described in the *Christianopolis* of Johann Valentin Andrea, a seventeenth-century Protestant theologian and Rosicrucian philosopher. 35–36. **New Atlantis**, see above, page 551.

1. **non . . . sumus**, we are not born for ourselves alone. 6–7. **alchemists.** "Not to make gold, but for matters of physic." (Burton) 25–26. **et sic . . . dicere**, and so they shall not squander the funds, which one is ashamed even to speak of. 48. **corrivations**, junctions of streams.

able to live of themselves. I will have such a proportion of ground belonging to every barony; he that buys the land shall buy the barony, he that by riot consumes his patrimony and ancient demesnes shall forfeit his honours. As some dignities shall be hereditary, so some again by election, or by gift (besides free offices, pensions, annuities), like our bishoprics, prebends, the bassas' palaces in Turkey, the procurators' houses and offices in Venice, which, like the golden apple, shall be given to the worthiest and best deserving both in war and peace, as a reward of their worth and good service, as so many goals for all to aim at (*honos alit artes*), and encouragement to others. For I hate these severe, unnatural, harsh, German, French, and Venetian decrees, which exclude plebeians from honours; be they never so wise, rich, virtuous, valiant, and well qualified, they must not be patricians, but keep their own rank; this is *naturae bellum inferre*, odious to God and men, I abhor it. My form of government shall be monarchical;

"*Nunquam libertas gratior exstat
Quam sub rege pio*, etc."

Few laws, but those severely kept, plainly put down, and in the mother tongue, that every man may understand. Every city shall have a peculiar trade or privilege, by which it shall be chiefly maintained: and parents shall teach their children, one of three at least, bring up and instruct them in the mysteries of their own trade. In each town these several tradesmen shall be so aptly disposed, as they shall free the rest from danger or offence: fire-trades, as smiths, forge-men, brewers, bakers, metal-men, etc. shall dwell apart by themselves: dyers, tanners, fellmongers, and such as use water, in convenient places by themselves: noisome or fulsome for bad smells, as butchers' slaughterhouses, chandlers, curriers, in remote places and some back lanes. Fraternities and companies I approve of, as merchants' bourses, colleges of druggers, physicians, musicians, etc., but all trades to be rated in the sale of wares, as our clerks of the market do bakers and brewers; corn itself, what scarcity soever shall come, not to exceed such a price. Of such wares as are transported or brought in, if they be necessary, commodious, and such as nearly concern man's life, as corn, wood, coal, etc., and such provision we cannot want, I will have little or no custom paid, no taxes; but for such things as are for pleasure, delight, or ornament, as wine, spice, tobacco, silk, velvet, cloth of gold, lace, jewels, etc., a greater impost. I will have certain ships sent out for new discoveries every year, and some discreet men appointed to travel into all neighbour kingdoms by land, which shall observe what artificial inventions and good laws are in other countries, customs, alterations, or aught else, concerning war or peace, which may tend to the common good. Ecclesiastical discipline, *penes episcopos*, subordinate as the other. No impropriations, no lay patrons of church livings, or one private man, but common societies, corporations, etc., and those rectors of benefices to be chosen out of the universities, examined and approved, as the *literati* in China. No parish to contain above a thousand auditors. If it were possible, I would have such priests as should imitate Christ, charitable lawyers should love their neighbours as themselves, temperate and modest physicians, politicians contemn the world, philosophers should know themselves, noblemen live honestly, tradesmen leave lying and cozening, magistrates corruption, etc.; but this is impossible, I must get such as I may. I will therefore have of lawyers, judges, advocates, physicians, chirurgeons, etc., a set number, and every man, if it be possible, to plead his own cause, to tell that tale to the judge which he doth to his advocate, as at Fez in Africa, Bantam, Aleppo, Ragusa, *suam quisque causam dicere tenetur*. Those advocates, chirurgeons, and physicians which are allowed, to be maintained out of the common treasure, no fees to be given or taken upon pain of losing their places; or if they do, very small fees, and when the cause is fully ended. He that sues any man shall put in a pledge, which, if it be proved he hath wrongfully sued his adversary, rashly or maliciously, he shall forfeit and lose. Or else, before any suit begin, the plaintiff shall have his complaint approved by a set delegacy to that purpose; if it be of moment, he shall be suffered as before to proceed, if otherwise, they shall determine it. All causes shall be pleaded *suppresso nomine*, the parties' names concealed, if some circumstances do not otherwise require. Judges and other officers shall be aptly disposed in each province, villages, cities, as common arbitrators to hear causes and end all controversies, and those not single, but three at least on the bench at once, to determine or give sentence, and those

---

5. forfeit his honours. "So it is in the kingdom of Naples and France." (Burton) **13. (honos alit artes),** honor fosters the arts. **19. naturae bellum inferre,** to make war on nature. **23–24. "Nunquam . . . pio."** "Liberty is never more gratifying than under a virtuous king." **36–37. fellmongers,** dealers in hides.

1. cannot want, cannot do without. **11–12. penes episcopos,** in the hands of the bishops. **16. as the literati in China,** that is, by competitive examinations. **30–31. suam . . . tenetur,** everyone is expected to plead his own cause. **38. forfeit and lose.** "It is so in most free cities in Germany." (Burton)

again to sit by turns or lots, and not to continue still in the same office. No controversy to depend above a year, but without all delays and further appeals to be speedily dispatched, and finally concluded in that time allotted. These and all other inferior magistrates to be chosen as the *literati* in China, or by those exact suffrages of the Venetians, and such again not to be eligible, or capable of magistracies, honours, offices, except they be sufficiently qualified for learning, manners, and that by the strict approbation of deputed examinators: first scholars to take place, then soldiers; for I am of Vegetius his opinion, a scholar deserves better than a soldier, because *unius aetatis sunt quae fortiter fiunt, quae vero pro utilitate reipub. scribuntur, aeterna:* a soldier's work lasts for an age, a scholar's for ever. If they misbehave themselves, they shall be deposed, and accordingly punished, and whether their offices be annual or otherwise, once a year they shall be called in question, and give an account; for men are partial and passionate, merciless, covetous, corrupt, subject to love, hate, fear, favour, etc., *omne sub regno graviore regnum:* like Solon's Areopagites, or those Roman censors, some shall visit others, and be visited *invicem* themselves, they shall oversee that no prowling officer, under colour of authority, shall insult over his inferiors, as so many wild beasts, oppress, domineer, flay, grind, or trample on, be partial or corrupt, but that there be *aequabile jus*, justice equally done, live as friends and brethren together; and which Seselius would have and so much desires in his kingdom of France, "a diapason and sweet harmony of kings, princes, nobles, and plebeians so mutually tied and involved in love, as well as laws and authority, as that they never disagree, insult or encroach one upon another." If any man deserve well in his office he shall be rewarded,

"*Quis enim virtutem amplectitur ipsam,
Praemia si tollas?*"

He that invents anything for public good in any art or science, writes a treatise, or performs any noble exploit at home or abroad, shall be accordingly enriched, honoured, and preferred. I say with Hannibal in Ennius, *Hostem qui feriet erit mihi Carthageniensis*, let him be of what condition he will, in all offices, actions, he that deserves best shall have best.
Tilianus in Philonius, out of a charitable mind no doubt, wished all his books were gold and silver, jewels and precious stones, to redeem captives, set free prisoners, and relieve all poor distressed souls that wanted means; religiously done, I deny not, but to what purpose? Suppose this were so well done, within a little after, though a man had Croesus' wealth to bestow, there would be as many more. Wherefore I will suffer no beggars, rogues, vagabonds, or idle persons at all, that cannot give an account of their lives how they maintain themselves. If they be impotent, lame, blind, and single, they shall be sufficiently maintained in several hospitals, built for that purpose; if married and infirm, past work, or by inevitable loss or some such-like misfortune cast behind, by distribution of corn, house-rent free, annual pensions or money, they shall be relieved, and highly rewarded for their good service they have formerly done; if able, they shall be enforced to work. "For I see no reason" (as he said) "why an epicure or idle drone, a rich glutton, a usurer, should live at ease, and do nothing, live in honour, in all manner of pleasures, and oppress others, whenas in the meantime a poor labourer, a smith, a carpenter, an husbandman that hath spent his time in continual labour, as an ass to carry burdens, to do the commonwealth good, and without whom we cannot live, shall be left in his old age to beg or starve, and lead a miserable life worse than a jument." As all conditions shall be tied to their task, so none shall be over-tired, but have their set times of recreations and holidays, *indulgere genio*, feasts and merry meetings, even to the meanest artificer, or basest servant, once a week to sing or dance (though not all at once), or do whatsoever he shall please; like that *Saccarum festum* amongst the Persians, those Saturnals in Rome, as well as his master. If any be drunk, he shall drink no more wine or strong drink in a twelvemonth after. A bankrupt shall be *catomidiatus in Amphitheatro*, publicly shamed, and he that cannot pay his debts, if by riot or negligence he have been impoverished, shall be for a twelvemonth imprisoned; if in that space his creditors be not satisfied, he shall be hanged. He that commits sacrilege shall lose his hands; he that bears false witness, or is of perjury convict, shall have his tongue cut out, except he redeem it with his head. Murder, adultery, shall be punished by death, but not theft, except it be some more grievous offence, or notorious offenders: otherwise they shall be condemned to the gal-

---

2. **depend**, be undecided.   22. **omne . . . regnum**, every throne is subject to a greater throne.   24. **invicem**, in turn.   39–40. "**Quis . . . tollas?**" For who would choose virtue for its own sake if you were to take away the reward?   46–47. **Hostem . . . Carthageniensis.** Whoever strikes down an enemy shall be to me a true Carthaginian.

19. (**as he said**). The passage is from Book II of Sir Thomas More's *Utopia*.   28–29. **jument**, mare.   31. **indulgere genio**, to follow their own bent.   38–39. **catomidiatus in Amphitheatro**, horsed and flogged in the amphitheater.   43. **shall be hanged.** "He that provides not for his family is more than a thief." (Burton)

leys, mines, be his slaves whom they have offended, during their lives. I hate all hereditary slaves, and that *duram Persarum legem*, as Brisonius calls it; or as Ammianus, *impendio formidatas et abominandas leges, per quas ob noxam unius omnis propinquitas perit*, hard law that wife and children, friends and allies, should suffer for the father's offence.

No man shall marry until he be 25, no woman till she be 20, *nisi aliter dispensatum fuerit*. If one die, the other party shall not marry till six months after; and because many families are compelled to live niggardly, exhaust and undone by great dowers, none shall be given at all, or very little, and that by supervisors rated; they that are foul shall have a greater portion; if fair, none at all, or very little: howsoever, not to exceed such a rate as those supervisors shall think fit. And when once they come to those years, poverty shall hinder no man from marriage, or any other respect, but all shall be rather enforced than hindered, except they be dismembered, or grievously deformed, infirm, or visited with some enormous hereditary disease in body or mind; in such cases upon a great pain or mulct, man or woman shall not marry, other order shall be taken for them to their content. If people overabound, they shall be eased by colonies.

No man shall wear weapons in any city. The same attire shall be kept, and that proper to several callings, by which they shall be distinguished. *Luxus funerum* shall be taken away, that intempestive expense moderated, and many others. Brokers, takers of pawns, biting usurers, I will not admit; yet because *hic cum hominibus non cum diis agitur*, we converse here with men, not with gods, and for the hardness of men's hearts, I will tolerate some kind of usury. If we were honest, I confess, *si probi essemus*, we should have no use of it, but being as it is, we must necessarily admit it. Howsoever most divines contradict it, *Dicimus inficias, sed vox ea sola reperta est*, it must be winked at by politicians. And yet some great doctors approve of it, Calvin, Bucer, Zanchius, P. Martyr, because by so many grand lawyers, decrees of emperors, princes' statutes, customs of commonwealths, churches' approbations, it is permitted, etc., I will therefore allow it. But to no private persons, nor to every man that will, to orphans only, maids, widows, or such as by reason of their age, sex, education, ignorance of trading, know not otherwise how to employ it; and those so approved, not to let it out apart, but to bring their money to a common bank which shall be allowed in every city, as in Genoa, Geneva, Nuremberg, Venice, at 5, 6, 7, not above 8 per centum, as the supervisors, or *aerarii praefecti*, shall think fit. And as it shall not be lawful for each man to be an usurer that will, so shall it not be lawful for all to take up money at use, not to prodigals and spendthrifts, but to merchants, young tradesmen, such as stand in need, or know honestly how to employ it, whose necessity, cause, and condition the said supervisors shall approve of.

I will have no private monopolies, to enrich one man and beggar a multitude, multiplicity of offices, of supplying by deputies; weights and measures the same throughout, and those rectified by the *Primum mobile* and sun's motion, threescore miles to a degree according to observation, 1000 geometrical paces to a mile, five foot to a pace, twelve inches to a foot, etc., and from measures known it is an easy matter to rectify weights, etc., to cast up all, and resolve bodies by algebra, stereometry. I hate wars if they be not *ad populi salutem*, upon urgent occasion. *Odimus accipitrem, quia semper vivit in armis*. Offensive wars, except the cause be very just, I will not allow of. For I do highly magnify that saying of Hannibal to Scipio, in Livy: "It had been a blessed thing for you and us, if God had given that mind to our predecessors, that you had been content with Italy, we with Africa. For neither Sicily nor Sardinia are worth such cost and pains, so many fleets and armies, or so many famous captains' lives." *Omnia prius tentanda*, fair means shall first be tried. *Peragit tranquilla potestas, Quod violenta nequit*. I will have them proceed with all moderation: but hear you, Fabius my general, not Minucius, *nam qui consilio nititur plus nostibus nocet, quam qui sine animi ratione, viribus*. And in such wars to abstain as much as is possible from depopulations, burning of towns, massacring of infants, etc. For defensive wars, I will have forces still ready at a small warning, by land and sea, a prepared navy, soldiers *in procinctu, et quam Bonfinius apud Hungaros suos vult, virgam ferream*,

---

3. **duram Persarum legem,** hard law of the Persians. 9. **nisi . . . fuerit,** unless it shall be otherwise arranged. 23. **mulct,** fine imposed for an offense. 24. **shall not marry.** "The Saxons exclude dumb, blind, leprous, and such like persons from all inheritance, as we do fools." (Burton) 27. **weapons in any city.** "So it is in most Italian cities." (Burton) 29–30. **Luxus funerum,** display at funerals. 30–31. **intempestive expense moderated.** "It hath ever been immoderate." (Burton) 39–40. **Dicimus . . . reperta est.** We say No, but it proves to be only a word.

18–19. **Primum mobile,** in the Ptolemaic system of astronomy, the tenth or outermost of the revolving spheres of the universe. 24. **stereometry,** the art of measuring solid bodies. 25–26. **ad populi salutem,** for the safety of the people. **Odimus . . . armis.** We hate the hawk because it always lives in battle. 35–36. **Peragit . . . nequit.** Peaceful strength accomplishes what violence cannot. 38–40. **nam . . . viribus.** For he who relies on strategy injures his enemy more than one who depends on unintelligent force. 44–45. **in procinctu . . . ferream,** ready for action, and what Bonfinius wants for his Hungarians, an iron rod.

and money, which is *nervus belli*, still in a readiness, and a sufficient revenue, a third part as in old Rome and Egypt, reserved for the commonwealth; to avoid those heavy taxes and impositions, as well to defray this charge of wars, as also all other public defalcations, expenses, fees, pensions, reparations, chaste sports, feasts, donaries, rewards, and entertainments. All things in this nature especially I will have maturely done, and with great deliberation: *ne quid temere, ne quid remisse ac timide fiat; Sed quo feror hospes?* To prosecute the rest would require a volume. *Manum de tabella*, I have been overtedious in this subject; I could have here willingly ranged, but these straits wherein I am included will not permit. . . .

George Herbert
1593-1633

In the history of the religious lyric in English, George Herbert occupies a unique and prominent place. There had been religious poems and lyrics before him, but Herbert more than any other poet developed and fashioned the devotional lyric into the literary type with which we have been familiar since his time. He is an author with whose character and personality one must be acquainted if one is to appreciate properly the poems he has left us. The details of his life furnish interesting proof of the fact that the ranks of the saints are not recruited wholly from the poor and the so-called lower classes of the world. He was born into one of the greatest houses in England. His older brother, Edward Lord Herbert of Cherbury, went as ambassador to Paris, and George's own training and natural abilities were such as to fit him to be an ambassador and a companion of princes. His mother, Magdalen Herbert, one of the most beautiful and able women of her day, took personal charge of the education of her sons. She followed Edward to Oxford, set up her household, and engaged tutors for George.

The next move was to London, and George was sent to Westminster School. Here began the friendship between Mrs. Herbert and John Donne, which was to be one of the most helpful influences in Donne's life, and which called forth his elegy "The Autumnal," in tribute to the lady. Herbert went to Trinity College, Cambridge, where he took his B.A. and M.A. degrees. He began to write religious verse while an undergraduate, and took up the study of divinity after receiving his Master's degree. He was made Public Orator of the university in 1619, when he was twenty-six, and the duties and privileges of the position brought him into close association with the rich and the great and with the King himself.

Herbert had been destined for the Church by his mother since his infancy, and while he perhaps never gave up entirely the idea of entering the priesthood, the associations induced by the oratorship were such as to make him think more of worldly preferment and a career at court. His tender conscience also made him feel unworthy of the priestly calling. A serious illness, and the deaths of his mother, his king, and several of his prominent friends, brought him to a realization of the transitoriness of persons and places, and led him eventually to the service of the Church. He resigned the oratorship in his thirty-fourth year. He married Jane Danvers two years later, and in the following year, 1630, he was ordained and became rector of St. Andrew's Church at Bemerton, near Salisbury, one of the smallest churches in England.

The story of the remaining years of his life is one of unstinted devotion to his church and his poor parishioners. Like the Good Parson of Chaucer's *Canterbury Tales*, he preached the gospel and followed it first himself. The countryside was full of stories of his kindness to the poor. He found time for his favorite recreation with the lute, to which he composed many of his poems; and there were frequent walks to Salisbury Cathedral to hear the music. In his prose work, *A Priest to the Temple*, 1632, he has given, after the fashion of the characterbooks, a picture of the ideal country parson, of whom he was himself unconsciously the model.

Herbert wrote some secular verse in his early days, but he destroyed it after his ordination. From his deathbed he sent the manuscript of his religious poems to his friend the pious Nicholas Ferrar, of

---

1. **nervus belli**, the sinews of war. 2. **ne quid . . . fiat,** that nothing be done rashly, nothing remissly, or timidly. 3. **Sed . . . hospes?** But where am I, a novice, drifting? 4. **Manum de tabella.** Hands off that paper.

the religious community of Little Gidding, near Bemerton, to be burned if they seemed unworthy, or to be printed if he thought they might "turn to the advantage of any dejected poor soul." Ferrar saw fit to have them printed in a volume entitled *The Temple* shortly after Herbert's death. The wisdom of his decision was proved by the many editions the book went into during the century. The influence of the book is to be seen in Crashaw's *Steps to the Temple* and in the poems of Henry Vaughan.

Herbert's poems show in many ways the influence of Donne. They have much of his elaborate figurativeness, the same wedding of the homely and colloquial to the "metaphysical" richness of image and analogy. Herbert's fondness for figures and conceits leads him into acrostics, anagrams, and verses shaped, as in "The Altar" and "Easter Wings," to represent the subject. His verses are more artistically constructed than Donne's, and they sing, as Donne's never could. They lack the fire and the fierceness of Donne, and the struggle which such poems as "The Collar" portray is, fortunately, not such a spiritual tumult as harassed the mind and soul of the older poet. Herbert's lyrics, more than any others, constitute the wood wind in the orchestra of seventeenth-century poetry.

EASTER WINGS

Poems in which the lines are arranged to form figures, and emblematic verse in general, were much in favor in the seventeenth century. Altars, crosses, and pyramids were especially popular in religious poetry. See Herrick's poem, "The Pillar of Fame," page 598. In the early editions of *The Temple*, the lines of "Easter Wings" were printed vertically, the first two stanzas on the left-hand page facing the last two on the right-hand page.

    Lord, who createdst man in wealth and store,
      Though foolishly he lost the same,
        Decaying more and more
          Till he became
            Most poor:
            ☩
           With thee
         O let me rise
       As larks, harmoniously,
     And sing this day thy victories:
   Then shall the fall further the flight in me.   10

1. store, abundance.

      My tender age in sorrow did begin:
        And still with sicknesses and shame
          Thou didst so punish sin
            That I became
              Most thin.
              ☩
            With thee
         Let me combine,
      And feel this day thy victory;
    For, if I imp my wing on thine,
Affliction shall advance the flight in me.   20

THE COLLAR

Herbert's titles illustrate his fondness for the "metaphysical" conceit and the emblematic style of writing. The collar is an emblem of the claim which God has on him, and of the restraint which it imposes. The poem is a portrayal of his struggles before he finally surrenders to his Master.

  I struck the board, and cried, "No more!
      I will abroad!
  What? Shall I ever sigh and pine?
My lines and life are free, free as the road,
  Loose as the wind, as large as store.
      Shall I be still in suit?
    Have I no harvest but a thorn
    To let me blood, and not restore
What I have lost with cordial fruit?
      Sure there was wine   10
  Before my sighs did dry it. There was corn
    Before my tears did drown it.
Is the year only lost to me?
    Have I no bays to crown it?
No flowers, no garlands gay? All blasted?
      All wasted?
Not so, my heart! But there is fruit,
    And thou hast hands.
Recover all thy sigh-blown age
On double pleasures. Leave thy cold dispute   20
Of what is fit and not. Forsake thy cage,
    Thy rope of sands,
Which petty thoughts have made, and made to thee

Easter Wings. **12. with sicknesses.** Herbert's naturally frail constitution was weakened by his studies and his devotion to his pastoral duties. He died at the age of forty. **19. imp,** a term from falconry; to mend the damaged wing of a hawk by grafting to it feathers from another bird. **1. board,** table. **5. as large as store,** as large as abundance itself. **6. in suit,** in attendance, as a suitor, for preferment or award. **9. cordial,** restorative. **14. bays,** the poet's wreaths of bay, or laurel. **22. rope of sands,** the teachings of the Church as they seem to the rebellious young man.

GEORGE HERBERT

    Good cable, to enforce and draw,
        And be thy law,
While thou didst wink and wouldst not see.
        Away! Take heed!
        I will abroad!
Call in thy death's head there! Tie up thy fears!
        He that forbears   30
        To suit and serve his need
        Deserves his load."
But as I raved, and grew more fierce and wild
        At every word,
Methoughts I heard one calling, "Child!"
        And I replied, "My Lord!"

THE QUIP

"Quip" is used in the sense of "sharp retort." See ll. 23–24.

    The merry World did on a day
      With his train-bands and mates agree
    To meet together where I lay,
      And all in sport to jeer at me.

    First Beauty crept into a rose;
      Which when I plucked not, "Sir," said she,
"Tell me, I pray, whose hands are those?"
      But Thou shalt answer, Lord, for me.

    Then Money came, and chinking still,
      "What tune is this, poor man?" said he;   10
"I heard in music you had skill."
      But Thou shalt answer, Lord, for me.

    Then came brave Glory puffing by
      In silks that whistled, who but he?
He scarce allowed me half an eye.
      But Thou shalt answer, Lord, for me.

    Then came quick Wit and Conversation,
      And he would needs a comfort be,
And, to be short, make an oration.
      But Thou shalt answer, Lord, for me.   20

    Yet when the hour of Thy design
      To answer these fine things shall come,
Speak not at large; say I am Thine;
      And then they have their answer home.

2. **train-bands,** citizen soldiers; here used in the sense of comrades.   4. **to jeer at me.** The poem depicts Herbert's qualities and accomplishments as a wealthy and cultured young gentleman, and the corresponding temptations. 7. **whose hands are those?"** that is, why do they not pluck the rose?   11. **in music you had skill."** Herbert was known to his friends as an "excellent master" in music.   13. **brave,** finely dressed.

THE PULLEY

The title is an emblem of the restlessness that, when all else fails, may raise man towards God.

    When God at first made man,
Having a glass of blessings standing by,
    "Let us," said He, "pour on him all we can.
Let the world's riches, which dispersèd lie,
    Contract into a span."

    So strength first made a way;
Then beauty flowed, then wisdom, honour, pleasure.
    When almost all was out, God made a stay,
Perceiving that, alone of all His treasure,
    Rest in the bottom lay.   10

    "For if I should," said He,
"Bestow this jewel also on my creature,
    He would adore my gifts instead of me
And rest in nature, not the God of nature;
    So both should losers be.

    "Yet let him keep the rest,
But keep them with repining restlessness.
    Let him be rich and weary, that at last,
If goodness lead him not, yet weariness
    May toss him to my breast."   20

THE ELIXIR

The elixir was the preparation sought by the alchemists whereby it was thought baser metals might be transmuted into gold. In the last stanza Herbert identifies it with the philosopher's stone.

    Teach me, my God and King,
      In all things Thee to see;
    And what I do in anything,
      To do it as for Thee.

    Not rudely, as a beast,
      To run into an actiòn;
But still to make Thee prepossessed,
      And give it his perfectiòn.

    A man that looks on glass
      On it may stay his eye,   10

The Pulley. 10. **Rest.** The poet characteristically plays on the word in the last two stanzas.   *The Elixir.* 7. **still to make Thee prepossessed,** always to make Thee possessed of me in advance.   8. **his,** its.

Or, if he pleaseth, through it pass,
    And then the heaven espy.

All may of Thee partake;
    Nothing can be so mean
Which with his tincture, "for Thy sake,"
    Will not grow bright and clean.

A servant with this clause
    Makes drudgery divine:
Who sweeps a room as for Thy laws
    Makes that and the action fine.   20

This is the famous stone
    That turneth all to gold;
For that which God doth touch and own
    Cannot for less be told.

DISCIPLINE

Throw away Thy rod,
Throw away Thy wrath.
    O my God,
Take the gentle path.

For my heart's desire
Unto Thine is bent;
    I aspire
To a full consent.

Not a word or look
I affect to own,   10
    But by book,
And Thy book alone.

Though I fail, I weep;
Though I halt in pace,
    Yet I creep
To the throne of grace.

Then let wrath remove;
Love will do the deed,
    For with love
Stony hearts will bleed.   20

Love is swift of foot.
Love's a man of war,
    And can shoot,
And can hit from far.

Who can scape his bow?
That which wrought on thee,
    Brought thee low,
Needs must work on me.

Throw away Thy rod;
Though man frailties hath,   30
    Thou art God.
Throw away Thy wrath.

LOVE

Love bade me welcome; yet my soul drew back,
    Guilty of dust and sin.
But quick-eyed Love, observing me grow slack
    From my first entrance in,
Drew nearer to me, sweetly questioning
    If I lacked anything.

"A guest," I answered, "worthy to be here."
    Love said, "You shall be he."
"I, the unkind, ungrateful? Ah my dear,
    I cannot look on Thee."   10
Love took my hand, and smiling, did reply,
    "Who made the eyes but I?"

"Truth, Lord, but I have marred them; let my shame
    Go where it doth deserve."
"And know you not," says Love, "who bore the blame?"
    "My dear, then I will serve."
"You must sit down," says Love, "and taste my meat."
    So I did sit and eat.

THE FLOWER

How fresh, O Lord, how sweet and clean
Are Thy returns! Even as the flowers in spring,
    To which, besides their own demean,
The late-past frosts tributes of pleasure bring.
    Grief melts away
    Like snow in May,
As if there were no such cold thing.

Who would have thought my shrivelled heart
Could have recovered greenness? It was gone
    Quite underground, as flowers depart   10

The Elixir. **15. his tincture,** its essential quality, used here to mean the philosopher's stone. **24. told,** counted. *Love.* **7. "A guest . . . worthy to be here."** "I lack being a worthy guest."—Palmer. **16. serve,"** at table. *The Flower.* **3. demean,** demeanor.

To see their mother-root, when they have blown;
    Where they together
    All the hard weather,
Dead to the world, keep house unknown.

These are Thy wonders, Lord of power,
Killing and quickening, bringing down to hell
  And up to heaven in an hour;
Making a chiming of a passing-bell.
    We say amiss
    This or that is;   20
Thy word is all, if we could spell.

Oh, that I once past changing were,
Fast in Thy paradise, where no flower can wither!
  Many a spring I shoot up fair,
Offering at heaven, growing and groaning thither;
    Nor doth my flower
    Want a spring shower,
My sins and I joining together.

But while I grow in a straight line,
Still upwards bent, as if heaven were mine own, 30
  Thy anger comes, and I decline.
What frost to that? What pole is not the zone
    Where all things burn,
    When Thou dost turn,
And the least frown of Thine is shown?

And now in age I bud again;
After so many deaths I live and write;
  I once more smell the dew and rain,

11. blown, bloomed.   **18. passing-bell,** the bell rung at the time of a death to obtain prayers for the departing soul. Professor George Herbert Palmer paraphrases the line, "Turning a funeral knell into a bridal peal."   **21. spell,** comprehend.   **25. Offering,** aiming.   **28. joining together,** to produce tears of contrition.   **32–35. What pole . . . shown?** The coldness of God's frown is, to a sensitive soul like Herbert, so intense as to make even the poles seem like the torrid zone.

And relish versing. O my only Light,
    It cannot be   40
    That I am he
On whom Thy tempests fell all night.

These are Thy wonders, Lord of love,
To make us see we are but flowers that glide;
  Which when we once can find and prove,
Thou hast a garden for us where to bide.
    Who would be more,
    Swelling through store,
Forfeit their paradise by their pride.

VIRTUE

Sweet day, so cool, so calm, so bright,
  The bridal of the earth and sky,
The dew shall weep thy fall to-night,
  For thou must die.

Sweet rose, whose hue, angry and brave,
  Bids the rash gazer wipe his eye,
Thy root is ever in its grave,
  And thou must die.

Sweet spring, full of sweet days and roses,
  A box where sweets compacted lie, 10
My music shows ye have your closes,
  And all must die.

Only a sweet and virtuous soul,
  Like seasoned timber, never gives;
But though the whole world turn to coal,
  Then chiefly lives.

48. store, abundance.   **11. closes.** "Close" is a technical term for the conclusion or resolution of a musical phrase.   **15. turn to coal,** be burned to embers at the Day of Judgment. See II Peter 3:10.

Robert Herrick
1591-1674

Herrick's life, although one of the longest in English literature, from the point of view of biography is one of the shortest. Most of the facts are missing, and much of what is known has been gathered from statements and hints in his poetry. These statements are often contradictory, for Herrick was a poet of many moods. Fortunately, however, the particular circumstances of his life, and the events of the fourscore and three years which he spent in this world, need concern us as little as they seem to have concerned him. It is of interest to reflect, and a temptation to point out, that he was born only three years after the Spanish Armada sailed against England, and he lived through the great days of Elizabeth, through the reigns of James I and Charles I, through the time of Cromwell and the Interregnum, on past the Restoration, and died in the same year with Milton. But nothing of the historical significance of all this panorama of men and events is reflected in his lyrics. Nor are the literary trends from Spenser to Dryden to be traced through the nearly thirteen hundred poems in his volume. No poet in any language ever showed more sublime indifference to the things which the world calls great, or set to more charming music the timeless commonplaces of the brevity of youth, the need for making the most of a moment, and the transitoriness of all lovely things.

Herrick was born in London, the son of a goldsmith in Cheapside. He was apprenticed to his uncle, also a goldsmith, for ten years. There is something of the delicacy of the goldsmith's art and the fineness of the lapidary's touch in Herrick's verse, and some of his little poems may indeed have been composed to be inscribed on wedding rings and pieces of jewelry. At a rather late age for that time, twenty-two, he went to St. John's College, Cambridge. (Bacon had gone to Cambridge at twelve.) He transferred to Trinity Hall to study law, and received his B.A. degree in 1617. The facts concerning the next ten years are lost to us, but we know from his book that a great part of them was spent in London with Ben Jonson—of whom he was the greatest admirer and pupil—and the other "Sons of Ben" at the taverns made famous by them. In addition to poets and wits, there were among his associates the musicians William and Henry Lawes, who set his verses to music, some of which were sung in the presence of the King and Queen at Whitehall. In the sixteenth and early seventeenth centuries, verse and music were closely interrelated, and more often than not one was considered the natural complement of the other. Herrick's lyrics can be more fully appreciated if it is remembered that many if not most of them were written to be sung, and some of them he composed probably with a melody in mind. His mastery of rhythmical cadences and his use of words and phrases indicate a knowledge of music as well as skill in versemaking. Unfortunately the musical settings of only a few of Herrick's lyrics have survived.

In 1627 Herrick entered the priesthood of the Church of England, for what reasons it is not known, and two years later this most accomplished of lyric poets became Vicar of Dean Prior in Devonshire. Here he lived for twenty years, preaching to the country people and fulfilling the other duties of his parson's calling. We know little of what happened, except as his poems show him now rebelling against the "warty incivility" of the country and yearning for the conversation and conviviality of London, and now delighting in the country sights and sounds and smells. There can be no doubt that this unwilling exile from London and hater of the country came at last to love the festivals, the hock carts, the wassails, the Maypoles, the fairies, and the folklore of the Devon countryside. For all its Englishness, however, his secular verse is full of classical overtones, just as his religious poems sound the pagan note as prominently as they do the Christian. He was not a countryman like Shakespeare, and his religious experience was a very different thing from that of Donne or Herbert or Crashaw or Vaughan. Herrick never married. Whether Julia and Corinna and the other charming creatures of whom he sings ever existed or were, as has been suggested, "the sirens of a lonely heart" can only be conjectured.

In 1647 he was ejected from his vicarage by the Roundheads, and returned to London and Westminster. He published his two books of poems, *Hesperides* and *Noble Numbers*, in one volume in 1648, the least propitious of years for a book singing "of brooks, of blossoms, birds, and bowers" and similar

ROBERT HERRICK

pleasant things. After a period of twelve years in London, of which again we know nothing, he was restored to Dean Prior by Charles II, and remained there until his death. If he wrote other poems after he returned to the country they have not survived.

from HESPERIDES

THE ARGUMENT OF HIS BOOK

"Argument" is the term formerly used for a brief summary of the contents of a book. See page 655.

I sing of brooks, of blossoms, birds, and bowers:
Of April, May, of June, and July flowers.
I sing of May-poles, hock-carts, wassails, wakes,
Of bridegrooms, brides, and of their bridal cakes.
I write of youth, of love, and have access
By these, to sing of cleanly wantonness.
I sing of dews, of rains, and piece by piece
Of balm, of oil, of spice, and ambergris.
I sing of times trans-shifting; and I write
How roses first came red, and lilies white.   10
I write of groves, of twilights, and I sing
The court of Mab, and of the Fairy King.
I write of hell; I sing (and ever shall)
Of heaven, and hope to have it after all.

CHERRY-RIPE

Cherry-ripe, ripe, ripe, I cry,
Full and fair ones; come and buy;
If so be you ask me where
They do grow, I answer: There,
Where my Julia's lips do smile;
There's the land, or Cherry-Isle:
Whose plantations fully show
All the year where cherries grow.

DELIGHT IN DISORDER

Compare this poem with Ben Jonson's "Still to Be Neat," page 560.

A sweet disorder in the dress
Kindles in clothes a wantonness;
A lawn about the shoulders thrown
Into a fine distraction;
An erring lace, which here and there
Enthralls the crimson stomacher;
A cuff neglectful, and thereby
Ribbands to flow confusèdly;
A winning wave (deserving note)
In the tempestuous petticoat;   10
A careless shoe-string, in whose tie
I see a wild civility;
Do more bewitch me, than when art
Is too precise in every part.

CORINNA'S GOING A-MAYING

Get, up, get up, for shame, the blooming morn
Upon her wings presents the god unshorn.
    See how Aurora throws her fair
    Fresh-quilted colours through the air!
    Get up, sweet slug-a-bed, and see
    The dew bespangling herb and tree.
Each flower has wept, and bowed toward the East,
Above an hour since; yet you not dressed,
    Nay! not so much as out of bed?
    When all the birds have matins said,   10
    And sung their thankful hymns: 'tis sin,
    Nay, profanation to keep in;
Whenas a thousand virgins on this day
Spring, sooner than the lark, to fetch in may.

Rise, and put on your foliage, and be seen
To come forth, like the spring-time, fresh and green
    And sweet as Flora. Take no care
    For jewels for your gown, or hair;
    Fear not, the leaves will strew
    Gems in abundance upon you;   20
Besides, the childhood of the day has kept,
Against you come, some orient pearls unwept;
    Come, and receive them while the light
    Hangs on the dew-locks of the night:
    And Titan on the eastern hill
    Retires himself, or else stands still
Till you come forth. Wash, dress, be brief in praying:
Few beads are best, when once we go a-maying.

The Argument of His Book. **3. hock-carts,** carts that brought in the last load of the harvest. The celebration of harvest home followed upon their arrival. **wakes,** times of merrymaking. They were formerly held on the anniversary of the dedication of a church, or on the day of the patron saint of the church. **8. ambergris,** a substance secreted by the sperm whale, and used in making perfumes. **12. Mab.** See Shakespeare's *Romeo and Juliet,* Act I, sc. 4, ll. 88 ff. **the Fairy King,** Oberon. See Shakespeare's *Midsummer Night's Dream. Delight in Disorder.* **2. wantonness,** mirthfulness.

Delight in Disorder. **3. lawn,** a scarf of lawn or linen. **4. distraction,** confusion. **5. erring,** straying. **6. stomacher,** a part of the dress forming the lower part of the bodice in front. **12. civility,** order, good breeding. *Corinna's Going a-Maying.* **2. god unshorn,** Apollo, god of the sun. **3. Aurora,** goddess of the dawn. **4. fresh-quilted,** freshly mingled, like colors in a newly made quilt. **13. Whenas,** when. **14. may,** hawthorn blossoms. **22. Against,** until. **orient,** shining. **25. Titan,** the sun. **28. beads,** prayers.

Come, my Corinna, come; and, coming, mark
How each field turns a street, each street a park   30
    Made green, and trimmed with trees; see how
    Devotion gives each house a bough,
    Or branch; each porch, each door, ere this,
    An ark, a tabernacle is,
Made up of white-thorn neatly interwove;
As if here were those cooler shades of love.
    Can such delights be in the street,
    And open fields, and we not see't?
    Come, we'll abroad; and let's obey
    The proclamation made for May: 40
And sin no more, as we have done, by staying;
But, my Corinna, come, let's go a-maying.

There's not a budding boy or girl this day
But is got up, and gone to bring in may.
    A deal of youth, ere this, is come
    Back, and with white-thorn laden home.
    Some have dispatched their cakes and cream,
    Before that we have left to dream;
And some have wept, and wooed, and plighted troth,
And chose their priest, ere we can cast off sloth.   50
    Many a green-gown has been given;
    Many a kiss, both odd and even:
    Many a glance too has been sent
    From out the eye, love's firmament;
Many a jest told of the keys betraying
This night, and locks picked, yet w'are not a-maying.

Come, let us go, while we are in our prime,
And take the harmless folly of the time.
    We shall grow old apace and die
    Before we know our liberty.   60
    Our life is short, and our days run
    As fast away as does the sun;
And as a vapour, or a drop of rain,
Once lost, can ne'er be found again:
    So when or you or I are made
    A fable, song, or fleeting shade,
    All love, all liking, all delight
    Lies drowned with us in endless night.
Then while time serves, and we are but decaying,
Come, my Corinna, come, let's go a-maying.   70

TO THE VIRGINS, TO MAKE MUCH OF TIME

Gather ye rose-buds while ye may,
    Old Time is still a-flying;
And this same flower that smiles to-day,
    To-morrow will be dying.

The glorious lamp of heaven, the sun,
    The higher he's a-getting;
The sooner will his race be run,
    And nearer he's to setting.

That age is best which is the first,
    When youth and blood are warmer;   10
But being spent, the worse, and worst
    Times, still succeed the former.

Then be not coy, but use your time;
    And while ye may, go marry:
For having lost but once your prime,
    You may for ever tarry.

TO ANTHEA, WHO MAY COMMAND HIM ANYTHING

Bid me to live, and I will live
    Thy protestant to be:
Or bid me love, and I will give
    A loving heart to thee.

A heart as soft, a heart as kind,
    A heart as sound and free,
As in the whole world thou canst find,
    That heart I'll give to thee.

Bid that heart stay, and it will stay,
    To honour thy decree;   10
Or bid it languish quite away,
    And't shall do so for thee.

Bid me to weep, and I will weep,
    While I have eyes to see;
And having none, yet I will keep
    A heart to weep for thee.

Bid me despair, and I'll despair,
    Under that cypress tree;
Or bid me die, and I will dare
    E'en death, to die for thee.   20

Thou art my life, my love, my heart,
    The very eyes of me;
And hast command of every part,
    To live and die for thee.

---

34. **ark,** basket. **48. left,** ceased. **51. Many a green-gown,** that is, many a gown made green by rolling on the grass.

2. protestant, one who protests devotion.

TO DAFFODILS

Fair daffodils, we weep to see
    You haste away so soon;
As yet the early-rising sun
    Has not attained his noon.
        Stay, stay,
    Until the hasting day
        Has run
    But to the even-song;
And, having prayed together, we
    Will go with you along.   10

We have short time to stay, as you;
    We have as short a spring;
As quick a growth to meet decay,
    As you, or any thing.
        We die,
As your hours do, and dry
        Away
Like to the summer's rain;
Or, as the pearls of morning dew,
    Ne'er to be found again.   20

THE MAD MAID'S SONG

Compare with this poem the mad song of "Old Tom o' Bedlam," page 600. Herrick's lyric inevitably suggests the mad song of Ophelia, *Hamlet*, Act IV, sc. 5.

Good morrow to the day so fair;
    Good morning, sir, to you;
Good morrow to mine own torn hair,
    Bedabbled with the dew.

Good morning to this primrose too;
    Good morrow to each maid,
That will with flowers the tomb bestrew,
    Wherein my love is laid.

Ah woe is me, woe, woe is me,
    Alack and welladay!   10
For pity, sir, find out that bee,
    Which bore my love away.

I'll seek him in your bonnet brave;
    I'll seek him in your eyes;
Nay, now I think they've made his grave
    I' the bed of strawberries.

I'll seek him there; I know, ere this,
    The cold, cold earth doth shake him;

The Mad Maid's Song. **13. brave,** beautiful.   **18. shake,** chill.

But I will go, or send a kiss
    By you, sir, to awake him.   20

Pray hurt him not; though he be dead,
    He knows well who do love him,
And who with green turfs rear his head,
    And who do rudely move him.

He's soft and tender; pray take heed;
    With bands of cowslips bind him,
And bring him home;—but 'tis decreed
    That I shall never find him.

MISTRESS SUSANNA SOUTHWELL, UPON HER FEET

    Her pretty feet
    Like snails did creep
A little out, and then,
    As if they started at bo-peep,
    Did soon draw in again.

MEAT WITHOUT MIRTH

Eaten I have; and though I had good cheer,
I did not sup, because no friends were there.
Where mirth and friends are absent when we dine
Or sup, there wants the incense and the wine.

HIS PRAYER TO BEN JONSON

This is one of half a dozen poems in which Herrick expresses his affection and admiration for Ben Jonson.

    When I a verse shall make,
        Know I have prayed thee,
    For old religion's sake,
        Saint Ben, to aid me.

    Make the way smooth for me,
        When I, thy Herrick,
    Honouring thee, on my knee
        Offer my lyric.

    Candles I'll give to thee,
        And a new altar;   10
    And thou, Saint Ben, shalt be
        Writ in my psalter.

Mistress Susanna Southwell, upon Her Feet. **2. Like snails.** Compare stanza 8 of Suckling's "A Ballad upon a Wedding," page 606.   **4. bo-peep,** peekaboo.   *Meat without Mirth.* **2. no friends were there.** This little poem was written probably in the early days of the poet's sojourn in Devonshire when he was keenly conscious of his separation from his fellows of the Tribe of Ben in London.

AN ODE FOR HIM

This ode was evidently written soon after Jonson's death in 1637, and probably composed at Dean Prior, where Herrick must often have thought of the "lyric feasts" which he had shared with Jonson and his group in London.

    Ah, Ben!
    Say how or when
    Shall we, thy guests,
    Meet at those lyric feasts
    Made at the Sun,
    The Dog, the Triple Tun,
    Where we such clusters had
As made us nobly wild, not mad;
    And yet each verse of thine
Outdid the meat, outdid the frolic wine.   10

    My Ben!
    Or come again,
    Or send to us
    Thy wit's great overplus;
    But teach us yet
    Wisely to husband it,
    Lest we that talent spend,
    And having once brought to an end
    That precious stock, the store
Of such a wit the world should have no more.   20

HIS CONTENT IN THE COUNTRY

Here, here I live with what my board
Can with the smallest cost afford;
Though ne'er so mean the viands be,
They well content my Prue and me.
Or pea, or bean, or wort, or beet,
Whatever comes, content makes sweet.
Here we rejoice because no rent
We pay for our poor tenement,
Wherein we rest, and never fear
The landlord or the usurer.   10
The quarter-day does ne'er affright
Our peaceful slumbers in the night.
We eat our own, and batten more
Because we feed on no man's score;
But pity those whose flanks grow great
Swelled with the lard of others' meat.

We bless our fortunes when we see
Our own belovèd privacy;
And like our living, where we're known
To very few, or else to none.   20

THE NIGHT-PIECE, TO JULIA

The stanzaic structure of this poem seems to have been suggested by that of Jonson's "The Faery Beam upon You," page 560.

    Her eyes the glow-worm lend thee;
    The shooting stars attend thee;
        And the elves also,
        Whose little eyes glow
Like the sparks of fire, befriend thee.

No will-o'-the-wisp mis-light thee;
No snake or slow-worm bite thee;
    But on, on thy way,
    Not making a stay,
Since ghost there's none to affright thee.   10

Let not the dark thee cumber;
What though the moon does slumber?
    The stars of the night
    Will lend thee their light,
Like tapers clear without number.

Then, Julia, let me woo thee,
Thus, thus to come unto me;
    And when I shall meet
    Thy silv'ry feet,
My soul I'll pour into thee.   20

THE HAG

    The hag is astride
    This night for to ride,
The Devil and she together;
    Through thick and through thin,
    Now out and then in,
Though ne'er so foul be the weather.

    A thorn or a burr
    She takes for a spur;
With a lash of a bramble she rides now;
    Through brakes and through briers,   10
    O'er ditches and mires,
She follows the spirit that guides now.

An Ode for Him. **7. clusters,** grapes, wine. *His Content in the Country.* **4. Prue,** Prudence Baldwin, the faithful servant of Herrick during his residence at Dean Prior. She is the subject of three other poems by him. See page 597. **5. wort,** a potherb.

The Night-Piece, to Julia. **7. slow-worm,** a small, snakelike lizard. **11. cumber,** trouble.

ROBERT HERRICK

    No beast for his food
    Dares now range the wood,
But hushed in his lair he lies lurking;
    While mischiefs by these,
    On lands and on seas,
At noon of night are a-working.

    The storm will arise
    And trouble the skies;   20
This night, and more for the wonder,
    The ghost from the tomb
    Affrighted shall come,
Called out by the clap of the thunder.

HIS GRANGE, OR PRIVATE WEALTH

    Though clock,
To tell me how the night draws hence, I've none,
    A cock
I have, to sing how day draws on.
    I have
A maid, my Prue, by good luck sent
    To save
That little Fates me gave or lent.
    A hen
I keep, which, creaking day by day,   10
    Tells when
She goes her long white egg to lay.
    A goose
I have, which with a jealous ear,
    Lets loose
Her tongue to tell what danger's near.
    A lamb
I keep, tame, with my morsels fed,
    Whose dam
An orphan left him, lately dead.   20
    A cat
I keep, that plays about my house,
    Grown fat
With eating many a miching mouse.
    To these
A Tracy I do keep, whereby
    I please
The more my rural privacy.
    Which are
But toys to give my heart some ease: 30
    Where care
None is, slight things do lightly please.

10. creaking, clucking.   **24. miching,** pilfering.
26. Tracy, Herrick's spaniel.

A TERNARY OF LITTLES

Upon a Pipkin of Jelly Sent to a Lady

A little saint best fits a little shrine,
A little prop best fits a little vine,
As my small cruse best fits my little wine.

A little seed best fits a little soil,
A little trade best fits a little toil,
As my small jar best fits my little oil.

A little bin best fits a little bread,
A little garland fits a little head,
As my small stuff best fits my little shed.

A little hearth best fits a little fire,   10
A little chapel fits a little quire,
As my small bell best fits my little spire.

A little stream best fits a little boat,
A little lead best fits a little float,
As my small pipe best fits my little note.

A little meat best fits a little belly,
As sweetly, lady, give me leave to tell ye,
This little pipkin fits this little jelly.

UPON JULIA'S CLOTHES

Whenas in silks my Julia goes,
Then, then, methinks, how sweetly flows
That liquefaction of her clothes.

Next, when I cast mine eyes and see
That brave vibration each way free,
O how that glittering taketh me!

UPON PRUE, HIS MAID

    In this little urn is laid
    Prudence Baldwin, once my maid,
    From whose happy spark here let
    Spring the purple violet.

CEREMONIES FOR CHRISTMAS

    Come, bring with a noise,
    My merry, merry boys,

18. pipkin, a small earthenware pot. *Upon Julia's Clothes.*
1. Whenas, when. **5. brave,** bright. *Ceremonies for Christmas.* **1. noise,** that is, a joyful noise, a melodious sound.

The Christmas log to the firing;
   While my good dame, she
   Bids ye all be free,
And drink to your hearts' desiring.

With the last year's brand
   Light the new block, and
For good success in his spending,
   On your psaltries play,   10
   That sweet luck may
Come while the log is a-teending.

Drink now the strong beer,
   Cut the white loaf here,
The while the meat is a-shredding;
   For the rare mince-pie
   And the plums stand by
To fill the paste that's a-kneading.

THE PILLAR OF FAME

This is one of the "shaped poems" of the period. See the note on Herbert's "Easter Wings," page 588.

Fame's pillar here at last we set,
Out-during marble, brass, or jet;
   Charmed and enchanted so
   As to withstand the blow
     Of overthrow;
     Nor shall the seas,
     Or outrages
     Of storms, o'erbear
     What we uprear;
    Tho' kingdoms fall,
   This pillar never shall
   Decline or waste at all;
But stand for ever by his own
Firm and well-fixed foundatiòn.

To his book's end this last line he'd have placed:
Jocund his Muse was, but his life was chaste.

from NOBLE NUMBERS

HIS LITANY TO THE HOLY SPIRIT

In the hour of my distress,
   When temptations me distress,
   And when I my sins confess,
     Sweet Spirit, comfort me!

Ceremonies for Christmas. **10. psaltries.** The psaltery was a medieval stringed instrument. **12. a-teending,** kindling.

When I lie within my bed,
Sick in heart and sick in head,
And with doubts discomforted,
   Sweet Spirit, comfort me!

When the house doth sigh and weep,
And the world is drowned in sleep,   10
Yet mine eyes the watch do keep,
   Sweet Spirit, comfort me!

When the artless doctor sees
No one hope, but of his fees,
And his skill runs on the lees,
   Sweet Spirit, comfort me!

When his potion and his pill
Has or none or little skill,
Meet for nothing but to kill,
   Sweet Spirit, comfort me!   20

When the passing-bell doth toll,
And the furies in a shoal
Come to fright a parting soul,
   Sweet Spirit, comfort me!

When the tapers now burn blue,
And the comforters are few,
And that number more than true,
   Sweet Spirit, comfort me!

When the priest his last hath prayed,
And I nod to what is said,   30
'Cause my speech is now decayed,
   Sweet Spirit, comfort me!

When, God knows, I'm tossed about,
Either with despair or doubt,
Yet, before the glass be out,
   Sweet Spirit, comfort me!

When the Tempter me pursu'th
With the sins of all my youth,
And half damns me with untruth,
   Sweet Spirit, comfort me!   40

When the flames and hellish cries
Fright mine ears and fright mine eyes,
And all terrors me surprise,
   Sweet Spirit, comfort me!

When the Judgment is revealed,
And that opened which was sealed,
When to Thee I have appealed,
   Sweet Spirit, comfort me!

13. artless, unskilled.

A THANKSGIVING TO GOD FOR HIS HOUSE

Lord, Thou hast given me a cell
    Wherein to dwell,
A little house, whose humble roof
    Is weather-proof;
Under the spars of which I lie
    Both soft and dry;
Where Thou, my chamber for to ward,
    Hast set a guard
Of harmless thoughts, to watch and keep
    Me while I sleep.
Low is my porch, as is my fate,
    Both void of state;
And yet the threshold of my door
    Is worn by the poor,
Who thither come and freely get
    Good words, or meat.
Like as my parlour, so my hall
    And kitchen's small;
A little buttery, and therein
    A little bin,
Which keeps my little loaf of bread
    Unchipped, unflead;
Some brittle sticks of thorn or brier
    Make me a fire,
Close by whose living coal I sit,
    And glow like it.
Lord, I confess too, when I dine,
    The pulse is Thine,
And all those other bits that be
    There placed by Thee;
The worts, the purslane, and the mess
    Of watercress,
Which of Thy kindness Thou hast sent;
    And my content
Makes those, and my belovèd beet
    To be more sweet.
'Tis Thou that crown'st my glittering hearth
    With guiltless mirth,
And giv'st me wassail bowls to drink,
    Spiced to the brink.
Lord, 'tis Thy plenty-dropping hand
    That soils my land,
And giv'st me, for my bushel sown,
    Twice ten for one;
Thou mak'st my teeming hen to lay
    Her egg each day;
Besides my healthful ewes to bear
    Me twins each year;
The while the conduits of my kine
    Run cream for wine.
All these, and better, Thou dost send
    Me, to this end,
That I should render for my part
    A thankful heart;
Which, fired with incense, I resign
    As wholly Thine;
But the acceptance, that must be,
    My Christ, by Thee.

TO DEATH

Thou bid'st me come away,
And I'll no longer stay
Than for to shed some tears
For faults of former years,
And to repent some crimes
Done in the present times;
And next, to take a bit
Of bread, and wine with it;
To don my robes of love,
Fit for the place above;
To gird my loins about
With charity throughout,
And so to travel hence
With feet of innocence:
These done, I'll only cry
God mercy, and so die.

ANOTHER GRACE FOR A CHILD

Here a little child I stand,
Heaving up my either hand;
Cold as paddocks though they be,
Here I lift them up to Thee,
For a benison to fall
On our meat and on us all. Amen.

THE BELLMAN

Along the dark and silent night,
With my lantern, and my light,
And the tinkling of my bell,
Thus I walk, and this I tell:
Death and dreadfulness call on
To the general Session;
To whose dismal bar, we there
All accounts must come to clear.

---

22. **unflead**, unflayed, unbroken. 28. **pulse**, peas, beans, and so on. 31. **purslane**, an herb formerly used for salads. 42. **soils**, fertilizes.

Another Grace for a Child. 3. **paddocks**, toads or frogs. 5. **benison**, blessing.

Scores of sins we've made here many,
Wiped out few, God knows, if any.   10
Rise ye debtors then, and fall

To make payment, while I call.
Ponder this when I am gone;
By the clock 'tis almost one.

Tom O' Bedlam's Song

"It is worth attention," says Bishop Percy in the prefatory note to the collection of mad songs in his *Reliques of Ancient English Poetry*, 1769, "that the English have more songs and ballads on the subject of madness than any of their neighbours."[1] In a footnote he adds, "Some explain this fact on the ground that after the dissolution of the religious houses, the poor were reduced to beggary, and to wander through the country in those disguises thought best to excite pity and to escape detection. Of these, the disguise of madness was found the most effectual."

One of the most distinctive and popular types of the mad song in the early seventeenth century was the "Tom o' Bedlam Song," the finest, and perhaps the original, example of which is given below. The famous London institution for the insane, under its corrupted name of "Bedlam," had by the seventeenth century become proverbial for both madness and cruelty. The capacity of the hospital was so limited that many chronic patients who were poor were regularly discharged by the governors of the hospital to provide accommodations for the more affluent, the more hopeful, and the more dangerous cases. Those who were allowed to go at large roamed aimlessly about the country, some of them provided with licenses permitting them to beg, and all of them living on the alms or the refuse of their more fortunate countrymen. These "Tom o' Bedlams," as they came to be known, in their outlandish garb, singing for their supper, were familiar sights on English roads during the greater part of the century.

In addition to the genuine Bedlamites, there were many impostors who, for one reason or another, joined their ranks or adopted their methods and manners. Edgar, in *King Lear*, who for his own purposes joins the fraternity, gives us a detailed description of the "Bedlam beggar."

By the seventeenth century a distinctive "Tom o' Bedlam Song" had evolved, and many poets of the time tried their hands at imitations of it. Izaak Walton refers in Chapter V of his *Compleat Angler* to "Mr. William Basse, one that hath made the choice songs of 'The Hunter in his Career' and of 'Tom of Bedlam,' and many others of note." Bishop Percy includes in his *Reliques* a song entitled "Old Tom of Bedlam," which has many elements in common with the song here printed, though it is not nearly so fine a composition.

Of the song here presented, the earliest extant version appears in a manuscript collection of lyrics in the British Museum entitled *Giles Earle his booke, 1615*, which was edited by Peter Warlock in 1932. The tune, arranged for the lute, was found in another manuscript in the British Museum. The words of the song were first printed in a collection of verse called *Wit and Drollery* in 1656. The tune was first published in John Playford's songbook, *Musick's Delight on the Cithren*, in 1666. It was reprinted by William Chappell in his *Popular Songs of Early England* in 1893. The name of neither the author of the poem nor the composer of the music is known. Of Giles Earle, the compiler of the book of lyrics in which the words were found, nothing is likewise known. Whether he was related to John Earle, the author of *Microcosmography*, cannot be ascertained. "He was evidently," says Mr. Warlock, "a man of taste, in close touch with the poets and musicians of his time."

In an interesting discussion of the poem and of the conditions in which the "Mad Tom" songs grew up, Albert Deutsch says: "It may have been the product of one mind or of many. Whatever its origin, the lyric has a remarkable, wild beauty, and certainly ranks as one of the finest anonymous pieces in English poetry. How much of it Tom really sang and how much was 'written in' is a moot question. It is quite obvious that a large part of it is too literary to have developed with the complete spontaneity of the folk ballads."[2]

The song is without title in the Earle manuscript, and is given here in Mr. Warlock's modernized transcription.

From the hag and hungry goblin
    That into rags would rend ye,
And the spirit that stands by the naked man
    In the book of moons, defend ye,
That of your five sound senses
    You never be forsaken,
Nor wander from yourselves with Tom,
    Abroad to beg your bacon.
      While I do sing: Any food,
        Any feeding, drink, or clothing?   10
      Come, dame or maid, be not afraid,
        Poor Tom will injure nothing.

Of thirty bare years have I
    Twice twenty been enragèd,
And of forty been three times fifteen
    In durance soundly cagèd
On the lordly lofts of Bedlam,
    With stubble soft and dainty,

---

[1] See, for the most artistic representative of the type, Herrick's "The Mad Maid's Song," page 595.

[2] "Tom o' Bedlam and His Song," *Yale Review*, Summer, 1940, pp. 856–61.

TOM O' BEDLAM'S SONG

Brave bracelets strong, sweet whips, ding-dong,
  With wholesome hunger plenty.   20
    And now I sing: Any food,
      Any feeding, drink, or clothing?
    Come, dame or maid, be not afraid,
      Poor Tom will injure nothing.

With a thought I took for Maudlin,
  And a cruse of cockle pottage,
With a thing thus tall, sky bless you all,
  I befell into this dotage.
I slept not since the Conquest,
  Till then I never wakèd,   30
Till the roguish boy of love where I lay
  Me found and stripped me naked.
    And now I sing: Any food,
      Any feeding, drink, or clothing?
    Come, dame or maid, be not afraid,
      Poor Tom will injure nothing.

When I short have shorn my sour-face,
  And swigged my horny barrel,
In an oaken inn I pound my skin,
  As a suit of gilt apparel.   40
The moon's my constant mistress,
  And the lowly owl my morrow;
The flaming drake and the night-crow make
  Me music to my sorrow.
    While I do sing: Any food,
      Any feeding, drink, or clothing?
    Come, dame or maid, be not afraid,
      Poor Tom will injure nothing.

The palsy plagues my pulses,
  When I prig your pigs or pullen,   50
Your culvers take, or matchless make
  Your chanticleer or sullen.
When I want provant, with Humphry
  I sup, and when benighted,
I repose in Powles with waking souls,
  Yet never am affrighted.
    But I do sing: Any food,
      Any feeding, drink, or clothing?
    Come, dame or maid, be not afraid,
      Poor Tom will injure nothing.   60

I know more than Apollo,
  For oft when he lies sleeping,
I see the stars at bloody wars
  In the wounded welkin weeping,
The moon embrace her shepherd,
  And the queen of love her warrior,
While the first doth horn the star of morn,
  And the next the heavenly Farrier.
    While I do sing: Any food,
      Any feeding, drink, or clothing?   70
    Come, dame or maid, be not afraid,
      Poor Tom will injure nothing.

The gipsy Snap and Pedro
  Are none of Tom's comradoes.
The punk I scorn, and the cutpurse sworn,
  And the roaring boys' bravadoes.
The meek, the white, the gentle,
  Me handle, touch, and spare not;
But those that cross Tom Rhinoceros
  Do what the panther dare not.   80
    Although I sing: Any food,
      Any feeding, drink, or clothing?
    Come, dame or maid, be not afraid
      Poor Tom will injure nothing.

With an host of furious fancies
  Whereof I am commander,
With a burning spear and a horse of air
  To the wilderness I wander.
By a knight of ghosts and shadows
  I summoned am to tourney   90
Ten leagues beyond the wide world's end,
  Methinks it is no journey.
    Yet will I sing: Any food,
      Any feeding, drink, or clothing?
    Come, dame or maid, be not afraid,
      Poor Tom will injure nothing.

25. Maudlin. "Poor Tom," says Mr. Deutsch, "was even provided with a female companion, 'Mad Bess,' or 'Maudlin Bess,' around whom other poems were written." **50. prig your . . . pullen,** steal your poultry. **51. culvers,** pigeons. **53–54. provant,** provender, food. **with Humphry I sup.** "To sup (or dine) with Duke Humphr(e)y" is an old expression meaning to go without supper. **55. Powles,** St. Paul's.

68. Farrier, Vulcan. **76. roaring boys,** a term applied to riotous fellows of the time of Elizabeth and James I.

Thomas Carew
1595?–1639?

Most of the facts of Carew's life have so far escaped the biographers, but it may perhaps be said of him, as has been remarked of another and very different character, that we have enough of his life to explain his reputation. He has achieved fame in English literature as one of the most brilliant of the "Sons of Ben," one of the most accomplished lyrists of the language, and arbiter of the elegants of the court of Charles I. He was born in Kent and was educated at Merton College, Oxford. After receiving his B.A. degree he was, ostensibly at least, engaged in the study of law at the Middle Temple in London, until it became as obvious to his father, Sir Matthew Carew, as it was to young Thomas that the son was not cut out to be a lawyer. He was next exposed to the diplomatic profession, and sent to join the staff of Sir Dudley Carleton, the ambassador to Venice. He seems to have been sufficiently successful to be allowed to continue as the ambassador's secretary when he was transferred in 1616 to The Hague. He did not last out the year in his secretaryship, however, as Sir Dudley found it necessary to get rid of him because of his slanderous remarks about the ambassador and his wife.

Carew returned home, and for the next three years was without employment, and with every prospect of going from bad to worse. His father gave him up as hopeless, and did what he could to hinder him. After his father's death he was fortunate enough to secure a place with the household of Lord Herbert of Cherbury when he went as ambassador to Paris in 1619. Of the events of the next nine years little is known. Whether he accompanied Herbert in his travels, and whether he stayed on with the embassy in Paris until Herbert's return, are not known. Some of his spare moments in France were devoted to writing love lyrics which were to be published later. After his return to England he succeeded in attaching himself to the court of Charles I, where he remained for the rest of his life. He was appointed Gentleman of the Privy Chamber and later was made Sewer in Ordinary, the official taster and server of the dishes for the royal table. There are anecdotes attesting the success of his wit and courtly manners in the royal household, and proving that, however lacking he may have been in more solid qualities, he was undoubtedly one of the most agreeable personalities of his time. He is reputed to have made a good end.

It is significant that Carew was one of the chief admirers and justest critics of both Donne and Jonson, for he knew and understood both personally, and the qualities of the two poets meet in his own verse more often than in that of any other poet of the day. He had been a parishioner of Donne's at St. Dunstan's-in-the-West, and probably knew him later in London. As one of the Tribe of Ben, he knew better than most of his contemporaries both the virtues and the failings of Jonson. Carew's poetry has none of the naïveté and spontaneity of Herrick's. He worked harder at his verse than any of his fellows, and had a hearty contempt for casual versifiers and "the abortive offspring of their hasty hours." He had the happy art, however, of being able to conceal his art and his labor, and few of the readers who enjoy the easy flow and exquisite rhythms and cadences of his lyrics are aware of the pains and "the dear expense of oil" that went into the making of them, or of the craftsmanship and structural unity that a careful study of them will reveal.

Carew is one of the greatest masters in the language of the octosyllabic couplet, and Tennyson, himself an artist in that kind, shows the influence of Carew in such verses as the lyrics in *The Princess* and elsewhere. It is not surprising that Carew should have been a discerning critic of poets and poetry. His "Elegy upon the Death of Dr. Donne, Dean of Paul's" contains the best contemporary analysis and description of "metaphysical" poetry and of the "giant fancy" of Donne, which had proved too stout for "the soft melting phrases" of more conventional poets. He was a just appraiser of his own work, also, and knew the capabilities and the limitations of his "lyric feet." If the times in which he lived and the circumstances of his own life could have been different, we might have had in Carew not only one of the most graceful lyrists and accomplished technicians but also one of the greatest poets of the language. Mr. Pope was more witty than just when he dismissed Carew contemptuously as one of

"the wits of either Charles's days,
The mob of gentlemen who wrote with ease."

UPON A RIBBON

This silken wreath, which circles in mine arm,
Is but an emblem of that mystic charm
Wherewith the magic of your beauties binds
My captive soul, and round about it winds
Fetters of lasting love. This hath entwined
My flesh alone; that hath empaled my mind.
Time may wear out these soft weak bands, but those
Strong chains of brass Fate shall not discompose.
This holy relic may preserve my wrist,
But my whole frame does by that power subsist;   10
To that my prayers and sacrifice, to this
I only pay a superstitious kiss.
This but the idol, that's the deity;
Religion there is due; here, ceremony;
That I receive by faith, this but in trust;
Here I may tender duty, there I must;
This order as a layman I may bear,
But I become Love's priest when that I wear;
This moves like air; that as the centre stands;
That knot your virtue tied, this but your hands;   20
That, Nature framed; but this was made by art;
This makes my arm your prisoner; that, my heart.

A SONG

Ask me no more where Jove bestows,
  When June is past, the fading rose;
For in your beauty's orient deep
  These flowers, as in their causes, sleep.

Ask me no more whither do stray
  The golden atoms of the day;
For in pure love heaven did prepare
  Those powders to enrich your hair.

Ask me no more whither doth haste
  The nightingale, when May is past;   10
For in your sweet dividing throat
  She winters, and keeps warm her note.

Ask me no more where those stars light,
  That downwards fall in dead of night;
For in your eyes they sit, and there
  Fixèd become, as in their sphere.

Ask me no more if east or west
  The phoenix builds her spicy nest;
For unto you at last she flies,
  And in your fragrant bosom dies.   20

DISDAIN RETURNED

He that loves a rosy cheek,
  Or a coral lip admires,
Or from star-like eyes doth seek
  Fuel to maintain his fires;
As old Time makes these decay,
So his flames must waste away.

But a smooth and stedfast mind,
  Gentle thoughts and calm desires,
Hearts with equal love combined,
  Kindle never-dying fires.   10
Where those are not, I despise
Lovely cheeks, or lips, or eyes.

No tears, Celia, now shall win
  My resolved heart to return;
I have searched thy soul within,
  And find nought but pride and scorn;
I have learned thy arts, and now
Can disdain as much as thou.
  Some power, in my revenge, convey
  That love to her I cast away.   20

Upon a Ribbon. **1. This silken wreath.** Compare Donne, "The Funeral," page 568, l. 3.   **19. the centre,** the earth, the center of the universe in the Ptolemaic cosmology.   *A Song.* **3. orient deep,** lustrous depth.   **4. causes,** the roots, seeds, or buds.   *A Song.* **11. dividing,** articulating harmoniously, singing.   **16. sphere,** an allusion, as often in seventeenth-century poetry, to the transparent globes or spheres of the Ptolemaic astronomy. The eighth of the concentric spheres was that of the fixed stars.   **18. phoenix,** the fabulous Arabian bird which, at the expiration of every five hundred years, built a funeral pyre of spices and died in its flames. From the ashes arose a new phoenix.

Sir John Suckling
1609–1642

Suckling and Lovelace have long been named together as the two Cavalier poets par excellence, and the tendency to contrast them at almost every point, to consider their most famous lines respectively as the "opposite poles" of Cavalier poetry, has proved irresistible. An examination of the facts of their lives will, indeed, disclose many dissimilarities in their characters and activities. It is inevitable that Suckling's dashing manners, gay flippancy, and devil-may-care attitude toward life should be set over against the sober courtliness and grace, the gentlemanly demeanor, and the more conventional and sentimental attitude of the author of the lines to Lucasta and Althea. One may take the liberty, however, to suspect that in Suckling's "Out upon it!" and "The devil take her!" and similar outbursts, the gentleman may be protesting rather too much, that he was perhaps not quite so inconstant in love or casual in composition as he boasts. Even Suckling had his more serious moments. There is Aubrey's story of his journey to Bath to take the waters, on which "he had a cartload of books carried down, and 'twas there at Bath that he writ the little tract in his book about Socinianism." It is less profitable, however, to catalogue the points and degrees of difference between the two Cavaliers than to consider them as complementary to each other, and to enjoy the verses that each contrived to write in his spare moments.

The thirty-three years of Suckling's life were packed as full of opportunities, adventure, and romance as ever befell a young man. He came of a family rich in land and titles. His father, Sir John, was made Secretary of State when the younger John was thirteen, and in the following year the son entered Trinity College, Cambridge. He was probably, as one of his earlier biographers opined, "a polite rather than a deep scholar," but he became one of the most accomplished linguists of his generation. In 1627 he was admitted to the study of law at Gray's Inn, but, his father dying in the same year, he inherited a fortune, gave up his studies, and made the grand tour. He was abroad for three years and on his return to England received his knighthood. He went as a gentleman soldier under the Marquis of Hamilton to serve in the army of Gustavus Adolphus. In a year or two he was back and at the center of courtly gaiety. He was equally at home in literary circles, and had begun to be known for his skill with his pen.

Suckling was easily the most spectacular young gentleman at court. The cost of the production of his play *Aglaura* in 1637 ran into hundreds of pounds, and the costumes were such as to dazzle even the court. Two years later when the King raised an army to send to Scotland, Suckling presented His Majesty with a troop of a hundred men, fitted out in scarlet and white, on which he spent £12,000. The brilliant company came back from the Scottish Border faster than it went, however, and Suckling was not allowed to forget the episode. He was hardly less spectacular in his private amusements. He became the most famous gambler of his time, and spent a large portion of his fortune on bowling, dice, and cards. Whenever public duty required, however, he could give money and energy to the cause, and leave pleasure and convenience as easily as any. He was one of the group who in 1641 conspired to rescue Strafford from the Tower after his impeachment, and had to escape to France. He died in Paris in 1642, by his own hand, according to the more commonly received account, although there is another story which makes him the victim of a servant. No one questions the likelihood of the splendid trifler's taking his own life rather than drawing out his years in exile and poverty. The volume of his poems, *Fragmenta Aurea*, was published in 1646, four years after his death, "by a friend, to perpetuate his memory."

Suckling never professed to be more than an amateur with the pen. He seems never to have worked over his lines, and he was at the farthest remove from such a finished artist as Carew. No verse in English smells less of the lamp than his. One never thinks of Suckling's poems in terms of schools, although he could not escape entirely the influence of such personalities and poems as those of Donne and Jonson. The reader of his verse will detect phrases and ideas which he imitated or lifted, more or less consciously, from the two poets. He is at his best and happiest when he is on his own, and not affected by "metaphysical" or other influences. His letters are as delightful as his lyrics, and for vivacity and heartiness they are equaled only by the letters

SIR JOHN SUCKLING

of Byron. Three hundred years have passed since his last gesture, but his readers find him still the same "natural, easy Suckling" that Congreve's Millamant quoted with such relish in *The Way of the World.*

SONG

This lyric occurs in Suckling's play *Aglaura.* Compare Wither's treatment of a similar theme in his "Sonnet," page 570.

    Why so pale and wan, fond lover?
        Prithee, why so pale?
    Will, when looking well can't move her,
        Looking ill prevail?
        Prithee, why so pale?

    Why so dull and mute, young sinner?
        Prithee, why so mute?
    Will, when speaking well can't win her,
        Saying nothing do't?
        Prithee, why so mute?   10

    Quit, quit, for shame; this will not move,
        This cannot take her.
    If of herself she will not love,
        Nothing can make her:
        The devil take her!

SONG

    Honest lover whatsoever,
    If in all thy love there ever
    Was one wavering thought, if thy flame
    Were not still even, still the same,
        Know this,
      Thou lov'st amiss;
      And to love true,
Thou must begin again, and love anew.

    If, when she appears i' the room,
    Thou dost not quake, and art struck dumb,   10
    And in striving this to cover,
    Dost not speak thy words twice over,
        Know this,
      Thou lov'st amiss;
      And to love true,
Thou must begin again, and love anew.

    If fondly thou dost not mistake,
    And all defects for graces take,
    Persuad'st thyself that jests are broken
    When she hath little or nothing spoken,   20
        Know this,
      Thou lov'st amiss;
      And to love true,
Thou must begin again, and love anew.

    If, when thou appear'st to be within,
    Thou let'st men not ask and ask again;
    And when thou answer'st, if it be
    To what was asked thee, properly,
        Know this,
      Thou lov'st amiss;   30
      And to love true,
Thou must begin again, and love anew.

    If, when thy stomach calls to eat,
    Thou cut'st not fingers, 'stead of meat,
    And with much gazing on her face
    Dost not rise hungry from the place,
        Know this,
      Thou lov'st amiss;
      And to love true,
Thou must begin again, and love anew.   40

    If by this thou dost discover
    That thou art no perfect lover,
    And, desiring to love true,
    Thou dost begin to love anew,
        Know this,
      Thou lov'st amiss;
      And to love true,
Thou must begin again, and love anew.

[CONSTANCY]

    Out upon it! I have loved
        Three whole days together;
    And am like to love three more,
        If it prove fair weather.

    Time shall moult away his wings,
        Ere he shall discover
    In the whole wide world again
        Such a constant lover.

    But the spite on it is, no praise
        Is due at all to me: 10

Song (Honest lover). **10. art struck.** "Not" is understood.   **17. fondly,** foolishly.   **19. persuad'st.** "Not" is understood. **jests are broken,** jokes are cracked.

Love with me had made no stays
  Had it any been but she.

Had it any been but she,
  And that very face,
There had been at least ere this
A dozen dozen in her place.

A BALLAD UPON A WEDDING

It is commonly supposed that this poem was written for the marriage of Roger Boyle, Baron Broghill, and the Lady Margaret Howard in 1641. The artistry and ingenuity with which the courtly author has identified himself with a naïve and hearty rustic has won the praise of readers for three centuries.

I tell thee, Dick, where I have been,
Where I the rarest things have seen,
  Oh, things without compare!
Such sights again cannot be found
In any place on English ground,
  Be it at wake or fair.

At Charing Cross, hard by the way
Where we (thou know'st) do sell our hay,
  There is a house with stairs;
And there I did see coming down   10
Such folk as are not in our town,
  Forty, at least, in pairs.

Amongst the rest, one pestilent fine
(His beard no bigger, though, than thine)
  Walked on before the rest.
Our landlord looks like nothing to him;
The king (God bless him!), 'twould undo him
  Should he go still so dressed.

At course-a-park, without all doubt,
He should have been the first taken out   20
  By all the maids i' the town,
Though lusty Roger there had been,
Or little George upon the Green,
  Or Vincent of the Crown.

But wot you what? the youth was going
To make an end of all his wooing;
  The parson for him stayed.
Yet by his leave, for all his haste,
He did not so much wish all past,
  Perchance, as did the maid.   30

The maid (and thereby hangs a tale),
For such a maid no Whitsun-ale
  Could ever yet produce;
No grape, that's kindly ripe, could be
So round, so plump, so soft as she,
  Nor half so full of juice.

Her finger was so small the ring
Would not stay on, which they did bring;
  It was too wide a peck:
And to say truth (for out it must),   40
It looked like the great collar (just)
  About our young colt's neck.

Her feet beneath her petticoat,
Like little mice stole in and out,
  As if they feared the light;
But oh, she dances such a way,
No sun upon an Easter day
  Is half so fine a sight!

He would have kissed her once or twice,
But she would not, she was so nice,   50
  She would not do't in sight;
And then she looked as who should say,
I will do what I list to-day,
  And you shall do't at night.

Her cheeks so rare a white was on,
No daisy makes comparison
  (Who sees them is undone),
For streaks of red were mingled there,
Such as are on a Catherine pear
  (The side that's next the sun).   60

Her lips were red, and one was thin
Compared to that was next her chin
  (Some bee had stung it newly);
But, Dick, her eyes so guard her face
I durst no more upon them gaze
  Than on the sun in July.

---

1. **Dick.** It has been suggested that "Dick" may be Suckling's friend Richard Lovelace. The author may have had particular individuals in mind in connection with the proper names of the poem, but they are mostly taken from popular tales and anecdotes, and are probably used as type names for rustics. 6. **wake.** See note on page 593. 7. **Charing Cross,** an open space near Haymarket, not far from the present Trafalgar Square. 18. **still,** always. 19. **course-a-park.** "A country game in which a girl called out one of the other sex to chase her."—*New English Dictionary.*

32. **Whitsun-ale.** A country merrymaking held at Whitsuntide, fifty days after Easter. 34. **kindly ripe,** naturally, fully, ripe. 44. **Like little mice.** See Herrick's simile in "Mistress Susanna Southwell, upon Her Feet," page 595. 47. **sun upon an Easter day.** "We shall not, I hope," says Sir Thomas Browne in his *Pseudodoxia Epidemica* (Book V, chap. 22), "disparage the Resurrection of our Redeemer, if we say the sun doth not dance on Easter Day." 59. **Catherine pear,** a small and early variety of pear.

SIR JOHN SUCKLING

Her mouth so small, when she does speak,
Thou'dst swear her teeth her words did break,
   That they might passage get;
But she so handled still the matter,   70
They came as good as ours, or better,
   And are not spent a whit.

If wishing should be any sin,
The parson himself had guilty been
   (She looked that day so purely);
And did the youth so oft the feat
At night, as some did in conceit,
   It would have spoiled him, surely.

Passion o' me, how I run on!
There's that that would be thought upon,   80
   I trow, besides the bride.
The business of the kitchen's great,
For it is fit that man should eat,
   Nor was it there denied.

Just in the nick the cook knocked thrice,
And all the waiters in a trice
   His summons did obey;
Each serving-man, with dish in hand,
Marched boldly up, like our trained band,
   Presented, and away.   90

When all the meat was on the table,
What man of knife or teeth was able
   To stay to be entreated?
And this the very reason was—
Before the parson could say grace,
   The company was seated.

Now hats fly off, and youths carouse;
Healths first go round, and then the house;
   The bride's came thick and thick:

89. trained band, the militia.   **99. The bride's,** the bride's health.

And when 'twas named another's health,   100
Perhaps he made it hers by stealth;
   And who could help it, Dick?

O' the sudden up they rise and dance;
Then sit again and sigh and glance;
   Then dance again and kiss;
Thus several ways the time did pass,
Till every woman wished her place,
   And every man wished his!

By this time all were stolen aside
To counsel and undress the bride,   110
   But that he must not know;
But yet 'twas thought he guessed her mind,
And did not mean to stay behind
   Above an hour or so.

When in he came, Dick, there she lay
Like new-fallen snow melting away
   ('Twas time, I trow, to part);
Kisses were now the only stay,
Which soon she gave, as who would say,
   "God be with ye, with all my heart."   120

But just as heavens would have to cross it,
In came the bridesmaids with the posset.
   The bridegroom eat in spite,
For had he left the women to't,
It would have cost two hours to do't,
   Which were too much that night.

At length the candle's out, and now
All that they had not done, they do.
   What that is, who can tell?
But I believe it was no more   130
Than thou and I have done before
   With Bridget and with Nell.

Richard Lovelace
1618–1657

Lovelace is probably the most romantic figure in English literature. All the elements that go to make up the beau ideal seem to have met in him, and legend and tradition have added to and re-enforced them. He is the best known of the "Cavalier Poets," and his own name and that of Cavalier have reflected color and glory on each other. He was born into a wealthy family, was educated at Charterhouse School and Gloucester Hall, now Worcester College, at Oxford, where Royalist traditions cluster thickest. He was described by contemporaries as an eminent "soldier, gentleman, and lover," and as "one of the handsomest men of England." He has the distinction, perhaps, of being the only Oxford undergraduate ever to be granted the M.A. degree in his second year—presumably because of his good looks and gracious manners. The award was made at the request of a great lady attending Queen Henrietta Maria when she and Charles I visited the university in 1636. The young Master of Arts left Oxford and took up his residence at the court.

Lovelace followed the tradition of his family and embarked upon a military career. He took part in the Scottish expeditions of 1639 and 1640. In 1642 he was chosen by the County of Kent to present to the Puritan Parliament a petition praying that the King and the Church might be restored to their rights. The Parliament was in no mood for such a petition, even from the bravest and handsomest man in England, and for his boldness in making the request he was thrown into prison for seven weeks. But stone walls and iron bars, though they kept Lovelace in, could not keep romance out, and he whiled away his time by writing songs, one of which, "To Althea, from Prison," has helped make him immortal. Out of prison, he naturally joined the King's forces, supplying equipment at his own charge, and serving as captain. When Oxford was captured in 1646, he served with the French army in Holland. His expedition thither was the occasion of his other famous verses, the farewells to Lucasta. He was wounded at Dunkirk, and from this circumstance the most romantic of the Lovelace legends takes its source. Anthony à Wood relates that a Miss Lucy Sacheverell, who was betrothed to Lovelace, heard a report that he had been killed at Dunkirk, and that the lady subsequently married another. Lovelace, so the story goes, returned to England to find her married, "became very poor in body and purse, was the object of charity, went in ragged clothes, and mostly lodged in obscure and dirty places," at last dying in an alley near Shoe Lane. How much, if any, of the story is true cannot be ascertained.

It is certain that Lovelace was soon back in England, took part in Royalist uprisings in Kent, and was again imprisoned. He took this occasion to prepare his verses for the press. He was released in 1649, and published a collection of his poems under the title *Lucasta*. Whether "Lucasta" was the Lucy Sacheverell of the legends, or whether she ever existed except as a creature of the poet's imagination, is uncertain. Dr. C. H. Wilkinson of Worcester College, the editor of Lovelace's poems, is inclined to identify her as a member of the family of Sir Charles Lucas. There is good reason to believe that Lovelace had spent his energy and his substance in the King's cause, and the gallant soldier of the King probably knew want in his last years.

To the general public, Lovelace is a two-poem poet, and the poems "To Althea, from Prison" and "To Lucasta, Going to the Wars" are the most perfect of their kind in the language. They are on a plane, however, which he never quite reached with any of his other poems. Much of his verse is uninspired, and some of it is downright slovenly in composition. He was enamored of the "metaphysical" conceit; the results are often far from happy, and betray the lack of the saving sense of humor. When, as in his best-known poems and a few others, he is not trying too hard to be poetical, and is content to express his feelings simply, he achieves a quality of verse which is unique and beautiful. In his life and in the three poems printed below, the best aspects of the spirit, the manner, and the way of life of the Cavaliers found their perfect expression.

TO ALTHEA, FROM PRISON

When Love with unconfinèd wings
   Hovers within my gates,
And my divine Althea brings
   To whisper at the grates;

When I lie tangled in her hair
    And fettered to her eye,
The gods that wanton in the air
    Know no such liberty.

When flowing cups run swiftly round,
    With no allaying Thames,   10
Our careless heads with roses bound,
    Our hearts with loyal flames;
When thirsty grief in wine we steep,
    When healths and draughts go free,
Fishes that tipple in the deep
    Know no such liberty.

When, like committed linnets, I
    With shriller throat shall sing
The sweetness, mercy, majesty,
    And glories of my king;   20
When I shall voice aloud how good
    He is, how great should be,
Enlargèd winds that curl the flood
    Know no such liberty.

Stone walls do not a prison make,
    Nor iron bars a cage:
Minds innocent and quiet take
    That for an hermitage.
If I have freedom in my love,
    And in my soul am free,   30
Angels alone, that soar above,
    Enjoy such liberty.

TO LUCASTA, GOING TO THE WARS

Tell me not, sweet, I am unkind,
    That from the nunnery
Of thy chaste breast and quiet mind
    To war and arms I fly.

7. gods. Most seventeenth-century manuscripts read "birds," which seems to be the meaning of "gods" here. **17. committed,** to prison; caged.

True, a new mistress now I chase,
    The first foe in the field;
And with a stronger faith embrace
    A sword, a horse, a shield.

Yet this inconstancy is such
    As you too shall adore;   10
I could not love thee, dear, so much,
    Loved I not honour more.

TO LUCASTA, GOING BEYOND THE SEAS

If to be absent were to be
    Away from thee;
Or that when I am gone,
    You or I were alone,
Then, my Lucasta, might I crave
Pity from blustering wind or swallowing wave.

But I'll not sigh one blast or gale
    To swell my sail,
Or pay a tear to 'suage
    The foaming blow-god's rage;   10
For whether he will let me pass
Or no, I'm still as happy as I was.

Though seas and land betwixt us both,
    Our faith and troth,
Like separated souls,
    All time and space controls:
Above the highest sphere we meet,
Unseen, unknown, and greet as angels greet.

So then we do anticipate
    Our after-fate,   20
And are alive i' the skies,
    If thus our lips and eyes
Can speak like spirits unconfined
In heaven, their earthly bodies left behind.

To Lucasta, Going Beyond the Seas. **9. 'suage,** assuage **10. blow-god's,** of Aeolus, god of the winds.

Edmund Waller
1606–1687

Waller, though he is today known chiefly as the author of only two or three charming little poems, was considered in the seventeenth and eighteenth centuries one of the greatest of English poets. His epitaph declares him *"facile princeps"*—easily first—among them. The "Preface to the Second Part of Mr. Waller's Poems," 1690, declares that "he was, indeed, the parent of English verse, and the first that showed us our tongue had beauty and numbers in it. Our language owes more to him than the French does to Cardinal Richelieu and the whole Academy." It is an interesting circumstance that Waller himself feared that the English language would soon become unintelligible because of the rapidity of its growth. In his poem "Of English Verse," he refers to English as "a daily changing tongue," and to English poets as writing in sand rather than carving, as did ancient poets, in the lasting marble of Latin or Greek. He was certainly the most polished and "correct" of English poets in his day, and Dryden and Pope never tired of praising the smoothness and the harmony of his verses. He was not, as is sometimes said, the father of the heroic couplet, but he did more than anyone of his time to illustrate its possibilities and beauties. He was, incidentally, the richest poet, and one of the wealthiest Englishmen, of his time.

He was born at Beaconsfield in Buckinghamshire, which he inherited as a boy, went to Eton, and thence to King's College, Cambridge. He entered Parliament at the age of sixteen. He was a cousin of John Hampden and a relative of Oliver Cromwell, and was for a while on the Parliamentary side. At the age of twenty-three he married, in the most romantic circumstances, and despite her guardians' disapproval, Anne Bankes, a London heiress, whose fortune, after some litigation and delay, was awarded to him. She died three years later, and there began soon afterwards his poetical courtship of "Sacharissa," Lady Dorothy Sidney, who married, doubtless very wisely, Lord Spencer, later Earl of Sunderland, at Penshurst, "the home of the Sidneys," in Kent.

Waller's early sympathies with the Parliamentary party, if they were ever sincere, soon evaporated, and he became one of the most ardent Royalists. His name has survived in Civil War annals in connection with "Waller's Plot" of 1643, the most famous seventeenth-century English version of what is today called "fifth-column" activity—an attempt to take London from the inside for Charles. The plot was discovered, Waller turned state's evidence, betraying his friends and associates, and thus escaped the block. He was imprisoned, fined heavily, and banished. For nearly ten years he was in France, acting as host to Royalist refugees, among whom were Abraham Cowley and other literary figures. He made his peace with Cromwell, came back to England, and wrote a panegyric on the Lord Protector, with whom he seems to have been friendly. At the Restoration he greeted Charles II with an "Address of Welcome." One of the best stories of the time has it that Charles in conversation with Waller remarked that his verses on Cromwell were much superior to those on himself. Waller, never at a loss for a reply, rejoined with "Poets, Sire, succeed much better in fiction than in truth." He was again in Parliament, where he sat from 1661 until his death at the age of eighty-one. He has, and justly, a reputation for superficial brilliance, but he had also a shrewd and penetrating insight into men and affairs. His prophecy that James II would be "left like a whale upon the strand" did not have long to wait for fulfillment. He died at Beaconsfield, and was there buried in the same graveyard where Edmund Burke lies.

"Waller was smooth," wrote Mr. Pope, and his words pretty effectively sum up the man's life and work. His verse is as free from the weighty subjects that Donne wrestled with in his poetry as it is from "metaphysical" conceits and fantastic imagery. Much of his verse was written for particular persons and on trivial occasions long since forgotten—"The Apology of Sleep, for Not Approaching the Lady Who Can Do Anything But Sleep When She Pleaseth," "To a Lady, from Whom He Received a Silver Pen," "On a Girdle." Perhaps he consoled himself with the thought that the English language in which he wrote would be as ephemeral as the trivial things and occasions he celebrated. No English poet ever wrote lyrics with greater charm and skill than Waller at his best, and few poets at eighty have produced anything comparable for ease and grace to "Of the Last Verses in the Book."

EDMUND WALLER

SAY, LOVELY DREAM

Say, lovely dream, where couldst thou find
    Shadows to counterfeit that face?
    Colours of this glorious kind
Come not from any mortal place.

In heaven itself thou sure wert drest
    With that angel-like disguise;
    Thus deluded am I blest,
And see my joy with closèd eyes.

But, ah, this image is too kind
    To be other than a dream!   10
    Cruel Sacharissa's mind
Never put on that sweet extreme.

Fair dream, if thou intend'st me grace,
    Change that heavenly face of thine;
    Paint despised love in thy face,
And make it to appear like mine.

Pale, wan, and meagre let it look,
    With a pity-moving shape,
    Such as wander by the brook
Of Lethe, or from graves escape.   20

Then to that matchless nymph appear,
    In whose shape thou shinest so,
    Softly in her sleeping ear,
With humble words express my woe.

Perhaps from greatness, state, and pride,
    Thus surprisèd she may fall:
    Sleep does disproportion hide,
And, death resembling, equals all.

ON A GIRDLE

That which her slender waist confined
Shall now my joyful temples bind;
No monarch but would give his crown
His arms might do what this has done.

It was my heaven's extremest sphere,
The pale which held that lovely deer;
My joy, my grief, my hope, my love
Did all within this circle move.

    20. **Lethe,** the stream in the lower world from which the shades drank and thus obtained forgetfulness of the past. *On a Girdle.* **5. extremest,** outermost. **6. pale,** enclosure.

A narrow compass, and yet there
Dwelt all that's good and all that's fair: 10
Give me but what this ribband bound,
Take all the rest the sun goes round!

GO, LOVELY ROSE

    This song, Waller's finest lyric, was set to music by Henry Lawes.

    Go, lovely rose,
Tell her that wastes her time and me,
    That now she knows,
When I resemble her to thee,
How sweet and fair she seems to be.

    Tell her that's young,
And shuns to have her graces spied,
    That hadst thou sprung
In deserts, where no men abide,
Thou must have uncommended died.   10

    Small is the worth
Of beauty from the light retired;
    Bid her come forth,
Suffer herself to be desired,
And not blush so to be admired.

    Then die, that she
The common fate of all things rare
    May read in thee;
How small a part of time they share,
That are so wondrous sweet and fair.   20

OF THE LAST VERSES IN THE BOOK

When we for age could neither read nor write,
The subject made us able to indite;
The soul, with nobler resolutions decked,
The body stooping, does herself erect.
No mortal parts are requisite to raise
Her that, unbodied, can her Maker praise.

The seas are quiet when the winds give o'er;
So, calm are we when passions are no more!
For then we know how vain it was to boast
Of fleeting things, so certain to be lost.   10
Clouds of affection from our younger eyes
Conceal that emptiness which age descries.

Of the Last Verses in the Book. **11. affection,** passion.

The soul's dark cottage, battered and decayed,
Lets in new light through chinks that time has made;
Stronger by weakness wiser men become

As they draw near to their eternal home.
Leaving the old, both worlds at once they view,
That stand upon the threshold of the new.

Richard Crashaw
1613?–1649

It fell to the lot of the father of Richard Crashaw, an Anglican clergyman of Puritan temperament and a violent crusader against the Roman Catholic Church in pamphlets, sermons, and even in his last will and testament, to give to English literature in his son the only distinguished Roman Catholic poet of the century. Doubtless the very violence of the father's hostility to the Roman Church had something to do with the son's becoming a convert to that church. But the son's instinctive love of the beauty of ritual, the splendor of Catholic art and architecture, and the rapturous expression in literature and music of religious devotion and spiritual exaltation, must in any event have led him to Rome. He went to school at Charterhouse and was later admitted to Pembroke Hall, Cambridge, where he took his B.A. degree in 1634. At Cambridge Crashaw made several literary acquaintances, chief of whom was Abraham Cowley, who was to remain his friend for life, and to write one of the most beautiful elegies in the language on his death.

Crashaw's first volume of verse, *Epigrammatum Sacrorum Liber*, a collection of Latin religious epigrams, was published in the year in which he took his degree. The following year he became a fellow of Peterhouse College at Cambridge, where he found a congenial religious atmosphere, and where his own devoutness and asceticism became a matter of comment. There were literary as well as religious associations and exercises at Peterhouse, and the young poet could have remained happy there had not the Civil War interfered. Cambridge was as sympathetic to the Parliamentary cause as Oxford was to that of the King, and Crashaw, a Royalist, was forced to leave.

He seems to have been received into the Roman Catholic Church about 1645, and in 1646 fled to Paris, which had become the center for Royalist refugees. He was found there in distress by his friend Cowley, by whom, probably, he was introduced to Queen Henrietta Maria. The Queen sent him with a recommendation to Cardinal Palotto, Governor of Rome, who received him and gave him a place in his household. The young man had enough of the English Puritan in him to be shocked by the laxity of the conduct of some members of the Cardinal's household, and he considered it his duty to make the conditions known to the Cardinal. The attitude toward Crashaw on the part of the accused was such that the Cardinal had to find him a place elsewhere, and he was sent to the Church of Our Lady of Loretto. He died a few weeks after his arrival, and was buried there.

His volume *Steps to the Temple* was published in 1646, and contains most of his religious verse and a section of secular verse entitled "The Delights of the Muses." A posthumous volume, *Carmen Deo Nostro*, which was published in 1652, contains a few new poems and reprints of some of his earlier religious verses. The first editor of *Steps to the Temple* referred to Crashaw as "Herbert's second, but equal," and it is interesting to note that the young Roman Catholic poet was introduced to the English reading public under the aegis of Herbert's *Temple*. But, though Crashaw sincerely admired Herbert, and may be said to be of the school of Herbert and Donne, there is little of the essential Herbert in his work, and there is nothing in the rapturous devotion and mystical splendor of his poetic cathedral which suggests the chaste simplicity of Herbert's parish church or of Herbert's English countryside.

Crashaw is in some ways the least English poet of seventeenth-century England. His fondness for the Italian poet Marino and his readings in the Spanish mystics led him to introduce elaborate conceits and enthusiasms which at times offend good taste, and at other times startle the reader with their exotic beauty. Such poems as the "Hymn to the Name and Honour of the Admirable Saint Teresa" and the concluding lines of "The Flaming Heart" are alive with wonder and worship, and in reading them one must confess with Crashaw that one has taken an angel by the wing.

The diversity of his gifts and the range of his

RICHARD CRASHAW

poetic themes may be illustrated by a comparison with these ecstatic lyrics of some of his secular verse, particularly the charming "Wishes: To His (Supposed) Mistress." No poet in the language has more glaring faults than Crashaw, and his love of elaborate conceits and lack of restraint resulted in some of the worst lines in the language. For all his faults, however, he belongs at his best with Shelley, and the enthusiasm which he has excited in modern poets and readers of poetry is not difficult to understand.

WISHES:

TO HIS (SUPPOSED) MISTRESS*

Whoe'er she be
That not impossible she
That shall command my heart and me;

Where'er she lie,
Locked up from mortal eye,
In shady leaves of destiny;

Till that ripe birth
Of studied fate stand forth,
And teach her fair steps to our earth;

Till that divine   10
Idea take a shrine
Of crystal flesh, through which to shine:

Meet you her, my wishes,
Bespeak her to my blisses,
And be ye called, my absent kisses.

I wish her beauty,
That owes not all his duty
To gaudy tire, or glist'ring shoe-tie.

Something more than
Taffeta or tissue can,   20
Or rampant feather, or rich fan.

More than the spoil
Of shop, or silkworm's toil,
Or a bought blush, or a set smile.

A face that's best
By its own beauty drest,
And can alone command the rest.

*From "The Delights of the Muses."
9. teach, guide.   17. his, its.   18. tire, attire.

A face made up
Out of no other shop
Than what Nature's white hand sets ope.   30

A cheek where youth
And blood, with pen of truth
Write what the reader sweetly ru'th.

A cheek where grows
More than a morning rose,
Which to no box his being owes.

Lips where all day
A lover's kiss may play,
Yet carry nothing thence away.

Looks that oppress   40
Their richest tires, but dress
Themselves in simple nakedness.

Eyes that displace
The neighbour diamond, and out-face
That sunshine by their own sweet grace.

Tresses that wear
Jewels, but to declare
How much themselves more precious are.

Whose native ray
Can tame the wanton day   50
Of gems, that in their bright shades play.

Each ruby there,
Or pearl that dares appear,
Be its own blush, be its own tear.

A well-tamed heart
For whose more noble smart
Love may be long choosing a dart.

Eyes that bestow
Full quivers on Love's bow,
Yet pay less arrows than they owe.   60

Smiles that can warm
The blood, yet teach a charm,
That chastity shall take no harm.

30. **ope**, open.   33. **Write what the reader sweetly ru'th**. Professor Kittredge paraphrases the line, "Depict that beauty which makes the beholder suffer the sweet sorrow of love."—F. E. Schelling, *Seventeenth Century Lyrics*, Ginn, 1899, p. 259.   36. **his**, its.   40–42. **Looks that . . . nakedness**. . . . "looks that *oppress*, overpower the richest apparel which decks them, which clothe and dress up the barest costume."—Schelling.   50. **tame the wanton day**, make dull the gay brilliance.

Blushes that bin
The burnish of no sin,
Nor flames of aught too hot within.

Joys that confess
Virtue their mistress,
And have no other head to dress.

Fears, fond and flight, 70
As the coy bride's, when night
First does the longing lover right.

Tears, quickly fled
And vain, as those are shed
For a dying maidenhead.

Days that need borrow
No part of their good morrow
From a fore-spent night of sorrow.

Days that, in spite
Of darkness, by the light 80
Of a clear mind are day all night.

Nights sweet as they,
Made short by lovers' play,
Yet long by the absence of the day.

Life that dares send
A challenge to his end,
And, when it comes, say, "Welcome, friend!"

Sidneian showers,
Of sweet discourse, whose powers
Can crown old Winter's head with flowers. 90

Soft silken hours,
Open suns, shady bowers;
'Bove all, nothing within that lours.

Whate'er delight
Can make Day's forehead bright,
Or give down to the wings of Night.

In her whole frame
Have Nature all the name,
Art and ornament all the shame.

Her flattery, 100
Picture and poesy:
Her counsel her own virtue be.

I wish her store
Of worth may leave her poor
Of wishes; and I wish—no more.

Now, if Time knows
That her, whose radiant brows
Weave them a garland of my vows;

Her whose just bays
My future hopes can raise 110
A trophy to her present praise;

Her that dares be
What these lines wish to see:
I seek no further—it is she.

'Tis she, and here
Lo! I unclothe and clear
My wishes' cloudy character.

May she enjoy it
Whose merit dare apply it,
But modesty dares still deny it. 120

Such worth as this is
Shall fix my flying wishes,
And determine them to kisses.

Let her full glory,
My fancies, fly before ye!
Be ye my fictions, but her story!

from THE HOLY NATIVITY OF OUR LORD GOD

A HYMN SUNG AS BY THE SHEPHERDS *

Gloomy night embraced the place
Where the noble Infant lay.
 The Babe looked up and showed His face;
In spite of darkness, it was day.
 It was Thy day, Sweet! and did rise,
Not from the east, but from Thine eyes. . . .

---

64. bin, are. **70. fond and flight,** foolish and fleeting. **88–90. Sidneian showers . . . flowers,** a reference probably to the elegant conversations of Sir Philip Sidney's prose romance *Arcadia*, which still retained its popularity as a ladies' book in Crashaw's day. **98. name,** repute.

100–02. Her flattery . . . be. However others may flatter her by painting and poetry, let her take counsel only of her own virtue. **104–05. poor of wishes,** that is, without need of wishes. **109. bays,** laurels. **123. determine them to,** terminate, or resolve, them into.
* From *Carmen Deo Nostro*.

RICHARD CRASHAW

We saw Thee in Thy balmy nest,
Young Dawn of our eternal Day!
We saw Thine eyes break from their east,
And chase the trembling shades away.   10
We saw Thee; and we blessed the sight,
We saw Thee by Thine own sweet light.

Poor world (said I), what wilt thou do
To entertain this starry Stranger?
Is this the best thou canst bestow?
A cold and not too cleanly manger?
Contend, the powers of heaven and earth,
To fit a bed for this huge birth.

Proud world (said I), cease your contest,
And let the mighty Babe alone.   20
The phoenix builds the phoenix' nest,
Love's architecture is his own.
The Babe whose birth embraves this morn
Made His own bed ere He was born.

I saw the curled drops, soft and slow,
Come hovering o'er the place's head;
Offering their whitest sheets of snow
To furnish the fair Infant's bed;
Forbear (said I); be not too bold,
Your fleece is white, but 'tis too cold. . . .   30

Welcome, all wonders in one sight!
Eternity shut in a span!
Summer in winter, day in night!
Heaven in earth, and God in man!
Great little One! whose all-embracing birth
Lifts earth to heaven, stoops heaven to earth. . . .

To Thee, meek Majesty! soft King
Of simple graces and sweet loves:
Each of us his lamb will bring,
Each his pair of silver doves;   40
Till burnt at last in fire of Thy fair eyes,
Ourselves become our own best sacrifice.

21. *phoenix.* See note on page 603.   23. *embraves,* beautifies.

from THE FLAMING HEART

The lines here printed are the last twenty-two of the hundred and eight lines of the poem, whose full title is "The Flaming Heart, upon the Book and Picture of the Seraphical Saint Teresa, as She Is Usually Expressed with a Seraphim beside Her" (from *Carmen Deo Nostro*). St. Teresa, the Spanish mystic, who died in 1582 and was canonized in 1622, exerted great influence on Crashaw, and, as in the lines here given, inspired him to unexcelled lyric rhapsody.

Let all thy scattered shafts of light, that play   87
Among the leaves of thy large books of day,
Combined against this breast, at once break in
And take away from me myself and sin!   90
This gracious robbery shall thy bounty be,
And my best fortunes such fair spoils of me.
O thou undaunted daughter of desires!
By all thy dower of lights and fires;
By all the eagle in thee, all the dove;
By all thy lives and deaths of love;
By thy large draughts of intellectual day,
And by thy thirsts of love more large than they;
By all thy brim-filled bowls of fierce desire,
By thy last morning's draught of liquid fire;   100
By the full kingdom of that final kiss
That seized thy parting soul, and sealed thee His;
By all the heavens thou hast in Him,
Fair sister of the seraphim,
By all of Him we have in thee;
Leave nothing of myself in me!
Let me so read thy life that I
Unto all life of mine may die!

Henry Vaughan
1622–1695

Vaughan was as much the poetic disciple of Herbert as Herbert was of Donne, though both disciples did their best work when they did not attempt to follow too closely the mannerisms of their masters. And none of the three would in his younger days have had reason to suppose that he would be best known three hundred years later as a poet. Vaughan is the first Welshman to find a place in the roster of English poets, and his peculiar contribution to English poetry is due in no small measure to his Welsh heritage. He was born in Brecknockshire, at Newton on the River Usk, in southeast Wales, and so devoted was he to his race and to the place of his nativity that he styled himself "the Silurist," after *Silures*, the old Roman name for the inhabitants of his district. He spoke only Welsh until he was twelve, and some of the expressions and locutions of his poems are attributable to his knowledge of his native tongue.

His early education was received in Wales, and from his childhood home he went with his twin brother, Thomas, to Jesus College, the headquarters of Welsh students at Oxford. He seems to have left without a degree, and is next heard of at the Inns of Court in London, studying law. Here he fell in with young poets and literary men, tried his hand at poetry, and continued his studies until the Civil War put an end to such peaceful pursuits. Not much is known of his life for the next few years, and indeed his biography is one of the most fragmentary in English literature. He probably served for a while in the King's army, and either before or after the war he studied medicine. After the war and for the rest of his life he was a country doctor in his native district in Wales.

Vaughan's earliest poems consisted probably of the literary exercises after the fashion of Donne which are addressed to "Amoret." Whether the lady so referred to was his first wife is not known. His greatest inspiration to poetry was to come not from the love of a lady, but from religion, and through sickness, the loss of friends, the execution of the King, the death of his wife, and, above all, the death of his twin brother. His volume *Silex Scintillans* (*The Sparkling Flint*), which was published in 1650, was devoted wholly to religious verse, much of it inspired by his brother's death, and most of it shot through with the mystical beliefs which he and his brother had shared. (The poems given here are all from this volume.) A second volume, *Olor Iscanus* (*The Swan of the Usk*), which was published in 1651, contains religious pieces as well as translations and early verse which, says the publisher's preface, the author had long ago condemned to obscurity.

The influence of Herbert on Vaughan has already been mentioned. Many of Vaughan's titles are taken directly or indirectly from Herbert, and one is constantly reminded in Vaughan's best verse of the rhythms of Herbert. He lacks, however, the artistic sense of Herbert, and is given to mixed metaphors and sudden transitions which never mar the calm flow of Herbert's verse. Vaughan's poetry is curiously uneven. Much of it is not above the level of verse that appears in a parish magazine. On the other hand there are unsurpassed flights of lyrical fancy and expressions of mystical experiences of which Herbert was not capable, and which only Crashaw among his contemporaries has equaled.

The twentieth century takes special note of Vaughan's interest in natural phenomena, and his perception of the presence of God in natural objects. This sense of the Divine immanence he believed to be particularly acute in children, and he strove to recapture for himself the state of mind and soul which would make possible communion with nature and the God of nature. In his best-known poem, "The Retreat," he looks backward to the early days of his "angel infancy," before the "white, celestial thought" of his fancy had become sullied with the wickedness of the world. The poem contains the germ of Wordsworth's thought in his "Ode: Intimations of Immortality from Recollections of Early Childhood," but there is no proof that Wordsworth ever heard of Vaughan or of "The Retreat."

Vaughan was spiritually farsighted. "The world of light" and the departed friends beyond the veil of physical experience were more real to him than the material things of this world. If his readers are continually reminded of what he drew from Donne and Herbert, they are as constantly impressed by the fact that at his best he transcends both. His is such poetry, says a distinguished critic, as Lazarus might have written after he had risen from the dead.

THE RETREAT

The thought of this poem should be compared with that of John Earle's character of "A Child," page 575, and of Wordsworth's "Ode: Intimations of Immortality," Vol. II, page 67.

Happy those early days, when I
Shined in my angel infancy;
Before I understood this place
Appointed for my second race,
Or taught my soul to fancy aught
But a white, celestial thought;
When yet I had not walked above
A mile or two from my first Love,
And looking back, at that short space,
Could see a glimpse of His bright face; 10
When on some gilded cloud or flower
My gazing soul would dwell an hour,
And in those weaker glories spy
Some shadows of eternity;
Before I taught my tongue to wound
My conscience with a sinful sound,
Or had the black art to dispense
A several sin to every sense,
But felt through all this fleshly dress
Bright shoots of everlastingness. 20
　Oh, how I long to travel back,
And tread again that ancient track!
That I might once more reach that plain
Where first I left my glorious train,
From whence the enlightened spirit sees
That shady city of palm trees.
But, ah! my soul with too much stay
Is drunk, and staggers in the way.
Some men a forward motion love;
But I by backward steps would move, 30
And when this dust falls to the urn,
In that state I came, return.

PEACE

My soul, there is a country
　Far beyond the stars,
Where stands a wingèd sentry
　All skilful in the wars.
There, above noise and danger,
　Sweet Peace sits crowned with smiles,
And One born in a manger
　Commands the beauteous files.

19. **fleshly dress**, earthly being.

He is thy gracious friend,
　And—O my soul, awake!— 10
Did in pure love descend
　To die here for thy sake.
If thou canst get but thither,
　There grows the flower of peace,
The rose that cannot wither,
　Thy fortress and thy ease.
Leave, then, thy foolish ranges;
　For none can thee secure
But One who never changes,
　Thy God, thy life, thy cure. 20

THE WORLD

I saw Eternity the other night
Like a great ring of pure and endless light,
　All calm as it was bright;
And round beneath it, Time, in hours, days, years,
　Driven by the spheres,
Like a vast shadow moved, in which the world
　And all her train were hurled.
The doting lover in his quaintest strain
　Did there complain;
Near him, his lute, his fancy, and his flights, 10
　Wit's sour delights,
With gloves and knots, the silly snares of pleasure,
　Yet his dear treasure,
All scattered lay, while he his eyes did pour
　Upon a flower.

The darksome statesman, hung with weights and woe,
Like a thick midnight fog, moved there so slow
　He did not stay nor go;
Condemning thoughts, like mad eclipses, scowl
　Upon his soul, 20
And crowds of crying witnesses without
　Pursued him with one shout.
Yet digged the mole, and lest his ways be found,
　Worked under ground,
Where he did clutch his prey. But one did see
　That policy:

Peace. 17. **ranges,** rovings (in search of peace). *The World.* 5. **spheres.** Vaughan is contrasting the great calm, unchanging ring of light above and the constantly revolving spheres of the Ptolemaic universe below with the feverish and vain activities and ambitions of human life at their center. 8. **quaintest,** decorated with the most elaborate conceits and fancies. 12. **knots,** love knots. 16. **darksome statesman,** possibly, but not certainly, a reference to Oliver Cromwell. It is most likely that Vaughan has in mind the typical unscrupulous politician. 26. **policy,** stratagem.

Churches and altars fed him; perjuries
    Were gnats and flies;
It rained about him blood and tears; but he
    Drank them as free.   30

The fearful miser on a heap of rust
    Sat pining all his life there, did scarce trust
        His own hands with the dust;
Yet would not place one piece above, but lives
        In fear of thieves.
Thousands there were as frantic as himself,
        And hugged each one his pelf:
The downright epicure placed heaven in sense,
        And scorned pretence;
While others, slipped into a wide excess,   40
        Said little less;
The weaker sort, slight trivial wares enslave,
        Who think them brave;
And poor, despisèd Truth sat counting by
        Their victory.

Yet some, who all this while did weep and sing,
    And sing and weep, soared up into the ring;
        But most would use no wing.
"O fools!" said I, "thus to prefer dark night
        Before true light!   50
To live in grots and caves, and hate the day
    Because it shows the way,
The way which from this dead and dark abode
    Leads up to God,
A way where you might tread the sun and be
    More bright than he!"
But, as I did their madness so discuss,
    One whispered thus:
"This ring the Bridegroom did for none provide,
    But for His bride."   60

THEY ARE ALL GONE INTO THE WORLD OF LIGHT

This poem was first printed in 1655, by which time, as Sir Edmund Chambers points out, Vaughan had lost his brother Thomas and other friends, and possibly also his first wife.

27. Churches and altars fed him, probably an allusion to the abolition of episcopacy by Parliament in 1642. **28. Were gnats and flies,** were of as little importance as gnats and flies.   **30. as free,** as freely and liberally as they rained about him.   **34. place one piece,** invest one coin. Compare Matthew 6:20: "Lay up for yourselves treasures in heaven, where . . . thieves do not break through nor steal." **43. brave,** fine, beautiful.   **44. counting by,** observing, taking note of.   **47. the ring.** See l. 2.   **59–60. the Bridegroom . . . His bride,"** Christ and his Church. See Revelation 21:9.

They are all gone into the world of light,
    And I alone sit lingering here!
Their very memory is fair and bright,
    And my sad thoughts doth clear.

It glows and glitters in my cloudy breast,
    Like stars upon some gloomy grove,
Or those faint beams in which this hill is dressed
    After the sun's remove.

I see them walking in an air of glory,
    Whose light doth trample on my days;   10
My days, which are at best but dull and hoary,
    Mere glimmerings and decays.

O holy hope, and high humility,
    High as the heavens above!
These are your walks, and you have showed them me
    To kindle my cold love.

Dear, beauteous death! the jewel of the just,
    Shining nowhere but in the dark;
What mysteries do lie beyond thy dust,
    Could man outlook that mark!   20

He that hath found some fledged bird's nest may know
    At first sight if the bird be flown;
But what fair well or grove he sings in now,
    That is to him unknown.

And yet, as angels in some brighter dreams
    Call to the soul when man doth sleep,
So some strange thoughts transcend our wonted themes,
    And into glory peep.

If a star were confined into a tomb,
    Her captive flames must needs burn there;   30
But when the hand that locked her up gives room,
    She'll shine through all the sphere.

O Father of eternal life, and all
    Created glories under Thee!
Resume Thy spirit from this world of thrall
    Into true liberty!

Either disperse these mists, which blot and fill
    My pèrspective still as they pass;
Or else remove me hence unto that hill
    Where I shall need no glass.   40

4. clear, brighten.   **5. It,** the memory of departed friends. **20. mark!** boundary.   **35. Resume Thy spirit,** that is, take back my spirit which Thou hast created.   **38. pèrspective,** telescope.

THE WATERFALL

This is another poem in which Vaughan suggests Wordsworth in his sympathetic interest in and watchfulness of natural phenomena.

With what deep murmurs through time's silent
    stealth
Doth thy transparent, cool, and watery wealth
    Here flowing fall,
    And chide, and call,
As if his liquid, loose retinue stayed
Lingering, and were of this steep place afraid,
    The common pass
    Where, clear as glass,
    All must descend—
    Not to an end,   10
But quickened by this steep and rocky grave,
Rise to a longer course more bright and brave.

  Dear stream! dear bank, where often I
  Have sat and pleased my pensive eye,
  Why, since each drop of thy quick store
  Runs thither whence it flowed before,
  Should poor souls fear a shade or night,
  Who came, sure, from a sea of light?
  Or since those drops are all sent back
  So sure to thee, that none doth lack,   20
  Why should frail flesh doubt any more
  That what God takes He'll not restore?

  O useful element and clear!
  My sacred wash and cleanser here,
  My first consigner unto those
  Fountains of life where the Lamb goes!
What sublime truths and wholesome themes
Lodge in thy mystical deep streams!
  Such as dull man can never find
  Unless that Spirit lead his mind   30
  Which first upon thy face did move,
  And hatched all with His quickening love.
As this loud brook's incessant fall
In streaming rings restagnates all,
Which reach by course the bank, and then
Are no more seen, just so pass men.
  O my invisible estate,
  My glorious liberty, still late!
  Thou art the channel my soul seeks,
  Not this with cataracts and creeks.   40

Sir Thomas Browne
1605–1682

Sir Thomas Browne is the best-known example in English literature of the physician as man of letters, the provincial doctor as philosopher and commentator on the universe and the mysteries of life and death. Like Burton, that other auditor of the world's accounts, he is also famous for the eccentricities of his genius, and for the exotic (though very different) quality of the prose in which he embalmed his meditations. Burton was "by his profession a divine, by his inclination a physician." Browne, we may say, though by profession a physician, was by his nature a divine and a metaphysician. Like both Burton and Donne, Browne was concerned with the intellectual and religious problems of the day—the seeming conflict between theology and science, the questions relating to man's place, limitations, and possibilities in the great scheme of the universe.

Sir Thomas, unlike the author of the *Anatomy*, saw a good part of the world before he began to philosophize upon it. He was born in London, went to school at Winchester, took his B.A. degree at Oxford in 1626, and his M.A. there in 1629. He was while at Oxford a member of Broadgates Hall, later Pembroke College, which was to shelter Dr. Johnson in the following century. He traveled in Ireland, France, Italy, and Flanders, and studied medicine at Montpellier, Padua, and Leyden, where he took his degree of Doctor of Medicine. He returned to England, and in 1637 settled in the market town of Norwich, where for nearly half a century he practiced his profession successfully, carried on his researches, and wrote his books. In 1641 he married Dorothy Mileham, a charming young woman of one of the county families of Norfolk. The domestic life of Sir Thomas and Dame Dorothy must have been singularly happy. His solicitude for the education and welfare of his children, especially of his sons, Edward and Thomas, and the tone of the correspondence between father and sons later, contrib-

32. **hatched all with His quickening love,** an allusion to the agency of the Spirit of God at the Creation. See Genesis 1:2.

ute to one of the pleasantest pictures of family life of the whole century. In 1665 he was made a fellow of the Royal College of Physicians. In 1671 he was knighted on a royal visit to Norwich by Charles II, who, says Dr. Johnson, writing of the incident, "with many frailties and vices, had yet skill to discover excellence, and virtue to reward it." He died on his seventy-sixth birthday, October 19, 1682.

Browne's first book, and the one which has remained most popular, is his *Religio Medici*, written when he was in his twenties, but not published by him until 1643, after two pirated editions had already appeared. It was written for himself and his friends, and is a young physician's confession of religious principles. The *Religio* is a rare exposition of the beliefs of a young man who combined a devout religious temper with an inquiring, skeptical, and scientific turn of mind. It is perhaps less a statement of faith than the revelation of a state of mind; an experiment in the deliberate suspension of judgment before the mysteries of revealed religion. It has been called the best answer of the age to the negativism and despair which tortured Donne and many another. The nobility and sweetness of Browne's character and the all-embracing tolerance of the man's mind are seen throughout the book.

His *Pseudodoxia Epidemica, or Vulgar Errors*, which he brought out in 1646, is an attempt to supply the "calendar of popular errors" which Bacon hoped would be drawn up in order that they might be convicted and disposed of. In it Browne brings together the most amazing array of "errors"—drawn from all the corners of his reading and research—and with more or less success confutes them. The poet and the scientist in him get in each other's way at times, and there are frequent struggles between his head and his heart in disposing of an error. No book was ever undertaken with more methodical gravity, but the modern reader finds it a constant source of amusement, thanks to the irrelevancies, the digressions, the bizarre fancies, and the whimsical speculations in which the author indulges.

Browne's most beautiful prose is to be found in the two pieces published in 1658, *Hydriotaphia: Urn Burial*, and *The Garden of Cyrus*, in which his antiquarian interests predominate. The discovery of some funerary urns leads Browne to the composition of an essay which, except for its companion piece, has not its equal in English for solemnly beautiful diction and rhythmical prose. Two other works, *A Letter to a Friend* and *Christian Morals*, were published posthumously in 1690 and 1716.

In all that he wrote Browne is an exponent of the genteel tradition in English literature, an aristocrat in the truest and best sense of the word. He was incapable of thinking or writing anything vulgar. He is the perfect specimen of the "magnanimous man" whose language, as Cardinal Newman says, "expresses not only his great thought, but his great self."

from RELIGIO MEDICI

THE SECOND PART

NOW for that other virtue of charity, without which faith is a mere notion, and of no existence, I have ever endeavoured to nourish the merciful disposition and humane inclination I borrowed from my parents, and regulate it to the written and prescribed laws of charity. And if I hold the true anatomy of myself, I am delineated and naturally framed to such a piece of virtue; for I am of a constitution so general that it consorts and sympathiseth with all things. I have no antipathy, or rather idiosyncrasy, in diet, humour, air, anything. I wonder not at the French for their dishes of frogs, snails and toadstools, nor at the Jews for locusts and grasshoppers; but being amongst them, make them my common viands, and I find they agree with my stomach as well as theirs. I could digest a salad gathered in a church-yard, as well as in a garden. I cannot start at the presence of a serpent, scorpion, lizard, or salamander: at the sight of a toad or viper, I find in me no desire to take up a stone to destroy them. I feel not in myself those common antipathies that I can discover in others: those national repugnances do not touch me, nor do I behold with prejudice the French, Italian, Spaniard, or Dutch: but where I find their actions in balance with my countrymen's, I honour, love, and embrace them in the same degree. I was born in the eighth climate, but seem for to be framed and constellated unto all. I am no plant that will not prosper out of a garden. All places, all airs, make unto me one country; I am in England everywhere, and under any meridian. I have been shipwrackt, yet am not enemy with the sea or winds; I can study, play, or sleep in a tempest. In brief, I am averse from nothing: my conscience would give me the lie if I should say I absolutely detest or hate any essence but the Devil: or so at least abhor anything, but that we might come to composition. If there be any among those common objects of hatred I do contemn and laugh at, it is that great enemy of reason, virtue and religion, the multitude: that numerous piece of monstrosity,

---

27. **eighth climate,** a zone measured on the earth's surface which included England.

which, taken asunder, seem men, and the reasonable creatures of GOD; but, confused together, make but one great beast, and a monstrosity more prodigious than Hydra. It is no breach of charity to call these *Fools;* it is the style all holy writers have afforded them, set down by Solomon in canonical Scripture, and a point of our Faith to believe so. Neither in the name of *Multitude* do I only include the base and minor sort of people; there is a rabble even amongst the gentry, a sort of plebeian heads, whose fancy moves with the same wheel as these; men in the same level with mechanics, though their fortunes do somewhat gild their infirmities, and their purses compound for their follies. But as, in casting account, three or four men together come short in account of one man placed by himself below them; so neither are a troop of these ignorant doradoes of that true esteem and value, as many a forlorn person, whose condition doth place him below their feet. Let us speak like politicians: there is a nobility without heraldry, a natural dignity, whereby one man is ranked with another, another filed before him, according to the quality of his desert, and pre-eminence of his good parts. Though the corruption of these times and the bias of present practice wheel another way, thus it was in the first and primitive commonwealths, and is yet in the integrity and cradle of well-ordered polities, till corruption getteth ground; ruder desires labouring after that which wiser considerations contemn, every one having a liberty to amass and heap up riches, and they a licence or faculty to do or purchase any thing. . . .

But to return from philosophy to charity: I hold not so narrow a conceit of this virtue, as to conceive that to give alms is only to be charitable, or think a piece of liberality can comprehend the total of charity. Divinity hath wisely divided the act thereof into many branches, and hath taught us in this narrow way many paths unto goodness; as many ways as we may do good, so many ways we may be charitable. There are infirmities not only of body, but of soul, and fortunes, which do require the merciful hand of our abilities. I cannot contemn a man for ignorance, but behold him with as much pity as I do Lazarus. It is no greater charity to clothe his body, than apparel the nakedness of his soul. It is an honourable object to see the reasons of other men wear our liveries, and their borrowed understandings do homage to the bounty of ours: it is the cheapest way of beneficence, and, like the natural charity of the sun, illuminates another without obscuring itself. To be reserved and caitiff in this part of goodness, is the sordidest piece of covetousness, and more contemptible than pecuniary avarice. To this (as calling myself a scholar) I am obliged by the duty of my condition: I make not therefore my head a grave, but a treasure, of knowledge; I intend no monopoly, but a community in learning; I study not for my own sake only, but for theirs that study not for themselves. I envy no man that knows more than myself, but pity them that know less. I instruct no man as an exercise of my knowledge, or with an intent rather to nourish and keep it alive in mine own head than beget and propagate it in his: and in the midst of all my endeavours there is but one thought that dejects me, that my acquired parts must perish with myself, nor can be legacied among my honoured friends. I cannot fall out or contemn a man for an error, or conceive why a difference in opinion should divide an affection; for controversies, disputes, and argumentations, both in philosophy and in divinity, if they meet with discreet and peaceable natures, do not infringe the laws of charity. In all disputes, so much as there is of passion, so much there is of nothing to the purpose; for then reason, like a bad hound, spends upon a false scent, and forsakes the question first started. And this is one reason why controversies are never determined; for, though they be amply proposed, they are scarce at all handled, they do so swell with unnecessary digressions; and the parenthesis on the party is often as large as the main discourse upon the subject. The foundations of religion are already established, and the principles of salvation subscribed unto by all: there remains not many controversies worth a passion; and yet never any disputed without, not only in divinity, but in inferior arts. What a βατραχομυομαχία and hot skirmish is betwixt S. and T. in Lucian! How do grammarians hack and slash for the genitive case in *Jupiter!* How do they break their own pates to salve that of Priscian!

"*Si foret in terris, rideret Democritus.*"

Yea, even amongst wiser militants, how many wounds have been given, and credits slain, for the poor victory of an opinion, or beggarly conquest of a distinction! Scholars are men of peace, they bear no arms, but their tongues are sharper than Actius

---

6. Solomon. See Proverbs 1:7 and so on. **10. plebeian heads,** base persons. **18. doradoes,** rich men (literally, goldfish). **47. Lazarus.** See Luke 16:19–21. **39.** βατραχομυομαχία, battle of frogs and mice. **43. Priscian!** the celebrated Roman grammarian. "To break Priscian's head" is to make a bad blunder in grammar. **44. "Si . . . Democritus."** "If he were on earth, how Democritus would laugh!"—Horace, *Epistles,* Book II, Ep. 1, l. 194

his razor; their pens carry farther, and give a louder report than thunder: I had rather stand the shock of a basilisco, than the fury of a merciless pen. It is not mere zeal to learning, or devotion to the muses, that wiser princes patron the arts, and carry an indulgent aspect unto scholars; but a desire to have their names eternized by the memory of their writings, and a fear of the revengeful pen of succeeding ages; for these are the men, that, when they have played their parts, and had their *exits*, must step out and give the moral of their scenes, and deliver unto posterity an Inventory of their virtues and vices. And surely there goes a great deal of conscience to the compiling of an history: there is no reproach to the scandal of a story; it is such an authentic kind of falsehood that with authority belies our good names to all nations and posterity.

There is another offence unto charity, which no author hath ever written of, and few take notice of; and that's the reproach, not of whole professions, mysteries, and conditions, but of whole nations, wherein by opprobrious epithets we miscall each other, and by an uncharitable logic, from a disposition in a few, conclude a habit in all.

"*Le mutin Anglois, et le bravache Escossois,*
Et le fol François,
Le poultron Romain, le larron de Gascongne,
L'Espagnol superbe, et l' Aleman yvrongne."

St. Paul, that calls the Cretians liars, doth it but indirectly, and upon quotation of their own poet. It is as bloody a thought in one way, as Nero's was in another; for by a word we wound a thousand, and at one blow assassine the honour of a nation. It is as complete a piece of madness to miscall and rave against the times, or think to recall men to reason by a fit of passion. Democritus, that thought to laugh the times into goodness, seems to me as deeply hypochondriac as Heraclitus, that bewailed them. It moves not my spleen to behold the multitude in their proper humours, that is, in their fits of folly and madness; as well understanding that wisdom is not profaned unto the world, and 'tis the privilege of a few to be virtuous. They that endeavour to abolish vice, destroy also virtue; for contraries, though they destroy one another, are yet the life of one another. Thus virtue (abolish vice) is an Idea. Again, the community of sin doth not disparage goodness; for when vice gains upon the major part, virtue, in whom it remains, becomes more excellent; and being lost in some, multiplies its goodness in others which remain untouched and persist entire in the general inundation. I can therefore behold vice without a satire, content only with an admonition, or instructive reprehension; for noble natures, and such as are capable of goodness, are railed into vice, that might as easily be admonished into virtue; and we should all be so far the orators of goodness, as to protect her from the power of vice, and maintain the cause of injured truth. No man can justly censure or condemn another, because indeed no man truly knows another. This I perceive in myself; for I am in the dark to all the world, and my nearest friends behold me but in a cloud. Those that know me but superficially, think less of me than I do of myself; those of my near acquaintance think more; God, who truly knows me, knows that I am nothing; for He only beholds me and all the world, who looks not on us through a derived ray, or a trajection of a sensible species, but beholds the substance without the helps of accidents, and the forms of things as we their operations. Further, no man can judge another, because no man knows himself: for we censure others but as they disagree from that humour which we fancy laudable in ourselves, and commend others but for that wherein they seem to quadrate and consent with us. So that, in conclusion, all is but that we all condemn, self-love. 'Tis the general complaint of these times, and perhaps of those past, that charity grows cold; which I perceive most verified in those which most do manifest the fires and flames of zeal; for it is a virtue that best agrees with coldest natures, and such as are complexioned for humility. But how shall we expect charity towards others, when we are uncharitable to our selves? *Charity begins at home,* is the voice of the world; yet is every man his greatest enemy, and, as it were, his own executioner. *Non occides,* is the commandment of God, yet scarce observed by any man; for I perceive every man is his own Atropos, and lends a hand to cut the thread of his own days. Cain was not therefore the first murtherer, but Adam, who brought in death; whereof he beheld the practice and example in his own son Abel, and saw that verified in the experience of another, which faith could not persuade him in the theory of himself.

There is, I think, no man that apprehends his own miseries less than myself, and no man that so nearly apprehends another's. I could lose an arm

---

3. **basilisco,** a large piece of ordnance, called after the fabled basilisk, whose breath, and even whose look, was fatal. 25–28. "**Le mutin . . . yvrongne.**" "The roistering Englishman, the swaggering Scotsman, and the mad Frenchman, the Roman coward, the Gascon thief, the arrogant Spaniard, and the drunken German." 30. **St. Paul.** See Titus 1:12.

22. **trajection . . . species,** transmission of a visible sort. 41. **Non occides.** Thou shalt not kill.

without a tear, and with few groans, methinks, be quartered into pieces; yet can I weep most seriously at a play, and receive with true passion the counterfeit grief of those known and professed impostures. It is a barbarous part of inhumanity to add unto any afflicted party's misery, or endeavour to multiply in any man a passion whose single nature is already above his patience. This was the greatest affliction of Job, and those oblique expostulations of his friends a deeper injury than the downright blows of the Devil. It is not the tears of our own eyes only, but of our friends also, that do exhaust the current of our sorrows; which, falling into many streams, runs more peaceably, and is contented with a narrower channel. It is an act within the power of charity, to translate a passion out of one breast into another, and to divide a sorrow almost out of itself; for an affliction, like a dimension, may be so divided, as, if not indivisible, at least to become insensible. Now with my friend I desire not to share or participate, but to engross, his sorrows; that, by making them mine own, I may more easily discuss them; for in mine own reason, and within myself, I can command that which I cannot entreat without myself, and within the circle of another. I have often thought those noble pairs and examples of friendship not so truly histories of what had been, as fictions of what should be; but I now perceive nothing in them but possibilities, nor any thing in the heroic examples of Damon and Pythias, Achilles and Patroclus, which methinks upon some grounds I could not perform within the narrow compass of myself. That a man should lay down his life for his friend, seems strange to vulgar affections, and such as confine themselves within that worldly principle, *Charity begins at home.* For mine own part I could never remember the relations that I held unto myself, nor the respect that I owe unto my own nature, in the cause of GOD, my country, and my friends. Next to these three, I do embrace myself. I confess I do not observe that order that the Schools ordain our affections, to love our parents, wives, children, and then our friends; for, excepting the injunctions of religion, I do not find in myself such a necessary and indissoluble sympathy to all those of my blood. I hope I do not break the fifth Commandment, if I conceive I may love my friend before the nearest of my blood, even those to whom I owe the principles of life. I never yet cast a true affection on a woman; but I have loved my friend as I do virtue, my soul, my GOD. From hence methinks I do conceive how GOD loves man, what happiness there is in the love of GOD. Omitting all other, there are three most mystical unions: 1. two natures in one person; 2. three persons in one nature; 3. one soul in two bodies; for though indeed they be really divided, yet are they so united, as they seem but one, and make rather a duality than two distinct souls.

There are wonders in true affection: it is a body of enigmas, mysteries, and riddles; wherein two so become one, as they both become two. I love my friend before myself, and yet methinks I do not love him enough: some few months hence my multiplied affection will make me believe I have not loved him at all. When I am from him, I am dead till I be with him; when I am with him, I am not satisfied, but would still be nearer him. United souls are not satisfied with embraces, but desire to be truly each other; which being impossible, their desires are infinite, and must proceed without a possibility of satisfaction. Another misery there is in affection, that whom we truly love like our own selves, we forget their looks, nor can our memory retain the idea of their faces; and it is no wonder, for they are ourselves, and our affection makes their looks our own. This noble affection falls not on vulgar and common constitutions, but on such as are marked for virtue: he that can love his friend with this noble ardour, will in a competent degree affect all. Now, if we can bring our affections to look beyond the body, and cast an eye upon the soul, we have found out the true object, not only of friendship, but charity; and the greatest happiness that we can bequeath the soul, is that wherein we all do place our last felicity, salvation; which though it be not in our power to bestow, it is in our charity and pious invocations to desire, if not procure and further. I cannot contentedly frame a prayer for myself in particular, without a catalogue for my friends; nor request a happiness, wherein my sociable disposition doth not desire the fellowship of my neighbour. I never hear the toll of a passing bell, though in my mirth, without my prayers and best wishes for the departing spirit; I cannot go to cure the body of my patient, but I forget my profession, and call unto GOD for his soul; I cannot see one say his prayers, but, instead of imitating him, I fall into a supplication for him, who perhaps is no more to me than a common nature: and if GOD hath vouchsafed an ear to my supplications, there are surely many happy that never saw me, and enjoy the blessing of mine unknown devotions. To pray for enemies, that is, for their salvation, is no harsh precept, but the practice of our daily and ordinary devotions. I cannot believe the story of the Italian: our bad wishes and uncharitable desires

52–53. the Italian. Sir Thomas refers more specifically in

proceed no further than this life; it is the Devil, and the uncharitable votes of Hell, that desire our misery in the World to come. . . .

I thank GOD, amongst those millions of vices I do inherit and hold from Adam, I have escaped one, and that a mortal enemy to charity, the first and father-sin, not only of man, but of the Devil, pride: a vice whose name is comprehended in a monosyllable, but in its nature not circumscribed with a world. I have escaped it in a condition that can hardly avoid it. Those petty acquisitions and reputed perfections that advance and elevate the conceits of other men, add no feathers unto mine. I have seen a grammarian tower and plume himself over a single line in Horace, and show more pride in the construction of one ode, than the author in the composure of the whole book. For my own part, besides the jargon and patois of several provinces, I understand no less than six languages; yet I protest I have no higher conceit of myself, than had our fathers before the confusion of Babel, when there was but one language in the world, and none to boast himself either linguist or critic. I have not only seen several countries, beheld the nature of their climes, the chorography of their provinces, topography of their cities, but understood their several laws, customs, and policies; yet cannot all this persuade the dulness of my spirit unto such an opinion of myself, as I behold in nimbler and conceited heads, that never looked a degree beyond their nests. I know the names, and somewhat more, of all the constellations in my horizon; yet I have seen a prating mariner, that could only name the pointers and the North Star, out-talk me, and conceit himself a whole sphere above me. I know most of the plants of my country, and of those about me; yet methinks I do not know so many as when I did but know a hundred, and had scarcely ever simpled further than Cheapside. For, indeed, heads of capacity, and such as are not full with a handful or easy measure of knowledge, think they know nothing till they know all; which being impossible, they fall upon the opinion of Socrates, and only know they know not any thing. I cannot think that Homer pined away upon the riddle of the fishermen; or that Aristotle, who understood the uncertainty of knowledge, and confessed so often the reason of man too weak for the works of nature, did ever drown himself upon the flux and reflux of Euripus. We do but learn to-day what our better advanced judgments will unteach to-morrow; and Aristotle doth but instruct us, as Plato did him; that is, to confute himself. I have run through all sorts, yet find no rest in any: though our first studies and junior endeavours may style us Peripatetics, Stoics, or Academics; yet I perceive the wisest heads prove, at last, almost all Sceptics, and stand like Janus in the field of knowledge. I have therefore one common and authentic philosophy I learned in the Schools, whereby I discourse and satisfy the reason of other men; another more reserved, and drawn from experience, whereby I content mine own. Solomon, that complained of ignorance in the height of knowledge, hath not only humbled my conceits, but discouraged my endeavours. There is yet another conceit that hath sometimes made me shut my books, which tells me it is a vanity to waste our days in the blind pursuit of knowledge; it is but attending a little longer, and we shall enjoy that by instinct and infusion, which we endeavour at here by labour and inquisition. It is better to sit down in a modest ignorance, and rest contented with the natural blessing of our own reasons, than buy the uncertain knowledge of this life with sweat and vexation, which Death gives every fool *gratis*, and is an accessary of our glorification.

I was never yet once, and commend their resolutions who never marry twice: not that I disallow of second marriage; as neither, in all cases, of polygamy, which, considering some times, and the unequal number of both sexes, may be also necessary. The whole world was made for man, but the twelfth part of man for woman: man is the whole world, and the breath of GOD; woman the rib and crooked piece of man. I could be content that we might procreate like trees, without conjunction, or that there were any way to perpetuate the world without this trivial and vulgar way of union: it is the foolishest act a wise man commits in all his life; nor is there any thing that will more deject his cooled imagination, when he shall consider what an odd and unworthy piece of folly he hath committed. I speak not in prejudice, nor am averse from that sweet sex, but naturally amorous of all that is beautiful. I can look a whole day with delight upon a handsome picture, though it be but of an horse. It is my temper, and I like it the better, to affect all harmony; and sure there is music even in the

his *Pseudodoxia*, Book VII, chap. 19, to this Italian, "who, after he had inveigled his enemy to disdain his faith for the redemption of his life, did presently poniard him, to prevent repentance, and assure his eternal death." **22. the confusion of Babel.** See Genesis 11:1–9. **26. chorography,** description of places and countries. **39. simpled,** botanized.

2. Euripus, the narrow channel between Euboea and Boeotia, opposite Chalcis. **15. Solomon.** See Ecclesiastes 7:23. **29. never yet once** (married). Browne was later to marry and have twelve children.

SIR THOMAS BROWNE

beauty, and the silent note which Cupid strikes, far sweeter than the sound of an instrument. For there is a music wherever there is a harmony, order, or proportion: and thus far we may maintain the music of the spheres; for those well-ordered motions, and regular paces, though they give no sound unto the ear, yet to the understanding they strike a note most full of harmony. Whosoever is harmonically composed delights in harmony; which makes me much distrust the symmetry of those heads which declaim against all church-music. For myself, not only from my obedience, but my particular genius, I do embrace it: for even that vulgar and tavern-music, which makes one man merry, another mad, strikes in me a deep fit of devotion, and a profound contemplation of the First Composer. There is something in it of divinity more than the ear discovers: it is an hieroglyphical and shadowed lesson of the whole world, and creatures of GOD; such a melody to the ear, as the whole world, well understood, would afford the understanding. In brief, it is a sensible fit of that harmony which intellectually sounds in the ears of GOD. I will not say, with Plato, the soul is an harmony, but harmonical, and hath its nearest sympathy unto music: thus some, whose temper of body agrees, and humours the constitution of their souls, are born poets, though indeed all are naturally inclined unto rhythm. This made Tacitus, in the very first line of his Story, fall upon a verse; and Cicero, the worst of poets, but declaiming for a poet, fall in the very first sentence upon a perfect hexameter. I feel not in me those sordid and unchristian desires of my profession; I do not secretly implore and wish for plagues, rejoice at famines, revolve ephemerides and almanacks in expectation of malignant aspects, fatal conjunctions, and eclipses. I rejoice not at unwholesome springs, nor unseasonable winters: my prayer goes with the husbandman's; I desire everything in its proper season, that neither men nor the times be put out of temper. Let me be sick myself, if sometimes the malady of my patient be not a disease unto me. I desire rather to cure his infirmities than my own necessities. Where I do him no good, methinks it is scarce honest gain; though I confess 'tis but the worthy salary of our well-intended endeavours. I am not only ashamed, but heartily sorry, that, besides death, there are diseases incurable: yet not for my own sake, or that they be beyond my art, but for the general cause and sake of humanity, whose common cause I apprehend as mine own. . . .

For my conversation, it is like the sun's, with all men, and with a friendly aspect to good and bad. Methinks there is no man bad, and the worst, best; that is, while they are kept within the circle of those qualities wherein they are good: there is no man's mind of such discordant and jarring a temper, to which a tunable disposition may not strike a harmony. *Magnae virtutes, nec minora vitia;* it is the posy of the best natures, and may be inverted on the worst; there are in the most depraved and venomous dispositions, certain pieces that remain untouch, which by an *antiperistasis* become more excellent, or by the excellency of their antipathies are able to preserve themselves from the contagion of their enemy vices, and persist entire beyond the general corruption. For it is also thus in nature: the greatest balsams do lie enveloped in the bodies of most powerful corrosives. I say, moreover, and I ground upon experience, that poisons contain within themselves their own antidote, and that which preserves them from the venom of themselves, without which they were not deleterious to others only, but to themselves also. But it is the corruption that I fear within me, not the contagion of commerce without me. 'Tis that unruly regiment within me, that will destroy me; 'tis I that do infect myself; the man without a navel yet lives in me; I feel that original canker and corrode and devour me; and therefore *Defenda me Dios de me,* "LORD deliver me from my self," is a part of my Litany, and the first voice of my retired imaginations. There is no man alone, because every man is a microcosm, and carries the whole world about him. *Nunquam minus solus quam cum solus,* though it be the apothegm of a wise man, is yet true in the mouth of a fool. Indeed, though in a wilderness, a man is never alone, not only because he is with himself and his own thoughts, but because he is with the Devil, who ever consorts with our solitude, and is that unruly rebel that musters up those disordered motions which accompany our sequestered imaginations. And to speak more narrowly, there is no such thing as solitude, nor any thing that can be said to be alone and by itself, but GOD, Who is His own circle, and can subsist by

---

5. music of the spheres. A music, imperceptible to human ears, was, according to an ancient belief, produced by the movement of the heavenly bodies. **16–17. First Composer,** God. **29–30. Tacitus . . . Story,** the *Annals.* **30–32. Cicero . . . hexameter,** *Pro Archia.* **35. ephemerides,** astronomical charts.

5. conversation, behavior. **12. Magnae . . . vitia.** Great virtues, and no smaller vices. **16. antiperistasis,** an opposition of contrary qualities by which one or both are intensified, or the intensification so produced. **21. balsams,** healing agents. **30–31. the man without a navel,** Adam. **37–38. Nunquam . . . solus.** Never less alone than when alone.—Cicero, *De Officiis,* Book III, sec. 1.

Himself; all others, besides their dissimilary and heterogeneous parts, which in a manner multiply their natures, cannot subsist without the concourse of GOD, and the society of that hand which doth uphold their natures. In brief, there can be nothing truly alone and by itself, which is not truly one; and such is only GOD: all others do transcend an unity, and so by consequence are many.

Now for my life, it is a miracle of thirty years, which to relate were not a history, but a piece of poetry, and would sound to common ears like a fable. For the world, I count it not an inn, but an hospital; and a place not to live, but to die in. The world that I regard is myself; it is the microcosm of my own frame that I cast mine eye on; for the other, I use it but like my globe, and turn it round sometimes for my recreation. Men that look upon my outside, perusing only my condition and fortunes, do err in my altitude; for I am above Atlas his shoulders. The earth is a point not only in respect of the heavens above us, but of that heavenly and celestial part within us; that mass of flesh that circumscribes me, limits not my mind: that surface that tells the heavens it hath an end, cannot persuade me I have any: I take my circle to be above three hundred and sixty; though the number of the arc do measure my body, it comprehendeth not my mind: whilst I study to find how I am a microcosm, or little world, I find myself something more than the great. There is surely a piece of Divinity in us, something that was before the elements, and owes no homage unto the sun. Nature tells me I am the image of GOD, as well as Scripture: he that understands not thus much, hath not his introduction or first lesson, and is yet to begin the alphabet of man. Let me not injure the felicity of others, if I say I am as happy as any: *Ruat coelum, fiat voluntas Tua*, salveth all; so that whatsoever happens, it is but what our daily prayers desire. In brief, I am content; and what should Providence add more? Surely this is it we call happiness, and this do I enjoy; with this I am happy in a dream, and as content to enjoy a happiness in a fancy, as others in a more apparent truth and realty. There is surely a nearer apprehension of anything that delights us in our dreams, than in our waked senses: without this I were unhappy; for my awaked judgment discontents me, ever whispering unto me, that I am from my friend; but my friendly dreams in the night requite me, and make me think I am within his arms. I thank GOD for my happy dreams, as I do for my good rest; for there is a satisfaction in them unto reasonable desires, and such as can be content with a fit of happiness: and surely it is not a melancholy conceit to think we are all asleep in this world, and that the conceits of this life are as mere dreams to those of the next; as the phantasms of the night to the conceits of the day. There is an equal delusion in both, and the one doth but seem to be the emblem or picture of the other: we are somewhat more than ourselves in our sleeps, and the slumber of the body seems to be but the waking of the soul. It is the ligation of sense, but the liberty of reason; and our waking conceptions do not match the fancies of our sleeps. At my nativity my ascendant was the watery sign of Scorpius; I was born in the planetary hour of Saturn, and I think I have a piece of that leaden planet in me. I am no way facetious, nor disposed for the mirth and galliardise of company; yet in one dream I can compose a whole comedy, behold the action, apprehend the jests, and laugh myself awake at the conceits thereof. Were my memory as faithful as my reason is then fruitful, I would never study but in my dreams; and this time also would I choose for my devotions: but our grosser memories have then so little hold of our abstracted understandings, that they forget the story, and can only relate to our awaked souls a confused and broken tale of that that hath passed. Aristotle, who hath written a singular tract *Of Sleep*, hath not, methinks, throughly defined it; nor yet Galen, though he seem to have corrected it; for those noctambuloes and night-walkers, though in their sleep, do yet enjoy the action of their senses. We must therefore say that there is something in us that is not in the jurisdiction of Morpheus; and that those abstracted and ecstatic souls do walk about in their own corpse as spirits with the bodies they assume, wherein they seem to hear, see, and feel, though indeed the organs are destitute of sense, and their natures of those faculties that should inform them. Thus it is observed, that men sometimes, upon the hour of their departure, do speak and reason above themselves; for then the soul, beginning to be freed from the ligaments of the body, begins to reason like herself, and to discourse in a strain above mortality.

We term sleep a death; and yet it is waking that kills us, and destroys those spirits that are the house

---

15. microcosm. The "microcosm," or "little world" of man, is contrasted with the "macrocosm," or "great world" of the universe. **20. Atlas,** the mythological giant who carried the world on his shoulders. **38. Ruat . . . Tua.** Though the heavens fall, Thy will be done.

5. conceit, fancy, opinion. **13–14. ligation,** binding. **16. ascendant,** the sign of the zodiac rising over the horizon. **20. galliardise,** excessive gaiety. **37. Morpheus,** the god of sleep.

of life. 'Tis indeed a part of life that best expresseth death; for every man truly lives, so long as he acts his nature, or some way makes good the faculties of himself. Themistocles, therefore, that slew his soldier in his sleep, was a merciful executioner: 'tis a kind of punishment the mildness of no laws hath invented: I wonder the fancy of Lucan and Seneca did not discover it. It is that death by which we may be literally said to die daily; a death which Adam died before his mortality; a death whereby we live a middle and moderating point between life and death: in fine, so like death, I dare not trust it without my prayers, and an half adieu unto the world, and take my farewell in a colloquy with God.

> The night is come, like to the day,
> Depart not Thou, great God, away.
> Let not my sins, black as the night,
> Eclipse the lustre of Thy light:
> Keep still in my horizon; for to me
> The sun makes not the day, but Thee.
> Thou, Whose nature cannot sleep,
> On my temples sentry keep;
> Guard me 'gainst those watchful foes,
> Whose eyes are open while mine close.
> Let no dreams my head infest,
> But such as Jacob's temples blest.
> While I do rest, my soul advance;
> Make my sleep a holy trance;
> That I may, my rest being wrought,
> Awake into some holy thought;
> And with as active vigour run
> My course, as doth the nimble sun.
> Sleep is a death; O make me try,
> By sleeping, what it is to die;
> And as gently lay my head
> On my grave, as now my bed.
> Howe'er I rest, great God, let me
> Awake again at last with Thee;
> And thus assur'd, behold I lie
> Securely, or to awake or die.
> These are my drowsy days; in vain
> I do now wake to sleep again:
> O come that hour, when I shall never
> Sleep again, but wake for ever.

This is the dormitive I take to bedward; I need no other laudanum than this to make me sleep; after which I close mine eyes in security, content to take my leave of the sun, and sleep unto the Resurrection....

48. **dormitive,** a medicine to induce sleep.

from HYDRIOTAPHIA: URN BURIAL

Chapter 5

NOW since these dead bones have already outlasted the living ones of Methuselah, and in a yard under ground, and thin walls of clay, out-worn all the strong and specious buildings above it; and quietly rested under the drums and tramplings of three conquests: what prince can promise such diuturnity unto his relics, or might not gladly say,

"Sic ego componi versus in ossa velim."

Time which antiquates antiquities, and hath an art to make dust of all things, hath yet spared these minor monuments.

In vain we hope to be known by open and visible conservatories, when to be unknown was the means of their continuation, and obscurity their protection. If they died by violent hands, and were thrust into their urns, these bones become considerable, and some old philosophers would honour them, whose souls they conceived most pure, which were thus snatched from their bodies, and to retain a stranger propension unto them; whereas they weariedly left a languishing corpse, and with faint desires of reunion. If they fell by long and aged decay, yet wrapt up in the bundle of time, they fall into indistinction, and make but one blot with infants. If we begin to die when we live, and long life be but a prolongation of death, our life is a sad composition. We live with death, and die not in a moment. How many pulses made up the life of Methuselah, were work for Archimedes: common counters sum up the life of Moses his man. Our days become considerable like petty sums by minute accumulations; where numerous fractions make up but small round numbers; and our days of a span long make not one little finger.

If the nearness of our last necessity brought a nearer conformity into it, there were a happiness in hoary hairs, and no calamity in half senses. But the long habit of living indisposeth us for dying; when avarice makes us the sport of death; when even David grew politicly cruel; and Solomon could hardly be said to be the wisest of men. But many are too early old, and before the date of age. Ad-

12. **diuturnity,** long duration. 14. **"Sic . . . velim."** "Thus, when I am turned to bones, would I be buried." 36. **the life of Moses his man.** "In the Psalm of Moses [Psalm 90:10]." (Browne) 40. **one little finger.** "According to the ancient arithmetic of the hand, wherein the little finger of the right hand contracted, signified an hundred. —*Pierius in Hieroglyph.*" (Browne)

versity stretcheth our days, misery makes Alcmena's nights, and time hath no wings unto it. But the most tedious being is that which can unwish itself, content to be nothing, or never to have been, which was beyond the malcontent of Job, who cursed not the day of his life, but his nativity; content to have so far been, as to have a title to future being, although he had lived here but in an hidden state of life, and as it were an abortion.

What song the sirens sang, or what name Achilles assumed when he hid himself among women, though puzzling questions, are not beyond all conjecture. What time the persons of these ossuaries entered the famous nations of the dead, and slept with princes and counsellours, might admit a wide solution. But who were the proprietaries of these bones, or what bodies these ashes made up, were a question above antiquarism. Not to be resolved by man, nor easily perhaps by spirits, except we consult the provincial guardians, or tutelary observators. Had they made as good provision for their names as they have done for their relics, they had not so grossly erred in the art of perpetuation. But to subsist in bones, and be but pyramidally extant, is a fallacy in duration. Vain ashes, which in the oblivion of names, persons, times, and sexes, have found unto themselves a fruitless continuation, and only arise unto late posterity, as emblems of mortal vanities; antidotes against pride, vainglory, and madding vices. Pagan vainglories which thought the world might last for ever, had encouragement for ambition, and, finding no Atropos unto the immortality of their names, were never dampt with the necessity of oblivion. Even old ambitions had the advantage of ours, in the attempts of their vainglories, who acting early, and before the probable meridian of time, have by this time found great accomplishment of their designs, whereby the ancient Heroes have already out-lasted their monuments, and mechanical preservations. But in this latter scene of time, we cannot expect such mummies unto our memories, when ambition may fear the prophecy of Elias, and Charles the Fifth can never hope to live within two Methuselahs of Hector.

And therefore restless inquietude for the diuturnity of our memories unto present considerations, seems a vanity almost out of date, and superannuated piece of folly. We cannot hope to live so long in our names, as some have done in their persons, one face of Janus holds no proportion unto the other. 'Tis too late to be ambitious. The great mutations of the world are acted, or time may be too short for our designs. To extend our memories by monuments, whose death we daily pray for, and whose duration we cannot hope, without injury to our expectations in the advent of the last day, were a contradiction to our beliefs. We whose generations are ordained in this setting part of time, are providentially taken off from such imaginations; and being necessitated to eye the remaining particle of futurity, are naturally constituted unto thoughts of the next world, and cannot excusably decline the consideration of that duration, which maketh pyramids pillars of snow, and all that's past a moment.

Circles and right lines limit and close all bodies, and the mortal right-lined circle must conclude and shut up all. There is no antidote against the opium of time, which temporally considereth all things. Our fathers find their graves in our short memories, and sadly tell us how we may be buried in our survivors. Grave-stones tell truth scarce forty years. Generations pass while some trees stand, and old families last not three oaks. To be read by bare inscriptions like many in Gruter, to hope for eternity by enigmatical epithets or first letters of our names, to be studied by antiquaries, who we were, and have new names given us like many of the mummies, are cold consolations unto the students of perpetuity, even by everlasting languages.

To be content that times to come should only know there was such a man, not caring whether they knew more of him, was a frigid ambition in Cardan: disparaging his horoscopal inclination and judgment of himself, who cares to subsist like Hippocrates' patients, or Achilles' horses in Homer, under naked nominations, without deserts and noble acts, which are the balsam of our memories, the *entelechia* and soul of our subsistences. To be nameless in worthy deeds exceeds an infamous his-

1–2. **Alcmena's nights.** "One night as long as three." (Browne)   5–6. **Job . . . nativity.** See Job 3.   12. **puzzling questions.** "The puzzling questions of Tiberius unto grammarians.—*Marcel. Donatus in Suet.*" (Browne)   13–14. **ossuaries,** repositories of bones.   16. **wide,** only roughly approximate.   20–21. **tutelary observators,** guardian spirits.   24–25. **pyramidally extant,** known by monuments only, like a mummy.   32. **Atropos,** the Fate whose duty it was to cut the thread of life.   33. **dampt,** dispirited.   37. **meridian,** noonday.   43. **prophecy of Elias.** "That the world may last but six thousand years." (Browne)   44. **two Methuselahs of Hector.** "Hector's fame lasting above two lives of Methuselah, before that famous prince was extant." (Browne)

6. **Janus,** the god of beginnings, who had two opposite faces.   21. **right,** straight. **close,** inclose.   22. **right-lined circle,** "Θ, the character of death." (Browne)   27. **scarce forty years.** "Old ones being taken up, and other bodies laid under them." (Browne)   30. **Gruter,** Jan Gruter (1560–1627), Dutch scholar who published a work on Latin inscriptions.   33–34. **mummies.** "Which men show in several countries, giving them what names they please; and unto some the names of the old Egyptian kings, out of Herodotus." (Browne)   39. **Cardan,** Girolamo (1501–1576). Italian mathematician and astrologer.   44. **entelechia,** being.

tory. The Canaanitish woman lives more happily without a name, than Herodias with one. And who had not rather have been the good thief, than Pilate?

But the iniquity of oblivion blindly scattereth her poppy, and deals with the memory of men without distinction to merit of perpetuity. Who can but pity the founder of the Pyramids? Herostratus lives that burnt the Temple of Diana, he is almost lost that built it. Time hath spared the epitaph of Adrian's horse, confounded that of himself. In vain we compute our felicities by the advantage of our good names, since bad have equal durations; and Thersites is like to live as long as Agamemnon. Who knows whether the best of men be known? or whether there be not more remarkable persons forgot, than any that stand remembered in the known account of time? Without the favour of the everlasting register, the first man had been as unknown as the last, and Methuselah's long life had been his only chronicle.

Oblivion is not to be hired. The greater part must be content to be as though they had not been, to be found in the register of God, not in the record of man. Twenty-seven names make up the first story before the flood, and the recorded names ever since contain not one living century. The number of the dead long exceedeth all that shall live. The night of time far surpasseth the day, and who knows when was the equinox? Every hour adds unto that current arithmetic which scarce stands one moment. And since death must be the Lucina of life, and even pagans could doubt, whether thus to live, were to die; since our longest sun sets at right descensions, and makes but winter arches, and therefore it cannot be long before we lie down in darkness, and have our light in ashes, since the brother of death daily haunts us with dying mementoes, and time that grows old in itself, bids us hope no long duration: diuturnity is a dream and folly of expectation.

Darkness and light divide the course of time, and oblivion shares with memory a great part even of our living beings; we slightly remember our felicities, and the smartest strokes of affliction leave but short smart upon us. Sense endureth no extremities, and sorrows destroy us or themselves. To weep into stones are fables. Afflictions induce callosities, miseries are slippery, or fall like snow upon us, which notwithstanding is no unhappy stupidity. To be ignorant of evils to come, and forgetful of evils past, is a merciful provision in nature, whereby we digest the mixture of our few and evil days, and our delivered senses not relapsing into cutting remembrances, our sorrows are not kept raw by the edge of repetitions. A great part of antiquity contented their hopes of subsistency with a transmigration of their souls. A good way to continue their memories, while having the advantage of plural successions, they could not but act something remarkable in such variety of beings, and enjoying the fame of their passed selves, make accumulation of glory unto their last durations. Others, rather than be lost in the uncomfortable night of nothing, were content to recede into the common being, and make one particle of the public soul of all things, which was no more than to return into their unknown and divine Original again. Egyptian ingenuity was more unsatisfied, contriving their bodies in sweet consistencies, to attend the return of their souls. But all was vanity, feeding the wind, and folly. The Egyptian mummies, which Cambyses or time hath spared, avarice now consumeth. Mummy is become merchandise, Mizraim cures wounds, and Pharaoh is sold for balsams.

In vain do individuals hope for immortality, or any patent from oblivion, in preservations below the moon; men have been deceived even in their flatteries above the sun, and studied conceits to perpetuate their names in heaven. The various cosmography of that part hath already varied the names of contrived constellations; Nimrod is lost in Orion, and Osiris in the Dog-star. While we look for incorruption in the heavens, we find they are but like the earth;—durable in their main bodies, alterable in their parts: whereof beside comets and new stars, perspectives begin to tell tales. And the spots that wander about the sun, with Phaeton's favour, would make clear conviction.

There is nothing strictly immortal, but immortality; whatever hath no beginning, may be confident of no end—which is the peculiar of that necessary Essence that cannot destroy itself; and the highest strain of omnipotency, to be so powerfully

---

1. Canaanitish woman. See Matthew 15:27-28.   **2. Herodias.** See Mark 6:22-25.   **3-4. good thief . . . Pilate?** See Luke 23.   **13-14. Thersites,** the most scurrilous of the Greeks before Troy.   **27. century,** hundred.   **30-31. that current arithmetic,** that steadily moving progression.   **32. Lucina,** the goddess of childbirth.   **33. pagans.** "Euripides." (Browne)   **37. ashes.** "According to the custom of the Jews, who place a lighted wax-candle in a pot of ashes by the corpse." (Browne)   **brother of death.** Sleep and Death are in Greek mythology the children of Night.

1. induce callosities, dull our sensitiveness.   **26-27. Mummy . . . merchandise.** In the seventeenth century, mummy powder was used as a specific for certain diseases.   **Mizraim,** Egypt.   **30. patent,** protection.   **40. perspectives,** telescopes.   **41. Phaeton's favour.** Phaëthon, in classical mythology, was the unlucky son of Helios (the Sun) who set heaven and earth on fire in the attempt to drive his father's chariot.   **45. peculiar,** peculiar characteristic.

constituted as not to suffer even from the power of itself: all others have a dependent being, and within the reach of destruction. But the sufficiency of Christian immortality frustrates all earthly glory, and the quality of either state after death makes a folly of posthumous memory. God who can only destroy our souls, and hath assured our resurrection, either of our bodies or names hath directly promised no duration. Wherein there is so much of chance, that the boldest expectants have found unhappy frustration; and to hold long subsistence, seems but a scape in oblivion. But man is a noble animal, splendid in ashes, and pompous in the grave, solemnizing nativities and deaths with equal lustre, nor omitting ceremonies of bravery in the infamy of his nature.

Life is a pure flame, and we live by an invisible sun within us. A small fire sufficeth for life, great flames seemed too little after death, while men vainly affected precious pyres, and to burn like Sardanapalus, but the wisdom of funeral laws found the folly of prodigal blazes, and reduced undoing fires unto the rule of sober obsequies, wherein few could be so mean as not to provide wood, pitch, a mourner, and an urn.

Five languages secured not the epitaph of Gordianus. The man of God lives longer without a tomb then any by one, invisibly interred by angels, and adjudged to obscurity, though not without some marks directing human discovery. Enoch and Elias without either tomb or burial, in an anomalous state of being, are the great examples of perpetuity, in their long and living memory, in strict account being still on this side death, and having a late part yet to act upon this stage of earth. If in the decretory term of the world we shall not all die but be changed, according to received translation; the last day will make but few graves; at least quick resurrections will anticipate lasting sepultures; some graves will be opened before they be quite closed, and Lazarus be no wonder. When many that feared to die shall groan that they can die but once, the dismal state is the second and living death, when life puts despair on the damned; when men shall wish the coverings of mountains, not of monuments, and annihilations shall be courted.

While some have studied monuments, others have studiously declined them: and some have been so vainly boisterous that they durst not acknowledge their graves; wherein Alaricus seems most subtle, who had a river turned to hide his bones at the bottom. Even Sylla, that thought himself safe in his urn, could not prevent revenging tongues, and stones thrown at his monument. Happy are they whom privacy makes innocent, who deal so with men in this world, that they are not afraid to meet them in the next, who when they die, make no commotion among the dead, and are not touched with that poetical taunt of Isaiah.

Pyramids, arches, obelisks, were but the irregularities of vain glory, and wild enormities of ancient magnanimity. But the most magnanimous resolution rests in the Christian religion, which trampleth upon pride, and sits on the neck of ambition, humbly pursuing that infallible perpetuity unto which all others must diminish their diameters, and be poorly seen in angles of contingency.

Pious spirits who passed their days in raptures of futurity made little more of this world than the world that was before it, while they lay obscure in the chaos of pre-ordination, and night of their fore-beings. And if any have been so happy as truly to understand Christian annihilation, extasis, exolution, liquefaction, transformation, the kiss of the Spouse, gustation of God, and ingression into the divine shadow, they have already had an handsome anticipation of heaven; the glory of the world is surely over, and the earth in ashes unto them.

To subsist in lasting monuments, to live in their productions, to exist in their names and predicament of chimaeras, was large satisfaction unto old expectations, and made one part of their Elysiums. But all this is nothing in the metaphysics of true belief. To live indeed is to be again ourselves, which being not only an hope but an evidence in noble believers, 'tis all one to lie in St. Innocent's churchyard, as in the sands of Egypt: ready to be anything, in the ecstasy of being ever, and as content with six foot as the Moles of Adrianus.

"——*Tabesne cadavera solvat*
An rogus haud refert."—LUCAN

12. taunt of Isaiah. See Isaiah 14:9. **20. angles of contingency.** "*Angulus contingentiae*, the least of angles." (Browne) **26–29. Christian annihilation . . . divine shadow**, terms used in mystical writings to express the mystical union with the divine. **39–40. St. Innocent's churchyard.** "In Paris, where bodies soon consume." (Browne) **42. the Moles of Adrianus.** "A stately mausoleum or sepulchral pile, built by Adrianus in Rome, where now standeth the Castle of St. Angelo." (Browne) **44–45. "Tabesne . . . refert."** "It matters little whether earth or the funeral pyre consumes the corpses."

6. can only, can alone. **12. scape in,** poor evasion of. **15. bravery,** ostentation. **26–27. epitaph of Gordianus.** "In Greek, Latin, Hebrew, Egyptian, Arabic; defaced by Licinius the emperor." (Browne) **man of God,** Moses. See Deuteronomy 34. **30–31. Enoch and Elias.** See Genesis 5:24 and II Kings 2:11. **36. decretory term,** the decreed end. **41. Lazarus be no wonder.** See John 11. **45. coverings of mountains.** See Luke 23:30 and Revelation 6:16.

Thomas Fuller
1608–1661

It is a great pity that almost all Fuller's works are out of print, except for the selections in anthologies, and all such selections put together would be hardly more than a straw in the great haystack of his writings. Nor could they give more than a hint of the richness and variety of his work, and the robust, whimsical, persistently good-natured spirit that produced them. He may be safely recommended as a cure for depression. Most of his books were produced in troubled years, and among them are several expressly designed to afford relief, with the characteristically humorous titles *Good Thoughts in Bad Times*, *Good Thoughts in Worse Times*, and *Mixed Contemplations in Better Times*.

He was born in the same year as Milton, and in the same village as John Dryden—Aldwinkle in Northamptonshire. He was at Cambridge while Milton was there, though not in Milton's college, and there is no proof that they knew each other. He gained high honors at college, and received his B.A. and M.A. degrees in 1625 and 1628. After leaving the university Fuller entered the Church, performed pastoral duties at Salisbury and elsewhere, and before the Civil War had risen to be "lecturer" at the Savoy Chapel in the Strand, where he became the most popular preacher in England. When war broke out, he joined the King's forces at Oxford as chaplain. He went to Exeter with the royal army and while there was made chaplain to the infant Princess Henrietta Ann. After the surrender of Exeter to the Parliamentarians in 1646, he returned to London, where, although he was a Royalist, he was allowed to preach at St. Clement's in Eastcheap. There were other changes of scene and fortune until the Restoration, when he was restored to the Savoy, appointed preacher at St. Bride's, Fleet Street, and made chaplain to Charles II. He would undoubtedly have been made a bishop had he not died untimely in the year following the Restoration.

During all these turns of Fortune's wheel, Fuller continued to produce books large and small, pamphlets, sermons, meditations, characters, biographies, and histories. The more important of them are his *History of the Holy War*, 1639, an account of the crusades; *The Holy State and the Profane State*, 1642, a collection of essays on types of characters and brief biographies; *The Church History of Britain* and *The History of the University of Cambridge*, 1655; and the monumental *History of the Worthies of England*, which was published the year after his death.

It would be impossible to sum up the character of Fuller and his writings in a few words. His was one of the most learned and most wayward fancies. "Quaint" is the word that most nineteenth-century critics fell back upon to describe him. He has been more often likened to Charles Lamb than to any other, and it was Lamb who, with excessive enthusiasm, introduced him to the last century. Fuller was as little troubled as Lamb by the exigencies of logic and the virtues of unity, coherence, and emphasis, and he has not escaped criticism for his perpetual playfulness and his incorrigible habit of introducing into his work anecdotes and odd bits of information, whether relevant or not. A contemporary of his, Dr. Peter Heylin, wrote a bitter attack on the *Church History*, ironically suggesting that the extraneous odds and ends of Fuller's book be put into a book by themselves as "a supplement to the old book entitled *Wits, Fits, and Fancies*." It is characteristic of Fuller that his *Appeal of Injured Innocence*, the reply to Heylin's caustic criticism, should end with a letter "To my Loving Friend, Dr. Peter Heylin."

In the history of English biography, Fuller's *History of the Worthies of England* stands as a sort of ancestor of the modern dictionaries of national biography. He was an antiquarian, with the most famous memory of the century, and gathered information of every kind, from all sorts and conditions of men, which he wove into a unique historical tapestry. His style is a fit medium for his thought. Of all the learned writers of his times, he uses the fewest Latin words and phrases. His English is homely and colloquial, and shot through with proverbial expressions and pithy sayings. He can be as ingeniously figurative as Donne and the other metaphysicals, and he has annoyed many of the more sober and literal-minded with his puns, his bizarre metaphors, quiddities, and conceits. If he is the most digressive of historians and the most gossipy of biographers, he is also the most kindly analyst of human character. A contemporary described him as a "walking library," but no scholar ever wore his learning so lightly, and by few others have so many true words been spoken in jest.

from THE HISTORY OF THE WORTHIES OF ENGLAND

DEVONSHIRE

Sir Walter Raleigh

THE sons of Heth said unto Abraham, thou art a great prince amongst us; in the choice of our sepulchres bury thy dead, none shall withhold them from thee." So may we say to the memory of this worthy knight, "Repose yourself in this our catalogue under what topic you please, of statesman, seaman, soldier, learned writer, and what not?" His worth unlocks our closest cabinets; and provides both room and welcome to entertain him.

He was born at Budeley in this County, of an ancient family, but decayed in estate, and he the youngest brother thereof. He was bred in Oriel College in Oxford; and thence coming to court, found some hopes of the queen's favours reflecting upon him. This made him write in a glass window, obvious to the queen's eye,

"Fain would I climb, yet fear I to fall."

Her majesty, either espying or being shown it, did underwrite,

"If thy heart fails thee, climb not at all."

However, he at last *climbed* up by the *stairs* of his own desert. But his introduction into the court bore an elder date; from this occasion. This captain Raleigh coming out of Ireland to the English Court in good habit (his clothes being then a considerable part of his estate) found the queen walking, till, meeting with a plashy place, she seemed to scruple going thereon. Presently Raleigh cast and spread his new plush cloak on the ground; whereon the queen trod gently, rewarding him afterwards with many suits, for his so free and seasonable a tender of so fair a foot-cloth. Thus an advantageous admission into the first notice of a prince is more than half a degree to preferment.

It is reported of the women in the Balearic Islands, that, to make their sons expert archers, they will not, when children, give them their breakfast before they hit the mark. Such the dealing of the queen with this knight, making him to earn his honour, and, by pain and peril, to purchase what places of credit or profit were bestowed upon him. Indeed it was true of him, what was said of Cato Uticensis, "that he seemed to be born to that only which he went about"; so dexterous was he in all his undertakings, in court, in camp, by sea, by land, with sword, with pen; witness in the last his "History of the World," wherein the only default (or defect rather) that it wanted one half thereof. Yet had he many enemies (which worth never wants) at court, his cowardly detractors, of whom Sir Walter was wont to say, "If any man accuseth me to my face, I will answer him with my mouth; but my tail is good enough to return an answer to such who traduceth me behind my back."

WESTMINSTER

Benjamin Jonson

Benjamin Jonson was born in this city. Though I cannot, with all my industrious inquiry, find him in his cradle, I can fetch him from his long coats. When a little child, he lived in Harts-horn-lane near Charing-cross, where his mother married a brick-layer for her second husband.

He was first bred in a private school in Saint Martin's Church; then in Westminster School; witness his own epigram;

"Camden, most reverend head, to whom I owe
All that I am in arts, all that I know;
How nothing's that to whom my country owes
The great renown and name wherewith she goes,"
etc.

He was statutably admitted into Saint John's College in Cambridge (as many years after incorporated an honorary member of Christ Church in Oxford), where he continued but a few weeks for want of further maintenance, being fain to return to the trade of his father-in-law. And let them blush not that have, but those who have not, a lawful calling. He helped in the new structure of Lincoln's Inn, when, having a trowel in his hand, he had a book in his pocket.

Some gentlemen, pitying that his parts should be buried under the rubbish of so mean a calling, did by their bounty manumise him freely to follow his own ingenious inclinations. Indeed his parts were not so ready to run of themselves as able to answer the spur; so that it may be truly said of him, that he had an elaborate wit wrought out in his own industry. He would sit silent in a learned company, and suck in (besides wine) their several humours into his observation. What was ore in others, he was able to refine to himself.

37. Presently, immediately.

25. his own epigram, Epigram 14.   44. manumise, set free.

He was paramount in the dramatic art of poetry, and taught the stage an exact conformity to the laws of comedians. His comedies were above the *volge* (which are only tickled with downright obscenity), and took not so well at the first stroke as at the rebound, when beheld the second time; yea, they will endure reading, and that with due commendation, so long as either ingenuity or learning are fashionable in our nation. If his later be not so spriteful and vigorous as his first pieces, all that are old will, and all that desire to be old should, excuse him therein.

He was not very happy in his children, and most happy in those which died first; though none lived to survive him. This be bestowed as part of an epitaph on his eldest son, dying in infancy:

"Rest in soft peace; and, asked, say here doth lie, Ben Jonson his best piece of poetry."

He died *anno Domini* 1638, and was buried about the belfry, in the abbey church at Westminster.

WARWICKSHIRE

William Shakespeare

William Shakespeare was born at Stratford-on-Avon in this county; in whom three eminent poets may seem in some sort to be compounded. 1. Martial, in the warlike sound of his surname (whence some may conjecture him of military extraction) *Hastivibrans*, or Shake-speare. 2. Ovid, the most natural and witty of all poets; and hence it was that Queen Elizabeth, coming into a grammar school, made this extemporary phrase,

"Persius a crab-staff, bawdy Martial, Ovid a fine wag."

3. Plautus, who was an exact comedian, yet never any exact scholar, as our Shakespeare (if alive) would confess himself. Add to all these, that though his genius generally was jocular, and inclining him to festivity, yet he could (when so disposed) be solemn and serious, as appears by his tragedies; so that Heraclitus himself (I mean if secret and unseen) might afford to smile at his comedies, they were so merry; and Democritus scarce forbear to sigh at his tragedies, they were so mournful.

He was an eminent instance of the truth of that rule, *Poeta non fit sed nascitur* (one is not made but born a poet). Indeed his learning was very little; so that, as Cornish diamonds are not polished by any lapidary, but are pointed and smooth even as they are taken out of the earth, so nature itself was all the art which was used upon him.

Many were the wit-combats betwixt him and Ben Jonson; which two I behold like a Spanish great galleon and an English man-of-war; Master Jonson (like the former) was built far higher in learning; solid, but slow, in his performances. Shakespeare, with the English man-of-war, lesser in bulk, but lighter in sailing, could turn with all tides, tack about, and take advantage of all winds, by the quickness of his wit and invention. He died *anno Domini* 1616, and was buried at Stratford-on-Avon, the town of his nativity.

17–18. "Rest . . . poetry," Epigram 45.

Izaak Walton
1593–1683

It is pleasant and reassuring to reflect that one of the quietest and most peace-loving men in English literature, and his *Compleat Angler*, surely the serenest of books, were products of one of the least peaceful of centuries. While England was rent with the conflicts of King and Parliament, Episcopalians and Presbyterians, Walton found time to go fishing. Within a short while after the Civil War came to a crisis in the execution of the King, he was writing on the mysteries of angling and the amenities of the angler's life. The little book was published in his sixtieth year, in May, 1653, a month after Cromwell's dismissal of the Long Parliament, and, as Andrew Lang has observed, just at the season when men expect the May fly.

As with Herrick, whose long life was almost exactly contemporaneous with Walton's, the known facts of his external life are few and relatively unimportant. He was born in Staffordshire, was apprenticed to an ironmonger, and practiced his trade in London. By his twenty-fifth year he was a freeman of the Ironmongers' Company, and retired from work when he was fifty. Walton lived in London most of his life, but his mind and heart were in the green pastures and beside the still waters of Staffordshire and Hampshire. He seems to have preferred the society of anglers and clergymen (whom he was always pleased to think of as fishers of souls) to that of ironmongers. His second wife was a half-sister of Bishop Thomas Ken, author of hymns still sung today, including the most familiar of English doxologies, "Praise God from Whom All Blessings Flow."

He was a Royalist, but of his activities during the Civil War only one that has any connection with the cause has been recorded. He was entrusted with the carrying of one of Charles II's Garter jewels to London after the Battle of Worcester in 1651. The mission was not without its risks, but Walton undertook it and carried it through. The intellectual and religious strains and perplexities of the time seem to have troubled him no more than did the political and economic issues. He studied to be quiet, and lived to be ninety. He lies buried, not far from Jane Austen, in Winchester Cathedral, and a memorial window has been erected to him by the anglers of England and America.

Walton, like every young man of his day, tried his hand at poetry, but he was past middle age when the first work of any consequence came from his pen. It was the *Life of Dr. John Donne*, which was prefixed to the 1640 edition of Donne's *Sermons*. Walton was a parishioner, as well as a friend and admirer, of Donne, and he had already written commendatory verses for the first two editions of Donne's poems. The success of his biography of Donne, and his inherent interest in and admiration for other distinguished men, led him a decade later to a further essay of the sort in his biography of his friend Sir Henry Wotton. This was followed over a period of years by his lives of Richard Hooker, George Herbert, and Bishop Robert Sanderson. The last appeared when he was eighty-five years old. As a biographer, Walton has been praised as the greatest, and certainly the most readable, in England before Boswell. Professor Saintsbury considers him unique "in having obtained and retained fame by a pair of books so different in character and treatment of subject as *The Compleat Angler* and the collection of short biographies."

Both the *Lives* and the *Compleat Angler* were more successful than he or his publishers could have hoped. All the biographies except that of Sanderson went into later editions during his life, and the *Angler* had attained to a fifth edition before his death. Walton's unpretentious little book on angling was one of the first English books to be advertised in a newspaper. The *Perfect Diurnal* and the *Mercurius Politicus* both contained notices of its appearance in May, 1653. Since then it has gone through more than a hundred editions, some of them so expensive that Walton would not be able to purchase them with a whole year's income from his ironmongering. Of the original editions only a very few copies have survived the hands of the anglers for whom they were intended. The price of *The Compleat Angler* in 1653 was eighteenpence. Nearly three centuries later, in 1940, in the midst of a war, savage beyond Walton's power to imagine, the five editions of the book which appeared in his lifetime were sold to an American for £1,600. It is not easy to say just why a technical treatise on fishing written for English anglers of three hundred years ago should have become one of the most popular and best-beloved books in the language. It seems to fulfill none of the requirements which a professional critic would prescribe for such a destiny. Perhaps it is because the more complex the world becomes, and the farther it removes from such streams and meadows and peaceful pursuits as Walton knew and described, the more appealing becomes the philosophy of a life and a book so simple, unified, and well ordered.

THE COMPLEAT ANGLER

Chapter 4

OBSERVATIONS OF THE NATURE AND BREEDING OF THE TROUT; AND HOW TO FISH FOR HIM. AND THE MILKMAID'S SONG

Piscator. The trout is a fish highly valued, both in this and foreign nations. He may be justly said, as the old poet said of wine and we English say of venison, to be a generous fish; a fish that is so like the buck that he also has his seasons, for it is observed that he comes in and goes out of his season with the stag and buck. Gesner says his name is of a German offspring, and says he is a fish that feeds cleanly and purely, in the swiftest streams and on

---

1. Piscator. *The Compleat Angler* is, for the most part, "A Conference betwixt an Angler [Piscator], a Falconer [Auceps], and a Hunter [Venator], each Commending His Recreation."   **7. Gesner**, Konrad Gesner (1516–1565), a learned physician and naturalist of Zurich. His principal works (which Walton knew only at third hand) were his *Historia Animalium* (*History of Animals*) and *De Piscibus et Aquatilibus* (*Of Fishes and Water Animals*).

the hardest gravel, and that he may justly contend with all fresh water fish, as the mullet may with all sea fish, for precedency and daintiness of taste; and that being in right season, the most dainty palates have allowed precedency to him.

And before I go farther in my discourse, let me tell you that you are to observe that as there be some barren does that are good in summer so there be some barren trouts that are good in winter; but there are not many that are so, for usually they be in their perfection in the month of May and decline with the buck. Now you are to take notice that in several countries, as in Germany and in other parts, compared to ours, fish do differ much in their bigness and shape and other ways; and so do trouts. It is well known that in the Lake Leman, the Lake of Geneva, there are trouts taken of three cubits long, as is affirmed by Gesner, a writer of good credit, and Mercator says the trouts that are taken in the Lake of Geneva are a great part of the merchandise of that famous city. And you are further to know that there be certain waters that breed trouts remarkable both for their number and smallness. I know a little brook in Kent that breeds them to a number incredible, and you may take them twenty or forty in an hour, but none greater than about the size of a gudgeon. There are also in divers rivers, especially that relate to or be near the sea, as Winchester or the Thames about Windsor, a little trout called a samlet or skegger trout, in both which places I have caught twenty or forty at a standing, that will bite as fast and as freely as minnows; these be by some taken to be young salmons, but in those waters they never grow to be bigger than a herring.

There is also in Kent near to Canterbury a trout called there a Fordidge trout, a trout that bears the name of the town where it is usually caught, that is accounted the rarest of fish, many of them near the bigness of a salmon, but known by their different color, and in their best season cut very white; and none of these have been known to be caught with an angle, unless it were one that was caught by Sir George Hastings, an excellent angler, now with God; and he hath told me, he thought that trout bit not for hunger but for wantonness; and it is the rather to be believed, because both he and many others before him have been curious to search into their bellies, what the food was by which they lived; and have found nothing by which they might satisfy their curiosity.

Concerning which you are to take notice that it is reported by good authors that grasshoppers and some fish have no mouths, but are nourished and take breath by the porousness of their gills, man knows not how; and this may be believed, if we consider that when the raven hath hatched her eggs, she takes no further care, but leaves her young ones to the care of the God of nature, who is said, in the Psalms, "to feed the young ravens that call upon him." And they be kept alive and fed by a dew, or worms that breed in their nests, or some other ways that we mortals know not. And this may be believed of the Fordidge trout which, as it is said of the stork that he knows his season, so he knows his times, I think almost his day, of coming into that river out of the sea, where he lives and, it is like, feeds nine months of the year, and about three in the river of Fordidge. And you are to note that those townsmen are very punctual in observing the very time of beginning to fish for them; and boast much that their river affords a trout that exceeds all others. And just so doth Sussex boast of several fish; as namely a Shelsey cockle, a Chichester lobster, an Arundel mullet, and an Amerly trout.

And now for some confirmation of the Fordidge trout: you are to know that this trout is thought to eat nothing in the fresh water; and it may be the better believed because it is well known that swallows and bats and wagtails, which are called half-year birds, and not seen to fly in England for six months in the year, but about Michaelmas leave us for a hotter climate, yet some of them that have been left behind their fellows, have been found, many thousands at a time, in hollow trees, where they have been observed to live and sleep out the whole winter without meat; and so Albertus observes that there is one kind of frog that hath her mouth naturally shut up about the end of August and that she lives so all the winter; and though it be strange to some, yet it is known to too many among us to be doubted.

And so much for these Fordidge trouts, which never afford an angler sport, but either live their time of being in the fresh water by their meat formerly gotten in the sea, not unlike the swallow or

17. cubits. The cubit, an ancient measure of length, represents the length of the forearm, 18 to 22 inches. **19. Mercator,** Gerard Mercator (1512–1594), a famous Flemish mathematician, geographer, and theologian. Walton, as in the case of other learned writers, is quoting him at third hand.

5. some fish have no mouths. The reader will not need to have pointed out to him either Walton's appetite for the strange and curious, or his amiable garrulity with respect to all sorts and conditions of fishes. **38. Albertus,** St. Albertus Magnus (1193?–1280), a German Dominican monk who became Bishop of Ratisbon. He wrote on many learned subjects, and his devotion to occult sciences got him the name among the vulgar of being a magician. Walton knew him only through quotations in other writers.

frog, or by virtue of the fresh water only; or as the birds of paradise and the chameleon are said to live, by the sun and the air.

There is also in Northumberland a trout called a bull-trout, of a much greater length and bigness than any in these southern parts; and there is in many rivers that relate to the sea salmon-trouts, as much different from others both in shape and in their spots, as we see sheep differ one from another in their shape and bigness, and in the fineness of their wool; and certainly, as some pastures breed larger sheep, so do some rivers by reason of the ground over which they run breed larger trouts.

Now the next thing that I will commend to your consideration is that the trout is of a more sudden growth than other fish. Concerning which you are also to take notice that he lives not so long as the perch and divers other fishes do, as Sir Francis Bacon hath observed in his *History of Life and Death*.

And next you are to take notice that he is not like the crocodile, which if he lives never so long, yet always thrives till his death; but 'tis not so with the trout, for after he is come to his full growth, he declines in his body, but keeps his bigness or thrives only in his head till his death. And you are to know that he will about (especially before) the time of his spawning get almost miraculously through weirs and flood-gates against the stream, even through such high and swift places as is almost incredible. Next, that the trout usually spawns about October or November, but in some rivers a little sooner or later. Which is the more observable because most other fish spawn in the spring or summer when the sun hath warmed both the earth and water and made it fit for generation. And you are to note that he continues for many months out of season; for it may be observed of the trout that he is like the buck or the ox that will not be fat in many months, though he go in the same pastures that horses do which will be fat in one month; and so you may observe that most other fishes recover strength and grow sooner fat and in season than the trout doth.

And next you are to note that till the sun gets to such a height as to warm the earth and the water the trout is sick, and lean, and lousy, and unwholesome; for you shall in winter find him to have a big head and then to be lank, and thin, and lean; at which time many of them have sticking on them sugs, or trout-lice, which is a kind of a worm in shape like a clove or pin with a big head, and sticks close to him and sucks his moisture; those, I think, the trout breeds himself, and never thrives till he free himself from them, which is when warm weather comes; and then, as he grows stronger, he gets from the dead, still water into the sharp streams and the gravel and there rubs off these worms or lice, and then as he grows stronger, so he gets himself into swifter and swifter streams, and there lies at the watch for any fly or minnow that comes near to him; and he especially loves the May-fly, which is bred of the cod-worm or caddis; and these make the trout bold and lusty, and he is usually fatter and better meat at the end of that month than at any time of the year.

Now you are to know that it is observed that usually the best trouts are either red or yellow, though some, as the Fordidge trout, be white and yet good; but that is not usual. And it is a note observable that the female trout hath usually a less head and a deeper body than the male trout, and is usually the better meat. And note, that a hog-back and a little head to either trout, salmon, or any other fish, is a sign that that fish is in season.

But yet you are to note, that as you see some willows or palm-trees bud and blossom sooner than others do, so some trouts be, in rivers, sooner in season; and as some hollies or oaks are longer before they cast their leaves, so are some trouts, in rivers, longer before they go out of season.

And you are to note, that there are several kinds of trouts. But these several kinds are not considered but by very few men; for they go under the general name of trouts; just as pigeons do, in most places, though it is certain there are tame and wild pigeons; and of the tame there be helmits and runts and carriers and cropers, and indeed too many to name. Nay, the Royal Society have found and published lately that there be thirty and three kinds of spiders; and yet all, for aught I know, go under that one general name of spider. And it is so with many kinds of fish, and of trouts especially, which differ in their bigness and shape and spots and colour. The great Kentish hens may be an instance, compared to other hens; and doubtless there is a kind of small trout which will never thrive to be big that breeds very many more than others do that be of a larger size. Which you may rather believe, if you consider that the little wren and titmouse will have twenty young ones at a time, when usually the noble hawk, or the musical throstle or blackbird, exceed not four or five.

And now you shall see me try my skill to catch a trout; and at my next walking, either this evening or to-morrow morning, I will give you direction how you yourself shall fish for him.

Venator. Trust me, master, I see now it is a harder matter to catch a trout than a chub; for I have put on patience and followed you these two hours and not seen a fish stir, neither at your minnow nor your worm.

Piscator. Well, scholar, you must endure worse luck sometime, or you will never make a good angler. But what say you now? There is a trout now, and a good one too, if I can but hold him; and two or three turns more will tire him. Now you see where he lies still, and the sleight is to land him. Reach me that landing-net. So, Sir, now he is mine own. What say you now? is not this worth all my labour and your patience?

Venator. On my word, master, this is a gallant trout; what shall we do with him?

Piscator. Marry, e'en eat him to supper. We'll go to my hostess from whence we came; she told me, as I was going out of door, that my brother Peter, a good angler and a cheerful companion, had sent word he would lodge there tonight and bring a friend with him. My hostess has two beds, and I know you and I may have the best. We'll rejoice with my brother Peter and his friend, tell tales, or sing ballads, or make a catch, or find some harmless sport to content us, and pass away a little time without offence to God or man.

Venator. A match, good master, let's go to that house, for the linen looks white and smells of lavender, and I long to lie in a pair of sheets that smell so. Let's be going, good master, for I am hungry again with fishing.

Piscator. Nay, stay a little, good scholar. I caught my last trout with a worm, now I will put on a minnow and try a quarter of an hour about yonder trees for another, and so walk towards our lodgings. Look you, scholar, thereabout we shall have a bite presently, or not at all. Have with you, Sir! O' my word, I have hold of him. Oh, it is a great loggerheaded chub! Come, hang him upon that willow twig, and let's be going. But turn out of the way a little, good scholar, towards yonder high honeysuckle hedge. There we'll sit and sing whilst this shower falls so gently upon the teeming earth and gives yet a sweeter smell to the lovely flowers that adorn these verdant meadows.

Look! under that broad beech-tree I sat down when I was last this way a-fishing; and the birds in the adjoining grove seemed to have a friendly contention with an echo whose dead voice seemed to live in a hollow tree near to the brow of that primrose-hill. There I sat viewing the silver streams glide silently towards their centre, the tempestuous sea, yet sometimes opposed by rugged roots and pebblestones, which broke their waves and turned them into foam. And sometimes I beguiled time by viewing the harmless lambs, some leaping securely in the cool shade, whilst others sported themselves in the cheerful sun; and saw others craving comfort from the swollen udders of their bleating dams. As I thus sat, these and other sights had so fully possessed my soul with content that I thought, as the poet has happily expressed it,

"I was for that time lifted above earth,
And possessed joys not promised in my birth."

As I left this place, and entered into the next field, a second pleasure entertained me; 'twas a handsome milkmaid that had not yet attained so much age and wisdom as to load her mind with any fears of many things that will never be, as too many men often do; but she cast away all care, and sung like a nightingale. Her voice was good, and the ditty fitted for it; 'twas that smooth song which was made by Kit Marlowe, now at least fifty years ago: and the milkmaid's mother sung an answer to it, which was made by Sir Walter Raleigh in his younger days.

They were old-fashioned poetry, but choicely good, I think much better than the strong lines that are now in fashion in this critical age. Look yonder! on my word, yonder they both be a-milking again. I will give her the chub, and persuade them to sing those two songs to us.

God speed you, good woman. I have been a-fishing, and am going to Bleak Hall to my bed, and having caught more fish than will sup myself and my friend, I will bestow this upon you and your daughter, for I use to sell none.

Milkwoman. Marry! God requite you, Sir, and we'll eat it cheerfully. And if you come this way a-fishing two months hence, a grace of God! I'll give you a syllabub of new verjuice, in a new-made hay-cock, for it. And my Maudlin shall sing you one of her best ballads, for she and I both love all anglers, they be such honest, civil, quiet men. In the meantime will you drink a draught of red cow's milk? You shall have it freely.

Piscator. No, I thank you, but I pray do us a courtesy that shall stand you and your daughter in nothing, and we will think ourselves still something in your debt. It is but to sing us a song that was sung by you and your daughter when I last passed over this meadow, about eight or nine days since.

Milkwoman. What song was it, I pray? Was it "Come, Shepherds, deck your herds" or "As at noon Dulcina rested" or "Phillida flouts me" or "Chevy Chase," or "Johnny Armstrong," or "Troy Town"?

37. **verjuice,** sour juice of green apples or grapes.

Piscator. No, it is none of those. It is a song that your daughter sung the first part, and you sung the answer to it.

Milkwoman. Oh, I know it now. I learned the first part in my golden age, when I was about the age of my poor daughter; and the latter part, which indeed fits me best now, but two or three years ago, when the cares of the world began to take hold of me. But you shall, God willing, hear them both; and sung as well as we can, for we both love anglers. Come, Maudlin, sing the first part to the gentlemen with a merry heart, and I'll sing the second, when you have done.

THE MILKMAID'S SONG

    Come live with me, and be my love,
    And we will all the pleasures prove
    That valleys, groves, or hills, or fields,
    Or woods, and steepy mountain yields.

    Where we will sit upon the rocks
    And see the shepherds feed our flocks
    By shallow rivers, to whose falls
    Melodious birds sing madrigals.

    And I will make thee beds of roses,
    And then a thousand fragrant posies,
    A cap of flowers, and a kirtle
    Embroidered all with leaves of myrtle;

    A gown made of the finest wool
    Which from our pretty lambs we pull,
    Slippers lined choicely for the cold
    With buckles of the purest gold;

    A belt of straw, and ivy-buds,
    With coral clasps, and amber studs;
    And if these pleasures may thee move,
    Come live with me, and be my love.

    Thy silver dishes for thy meat,
    As precious as the gods do eat,
    Shall on an ivory table be
    Prepared each day for thee and me.

    The shepherd swains shall dance and sing
    For thy delight each May morning:
    If these delights thy mind may move,
    Then live with me, and be my love.

Venator. Trust me, master, it is a choice song, and sweetly sung by honest Maudlin. I see now it was not without cause that our good Queen Elizabeth did so often wish herself a milkmaid all the month of May, because they are not troubled with fears and cares, but sing sweetly all the day and sleep securely all the night. And without doubt honest, innocent, pretty Maudlin does so. I'll bestow Sir Thomas Overbury's milkmaid's wish upon her, "that she may die in the spring; and have good store of flowers stuck round about her winding-sheet."

THE MILKMAID'S MOTHER'S ANSWER

    If all the world and love were young,
    And truth in every shepherd's tongue,
    These pretty pleasures might me move
    To live with thee, and be thy love.

    But time drives flocks from field to fold,
    When rivers rage, and rocks grow cold,
    Then Philomel becometh dumb,
    And age complains of cares to come.

    The flowers do fade, and wanton fields
    To wayward winter reckoning yields.
    A honey tongue, a heart of gall,
    Is fancy's spring, but sorrow's fall.

    Thy gowns, thy shoes, thy beds of roses,
    Thy cap, thy kirtle, and thy posies,
    Soon break, soon wither, soon forgotten,
    In folly ripe, in reason rotten.

    Thy belt of straw, and ivy-buds,
    Thy coral clasps, and amber studs,
    All these in me no means can move
    To come to thee, and be thy love.

    What should we talk of dainties then,
    Of better meat than's fit for men?
    These are but vain; that's only good
    Which God hath blessed, and sent for food.

    But could youth last, and love still breed,
    Had joys no date, nor age no need;
    Then those delights my mind might move
    To live with thee, and be thy love.

Mother. Well, I have done my song. But stay, honest anglers; for I will make Maudlin to sing you one short song more. Maudlin! sing that song that you sung last night, when young Coridon the shepherd played so purely on his oaten pipe to you and your cousin Betty.

Maudlin. I will, mother.

> I married a wife of late,
> The more's my unhappy fate:
>   I married her for love,
>   As my fancy me did move,
> And not for a worldly estate:
>   But oh! the green-sickness
>   Soon changed her likeness;
> And all her beauty did fail.
>   But 'tis not so
>   With those that go
> Through frost and snow,
>   As all men know,
> And carry the milking-pail.

Piscator. Well sung, good woman; I thank you. I'll give you another dish of fish one of these days; and then beg another song of you. Come, scholar! let Maudlin alone: do not you offer to spoil her voice. Look! yonder comes mine hostess, to call us to supper. How now! is my brother Peter come?

Hostess. Yes, and a friend with him. They are both glad to hear that you are in these parts, and long to see you, and long to be at supper, for they be very hungry.

John Milton
1608–1674

If Milton reached greater heights in poetry than others, it is partly because he prepared himself as few others ever did for his life's work, the writing of great poetry. Only Wordsworth in English literature ever gave himself so wholly to the cultivation of his art, and only Dante, perhaps, in the greater circle of poets, ever lived and wrote with such religious devotion and such keen awareness of his great Taskmaster's eye. His life is an almost unique example of a precocious youth, followed by a young manhood of brilliant performance, a middle age of unrelenting labor for the public welfare, and an old age of vigorous intellectual and poetic achievement.

He was born in London, the son of John and Sarah Milton. His father, a scrivener, had made a comfortable fortune in his business of drawing up business contracts, and was a musician and composer of songs. The mother, of whom little is known, destined her son for the Church, and devoted herself to his religious training. Milton's education was begun at home, and the boy took to his studies with such zeal that, as he says, "from my twelfth year I scarcely ever went to bed before midnight, which was the first cause of injury to my eyes." He later went to St. Paul's School and to Christ's College, Cambridge. Outside his studies, the most important circumstances in his early life was his friendship with Charles Diodati, a schoolfellow at St. Paul's. Milton had too much a mind of his own to be an entirely docile student. He objected to much in the curriculum, and had some difficulty in getting on with both his fellow students and with his tutor. The former, because of his domineering ways and his handsome face, dubbed him *Domina Christi*—the Lady of Christ's. The tutor had him disciplined and suspended for a term. He enjoyed his enforced holiday, and came back to college, where he won the esteem of the students, as much, perhaps, for his ability at fencing as for his intellectual eminence. He received his B.A. degree at twenty-one, in 1629. The most important of his early poems, the ode "On the Morning of Christ's Nativity," was composed in this year.

He left the university after taking his M.A. degree in 1632, and spent the next five years in study at his father's country house at Horton. The ripening of his poetic genius is shown in his chief compositions of this period—"L'Allegro," "Il Penseroso," *Comus*, and "Lycidas." The deepening of his religious convictions, and the entry of the Puritan seriousness into his poetry, are also to be noted in the latter two poems. During 1638 and 1639 he traveled on the Continent, where he met and was well received by distinguished men in letters, politics, and science. His travels were cut short by the news of the disputes between the King and Parliament, and his homecoming was saddened by the death of his friend Diodati.

Back in London, Milton expressed his grief for his lost friend in the Latin elegy "*Epitaphium Damonis*," the last of his early poems. He now settled down to teaching his two nephews and a few other young gentlemen. Out of this experience came in 1644 his tractate *On Education*, with its outline of an encyclopedic course of study, and its noble statement of the aims of "a complete and generous education."

During these middle years Milton's thoughts and energy were more and more taken up with problems of his own. He married in 1642 Mary Powell, the young daughter of a Royalist gentleman. The relations between them were not happy. Out of the unrest occasioned by his marriage came a series of divorce tracts arguing, in a daring way, for dissolution of marriage when husband and wife are spiritually and temperamentally incompatible.

His belief in the necessity of freedom of speech and the press produced in 1644 the *Areopagitica*, the noblest expression in the language of the essential goodness of man and of his possibilities when guided by reason and unhampered by the restrictions of an unwise censorship. In 1649 Cromwell appointed him Foreign Secretary, and for the next eleven years he gave to the Commonwealth his time, his talents, and his eyesight.

With the Restoration all that he had hoped and worked for seemed lost. He was arrested and heavily fined, but was released after a short while. The last ten years had also brought domestic changes and sorrows. Death had taken his infant son, his first wife, Mary Powell, and his second wife, Katherine Woodcock. In 1663 he married Elizabeth Minshull, and retired to a small house, where he again took up his poetry, which, except for a few sonnets, he had had to lay aside. In spite of circumstances that would have reduced most men to inactivity, he completed the work to which he had dedicated himself. *Paradise Lost*, 1667, *Paradise Regained*, 1671, and *Samson Agonistes*, 1671, though different in plan, structure, and content, constitute a great poetic trilogy in which finally and magnificently Milton restates and re-enforces his lifelong belief in the benevolent providence of God, under which man is essentially the master of his own fate, and by which man, though he may lose his earthly Paradise when passion gets the upper hand, may, through the exercise of reason and the aid of a Greater Man, restore his loss and regain the Paradise within.

ON THE MORNING OF CHRIST'S NATIVITY

This ode was composed in December, 1629, as a "birthday gift to Christ." Milton had come of age in that month, and was in his fourth year at Cambridge. It was first printed in the 1645 edition of Milton's poems. It is the finest production of his early maturity, and the first example of the serious and lofty style of which he was later to be the master. It is still, nevertheless, the poem of a young man who has not outgrown his fondness for the conceits and other literary devices of the Spenserians and the Elizabethan sonneteers in general. The erudition of the youthful author is evident throughout the poem. It is as Protestant in feeling as Crashaw's hymn "The Holy Nativity of Our Lord God" (page 614) is Catholic.

This is the month, and this the happy morn,
Wherein the Son of Heaven's eternal King,
Of wedded Maid and Virgin Mother born,
Our great redemption from above did bring;
For so the holy sages once did sing,
  That he our deadly forfeit should release,
And with his Father work us a perpetual peace.

That glorious form, that light unsufferable,
And that far-beaming blaze of majesty,   9
Wherewith he wont at Heaven's high council-table
To sit the midst of Trinal Unity,
He laid aside, and, here with us to be,
  Forsook the courts of everlasting day,
And chose with us a darksome house of mortal clay.

Say, Heavenly Muse, shall not thy sacred vein
Afford a present to the Infant God?
Hast thou no verse, no hymn, or solemn strain,
To welcome him to this his new abode,
Now while the heaven, by the sun's team untrod,
  Hath took no print of the approaching light, 20
And all the spangled host keep watch in squadrons bright?

See how from far upon the eastern road
The star-led wizards haste with odours sweet!
Oh! run; prevent them with thy humble ode,
And lay it lowly at his blessèd feet;
Have thou the honour first thy Lord to greet,
  And join thy voice unto the angel quire,
From out his secret altar touched with hallowed fire.

THE HYMN

It was the winter wild,
While the Heaven-born Child   30
  All meanly wrapt in the rude manger lies;

5. the holy sages, the Old Testament prophets. **6. he our deadly forfeit should release**, he should remit the fine or penalty of death which resulted from Adam's sin. **10. wont**, was wont, accustomed. **15. Say, Heavenly Muse.** Compare the invocation of the "Heavenly Muse" in *Paradise Lost*, Book I, ll. 6–7. **23. The star-led wizards**, the "Wise Men from the East." See Matthew 2:1–11. **24. prevent**, anticipate. **28. altar . . . fire.** See Isaiah 6:6. Milton's lips, purified by the hallowed fire, would join the "angel quire" in greeting Christ's birth. See Luke 2:13–14.

Nature in awe to him
Had doffed her gaudy trim,
　　With her great Master so to sympathize:
It was no season then for her
To wanton with the sun her lusty paramour.

Only with speeches fair
She woos the gentle air
　　To hide her guilty front with innocent snow,
And on her naked shame, 40
Pollute with sinful blame,
　　The saintly veil of maiden white to throw,
Confounded, that her Maker's eyes
Should look so near upon her foul deformities.

But he, her fears to cease,
Sent down the meek-eyed Peace;
　　She crowned with olive green came softly sliding
Down through the turning sphere,
His ready harbinger,
　　With turtle wing the amorous clouds dividing, 50
And waving wide her myrtle wand,
She strikes a universal peace through sea and land.

No war, or battle's sound,
Was heard the world around;
　　The idle spear and shield were high uphung;
The hookèd chariot stood,
Unstained with hostile blood;
　　The trumpet spake not to the armèd throng;
And kings sat still with awful eye,
As if they surely knew their sovran Lord was by. 60

But peaceful was the night
Wherein the Prince of Light
　　His reign of peace upon the earth began.
The winds, with wonder whist,
Smoothly the waters kissed,
　　Whispering new joys to the mild oceàn,
Who now hath quite forgot to rave,
While birds of calm sit brooding on the charmèd wave.

The stars, with deep amaze,
Stand fixed in steadfast gaze, 70
　　Bending one way their precious influence,
And will not take their flight,
For all the morning light,
　　Or Lucifer that often warned them thence;
But in their glimmering orbs did glow,
Until their Lord himself bespake, and bid them go.

And, though the shady gloom
Had given day her room,
　　The sun himself withheld his wonted speed,
And hid his head for shame, 80
As his inferior flame
　　The new-enlightened world no more should need:
He saw a greater Sun appear
Than his bright throne or burning axletree could bear.

The shepherds on the lawn,
Or ere the point of dawn,
　　Sat simply chatting in a rustic row;
Full little thought they than
That the mighty Pan
　　Was kindly come to live with them below; 90
Perhaps their loves or else their sheep,
Was all that did their silly thoughts so busy keep.

When such music sweet
Their hearts and ears did greet,
　　As never was by mortal finger strook,
Divinely warbled voice
Answering the stringèd noise,
　　As all their souls in blissful rapture took:
The air such pleasure loth to lose,
With thousand echoes still prolongs each heavenly close. 100

Nature that heard such sound
Beneath the hollow round
　　Of Cynthia's seat, the airy region thrilling,

---

39. guilty front. Nature is, like man, thought of as under a curse as the result of the Fall of Man. **46. Sent down the meek-eyed Peace.** Milton doubtless had in mind the representation of Peace in an allegorical masque or painting. **48. the turning sphere,** the whole globe of the stars, which, in the Ptolemaic conception of the universe, revolved daily about the earth. **50. turtle,** turtledove. **53–60. No war . . . by,** an allusion to the (relatively) peaceful interlude throughout the Roman Empire at the time of Christ's birth. **56. hookèd,** having hooks, or scythes, projecting from the axles. **59. awful,** full of awe. **64. whist,** hushed. **68. birds of calm,** an allusion to the halcyons, who, according to classical mythology, bred during a calm period at the winter solstice.

69. amaze, amazement, wonder. **71. influence.** The stars were supposed, in astrology, to affect or "influence" the lives of human beings. Milton represents their influence at the time of the birth of Christ as altogether beneficent. **74. Lucifer,** literally "Light-bearer." Either the morning star or the sun. **76. bespake,** spoke. **85. lawn,** field or pasture. **86. Or ere,** before. **88. than,** then. **89. the mighty Pan,** Christ. The Greek god Pan, the deity of universal nature, was frequently identified in the Renaissance poetry with Christ. **92. silly,** simple, innocent. **95. strook,** struck. **97. noise,** harmonious sound. **98. took,** captivated, bewitched. **100. close,** cadence. **102–03. the hollow round of Cynthia's seat,** the sphere of the moon. **thrilling,** penetrating.

Now was almost won
To think her part was done,
    And that her reign had here its last fulfilling;
She knew such harmony alone
Could hold all Heaven and Earth in happier union.

At last surrounds their sight
A globe of circular light,   110
    That with long beams the shame-faced night arrayed,
The helmèd cherubim
And swordèd seraphim
    Are seen in glittering ranks with wings displayed,
Harping in loud and solemn quire,
With unexpressive notes to Heaven's new-born Heir.

Such music (as 'tis said)
Before was never made,
    But when of old the Sons of Morning sung,
While the Creator great   120
His constellations set,
    And the well balanced world on hinges hung,
And cast the dark foundations deep,
And bid the weltering waves their oozy channel keep.

Ring out, ye crystal spheres!
Once bless our human ears,
    If ye have power to touch our senses so;
And let your silver chime
Move in melodious time;
    And let the bass of heaven's deep organ blow; 130
And with your ninefold harmony
Make up full consort to the angelic symphony.

For, if such holy song
Enwrap our fancy long,
    Time will run back and fetch the Age of Gold;
And speckled Vanity
Will sicken soon and die;
    And leprous Sin will melt from earthly mould;
And Hell itself will pass away,
And leave her dolorous mansions to the peering day.   140

Yea, Truth and Justice then
Will down return to men,
    Orbed in a rainbow; and, like glories wearing,
Mercy will sit between,
Throned in celestial sheen,
    With radiant feet the tissued clouds down steering;
And Heaven, as at some festival,
Will open wide the gates of her high palace-hall.

But wisest Fate says No,
This must not yet be so,   150
    The Babe lies yet in smiling infancy,
That on the bitter cross
Must redeem our loss,
    So both himself and us to glorify:
Yet first to those ychained in sleep,
The wakeful trump of doom must thunder through the deep,

With such a horrid clang
As on Mount Sinai rang,
    While the red fire and smould'ring clouds outbrake:
The agèd Earth aghast   160
With terror of that blast
    Shall from the surface to the centre shake;
When at the world's last session,
The dreadful Judge in middle air shall spread his throne.

And then at last our bliss
Full and perfect is,
    But now begins; for from this happy day
The old Dragon under ground
In straiter limits bound,
    Not half so far casts his usurpèd sway,   170
And, wroth to see His kingdom fail,
Swinges the scaly horror of his folded tail.

The oracles are dumb,
No voice or hideous hum
    Runs through the archèd roof in words deceiving.
Apollo from his shrine
Can no more divine,
    With hollow shriek the steep of Delphos leaving.

---

107. alone, of itself, without the aid of "Nature" and her system of spheres and so forth.   **116. unexpressive,** inexpressible.   **119–24. the Sons of Morning sung . . . keep.** See Job 38, page 540.   **125–27. Ring out . . . so.** "Let the music made by the turning of the nine celestial spheres become for once audible to human ears."—Hanford   **132. consort to,** union with.   **133–48. For, if such holy song . . . palace-hall.** Milton here makes a composite picture of the Christian millennium at the end of the world (Revelation 20–22) and the Golden Age of classical mythology, in which Astraea, goddess of justice, "will down return to man." **136. speckled,** plague-spotted.

143. like, similar.   **146. tissued,** as if made of "tissue," a cloth interwoven with silver.   **155. ychained,** chained. The "y," as often in Chaucer, is a survival of the Old English past-participial prefix, "ge." **sleep,** death.   **156. The wakeful trump of doom.** The awakening trumpet of the Day of Doom.   **157. horrid,** terrifying.   **158. As on Mount Sinai.** See Exodus 19:16.   **168. The old Dragon,** Satan. See Revelation 12:9.   **172. Swinges,** lashes.   **173–80. The oracles . . . cell.** Milton refers to the legend that at the time of Christ's birth pagan oracles ceased to make prophecies. **178. Delphos,** Delphi, the seat of the famous oracle of Apollo.

No nightly trance or breathèd spell
Inspires the pale-eyed priest from the prophetic cell.

The lonely mountains o'er, 181
And the resounding shore,
   A voice of weeping heard, and loud lament;
From haunted spring and dale,
Edged with poplar pale,
   The parting Genius is with sighing sent;
With flower-inwoven tresses torn
The nymphs in twilight shade of tangled thickets mourn.

In consecrated earth,
And on the holy hearth, 190
   The Lars and Lemures moan with midnight plaint;
In urns and altars round,
A drear and dying sound
   Affrights the Flamens at their service quaint;
And the chill marble seems to sweat,
While each peculiar power forgoes his wonted seat.

Peor and Baälim
Forsake their temples dim,
   With that twice-battered god of Palestine;
And moonèd Ashtaroth, 200
Heaven's queen and mother both,
   Now sits not girt with tapers' holy shine;
The Libyc Hammon shrinks his horn,
In vain the Tyrian maids their wounded Thammuz mourn.

And sullen Moloch fled,
Hath left in shadows dread
   His burning idol all of blackest hue;
In vain with cymbals' ring
They call the grisly king,
   In dismal dance about the furnace blue; 210
The brutish gods of Nile as fast,
Isis and Orus, and the dog Anubis, haste.

Nor is Osiris seen
In Memphian grove or green,
   Trampling the unshowered grass with lowings loud;
Nor can he be at rest
Within his sacred chest;
   Nought but profoundest Hell can be his shroud;
In vain, with timbrelled anthems dark,
The sable-stolèd sorcerers bear his worshipped ark. 220

He feels from Juda's land
The dreaded Infant's hand;
   The rays of Bethlehem blind his dusky eyn;
Nor all the gods beside
Longer dare abide,
   Not Typhon huge ending in snaky twine:
Our Babe, to show his Godhead true,
Can in his swaddling bands control the damnèd crew.

So, when the sun in bed,
Curtained with cloudy red, 230
   Pillows his chin upon an orient wave,
The flocking shadows pale
Troop to the infernal jail,
   Each fettered ghost slips to his several grave,
And the yellow-skirted fays
Fly after the night-steeds, leaving their moon-loved maze.

But see! the Virgin blest
Hath laid her Babe to rest.
   Time is our tedious song should here have ending:

---

186. Genius, the guardian spirit of a locality. **191. The Lars and Lemures,** in Roman mythology the household gods and spirits of the dead. **194. the Flamens at their service quaint,** the priests at their curious (or elaborate) service. **195. marble seems to sweat,** as a portent of the ill fate about to overtake the gods (**marble,** statue). **197-204. Peor and Baälim . . . mourn.** This and the next two stanzas are specially interesting as anticipating Milton's treatment of the demons in *Paradise Lost*. **Peor** is one of the sun gods, called Baals or **Baälim** (the Hebrew masculine plural), whose shrine was on Mount Peor in Moab. See Numbers 23:28. **199. that twice-battered god,** Dagon, the fish god, whose image was thrown down twice before the Ark of the Covenant. See I Samuel 5:4 and *Paradise Lost*, Book I, ll. 457-66. **200. Ashtaroth,** the Hebew feminine plural of Ashtoreth, or Astarte, identified with the moon. **203. Libyc Hammon,** or Ammon, the Egyptian deity, a ram god, whose shrine was in the Libyan desert. **204. Thammuz,** a Syrian god identified by the Greeks with Adonis, who was slain by a boar. See *Paradise Lost*, Book I, ll. 446-57. **205. Moloch,** a god of the Ammonites, in whose idol children were said to be burned. See *Paradise Lost*, Book I, l. 392.

212-13. Isis and Orus . . . Osiris. Isis was the sister and wife of Osiris, and mother of Orus (Horus). Isis was represented with cow's horns and the disk of the sun between them; Orus, with a hawk's head; and Osiris, the chief Egyptian deity, whose shrine was at Memphis, as a bull. **215. unshowered,** a reference to the lack of rain in Egypt. **220. his worshipped ark,** a small ark or chest in which a figure of the god was kept and carried in processions. **223. eyn,** the old plural of "eye." **226. Typhon,** the monster of Greek mythology, half man and half serpent, vanquished by Zeus and Hercules. **227-28. Our Babe . . . crew.** "The implication here is that Christ slew, or routed, Typhon, as Hercules strangled serpents in his cradle."— A. S. Cook. **231. orient,** lustrous, pearllike. **236. moon-loved maze,** the forests loved by Diana and the other gods.

Heaven's youngest-teemèd star 240
Hath fixed her polished car,
  Her sleeping Lord with handmaid lamp attending;
And all about the courtly stable
Bright-harnessed angels sit in order serviceable.

ON SHAKESPEARE

This poem, dated 1630 by Milton, was the first of his compositions to appear in print. It was among the commendatory poems prefixed to the Second Folio of Shakespeare's plays in 1632. It should be compared with Jonson's lines on Shakespeare in the First Folio, which perhaps suggested the theme to Milton. It is full of echoes from other poets, and the "conceit" in ll. 13–16 is in the best (or worst) manner of the fashionable verse of the time.

What needs my Shakespeare for his honoured bones
The labour of an age in pilèd stones?
Or that his hallowed reliques should be hid
Under a star-ypointing pyramid?
Dear son of memory, great heir of fame,
What need'st thou such weak witness of thy name?
Thou in our wonder and astonishment
Hast built thyself a livelong monument.
For whilst, to the shame of slow-endeavouring art,
Thy easy numbers flow, and that each heart 10
Hath from the leaves of thy unvalued book
Those Delphic lines with deep impression took,
Then thou, our fancy of itself bereaving,
Dost make us marble with too much conceiving,
And so sepùlchred in such pomp dost lie
That kings for such a tomb would wish to die.

HOW SOON HATH TIME

This sonnet was written either on or shortly after Milton's twenty-third birthday, December 9, 1631, and was first printed in 1645. He took his M.A. degree and left Cambridge about the time of its composition. Like other young men, he was faced with the problem of a future career, and was meeting with some criticism for not having already settled that problem. To a friend who had apparently expostulated with him for dreaming away his years "in the arms of studious retirement," Milton sent this sonnet, together with a letter which is preserved in the Trinity College MS. at Cambridge. "I am something suspicious of myself," he writes, "and do take notice of a certain belatedness in me," but he declares that his chief concern is the consideration of "how *best* to undergo, not taking thought of being *late*, so it give advantage to be more *fit*." For a similar expression of this philosophy of life see his sonnet "When I Consider How My Light Is Spent," page 735.

How soon hath Time, the subtle thief of youth,
  Stolen on his wing my three-and-twentieth year!
  My hasting days fly on with full career,
  But my late spring no bud or blossom shew'th.
Perhaps my semblance might deceive the truth
  That I to manhood am arrived so near;
  And inward ripeness doth much less appear,
  That some more timely-happy spirits endu'th.
Yet, be it less or more, or soon or slow,
  It shall be still in strictest measure even 10
  To that same lot, however mean or high,
Toward which Time leads me, and the will of Heaven.
  All is, if I have grace to use it so,
  As ever in my great Task-Master's eye.

L'ALLEGRO

The date of the two companion lyrics, "L'Allegro" and "Il Penseroso," is uncertain. Professor E. M. W. Tillyard assigns them to the summer of 1631 (*The Miltonic Setting*, Macmillan, 1938, p. 26), and recent scholarship connects them with Milton's university career rather than with the years of his retirement at Horton. They are the best known and best loved of Milton's poems. It has been estimated that more words, phrases, and expressions from them have entered into ordinary English speech than from any other poems of similar length.

The structure of the two poems follows the same general plan. They represent two contrasting, but not mutually exclusive or incompatible, poetic moods, and their author obviously takes as keen delight in depicting one series of experiences as the other. In them scholars have detected echoes of many poets and poems from Theocritus down to Milton's own contemporaries, but a comparison of Milton's lines and phrases with those of his suggested sources only serves to illustrate his genius and

---

240. **youngest-teemèd star,** newest-born star (the star of Bethlehem). 243. **courtly,** because serving as a king's residence. 244. **Bright-harnessed,** in bright armor. 3. **reliques,** remains. 4. **star-ypointing.** See note 155 on "ychained" on page 642. Milton has here prefixed the "y" to the present participle for the sake of the rhythm. 10. **numbers,** verses. Milton contrasts Shakespeare's spontaneous genius with the labor and pain of conscious artists. Compare "L'Allegro," ll. 134–35. 11. **unvalued,** invaluable. 12. **Delphic,** inspired (as by the oracle of Apollo at Delphi). 14. **conceiving,** thinking, imagining. Compare "Il Penseroso," l. 42.

5. **semblance,** outward appearance. 8. **timely-happy,** happy in the early maturity of their powers. **endu'th,** endows, supplies with intellectual vigor. 9. **it,** inward ripeness. 10. **still,** always. **even,** comfortable to. 13. **All,** all the affairs of life.

JOHN MILTON

to emphasize the originality of his mind and art. The title is Italian for "The Cheerful Man."

Hence, loathèd Melancholy,
   Of Cerberus and blackest Midnight born
In Stygian cave forlorn,
   'Mongst horrid shapes, and shrieks, and sights unholy!
Find out some uncouth cell,
   Where brooding Darkness spreads his jealous wings,
And the night-raven sings;
   There, under ebon shades and low-browed rocks,
As ragged as thy locks,
   In dark Cimmerian desert ever dwell.   10
But come, thou Goddess fair and free,
In heaven yclept Euphrosyne,
And by men heart-easing Mirth;
Whom lovely Venus, at a birth,
With two sister Graces more,
To ivy-crownèd Bacchus bore:
Or whether (as some sager sing)
The frolic wind that breathes the spring,
Zephyr, with Aurora playing,
As he met her once a-Maying,   20
There, on beds of violets blue,
And fresh-blown roses washed in dew,
Filled her with thee, a daughter fair,
So buxom, blithe, and debonair.
Haste thee, Nymph, and bring with thee
Jest, and youthful Jollity,
Quips and cranks and wanton wiles,
Nods and becks and wreathèd smiles,
Such as hang on Hebe's cheek,
And love to live in dimple sleek;   30
Sport that wrinkled Care derides,
And Laughter holding both his sides.
Come, and trip it, as you go,
On the light fantastic toe;
And in thy right hand lead with thee
The mountain-nymph, sweet Liberty;
And, if I give thee honour due,
Mirth, admit me of thy crew,
To live with her, and live with thee,
In unreprovèd pleasures free;   40
To hear the lark begin his flight,
And, singing, startle the dull night,
From his watch-tower in the skies,
Till the dappled dawn doth rise;
Then to come, in spite of sorrow,
And at my window bid good-morrow,
Through the sweet-briar or the vine,
Or the twisted eglantine;
While the cock, with lively din,
Scatters the rear of darkness thin;   50
And to the stack or the barn door,
Stoutly struts his dames before:
Oft listening how the hounds and horn
Cheerly rouse the slumbering morn,
From the side of some hoar hill,
Through the high wood echoing shrill:
Sometime walking, not unseen,
By hedgerow elms, on hillocks green,
Right against the eastern gate
Where the great sun begins his state,   60
Robed in flames and amber light,
The clouds in thousand liveries dight;
While the ploughman, near at hand,
Whistles o'er the furrowed land,
And the milkmaid singeth blithe,
And the mower whets his scythe,
And every shepherd tells his tale
Under the hawthorn in the dale.
Straight mine eye hath caught new pleasures,
Whilst the landskip round it measures: 70
Russet lawns, and fallows grey,
Where the nibbling flocks do stray;
Mountains on whose barren breast
The labouring clouds do often rest;
Meadows trim with daisies pied;
Shallow brooks, and rivers wide;
Towers and battlements it sees
Bosomed high in tufted trees,
Where perhaps some beauty lies,
The cynosure of neighbouring eyes.   80

1. Melancholy. The genealogy is invented by the poet. **2. Cerberus,** the three-headed watchdog of Hades. **3. Stygian cave.** The cave of Cerberus was on the Styx, one of the four rivers of Hades. **5. uncouth,** unfamiliar, uncanny. **10. Cimmerian.** The Cimmerians, according to Homer, dwelt in "eternal cloud and darkness" beyond the "ocean-stream." **12. yclept,** called. For the prefix "y" see note 155 on page 642. **19. Zephyr . . . Aurora,** the west wind and the dawn. Milton again invents the genealogy to suit his own purposes. **24. buxom,** gracious, lively. **debonair,** courteous. **27. Quips and cranks,** witty turns of speech. **29. Hebe's.** Hebe was goddess of youth and cupbearer of the gods. **40. unprovèd,** innocent. **45-53. Then to come . . .** This is a much-disputed passage. "To come" would seem to be co-ordinate with "To live" in l. 39, "To hear" in l. 41, and "oft listening" in l. 53. **48. twisted eglantine.** Since eglantine is another name for the sweetbrier, it is commonly assumed that Milton here means the woodbine or honeysuckle. **55. hoar.** "Grey from absence of foliage."—*New English Dictionary* **57. not unseen.** See the contrasting circumstance in "Il Penseroso," l. 65. **59. against,** toward. **60. state,** stately progress. **62. dight,** arrayed. **67. tells his tale,** counts his number (of sheep). **70. landskip,** an old spelling of "landscape." **71. fallows,** plowed fields. **75. pied,** of variegated colors. **80. cynosure,** literally, "dog's tail." The name was given to the Polestar, by which ancient seamen guided their ships; hence, an object of attention by reason of its brilliancy or position.

Hard by a cottage chimney smokes
From betwixt two aged oaks,
Where Corydon and Thyrsis met
Are at their savoury dinner set
Of herbs and other country messes,
Which the neat-handed Phillis dresses;
And then in haste her bower she leaves,
With Thestylis to bind the sheaves;
Or, if the earlier season lead,
To the tanned haycock in the mead.   90
Sometimes, with secure delight,
The upland hamlets will invite,
When the merry bells ring round,
And the jocund rebecks sound
To many a youth and many a maid
Dancing in the chequered shade,
And young and old come forth to play
On a sunshine holiday,
Till the livelong daylight fail:
Then to the spicy nut-brown ale: 100
With stories told of many a feat,
How Faery Mab the junkets eat.
She was pinched and pulled, she said;
And he, by friar's lantern led,
Tells how the drudging goblin sweat
To earn his cream-bowl duly set,
When in one night, ere glimpse of morn,
His shadowy flail hath threshed the corn
That ten day-labourers could not end;
Then lies him down, the lubber fiend,   110
And, stretched out all the chimney's length
Basks at the fire his hairy strength,
And crop-full out of doors he flings,
Ere the first cock his matin rings.
Thus done the tales, to bed they creep,
By whispering winds soon lulled asleep.
Towered cities please us then,
And the busy hum of men,
Where throngs of knights and barons bold,
In weeds of peace, high triumphs hold,   120
With store of ladies, whose bright eyes
Rain influence, and judge the prize
Of wit or arms, while both contend
To win her grace whom all commend.
There let Hymen oft appear
In saffron robe, with taper clear,
And pomp, and feast, and revelry,
With mask and antique pageantry;
Such sights as youthful poets dream
On summer eves by haunted stream.   130
Then to the well-trod stage anon,
If Jonson's learnèd sock be on,
Or sweetest Shakespeare, Fancy's child,
Warble his native wood-notes wild.
And ever, against eating cares,
Lap me in soft Lydian airs,
Married to immortal verse,
Such as the meeting soul may pierce,
In notes with many a winding bout
Of linkèd sweetness long drawn out   140
With wanton heed and giddy cunning,
The melting voice through mazes running,
Untwisting all the chains that tie
The hidden soul of harmony;
That Orpheus' self may heave his head
From golden slumber on a bed
Of heaped Elysian flowers, and hear
Such strains as would have won the ear
Of Pluto to have quite set free
His half-regained Eurydice.   150
    These delights if thou canst give,
Mirth, with thee I mean to live.

IL PENSEROSO

Milton very probably received suggestions for his poem from Robert Burton's "The Author's Abstract of Melancholy," prefixed in 1628 to his *Anatomy of Melancholy*. The "melancholy" of "Il Penseroso," however, is not that of the *Anatomy*, with its brood of mental, spiritual, and physical disturbances. "As employed in this poem," says Professor Hanford, "it designates a pensive and contemplative mood favorable to reverie and to the more inward kind of poetic feeling." The title is seventeenth-century Italian for "The Meditative Man."

83–88. **Corydon . . . Thyrsis . . . Phillis . . . Thestylis,** type names in pastoral poetry for shepherds and shepherdesses.   87. **bower,** cottage.   91. **secure,** carefree.   94. **rebecks,** primitive fiddles.   102. **junkets,** sweet curds.   103–04. **She . . . he,** individuals in the company. **friar's lantern,** jack-o'-lantern, will-o'-the-wisp.   105. **the drudging goblin,** Robin Goodfellow of the country legends, referred to frequently as Hobgoblin.   110. **lubber,** clumsy, drudging.   111. **chimney's,** that is, the fireplace's.   113. **crop-full,** with a full stomach.   114. **matin,** morning song.   117. **Towered cities.** The passage which follows shifts the scene to the city, and describes typical experiences there.   120. **weeds,** garments. **triumphs,** festivals.   121. **store,** abundance.   122. **Rain influence,** an astrological term, referring to the power of the stars over human beings.

125. **Hymen,** the god of marriage, a common figure in masques.   132. **sock.** See note 36–37 on page 563.   136. **Lydian.** The Lydian "mode" of ancient music was characterized by softness and delicacy, in contrast to the Dorian (stateliness) and the Phrygian (liveliness).   138. **meeting,** responsive. **pierce,** then pronounced "perse."   139. **bout,** turn, passage.   145–50. **Orpheus . . . Eurydice,** the legendary poet and musician of Thrace, who, when his wife **Eurydice** died, descended to the underworld to seek her. He so charmed **Pluto** by his music that he gained her release on condition that he should not look back at her on the return journey through the shades. Unable to restrain himself, he looked behind him, and lost her. **Elysian.** Orpheus is represented as with the shades of the blessed in Elysium.

JOHN MILTON

Hence, vain deluding Joys,
   The brood of Folly without father bred!
How little you bested,
   Or fill the fixed mind with all your toys;
Dwell in some idle brain,
   And fancies fond with gaudy shapes possess,
As thick and numberless
   As the gay motes that people the sunbeams,
Or likest hovering dreams,
   The fickle pensioners of Morpheus' train.   10
But, hail! thou Goddess sage and holy,
Hail, divinest Melancholy!
Whose saintly visage is too bright
To hit the sense of human sight,
And therefore to our weaker view
O'erlaid with black, staid Wisdom's hue;
Black, but such as in esteem
Prince Memnon's sister might beseem,
Or that starred Ethiop queen that strove
To set her beauty's praise above   20
The Sea-Nymphs, and their powers offended.
Yet thou art higher far descended:
Thee bright-haired Vesta long of yore
To solitary Saturn bore;
His daughter she; in Saturn's reign
Such mixture was not held a stain.
Oft in glimmering bowers and glades
He met her, and in secret shades
Of woody Ida's inmost grove,
Whilst yet there was no fear of Jove.   30
Come, pensive Nun, devout and pure,
Sober, steadfast, and demure,
All in a robe of darkest grain,
Flowing with majestic train,
And sable stole of cypress lawn
Over thy decent shoulders drawn.

Come; but keep thy wonted state,
With even step, and musing gait,
And looks commercing with the skies,
Thy wrapt soul sitting in thine eyes: 40
There, held in holy passion still,
Forget thyself to marble, till
With a sad leaden downward cast
Thou fix them on the earth as fast.
And join with thee calm Peace and Quiet,
Spare Fast, that oft with gods doth diet,
And hears the Muses in a ring
Aye round about Jove's altar sing;
And add to these retirèd Leisure,
That in trim gardens takes his pleasure;   50
But, first and chiefest, with thee bring
Him that yon soars on golden wing,
Guiding the fiery-wheelèd throne,
The Cherub Contemplation;
And the mute Silence hist along,
'Less Philomel will deign a song,
In her sweetest saddest plight,
Smoothing the rugged brow of Night,
While Cynthia checks her dragon yoke,
Gently o'er the accustomed oak.   60
Sweet bird that shunn'st the noise of folly,
Most musical, most melancholy!
Thee, chauntress, oft the woods among
I woo, to hear thy even-song;
And, missing thee, I walk unseen
On the dry smooth-shaven green
To behold the wandering moon,
Riding near her hightest noon,
Like one that had been led astray
Through the heaven's wide pathless way,   70
And oft, as if her head she bowed,
Stooping through a fleecy cloud.
Oft, on a plat of rising ground,
I hear the far-off curfew sound,
Over some wide-watered shore,
Swinging slow with sullen roar;
Or, if the air will not permit,
Some still removèd place will fit,
Where glowing embers through the room
Teach light to counterfeit a gloom,   80
Far from all resort of mirth,
Save the cricket on the hearth,
Or the bellman's drowsy charm
To bless the doors from nightly harm.
Or let my lamp, at midnight hour,

---

1. vain deluding Joys. It is to be noted that these are not exactly identical with the pleasures invoked and described in "L'Allegro," nor is the mood that is the theme of "Il Penseroso" the "loathèd Melancholy" of its companion poem.   **3. bested,** bestead, avail.   **6. fond,** foolish.   **10. pensioners,** retinue.   **14. hit,** to be congenial or endurable to.   **18. Prince Memnon's sister,** Hemera, sister of the beautiful Ethiopian prince who fought with the Trojans (*Odyssey*, Book XI, l. 552).   **19. that starred Ethiop queen,** Cassiopeia, mother of Andromeda, whose boasting about her beauty and that of her daughter led to a feud with the Nereids. After death they were placed in the constellations that bear their names.   **23–24. Vesta . . . Saturn.** The genealogy is Milton's own, and represents pensiveness as springing from Vesta, the chaste goddess of the hearth, and Saturn, the solitary god and introducer of civilization. There are implications of the moroseness supposed by the astrologers to be the result of the influence of the planet Saturn, and of the golden age of Saturn's reign, brought to an end by the aggressive **Jove** (l. 30).   **29. Ida's inmost grove,** Mt. Ida on the island of Crete, home of Saturn and birthplace of Jupiter, noted for its forests.   **33. grain,** color, in this case probably dark purple.   **35. stole,** shawl or veil. **cypress lawn,** black linen or crape.   **36. decent,** comely.

37. state, stateliness, dignity.   **39. commercing,** communing.   **43. sad,** sober, serious.   **54. The Cherub Contemplation.** Milton has given the name "Contemplation" to one of the cherubs of Ezekiel's vision. See Ezekiel 10.   **55. hist along,** bring along silently.   **56. Philomel,** the nightingale.   **59. Cynthia,** the moon.   **73. plat,** plot.

Be seen in some high lonely tower,
Where I may oft outwatch the Bear,
With thrice great Hermes, or unsphere
The spirit of Plato, to unfold
What worlds or what vast regions hold   90
The immortal mind that hath forsook
Her mansion in this fleshly nook;
And of those demons that are found
In fire, air, flood, or underground,
Whose power hath a true consent
With planet or with element.
Sometime let gorgeous Tragedy
In sceptred pall come sweeping by,
Presenting Thebes, or Pelops' line,
Or the tale of Troy divine,   100
Or what (though rare) of later age
Ennobled hath the buskined stage,
  But, O sad Virgin! that thy power
Might raise Musaeus from his bower;
Or bid the soul of Orpheus sing
Such notes as, warbled to the string,
Drew iron tears down Pluto's cheek,
And made Hell grant what love did seek;
Or call up him that left half-told
The story of Cambuscan bold,   110
Of Camball, and of Algarsife,
And who had Canace to wife,
That owned the virtuous ring and glass,
And of the wondrous horse of brass
On which the Tartar king did ride;
And if aught else great bards beside
In sage and solemn tunes have sung,
Of tourneys, and of trophies hung,
Of forests, and enchantments drear,
Where more is meant than meets the ear.   120
Thus, Night, oft see me in thy pale career,

Till civil-suited Morn appear,
Not tricked and frounced, as she was wont
With the Attic boy to hunt,
But kerchieft in a comely cloud,
While rocking winds are piping loud,
Or ushered with a shower still,
When the gust hath blown his fill,
Ending on the rustling leaves,
With minute-drops from off the eaves.   130
And, when the sun begins to fling
His flaring beams, me, Goddess, bring
To archèd walks of twilight groves,
And shadows brown, that Sylvan loves,
Of pine, or monumental oak,
Where the rude axe with heavèd stroke
Was never heard the nymphs to daunt,
Or fright them from their hallowed haunt.
There, in close covert, by some brook,
Where no profaner eye may look,   140
Hide me from day's garish eye,
While the bee with honeyed thigh,
That at her flowery work doth sing,
And the waters murmuring,
With such consort as they keep,
Entice the dewy-feathered Sleep.
And let some strange mysterious dream
Wave at his wings, in airy stream
Of lively portraiture displayed,
Softly on my eyelids laid;   150
And, as I wake, sweet music breathe
Above, about, or underneath,
Sent by some Spirit to mortals good,
Or the unseen Genius of the wood.
But let my due feet never fail
To walk the studious cloister's pale,
And love the high embowèd roof,
With antique pillars massy-proof,
And storied windows richly dight,
Casting a dim religious light.   160
There let the pealing organ blow,
To the full-voiced quire below,
In service high and anthems clear,

87. **the Bear,** the constellation of the Great Dipper, which in northern latitudes does not set, but disappears only with dawn.   88–89. **thrice great Hermes,** Hermes Trismegistus, as the Greeks called the Egyptian Thoth, the god of wisdom. **unsphere The spirit of Plato,** bring down from its sphere the spirit of Plato, greatest of philosophers and exponent of the theory of the immortality of the soul.   95. **a true consent,** a complete agreement; another reference to astrology. 98. **sceptred pall,** royal robe. Ancient tragedy concerned itself chiefly with the "falls of princes."   99–100. **Thebes . . . Pelops' line . . . Troy,** allusions to the chief themes of Greek tragedy and epic poetry.   102. **buskined.** See the note on Jonson's "To the Memory of . . . Shakespeare," l. 36 (page 563). 104. **Musaeus,** a mythical Greek poet, sometimes referred to as the son of Orpheus. See "L'Allegro," l. 145.   110–15. **The story of Cambuscan . . . ride,** Chaucer's unfinished "Squire's Tale." Cambuscan (Ghengis Khan), the Tatar king, is represented as the father of two sons, Camball and Algarsife, and a daughter, Canace. The father and the daughter received from the king of Arabia and India the magic gifts here mentioned. Chaucer left untold the name of him "who had Canace to wife."   116–20. **And if aught else . . . ear.** The passage probably refers to such works as Spenser's *Faerie Queene* with its allegories, "where more is meant than meets the ear."

122. **civil-suited,** quietly dressed, in contrast with the flaming "liveries" of the morning in "L'Allegro," l. 62. 123. **tricked and frounced,** adorned and becurled like a fop. 124. **the Attic boy,** Cephalus of Attica, of whom Eos, goddess of the dawn, became enamored.   130. **minute-drops,** drops falling at intervals of a minute.   134. **Sylvan,** the woodland god, Sylvanus. See Spenser's *Faerie Queene*, Book I, Canto 6.   145. **consort,** company.   147–50. **And let . . . laid.** "Let some dream float with undulating motion (*i.e. wave*) at the wings of Sleep, amid a stream of vivid pictures which rest lightly on the eyelids."—Verity   154. **Genius,** guardian spirit.   155. **due,** accustomed, expected.   156. **pale,** enclosure.   157. **embowèd,** vaulted.   158. **massy-proof,** proof against mass, strong enough to support the roof.   159. **storied,** with stained glass representing episodes from the Bible. **dight,** adorned.

JOHN MILTON

As may with sweetness, through mine ear,
Dissolve me into ecstasies,
And bring all Heaven before mine eyes.
And may at last my weary age
Find out the peaceful hermitage,
The hairy gown and mossy cell,
Where I may sit and rightly spell   170
Of every star that heaven doth shew,
And every herb that sips the dew,
Till old experience do attain
To something like prophetic strain.
    These pleasures, Melancholy, give;
And I with thee will choose to live.

ON TIME

In the Trinity College MS. at Cambridge, where this poem is written in Milton's hand, a subtitle, later crossed out, states that the lines were "to be set on a clock case."

Fly, envious Time, till thou run out thy race:
Call on the lazy leaden-stepping Hours,
Whose speed is but the heavy plummet's pace;
And glut thyself with what thy womb devours,
Which is no more than what is false and vain,
And merely mortal dross;
So little is our loss,
So little is thy gain!
For, when as each thing bad thou hast entombed,
And, last of all, thy greedy self consumed,   10
Then long Eternity shall greet our bliss
With an individual kiss;
And Joy shall overtake us as a flood,
When every thing that is sincerely good
And perfectly divine,
With Truth, and Peace, and Love, shall ever shine
About the supreme throne
Of him, to whose happy-making sight alone
When once our heavenly-guided soul shall climb,
Then, all this earthly grossness quit,   20
Attired with stars we shall for ever sit,
    Triumphing over Death, and Chance, and thee,
    O Time!

AT A SOLEMN MUSIC

The theme of the poem is essentially that of the Platonic doctrine of the music of the spheres sung by the celestial Sirens, which cannot be heard by the gross ears of sinful humanity. With the Platonic elements are mingled, as Professor Tillyard points out, the mythology and mysticism of the Old and New Testaments. Milton's aspiration to hear and "answer that melodious noise," and his contemplation of heaven and immortality, are characteristic of his early thought, and a foreshadowing of the philosophy of his later poetry.

Blest pair of Sirens, pledges of Heaven's joy,
Sphere-born harmonious sisters, Voice and Verse,
Wed your divine sounds, and mixed power employ,
Dead things with inbreathed sense able to pierce;
And to our high-raised phantasy present
That undisturbèd song of pure concent,
Aye sung before the sapphire-coloured throne
To him that sits thereon,
With saintly shout and solemn jubilee;
Where the bright Seraphim in burning row   10
Their loud uplifted angel-trumpets blow,
And the Cherubic host in thousand quires
Touch their immortal harps of golden wires,
With those just Spirits that wear victorious palms,
Hymns devout and holy psalms
Singing everlastingly:
That we on Earth, with undiscording voice,
May rightly answer that melodious noise;
As once we did, till disproportioned sin
Jarred against nature's chime, and with harsh din   20
Broke the fair music that all creatures made
To their great Lord, whose love their motion swayed
In perfect diapason, whilst they stood
In first obedience, and their state of good.
O, may we soon again renew that song,
And keep in tune with Heaven, till God ere long
To his celestial consort us unite,
To live with him, and sing in endless morn of light!

170. spell, study, ponder.   **3. the heavy plummet's pace.** The allusion is to the weight of lead suspended on a string, which operated the works of the clock.   **12. individual**, undividable. "The kiss symbolizes the union of the 'individual soul For ever happy' (*P. L.*, V, 610–11) to God."—M. Y. Hughes   **16. Truth, and Peace, and Love.** Compare "On the Morning of Christ's Nativity," ll. 141–44 (page 642).   **20. quit**, discarded.

1–2. Blest pair of Sirens . . . Voice and Verse. Milton mentions only two of the eight Sirens described by Plato at the close of his *Republic*, and gives them names of his own devising.   **5. phantasy**, imagination.   **6. concent**, harmony.   **7. the sapphire-coloured throne**, from the vision described in Ezekiel 1 : 26.   **10. burning**, shining.   **14. those just Spirits**, a reference to the redeemed souls in heaven as St. John saw them in his vision, Revelation 7 : 9.   **16. Singing everlastingly.** See Revelation 14 : 3–4. The song is known only to the pure in heart.   **18. rightly answer**, sing in complete accord with.   **23. perfect diapason**, the "concord of the octave"; the entire compass of harmonious tones. The words are used in both a literal and a spiritual sense.   **24. In first obedience . . . good**, an interesting anticipation of the theme of *Paradise Lost*.   **27. consort**, company of musicians.

LYCIDAS

"Lycidas" appeared first in 1638 in a volume of memorial verses on Edward King, a college mate of Milton's who was drowned off the coast of Wales on August 10, 1637. Milton and King were probably not close friends, but the untimely death of a young poet gave Milton an opportunity to lament the uncertainty of life, to question the value of long and earnest preparation for a career which might be cut short just as it was beginning, and to attack the unworthy members of the clergy of the Church of England. In form the poem shows Milton's familiarity with the pastoral elegies of the Greeks—Theocritus, Bion, and Moschus—and the pastoral poetry of Virgil, but it is in no real sense a slavish imitation of the classic elegy or of any of the Renaissance forms which were based on that type of elegy. "Lycidas" is the happiest illustration in the language of the combination of tradition and individual talent, of passionate feeling kept in check by a highly developed sense of form. It has probably more often than any other poem in the language been called the perfect poem.

In This Monody the Author Bewails a Learned Friend, Unfortunately Drowned in His Passage from Chester on the Irish Seas, 1637; and, by Occasion, Foretells the Ruin of Our Corrupted Clergy, Then in Their Height.

Yet once more, O ye laurels, and once more,
Ye myrtles brown, with ivy never sere,
I come to pluck your berries harsh and crude,
And with forced fingers rude
Shatter your leaves before the mellowing year.
Bitter constraint, and sad occasion dear
Compels me to disturb your season due;
For Lycidas is dead, dead ere his prime,
Young Lycidas, and hath not left his peer.
Who would not sing for Lycidas? he well knew   10
Himself to sing, and build the lofty rhyme.
He must not float upon his watery bier
Unwept, and welter to the parching wind,
Without the meed of some melodious tear.
  Begin, then, Sisters of the sacred well
That from beneath the seat of Jove doth spring;
Begin, and somewhat loudly sweep the string.
Hence with denial vain and coy excuse:
So may some gentle Muse
With lucky words favour my destined urn,   20
And as he passes turn,
And bid fair peace be to my sable shroud!
For we were nursed upon the self-same hill,
Fed the same flock, by fountain, shade, and rill.
  Together both, ere the high lawns appeared
Under the opening eyelids of the Morn,
We drove a-field, and both together heard
What time the gray-fly winds her sultry horn,
Battening our flocks with the fresh dews of night,
Oft till the star that rose, at evening, bright   30
Toward heaven's descent had sloped his westering wheel.
Meanwhile the rural ditties were not mute;
Tempered to the oaten flute,
Rough Satyrs danced, and Fauns with cloven heel
From the glad sound would not be absent long;
And old Damoetas loved to hear our song.
  But, oh! the heavy change, now thou art gone,
Now thou art gone and never must return!
Thee, Shepherd, thee the woods and desert caves,
With wild thyme and the gadding vine o'ergrown,
And all their echoes, mourn.   41
The willows, and the hazel copses green,
Shall now no more be seen
Fanning their joyous leaves to thy soft lays.
As killing as the canker to the rose,
Or taint-worm to the weanling herds that graze,
Or frost to flowers, that their gay wardrobe wear,
When first the white-thorn blows;
Such, Lycidas, thy loss to shepherd's ear.

1–2. Yet once more. An interval of four years separates "Lycidas" from *Comus*, Milton's most ambitious poem before "Lycidas." **laurels . . . myrtles . . . ivy**, evergreens with which poets were traditionally crowned. The lines are interesting as suggestive both of Milton's reluctance to write and of his chief concern in the poem with the poet's calling. **brown**, in the sense of dark. **never sere**, ever green.   **3–5. I come . . . year**, before my genius has been matured by time.   **6. dear**, keenly felt.   **8. Lycidas**, a typical shepherd's name in the pastoral elegies.   **9. peer**, equal.   **10. knew**, knew how.   **13. welter**, toss about. King's body was never recovered.   **14. meed**, tribute. **melodious tear**, a conventional figure for elegiac verse.   **15–16. Sisters . . . spring**, the Muses, to whom certain springs (wells) were sacred. Compare *Paradise Lost*, Book I, l. 11.   **17. somewhat loudly**, "allegro ma non troppo," as it were!   **18. coy**, modest.   **19–22. So may some gentle Muse . . . shroud!** an obscure passage which has been variously interpreted. Mr. G. M. Gathorne-Hardy, writing in the London *Times Literary Supplement*, Jan. 18, 1934, suggests that the poet's meaning is that since Lycidas is denied an ordinary funeral, the poem now being written shall take its place. "My destined urn" would then mean "the memorial I am now, under inspiration of the Muses, preparing for Lycidas. . . . Similarly the shroud, at an earlier stage of the funeral procession, in which Lycidas is metaphorically envisaged as 'passing.' 'He' [l. 21] is Lycidas." A more usual but less satisfactory interpretation is that "Muse" in l. 19 must be read "poet," and that Milton is expressing the wish that after his death some poet will write memorial verses for him as he is now writing them for King.   **23–36. the self-same hill . . . song**, conventionally pastoral references to Milton's associations with King at Cambridge.   **27–28. heard What time the gray-fly**, heard the grayfly when.   **sultry**, in the heat of noon.   **29. Battening**, feeding.   **32. rural ditties**, a reference probably to their undergraduate poetical exercises.   **33. Tempered**, modulated.   **36. Damoetas**, another type name from pastoral poetry. Possibly the reference is to some tutor at the university.   **40. gadding**, straggling.   **45. canker**, the canker worm.   **48. white-thorn**, hawthorn.

Where were ye, Nymphs, when the remorseless deep 50
Closed o'er the head of your loved Lycidas?
For neither were ye playing on the steep
Where your old bards, the famous Druids, lie,
Nor on the shaggy top of Mona high,
Nor yet where Deva spreads her wizard stream.
Ay me! I fondly dream
"Had ye been there," . . . for what could that have done?
What could the Muse herself that Orpheus bore,
The Muse herself, for her enchanting son,
Whom universal nature did lament, 60
When, by the rout that made the hideous roar,
His gory visage down the stream was sent,
Down the swift Hebrus to the Lesbian shore?
   Alas! what boots it with uncessant care
To tend the homely, slighted, shepherd's trade,
And strictly meditate the thankless Muse?
Were it not better done, as others use,
To sport with Amaryllis in the shade,
Or with the tangles of Neaera's hair?
Fame is the spur that the clear spirit doth raise 70
(That last infirmity of noble mind)
To scorn delights, and live laborious days;
But the fair guerdon when we hope to find,
And think to burst out into sudden blaze,
Comes the blind Fury with the abhorrèd shears,
And slits the thin-spun life. "But not the praise,"
Phoebus replied, and touched my trembling ears:
"Fame is no plant that grows on mortal soil,
Nor in the glistering foil
Set off to the world, nor in broad rumour lies, 80
But lives and spreads aloft by those pure eyes,
And perfect witness of all-judging Jove;
As he pronounces lastly on each deed,
Of so much fame in heaven expect thy meed."
   O fountain Arethuse, and thou honoured flood,
Smooth-sliding Mincius, crowned with vocal reeds,
That strain I heard was of a higher mood.
But now my oat proceeds,
And listens to the Herald of the Sea
That came in Neptune's plea. 90
He asked the waves, and asked the felon winds,
What hard mishap hath doomed this gentle swain?
And questioned every gust of rugged wings
That blows from off each beakèd promontory.
They knew not of his story;
And sage Hippotades their answer brings;
That not a blast was from his dungeon strayed,
The air was calm, and on the level brine
Sleek Panope with all her sisters played.
It was that fatal and perfidious bark, 100
Built in the eclipse, and rigged with curses dark,
That sunk so low that sacred head of thine.
   Next, Camus, reverend sire, went footing slow,
His mantle hairy, and his bonnet sedge,
Inwrought with figures dim, and on the edge
Like to that sanguine flower inscribed with woe.
"Ah! who hath reft," quoth he, "my dearest pledge?"
Last came, and last did go,
The Pilot of the Galilean Lake;
Two massy keys he bore of metals twain 110
(The golden opes, the iron shuts amain).

---

50. Nymphs. The sea nymphs are here identified, as in other pastoral elegies, with the Muses. **52. steep**, mountain. **53. Druids,** the minstrel-priests of the ancient Celts of Britain. **54. Mona,** the Roman name for the isle of Anglesey, off the Welsh coast. **55. Deva,** the river Dee, which flows between England and Wales into the Irish Sea. The adjective **wizard** indicates the supernatural associations connected with the stream. **56. fondly,** foolishly. **58. the Muse,** Calliope, the Muse of epic poetry. **59. enchanting,** given to use enchantments. **61. the rout,** the band of frenzied women of Thrace who, because of Orpheus' slight to them after the loss of Eurydice, tore him in pieces. The story is found in Ovid's *Metamorphoses,* Book XI, ll. 1–60. **64–84. Alas! what boots it . . . meed.**" Milton digresses from his principal theme to consider whether the incessant labor and pain of the poet's preparation are, after all, worth while. **boots,** profits. **65. shepherd's trade,** the writing of verse. **66. meditate the . . . Muse,** to give oneself to the composition of poetry. Milton borrows the phrase from Virgil. **67. use,** are accustomed to do. **68–69. Amaryllis . . . Neaera's,** typical names of maidens in pastoral poetry. **70. clear,** pure, noble. **71. (That last infirmity,** that is, the last to be abandoned. **73. guerdon,** reward. **75. blind Fury.** In classical mythology it is Atropos, one of the three Fates, who cuts the thread of life. Milton has purposely identified the Fates with the Furies here to re-enforce the idea of the blind and senseless working of the forces which carried young King off. **77. Phoebus,** Apollo, god of poetic inspiration. **touched my trembling ears,** a Virgilian figure meaning to recall something to one's mind.

79. glistering foil, glittering gold or silver leaf, placed under transparent gems to enhance their brilliance. **82. perfect witness of all-judging Jove.** Compare 1 Samuel 16:7: "The Lord seeth not as man seeth; for man looketh on the outward appearance, but the Lord looketh on the heart." **85–86. fountain Arethuse . . . Mincius.** Arethusa, a spring in Sicily, the country of Theocritus, represents the Greek tradition of pastoral poetry, as Mincius, the river near which Virgil was born, does the Latin. **88. oat,** the shepherd's pipe of oat straw. **89–90. the Herald of the Sea,** Triton, the herald and agent of Neptune, who comes **in Neptune's plea** of innocence of the guilt of having drowned Lycidas. **96. Hippotades,** Aeolus (son of Hippotes), god of the winds. **99. Panope,** one of the fifty Nereids, or sea nymphs. **101. the eclipse,** the proverbial omen of ill fortune. **103. Camus,** a personification of the river Cam, which flows through Cambridge. **106. sanguine,** literally, "bloody." The flower referred to is the purple hyacinth, named for the youth Hyacinthus, slain by Apollo. The hyacinth was reputed to be marked *ai, ai* (woe! woe!). **107. reft,**" snatched away. **pledge?**" child. **109. The Pilot,** St. Peter, the legendary keeper of the keys of heaven. See Matthew 16:19. He is introduced here as the earthly founder and chief pastor of the Church, of which young King was to have been a pastor (shepherd). **111. amain,** with force.

He shook his mitred locks, and stern bespake:—
"How well could I have spared for thee, young swain,
Enow of such as, for their bellies' sake,
Creep, and intrude, and climb into the fold!
Of other care they little reckoning make
Than how to scramble at the shearers' feast,
And shove away the worthy bidden guest.
Blind mouths! that scarce themselves know how to hold
A sheep-hook, or have learnt aught else the least 120
That to the faithful herdman's art belongs!
What recks it them? What need they? They are sped;
And, when they list, their lean and flashy songs
Grate on their scrannel pipes of wretched straw;
The hungry sheep look up, and are not fed,
But, swoln with wind and the rank mist they draw,
Rot inwardly, and foul contagion spread;
Besides what the grim wolf with privy paw
Daily devours apace, and nothing said.
But that two-handed engine at the door 130
Stands ready to smite once, and smite no more."
   Return, Alpheus; the dread voice is past
That shrunk thy streams; return, Sicilian Muse,
And call the vales, and bid them hither cast
Their bells and flowerets of a thousand hues.
Ye valleys low, where the mild whispers use
Of shades, and wanton winds, and gushing brooks,
On whose fresh lap the swart star sparely looks,
Throw hither all your quaint enamelled eyes,
That on the green turf suck the honeyed showers, 140
And purple all the ground with vernal flowers.
Bring the rathe primrose that forsaken dies,
The tufted crow-toe, and pale jessamine,
The white pink, and the pansy freaked with jet,
The glowing violet,
The musk rose, and the well-attired woodbine,
With cowslips wan that hang the pensive head,
And every flower that sad embroidery wears;
Bid amaranthus all his beauty shed,
And daffadillies fill their cups with tears, 150
To strew the laureate hearse where Lycid lies.
For so, to interpose a little ease,
Let our frail thoughts dally with false surmise.
Ay me! whilst thee the shores and sounding seas
Wash far away, where'er thy bones are hurled;
Whether beyond the stormy Hebrides,
Where thou perhaps under the whelming tide
Visit'st the bottom of the monstrous world;
Or whether thou, to our moist vows denied,
Sleep'st by the fable of Bellerus old, 160
Where the great Vision of the guarded mount
Looks toward Namancos and Bayona's hold.
Look homeward, Angel, now, and melt with ruth:
And, O ye dolphins, waft the hapless youth.
   Weep no more, woeful shepherds, weep no more,
For Lycidas, your sorrow, is not dead,
Sunk though he be beneath the watery floor.
So sinks the day-star in the ocean bed,
And yet anon repairs his drooping head,
And tricks his beams, and with new-spangled ore 170
Flames in the forehead of the morning sky:
So Lycidas sunk low, but mounted high,
Through the dear might of Him that walked the waves,
Where, other groves and other streams along,
With nectar pure his oozy locks he laves,
And hears the unexpressive nuptial song,
In the blest kingdoms meek of joy and love.
There entertain him all the Saints above,
In solemn troops, and sweet societies,
That sing, and singing in their glory move, 180
And wipe the tears for ever from his eyes.
Now, Lycidas, the shepherds weep no more;
Henceforth thou art the Genius of the shore,

---

112. mitred, wearing a miter (as a bishop). **114. Enow,** enough. **115–27. Creep . . . spread.** For an interesting analysis of this passage see Ruskin, *Sesame and Lilies*, Secs. 20–24. **122. What recks it them?** What matters it to them? **They are sped,** they have succeeded in getting what they wanted. **124. scrannel,** thin, harsh. **126. rank,** pestilential. **128. the grim wolf,** the Roman Catholic Church. **privy paw,** secret proselytizing. **130. that two-handed engine,** the most celebrated crux in Milton's poetry. Just what particular "engine" or instrument of reform was referred to by Milton is uncertain. The two Houses of Parliament have been suggested, among others. The figure seems to imply a sword or ax, and may have been suggested by such Biblical passages as Revelation 1:16 and Matthew 3:10. **132. Alpheus,** a river whose god was the lover of Arethusa, referred to in l. 85. The invocation to Alpheus and the **Sicilian Muse** signifies Milton's return to the pastoral strain after the digression on the corruption of the Church. **136. use,** are accustomed to dwell. **138. swart star,** the Dog Star, Sirius, whose baleful influence blasts or makes "swart" the summer's flowers. **sparely,** rarely. **139. quaint enamelled eyes,** pretty varicolored blossoms. **142. rathe,** early.

151. hearse, bier. **153. frail,** unable or unwilling to face the fact that the body of Lycidas is not on a flower-decked bier, but tossing in the sea. **158. monstrous,** teeming with monsters. **159. moist vows,** tearful devotions. **160. fable of Bellerus,** of the abode of the fabulous Bellerus—Land's End, the southwestern extremity of England. **161. the guarded mount,** St. Michael's Mount in Cornwall, under the protection of the sword of St. Michael the Archangel. **162. Namancos and Bayona's hold,** in Spain; **hold,** stronghold. **163. Look homeward,** be on guard against internal enemies and dangers. **168. day-star,** the sun. **170. tricks,** dresses. **ore,** gold, radiance. **176. unexpressive,** inexpressible. Compare "At a Solemn Music," ll. 27–28 (page 649). **nuptial song,** at "the marriage supper of the Lamb." See Revelation 19:9. **183. Genius,** guardian spirit.

JOHN MILTON

In thy large recompense, and shalt be good
To all that wander in that perilous flood.

Thus sang the uncouth swain to the oaks and rills,
While the still morn went out with sandals grey:
He touched the tender stops of various quills,
With eager thought warbling his Doric lay:
And now the sun had stretched out all the hills, 190
And now was dropt into the western bay;
At last he rose, and twitched his mantle blue:
To-morrow to fresh woods, and pastures new.

SONNETS

WHEN I CONSIDER

This sonnet seems to have been written in the early days of Milton's total blindness, and is therefore assigned by Tillyard to 1652, or a slightly later date.

When I consider how my light is spent
  Ere half my days in this dark world and wide,
  And that one talent which is death to hide
  Lodged with me useless, though my soul more bent
To serve therewith my Maker, and present
  My true account, lest He returning chide,
  "Doth God exact day-labour, light denied?"
  I fondly ask. But Patience, to prevent
That murmur, soon replies, "God doth not need
  Either man's work or his own gifts. Who best   10
  Bear his mild yoke, they serve him best. His state
Is kingly: thousands at his bidding speed,
  And post o'er land and ocean without rest;
  They also serve who only stand and wait."

ON THE LATE MASSACRE IN PIEMONT

"Piemont" is the French form of "Piedmont," now a part of Italy. In 1655, the Waldensians, a Protestant religious sect living in the Piedmontese Alps, were cruelly persecuted by the Duke of Savoy. A wave of indignation swept over England, which elicited official protests from Cromwell, and called forth this most vigorous of Milton's sonnets.

Avenge, O Lord, thy slaughtered saints, whose bones
  Lie scattered on the Alpine mountains cold;
Even them who kept thy truth so pure of old,
  When all our fathers worshipped stocks and stones,
Forget not: in thy book record their groans
  Who were thy sheep, and in their ancient fold
  Slain by the bloody Piemontese, that rolled
Mother with infant down the rocks. Their moans
The vales redoubled to the hills, and they 9
  To heaven. Their martyred blood and ashes sow
  O'er all the Italian fields, where still doth sway
The triple Tyrant; that from these may grow
  A hundredfold, who, having learnt thy way,
  Early may fly the Babylonian woe.

CYRIACK, THIS THREE YEARS' DAY

This sonnet was probably written in 1655, to Cyriack Skinner, a former pupil of Milton's who had become one of his most intimate friends.

Cyriack, this three years' day these eyes, though clear
  To outward view of blemish or of spot,
  Bereft of light, their seeing have forgot;
  Nor to their idle orbs doth sight appear
Of sun, or moon, or star, throughout the year,
  Or man, or woman. Yet I argue not
  Against Heaven's hand or will, nor bate a jot
  Of heart or hope; but still bear up and steer
Right onward. What supports me, dost thou ask?
  The conscience, friend, to have lost them overplied   10
  In Liberty's defence, my noble task,
Of which all Europe talks from side to side.
  This thought might lead me through the world's vain mask
  Content, though blind, had I no better guide.

---

186. **uncouth,** in the original sense of unknown, or rustic. 189. **Doric,** the dialect in which the Sicilian pastoral poets wrote.   3. **that one talent.** See Matthew 25:14–30. Compare the determination expressed in his sonnet "How Soon Hath Time," ll. 9–14 (page 644).   8. **fondly,** foolishly.   12. **thousands . . . speed,** the angelic messengers.

On the Late Massacre in Piemont. 3. **them who kept . . . of old.** The Waldensians had from the twelfth century maintained the simple practices of the primitive Christians. 4. **all our fathers,** the Englishmen and Europeans of pre-Reformation days. **stocks and stones,** images of wood and stone.   5. **thy book,** the Book of Life. See Revelation 20:12. 12. **The triple Tyrant,** the Pope, who wears a tiara with three crowns.   14. **the Babylonian woe,** the punishment reserved for the Church of Rome. The seventeenth-century Protestants identified the Babylon of the Book of Revelation with the Roman Catholic Church. See Revelation 14:8; 17:5; and 18:2.   *Cyriack, This Three Years' Day.* 1. **this three years' day,** for the past three years.   8. **bear up,** a nautical term, meaning "to put the helm 'up' so as to bring the vessel into the direction of the wind."—*New English Dictionary*   10. **conscience,** consciousness.   11. **my noble task.** Milton refers to his *Defence of the English People,* 1651, which he had given his days and nights to, despite his physicians' orders and warnings.   14. **had I no better guide,** that is, than my faith in God and my consciousness of Divine approval.

METHOUGHT I SAW

This is Milton's last sonnet, written supposedly soon after the death in childbirth of his second wife, Katherine Woodcock, in February, 1658. He had presumably never seen her, as he married her several years after he had lost his sight.

Methought I saw my late espousèd saint
  Brought to me like Alcestis from the grave,
  Whom Jove's great son to her glad husband gave,
  Rescued from Death by force, though pale and faint.
Mine, as whom washed from spot of child-bed taint
  Purification in the Old Law did save,
  And such as yet once more I trust to have
  Full sight of her in Heaven without restraint,
Came vested all in white, pure as her mind.
  Her face was veiled; yet to my fancied sight   10
  Love, sweetness, goodness, in her person shined
So clear as in no face with more delight.
  But, oh! as to embrace me she inclined,
  I waked, she fled, and day brought back my night.

from PARADISE LOST

From his nineteenth year, at least, Milton had the ambition to write a great poem in his native language, and by the time he returned from Italy in 1639 he had resolved to do for his own nation something of what Virgil had done for ancient Rome, and Tasso and Ariosto for Italy. King Arthur was his first hero, but the more Milton studied the records of the ancient British chieftain, the less he felt drawn to the subject. Other ideas came to him as he read, and in the Trinity MS. at Cambridge there are listed some ninety-nine possible subjects, about two-thirds of which have to do with Biblical themes. It is as material for dramatic treatment that they were jotted down, and there are rather detailed outlines of a projected drama on the subject of the Fall of Man. After years of consideration, Milton finally discarded the dramatic for the epic form, and of all the subjects pondered over he chose that which he made the theme of *Paradise Lost*. "Long choosing, and beginning late," as he says near the beginning of Book IX, he completed the poem probably in 1663, when he was fifty-four years old. It was first published in 1667.

Paradise Lost, however considered, is one of the world's greatest poetical compositions. In theme, in scope, and in the success of its execution, it has no equal in English, nor perhaps in any other language. As an epic poem, it conforms in general to the requirements and conventions of the classical epic, without which, of course, it could not have been fashioned. If it misses something of the formal perfection of Virgil's *Aeneid*, it makes up for the loss in depth of religious thought and feeling. The spiritual horizon of mankind was larger and wider in seventeenth-century England than in Augustan Rome, even if it was a good deal less clear.

The elements of *Paradise Lost* are drawn from all Milton's experience and all his reading and thinking. The Biblical matter is supplemented by illustrations and interpretations from rabbinical writings. The Christian material is a composite of modern and medieval, Protestant and patristic, doctrines and dogmas. The Hebraic and the Christian elements are fused and molded in accordance with a thorough knowledge of the Greek and Latin classics and an artistic sense derived from their study.

Paradise Lost is, more than any other poem ever written perhaps, cosmological in setting and theme. Milton was aware of and accepted the implications of the Copernican theory of the universe, as his spokesman, the Archangel Raphael, indicates on occasion; but for philosophical and poetic reasons he chooses as his mise en scène the old Ptolemaic universe of nine concentric spheres with the earth at its center. He is purposely indefinite in his cosmic spaces and dimensions, and does not attempt to be altogether consistent in such details as he does supply. For all its cosmic scope, however, embracing as it does all time—past, present, and future—and all conceivable space, the poem has, in many respects, a surprisingly local and intimate quality. The whole starry universe of our world, in which Man is the most important creature, hangs suspended by a golden chain from the floor of Heaven. Man is the center of the attention of all the powers of Heaven and of all the devils of Hell.

The purpose of the poem is to "assert Eternal Providence" with respect to man, and to "justify the ways of God to men." All the characters of the poem, from the Almighty Father and the Divine Son to the humblest angels in the heavenly hierarchy, are part of the grand plot which centers in the two human beings in the Garden. In every real sense, therefore, the hero of the piece is Man, created, preserved, counseled, punished, and restored by Divine Power; tempted, betrayed, and banished from Paradise through the machinations of the incomparable and irresistible Satan, the villain of the poem. Like Shakespeare's Iago, Milton's Satan is, from the point of view of dramatic interest, the author's most brilliant creation. "The greatness of Iago," said Professor Raleigh, "is shown in this—that Othello never loses our sympathy." Something of that same sympathy, and for a similar reason, may be claimed for Milton's Adam and Eve. The excerpts from the poem given here

---

1. **saint,** in the sense of a soul in heaven.   2. **Alcestis,** the wife of Admetus, king of Thessaly, who offered to die for her husband, but was rescued from death by Hercules, son of Zeus. Milton is thought to have in mind the *Alcestis* of Euripides.

6. **Purification in the Old Law.** See Leviticus 12:2–8.

present Milton's account of the supernatural forces which converged on his hero and heroine in their happy garden, and their expulsion from it into the workaday world of toil and pain and hope.

The Verse*

The measure is English heroic verse without rime, as that of Homer in Greek, and of Virgil in Latin—rime being no necessary adjunct or true ornament of poem or good verse, in longer works especially, but the invention of a barbarous age, to set off wretched matter and lame metre; graced indeed since by the use of some famous modern poets, carried away by custom, but much to their own vexation, hindrance, and constraint to express many things otherwise, and for the most part worse, than else they would have expressed them. Not without cause, therefore, some both Italian and Spanish poets of prime note have rejected rime both in longer and shorter works, as have also long since our best English tragedies, as a thing of itself, to all judicious ears, trivial and of no true musical delight; which consists only in apt numbers, fit quantity of syllables, and the sense variously drawn out from one verse into another, not in the jingling sound of like endings—a fault avoided by the learned ancients both in poetry and all good oratory. This neglect then of rime so little is to be taken for a defect, though it may seem so perhaps to vulgar readers, that it rather is to be esteemed an example set, the first in English, of ancient liberty recovered to heroic poem from the troublesome and modern bondage of riming.

BOOK I

The Argument

This First Book proposes, first in brief, the whole subject: Man's disobedience, and the loss thereupon of Paradise, wherein he was placed: then touches the prime cause of his fall—the Serpent, or rather Satan in the Serpent; who, revolting from God, and drawing to his side many legions of Angels, was by the command of God driven out of Heaven with all his crew into the great Deep. Which action passed over, the poem hastens into the midst of things; presenting Satan with his Angels now fallen into Hell—described here, not in the Center (for Heaven and Earth may be supposed as yet not made, certainly not yet accursed), but in a place of utter darkness, fitliest called Chaos: here Satan with his Angels lying on the burning lake, thunder-struck and astonished, after a certain space recovers, as from confusion; calls up him who, next in order and dignity, lay by him; they confer of their miserable fall. Satan awakens all his legions, who lay till then in the same manner confounded. They rise: their numbers, array of battle, their chief leaders named, according to the idols known afterwards in Canaan and the countries adjoining. To these Satan directs his speech; comforts them with hope yet of regaining Heaven; but tells them lastly of a new world and new kind of creature to be created, according to an ancient prophecy or report in Heaven; for that Angels were long before this visible creation was the opinion of many ancient Fathers. To find out the truth of this prophecy, and what to determine thereon, he refers to a full council. What his associates thence attempt. Pandemonium, the palace of Satan, rises, suddenly built out of the Deep: the infernal peers there sit in council.

Of man's first disobedience, and the fruit
Of that forbidden tree, whose mortal taste
Brought death into the world, and all our woe,
With loss of Eden, till one greater Man
Restore us, and regain the blissful seat,
Sing, Heavenly Muse, that, on the secret top
Of Oreb or of Sinai, didst inspire
That shepherd, who first taught the chosen seed,
In the beginning how the Heavens and Earth
Rose out of Chaos; or, if Sion hill 10
Delight thee more, and Siloa's brook that flowed
Fast by the oracle of God, I thence
Invoke thy aid to my adventurous song,
That with no middle flight intends to soar
Above the Aonian mount, while it pursues
Things unattempted yet in prose or rhyme.
And chiefly thou, O Spirit, that dost prefer
Before all temples the upright heart and pure,
Instruct me, for thou know'st; thou from the first
Wast present, and, with mighty wings outspread, 20

---

*Milton's forthright statement of why his verse is unrhymed was not in the first edition of 1667, but was added in 1668. It contains obvious hits at Dryden, who was the chief defender of rhyme. Milton's contention that his epic is the first important English poem of a nondramatic type written in blank verse is substantially true, as only a few scattered nondramatic pieces in unrhymed pentameter had appeared before *Paradise Lost*.

The Argument, the subject matter of what follows.

2. mortal, deadly. **5. seat,** abode. **6. Sing, Heavenly Muse.** The invocation, or address to the Muse of poetry, is an epic convention, which Milton borrows from Virgil and the classic authors. Milton identifies the Muse of the classical epics with the Holy Spirit of the Bible and Christian theology. **secret,** remote, and therefore mysterious. **7. Oreb . . . Sinai.** Oreb (Horeb) and Sinai are mountains or mountain ranges on which Moses received communications from God. **8. That shepherd,** Moses. See Exodus 3 and 19–31. **9–10. In the beginning . . . Chaos.** See Genesis 1. The first five books of the Bible were supposed to have been written by Moses. **Sion,** one of the hills on which Jerusalem was built, and thus the abode of David, the "sweet singer of Israel." **12. Fast by,** close by. **the oracle,** Solomon's temple. **15. the Aonian mount,** Helicon, the mountain of the classic Muses. Milton is contrasting his great theme with the more earthly subjects of the classic poets. **16. rhyme.** Milton seems to distinguish between "rhyme" as meaning "verse" and "rime" (see "The Verse," first column of this page), "the jingling sound of like endings." **17. thou, O Spirit,** the Holy Spirit of the New Testament.

Dove-like sat'st brooding on the vast Abyss,
And mad'st it pregnant: what in me is dark,
Illumine; what is low, raise and support;
That to the highth of this great argument
I may assert Eternal Providence,
And justify the ways of God to men.

    Say first—for Heaven hides nothing from Thy view,
Nor the deep tract of Hell—say first what cause
Moved our grand parents, in that happy state,
Favoured of Heaven so highly, to fall off   30
From their Creator, and transgress his will
For one restraint, lords of the world besides.
Who first seduced them to that foul revolt?

    The infernal Serpent; he it was, whose guile,
Stirred up with envy and revenge, deceived
The Mother of Mankind, what time his pride
Had cast him out from Heaven, with all his host
Of rebel Angels, by whose aid, aspiring
To set himself in glory above his peers,
He trusted to have equalled the Most High,   40
If he opposed; and with ambitious aim
Against the throne and monarchy of God
Raised impious war in Heaven, and battle proud,
With vain attempt. Him the Almighty Power
Hurled headlong flaming from the ethereal sky,
With hideous ruin and combustion, down
To bottomless perdition; there to dwell
In adamantine chains and penal fire,
Who durst defy the Omnipotent to arms.   49

    Nine times the space that measures day and night
To mortal men, he with his horrid crew
Lay vanquished, rolling in the fiery gulf,
Confounded, though immortal. But his doom
Reserved him to more wrath; for now the thought
Both of lost happiness and lasting pain
Torments him; round he throws his baleful eyes,
That witnessed huge affliction and dismay,
Mixed with obdúrate pride and stedfast hate.
At once, as far as Angels ken, he views
The dismal situation waste and wild: 60
A dungeon horrible on all sides round
As one great furnace flamed; yet from those flames
No light; but rather darkness visible
Served only to discover sights of woe,
Regions of sorrow, doleful shades, where peace
And rest can never dwell, hope never comes
That comes to all; but torture without end
Still urges, and a fiery deluge, fed
With ever-burning sulphur unconsumed.
Such place Eternal Justice had prepared   70
For those rebellious; here their prison ordained
In utter darkness, and their portion set,
As far removed from God and light of Heaven,
As from the center thrice to the utmost pole.
Oh, how unlike the place from whence they fell!
There the companions of his fall, o'erwhelmed
With floods and whirlwinds of tempestuous fire,
He soon discerns, and, weltering by his side,
One next himself in power and next in crime,
Long after known in Palestine and named   80
Beëlzebub. To whom the Arch-Enemy,—
And thence in Heaven called Satan,—with bold words
Breaking the horrid silence, thus began:

    "If thou beest he,—but O, how fallen! how changed
From him, who, in the happy realms of light,
Clothed with transcendent brightness, didst outshine
Myriads though bright!—if he, whom mutual league,
United thoughts and counsels, equal hope
And hazard in the glorious enterprise,
Joined with me once, now misery hath joined   90
In equal ruin; into what pit, thou seest,
From what highth fallen! so much the stronger proved
He with his thunder; and till then who knew
The force of those dire arms? Yet not for those,
Nor what the potent Victor in his rage
Can else inflict, do I repent or change,
Though changed in outward lustre, that fixed mind,
And high disdain from sense of injured merit,

---

21. Dove-like sat'st brooding, a happy combination of the New Testament conception of the Holy Spirit "descending like a dove" (Matthew 3:16) and the statement in Genesis 1:2, "the Spirit of God moved upon the face of the waters."   **24. highth**, the older form of the word. **argument**, subject.   **25. assert**, vindicate, defend.   **29. grand**, first, original.—**32. For**, because of. **besides**, in all other respects.   **34. The infernal Serpent.** Milton is here anticipating the final condition and appearance of Satan, a very different appearance from that of the great archangel of Books I and II.   **36. what time**, at the time when.   **39. his peers**, his equals, the other archangels.   **50-53. Nine times the space . . . immortal.** Milton in Book VI, l. 871, represents the angels as having fallen for nine days, after which for nine days they **lay vanquished. doom**, judgment.   **56. baleful**, woeful, full of pain.   **59. as far as Angels ken**, as far as the knowledge and perceptive faculties of angels extend.

68. urges, afflicts, presses on.   **72. utter**, outer. Milton represents Hell as being at the farthest remove from Heaven. **74. from the center . . . pole.** Milton seems to imply that the distance from Heaven (or the Empyrean) to the gate of Hell is three times the radius of the starry universe. The vast and indeterminate region called Chaos is represented as extending round and below the universe. Hell, the region "prepared for the devil and his angels," is at the bottom of Chaos.   **78. weltering**, rolling about.   **82. Satan.** Satan in Hebrew means "adversary" or "opposer."   **93. He**, God. **thunder**, thunderbolt.

That with the Mightiest raised me to contend,
And to the fierce contention brought along   100
Innumerable force of spirits armed,
That durst dislike his reign, and, me preferring,
His utmost power with adverse power opposed
In dubious battle on the plains of Heaven,
And shook his throne. What though the field be lost?
All is not lost; the unconquerable will,
And study of revenge, immortal hate,
And courage never to submit or yield:
And what is else not to be overcome?
That glory never shall his wrath or might   110
Extort from me. To bow and sue for grace
With suppliant knee, and deify his power,
Who, from the terror of this arm, so late
Doubted his empire,—that were low indeed,
That were an ignominy and shame beneath
This downfall; since, by fate, the strength of gods
And this empyreal substance cannot fail,
Since, through experience of this great event,
In arms not worse, in foresight much advanced,
We may with more successful hope resolve   120
To wage by force or guile eternal war,
Irreconcilable to our grand foe,
Who now triumphs, and in the excess of joy
Sole reigning holds the tyranny of Heaven."

So spake the apostate Angel, though in pain,
Vaunting aloud, but racked with deep despair;
And him thus answered soon his bold compeer:
"O Prince! O Chief of many thronèd Powers!
That led the embattled Seraphim to war
Under thy conduct, and, in dreadful deeds   130
Fearless, endangered Heaven's perpetual King,
And put to proof his high supremacy,
Whether upheld by strength, or chance, or fate!
Too well I see and rue the dire event
That with sad overthrow and foul defeat
Hath lost us Heaven, and all this mighty host
In horrible destruction laid thus low,
As far as gods and Heavenly essences
Can perish: for the mind and spirit remains
Invincible, and vigour soon returns,   140
Though all our glory extinct, and happy state
Here swallowed up in endless misery.
But what if he our Conqueror (whom I now
Of force believe almighty, since no less
Than such could have o'erpowered such force as ours)
Have left us this our spirit and strength entire,
Strongly to suffer and support our pains,
That we may so suffice his vengeful ire;
Or do him mightier service, as his thralls
By right of war, whate'er his business be,   150
Here in the heart of Hell to work in fire,
Or do his errands in the gloomy Deep?
What can it then avail, though yet we feel
Strength undiminished, or eternal being
To undergo eternal punishment?"

Whereto with speedy words the Arch-Fiend replied:—
"Fallen Cherub, to be weak is miserable,
Doing or suffering: but of this be sure—
To do aught good never will be our task,
But ever to do ill our sole delight,   160
As being the contrary to his high will
Whom we resist. If then his Providence
Out of our evil seek to bring forth good,
Our labour must be to pervert that end,
And out of good still to find means of evil;
Which ofttimes may succeed, so as perhaps
Shall grieve him, if I fail not, and disturb
His inmost counsels from their destined aim.
But see! the angry Victor hath recalled
His ministers of vengeance and pursuit   170
Back to the gates of Heaven; the sulphurous hail,
Shot after us in storm, o'erblown hath laid
The fiery surge, that from the precipice
Of Heaven received us falling; and the thunder,
Winged with red lightning and impetuous rage,
Perhaps hath spent his shafts, and ceases now
To bellow through the vast and boundless Deep.
Let us not slip the occasion, whether scorn
Or satiate fury yield it from our foe.
Seest thou yon dreary plain, forlorn and wild,   180
The seat of desolation, void of light,
Save what the glimmering of these livid flames
Casts pale and dreadful? Thither let us tend
From off the tossing of these fiery waves,
There rest, if any rest can harbour there,

---

104. In dubious battle. The description of the war in Heaven occurs in Book VI.   **107. study,** pursuit, endeavor.   **109. And what . . . overcome?** The line, somewhat obscure, is interpreted by Verity: "To retain one's hate, one's courage, etc., is not that to be still unsubdued: in what else but this lies the test of being not overcome?"   **110. That glory,** the glory which would redound to God from Satan's submission.   **114. Doubted his empire,** doubted whether his power were still his.   **127. compeer,** companion.   **129. Seraphim.** Milton throughout the poem uses such terms as "Seraphim," "Cherubim," "archangel," and so on loosely, both to obtain variety and to avoid the limitations that would be imposed by a strict adherence to the angelic hierarchy of the medieval Schoolmen.   **134. event,** outcome.   **138. essences,** beings.

144. Of force, of necessity.   **148. suffice,** satisfy.   **152. Deep?** Chaos.   **156. Arch-Fiend.** The old meaning of "fiend" is "one who hates"—the opposite of "friend."   **158. suffering,** enduring.   **165. still,** always.   **167. fail,** mistake.   **176. his,** its.   **178. slip,** let slip.   **179. satiate,** satiated.

And, reassembling our afflicted powers,
Consult how we may henceforth most offend
Our Enemy, our own loss how repair,
How overcome this dire calamity,
What reinforcement we may gain from hope,   190
If not, what resolution from despair."

   Thus Satan, talking to his nearest mate,
With head uplift above the wave, and eyes
That sparkling blazed; his other parts besides
Prone on the flood, extended long and large,
Lay floating many a rood, in bulk as huge
As whom the fables name of monstrous size,
Titanian, or Earth-born, that warred on Jove,
Briareos or Typhon, whom the den
By ancient Tarsus held, or that sea-beast   200
Leviathan, which God of all his works
Created hugest that swim the ocean stream;
Him, haply, slumbering on the Norway foam,
The pilot of some small night-foundered skiff
Deeming some island, oft, as seamen tell,
With fixèd anchor in his scaly rind
Moors by his side under the lee, while night
Invests the sea, and wishèd morn delays:
So stretched out huge in length the Arch-Fiend lay,
Chained on the burning lake; nor ever thence   210
Had risen, or heaved his head, but that the will
And high permission of all-ruling Heaven
Left him at large to his own dark designs,
That with reiterated crimes he might
Heap on himself damnation, while he sought
Evil to others, and, enraged, might see
How all his malice served but to bring forth
Infinite goodness, grace, and mercy, shewn
On Man by him seduced; but on himself   219
Treble confusion, wrath, and vengeance poured.

   Forthwith upright he rears from off the pool
His mighty stature; on each hand the flames
Driven backward slope their pointing spires, and rolled
In billows, leave in the midst a horrid vale.
Then with expanded wings he steers his flight
Aloft, incumbent on the dusky air
That felt unusual weight; till on dry land
He lights—if it were land that ever burned
With solid, as the lake with liquid fire,
And such appeared in hue; as when the force   230
Of subterranean wind transports a hill
Torn from Pelorus, or the shattered side
Of thundering Aetna, whose combustible
And fuelled entrails thence conceiving fire,
Sublimed with mineral fury, aid the winds,
And leave a singèd bottom all involved
With stench and smoke: such resting found the sole
Of unblest feet. Him followed his next mate,
Both glorying to have scaped the Stygian flood
As gods, and by their own recovered strength,   240
Not by the sufferance of supernal power.

   "Is this the region, this the soil, the clime,"
Said then the lost Archangel, "this the seat
That we must change for Heaven? this mournful gloom
For that celestial light? Be it so, since he
Who now is sovran can dispose and bid
What shall be right: farthest from him is best,
Whom reason hath equalled, force hath made supreme
Above his equals. Farewell, happy fields,
Where joy for ever dwells! Hail, horrors! hail,   250
Infernal world! and thou, profoundest Hell,
Receive thy new possessor; one who brings
A mind not to be changed by place or time.
The mind is its own place, and in itself
Can make a Heaven of Hell, a Hell of Heaven.
What matter, where, if I be still the same,
And what I should be, all but less than he
Whom thunder hath made greater? Here at least
We shall be free; the Almighty hath not built
Here for his envy, will not drive us hence: 260
Here we may reign secure; and in my choice
To reign is worth ambition, though in Hell:
Better to reign in Hell than serve in Heaven.
But wherefore let we then our faithful friends,
The associates and copartners of our loss,
Lie thus astonished on the oblivious pool,
And call them not to share with us their part

---

186. afflicted, overthrown. **powers,** forces (the other angels). **187. offend,** do violence to. **197. As whom,** as those whom. **198-99. Titanian . . . Briareos or Typhon.** The Titans were the older deities of Greek mythology, who waged war on the usurper Zeus (or Jove). The Giants were the offspring of Ge (Earth). Briareus, a hundred-handed Giant, assisted Zeus in his battle with the Titans. Typhon, a fire-breathing giant, with a hundred heads, after a fearful struggle with Zeus was subdued by thunderbolts, and was buried in Tartarus under Mt. Aetna. **201. Leviathan,** a reference to the mysterious sea monster of the Bible, and probably to Isaiah 27:1. Milton, in common with others of his day, doubtless thought of it as a whale. **204. night-foundered,** overtaken by night. **207. lee,** sheltered side. **208. Invests,** clothes, covers. **209. in length.** Notice that it is only in length or bulk, not in appearance, that Satan resembles the sea monster. **217-18. to bring forth . . . mercy.** In Book XII Adam in a vision is shown how the Redemption of man is to be accomplished. **223. spires,** tongues of flame.

226. incumbent, lying upon. **232-33. Pelorus . . . Aetna,** mountains in Sicily, the latter the famous volcano. **235. Sublimed,** a technical term from alchemy, meaning here "turned to flame." **238. next,** nearest. **241. sufferance,** permission. **248. Whom reason hath equalled.** Satan likes to think that in every respect but power he is quite equal to God. **251. profoundest,** lowest. **254. its,** one of the few occasions on which Milton uses this word. **257. all but less than he,** second only to him (God). **266. astonished,** thunderstruck, dazed. **oblivious,** producing forgetfulness.

In this unhappy mansion, or once more,
With rallied arms, to try what may be yet   269
Regained in Heaven, or what more lost in Hell?"
   So Satan spake, and him Beëlzebub
Thus answered: "Leader of those armies bright
Which but the Omnipotent none could have foiled,
If once they hear that voice, their liveliest pledge
Of hope in fears and dangers—heard so oft
In worst extremes, and on the perilous edge
Of battle when it raged, in all assaults
Their surest signal—they will soon resume
New courage and revive, though now they lie
Grovelling and prostrate on yon lake of fire,   280
As we erewhile, astounded and amazed;
No wonder, fallen such a pernicious highth!"
   He scarce had ceased when the superior Fiend
Was moving toward the shore; his ponderous shield
Ethereal temper, massy, large, and round,
Behind him cast. The broad circumference
Hung on his shoulders like the moon, whose orb
Through optic glass the Tuscan artist views
At evening from the top of Fesole,
Or in Valdarno, to descry new lands,   290
Rivers, or mountains, in her spotty globe.
His spear—to equal which the tallest pine
Hewn on Norwegian hills, to be the mast
Of some great ammiral, were but a wand—
He walked with, to support uneasy steps
Over the burning marle, not like those steps
On Heaven's azure; and the torrid clime
Smote on him sore besides, vaulted with fire.
Nathless he so endured, till on the beach
Of that inflamèd sea he stood, and called   300
His legions, Angel forms, who lay entranced,
Thick as autumnal leaves that strew the brooks
In Vallombrosa, where the Etrurian shades
High over-arched embower; or scattered sedge
Afloat, when with fierce winds Orion armed
Hath vexed the Red-Sea coast, whose waves o'erthrew
Busiris and his Memphian chivalry,
While with perfidious hatred they pursued

The sojourners of Goshen, who beheld
From the safe shore their floating carcasses   310
And broken chariot wheels: so thick bestrewn,
Abject and lost lay these, covering the flood,
Under amazement of their hideous change.
He called so loud, that all the hollow deep
Of Hell resounded: "Princes, Potentates,
Warriors, the flower of Heaven, once yours, now lost,
If such astonishment as this can seize
Eternal spirits! Or have ye chosen this place
After the toil of battle to repose
Your wearied virtue, for the ease you find   320
To slumber here as in the vales of Heaven?
Or in this abject posture have ye sworn
To adore the Conqueror—who now beholds
Cherub and Seraph rolling in the flood,
With scattered arms and ensigns, till anon
His swift pursuers from Heaven gates discern
The advantage, and, descending, tread us down
Thus drooping, or with linkèd thunderbolts
Transfix us to the bottom of this gulf?—
Awake, arise, or be for ever fallen!"   330
   They heard, and were abashed, and up they
      sprung
Upon the wing, as when men wont to watch,
On duty sleeping found by whom they dread,
Rouse and bestir themselves ere well awake.
Nor did they not perceive the evil plight
In which they were, or the fierce pains not feel;
Yet to their General's voice they soon obeyed,
Innumerable. As when the potent rod
Of Amram's son, in Egypt's evil day,
Waved round the coast, up called a pitchy cloud   340
Of locusts, warping on the eastern wind,
That o'er the realm of impious Pharaoh hung
Like night, and darkened all the land of Nile:
So numberless were those bad Angels seen
Hovering on wing under the cope of Hell,
'Twixt upper, nether, and surrounding fires;
Till, as a signal given, the uplifted spear
Of their great Sultan waving to direct
Their course, in even balance down they light
On the firm brimstone, and fill all the plain: 350
A multitude like which the populous North
Poured never from her frozen loins, to pass
Rhene or the Danaw, when her barbarous sons
Came like a deluge on the South, and spread

---

281. **amazed**, stupefied, bewildered.   282. **pernicious**, harmful, destructive.   285. **Ethereal**, heavenly.   288. **optic glass**, telescope. **the Tuscan artist,** Galileo, whom Milton had met at Florence.   289. **Fesole**, Fiesole, on a hill overlooking Florence, in the valley of the Arno (**Valdarno**).   294. **ammiral** (admiral), flagship. Milton preferred, when possible, to use the Italian forms or equivalents of certain English words.   296. **marle**, soil.   299. **Nathless**, nevertheless.   300. **inflamèd**, flaming.   303. **Vallombrosa**, "Shady Valley,"—about 18 miles from Florence.   305. **Orion**, the constellation Orion, the rising and setting of which were attended often by severe storms.   306. **Red-Sea.** The Hebrew original means "Reed Sea" or "Sea of Sedge," hence the **scattered sedge** of l. 304.   307. **Busiris**, the name of a legendary Egyptian ruler; used here instead of the official title Pharaoh. **Memphian**, of Memphis, one of the capitals of Egypt. **chivalry**, in the sense of cavalry.

309. **sojourners of Goshen**, the Israelites. See Exodus 14. 312. **Abject**, hurled down.   315–30. **"Princes, Potentates . . . fallen!"** The irony of Satan's opening remarks is as clever as it is effective.   320. **virtue**, valor.   339. **Amram's son**, Moses. See Exodus 10:12–15.   340. **pitchy**, black as pitch.   341. **warping**, undulating.   345. **cope**, covering, dome.   353. **Rhene . . . Danaw**, Rhine, Danube. These rivers formed the boundary of the Roman Empire, which was invaded by the northern Teutonic tribes.

Beneath Gibraltar to the Libyan sands.
Forthwith, from every squadron and each band,
The heads and leaders thither haste where stood
Their great Commander; godlike shapes, and forms
Excelling human, princely Dignities,
And Powers that erst in Heaven sat on thrones; 360
Though of their names in Heavenly records now
Be no memorial, blotted out and rased
By their rebellion from the Books of Life.
Nor had they yet among the sons of Eve
Got them new names, till, wandering o'er the Earth,
Through God's high sufferance for the trial of man,
By falsities and lies the greatest part
Of mànkind they corrupted to forsake
God their Creator; and the invisible
Glory of him that made them, to transform 370
Oft to the image of a brute, adorned
With gay religions full of pomp and gold,
And devils to adore for deities:
Then were they known to men by various names,
And various idols through the heathen world.
    Say, Muse, their names then known, who first, who last,
Roused from the slumber on that fiery couch,
At their great Emperor's call, as next in worth,
Came singly where he stood on the bare strand,
While the promiscuous crowd stood yet aloof. 380
    The chief were those, who, from the pit of Hell
Roaming to seek their prey on earth, durst fix
Their seats long after next the seat of God,
Their altars by his altar, gods adored
Among the nations round, and durst abide
Jehovah thundering out of Sion, throned
Between the Cherubim: yea, often placed
Within his sanctuary itself their shrines,
Abominations; and with cursèd things
His holy rites and solemn feasts profaned, 390
And with their darkness durst affront his light.
    First Moloch, horrid king, besmeared with blood
Of human sacrifice, and parents' tears,
Though, for the noise of drums and timbrels loud,
Their children's cries unheard, that passed through fire
To his grim idol. Him the Ammonite
Worshipped in Rabba and her watery plain,
In Argob, and in Basan, to the stream
Of utmost Arnon. Nor content with such
Audacious neighbourhood, the wisest heart 400
Of Solomon he led by fraud to build
His temple right against the temple of God
On that opprobrious hill, and made his grove
The pleasant valley of Hinnom, Tophet thence
And black Gehenna called, the type of Hell.
    Next, Chemos, the obscene dread of Moab's sons,
From Aroar to Nebo and the wild
Of southmost Abarim; in Heseboh
And Horonaim, Seon's realm, beyond
The flowery dale of Sibma clad with vines, 410
And Eleale to the Asphaltic Pool—
Peor his other name, when he enticed
Israel in Sittim, on their march from Nile,
To do him wanton rites, which cost them woe.
Yet thence his lustful orgies he enlarged
Even to that hill of scandal, by the grove
Of Moloch homicide, lust hard by hate;
Till good Josiah drove them thence to Hell.
With these came they who, from the bordering flood
Of old Euphrates to the brook that parts 420
Egypt from Syrian ground, had general names
Of Baälim and Ashtaroth—those male,
These feminine. For spirits, when they please,
Can either sex assume, or both; so soft
And uncompounded is their essence pure,
Not tied or manacled with joint or limb,
Nor founded on the brittle strength of bones,
Like cumbrous flesh; but, in what shape they choose,
Dilated or condensed, bright or obscure,
Can execute their aery purposes, 430
And works of love or enmity fulfil.
For those the race of Israel oft forsook
Their living Strength, and unfrequented left
His righteous altar, bowing lowly down
To bestial gods; for which their heads as low
Bowed down in battle, sunk before the spear

403. **opprobrious hill,** the Mount of Olives. Because of the pagan shrines upon it, it was called "hill of scandal" (see l. 416). 404. **Tophet,** from the Hebrew *toph*, drum. See above, l. 394. 404–05. **valley of Hinnom . . . Gehenna.** The Jewish reformers turned the beautiful valley, which had been polluted by pagan rites, into a place for casting rubbish. The fires, kept constantly burning to destroy the rubbish, caused the valley to become **the type of Hell;** hence the modern meanings of "Tophet" and "Gehenna." 406. **dread,** dreaded god. **Chemos,** another form of Moloch as he was worshiped by the Moabites. 411. **the Asphaltic Pool,** the Dead Sea, on the shores of which are asphaltic or bituminous deposits. The towns and sites mentioned in the preceding lines are in its neighborhood. 413. **Israel in Sittim.** See Numbers 25. 417. **hard,** near. 418. **good Josiah drove them thence.** See II Kings 23:13–14. 422. **Baälim and Ashtaroth.** See notes on ll. 197–200 of "On the Morning of Christ's Nativity" (page 640). 423–31. **spirits . . . fulfil.** Milton in these lines is preparing for important developments later in the poem. **bright or obscure** (l. 429), visible or invisible.

362. **rased,** erased. 364–75. **Nor had they yet . . . world.** Milton follows the belief of the Church Fathers that the fallen angels had, in process of time, become pagan deities. 372. **religions,** rites. 392. **Moloch,** a sun god worshiped in the form of a bull. For Biblical references to his sacrifices, see Psalm 106:36–38; Jeremiah 7:31; and Ezekiel 16:21. 394. **for,** because of.

Of despicable foes. With these in troop
Came Astoreth, whom the Phoenicians called
Astarte, Queen of Heaven, with crescent horns;
To whose bright image nightly by the moon   440
Sidonian virgins paid their vows and songs;
In Sion also not unsung, where stood
Her temple on the offensive mountain, built
By that uxorious king whose heart, though large,
Beguiled by fair idolatresses, fell
To idols foul. Thammuz came next behind,
Whose annual wound in Lebanon allured
The Syrian damsels to lament his fate
In amorous ditties all a summer's day;
While smooth Adonis from his native rock   450
Ran purple to the sea, supposed with blood
Of Thammuz yearly wounded. The love-tale
Infected Sion's daughters with like heat,
Whose wanton passions in the sacred porch
Ezekiel saw, when, by the vision led,
His eye surveyed the dark idolatries
Of alienated Judah. Next came one
Who mourned in earnest, when the captive ark
Maimed his brute image, head and hands lopt off
In his own temple, on the grunsel edge,   460
Where he fell flat, and shamed his worshippers:
Dagon his name, sea monster, upward man
And downward fish; yet had his temple high
Reared in Azotus, dreaded through the coast
Of Palestine, in Gath, and Ascalon,
And Accaron, and Gaza's frontier bounds.
Him followed Rimmon, whose delightful seat
Was fair Damascus, on the fertile banks
Of Abbana, and Pharphar, lucid streams.
He also against the house of God was bold: 470
A leper once he lost and gained a king,
Ahaz, his sottish conqueror, whom he drew
God's altar to disparage and displace
For one of Syrian mode, whereon to burn
His odious offerings, and adore the gods
Whom he had vanquished. After these appeared
A crew, who, under names of old renown,
Osiris, Isis, Orus, and their train,
With monstrous shapes and sorceries abused
Fanatic Egypt and her priests to seek   480
Their wandering gods disguised in brutish forms
Rather than human. Nor did Israel scape
The infection, when their borrowed gold composed
The calf in Oreb; and the rebel king
Doubled that sin in Bethel and in Dan,
Likening his Maker to the grazèd ox—
Jehovah, who, in one night, when he passed
From Egypt marching, equalled with one stroke
Both her first-born and all her bleating gods.
Belial came last, than whom a spirit more lewd   490
Fell not from Heaven, or more gross to love
Vice for itself. To him no temple stood
Or altar smoked; yet who more oft than he
In temples and at altars, when the priest
Turns atheist, as did Eli's sons, who filled
With lust and violence the house of God?
In courts and palaces he also reigns,
And in luxurious cities, where the noise
Of riot ascends above their loftiest towers,
And injury and outrage; and when night   500
Darkens the streets, then wander forth the sons
Of Belial, flown with insolence and wine.
Witness the streets of Sodom, and that night
In Gibeah, when the hospitable door
Exposed a matron, to avoid worse rape.
  These were the prime in order and in might;
The rest were long to tell; though far renowned
The Ionian gods—of Javan's issue held
Gods, yet confessed later than Heaven and Earth,
Their boasted parents—Titan, Heaven's first-born
With his enormous brood, and birthright seized   511
By younger Saturn; he from mightier Jove,
His own and Rhea's son, like measure found;
So Jove usurping reigned. These, first in Crete
And Ida known, thence on the snowy top
Of cold Olympus ruled the middle air,

438. **Astoreth,** singular of Ashtaroth. See "On the Morning of Christ's Nativity," l. 200 (page 643). 441. **Sidonian.** Tyre and Sidon were the chief coast towns of the Phoenicians. 443. **offensive mountain.** See ll. 403 and 416 above. 444. **uxorious king,** Solomon. See I Kings 11:1–8. 446. **Thammuz,** the Greek Adonis. See "On the Morning of Christ's Nativity," l. 204 (page 643). 450. **smooth Adonis,** the Phoenician river, named after the god, the waters of which were in the spring reddened with mud. 455. **Ezekiel saw.** See Ezekiel 8:14–15. 456. **dark,** secret. 459. **his brute image,** Dagon the fish god. See "On the Morning of Christ's Nativity," l. 199 (page 643). 460. **grunsel,** groundsel, threshold. 464. **dreaded,** worshiped. 471. **A leper,** Naaman. See II Kings 5. 474. **Syrian mode.** See II Kings 16; II Chronicles 28:20–24. 478. **Osiris, Isis, Orus.** See "On the Morning of Christ's Nativity," ll. 210–13 (page 643). 479. **monstrous,** that is, of animals. **abused,** deceived. 483. **borrowed gold.** See Exodus 12:35–36 and chap. 32. 484–85. **rebel king . . . sin.** Jeroboam made *two* golden calves. I Kings 12:28–30. 487. **when he passed.** See Exodus 12:12. 489. **her first-born.** A reference to the tenth of the Egyptian plagues. See Exodus 12. 490. **Belial,** not, strictly speaking, a god, but in the original Hebrew an abstract term signifying worthlessness, baseness, "of no account." 495. **Eli's sons.** See I Samuel 2:12, 22. 498. **luxurious,** lewd. 501–03. **the sons Of Belial.** Milton undoubtedly had in mind the bands of roistering young men who roamed the streets of London at night, committing outrages upon citizens. **flown,** flushed. **Sodom.** See Genesis 19:4–8. 504. **Gibeah.** See Judges 19:16–25. 506. **prime,** chief. 508. **Javan's issue,** the Ionians, or Greeks, offspring of Javan, son of Japhet. See Genesis 10:2. **held,** considered. 509. **later,** to be later. 513. **measure,** treatment. 515. **Ida,** Mt. Ida, in Crete.

Their highest Heaven; or on the Delphian cliff,
Or in Dodona, and through all the bounds
Of Doric land; or who with Saturn old
Fled over Adria to the Hesperian fields,   520
And o'er the Celtic roamed the utmost isles.

All these and more came flocking; but with looks
Downcast and damp, yet such wherein appeared
Obscure some glimpse of joy to have found their chief
Not in despair, to have found themselves not lost
In loss itself; which on his countenance cast
Like doubtful hue. But he, his wonted pride
Soon recollecting, with high words, that bore
Semblance of worth, not substance, gently raised
Their fainted courage, and dispelled their fears: 530
Then straight commands, that at the warlike sound
Of trumpets loud and clarions, be upreared
His mighty standard. That proud honour claimed
Azazel as his right, a Cherub tall:
Who forthwith from the glittering staff unfurled
The imperial ensign, which, full high advanced,
Shone like a meteor, streaming to the wind,
With gems and golden lustre rich emblazed,
Seraphic arms and trophies; all the while
Sonorous metal blowing martial sounds: 540
At which the universal host upsent
A shout that tore Hell's concave, and beyond
Frighted the reign of Chaos and old Night.
All in a moment through the gloom were seen
Ten thousand banners rise into the air,
With orient colours waving: with them rose
A forest huge of spears; and thronging helms
Appeared, and serried shields in thick array
Of depth immeasurable. Anon they move
In perfect phalanx to the Dorian mood   550
Of flutes and soft recorders; such as raised
To highth of noblest temper heroes old
Arming to battle, and, instead of rage,
Deliberate valour breathed, firm and unmoved
With dread of death to flight or foul retreat;
Nor wanting power to mitigate and suage
With solemn touches troubled thoughts, and chase
Anguish and doubt and fear and sorrow and pain
From mortal or immortal minds. Thus they,
Breathing united force with fixèd thought,   560
Moved on in silence to soft pipes, that charmed
Their painful steps o'er the burnt soil: and now,
Advanced in view, they stand, a horrid front
Of dreadful length and dazzling arms, in guise
Of warriors old with ordered spear and shield,
Awaiting what command their mighty chief
Had to impose. He through the armèd files
Darts his experienced eye, and soon traverse
The whole battalion views, their order due,
Their visages and stature as of gods;   570
Their number last he sums. And now his heart
Distends with pride, and hardening in his strength
Glories; for never, since created man,
Met such embodied force as named with these
Could merit more than that small infantry
Warred on by cranes: though all the giant brood
Of Phlegra with the heroic race were joined
That fought at Thebes and Ilium, on each side
Mixed with auxiliar gods; and what resounds
In fable or romance of Uther's son,   580
Begirt with British and Armoric knights;
And all who since, baptized or infidel,
Jousted in Aspramont, or Montalban,
Damasco, or Marocco, or Trebisond;
Or whom Biserta sent from Afric shore
When Charlemain with all his peerage fell
By Fontarabbia. Thus far these beyond
Compare of mortal prowess, yet observed
Their dread commander. He, above the rest
In shape and gesture proudly eminent,   590
Stood like a tower; his form had yet not lost
All her original brightness, nor appeared
Less than Archangel ruined, and the excess

517. **Delphian.** The oracle of Apollo was at Delphi, on Mt. Parnassus.   518. **Dodona,** the oracle of Zeus (Jove) in Epirus.   519. **Doric,** that is, Greek.   520. **Adria,** the Adriatic Sea. **the Hesperian fields,** Italy. According to Latin legends, Saturn, driven out by Jupiter, had established his sovereignty and the "Age of Gold" in Italy and Iberia (Spain).   521. **the Celtic,** France and Northwestern Europe. **the utmost isles,** the British Isles.   523. **damp,** depressed.   526–27. **cast Like doubtful hue,** that is, their discouragement was at first reflected in Satan's countenance. 528. **recollecting,** re-collecting.   531. **straight,** straightway, immediately.   536. **advanced,** uplifted.   538. **emblazed,** emblazoned.   542. **concave,** vault, dome.   543. **reign,** realm. **Chaos and old Night.** Chaos here is a person, ruler of the great Deep, also called Chaos, and, with "grandmother Night," as Spenser calls her, ancestor of all things. An interesting analogue to this classical conception is found in Genesis 1:2; "And the earth was *without form, and void,* and *darkness* was upon the face of the *deep.*"   546. **orient,** bright.   548. **serried,** interlocked.   550. **the Dorian mood.** See note 136 on page 646.   551. **recorders,** flageolets.

554. **unmoved,** immovable.   556–59. **power to mitigate . . . minds.** Could there be a happier statement of the function and effect of noble music than is contained in these lines? **suage,** assuage.   561. **charmed.** The word has connotations of both song and magic (en*chant*ment).   563. **horrid,** bristling.   568. **traverse,** across.   573. **since created man,** a Latinism; the English form would be "since man was created."   574. **embodied,** collected. **named with,** compared with.   575–76. **that small infantry . . . cranes,** the Pigmies, whose battles with the cranes form the subject of one of the Homeric poems.   577. **Phlegra,** the site, in Macedonia, where the giants were conquered by the gods. **the heroic race,** the heroes who fought at Thebes and in the Trojan War.   580. **Uther's son,** Arthur.   581. **Begirt with,** surrounded by. **Armoric,** of Brittany.   583–87. **Aspramont . . . Fontarabbia,** names from the chivalric romances, and intended, doubtless, to induce a romantic sensation in the reader.   588. **observed,** did homage to.   592. **her.** *Forma* in Latin is feminine; hence the pronoun "her."

Of glory obscured: as when the sun new risen
Looks through the horizontal misty air
Shorn of his beams, or, from behind the moon,
In dim eclipse disastrous twilight sheds
On half the nations, and with fear of change
Perplexes monarchs: darkened so, yet shone
Above them all the Archangel; but his face 600
Deep scars of thunder had intrenched, and care
Sat on his faded cheek, but under brows
Of dauntless courage, and considerate pride
Waiting revenge. Cruel his eye, but cast
Signs of remorse and passion to behold
The fellows of his crime, the followers rather
(Far other once beheld in bliss), condemned
For ever now to have their lot in pain;
Millions of spirits for his fault amerced
Of Heaven, and from eternal splendours flung 610
For his revolt: yet faithful how they stood,
Their glory withered; as when Heaven's fire
Hath scathed the forest oaks or mountain pines,
With singèd top their stately growth, though bare,
Stands on the blasted heath. He now prepared
To speak; whereat their doubled ranks they bend
From wing to wing, and half enclose him round
With all his peers; attention held them mute.
Thrice he assayed, and thrice, in spite of scorn,
Tears, such as angels weep, burst forth: at last 620
Words, interwove with sighs, found out their way:
  "O myriads of immortal Spirits! O Powers
Matchless, but with the Almighty!—and that strife
Was not inglorious, though the event was dire,
As this place testifies, and this dire change,
Hateful to utter. But what power of mind,
Foreseeing or presaging, from the depth
Of knowledge past or present, could have feared
How such united force of gods, how such
As stood like these, could ever know repulse? 630
For who can yet believe, though after loss,
That all these puissant legions, whose exile
Hath emptied Heaven, shall fail to reascend,
Self-raised, and repossess their native seat?
For me, be witness all the host of Heaven,
If counsels different, or dangers shunned
By me, have lost our hopes. But he who reigns
Monarch in Heaven, till then as one secure
Sat on his throne, upheld by old repute,
Consent or custom, and his regal state 640
Put forth at full, but still his strength concealed;
Which tempted our attempt, and wrought our fall.

Henceforth his might we know, and know our own,
So as not either to provoke, or dread
New war provoked. Our better part remains
To work in close design, by fraud or guile,
What force effected not; that he no less
At length from us may find, who overcomes
By force hath overcome but half his foe.
Space may produce new worlds; whereof so rife 650
There went a fame in Heaven that he ere long
Intended to create, and therein plant
A generation whom his choice regard
Should favour equal to the Sons of Heaven.
Thither, if but to pry, shall be perhaps
Our first eruption: thither or elsewhere;
For this infernal pit shall never hold
Celestial spirits in bondage, nor the Abyss
Long under darkness cover. But these thoughts
Full counsel must mature. Peace is despaired; 660
For who can think submission? War then, war
Open or understood, must be resolved."
  He spake; and, to confirm his words, out flew
Millions of flaming swords, drawn from the thighs
Of mighty Cherubim; the sudden blaze
Far round illumined Hell. Highly they raged
Against the Highest, and fierce, with graspèd arms,
Clashed on their sounding shields the din of war,
Hurling defiance toward the vault of Heaven.
  There stood a hill not far, whose grisly top 670
Belched fire and rolling smoke; the rest entire
Shone with a glossy scurf, undoubted sign
That in his womb was hid metallic ore,
The work of sulphur. Thither, winged with speed,
A numerous brigad hastened: as when bands
Of pioneers, with spade and pickaxe armed,
Forerun the royal camp, to trench a field,
Or cast a rampart. Mammon led them on,
Mammon, the least erected spirit that fell
From Heaven; for even in Heaven his looks and thoughts 680
Were always downward bent, admiring more
The riches of Heaven's pavement, trodden gold,
Than aught divine or holy else enjoyed
In vision beatific. By him first
Men also, and by his suggestion taught,

597. **disastrous,** portending disaster. 601. **intrenched,** cut into. 603. **considerate,** thoughtful. 605. **passion,** deep feeling. 609. **amerced,** punished by loss. 619. **assayed,** essayed, attempted. 624. **event,** outcome. 633. **Hath emptied Heaven,** one of Satan's many vain boasts. 636. **different,** differing from yours; selfish. 645. **better part,** wiser course of action. 646. **work,** bring about. **close,** secret. 650. **rife,** commonly reported. 651. **fame,** rumor. 660. **despaired,** despaired of. 662. **understood,** among ourselves; secret. 670. **grisly,** horrible. 672. **scurf,** incrustation. 673. **his,** its. 674. **The work of sulphur,** a reference to the ancient theory that metals were compounded of sulphur and mercury. 676. **pioneers,** miners, sappers. 678. **Mammon.** Like Belial, Mammon is not the name of a god, but a Chaldaic abstract term for "riches." See Matthew 6:24. 679. **erected,** elevated.

Ransacked the Center, and with impious hands
Rifled the bowels of their mother Earth
For treasures better hid. Soon had his crew
Opened into the hill a spacious wound,
And digged out ribs of gold. Let none admire   690
That riches grow in Hell; that soil may best
Deserve the precious bane. And here let those
Who boast in mortal things, and wondering tell
Of Babel, and the works of Memphian kings,
Learn how their greatest monuments of fame,
And strength, and art, are easily outdone
By spirits reprobate, and in an hour
What in an age they, with incessant toil
And hands innumerable, scarce perform.
Nigh on the plain, in many cells prepared,   700
That underneath had veins of liquid fire
Sluiced from the lake, a second multitude
With wondrous art founded the massy ore,
Severing each kind, and scummed the bullion dross.
A third as soon had formed within the ground
A various mould, and from the boiling cells
By strange conveyance filled each hollow nook:
As in an organ, from one blast of wind,
To many a row of pipes the sound-board breathes.
Anon out of the earth a fabric huge   710
Rose like an exhalation, with the sound
Of dulcet symphonies and voices sweet—
Built like a temple, where pilasters round
Were set, and Doric pillars overlaid
With golden architrave; nor did there want
Cornice or frieze, with bossy sculptures graven:
The roof was fretted gold. Not Babylon,
Nor great Alcairo, such magnificence
Equalled in all their glories, to enshrine
Belus or Serapis their gods, or seat   720
Their kings, when Egypt with Assyria strove
In wealth and luxury. The ascending pile
Stood fixed her stately highth, and straight the doors,
Opening their brazen folds, discover, wide
Within, her ample spaces o'er the smooth
And level pavement: from the archèd roof,
Pendent by subtle magic, many a row
Of starry lamps and blazing cressets, fed
With naphtha and asphaltus, yielded light
As from a sky. The hasty multitude   730
Admiring entered, and the work some praise,

And some the architect. His hand was known
In Heaven by many a towered structure high,
Where sceptred Angels held their residence,
And sat as princes, whom the supreme King
Exalted to such power, and gave to rule,
Each in his hierarchy, the orders bright.
Nor was his name unheard, or unadored,
In ancient Greece, and in Ausonian land
Men called him Mulciber: and how he fell   740
From Heaven they fabled, thrown by angry Jove
Sheer o'er the crystal battlements; from morn
To noon he fell, from noon to dewy eve,
A summer's day; and with the setting sun
Dropt from the zenith like a falling star,
On Lemnos, the Aegean isle. Thus they relate,
Erring; for he with this rebellious rout
Fell long before; nor aught availed him now
To have built in Heaven high towers; nor did he scape
By all his engines, but was headlong sent   750
With his industrious crew to build in Hell.
    Meanwhile the wingèd haralds, by command
Of sovran power, with awful ceremony
And trumpet's sound, throughout the host proclaim
A solemn council forthwith to be held
At Pandaemonium, the high capitol
Of Satan and his peers. Their summons called
From every band and squarèd regiment
By place or choice the worthiest; they anon   759
With hundreds and with thousands trooping came
Attended. All access was thronged, the gates
And porches wide, but chief the spacious hall
(Though like a covered field, where champions bold
Wont ride in armed, and at the Soldan's chair
Defied the best of Panim chivalry
To mortal combat, or career with lance)
Thick swarmed, both on the ground and in the air,
Brushed with the hiss of rustling wings. As bees
In spring time, when the Sun with Taurus rides,
Pour forth their populous youth about the hive   770
In clusters; they among fresh dews and flowers
Fly to and fro, or on the smoothèd plank,

---

686. **Center**, the earth.   690. **admire**, wonder.   692. **bane**, evil, blight.   694. **works of Memphian kings**, the Pyramids.   703. **founded**, melted.   704. **bullion dross**, slag.   716. **bossy**, in high relief; embossed.   717. **fretted**, wrought with designs.   718. **Alcairo**, Cairo.   720. **Belus**, Bel, or Baal. **Serapis**, the Egyptian god of the underworld.   723. **fixed**, completed. **straight**, straightway.   728. **cressets**, hanging lamps.

732. **the architect.** Whether the architect is Mammon, and therefore identical with **Mulciber** (l. 740), is not certain. Since Milton has already sufficiently characterized Mammon (ll. 678 ff.), and since the account of Mulciber's activities which follows is quite dissimilar to that of Mammon's, there seems to be good reason for considering Mulciber, the architect, a distinct person from Mammon. (Mulciber is Vulcan.)   739. **Ausonian**, Italian.   747. **rout**, crew.   750. **engines**, devices.   752. **haralds**, heralds.   753. **awful**, awe-inspiring.   756. **Pandaemonium**, literally, "the place of all the demons."   757. **peers.** The word has here the meaning of "nobility," as in modern English.   764. **Soldan's**, Sultan's.   765. **Panim**, pagan.   769. **with Taurus**, in the sign of the Bull, one of the signs of the Zodiac (April 19–May 20).

JOHN MILTON

The suburb of their straw-built citadel,
New rubbed with balm, expatiate and confer
Their state affairs. So thick the aery crowd
Swarmed and were straitened; till, the signal given,
Behold a wonder! they but now who seemed
In bigness to surpass Earth's giant sons,
Now less than smallest dwarfs, in narrow room
Throng numberless, like that Pygmean race   780
Beyond the Indian mount; or faery elves,
Whose midnight revels, by a forest side
Or fountain, some belated peasant sees,
Or dreams he sees, while overhead the Moon
Sits arbitress, and nearer to the Earth
Wheels her pale course; they, on their mirth and dance
Intent, with jocund music charm his ear;
At once with joy and fear his heart rebounds.
Thus incorporeal spirits to smallest forms   789
Reduced their shapes immense, and were at large,
Though without number still, amidst the hall
Of that infernal court. But far within,
And in their own dimensions like themselves,
The great Seraphic Lords and Cherubim
In close recess and secret conclave sat,
A thousand demi-gods on golden seats,
Frequent and full. After short silence then,
And summons read, the great consùlt began.

BOOK II

The Argument

The consultation begun, Satan debates whether another battle be to be hazarded for the recovery of Heaven: some advise it, others dissuade. A third proposal is preferred, mentioned before by Satan, to search the truth of that prophecy or tradition in Heaven concerning another world, and another kind of creature, equal or not much inferior to themselves, about this time to be created. Their doubt who shall be sent on this difficult search; Satan, their chief, undertakes alone the voyage; is honoured and applauded. The council thus ended, the rest betake them several ways and to several employments, as their inclinations lead them, to entertain the time till Satan return. He passes on his journey to Hell Gates, finds them shut, and who sat there to guard them; by whom at length they are opened, and discover to him the great gulf between Hell and Heaven; with what difficulty he passes through, directed by Chaos, the Power of that place, to the sight of this new World which he sought.

774. **expatiate,** spread out. **confer,** discuss. 776. **straitened,** crowded. 785. **arbitress,** witness. 790. **at large,** uncrowded. 793. **like themselves.** The angels, though having power to change shape and sex at will, are represented as having each his own special form and nature. 797. **Frequent,** crowded. 798. **consùlt,** consultation.

High on a throne of royal state, which far
Outshone the wealth of Ormus and of Ind,
Or where the gorgeous East, with richest hand,
Showers on her kings barbaric pearl and gold,
Satan exalted sat, by merit raised
To that bad eminence; and, from despair
Thus high uplifted beyond hope, aspires
Beyond thus high, insatiate to pursue
Vain war with Heaven, and, by success untaught,
His proud imaginations thus displayed: 10
"Powers and Dominions, Deities of Heaven!
For, since no deep within her gulf can hold
Immortal vigour, though oppressed and fallen,
I give not Heaven for lost. From this descent
Celestial Virtues rising will appear
More glorious and more dread than from no fall,
And trust themselves to fear no second fate.
Me, though just right, and the fixed laws of Heaven,
Did first create your leader, next, free choice,
With what besides, in council or in fight,   20
Hath been achieved of merit, yet this loss,
Thus far at least recovered, hath much more
Established in a safe unenvied throne,
Yielded with full consent. The happier state
In Heaven, which follows dignity, might draw
Envy from each inferior; but who here
Will envy whom the highest place exposes
Foremost to stand against the Thunderer's aim
Your bulwark, and condemns to greatest share
Of endless pain? Where there is then no good   30
For which to strive, no strife can grow up there
From faction; for none sure will claim in Hell
Precedence, none whose portion is so small
Of present pain, that with ambitious mind
Will covet more. With this advantage then
To union, and firm faith, and firm accord,
More than can be in Heaven, we now return
To claim our just inheritance of old,
Surer to prosper than prosperity
Could have assured us; and by what best way,   40
Whether of open war or covert guile,
We now debate; who can advise may speak."
   He ceased; and next him Moloch, sceptred king,
Stood up, the strongest and the fiercest spirit
That fought in Heaven, now fiercer by despair.
His trust was with the Eternal to be deemed
Equal in strength, and rather than be less
Cared not to be at all; with that care lost

2. **Ormus** a town on an island in the Persian Gulf, famous for its diamond trade. **Ind,** India. 4. **barbaric,** barbarously magnificent. 9. **success,** issue, result, experience. 11. **"Powers, and Dominions, . . ."** two of the angelic orders. Milton uses the titles in the general sense of "powers of Heaven." 14. **give . . . for lost,** consider as lost. 15. **Virtues,** one of the orders of angels; used here in a general sense. 16. **dread,** to be dreaded.

Went all his fear: of God, or Hell, or worse,
He recked not, and these words thereafter spake: 50
"My sentence is for open war. Of wiles,
More unexpert, I boast not: them let those
Contrive who need, or when they need; not now.
For while they sit contriving, shall the rest—
Millions that stand in arms, and longing wait
The signal to ascend—sit lingering here,
Heaven's fugitives, and for their dwelling-place
Accept this dark opprobrious den of shame,
The prison of his tyranny who reigns
By our delay? No! let us rather choose, 60
Armed with Hell flames and fury, all at once
O'er Heaven's high towers to force resistless way,
Turning our tortures into horrid arms
Against the Torturer; when to meet the noise
Of his almighty engine he shall hear
Infernal thunder, and for lightning see
Black fire and horror shot with equal rage
Among his Angels, and his throne itself
Mixed with Tartarean sulphur and strange fire,
His own invented torments. But perhaps 70
The way seems difficult and steep to scale
With upright wing against a higher foe.
Let such bethink them, if the sleepy drench
Of that forgetful lake benumb not still,
That in our proper motion we ascend
Up to our native seat; descent and fall
To us is adverse. Who but felt of late,
When the fierce foe hung on our broken rear
Insulting, and pursued us through the deep,
With what compulsion and laborious flight 80
We sunk thus low? The ascent is easy then.
The event is feared: should we again provoke
Our stronger, some worse way his wrath may find
To our destruction—if there be in Hell
Fear to be worse destroyed! What can be worse
Than to dwell here, driven out from bliss, condemned
In this abhorrèd deep to utter woe;
Where pain of unextinguishable fire
Must exercise us, without hope of end,
The vassals of his anger, when the scourge 90
Inexorably, and the torturing hour,
Calls us to penance? More destroyed than thus,
We should be quite abolished, and expire.
What fear we then? what doubt we to incense
His utmost ire? which, to the highth enraged,
Will either quite consume us, and reduce
To nothing this essential—happier far
Than miserable to have eternal being!
Or if our substance be indeed divine,
And cannot cease to be, we are at worst 100
On this side nothing; and by proof we feel
Our power sufficient to disturb his Heaven,
And with perpetual inroads to alarm,
Though inaccessible, his fatal throne;
Which, if not victory, is yet revenge."
 He ended frowning, and his look denounced
Desperate revenge, and battle dangerous
To less than gods. On the other side up rose
Belial, in act more graceful and humane;
A fairer person lost not heaven; he seemed 110
For dignity composed and high exploit.
But all was false and hollow; though his tongue
Dropt manna, and could make the worse appear
The better reason, to perplex and dash
Maturest counsels: for his thoughts were low,
To vice industrious, but to nobler deeds
Timorous and slothful. Yet, he pleased the ear,
And with persuasive accent thus began:
 "I should be much for open war, O Peers!
As not behind in hate, if what was urged 120
Main reason to persuade immediate war
Did not dissuade me most, and seem to cast
Ominous conjecture on the whole success;
When he who most excels in fact of arms,
In what he counsels and in what excels
Mistrustful, grounds his courage on despair
And utter dissolution, as the scope
Of all his aim, after some dire revenge.
First, what revenge? The towers of Heaven are filled
With armèd watch, that render all access 130
Impregnable; oft on the bordering Deep
Encamp their legions; or with òbscure wing
Scout far and wide into the realm of Night,
Scorning surprise. Or could we break our way
By force, and at our heels all Hell should rise
With blackest insurrection, to confound
Heaven's purest light, yet our great Enemy,
All incorruptible, would on his throne
Sit unpolluted, and the ethereal mould,
Incapable of stain, would soon expel 140
Her mischief, and purge off the baser fire,
Victorious. Thus repulsed, our final hope

50. **recked,** cared. 51. **sentence,** vote, opinion. 52. **More unexpert,** less experienced in **wiles** (l. 51); without skill in speech and theoretical strategy. 65. **engine,** the thunderbolt. See Book I, l. 174. 69. **Mixed,** convulsed. 73. **sleepy drench,** sleep-producing draught. 74. **forgetful lake.** Compare "oblivious pool," Book I, l. 26. 75. **proper motion,** the motion "proper" or natural to us. 77. **adverse,** unnatural. 82. **event,** outcome. 89. **exercise,** torment. 94. **What,** why.

97. **esssential,** existence, essence. 100–01. **at worst . . . nothing,** at the worst possible point short of annihilation. 104. **fatal,** ordained by fate. 106. **denounced,** proclaimed, threatened. 109. **humane,** urbane, polished. 113. **manna,** honey. 114. **dash,** frustrate. 124. **fact,** feat. 132. **òbscure,** invisible. 139. **mould,** substance.

Is flat despair: we must exasperate
The Almighty Victor to spend all his rage;
And that must end us, that must be our cure—
To be no more. Sad cure! for who would lose,
Though full of pain, this intellectual being,
Those thoughts that wander through eternity,
To perish rather, swallowed up and lost
In the wide womb of uncreated Night,   150
Devoid of sense and motion? And who knows,
Let this be good, whether our angry Foe
Can give it, or will ever? How he can
Is doubtful; that he never will is sure.
Will he, so wise, let loose at once his ire,
Belike through impotence, or unaware,
To give his enemies their wish, and end
Them in his anger, whom his anger saves
To punish endless? 'Wherefore cease we, then?'
Say they who counsel war; 'we are decreed,   160
Reserved, and destined to eternal woe;
Whatever doing, what can we suffer more,
What can we suffer worse?' Is this then worst,
Thus sitting, thus consulting, thus in arms?
What when we fled amain, pursued and strook
With Heaven's afflicting thunder, and besought
The Deep to shelter us? This Hell then seemed
A refuge from those wounds. Or when we lay
Chained on the burning lake? That sure was worse.
What if the breath that kindled those grim fires, 170
Awaked, should blow them into sevenfold rage,
And plunge us in the flames? or, from above,
Should intermitted vengeance arm again
His red right hand to plague us? What if all
Her stores were opened, and this firmament
Of Hell should spout her cataracts of fire,
Impendent horrors, threatening hideous fall
One day upon our heads? while we, perhaps,
Designing or exhorting glorious war,
Caught in a fiery tempest, shall be hurled,   180
Each on his rock transfixed, the sport and prey
Of racking whirlwinds, or for ever sunk
Under yon boiling ocean, wrapt in chains,
There to converse with everlasting groans,
Unrespited, unpitied, unreprieved,
Ages of hopeless end! This would be worse.
War therefore, open or concealed, alike
My voice dissuades; for what can force or guile
With him, or who deceive his mind, whose eye
Views all things at one view? He from Heaven's
    highth   190
All these our motions vain sees and derides;
Not more almighty to resist our might
Than wise to frustrate all our plots and wiles.
Shall we then live thus vile, the race of Heaven
Thus trampled, thus expelled, to suffer here
Chains and these torments? Better these than worse,
By my advice; since fate inevitable
Subdues us, and omnipotent decree,
The Victor's will. To suffer, as to do,
Our strength is equal, nor the law unjust   200
That so ordains. This was at first resolved,
If we were wise, against so great a foe
Contending, and so doubtful what might fall.
I laugh, when those who at the spear are bold
And venturous, if that fail them, shrink, and fear
What yet they know must follow—to endure
Exile, or ignominy, or bonds, or pain,
The sentence of their conqueror. This is now
Our doom; which if we can sustain and bear,
Our Sùpreme Foe in time may much remit   210
His anger, and perhaps, thus far removed,
Not mind us not offending, satisfied
With what is punished; whence these raging fires
Will slacken, if his breath stir not their flames.
Our purer essence then will overcome
Their noxious vapour, or, inured, not feel;
Or, changed at length, and to the place conformed
In temper and in nature, will receive
Familiar the fierce heat; and, void of pain,
This horror will grow mild, this darkness light; 220
Besides what hope the never-ending flight
Of future days may bring, what chance, what
    change
Worth waiting,—since our present lot appears
For happy though but ill, for ill not worst,
If we procure not to ourselves more woe."
   Thus Belial, with words clothed in reason's garb,
Counselled ignoble ease, and peaceful sloth,
Not peace; and after him thus Mammon spake:
"Either to disenthrone the King of Heaven
We war, if war be best, or to regain   230
Our own right lost. Him to unthrone we then
May hope, when everlasting Fate shall yield
To fickle Chance, and Chaos judge the strife.
The former, vain to hope, argues as vain
The latter; for what place can be for us
Within Heaven's bound, unless Heaven's Lord Su-
    preme

---

152. Let this be, grant this to be.   **156. Belike,** used ironically, in the sense of "Doubtless!" **impotence,** inability to restrain himself. **unaware,** in ignorance of his enemies' desires.   **165. amain,** with all speed. **strook,** struck.   **173. intermitted,** temporarily suspended.   **175. Her stores,** those of Hell.   **177. Impendent,** overhanging.   **182. racking,** torturing.   **184. converse,** dwell with.   **188. what can force,** what can force achieve?

191. motions, schemes.   **199. suffer,** endure.   **203. fall,** befall, happen.   **216. inured,** accustomed to it.   **219. Familiar,** as familiar, and thus not uncomfortable.   **223. waiting,** waiting for.   **234. argues,** shows.

We overpower? Suppose he should relent,
And publish grace to all, on promise made
Of new subjection; with what eyes could we
Stand in his presence humble, and receive   240
Strict laws imposed, to celebrate his throne
With warbled hymns, and to his Godhead sing
Forced halleluiahs; while he lordly sits
Our envied sovran, and his altar breathes
Ambrosial odours and ambrosial flowers,
Our servile offerings? This must be our task
In Heaven, this our delight. How wearisome
Eternity so spent, in worship paid
To whom we hate! Let us not then pursue
By force impossible, by leave obtained   250
Unacceptable, though in Heaven, our state
Of splendid vassalage; but rather seek
Our own good from ourselves, and from our own
Live to ourselves, though in this vast recess,
Free and to none accountable, preferring
Hard liberty before the easy yoke
Of servile pomp. Our greatness will appear
Then most conspicuous, when great things of small,
Useful of hurtful, prosperous of adverse,
We can create; and in what place soe'er   260
Thrive under evil, and work ease out of pain
Through labour and endurance. This deep world
Of darkness do we dread? How oft amidst
Thick clouds and dark doth Heaven's all-ruling Sire
Choose to reside, his glory unobscured,
And with the majesty of darkness round
Covers his throne, from whence deep thunders roar
Mustering their rage, and Heaven resembles Hell?
As he our darkness, cannot we his light
Imitate when we please? This desert soil   270
Wants not her hidden lustre, gems and gold;
Nor want we skill or art, from whence to raise
Magnificence; and what can Heaven show more?
Our torments also may in length of time
Become our elements, these piercing fires
As soft as now severe, our temper changed
Into their temper; which must needs remove
The sensible of pain. All things invite
To peaceful counsels, and the settled state
Of order, how in safety best we may   280
Compose our present evils, with regard
Of what we are and where, dismissing quite
All thoughts of war. Ye have what I advise."
   He scarce had finished, when such murmur filled
The assembly, as when hollow rocks retain
The sound of blustering winds, which all night long
Had roused the sea, now with hoarse cadence lull
Seafaring men o'erwatched, whose bark by chance,
Or pinnace, anchors in a craggy bay
After the tempest: such applause was heard   290
As Mammon ended, and his sentence pleased,
Advising peace; for such another field
They dreaded worse than Hell; so much the fear
Of thunder and the sword of Michaël
Wrought still within them; and no less desire
To found this nether empire, which might rise
By policy, and long process of time,
In emulation opposite to Heaven.
Which when Beëlzebub perceived, than whom,
Satan except, none higher sat, with grave   300
Aspect he rose, and in his rising seemed
A pillar of state; deep on his front engraven
Deliberation sat and public care;
And princely counsel in his face yet shone,
Majestic, though in ruin. Sage he stood,
With Atlantean shoulders fit to bear
The weight of mightiest monarchies; his look
Drew audience and attention still as night
Or summer's noon-tide air, while thus he spake:
   "Thrones and Imperial Powers, offspring of Heaven, 310
Ethereal Virtues! or these titles now
Must we renounce, and, changing style, be called
Princes of Hell? for so the popular vote
Inclines, here to continue, and build up here
A growing empire; doubtless, while we dream,
And know not that the King of Heaven hath doomed
This place our dungeon, not our safe retreat
Beyond his potent arm, to live exempt
From Heaven's high jurisdiction, in new league
Banded against his throne, but to remain   320
In strictest bondage, though thus far removed
Under the inevitable curb, reserved
His captive multitude. For he, be sure,
In highth or depth, still first and last will reign
Sole King, and of his kingdom lose no part
By our revolt, but over Hell extend
His empire, and with iron sceptre rule
Us here, as with his golden those in Heaven.
What sit we then projecting peace and war?
War hath determined us, and foiled with loss   330
Irreparable; terms of peace yet none
Vouchsafed or sought; for what peace will be given

249. **pursue**, strive to regain.   271. **Wants**, lacks.   275. **elements**, congenial surroundings.   278. **sensible**, sensibility.   288. **o'erwatched**, weary with watching.   291. **sentence**, opinion, advice.   294. **Michaël**, the leader of the heavenly army. "Michael" means "the sword of God."   296. **nether**, lower.   302. **front**, countenance.   306. **Atlantean**. Atlas, one of the Titans, was condemned to bear heaven upon his shoulders.   312. **style**, title.   329. **What**, why.   330. **determined**, put an end to.

JOHN MILTON

To us enslaved, but custody severe,
And stripes, and arbitrary punishment
Inflicted? and what peace can we return,
But, to our power, hostility and hate,
Untamed reluctance, and revenge, though slow,
Yet ever plotting how the Conqueror least
May reap his conquest, and may least rejoice
In doing what we most in suffering feel?   340
Nor will occasion want, nor shall we need
With dangerous expedition to invade
Heaven, whose high walls fear no assault or siege,
Or ambush from the Deep. What if we find
Some easier enterprise? There is a place
(If ancient and prophetic fame in Heaven
Err not), another World, the happy seat
Of some new race called Man, about this time
To be created like to us, though less
In power and excellence, but favoured more   350
Of him who rules above; so was his will
Pronounced among the gods, and by an oath,
That shook Heaven's whole circumference, confirmed.
Thither let us bend all our thoughts, to learn
What creatures there inhabit, of what mould
Or substance, how endued, and what their power,
And where their weakness, how attempted best,
By force or subtlety. Though Heaven be shut,
And Heaven's high Arbitrator sit secure
In his own strength, this place may lie exposed, 360
The utmost border of his kingdom, left
To their defence who hold it. Here perhaps
Some advantageous act may be achieved
By sudden onset: either with Hell fire
To waste his whole creation, or possess
All as our own, and drive, as we were driven,
The puny habitants; or, if not drive,
Seduce them to our party, that their God
May prove their foe, and with repenting hand
Abolish his own works. This would surpass   370
Common revenge, and interrupt his joy
In our confusion, and our joy upraise
In his disturbance; when his darling sons,
Hurled headlong to partake with us, shall curse
Their frail original, and faded bliss,
Faded so soon. Advise, if this be worth
Attempting, or to sit in darkness here
Hatching vain empires." Thus Beëlzebub
Pleaded his devilish counsel, first devised
By Satan, and in part proposed; for whence,   380
But from the author of all ill, could spring

So deep a malice, to confound the race
Of mankind in one root, and Earth with Hell
To mingle and involve, done all to spite
The great Creator? But their spite still serves
His glory to augment. The bold design
Pleased highly those infernal States, and joy
Sparkled in all their eyes: with full assent
They vote; whereat his speech he thus renews:
   "Well have ye judged, well ended long debate, 390
Synod of gods! and, like to what ye are,
Great things resolved; which from the lowest deep
Will once more lift us up, in spite of fate,
Nearer our ancient seat—perhaps in view
Of those bright confines, whence, with neighbouring arms
And opportune excursion, we may chance
Re-enter Heaven; or else in some mild zone
Dwell not unvisited of Heaven's fair light,
Secure, and at the brightening orient beam
Purge off this gloom; the soft delicious air,   400
To heal the scar of these corrosive fires,
Shall breathe her balm. But first, whom shall we send
In search of this new World? whom shall we find
Sufficient? who shall tempt with wandering feet
The dark, unbottomed, infinite Abyss,
And through the palpable obscure find out
His uncouth way, or spread his aery flight,
Upborne with indefatigable wings
Over the vast abrupt, ere he arrive
The happy isle? What strength, what art, can then 410
Suffice, or what evasion bear him safe
Through the strict senteries and stations thick
Of Angels watching round? Here he had need
All circumspection: and we now no less
Choice in our suffrage; for on whom we send,
The weight of all, and our last hope, relies."
   This said, he sat; and expectation held
His look suspense, awaiting who appeared
To second, or oppose, or undertake
The perilous attempt; but all sat mute,   420
Pondering the danger with deep thoughts; and each
In other's countenance read his own dismay,
Astonished. None among the choice and prime
Of those Heaven-warring champions could be found

---

382. **confound**, ruin utterly.   404. **tempt**, attempt, essay.
406. **palpable obscure**, "darkness which may be felt," as in the Egyptian plague. See Exodus 10:21.   407. **uncouth**, unknown.   409. **abrupt**, the abyss of Chaos. **arrive**, arrive at.   410. **The happy isle?** The reference is, of course, not to the earth but to the universe, of the structure of which the fallen angels have as yet no knowledge.   412. **senteries**, old spelling of "sentries."   414. **we now**, we now need.
415. **Choice in our suffrage**, care in our voting.   418. **suspense**, fixed in suspense.

336. **to**, according to.   337. **reluctance**, resistance.
341. **want**, be lacking.   346. **fame**, report, rumor.
357. **attempted**, attacked.   365. **waste**, lay waste.
367. **puny**, younger, and therefore weaker.   375. **original**, him who was their origin, Adam.   376. **Advise**, consider.

So hardy as to proffer or accept,
Alone, the dreadful voyage; till at last
Satan, whom now transcendent glory raised
Above his fellows, with monarchal pride
Conscious of highest worth, unmoved thus spake:
"O Progeny of Heaven! Empyreal Thrones! 430
With reason hath deep silence and demur
Seized us, though undismayed. Long is the way
And hard, that out of Hell leads up to light;
Our prison strong, this huge convex of fire,
Outrageous to devour, immures us round
Ninefold; and gates of burning adamant,
Barred over us, prohibit all egress.
These passed, if any pass, the void profound
Of unessential Night receives him next,
Wide-gaping, and with utter loss of being 440
Threatens him, plunged in that abortive gulf.
If thence he scape into whatever world,
Or unknown region, what remains him less
Than unknown dangers and as hard escape?
But I should ill become this throne, O Peers,
And this imperial sovranty, adorned
With splendour, armed with power, if aught proposed
And judged of public moment, in the shape
Of difficulty or danger, could deter
Me from attempting. Wherefore do I assume 450
These royalties, and not refuse to reign,
Refusing to accept as great a share
Of hazard as of honour, due alike
To him who reigns, and so much to him due
Of hazard more, as he above the rest
High honoured sits? Go, therefore, mighty Powers,
Terror of Heaven, though fallen! intend at home,
While here shall be our home, what best may ease
The present misery, and render Hell
More tolerable; if there be cure or charm 460
To respite, or deceive, or slack the pain
Of this ill mansion. Intermit no watch
Against a wakeful foe, while I abroad
Through all the coasts of dark destruction seek
Deliverance for us all. This enterprise
None shall partake with me." Thus saying, rose
The Monarch, and prevented all reply;
Prudent, lest, from his resolution raised,
Others among the chief might offer now
(Certain to be refused) what erst they feared; 470
And, so refused, might in opinion stand
His rivals, winning cheap the high repute,
Which he, through hazard huge, must earn. But they
Dreaded not more the adventure than his voice
Forbidding; and at once with him they rose.
Their rising all at once was as the sound
Of thunder heard remote. Towards him they bend
With awful reverence prone; and as a god
Extol him equal to the Highest in Heaven: 479
Nor failed they to express how much they praised
That for the general safety he despised
His own; for neither do the spirits damned
Lose all their virtue; lest bad men should boast
Their specious deeds on Earth, which glory excites,
Or close ambition varnished o'er with zeal.
  Thus they their doubtful consultations dark
Ended, rejoicing in their matchless Chief;
As when from the mountain-tops the dusky clouds
Ascending, while the North wind sleeps, o'erspread
Heaven's cheerful face, the louring element 490
Scowls o'er the darkened landskip snow or shower;
If chance the radiant sun with farewell sweet
Extend his evening beam, the fields revive,
The birds their notes renew, and bleating herds
Attest their joy, that hill and valley rings.
O shame to men! Devil with devil damned
Firm concord holds; men only disagree
Of creatures rational, though under hope
Of heavenly grace; and, God proclaiming peace,
Yet lived in hatred, enmity, and strife 500
Among themselves, and levy cruel wars,
Wasting the Earth, each other to destroy:
As if (which might induce us to accord)
Man had not hellish foes enow besides,
That day and night for his destruction wait!
  The Stygian council thus dissolved; and forth
In order came the grand Infernal Peers;
Midst came their mighty Paramount, and seemed
Alone the antagonist of Heaven, nor less 509
Than Hell's dread Emperor, with pomp supreme,
And god-like imitated state; him round
A globe of fiery Seraphim enclosed
With bright emblazonry, and horrent arms.
Then of their session ended they bid cry
With trumpet's regal sound the great result:
Toward the four winds four speedy Cherubim
Put to their mouths the sounding alchymy,
By harald's voice explained; the hollow Abyss
Heard far and wide, and all the host of Hell
With deafening shout returned them loud acclaim. . . . 520

431. **demur**, delay.   439. **unessential**, without substance.   443. **remains**, awaits.   457. **intend**, endeavor.   461. **deceive**, beguile.   467. **prevented**, forestalled.   468. **Prudent**, watchful. **from his resolution raised**, encouraged by his fortitude.   470. **erst**, at first.   471. **opinion**, public opinion.

478. **awful**, full of awe.   484. **specious**, seemingly virtuous. **glory**, love of glory.   485. **close**, secret.   490. **element**, sky.   504. **enow**, enough.   508–09. **Paramount**, supreme lord. **seemed Alone the antagonist**, seemed in himself alone to be a sufficient antagonist.   513. **horrent**, bristling.   517. **sounding alchymy**, brass trumpets.

JOHN MILTON

BOOK III

The Argument

God, sitting on his throne, sees Satan flying towards this World, then newly created; shows him to the Son, who sat at his right hand; foretells the success of Satan in perverting mankind; clears his own justice and wisdom from all imputation, having created Man free, and able enough to have withstood his Tempter; yet declares his purpose of grace towards him, in regard he fell not of his own malice, as did Satan, but by him seduced. The Son of God renders praises to his Father for the manifestation of his gracious purpose towards Man: but God again declares that Grace cannot be extended towards Man without the satisfaction of Divine Justice; Man hath offended the majesty of God by aspiring to Godhead, and therefore, with all his progeny, devoted to death, must die, unless some one can be found sufficient to answer for his offence, and undergo his punishment. The Son of God freely offers himself a ransom for man: the Father accepts him, ordains his incarnation, pronounces his exaltation above all Names in Heaven and Earth; commands all the Angels to adore him. They obey, and, hymning to their harps in full choir, celebrate the Father and the Son. Meanwhile Satan alights upon the bare convex of this World's outermost orb; where wandering he first finds a place since called the Limbo of Vanity; what persons and things fly up thither: thence comes to the gate of Heaven, described ascending by stairs, and the waters above the firmament that flow about it. His passage thence to the orb of the Sun: he finds there Uriel, the regent of that orb, but first changes himself into the shape of a meaner Angel, and, pretending a zealous desire to behold the new Creation, and Man whom God had placed here, inquires of him the place of his habitation, and is directed: alights first on Mount Niphates.

BOOK IV

The Argument

Satan, now in prospect of Eden, and nigh the place where he must now attempt the bold enterprise which he undertook alone against God and Man, falls into many doubts with himself, and many passions—fear, envy, and despair; but at length confirms himself in evil; journeys on to Paradise, whose outward prospect and situation is described; overleaps the bounds; sits, in the shape of a cormorant, on the Tree of Life, as highest in the Garden, to look about him. The Garden described; Satan's first sight of Adam and Eve; his wonder at their excellent form and happy state, but with resolution to work their fall; overhears their discourse: thence gathers that the Tree of Knowledge was forbidden them to eat of under penalty of death, and thereon intends to found his temptation by seducing them to transgress; then leaves them a while, to know further of their state by some other means. Meanwhile Uriel, descending on a sun-beam, warns Gabriel, who had in charge the gate of Paradise, that some evil spirit had escaped the Deep, and passed at noon by his sphere, in the shape of a good Angel, down to Paradise, discovered after by his furious gestures in the mount. Gabriel promises to find him ere morning. Night coming on, Adam and Eve discourse of going to their rest: their bower described; their evening worship. Gabriel, drawing forth his band of night-watch to walk the round of Paradise, appoints two strong Angels to Adam's bower, lest the evil Spirit should be there doing some harm to Adam or Eve sleeping: there they find him at the ear of Eve, tempting her in a dream, and bring him, though unwilling, to Gabriel; by whom questioned, he scornfully answers; prepares resistance; but, hindered by a sign from Heaven, flies out of Paradise.

BOOK V

The Argument

Morning approached, Eve relates to Adam her troublesome dream; he likes it not, yet comforts her: they come forth to their day labours: their morning hymn at the door of their bower. God, to render Man inexcusable, sends Raphael to admonish him of his obedience, of his free estate, of his enemy near at hand, who he is, and why his enemy, and whatever else may avail Adam to know. Raphael comes down to Paradise; his appearance described; his coming discerned by Adam afar off, sitting at the door of his bower; he goes out to meet him, brings him to his lodge, entertains him with the choicest fruits of Paradise, got together by Eve; their discourse at table. Raphael performs his message, minds Adam of his state and of his enemy; relates, at Adam's request, who that enemy is, and how he came to be so, beginning from his first revolt in Heaven, and the occasion thereof; how he drew his legions after him to the parts of the North, and there incited them to rebel with him, persuading all but Abdiel, a Seraph, who in argument dissuades and opposes him, then forsakes him.

BOOK VI

The Argument

Raphael continues to relate how Michael and Gabriel were sent forth to battle against Satan and his Angels. The first fight described: Satan and his Powers retire under night. He calls a council; invents devilish engines, which, in the second day's fight, put Michael and his Angels to some disorder; but they at length, pulling up mountains, overwhelmed both the force and machines of Satan. Yet, the tumult not so ending, God, on the third day, sends Messiah his Son, for whom he had reserved the glory of that victory. He, in the power of his Father, coming to the place, and causing all his legions to stand still on either side, with his chariot and thunder driving into the midst of his enemies, pursues them, unable to resist, towards the wall of Heaven; which opening, they leap down with horror and confusion into the place of punishment prepared for them in the Deep. Messiah returns with triumph to his Father.

BOOK VII

The Argument

Raphael, at the request of Adam, relates how and wherefore this World was first created: that God, after the expelling of Satan and his Angels out of Heaven, declared his pleasure to create another World, and other creatures to dwell therein; sends his Son with glory, and attendance of Angels, to perform the work of Creation in six days: the Angels celebrate with hymns the performance thereof, and his reascension into Heaven.

BOOK VIII

The Argument

Adam inquires concerning celestial motions; is doubtfully answered, and exhorted to search rather things more worthy of knowledge. Adam assents, and, still desirous to detain Raphael, relates to him what he remembered since his own creation—his placing in Paradise; his talk with God concerning solitude and fit society; his first meeting and nuptials with Eve. His discourse with the Angel thereupon; who, after admonitions repeated, departs.

BOOK IX

The Argument

Satan, having compassed the Earth, with meditated guile returns as a mist by night into Paradise; enters into the Serpent sleeping. Adam and Eve in the morning go forth to their labours, which Eve proposes to divide in several places, each labouring apart: Adam consents not, alleging the danger lest that enemy of whom they were forewarned should attempt her found alone. Eve, loth to be thought not circumspect or firm enough, urges her going apart, the rather desirous to make trial of her strength; Adam at last yields. The Serpent finds her alone: his subtle approach, first gazing, then speaking, with much flattery extolling Eve above all other creatures. Eve, wondering to hear the Serpent speak, asks how he attained to human speech and such understanding not till now; the Serpent answers that by tasting of a certain tree in the Garden he attained both to speech and reason, till then void of both. Eve requires him to bring her to that tree, and finds it to be the Tree of Knowledge forbidden: the Serpent, now grown bolder, with many wiles and arguments induces her at length to eat. She, pleased with the taste, deliberates a while whether to impart thereof to Adam or not; at last brings him of the fruit; relates what persuaded her to eat thereof. Adam, at first amazed, but perceiving her lost, resolves, through vehemence of love, to perish with her, and, extenuating the trespass, eats also of the fruit. The effects thereof in them both; they seek to cover their nakedness; then fall to variance and accusation of one another.

. . . To whom thus Adam fervently replied:
"O Woman, best are all things as the will
Of God ordained them; his creating hand
Nothing imperfect or deficient left
Of all that he created—much less Man,
Or aught that might his happy state secure,
Secure from outward force. Within himself
The danger lies, yet lies within his power;
Against his will he can receive no harm. 350
But God left free the Will; for what obeys
Reason is free; and Reason he made right,
But bid her well be ware, and still erect,
Lest, by some fair appearing good surprised,
She dictate false, and misinform the Will
To do what God expressly hath forbid.
Not then mistrust, but tender love, enjoins
That I should mind thee oft; and mind thou me.
Firm we subsist, yet possible to swerve,
Since Reason not impossibly may meet 360
Some specious object by the foe suborned,
And fall into deception unaware,
Not keeping strictest watch, as she was warned.
Seek not temptation, then, which to avoid
Were better, and most likely if from me
Thou sever not: trial will come unsought.
Wouldst thou approve thy constancy, approve
First thy obedience; the other who can know,
Not seeing thee attempted, who attest?
But if thou think trial unsought may find 370
Us both securer than thus warned thou seem'st,
Go; for thy stay, not free, absents thee more.
Go in thy native innocence; rely

353. **and still erect,** and be always alert. 358. **mind,** remind. 361. **suborned,** literally, "secretly equipped," tricked out. 367. **approve,** prove. 369. **attempted,** tempted. 371. **securer,** less careful, less watchful.

On what thou hast of virtue; summon all;
For God towards thee hath done his part: do thine."
   So spake the Patriarch of Mankind; but Eve
Persisted; yet submiss, though last, replied:
"With thy permission, then, and thus forewarned,
Chiefly by what thy own last reasoning words
Touched only, that our trial, when least sought, 380
May find us both perhaps far less prepared,
The willinger I go, nor much expect
A foe so proud will first the weaker seek;
So bent, the more shall shame him his repulse."
   Thus saying, from her husband's hand her hand
Soft she withdrew, and, like a wood-nymph light,
Oread or Dryad, or of Delia's train,
Betook her to the groves, but Delia's self
In gait surpassed and goddess-like deport,
Though not as she with bow and quiver armed, 390
But with such gardening tools as art, yet rude,
Guiltless of fire had formed, or Angels brought.
To Pales, or Pomona, thus adorned,
Likest she seemed—Pomona when she fled
Vertumnus—or to Ceres in her prime,
Yet virgin of Proserpina from Jove.
   Her long with ardent look his eye pursued
Delighted, but desiring more her stay.
Oft he to her his charge of quick return
Repeated; she to him as oft engaged 400
To be returned by noon amid the bower,
And all things in best order to invite
Noontide repast, or afternoon's repose.
O much deceived, much failing, hapless Eve,
Of thy presumed return! event perverse!
Thou never from that hour in Paradise
Found'st either sweet repast or sound repose;
Such ambush, hid among sweet flowers and shades,
Waited, with hellish rancour imminent,
To intercept thy way, or send thee back 410
Despoiled of innocence, of faith, of bliss.
For now, and since first break of dawn, the Fiend,
Mere serpent in appearance, forth was come,
And on his quest where likeliest he might find
The only two of mankind, but in them
The whole included race, his purposed prey.
In bower and field he sought, where any tuft
Of grove or garden-plot more pleasant lay,
Their tendance or plantation for delight;
By fountain or by shady rivulet 420
He sought them both, but wished his hap might find
Eve separate; he wished, but not with hope
Of what so seldom chanced, when to his wish,
Beyond his hope, Eve separate he spies,
Veiled in a cloud of fragrance, where she stood,
Half-spied, so thick the roses bushing round
About her glowed, oft stooping to support
Each flower of slender stalk, whose head, though gay
Carnation, purple, azure, or specked with gold,
Hung drooping unsustained. Them she upstays 430
Gently with myrtle band, mindless the while
Herself, though fairest unsupported flower,
From her best prop so far, and storm so nigh.
Nearer he drew, and many a walk traversed
Of stateliest covert, cedar, pine, or palm;
Then voluble and bold, now hid, now seen
Among thick-woven arborets, and flowers
Imbordered on each bank, the hand of Eve:
Spot more delicious than those gardens feigned
Or of revived Adonis, or renowned 440
Alcinous, host of old Laertes' son,
Or that, not mystic, where the sapient king
Held dalliance with his fair Egyptian spouse.
Much he the place admired, the person more.
As one who, long in populous city pent,
Where houses thick and sewers annoy the air,
Forth issuing on a summer's morn, to breathe
Among the pleasant villages and farms
Adjoined, from each thing met conceives delight—
The smell of grain, or tedded grass, or kine, 450
Or dairy, each rural sight, each rural sound—
If chance with nymph-like step fair virgin pass,
What pleasing seemed, for her now pleases more,
She most, and in her look sums all delight:
Such pleasure took the Serpent to behold
This flowery plat, the sweet recess of Eve
Thus early, thus alone. Her heavenly form
Angelic, but more soft and feminine,
Her graceful innocence, her every air
Of gesture or least action, overawed 460

---

419. **Their tendance,** the object of their attention or care.   431. **mindless,** heedless, unmindful.   436. **voluble,** rolling, turning.   437. **arborets,** small trees, shrubs.   438. **hand,** handiwork.   440. **revived Adonis.** See Book I, l. 450. For Spenser's description of the Garden of Adonis, see *The Faerie Queene*, Book III, Canto 6.   441. **Laertes' son,** Ulysses. See *Odyssey*, Book VII, ll. 25 ff.   442. **not mystic,** not a mystical, and therefore fanciful, garden of pagan allegory, but the real garden referred to in the history of Solomon in the Bible. See I Kings 3 and the Song of Solomon. 446. **annoy,** make noisome, pollute.   450. **tedded,** spread out to dry for hay. **kine,** cattle.   453. **for her,** because of **her.** 454. **sums,** comprises, completes.   456. **plat,** plot.

377. **submiss,** submissively.   384. **So bent,** on seeking the weaker first.   387. **Oread or Dryad,** mountain nymph or wood nymph. **Delia's train,** the nymphs who attended the huntress Diana, called Delia from her birthplace, the isle of Delos.   389. **deport,** deportment, manner.   393. **Pales,** a Roman goddess of flocks and shepherds. **Pomona,** the Roman goddess of fruit.   395. **Ceres,** goddess of the earth and protectress of agriculture.   396. **Yet virgin of,** not yet mother of.   397. **Her . . . his,** Eve's . . . Adam's. 405. **event,** outcome.   413. **Mere,** pure.   418. **more pleasant,** most pleasant.

His malice, and with rapine sweet bereaved
His fierceness of the fierce intent it brought.
That space the Evil One abstracted stood
From his own evil, and for the time remained
Stupidly good, of enmity disarmed,
Of guile, of hate, of envy, of revenge.
But the hot Hell that always in him burns,
Though in mid Heaven, soon ended his delight
And tortures him now more, the more he sees
Of pleasure not for him ordained. Then soon   470
Fierce hate he recollects, and all his thoughts
Of mischief, gratulating, thus excites:
  "Thoughts, whither have ye led me? with what sweet
Compulsion thus transported to forget
What hither brought us? hate, not love, nor hope
Of Paradise for Hell, hope here to taste
Of pleasure, but all pleasure to destroy,
Save what is in destroying; other joy
To me is lost. Then let me not let pass
Occasion which now smiles: behold alone   480
The Woman, opportune to all attempts;
Her husband, for I view far round, not nigh,
Whose higher intellectual more I shun,
And strength, of courage haughty, and of limb
Heroic built, though of terrestrial mould;
Foe not informidable, exempt from wound,
I not; so much hath Hell debased, and pain
Enfeebled me, to what I was in Heaven.
She fair, divinely fair, fit love for gods,
Not terrible, though terror be in love,   490
And beauty, not approached by stronger hate,
Hate stronger under show of love well feigned,
The way which to her ruin now I tend."
  So spake the Enemy of Mankind, enclosed
In serpent, inmate bad, and toward Eve
Addressed his way: not with indented wave,
Prone on the ground, as since, but on his rear,
Circular base of rising folds, that towered
Fold above fold, a surging maze; his head
Crested aloft, and carbuncle his eyes;   500
With burnished neck of verdant gold, erect
Amidst his circling spires, that on the grass
Floated redundant. Pleasing was his shape
And lovely; never since of serpent kind
Lovelier—not those that in Illyria changed
Hermione and Cadmus, or the god
In Epidaurus; nor to which transformed
Ammonian Jove, or Capitoline, was seen,
He with Olympias, this with her who bore
Scipio, the highth of Rome. With tract oblique   510
At first, as one who sougnt access but feared
To interrupt, sidelong he works his way.
As when a ship, by skilful steersman wrought
Nigh river's mouth or foreland, where the wind
Veers oft, as oft so steers, and shifts her sail,
So varied he, and of his tortuous train
Curled many a wanton wreath in sight of Eve,
To lure her eye; she, busied, heard the sound
Of rustling leaves, but minded not, as used
To such disport before her through the field   520
From every beast, more duteous at her call
Than at Circean call the herd disguised.
He, bolder now, uncalled before her stood,
But as in gaze admiring. Oft he bowed
His turret crest and sleek enamelled neck,
Fawning, and licked the ground whereon she trod.
His gentle dumb expression turned at length
The eye of Eve to mark his play; he, glad
Of her attention gained, with serpent tongue
Organic, or impulse of vocal air,   530
His fraudulent temptation thus began:
  "Wonder not, sovran mistress (if perhaps
Thou canst who art sole wonder), much less arm
Thy looks, the heaven of mildness, with disdain,
Displeased that I approach thee thus, and gaze
Insatiate, I thus single, nor have feared
Thy awful brow, more awful thus retired.
Fairest resemblance of thy Maker fair,
Thee all things living gaze on, all things thine
By gift, and thy celestial beauty adore,   540
With ravishment beheld—there best beheld
Where universally admired. But here,
In this enclosure wild, these beasts among,
Beholders rude, and shallow to discern
Half what in thee is fair, one man except,
Who sees thee (and what is one!) who shouldst be seen
A Goddess among Gods, adored and served
By Angels numberless, thy daily train?"

461. **rapine,** robbery.   472. **gratulating,** rejoicing.   491. **not,** when not.   500. **carbuncle,** deep red.   502. **spires,** coils. Compare the modern "spiral."   505–06. **changed . . . Cadmus,** took the place of. Cadmus and his wife Harmonia (**Hermione**), were, at their own request, transformed into serpents. Milton has in mind Ovid's account in *Metamorphoses*, Book IV, ll. 563 ff.   506. **the god,** Aesculapius, the god of healing, who took a serpent's form on occasion. See Ovid, *Metamorphoses*, Book XV, ll. 670 ff.   507. **to which transformed,** into which was transformed.   508. **Ammonian Jove.** Jove (Jupiter Ammon), according to the legend, appeared to Olympias, the mother of Alexander the Great, in the form of a serpent. **Capitoline,** Jupiter, called Capitoline from his temple, the Capitol.   510. **Scipio.** Scipio Africanus was said to have been the son of Jupiter by Sempronia.   517. **wanton,** playful.   522. **Circean.** The enchantress Circe had at her call the herd of men whom she had disguised as beasts. See *Odyssey*, Book X, ll. 214 ff.   525. **turret,** towerlike.   530. **Organic . . . air,** by direct motion of the serpent's speech organs, or by making the air **vocal** with some other impulse or vibration.   532–33. "**Wonder not . . . sole wonder**). Satan begins by appealing to Eve's vanity.

So glozed the Tempter, and his proem tuned.
Into the heart of Eve his words made way, 550
Though at the voice much marvelling; at length,
Not unamazed, she thus in answer spake:
   "What may this mean? Language of Man pronounced
By tongue of brute, and human sense expressed!
The first at least of these I thought denied
To beasts, whom God on their creation-day
Created mute to all articulate sound;
The latter I demur, for in their looks
Much reason, and in their actions, oft appears.
Thee, Serpent, subtlest beast of all the field 560
I knew, but not with human voice endued;
Redouble, then, this miracle, and say,
How cam'st thou speakable of mute, and how
To me so friendly grown above the rest
Of brutal kind that daily are in sight:
Say, for such wonder claims attention due."
   To whom the guileful Tempter thus replied:
"Empress of this fair World, resplendent Eve!
Easy to me it is to tell thee all
What thou command'st, and right thou shouldst be obeyed. 570
I was at first as other beasts that graze
The trodden herb, of abject thoughts and low,
As was my food, nor aught but food discerned
Or sex, and apprehended nothing high:
Till on a day, roving the field, I chanced
A goodly tree far distant to behold,
Loaden with fruit of fairest colours mixed,
Ruddy and gold: I nearer drew to gaze;
When from the boughs a savoury odour blown,
Grateful to appetite, more pleased my sense 580
Than smell of sweetest fennel, or the teats
Of ewe or goat dropping with milk at even,
Unsucked of lamb or kid, that tend their play.
To satisfy the sharp desire I had
Of tasting those fair apples, I resolved
Not to defer; hunger and thirst at once,
Powerful persuaders, quickened at the scent
Of that alluring fruit, urged me so keen.
About the mossy trunk I wound me soon; 589
For, high from ground, the branches would require
Thy utmost reach, or Adam's: round the tree
All other beasts that saw, with like desire
Longing and envying stood, but could not reach.
Amid the tree now got, where plenty hung
Tempting so nigh, to pluck and eat my fill
I spared not; for such pleasure till that hour
At feed or fountain never had I found.
Sated at length, ere long I might perceive
Strange alteration in me, to degree
Of reason in my inward powers, and speech 600
Wanted not long, though to this shape retained.
Thenceforth to speculations high or deep
I turned my thoughts, and with capacious mind
Considered all things visible in Heaven,
Or Earth, or Middle, all things fair and good.
But all that fair and good in thy divine
Semblance and in thy beauty's heavenly ray,
United I beheld—no fair to thine
Equivalent or second; which compelled
Me thus, though importune perhaps, to come 610
And gaze, and worship thee of right declared
Sovran of creatures, universal Dame!"
   So talked the spirited sly Snake; and Eve,
Yet more amazed, unwary thus replied:
   "Serpent, thy overpraising leaves in doubt
The virtue of that fruit, in thee first proved.
But say, where grows the tree? from hence how far?
For many are the trees of God that grow
In Paradise, and various, yet unknown
To us; in such abundance lies our choice 620
As leaves a greater store of fruit untouched,
Still hanging incorruptible, till men
Grow up to their provision, and more hands
Help to disburden Nature of her bearth."
   To whom the wily Adder, blithe and glad:—
"Empress, the way is ready, and not long—
Beyond a row of myrtles, on a flat,
Fast by a fountain, one small thicket past
Of blowing myrrh and balm. If thou accept
My conduct, I can bring thee thither soon." 630
   "Lead, then," said Eve. He, leading, swiftly rolled
In tangles, and made intricate seem straight,
To mischief swift. Hope elevates, and joy
Brightens his crest. As when a wandering fire,
Compact of unctuous vapour, which the night
Condenses, and the cold environs round,
Kindled through agitation to a flame
(Which oft, they say, some evil spirit attends),
Hovering and blazing with delusive light, 639
Misleads the amazed night-wanderer from his way
To bogs and mires, and oft through pond or pool,
There swallowed up and lost, from succour far:

   549. **glozed,** flattered. **proem,** preamble.   558. **demur,** have doubts about (whether reason is denied to brutes).   563. **of mute,** from being mute.   581. **fennel . . . teats.** Popular belief had it that fennel was a favorite food of serpents, and that they sucked the teats of sheep.   599–600. **to degree Of reason,** to the extent of inducing in me some degree of reason.   605. **Middle,** the air.   608. **fair,** fairness, beauty.   612. **Dame!"** mistress (of the universe).   613. **spirited,** inspired (by Satan).   624. **bearth,"** that which she bears; fruit.   629. **blowing,** blossoming.   634. **wandering fire,** will-o'-the-wisp, jack-o'-lantern. Compare "L'Allegro," l. 104.   635. **Compact,** composed. **unctuous,** oily.

So glistered the dire Snake, and into fraud
Led Eve, our credulous mother, to the Tree
Of Prohibition, root of all our woe;
Which when she saw, thus to her guide she spake:
  "Serpent, we might have spared our coming hither,
Fruitless to me, though fruit be here to excess,
The credit of whose virtue rest with thee—
Wondrous, indeed, if cause of such effects!   650
But of this tree we may not taste nor touch;
God so commanded, and left that command
Sole daughter of his voice: the rest, we live
Law to ourselves; our reason is our law."
  To whom the Tempter guilefully replied:
"Indeed! Hath God then said that of the fruit
Of all these garden-trees ye shall not eat,
Yet lords declared of all in earth or air?"
  To whom thus Eve, yet sinless: "Of the fruit
Of each tree in the garden we may eat;   660
But of the fruit of this fair tree, amidst
The garden, God hath said, 'Ye shall not eat
Thereof, nor shall ye touch it, lest ye die.'"
  She scarce had said, though brief, when now more bold
The Tempter, but with show of zeal and love
To Man, and indignation at his wrong,
New part puts on, and, as to passion moved,
Fluctuates disturbed, yet comely, and in act
Raised, as of some great matter to begin.
As when of old some orator renowned   670
In Athens or free Rome, where eloquence
Flourished, since mute, to some great cause addressed,
Stood in himself collected, while each part,
Motion, each act, won audience ere the tongue
Sometimes in highth began, as no delay
Of preface brooking through his zeal of right:
So standing, moving, or to highth upgrown,
The Tempter, all impassioned, thus began:
  "O sacred, wise, and wisdom-giving Plant,
Mother of science! now I feel thy power   680
Within me clear, not only to discern
Things in their causes, but to trace the ways
Of highest agents, deemed however wise.
Queen of this Universe! do not believe
Those rigid threats of death; ye shall not die.
How should ye? by the fruit? it gives you life
To knowledge. By the Threatener? look on me,
Me who have touched and tasted, yet both live,
And life more perfect have attained than Fate
Meant me, by venturing higher than my lot.   690
Shall that be shut to Man which to the Beast
Is open? or will God incense his ire
For such a petty trespass, and not praise
Rather your dauntless virtue, whom the pain
Of death denounced, whatever thing Death be,
Deterred not from achieving what might lead
To happier life, knowledge of Good and Evil?
Of good, how just! of evil—if what is evil
Be real, why not known, since easier shunned?
God therefore cannot hurt ye, and be just;   700
Not just, not God; not feared then, nor obeyed;
Your fear itself of death removes the fear.
Why, then, was this forbid? Why but to awe,
Why but to keep ye low and ignorant,
His worshippers? He knows that in the day
Ye eat thereof your eyes, that seem so clear,
Yet are but dim, shall perfectly be then
Opened and cleared, and ye shall be as Gods,
Knowing both good and evil, as they know.
That ye should be as Gods, since I as Man,   710
Internal Man, is but proportion meet—
I, of brute, human; ye, of human, Gods.
So ye shall die perhaps, by putting off
Human, to put on Gods—death to be wished,
Though threatened, which no worse than this can bring!
And what are Gods, that Man may not become
As they, participating god-like food?
The Gods are first, and that advantage use
On our belief, that all from them proceeds.
I question it; for this fair Earth I see,   720
Warmed by the Sun, producing every kind;
Them nothing. If they all things, who enclosed
Knowledge of good and evil in this tree,
That whoso eats thereof forthwith attains
Wisdom without their leave? and wherein lies
The offence, that Man should thus attain to know?
What can your knowledge hurt him, or this tree
Impart against his will, if all be his?
Or is it envy? and can envy dwell   729

---

643. **glistered**, glittered. **fraud**, harm, evil-doing. 644–45. **Tree Of Prohibition**, the Forbidden Tree. 649. **The credit . . . thee.** The proof of whose wonder-working powers may be retained by thee alone. 653. **daughter of his voice**, one of the many Hebraisms of the poem. Compare Wordsworth's "Ode to Duty," Vol. II, page 64. **the rest**, as for the rest of the trees. 667. **New part puts on**, assumes a new role. 668. **Fluctuates**, moves his body to and fro. 673. **part**, of his body. 674. **audience**, hearing. 675. **highth**, of feeling. 676. **brooking**, enduring, "putting up with." 679 ff. **"O sacred, wise ff.** The shrewdness and persuasiveness of the serpent's speech might well have deceived a person of far greater experience and knowledge than Eve. 680. **science!** knowledge.

687. **To knowledge**, in addition to knowledge. 692. **incense**, kindle. 695. **denounced**, proclaimed, threatened. 710. **Gods.** "Satan speaks like a polytheist, and Eve later falls into the same idolatrous and pagan way of thought."—Hanford 711. **Internal Man**, internally, with manlike faculties, though externally a serpent. 714. **to put on**, to assume the nature of. 722. **If they**, if they produced.

In heavenly breasts? These, these and many more
Causes import your need of this fair fruit.
Goddess humane, reach, then, and freely taste!"
   He ended; and his words, replete with guile,
Into her heart too easy entrance won:
Fixed on the fruit she gazed, which to behold
Might tempt alone; and in her ears the sound
Yet rung of his persuasive words, impregned
With reason, to her seeming, and with truth.
Meanwhile the hour of noon drew on, and waked
An eager appetite, raised by the smell   740
So savoury of that fruit, which with desire,
Inclinable now grown to touch or taste,
Solicited her longing eye; yet first,
Pausing a while, thus to herself she mused:
   "Great are thy virtues, doubtless, best of fruits,
Though kept from Man, and worthy to be admired,
Whose taste, too long forborne, at first assay
Gave elocution to the mute, and taught
The tongue not made for speech to speak thy praise.
Thy praise he also who forbids thy use   750
Conceals not from us, naming thee the Tree
Of Knowledge, knowledge both of good and evil;
Forbids us then to taste; but his forbidding
Commends thee more, while it infers the good
By thee communicated, and our want;
For good unknown sure is not had, or, had
And yet unknown, is as not had at all.
In plain, then, what forbids he but to know,
Forbids us good, forbids us to be wise?
Such prohibitions bind not. But, if Death   760
Bind us with after-bands, what profits then
Our inward freedom? In the day we eat
Of this fair fruit, our doom is we shall die!
How dies the Serpent? He hath eaten, and lives,
And knows, and speaks, and reasons, and discerns,
Irrational till then. For us alone
Was death invented? or to us denied
This intellectual food, for beasts reserved?
For beasts it seems; yet that one beast which first
Hath tasted envies not, but brings with joy   770
The good befallen him, author unsuspect,
Friendly to Man, far from deceit or guile.
What fear I, then? rather, what know to fear
Under this ignorance of good and evil,
Of God or Death, of law or penalty?
Here grows the cure of all, this fruit divine,
Fair to the eye, inviting to the taste,
Of virtue to make wise. What hinders, then,
To reach, and feed at once both body and mind?"
   So saying, her rash hand in evil hour   780
Forth reaching to the fruit, she plucked, she eat.
Earth felt the wound, and Nature from her seat,
Sighing through all her works, gave signs of woe
That all was lost. Back to the thicket slunk
The guilty Serpent, and well might, for Eve,
Intent now only on her taste, naught else
Regarded; such delight till then, as seemed,
In fruit she never tasted, whether true,
Or fancied so through expectation high   789
Of knowledge; nor was Godhead from her thought.
Greedily she ingorged without restraint,
And knew not eating death. Satiate at length,
And heightened as with wine, jocund and boon,
Thus to herself she pleasingly began:
   "O sovran, virtuous, precious of all trees
In Paradise! of operation blest
To sapience, hitherto obscured, infamed,
And thy fair fruit let hang, as to no end
Created! but henceforth my early care,   799
Not without song, each morning, and due praise,
Shall tend thee, and the fertile burden ease
Of thy full branches, offered free to all;
Till, dieted by thee, I grow mature
In knowledge, as the Gods who all things know.
Though others envy what they cannot give—
For, had the gift been theirs, it had not here
Thus grown! Experience, next to thee I owe,
Best guide: not following thee, I had remained
In ignorance; thou open'st Wisdom's way,
And giv'st access, though secret she retire.   810
And I perhaps am secret: Heaven is high—
High, and remote to see from thence distinct
Each thing on Earth; and other care perhaps
May have diverted from continual watch
Our great Forbidder, safe with all his spies
About him. But to Adam in what sort
Shall I appear? Shall I to him make known
As yet my change, and give him to partake
Full happiness with me, or rather not,

---

731. import, indicate.   **732. humane,** gentle, gracious.   **737. impregned,** impregnated.   **742. Inclinable,** easily inclined.   **754. infers,** implies.   **758. In plain,** in plain terms.   **771. author unsuspect,** the authority for which information (that is, the serpent), not to be suspected.   **778. virtue,** power.   **781. eat,** past tense (pronounced ĕt).   **782–84. Earth . . . lost.** Milton's musicianship, in having **Nature** provide a solemn orchestral punctuation of the fatal climaxes in the poem (the moments when Adam and Eve taste the forbidden fruit) has been likened to that of Wagner in his music dramas, especially in the potion scene in *Tristan und Isolde.*   **792. knew not eating,** knew not that she was eating.   **793. boon,** gay.   **795. sovran,** most sovereign.   **796–97. blest To sapience,** blest with the power of conferring wisdom. **infamed,** not known (or, perhaps, falsely reputed). **805 ff. Though others envy ff.** The Devil's first earthly disciple has learned her lesson well!   **811. I perhaps . . . high.** Eve's words betray the dawn of a guilty conscience.   **815. safe,** not dangerous.   **817 ff. Shall I to him ff.** Envy and jealousy are among the chief results of the forbidden fruit.

But keep the odds of knowledge in my power 820
Without copartner? so to add what wants
In female sex, the more to draw his love,
And render me more equal, and perhaps—
A thing not undesirable—sometime
Superior; for, inferior, who is free?
This may be well; but what if God have seen,
And death ensue? Then I shall be no more;
And Adam, wedded to another Eve,
Shall live with her enjoying, I extinct!
A death to think! Confirmed, then, I resolve 830
Adam shall share with me in bliss or woe.
So dear I love him that with him all deaths
I could endure, without him live no life."

   So saying, from the tree her step she turned,
But first low reverence done, as to the power
That dwelt within, whose presence had infused
Into the plant scientual sap, derived
From nectar, drink of Gods. Adam the while,
Waiting desirous her return, had wove
Of choicest flowers a garland, to adorn 840
Her tresses, and her rural labours crown,
As reapers oft are wont their harvest queen.
Great joy he promised to his thoughts, and new
Solace in her return, so long delayed;
Yet oft his heart, divine of something ill,
Misgave him. He the faltering measure felt,
And forth to meet her went, the way she took
That morn when first they parted; by the Tree
Of Knowledge he must pass; there he her met,
Scarce from the tree returning; in her hand 850
A bough of fairest fruit, that downy smiled,
New gathered, and ambrosial smell diffused.
To him she hasted; in her face excuse
Came prologue, and apology to prompt,
Which, with bland words at will, she thus addressed:

   "Hast thou not wondered, Adam, at my stay?
Thee I have missed, and thought it long, deprived
Thy presence—agony of love till now
Not felt, nor shall be twice; for never more
Mean I to try, what rash untried I sought, 860
The pain of absence from thy sight. But strange
Hath been the cause, and wonderful to hear.
This tree is not, as we are told, a tree
Of danger tasted, nor to evil unknown
Opening the way, but of divine effect

   835. low reverence . . . to the power, the first manifestation of idolatry.   **837. sciential,** conferring knowledge.   **845. divine of,** divining, foreboding.   **846. faltering measure,** irregular beat.   **853–54. excuse Came prologue.** The expression on her face was a suitable prologue to the apology and the hypocritical scene she was about to rehearse.   **860. what rash . . . sought,** what I rashly sought after because it was untried and therefore not experienced.   **864. tasted,** when tasted.

To open eyes, and make them Gods who taste;
And hath been tasted such. The Serpent wise,
Or not restrained as we, or not obeying,
Hath eaten of the fruit, and is become
Not dead, as we are threatened, but thenceforth 870
Endued with human voice and human sense,
Reasoning to admiration, and with me
Persuasively hath so prevailed that I
Have also tasted, and have also found
The effects to correspond—opener mine eyes,
Dim erst, dilated spirits, ampler heart,
And growing up to Godhead; which for thee
Chiefly I sought, without thee can despise.
For bliss, as thou hast part, to me is bliss;
Tedious, unshared with thee, and odious soon. 880
Thou, therefore, also taste, that equal lot
May join us, equal joy, as equal love;
Lest, thou not tasting, different degree
Disjoin us, and I then too late renounce
Deity for thee, when fate will not permit."

   Thus Eve with countenance blithe her story told;
But in her cheek distemper flushing glowed.
On the other side, Adam, soon as he heard
The fatal trespass done by Eve, amazed,
Astonied stood and blank, while horror chill 890
Ran through his veins, and all his joints relaxed.
From his slack hand the garland wreathed for Eve
Down dropt, and all the faded roses shed.
Speechless he stood and pale, till thus at length
First to himself he inward silence broke:

   "O fairest of Creation, last and best
Of all God's works, creature in whom excelled
Whatever can to sight or thought be formed,
Holy, divine, good, amiable, or sweet!
How art thou lost! how on a sudden lost, 900
Defaced, deflowered, and now to death devote!
Rather, how hast thou yielded to transgress
The strict forbiddance, how to violate
The sacred fruit forbidden? Some cursèd fraud
Of enemy hath beguiled thee, yet unknown,
And me with thee hath ruined; for with thee
Certain my resolution is to die.
How can I live without thee? how forgo
Thy sweet converse and love so dearly joined,
To live again in these wild woods forlorn? 910
Should God create another Eve, and I
Another rib afford, yet loss of thee
Would never from my heart. No, no! I feel

   867. tasted such, found by tasting to be such.   **872. to admiration,** in a manner to be wondered at.   **876. erst,** formerly.   **877 ff. which for thee ff.** Eve now adds a palpable falsehood to her sins.   **884. renounce,** try to renounce.   **901. devote!** doomed.

JOHN MILTON

The link of nature draw me: flesh of flesh,
Bone of my bone thou art, and from thy state
Mine never shall be parted, bliss or woe."
    So having said, as one from sad dismay
Recomforted, and, after thoughts disturbed,
Submitting to what seemed remediless,
Thus in calm mood his words to Eve he turned: 920
    "Bold deed thou hast presumed, adventurous Eve,
And peril great provoked, who thus hast dared,
Had it been only coveting to eye
That sacred fruit, sacred to abstinence,
Much more to taste it, under ban to touch.
But past who can recall, or done undo?
Not God Omnipotent, nor Fate! Yet so
Perhaps thou shalt not die; perhaps the fact
Is not so heinous now—foretasted fruit,
Profaned first by the Serpent, by him first   930
Made common and unhallowed ere our taste,
Nor yet on him found deadly; he yet lives—
Lives, as thou saidst, and gains to live, as Man,
Higher degree of life: inducement strong
To us, as likely, tasting, to attain
Proportional ascent; which cannot be
But to be Gods, or Angels, demi-gods.
Nor can I think that God, Creator wise,
Though threatening, will in earnest so destroy
Us, his prime creatures, dignified so high,   940
Set over all his works; which, in our fall,
For us created, needs with us must fail,
Dependent made. So God shall uncreate,
Be frustrate, do, undo, and labour lose—
Not well conceived of God; who, though his power
Creation could repeat, yet would be loth
Us to abolish, lest the Adversary
Triumph and say: 'Fickle their state whom God
Most favours; who can please him long? Me first
He ruined, now Mankind; whom will he next?'   950
Matter of scorn not to be given the Foe.
However, I with thee have fixed my lot,
Certain to undergo like doom. If death
Consort with thee, death is to me as life;
So forcible within my heart I feel
The bond of Nature draw me to my own—
My own in thee; for what thou art is mine.
Our state cannot be severed; we are one,
One flesh; to lose thee were to lose myself."
    So Adam; and thus Eve to him replied: 960
"O glorious trial of exceeding love,
Illustrious evidence, example high!
Engaging me to emulate; but, short
Of thy perfection, how shall I attain,
Adam? from whose dear side I boast me sprung,
And gladly of our union hear thee speak,
One heart, one soul in both; whereof good proof
This day affords, declaring thee resolved,
Rather than death, or aught than death more dread,
Shall separate us, linked in love so dear,   970
To undergo with me one guilt, one crime,
If any be, of tasting this fair fruit;
Whose virtue (for of good still good proceeds,
Direct, or by occasion) hath presented
This happy trial of thy love, which else
So eminently never had been known.
Were it I thought death menaced would ensue
This my attempt, I would sustain alone
The worst, and not persuade thee—rather die
Deserted than oblige thee with a fact   980
Pernicious to thy peace, chiefly assured
Remarkably so late of thy so true,
So faithful, love unequalled. But I feel
Far otherwise the event—not death, but life
Augmented, opened eyes, new hopes, new joys,
Taste so divine that what of sweet before
Hath touched my sense, flat seems to this and harsh.
On my experience, Adam, freely taste,
And fear of death deliver to the winds."
    So saying, she embraced him, and for joy   990
Tenderly wept, much won that he his love
Had so ennobled as of choice to incur
Divine displeasure for her sake, or death.
In recompense (for such compliance bad
Such recompense best merits), from the bough
She gave him of that fair enticing fruit
With liberal hand. He scrupled not to eat,
Against his better knowledge, not deceived,
But fondly overcome with female charm.
Earth trembled from her entrails, as again   1000
In pangs, and Nature gave a second groan;
Sky loured, and, muttering thunder, some sad drops
Wept at completing of the mortal sin
Original; while Adam took no thought,
Eating his fill, nor Eve to iterate
Her former trespass feared, the more to soothe
Him with her loved society; that now,
As with new wine intoxicated both,
They swim in mirth, and fancy that they feel
Divinity within them breeding wings   1010
Wherewith to scorn the Earth: but that false fruit
Far other operation first displayed,
Carnal desire inflaming; he on Eve

914–15. **flesh . . . bone.** See Genesis 2:23.   **928. fact,** deed.   **945. Not well conceived of God.** That is, it is not easily conceivable that God should undo and lose his work.   **953. Certain,** resolved.

980. oblige, involve. **fact,** deed.   **984. event,** outcome.

Began to cast lascivious eyes; she him
As wantonly repaid; in lust they burn,
Till Adam thus 'gan Eve to dalliance move:
   "Eve, now I see thou art exact of taste
And elegant—of sapience no small part;
Since to each meaning savour we apply,
And palate call judicious. I the praise   1020
Yield thee, so well this day thou hast purveyed.
Much pleasure we have lost, while we abstained
From this delightful fruit, nor known till now
True relish, tasting. If such pleasure be
In things to us forbidden, it might be wished
For this one tree had been forbidden ten.
But come; so well refreshed, now let us play,
As meet is, after such delicious fare;
For never did thy beauty, since the day
I saw thee first and wedded thee, adorned   1030
With all perfections, so inflame my sense
With ardour to enjoy thee, fairer now
Than ever—bounty of this virtuous tree!"
   So said he, and forbore not glance or toy
Of amorous intent, well understood
Of Eve, whose eye darted contagious fire.
Her hand he seized, and to a shady bank,
Thick overhead with verdant roof embowered,
He led her, nothing loth; flowers were the couch,
Pansies, and violets, and asphodel,   1040
And hyacinth—Earth's freshest, softest lap.
There they their fill of love and love's disport
Took largely, of their mutual guilt the seal,
The solace of their sin, till dewy sleep
Oppressed them, wearied with their amorous play.
   Soon as the force of that fallacious fruit,
That with exhilarating vapour bland
About their spirits had played, and inmost powers
Made err, was now exhaled, and grosser sleep,
Bred of unkindly fumes, with conscious dreams   1050
Encumbered, now had left them, up they rose
As from unrest, and each the other viewing,
Soon found their eyes how opened, and their minds
How darkened. Innocence, that as a veil
Had shadowed them from knowing ill, was gone;
Just confidence, and native righteousness,
And honour, from about them, naked left
To guilty Shame: he covered, but his robe
Uncovered more. So rose the Danite strong,
Herculean Samson, from the harlot-lap   1060
Of Philistean Dálilah, and waked
Shorn of his strength; they destitute and bare
Of all their virtue. Silent, and in face
Confounded, long they sat, as stricken mute;
Till Adam, though not less than Eve abashed,
At length gave utterance to these words constrained:
   "O Eve, in evil hour thou didst give ear
To that false Worm, of whomsoever taught
To counterfeit Man's voice—true in our fall,
False in our promised rising; since our eyes   1070
Opened we find indeed, and find we know
Both good and evil, good lost and evil got:
Bad fruit of knowledge, if this be to know,
Which leaves us naked thus, of honour void,
Of innocence, of faith, of purity,
Our wonted ornaments now soiled and stained,
And in our faces evident the signs
Of foul concupiscence; whence evil store,
Even shame, the last of evils; of the first
Be sure then. How shall I behold the face   1080
Henceforth of God or Angel, erst with joy
And rapture so oft beheld? Those heavenly shapes
Will dazzle now this earthly with their blaze
Insufferably bright. Oh, might I here
In solitude live savage, in some glade
Obscured, where highest woods, impenetrable
To star or sunlight, spread their umbrage broad,
And brown as evening! Cover me, ye pines!
Ye cedars, with innumerable boughs
Hide me, where I may never see them more!   1090
But let us now, as in bad plight, devise
What best may, for the present, serve to hide
The parts of each from other that seem most
To shame obnoxious, and unseemliest seen—
Some tree, whose broad smooth leaves, together sewed,
And girded on our loins, may cover round
Those middle parts, that this new comer, Shame,
There sit not, and reproach us as unclean."
   So counselled he, and both together went
Into the thickest wood, there soon they chose   1100
The fig-tree—not that kind for fruit renowned,
But such as at this day, to Indians known,
In Malabar or Deccan spreads her arms
Branching so broad and long that in the ground
The bended twigs take root, and daughters grow
About the mother tree, a pillared shade

   1017. exact of taste. Adam begins with an elaborate pun or series of puns depending on the Latin word *sapere*, which means both "to taste" and "to be wise." "Savour," he says, is applied "to each meaning." Good "taste" is used in speaking of intellectual matters, and likewise we call the palate "judicious."   **1026. For,** instead of.   **1034. toy,** caress.   **1050. unkindly,** unnatural.   **1058–59. he covered . . . more.** The very robe that covered them revealed to them their nakedness.   **the Danite.** See Judges 16: 4–20.   **1068. Worm,** serpent.   **1078. evil store,** abundance of evil.   **1079. last of evils,** a Latinism meaning "worst of evils." **the first,** that is, the lesser evils.   **1087. umbrage,** shade.   **1088. brown,** dark.   **1094. obnoxious,** liable; a Latinism.   **1101. The fig-tree,** the Indian fig tree, or banyan.   **1103. Malabar or Deccan.** Malabar is the southwestern coast of India. Deccan refers to the whole peninsula of India, especially to the south-central portion.

JOHN MILTON

High overarched, and echoing walks between:
There oft the Indian herdsman, shunning heat,
Shelters in cool, and tends his pasturing herds
At loopholes cut through thickest shade. Those leaves   1110
They gathered, broad as Amazonian targe,
And with what skill they had together sewed,
To gird their waist—vain covering, if to hide
Their guilt and dreaded shame! O how unlike
To that first naked glory! Such of late
Columbus found the American, so girt
With feathered cincture, naked else and wild,
Among the trees on isles and woody shores.
Thus fenced, and, as they thought, their shame in part
Covered, but not at rest or ease of mind,   1120
They sat them down to weep. Nor only tears
Rained at their eyes, but high winds worse within
Began to rise, high passions—anger, hate,
Mistrust, suspicion, discord—and shook sore
Their inward state of mind, calm region once
And full of peace, now tost and turbulent:
For Understanding ruled not, and the Will
Heard not her lore, both in subjection now
To sensual Appetite, who, from beneath
Usurping over sovran Reason, claimed   1130
Superior sway. From thus distempered breast
Adam, estranged in look and altered style,
Speech intermitted thus to Eve renewed:

  "Would thou hadst hearkened to my words, and stayed
With me, as I besought thee, when that strange
Desire of wandering, this unhappy morn,
I know not whence possessed thee! We had then
Remained still happy—not, as now, despoiled
Of all our good, shamed, naked, miserable!   1139
Let none henceforth seek needless cause to approve
The faith they owe; when earnestly they seek
Such proof, conclude they then begin to fail."

  To whom soon moved with touch of blame, thus Eve:
"What words have passed thy lips, Adam severe?
Imput'st thou that to my default, or will
Of wandering, as thou call'st it, which who knows
But might as ill have happened thou being by,
Or to thyself perhaps? Hadst thou been there,
Or here the attempt, thou couldst not have discerned
Fraud in the Serpent, speaking as he spake;   1150
No ground of enmity between us known,
Why he should mean me ill or seek to harm.
Was I to have never parted from thy side?
As good have grown there still, a lifeless rib.
Being as I am, why didst not thou, the head,
Command me absolutely not to go,
Going into such danger, as thou saidst?
Too facile then, thou didst not much gainsay,
Nay, didst permit, approve, and fair dismiss.
Hadst thou been firm and fixed in thy dissent,   1160
Neither had I transgressed, nor thou with me."

  To whom, then first incensed, Adam replied:—
"Is this the love, is this the recompense
Of mine to thee, ingrateful Eve, expressed
Immutable when thou wert lost, not I—
Who might have lived, and joyed immortal bliss,
Yet willingly chose rather death with thee?
And am I now upbraided as the cause
Of thy transgressing? not enough severe,
It seems, in thy restraint! What could I more?   1170
I warned thee, I admonished thee, foretold
The danger, and the lurking enemy
That lay in wait; beyond this had been force,
And force upon free will hath here no place.
But confidence then bore thee on, secure
Either to meet no danger, or to find
Matter of glorious trial; and perhaps
I also erred in overmuch admiring
What seemed in thee so perfect that I thought
No evil durst attempt thee. But I rue   1180
That error now, which is become my crime,
And thou the accuser. Thus it shall befall
Him who, to worth in women overtrusting,
Lets her will rule: restraint she will not brook;
And, left to herself, if evil thence ensue,
She first his weak indulgence will accuse."

  Thus they in mutual accusation spent
The fruitless hours, but neither self-condemning;
And of their vain contèst appeared no end.

BOOK X

The Argument

Man's transgression known, the guardian Angels forsake Paradise, and return up to Heaven to approve their vigilance, and are approved; God declaring that the entrance of Satan could not be by them prevented. He sends his Son to judge the transgressors; who descends, and gives sentence accordingly; then, in pity, clothes them both, and reascends. Sin and Death, sitting till then at the gates of Hell, by wondrous sympathy feeling the success of Satan in this new World, and the sin by Man there committed, resolve to sit no longer confined in Hell, but to follow Satan, their sire, up

---

1111. **Amazonian targe,** the shield of the Amazons, the female warriors of Greek mythology.   1117. **cincture,** belt.
1132. **altered style,** changed manner.   1141. **owe,** own, possess.

1164–65. **expressed Immutable,** demonstrated to be immutable.   1184. **brook,** endure.

to the place of Man. To make the way easier from Hell to this World to and fro, they pave a broad highway or bridge over Chaos, according to the track that Satan first made; then, preparing for Earth, they meet him, proud of his success, returning to Hell; their mutual gratulation. Satan arrives at Pandemonium; in full assembly relates, with boasting, his success against Man; instead of applause is entertained with a general hiss by all his audience, transformed, with himself also, suddenly into Serpents, according to his doom given in Paradise; then, deluded with a show of the Forbidden Tree springing up before them, they, greedily reaching to take of the fruit, chew dust and bitter ashes. The proceedings of Sin and Death: God foretells the final victory of his Son over them, and the renewing of all things; but, for the present, commands his Angels to make several alterations in the Heavens and elements. Adam, more and more perceiving his fallen condition, heavily bewails, rejects the condolement of Eve; she persists, and at length appeases him: then, to evade the curse likely to fall on their offspring, proposes to Adam violent ways; which he approves not, but, conceiving better hope, puts her in mind of the late promise made them, that her seed should be revenged on the Serpent, and exhorts her, with him, to seek peace of the offended Deity, by repentance and supplication.

BOOK XI

The Argument

The Son of God presents to his Father the prayers of our first parents now repenting, and intercedes for them. God accepts them, but declares that they must no longer abide in Paradise; sends Michael with a band of Cherubim to dispossess them, but first to reveal to Adam future things: Michael's coming down. Adam shows to Eve certain ominous signs: he discerns Michael's approach; goes out to meet him: the Angel denounces their departure. Eve's lamentation. Adam pleads, but submits: The Angel leads him up to a high hill; sets before him in vision what shall happen till the Flood.

BOOK XII

The Argument

The Angel Michael continues, from the Flood, to relate what shall succeed; then, in the mention of Abraham, comes by degrees to explain who that Seed of the Woman shall be which was promised Adam and Eve in the Fall: his Incarnation, Death, Resurrection, and Ascension; the state of the Church till his second coming. Adam, greatly satisfied and recomforted by these relations and promises, descends the hill with Michael; wakens Eve, who all this while had slept, but with gentle dreams composed to quietness of mind and submission. Michael in either hand leads them out of Paradise, the fiery sword waving behind them, and the Cherubim taking their stations to guard the place.

. . . He ended; and thus Adam last replied: 552
"How soon hath thy prediction, Seer blest,
Measured this transient World, the race of Time,
Till Time stand fixed! Beyond is all abyss—
Eternity, whose end no eye can reach.
Greatly instructed I shall hence depart,
Greatly in peace of thought, and have my fill
Of knowledge, what this vessel can contain;
Beyond which was my folly to aspire. 560
Henceforth I learn that to obey is best,
And love with fear the only God, to walk
As in his presence, ever to observe
His providence, and on him sole depend,
Merciful over all his works, with good
Still overcoming evil, and by small
Accomplishing great things—by things deemed weak
Subverting worldly strong, and worldly wise
By simply meek; that suffering for Truth's sake
Is fortitude to highest victory, 570
And to the faithful death the gate of life—
Taught this by his example whom I now
Acknowledge my Redeemer ever blest."
    To whom thus also the Angel last replied:
"This having learned, thou hast attained the sum
Of wisdom; hope no higher, though all the stars
Thou knew'st by name, and all the ethereal powers,
All secrets of the Deep, all Nature's works,
Or works of God in heaven, air, earth, or sea,
And all the riches of this world enjoy'dst, 580
And all the rule, one empire. Only add
Deeds to thy knowledge answerable; add faith;
Add virtue, patience, temperance; add love,
By name to come called Charity, the soul
Of all the rest: then wilt thou not be loth
To leave this Paradise, but shalt possess
A Paradise within thee, happier far.
Let us descend now, therefore, from this top
Of speculation; for the hour precise
Exacts our parting hence; and, see! the guards, 590
By me encamped on yonder hill, expect
Their motion, at whose front a flaming sword,
In signal of remove, waves fiercely round.
We may no longer stay. Go, waken Eve;
Her also I with gentle dreams have calmed,
Portending good, and all her spirits composed
To meek submission: thou, at season fit,

32. **denounces**, announces, proclaims.

552. **He**, the Angel Michael. **last**, for the last time.
554. **Measured**, surveyed. 559. **this vessel**, this mind. 584. **Charity.** See I Corinthians 13. 588–89. **top Of speculation.** "Top" is used in a double sense. "Speculation" means observation (from the Latin *specula*, "watchtower").

JOHN MILTON

Let her with thee partake what thou hast heard—
Chiefly what may concern her faith to know,
The great deliverance by her seed to come   600
(For by the Woman's Seed) on all mankind—
That ye may live, which will be many days,
Both in one faith unanimous; though sad
With cause for evils past, yet much more cheered
With meditation on the happy end."
   He ended, and they both descend the hill.
Descended, Adam to the bower where Eve
Lay sleeping ran before, but found her waked;
And thus with words not sad she him received:
   "Whence thou return'st and whither went'st I
     know;   610
For God is also in sleep, and dreams advise,
Which he hath sent propitious, some great good
Presaging, since, with sorrow and heart's distress
Wearied, I fell asleep: but now lead on;
In me is no delay; with thee to go
Is to stay here; without thee here to stay
Is to go hence unwilling; thou to me
Art all things under Heaven, all places thou,
Who for my wilful crime art banished hence.
This further consolation yet secure   620
I carry hence: though all by me is lost,
Such favour I unworthy am vouchsafed,
By me the Promised Seed shall all restore."
   So spake our mother Eve; and Adam heard
Well pleased, but answered not; for now too nigh
The Archangel stood, and from the other hill
To their fixed station, all in bright array
The Cherubim descended, on the ground
Gliding meteorous, as evening mist,
Risen from a river, o'er the marish glides,   630
And gathers ground fast at the labourer's heel
Homeward returning. High in front advanced,
The brandished sword of God before them blazed
Fierce as a comet, which with torrid heat,
And vapour as the Libyan air adust,
Began to parch that temperate clime; whereat
In either hand the hast'ning Angel caught
Our lingering parents, and to the eastern gate
Led them direct, and down the cliff as fast
To the subjected plain; then disappeared.   640
They, looking back, all the eastern side beheld
Of Paradise, so late their happy seat,
Waved over by that flaming brand, the gate
With dreadful faces thronged and fiery arms:
Some natural tears they dropped, but wiped them soon;
The world was all before them, where to choose
Their place of rest, and Providence their guide:
They, hand in hand, with wandering steps and slow,
Through Eden took their solitary way.

The End.

---

from AREOPAGITICA

A SPEECH OF MR. JOHN MILTON FOR THE LIBERTY OF UNLICENSED PRINTING TO THE PARLIAMENT OF ENGLAND

On June 14, 1643, Parliament passed an act requiring all books and pamphlets to be licensed by an official censor before publication. Milton saw in this act and in its implications a denial of liberty disastrous to the nation as a whole and unworthy of those who had fought to overthrow the Stuart tyranny. He had also a very personal interest in the matter, since his divorce pamphlets were being published without official license, and were scandalizing many both in and out of Parliament. In the summer of 1644 Parliament ordered a search for the author of the divorce pamphlets. In November, 1644, Milton published this most famous plea on behalf of free speech and the freedom of the press. His own account of the circumstances in which the *Areopagitica* was written is to be found in his *Second Defence of the People of England,* 1654.

602. **many days,** an allusion to Adam's long life of 930 years. See Genesis 5: 5.

The title is taken from the speech addressed by Isocrates, a contemporary of Plato, to the Areopagus, or Great Council, of Athens. Like Milton's, the Areopagitic Oration of Isocrates appeals to the highest instincts of the Athenian Council, and urges its members to reconsider certain of their acts.

THEY who to states and governors of the Commonwealth direct their speech, High Court of Parliament, or wanting such access in a private condition, write that which they foresee may advance the public good; I suppose them as at the beginning of no mean endeavour, not a little altered and moved inwardly in their minds: some with doubt of what will be the success, others with fear of what will be the censure; some with hope, others 10 with confidence of what they have to speak. And

629. **meteorous,** like meteors.   630. **marish,** marsh.
635. **adust,** scorched.   640. **subjected,** lying below.
1. **states,** heads of states, statesmen.   3. **wanting,** lacking.
6. **altered,** disturbed.   8. **success,** outcome.   9. **censure,** judgment.

me perhaps each of these dispositions, as the subject was whereon I entered, may have at other times variously affected; and likely might in these foremost expressions now also disclose which of them swayed most, but that the very attempt of this address thus made, and the thought of whom it hath recourse to, hath got the power within me to a passion, far more welcome than incidental to a preface. Which though I stay not to confess ere any ask, I shall be blameless, if it be no other than the joy and gratulation which it brings to all who wish and promote their country's liberty; whereof this whole discourse proposed will be a certain testimony, if not a trophy. For this is not the liberty which we can hope, that no grievance ever should arise in the Commonwealth, that let no man in this world expect; but when complaints are freely heard, deeply considered, and speedily reformed, then is the utmost bound of civil liberty attained that wise men look for. To which if I now manifest by the very sound of this which I shall utter, that we are already in good part arrived, and yet from such a steep disadvantage of tyranny and superstition grounded into our principles as was beyond the manhood of a Roman recovery, it will be attributed first, as is most due, to the strong assistance of God our deliverer, next to your faithful guidance and undaunted wisdom, Lords and Commons of England. Neither is it in God's esteem the diminution of his glory, when honourable things are spoken of good men and worthy magistrates; which if I now first should begin to do, after so fair a progress of your laudable deeds, and such a long obligement upon the whole realm to your indefatigable virtues, I might be justly reckoned among the tardiest, and the unwillingest of them that praise ye. . . .

If I should thus far presume upon the meek demeanour of your civil and gentle greatness, Lords and Commons, as what your published Order hath directly said, that to gainsay, I might defend myself with ease, if any should accuse me of being new or insolent, did they but know how much better I find ye esteem it to imitate the old and elegant humanity of Greece, than the barbaric pride of a Hunnish and Norwegian stateliness. And out of those ages, to whose polite wisdom and letters we owe that we are not yet Goths and Jutlanders, I could name him who from his private house wrote that discourse to the parliament of Athens, that persuades them to change the form of democracy which was then established. Such honour was done in those days to men who professed the study of wisdom and eloquence, not only in their own country, but in other lands, that cities and signiories heard them gladly, and with great respect, if they had aught in public to admonish the state. Thus did Dion Prusaeus, a stranger and a private orator, counsel the Rhodians against a former edict: and I abound with other like examples, which to set here would be superfluous. But if from the industry of a life wholly dedicated to studious labours, and those natural endowments haply not the worst for two and fifty degrees of northern latitude, so much must be derogated, as to count me not equal to any of those who had this privilege, I would obtain to be thought not so inferior, as yourselves are superior to the most of them who received their counsel: and how far you excel them, be assured, Lords and Commons, there can no greater testimony appear, than when your prudent spirit acknowledges and obeys the voice of reason from what quarter soever it be heard speaking; and renders ye as willing to repeal any Act of your own setting forth, as any set forth by your predecessors.

If ye be thus resolved, as it were injury to think ye were not, I know not what should withhold me from presenting ye with a fit instance wherein to show both that love of truth which ye eminently profess, and that uprightness of your judgment which is not wont to be partial to yourselves; by judging over again that Order which ye have ordained *to regulate printing. That no book, pamphlet, or paper shall be henceforth printed, unless the same be first approved and licensed by such,* or at least one of such as shall be thereto appointed. For that part which preserves justly every man's copy to himself, or provides for the poor, I touch not, only wish they be not made pretences to abuse and persecute honest and painful men, who offend not in either of these particulars. But that other clause of licensing books, which we thought had died with his

---

1–2. dispositions . . . entered. Milton's five pamphlets on church reform, his treatise on education, and two of his pamphlets on divorce had preceded the *Areopagitica*. **14. if not a trophy,** that is, he may perhaps not win the trophy of victory in his argument for the freedom of the press, but he will have put his own feelings on record. **25. a Roman recovery.** England's recovery from her low estate under the Stuart tyranny had surpassed Rome's recovery from her numerous misfortunes.

3. him, Isocrates. **12. Dion Prusaeus,** surnamed Chrysostomus (golden mouthed) because of his eloquence. He attempted to dissuade the Rhodians from altering the names on their public statues in order to inscribe the names of the men then in power. He flourished in the first century B.C. **18. northern latitude.** Milton believed that cold climates were not conducive to literary activity. **19. derogated,** subtracted. **42. copy,** copyright. **45. painful,** painstaking.

JOHN MILTON

brother quadragesimal and matrimonial when the prelates expired, I shall now attend with such a homily, as shall lay before ye, first the inventors of it to be those whom ye will be loth to own; next what is to be thought in general of reading, whatever sort the books be; and that this Order avails nothing to the suppressing of scandalous, seditious, and libellous books, which were mainly intended to be suppressed. Last, that it will be primely to the discouragement of all learning, and the stop of truth, not only by disexercising and blunting our abilities in what we know already, but by hindering and cropping the discovery that might be yet further made both in religious and civil wisdom.

I deny not, but that it is of greatest concernment in the Church and Commonwealth, to have a vigilant eye how books demean themselves, as well as men; and thereafter to confine, imprison, and do sharpest justice on them as malefactors. For books are not absolutely dead things, but do contain a potency of life in them to be as active as that soul was whose progeny they are; nay, they do preserve as in a vial the purest efficacy and extraction of that living intellect that bred them. I know they are as lively, and as vigorously productive, as those fabulous dragon's teeth; and being sown up and down, may chance to spring up armed men. And yet, on the other hand, unless wariness be used, as good almost kill a man as kill a good book; who kills a man kills a reasonable creature, God's image; but he who destroys a good book, kills reason itself, kills the image of God, as it were in the eye. Many a man lives a burden to the earth; but a good book is the precious life-blood of a master-spirit, embalmed and treasured up on purpose to a life beyond life. 'Tis true, no age can restore a life, whereof perhaps there is no great loss; and revolutions of ages do not oft recover the loss of a rejected truth, for the want of which whole nations fare the worse. We should be wary therefore what persecution we raise against the living labours of public men, how we spill that seasoned life of man preserved and stored up in books; since we see a kind of homicide may be thus committed, sometimes a martyrdom, and if it extend to the whole impression, a kind of massacre, whereof the execution ends not in the slaying of an elemental life, but strikes at that ethereal and fifth essence, the breath of reason itself, slays an immortality rather than a life. . . .

Good and evil we know in the field of this world grow up together almost inseparably; and the knowledge of good is so involved and interwoven with the knowledge of evil, and in so many cunning resemblances hardly to be discerned, that those confused seeds which were imposed on Psyche as an incessant labour to cull out, and sort asunder, were not more intermixed. It was from out the rind of one apple tasted, that the knowledge of good and evil as two twins cleaving together leaped forth into the world. And perhaps this is that doom which Adam fell into of knowing good and evil, that is to say of knowing good by evil.

As therefore the state of man now is, what wisdom can there be to choose, what continence to forbear without the knowledge of evil? He that can apprehend and consider vice with all her baits and seeming pleasures, and yet abstain, and yet distinguish, and yet prefer that which is truly better, he is the true wayfaring Christian. I cannot praise a fugitive and cloistered virtue, unexercised and unbreathed, that never sallies out and sees her adversary, but slinks out of the race, where that immortal garland is to be run for, not without dust and heat. Assuredly we bring not innocence into the world, we bring impurity much rather: that which purifies us is trial, and trial is by what is contrary. That virtue therefore which is but a youngling in the contemplation of evil, and knows not the utmost that vice promises to her followers, and rejects it, is but a blank virtue, not a pure; her whiteness is but an excremental whiteness. Which was the reason why our sage and serious poet Spenser, whom I dare be known to think a better teacher than Scotus or Aquinas, describing true temperance under the person of Guion, brings

---

1. **quadragesimal**, Lenten license regulating the observance of fast days. **matrimonial.** Milton upheld the theory that marriage was wholly a civil ceremony and contract, in which the Church had properly no part. 2. **expired.** The bishops had been deprived of their power by the bill which excluded them from Parliament in 1642. 27. **dragon's teeth.** Jason, according to the story in Ovid's *Metamorphoses*, by Medea's direction sowed the teeth of the Colchian dragon, whence armed men sprang up. 33. **in the eye.** Reason seems to be referred to as the image of God within the pupil of the eye. 38-39. **revolutions,** cycles.

1-2. **the whole impression,** the total number of copies printed. 3-4. **elemental life . . . fifth essence.** An "elemental" life is an earthly, material existence, depending on the four elements; the fifth essence (*quinta essentia*) is not material, but spiritual. 13-15. **Psyche . . . intermixed.** The famous story of Cupid and Psyche is an incidental tale in *The Golden Ass* of Apuleius, Books IV-VI. Walter Pater's translation of the story is the best known. 30-31. **that immortal garland.** See I Corinthians 9:24. 39. **excremental,** superficial. 42. **Scotus or Aquinas.** Duns Scotus (1265-1308), the great British Franciscan Schoolman, was the chief opponent of St. Thomas Aquinas (1225?-1274), "the Seraphic Doctor" and greatest of medieval metaphysicians.

him in with his palmer through the cave of Mammon, and the bower of earthly bliss that he might see and know, and yet abstain. Since therefore the knowledge and survey of vice is in this world so necessary to the constituting of human virtue, and the scanning of error to the confirmation of truth, how can we more safely and with less danger scout into the regions of sin and falsity than by reading all manner of tractates, and hearing all manner of reason? And this is the benefit which may be had of books promiscuously read. . . .

Seeing therefore that those books, and those in great abundance which are likeliest to taint both life and doctrine, cannot be suppressed without the fall of learning, and of all ability in disputation, and that these books of either sort are most and soonest catching to the learned, from whom to the common people whatever is heretical or dissolute may quickly be conveyed, and that evil manners are as perfectly learnt without books a thousand other ways which cannot be stopped, and evil doctrine not with books can propagate, except a teacher guide, which he might also do without writing, and so beyond prohibiting, I am not able to unfold, how this cautelous enterprise of licensing can be exempted from the number of vain and impossible attempts. And he who were pleasantly disposed could not well avoid to liken it to the exploit of that gallant man who thought to pound up the crows by shutting his park gate.

Besides another inconvenience, if learned men be the first receivers out of books, and dispreaders both of vice and error, how shall the licensers themselves be confided in, unless we can confer upon them, or they assume to themselves above all others in the land, the grace of infallibility, and uncorruptedness? And again if it be true that a wise man like a good refiner can gather gold out of the drossiest volume, and that a fool will be a fool with the best book, yea or without book, there is no reason that we should deprive a wise man of any advantage to his wisdom, while we seek to restrain from a fool that which being restrained will be no hindrance to his folly. For if there should be so much exactness always used to keep that from him which is unfit for his reading, we should in the judgment of Aristotle not only, but of Solomon, and of our Saviour, not vouchsafe him good precepts, and by consequence not willingly admit him to good books; as being certain that a wise man will make better use of an idle pamphlet than a fool will do of sacred Scripture.

'Tis next alleged we must not expose ourselves to temptations without necessity, and next to that, not employ our time in vain things. To both these objections one answer will serve, out of the grounds already laid, that to all men such books are not temptations, nor vanities; but useful drugs and materials wherewith to temper and compose effective and strong medicines, which man's life cannot want. The rest, as children and childish men, who have not the art to qualify and prepare these working minerals, well may be exhorted to forbear, but hindered forcibly they cannot be by all the licensing that sainted Inquisition could ever yet contrive; which is what I promised to deliver next, that this order of licensing conduces nothing to the end for which it was framed; and hath almost prevented me by being clear already while thus much hath been explaining. See the ingenuity of Truth, who when she gets a free and willing hand, opens herself faster than the pace of method and discourse can overtake her. It was the task which I began with, to shew that no Nation, or well-instituted State, if they valued books at all, did ever use this way of licensing. . . .

If we think to regulate printing, thereby to rectify manners, we must regulate all recreations and pastimes, all that is delightful to man. No music must be heard, no song be set or sung, but what is grave and Doric. There must be licensing dancers, that no gesture, motion, or deportment be taught our youth but what by their allowance shall be thought honest; for such Plato was provided of. It will ask more than the work of twenty licensers to examine all the lutes, the violins, and the guitars in every house; they must not be suffered to prattle as they do, but must be licensed what they may say. And who shall silence all the airs and madrigals, that whisper softness in chambers? The windows also, and the balconies must be thought on, there are shrewd books, with dangerous frontispieces set to sale; who shall prohibit them, shall twenty licensers? The villages also must have their visitors to inquire what lectures the bagpipe and the rebeck reads even to the ballatry, and the gamut of every municipal fiddler, for these are the countryman's Arcadias, and his Monte Mayors. Next, what more

---

1-2. **the cave of Mammon.** See *The Faerie Queene*, Book II, Canto VII. **the bower of earthly bliss.** See *ibid.*, Canto XII.   26. **cautelous,** crafty.   48. **Solomon.** See Proverbs 26:5.   49. **our Saviour.** See Matthew 7:6.

12. **want,** dispense with.   19-20. **prevented me,** anticipated my proofs.   32. **Doric.** See note 136 on page 646.   43. **shrewd,** mischievous.   49. **Monte Mayors.** Jorge de Montemayor (1520?-1561), Portuguese poet, was author of the prose pastoral *Diana Enamorada*, written in imitation of the Italian Sanazzaro's *Arcadia*.

national corruption, for which England hears ill abroad, than household gluttony; who shall be the rectors of our daily rioting? and what shall be done to inhibit the multitudes that frequent those houses where drunkenness is sold and harboured? Our garments also should be referred to the licensing of some more sober work-masters to see them cut into a less wanton garb. Who shall regulate all the mixed conversation of our youth, male and female together, as is the fashion of this country, who shall still appoint what shall be discoursed, what presumed, and no further? Lastly, who shall forbid and separate all idle resort, all evil company? These things will be, and must be; but how they shall be least hurtful, how least enticing, herein consists the grave and governing wisdom of a State.

To sequester out of the world into Atlantic and Utopian polities, which never can be drawn into use, will not mend our condition; but to ordain wisely as in this world of evil, in the midst whereof God hath placed us unavoidably. Nor is it Plato's licensing of books will do this, which necessarily pulls along with it so many other kinds of licensing, as will make us all both ridiculous and weary, and yet frustrate; but those unwritten, or at least unconstraining laws of virtuous education, religious and civil nurture, which Plato there mentions as the bonds and ligaments of the Commonwealth, the pillars and the sustainers of every written statute; these they be which will bear chief sway in such matters as these, when all licensing will be easily eluded. Impunity and remissness, for certain, are the bane of a Commonwealth, but here the great art lies to discern in what the law is to bid restraint and punishment, and in what things persuasion only is to work.

If every action which is good or evil in man at ripe years were to be under pittance, and prescription, and compulsion, what were virtue but a name, what praise could be then due to well-doing, what gramercy to be sober, just or continent? Many there be that complain of divine Providence for suffering Adam to transgress; foolish tongues! When God gave him reason, he gave him freedom to choose, for reason is but choosing; he had been else a mere artificial Adam, such an Adam as he is in the motions. We ourselves esteem not of that obedience, or love, or gift, which is of force: God therefore left him free, set before him a provoking object, ever almost in his eyes herein consisted his merit, herein the right of his reward, the praise of his abstinence. Wherefore did he create passions within us, pleasures round about us, but that these rightly tempered are the very ingredients of virtue?

They are not skilful considerers of human things, who imagine to remove sin by removing the matter of sin; for, besides that it is a huge heap increasing under the very act of diminishing, though some part of it may for a time be withdrawn from some persons, it cannot from all, in such a universal thing as books are; and when this is done, yet the sin remains entire. Though ye take from a covetous man all his treasure, he has yet one jewel left, ye cannot bereave him of his covetousness. Banish all objects of lust, shut up all youth into the severest discipline that can be exercised in any hermitage, ye cannot make them chaste that came not thither so: such great care and wisdom is required to the right managing of this point. Suppose we could expel sin by this means; look how much we thus expel of sin, so much we expel of virtue: for the matter of them both is the same; remove that, and ye remove them both alike.

This justifies the high providence of God, who though he commands us temperance, justice, continence, yet pours out before us even to a profuseness all desirable things, and gives us minds that can wander beyond all limit and satiety. Why should we then affect a rigour contrary to the manner of God and of nature, by abridging or scanting those means, which books freely permitted are, both to the trial of virtue, and the exercise of truth. It would be better done to learn that the law must needs be frivolous which goes to restrain things, uncertainly and yet equally working to good, and to evil. And were I the chooser, a dram of well-doing should be preferred before many times as much the forcible hindrance of evil-doing. For God sure esteems the growth and completing of one virtuous person, more than the restraint of ten vicious. . . .

Lords and Commons of England, consider what nation it is whereof ye are, and whereof ye are the governors: a nation not slow and dull, but of a quick, ingenious, and piercing spirit, acute to invent, subtle and sinewy to discourse, not beneath the reach of any point the highest that human capacity can soar to. Therefore the studies of learning in her deepest sciences have been so ancient, and so eminent among us, that writers of good antiquity, and ablest judgment, have been persuaded that

---

1. **hears ill,** is ill spoken of.   **17–18. Atlantic and Utopian polities,** such fabulous governments as those of Plato's island of Atlantis and Sir Thomas More's Utopia.   **41. gramercy,** thanks.   **47. motions,** puppet shows.   **49. provoking,** enticing.

4. tempered, moderated.   **29. affect a rigour,** adopt a strictness.

even the school of Pythagoras, and the Persian wisdom, took beginning from the old philosophy of this island. And that wise and civil Roman, Julius Agricola, who governed once here for Caesar, preferred the natural wits of Britain before the laboured studies of the French. Nor is it for nothing that the grave and frugal Transylvanian sends out yearly from as far as the mountainous borders of Russia, and beyond the Hercynian wilderness, not their youth, but their staid men, to learn our language, and our theologic arts.

Yet that which is above all this, the favour and the love of Heaven, we have great argument to think in a peculiar manner propitious and propending towards us. Why else was this nation chosen before any other, that out of her as out of Sion should be proclaimed and sounded forth the first tidings and trumpet of Reformation to all Europe? And had it not been the obstinate perverseness of our prelates against the divine and admirable spirit of Wickliffe, to suppress him as a schismatic and innovator, perhaps neither the Bohemian Huss and Jerome, no, nor the name of Luther, or of Calvin had been ever known: the glory of reforming all our neighbours had been completely ours. But now, as our obdurate clergy have with violence demeaned the matter, we are become hitherto the latest and the backwardest scholars, of whom God offered to have made us the teachers. Now once again by all concurrence of signs, and by the general instinct of holy and devout men, as they daily and solemnly express their thoughts, God is decreeing to begin some new and great period in his Church, even to the reforming of Reformation itself: what does he then but reveal himself to his servants, and as his manner is, first to his Englishmen? I say, as his manner is, first to us, though we mark not the method of his counsels, and are unworthy. Behold now this vast city; a city of refuge, the mansion-house of liberty, encompassed and surrounded with his protection; the shop of war hath not there more anvils and hammers waking, to fashion out the plates and instruments of armed Justice in defence of beleaguered Truth, than there be pens and heads there, sitting by their studious lamps, musing, searching, revolving new notions and ideas wherewith to present, as with their homage and their fealty, the approaching Reformation: others as fast reading, trying all things, assenting to the force of reason and convincement. What could a man require more from a nation so pliant and so prone to seek after knowledge? What wants there to such a towardly and pregnant soil, but wise and faithful labourers, to make a knowing people, a nation of prophets, of sages, and of worthies? We reckon more than five months yet to harvest; there need not be five weeks, had we but eyes to lift up, the fields are white already.

Where there is much desire to learn, there of necessity will be much arguing, much writing, many opinions; for opinion in good men is but knowledge in the making. Under these fantastic terrors of sect and schism, we wrong the earnest and zealous thirst after knowledge and understanding which God hath stirred up in this city. What some lament of, we rather should rejoice at, should rather praise this pious forwardness among men, to reassume the ill-deputed care of their religion into their own hands again. A little generous prudence, a little forbearance of one another, and some grain of charity might win all these diligences to join, and unite into one general and brotherly search after Truth; could we but forego this prelatical tradition of crowding free consciences and Christian liberties into canons and precepts of men. I doubt not, if some great and worthy stranger should come among us, wise to discern the mould and temper of a people, and how to govern it, observing the high hopes and aims, the diligent alacrity of our extended thoughts and reasonings in the pursuance of truth and freedom, but that he would cry out as Pyrrhus did, admiring the Roman docility and courage, "If such were my Epirots, I would not despair the greatest design that could be attempted to make a Church or Kingdom happy."

Yet these are the men cried out against for schismatics and sectaries; as if, while the temple of the Lord was building, some cutting, some squaring the marble, others hewing the cedars, there should be a sort of irrational men who could not consider there must be many schisms and many dissections made in the quarry and in the timber, ere the house of God can be built. And when every stone is laid artfully together, it cannot be united into a continuity, it can but be contiguous in this world; neither can every piece of the building be of one form; nay, rather the perfection consists in this, that out of many moderate varieties and brotherly dissimilitudes that are not vastly disproportional arises the goodly and the graceful symmetry that commends the whole pile and structure.

---

3. **civil,** cultured.   9. **Hercynian wilderness,** the Roman term for the forests and hills of southern and central Germany.   14–15. **propending,** favorably inclined.   26–27. **demeaned,** conducted.

3. **towardly,** favorable.   21. **diligences,** exertions.   32. **Pyrrhus,** the king of Epirus who defeated the Romans at Heraclea in 280 B.C.   40. **sort,** set.

Let us therefore be more considerate builders, more wise in spiritual architecture, when great reformation is expected. For now the time seems come, wherein Moses the great prophet may sit in heaven rejoicing to see that memorable and glorious wish of his fulfilled, when not only our seventy elders, but all the Lord's people are become prophets. No marvel then though some men, and some good men too perhaps, but young in goodness, as Joshua then was, envy them. They fret, and out of their own weakness are in agony, lest these divisions and subdivisions will undo us. The adversary again applauds, and waits the hour, when they have branched themselves out, saith he, small enough into parties and partitions, then will be our time. Fool! he sees not the firm root, out of which we all grow, though into branches: nor will beware until he see our small divided maniples cutting through at every angle of his ill-united and unwieldy brigade. And that we are to hope better of all these supposed sects and schisms, and that we shall not need that solicitude, honest, perhaps, though over-timorous, of them that vex in this behalf, but shall laugh in the end at those malicious applauders of our differences, I have these reasons to persuade me.

First, when a city shall be as it were besieged and blocked about, her navigable river infested, inroads and incursions round, defiance and battle oft rumoured to be marching up even to her walls, and suburb trenches, that then the people, or the greater part, more than at other times, wholly taken up with the study of highest and most important matters to be reformed, should be disputing, reasoning, reading, inventing, discoursing, even to a rarity, and admiration, things not before discoursed or written of, argues first a singular good will, contentedness, and confidence in your prudent foresight, and safe government, Lords and Commons; and from thence derives itself to a gallant bravery and well-grounded contempt of their enemies, as if there were no small number of as great spirits among us, as his was, who when Rome was nigh besieged by Hannibal, being in the city, bought that piece of ground at no cheap rate whereon Hannibal himself encamped his own regiment.

Next it is a lively and cheerful presage of our happy success and victory. For as in a body, when the blood is fresh, the spirits pure and vigorous, not only to vital, but to rational faculties, and those in the acutest, and the pertest operations of wit and subtlety, it argues in what good plight and constitution the body is, so when the cheerfulness of the people is so sprightly up, as that it has, not only wherewith to guard well its own freedom and safety, but to spare, and to bestow upon the solidest and sublimest points of controversy, and new invention, it betokens us not degenerated, nor drooping to a fatal decay, but casting off the old and wrinkled skin of corruption to outlive these pangs and wax young again, entering the glorious ways of Truth and prosperous virtue destined to become great and honourable in these latter ages. Methinks I see in my mind a noble and puissant nation rousing herself like a strong man after sleep, and shaking her invincible locks. Methinks I see her as an eagle mewing her mighty youth, and kindling her undazzled eyes at the full mid-day beam; purging and unscaling her long-abused sight at the fountain itself of heavenly radiance; while the whole noise of timorous and flocking birds, with those also that love the twilight, flutter about, amazed at what she means, and in their envious gabble would prognosticate a year of sects and schisms.

What should ye do then, should ye suppress all this flowery crop of knowledge and new light sprung up and yet springing daily in this city, should ye set an oligarchy of twenty engrossers over it, to bring a famine upon our minds again, when we shall know nothing but what is measured to us by their bushel? Believe it, Lords and Commons, they who counsel ye to such a suppressing do as good as bid ye suppress yourselves; and I will soon show how. If it be desired to know the immediate cause of all this free writing and free speaking, there cannot be assigned a truer than your own mild, and free, and humane government. It is the liberty, Lords and Commons, which your own valorous and happy counsels have purchased us, liberty which is the nurse of all great wits; this is that which hath rarefied and enlightened our spirits like the influence of heaven; this is that which hath enfranchised, enlarged and lifted up our apprehensions degrees above themselves.

Ye cannot make us now less capable, less knowing, less eagerly pursuing of the truth, unless ye first make yourselves, that made us so, less the lovers, less the founders of our true liberty. We can grow ignorant again, brutish, formal, and slavish, as ye found us; but you then must first become that which ye cannot be, oppressive, arbitrary, and tyrannous, as they were from whom ye have freed us. That our hearts are now more capacious, our

---

7–8. **prophets.** See Numbers 11:27–29. **18. maniples,** small companies. **52. pertest,** sprightliest.

16. mewing, renewing. **27. engrossers,** those who get a monopoly by buying up large quantities and thus command the market.

thoughts more erected to the search and expectation of greatest and exactest things, is the issue of your own virtue propagated in us; ye cannot suppress that unless ye reinforce an abrogated and merciless law, that fathers may dispatch at will their own children. And who shall then stick closest to ye, and excite others? Not he who takes up arms for coat and conduct, and his four nobles of Danegelt. Although I dispraise not the defence of just immunities, yet love my peace better, if that were all. Give me the liberty to know, to utter, and to argue freely according to conscience, above all liberties.

What would be best advised, then, if it be found so hurtful and so unequal to suppress opinions for the newness, or the unsuitableness to a customary acceptance, will not be my task to say. I only shall repeat what I have learned from one of your own honourable number, a right noble and pious Lord, who had he not sacrificed his life and fortunes to the Church and Commonwealth, we had not now missed and bewailed a worthy and undoubted patron of this argument. Ye know him I am sure; yet I for honour's sake, and may it be eternal to him, shall name him, the Lord Brooke. He, writing of episcopacy, and by the way treating of sects and schisms, left ye his vote, or rather now the last words of his dying charge, which I know will ever be of dear and honoured regard with ye, so full of meekness and breathing charity that, next to His last testament, who bequeathed love and peace to His disciples, I cannot call to mind where I have read or heard words more mild and peaceful. He there exhorts us to hear with patience and humility those, however they be miscalled, that desire to live purely, in such a use of God's ordinances as the best guidance of their conscience gives them, and to tolerate them, though in some disconformity to ourselves. The book itself will tell us more at large being published to the world, and dedicated to the Parliament by him who both for his life and for his death deserves that what advice he left be not laid by without perusal.

And now the time in special is, by privilege to write and speak what may help to the further discussing of matters in agitation. The temple of Janus with his two controversal faces might now not unsignificantly be set open. And though all the winds of doctrine were let loose to play upon the earth, so Truth be in the field, we do injuriously by licensing and prohibiting to misdoubt her strength. Let her and Falsehood grapple; who ever knew Truth put to the worse, in a free and open encounter? Her confuting is the best and surest suppressing. He who hears what praying there is for light and clearer knowledge to be sent down among us, would think of other matters to be constituted beyond the discipline of Geneva, framed and fabricked already to our hands.

Yet when the new light which we beg for shines in upon us, there be who envy, and oppose, if it come not first in at their casements. What a collusion is this, whenas we are exhorted by the wise man to use diligence, to seek for wisdom as for hidden treasures early and late, that another order shall enjoin us to know nothing but by statute. When a man hath been labouring the hardest labour in the deep mines of knowledge, hath furnished out his findings in all their equipage, drawn forth his reasons as it were a battle ranged, scattered and defeated all objections in his way, calls out his adversary into the plain, offers him the advantage of wind and sun, if he please, only that he may try the matter by dint of argument, for his opponents then to skulk, to lay ambushments, to keep a narrow bridge of licensing where the challenger should pass, though it be valour enough in soldiership, is but weakness and cowardice in the wars of Truth. For who knows not that Truth is strong next to the Almighty; she needs no policies, nor stratagems, nor licensings to make her victorious, those are the shifts and the defences that error uses against her power. Give her but room, and do not bind her when she sleeps, for then she speaks not true, as the old Proteus did, who spake oracles only when he was caught and bound, but then rather she turns herself into all shapes, except her own, and perhaps tunes her voice according to the time, as Micaiah did before Ahab, until she be adjured into her own likeness.

Yet is it not impossible that she may have more shapes than one. What else is all that rank of things indifferent, wherein Truth may be on this side, or on the other, without being unlike herself? What but a vain shadow else is the abolition of those ordinances, that hand-writing nailed to the cross, what

8. Danegelt, probably an allusion to John Hampden's refusal to pay ship money. Danegelt was the old land tax levied in order to protect the country from the Danes. Charles I appealed to the precedent of Danegelt in his attempts to impose ship money. A noble was a coin worth 6s. 8d.   **10. if that were all,** if it were merely a question of being immune from paying a tax.   **14. unequal,** unjust.   **24. Lord Brooke,** Robert, adopted son of Fulke Greville, Lord Brooke. He was a general in the Parliamentary army and was killed on March 1, 1643, during an attack on Lichfield Cathedral, which was held by the Royalists. His book was *A Discourse on Episcopacy,* 1641.

11-12. discipline of Geneva, the system of church government instituted by John Calvin.   **29. bridge of licensing.** The allusion is to the tales of chivalry, in which knights often held a bridge in the manner described.   **38. Proteus,** the old man of the sea in Greek mythology, who, to avoid having to prophesy, assumed many different shapes until he was finally caught and bound.   **41-42. Micaiah . . . Ahab.** See I Kings 22.

great purchase is this Christian liberty which Paul so often boasts of? His doctrine is, that he who eats or eats not, regards a day, or regards it not, may do either to the Lord. How many other things might be tolerated in peace, and left to conscience, had we but charity, and were it not the chief stronghold of our hypocrisy to be ever judging one another. I fear yet this iron yoke of outward conformity hath left a slavish print upon our necks; the ghost of a linen decency yet haunts us. We stumble and are impatient at the least dividing of one visible congregation from another, though it be not in fundamentals; and through our forwardness to suppress, and our backwardness to recover any enthralled piece of truth out of the gripe of custom, we care not to keep truth separated from truth, which is the fiercest rent and disunion of all. We do not see that while we still affect by all means a rigid external formality, we may as soon fall again into a gross conforming stupidity, a stark and dead congealment of wood and hay and stubble forced and frozen together, which is more to the sudden degenerating of a Church than many subdichotomies of petty schisms.

Not that I can think well of every light separation, or that all in a Church is to be expected gold and silver and precious stones: it is not possible for man to sever the wheat from the tares, the good fish from the other fry; that must be the angels' ministry at the end of mortal things. Yet if all cannot be of one mind (as who looks they should be?) this doubtless is more wholesome, more prudent, and more Christian that many be tolerated, rather than all compelled. I mean not tolerated popery, and open superstition, which as it extirpates all religions and civil supremacies, so itself should be extirpate, provided first that all charitable and compassionate means be used to win and regain the weak and the misled: that also which is impious or evil absolutely either against faith or manners no law can possibly permit, that intends not to unlaw itself: but those neighbouring differences, or rather indifferences, are what I speak of, whether in some point of doctrine or of discipline, which though they may be many, yet need not interrupt the unity of Spirit, if we could but find among us the bond of peace.

In the meanwhile if any one would write, and bring his helpful hand to the slow-moving reformation which we labour under, if Truth have spoken to him before others, or but seemed at least to speak, who hath so bejesuited us that we should trouble that man with asking licence to do so worthy a deed? and not consider this, that if it come to prohibiting, there is not aught more likely to be prohibited than truth itself; whose first appearance to our eyes bleared and dimmed with prejudice and custom, is more unsightly and unplausible than many errors, even as the person is of many a great man slight and contemptible to see to. And what do they tell us vainly of new opinions, when this very opinion of theirs, that none must be heard but whom they like, is the worst and newest opinion of all others; and is the chief cause why sects and schisms do so much abound, and true knowledge is kept at distance from us; besides yet a greater danger which is in it.

For when God shakes a kingdom with strong and healthful commotions to a general reforming, 'tis not untrue that many sectaries and false teachers are then busiest in seducing; but yet more true it is, that God then raises to his own work men of rare abilities, and more than common industry not only to look back and revise what hath been taught heretofore, but to gain further and go on to some new enlightened steps in the discovery of truth. For such is the order of God's enlightening his Church, to dispense and deal out by degrees his beam, so as our earthly eyes may best sustain it. Neither is God appointed and confined, where and out of what place these his chosen shall be first heard to speak; for he sees not as man sees, chooses not as man chooses, lest we should devote ourselves again to set places, and assemblies, and outward callings of men; planting our faith one while in the old Convocation house, and another while in the Chapel at Westminster; when all the faith and religion that shall be there canonized, is not sufficient without plain convincement, and the charity of patient instruction to supple the least bruise of conscience, to edify the meanest Christian, who desires to walk in the Spirit, and not in the letter of human trust, for all the number of voices that can be there made; no though Harry the Seventh himself there, with all his liege tombs about him, should lend them voices from the dead, to swell their number.

And if the men be erroneous who appear to be the leading schismatics, what withholds us but our

---

9–10. **linen decency**, a sarcastic reference to the controversies over ecclesiastical vestments, ceremonies, and so forth. 23. **subdichotomies**, subdivisions. 33. **I mean not tolerated popery.** Because of the political claims of the Pope as a temporal sovereign, Milton was unwilling to extend the benefits of religious toleration to Roman Catholics.

34–35. **Convocation house.** The Convocation of the Church of England had been held in the Chapter House of Westminster Abbey. 35–36. **the Chapel at Westminster.** When Presbyterianism was made the state religion in 1643, Parliament gave to the Assembly of Divines of the Presbyterian Church the powers and privileges formerly held by the Convocation, and set aside Henry VII's Chapel in Westminster Abbey for its meeting-place. 37. **canonized,** pronounced to be orthodox.

sloth, our self-will, and distrust in the right cause, that we do not give them gentle meetings and gentle dismissions, that we debate not and examine the matter thoroughly with liberal and frequent audience; if not for their sakes, yet for our own? seeing no man who hath tasted learning, but will confess the many ways of profiting by those who not contented with stale receipts are able to manage, and set forth new positions to the world. And were they but as the dust and cinders of our feet, so long as in that notion they may yet serve to polish and brighten the armoury of Truth, even for that respect they were not utterly to be cast away. But if they be of those whom God hath fitted for the special use of these times with eminent and ample gifts, and those perhaps neither among the priests, nor among the Pharisees, and we in the haste of a precipitant zeal shall make no distinction, but resolve to stop their mouths, because we fear they come with new and dangerous opinions, as we commonly forejudge them ere we understand them, no less than woe to us, while thinking thus to defend the Gospel, we are found the persecutors.

There have been not a few since the beginning of this Parliament, both of the presbytery and others who by their unlicensed books to the contempt of an Imprimatur first broke that triple ice clung about our hearts, and taught the people to see day: I hope that none of those were the persuaders to renew upon us this bondage which they themselves have wrought so much good by contemning. But if neither the check that Moses gave to young Joshua, nor the countermand which our Saviour gave to young John, who was so ready to prohibit those whom he thought unlicensed, be not enough to admonish our elders how unacceptable to God their testy mood of prohibiting is, if neither their own remembrance what evil hath abounded in the Church by this let of licensing, and what good they themselves have begun by transgressing it, be not enough, but that they will persuade, and execute the most Dominican part of the Inquisition over us, and are already with one foot in the stirrup so active at suppressing, it would be no unequal distribution in the first place to suppress the suppressors themselves; whom the change of their condition hath puffed up, more than their late experience of harder times hath made wise.

And as for regulating the Press, let no man think to have the honour of advising ye better than yourselves have done in that Order published next before this, that no book be printed, unless the printer's and the author's name, or at least the printer's be registered. Those which otherwise come forth, if they be found mischievous and libellous, the fire and the executioner will be the timeliest and the most effectual remedy that man's prevention can use. For this authentic Spanish policy of licensing books, if I have said aught, will prove the most unlicensed book itself within a short while; and was the immediate image of a Star Chamber decree to that purpose made in those very times when that court did the rest of those her pious works, for which she is now fallen from the stars with Lucifer. Whereby ye may guess what kind of state prudence, what love of the people, what care of religion or good manners there was at the contriving, although with singular hypocrisy it pretended to bind books to their good behaviour. And how it got the upper hand of your precedent Order so well constituted before, if we may believe those men whose profession gives them cause to inquire most, it may be doubted there was in it the fraud of some old patentees and monopolizers in the trade of bookselling; who under pretence of the poor in their Company not to be defrauded, and the just retaining of each man his several copy, which God forbid should be gainsaid, brought divers glossing colours to the House, which were indeed but colours, and serving to no end except it be to exercise a superiority over their neighbours, men who do not therefore labour in an honest profession to which learning is indebted, that they should be made other men's vassals. Another end is thought was aimed at by some of them in procuring by petition this Order, that having power in their hands, malignant books might the easier escape abroad, as the event shows.

But of these sophisms and elenchs of merchandise I skill not. This I know, that errors in a good government and in a bad are equally almost incident; for what magistrate may not be misinformed, and much the sooner, if liberty of printing be reduced into the power of a few. But to redress willingly and speedily what hath been erred, and in highest authority to esteem a plain advertisement more than others have done a sumptuous bribe, is a virtue (honoured Lords and Commons) answerable to your highest actions, and whereof none can participate but greatest and wisest men.

---

27. **Imprimatur.** "Let it be printed"—the formula which authorized the printing of a book. 32–33. **Moses . . . Joshua.** See Exodus 32:17–18. 34. **Saviour . . . John.** See Mark 9:38–39. 39. **let,** hindrance.

1–2. **published next before this,** in January, 1642. 8. **authentic,** characteristic. 28. **copy,** copyright. 39. **sophisms and elenchs,** fallacious arguments. 46–47. **advertisement,** notification.

Andrew Marvell
1621–1678

On the statue of Marvell which stands in the city of Hull, an inscription pays tribute to him as "an incorruptible patriot, a wise statesman, and a zealous and energetic representative of this his native town." The writer of the tribute seems not to have known that Marvell was also a poet, and he forgot, or did not know, that he was born not at Hull but at Winestead, thirteen miles away, where his father was rector of the parish. It was as a politician and a public servant that Marvell was known during his lifetime, for his poems were not published until three years after his death. Few if any of his contemporaries knew that he was one of the most gifted lyric poets of England. Marvell is one of the most extraordinary combinations of opposites in English literature. That the homespun original, M.P. for Hull, author of the businesslike letters to his constituents, should be the same person who wrote the charming lyrics on the garden, and the remote Bermudas, the nymph and the fawn, seems impossible. That the author of the lyrics was the author of the savage satires of his later years; that the writer of the lines "To His Coy Mistress" was a Puritan; that the Puritan Marvell was a friend of Royalists and paid one of the finest tributes to Charles I—these are but a few of the paradoxes that meet one everywhere in his life and works.

Marvell had probably learned a good deal about life in the busy shipping town of Hull and in the local grammar school before he entered Trinity College, Cambridge, at the age of twelve. At the university he became proficient in half a dozen ancient languages. He also learned a good deal about poetry, and his verses on the birth of the Princess Anne were published with similar tributes by other undergraduates before he left. While at Cambridge he became for a short period a Roman Catholic, but returned to his father's faith soon afterwards. In 1641, two years after his graduation, his father died, and he began to make his own living as a clerk in a business house in Hull. A period of four years was spent on the Continent, where he may have been a tutor, and where he acquired the principal modern languages. In 1651, in his thirtieth year, happily for him and for English poetry, he was made tutor to the twelve-year-old daughter of Cromwell's Lord General Fairfax at his beautiful estate, Nun Appleton, in Yorkshire. For two years, while Cromwell was making the country safe for Puritanism, Marvell, "easy philosopher," was reading in Nature's book and conferring among the birds and trees. It was not cowardice, or a lack of interest in what was going on, that led Marvell to serve as tutor and write verses while his contemporaries were fighting. He is on record as having said that "the cause was too good to have been fought for," and the twentieth century is inclined to agree with him. The garden at Nun Appleton was the inspiration for Marvell's happiest and best-known lyrics. In 1653 he removed to Eton to become the tutor of William Dutton, a ward of Cromwell's in the home of the Rev. John Oxenbridge. The latter had served as a minister in the Bermudas, and there is no doubt that it was from him that Marvell got the inspiration for his poem on Bermuda.

Four years later Marvell entered public life as assistant to Milton, who was Cromwell's Latin Secretary. It is interesting to think of the two Puritan poets of the century, both of them having laid aside their singing robes, working together over state papers. In 1659 he was elected to Richard Cromwell's Parliament, and remained in Parliament to represent Hull for the rest of his life. It was due partly to his influence that Milton escaped imprisonment and perhaps even death after the Restoration. As a statesman he was a far more flexible and more practical man than Milton. Unlike Milton, Marvell could distinguish between the system and those who served the system. What he asked of public government was that it should deal justly and efficiently with the practical side of living, and so leave men free to pursue the life of sensibility and contemplation and culture. His verse after the Restoration consists of political satires, which were published in 1689.

It is only in the twentieth century that Marvell has come to be appreciated as the remarkable poet he is. It is hardly too much to say that today he is more often than any other poet chosen as the best representative of the peculiar qualities of seventeenth-century poetry. He combined in his verse the best the "metaphysical" tradition had to offer, the Cavalier richness of image and rhythm, and the smoothness and classical precision of Waller and Dryden. He "discovered nature" a century and a half before Wordsworth and the Romantic poets, though his reactions to natural phenomena were not the same as theirs. It has been said of him that he sees nature with the eye of Walton rather than with the eye of Wordsworth. He enjoyed nature as a present good, without regrets or retrospection. More than anyone before him he possessed the power to describe his own moods at the same time and in the same words as he described the external natural conditions that conduced the moods. Thus he portrays not only a scene but a state of mind, as in the famous lines of "The Garden"—a scene as it is envisaged by a selective poetic fancy, and by a fancy that has the rare gift of selecting essence rather than detail. He looked at life at times with the surprise of a schoolboy returning to the country on a holiday, at times with the detachment of a god, and from both points of view he saw that it was good.

THE GARDEN

This poem in particular, and Marvell's other poems in which he celebrates the "happy garden-state," have won for him the title "Poet Laureate of the Garden."

    How vainly men themselves amaze
    To win the palm, the oak, or bays,
    And their incessant labours see
    Crowned from some single herb, or tree,
    Whose short and narrow-vergèd shade
    Does prudently their toils upbraid;
    While all flowers and all trees do close
    To weave the garlands of repose!

    Fair Quiet, have I found thee here,
    And Innocence, thy sister dear?   10
    Mistaken long, I sought you then
    In busy companies of men.
    Your sacred plants, if here below,
    Only among the plants will grow;
    Society is all but rude
    To this delicious solitude.

    No white nor red was ever seen
    So amorous as this lovely green.
    Fond lovers, cruel as their flame,
    Cut in these trees their mistress' name: 20

1. **amaze**, perplex.   6. **prudently**, by its wisdom. 7. **close**, unite.   16. **To**, in comparison to.   17. **white . . . red**, of a lady's complexion.   18. **amorous**, lovable. beautiful.

    Little, alas, they know or heed
    How far these beauties hers exceed!
    Fair trees, wheresoe'er your barks I wound,
    No name shall but your own be found.

    When we have run our passion's heat,
    Love hither makes his best retreat.
    The gods, that mortal beauty chase,
    Still in a tree did end their race:
    Apollo hunted Daphne so,
    Only that she might laurel grow;   30
    And Pan did after Syrinx speed,
    Not as a nymph, but for a reed.

    What wondrous life is this I lead!
    Ripe apples drop about my head;
    The luscious clusters of the vine
    Upon my mouth do crush their wine;
    The nectarine and curious peach
    Into my hands themselves do reach;
    Stumbling on melons, as I pass,
    Insnared with flowers, I fall on grass.   40

    Meanwhile the mind, from pleasure less
    Withdraws into its happiness;
    The mind, that ocean where each kind
    Does straight its own resemblance find;
    Yet it creates, transcending these,
    Far other worlds and other seas,
    Annihilating all that's made
    To a green thought in a green shade.

    Here at the fountain's sliding foot,
    Or at some fruit-tree's mossy root,   50
    Casting the body's vest aside,
    My soul into the boughs does glide:
    There, like a bird, it sits and sings,
    Then whets and combs its silver wings,
    And, till prepared for longer flight,
    Waves in its plumes the various light.

    Such was that happy garden-state,
    While man there walked without a mate:
    After a place so pure and sweet,
    What other help could yet be meet!   60
    But 'twas beyond a mortal's share
    To wander solitary there:

27–32. **The gods . . . reed.** The stories of the pursuit and transformation of Daphne and Syrinx are told in Book I of Ovid's *Metamorphoses*.   37. **curious**, rare, exquisite. 41. **from pleasure less.** The meaning is, apparently, "from lesser pleasure." For a careful analysis and interpretation of this stanza, as well as of the poem, see "Marvell's Garden," in William Empson's *English Pastoral Poetry*, Norton, 1938. 51. **the body's vest**, the body's garment of flesh.   54. **whets**, preens.

Two paradises 'twere in one
To live in paradise alone.

   How well the skilful gardener drew,
Of flowers and herbs, this dial new;
Where, from above, the milder sun
Does through a fragrant zodiac run;
And, as it works, the industrious bee
Computes its time as well as we!   70
How could such sweet and wholesome hours
Be reckoned but with herbs and flowers?

THE DEFINITION OF LOVE

My love is of a birth as rare
As 'tis, for object, strange and high;
It was begotten by Despair
Upon Impossibility.

Magnanimous Despair alone
Could show me so divine a thing,
Where feeble Hope could ne'er have flown
But vainly flapped its tinsel wing.

And yet I quickly might arrive
Where my extended soul is fixed;   10
But Fate does iron wedges drive,
And always crowds itself betwixt.

For Fate with jealous eyes does see
Two perfect loves, nor lets them close;
Their union would her ruin be,
And her tyrannic power depose.

And therefore her decrees of steel
Us as the distant poles have placed,
(Though Love's whole world on us doth wheel),
Not by themselves to be embraced;   20

Unless the giddy heaven fall,
And earth some new convulsion tear,
And, us to join, the world should all
Be cramped into a planisphere.

As lines, so loves, oblique may well
Themselves in every angle greet;
But ours, so truly parallel,
Though infinite, can never meet.

Therefore the love which us doth bind,
But Fate so enviously debars,   30

  66. **this dial new,** this garden plot designed in the form of a sundial.   **14. close,** unite.   **24. planisphere,** a map of the globe projected on a plane surface; a "flat globe."

Is the conjunction of the mind,
And opposition of the stars.

TO HIS COY MISTRESS

Had we but world enough, and time,
This coyness, lady, were no crime.
We would sit down, and think which way
To walk, and pass our long love's day.
Thou by the Indian Ganges' side
Shouldst rubies find; I by the tide
Of Humber would complain. I would
Love you ten years before the flood,
And you should, if you please, refuse
Till the conversion of the Jews.   10
My vegetable love should grow
Vaster than empires and more slow;
An hundred years should go to praise
Thine eyes, and on thy forehead gaze;
Two hundred to adore each breast,
But thirty thousand to the rest;
An age at least to every part,
And the last age should show your heart.
For, lady, you deserve this state,
Nor would I love at lower rate.   20
   But at my back I always hear
Time's wingèd chariot hurrying near;
And yonder all before us lie
Deserts of vast eternity.
Thy beauty shall no more be found,
Nor, in thy marble vault, shall sound
My echoing song; then worms shall try
That long-preserved virginity,
And your quaint honour turn to dust,
And into ashes all my lust: 30
The grave's a fine and private place,
But none, I think, do there embrace.
   Now therefore, while the youthful hue
Sits on thy skin like morning lew,
And while thy willing soul transpires
At every pore with instant fires,
Now let us sport us while we may,
And now, like amorous birds of prey,
Rather at once our time devour
Than languish in his slow-chapped power. 40
Let us roll all our strength and all

  The Definition of Love. **31–32. conjunction . . . opposition,** a very happy use of technical terms from astronomy. **7. Humber,** the river on which is situated Marvell's town of Hull. **complain,** sing plaintively of love, in the fashion of the medieval courtly lover. **11. vegetable,** growing in the manner of plants. **19. state,** dignified treatment. **29. quaint,** fastidious; perhaps there is, also, a suggestion of "old-fashioned." **34. lew,** "warmth."—Margoliouth **35. transpires,** comes forth. **36. instant,** eager. **40. slow-chapped,** slow-jawed; that is, slowly devouring.

Our sweetness up into one ball,
And tear our pleasures with rough strife
Thorough the iron gates of life;
Thus, though we cannot make our sun
Stand still, yet we will make him run.

BERMUDAS

The Bermudas, discovered by Juan Bermudez in 1522, were settled in the early seventeenth century by religious exiles from England, who are represented as singing the poem.

Where the remote Bermudas ride,
In the ocean's bosom unespied,
From a small boat that rowed along,
The listening winds received this song:

"What should we do but sing His praise,
That led us through the watery maze
Unto an isle so long unknown,
And yet far kinder than our own?
Where He the huge sea-monsters wracks,
That lift the deep upon their backs;   10
He lands us on a grassy stage,
Safe from the storms' and prelates' rage.
He gave us this eternal spring
Which here enamels every thing,
And sends the fowls to us in care,
On daily visits through the air;
He hangs in shades the orange bright,
Like golden lamps in a green night,
And does in the pomegranates close
Jewels more rich than Ormus shows;   20
He makes the figs our mouths to meet,
And throws the melons at our feet;
But apples plants of such a price,
No tree could ever bear them twice;
With cedars, chosen by His hand,
From Lebanon, He stores the land;
And makes the hollow seas, that roar,
Proclaim the ambergris on shore;
He cast (of which we rather boast)
The Gospel's pearl upon our coast,   30
And in these rocks for us did frame
A temple, where to sound His name.
Oh! let our voice His praise exalt,
Till it arrive at heaven's vault,
Which, thence (perhaps) rebounding, may
Echo beyond the Mexique Bay."

Thus sung they in the English boat,
An holy and a cheerful note;
And all the way, to guide their chime,
With falling oars they kept the time.   40

44. Thorough, through.   **9. wracks,** wrecks.   **20. Ormus,** an island in the Persian Gulf, famous for its diamond mart and proverbial for its wealth. See *Paradise Lost*, Book II, l. 2 (page 665).   **23. apples,** pineapples. **28. ambergris.** See note 8 on page 593.

Abraham Cowley
1618–1667

Cowley was one of the most precocious of the seventeenth century's children. He attained fame at an earlier age than any of his contemporaries, was one of the most popular poets of his generation, and went into eclipse sooner than any major poet of his day. He had from his birth all the advantages that wealth and a cultured family could provide. By the time he was ten he had fallen under the spell of Spenser's *Faerie Queene* at home, and had written an epical romance of his own. At twelve he was composing an epic. At Westminster School, where he was King's Scholar, he spent over twelve hours a day studying languages and writing verses. He published his first volume, *Poetical Blossoms*, in 1633, at the age of fifteen. By the time he was admitted to Trinity College, Cambridge, his volume had gone through a second edition. A third appeared in 1637, and in the following year a pastoral play, *Love's Riddle*, and a Latin comedy, written for production at the university, came out. When he was twenty-three he produced a prose comedy, *The Guardian*, a mild satire upon the Puritans, which was acted at Cambridge, and later published as *Cutter of Coleman Street*. He was ejected from Cambridge by the Parliamentarians, and moved to Oxford, the Royalist headquarters. When the Queen, Henrietta Maria, went into exile at Paris, Cowley went with her, and for twelve years acted as her secretary. Among his duties were those of writing letters in cipher to Charles I and discharging various delicate diplomatic commissions.

Cowley's work as court secretary was doubtless of the greatest help in developing the gracefulness and ease of his prose style. There was also plenty of literary conversation with the other poets who had followed the court to France, among them Waller and Crashaw. To the latter he became especially attached, and proved himself a friend by generous financial assistance. He found time in the midst of his duties to write verse, and in 1647 published his best-known volume, *The Mistress*, a cycle of love poems. After several years he returned to England, and probably served as a Royalist spy. He was imprisoned for a while, was released on bail, and retired to Oxford, ostensibly to study medicine but still in the service of the court. Nevertheless he received his degree in medicine in 1657. He had contracted a serious interest in natural science, especially in botany, and produced a bulky treatise on plants. He was made president of the Royal Society, wrote a *Proposition for the Advancement of Experimental Philosophy*, 1661, and a poetical tribute to the society. In 1656 he published a collection of his poems in folio.

The Restoration, for which he had worked so faithfully, and which he celebrated in verse, brought him sincere joy, but did not bring him the rewards and preferment he had been promised for his services. In the Preface to the edition of his works published the year following his death he mentions his desire "to retire myself to some American plantations . . . to forsake this world for ever, with all the vanities and vexations of it, and to bury myself there in some obscure retreat." His friend the Queen and the Duke of Buckingham made him some small gifts of land, and he retired to the country for the rest of his life. It was in this retirement that he wrote his familiar essays, which are today his most widely read compositions. They are among the pleasantest of the kind in English, and were without rivals until Lamb's *Essays of Elia* appeared. Pope loved them for "the language of his heart," and Dr. Johnson remarked of Cowley's prose, "All is easy without feebleness, and familiar without grossness."

Dr. Johnson began his *Lives of the Poets* with Cowley, and in his *Life of Cowley* he coined the phrase "metaphysical poets," declaring that he was "undoubtedly the best" of the group. Cowley is a "Metaphysical" with respect to externals, such as ingenious conceits, clever phrases, and abrupt beginnings, but his verses have a smoothness which Donne never attempted or achieved, and there is in his verse hardly a trace of the sinewy intellectualism of Donne. He was happiest in his *Anacreontics*, and he wrote heroic couplets with ease. Cowley himself considered his odes his best work. He is historically important as having anticipated Milton in producing an epic on a Biblical theme cast in the mold of Homer and Virgil, and for having given to the language the irregular ode. It is in his informal essays, however, where he is not competing with the ancients or with the great poets of his own day, that the essential goodness and charm of his personality are best to be seen.

from SEVERAL DISCOURSES BY WAY OF ESSAYS, IN VERSE AND PROSE

OF LIBERTY

THE liberty of a people consists in being governed by laws which they have made themselves, under whatsoever form it be of government; the liberty of a private man, in being master of his own time and actions, as far as may consist with the laws of God and of his country. Of this latter only are we here to discourse, and to enquire what estate of life does best seat us in the possession of it. This liberty of our own actions is such a fundamental privilege of human nature, that God himself, notwithstanding all his infinite power and right over us, permits us to enjoy it, and that, too, after a forfeiture made by the rebellion of Adam. He takes so much care for the entire preservation of it to us, that he suffers neither his Providence nor eternal decree to break or infringe it. Now for our time, the same God, to whom we are but tenants-at-will for the whole, requires but the seventh part to be paid to him as a small quit-rent in acknowledgment of his title. It is man only that has the impudence to demand our whole time, though he neither gave it, nor can restore it, nor is able to pay any considerable value for the least part of it. This birth-right of mankind above all other creatures some are forced by hunger to sell, like Esau, for bread and broth; but the greatest part of men make such a bargain for the delivery up of themselves, as Thamar did with Judah; instead of a kid, the necessary provisions for human life, they are contented to do it for rings and bracelets. The great dealers in this world may be divided into the ambitious, the covetous, and the voluptuous, and that all these men sell themselves to be slaves, though to the vulgar it may

26. **Esau.** See Genesis 25:29–34. 28. **Thamar.** See Genesis 38:18.

seem a Stoical paradox, will appear to the wise so plain and obvious, that they will scarce think it deserves the labour of argumentation. Let us first consider the ambitious, and those both in their progress to greatness, and after the attaining of it. There is nothing truer that what Sallust says, *Dominationis in alios servitium suum mercedem dant:* They are content to pay so great a price as their own servitude to purchase the domination over others. The first thing they must resolve to sacrifice is their whole time; they must never stop, nor ever turn aside whilst they are in the race of glory, no, not like Atalanta for golden apples. Neither, indeed, can a man stop himself if he would when he's in this career. *Fertur equis auriga neque audit currus habenas.*

Pray let us but consider a little what mean servile things men do for this imaginary food. We cannot fetch a greater example of it, than from the chief men of that nation which boasted most of liberty. To what pitiful baseness did the noblest Romans submit themselves for the obtaining of a praetorship, or the consular dignity! They put on the habit of suppliants, and ran about on foot, and in dirt, through all the tribes to beg voices; they flattered the poorest artisans, and carried a *nomenclator* with them, to whisper in their ear every man's name, lest they should mistake it in their salutations; they shook the hand and kissed the cheek of every popular tradesman; they stood all day at every market in the public places to show and ingratiate themselves to the rout; they employed all their friends to solicit for them; they kept open tables in every street; they distributed wine and bread and money, even to the vilest of the people. *En Romanos rerum dominos!* Behold the masters of the world begging from door to door. This particular humble way to greatness is now out of fashion, but yet every ambitious person is still in some sort a Roman candidate. He must feast and bribe, and attend and flatter, and adore many beasts, though not the beast with many heads. Catiline, who was so proud that he could not content himself with a less power than Sylla's, was yet so humble for the attaining of it as to make himself the most contemptible of all servants, to be a public bawd, to provide whores, and something worse, for all the young gentlemen of Rome, whose hot lusts and courages and heads he thought he might make use of. And since I happen here to propose Catiline for my instance (though there be thousand of examples for the same thing), give me leave to transcribe the character which Cicero gives of this noble slave, because it is a general description of all ambitious men, and which Machiavel, perhaps, would say ought to be the rule of their life and actions. "This man" (says he, as most of you may well remember) "had many artificial touches and strokes that looked like the beauty of great virtues; his intimate conversation was with the worst of men, and yet he seemed an admirer and lover of the best; he was furnished with all the nets of lust and luxury, and yet wanted not the arms of labour and industry; neither do I believe that there was ever any monster in nature composed out of so many different and disagreeing parts. Who more acceptable sometimes to the most honourable persons, who more a favourite to the most infamous? Who sometimes appeared a braver champion, who at other times a bolder enemy to his country? Who more dissolute in his pleasures, who more patient in his toils? Who more rapacious in robbing, who more profuse in giving? Above all things, this was remarkable and admirable in him: the arts he had to acquire the good opinion and kindness of all sorts of men, to retain it with great complaisance, to communicate all things to them, to watch and serve all the occasions of their fortune, both with his money and his interest, and his industry; and if need were, not by sticking at any wickedness whatsoever that might be useful to them, to bend and turn about his own nature and laveer with every wind, to live severely with the melancholy, merrily with the pleasant, gravely with the aged, wantonly with the young, desperately with the bold, and debauchedly with the luxurious; with this variety and multiplicity of his nature, as he had made a collection of friendships with all the wicked and most reckless of all nations, so by the artificial simulation of some virtues, he made a shift to ensnare some honest and eminent persons into his familiarity. Neither could so vast a design as the destruction of this empire have been undertaken by him, if the immanity of so many vices had not been covered and disguised by the appearances of some excellent qualities."

---

1. **Stoical paradox.** The Stoics made use of arguments and maxims, called paradoxes, which on the face of them seemed untrue.   6. **Sallust says.** The quotation is from the fragments of Sallust (86–34 B.C.).   15–16. **Fertur . . . habenas.** The charioteer is carried on by his steed, nor does the team heed the reins.—Virgil, *Georgics* I, l. 514.   24. **habit,** the white toga, whence is derived the term *candidati.*   32. **rout,** crowd.   36. **En . . . dominos!** See Virgil's *Aeneid,* Book I, l. 282.   42. **beast with many heads,** the populace. **Catiline,** Lucius Sergius Catilina, against whom some of Cicero's most bitter philippics were delivered.   44. **Sylla's,** of Lucius Cornelius Sulla, the dictator.

12. **says he.** See Cicero's oration *Pro Coelio,* Secs. 5 and 6.   38. **laveer,** a term borrowed from the Dutch, meaning to sail so as to catch the wind, to tack.   49. **immanity,** enormity.

I see, methinks, the character of an Anti-Paul, who became all things to all men, that he might destroy all; who only wanted the assistance of fortune to have been as great as his friend Caesar was a little after him. And the ways of Caesar to accomplish the same ends (I mean till the civil war, which was but another manner of setting his country on fire) were not unlike these, though he used afterward his unjust dominion with more moderation than I think the other would have done. Sallust therefore who was well acquainted with them both, and with many such like gentlemen of his time, says, "That it is the nature of ambition (*ambitio multos mortales falsos fieri coegit*, etc.) to make men liars and cheaters, to hide the truth in their breasts, and show, like jugglers, another thing in their mouths, to cut all friendships and enmities to the measure of their own interest, and to make a good countenance without the help of good will." And can there be freedom with this perpetual constraint? What is it but a kind of rack that forces men to say what they have no mind to? I have wondered at the extravagant and barbarous stratagem of Zopyrus, and more at the praises which I find of so deformed an action; who, though he was one of the seven grandees of Persia, and the son of Megabyzus, who had freed before his country from an ignoble servitude, slit his own nose and lips, cut off his own ears, scourged and wounded his whole body, that he might, under pretence of having been mangled so inhumanely by Darius, be received into Babylon (then besieged by the Persians) and get into the command of it by the recommendation of so cruel a sufferance, and their hopes of his endeavouring to revenge it. It is great pity the Babylonians suspected not his falsehood, that they might have cut off his hands too, and whipped him back again. But the design succeeded, he betrayed the city, and was made governor of it. What brutish master ever punished his offending slave with so little mercy as ambition did this Zopyrus? And yet how many are there in all nations who imitate him in some degree for a less reward; who, though they endure not so much corporal pain for a small preferment, or some honour (as they call it), yet stick not to commit actions, by which they are more shamefully and more lastingly stigmatized! But you may say, though these be the most ordinary and open ways to greatness, yet there are narrow, thorny, and little-trodden paths too, through which some men find a passage by virtuous industry. I grant, sometimes they may; but then that industry must be such as cannot consist with liberty, though it may with honesty. Thou'rt careful, frugal, painful; we commend a servant so, but not a friend.

Well then, we must acknowledge the toil and drudgery which we are forced to endure in this ascent, but we are epicures and lords when once we are gotten up into the high places. This is but a short apprenticeship, after which we are made free of a royal company. If we fall in love with any beauteous women, we must be content that they should be our mistresses while we woo them; as soon as we are wedded and enjoy, 'tis we shall be the masters.

I am willing to stick to this similitude in the case of greatness; we enter into the bonds of it, like those of matrimony; we are bewitched with the outward and painted beauty, and take it for better or for worse, before we know its true nature and interior inconveniences. A great fortune (says Seneca) is a great servitude; but many are of the opinion which Brutus imputes (I hope untruly) even to that patron of liberty, his friend Cicero: "We fear" (says he to Atticus) "death, and banishment, and poverty, a great deal too much. Cicero, I am afraid, thinks these to be the worst of evils, and if he have but some persons from whom he can obtain what he has a mind to, and others who will flatter and worship him, seems to be well enough contented with an honourable servitude, if indeed anything ought to be called honourable in so base and contumelious a condition." This was spoken as became the bravest man who was ever born in the bravest commonwealth. But with us generally no condition passes for servitude, that is accompanied with great riches, with honours, and with the service of many inferiors. This is but a deception of the sight through a false medium; for if a groom serve a gentleman in his chamber, that gentleman a lord, and that lord a prince, the groom, the gentleman, and the lord are as much servants one as the other; the circumstantial difference of the one's getting only his bread and wages, the second a plentiful, and the third a superfluous estate, is no more intrinsical to this matter than the difference between a plain, a rich, and a gaudy livery. I do not say that he who sells his whole time and his own will for one hundred thousand is not a

---

1. **Anti-Paul.** See the Apostle Paul's statement, "I am made all things to all men, that I might by all means save some."—I Corinthians 9:22.   11–13. **Sallust . . . says.** See Sallust's *De Catilinae Conjuratione*, Sec. x.   24. **Zopyrus.** The story of Zopyrus is in Herodotus, Book III, Secs. 153–59.   34–35. **sufferance,** suffering.

7. **painful,** painstaking.   24. **Seneca,** Seneca the Younger, *Liber de Consolatione*, Sec. 26.

wiser merchant than he who does it for one hundred pounds; but I will swear they are both merchants, and that he is happier than both, who can live contentedly without selling the estate to which he was born. But his dependence upon superiors is but one chain of the lovers of power: *Amatorem trecentae Pirithoum cohibent catenae.* Let's begin with him by break of day: for by that time he's besieged by two or three hundred suitors; and the hall and the antechambers (all the outworks) possessed by the enemy; as soon as his chamber opens, they are ready to break into that, or to corrupt the guards, for entrance. This is so essential a part of greatness, that whosoever is without it looks like a fallen favourite, like a person disgraced, and condemned to do what he please all the morning. There are some who, rather than want this, are contented to have their rooms filled up every day with murmuring and cursing creditors, and to charge bravely through a body of them to get to their coach. Now I would fain know which is the worst duty, that of any one particular person who waits to speak with the great man, or the great man's, who waits every day to speak with all the company. *Aliena negotia centum per caput et circum saliunt latus;* a hundred businesses of other men (many unjust and most impertinent) fly continually about his head and ears, and strike him in the face like dors. Let's contemplate him a little at another special scene of glory; and that is, his table. Here he seems to be the lord of all nature: the earth affords him her best metals for dishes, her best vegetables and animals for his food; the air and sea supply him with their choicest birds and fishes; and a great many men, who look like masters, attend upon him; and yet when all this is done, even all this is but a *table d'hoste;* 'tis crowded with people for whom he cares not, with many parasites, and some spies, with the most burdensome sort of guests, the endeavourers to be witty.

But everybody pays him great respect, everybody commends his meat, that is, his money; everybody admires the exquisite dressing and ordering of it, that is, his clerk of the kitchen, or his cook; everybody loves his hospitality, that is, his vanity. But I desire to know why the honest innkeeper, who provides a public table for his profit, should be but of a mean profession; and he who does it for his honour, a munificent prince. You'll say, because one sells, and the other gives. Nay, both sell, though for different things; the one for plain money, the other for I know not what jewels, whose value is in custom and in fancy. If then his table be made a snare (as the Scripture speaks) to his liberty, where can there be hope for freedom? There is always and everywhere some restraint upon him. He's guarded with crowds, and shackled with formalities. The half hat, the whole hat, the half smile, the whole smile, the nod, the embrace, the positive parting with a little bow, the comparative at the middle of the room, the superlative at the door; and if the person be *Pan huper sebastos*, there's a *hupersuperlative* ceremony then of conducting him to the bottom of the stairs, or to the very gate; as if there were such rules set to these leviathans as are to the sea, "Hitherto shalt thou go, and no further." *Perditur haec inter misero lux,* Thus wretchedly the precious day is lost.

How many impertinent letters and visits must he receive, and sometimes answer, both too as impertinently! He never sets his foot beyond his threshold, unless, like a funeral, he have a train to follow him; as if, like the dead corpse, he could not stir till the bearers were all ready. "My life" (says Horace, speaking to one of these magnificos) "is a great deal more easy and commodious than thine, in that I can go into the market and cheapen what I please without being wondered at; and take my horse and ride as far as Tarentum, without being missed." 'Tis an unpleasant constraint to be always under the sight and observation and censure of others; as there may be vanity in it, so, methinks, there should be vexation too of spirit. And I wonder how princes can endure to have two or three hundred men stand gazing upon them while they are at dinner, and take notice of every bit they eat. Nothing seems greater and more lordly than the multitude of domestic servants; but even this too, if weighed seriously, is a piece of servitude. Unless you be a servant to them (as many men are), the trouble and care of yours in the government of them all is much more than that of every one of them in their observance of you. I take the profession of a school-master to be one of the most useful, and which ought to be of the most honourable in a commonwealth; yet certainly all his fasces and tyrannical authority over so many boys takes away his own liberty more than theirs.

I do but slightly touch upon all these particulars of the slavery of greatness; I shake but a few of

---

6–7. Amatorem . . . catenae. Three hundred chains bind the lover Pirithous.—Horace, *Odes*, Book III, Ode 4, l. 79.   **25. Aliena . . . latus.** See Horace's *Satires*, Book II, Sat. 6, ll. 33–34.   **28. like dors.** A dor is a species of beetle.   **4. Scripture.** See Psalm 69:22.   **12–13. Pan huper sebastos,** altogether superlatively reverend and august.   **16–17. "Hitherto . . . further."** See Job 38:11.   **Perditur . . . lux.** See Horace, *Satires*, Book II, Sat. 6, l. 59   **24–25. says Horace,** *ibid*, ll. 104–17.   **27. cheapen,** bargain for.

their outward chains. Their anger, hatred, jealousy, fear, envy, grief, and all the *et caetera* of their passions, which are the secret but constant tyrants and torturers of their life, I omit here, because, though they be symptoms most frequent and violent in this disease, yet they are common, too, in some degree, to the epidemical disease of life itself. But the ambitious man, though he be so many ways a slave (*O toties servus!*), yet he bears it bravely and heroically! he struts and looks big upon the stage; he thinks himself a real prince in his masking-habit, and deceives, too, all the foolish part of his spectators. He's a slave *in Saturnalibus*. The covetous man is a downright servant, a draught-horse without bells or feathers; *ad metalla damnatus*, a man condemned to work in mines, which is the lowest and hardest condition of servitude; and, to increase his misery, a worker there for he knows not whom: "He heapeth up riches and knows not who shall enjoy them"; 'tis only sure that he himself neither shall nor can enjoy them. He's an indigent needy slave; he will hardly allow himself clothes and board-wages; *Unciatim vix demenso de suo suum defraudans genium comparsit miser;* he defrauds not only other men, but his own genius; he cheats himself for money. But the servile and miserable condition of this wretch is so apparent, that I leave it, as evident to every man's sight, as well as judgment.

It seems a more difficult work to prove that the voluptuous man too is but a servant. What can be more the life of a free man, or, as we say ordinarily, of a gentleman, than to follow nothing but his own pleasures? Why, I'll tell you who is that true free man, and true gentleman. Not he who blindly follows all his pleasures (the very name of follower is servile), but he who rationally guides them, and is not hindered by outward impediments in the conduct and enjoyment of them. If I want skill or force to restrain the beast that I ride upon, though I bought it, and call it my own, yet in the truth of the matter I am at that time rather his man, than he my horse. The voluptuous man (whom we are fallen upon) may be divided, I think, into the lustful and luxurious, who are both servants of the belly; the other, whom we spoke of before, the ambitious and the covetous, were κακὰ θηρία, evil wild beasts; these are γαστέρες ἀργαί, slow bellies, as our translation renders it; but the word ἀργαί (which is a fantastical word, with two directly opposite significations) will bear as well the translation of quick or diligent bellies; and both interpretations may be applied to these men. Metrodorus said that he had learnt Ἀληθῶς γαστρὶ χαρίξεσθαι, to give his belly just thanks for all his pleasures. This, by the calumniators of Epicurus his philosophy, was objected as one of the most scandalous of all their sayings; which, according to my charitable understanding, may admit a very virtuous sense, which is, that he thanked his own belly for that moderation in the customary appetites of it, which can only give a man liberty and happiness in this world. Let this suffice at present to be spoken of those great *triumviri* of the world; the covetous man, who is a mean villain, like Lepidus; the ambitious, who is a brave one, like Octavius, and the voluptuous, who is a loose and debauched one, like Mark Antony. *Quisnam igitur liber? Sapiens, sibique imperiosus.* Not Oenomaus, who commits himself wholly to a charioteer, that may break his neck, but the man,

Who governs his own course with steady hand,
Who does himself with sovereign power command;
Whom neither death nor poverty does fright,
Who stands not awkwardly in his own light
Against the truth: who can, when pleasures knock
Loud at his door, keep firm the bolt and lock.
Who can, though honour at his gate should stay
In all her masking clothes, send her away,
And cry, Be gone, I have no mind to play.

This I confess is a freeman: but it may be said, that many persons are so shackled by their fortune, that they are hindered from enjoyment of that manumission which they have obtained from virtue. I do both understand, and in part feel, the weight of this objection. All I can answer to it is, that we must get as much liberty as we can; we must use our utmost endeavours, and when all that is done, be contented with the length of that line which is allowed us. If you ask me what condition of life I think the most allowed, I should pitch upon that sort of people whom King James was wont to call the happiest of our nation; the men placed in the country by their fortune above an high-constable, and yet beneath the trouble of a justice of peace, in a moderate plenty, without any just argument

---

13. a slave in Saturnalibus. Slaves were allowed great freedom and general license during the Roman feast of Saturnalia, held in December in honor of Saturn. **19–20. "He . . . them."** See Psalm 39:6. **23–24. Unciatim . . . miser.** See Terence's *Phormio*, Act I, sc. 1, l. 33. **47. slow bellies.** The words are quoted from Paul's Epistle to Titus 1:12.

4. Metrodorus, an Epicurean philosopher who flourished during the third century B.C. **19–20. Quisnam . . . imperiosus.** Who then is free? The wise man, and the man who is able to govern himself. **Oenomaus,** king of Pisa in Elis, the father of Hippodamia. He announced that he would bestow his daughter on the suitor who conquered him in a chariot race. His charioteer was at last overcome by Pelops.

for the desirement of increasing it by the care of many relations, and with so much knowledge and love of piety and philosophy (that is of the study of God's laws, and of his creatures) as may afford him matter enough never to be idle though without business, and never to be melancholy though without sin or vanity.

I shall conclude this tedious discourse of mine with a prayer of mine in a copy of Latin verses, of which I remember no other part, and (*pour faire bonne bouche*) with some other verses upon the same subject.

> *Magne Deus, quod ad has vitae brevis attinet horas,*
> *Da mihi, da panem libertatemque, nec ultra*
> *Sollicitas effundo preces, si quid datur ultra*
> *Accipiam gratus; si non, contentus abibo.*

> For the few hours of life allotted me,
> Give me (Great God) but bread and liberty,
> I'll beg no more; if more thou'rt pleased to give,
> I'll thankfully that overplus receive;
> If beyond this no more be freely sent,
> I'll thank for this, and go away content.

OF MYSELF

It is a hard and nice subject for a man to write of himself; it grates his own heart to say anything of disparagement, and the reader's ears to hear anything of praise from him. There is no danger from me of offending him in this kind; neither my mind, nor body, nor my fortune, allow me any materials for that vanity. It is sufficient, for my own contentment, that they have preserved me from being scandalous, or remarkable on the defective side. But besides that, I shall here speak of myself, only in relation to the subject of these precedent discourses, and shall be likelier thereby to fall into the contempt, than rise up to the estimation, of most people.

As far as my memory can return back into my past life, before I knew or was capable of guessing what the world, or glories, or business of it were, the natural affection of my soul gave me a secret bent of aversion from them, as some plants are said to turn away from others, by an antipathy imperceptible to themselves, and inscrutable to man's understanding. Even when I was a very young boy at school, instead of running about on holidays and playing with my fellows, I was wont to steal from them, and walk into the fields, either alone with a book, or with some one companion, if I could find any of the same temper. I was then, too, so much an enemy to all constraint, that my masters could never prevail upon me by any persuasions or encouragements to learn without book the common rules of grammar, in which they dispensed with me alone, because they found I made a shift to do the usual exercise out of my own reading and observation. That I was then of the same mind as I am now (which I confess, I wonder at myself) may appear by the latter end of an ode, which I made when I was but thirteen years old, and which was then printed with many other verses. The beginning of it is boyish, but of this part which I here set down (if a very little were corrected) I should hardly now be much ashamed.

9.

> This only grant me, that my means may lie
> Too low for envy, for contempt too high.
>   Some honour would I have
> Not from great deeds, but good alone.
> The unknown are better than ill known.
>   Rumour can ope the grave.
> Acquaintance would I have, but when 't depends
> Not on the number, but the choice of friends.

10.

> Books should, not business, entertain the light,
> And sleep, as undisturbed as death, the night.
>   My house a cottage, more
> Than palace; and should fitting be
> For all my use, no luxury.
>   My garden painted o'er
> With nature's hand, not art's; and pleasures yield,
> Horace might envy in his Sabine field.

11.

> Thus would I double my life's fading space,
> For he that runs it well, twice runs his race.
>   And in this true delight,
> These unbought sports, this happy state,
> I would not fear nor wish my fate,
>   But boldly say each night:
> "Tomorrow let my sun his beams display,
> Or in clouds hide them; I have lived today."

You may see by it, I was even then acquainted with the poets (for the conclusion is taken out of Horace), and perhaps it was the immature and immoderate love of them which stamped first, or

---

10–11. **pour faire bonne bouche,** to give a pleasant taste. 26. **nice,** delicate, ticklish.

10. **end of an ode.** The poem from which Cowley quotes is entitled "A Vote" (that is, a wish, or prayer), and was included in his *Sylva*, 1636. 47–48. **out of Horace.** See Horace's *Odes*, Book III, Ode 29, ll. 41–45.

rather engraved, these characters in me; they were like letters cut into the bark of a young tree, which with the tree still grow proportionably. But, how this love came to be produced in me so early is a hard question. I believe I can tell the particular little chance that first filled my head with such chimes of verse as have never since left ringing there: for I remember when I began to read, and to take some pleasure in it, there was wont to lie in my mother's parlour (I know not by what accident, for she herself never in her life read any book but of devotion), but there was wont to lie Spenser's works; this I happened to fall upon, and was infinitely delighted with the stories of the knights, and giants, and monsters, and brave houses, which I found everywhere there, though my understanding had little to do with all this; and by degrees with the tinkling of the rhyme and dance of the numbers, so that I think I had read him all over before I was twelve years old, and thus was made a poet as irremediably as a child is made a eunuch. With these affections of mind, and my heart wholly set upon letters, I went to the university, but was soon torn from thence by that violent public storm, which could suffer nothing to stand where it did, but rooted up every plant, even from the princely cedars to me, the hyssop. Yet I had as good fortune as could have befallen me in such a tempest; for I was cast by it into the family of one of the best persons, and into the court of one of the best princesses of the world. Now though I was here engaged in ways most contrary to the original design of my life, that is, into much company and no small business, and into a daily sight of greatness, both militant and triumphant (for that was the state then of the English and French courts), yet all this was so far from altering my opinion, that it only added the confirmation of reason to that which was before but natural inclination. I saw plainly all the paint of that kind of life, the nearer I came to it; and that beauty which I did not fall in love with, when, for aught I knew, it was real, was not like to bewitch or entice me when I saw that it was adulterate. I met with several great persons, whom I liked very well, but could not perceive that any part of their greatness was to be liked or desired, no more than I would be glad or content to be in a storm, though I saw many ships which rid safely and bravely in it; a storm would not agree with my stomach, if it did with my courage. Though I was in a crowd of as good company as could be found anywhere, though I was in business of great and honourable trust, though I ate at the best table, and enjoyed the best conveniences for present subsistence that ought to be desired by a man of my condition in banishment and public distresses; yet I could not abstain from renewing my old school-boy's wish in a copy of verses to the same effect.

Well then; I now do plainly see
This busy world and I shall ne'er agree, etc.

And I never then proposed to myself any other advantage from his Majesty's happy restoration, but the getting into some moderately convenient retreat in the country; which I thought in that case I might easily have compassed, as well as some others, with no greater probabilities or pretences, have arrived to extraordinary fortunes. But I had before written a shrewd prophecy against myself, and I think Apollo inspired me in the truth, though not in the elegance of it.

Though, neither great at Court nor in the war,
Nor at the Exchange shalt be, nor at the wrangling
    bar:
Content thyself with the small barren praise
Which neglected verse does raise, etc.

However, by the failing of the forces which I had expected, I did not quit the design which I had resolved on: I cast myself into it *à corps perdu*, without making capitulations, or taking counsel of fortune. But God laughs at a man who says to his soul, Take thy ease. I met presently not only with many little encumbrances and impediments, but with so much sickness (a new misfortune to me) as would have spoiled the happiness of an emperor as well as mine. Yet I do neither repent nor alter my course, *Non ego perfidum dixi sacramentum*. Nothing shall separate me from a mistress, which I have loved so long, and have now at last married; though she neither has brought me a rich portion, nor lived yet so quietly with me as I hoped from her.

Nec vos, dulcissima mundi
Nomina, vos Musae, libertas, otia, libri,
Hortique, sylvaeque anima remanente relinquam.

24. **violent . . . storm**, the Civil War, which began in 1642. 29–31. **one of the best persons**, Lord Jermyn, later Earl of St. Albans. **one of . . . princesses**, Queen Henrietta Maria, wife of Charles I.

10–11. **Well then . . . etc.**, from the poem entitled "The Wish" in Cowley's *The Mistress*. 23–27. **Though . . . etc.**, from Cowley's poem "Destiny," in his *Pindaric Odes*. 31. **à corps perdu**, headlong. 34. **Take thy ease.** See Luke 12:16–21. 39. **Non ego . . . sacramentum**. I have not sworn a faithless oath.—Horace, *Odes*, Book II, Ode 17, ll. 9–10. 45–47. **Nec vos . . . relinquam**, presumably Cowley's own lines.

Nor by me e'er shall you,
You of all names the sweetest and the best,
You Muses, books, and liberty and rest,

Your gardens, fields, and woods forsaken be,
As long as life itself forsakes not me. . . .

John Bunyan
1628–1688

The annals of Bunyan's life, it will be noted, are very different from those of most of his contemporaries who are represented in this volume. There was no cultured home for him to be born into, no private tutor to guide him, no great public school or university to provide him with a formal—or informal—education. He went through life without the "rights and privileges" of academic degrees. He was the son of a tinsmith, and after learning to read and write at the village school of Elstow in Bedfordshire, where he was born, he began work at his father's trade.

From his earliest years he was possessed of an extraordinary power of imagination and of an acute sense of sinfulness, and the two, acting together, made his boyhood and young manhood miserable almost to insanity. He seemed to himself to be the chief of sinners in his village, and as he was familiar with the Bible, and particularly with the portions of it which describe the punishments reserved for the wicked, his imagination was constantly creating images of fear and apprehensions of danger. The accounts of signs and portents in the Bible led him to look for them in even the most commonplace events of daily life. He served, from sixteen to nineteen, in the Parliamentary army, and was much affected on one occasion when another soldier, who had taken his place during a siege, was shot and killed. His marriage to a poor woman, whose name he does not give us, was an important event, because, although they married "without so much household stuff as a dish or a spoon," she did bring him two religious books, one of which, *The Plain Man's Pathway to Heaven*, was to influence greatly his life and writing. The story of his life up to his conversion, as he tells it in his autobiography, *Grace Abounding to the Chief of Sinners*, is largely one of mental and spiritual torture. Happily, at the age of twenty-seven he heard comfortable words from Heaven, and the struggle was over.

After his conversion he joined the congregation of Baptists in Bedford, and was soon taking a prominent part among them as a preacher. At the Restoration he was arrested for preaching at Nonconformist meetings. He was kept in prison in Bedford for the greater part of twelve years, until the Declaration of Indulgence was issued by Charles II. During his imprisonment he supported himself by making laces, and his vigorous mind found employment in preaching to the other prisoners and in writing. His *Grace Abounding*, 1666, was the chief product of this period. In 1672 he was released and granted a license to preach, and became the pastor of the Baptists at Bedford. In 1675 he was again imprisoned for a short period, during which he wrote the first part of *The Pilgrim's Progress*. This, his twenty-fourth book, was published in 1678. Part II of the book was brought out in 1684. Between those two dates he had published two other important works, *The Life and Death of Mr. Badman*, 1680, which portrays the opposite of the picture in *Grace Abounding*, and *The Holy War*, 1682, an allegory of the "losing and taking again of the town of Mansoul."

Bunyan's writings are all based on his own vivid and varied experiences, physical and spiritual. The faculty of imagination which had caused him so much anguish in his youth he employed in his *Pilgrim's Progress* so effectively that it long ago took its place among the greatest imaginative works of the world. With great skill he translated and sublimated his own experiences into allegories and symbols, providing at once a manual of Christian doctrine, a work of art, and a lively picture of seventeenth-century life and circumstances. To the student of English literature, Bunyan's narrative and descriptive powers, and his ability in handling dialogue, are of great importance in the early development of the novel. In earlier days and different circumstances, he might have taken his place among the Elizabethan dramatists. In the eighteenth century he would, perhaps, with such powers, have been able to compete with such novelists as Fielding and Smollett. As it was, he looked with distrust upon what the world calls art, and yet he achieved, in spite of himself, a permanent and unique place among literary artists.

The simple, homely style of his book, deriving as it does from the speech of the common people and the vocabulary of the King James Bible, has made *The Pilgrim's Progress* accessible to men, women, and children of all classes. It was one of the first books printed in America, and has gone into more editions and translations than any other English book except the Bible. It is the best proof in literature that the secret of success in writing lies not so much in a conscious striving after artistic effect as in having something to say and saying it simply and directly.

from THE PILGRIM'S PROGRESS

FROM THIS WORLD TO THAT WHICH IS TO COME,
DELIVERED UNDER THE SIMILITUDE OF A DREAM

THE FIRST PART

[Christian Escapes from the City of Destruction]

AS I walked through the wilderness of this world, I lighted on a certain place where was a den, and I laid me down in that place to sleep: and, as I slept, I dreamed a dream. I dreamed, and behold I saw a man clothed with rags, standing in a certain place, with his face from his own house, a book in his hand, and a great burden upon his back. I looked, and saw him open the book and read therein; and, as he read, he wept, and trembled; and not being able longer to contain, he brake out with a lamentable cry, saying, "What shall I do?"

In this plight, therefore, he went home and refrained himself as long as he could, that his wife and children should not perceive his distress; but he could not be silent long, because that his trouble increased. Wherefore at length he brake his mind to his wife and children; and thus he began to talk to them. "O my dear wife," said he, "and you the children of my bowels, I, your dear friend, am in myself undone by reason of a burden that lieth hard upon me; moreover, I am for certain informed that this our city will be burned with fire from heaven, in which fearful overthrow both myself, with thee, my wife, and you my sweet babes, shall miserably come to ruin, except (the which yet I see not) some way of escape can be found, whereby we may be delivered." At this his relations were sore amazed; not for that they believed that what he had said to them was true, but because they thought that some frenzy distemper had got into his head; therefore, it drawing towards night, and they hoping that sleep might settle his brains, with all haste they got him to bed. But the night was as troublesome to him as the day; wherefore, instead of sleeping, he spent it in sighs and tears. So, when the morning was come, they would know how he did. He told them, "Worse and worse." He also set to talking to them again: but they began to be hardened. They also thought to drive away his distemper by harsh and surly carriages to him; sometimes they would deride, sometimes they would chide, and sometimes they would quite neglect him. Wherefore he began to retire himself to his chamber, to pray for and pity them, and also to condole his own misery; he would also walk solitarily in the fields, sometimes reading, and sometimes praying: and thus for some days he spent his time.

Now, I saw, upon a time, when he was walking in the fields, that he was, as he was wont, reading in his book, and greatly distressed in his mind; and as he read, he burst out, as he had done before, crying, "What shall I do to be saved?"

I saw also that he looked this way and that way, as if he would run; yet he stood still, because, as I perceived, he could not tell which way to go. I looked then, and saw a man named Evangelist coming to him, who asked, "Wherefore dost thou cry?"

He answered, "Sir, I perceive by the book in my hand that I am condemned to die, and after that to come to judgment, and I find that I am not willing to do the first, nor able to do the second."

Then said Evangelist, "Why not willing to die, since this life is attended with so many evils?" The man answered, "Because I fear that this burden that is upon my back will sink me lower than the grave, and I shall fall into Tophet. And, sir, if I be not fit to go to prison, I am not fit to go to judg-

---

7. I dreamed a dream. From the first sentence of *The Pilgrim's Progress* to the last, almost every line of the book, as, indeed, of all Bunyan's work, shows the influence of the King James Bible. Bunyan knew the Bible by heart, and both consciously and unconsciously used its language. In the original editions, as in all complete modern editions, the quotations from the Bible are indicated in the notes. These are generally omitted here, to simplify the reading. **34. frenzy,** a rare and colloquial use of the noun as adjective.

10-11. surly carriages, surly behavior.   **38. Tophet,** Hell.

ment, and from thence to execution; and the thoughts of these things make me cry."

Then said Evangelist, "If this be thy condition, why standest thou still?" He answered, "Because I know not whither to go." Then he gave him a parchment roll, and there was written within, "Fly from the wrath to come."

The man therefore read it, and looking upon Evangelist very carefully, said, "Whither must I fly?" Then said Evangelist, pointing with his finger over a very wide field, "Do you see yonder wicket-gate?" The man said, "No." Then said the other, "Do you see yonder shining light?" He said, "I think I do." Then said Evangelist, "Keep that light in your eye, and go up directly thereto: so shalt thou see the gate; at which when thou knockest it shall be told thee what thou shalt do." So I saw in my dream that the man began to run. Now, he had not run far from his own door, but his wife and children perceiving it, began to cry after him to return; but the man put his fingers in his ears, and ran on, crying, "Life! life! eternal life!" So he looked not behind him, but fled towards the middle of the plain.

The neighbours also came out to see him run; and as he ran, some mocked, others threatened, and some cried after him to return; and, among those that did so, there were two that resolved to fetch him back by force. The name of the one was Obstinate, and the name of the other Pliable. Now by this time, the man was got a good distance from them; but, however, they were resolved to pursue him, which they did, and in a little time they overtook him. Then said the man, "Neighbours, wherefore are ye come?" They said, "To persuade you to go back with us." But he said, "That can by no means be; you dwell," said he, "in the City of Destruction, the place also where I was born. I see it to be so; and dying there, sooner or later, you will sink lower than the grave, into a place that burns with fire and brimstone: be content, good neighbours, and go along with me."

Obst. What! said Obstinate, and leave our friends and our comforts behind us?

Chr. Yes, said Christian (for that was his name), because that all which you shall forsake is not worthy to be compared with a little of that which I am seeking to enjoy; and if you will go along with me, and hold it, you shall fare as I myself; for there, where I go, is enough and to spare. Come away, and prove my words.

12. **wicket-gate?"** a small gate, often one set into a larger gate.

Obst. What are the things you seek, since you leave all the world to find them?

Chr. I seek an inheritance incorruptible, undefiled, and that fadeth not away, and it is laid up in heaven, and safe there, to be bestowed, at the time appointed, on them that diligently seek it. Read it so, if you will, in my book.

Obst. Tush! said Obstinate, away with your book. Will you go back with us or no?

Chr. No, not I, said the other, because I have laid my hand to the plough.

Obst. Come then, Neighbour Pliable, let us turn again, and go home without him; there is a company of these crazy-headed coxcombs, that, when they take a fancy by the end, are wiser in their own eyes than seven men that can render a reason.

Pli. Then said Pliable, Don't revile; if what the good Christian says is true, the things he looks after are better than ours: my heart inclines to go with my neighbour.

Obst. What! more fools still! Be ruled by me, and go back; who knows whither such a brain-sick fellow will lead you? Go back, go back, and be wise.

Chr. Nay, but do thou come with thy neighbour, Pliable; there are such things to be had which I spoke of, and many more glories besides. If you believe not me, read here in this book; and for the truth of what is expressed therein, behold all is confirmed by the blood of Him that made it.

Pli. Well, Neighbour Obstinate, said Pliable, I begin to come to a point; I intend to go along with this good man, and to cast in my lot with him; but, my good companion, do you know the way to this desired place?

Chr. I am directed by a man, whose name is Evangelist, to speed me to a little gate that is before us, where we shall receive instructions about the way.

Pli. Come, then, good neighbour, let us be going. Then they went both together.

Obst. And I will go back to my place, said Obstinate; I will be no companion of such misled, fantastical fellows.

Now, I saw in my dream, that, when Obstinate was gone back, Christian and Pliable went talking over the plain; and thus they began their discourse.

Chr. Come, Neighbour Pliable, how do you do? I am glad you are persuaded to go along with me. Had even Obstinate himself but felt what I have felt of the powers and terrors of what is yet unseen, he would not thus lightly have given us the back.

Pli. Come, Neighbour Christian, since there are none but us two here, tell me now further what the things are, and how to be enjoyed, whither we are going.

Chr. I can better conceive of them with my mind, than speak of them with my tongue; but yet, since you are desirous to know, I will read of them in my book.

Pli. And do you think that the words of your book are certainly true?

Chr. Yes, verily; for it was made by Him that cannot lie.

Pli. Well said; what things are they?

Chr. There is an endless kingdom to be inhabited, and everlasting life to be given us, that we may inhabit that kingdom for ever.

Pli. Well said; and what else?

Chr. There are crowns of glory to be given us, and garments that will make us shine like the sun in the firmament of heaven.

Pli. This is very pleasant; and what else?

Chr. There shall be no more crying, nor sorrow; for He that is owner of the place will wipe all tears from our eyes.

Pli. And what company shall we have there?

Chr. There we shall be with seraphims and cherubims, creatures that will dazzle your eyes to look on them. There also you shall meet with thousands and ten thousands that have gone before us to that place; none of them are hurtful, but loving and holy; every one walking in the sight of God, and standing in his presence with acceptance for ever. In a word, there we shall see the elders with their golden crowns; there we shall see the holy virgins with their golden harps; there we shall see men that by the world were cut in pieces, burnt in flames, eaten of beasts, drowned in the seas, for the love that they bare to the Lord of the place, all well, and clothed with immortality as with a garment.

Pli. The hearing of this is enough to ravish one's heart. But are these things to be enjoyed? How shall we get to be sharers thereof?

Chr. The Lord, the Governor of the country, hath recorded that in this book; the substance of which is, If we be truly willing to have it, he will bestow it upon us freely.

Pli. Well, my good companion, glad am I to hear of these things; come on, let us mend our pace.

Chr. I cannot go so fast as I would, by reason of this burden that is on my back.

Now, I saw in my dream, that just as they had ended this talk they drew near to a very miry slough, that was in the midst of the plain; and they, being heedless, did both fall suddenly into the bog. The name of the slough was Despond. Here, therefore, they wallowed for a time, being grievously bedaubed with the dirt; and Christian, because of the burden that was on his back, began to sink in the mire.

Pli. Then said Pliable, Ah! Neighbour Christian, where are you now?

Chr. Truly, said Christian, I do not know.

Pli. At this Pliable began to be offended, and angrily said to his fellow, Is this the happiness you have told me all this while of? If we have such ill speed at our first setting out, what may we expect betwixt this and our journey's end? May I get out again with my life, you shall possess the brave country alone for me. And, with that, he gave a desperate struggle or two, and got out of the mire on that side of the slough which was next to his own house: so away he went, and Christian saw him no more.

Wherefore Christian was left to tumble in the Slough of Despond alone: but still he endeavoured to struggle to that side of the slough that was still further from his own house, and next to the wicket-gate; the which he did, but could not get out, because of the burden that was upon his back: but I beheld in my dream, that a man came to him, whose name was Help, and asked him what he did there.

Chr. Sir, said Christian, I was bid go this way by a man called Evangelist, who directed me also to yonder gate, that I might escape the wrath to come; and as I was going thither I fell in here.

Help. But why did not you look for the steps?

Chr. Fear followed me so hard, that I fled the next way and fell in.

Help. Then said he, Give me thy hand: so he gave him his hand, and he drew him out, and set him upon sound ground, and bid him go on his way.

Then I stepped to him that plucked him out, and said, "Sir, wherefore, since over this place is the way from the City of Destruction to yonder gate, is it that this plat is not mended, that poor travellers might go thither with more security?" And he said unto me, "This miry slough is such a place as cannot be mended; it is the descent whither the scum and filth that attends conviction for sin doth continually run, and therefore it is called the Slough of Despond; for still, as the sinner

---

24-25. seraphims and cherubims. "Seraphim" and "cherubim" are the Hebrew plural forms for "seraph" and "cherub." The "s" was mistakenly added to the words by many older writers.

18. alone for me, alone for all I care. **20. next,** nearest, as elsewhere in this context. **45. plat,** plot, small piece of ground.

is awakened about his lost condition, there ariseth in his soul many fears, and doubts, and discouraging apprehensions, which all of them get together, and settle in this place. And this is the reason of the badness of this ground.

"It is not the pleasure of the King that this place should remain so bad. His labourers also have, by the direction of His Majesty's surveyors, been for above these sixteen hundred years employed about this patch of ground, if perhaps it might have been mended: yea, and to my knowledge, said he, here have been swallowed up at least twenty thousand cart-loads, yea, millions of wholesome instructions, that have at all seasons been brought from all places of the King's dominions, and they that can tell, say they are the best materials to make good ground of the place; if so be, it might have been mended, but it is the Slough of Despond still, and so will be when they have done what they can.

"True, there are, by the direction of the Lawgiver, certain good and substantial steps, placed even through the very midst of the slough; but at such time as this place doth much spew out its filth, as it doth against change of weather, these steps are hardly seen; or, if they be, men, through the dizziness of their heads, step beside, and then they are bemired to purpose, notwithstanding the steps be there; but the ground is good when they are once got in at the gate."

Now, I saw in my dream, that by this time Pliable was got home to his house again, so that his neighbours came to visit him; and some of them called him wise man for coming back, and some called him fool for hazarding himself with Christian: others, again, did mock at his cowardliness; saying, "Surely, since you began to venture, I would not have been so base to have given out for a few difficulties." So Pliable sat sneaking among them. But at last he got more confidence, and then they all turned their tales, and began to deride poor Christian behind his back. And thus much concerning Pliable. . . .

[Christian and Apollyon]

But now in this Valley of Humiliation poor Christian was hard put to it; for he had gone but a little way, before he espied a foul fiend coming over the field to meet him; his name is Apollyon. Then did Christian begin to be afraid, and to cast in his mind whether to go back or to stand his ground. But he considered again that he had no armour for his back; and therefore thought that to turn the back to him might give him the greater advantage with ease to pierce him with his darts. Therefore he resolved to venture and stand his ground; for, thought he, had I no more in mine eye than the saving of my life, it would be the best way to stand.

So he went on, and Apollyon met him. Now the monster was hideous to behold; he was clothed with scales, like a fish (and they are his pride), he had wings like a dragon, feet like a bear, and out of his belly came fire and smoke, and his mouth was as the mouth of a lion. When he was come up to Christian, he beheld him with a disdainful countenance, and thus began to question with him.

Apol. Whence come you? and whither are you bound?

Chr. I am come from the City of Destruction, which is the place of all evil, and am going to the City of Zion.

Apol. By this I perceive thou art one of my subjects, for all that country is mine, and I am the prince and god of it. How is it, then, that thou hast run away from thy king? Were it not that I hope thou mayest do me more service, I would strike thee now, at one blow, to the ground.

Chr. I was born, indeed, in your dominions, but your service was hard, and your wages such as a man could not live on, "for the wages of sin is death"; therefore, when I was come to years, I did as other considerate persons do, look out, if, perhaps, I might mend myself.

Apol. There is no prince that will thus lightly lose his subjects, neither will I as yet lose thee; but since thou complainest of thy service and wages, be content to go back: what our country will afford, I do here promise to give thee.

Chr. But I have let myself to another, even to the King of princes; and how can I, with fairness, go back with thee?

Apol. Thou hast done in this, according to the proverb, "Changed a bad for a worse"; but it is ordinary for those that have professed themselves his servants, after a while to give him the slip, and return again to me. Do thou so too, and all shall be well.

Chr. I have given him my faith, and sworn my

---

8. **His Majesty's surveyors,** the writers and teachers of the Bible.   9. **sixteen hundred years,** the period that had elapsed from the time of Jesus to that of Bunyan.   28. **to purpose,** to good purpose, thoroughly.   39. **Pliable sat sneaking among them,** one of the many vivid and realistic touches which give to Bunyan's allegory the quality of good fiction.   41. **turned their tales,** turned their talk from Pliable to Christian.

2. **Apollyon,** destroyer (Greek). See Revelation 9:11 and 13:2.

allegiance to him; how, then, can I go back from this, and not be hanged as a traitor?

Apol. Thou didst the same to me, and yet I am willing to pass by all, if now thou wilt yet turn again and go back.

Chr. What I promised thee was in my nonage; and, besides, I count the Prince under whose banner now I stand is able to absolve me; yea, and to pardon also what I did as to my compliance with thee; and besides, O thou destroying Apollyon! to speak truth, I like his service, his wages, his servants, his government, his company, and country better than thine; and therefore leave off to persuade me further; I am his servant, and I will follow him.

Apol. Consider, again, when thou art in cool blood, what thou art like to meet with in the way that thou goest. Thou knowest that, for the most part, his servants come to an ill end, because they are transgressors against me and my ways. How many of them have been put to shameful deaths; and, besides, thou countest his service better than mine, whereas he never came yet from the place where he is to deliver any that served him out of their hands; but as for me, how many times, as all the world very well knows, have I delivered, either by power or fraud, those that have faithfully served me, from him and his, though taken by them; and so I will deliver thee.

Chr. His forbearing at present to deliver them is on purpose to try their love, whether they will cleave to him to the end; and as for the ill end thou sayest they come to, that is most glorious in their account; for, for present deliverance, they do not much expect it, for they stay for their glory, and then they shall have it, when their Prince comes in his, and the glory of the angels.

Apol. Thou hast already been unfaithful in thy service to him; and how dost thou think to receive wages of him?

Chr. Wherein, O Apollyon! have I been unfaithful to him?

Apol. Thou didst faint at first setting out, when thou wast almost choked in the Gulf of Despond; thou didst attempt wrong ways to be rid of thy burden, whereas thou shouldest have stayed till thy Prince had taken it off; thou didst sinfully sleep and lose thy choice thing; thou wast, also, almost persuaded to go back, at the sight of the lions; and when thou talkest of thy journey, and of what thou hast heard and seen, thou art inwardly desirous of vain-glory in all that thou sayest or doest.

Chr. All this is true, and much more which thou hast left out; but the Prince whom I serve and honour is merciful, and ready to forgive; but, besides, these infirmities possessed me in thy country, for there I sucked them in; and I have groaned under them, been sorry for them, and have obtained pardon of my Prince.

Apol. Then Apollyon broke out into a grievous rage, saying, I am an enemy to this Prince; I hate his person, his laws, and people; I am come out on purpose to withstand thee.

Chr. Apollyon, beware what you do; for I am in the King's highway, the way of holiness; therefore take heed to yourself.

Apol. Then Apollyon straddled quite over the whole breadth of the way, and said, I am void of fear in this matter: prepare thyself to die; for I swear by my infernal den, that thou shalt go no further; here will I spill thy soul.

And with that he threw a flaming dart at his breast; but Christian had a shield in his hand, with which he caught it, and so prevented the danger of that.

Then did Christian draw, for he saw it was time to bestir him: and Apollyon as fast made at him, throwing darts as thick as hail; by the which, notwithstanding all that Christian could do to avoid it, Apollyon wounded him in his head, his hand, and foot. This made Christian give a little back; Apollyon, therefore, followed his work amain, and Christian again took courage, and resisted as manfully as he could. This sore combat lasted for above half a day, even till Christian was almost quite spent; for you must know that Christian, by reason of his wounds, must needs grow weaker and weaker.

Then Apollyon, espying his opportunity, began to gather up close to Christian, and wrestling with him, gave him a dreadful fall; and with that Christian's sword flew out of his hand. Then said Apollyon, "I am sure of thee now." And with that he had almost pressed him to death, so that Christian began to despair of life: but as God would have it, while Apollyon was fetching of his last blow, thereby to make a full end of this good man, Christian nimbly stretched out his hand for his sword, and caught it, saying, "Rejoice not against me, O mine enemy: when I fall I shall arise"; and with that gave him a deadly thrust, which made him give back, as one that had received his mortal wound. Christian perceiving that, made at him again, saying, "Nay, in all these things we are more

---

6. nonage, minority; the time of life before legal maturity, during which no contracts binding at law can be made.
48. thy choice thing, the parchment roll with a seal, which had been given to Christian by one of the Shining Ones, and which was to admit him to the Celestial City. Christian had already recovered it.

than conquerors through him that loved us." And with that Apollyon spread forth his dragon's wings, and sped him away, that Christian for a season saw him no more. . . .

[*Christian and Faithful at Vanity Fair*]

Then I saw in my dream, that when they were got out of the wilderness, they presently saw a town before them, and the name of that town is Vanity; and at the town there is a fair kept, called Vanity Fair: it is kept all the year long; it beareth the name of Vanity Fair, because the town where it is kept is lighter than vanity; and also because all that is there sold, or that cometh thither, is vanity. As is the saying of the wise, "all that cometh is vanity."

This fair is no new-erected business, but a thing of ancient standing; I will show you the original of it.

Almost five thousand years agone, there were pilgrims walking to the Celestial City, as these two honest persons are: and Beelzebub, Apollyon, and Legion, with their companions, perceiving by the path that the pilgrims made, that their way to the city lay through this town of Vanity, they contrived here to set up a fair; a fair wherein should be sold all sorts of vanity, and that it should last all the year long: therefore at this fair are all such merchandise sold, as houses, lands, trades, places, honours, preferments, titles, countries, kingdoms, lusts, pleasures, and delights of all sorts, as whores, bawds, wives, husbands, children, masters, servants, lives, blood, bodies, souls, silver, gold, pearls, precious stones, and what not.

And, moreover, at this fair there is at all times to be seen juggling, cheats, games, plays, fools, apes, knaves, and rogues, and that of every kind.

Here are to be seen, too, and that for nothing, thefts, murders, adulteries, false swearers, and that of a blood-red colour.

And as in other fairs of less moment, there are the several rows and streets, under their proper names, where such and such wares are vended; so here likewise you have the proper places, rows, streets (viz. countries and kingdoms), where the wares of this fair are soonest to be found. Here is the Britain Row, the French Row, the Italian Row, the Spanish Row, the German Row, where several sorts of vanities are to be sold. But, as in other fairs, some one commodity is as the chief of all the fair, so the ware of Rome and her merchandise is greatly promoted in this fair; only our English nation, with some others, have taken a dislike thereat.

Now, as I said, the way to the Celestial City lies just through this town where this lusty fair is kept; and he that will go to the City, and yet not go through this town, must needs "go out of the world." The Prince of princes himself, when here, went through this town to his own country, and that upon a fair day too; yea, and as I think, it was Beelzebub, the chief lord of this fair, that invited him to buy of his vanities; yea, would have made him lord of the fair, would he but have done him reverence as he went through the town. Yea, because he was such a person of honour, Beelzebub had him from street to street, and showed him all the kingdoms of the world in a little time, that he might, if possible, allure the Blessed One to cheapen and buy some of his vanities; but he had no mind to the merchandise, and therefore left the town without laying out so much as one farthing upon these vanities. This fair, therefore, is an ancient thing, of long standing, and a very great fair. Now these pilgrims, as I said, must needs go through this fair. Well, so they did: but, behold, even as they entered into the fair, all the people in the fair were moved, and the town itself as it were in a hubbub about them; and that for several reasons: for—

First, The pilgrims were clothed with such kind of raiment as was diverse from the raiment of any that traded in that fair. The people, therefore, of the fair, made a great gazing upon them: some said they were fools, some they were bedlams, and some they are outlandish men.

Secondly, And as they wondered at their apparel, so they did likewise at their speech; for few could understand what they said; they naturally spoke the language of Canaan, but they that kept the fair were the men of this world; so that, from one end of the fair to the other, they seemed barbarians each to the other.

Thirdly, But that which did not a little amuse the merchandisers was, that these pilgrims set very light by all their wares; they cared not so much as

---

12. **Vanity Fair.** Bunyan here coins one of the most famous phrases in the language. In the description of the fair he provides us with an unrivaled and realistic picture of the ancient fairs of England, with all their hubbub, riot, and noise, and, from a moralist's point of view, their thousand and one opportunities to waste time and money on "vanities." Bunyan probably has in mind the largest of all the fairs of his day, that of Stourbridge, which was held for weeks at a time in a large field near Cambridge. Ben Jonson has immortalized its chief rival, Bartholomew Fair, in his play of that name. 24. **Legion.** See Mark 5: 9.

11. **lusty,** joyous. 24. **cheapen,** bargain for. 40. **outlandish men,** foreigners. 44. **the language of Canaan,** that is, the language of the chosen people. 46–47. **barbarians,** used in the classical and Biblical sense of "those who speak foreign tongues."

to look upon them; and if they called upon them to buy, they would put their fingers in their ears, and cry, "Turn away mine eyes from beholding vanity," and look upwards, signifying that their trade and traffic was in heaven.

One chanced mockingly, beholding the carriage of the men, to say unto them, "What will ye buy?" But they, looking gravely upon him, answered, "We buy the truth." At that there was an occasion taken to despise the men the more; some mocking, some taunting, some speaking reproachfully, and some calling upon others to smite them. At last things came to a hubbub and great stir in the fair, insomuch that all order was confounded. Now was word presently brought to the great one of the fair, who quickly came down, and deputed some of his most trusty friends to take these men into examination, about whom the fair was almost overturned. So the men were brought to examination; and they that sat upon them asked them whence they came, whither they went, and what they did there, in such an unusual garb? The men told them that they were pilgrims and strangers in the world, and that they were going to their own country, which was the heavenly Jerusalem; and that they had given no occasion to the men of the town, nor yet to the merchandisers, thus to abuse them, and to let them in their journey, except it was for that, when one asked them what they would buy, they said they would buy the truth. But they that were appointed to examine them did not believe them to be any other than bedlams and mad, or else such as came to put all things into a confusion in the fair. Therefore they took them and beat them, and besmeared them with dirt, and then put them into the cage, that they might be made a spectacle to all the men of the fair.

There, therefore, they lay for some time, and were made the objects of any man's sport, or malice, or revenge, the great one of the fair laughing still at all that befell them. But the men being patient, and not rendering railing for railing, but contrariwise, blessing, and giving good words for bad, and kindness for injuries done, some men in the fair that were more observing, and less prejudiced than the rest, began to check and blame the baser sort for their continual abuses done by them to the men; they, therefore, in angry manner, let fly at them again, counting them as bad as the men in the cage, and telling them that they seemed confederates, and should be made partakers of their misfortunes. The other replied, that for aught they could see, the men were quiet, and sober, and intended nobody any harm; and that there were many that traded in their fair that were more worthy to be put into the cage, yea, and pillory too, than were the men they had abused. Thus, after divers words had passed on both sides, the men behaving themselves all the while very wisely and soberly before them, they fell to some blows among themselves, and did harm one to another. Then were these two poor men brought before their examiners again, and there charged as being guilty of the late hubbub that had been in the fair. So they beat them pitifully, and hanged irons upon them, and led them in chains up and down the fair, for an example and a terror to others, lest any should speak in their behalf, or join themselves unto them. But Christian and Faithful behaved themselves yet more wisely, and received the ignominy and shame that was cast upon them, with so much meekness and patience, that it won to their side, though but few in comparison of the rest, several of the men in the fair. This put the other party yet into greater rage, insomuch that they concluded the death of these two men. Wherefore they threatened, that neither cage nor irons should serve their turn, but that they should die, for the abuse they had done, and for deluding the men of the fair.

Then were they remanded to the cage again, until further order should be taken with them. So they put them in, and made their feet fast in the stocks.

Here, therefore, they called again to mind what they had heard from their faithful friend Evangelist, and were the more confirmed in their way and sufferings, by what he told them would happen to them. They also now comforted each other, that whose lot it was to suffer, even he should have the best of it; therefore each man secretly wished that he might have that preferment: but committing themselves to the all-wise disposal of him that ruleth all things, with much content, they abode in the condition in which they were, until they should be otherwise disposed of.

Then a convenient time being appointed, they brought them forth to their trial, in order to their condemnation. When the time was come, they were brought before their enemies and arraigned. The Judge's name was Lord Hate-good. Their indictment was one and the same in substance,

6. **carriage,** behavior. 28. **let,** hinder.

23. **concluded,** determined upon. 45. **to their trial.** The scene which follows is a vivid and realistic portrayal of a Restoration courtroom. Bunyan's mastery of the art of satire, as well as his ability to describe experiences with which he was familiar, is illustrated in his account of the jury, the witnesses, and the judge.

though somewhat varying in form, the contents whereof were this:—

"That they were enemies to and disturbers of their trade; that they had made commotions and divisions in the town, and had won a party to their own most dangerous opinions, in contempt of the law of their prince."

Then Faithful began to answer, that he had only set himself against that which hath set itself against him that is higher than the highest. "And," said he, "as for disturbance, I make none, being myself a man of peace; the parties that were won to us, were won by beholding our truth and innocence, and they are only turned from the worse to the better. And as to the king you talk of, since he is Beelzebub, the enemy of our Lord, I defy him and all his angels."

Then proclamation was made, that they that had aught to say for their lord the king against the prisoner at the bar, should forthwith appear and give in their evidence. So there came in three witnesses, to wit, Envy, Superstition, and Pickthank. They were then asked if they knew the prisoner at the bar; and what they had to say for their lord the king against him.

Then stood forth Envy, and said to this effect: "My Lord, I have known this man a long time, and will attest upon my oath before this honourable bench that he is——"

Judge. Hold! Give him his oath. So they sware him. Then he said:

Envy. My lord, this man, notwithstanding his plausible name, is one of the vilest men in our country. He neither regardeth prince nor people, law nor custom; but doth all that he can to possess all men with certain of his disloyal notions, which he in the general calls principles of faith and holiness. And, in particular, I heard him once myself affirm that Christianity and the customs of our town of Vanity were diametrically opposite, and could not be reconciled. By which saying, my lord, he doth at once not only condemn all our laudable doings, but us in the doing of them.

Judge. Then did the judge say to him, Hast thou any more to say?

Envy. My lord, I could say much more, only I would not be tedious to the court. Yet, if need be, when the other gentlemen have given in their evidence, rather than anything shall be wanting that will despatch him, I will enlarge my testimony against him. So he was bid to stand by.

Then they called Superstition, and bid him look upon the prisoner. They also asked, what he could say for their lord the king against him. Then they sware him; so he began.

Super. My lord, I have no great acquaintance with this man, nor do I desire to have further knowledge of him; however, this I know, that he is a very pestilent fellow, from some discourse that, the other day, I had with him in this town; for then, talking with him, I heard him say, that our religion was naught, and such by which a man could by no means please God. Which sayings of his, my Lord, your Lordship very well knows, what necessarily thence will follow, to wit, that we do still worship in vain, are yet in our sins, and finally shall be damned; and this is that which I have to say.

Then was Pickthank sworn, and bid say what he knew, in behalf of their lord the king, against the prisoner at the bar.

Pick. My Lord, and you gentlemen all, This fellow I have known of a long time, and have heard him speak things that ought not to be spoke; for he hath railed on our noble prince Beelzebub, and hath spoken contemptibly of his honourable friends, whose names are the Lord Old Man, the Lord Carnal Delight, the Lord Luxurious, the Lord Desire-of-Vain-Glory, my old Lord Lechery, Sir Having Greedy, with all the rest of our nobility; and he hath said, moreover, That if all men were of his mind, if possible, there is not one of these noblemen should have any longer a being in this town. Besides, he hath not been afraid to rail on you, my Lord, who are now appointed to be his judge, calling you an ungodly villain, with many other such like vilifying terms, with which he hath bespattered most of the gentry of our town.

When this Pickthank had told his tale, the Judge directed his speech to the prisoner at the bar, saying, "Thou runagate, heretic, and traitor, hast thou heard what these honest gentlemen have witnessed against thee?"

Faith. May I speak a few words in my own defence?

Judge. Sirrah! Sirrah! thou deservest to live no longer, but to be slain immediately upon the place; yet, that all men may see our gentleness towards thee, let us hear what thou, vile runagate, hast to say.

Faith. 1. I say, then, in answer to what Mr. Envy hath spoken, I never said aught but this, That what rule, or laws, or customs, or people, were flat against the Word of God, are diametrically opposite to Christianity. If I have said amiss in this, convince me of my error, and I am ready here before you to make my recantation.

2. As to the second, to wit, Mr. Superstition, and his charge against me, I said only this, That in the worship of God there is required a divine faith; but

there can be no divine faith without a divine revelation of the will of God. Therefore, whatever is thrust into the worship of God that is not agreeable to divine revelation, cannot be done but by a human faith, which faith will not be profitable to eternal life.

3. As to what Mr. Pickthank hath said, I say (avoiding terms, as that I am said to rail, and the like), That the prince of this town, with all the rabblement, his attendants, by this gentleman named, are more fit for a being in hell, than in this town and country: and so, the Lord have mercy upon me!

Then the Judge called to the jury (who all this while stood by, to hear and observe): "Gentlemen of the jury, you see this man about whom so great an uproar hath been made in this town. You have also heard what these worthy gentlemen have witnessed against him. Also you have heard his reply and confession. It lieth now in your breasts to hang him or save his life; but yet I think meet to instruct you into our law.

"There was an act made in the days of Pharaoh the Great, servant to our prince, that lest those of a contrary religion should multiply and grow too strong for him, their males should be thrown into the river. There was also an act made in the days of Nebuchadnezzar the Great, another of his servants, that whosoever would not fall down and worship his golden image, should be thrown into a fiery furnace. There was also an act made in the days of Darius, that whoso, for some time, called upon any god but him, should be cast into the lions' den. Now the substance of these laws this rebel has broken, not only in thought (which is not to be borne), but also in word and deed; which must therefore needs be intolerable.

"For that of Pharaoh, his law was made upon a supposition, to prevent mischief, no crime being yet apparent; but here is a crime apparent. For the second and third, you see he disputeth against our religion; and for the treason he hath confessed, he deserveth to die the death."

Then went the jury out, whose names were, Mr. Blind-man, Mr. No-good, Mr. Malice, Mr. Love-lust, Mr. Live-loose, Mr. Heady, Mr. High-mind, Mr. Enmity, Mr. Liar, Mr. Cruelty, Mr. Hate-light, and Mr. Implacable; who every one gave in his private verdict against him among themselves, and afterwards unanimously concluded to bring him in guilty before the Judge. And first, among themselves, Mr. Blind-man, the foreman, said, "I see clearly that this man is a heretic." Then said Mr. No-good, "Away with such a fellow from the earth." "Ay," said Mr. Malice, "for I hate the very looks of him." Then said Mr. Love-lust, "I could never endure him." "Nor I," said Mr. Live-loose, "for he would always be condemning my way." "Hang him, hang him," said Mr. Heady. "A sorry scrub," said Mr. High-mind. "My heart riseth against him," said Mr. Enmity. "He is a rogue," said Mr. Liar. "Hanging is too good for him," said Mr. Cruelty. "Let us despatch him out of the way," said Mr. Hate-light. Then said Mr. Implacable, "Might I have all the world given me, I could not be reconciled to him; therefore, let us forthwith bring him in guilty of death." And so they did; therefore he was presently condemned to be had from the place where he was, to the place from whence he came, and there to be put to the most cruel death that could be invented.

They, therefore, brought him out, to do with him according to their law; and, first, they scourged him, then they buffeted him, then they lanced his flesh with knives; after that, they stoned him with stones, then pricked him with their swords; and, last of all, they burned him to ashes at the stake. Thus came Faithful to his end.

Now I saw that there stood behind the multitude a chariot and a couple of horses, waiting for Faithful, who (so soon as his adversaries had despatched him) was taken up into it, and straightway was carried up through the clouds, with sound of trumpet, the nearest way to the celestial gate.

But as for Christian, he had some respite, and was remanded back to prison. So he there remained for a space; but he that overrules all things, having the power of their rage in his own hand, so wrought it about, that Christian for that time escaped them, and went his way. . . .

[*Christian and Hopeful in Doubting Castle*]

Now there was, not far from the place where they lay, a castle called Doubting Castle, the owner whereof was Giant Despair; and it was in his grounds they now were sleeping. Wherefore he, getting up in the morning early, and walking up and down in his fields, caught Christian and Hopeful asleep in his grounds. Then, with a grim and surly voice, he bid them awake; and asked them whence they were, and what they did in his

---

26–27. **males should be thrown into the river.** See the story of the oppression of the children of Israel in Egypt, Exodus I.   30–31. **into a fiery furnace.** See the story of the three Hebrew children, Daniel 3.   33. **the lions' den.** See the story of Daniel, Daniel 6.

30. **a chariot and . . . horses.** See the story of Elijah II Kings 2:11.

grounds. They told him they were pilgrims, and that they had lost their way. Then said the Giant, "You have this night trespassed on me, by trampling in and lying on my grounds, and therefore you must go along with me." So they were forced to go, because he was stronger than they. They also had but little to say, for they knew themselves in a fault. The Giant, therefore, drove them before him, and put them into his castle, into a very dark dungeon, nasty and stinking to the spirits of these two men. Here, then, they lay from Wednesday morning till Saturday night, without one bit of bread, or drop of drink, or light, or any to ask how they did; they were, therefore, here in evil case, and were far from friends and acquaintance. Now in this place Christian had double sorrow, because it was through his unadvised counsel that they were brought into this distress.

Now, Giant Despair had a wife, and her name was Diffidence. So when he was gone to bed, he told his wife what he had done; to wit, that he had taken a couple of prisoners and cast them into his dungeon, for trespassing on his grounds. Then he asked her also what he had best to do further to them. So she asked him what they were, whence they came, and whither they were bound; and he told her. Then she counselled him that when he arose in the morning he should beat them without any mercy. So, when he arose, he getteth him a grievous crab-tree cudgel, and goes down into the dungeon to them, and there first falls to rating of them as if they were dogs, although they never gave him a word of distaste. Then he falls upon them, and beats them fearfully, in such sort, that they were not able to help themselves, or to turn them upon the floor. This done, he withdraws and leaves them, there to condole their misery, and to mourn under their distress. So all that day they spent the time in nothing but sighs and bitter lamentations. The next night, she, talking with her husband about them further, and understanding they were yet alive, did advise him to counsel them to make away themselves. So when morning was come, he goes to them in a surly manner as before, and perceiving them to be very sore with the stripes that he had given them the day before, he told them, that since they were never like to come out of that place, their only way would be forthwith to make an end of themselves, either with knife, halter, or poison, "for why," said he, "should you choose life, seeing it is attended with so much bitterness?" But they desired him to let them go. With that he looked ugly upon them, and, rushing to them, had doubtless made an end of them himself, but that he fell into one of his fits (for he sometimes, in sunshiny weather, fell into fits), and lost for a time the use of his hand; wherefore he withdrew, and left them as before, to consider what to do. Then did the prisoners consult between themselves, whether 'twas best to take his counsel or no; and thus they began to discourse:—

Chr. Brother, said Christian, what shall we do? The life that we now live is miserable. For my part I know not whether is best, to live thus, or to die out of hand. "My soul chooseth strangling rather than life," and the grave is more easy for me than this dungeon. Shall we be ruled by the Giant?

Hope. Indeed, our present condition is dreadful, and death would be far more welcome to me than thus for ever to abide; but yet, let us consider, the Lord of the country to which we are going hath said, Thou shalt do no murder: no, not to another man's person; much more, then, are we forbidden to take his counsel to kill ourselves. Besides, he that kills another, can but commit murder upon his body; but for one to kill himself is to kill body and soul at once. And, moreover, my brother, thou talkest of ease in the grave; but hast thou forgotten the hell, whither for certain the murderers go? For "no murderer hath eternal life," &c. And let us consider, again, that all the law is not in the hand of Giant Despair. Others, so far as I can understand, have been taken by him, as well as we; and yet have escaped out of his hand. Who knows, but that God that made the world may cause that Giant Despair may die? or that, at some time or other, he may forget to lock us in? or that he may, in a short time, have another of his fits before us, and may lose the use of his limbs? and if ever that should come to pass again, for my part, I am resolved to pluck up the heart of a man, and to try my utmost to get from under his hand. I was a fool that I did not try to do it before; but, however, my brother, let us be patient, and endure a while. The time may come that may give us a happy release; but let us not be our own murderers. With these words, Hopeful at present did moderate the mind of his brother; so they continued together (in the dark) that day, in their sad and doleful condition.

---

9. dark dungeon. Bunyan wrote *The Pilgrim's Progress* in Bedford jail, and his description of the dungeon was undoubtedly based in part upon his own experience. The adventures of Christian and Hopeful with Giant Despair may have been suggested in part by those of Spenser's Red Cross Knight in the Cave of Despair (see *The Faerie Queene*, Book I, Canto IX). **20. Diffidence.** The word in Bunyan's day meant "distrust, want of confidence in others," rather than "bashfulness."

17. whether. In the seventeenth century the word meant "which" (of two).

Well, towards evening, the Giant goes down into the dungeon again, to see if his prisoners had taken his counsel; but when he came there he found them alive; and truly, alive was all; for now, what for want of bread and water, and by reason of the wounds they received when he beat them, they could do little but breathe. But, I say, he found them alive; at which he fell into a grievous rage, and told them that, seeing they had disobeyed his counsel, it should be worse with them than if they had never been born.

At this they trembled greatly, and I think that Christian fell into a swoon; but, coming a little to himself again, they renewed their discourse about the Giant's counsel; and whether yet they had best to take it or no. Now Christian again seemed to be for doing it, but Hopeful made his second reply as followeth:—

Hope, My brother, said he, rememberest thou not how valiant thou hast been heretofore? Apollyon could not crush thee, nor could all that thou didst hear, or see, or feel, in the Valley of the Shadow of Death. What hardship, terror, and amazement hast thou already gone through, and art thou now nothing but fear! Thou seest that I am in the dungeon with thee, a far weaker man by nature than thou art; also, this Giant has wounded me as well as thee, and hath also cut off the bread and water from my mouth; and with thee I mourn without the light. But let us exercise a little more patience; remember how thou playedst the man at Vanity Fair, and wast neither afraid of the chain, nor cage, nor yet of bloody death. Wherefore let us (at least to avoid the shame, that becomes not a Christian to be found in) bear up with patience as well as we can.

Now, night being come again, and the Giant and his wife being in bed, she asked him concerning the prisoners, and if they had taken his counsel. To which he replied, "They are sturdy rogues, they choose rather to bear all hardship, than to make away themselves." Then said she, "Take them into the castle-yard to-morrow, and show them the bones and skulls of those that thou hast already despatched, and make them believe, ere a week comes to an end, thou also wilt tear them in pieces, as thou hast done their fellows before them."

So when the morning was come, the Giant goes to them again, and takes them into the castle-yard, and shows them, as his wife had bidden him. "These," said he, "were pilgrims as you are, once, and they trespassed in my grounds, as you have done; and when I thought fit, I tore them in pieces, and so, within ten days, I will do you. Go, get you down to your den again"; and with that he beat them all the way thither. They lay, therefore, all day on Saturday in a lamentable case, as before. Now, when night was come, and when Mrs. Diffidence and her husband, the Giant, were got to bed, they began to renew their discourse of their prisoners; and withal the old Giant wondered, that he could neither by his blows nor his counsel bring them to an end. And with that his wife replied, "I fear," said she, "that they live in hope that some will come to relieve them, or that they have picklocks about them, by the means of which they hope to escape." "And sayest thou so, my dear?" said the Giant; "I will, therefore, search them in the morning."

Well, on Saturday, about midnight, they began to pray, and continued in prayer till almost break of day.

Now, a little before it was day, good Christian, as one half amazed, brake out in this passionate speech: "What a fool," quoth he, "am I, thus to lie in a stinking dungeon, when I may as well walk at liberty! I have a key in my bosom, called Promise, that will, I am persuaded, open any lock in Doubting Castle." Then said Hopeful, "That is good news, good brother; pluck it out of thy bosom, and try."

Then Christian pulled it out of his bosom, and began to try at the dungeon door, whose bolt (as he turned the key) gave back, and the door flew open with ease, and Christian and Hopeful both came out. Then he went to the outward door that leads into the castle-yard, and, with his key, opened that door also. After, he went to the iron gate, for that must be opened too; but that lock went damnable hard, yet the key did open it. Then they thrust open the gate to make their escape with speed, but that gate, as it opened, made such a creaking that it waked Giant Despair, who, hastily rising to pursue his prisoners, felt his limbs to fail, for his fits took him again, so that he could by no means go after them. Then they went on, and came to the King's highway, and so were safe, because they were out of his jurisdiction. . . .

[*The Pilgrims Welcomed to the Celestial City*]

Now while they were thus drawing towards the gate, behold a company of the heavenly host came out to meet them; to whom it was said, by the other two Shining Ones, "These are the men that have

---

1. **Well, towards evening.** Note the conversational style of Bunyan's narrative.

6. **Mrs.**, pronounced "Mistress" in Bunyan's day.

loved our Lord when they were in the world, and that have left all for his holy name; and he hath sent us to fetch them, and we have brought them thus far on their desired journey, that they may go in and look their Redeemer in the face with joy." Then the heavenly host gave a great shout, saying, "Blessed are they which are called unto the marriage supper of the Lamb." There came out also at this time to meet them, several of the King's trumpeters, clothed in white and shining raiment, who, with melodious noises, and loud, made even the heavens to echo with their sound. These trumpeters saluted Christian and his fellow with ten thousand welcomes from the world; and this they did with shouting, and sound of trumpet.

This done, they compassed them round on every side; some went before, some behind, and some on the right hand, some on the left (as it were to guard them through the upper regions), continually sounding as they went, with melodious noise, in notes on high: so that the very sight was to them that could behold it, as if heaven itself was come down to meet them. Thus, therefore, they walked on together; and as they walked, ever and anon these trumpeters, even with joyful sound, would, by mixing their music with looks and gestures, still signify to Christian and his brother, how welcome they were into their company, and with what gladness they came to meet them; and now were these two men, as it were, in heaven, before they came at it, being swallowed up with the sight of angels, and with hearing of their melodious notes. Here also they had the city itself in view, and they thought they heard all the bells therein to ring, to welcome them thereto. But above all, the warm and joyful thoughts that they had about their own dwelling there, with such company, and that for ever and ever. Oh, by what tongue or pen can their glorious joy be expressed! And thus they came up to the gate.

Now, when they were come up to the gate, there was written over it in letters of gold, "Blessed are they that do his commandments, that they may have right to the tree of life, and may enter in through the gates into the city."

Then I saw in my dream, that the Shining Men bid them call at the gate; the which, when they did, some looked from above over the gate, to wit, Enoch, Moses, and Elijah, &c., to whom it was said, "These pilgrims are come from the City of Destruction, for the love that they bear to the King of this place." And then the pilgrims gave in unto them each man his certificate, which they had received in the beginning; those, therefore, were carried in to the King, who, when he had read them, said, "Where are the men?" To whom it was answered, "They are standing without the gate." The King then commanded to open the gate, "That the righteous nation," said he, "which keepeth the truth may enter in."

Now I saw in my dream that these two men went in at the gate: and lo, as they entered, they were transfigured, and they had raiment put on that shone like gold. There were also that met them with harps and crowns, and gave them to them—the harps to praise withal, and the crowns in token of honour. Then I heard in my dream that all the bells in the city rang again for joy, and that it was said unto them, "ENTER YE INTO THE JOY OF YOUR LORD." I also heard the men themselves, that they sang with a loud voice, saying, "BLESSING AND HONOUR, AND GLORY, AND POWER, BE UNTO HIM THAT SITTETH UPON THE THRONE, AND UNTO THE LAMB, FOR EVER AND EVER."

Now, just as the gates were opened to let in the men, I looked in after them, and, behold, the City shone like the sun; the streets also were paved with gold, and in them walked many men, with crowns on their heads, palms in their hands, and golden harps to sing praises withal.

There were also of them that had wings, and they answered one another without intermission, saying, "Holy, holy, holy is the Lord." And after that they shut up the gates; which, when I had seen, I wished myself among them. . . .

from THE SECOND PART

[*Mr. Great-heart and Mr. Valiant-for-truth*]

Great-heart. Then this was your victory, even your faith.

Valiant. It was so. I believed, and therefore came out, got into the way, fought all that set themselves against me, and, by believing, am come to this place.

> Who would true valour see,
>   Let him come hither;
> One here will constant be,
>   Come wind, come weather.
> There's no discouragement
> Shall make him once relent,
> His first avowed intent
>   To be a pilgrim.

42. **Who would true valour see.** Bunyan seems here to be parodying the song "Under the Greenwood Tree," in Shakespeare's *As You Like It*, Act II, sc. 5, with which it should be compared. If he has Shakespeare's song in mind, it is one of the very few instances in which literary influence other than that of the Bible and the religious chapbooks of the day can be detected in his works.

Who so beset him round
  With dismal stories,
Do but themselves confound,—
  His strength the more is;
No lion can him fright,
He'll with a giant fight,
But he will have a right
  To be a pilgrim.

Hobgoblin nor foul fiend
  Can daunt his spirit;
He knows he at the end
  Shall life inherit.
Then fancies fly away,
He'll fear not what men say;
He'll labour night and day
  To be a pilgrim.

By this time they were got to the Enchanted Ground, where the air naturally tended to make one drowsy; and that place was all grown over with briars and thorns, excepting here and there, where was an Enchanted Arbour, upon which, if a man sits, or in which, if a man sleeps, it is a question, say some, whether ever he shall rise or wake again in this world. Over this forest, therefore, they went, both one and the other, and Mr. Great-heart went before, for that he was the guide; and Mr. Valiant-for-truth, he came behind, being there a guard, for fear, lest peradventure some fiend, or dragon, or giant, or thief, should fall upon their rear, and so do mischief. . . .

After this it was noised abroad, that Mr. Valiant-for-truth was taken with a summons by the same post as the other; and had this for a token that the summons was true, "That his pitcher was broken at the fountain." When he understood it, he called for his friends, and told them of it. "Then," said he, "I am going to my Father's; and though with great difficulty I am got hither, yet now I do not repent me of all the trouble I have been at to arrive where I am. My sword I give to him that shall succeed me in my pilgrimage, and my courage and skill to him that can get it. My marks and scars I carry with me, to be a witness for me, that I have fought his battles who now will be my rewarder." When the day that he must go hence was come, many accompanied him to the river side, into which as he went he said, "Death, where is thy sting?" And as he went down deeper, he said, "Grave, where is thy victory?" So he passed over, and all the trumpets sounded for him on the other side. . . .

Samuel Pepys
1633–1703

Mr. Pepys came late to his unique place in English literature. At the beginning of the nineteenth century he was hardly known at all outside British naval circles, but in them he was held in the highest esteem. In 1805, when England was in greater danger of invasion than she had been since 1066, a commission for the investigation of naval affairs reported that the general methods of defense instituted in the time of Samuel Pepys's Secretaryship to the Admiralty were still in force, and highly satisfactory. Twenty years later an entirely different Samuel Pepys burst upon the world in the pages of his diary. Successive editions of the diary gave more and more of its contents to an increasingly delighted world. By the twentieth century Pepys's place in the literature and in the affections of English-speaking people was as secure as Shakespeare's, although, strictly speaking, he was not a man of letters, and only in its very artlessness can his record of daily events be called a work of art.

He was born in London, the son of John Pepys, a tailor—this may account somewhat for his unceasing interest in clothes. He went to Westminster School and Magdalene College, Cambridge. The most significant event of his early years was his marriage, at twenty-two, to Elizabeth le Marchant de St. Michel, aged fifteen, the daughter of a French Huguenot refugee. He was fortunate to have as a first cousin of his father's Sir Edward Montagu, later Earl of Sandwich, and his rise in the world began with his secretaryship to Montagu. Through his influence Pepys became, after the Restoration, Clerk of the Acts in the Navy Office, and subsequently Clerk of the Privy Seal and Secretary to the Admiralty. No public servant was ever more assiduous in his duties than Mr. Pepys. He found the navy in a bad way and put it on a sound financial basis, introducing efficiency and strict

---

10–11. **broken at the fountain."** For the context see Ecclesiastes 12.

economy in the victualing of seamen and in the building and equipping of ships. It cannot be denied that he did well by himself also in the management of naval affairs, but the "honest graft" he got out of it was as nothing compared to the money he saved for the nation. There were other activities and honors outside the Navy Office. His interest in natural science led him in 1664 to join the Royal Society, of which he was later president, and in 1679 he was chosen M.P. for Harwich.

The years which saw Pepys's steady rise were not smooth or peaceful, and his own life was not unaffected by the alarms and disturbances. After the Dutch war he was called before the House of Commons to give an accounting, but came off with his own prestige increased. After the "Popish Plot," he was put into the Tower on charges of popery and treason, but was acquitted. He was reappointed in 1684, and threw himself into his tasks with his old vigor. His career in the Navy Office ended in 1688 when his lifelong friend, King James II, went into exile. Once again, in 1690, he was in prison for a brief while on an unproved charge of Jacobite intrigue. His remaining thirteen years were spent in retirement with his friends and his books and his music. He published several volumes dealing with the history and affairs of the navy.

The diary was begun on January 1, 1660, and was written mostly in a system of shorthand devised thirty years before by Thomas Shelton. Passages for which Mr. Pepys wished special secrecy he inscribed in foreign words or in signs of his own invention. His principal desire in all this seems to have been to prevent his wife and servants from reading the contents of his journal. He brought the diary sadly to an end on May 31, 1669, when his failing eyesight forced him to give it up. Mrs. Pepys died later in the same year. Pepys seems to have intended the diary for no eye but his own, but it was so much a part of him that he could not bring himself to destroy it in later years, and at his death he bequeathed it, in six manuscript volumes, containing three thousand and twelve pages and over eight hundred thousand words, with his other books to Magdalene College. Here it lay, all but forgotten, until 1819, when an undergraduate, John Smith, later a clergyman, began the work of transcription, which he finished in 1822. Parts of it were edited and published for the first time, in two volumes, by Lord Braybrooke, in 1825.

The Diary has become so well known that it needs no lengthy description. It should be remembered that it is the diary of a young man (he began it when he was twenty-six), and that it was not intended for publication. It reveals, as everybody knows, the Pepys who was a bon vivant, a mixture of good and bad, a lover of trifles, a philanderer, an insatiably curious man who was interested in every phase of life in a decade full to overflowing with exciting persons and events. But it also reveals, as many seem to forget, a young man who was as enthusiastic about his work as about his play, and who enjoyed his leisure moments all the more because he had earned them with hours of labor. It is as much the diary of Pepys the bee as of Pepys the butterfly. But he speaks for himself in its pages, and his case may be left in his own hands.

from THE DIARY

The text of *The Diary* from which these extracts are taken is, by permission, that of the standard edition of Henry B. Wheatley, published by G. Bell and Sons, Ltd., London, and Harcourt, Brace and Company, New York.

September 1st. [1666] Up and at the office all morning, and then dined at home. Got my new closet made mighty clean against tomorrow. Sir W. Penn and my wife and Mercer and I to "Polichinelly," but were there horribly frighted to see young Killigrew come in with a great many more young sparks; but we hid ourselves, so as we think they did not see us. By and by they went away, and then we were at rest again; and so, the play being done, we to Islington, and there eat and drink and mighty merry; and so home singing, and, after a letter or two at the office, to bed.

2nd (Lord's day). Some of our maids sitting up late last night to get things ready against our feast to-day, Jane called us up about three in the morn-

3–5. **Sir W. Penn,** Sir William Penn, father of William Penn, founder of Pennsylvania. Sir William, with whom Pepys was very intimate, had had a distinguished career. He was Vice-Admiral of England and a general in the first Dutch war at the age of thirty-two. His son, who turned Quaker and was to have so prominent a part in American history, is often alluded to in *The Diary*. **Mercer,** Mary Mercer, Mrs. Pepys's woman, whom, just about a month before, Mr. Pepys had taught to sing. He writes on July 30, 1666: "Thence home; and coming in I find my wife plainly dissatisfied with me that I can spend so much time with Mercer, teaching her to sing, and could never take the pains with her. Which I acknowledge; but it is because that the girl do take music mighty readily, and she do not, and music is the thing of the world that I love most, and all the pleasure almost that I can now take." **"Polichinelly,"** Polichinello (the Italian Punch), the most popular of the puppet shows of the day. Pepys mentions it nine times in his *Diary*. 6. **young Killigrew,** Thomas Killigrew, "the King's Fool or Jester," the author of a scandalous play, a notorious scapegrace, and young man about town.

ing, to tell us of a great fire they saw in the City. So I rose and slipped on my night-gown, and went to her window, and thought it to be on the back-side of Mark-lane at the farthest; but, being unused to such fires as followed, I thought it far enough off; and so went to bed again and to sleep. About seven rose again to dress myself, and there looked out at the window, and saw the fire not so much as it was and further off. So to my closet to set things to rights after yesterday's cleaning. By and by Jane comes and tells me that she hears that above 300 houses have been burned down to-night by the fire we saw, and that it is now burning down all Fish-street, by London Bridge. So I made myself ready presently, and walked to the Tower, and there got up upon one of the high places, Sir J. Robinson's little son going up with me; and there I did see the houses at that end of the bridge all on fire, and an infinite great fire on this and the other side the end of the bridge; which, among other people, did trouble me for poor little Michell and our Sarah on the bridge. So down, with my heart full of trouble, to the Lieutenant of the Tower, who tells me that it begun this morning in the King's baker's house in Pudding-lane, and that it hath burned St. Magnus's Church and most part of Fish-street already. So I down to the water-side, and there got a boat and through bridge, and there saw a lamentable fire. Poor Michell's house, as far as the Old Swan, already burned that way, and the fire running further, that in a very little time it got as far as the Steel-yard, while I was there. Everybody endeavouring to remove their goods, and flinging into the river or bringing them into lighters that lay off; poor people staying in their houses as long as till the very fire touched them, and then running into boats, or clambering from one pair of stairs by the water-side to another. And among other things, the poor pigeons, I perceive, were loth to leave their houses, but hovered about the windows and balconies till they were, some of them, burned, their wings, and fell down. Having stayed, and in an hour's time seen the fire rage every way, and nobody, to my sight, endeavouring to quench it, but to remove their goods, and leave all to the fire, and having seen it get as far as the Steel-yard, and the wind mighty high and driving it into the City; and every thing, after so long a drought, proving combustible, even the very stones of churches, and among other things the poor steeple by which pretty Mrs. —— lives, and whereof my old school-fellow Elborough is parson, taken fire in the very top, and there burned till it fell down: I to Whitehall (with a gentleman with me who desired to go off from the Tower, to see the fire, in my boat); to Whitehall, and there up to the King's closet in the Chapel, where people come about me, and I did give them an account dismayed them all, and word was carried in to the King. So I was called for, and did tell the King and Duke of York what I saw, and that unless His Majesty did command houses to be pulled down nothing could stop the fire. They seemed much troubled, and the King commanded me to go to my Lord Mayor from him, and command him to spare no houses, but to pull down before the fire every way. The Duke of York bid me tell him that if he would have any more soldiers he shall; and so did my Lord Arlington afterwards, as a great secret. Here meeting with Captain Cocke, I in his coach, which he lent me, and Creed with me to Paul's, and there walked along Watling-street, as well as I could, every creature coming away loaden with goods to save, and here and there sick people carried away in beds. Extraordinary good goods carried in carts and on backs. At last met my Lord Mayor in Canning-street, like a man spent, with a handkerchief about his neck. To the King's message he cried, like a fainting woman, "Lord! what can I do? I am spent: people will not obey me. I have been pulling down houses; but the fire overtakes us faster than we can do it." That he needed no more soldiers; and that, for himself, he must go and refresh himself, having been up all night. So he left me, and I him, and walked home, seeing people all almost distracted, and no manner of means used to quench the fire. The houses, too, so very thick thereabouts, and full of matter for burning, as pitch and tar, in Thames-street; and warehouses of oil, and wines, and brandy, and other things. Here I saw Mr. Isaac Houblon, the handsome man, prettily dressed and dirty, at his door at Dowgate, receiving some of his brothers' things, whose houses were on fire; and, as he says, have been removed twice already; and he doubts (as it soon proved) that they must be in a little time removed from his house also, which was a sad consideration. And to see the churches all filling with goods by people who themselves should have been quietly there at this time. By this time it was about twelve o'clock; and so home, and there find my guests, which was Mr. Wood and his wife Barbary

---

37. pair, set. Compare the expression, "pair of virginals," on page 720, and the "peyre of bedes" of Chaucer's Prioress, page 175.

3. Whitehall, the royal palace. **10. Duke of York,** Pepys's patron, the brother of Charles II, afterwards King James II. **21. Paul's,** St. Paul's Cathedral.

Sheldon, and also Mr. Moone: she mighty fine, and her husband, for aught I see, a likely man. But Mr. Moone's design and mine, which was to look over my closet and please him with the sight thereof, which he hath long desired, was wholly disappointed; for we were in great trouble and disturbance at this fire, not knowing what to think of it. However, we had an extraordinary good dinner, and as merry as at this time we could be. While at dinner Mrs. Batelier come to enquire after Mr. Woolfe and Stanes (who, it seems, are related to them), whose houses in Fish-street are all burned, and they in a sad condition. She would not stay in the fright. Soon as dined, I and Moone away, and walked through the City, the streets full of nothing but people and horses and carts loaden with goods, ready to run over one another, and removing goods from one burned house to another. They now removing out of Canning-street (which received goods in the morning) into Lombard-street, and further; and among others I now saw my little goldsmith, Stokes, receiving some friend's goods, whose house itself was burned the day after. We parted at Paul's; he home, and I to Paul's Wharf, where I had appointed a boat to attend me, and took in Mr. Carcasse and his brother, whom I met in the street, and carried them below and above bridge too. And again to see the fire, which was now got further, both below and above, and no likelihood of stopping it. Met with the King and Duke of York in their barge, and with them to Queenhithe, and there called Sir Richard Browne to them. Their order was only to pull down houses apace, and so below bridge at the water-side; but little was or could be done, the fire coming upon them so fast. Good hopes there was of stopping it at the Three Cranes above, and at Buttolph's Wharf below bridge, if care be used; but the wind carries it into the City, so as we know not by the water-side what it do there. River full of lighters and boats taking in goods, and good goods swimming in the water, and only I observed that hardly one lighter or boat in three that had the goods of a house in, but there was a pair of virginals in it. Having seen as much as I could now, I away to Whitehall by appointment, and there walked to St. James's Park, and there met my wife and Creed and Wood and his wife, and walked to my boat; and there upon the water again, and to the fire up and down, it still increasing, and the wind great. So near the fire as we could for smoke; and all over the Thames, with one's face in the wind, you were almost burned with a shower of fire-drops. This is very true: so as houses were burned by these drops and flakes of fire, three or four, nay, five or six houses, one from another. When we could endure no more upon the water, we to a little ale-house on the Bankside, over against the Three Cranes, and there stayed till it was dark almost, and saw the fire grow; and, as it grew darker, appeared more and more, and in corners and upon steeples, and between churches and houses, as far as we could see up the hill of the City, in a most horrid malicious bloody flame, not like the flame of an ordinary fire. Barbary and her husband away before us. We stayed till, it being darkish, we saw the fire as only one entire arch of fire from this to the other side the bridge, and in a bow up the hill for an arch of above a mile long: it made me weep to see it. The churches, houses, and all on fire and flaming at once; and a horrid noise the flames made, and the cracking of houses at their ruin. So home with a sad heart, and there find everybody discoursing and lamenting the fire; and poor Tom Hater come with some few of his goods saved out of his house, which is burned upon Fish-street Hill. I invited him to lie at my house, and did receive his goods, but was deceived in his lying there, the news coming every moment of the growth of the fire; so as we were forced to begin to pack up our own goods, and prepare for their removal; and did by moonshine (it being brave dry and moonshine and warm weather) carry much of my goods into the garden, and Mr. Hater and I did remove my money and iron chests into my cellar, as thinking that the safest place. And got my bags of gold into my office, ready to carry away, and my chief papers of accounts also there, and my tallies into a box by themselves. So great was our fear, as Sir W. Batten hath carts come out of the country to fetch away his goods this night. We did put Mr. Hater, poor man, to bed a little; but he got but very little rest, so much noise being in my house, taking down of goods.

3rd. About four o'clock in the morning, my Lady Batten sent me a cart to carry away all my money, and plate, and best things, to Sir W. Rider's at Bednall-green. Which I did, riding myself in my

---

4. closet, a small private chamber for valuables or rarities. **40. lighters,** barges. **44. pair of virginals.** See note to "pair of stairs," page 719. The virginal was a small square legless spinet. The spinet proper was triangular in form. The instrument may have received its name from the circumstance that young women usually played on it.

39. tallies. A tally was a strip of wood notched to indicate the amount of a debt. The tally was then split lengthwise through the notches, so that the parts exactly corresponded, and each party to the transaction retained one half. When payment was to be made, the creditor presented his half as evidence of the amount due.

night-gown in the cart; and, Lord! to see how the streets and the highways are crowded with people running and riding, and getting of carts at any rate to fetch away things. I find Sir W. Rider tired with being called up all night, and receiving things from several friends. His house full of goods, and much of Sir W. Batten's and Sir W. Penn's. I am eased at my heart to have my treasure so well secured. Then home, with much ado to find a way, nor any sleep all this night to me nor my poor wife. But then and all this day she and I, and all my people labouring to get away the rest of our things, and did get Mr. Tooker to get me a lighter to take them in, and we did carry them (myself some) over Tower Hill, which was by this time full of people's goods, bringing their goods thither; and down to the lighter, which lay at the next quay, above the Tower Dock. And here was my neighbour's wife, Mrs. ——, with her pretty child, and some few of her things, which I did willingly give way to be saved with mine; but there was no passing with anything through the postern, the crowd was so great. The Duke of York come this day by the office, and spoke to us, and did ride with his guard up and down the City to keep all quiet (he being now General, and having the care of all). This day, Mercer being not at home, but against her mistress's order gone to her mother's, and my wife going thither to speak with W. Hewer, met her there, and was angry; and her mother saying that she was not a 'prentice girl, to ask leave every time she goes abroad, my wife with good reason was angry, and, when she came home, bid her be gone again. And so she went away, which troubled me, but yet less than it would, because of the condition we are in, fear of coming into a little time of being less able to keep one in her quality. At night lay down a little upon a quilt of W. Hewer's in the office, all my own things being packed up or gone; and after me my poor wife did the like, we having fed upon the remains of yesterday's dinner, having no fire nor dishes, nor any opportunity of dressing anything.

4th. Up by break of day to get away the remainder of my things; which I did by a lighter at the Iron gate: and my hands so full, that it was the afternoon before we could get them all away. Sir W. Penn and I to Tower-street, and there met the fire burning three or four doors beyond Mr. Howell's, whose goods, poor man, his trays, and dishes, shovels, etc., were flung all along Tower-street in the kennels, and people working therewith from one end to the other; the fire coming on in that narrow street, on both sides, with infinite fury. Sir W. Batten not knowing how to remove his wine, did dig a pit in the garden, and laid it in there; and I took the opportunity of laying all the papers of my office that I could not otherwise dispose of. And in the evening Sir W. Penn and I did dig another, and put our wine in it; and I my Parmazan cheese, as well as my wine and some other things. The Duke of York was at the office this day, at Sir W. Penn's; but I happened not to be within. This afternoon, sitting melancholy with Sir W. Penn in our garden, and thinking of the certain burning of this office, without extraordinary means, I did propose for the sending up of all our workmen from Woolwich and Deptford yards (none whereof yet appeared), and to write to Sir W. Coventry to have the Duke of York's permission to pull down houses, rather than lose this office, which would much hinder the King's business. So Sir W. Penn he went down this night, in order to the sending them up to-morrow morning; and I wrote to Sir W. Coventry about the business, but received no answer. This night Mrs. Turner (who, poor woman, was removing her goods all this day, good goods into the garden, and knows not how to dispose of them), and her husband supped with my wife and I at night, in the office, upon a shoulder of mutton from the cook's, without napkin or any thing, in a sad manner, but were merry. Only now and then walking into the garden, and saw how horridly the sky looks, all on a fire in the night, was enough to put us out of our wits; and, indeed, it was extremely dreadful, for it looks just as if it was at us, and the whole heaven on fire. I after supper walked in the dark down to Tower-street, and there saw it all on fire, at the Trinity House on that side, and the Dolphin Tavern on this side, which was very near us; and the fire with extraordinary vehemence. Now begins the practice of blowing up of houses in Tower-street, those next the Tower, which at first did frighten people more than anything; but it stopped the fire where it was done, it bringing down the houses to the ground in the same places they stood, and then it was easy to quench what little fire was in it, though it kindled nothing almost. W. Hewer this day went to see how his mother did, and comes late home, telling us how he hath been forced to remove her to Islington, her house in Pie-corner being burned; so the fire is got so far that way, and all the Old Bailey, and was run-

52. **kennels,** gutters.

8. **Parmazan cheese,** made in Parma, Italy; now spelled "Parmesan."   50. **the Old Bailey,** the London Central Criminal Court, so called because it stood within the ancient bailey (inner circuit of the city wall).

ning down to Fleet-street; and Paul's is burned, and all Cheapside. I wrote to my father this night, but the post-house being burned, the letter could not go.

5th. I lay down in the office again upon W. Hewer's quilt, being mighty weary, and sore in my feet with going till I was hardly able to stand. About two in the morning my wife calls me up and tells me of new cries of fire, it being come to Barking Church, which is the bottom of our lane. I up, and finding it so, resolved presently to take her away, and did, and took my gold, which was about £2,350, W. Hewer, and Jane, down by Proundy's boat to Woolwich; but, Lord! what a sad sight it was by moonlight to see the whole City almost on fire, that you might see it plain at Woolwich, as if you were by it. There, when I come, I find the gates shut, but no guard kept at all, which troubled me, because of discourse now begun, that there is plot in it, and that the French had done it. I got the gates open, and to Mr. Sheldon's, where I locked up my gold, and charged my wife and W. Hewer never to leave the room without one of them in it, night or day. So back again, by the way seeing my goods well in the lighters at Deptford, and watched well by people. Home, and whereas I expected to have seen our house on fire, it being now about seven o'clock, it was not. But to the fire, and there find greater hopes than I expected; for my confidence of finding our office on fire was such, that I durst not ask anybody how it was with us, till I come and saw it not burned. But going to the fire, I find by the blowing up of houses, and the great help given by the workmen out of the King's yards, sent up by Sir W. Penn, there is a good stop given to it, as well at Mark-lane end as at ours; it having only burned the dial of Barking Church, and part of the porch, and was there quenched. I up to the top of Barking steeple, and there saw the saddest sight of desolation that I ever saw; everywhere great fires, oil-cellars, and brimstone, and other things burning. I became afeared to stay there long, and therefore down again as fast as I could, the fire being spread as far as I could see it; and to Sir W. Penn's, and there eat a piece of cold meat, having eaten nothing since Sunday, but the remains of Sunday's dinner. Here I met with Mr. Young and Whistler; and having removed all my things, and received good hopes that the fire at our end is stopped, they and I walked into the town, and find Fanchurch-street, Gracious-street, and Lombard-street all in dust. The Exchange a sad sight, nothing standing there, of all the statues or pillars, but Sir Thomas Gresham's picture in the corner. Walked into Moore fields (our feet ready to burn, walking through the town among the hot coals), and find that full of people, and poor wretches carrying their goods there, and everybody keeping his goods together by themselves (and a great blessing it is to them that it is fair weather for them to keep abroad night and day); drank there, and paid twopence for a plain penny loaf. Thence homeward, having passed through Cheapside and Newgate Market, all burned, and seen Anthony Joyce's house in fire. And took up (which I keep by me) a piece of glass of Mercers' Chapel in the street, where much more was, so melted and buckled by the heat of the fire like parchment. I also did see a poor cat taken out of a hole in the chimney, joining to the wall of the Exchange, with the hair all burned off the body, and yet alive. So home at night, and find there good hopes of saving our office; but great endeavours of watching all night, and having men ready; and so we lodged them in the office, and had drink and bread and cheese for them. And I lay down and slept a good night about midnight, though when I rose I heard that there had been a great alarm of French and Dutch being risen, which proved nothing. But it is a strange thing to see how long this time of life did look since Sunday, having been always full of variety of actions, and little sleep, that it looked like a week or more, and I had forgot almost the day of the week.

6th. Up about five o'clock, and there met Mr. Gawden at the gate of the office (I intending to go out, as I used, every now and then to-day, to see how the fire is) to call our men to Bishop's-gate, where no fire had yet been near, and there is now one broke out: which did give great grounds to people, and to me too, to think that there is some kind of plot in this (on which many by this time have been taken, and it hath been dangerous for any stranger to walk in the streets), but I went with the men, and we did put it out in a little time; so that that was well again. It was pretty to see how hard the women did work in the cannells, sweeping

---

12. **about £2,350.** For its approximate value in present-day money, this figure should be multiplied by four. There were, of course, no banks in which Mr. Pepys might deposit his gold. 45. **having eaten nothing.** Mr. Pepys has forgotten, as his editors delight to point out, the shoulder of mutton from the cook's the day before.

5. **picture,** statue. 42–43. **some kind of plot.** "The terrible disaster which overtook London was borne by the inhabitants of the city with great fortitude, but foreigners and Roman Catholics had a bad time. As no cause for the outbreak of the fire could be traced, a general cry was raised that it owed its origin to a plot."—Wheatley 48. **cannells,** gutters.

of water; but then they would scold for drink, and be as drunk as devils. I saw good butts of sugar broke open in the street, and people go and take handfuls out, and put into beer, and drink it. And now all being pretty well, I took boat, and over to Southwark, and took boat on the other side the bridge, and so to Westminster, thinking to shift myself, being all in dirt from top to bottom; but could not there find any place to buy a shirt or pair of gloves, Westminster Hall being full of people's goods, those in Westminster having removed all their goods, and the Exchequer money being put into vessels to carry to Nonsuch; but to the Swan, and there was trimmed; and then to Whitehall, but saw nobody; and so home. A sad sight to see how the river looks: no houses nor churches near it, to the Temple, where it stopped. At home, did go with Sir W. Batten, and our neighbour, Knightly (who, with one more, was the only man of any fashion left in all the neighbourhood thereabouts, they all removing their goods and leaving their houses to the mercy of the fire), to Sir R. Ford's, and there dined in an earthen platter—a fried breast of mutton; a great many of us, but very merry, and indeed as good a meal, though as ugly a one, as ever I had in my life. Thence down to Deptford, and there with great satisfaction landed all my goods at Sir G. Carteret's safe, and nothing missed I could see, or hurt. This being done to my great content, I home, and to Sir W. Batten's, and there with Sir R. Ford, Mr. Knightly, and one Withers, a professed lying rogue, supped well, and mighty merry, and our fears over. From them to the office, and there slept with the office full of labourers, who talked, and slept, and walked all night long there. But strange it was to see Clothworkers' Hall on fire these three days and nights in one body of flame, it being the cellar full of oil.

7th. Up by five o'clock; and, blessed be God! find all well; and by water to Paul's Wharf. Walked thence, and saw all the town burned, and a miserable sight of Paul's church, with all the roofs fallen, and the body of the choir fallen into St. Faith's; Paul's school also, Ludgate, and Fleet-street, my father's house and the church and a good part of the Temple the like. So to Creed's lodging, near the New Exchange, and there find him laid down upon a bed; the house all unfurnished, there being fears of the fire's coming to them. There borrowed a shirt of him, and washed. To Sir W. Coventry, at St. James's, who lay without curtains, having removed all his goods; as the King at Whitehall and every body had done and was doing. He hopes that we shall have no public distractions upon this fire, which is what every body fears, because of the talk of the French having a hand in it. And it is a proper time for discontents; but all men's minds are full of care to protect themselves, and save their goods: the militia is in arms every where. Our fleets, he tells me, have been in sight one of another, and most unhappily by foul weather were parted, to our great loss, as in reason they do conclude; the Dutch being come out only to make a show, and please their people; but in very bad condition as to stores, victuals, and men. They are at Bullen, and our fleet come to St. Ellen's. We have got nothing, but have lost one ship, but he knows not what. Thence to the Swan, and there drank: and so home, and find all well. My Lord Bruncker, at Sir W. Batten's, and tells us the General is sent for up, to come to advise with the King about business at this juncture, and to keep all quiet; which is great honour to him, but I am sure is but a piece of dissimulation. So home, and did give orders for my house to be made clean; and then down to Woolwich, and there find all well. Dined, and Mrs. Markham come to see my wife. So I up again, and calling at Deptford for some things of W. Hewer's, he being with me, and then home and spent the evening with Sir R. Ford, Mr. Knightly, and Sir W. Penn at Sir W. Batten's. This day our merchants first met at Gresham College, which, by proclamation, is to be their Exchange. Strange to hear what is bid for houses all up and down here; a friend of Sir W. Rider's having £150 for what he used to let for £40 per annum. Much dispute where the Custom-house shall be; thereby the growth of the City again to be foreseen. My Lord Treasurer, they say, and others, would have it at the other end of the town. I home late to Sir W. Penn's, who did give me a bed; but without curtains or hangings, all being down. So here I went the first time into a naked bed, only my drawers on; and did sleep pretty well: but still both sleeping and waking had a fear of fire in my heart, that I took little rest. People do all the world over cry out of the simplicity of my Lord Mayor in general; and more particularly in this business of the fire, laying it all upon him. A proclamation is come out for markets to be kept at Leadenhall and Mile-end-green, and several other places about the town; and Tower-hill, and all churches be set open to receive poor people. . . .

9th (Sunday). Up; and was trimmed, and sent my brother to Woolwich to my wife, to dine with

---

43. **St. Faith's**, the crypt under the choir of St. Paul's.   12. **Bullen**, Boulogne.   13. **St. Ellen's**, St. Helen's, or Watch-house Point, on the Isle of Wight.

her. I to church, where our parson made a melancholy but good sermon; and many and most in church cried, specially the women. The church mighty full; but few of fashion, and most strangers. I walked to Bednall Green, and there dined well, but a bad venison pasty at Sir W. Rider's. Good people they are, and good discourse; and his daughter, Middleton, a fine woman, discreet. Thence home, and to church again, and there preached Dean Harding; but, methinks, a bad, poor sermon, though proper for the time; nor eloquent, in saying at this time that the City is reduced from a large folio to a decimo-tertio. So to my office, there to write down my journal, and take leave of my brother, whom I sent back this afternoon, though rainy; which it hath not done a good while before. But I had no room or convenience for him here till my house is fitted; but I was very kind to him, and do take very well of him his journey. I did give him 40s. for his pocket, and so, he being gone, and, it presently raining, I was troubled for him, though it is good for the fire. Anon to Sir W. Penn's to bed, and made my boy Tom read me asleep.

10th. All the morning clearing our cellars, and breaking in pieces all my old lumber, to make room, and to prevent fire. And then to Sir W. Batten's, and dined; and there to hear that Sir W. Rider says that the town is full of the report of the wealth that is in his house, and would be glad that his friends would provide for the safety of their goods there. This made me get a cart; and thither, and there brought my money all away. Took a hackney-coach myself (the hackney-coaches now standing at Allgate). Much wealth indeed there is at his house. Blessed be God, I got all mine well thence, and lodged it in my office; but vexed to have all the world see it. . . .

17th. Up betimes, and shaved myself after a week's growth; but Lord! how ugly I was yesterday and how fine to-day! By water, seeing the City all the way, a sad sight indeed, much fire being still in. . . . Thence home a little to look after my people at work and back to Sir G. Carteret's to dinner; and thence, after some discourse with him upon our public accounts, I back home, and all the day with Harman and his people finishing the hangings and beds in my house, and the hangings will be as good as ever, and particularly in my new closet. They gone and I weary, my wife and I, and Balty and his wife, who come hither to-day to help us, to a barrel of oysters I sent from the river to-day, and so to bed.

[*Mr. Pepys at the Theatre*]

For a thorough and very interesting discussion of Mr. Pepys's theatergoing and the plays which he saw, see Helen McAfee, *Pepys on the Restoration Stage*, Yale University Press, 1916.

Jan. 3rd [1661]. . . . Thence to Will's, where Spicer and I eat our dinner of a roasted leg of pork which Will did give us, and after that to the theatre, where was acted "Beggar's Bush," it being very well done; and here the first time that ever I saw women come upon the stage. . . .

Jan. 28th. At the office all the morning; dine at home, and after dinner to Fleet Street, with my sword to Mr. Brigden (lately made Captain of the Auxiliaries) to be refreshed, and with him to an alehouse, where I met Mr. Davenport, and after some talk of Cromwell, Ireton, and Bradshaw's bodies being taken out of their graves to-day, I went to Mr. Crew's and thence to the theatre, where I saw again "The Lost Lady," which do now please me better than before; and here I sitting in a dark place, a lady spit backward upon me by a mistake, not seeing me, but after seeing her to be a very pretty lady, I was not troubled at it at all. . . .

Sept. 25th. . . . Hence, much against my nature and will, yet such is the power of the Devil over me I could not refuse it, to the theatre, and saw "The Merry Wives of Windsor," ill done. And that ended, with Sir W. Penn and Sir G. More to the tavern, and so home with him by coach, and after supper to prayers and to bed. . . .

Sept. 29th (Michaelmas Day) [1662]. . . . I sent for some dinner and there dined, Mrs. Margaret Penn being by, to whom I had spoke to go along with us to a play this afternoon, and then to the King's Theatre, where we saw "Midsummer Night's Dream," which I had never seen before, nor shall ever again, for it is the most insipid ridiculous play

11. **"Beggar's Bush,"** a comedy by Beaumont and Fletcher, 1622. 13. **women . . . upon the stage.** The first English professional actress was Mrs. Coleman, who took the part of Ianthe in Davenant's *The Siege of Rhodes*, at Rutland House, in 1656. The acting of female characters by women became increasingly common after the Restoration. Boys continued, however, to appear in female roles in some companies. 20. **Cromwell, Ireton, and Bradshaw's bodies.** Henry Ireton was a son-in-law of Cromwell and a general in the Parliamentary army. John Bradshaw was one of the judges who sentenced Charles I. The three bodies had been buried in Westminster Abbey. 23. **"The Lost Lady,"** a tragicomedy by Sir William Berkeley, who subsequently became Governor of Virginia.

that ever I saw in my life. I saw, I confess, some good dancing and some handsome women, which was all my pleasure.

Feb. 18th [1667]. . . . Thence away, and with my wife by coach to the Duke of York's playhouse, expecting a new play, and so stayed not no more than other people, but to the King's house, to "The Maid's Tragedy"; but vexed all the while with two talking ladies and Sir Charles Sedley; yet pleased to hear their discourse, he being a stranger. And one of the ladies would and did sit with her mask on, all the play, and, being exceeding witty as ever I heard woman, did talk most pleasantly with him; but was, I believe, a virtuous woman, and of quality. He would fain know who she was, but she would not tell; yet did give him many pleasant hints of her knowledge of him, by that means setting his brains at work to find out who she was, and did give him leave to use all means to find out who she was, but pulling off her mask. He was mighty witty, and she also making sport with him very inoffensively, that a more pleasant *rencontre* I never heard. But by that means lost the pleasure of the play wholly, to which now and then Sir Charles Sedley's exceptions against both words and pronouncing were very pretty. So home and to the office, did much business, then home, to supper, and to bed.

Nov. 2nd. Up, and to the office, where busy all the morning; at noon home, and after dinner my wife and Willett and I to the King's playhouse, and there saw "Henry the Fourth": and contrary to expectation, was pleased in nothing more than in Cartwright's speaking of Falstaff's "What is honour?" The house full of Parliament men, it being holiday with them: and it was observable how a gentleman of good habit, sitting just before us, eating of some fruit in the midst of the play, did drop down as dead, being choked; but with much ado Orange Moll did thrust her finger down his throat, and brought him to life again. After the play, we home, and I busy at the office late, and then home to supper and to bed.

John Dryden
1631–1700

There are greater poets than Dryden, but certainly none more versatile. Pope remarked that he could select from Dryden's works better specimens of every mode of poetry than any other English writer could supply. He was equally at home in dramatic, satiric, narrative, and didactic poetry, was one of the greatest of English translators, and one of the most accomplished writers of English prose. Dr. Johnson called him the father of English criticism. He was the undisputed king of English letters at his death. And yet, in spite of his prominence, we have surprisingly few facts about him outside of his own writings, and if he had died before he was fifty he would probably not be just now the subject of our consideration.

He was born at Aldwinkle, Northamptonshire, of a Puritan family, and was educated at Westminster School and at Trinity College, Cambridge. He began to try his hand at verse while at school, and produced some exercises in the "metaphysical" style. Shortly after his graduation he came to London to seek his fortune, and became secretary to his cousin, Sir Gilbert Pickering, Cromwell's chamberlain. He began his literary career in 1659 with his *Heroic Stanzas* on the death of Cromwell. It is interesting that the restoration of Charles II in the following year gave him his next occasion for a poem, *Astraea Redux*, in which he celebrated the return of peace and the King. He now settled down to writing plays for a living, and may fairly be called our first professional man of letters. His first play, *The Wild Gallant*, 1663, was a complete failure, but in 1665 he gained fame with *The Indian Emperor*, in which Nell Gwyn made her first appearance at the age of fifteen. He had meanwhile married Lady Elizabeth Howard, the sister of his friend and patron Sir Robert Howard, the "Crites" of his later *Essay of Dramatic Poesy*. A combination of important events furnished the occasion of his first long poem, *Annus Mirabilis*, 1667, in which he describes the war with the Dutch and the Great Fire of London. The

---

8–9. "The Maid's Tragedy," by Beaumont and Fletcher.

13. Cartwright's speaking. William Cartwright was one of Thomas Killigrew's company at the original establishment in Drury Lane. He died respectable and wealthy in 1678.
19. Orange Moll. Oranges were the chief refreshment in the Restoration theater. They were sold, usually for sixpence apiece, before the play and between the acts by the "orange women." "Orange Moll" was the name generally given to the head orange woman.

next year he achieved fame as a critic in his *Essay of Dramatic Poesy*, which is said to have been written during his absences from London on account of the plague.

The need of money kept Dryden's pen busy, and his life from now on has been described as "one long literary labor." He produced plays at the rate of three a year for an annual salary of about £300. In 1670 he was appointed poet laureate, and no holder of the laureateship ever did more to earn his salary. With it came also his appointment as Historiographer Royal. The stipends did not relieve him from the necessity of continuing his hack writing. In addition to new plays, he rewrote, or helped in revamping, several of Shakespeare's. He turned *Paradise Lost* into a rhymed opera, *The State of Innocence*, which, however, was never produced. Most of Dryden's plays are of the type known as heroic drama, in which the themes of beauty, love, and honor, and the struggles between them in the breasts of noble warrior-heroes and angelic heroines, are presented against a background of foreign battlefields, and with the rhetorical declamation of exaggerated emotions. The literary medium was the rhymed couplet, and careful attention was paid to the dramatic unities. In 1678, as if he were weary of heroics and rhymes, he produced in blank verse his greatest drama, *All for Love*, on the theme of Antony and Cleopatra.

It was in 1681, and in the midst of another national crisis, that his greatest satire was produced. Feeling was running strong against the Roman Catholic Duke of York, brother of the King and heir presumptive to the throne. The Earl of Shaftesbury became the leader of a plot to depose Charles in favor of his illegitimate son, the Duke of Monmouth. Dryden ingeniously adapted the Biblical story of David and his son Absalom to the circumstances, and published his first and greatest satire, the first part of *Absalom and Achitophel*, a few days before the trial of Shaftesbury for high treason. Other satires arose out of this, culminating in Dryden's *Mac Flecknoe*, 1682.

From political controversy Dryden turned in 1682 to religious and theological debate. His *Religio Laici*, published that year, is an exposition in verse of the reasons in favor of the Church of England. In 1687 he published *The Hind and the Panther*, in defense of the Roman Catholic faith, to which he had meanwhile become converted. Of the sincerity of his conversion, which took place about the time the Roman Catholic James II became king, there has naturally been some doubt. It must be said in his favor that he did not revert to Protestantism when William and Mary came in, although by doing so he could have retained both his laureateship and his pension. In his last years, out of pocket and out of favor, he busied himself with translations of the classics. At sixty-six, and in a single sitting, he wrote his ode "Alexander's Feast." His last poem, the *Secular Masque*, published in the year of his death, contains some of his most vigorous verse. He was, although a Roman Catholic, given burial by the side of Chaucer in Westminster Abbey, where his bust is among the most conspicuous in the Poets' Corner.

AH, FADING JOY

Ah, fading joy, how quickly art thou past!
   Yet we thy ruin haste.
As if the cares of human life were few,
   We seek out new;
And follow fate, that does too fast pursue.

See how on every bough the birds express
   In their sweet notes their happiness.
   They all enjoy and nothing spare,
But on their mother nature lay their care:
Why then should man, the lord of all below,   10
   Such troubles choose to know
As none of all his subjects undergo?

Hark, hark, the waters fall, fall, fall,
   And with a murmuring sound
Dash, dash, upon the ground,
   To gentle slumbers call.
          —from *The Indian Emperor*

YOU PLEASING DREAMS

You pleasing dreams of love and sweet delight,
Appear before this slumbering virgin's sight;
Soft visions set her free
From mournful piety.
Let her sad thoughts from heaven retire;
And let the melancholy love
Of those remoter joys above
Give place to your more sprightly fire.
Let purling streams be in her fancy seen,
And flowery meads, and vales of cheerful green;   10
And in the midst of deathless groves
Soft sighing wishes lie,
And smiling hopes fast by,
And just beyond 'em ever-laughing loves.
          —from *Tyrannic Love*

from ABSALOM AND ACHITOPHEL

Dryden, with great ingenuity, applies the Biblical story of the revolt of Absalom against his father, King David (II Samuel 13-18), to the plot of the young Duke of Monmouth against his father, Charles II. (See above, page 726.) The Earl of Shaftesbury, the leader of the Whigs, who instigated the plot, is Achitophel; Charles II is David; England is Israel; the English, the Jews; and so on. Dryden in his satire defends the King, at whose request he wrote the poem, and the Tories.

. . . The Jews, a headstrong, moody, murmuring race,   45
As ever tried the extent and stretch of grace;
God's pampered people, whom, debauched with ease,
No king could govern, nor no God could please
(Gods they had tried of every shape and size
That god-smiths could produce, or priests devise);   50
These Adam-wits, too fortunately free,
Began to dream they wanted liberty;
And when no rule, no precedent was found,
Of men by laws less circumscribed and bound,
They led their wild desires to woods and caves,
And thought that all but savages were slaves.
They too, when Saul was dead, without a blow,
Made foolish Ishbosheth the crown forego;
Who banished David did from Hebron bring,
And with a general shout proclaimed him King: 60
Those very Jews, who, at their very best,
Their humour more than loyalty expressed,
Now wondered why so long they had obeyed
An idol monarch, which their hands had made;
Thought they might ruin him they could create,
Or melt him to that golden calf, a State.
But these were random bolts; no formed design,
Nor interest made the factious crowd to join:
The sober part of Israel, free from stain,
Well knew the value of a peaceful reign;   70
And, looking backward with a wise affright,
Saw seams of wounds, dishonest to the sight:
In contemplation of whose ugly scars
They cursed the memory of civil wars.
The moderate sort of men, thus qualified,
Inclined the balance to the better side;
And David's mildness managed it so well,
The bad found no occasion to rebel.
But when to sin our biassed nature leans,
The careful Devil is still at hand with means;   80
And providently pimps for ill desires:
The Good Old Cause revived, a plot requires.
Plots, true or false, are necessary things,
To raise up commonwealths and ruin kings. . . .

This plot, which failed for want of common sense,   134
Had yet a deep and dangerous consequence:
For, as when raging fevers boil the blood,
The standing lake soon floats into a flood,
And every hostile humour, which before
Slept quiet in its channels, bubbles o'er;
So several factions from this first ferment   140
Work up to foam, and threat the government.
Some by their friends, more by themselves thought wise,
Opposed the power to which they could not rise.
Some had in courts been great, and thrown from thence,
Like fiends were hardened in impenitence;
Some, by their Monarch's fatal mercy, grown
From pardoned rebel kinsmen to the throne,
Were raised in power and public office high;
Strong bands, if bands ungrateful men could tie.
Of these the false Achitophel was first;   150
A name to all succeeding ages curst:
For close designs and crooked counsels fit;
Sagacious, bold, and turbulent of wit;
Restless, unfixed in principles and place;
In power unpleased, impatient of disgrace:
A fiery soul, which, working out its way,
Fretted the pigmy body to decay,
And o'er-informed the tenement of clay.
A daring pilot in extremity;
Pleased with the danger, when the waves went high,   160
He sought the storms; but, for a calm unfit,
Would steer too near the sands, to boast his wit.
Great wits are sure to madness near allied,
And thin partitions do their bounds divide;
Else why should he, with wealth and honour blest,
Refuse his age the needful hours of rest?
Punish a body which he could not please;
Bankrupt of life, yet prodigal of ease?

---

51. Adam-wits, persons who, like Adam in the Garden of Eden, were not contented with their fortunate lot. **57. Saul,** Oliver Cromwell. **58. Ishbosheth,** Richard Cromwell, who succeeded Oliver. **59. Hebron,** probably Scotland, where Charles was crowned king before his coronation in London (Jerusalem). **66. golden calf.** See Exodus 32:1-6. **75. thus qualified,** of such a disposition.

82. The Good Old Cause, that of the Commonwealth. **134. This plot,** the alleged Popish Plot of 1678, about which the Whigs were, or pretended to be, so concerned. See page 529. **150. the false Achitophel.** The Earl of Shaftesbury (Anthony Ashley Cooper), who was leading the plot against Charles, had once been a trusted adviser of the King.

And all to leave what with his toil he won,
To that unfeathered two-legged thing, a son; 170
Got, while his soul did huddled notions try,
And born a shapeless lump, like anarchy.
In friendship false, implacable in hate;
Resolved to ruin or to rule the State.
To compass this the triple bond he broke,
The pillars of the public safety shook,
And fitted Israel for a foreign yoke;
Then seized with fear, yet still affecting fame,
Usurped a patriot's all-atoning name.
So easy still it proves in factious times, 180
With public zeal to cancel private crimes.
How safe is treason, and how sacred ill,
Where none can sin against the people's will!
Where crowds can wink, and no offence be known,
Since in another's guilt they find their own!
Yet fame deserved no enemy can grudge;
The statesman we abhor, but praise the judge.
In Israel's courts ne'er sat an Abbethdin
With more discerning eyes, or hands more clean;
Unbribed, unsought, the wretched to redress; 190
Swift of despatch, and easy of access.
Oh, had he been content to serve the crown,
With virtues proper only to the gown;
Or had the rankness of the soil been freed
From cockle, that oppressed the noble seed;
David for him his tuneful harp had strung,
And Heaven had wanted one immortal song.
But wild Ambition loves to slide, not stand,
And Fortune's ice prefers to Virtue's land.
Achitophel, grown weary to possess 200
A lawful fame, and lazy happiness,
Disdained the golden fruit to gather free,
And lent the crowd his arm to shake the tree.
Now, manifest of crimes contrived long since,
He stood at bold defiance with his Prince;
Held up the buckler of the people's cause
Against the crown, and skulked behind the laws.
The wished occasion of the Plot he takes;
Some circumstances finds, but more he makes.
By buzzing emissaries fills the ears 210
Of listening crowds with jealousies and fears
Of arbitrary counsels brought to light,
And proves the King himself a Jebusite.
Weak arguments! which yet he knew full well
Were strong with people easy to rebel.
For, governed by the moon, the giddy Jews
Tread the same track when she the prime renews;
And once in twenty years, their scribes record,
By natural instinct they change their lord.
Achitophel still wants a chief, and none 220
Was found so fit as warlike Absalom:
Not that he wished his greatness to create
(For politicians neither love nor hate),
But, for he knew his title not allowed,
Would keep him still depending on the crowd,
That kingly power, thus ebbing out, might be
Drawn to the dregs of a democracy.
Him he attempts with studied arts to please,
And sheds his venom with such words as these:
"Auspicious prince, at whose nativity 230
Some royal planet ruled the southern sky;
Thy longing country's darling and desire;
Their cloudy pillar and their guardian fire,
Their second Moses, whose extended wand
Divides the seas and shows the promised land;
Whose dawning day in every distant age
Has exercised the sacred prophet's rage:
The people's prayer, the glad diviners' theme,
The young men's vision, and the old men's dream!
Thee, Saviour, thee, the nation's vows confess, 240
And, never satisfied with seeing, bless:
Swift unbespoken pomps thy steps proclaim,
And stammering babes are taught to lisp thy name.
How long wilt thou the general joy detain,
Starve and defraud the people of thy reign?
Content ingloriously to pass thy days
Like one of virtue's fools that feeds on praise;
Till thy fresh glories, which now shine so bright,
Grow stale and tarnish with our daily sight.
Believe me, royal youth, thy fruit must be 250
Or gathered ripe, or rot upon the tree.
Heaven has to all allotted, soon or late,
Some lucky revolution of their fate;
Whose motions if we watch and guide with skill
(For human good depends on human will),
Our fortune rolls as from a smooth descent,
And from the first impression takes the bent;
But if unseized she glides away like wind,
And leaves repenting folly far behind.
Now, now she meets you with a glorious prize, 260
And spreads her locks before her as she flies.
Had thus old David, from whose loins you spring,
Not dared, when Fortune called him, to be King,
At Gath an exile he might still remain,
And Heaven's anointing oil had been in vain.
Let his successful youth your hopes engage;
But shun the example of declining age:
Behold him setting in his western skies,
The shadows lengthening as the vapours rise.

171. Got, begot. **huddled,** confused. **175. triple bond,** the alliance, formed in 1667, which bound England, Sweden, and the Dutch Republic against France. It was broken in 1670 by Charles, when England allied herself with France against Holland. Dryden's accusaton of Shaftesbury is, in this instance, unjust. **188. Abbethdin,** chief justice of the Jewish court. Shaftesbury had been Lord Chancellor.

264. Gath, Brussels.

JOHN DRYDEN

He is not now, as when on Jordan's sand 270
The joyful people thronged to see him land,
Covering the beach, and blackening all the strand;
But, like the Prince of Angels, from his height
Comes tumbling downward with diminished light;
Betrayed by one poor Plot to public scorn
(Our only blessing since his curst return),
Those heaps of people which one sheaf did bind,
Blown off and scattered by a puff of wind.
What strength can he to your designs oppose,
Naked of friends, and round beset with foes? 280
If Pharaoh's doubtful succour he should use,
A foreign aid would more incense the Jews;
Proud Egypt would dissembled friendship bring,
Foment the war, but not support the King:
Nor would the royal party e'er unite
With Pharaoh's arms to assist the Jebusite;
Or if they should, their interest soon would break,
And with such odious aid make David weak.
All sorts of men by my successful arts,
Abhorring kings, estrange their altered hearts 290
From David's rule: and 'tis the general cry,
'Religion, commonwealth, and liberty.'
If you, as champion of the public good,
Add to their arms a chief of royal blood,
What may not Israel hope, and what applause
Might such a general gain by such a cause?
Not barren praise alone, that gaudy flower
Fair only to the sight, but solid power;
And nobler is a limited command,
Given by the love of all your native land, 300
Than a successive title, long and dark,
Drawn from the mouldy rolls of Noah's ark."

 What cannot praise effect in mighty minds,
When flattery soothes, and when ambition blinds!
Desire of power, on earth a vicious weed,
Yet, sprung from high, is of celestial seed;
In God 'tis glory; and when men aspire,
'Tis but a spark too much of heavenly fire.
The ambitious youth, too covetous of fame,
Too full of angels' metal in his frame, 310
Unwarily was led from virtues ways,
Made drunk with honour, and debauched with praise.
Half loth and half consenting to the ill
(For loyal blood within him struggled still),
He thus replied: "And what pretence have I
To take up arms for public liberty?
My father governs with unquestioned right;
The faith's defender, and mankind's delight;
Good, gracious, just, observant of the laws:
And Heaven by wonders has espoused his cause. 320
Whom has he wronged in all his peaceful reign?
Who sues for justice to his throne in vain?
What millions has he pardoned of his foes
Whom just revenge did to his wrath expose?
Mild, easy, humble, studious of our good,
Inclined to mercy, and averse from blood;
If mildness ill with stubborn Israel suit,
His crime is God's belovèd attribute.
What could he gain, his people to betray
Or change his right for arbitrary sway? 330
Let haughty Pharaoh curse with such a reign
His fruitful Nile, and yoke a servile train.
If David's rule Jerusalem displease,
The dog-star heats their brains to this disease.
Why then should I, encouraging the bad,
Turn rebel and run popularly mad?
Were he a tyrant, who by lawless might
Oppressed the Jews and raised the Jebusite,
Well might I mourn; but nature's holy bands
Would curb my spirits and restrain my hands: 340
The people might assert their liberty,
But what was right in them were crime in me.
His favour leaves me nothing to require,
Prevents my wishes, and outruns desire.
What more can I expect while David lives?
All but his kingly diadem he gives:
And that"—but there he paused; then sighing said—
"Is justly destined for a worthier head.
For when my father from his toils shall rest
And late augment the number of the blest, 350
His lawful issue shall the throne ascend,
Or the collateral line, where that shall end.
His brother, though oppressed with vulgar spite,
Yet dauntless, and secure of native right,
Of every royal virtue stands possessed;
Still dear to all the bravest and the best.
His courage foes, his friends his truth proclaim;
His loyalty the King, the world his fame.
His mercy even the offending crowd will find,
For sure he comes of a forgiving kind. 360
Why should I then repine at Heaven's decree,
Which gives me no pretence to royalty?
Yet oh that fate, propitiously inclined,
Had raised my birth, or had debased my mind;
To my large soul not all her treasure lent,
And then betrayed it to a mean descent!
I find, I find my mounting spirits bold,
And David's part disdains my mother's mould.
Why am I scanted by a niggard birth?
My soul disclaims the kindred of her earth 370
And, made for empire, whispers me within,

 270. **on Jordan's sand,** a reference to the landing of Charles at Dover on May 1, 1660. 281. **Pharaoh's doubtful succour.** Charles was a pensioner of Louis XIV (Pharaoh), whose financial aid helped to make him independent of Parliament.

'Desire of greatness is a god-like sin.'"
  Him staggering so when Hell's dire agent found,
While fainting Virtue scarce maintained her ground,
He pours fresh forces in, and thus replies:
  "The eternal God, supremely good and wise,
Imparts not these prodigious gifts in vain:
What wonders are reserved to bless your reign!
Against your will, your arguments have shown,
Such virtue's only given to guide a throne.   380
Not that your father's mildness I contemn;
But manly force becomes the diadem.
'Tis true he grants the people all they crave
And more, perhaps, than subjects ought to have:
For lavish grants suppose a monarch tame,
And more his goodness than his wit proclaim.
But when should people strive their bonds to break,
If not when kings are negligent or weak?
Let him give on till he can give no more,
The thrifty Sanhedrin shall keep him poor;   390
And every shekel which he can receive,
Shall cost a limb of his prerogative.
To ply him with new plots shall be my care;
Or plunge him deep in some expensive war;
Which when his treasury can no more supply,
He must, with the remains of kingship, buy.
His faithful friends, our jealousies and fears
Call Jebusites, and Pharaoh's pensioners;
Whom when our fury from his aid has torn,
He shall be naked left to public scorn.   400
The next successor, whom I fear and hate,
My arts have made obnoxious to the state;
Turned all his virtues to his overthrow,
And gained our elders to pronounce a foe.
His right, for sums of necessary gold,
Shall first be pawned, and afterward be sold;
Till time shall ever-wanting David draw,
To pass your doubtful title into law:
If not, the people have a right supreme
To make their kings; for kings are made for them.   410
All empire is no more than power in trust,
Which, when resumed, can be no longer just.
Succession, for the general good designed,
In its own wrong a nation cannot bind;
If altering that the people can relieve,
Better one suffer than a nation grieve.
The Jews well know their power: ere Saul they chose,
God was their King, and God they durst depose.
Urge now your piety, your filial name,
A father's right, and fear of future fame;   420

    390. **Sanhedrin**, the supreme council in ancient Jerusalem. Here, of course, it signifies the British Parliament.

The public good, that universal call,
To which even Heaven submitted, answers all.
Nor let his love enchant your generous mind;
'Tis Nature's trick to propagate her kind.
Our fond begetters, who would never die,
Love but themselves in their posterity.
Or let his kindness by the effects be tried,
Or let him lay his vain pretence aside.
God said he loved your father; could he bring
A better proof, than to anoint him King?   430
It surely showed he loved the shepherd well,
Who gave so fair a flock as Israel.
Would David have you thought his darling son?
What means he, then, to alienate the crown?
The name of godly he may blush to bear:
'Tis after God's own heart to cheat his heir.
He to his brother gives supreme command;
To you a legacy of barren land,
Perhaps the old harp, on which he thrums his lays,
Or some dull Hebrew ballad in your praise.   440
Then the next heir, a prince severe and wise,
Already looks on you with jealous eyes;
Sees through the thin disguises of your arts,
And marks your progress in the people's hearts.
Though now his mighty soul its grief contains,
He meditates revenge who least complains;
And, like a lion, slumbering in the way,
Or sleep dissembling, while he waits his prey,
His fearless foes within his distance draws,
Constrains his roaring, and contracts his paws;   450
Till at the last, his time for fury found,
He shoots with sudden vengeance from the ground;
The prostrate vulgar passes o'er and spares,
But with a lordly rage his hunter tears.
Your case no tame expedients will afford:
Resolve on death, or conquest by the sword,
Which for no less a stake than life you draw;
And self-defence is Nature's eldest law.
Leave the warm people no considering time;
For then rebellion may be thought a crime.   460
Prevail yourself of what occasion gives,
But try your title while your father lives;
And that your arms may have a fair pretence,
Proclaim you take them in the King's defence;
Whose sacred life each minute would expose
To plots, from seeming friends, and secret foes.
And who can sound the depth of David's soul?
Perhaps his fear his kindness may control.
He fears his brother, though he loves his son,
For plighted vows too late to be undone.   470
If so, by force he wishes to be gained,
Like women's lechery, to seem constrained:
Doubt not; but when he most affects the frown,
Commit a pleasing rape upon the crown.

JOHN DRYDEN

Secure his person to secure your cause:
They who possess the Prince, possess the laws."
    He said, and this advice above the rest,
With Absalom's mild nature suited best:
Unblamed of life (ambition set aside),
Not stained with cruelty, nor puffed with pride, 480
How happy had he been, if destiny
Had higher placed his birth, or not so high!
His kingly virtues could have claimed a throne,
And blest all other countries but his own.
But charming greatness since so few refuse,
'Tis juster to lament him than accuse.
Strong were his hopes a rival to remove,
With blandishments to gain the public love;
To head the faction while their zeal was hot,
And popularly prosecute the plot. 490
To further this, Achitophel unites
The malcontents of all the Israelites;
Whose differing parties he could wisely join,
For several ends, to serve the same design:
The best (and of the princes some were such),
Who thought the power of monarchy too much;
Mistaken men, and patriots in their hearts;
Not wicked, but seduced by impious arts.
By these the springs of property were bent,
And wound so high, they cracked the government. . . . 500

Some of their chiefs were princes of the land: 543
In the first rank of these did Zimri stand;
A man so various, that he seemed to be
Not one, but all mankind's epitome:
Stiff in opinions, always in the wrong;
Was everything by starts, and nothing long;
But, in the course of one revolving moon,
Was chemist, fiddler, statesman, and buffoon: 550
Then all for women, painting, rhyming, drinking,
Besides ten thousand freaks that died in thinking.
Blest madman, who could every hour employ,
With something new to wish, or to enjoy!
Railing and praising were his usual themes;
And both (to show his judgment) in extremes:
So over-violent, or over-civil,
That every man, with him, was God or Devil.
In squandering wealth was his peculiar art:
Nothing went unrewarded but desert. 560
Beggared by fools, whom still he found too late,
He had his jest, and they had his estate.
He laughed himself from court; then sought relief
By forming parties, but could ne'er be chief;

For, spite of him, the weight of business fell
On Absalom and wise Achitophel:
Thus, wicked but in will, of means bereft,
He left not faction, but of that was left. . . .

from THRENODIA AUGUSTALIS

A FUNERAL PINDARIC POEM TO THE HAPPY MEMORY OF KING CHARLES II

15

A warlike Prince ascends the regal state,
A Prince long exercised by Fate: 430
Long may he keep, though he obtains it late.
Heroes in Heaven's peculiar mould are cast,
They and their poets are not formed in haste;
Man was the first in God's design, and man was made the last.
False heroes, made by flattery so,
Heaven can strike out, like sparkles, at a blow;
But ere a Prince is to perfection brought,
He costs Omnipotence a second thought.
    With toil and sweat,
    With hardening cold and forming heat 440
    The Cyclops did their strokes repeat,
Before the impenetrable shield was wrought.
    It looks as if the Maker would not own
    The noble work for his,
Before 'twas tried and found a masterpiece.

LINES PRINTED UNDER THE ENGRAVED PORTRAIT OF MILTON

These lines were engraved, without the author's name, under the portrait of Milton in the frontispiece of Tonson's folio edition (the fourth edition) of *Paradise Lost* in 1688.

Three poets, in three distant ages born,
Greece, Italy, and England did adorn.
The first in loftiness of thought surpassed,
The next in majesty, in both the last:
The force of Nature could no farther go;
To make a third she joined the former two.

---

544. **Zimri,** George Villiers, Duke of Buckingham, whose political and literary philosophies were equally disliked by Dryden. The author thought his character of Zimri "worth the whole poem."

429. **A warlike Prince,** James II, who succeeded his brother, Charles II, in 1685. James's reign, in spite of Dryden's prayer, was one of the shortest in English history He was deposed in 1688 and fled to France. 441. **The Cyclops,** the giants or Titans of Greek mythology who had only one eye, in their foreheads. They are represented in various legends as assistants of Hephaestus (Vulcan) and makers of the metal armor and ornaments of gods and heroes.

ALEXANDER'S FEAST;

OR, THE POWER OF MUSIC

An Ode in Honour of St. Cecilia's Day

This ode was composed in 1697 at the request of a London society which had been organized in 1683 to celebrate annually the day of St. Cecilia (November 22), patron saint of music. Dryden had already composed an earlier ode for the society in 1687.

1

'Twas at the royal feast, for Persia won
    By Philip's warlike son:
    Aloft in awful state,
    The godlike hero sate
    On his imperial throne;
His valiant peers were placed around,
Their brows with roses and with myrtles bound
(So should desert in arms be crowned).
The lovely Thais, by his side,
Sat like a blooming Eastern bride,   10
In flower of youth and beauty's pride.
    Happy, happy, happy pair!
      None but the brave,
      None but the brave,
    None but the brave deserves the fair.

Chorus

Happy, happy, happy pair!
  None but the brave,
  None but the brave,
None but the brave deserves the fair.

2

    Timotheus, placed on high   20
      Amid the tuneful quire,
With flying fingers touched the lyre:
  The trembling notes ascend the sky,
    And heavenly joys inspire.
The song began from Jove,
Who left his blissful seats above,
(Such is the power of mighty love).
A dragon's fiery form belied the god:
Sublime on radiant spires he rode,
When he to fair Olympia pressed;   30
  And while he sought her snowy breast,
Then round her slender waist he curled,
And stamped an image of himself, a sovereign of the world.
  The listening crowd admire the lofty sound:
"A present deity!" they shout around;
"A present deity!" the vaulted roofs rebound.
    With ravished ears
    The monarch hears;
    Assumes the god,
    Affects to nod,   40
And seems to shake the spheres.

Chorus

    With ravished ears
    The monarch hears;
    Assumes the god,
    Affects to nod,
And seems to shake the spheres.

3

The praise of Bacchus then the sweet musician sung,
  Of Bacchus ever fair and ever young.
    The jolly god in triumph comes:
    Sound the trumpets, beat the drums!   50
    Flushed with a purple grace,
    He shows his honest face:
Now give the hautboys breath! he comes, he comes!
  Bacchus, ever fair and young,
  Drinking joys did first ordain:
Bacchus' blessings are a treasure;
Drinking is the soldier's pleasure;
    Rich the treasure,
    Sweet the pleasure,
  Sweet is pleasure after pain.   60

Chorus

Bacchus' blessings are a treasure;
Drinking is the soldier's pleasure;
    Rich the treasure,
    Sweet the pleasure;
  Sweet is pleasure after pain.

4

  Soothed with the sound, the king grew vain,
    Fought all his battles o'er again,
And thrice he routed all his foes, and thrice he slew the slain.
The master saw the madness rise,
His glowing cheeks, his ardent eyes;   70
And while he heaven and earth defied,
Changed his hand and checked his pride.
    He chose a mournful Muse,
    Soft pity to infuse:

---

1. royal feast, in celebration of Alexander's victory at Arbela, 351 B.C.   **9. Thais**, the Greek courtesan who accompanied Alexander back to Asia.   **20. Timotheus**, Alexander's favorite musician.   **25. began from Jove**, proceeded from the story about Jove which immediately follows.   **28. belied**, disguised, concealed.   **29. Sublime on radiant spires**, aloft on radiant spirals, or coils.   **30. Olympia**, Olympias, the mother of Alexander.

41. seems to shake the spheres, seems, like Jove, to shake the heavens with his nod.   **52. honest**, handsome.   **53. hautboys**, oboes.   **72. his pride**, Alexander's pride.

He sung Darius great and good,
　By too severe a fate,
Fallen, fallen, fallen, fallen,
　Fallen from his high estate,
And weltering in his blood;
Deserted at his utmost need　　　　　　　　　80
By those his former bounty fed,
On the bare earth exposed he lies,
With not a friend to close his eyes.
With downcast looks the joyless victor sate,
　Revolving in his altered soul
　　The various turns of chance below;
　And now and then a sigh he stole,
　　And tears began to flow.

Chorus

　Revolving in his altered soul
　　The various turns of chance below;　　　90
　And now and then a sigh he stole,
　　And tears began to flow.

5

The mighty master smiled to see
That love was in the next degree;
'Twas but a kindred sound to move,
For pity melts the mind to love.
　Softly sweet, in Lydian measures,
　Soon he soothed his soul to pleasures.
"War," he sung, "is toil and trouble;
Honour, but an empty bubble;　　　　　　　100
　Never ending, still beginning,
　Fighting still, and still destroying:
　If the world be worth thy winning,
　Think, O think it worth enjoying.
　Lovely Thais sits beside thee,
　Take the good the gods provide thee."
The many rend the skies with loud applause;
So Love was crowned, but Music won the cause.
　The prince, unable to conceal his pain,
　　Gazed on the fair,　　　　　　　　　110
　　Who caused his care,
　And sighed and looked, sighed and looked,
　Sighed and looked, and sighed again;
At length, with love and wine at once oppressed,
The vanquished victor sunk upon her breast.

Chorus

　The prince, unable to conceal his pain,
　　Gazed on the fair,
　　Who caused his care,
　And sighed and looked, sighed and looked,
　Sighed and looked, and sighed again;　　120
At length, with love and wine at once oppressed,
The vanquished victor sunk upon her breast.

6

Now strike the golden lyre again:
A louder yet, and yet a louder strain.
Break his bands of sleep asunder,
And rouse him, like a rattling peal of thunder.
　Hark, hark! the horrid sound
　　Has raised up his head;
　　As awaked from the dead,
　And amazed, he stares around.　　　　　130
"Revenge, revenge!" Timotheus cries;
　"See the Furies arise!
　See the snakes that they rear,
　How they hiss in their hair,
And the sparkles that flash from their eyes!
　Behold a ghastly band,
　Each a torch in his hand!
Those are Grecian ghosts, that in battle were slain,
　　And unburied remain
　　Inglorious on the plain:　　　　　　140
　　Give the vengeance due
　　To the valiant crew!
Behold how they toss their torches on high,
　How they point to the Persian abodes,
And glittering temples of their hostile gods!"
The princes applaud with a furious joy,
And the king seized a flambeau with zeal to destroy;
　Thais led the way,
　To light him to his prey,
And, like another Helen, fired another Troy.　150

Chorus

And the king seized a flambeau with zeal to destroy;
　Thais led the way,
　To light him to his prey,
And, like another Helen, fired another Troy.

7

　Thus, long ago,
Ere heaving bellows learned to blow,
　While organs yet were mute,
　Timotheus, to his breathing flute
　　And sounding lyre,
Could swell the soul to rage or kindle soft desire.　160
　At last divine Cecilia came,
　Inventress of the vocal frame:

148. Thais led the way. After the capture of Persepolis Alexander set fire to the palace of the city. There is little authority for the legend that it was in the revelry of a banquet and at the instigation of Thais.　**162. Inventress of the vocal frame.** Although St. Cecilia had long been associated with the organ in art and legend, no one before Dryden seems to have credited her with its invention.

75. Darius, king of Persia, conquered by Alexander. The unfortunate king was stabbed by one of his companions as Alexander was on the point of capturing him.　**97. Lydian measures.** See note 136 on page 646.

The sweet enthusiast, from her sacred store,
   Enlarged the former narrow bounds,
   And added length to solemn sounds,
With Nature's mother-wit, and arts unknown before.
   Let old Timotheus yield the prize,
   Or both divide the crown:
   He raised a mortal to the skies;
     She drew an angel down.   170

Grand Chorus

   At last divine Cecilia came,
   Inventress of the vocal frame:
The sweet enthusiast, from her sacred store,
   Enlarged the former narrow bounds,
   And added length to solemn sounds,
With Nature's mother-wit, and arts unknown before.
   Let old Timotheus yield the prize,
   Or both divide the crown:
   He raised a mortal to the skies;
     She drew an angel down.   180

from AN ESSAY OF DRAMATIC POESY

The essay takes the form of a conversation among four friends: Eugenius (Sir Charles Sackville, later Earl of Dorset); Crites (Sir Robert Howard, Dryden's brother-in-law); Lisideius (Sir Charles Sedley); and Neander (Dryden). They are represented as boating on the Thames on the day that the English and the Dutch fleets were fighting in the mouth of the river (June 3, 1665). As they leave the sound of the guns behind, the conversation turns on the respective merits of the French and the English drama and of the earlier and later English drama. This extract, in which Neander is speaking, is taken from the last third of the essay.

TO begin, then, with Shakespeare. He was the man who of all modern, and perhaps ancient poets, had the largest and most comprehensive soul. All the images of Nature were still present to him, and he drew them, not laboriously, but luckily; when he describes anything, you more than see it, you feel it too. Those who accuse him to have wanted learning give him the greater commendation: he was naturally learned. He needed not the spectacles of books to read Nature; he looked inwards, and found her there. I cannot say he is everywhere alike; were he so, I should do him injury to compare him with the greatest of mankind. He is many times flat, insipid; his comic wit degenerating into clenches, his serious swelling into bombast. But he is always great when some great occasion is presented to him; no man can say he ever had a fit subject for his wit and did not raise himself as high above the rest of poets,

Quantum lenta solent inter viburna cupressi.

The consideration of this made Mr. Hales of Eton say, that there is no subject of which any poet ever writ, but he would produce it much better done in Shakespeare; and however others are now more generally preferred before him, yet the age wherein he lived, which had contemporaries with him Fletcher and Jonson, never equalled them to him in their esteem: and in the last King's court, when Ben's reputation was at highest, Sir John Suckling, and with him the greater part of the courtiers, set our Shakespeare far above him.

"Beaumont and Fletcher, of whom I am next to speak, had, with the advantage of Shakespeare's wit, which was their precedent, great natural gifts, improved by study: Beaumont especially being so accurate a judge of plays, that Ben Jonson, while he lived, submitted all his writings to his censure, and, 'tis thought, used his judgment in correcting, if not contriving, all his plots. What value he had for him, appears by the verses he writ to him; and therefore I need speak no farther of it. The first play that brought Fletcher and him in esteem was their *Philaster:* for, before that, they had written two or three very unsuccessfully, as the like is reported of Ben Jonson, before he writ *Every Man in His Humour.* Their plots were generally more regular than Shakespeare's, especially those that were made before Beaumont's death; and they understood and imitated the conversation of gentlemen much better; whose wild debaucheries, and quickness of wit in repartees, no poet before them could paint as they have done. Humour, which Ben Jonson derived from particular persons, they made it their business not to describe: they represented all the passions very lively, but above all, love. I am apt to believe the English language in them arrived to its highest perfection: what words have since been taken in are rather superfluous than ornamental. Their plays are now the most pleasant and frequent entertainments of the stage; two of theirs being acted through

---

170. **She drew an angel down.** No authority has been found for Dryden's representation of St. Cecilia as having the power to draw an angel to her by her music.   **42. still,** always.   **4. clenches,** puns.   **9. Quantum . . . cupressi.** As cypresses tower among the humbler trees of the wayside. **10. Mr. Hales,** John Hales, fellow of Eton, and author of *The Golden Remains,* 1659.   **41. Humour,** the portrayal of eccentricities of character.

the year for one of Shakespeare's or Jonson's: the reason is, because there is a certain gaiety in their comedies, and pathos in their more serious plays, which suit generally with all men's humours. Shakespeare's language is likewise a little obsolete, and Ben Jonson's wit comes short of theirs.

"As for Jonson, to whose character I am now arrived, if we look upon him while he was himself (for his last plays were but his dotages), I think him the most learned and judicious writer which any theatre ever had. He was a most severe judge of himself, as well as others. One cannot say he wanted wit, but rather that he was frugal of it. In his works you find little to retrench or alter. Wit, and language, and humour also in some measure we had before him; but something of art was wanting to the drama till he came. He managed his strength to more advantage than any who preceded him. You seldom find him making love in any of his scenes, or endeavouring to move the passions; his genius was too sullen and saturnine to do it gracefully, especially when he knew he came after those who had performed both to such an height. Humour was his proper sphere; and in that he delighted most to represent mechanic people. He was deeply conversant in the ancients, both Greek and Latin, and he borrowed boldly from them: there is scarcely a poet or historian among the Roman authors of those times whom he has not translated in *Sejanus* and *Catiline*. But he has done his robberies so openly, that one may see he fears not to be taxed by any law. He invades authors like a monarch; and what would be theft in other poets is only victory in him. With the spoils of these writers he so represents old Rome to us, in its rites, ceremonies, and customs, that if one of their poets had written either of his tragedies, we had seen less of it than in him. If there was any fault in his language, 'twas that he weaved it too closely and laboriously, in his comedies especially: perhaps, too, he did a little too much to Romanize our tongue, leaving the words which he translated almost as much Latin as when he found them: wherein, though he learnedly followed their language, he did not enough comply with the idiom of ours. If I would compare him with Shakespeare, I must acknowledge him the more correct poet, but Shakespeare the greater wit. Shakespeare was the Homer, or father of our dramatic poets; Jonson was the Virgil, the pattern of elaborate writing; I admire him, but I love Shakespeare. To conclude of him; as he has given us the most correct plays, so in the precepts which he has laid down in his *Discoveries*, we have as many and profitable rules for perfecting the stage, as any wherewith the French can furnish us. . . ."

from PREFACE TO THE FABLES

I PROCEED to Ovid and Chaucer, considering the former only in relation to the latter. With Ovid ended the Golden Age of the Roman tongue; from Chaucer the purity of the English tongue began. The manners of the poets were not unlike. Both of them were well-bred, well-natured, amorous, and libertine, at least in their writings; it may be also in their lives. Their studies were the same, philosophy and philology. Both of them were knowing in astronomy; of which Ovid's books of the *Roman Feasts* and Chaucer's *Treatise of the Astrolabe* are sufficient witnesses. But Chaucer was likewise an astrologer, as were Virgil, Horace, Persius, and Manilius. Both writ with wonderful facility and clearness; neither were great inventors: for Ovid only copied the Grecian fables, and most of Chaucer's stories were taken from his Italian contemporaries, or their predecessors. Boccace his *Decameron* was first published, and from thence our Englishman has borrowed many of his *Canterbury Tales;* yet that of Palamon and Arcite was written, in all probability, by some Italian wit, in a former age, as I shall prove hereafter. The tale of Griselda was the invention of Petrarch; by him sent to Boccace, from whom it came to Chaucer. *Troilus and Criseyde* was also written by a Lombard author, but much amplified by our English translator, as well as beautified; the genius of our countrymen, in general, rather being to improve an invention than to invent themselves, as is evident not only in our poetry but in many of our manufactures. I find I have anticipated already, and taken up from Boccace before I come to him; but there is so much less behind; and I am of the temper of most kings, who love to be in debt, are all for present money, no matter how they pay it afterwards; besides, the nature of a preface is rambling, never wholly out of the way, nor in it.

25. **mechanic people,** working people, tradesmen.

6. **Ovid . . . Chaucer.** The discussion of Ovid and Chaucer follows that of Homer.   14. **philology.** Philology here has not its present meaning, but connotes the study of literature and polite learning in general.   24–25. **from thence . . . borrowed.** Modern scholarship has shown that Chaucer probably did not know the *Decameron*, although he was acquainted with other works of Boccaccio.   29. **the invention of Petrarch.** Dryden is also in error here. Petrarch, as is now well known, took the story of Griselda from the last novella of the *Decameron*, and Chaucer's version is based on Petrarch's Latin version, or possibly some French translation of it.   30–31. **Troilus and Criseyde.** The main elements of Chaucer's poem came from Boccaccio's *Filostrato*. Dryden is misled by Chaucer's statement that he is following "myn auctor called Lollius," who remains unidentified. It has been suggested that Chaucer did not know who the author of *Filostrato* was.

This I have learned from the practice of honest Montaigne, and return at my pleasure to Ovid and Chaucer, of whom I have little more to say.

Both of them built on the inventions of other men; yet since Chaucer had something of his own, as *The Wife of Bath's Tale*, *The Cock and the Fox*, which I have translated, and some others, I may justly give our countryman the precedence in that part; since I can remember nothing of Ovid which was wholly his. Both of them understood the manners, under which name I comprehend the passions, and, in a larger sense the descriptions of persons, and their very habits. For an example, I see Baucis and Philemon as perfectly before me, as if some ancient painter had drawn them; and all the pilgrims in the *Canterbury Tales*, their humours, their features, and the very dress, as distinctly as if I had supped with them at the Tabard in Southwark. Yet even there, too, the figures of Chaucer are much more lively, and set in a better light; which though I have not time to prove, yet I appeal to the reader, and am sure he will clear me from partiality. The thoughts and words remain to be considered in the comparison of the two poets, and I have saved myself one half of that labour, by owning that Ovid lived when the Roman tongue was in its meridian; Chaucer, in the dawning of our language; therefore that part of the comparison stands not on an equal foot, any more than the diction of Ennius and Ovid, or of Chaucer and our present English. The words are given up, as a post not to be defended in our poet, because he wanted the modern art of fortifying. The thoughts remain to be considered; and they are to be measured only by their propriety; that is, as they flow more or less naturally from the persons described, on such and such occasions. The vulgar judges, which are nine parts in ten of all nations, who call conceits and jingles wit, who see Ovid full of them, and Chaucer altogether without them, will think me little less than mad for preferring the Englishman to the Roman. Yet, with their leave, I must presume to say, that the things they admire are only glittering trifles, and so far from being witty, that in a serious poem they are nauseous, because they are unnatural. Would any man who is ready to die for love describe his passion like Narcissus? Would he think of *inopem me copia fecit*, and a dozen more of such expressions, poured on the neck of one another, and signifying all the same thing? If this were wit, was this a time to be witty, when the poor wretch was in the agony of death?

This is just John Littlewit, in *Bartholomew Fair*, who had a conceit (as he tells you) left him in his misery; a miserable conceit. On these occasions the poet should endeavour to raise pity; but, instead of this, Ovid is tickling you to laugh. Virgil never made use of such machines when he was moving you to commiserate the death of Dido: he would not destroy what he was building. Chaucer makes Arcite violent in his love, and unjust in the pursuit of it; yet when he came to die, he made him think more reasonably; he repents not of his love, for that had altered his character; but acknowledges the injustice of his proceedings, and resigns Emilia to Palamon. What would Ovid have done on this occasion? He would certainly have made Arcite witty on his death-bed; he had complained he was further off from possession, by being so near, and a thousand such boyisms, which Chaucer rejected as below the dignity of the subject. They who think otherwise, would, by the same reason, prefer Lucan and Ovid to Homer and Virgil, and Martial to all four of them. As for the turn of words, in which Ovid particularly excels all poets, they are sometimes a fault, and sometimes a beauty, as they are used properly or improperly; but in strong passions always to be shunned, because passions are serious, and will admit no playing. The French have a high value for them; and, I confess, they are often what they call delicate, when they are introduced with judgment; but Chaucer writ with more simplicity, and followed nature more closely than to use them. I have thus far, to the best of my knowledge, been an upright judge betwixt the parties in competition, not meddling with the design nor the disposition of it; because the design was not their own; and in the disposing of it they were equal. It remains that I say somewhat of Chaucer in particular.

In the first place, as he is the father of English poetry, so I hold him in the same degree of veneration as the Grecians held Homer, or the Romans Virgil. He is a perpetual fountain of good sense; learned in all sciences; and, therefore, speaks properly on all subjects. As he knew what to say, so he knows also when to leave off; a continence, which is practised by few writers, and scarcely by any of the ancients, excepting Virgil and Horace. One of our late great poets is sunk in his reputation, because he could never forgive any conceit which came in his way; but swept, like a drag-net, great and small. There was plenty enough, but the dishes were ill-sorted; whole pyramids of sweet-meats for boys and women, but little of solid meat for men. All this

---

6. **The Cock and the Fox,** *The Nun's Priest's Tale.* 47. **inopem me copia fecit,** my abundance has made me poor.—*Metamorphoses.* Book III. l. 466

1. **Bartholomew Fair,** by Ben Jonson. 46-47. **One of our late great poets,** Abraham Cowley. See page 696.

proceeded not from any want of knowledge, but of judgment. Neither did he want that in discerning the beauties and faults of other poets, but only indulged himself in the luxury of writing; and perhaps knew it was a fault, but hoped the reader would not find it. For this reason, though he must always be thought a great poet, he is no longer esteemed a good writer; and for ten impressions which his works have had in so many successive years, yet at present a hundred books are scarcely purchased once a twelve-month; for, as my last Lord Rochester said, though somewhat profanely, "Not being of God, he could not stand."

Chaucer followed Nature everywhere, but was never so bold to go beyond her; and there is a great difference of being *poeta* and *nimis poeta*, if we may believe Catullus, as much as betwixt a modest behaviour and affectation. The verse of Chaucer, I confess, is not harmonious to us; but 'tis like the eloquence of one whom Tacitus commends, it was *auribus istius tempora accommodata:* they who lived with him, and some time after him, thought it musical; and it continues so, even in our judgment, if compared with the numbers of Lidgate and Gower, his contemporaries; there is the rude sweetness of a Scotch tune in it, which is natural and pleasing, though not perfect. 'Tis true, I cannot go so far as he who published the last edition of him; for he would make us believe the fault is in our ears, and that there were really ten syllables in a verse where we find but nine; but this opinion is not worth confuting; 'tis so gross and obvious an error, that common sense (which is a rule in everything but matters of faith and revelation) must convince the reader, that equality of numbers, in every verse which we call heroic, was either not known, or not always practised, in Chaucer's age. It were an easy matter to produce some thousands of his verses, which are lame for want of half a foot, and sometimes a whole one, and which no pronunciation can make otherwise. We can only say, that he lived in the infancy of our poetry, and that nothing is brought to perfection at the first. We must be children before we grow men. There was an Ennius, and in process of time a Lucilius, and a Lucretius, before Virgil and Horace; even after Chaucer there was a Spenser, a Harington, a Fairfax, before Waller and Denham were in being; and our numbers were in their nonage till these last appeared. I need say little of his parentage, life, and fortunes; they are to be found at large in all the editions of his works. He was employed abroad, and favoured, by Edward the Third, Richard the Second, and Henry the Fourth, and was poet, as I suppose, to all three of them. In Richard's time, I doubt, he was a little dipped in the rebellion of the Commons; and being brother-in-law to John of Gaunt, it was no wonder if he followed the fortunes of that family; and was well with Henry the Fourth when he had deposed his predecessor. Neither is it to be admired, that Henry, who was a wise as well as a valiant prince, who claimed by succession, and was sensible that his title was not sound, but was rightfully in Mortimer, who had married the heir of York; it was not to be admired, I say, if that great politician should be pleased to have the greatest wit of those times in his interests, and to be the trumpet of his praises. Augustus had given him the example, by the advice of Maecenas, who recommended Virgil and Horace to him; whose praises helped to make him popular while he was alive, and after his death have made him precious to posterity. As for the religion of our poet, he seems to have some little bias towards the opinions of Wycliffe, after John of Gaunt his patron; somewhat of which appears in the tale of Piers Plowman; yet I cannot blame him for inveighing so sharply against the vices of the clergy in his age; their pride, their ambition, their pomp, their avarice, their worldly interest, deserved the lashes which he gave them, both in that, and in most of his *Canterbury Tales*. Neither has his contemporary Boccace spared them: yet both those poets lived in much esteem with good and holy men in orders; for the scandal which is given by particular priests reflects not on the sacred function. Chaucer's Monk, his Canon, and his Friar, took not from the character of his Good Parson. A satirical poet is the check of the laymen on bad priests. We are only to take care that we involve not the innocent with the guilty in the same condemnation. The good cannot be too much honoured, nor the bad too coarsely used; for the corruption of the best becomes the worst. When a clergyman is whipped, his gown is first taken off,

---

16. **poeta and nimis poeta,** a poet and too much a poet. Dryden is nodding here. He has in mind a line from Martial. 21. **auribus . . . accommodata,** adapted to the ears of that time. 28. **he who published the last edition.** Dryden refers to the edition of Thomas Speght, reprinted in 1687. The proper pronunciation of Chaucer's Middle English was not understood in Dryden's time. Furthermore, in Speght's edition the final "e" in many words was omitted, and Dryden can hardly be blamed for failing to appreciate the melodious quality of Chaucer's lines as he wrote them and as we have them today.

2. **Harington,** Sir John Harington, whose translation of Ariosto's *Orlando Furioso* was published in 1591. **Fairfax,** Edward Fairfax, translator of Tasso's *Gerusalemme liberata*, 1604. 15. **admired,** wondered at. 30. **the tale of Piers Plowman.** Dryden has in mind *The Plowman's Tale*, formerly thought to be Chaucer's and printed at the end of the *Canterbury Tales*.

by which the dignity of his order is secured. If he be wrongfully accused, he has his action of slander; and 'tis at the poet's peril if he transgress the law. But they will tell us that all kind of satire, though never so well deserved by particular priests, yet brings the whole order into contempt. Is then the peerage of England anything dishonoured when a peer suffers for his treason? If he be libelled, or any way defamed, he has his *scandalum magnatum* to punish the offender. They who use this kind of argument seem to be conscious to themselves of somewhat which has deserved the poet's lash, and are less concerned for their public capacity than for their private; at least there is pride at the bottom of their reasoning. If the faults of men in orders are only to be judged among themselves, they are all in some sort parties; for, since they say the honour of their order is concerned in every member of it, how can we be sure that they will be impartial judges? How far I may be allowed to speak my opinion in this case I know not; but I am sure a dispute of this nature caused mischief in abundance betwixt a King of England and an Archbishop of Canterbury; one standing up for the laws of his land, and the other for the honour (as he called it) of God's Church; which ended in the murder of the prelate, and in the whipping of his Majesty from post to pillar for his penance. The learned and ingenious Dr. Drake has saved me the labour of inquiring into the esteem and reverence which the priests have had of old; and I would rather extend than diminish any part of it; yet I must needs say, that when a priest provokes me without occasion given him, I have no reason, unless it be the charity of a Christian, to forgive him: *prior laesit* is justification sufficient in the civil law. If I answer him in his own language, self-defence I am sure must be allowed me; and if I carry it further, even to a sharp recrimination, somewhat may be indulged to human frailty. Yet my resentment has not wrought so far but that I have followed Chaucer in his character of a holy man, and have enlarged on that subject with some pleasure; reserving to myself the right, if I shall think fit hereafter, to describe another sort of priests, such as are more easily to be found than the Good Parson; such as have given the last blow to Christianity in this age, by a practice so contrary to their doctrine. But this will keep cold till another time. In the meanwhile, I take up Chaucer where I left him.

He must have been a man of a most wonderful comprehensive nature, because, as it has been truly observed of him, he has taken into the compass of his *Canterbury Tales* the various manners and humours (as we now call them) of the whole English nation, in his age. Not a single character has escaped him. All his pilgrims are severally distinguished from each other; and not only in their inclinations but in their very physiognomies and persons. Baptista Porta could not have described their natures better, than by the marks which the poet gives them. The matter and manner of their tales, and of their telling, are so suited to their different educations, humours, and callings, that each of them would be improper in any other mouth. Even the grave and serious characters are distinguished by their several sorts of gravity: their discourses are such as belong to their age, their calling, and their breeding; such as are becoming of them, and of them only. Some of his persons are vicious, and some virtuous; some are unlearned, or (as Chaucer calls them) lewd, and some are learned. Even the ribaldry of the low characters is different: the Reeve, the Miller, and the Cook, are several men, and distinguished from each other as much as the mincing Lady-Prioress and the broad-speaking, gap-toothed Wife of Bath. But enough of this; there is such a variety of game springing up before me, that I am distracted in my choice, and know not which to follow. 'Tis sufficient to say, according to the proverb, that here is God's plenty. We have our forefathers and great-grand-dames all before us, as they were in Chaucer's days: their general characters are still remaining in mankind, and even in England, though they are called by other names than those of monks, and friars, and canons, and lady-abbesses, and nuns; for mankind is ever the same, and nothing lost out of nature, though everything is altered. . . .

9. **scandalum magnatum,** the offense of slandering those in power.   22–23. **a King . . . and an Archbishop,** Henry II and Thomas à Becket.   28. **Dr. Drake,** James Drake, whose reply to Jeremy Collier's *Short View of the English Stage,* 1698, was published in 1699.   35. **prior laesit,** "he hit me first."

16. **Baptista Porta,** the famous Italian physiognomist (1538–1615).

William Congreve
1670-1729

Of the five authors who are considered the best representatives of the Restoration comedy of manners—Etherege, Wycherley, Congreve, Vanbrugh, and Farquhar—Congreve may safely be said to have written the wittiest and most graceful plays of them all. *The Way of the World*, which had its initial performance in the last year of the century, is as certainly his most brilliant composition. Like all the best comedies of the time, Congreve's plays were the productions of a young man. His five plays were all written in his twenties, within less than a decade of a life that extended to almost sixty years.

Congreve came of the landed gentry of Staffordshire, but was brought up in Ireland, and was educated at Trinity College, Dublin, a college mate and friend of Jonathan Swift. He came to London as an impecunious young law student with the manuscript of a play in his pocket. This was the comedy *The Old Bachelor*, which was produced when he was twenty-three, and was an immediate success. The chief admirer of the play was the aging Dryden, who became his friend and sponsor, and the first of a group of distinguished literary men, including Southerne, Addison, Steele, Pope, and later Voltaire, who praised him, often with more extravagance than wisdom. The success of his first play led Congreve to bring out within a few months a second and less successful comedy, *The Double-Dealer*. Two years later, in 1695, his most successful comedy, *Love for Love*, was produced as the opening play at the new Lincoln's Inn Fields Theatre, with the great actor Thomas Betterton in the leading role. He was fortunate enough about this time to secure the patronage of Charles Montagu, later Earl of Halifax, who appointed him to various sinecures and relieved him of all financial burdens.

In 1697 Congreve changed his mood temporarily and brought out a tragedy, *The Mourning Bride*, the only tragic composition by any of the leading comic writers of the Restoration theater. It is in blank verse, in which Sir Edmund Gosse and others have detected the influence of Milton. It was, oddly enough, more successful in its day than any of his comedies, and its popularity continued throughout the eighteenth century. Though unread today, it begins with the one line of Congreve's that everybody knows, and usually misquotes: "Music has charms to soothe a savage breast." Congreve's next play, *The Way of the World*, came five years later, and was received at the time with disappointment. It was, indeed, so unsuccessful that its author retired in pique from the theater, and never wrote another play, though he lived on in elegance and leisure for nearly thirty years.

Congreve belonged to the genteel tradition in English letters and, as he told Voltaire, preferred to be considered a gentleman rather than a playwright. He could condescend to amuse himself by writing plays that would amuse the aristocracy of London, but he would not be so vulgar as to try to entertain aristocrats against their will. In 1717 he acknowledged his early debt to his friend Dryden by editing Dryden's plays in six volumes. He seems not to have given any attention to the later editions of his own plays, partly because of increasing blindness and partly on account of his offended pride at the reception of *The Way of the World*. Both the latter play and *Love for Love* have been successfully revived from time to time in the twentieth century in England and America.

The Way of the World has hardly its equal in the language for ease and wit and brilliance. In fact, the abundance of Congreve's wit is, as every critic has pointed out, both his strength and his weakness. The dialogue flourishes at the expense of the plot, and the dullest characters, if they can be called dull, would sufficiently illuminate many another play. Pope, in his "Epistle to Augustus," asked knowingly, "Tell me if Congreve's fools are fools indeed?" The reader of their repartee may supply the answer. Of Millamant, too, the reader may form his own opinion, but it can hardly differ from that of her lover Mirabell and of the critics of two hundred years who have united to applaud her sparkling sallies and to "like her with all her faults; nay, like her for her faults."

The Way of the World does not provide an object lesson in moral conduct, but it is refreshingly free from the gross obscenities of much of Restoration comedy. Its characters are oversophisticated, and, like others of the drama of the period, they live and move, as Lamb remarked in his essay "On the Artificial Comedy of the Last Century," in a "Utopia of gallantry, where pleasure is duty, and the manners perfect freedom." Congreve was presenting in the play a panorama of the broad "way of the world," and not dramatizing the narrow way of *The Pilgrim's Progress*. It is a portrayal of Vanity Fair, not of the Celestial City, and no picture of seventeenth-century England or of life would be complete, as Bunyan when he coined the phrase realized, which ignored the existence and the tempting, if unsubstantial, wares of Vanity Fair.

THE WAY OF THE WORLD

DRAMATIS PERSONAE

MEN

FAINALL, in love with MRS. MARWOOD
[EDWARD] MIRABELL, in love with MRS. MILLAMANT
[ANTHONY] WITWOUD, } followers of MRS. MILLAMANT
PETULANT,
SIR WILFULL WITWOUD, half-brother to WITWOUD, nephew to LADY WISHFORT
WAITWELL, servant to MIRABELL

WOMEN

LADY WISHFORT, enemy to MIRABELL, for having falsely pretended love to her
MRS.[1] MILLAMANT, a fine lady, niece to LADY WISHFORT, and loves MIRABELL
MRS. MARWOOD, friend to MR. FAINALL, and likes MIRABELL
MRS. [ARABELLA] FAINALL, daughter to LADY WISHFORT, and wife to FAINALL, formerly friend to MIRABELL
FOIBLE, woman to LADY WISHFORT
MINCING, woman to MRS. MILLAMANT
[BETTY, servant in a chocolate-house]
[PEG, servant to LADY WISHFORT]
Dancers, Footmen, and Attendants

SCENE.—London. The time equal to that of the presentation.[2]

ACT I

SCENE.—*A chocolate-house.* MIRABELL *and* FAINALL, *rising from cards.* BETTY *waiting.*

Mira. You are a fortunate man, Mr. Fainall.
Fain. Have we done?
Mira. What you please. I'll play on to entertain you.
Fain. No, I'll give you your revenge another time, when you are not so indifferent; you are thinking of something else now, and play too negligently; the coldness of a losing gamester lessens the pleasure of the winner. I'd no more play with a man that slighted his ill fortune, than I'd make love to a woman who undervalued the loss of her reputation.
Mira. You have a taste extremely delicate, and are for refining on your pleasures.
Fain. Prithee, why so reserved? Something has put you out of humour.
Mira. Not at all: I happen to be grave to-day; and you are gay; that's all.
Fain. Confess, Millamant and you quarrelled last night, after I left you; my fair cousin has some humours that would tempt the patience of a Stoic. What! some coxcomb came in, and was well received by her, while you were by.
Mira. Witwoud and Petulant; and what was worse, her aunt, your wife's mother, my evil genius; or to sum up all in her own name, my old Lady Wishfort came in—
Fain. Oh, there it is then—she has a lasting passion for you, and with reason.—What! then my wife was there?
Mira. Yes, and Mrs. Marwood and three or four more, whom I never saw before; seeing me, they all put on their grave faces, whispered one another, then complained aloud of the vapours, and after fell into a profound silence.
Fain. They had a mind to be rid of you.
Mira. For which reason I resolved not to stir. At last the good old lady broke through her painful taciturnity, with an invective against long visits. I would not have understood her, but Millamant joining in the argument, I rose and with a constrained smile told her I thought nothing was so easy as to know when a visit began to be troublesome; she reddened and I withdrew, without expecting her reply.
Fain. You were to blame to resent what she spoke only in compliance with her aunt.
Mira. She is more mistress of herself than to be under the necessity of such a resignation.
Fain. What? though half her fortune depends upon her marrying with my lady's approbation?

---

[1] **Mrs.** "Mrs." was commonly used in addressing unmarried women and even girls, as well as married women. The term "Miss" had a derogatory significance. [2] **The time ... presentation.** "Time, the present."

36–37. **expecting,** awaiting.

Mira. I was then in such a humour, that I should have been better pleased if she had been less discreet.

Fain. Now I remember, I wonder not they were weary of you; last night was one of their cabal-nights; they have 'em three times a week, and meet by turns, at one another's apartments, where they come together like the coroner's inquest, to sit upon the murdered reputations of the week. You and I are excluded; and it was once proposed that all the male sex should be excepted; but somebody moved that to avoid scandal there might be one man of the community; upon which motion Witwoud and Petulant were enrolled members.

Mira. And who may have been the foundress of this sect? My Lady Wishfort, I warrant, who publishes her detestation of mankind; and full of the vigour of fifty-five, declares for a friend and ratafia; and let posterity shift for itself, she'll breed no more.

Fain. The discovery of your sham addresses to her, to conceal your love to her niece, has provoked this separation: had you dissembled better, things might have continued in the state of nature.

Mira. I did as much as man could, with any reasonable conscience; I proceeded to the very last act of flattery with her, and was guilty of a song in her commendation. . . . But for the discovery of this amour, I am indebted to your friend, or your wife's friend, Mrs. Marwood.

Fain. What should provoke her to be your enemy, unless she has made you advances, which you have slighted? Women do not easily forgive omissions of that nature.

Mira. She was always civil to me, till of late. I confess I am not one of those coxcombs who are apt to interpret a woman's good manners to her prejudice; and think that she who does not refuse 'em everything, can refuse 'em nothing.

Fain. You are a gallant man, Mirabell; and though you may have cruelty enough not to satisfy a lady's longing, you have too much generosity not to be tender of her honour. Yet you speak with an indifference which seems to be affected, and confesses you are conscious of a negligence.

Mira. You pursue the argument with a distrust that seems to be unaffected, and confesses you are conscious of a concern for which the lady is more indebted to you than your wife.

Fain. Fie, fie, friend, if you grow censorious I must leave you. I'll look upon the gamesters in the next room.

Mira. Who are they?

Fain. Petulant and Witwoud. (*To* BETTY.) Bring me some chocolate. [*Exit.*

17. *ratafia,* a liqueur flavored with fruit.

Mira. Betty, what says your clock?

Bet. Turned of the last canonical hour, sir.

Mira. How pertinently the jade answers me! Ha! almost one o'clock! (*Looking on his watch.*) Oh, y'are come—

[*Enter a* Servant.]

Mira. Well, is the grand affair over? You have been something tedious.

Serv. Sir, there's such coupling at Pancras that they stand behind one another, as 'twere in a country dance. Ours was the last couple to lead up; and no hopes appearing of dispatch, besides, the parson growing hoarse, we were afraid his lungs would have failed before it came to our turn; so we drove round to Duke's Place; and there they were rivetted in a trice.

Mira. So, so, you are sure they are married.

Serv. Married and bedded, sir: I am witness.

Mira. Have you the certificate?

Serv. Here it is, sir.

Mira. Has the tailor brought Waitwell's clothes home, and the new liveries?

Serv. Yes, sir.

Mira. That's well. Do you go home again, d'ye hear, and adjourn the consummation till farther order; bid Waitwell shake his ears, and Dame Partlet rustle up her feathers, and meet me at one o'clock by Rosamond's Pond; that I may see her before she returns to her lady: and as you tender your ears, be secret. [*Exit* Servant.

[*Re-enter* FAINALL.]

Fain. Joy of your success, Mirabell; you look pleased.

Mira. Ay; I have been engaged in a matter of some sort of mirth, which is not yet ripe for discovery. I am glad this is not a cabal-night. I wonder, Fainall, that you who are married, and of consequence should be discreet, will suffer your wife to be of such a party.

Fain. Faith, I am not jealous. Besides, most who are engaged are women and relations; and for the men, they are of a kind too contemptible to give scandal.

Mira. I am of another opinion. The greater the coxcomb, always the more the scandal: for a woman

2. **canonical hour.** Marriage might not be legally performed in any parish church except during the canonical hours, which were, at that date, from eight to twelve in the morning. 10. **Pancras.** St. Pancras Church and St. James's Church in Duke's Place, referred to later, were notorious for marriages celebrated without special license or publication of banns. 27–28. **Dame Partlet,** the wife of Chanticleer in the old tale of the Cock and the Fox. 29. **Rosamond's Pond,** in St. James's Park.

who is not a fool can have but one reason for associating with a man who is one.

Fain. Are you jealous as often as you see Witwoud entertained by Millamant?

Mira. Of her understanding I am, if not of her person.

Fain. You do her wrong; for to give her her due, she has wit.

Mira. She has beauty enough to make any man think so; and complaisance enough not to contradict him who shall tell her so.

Fain. For a passionate lover, methinks you are a man somewhat too discerning in the failings of your mistress.

Mira. And for a discerning man, somewhat too passionate a lover; for I like her with all her faults; nay, like her for her faults. Her follies are so natural, or so artful, that they become her; and those affectations which in another woman would be odious, serve but to make her more agreeable. I'll tell thee, Fainall, she once used me with that insolence, that in revenge I took her to pieces; sifted her, and separated her failings; I studied 'em, and got 'em by rote. The catalogue was so large, that I was not without hopes, one day or other, to hate her heartily: to which end I so used myself to think of 'em, that at length, contrary to my design and expectation, they gave me every hour less and less disturbance; till in a few days it became habitual to me to remember 'em without being displeased. They are now grown as familiar to me as my own frailties; and in all probability in a little time longer I shall like 'em as well.

Fain. Marry her, marry her; be half as well acquainted with her charms as you are with her defects, and my life on't, you are your own man again.

Mira. Say you so?

Fain. Ay, ay; I have experience: I have a wife, and so forth.

[*Enter* Messenger.]

Mess. Is one Squire Witwoud here?

Bet. Yes; what's your business?

Mess. I have a letter for him, from his brother, Sir Wilfull, which I am charged to deliver into his own hands.

Bet. He's in the next room, friend—that way.

[*Exit* Messenger.

Mira. What, is the chief of that noble family in town, Sir Wilfull Witwoud?

Fain. He is expected to-day. Do you know him?

Mira. I have seen him, he promises to be an extraordinary person; I think you have the honour to be related to him.

Fain. Yes; he is half-brother to this Witwoud by a former wife, who was sister to my Lady Wishfort, my wife's mother. If you marry Millamant, you must call cousins too.

Mira. I had rather be his relation than his acquaintance.

Fain. He comes to town in order to equip himself for travel.

Mira. For travel! Why the man that I mean is above forty.

Fain. No matter for that; 'tis for the honour of England that all Europe should know we have blockheads of all ages.

Mira. I wonder there is not an act of Parliament to save the credit of the nation, and prohibit the exportation of fools.

Fain. By no means, 'tis better as 'tis; 'tis better to trade with a little loss than to be quite eaten up, with being overstocked.

Mira. Pray, are the follies of this knight-errant, and those of the squire his brother, anything related?

Fain. Not at all; Witwoud grows by the knight, like a medlar grafted on a crab. One will melt in your mouth, and t'other set your teeth on edge; one is all pulp, and the other all core.

Mira. So one will be rotten before he be ripe, and the other will be rotten without ever being ripe at all.

Fain. Sir Wilfull is an odd mixture of bashfulness and obstinacy.—But when he's drunk, he's as loving as the monster in *The Tempest*, and much after the same manner. To give t'other his due, he has something of good nature, and does not always want wit.

Mira. Not always; but as often as his memory fails him, and his commonplace of comparisons. He is a fool with a good memory, and some few scraps of other folks' wit. He is one whose conversation can never be approved, yet it is now and then to be endured. He has indeed one good quality, he is not exceptious; for he so passionately affects the reputation of understanding raillery, that he will construe an affront into a jest; and call downright rudeness and ill language, satire and fire.

Fain. If you have a mind to finish his picture, you have an opportunity to do it at full length. Behold the original.

[*Enter* WITWOUD.]

Wit. Afford me your compassion, my dears; pity me, Fainall, Mirabell, pity me.

10. **above forty,** an unusually late time in life for a gentleman to make the "grand tour." 23. **medlar grafted on a crab,** a medlar (a soft, pulpy fruit) grafted on a crabapple. 30. **The Tempest.** The reference is probably to the description of Caliban in Act II, sc. 2. 39. **exceptious,** disposed to take exceptions.

Mira. I do from my soul.

Fain. Why, what's the matter?

Wit. No letters for me, Betty?

Bet. Did not the messenger bring you one but now, sir?

Wit. Ay, but no other?

Bet. No, sir.

Wit. That's hard, that's very hard;—a messenger, a mule, a beast of burden: he has brought me a letter from the fool my brother, as heavy as a panegyric in a funeral sermon, or a copy of commendatory verses from one poet to another. And what's worse, 'tis as sure a forerunner of the author as an epistle dedicatory.

Mira. A fool, and your brother, Witwoud!

Wit. Ay, ay, my half-brother. My half-brother he is, no nearer upon honour.

Mira. Then 'tis possible he may be but half a fool.

Wit. Good, good, Mirabell, *le drôle!* Good, good!—hang him, don't let's talk of him.—Fainall, how does your lady? Gad, I say anything in the world to get this fellow out of my head. I beg pardon that I should ask a man of pleasure, and the town, a question at once so foreign and domestic. But I talk like an old maid at a marriage, I don't know what I say; but she's the best woman in the world.

Fain. 'Tis well you don't know what you say, or else your commendation would go near to make me either vain or jealous.

Wit. No man in town lives well with a wife but Fainall. Your judgment, Mirabell.

Mira. You had better step and ask his wife if you would be credibly informed.

Wit. Mirabell.

Mira. Ay.

Wit. My dear, I ask ten thousand pardons.—Gad, I have forgot what I was going to say to you.

Mira. I thank you heartily, heartily.

Wit. No, but prithee excuse me—my memory is such a memory.

Mira. Have a care of such apologies, Witwoud; for I never knew a fool but he affected to complain, either of the spleen or his memory.

Fain. What have you done with Petulant?

Wit. He's reckoning his money—my money it was; I have no luck to-day.

Fain. You may allow him to win of you at play, for you are sure to be too hard for him at repartee: since you monopolize the wit that is between you, the fortune must be his, of course.

Mira. I don't find that Petulant confesses the superiority of wit to be your talent, Witwoud.

19. **le drôle!** the witty fellow.

Wit. Come, come, you are malicious now, and would breed debates. Petulant's my friend, and a very honest fellow, and a very pretty fellow, and has a smattering—faith and troth, a pretty deal of an odd sort of a small wit. Nay, I'll do him justice. I'm his friend, I won't wrong him, neither. And if he had but any judgment in the world, he would not be altogether contemptible. Come, come, don't detract from the merits of my friend.

Fain. You don't take your friend to be over-nicely bred.

Wit. No, no, hang him, the rogue has no manners at all, that I must own—no more breeding than a bum-baily, that I grant you. 'Tis pity, faith; the fellow has fire and life.

Mira. What, courage?

Wit. Hum, faith, I don't know as to that—I can't say as to that. Yes, faith, in a controversy he'll contradict anybody.

Mira. Though 'twere a man whom he feared, or a woman whom he loved.

Wit. Well, well, he does not always think before he speaks. We have all our failings; you're too hard upon him, you are, faith. Let me excuse him—I can defend most of his faults, except one or two; one he has, that's the truth on't, if he were my brother, I could not acquit him. That, indeed, I could wish were otherwise.

Mira. Ay, marry, what's that, Witwoud?

Wit. Oh, pardon me! Expose the infirmities of my friend? No, my dear, excuse me there.

Fain. What! I warrant he's unsincere, or 'tis some such trifle.

Wit. No, no, what if he be? 'Tis no matter for that, his wit will excuse that: a wit should no more be sincere than a woman constant; one argues a decay of parts, as t'other of beauty.

Mira. Maybe you think him too positive?

Wit. No, no, his being positive is an incentive to argument, and keeps up conversation.

Fain. Too illiterate.

Wit. That! that's his happiness. His want of learning gives him the more opportunities to show his natural parts.

Mira. He wants words.

Wit. Ay; but I like him for that now; for his want of words gives me the pleasure very often to explain his meaning.

Fain. He's impudent.

Wit. No, that's not it.

Mira. Vain.

Wit. No.

14. **bum-baily,** the lowest kind of bailiff or sheriff's officer, employed in arrests.

Mira. What, he speaks unseasonable truths sometimes, because he has not wit enough to invent an evasion!

Wit. Truths! Ha, ha, ha! No, no, since you will have it—I mean, he never speaks truth at all—that's all. He will lie like a chambermaid, or a woman of quality's porter. Now that is a fault.

[*Enter* Coachman.]

Coach. Is Master Petulant here, mistress?
Bet. Yes.
Coach. Three gentlewomen in a coach would speak with him.
Fain. O brave Petulant, three!
Bet. I'll tell him.
Coach. You must bring two dishes of chocolate and a glass of cinnamon-water.

[*Exeunt* BETTY *and* Coachman.

Wit. That should be for two fasting strumpets, and a bawd troubled with wind. Now you may know what the three are.

Mira. You are very free with your friend's acquaintance.

Wit. Ay, ay, friendship without freedom is as dull as love without enjoyment, or wine without toasting; but to tell you a secret, these are trulls whom he allows coach-hire, and something more by the week, to call on him once a day at public places.

Mira. How!

Wit. You shall see he won't go to 'em because there's no more company here to take notice of him—Why, this is nothing to what he used to do;—before he found out this way, I have known him call for himself—

Fain. Call for himself? What dost thou mean?

Wit. Mean? why he would slip you out of this chocolate-house, just when you had been talking to him—as soon as your back was turned—whip he was gone;—then trip to his lodging, clap on a hood and scarf, and a mask, slap into a hackney-coach, and drive hither to the door again in a trice; where he would send in for himself, that I mean, call for himself, wait for himself, nay and what's more, not finding himself, sometimes leave a letter for himself.

Mira. I confess this is something extraordinary—I believe he waits for himself now, he is so long a coming. Oh, I ask his pardon.

[*Enter* PETULANT *and* BETTY.]

Bet. Sir, the coach stays.
Pet. Well, well; I come.— 'Sbud, a man had as good be a professed midwife as a professed whore- [*Exit.*

master, at this rate; to be knocked up and raised at all hours, and in all places! Pox on 'em, I won't come.—D'ee hear, tell 'em I won't come. Let 'em snivel and cry their hearts out.

Fain. You are very cruel, Petulant.
Pet. All's one, let it pass—I have a humour to be cruel.

Mira. I hope they are not persons of condition that you use at this rate.

Pet. Condition! condition's a dried fig, if I am not in humour. By this hand, if they were your—a—a—your what-d'ee-call-'ems themselves, they must wait or rub off, if I want appetite.

Mira. What-d'ee-call-'ems! What are they, Witwoud?

Wit. Empresses, my dear—by your what-d'ee-call-'ems he means sultana queens.

Pet. Ay, Roxolanas.
Mira. Cry you mercy.
Fain. Witwoud says they are—
Pet. What does he say th' are?
Wit. I—fine ladies, I say.

Pet. Pass on, Witwoud.—Hark 'ee, by this light, his relations—two co-heiresses his cousins, and an old aunt, that loves caterwauling better than a conventicle.

Wit. Ha, ha, ha! I had a mind to see how the rogue would come off. Ha, ha, ha! Gad, I can't be angry with him, if he said they were my mother and my sisters.

Mira. No!

Wit. No, the rogue's wit and readiness of invention charm me: dear Petulant!

[*Re-enter* BETTY.]

Bet. They are gone, sir, in great anger.

Pet. Enough, let 'em trundle. Anger helps complexion, saves paint.

Fain. This continence is all dissembled; this is in order to have something to brag of the next time he makes court to Millamant, and swears he has abandoned the whole sex for her sake.

Mira. Have you not left off your impudent pretensions there yet? I shall cut your throat, sometime or other, Petulant, about that business.

Pet. Ay, ay, let that pass—there are other throats to be cut.

Mira. Meaning mine, sir?

Pet. Not I—I mean nobody—I know nothing.—But there are uncles and nephews in the world—and they may be rivals. What then? All's one for that—

---

51. 'Sbud, a contraction of 'sbodikins, meaning "God's dear body."

13. **rub off,** go away.   18. **Roxolana,** the wife of Solyman the Magnificent in Davenant's *The Siege of Rhodes.*
25–26. **conventicle,** assembly for religious worship.

Mira. How! Harkee, Petulant, come hither. Explain, or I shall call your interpreter.

Pet. Explain! I know nothing.—Why, you have an uncle, have you not, lately come to town, and lodges by my Lady Wishfort's?

Mira. True.

Pet. Why, that's enough—you and he are not friends; and if he should marry and have a child, you may be disinherited, ha?

Mira. Where hast thou stumbled upon all this truth?

Pet. All's one for that; why, then say I know something.

Mira. Come, thou art an honest fellow, Petulant, and shalt make love to my mistress, thou shalt, faith. What hast thou heard of my uncle?

Pet. I? nothing I. If throats are to be cut, let swords clash; snug's the word, I shrug and am silent.

Mira. Oh, raillery, raillery. Come, I know thou art in the women's secrets.—What, you're a cabalist, I know you stayed at Millamant's last night, after I went. Was there any mention made of my uncle or me? Tell me; if thou hadst but good nature equal to thy wit, Petulant, Tony Witwoud, who is now thy competitor in fame, would show as dim by thee as a dead whiting's eye by a pearl of Orient; he would no more be seen by thee, than Mercury is by the sun: Come, I'm sure thou wo't tell me.

Pet. If I do, will you grant me common sense then, for the future?

Mira. Faith, I'll do what I can for thee, and I'll pray that Heaven may grant it thee in the meantime.

Pet. Well, hark 'ee.

[*They converse aside.*]

Fain. Petulant and you both will find Mirabell as warm a rival as a lover.

Wit. Pshaw, pshaw, that she laughs at Petulant is plain. And for my part—but that it is almost a fashion to admire her, I should—hark'ee—to tell you a secret, but let it go no further—between friends, I shall never break my heart for her.

Fain. How!

Wit. She's handsome; but she's a sort of an uncertain woman.

Fain. I thought you had died for her.

Wit. Umh—no—

Fain. She has wit.

Wit. 'Tis what she will hardly allow anybody else. Now, demme, I should hate that, if she were as handsome as Cleopatra. Mirabell is not so sure of her as he thinks for.

Fain. Why do you think so?

Wit. We stayed pretty late there last night; and heard something of an uncle to Mirabell, who is lately come to town—and is between him and the best part of his estate. Mirabell and he are at some distance, as my Lady Wishfort has been told; and you know she hates Mirabell, worse than a Quaker hates a parrot, or than a fishmonger hates a hard frost. Whether this uncle has seen Mrs. Millamant or not, I cannot say; but there were items of such a treaty being in embryo; and if it should come to life, poor Mirabell would be in some sort unfortunately fobbed, i'faith.

Fain. 'Tis impossible Millamant should hearken to it.

Wit. Faith, my dear, I can't tell; she's a woman and a kind of a humourist.

Mira. (*conversing apart with* PETULANT). And this is the sum of what you could collect last night.

Pet. The quintessence. Maybe Witwoud knows more, he stayed longer.—Besides, they never mind him; they say anything before him.

Mira. I thought you had been the greatest favourite.

Pet. Ay, *tête-à-tête;* but not in public, because I make remarks.

Mira. You do?

Pet. Ay, ay, pox, I'm malicious, man. Now he's soft, you know, they are not in awe of him—the fellow's well bred, he's what you call a—what-d'ee-call-'em. A fine gentleman, but he's silly withal.

Mira. I thank you, I know as much as my curiosity requires. Fainall, are you for the Mall?

Fain. Ay, I'll take a turn before dinner.

Wit. Ay, we'll all walk in the Park, the ladies talked of being there.

Mira. I thought you were obliged to watch for your brother Sir Wilfull's arrival.

Wit. No, no, he comes to his aunt's, my Lady Wishfort; pox on him, I shall be troubled with him too; what shall I do with the fool?

Pet. Beg him for his estate; that I may beg you afterwards; and so have but one trouble with you both.

Wit. O rare Petulant! thou art as quick as fire in a frosty morning; thou shalt to the Mall with us; and we'll be very severe.

Pet. Enough! I'm in a humour to be severe.

Mira. Are you? Pray then walk by yourselves,— let not us be accessory to your putting the ladies out of countenance, with your senseless ribaldry, which you roar out aloud as often as they pass by you; and

13. **fobbed,** tricked.   34. **the Mall,** in St. James's Park.

when you have made a handsome woman blush, then you think you have been severe.

Pet. What, what? Then let 'em either show their innocence by not understanding what they hear, or else show their discretion by not hearing what they would not be thought to understand.

Mira. But hast not thou then sense enough to know that thou ought'st to be most ashamed of thyself, when thou hast put another out of countenance?

Pet. Not I, by this hand—I always take blushing either for a sign of guilt, or ill breeding.

Mira. I confess you ought to think so. You are in the right, that you may plead the error of your judgment in defence of your practice.

>   Where modesty's ill manners, 'tis but fit
>   That impudence and malice pass for wit.
>   [*Exeunt.*

ACT II

SCENE.—*St. James's Park.*

Enter MRS. FAINALL *and* MRS. MARWOOD.

Mrs. Fain. Ay, ay, dear Marwood, if we will be happy, we must find the means in ourselves, and among ourselves. Men are ever in extremes, either doting or averse. While they are lovers, if they have fire and sense, their jealousies are insupportable; and when they cease to love (we ought to think at least) they loathe; they look upon us with horror and distaste; they meet us like the ghosts of what we were, and as from such, fly from us.

Mrs. Mar. True, 'tis an unhappy circumstance of life, that love should ever die before us; and that the man so often should outlive the lover. But say what you will, 'tis better to be left than never to have been loved. To pass our youth in dull indifference, to refuse the sweets of life because they once must leave us, is as preposterous as to wish to have been born old, because we one day must be old. For my part, my youth may wear and waste, but it shall never rust in my possession.

Mrs. Fain. Then it seems you dissemble an aversion to mankind only in compliance to my mother's humour.

Mrs. Mar. Certainly. To be free; I have no taste of those insipid dry discourses, with which our sex of force must entertain themselves, apart from men. We may affect endearments to each other, profess eternal friendships, and seem to dote like lovers; but 'tis not in our natures long to persevere. Love will resume his empire in our breasts, and every heart, or soon or late, receive and readmit him as its lawful tyrant.

Mrs. Fain. Bless me, how have I been deceived! Why, you profess a libertine.

Mrs. Mar. You see my friendship by my freedom. Come, be as sincere, acknowledge that your sentiments agree with mine.

Mrs. Fain. Never.

Mrs. Mar. You hate mankind?

Mrs. Fain. Heartily, inveterately.

Mrs. Mar. Your husband?

Mrs. Fain. Most transcendently; ay, though I say it, meritoriously.

Mrs. Mar. Give me your hand upon it.

Mrs. Fain. There.

Mrs. Mar. I join with you; what I have said has been to try you.

Mrs. Fain. Is it possible? Dost thou hate those vipers, men?

Mrs. Mar. I have done hating 'em, and am now come to despise 'em; the next thing I have to do, is eternally to forget 'em.

Mrs. Fain. There spoke the spirit of an Amazon, a Penthesilea.

Mrs. Mar. And yet I am thinking sometimes to carry my aversion further.

Mrs. Fain. How?

Mrs. Mar. Faith, by marrying; if I could but find one that loved me very well, and would be thoroughly sensible of ill usage, I think I should do myself the violence of undergoing the ceremony.

Mrs. Fain. You would not make him a cuckold?

Mrs. Mar. No; but I'd make him believe I did, and that's as bad.

Mrs. Fain. Why had not you as good do it?

Mrs. Mar. Oh, if he should ever discover it, he would then know the worst, and be out of his pain; but I would have him ever to continue upon the rack of fear and jealousy.

Mrs. Fain. Ingenious mischief! Would thou wert married to Mirabell.

Mrs. Mar. Would I were!

Mrs. Fain. You change colour.

Mrs. Mar. Because I hate him.

Mrs. Fain. So do I; but I can hear him named. But what reason have you to hate him in particular?

Mrs. Mar. I never loved him; he is, and always was, insufferably proud.

Mrs. Fain. By the reason you give for your aversion, one would think it dissembled; for you have laid a fault to his charge of which his enemies must acquit him.

Mrs. Mar. Oh, then it seems you are one of his favourable enemies. Methinks you look a little pale, and now you flush again.

22. **Penthesilea,** queen of the **Amazons.**

Mrs. Fain. Do I? I think I am a little sick o' the sudden.

Mrs. Mar. What ails you?

Mrs. Fain. My husband. Don't you see him? He turned short upon me unawares, and has almost overcome me.

[*Enter* FAINALL *and* MIRABELL.]

Mrs. Mar. Ha, ha, ha! he comes opportunely for you.

Mrs. Fain. For you, for he has brought Mirabell with him.

Fain. My dear.

Mrs. Fain. My soul.

Fain. You don't look well to-day, child.

Mrs. Fain. D'ee think so?

Mira. He is the only man that does, madam.

Mrs. Fain. The only man that would tell me so, at least; and the only man from whom I could hear it without mortification.

Fain. O my dear, I am satisfied of your tenderness; I know you cannot resent anything from me; especially what is an effect of my concern.

Mrs. Fain. Mr. Mirabell, my mother interrupted you in a pleasant relation last night: I would fain hear it out.

Mira. The persons concerned in that affair have yet a tolerable reputation.—I am afraid Mr. Fainall will be censorious.

Mrs. Fain. He has a humour more prevailing than his curiosity, and will willingly dispense with the hearing of one scandalous story, to avoid giving an occasion to make another by being seen to walk with his wife. This way, Mr. Mirabell, and I dare promise you will oblige us both.

[*Exeunt* MRS. FAINALL *and* MIRABELL.

Fain. Excellent creature! Well, sure if I should live to be rid of my wife, I should be a miserable man.

Mrs. Mar. Ay!

Fain. For having only that one hope, the accomplishment of it, of consequence, must put an end to all my hopes; and what a wretch is he who must survive his hopes! Nothing remains when that day comes, but to sit down and weep like Alexander, when he wanted other worlds to conquer.

Mrs. Mar. Will you not follow 'em?

Fain. I think not.

Mrs. Mar. Pray let us; I have a reason.

Fain. You are not jealous?

Mrs. Mar. Of whom?

Fain. Of Mirabell.

Mrs. Mar. If I am, is it inconsistent with my love to you that I am tender of your honour?

Fain. You would intimate, then, as if there were a fellow-feeling between my wife and him.

Mrs. Mar. I think she does not hate him to that degree she would be thought.

Fain. But he, I fear, is too insensible.

Mrs. Mar. It may be you are deceived.

Fain. It may be so. I do now begin to apprehend it.

Mrs. Mar. What?

Fain. That I have been deceived, madam, and you are false.

Mrs. Mar. That I am false! What mean you?

Fain. To let you know I see through all your little arts. Come, you both love him; and both have equally dissembled your aversion. Your mutual jealousies of one another have made you clash till you have both struck fire. I have seen the warm confession reddening on your cheeks, and sparkling from your eyes.

Mrs. Mar. You do me wrong.

Fain. I do not—'twas for my ease to oversee and wilfully neglect the gross advances made him by my wife; that by permitting her to be engaged, I might continue unsuspected in my pleasures; and take you oftener to my arms in full security. But could you think, because the nodding husband would not wake, that e'er the watchful lover slept?

Mrs. Mar. And wherewithal can you reproach me?

Fain. With infidelity, with loving another, with love of Mirabell.

Mrs. Mar. 'Tis false. I challenge you to show an instance that can confirm your groundless accusation. I hate him.

Fain. And wherefore do you hate him? He is insensible, and your resentment follows his neglect. An instance? The injuries you have done him are a proof: your interposing in his love. What cause had you to make discoveries of his pretended passion? To undeceive the credulous aunt, and be the officious obstacle of his match with Millamant?

Mrs. Mar. My obligations to my lady urged me: I had professed a friendship to her, and could not see her easy nature so abused by that dissembler.

Fain. What, was it conscience, then? Professed a friendship! Oh, the pious friendships of the female sex!

Mrs. Mar. More tender, more sincere, and more enduring, than all the vain and empty vows of men, whether professing love to us, or mutual faith to one another.

Fain. Ha, ha, ha! you are my wife's friend too.

Mrs. Mar. Shame and ingratitude! Do you reproach me? You, you upbraid me! Have I been false to her, through strict fidelity to you, and sacrificed my friendship to keep my love inviolate? And have you the baseness to charge me with the guilt, unmindful of the merit! To you it should be meritorious, that I have been vicious. And do you reflect that guilt upon me which should lie buried in your bosom?

Fain. You misinterpret my reproof. I meant but to remind you of the slight account you once could make of strictest ties, when set in competition with your love to me.

Mrs. Mar. 'Tis false, you urged it with deliberate malice—'twas spoke in scorn, and I never will forgive it.

Fain. Your guilt, not your resentment, begets your rage. If yet you loved, you could forgive a jealousy; but you are stung to find you are discovered.

Mrs. Mar. It shall be all discovered. You too shall be discovered; be sure you shall. I can but be exposed—if I do it myself I shall prevent your baseness.

Fain. Why, what will you do?

Mrs. Mar. Disclose it to your wife; own what has passed between us.

Fain. Frenzy!

Mrs. Mar. By all my wrongs I'll do't—I'll publish to the world the injuries you have done me, both in my fame and fortune. With both I trusted you, you bankrupt in honour, as indigent of wealth.

Fain. Your fame I have preserved. Your fortune has been bestowed as the prodigality of your love would have it, in pleasures which we both have shared. Yet, had not you been false, I had ere this repaid it. 'Tis true—had you permitted Mirabell with Millamant to have stolen their marriage, my lady had been incensed beyond all means of reconcilement; Millamant had forfeited the moiety of her fortune, which then would have descended to my wife. And wherefore did I marry, but to make lawful prize of a rich widow's wealth, and squander it on love and you?

Mrs. Mar. Deceit and frivolous pretence!

Fain. Death, am I not married? What's pretence? Am I not imprisoned, fettered? Have I not a wife? Nay, a wife that was a widow, a young widow, a handsome widow; and would be again a widow, but that I have a heart of proof, and something of a constitution to bustle through the ways of wedlock and this world. Will you yet be reconciled to truth and me?

Mrs. Mar. Impossible. Truth and you are inconsistent—I hate you, and shall for ever.

21. **prevent,** anticipate.

Fain. For loving you?

Mrs. Mar. I loathe the name of love after such usage; and next to the guilt with which you would asperse me, I scorn you most. Farewell.

Fain. Nay, we must not part thus.

Mrs. Mar. Let me go.

Fain. Come, I'm sorry.

Mrs. Mar. I care not—let me go—break my hands, do—I'd leave 'em to get loose.

Fain. I would not hurt you for the world. Have I no other hold to keep you here?

Mrs. Mar. Well, I have deserved it all.

Fain. You know I love you.

Mrs. Mar. Poor dissembling!—Oh, that—well, it is not yet—

Fain. What? What is it not? What is it not yet? It is not yet too late—

Mrs. Mar. No, it is not yet too late—I have that comfort.

Fain. It is, to love another.

Mrs. Mar. But not to loathe, detest, abhor mankind, myself, and the whole treacherous world.

Fain. Nay, this is extravagance.—Come, I ask your pardon—no tears—I was to blame, I could not love you and be easy in my doubts. Pray forbear—I believe you; I'm convinced I've done you wrong; and any way, every way will make amends;—I'll hate my wife yet more, damn her, I'll part with her, rob her of all she's worth, and we'll retire somewhere, anywhere, to another world. I'll marry thee—be pacified.—'Sdeath, they come, hide your face, your tears. You have a mask, wear it a moment. This way, this way, be persuaded. [*Exeunt.*

[*Enter* MIRABELL *and* MRS. FAINALL.]

Mrs. Fain. They are here yet.

Mira. They are turning into the other walk.

Mrs. Fain. While I only hated my husband, I could bear to see him; but since I have despised him, he's too offensive.

Mira. Oh, you should hate with prudence.

Mrs. Fain. Yes, for I have loved with indiscretion.

Mira. You should have just so much disgust for your husband as may be sufficient to make you relish your lover.

Mrs. Fain. You have been the cause that I have loved without bounds, and would you set limits to that aversion, of which you have been the occasion? Why did you make me marry this man?

Mira. Why do we daily commit disagreeable and dangerous actions? To save that idol, reputation. If the familiarities of our loves had produced that consequence of which you were apprehensive, where could you have fixed a father's name with credit, but on a husband? I knew Fainall to be a man lavish of his morals, an interested and professing friend, a false and a designing lover; yet one whose wit and outward fair behaviour have gained a reputation with the town, enough to make that woman stand excused who has suffered herself to be won by his addresses. A better man ought not to have been sacrificed to the occasion; a worse had not answered to the purpose. When you are weary of him, you know your remedy.

Mrs. Fain. I ought to stand in some degree of credit with you, Mirabell.

Mira. In justice to you, I have made you privy to my whole design, and put it in your power to ruin or advance my fortune.

Mrs. Fain. Whom have you instructed to represent your pretended uncle?

Mira. Waitwell, my servant.

Mrs. Fain. He is an humble servant to Foible, my mother's woman, and may win her to your interest.

Mira. Care is taken for that—she is won and worn by this time. They were married this morning.

Mrs. Fain. Who?

Mira. Waitwell and Foible. I would not tempt my servant to betray me by trusting him too far. If your mother, in hopes to ruin me, should consent to marry my pretended uncle, he might, like Mosca in *The Fox*, stand upon terms; so I made him sure beforehand.

Mrs. Fain. So, if my poor mother is caught in a contract, you will discover the imposture betimes; and release her by producing a certificate of her gallant's former marriage.

Mira. Yes, upon condition that she consent to my marriage with her niece, and surrender the moiety of her fortune in her possession.

Mrs. Fain. She talked last night of endeavouring at a match between Millamant and your uncle.

Mira. That was by Foible's direction, and my instruction, that she might seem to carry it more privately.

Mrs. Fain. Well, I have an opinion of your success; for I believe my lady will do anything to get an husband; and when she has this, which you have provided for her, I suppose she will submit to anything to get rid of him.

Mira. Yes, I think the good lady would marry anything that resembled a man, though 'twere no more than what a butler could pinch out of a napkin.

Mrs. Fain. Female frailty! We must all come to it, if we live to be old, and feel the craving of a false appetite when the true is decayed.

Mira. An old woman's appetite is depraved like that of a girl—'tis the green-sickness of a second childhood; and like the faint offer of a latter spring, serves but to usher in the fall, and withers in an affected bloom.

Mrs. Fain. Here's your mistress.

[*Enter* MRS. MILLAMANT, WITWOUD, *and* MINCING.]

Mira. Here she comes, i'faith, full sail, with her fan spread and streamers out, and a shoal of fools for tenders. Ha, no, I cry her mercy!

Mrs. Fain. I see but one poor empty sculler; and he tows her woman after him.

Mira. You seem to be unattended, madam—you used to have the *beau-monde* throng after you; and a flock of gay fine perukes hovering round you.

Wit. Like moths about a candle.—I had like to have lost my comparison for want of breath.

Milla. Oh, I have denied myself airs to-day. I have walked as fast through the crowd—

Wit. As a favourite just disgraced, and with as few followers.

Milla. Dear Mr. Witwoud, truce with your similitudes; for I am as sick of 'em—

Wit. As a physician of a good air.—I cannot help it, madam, though 'tis against myself.

Milla. Yet again! Mincing, stand between me and his wit.

Wit. Do, Mrs. Mincing, like a screen before a great fire. I confess I do blaze to-day, I am too bright.

Mrs. Fain. But, dear Millamant, why were you so long?

Milla. Long! Lord, have I not made violent haste? I have asked every living thing I met for you; I have enquired after you, as after a new fashion.

Wit. Madam, truce with your similitudes.—No, you met her husband, and did not ask him for her.

Mira. By your leave, Witwoud, that were like enquiring after an old fashion, to ask a husband for his wife.

Wit. Hum, a hit, a hit, a palpable hit, I confess it.

Mrs. Fain. You were dressed before I came abroad.

Milla. Ay, that's true—Oh, but then I had—Mincing, what had I? Why was I so long?

Minc. O mem, your la'ship stayed to peruse a pecquet of letters.

Milla. Oh ay, letters—I had letters—I am persecuted with letters—I hate letters—nobody knows

---

28. **The Fox,** Ben Jonson's *Volpone, or The Fox*. In the play, Mosca, the servant of the swindler, Volpone, blackmails his master by threatening to expose him.

50. **pecquet.** Mincing uses "e" for "a" in order to attain a "refined" pronunciation.

how to write letters; and yet one has 'em, one does not know why.—They serve one to pin up one's hair.

Wit. Is that the way? Pray, madam, do you pin up your hair with all your letters? I find I must keep copies.

Milla. Only with those in verse, Mr. Witwoud. I never pin up my hair with prose. I think I tried once, Mincing.

Minc. O mem, I shall never forget it.

Milla. Ay, poor Mincing tift and tift all the morning.

Minc. 'Till I had the cremp in my fingers, I'll vow, mem. And all to no purpose. But when your la'ship pins it up with poetry, it sits so pleasant the next day as anything, and is so pure and so crips.

Wit. Indeed, so crips?

Minc. You're such a critic, Mr. Witwoud.

Milla. Mirabell, did not you take exceptions last night? Oh ay, and went away.—Now I think on't I'm angry—no, now I think on't I'm pleased—for I believe I gave you some pain.

Mira. Does that please you?

Milla. Infinitely; I love to give pain.

Mira. You would affect a cruelty which is not in your nature; your true vanity is in the power of pleasing.

Milla. Oh, I ask your pardon for that—one's cruelty is one's power, and when one parts with one's cruelty, one parts with one's power; and when one has parted with that, I fancy one's old and ugly.

Mira. Ay, ay, suffer your cruelty to ruin the object of your power, to destroy your lover—and then how vain, how lost a thing you'll be! Nay, 'tis true: you are no longer handsome when you've lost your lover; your beauty dies upon the instant. For beauty is the lover's gift; 'tis he bestows your charms—your glass is all a cheat. The ugly and the old, whom the looking-glass mortifies, yet after commendation can be flattered by it, and discover beauties in it; for that reflects our praises, rather than your face.

Milla. Oh, the vanity of these men! Fainall, d'ee hear him? If they did not commend us, we were not handsome! Now you must know they could not commend one, if one was not handsome. Beauty the lover's gift—Lord, what is a lover, that it can give? Why, one makes lovers as fast as one pleases, and they live as long as one pleases, and they die as soon as one pleases; and then if one pleases, one makes more.

Wit. Very pretty. Why you make no more of making of lovers, madam, than of making so many card-matches.

Milla. One no more owes one's beauty to a lover than one's wit to an echo; they can but reflect what we look and say, vain empty things if we are silent or unseen, and want a being.

Mira. Yet, to those two vain empty things, you owe two the greatest pleasures of your life.

Milla. How so?

Mira. To your lover you owe the pleasure of hearing yourselves praised, and to an echo the pleasure of hearing yourselves talk.

Wit. But I know a lady that loves talking so incessantly, she won't give an echo fair play; she has that everlasting rotation of tongue, that an echo must wait till she dies before it can catch her last words.

Milla. Oh, fiction! Fainall, let us leave these men.

Mira. (*aside to* MRS. FAINALL). Draw off Witwoud.

Mrs. Fain. (*aside*). Immediately.—I have a word or two for Mr. Witwoud.

Mira. I would beg a little private audience too. (*Exeunt* WITWOUD *and* MRS. FAINALL.) You had the tyranny to deny me last night; though you knew I came to impart a secret to you that concerned my love.

Milla. You saw I was engaged.

Mira. Unkind. You had the leisure to entertain a herd of fools, things who visit you from their excessive idleness, bestowing on your easiness that time which is the incumbrance of their lives. How can you find delight in such society? It is impossible they should admire you, they are not capable; or if they were, it should be to you as a mortification, for sure to please a fool is some degree of folly.

Milla. I please myself—besides, sometimes to converse with fools is for my health.

Mira. Your health! Is there a worse disease than the conversation of fools?

Milla. Yes, the vapours; fools are physic for it, next to asafetida.

Mira. You are not in a course of fools?

Milla. Mirabell, if you persist in this offensive freedom, you'll displease me. I think I must resolve, after all, not to have you—we shan't agree.

Mira. Not in our physic, it may be.

Milla. And yet our distemper in all likelihood will be the same; for we shall be sick of one another. I

---

11. **tift,** "struggled with my hair."   16. **crips,** Mincing's pronunciation of "crisp."
3. **card-matches,** strips of card dipped in melted sulphur. 45. **a course of fools,** by analogy, that is, with a prescribed course of physic.

shan't endure to be reprimanded, nor instructed; 'tis so dull to act always by advice, and so tedious to be told of one's faults—I can't bear it. Well, I won't have you, Mirabell—I'm resolved—I think—you may go—ha, ha, ha! What would you give, that you could help loving me?

Mira. I would give something that you did not know I could not help it.

Milla. Come, don't look grave, then. Well, what do you say to me?

Mira. I say that a man may as soon make a friend by his wit, or a fortune by his honesty, as win a woman with plain dealing and sincerity.

Milla. Sententious Mirabell! Prithee don't look with that violent and inflexible wise face, like Solomon at the dividing of the child in an old tapestry hanging.

Mira. You are merry, madam, but I would persuade you for a moment to be serious.

Milla. What, with that face? No, if you keep your countenance, 'tis impossible I should hold mine. Well, after all, there is something very moving in a lovesick face. Ha, ha, ha!—Well I won't laugh, don't be peevish.—Heigho! Now I'll be melancholy, as melancholy as a watch-light. Well, Mirabell, if ever you will win me, woo me now.—Nay, if you are so tedious, fare you well—I see they are walking away.

Mira. Can you not find in the variety of your disposition one moment—

Milla. To hear you tell me Foible's married, and your plot like to speed?—No.

Mira. But how you came to know it—

Milla. Without the help of the devil, you can't imagine; unless she should tell me herself. Which of the two it may have been, I will leave you to consider; and when you have done thinking of that, think of me. [*Exit.*

Mira. I have something more—Gone!—Think of you! To think of a whirlwind, though 'twere in a whirlwind, were a case of more steady contemplation; a very tranquillity of mind and mansion. A fellow that lives in a windmill has not a more whimsical dwelling than the heart of a man that is lodged in a woman. There is no point of the compass to which they cannot turn, and by which they are not turned; and by one as well as another, for motion, not method, is their occupation. To know this, and yet continue to be in love, is to be made wise from the dictates of reason, and yet persevere to play the fool by the force of instinct.—Oh, here come my pair of turtles.—What, billing so sweetly! Is not Valentine's Day over with you yet?

25. **watch-light,** night light. 52. **turtles,** turtledoves.

[*Enter* WAITWELL *and* FOIBLE.]

Mira. Sirrah, Waitwell, why sure you think you were married for your own recreation, and not for my conveniency.

Wait. Your pardon, sir. With submission, we have indeed been solacing in lawful delights; but still with an eye to business, sir. I have instructed her as well as I could. If she can take your directions as readily as my instructions, sir, your affairs are in a prosperous way.

Mira. Give you joy, Mrs. Foible.

Foib. Oh 'las, sir, I'm so ashamed—I'm afraid my lady has been in a thousand inquietudes for me. But I protest, sir, I made as much haste as I could.

Wait. That she did indeed, sir. It was my fault that she did not make more.

Mira. That I believe.

Foib. But I told my lady as you instructed me, sir. That I had a prospect of seeing Sir Rowland your uncle; and that I would put her ladyship's picture in my pocket to show him; which I'll be sure to say has made him so enamoured of her beauty that he burns with impatience to lie at her ladyship's feet and worship the original.

Mira. Excellent Foible! Matrimony has made you eloquent in love.

Wait. I think she has profited, sir. I think so.

Foib. You have seen Madam Millamant, sir?

Mira. Yes.

Foib. I told her, sir, because I did not know that you might find an opportunity; she had so much company last night.

Mira. Your diligence will merit more.—In the meantime—(*Gives money.*)

Foib. O dear sir, your humble servant.

Wait. Spouse!

Mira. Stand off, sir, not a penny.—Go on and prosper, Foible—the lease shall be made good and the farm stocked, if we succeed.

Foib. I don't question your generosity, sir; and you need not doubt of success. If you have no more commands, sir, I'll be gone; I'm sure my lady is at her toilet, and can't dress till I come.—Oh dear, I'm sure that (*Looking out.*) was Mrs. Marwood that went by in a mask; if she has seen me with you I'm sure she'll tell my lady. I'll make haste home and prevent her. Your servant, sir. B'w'y, Waitwell.

[*Exit* FOIBLE.

Wait. Sir Rowland, if you please. The jade's so pert upon her preferment she forgets herself.

Mira. Come, sir, will you endeavour to forget yourself—and transform into Sir Rowland.

47–48. **prevent,** anticipate.

Wait. Why, sir, it will be impossible I should remember myself—married, knighted, and attended all in one day! 'Tis enough to make any man forget himself. The difficulty will be how to recover my acquaintance and familiarity with my former self, and fall from my transformation to a reformation into Waitwell. Nay, I shan't be quite the same Waitwell neither—for now I remember me, I'm married, and can't be my own man again.

Ay there's my grief; that's the sad change of life;
To lose my title, and yet keep my wife. [*Exeunt.*

ACT III

SCENE.—*A room in* LADY WISHFORT'S *house.*

LADY WISHFORT *at her toilet,* PEG *waiting.*

Lady W. Merciful, no news of Foible yet?

Peg. No, madam.

Lady W. I have no more patience. If I have not fretted myself till I am pale again, there's no veracity in me. Fetch me the red—the red, do you hear, sweetheart? An arrant ash colour, as I'm a person. Look you how this wench stirs! Didst thou not hear me, mopus?

Peg. The red ratafia, does your ladyship mean, or the cherry brandy?

Lady W. Ratafia, fool! No, fool. Not the ratafia, fool—grant me patience! I mean the Spanish paper, idiot—complexion, darling. Paint, paint, paint, dost thou understand that, changeling, dangling thy hands like bobbins before thee? Why dost thou not stir, puppet?—thou wooden thing upon wires!

Peg. Lord, madam, your ladyship is so impatient. I cannot come at the paint, madam; Mrs. Foible has locked it up, and carried the key with her.

Lady W. A pox take you both! Fetch me the cherry brandy, then. (*Exit* PEG.) I'm as pale and as faint, I look like Mrs. Qualmsick the curate's wife, that's always breeding.—Wench, come, come, wench, what art thou doing, sipping? tasting? Save thee, dost thou not know the bottle?

[*Enter* PEG *with a bottle and china cup.*]

Peg. Madam, I was looking for a cup.

Lady W. A cup, save thee, and what a cup hast thou brought! Dost thou take me for a fairy, to drink out of an acorn? Why didst thou not bring thy thimble? Hast thou ne'er a brass thimble clinking in thy pocket with a bit of nutmeg? I warrant thee. Come, fill, fill.—So—again. (*One knocks.*) See who that is.—Set down the bottle first. Here, here, under the table. What, wouldst thou go with the bottle in thy hand like a tapster? (*Exit* PEG.) As I'm a person, this wench has lived in an inn upon the road, before she came to me, like Maritornes the Asturian in *Don Quixote*. (*Re-enter* PEG.) No Foible yet?

Peg. No, madam—Mrs. Marwood.

Lady W. Oh, Marwood! let her come in. Come in, good Marwood.

[*Enter* MRS. MARWOOD.]

Mrs. Mar. I'm surprised to find your ladyship in dishabille at this time of day.

Lady W. Foible's a lost thing; has been abroad since morning, and never heard of since.

Mrs. Mar. I saw her but now, as I came masked through the Park, in conference with Mirabell.

Lady W. With Mirabell! You call my blood into my face, with mentioning that traitor. She durst not have the confidence. I sent her to negotiate an affair, in which if I'm detected I'm undone. If that wheedling villain has wrought upon Foible to detect me, I'm ruined. Oh, my dear friend, I'm a wretch of wretches if I'm detected.

Mrs. Mar. O madam, you cannot suspect Mrs. Foible's integrity.

Lady W. Oh, he carries poison in his tongue that would corrupt integrity itself. If she has given him an opportunity, she has as good as put her integrity into his hands. Ah, dear Marwood, what's integrity to an opportunity?—Hark! I hear her.—Dear friend, retire into my closet, that I may examine her with more freedom.—You'll pardon me, dear friend, I can make bold with you.—There are books over the chimney—Quarles and Prynne, and the *Short View of the Stage*, with Bunyan's works to entertain you. (*To* PEG.) Go, you thing, and send her in. [*Exeunt* MARWOOD *and* PEG.

[*Enter* FOIBLE.]

Lady W. O Foible, where hast thou been? what hast thou been doing?

Foib. Madam, I have seen the party.

---

17. Merciful, "heaven" or "goodness" understood. 24. mopus, stupid person. 28. Spanish paper, a Spanish cosmetic preparation. 1–2. thimble . . . nutmeg, good-luck charms. 37–38. Quarles, Francis Quarles (1592–1644), whose *Emblems*, published in 1635, was one of the most popular religious works of the century. Prynne, William Prynne (1600–1669), a Puritan author of many pamphlets and books, including *Histrio-Mastix, or The Players' Scourge*, 1633. Short View of the Stage, Jeremy Collier's *A Short View of the Immorality and Profaneness of the English Stage*, 1698, the most famous of the contemporary attacks on the stage.

Lady W. But what hast thou done?

Foib. Nay, 'tis your ladyship has done, and are to do; I have only promised. But a man so enamoured—so transported! Well, if worshipping of pictures be a sin—poor Sir Rowland, I say.

Lady W. The miniature has been counted like—but hast thou not betrayed me, Foible? Hast thou not detected me to that faithless Mirabell? What hadst thou to do with him in the park? Answer me, has he got nothing out of thee?

Foib. (*aside*). So, the devil has been beforehand with me; what shall I say?—Alas, madam, could I help it, if I met that confident thing? Was I in fault? If you had heard how he used me, and all upon your ladyship's account, I'm sure you would not suspect my fidelity. Nay, if that had been the worst, I could have borne: but he had a fling at your ladyship, too; and then I could not hold, but, i' faith, I gave him his own.

Lady W. Me? What did the filthy fellow say?

Foib. O madam, 'tis a shame to say what he said—with his taunts and his fleers, tossing up his nose. "Humh!" says he, "what, you are a hatching some plot," says he, "you are so early abroad, or catering," says he, "ferreting for some disbanded officer, I warrant—half pay is but thin subsistence," says he. "Well, what pension does your lady propose? Let me see," says he; "what, she must come down pretty deep now: she's superannuated," says he, "and—"

Lady W. Ods my life, I'll have him—I'll have him murdered. I'll have him poisoned. Where does he eat? I'll marry a drawer to have him poisoned in his wine. I'll send for Robin from Locket's immediately.

Foib. Poison him? Poisoning's too good for him. Starve him, madam, starve him; marry Sir Rowland and get him disinherited. Oh, you would bless yourself, to hear what he said.

Lady W. A villain! "superannuated!"

Foib. "Humh!" says he; "I hear you are laying designs against me, too," says he, "and Mrs. Millamant is to marry my uncle,"—(he does not suspect a word of your ladyship)—"but," says he, "I'll fit you for that, I warrant you," says he, "I'll hamper you for that," says he, "you and your old frippery, too," says he, "I'll handle you—"

Lady W. Audacious villain! handle me! would he durst! "Frippery? old frippery!" Was there ever such a foul-mouthed fellow? I'll be married to-morrow, I'll be contracted to-night.

Foib. The sooner the better, madam.

Lady W. Will Sir Rowland be here, say'st thou? When, Foible?

Foib. Incontinently, madam. No new sheriff's wife expects the return of her husband after knighthood with that impatience in which Sir Rowland burns for the dear hour of kissing your ladyship's hands after dinner.

Lady W. "Frippery? superannuated frippery!" I'll frippery the villain; I'll reduce him to frippery and rags. A tatterdemalion!—I hope to see him hung with tatters, like a Long Lane pent-house, or a gibbet-thief. A slander-mouthed railer. I warrant the spendthrift prodigal's in debt as much as the million lottery, or the whole court upon a birthday. I'll spoil his credit with his tailor. Yes, he shall have my niece with her fortune, he shall.

Foib. He! I hope to see him lodge in Ludgate first, and angle into Blackfriars for brass farthings, with an old mitten.

Lady W. Ay, dear Foible; thank thee for that, dear Foible. He has put me out of all patience. I shall never recompose my features to receive Sir Rowland with any economy of face. This wretch has fretted me that I am absolutely decayed. Look, Foible.

Foib. Your ladyship has frowned a little too rashly, indeed, madam. There are some cracks discernible in the white varnish.

Lady W. Let me see the glass.—Cracks, say'st thou? Why, I am arrantly flayed. I look like an old peeled wall. Thou must repair me, Foible, before Sir Rowland comes, or I shall never keep up to my picture.

Foib. I warrant you, madam; a little art once made your picture like you, and now a little of the same art must make you like your picture. Your picture must sit for you, madam.

Lady W. But art thou sure Sir Rowland will not fail to come? Or will a' not fail when he does come? Will he be importunate, Foible, and push? For if he should not be importunate—I shall never break decorums—I shall die with confusion, if I am forced to advance—Oh no, I can never advance—I shall swoon if he should expect advances. No, I hope Sir Rowland is better bred than to put a lady to the necessity of breaking her forms. I won't be too coy neither.—I won't give him despair—but a little disdain is not amiss; a little scorn is alluring.

Foib. A little scorn becomes your ladyship.

---

33. **drawer,** tapster, or waiter in a taproom. 34. **Robin from Locket's,** presumably a tapster at Locket's, a fashionable tavern. 12. **Long Lane pent-house,** where old clothes were sold. 18–19. **Ludgate . . . Blackfriars.** The Fleet Prison in Ludgate, in the district of Blackfriars, was the most notorious place of confinement for persons arrested for debt. 40. **a',** he.

Lady W. Yes, but tenderness becomes me best—a sort of a dyingness.—You see that picture has a sort of a—ha, Foible? A swimmingness in the eyes.—Yes, I'll look so—my niece affects it, but she wants features. Is Sir Rowland handsome? Let my toilet be removed—I'll dress above. I'll receive Sir Rowland here. Is he handsome? Don't answer me. I won't know; I'll be surprised. I'll be taken by surprise.

Foib. By storm, madam. Sir Rowland's a brisk man.

Lady W. Is he! Oh, then he'll importune, if he's a brisk man. I shall save decorums if Sir Rowland importunes. I have a mortal terror at the apprehension of offending against decorums. Oh, I'm glad he's a brisk man. Let my things be removed, good Foible. [*Exit.*

[*Enter* MRS. FAINALL.]

Mrs. Fain. O Foible, I have been in a fright, lest I should come too late. That devil, Marwood, saw you in the Park with Mirabell, and I'm afraid will discover it to my lady.

Foib. Discover what, madam?

Mrs. Fain. Nay, nay, put not on that strange face. I am privy to the whole design, and know that Waitwell, to whom thou wert this morning married, is to personate Mirabell's uncle, and as such, winning my lady, to involve her in those difficulties from which Mirabell only must release her, by his making his conditions to have my cousin and her fortune left to her own disposal.

Foib. O dear madam, I beg your pardon. It was not my confidence in your ladyship that was deficient; but I thought the former good correspondence between your ladyship and Mr. Mirabell might have hindered his communicating this secret.

Mrs. Fain. Dear Foible, forget that.

Foib. O dear madam, Mr. Mirabell is such a sweet winning gentleman!—But your ladyship is the pattern of generosity.—Sweet lady, to be so good! Mr. Mirabell cannot choose but be grateful. I find your ladyship has his heart still. Now, madam, I can safely tell your ladyship our success. Mrs. Marwood had told my lady, but I warrant I managed myself. I turned it all for the better. I told my lady that Mr. Mirabell railed at her. I laid horrid things to his charge, I'll vow; and my lady is so incensed, that she'll be contracted to Sir Rowland to-night, she says.—I warrant I worked her up, that he may have her for asking for, as they say of a Welsh maidenhead.

Mrs. Fain. O rare Foible!

Foib. Madam, I beg your ladyship to acquaint Mr. Mirabell of his success. I would be seen as little as possible to speak to him—besides, I believe Madam Marwood watches me.—She has a month's mind; but I know Mr. Mirabell can't abide her.—(*Calls.*) John—remove my lady's toilet. Madam, your servant. My lady is so impatient, I fear she'll come for me if I stay.

Mrs. Fain. I'll go with you up the back stairs, lest I should meet her. [*Exeunt.*

[*Enter* MRS. MARWOOD.]

Mrs. Mar. Indeed, Mrs. Engine, is it thus with you? Are you become a go-between of this importance? Yes, I shall watch you. Why this wench is the *passe-partout*, a very master-key to everybody's strongbox. My friend Fainall, have you carried it so swimmingly? I thought there was something in it; but it seems it's over with you. Your loathing is not from a want of appetite, then, but from a surfeit. Else you could never be so cool to fall from a principal to be an assistant; to procure for him! A pattern of generosity, that I confess. Well, Mr. Fainall, you have met with your match.—O man, man! Woman, woman! The devil's an ass: if I were a painter, I would draw him like an idiot, a driveler with a bib and bells. Man should have his head and horns, and woman the rest of him. Poor simple fiend! "Madam Marwood has a month's mind, but he can't abide her."—'Twere better for him you had not been his confessor in that affair, without you could have kept his counsel closer. I shall not prove another pattern of generosity—he has not obliged me to that with those excesses of himself; and now I'll have none of him. Here comes the good lady, panting ripe; with a heart full of hope, and a head full of care, like any chemist upon the day of projection.

[*Enter* LADY WISHFORT.]

Lady W. O dear Marwood, what shall I say for this rude forgetfulness?—but my dear friend is all goodness.

Mrs. Mar. No apologies, dear madam. I have been very well entertained.

Lady W. As I'm a person I am in a very chaos to think I should so forget myself—but I have such an olio of affairs really I know not what to do.—(*Calls.*)—Foible!—I expect my nephew Sir Wilfull every moment too.—Why, Foible!—He means to travel for improvement.

4-5. **a month's mind,** an intense longing. 13. **Mrs. Engine,** "Mrs. Trickery." 37. **chemist . . . projection.** "Projection," in alchemy, was the term applied to the transmutation of the base metal into gold. 47. **olio,** hotchpotch.

Mrs. Mar. Methinks Sir Wilfull should rather think of marrying than travelling at his years. I hear he is turned of forty.

Lady W. Oh, he's in less danger of being spoiled by his travels.—I am against my nephew's marrying too young. It will be time enough when he comes back, and has acquired discretion to choose for himself.

Mrs. Mar. Methinks Mrs. Millamant and he would make a very fit match. He may travel afterwards. 'Tis a thing very usual with young gentlemen.

Lady W. I promise you I have thought on't—and since 'tis your judgment, I'll think on't again. I assure you I will; I value your judgment extremely. On my word I'll propose it. (*Enter* FOIBLE.) Come, come, Foible—I had forgot my nephew will be here before dinner—I must make haste.

Foib. Mr. Witwoud and Mr. Petulant are come to dine with your ladyship.

Lady W. Oh, dear, I can't appear till I am dressed. Dear Marwood, shall I be free with you again, and beg you to entertain 'em? I'll make all imaginable haste. Dear friend, excuse me.

[*Exeunt* LADY WISHFORT *and* FOIBLE.

[*Enter* MRS. MILLAMANT *and* MINCING.]

Milla. Sure never anything was so unbred as that odious man.—Marwood, your servant.

Mrs. Mar. You have a colour, what's the matter?

Milla. That horrid fellow Petulant has provoked me into a flame—I have broke my fan.—Mincing, lend me yours.—Is not all the powder out of my hair?

Mrs. Mar. No. What has he done?

Milla. Nay, he has done nothing; he has only talked.—Nay, he has said nothing neither, but he has contradicted everything that has been said. For my part, I thought Witwoud and he would have quarrelled.

Minc. I vow, mem, I thought once they would have fit.

Milla. Well, 'tis a lamentable thing I swear, that one has not the liberty of choosing one's acquaintance as one does one's clothes.

Mrs. Mar. If we had that liberty, we should be as weary of one set of acquaintance, though never so good, as we are of one suit, though never so fine. A fool and a doily stuff would now and then find days of grace, and be worn for variety.

Milla. I could consent to wear 'em, if they would wear alike; but fools never wear out—they are such drap-de-Berry things! Without one could give 'em to one's chambermaid after a day or two.

47. **doily stuff,** a light, cheap woolen material. 51. **drap-de-Berry,** a heavier woolen cloth.

Mrs. Mar. 'Twere better so indeed. Or what think you of the play-house? A fine gay glossy fool should be given there, like a new masking habit, after the masquerade is over, and we have done with the disguise. For a fool's visit is always a disguise, and never admitted by a woman of wit but to blind her affair with a lover of sense. If you would but appear bare-faced now, and own Mirabell, you might as easily put off Petulant and Witwoud as your hood and scarf. And indeed 'tis time, for the town has found it: the secret is grown too big for the pretence: 'tis like Mrs. Primly's great belly; she may lace it down before, but it burnishes on her hips. Indeed, Millamant, you can no more conceal it than my Lady Strammel can her face, that goodly face, which in defiance of her Rhenish-wine tea, will not be comprehended in a mask.

Milla. I'll take my death, Marwood, you are more censorious than a decayed beauty, or a discarded toast. Mincing, tell the men they may come up. My aunt is not dressing here; their folly is less provoking than your malice. (*Exit* MINCING.) "The town has found it." What has it found? That Mirabell loves me is no more a secret than it is a secret that you discovered it to my aunt, or than the reason why you discovered it is a secret.

Mrs. Mar. You are nettled.

Milla. You're mistaken. Ridiculous!

Mrs. Mar. Indeed, my dear, you'll tear another fan if you don't mitigate those violent airs.

Milla. O silly! Ha, ha, ha! I could laugh immoderately. Poor Mirabell! His constancy to me has quite destroyed his complaisance for all the world beside. I swear, I never enjoined it him, to be so coy. If I had the vanity to think he would obey me, I would command him to show more gallantry—'tis hardly well bred to be so particular on one hand, and so insensible on the other. But I despair to prevail, and so let him follow his own way. Ha, ha, ha! Pardon me, dear creature, I must laugh, ha, ha, ha! though I grant you 'tis a little barbarous, ha, ha, ha!

Mrs. Mar. What pity 'tis, so much fine raillery, and delivered with so significant gesture, should be so unhappily directed to miscarry.

Milla. Heh? Dear creature, I ask your pardon—I swear I did not mind you.

Mrs. Mar. Mr. Mirabell and you both may think it a thing impossible, when I shall tell him by telling you—

Milla. Oh, dear, what? for it is the same thing if I hear it—ha, ha, ha!

Mrs. Mar. That I detest him, hate him, madam.

46. **mind you,** pay attention to you.

Milla. O madam, why so do I—and yet the creature loves me, ha, ha, ha! How can one forbear laughing to think of it—I am a sibyl if I am not amazed to think what he can see in me. I'll take my death, I think you are handsomer—and within a year or two as young. If you could but stay for me, I should overtake you—but that cannot be. Well, that thought makes me melancholic—now I'll be sad.

Mrs. Mar. Your merry note may be changed sooner than you think.

Milla. D'ee say so? Then I'm resolved I'll have a song to keep up my spirits.

[*Enter* MINCING.]

Minc. The gentlemen stay but to comb, madam, and will wait on you.

Milla. Desire Mrs. —— that is in the next room to sing the song I would have learnt yesterday. You shall hear it, madam.—Not that there's any great matter in it—but 'tis agreeable to my humour.

SONG

Set by Mr. John Eccles, and sung by Mrs. Hodgson.

1

Love's but the frailty of the mind,
When 'tis not with ambition joined;
A sickly flame, which if not fed expires;
And feeding, wastes in self-consuming fires.

2

'Tis not to wound a wanton boy
Or amorous youth, that gives the joy;
But 'tis the glory to have pierced a swain,
For whom inferior beauties sighed in vain.

3

Then I alone the conquest prize,
When I insult a rival's eyes:
If there's delight in love, 'tis when I see
That heart which others bleed for, bleed for me.

[*Enter* PETULANT *and* WITWOUD.]

Milla. Is your animosity composed, gentlemen?

Wit. Raillery, raillery, madam; we have no animosity—we hit off a little wit now and then, but no animosity. The falling out of wits is like the falling out of lovers. We agree in the main, like treble and bass. Ha, Petulant?

Pet. Ay, in the main—but when I have a humour to contradict—

Wit. Ay, when he has a humour to contradict, then I contradict too. What, I know my cue. Then we contradict one another like two battledores; for contradictions beget one another like Jews.

Pet. If he says black's black—if I have a humour to say 'tis blue—let that pass—all's one for that. If I have a humour to prove it, it must be granted.

Wit. Not positively must—but it may—it may.

Pet. Yes, it positively must, upon proof positive.

Wit. Ay, upon proof positive it must; but upon proof presumptive it only may. That's a logical distinction now, madam.

Mrs. Mar. I perceive your debates are of importance, and very learnedly handled.

Pet. Importance is one thing, and learning's another; but a debate's a debate, that I assert.

Wit. Petulant's an enemy to learning; he relies altogether on his parts.

Pet. No, I'm no enemy to learning; it hurts not me.

Mrs. Mar. That's a sign indeed it's no enemy to you.

Pet. No, no, it's no enemy to anybody, but them that have it.

Milla. Well, an illiterate man's my aversion. I wonder at the impudence of any illiterate man, to offer to make love.

Wit. That I confess I wonder at too.

Milla. Ah! to marry an ignorant! that can hardly read or write.

Pet. Why should a man be any further from being married though he can't read, than he is from being hanged? The ordinary's paid for setting the psalm, and the parish-priest for reading the ceremony. And for the rest which is to follow in both cases, a man may do it without book—so all's one for that.

Milla. D'ee hear the creature? Lord, here's company, I'll be gone. [*Exeunt* MILLAMANT *and* MINCING.]

Wit. In the name of Bartlemew and his fair, what have we here?

Mrs. Mar. 'Tis your brother, I fancy. Don't you know him?

Wit. Not I—yes, I think it is he—I've almost forgot him; I have not seen him since the Revolution.

[*Enter* SIR WILFULL WITWOUD *in a country riding habit, and* Servant *to* LADY WISHFORT.]

Serv. Sir, my lady's dressing. Here's company, if you please to walk in, in the meantime.

Sir Wil. Dressing! What, it's but morning here, I warrant, with you in London; we should count it towards afternoon in our parts, down in Shropshire.

30. ordinary's . . . psalm. A psalm was read by the ordinary (the prison chaplain) before the execution of a criminal. **36. Bartlemew . . . fair.** The most popular of all English fairs, held in Smithfield about St. Bartholomew's Day, August 24, until 1855. **41. Revolution,** of 1688.

WILLIAM CONGREVE

Why then belike my aunt han't dined yet—ha, friend?

Serv. Your aunt, sir?

Sir Wil. My aunt, sir, yes, my aunt, sir, and your lady, sir; your lady is my aunt, sir.—Why, what, dost thou not know me, friend? Why, then send somebody hither that does. How long hast thou lived with thy lady, fellow, ha?

Serv. A week, sir; longer than anybody in the house, except my lady's woman.

Sir Wil. Why, then belike thou dost not know thy lady, if thou see'st her, ha, friend?

Serv. Why truly, sir, I cannot safely swear to her face in a morning, before she is dressed. 'Tis like I may give a shrewd guess at her by this time.

Sir Wil. Well, prithee try what thou canst do; if thou canst not guess, enquire her out, dost hear, fellow? And tell her, her nephew, Sir Wilfull Witwoud, is in the house.

Serv. I shall, sir.

Sir Wil. Hold ye, hear me, friend; a word with you in your ear, prithee who are these gallants?

Serv. Really, sir, I can't tell; here come so many here, 'tis hard to know 'em all. [*Exit* Servant.

Sir Wil. Oons, this fellow knows less than a starling; I don't think a' knows his own name.

Mrs. Mar. Mr. Witwoud, your brother is not behindhand in forgetfulness—I fancy he has forgot you too.

Wit. I hope so—the devil take him that remembers first, I say.

Sir Wil. Save you, gentlemen and lady.

Mrs. Mar. For shame, Mr. Witwoud; why won't you speak to him?—And you, sir.

Wit. Petulant, speak.

Pet. And you, sir.

Sir Wil. No offence, I hope. (*Salutes* MARWOOD.)

Mrs. Mar. No, sure, sir.

Wit. This is a vile dog, I see that already. No offence! Ha, ha, ha! To him; to him, Petulant, smoke him.

Pet. It seems as if you had come a journey, sir; hem, hem. (*Surveying him round.*)

Sir Wil. Very likely, sir, that it may seem so.

Pet. No offence, I hope, sir.

Wit. Smoke the boots, the boots; Petulant, the boots; ha, ha, ha!

Sir Wil. Maybe not, sir; thereafter as 'tis meant, sir.

Pet. Sir, I presume upon the information of your boots.

Sir Wil. Why, 'tis like you may, sir. If you are not satisfied with the information of my boots, sir, if you will step to the stable, you may enquire further of my horse, sir.

Pet. Your horse, sir! Your horse is an ass, sir!

Sir Wil. Do you speak by way of offence, sir?

Mrs. Mar. The gentleman's merry, that's all, sir. (*Aside.*)—S'life, we shall have a quarrel betwixt an horse and an ass, before they find one another out. (*Aloud.*) You must not take anything amiss from your friends, sir. You are among your friends here, though it may be you don't know it.—If I am not mistaken, you are Sir Wilfull Witwoud.

Sir Wil. Right, lady; I am Sir Wilfull Witwoud, so I write myself; no offence to anybody, I hope; and nephew to the Lady Wishfort of this mansion.

Mrs. Mar. Don't you know this gentleman, sir?

Sir Wil. Hum! What, sure 'tis not—Yea, by'r lady, but 'tis—'Sheart, I know not whether 'tis or no.—Yea, but 'tis, by the Wrekin. Brother Antony! What, Tony, i' faith! What, dost thou not know me? By'r Lady, nor I thee, thou art so becravated, and so beperriwigged—'Sheart, why dost not speak? Art thou o'erjoyed?

Wit. Odso, brother, is it you? Your servant, brother.

Sir Wil. Your servant! Why, yours, sir. Your servant again.—'Sheart, and your friend and servant to that—and a—(*Puff.*) and a flap-dragon for your service, sir: and a hare's foot, and a hare's scut for your service, sir; an you be so cold and so courtly!

Wit. No offence, I hope, brother.

Sir Wil. 'Sheart, sir, but there is, and much offence.—A pox, is this your Inns o' Court breeding, not to know your friends and your relations, your elders, and your betters?

Wit. Why, brother Wilfull of Salop, you may be as short as a Shrewsbury cake, if you please. But I tell you 'tis not modish to know relations in town. You think you're in the country, where great lubberly brothers slabber and kiss one another when they meet, like a call of serjeants.—'Tis not the fashion here; 'tis not indeed, dear brother.

Sir Wil. The fashion's a fool; and you're a fop, dear brother. 'Sheart, I've suspected this.—By'r Lady, I conjectured you were a fop, since you began to change the style of your letters, and write in a scrap of paper gilt round the edges, no bigger than a subpoena. I might expect this when you left off, "Honoured Brother," and "hoping you are in good

---

25. Oons, a vulgar contraction of "God's wounds!" **41. smoke,** make fun of. **19. Wrekin,** a hill in Shropshire. **24. Odso,** a contraction of "Godso!" from "God's soul!" **30. scut,** tail. **an,** if. **34. Inns o' Court,** the four legal societies admitting persons to practice at the bar. **37. Salop,** the abbreviation for Shropshire.

health," and so forth—to begin with a "Rat me, knight, I'm so sick of a last night's debauch."—'Odsheart, and then tell a familiar tale of a cock and a bull, and a whore and a bottle, and so conclude.—You could write news before you were out of your time, when you lived with honest Pumple-Nose, the attorney of Furnival's Inn.—You could intreat to be remembered then to your friends round the Wrekin. We could have gazettes then, and Dawks's Letter, and the weekly bill, 'till of late days.

Pet. 'Slife, Witwoud, were you ever an attorney's clerk? of the family of the Furnivals. Ha, ha, ha!

Wit. Ay, ay, but that was for a while. Not long, not long. Pshaw! I was not in my own power then. An orphan, and this fellow was my guardian; ay, ay, I was glad to consent to that man to come to London. He had the disposal of me then. If I had not agreed to that, I might have been bound prentice to a felt maker in Shrewsbury; this fellow would have bound me to a maker of felts.

Sir Wil. 'Sheart, and better than to be bound to a maker of fops; where, I suppose, you have served your time, and now you may set up for yourself.

Mrs. Mar. You intend to travel, sir, as I'm informed.

Sir Wil. Belike I may, madam. I may chance to sail upon the salt seas, if my mind hold.

Pet. And the wind serve.

Sir Wil. Serve or not serve, I shan't ask licence of you, sir, nor the weather-cock your companion. I direct my discourse to the lady, sir. 'Tis like my aunt may have told you, madam—yes, I have settled my concerns, I may say now, and am minded to see foreign parts. If an' how that the peace holds, whereby, that is, taxes abate.

Mrs. Mar. I thought you had designed for France at all adventures.

Sir Wil. I can't tell that; 'tis like I may, and 'tis like I may not. I am somewhat dainty in making a resolution,—because when I make it I keep it. I don't stand shill I, shall I, then; if I say't, I'll do't: but I have thoughts to tarry a small matter in town, to learn somewhat of your lingo first, before I cross the seas. I'd gladly have a spice of your French, as they say, whereby to hold discourse in foreign countries.

Mrs. Mar. Here is an academy in town for that use.

Sir Wil. There is? 'Tis like there may.

10. Dawks's Letter ... weekly bill. *Dawks's News-Letter* was a weekly digest of the news. Weekly bills of mortality (lists of deaths) were published in London. **35. taxes abate.** The war with France, which had raised English taxes considerably, had been temporarily halted by the Peace of Ryswick, 1697.

Mrs. Mar. No doubt you will return very much improved.

Wit. Yes, refined, like a Dutch skipper from a whale-fishing.

[*Enter* LADY WISHFORT *and* FAINALL.]

Lady W. Nephew, you are welcome.

Sir Wil. Aunt, your servant.

Fain. Sir Wilfull, your most faithful servant.

Sir Wil. Cousin Fainall, give me your hand.

Lady W. Cousin Witwoud, your servant; Mr. Petulant, your servant—nephew, you are welcome again. Will you drink anything after your journey, nephew, before you eat? Dinner's almost ready.

Sir Wil. I'm very well, I thank you, aunt—however, I thank you for your courteous offer. 'Sheart, I was afraid you would have been in the fashion too, and have remembered to have forgot your relations. Here's your Cousin Tony, belike, I mayn't call him brother for fear of offence.

Lady W. Oh, he's a rallier, nephew—my cousin's a wit; and your great wits always rally their best friends to choose. When you have been abroad, nephew, you'll understand raillery better.

[FAINALL *and* MRS. MARWOOD *talk apart.*]

Sir Wil. Why then, let him hold his tongue in the meantime, and rail when that day comes.

[*Enter* MINCING.]

Minc. Mem, I come to acquaint your la'ship that dinner is impatient.

Sir Wil. Impatient? Why then belike it won't stay till I pull off my boots. Sweetheart, can you help me to a pair of slippers? My man's with his horses, I warrant.

Lady W. Fie, fie, nephew, you would not pull off your boots here. Go down into the hall—dinner shall stay for you.—My nephew's a little unbred, you'll pardon him, madam. Gentlemen, will you walk? Marwood—

Mrs. Mar. I'll follow you, madam, before Sir Wilfull is ready. [*Exeunt.*

[*Manent* MRS. MARWOOD *and* FAINALL.]

Fain. Why then Foible's a bawd, an arrant, rank, match-making bawd. And I, it seems, am a husband, a rank husband; and my wife a very arrant, rank wife—all in the way of the world. 'Sdeath, to be a cuckold by anticipation, a cuckold in embryo? Sure I was born with budding antlers like a young satyr, or a citizen's child. 'Sdeath, to be outwitted, to be out-jilted—out-matrimonied!—If I had kept my speed like a stag, 'twere somewhat—but to crawl after, with my horns like a snail, and be outstripped by my wife—'tis scurvy wedlock.

Mrs. Mar. Then shake it off, you have often wished for an opportunity to part—and now you have it. But first prevent their plot—the half of Millamant's fortune is too considerable to be parted with, to a foe, to Mirabell.

Fain. Damn him, that had been mine, had you not made that fond discovery—that had been forfeited, had they been married. My wife had added lustre to my horns, by that increase of fortune. I could have worn 'em tipt with gold, though my forehead had been furnished like a deputy-lieutenant's hall.

Mrs. Mar. They may prove a cap of maintenance to you still, if you can away with your wife. And she's no worse than when you had her—I dare swear she had given up her game, before she was married.

Fain. Hum! That may be—

Mrs. Mar. You married her to keep you; and if you can contrive to have her keep you better than you expected, why should you not keep her longer than you intended?

Fain. The means, the means!

Mrs. Mar. Discover to my lady your wife's conduct; threaten to part with her—my lady loves her, and will come to any composition to save her reputation. Take the opportunity of breaking it, just upon the discovery of this imposture. My lady will be enraged beyond bounds, and sacrifice niece, and fortune, and all at that conjuncture. And let me alone to keep her warm; if she should flag in her part, I will not fail to prompt her.

Fain. Faith, this has an appearance.

Mrs. Mar. I'm sorry I hinted to my lady to endeavour a match between Millamant and Sir Wilfull; that may be an obstacle.

Fain. Oh, for that matter leave me to manage him; I'll disable him for that, he will drink like a Dane—after dinner, I'll set his hand in.

Mrs. Mar. Well, how do you stand affected towards your lady?

Fain. Why, faith I'm thinking of it.—Let me see—I am married already; so that's over.—My wife has played the jade with me—well, that's over too—I never loved her, or if I had, why that would have been over too by this time.—Jealous of her I cannot be, for I am certain; so there's an end of jealousy. Weary of her, I am and shall be.—No, there's no end of that; no, no, that were too much to hope. Thus far concerning my repose. Now for my reputation.—As to my own, I married not for it; so that's out of the question.—And as to my part in my wife's—why, she had parted with hers before; so bringing none to me, she can take none from me; 'tis against all rule of play that I should lose to one who has not wherewithal to stake.

Mrs. Mar. Besides, you forget, marriage is honourable.

Fain. Hum! Faith, and that's well thought on; marriage is honourable, as you say; and if so, wherefore should cuckoldom be a discredit, being derived from so honourable a root?

Mrs. Mar. Nay, I know not; if the root be honourable, why not the branches?

Fain. So, so, why this point's clear.—Well, how do we proceed?

Mrs. Mar. I will contrive a letter which shall be delivered to my lady at the time when that rascal who is to act Sir Rowland is with her. It shall come as from an unknown hand—for the less I appear to know of the truth, the better I can play the incendiary. Besides, I would not have Foible provoked if I could help it—because you know she knows some passages—nay, I expect all will come out—but let the mine be sprung first, and then I care not if I am discovered.

Fain. If the worst come to the worst, I'll turn my wife out to grass—I have already a deed of settlement of the best part of her estate, which I wheedled out of her; and that you shall partake at least.

Mrs. Mar. I hope you are convinced that I hate Mirabell now: you'll be no more jealous?

Fain. Jealous, no,—by this kiss—let husbands be jealous; but let the lover still believe; or if he doubt, let it be only to endear his pleasure, and prepare the joy that follows, when he proves his mistress true. But let husbands' doubts convert to endless jealousy; or if they have belief, let it corrupt to superstition, and blind credulity. I am single, and will herd no more with 'em. True, I wear the badge, but I'll disown the order. And since I take my leave of 'em, I care not if I leave 'em a common motto to their common crest.

All husbands must, or pain, or shame, endure;
The wise too jealous are, fools too secure.

[*Exeunt.*

ACT IV

SCENE.—*Scene continues.*

LADY WISHFORT *and* FOIBLE.

Lady W. Is Sir Rowland coming, say'st thou, Foible? and are things in order?

---

15. **cap of maintenance**, a cap worn as a symbol of official dignity or carried before a king or high official. Marwood is, of course, playing on the words.

Foib. Yes, madam. I have put wax-lights in the sconces; and placed the footmen in a row in the hall, in their best liveries, with the coachman and postilion to fill up the equipage.

Lady W. Have you pulvilled the coachman and postilion, that they may not stink of the stable when Sir Rowland comes by?

Foib. Yes, madam.

Lady W. And are the dancers and the music ready, that he may be entertained in all points with correspondence to his passion?

Foib. All is ready, madam.

Lady W. And—well—and how do I look, Foible?

Foib. Most killing well, madam.

Lady W. Well, and how shall I receive him? In what figure shall I give his heart the first impression? There is a great deal in the first impression. Shall I sit?—No, I won't sit—I'll walk—ay, I'll walk from the door upon his entrance; and then turn full upon him.—No, that will be too sudden. I'll lie—ay, I'll lie down—I'll receive him in my little dressing-room, there's a couch—yes, yes, I'll give the first impression on a couch—I won't lie neither, but loll and lean upon one elbow, with one foot a little dangling off, jogging in a thoughtful way—yes—and then as soon as he appears, start, ay, start and be surprised, and rise to meet him in a pretty disorder— yes—oh, nothing is more alluring than a levee from a couch in some confusion—it shows the foot to advantage, and furnishes with blushes, and re-composing airs beyond comparison. Hark! There's a coach.

Foib. 'Tis he, madam.

Lady W. Oh, dear, has my nephew made his addresses to Millamant? I ordered him.

Foib. Sir Wilfull is set in to drinking, madam, in the parlour.

Lady W. Ods my life, I'll send him to her. Call her down, Foible; bring her hither. I'll send him as I go.—When they are together, then come to me, Foible, that I may not be too long alone with Sir Rowland. [*Exit.*

[*Enter* MRS. MILLAMANT *and* MRS. FAINALL.]

Foib. Madam, I stayed here, to tell your ladyship that Mr. Mirabell has waited this half-hour for an opportunity to talk with you. Though my lady's orders were to leave you and Sir Wilfull together. Shall I tell Mr. Mirabell that you are at leisure?

Milla. No—what would the dear man have? I am thoughtful, and would amuse myself—bid him come another time.

5. **pulvilled,** powdered.

There never yet was woman made,
Nor shall, but to be cursed.

(*Repeating and walking about.*) That's hard!

Mrs. Fain. You are very fond of Sir John Suckling to-day, Millamant, and the poets.

Milla. Heh? Ay, and filthy verses—so I am.

Foib. Sir Wilfull is coming, madam. Shall I send Mr. Mirabell away?

Milla. Ay, if you please, Foible, send him away— or send him hither—just as you will, dear Foible.—I think I'll see him.—Shall I? Ay, let the wretch come. (*Repeating.*)

Thyrsis, a youth of the inspirèd train.

Dear Fainall, entertain Sir Wilfull—thou hast philosophy to undergo a fool, thou art married and hast patience—I would confer with my own thoughts.

Mrs. Fain. I am obliged to you, that you would make me your proxy in this affair; but I have business of my own.

[*Enter* SIR WILFULL.]

Mrs. Fain. Oh, Sir Wilfull; you are come at the critical instant. There's your mistress up to the ears in love and contemplation; pursue your point, now or never.

Sir Wil. Yes, my aunt will have it so—I would gladly have been encouraged with a bottle or two, because I'm somewhat wary at first, before I am acquainted—(*This while* MILLAMANT *walks about repeating to herself.*) But I hope, after a time, I shall break my mind—that is upon further acquaintance.—So for the present, cousin, I'll take my leave—if so be you'll be so kind to make my excuse. I'll return to my company—

Mrs. Fain. Oh, fie, Sir Wilfull! What, you must not be daunted.

Sir Wil. Daunted! no, that's not it, it is not so much for that—for if so be that I set on't, I'll do't. But only for the present, 'tis sufficient 'till further acquaintance, that's all—your servant.

Mrs. Fain. Nay, I'll swear you shall never lose so favourable an opportunity, if I can help it. I'll leave you together, and lock the door. [*Exit.*

Sir Wil. Nay, nay, cousin,—I have forgot my gloves.—What d'ee do? 'Sheart, a' has locked the door indeed, I think.—Nay, Cousin Fainall, open the door.—Pshaw, what a vixen trick is this?—Nay,

1–2. **There never . . . cursed,** the opening lines of a poem by Sir John Suckling. 14. **Thyrsis . . . train,** the opening lines of Edmund Waller's poem "The Story of Phoebus and Daphne, Applied."

now a' has seen me too—cousin, I made bold to pass through as it were—I think this door's enchanted—

Milla. (*repeating*).

> I prithee spare me, gentle boy,
> Press me no more for that slight toy—

Sir Wil. Anan? Cousin, your servant.

Milla. That foolish trifle of a heart—

Sir Wilfull!

Sir Wil. Yes—your servant. No offence, I hope, cousin.

Milla. (*repeating*).

> I swear it will not do its part,
> Though thou dost thine, employ'st thy power and art.

Natural, easy Suckling!

Sir Wil. Anan? Suckling? No such suckling neither, cousin, nor stripling. I thank Heaven, I'm no minor.

Milla. Ah, rustic, ruder than Gothic.

Sir Wil. Well, well, I shall understand your lingo one of these days, cousin; in the meanwhile I must answer in plain English.

Milla. Have you any business with me, Sir Willful?

Sir Wil. Not at present, cousin.—Yes, I made bold to see, to come and know if that how you were disposed to fetch a walk this evening; if so be that I might not be troublesome, I would have sought a walk with you.

Milla. A walk? What then?

Sir Wil. Nay, nothing—only for the walk's sake, that's all—

Milla. I nauseate walking; 'tis a country diversion, I loathe the country and everything that relates to it.

Sir Wil. Indeed! Hah! Look ye, look ye, you do? Nay, 'tis like you may.—Here are choice of pastimes here in town, as plays and the like, that must be confessed indeed—

Milla. Ah, *l'étourdie!* I hate the town too.

Sir Wil. Dear heart, that's much—Hah! that you should hate 'em both! Hah! 'tis like you may; there are some can't relish the town, and others can't away with the country—'tis like you may be one of those, cousin.

Milla. Ha, ha, ha! Yes, 'tis like I may.—You have nothing further to say to me?

Sir Wil. Not at present, cousin.—'Tis like when I have an opportunity to be more private, I may break my mind in some measure—I conjecture you partly guess.—However, that's as time shall try—but spare to speak and spare to speed, as they say.

Milla. If it is of no great importance, Sir Wilfull, you will oblige me to leave me. I have just now a little business—

Sir Wil. Enough, enough, cousin; yes, yes, all a case—when you're disposed, when you're disposed. Now's as well as another time; and another time as well as now. All's one for that.—Yes, yes, if your concerns call you, there's no haste; it will keep cold, as they say.—Cousin, your servant.—I think this door's locked.

Milla. You may go this way, sir.

Sir Wil. Your servant! then with your leave I'll return to my company.

Milla. Ay, ay; ha, ha, ha!

> Like Phoebus sung the no less amorous boy.

[*Enter* MIRABELL.]

Mira. Like Daphne she, as lovely and as coy. Do you lock yourself up from me, to make my search more curious? Or is this pretty artifice contrived to signify that here the chase must end, and my pursuit be crowned, for you can fly no further?

Milla. Vanity! No—I'll fly and be followed to the last moment; though I am upon the very verge of matrimony, I expect you should solicit me as much as if I were wavering at the grate of a monastery, with one foot over the threshold. I'll be solicited to the very last, nay, and afterwards.

Mira. What, after the last?

Milla. Oh, I should think I was poor and had nothing to bestow, if I were reduced to an inglorious ease, and freed from the agreeable fatigues of solicitation.

Mira. But do not you know, that when favours are conferred upon instant and tedious solicitation, that they diminish in their value, and that both the giver loses the grace, and the receiver lessens his pleasure?

Milla. It may be in things of common application, but never sure in love. Oh, I hate a lover that can dare to think he draws a moment's air, independent on the bounty of his mistress. There is not so impudent a thing in nature as the saucy look of an assured man, confident of success. The pedantic arrogance of a very husband has not so pragmatical

---

4-5. **I prithee . . . toy.** These lines and the others quoted by Millamant here constitute the first stanza of a song by Suckling. 21. **Gothic,** used in its seventeenth-century connotation of "barbarous." 42. **Ah, l'étourdie!** Ah, the giddy (town)! 20. **Like Phoebus . . . boy,** the third line of Waller's poem which Millamant has previously quoted. Mirabell, coming in, caps it with the fourth line. 25. **curious,** complicated. 31. **grate,** grated window. The word **monastery** was sometimes used for "convent." 49. **pragmatical,** conceited.

an air. Ah! I'll never marry, unless I am first made sure of my will and pleasure.

Mira. Would you have 'em both before marriage? Or will you be contented with the first now, and stay for the other till after grace?

Milla. Ah, don't be impertinent.—My dear liberty, shall I leave thee? My faithful solitude, my darling contemplation, must I bid you then adieu? Ay-h, adieu—my morning thoughts, agreeable wakings, indolent slumbers, all ye *douceurs*, ye *sommeils du matin*, adieu—I can't do't, 'tis more than impossible.—Positively, Mirabell, I'll lie abed in a morning as long as I please.

Mira. Then I'll get up in a morning as early as I please.

Milla. Ah! Idle creature, get up when you will.—And d'ee hear, I won't be called names after I'm married; positively I won't be called names.

Mira. Names!

Milla. Ay, as wife, spouse, my dear, joy, jewel, love, sweetheart, and the rest of that nauseous cant, in which men and their wives are so fulsomely familiar—I shall never bear that.—Good Mirabell, don't let us be familiar or fond, nor kiss before folks, like my Lady Fadler and Sir Francis; nor go to Hyde Park together the first Sunday in a new chariot, to provoke eyes and whispers; and then never be seen there together again, as if we were proud of one another the first week, and ashamed of one another ever after. Let us never visit together, nor go to a play together, but let us be very strange and well bred: let us be as strange as if we had been married a great while, and as well bred as if we were not married at all.

Mira. Have you any more conditions to offer? Hitherto your demands are pretty reasonable.

Milla. Trifles—as liberty to pay and receive visits to and from whom I please; to write and receive letters, without interrogatories or wry faces on your part; to wear what I please; and choose conversation with regard only to my own taste; to have no obligation upon me to converse with wits that I don't like, because they are your acquaintance; or to be intimate with fools because they may be your relations. Come to dinner when I please, dine in my dressing-room when I'm out of humour, without giving a reason. To have my closet inviolate; to be sole empress of my tea-table, which you must never presume to approach without first asking leave. And lastly, wherever I am, you shall always knock at the door before you come in. These articles subscribed, if I continue to endure you a little longer, I may by degrees dwindle into a wife.

Mira. Your bill of fare is something advanced in this latter account. Well, have I liberty to offer conditions—that when you are dwindled into a wife, I may not be beyond measure enlarged into a husband?

Milla. You have free leave, propose your utmost, speak and spare not.

Mira. I thank you. *Imprimis* then, I covenant that your acquaintance be general; that you admit no sworn confident, or intimate of your own sex; no she-friend to screen her affairs under your countenance, and tempt you to make trial of a mutual secrecy. No decoy-duck to wheedle you a fop-scrambling to the play in a mask—then bring you home in a pretended fright, when you think you shall be found out—and rail at me for missing the play, and disappointing the frolic which you had, to pick me up and prove my constancy.

Milla. Detestable *imprimis!* I go to the play in a mask!

Mira. Item, I article, that you continue to like your own face as long as I shall: and while it passes current with me, that you endeavour not to new-coin it. To which end, together with all vizards for the day, I prohibit all masks for the night, made of oiled-skins and I know not what—hog's bones, hare's gall, pig-water, and the marrow of a roasted cat. In short, I forbid all commerce with the gentlewoman in what-d'ee-call-it Court. *Item*, I shut my doors against all bawds with baskets, and pennyworths of muslin, china, fans, atlases, etc.—*Item*, when you shall be breeding—

Milla. Ah! name it not.

Mira. Which may be presumed, with a blessing on our endeavours—

Milla. Odious endeavours!

Mira. I denounce against all strait lacing, squeezing for a shape, till you mould my boy's head like a sugar-loaf; and instead of a man-child, make me father to a crooked billet. Lastly, to the dominion of the tea-table I submit.—But with proviso, that you exceed not in your province, but restrain yourself to native and simple tea-table drinks, as tea, chocolate, and coffee. As likewise to genuine and authorised tea-table talk—such as mending of fashions, spoiling reputations, railing at absent friends, and so forth—but that on no account you encroach upon the men's prerogative, and presume to drink healths, or toast fellows; for prevention of which, I banish all foreign forces, all auxiliaries to the tea-table, as orange-brandy, all aniseed, cinnamon, citron and

---

10–11. douceurs, pleasant indulgences. **sommeils du matin,** morning slumbers.   **25. Fadler,** Fondler. **31. strange,** reserved.   **47. closet,** private chamber.

23. article, stipulate.   **33. atlases,** rich silks.

Barbadoes waters, together with ratafia and the most noble spirit of clary. But for cowslip-wine, poppy-water, and all dormitives, those I allow.—These provisos admitted, in other things I may prove a tractable and complying husband.

Milla. O horrid provisos! filthy strong waters! I toast fellows, odious men! I hate your odious provisos.

Mira. Then we're agreed. Shall I kiss your hand upon the contract? and here comes one to be a witness to the sealing of the deed.

[*Enter* MRS. FAINALL.]

Milla. Fainall, what shall I do? Shall I have him? I think I must have him.

Mrs. Fain. Ay, ay, take him, take him, what should you do?

Milla. Well then—I'll take my death I'm in a horrid fright.—Fainall, I shall never say it—well—I think—I'll endure you.

Mrs. Fain. Fie, fie! have him, have him, and tell him so in plain terms; for I am sure you have a mind to him.

Milla. Are you? I think I have—and the horrid man looks as if he thought so too.—Well, you ridiculous thing you, I'll have you—I won't be kissed, nor I won't be thanked.—Here, kiss my hand though—so, hold your tongue now, don't say a word.

Mrs. Fain. Mirabell, there's a necessity for your obedience;—you have neither time to talk nor stay. My mother is coming; and in my conscience, if she should see you, would fall into fits, and maybe not recover time enough to return to Sir Rowland; who, as Foible tells me, is in a fair way to succeed. Therefore spare your ecstasies for another occasion, and slip down the back stairs, where Foible waits to consult you.

Milla. Ay, go, go! In the meantime I suppose you have said something to please me.

Mira. I am all obedience. [*Exit* MIRABELL.

Mrs. Fain. Yonder Sir Wilfull's drunk; and so noisy that my mother has been forced to leave Sir Rowland to appease him; but he answers her only with singing and drinking.—What they may have done by this time I know not, but Petulant and he were upon quarrelling as I came by.

Milla. Well, if Mirabell should not make a good husband, I am a lost thing; for I find I love him violently.

Mrs. Fain. So it seems; for you mind not what's said to you.—If you doubt him, you had best take up with Sir Wilfull.

3. **dormitives,** sleep-inducing drinks.

Milla. How can you name that superannuated lubber? foh!

[*Enter* WITWOUD *from drinking*.]

Mrs. Fain. So, is the fray made up, that you have left 'em?

Wit. Left 'em? I could stay no longer—I have laughed like ten christ'nings—I am tipsy with laughing—if I had stayed any longer I should have burst—I must have been let out and pieced in the sides like an unsized camlet.—Yes, yes, the fray is composed; my lady came in like a *nolle prosequi*, and stopped the proceedings.

Milla. What was the dispute?

Wit. That's the jest; there was no dispute. They could neither of 'em speak for rage, and so fell a sputtering at one another like two roasting apples. . . .

[*Enter* LADY WISHFORT, *and* SIR WILFULL, *drunk.*]

Lady W. Out upon't, out upon't, at years of discretion, and comport yourself at this rantipole rate.

Sir Wil. No offence, aunt.

Lady W. Offence? As I'm a person, I'm ashamed of you.—Fogh! how you stink of wine! D'ye think my niece will ever endure such a *borachio!* you're an absolute *borachio*.

Sir Wil. Borachio!

Lady W. At a time when you should commence an amour, and put your best foot foremost—

Sir Wil. 'Sheart, an you grutch me your liquor, make a bill—give me more drink, and take my purse. (*Sings.*)

> Prithee fill me the glass
> 'Till it laugh in my face.
> With ale that is potent and mellow;
> He that whines for a lass
> Is an ignorant ass,
> For a bumper has not its fellow.

But if you would have me marry my cousin, say the word, and I'll do't—Wilfull will do't, that's the word—Wilfull will do't, that's my crest—my motto I have forgot.

Lady W. My nephew's a little overtaken, cousin— but 'tis with drinking your health.—O' my word you are obliged to him—

Sir Wil. *In vino veritas*, aunt:—If I drunk your health to-day, cousin, I am a *borachio*. But if you have a mind to be married say the word, and send for the

11. **camlet,** garment made of a cloth woven of wool and silk. 12. **nolle prosequi,** a motion in a legal action denoting that the prosecutor or plaintiff will proceed no further in his suit. 26. **borachio!** drunkard; literally, wineskin. 48. **In vino veritas.** In wine there is truth.

piper, Wilfull will do't. If not, dust it away, and let's have t'other round—Tony, 'odsheart, where's Tony?—Tony's an honest fellow, but he spits after a bumper, and that's a fault. (*Sings.*)

> We'll drink and we'll never ha' done, boys,
> Put the glass then around with the sun, boys,
> Let Apollo's example invite us;
> For he's drunk every night,
> And that makes him so bright,
> That he's able next morning to light us.

The sun's a good pimple, an honest soaker, he has a cellar at your Antipodes. If I travel, aunt, I touch at your Antipodes—your Antipodes are a good rascally sort of topsy-turvy fellows—if I had a bumper I'd stand upon my head and drink a health to 'em.—A match or no match, cousin, with the hard name—aunt, Wilfull will do't. . . .

Milla. Your pardon, madam, I can stay no longer—Sir Wilfull grows very powerful. Egh! how he smells! I shall be overcome if I stay. Come, cousin. [*Exeunt* MILLAMANT *and* MRS. FAINALL.

Lady W. Smells! he would poison a tallow-chandler and his family. Beastly creature, I know not what to do with him.—Travel, quoth a; ay, travel, travel, get thee gone, get thee but far enough, to the Saracens, or the Tartars, or the Turks—for thou art not fit to live in a Christian commonwealth, thou beastly pagan.

Sir Wil. Turks, no; no Turks, aunt: your Turks are infidels, and believe not in the grape. Your Mahometan, your Mussulman, is a dry stinkard—no offence, aunt. My map says that your Turk is not so honest a man as your Christian—I cannot find by the map that your Mufti is orthodox—whereby it is a plain case, that orthodox is a hard word, aunt, and (*Hiccup.*) Greek for claret. (*Sings.*)

> To drink is a Christian diversion,
> Unknown to the Turk and the Persian:
>   Let Mahometan fools
>   Live by heathenish rules,
> And be damned over tea-cups and coffee.
>   But let British lads sing,
>   Crown a health to the king,
> And a fig for your sultan and sophy.

Ah, Tony!

[*Enter* FOIBLE *and whispers* LADY WISHFORT.]

Lady W. Sir Rowland impatient? Good lack! what shall I do with this beastly tumbril?—Go lie down and sleep, you sot—or as I'm a person, I'll have you bastinadoed with broomsticks. Call up the wenches. [*Exit* FOIBLE.

Sir Wil. Ahey! Wenches, where are the wenches?

Lady W. Dear Cousin Witwoud, get him away, and you will bind me to you inviolably. I have an affair of moment that invades me with some precipitation.—You will oblige me to all futurity.

Wit. Come, knight.—Pox on him, I don't know what to say to him.—Will you go to a cock-match?

Sir Wil. With a wench, Tony? Is she a shake-bag, sirrah? Let me bite your cheek for that.

Wit. Horrible! He has a breath like a bagpipe.—Ay, ay; come, will you march, my Salopian?

Sir Wil. Lead on, little Tony—I'll follow thee, my Antony, my Tantony. Sirrah, thou sha't be my Tantony; and I'll be thy pig.

—And a fig for your sultan and sophy.

[*Exit singing with* WITWOUD.

Lady W. This will never do. It will never make a match.—At least before he has been abroad. (*Enter* WAITWELL, *disguised as for Sir Rowland.*) Dear Sir Rowland, I am confounded with confusion at the retrospection of my own rudeness—I have more pardons to ask than the pope distributes in the year of jubilee. But I hope where there is likely to be so near an alliance, we may unbend the severity of decorum, and dispense with a little ceremony.

Wait. My impatience, madam, is the effect of my transport;—and till I have the possession of your adorable person, I am tantalised on the rack; and do but hang, madam, on the tenter of expectation.

Lady. W. You have excess of gallantry, Sir Rowland, and press things to a conclusion, with a most prevailing vehemence.—But a day or two for decency of marriage—

Wait. For decency of funeral, madam. The delay will break my heart—or if that should fail, I shall be poisoned. My nephew will get an inkling of my designs, and poison me—and I would willingly starve him before I die—I would gladly go out of the world with that satisfaction.—That would be some comfort to me, if I could but live so long as to be revenged on that unnatural viper.

Lady W. Is he so unnatural, say you? Truly I would contribute much both to the saving of your life, and the accomplishment of your revenge—not that I respect myself, though he has been a perfidious wretch to me.

Wait. Perfidious to you!

---

12. **pimple,** boon companion.   35. **Mufti,** the Grand Mufti, the head of the Mahometan religion in Turkey.   45. **sophy,** the Shah of Persia; the word is derived from the Sufi dynasty.   51. **tumbril?** here, drunken person.

11. **shake-bag,** a lazy person.   14. **Salopian,** native of Shropshire.   17. **pig.** St. Antony, or Tantony, was the patron of swineherds.   33. **tenter,** tenterhook.   49. **respect,** consider.

Lady W. O Sir Rowland, the hours that he has died away at my feet, the tears that he has shed, the oaths that he has sworn, the palpitations that he has felt, the trances and the tremblings, the ardours and the ecstasies, the kneelings and the risings, the heart-heavings and the hand-grippings, the pangs and the pathetic regards of his protesting eyes! Oh, no memory can register.

Wait. What, my rival! Is the rebel my rival? a' dies.

Lady W. No, don't kill him at once, Sir Rowland, starve him gradually inch by inch.

Wait. I'll do't. In three weeks he shall be barefoot; in a month out at knees with begging an alms—he shall starve upward and upward, till he has nothing living but his head, and then go out in a stink like a candle's end upon a save-all.

Lady W. Well, Sir Rowland, you have the way—you are no novice in the labyrinth of love—you have the clue.—But as I am a person, Sir Rowland, you must not attribute my yielding to any sinister appetite, or indigestion of widowhood; nor impute my complacency to any lethargy of continence.—I hope you do not think me prone to any iteration of nuptials—

Wait. Far be it from me—

Lady W. If you do, I protest I must recede—or think that I have made a prostitution of decorums, but in the vehemence of compassion, and to save the life of a person of so much importance—

Wait. I esteem it so—

Lady W. Or else you wrong my condescension—

Wait. I do not, I do not—

Lady W. Indeed you do.

Wait. I do not, fair shrine of virtue.

Lady W. If you think the least scruple of carnality was an ingredient—

Wait. Dear madam, no. You are all camphire and frankincense, all chastity and odour.

Lady W. Or that—

[*Enter* FOIBLE.]

Foib. Madam, the dancers are ready, and there's one with a letter, who must deliver it into your own hands.

Lady W. Sir Rowland, will you give me leave? Think favourably, judge candidly, and conclude you have found a person who would suffer racks in honour's cause, dear Sir Rowland, and will wait on you incessantly. [*Exit.*

Wait. Fie, fie!—What a slavery have I undergone; spouse, hast thou any cordial?—I want spirits.

Foib. What a washy rogue art thou, to pant thus for a quarter of an hour's lying and swearing to a fine lady?

Wait. Oh, she is the antidote to desire. Spouse, thou wilt fare the worse for't—I shall have no appetite to iteration of nuptials this eight and forty hours.—By this hand, I'd rather be a chairman in the dog-days, than act Sir Rowland 'till this time tomorrow.

[*Enter* LADY WISHFORT *with a letter.*]

Lady W. Call in the dancers;—Sir Rowland, we'll sit, if you please, and see the entertainment.

[*Dance.*]

Now with your permission, Sir Rowland, I will peruse my letter—I would open it in your presence, because I would not make you uneasy. If it should make you uneasy I would burn it—speak if it does—but you may see, the superscription is like a woman's hand.

Foib. (*to him*). By heaven! Mrs. Marwood's, I know it—my heart aches—get it from her—

Wait. A woman's hand? No, madam, that's no woman's hand, I see that already. That's somebody whose throat must be cut.

Lady W. Nay, Sir Rowland, since you give me a proof of your passion by your jealousy, I promise you I'll make a return, by a frank communication.—You shall see it—we'll open it together—look you here. (*Reads.*)

"Madam, though unknown to you,"—Look you there, 'tis from nobody that I know—"I have that honour for your character, that I think myself obliged to let you know you are abused. He who pretends to be Sir Rowland is a cheat and a rascal—" Oh heavens! what's this?

Foib. (*aside*). Unfortunate, all's ruined.

Wait. How, how, let me see, let me see! (*Reading.*) "A rascal and disguised, and suborned for that imposture."—Oh, villainy! Oh, villainy!—"by the contrivance of—"

Lady W. I shall faint, I shall die, oh!

Foib. (*to him*). Say 'tis your nephew's hand.—Quickly, his plot, swear, swear it.

Wait. Here's a villain! Madam, don't you perceive it, don't you see it?

Lady W. Too well, too well. I have seen too much.

Wait. I told you at first I knew the hand.—A woman's hand? The rascal writes a sort of a large hand; your Roman hand—I saw there was a throat to be cut presently. If he were my son, as he is my nephew, I'd pistol him—

Foib. Oh, treachery! But are you sure, Sir Rowland, it is his writing?

Wait. Sure? Am I here? do I live? do I love this

---

16. **save-all,** a small pan inserted into a candlestick to save the drips and ends of candles.

pearl of India? I have twenty letters in my pocket from him, in the same character.

Lady W. How!

Foib. Oh, what luck it is, Sir Rowland, that you were present at this juncture! This was the business that brought Mr. Mirabell disguised to Madam Millamant this afternoon. I thought something was contriving, when he stole by me and would have hid his face.

Lady W. How, how!—I heard the villain was in the house indeed; and now I remember, my niece went away abruptly, when Sir Wilfull was to have made his addresses.

Foib. Then, then, madam, Mr. Mirabell waited for her in her chamber: but I would not tell your ladyship to discompose you when you were to receive Sir Rowland.

Wait. Enough, his date is short.

Foib. No, good Sir Rowland, don't incur the law.

Wait. Law! I care not for law. I can but die, and 'tis in a good cause—my lady shall be satisfied of my truth and innocence, though it cost me my life.

Lady W. No, dear Sir Rowland, don't fight; if you should be killed I must never show my face; or hanged—oh consider my reputation, Sir Rowland.—No, you shan't fight.—I'll go in and examine my niece; I'll make her confess. I conjure you, Sir Rowland, by all your love, not to fight.

Wait. I am charmed, madam, I obey. But some proof you must let me give you.—I'll go for a black box, which contains the writings of my whole estate, and deliver that into your hands.

Lady W. Ay, dear Sir Rowland, that will be some comfort, bring the black box.

Wait. And may I presume to bring a contract to be signed this night? May I hope so far?

Lady W. Bring what you will; but come alive, pray come alive. Oh, this is a happy discovery.

Wait. Dead or alive I'll come—and married we will be in spite of treachery; ay, and get an heir that shall defeat the last remaining glimpse of hope in my abandoned nephew. Come, my buxom widow:

E'er long you shall substantial proof receive
That I'm an arrant knight—

Foib. (*aside*). Or arrant knave.

ACT V

SCENE.—*Scene continues*.

LADY WISHFORT *and* FOIBLE.

Lady W. Out of my house, out of my house, thou viper, thou serpent, that I have fostered! thou bosom traitress, that I raised from nothing!—begone, begone, begone, go, go!—that I took from washing of old gauze and weaving of dead hair, with a bleak blue nose, over a chafing-dish of starved embers, and dining behind a traverse rag, in a shop no bigger than a bird-cage,—go, go, starve again, do, do!

Foib. Dear madam, I'll beg pardon on my knees.

Lady W. Away, out, out, go set up for yourself again!—do, drive a trade, do, with your three-penny-worth of small ware, flaunting upon a packthread, under a brandy-seller's bulk, or against a dead wall by a ballad-monger. Go, hang out an old Frisoneer gorget with a yard of yellow colberteen again! do! an old gnawed mask, two rows of pins and a child's fiddle; a glass necklace with the beads broken, and a quilted nightcap with one ear. Go, go, drive a trade!—These were your commodities, you treacherous trull, this was the merchandise you dealt in, when I took you into my house, placed you next myself, and made you governante of my whole family. You have forgot this, have you, now you have feathered your nest?

Foib. No, no, dear madam. Do but hear me, have but a moment's patience—I'll confess all. Mr. Mirabell seduced me; I am not the first that he has wheedled with his dissembling tongue; your ladyship's own wisdom has been deluded by him, then how should I, a poor ignorant, defend myself? O madam, if you knew but what he promised me, and how he assured me your ladyship should come to no damage—or else the wealth of the Indies should not have bribed me to conspire against so good, so sweet, so kind a lady as you have been to me.

Lady W. No damage? What, to betray me, to marry me to a cast-serving-man; to make me a receptacle, an hospital for a decayed pimp? No damage? O thou frontless impudence, more than a big-bellied actress.

Foib. Pray do but hear me, madam, he could not marry your ladyship, madam, no indeed, his marriage was to have been void in law; for he was married to me first, to secure your ladyship. . . . Yes indeed, I enquired of the law in that case before I would meddle or make.

Lady W. What, then I have been your property, have I? I have been convenient to you, it seems,—while you were catering for Mirabell; I have been broker for you? What, have you made a passive bawd of me?—This exceeds all precedent; I am brought to fine uses, to become a botcher of second-

---

3. **weaving of dead hair,** making wigs.   14. **colberteen,** a kind of French lace.   21. **governante,** housekeeper.
38. **frontless,** shameless.

hand marriages between Abigails and Andrews! I'll couple you. Yes, I'll baste you together, you and your Philander. I'll Duke's Place you, as I'm a person. Your turtle is in custody already; you shall coo in the same cage, if there be constable of warrant in the parish. [*Exit.*

Foib. Oh, that ever I was born! Oh, that I was ever married!—a bride, ay, I shall be a Bridewell-bride. Oh!

[*Enter* MRS. FAINALL.]

Mrs. Fain. Poor Foible, what's the matter?

Foib. O madam, my lady's gone for a constable; I shall be had to a justice, and put to Bridewell to beat hemp; poor Waitwell's gone to prison already.

Mrs. Fain. Have a good heart, Foible, Mirabell's gone to give security for him. This is all Marwood's and my husband's doing.

Foib. Yes, yes, I know it, madam; she was in my lady's closet, and overheard all that you said to me before dinner. She sent the letter to my lady; and that missing effect, Mr. Fainall laid this plot to arrest Waitwell, when he pretended to go for the papers; and in the meantime Mrs. Marwood declared all to my lady.

Mrs. Fain. Was there no mention made of me in the letter?—My mother does not suspect my being in the confederacy? I fancy Marwood has not told her, though she has told my husband.

Foib. Yes, madam; but my lady did not see that part. We stifled the letter before she read so far. Has that mischievous devil told Mr. Fainall of your ladyship, then?

Mrs. Fain. Ay, all's out, my affair with Mirabell, everything discovered. This is the last day of our living together, that's my comfort.

Foib. Indeed, madam, and so 'tis a comfort if you knew all—he has been even with your ladyship; which I could have told you long enough since, but I love to keep peace and quietness by my good will. I had rather bring friends together than set 'em at distance. But Mrs. Marwood and he are nearer related than ever their parents thought for.

Mrs. Fain. Say'st thou so, Foible? Canst thou prove this?

Foib. I can take my oath of it, madam, so can Mrs. Mincing; we have had many a fair word from Madam Marwood, to conceal something that passed in our chamber one evening when you were at Hyde Park—and we were thought to have gone a walking; but we went up unawares—though we were sworn to secrecy too. Madam Marwood took a book and swore us upon it: but it was but a book of poems—so long as it was not a Bible-oath, we may break it with a safe conscience.

Mrs. Fain. This discovery is the most opportune thing I could wish. Now, Mincing?

[*Enter* MINCING.]

Minc. My lady would speak with Mrs. Foible, mem. Mr. Mirabell is with her; he has set your spouse at liberty, Mrs. Foible, and would have you hide yourself in my lady's closet, till my old lady's anger is abated. Oh, my old lady is in a perilous passion at something Mr. Fainall has said; he swears, and my old lady cries. There's a fearful hurricane, I vow. He says, mem, how that he'll have my lady's fortune made over to him, or he'll be divorced.

Mrs. Fain. Does your lady or Mirabell know that?

Minc. Yes, mem, they have sent me to see if Sir Wilfull be sober, and to bring him to them. My lady is resolved to have him, I think, rather than lose such a vast sum as six thousand pound. Oh, come, Mrs. Foible, I hear my old lady.

Mrs. Fain. Foible, you must tell Mincing that she must prepare to vouch when I call her.

Foib. Yes, yes, madam.

Minc. Oh yes, mem, I'll vouch anything for your ladyship's service, be what it will.

[*Exeunt* MINCING *and* FOIBLE.

[*Enter* LADY WISHFORT *and* MRS. MARWOOD.]

Lady W. O my dear friend, how can I enumerate the benefits that I have received from your goodness? To you I owe the timely discovery of the false vows of Mirabell; to you I owe the detection of the impostor Sir Rowland. And now you are become an intercessor with my son-in-law, to save the honour of my house, and compound for the frailties of my daughter. Well, friend, you are enough to reconcile me to the bad world, or else I would retire to deserts and solitudes; and feed harmless sheep by groves and purling streams. Dear Marwood, let us leave the world, and retire by ourselves and be shepherdesses.

Mrs. Mar. Let us first dispatch the affair in hand, madam. We shall have leisure to think of retirement afterwards. Here is one who is concerned in the treaty.

Lady W. O daughter, daughter, is it possible thou shouldst be my child, bone of my bone, and flesh of my flesh, and as I may say, another me, and yet transgress the most minute particle of severe virtue?

---

1. Abigails and Andrews! lady's maids and valets.
3. Duke's Place. Compare above, Act I, sc. 1, l. 16, page 741.
8. Bridewell, a prison where vagabonds and loose women were confined.   **22. missing effect,** failing of its purpose.

Is it possible you should lean aside to iniquity, who have been cast in the direct mould of virtue? I have not only been a mould but a pattern for you, and a model for you, after you were brought into the world.

Mrs. Fain. I don't understand your ladyship.

Lady W. Not understand? Why, have you not been naught? Have you not been sophisticated? Not understand? Here I am ruined to compound for your caprices and your cuckoldoms. I must pawn my plate and my jewels, and ruin my niece, and all little enough—

Mrs. Fain. I am wronged and abused, and so are you. 'Tis a false accusation, as false as hell, as false as your friend there, ay, or your friend's friend, my false husband.

Mrs. Mar. My friend, Mrs. Fainall? Your husband my friend, what do you mean?

Mrs. Fain. I know what I mean, madam, and so do you; and so shall the world at a time convenient.

Mrs. Mar. I am sorry to see you so passionate, madam. More temper would look more like innocence. But I have done. I am sorry my zeal to serve your ladyship and family should admit of misconstruction, or make me liable to affronts. You will pardon me, madam, if I meddle no more with an affair in which I am not personally concerned.

Lady W. O dear friend, I am so ashamed that you should meet with such returns. (*To* MRS. FAINALL.) You ought to ask pardon on your knees, ungrateful creature; she deserves more from you, than all your life can accomplish. (*To* MRS. MARWOOD.) Oh, don't leave me destitute in this perplexity—no, stick to me, my good genius.

Mrs. Fain. I tell you, madam, you're abused.—Stick to you? ay, like a leech, to suck your best blood—she'll drop off when she's full. Madam, you shan't pawn a bodkin, nor part with a brass counter, in composition for me. I defy 'em all. Let 'em prove their aspersions: I know my own innocence, and dare stand a trial. [*Exit.*

Lady W. Why, if she should be innocent, if she should be wronged after all, ha? I don't know what to think—and I promise you, her education has been unexceptionable—I may say it; for I chiefly made it my own care to initiate her very infancy in the rudiments of virtue, and to impress upon her tender years a young odium and aversion to the very sight of men—ay, friend, she would ha' shrieked if she had but seen a man, till she was in her teens. As I'm a person 'tis true.—She was never suffered to play with a male-child, though but in coats; nay, her very babies were of the feminine gender.—Oh, she never looked a man in the face but her own father, or the chaplain, and him we made a shift to put upon her for a woman, by the help of his long garments, and his sleek face; till she was going in her fifteen.

Mrs. Mar. 'Twas much she should be deceived so long.

Lady W. I warrant you, or she would never have borne to have been catechised by him; and have heard his long lectures against singing and dancing, and such debaucheries; and going to filthy plays; and profane music-meetings, where the lewd trebles squeak nothing but bawdy, and the basses roar blasphemy. Oh, she would have swooned at the sight or name of an obscene play-book—and can I think after all this, that my daughter can be naught? What, a whore? And thought it excommunication to set her foot within the door of a play-house. O dear friend, I can't believe it, no, no; as she says, let him prove it, let him prove it.

Mrs. Mar. Prove it, madam? What, and have your name prostituted in a public court; yours and your daughter's reputation worried at the bar by a pack of bawling lawyers? To be ushered in with an "Oyez" of scandal; and have your case opened by an old fumbling lecher in a quoif like a man midwife, to bring your daughter's infamy to light; to be a theme for legal punsters, and quibblers by the statute; and become a jest, against a rule of court, where there is no precedent for a jest in any record; not even in Doomsday Book: to discompose the gravity of the bench, and provoke naughty interrogatories in more naughty law Latin; while the good judge, tickled with the proceeding, simpers under a grey beard, and fidges off and on his cushion as if he had swallowed cantharides, or sat upon cowitch.

Lady W. Oh, 'tis very hard!

Mrs. Mar. And then to have my young revellers of the Temple take notes, like prentices at a conventicle; and after talk it over again in Commons, or before drawers in an eating-house.

Lady W. Worse and worse.

Mrs. Mar. Nay, this is nothing; if it would end here 'twere well. But it must after this be consigned by the shorthand writers to the public press; and from thence be transferred to the hands, nay, into the throats and lungs of hawkers, with voices more licentious than the loud flounder-man's: and this you must hear 'till you are stunned; nay, you must hear nothing else for some days.

---

8. **naught?** immoral. **sophisticated?** corrupted. 22. **temper,** equanimity. 1. **babies,** dolls. 27. **quoif,** white cap worn by lawyers. 37. **cowitch,** cowage, a tropical vine, the pods of which are covered with barbed hairs.

Lady W. Oh, 'tis insupportable. No, no, dear friend, make it up, make it up; ay, ay, I'll compound. I'll give up all, myself and my all, my niece and her all—anything, everything for composition.

Mrs. Mar. Nay, madam, I advise nothing, I only lay before you, as a friend, the inconveniencies which perhaps you have overseen. Here comes Mr. Fainall, if he will be satisfied to huddle up all in silence, I shall be glad. You must think I would rather congratulate than condole with you.

[*Enter* FAINALL.]

Lady W. Ay, ay, I do not doubt it, dear Marwood; no, no, I do not doubt it.

Fain. Well, madam, I have suffered myself to be overcome by the importunity of this lady, your friend; and am content you shall enjoy your own proper estate during life—on condition you oblige yourself never to marry, under such penalty as I think convenient.

Lady W. Never to marry?

Fain. No more Sir Rowlands—the next imposture may not be so timely detected.

Mrs. Mar. That condition, I dare answer, my lady will consent to, without difficulty; she has already but too much experienced the perfidiousness of men. Besides, madam, when we retire to our pastoral solitude we shall bid adieu to all other thoughts.

Lady W. Ay, that's true; but in case of necessity; as of health, or some such emergency—

Fain. Oh, if you are prescribed marriage, you shall be considered; I will only reserve to myself the power to choose for you. If your physic be wholesome, it matters not who is your apothecary. Next, my wife shall settle on me the remainder of her fortune, not made over already, and for her maintenance depend entirely on my discretion.

Lady W. This is most inhumanly savage, exceeding the barbarity of a Muscovite husband.

Fain. I learned it from his czarish majesty's retinue, in a winter evening's conference over brandy and pepper, amongst other secrets of matrimony and policy, as they are at present practised in the northern hemisphere. But this must be agreed unto, and that positively. Lastly, I will be endowed, in right of my wife, with that six thousand pound, which is the moiety of Mrs. Millamant's fortune in your possession, and which she has forfeited (as will appear by the last will and testament of your deceased husband, Sir Jonathan Wishfort) by her disobedience in contracting herself against your consent or knowledge, and by refusing the offered match with Sir Wilfull Witwoud, which you, like a careful aunt, had provided for her.

Lady W. My nephew was *non compos;* and could not make his addresses.

Fain. I come to make demands—I'll hear no objections.

Lady W. You will grant me time to consider?

Fain. Yes, while the instrument is drawing, to which you must set your hand till more sufficient deeds can be perfected, which I will take care shall be done with all possible speed. In the meanwhile I will go for the said instrument, and till my return you may balance this matter in your own discretion.

[*Exit* FAINALL.

Lady W. This insolence is beyond all precedent, all parallel; must I be subject to this merciless villain?

Mrs. Mar. 'Tis severe indeed, madam, that you should smart for your daughter's wantonness.

Lady W. 'Twas against my consent that she married this barbarian, but she would have him, though her year was not out.—Ah! her first husband, my son Languish, would not have carried it thus. Well, that was my choice, this is hers; she is matched now with a witness.—I shall be mad, dear friend, is there no comfort for me? Must I live to be confiscated at this rebel-rate?—Here come two more of my Egyptian plagues, too.

[*Enter* MILLAMANT *and* SIR WILFULL.]

Sir Wil. Aunt, your servant.

Lady W. Out, caterpillar, call not me aunt; I know thee not.

Sir Wil. I confess I have been a little in disguise, as they say—'Sheart! and I'm sorry for't. What would you have? I hope I committed no offence, aunt—and if I did I am willing to make satisfaction; and what can a man say fairer? If I have broke anything I'll pay for't, an it cost a pound. And so let that content for what's past, and make no more words. For what's to come, to pleasure you I'm willing to marry my cousin. So pray let's all be friends; she and I are agreed upon the matter before a witness.

Lady W. How's this, dear niece? Have I any comfort? Can this be true?

Milla. I am content to be a sacrifice to your repose, madam; and to convince you that I had no hand in the plot, as you were misinformed, I have laid my commands on Mirabell to come in person,

---

7. overseen, overlooked. **3. non compos,** non compos mentis, not in his right mind. **22. her year,** her first year of widowhood. **25. with a witness,** without a doubt. **34. a little in disguise,** a euphemism for "drunk."

and be a witness that I give my hand to this flower of knighthood; and for the contract that passed between Mirabell and me, I have obliged him to make a resignation of it in your ladyship's presence—he is without, and waits your leave for admittance.

Lady W. Well, I'll swear I am something revived at this testimony of your obedience; but I cannot admit that traitor.—I fear I cannot fortify myself to support his appearance. He is as terrible to me as a Gorgon; if I see him I fear I shall turn to stone, petrify incessantly.

Milla. If you disoblige him he may resent your refusal, and insist upon the contract still. Then, 'tis the last time he will be offensive to you.

Lady W. Are you sure it will be the last time?—If I were sure of that—shall I never see him again?

Milla. Sir Wilfull, you and he are to travel together, are you not?

Sir Wil. 'Sheart, the gentleman's a civil gentleman, aunt, let him come in; why, we are sworn brothers and fellow-travellers.—We are to be Pylades and Orestes, he and I—he is to be my interpreter in foreign parts. He has been overseas once already; and with proviso that I marry my cousin, will cross 'em once again, only to bear me company.—'Sheart, I'll call him in—an I set on't once, he shall come in, and see who'll hinder him. [*Exit.*

Mrs. Mar. (*aside*). This is precious fooling, if it would pass; but I'll know the bottom of it.

Lady W. O dear Marwood, you are not going?

Mar. Not far, madam; I'll return immediately. [*Exit.*

[*Re-enter* SIR WILFULL *and* MIRABELL.]

Sir Wil. Look up, man, I'll stand by you, 'sbud, an she do frown, she can't kill you.—Besides—hark'ee, she dare not frown desperately, because her face is none of her own; 'sheart, an she should, her forehead would wrinkle like the coat of a cream-cheese; but mum for that, fellow-traveller.

Mira. If a deep sense of the many injuries I have offered to so good a lady, with a sincere remorse, and a hearty contrition, can but obtain the least glance of compassion, I am too happy.—Ah, madam, there was a time—but let it be forgotten—I confess I have deservedly forfeited the high place I once held, of sighing at your feet; nay, kill me not, by turning from me in disdain—I come not to plead for favour—nay, not for pardon; I am a suppliant only for pity—I am going where I never shall behold you more—

Sir Wil. How, fellow-traveller!—You shall go by yourself then.

Mira. Let me be pitied first; and afterwards forgotten—I ask no more.

Sir Wil. By'r Lady, a very reasonable request, and will cost you nothing, aunt.—Come, come, forgive and forget, aunt, why, you must an you are a Christian.

Mira. Consider, madam, in reality, you could not receive much prejudice; it was an innocent device; though I confess it had a face of guiltiness, it was at most an artifice which love contrived—and errors which love produces have ever been accounted venial. At least think it is punishment enough that I have lost what in my heart I hold most dear, that to your cruel indignation I have offered up this beauty, and with her my peace and quiet; nay, all my hopes of future comfort.

Sir Wil. An he does not move me, would I may never be o' the quorum—an it were not as good a deed as to drink, to give her to him again, I would I might never take shipping!—Aunt, if you don't forgive quickly, I shall melt, I can tell you that. My contract went no farther than a little mouth-glue, and that's hardly dry—one doleful sigh more from my fellow-traveller and 'tis dissolved.

Lady W. Well, nephew, upon your account.—Ah, he has a false insinuating tongue!—Well, sir, I will stifle my just resentment at my nephew's request.—I will endeavour what I can to forget—but on proviso that you resign the contract with my niece immediately.

Mira. It is in writing and with papers of concern; but I have sent my servant for it, and will deliver it to you, with all acknowledgments for your transcendent goodness.

Lady W. (*apart*). Oh, he has witchcraft in his eyes and tongue!—When I did not see him I could have bribed a villain to his assassination; but his appearance rakes the embers which have so long lain smothered in my breast.—

[*Enter* FAINALL *and* MRS. MARWOOD.]

Fain. Your date of deliberation, madam, is expired. Here is the instrument; are you prepared to sign?

Lady W. If I were prepared, I am not impowered. My niece exerts a lawful claim, having matched herself by my direction to Sir Wilfull.

Fain. That sham is too gross to pass on me—though 'tis imposed on you, madam.

22-23. **Pylades and Orestes,** the proverbial pair of friends in the Greek legends. Pylades accompanied Orestes when, after he had murdered his mother, he was seized with madness and fled from land to land, pursued by the Furies.

22. **quorum,** the bench of county magistrates. 26. **mouth-glue,** an oral promise.

Milla. Sir, I have given my consent.

Mira. And, sir, I have resigned my pretensions.

Sir Wil. And, sir, I assert my right; and will maintain it in defiance of you, sir, and of your instrument. 'Sheart, an you talk of an instrument, sir, I have an old fox by my thigh shall hack your instrument of ram vellum to shreds, sir. It shall not be sufficient for a mittimus or a tailor's measure; therefore withdraw your instrument, sir, or by'r Lady I shall draw mine.

Lady W. Hold, nephew, hold.

Milla. Good Sir Wilfull, respite your valour.

Fain. Indeed? Are you provided of your guard, with your single beef-eater there? But I'm prepared for you, and insist upon my first proposal. You shall submit your own estate to my management, and absolutely make over my wife's to my sole use, as pursuant to the purport and tenor of this other covenant.—I suppose, madam, your consent is not requisite in this case; nor, Mr. Mirabell, your resignation; nor, Sir Wilfull, your right—you may draw your fox if you please, sir, and make a bear-garden flourish somewhere else, for here it will not avail. This, my Lady Wishfort, must be subscribed, or your darling daughter's turned adrift, like a leaky hulk to sink or swim, as she and the current of this lewd town can agree.

Lady W. Is there no means, no remedy, to stop my ruin? Ungrateful wretch! dost thou not owe thy being, thy subsistence, to my daughter's fortune?

Fain. I'll answer you when I have the rest of it in my possession.

Mira. But that you would not accept of a remedy from my hands—I own I have not deserved you should owe any obligation to me; or else perhaps I could advise—

Lady W. Oh, what? what? to save me and my child from ruin, from want, I'll forgive all that's past; nay, I'll consent to anything to come, to be delivered from this tyranny.

Mira. Ay, madam; but that is too late, my reward is intercepted. You have disposed of her, who only could have made me a compensation for all my services—but be it as it may, I am resolved I'll serve you, you shall not be wronged in this savage manner.

Lady W. How! Dear Mr. Mirabell, can you be so generous at last! But it is not possible. Hark'ee, I'll break my nephew's match, you shall have my niece yet, and all her fortune, if you can but save me from this imminent danger.

Mira. Will you? I take you at your word. I ask no more. I must have leave for two criminals to appear.

Lady W. Ay, ay, anybody, anybody!

Mira. Foible is one, and a penitent.

[*Enter* MRS. FAINALL, FOIBLE, *and* MINCING.]

Mrs. Mar. (*to* FAINALL). Oh, my shame! these corrupt things are brought hither to expose me.

Fain. If it must all come out, why let 'em know it, 'tis but *the way of the world*. That shall not urge me to relinquish or abate one title of my terms, no; I will insist the more.

Foib. Yes indeed, madam, I'll take my Bible-oath of it.

Minc. And so will I, mem.

Lady W. O Marwood, Marwood, art thou false? my friend deceive me? Hast thou been a wicked accomplice with that profligate man?

Mrs. Mar. Have you so much ingratitude and injustice, to give credit against your friend, to the aspersions of two such mercenary trulls?

Minc. Mercenary, mem? I scorn your words. 'Tis true we found you and Mr. Fainall in the blue garret; by the same token, you swore us to secrecy upon Messalinas's poems. Mercenary? No, if we would have been mercenary, we should have held our tongues; you would have bribed us sufficiently.

Fain. Go, you are an insignificant thing!—Well, what are you the better for this! Is this Mr. Mirabell's expedient? I'll be put off no longer.—You, thing, that was a wife, shall smart for this. I will not leave thee wherewithal to hide thy shame; your body shall be naked as your reputation.

Mrs. Fain. I despise you, and defy your malice—you have aspersed me wrongfully—I have proved your falsehood—go you and your treacherous—I will not name it, but starve together—perish!

Fain. Not while you are worth a groat, indeed, my dear. Madam, I'll be fooled no longer.

Lady W. Ah, Mr. Mirabell, this is small comfort, the detection of this affair.

Mira. Oh, in good time.—Your leave for the other offender and penitent to appear, madam.

[*Enter* WAITWELL *with a box of writings.*]

Lady W. O Sir Rowland!—Well, rascal!

Wait. What your ladyship pleases.—I have brought the black box at last, madam.

Mira. Give it me. Madam, you remember your promise.

Lady W. Ay, dear sir.

6. **fox,** a sword, perhaps so named because engraved with a fox.   8. **mittimus,** a warrant by which an arrest is made.

25. **Messalinas's poems.** Mincing is unintentionally witty here. She means "miscellaneous," of course. Messalina was the notoriously profligate wife of the Emperor Claudius.

Mira. Where are the gentlemen?

Wait. At hand, sir, rubbing their eyes—just risen from sleep.

Fain. 'Sdeath, what's this to me? I'll not wait your private concerns.

[*Enter* PETULANT *and* WITWOUD.]

Pet. How now? what's the matter? whose hand's out?

Wit. Heyday! what, are you all got together, like players at the end of the last act?

Mira. You may remember, gentlemen, I once requested your hands as witnesses to a certain parchment.

Wit. Ay, I do, my hand I remember—Petulant set his mark.

Mira. You wrong him, his name is fairly written, as shall appear.—You do not remember, gentlemen, anything of what that parchment contained? (*Undoing the box.*)

Wit. No.

Pet. Not I. I writ, I read nothing.

Mira. Very well, now you shall know.—Madam, your promise.

Lady W. Ay, ay, sir, upon my honour.

Mira. Mr. Fainall, it is now time that you should know that your lady, while she was at her own disposal, and before you had by your insinuations wheedled her out of a pretended settlement of the greatest part of her fortune—

Fain. Sir! pretended!

Mira. Yes, sir. I say that this lady while a widow, having, it seems, received some cautions respecting your inconstancy and tyranny of temper, which from her own partial opinion and fondness of you she could never have suspected—she did, I say, by the wholesome advice of friends and of sages learned in the laws of this land, deliver this same as her act and deed to me in trust, and to the uses within mentioned. You may read if you please—(*Holding out the parchment.*) though perhaps what is written on the back may serve your occasions.

Fain. Very likely, sir. What's here? Damnation! (*Reads.*) "A deed of conveyance of the whole estate real of Arabella Languish, widow, in trust to Edward Mirabell."—Confusion!

Mira. Even so, sir, 'tis *the way of the world*, sir; of the widows of the world. I suppose this deed may bear an elder date than what you have obtained from your lady.

Fain. Perfidious fiend! then thus I'll be revenged.—(*Offers to run at* MRS. FAINALL.)

Sir Wil. Hold, sir, now you may make your bear-garden flourish somewhere else, sir.

Fain. Mirabell, you shall hear of this, sir, be sure you shall.—Let me pass, oaf. [*Exit.*

Mrs. Fain. Madam, you seem to stifle your resentment: you had better give it vent.

Mrs. Mar. Yes, it shall have vent—and to your confusion, or I'll perish in the attempt. [*Exit.*

Lady W. O daughter, daughter, 'tis plain thou hast inherited thy mother's prudence.

Mrs. Fain. Thank Mr. Mirabell, a cautious friend, to whose advice all is owing.

Lady W. Well, Mr. Mirabell, you have kept your promise—and I must perform mine.—First, I pardon for your sake Sir Rowland there and Foible—the next thing is to break the matter to my nephew—and how to do that—

Mira. For that, madam, give yourself no trouble,—let me have your consent.—Sir Wilfull is my friend; he has had compassion upon lovers, and generously engaged a volunteer in this action, for our service; and now designs to prosecute his travels.

Sir Wil. 'Sheart, aunt, I have no mind to marry. My cousin's a fine lady, and the gentleman loves her, and she loves him, and they deserve one another; my resolution is to see foreign parts—I have set on't—and when I'm set on't, I must do't. And if these two gentlemen would travel too, I think they may be spared.

Pet. For my part, I say little—I think things are best off or on.

Wit. I gad, I understand nothing of the matter—I'm in a maze yet, like a dog in a dancing-school.

Lady W. Well, sir, take her, and with her all the joy I can give you.

Milla. Why does not the man take me? Would you have me give myself to you over again?

Mira. Ay, and over and over again. (*Kisses her hand.*) I would have you as often as possibly I can. Well, Heaven grant I love you not too well, that's all my fear.

Sir Wil. 'Sheart, you'll have time enough to toy after you're married; or if you will toy now, let us have a dance in the meantime, that we who are not lovers may have some other employment, besides looking on.

Mira. With all my heart, dear Sir Wilfull. What shall we do for music?

Foib. O sir, some that were provided for Sir Rowland's entertainment are yet within call.

[*A dance.*]

Lady W. As I am a person, I can hold out no longer—I have wasted my spirits so to-day already, that I am ready to sink under the fatigue; and I cannot but have some fears upon me yet, that my son Fainall will pursue some desperate course.

Mira. Madam, disquiet not yourself on that account; to my knowledge his circumstances are such, he must of force comply. For my part, I will contribute all that in me lies to a reunion; in the meantime, madam (*To* MRS. FAINALL.), let me before these witnesses restore to you this deed of trust; it may be a means, well managed, to make you live easily together.

From hence let those be warned, who mean to wed;
Lest mutual falsehood stain the bridal-bed:
For each deceiver to his cost may find,
That marriage frauds too oft are paid in kind.

[*Exeunt omnes.*

SUGGESTIONS FOR FURTHER READING

GENERAL

Clark, G. N., *The Seventeenth Century*, Oxford Press, 1929. The best one-volume survey of seventeenth-century life, thought, religion, politics, art

Trevelyan, G. M., *England under the Stuarts*, Putnam, 1928

Bryant, Arthur, *The England of Charles II*, Longmans, Green, 1934. "What happened to ordinary people on ordinary days in the reign of Charles II"

Willey, Basil, *The Seventeenth Century Background: Studies in the Thought of the Age in Relation to Poetry and Religion*, Chatto & Windus, 1934

Pinto, V de Sola, *The English Renaissance*, 1510–1688, McBride, 1938. The best one-volume introduction to all phases of Elizabethan and seventeenth-century literature, with a chapter on "Literature and Music" by Bruce Pattison

Reed, E. B., *English Lyrical Poetry*, Yale University Press, 1912. Comments on Carew, Suckling, Herrick, Lovelace, Crashaw, Vaughan

Coffin, R. P. T., and Witherspoon, A. M., eds., *A Book of Seventeenth-Century Prose*, Harcourt, Brace, 1929. Selections from the more important authors, with introductions and notes

THE AUTHORIZED VERSION OF THE BIBLE

Skinner, Conrad, *Concerning the Bible: A Brief Sketch of Its Origin, Growth, and Contents*, Abingdon Press, 1934

Crook, M. B., and others, *The Bible and Its Literary Associations*, Abingdon Press, 1937

FRANCIS BACON

Essays, Advancement of Learning, New Atlantis, and Other Pieces, ed. by R. F. Jones, Doubleday, Doran, 1937. An inexpensive and well-annotated edition

Steel, Byron, *Sir Francis Bacon*, Doubleday, Doran, 1930

BEN JONSON

Selected Works, ed. with an introduction by Harry Levin, Random House, 1938. The best and most recent one-volume anthology of Jonson's poems and prose

Palmer, John, *Ben Jonson*, Viking Press, 1934

THE METAPHYSICAL POETS

Grierson, H. J. C., "The Metaphysical Poets," in *The Background of English Literature*, Holt, 1925

Bennett, Joan, *Four Metaphysical Poets: Donne, Herbert, Vaughan, and Crashaw*, Macmillan, 1934

JOHN DONNE

Poems, ed. by H. I'A. Fausset, Dutton, 1931 (Everyman's Library)

Complete Poetry and Selected Prose, ed. by John Hayward, Random House, 1929. The best inexpensive modern edition

Walton, Izaak, *The Lives of Dr. John Donne and Others*, Oxford Press, 1927 (World's Classics)

Fausset, H. I'A., *John Donne: A Study in Discord*, Harcourt, Brace, 1925

THE CHARACTER BOOKS

Aldington, Richard, *A Book of Characters*, Dutton, 1924. Contains a valuable introduction, and characters from Theophrastus, La Bruyère, and other foreign authors, in addition to a generous selection of English characters.

Murphy, Gwendolen, *A Cabinet of Characters*, Oxford Press, 1925

ROBERT BURTON

The Anatomy of Melancholy, ed. by Holbrook Jackson, 3 vols., Dutton, 1932 (Everyman's Library)

GEORGE HERBERT

Poems, ed. by Dr. A. B. Grosart, with an introduction by Arthur Waugh, Oxford Press, 1912 (World's Classics)

Walton, Izaak, "The Life of Mr. George Herbert," in *The Lives of Dr. John Donne and Others*, Oxford Press, 1927 (World's Classics)

ROBERT HERRICK

Poems, ed. by F. W. Moorman, Oxford Press, 1933 (World's Classics)

Macaulay, Rose, *The Shadow Flies*, Harper, 1932. A biographical study of the life and times of Herrick in the form of a novel

THE CAVALIER POETS

Minor Poets of the Seventeenth Century, ed. by R. G. Howarth, Dutton, 1931 (Everyman's Library). Contains the poems of Carew, Suckling, Lovelace, and Herbert of Cherbury.

Hartmann, C. H., *The Cavalier Spirit and Its Influence on the Life and Work of Richard Lovelace*, Dutton, 1925

EDMUND WALLER

Poems, ed. by G. Thorn Drury, Dutton, 1901 (Muses Library)

RICHARD CRASHAW

Poems, ed. by J. R. Tutin, with an introduction by Canon Beeching, Dutton, 1913 (Muses Library)

HENRY VAUGHAN

Poems, ed. by E. K. Chambers, 2 vols., Dutton, 1913 (Muses Library)

Ashton, Helen, *The Swan of Usk*, Macmillan, 1940. A biography of Vaughan in the form of a novel

SIR THOMAS BROWNE

Religio Medici and Other Writings (*Hydriotaphia, Brampton Urns, Letter to a Friend, The Garden of Cyrus, Christian Morals*), with an introduction by C. H. Herford, Dutton, 1906 (Everyman's Library)

IZAAK WALTON

Lives, with an introduction by George Saintsbury, Oxford Press, 1927 (World's Classics)

The Compleat Angler, with an introduction by Andrew Lang, Dutton, 1906 (Everyman's Library)

JOHN MILTON

Poems, ed. by J. H. Hanford, Nelson, 1936. The most conveniently arranged and inexpensive one-volume edition of Milton's poems

Paradise Lost, ed. by M. Y. Hughes, Doubleday, Doran, 1935. A well-annotated one-volume edition

Paradise Regained, the Minor Poems, and Samson Agonistes, ed. by M. Y. Hughes, Doubleday, Doran, 1937. A companion volume to the editor's *Paradise Lost*

Milton's Prose, selected and ed. by M. W. Wallace, Oxford Press, 1937 (World's Classics)

Tillyard, E. M. W., *Milton*, Dial Press, 1930. The best one-volume study of the life and works of Milton

Macaulay, Rose, *Milton*, Harper, 1935. A short but illuminating study

Hanford, J. H., *A Milton Handbook*, rev. ed., Crofts, 1939. The best general guide to the study of Milton, with extensive bibliographies

ANDREW MARVELL

Poems and Satires, ed. by G. A. Aitken, 2 vols., Dutton, 1901 (Muses Library)

Birrell, Augustine, *Andrew Marvell*, Macmillan, 1905

ABRAHAM COWLEY

English Writings, ed. by A. R. Waller, 2 vols., Macmillan, 1907

Nethercot, A. H., *Abraham Cowley, the Muses' Hannibal*, Oxford Press, 1931

JOHN BUNYAN

The Pilgrim's Progress, with an introduction by Rev. H. E. Lewis, Dutton, 1937 (Everyman's Library)

SAMUEL PEPYS

The Diary, ed. by Richard, Lord Braybrooke, with a note by Richard Garnett, 2 vols. Dutton, 1924 (Everyman's Library)

Everybody's Pepys, ed. by O. F. Morshead, Harcourt, Brace, 1926. An excellent abridged edition, illustrated by E. H. Shepard

Arthur Ponsonby, *Samuel Pepys*, Macmillan, 1928.

Tanner, J. R., *Mr. Pepys: An Introduction to the Diary of Samuel Pepys*, Harcourt, Brace, 1924

Fagan, J. B., *And So to Bed*, Holt, 1926. A comedy in three acts with Mr. Pepys the central figure

JOHN DRYDEN

Poems, ed. by B. Dobrée, Dutton, 1934 (Everyman's Library)

Essays, ed. by W. P. Ker, 2 vols., Oxford Press, 1928

The Essay of Dramatic Poesy and Other Essays, with an introduction by W. H. Hudson, Dutton, 1912 (Everyman's Library)

Eliot, T. S., *John Dryden*, Holliday, 1932

Van Doren, Mark, *The Poetry of John Dryden*, Harcourt, Brace, 1920

RESTORATION DRAMA

Nettleton, G. H., *English Drama of the Restoration and the Eighteenth Century*, Macmillan, 1914

Krutch, J. W., *Comedy and Conscience after the Restoration*, Columbia University Press, 1924

WILLIAM CONGREVE

Comedies, ed. by Bonamy Dobrée, Oxford Press, 1925 (World's Classics)

The Eighteenth Century

Wood Eaton, near Oxford — a village that has changed little since the beginning of the eighteenth century. (Photograph by Odell Shepard)

Blenheim Palace, designed in the classical style, about 1705, by the dramatist Sir John Vanbrugh, and built at public expense for the Duke of Marlborough as a reward for his victory over the French and Bavarians in the battle of Blenheim. (New York Public Library)

The church and churchyard at Stoke Poges, scene of Thomas Gray's Elegy. (Ewing Galloway)

During the rapid expansion of London in the eighteenth century a number of large public squares surrounded by substantial buildings were planned and constructed. These contributed much toward the appearance of solid and unostentatious dignity which England's capital had never presented before but which it retains to the present day. (Metropolitan Museum of Art)

Throughout the eighteenth century the Drury Lane Theater, first constructed in the time of James I and rebuilt by Christopher Wren in 1674, was London's dramatic and histrionic center. (Bettmann Archive)

The formality and decorum of the period were shown almost as much in London's pleasure gardens and promenades as in its drawing-rooms. (Culver)

Above left. "When the morning stars sang together, and all the Sons of God shouted for joy" — one of the water-color designs made by William Blake (1757–1827) for his *Illustrations on the Book of Job*. The audacious force of Blake's imagination is quite as evident in his designs as in his poems. (From the original in the Pierpont Morgan Library)

Above right. The old East India wharf at London Bridge, from a painting by Peter Monamy. In the eighteenth century England expanded from an island to an Empire; trade, manifest in warehouses and counting-houses, docks and laden ships was turning London into the financial and business center of the world. (Bettmann Archive)

Below left. The Mall in St. James's Park, from the painting by Thomas Gainsborough (1727–1788), one of the chief landscape and portrait painters of his time. (© The Frick Collection, New York)

Below right. In *The Cockpit* and scores of other engravings of the same satiric vigor William Hogarth (1697–1764) revealed the "seamy side" of England's tapestry. (Culver)

JONATHAN SWIFT
After the portrait by Jervas

ALEXANDER POPE
After the portrait by William Hoare

DR. SAMUEL JOHNSON
After a painting by Sir Joshua Reynolds

OLIVER GOLDSMITH
After a painting by Sir Joshua Reynolds

THE EIGHTEENTH CENTURY

The Literary Stream

A SPORTSMAN who has leased the fishing rights along some part of a trout stream is allowed to stretch wires across the water, if he likes, to mark his upper and lower boundaries. Having done this, he may begin to feel that the reach of stream his wires mark off has a special beauty and excellence. He learns by heart, and he learns to love, each pool and eddy and curve within his domain. Yet he must be a dull sportsman, and hardly a sportsman at all, if he forgets that the water he fishes comes down from the miles above him and flows into miles below. He does not own this water. His wires leave the stream unchanged. The trout he would call his own glide under his boundary lines as though no lines were there.

It is an equally artificial separation that we make between one century and another. However well they may serve the geologist and the astronomer, centuries were not devised for the convenience of historians, critics, or those unclassifiable persons who write introductions to literary periods. We compute time in bundles of a hundred years for no profounder reason than that every human being is normally equipped with ten fingers, and there seems to be no close correlation between the contents of history and this anatomical fact.

The river of English literature swept out of the seventeenth and into the eighteenth century without perceptible change. It merely went floating on, bearing forward and braiding together the hundreds of tributaries that it had gathered on its way from the far-off springs of *Beowulf*. Something of the Middle Ages there was in it, and more of the Renaissance. The seventeenth century's turmoil of mind and heart, the furies and fervors of the Civil War, and the political excitements of the Protectorate, the Restoration, and the Revolution, were still bubbling and boiling just below its surface. To a superficial view, however, the stream was quieting down, and the time did not seem distant when it would become

"Though deep, yet clear; though gentle, yet **not** dull;
Strong without rage, without o'erflowing full."

Some such calming of the national life, thought, and expression was vaguely desired by the English people of about the year 1702, the year in which King William III was killed by a fall from his horse and was succeeded by Anne, daughter of James II. For these people were in a cautious if not a chastened mood. Their country, with a population of some six millions, was at war with the twenty millions of France, and it was not yet known that she had in the mighty Duke of Marlborough a man far more than a match for the generals of Louis XIV.

The English people, moreover, still kept a vivid recollection of domestic storms in which they had recently averted national catastrophe by a narrow margin, and they hoped henceforth to avoid such excesses of emotion and "enthusiasm" as those out of which the dangers of the past had sprung. There were dreams they could no longer trust in, and hopes that they would not indulge. Reason, moderation, and good sense were the objects of their somewhat humbled ambition. Having once for all vindicated the rights of the subject against a threat of tyranny from the throne, they were well disposed toward legitimate power and authority. After a long period of somewhat wild and chaotic innovation they began to think more favorably of the tried traditions of the past. Because they were so deeply acquainted with danger, they began to care rather more than English people have usually done for peace, order, and safety. Those Elizabethan sails had reached their distant bournes by now, and were beating homeward again. The dust and debris of Jacobean, Caroline, and Cromwellian explosion were slowly settling down. England began to hope for a long period of quiet.

It is one of the more remarkable things about eighteenth-century England that this liking for security, crossed and countered to be sure by many an outbreak of an older and more native adventurous spirit, steadily persisted from the timid accession of Queen Anne to the last passionate peroration of Edmund Burke. One might even say—of course with many doubts and qualifications—that the mood of cautious conservatism ruled English public and private life from the Revolution Settlement of 1689 to the first Reform Bill, belatedly passed in 1832. During these hundred-and-forty-three years most Englishmen felt that they had gone far enough along the ways of freedom, that in their "matchless constitution" they had struck an almost perfect balance between the liberties of the individual and centralized authority, and that it was their main business to use and defend those blessings secured to them in the strife of the past. They looked back to the Revolutionary Settlement as a final victory of political truth and justice and right, never to be altered without loss. Those chartered privileges of Parliament, of the Established Church, of the universities, and of private property, which had been threatened by James II and gloriously defended by the patriots of 1688–89, were to them like the Tables of the Law handed down from the Holy Mountain.

Most English institutions remained unchanged, even unchallenged, during the eighteenth century, and English laws remained for the most part unaltered. In literature and the other arts the same tendencies and tastes are discernible at the end of the century as those that we find at its beginning. Viewed from our distance, the thought and art and life of this time may seem to be standing still. This particular reach in the river of English literature, as seen from our far-off hilltop, often looks to us as though it were carved in some bright metal.

A Distant View

Many of us have somehow acquired a set of fairly definite opinions—true and false, favorable and adverse—about the eighteenth century as a whole. Indeed, there is no equal stretch of English history about which thoughtful people are more ready to indulge in easy and sweeping generalizations. We do not feel entirely strange in this period. It is like a country home, lying neither too near nor too far away. A few of its people, at least, are friends of ours, familiar since our childhood. Dr. Johnson, Oliver Goldsmith, Lemuel Gulliver, and Sir Roger De Coverley are not mysterious foreigners to us, like the men of the preceding age. We feel that we understand them, and also the world in which they lived.

The eighteenth century, we say, was a time in which the English people restrained their habitual ecstasies and fervors, a time in which reason held imagination and enthusiasm on a tight rein, so that prose grew clear at last and poets talked like people of this world. We say that it was a period in which men trusted the five senses chiefly, although they had much to say about "good sense" and "common sense" and what they called "the Reason." They tended, we think, to look away from life's mystery, strangeness, and wonder as though it were not there, feeling that what they could not readily comprehend could scarcely be said to exist. The rational, to their thinking, was almost equivalent to the true.

Again, we say that the people of this age liked to live and work within strictly defined limits—witness their architecture, their gardening, their heroic couplets, their essays never too long or too short, their sermons never too gay or too dull, their poems never too poetical, their ladies and gentlemen always observing the bounds of decorum. We feel that the eighteenth century was more coherent in its intellectual life, in its basic beliefs, and in its tastes and esthetic preferences than the world in which we live. It had, we think, a more educated feeling for symmetry, pattern, and form, together with a stronger "sense of the whole," than we commonly find in the culture of our day. More steadily than we do it remembered the limitations of human powers, and attended chiefly to the tasks for which those powers are fit. Regarded from our distance, its leading people seem to have achieved a greater harmony of the inner and outer life than the men and women that we know. We feel that they must all have been shaped by the same disciplines, that they shared the same body of knowledge, and that they spoke the same intellectual language. We say that this was a strongly social and conventional time. It regarded convention—that is, "coming together"—as a source and a sign of strength.

When we affirm that the eighteenth century was socially minded we do not mean that it was committed, at least during its first fifty years, to humanitarian effort. We mean, rather, that its effort was humanistic, and that it strove to bring men together at the top rather than at the bottom of the intellectual and cultural scale. The significant minds of this epoch did not try to find out and to express their differences from one another. They were not concerned to exploit their peculiarities. They tried to discover those thoughts, feelings, and beliefs which they held in common not merely with their foremost contemporaries but also with the nobler persons of the past. Their ambition was, in the comprehensive phrase of Irving Babbitt, to make themselves "normally and representatively human." And one sees that this ambition would bring about a greater cohesion and esprit de corps among the exponents and defenders of the national culture than we commonly find today.

It would be absurd, of course, to suggest that the age of Swift, of Pope, and of Dr. Johnson discouraged individualism. On the contrary, it set the individual free as few other ages have done—but free, we should carefully observe, not for eccentric, irresponsible, and self-seeking action but for a co-operative execution of duty. It set him free as a member of an old, intricate, delicately organized society which had been made by ages of human effort and might be wrecked in a day. All the liberty that could be given by a society that did not feel itself entirely safe, it gave him. But this society expected him to re-enact in his own inward senate chamber those laws of decency, decorum, and good sense which had been promulgated in the world without, and especially in the great civilizations of the past. It hoped that he would make the basic moral law his own law, and it wished him to consider how long had been the task of getting that law established.

And the age went beyond mere wishing and hoping. A large part of its literature, in prose and verse, is unashamedly devoted to moral and social instruction. Always remembering the Horatian maxim that literature should mingle the useful with the pleasing, the eighteenth century believed that utility is the more important of these ingredients. It revealed its Puritan backgrounds in its conviction that literature is no mere decoration of the fringe of life, that creative writing has a more important function than the amusement of lazy ladies and gentlemen, and that any writer worth his salt will of course be a teacher, a warner, an upholder of things found true, a defender of the society that supports him against all destructive forces. Therefore it was a sober and responsible kind of literature that the eighteenth century, as a whole, tried to write. For those who would not accept its doctrines of moderation, good sense, and decorum—all of them looking toward the safety of the social fabric—it provided the punitive lash of satire.

Didacticism and satire are the literary insignia of an age which does not feel itself to be secure. We have already seen that England's eighteenth century began with the conviction that it was not safe; and this conviction, in spite of prevailing good fortune and prosperity, it never quite overcame. The sense of danger and the longing for safety count for more than one would at first suppose in the continuity and also in the changes of these hundred years.

The Town

That social-mindedness, for example, which we have already named as a characteristic of the age—may it not have been partly due to a feeling that English people, as a rule not remarkable for sociability, ought to stand together in a time of stress? While the Court declined in social and intellectual influence, the coffeehouses and drawing-rooms increased their sway. In London, still the literary capital, there grew up that unorganized, ever shifting, shapeless, and yet strangely coherent society of cultivated men and women which called itself "the Town." This important body of persons, never numbering more than a few hundreds, would seem, at least from our distance, to have dictated the fashionable tastes and opinions of the age of Pope. We think of it as wielding almost the power of life and death over literary, political, and social reputations. It is to the Town that we look for those traits of extreme conventionality which are sometimes mistakenly attributed to eighteenth-century England as a whole. Yet we ought not to conclude, in spite of such suggestions to the contrary as we find in Pope's "Rape of the Lock," that this was either a wholly conventional or a merely frivolous society. The presence in it of many gifted persons and the constant circulation of enlightened ideas preserved it both from triviality and from dullness. The gradual infiltration of people who would once have been known as Puritans tended to make it increasingly sober.

Unorganized though it was, and therefore incapable of shaping any detailed program, the Town did perform several functions of high literary significance. It drew together a considerable number of writers who might otherwise have lived and worked alone, thus giving them some sense of co-operation in a common task. It enabled these writers to study at close range the audience which they chiefly addressed, and it subjected them to a criticism which was upon the whole well-informed without being professional, a criticism none the less effective because it was chiefly expressed by word of mouth. It corrected the pedantries and egotisms of these writers, smoothed down their eccentricities, and, in a word, made them more urbane. It gave them the cultivated talk of every day as a model for their prose style, and taught the verse-writers among them to strive not so much for full emotional expression as for the intellectual effects of epigram, wit, sententiousness, and "point." The Town did its favorite writers the high honor, seldom accorded in other periods of English history, of taking them into good and regular social standing, and so it felt free to lay upon them that same eleventh commandment which was binding upon all its other members: "Thou shalt not bore."

No doubt we are in some danger, today, of exaggerating the unanimity of the Town, and certainly the extent to which it represented the country as a whole has been greatly overestimated. Yet no one can read the standard literature produced in England during the first fifty years of the eighteenth century without observing that the opinion and taste of the Town is frequently referred to, even deferred to, as a norm, a criterion, almost an authority. Thus Joseph Addison aspires to be the spokesman of the Town at the same time that he is trying, in a mild and somewhat deprecating way, to instruct it. The tone of almost complete self-confidence that rings in every couplet of Alexander Pope is due not so much to Pope's unquestionable egotism as to his belief that he speaks not for himself alone. The dogmatism of Dr. Johnson, frequently almost ludicrous to a modern reader who does not understand its social backgrounds, is to be explained in much the same way. All three of these men, together with most of their contemporaries, believed that the consensus of a cultivated society such as the Town was likely to be wiser than any one of the members of that society.

The Common Mind of Man

But these men believed also that the concerted opinion of the ages upon any given problem, if only one could find out what that opinion was, would probably be wiser than that of any single age, including their own. For their chief authority and guidance, therefore, they looked to the past. Without being antiquarian, they were more retrospective than we. They knew far less about the past than we do, but they cared about it far more. Their sense of time and change was not so acute as ours, and they tended to think of the ancient classical past as a period in which time had stood still; yet they took up much more of the ancient world into their lives than we do. History, to them, and especially the history of ancient Greece and Rome, was not a mere learning but a hoard of experience, a treasury of human example, from which to draw warning and wisdom. They looked to it for their models of character and conduct, for their ideals of private and public life, even for the bases of their literary "rules." In so doing they were true to a belief which seemed to them axiomatic, that human nature remains throughout the ages essentially one and the same.

This confidence of theirs in the authority of the ancients and in the "common mind of man" made for an assurance in matters of morality, thought, and taste, to which we, with our greatly increased knowledge of human differences, can no longer pretend. The people of the eighteenth century felt sure that they understood many things about which we, although much better informed, are equally sure that we know almost nothing. Fundamentally they felt, like the ancient Greeks, that "man is the measure of all things," and they seldom doubted that man's mind is able to comprehend and control his world.

An age, like a man, must pay in full for its peculiar qualities by suffering the defects which those qualities entail. That same trust in authority which made the thought of this period prevailingly serene often left it shallow and derivative as well. Too often it lacked tension, intensity, the strength that comes of struggle and the courage that ventures forth alone.

Much of this century's effort was made with the

crippling conviction that nearly everything worth doing and saying had already been perfectly said and done. There was a feeling abroad, as a French critic of the preceding age had phrased it, that "all the verses are already written," so that nothing was left for the modern world except a rather hopeless imitation. The Earl of Chatham or Edmund Burke, speaking before Parliament, could hardly hope to do more than remind their listeners of the triumphs achieved by Cicero before the Roman Senate. Samuel Johnson, writing a poem about his beloved London, felt obliged to pretend that he hated that city, for no better reason than that his model, the ancient satiric poet Juvenal, had pretended to hate ancient Rome. Alexander Pope, for all his vaulting ambition, aspired to no greater glory than that of being known as the Horace of his age. And this imitative docility was shown not only in matters of style and thought but in the choice of literary forms as well. One reason, at least, for the popularity of satire in this period is the simple one that satire had been a popular form in that period of Roman civilization, the Augustan, which the eighteenth century most admired. As for that totally different poetic form or mood, the ode, one sees no particular reason why it too should have been extensively cultivated in this time aside from the fact that it had the sanction of the ancients. The grand simplicities of epic poetry lay, of course, far beyond the emotional range of eighteenth-century writers, but in the mock epic, with its combination of a grandiose theme and a spirit of ridicule, these writers found a form entirely to their minds.

In trying to understand this veneration for the ancient classical past we ought to keep in mind the influence of the English school curriculum and the effect of that severely restricted diet upon which almost every leading mind of the time was reared. By precept and by birch rod, from the beginning of the century until its end, the schoolmasters of England kept England's future rulers and writers to their task of learning by heart what the Greeks and Romans had said, and of imitating in the original tongues their ways of saying it. Little else was thought necessary for the education of a gentleman, but this was considered indispensable.

Influences of the Past

Largely on account of the imitative and retrospective tendencies so apparent in this period, many critics have asserted that there was a close relationship between it and the Renaissance. The relationship, though traceable, is remote. In the great years of the Renaissance men's minds were fired by a passionate delight in the ancient grandeurs and glories, and by an overmastering desire not merely to know and understand and record that earlier world but to bring it alive again. The true Renaissance, we should always remember, was not mainly a literary movement, nor was it primarily an affair of scholarship. Rather it was a period of free creative activity ranging through all the arts and up and down the whole gamut of human powers. It revived and amplified the Hellenic ideal of the harmonized, fully developed, widely experienced man. It held that the best of life is not found in a cautious avoidance of error but in a bold adventuring.

Little of this tradition was preserved or exemplified in the English eighteenth century, which tended to distrust all passion, whether of delight or of desire. Exaggerating a most unfortunate error of the earlier Renaissance, it paid far more attention to the Roman than to the Hellenic elements in classical antiquity, thus inclining to the imitation of a culture which had itself been imitative. Even the Roman element it trimmed down to its literary, or rather to its rhetorical, aspects. In Dr. Samuel Johnson, one of the more favorable examples of what the eighteenth century could do in the development of personality, no one can fail to see the results of this dwindling. Painting, sculpture, architecture, dancing, and acting he cared little for. Music he defined as the least unpleasant form of noise. About most of what we refer to by the word "nature" he knew little and cared less. To that health, beauty, strength, and skill of the body which the wiser ancients had thought to be almost the highest good he did not even aspire. He was gross in appearance and in physical habits. He was often boorish in manners. Out of the total wealth of knowledge and experience which the classic mind had comprised and the mind of the Renaissance had striven to recapture he chose the literary elements almost exclusively. He did his best literary work in the field of criticism, and even there his judgments were often shaped not by true literary standards but by a dogmatic morality.

Rhetoric

The men of the eighteenth century did not inherit so much from the Renaissance as they did from the declining period of Roman culture. They remind one of the later Romans in the fact that they cared more for rhetoric than for literature. Too often, that is, their main concern was rather for expression, form, and phraseology than for the thought and feeling their phrases were supposed to present.

One sees how this came about. Subject matter, these men believed, was everyone's property. In proportion as it was important it was also commonplace. All the great themes had been used by the ancients, and the attempt to find a new one would only lead one away from "the common mind of man" into the dangerous bypaths of eccentricity. Thus, with nearly all that we now mean by "invention" and "originality" made to seem impossible, the writers of this period devoted most of their energy to literary form, to style, to manner—in a word, to rhetoric. And it was in these matters that their work really excelled.

Pope's *Essay on Man*, to choose a single example, is not remarkable for the novelty of its thought. As an original thinker, indeed, Pope does not take high rank among the poets of the world, and we may well doubt whether he even aspired to intellectual originality. On the other hand, his poem is clearly a triumph of manner and style. It contains much of "what oft was thought but ne'er so well expressed." On that account it stands high among the characteristic achievements of its time.

We in our day, to be sure, commonly do far less than justice to style and manner. We suspect that when a man turns a sentence twenty ways before he lets it stand, as Pope often did, he can scarcely care what the sentence means or whether he believes it. But this does not follow. Extreme elaboration of manner and utmost concern about the form of expression are not signs of carelessness about anything. Pope did believe in the ideas of his *Essay on Man*, and probably all the more because he knew that they had not been born in his own clever head. Precisely for the reason that they had come, as he thought, out of the oldest granaries of human experience, he wished to give them the corroboration of his utmost rhetorical skill.

Perhaps it is our fundamental complaint against the literature of the eighteenth century that it only tells us, like Mark Antony's speech to the Roman plebeians, what we ourselves do know. Solidly based upon those beliefs in which all civilized ages have agreed, distrusting the odd and suspicious of all novelty, this literature never shocks and seldom surprises us. We are tempted, therefore, to call it shallow and platitudinous.

Yet here too we should keep in mind our own shortcomings while passing judgment upon those of another age. Certain it is that platitudes, grandly or gracefully expressed, won more applause in the eighteenth century than they do today, but from this fact we should not too hastily infer that the mind of the eighteenth century was less profound or less energetic than our own. It may have been only more patient and sober, more fully aware than we are that most of the little wisdom mankind has gathered can be expressed in few, familiar, and simple words.

The best writers of this period strove always to be clear in thought and simple in style. Clarity and simplicity were to them the chief marks of good taste, and the trophies, also, of intellectual triumph. They felt that a writer had finished his task only when he had completely lifted a beautiful order out of chaos, had cut every facet of his diamond sharp and true and blown the dust away. They came closest to the classic ideal which they admired from a distance in their labor to impose the patterns of mind upon the outer world, in their struggle to subject the wild miscellaneity of man's surroundings to the laws of human thought. We miss their secret if we confuse the simplicity which they often attained with the crude, the naïve, the elementary. Above all, they were lovers of order.

Prose and Poetry

Here lies one reason, at least, for this period's most important literary achievement—its rapid perfection of a clear and simple prose style. Other explanations of this feat have, to be sure, been given. For one thing, the new interest in natural science brought a demand for a more precise use of language. Moreover, the rapid growth of the reading public made it necessary for writers to address a multitude of persons to whom the intricate prose of the past would have been unintelligible. The growth of newspapers, the increase in the number and importance of political pamphlets, the influence of the coffeehouses, and the example of French literature all made in the same direction. Yet it seems likely that even without these influences the eighteenth century would have worked out for itself the direct and straight-grained prose which we see at its best in the pages of Jonathan Swift. And this it would have done because its master passion was for clarity and order.

These are among the highest virtues of prose, but they are not sufficient to produce poetry as we now understand that term. They did not do so in the eighteenth century. In reading the literature of that century we are often tempted to doubt whether the writers of its first few decades, at any rate, quite knew what poetry is, or is good for. Certainly they wrote some of the neatest verse in our language, and in this verse they were often admirably eloquent, sententious, edifying, and instructive; but all this, we tend to feel, is of slight importance in comparison with the fact that their so-called poetry is seldom, to our thinking, poetic. In their frequent use of flat and dull personifications, in their anxious avoidance of homebred and blood-warm words, most clearly of all in their steady preference for the generalized or universal statement as opposed to the precise and particular, they strained deliberately away from poetry as we know it.

"The business of a poet," said Dr. Johnson in his *Rasselas*, "is to examine not the individual but the species, to remark general properties and large appearances. He does not number the streaks of the tulip or describe the different shades in the verdure of the forest. He is to exhibit in his portraits of nature such prominent and striking features as recall the original to every mind, and must neglect the minuter discriminations, which one may have remarked and another neglected, for those characteristics which are alike obvious to vigilance and carelessness."

A twentieth-century critic feels compelled to say that almost every statement in this passage, written by the most influential literary critic of the eighteenth century, is completely and viciously wrong. The passage reveals a total ignorance of the fact that sensory images, which can never be too precise and clear, are not the "ornament" of poetry, as Johnson and his congeners took them to be, but its very stuff and substance. This effort to sink the concrete and specific—"all singular forms, local customs, particularities, and details of every kind"—in seas of abstraction, was really, however it may have been intended, an effort to drown poetry itself. It was by such means, Dr. Johnson thought, that a poet might secure what he elsewhere calls "the grandeur of generality." But the first true poet who looked squarely at this doctrine brushed it contemptuously aside. "To generalize," said William Blake, "is to be an idiot. To particularize is the great distinction of merit. . . . Grandeur of ideas is founded on precision of ideas."

Dr. Johnson's wrong opinions, however, are often more interesting than other men's right ones; and here we ought not to ignore the motives, conscious and unconscious, that suggested all this havoc in the forest of poetry. The motive of which Johnson was aware may be called a social one: his purpose was to make poetry—to call it that—more widely accessible. The poet is told to say "tree" rather than "oak" in order that "every mind" may find its account in the poem he writes. The forest of poetry is being improved into a public park.

And the motives of which Dr. Johnson and his like-minded fellows were probably unaware were social too, although in a different sense. These writers held the mistaken opinion, deviously inherited from the aristocratic past, that general and abstract ideas are, in some way which they never made quite clear even to themselves, more dignified and genteel than particular ideas. A study of their social origins will suggest the reason why most of them wished to appear as genteel and dignified as possible. To this end they carefully avoided the themes, the thoughts, and, even more carefully, the language of those lower classes from which many of them came; they scorned the speech of the people as "low" and "vulgar"; they bedizened their language with tasteless circumlocutions and overloaded it with a cumbrous Latinity. For all this they gave themselves plausible excuses. "Since it often happens," says Addison, "that the most obvious phrases, and those which are used in ordinary conversations, become too familiar to the ear, and contract a kind of meanness by passing through the mouths of the vulgar, a poet should take particular care to guard himself against idiomatic ways of speaking." And Dr. Johnson chimed in, fifty years later, with the assertion that "the most heroic sentiments will lose their efficacy, and the most splendid ideas drop their magnificence, if they are conveyed by words used commonly upon low and trivial occasions, debased by vulgar mouths and contaminated by inelegant applications."

These opinions, we ought perhaps to remember, were not peculiar to the English eighteenth century. Like many other critical doctrines and attitudes of the time, they were derived more or less directly from France, which had taken them, in turn, from Italy. Nevertheless, they are based, wherever found, upon unconscious social considerations. The pompous poetic diction of the eighteenth century reminds us that, however it might be with prose, the fashionable poetry of the time was not meant for the English people as a whole. Like most art of the Renaissance, it was produced by persons not sure of their social rating, as a part of the great and sometimes lucrative business of "making life pleasant for the upper classes." Nothing short of the French Revolution, with all its leveling tendencies, could have enabled even a Wordsworth to shake the conviction that poetry is something luxurious, highly dignified, and essentially aristocratic, which must be kept unspotted from the world of every day.

Along the Banks

We have now considered some part of what can be said about the eighteenth century on the supposition that it was a quiet if not a static time, like a stream that paces evenly forward with no turbulence, glassing a serene sky. But every actual river, we know, moves through many a changing landscape. Even in his single mile of trout stream our imaginary sportsman is likely to find a wide variety. At the upper end of it, let us say, he fishes a flashing and arrowy water that plunges among steep hills; midway in his mile he comes into level meadows where the currents circle slowly, filled with slumbering sunlight, between low banks; and then at last, close to his lower wire, he may have gorges to clamber down before he comes to where the unleashed stream roars by through a daylong dusk. Such changes in speed, in color and depth, and in the surrounding landscape, will make for variety in his sport. He will not cast in the same way, or use the same flies, on the water that runs through meadows as on that of the hills or the gorges. Neither will he take the same kinds of trout.

To a lover of streams it is always a marvel how they vary and transmute themselves from place to place. In trying to explain their infinite variety one is forced back upon the notion of numberless local gods, *genii loci*, who were anciently supposed to lend every spot of earth its peculiar character. This was a helpful idea; and we in our turn might be helped by the fancy that every distinguishable period of time takes its character from a separate *Zeitgeist* or time spirit. Thus we should be reminded that although time is forever one and the same continuous stream, yet it is always changing.

Thus far we have been taking a distant view of the eighteenth century, trying to see it all in one glance as though we were looking out from a hilltop over a river. We have been trying to imagine that it was ruled from end to end by a single temporal god. But now, as we step closer down, coming in sight of its conflict of currents and hearing its actual uproar of warring voices, we begin to wonder what we could have been thinking of when we called this a placid stream.

What leisure for retrospection can there have been, and what peace for the imitation of ancient amenities, during a hundred-year spell in which England, though constantly torn by strife of party and class, yet founded our modern industry and finance, led the world in science and invention, fought half a dozen triumphant wars, and grew from the size of Illinois into the widest empire the world has ever seen? Instead of being the end of the Renaissance, was not this the birth time of modernity? Rather than being poised, serene, conservative, and a little languid, was it not really a time of explosive forces? How can we assert that the eighteenth century was mainly concerned with the ancient world in view of its ever growing delight in the Middle Ages, in popular ballads and folklore, in the life and literature of the English past, and even in wild nature? How can we call this essentially a social time, considering that the praise of solitude rings through it from end to end? With what reason can we say that it emphasized chiefly "the common mind of man" when one of its most characteristic products was the modern novel, dedicated to the presentation not of "Man" in the abstract but of highly individual men and women? What of the declaration that in this time the mouths of reformers were stopped? John Howard was not silenced in his campaign for the reform of British prisons, and neither were Wilberforce and Clarkson in their determined attack upon slavery. What is to be made of the statement that Englishmen "retrained their habitual ecstasies and fervors" during that century which saw, in the "Methodist" or Wesleyan revival, as great an emotional upheaval as England has ever known? And how, finally, can we maintain that this was a period of docile imitation when we recall that it produced such audacities as Smart's "Song to David," the poems and paintings of Blake, and the lyrics of Robert Burns?

Romanticism and Classicism

It is clear that more than one time spirit held sway along this reach of the river. Academic critics have singled out at least two such, and have pasted on their statues the labels "Classic" and "Romantic." Properly understood and used, these are helpful labels, and they can do no harm so long as we remember that they are nothing more. We should remember, too, that Classicism did not end in the eighteenth century, and that Romanticism certainly did not begin there. Both of them are easily discoverable in every one of these ten decades, as they are also in our own time—and, for that matter, in ancient China, in the Egypt that built the pyramids, and in the Athens of Pericles. We should remember always that Classicism and Romanticism are not "mutually exclusive." They overlap, and often they seem to lie side by side in an age, in a given book or poem, and even—most perplexingly—in an individual mind. They

THE EIGHTEENTH CENTURY

make one think of that endless dialogue which the left lobe of a man's brain carries on with the right. They remind one of the Chinese gentleman's desire to be Confucian in the morning, at his business, but Taoist in the leisure of the afternoon when he retires to his garden for meditation.

Literary critics and historians have long worked upon the assumption that the feelings and thoughts underlying the English "Romantic Movement" were new discoveries toward which the men of the preceding period had groped their way as though out of darkness into light. Until recent years, in fact, an accepted way of praising certain minor writers of the eighteenth century has been to say that they "anticipated" or that they "heralded" Romanticism. The truth is, however, as we have said, that the Romantic temper is discernible in every decade of this century. Unmistakably Romantic traits are to be found not only in those whom we have chosen to call "minor writers" but in such thoroughly representative figures, often considered completely "Classical" or "Neoclassical," as Addison, Swift, and Pope. It follows that such a phrase as "the beginnings of Romanticism" is absurdly inapplicable to any part of the English eighteenth century, and that the segregation of fifty or sixty years of that century as the period of such alleged "beginnings" leads into serious error.

We do well to recognize that the English people are naturally—or perhaps one should say incorrigibly—romantic; but this need not mean that they are exclusively so. Special circumstances such as those in which they found themselves after the Restoration may cause them to incline for a time toward the opposite side. And concerning the eighteenth century one may say that the Classical tendency predominated, although as a declining force, during its first fifty years, and that the Romantic tendency increased during its second half.—Even this statement one makes with a host of exceptions in mind, and yet with the belief that it may be helpful if rightly understood and applied.

The chief cause of the hesitancy that one feels in making such a statement is due to the realization that the Classical and Romantic regimes were not separated from each other in time alone but also in space. Classicism ruled, while it ruled at all, in the Town, but never in the country—and the country has always been the home of English hearts. The tension of Neoclassical authority decreased, one might say, as the square of the distance from London. In the northern counties, and in the western, it was scarcely perceptible.

In studying the interplay of Classicism and Romanticism during the eighteenth century, moreover, we need to keep in mind the distinctions of social rank, which meant far more to the English of this period than Americans of the twentieth century are likely to realize. The literature of the Town was composed not so much for a true aristocracy, assured of its position and therefore unafraid of natural simplicity, as for a new upper middle class extremely anxious about matters of fashion and vogue precisely because it was not to the manner born. And a similar thing must be said, with suitable qualifications, about most of the men who wrote this literature. Their sedulous avoidance of everything that they called "low" is to be understood, as we have seen, at least partly in terms of their social origins and aspirations. They seldom brought a purely creative purpose to their literary tasks. They were far less disinterested than those lonely minds that have shaped the world's greater structures of thought and woven its fabric of beauty.

We see, then, that many characteristics of this period which have been attributed largely to intellectual causes may be traced back to a cultural timidity and to a social ambition which, distrusting the homely English ways, looked abroad for guidance and support. Fashionable people who went up to the Town in the Season were not content with importing their literary opinions alone. It was from Europe that they learned what paintings to admire, what music they ought to like, what dances were most genteel, and how to lay out their gardens. To call them "cosmopolitan" is to do them more than justice. They were, in fact, not wholly unlike those Americans who, until the occurrence of a recent catastrophe, hardly knew what they ought to wear before the Parisian dictators of style had spoken.

But although the Town had grown a little ashamed of native English traditions, the central mind and heart of England as they lived on in the country were not abashed at all. During this period, as in every other, the great body of English people remained unaffected by foreign fashions. John Bunyan was a greater name to hosts of them than that of Pope himself; they loved and admired their English Shakespeare in defiance, often in simple ignorance, of the rules for poetic composition laid down by Boileau and Horace and Aristotle; and they were never shaken in their conviction that the greatest literature in the world was that of the English Bible. Thus the older, the native, or what we now call the "Romantic," tradition lasted on, by no means overcome or even checked, but only, for a time, submerged. It flowed onward as a lower current in the stream; and the "Romantic Movement," when it came, was but the re-emergence of a mood and manner so very old that they seemed new.

Evidently, then, this period was not so simple as we have taken it to be. It was, at least, duplex. And therefore those easy generalizations with which we began are in need of some revision. They are valid enough, to be sure, for the fashionable literature of the Town as written during the time of the Town's dominance, but they go wrong in the assumption that the Town ruled the whole of this century and dominated all of England.

London literature did not speak for England as a whole in any part of our period. It did not speak even for all of London. It gave little hint that the English village was coming at just this time to its final and perfect flower, winning a devotion from painters and poets, from diarists and storytellers and students of nature, as deep as any that London could claim. We have called this, not incorrectly, a time of tradition and of imitation; but it was also a time in which men trusted as firmly as ever before or since in "original genius." We have called it a social time, and it was that; and yet through all these hundred years there rises, as though from ten thousand aeolian harps, the music of romantic solitude.

Changing Currents

Our general statements about the century as a whole, moreover, will be found to apply more closely to the first half of the period than they do to the second. The common error of interpreting the entire century in terms that apply to scarcely more than half of it is due, partly, to the fact that Dr. Johnson—upon the whole a Neoclassical and of course a dominant mind—maintained and imposed until his death in 1784 the opinions and standards of an earlier time. He imposed them, however, upon a dwindling circle. He might still be the chief literary voice of London; but literature, during his old age, was moving into the country.

This suggestion that English literature underwent a change of mood at about the middle of the eighteenth century need not rest upon the literary evidence alone. It is in keeping with what we might expect, for England herself was rapidly changing in this time. Her social, political, and industrial history shows many swift transformations.

During the reign of Queen Anne (1702–14) and the reigns of the first two Georges, extending to 1760, the Court lost that leadership in the arts and in society which it had held since the time of Henry the Eighth. Little by little the Crown let slip even such influence upon public affairs as was still available to it after the "Revolution" of 1688. Political power was taken over by Parliament and the Ministers of the Crown, many of whom were men of exceptional abilities. During the first half of the century this power was wielded chiefly by the Whigs— that is, by a party of great landowners, London merchants, and wealthy tradesmen whose primary interests were commercial and mercantile. Sir Robert Walpole, at the head of a Whig Ministry, gave England the sort of "businessman's administration" that its wealthy classes wanted, together with a long peace, a steadily growing prosperity for those who prospered at all, and a government as strong and able as it was corrupt. Although not a few of the old and noble families were glad to share the profits of this regime, the general social tone was that which we now associate with the "high bourgeoisie" or upper middle class. The main requirement of this class was, then as now, that one must get rich and remain so. If one could not be rich, then one should imitate and cultivate those who were. To this end one should avoid all extremes and eccentricities of thought, feeling, and behavior. One should do what was done, say what was said, like what was liked, and wear what was worn. Not otherwise could one be "respectable"—a word of steadily increasing overtones, connotations, and, from an impartial point of view, even humor. Undoubtedly there lingered on through the time of Anne, and even into that of her two thoroughly stupid successors, an aristocratic recognition that getting rich is not in itself sufficient, that it is not a goal of life, but a means of living rightly. It would not do to suggest that the last true aristocrat slunk away before the bland stare of the first successful businessman. Rather, being an Englishman, he proposed a compromise. He seems to have hinted that if only the businessman would let him become or remain very rich, then he, the aristocrat, would spread the notion abroad that being extremely rich is almost the same thing as being aristocratic. And it would appear that the businessman, trying not to look overjoyed, accepted this proposal.

But the consequences are numerous and grave, of course, whenever the aristocrat or the man who works with his hands or brain surrenders to the middleman. For the middleman's thought is seldom about what things cost in terms of nature's gift and man's earnest effort upon it. He is chiefly concerned with what he can collect. And just that is what too many of the leading men were mainly concerned about during England's eighteenth century. Seats in Parliament were for sale to those who could pay the price. Dignified positions on the bench of bishops were provided for those who could be trusted to vote in the interests of their Whig patrons. Comfortable professorships at Oxford and Cambridge went usually to those who could be counted upon to inculcate "sound" opinions. The Bank of England, founded in 1694, and a new and greatly strengthened East India Company, became powerful forces of political corruption. Not only did wealth accumulate rapidly during these hundred years, and not only was it drawn into ever fewer hands, but it was given an influence in the national life such as it had never known before. One might say that all the other members of Chaucer's pilgrimage, certainly including the Knight, were now falling back to subordinate positions, and that the Merchant was jogging briskly to the head of the procession, "souning alway th' encrees of his winning."

The results of this change in leadership looked, at first, satisfactory enough. England's agricultural methods were greatly improved—as indeed they had to be if the growing population was to be supported. Her manufactures, carried in her own ships, began to appear in the most distant markets of the world. Her arms were almost everywhere triumphant. She became the almost unchallenged mistress of the seven seas. Before the first half of the century was out she began to regard herself, with reason, as the wealthiest and most powerful nation on earth.

This prosperity and sense of power affected the English people in several ways. By alleviating the feeling of insecurity with which the century began, it caused a rapidly increasing tolerance of eccentricities which had formerly seemed dangerous. The individual was more and more set free, as the decades passed, from social control, and the "rules" of literary composition to which the writers of the Age of Pope had willingly subjected themselves were gradually relaxed. A less fortunate effect of England's growth in wealth and power was that the graceful gaiety which had been the charm of Elizabethan gentlemen and of the Cavaliers was lost to Englishmen, at about this time, forever. A certain national arrogance, never to be confused with true patriotism, took for a while its place. One might hazard a guess that John Bull was born at about the time when George III, in 1760, came to the throne.

In spite of all its concentration upon the "humanities," the age of Pope was not, in our changed sense of the word, remarkably humane. Social though it was in several important respects, this period is likely to seem to us deficient in social imagination. It could and did tacitly exclude ninety-nine in the hundred of human beings as though, for literary and intellectual purposes at any rate, they did not fully exist.

Something like this, indeed, really was the belief of many influential persons. Since the beginning of the Renaissance the conviction had been fairly common that a full and complete humanity is by no means conferred by birth, but is to be attained only by long subjection to the humanizing discipline of classical culture and polite society. Germs of the old Stoic idea that all men are born free and equal were, to be sure, in the air, but there was as yet little thought of giving a practical application to that notion. When Pope declared that "the proper study of mankind is man" he did not refer to the whole human race, nor was he recommending the pursuit of the science we now call anthropology. When he and his fellows used their significant expression "the Town" they did not mean to include the total population of London. And even Dr. Johnson, in some sense a man of the people, when he said that poetry should be made intelligible to "every mind" was probably not thinking of the millions of English people who in his time could neither read nor write.

We have seen that the true aristocracy of England, which had for centuries maintained the aristocrat's traditional sense of responsibility for the poor, was trying now to sell its birthright for a mess of prosperity, and that the place of this aristocracy was being taken by a rich upper class determined to grow richer. Immemorial rights of the peasantry were giving way to "poor laws"—a very different thing. The ancient system of open-field or communal farming, to which both Old and New England owe much of their essential nature, was being slowly obliterated by the Enclosure Acts. Long-established patterns of social structure were breaking up. The rural population, torn loose from its moorings of traditional use and wont, drifted helplessly into cities where no effort had yet been made for its educational, moral, religious, or even economic maintenance. A new poverty, more dismal and brutalizing by far than any that English people had ever known in their village homes, increased step by step with the new wealth. The drunkenness of the London poor, made possible by the introduction of a cheap gin of English manufacture, became a major problem of legislators who were not themselves perfect models of sobriety. A gambling frenzy, taking its impetus from the "Mississippi Bubble" of 1720, swept through the nation from high to low. Bull-baiting, the cockpit, and prize fighting with bare knuckles contributed to the degradation of the people. The country clergy, obsequiously following the country squires, did all they could to keep down the pest of foxes. Penal codes of ever increasing severity could not check the growth of crime. Twenty convicted men and women might be hanged in a day at Tyburn Tree or in front of Newgate Prison—hanged on charges ranging from murder to theft of a loaf of bread; yet highwaymen continued to rule the country roads, and organized gangs of thugs defied the feeble London constabulary.

"Everyone laughs if you talk of religion," Montesquieu wrote home from England about the year 1730, having in mind the fashionable society of London. He may have been unfortunate in his introductions, but if the word "religion" was meant to refer to the Established Church, then this laughter was not unwarranted. At no time has that Church fallen farther below its opportunities and obligations. Having abandoned the mystical elements of belief that lie at the core of Christianity, it degenerated into an ethical society, a tool of the State, and a means of keeping poor people quiet. Too often the bishops and clergy lent their voices to whatever seemed the most respectable contemporary cry. It contained, of course, many good and earnest persons, yet the Church did little in this time to point out or to correct the corruptions of public life, the depravity of highly placed individuals, and the widespread miseries of the poor.

The Church, to be sure, was not alone in taking advantage of England's feeling that all institutions whatsoever—dangerously attacked as they had been by James II and gloriously defended in the Revolution Settlement of 1689—ought to be held forever exempt even from criticism. The same dry rot that corroded the Church was discernible also in the universities and in the great public schools. It ate into the courts of law, even though this was the century of Sir William Blackstone, and into Parliament and high finance. Most sacred of all, in this age of merchants and bankers, were the rights of private property. A very rich man, it was tacitly agreed, could scarcely do anything wrong. A rich man must be a good man because God had so obviously blessed him. Conversely, there was already growing up the sage opinion of Tennyson's Northern Farmer that "the poor, in the lump, is bad." Why, then, should they not suffer a few anticipatory pangs of punishment in the slums of London and in the frightful new factory towns of the Black Country? "Let well enough alone" might have been the motto of the ruling classes. Alexander Pope was their mouthpiece when he set down his blatantly optimistic line

"One truth is clear, WHATEVER IS, IS RIGHT."

We are not so sure of that, two hundred years later. Pope himself might not be quite so sure if he could see the delicate grotto of shells that he built at Twickenham now lying under the random rain of bombs. James Thomson, if he could revisit that Richmond Terrace whence he once admired the view, might not be so confident that "Britons never will be slaves." The ghosts of Gibbon and Gray, looking down in 1942 upon the time-eaten towers of their Oxford and Cambridge, may be wondering how they ever took these beautiful cities of the mind to be eternal. Even Dr. Johnson, if he now cares at all about the right little island that he once so fiercely loved, may be asking how he could go on talking to Boswell and Burke and Reynolds and Mrs. Thrale with the premonitory hum in his ears of the engines and machines that would soon tear his comfortable world to bits.—We have said, correctly, that the people of the eighteenth century felt insecure, but in comparison with our own uncertainties they may be said to have lived in a fool's paradise.

Yet even here we should remember that Pope spoke for only the first half of these hundred years and for a small minority of the people living in that. Even while he spoke, the yeast of a profound change was working. Within the Established Church itself there developed, in the fourth and fifth decades of the century, a movement nicknamed "Methodism" which amounted to a gradual revolution. Co-operating or coalescing with other tendencies variously called sentimentalism, sensibility, enthusiasm, and humanitarianism, this movement was either the source or a main support of many long-needed reforms. The thought and spirit and organizing power of John Wesley, the hymns of his brother Charles, and the mighty preaching of his coadjutor George Whitefield, reverberated into every nook of English and American life until they reached the banks of the Mississippi. Remote as the Methodist revival may seem from the work of English poets and prosemen, no one can understand the English literature of this time if he leaves that revival out of account. In no small degree it was the spread of Methodism that gave the second half of this century, as represented in literature, a tone increasingly different from that of the foregoing fifty years.

One may guess at the nature and estimate the need of this movement from a letter written by the Duchess of Buckingham to the Countess of Huntington, a strong supporter of the Methodists who had invited the Duchess to hear the great preacher Whitefield. "I thank your Ladyship," ran the haughty reply, "for your information concerning the Methodist preachers. Their doctrines are most repulsive and tinctured with impertinence and disrespect towards their superiors, in perpetually endeavouring to level all ranks and do away with all social distinctions. It is monstrous to be told that you have a heart as sinful as the common wretches that crawl the earth. This is highly offensive and insulting, and I cannot but wonder that your Ladyship should relish any sentiments so much at variance with high rank and good breeding."

Here is all the evidence one needs for the assertion that the English eighteenth century comprised at least two sharply different kinds of people. This "tough-minded" insistence upon social stratifications was addressed to a "tender-minded" woman, quite as representative as her correspondent, who devoted her life and fortune to the very forces that were breaking down the barriers between class and class. People of both kinds lived in every decade of the century, yet there would be truth in the assertion that this letter, written about the year 1750, spoke out of an age that was dying to one that was coming to be. At just the time when the Duchess of Buckingham was thus exhibiting her own "high rank and good breeding," an obscure scholar and poet called Thomas Gray was delivering a mild rebuke to

"The boast of heraldry, the pomp of power,
And all that beauty, all that wealth e'er gave."

Hackneyed and commonplace though his words now sound to us, Gray was making a really bold suggestion when he implied that the differences between the humblest and the most exalted of mankind are not, after all, intrinsic, but only accidental. Once that opinion, so quietly and plausibly insinuated, had become a fairly general belief, there would have to be considerable changes made in the whole structure of society. And the immediate popularity of Gray's poem seemed to show that many people were already feeling, at the middle of the century, somewhat as he did. Long before the century was over a young British subject living in Virginia was to declare, as though stating an axiom, that "all men are born free and equal," and another, living in Scotland, would assert before the century waned that "A man's a man for a' that."

Without meaning to suggest that Gray's "Elegy" changed anything whatever, or even that it was the first indication of changes already going on, one may regard it, for purposes of clarification, as though it were the central pivot upon which this century swung. Halfway between the last work of Dryden and the *Lyrical Ballads* of Wordsworth and Coleridge, it looked before and after. Learned, retrospective, imitative, and rhetorical in high degree, the poem had in it much of the past, but it held quite as much of the future. While recognizing the solid and perhaps everlasting discriminations of social rank and privilege, it set thousands of readers to wondering whether these discriminations have an everlasting warrant. The new thing in it, or the thing that in 1751 must have seemed new, was human sympathy, fellow feeling, the reminder that for the little time in which we are huddled here together on this second-rate planet we should do well to make what warmth and comfort and love we have go all round. As for the old things, it had enough of that "grandeur of generality" which Dr. Johnson was so pontifically to desiderate, but also it had its soberly tinted vignettes of cottage scenes, of tired laborers going home across the twilight fields, of lowing herds, of the owl in the ivy tod and the "swallow twittering from the straw-built shed." These secret messages were written, one might say, in onion ink, by an old-fashioned bachelor of the eighteenth century to men and women not yet born. One has to hold them up before the fire of imagination to read them at all; but when they are so held they begin to grow and glow. More clearly than all the writings of Alexander Pope together they show us how the nineteenth and twentieth centuries could grow out of that earlier English time. After brooding over them long, and learning them all by heart, one sees what young General James Wolfe may have meant when he said at the base of the Heights of Abraham on the night before his death: "I had rather be the author of that poem than take Quebec."

The capture of Quebec in 1759 turned the North American continent away from the French and toward the English tradition. Gray's "Elegy," published eight years before, has helped to turn the English-speaking people of two continents away from French and Roman urbanism toward the ageless dignity of labor and the everlasting companionship of earth. Here was a society, it seemed to say, immensely greater and grander than that of those who merely know Latin and Greek. Here were castle and cottage brought together with the beasts and the glimmering fields, with the dim memorials of the dead and the night that surrounds us all. And here, quietly and unerringly uttered, is the human pathos and tragedy on which the stars are always looking down. Here is the common heart of man. Though not the greatest, this is the central and the most widely representative poem that the eighteenth century made. The thoughts and feelings, the fears and hopes, of a hundred years drain into it. And no one can fail to see how it reaches toward the lines that Wordsworth was to write before the century closed:

"To her fair forms did Nature link
 The human soul that through me ran;
And much it grieved my heart to think
 What man has made of man."

Wading

From a distant hill, using all the advantages of ignorance, one may conclude that the stream of English literature in the eighteenth century is all one kind of water. At half the distance one sees that it must be ruled by two temporal gods at least. Closer than that no sensible writer of introductions, realizing that every one must do his own fishing, will go. It may be his own experience that when he gets down to the water itself and begins to lay out his line along these guttural reaches, every bend of the bank seems to have its peculiar genius and every eddy and pool its own kind of trout. However that may be, he knows that the study of streams is one thing and actual fishing is another. He remembers that fishing is a solitary sport, best done without a guide.

The young sportsman who is wading out for the first time into these riffles will not ask to have the fish attached to his hook or held up one by one for his admiration. And he has now been told enough of what he may expect. Far up toward the seventeenth-century wire the trout are darting and voracious, living as they do in a dangerous, tumbling water. Lower down, they fatten a little, and brighten; they burnish themselves on the gravel; they gather into groups. Still farther on they darken again with the deepening stream, they grow more shy and swifter, lurking behind reeds and rocks, each swimming alone in "the glassy, cool, translucent wave." At last, after many a pool and stickle and slide, they move smoothly under the wire that is stretched across the water below.

And now to that young sportsman one can only wish many long musical hours of alternate sun and shade, a breeze that ruffles from the southwest, and a bulging creel at nightfall. May he cast his flies all day into beauty, and draw them back over waters of peace.

Daniel Defoe
1660?–1731

The bare facts of Daniel Defoe's career, if he had ever thought it safe to write them down, would have made a book much harder to believe than any of the fictitious narratives to which he did set his hand. Our knowledge of Defoe has grown rapidly in recent years, but the more we know about him the less credible he becomes.

The son of a London butcher, Defoe was educated at an excellent Nonconformist academy. His start in life was that of what we should call a businessman, and it seems likely that after his marriage in 1684 he spent some time in Europe as a commission merchant. At the age of thirty-two he went into bankruptcy for a great sum, most of which he afterward repaid. Eleven years later he failed in business again. By that time, however, he had attracted the favorable attention of the Tory leaders and had begun to work for them as a political agent, mainly in Scotland. In this work, involving constant deceit and subterfuge, he soon grew callous enough, his chief biographer says, "to write, presumably for pay, on all sides of any given subject. Within the arena of journalism he was a treacherous mercenary who fought all comers with any weapon and stratagem he could command."

To the student of literature it is one of the most remarkable things about Defoe that he was able while carrying on this exacting political activity to turn out books and pamphlets by the scores and hundreds. More than half his life was spent before he definitely began his work as a writer, but during his last thirty years he must have lived with his quill almost constantly in hand. We know of some two hundred and fifty publications produced by him in these years, and this is to say nothing of the eight or ten periodicals which he wrote, or of his own paper, the *Review*, which he founded and kept going, almost unaided, for nearly a decade.

The range of Defoe's interests is as remarkable as his fecundity. This is indicated in one of his earliest works, the *Essay on Projects*, 1697, in which, among other matters, he discusses banking systems, the care of idiots, insurance of various kinds, road-building, proposals for an income tax, and higher education. He had many advanced notions upon what we now call political economy, and he wrote the best book of his time about business life and business methods. His three-volume *Tour through the Whole Island of Great Britain*, written when he was well over sixty, is a mine of miscellaneous information.

Always a journalist and a businessman rather than a free creative artist, Defoe studied his literary market with great care and acumen. He wrote only what he knew would sell. It should be remembered, however, that his public was by no means the same as that to which writers such as Swift and Pope addressed themselves. He spoke always to the class out of which he came—to a class, that is, which knew little and cared less for matters of literary form, elegant diction, critical theory, and the authority of the ancients. What it chiefly wanted was to be informed, although it did not object to a certain amount of moral edification. It distrusted fiction, but had a profound respect for facts. Defoe supplied it with facts in great abundance, and when he turned to fiction, as in *The True Relation of the Apparition of one Mrs. Veal* and in *The Life and Strange Surprizing Adventures of Robinson Crusoe*, he showed great skill in giving the effect of actuality by the invention of minute convincing details. He had a positive genius for "lying like the truth." Twenty years of journalism, pamphleteering, and political intrigue had strengthened this natural gift before, at the age of sixty, he began to write the fiction upon which his fame now chiefly rests. The success of *Robinson Crusoe*, which appeared in 1719, led him on to write his *Memoirs of a Cavalier*, his *Captain Singleton*, *The Fortunes and Misfortunes of Moll Flanders*, *The History of Colonel Jack*, and *Roxana*, all of which are still living books. One of his chief performances was his *Journal of the Plague Year*, an account of the London Plague of 1666 so minutely particular that it was long regarded as an account of the author's personal experience.

Defoe had no place in the literary circles of the early eighteenth century. He did not belong to "the Town," nor did he address it. Yet he paved the way for the *Tatler* and the *Spectator*. In such satirical writing as his *Shortest Way with the Dissenters* he gave the example for Swift's *Modest Proposal*. He extended and enlarged the British reading public. Finally, although not a novelist in the full sense of the word, he provided just the impulse that was needed in order to set the modern novel on its way.

from AN ESSAY ON PROJECTS

OF ACADEMIES

An Academy for Women

I HAVE often thought of it as one of the most barbarous customs in the world, considering us as a civilized and a Christian country, that we deny the advantages of learning to women. We reproach the sex every day with folly and impertinence, while I am confident, had they the advantages of education equal to us, they would be guilty of less than ourselves.

One would wonder, indeed, how it should happen that women are conversible at all, since they are only beholden to natural parts for all their knowledge. Their youth is spent to teach them to stitch and sew, or make baubles! They are taught to read, indeed, and perhaps to write their names, or so, and that is the height of a woman's education! And I would but ask any who slight the sex for their understanding, what is a man (a gentleman I mean) good for, that is taught no more?

I need not give instances, or examine the character of a gentleman with a good estate, of a good family, and with tolerable parts, and examine what figure he makes for want of education.

The soul is placed in the body like a rough diamond, and must be polished, or the lustre of it will never appear: and 'tis manifest, that as the rational soul distinguishes us from brutes, so education carries on the distinction and makes some less brutish than others. This is too evident to need any demonstration. But why, then, should women be denied the benefit of instruction? If knowledge and understanding had been useless additions to the sex, God Almighty would never have given them capacities; for He made nothing needless. Besides, I would ask such what they can see in ignorance that they should think it a necessary ornament to a woman? Or how much worse is a wise woman than a fool? Or what has the woman done to forfeit the privilege of being taught? Does she plague us with her pride and impertinence? Why did we not let her learn, that she might have had more wit? Shall we upbraid women with folly, when 'tis only the error of this inhuman custom that hindered them being made wiser?

The capacities of women are supposed to be greater and their senses quicker than those of the men; and what they might be capable of being bred to is plain from some instances of female wit, which this age is not without; which upbraids us with injustice, and looks as if we denied women the advantages of education for fear they should vie with the men in their improvements. . . .

[They] should be taught all sorts of breeding suitable to both their genius and their quality, and in particular music and dancing, which it would be cruelty to bar the sex of, because they are their darlings; but besides this, they should be taught languages, as particularly French and Italian; and I would venture the injury of giving a woman more tongues than one.

They should as a particular study be taught all the graces of speech and all the necessary air of conversation, which our common education is so defective in that I need not expose it. They should be brought to read books, and especially history, and so to read as to make them understand the world, and be able to know and judge of things when they hear of them.

To such whose genius would lead them to it I would deny no sort of learning; but the chief thing in general is to cultivate the understandings of the sex, that they may be capable of all sorts of conversation; that their parts and judgments being improved, they may be as profitable in their conversation as they are pleasant.

Women, in my observation, have little or no difference in them, but as they are or are not distinguished by education. Tempers, indeed, may in some degree influence them, but the main distinguishing part is their breeding.

The whole sex are generally quick and sharp. I believe I may be allowed to say generally so, for you rarely see them lumpish and heavy when they are children, as boys will often be. If a woman be well-bred, and taught the proper management of her natural wit, she proves generally very sensible and retentive; and without partiality, a woman of sense and manners is the finest and most delicate part of God's creation; the glory of her Maker, and the great instance of His singular regard to man, His darling creature, to whom He gave the best gift either God could bestow or man receive. And it is the sordidest piece of folly and ingratitude in the world to withhold from the sex the due lustre which the advantages of education give to the natural beauty of their minds.

A woman well bred and well taught, furnished with the additional accomplishments of knowledge and behaviour, is a creature without comparison; her society is the emblem of sublimer enjoyments; her person is angelic, and her conversation heavenly; she is all softness and sweetness, peace, love, wit, and delight. She is every way suitable to the sublimest wish, and the man that has such a one to his portion has nothing to do but to rejoice in her and be thankful.

On the other hand, suppose her to be the very same woman, and rob her of the benefit of education, and it follows thus:—

If her temper be good, want of education makes her soft and easy.

Her wit, for want of teaching, makes her impertinent and talkative.

Her knowledge, for want of judgment and experience, makes her fanciful and whimsical.

If her temper be bad, want of breeding makes her worse, and she grows haughty, insolent, and loud.

If she be passionate, want of manners makes her termagant and a scold, which is much at one with lunatic.

If she be proud, want of discretion (which still is breeding) makes her conceited, fantastic, and ridiculous.

And from these she degenerates to be turbulent, clamorous, noisy, nasty, and the devil.

. Methinks mankind, for their own sakes, since say what we will of the women, we all think fit one time or other to be concerned with them, should take some care to breed them up to be suitable and serviceable, if they expected no such thing as delight from them. Bless us! what care do we take to breed up a good horse, and to break him well! and what a value do we put upon him when it is done, and all because he should be fit for our use. And why not a woman? since all her ornaments and beauty, without suitable behaviour, is a cheat in nature, like the false tradesman, who puts the best of his goods uppermost that the buyer may think the rest are of the same goodness.

Beauty of the body, which is the women's glory, seems to be now unequally bestowed, and nature, or rather Providence, to lie under some scandal about it, as if it was given a woman for a snare to men, and so make a kind of a she-devil of her. Because, they say, exquisite beauty is rarely given with wit, more rarely with goodness of temper, and never at all with modesty. And some, pretending to justify the equity of such a distribution, will tell us 'tis the effect of the justice of Providence in dividing particular excellences among all His creatures, share and share alike, as it were, that all might for something or other be acceptable to one another, else some would be despised.

I think both these notions false, and yet the last, which has the show of respect to Providence, is the worst, for it supposes Providence to be indigent and empty, as if it had not wherewith to furnish all the creatures it had made, but was fain to be parsimonious in its gifts, and distribute them by piece-meal for fear of being exhausted.

If I might venture my opinion against an almost universal notion, I would say, most men mistake the proceedings of Providence in this case, and all the world at this day are mistaken in their practice about it; and because the assertion is very bold, I desire to explain myself.

That Almighty First Cause which made us all is certainly the fountain of excellence, as it is of being, and by an invisible influence could have diffused equal qualities and perfections to all the creatures it has made, as the sun does its light, without the least ebb or diminution to Himself; and has given indeed to every individual sufficient to the figure His providence had designed him in the world.

I believe it might be defended, if I should say that I do suppose God has given to all mankind equal gifts and capacities in that He has given them all souls equally capable; and that the whole difference in mankind proceeds either from accidental difference in the make of their bodies or from the foolish difference of education.

1. From accidental difference in bodies.—I would avoid discoursing here of the philosophical position of the soul in the body. But if it be true, as philosophers do affirm, that the understanding and memory is dilated or contracted according to the accidental dimensions of the organ through which it is conveyed, then, though God has given a soul as capable to me as another, yet if I have any natural defect in those parts of the body by which the soul should act, I may have the same soul infused as another man, and yet he be a wise man, and I a very fool. For example, if a child naturally have a defect in the organ of hearing, so that he could never distinguish any sound, that child shall never be able to speak or read, though it have a soul capable of all the accomplishments in the world. The brain is the centre of the soul's actings, where all the distinguishing faculties of it reside; and it is observable, a man who has a narrow, contracted head, in which there is not room for the due and necessary operations of nature by the brain, is never a man of very great judgment; and that proverb, "A great head and little wit," is not meant by nature, but is a reproof upon sloth, as if one should, by way of wonder, say, "Fie, fie! you that have a great head, have but little wit; that is strange! that must certainly be your own fault." From this notion I do believe there is a great matter in the breed of men and women—not that wise men shall always get wise children, but I believe strong and healthy bodies have the wisest children; and sickly, weakly bodies affect the wits as well as the bodies of their children. We are easily persuaded to believe this in the breeds of horses, cocks, dogs, and other creatures, and I believe it is as visible in men.

But to come closer to the business; the great distinguishing difference which is seen in the world between men and women, is in their education, and this is manifested by comparing it with the difference between one man or woman and another.

And herein it is that I take upon me to make such a bold assertion, that all the world are mistaken in their practice about women; for I cannot think that God Almighty ever made them so delicate, so glorious creatures, and furnished them with such charms, so agreeable and so delightful to mankind, with souls capable of the same accomplishments with men, and all to be only stewards of our houses, cooks, and slaves.

Not that I am for exalting the female government in the least; but, in short, I would have men take women for companions, and educate them to be fit for it. A woman of sense and breeding will scorn as much to encroach upon the prerogative of the man as a man of sense will scorn to oppress the weakness of the woman. But if the women's souls were refined and improved by teaching, that word would be lost; to say, the weakness of the sex, as to judgment, would be nonsense; for ignorance and folly would be no more to be found among women than men. I remember a passage which I heard from a very fine woman; she had wit and capacity enough, an extraordinary shape and face, and a great fortune, but had been cloistered up all her time, and for fear of being stolen, had not had the liberty of being taught the common necessary knowledge of women's affairs; and when she came to converse in the world, her natural wit made her so sensible of the want of education, that she gave this short reflection on herself: —"I am ashamed to talk with my very maids," says she, "for I don't know when they do right or wrong. I had more need go to school than be married."

I need not enlarge on the loss the defect of education is to the sex, nor argue the benefit of the contrary practice; it is a thing will be more easily granted than remedied. This chapter is but an essay at the thing, and I refer the practice to those happy days, if ever they shall be, when men shall be wise enough to mend it.

THE SHORTEST WAY WITH THE DISSENTERS

This pamphlet, appearing in 1702, marked a turning-point in the career of Daniel Defoe. He was himself a dissenter against the Established Church of England, and in his ironical demand that dissent be suppressed and crushed out by any necessary severity he was trying to bring ecclesiastical intolerance into ridicule. Irony, however, always a dangerous two-edged weapon, has seldom been well understood by English-speaking people. At first the pamphlet was taken seriously by all parties, but when it became clear what Defoe's real purpose had been, he was brought to trial and was heavily fined, condemned to stand in the pillory three times, and to be imprisoned indefinitely.

SIR Roger L'Estrange tells us a story in his collection of fables, of the cock and the horses. The cock was gotten to roost in the stable among the horses, and there being no racks or other conveniences for him, it seems he was forced to roost upon the ground. The horses jostling about for room and putting the cock in danger of his life, he gives them this grave advice: "Pray, gentlefolks, let us stand still, for fear we should tread upon one another."

There are some people in the world, who, now they are unperched and reduced to an equality with other people, and under strong and very just apprehensions of being further treated as they deserve, begin, with Esop's cock, to preach up peace and union and the Christian duty of moderation; forgetting that when they had the power in their hands, those graces were strangers in their gates.

It is now near fourteen years that the glory and peace of the purest and most flourishing church in the world has been eclipsed, buffeted, and disturbed by a sort of men whom God in His Providence has suffered to insult over her, and bring her down. These have been the days of her humiliation and tribulation. She has borne with an invincible patience the reproach of the wicked; and God has at last heard her prayers, and delivered her from the oppression of the stranger.

And now, they find their day is over, their power gone, and the throne of this nation possessed by a Royal, English, true, and ever constant member of and friend to the Church of England. Now they find that they are in danger of the Church of England's just resentments. Now they cry out "Peace!" "Union!" "Forbearance!" and "Charity!" as if the Church had not too long harboured her enemies under her wing, and nourished the viperous brood, till they hiss and fly in the face of the mother that cherished them!

No, gentlemen, the time of mercy is past; your day of grace is over; you should have practised peace, and moderation, and charity, if you expected any yourselves.

We have heard none of this lesson for fourteen years past. We have been huffed and bullied with your Act of Toleration; you have told us you are the Church established by law, as well as others; have set up your canting synagogues at our church doors; and the Church and members have been loaded with reproaches, with oaths, associations, abjurations, and what not. Where has been the mercy, the forbearance, the charity you have shown to tender consciences of the Church of England, that could not take oaths as fast as you made them; that, having sworn allegiance to their lawful and rightful king, could not dispense with that oath, their king being still alive, and swear to your new hodge-podge of a Dutch government? These have been turned out of their livings, and they and their families left to starve; their estates double taxed to carry on a war they had no hand in, and you got nothing by. What account can you give of the multitudes you have forced to comply, against their consciences, with your new sophistical politics, who, like new converts in France, sin because they cannot starve? And now the tables are turned upon you, you must not be persecuted! It is not a Christian spirit!

You have butchered one king, deposed another king, and made a mock king of a third, and yet you could have the face to expect to be employed and trusted by the fourth! Anybody that did not know the temper of your party would stand amazed at the impudence as well as the folly to think of it!

Your management of your Dutch monarch, whom you reduced to a mere King of Clubs, is enough to give any future princes such an idea of your principles as to warn them sufficiently from coming into your clutches; and, God be thanked, the Queen is out of your hands, knows you, and will have a care of you.

There is no doubt but the supreme authority of a nation has in itself a power, and a right to that power, to execute the laws upon any part of that nation it governs. The execution of the known laws of the land, and that with but a gentle hand neither,

---

17. **L'Estrange,** an English journalist and pamphleteer (1616–1704) whose translation of Aesop's *Fables* contains many tales of his own.   26. **people,** the Dissenters from the Church of England.   34. **years,** since the Revolution of 1688.   35. **church,** the Church of England.   46–47. **Royal . . . friend.** Queen Anne, who ascended the throne in March, 1702.

25. **Dutch government,** that of William of Orange, to which Defoe, in fact, was entirely loyal.

was all that the fanatical party of this land have ever called persecution. This they have magnified to a height that the sufferings of the Huguenots in France were not to be compared with. Now to execute the known laws of a nation upon those who transgress them, after voluntarily consenting to the making of those laws, can never be called persecution, but justice. But justice is always violence to the party offending, for every man is innocent in his own eyes.

The first execution of the laws against Dissenters in England was in the days of King James I; and what did it amount to? Truly, the worst they suffered was at their own request, to let them go to New England and erect a new colony, and give them great privileges, grants, and suitable powers, keep them under protection, and defend them against all invaders, and receive no taxes or revenue from them. This was the cruelty of the Church of England! Fatal lenity! It was the ruin of that excellent prince, King Charles I. Had King James sent all the Puritans in England away to the West Indies we had been a national, unmixed church. The Church of England had been kept undivided and entire.

To requite the lenity of the father, they take up arms against the son; conquer, pursue, take, imprison, and at last put to death the anointed of God, and destroy the very being and nature of government; setting up a sordid impostor who had neither title to govern nor understanding to manage, but supplied that want with power, bloody and desperate counsels and craft, without conscience.

Had not King James I withheld the full execution of the laws, had he given them strict justice, he had cleared the nation of them, and the consequences had been plain: his son had never been murdered by them, nor the monarchy overwhelmed. It was too much mercy shown them that was the ruin of his posterity and the ruin of the nation's peace. One would think the Dissenters should not have the face to believe that we are to be wheedled and canted into peace and toleration when they know that they have once requited us with a civil war, and once with an intolerable and unrighteous persecution for our former civility.

Nay, to encourage us to be easy with them, it is apparent that they never had the upper hand of the Church but they treated her with all the severity, with all the reproach and contempt as was possible. What peace and what mercy did they show the loyal gentry of the Church of England in the time of their triumphant Commonwealth? How did they put all the gentry of England to ransom, whether they were actually in arms for the king or not, making people compound for their estates and starve their families? How did they treat the clergy of the Church of England, sequester the ministers, devour the patrimony of the Church and divide the spoil, by sharing the Church lands among their soldiers, and turning her clergy out to starve? Just such measure as they have meted should be measured them again!

Charity and love is the known doctrine of the Church of England, and it is plain she has put it in practice towards the Dissenters, even beyond what they ought, till she has been wanting to herself and, in effect, unkind to her own sons, particularly in the too much lenity of King James I, mentioned before. Had he so rooted the Puritans from the face of the land, which he had an opportunity early to have done, they had not had the power to vex the Church as since they have done.

In the days of King Charles II how did the Church reward their bloody doings with lenity and mercy! Except the barbarous regicides of the pretended court of justice, not a soul suffered for all the blood in an unnatural war. King Charles came in all mercy and love, cherished them, preferred them, employed them, withheld the rigour of the law, and oftentimes, even against the advice of his Parliament, gave them liberty of conscience. And how did they requite him? With the villainous contrivance to depose and murder him and his successor at the Rye Plot!

King James II, as if mercy was the inherent quality of the family, began his reign with unusual favour to them, nor could their joining with the Duke of Monmouth against him move him to do himself justice upon them. But that mistaken prince, thinking to win them by gentleness and love, proclaimed an universal liberty to them, and rather discountenanced the Church of England than them. How they requited him, all the world knows.

The late reign is too fresh in the memory of all the world to need a comment—how, under pretence of joining with the Church in redressing some grievances, they pushed things to that extremity, in conjunction with some mistaken gentlemen, as to depose the late king, as if the grievance of the nation could not have been redressed but by the absolute ruin of the prince. Here is an instance of their temper, their peace and charity! To what height they carried themselves during the reign of a king of

---

30. impostor, Oliver Cromwell.

32. Rye Plot! a conspiracy to assassinate Charles II.
36. Monmouth. Defoe himself took part in Monmouth's Rebellion, 1688.

their own; how they crept into all places of trust and profit; how they insinuated themselves into the favour of the king, and were at first preferred to the highest places in the nation; how they engrossed the ministry, and above all, how pitifully they managed, is too plain to need any remarks.

But particularly their mercy and charity, the spirit of union, they tell us so much of, has been remarkable in Scotland. If any man would see the spirit of a Dissenter, let him look into Scotland. There, they made entire conquest of the Church, trampled down the sacred orders and suppressed the episcopal government with an absolute, and, as they supposed, irretrievable victory; though it is possible they may find themselves mistaken. Now it would be a very proper question to ask their impudent advocate, the Observator, pray how much mercy and favour did the members of the Episcopal Church find in Scotland from the Scotch Presbyterian government? And I shall undertake for the Church of England, that the Dissenters shall still receive as much here, though they deserve but little.

In a small treatise of the sufferings of the Episcopal clergy in Scotland, it will appear what usage they met with, how they not only lost their livings, but in several places were plundered and abused in their persons; the ministers that could not conform turned out with numerous families and no maintenance, and hardly charity enough left to relieve them with a bit of bread; and the cruelties of the party were innumerable, and not to be attempted in this short piece.

And now, to prevent the distant cloud which they perceive to hang over their heads from England, with a true Presbyterian policy, they put in for a union of nations, that England might unite their Church with the Kirk of Scotland, and their Presbyterian members sit in our House of Commons, and their assembly of Scotch canting long-cloaks in our convocation! What might have been if our fanatic, Whiggish statesmen continued, God only knows; but we hope we are out of fear of that now.

It is alleged by some of the faction, and they have begun to bully us with it, that if we will not unite with them, they will not settle the Crown with us again, but when her Majesty dies will choose a king for themselves.

If they won't, we must make them; and it is not the first time we have let them know that we are able. The crowns of these kingdoms have not so far disowned the right of succession but they may retrieve it again, and if Scotland thinks to come off from a successive to an elective state of government, England has not promised not to assist the right heir, and put him into possession, without any regards to their ridiculous settlements.

These are the gentlemen! These their ways of treating the Church both at home and abroad. Now let us examine the reasons they pretend to give why we should be favourable to them, why we should continue and tolerate them among us.

First. They are very numerous, they say. They are a great part of the nation, and we cannot suppress them.

To this, may be answered:

First. They are not so numerous as the Protestants in France, and yet the French king effectually cleared the nation of them at once, and we do not find he misses them at home.

But I am not of the opinion they are so numerous as is pretended. Their party is more numerous than their persons, and those mistaken people of the Church, who are misled and deluded by their wheedling artifices to join with them, make their party the greater; but those will open their eyes when the government shall set heartily about the work, and come off from them as some animals, which they say, always desert a house when it is likely to fall.

Secondly. The more numerous the more dangerous, and therefore the more need to suppress them; and God has suffered us to bear them as goads in our sides for not utterly extinguishing them long ago.

Thirdly. If we are to allow them, only because we cannot suppress them, then it ought to be tried whether we can or no; and I am of opinion it is easy to be done, and could prescribe ways and means, if it were proper, but I doubt not the government will find effectual methods for the rooting of the contagion from the face of this land.

Another argument they use, which is this. That this is a time of war, and we have need to unite against the common enemy.

We answer, this common enemy had been no enemy, if they had not made him so. He was quiet in peace, and no way disturbed and encroached upon us, and we know no reason we had to quarrel with him.

But further, we make no question but we are able to deal with this common enemy without their help. But why must we unite with them because of the enemy? Will they go over to the enemy if we do not prevent it by a union with them? We are very well contented they should, and make no question we

14. **once**, referring to the Massacre of St. Bartholomew, August 24, 1572, in which many French Protestants were killed.

shall be ready to deal with them and the common enemy too, and better without them than with them.

Besides, if we have a common enemy, there is the more need to be secure against our private enemies; if there is one common enemy, we have the less need to have an enemy in our bowels.

It was a great argument some people used against suppressing the old money, that it was a time of war, and it was too great a risk for the nation to run, if we should not master it, we should be undone; and yet the sequel proved the hazard was not so great but it might be mastered, and the success was answerable. The suppressing the Dissenters is not a harder work, nor a work of less necessity to the public. We can never enjoy a settled, uninterrupted union and tranquillity in this nation, till the spirit of Whiggism, faction, and schism is melted down like the old money.

To talk of difficulty is to frighten ourselves with chimeras and notions of a powerful party, which are indeed a party without power. Difficulties often appear greater at a distance than when they are searched into with judgment and distinguished from the vapours and shadows that attend them.

We are not to be frightened with it. This age is wiser than that by all our own experience and theirs too. King Charles the First had early suppressed this party if he had taken more deliberate measures. In short, it is not worth arguing, to talk of their arms. Their Monmouths and Shaftesburys and Argyles are gone, their Dutch sanctuary is at an end. Heaven has made way for their destruction, and if we do not close with the divine occasion we are to blame ourselves, and may remember that we had once an opportunity to serve the Church of England by extirpating her implacable enemies, and having let slip the minute that heaven presented, may experimentally complain, *Post est occasio calva.*

Here are some popular objections in the way.

As first, the Queen has promised them to continue them in their tolerated liberty; and has told us she will be a religious observer of her word.

What her Majesty will do we cannot help, but what, as the head of the Church she ought to do is another case. Her Majesty has promised to protect and defend the Church of England, and if she cannot effectually do that without the destruction of the Dissenters, she must, of course, dispense with one promise to comply with another.

But to answer this cavil more effectually: Her Majesty did never promise to maintain the toleration to the destruction of the Church; but it was upon supposition that it may be compatible with the well-being and safety of the Church which she had declared she would take especial care of. Now if these two interests clash, it is plain her Majesty's intentions are to uphold, protect, defend, and establish the Church; and this we conceive is impossible.

Perhaps it may be said, that the Church is in no immediate danger from the Dissenters, and therefore it is time enough; but this is a weak answer.

For first, if a danger be real, the distance of it is no argument against, but rather a spur to quicken us to prevention, lest it be too late hereafter.

And secondly, here is the opportunity, and the only one perhaps that ever the Church had to secure herself and destroy her enemies.

The representatives of the nation have now an opportunity, the time is come which all good men have wished for, that the gentlemen of England may serve the Church of England, now they are protected and encouraged by a Church of England Queen.

What will you do for your sister in the day that she shall be spoken for?

If ever you will establish the best Christian Church in the world; if ever you will suppress the spirit of enthusiasm; if ever you will free the nation from the viperous brood that have so long sucked the blood of their mother; if ever you will leave your posterity free from faction and rebellion, this is the time! This is the time to pull up this heretical weed of sedition, that has so long disturbed the peace of our church, and poisoned the good corn!

But, says another hot and cold objector, this is renewing fire and faggot, reviving the Act *de heretico comburendo.* This will be cruelty in its nature and barbarous to all the world.

I answer, it is cruelty to kill a snake or a toad in cold blood, but the poison of their nature makes it a charity to our neighbours to destroy those creatures, not for any personal injury received, but for prevention; not for the evil they have done, but the evil they may do. Serpents, toads, vipers, etc., are noxious to the body, and poison the sensitive life; these poison the soul, corrupt our posterity, ensnare our children, destroy the vitals of our happiness, our future felicity, and contaminate the whole mass.

Shall any law be given to such wild creatures? Some beasts are for sport, and the huntsmen give them the advantages of ground; but some are knocked on the head by all possible ways of violence and surprise.

I do not prescribe fire and faggot; but as Scipio

---

39. **Post . . . calva.** Opportunity is bald behind.   25. **enthusiasm,** fanaticism.   33–34. **de . . . comburendo,** on the burning of heretics.

said of Carthage, *Delenda est Carthago!* They are to be rooted out of this nation, if ever we will live in peace, serve God, or enjoy our own. As for the manner, I leave it to those hands who have a right to execute God's justice on the nation's and the Church's enemies.

But if we must be frighted from this justice, under these specious pretences and odious sense of cruelty, nothing will be effected. It will be more barbarous to our own children and dear posterity, when they shall reproach their fathers, as we ours, and tell us, "You had an opportunity to root out this cursed race from the world, under the favour and protection of a true Church of England queen; and out of your foolish pity you spared them, because, forsooth, you would not be cruel! And now our Church is suppressed and persecuted, our religion trampled under foot, our estates plundered, our persons imprisoned and dragged to gaols, gibbets, and scaffolds! Your sparing this Amalekite race is our destruction. Your mercy to them proves cruelty to your poor posterity."

How just will such reflections be when our posterity shall fall under the merciless clutches of this uncharitable generation; when our Church shall be swallowed up in schism, faction, enthusiasm, and confusion; when our government shall be devolved upon foreigners, and our monarchy dwindled into a republic!

It would be more rational for us, if we must spare this generation, to summon our own to a general massacre; and as we have brought them into the world free, to send them out so, and not betray them to destruction by our supine negligence; and then cry, "It is mercy."

Moses was a merciful, meek man; and yet with what fury did he run through the camp and cut the throats of three and thirty thousand of his dear Israelites that were fallen into idolatry. What was the reason? It was mercy to the rest to make these examples, to prevent the destruction of the whole army.

How many millions of future souls we save from infection and delusion if the present race of poisoned spirits were purged from the face of the land!

It is vain to trifle in this matter. The light, foolish handling of them by mulcts, fines, etc., 'tis their glory and their advantage! If the gallows instead of the counter, and the galleys instead of the fines, were the reward of going to a conventicle to preach or hear, there would not be so many sufferers. The spirit of martyrdom is over. They that will go to church to be chosen sheriffs and mayors would go to forty churches rather than be hanged.

If one severe law were made, and punctually executed, that whoever was found at a conventicle should be banished the nation, and the preacher be hanged, we should soon see an end of the tale. They would all come to church again, and one age would make us all one again.

To talk of five shillings a month for not coming to the sacrament, and one shilling per week, for not coming to church, this is such a way of converting people as was never known; this is selling them a liberty to transgress for so much money.

If it be not a crime, why do not we give them full licence? And if it be, no price ought to compound for the committing it, for that is selling a liberty to people to sin against God and the government.

If it be a crime of the highest consequence both against the peace and welfare of the nation, the glory of God, the good of the Church, and the happiness of the soul, let us rank it among capital offences, and let it receive a punishment in proportion to it.

We hang men for trifles, and banish them for things not worth naming, but that an offence against God and the Church, against the welfare of the world and the dignity of religion, shall be bought off for five shillings, this is such a shame to a Christian government, that it is with regret I transmit it to posterity.

If men sin against God, affront His ordinances, rebel against His Church, and disobey the precepts of their superiors, let them suffer as such capital crimes deserve. So will religion flourish, and this divided nation be once again united.

And yet the title of barbarous and cruel will soon be taken off from this law too. I am not supposing that all the Dissenters in England should be hanged or banished. But as in cases of rebellions and insurrections, if a few of the ringleaders suffer, the multitude are dismissed, so, a few obstinate people being made examples, there is no doubt but the severity of the law would find a stop in the compliance of the multitude.

To make the reasonableness of this matter out of question, and more unanswerably plain, let us examine for what it is that this nation is divided into parties and factions; and let us see how they can justify a separation, or we of the Church of England can justify our bearing the insults and inconveniences of the party.

One of their leading pastors, and a man of as much learning as most among them, in his answer to a pamphlet entitled *An Enquiry into the Occasional*

---

1. Delenda est Carthago! Carthage must be destroyed. 49. counter, a prison. 50. conventicle, a meeting of Dissenters.

Conformity, hath these words, p. 27: "Do the religion of the Church and the meeting-houses make two religions? Wherein do they differ? The substance of the same religion is common to them both, and the modes and accidents are the things in which only they differ." P. 28: "Thirty-nine articles are given us for the summary of our religion; thirty-six contain the substance of it, wherein we agree; three the additional appendices, about which we have some differences."

Now if, as by their own acknowledgment, the Church of England is a true church, and the difference is only in a few modes and accidents, why should we expect that they will suffer the gallows and galleys, corporal punishment, and banishment, for these trifles? There is no question but they will be wiser. Even their own principles will not bear them out in it.

They will certainly comply with the laws, and with reason. And though at the first severity may seem hard, the next age will feel nothing of it, the contagion will be rooted out. The disease being cured there will be no need of the operation. But if they should venture to transgress, and fall into the pit, all the world must condemn their obstinacy, as being without ground from their own principles.

Thus the pretence of cruelty will be taken off, and the party actually suppressed, and the disquiets they have so often brought upon the nation, prevented.

Their numbers and their wealth make them haughty, and that is so far from being an argument to persuade us to forbear them, that it is a warning to us, without any more delay, to reconcile them to the unity of the Church, or remove them from us.

At present, Heaven be praised, they are not so formidable as they have been, and it is our own fault if ever we suffer them to be so. Providence and the Church of England seem to join in this particular, that now the destroyers of the nation's peace may be overturned, and to this end, the present opportunity seems to be put into our hands.

To this end her present Majesty seems reserved to enjoy the crown, that the ecclesiastic as well as civil rights of the nation may be restored by her hand.

To this end the face of affairs has received such a turn in the process of a few months as never has been before. The leading men of the nation, the universal cry of the people, the unanimous request of the clergy, agree in this, that the deliverance of our Church is at hand.

For this end has Providence given such a parliament, such a convocation, such a gentry, and such a queen as we never had before.

And what may be the consequences of a neglect of such opportunities? The succession of the crown has but a dark prospect. Another Dutch turn may make the hopes of it ridiculous, and the practice impossible. Be the house of our future princes ever so well inclined, they will be foreigners, and many years will be spent in suiting the genius of strangers to this crown and the interests of the nation; and how many ages it may be before the English throne be filled with so much zeal and candour, so much tenderness and hearty affection to the Church as we see it now covered with, who can imagine?

It is high time, then, for the friends of the Church of England to think of building up and establishing her in such a manner, that she may be no more invaded by foreigners, nor divided by factions, schisms, and error.

If this could be done by gentle and easy methods, I should be glad; but the wound is corroded, the vitals begin to mortify, and nothing but amputation of members can complete the cure. All the ways of tenderness and compassion, all persuasive arguments, have been made use of in vain.

The humour of the Dissenters has so increased among the people that they hold the Church in defiance, and the house of God is an abomination among them. Nay, they have brought up their posterity in such prepossessed aversions to our holy religion, that the ignorant mob think we are all idolators and worshippers of Baal, and account it a sin to come within the walls of our churches.

The primitive Christians were not more shy of a heathen temple, or of meat offered to idols, nor the Jews of swine's flesh, than some of our Dissenters are of the Church and the divine service solemnized therein.

The obstinacy must be rooted out with the profession of it. While the generation are left at liberty daily to affront God Almighty and dishonour his holy worship, we are wanting in our duty to God, and to our mother, the Church of England.

How can we answer it to God, to the Church, and to our posterity, to leave them entangled with fanaticism, error, and obstinacy in the bowels of the nation; to leave them an enemy in their streets that, in time, may involve them in the same crimes, and endanger the utter extirpation of the religion in the nation?

What is the difference betwixt this and being subject to the power of the Church of Rome, from whence we have reformed? If one be an extreme on one hand and one on another, it is equally destructive to the truth to have errors settled among us, let them be of what nature they will.

Both are enemies of our Church and of our peace, and why should it not be as criminal to admit an enthusiast as a Jesuit? Why should the Papist with his seven sacraments be worse than the Quaker with no sacraments at all? Why should religious houses be more intolerable than meeting-houses?

Alas! the Church of England! What with Popery on one hand and schismatics on the other, how has she been crucified between two thieves!

Now, let us crucify the thieves! Let her foundations be established upon the destruction of her enemies! The doors of mercy being always open to the returning part of the deluded people, let the obstinate be ruled with the rod of iron!

Let all true sons of so holy and oppressed a mother, exasperated by her afflictions, harden their hearts against those who have oppressed her.

And may God Almighty put it into the hearts of all the friends of truth to lift up a standard against pride and Antichrist, that the posterity of the sons of error may be rooted out from the face of this land, for ever!

A TRUE RELATION OF THE APPARITION OF ONE MRS. VEAL,

THE NEXT DAY AFTER HER DEATH, TO ONE MRS. BARGRAVE, AT CANTERBURY, THE 8TH OF SEPTEMBER, 1705.

THE PREFACE

This relation is matter of fact, and attended with such circumstances as may induce any reasonable man to believe it. It was sent by a gentleman, a Justice of Peace at Maidstone, in Kent, and a very intelligent person, to his friend in London, as it is here worded; which discourse is attested by a very sober and understanding gentleman, who had it from his kinswoman, who lives in Canterbury, within a few doors of the house in which the within-named Mrs. Bargrave lived; and who he believes to be of so discerning a spirit, as not to be put upon by any fallacy, and who positively assured him that the whole matter as it is related and laid down is really true, and what she herself had in the same words, as near as may be, from Mrs. Bargrave's own mouth, who, she knows, had no reason to invent and publish such a story, or any design to forge and tell a lie, being a woman of much honesty and virtue, and her whole life a course, as it were, of piety. The use which we ought to make of it is to consider that there is a life to come after this, and a just God who will retribute to every one according to the deeds done in the body, and therefore to reflect upon our past course of life we have led in the world; that our time is short and uncertain; and that if we would escape the punishment of the ungodly and receive the reward of the righteous, which is the laying hold of eternal life, we ought for the time to come to return to God by a speedy repentance, ceasing to do evil, and learning to do well; to seek after God early, if haply He may be found of us, and lead such lives for the future as may well be pleasing in His sight.

THE RELATION

THIS thing is so rare in all its circumstances, and on so good authority, that my reading and conversation have not given me anything like it. It is fit to gratify the most ingenious and serious inquirer. Mrs. Bargrave is the person to whom Mrs. Veal appeared after her death; she is my intimate friend, and I can avouch for her reputation for these last fifteen or sixteen years, on my own knowledge; and I can confirm the good character she had from her youth to the time of my acquaintance; though, since this relation, she is calumniated by some people that are friends to the brother of Mrs. Veal who appeared, who think the relation of this appearance to be a reflection, and endeavour what they can to blast Mrs. Bargrave's reputation, and to laugh the story out of countenance. But by the circumstances thereof, and the cheerful disposition of Mrs. Bargrave, notwithstanding the ill-usage of a very wicked husband, there is not the least sign of dejection in her face; nor did I ever hear her let fall a desponding or murmuring expression; nay, not when actually under her husband's barbarity, which I have been witness to, and several other persons of undoubted reputation.

Now you must know Mrs. Veal was a maiden gentlewoman of about thirty years of age, and for some years last past had been troubled with fits, which were perceived coming on her, by her going off from her discourses very abruptly to some impertinence. She was maintained by an only brother, and kept his house in Dover. She was a very pious woman, and her brother a very sober man, to all appearance; but now he does all he can to null or quash the story. Mrs. Veal was intimately acquainted with Mrs. Bargrave from her childhood. Mrs. Veal's circumstances were then mean; her father did not take care of his children as he ought, so that they were exposed to hardships; and Mrs. Bargrave in those days had as unkind a father, though she wanted neither for food nor clothing, whilst Mrs. Veal wanted for both, insomuch that she would often say, "Mrs. Bargrave, you are not only the best, but the only friend I have in the world; and no circumstance in life shall ever dissolve my friendship." They would often condole each other's adverse fortunes, and read together *Drelincourt upon Death*, and other good books; and so,

9. **Mrs.**, Mistress. The title in Defoe's time was one of respect, and was not confined to married women. 33–34. **impertinence.** topic beside the point.

like two Christian friends, they comforted each other under their sorrow.

Some time after, Mr. Veal's friends got him a place in the custom-house at Dover, which occasioned Mrs. Veal, by little and little, to fall off from her intimacy with Mrs. Bargrave, though there never was any such thing as a quarrel; but an indifferency came on by degrees, till at last Mrs. Bargrave had not seen her in two years and a half; though about a twelvemonth of the time Mrs. Bargrave had been absent from Dover, and this last half-year had been in Canterbury about two months of the time, dwelling in a house of her own.

In this house, on the 8th of September 1705, she was sitting alone, in the forenoon, thinking over her unfortunate life, and arguing herself into a due resignation to Providence, though her condition seemed hard. "And," said she, "I have been provided for hitherto, and doubt not but I shall be still; and am well satisfied that my afflictions shall end when it is most fit for me"; and then took up her sewing-work, which she had no sooner done but she hears a knocking at the door. She went to see who was there, and this proved to be Mrs. Veal, her old friend, who was in a riding-habit. At that moment of time the clock struck twelve at noon.

"Madam," says Mrs. Bargrave, "I am surprised to see you, you have been so long a stranger"; but told her she was glad to see her, and offered to salute her; which Mrs. Veal complied with, till their lips almost touched; and then Mrs. Veal drew her hand across her own eyes, and said, "I am not very well"; and so waived it. She told Mrs. Bargrave she was going a journey, and had a great mind to see her first. "But," says Mrs. Bargrave, "how came you to take a journey alone? I am amazed at it, because I know you have a fond brother." "Oh," says Mrs. Veal, "I gave my brother the slip, and came away because I had so great a desire to see you before I took my journey." So Mrs. Bargrave went in with her, into another room within the first, and Mrs. Veal sat her down in an elbow-chair, in which Mrs. Bargrave was sitting when she heard Mrs. Veal knock. Then says Mrs. Veal, "My dear friend, I am come to renew our old friendship again, and beg your pardon for my breach of it; and if you can forgive me, you are the best of women." "Oh," says Mrs. Bargrave, "do not mention such a thing. I have not had an uneasy thought about it; I can easily forgive it." "What did you think of me?" said Mrs. Veal. Says Mrs. Bargrave, "I thought you were like the rest of the world, and that prosperity had made you forget yourself and me." Then Mrs. Veal reminded Mrs. Bargrave of the many friendly offices she did in her former days, and much of the conversation they had with each other in the times of their adversity; what books they read, and what comfort, in particular, they received from *Drelincourt's Book of Death*, which was the best, she said, on that subject ever written. She also mentioned Dr. Sherlock, the two Dutch books which were translated, written upon death, and several others. But Drelincourt, she said, had the clearest notions of death, and of the future state, of any who had handled that subject. Then she asked Mrs. Bargrave whether she had Drelincourt. She said, "Yes." Says Mrs. Veal, "Fetch it." And so Mrs. Bargrave goes up stairs and brings it down. Says Mrs. Veal, "Dear Mrs. Bargrave, if the eyes of our faith were as open as the eyes of our body, we should see numbers of angels about us for our guard. The notions we have of heaven now are nothing like to what it is, as Drelincourt says; therefore be comforted under your afflictions, and believe that the Almighty has a particular regard to you; and that your afflictions are marks of God's favour; and when they have done the business they are sent for, they shall be removed from you. And, believe me, my dear friend, believe what I say to you, one minute of future happiness will infinitely reward you for all your sufferings. For I can never believe (and claps her hands upon her knees with great earnestness, which, indeed, ran through most of her discourse) that ever God will suffer you to spend all your days in this afflicted state; but be assured that your afflictions shall leave you, or you them, in a short time." She spake in that pathetical and heavenly manner that Mrs. Bargrave wept several times, she was so deeply affected with it.

Then Mrs. Veal mentioned Dr. Horneck's *Ascetic*, at the end of which he gives an account of the lives of the primitive Christians. Their pattern she recommended to our imitation, and said, "Their conversation was not like this of our age; for now," says she, "there is nothing but frothy, vain discourse, which is far different from theirs. Theirs was to edification, and to build one another up in faith; so that they were not as we are, nor are we as they were. But," said she, "we ought to do as they did. There was an hearty friendship among them; but where is it now to be found?" Says Mrs. Bargrave, "It is hard indeed to find a true friend in these days." Says Mrs. Veal, "Mr. Norris has a fine copy

5. Book of Death. This book, first published in French, appeared in an English translation in 1675. Its real title was *The Christian's Defense against the Fears of Death*. **36. Ascetic,** *The Happy Ascetick,* 1681, by Dr. Anthony Horneck (1641–1697). **49. Norris,** John Norris of Bemerton (1657–1711), a country parson and mystical poet.

of verses, called 'Friendship in Perfection,' which I wonderfully admire. Have you seen the book?" says Mrs. Veal. "No," says Mrs. Bargrave, "but I have the verses of my own writing out." "Have you?" says Mrs. Veal, "then fetch them." Which she did from above stairs, and offered them to Mrs. Veal to read, who refused, and waived the thing, saying holding down her head would make it ache; and then desired Mrs. Bargrave to read them to her, which she did. As they were admiring "Friendship," Mrs. Veal said, "Dear Mrs. Bargrave, I shall love you for ever." In these verses there is twice used the word 'Elysian.' "Ah!" says Mrs. Veal, "these poets have such names for heaven." She would often draw her hand across her own eyes, and say, "Mrs. Bargrave, do not you think I am mightily impaired by my fits?" "No," says Mrs. Bargrave, "I think you look as well as ever I knew you."

After all this discourse, which the apparition put in much finer words than Mrs. Bargrave said she could pretend to, and as much more as she could remember (for it cannot be thought that an hour and three-quarters' conversation could be retained, though the main of it she thinks she does), she said to Mrs. Bargrave she would have her write a letter to her brother, and tell him she would have him give rings to such and such; and that there was a purse of gold in her cabinet, and that she would have two broad pieces given to her cousin Watson.

Talking at this rate, Mrs. Bargrave thought that a fit was coming upon her, and so placed herself in a chair just before her knees, to keep her from falling to the ground, if her fits should occasion it; for the elbow-chair, she thought, would keep her from falling on either side; and to divert Mrs. Veal, as she thought, took hold of her gown-sleeve several times and commended it. Mrs. Veal told her it was a scoured silk, and newly made up. But for all this Mrs. Veal persisted in her request, and told Mrs. Bargrave she must not deny her; and she would have her tell her brother all their conversation, when she had opportunity. "Dear Mrs. Veal," said Mrs. Bargrave, "this seems so impertinent that I cannot tell how to comply with it; and what a mortifying story will our conversation be to a young gentleman! Why," says Mrs. Bargrave, "it is much better, methinks, to do it yourself." "No," says Mrs. Veal, "though it seems impertinent to you now, you will see more reason for it hereafter." Mrs. Bargrave then, to satisfy her importunity, was going to fetch a pen and ink, but Mrs. Veal said, "Let it alone now, but do it when I am gone; but you must be sure to do it"; which was one of the last things she enjoined her at parting. So she promised her.

Then Mrs. Veal asked for Mrs. Bargrave's daughter. She said she was not at home, "But if you have a mind to see her," says Mrs. Bargrave, "I'll send for her." "Do," says Mrs. Veal. On which she left her, and went to a neighbour's, to send for her; and by the time Mrs. Bargrave was returning, Mrs. Veal was got without the door into the street, in the face of the beast-market, on a Saturday, which is market-day, and stood ready to part, as soon as Mrs. Bargrave came to her. She asked her why she was in such haste. She said she must be going, though perhaps she might not go her journey till Monday; and told Mrs. Bargrave she hoped she should see her again at her cousin Watson's before she went whither she was going. Then she said she would take her leave of her, and walked from Mrs. Bargrave in her view, till a turning interrupted the sight of her, which was three-quarters after one in the afternoon.

Mrs. Veal died the 7th of September, at twelve o'clock at noon, of her fits, and had not above four hours' senses before her death, in which time she received the sacrament. The next day after Mrs. Veal's appearing, being Sunday, Mrs. Bargrave was so mightily indisposed with a cold and a sore throat that she could not go out that day; but on Monday morning she sent a person to Captain Watson's, to know if Mrs. Veal was there. They wondered at Mrs. Bargrave's inquiry, and sent her word that she was not there, nor was expected. At this answer, Mrs. Bargrave told the maid she had certainly mistook the name or made some blunder. And though she was ill, she put on her hood, and went herself to Captain Watson's, though she knew none of the family, to see if Mrs. Veal was there or not. They said they wondered at her asking, for that she had not been in town; they were sure, if she had, she would have been there. Says Mrs. Bargrave, "I am sure she was with me on Saturday almost two hours." They said it was impossible; for they must have seen her if she had. In comes Captain Watson, while they are in dispute, and said that Mrs. Veal was certainly dead, and her escutcheons were making. This strangely surprised Mrs. Bargrave, when she sent to the person immediately who had the care of them, and found it true. Then she related the whole story to Captain Watson's family, and what gown she had on, and how striped; and that Mrs. Veal told her it was scoured. Then Mrs. Watson cried out, "You have seen her indeed, for none knew but Mrs. Veal and myself that the gown was

44. **escutcheons**, shields with armorial bearings, used at funerals in Defoe's time even by the middle classes.

scoured." And Mrs. Watson owned that she described the gown exactly: "For," said she, "I helped her to make it up." This Mrs. Watson blazed all about the town, and avouched the demonstration of the truth of Mrs. Bargrave's seeing Mrs. Veal's apparition. And Captain Watson carried two gentlemen immediately to Mrs. Bargrave's house to hear the relation from her own mouth. And when it spread so fast that gentlemen and persons of quality, the judicious and sceptical part of the world, flocked in upon her, it at last became such a task that she was forced to go out of the way. For they were, in general, extremely satisfied of the truth of the thing, and plainly saw that Mrs. Bargrave was no hypochondriac; for she always appears with such a cheerful air and pleasing mien, that she has gained the favour and esteem of all the gentry, and it is thought a great favour if they can but get the relation from her own mouth. I should have told you before that Mrs. Veal told Mrs. Bargrave that her sister and brother-in-law were just come down from London to see her. Says Mrs. Bargrave, "How came you to order matters so strangely?" "It could not be helped," said Mrs. Veal. And her brother and sister did come to see her, and entered the town of Dover just as Mrs. Veal was expiring. Mrs. Bargrave asked her whether she would drink some tea. Says Mrs. Veal, "I do not care if I do; but I'll warrant you this mad fellow (meaning Mrs. Bargrave's husband) has broken all your trinkets." "But," says Mrs. Bargrave, "I'll get something to drink in for all that"; but Mrs. Veal waived it, and said, "It is no matter; let it alone"; and so it passed.

All the time I sat with Mrs. Bargrave, which was some hours, she recollected fresh sayings of Mrs. Veal. And one material thing more she told Mrs. Bargrave, that old Mr. Breton allowed Mrs. Veal ten pounds a year, which was a secret, and unknown to Mrs. Bargrave, till Mrs. Veal told it her.

Mrs. Bargrave never varies in her story, which puzzles those who doubt of the truth, or are unwilling to believe it. A servant in the neighbour's yard adjoining to Mrs. Bargrave's house, heard her talking to somebody an hour of the time Mrs. Veal was with her. Mrs. Bargrave went out to her next neighbour's the very moment she parted with Mrs. Veal, and told her what ravishing conversation she had with an old friend, and told the whole of it. *Drelincourt's Book of Death* is, since this happened, bought up strangely. And it is to be observed, that notwithstanding all the trouble and fatigue Mrs. Bargrave has undergone upon this account, she never took the value of a farthing, nor suffered her daughter to take anything of anybody, and therefore can have no interest in telling the story.

But Mr. Veal does what he can to stifle the matter, and said he would see Mrs. Bargrave; but yet it is certain matter of fact that he has been at Captain Watson's since the death of his sister, and yet never went near Mrs. Bargrave; and some of his friends report her to be a liar, and that she knew of Mr. Breton's ten pounds a year. But the person who pretends to say so has the reputation of a notorious liar among persons whom I know to be of undoubted credit. Now, Mr. Veal is more of a gentleman than to say she lies; but says a bad husband has crazed her. But she needs only present herself, and it will effectually confute that pretence. Mr. Veal says he asked his sister on her death-bed whether she had a mind to dispose of anything, and she said no. Now, the things which Mrs. Veal's apparition would have disposed of were so trifling, and nothing of justice aimed at in their disposal, that the design of it appears to me to be only in order to make Mrs. Bargrave so to demonstrate the truth of her appearance as to satisfy the world of the reality thereof, as to what she had seen and heard, and to secure her reputation among the reasonable and understanding part of mankind. And then again, Mr. Veal owns that there was a purse of gold; but it was not found in her cabinet, but in a comb-box. This looks improbable; for that Mrs. Watson owned that Mrs. Veal was so very careful of the key of the cabinet that she would trust nobody with it; and if so, no doubt she would not trust her gold out of it. And Mrs. Veal's often drawing her hand over her eyes, and asking Mrs. Bargrave whether her fits had not impaired her, looks to me as if she did it on purpose to remind Mrs. Bargrave of her fits, to prepare her not to think it strange that she should put her upon writing to her brother to dispose of rings and gold, which looked so much like a dying person's request; and it took accordingly with Mrs. Bargrave, as the effects of her fits coming upon her; and was one of the many instances of her wonderful love to her, and care of her, that she should not be affrighted; which indeed appears in her whole management, particularly in her coming to her in the day-time, waiving the salutation, and when she was alone; and then the manner of her parting to prevent a second attempt to salute her.

Now, why Mr. Veal should think this relation a reflection, as it is plain he does, by his endeavouring to stifle it, I cannot imagine, because the generality believe her to be a good spirit, her discourse was so heavenly. Her two great errands were to comfort Mrs. Bargrave in her affliction, and to ask her for-

---

3. blazed, spread the report of.

giveness for the breach of friendship, and with a pious discourse to encourage her. So that, after all, to suppose that Mrs. Bargrave could hatch such an invention as this from Friday noon to Saturday noon, supposing that she knew of Mrs. Veal's death the very first moment, without jumbling circumstances, and without any interest too, she must be more witty, fortunate, and wicked too, than any indifferent person, I dare say, will allow. I asked Mrs. Bargrave several times, if she was sure she felt the gown. She answered modestly, "If my senses are to be relied on, I am sure of it." I asked her if she heard a sound when she clapped her hands upon her knee. She said she did not remember she did; but said she appeared to be as much a substance as I did, who talked with her. "And I may," said she, "be as soon persuaded that your apparition is talking to me now, as that I did not really see her; for I was under no manner of fear, and received her as a friend, and parted with her as such. I would not," says she, "give one farthing to make any one believe it; I have no interest in it. Nothing but trouble is entailed upon me for a long time, for aught I know; and had it not come to light by accident, it would never have been made public." But now, she says, she will make her own private use of it, and keep herself out of the way as much as she can; and so she has done since. She says she had a gentleman who came thirty miles to her to hear the relation; and that she had told it to a room full of people at a time. Several particular gentlemen have had the story from Mrs. Bargrave's own mouth.

This thing has very much affected me, and I am as well satisfied as I am of the best-grounded matter of fact. And why we should dispute matter of fact because we cannot solve things of which we have no certain or demonstrative notions, seems strange to me. Mrs. Bargrave's authority and sincerity alone would have been undoubted in any other case.

Jonathan Swift
1667–1745

In any effort to face the riddle of Jonathan Swift one must begin with some consideration, however brief, of the man's outward career. One should know that he was born and bred in Ireland, a country for which he had great compassion but little liking. It is significant that his childhood and youth were spent in poverty and dependence. His years in the household of Sir William Temple, although they brought him a fruitful leisure and influential acquaintances, were years of subserviency. The fact is not to be forgotten that he became a clergyman less for religious reasons than in the hope of a "preferment" which was long in coming, and neither should one forget that his eager political activity in London during the last years of Queen Anne led to ultimate disappointment.

One would not suggest that Swift turned against the world because he came to feel that the world was against him. Although embittered, he was not petty, and his satirical writing—which began, one should remember, long before the defeat of his political hopes—does not suggest the spite of a little man with a grievance. On the other hand, one cannot believe that his "savage indignation" at mankind was arrived at by a wholly disinterested observation of the human show, for such an observation leads not to wrath but to pity. The fact appears to be, then, that Jonathan Swift, for all the nobleness of his nature, the tenderness of his heart, and the glorious powers of his mind, was after all a worldly man disappointed in his worldliness.

What Swift chiefly wanted was power, and pride was his master passion. It was a main, though not a conscious, effort of his mature life to vindicate his pride against those indignities which he thought his childhood and youth had suffered. Of such an effort there can be no end and no final success.

These moral considerations have a literary bearing. Upon discovering that Swift never set his own mental house in order one is led to ask whether he really was, even in his writings, what his critics have often called him, an exponent of reason and common sense. One begins to doubt his alleged distrust of the passions when one learns to what degree he was governed by anger and pride. The "wisdom" often attributed to him is brought into question when one sees how grievously he failed in his "great task of happiness."

But perhaps it is not so much of Swift's matter as of his manner that critics are thinking when they speak of his clarity and good sense. His manner is nearly always that of plain unadorned statement. It is that of a man who wishes at all cost to be clearly understood. Yet the cost, one should not forget, is considerable. This universally admired prose style is indeed admirably suited to Swift's somewhat restricted needs and occasions. In the high virtue of clarity it has seldom been surpassed; but there are other prose virtues, and high ones, which Swift and his fellows either did not know or else decided to abandon. Among these one may mention grandeur, rhythmical subtlety, musical range and depth, surprise, glamour, and the suggestion by ways hardly namable of "thoughts that break through language and escape."

When we test the "reason" and "good sense" of Swift in his own peculiar territory, that of prose satire, we find at once that he does not attack individual persons, or even particular follies and vices, but mankind in general. His, we are told, is a "universal satire." "I have ever hated all nations, professions, and communities," he once wrote to Pope, "and all my love is toward individuals. . . . I hate and detest that animal called man, although I heartily love John, Peter, Thomas, and so forth." Yet clearly there is something even more absurd in a satirical attack upon the human race than there is in the effort to indict a nation. The human race is "as the air, invulnerable," so that if it is really execution that a satirist is seeking, he does better to use a rifle, in the way of Alexander Pope, than to spray the surrounding landscape with bird shot. The satire of Swift is too often dispersed, digressive, and miscellaneous. Only once or twice, as in *A Modest Proposal*, does he deliver his total force in a single well-aimed blow.

Anger, if not pride, makes an artist's hand tremble, but neither the one nor the other is an unheroic passion. It has been justly said that Jonathan Swift was the only English writer of his time who might have been the hero of a Shakespearian tragedy, and this is a way of reminding us that the faults and failures of the man were closely related to magnificent powers. He reached nearer to greatness than any of his contemporaries. The mystery of his life and of his mind has fascinated thousands. If he could know how his imaginings and indignations have worked upon the thought of the last two hundred years, even his pride might find some satisfaction.

from GULLIVER'S TRAVELS

Swift once said that he wrote *Gulliver's Travels*, his most famous work, "to vex the world rather than to divert it." In that case he failed in his purpose, for millions of readers, including great numbers of children, have been diverted by the adventures and observations of his imaginary traveler, and not one, it seems likely, has ever been seriously vexed. Indeed, there was something strangely naïve in Swift's assumption that "the world" would be aggrieved by his attack upon human nature in general. In reading the more frantic pages of his libel upon humanity one feels only a compassionate sorrow—for Jonathan Swift. The ageless charm of *Gulliver's Travels* is in its boldness of conception and its ingenuity of execution. It fails as satire partly because it explodes into a scream of hatred and partly for the reason that it tries to ridicule too many absurdities at once.

The first of Lemuel Gulliver's voyages—the one that takes him to Lilliput, the land of little people—is the most interesting and the most familiar. Later he visits a land of giants called Brobdingnag, a realm of learned fools by the name of Laputa, and a country of noble horses. The first voyage is here given almost entire.

PART I: A VOYAGE TO LILLIPUT

Chapter 1

The Author gives some account of himself and family, his first inducements to travel. He is shipwrecked, and swims for his life, gets safe on shore in the country of Lilliput, *is made a prisoner, and is carried up country.*

MY father had a small estate in Nottinghamshire; I was the third of five sons. He sent me to Emanuel College in Cambridge, at fourteen years old, where I resided three years, and applied myself close to my studies; but the charge of maintaining me (although I had a very scanty allowance) being too great for a narrow fortune, I was bound apprentice to Mr. James Bates, an eminent surgeon in London, with whom I continued four years; and my father now and then sending me small sums of money, I laid them out in learning navigation, and other parts of the mathematics, useful to those who intend to travel, as I always believed it would be some time or other my fortune to do. When I left Mr. Bates, I went down to my father; where, by the assistance of him and my uncle John, and some other relations, I got forty pounds, and a promise of thirty pounds a year to maintain me at Leyden: there I studied physic two years and seven months, knowing it would be useful in long voyages.

Soon after my return from Leyden, I was recommended by my good master, Mr. Bates, to be surgeon to the *Swallow*, Captain Abraham Pannell, commander; with whom I continued three years and a half, making a voyage or two into the Levant, and some other parts. When I came back I resolved to settle in London, to which Mr. Bates, my master, encouraged me, and by him I was recommended to several patients. I took part of a small house in the Old Jury; and being advised to alter my condition, I married Mrs. Mary Burton, second daughter to Mr. Edmund Burton, hosier, in Newgate-street, with whom I received four hundred pounds for a portion.

But, my good master Bates dying in two years after, and I having few friends, my business began to fail; for my conscience would not suffer me to imitate the bad practice of too many among my brethren. Having therefore consulted with my wife, and some of my acquaintance, I determined to go again to sea. I was surgeon successively in two ships, and made several voyages, for six years, to the East and West-Indies, by which I got some addition to my fortune. My hours of leisure I spent in reading the best authors, ancient and modern, being always provided with a good number of books; and when I was ashore, in observing the manners and dispositions of the people, as well as learning their language, wherein I had a great facility by the strength of my memory.

The last of these voyages not proving very fortunate, I grew weary of the sea, and intended to stay at home with my wife and family. I removed from the Old Jury to Fetter-Lane, and from thence to Wapping, hoping to get business among the sailors; but it would not turn to account. After three years expectation that things would mend, I accepted an advantageous offer from Captain William Prichard, master of the *Antelope*, who was making a voyage to the South-Sea. We set sail from Bristol, May 4, 1699, and our voyage at first was very prosperous.

It would not be proper, for some reasons, to trouble the reader with the particulars of our adventures in those seas: let it suffice to inform him, that in our passage from thence to the East-Indies, we were driven by a violent storm to the north-west of Van Diemen's Land. By an observation, we found ourselves in the latitude of 30 degrees 2 minutes south. Twelve of our crew were dead by immoderate labour, and ill food; the rest were in a very weak condition. On the fifth of November, which was the beginning of summer in those parts, the weather being very hazy, the seamen spied a rock, within half a cable's length of the ship; but the wind was so strong, that we were driven directly upon it, and immediately split. Six of the crew, of whom I was one, having let down the boat into the sea, made a shift to get clear of the ship, and the rock. We rowed, by my computation, about three leagues, till we were able to work no longer, being already spent with labour while we were in the ship. We therefore trusted ourselves to the mercy of the waves, and in about half an hour the boat was overset by a sudden flurry from the north. What became of my companions in the boat, as well as of those who escaped on the rock, or were left in the vessel, I cannot tell; but conclude they were all lost. For my own part, I swam as fortune directed me, and was pushed forward by wind and tide. I often let my legs drop, and could feel no bottom: but when I was almost gone, and able to struggle no longer, I found myself within my depth; and by this time the storm was much abated. The declivity was so small, that I walked near a mile before I got to the shore, which I conjectured was about eight a clock in the evening. I then advanced forward near half a mile, but could not discover any sign of houses or inhabitants; at least I was in so weak a condition, that I did not observe them. I was extremely tired, and with that, and the heat of the weather, and about half a pint of brandy that I drank as I left the ship, I found myself much inclined to sleep. I lay down on the grass, which was very short and soft, where I slept sounder than ever I remember to have done in my life, and, as I reckoned, about nine hours; for when I awaked, it was just day-light. I attempted to rise, but was not able to stir: for as I happened to lie on my back, I found my arms and legs were strongly fastened on each side to the ground; and my hair, which was long and thick, tied down in the same manner. I likewise felt several slender ligatures across my body, from my arm-pits to my thighs. I could only look upwards, the sun began to grow hot, and the light offended my eyes. I heard a confused noise about me, but in the posture I lay, could see nothing except the sky. In a little time I felt something alive moving on my left leg, which advancing gently forward over my breast, came almost up to my chin; when bending my eyes downwards as much as I could, I perceived it to be a human creature not six inches high, with a bow and arrow in his hands, and a quiver at his back. In the mean time, I felt at least forty more of the same kind (as I conjectured) following the first. I was in the utmost astonishment, and roared so loud, that they all ran back in a fright; and some of them, as I was afterwards told, were hurt with the falls they got by leaping from my sides upon the ground. However, they soon returned, and one of them, who ventured so far as to get a full sight of my face, lifting up his hands and eyes by way of admiration, cried out in a shrill, but

---

4. **Mrs.**, again for an unmarried woman. 43. **south.** This would be in the region of Tasmania.

17. **a clock**, old form.

distinct voice, *Hekinah degul:* the others repeated the same words several times, but then I knew not what they meant. I lay all this while, as the reader may believe, in great uneasiness: at length, struggling to get loose, I had the fortune to break the strings, and wrench out the pegs that fastened my left arm to the ground: for, by lifting it up to my face, I discovered the methods they had taken to bind me, and at the same time with a violent pull, which gave me excessive pain, I a little loosened the strings that tied down my hair on the left side, so that I was just able to turn my head about two inches. But the creatures ran off a second time, before I could seize them; whereupon there was a great shout in a very shrill accent, and after it ceased, I heard one of them cry aloud *Tolgo phonac;* when in an instant I felt above an hundred arrows discharged on my left hand, which pricked me like so many needles; and besides, they shot another flight into the air, as we do bombs in Europe, whereof many, I suppose, fell on my body, (though I felt them not) and some on my face, which I immediately covered with my left hand. When this shower of arrows was over, I fell a groaning with grief and pain, and then striving again to get loose, they discharged another volley larger than the first, and some of them attempted with spears to stick me in the sides; but, by good luck, I had on a buff jerkin, which they could not pierce. I thought it the most prudent method to lie still, and my design was to continue so till night, when, my left hand being already loose, I could easily free myself: and as for the inhabitants, I had reason to believe I might be a match for the greatest armies they could bring against me, if they were all of the same size with him that I saw. But fortune disposed otherwise of me. When the people observed I was quiet, they discharged no more arrows; but, by the noise I heard, I knew their numbers increased; and about four yards from me, over-against my right ear, I heard a knocking for above an hour, like that of people at work; when turning my head that way, as well as the pegs and strings would permit me, I saw a stage erected, about a foot and a half from the ground, capable of holding four of the inhabitants, with two or three ladders to mount it: from whence one of them, who seemed to be a person of quality, made me a long speech, whereof I understood not one syllable. But I should have mentioned, that before the principal person began his oration, he cried out three times, *Langro dehul san:* (these words and the former were afterwards repeated and explained to me). Whereupon immediately about fifty of the inhabitants came and cut the strings that fastened the left side of my head, which gave me the liberty of turning it to the right, and of observing the person and gesture of him that was to speak. He appeared to be of a middle age, and taller than any of the other three who attended him, whereof one was a page that held up his train, and seemed to be somewhat longer than my middle finger; the other two stood one on each side to support him. He acted every part of an orator, and I could observe many periods of threatenings, and others of promises, pity, and kindness. I answered in a few words, but in the most submissive manner, lifting up my left hand, and both my eyes to the sun, as calling him for a witness; and being almost famished with hunger, having not eaten a morsel for some hours before I left the ship, I found the demands of nature so strong upon me, that I could not forbear showing my impatience (perhaps against the strict rules of decency) by putting my finger frequently on my mouth, to signify that I wanted food. The *Hurgo* (for so they call a great lord, as I afterwards learnt) understood me very well. He descended from the stage, and commanded that several ladders should be applied to my sides, on which above an hundred of the inhabitants mounted and walked towards my mouth, laden with baskets full of meat, which had been provided and sent thither by the King's orders, upon the first intelligence he received of me. I observed there was the flesh of several animals, but could not distinguish them by the taste. There were shoulders, legs, and loins, shaped like those of mutton, and very well dressed, but smaller than the wings of a lark. I eat them by two or three at a mouthful, and took three loaves at a time, about the bigness of musket bullets. They supplied me as fast as they could, showing a thousand marks of wonder and astonishment at my bulk and appetite. I then made another sign that I wanted drink. They found by my eating, that a small quantity would not suffice me; and being a most ingenious people, they slung up with great dexterity one of their largest hogsheads, then rolled it towards my hand, and beat out the top; I drank it off at a draught, which I might well do, for it did not hold half a pint, and tasted like a small wine of Burgundy, but much more delicious. They brought me a second hogshead, which I drank in the same manner, and made signs for more, but they had none to give me. When I had performed these wonders, they shouted for joy, and danced upon my breast, repeating several times as they did at first, *Hekinah degul.* They made me a sign that I should throw down the two hogsheads, but first warning the people below to stand out of the way, crying aloud, *Borach mivola,* and when they saw the vessels in the air, there was an universal shout of *Hekinah degul*. I confess I was often tempted, while they were passing backwards and forwards on my body, to seize forty or fifty of the first that came in my reach, and dash them against the ground. But the remembrance of what I had felt, which probably might not be the worst they could do, and the promise of honour I made them, for so I interpreted my submissive behaviour, soon drove out these imaginations. Besides, I now considered myself as bound by the laws of hospitality to a people who had treated me with so much expense and magnificence. However, in my thoughts, I could not sufficiently wonder at the intrepidity of these diminutive mortals, who durst venture to mount and walk upon my body, while one of my hands was at liberty, without trembling at the very sight of so prodigious a creature as I must appear to them. After some time, when they observed that I made no more demands for meat, there appeared before me a person of high rank from his Imperial Majesty. His Excellency, having mounted on the small of my right leg, advanced forwards up to my face, with about a dozen of his retinue. And producing his credentials under the Signet Royal, which he applied close to my eyes, spoke about ten minutes, without any signs of anger, but with a kind of determinate resolution; often pointing forwards, which, as I afterwards found, was toward the capital city, about half a mile distant, whither it was agreed by his Majesty in council that I must be conveyed. I answered in few words, but to no purpose, and made a sign with my hand that was loose, putting it to the other (but over his Excellency's head for fear of hurting him or his train) and then to my own head and body, to signify that I desired my liberty. It appeared that he understood me well enough, for he shook his head by way of disapprobation, and held his hand in a posture to show that I must be carried as a prisoner. However, he made other signs to let me understand that I should have meat and drink enough, and very good treatment. Whereupon I once more thought of attempting to break my bonds; but again, when I felt the smart of their arrows, upon my face and hands, which were all in blisters, and many of the darts still sticking in them, and observing likewise that the number of my enemies increased, I gave tokens to let them know that they might do with me what they pleased. Upon this, the *Hurgo* and his train withdrew, with much civility and cheerful countenances. Soon after I heard a general shout, with frequent repetitions of the words, *Peplom selan*, and I felt great numbers of people on my left side relaxing the cords to such a degree, that I was able to turn upon my right, and to ease myself with making water; which I very plentifully did, to the great astonishment of the people, who conjecturing by my motions what I was going to do, immediately opened to the right and left on that side, to avoid the torrent which fell with such noise and violence from me. But before this, they had daubed my face and both my hands with a sort of ointment very pleasant to the smell, which in a few minutes removed all the smart of their arrows. These circumstances, added to the refreshment I had received by their victuals and drink, which were very nourishing, disposed me to sleep. I slept about eight hours, as I was afterwards assured; and it was no wonder, for the physicians, by the Emperor's order, had mingled a sleepy potion in the hogshead of wine.

It seems that upon the first moment I was discovered sleeping on the ground after my landing, the Emperor had early notice of it by an express; and determined in council that I should be tied in the manner I have related, (which was done in the night while I slept) that plenty of meat and drink should be sent to me, and a machine prepared to carry me to the capital city.

This resolution perhaps may appear very bold and dangerous, and I am confident would not be imitated by any prince in Europe on the like occasion; however, in my opinion, it was extremely prudent, as well as generous: for supposing these people had endeavoured to kill me with their spears and arrows while I was asleep, I should certainly have awaked with the first sense of smart, which might so far have roused my rage and strength, as to have enabled me to break the strings wherewith I was tied; after which, as they were not able to make resistance, so they could expect no mercy.

These people are most excellent mathematicians, and arrived to a great perfection in mechanics, by the countenance and encouragement of the Emperor, who is a renowned patron of learning. This prince hath several machines fixed on wheels, for the carriage of trees and other great weights. He often builds his largest men of war, whereof some are nine foot long, in the woods where the timber grows, and has them carried on these engines three or four hundred yards to the sea. Five hundred carpenters and engineers were immediately set at work to prepare the greatest engine they had. It was a frame of wood raised three inches from the ground, about seven foot long and four wide, moving upon twenty-two wheels. The shout I heard was upon the arrival of this engine, which it seems set out in four hours after my landing. It was brought parallel to me as I lay. But the principal difficulty was to raise and place me in this vehicle. Eighty poles, each of one foot high, were erected for this purpose, and very strong cords of the bigness of packthread were fastened by hooks to many bandages, which the workmen had girt round my neck, my hands, my body, and my legs. Nine hundred of the strongest men were employed to draw up these cords by many pulleys fastened on the poles, and thus, in less than three hours, I was raised and slung into the engine, and there tied fast. All this I was told, for, while the whole operation was performing, I lay in a profound sleep, by the force of that soporiferous medicine infused into my liquor. Fifteen hundred of the Emperor's largest horses, each about four inches and a half high, were employed to draw me towards the metropolis, which, as I said, was half a mile distant.

About four hours after we began our journey, I awaked by a very ridiculous accident; for the carriage being stopped a while to adjust something that was out of order, two or three of the young natives had the curiosity to see how I looked when I was asleep; they climbed up into the engine, and advancing very softly to my face, one of them, an officer in the guards, put the sharp end of his half-pike a good way up into my left nostril, which tickled my nose like a straw, and made me sneeze violently: whereupon they stole off unperceived, and it was three weeks before I knew the cause of my awaking so suddenly. We made a long march the remaining part of that day, and rested at night with five hundred guards on each side of me, half with torches, and half with bows and arrows, ready to shoot me if I should offer to stir. The next morning at sunrise we continued our march, and arrived within two hundred yards of the city gates about noon. The Emperor, and all his court, came out to meet us; but his great officers would by no means suffer his Majesty to endanger his person by mounting on my body.

At the place where the carriage stopped, there stood an ancient temple, esteemed to be the largest in the whole kingdom; which having been polluted some years before by an unnatural murder, was, according to the zeal of those people, looked upon as profane, and therefore had been applied to common uses, and all the ornaments and furniture carried away. In this edifice it was determined I should lodge. The great gate fronting to the north was about four foot high, and almost two foot wide, through which I could easily creep. On each side of the gate was a small window not above six inches from the ground: into that on the left side, the King's smiths conveyed fourscore and eleven chains, like those that hang to a lady's watch in Europe, and almost as large, which were locked to my left leg with six and thirty padlocks. Over against this temple, on the other side of the great highway, at twenty foot distance, there was a turret at least five foot high. Here the Emperor ascended, with many principal lords of his court, to have an opportunity of viewing me, as I was told, for I could not see them. It was reckoned that above an hundred thousand inhabitants came out of the town upon the same errand; and, in spite of my guards, I believe there could not be fewer than ten thousand at several times, who mounted my body by the help of ladders. But a proclamation was soon issued to forbid it upon pain of death. When the workmen found it was impossible for me to break loose, they cut all the strings that bound me; whereupon I rose up, with as melancholy a disposition as ever I had in my life. But the noise and astonishment of the people at seeing me rise and walk, are not to be expressed. The chains that held my left leg were about two yards long, and gave me not only the liberty of walking backwards and forwards in a semicircle; but, being fixed within four inches of the gate, allowed me to creep in, and lie at my full length in the temple.

Chapter 2

The Emperor of Lilliput, *attended by several of the nobility, comes to see the Author in his confinement. The Emperor's person and habit described. Learned men appointed to teach the Author their language. He gains favour by his mild disposition. His pockets are searched, and his sword and pistols taken from him.*

WHEN I found myself on my feet, I looked about me, and must confess I never beheld a more entertaining prospect. The country round appeared like a continued garden, and the inclosed fields, which were generally forty foot square, resembled so many beds of flowers. These fields were intermingled with woods of half a stang, and the tallest trees, as I could judge, appeared to be seven foot high. I viewed the town on my left hand, which looked like the painted scene of a city in a theatre.

I had been for some hours extremely pressed by the necessities of nature; which was no wonder, it being almost two days since I had last disburthened myself. I was under great difficulties between urgency and shame. The best expedient I could think on, was to creep into my house, which I accordingly did; and shutting the gate after me, I went as far as

43. **stang,** a pole or perch, 16½ feet.

the length of my chain would suffer, and discharged my body of that uneasy load. But this was the only time I was ever guilty of so uncleanly an action; for which I cannot but hope the candid reader will give some allowance, after he hath maturely and impartially considered my case, and the distress I was in. From this time my constant practice was, as soon as I rose, to perform that business in open air, at the full extent of my chain, and due care was taken every morning before company came, that the offensive matter should be carried off in wheelbarrows, by two servants appointed for that purpose. I would not have dwelt so long upon a circumstance, that perhaps at first sight may appear not very momentous, if I had not thought it necessary to justify my character in point of cleanliness to the world; which I am told some of my maligners have been pleased, upon this and other occasions, to call in question.

When this adventure was at an end, I came back out of my house, having occasion for fresh air. The Emperor was already descended from the tower, and advancing on horseback towards me, which had like to have cost him dear; for the beast, though very well trained, yet wholly unused to such a sight, which appeared as if a mountain moved before him, reared up on his hinder feet: but that prince, who is an excellent horseman, kept his seat, till his attendants ran in, and held the bridle, while his Majesty had time to dismount. When he alighted, he surveyed me round with great admiration, but kept beyond the length of my chain. He ordered his cooks and butlers, who were already prepared, to give me victuals and drink, which they pushed forward in a sort of vehicles upon wheels, till I could reach them. I took these vehicles, and soon emptied them all; twenty of them were filled with meat, and ten with liquor; each of the former afforded me two or three good mouthfuls, and I emptied the liquor of ten vessels, which was contained in earthen vials, into one vehicle, drinking it off at a draught; and so I did with the rest. The Empress, and young Princes of the blood of both sexes, attended by many ladies, sat at some distance in their chairs; but upon the accident that happened to the Emperor's horse, they alighted, and came near his person, which I am now going to describe. He is taller by almost the breadth of my nail, than any of his court; which alone is enough to strike an awe into the beholders. His features are strong and masculine, with an Austrian lip and arched nose, his complexion olive, his countenance erect, his body and limbs well proportioned, all his motions graceful, and his deportment majestic. He was then past his prime, being twenty-eight years and three quarters old, of which he had reigned about seven, in great felicity, and generally victorious. For the better convenience of beholding him, I lay on my side, so that my face was parallel to his, and he stood but three yards off: however, I have had him since many times in my hand, and therefore cannot be deceived in the description. His dress was very plain and simple, and the fashion of it between the Asiatic and the European: but he had on his head a light helmet of gold, adorned with jewels, and a plume on the crest. He held his sword drawn in his hand, to defend himself, if I should happen to break loose; it was almost three inches long, the hilt and scabbard were gold enriched with diamonds. His voice was shrill, but very clear and articulate, and I could distinctly hear it when I stood up. The ladies and courtiers were all most magnificently clad, so that the spot they stood upon seemed to resemble a petticoat spread on the ground, embroidered with figures of gold and silver. His Imperial Majesty spoke often to me, and I returned answers, but neither of us could understand a syllable. There were several of his priests and lawyers present (as I conjectured by their habits) who were commanded to address themselves to me, and I spoke to them in as many languages as I had the least smattering of, which were High and Low Dutch, Latin, French, Spanish, Italian, and Lingua Franca; but all to no purpose. After about two hours the court retired, and I was left with a strong guard, to prevent the impertinence, and probably the malice of the rabble, who were very impatient to crowd about me as near as they durst, and some of them had the impudence to shoot their arrows at me as I sat on the ground by the door of my house, whereof one very narrowly missed my left eye. But the colonel ordered six of the ringleaders to be seized, and thought no punishment so proper as to deliver them bound into my hands, which some of his soldiers accordingly did, pushing them forwards with the butt-ends of their pikes into my reach; I took them all in my right hand, put five of them into my coat-pocket, and as to the sixth, I made a countenance as if I would eat him alive. The poor man squalled terribly, and the colonel and his officers were in much pain, especially when they saw me take out my penknife: but I soon put them out of fear: for, looking mildly, and immediately cutting the strings he was bound with, I set him gently on the ground, and away he ran. I treated the rest in the same manner, taking them one by one out of my pocket, and I ob-

31-32. admiration, wonder.

served both the soldiers and people were highly obliged at this mark of my clemency, which was represented very much to my advantage at court.

Towards night I got with some difficulty into my house, where I lay on the ground, and continued to do so about a fortnight; during which time the Emperor gave orders to have a bed prepared for me. Six hundred beds of the common measure were brought in carriages, and worked up in my house; an hundred and fifty of their beds sewn together made up the breadth and length, and these were four double, which however kept me but very indifferently from the hardness of the floor, that was of smooth stone. By the same computation they provided me with sheets, blankets, and coverlets, tolerable enough for one who had been so long inured to hardships as I.

As the news of my arrival spread through the kingdom, it brought prodigious numbers of rich, idle, and curious people to see me; so that the villages were almost emptied, and great neglect of tillage and household affairs must have ensued, if his Imperial Majesty had not provided, by several proclamations and orders of state, against this inconveniency. He directed that those who had already beheld me should return home, and not presume to come within fifty yards of my house without licence from court; whereby the secretaries of state got considerable fees.

In the meantime, the Emperor held frequent councils to debate what course should be taken with me; and I was afterwards assured by a particular friend, a person of great quality, who was looked upon to be as much in the secret as any, that the court was under many difficulties concerning me. They apprehended my breaking loose, that my diet would be very expensive, and might cause a famine. Sometimes they determined to starve me, or at least to shoot me in the face and hands with poisoned arrows, which would soon dispatch me; but again they considered, that the stench of so large a carcass might produce a plague in the metropolis, and probably spread through the whole kingdom. In the midst of these consultations, several officers of the army went to the door of the great council-chamber; and two of them being admitted, gave an account of my behaviour to the six criminals above-mentioned, which made so favourable an impression in the breast of his Majesty and the whole board, in my behalf, that an Imperial Commission was issued out, obliging all the villages nine hundred yards around the city, to deliver in every morning six beeves, forty sheep, and other victuals for my sustenance; together with a proportionable quantity of bread, and wine, and other liquors; for the due payment of which his Majesty gave assignments upon his treasury. For this prince lives chiefly upon his own demesnes, seldom, except upon great occasions, raising any subsidies upon his subjects, who are bound to attend him in his wars at their own expense. An establishment was also made of six hundred persons to be my domestics, who had board-wages allowed for their maintenance, and tents built for them very conveniently on each side of my door. It was likewise ordered, that three hundred tailors should make me a suit of clothes after the fashion of the country: that six of his Majesty's greatest scholars should be employed to instruct me in their language: and, lastly, that the Emperor's horses, and those of the nobility, and troops of guards, should be frequently exercised in my sight, to accustom themselves to me. All these orders were duly put in execution, and in about three weeks I made a great progress in learning their language; during which time, the Emperor frequently honoured me with his visits, and was pleased to assist my masters in teaching me. We began already to converse together in some sort; and the first words I learnt were to express my desire that he would please to give me my liberty, which I every day repeated on my knees. His answer, as I could comprehend it, was, that this must be a work of time, not to be thought on without the advice of his council, and that first I must *Lumos kelmin pesso desmar lon Emposo;* that is, swear a peace with him and his kingdom. However, that I should be used with all kindness; and he advised me to acquire, by my patience and discreet behaviour, the good opinion of himself and his subjects. He desired I would not take it ill, if he gave orders to certain proper officers to search me; for probably I might carry about me several weapons, which must needs be dangerous things, if they answered the bulk of so prodigious a person. I said, his Majesty should be satisfied, for I was ready to strip myself, and turn up my pockets before him. This I delivered part in words, and part in signs. He replied, that by the laws of the kingdom I must be searched by two of his officers; that he knew this could not be done without my consent and assistance; that he had so good an opinion of my generosity and justice, as to trust their persons in my hands: that whatever they took from me should be returned when I left the country, or paid for at the rate which I would set upon them. I took up the two officers in my hands, put them first into my coat-pockets, and then into every other pocket about me, except my two fobs, and another secret pocket which I had no mind should be searched, wherein I had some little necessaries that were of no consequence to any but myself. In one of my fobs there was a silver watch, and in the other a small quantity of gold in a purse. These gentlemen, having pen, ink, and paper about them, made an exact inventory of every thing they saw; and when they had done, desired I would set them down, that they might deliver it to the Emperor. This inventory I afterwards translated into English, and is word for word as follows:

Imprimis, In the right coat-pocket of the Great Man-Mountain (for so I interpret the words *Quinbus Flestrin*) after the strictest search, we found only one great piece of coarse cloth, large enough to be a foot-cloth for your Majesty's chief room of state. In the left pocket we saw a huge silver chest, with a cover of the same metal, which we, the searchers, were not able to lift. We desired it should be opened, and one of us stepping into it, found himself up to the mid leg in a sort of dust, some part whereof flying up to our faces, set us both a sneezing for several times together. In his right waistcoat-pocket we found a prodigious bundle of white thin substances, folded one over another, about the bigness of three men, tied with a strong cable, and marked with black figures; which we humbly conceive to be writings, every letter almost half as large as the palm of our hands. In the left there was a sort of engine, from the back of which were extended twenty long poles, resembling the pallisadoes before your Majesty's court; wherewith we conjecture the Man-Mountain combs his head; for we did not always trouble him with questions, because we found it a great difficulty to make him understand us. In the large pocket on the right side of his middle cover (so I translate the word *ranfu-lo*, by which they meant my breeches) we saw a hollow pillar of iron, about the length of a man, fastened to a strong piece of timber, larger than the pillar; and upon one side of the pillar were huge pieces of iron sticking out, cut into strange figures, which we know not what to make of. In the left pocket, another engine of the same kind. In the smaller pocket on the right side, were several round flat pieces of white and red metal, of different bulk; some of the white, which seemed to be silver, were so large and heavy, that my comrade and I could hardly lift them. In the left pocket were two black pillars irregularly shaped: we could not, without difficulty, reach the top of them as we stood at the bottom of his pocket. One of them was covered, and seemed all of a piece: but at the upper end of the other, there appeared a white round substance, about twice the bigness of our heads. Within each of these was enclosed a prodigious plate of steel; which, by our orders, we obliged him to show us, because we apprehended they might be dangerous engines. He took them out of their cases, and told us, that in his own country his practice was to shave his beard with one of these, and cut his meat with the other. There were two pockets which we could not enter: these he called his fobs; they were two large slits cut into the top of his middle cover, but squeezed close by the pressure of his belly. Out of the right fob hung a great silver chain, with a wonderful kind of engine at the bottom. We directed him to draw out whatever was fastened to that chain; which appeared to be a globe, half silver, and half of some transparent metal; for, on the transparent side, we saw certain strange figures circularly drawn, and thought we could touch them, till we found our fingers stopped by that lucid substance. He put this engine to our ears, which made an incessant noise like that of a water-mill. And we conjecture it is either some unknown animal, or the god that he worships; but we are more inclined to the latter opinion, because he assured us, (if we understood him right, for he expressed himself very imperfectly) that he seldom did any thing without consulting it. He called it his oracle, and said it pointed out the time for every action of his life. From the left fob he took out a net almost large enough for a fisherman, but contrived to open and shut like a purse, and served him for the same use: we found therein several massy pieces of yellow metal, which, if they be real gold, must be of immense value.

Having thus, in obedience to your Majesty's commands, diligently searched all his pockets, we observed a girdle about his waist made of the hide of some prodigious animal; from which, on the left side, hung a sword of the length of five men; and on the right, a bag or pouch divided into two cells, each capable of holding three of your Majesty's subjects. In one of these cells were several globes or balls of a most ponderous metal, about the bigness of our heads, and requiring a strong hand to lift them: the other cell contained a heap of certain black grains, but of no great bulk or weight, for we could hold about fifty of them in the palms of our hands.

This is an exact inventory of what we found about the body of the Man-Mountain, who used us with great civility, and due respect to your Majesty's Commission. Signed and sealed on the fourth day of the eighty-ninth moon of your Majesty's auspicious reign.

CLEFRIN FRELOCK, MARSI FRELOCK.

When this inventory was read over to the Emperor, he directed me, although in very gentle terms, to deliver up the several particulars. He first called for my scimitar, which I took out, scabbard and all. In the mean time he ordered three thousand of his choicest troops (who then attended him) to surround me at a distance, with their bows and arrows just ready to discharge: but I did not observe it, for my eyes were wholly fixed upon his Majesty. He then desired me to draw my scimitar, which, although it had got some rust by the sea-water, was in most parts exceeding bright. I did so, and immediately all the troops gave a shout between terror and surprise; for the sun shone clear, and the reflection dazzled their eyes, as I waved the scimitar to and fro in my hand. His Majesty, who is a most magnanimous prince, was less daunted than I could expect; he ordered me to return it into the scabbard, and cast it on the ground as gently as I could, about six foot from the end of my chain. The next thing he demanded, was one of the hollow iron pillars, by which he meant my pocket-pistols. I drew it out, and at his desire, as well as I could, expressed to him the use of it; and charging it only with powder, which, by the closeness of my pouch, happened to escape wetting in the sea (an inconvenience against which all prudent mariners take special care to provide,) I first cautioned the Emperor not to be afraid, and then I let it off in the air. The astonishment here was much greater than at the sight of my scimitar. Hundreds fell down as if they had been struck dead; and even the Emperor, although he stood his ground, could not recover himself in some time. I delivered up both my pistols in the same manner as I had done my scimitar, and then my pouch of powder and bullets; begging him that the former might be kept from fire, for it would kindle with the smallest spark, and blow up his imperial palace into the air. I likewise delivered up my watch, which the Emperor was very curious to see, and commanded two of his tallest yeomen of the guards to bear it on a pole upon their shoulders, as draymen in England do a barrel of ale. He was amazed at the continual noise it made, and the motion of the minute-hand, which he could easily discern; for their sight is much more acute than ours: and asked the opinions of his learned men about him, which were various and remote, as the reader may well imagine without my repeating; although indeed I could not very perfectly understand them. I then gave up my silver and copper money, my purse, with nine large pieces of gold, and some smaller ones; my knife and razor, my comb and silver snuff-box, my handkerchief and journal-book. My scimitar, pistols, and pouch, were conveyed in carriages to his Majesty's stores; but the rest of my goods were returned to me.

I had, as I before observed, one private pocket which escaped their search, wherein there was a pair of spectacles, (which I sometimes use for the weakness of my eyes) a pocket perspective, and several other little conveniences; which being of no consequence to the Emperor, I did not think myself bound in honour to discover, and I apprehended they might be lost or spoiled if I ventured them out of my possession.

Chapter 3

The Author diverts the Emperor, and his nobility of both sexes, in a very uncommon manner. The diversions of the court of Lilliput described. The Author has his liberty granted him upon certain conditions.

MY gentleness and good behaviour had gained so far on the Emperor and his court, and indeed upon the army and people in general, that I began to conceive hopes of getting my liberty in a short time. I took all possible methods to cultivate this favourable disposition. The natives came by degrees to be less apprehensive of any danger from me. I would sometimes lie down, and let five or six of them dance on my hand. And at last the boys and girls would venture to come and play at hide and seek in my hair. I had now made a good progress in understanding and speaking their language. The Emperor had a mind one day to entertain me with several of the country shows, wherein they exceed all nations I have known, both for dexterity and magnificence. I was diverted with none so much as that of the rope-dancers, performed upon a slender white thread, extended about two foot and twelve inches from the ground. Upon which I shall desire liberty, with the reader's patience, to enlarge a little.

This diversion is only practised by those persons who are candidates for great employments, and high favour, at court. They are trained in this art from their youth, and are not always of noble birth, or liberal education. When a great office is vacant, either by death or disgrace, (which often happens) five or six of those candidates petition the Emperor to entertain his Majesty and the court with a dance on the rope, and whoever jumps the highest without falling, succeeds in the office. Very often the chief ministers themselves are commanded to show their

---

44. **court.** The following passage is a satire upon the court of England.

skill, and to convince the Emperor that they have not lost their faculty. Flimnap, the Treasurer, is allowed to cut a caper on the straight rope, at least an inch higher than any other lord in the whole empire. I have seen him do the summerset several times together upon a trencher fixed on the rope, which is no thicker than a common packthread in England. My friend Reldresal, principal Secretary for Private Affairs, is, in my opinion, if I am not partial, the second after the Treasurer; the rest of the great officers are much upon a par.

These diversions are often attended with fatal accidents, whereof great numbers are on record. I myself have seen two or three candidates break a limb. But the danger is much greater when the ministers themselves are commanded to show their dexterity; for, by contending to excel themselves and their fellows, they strain so far, that there is hardly one of them who hath not received a fall, and some of them two or three. I was assured that a year or two before my arrival, Flimnap would have infallibly broke his neck, if one of the King's cushions, that accidentally lay on the ground, had not weakened the force of his fall.

There is likewise another diversion, which is only shown before the Emperor and Empress, and first minister, upon particular occasions. The Emperor lays on the table three fine silken threads of six inches long. One is blue, the other red, and the third green. These threads are proposed as prizes for those persons whom the Emperor hath a mind to distinguish by a peculiar mark of his favour. The ceremony is performed in his Majesty's great chamber of state, where the candidates are to undergo a trial of dexterity very different from the former, and such as I have not observed the least resemblance of in any other country of the old or the new world. The Emperor holds a stick in his hands, both ends parallel to the horizon, while the candidates advancing one by one, sometimes leap over the stick, sometimes creep under it backwards and forwards several times, according as the stick is advanced or depressed. Sometimes the Emperor holds one end of the stick, and his first minister the other; sometimes the minister has it entirely to himself. Whoever performs his part with most agility, and holds out the longest in leaping and creeping, is rewarded with the blue-coloured silk; the red is given to the next, and the green to the third, which they all wear girt twice round about the middle; and you see few great persons about this court, who are not adorned with one of these girdles.

The horses of the army, and those of the royal stables, having been daily led before me, were no longer shy, but would come up to my very feet without starting. The riders would leap them over my hand as I held it on the ground, and one of the Emperor's huntsmen, upon a larger courser, took my foot, shoe and all; which was indeed a prodigious leap. I had the good fortune to divert the Emperor one day after a very extraordinary manner. I desired he would order several sticks of two foot high, and the thickness of an ordinary cane, to be brought me; whereupon his Majesty commanded the master of his woods to give directions accordingly; and the next morning six woodmen arrived with as many carriages, drawn by eight horses to each. I took nine of these sticks, fixing them firmly in the ground in a quadrangular figure, two foot and a half square. I took four other sticks, and tied them parallel at each corner, about two foot from the ground; then I fastened my handkerchief to the nine sticks that stood erect, and extended it on all sides, till it was tight as the top of a drum; and the four parallel sticks rising about five inches higher than the handkerchief, served as ledges on each side. When I had finished my work, I desired the Emperor to let a troop of his best horse, twenty-four in number, come and exercise upon this plain. His Majesty approved of the proposal, and I took them up, one by one, in my hands, ready mounted and armed, with the proper officers to exercise them. As soon as they got into order, they divided into two parties, performed mock skirmishes, discharged blunt arrows, drew their swords, fled and pursued, attacked and retired, and in short discovered the best military discipline I ever beheld. The parallel sticks secured them and their horses from falling over the stage; and the Emperor was so much delighted that he ordered this entertainment to be repeated several days, and once was pleased to be lifted up and give the word of command; and, with great difficulty, persuaded even the Empress herself to let me hold her in her close chair within two yards of the stage, from whence she was able to take a full view of the whole performance. It was my good fortune that no ill accident happened in these entertainments, only once a fiery horse, that belonged to one of the captains, pawing with his hoof, struck a hole in my handkerchief, and his foot slipping, he overthrew his rider and himself; but I immediately relieved them both, and covering the hole with one hand, I set down the troop with the other, in the same manner as I took

---

2. **Flimnap,** probably meant for Sir Robert Walpole.
28. **threads,** corresponding to the English orders of the Garter, the Bath, and the Thistle.

them up. The horse that fell was strained in the left shoulder, but the rider got no hurt, and I repaired my handkerchief as well as I could: however, I would not trust to the strength of it any more in such dangerous enterprises.

About two or three days before I was set at liberty, as I was entertaining the court with these kind of feats, there arrived an express to inform his Majesty, that some of his subjects riding near the place where I was first taken up, had seen a great black substance lying on the ground, very oddly shaped, extending its edges round as wide as his Majesty's bedchamber, and rising up in the middle as high as a man; that it was no living creature, as they at first apprehended, for it lay on the grass without motion, and some of them had walked round it several times: that by mounting upon each other's shoulders, they had got to the top, which was flat and even, and stamping upon it they found it was hollow within; that they humbly conceived it might be something belonging to the Man-Mountain; and if his Majesty pleased, they would undertake to bring it with only five horses. I presently knew what they meant, and was glad at heart to receive this intelligence. It seems upon my first reaching the shore after our shipwreck, I was in such confusion, that before I came to the place where I went to sleep, my hat, which I had fastened with a string to my head while I was rowing, and had stuck on all the time I was swimming, fell off after I came to land; the string, as I conjecture, breaking by some accident which I never observed, but thought my hat had been lost at sea. I intreated his Imperial Majesty to give orders it might be brought to me as soon as possible, describing to him the use and the nature of it: and the next day the waggoners arrived with it, but not in a very good condition; they had bored two holes in the brim, within an inch and half of the edge, and fastened two hooks in the holes; these hooks were tied by a long cord to the harness, and thus my hat was dragged along for above half an English mile; but the ground in that country being extremely smooth and level, it received less damage than I expected.

Two days after this adventure, the Emperor having ordered that part of his army which quarters in and about his metropolis to be in readiness, took a fancy of diverting himself in a very singular manner. He desired I would stand like a Colossus, with my legs as far asunder as I conveniently could. He then commanded his General (who was an old experienced leader, and a great patron of mine) to draw up the troops in close order, and march them under me; the foot by twenty-four in a breast, and the horse by sixteen, with drums beating, colours flying, and pikes advanced. This body consisted of three thousand foot, and a thousand horse. His Majesty gave orders, upon pain of death, that every soldier in his march should observe the strictest decency with regard to my person; which, however, could not prevent some of the younger officers from turning up their eyes as they passed under me. And, to confess the truth, my breeches were at that time in so ill a condition, that they afforded some opportunities for laughter and admiration.

I had sent so many memorials and petitions for my liberty, that his Majesty at length mentioned the matter, first in his cabinet, and then in a full council; where it was opposed by none, except Skyresh Bolgolam, who was pleased, without any provocation, to be my mortal enemy. But it was carried against him by the whole board, and confirmed by the Emperor. That minister was *Galbet*, or Admiral of the Realm, very much in his master's confidence, and a person well versed in affairs, but of a morose and sour complexion. However, he was at length persuaded to comply; but prevailed that the articles and conditions upon which I should be set free, and to which I must swear, should be drawn up by himself. These articles were brought to me by Skyresh Bolgolam in person, attended by two under-secretaries, and several persons of distinction. After they were read, I was demanded to swear to the performance of them; first in the manner of my own country, and afterwards in the method prescribed by their laws; which was to hold my right foot in my left hand, to place the middle finger of my right hand on the crown of my head, and my thumb on the tip of my right ear. But because the reader may be curious to have some idea of the style and manner of expression peculiar to that people, as well as to know the articles upon which I recovered my liberty, I have made a translation of the whole instrument word for word, as near as I was able, which I here offer to the public.

GOLBASTO MOMAREM EVLAME GURDILO SHEFIN MULLY ULLY GUE, most mighty Emperor of Lilliput, delight and terror of the universe, whose dominions extend five thousand *blustrugs* (about twelve miles in circumference) to the extremities of the globe; monarch of all monarchs, taller than the sons of men; whose feet press down to the centre, and whose head strikes against the sun; at whose nod the princes of the earth shake their knees; pleasant as the spring, comfortable as the summer, fruitful as autumn, dreadful as winter. His most sublime Majesty proposeth to the Man-Mountain, lately arrived to our celestial dominions, the following articles, which by a solemn oath he shall be obliged to perform.

First, The Man-Mountain shall not depart from our dominions, without our licence under our great seal.

2d, He shall not presume to come into our metropolis, without our express order; at which time, the inhabitants shall have two hours warning to keep within their doors.

3rd, The said Man-Mountain shall confine his walks to our principal high roads, and not offer to walk or lie down in a meadow or field of corn.

4th, As he walks the said roads, he shall take the utmost care not to trample upon the bodies of any of our loving subjects, their horses, or carriages, nor take any of our subjects into his hands, without their own consent.

5th, If an express requires extraordinary dispatch, the Man-Mountain shall be obliged to carry in his pocket the messenger and horse a six days journey once in every moon, and return the said messenger back (if so required) safe to our Imperial Presence.

6th, He shall be our ally against our enemies in the Island of Blefuscu and do his utmost to destroy their fleet, which is now preparing to invade us.

7th, That the said Man-Mountain shall, at his times of leisure, be aiding and assisting to our workmen, in helping to raise certain great stones, towards covering the wall of the principal park, and other our royal buildings.

8th, That the said Man-Mountain shall, in two moons' time, deliver in an exact survey of the circumference of our dominions by a computation of his own paces round the coast.

Lastly, That upon his solemn oath to observe all the above articles, the said Man-Mountain shall have a daily allowance of meat and drink sufficient for the support of 1728 of our subjects, with free access to our Royal Person, and other marks of our favour. Given at our Palace at Belfaborac the twelfth day of the ninety-first moon of our reign.

I swore and subscribed to these articles with great cheerfulness and content, although some of them were not so honourable as I could have wished; which proceeded wholly from the malice of Skyresh Bolgolam, the High-Admiral: whereupon my chains were immediately unlocked, and I was at full liberty; the Emperor himself in person did me the honour to be by at the whole ceremony.

27. Blefuscu, France.

I made my acknowledgements by prostrating myself at his Majesty's feet: but he commanded me to rise; and after many gracious expressions, which, to avoid the censure of vanity, I shall not repeat, he added, that he hoped I should prove a useful servant, and well deserve all the favours he had already conferred upon me, or might do for the future.

The reader may please to observe, that in the last article for the recovery of my liberty, the Emperor stipulates to allow me a quantity of meat and drink sufficient for the support of 1728 Lilliputians. Some time after, asking a friend at court how they came to fix on that determinate number, he told me that his Majesty's mathematicians, having taken the height of my body by the help of a quadrant, and finding it to exceed theirs in the proportion of twelve to one they concluded from the similarity of their bodies, that mine must contain at least 1728 of theirs, and consequently would require as much food as was necessary to support that number of Lilliputians. By which, the reader may conceive an idea of the ingenuity of that people, as well as the prudent and exact economy of so great a prince.

Chapter 4

Mildendo, *the metropolis of* Lilliput, *described, together with the Emperor's palace. A conversation between the Author and a principal Secretary, concerning the affairs of that empire. The Author's offer to serve the Emperor in his wars.*

THE first request I made after I had obtained my liberty, was, that I might have licence to see Mildendo, the metropolis; which the Emperor easily granted me, but with a special charge to do no hurt either to the inhabitants or their houses. The people had notice by proclamation of my design to visit the town. The wall which encompassed it, is two foot and a half high, and at least eleven inches broad, so that a coach and horses may be driven very safely round it; and it is flanked with strong towers at ten foot distance. I stepped over the great Western Gate, and passed very gently, and sideling through the two principal streets, only in my short waistcoat, for fear of damaging the roofs and eaves of the houses with the skirts of my coat. I walked with the utmost circumspection, to avoid treading on any stragglers, that might remain in the streets, although the orders were very strict, that all people should keep in their houses, at their own peril. The garret windows and tops of houses were so crowded with spectators, that I thought in

45. sideling, old form.

all my travels I had not seen a more populous place. The city is an exact square, each side of the wall being five hundred foot long. The two great streets, which run cross and divide it into four quarters, are five foot wide. The lanes and alleys, which I could not enter, but only viewed them as I passed, are from twelve to eighteen inches. The town is capable of holding five hundred thousand souls. The houses are from three to five stories. The shops and markets well provided.

The Emperor's palace is in the centre of the city, where the two great streets meet. It is inclosed by a wall of two foot high, and twenty foot distant from the buildings. I had his Majesty's permission to step over this wall; and the space being so wide between that and the palace, I could easily view it on every side. The outward court is a square of forty foot, and includes two other courts: in the inmost are the royal apartments, which I was very desirous to see, but found it extremely difficult; for the great gates, from one square into another, were but eighteen inches high, and seven inches wide. Now the buildings of the outer court were at least five foot high, and it was impossible for me to stride over them without infinite damage to the pile, though the walls were strongly built of hewn stone, and four inches thick. At the same time the Emperor had a great desire that I should see the magnificence of his palace; but this I was not able to do till three days after, which I spent in cutting down with my knife some of the largest trees in the royal park, about an hundred yards distant from the city. Of these trees I made two stools, each about three foot high, and strong enough to bear my weight. The people having received notice a second time, I went again through the city to the palace, with my two stools in my hands. When I came to the side of the outer court, I stood upon one stool, and took the other in my hand: this I lifted over the roof, and gently set it down on the space between the first and second court, which was eight foot wide. I then stept over the buildings very conveniently from one stool to the other, and drew up the first after me with a hooked stick. By this contrivance I got into the inmost court; and lying down upon my side, I applied my face to the windows of the middle stories, which were left open on purpose, and discovered the most splendid apartments that can be imagined. There I saw the Empress and the young Princes, in their several lodgings, with their chief attendants about them. Her Imperial Majesty was pleased to smile very graciously upon me, and gave me out of the window her hand to kiss.

But I shall not anticipate the reader with farther descriptions of this kind, because I reserve them for a greater work, which is now almost ready for the press, containing a general description of this empire, from its first erection, through a long series of princes, with a particular account of their wars and politics, laws, learning, and religion: their plants and animals, their peculiar manners and customs, with other matters very curious and useful; my chief design at present being only to relate such events and transactions as happened to the public, or to myself, during a residence of about nine months in that empire.

One morning, about a fortnight after I had obtained my liberty, Reldresal, principal Secretary (as they style him) of Private Affairs, came to my house attended only by one servant. He ordered his coach to wait at a distance, and desired I would give him an hour's audience; which I readily consented to, on account of his quality and personal merits, as well as the many good offices he had done me during my solicitations at court. I offered to lie down, that he might the more conveniently reach my ear; but he chose rather to let me hold him in my hand during our conversation. He began with compliments on my liberty; said he might pretend to some merit in it: but, however, added, that if it had not been for the present situation of things at court, perhaps I might not have obtained it so soon. "For," said he, "as flourishing a condition as we may appear to be in to foreigners, we labour under two mighty evils; a violent faction at home, and the danger of an invasion by a most potent enemy from abroad. As to the first, you are to understand, that for about seventy moons past there have been two struggling parties in this empire, under the names of *Tramecksan* and *Slamecksan*, from the high and low heels on their shoes, by which they distinguish themselves. It is alleged indeed, that the high heels are most agreeable to our ancient constitution: but however this be, his Majesty hath determined to make use of only low heels in the administration of the government, and all offices in the gift of the Crown, as you cannot but observe; and particularly, that his Majesty's Imperial heels are lower at least by a *drurr* than any of his court; (*drurr* is a measure about the fourteenth part of an inch). The animosities between these two parties run so high, that they will neither eat nor drink, nor talk with each other. We compute the *Tramecksan*, or High-Heels, to exceed us in number; but the power is wholly on our side. We apprehend

39. **themselves,** the English Tories and Whigs.   42. **low heels,** the Whigs, whom King George I of England favored.

his Imperial Highness, the Heir to the Crown, to have some tendency towards the High-Heels; at least we can plainly discover one of his heels higher than the other, which gives him a hobble in his gait. Now, in the midst of these intestine disquiets, we are threatened with an invasion from the Island of Blefuscu, which is the other great empire of the universe, almost as large and powerful as this of his Majesty. For as to what we have heard you affirm, that there are other kingdoms and states in the world inhabited by human creatures as large as yourself, our philosophers are in much doubt, and would rather conjecture that you dropped from the moon, or one of the stars; because it is certain, that an hundred mortals of your bulk would, in a short time, destroy all the fruits and cattle of his Majesty's dominions. Besides, our histories of six thousand moons make no mention of any other regions, than the two great empires of Lilliput and Blefuscu. Which two mighty powers have, as I was going to tell you, been engaged in a most obstinate war for six and thirty moons past. It began upon the following occasion. It is allowed on all hands, that the primitive way of breaking eggs, before we eat them, was upon the larger end: but his present Majesty's grandfather, while he was a boy, going to eat an egg, and breaking it according to the ancient practice, happened to cut one of his fingers. Whereupon the Emperor his father published an edict, commanding all his subjects, upon great penalties, to break the smaller end of their eggs. The people so highly resented this law, that our histories tell us there have been six rebellions raised on that account; wherein one Emperor lost his life, and another his crown. These civil commotions were constantly fomented by the monarchs of Blefuscu; and when they were quelled, the exiles always fled for refuge to that empire. It is computed, that eleven thousand persons have, at several times, suffered death, rather than submit to break their eggs at the smaller end. Many hundred large volumes have been published upon this controversy: but the books of the Big-Endians have been long forbidden, and the whole party rendered incapable by law of holding employments. During the course of these troubles, the Emperors of Blefuscu did frequently expostulate by their ambassadors, accusing us of making a schism of religion, by offending against a fundamental doctrine of our great prophet Lustrog, in the fifty-fourth chapter of the Blundecral (which is their Alcoran). This, however, is thought to be a mere strain upon the text: for the words are these; *That all true believers break their eggs at the convenient end:* and which is the convenient end, seems, in my humble opinion, to be left to every man's conscience, or at least in the power of the chief magistrate to determine. Now the Big-Endian exiles have found so much credit in the Emperor of Blefuscu's court, and so much private assistance and encouragement from their party here at home, that a bloody war has been carried on between the two empires for six and thirty moons with various success; during which time we have lost forty capital ships, and a much greater number of smaller vessels, together with thirty thousand of our best seamen and soldiers; and the damage received by the enemy is reckoned to be somewhat greater than ours. However, they have now equipped a numerous fleet, and are just preparing to make a descent upon us; and his Imperial Majesty, placing great confidence in your valour and strength, has commanded me to lay this account of his affairs before you."

I desired the Secretary to present my humble duty to the Emperor, and to let him know, that I thought it would not become me, who was a foreigner, to interfere with parties; but I was ready, with the hazard of my life, to defend his person and state against all invaders.

Chapter 5

The Author, by an extraordinary stratagem, prevents an invasion. A high title of honour is conferred upon him. Ambassadors arrive from the Emperor of Blefuscu, *and sue for peace. The Empress's apartment on fire by an accident; the Author instrumental in saving the rest of the palace.*

THE Empire of Blefuscu is an island situated to the north north-east side of Lilliput, from whence it is parted only by a channel of eight hundred yards wide. I had not yet seen it, and upon this notice of an intended invasion, I avoided appearing on that side of the coast, for fear of being discovered by some of the enemy's ships, who had received no intelligence of me, all intercourse between the two empires having been strictly forbidden during the war, upon pain of death, and an embargo laid by our Emperor upon all vessels whatsoever. I communicated to his Majesty a project I had formed of seizing the enemy's whole fleet: which, as our scouts assured us, lay at anchor in the harbour ready to sail with the first fair wind. I consulted the most experienced seamen, upon the depth of the channel, which they had often

---

26. **grandfather,** Henry VIII.   34–35. **one Emperor . . . another,** Charles I and James II.   43. **Big-Endians,** Roman Catholics; **Little Endians,** Protestants.

plumbed, who told me, that in the middle at high-water it was seventy *glumgluffs* deep, which is about six foot of European measure; and the rest of it fifty *glumgluffs* at most. I walked towards the north-east coast over against Blefuscu; and lying down behind a hillock, took out my small pocket perspective-glass, and viewed the enemy's fleet at anchor, consisting of about fifty men of war, and a great number of transports: I then came back to my house, and gave order (for which I had a warrant) for a great quantity of the strongest cable and bars of iron. The cable was about as thick as packthread, and the bars of the length and size of a knitting-needle. I trebled the cable to make it stronger, and for the same reason I twisted three of the iron bars together, binding the extremities into a hook. Having thus fixed fifty hooks to as many cables, I went back to the north-east coast, and putting off my coat, shoes, and stockings, walked into the sea in my leathern jerkin, about half an hour before high water. I waded with what haste I could, and swam in the middle about thirty yards till I felt ground; I arrived at the fleet in less than half an hour. The enemy was so frighted when they saw me, that they leaped out of their ships, and swam to shore, where there could not be fewer than thirty thousand souls. I then took my tackling, and fastening a hook to the hole at the prow of each, I tied all the cords together at the end. While I was thus employed, the enemy discharged several thousand arrows, many of which stuck in my hands and face; and besides the excessive smart, gave me much disturbance in my work. My greatest apprehension was for my eyes, which I should have infallibly lost, if I had not suddenly thought of an expedient. I kept among other little necessaries a pair of spectacles in a private pocket, which, as I observed before, had scaped the Emperor's searchers. These I took out and fastened as strongly as I could upon my nose, and thus armed went on boldly with my work in spite of the enemy's arrows, many of which struck against the glasses of my spectacles, but without any other effect, further than a little to discompose them. I had now fastened all the hooks, and taking the knot in my hand, began to pull; but not a ship would stir, for they were all too fast held by their anchors, so that the boldest part of my enterprise remained. I therefore let go the cord, and leaving the hooks fixed to the ships, I resolutely cut with my knife the cables that fastened the anchors, receiving about two hundred shots in my face and hands; then I took up the knotted end of the cables, to which my hooks were tied, and with great ease drew fifty of the enemy's largest men of war after me.

The Blefuscudians, who had not the least imagination of what I intended, were at first confounded with astonishment. They had seen me cut the cables, and thought my design was only to let the ships run a-drift, or fall foul on each other: but when they perceived the whole fleet moving in order, and saw me pulling at the end, they set up such a scream of grief and despair, that it is almost impossible to describe or conceive. When I had got out of danger, I stopped awhile to pick out the arrows that stuck in my hands and face; and rubbed on some of the same ointment that was given me at my first arrival, as I have formerly mentioned. I then took off my spectacles, and waiting about an hour, till the tide was a little fallen, I waded through the middle with my cargo, and arrived safe at the royal port of Lilliput.

The Emperor and his whole court stood on the shore, expecting the issue of this great adventure. They saw the ships move forward in a large half-moon, but could not discern me, who was up to my breast in water. When I advanced in the middle of the channel, they were yet in more pain, because I was under water to my neck. The Emperor concluded me to be drowned, and that the enemy's fleet was approaching in a hostile manner: but he was soon eased of his fears, for the channel growing shallower every step I made, I came in a short time within hearing, and holding up the end of the cable by which the fleet was fastened, I cried in a loud voice, *Long live the most puissant Emperor of Lilliput!* This great prince received me at my landing with all possible encomiums, and created me a *Nardac* upon the spot, which is the highest title of honour among them.

His Majesty desired I would take some other opportunity of bringing all the rest of his enemy's ships into his ports. And so unmeasureable is the ambition of princes, that he seemed to think of nothing less than reducing the whole empire of Blefuscu into a province and governing it by a viceroy; of destroying the Big-Endian exiles, and compelling the people to break the smaller end of their eggs, by which he would remain the sole monarch of the whole world. But I endeavoured to divert him from this design, by many arguments drawn from the topics of policy as well as justice; and I plainly protested, that I would never be an instrument of bringing a free and brave people into slavery. And when the matter was debated in council, the wisest part of the ministry were of my opinion.

38. **scaped,** old form.

This open bold declaration of mine was so opposite to the schemes and politics of his Imperial Majesty, that he could never forgive it; he mentioned it in a very artful manner at council, where I was told that some of the wisest appeared, at least by their silence, to be of my opinion; but others, who were my secret enemies, could not forbear some expressions, which by a side-wind reflected on me. And from this time began an intrigue between his Majesty and a junto of ministers maliciously bent against me, which broke out in less than two months, and had like to have ended in my utter destruction. Of so little weight are the greatest services to princes, when put into the balance with a refusal to gratify their passions.

About three weeks after this exploit, there arrived a solemn embassy from Blefuscu, with humble offers of a peace; which was soon concluded upon conditions very advantageous to our Emperor, wherewith I shall not trouble the reader. There were six ambassadors, with a train of about five hundred persons, and their entry was very magnificent, suitable to the grandeur of their master, and the importance of their business. When their treaty was finished, wherein I did them several good offices by the credit I now had, or at least appeared to have at court, their Excellencies, who were privately told how much I had been their friend, made me a visit in form. They began with many compliments upon my valour and generosity, invited me to that kingdom in the Emperor their master's name, and desired me to show them some proofs of my prodigious strength, of which they had heard so many wonders; wherein I readily obliged them, but shall not trouble the reader with the particulars.

When I had for some time entertained their Excellencies, to their infinite satisfaction and surprise, I desired they would do me the honour to present my most humble respects to the Emperor their master, the renown of whose virtues had so justly filled the whole world with admiration, and whose royal person I resolved to attend before I returned to my own country: accordingly, the next time I had the honour to see our Emperor, I desired his general licence to wait on the Blefuscudian monarch, which he was pleased to grant me, as I could perceive, in a very cold manner; but could not guess the reason, till I had a whisper from a certain person, that Flimnap and Bolgolam had represented my intercourse with those ambassadors as a mark of disaffection, from which I am sure my heart was wholly free. And this was the first time I began to conceive some imperfect idea of courts and ministers.

It is to be observed, that these ambassadors spoke to me by an interpreter, the languages of both empires differing as much from each other as any two in Europe, and each nation priding itself upon the antiquity, beauty, and energy of their own tongues, with an avowed contempt for that of their neighbour; yet our Emperor, standing upon the advantage he had got by seizure of their fleet, obliged them to deliver their credentials, and make their speech in the Lilliputian tongue. And it must be confessed, that from the great intercourse of trade and commerce between both realms, from the continual reception of exiles, which is mutual among them, and from the custom in each empire to send their young nobility and richer gentry to the other, in order to polish themselves by seeing the world, and understanding men and manners; there are few persons of distinction, or merchants, or seamen, who dwell in the maritime parts, but what can hold conversation in both tongues; as I found some weeks after, when I went to pay my respects to the Emperor of Blefuscu, which in the midst of great misfortunes, through the malice of my enemies, proved a very happy adventure to me, as I shall relate in its proper place.

The reader may remember, that when I signed those articles upon which I recovered my liberty, there were some which I disliked upon account of their being too servile, neither could anything but an extreme necessity have forced me to submit. But being now a *Nardac* of the highest rank in that empire, such offices were looked upon as below my dignity, and the Emperor (to do him justice) never once mentioned them to me. However, it was not long before I had an opportunity of doing his Majesty, at least, as I then thought, a most signal service. I was alarmed at midnight with the cries of many hundred people at my door; by which being suddenly awaked, I was in some kind of terror. I heard the word *burglum* repeated incessantly: several of the Emperor's court, making their way through the crowd, entreated me to come immediately to the palace, where her Imperial Majesty's apartment was on fire, by the carelessness of a maid of honour, who fell asleep while she was reading a romance. I got up in an instant; and orders being given to clear the way before me, and it being likewise a moonshine night, I made a shift to get to the Palace without trampling on any of the people. I found they had already applied ladders to the walls of the apartment, and were well provided with buckets, but the water was at some distance. These buckets were about the size of a large thimble, and the poor people supplied me with them as fast as they could; but the flame was so violent that they did little good. I might easily have stifled it with my coat, which I unfortunately left behind me for haste, and came away only in my leathern jerkin. The case seemed wholly desperate and deplorable; and this magnificent palace would have infallibly been burnt down to the ground, if, by a presence of mind, unusual to me, I had not suddenly thought of an expedient. I had the evening before drunk plentifully of a most delicious wine, called *glimigrim*, (the Blefuscudians call it *flunec*, but ours is esteemed the better sort) which is very diuretic. By the luckiest chance in the world, I had not discharged myself of any part of it. The heat I had contracted by coming very near the flames, and by labouring to quench them, made the wine begin to operate by urine; which I voided in such a quantity, and applied so well to the proper places, that in three minutes the fire was wholly extinguished, and the rest of that noble pile, which had cost so many ages in erecting, preserved from destruction.

It was now day-light, and I returned to my house without waiting to congratulate with the Emperor: because, although I had done a very eminent piece of service, yet I could not tell how his Majesty might resent the manner by which I had performed it: for, by the fundamental laws of the realm, it is capital in any person, of what quality soever, to make water within the precincts of the palace. But I was a little comforted by a message from his Majesty, that he would give orders to the Grand Justiciary for passing my pardon in form; which, however, I could not obtain. And I was privately assured, that the Empress, conceiving the greatest abhorrence of what I had done, removed to the most distant side of the court, firmly resolved that those buildings should never be repaired for her use; and, in the presence of her chief confidents could not forbear vowing revenge.

Chapter 6

Of the inhabitants of Lilliput; *their learning, laws, and customs, the manner of educating their children. The Author's way of living in that country. His vindication of a great lady.*

ALTHOUGH I intend to leave the description of this empire to a particular treatise, yet in the mean time I am content to gratify the curious reader with some general ideas. As the common size of the natives is somewhat under six inches high, so there is an exact proportion in all other animals, as well as plants and trees: for instance, the tallest horses and oxen are between four and five inches in height, the sheep an inch and a half, more or less: their geese about the bigness of a sparrow, and so the several gradations downwards till you come to the smallest, which, to my sight, were almost invisible; but nature hath adapted the eyes of the Lilliputians to all objects proper for their view: they see with great exactness, but at no great distance. And to show the sharpness of their sight towards objects that are near, I have been much pleased with observing a cook pulling a lark, which was not so large as a common fly; and a young girl threading an invisible needle with invisible silk. Their tallest trees are about seven foot high: I mean some of those in the great royal park, the tops whereof I could but just reach with my fist clinched. The other vegetables are in the same proportion; but this I leave to the reader's imagination.

I shall say but little at present of their learning, which for many ages hath flourished in all its branches among them: but their manner of writing is very peculiar, being neither from the left to the right, like the Europeans; nor from the right to the left, like the Arabians; nor from up to down, like the Chinese; nor from down to up, like the Cascagians; but aslant from one corner of the paper to the other, like ladies in England.

They bury their dead with their heads directly downwards, because they hold an opinion, that in eleven thousand moons they are all to rise again, in which period the earth (which they conceive to be flat) will turn upside down, and by this means they shall, at their resurrection, be found ready standing on their feet. The learned among them confess the absurdity of this doctrine, but the practice still continues, in compliance to the vulgar.

There are some laws and customs in this empire very peculiar; and if they were not so directly contrary to those of my own dear country, I should be tempted to say a little in their justification. It is only to be wished, that they were as well executed. The first I shall mention, relates to informers. All crimes against the state are punished here with the utmost severity; but if the person accused maketh his innocence plainly to appear upon his trial, the accuser is immediately put to an ignominious death; and out of his goods or lands, the innocent person is quadruply recompensed for the loss of his time, for the danger he underwent, for the hardship of his imprisonment, and for all the charges he hath been at in making his defence. Or, if that fund be deficient, it is largely supplied by the Crown. The Emperor does also confer on him some public mark of his favour, and proclamation is made of his innocence through the whole city.

They look upon fraud as a greater crime than theft, and therefore seldom fail to punish it with death; for they allege, that care and vigilance, with a very common understanding, may preserve a man's goods from thieves, but honesty has no fence against superior cunning; and since it is necessary that there should be a perpetual intercourse of buying and selling, and dealing upon credit, where fraud is permitted and connived at, or hath no law to punish it, the honest dealer is always undone, and the knave gets the advantage. I remember when I was once interceding with the Emperor for a criminal who had wronged his master of a great sum of money, which he had received by order, and ran away with; and happening to tell his Majesty, by way of extenuation, that it was only a breach of trust; the Emperor thought it monstrous in me to offer, as a defence, the greatest aggravation of the crime: and truly I had little to say in return, farther than the common answer, that different nations had different customs; for, I confess, I was heartily ashamed.

Although we usually call reward and punishment the two hinges upon which all government turns, yet I could never observe this maxim to be put in practice by any nation except that of Lilliput. Whoever can there bring sufficient proof that he hath strictly observed the laws of his country for seventy-three moons, hath a claim to certain privileges, according to his quality and condition of life, with a proportionable sum of money out of a fund appropriated for that use: he likewise acquires the title of *Snilpall*, or Legal, which is added to his name, but does not descend to his posterity. And these people thought it a prodigious defect of policy among us, when I told them that our laws were enforced only by penalties, without any mention of reward. It is upon this account that the image of Justice, in their courts of judicature, is formed with six eyes, two before, as many behind, and on each side one, to signify circumspection; with a bag of gold open in her right hand, and a sword sheathed in her left, to show she is more disposed to reward than to punish.

In choosing persons for all employments, they have more regard to good morals than to great abilities; for, since government is necessary to mankind, they believe that the common size of human understandings is fitted to some station or other, and that Providence never intended to make the management of public affairs a mystery, to be comprehended only by a few persons of sublime genius, of which there seldom are three born in an age: but they suppose truth, justice, temperance, and the like, to be in every man's power; the practice of which virtues, assisted by experience and a good intention, would qualify any man for the service of his country, except where a course of study is required. But they thought the want of moral virtues was so far from being supplied by superior endowments of the mind, that employments could never be put into such dangerous hands as those of persons so qualified; and at least, that the mistakes committed by ignorance in a virtuous disposition, would never be of such fatal consequence to the public weal, as the practices of a man whose inclinations led him to be corrupt, and had great abilities to manage, and multiply, and defend his corruptions.

In like manner, the disbelief of a Divine Providence renders a man uncapable of holding any public station; for, since kings avow themselves to be the deputies of Providence, the Lilliputians think nothing can be more absurd than for a prince to employ such men as disown the authority under which he acts.

In relating these and the following laws, I would only be understood to mean the original institutions, and not the most scandalous corruptions into which these people are fallen by the degenerate nature of man. For as to that infamous practice of acquiring great employments by dancing on the ropes, or badges of favour and distinction by leaping over sticks and creeping under them, the reader is to observe, that they were first introduced by the grandfather of the Emperor now reigning, and grew to the present height, by the gradual increase of party and faction.

Ingratitude is among them a capital crime, as we read it to have been in some other countries: for they reason thus, that whoever makes ill returns to his benefactor, must needs be a common enemy to the rest of mankind, from whom he hath received no obligation, and therefore such a man is not fit to live.

Their notions relating to the duties of parents and children differ extremely from ours. For, since the conjunction of male and female is founded upon the great law of nature, in order to propagate and continue the species, the Lilliputians will needs have it, that men and women are joined together like other animals, by the motives of concupiscence; and that their tenderness towards their young proceeds from the like natural principle: for which reason they will never allow, that a child is under any obligation to his father for begetting him, or to his mother for bringing him into the world, which, considering the

33. **grandfather,** James I.

miseries of human life, was neither a benefit in itself, nor intended so by his parents, whose thoughts in their love-encounters were otherwise employed. Upon these, and the like reasonings, their opinion is, that parents are the last of all others to be trusted with the education of their own children; and therefore they have in every town public nurseries, where all parents, except cottagers and labourers, are obliged to send their infants of both sexes to be reared and educated when they come to the age of twenty moons, at which time they are supposed to have some rudiments of docility. These schools are of several kinds, suited to different qualities, and to both sexes. They have certain professors well skilled in preparing children for such a condition of life as befits the rank of their parents, and their own capacities as well as inclinations. I shall first say something of the male nurseries, and then of the female.

The nurseries for males of noble or eminent birth, are provided with grave and learned professors, and their several deputies. The clothes and food of the children are plain and simple. They are bred up in the principles of honour, justice, courage, modesty, clemency, religion, and love of their country; they are always employed in some business, except in the times of eating and sleeping, which are very short, and two hours for diversions, consisting of bodily exercises. They are dressed by men till four years of age, and then are obliged to dress themselves, although their quality be ever so great; and the women attendants, who are aged proportionably to ours at fifty, perform only the most menial offices. They are never suffered to converse with servants, but go together in small or greater numbers to take their diversions, and always in the presence of a professor, or one of his deputies; whereby they avoid those early bad impressions of folly and vice to which our children are subject. Their parents are suffered to see them only twice a year; the visit is to last but an hour. They are allowed to kiss the child at meeting and parting; but a professor, who always stands by on those occasions, will not suffer them to whisper, or use any fondling expressions, or bring any presents of toys, sweetmeats, and the like.

The pension from each family for the education and entertainment of a child, upon failure of due payment, is levied by the Emperor's officers.

The nurseries for children of ordinary gentlemen, merchants, traders, and handicrafts, are managed proportionably after the same manner; only those designed for trades, are put out apprentices at eleven years old, whereas those of persons of quality continue in their exercises till fifteen, which answers to one and twenty with us: but the confinement is gradually lessened for the last three years.

In the female nurseries, the young girls of quality are educated much like the males, only they are dressed by orderly servants of their own sex; but always in the presence of a professor or deputy, till they come to dress themselves, which is at five years old. And if it be found that these nurses ever presume to entertain the girl with frightful or foolish stories, or the common follies practised by chambermaids among us, they are publicly whipped thrice about the city, imprisoned for a year, and banished for life to the most desolate part of the country. Thus the young ladies there are as much ashamed of being cowards and fools, as the men, and despise all personal ornaments beyond decency and cleanliness: neither did I perceive any difference in their education, made by their difference of sex, only that the exercises of the females were not altogether so robust; and that some rules were given them relating to domestic life, and a smaller compass of learning was enjoined them: for their maxim is, that among people of quality, a wife should be always a reasonable and agreeable companion, because she cannot always be young. When the girls are twelve years old, which among them is the marriageable age, their parents or guardians take them home, with great expressions of gratitude to the professors, and seldom without tears of the young lady and her companions.

In the nurseries of females of the meaner sort, the children are instructed in all kinds of works proper for their sex, and their several degrees: those intended for apprentices, are dismissed at seven years old, the rest are kept to eleven.

The meaner families who have children at these nurseries, are obliged, besides their annual pension, which is as low as possible, to return to the steward of the nursery a small monthly share of their gettings, to be a portion for the child; and therefore all parents are limited in their expenses by the law. For the Lilliputians think nothing can be more unjust, than for people, in subservience to their own appetites, to bring children into the world, and leave the burthen of supporting them on the public. As to persons of quality, they give security to appropriate a certain sum for each child, suitable to their condition; and these funds are always managed with good husbandry, and the most exact justice.

The cottagers and labourers keep their children at home, their business being only to till and cultivate the earth, and therefore their education is of little consequence to the public; but the old and dis-

---

12. **docility,** teachableness.   46. **pension,** tuition.

eased among them are supported by hospitals: for begging is a trade unknown in this empire.

And here it may perhaps divert the curious reader, to give some account of my domestic, and my manner of living in this country, during a residence of nine months and thirteen days. Having a head mechanically turned, and being likewise forced by necessity, I had made for myself a table and chair convenient enough, out of the largest trees in the royal park. Two hundred sempstresses were employed to make me shirts, and linen for my bed and table, all of the strongest and coarsest kind they could get; which, however, they were forced to quilt together in several folds, for the thickest was some degrees finer than lawn. Their linen was usually three inches wide, and three foot make a piece. The sempstresses took my measure as I lay on the ground, one standing at my neck, and another at my mid-leg, with a strong cord extended, that each held by the end, while the third measured the length of the cord with a rule an inch long. Then they measured my right thumb, and desired no more; for by a mathematical computation, that twice round the thumb is once round the wrist, and so on to the neck and the waist, and by the help of my old shirt, which I displayed on the ground before them for a pattern, they fitted me exactly. Three hundred tailors were employed in the same manner to make me clothes; but they had another contrivance for taking my measure. I kneeled down, and they raised a ladder from the ground to my neck; upon this ladder one of them mounted, and let fall a plumb-line from my collar to the floor, which just answered the length of my coat: but my waist and arms I measured myself. When my clothes were finished, which was done in my house, (for the largest of theirs would not have been able to hold them) they looked like the patch-work made by the ladies in England, only that mine were all of a color.

I had three hundred cooks to dress my victuals, in little convenient huts built about my house, where they and their families lived, and prepared me two dishes a-piece. I took up twenty waiters in my hand, and placed them on the table: an hundred more attended below on the ground, some with dishes of meat, and some with barrels of wine, and other liquors, slung on their shoulders; all which the waiters above drew up as I wanted, in a very ingenious manner, by certain cords, as we draw the bucket up a well in Europe. A dish of their meat was a good mouthful, and a barrel of their liquor a reasonable draught. Their mutton yields to ours, but their beef is excellent. I have had a sirloin so large, that I have been forced to make three bits of it; but this is rare. My servants were astonished to see me eat it bones and all, as in our country we do the leg of a lark. Their geese and turkeys I usually eat at a mouthful, and I must confess they far exceed ours. Of their smaller fowl I could take up twenty or thirty at the end of my knife.

One day his Imperial Majesty, being informed of my way of living, desired that himself and his Royal Consort, with the young Princes of the blood of both sexes, might have the happiness (as he was pleased to call it) of dining with me. They came accordingly, and I placed them in chairs of state on my table, just over against me, with their guards about them. Flimnap, the Lord High Treasurer, attended there likewise with his white staff; and I observed he often looked on me with a sour countenance, which I would not seem to regard, but eat more than usual, in honour to my dear country, as well as to fill the court with admiration. I have some private reasons to believe, that this visit from his Majesty gave Flimnap an opportunity of doing me ill offices to his master. That minister had always been my secret enemy, though he outwardly caressed me more than was usual to the moroseness of his nature. He represented to the Emperor the low condition of his treasury; that he was forced to take up money at great discount; that exchequer bills would not circulate under nine per cent. below par; that in short I had cost his Majesty above a million and a half of *sprugs* (their greatest gold coin, about the bigness of a spangle); and upon the whole, that it would be advisable in the Emperor to take the first fair occasion of dismissing me.

I am here obliged to vindicate the reputation of an excellent lady, who was an innocent sufferer upon my account. The Treasurer took a fancy to be jealous of his wife, from the malice of some evil tongues, who informed him that her Grace had taken a violent affection for my person; and the court-scandal ran for some time, that she once came privately to my lodging. This I solemnly declare to be a most infamous falsehood, without any grounds, farther than that her Grace was pleased to treat me with all innocent marks of freedom and friendship. I own she came often to my house, but always publicly, nor ever without three more in the coach, who were usually her sister and young daughter, and some particular acquaintance; but this was common to many other ladies of the court. And I still appeal to my servants round, whether they at any time saw a coach at my door without knowing what persons were in it. On those occasions, when a servant had given me notice, my custom was to go immediately to the door; and, after paying my respects, to take up the coach and two horses very carefully in my hands, (for, if there were six horses, the postillion always unharnessed four) and place them on a table, where I had fixed a moveable rim quite round, of five inches high, to prevent accidents. And I have often had four coaches and horses at once on my table full of company, while I sat in my chair leaning my face towards them; and when I was engaged with one set, the coachmen would gently drive the others round my table. I have passed many an afternoon very agreeably in these conversations. But I defy the Treasurer, or his two informers (I will name them, and let them make their best of it) Clustril and Drunlo, to prove that any person ever came to me *incognito*, except the secretary Reldresal, who was sent by express command of his Imperial Majesty, as I have before related. I should not have dwelt so long upon this particular, if it had not been a point wherein the reputation of a great lady is so nearly concerned, to say nothing of my own; though I then had the honour to be a *Nardac*, which the Treasurer himself is not; for all the world knows he is only a *Glumglum*, a title inferior by one degree, as that of a Marquis is to a Duke in England, although I allow he preceded me in right of his post. These false informations, which I afterwards came to the knowledge of, by an accident not proper to mention, made Flimnap, the Treasurer, show his lady for some time an ill countenance, and me a worse; and although he were at last undeceived and reconciled to her, yet I lost all credit with him, and found my interest decline very fast with the Emperor himself, who was indeed too much governed by that favourite.

Chapter 7

The Author, being informed of a design to accuse him of high-treason, makes his escape to Blefuscu. *His reception there.*

BEFORE I proceed to give an account of my leaving this kingdom, it may be proper to inform the reader of a private intrigue which had been for two months forming against me.

I had been hitherto all my life a stranger to courts, for which I was unqualified by the meanness of my condition. I had indeed heard and read enough of the dispositions of great princes and ministers; but never expected to have found such terrible effects of them in so remote a country, governed, as I thought, by very different maxims from those in Europe.

When I was just preparing to pay my attendance on the Emperor of Blefuscu, a considerable person at court (to whom I had been very serviceable at a time when he lay under the highest displeasure of his Imperial Majesty) came to my house very privately at night in a close chair, and without sending his name, desired admittance. The chair-men were dismissed; I put the chair, with his Lordship in it, into my coat-pocket: and giving orders to a trusty servant to say I was indisposed and gone to sleep, I fastened the door of my house, placed the chair on the table, according to my usual custom, and sat down by it. After the common salutations were over, observing his Lordship's countenance full of concern, and enquiring into the reason, he desired I would hear him with patience in a matter that highly concerned my honour and my life. His speech was to the following effect, for I took notes of it as soon as he left me:

"You are to know," said he, "that several Committees of Council have been lately called in the most private manner on your account; and it is but two days since his Majesty came to a full resolution.

"You are very sensible that Skyresh Bolgolam (*Galbet*, or High-Admiral) hath been your mortal enemy almost ever since your arrival. His original reasons I know not; but his hatred is much increased since your great success against Blefuscu, by which his glory, as Admiral, is obscured. This Lord, in conjunction with Flimnap the High-Treasurer, whose enmity against you is notorious on account of his lady, Limtoc the General, Lalcon the Chamberlain, and Balmuff the Grand Justiciary, have prepared articles of impeachment against you, for treason, and other capital crimes."

This preface made me so impatient, being conscious of my own merits and innocence, that I was going to interrupt; when he entreated me to be silent, and thus proceeded:

"Out of gratitude for the favours you have done me, I procured information of the whole proceedings, and a copy of the articles, wherein I venture my head for your service.

Articles of Impeachment against Quinbus Flestrin (*the* Man-Mountain.)

ARTICLE I

"'Whereas, by a statute made in the reign of his Imperial Majesty Calin Deffar Plune, it is enacted, that whoever shall make water within the precincts of the royal palace, shall be liable to the pains and penalties of high treason; notwithstanding, the said Quinbus Flestrin, in open breach of the said law, under colour of extinguishing the fire kindled in the apartment of his Majesty's most dear Imperial Consort, did maliciously, traitorously, and devilishly, by discharge of his urine, put out the said fire kindled in the said apartment, lying and being within the precincts of the said royal palace, against the statute in that case provided, *etc.* against the duty, *etc.*

ARTICLE II

"'That the said Quinbus Flestrin having brought the imperial fleet of Blefuscu into the royal port, and being afterwards commanded by his Imperial Majesty to seize all the other ships of the said empire of Blefuscu, and reduce that empire to a province, to be governed by a viceroy from hence, and to destroy and put to death not only all the Big-Endian exiles, but likewise all the people of that empire, who would not immediately forsake the Big-Endian heresy: He, the said Flestrin, like a false traitor against his most Auspicious, Serene, Imperial Majesty, did petition to be excused from the said service, upon pretence of unwillingness to force the consciences, or destroy the liberties and lives of an innocent people.

ARTICLE III

"'That, whereas certain ambassadors arrived from the court of Blefuscu, to sue for peace in his Majesty's court: He, the said Flestrin, did, like a false traitor, aid, abet, comfort, and divert the said ambassadors, although he knew them to be servants to a Prince who was lately an open enemy to his Imperial Majesty, and in open war against his said Majesty.

ARTICLE IV

"'That the said Quinbus Flestrin, contrary to the duty of a faithful subject, is now preparing to make a voyage to the court and empire of Blefuscu, for which he hath received only verbal licence from his Imperial Majesty; and under colour of the said licence, doth falsely and traitorously intend to take the said voyage, and thereby to aid, comfort, and abet the Emperor of Blefuscu, so late an enemy, and in open war with his Imperial Majesty aforesaid.'

"There are some other articles, but these are the most important, of which I have read you an abstract.

"In the several debates upon this impeachment, it must be confessed that his Majesty gave many marks of his great lenity, often urging the services you had done him, and endeavouring to extenuate your crimes. The Treasurer and Admiral insisted that you should be put to the most painful and ignominious death, by setting fire on your house at night, and the General was to attend with twenty thousand men armed with poisoned arrows to shoot you on the face and hands. Some of your servants were to have private orders to strew a poisonous juice on your shirts, which would soon make you tear your own flesh, and die in the utmost torture. The General came into the same opinion; so that for a long time there was a majority against you. But his Majesty resolving, if possible, to spare your life, at last brought off the Chamberlain.

"Upon this incident, Reldresal, principal Secretary for Private Affairs, who always approved himself your true friend, was commanded by the Emperor to deliver his opinion, which he accordingly did; and therein justified the good thoughts you have of him. He allowed your crimes to be great, but that still there was room for mercy, the most commendable virtue in a prince, and for which his Majesty was so justly celebrated. He said, the friendship between you and him was so well known to the world, that perhaps the most honourable board might think him partial: however, in obedience to the command he had received, he would freely offer his sentiments. That if his Majesty, in consideration of your services, and pursuant to his own merciful disposition, would please to spare your life, and only give orders to put out both your eyes, he humbly conceived, that by this expedient, justice might in some measure be satisfied, and all the world would applaud the lenity of the Emperor, as well as the fair and generous proceedings of those who have the honour to be his counsellors. That the loss of your eyes would be no impediment to your bodily strength, by which you might still be useful to his Majesty. That blindness is an addition to courage, by concealing dangers from us; that the fear you had for your eyes, was the greatest difficulty in bringing over the enemy's fleet, and it would be sufficient for you to see by the eyes of the ministers, since the greatest princes do no more.

"This proposal was received with the utmost disapprobation by the whole board. Bolgolam, the Admiral, could not preserve his temper; but rising up in fury, said, he wondered how the Secretary durst presume to give his opinion for preserving the life of a traitor: that the services you had performed, were, by all true reasons of state, the great aggravation of your crimes; that you, who were able to extinguish the fire, by discharge of urine in her Majesty's apartment (which he mentioned with horror), might, at another time, raise an inundation by the same means, to drown the whole palace; and the same strength which enabled you to bring over the enemy's fleet, might serve, upon the first discontent, to carry it back: that he had good reasons to think you were a Big-Endian in your heart; and as treason begins in the heart, before it appears in overt acts, so he accused you as a traitor on that account, and therefore insisted you should be put to death.

"The Treasurer was of the same opinion; he showed to what straits his Majesty's revenue was reduced by the charge of maintaining you, which would soon grow insupportable: that the Secretary's expedient of putting out your eyes was so far from being a remedy against this evil, that it would probably increase it, as it is manifest from the common practice of blinding some kind of fowl, after which they fed the faster, and grew sooner fat: that his sacred Majesty and the Council, who are your judges, were in their own consciences fully convinced of your guilt, which was a sufficient argument to condemn you to death, without the formal proofs required by the strict letter of the law.

"But his Imperial Majesty, fully determined against capital punishment, was graciously pleased to say, that since the Council thought the loss of your eyes too easy a censure, some other may be inflicted hereafter. And your friend the Secretary humbly desiring to be heard again, in answer to what the Treasurer had objected concerning the great charge his Majesty was at in maintaining you, said, that his Excellency, who had the sole disposal of the Emperor's revenue, might easily provide against that evil, by gradually lessening your establishment; by which, for want of sufficient food, you would grow weak and faint, and lose your appetite, and consequently decay and consume in a few months; neither would the stench of your carcass be then so dangerous, when it should become more than half diminished; and immediately upon your death, five or six thousand of his Majesty's subjects might, in two or three days, cut your flesh from your bones, take it away by cart-loads, and bury it in distant parts to prevent infection, leaving the skeleton as a monument of admiration to posterity.

"Thus by the great friendship of the Secretary, the whole affair was compromised. It was strictly enjoined, that the project of starving you by degrees should be kept a secret, but the sentence of putting out your eyes was entered on the books; none dissenting except Bolgolam the Admiral, who, being a creature of the Empress, was perpetually instigated by her Majesty to insist upon your death, she having borne perpetual malice against you, on account of that infamous and illegal method you took to extinguish the fire in her apartment.

"In three days your friend the Secretary will be directed to come to your house, and read before you the articles of impeachment; and then to signify the great lenity and favour of his Majesty and Council, whereby you are only condemned to the loss of your eyes, which his Majesty doth not question you will gratefully and humbly submit to; and twenty of his Majesty's surgeons will attend, in order to see the operation well performed, by discharging very sharp-pointed arrows into the balls of your eyes, as you lie on the ground.

"I leave to your prudence what measures you will take; and to avoid suspicion, I must immediately return in as private a manner as I came."

His Lordship did so, and I remained alone, under many doubts and perplexities of mind.

It was a custom introduced by this prince and his ministry (very different, as I have been assured, from the practices of former times,) that after the court had decreed any cruel execution, either to gratify the monarch's resentment, or the malice of a favourite, the Emperor always made a speech to his whole Council, expressing his great lenity and tenderness, as qualities known and confessed by all the world. This speech was immediately published through the kingdom; nor did any thing terrify the people so much as those encomiums on his Majesty's mercy; because it was observed, that the more these praises were enlarged and insisted on, the more inhuman was the punishment, and the sufferer more innocent. And as to myself, I must confess, having never been designed for a courtier either by my birth or education, I was so ill a judge of things, that I could not discover the lenity and favour of his sentence, but conceived it (perhaps erroneously) rather to be rigorous than gentle. I sometimes thought of standing my trial, for although I could not deny the facts alleged in the several articles, yet I hoped they would admit of some extenuations. But having in my life perused many state-trials, which I ever observed to terminate as the judges thought fit to direct, I durst not rely on so dangerous a decision, in so critical a juncture, and against such powerful enemies. Once I was strongly bent upon resistance, for while I had liberty, the whole strength of that empire could hardly subdue me, and I might easily with stones pelt the metropolis to pieces; but I soon rejected that project with horror, by remembering the oath I had made to the Emperor, the favours I received from him, and the high title of *Nardac* he conferred upon me. Neither had I so soon learned the gratitude of courtiers, to persuade myself that his Majesty's present severities acquitted me of all past obligations.

At last I fixed upon a resolution, for which it is probable I may incur some censure, and not unjustly; for I confess I owe the preserving my eyes, and consequently my liberty, to my own great rashness and want of experience: because if I had then known the nature of princes and ministers, which I have since observed in many other courts, and their methods of treating criminals less obnoxious than myself, I should with great alacrity and readiness have submitted to so easy a punishment. But hurried on by the precipitancy of youth, and having his Imperial Majesty's licence to pay my attendance upon the Emperor of Blefuscu, I took this opportunity, before the three days were elapsed, to send a letter to my friend the Secretary, signifying my resolution of setting out that morning for Blefuscu pursuant to the leave I had got; and without waiting for an answer, I went to that side of the island where our fleet lay. I seized a large man of war, tied a cable to the prow, and, lifting up the anchors, I stripped myself, put my clothes (together with my coverlet, which I brought under my arm) into the vessel, and drawing it after me between wading and swimming, arrived at the royal port of Blefuscu, where the people had long expected me: they lent me two guides to direct me to the capital city, which is of the same name. I held them in my hands till I came within two hundred yards of the gate, and desired them to signify my arrival to one of the secretaries, and let him know, I there waited his Majesty's command. I had an answer in about an hour, that his Majesty, attended by the Royal Family, and great officers of the court, was coming out to receive me. I advanced a hundred yards. The Emperor and his train alighted from their horses, the Empress and ladies from their coaches, and I did not perceive they were in any fright or concern. I lay on the ground to kiss his Majesty's and the Empress's hands. I told his Majesty, that I was come according to my promise, and with the licence of the Emperor my master, to have the honour of seeing so mighty a monarch, and to offer him any service in my power, consistent with my duty to my own prince; not mentioning a word of my disgrace, because I had hitherto no regular information of it, and might suppose myself wholly ignorant of any such design; neither could I reasonably conceive that the Emperor would discover the secret while I was out of his power; wherein, however, it soon appeared I was deceived.

I shall not trouble the reader with the particular account of my reception at this court, which was suitable to the generosity of so great a prince; nor of the difficulties I was in for want of a house and bed, being forced to lie on the ground, wrapped up in my coverlet.

Chapter 8

The Author, by a lucky accident, finds means to leave Blefuscu; *and, after some difficulties, returns safe to his native country.*

THREE days after my arrival, walking out of curiosity to the north-east coast of the island, I observed, about half a league off, in the sea, somewhat that looked like a boat overturned. I pulled off my shoes and stockings, and wading two or three hundred yards, I found the object to approach nearer by force of the tide; and then plainly saw it to be a real boat, which I supposed might, by some tempest, have been driven from a ship; whereupon I returned immediately towards the city, and desired his Imperial Majesty to lend me twenty of the tallest vessels he had left after the loss of his fleet, and three thousand seamen under the command of his Vice-Admiral. This fleet sailed round, while I went back the shortest way to the coast where I first discovered the boat; I found the tide had driven it still nearer. The seamen were all provided with cordage, which I had beforehand twisted to a sufficient strength. When the ships came up, I stripped myself, and waded till I came within an hundred yards of the boat, after which I was forced to swim till I got up to it. The seamen threw me the end of the cord, which I fastened to a hole in the fore-part of the boat, and the other end to a man of war; but I found all my labour to little purpose; for being out of my depth, I was not able to work. In this necessity, I was forced to swim behind, and push the boat forwards as often as I could, with one of my hands; and the tide favouring me, I advanced so far, that I could just hold up my chin and feel the ground. I rested two or three minutes, and then gave the boat another shove, and so on till the sea was no higher than my arm-pits; and now the most laborious part being over, I took out my other cables, which were stowed in one of the ships, and fastening them first to the boat, and then to nine of the vessels which attended me; the wind being favourable, the seamen towed, and I shoved till we arrived within forty yards of the shore; and waiting till the tide was out, I got dry to the boat, and by the assistance of two thousand men, with ropes and engines, I made a shift to turn it on its bottom, and found it was but little damaged.

I shall not trouble the reader with the difficulties I was under by the help of certain paddles, which cost me ten days making, to get my boat to the royal port of Blefuscu, where a mighty concourse of people appeared upon my arrival, full of wonder at the sight of so prodigious a vessel. I told the Emperor that my good fortune had thrown this boat in my way, to carry me to some place from whence I might return into my native country, and begged his Majesty's orders for getting materials to fit it up, together with his licence to depart; which, after some kind expostulations, he was pleased to grant.

I did very much wonder, in all this time, not to have heard of any express relating to me from our Emperor to the court of Blefuscu. But I was afterwards given privately to understand, that his Imperial Majesty, never imagining I had the least notice of his designs, believed I was only gone to Blefuscu in performance of my promise, according to the licence he had given me, which was well known at our court, and would return in a few days when that ceremony was ended. But he was at last in pain at my long absence; and after consulting with the Treasurer, and the rest of that cabal, a person of quality was dispatched with the copy of the articles against me. This envoy had instructions to represent to the monarch of Blefuscu, the great lenity of his master, who was content to punish me no farther than with the loss of my eyes; that I had fled from justice, and if I did not return in two hours, I should be deprived of my title of *Nardac*, and declared a traitor. The envoy further added, that in order to maintain the peace and amity between both empires, his master expected, that his brother of Blefuscu would give orders to have me sent back to Lilliput, bound hand and foot, to be punished as a traitor.

The Emperor of Blefuscu having taken three days to consult, returned an answer consisting of many civilities and excuses. He said, that as for sending me bound, his brother knew it was impossible; that although I had deprived him of his fleet, yet he owed great obligations to me for many good offices I had done him in making the peace. That however both their Majesties would soon be made easy; for I had found a prodigious vessel on the shore, able to carry me on the sea, which he had given order to fit up with my own assistance and direction; and he hoped in a few weeks both empires would be freed from so insupportable an incumbrance.

With this answer the envoy returned to Lilliput, and the monarch of Blefuscu related to me all that had passed; offering me at the same time (but under the strictest confidence) his gracious protection, if I would continue in his service; wherein although I believed him sincere, yet I resolved never more to put any confidence in princes or ministers, where I could possibly avoid it; and therefore, with all due acknowledgements for his favourable intentions, I humbly begged to be excused. I told him, that since fortune, whether good or evil, had thrown a vessel in my way, I was resolved to venture myself in the ocean, rather than be an occasion of difference between two such mighty monarchs. Neither did I find the Emperor at all displeased; and I discovered by a certain accident, that he was very glad of my resolution, and so were most of his ministers.

These considerations moved me to hasten my departure somewhat sooner than I intended; to which the court, impatient to have me gone, very readily contributed. Five hundred workmen were employed to make two sails to my boat, according to my directions, by quilting thirteen fold of their strongest linen together. I was at the pains of making ropes and cables, by twisting ten, twenty or thirty of the thickest and strongest of theirs. A great stone that I happened to find, after a long search, by the sea-shore, served me for an anchor. I had the tallow of three hundred cows for greasing my boat, and other uses. I was at incredible pains in cutting down some of the largest timber-trees for oars and masts, wherein I was, however, much assisted by his Majesty's ship-carpenters, who helped me in smoothing them, after I had done the rough work.

In about a month, when all was prepared, I sent to receive his Majesty's commands, and take my leave. The Emperor and Royal Family came out of the palace; I lay down on my face to kiss his hand, which he very graciously gave me: so did the Empress and young Princes of the blood. His Majesty presented me with fifty purses of two hundred *sprugs* a-piece, together with his picture at full length, which I put immediately into one of my gloves, to keep it from being hurt. The ceremonies at my departure were too many to trouble the reader with at this time.

I stored the boat with the carcasses of an hundred oxen, and three hundred sheep, with bread and drink proportionable, and as much meat ready dressed as four hundred cooks could provide. I took with me six cows and two bulls alive, with as many ewes and rams, intending to carry them into my own country, and propagate the breed. And to feed them on board, I had a good bundle of hay, and a bag of corn. I would gladly have taken a dozen of the natives, but this was a thing the Emperor would by no means permit; and besides a diligent search into my pockets, his Majesty engaged my honour not to carry away any of his subjects, although with their own consent and desire.

Having thus prepared all things as well as I was able, I set sail on the twenty-fourth day of September 1701, at six in the morning; and when I had gone about four leagues to the northward, the wind being at south-east, at six in the evening I descried a small island about half a league to the north-west. I advanced forward, and cast anchor on the lee-side of the island, which seemed to be uninhabited. I then took some refreshment, and went to my rest. I slept well, and as I conjecture at least six hours, for I found the day broke in two hours after I awaked. It was a clear night. I eat my breakfast before the sun was up; and heaving anchor, the wind being favourable, I steered the same course that I had done the day before, wherein I was directed by my pocket-compass. My intention was to reach, if possible, one of those islands, which I had reason to believe lay to the north-east of Van Diemen's Land. I discovered nothing all that day; but upon the next, about three in the afternoon, when I had by my computation made twenty-four leagues from Blefuscu, I descried a sail steering to the south-east; my course was due east. I hailed her, but could get no answer; yet I found I gained upon her, for the wind slackened. I made all the sail I could, and in half an hour she spied me, then hung out her ancient, and discharged a gun. It is not easy to express the joy I was in upon the unexpected hope of once more seeing my beloved country, and the dear pledges I had left in it. The ship slackened her sails, and I came up with her between five and six in the evening, September 26; but my heart leaped within me to see her English colours. I put my cows and sheep into my coat-pockets, and got on board with all my little cargo of provisions. The vessel was an English merchantman, returning from Japan by the North and South Seas; the Captain, Mr. John Biddel of Deptford, a very civil man, and an excellent sailor. We were now in the latitude of 30 degrees south; there were about fifty men in the ship; and here I met an old comrade of mine, one Peter Williams, who gave me a good character to the Captain. This gentleman treated me with kindness, and desired I would let him know what place I came from last, and whither I was bound; which I did in a few words, but he thought I was raving, and that the dangers I underwent had disturbed my head; whereupon I took my black cattle and sheep out of my pocket, which, after great astonishment, clearly convinced him of my veracity. I then showed him the gold given me by the Emperor of Blefuscu, together with his Majesty's picture at full length, and some other rarities of that country. I gave him two purses of two hundred *sprugs* each, and promised, when we arrived in England, to make him a present of a cow and a sheep big with young.

I shall not trouble the reader with a particular ac-

22. **ancient,** flag, or ensign.

count of this voyage, which was very prosperous for the most part. We arrived in the Downs on the 13th of April, 1702. I had only one misfortune, that the rats on board carried away one of my sheep; I found her bones in a hole, picked clean from the flesh. The rest of my cattle I got safe on shore, and set them a grazing in a bowling-green at Greenwich, where the fineness of the grass made them feed very heartily, though I had always feared the contrary: neither could I possibly have preserved them in so long a voyage, if the Captain had not allowed me some of his best biscuit, which, rubbed to powder, and mingled with water, was their constant food. The short time I continued in England, I made a considerable profit by showing my cattle to many persons of quality, and others: and before I began my second voyage, I sold them for six hundred pounds. Since my last return, I find the breed is considerably increased, especially the sheep; which I hope will prove much to the advantage of the woollen manufacture, by the fineness of the fleeces. . . .

THOUGHTS ON VARIOUS SUBJECTS

The following epigrams are selected from a considerably larger number of detached "thoughts" set down by Swift about the year 1706. They are related in style to the *pensées* in which many French writers have excelled, and in their emphasis upon the theme of self-love they resemble the *Maximes* of La Rochefoucauld.

We have just enough religion to make us hate, but not enough to make us love one another.

Positiveness is a good quality for preachers and orators, because he that would obtrude his thoughts and reasons upon a multitude, will convince others the more, as he appears convinced himself.

How is it possible to expect that mankind will take advice, when they will not so much as take warning?

No preacher is listened to but time, which gives us the same train and turn of thought that elder people have tried in vain to put into our heads before.

Religion seems to have grown an infant with age, and requires miracles to nurse it, as it had in its infancy.

Would a writer know how to behave himself with relation to posterity, let him consider in old books what he finds that he is glad to know, and what omissions he most laments.

When a true genius appears in the world, you may know him by this sign, that the dunces are in confederacy against him.

I am apt to think, that in the day of judgment there will be small allowance given to the wise for their want of morals, and to the ignorant for their want of faith, because both are without excuse. This renders the advantages equal of ignorance and knowledge. But some scruples in the wise, and some vices in the ignorant, will perhaps be forgiven, upon the strength of temptation to each.

The chameleon, who is said to feed upon nothing but air, has of all animals the nimblest tongue.

There are but three ways for a man to revenge himself of the censure of the world; to despise it, to return the like, or to endeavour to live so as to avoid it: the first of these is usually pretended, the last is almost impossible, the universal practice is for the second.

What they do in Heaven we are ignorant of; what they do not we are told expressly, that they neither marry, nor are given in marriage.

The stoical scheme of supplying our wants, by lopping off our desires, is like cutting off our feet when we want shoes.

The reason why so few marriages are happy, is, because young ladies spend their time in making nets, not in making cages.

If a man will observe as he walks the streets, I believe he will find the merriest countenances in mourning coaches.

No wise man ever wished to be younger.

Complaint is the largest tribute heaven receives, and the sincerest part of our devotion.

The common fluency of speech in many men, and most women, is owing to a scarcity of matter, and a scarcity of words; for whoever is a master of language, and has a mind full of ideas, will be apt in speaking to hesitate upon the choice of both; whereas common speakers have only one set of ideas, and one set of words to clothe them in; and these are always ready at the mouth: so people come faster out of church when it is almost empty, than when a crowd is at the door.

To be vain, is rather a mark of humility than pride. Vain men delight in telling what honours have been done them, what great company they have kept, and the like, by which they plainly confess that these honours were more than their due, and such as their friends would not believe, if they had not been told: whereas a man truly proud, thinks the greatest honours below his merit, and consequently scorns to boast. I therefore deliver it as a maxim, that whoever desires the character of a proud man, ought to conceal his vanity.

A very little wit is valued in a woman, as we are pleased with a few words spoken plain by a parrot.

A nice man is a man of nasty ideas.

Apollo was held the god of physic, and sender of diseases. Both were originally the same trade, and still continue.

Most sorts of diversion in men, children, and other animals, are in imitation of fighting.

That was excellently observed, say I, when I read a passage in an author, where his opinion agrees with mine. When we differ, there I pronounce him to be mistaken.

Very few men, properly speaking, live at present, but are providing to live another time.

As universal a practice as lying is, and as easy a one as it seems, I do not remember to have heard three good lies in all my conversation, even from those who were most celebrated in that faculty.

A man seeing a wasp creeping into a vial filled with honey, that was hung on a fruit tree, said thus: "Why, thou sottish animal, art thou mad to go into the vial, where you see many hundred of your kind dying before you?"—"The reproach is just," answered the wasp, "but not from you men, who are so far from taking example by other people's follies, that you will not take warning by your own. If after falling several times into this vial, and escaping by chance, I should fall in again, I should then but resemble you."

Sometimes I read a book with pleasure, and detest the author.

Men of great parts are often unfortunate in the management of public business, because they are apt to go out of the common road by the quickness of their imagination. This I once said to my lord Bolingbroke, and desired he would observe, that the clerks in his office used a sort of ivory knife with a blunt edge to divide a sheet of paper, which never failed to cut it even, only requiring a steady hand: whereas if they should make use of a sharp penknife, the sharpness would make it go often out of the crease and disfigure the paper.

Vision is the art of seeing things invisible.

When I am reading a book, whether wise or silly, it seems to me to be alive and talking to me.

Whoever live at a different end of the town from me, I look upon as persons out of the world, and only myself and the scene about me to be in it.

Elephants are always drawn smaller than life; but a flea always larger.

from JOURNAL TO STELLA

Esther Johnson, commonly known as Stella, was Swift's pupil during the years in which he served Sir William Temple at Moor Park in England. The whole story of the relationship between the two may never be known, but it is certain that they were bound together by mutual respect and ardent friendship. During Swift's absences from Ireland they maintained a correspondence in which the part of Swift is now known as the *Journal to Stella*. Each wrote to the other nearly every day, and sent his or her letters in fortnightly installments. Obviously, Swift had no expectation or wish that his letters to Esther Johnson might ever be published. They reveal a phase of his life, mind, and character which is not discernible in his other writings.

The present extract is one complete letter, written at a time when Swift was deeply engaged in the social and political life of London.

LETTER XIX

London, March 24, 1710–11

IT was a little cross in Presto not to send to-day to the coffeehouse to see whether there was a letter from MD before I sent away mine; but faith I did it on purpose, because I would scorn to answer two letters of yours successively. This way of journal is the worst in the world for writing of news, unless one does it the last day; and so I will observe henceforward, if there be any politics or stuff worth sending. My shin mends in spite of the scratching last night. I dined to-day at Ned Southwell's with the Bishop of Ossory and a parcel of Irish gentlemen. Have you yet seen any of the Spectators? Just three weeks to-day since I had your last, N. 11. I am afraid I have lost one by the packet that was taken; that will vex me, considering the pains MD take to write, especially poor pretty Stella, and her weak eyes: God bless them and the owner, and send them well, and little me together, I hope ere long. This illness of Mr Harley puts everything backwards, and he is still down, and like to be so, by that extravasated blood which comes from his breast to the wound; it was by the second blow Guiscard gave him after the penknife was broken. I am shocked at that villainy whenever I think of it. Biddy Floyd is past danger but will lose all her beauty: she had them mighty thick, especially about her nose.

25. Morning. I wish you a merry new year: this is the first day of the year, you know, with us, and 'tis Lady-day. I must rise and go to my Lord-Keeper: it is not shaving day to-day, so I shall be early. I am to dine with Mr Secretary St. John. Good morrow, my mistresses both, good morrow. Stella will be peeping out of her room at Mrs de Caudres' down upon the folks as they come from church; and there comes Mrs Proby, and that's my Lady Southwell, and there's Lady Betty Rochfort. I long to hear how you are settled in you new lodgings. I wish I were rid of my old ones, and that Mrs Brent could contrive to put my books in boxes, and lodge them in some safe place, and you keep my papers of importance. But I must rise, I tell you.— At night. So I visited and dined as I told you, and what of that? We have let Guiscard be buried at last, after showing him pickled in a trough this fortnight for twopence a piece; and the fellow that showed would point to his body, and, See, gentlemen, this is the wound that was given him by his Grace the Duke of Ormond; and this is the wound, &c. and then the show was over, and another set of rabble came in. 'Tis hard that our laws would not suffer us to hang his body in chains, because he was not tried;

49. **Presto,** Italian for Swift. 51. **MD,** my dears—that is, Esther Johnson, or Stella, and her companion, Rebecca Dingley.

16. **Harley,** Chancellor of the Exchequer; later, Lord Oxford. 19. **Guiscard,** a Frenchman who had recently stabbed Harley. 21. **Biddy Floyd,** a reigning beauty who had been down with smallpox. 24. **new year.** By the old calendar the year began on March 25. 26. **Lady-day,** the Feast of the Annunciation, March 25. 26–27. **Lord-Keeper,** Sir Simon Harcourt, Keeper of the Great Seal. 28. **St. John,** Viscount Bolingbroke, Secretary of State.

and in the eye of our law every man is innocent till then.—Mr Harley is still very weak and never out of bed.

26. This was a most delicious day; and my shin being past danger, I walked like lightning above two hours in the Park. We have generally one fair day, and then a great deal of rain for three or four days together. All things are at a stop in Parliament for want of Mr Harley; they cannot stir an inch without him in their most material affairs: and we fear by the caprice of Radcliffe, who will admit none but his own surgeon, he has not been well looked after. I dined at an ale-house with Mr Lewis, but had his wine. Don't you begin to see the flowers and blossoms of the field? How busy should I now be at Laracor? No news of your box? I hope you have it, and are this minute drinking the chocolate, and that the smell of the Brazil tobacco has not affected it. I would be glad to know whether you like it, because I would send you more by people that are now every day thinking of going to Ireland; therefore pray tell me, and tell me soon; and I will have the strong box.

27. A rainy wretched scurvy day from morning till night: and my neighbour Vanhomrigh invited me to dine with them: and this evening I passed at Mr Prior's with Dr Freind; and 'tis now past twelve, so I must go to sleep.

28. Morning. O faith, you're an impudent saucy couple of sluttekins, for presuming to write so soon, said I to myself this morning; who knows but there may be a letter from MD at the coffeehouse? Well, you must know, and so, I just now sent Patrick, and he brought me three letters, but not one from MD, no indeed, for I read all the superscriptions; and not one from MD. One I opened, it was from the Archbishop; t'other I opened, it was from Staunton; the third I took, and looked at the hand. Whose hand is this? says I: yes, says I, whose hand is this? then there was wax between the folds; then I began to suspect; then I peeped; faith, it was Walls's hand after all: then I opened it in a rage, and then it was little MD's hand, dear, little, pretty, charming, MD's sweet hand again. O Lord, en't here a clutter and a stir, and a bustle, never saw the like. Faith I believe yours lay some days at the post-office, and that it came before my eighteenth went, but that I did not expect it, and I hardly ever go there. Well, and so you think I'll answer this letter now? no, faith, and so I won't. I'll make you wait, young woman; but I'll inquire immediately about poor Dingley's exchequer trangum. What, is that Vedel again a soldier? Was he broke? I'll put it in Ben Tooke's hand. I hope Vedel could not sell it.—At night. Vedel, Vedel, poh, pox, I think it is Vedeau, ay, Vedeau, now I have it: let me see, do you name him in yours? Yes, Mr John Vedeau is the brother; but where does this brother live? I'll inquire. This was a fast-day for the public; so I dined late with Sir Matthew Dudley, whom I have not been with a great while. He is one of those that must lose his employment whenever the great shake comes; and I can't contribute to keep him in, though I have dropped words in his favour to the ministry; but he has been too violent a Whig, and friend to the Lord Treasurer, to stay in. 'Tis odd to think how long they let those people keep their places; but the reason is that they have not enough to satisfy all expecters, and so they keep them all in hopes, that they may be good boys in the mean time; and thus the old ones hold in still. The Comptroller told me that there are eight people expect his staff. I walked after dinner to-day round the Park.—What, do I write politics to little young women? Hold your tongue, and go to your Dean's.

29. Morning. If this be a fine day, I will walk into the city, and see Charles Barnard's library. What care I for your letter, your saucy N. 12? I will say nothing to it yet: faith, I believe this will be full before its time, and then go it must. I will always write once a-fortnight; and if it goes sooner by filling sooner, why then there is so much clear gain. Morrow, morrow, rogues and lasses both, I can't lie scribbling here in bed for your play; I must rise, and so morrow again.—At night. Your friend Montgomery and his sister are here, as I am told by Patrick; I have seen him often, but take no notice of him: he is grown very ugly and pimpled. They tell me he is a gamester, and wins money. How could I help it, pray? Patrick snuffed the candle too short, and the grease ran down upon the paper. It en't my fault, 'tis Patrick's fault; pray now don't blame Presto. I walked to-day in the city, and dined at a private house, and went to see the auction of poor Charles Barnard's books; they were in the middle of the physic books; so I bought none; and they are so dear, I believe I shall buy none, and there's an end; and go to Stoyte's, and I'll go sleep.

30. Morning. This is Good-Friday, you must know, and I must rise and go to Mr Secretary about some business, and Mrs Vanhomrigh desires me to breakfast with her, because she is to intercede for

---

11. **Radcliffe,** John Radcliffe (1650–1714), a famous physician.   16. **Laracor,** Swift's home in Ireland. 27. **Prior,** Matthew Prior (1664–1671), the poet.   33. **Patrick,** Swift's Irish servant.   41. **Walls's,** of Archdeacon Walls.

2. **trangum,** trifle; here probably a tally.   3–4. **Ben Tooke,** publisher of *A Tale of a Tub*.

Patrick, who is so often drunk and quarrelsome in the house, that I was resolved to send him over; but he knows all the places where I send, and is so used to my ways, that it would be inconvenient to me; but when I come to Ireland, I will discharge him. [At night] Sir Thomas Mansel, one of the Lords of the Treasury, setting me down at my door to-day, saw Patrick, and swore he was a Teaguelander. I am so used to his face, I never observed it, but thought him a pretty fellow. Sir Andrew Fountaine and I supped this fast-day with Mrs Vanhomrigh. We were afraid Mr Harley's wound would turn to a fistula; but we think the danger is now past. He rises every day and walks about his room, and we hope he will be out in a fortnight. Prior showed me a handsome paper of verses he has writ on Mr Harley's accident: they are not out; I will send them to you, if he will give me a copy.

31. Morning. What shall we do to make April fools this year, now it happens on Sunday? Patrick brings word that Mr Harley still mends, and is up every day. I design to see him in a few days: and he brings me word too that he has found out Vedeau's brother's shop: I shall call there in a day or two. It seems the wife lodges next door to the brother. I doubt the scoundrel was broke, and got a commission, or perhaps is a volunteer gentleman, and expects to get one by his valour. Morrow, sirrahs, let me rise.—At night. I dined to-day with Sir Thomas Mansel. We were walking in the Park, and Mr Lewis came to us. Mansel asked where we dined? We said, together. He said, we should dine with him, only his wife desired him to bring nobody, because she had only a leg of mutton. I said, I would dine with him to choose; but he would send a servant to order a plate or two; yet this man has ten thousand pounds a-year in land, and is a Lord of the Treasury, and is not covetous neither, but runs out merely by slattering and negligence. The worst dinner I ever saw at the Dean's was better: but so it is with abundance of people here. I called at night at Mr Harley's, who begins to walk in his room with a stick, but is mighty weak. See how much I have lost with that ugly grease. 'Tis your fault, pray; and I'll go to bed.

April 1. The Duke of Buckingham's house fell down last night with an earthquake, and is half swallowed up;—Won't you go and see it?—An April fool, an April fool, O ho, young women.— Well, don't be angry, I'll make you an April fool no more till the next time: we had no sport here because it is Sunday, and Easter Sunday. I dined with the Secretary, who seemed terribly down and melancholy, which Mr Prior and Lewis observed as well as I: perhaps something is gone wrong; perhaps there is nothing in it. God bless my own dearest MD, and all is well.

2. We have such windy weather, 'tis troublesome walking, yet all the rabble have got into our Park these Easter holidays. I am plagued with one Richardson, an Irish parson, and his project of printing Irish Bibles, &c. to make you Christians in that country: I befriend him what I can, on account of the Archbishop and Bishop of Clogher. But what business have I to meddle? &c. Don't you remember that, sirrah Stella? what was that about, when you thought I was meddling with something that was not my business? O faith, you are an impudent slut, I remember your doings, I'll never forget you as long as I live. Lewis and I dined together at his lodgings. But where's the answer to this letter of MD's? O faith, Presto, you must think of that. Time enough, says saucy Presto.

3. I was this morning to see Mrs Barton; I love her better than any body here, and see her seldomer. Why, really now, so it often happens in the world, that where one loves a body best—pshah, pshah, you are so silly with your moral observations.—Well, but she told me a very good story. An old gentlewoman died here two months ago, and left in her will to have eight men and eight maids bearers, who should have two guineas a-piece, ten guineas to the parson for a sermon, and two guineas to the clerk. But bearers, parson, and clerk, must be all true virgins; and not to be admitted till they took their oaths of virginity: so the poor woman lies still unburied, and so must do till the general resurrection. I called at Mr Secretary's to see what the D—— ailed him on Sunday; I made him a very proper speech, told him I observed he was much out of temper: that I did not expect he would tell me the cause, but would be glad to see he was in better; and one thing I warned him of, never to appear cold to me, for I would not be treated like a schoolboy; that I had felt too much of that in my life already, (meaning from Sir William Temple,) that I expected every great minister, who honoured me with his acquaintance, if he heard or saw any thing to my disadvantage, would let me know in plain words, and not put me in pain to guess by the change or coldness of his countenance or behaviour; for it was what I would hardly bear from a crowned head, and I thought no subject's favour was worth

---

8. **Teaguelander,** Irishman. 38–39. **runs out . . . by slattering,** loses money by being wasteful. 44. **grease,** the candle grease already mentioned.

23. **Mrs Barton,** a niece of Sir Isaac Newton, and a famous beauty.

it; and that I designed to let my Lord-Keeper and Mr Harley know the same thing, that they might use me accordingly. He took all right; said I had reason; vowed nothing ailed him but sitting up whole nights at business, and one night at drinking; would have had me dine with him and Mrs Masham's brother to make up matters; but I would not. I don't know, but I would not. But indeed I was engaged with my old friend Rollinson; you never heard of him before.

4. I sometimes look a line or two back, and see plaguy mistakes of the pen; how do you get over them? you are puzzled sometimes. Why, I think what I said to Mr Secretary was right. Don't you remember how I used to be in pain when Sir William Temple would look cold and out of humour for three or four days, and I used to suspect a hundred reasons. I have plucked up my spirit since then, faith; he spoiled a fine gentleman. I dined with my neighbour Vanhomrigh, and MD, poor MD, at home on a loin of mutton, and half a pint of wine, and the mutton was raw, poor Stella could not eat, poor dear rogue, and Dingley was so vexed; but we'll dine at Stoyte's to-morrow. Mr Harley promised to see me in a day or two; so I called this evening; but his son and others were abroad, and he asleep, so I came away and found out Mrs Vedeau. She drew out a letter from Dingley, and said she would get a friend to receive the money. I told her I would employ Mr Tooke in it henceforward. Her husband bought a lieutenancy of foot, and is gone to Portugal. He sold his share of the shop to his brother, and put out the money to maintain her, all but what bought the commission. She lodges within two doors of her brother. She told me it made her very melancholy to change the manner of her life thus, but trade was dead, &c. She says she will write to you soon. I design to engage Ben Tooke, and then receive the parchment from her. I give Mr Dopping a copy of Prior's verses on Mr Harley, he sent them yesterday to Ireland, so go look for them, for I won't be at the trouble to transcribe them there.—They will be printed in a day or two. Give my hearty service to Stoyte and Catherine; upon my word I love them dearly, and desire you will tell them so: pray desire Goody Stoyte not to let Mrs Walls and Mrs Johnson cheat her of her money at ombre, but assure her from me, that she is a bungler. Dine with her to-day, and tell her so, and drink my health, and good voyage, and speedy return, and so you're a rogue.

5. Morning. Now let us proceed to examine a saucy letter from one Madam MD. God Almighty bless poor dear Stella, and send her a great many birthdays, all happy and healthy, and wealthy, and with me ever together, and never asunder again, unless by chance. When I find you are happy or merry there, it makes me so here, and I can hardly imagine you absent when I am reading your letter or writing to you. No, faith, you are just here upon this little paper, and therefore I see and talk with you every evening constantly, and sometimes in the morning, but not always in the morning because that is not so modest to young ladies. What, you would fain palm a letter upon me more than you sent; and I, like a fool, must look over all yours to see whether this was really N. 12, or more. Patrick has this moment brought me letters from the Bishop of Clogher and Parvisol; my heart was at my mouth for fear of one from MD; what a disgrace would it be to have two of yours to answer together? but faith this shall go to-night, for fear, and then come when it will, I defy it. No, you are not naughty at all, write when you are disposed. And so the Dean told you the story of Mr Harley, from the Archbishop; I warrant it never spoiled your supper, or broke off your game. Nor yet, have not you the box; I wish Mrs Edgworth had the———. But you have it now, I suppose: and is the chocolate good, or has the tobacco spoiled it? Leigh stays till Sterne has done his business, no longer; and when that will be, God knows: I befriend him as much as I can, but Mr Harley's accident stops that as well as all things else. You guess, Madam Dingley, that I shall stay a round twelvemonth; as hope saved, I would come over, if I could, this minute; but we will talk of that by and by. Your affair of Vedeau I have told you of already; now to the next, turn over the leaf. Mrs Dobbins lies; I have no more provision here or in Ireland than I had. I am pleased that Stella the conjurer approves what I did with Mr Harley; but your generosity makes me mad; I know you repine inwardly at Presto's absence; you think he has broken his word, of coming in three months, and that this is always his trick: and now Stella says, she does not see possibly how I can come away in haste, and that MD is satisfied, &c. An't you a rogue to overpower me thus? I did not expect to find such friends as I have done. They may indeed deceive me too. But there are important reasons [pox on this grease, this candle tallow!] why they

6–7. Mrs Masham, a favorite of Queen Anne.
24. Stoyte, alderman, and later Lord Mayor, of Dublin.
40. Dopping, an Irish friend of Stella's.

18. Parvisol, Swift's agent at Laracor.   **27. Mrs Edgworth,** a friend by whom Swift had sent a box to Ireland.
40. Harley. Swift had returned a banknote for £50, saying that he was not a hired writer.

should not. I have been used barbarously by the late ministry; I am a little piqued in honour to let people see I am not to be despised. The assurances they give me, without any scruple or provocation, are such as are usually believed in the world; they may come to nothing, but the first opportunity that offers, and is neglected, I shall depend no more, but come away. I could say a thousand things on this head, if I were with you. I am thinking why Stella should not go to the Bath, if she be told it will do her good; I will make Parvisol get up fifty pounds, and pay it you; and you may be good housewives, and live cheap there some months, and return in autumn, or visit London, as you please: pray think of it. I writ to Bernage, directed to Curry's; I wish he had the letter. I will send the bohea tea, if I can. The Bishop of Kilmore, I don't keep such company; an old dying fool, whom I was never with in my life. So I am no godfather; all the better. Pray, Stella, explain those two words of yours to me, what you mean by *Villain and Dainger*, and you, Madam Dingley, what is *Christianing?*—Lay your letters *this way*, *this way*, and the devil a bit of difference between this way and t'other way. No; I'll show you, lay them *this way, this way, and not that way, that way.*— You shall have your aprons; and I'll put all your commissions as they come, in a paper together, and don't think I'll forget MD's orders, because they are friends; I'll be as careful as if they were strangers. I know not what to do about this Clements. Walls will not let me say any thing, as if Mr Pratt was against him; and now the Bishop of Clogher has written to me in his behalf. This thing does not rightly fall in my way, and that people never consider: I always give my good offices where they are proper, and that I am judge of; however, I will do what I can. But if he has the name of a Whig, it will be hard, considering my Lord Anglesea and Hyde are very much otherwise, and you know they have the employment of Deputy-Treasurer. If the frolic should take you of going to the Bath, I here send you a note on Parvisol; if not, you may tear it, and there's an end. Farewell.

If you have an imagination that the Bath will do you good, I say again, I would have you go; if not, or if it be inconvenient, burn this note. Or, if you would go, and not take so much money, take thirty pounds, and I will return you twenty from hence. Do as you please, sirrahs. I suppose it will not be too late for the first season; if it be, I would have you resolve, however, to go the second season, if the doctors say it will do you good, and you fancy so.

22. **this way.** Swift is giving the girls a lesson in handwriting.

AN ARGUMENT

TO PROVE THAT THE ABOLISHING OF
CHRISTIANITY IN ENGLAND
MAY, AS THINGS NOW STAND, BE ATTENDED WITH SOME INCONVENIENCES, AND PERHAPS NOT PRODUCE THOSE MANY GOOD EFFECTS PROPOSED THEREBY

Swift's irony is here directed in part against the Deists and freethinkers of his time, but his main attack is against those who profess Christianity merely for the worldly advantages which outward professions may bring.

I AM very sensible what a weakness and presumption it is to reason against the general humour and disposition of the world. I remember it was with great justice, and due regard to the freedom both of the public and the press, forbidden upon several penalties to write, or discourse, or lay wagers against the Union, even before it was confirmed by parliament, because that was looked upon as a design, to oppose the current of the people, which, besides the folly of it, is a manifest breach of the fundamental law that makes this majority of opinion the voice of God. In like manner, and for the very same reasons, it may perhaps be neither safe nor prudent to argue against the abolishing of Christianity, at a juncture when all parties appear so unanimously determined upon the point, as we cannot but allow from their actions, their discourses, and their writings. However, I know not how, whether from the affectation of singularity, or the perverseness of human nature, but so it unhappily falls out, that I cannot be entirely of this opinion. Nay, though I were sure an order were issued for my immediate prosecution by the Attorney-General, I should still confess that in the present posture of our affairs at home or abroad, I do not yet see the absolute necessity of extirpating the Christian religion from among us.

This perhaps may appear too great a paradox even for our wise and paradoxical age to endure; therefore I shall handle it with all tenderness, and with the utmost deference to that great and profound majority which is of another sentiment.

And yet the curious may please to observe, how much the genius of a nation is liable to alter in half an age. I have heard it affirmed for certain by some very old people, that the contrary opinion was even in their memories as much in vogue as the other is now; and that a project for the abolishing of Chris-

22. **Union,** the union of England and Scotland, 1707.

tianity would then have appeared as singular, and been thought as absurd, as it would be at this time to write or discourse in its defence.

Therefore I freely own that all appearances are against me. The system of the Gospel, after the fate of other systems, is generally antiquated and exploded; and the mass or body of the common people, among whom it seems to have had its latest credit, are now grown as much ashamed of it as their betters; opinions, like fashions, always descending from those of quality to the middle sort, and thence to the vulgar, where at length they are dropped and vanish.

But here I would not be mistaken, and must therefore be so bold as to borrow a distinction from the writers on the other side, when they make a difference between nominal and real Trinitarians. I hope no reader imagines me so weak as to stand up in the defence of real Christianity, such as used in primitive times (if we may believe the authors of those ages) to have an influence upon men's belief and actions. To offer at the restoring of that would indeed be a wild project; it would be to dig up foundations; to destroy at one blow all the wit, and half the learning of the kingdom; to break the entire frame and constitution of things; to ruin trade, extinguish arts and sciences with the professors of them; in short, to turn our courts, exchanges, and shops into deserts; and would be full as absurd as the proposal of Horace, where he advises the Romans all in a body to leave their city, and seek a new seat in some remote part of the world, by way of cure for the corruption of their manners.

Therefore I think this caution was in itself altogether unnecessary (which I have inserted only to prevent all possibility of cavilling) since every candid reader will easily understand my discourse to be intended only in defence of nominal Christianity; the other having been for some time wholly laid aside by general consent, as utterly inconsistent with our present schemes of wealth and power.

But why we should therefore cast off the name and title of Christians, although the general opinion and resolution be so violent for it, I confess I cannot (with submission) apprehend, nor is the consequence necessary. However, since the undertakers propose such wonderful advantages to the nation by this project, and advance many plausible objections against the system of Christianity, I shall briefly consider the strength of both, fairly allow them their greatest weight, and offer such answers as I think most reasonable. After which I will beg leave to show what inconveniences may possibly happen by such an innovation, in the present posture of our affairs.

First, One great advantage proposed by the abolishing of Christianity is, that it would very much enlarge and establish liberty of conscience, that great bulwark of our nation, and of the Protestant Religion, which is still too much limited by priestcraft, notwithstanding all the good intentions of the legislature, as we have lately found by a severe instance. For it is confidently reported, that two young gentlemen of real hopes, bright wit, and profound judgment, who upon a thorough examination of causes and effects, and by the mere force of natural abilities, without the least tincture of learning, having made a discovery, that there was no God, and generously communicating their thoughts for the good of the public, were some time ago, by an unparalleled severity, and upon I know not what obsolete law, broke for blasphemy. And as it hath been wisely observed, if persecution once begins, no man alive knows how far it may reach, or where it will end.

In answer to all which, with deference to wiser judgments, I think this rather shows the necessity of a nominal religion among us. Great wits love to be free with the highest objects; and if they cannot be allowed a God to revile or renounce, they will speak evil of dignities, abuse the government, and reflect upon the ministry; which I am sure few will deny to be of much more pernicious consequence, according to the saying of Tiberius, *deorum offensa diis curae*. As to the particular fact related, I think it is not fair to argue from one instance. Perhaps another cannot be produced; yet (to the comfort of all those who may be apprehensive of persecution) blasphemy, we know, is freely spoken a million of times in every coffeehouse and tavern, or wherever else good company meet. It must be allowed, indeed, that, to break an English free-born officer only for blasphemy, was, to speak the gentlest of such an action, a very high strain of absolute power. Little can be said in excuse for the general; perhaps he was afraid it might give offence to the allies, among whom, for aught we know, it may be the custom of the country to believe a God. But if he argued, as some have done, upon a mistaken principle, that an officer who is guilty of speaking blasphemy, may some time or other proceed so far as to raise a mutiny, the consequence is by no means to be admitted; for, surely the commander of an English army is likely to be but ill obeyed whose soldiers fear and reverence him as little as they do a Deity.

30. Horace, *Epodes*, Ode 16.

19. **broke**, dismissed. 31. **deorum . . . curae.** The offenses of the gods are the concern of the gods.

It is further objected against the Gospel System, that it obliges men to the belief of things too difficult for freethinkers, and such who have shaken off the prejudices that usually cling to a confined education. To which I answer, that men should be cautious how they raise objections which reflect upon the wisdom of the nation. Is not every body freely allowed to believe whatever he pleases, and to publish his belief to the world whenever he thinks fit, especially if it serves to strengthen the party which is in the right? Would any indifferent foreigner, who should read the trumpery lately written by Asgil, Tindal, Toland, Coward, and forty more, imagine the Gospel to be our rule of faith, and confirmed by parliaments? Does any man either believe, or say he believes, or desire to have it thought that he says he believes, one syllable of the matter? And is any man worse received upon that score, or does he find his want of nominal faith a disadvantage to him in the pursuit of any civil or military employment? What if there be an old dormant statute or two against him, are they not now obsolete, to a degree, that Empson and Dudley themselves if they were now alive, would find it impossible to put them in execution?

It is likewise urged that there are, by computation, in this kingdom, above ten thousand parsons, whose revenues, added to those of my lords the bishops, would suffice to maintain at least two hundred young gentlemen of wit and pleasure and freethinking, enemies to priestcraft, narrow principles, pedantry, and prejudices, who might be an ornament to the Court and Town: and then, again, so great a number of able[-bodied] divines might be a recruit to our fleet and armies. This, indeed appears to be a consideration of some weight: but then, on the other side, several things deserve to be considered likewise: as, first, whether it may not be thought necessary that in certain tracts of country, like what we call parishes, there shall be one man at least of abilities to read and write. Then it seems a wrong computation, that the revenues of the Church throughout this island would be large enough to maintain two hundred young gentlemen, or even half that number, after the present refined way of living; that is, to allow each of them such a rent as, in the modern form of speech, would make them easy. But still there is in this project a greater mischief behind; and we ought to beware of the woman's folly, who killed the hen that every morning laid her a golden egg. For, pray what would become of the race of men in the next age, if we had nothing to trust to beside the scrofulous, consumptive productions, furnished by our men of wit and pleasure, when, having squandered away their vigour, health, and estates, they are forced by some disagreeable marriage to piece up their broken fortunes, and entail rottenness and politeness on their posterity? Now, here are ten thousand persons reduced by the wise regulations of Henry the Eighth, to the necessity of a low diet and moderate exercise, who are the only great restorers of our breed, without which the nation would in an age or two become one great hospital.

Another advantage proposed by the abolishing of Christianity, is the clear gain of one day in seven, which is now entirely lost, and consequently the kingdom one-seventh less considerable in trade, business, and pleasure; besides the loss to the public of so many stately structures, now in the hands of the Clergy, which might be converted into playhouses, market-houses, exchanges, common dormitories, and other public edifices.

I hope I shall be forgiven a hard word, if I call this a perfect *cavil*. I readily own there has been an old custom, time out of mind, for people to assemble in the churches every Sunday, and that shops are still frequently shut, in order, as it is conceived, to preserve the memory of that ancient practice; but how this can prove a hindrance to business or pleasure is hard to imagine. What if the men of pleasure are forced one day in the week, to game at home instead of the chocolate houses? Are not the taverns and coffeehouses open? Can there be a more convenient season for taking a dose of physic? Are fewer claps got upon Sundays than other days? Is not that the chief day for traders to sum up the accounts of the week, and for lawyers to prepare their briefs? But I would fain know how it can be pretended that the churches are misapplied? Where are more appointments and rendezvouses of gallantry? Where more care to appear in the foremost box with greater advantage of dress? Where more meetings for business? Where more bargains driven of all sorts? And where so many conveniences or incitements to sleep?

There is one advantage greater than any of the foregoing, proposed by the abolishing of Christianity: that it will utterly extinguish parties among us, by removing those factious distinctions of High and Low church, of Whig and Tory, Presbyterian and Church of England, which are now so many mutual clogs upon public proceedings, and are apt

---

12–13. **Asgil . . . Coward,** deists and freethinkers. 23. **Empson and Dudley,** tyrannical state officers of the time of Henry VII.

9. **Henry the Eighth,** who seized the revenues of the Church. 35. **claps,** venereal infections.

to dispose men to prefer the gratifying themselves, or depressing of their adversaries, before the most important interests of the state.

I confess, if it were certain that so great an advantage would redound to the nation by this expedient, I would submit and be silent. But will any man say, that if the words *whoring*, *drinking*, *cheating*, *lying*, *stealing* were by act of parliament ejected out of the English tongue and dictionaries, we should all awake next morning chaste and temperate, honest and just, and lovers of truth? Is this a fair consequence? Or, if the physicians would forbid us to pronounce the words *pox*, *gout*, *rheumatism*, and *stone*, would that expedient serve like so many talismans to destroy the diseases themselves? Are party and faction rooted in men's hearts no deeper than phrases borrowed from religion, or founded upon no firmer principles? And is our language so poor that we cannot find other terms to express them? Are *envy*, *pride*, *avarice*, and *ambition* such ill nomenclators, that they cannot furnish appellations for their owners? Will not *heydukes* and *mamalukes*, *mandarins* and *pashaws*, or any other words formed at pleasure, serve to distinguish those who are in the ministry from others who would be in it if they could? What, for instance, is easier than to vary the form of speech, and instead of the word church, make it a question in politics whether the Monument be in danger? Because religion was nearest at hand to furnish a few convenient phrases, is our invention so barren, we can find no other? Suppose, for argument sake, that the Tories favored Margarita, the Whigs Mrs. Tofts, and the Trimmers Valentini, would not *Margaritians*, *Toftians*, and *Valentinians* be very tolerable marks of distinction? The *Prasini* and *Veniti*, two most virulent factions in Italy, began (if I remember right) by a distinction of colours in ribbons; and we might contend with as good a grace about the dignity of the blue and the green, which would serve as properly to divide the Court, the Parliament, and the Kingdom between them, as any terms of art whatsoever, borrowed from religion. And therefore I think, there is little force in this objection against Christianity, or prospect of so great an advantage, as is proposed in the abolishing of it.

It is again objected, as a very absurd ridiculous custom, that a set of men should be suffered, much less employed and hired, to bawl one day in seven against the lawfulness of those methods most in use toward the pursuit of greatness, riches, and pleasure, which are the constant practice of all men alive on the other six. But this objection is, I think, a little unworthy so refined an age as ours. Let us argue this matter calmly: I appeal to the breast of any polite freethinker, whether in the pursuit of gratifying a predominant passion, he hath not always felt a wonderful incitement, by reflecting it was a thing forbidden; and therefore we see, in order to cultivate this taste, the wisdom of the nation has taken special care, that the ladies should be furnished with prohibited silks, and the men with prohibited wine. And indeed it were to be wished, that some other prohibitions were promoted, in order to improve the pleasures of the town; which, for want of such expedients begin already, as I am told, to flag and grow languid, giving way daily to cruel inroads from the spleen.

It is likewise proposed as a great advantage to the public, that if we once discard the system of the Gospel, all religion will of course be banished for ever; and consequently, along with it, those grievous prejudices of education, which under the names of *virtue*, *conscience*, *honour*, *justice*, and the like, are so apt to disturb the peace of human minds, and the notions whereof are so hard to be eradicated by right reason or freethinking, sometimes during the whole course of our lives.

Here first, I observe how difficult it is to get rid of a phrase, which the world is once grown fond of, though the occasion that first produced it, be entirely taken away. For several years past, if a man had but an ill-favoured nose, the deep-thinkers of the age would some way or other contrive to impute the cause to the prejudice of his education. From this fountain were said to be derived all our foolish notions of justice, piety, love of our country; all our opinions of God, or a future state, Heaven, Hell, and the like. And there might formerly perhaps have been some pretence for this charge. But so effectual care has been taken to remove those prejudices by an entire change in the methods of education, that (with honour I mention it to our polite innovators) the young gentlemen who are now on the scene seem to have not the least tincture of those infusions, or string of those weeds; and, by consequence, the reason for abolishing nominal Christianity upon that pretext, is wholly ceased.

For the rest, it may perhaps admit a controversy, whether the banishing of all notions of religion whatsoever, would be convenient for the vulgar. Not that I am in the least of opinion with those who hold religion to have been the invention of politicians, to keep the lower part of the world in awe by the fear of invisible powers; unless mankind were then very

---

22. heydukes, Slavic name for foot soldiers. 32-34. Margarita . . . Valentini, stage favorites. 33. Trimmers, a political party in the time of Charles II.

different to what it is now. For I look upon the mass or body of our people here in England, to be as freethinkers, that is to say, as staunch unbelievers, as any of the highest rank. But I conceive some scattered notions about a superior power to be of singular use for the common people, as furnishing excellent materials to keep children quiet when they grow peevish, and providing topics of amusement in a tedious winter-night.

Lastly, 'tis proposed as a singular advantage, that the abolishing of Christianity will very much contribute to the uniting of Protestants, by enlarging the terms of communion so as to take in all sorts of dissenters, who are now shut out of the pale upon account of a few ceremonies which all sides confess to be things indifferent: that this alone will effectually answer the great ends of a scheme for comprehension, by opening a large noble gate, at which all bodies may enter; whereas the chaffering with dissenters, and dodging about this or t'other ceremony, is but like opening a few wickets, and leaving them at jar, by which no more than one can get in at a time, and that, not without stooping, and sideling, and squeezing his body.

To all this I answer; that there is one darling inclination of mankind, which usually affects to be a retainer to religion, though she be neither its parent, its godmother, or its friend; I mean the spirit of opposition, that lived long before Christianity, and can easily subsist without it. Let us, for instance, examine wherein the opposition of sectaries among us consists. We shall find Christianity to have no share in it at all. Does the Gospel any where prescribe a starched, squeezed countenance, a stiff, formal gait, a singularity of manners and habit, or any affected modes of speech different from the reasonable part of mankind? Yet, if Christianity did not lend its name to stand in the gap, and to employ or divert these humours, they must of necessity be spent in contraventions to the laws of the land, and disturbance of the public peace. There is a portion of enthusiasm assigned to every nation, which, if it hath not proper objects to work on, will burst out, and set all in a flame. If the quiet of a state can be bought by only flinging men a few ceremonies to devour, it is a purchase no wise man would refuse. Let the mastiffs amuse themselves about a sheep's skin stuffed with hay, provided it will keep them from worrying the flock. The institution of convents abroad, seems in one point a strain of great wisdom, there being few irregularities in human passions, which may not have recourse to vent themselves in some of those orders, which are so many retreats for the speculative, the melancholy, the proud, the silent, the politic, and the morose, to spend themselves, and evaporate the noxious particles; for each of whom we in this island are forced to provide a several sect of religion, to keep them quiet; and whenever Christianity shall be abolished, the legislature must find some other expedient to employ and entertain them. For what imports it how large a gate you open, if there will be always left a number who place a pride and a merit in refusing to enter?

Having thus considered the most important objections against Christianity, and the chief advantages proposed by the abolishing thereof; I shall now, with equal deference and submission to wiser judgments, as before, proceed to mention a few inconveniences that may happen, if the Gospel should be repealed; which perhaps the projectors may not have sufficiently considered.

And first, I am very sensible how much the gentlemen of wit and pleasure are apt to murmur, and be choqued at the sight of so many daggled-tail parsons, that happen to fall in their way, and offend their eyes; but at the same time, these wise reformers do not consider what an advantage and felicity it is, for great wits to be always provided with objects of scorn and contempt, in order to exercise and improve their talents, and divert their spleen from falling on each other or on themselves; especially when all this may be done without the least imaginable danger to their persons.

And to urge another argument of a parallel nature: if Christianity were once abolished, how could the freethinkers, the strong reasoners, and the men of profound learning, be able to find another subject so calculated in all points whereon to display their abilities? What wonderful productions of wit should we be deprived of, from those whose genius by continual practice hath been wholly turned upon raillery and invectives against religion, and would therefore never be able to shine or distinguish themselves upon any other subject! We are daily complaining of the great decline of wit among us, and would we take away the greatest, perhaps the only topic we have left? Who would ever have suspected Asgil for a wit, or Toland for a philosopher, if the inexhaustible stock of Christianity had not been at hand to provide them with materials? What other subject, through all art or nature, could have produced Tindal for a profound author, or furnished him with readers? It is the wise choice of the subject that alone adorns and distinguishes the writer. For, had a hundred such pens as these been em-

42. **enthusiasm,** fanaticism.

22. **choqued,** shocked.

ployed on the side of religion, they would have immediately sunk into silence and oblivion.

Nor do I think it wholly groundless, or my fears altogether imaginary, that the abolishing Christianity may perhaps bring the Church into danger, or at least put the senate to the trouble of another securing vote. I desire I may not be mistaken; I am far from presuming to affirm or think that the Church is in danger at present, or as things now stand; but we know not how soon it may be so when the Christian religion is repealed. As plausible as this project seems, there may be a dangerous design lurking under it. Nothing can be more notorious, than that the Atheists, Deists, Socinians, Anti-trinitarians, and other subdivisions of freethinkers, are persons of little zeal for the present ecclesiastical establishment: their declared opinion is for repealing the Sacramental Test; they are very indifferent with regard to ceremonies; nor do they hold the *jus divinum* of Episcopacy. Therefore this may be intended as one politic step toward altering the constitution of the Church established, and setting up Presbytery in the stead, which I leave to be further considered by those at the helm.

In the last place, I think nothing can be more plain, than that by this expedient, we shall run into the evil we chiefly pretend to avoid; and that the abolishment of the Christian religion will be the readiest course we can take to introduce popery. And I am the more inclined to this opinion, because we know it has been the constant practice of the Jesuits to send over emissaries, with instructions to personate themselves members of the several prevailing sects among us. So it is recorded, that they have at sundry times appeared in the disguise of Presbyterians, Anabaptists, Independents and Quakers, according as any of these were most in credit; so, since the fashion has been taken up of exploding religion, the popish missionaries have not been wanting to mix with the freethinkers; among whom, Toland the great oracle of the Antichristians, is an Irish priest, the son of an Irish priest; and the most learned and ingenious author of a book called "The Rights of the Christian Church," was in a proper juncture reconciled to the Romish faith, whose true son, as appears by a hundred passages in his treatise, he still continues. Perhaps I could add some others to the number; but the fact is beyond dispute, and the reasoning they proceed by is right: for, supposing Christianity to be extinguished, the people will never be at ease till they find out some other method of worship; which will as infallibly produce superstition, as this will end in popery.

And therefore if, notwithstanding all I have said, it still be thought necessary to have a bill brought in for repealing Christianity, I would humbly offer an amendment; that instead of the word *Christianity,* may be put *religion in general;* which I conceive will much better answer all the good ends proposed by the projectors of it. For, as long as we leave in being a God and his providence, with all the necessary consequences which curious and inquisitive men will be apt to draw from such premises, we do not strike at the root of the evil, though we should ever so effectually annihilate the present scheme of the Gospel: for of what use is freedom of thought, if it will not produce freedom of action, which is the sole end, how remote soever in appearance, of all objections against Christianity? And therefore, the freethinkers consider it as a sort of edifice, wherein all the parts have such a mutual dependence on each other, that if you happen to pull out one single nail, the whole fabric must fall to the ground. This was happily expressed by him who had heard of a text brought for proof of the Trinity, which in an ancient manuscript was differently read; he thereupon immediately took the hint, and by a sudden deduction of a long *sorites* most logically concluded; "Why, if it be as you say, I may safely whore and drink on, and defy the parson." From which, and many the like instances easy to be produced, I think nothing can be more manifest, than that the quarrel is not against any particular points of hard digestion in the Christian system, but against religion in general; which, by laying restraints on human nature, is supposed the great enemy to the freedom of thought and action.

Upon the whole, if it shall still be thought for the benefit of Church and State, that Christianity be abolished, I conceive however, it may be more convenient to defer the execution to a time of peace, and not venture in this conjuncture to disoblige our allies, who, as it falls out, are all Christians, and many of them, by the prejudices of their education, so bigoted, as to place a sort of pride in the appellation. If upon being rejected by them, we are to trust to an alliance with the Turk, we shall find ourselves much deceived: for, as he is too remote, and generally engaged in war with the Persian emperor, so his people would be more scandalized at our infidelity, than our Christian neighbours. For they [the Turks] are not only strict observers of religious worship, but what is worse, believe a God; which is more than is required of us even while we preserve the name of Christians.

---

14. **Socinians,** deniers of the divinity of Christ.   19. **jus divinum,** divine right.   43. **author,** Matthew Tindal (d. 1733), an English Deist.

27. **sorites,** a chain of syllogisms.

To conclude: Whatever some may think of the great advantages to trade by this favourite scheme, I do very much apprehend, that in six months time after the act is passed for the extirpation of the Gospel, the Bank, and East India Stock may fall at least one *per cent*. And since that is fifty times more than ever the wisdom of our age thought fit to venture for the preservation of Christianity, there is no reason we should be at so great a loss, merely for the sake of destroying it.

A MODEST PROPOSAL

FOR PREVENTING THE CHILDREN OF POOR PEOPLE IN IRELAND FROM BEING A BURTHEN TO THEIR PARENTS OR COUNTRY, AND FOR MAKING THEM BENEFICIAL TO THE PUBLIC
1729

Swift's hatred of all cruelty is clearly shown by the fact that in this, his most powerful pamphlet, he attacks his own people, the English, for their brutally tyrannical treatment of a people, the Irish, whom he despised.

IT is a melancholy object to those who walk through this great town or travel in the country, when they see the streets, the roads, and cabin-doors, crowded with beggars of the female sex, followed by three, four, or six children, *all in rags*, and importuning every passenger for an alms. These mothers, instead of being able to work for their honest livelihood, are forced to employ all their time in strolling, to beg sustenance for their helpless infants, who, as they grow up, either turn thieves for want of work, or leave their dear native country to fight for the Pretender in Spain, or sell themselves to the Barbadoes.

I think it is agreed by all parties that this prodigious number of children, in the arms, or on the backs, or at the heels of their mothers, and frequently of their fathers, is in the present deplorable state of the kingdom a very great additional grievance; and therefore whoever could find out a fair, cheap, and easy method of making these children sound, useful members of the commonwealth, would deserve so well of the public as to have his statue set up for a preserver of the nation.

But my intention is very far from being confined to provide only for the children of professed beggars; it is of a much greater extent, and shall take in the whole number of infants at a certain age, who are born of parents in effect as little able to support them as those who demand our charity in the streets.

As to my own part, having turned my thoughts for many years upon this important subject, and maturely weighed the several schemes of other projectors, I have always found them grossly mistaken in their computation. It is true, a child, just dropped from its dam, may be supported by her milk for a solar year with little other nourishment, at most not above the value of two shillings, which the mother may certainly get, or the value in scraps, by her lawful occupation of begging; and it is exactly at one year old that I propose to provide for them in such a manner as instead of being a charge upon their parents or the parish, or wanting food and raiment for the rest of their lives, they shall, on the contrary, contribute to the feeding and partly to the clothing of many thousands.

There is likewise another great advantage in my scheme, that it will prevent those voluntary abortions, and that horrid practice of women murdering their bastard children, alas, too frequent among us, sacrificing the poor innocent babes, I doubt, more to avoid the expense than the shame, which would move tears and pity in the most savage and inhuman breast.

The number of souls in this kingdom being usually reckoned one million and a half, of these I calculate there may be about two hundred thousand couple whose wives are breeders; from which number I subtract thirty thousand couple who are able to maintain their own children, although I apprehend there cannot be so many under the present distresses of the kingdom; but this being granted, there will remain an hundred and seventy thousand breeders. I again subtract fifty thousand for those women who miscarry, or whose children die by accident or disease within the year. There only remain an hundred and twenty thousand children of poor parents annually born. The question therefore is, how this number shall be reared and provided for, which, as I have already said, under the present situation of affairs, is utterly impossible by all the methods hitherto proposed, for we can neither employ them in handicraft or agriculture; we neither build houses (I mean in the country) nor cultivate land; they can very seldom pick up a livelihood by stealing till they arrive at six years old, except where they are of towardly parts, although I confess they learn the rudiments much earlier, during which time, they can however be properly looked upon only as *probationers*; as I have been informed by a principal gentleman in the County of Cavan, who protested to me, that he never knew above one or two instances

27. this . . . town, Dublin.

under the age of six, even in a part of the kingdom so renowned for the quickest proficiency in that art.

I am assured by our merchants that a boy or a girl before twelve years old is no saleable commodity, and even when they come to this age, they will not yield above three pounds, or three pounds and half-a-crown at most on the Exchange, which cannot turn to account either to the parents or kingdom, the charge of nutriment and rags having been at least four times that value.

I shall now therefore humbly propose my own thoughts, which I hope will not be liable to the least objection.

I have been assured by a very knowing American of my acquaintance in London, that a young healthy child well nursed is at a year old a most delicious, nourishing, and wholesome food, whether stewed, roasted, baked, or boiled, and I make no doubt that it will equally serve in a fricassee or a ragout.

I do therefore humbly offer it to public consideration that of the hundred and twenty thousand children already computed, twenty thousand may be reserved for breed, whereof only one fourth part to be males, which is more than we allow to sheep, black cattle, or swine; and my reason is that these children are seldom the fruits of marriage, a circumstance not much regarded by our savages. Therefore one male will be sufficient to serve four females. That the remaining hundred thousand may at a year old be offered in sale to the persons of quality and fortune through the kingdom, always advising the mother to let them suck plentifully in the last month, so as to render them plump and fat for a good table. A child will make two dishes at an entertainment for friends, and when the family dines alone, the fore or hind quarter will make a reasonable dish, and seasoned with a little pepper or salt will be very good boiled on the fourth day, especially in winter.

I have reckoned, upon a medium, that a child just born will weigh 12 pounds, and in a solar year if tolerably nursed will increase to 28 pounds.

I grant this food will be somewhat dear, and therefore very proper for landlords, who, as they have already devoured most of the parents, seem to have the best title to the children.

Infants' flesh will be in season throughout the year, but more plentiful in March, and a little before and after, for we are told by a grave author, an eminent French physician, that fish being a prolific diet, there are more children born in Roman Catholic countries about nine months after Lent, than at any other season; therefore reckoning a year after Lent, the markets will be more glutted than usual, because the number of Popish infants is at least three to one in this kingdom, and therefore it will have one other collateral advantage, by lessening the number of Papists among us.

I have already computed the charge of nursing a beggar's child (in which list I reckon all cottagers, labourers, and four-fifths of the farmers) to be about two shillings *per annum*, rags included, and I believe no gentleman would repine to give ten shillings for the carcass of a good fat child, which, as I have said, will make four dishes of excellent nutritive meat, when he has only some particular friend or his own family to dine with him. Thus the squire will learn to be a good landlord, and grow popular among his tenants, the mother will have eight shillings net profit, and be fit for work till she produces another child.

Those who are more thrifty (as I must confess the times require) may flay the carcass; the skin of which, artificially dressed, will make admirable gloves for ladies, and summer boots for fine gentlemen.

As to our city of Dublin, shambles may be appointed for this purpose in the most convenient parts of it, and butchers we may be assured will not be wanting, although I rather recommend buying the children alive, and dressing them hot from the knife, as we do roasting pigs.

A very worthy person, a true lover of his country, and whose virtues I highly esteem, was lately pleased, in discoursing on this matter, to offer a refinement upon my scheme. He said, that many gentlemen of this kingdom having of late destroyed their deer, he conceived that the want of venison might be well supplied by the bodies of young lads and maidens, not exceeding fourteen years of age, nor under twelve, so great a number of both sexes in every country being now ready to starve, for want of work and service, and these to be disposed of by their parents if alive, or otherwise by their nearest relations. But with due deference to so excellent a friend, and so deserving a patriot, I cannot be altogether in his sentiments; for as to the males, my American acquaintance assured me from frequent experience, that their flesh was generally tough and lean, like that of our schoolboys, by continual exercise, and their taste disagreeable, and to fatten them would not answer the charge. Then as to the females, it would, I think with humble submission, be a loss to the public, because they soon would become breeders themselves. And besides, it is not improbable that some scrupulous people might be apt to censure such a practice, (although indeed very unjustly) as a little bordering upon cruelty, which,

I confess, has always been with me the strongest objection against any project, however so well intended.

But in order to justify my friend, he confessed that this expedient was put into his head by the famous Psalmanazar, a native of the island Formosa, who came from thence to London, above twenty years ago, and in conversation told my friend, that in his country when any young person happened to be put to death, the executioner sold the carcass to persons of quality, as a prime dainty, and that, in his time, the body of a plump girl of fifteen, who was crucified for an attempt to poison the emperor, was sold to his Imperial Majesty's Prime Minister of State, and other great Mandarins of the Court, in joints from the gibbet, at four hundred crowns. Neither indeed can I deny, that if the same use were made of several plump young girls in this town, who, without one single groat to their fortunes, cannot stir abroad without a chair, and appear at the playhouse and assemblies in foreign fineries, which they never will pay for, the kingdom would not be the worse.

Some persons of a desponding spirit are in great concern about that vast number of poor people who are aged, diseased, or maimed, and I have been desired to employ my thoughts what course may be taken, to ease the nation of so grievous an encumbrance. But I am not in the least pain upon that matter, because it is very well known that they are every day dying and rotting, by cold, and famine, and filth, and vermin, as fast as can be reasonably expected. And as to the young labourers, they are now in as hopeful a condition. They cannot get work, and consequently pine away for want of nourishment, to a degree that if at any time they are accidentally hired to common labour, they have not strength to perform it; and thus the country and themselves are happily delivered from the evils to come.

I have too long digressed, and therefore shall return to my subject. I think the advantages by the proposal which I have made are obvious and many, as well as of the highest importance.

For first, as I have already observed, it would greatly lessen the number of Papists, with whom we are yearly over-run, being the principal breeders of the nation, as well as our most dangerous enemies, and who stay at home on purpose to deliver the kingdom to the Pretender, hoping to take their advantage by the absence of so many good Protestants, who have chosen rather to leave their country, than stay at home, and pay tithes against their conscience, to an Episcopal curate.

Secondly, The poor tenants will have something valuable of their own, which by law may be made liable to distress, and help to pay their landlord's rent, their corn and cattle being already seized, and *money a thing unknown.*

Thirdly, Whereas the maintenance of an hundred thousand children, from two years old and upward, cannot be computed at less than ten shillings a piece per annum, the nation's stock will be thereby increased fifty thousand pounds *per annum*, besides the profit of a new dish, introduced to the tables of all gentlemen of fortune in the kingdom who have any refinement in taste, and the money will circulate among ourselves, the goods being entirely of our own growth and manufacture.

Fourthly, The constant breeders, beside the gain of eight shillings sterling *per annum*, by the sale of their children, will be rid of the charge of maintaining them after the first year.

Fifthly, This food would likewise bring great custom to taverns, where the vintners will certainly be so prudent as to procure the best receipts for dressing it to perfection, and consequently have their houses frequented by all the fine gentlemen who justly value themselves upon their knowledge in good eating; and a skilful cook, who understands how to oblige his guests, will contrive to make it as expensive as they please.

Sixthly, This would be a great inducement to marriage, which all wise nations have either encouraged by rewards, or enforced by laws and penalties. It would increase the care and tenderness of mothers toward their children, when they were sure of a settlement for life, to the poor babes, provided in some sort by the public, to their annual profit instead of expense. We should see an honest emulation among the married women, which of them could bring the fattest child to the market. Men would become as fond of their wives, during the time of their pregnancy, as they are now of their mares in foal, their cows in calf, their sows when they are ready to farrow, nor offer to beat or kick them (as is too frequent a practice) for fear of a miscarriage.

Many other advantages might be enumerated. For instance, the addition of some thousand carcasses in our exportation of barrelled beef, the propagation of swine's flesh, and improvement in the art of making good bacon, so much wanted among us by the great destruction of pigs, too frequent at our table, which are no way comparable in taste, or magnificence, to a well-grown, fat yearling child, which roasted whole will make a considerable figure

---

6. **Psalmanazar,** really a Frenchman, who published in 1704 a fictitious description of Formosa

at a Lord Mayor's feast, or any other public entertainment. But this and many others I omit, being studious of brevity.

Supposing that one thousand families in this city would be constant customers for infants' flesh, beside others who might have it at merry-meetings, particularly at weddings and christenings, I compute that Dublin would take off annually about twenty thousand carcasses; and the rest of the kingdom (where probably they will be sold somewhat cheaper) the remaining eighty thousand.

I can think of no one objection, that will possibly be raised against this proposal, unless it should be urged that the number of people will be thereby much lessened in the kingdom. This I freely own, and it was indeed one principal design in offering it to the world. I desire the reader will observe, that I calculate my remedy *for this one individual kingdom of Ireland, and for no other that ever was, is, or, I think, ever can be upon earth.* Therefore let no man talk to me of other expedients: *Of taxing our absentees at five shillings a pound: Of using neither clothes, nor household furniture, except what is of our own growth and manufacture: Of utterly rejecting the materials and instruments that promote foreign luxury: Of curing the expensiveness of pride, vanity, idleness, and gaming in our women: Of introducing a vein of parsimony, prudence and temperance: Of learning to love our Country, wherein we differ even from* Laplanders, *and the inhabitants of* Topinamboo: *Of quitting our animosities and factions, nor act any longer like the Jews, who were murdering one another at the very moment their city was taken: Of being a little cautious not to sell our country and conscience for nothing: Of teaching landlords to have at least one degreee of mercy toward thir tenants. Lastly of putting a spirit of honesty, industry, and skill into our shopkeepers, who, if a resolution could now be taken to buy only our native goods, would immediately unite to cheat and exact upon us in the price, the measure, and the goodness, nor could ever yet be brought to make one fair proposal of just dealing, though often and earnestly invited to it.*

Therefore I repeat, let no man talk to me of these and the like expedients till he hath at least some glimpse of hope that there will ever be some hearty and sincere attempt to put them in practice.

But as to myself, having been wearied out for many years with offering vain, idle, visionary thoughts, and at length utterly despairing of success, I fortunately fell upon this proposal, which as it is wholly new, so it hath something solid and real, of no expense and little trouble, full in our own power, and whereby we can incur no danger in *disobliging* ENGLAND. For this kind of commodity will not bear exportation, the flesh being of too tender a consistence to admit a long continuance in salt, *although perhaps I could name a country which would be glad to eat up our whole nation without it.*

After all, I am not so violently bent upon my own opinion as to reject any offer, proposed by wise men, which shall be found equally innocent, cheap, easy and effectual. But before something of that kind shall be advanced in contradiction to my scheme, and offering a better, I desire the author or authors will be pleased maturely to consider two points. First, as things now stand, how they will be able to find food and raiment for an hundred thousand useless mouths and backs. And secondly, there being a round million of creatures in human figure throughout this kingdom, whose whole subsistence put into a common stock would leave them in debt two million pounds sterling, adding those who are beggars by profession to the bulk of farmers, cottagers and labourers, with their wives and children, who are beggars in effect, I desire those politicians, who dislike my overture, and may perhaps be so bold as to attempt an answer, that they will first ask the parents of these mortals, whether they would not at this day think it a great happiness to have been sold for food at a year old, in the manner I prescribe, and thereby have avoided such a perpetual scene of misfortunes as they have since gone through by the oppression of landlords, the impossibility of paying rent without money or trade, the want of common sustenance, with neither house nor clothes to cover them from the inclemencies of the weather, and the most inevitable prospect of entailing the like or greater miseries upon their breed for ever.

I profess, in the sincerity of my heart, that I have not the least personal interest in endeavouring to promote this necessary work, having no other motive than the *public good of my country, by advancing our trade, providing for infants, relieving the poor, and giving some pleasure to the rich.* I have no children by which I can propose to get a single penny; the youngest being nine years old, and my wife past child-bearing.

---

29. **Topinamboo,** a district of Brazil supposedly inhabited by savages.

4–5. **not bear exportation.** "So that there would be no danger of an objection from England that the English were suffering from Irish competition."—Temple Scott

Joseph Addison and Richard Steele
1672–1719   1672–1729

The lives of Addison and Steele were so closely interrelated, aside from the fact that the two were born within a few weeks of each other, that we can now scarcely think of either man without some thought of his companion. Steele was born in Dublin and Addison in a Wiltshire village, but both attended the Charterhouse School in London and went from there to Oxford University.

It was characteristic of Addison that after taking his degree he secured a fellowship at Magdalen College and lingered on there in the not very laborious life of a college fellow—reading widely, conversing shyly, strolling every day along the path still known as Addison's Walk, drinking expensive wines, and writing unexceptionable verses in Latin and English. This, so far as his ambitions were concerned, might have gone on indefinitely, but the young man's somewhat uncommon ability as a versifier attracted the attention of a few leading Whigs when he was about twenty-seven, with the result that he was granted a comfortable pension in order that the Whig party might retain his literary services.

On the funds thus provided Addison spent some four years in European travel and study, thus making himself, according to the easy standards of his age, a rather learned and certainly a very cultivated man. Upon his return to England he repaid the generosity of the Whigs by writing for them a poem called "The Campaign" in celebration of the Duke of Marlborough's recent victory in the Battle of Blenheim. This poem, to our taste a cold and stilted performance, made his political and literary fortune. In the year 1713 he followed it with a tragedy called *Cato*, equally lifeless, and equally successful because of the sound political doctrines it was thought to uphold. The unhappiness of his last years was not alleviated by his growing indulgence in expensive wines, by his appointment to the Secretaryship of State, or by his emptily splendid marriage to the Dowager Countess of Warwick.

Richard Steele, meanwhile, taking the very different path through life of a gay and companionable man, left Oxford without a degree to enter the army. Instead of an academic fellowship he won, before he was thirty, a captaincy. A little after the turn of the century he began to write for the London stage, where his *Lying Lover* and *Tender Husband*, both of them decent yet blithe and gay-hearted comedies, were well received. He held some minor offices of state during the later years of Queen Anne, but shortly after the accession of George I he was elected a member of Parliament, was dubbed a knight, and was granted several sinecures in the gift of the ruling Whig party. Perhaps the greatest honor of his life came in 1715, when he was made manager of Drury Lane Theatre. This prosperity, however, only increased his temptations to the reckless and spendthrift living which had always been his natural tendency. Financial and other troubles obliged him to leave London in 1723, and the last six years of his life were spent rather dismally in various provincial towns.

Addison and Steele came together in their most fruitful partnership in their work on the *Tatler* and the *Spectator*, lasting from April, 1709, to December, 1712. It has long been a pretty question as between academic persons and those who plump for spermatic vigor, which of the two did the better work. Every reader is entitled to his own opinion, but no one should forget that Steele thought out the plan for these two papers—he who had always shown in his writing, if not in his conduct, a deep concern for the morals of London and England. He and Addison agreed—and so, no doubt, did the fifty or more miscellaneous persons who occasionally contributed essays or letters—that the main purpose of the *Tatler* and the *Spectator* was to improve, to mollify and urbanize, to reform, the manners if not the morals of the English people. These two periodicals, the first of which appeared thrice a week and the second six times, have an important place in the history of English journalism, but they were concerned to only a slight extent with anything that we should now call news. What they mainly tried to do was to uplift; and this, it was felt, could be managed not so well by the harsh methods of satire as by a gentle, good-humored raillery, a steady application of friendly laughter and common sense. It seems probable that Addison and Steele had some success in their well-considered effort. There is no doubt whatever that they succeeded in other regards to which they gave less conscious attention. Certainly they succeeded in presenting a vivid picture of the English social life of their day, in drawing a dozen or more indelible imaginary portraits of typical English persons, and, not least, in showing once and for all that English prose may be simple without loss of beauty and idiomatic without being "low."

from THE TATLER

NO. 25. TUESDAY, JUNE 7, 1709 (Steele)

*Quicquid agunt homines—
nostri est farrago libelli.*   Juv. Sat. i. 85, 86.

Whate'er men do, or say, or think, or dream,
Our motley paper seizes for its theme.—P[ope]

A LETTER from a young lady, written in the most passionate terms, wherein she laments the misfortune of a gentleman, her lover, who was lately wounded in a duel, has turned my thoughts to that subject, and inclined me to examine into the causes which precipitate men into so fatal a folly. And as it has been proposed to treat of subjects of gallantry in the article from hence, and no one point in nature is more proper to be considered by the company who frequent this place than that of duels, it is worth our consideration to examine into this chimerical groundless humour, and to lay every other thought aside until we have stripped it of all its false pretences to credit and reputation amongst men.

But I must confess, when I consider what I am going about, and run over in my imagination all the endless crowd of men of honour who will be offended at such a discourse, I am undertaking, methinks, a work worthy an invulnerable hero in romance, rather than a private gentleman with a single rapier: but as I am pretty well acquainted by great opportunities with the nature of man, and know of a truth that all men fight *against their will*, the danger vanishes, and resolution rises upon this subject. For this reason I shall talk very freely on a custom which all men wish exploded, though no man has courage enough to resist it.

But there is one unintelligible word which I fear will extremely perplex my dissertation; and I confess to you I find very hard to explain, which is, the term *satisfaction*. An honest country gentleman had the misfortune to fall into company with two or three modern men of honour, where he happened to be very ill treated; and one of the company, being conscious of his offence, sends a note to him in the morning, and tells him, he was ready to give him satisfaction. This is fine doing (says the plain fellow), last night he sent me away cursedly out of humour, and this morning he fancies it would be a satisfaction to be run through the body.

As the matter at present stands, it is not to do handsome actions denominates a man of honour; it is enough if he dares to defend ill ones. Thus you often see a common sharper in competition with a gentleman of the first rank; though all mankind is convinced, that a fighting gamester is only a pickpocket with the courage of a highway-man. One cannot with any patience reflect on the unaccountable jumble of persons and things in this town and nation, which occasions very frequently that a brave man falls by a hand below that of a common hangman, and yet his executioner escapes the clutches of the hangman for doing it. I shall therefore hereafter consider, how the bravest men in other ages and nations have behaved themselves upon such incidents as we decide by combat; and show, from their practice, that this resentment neither has its foundation from true reason, or solid fame; but is an imposture made up of cowardice, falsehood, and want of understanding. For this work, a good history of quarrels would be very edifying to the public, and I apply my self to the town for particulars and circumstances within their knowledge, which may serve to embellish the dissertation with proper cuts. Most of the quarrels I have ever known, have proceeded from some valiant coxcomb's persisting in the wrong, to defend some prevailing folly, and preserve himself from the ingenuity of owning a mistake.

By this means it is called *giving a man satisfaction*, to urge your offence against him with your sword; which puts me in mind of Peter's order to the keeper, in *The Tale of a Tub: If you neglect to do all this, damn you and your generation for ever; and so we bid you heartily farewell.* If the contradiction in the very terms of one of our challenges were as well explained and turned into downright *English*, would it not run after this manner?

"Sir,

"Your extraordinary behaviour last night, and the liberty you were pleased to take with me, makes me this morning give you this, to tell you, because you are an ill-bred puppy, I will meet you in *Hide-park*, an hour hence; and because you want both breeding and humanity, I desire you would come with a pistol in your hand, on horseback, and endeavour to shoot me through the head; to teach you more manners. If you fail of doing me this pleasure, I

---

24. **hence.** This number of the *Tatler* is dated from "White's Chocolate-house."

32. **ingenuity,** ingenuousness.

shall say, you are a rascal, on every post in town: and so, Sir, if you will not injure me more, I shall never forgive what you have done already. Pray Sir, do not fail of getting every thing ready, and you will infinitely oblige,

SIR

"*Your most obedient, humble servant, &c.*". . .

NO. 158. THURSDAY, APRIL 13, 1710 (Addison)

Faciunt nae intelligendo, ut nihil intelligant.—Ter.

TOM Folio is a broker in learning, employed to get together good editions, and stock the libraries of great men. There is not a sale of books begins until *Tom Folio* is seen at the door. There is not an auction where his name is not heard, and that too in the very nick of time, in the critical moment, before the last decisive stroke of the hammer. There is not a subscription goes forward in which *Tom* is not privy to the first rough draught of the proposals; nor a catalogue printed, that doth not come to him wet from the press. He is a universal scholar, so far as the title-page of all authors, knows the manuscripts in which they were discovered, the editions through which they have passed, with the praises or censures which they have received from the several members of the learned world. He has a greater esteem for *Aldus* and *Elzevir*, than for *Virgil* and *Horace*. If you talk of *Herodotus*, he breaks out into a panegyric upon *Harry Stephens*. He thinks he gives you an account of an author, when he tells you the subject he treats of, the name of the editor, and the year in which it was printed. Or if you draw him into further particulars, he cries up the goodness of the paper, extols the diligence of the corrector, and is transported with the beauty of the letter. This he looks upon to be sound learning and substantial criticism. As for those who talk of the fineness of style, and the justness of thought, or describe the brightness of any particular passages; nay, though they themselves write in the genius and spirit of the author they admire, *Tom* looks upon them as men of superficial learning, and flashy parts.

I had yesterday morning a visit from this learned idiot, (for that is the light in which I consider every pedant) when I discovered in him some little touches of the coxcomb, which I had not before observed. Being very full of the figure which he makes in the republic of letters, and wonderfully satisfied with his great stock of knowledge, he gave me broad intimations, that he did not *believe* in all points as his forefathers had done. He then communicated to me a thought of a certain author upon a passage of *Virgil's* account of the dead, which I made the subject of a late paper. This thought hath taken very much among men of *Tom's* pitch and understanding, though universally exploded by all that know how to construe *Virgil*, or have any relish of antiquity. Not to trouble my reader with it, I found upon the whole, that *Tom* did not believe [in] a future state of rewards and punishments, because *Aeneas*, at his leaving the empire of the dead, passed through the gate of ivory, and not through that of horn. Knowing that *Tom* had not sense enough to give up an opinion which he had once received, that he might avoid wrangling, I told him, that *Virgil* possibly had his oversights as well as another author. Ah! Mr. *Bickerstaff*, says he, you would have another opinion of him, if you would read him in *Daniel Heinsius's* edition. I have perused him my self several times in that edition, continued he; and after the strictest and most malicious examination, could find but two faults in him: one of them is in the *Aeneids*, where there are two commas instead of a parenthesis; and another in the third *Georgic*, where you may find a semicolon turned upside-down. Perhaps, said I, these were not *Virgil's* faults, but those of the transcriber. I do not design it, says *Tom*, as a reflection on *Virgil:* on the contrary, I know that all the manuscripts declaim against such a punctuation. Oh! Mr. *Bickerstaff*, says he, what would a man give to see one simile of *Virgil* writ in his own hand? I asked him which was the simile he meant; but was answered, any simile in *Virgil*. He then told me all the secret history in the commonwealth of learning; of modern pieces that had the names of ancient authors annexed to them; of all the books that were now writing or printing in the several parts of Europe; of many amendments which are made, and not yet published; and a thousand other particulars, which I would not have my memory burthened with for a Vatican.

At length, being fully persuaded that I thoroughly admired him, and looked upon him as a prodigy of learning, he took his leave. I know several of *Tom's* class who are professed admirers of *Tasso*, without understanding a word of *Italian:* and one in particular, that carries a *Pastor Fido* in his pocket, in which,

---

11. Faciunt . . . intelligant. While they pretend to know more than others, they know nothing in reality.—Terence, *Andria*, Prologue. **29. Aldus and Elzevir,** famous early printers. **31. Harry Stephens,** Henri Estienne (1531–1598), a learned publisher of the ancient classics.

22. Heinsius, a learned Dutch poet and editor of the classics (1580–1655). **44. Vatican,** that is, for all the books in the Vatican library. **50. Pastor Fido,** a pastoral drama by Giovanni Guarini (1537–1612).

I am sure he is acquainted with no other beauty but the clearness of the character.

There is another kind of pedant, who, with all *Tom Folio's* impertinences, hath greater superstructures and embellishments of *Greek* and *Latin*, and is still more insupportable than the other, in the same degree as he is more learned. Of this kind very often are editors, commentators, interpreters, scholiasts, and criticks; and in short, all men of deep learning without common sense. These persons set a greater value on themselves for having found out the meaning of a passage in *Greek*, than upon the author for having written it; nay, will allow the passage it self not to have any beauty in it, at the same time that they would be considered as the greatest men of the age, for having interpreted it. They will look with contempt on the most beautiful poems that have been composed by any of their contemporaries; but will lock themselves up in their studies for a twelve-month together, to correct, publish, and expound such trifles of antiquity, as a modern author would be contemned for. Men of the strictest morals, severest lives, and the gravest professions, will write volumes upon an idle sonnet, that is originally in *Greek* or *Latin;* give editions of the most immoral authors; and spin out whole pages upon the various readings of a lewd expression. All that can be said in excuse for them, is, that their works sufficiently shew they have no taste of their authors; and that what they do in this kind, is out of their great learning, and not out of any levity or lasciviousness of temper. . . .

NO. 181. JUNE 6, 1710 (Steele)

*—Dies, ni fallor, adest, quem semper acerbum,
Semper honoratum, sic Dii voluistis, habebo.*
—Virg.

THERE are those among mankind, who can enjoy no relish of their being, except the world is made acquainted with all that relates to them, and think every thing lost that passes unobserved; but others find a solid delight in stealing by the crowd, and modelling their life after such a manner, as is as much above the approbation as the practice of the vulgar. Life being too short to give instances great enough of true friendship or good-will, some sages have thought it pious to preserve a certain reverence for the manes of their deceased friends, and have withdrawn themselves from the rest of the world at certain seasons to commemorate in their own thoughts such of their acquaintance who have gone before them out of this life: and indeed, when we are advanced in years, there is not a more pleasing entertainment, than to recollect in a gloomy moment the many we have parted with that have been dear and agreeable to us, and to cast a melancholy thought or two after those, with whom, perhaps, we have indulged our selves in whole nights of mirth and jollity. With such inclinations in my heart I went to my closet yesterday in the evening, and resolved to be sorrowful; upon which occasion I could not but look with disdain upon my self, that though all the reasons which I had to lament the loss of many of my friends are now as forcible as at the moment of their departure, yet did not my heart swell with the same sorrow which I felt at that time; but I could, without tears, reflect upon many pleasing adventures I have had with some, who have long been blended with common earth. Though it is by the benefit of nature that length of time thus blots out the violence of afflictions, yet with tempers too much given to pleasure, it is almost necessary to revive the old places of grief in our memory, and ponder step by step on past life, to lead the mind into that sobriety of thought which poises the heart, and makes it beat with due time, without being quickened with desire, or retarded with despair, from its proper and equal motion. When we wind up a clock that is out of order, to make it go well for the future, we do not immediately set the hand to the present instant, but we make it strike the round of all its hours, before it can recover the regularity of its time. Such, thought I, shall be my method this evening; and since it is that day of the year which I dedicate to the memory of such in another life as I much delighted in when living, an hour or two shall be sacred to sorrow and their memory, while I run over all the melancholy circumstances of this kind which have occurred to me in my whole life.

The first sense of sorrow I ever knew was upon the death of my father, at which time I was not quite five years of age; but was rather amazed at what all the house meant, than possessed with a real understanding why no body was willing to play with me. I remember I went into the room where his body lay, and my mother sate weeping alone by it. I had my battledore in my hand, and fell a-beating the coffin, and calling "Papa"; for, I know not how, I had some slight idea that he was locked up there. My mother catched me in her arms, and transported

---

2. **character,** lettering.   25. **sonnet,** not used here in the strict sense but to mean any short poem.   37–38. **Dies . . . habebo.**
And now the rising day renews the year;
A day for ever sad, for ever dear.—Dryden's trans. of the *Æneid*, Book V, ll. 49–50.   1. **manes,** spirits.   13. **closet,** small room for retirement.

beyond all patience of the silent grief she was before in, she almost smothered me in her embraces; and told me in a flood of tears, Papa could not hear me, and would play with me no more, for they were going to put him under ground whence he could never come to us again. She was a very beautiful woman, of a noble spirit, and there was a dignity in her grief amidst all the wildness of her transport, which, methought, struck me with an instinct of sorrow, which, before I was sensible of what it was to grieve, seized my very soul, and has made pity the weakness of my heart ever since. The mind in infancy is, methinks, like the body in embryo, and receives impressions so forcible that they are as hard to be removed by reason, as any mark with which a child is born is to be taken away by any future application. Hence it is that good nature in me is no merit; but, having been so frequently overwhelmed with her tears before I knew the cause of any affliction, or could draw defences from my own judgment, I imbibed commiseration, remorse, and an unmanly gentleness of mind, which has since insnared me into ten thousand calamities; and from whence I can reap no advantage, except it be that, in such a humour as I am now in, I can the better indulge my self in the softnesses of humanity, and enjoy that sweet anxiety which arises from the memory of past afflictions. . .

from THE SPECTATOR

NO. 2. FRIDAY, MARCH 2, 1711 (Steele)

——*Haec alii sex*
Vel plures uno conclamant ore.
Juv., Sat. VII, 167–8.

THE first of our society is a gentleman of Worcestershire, of ancient descent, a baronet, his name is Sir ROGER DE COVERLEY. His great grandfather was inventor of that famous country-dance which is called after him. All who know that shire are very well acquainted with the parts and merits of Sir ROGER. He is a gentleman that is very singular in his behaviour, but his singularities proceed from his good sense, and are contradictions to the manners of the world only as he thinks the world is in the wrong. However, this humour creates him no enemies, for he does nothing with sourness or obstinacy; and his being unconfined to modes and forms, makes him but the readier and more capable to please and oblige all who know him. When he is in town, he lives in Soho Square: It is said, he keeps himself a batchelour by reason he was crossed in love by a perverse beautiful widow of the next county to him. Before this disappointment, Sir ROGER was what you call a fine gentleman, had often supped with my Lord *Rochester* and *Sir George Etherege*, fought a duel upon his first coming to town, and kicked *Bully Dawson* in a public coffee-house for calling him youngster. But, being ill used by the above-mentioned widow, he was very serious for a year and a half; and though, his temper being naturally jovial, he at last got over it, he grew careless of himself, and never dressed afterwards. He continues to wear a coat and doublet of the same cut that were in fashion at the time of his repulse, which, in his merry humours, he tells us, has been in and out twelve times since he first wore it. . . . He is now in his fifty-sixth year, cheerful, gay, and hearty; keeps a good house in both town and country; a great lover of mankind: but there is such a mirthful cast in his behaviour, that he is rather beloved than esteemed. His tenants grow rich, his servants look satisfied, all the young women profess love to him, and the young men are glad of his company. When he comes into a house he calls the servants by their names, and talks all the way up stairs to a visit. I must not omit, that Sir ROGER is a justice of the *quorum;* that he fills the chair at a quarter-session with great abilities, and three months ago, gained universal applause by explaining a passage in the game-act.

The gentleman next in esteem and authority among us is another batchelour, who is a member of the Inner Temple; a man of great probity, wit, and understanding; but he has chosen his place of residence rather to obey the direction of an old humoursome father, than in pursuit of his own inclinations. He was placed there to study the laws of the land, and is the most learned of any of the house in those of the stage. *Aristotle* and *Longinus* are much better understood by him than *Littleton* or *Cooke*. The father sends up every post questions relating to marriage-articles, leases, and tenures, in the neighbourhood; all which questions he agrees with an attorney to answer and take care of in the lump. He is studying the passions themselves, when he should be inquiring into the debates among men which arise from them. He knows the argument of each of the orations of *Demosthenes* and *Tully;* but not one case in the reports of our own courts. No one ever took him for a fool, but none, except his intimate

---

33–34. **Haec . . . ore.** Six others or more cry out with one voice. 52. **Soho Square,** at the time, a fashionable district. 5. **Rochester . . . Etherege,** wits and men of letters of the Restoration period. 7. **Dawson,** a notorious gambler. 33. **Inner Temple,** one of the Inns of Court, a haunt of lawyers. 40. **Littleton . . . Cooke** (Coke), authorities on matters of law. 48. **Tully,** Cicero.

friends, know he has a great deal of wit. This turn makes him at once both disinterested and agreeable. As few of his thoughts are drawn from business, they are most of them fit for conversation. His taste of books is a little too just for the age he lives in; he has read all, but approves of very few. His familiarity with the customs, manners, actions, and writings of the ancients, makes him a very delicate observer of what occurs to him in the present world. He is an excellent critick, and the time of the play is his hour of business; exactly at five he passes through New Inn, crosses through Russell Court, and takes a turn at Will's till the play begins; he has his shoes rubbed, and his periwig powdered at the barber's as you go into the Rose. It is for the good of the audience when he is at a play; for the actors have an ambition to please him.

The person of next consideration is Sir ANDREW FREEPORT, a merchant of great eminence in the city of London: a person of indefatigable industry, strong reason, and great experience. His notions of trade are noble and generous, and (as every rich man has usually some sly way of jesting, which would make no great figure were he not a rich man) he calls the sea the *British Common*. He is acquainted with commerce in all its parts, and will tell you that it is a stupid and barbarous way to extend dominion by arms, for true power is to be got by arts and industry. He will often argue, that if this part of our trade were well cultivated, we should gain from one nation; and if another, from another. I have heard him prove that diligence makes more lasting acquisitions than valour, and that sloth has ruined more nations than the sword. He abounds in several frugal maxims, amongst which the greatest favourite is, "A penny saved is a penny got." A general trader of good sense is pleasanter company than a general scholar; and Sir ANDREW having a natural unaffected eloquence, the perspicuity of his discourse gives the same pleasure that wit would in another man. He has made his fortunes himself; and says that England may be richer than other kingdoms, by as plain methods as he himself is richer than other men; though at the same time I can say this of him, that there is not a point in the compass, but blows home a ship in which he is an owner.

Next to Sir ANDREW in the club-room sits Captain SENTRY, a gentleman of great courage, good understanding, but invincible modesty. He is one of those that deserve very well, but are very awkward at putting their talents within the observation of such as should take notice of them. He was some years a captain, and behaved himself with great gallantry in several engagements and at several sieges; but having a small estate of his own, and being next heir to Sir ROGER, he has quitted a way of life in which no man can rise suitably to his merit who is not something of a courtier as well as a soldier. I have heard him often lament, that in a profession where merit is placed in so conspicuous a view, impudence should get the better of modesty. When he has talked to this purpose, I never heard him make a sour expression, but frankly confess that he left the world, because he was not fit for it. A strict honesty and an even regular behaviour are in themselves obstacles to him that must press through crowds who endeavour at the same end with himself, the favour of a commander. He will, however, in this way of talk, excuse generals, for not disposing according to men's desert, or enquiring into it: for, says he, that great man who has a mind to help me, has as many to break through to come at me as I have to come at him: therefore, he will conclude, that the man who would make a figure, especially in a military way, must get over all false modesty, and assist his patron against the importunity of other pretenders, by a proper assurance in his own vindication. He says it is a civil cowardice to be backward in asserting what you ought to expect, as it is a military fear to be slow in attacking when it is your duty. With this candour does the gentleman speak of himself and others. The same frankness runs through all his conversation. The military part of his life has furnished him with many adventures, in the relation of which he is very agreeable to the company; for he is never overbearing, though accustomed to command men in the utmost degree below him; nor ever too obsequious, from an habit of obeying men highly above him.

But that our society may not appear a set of humourists unacquainted with the gallantries and pleasures of the age, we have among us the gallant WILL. HONEYCOMB, a gentleman who, according to his years, should be in the decline of his life, but having ever been very careful of his person, and always had a very easy fortune, time has made but very little impression, either by wrinkles on his forehead, or traces on his brain. His person is well turned, of a good height. He is very ready at that sort of discourse with which men usually entertain women. He has all his life dressed very well, and remembers habits as others do men. He can smile when one speaks to him, and laughs easily. He knows the history of every mode, and can inform you from which of the French king's wenches our wives and daughters had this manner of curling

13. Will's, a coffeehouse.

their hair, that way of placing their hoods . . . and whose vanity to shew her foot made that part of the dress so short in such a year. In a word, all his conversation and knowledge have been in the female world: as other men of his age will take notice to you what such a minister said upon such and such an occasion, he will tell you when the Duke of *Monmouth* danced at court, such a woman was then smitten, another was taken with him at the head of his troop in the Park. In all these important relations, he has ever about the same time received a kind glance, or a blow of a fan, from some celebrated beauty, mother of the present lord such-a-one. . . . This way of talking of his, very much enlivens the conversation among us of a more sedate turn; and I find there is not one of the company but myself, who rarely speaks at all, but speaks of him as of that sort of man who is usually called a well-bred fine gentleman. To conclude his character, where women are not concerned, he is an honest worthy man.

I cannot tell whether I am to account him whom I am next to speak of, as one of our company; for he visits us but seldom, but when he does, it adds to every man else a new enjoyment of himself. He is a clergyman, a very philosophick man, of general learning, great sanctity of life, and the most exact good breeding. He has the misfortune to be of a very weak constitution; and consequently cannot accept of such cares and business as preferments in his function would oblige him to. He is therefore among divines what a chamber-counsellor is among lawyers. The probity of his mind, and the integrity of his life, create him followers, as being eloquent or loud advances others. He seldom introduces the subject he speaks upon; but we are so far gone in years, that he observes when he is among us, an earnestness to have him fall on some divine topick, which he always treats with much authority, as one who has no interests in this world, as one who is hastening to the object of all his wishes, and conceives hope from his decays and infirmities. These are my ordinary companions.   R.

NO. 10. MONDAY, MARCH 12, 1711 (Addison)

Non aliter quàm qui adverso vix flumine lembum
Remigiis subigit; si brachia forte remisit,
Atque illum in praeceps prono rapit alveus amni.

47–49. Non . . . amni.
So the boat's brawny crew the current stem,
And, slow advancing, struggle with the stream;
But if they slack their hands, or cease to strive,
Then down the flood with headlong haste they drive.
—Dryden's translation of Virgil, *Georgics*, I, l. 201.

IT is with much satisfaction that I hear this great city inquiring day by day after these my papers, and receiving my morning lectures with a becoming seriousness and attention. My publisher tells me, that there are already three thousand of them distributed every day: so that if I allow twenty readers to every paper, which I look upon as a modest computation, I may reckon about threescore thousand disciples in *London* and *Westminster*, who I hope will take care to distinguish themselves from the thoughtless herd of their ignorant and inattentive brethren. Since I have raised to myself so great an audience, I shall spare no pains to make their instruction agreeable, and their diversion useful. For which reasons I shall endeavour to enliven morality with wit, and to temper wit with morality, that my readers may, if possible, both ways find their account in the speculation of the day. And to the end that their virtue and discretion may not be short, transient, intermitting starts of thought, I have resolved to refresh their memories from day to day, till I have recovered them out of that desperate state of vice and folly, into which the age is fallen. The mind that lies fallow for a single day, sprouts up in follies that are only to be killed by a constant and assiduous culture. It was said of *Socrates*, that he brought philosophy down from heaven, to inhabit among men; and I shall be ambitious to have it said of me, that I have brought philosophy out of closets and libraries, schools and colleges, to dwell in clubs and assemblies, at tea-tables, and in coffee-houses.

I would therefore in a very particular manner recommend these my speculations to all well-regulated families, that set apart an hour in every morning for tea and bread and butter; and would earnestly advise them for their good to order this paper to be served up, and to be looked upon as a part of the tea equipage.

Sir *Francis Bacon* observes, that a well-written book, compared with its rivals and antagonists, is like *Moses's* serpent, that immediately swallowed up and devoured those of the *Aegyptians*. I shall not be so vain as to think, that where the SPECTATOR appears, the other publick prints will vanish; but shall leave it to my reader's consideration, whether it is not much better to be let into the knowledge of one's-self, than to hear what passes in *Muscovy* or *Poland;* and to amuse our selves with such writings as tend to the wearing out of ignorance, passion, and prejudice, than such as naturally conduce to inflame hatreds, and make enmities irreconcilable.

In the next place, I would recommend this paper to the daily persual of those gentlemen whom I cannot but consider as my good brothers and allies, I mean the fraternity of Spectators, who live in the world without having any thing to do in it; and either by the affluence of their fortunes, or laziness of their dispositions, have no other business with the rest of mankind but to look upon them. Under this class of men are comprehended all contemplative tradesmen, titular physicians, fellows of the Royal Society, Templars that are not given to be contentious, and statesmen that are out of business. In short, every one that considers the world as a theatre, and desires to form a right judgment of those who are the actors on it.

There is another set of men that I must likewise lay a claim to, whom I have lately called the blanks of society, as being altogether unfurnished with ideas, till the business and conversation of the day has supplied them. I have often considered these poor souls with an eye of great commiseration, when I have heard them asking the first man they have met with, whether there was any news stirring, and by that means gathering together materials for thinking. These needy persons do not know what to talk of, till about twelve a'clock in the morning; for by that time they are pretty good judges of the weather, know which way the wind sits, and whether the Dutch mail be come in. As they lie at the mercy of the first man they meet, and are grave or impertinent all the day long, according to the notions which they have imbibed in the morning, I would earnestly entreat them not to stir out of their chambers till they have read this paper, and do promise them that I will daily instil into them such sound and wholesome sentiments, as shall have a good effect upon their conversation for the ensuing twelve hours.

But there are none to whom this paper will be more useful than to the female world. I have often thought there has not been sufficient pains taken in finding out proper employment and diversions for the fair ones. Their amusements seem contrived for them rather as they are women, than as they are reasonable creatures; and are more adapted to the sex than to the species. The toilet is their great scene of business, and the right adjusting of their hair the principal employment of their lives. The sorting of a suit of ribbons is reckoned a very good morning's work; and if they make an excursion to a mercer's or a toy-shop, so great a fatigue makes them unfit for any thing else all the day after. Their more serious occupations are sewing and embroidery, and their greatest drudgery the preparation of jellies and sweet-meats. This, I say, is the state of ordinary women; though I know there are multitudes of those of a more elevated life and conversation, that move in an exalted sphere of knowledge and virtue, that join all the beauties of the mind to the ornaments of dress, and inspire a kind of awe and respect, as well as love, into their male-beholders. I hope to increase the number of these by publishing this daily paper, which I shall always endeavour to make an innocent if not an improving entertainment, and by that means at least divert the minds of my female readers from greater trifles. At the same time, as I would fain give some finishing touches to those which are already the most beautiful pieces in humane nature, I shall endeavour to point out all those imperfections that are the blemishes, as well as those virtues which are the embellishments, of the sex. In the mean while I hope these my gentle readers, who have so much time on their hands, will not grudge throwing away a quarter of an hour in a day upon this paper, since they may do it without any hindrance to business.

I know several of my friends and well-wishers are in great pain for me, lest I should not be able to keep up the spirit of a paper which I oblige myself to furnish every day: but to make them easy in this particular, I will promise them faithfully to give it over as soon as I grow dull. This I know will be a matter of great raillery to the small wits; who will frequently put me in mind of my promise, desire me to keep my word, assure me that it is high time to give over, with many other little pleasantries of the like nature, which men of a little smart genius cannot forbear throwing out against their best friends when they have such a handle given them of being witty. But let them remember, that I do hereby enter my caveat against this piece of raillery.

NO. 109. THURSDAY, JULY 5, 1711 (Steele)

Abnormis sapiens—Hor., 2 Sat. ii, 3.

I WAS this morning walking in the gallery, when Sir ROGER entered at the end opposite to me, and, advancing towards me, said he was glad to meet me among his relations the DE COVERLEYS, and hoped I liked the conversation of so much good company, who were as silent as myself. I knew he alluded to the pictures, and as he is a gentleman who does not a little value himself upon his ancient descent, I expected he would give me some ac-

---

8. **Templars**, students of law, or lawyers, so called because of living in the Temple in London.

37. **caveat**, warning—"let him beware." 41. **Abnormis sapiens.** Of plain good sense, untutored in the schools. 43. **gallery**, at Sir Roger's country house.

count of them. We were now arrived at the upper end of the gallery, when the Knight faced towards one of the pictures, and as we stood before it, he entered into the matter, after his blunt way of saying things, as they occur to his imagination, without regular introduction, or care to preserve the appearance of chain of thought.

"It is," said he, "worth while to consider the force of dress; and how the persons of one age differ from those of another, merely by that only. One may observe also, that the general fashion of one age has been followed by one particular set of people in another, and by them preserved from one generation to another. Thus the vast jetting coat and small bonnet, which was the habit in Harry the Seventh's time, is kept on the Yeomen of the Guard; not without a good and politick view, because they look a foot taller, and a foot and a half broader: besides that the cap leaves the face expanded, and consequently more terrible, and fitter to stand at the entrance of palaces.

"This predecessor of ours, you see, is dressed after this manner, and his cheeks would be no larger than mine, were he in a hat as I am. He was the last man that won a prize in the Tilt-yard (which is now a common street before Whitehall). You see the broken lance that lies there by his right foot. He shivered that lance of his adversary all to pieces; and bearing himself, look you, Sir, in this manner, at the same time he came within the target of the gentleman who rode against him, and taking him with incredible force before him on the pommel of his saddle, he in that manner rid the tournament over, with an air that showed he did it rather to perform the rule of the lists, than expose his enemy; however, it appeared he knew how to make use of a victory, and with a gentle trot he marched up to a gallery where their mistress sat (for they were rivals) and let him down with laudable courtesy and pardonable insolence. I do not know but it might be exactly where the coffee-house is now.

"You are to know this my ancestor was not only of a military genius, but fit also for the arts of peace, for he played on the base-viol as well as any gentleman at court; you see where his viol hangs by his basket-hilt sword. The action at the Tilt-yard you may be sure won the fair lady, who was a maid of honour and the greatest beauty of her time; here she stands, the next picture. You see, Sir, my great-great-great-grandmother has on the new-fashioned petticoat, except that the modern is gathered at the waist; my grandmother appears as if she stood in a large drum, whereas the ladies now walk as if they were in a go-cart. For all this lady was bred at court, she made an excellent country-wife; she brought ten children, and when I shew you the library, you shall see in her own hand (allowing for the difference of the language) the best receipt now in England for a hasty-pudding and a white-pot.

"If you please to fall back a little, because 'tis necessary to look at the three next pictures at one view; these are three sisters. She on the right hand, who is so very beautiful, died a maid; the next to her, still handsomer, had the same fate, against her will; this homely thing in the middle had both their portions added to her own, and was stolen by a neighbouring gentleman, a man of strategem and resolution; for he poisoned three mastiffs to come at her, and knocked down two deer-stealers in carrying her off. Misfortunes happen in all families. The theft of this romp and so much money, was no great matter to our estate. But the next heir that possessed it was this soft gentleman, whom you see there. Observe the small buttons, the little boots, the laces, the slashes about his clothes, and above all the posture he is drawn in (which to be sure was his own choosing); you see he sits with one hand on a desk, writing, and looking as it were another way, like an easy writer, or a sonneteer. He was one of those that had too much wit to know how to live in the world. He was a man of no justice, but great good manners; he ruined every body that had any thing to do with him, but never said a rude thing in his life; the most indolent person in the world, he would sign a deed that passed away half his estate with his gloves on, but would not put on his hat before a lady if it were to save his country. He is said to be the first that made love by squeezing the hand. He left the estate with ten thousand pounds debt upon it, but however by all hands I have been informed, that he was every way the finest gentleman in the world. That debt lay heavy on our house for one generation, but it was retrieved by a gift from that honest man you see there, a citizen of our name, but nothing at all a-kin to us. I know Sir ANDREW FREEPORT has said behind my back, that this man was descended from one of the ten children of the maid of honour I shewed you above; but it was never made out. We winked at the thing indeed, because money was wanting at that time."

Here I saw my friend a little embarrassed, and turned my face to the next portraiture.

Sir ROGER went on with his account of the gallery in the following manner. "This man (pointing to him I looked at) I take to be the honour of our

17. **Guard,** the bodyguard of the English sovereign. 33. **rid,** rode.

7. **white-pot,** a dish somewhat like a bread pudding.

house, Sir HUMPHREY DE COVERLEY. He was in his dealings as punctual as a tradesman, and as generous as a gentleman. He would have thought himself as much undone by breaking his word, as if it were to be followed by bankruptcy. He served his country as a knight of the shire to his dying day. He found it no easy matter to maintain an integrity in his words and actions, even in things that regarded the offices which were incumbent upon him, in the care of his own affairs and relations of life; and therefore dreaded (though he had great talents) to go into employments of state, where he must be exposed to the snares of ambition. Innocence of life and great ability were the distinguishing parts of his character; the latter, he had often observed, had led to the destruction of the former, and he used frequently to lament that great and good had not the same signification. He was an excellent husbandman, but had resolved not to exceed such a degree of wealth; all above it he bestowed in secret bounties many years after the sum he aimed at for his own use was attained. Yet he did not slacken his industry, but to a decent old age spent the life and fortune which were superfluous to himself, in the service of his friends and neighbours."

Here we were called to dinner, and Sir ROGER ended the discourse of this gentleman, by telling me, as we followed the servant, that this his ancestor was a brave man, and narrowly escaped being killed in the civil wars; "for," said he, "he was sent out of the field with a private message, the day before the battle of Worcester." The whim of narrowly escaping by having been within a day of danger, with other matters above-mentioned, mixed with good sense, left me at a loss whether I was more delighted with my friend's wisdom or simplicity.

NO. 112. MONDAY, JULY 9, 1711 (Addison)

'Αθανάτους μὲν πρῶτα θεοὺς, νόμῳ ὡς διάκειται,
Τίμα.   —Pyth.

I AM always very well pleased with a country Sunday, and think, if keeping holy the seventh day were only a human institution, it would be the best method that could have been thought of for the polishing and civilizing of mankind. It is certain the country-people would soon degenerate into a kind of savages and barbarians, were there not such frequent returns of a stated time, in which the whole village meet together with their best faces, and in their cleanliest habits, to converse with one another upon indifferent subjects, hear their duties explained to them, and join together in adoration of the Supreme Being. Sunday clears away the rust of the whole week, not only as it refreshes in their minds the notions of religion, but as it puts both the sexes upon appearing in their most agreeable forms, and exerting all such qualities as are apt to give them a figure in the eye of the village. A country-fellow distinguishes himself as much in the church-yard, as a citizen does upon the Change, the whole parish-politicks being generally discussed in that place either after sermon or before the bell rings.

My friend Sir ROGER, being a good churchman, has beautified the inside of his church with several texts of his own chusing: he has likewise given a handsome pulpit-cloth, and railed in the communion-table at his own expence. He has often told me that at his coming to his estate he found his parishioners very irregular; and that in order to make them kneel and join in the responses, he gave every one of them a hassock and a common-prayer book: and at the same time employed an itinerant singing-master, who goes about the country for that purpose, to instruct them rightly in the tunes of the psalms; upon which they now very much value themselves, and indeed out-do most of the country churches that I have ever heard.

As Sir ROGER is landlord to the whole congregation, he keeps them in very good order, and will suffer no body to sleep in it besides himself; for if by chance he has been surprised into a short nap at sermon, upon recovering out of it he stands up and looks about him, and if he sees any body else nodding, either wakes them himself, or sends his servant to them. Several other of the old Knight's particularities break out upon these occasions: sometimes he will be lengthening out a verse in the singing-psalms, half a minute after the rest of the congregation have done with it; sometimes, when he is pleased with the matter of his devotion, he pronounces *Amen* three or four times to the same prayer; and sometimes stands up when every body else is upon their knees, to count the congregation, or see if any of his tenants are missing.

I was yesterday very much surprised to hear my old friend, in the midst of the service, calling out to one *John Matthews* to mind what he was about, and not disturb the congregation. This *John Matthews* it seems is remarkable for being an idle fellow, and at that time was kicking his heels for his diversion. This authority of the Knight, though exerted in that odd manner which accompanies him in all circumstances of life, has a very good effect upon the par-

---

41-2. 'Αθανάτους . . . Τίμα. "First, in obedience to thy country's rites, worship the immortal gods."—Pythagoras

ish, who are not polite enough to see any thing ridiculous in his behaviour; besides that the general good sense and worthiness of his character makes his friends observe these little singularities as foils that rather set off than blemish his good qualities.

As soon as the sermon is finished, no body presumes to stir till Sir ROGER is gone out of the church. The Knight walks down from his seat in the chancel between a double row of his tenants, that stand bowing to him on each side; and every now and then enquires how such an one's wife, or mother, or son, or father do, whom he does not see at church; which is understood as a secret reprimand to the person that is absent.

The chaplain has often told me, that upon a catechising-day, when Sir ROGER has been pleased with a boy that answers well, he has ordered a Bible to be given him next day for his encouragement; and sometimes accompanies it with a flitch of bacon to his mother. Sir ROGER has likewise added five pounds a year to the clerk's place; and that he may encourage the young fellows to make themselves perfect in the church-service, has promised, upon the death of the present incumbent, who is very old, to bestow it according to merit.

The fair understanding between Sir ROGER and his chaplain, and their mutual concurrence in doing good, is the more remarkable, because the very next village is famous for the differences and contentions that rise between the parson and the 'squire, who live in a perpetual state of war. The parson is always preaching at the 'squire, and the 'squire to be revenged on the parson never comes to church. The 'squire has made all his tenants atheists, and tithe-stealers; while the parson instructs them every Sunday in the dignity of his order, and insinuates to them in almost every sermon, that he is a better man than his patron. In short matters have come to such an extremity, that the 'squire has not said his prayers either in publick or private this half year; and that the parson threatens him, if he does not mend his manners, to pray for him in the face of the whole congregation.

Feuds of this nature, though too frequent in the country, are very fatal to the ordinary people; who are so used to be dazzled with riches, that they pay as much deference to the understanding of a man of an estate, as of a man of learning; and are very hardly brought to regard any truth, how important soever it may be, that is preached to them, when they know there are several men of five hundred a year who do not believe it.

1. **polite,** polished, sophisticated.

NO. 122. FRIDAY, JULY 29, 1711 (Addison)

Comes jucundus in via pro vehiculo est.—Publ. Syr., Frag.

A MAN'S first care should be to avoid the reproaches of his own heart; his next, to escape the censures of the world. If the last interferes with the former, it ought to be entirely neglected; but otherwise, there cannot be a greater satisfaction to an honest mind, than to see those approbations which it gives it self seconded by the applauses of the publick: a man is more sure of his conduct, when the verdict which he passes upon his own behaviour is thus warranted and confirmed by the opinion of all that know him.

My worthy friend Sir ROGER is one of those who is not only at peace within himself, but beloved and esteemed by all about him. He receives a suitable tribute for his universal benevolence to mankind, in the returns of affection and good-will, which are paid him by every one that lives within his neighbourhood. I lately met with two or three odd instances of that general respect which is shewn to the good old Knight. He would needs carry *Will. Wimble* and myself with him to the county assizes. As we were upon the road *Will. Wimble* joined a couple of plain men who rid before us, and conversed with them for some time; during which my friend Sir ROGER acquainted me with their characters.

"The first of them," says he, "that has a spaniel by his side, is a yeoman of about an hundred pounds a year, an honest man: he is just within the game-act, and qualified to kill an hare or a pheasant: he knocks down a dinner with his gun twice or thrice a week: and by that means lives much cheaper than those who have not so good an estate as himself. He would be a good neighbour if he did not destroy so many partridges: in short he is a very sensible man, shoots flying; and has been several times foreman of the petty-jury.

"The other that rides along with him is *Tom Touchy*, a fellow famous for taking the law of every body. There is not one in the town where he lives that he has not sued at a quarter-sessions. The rogue had once the impudence to go to law with the widow. His head is full of costs, damages, and ejectments: he plagued a couple of honest gentlemen so

4. **Comes ... est.** A merry companion is as good on the road as a coach. 26. **assizes,** periodical sessions of a local court. 33. **yeoman,** small landowner. 46. **quarter-sessions,** a court of limited jurisdiction held in English counties every three months. 48. **widow,** a woman with whom Sir Roger had once been in love.

long for a trespass in breaking one of his hedges, till he was forced to sell the ground it enclosed to defray the charges of the prosecution: his father left him fourscore pounds a year; but he has cast and been cast so often, that he is not now worth thirty. I suppose he is going upon the old business of the willow-tree."

As Sir ROGER was giving me this account of *Tom Touchy*, *Will. Wimble* and his two companions stopped short till we came up to them. After having paid their respects to Sir ROGER, *Will.* told him that Mr. *Touchy* and he must appeal to him upon a dispute that arose between them. *Will.* it seems had been giving his fellow-traveller an account of his angling one day in such a hole; when *Tom Touchy*, instead of hearing out his story, told him that Mr. such an one, if he pleased, might take the law of him for fishing in that part of the river. My friend Sir ROGER heard them both upon a round trot; and after having paused some time told them, with the air of a man who would not give his judgment rashly, that *much might be said on both sides*. They were neither of them dissatisfied with the Knight's determination, because neither of them found himself in the wrong by it; upon which we made the best of our way to the assizes.

The court was sat before Sir ROGER came; but, notwithstanding all the justices had taken their places upon the bench, they made room for the old Knight at the head of them; who for his reputation in the country took occasion to whisper in the judge's ear that he was glad his lordship had met with so much good weather in his circuit. I was listening to the proceedings of the court with much attention, and infinitely pleased with that great appearance and solemnity which so properly accompanies such a publick administration of our laws; when, after about an hour's sitting, I observed to my great surprize, in the midst of a trial, that my friend Sir ROGER was getting up to speak. I was in some pain for him, till I found he had acquitted himself of two or three sentences with a look of much business and great intrepidity.

Upon his first rising the court was hushed, and a general whisper ran among the country people that Sir ROGER *was up*. The speech he made was so little to the purpose, that I shall not trouble my readers with an account of it; and I believe was not so much designed by the Knight himself to inform the court as to give him a figure in my eye, and keep up his credit in the country.

I was highly delighted, when the court rose, to see the gentlemen of the country gathering about my old friend, and striving who should compliment him most; at the same time that the ordinary people gazed upon him at a distance, not a little admiring his courage, that was not afraid to speak to the judge.

In our return home we met with a very odd accident; which I cannot forbear relating, because it shews how desirous all who know Sir ROGER are of giving him marks of their esteem. When we were arrived upon the verge of his estate, we stopped at a little inn to rest our selves and our horses. The man of the house had it seems been formerly a servant in the Knight's family; and to do honour to his old master, had some time since, unknown to Sir ROGER, put him up in a sign-post before the door; so that the *Knight's Head* had hung out upon the road about a week before he himself knew anything of the matter. As soon as Sir ROGER was acquainted with it, finding that his servant's indiscretion proceeded wholly from affection and good-will, he only told him that he had made him too high a compliment, and when the fellow seemed to think that could hardly be, added with a more decisive look, that it was too great an honour for any man under a duke; but told him at the same time, that it might be altered with a very few touches, and that he himself would be at the charge of it. Accordingly they got a painter by the Knight's directions to add a pair of whiskers to the face, and by a little aggravation to the features to change it into the *Saracen's Head*. I should not have known this story had not the innkeeper, upon Sir ROGER's alighting, told him in my hearing, that his honour's head was brought back last night with the alterations that he had ordered to be made in it. Upon this my friend with his usual cheerfulness related the particulars above-mentioned, and ordered the head to be brought into the room. I could not forbear discovering greater expressions of mirth than ordinary upon the appearance of this monstrous face, under which, notwithstanding it was made to frown and stare in a most extraordinary manner, I could still discover a distant resemblance of my old friend. Sir ROGER, upon seeing me laugh, desired me to tell him truly if I thought it possible for people to know him in that disguise. I at first kept my usual silence; but upon the Knight's conjuring me to tell him whether it was not still more like himself than a Saracen, I composed my countenance in the best manner I could, and replied that *much might be said on both sides*.

These several adventures, with the Knight's behaviour in them, gave me as pleasant a day as ever I met with in any of my travels.

4. cast, to defeat in a lawsuit.

NO. 159. SATURDAY, SEPTEMBER 1, 1711
(Addison)

> . . . *omnem, quae nunc obducta tuenti*
> *Mortales hebetat visus tibi, et humida circum*
> *Caligat, nubem eripiam.* . . .
> —Virg. *Æneid.*

When I was at *Grand Cairo*, I picked up several Oriental manuscripts, which I have still by me. Among others I met with one, entitled *The Visions of Mirzah*, which I have read over with great pleasure. I intend to give it to the publick when I have no other entertainment for them; and shall begin with the first vision, which I have translated word for word as follows:

"On the fifth day of the moon, which according to the custom of my forefathers I always keep holy, after having washed myself, and offered up my morning devotions, I ascended the high hills of *Bagdat*, in order to pass the rest of the day in meditation and prayer. As I was here airing myself on the tops of the mountains, I fell into a profound contemplation on the vanity of human life; and passing from one thought to another, Surely, said I, man is but a shadow and life a dream. Whilst I was thus musing, I cast my eyes towards the summit of a rock that was not far from me, where I discovered one in the habit of a shepherd, with a little musical instrument in his hand. As I looked upon him he applied it to his lips, and began to play upon it. The sound of it was exceeding sweet, and wrought into a variety of tunes that were inexpressibly melodious, and altogether different from any thing I had ever heard. They put me in mind of those heavenly airs that are played to the departed souls of good men upon their first arrival in Paradise, to wear out the impressions of the last agonies, and qualify them for the pleasures of that happy place. My heart melted away in secret raptures.

"I had been often told that the rock before me was the haunt of a Genius; and that several had been entertained with musick who had passed by it, but never heard that the musician had before made himself visible. When he had raised my thoughts, by those transporting airs which he played, to taste the pleasures of his conversation, as I looked upon him like one astonished, he beckoned to me, and by the waving of his hand directed me to approach the place where he sat. I drew near with that reverence which is due to a superior nature; and as my heart was entirely subdued by the captivating strains I had heard, I fell down at his feet and wept. The Genius smiled upon me with a look of compassion and affability that familiarized him to my imagination, and at once dispelled all the fears and apprehensions with which I approached him. He lifted me from the ground, and taking me by the hand, *Mirzah*, said he, I have heard thee in thy soliloquies; follow me.

"He then led me to the highest pinnacle of the rock, and placing me on the top of it, Cast thy eyes eastward, said he, and tell me what thou seest. I see, said I, a huge valley and a prodigious tide of water rolling through it. The valley that thou seest, said he, is the vale of misery, and the tide of water that thou seest is part of the great tide of eternity. What is the reason, said I, that the tide I see rises out of a thick mist at one end, and again loses itself in a thick mist at the other? What thou seest, said he, is that portion of eternity which is called time, measured out by the sun, and reaching from the beginning of the world to its consummation. Examine now, said he, this sea that is bounded with darkness at both ends, and tell me what thou discoverest in it. I see a bridge, said I, standing in the midst of the tide. The bridge thou seest, said he, is human life: consider it attentively. Upon a more leisurely survey of it, I found that it consisted of threescore and ten entire arches, with several broken arches, which, added to those that were entire, made up the number about an hundred. As I was counting the arches, the Genius told me that this bridge consisted at first of a thousand arches; but that a great flood swept away the rest, and left the bridge in the ruinous condition I now beheld it. But tell me further, said he, what thou discoverest on it. I see multitudes of people passing over it, said I, and a black cloud hanging on each end of it. As I looked more attentively, I saw several of the passengers dropping through the bridge, into the great tide that flowed underneath it; and upon farther examination, perceived there were innumerable trap-doors that lay concealed in the bridge, which the passengers no sooner trod upon, but they fell through them into the tide and immediately disappeared. These hidden pit-falls were set very thick at the entrance of the bridge, so that throngs of people no sooner broke through the cloud, but many of them fell into them. They grew thinner towards the middle, but multiplied and lay closer together towards the end of the arches that were entire.

"There were indeed some persons, but their number was very small, that continued a kind of hobbling march on the broken arches, but fell through one after another, being quite tired and spent with so long a walk.

3–5. **omnem . . . eripiam.** I shall snatch away all the cloud which, now drawn across your eyes, obscures your mortal vision. *Aeneid*, Book II, ll. 604–06.

"I passed some time in the contemplation of this wonderful structure, and the great variety of objects which it presented. My heart was filled with a deep melancholy to see several dropping unexpectedly in the midst of mirth and jollity, and catching at every thing that stood by them to save themselves. Some were looking up towards the heavens in a thoughtful posture, and, in the midst of a speculation, stumbled and fell out of sight. Multitudes were very busy in the pursuit of bubbles that glittered in their eyes and danced before them; but often when they thought themselves within the reach of them their footing failed and down they sunk. In this confusion of objects, I observed some with scimitars in their hands, and others with urinals, who ran to and fro upon the bridge, thrusting several persons on trap-doors which did not seem to lie in their way, and which they might have escaped had they not been thus forced upon them.

"The Genius seeing me indulge my self in this melancholy prospect, told me I had dwelt long enough upon it. Take thine eyes off the bridge, said he, and tell me if thou yet seest any thing thou dost not comprehend. Upon looking up, What mean, said I, those great flights of birds that are perpetually hovering about the bridge, and settling upon it from time to time? I see vultures, harpies, ravens, cormorants; and among many other feathered creatures several little winged boys, that perch in great numbers upon the middle arches. These, said the Genius, are envy, avarice, superstition, despair, love, with the like cares and passions that infest human life.

"I here fetched a deep sigh. Alas, said I, man was made in vain! How is he given away to misery and mortality, tortured in life, and swallowed up in death! The Genius, being moved with compassion towards me, bid me quit so uncomfortable a prospect. Look no more, said he, on man in the first stage of his existence, in his setting out for eternity; but cast thine eye on that thick mist into which the tide bears the several generations of mortals that fall into it. I directed my sight as I was ordered, and (whether or no the good Genius strengthened it with any supernatural force, or dissipated part of the mist that was before too thick for the eye to penetrate) I saw the valley opening at the farther end, and spreading forth into an immense ocean, that had a huge rock of adamant running through the midst of it, and dividing it into two equal parts. The clouds still rested on one half of it, insomuch that I could discover nothing in it; but the other appeared to me a vast ocean planted with innumerable islands, that were covered with fruits and flowers, and interwoven with a thousand little shining seas that ran among them. I could see persons dressed in glorious habits, with garlands upon their heads, passing among the trees, lying down by the side of fountains, or resting on beds of flowers; and could hear a confused harmony of singing birds, falling waters, human voices, and musical instruments. Gladness grew in me upon the discovery of so delightful a scene. I wished for the wings of an eagle, that I might fly away to those happy seats; but the Genius told me there was no passage to them, except through the gates of death that I saw opening every moment upon the bridge. The islands, said he, that lie so fresh and green before thee, and with which the whole face of the ocean appears spotted as far as thou canst see, are more in number than the sands on the sea-shore; there are myriads of islands behind those which thou here discoverest, reaching further than thine eye or even thine imagination can extend it self. These are the mansions of good men after death, who according to the degree and kinds of virtue in which they excelled, are distributed among these several islands, which abound with pleasures of different kinds and degrees, suitable to the relishes and perfections of those who are settled in them; every island is a paradise accommodated to its respective inhabitants. Are not these, O *Mirzah*, habitations worth contending for? Does life appear miserable, that gives thee opportunities of earning such a reward? Is death to be feared, that will convey thee to so happy an existence? Think not man was made in vain, who has such an eternity reserved for him. I gazed with inexpressible pleasure on these happy islands. At length, said I, shew me now, I beseech thee, the secrets that lie hid under those dark clouds which cover the ocean on the other side of the rock of adamant. The Genius making me no answer, I turned about to address myself to him a second time, but I found that he had left me; I then turned again to the vision which I had been so long contemplating; but instead of the rolling tide, the arched bridge, and the happy islands, I saw nothing but the long hollow valley of Bagdat, with oxen, sheep, and camels grazing upon the sides of it."

NO. 160. MONDAY, SEPTEMBER 3, 1711 (Addison)

———*Cui mens divinior, atque os*
Magna sonaturum, des nominis hujus honorem.—Hor.

49–50. Cui mens . . . honorem.
   On him confer the Poet's sacred name,
   Whose lofty voice proclaims the heavenly flame.
—Pope's translation of *Satires*, Book I, Sat. 4, ll. 43–44.

14–15. scimitars . . . urinals, representing warriors and physicians.   **43. it,** that is, the beholder's "sight."

THERE is no character more frequently given to a writer than that of being a "genius." I have heard many a little sonneteer called a *fine genius*. There is not an heroick scribbler in the nation that has not his admirers who think him a *great genius;* and as for your smatterers in tragedy, there is scarce a man among them who is not cried up by one or other for a *prodigious genius*.

My design in this paper is to consider what is properly a great genius, and throw some thoughts together on so uncommon a subject.

Among great geniuses those few draw the admiration of all the world upon them, and stand up as the prodigies of mankind, who by the mere strength of natural parts, and without the assistance of arts or learning, have produced works that were the delight of their own times and the wonder of posterity. There appears something nobly wild and extravagant in these great natural geniuses that is infinitely more beautiful than all the turn and polishing of what the French call a *bel esprit*, by which they would express a genius refined by conversation, reflection, and the reading of the most polite authors. The greatest genius which runs through the arts and sciences, takes a kind of tincture from them, and falls unavoidably into imitation.

Many of these great natural geniuses that were never disciplined and broken by rules of art, are to be found among the ancients, and in particular among those of the more eastern parts of the world. *Homer* has innumerable flights that *Virgil* was not able to reach, and in the Old Testament we find several passages more elevated and sublime than any in *Homer*. At the same time that we allow a greater and more daring genius to the ancients, we must own that the greatest of them very much failed in, or, if you will, that they were much above the nicety and correctness of the moderns. In their similitudes and allusions, provided there was a likeness, they did not much trouble themselves about the decency of the comparison. Thus *Solomon* resembles the nose of his beloved to the tower of *Lebanon* which looketh toward *Damascus;* as the coming of a thief in the night, is a similitude of the same kind in the New Testament. It would be endless to make collections of this nature. *Homer* illustrates one of his heroes encompassed by the enemy by an ass in a field of corn that has his sides belaboured by all the boys of the village without stirring a foot for it; and another of them tossing to and fro in his bed and burning with resentment, to a piece of flesh broiled on the coals. This particular failure in the ancients opens a large field of raillery to the little wits, who can laugh at an indecency but not relish the sublime in these sorts of writings. The present emperor of Persia, conformable to this Eastern way of thinking, amidst a great many pompous titles, denominates himself the sun of glory and the nutmeg of delight. In short, to cut off all cavilling against the ancients and particularly those of the warmer climates who had most heat and life in their imaginations, we are to consider that the rule of observing what the French call the *bienséance* in an allusion has been found out of latter years, and in the colder regions of the world; where we could make some amends for our want of force and spirit, by a scrupulous nicety and exactness in our compositions. Our countryman Shakespear was a remarkable instance of this first kind of great geniuses.

I cannot quit this head without observing that *Pindar* was a great genius of the first class, who was hurried on by a natural fire and impetuosity to vast conceptions of things and noble sallies of imagination. At the same time, can any thing be more ridiculous than for men of a sober and moderate fancy to imitate this poet's way of writing in those monstrous compositions which go among us under the name of Pindaricks? When I see people copying works which, as *Horace* has represented them, are singular in their kind, and inimitable; when I see men following irregularities by rule, and by the little tricks of art straining after the most unbounded flights of nature, I cannot but apply to them that passage in *Terence:*

"———*Incerta haec si tu postules
Ratione certâ facere, nikilo plus agas,
Quam si des operam, ut cum ratione insanias.*"

In short a modern Pindarick writer, compared with *Pindar*, is like a sister among the *Camisars* compared with *Virgil's* Sibyl. There is the distortion, grimace, and outward figure, but nothing of that divine impulse which raises the mind above its self, and makes the sounds more than human.

There is another kind of great geniuses which I shall place in a second class, not as I think them inferior to the first, but only for distinction's sake, as they are of a different kind. This second class of great geniuses are those that have formed themselves by rules, and submitted the greatness of their natural

---

40–41. **decency,** fitness.   46–47. **one of his heroes,** Ajax. See *Iliad*, Book II, l. 558.   50. **another,** Odysseus. See *Odyssey*, Book XX, l. 25.

27. **Pindaricks,** irregular odes of the sort written by Cowley and others in the seventeenth century.   34–36. "**Incerta . . . insanias.**" "You may as well pretend to be mad and in your senses at the same time, as to think of reducing these uncertain things to any certainty by reason"—*Eunuchus,* Act I, sc. 1, ll. 16–18   39. **Camisars,** French Calvinists.

talents to the corrections and restraints of art. Such among the Greeks were *Plato* and *Aristotle;* among the Romans, *Virgil* and *Tully;*. among the English, *Milton* and *Sir Francis Bacon.*

The genius in both these classes of authors may be equally great, but shews it self after a different manner. In the first it is like a rich soil in a happy climate, that produces a whole wilderness of noble plants rising in a thousand beautiful landskips without any certain order or regularity. In the other it is the same rich soil under the same happy climate, that has been laid out in walks and parterres, and cut into shape and beauty by the skill of the gardener.

The great danger in the latter kind of geniuses is lest they cramp their own abilities too much by imitation, and form themselves altogether upon models, without giving the full play to their own natural parts. An imitation of the best authors is not to compare with a good original; and I believe we may observe that very few writers make an extraordinary figure in the world, who have not something in their way of thinking or expressing themselves, that is peculiar to them, and entirely their own.

It is odd to consider what great geniuses are sometimes thrown away upon trifles.

I once saw a shepherd, says a famous Italian author, who used to divert himself in his solitudes with tossing up eggs and catching them again without breaking them; in which he had arrived to so great a degree of perfection, that he would keep up four at a time for several minutes together playing in the air, and falling into his hand by turns. I think, says the author, I never saw a greater severity than in this man's face; for by his wonderful perseverance and application, he had contracted the seriousness and gravity of a privy-councillor; and I could not but reflect with my self, that the same assiduity and attention, had they been rightly applied, might have made him a greater mathematician than *Archimedes.*

NO. 291. SATURDAY, FEB. 2, 1712 (Addison)

——Ubi plura nitent in carmine, non ego paucis
Offendar maculis, quas aut incuria fudit,
Aut humana parum cavit natura.— Hor.

I HAVE now considered Milton's *Paradise Lost* under those four great heads of the fable, the characters, the sentiments, and the language; and have shewn that he excels, in general, under each of these heads. I hope that I have made several discoveries which may appear new, even to those who are versed in critical learning. Were I indeed to chuse my readers, by whose judgment I would stand or fall, they should not be such as are acquainted only with the French and Italian criticks, but also with the ancient and moderns who have written in either of the learned languages. Above all, I would have them well versed in the Greek and Latin poets, without which a man very often fancies that he understands a critick, when in reality he does not comprehend his meaning.

It is in criticism, as in all other sciences and speculations; one who brings with him any implicit notions and observations which he has made in his reading of the poets, will find his own reflections methodized and explained, and perhaps several little hints that have passed in his mind, perfected and improved in the works of a good critick; whereas one who has not these previous lights is often an utter stranger to what he reads, and apt to put a wrong interpretation upon it.

Nor is it sufficient, that a man who sets up for a judge in criticism should have perused the authors above mentioned, unless he has also a clear and logical head. Without this talent he is perpetually puzzled and perplexed amidst his own blunders, mistakes the sense of those he would confute, or if he chances to think right, does not know how to convey his thoughts to another with clearness and perspicuity. *Aristotle*, who was the best critick, was also one of the best logicians that ever appeared in the world.

Mr. Locke's Essay on Human Understanding would be thought a very odd book for a man to make himself master of, who would get a reputation by critical writings; though at the same time it is very certain, that an author who has not learned the art of distinguishing between words and things, and of ranging his thoughts, and setting them in proper lights, whatever notions he may have, will lose himself in confusion and obscurity. I might further observe, that there is not a Greek or Latin critick who has not shewn, even in the style of his criticisms, that he was a master of all the elegance and delicacy of his native tongue.

The truth of it is, there is nothing more absurd, than for a man to set up for a critick, without a good insight into all the parts of learning; whereas many of those who have endeavoured to signalize themselves by works of this nature among our English writers, are not only defective in the above-mentioned particulars, but plainly discover, by the

---

44–46. Ubi . . . natura.
    But in a poem elegantly writ,
    I will not quarrel with a slight mistake,
    Such as our nature's frailty may excuse.
      —Roscommon's translation of Horace, *Ars Poetica*, ll. 351–53.

phrases which they make use of, and by their confused way of thinking, that they are not acquainted with the most common and ordinary systems of arts and sciences. A few general rules extracted out of the French authors, with a certain cant of words, has sometimes set up an illiterate heavy writer for a most judicious and formidable critick.

One great mark, by which you may discover a critick who has neither taste nor learning, is this, that he seldom ventures to praise any passage in an author which has not been before received and applauded by the publick, and that his criticism turns wholly upon little faults and errors. This part of a critick is so very easy to succeed in, that we find every ordinary reader, upon the publishing of a new poem, has wit and ill-nature enough to turn several passages of it into ridicule, and very often in the right place. This Mr. Dryden has very agreeably remarked in these two celebrated lines:

"Errors, like Straws, upon the Surface flow;
He who would search for Pearls must dive below."

A true critic ought to dwell rather upon excellencies than imperfections, to discover the concealed beauties of a writer, and communicate to the world such things as are worth their observation. The most exquisite words and finest strokes of an author are those which very often appear the most doubtful and exceptionable to a man who wants a relish for polite learning; and they are these, which a sour undistinguishing critick generally attacks with the greatest violence. *Tully* observes, that it is very easy to brand or fix a mark upon what he calls *verbum ardens*, or, as it may be rendered into English, *a glowing, bold expression*, and to turn it into ridicule by a cold ill-natured criticism. A little wit is equally capable of exposing a beauty, and of aggravating a fault; and though such a treatment of an author naturally produces indignation in the mind of an understanding reader, it has however its effect among the generality of those whose hands it falls into, the rabble of mankind being very apt to think that anything which is laughed at with any mixture of wit is ridiculous in it self.

Such a mirth as this is always unseasonable in a critic, as it rather prejudices the reader than convinces him, and is capable of making a beauty, as well as a blemish, the subject of derision. A man who cannot write with wit on a proper subject is dull and stupid, but one who shews it in an improper place, is as impertinent and absurd. Besides, a man who has the gift of ridicule is apt to find fault with any thing that gives him an opportunity of exerting his beloved talent, and very often censures a passage, not because there is any fault in it, but because he can be merry upon it. Such kinds of pleasantry are very unfair and disingenuous in works of criticism, in which the greatest masters, both ancient and modern, have always appeared with a serious and instructive air.

As I intend in my next paper to show the defects in Milton's *Paradise Lost*, I thought fit to premise these few particulars, to the end that the reader may know I enter upon it, as on a very ungrateful work, and that I shall just point at the imperfections, without endeavouring to enflame them with ridicule. I must also observe, with *Longinus*, that the productions of a great genius, with many lapses and inadvertences, are infinitely preferable to the works of an inferior kind of author which are scrupulously exact, and conformable to all the rules of correct writing.

I shall conclude my paper with a story out of *Boccalini*, which sufficiently shews us the opinion that judicious author entertained of the sort of criticks I have been here mentioning. A famous critick, says he, having gathered together all the faults of an eminent poet, made a present of them to *Apollo*, who received them very graciously, and resolved to make the author a suitable return for the trouble he had been at in collecting them. In order to this, he set before him a sack of wheat, as it had been just threshed out of the sheaf. He then bid him pick out the chaff from among the corn, and lay it aside by it self. The critick applied himself to the task with great industry and pleasure, and, after having made the due separation, was presented by *Apollo* with the chaff for his pains.

NO. 323. TUESDAY, MARCH 11, 1712 (Addison)

———*Modo vir, modo foemina.*—Virg.

THE journal with which I presented my reader on Tuesday last, has brought me in several letters, with accounts of many private lives cast into that form. I have the *Rake's Journal*, the *Sot's Journal*, the *Whoremaster's Journal*, and, among several others a very curious piece, entituled, *The Journal of a Mohock*. By these instances I find that the intention of my last Tuesday's paper has been mistaken by many of my readers. I did not design so much to

13. **Longinus**, Greek critic (c. A.D. 213–273). 19–20. **Boccalini**, Trajano Boccalini (1556–1613), an Italian critic and satirist. 39. **Modo . . . foemina.** Sometimes a man, sometimes a woman.—*Aeneid*, Book IV, l. 448. 41. **last.** This *Spectator* had advised the keeping of private diaries. 46. **Mohock**, a ruffian of the sort that infested London streets in Addison's time.

expose vice as idleness, and aimed at those persons who pass away their time rather in trifle and impertinence, than in crimes and immoralities. Offences of this latter kind are not to be dallied with, or treated in so ludicrous a manner. In short, my journal only holds up folly to the light, and shows the disagreeableness of such actions as are indifferent in themselves, and blameable only as they proceed from creatures endowed with reason.

My following correspondent, who calls herself *Clarinda*, is such a journalist as I require. She seems by her letter to be placed in a modish state of indifference between vice and virtue, and to be susceptible of either, were there proper pains taken with her. Had her journal been filled with gallantries, or such occurrences as had shown her wholly divested of her natural innocence, notwithstanding it might have been more pleasing to the generality of readers, I should not have published it; but as it is only the picture of a life filled with a fashionable kind of gaiety and laziness, I shall set down five days of it, as I have received it from the hand of my fair correspondent.

"Dear Mr. Spectator,

"You having set your readers an exercise in one of your last week's papers, I have performed mine according to your orders, and herewith send it you enclosed. You must know, *Mr. Spectator*, that I am a maiden lady of a good fortune, who have had several matches offered me for these ten years last past, and have at present warm applications made to me by a very pretty fellow. As I am at my own disposal, I come up to town every winter, and pass my time in it after the manner you will find in the following journal, which I begun to write the very day after your *Spectator* upon that subject.

Tuesday night. Could not go to sleep till one in the morning for thinking of my journal.

Wednesday. From eight 'till ten. Drank two dishes of chocolate in bed, and fell asleep after 'em.

From ten to eleven. Eat a slice of bread and butter, drank a dish of bohea, read the *Spectator*.

From eleven to one. At my toilet, tried a new head. Gave orders for *Veny* to be combed and washed. *Mem.* I look best in blue.

From one till half an hour after two. Drove to the Change. Cheapened a couple of fans.

Till four. At dinner. *Mem.* Mr. *Froth* passed by in his new liveries.

From four to six. Dressed, paid a visit to old Lady *Blithe* and her sister, having before heard they were gone out of town that day.

From six to eleven. At basset. *Mem.* Never set again upon the ace of diamonds.

Thursday. From eleven at night to eight in the morning. Dreamed that I punted to Mr. *Froth*.

From eight to ten. Chocolate. Read two acts in *Aurenzebe* abed.

From ten to eleven. Tea-table. Sent to borrow Lady *Faddle's* Cupid for *Veny*. Read the play-bills. Received a letter from Mr. *Froth*. *Mem.* Locked it up in my strong box.

Rest of the morning. Fontange, the tire-woman, her account of my Lady *Blithe's* wash. Broke a tooth in my little tortoise-shell comb. Sent *Frank* to know how my Lady *Hectick* rested after her monky's leaping out at window. Looked pale. *Fontange* tells me my glass is not true. Dressed by three.

From three to four. Dinner cold before I sat down.

From four to eleven. Saw company. Mr. *Froth's* opinion of *Milton*. His accounts of the *Mohocks*. His fancy for a pin-cushion. Picture in the lid of his snuff-box. Old Lady *Faddle* promises me her woman to cut my hair. Lost five guineas at crimp.

Twelve a-clock at night. Went to bed.

Friday. Eight in the morning. Abed. Read over all Mr. *Froth's* letters. *Cupid* and *Veny*.

Ten a-clock. Stayed within all day, not at home.

From ten to twelve. In conference with my mantua-maker. Sorted a suit of ribbands. Broke my blue china cup.

From twelve to one. Shut myself up in my chamber, practised Lady *Betty Modely's* skuttle.

One in the afternoon. Called for my flowered handkerchief. Worked half a violet-leaf in it. Eyes ached and head out of order. Threw by my work, and read over the remaining part of *Aurenzebe*.

From three to four. Dined.

From four to twelve. Changed my mind, dressed, went abroad, and played at crimp till midnight. Found Mrs. *Spitely* at home. Conversation: Mrs. *Brilliant's* necklace false stones. Old Lady *Loveday* going to be married to a young fellow that is not worth a groat. Miss *Prue* gone into the country. *Tom Townley* has red hair. *Mem.* Mrs. *Spitely* whispered in my ear that she had something to tell me about Mr. *Froth*, I am sure it is not true.

Between twelve and one. Dreamed that Mr. *Froth* lay at my feet, and called me *Indamora*.

---

6. punted, played at ombre or basset. **8. Aurenzebe,** *Aurengzebe*, a tragedy by Dryden, published in 1676. **14. wash,** a cosmetic. **24. crimp,** a game of cards. **29–30. mantua-maker,** dressmaker. **33. skuttle,** a mincing, affected way of walking. **49. Indamora,** the heroine of *Aurengzebe*. **45. head,** coiffure or headdress. **46. Veny,** a pet lapdog. **49. Cheapened,** bought. **51. liveries,** uniform.

Saturday. Rose at eight a-clock in the morning. Sate down to my toilet.

From eight to nine. Shifted a patch for half an hour before I could determine it. Fixed it above my left eye-brow.

From nine to twelve. Drank my tea, and dressed.

From twelve to two. At chappel. A great deal of good company. *Mem.* The third air in the new opera. Lady *Blithe* dressed frightfully.

From three to four. Dined. Miss *Kitty* called upon me to go to the opera before I was risen from table.

From dinner to six. Drank tea. Turned off a footman for being rude to *Veny.*

Six a-clock. Went to the opera. I did not see Mr. *Froth* till the beginning of the second act. Mr. *Froth* talked to a gentleman in a black wig; bowed to a lady in the front box. Mr. *Froth* and his friend clapped *Nicolini* in the third act. Mr. *Froth* cried out *Ancora.* Mr. *Froth* led me to my chair. I think he squeezed my hand.

Eleven at night. Went to bed. Melancholy dreams. Methought *Nicolini* said he was Mr. *Froth.*

Sunday. Indisposed.

Monday. Eight a-clock. Waked by Miss *Kitty. Aurenzebe* lay upon the chair by me. *Kitty* repeated without book the eight best lines in the play. Went in our mobbs to the dumb man, according to appointment. Told me that my lover's name began with a *G. Mem.* The conjurer was within a letter of Mr. *Froth's* name, &c.

"Upon looking back into this journal, I find that I am at a loss to know whether I pass my time well or ill; and indeed never thought of considering how I did it before I perused your speculations upon that subject. I scarce find a single action in these five days that I can thoroughly approve of, except the working upon the violet-leaf, which I am resolved to finish the first day I am at leisure. As for Mr. *Froth* and *Veny,* I did not think they took up so much of my time and thoughts, as I find they do upon my journal. The latter of them I will turn off, if you insist upon it; and if Mr. *Froth* does not bring matters to a conclusion very suddenly, I will not let my life run away in a dream.

"*Your humble servant,*
"*Clarinda.*"

To resume one of the morals of my first paper, and to confirm *Clarinda* in her good inclinations, I would have her consider what a pretty figure she would make among posterity, were the history of her whole life published like these five days of it. I shall conclude my paper with an epitaph written by an uncertain author on Sir *Philip Sidney's* sister, a lady who seems to have been of a temper very much different from that of *Clarinda.* The last thought of it is so very noble, that I dare say my reader will pardon me the quotation.

On the Countess Dowager of *Pembroke*
Underneath this Marble Hearse
Lies the Subject of all Verse,
Sidney's *Sister,* Pembroke's *Mother:*
Death, ere thou hast killed another,
Fair, and learned, and good as she,
Time shall throw a Dart at thee.

NO. 335. TUESDAY, MARCH 25, 1712 (Addison)

Respicere exemplar vitae morumque jubebo
Doctum imitatorem, et vivas hinc ducere voces.—Hor.

MY friend Sir ROGER DE COVERLEY, when we last met together at the club, told me he had a great mind to see the new tragedy with me, assuring me at the same time, that he had not been at a play these twenty years. The last I saw, said Sir ROGER, was the *Committee,* which I should not have gone to neither, had not I been told beforehand that it was a good Church-of-England comedy. He then proceeded to enquire of me who this *Distrest Mother* was; and upon hearing that she was *Hector's* widow, he told me that her husband was a brave man, and that when he was a schoolboy he had read his life at the end of the dictionary. My friend asked me, in the next place, if there would not be some danger in coming home late, in case the *Mohocks* should be abroad. I assure you, says he, I thought I had fallen into their hands last night; for I observed two or three lusty black men that followed me half way up Fleet-street, and mended their pace behind me, in proportion as I put on to get away from them. You must know, continued the Knight with a smile, I fancied they had a mind to *hunt* me; for I remember an honest gentleman in my neighbourhood, who was served such a trick in King Charles the Second's time; for which reason he has not ventured himself in town ever since. I might have shown them very good

---

18. **Nicolini,** Nicolino Grimaldi, an Italian operatic singer. 27. **mobbs,** mobcaps, used for informal occasions. 3. **author,** now known to have been William Browne (1591–1643), the author of *Britannia's Pastorals.* 19–20. **Respicere . . . voces.**
Keep Nature's great original in view,
And thence the living images pursue.
—Francis's translation of *Ars Poetica,* ll. 317–18
26. **the Committee,** a comedy by Sir Robert Howard, first performed in 1663. 30. **Distrest Mother,** referring to a tragedy of this title by Ambrose Philips, first acted in 1712.

sport, had this been their design; for as I am an old fox-hunter, I should have turned and dodged, and have played them a thousand tricks they had never seen in their lives before. Sir ROGER added, that if these gentlemen had any such intention, they did not succeed very well in it; for I threw them out, says he, at the end of Norfolk street, where I doubled the corner, and got shelter in my lodgings before they could imagine what was become of me. However, says the Knight, if Captain *Sentry* will make one with us to-morrow night, and you will both of you call upon me about four a-clock, that we may be at the house before it is full, I will have my own coach in readiness to attend you, for *John* tells me he has got the fore-wheels mended.

The Captain, who did not fail to meet me there at the appointed hour, bid Sir ROGER fear nothing, for that he had put on the same sword which he made use of at the battle of Steenkirk. Sir ROGER's servants, and among the rest my old friend the butler, had, I found, provided themselves with good oaken plants, to attend their master upon this occasion. When we had placed him in his coach, with my self at his left-hand, the Captain before him, and his butler at the head of his footmen in the rear, we convoyed him in safety to the play-house, where, after having marched up the entry in good order, the Captain and I went in with him, and seated him betwixt us in the pit. As soon as the house was full, and the candles lighted, my old friend stood up and looked about him with that pleasure, which a mind seasoned with humanity naturally feels in its self, at the sight of a multitude of people who seem pleased with one another, and partake of the same common entertainment. I could not but fancy to myself, as the old man stood up in the middle of the pit, that he made a very proper center to a tragick audience. Upon the entering of *Pyrrhus*, the Knight told me, that he did not believe the king of France himself had a better strut. I was indeed very attentive to my old friend's remarks, because I looked upon them as a piece of natural criticism, and was well pleased to hear him at the conclusion of almost every scene, telling me that he could not imagine how the play would end. One while he appeared much concerned for *Andromache;* and a little while after as much for *Hermione;* and was extremely puzzled to think what would become of *Pyrrhus*.

When Sir ROGER saw *Andromache*'s obstinate refusal to her lover's importunities he whispered me in the ear, that he was sure she would never have him; to which he added, with a more than ordinary vehemence, You can't imagine, Sir, what 'tis to have to do with a widow. Upon *Pyrrhus* his threatening afterwards to leave her, the Knight shook his head, and muttered to himself, Ay, do if you can. This part dwelt so much upon my friend's imagination, that at the close of the third act, as I was thinking of something else, he whispered me in my ear, These widows, Sir, are the most perverse creatures in the world. But pray, says he, you that are a critick, is this play according to your dramatick rules, as you call them? Should your people in tragedy always talk to be understood? Why, there is not a single sentence in this play that I do not know the meaning of.

The fourth act very luckily begun before I had time to give the old gentleman an answer: Well, says the Knight, sitting down with great satisfaction, I suppose we are now to see *Hector's* ghost. He then renewed his attention, and, from time to time, fell a-praising the widow. He made, indeed, a little mistake as to one of her pages, whom at his first entering, he took for *Astyanax;* but he quickly set himself right in that particular, though, at the same time, he owned he should have been very glad to have seen the little boy, who, says he, must needs be a very fine child by the account that is given of him. Upon *Hermione's* going off with a menace to *Pyrrhus*, the audience gave a loud clap, to which Sir ROGER added, On my word, a notable young baggage!

As there was a very remarkable silence and stillness in the audience during the whole action, it was natural for them to take the opportunity of the intervals between the acts, to express their opinion of the players, and of their respective parts. Sir ROGER, hearing a cluster of them praise *Orestes*, struck in with them, and told them, that he thought his friend *Pylades* was a very sensible man; as they were afterwards applauding *Pyrrhus*, Sir ROGER put in a second time; And let me tell you, says he, though he speaks but little, I like the old fellow in whiskers as well as any of them. Captain Sentry, seeing two or three waggs who sat near us, lean with an attentive ear toward Sir ROGER, and fearing lest they should smoke the Knight, plucked him by the elbow, and whispered something in his ear, that lasted till the opening of the fifth act. The Knight was wonderfully attentive to the account which *Orestes* gives of *Pyrrhus* his death, and at the conclusion of it, told me it was such a bloody piece of work, that he was glad it was not done upon the stage. Seeing afterward *Orestes* in his raving fit, he grew

---

19. Steenkirk, a battle fought in Belgium in 1692 between the English and the French.   **22. plants,** cudgels.   **38. Pyrrhus,** a character in the play.

46. smoke, find out and turn to ridicule.

more than ordinary serious, and took occasion to moralize (in his way) upon an evil conscience, adding, that *Orestes, in his madness, looked as if he saw something.*

As we were the first that came into the house, so we were the last that went out of it; being resolved to have a clear passage for our old friend, whom we did not care to venture among the jostling of the crowd. Sir ROGER went out fully satisfied with his entertainment, and we guarded him to his lodging in the same manner that we brought him to the play-house; being highly pleased, for my own part, not only with the performance of the excellent piece which had been presented, but with the satisfaction which it had given to the good old man.

NO. 454. MONDAY, AUGUST 11, 1712 (Steele)

Sine me, vacivum tempus ne quod dem mihi Laboris. —Ter. Heau.

IT is an inexpressible pleasure to know a little of the world, and be of no character or significancy in it.

To be ever unconcerned, and ever looking on new objects with an endless curiosity, is a delight known only to those who are turned for speculation: nay, they who enjoy it must value things only as they are the objects of speculation, without drawing any worldly advantage to themselves from them, but just as they are what contribute to their amusement, or the improvement of the mind. I lay one night last week at Richmond; and being restless, not out of dissatisfaction, but a certain busy inclination one sometimes has, I rose at four in the morning, and took boat for London, with a resolution to rove by boat and coach for the next four and twenty hours, till the many different objects I must needs meet with should tire my imagination, and give me an inclination to a repose more profound than I was at that time capable of. I beg people's pardon for an odd humour I am guilty of, and was often that day, which is saluting any person whom I like, whether I know him or not. This is a particularity would be tolerated in me, if they considered that the greatest pleasure I know I receive at my eyes, and that I am obliged to an agreeable person for coming abroad into my view, as another is for a visit of conversation at their own houses.

The hours of the day and night are taken up in the cities of London and Westminster by people as different from each other as those who are born in different centuries. Men of six a clock give way to those of nine, they of nine to the generation of twelve, and they of twelve disappear, and make room for the fashionable world, who have made two a clock the noon of the day.

When we first put off from shore, we soon fell in with a fleet of gardeners bound for the several market-ports of London; and it was the most pleasing scene imaginable to see the cheerfulness with which those industrious people plied their way to a certain sale of their goods. The banks on each side are as well peopled, and beautified with as agreeable plantations, as any spot on the earth; but the Thames it self, loaded with the product of each shore, added very much to the landskip. It was very easy to observe by their sailing, and the countenances of the ruddy virgins who were supercargoes, the parts of the town to which they were bound. There was an air in the purveyors for Covent Garden who frequently converse with morning rakes, very unlike the seemly sobriety of those bound for Stocks Market.

Nothing remarkable happened in our voyage; but I landed with ten sail of apricock-boats at Strand Bridge, after having put in at Nine Elms, and taken in melons, consigned by Mr. *Cuffe* of that place, to *Sarah Sewell* and Company, at their stall in Covent Garden. We arrived at Strand Bridge at six of the clock, and were unloading when the hackney-coachmen of the foregoing night took their leave of each other at the Dark House, to go to bed before the day was too far spent. Chimney-sweepers passed by us as we made up to the market, and some raillery happened between one of the fruit wenches and those black men, about the Devil and *Eve*, with allusion to their several professions. I could not believe any place more entertaining than Covent Garden; where I strolled from one fruit-shop to another, with crowds of agreeable young women around me, who were purchasing fruit for their respective families. It was almost eight of the clock before I could leave that variety of objects. I took coach and followed a young lady, who tripped into another just before me, attended by her maid. I saw immediately she was of the family of the *Vainloves*. There are a set of these, who of all things affect the play of blindman's-buff, and leading men into love for they know not whom, who are fled they know not where. This sort of woman is usually a jaunty slattern; she hangs on her clothes, plays her head, varies her posture, and changes place incessantly,

---

21–22. Sine ... Laboris. Give me leave to allow myself no respite from labor.—*Heautontimorumenos*. Act I, sc. 1.

38–39. Covent Garden, a vegetable and flower market, opening very early.

and all with an appearance of striving at the same time to hide her self, and yet give you to understand she is in humour to laugh at you. You must have often seen the coachmen make signs with their fingers as they drive by each other, to intimate how much they have got that day. They can carry on that language to give intelligence where they are driving. In an instant my coachman took the wink to pursue, and the lady's driver gave the hint that he was going through Longacre toward St. James's: while he whipped up James Street, we drove for King Street, to save the pass at St. Martin's Lane. The coachmen took care to meet, jostle, and threaten each other for way, and be entangled at the end of Newport Street and Longacre. The fright, you must believe, brought down the lady's coach door, and obliged her, with her mask off, to enquire into the bustle, when she sees the man she would avoid. The tackle of the coach-window is so bad she cannot draw it up again, and she drives on sometimes wholly discovered, and sometimes half escaped, according to the accident of carriages in her way. One of these ladies keeps her seat in a hackney-coach, as well as the best rider does on a managed horse. The laced shoe on her left foot, with a careless gesture, just appearing on the opposite cushion, held her both firm, and in a proper attitude to receive the next jolt.

As she was an excellent coach woman, many were the glances at each other which we had for an hour and an half in all parts of the town by the skill of our drivers; till at last my lady was conveniently lost with notice from her coachman to ours to make off, and he should hear where she went. This chase was now at an end, and the fellow who drove her came to us, and discovered that he was ordered to come again in an hour, for that she was a silk-worm. I was surprized with this phrase, but found it was a cant among the hackney fraternity for their best customers, women who ramble twice or thrice a week from shop to shop, to turn over all the goods in town without buying any thing. The silk-worms are, it seems, indulged by the tradesmen; for though they never buy, they are ever talking of new silks, laces and ribbands, and serve the owners in getting them customers, as their common dunners do in making them pay.

The day of people of fashion began now to break, and carts and hacks were mingled with equipages of show and vanity; when I resolved to walk it, out of cheapness; but my unhappy curiosity is such, that I find it always my interest to take coach, for some odd adventure among beggars, ballad-singers, or the like, detains and throws me into expense. It happened so immediately; for at the corner of Warwick Street, as I was listening to a new ballad, a ragged rascal, a beggar who knew me, came up to me, and began to turn the eyes of the good company upon me, by telling me he was extreme poor, and should die in the street for want of drink, except I immediately would have the charity to give him sixpence to go into the next ale-house and save his life. He urged with a melancholy face, that all his family had died of thirst. All the mob have humour, and two or three began to take the jest; by which Mr. *Sturdy* carried his point, and let me sneak off to a coach. As I drove along, it was a pleasing reflection to see the world so prettily chequered since I left Richmond, and the scene still filling with children of a new hour. This satisfaction increased as I moved towards the city; and gay signs, well disposed streets, magnificent publick structures, and wealthy shops, adorned with contented faces, made the joy still rising till we came into the centre of the city, and centre of the world of trade, the Exchange of London. As other men in the crowds about me were pleased with their hopes and bargains, I found my account in observing them, in attention to their several interests. I, indeed, looked upon my self as the richest man that walked the Exchange that day; for my benevolence made me share the gains of every bargain that was made. It was not the least of my satisfactions in my survey, to go up stairs and pass the shops of agreeable females; to observe so many pretty hands busy in the foldings of ribbands, and the utmost eagerness of agreeable faces in the sale of patches, pins, and wires, on each side of the counters, was an amusement in which I could longer have indulged my self, had not the dear creatures called to me to ask what I wanted, when I could not answer, only *to look at you.* I went to one of the windows which opened to the area below, where all the several voices lost their distinction, and rose up in a confused humming; which created in me a reflection that could not come into the mind of any but of one a little too studious; for I said to my self, with a kind of pun in thought, *What nonsense is all the hurry of this world to those who are above it?* In these, or not much wiser thoughts, I had like to have lost my place at the chop-house, where every man according to the natural bashfulness or sullenness of our nation, eats in a publick room a mess of broth, or chop of meat, in dumb silence, as if they had no pretence to speak to each other on the foot of being men, except they were of each other's acquaintance.

I went afterward to Robin's, and saw people who

12. Sturdy, that is, sturdy beggar.

had dined with me at the five-penny ordinary just before, give bills for the value of large estates; and could not but behold with great pleasure, property lodged in, and transferred in a moment from, such as would never be masters of half as much as is seemingly in them, and given from them every day they live. But before five in the afternoon I left the city, came to my common scene of Covent Garden, and passed the evening at Will's in attending the discourses of several sets of people, who relieved each other within my hearing on the subjects of cards, dice, love, learning, and politicks. The last subject kept me till I heard the streets in the possession of the bellman, who had now the world to himself, and cried, *Past two of clock.* This roused me from my seat, and I went to my lodging, led by a light, whom I put into the discourse of his private economy, and made him give me an account of the charge, hazard, profit, and loss of a family that depended upon a link, with a design to end my trivial day with the generosity of six-pence, instead of a third part of that sum. When I came to my chambers I writ down these minutes; but was at a loss what instruction I should propose to my reader from the enumeration of so many insignificant matters and occurrences; and I thought it of great use, if they could learn with me to keep their minds open to gratification, and ready to receive it from any thing it meets with. This one circumstance will make every face you see give you the satisfaction you now take in beholding that of a friend; will make every object a pleasing one; will make all the good which arrives to any man, an increase of happiness to your self.

Philip Dormer Stanhope, Earl of Chesterfield
1694–1773

During the period which we have agreed, perhaps too hastily, to call the age of Pope, England produced one man who summed up in his own person and accomplishment nearly everything to which other representative men of the time aspired. The fourth Earl of Chesterfield, an aristocrat by birth and breeding, was a cosmopolite, as much at home in Europe as in England. He was a famous wit and orator, a literary patron, a man at home in the literature of the ancient world but entirely free from pedantry, a leader in society, and a power in politics. He was an ambassador to Holland, an efficient Lord Lieutenant of Ireland, a Secretary of State, and a son-in-law of the King. Moreover, he had precisely the right amount of fashionable cynicism. His manners were exquisitely suave, his dress was both rich and decorous, and in all respects he was a model of grace and elegance.—All things considered, we should have done well to name the period in which he flourished the age of Chesterfield.

The title would not be disparaging, for Lord Chesterfield was in several ways an admirable person. He had good taste, worldly wisdom, courtesy, and refinement of feeling. Throughout his life he exemplified the ideal of the gentleman as he, mistakenly in some regards, understood it. He has been called contemptuous, calculating, hardhearted, and selfish, but against these charges there is positive evidence in plenty that he was capable of strong affection, at least where his pride was involved.

This evidence is to be found in the series of four hundred and thirteen letters that Lord Chesterfield wrote, during more than thirty years, to his illegitimate son, Philip Stanhope. These famous letters, beginning when the son was five years of age, are concerned for the most part with matters of education, deportment, good breeding, and all that went to the making of an eighteenth-century gentleman. In the course of them, however, Chesterfield touches upon or discusses most of the main ideas current in his time, and this he does so thoughtfully that one must regard him as one of the chief exponents of the Neoclassical mind and spirit. However vigorously we may disagree with some of the advice he gives to his son, there can be no doubt of his fatherly kindness and affection. He had no thought, we may be sure, that his letters would ever be published, and yet they are models of clarity, charm, and graceful ease. The plain and yet dignified prose in which they are written has never, in its own kind, been surpassed.

His only son, Philip Stanhope, to whom the letters were written, died five years before his father, and the letters were first published by Stanhope's widow, in 1774.

1. **ordinary,** table d'hôte.
3. **link,** torch.

from LETTERS TO HIS SON

Bath, February 22, O.S. 1748

Dear Boy:

Every excellency, and every virtue, has its kindred vice or weakness; and, if carried beyond certain bounds, sinks into one or the other. Generosity often runs into profusion, economy into avarice, courage into rashness, caution into timidity, and so on:—insomuch that, I believe, there is more judgment required, for the proper conduct of our virtues, than for avoiding their opposite vices. Vice, in its true light, is so deformed, that it shocks us at first sight, and would hardly ever seduce us, if it did not, at first, wear the mask of some virtue. But virtue is, in itself, so beautiful, that it charms us at first sight; engages us more and more upon further acquaintance; and, as with other beauties, we think excess impossible; it is here that judgment is necessary, to moderate and direct the effects of an excellent cause. I shall apply this reasoning, at present, not to any particular virtue, but to an excellency, which, for want of judgment, is often the cause of ridiculous and blamable effects; I mean, great learning; which, if not accompanied with sound judgment, frequently carries us into error, pride, and pedantry. As, I hope, you will possess that excellency in its utmost extent, and yet without its too common failings, the hints, which my experience can suggest, may probably not be useless to you.

Some learned men, proud of their knowledge, only speak to decide, and give judgment without appeal; the consequence of which is, that mankind, provoked by the insult, and injured by the oppression, revolt; and, in order to shake off the tyranny, even call the lawful authority in question. The more you know, the modester you should be: and (by the bye) that modesty is the surest way of gratifying your vanity. Even when you are sure, seem rather doubtful; represent, but do not pronounce, and, if you would convince others, seem open to conviction yourself.

Others, to show their learning, or often from the prejudices of a school-education, where they hear of nothing else, are always talking of the ancients, as something more than men, and of the moderns, as something less. They are never without a classic or two in their pockets; they stick to the old good sense; they read none of the modern trash; and will show you, plainly, that no improvement has been made, in any one art or science, these last seventeen hundred years. I would by no means have you disown your acquaintance with the ancients: but still less would I have you brag of an exclusive intimacy with them. Speak of the moderns without contempt, and of the ancients without idolatry; judge them all by their merits, but not by their ages; and if you happen to have an Elzevir classic in your pocket neither show it nor mention it.

Some great scholars, most absurdly, draw all their maxims, both for public and private life, from what they call parallel cases in the ancient authors; without considering, that, in the first place, there never were, since the creation of the world, two cases exactly parallel; and, in the next place, that there never was a case stated, or even known, by any historian, with every one of its circumstances; which, however, ought to be known, in order to be reasoned from. Reason upon the case itself, and the several circumstances that attend it, and act accordingly; but not from the authority of ancient poets, or historians. Take into your consideration, if you please, cases seemingly analogous; but take them as helps only, not as guides. We are really so prejudiced by our education, that, as the ancients deified their heroes, we deify their madmen; of which, with all due regard for antiquity, I take Leonidas and Curtius to have been two distinguished ones. And yet a solid pedant would, in a speech in Parliament, relative to a tax of two-pence in the pound upon some commodity or other, quote those two heroes as examples of what we ought to do and suffer for our country. I have known these absurdities carried so far by people of injudicious learning, that I should not be surprised, if some of them were to propose, while we are at war with the Gauls, that a number of geese should be kept in the Tower, upon account of the infinite advantage which Rome received *in a parallel case*, from a certain number of geese in the Capitol. This way of reasoning, and this way of speaking, will always form a poor politician, and a puerile declaimer.

There is another species of learned men who, though less dogmatical and supercilious, are not less impertinent. These are the communicative and shining pedants, who adorn their conversation, even with women, by happy quotations of Greek and Latin; and who have contracted such a familiarity with the Greek and Roman authors, that they call them by certain names or epithets denoting intimacy. As *old* Homer; that *sly rogue* Horace; *Maro*, instead of Virgil; and *Naso*, instead of Ovid. These are often imitated by coxcombs, who have no learning at all; but who have got some names and some scraps of ancient authors by heart, which they improperly and impertinently retail in all companies, in hopes of passing for scholars. If, therefore, you would avoid the accusation of pedantry on one hand, or the suspicion of ignorance on the other, abstain from learned ostentation. Speak the language of the company that you are in; speak it purely, and unlarded with any other. Never seem wiser, nor more learned, than the people you are with. Wear your learning, like your watch, in a private pocket: and do not pull it out and strike it, merely to show that you have one. If you are asked what o'clock it is, tell it; but do not proclaim it hourly and unasked, like the watchman.

Upon the whole, remember that learning (I mean Greek and Roman learning) is a most useful and necessary ornament, which it is shameful not to be master of; but, at the same time most carefully avoid those errors and abuses which I have mentioned, and which too often attend it. Remember, too, that great modern knowledge is still more necessary than ancient; and that you had better know perfectly the present, than the old state of Europe; though I would have you well acquainted with both. . . .

London, December 12, O.S. 1749

Dear Boy:

Lord Clarendon in his history says of Mr. John Hampden, *that he had a head to contrive, a tongue to persuade, and a hand to execute, any mischief.* I shall not now enter into the justness of this character of Mr. Hampden, to whose brave stand against the illegal demand of ship-money we owe our present liberties; but I mention it to you as the character, which with the alteration of one single word, *Good* instead of *Mischief*, I would have you aspire to, and use your utmost endeavours to deserve. The head to contrive, God must to a certain degree have given you; but it is in your own power greatly to improve it by study, observation, and reflection. As for the tongue to persuade, it wholly depends upon yourself; and without it the best head will contrive to very little purpose. The hand to execute depends likewise, in my opinion, in a great measure upon yourself. Serious reflection will always give courage in a good cause; and the courage arising from reflection is of a much superior nature to the animal and constitutional courage of a foot soldier. The former is steady and unshaken, where the *nodus* is *dignus vindice;* the latter is oftener improperly than properly exerted, but always brutally.

The second member of my text (to speak ecclesiastically) shall be the subject of my following discourse: *the tongue to persuade*, as judicious preachers recommend those virtues which they think their several audiences want the most: such as truth and continence at Court; disinterestedness in the City; and sobriety in the Country.

You must certainly, in the course of your little experience, have felt the different effects of elegant and inelegant speaking. Do you not suffer, when people accost you in a stammering or hesitant manner, in an untuneful voice, with false accents and cadences; puzzling and blundering through solecisms, barbarisms, and vulgarisms; misplacing even their bad words, and inverting all method? Does not this prejudice you against their matter, be it what it will; nay, even against their persons? I am sure it does me. On the other hand, do you not feel yourself inclined, prepossessed, nay, even engaged in favour of those who address you in the direct contrary manner? The effects of a correct and adorned style, of method and perspicuity, are incredible towards persuasion; they often supply the want of reason and argument; but when used in support of reason and argument, they are irresistible. The French attend very much to the purity and elegancy of their style, even in common conversation; insomuch, that it is a character to say of a man, *qu'il narre bien*. Their conversations frequently turn upon the delicacies of their language, and an Academy is employed in fixing it. The *Crusca*, in Italy, has the same object; and I have met with very few Italians who did not speak their own language correctly and elegantly. How much more necessary is it for an Englishman to do so who is to speak it in a public assembly, where the laws and liberties of his country are the subjects of his deliberation? The tongue that would persuade, there, must not content itself with mere articulation. You know what pains Demosthenes took to correct his naturally bad elocution; you know that he declaimed by the sea-side in storms, to prepare himself for the noise of the tumultuous assemblies he was to speak to; and you can now judge of the correctness and elegancy of his style. He thought all these things of consequence, and he thought right; pray do you think so too. It is of the utmost consequence to you to be of that opinion. If you have the least defect in your elocution, take the utmost care and pains to correct it. Do not neglect your style, whatever language you speak in, or whomever you

27. **Clarendon**, Edward Hyde, Earl of Clarendon, whose *History of the Rebellion and Civil Wars in England* was begun in 1641 and published in 1702–04.   48–49. **nodus . . . dignus vindice**, difficulty . . . deserving a defender.

29. **qu'il narre bien**, that he tells a story well. 31. **Academy**, the Académie Française, founded in 1635. 32. **Crusca**. See note on page 949.

speak to, were it your footman. Seek always for the best words and the happiest expressions you can find. Do not content yourself with being barely understood, but adorn your thoughts, and dress them as you would your person; which, however well proportioned it might be, it would be very improper and indecent to exhibit naked, or even worse dressed than people of your sort are.

I have sent you, in a packet which your Leipsig acquaintance, Duval, sends to his correspondent at Rome, Lord Bolingbroke's book, which he published about a year ago. I desire that you will read it over and over again, with particular attention to the style, and to all those beauties of oratory with which it is adorned. Till I read that book, I confess I did not know all the extent and powers of the English language. Lord Bolingbroke has both a tongue and a pen to persuade; his manner of speaking in private conversation is full as elegant as his writings; whatever subject he either speaks or writes upon, he adorns it with the most splendid eloquence; not a studied or laboured eloquence, but such a flowing happiness of diction, which (from care perhaps at first) is become so habitual to him, that even his most familiar conversations, if taken down in writing, would bear the press, without the least correction either as to method or style. If his conduct, in the former part of his life, had been equal to all his natural and acquired talents, he would most justly have merited the epithet of all-accomplished. He is himself sensible of his past errors: those violent passions, which seduced him in his youth, have now been subsided by age; and take him as he is now, the character of all-accomplished is more his due than any man's I ever knew in my life.

But he has been a most mortifying instance of the violence of human passions, and of the weakness of the most exalted human reason. His virtues and his vices, his reason and his passions, did not blend themselves by a graduation of tints, but formed a shining and sudden contrast. Here the darkest, there the most splendid colours, and both rendered more shining from their proximity. Impetuosity, excess, and almost extravagancy, characterised not only his passions, but even his senses. His youth was distinguished by all the tumult and storm of pleasures, in which he most licentiously triumphed, disdaining all decorum. His fine imagination has often been heated and exhausted with his body, in celebrating and deifying the prostitute of the night; and his convivial joys were pushed to all the extravagancy of frantic Bacchanals. Those passions were interrupted but by a stronger ambition. The former impaired both his constitution and his character, but the latter destroyed both his fortune and his reputation.

He has noble and generous sentiments, rather than fixed reflected principles of good nature and friendship; but they are more violent than lasting, and suddenly and often varied to their opposite extremes, with regard to the same persons. He receives the common attentions of civility as obligations, which he returns with interest; and resents with passion the little inadvertencies of human nature, which he repays with interest too. Even a difference of opinion upon a philosophical subject would provoke, and prove him no practical philosopher at least.

Notwithstanding the dissipation of his youth, and the tumultuous agitation of his middle age, he has an infinite fund of various and almost universal knowledge, which, from the clearest and quickest conception, and happiest memory, that ever man was blessed with, he always carries about him. It is his pocket-money, and he never has occasion to draw upon a book for any sum. He excels more particularly in history, as his historical works plainly prove. The relative political and commercial interests of every country in Europe, particularly his own, are better known to him than perhaps to any man in it; but how steadily he has pursued the latter, in his public conduct, his enemies, of all parties and denominations, tell with joy.

He engaged young, and distinguished himself in business; and his penetration was almost intuition. I am old enough to have heard him speak in Parliament. And I remember that, though prejudiced against him by party, I felt all the force and charms of his eloquence. Like Belial in Milton, "he made the worse appear the better cause." All the internal and external advantages and talents of an orator are undoubtedly his. Figure, voice, elocution, knowledge; and, above all, the purest and most florid diction, with the justest metaphors and happiest images, had raised him to the post of Secretary at War, at four-and-twenty years old, an age at which others are hardly thought fit for the smallest employments.

During his long exile in France, he applied himself to study with his characteristical ardour; and there he formed, and chiefly executed, the plan of a great philosophical work. The common bounds of

---

11. book, probably *The Patriot King*.   **34. character.** This glowing praise is now difficult to understand, partly because Bolingbroke's public speeches have not been preserved. He and Lord Chesterfield, however, had much in common.

35. business, public affairs.   **39–40. "he . . . cause,"** misquoted from *Paradise Lost*, II, ll. 113–14.

human knowledge are too narrow for his warm and aspiring imagination. He must go *extra flammantia moenia Mundi*, and explore the unknown and unknowable regions of metaphysics; which open an unbounded field for the excursions of an ardent imagination, where endless conjectures supply the defect of unattainable knowledge, and too often usurp both its name and influence.

He has had a very handsome person, with a most engaging address in his air and manners; he has all the dignity and good-breeding which a man of quality should or can have, and which so few, in this country at least, really have.

He professes himself a Deist; believing in a general Providence, but doubting of, though by no means rejecting, (as is commonly supposed,) the immortality of the soul, and a future state.

Upon the whole, of this extraordinary man, what can we say, but alas, poor human nature!

In your destination, you will have frequent occasions to speak in public; to Princes and States abroad; to the House of Commons, at home. Judge, then, whether eloquence is necessary for you or not; not only common eloquence, which is rather free from faults, than adorned by beauties, but the highest, the most shining degree of eloquence. For God's sake, have this object always in your view, and in your thoughts. Tune your tongue early to persuasion; and let no jarring, dissonant accents ever fall from it. Contract an habit of speaking well, upon every occasion, and neglect yourself in no one. Eloquence and good-breeding, alone, with an exceeding small degree of parts and knowledge, will carry a man a great way. With your parts and knowledge, then how far will they not carry you? Adieu.

London, January 8, O.S. 1750

Dear Boy:

I have seldom or never written to you upon the subject of religion and morality: your own reason, I am persuaded, has given you true notions of both; they speak best for themselves; but, if they wanted assistance, you have Mr. Harte at hand, both for precept and example. To your own reason, therefore, and to Mr. Harte, shall I refer you, for the reality of both; and confine myself, in this letter, to the decency, the utility, and the necessity, of scrupulously preserving the appearances of both. When I say the appearances of religion, I do not mean that you should talk or act like a missionary, or an enthusiast, nor that you should take up a controversial cudgel against whoever attacks the sect you are of; this would be both useless and unbecoming your age: but I mean that you should by no means seem to approve, encourage, or applaud, those libertine notions, which strike at religions equally, and which are the poor threadbare topics of half wits, and minute philosophers. Even those who are silly enough to laugh at their jokes, are still wise enough to distrust and detest their characters; for, putting moral virtues at the highest, and religion at the lowest, religion must still be allowed to be a collateral security, at least, to virtue; and every prudent man will sooner trust to two securities than to one. . . .

There is nothing so delicate as your moral character, and nothing which it is your interest so much to preserve pure. Should you be suspected of injustice, malignity, perfidy, lying, &c., all the parts and knowledge in the world will never procure you esteem, friendship, or respect. A strange concurrence of circumstances has sometimes raised very bad men to high stations; but they have been raised like criminals to a pillory, where their persons and their crimes, by being more conspicuous, are only the more known, the more detested, and the more pelted and insulted. If, in any case whatsoever, affectation and ostentation are pardonable, it is in the case of morality; though, even there, I would not advise you to a pharisaical pomp of virtue. But I will recommend to you a most scrupulous tenderness for your moral character, and the utmost care not to say or do the least thing that may, ever so slightly, taint it. Show yourself, upon all occasions, the advocate, the friend, but not the bully, of Virtue. Colonel Chartres, whom you have certainly heard of, (who was, I believe, the most notorious blasted rascal in the world, and who had, by all sorts of crimes, amassed immense wealth) was so sensible of the disadvantage of a bad character, that I heard him once say, in his impudent profligate manner, that, though he would not give one farthing for virtue, he would give ten thousand pounds for a character; because he should get a hundred thousand by it: whereas he was so blasted that he had no longer an opportunity of cheating people. Is it possible then that an honest man can neglect what a wise rogue would purchase so dear?

There is one of the vices above-mentioned, into which people of good education, and, in the main, of good principles, sometimes fall, from mistaken notions of skill, dexterity, and self-defence; I mean

---

2–3. **extra . . . Mundi**, beyond the flaming walls of the world—from Lucretius.   20. **destination**, what we should now call the consular service.

17–18. **character**, reputation.

lying; though it is inseparably attended with more infamy and loss than any other. The prudence and necessity of often concealing the truth, insensibly seduces people to violate it. It is the only art of mean capacities, and the only refuge of mean spirits. Whereas concealing the truth, upon proper occasion, is as prudent and as innocent, as telling a lie, upon any occasion, is infamous and foolish. I will state you a case in your own department. Suppose you are employed at a foreign Court, and that the Minister of that Court is absurd or impertinent enough to ask you what your instructions are. Will you tell him a lie; which, as soon as found out, and found out it certainly will be, must destroy your credit, blast your character, and render you useless there? No. Will you tell him the truth then, and betray your trust? As certainly, no. But you will answer with firmness, that you are surprised at such a question; that you are persuaded he does not expect an answer to it; but that, at all events, he certainly will not have one. Such an answer will give him confidence in you; he will conceive an opinion of your veracity, of which opinion you may afterwards make very honest and fair advantages. But if, in negotiations, you are looked upon as a liar, and a trickster, no confidence will be placed in you, nothing will be communicated to you, and you will be in the situation of a man who has been burnt in the cheek; and who, from that mark, cannot afterwards get an honest livelihood if he would, but must continue a thief. . . .

Alexander Pope
1688–1744

Classical and Neoclassical times think well of themselves and of their poetry. It is only in Romantic and antiquarian periods that poetry comes to seem a thing remote, queer, bygone, and outlived.

This fact, so little recognized, is vividly illustrated by the career and reputation of Alexander Pope, who was universally regarded two hundred years ago, while he was still alive, as the prince of English poets. We no longer think of him in quite that way, but it is worth our while to consider why his contemporaries did so.

Primarily this was because he so triumphantly achieved in his writing what others aspired to. He was the spokesman of his time, providing a compact and crystal-clear expression for its most characteristic thought and feeling. To think of the English Neoclassical Period is to think of him. True it is that a close examination of his text reveals several tendencies which are now called Romantic, but this is only what may be said of any other man of his day. In most essential respects he belonged to his epoch and was its voice.

Critics have long disagreed as to whether Pope had poetic genius, but no one has ever doubted, after a glance at the evidence, that he had indomitable will. Pope won his fame and influence in spite of many difficulties. He was born a physical weakling, and his whole life, as he said toward the end of it, was "one long disease." He was the son of a Roman Catholic family, and this meant in his time that he could neither attend an English university nor hold public office. The consequence was that he had no regular education. From early boyhood, however, he read voraciously, rapidly gaining a sufficient command of Latin, Greek, French, and Italian. He was a good deal assisted during his youth by members of the cultivated Roman Catholic families near his father's home at Binfield in Windsor Forest. His determination to be a great and famous poet began almost in his childhood. "About fifteen," he once said, "I got acquainted with Mr. Walsh. He used to encourage me much, and used to tell me that there was one way left of excelling; for, though we had several great poets, we never had any one great poet that was correct, and he desired me to make that my study and aim."

It was the eager study of "correctness," no doubt, that enabled Pope to write the better part of his brilliant *Essay on Criticism* before he was twenty-one, thereby making a connection with the circle of Addison which he was later to abandon in favor of Swift and the Scriblerus Club. It was characteristic of him, and of his age as well, that his study of critical theory preceded his more creative writing. Always he wished to know the law before he tried his liberty. It was always his intention and effort to have the weight of authority on his side. Correctness, orthodoxy, tradition, and the consensus of the past were what he sought from his youth up, so that he

12. burnt, branded.

gives the impression of never having been really young. At the best, he had an old head on young shoulders. We do not look to him for boyish rebellion or for youthful enthusiasm. While still a boy in years he spoke in the language of age.

The fame of Pope, which came to him before his youth was past and grew throughout his life, was partly due to his single-minded devotion. Other writers of his time, dominated as many of them were by the current notion of the gentleman as one who never worked hard at anything, gave most of their energies to politics, journalism, society, or amiable trifling. Pope was a professional writer, and, though he usually tried to give the impression that his most polished productions were tossed off in his idle hours, it is demonstrable that he worked hard at his profession. He worked at nothing else. He made a good living by poetry because he lived for it. On the proceeds of his verse translation of Homer's *Iliad* he was able to buy himself a small estate near Richmond and to live there during the rest of his life, courted and feared, in security and ease. Thus he needed no patron, and he had none. His independence, because it was recognized by everyone, did much for the dignity of the profession of letters.

The reputation of Alexander Pope is probably higher at present than it has been at any time during the last hundred and fifty years. We do not think of him as a great or a magnanimous man. Neither do we regard him as profound or in any high degree original. It is quite clear to us that in the vast terrain of poetry he cultivated only a tiny garden. We do not enjoy his unquestionable spitefulness, nor do we admire the animating spirit of his satire, however much we may delight in its flashing skill. It is more and more recognized, moreover, that all his effort for "correctness" did not give him a secure sense of form or develop the architectonic power of laying out his materials in an orderly way. The question whether he was a poet, considering how rapidly and widely that word has shifted, is now felt to have little meaning. What we do know about Alexander Pope is that in the precise, economical, vivid, and musical use of English words he was one of the most consummate artists that have ever lived.

from AN ESSAY ON CRITICISM

Pope's effort in this brilliant though somewhat discursive poem is not to contribute his own opinions upon an old and much-debated theme but to bring together the tried and accepted doctrines of Aristotle, Horace, and Longinus among the ancients, and of Boileau, chiefly, among critics of more recent times. Although his assertions may seem to a twentieth-century reader highly dogmatic, he is in fact decidedly liberal in his attitude toward the "rules," and it will be seen that he leaves much room for what we call "inspiration." The word "essay" in his title is intended, of course, to suggest an informal and somewhat tentative handling of his theme.

PART I

Introduction: *That 'tis as great a fault to judge ill, as to write ill, and a more dangerous one to the public. That a true Taste is as rare to be found, as a true Genius. That most men are born with some Taste, but spoiled by false Education. The multitude of Critics, and causes of them. That we are to study our own Taste, and know the Limits of it. Nature the best guide of Judgment. Improved by Art and Rules, which are but methodised Nature. Rules derived from the Practice of the Ancient Poets. That therefore the Ancients are necessary to be studied, by a Critic, particularly Homer and Virgil. Of Licences, and the use of them by the Ancients. Reverence due to the Ancients, and praise of them.*

'Tis hard to say, if greater want of skill
Appear in writing or in judging ill;
But, of the two, less dangerous is the offence
To tire our patience, than mislead our sense.
Some few in that, but numbers err in this,
Ten censure wrong for one who writes amiss;
A fool might once himself alone expose,
Now one in verse makes many more in prose.
   'Tis with our judgments as our watches, none
Go just alike, yet each believes his own.   10
In Poets as true genius is but rare,
True Taste as seldom is the Critic's share;
Both must alike from Heaven derive their light,
These born to judge, as well as those to write.
Let such teach others who themselves excel,
And censure freely who have written well.
Authors are partial to their wit, 'tis true,
But are not Critics to their judgment too?
   Yet if we look more closely, we shall find
Most have the seeds of judgment in their mind: 20
Nature affords at least a glimmering light;
The lines, though touched but faintly, are drawn right.
But as the slightest sketch, if justly traced,
Is by ill-colouring but the more disgraced,
So by false learning is good sense defaced:
Some are bewildered in the maze of schools,
And some made coxcombs Nature meant but fools.
In search of wit these lose their common sense,
And then turn Critics in their own defence:
Each burns alike, who can, or cannot write,   30
Or with a Rival's, or an Eunuch's spite.

6. censure, judge.

All fools have still an itching to deride,
And fain would be upon the laughing side.
If Maevius scribble in Apollo's spite,
There are who judge still worse than he can write.
   Some have at first for Wits, then Poets passed,
Turned Critics next, and proved plain fools at last.
Some neither can for Wits nor Critics pass,
As heavy mules are neither horse nor ass.
Those half-learned witlings, numerous in our isle, 40
As half-formed insects on the banks of Nile;
Unfinished things, one knows not what to call,
Their generation's so equivocal;
To tell 'em, would a hundred tongues require,
Or one vain wit's, that might a hundred tire.
   But you who seek to give and merit fame,
And justly bear a Critic's noble name,
Be sure yourself and your own reach to know,
How far your genius, taste, and learning go;
Launch not beyond your depth, but be discreet, 50
And mark that point where sense and dulness meet.
   Nature to all things fixed the limits fit,
And wisely curbed proud man's pretending wit.
As on the land while here the ocean gains,
In other parts it leaves wide sandy plains;
Thus in the soul while memory prevails,
The solid power of understanding fails;
Where beams of warm imagination play,
The memory's soft figures melt away.
One science only will one genius fit; 60
So vast is art, so narrow human wit:
Not only bounded to peculiar arts,
But oft in those confined to single parts.
Like kings we lose the conquests gained before,
By vain ambition still to make them more;
Each might his several province well command,
Would all but stoop to what they understand.
   First follow Nature, and your judgment frame
By her just standard, which is still the same:
Unerring Nature, still divinely bright, 70
One clear, unchanged, and universal light,
Life, force, and beauty, must to all impart,
At once the source, and end, and test of Art.
Art from that fund each just supply provides,
Works without show, and without pomp presides:
In some fair body thus the informing soul
With spirits feeds, with vigour fills the whole,
Each motion guides, and every nerve sustains;
Itself unseen, but in the effects, remains.

  34. **Maevius**, a poet contemporary with Virgil, a classic example of the bad poet. 44. **tell**, count. 53. **wit**, intelligence. In later lines the word is used in several slightly differing senses. 68. **Nature**. Pope's varying use of this difficult word should be carefully studied. Usually, as here, he intends it to mean universal, representative, and normal—though not average—human nature, as shown in feeling, thought, taste, and conduct.

Some, to whom Heaven in wit has been profuse, 80
Want as much more, to turn it to its use;
For wit and judgment often are at strife,
Though meant each other's aid, like man and wife.
'Tis more to guide, than spur the Muse's steed,
Restrain his fury, than provoke his speed;
The wingèd courser, like a generous horse,
Shows most true mettle when you check his course.
   Those Rules of old discovered, not devised,
Are Nature still, but Nature methodized;
Nature, like liberty, is but restrained 90
By the same laws which first herself ordained.
   Hear how learned Greece her useful rules indites,
When to repress, and when indulge our flights:
High on Parnassus' top her sons she showed,
And pointed out those arduous paths they trod;
Held from afar, aloft, the immortal prize,
And urged the rest by equal steps to rise.
Just precepts thus from great examples given,
She drew from them what they derived from Heaven.
The generous Critic fanned the Poet's fire, 100
And taught the world with reason to admire.
Then Criticism the Muses' handmaid proved,
To dress her charms, and make her more beloved:
But following wits from that intention strayed;
Who could not win the mistress, wooed the maid;
Against the Poets their own arms they turned,
Sure to hate most the men from whom they learned.
So modern 'Pothecaries, taught the art
By Doctor's bills to play the Doctor's part,
Bold in the practice of mistaken rules, 110
Prescribe, apply, and call their masters fools.
Some on the leaves of ancient authors prey,
Nor time nor moths e'er spoiled so much as they.
Some drily plain, without invention's aid,
Write dull receipts how poems may be made.
These leave the sense, their learning to display,
And those explain the meaning quite away.
   You then whose judgment the right course would steer,
Know well each Ancient's proper character;
His fable, subject, scope in every page; 120
Religion, Country, genius of his Age:
Without all these at once before your eyes,
Cavil you may, but never criticize.
Be Homer's works your study and delight,
Read them by day, and meditate by night;
Thence form your judgment, thence your maxims bring,
And trace the Muses upward to their spring.
Still with itself compared, his text peruse,

  88. **discovered**, by Aristotle. 120. **fable**, story or plot.

And let your comment be the Mantuan Muse.
    When first young Maro in his boundless mind 130
A work to outlast immortal Rome designed,
Perhaps he seemed above the critic's law,
And but from Nature's fountains scorned to draw;
But when to examine every part he came,
Nature and Homer were, he found, the same.
Convinced, amazed, he checks the bold design;
And rules as strict his laboured work confine,
As if the Stagirite o'erlooked each line.
Learn hence for ancient rules a just esteem;
To copy nature is to copy them. 140
    Some beauties yet no Precepts can declare,
For there's a happiness as well as care.
Music resembles Poetry, in each
Are nameless graces which no methods teach,
And which a master-hand alone can reach.
If, where the rules not far enough extend,
(Since rules were made but to promote their end)
Some lucky Licence answer to the full
The intent proposed, that Licence is a rule.
Thus Pegasus, a nearer way to take, 150
May boldly deviate from the common track;
From vulgar bounds with brave disorder part,
And snatch a grace beyond the reach of art,
Which without passing through the judgment, gains
The heart, and all its end at once attains.
In prospects thus, some objects please our eyes,
Which out of nature's common order rise,
The shapeless rock, or hanging precipice.
Great wits sometimes may gloriously offend,
And rise to faults true Critics dare not mend. 160
But though the Ancients thus their rules invade,
(As Kings dispense with laws themselves have made)
Moderns, beware! or if you must offend
Against the precept, ne'er transgress its End;
Let it be seldom, and compelled by need;
And have, at least, their precedent to plead.
The Critic else proceeds without remorse,
Seizes your fame, and puts his laws in force.
    I know there are, to whose presumptuous thoughts
Those freer beauties, even in them, seem faults. 170
Some figures monstrous and mis-shaped appear,
Considered singly, or beheld too near,
Which, but proportioned to their light, or place,
Due distance reconciles to form and grace.
A prudent chief not always must display
His powers in equal ranks, and fair array,
But with the occasion and the place comply,
Conceal his force, nay seem sometimes to fly.
Those oft are stratagems which error seem,
Nor is it Homer nods, but we that dream. 180
    Still green with bays each ancient Altar stands,
Above the reach of sacrilegious hands,
Secure from Flames, from Envy's fiercer rage,
Destructive War, and all-involving Age.
See, from each clime the learned their incense bring!
Hear, in all tongues consenting Paeans ring!
In praise so just let every voice be joined,
And fill the general chorus of mankind.
Hail, Bards triumphant! born in happier days;
Immortal heirs of universal praise! 190
Whose honours with increase of ages grow,
As streams roll down, enlarging as they flow;
Nations unborn your mighty names shall sound,
And worlds applaud that must not yet be found!
Oh may some spark of your celestial fire,
The last, the meanest of your sons inspire,
(That on weak wings, from far, pursues your flights;
Glows while he reads, but trembles as he writes)
To teach vain Wits a science little known,
To admire superior sense, and doubt their own! 200

PART II

Introduction: *Causes hindering a true Judgment:* 1. *Pride.* 2. *Imperfect Learning.* 3. *Judging by parts, and not by the whole. Critics in Wit, Language, Versification, only.* 4. *Being too hard to please, or too apt to admire.* 5. *Partiality—too much Love to a Sect, to the Ancients or Moderns.* 6. *Prejudice or Prevention.* 7. *Singularity.* 8. *Inconstancy.* 9. *Party Spirit.* 10. *Envy. Against Envy, and in praise of Good-nature. When Severity is chiefly to be used by Critics.*

    Of all the Causes which conspire to blind
Man's erring judgment, and misguide the mind,
What the weak head with strongest bias rules,
Is *Pride,* the never-failing vice of fools.
Whatever nature has in worth denied,
She gives in large recruits of needful pride;
For as in bodies, thus in souls, we find
What wants in blood and spirits, swelled with wind:
Pride, where wit fails, steps in to our defence,
And fills up all the mighty Void of sense. 210
If once right reason drives that cloud away,
Truth breaks upon us with resistless day.
Trust not yourself; but your defects to know,
Make use of every friend—and every foe.

---

129. Mantuan, Virgil, whose surname was **Maro,** was born in Mantua. **138. Stagirite,** Aristotle, born in Stagira, Macedonia. His *Art of Poetry* has been the most influential of all critical documents, for upon it, rightly and wrongly interpreted, the so-called rules of which Neoclassicism made so much were based. **142. happiness,** good fortune in writing, inspiration. **150. Pegasus,** the winged horse of Greek myth, emblem of poetic inspiration and power. **164. End,** purpose or intention.

187. joined. In the pronunciation of Pope's time this word rhymed exactly with "kind," as the word "faults," in l. 170 above, did with "thoughts."

A *little learning* is a dangerous thing;
Drink deep, or taste not the Pierian spring.
There shallow draughts intoxicate the brain,
And drinking largely sobers us again.
Fired at first sight with what the Muse imparts,
In fearless youth we tempt the heights of Arts,   220
While from the bounded level of our mind
Short views we take, nor see the lengths behind;
But more advanced, behold with strange surprise
New distant scenes of endless science rise!
So pleased at first the towering Alps we try,
Mount o'er the vales, and seem to tread the sky,
The eternal snows appear already past,
And the first clouds and mountains seem the last;
But, those attained, we tremble to survey
The growing labours of the lengthened way,   230
The increasing prospects tire our wandering eyes,
Hills peep o'er hills, and Alps on Alps arise!

A perfect Judge will read each work of Wit
With the same spirit that its author writ:
Survey the Whole, nor seek slight faults to find
Where nature moves, and rapture warms the mind;
Nor lose, for that malignant dull delight,
The generous pleasure to be charmed with Wit.
But in such lays as neither ebb, nor flow,
Correctly cold, and regularly low,   240
That, shunning faults, one quiet tenour keep,
We cannot blame indeed—but we may sleep.
In wit, as nature, what affects our hearts
Is not the exactness of peculiar parts;
'Tis not a lip, or eye, we beauty call,
But the joint force and full result of all.
Thus when we view some well-proportioned dome,
(The world's just wonder, and even thine, O Rome!)
No single parts unequally surprize,
All comes united to the admiring eyes;   250
No monstrous height, or breadth, or length appear;
The Whole at once is bold, and regular.

Whoever thinks a faultless piece to see,
Thinks what ne'er was, nor is, nor e'er shall be.
In every work regard the writer's End,
Since none can compass more than they intend;
And if the means be just, the conduct true,
Applause, in spite of trivial faults, is due;
As men of breeding, sometimes men of wit,
To avoid great errors, must the less commit: 260
Neglect the rules each verbal Critic lays,
For not to know some trifles, is a praise.
Most Critics, fond of some subservient art,
Still make the Whole depend upon a Part;
They talk of principles, but notions prize,
And all to one loved Folly sacrifice.

Once on a time, La Mancha's Knight, they say,
A certain bard encountering on the way,
Discoursed in terms as just, with looks as sage,
As e'er could Dennis of the Grecian stage;   270
Concluding all were desperate sots and fools,
Who durst depart from Aristotle's rules.
Our Author, happy in a judge so nice,
Produced his Play, and begged the Knight's advice;
Made him observe the subject, and the plot,
The manners, passions, unities—what not?
All which, exact to rule, were brought about,
Were but a Combat in the lists left out.
"What! leave the Combat out?" exclaims the Knight;
Yes, or we must renounce the Stagirite.   280
"Not so, by Heaven" (he answers in a rage),
"Knights, squires, and steeds, must enter on the stage."
So vast a throng the stage can ne'er contain.
"Then build a new, or act it in a plain."
Thus Critics, of less judgment than caprice,
Curious not knowing, not exact but nice,
Form short Ideas, and offend in arts
(As most in manners) by a love to parts.

Some to *Conceit* alone their taste confine,
And glittering thoughts struck out at every line;   290
Pleased with a work where nothing's just or fit,
One glaring Chaos and wild heap of wit.
Poets like painters, thus, unskilled to trace
The naked nature and the living grace,
With gold and jewels cover every part,
And hide with ornaments their want of art.
True Wit is Nature to advantage dressed,
What oft was thought, but ne'er so well expressed;
Something, whose truth convinced at sight we find,
That gives us back the image of our mind.   300
As shades more sweetly recommend the light,
So modest plainness sets off sprightly wit.
For works may have more wit than does 'em good,
As bodies perish through excess of blood.

Others for *Language* all their care express,
And value books, as women men, for Dress:
Their praise is still,—the Style is excellent:
The Sense, they humbly take upon content.
Words are like leaves; and where they most abound,
Much fruit of sense beneath is rarely found,   310
False Eloquence, like the prismatic glass,
Its gaudy colours spreads on every place;
The face of Nature we no more survey,
All glares alike, without distinction gay:
But true expression, like the unchanging Sun,

216. **Pierian spring,** Hippocrene, at Pieria in Thessaly, birthplace of the Muses.
267. **La Mancha's Knight,** Don Quixote de La Mancha.
270. **Dennis,** John (1657–34), an English critic.   289. **Conceit,** a far-fetched metaphor of the kind favored by English poets of the seventeenth century.

Clears and improves whate'er it shines upon,
It gilds all objects, but it alters none.
Expression is the dress of thought, and still
Appears more decent, as more suitable;
A vile conceit in pompous words expressed, 320
Is like a clown in regal purple dressed:
For different styles with different subjects sort,
As several garbs with country, town, and court.
Some by old words to fame have made pretence,
Ancients in phrase, mere moderns in their sense;
Such laboured nothings, in so strange a style,
Amaze the unlearned, and make the learnèd smile.
Unlucky, as Fungoso in the play,
These sparks with awkward vanity display
What the fine gentleman wore yesterday; 330
And but so mimic ancient wits at best,
As apes our grandsires, in their doublets drest.
In words, as fashions, the same rule will hold;
Alike fantastic, if too new, or old:
Be not the first by whom the new are tried,
Nor yet the last to lay the old aside.

  But most by Numbers judge a Poet's song;
And smooth or rough, with them is right or wrong:
In the bright Muse though thousand charms conspire,
Her voice is all these tuneful fools admire, 340
Who haunt Parnassus but to please their ear,
Not mend their minds; as some to Church repair,
Not for the doctrine, but the music there.
These equal syllables alone require,
Though oft the ear the open vowels tire;
While expletives their feeble aid do join,
And ten low words oft creep in one dull line:
While they ring round the same unvaried chimes,
With sure returns of still expected rhymes; 349
Wher-e'er you find "the cooling western breeze,"
In the next line, it "whispers through the trees":
If crystal streams "with pleasing murmurs creep,"
The reader's threatened (not in vain) with "sleep":
Then, at the last and only couplet fraught
With some unmeaning thing they call a thought,
A needless Alexandrine ends the song
That, like a wounded snake, drags its slow length along.
Leave such to tune their own dull rhymes, and know
What's roundly smooth or languishingly slow;
And praise the easy vigour of a line, 360
Where Denham's strength, and Waller's sweetness join.

---

328. Fungoso, in Ben Jonson's *Every Man out of His Humour*. **344. require.** In this and in several following lines Pope illustrates the effects of versification that he is discussing. **361. Denham . . . Waller**, poets of the seventeenth century admired by Pope's contemporaries for the vigor, ease, and correctness of their versification.

True ease in writing comes from art, not chance,
As those move easiest who have learned to dance.
'Tis not enough no harshness gives offence;
The sound must seem an Echo to the sense:
Soft is the strain when Zephyr gently blows,
And the smooth stream in smoother numbers flows;
But when loud surges lash the sounding shore,
The hoarse, rough verse should like the torrent roar:
When Ajax strives some rock's vast weight to throw,
The line too labours, and the words move slow; 371
Not so, when swift Camilla scours the plain,
Flies o'er the unbending corn, and skims along the main.
Hear how Timotheus' varied lays surprize,
And bid alternate passions fall and rise!
While, at each change, the son of Libyan Jove
Now burns with glory, and then melts with love,
Now his fierce eyes with sparkling fury glow,
Now sighs steal out, and tears begin to flow:
Persians and Greeks like turns of nature found, 380
And the world's victor stood subdued by Sound!
The power of Music all our hearts allow,
And what Timotheus was, is DRYDEN now.

  Avoid Extremes, and shun the fault of such,
Who still are pleased too little or too much.
At every trifle scorn to take offence;
That always shows great pride, or little sense;
Those heads, as stomachs, are not sure the best,
Which nauseate all, and nothing can digest.
Yet let not each gay turn thy rapture move; 390
For fools admire, but men of sense approve:
As things seem large which we through mists descry,
Dulness is ever apt to magnify.

  Some foreign writers, some our own despise;
The Ancients only, or the Moderns prize.
Thus Wit, like Faith, by each man is applied
To one small sect, and all are damned beside.
Meanly they seek the blessing to confine,
And force that sun but on a part to shine,
Which not alone the southern wit sublimes, 400
But ripens spirits in cold northern climes;
Which from the first has shone on ages past,
Enlights the present, and shall warm the last;
Though each may feel increases and decays,
And see now clearer and now darker days.
Regard not then if Wit be old or new,
But blame the false, and value still the true.

  Some ne'er advance a Judgment of their own,
But catch the spreading notion of the Town;

---

374. Timotheus. See Dryden's "Alexander's Feast." **380. turns,** tropes, or figures of speech. **391. admire,** wonder at.

They reason and conclude by precedent, 410
And own stale nonsense which they ne'er invent.
Some judge of authors' names, not works, and then
Nor praise nor blame the writings, but the men.
Of all this servile herd the worst is he
That in proud dulness joins with Quality;
A constant Critic at the great man's board,
To fetch and carry nonsense for my lord.
What woful stuff this madrigal would be,
In some starved hackney sonneteer, or me?
But let a Lord once own the happy lines, 420
How the wit brightens! how the style refines!
Before his sacred name flies every fault,
And each exalted stanza teems with thought!
   The Vulgar thus through Imitation err;
As oft the Learned by being singular;
So much they scorn the crowd, that if the throng
By chance go right, they purposely go wrong;
So Schismatics the plain believers quit,
And are but damned for having too much wit.
Some praise at morning what they blame at night;
But always think the last opinion right. 431
A Muse by these is like a mistress used,
This hour she's idolized, the next abused;
While their weak heads like towns unfortified,
'Twixt sense and nonsense daily change their side.
Ask them the cause; they're wiser still, they say;
And still to-morrow's wiser than to-day.
We think our fathers fools, so wise we grow,
Our wiser sons, no doubt, will think us so.
Once School-divines this zealous isle o'erspread; 440
Who knew most Sentences, was deepest read;
Faith, Gospel, all, seemed made to be disputed,
And none had sense enough to be confuted:
Scotists and Thomists, now, in peace remain,
Amidst their kindred cobwebs in Duck-lane.
If Faith itself has different dresses worn,
What wonder modes in Wit should take their turn?
Oft, leaving what is natural and fit,
The current folly proves the ready wit;
And authors think their reputation safe, 450
Which lives as long as fools are pleased to laugh.
   Some, valuing those of their own side or mind,
Still make themselves the measure of mankind:
Fondly we think we honour merit then,
When we but praise ourselves in other men.
Parties in Wit attend on those of State,
And public faction doubles private hate.
Pride, Malice, Folly, against Dryden rose,
In various shapes of Parsons, Critics, Beaux;
But sense survived, when merry jests were past; 460

For rising merit will buoy up at last.
Might he return, and bless once more our eyes,
New Blackmores and new Milbourns must arise:
Nay, should great Homer lift his awful head,
Zoilus again would start up from the dead.
Envy will merit, as its shade, pursue;
But like a shadow, proves the substance true;
For envyed Wit, like Sol eclipsed, makes known
The opposing body's grossness, not its own.
When first that sun too powerful beams displays,
It draws up vapours which obscure its rays; 471
But even those clouds at last adorn its way,
Reflect new glories, and augment the day.
   Be thou the first true merit to befriend;
His praise is lost, who stays till all commend.
Short is the date, alas, of modern rhymes,
And 'tis but just to let them live betimes.
No longer now that golden age appears,
When Patriarch-wits survived a thousand years:
Now length of Fame (our second life) is lost, 480
And bare threescore is all even that can boast;
Our sons their fathers' failing language see,
And such as Chaucer is, shall Dryden be.
So when the faithful pencil has designed
Some bright Idea of the master's mind,
Where a new world leaps out at his command,
And ready Nature waits upon his hand;
When the ripe colours soften and unite,
And sweetly melt into just shade and light;
When mellowing years their full perfection give, 490
And each bold figure just begins to live,
The treacherous colours the fair art betray,
And all the bright creation fades away!
   Unhappy Wit, like most mistaken things,
Atones not for that envy which it brings.
In youth alone its empty praise we boast,
But soon the short-lived vanity is lost:
Like some fair flower the early spring supplies,
That gaily blooms, but even in blooming dies.
What is this Wit, which must our cares employ? 500
The owner's wife, that other men enjoy;
Then most our trouble still when most admired,
And still the more we give, the more required;
Whose fame with pains we guard, but lose with ease,
Sure some to vex, but never all to please;
'Tis what the vicious fear, the virtuous shun,
By fools 'tis hated, and by knaves undone!
   If Wit so much from Ignorance undergo,
Ah, let not Learning too commence its foe!
Of old, those met rewards who could excel, 510
And such were praised who but endeavoured well:

---

444. **Scotists and Thomists,** followers of Duns Scotus and Thomas Aquinas.   445. **Duck-lane,** a street in which secondhand books were sold.

463. **Blackmores** ... **Milbourns,** literary foes of Dryden.   465. **Zoilus,** a Greek critic (c. 400–320 B.C.) who assailed the literary reputation of Homer.

Though triumphs were to generals only due,
Crowns were reserved to grace the soldiers too.
Now they who reach Parnassus' lofty crown
Employ their pains to spurn some others down;
And while self-love each jealous writer rules,
Contending wits become the sport of fools:
But still the worst with most regret commend,
For each ill Author is as bad a Friend.
To what base ends, and by what abject ways,   520
Are mortals urged through sacred lust of praise!
Ah, ne'er so dire a thirst of glory boast,
Nor in the Critic let the Man be lost.
Good-nature and good-sense must ever join;
To err is human, to forgive, divine.
   But if in noble minds some dregs remain
Not yet purged off, of spleen and sour disdain,
Discharge that rage on more provoking crimes,
Nor fear a dearth in these flagitious times.
No pardon vile Obscenity should find,   530
Though wit and art conspire to move your mind;
But Dulness with Obscenity must prove
As shameful sure as Impotence in love.
In the fat age of pleasure, wealth, and ease,
Sprung the rank weed, and thrived with large increase:
When love was all an easy Monarch's care;
Seldom at council, never in a war:
Jilts ruled the state, and statesmen farces writ;
Nay wits had pensions, and young Lords had wit:
The Fair sate panting at a Courtier's play,   540
And not a Mask went unimproved away:
The modest fan was lifted up no more,
And Virgins smiled at what they blushed before.
The following licence of a Foreign reign
Did all the dregs of bold Socinus drain;
Then unbelieving priests reformed the nation,
And taught more pleasant methods of salvation;
Where Heaven's free subjects might their rights dispute,
Lest God himself should seem too absolute:
Pulpits their sacred satire learned to spare,   550
And Vice admired to find a flatterer there!
Encouraged thus, Wit's Titans braved the skies,
And the press groaned with licensed blasphemies.
These monsters, Critics! with your darts engage,
Here point your thunder, and exhaust your rage!
Yet shun their fault, who, scandalously nice,
Will needs mistake an author into vice;
All seems infected that the infected spy,
As all looks yellow to the jaundiced eye. . . .

536. **easy . . . care,** of Charles II.   541. **Mask,** a woman wearing a mask.   544. **Foreign reign,** of William and Mary.   545. **Socinus,** Lelio Francisco Maria Sozini (1525–1562), an Italian Protestant theologian.

from AN ESSAY ON MAN

Although it is in some respects the most ambitious of his undertakings, Pope's *Essay on Man* does not represent an original philosophical effort on the poet's part. Many if not most of the ideas it contains were derived, probably in conversation, from the remarkable politician, philosopher, and writer whom we now know as Lord Bolingbroke. These ideas are "Deistic" in tendency. That is to say, they find the evidence for their "natural religion" rather in the study of nature and in human reason than in direct revelation.

The poem in its entirety comprises four epistles, of which only the first two are printed here. It is more remarkable for its brilliant passages than for coherence of thought.

EPISTLE I

Awake, my St. John! leave all meaner things
To low ambition, and the pride of Kings.
Let us (since Life can little more supply
Than just to look about us and to die)
Expatiate free o'er all this scene of Man;
A mighty maze! but not without a plan;
A Wild, where weeds and flowers promiscuous shoot;
Or Garden, tempting with forbidden fruit.
Together let us beat this ample field,
Try what the open, what the covert yield;   10
The latent tracts, the giddy heights, explore
Of all who blindly creep, or sightless soar;
Eye Nature's walks, shoot Folly as it flies,
And catch the Manners living as they rise;
Laugh where we must, be candid where we can,
But vindicate the ways of God to Man.
   1. Say first, of God above, or Man below,
What can we reason, but from what we know?
Of Man, what see we but his station here,
From which to reason, or to which refer?   20
Through worlds unnumbered though the God be known,
'Tis ours to trace him only in our own.
He, who through vast immensity can pierce,
See worlds on worlds compose one universe,
Observe how system into system runs,
What other planets circle other suns,
What varied Being peoples every star,
May tell why Heaven has made us as we are.
But of this frame the bearings, and the ties,
The strong connexions, nice dependencies,   30

1. **St. John!** Henry St. John, Viscount Bolingbroke (1678–1751). See the vivid characterization of him in Lord Chesterfield's letter of December 12, 1749, page 869.   5. **Expatiate,** roam.

Gradations just, has thy pervading soul
Looked through? or can a part contain the whole?
  Is the great chain, that draws all to agree,
And drawn supports, upheld by God, or thee?
    2. Presumptuous Man! the reason wouldst thou find,
Why formed so weak, so little, and so blind?
First, if thou canst, the harder reason guess,
Why formed no weaker, blinder, and no less?
Ask of thy mother earth, why oaks are made
Taller or stronger than the weeds they shade!   40
Or ask of yonder argent fields above,
Why Jove's satellites are less than Jove!
  Of Systems possible, if 'tis confesst
That Wisdom infinite must form the best,
Where all must full or not coherent be,
And all that rises, rise in due degree;
Then, in the scale of reasoning life, 'tis plain,
There must be, somewhere, such a rank as Man:
And all the question (wrangle e'er so long)
Is only this, if God has placed him wrong?   50
  Respecting Man, whatever wrong we call,
May, must be right, as relative to all.
In human works, though laboured on with pain,
A thousand movements scarce one purpose gain;
In God's, one single can its end produce;
Yet serves to second too some other use.
So Man, who here seems principal alone,
Perhaps acts second to some sphere unknown,
Touches some wheel, or verges to some goal.
'Tis but a part we see, and not a whole.   60
    When the proud steed shall know why Man restrains
His fiery course, or drives him o'er the plains:
When the dull Ox, why now he breaks the clod,
Is now a victim, and now Aegypt's god:
Then shall Man's pride and dulness comprehend
His actions', passions', being's, use and end;
Why doing, suffering, checked, impelled; and why
This hour a slave, the next a deity.
  Then say not Man's imperfect, Heaven in fault;
Say rather, Man's as perfect as he ought: 70
His knowledge measured to his state and place;
His time a moment, and a point his space.
If to be perfect in a certain sphere,
What matter, soon or late, or here or there?
The blest to-day is as completely so,
As who began a thousand years ago.
    3. Heaven from all creatures hides the book of Fate,
All but the page prescribed, their present state:
From brutes what men, from men what spirits know,

Or who could suffer Being here below?   80
The lamb thy riot dooms to bleed to-day,
Had he thy Reason, would he skip and play?
Pleased to the last, he crops the flowery food,
And licks the hand just raised to shed his blood.
Oh blindness to the future! kindly given,
That each may fill the circle marked by Heaven,
Who sees with equal eye, as God of all,
A hero perish, or a sparrow fall,
Atoms or systems into ruin hurled,
And now a bubble burst, and now a world.   90
  Hope humbly then; with trembling pinions soar;
Wait the great teacher Death; and God adore.
What future bliss, he gives not thee to know,
But gives that Hope to be thy blessing now.
Hope springs eternal in the human breast:
Man never Is, but always To be blessed;
The soul, uneasy and confined from home,
Rests and expatiates in a life to come.
  Lo, the poor Indian! whose untutored mind
Sees God in clouds, or hears him in the wind;   100
His soul, proud Science never taught to stray
Far as the solar walk, or milky way;
Yet simple Nature to his hope has given,
Behind the cloud-toppt hill, an humbler heaven;
Some safer world in depth of woods embraced,
Some happier island in the watry waste,
Where slaves once more their native land behold,
No fiends torment, no Christians thirst for gold.
To Be, contents his natural desire;
He asks no Angel's wing, no Seraph's fire;   110
But thinks, admitted to that equal sky,
His faithful dog shall bear him company.
    4. Go, wiser thou! and, in thy scale of sense,
Weigh thy Opinion against Providence;
Call imperfection what thou fanciest such;
Say, here he gives too little, there too much:
Destroy all Creatures for thy sport or gust,
Yet cry, If Man's unhappy, God's unjust;
If Man alone engross not Heaven's high care,
Alone made perfect here, immortal there: 120
Snatch from his hand the balance and the rod,
Re-judge his justice, be the GOD of GOD.
In Pride, in reasoning Pride, our error lies;
All quit their sphere, and rush into the skies.
Pride still is aiming at the blest abodes,
Men would be Angels, Angels would be Gods.
Aspiring to be Gods, if Angels fell,
Aspiring to be Angels, Men rebel:
And who but wishes to invert the laws
Of Order, sins against the Eternal Cause.   130
    5. Ask for what end the heavenly bodies shine,
Earth for whose use? Pride answers, "'Tis for mine:

42. **satellites**, pronounced as in Latin, să-tĕl′ĭ-tēz.

117. **gust**, pleasure.

For me kind Nature wakes her genial Power,
Suckles each herb, and spreads out every flower;
Annual for me, the grape, the rose renew
The juice nectareous, and the balmy dew;
For me, the mine a thousand treasures brings;
For me, health gushes from a thousand springs;
Seas roll to waft me, suns to light me rise;
My foot-stool earth, my canopy the skies."   140

  But errs not Nature from this gracious end,
From burning suns when living death descend,
When earthquakes swallow, or when tempests sweep
Towns to one grave, whole nations to the deep?
"No," ('tis replied), "the first Almighty Cause
Acts not by partial, but by general laws;
The exceptions few; some change since all began:
And what created perfect?"—Why then Man?
If the great end be human Happiness,
Then Nature deviates; and can Man do less?   150
As much that end a constant course requires
Of showers and sunshine, as of Man's desires;
As much eternal springs and cloudless skies,
As Men forever temperate, calm, and wise.
If plagues or earthquakes break not Heaven's design,
Why then a Borgia, or a Catiline?
Who knows but he, whose hand the lightning forms,
Who heaves old Ocean, and who wings the storms;
Pours fierce ambition in a Caesar's mind,   159
Or turns young Ammon loose to scourge mankind?
From pride, from pride, our very reasoning springs;
Account for moral, as for natural things:
Why charge we Heaven in those, in these acquit?
In both, to reason right is to submit.

  Better for us, perhaps, it might appear,
Were there all harmony, all virtue here;
That never air or ocean felt the wind;
That never passion discomposed the mind.
But All subsists by elemental strife,
And passions are the elements of life.   170
The general Order, since the whole began,
Is kept in Nature, and is kept in Man.

  6. What would this Man? Now upward will he soar,
And little less than Angel, would be more;
Now looking downwards, just as grieved appears
To want the strength of bulls, the fur of bears.
Made for his use all creatures if he call,
Say what their use, had he the powers of all?
Nature to these, without profusion, kind,
The proper organs, proper powers assigned;   180
Each seeming want compensated of course,
Here with degrees of swiftness, there of force;
All in exact proportion to the state;
Nothing to add, and nothing to abate.
Each beast, each insect, happy in its own:
Is Heaven unkind to Man, and Man alone?
Shall he alone, whom rational we call,
Be pleased with nothing, if not blessed with all?

  The bliss of Man (could Pride that blessing find)
Is not to act or think beyond mankind;   190
No powers of body or of soul to share,
But what his nature and his state can bear.
Why has not Man a microscopic eye?
For this plain reason, Man is not a Fly.
Say what the use, were finer optics given,
To inspect a mite, not comprehend the heaven?
Or touch, if tremblingly alive all o'er,
To smart and agonize at every pore?
Or quick effluvia darting through the brain,
Die of a rose in aromatic pain?   200
If nature thundered in his opening ears,
And stunned him with the music of the spheres,
How would he wish that Heaven had left him still
The whispering Zephyr, and the purling rill?
Who finds not Providence all good and wise,
Alike in what it gives, and what denies?

  7. Far as Creation's ample range extends,
The scale of sensual, mental powers ascends:
Mark how it mounts, to Man's imperial race,
From the green myriads in the peopled grass: 210
What modes of sight betwixt each wide extreme,
The mole's dim curtain and the lynx's beam:
Of smell, the headlong lioness between,
And hound sagacious on the tainted green:
Of hearing, from the life that fills the flood,
To that which warbles through the vernal wood:
The spider's touch, how exquisitely fine!
Feels at each thread, and lives along the line:
In the nice bee, what sense so subtly true
From poisonous herbs extracts the healing dew?   220
How Instinct varies in the grovelling swine,
Compared, half-reasoning elephant, with thine!
'Twixt that, and Reason, what a nice barrier,
Forever separate, yet forever near!
Remembrance and Reflection how allied;
What thin partitions Sense from Thought divide:
And Middle natures, how they long to join,
Yet never pass the insuperable line!
Without this just gradation, could they be
Subjected, these to those, or all to thee?   230
The powers of all subdued by thee alone,
Is not thy reason all these powers in one?

  8. See, through this air, this ocean, and this earth,

---

133. **genial**, life-giving.   156. **Borgia . . . Catiline**, examples of human depravity.   160. **Ammon**, Alexander the Great.   208. **sensual**, sensory.

All matter quick, and bursting into birth.
Above, how high progressive life may go!
Around, how wide! how deep extend below!
Vast chain of Being! which from God began,
Natures ethereal, human, angel, man,
Beast, bird, fish, insect, what no eye can see,
No glass can reach; from Infinite to thee,   240
From thee to Nothing.—On superior powers
Were we to press, inferior might on ours:
Or in the full creation leave a void,
Where, one step broken, the great scale's destroyed:
From Nature's chain whatever link you strike,
Tenth or ten thousandth, breaks the chain alike.

    And, if each system in gradation roll
Alike essential to the amazing Whole,
The least confusion but in one, not all
That system only, but the Whole must fall.   250
Let Earth unbalanced from her orbit fly,
Planets and Suns run lawless through the sky;
Let ruling angels from their spheres be hurled,
Being on Being wrecked, and world on world;
Heaven's whole foundations to their centre nod,
And Nature tremble to the throne of God.
All this dread Order break—for whom? for thee?
Vile worm!—Oh Madness! Pride! Impiety!

    9. What if the foot, ordained the dust to tread,
Or hand, to toil, aspired to be the head?   260
What if the head, the eye, or ear repined
To serve mere engines to the ruling Mind?
Just as absurd for any part to claim
To be another, in this general frame:
Just as absurd, to mourn the tasks or pains
The great directing Mind of All ordains.

    All are but parts of one stupendous whole,
Whose body Nature is, and God the soul;
That, changed through all, and yet in all the same,
Great in the earth, as in the ethereal frame,   270
Warms in the sun, refreshes in the breeze,
Glows in the stars, and blossoms in the trees,
Lives through all life, extends through all extent,
Spreads undivided, operates unspent;
Breathes in our soul, informs our mortal part,
As full, as perfect, in a hair as heart:
As full, as perfect, in vile Man that mourns,
As the rapt Seraph that adores and burns:
To him no high, no low, no great, no small;
He fills, he bounds, connects, and equals all.   280

    10. Cease then, nor Order imperfection name;
Our proper bliss depends on what we blame.
Know thy own point: this kind, this due degree
Of blindness, weakness, Heaven bestows on thee.
Submit.—In this, or any other sphere,
Secure to be as blessed as thou canst bear:
Safe in the hand of one disposing Power,
Or in the natal or the mortal hour.
All Nature is but Art, unknown to thee;
All Chance, Direction, which thou canst not see;
All Discord, Harmony not understood;   291
All partial Evil, universal Good:
And, spite of Pride, in erring Reason's spite,
One truth is clear, WHATEVER IS, IS RIGHT.

EPISTLE II

    1. Know then thyself, presume not God to scan;
The proper study of Mankind is Man.
Placed on this isthmus of a middle state,
A Being darkly wise, and rudely great:
With too much knowledge for the Sceptic side,
With too much weakness for the Stoic's pride,
He hangs between; in doubt to act, or rest;
In doubt to deem himself a God, or Beast;
In doubt his Mind or Body to prefer;
Born but to die, and reasoning but to err;   10
Alike in ignorance, his reason such,
Whether he thinks too little, or too much:
Chaos of Thought and Passion, all confused;
Still by himself abused, or disabused;
Created half to rise, and half to fall;
Great lord of all things, yet a prey to all;
Sole judge of Truth, in endless Error hurled:
The glory, jest, and riddle of the world!

    Go, wondrous creature! mount where Science guides;
Go, measure earth, weigh air, and state the tides;
Instruct the planets in what orbs to run,   21
Correct old Time, and regulate the Sun;
Go, soar with Plato to the empyreal sphere,
To the first good, first perfect, and first fair;
Or tread the mazy round his followers trod,
And quitting sense call imitating God;
As Eastern priests in giddy circles run,
And turn their heads to imitate the Sun.
Go, teach Eternal Wisdom how to rule—
Then drop into thyself, and be a fool!   30

    Superior beings, when of late they saw
A mortal Man unfold all Nature's law,
Admired such wisdom in an earthly shape,
And shewed a Newton as we show an Ape.

    Could he, whose rules the rapid Comet bind,
Describe or fix one movement of his Mind?
Who saw its fires here rise, and there descend,
Explain his own beginning, or his end?
Alas, what wonder! Man's superior part
Unchecked may rise, and climb from art to art;

    234. **quick**, alive.

    17. **hurled**, whirled.   27. **priests,** of the sun god Baal.

But when his own great work is but begun, 41
What Reason weaves, by Passion is undone.
    Trace Science then, with Modesty thy guide;
First strip off all her equipage of Pride;
Deduct what is but Vanity, or Dress,
Or Learning's Luxury, or Idleness;
Or tricks to show the stretch of human brain,
Mere curious pleasure, or ingenious pain;
Expunge the whole, or lop the excrescent parts
Of all our Vices have created Arts; 50
Then see how little the remaining sum,
Which served the past, and must the times to come!
    2. Two Principles in human nature reign:
Self-love, to urge, and Reason, to restrain;
Nor this a good, nor that a bad we call,
Each works its end, to move or govern all:
And to their proper operation still,
Ascribe all Good; to their improper Ill.
    Self-love, the spring of motion, acts the soul;
Reason's comparing balance rules the whole. 60
Man, but for that, no action could attend,
And but for this, were active to no end:
Fixed like a plant on his peculiar spot,
To draw nutrition, propagate, and rot;
Or, meteor-like, flame lawless through the void,
Destroying others, by himself destroyed.
    Most strength the moving principle requires;
Active its task, it prompts, impels, inspires.
Sedate and quiet the comparing lies,
Formed but to check, deliberate, and advise. 70
Self-love still stronger, as its objects nigh;
Reason's at distance, and in prospect lie:
That sees immediate good by present sense;
Reason, the future and the consequence.
Thicker than arguments, temptations throng,
At best more watchful this, but that more strong.
The action of the stronger to suspend,
Reason still use, to Reason still attend.
Attention, habit and experience gains;
Each strengthens Reason, and Self-love restrains.
    Let subtle schoolmen teach these friends to fight,
More studious to divide than to unite; 82
And Grace and Virtue, Sense and Reason split,
With all the rash dexterity of wit.
Wits, just like Fools, at war about a name,
Have full as oft no meaning, or the same.
Self-love and Reason to one end aspire,
Pain their aversion, Pleasure their desire;
But greedy that, its object would devour;
This taste the honey, and not wound the flower:
Pleasure, or wrong or rightly understood,
Our greatest evil, or our greatest good. 90

    3. Modes of Self-love the Passions we may call;
'Tis real good, or seeming, moves them all;
But since not every good we can divide,
And Reason bids us for our own provide,
Passions, though selfish, if their means be fair,
List under Reason, and deserve her care;
Those, that imparted, court a nobler aim,
Exalt their kind, and take some Virtue's name. 100
    In lazy Apathy let Stoics boast
Their Virtue fixed; 'tis fixed as in a frost;
Contracted all, retiring to the breast;
But strength of mind is Exercise, not rest:
The rising tempest puts in act the soul,
Parts it may ravage, but preserves the whole.
On life's vast ocean diversely we sail,
Reason the card, but Passion is the gale;
Nor God alone in the still calm we find;
He mounts the storm, and walks upon the wind.
    Passions, like Elements, though born to fight, 111
Yet, mixed and softened, in his work unite:
These 'tis enough to temper and employ;
But what composes Man, can Man destroy?
Suffice that Reason keep to Nature's road,
Subject, compound them, follow her and God.
Love, Hope, and Joy, fair pleasure's smiling train,
Hate, Fear, and Grief, the family of pain,
These mixed with art, and to due bounds confined,
Make and maintain the balance of the mind: 120
The lights and shades, whose well accorded strife
Gives all the strength and colour of our life.
    Pleasures are ever in our hands or eyes;
And when in act they cease, in prospect rise;
Present to grasp, and future still to find,
The whole employ of body and of mind.
All spread their charms, but charm not all alike;
On different senses different objects strike;
Hence different Passions more or less inflame,
As strong or weak, the organs of the frame; 130
And hence one Master Passion in the breast,
Like Aaron's serpent, swallows up the rest.
    As Man, perhaps, the moment of his breath,
Receives the lurking principle of death;
The young disease, that must subdue at length,
Grows with his growth, and strengthens with his strength:
So, cast and mingled with his very frame,
The Mind's disease, its Ruling Passion, came;
Each vital humour which should feed the whole
Soon flows to this, in body and in soul: 140

    50. **Vices,** after this word supply "which."   **59. acts,** actuates, sets in motion.   **69. comparing,** reason.

    98. List, enlist.   **101. Stoics.** This passage gives a false view of the Stoic philosophy.   **108. card,** mariner's compass.   **131. Master Passion.** This is the "humor" of Elizabethan times and the "genius" of the later eighteenth century. Today we call it individuality, and regard it as a thing to be trusted and encouraged.

Whatever warms the heart, or fills the head,
As the mind opens, and its functions spread,
Imagination plies her dangerous art,
And pours it all upon the peccant part.
    Nature its mother, Habit is its nurse;
Wit, Spirit, Faculties, but make it worse;
Reason itself but gives it edge and power,
As Heaven's blest beam turns vinegar more sour.
    We, wretched subjects though to lawful sway,
In this weak queen some favourite still obey: 150
Ah! if she lend not arms, as well as rules,
What can she more than tell us we are fools?
Teach us to mourn our Nature, not to mend,
A sharp accuser, but a helpless friend!
Or from a judge turn pleader, to persuade
The choice we make, or justify it made;
Proud of an easy conquest all along,
She but removes weak passions for the strong:
So, when small humours gather to a gout,
The doctor fancies he has driven them out.   160
    Yes, Nature's road must ever be preferred;
Reason is here no guide, but still a guard;
'Tis hers to rectify, not overthrow.
And treat this passion more as friend than foe:
A mightier Power the strong direction sends,
And several Men impels to several ends:
Like varying winds, by other passions tost,
This drives them constant to a certain coast.
Let power or knowledge, gold or glory, please,
Or (oft more strong than all) the love of ease;   170
Through life 'tis followed, even at life's expense;
The merchant's toil, the sage's indolence,
The monk's humility, the hero's pride,
All, all alike, find Reason on their side.
    The Eternal Art, educing good from ill,
Grafts on this Passion our best principle:
'Tis thus the Mercury of Man is fixed,
Strong grows the Virtue with his nature mixed;
The dross cements what else were too refined,
And in one interest body acts with mind.   180
    As fruits, ungrateful to the planter's care,
On savage stocks inserted, learn to bear;
The surest Virtues thus from Passions shoot,
Wild Nature's vigour working at the root.
What crops of wit and honesty appear
From spleen, from obstinacy, hate, or fear!
See anger, zeal and fortitude supply;
Even avarice, prudence; sloth, philosophy;
Lust, through some certain strainers well refined,
Is gentle love, and charms all womankind;   190

Envy, to which the ignoble mind's a slave,
Is emulation in the learned or brave;
Nor Virtue, male or female, can we name,
But what will grow on Pride, or grow on Shame.
    Thus Nature gives us (let it check our pride)
The virtue nearest to our vice allied:
Reason the bias turns to good from ill,
And Nero reigns a Titus, if he will.
The fiery soul abhorred in Catiline,
In Decius charms, in Curtius is divine: 200
The same ambition can destroy or save,
And makes a patriot as it makes a knave.
    4. This light and darkness in our chaos joined,
What shall divide? The God within the mind.
    Extremes in Nature equal ends produce;
In Man they join to some mysterious use;
Though each by turns the other's bound invade,
As, in some well-wrought picture, light and shade,
And oft so mix, the difference is too nice
Where ends the Virtue, or begins the Vice.   210
    Fools! who from hence into the notion fall,
That Vice or Virtue there is none at all.
If white and black blend, soften, and unite
A thousand ways, is there no black or white?
Ask your own heart, and nothing is so plain;
'Tis to mistake them, costs the time and pain.
    5. Vice is a monster of so frightful mien,
As, to be hated, needs but to be seen;
Yet seen too oft, familiar with her face,
We first endure, then pity, then embrace.   220
But where the Extreme of Vice, was ne'er agreed:
Ask where's the North? at York, 'tis on the *Tweed*;
In Scotland, at the Orcades; and there,
At Greenland, Zembla, or the Lord knows where.
No creature owns it in the first degree,
But thinks his neighbour further gone than he;
Even those who dwell beneath its very zone,
Or never feel the rage, or never own;
What happier natures shrink at with affright,
The hard inhabitant contends is right.   230
    6. Virtuous and vicious every Man must be,
Few in the extreme, but all in the degree;
The rogue and fool by fits is fair and wise;
And even the best, by fits, what they despise.
'Tis but by parts we follow good or ill,
For, Vice or Virtue, Self directs it still;
Each individual seeks a several goal,
But Heaven's great view is One, and that the Whole.
That counter-works each folly and caprice;
That disappoints the effect of every vice;   240
That, happy frailties to all ranks applied,

---

144. peccant, diseased.   **150. queen,** that is, Reason, which is itself subject to the "ruling passion."   **161. road.** Compare l. 115, above.   **174. find . . . side,** can find reasons for what they wish to do. In our day this is sometimes called "rationalizing."

209. nice, too delicate or minute to be discerned.
227. zone, track of the sun.

Shame to the virgin, to the matron pride,
Fear to the statesman, rashness to the chief,
To kings presumption, and to crowds belief:
That, Virtue's ends from Vanity can raise,
Which seeks no interest, no reward but praise;
And build on wants, and on defects of mind,
The joy, the peace, the glory of Mankind.
    Heaven forming each on other to depend,
A master, or a servant, or a friend,   250
Bids each on other for assistance call,
Till one man's weakness grows the strength of all.
Wants, frailties, passions, closer still ally
The common interest, or endear the tie.
To these we owe true friendship, love sincere,
Each home-felt joy that life inherits here;
Yet from the same we learn, in its decline,
Those joys, those loves, those interests to resign;
Taught half by Reason, half by mere decay,
To welcome death, and calmly pass away.   260
    Whate'er the Passion, knowledge, fame, or pelf,
Not one will change his neighbour with himself.
The learned is happy nature to explore.
The fool is happy that he knows no more,
The rich is happy in the plenty given,
The poor contents him with the care of Heaven.
See the blind beggar dance, the cripple sing,
The sot a hero, lunatic a king;
The starving chemist in his golden views
Supremely blest, the poet in his Muse.   270
    See some strange comfort every state attend,
And Pride bestowed on all, a common friend;
See some fit Passion every age supply.
Hope travels through, nor quits us when we die.
    Behold the child, by Nature's kindly law,
Pleased with a rattle, tickled with a straw;
Some livelier play-thing gives his youth delight,
A little louder, but as empty quite:
Scarfs, garters, gold, amuse his riper stage,
And beads and prayer-books are the toys of age: 280
Pleased with this bauble still, as that before;
'Till tired he sleeps, and Life's poor play is o'er.
    Mean-while Opinion gilds with varying rays
Those painted clouds that beautify our days;
Each want of happiness by hope supplied,
And each vacuity of sense by Pride.
These build as fast as knowledge can destroy;
In Folly's cup still laughs the bubble, joy;
One prospect lost, another still we gain,
And not a vanity is given in vain;   290
Even mean Self-love becomes, by force divine,
The scale to measure others' wants by thine.

269. **chemist,** alchemist, with his hope of making gold out of the baser metals.

See! and confess, one comfort still must rise.
'Tis this, Though Man's a fool, yet GOD IS WISE.

THE UNIVERSAL PRAYER

DEO OPT. MAX.

This poem was written, on the model of the Lord's Prayer, to sum up the Essay on Man *and to show that the thought of that poem was based upon a belief in free will. The Latin subtitle means "To God the best and greatest."*

    Father of All! in every Age,
        In every Clime adored,
    By Saint, by Savage, and by Sage,
        Jehovah, Jove, or Lord!

    Thou Great First Cause, least understood:
        Who all my Sense confined
    To know but this, that Thou art Good,
        And that myself am blind;

    Yet gave me, in this dark Estate,
        To see the Good from Ill;   10
    And binding Nature fast in Fate,
        Left free the Human Will.

    What Conscience dictates to be done,
        Or warns me not to do,
    This, teach me more than Hell to shun,
        That, more than Heaven pursue.

    What Blessings thy free Bounty gives,
        Let me not cast away;
    For God is payed when Man receives;
        To enjoy is to obey.   20

    Yet not to Earth's contracted Span
        Thy Goodness led me bound,
    Or think Thee Lord alone of Man,
        When thousand Worlds are round:

    Let not this weak, unknowing hand
        Presume thy bolts to throw,
    And deal damnation round the land,
        On each I judge thy Foe.

    If I am right, thy grace impart,
        Still in the right to stay;   30
    If I am wrong, oh teach my heart
        To find that better way.

Save me alike from foolish Pride
   Or impious Discontent,
At aught thy Wisdom has denied,
   Or aught thy Goodness lent.

Teach me to feel another's Woe,
   To hide the Fault I see;
That Mercy I to others show,
   That Mercy show to me.   40

Mean though I am, not wholly so,
   Since quickened by thy Breath;
Oh lead me wheresoe'er I go,
   Through this day's Life or Death.

This day, be Bread and Peace my Lot:
   All else beneath the Sun,
Thou know'st if best bestowed or not;
   And let Thy Will be done.

To thee, whose Temple is all Space,
   Whose Altar Earth, Sea, Skies,   50
One Chorus let all Being raise,
   All Nature's Incense rise!

THE RAPE OF THE LOCK

AN HEROIC-COMICAL POEM

Published at first in two parts and then, two years later, reissued in its present enlarged form, *The Rape of the Lock* has always been by far the most popular of Pope's writings. It is based upon an actual event in which an acquaintance of Pope's, Lord Petre, cut a lock of hair from the head of a Miss Arabella Fermor. Much more was made of this by the families of the two young people than the incident warranted, and this fact may have suggested to Pope the "mock heroic" style of his poem, in which "the little is made great and the great little."

Pope's letter of dedication to "Mrs. Arabella Fermor," the original of "Belinda," was intended not chiefly to placate her wrath at the freedom with which he had treated the incident but to give necessary information to his readers. *Madam*, he says, *It will be in vain to deny that I have some regard for this piece, since I dedicate it to You. Yet you may bear me witness, it was intended only to divert a few young Ladies, who have good sense and good humour enough to laugh not only at their sex's little unguarded follies, but at their own. But as it was communicated with the air of a Secret, it soon found its way into the world. An imperfect copy having been offered to a Bookseller, you had the good-nature for my sake to consent to the publication of one more correct: This I was forced to before I had executed half my design, for the Machinery was entirely wanting to complete it.*

The Machinery, Madam, is a term invented by the Critics to signify that part which the Deities, Angels, or Daemons are made to act in a Poem; For the ancient Poets are in one respect like modern Ladies: let an action be never so trivial in itself, they always make it appear of the utmost importance. These Machines I determined to raise on a very new and odd foundation, the Rosicrucian doctrine of Spirits.

I know how disagreeable it is to make use of hard words before a Lady, but 't is so much the concern of a Poet to have his works understood, and particularly by your Sex, that you must give me leave to explain two or three difficult terms.

The Rosicrucians are a people I must bring you acquainted with. The best account I know of them is in a French book called Le Comte de Gabalis, which both by its title and size is so like a Novel, that many of the Fair Sex have read it for one by mistake. According to these Gentlemen, the four Elements are inhabited by Spirits, which they call Sylphs, Gnomes, Nymphs, and Salamanders. The Gnomes or Daemons of Earth delight in mischief; but the Sylphs, whose habitation is in the Air, are the best-conditioned creatures imaginable. For they say, any mortals may enjoy the most intimate familiarities with these gentle Spirits, upon a condition very easy to all true Adepts, an inviolate preservation of Chastity.

As to the following Cantos, all the passages of them are as fabulous, as the Vision at the beginning, or the Transformation at the end (except the loss of your Hair, which I always mention with reverence). The Human persons are as fictitious as the airy ones, and the character of Belinda, as it is now managed, resembles you in nothing but in Beauty.

If this Poem had as many Graces as there are in your Person, or in your Mind, yet I could never hope it should pass through the world half so Uncensured as You have done. But let its fortune be what it will, mine is happy enough to have given me this occasion of assuring you that I am, with the truest esteem, Madam,

Your most obedient, Humble Servant,

A. Pope.

CANTO I

What dire offence from amorous causes springs,
What mighty contests rise from trivial things,
I sing—This verse to CARYL, Muse! is due:
This, even Belinda may vouchsafe to view:
Slight is the subject, but not so the praise,
If She inspire, and He approve my lays.
   Say what strange motive, Goddess! could compel
A well-bred Lord to assault a gentle Belle?
O say what stranger cause, yet unexplored,
Could make a gentle Belle reject a Lord?   10
In tasks so bold, can little men engage,
And in soft bosoms dwells such mighty Rage?
   Sol through white curtains shot a timorous ray,
And oped those eyes that must eclipse the day:
Now lap-dogs give themselves the rousing shake,

3. Caryl, John Caryll, a common friend of Pope, Lord Petre (the "Baron"), and Arabella Fermor (Belinda). He suggested the present poem to Pope.   **12. Rage,** compare the *Aeneid*, Book I, l. 11.

And sleepless lovers, just at twelve, awake:
Thrice rung the bell, the slipper knocked the ground,
And the pressed watch returned a silver sound.
Belinda still her downy pillow prest,
Her guardian SYLPH prolonged the balmy rest: 20
'Twas He had summoned to her silent bed
The morning-dream that hovered o'er her head;
A Youth more glittering than a Birth-night Beau,
(That even in slumber caused her cheek to glow)
Seemed to her ear his winning lips to lay,
And thus in whispers said, or seemed to say:

"Fairest of mortals, thou distinguished care
Of thousand bright Inhabitants of Air!
If e'er one vision touched thy infant thought,
Of all the Nurse and all the Priest have taught; 30
Of airy Elves by moonlight shadows seen,
The silver token, and the circled green,
Or virgins visited by Angel-powers,
With golden crowns and wreaths of heavenly flowers;
Hear and believe! thy own importance know,
Nor bound thy narrow views to things below.
Some secret truths, from learnèd pride concealed,
To Maids alone and Children are revealed:
What though no credit doubting Wits may give?
The Fair and Innocent shall still believe. 40
Know, then, unnumbered Spirits round thee fly,
The light Militia of the lower sky:
These, though unseen, are ever on the wing,
Hang o'er the Box, and hover round the Ring.
Think what an equipage thou hast in Air,
And view with scorn two Pages and a Chair.
As now your own, our beings were of old,
And once inclosed in Woman's beauteous mould;
Thence, by a soft transition, we repair
From earthly Vehicles to these of air. 50
Think not, when Woman's transient breath is fled,
That all her vanities at once are dead;
Succeeding vanities she still regards,
And though she plays no more, o'erlooks the cards.
Her joy in gilded Chariots, when alive,
And love of Ombre, after death survive.
For when the Fair in all their pride expire,
To their first Elements their Souls retire:
The Sprites of fiery Termagants in Flame
Mount up, and take a Salamander's name. 60
Soft yielding minds to Water glide away,
And sip, with Nymphs, their elemental Tea.
The graver Prude sinks downward to a Gnome,
In search of mischief still on Earth to roam.

The light Coquettes in Sylphs aloft repair,
And sport and flutter in the fields of Air.

"Know further yet: whoever fair and chaste
Rejects mankind, is by some Sylph embraced:
For Spirits, freed from mortal laws, with ease
Assume what sexes and what shapes they please. 70
What guards the purity of melting Maids,
In courtly balls, and midnight masquerades,
Safe from the treacherous friend, the daring spark,
The glance by day, the whisper in the dark,
When kind occasion prompts their warm desires,
When music softens, and when dancing fires?
'Tis but their Sylph, the wise Celestials know,
Though Honour is the word with Men below.

"Some nymphs there are, too conscious of their face,
For life predestined to the Gnomes' embrace. 80
These swell their prospects and exalt their pride,
When offers are disdained, and love denied:
Then gay Ideas crowd the vacant brain,
While Peers, and Dukes, and all their sweeping train,
And Garters, Stars, and Coronets appear,
And in soft sounds, Your Grace salutes their ear.
'Tis these that early taint the female soul,
Instruct the eyes of young Coquettes to roll,
Teach Infant-cheeks a bidden blush to know,
And little hearts to flutter at a Beau. 90

"Oft, when the world imagine women stray,
The Sylphs through mystic mazes guide their way;
Through all the giddy circle they pursue,
And old impertinence expel by new.
What tender maid but must a victim fall
To one man's treat, but for another's ball?
When Florio speaks what virgin could withstand,
If gentle Damon did not squeeze her hand?
With varying vanities, from every part,
They shift the moving Toyshop of their heart; 100
Where wigs with wigs, with sword-knots sword-knots strive,
Beaux banish beaux, and coaches coaches drive.
This erring mortals Levity may call;
Oh blind to truth! the Sylphs contrive it all.

"Of these am I, who thy protection claim,
A watchful sprite, and Ariel is my name.
Late, as I ranged the crystal wilds of air,
In the clear Mirror of thy ruling Star
I saw, alas! some dread event impend,
Ere to the main this morning sun descend, 110
But heaven reveals not what, or how, or where:
Warned by the Sylph, oh pious maid, beware!
This to disclose is all thy guardian can:
Beware of all, but most beware of man!"

---

17. **knocked the ground**, to call the maid. 30. **Priest.** Miss Fermor, like the other members of the group here presented, was a Roman Catholic. 44. **Ring**, in Hyde Park.

He said; when Shock, who thought she slept too long,
Leaped up, and waked his mistress with his tongue.
'Twas then, Belinda, if report say true,
Thy eyes first opened on a Billet-doux;
Wounds, Charms, and Ardors were no sooner read,
But all the vision vanished from thy head.   120
   And now, unveiled, the Toilet stands displayed,
Each silver Vase in mystic order laid.
First, robed in white, the Nymph intent adores,
With head uncovered, the Cosmetic powers.
A heavenly image in the glass appears,
To that she bends, to that her eyes she rears;
Th' inferior Priestess, at her altar's side,
Trembling begins the sacred rites of Pride.
Unnumbered treasures ope at once, and here
The various offerings of the world appear;   130
From each she nicely culls with curious toil,
And decks the Goddess with the glittering spoil.
This casket India's glowing gems unlocks,
And all Arabia breathes from yonder box.
The Tortoise here and Elephant unite,
Transformed to combs, the speckled, and the white.
Here files of pins extend their shining rows,
Puffs, Powders, Patches, Bibles, Billet-doux.
Now awful Beauty puts on all its arms;
The fair each moment rises in her charms,   140
Repairs her smiles, awakens every grace,
And calls forth all the wonders of her face;
Sees by degrees a purer blush arise,
And keener lightnings quicken in her eyes.
The busy Sylphs surround their darling care,
These set the head, and those divide the hair,
Some fold the sleeve, whilst others plait the gown;
And Betty's praised for labours not her own.

CANTO II

Not with more glories, in the ethereal plain,
The Sun first rises o'er the purpled main,
Than, issuing forth, the rival of his beams
Launched on the bosom of the silver Thames.
Fair Nymphs and well-drest Youths around her shone,
But every eye was fixed on her alone.
On her white breast a sparkling Cross she wore.
Which Jews might kiss, and Infidels adore.
Her lively looks a sprightly mind disclose,
Quick as her eyes, and as unfixed as those: 10
Favours to none, to all she smiles extends;
Oft she rejects, but never once offends.
Bright as the sun, her eyes the gazers strike,
And, like the sun, they shine on all alike.
Yet graceful ease, and sweetness void of pride,

127. **Priestess,** that is, the maid, Betty.

Might hide her faults, if Belles had faults to hide:
If to her share some female errors fall,
Look on her face, and you'll forget 'em all.
   This Nymph, to the destruction of mankind,   19
Nourished two Locks, which graceful hung behind
In equal curls, and well conspired to deck
With shining ringlets the smooth ivory neck.
Love in these labyrinths his slaves detains,
And mighty hearts are held in slender chains.
With hairy springes we the birds betray,
Slight lines of hair surprise the finny prey,
Fair tresses man's imperial race ensnare,
And beauty draws us with a single hair.
   The adventurous Baron the bright locks admired;
He saw, he wished, and to the prize aspired.   30
Resolved to win, he meditates the way,
By force to ravish, or by fraud betray;
For when success a Lover's toil attends,
Few ask, if fraud or force attained his ends.
   For this, ere Phoebus rose, he had implored
Propitious heaven, and every power adored,
But chiefly Love—to Love an Altar built,
Of twelve vast French Romances, neatly gilt.
There lay three garters, half a pair of gloves;
And all the trophies of his former loves;   40
With tender Billet-doux he lights the pyre,
And breathes three amorous sighs to raise the fire.
Then prostrate falls, and begs with ardent eyes
Soon to obtain, and long possess the prize;
The powers gave ear, and granted half his prayer,
The rest, the winds dispersed in empty air.
   But now secure the painted vessel glides,
The sun-beams trembling on the floating tides:
While melting music steals upon the sky,
And softened sounds along the waters die;   50
Smooth flow the waves, the Zephyrs gently play,
Belinda smiled, and all the world was gay.
All but the Sylph—with careful thoughts opprest,
The impending woe sat heavy on his breast.
He summons straight his Denizens of air;
The lucid squadrons round the sails repair;
Soft o'er the shrouds aërial whispers breathe,
That seemed but Zephyrs to the train beneath.
Some to the sun their insect-wings unfold,
Waft on the breeze, or sink in clouds of gold;   60
Transparent forms, too fine for mortal sight,
Their fluid bodies half dissolved in light,
Loose to the wind their airy garments flew,
Thin glittering textures of the filmy dew,
Dipt in the richest tincture of the skies,
Where light disports in ever-mingling dyes,
While every beam new transient colours flings,
Colours that change whene'er they wave their wings.
Amid the circle, on the gilded mast,

Superior by the head, was Ariel placed; 70
His purple pinions opening to the sun,
He raised his azure wand, and thus begun.
    "Ye Sylphs and Sylphids, to your chief give ear!
Fays, Fairies, Genii, Elves, and Daemons, hear!
Ye know the spheres and various tasks assigned
By laws eternal to the aërial kind.
Some in the fields of purest Aether play,
And bask and whiten in the blaze of day.
Some guide the course of wandering orbs on high,
Or roll the planets through the boundless sky. 80
Some less refined, beneath the moon's pale light
Pursue the stars that shoot athwart the night,
Or suck the mists in grosser air below,
Or dip their pinions in the painted bow,
Or brew fierce tempests on the wintry main,
Or o'er the glebe distil the kindly rain.
Others on earth o'er human race preside,
Watch all their ways, and all their actions guide:
Of these the chief the care of Nations own,
And guard with Arms divine the British throne. 90
    "Our humbler province is to tend the Fair,
Not a less pleasing, though less glorious care;
To save the powder from too rude a gale,
Nor let the imprisoned essences exhale;
To draw fresh colours from the vernal flowers;
To steal from rainbows e'er they drop in showers
A brighter wash; to curl their waving hairs,
Assist their blushes, and inspire their airs;
Nay oft, in dreams, invention we bestow,
To change a Flounce, or add a Furbelow. 100
    "This day, black Omens threat the brightest Fair
That e'er deserved a watchful spirit's care;
Some dire disaster, or by force, or slight;
But what, or where, the fates have wrapt in night.
Whether the nymph shall break Diana's law,
Or some frail China jar receive a flaw;
Or stain her honour or her new brocade;
Forget her prayers, or miss a masquerade;
Or lose her heart, or necklace, at a ball;
Or whether Heaven has doomed that Shock must fall. 110
Haste, then, ye spirits! to your charge repair:
The fluttering fan be Zephyretta's care;
The drops to thee, Brillante, we consign;
And, Momentilla, let the watch be thine;
Do thou, Crispissa, tend her favourite Lock;
Ariel himself shall be the guard of Shock.
    "To fifty chosen Sylphs, of special note,
We trust the important charge, the Petticoat:
Oft have we known that seven-fold fence to fail,
Though stiff with hoops, and armed with ribs of whale; 120
Form a strong line about the silver bound,
And guard the wide circumference around.
    "Whatever spirit, careless of his charge,
His post neglects, or leaves the fair at large,
Shall feel sharp vengeance soon o'ertake his sins,
Be stopped in vials, or transfixed with pins;
Or plunged in lakes of bitter washes lie,
Or wedged whole ages in a bodkin's eye:
Gums and Pomatums shall his flight restrain,
While clogged he beats his silken wings in vain; 130
Or Alum styptics with contracting power
Shrink his thin essence like a rivelled flower:
Or, as Ixion fixed, the wretch shall feel
The giddy motion of the whirling Mill,
In fumes of burning Chocolate shall glow,
And tremble at the sea that froths below!"
    He spoke; the spirits from the sails descend;
Some, orb in orb, around the nymph extend;
Some thrid the mazy ringlets of her hair;
Some hang upon the pendants of her ear; 140
With beating hearts the dire event they wait,
Anxious, and trembling for the birth of Fate.

CANTO III

    Close by those meads, for ever crowned with flowers,
Where Thames with pride surveys his rising towers,
There stands a structure of majestic frame,
Which from the neighbouring Hampton takes its name.
Here Britain's statesmen oft the fall foredoom
Of foreign Tyrants and of Nymphs at home;
Here thou, great ANNA! whom three realms obey,
Dost sometimes counsel take—and sometimes Tea.
    Hither the heroes and the nymphs resort,
To taste awhile the pleasures of a Court; 10
In various talk the instructive hours they passed,
Who gave the ball, or paid the visit last;
One speaks the glory of the British Queen,
And one describes a charming Indian screen;
A third interprets motions, looks, and eyes;
At every word a reputation dies.
Snuff, or the fan, supply each pause of chat,
With singing, laughing, ogling, *and all that*.
    Mean while, declining from the noon of day,
The sun obliquely shoots his burning ray; 20
The hungry Judges soon the Sentence sign,
And wretches hang that jury-men may dine;
The merchant from the Exchange returns in peace,
And the long labours of the Toilet cease.
Belinda now, whom thirst of fame invites,

---

132. **rivelled,** shriveled, faded. *Canto III.* **3. structure,** the royal palace of Hampton Court. **8. Tea,** pronounced so as to rhyme exactly with "obey."

Burns to encounter two adventurous Knights,
At Ombre singly to decide their doom;
And swells her breast with conquests yet to come.
Straight the three bands prepare in arms to join,
Each band the number of the sacred nine.   30
Soon as she spreads her hand, the aërial guard
Descend, and sit on each important card:
First Ariel perched upon a Matadore,
Then each, according to the rank they bore;
For Sylphs, yet mindful of their ancient race,
Are, as when women, wondrous fond of place.
    Behold, four Kings in majesty revered,
With hoary whiskers and a forky beard;
And four fair Queens whose hands sustain a flower,
The expressive emblem of their softer power;   40
Four Knaves in garbs succinct, a trusty band,
Caps on their heads, and halberts in their hand;
And particoloured troops, a shining train,
Draw forth to combat on the velvet plain.
    The skilful nymph reviews her force with care:
"Let Spades be trumps!" she said, and trumps they were.
    Now move to war her sable Matadores,
In show like leaders of the swarthy Moors.
Spadillio first, unconquerable Lord!
Led off two captive trumps, and swept the board.   50
As many more Manillio forced to yield,
And marched a victor from the verdant field.
Him Basto followed, but his fate more hard
Gained but one trump and one Plebeian card.
With his broad sabre next, a chief in years,
The hoary Majesty of Spades appears,
Puts forth one manly leg, to sight revealed;
The rest, his many-coloured robe concealed.
The rebel Knave, who dares his prince engage,
Proves the just victim of his royal rage.   60
Even mighty Pam, that Kings and Queens o'erthrew
And mowed down armies in the fights of Lu,
Sad chance of war! now destitute of aid,
Falls undistinguished by the victor spade!
    Thus far both armies to Belinda yield;
Now to the Baron fate inclines the field.
His warlike Amazon her host invades,
The imperial consort of the crown of Spades.
The Club's black Tyrant first her victim died,
Spite of his haughty mien, and barbarous pride: 70
What boots the regal circle on his head,
His giant limbs, in state unwieldy spread;
That long behind he trails his pompous robe,
And, of all monarchs, only grasps the globe?
    The Baron now his Diamonds pours apace;
The embroidered King who shows but half his face,
And his refulgent Queen, with powers combined
Of broken troops an easy conquest find.
Clubs, Diamonds, Hearts, in wild disorder seen,
With throngs promiscuous strow the level green.   80
Thus when dispersed a routed army runs,
Of Asia's troops, and Afric's sable sons,
With like confusion different nations fly,
Of various habit, and of various dye;
The pierced battalions dis-united fall,
In heaps on heaps; one fate o'erwhelms them all.
    The Knave of Diamonds tries his wily arts,
And wins (oh shameful chance!) the Queen of Hearts.
At this, the blood the virgin's cheek forsook,
A livid paleness spreads o'er all her look;   90
She sees, and trembles at the approaching ill,
Just in the jaws of ruin, and Codille.
And now (as oft in some distempered State)
On one nice Trick depends the general fate.
An Ace of Hearts steps forth: The King unseen
Lurked in her hand, and mourned his captive Queen:
He springs to Vengeance with an eager pace,
And falls like thunder on the prostrate Ace.
The nymph exulting fills with shouts the sky;
The walls, the woods, and long canals reply.   100
    Oh thoughtless mortals! ever blind to fate,
Too soon dejected, and too soon elate.
Sudden, these honours shall be snatched away,
And cursed forever this victorious day.
    For lo! the board with cups and spoons is crowned,
The berries crackle, and the mill turns round;
On shining Altars of Japan they raise
The silver lamp; the fiery spirits blaze:
From silver spouts the grateful liquors glide,
While China's earth receives the smoking tide: 110
At once they gratify their scent and taste,
And frequent cups prolong the rich repast.
Straight hover round the Fair her airy band;
Some, as she sipped, the fuming liquor fanned,
Some o'er her lap their careful plumes displayed,
Trembling, and conscious of the rich brocade.
Coffee, (which makes the politician wise,
And see through all things with his half-shut eyes)
Sent up in vapours to the Baron's brain
New Stratagems, the radiant Lock to gain.   120

27. Ombre, a three-handed game in which each player held nine cards. The three principal trumps, called "matadores," were, first, the ace of spades ("spadillio"), the deuce of trumps when black or the seven of trumps when red ("Manillio"), and the ace of clubs ("Basto"). **62. Lu,** the game in which **Pam** is the highest card (the knave of clubs). **92. Codille,** the term used at Ombre when the challenger loses the game. **106. berries,** coffee beans. **107. Altars of Japan,** japanned tables.

Ah cease, rash youth! desist ere 'tis too late,
Fear the just Gods, and think of Scylla's Fate!
Changed to a bird, and sent to flit in air,
She dearly pays for Nisus' injured hair!
  But when to mischief mortals bend their will,
How soon they find fit instruments of ill!
Just then, Clarissa drew with tempting grace
A two-edged weapon from her shining case:
So Ladies in Romance assist their Knight,
Present the spear, and arm him for the fight.   130
He takes the gift with reverence, and extends
The little engine on his fingers' ends;
This just behind Belinda's neck he spread,
As o'er the fragrant steams she bends her head.
Swift to the Lock a thousand Sprites repair,
A thousand wings, by turns, blow back the hair;
And thrice they twitched the diamond in her ear;
Thrice she looked back, and thrice the foe drew near.
Just in that instant, anxious Ariel sought
The close recesses of the Virgin's thought;   140
As on the nosegay in her breast reclined,
He watched the Ideas rising in her mind.
Sudden he viewed, in spite of all her art,
An earthly Lover lurking at her heart.
Amazed, confused, he found his power expired,
Resigned to fate, and with a sigh retired.
  The Peer now spreads the glittering Forfex wide,
To inclose the Lock; now joins it, to divide.
Even then, before the fatal engine closed,
A wretched Sylph too fondly interposed;   150
Fate urged the shears, and cut the Sylph in twain
(But airy substance soon unites again).
The meeting points the sacred hair dissever
From the fair head, for ever, and for ever!
  Then flashed the living lightning from her eyes,
And screams of horror rend the affrighted skies.
Not louder shrieks to pitying Heaven are cast,
When husbands, or when lap-dogs breathe their last;
Or when rich China vessels fallen from high,
In glittering dust and painted fragments lie!   160
"Let wreaths of triumph now my temples twine,"
The victor cried; "the glorious Prize is mine!
While fish in streams, or birds delight in air,
Or in a coach and six the British Fair,
As long as Atalantis shall be read,
Or the small pillow grace a Lady's bed,
While visits shall be paid on solemn days,
When numerous wax-lights in bright order blaze,
While nymphs take treats, or assignations give,   169
So long my honour, name, and praise shall live!

147. **Forfex**, scissors. 165. **Atalantis**, *The New Atalantis*, 1709, by Mrs. Manley, a book dealing in contemporary scandal.

What Time would spare, from Steel receives its date,
And monuments, like men, submit to fate!
Steel could the labour of the Gods destroy,
And strike to dust the imperial towers of Troy;
Steel could the works of mortal pride confound,
And hew triumphal arches to the ground.
What wonder then, fair nymph! thy hairs should feel
The conquering force of unresisted steel?"

CANTO IV

But anxious cares the pensive nymph oppressed,
And secret passions laboured in her breast.
Not youthful kings in battle seized alive,
Not scornful virgins who their charms survive,
Not ardent lovers robbed of all their bliss,
Not ancient ladies when refused a kiss,
Not tyrants fierce that unrepenting die,
Not Cynthia when her manteau's pinned awry,
E'er felt such rage, resentment, and despair,
As thou, sad Virgin! for thy ravished Hair.   10
  For, that sad moment, when the Sylphs withdrew
And Ariel weeping from Belinda flew,
Umbriel, a dusky, melancholy sprite,
As ever sullied the fair face of light,
Down to the central earth, his proper scene,
Repaired to search the gloomy Cave of Spleen.
  Swift on his sooty pinions flits the Gnome,
And in a vapour reached the dismal dome.
No cheerful breeze this sullen region knows,
The dreaded East is all the wind that blows.   20
Here in a grotto, sheltered close from air,
And screened in shades from day's detested glare,
She sighs for ever on her pensive bed,
Pain at her side, and Megrim at her head.
  Two handmaids wait the throne: alike in place,
But differing far in figure and in face.
Here stood Ill-nature like an ancient maid,
Her wrinkled form in black and white arrayed;
With store of prayers, for mornings, nights, and noons,
Her hand is filled; her bosom with lampoons.   30
  There Affectation, with a sickly mien,
Shows in her cheek the roses of eighteen,
Practised to lisp, and hang the head aside,
Faints into airs, and languishes with pride,
On the rich quilt sinks with becoming woe,
Wrapt in a gown, for sickness, and for show.
The fair ones feel such maladies as these,
When each new night-dress gives a new disease.

16. **Spleen**, bad temper. The **Cave** represents the lower world or hell of classical epic. 24. **Megrim**, headache.

A constant Vapour o'er the palace flies;
Strange phantoms rising as the mists arise; 40
Dreadful, as hermit's dreams in haunted shades,
Or bright, as visions of expiring maids.
Now glaring fiends, and snakes on rolling spires,
Pale spectres, gaping tombs, and purple fires:
Now lakes of liquid gold, Elysian scenes,
And crystal domes, and angels in machines.
Unnumbered throngs on every side are seen,
Of bodies changed to various forms by Spleen.
Here living Tea-pots stand, one arm held out,
One bent; the handle this, and that the spout: 50
A Pipkin there, like Homer's Tripod walks;
Here sighs a Jar, and there a Goose-pie talks;
Men prove with child, as powerful fancy works,
And maids turned bottles, call aloud for corks.
  Safe passed the Gnome through this fantastic band,
A branch of healing Spleenwort in his hand,
Then thus addressed the Power: "Hail, wayward Queen!
Who rule the sex to fifty from fifteen:
Parent of vapours and of female wit,
Who give the hysteric or poetic fit, 60
On various tempers act by various ways,
Make some take physic, others scribble plays;
Who cause the proud their visits to delay,
And send the godly in a pet to pray.
A nymph there is, that all thy power disdains,
And thousands more in equal mirth maintains.
But oh! if e'er thy Gnome could spoil a grace,
Or raise a pimple on a beauteous face,
Like Citron-waters matrons cheeks inflame,
Or change complexions at a losing game; 70
If e'er with airy horns I planted heads,
Or rumpled petticoats, or tumbled beds,
Or caused suspicion when no soul was rude,
Or discomposed the head-dress of a Prude,
Or e'er to costive lap-dog gave disease,
Which not the tears of brightest eyes could ease:
Hear me, and touch Belinda with chagrin;
That single act gives half the world the spleen."
  The Goddess with a discontented air 79
Seems to reject him, though she grants his prayer.
A wondrous Bag with both her hands she binds,
Like that where once Ulysses held the winds;
There she collects the force of female lungs,
Sighs, sobs, and passions, and the war of tongues.
A Vial next she fills with fainting fears,
Soft sorrows, melting griefs, and flowing tears.

The Gnome rejoicing bears her gifts away,
Spreads his black wings, and slowly mounts to day.
  Sunk in Thalestris' arms the nymph he found,
Her eyes dejected and her hair unbound. 90
Full o'er their heads the swelling bag he rent,
And all the Furies issued at the vent.
Belinda burns with more than mortal ire,
And fierce Thalestris fans the rising fire.
"O wretched maid!" she spread her hands, and cried,
(While Hampton's echoes, "Wretched maid!" replied)
"Was it for this you took such constant care
The bodkin, comb, and essence to prepare?
For this your locks in paper durance bound,
For this with torturing irons wreathed around? 100
For this with fillets strained your tender head,
And bravely bore the double loads of lead?
Gods! shall the ravisher display your hair,
While the Fops envy, and the Ladies stare!
Honour forbid! at whose unrivalled shrine
Ease, pleasure, virtue, all our sex resign.
Methinks already I your tears survey,
Already hear the horrid things they say,
Already see you a degraded toast,
And all your honour in a whisper lost! 110
How shall I, then, your helpless fame defend?
'Twill then be infamy to seem your friend!
And shall this prize, the inestimable prize,
Exposed through crystal to the gazing eyes,
And heightened by the diamond's circling rays,
On that rapacious hand for ever blaze?
Sooner shall grass in Hyde-park Circus grow,
And wits take lodgings in the sound of Bow;
Sooner let earth, air, sea, to Chaos fall,
Men, monkeys, lap-dogs, parrots, perish all!" 120
  She said; then raging to Sir Plume repairs,
And bids her Beau demand the precious hairs:
(Sir Plume of amber snuff-box justly vain,
And the nice conduct of a clouded cane)
With earnest eyes, and round unthinking face,
He first the snuff-box opened, then the case,
And thus broke out—"My Lord, why, what the devil?
Z—ds! damn the lock! 'fore Gad, you must be civil!
Plague on't! 'tis past a jest—nay prithee, pox! 129
Give her the hair"—he spoke, and rapped his box.
  "It grieves me much" (replied the Peer again)
"Who speaks so well should ever speak in vain.
But by this Lock, this sacred Lock, I swear,

---

39. Vapour. A fashionable disease of Pope's time was the "vapours," or hypochondria, closely related to the "blues" of later generations and to the "melancholy" of the Elizabethans. It induced morbid fancies like those listed below. **109. toast,** a woman whose health was drunk in celebration of her beauty. **118. Bow.** The church of St. Mary le Bow, which had a famous peal of bells, was in an unfashionable part of London. **121. Sir Plume,** Sir George Brown, brother of Mrs. Morley, or "Thalestris."

(Which never more shall join its parted hair;
Which never more its honours shall renew,
Clipped from the lovely head where late it grew)
That while my nostrils draw the vital air,
This hand, which won it, shall for ever wear."
He spoke, and speaking, in proud triumph spread
The long-contended honours of her head.   140

    But Umbriel, hateful Gnome! forbears not so;
He breaks the Vial whence the sorrows flow.
Then see! the nymph in beauteous grief appears,
Her eyes half-languishing, half-drowned in tears;
On her heaved bosom hung her drooping head,
Which, with a sigh, she raised; and thus she said:
    "For ever curst be this detested day,
Which snatched my best, my favourite curl away!
Happy! ah ten times happy had I been,
If Hampton-Court these eyes had never seen!   150
Yet am not I the first mistaken maid,
By love of Courts to numerous ills betrayed.
Oh had I rather unadmired remained
In some lone isle, or distant Northern land;
Where the gilt Chariot never marks the way,
Where none learn Ombre, none e'er taste Bohea!
There kept my charms concealed from mortal eye,
Like roses, that in deserts bloom and die.
What moved my mind with youthful Lords to roam?
Oh had I stayed, and said my prayers at home!   160
'Twas this, the morning omens seemed to tell,
Thrice from my trembling hand the patch-box fell;
The tottering China shook without a wind,
Nay, Poll sat mute, and Shock was most unkind!
A Sylph too warned me of the threats of fate,
In mystic visions, now believed too late!
See the poor remnants of these slighted hairs!
My hands shall rend what e'en thy rapine spares:
These in two sable ringlets taught to break,
Once gave new beauties to the snowy neck;   170
The sister-lock now sits uncouth, alone,
And in its fellow's fate foresees its own;
Uncurled it hangs, the fatal shears demands,
And tempts once more, thy sacrilegious hands.
Oh hadst thou, cruel! been content to seize
Hairs less in sight, or any hairs but these!"

CANTO V

She said: the pitying audience melt in tears;
But Fate and Jove had stopped the Baron's ears.
In vain Thalestris with reproach assails,
For who can move when fair Belinda fails?
Not half so fixed the Trojan could remain,
While Anna begged and Dido raged in vain.
Then grave Clarissa graceful waved her fan;
Silence ensued, and thus the nymph began:

   5. **Trojan**, Aeneas.

    "Say why are Beauties praised and honoured most,   9
The wise man's passion, and the vain man's toast?
Why decked with all that land and sea afford,
Why Angels called, and Angel-like adored?
Why round our coaches crowd the white-gloved Beaux,
Why bows the side-box from its inmost rows;
How vain are all these glories, all our pains,
Unless good sense preserve what beauty gains:
That men may say, when we the front-box grace:
'Behold the first in virtue as in face!'
Oh! if to dance all night, and dress all day,   19
Charmed the small-pox, or chased old-age away;
Who would not scorn what housewife's cares produce,
Or who would learn one earthly thing of use?
To patch, nay ogle, might become a saint,
Nor could it sure be such a sin to paint.
But since, alas! frail beauty must decay,
Curled or uncurled, since locks will turn to grey;
Since painted, or not painted, all shall fade,
And she who scorns a man, must die a maid;
What then remains but well our power to use,
And keep good-humour still whate'er we lose?   30
And trust me, dear! good-humour can prevail,
When airs, and flights, and screams, and scolding fail.
Beauties in vain their pretty eyes may roll;
Charms strike the sight, but merit wins the soul."
    So spoke the Dame, but no applause ensued;
Belinda frowned, Thalestris called her Prude.
"To arms, to arms!" the fierce Virago cries,
And swift as lightning to the combat flies.
All side in parties, and begin the attack;   39
Fans clap, silks rustle, and tough whalebones crack;
Heroes' and Heroines' shouts confusedly rise,
And bass, and treble voices strike the skies.
No common weapons in their hands are found,
Like Gods they fight, nor dread a mortal wound.
    So when bold Homer makes the Gods engage,
And heavenly breasts with human passions rage;
'Gainst Pallas, Mars; Latona, Hermes arms;
And all Olympus rings with loud alarms:
Jove's thunder roars, heaven trembles all around,   49
Blue Neptune storms, the bellowing deeps resound:
Earth shakes her nodding towers, the ground gives way,
And the pale ghosts start at the flash of day!
    Triumphant Umbriel on a sconce's height
Clapped his glad wings, and sate to view the fight:
Propped on their bodkin spears, the Sprites survey
The growing combat, or assist the fray.

   53. **sconce**, a candleholder attached to the wall.

While through the press enraged Thalestris flies,
And scatters death around from both her eyes,
A Beau and Witling perished in the throng,
One died in metaphor, and one in song.　　60
"O cruel nymph! a living death I bear,"
Cried Dapperwit, and sunk beside his chair.
A mournful glance Sir Fopling upwards cast,
"Those eyes are made so killing"—was his last.
Thus on Maeander's flowery margin lies
The expiring Swan, and as he sings he dies.

When bold Sir Plume had drawn Clarissa down,
Chloe stepped in, and killed him with a frown;
She smiled to see the doughty hero slain,
But, at her smile, the Beau revived again.　　70

Now Jove suspends his golden scales in air,
Weighs the Men's wits against the Lady's hair;
The doubtful beam long nods from side to side;
At length the wits mount up, the hairs subside.

See, fierce Belinda on the Baron flies,
With more than usual lightning in her eyes:
Nor feared the Chief the unequal fight to try,
Who sought no more than on his foe to die.
But this bold Lord with manly strength endued,
She with one finger and a thumb subdued:　　80
Just where the breath of life his nostrils drew,
A charge of snuff the wily virgin threw;
The Gnomes direct, to every atom just,
The pungent grains of titillating dust.
Sudden, with starting tears each eye o'erflows,
And the high dome re-echoes to his nose.

"Now meet thy fate," incensed Belinda cried,
And drew a deadly bodkin from her side.
(The same, his ancient personage to deck,
Her great great grandsire wore about his neck,　　90
In three seal-rings; which after, melted down,
Formed a vast buckle for his widow's gown:
Her infant grandame's whistle next it grew,
The bells she jingled, and the whistle blew;
Then in a bodkin graced her mother's hairs,
Which long she wore, and now Belinda wears.)

"Boast not my fall," (he cried) "insulting foe!
Thou by some other shalt be laid as low,
Nor think, to die dejects my lofty mind:
All that I dread is leaving you behind!　　100
Rather than so, ah let me still survive,
And burn in Cupid's flames—but burn alive."

"Restore the Lock!" she cries; and all around
"Restore the Lock!" the vaulted roofs rebound.
Not fierce Othello in so loud a strain
Roared for the handkerchief that caused his pain.
But see how oft ambitious aims are crossed,
And chiefs contend 'till all the prize is lost!
The Lock, obtained with guilt, and kept with pain,
In every place is sought, but sought in vain:　　110

With such a prize no mortal must be blest,
So heaven decrees! With heaven who can contest?

Some thought it mounted to the Lunar sphere,
Since all things lost on earth are treasured there.
There Hero's wits are kept in ponderous vases,
And beaux' in snuff-boxes and tweezer-cases.
There broken vows and death-bed alms are found,
And lovers' hearts with ends of riband bound,
The courtier's promises, and sick man's prayers,
The smiles of harlots, and the tears of heirs,　　120
Cages for gnats, and chains to yoke a flea,
Dried butterflies, and tomes of casuistry.

But trust the Muse—she saw it upward rise,
Though marked by none but quick, poetic eyes
(So Rome's great founder to the heavens withdrew,
To Proculus alone confessed in view);
A sudden Star, it shot through liquid air,
And drew behind a radiant trail of hair.
Not Berenice's Locks first rose so bright,
The heavens bespangling with dishevelled light.　　130
The Sylphs behold it kindling as it flies,
And pleased pursue its progress through the skies.

This the beau monde shall from the Mall survey,
And hail with music its propitious ray.
This the blest Lover shall for Venus take,
And send up vows from Rosamonda's lake.
This Partridge soon shall view in cloudless skies,
When next he looks through Galileo's eyes;
And hence the egregious wizard shall foredoom
The fate of Louis, and the fall of Rome.　　140

Then cease, bright Nymph! to mourn thy ravished hair,
Which adds new glory to the shining sphere!
Not all the tresses that fair head can boast,
Shall draw such envy as the Lock you lost.
For, after all the murders of your eye,
When, after millions slain, yourself shall die:
When those fair suns shall set, as set they must,
And all those tresses shall be laid in dust,
This Lock, the Muse shall consecrate to fame,
And 'midst the stars inscribe Belinda's name.　　150

ELOÏSA TO ABELARD

ARGUMENT

Abelard and Eloïsa flourished in the twelfth Century; they were two of the most distinguished Persons of their age in learning and beauty, but for nothing more famous than for their unfortunate passion. After a long course of calamities, they retired each to a

129. Berenice's Locks. The Egyptian queen pledged a lock of hair for her husband's safe return. It became a constellation. **133. Mall,** a fashionable walk in St. James's Park. **136. lake,** in St. James's Park. **137. Partridge,** a London astrologer. **138. Galileo's eyes,** the telescope.

several Convent, and consecrated the remainder of their days to religion. It was many years after this separation, that a letter of Abelard's to a Friend fell into the hands of Eloïsa. This awakening all her Tenderness, occasioned those celebrated letters (out of which the following is partly extracted) which gives [sic] so lively a picture to the struggles of grace and nature, virtue and passion.

In these deep solitudes and awful cells,
Where heavenly-pensive Contemplation dwells,
And ever musing Melancholy reigns;
What means this tumult in a Vestal's veins?
Why rove my thoughts beyond this last retreat?
Why feels my heart its long-forgotten heat?
Yet, yet I love!—From Abelard it came,
And Eloïsa yet must kiss the name.
   Dear fatal name! rest ever unrevealed,
Nor pass these lips in holy silence sealed: 10
Hide it, my heart, within that close disguise,
Where mixed with God's, his loved Idea lies:
O write it not, my hand—the name appears
Already written—wash it out, my tears!
In vain lost Eloïsa weeps and prays,
Her heart still dictates, and her hand obeys.
   Relentless walls! whose darksome round contains
Repentant sighs, and voluntary pains:
Ye rugged rocks! which holy knees have worn;
Ye grots and caverns shagged with horrid thorn!   20
Shrines! where their vigils pale-eyed virgins keep,
And pitying saints, whose statues learn to weep!
Though cold like you, unmoved and silent grown,
I have not yet forgot myself to stone.
All is not Heaven's while Abelard has part,
Still rebel nature holds out half my heart;
Nor prayers nor fasts its stubborn pulse restrain,
Nor tears for ages taught to flow in vain.
   Soon as thy letters trembling I unclose,
That well-known name awakens all my woes.   30
Oh name for ever sad! for ever dear!
Still breathed in sighs, still ushered with a tear.
I tremble too, where'er my own I find,
Some dire misfortune follows close behind.
Line after line my gushing eyes o'erflow,
Led through a sad variety of woe:
Now warm in love, now withering in my bloom,
Lost in a convent's solitary gloom!
There stern Religion quenched the unwilling flame,
There died the best of passions, Love and Fame.   40
   Yet write, oh write me all, that I may join
Griefs to thy griefs, and echo sighs to thine.
Nor foes nor fortune take this power away;
And is my Abelard less kind than they?
Tears still are mine, and those I need not spare,
Love but demands what else were shed in prayer;
No happier task these faded eyes pursue;
To read and weep is all they now can do.
   Then share thy pain, allow that sad relief;
Ah, more than share it, give me all thy grief.   50
Heaven first taught letters for some wretch's aid,
Some banished lover or some captive maid;
They live, they speak, they breathe what love inspires,
Warm from the soul, and faithful to its fires,
The virgin's wish without her fears impart,
Excuse the blush, and pour out all the heart,
Speed the soft intercourse from soul to soul,
And waft a sigh from Indus to the Pole.
   Thou know'st how guiltless first I met thy flame,
When Love approached me under Friendship's name;   60
My fancy formed thee of angelic kind,
Some emanation of the all-beauteous Mind.
Those smiling eyes, attempering every ray,
Shone sweetly lambent with celestial day.
Guiltless I gazed; heaven listened while you sung;
And truths divine came mended from that tongue.
From lips like those what precept failed to move?
Too soon they taught me 'twas no sin to love:
Back through the paths of pleasing sense I ran,
Nor wished an Angel whom I loved a Man.   70
Dim and remote the joys of saints I see,
Nor envy them that heaven I lose for thee.
   How oft, when pressed to marriage, have I said,
Curse on all laws but those which love has made?
Love, free as air, at sight of human ties,
Spreads his light wings, and in a moment flies.
Let wealth, let honour, wait the wedded dame,
August her deed, and sacred be her fame;
Before true passion all those views remove.   79
Fame, wealth, and honour! what are you to Love?
The jealous God, when we profane his fires,
Those restless passions in revenge inspires,
And bids them make mistaken mortals groan,
Who seek in love for aught but love alone.
Should at my feet the world's great master fall,
Himself, his throne, his world, I'd scorn 'em all:
Not Caesar's empress would I deign to prove;
No, make me mistress to the man I love;
If there be yet another name more free,
More fond than mistress, make me that to thee!   90
Oh! happy state! when souls each other draw,
When love is liberty, and nature law:
All then is full, possessing, and possessed,
No craving void left aching in the breast:
Even thought meets thought, ere from the lips it part,
And each warm wish springs mutual from the heart.
This sure is bliss (if bliss on earth there be)
And once the lot of Abelard and me.

24. stone. Compare Milton's "Il Penseroso," l. 42.

66. mended, improved.

Alas, how changed! what sudden horrors rise!
A naked Lover bound and bleeding lies!   100
Where, where was Eloïse? her voice, her hand,
Her poniard, had opposed the dire command.
Barbarian, stay! that bloody stroke restrain;
The crime was common, common be the pain.
I can no more; by shame, by rage suppressed,
Let tears, and burning blushes speak the rest.
   Canst thou forget that sad, that solemn day,
When victims at yon altar's foot we lay?
Canst thou forget what tears that moment fell,
When, warm in youth, I bade the world farewell?   110
As with cold lips I kissed the sacred veil,
The shrines all trembled, and the lamps grew pale:
Heaven scarce believed the Conquest it surveyed,
And Saints with wonder heard the vows I made.
Yet then, to those dread altars as I drew,
Not on the Cross my eyes were fixed, but you:
Not grace, or zeal, love only was my call,
And if I lose thy love, I lose my all.
Come! with thy looks, thy words, relieve my woe;
Those still at least are left thee to bestow.   120
Still on that breast enamoured let me lie,
Still drink delicious poison from thy eye,
Pant on thy lip, and to thy heart be pressed;
Give all thou canst—and let me dream the rest.
Ah no! instruct me other joys to prize,
With other beauties charm my partial eyes,
Full in my view set all the bright abode,
And make my soul quit Abelard for God.
   Ah, think at least thy flock deserves thy care,
Plants of thy hand, and children of thy prayer.   130
From the false world in early youth they fled,
By thee to mountains, wilds, and deserts led.
You raised these hallowed walls; the desert smiled,
And Paradise was opened in the wild.
No weeping orphan saw his father's stores
Our shrines irradiate, or emblaze the floors;
No silver saints, by dying misers given,
Here bribed the rage of ill-requited heaven:
But such plain roofs as Piety could raise,
And only vocal with the Maker's praise.   140
In these lone walls (their days eternal bound)
These moss-grown domes with spiry turrets crowned,
Where awful arches make a noon-day night,
And the dim windows shed a solemn light;
Thy eyes diffused a reconciling ray,
And gleams of glory brightened all the day.
But now no face divine contentment wears,
'Tis all blank sadness, or continual tears.
See how the force of others' prayers I try,
(O pious fraud of amorous charity!)   150
But why should I on others' prayers depend?
Come thou, my father, brother, husband, friend!
Ah let thy handmaid, sister, daughter move,
And all those tender names in one, thy love!
The darksome pines that o'er yon rocks reclined
Wave high, and murmur to the hollow wind,
The wandering streams that shine between the hills,
The grots that echo to the tinkling rills,
The dying gales that pant upon the trees,
The lakes that quiver to the curling breeze;   160
No more these scenes my meditation aid,
Or lull to rest the visionary maid.
But o'er the twilight groves and dusky caves,
Long-sounding aisles, and intermingled graves,
Black Melancholy sits, and round her throws
A death-like silence, and a dead repose:
Her gloomy presence saddens all the scene,
Shades every flower, and darkens every green,
Deepens the murmur of the falling floods,
And breathes a browner horror on the woods.   170
   Yet here for ever, ever must I stay;
Sad proof how well a lover can obey!
Death, only death, can break the lasting chain;
And here, even then, shall my cold dust remain,
Here all its frailties, all its flames resign,
And wait till 'tis no sin to mix with thine.
   Ah wretch! believed the spouse of God in vain,
Confessed within the slave of love and man.
Assist me, Heaven! But whence arose that prayer?
Sprung it from piety, or from despair?   180
Even here, where frozen chastity retires,
Love finds an altar for forbidden fires.
I ought to grieve, but cannot what I ought;
I mourn the lover, not lament the fault;
I view my crime, but kindle at the view,
Repent old pleasures, and solicit new;
Now turned to heaven, I weep my past offence,
Now think of thee, and curse my innocence.
Of all affliction taught a lover yet,
'Tis sure the hardest science to forget!   190
How shall I lose the sin, yet keep the sense,
And love the offender, yet detest the offence?
How the dear object from the crime remove,
Or how distinguish penitence from love?
Unequal task! a passion to resign,
For hearts so touched, so pierced, so lost as mine.
Ere such a soul regains its peaceful state,
How often must it love, how often hate!
How often hope, despair, resent, regret,
Conceal, disdain,—do all things but forget.   200
But let heaven seize it, all at once 'tis fired:
Not touched, but rapt; not wakened, but inspired!

   133. **You raised . . . walls.** Abelard had founded the monastery, called Paraclete, to which Eloïsa retired.

   170. **browner,** darker.

Oh come! oh teach me nature to subdue,
Renounce my love, my life, myself—and you.
Fill my fond heart with God alone, for he
Alone can rival, can succeed to thee.
 How happy is the blameless Vestal's lot!
The world forgetting, by the world forgot:
Eternal sunshine of the spotless mind!
Each prayer accepted, and each wish resigned;   210
Labour and rest, that equal periods keep;
"Obedient slumbers that can wake and weep";
Desires composed, affections ever even;
Tears that delight, and sighs that waft to heaven.
Grace shines around her with serenest beams,
And whispering Angels prompt her golden dreams.
For her the unfading rose of Eden blooms,
And wings of Seraphs shed divine perfumes;
For her the Spouse prepares the bridal ring,
For her white virgins Hymenaeals sing,   220
To sounds of heavenly harps she dies away,
And melts in visions of eternal day.
 Far other dreams my erring soul employ,
Far other raptures, of unholy joy:
When at the close of each sad, sorrowing day,
Fancy restores what vengeance snatched away,
Then conscience sleeps, and leaving nature free,
All my loose soul unbounded springs to thee.
Oh curst, dear horrors of all-conscious night!
How glowing guilt exalts the keen delight!   230
Provoking Daemons all restraint remove,
And stir within me every source of love.
I hear thee, view thee, gaze o'er all thy charms,
And round thy phantom glue my clasping arms.
I wake:—no more I hear, no more I view,
The phantom flies me, as unkind as you.
I call aloud; it hears not what I say:
I stretch my empty arms; it glides away.
To dream once more I close my willing eyes;
Ye soft illusions, dear deceits, arise!   240
Alas, no more! methinks we wandering go
Through dreary wastes, and weep each other's woe,
Where round some mouldering tower pale ivy creeps,
And low-browed rocks hang nodding o'er the deeps.
Sudden you mount, you beckon from the skies;
Clouds interpose, waves roar, and winds arise.
I shriek, start up, the same sad prospect find,
And wake to all the griefs I left behind.
 For thee the fates, severely kind, ordain
A cool suspense from pleasure and from pain;   250
Thy life a long dead calm of fixed repose;
No pulse that riots, and no blood that glows.
Still as the sea, ere winds were taught to blow,

212. "Obedient ... weep," quoted from Crashaw.
220. Hymenaeals, wedding songs.

Or moving spirit bade the waters flow;
Soft as the slumbers of a saint forgiven,
And mild as opening gleams of promised heaven.
 Come, Abelard! for what hast thou to dread?
The torch of Venus burns not for the dead.
Nature stands checked; Religion disapproves;
Even thou art cold—yet Eloïsa loves.   260
Ah hopeless, lasting flames! like those that burn
To light the dead, and warm the unfruitful urn.
 What scenes appear where'er I turn my view?
The dear Ideas, where I fly, pursue,
Rise in the grove, before the altar rise,
Stain all my soul, and wanton in my eyes.
I waste the Matin lamp in sighs for thee,
Thy image steals between my God and me,
Thy voice I seem in every hymn to hear,
With every bead I drop too soft a tear.   270
When from the censer clouds of fragrance roll,
And swelling organs lift the rising soul,
One thought of thee puts all the pomp to flight,
Priests, tapers, temples, swim before my sight:
In seas of flame my plunging soul is drowned,
While Altars blaze, and Angels tremble round.
 While prostrate here in humble grief I lie,
Kind, virtuous drops just gathering in my eye,
While praying, trembling, in the dust I roll,
And dawning grace is opening on my soul: 280
Come, if thou dar'st, all charming as thou art!
Oppose thyself to heaven; dispute my heart;
Come, with one glance of those deluding eyes
Blot out each bright Idea of the skies;
Take back that grace, those sorrows, and those tears;
Take back my fruitless penitence and prayers;
Snatch me, just mounting, from the blest abode;
Assist the fiends, and tear me from my God!
 No, fly me, fly me, far as Pole from Pole;
Rise Alps between us! and whole oceans roll!   290
Ah, come not, write not, think not once of me,
Nor share one pang of all I felt for thee.
Thy oaths I quit, thy memory resign;
Forget, renounce me, hate whate'er was mine.
Fair eyes, and tempting looks (which yet I view!)
Long loved, adored ideas, all adieu!
Oh Grace serene! oh virtue heavenly fair!
Divine oblivion of low-thoughted care!
Fresh blooming Hope, gay daughter of the sky!
And Faith, our early immortality!   300
Enter, each mild, each amicable guest;
Receive, and wrap me in eternal rest!
 See in her cell sad Eloïsa spread,
Propped on some tomb, a neighbour of the dead.
In each low wind methinks a Spirit calls,
And more than Echoes talk along the walls.
Here, as I watched the dying lamps around,

From yonder shrine I heard a hollow sound.
"Come, sister, come!" (it said, or seemed to say)
"Thy place is here, sad sister, come away!   310
Once like thyself, I trembled, wept, and prayed,
Love's victim then, though now a sainted maid:
But all is calm in this eternal sleep;
Here grief forgets to groan, and love to weep;
Even superstition loses every fear,
For God, not man, absolves our frailties here."
   I come, I come! prepare your roseate bowers,
Celestial palms, and ever-blooming flowers.
Thither, where sinners may have rest, I go,
Where flames refined in breasts seraphic glow: 320
Thou, Abelard! the last sad office pay,
And smooth my passage to the realms of day;
See my lips tremble, and my eye-balls roll,
Suck my last breath, and catch my flying soul!
Ah no—in sacred vestments may'st thou stand,
The hallowed taper trembling in thy hand,
Present the Cross before my lifted eye,
Teach me at once, and learn of me to die.
Ah then, thy once loved Eloïsa see!
It will be then no crime to gaze on me.   330
See from my cheek the transient roses fly!
See the last sparkle languish in my eye!
Till every motion, pulse, and breath be o'er;
And even my Abelard be loved no more.
O Death all-eloquent! you only prove
What dust we dote on, when 'tis man we love.
   Then too, when fate shall thy fair frame destroy,
(That cause of all my guilt, and all my joy)
In trance ecstatic may thy pangs be drowned,
Bright clouds descend, and Angels watch thee round,   340
From opening skies may streaming glories shine,
And saints embrace thee with a love like mine.
   May one kind grave unite each hapless name,
And graft my love immortal on thy fame!
Then, ages hence, when all my woes are o'er,
When this rebellious heart shall beat no more;
If ever chance two wandering lovers brings
To Paraclete's white walls and silver springs,
O'er the pale marble shall they join their heads,
And drink the falling tears each other sheds;   350
Then sadly say, with mutual pity moved,
"Oh may we never love as these have loved!"
From the full choir when loud Hosannas rise,
And swell the pomp of dreadful sacrifice,
Amid that scene if some relenting eye
Glance on the stone where our cold relics lie,
Devotion's self shall steal a thought from heaven,
One human tear shall drop and be forgiven.
And sure, if fate some future bard shall join
In sad similitude of griefs to mine,   360
Condemned whole years in absence to deplore,
And image charms he must behold no more;
Such if there be, who loves so long, so well,
Let him our sad, our tender story tell;
The well-sung woes will soothe my pensive ghost;
He best can paint 'em who shall feel 'em most.

James Thomson
1700–1748

One of the clearest proofs that Romanticism never died out in England during the period of Neo-classical domination is seen in the poetry of James Thomson, a Scotchman who went up to London in 1725 with a manuscript called "Winter" in his pocket. This poem was one of four which, when the series was completed in 1730, he called *The Seasons*. They made him famous at thirty. Concerned as they are with typical scenes and events of the Scottish and English countryside, they constitute a voluble answer to Pope's declaration that "the proper study of mankind is Man." Thomson held that "there is no subject more elevating, more amusing, more ready to awake poetical enthusiasm, philosophic reflection, and moral sentiment, than the works of Nature."

As a somewhat indolent man who wished to please everyone, Thomson did not oppose Neo-classical practice and doctrine. He was a friend of Pope's, and found several patrons, so it is not surprising that he allowed his natural gift for sharp delineation to be blurred by that "grandeur of generality" for which all fashionable poets were in his time trying. His blank verse wavers between the sonorous periods of Milton and the brisk staccato distich of Pope. Worst of all, with a subject matter crying out for the simplest language, he often indulges himself in pomposities

343. one kind grave. "Abélard and Eloïsa were interred in the same grave, or in monuments adjoining, in the Monastery of the **Paraclete**; he died in the year 1142, she in 1163." (Pope)   **359. bard.** Pope here refers to himself, with reference to Lady Mary Wortley Montague.

of circumlocution which, to our taste, are merely ludicrous.

Yet James Thomson is a poet whose voice thrills through all the "static" of his time and place. The sunsets that he watched two centuries ago from Richmond Hill are lingering faintly even now upon his pages. His English robin redbreast will live as long in memory as Lesbia's sparrow, mourned by Catullus. We feel today, as many readers did in Germany and France and England long ago, the delight that came to this little lazy Scotchman, "more fat than bard beseems," while he watched the pageant of the rounded year.

Thomson, in fact, helped to shape the modern mind and temper. He has his honorable place in the tradition of the Western world. More than most of the vocal persons of his time, he knew how we are linked with earth. He had a sense of the vast spatial backgrounds and the huge natural panorama against which our little lives are led. Most of his contemporaries thought and fancied in terms of a single city as though it were the universe, but he in terms of land and sea and the cloud-laden air.

One feels that Thomson had a wider range of emotion and more freedom of mood than most of the famous men among whom he lived. The contrast is sharp and clear, for example, between the enthusiastic vision of his remarkable ode "To the Memory of Sir Isaac Newton" and Jonathan Swift's ignorant contempt for natural science. He wrote, moreover, not out of his hatreds, if we may suppose that he had any, but always in praise of things he loved, admired, or adored. The precious gift of song, denied to most other poets of his time, was not wholly lacking in him. Now and then we find in his pages a gleam of pure magic—it may be some glamorous stanza of *The Castle of Indolence*, a single phrase such as that in which the Arctic whales are said to "tempest the loosened brine," or some heart-easing cadence worthy of Keats, like that in his "Hymn on the Seasons":

> . . . "ye harvests, wave to Him—
> Breathe your still song into the reaper's heart
> As home he goes beneath the joyous moon."

A HYMN ON THE SEASONS

English Deism, a body of religious and philosophical doctrine prominent in Thomson's time, asserted that there is to be found in the natural world a sufficient revelation not only of God but also of moral truth. From this doctrine it followed that the human mind may proceed "through nature to nature's God," and the opinion was sometimes advanced that in the contemplation or study of nature one is really engaged in divine worship. Although James Thomson was not himself an avowed Deist, one sees in the present poem, written to complete his series of poems on the four seasons, that he was affected by Deistic thought. The same influence is to be discerned in Joseph Addison's hymn "The Spacious Firmament on High," and also in Coleridge's "Hymn before Sunrise in the Vale of Chamouni."

These, as they change, Almighty Father! these
Are but the varied God. The rolling year
Is full of thee. Forth in the pleasing Spring
Thy beauty walks, thy tenderness and love.
Wide flush the fields; the softening air is balm;
Echo the mountains round; the forest smiles;
And every sense, and every heart, is joy.
Then comes thy glory in the Summer-months,
With light and heat refulgent. Then thy sun
Shoots full perfection through the swelling year: 10
And oft thy voice in dreadful thunder speaks,
And oft, at dawn, deep noon, or falling eve,
By brooks and groves, in hollow-whispering gales.
Thy bounty shines in Autumn unconfined,
And spreads a common feast for all that lives.
In Winter awful thou! with clouds and storms
Around thee thrown, tempest o'er tempest rolled,
Majestic darkness! On the whirlwind's wing
Riding sublime, thou bidst the world adore,
And humblest nature with thy northern blast.   20

Mysterious round! what skill, what force divine,
Deep-felt in these appear! a simple train,
Yet so delightful mixed, with such kind art,
Such beauty and beneficence combined,
Shade unperceived so softening into shade,
And all so forming an harmonious whole
That, as they still succeed, they ravish still.
But, wandering oft with brute unconscious gaze,
Man marks not thee, marks not the mighty hand
That, ever busy, wheels the silent spheres,   30
Works in the secret deep, shoots steaming thence
The fair profusion that o'erspreads the Spring,
Flings from the sun direct the flaming day,
Feeds every creature, hurls the tempest forth,
And, as on earth this grateful change revolves,
With transport touches all the springs of life.

Nature, attend! join every living soul
Beneath the spacious temple of the sky,
In adoration join; and ardent raise
One general song! To Him, ye local gales,   40
Breathe soft, whose spirit in your freshness breathes:

1. **These,** the seasons of the year.   21. **round,** the circle of the year.   22. **train,** succession.

Oh! talk of Him in solitary glooms,
Where, o'er the rock, the scarcely-waving pine
Fills the brown shade with a religious awe.
And ye, whose bolder note is heard afar,
Who shake the astonished world, lift high to Heaven
The impetuous song, and say from whom you rage.
His praise, ye brooks, attune, ye trembling rills;
And let me catch it as I muse along.
Ye headlong torrents, rapid and profound; 50
Ye softer floods, that lead the humid maze
Along the vale; and thou, majestic main,
A secret world of wonders in thyself,
Sound His stupendous praise, whose greater voice
Or bids you roar or bids your roarings fall.
Soft roll your incense, herbs, and fruits, and flowers,
In mingled clouds to Him, whose sun exalts,
Whose breath perfumes you, and whose pencil paints.
Ye forests, bend; ye harvests wave to Him—
Breathe your still song into the reaper's heart 60
As home he goes beneath the joyous moon.
Ye that keep watch in heaven, as earth asleep
Unconscious lies, effuse your mildest beams,
Ye constellations! while your angels strike
Amid the spangled sky the silver lyre.
Great source of day! best image here below
Of thy Creator, ever pouring wide
From world to world the vital ocean round!
On nature write with every beam His praise. 69
The thunder rolls: be hushed the prostrate world,
While cloud to cloud returns the solemn hymn.
Bleat out afresh, ye hills; ye mossy rocks,
Retain the sound; the broad responsive low,
Ye valleys, raise; for the Great Shepherd reigns,
And His unsuffering kingdom yet will come.
Ye woodlands all, awake: a boundless song
Burst from the groves; and, when the restless day,
Expiring, lays the warbling world asleep,
Sweetest of birds, sweet Philomela! charm 79
The listening shades, and teach the night His praise!
Ye, chief, for whom the whole creation smiles,
At once the head, the heart, the tongue of all,
Crown the great hymn! In swarming cities vast,
Assembled men, to the deep organ join
The long-resounding voice, oft breaking clear
At solemn pauses through the swelling bass;
And, as each mingling flame increases each,
In one united ardour rise to heaven.
Or, if you rather choose the rural shade,
And find a fane in every sacred grove, 90
There let the shepherd's flute, the virgin's lay,
The prompting seraph, and the poet's lyre
Still sing the God of Seasons as they roll.

For me, when I forget the darling theme,
Whether the blossom blows, the summer-ray
Russets the plain, inspiring autumn gleams,
Or winter rises in the blackening east,
Be my tongue mute, may fancy paint no more,
And, dead to joy, forget my heart to beat!

Should fate command me to the farthest verge 100
Of the green earth, to distant barbarous climes,
Rivers unknown to song, where first the sun
Gilds Indian mountains, or his setting beam
Flames on the Atlantic isles, 'tis naught to me;
Since God is ever present, ever felt,
In the void waste as in the city full,
And where He vital spreads there must be joy.
When even at last the solemn hour shall come,
And wing my mystic flight to future worlds,
I cheerful will obey; there, with new powers, 110
Will rising wonders sing: I cannot go
Where universal love not smiles around,
Sustaining all yon orbs and all their sons;
From seeming evil still educing good,
And better thence again, and better still,
In infinite progression. But I lose
Myself in Him, in light ineffable!
Come then, expressive Silence. muse His praise.

TO THE MEMORY OF SIR ISAAC NEWTON

Newton's importance in English thought and literature is due to the support given by his scientific achievements to those who held that human reason alone, without supernatural revelation, is able to comprehend and control the world. Thomson's ode is an enthusiastic expression of the hopes thus awakened. In a time when many leading minds were still contemptuous of scientific study it celebrates the inherent beauty of science and proclaims its high imaginative value.

Shall the great soul of Newton quit this earth
To mingle with his stars, and every Muse,
Astonished into silence, shun the weight
Of honours due to his illustrious name?
But what can man? Even now the sons of light,
In strains high warbled to seraphic lyre,
Hail his arrival on the coast of bliss.
Yet am not I deterred, though high the theme,
And sung to harps of angels, for with you,
Ethereal flames! ambitious, I aspire 10
In Nature's general symphony to join.

1. Newton. He died March 20, 1727. The present poem appeared three months later. **2. his,** in the sense that he understood them. **6. strains,** the "music of the spheres."

And what new wonders can ye show your guest!
Who, while on this dim spot where mortals toil
Clouded in dust, from motion's simple laws
Could trace the secret hand of Providence,
Wide-working through this universal frame?
    Have ye not listened while he bound the suns
And planets to their spheres! the unequal task
Of humankind till then? Oft had they rolled
O'er erring man the year, and oft disgraced   20
The pride of schools, before their course was known
Full in its causes and effects to him.
All-piercing sage! who sat not down and dreamed
Romantic schemes, defended by the din
Of specious words, and tyranny of names;
But, bidding his amazing mind attend,
And with heroic patience years on years
Deep-searching, saw at last the system dawn,
And shine, of all his race, on him alone.
    What were his raptures then! how pure! how
        strong!   30
And what the triumphs of old Greece and Rome,
By his diminished, but the pride of boys
In some small fray victorious! when instead
Of shattered parcels of this earth usurped
By violence unmanly, and sore deeds
Of cruelty and blood, Nature herself
Stood all subdued by him, and open laid
Her every latent glory to his view.
    All intellectual eye, our solar round
First gazing through, he, by the blended power   40
Of gravitation and projection, saw
The whole in silent harmony revolve.
From unassisted vision hid, the moons
To cheer remoter planets numerous formed,
By him in all their mingled tracts were seen.
He also fixed the wandering Queen of Night,
Whether she wanes into a scanty orb,
Or, waxing broad, with her pale shadowy light,
In a soft deluge overflows the sky.
Her every motion clear-discerning, he   50
Adjusted to the mutual main, and taught
Why now the mighty mass of waters swells
Resistless, heaving on the broken rocks,
And the full river turning—till again
The tide revertive, unattracted, leaves
A yellow waste of idle sands behind.
    Then, breaking hence, he took his ardent flight
Through the blue infinite; and every star
Which the clear concave of a winter's night
Pours on the eye, or astronomic tube,   60
Far stretching, snatches from the dark abyss,
Or such as further in successive skies
To fancy shine alone, at his approach
Blazed into suns, the living centre each
Of an harmonious system—all combined,
And ruled unerring by that single power
Which draws the stone projected to the ground.
    O unprofuse magnificence divine!
O wisdom truly perfect! thus to call
From a few causes such a scheme of things,   70
Effects so various, beautiful, and great,
An universe complete! And O beloved
Of Heaven! whose well purged penetrative eye
The mystic veil transpiercing, inly scanned
The rising, moving, wide-established frame.
    He, first of men, with awful wing pursued
The comet through the long elliptic curve,
As round innumerous worlds he wound his way,
Till, to the forehead of our evening sky
Returned, the blazing wonder glares anew,   80
And o'er the trembling nations shakes dismay.
    The heavens are all his own, from the wide rule
Of whirling vortices and circling spheres
To their first great simplicity restored.
The schools astonished stood; but found it vain
To keep at odds with demonstration strong,
And, unawakened, dream beneath the blaze
Of truth. At once their pleasing visions fled,
With the gay shadows of the morning mixed,
When Newton rose, our philosophic sun!   90
    The aerial flow of sound was known to him,
From whence it first in wavy circles breaks,
Till the touched organ takes the meaning in.
Nor could the darting beam of speed immense
Escape his swift pursuit and measuring eye.
Even light itself, which every thing displays,
Shone undiscovered, till his brighter mind
Untwisted all the shining robe of day;
And from the whitening undistinguished blaze,
Collecting every ray into his kind,   100
To the charmed eye educed the gorgeous train
Of parent colours. First the flaming red
Sprung vivid forth; the tawny orange next;
And next delicious yellow; by whose side
Fell the kind beams of all-refreshing green;
Then the pure blue, that swells autumnal skies,
Ethereal played; and then, of sadder hue,
Emerged the deepened indigo, as when
The heavy-skirted evening droops with frost;
While the last gleamings of refracted light   110
Died in the fainting violet away.
These, when the clouds distil the rosy shower,
Shine out distinct adown the watery bow;

18. **unequal,** too difficult.   45. **tracts,** orbits.   51. **main,** the sea, as affected by the moon.   88. **pleasing,** flattering to humanity's sense of its own importance. After Newton's discoveries "the scenery became too wide for the drama."   100. **his,** its.

While o'er our heads the dewy vision bends
Delightful, melting on the fields beneath.
Myriads of mingling dyes from these result,
And myriads still remain—infinite source
Of beauty, ever flushing, ever new.
    Did ever poet image aught so fair,
Dreaming in whispering groves by the hoarse brook?   120
Or prophet, to whose rapture heaven descends?
Even now the setting sun and shifting clouds,
Seen, Greenwich, from thy lovely heights, declare
How just, how beauteous the refractive law.
    The noiseless tide of time, all bearing down
To vast eternity's unbounded sea,
Where the green islands of the happy shine,
He stemmed alone: and to the source (involved
Deep in primeval gloom) ascending, raised
His lights at equal distances, to guide   130
Historian wildered on his darksome way.
    But who can number up his labours? who
His high discoveries sing? When but a few
Of the deep-studying race can stretch their minds
To what he knew—in fancy's lighter thought
How shall the Muse then grasp the mighty theme?
    What wonder thence that his devotion swelled
Responsive to his knowledge? For could he
Whose piercing mental eye diffusive saw
The finished university of things   140
In all its order, magnitude, and parts,
Forbear incessant to adore that Power
Who fills, sustains, and actuates the whole?
    Say, ye who best can tell, ye happy few,
Who saw him in the softest lights of life,
All unwithheld, indulging to his friends
The vast unborrowed treasures of his mind,
Oh, speak the wondrous man! how mild, how calm,
How greatly humble, how divinely good,
How firm established on eternal truth;   150
Fervent in doing well, with every nerve
Still pressing on, forgetful of the past,
And panting for perfection; far above
Those little cares and visionary joys
That so perplex the fond impassioned heart
Of ever cheated, ever trusting man.
This, Conduitt, from thy rural hours we hope,
As through the pleasing shade where nature pours
Her every sweet in studious ease you walk,
The social passions smiling at thy heart,   160
That glows with all the recollected sage.
    And you, ye hopeless gloomy-minded tribe,
You who, unconscious of those nobler flights
That reach impatient at immortal life,
Against the prime endearing privilege
Of being dare contend,—say, can a soul
Of such extensive, deep, tremendous powers,
Enlarging still, be but a finer breath
Of spirits dancing through their tubes awhile,
And then forever lost in vacant air?   170
    But hark! methinks I hear a warning voice,
Solemn as when some awful change is come,
Sound through the world—"'Tis done!—the measure's full;
And I resign my charge."—Ye mouldering stones
That build the towering pyramid, the proud
Triumphal arch, the monument effaced
By ruthless ruin, and what'er supports
The worshipped name of hoar antiquity—
Down to the dust! What grandeur can ye boast
While Newton lifts his column to the skies,   180
Beyond the waste of time? Let no weak drop
Be shed for him. The virgin in her bloom
Cut off, the joyous youth, and darling child—
These are the tombs that claim the tender tear
And elegiac song. But Newton calls
For other notes of gratulation high,
That now he wanders through those endless worlds
He here so well descried, and wondering talks,
And hymns their Author with his glad compeers.
O Britain's boast! whether with angels thou   190
Sittest in dread discourse, or fellow-blessed,
Who joy to see the honour of their kind;
Or whether, mounted on cherubic wing,
Thy swift career is with the whirling orbs,
Comparing things with things, in rapture lost,
And grateful adoration for that light
So plenteous rayed into thy mind below
From Light Himself; oh, look with pity down
On humankind, a frail erroneous race!
Exalt the spirit of a downward world!   200
O'er thy dejected country chief preside,
And be her Genius called! her studies raise,
Correct her manners, and inspire her youth;
For, though depraved and sunk, she brought thee forth,
And glories in thy name! she points thee out
To all her sons, and bids them eye thy star;
While in expectance of the second life,
When time shall be no more, thy sacred dust
Sleeps with her kings and dignifies the scene.

118. **new.** With this passage compare Keats's "Lamia," Part II, ll. 231–38.   131. **way,** a reference to Newton's *Chronology of Ancient Kingdoms.*   142–43. **adore . . . whole?** Newton gave his last years to the study of theology.   157. **Conduitt,** Newton's deputy as Warden of the Mint, who had promised to write a biography of the scientist.   165. **privilege,** immortality.   209. **Sleeps with her kings.** Newton was buried in Westminster Abbey.

from THE CASTLE OF INDOLENCE

Thomson's imitation of Edmund Spenser's style and stanza shows the skill in painting vignettes of landscape which one would expect from the author of *The Seasons* and which Spenser himself also possessed. The eighteenth-century poet comes closest to his original, however, in the ample, rich, and always somewhat indolent music of his verse. This music, the charm of the theme, and the poet's prevailing mood combine to produce one of the minor masterpieces of the century. The poem is in two cantos, of which the first is here given entire.

ADVERTISEMENT

This Poem being writ in the manner of Spenser, the obsolete words, and a simplicity of diction in some of the lines which borders on the ludicrous, were necessary to make the imitation more perfect. And the style of that admirable poet, as well as the measure in which he wrote, are as it were appropriated by custom to all allegorical poems writ in our language—just as in French the style of Marot, who lived under Francis I, has been used in tales and familiar epistles by the politest writers of the age of Louis XIV.—Thomson.

CANTO I

The Castle hight of Indolence,
And its false luxury;
Where for a little time, alas!
We lived right jollily.

1

O mortal man, who livest here by toil,
Do not complain of this thy hard estate;
That like an emmet thou must ever moil
Is a sad sentence of an ancient date:
And, certes, there is for it reason great;
For though sometimes it makes thee weep and wail,
And curse thy stars, and early drudge and late,
Withouten that would come an heavier bale,
Loose life, unruly passions, and diseases pale.

2

In lowly dale, fast by a river's side, 10
With woody hill o'er hill encompassed round,
A most enchanting wizard did abide,
Than whom a fiend more fell is nowhere found.
It was, I ween, a lovely spot of ground;
And there a season atween June and May,
Half prankt with spring, with summer half imbrowned,
A listless climate made, where, sooth to say,
No living wight could work, ne carèd even for play.

3

Was naught around but images of rest:
Sleep-soothing groves, and quiet lawns between; 20
And flowery beds that slumbrous influence kest,
From poppies breathed; and beds of pleasant green,
Where never yet was creeping creature seen.
Meantime unnumbered glittering streamlets played,
And hurlèd everywhere their waters sheen;
That, as they bickered through the sunny glade,
Though restless still themselves, a lulling murmur made.

4

Joined to the prattle of the purling rills,
Were heard the lowing herds along the vale,
And flocks loud-bleating from the distant hills, 30
And vacant shepherds piping in the dale:
And now and then sweet Philomel would wail,
Or stock-doves plain amid the forest deep,
That drowsy rustled to the sighing gale;
And still a coil the grasshopper did keep;
Yet all these sounds yblent inclinèd all to sleep.

5

Full in the passage of the vale, above,
A sable, silent, solemn forest stood;
Where naught but shadowy forms were seen to move,
As Idless fancied in her dreaming mood. 40
And up the hills, on either side, a wood
Of blackening pines, ay waving to and fro,
Sent forth a sleepy horror through the blood;
And where this valley winded out, below,
The murmuring main was heard, and scarcely heard, to flow.

6

A pleasing land of drowsyhed it was:
Of dreams that wave before the half-shut eye;
And of gay castles in the clouds that pass,
Forever flushing round a summer sky:
There eke the soft delights, that witchingly 50
Instil a wanton sweetness through the breast,
And the calm pleasures always hovered nigh;
But whate'er smacked of noyance, or unrest,
Was far far off expelled from this delicious nest.

Prefatory stanza. **1. hight,** called. *Sec. 1.* **3. emmet,** ant. **moil,** labor. **4. sentence,** laid upon Adam. **8. bale,** evil. **10. dale . . . side.** Compare Spenser, *The Faerie Queene,* Book I, Canto I, l. 34. **18. wight,** creature. **ne,** nor. **21. kest,** cast. **25. sheen,** shining. **27. still,** continually. **31. vacant,** idle. **35. coil,** disturbance. **keep,** maintain. **36. yblent.** The "y" is the old sign of the past participle. **40. Idless,** idleness. **46. drowsyhed,** the suffix is equivalent to "-ness."

7

The landskip such, inspiring perfect ease;
Where INDOLENCE (for so the wizard hight)
Close-hid his castle mid embowering trees,
That half shut out the beam of Phoebus bright,
And made a kind of checkered day and night.
Meanwhile, unceasing at the massy gate, 60
Beneath a spacious palm, the wicked wight
Was placed; and, to his lute, of cruel fate
And labour harsh complained, lamenting man's estate.

8

Thither continual pilgrims crowded still
From all the roads of earth that pass thereby:
For, as they chaunced to breathe on neighbouring hill,
The freshness of this valley smote their eye,
And drew them ever and anon more nigh,
Till clustering round the enchanter false they hung,
Ymolten with his syren melody; 70
While o'er the enfeebling lute his hand he flung,
And to the trembling chord these tempting verses sung:

9

"Behold! ye pilgrims of this earth, behold!
See all but man with unearned pleasure gay.
See her bright robes the butterfly unfold,
Broke from her wintry tomb in prime of May.
What youthful bride can equal her array?
Who can with her for easy pleasure vie?
From mead to mead with gentle wing to stray,
From flower to flower on balmy gales to fly, 80
Is all she has to do beneath the radiant sky.

10

"Behold the merry minstrels of the morn,
The swarming songsters of the careless grove,
Ten thousand throats that, from the flowering thorn,
Hymn their good God, and carol sweet of love,
Such grateful kindly raptures them emove!
They neither plough nor sow; ne, fit for flail,
E'er to the barn the nodding sheaves they drove;
Yet theirs each harvest dancing in the gale,
Whatever crowns the hill, or smiles along the vale. 90

11

"Outcast of Nature, man! the wretched thrall
Of bitter-dropping sweat, of sweltry pain,
Of cares that eat away thy heart with gall,
And of the vices, an inhuman train,
That all proceed from savage thirst of gain:
For when hard-hearted Interest first began
To poison earth, Astraea left the plain;
Guile, Violence, and Murder seized on man,
And, for soft milky streams, with blood the rivers ran.

12

"Come, ye, who still the cumbrous load of life 100
Push hard up hill; but, as the farthest steep
You trust to gain, and put an end to strife,
Down thunders back the stone with mighty sweep,
And hurls your labours to the valley deep,
Forever vain: come, and withouten fee
I in oblivion will your sorrows steep,
Your cares, your toils; will steep you in a sea
Of full delight—O come, ye weary wights, to me!

13

"With me, you need not rise at early dawn,
To pass the joyless day in various stounds; 110
Or, louting low, on upstart fortune fawn,
And sell fair honour for some paltry pounds;
Or through the city take your dirty rounds,
To cheat, and dun, and lie, and visit pay,
Now flattering base, now giving secret wounds;
Or prowl in courts of law for human prey,
In venal senate thieve, or rob on broad highway.

14

"No cocks, with me, to rustic labour call,
From village on to village sounding clear; 119
To tardy swain no shrill-voiced matrons squall;
No dogs, no babes, no wives to stun your ear;
No hammers thump; no horrid blacksmith sear,
Ne noisy tradesman your sweet slumbers start
With sounds that are a misery to hear:
But all is calm as would delight the heart
Of Sybarite of old, all nature, and all art.

15

"Here naught but candour reigns, indulgent ease,
Good-natured lounging, sauntering up and down:

---

55. landskip, the common form of the word in Thomson's time, and more correct than "landscape." After this word supply "was." **70. Ymolten,** melted. **86. emove,** move, suggested by "emotion." **96. Interest,** self-interest, private profit. **97. Astraea,** the "star maid," last deity to leave earth when the Iron Age succeeded the Golden. **103. sweep,** alluding to the myth of Sisyphus. **110. stounds,** pangs of pain. **111. louting,** bowing. **126. Sybarite,** a citizen of Sybaris, famous for its luxury.

They who are pleased themselves must always
    please;
On others' ways they never squint a frown,   130
Nor heed what haps in hamlet or in town.
Thus, from the source of tender Indolence,
With milky blood the heart is overflown,
Is soothed and sweetened by the social sense;
For interest, envy, pride, and strife are banished
    hence.

16

"What, what is virtue but repose of mind?
A pure ethereal calm that knows no storm,
Above the reach of wild ambition's wind,
Above those passions that this world deform,
And torture man, a proud malignant worm!   140
But here, instead, soft gales of passion play,
And gently stir the heart, thereby to form
A quicker sense of joy; as breezes stray
Across the enlivened skies, and make them still more
    gay.

17

"The best of men have ever loved repose:
They hate to mingle in the filthy fray;
Where the soul sours, and gradual rancour
    grows,
Imbittered more from peevish day to day.
Even those whom Fame has lent her fairest ray,
The most renowned of worthy wights of yore,   150
From a base world at last have stolen away:
So Scipio, to the soft Cumaean shore
Retiring, tasted joy he never knew before.

18

"But if a little exercise you chuse,
Some zest for ease, 'tis not forbidden here.
Amid the groves you may indulge the Muse,
Or tend the blooms, and deck the vernal year;
Or softly stealing, with your watery gear,
Along the brooks, the crimson-spotted fry
You may delude: the whilst, amused, you
    hear   160
Now the hoarse stream, and now the zephyr's
    sigh,
Attunèd to the birds, and woodland melody.

19

"O grievous folly! to heap up estate,
Losing the days you see beneath the sun;
When, sudden, comes blind unrelenting fate,
And gives the untasted portion you have won
With ruthless toil, and many a wretch undone,
To those who mock you, gone to Pluto's reign,
There with sad ghosts to pine and shadows dun:
But sure it is of vanities most vain,   170
To toil for what you here untoiling may obtain."

20

He ceased. But still their trembling ears retained
The deep vibrations of his witching song;
That, by a kind of magic power, constrained
To enter in, pell-mell, the listening throng.
Heaps poured on heaps, and yet they slipped
    along
In silent ease: as when, beneath the beam
Of summer moons, the distant woods among,
Or by some flood all silvered with the gleam,
The soft-embodied fays through airy portal
    stream.   180

21

By the smooth demon so it ordered was,
And here his baneful bounty first began;
Though some there were who would not further
    pass,
And his alluring baits suspected han.
The wise distrust the too fair-spoken man.
Yet through the gate they cast a wishful eye:
Not to move on, perdie, is all they can;
For, do their very best, they cannot fly,
But often each way look, and often sorely sigh.

22

When this the watchful wicked wizard saw,   190
With sudden spring he leaped upon them strait;
And, soon as touched by his unhallowed paw,
They found themselves within the cursèd gate,
Full hard to be repassed, like that of Fate.
Not stronger were of old the giant-crew,
Who sought to pull high Jove from regal state,
Though feeble wretch he seemed, of sallow hue:
Certes, who bides his grasp, will that encounter rue.

23

For whomsoe'er the villain takes in hand,
Their joints unknit, their sinews melt apace; 200
As lithe they grow as any willow-wand,
And of their vanished force remains no trace:
So when a maiden fair, of modest grace,
In all her buxom blooming May of charms,
Is seizèd in some losel's hot embrace,
She waxeth very weakly as she warms,
Then sighing yields her up to love's delicious
    harms.

152. Scipio, surnamed Africanus, conqueror of Hannibal. **Cumaean**, Campanian, in southern Italy. **159. fry**, trout. **172. trembling.** See Milton's "Lycidas," l. 77. **184. han**, have. **187. perdie**, *par dieu*, by God, an old oath. **195. giant-crew**, the Titans. **205. losel**, a loose, idle fellow.

24

Waked by the crowd, slow from his bench arose
A comely full-spread porter, swoln with sleep:
His calm, broad, thoughtless aspect breathed repose;   210
And in sweet torpor he was plungèd deep,
Ne could himself from ceaseless yawning keep;
While o'er his eyes the drowsy liquor ran,
Through which his half-waked soul would faintly peep.
Then, taking his black staff, he called his man,
And roused himself as much as rouse himself he can.

25

The lad leaped lightly at his master's call.
He was, to weet, a little roguish page,
Save sleep and play who minded naught at all,
Like most the untaught striplings of his age.   220
This boy he kept each band to disengage,
Garters and buckles, task for him unfit,
But ill-becoming his grave personage,
And which his portly paunch would not permit.
So this same limber page to all performèd it.

26

Meantime the master-porter wide displayed
Great store of caps, of slippers, and of gowns,
Wherewith he those who entered in arrayed,
Loose as the breeze that plays along the downs,
And waves the summer woods when evening frowns.   230
O fair undress, best dress! it checks no vein,
But every flowing limb in pleasure drowns,
And heightens ease with grace. This done, right fain
Sir Porter sat him down, and turned to sleep again.

27

Thus easy robed, they to the fountain sped,
That in the middle of the court up-threw
A stream, high-spouting from its liquid bed,
And falling back again in drizzly dew:
There each deep draughts, as deep he thirsted, drew;
It was a fountain of Nepenthe rare: 240
Whence, as Dan Homer sings, huge pleasaunce grew,
And sweet oblivion of vile earthly care,
Fair gladsome waking thoughts, and joyous dreams more fair.

28

This rite performed, all inly pleased and still,
Withouten trump was proclamation made:—
"Ye sons of Indolence, do what you will;
And wander where you list, through hall or glade:
Be no man's pleasure for another's staid:
Let each as likes him best his hours employ,
And curst be he who minds his neighbour's trade!   250
Here dwells kind ease, and unreproving joy:
He little merits bliss who others can annoy."

29

Strait of these endless numbers, swarming round
As thick as idle motes in sunny ray,
Not one eftsoons in view was to be found,
But every man strolled off his own glad way.
Wide o'er this ample court's blank area,
With all the lodges that thereto pertained,
No living creature could be seen to stray;
While solitude and perfect silence reigned: 260
So that to think you dreamt you almost was constrained.

30

As when a shepherd of the Hebrid Isles,
Placed far amid the melancholy main,
(Whether it be lone fancy him beguiles,
Or that aerial beings sometimes deign
To stand embodied to our senses plain)
Sees on the naked hill, or valley low,
The whilst in ocean Phoebus dips his wain,
A vast assembly moving to and fro;
Then all at once in air dissolves the wondrous show.   270

31

Ye gods of quiet, and of sleep profound,
Whose soft dominion o'er this castle sways,
And all the widely-silent places round,
Forgive me, if my trembling pen displays
What never yet was sung in mortal lays.
But how shall I attempt such arduous string?
I who have spent my nights and nightly days
In this soul-deadening place, loose-loitering—
Ah! how shall I for this uprear my moulted wing?

32

Come on, my Muse, nor stoop to low despair,   280
Thou imp of Jove, touched by celestial fire!

218. **to weet**, to wit.   233. **fain**, gladly.   240. **Nepenthe**, a pain-killing drug.   241. **Dan**, Master, a short form of *Dominus*. **sings**, in the *Odyssey*, Book IV, l. 228.   245. **trump**, sound of a trumpet.   246–52. "**Ye . . . annoy**," motto of the Abbey of Theleme, described in Rabelais's *Gargantua*, chap. 57.   268. **wain**, wagon, chariot.   281. **imp**, child.

Thou yet shalt sing of war, and actions fair,
Which the bold sons of Britain will inspire;
Of ancient bards thou yet shalt sweep the lyre;
Thou yet shalt tread in tragic pall the stage,
Paint love's enchanting woes, the hero's ire,
The sage's calm, the patriot's noble rage,
Dashing corruption down through every worthless age.

33

The doors, that knew no shrill alarming bell,
Ne cursèd knocker plied by villain's hand, 290
Self-opened into halls, where, who can tell
What elegance and grandeur wide expand
The pride of Turkey and of Persia land?
Soft quilts on quilts, on carpets carpets spread,
And couches stretched around in seemly band;
And endless pillows rise to prop the head;
So that each spacious room was one full-swelling bed.

34

And everywhere huge covered tables stood,
With wines high-flavoured and rich viands crowned;
Whatever sprightly juice or tasteful food 300
On the green bosom of this Earth are found,
And all old Ocean genders in his round—
Some hand unseen these silently displayed,
Even undemanded by a sign or sound;
You need but wish, and, instantly obeyed,
Fair-ranged the dishes rose, and thick the glasses played.

35

Here freedom reigned without the least alloy;
Nor gossip's tale, nor ancient maiden's gall,
Nor saintly spleen durst murmur at our joy,
And with envenomed tongue our pleasures pall. 310
For why? There was but one great rule for all;
To wit, that each should work his own desire,
And eat, drink, study, sleep, as it may fall,
Or melt the time in love, or wake the lyre,
And carol what, unbid, the Muses might inspire.

36

The rooms with costly tapestry were hung,
Where was inwoven many a gentle tale,
Such as of old the rural poets sung
Or of Arcadian or Sicilian vale:
Reclining lovers, in the lonely dale, 320
Poured forth at large the sweetly tortured heart;
Or, looking tender passion, swelled the gale,
And taught charmed echo to resound their smart;
While flocks, woods, streams around, repose and peace impart.

37

Those pleased the most, where, by a cunning hand,
Depeinten was the patriarchal age;
What time Dan Abraham left the Chaldee land,
And pastured on from verdant stage to stage,
Where fields and fountains fresh could best engage.
Toil was not then. Of nothing took they heed, 330
But with wild beasts the silvan war to wage,
And o'er vast plains their herds and flocks to feed:
Blest sons of nature they! true golden age indeed!

38

Sometimes the pencil, in cool airy halls,
Bade the gay bloom of vernal landskips rise,
Or Autumn's varied shades imbrown the walls:
Now the black tempest strikes the astonished eyes;
Now down the steep the flashing torrent flies;
The trembling sun now plays o'er ocean blue, 339
And now rude mountains frown amid the skies;
Whate'er Lorrain light-touched with softening hue,
Or savage Rosa dashed, or learnèd Poussin drew.

39

Each sound too here to languishment inclined,
Lulled the weak bosom, and inducèd ease,
Aerial music in the warbling wind,
At distance rising oft, by small degrees
Nearer and nearer came, till o'er the trees
It hung, and breathed such soul-dissolving airs
As did, alas! with soft perdition please:
Entangled deep in its enchanting snares, 350
The listening heart forgot all duties and all cares.

40

A certain music, never known before,
Here lulled the pensive melancholy mind;

286–88. **Paint . . . age,** an outline of Thomson's literary plans. **306. played.** Compare Keats's "Eve of St. Agnes," stanzas 29–31. **312. desire.** Compare l. 246.

326. Depeinten, depicted. **334. pencil,** artists' paintbrush. **341. Lorrain,** Claude of Lorraine (Claude Gelée; 1600–1682), French landscape-painter. **342. Rosa,** Salvator Rosa (1615–1673), Italian painter of the Neapolitan school. **Poussin,** Nicolas Poussin (1594–1665), a famous French painter. **352. music . . . before,** scarcely true. The aeolian harp was first described in 1650. It became known in England, however, in the time of Thomson, who wrote a poem about it.

Full easily obtained. Behoves no more,
But sidelong to the gently-waving wind
To lay the well-tuned instrument reclined;
From which, with airy flying fingers light,
Beyond each mortal touch the most refined,
The god of winds drew sounds of deep delight:
Whence, with just cause, The Harp of Aeolus it hight. 360

41

Ah me! what hand can touch the strings so fine?
Who up the lofty diapson roll
Such sweet, such sad, such solemn airs divine,
Then let them down again into the soul?
Now rising love they fanned; now pleasing dole
They breathed, in tender musings, through the heart;
And now a graver sacred strain they stole,
As when seraphic hands an hymn impart:
Wild warbling nature all, above the reach of art!

42

Such the gay splendour, the luxurious state, 370
Of Caliphs old, who on the Tygris' shore,
In mighty Bagdat, populous and great,
Held their bright court, where was of ladies store;
And verse, love, music still the garland wore:
When sleep was coy, the bard in waiting there
Cheered the lone midnight with the Muse's lore;
Composing music bade his dreams be fair,
And music lent new gladness to the morning air.

43

Near the pavilions where we slept, still ran
Soft-tinkling streams, and dashing waters fell, 380
And sobbing breezes sighed, and oft began
(So worked the wizard) wintry storms to swell,
As heaven and earth they would together mell:
At doors and windows, threatening, seemed to call
The demons of the tempest, growling fell;
Yet the least entrance found they none at all;
Whence sweeter grew our sleep, secure in massy hall.

44

And hither Morpheus sent his kindest dreams,
Raising a world of gayer tinct and grace; 389
O'er which were shadowy cast Elysian gleams,
That played in waving lights from place to place,
And shed a roseate smile on nature's face.
Not Titian's pencil e'er could so array,

383. **mell**, mingle. 393. **Titian**, Tiziano Vecellio (1477–1576), Venetian painter.

So fleece with clouds the pure ethereal space;
Ne could it e'er such melting forms display,
As loose on flowery beds all languishingly lay.

45

No, fair illusions! artful phantoms, no!
My Muse will not attempt your fairy-land:
She has no colours that like you can glow;
To catch your vivid scenes too gross her hand. 400
But sure it is, was ne'er a subtler band
Than these same guileful angel-seeming sprites,
Who thus in dreams voluptuous, soft, and bland,
Poured all the Arabian heaven upon our nights,
And blessed them oft besides with more refined delights.

46

They were in sooth a most enchanting train,
Even feigning virtue; skilful to unite
With evil good, and strew with pleasure pain.
But, for those fiends whom blood and broils delight,
Who hurl the wretch as if to hell outright 410
Down, down black gulfs where sullen waters sleep,
Or hold him clambering all the fearful night
On beetling cliffs, or pent in ruins deep—
They, till due time should serve, were bid far hence to keep.

47

Ye guardian spirits, to whom man is dear,
From these foul demons shield the midnight gloom!
Angels of fancy and of love, be near,
And o'er the wilds of sleep diffuse a bloom;
Evoke the sacred shades of Greece and Rome,
And let them virtue with a look impart! 420
But chief, a while, O! lend us from the tomb
Those long-lost friends for whom in love we smart,
And fill with pious awe and joy-mixt woe the heart!

48

Or are you sportive?— bid the morn of youth
Rise to new light, and beam afresh the days
Of innocence, simplicity, and truth,
To cares estranged, and manhood's thorny ways.
What transport to retrace our boyish plays,
Our easy bliss, when each thing joy supplied—
The woods, the mountains, and the warbling maze 430
Of the wild brooks! But, fondly wandering wide,
My Muse, resume the task that yet doth thee abide.

432. **abide**, await.

49

One great amusement of our household was
In a huge crystal magic globe to spy,
Still as you turned it, all things that do pass
Upon this ant-hill earth; where constantly
Of idly-busy men the restless fry
Run bustling to and fro with foolish haste
In search of pleasures vain, that from them fly,
Or which, obtained, the caitiffs dare not taste: 440
When nothing is enjoyed, can there be greater waste?

50

Of Vanity the Mirror this was called.
Here you a muckworm of the town might see
At his dull desk, amid his ledgers stalled,
Eat up with carking care and penurie,
Most like to carcase parched on gallow-tree.
"A penny savèd is a penny got"—
Firm to this scoundrel maxim keepeth he,
Ne of its rigour will he bate a jot,
Till it has quenched his fire, and banishèd his pot. 450

51

Strait from the filth of this low grub, behold!
Comes fluttering forth a gaudy spendthrift heir,
All glossy gay, enamelled all with gold,
The silly tenant of the summer-air.
In folly lost, of nothing takes he care;
Pimps, lawyers, stewards, harlots, flatterers vile,
And thieving tradesmen him among them share:
His father's ghost from Limbo-lake the while
Sees this, which more damnation does upon him pile.

52

This globe portrayed the race of learnèd men, 460
Still at their books, and turning o'er the page
Backwards and forwards: oft they snatch the pen
As if inspired, and in a Thespian rage;
Then write, and blot, as would your ruth engage.
Why, authors, all this scrawl and scribbling sore?
To lose the present, gain the future age,
Praisèd to be when you can hear no more,
And much enriched with fame when useless worldly store!

53

Then would a splendid city rise to view,
With carts, and cars, and coaches roaring all: 470
Wide-poured abroad, behold the prowling crew;
See how they dash along from wall to wall!
At every door, hark how they thundering call!
Good Lord! what can this giddy rout excite?
Why? each on each to prey, by guile or gall;
With flattery these, with slander those to blight;
And make new tiresome parties for the coming night.

54

The puzzling sons of party next appeared,
In dark cabals and nightly juntos met;
And now they whispered close, now shrugging reared 480
The important shoulder; then, as if to get
New light, their twinkling eyes were inward set.
No sooner Lucifer recalls affairs,
Than forth they various rush in mighty fret;
When lo! pushed up to power, and crowned their cares,
In comes another set, and kicketh them down stairs.

55

But what most showed the vanity of life
Was to behold the nations all on fire,
In cruel broils engaged, and deadly strife:
Most Christian kings, inflamed by black desire, 490
With honourable ruffians in their hire,
Cause war to rage, and blood around to pour.
Of this sad work when each begins to tire,
They sit them down just where they were before,
Till for new scenes of woe peace shall their force restore.

56

To number up the thousands dwelling here,
An useless were, and eke an endless task—
From kings, and those who at the helm appear,
To gipsies brown in summer-glades who bask.
Yea, many a man, perdie, I could unmask, 500
Whose desk and table make a solemn show
With tape-tied trash, and suits of fools that ask
For place or pension, laid in decent row;
But these I passen by, with nameless numbers moe.

57

Of all the gentle tenants of the place,
There was a man of special grave remark:
A certain tender gloom o'erspread his face,
Pensive, not sad; in thought involved, not dark:
As soote this man could sing as morning-lark,

---

450. **pot**, of ale. 463. **Thespian,** from Thespis a Greek poet (6th century B.C.), supposed inventor of tragedy. 474. **rout**, crowd. 504. **moe**, more. 506. **man,** probably the poet Collins. 509. **soote,** sweetly.

58

And teach the noblest morals of the heart;   510
But these his talents were yburied stark;
Of the fine stores he nothing would impart,
Which or boon nature gave or nature-painting art.

58

To noontide shades incontinent he ran
Where purls the brook with sleep-inviting sound;
Or, when Dan Sol to slope his wheels began,
Amid the broom he basked him on the ground,
Where the wild thyme and camomil are found:
There would he linger till the latest ray
Of light sat quivering on the welkin's bound; 520
Then homeward through the twilight shadows stray,
Sauntering and slow. So had he passèd many a day.

59

Yet not in thoughtless slumber were they past:
For oft the heavenly fire, that lay concealed
Emongst the sleeping embers, mounted fast,
And all its native light anew revealed.
Oft as he traversed the cerulean field,
And marked the clouds that drove before the wind,
Ten thousand glorious systems would he build,
Ten thousand great ideas filled his mind; 530
But with the clouds they fled, and left no trace behind.

60

With him was sometimes joined in silent walk
(Profoundly silent, for they never spoke)
One shyer still, who quite detested talk:
Oft, stung by spleen, at once away he broke
To groves of pine and broad o'ershadowing oak;
There, inly thrilled, he wandered all alone,
And on himself his pensive fury wroke,
Ne ever uttered word, save when first shone
The glittering star of eve—"Thank Heaven! the day is done." 540

61

Here lurked a wretch who had not crept abroad
For forty years, ne face of mortal seen—
In chamber brooding like a loathly toad;
And sure his linen was not very clean.
Through secret loophole, that had practised been
Near to his bed, his dinner vile he took;
Unkempt, and rough, of squalid face and mien,
Our castle's shame! whence, from his filthy nook,
We drove the villain out for fitter lair to look.

62

One day there chanced into these halls to rove 550
A joyous youth, who took you at first sight;
Him the wild wave of pleasure hither drove,
Before the sprightly tempest tossing light:
Certes, he was a most engaging wight,
Of social glee, and wit humane though keen,
Turning the night to day and day to night:
For him the merry bells had rung, I ween,
If, in this nook of quiet, bells had ever been.

63

But not even pleasure to excess is good:
What most elates then sinks the soul as low: 560
When spring-tide joy pours in with copious flood,
The higher still the exulting billows flow,
The farther back again they flagging go
And leave us grovelling on the dreary shore.
Taught by this son of joy, we found it so;
Who, whilst he staid, kept in a gay uproar
Our maddened Castle all, the abode of sleep no more;

64

As when in prime of June a burnished fly,
Sprung from the meads, o'er which he sweeps along,
Cheered by the breathing bloom and vital sky,
Tunes up amid these airy halls his song, 571
Soothing at first the gay reposing throng:
And oft he sips their bowl; or, nearly drowned,
He, thence recovering, drives their beds among,
And scares their tender sleep with trump profound;
Then out again he flies, to wing his mazy round.

65

Another guest there was, of sense refined,
Who felt each worth,—for every worth he had;
Serene yet warm, humane yet firm his mind,
As little touched as any man's with bad: 580
Him through their inmost walks the Muses lad,
To him the sacred love of Nature lent;
And sometimes would he make our valley glad.
Whenas we found he would not here be pent,
To him the better sort this friendly message sent:—

---

513. boon, generous.   **514. incontinent**, immediately.   **517. broom**, a yellow-flowered shrub.   **534. One**, the poet and physician John Armstrong (1709–1779).   **538. wroke**, wreaked.   **541. wretch**, Henry Welby, an eccentric solitary.   **551. youth**, John Forbes.   **577. guest**, George Lyttleton (1709–1773), statesman and man of letters. He was Thomson's patron.   **581. lad**, led.

66

"Come, dwell with us! true son of virtue, come!
But if, alas! we cannot thee persuade
To lie content beneath our peaceful dome,
Ne ever more to quit our quiet glade;
Yet, when at last thy toils, but ill apaid,   590
Shall dead thy fire and damp its heavenly spark,
Thou wilt be glad to seek the rural shade,
There to indulge the Muse, and Nature mark:
We then a lodge for thee will rear in Hagley Park."

67

Here whilom ligged the Esopus of the age;
But, called by fame, in soul yprickèd deep,
A noble pride restored him to the stage,
And roused him like a giant from his sleep.
Even from his slumbers we advantage reap: 599
With double force the astonished scene he wakes,
Yet quits not nature's bounds. He knows to keep
Each due decorum: now the heart he shakes,
And now with well-urged sense the enlightened judgement takes.

68

A bard here dwelt, more fat than bard beseems,
Who, void of envy, guile, and lust of gain,
On virtue still, and nature's pleasing themes,
Poured forth his unpremeditated strain,
The world forsaking with a calm disdain:
Here laughed he careless in his easy seat;
Here quaffed, encircled with the joyous train;   610
Oft moralizing sage; his ditty sweet
He loathèd much to write, ne carèd to repeat.

69

Full oft by holy feet our ground was trod;
Of clerks good plenty here you mote espy.
A little, round, fat, oily man of God
Was one I chiefly marked among the fry:
He had a roguish twinkle in his eye,
And shone all glittering with ungodly dew,
If a tight damsel chanced to trippen by;
Which when observed, he shrunk into his mew,   620
And straight would recollect his piety anew.

70

Nor be forgot a tribe who minded nought
(Old inmates of the place) but state affairs:

590. **apaid**, satisfied.   594. **Hagley Park,"** Lyttleton's estate in Worcestershire.   595. **whilom ligged**, formerly lay. **Esopus of the age**, James Quin (1693-1766), a famous actor.   604. **bard**, Thomson himself. The stanza was written by Lyttleton.   614. **mote**, might.   615. **man of God**, the Rev. Patrick Murdoch, Thomson's first biographer.   619. **tight**, neat.

They looked, perdie, as if they deeply thought,
And on their brow sat every nation's cares.
The world by them is parcelled out in shares,
When in the Hall of Smoke they congress hold,
And the sage berry sun-burnt Mocha bears
Has cleared their inward eye: then, smoke-enrolled,
Their oracles break forth, mysterious as of old.   630

71

Here languid Beauty kept her pale-faced court:
Bevies of dainty dames of high degree
From every quarter hither made resort;
Where, from gross mortal care and business free,
They lay poured out in ease and luxury.
Or, should they a vain show of work assume,
Alas! and well-a-day! what can it be?
To knot, to twist, to range the vernal bloom;
But far is cast the distaff, spinning-wheel, and loom.

72

Their only labour was to kill the time;   640
And labour dire it is, and weary woe.
They sit, they loll, turn o'er some idle rhyme;
Then, rising sudden, to the glass they go,
Or saunter forth with tottering step and slow:
This soon too rude an exercise they find;
Strait on the couch their limbs again they throw,
Where, hours on hours, they sighing lie reclined,
And court the vapoury god soft-breathing in the wind.

73

Now must I mark the villainy we found,
But ah! too late, as shall eftsoons be shown.   650
A place here was, deep, dreary, under ground,
Where still our inmates, when unpleasing grown,
Diseased, and loathsome, privily were thrown.
Far from the light of heaven they languished there,
Unpitied, uttering many a bitter groan;
For of these wretches taken was no care:
Fierce fiends and hags of hell their only nurses were.

74

Alas the change! from scenes of joy and rest
To this dark den, where sickness tossed alway.
Here Lethargy, with deadly sleep opprest,   660
Stretched on his back, a mighty lubbard lay,
Heaving his sides, and snorèd night and day:
To stir him from his traunce it was not eath,

658. **change!** The following stanzas were written by Dr. Armstrong.   661. **lubbard**, old form of lubber.   663. **eath**, easy.

And his half-opened eyne he shut straitway;
He led, I wot, the softest way to death,
And taught withouten pain and strife to yield the breath.

75

Of limbs enormous, but withal unsound,
Soft-swoln and pale, here lay the Hydropsy:
Unwieldy man! with belly monstrous round,
Forever fed with watery supply; 670
For still he drank, and yet he still was dry.
And moping here did Hypochondria sit,
Mother of Spleen, in robes of various dye,
Who vexèd was full oft with ugly fit;
And some her frantic deemed, and some her deemed a wit.

76

A lady proud she was, of ancient blood,
Yet oft her fear her pride made crouchen low:
She felt, or fancied in her fluttering mood,
All the diseases which the spittles know, 679
And sought all physic which the shops bestow,
And still new leeches and new drugs would try,
Her humour ever wavering to and fro;
For sometimes she would laugh, and sometimes cry,
Then sudden waxèd wroth; and all she knew not why.

77

Fast by her side a listless maiden pined,
With aching head and squeamish heart-burnings;
Pale, bloated, cold, she seemed to hate mankind,
Yet loved in secret all forbidden things.
And here the Tertian shakes his chilling wings;
The sleepless Gout here counts the crowing cocks— 690
A wolf now gnaws him, now a serpent stings:
Whilst Apoplexy crammed Intemperance knocks
Down to the ground at once, as butcher felleth ox.

Thomas Gray
1716–1771

The life of Thomas Gray was that of a retired scholar. Insofar as it is possible for anyone to be that, he was a poet of the library. One thinks of him as usually immured in ivied academic walls, reading enormously. In his youth, to be sure, he saw a good deal of Europe, making the "grand tour" of France and Switzerland and Italy with his friend Horace Walpole. Later, he discovered the "picturesque" landscapes of the Lake District, Scotland, and Wales. Yet it was always his tendency, perhaps in part on account of his frail health, to seek seclusion and quiet. This he found chiefly in a corner with a book.

Born in London on December 26, 1716—the only one in a family of twelve children to reach maturity—Gray had his schooling at Eton and entered Cambridge University. There he remained during the greater part of his life, hating the place for its dullness and ignorance but doing little to reduce its tedium. It was at least a place in which one could read a great many old books, as the newly founded library of the British Museum was also. Gray read old books in great numbers. He attained a scholarship of the white-blooded, miserly kind which has been equaled by only two or three of the English poets. His reading won him, at last, a professorship in modern history, and out of it came also his few, fastidious, and painfully wrought poems.

And yet it will not quite do to suggest that no red corpuscles whatever circulated in the veins of this bibliolatrous old bachelor. Gray's letters alone would show that he was not wholly a cold, withdrawn, and self-centered person. He bound a few friends to him with hoops of steel. Looking closely into his later years, one comes to the conclusion that the early loss of his dearest friend, Richard West, darkened his whole life. Undoubtedly he understood the warmth of human affection, and in some degree he shared it. One can only say that there was little passion in him—or, at any rate, that he never spoke it out. And this may have been for the reason that, born the son of a London scrivener, he was all his life consumed with a yearning for respectability.

One can understand that a man like Gray would be a special darling of scholarly and academic critics—of the same persons, that is, who have for

---

675. frantic, insane. Compare *The Rape of The Lock*, stanza 4, ll. 16–78.   679. spittles, hospitals.   689. Tertian, a fever returning every third day.

two centuries almost ignored the greatly superior creative powers of Gray's fellow collegian Christopher Smart. Examining the scanty text of their hero's poems as it were with a microscope, these gentry have shown to their own satisfaction that Gray's verse falls into three periods: a Neoclassical, a transitional, and a Romantic. But this, if common sense may make bold to say so, is to consider somewhat too curiously. It is to succumb to the temptation of mere labels. We should do better to say that Thomas Gray was all his life conservative and yet also timidly adventurous. He wished to include the past, but not to be imprisoned by it. He loved and needed the changeless peace of antiquity and all the safety of the ancient rules, but yet he was sensitive always to whatever germs of novelty and revolt there might be floating in the intellectual air. In his mind and work, therefore, the terms "Neoclassical" and "Romantic" collide—and are obliterated.

ODE ON A DISTANT PROSPECT OF ETON COLLEGE

The spires of Eton and of Windsor Castle were visible in Gray's time from the village of Stoke Poges, where, in the summer of 1742, this poem was written. Gray's recollection of the brief happiness he had enjoyed in his school days at Eton was darkened at this time by the fact that he had recently lost the dearest of his boyhood companions, Richard West, and that he was temporarily estranged from two other friends, Thomas Ashton and Horace Walpole, who were also fellow Etonians.

Ye distant spires, ye antique towers,
That crown the watery glade,
Where grateful Science still adores
Her HENRY's holy Shade;
And ye, that from the stately brow
Of WINDSOR's heights the expanse below
Of grove, of lawn, of mead survey,
Whose turf, whose shade, whose flowers among
Wanders the hoary Thames along
His silver-winding way: 10

Ah happy hills, ah, pleasing shade,
Ah fields beloved in vain,
Where once my careless childhood strayed,
A stranger yet to pain!
I feel the gales that from ye blow
A momentary bliss bestow,
As, waving fresh their gladsome wing,
My weary soul they seem to sooth,
And, redolent of joy and youth,
To breathe a second spring.   20

4. Henry, Henry VI, founder of Eton College.

Say, Father THAMES, for thou hast seen
Full many a sprightly race
Disporting on thy margent green
The paths of pleasure trace,
Who foremost now delight to cleave
With pliant arm thy glassy wave?
The captive linnet which enthrall?
What idle progeny succeed
To chase the rolling circle's speed,
Or urge the flying ball?   30

While some on earnest business bent
Their murmuring labours ply
'Gainst graver hours, that bring constraint
To sweeten liberty:
Some bold adventurers disdain
The limits of their little reign,
And unknown regions dare descry:
Still as they run they look behind,
They hear a voice in every wind,
And snatch a fearful joy.   40

Gay hope is theirs, by fancy fed,
Less pleasing when possest;
The tear forgot as soon as shed,
The sunshine of the breast;
Theirs buxom health of rosy hue,
Wild wit, invention ever new,
And lively cheer of vigour born;
The thoughtless day, the easy night,
The spirits pure, the slumbers light,
That fly the approach of morn.   50

Alas, regardless of their doom,
The little victims play!
No sense have they of ills to come,
Nor care beyond to-day:
Yet see how all around 'em wait
The Ministers of human fate,
And black Misfortune's baleful train!
Ah, shew them where in ambush stand
To seize their prey the murtherous band!
Ah, tell them, they are men!   60

These shall the fury Passions tear,
The vultures of the mind,
Disdainful Anger, pallid Fear,
And Shame that skulks behind;
Or pining Love shall waste their youth,
Or Jealousy with rankling tooth,
That inly gnaws the secret heart,
And Envy wan, and faded Care,
Grim-visaged comfortless Despair,
And Sorrow's piercing dart.   70

29. circle, hoop.

Ambition this shall tempt to rise,
Then whirl the wretch from high,
To bitter Scorn a sacrifice,
And grinning Infamy.
The stings of Falsehood those shall try,
And hard Unkindness' altered eye,
That mocks the tear it forced to flow;
And keen Remorse with blood defiled,
And moody Madness laughing wild
Amid severest woe.   80

Lo, in the vale of years beneath
A grisly troop are seen,
The painful family of Death,
More hideous than their Queen:
This racks the joints, this fires the veins,
That every labouring sinew strains,
Those in the deeper vitals rage:
Lo, Poverty, to fill the band,
That numbs the soul with icy hand,
And slow-consuming Age.   90

To each his sufferings: all are men,
Condemned alike to groan,
The tender for another's pain;
The unfeeling for his own.
Yet ah! why should they know their fate?
Since sorrow never comes too late,
And happiness too swiftly flies.
Thought would destroy their paradise.
No more; where ignorance is bliss,
'Tis folly to be wise.

ELEGY WRITTEN IN A COUNTRY CHURCH-YARD

Gray began the best and most famous of his poems at Stoke Poges, near Windsor, in the summer of 1742, shortly after the death of his dearest friend, Richard West. The scene of the poem is probably the Stoke Poges churchyard, with which he had been familiar from boyhood. Finally published in 1751, the *Elegy* was immediately successful. It has long been one of the most widely familiar poems in the language.

Sir Edmund Gosse expressed the common belief in saying that Gray's *Elegy* "belongs to a class apart, as it is not addressed to the memory of any particular person." The fact is demonstrable, however, that the last nine stanzas of the poem were written with Richard West in mind. We should not, therefore, read the "Epitaph" at the end with the awkward, and indeed the rather absurd, supposition that Gray is there referring to himself.

Although its sympathetic treatment of obscure and humble lives does mark a new departure of high importance, the *Elegy* is a triumph not of genius but of learned and patient artistry. Its thought is commonplace, and it contains no single stanza, hardly a line or an image, for which no literary source can be found. It is a masterly arrangement of old materials.

The Curfew tolls the knell of parting day,
The lowing herd wind slowly o'er the lea,
The plowman homeward plods his weary way,
And leaves the world to darkness and to me.

Now fades the glimmering landscape on the sight,
And all the air a solemn stillness holds,
Save where the beetle wheels his droning flight,
And drowsy tinklings lull the distant folds;

Save that from yonder ivy-mantled tower
The moping owl does to the moon complain   10
Of such as, wandering near her secret bower,
Molest her ancient solitary reign.

Beneath those rugged elms, that yew-tree's shade,
Where heaves the turf in many a mouldering heap,
Each in his narrow cell for ever laid,
The rude Forefathers of the hamlet sleep.

The breezy call of incense-breathing Morn,
The swallow twittering from the straw-built shed,
The cock's shrill clarion, or the echoing horn,
No more shall rouse them from their lowly bed.   20

For them no more the blazing hearth shall burn,
Or busy housewife ply her evening care:
No children run to lisp their sire's return,
Or climb his knees the envied kiss to share.

Oft did the harvest to their sickle yield,
Their furrow oft the stubborn glebe has broke;
How jocund did they drive their team afield!
How bowed the woods beneath their sturdy stroke!

Let not Ambition mock their useful toil,
Their homely joys, and destiny obscure;   30
Nor Grandeur hear with a disdainful smile
The short and simple annals of the poor.

The boast of heraldry, the pomp of power,
And all that beauty, all that wealth e'er gave,
Awaits alike the inevitable hour.
The paths of glory lead but to the grave.

Nor you, ye Proud, impute to These the fault,
If Memory o'er their Tomb no Trophies raise,

16. **rude,** unlettered.   33. **heraldry,** noble lineage.
35. **Awaits.** The hour of death lies in wait for **beauty, wealth, glory.**

Where through the long-drawn aisle and fretted vault
The pealing anthem swells the note of praise.   40

Can storied urn or animated bust
Back to its mansion call the fleeting breath?
Can Honour's voice provoke the silent dust,
Or Flattery soothe the dull cold ear of Death?

Perhaps in this neglected spot is laid
Some heart once pregnant with celestial fire;
Hands, that the rod of empire might have swayed,
Or waked to extasy the living lyre.

But Knowledge to their eyes her ample page
Rich with the spoils of time did ne'er unroll;   50
Chill Penury repressed their noble rage,
And froze the genial current of the soul.

Full many a gem of purest ray serene,
The dark unfathomed caves of ocean bear:
Full many a flower is born to blush unseen,
And waste its sweetness on the desert air.

Some village-Hampden, that with dauntless breast
The little Tyrant of his fields withstood;
Some mute, inglorious Milton here may rest,
Some Cromwell guiltless of his country's blood.   60

The applause of listening senates to command,
The threats of pain and ruin to despise,
To scatter plenty o'er a smiling land,
And read their history in a nation's eyes,

Their lot forbad: nor circumscribed alone
Their growing virtues, but their crimes confined;
Forbad to wade through slaughter to a throne,
And shut the gates of mercy on mankind;

The struggling pangs of conscious truth to hide,
To quench the blushes of ingenuous shame,   70
Or heap the shrine of Luxury and Pride
With incense kindled at the Muse's flame.

Far from the madding crowd's ignoble strife,
Their sober wishes never learned to stray;
Along the cool sequestered vale of life
They kept the noiseless tenor of their way.

Yet ev'n these bones from insult to protect,
Some frail memorial still erected nigh,
With uncouth rhimes and shapeless sculpture decked,
Implores the passing tribute of a sigh.   80

Their name, their years, spelt by the unlettered Muse,
The place of fame and elegy supply;
And many a holy text around she strews,
That teach the rustic moralist to die.

For who to dumb Forgetfulness a prey,
This pleasing anxious being e'er resigned,
Left the warm precincts of the chearful day,
Nor cast one longing lingering look behind?

On some fond breast the parting soul relies,
Some pious drops the closing eye requires;   90
Ev'n from the tomb the voice of Nature cries,
Ev'n in our Ashes live their wonted Fires.

For thee who, mindful of the unhonoured Dead,
Dost in these lines their artless tale relate;
If chance, by lonely contemplation led,
Some kindred Spirit shall inquire thy fate,

Haply some hoary-headed Swain may say,
"Oft have we seen him at the peep of dawn
Brushing with hasty steps the dews away,
To meet the sun upon the upland lawn.   100

"There at the foot of yonder nodding beech
That wreathes its old fantastic roots so high,
His listless length at noontide would he stretch,
And pore upon the brook that babbles by.

"Hard by yon wood, now smiling as in scorn,
Muttering his wayward fancies he would rove;
Now drooping, woeful wan, like one forlorn,
Or crazed with care, or crossed in hopeless love.

"One morn I missed him on the customed hill,
Along the heath, and near his favourite tree;   110
Another came; nor yet beside the rill,
Nor up the lawn, nor at the wood was he;

"The next with dirges due in sad array,
Slow through the church-way path we saw him borne.
Approach and read (for thou can'st read) the lay,
Graved on the stone beneath yon agèd thorn."

---

39. fretted, decorated. **41. storied urn**, a funeral urn with an inscription. **animated**, like life. **43. provoke**, call forth. **51. rage**, enthusiasm. **52. genial**, giving life. **57. Hampden**, John Hampden, English patriot (1595–1643). **78. still**, always.

82. elegy, versified praise. **98. him**, usually taken to refer to Gray. More probably the person described in the following lines and in the Epitaph is Richard West.

THE EPITAPH

Here rests his head upon the lap of Earth,
A Youth to Fortune and to Fame unknown.
Fair Science frowned not on his humble birth,
And Melancholy marked him for her own. 120

Large was his bounty, and his soul sincere,
Heaven did a recompence as largely send:
He gave to Misery all he had, a tear,
He gained from Heaven ('twas all he wished) a friend.

No farther seek his merits to disclose,
Or draw his frailties from their dread abode,
(There they alike in trembling hope repose,)
The bosom of his Father and his God.

SONNET

ON THE DEATH OF MR. RICHARD WEST

In vain to me the smiling Mornings shine,
   And reddening Phoebus lifts his golden Fire:
The Birds in vain their amorous Descant joyn,
   Or chearful Fields resume their green Attire:
These Ears, alas! for other Notes repine,
   A different Object do these Eyes require.
My lonely Anguish melts no Heart but mine;
   And in my Breast the imperfect Joys expire.
Yet Morning smiles the busy Race to chear, 9
   And new-born Pleasure brings to happier Men:
The Fields to all their wonted Tribute bear:
   To warm their little Loves the Birds complain:
I fruitless mourn to him, that cannot hear,
   And weep the more because I weep in vain.

HYMN TO ADVERSITY

This poem, based upon one of the *Odes* of Horace and resting mainly upon ancient Stoical thought, is chiefly important, perhaps, because it suggested Wordsworth's "Ode to Duty."

   Daughter of Jove, relentless Power,
   Thou Tamer of the human breast,
   Whose iron scourge and torturing hour,
   The Bad affright, afflict the Best!
   Bound in thy adamantine chain
   The Proud are taught to taste of pain,
   And purple Tyrants vainly groan
   With pangs unfelt before, unpitied and alone.

When first thy Sire to send on earth
Virtue, his darling Child, designed, 10
To thee he gave the heavenly Birth,
And bad to form her infant mind.
Stern rugged Nurse! thy rigid lore
With patience many a year she bore:
What sorrow was, thou bad'st her know,
And from her own she learned to melt at others' woe.

Scared at thy frown terrific, fly
Self-pleasing Folly's idle brood,
Wild Laughter, Noise, and thoughtless Joy,
And leave us leisure to be good. 20
Light they disperse, and with them go
The summer Friend, the flattering Foe;
By vain Prosperity received,
To her they vow their truth, and are again believed.

Wisdom in sable garb arrayed,
Immersed in rapturous thought profound,
And Melancholy, silent maid
With leaden eye, that loves the ground,
Still on thy solemn steps attend:
Warm Charity, the general Friend, 30
With Justice to herself severe,
And Pity, dropping soft the sadly-pleasing tear.

Oh, gently on thy Suppliant's head,
Dread Goddess, lay thy chastening hand!
Not in thy Gorgon terrors clad,
Nor circled with the vengeful Band
(As by the Impious thou art seen)
With thundering voice, and threatening mien,
With screaming Horror's funeral cry,
Despair, and fell Disease, and ghastly Poverty. 40

Thy form benign, oh Goddess, wear,
Thy milder influence impart,
Thy philosophic Train be there
To soften, not to wound my heart.
The generous spark extinct revive,
Teach me to love and to forgive,
Exact my own defects to scan,
What others are to feel, and know myself a Man.

THE PROGRESS OF POESY

A PINDARIC ODE

This poem and "The Bard" are obviously the work of one who cares more for scholarship than he does for po-

---

Hymn to Adversity. **7. purple,** a kind of crimson worn by ancient emperors. **8. pangs unfelt before,** from *Paradise Lost*, Book II, l. 703.

21. Light, swiftly. **28. leaden,** suggested by Milton's "Il Penseroso." **36. vengeful Band,** the Furies. **37. Impious,** undutiful to parents. **43. Train,** as enumerated in the fourth stanza. **47. Exact,** an adjective.

etry. The tripartite divisions are worked out in imitation of the strict though intricate symmetry of the odes of Pindar, and the style of the two poems is also intended to be Pindaric. Dr. Johnson said of them that "they are marked by a glittering accumulation of ungraceful ornaments." Gray himself admitted that they were "on stilts."

$$\text{Φωνᾶντα συνετοῖσιν ἐς}$$
$$\text{Δὲ τὸ πᾶν ἑρμηνέων χατίζει.}$$
Pindar, Olymp. II

I. 1.

Awake, Aeolian lyre, awake,
And give to rapture all thy trembling strings.
From Helicon's harmonious springs
A thousand rills their mazy progress take:
The laughing flowers, that round them blow,
Drink life and fragrance as they flow.
Now the rich stream of music winds along
Deep, majestic, smooth, and strong,
Through verdant vales, and Ceres' golden reign:
Now rolling down the steep amain,   10
Headlong, impetuous, see it pour:
The rocks, and nodding groves rebellow to the roar.

I. 2.

Oh! Sovereign of the willing soul,
Parent of sweet and solemn-breathing airs,
Enchanting shell! the sullen Cares
And frantic Passions hear thy soft controul.
On Thracia's hills the Lord of War
Has curbed the fury of his car,
And dropped his thirsty lance at thy command.
Perching on the sceptered hand   20
Of Jove, thy magic lulls the feathered king,
With ruffled plumes, and flagging wing;
Quenched in dark clouds of slumber lie
The terror of his beak, and lightnings of his eye.

I. 3.

Thee the voice, the dance, obey,
Tempered to thy warbled lay.
O'er Idalia's velvet-green
The rosy-crownèd Loves are seen
On Cytherea's day
With antic Sports, and blue-eyed Pleasures,   30
Frisking light in frolic measures;
Now pursuing, now retreating,
Now in circling troops they meet:
To brisk notes in cadence beating
Glance their many-twinkling feet.
Slow melting strains their Queen's approach declare:
Where'er she turns the Graces homage pay.
With arms sublime, that float upon the air,
In gliding state she wins her easy way:
O'er her warm cheek, and rising bosom, move   40
The bloom of young Desire and purple light of Love.

II. 1.

Man's feeble race what Ills await,
Labour, and Penury, the racks of Pain,
Disease, and Sorrow's weeping train,
And Death, sad refuge from the storms of Fate!
The fond complaint, my Song, disprove,
And justify the laws of Jove.
Say, has he given in vain the heavenly Muse?
Night, and all her sickly dews,
Her Spectres wan, and Birds of boding cry   50
He gives to range the dreary sky:
Till down the eastern cliffs afar
Hyperion's march they spy, and glittering shafts of war.

II. 2.

In climes beyond the solar road,
Where shaggy forms o'er ice-built mountains roam,
The Muse has broke the twilight-gloom
To cheer the shivering Native's dull abode.
And oft, beneath the odorous shade
Of Chili's boundless forests laid,
She deigns to hear the savage Youth repeat   60
In loose numbers wildly sweet
Their feathered-cinctured Chiefs and dusky Loves.
Her track, where'er the Goddess roves,
Glory pursue, and generous Shame,
The unconquerable Mind, and Freedom's holy flame.

II. 3.

Woods, that wave o'er Delphi's steep,
Isles, that crown the Egaean deep,
Fields, that cool Ilissus laves,
Or where Maeander's amber waves
In lingering Labyrinths creep,   70
How do your tuneful Echoes languish,
Mute, but to the voice of Anguish?

Φωνᾶντα ... χατίζει. A voice understood by the wise, but needing interpretation to the ignorant.
   1. lyre, the lyre of Pindar, who called his verse **Aeolian**. **3. Helicon's**, of a mountain range in Boeotia, home of the Muses. **9. reign**, realm. **15. shell!** the lyre, first made of a tortoise shell. **21. king**, the eagle of Jove. **27. Idalia**, a town sacred to Venus, in Cyprus.

   38. sublime, held high. **46. fond**, foolish. **53. Hyperion's march**, sunrise. **54. In climes ... road**, translation of the *Aeneid*, Book VI, l. 796. **66. steep**, Parnassus which rises above the Delphic oracle. **68. Ilissus**, a river near Athens. **69. Maeander**, a winding river in Asia Minor.

Where each old poetic Mountain
Inspiration breathed around:
Every shade and hallowed Fountain
Murmured deep a solemn sound:
Till the sad Nine in Greece's evil hour
Left their Parnassus for the Latian plains.
Alike they scorn the pomp of tyrant-Power,
And coward Vice, that revels in her chains. 80
When Latium had her lofty spirit lost,
They sought, oh Albion! next, thy sea-encircled coast.

III. 1.

Far from the sun and summer-gale,
In thy green lap was Nature's Darling laid,
What time, where lucid Avon strayed,
To Him the mighty Mother did unveil
Her aweful face: The dauntless Child
Stretched forth his little arms, and smiled.
This pencil take (she said) whose colours clear
Richly paint the vernal year: 90
Thine too these golden keys, immortal Boy!
This can unlock the gates of Joy;
Of Horrour that, and thrilling Fears,
Or ope the sacred source of sympathetic Tears.

III. 2.

Nor second He, that rode sublime
Upon the seraph-wings of Extasy,
The secrets of the Abyss to spy.
He passed the flaming bounds of Place and Time:
The living Throne, the sapphire-blaze,
Where Angels tremble while they gaze, 100
He saw; but blasted with excess of light,
Closed his eyes in endless night.
Behold where Dryden's less presumptuous car,
Wide o'er the fields of Glory bear
Two Coursers of ethereal race,
With necks in thunder cloathed, and long-resounding pace.

III. 3.

Hark, his hands the lyre explore!
Bright-eyed **Fancy** hovering o'er,
Scatters from her pictured urn
Thoughts that breathe, and words that burn 110
But ah! 'tis heard no more—
Oh! Lyre divine, what daring Spirit
Wakes thee now? Though he inherit
Nor the pride, nor ample pinion,

84. Darling, Shakespeare. **95. He,** Milton. **98. flaming bounds,** imitated from Lucretius. **105. Two Coursers,** suggesting Dryden's mastery of the heroic couplet. **112. Spirit,** Thomas Gray.

That the Theban Eagle bear,
Sailing with supreme dominion
Through the azure deep of air:
Yet oft before his infant eyes would run
Such forms, as glitter in the Muse's ray
With orient hues, unborrowed of the Sun; 120
Yet shall he mount, and keep his distant way
Beyond the limits of a vulgar fate,
Beneath the Good how far—but far above the great.

THE BARD

A PINDARIC ODE

"The Bard" is based upon a legend that King Edward I of England, when he overran Wales in 1276–84, ordered that all the Welsh bards should be put to death.

Gray gives the following plan:

The army of Edward I, as they march through a deep valley and approach Mount Snowdon, are suddenly stopped by the appearance of a venerable figure seated on the summit of an inaccessible rock, who, with a voice more than human, reproaches the king with all the desolation and misery which he had brought upon his country, foretells the misfortunes of the Norman race, and with prophetic spirit declares that all his cruelty shall never extinguish the noble ardour of poetic genius in this island, and that men shall never be wanting to celebrate true virtue and valour in immortal strains, to expose vice and infamous pleasure, and boldly censure tyranny and oppression. His song ended, he precipitates himself from the mountain and is swallowed up in the river that rolls at its foot.

I. 1.

"Ruin seize thee, ruthless King!
Confusion on thy banners wait,
Though fanned by Conquest's crimson wing
They mock the air with idle state.
Helm, nor Hauberk's twisted mail,
Nor e'en thy virtues, Tyrant, shall avail
To save thy secret soul from nightly fears,
From Cambria's curse, from Cambria's tears!"
Such were the sounds, that o'er the crested pride
Of the first Edward scattered wild dismay, 10
As down the steep of Snowdon's shaggy side
He wound with toilsome march his long array.
Stout Glo'ster stood aghast in speechless trance:
To arms! cried Mortimer, and couched his quivering lance.

I. 2.

On a rock, whose haughty brow
Frowns o'er old Conway's foaming flood,

115. Theban Eagle, Pindar. *The Bard.* **8. Cambria,** Wales. **13. Glo'ster,** The Earl of Gloucester and Hereford, King Edward's son-in-law.

Robed in the sable garb of woe,
With haggard eyes the Poet stood
(Loose his beard, and hoary hair
Streamed, like a meteor, to the troubled air)   20
And with a Master's hand and Prophet's fire
Struck the deep sorrows of his lyre.
"Hark, how each giant-oak, and desert cave,
Sighs to the torrent's aweful voice beneath!
O'er thee, oh King! their hundred arms they wave,
Revenge on thee in hoarser murmurs breath;
Vocal no more, since Cambria's fatal day,
To high-born Hoel's harp, or soft Llewellyn's lay.

I. 3.

"Cold is Cadwallo's tongue,
That hushed the stormy main;   30
Brave Urien sleeps upon his craggy bed:
Mountains, ye mourn in vain
Modred, whose magic song
Made huge Plinlimmon bow his cloud-topped head.
On dreary Arvon's shore they lie,
Smeared with gore, and ghastly pale:
Far, far aloof the affrighted ravens sail;
The famished Eagle screams, and passes by.
Dear lost companions of my tuneful art,
Dear as the light that visits these sad eyes,   40
Dear as the ruddy drops that warm my heart,
Ye died amidst your dying country's cries—
No more I weep. They do not sleep.
On yonder cliffs, a griesly band,
I see them sit; they linger yet,
Avengers of their native land:
With me in dreadful harmony they join,
And weave with bloody hands the tissue of thy line.

II. 1.

" 'Weave the warp, and weave the woof,
The winding-sheet of Edward's race.   50
Give ample room, and verge enough
The characters of hell to trace.
Mark the year, and mark the night,
When Severn shall re-echo with affright
The shrieks of death, through Berkley's roofs that ring,
Shrieks of an agonizing King!
She-Wolf of France, with unrelenting fangs,
That tear'st the bowels of thy mangled Mate,
From thee be born, who o'er thy country hangs
The scourge of Heaven. What Terrors round him wait!   60

Amazement in his van, with Flight combined,
And sorrow's faded form, and solitude behind.

II. 2.

" 'Mighty Victor, mighty Lord,
Low on his funeral couch he lies!
No pitying heart, no eye, afford
A tear to grace his obsequies.
Is the sable Warriour fled?
Thy son is gone. He rests among the Dead.
The Swarm that in thy noon-tide beam were born?
Gone to salute the rising Morn.   70
Fair laughs the Morn, and soft the Zephyr blows,
While proudly riding o'er the azure realm
In gallant trim the gilded Vessel goes;
Youth on the prow, and Pleasure at the helm;
Regardless of the sweeping Whirlwind's sway,
That, hushed in grim repose, expects his evening-prey.

II. 3.

" 'Fill high the sparkling bowl,
The rich repast prepare,
Reft of a crown, he yet may share the feast:
Close by the regal chair   80
Fell Thirst and Famine scowl
A baleful smile upon their baffled Guest.
Heard ye the din of battle bray,
Lance to lance, and horse to horse?
Long Years of havock urge their destined course,
And through the kindred squadrons mow their way.
Ye Towers of Julius, London's lasting shame,
With many a foul and midnight murther fed,
Revere his Consort's faith, his Father's fame,
And spare the meek Usurper's holy head.   90
Above, below, the rose of snow,
Twined with her blushing foe, we spread:
The bristled Boar in infant-gore
Wallows beneath the thorny shade.
Now, Brothers, bending o'er the accursèd loom,
Stamp we our vengeance deep, and ratify his doom.

III. 1.

" 'Edward, lo! to sudden fate
(Weave we the woof. The thread is spun)
Half of thy heart we consecrate.
(The web is wove. The work is done.)' "   100
"Stay, oh stay! nor thus forlorn

28. **Hoel,** a royal poet of the twelfth century. **lay,** poem. 34. **Plinlimmon,** a mountain in Wales. 35. **shore,** opposite Anglesea. 56. **King!** Edward II, murdered at Berkeley Castle. 57. **She-Wolf,** Isabel of France, wife of Edward II. 60. **him,** Edward III. 67. **sable Warriour,** Edward the Black Prince. 85. **havock,** the Wars of the Roses. 89. **Consort,** Margaret of Anjou, wife of Henry VI. **Father,** Henry V. 90. **Usurper,** Henry VI. 92. **foe,** the red rose of Lancaster, foe to the white rose of York. 93. **Boar,** emblem of Richard III. 101. **Stay.** From this point the Bard speaks only for himself.

Leave me unblessed, unpitied, here to mourn:
In yon bright track, that fires the western skies,
They melt, they vanish from my eyes.
But oh! what solemn scenes on Snowdon's height
Descending slow their glittering skirts unroll?
Visions of glory, spare my aching sight,
Ye unborn Ages, crowd not on my soul!
No more our long-lost Arthur we bewail.   109
All-hail, ye genuine Kings, Britannia's Issue, hail!

III. 2.

"Girt with many a baron bold
Sublime their starry fronts they rear;
And gorgeous Dames, and Statesman old
In bearded majesty, appear.
In the midst a Form divine!
Her eye proclaims her of the Briton-Line;
Her lyon-port, her awe-commanding face,
Attempered sweet to virgin-grace.
What strings symphonious tremble in the air,
What strains of vocal transport round her play! 120
Hear from the grave, great Taliessin, hear;
They breathe a soul to animate thy clay.
Bright Rapture calls, and soaring, as she sings,
Waves in the eye of Heaven her many-coloured wings.

III. 3.

"The verse adorn again
Fierce War, and faithful Love,
And Truth severe, by fairy Fiction drest.
In buskined measures move
Pale Grief, and pleasing Pain,
With Horrour, tyrant of the throbbing breast.   130
A Voice, as of the Cherub-Choir,
Gales from blooming Eden bear;
And distant warblings lessen on my ear,
That lost in long futurity expire.
Fond impious Man, think'st thou, yon sanguine cloud,
Raised by thy breath, has quenched the Orb of day?
To-morrow he repairs the golden flood,
And warms the nations with redoubled ray.
Enough for me: with joy I see
The different doom our Fates assign.   140
Be thine Despair, and sceptered Care;
To triumph, and to die, are mine."

_{109. **Arthur,** regarded by the Welsh as still living. 110. **Kings,** of the House of Tudor, which was of Welsh origin.   115. **Form divine!** Queen Elizabeth.   120. **strains,** Elizabethan poetry.   121. **Taliessin,** a Welsh bard. 127. **drest,** in Spenser's *Faerie Queene*.   128. **measures,** of Shakespeare's tragedies.   131. **Voice,** Milton.   133. **warblings,** of poets following Milton.   135. **Man,** Edward I.}

He spoke, and headlong from the mountain's height
Deep in the roaring tide he plunged to endless night.

THE FATAL SISTERS

AN ODE

Most of the difficulties in this poem are cleared up by Gray's prefatory note:

In the eleventh century, Sigurd, Earl of the Orkney Islands, went with a fleet of ships and a considerable body of troops into Ireland, to the assistance of Sictryg with the Silken Beard, who was then making war on his father-in-law, Brian, king of Dublin. The earl and all his forces were cut to pieces, and Sictryg was in danger of a total defeat; but the enemy had a greater loss by the death of Brian, their king, who fell in the action. On Christmas Day (the day of the battle) a native of Caithness, in Scotland, saw at a distance a number of persons on horseback riding full speed towards a hill, and seeming to enter it. Curiosity led him to follow them, till, looking through an opening in the rocks, he saw twelve gigantic figures resembling women. They were all employed about a loom, and, as they wove, they sung the following dreadful song; which when they had finished, they tore the web into twelve pieces and, each taking her own portion, galloped six to the north and as many to the south.

Gray gives the impression elsewhere in this note that he had translated the poem directly from the Norse tongue, but it is now known that he could scarcely read Old Norse and that he must have depended upon a Latin version.

The Fatal Sisters of the poem are Valkyries, or choosers of the slain.

Now the storm begins to lower,
  (Haste, the loom of Hell prepare,)
Iron-sleet of arrowy shower
  Hurtles in the darkened air.

Glittering lances are the loom,
  Where the dusky warp we strain,
Weaving many a Soldier's doom,
  Orkney's woe, and *Randver's* bane.

See the griesly texture grow,
  ('Tis of human entrails made,)   10
And the weights that play below,
  Each a gasping Warriour's head.

Shafts for shuttles, dipt in gore,
  Shoot the trembling cords along.
Sword, that once a Monarch bore,
  Keep the tissue close and strong.

Mista black, terrific Maid,
Sangrida, and *Hilda* see,
Join the wayward work to aid:
'Tis the woof of victory.   20

Ere the ruddy sun be set,
Pikes must shiver, javelins sing,
Blade with clattering buckler meet,
Hauberk crash, and helmet ring.

(Weave the crimson web of war.)
Let us go, and let us fly,
Where our Friends the conflict share,
Where they triumph, where they die.

As the paths of fate we tread,
Wading through the ensanguined field: 30
Gondula and *Geira*, spread
O'er the youthful King your shield.

We the reins to slaughter give,
Ours to kill, and ours to spare:
Spite of danger he shall live.
(Weave the crimson web of war.)

They whom once the desart-beach
Pent within its bleak domain,
Soon their ample sway shall stretch
O'er the plenty of the plain.   40

Low the dauntless Earl is laid,
Gored with many a gaping wound:
Fate demands a nobler head;
Soon a King shall bite the ground.

Long his loss shall Eirin weep,
Ne'er again his likeness see;
Long her strains in sorrow steep,
Strains of Immortality!

Horror covers all the heath,
Clouds of carnage blot the sun.   50
Sisters, weave the web of death;
Sisters, cease, the work is done.

Hail the task, and hail the hands!
Songs of joy and triumph sing!
Joy to the victorious bands;
Triumph to the younger King.

Mortal, thou that hear'st the tale,
Learn the tenour of our song.

Scotland, through each winding vale
Far and wide the notes prolong.   60

Sisters, hence with spurs of speed:
Each her thundering faulchion wield;
Each bestride her sable steed.
Hurry, hurry to the field.

LETTERS

TO RICHARD WEST

YOU must know that I do not take degrees, and, after this term, shall have nothing more of college impertinences to undergo, which I trust will be some pleasure to you, as it is a great one to me. I have endured lectures daily and hourly since I came last, supported by the hopes of being shortly at full liberty to give myself up to my friends and classical companions, who, poor souls! though I see them fallen into great contempt with most people here, yet I cannot help sticking to them, and out of a spirit of obstinacy (I think) love them the better for it; and indeed, what can I do else? Must I plunge into metaphysics? Alas, I cannot see in the dark; nature has not furnished me with the optics of a cat. Must I pore upon mathematics? Alas, I cannot see in too much light; I am no eagle. It is very possible that two and two make four, but I would not give four farthings to demonstrate this ever so clearly; and if these be the profits of life, give me the amusements of it. The people I behold all around me, it seems, know all this and more, and yet I do not know one of them who inspires me with any ambition of being like him. Surely it was of this place, now Cambridge, but formerly known by the name of Babylon, that the prophet spoke when he said, "the wild beasts of the desert shall dwell there, and their houses shall be full of doleful creatures, and owls shall build there, and satyrs shall dance there; their forts and towers shall be a den for ever, a joy of wild asses; there shall the great owl make her nest, and lay and hatch and gather under her shadow; it shall be a court of dragons; the screech owl also shall rest there, and find for herself a place of rest." You see here is a pretty collection of desolate animals, which is verified in this town to a tittle, and perhaps it may also allude to your habitation, for you know all types may be taken by abundance of handles; however, I defy your owls to match mine.

If the default of your spirits and nerves be nothing but the effect of the hyp, I have no more to say.

32. **King,** Sictryg.   37. **They,** the Norse.   40. **plain,** near Dublin.   41. **Earl,** Sigurd.   44. **King,** Brian.   56. **King,** Sictryg.

36. **habitation,** Oxford.   41. **hyp,** hypochondria.

We all must submit to that wayward queen; I too in no small degree own her sway,

"I feel her influence while I speak her power."

But if it be a real distemper, pray take more care of your health, if not for your own at least for our sakes, and do not be so soon weary of this little world. I do not know what refined friendships you may have contracted in the other, but pray do not be in a hurry to see your acquaintance above; among your terrestrial familiars, however, though I say it, that should not say it, there positively is not one that has a greater esteem for you than yours most sincerely, etc.

Peterhouse, December, 1736.

TO HORACE WALPOLE

I WAS hindered in my last, and so could not give you all the trouble I would have done. The description of a road, which your coach wheels have so often honoured, it would be needless to give you; suffice it that I arrived safe at my Uncle's, who is a great hunter in imagination; his dogs take up every chair in the house, so I am forced to stand at this present writing; and though the gout forbids him galloping after them in the field, yet he continues still to regale his ears and nose with their comfortable noise and stink. He holds me mighty cheap, I perceive, for walking when I should ride, and reading when I should hunt. My comfort amidst all this is, that I have at the distance of half a mile, through a green lane, a forest (the vulgar call it a common) all my own, at least as good as so, for I spy no human thing in it but myself. It is a little chaos of mountains and precipices; mountains, it is true, that do not ascend much above the clouds, nor are the declivities quite so amazing as Dover cliff; but just such hills as people who love their necks as well as I do may venture to climb, and craggs that give the eye as much pleasure as if they were more dangerous. Both vale and hill are covered with most venerable beeches, and other very reverend vegetables, that, like most other ancient people, are always dreaming out their old stories to the winds,

"And as they bow their hoary tops relate,
In murmuring sounds, the dark decrees of fate;
While visions, as poetic eyes avow,
Cling to each leaf, and swarm on every bough."

At the foot of one of these squats ME I, (il penseroso) and there grow to the trunk for a whole morning. The timorous hare and sportive squirrel gambol

33. **forest,** Burnham Beeches.

around me like Adam in Paradise, before he had an Eve; but I think he did not use to read Virgil, as I commonly do there. In this situation I often converse with my Horace, aloud too, that is talk to you, but I do not remember that I ever heard you answer me. I beg pardon for taking all the conversation to myself, but it is entirely your own fault. We have old Mr. Southern at a Gentleman's house a little way off, who often comes to see us; he is now seventy-seven years old, and has almost wholly lost his memory; but is as agreeable as an old man can be, at least I persuade myself so when I look at him, and think of Isabella and Oroonoko. I shall be in Town in about three weeks. Adieu.

September, 1737.

TO RICHARD WEST

London, April, Thursday [1742].

YOU are the first who ever made a Muse of a Cough; to me it seems a much more easy task to versify in one's sleep, (that indeed you were of old famous for) than for want of it. Not the wakeful nightingale (when she had a cough) ever sung so sweetly. I give you thanks for your warble, and wish you could sing yourself to rest. These wicked remains of your illness will sure give way to warm weather and gentle exercise; which I hope you will not omit as the season advances. Whatever low spirits and indolence, the effect of them, may advise to the contrary, I pray you add five steps to your walk daily for my sake; by the help of which, in a month's time, I propose to set you on horseback.

I talked of the Dunciad as concluding you had seen it; if you have not, do you choose I should get and send it you? I have myself, upon your recommendation, been reading Joseph Andrews. The incidents are ill laid and without invention; but the characters have a great deal of nature, which always pleases even in her lowest shapes. Parson Adams is perfectly well; so is Mrs. Slipslop, and the story of Wilson; and throughout he shews himself well read in Stage-Coaches, Country Squires, Inns, and Inns of Court. His reflections upon high people and low people, and misses and masters, are very good. However the exaltedness of some minds (or rather as I shrewdly suspect their insipidity and want of feeling or observation) may make them insensible to these light things, (I mean such as characterize and

13. **Isabella . . . Oroonoko,** plays by Thomas **Southerne** (1660–1746). 35. **Dunciad.** The fourth book appeared in 1742. 38. **Joseph Andrews,** the novel by Fielding, published in 1742.

paint nature) yet surely they are as weighty and much more useful than your grave discourses upon the mind, the passions, and what not. Now as the paradisiacal pleasures of the Mahometans consist in playing upon the flute and lying with Houris, be mine to read eternal new romances of Marivaux and Crébillon.

You are very good in giving yourself the trouble to read and find fault with my long harangues. Your freedom (as you call it) has so little need of apologies, that I would scarce excuse your treating me any otherwise; which, whatever compliment it might be to my vanity, would be making a very ill one to my understanding. As to matter of stile, I have this to say: The language of the age is never the language of poetry; except among the French, whose verse, where the thought or image does not support it, differs in nothing from prose. Our poetry, on the contrary, has a language peculiar to itself; to which almost every one, that has written, has added something by enriching it with foreign idioms and derivatives: Nay sometimes words of their own composition or invention. Shakespear and Milton have been great creators this way; and no one more licentious than Pope or Dryden, who perpetually borrow expressions from the former. Let me give you some instances from Dryden, whom everybody reckons a great master of our poetical tongue.—Full of *museful mopeings*—unlike the *trim of love*—a pleasant *beverage*—a *roundelay* of love—stood silent in his *mood*—with knots and *knares* deformed—his *ireful mood*—in proud *array*—his *boon* was granted—and *disarray* and shameful rout—*wayward* but wise—*furbished* for the field—the *foiled dodderd* oaks——*disherited*—*smouldering* flames—*retchless* of laws—*crones* old and ugly—the *beldam* at his side—the *grandam-hag*—*villanize* his Father's fame. ——But they are infinite: And our language not being a settled thing (like the French) has an undoubted right to words of an hundred years old, provided antiquity have not rendered them unintelligible. In truth, Shakespear's language is one of his principal beauties; and he has no less advantage over your Addisons and Rowes in this, than in those other great excellences you mention. Every word in him is a picture. Pray put me the following lines into the tongue of our modern Dramatics:

"But I, that am not shaped for sportive tricks,
Nor made to court an amorous looking-glass:
I, that am rudely stampt, and want love's majesty
To strut before a wanton ambling nymph:
I, that am curtailed of this fair proportion,
Cheated of feature by dissembling nature,
Deformed, unfinished, sent before my time
Into this breathing world, scarce half made up—"

and what follows. To me they appear untranslatable; and if this be the case, our language is greatly degenerated. However, the affectation of imitating Shakespear may doubtless be carried too far; and is no sort of excuse for sentiments ill-suited or speeches ill-timed, which I believe is a little the case with me. I guess the most faulty expressions may be these—*silken son* of *dalliance*—*drowsier* pretensions—*wrinkled beldams*—*arched* the hearer's brow and *riveted* his eyes in *fearful extasie*. These are easily altered or omitted: and indeed if the thoughts be wrong or superfluous, there is nothing easier than to leave out the whole. The first ten or twelve lines are, I believe, the best; and as for the rest, I was betrayed into a good deal of it by Tacitus; only what he has said in five words, I imagine I have said in fifty lines. Such is the misfortune of imitating the inimitable. Now, if you are of my opinion, una litura may do the business better than a dozen; and you need not fear unravelling my web. I am a sort of spider; and have little else to do but spin it over again, or creep to some other place and spin there. Alas! for one who has nothing to do but amuse himself, I believe my amusements are as little amusing as most folks. But no matter; it makes the hours pass; and is better than ἐν ἀμαθίᾳ καὶ ἀμουσίᾳ καταβιῶναι. Adieu.

TO HORACE WALPOLE

Cambridge, February 11, 1751.

AS you have brought me into a little sort of distress, you must assist me, I believe, to get out of it as well as I can. Yesterday I had the misfortune of receiving a letter from certain gentlemen (as their bookseller expresses it), who have taken the Magazine of Magazines into their hands. They tell me that an *ingenious* Poem, called reflections in a Country Church-yard, has been communicated to them, which they are printing forthwith; that they are informed that the *excellent* author of it is I by name, and that they beg not only his *indulgence*, but the *honour* of his correspondence, etc. As I am not at all disposed to be either so indulgent, or so correspondent, as they desire, I have but one bad way left

---

6-7. **Marivaux and Crébillon,** French novelists of the eighteenth century.   49. **"But I . . . up"** (*next column, line 5*). The quotation is from Shakespeare's *Richard III*, Act I, sc. 1, ll. 14–21.

13. **expressions,** in the lines he has sent to West.   24. **una litura,** one erasure.   32. **ἐν . . . καταβιῶναι,** in ignorance and without art to waste one's life.

to escape the honour they would inflict upon me; and therefore am obliged to desire you would make Dodsley print it immediately (which may be done in less than a week's time) from your copy, but without my name, in what form is most convenient for him, but on his best paper and character; he must correct the press himself, and print it without any interval between the stanzas, because the sense is in some places continued beyond them; and the title must be,—Elegy, written in a Country Churchyard. If he would add a line or two to say it came into his hands by accident, I should like it better. If you behold the Magazine of Magazines in the light that I do, you will not refuse to give yourself this trouble on my account, which you have taken of your own accord before now. If Dodsley do not do this immediately, he may as well let it alone.

William Collins
1721–1759

The short and rather pitiful life of William Collins began in the cathedral city of Chichester, near the southern coast of England. He began to write verse while yet a schoolboy at Winchester College and continued to do so during his years at Oxford. After taking his degree he spent some time in the literary circles of London, apparently with a vague intention of trying to make a living by his pen. Several ambitious literary plans were brought to nothing by his indolence, intemperance, and fits of despondency. His *Persian Eclogues*, 1742, and his *Odes on Several Descriptive and Allegoric Subjects*, 1746, failed so dismally that when, at the age of twenty-eight, he inherited a small fortune from an uncle, he was glad to return to his native town. A main reason for his retirement from London, probably, was the gradual increase of a nervous and mental disorder which darkened the last decade of his life.

The earliest important judgment passed upon the poetry of Collins, and even today one of the soundest, is that of Dr. Samuel Johnson:

"His diction was often harsh, unskillfully laboured and injudiciously selected. He affected the obsolete when it was not worthy of revival; and he puts his words out of the common order, seeming to think . . . that not to write prose is certainly to write poetry. His lines commonly are slow of motion, clogged and impeded with clusters of consonants. As men are often esteemed who cannot be loved, so the poetry of Collins may sometimes extort praise where it gives little pleasure."

As an estimate of Collins's average accomplishment this opinion is fair enough, but it is not the opinion that is held today. Collins won his modest but secure position in English literature by some five or six poems, most of them short and all of them written before he was twenty-nine. He did indeed turn out a number of frigid, awkward, and scarcely readable verses that were quite as bad as his friend Dr. Johnson thought them, but the world has wisely chosen to remember the exquisite though never quite flawless beauty of the few things he did surpassingly well.

ODE TO SIMPLICITY

   O thou by *Nature* taught
   To breathe her genuine Thought,
In Numbers warmly pure, and sweetly strong;
   Who first on Mountains wild,
   In *Fancy*, loveliest Child,
Thy Babe, or *Pleasure's*, nursed the Powers of Song!

   Thou, who with Hermit Heart
   Disdain'st the Wealth of Art,
And Gauds, and pageant Weeds, and trailing Pall;
   But com'st a decent Maid,   10
   In *Attic* Robe arrayed,
O chaste unboastful Nymph, to Thee I call!

   By all the honeyed Store
   On Hybla's Thymy Shore,
By all her Blooms and mingled Murmurs dear,

Letters. **7. Dodsley,** Robert Dodsley (1703–1764), a poet and publisher. **8. let it alone.** Dodsley published the *Elegy*, without Gray's name, five days after this letter was written. *Ode to Simplicity.* **9. Gauds,** ornaments. **Weeds,** garments. **Pall,** a long cloak. **10. decent,** decorous. **14. Hybla,** a region in Sicily famous for honey.

By Her, whose Love-born Woe
　　　In Evening Musings slow,
Soothed sweetly sad *Electra*'s Poet's Ear:

　　By old *Cephisus* deep,
　　　Who spread his wavy Sweep　　　　20
In warbled Wanderings round thy green Retreat,
　　　On whose enamelled Side,
　　　When holy *Freedom* died,
No equal Haunt allured thy future Feet:

　　O Sister meek of Truth,
　　　To my admiring Youth,
Thy sober Aid and native Charms infuse!
　　　The Flowers that sweetest breathe,
　　　Though Beauty culled the Wreath,
Still ask thy Hand to range their ordered Hues.　30

　　While *Rome* could none esteem
　　　But Virtue's Patriot Theme,
You loved her Hills, and led her Laureate Band;
　　　But staid to sing alone
　　　To one distinguished Throne,
And turned Thy face, and fled her altered Land.

　　No more, in Hall or Bower,
　　　The Passions own thy Power;
Love, only Love her forceless Numbers mean:
　　　For Thou hast left her Shrine;　　　　40
　　　Nor Olive more, nor Vine,
Shall gain thy Feet to bless the servile Scene.

　　Though Taste, though Genius bless,
　　　To some divine Excess,
Faints the cold Work till Thou inspire the whole;
　　　What each, what all supply,
　　　May court, may charm, our Eye;
Thou, only Thou, canst raise the meeting Soul!

　　Of These let others ask,
　　　To aid some mighty Task;　　　　50
I only seek to find thy temperate Vale,
　　　Where oft my Reed might sound
　　　To Maids and Shepherds round,
And all thy Sons, O *Nature*, learn my Tale.

16. Her, the nightingale, praised by Electra in Sophocles' tragedy of that name.　**18. Poet's Ear,** from Milton's sonnet "When the Assault Was Intended to the City."　**19. Cephisus,** a river in Attica.　**21. Retreat,** Athens.　**33. Band,** of poets.　**35. Throne,** of Augustus, patron of poets.　**37. Bower,** the private apartment of a castle.　**39. her,** Rome's, or Italy's.　**42. servile Scene,** the typical British attitude of the time toward Italian poetry and drama.　**49. These,** taste and genius.

ODE TO EVENING

If aught of oaten stop, or pastoral song,
May hope, chaste Eve, to soothe thy modest ear,
　　Like thy own solemn springs,
　　Thy springs, and dying gales,
O Nymph reserved, while now the bright-haired sun
Sits in yon western tent, whose cloudy skirts,
　　With brede ethereal wove,
　　O'erhang his wavy bed:
Now air is hushed, save where the weak-eyed bat,
With short shrill shriek flits by on leathern wing, 10
　　Or where the Beetle winds
　　His small but sullen horn,
As oft he rises 'midst the twilight path,
Against the pilgrim born in heedless hum:
　　Now teach me, Maid composed,
　　To breathe some softened strain,
Whose numbers stealing through thy darkening vale,
May not unseemly with its stillness suit,
　　As musing slow, I hail
　　Thy genial loved return!　　　　20
For when thy folding star arising shews
His paly circlet, at his warning lamp
　　The fragrant Hours, and Elves
　　Who slept in flowers the day,
And many a Nymph who wreaths her brows with sedge,
And sheds the freshening dew, and lovelier still,
　　The Pensive Pleasures sweet
　　Prepare thy shadowy car.
Then lead, calm Votaress, where some sheety lake
Cheers the lone heath, or some time-hallowed pile,
　　Or up-land fallows grey　　　　31
　　Reflect its last cool gleam.
But when chill blustering winds, or driving rain,
Forbid my willing feet, be mine the hut,
　　That from the mountain's side
　　Views wilds, and swelling floods,
And hamlets brown, and dim-discovered spires,
And hears their simple bell, and marks o'er all
　　Thy dewy fingers draw
　　The gradual dusky veil.　　　　40
While Spring shall pour his showers, as oft he wont,
And bathe thy breathing tresses, meekest Eve!
　　While Summer loves to sport,
　　Beneath thy lingering light;
While sallow Autumn fills thy lap with leaves;
Or Winter, yelling thro' the troublous air,

1. If aught . . . song. If any music from a shepherd's flute.　**7. brede,** embroidery.　**9. Now.** Supply "while."　**21. folding star,** at the rising of which shepherds fold their sheep.　**28. car,** triumphal chariot.　**32. gleam,** reflection from the lake.　**41. wont,** is accustomed to.

Affrights thy shrinking train,
And rudely rends thy robes;
So long, sure-found beneath the Sylvan shed,
Shall FANCY, FRIENDSHIP, SCIENCE, rose-lipped
    HEALTH, 50
    Thy gentlest influence own,
    And hymn thy favorite name!

THE PASSIONS: AN ODE FOR MUSIC

When Music, Heavenly Maid, was young,
While yet in early *Greece* she sung,
The Passions oft, to hear her Shell,
Thronged around her magic Cell,
Exulting, trembling, raging, fainting,
Possessed beyond the Muse's Painting;
By turns they felt the glowing Mind,
Disturbed, delighted, raised, refined,
Till once, 'tis said, when all were fired,
Filled with Fury, rapt, inspired, 10
From the supporting Myrtles round
They snatched her Instruments of Sound,
And as they oft had heard a-part
Sweet Lessons of her forceful Art,
Each, for Madness ruled the Hour,
Would prove his own expressive Power.

First *Fear* his Hand, its Skill to try,
    Amid the Chords bewildered laid,
And back recoiled, he knew not why,
    Ev'n at the Sound himself had made. 20

Next *Anger* rushed; his Eyes on fire
    In Lightnings owned his secret Stings:
In one rude Clash he struck the Lyre,
    And swept with hurried Hand the Strings.

With woeful Measures wan *Despair*
    Low sullen Sounds his Grief beguiled,
A solemn, strange, and mingled Air,
    'Twas sad by Fits, by Starts 'twas wild.

But thou, O *Hope*, with Eyes so fair,
    What was thy delightful Measure? 30
Still it whispered promised Pleasure,
    And bade the lovely Scenes at distance hail!
Still would Her Touch the Strain prolong,
    And from the Rocks, the Woods, the Vale,
She called on Echo still through all the Song;

3. Passions, emotions. **Shell,** lyre.

And, where Her sweetest Theme She chose,
    A soft responsive Voice was heard at every
    Close,
And *Hope* enchanted smiled, and waved Her golden
    Hair.

And longer had She sung,—but with a Frown
    Revenge impatient rose, 40
He threw his blood-stained Sword in Thunder
    down,
    And with a withering Look,
    The War-denouncing Trumpet took,
And blew a Blast so loud and dread,
Were ne'er Prophetic Sounds so full of Woe.
    And ever and anon he beat
    The doubling Drum with furious Heat;
And though sometimes, each dreary Pause between,
    Dejected *Pity* at his Side
    Her Soul-subduing Voice applied, 50
Yet still He kept his wild unaltered Mien,
While each strained Ball of Sight seemed bursting
    from his Head.

Thy Numbers, *Jealousy*, to nought were fixed,
    Sad Proof of thy distressful State;
Of differing Themes the veering Song was mixed,
    And now it courted *Love*, now raving called on
    Hate.

With Eyes upraised, as one inspired,
Pale *Melancholy* sate retired,
And from her wild sequestered Seat,
In notes by distance made more sweet, 60
Poured through the mellow *Horn* her pensive
    Soul:
    And dashing soft from Rocks around,
    Bubbling Runnels joined the Sound;
Through Glades and Glooms the mingled Measure
    stole,
Or o'er some haunted Stream with fond Delay,
    Round an holy Calm diffusing,
    Love of Peace and lonely Musing,
In hollow Murmurs died away.
But O how altered was its sprightlier Tone!
When *Chearfulness*, a Nymph of healthiest Hue, 70
    Her Bow a-cross her Shoulder flung,
    Her Buskins gemmed with Morning Dew,
Blew an inspiring Air, that Dale and Thicket
    rung,
    The Hunter's Call to *Faun* and *Dryad* known!

36. Theme, that of love. **43. War-denouncing,** war-announcing.

The Oak-crowned *Sisters*, and their chaste-eyed *Queen*,
  Satyrs and sylvan Boys were seen,
  Peeping from forth their Alleys green;
Brown *Exercise* rejoiced to hear,
  And *Sport* leaped up, and seized his Beechen Spear.

Last came *Joy's* Ecstatic Trial,   80
He, with viny Crown advancing,
  First to the lively Pipe his Hand addrest,
But soon he saw the brisk awakening Viol,
  Whose sweet entrancing Voice he loved the best.
    They would have thought who heard the Strain,
    They saw in *Tempe's* Vale her native Maids,
  Amidst the festal sounding Shades,
To some unwearied Minstrel dancing,
  While, as his flying Fingers kissed the Strings,
Love framed with *Mirth* a gay fantastic Round.   90
Loose were Her Tresses seen, her Zone unbound,
And He amidst his frolic Play,
As if he would the charming Air repay,
Shook thousand Odours from his dewy Wings.

O *Music*, sphere-descended Maid,
Friend of Pleasure, *Wisdom's* Aid,
Why, Goddess, why to us denyed?
Lay'st thou thy antient Lyre aside?
As in that loved *Athenian* Bower,
You learned an all-commanding Power,   100
Thy mimic Soul, O Nymph endeared,
Can well recall what then it heard.
Where is thy native simple Heart,
Devote to Virtue, Fancy, Art?
Arise as in that elder Time,
Warm, Energic, Chaste, Sublime!
Thy Wonders, in that God-like Age,
Fill thy recording *Sister's* Page—
'Tis said, and I believe the Tale,
Thy humblest *Reed* could more prevail,   110
Had more of Strength, diviner Rage,
Than all which charms this laggard Age,
Ev'n all at once together found,
Caecilia's mingled World of Sound—
O bid our vain Endeavors cease,
Revive the just Designs of *Greece*,
Return in all thy simple State!
Confirm the Tales Her Sons relate!

75. Sisters, wood nymphs. **Queen,** Diana. **81. viny,** suggesting that Joy is the same as Bacchus. **86. Vale,** in Thessaly. **108. Sister,** poetry. **110. Reed,** flute. **114. World of Sound,** the pipe organ. **115. Endeavors,** in Italian opera.

ODE

WRITTEN IN THE BEGINNING OF THE YEAR 1746

How sleep the Brave, who sink to Rest,
  By all their Country's Wishes blest!
When *Spring*, with dewy Fingers cold,
  Returns to deck their hallowed Mold,
She there shall dress a sweeter Sod,
  Than Fancy's Feet have ever trod.

By Fairy Hands their Knell is rung,
  By Forms unseen their Dirge is sung;
There *Honour* comes, a Pilgrim grey,
  To bless the Turf that wraps their Clay,   10
And *Freedom* shall a-while repair,
  To dwell a weeping Hermit there!

A SONG FROM SHAKESPEAR'S CYMBELINE

SUNG BY GUIDERUS AND ARVIRAGUS OVER FIDELE, SUPPOSED TO BE DEAD

To fair Fidele's grassy tomb
  Soft maids and village hinds shall bring
Each opening sweet, of earliest bloom,
  And rifle all the breathing Spring.

No wailing ghost shall dare appear
  To vex with shrieks this quiet grove:
But shepherd lads assemble here,
  And melting virgins own their love.

No withered witch shall here be seen,
  No goblins lead their nightly crew: 10
The female fays shall haunt the green,
  And dress thy grave with pearly dew!

The red-breast oft at evening hours
  Shall kindly lend his little aid:
With hoary moss, and gathered flowers,
  To deck the ground where thou art laid.

When howling winds, and beating rain,
  In tempests shake the sylvan cell:
Or midst the chace on every plain,
  The tender thought on thee shall dwell.   20

Ode . . . 1746, written in honor of the English soldiers who fell at Fontenoy in May, 1745, at Preston Pans in September of that year, and at Falkirk in January, 1746. The English were defeated in all of these battles. **DEAD.** See Shakespeare's *Cymbeline*, Act IV, sc. 2.

WILLIAM COLLINS

    Each lonely scene shall thee restore,
        For thee the tear be duly shed:
    Beloved till life can charm no more,
        And mourned, till Pity's self be dead.

ODE ON THE DEATH OF MR. THOMSON

The Scene of the following STANZAS is supposed to lie on the *Thames* near *Richmond*.—Collins.

1

In yonder Grave a DRUID lies
    Where slowly winds the stealing Wave!
The Year's best Sweets shall duteous rise
    To deck *its* POET's sylvan Grave!

2

In yon deep Bed of whispering Reeds
    His airy Harp shall now be laid,
That He, whose Heart in Sorrow bleeds,
    May love through Life the soothing Shade.

3

Then Maids and Youths shall linger here,
    And while its Sounds at distance swell,   10
Shall sadly seem in Pity's Ear
    To hear the WOODLAND PILGRIM'S KNELL.

4

REMEMBRANCE oft shall haunt the Shore
    When THAMES in Summer-wreaths is drest,
And oft suspend the dashing Oar
    To bid his gentle Spirit rest!

5

And oft, as EASE and HEALTH retire
    To breezy Lawn, or Forest deep,
The Friend shall view yon whitening Spire,
    And 'mid the varied Landscape weep.   20

6

But Thou, who own'st that Earthy Bed,
    Ah! what will every Dirge avail?
Or Tears, which LOVE and PITY shed,
    That mourn beneath the gliding Sail!

7

Yet lives there one, whose heedless Eye
    Shall scorn thy pale Shrine glimmering near?
With Him, sweet Bard, may FANCY die,
    And JOY desert the blooming Year.

8

But thou, lorn STREAM, whose sullen Tide
    No sedge-crowned SISTERS now attend,   30
Now waft me from the green Hill's Side
    Whose cold Turf hides the buried FRIEND!

9

And see, the Fairy Valleys fade,
    Dun *Night* has veiled the solemn View!
—Yet once again, Dear parted Shade,
    Meek NATURE'S CHILD again adieu!

10

The genial Meads, assigned to bless
    Thy Life, shall mourn thy early Doom,
Their Hinds, and Shepherd-Girls shall dress
    With simple Hands thy rural Tomb.   40

11

Long, long, thy Stone and pointed Clay
    Shall melt the musing BRITON'S Eyes,
O! VALES and WILD WOODS, shall HE say
    In yonder Grave YOUR DRUID lies!

19. **Spire**, of Richmond church.

Christopher Smart

1722-1771

A university wit and scholar, a translator of Horace, a Grub Street hack, a drunkard, a Bedlamite, and a radiantly happy Christian who died in debtor's prison, Christopher Smart was one of the strangest and most enigmatic apparitions among English writers of the eighteenth century. The few facts that we know about Smart's life do not easily fit into a coherent picture, and his best work does not seem to have come from the same mind as that which produced his worst. It has been unfortunate, moreover, that the many third-rate things he wrote won a moderate success in his lifetime, and that his one really superb performance was omitted from the first collected edition of his poems on the ground that it bore "melancholy proofs of the recent estrangement of his mind."

It is true that Smart's *Song to David* does show some signs of abnormal mentality, as his recently discovered and almost equally remarkable *Rejoice in the Lamb* also does. In the *Song*, however, these aberrations amount to no more than a "noble wildness," as Palgrave called them, and they did not prevent Churton Collins from calling this poem "the most extraordinary phenomenon, perhaps, in our literature; the one rapt strain in the poetry of the eighteenth century." Robert Browning too ignored Smart's alleged insanity when he said that between the time of Milton and that of Keats only this one poet had "pierced the screen 'twixt thing and word, lit language straight from soul."

Smart was closer to Keats than to Milton. He forced words to work three shifts. While his mind was on fire with the *Song to David* his thought linked heaven to earth like a lightning flash. Yet he did not see nature in Keats's way, as a mere spectacle. He saw it with the ecstatic innocence and childlike gratitude of Vaughan and Blake. He took a religious delight, one sees, in the mere naming of God's creatures, from worm to star. In the one Pisgah sight which he attained—or, at any rate, recorded —he saw all creation on its knees in adoring prayer.

There is no period of English literature in which Smart could have been less at home than he was in the eighteenth century. Those qualities of imaginative intensity, audacious speed of thought and utterance, and great masculine vigor in which his chief poem excels are just the qualities in which his generation was most clearly deficient. The *Song to David* is a magnificent lyric composed at a time when the lyric mode had almost died. It is a song of adoration fearlessly chanted at a time when most men had forgotten how to worship and to sing.

Some two-thirds of the eighty-six stanzas in the *Song* are here given, together with a few lines from the recently published *Rejoice in the Lamb*.

A SONG TO DAVID

Excepting only the works of William Blake, Smart's masterpiece lays a greater strain upon the reader than any other poem written in the eighteenth century. The difficulties of it are due in part to the author's erudition, especially in the Bible, in Masonic and Rosicrucian lore, and in natural science. These, however, are not so apparent in the passages here given as in certain stanzas that have been omitted. Yet even when Smart's recondite allusions are understood, there remains the task of discovering precisely what poetic plan lay before him in this poem, what his main topics are, and what were the moods in which he presented them.

The poem begins, one sees, with direct praise of David as king, warrior, man of God, and poet; but the thought of David's poetry draws Smart aside into an ecstatic naming of God's creatures more or less reminiscent of the Psalms. In this passage all the beauty, power, speed, and ingenuity of the lower creation is interpreted as a prayer of praise to the Maker. Then, by a beautifully wrought transition, the *Song* passes on to the prayer of man, to that of David, and finally to the prayer of Christ's life and death, which "brought salvation down."

Having seen this much, one may recall that Christopher Smart was regarded as insane by the people of his time because he insisted upon carrying out the Biblical injunction that all men should "pray unceasingly."

For comprehension of the poem's rich details a reader needs the power of raising into sharp visual focus Smart's startling images of the lion, the crocus, the whale, and a hundred other creatures. This takes time, for the picture in the mind does not instantly form and glow and burn. It is also a matter of imaginative intensity and concentration.

If one finds, after a tenth or a hundredth reading, that the *Song to David* is inexhaustible, that ever new and larger significances crowd upon the mind at each return, then one may conclude that here is a work of sheer genius and one of the supreme achievements in the history of

CHRISTOPHER SMART

English song. Robert Browning seems to have suspected this when he wrote his "Parleying" with Christopher Smart, and also when he based his own poem "Saul" upon the *Song to David*.

O thou, that sit'st upon a throne,
With harp of high majestic tone,
    To praise the King of kings:
And voice of heaven-ascending swell,
Which, while its deeper notes excell,
    Clear, as a clarion, rings:

To bless each valley, grove and coast,
And charm the cherubs to the post
    Of gratitude in throngs;
To keep the days on Zion's mount,   10
And send the year to his account,
    With dances and with songs:

O Servant of God's holiest charge,
The minister of praise at large,
    Which thou may'st now receive;
From thy blest mansion hail and hear,
From topmost eminence appear
    To this the wreath I weave. . . .

He sung of God—the mighty source
Of all things—the stupendous force   20
    On which all strength depends;
From whose right arm, beneath whose eyes,
All period, power, and enterprize
    Commences, reigns, and ends.

Angels—their ministry and meed,
Which to and fro with blessings speed,
    Or with their citterns wait:
Where Michael with his millions bows,
Where dwells the seraph and his spouse,
    The cherub and her mate.   30

Of man—the semblance and effect
Of God and Love—the Saint elect
    For infinite applause—
To rule the land, and briny broad,
To be laborious in his laud,
    And heroes in his cause.

The world—the clustring spheres he made,
The glorious light, the soothing shade,
    Dale, champaign, grove, and hill;

The multitudinous abyss,   40
Where secrecy remains in bliss,
    And wisdom hides her skill.

Trees, plants, and flowers—of virtuous root;
Gem yielding blossom, yielding fruit,
    Choice gums and precious balm;
Bless ye the nosegay in the vale,
And with the sweetners of the gale
    Enrich the thankful psalm;

Of fowl—e'en every beak and wing
Which cheer the winter, hail the spring,   50
    That live in peace or prey;
They that make music, or that mock,
The quail, the brave domestic cock,
    The raven, swan, and jay.

Of fishes—every size and shape,
Which nature frames of light escape,
    Devouring man to shun:
The shells are in the wealthy deep,
The shoals upon the surface leap,
    And love the glancing sun.   60

Of beasts—the beaver plods his task;
While the sleek tygers roll and bask,
    Nor yet the shades arouse:
Her cave the mining coney scoops;
Where o'er the mead the mountain stoops,
    The kids exult and browse:

Of gems—their virtue and their price,
Which hid in earth from man's device,
    Their darts of lustre sheathe;
The jasper of the master's stamp,   70
The topaz blazing like a lamp
    Among the mines beneath.

Blest was the tenderness he felt
When to his graceful harp he knelt,
    And did for audience call;
When satan with his hand he quelled,
And in serene suspense he held
    The frantic throes of Saul. . . .

O DAVID, highest in the list
Of worthies, on God's ways insist,   80
    The genuine word repeat.

1. **thou**, David.   13. **charge**, duty.   19. **sung**. The following nine stanzas all depend upon this verb. They refer to the poetry in the Psalms of David.   25. **meed**, reward.   27. **citterns**, lutes.   32. **elect**, chosen.   34. **briny broad**, the sea.   35. **his**, God's.   43. **virtuous**, having medicinal virtue.   44. **Gem**, bud.   59. **shoals**, schools.   64. **coney**, in England, the rabbit; in Biblical usage, the rock badger.   67. **virtue**, magical power.   68. **device**, skill, in discovery.   78. **Saul**. See I Samuel 16:23.

Vain are the documents of men,
And vain the flourish of the pen
    That keeps the fool's conceit.

PRAISE above all—for praise prevails;
Heap up the measure, load the scales,
    And good to goodness add:
The generous soul her Saviour aids,
But peevish obloquy degrades;
    The Lord is great and glad.   90

For ADORATION all the ranks
Of angels yield eternal thanks,
    And DAVID in the midst;
With God's good poor, which, last and least
In man's esteem, thou to thy feast,
    O blessed bridegroom, bidst.

For ADORATION seasons change,
And order, truth, and beauty range,
    Adjust, attract, and fill:
The grass the polyanthus cheques;   100
And polished porphyry reflects
    By the descending rill.

Rich almonds colour to the prime
For ADORATION; tendrils climb,
    And fruit-trees pledge their gems;
And Ivis with her gorgeous vest
Builds for her eggs her cunning nest,
    And bell-flowers bow their stems.

With vinous syrups cedars spout;
From rocks pure honey gushing out,   110
    For ADORATION springs:
All scenes of painting crowd the map
Of nature; to the mermaid's pap
    The scalèd infant clings.

The spotted ounce and playsome cubs
Run rustling 'mongst the flowering shrubs,
    And lizards feed the moss;
For ADORATION beasts embark,
While waves upholding halycon's ark
    No longer roar and toss.   120

While Israel sits beneath his fig,
With coral root and amber sprig
    The weaned adventurer sports;
Where to the palm the jasmin cleaves,
For ADORATION 'mongst the leaves
    The gale his peace reports.

Increasing days their reign exalt,
Nor in the pink and mottled vault
    The opposing spirits tilt;
And, by the coasting reader spied,   130
The silverlings and crusions glide
    For ADORATION gilt.

For ADORATION ripening canes
And cocoa's purest milk detains
    The western pilgrim's staff;
Where rain in clasping boughs enclosed,
And vines with oranges disposed,
    Embower the social laugh.

Now labour his reward receives,
For ADORATION counts his sheaves   140
    To peace, her bounteous prince;
The nectarine his strong tint imbibes,
And apples of ten thousand tribes,
    And quick peculiar quince.

The wealthy crops of whitening rice
'Mongst thyine woods and groves of spice,
    For ADORATION grow;
And, marshalled in the fencèd land,
The peaches and pomegranates stand,
    Where wild carnations blow.   150

The laurels with the winter strive;
The crocus burnishes alive
    Upon the snow-clad earth.
For ADORATION myrtles stay
To keep the garden from dismay,
    And bless the sight from dearth.

The pheasant shows his pompous neck;
And ermine, jealous of a speck,
    With fear eludes offence:
The sable, with his glossy pride,   160
For ADORATION is descried,
    Where frosts the wave condense.

---

100. **cheques,** checkers.   103. **prime,** ripeness.   106. **Ivis,** the hummingbird.   108. **bell-flowers,** either daffodils or campanulas.   115. **ounce,** the snow leopard or mountain panther.   117. **feed,** supply "upon."   118. **embark.** "There is a large quadruped that preys upon fish, and provides himself with a piece of timber for that purpose, with which he is very handy." (Smart)   119. **ark,** the nest of the halcyon or kingfisher, which was supposed to build on the waves and to charm them into quiet.

121. **fig.** See Micah 4:4.   129. **spirits tilt,** spirits of the seasons contend.   130. **coasting reader,** observer of God's works moving along the coast.   131. **silverlings,** tarpons. **crusions,** fish of the carp family.   146. **thyine,** precious or sweet—taken from Revelation 18:12.

The cheerful holly, pensive yew,
And holy thorn, their trim renew;
    The squirrel hoards his nuts:
All creatures batten o'er their stores,
And careful nature all her doors
    For ADORATION shuts.

For ADORATION, DAVID's Psalms
Lift up the heart to deeds of alms;   170
    And he who kneels and chants,
Prevails his passions to control,
Finds meat and medicine to the soul,
    Which for translation pants.

For ADORATION, beyond match,
The scholar bulfinch aims to catch
    The soft flute's ivory touch;
And, careless on the hazel spray,
The daring redbreast keeps at bay
    The damsel's greedy clutch.   180

For ADORATION, in the skies,
The Lord's philosopher espies
    The Dog, the Ram, and Rose;
The planet's ring, Orion's sword;
Nor is his greatness less adored
    In the vile worm that glows.

For ADORATION on the strings
The western breezes work their wings,
    The captive ear to sooth.—
Hark! 'tis a voice—how still, and small—   190
That makes the cataracts to fall,
    Or bids the sea be smooth.

For ADORATION, incense comes
From bezoar, and Arabian gums;
    And on the civet's furr:
But as for prayer, or e'er it faints,
Far better is the breath of saints
    Than galbanum and myrrh.

For ADORATION, from the down
Of damsons to the anana's crown,   200
    God sends to tempt the taste;

And while the luscious zest invites
The sense, that in the scene delights,
    Commands desire be chaste.

For ADORATION, all the paths
Of grace are open, all the baths
    Of purity refresh;
And all the rays of glory beam
To deck the man of God's esteem,
    Who triumphs o'er the flesh.   210

For ADORATION, in the dome
Of Christ the sparrows find an home;
    And on his olives perch:
The swallow also dwells with thee,
O man of God's humility,
    Within his Saviour's CHURCH.

Sweet is the dew that falls betimes,
And drops upon the leafy limes;
    Sweet Hermon's fragrant air:
Sweet is the lilly's silver bell,   220
And sweet the wakeful tapers smell
    That watch for early prayer.

Sweet the young nurse with love intense,
Which smiles o'er sleeping innocence;
    Sweet when the lost arrive:
Sweet the musician's ardour beats,
While his vague mind's in quest of sweets,
    The choicest flowers to hive.

Sweeter in all the strains of love,
The language of thy turtle dove,   230
    Paired to thy swelling chord;
Sweeter with every grace endued,
The glory of thy gratitude,
    Respired unto the Lord.

Strong is the horse upon his speed;
Strong in pursuit the rapid glede,
    Which makes at once his game;
Strong the tall ostrich on the ground;
Strong through the turbulent profound
    Shoots xiphias to his aim.   240

Strong is the lion—like a coal
His eyeball—like a bastion's mole
    His chest against the foes:
Strong the gier-eagle on his sail,
Strong against tide, the enormous whale
    Emerges, as he goes.

164. thorn, the hawthorn, called **holy** because of its association with Christ and St. Joseph of Arimathea. **174. translation,** to heaven. **176. bulfinch,** bullfinch, a European bird that can be taught to whistle a tune. **182. philosopher,** a student of science—here, of astronomy—who tries to read the mind of God through his natural works. **184. ring,** of Saturn. **187. strings,** of the aeolian harp. **190. voice,** of God. **194. bezoar,** a concretion found in the intestines of ruminating animals, once used in magic and medicine, but not for incense. **198. galbanum,** a Persian gum. **200. crown,** the tuft of leaves on the pineapple, called **anana** in the tropics. **216. church.** See Psalm 84:3. **236. glede,** hawk. **240. xiphias,** swordfish. **242. mole,** a mound of earth or stone. **244. gier-eagle,** vulture.

But stronger still, in earth and air,
And in the sea, the man of prayer;
    And far beneath the tide;
And in the seat to faith assigned,   250
Where ask is have, where seek is find,
    Where knock is open wide.

Beauteous the fleet before the gale;
Beauteous the multitudes in mail,
    Ranked arms and crested heads:
Beauteous the garden's umbrage mild,
Walk, water, meditated wild,
    And all the bloomy beds.

Beauteous the moon full on the lawn;
And beauteous, when the veil's withdrawn,   260
    The virgin to her spouse:
Beauteous the temple decked and filled,
When to the heaven of heavens they build
    Their heart-directed vows.

Beauteous, yea beauteous more than these,
The shepherd king upon his knees,
    For his momentous trust;
With wish of infinite conceit,
For man, beast, mute, the small and great,
    And prostrate dust to dust.   270

Precious the bounteous widow's mite;
And precious, for extreme delight,
    The largess from the churl:
Precious the ruby's blushing blaze,
And alba's blest imperial rays,
    And pure cerulean pearl,

Precious the penitential tear;
And precious is the sigh sincere,
    Acceptable to God:
And precious are the winning flowers,   280
In gladsome Israel's feast of bowers,
    Bound on the hallowed sod.

More precious that diviner part
Of David, ev'n the Lord's own heart,
    Great, beautiful, and new:
In all things where it was intent,
In all extremes, in each event,
    Proof—answering true to true.

Glorious the sun in mid career;
Glorious the assembled fires appear;   290
    Glorious the comet's train:
Glorious the trumpet and alarm;
Glorious the almighty stretched-out arm;
    Glorious the enraptured main:

Glorious the northern lights astream;
Glorious the song, when God's the theme;
    Glorious the thunder's roar:
Glorious hosanna from the den;
Glorious the catholic amen;
    Glorious the martyr's gore: 300

Glorious—more glorious is the crown
Of Him that brought salvation down
    By meekness, called thy Son;
Thou that stupendous truth believed,
And now the matchless deed's achieved,
    DETERMINED, DARED, and DONE.

from REJOICE IN THE LAMB[1]

The recent discovery and publication of a long, hitherto unknown manuscript by Christopher Smart has shed new light upon this fascinating poet and upon his chief production. *Rejoice in the Lamb* is really what the "Song to David" was long thought to be, the work of a disordered mind. In fact it was actually composed in a madhouse, at some time between 1756 and 1763. It has almost no discernible continuity of thought, and such artistic form as one can find in it consists largely in the fact that about half of the long and unrhymed lines of which it is composed begin with the word "Let" and the other half with the word "For." And yet, little by little, out of this rubbish there slowly emerges just the same profoundly religious thought that animates the "Song"—the thought, namely, that all God's creatures worship Him by their beauty, power, speed, and various skill. This thought is most affectingly presented in a passage about the cat that shared Smart's otherwise solitary confinement.

For I will consider my Cat Jeoffry.
For he is the servant of the Living God, duly and daily serving him.
For at the first glance of the glory of God in the East he worships in his way.
For is this done by wreathing his body seven times round with elegant quickness.

---

249. **beneath the tide,** Jonah.   251–52. **Where . . . wide.** See St. Matthew 7:7.   257. **meditated wild,** left uncultivated by design.   268. **conceit,** understanding.   275. **alba's.** See Revelation 11:17.

306. **done,** referring to the life and death of Christ primarily, but also, it may be, to Smart's composition of the present poem.

[1] The selection from Smart's *Rejoice in the Lamb* is here reprinted by special permission of Jonathan Cape and Company, London. The book is published in the United States by Henry Holt and Company.

For then he leaps up to catch the musk, which is the blessing of God upon his prayer.
For he rolls upon prank to work it in.
For having done duty and received blessing he begins to consider himself.
For this he performs in ten degrees.
For first he looks upon his fore-paws to see if they are clean.
For secondly he kicks up behind to clear away there.
For thirdly he works it upon stretch with the fore paws extended.
For fourthly he sharpens his paws by wood.
For fifthly he washes himself.
For sixthly he rolls upon wash.
For Seventhly he fleas himself, that he may not be interrupted upon the beat.
For Eighthly he rubs himself against a post.
For Ninthly he looks up for his instructions.
For Tenthly he goes in quest of food.
For having considered God and himself he will consider his neighbour.
For if he meets another cat he will kiss her in kindness.
For when he takes his prey he plays with it to give it [a] chance.
For one mouse in seven escapes by his dallying.
For when his day's work is done his business more properly begins.
For he keeps the Lord's watch in the night against the adversary.
For he counteracts the powers of darkness by his electrical skin & glaring eyes.
For he counteracts the Devil, who is death, by brisking about the life.
For in his morning orisons he loves the sun and the sun loves him.
For he is of the tribe of Tiger.
For the Cherub Cat is a term of the Angel Tiger.
For he has the subtlety and hissing of a serpent, which in goodness he suppresses.
For he will not do destruction, if he is well-fed, neither will he spit without provocation.
For he purrs in thankfulness, when God tells him he's a good Cat.
For he is an instrument for the children to learn benevolence upon.
For every house is incompleat without him & a blessing is lacking in the spirit.
For the Lord commanded Moses concerning the cats at the departure of the Children of Israel from Egypt.
For every family had one cat at least in the bag.

For the English Cats are the best in Europe.
For he is the cleanest in the use of his fore-paws of any quadrupede.
For the dexterity of his defence is an instance of the love of God to him exceedingly.
For he is the quickest to his mark of any creature.
For he is tenacious of his point.
For he is a mixture of gravity and waggery.
For he knows that God is his Saviour.
For there is nothing sweeter than his peace when at rest.
For there is nothing brisker than his life when in motion.
For he is of the Lord's poor and so indeed is he called by benevolence perpetually—
Poor Jeoffry! poor Jeoffry! the rat has bit thy throat.
For I bless the name of the Lord Jesus that Jeoffry is better.
For the divine spirit comes about his body to sustain it in compleat cat.
For his tongue is exceeding pure so that it has in purity what it wants in musick.
For he is docile and can learn certain things.
For he can set up with gravity which is patience upon approbation.
For he can fetch and carry, which is patience in employment.
For he can jump over a stick which is patience upon proof positive.
For he can spraggle upon waggle at the word of command.
For he can jump from an eminence into his master's bosom.
For he can catch the cork and toss it again.
For he is hated by the hypocrite and miser.
For the former is affraid of detection.
For the latter refuses the charge.
For he camels his back to bear the first notion of business.
For he is good to think on, if a man would express himself neatly.
For he made a great figure in Egypt for his signal services.
For he killed the Icneumon-rat very pernicious by land.
For his ears are so acute that they sting again.
For from this proceeds the passing quickness of his attention.
For by stroking him I have found out electricity.
For I perceived God's light about him both wax and fire.
For the Electrical fire is the spiritual substance,

which God sends from heaven to sustain the bodies both of man and beast.
For God has blessed him in the variety of his movements. 70
For, though he cannot fly, he is an excellent clamberer.
For his motions upon the face of the earth are more than any other quadrupede.
For he can tread to all measures upon the musick.
For he can swim for life.
For he can creep.

James Macpherson
1736-1796

The literary circles of Great Britain were electrified in 1760 by the publication of a small volume entitled *Fragments of Ancient Poetry Collected in the Highlands of Scotland*, bearing the then unknown name of James Macpherson on its title page. Within a few weeks after the appearance of these "Fragments" Thomas Gray was writing to a friend: "I am gone mad about them. They are said to be translations, literal, and in prose, from the Erse tongue, done by one Macpherson, a young clergyman in the Highlands. He means to publish a collection he has of these specimens of antiquity—if it be antiquity; but what plagues me is, I cannot come to any certainty on that head."

In the following year Macpherson put forth *Fingal, an Ancient Epic Poem, with Other Poems Composed by Ossian*. Two years later still he produced *Temora, an Epic Poem*, and with this publication closed his connection with "Ossian," the third-century Gaelic bard. Macpherson never showed any original manuscripts, although they were often demanded of him, to prove that his alleged translations were genuine, and the opinion slowly grew, assisted by the emphatic assertions of Dr. Johnson, that they were not so. In our own time, however, it is no longer doubted that Macpherson drew upon some original sources, whether oral or written, although his treatment of these was certainly not that of a translator.

The so-called Ossianic poems exerted an influence in Europe and America that was out of proportion to their actual worth. Echoes of them are to be heard in the poems of William Blake, in Byron and Lamartine and Chateaubriand. In the Italian translation they were Napoleon Bonaparte's favorite reading, and in the German version they had a deep effect upon Herder and Goethe. Both in England and throughout Europe they helped to hasten the oncoming of the Romantic movement. Considering that Macpherson was only twenty-four when the first of the "Ossian" books appeared and that he produced the last of them at twenty-seven, the range and the endurance of his literary influence were phenomenal.

During recent decades the common opinion has been that this influence was unjustified by any intrinsic merit in the writings themselves. Macpherson's prose, once so much admired and imitated, is now thought to be tawdry and pretentious. To those readers, however, who do it the justice of reading it very slowly aloud, listening for its cadences and trying to lift every simple picture into a clear mental image, this prose, formed chiefly upon the Bible and Homer, is still impressive. "Choose any one of the better passages," Matthew Arnold remarked, "and you can see at this day what an apparition of newness and of power such a strain must have been in the eighteenth century."

CARTHON: A POEM

ARGUMENT

This poem is complete, and the subject of it, as of most of Ossian's compositions, tragical. In the time of Comhal, the son of Trathal, and father of the celebrated Fingal, Clessámmor, the son of Thaddu, and brother of Morna, Fingal's mother, was driven by a storm into the river Clyde [Clutha], on the banks of which stood Balclutha, a town belonging to the Britons between the walls. He was hospitably received by Reuthámir, the principal man in the place, who gave him Moina his only daughter in marriage. Reuda, the son of Cormo, a Briton who was in love with Moina, came to Reuthámir's house, and behaved haughtily towards Clessámmor. A quarrel ensued, in which Reuda was killed; the Britons, who attended him, pressed so hard on Clessámmor, that he was obliged to throw himself into the Clyde, and swim to his ship. He hoisted sail, and the wind being favourable, bore him out to sea. He often endeavoured to return, and carry off his beloved Moina by night; but the wind continuing contrary, he was forced to desist.

Moina, who had been left with child by her husband, brought forth a son, and died soon after.—Reuthámir named the child

Carthon—*i.e. the murmur of waves, from the storm which carried off Clessámmor his father, who was supposed to have been cast away. When Carthon was three years old, Comhal, the father of Fingal, in one of his expeditions against the Britons, took and burned Balclutha. Reuthámir was killed in the attack: and Carthon was carried safe away by his nurse, who fled farther into the country of the Britons. Carthon, coming to man's estate, was resolved to revenge the fall of Balclutha on Comhal's posterity. He set sail from the Clyde, and, falling on the coast of Morven, defeated two of Fingal's heroes who came to oppose his progress. He was, at last, unwittingly killed by his father Clessámmor, in a single combat. This story is the foundation of the present poem, which opens on the night preceding the death of Carthon, so that what passed before is introduced by way of episode. The poem is addressed to Malvina, the daughter of Toscar.*

A TALE of the times of old! The deeds of days of other years!

The murmur of thy streams, O Lora! brings back the memory of the past. The sound of thy woods, Garmallar, is lovely in mine ear. Dost thou not behold, Malvina, a rock with its head of heath? Three aged pines bend from its face; green is the narrow plain at its feet; there the flower of the mountain grows, and shakes its white head in the breeze. The thistle is there alone, shedding its aged beard. Two stones, half sunk in the ground, show their heads of moss. The deer of the mountain avoids the place, for he beholds a dim ghost standing there. The mighty lie, O Malvina! in the narrow plain of the rock.

A tale of the times of old! the deeds of days of other years!

Who comes from the land of strangers, with his thousands around him? The sun-beam pours its bright stream before him; his hair meets the wind of his hills. His face is settled from war. He is calm as the evening beam that looks, from the cloud of the west, on Cona's silent vale. Who is it but Comhal's son, the king of mighty deeds! He beholds his hills with joy, he bids a thousand voices rise. "Ye have fled over your fields, ye sons of the distant land! The king of the world sits in his hall, and hears of his people's flight. He lifts his red eye of pride; he takes his father's sword. Ye have fled over your fields, sons of the distant land!"

Such were the words of the bards, when they came to Selma's halls. A thousand lights from the stranger's land rose, in the midst of the people. The feast is spread around; the night passed away in joy. "Where is the noble Clessámmor?" said the fair-haired Fingal. "Where is the brother of Morna, in the hour of my joy? Sullen and dark he passes his days in the vale of echoing Lora: but, behold, he comes from the hill, like a steed in his strength, who finds his companions in the breeze; and tosses his bright mane in the wind. Blessed be the soul of Clessámmor, why so long from Selma?"

"Returns the chief," said Clessámmor, "in the midst of his fame? Such was the renown of Comhal in the battles of his youth. Often did we pass over Carun to the land of the strangers: our swords returned, not unstained with blood: nor did the kings of the world rejoice. Why do I remember the times of our war? My hair is mixed with grey. My hand forgets to bend the bow: I lift a lighter spear. O that my joy would return, as when I first beheld the maid; the white-bosomed daughter of strangers, Moina, with the dark-blue eyes!"

"Tell," said the mighty Fingal, "the tale of thy youthful days. Sorrow, like a cloud on the sun, shades the soul of Clessámmor. Mournful are thy thoughts, alone on the banks of the roaring Lora. Let us hear the sorrow of thy youth, and the darkness of thy days!"

"It was in the days of peace," replied the great Clessámmor. "I came, in my bounding ship, to Balclutha's walls of towers. The winds had roared behind my sails, and Clutha's streams received my dark-bosomed ship. Three days I remained in Reuthámir's halls, and saw his daughter, that beam of light. The joy of the shell went round, and the aged hero gave the fair. Her breasts were like foam on the wave, and her eyes like stars of light: her hair was dark as the raven's wing: her soul was generous and mild. My love for Moina was great: my heart poured forth in joy.

"The son of a stranger came; a chief who loved the white-bosomed Moina. His words were mighty in the hall; he often half-unsheathed his sword. Where, said he, is the mighty Comhal, the restless wanderer of the heath? Comes he, with his host, to Balclutha, since Clessámmor is so bold? My soul, I replied, O warrior! burns in a light of its own. I stand without fear in the midst of thousands, though the valiant are distant far. Stranger! thy words are mighty, for Clessámmor is alone. But my sword trembles by my side, and longs to glitter in my hand. Speak no more of Comhal, son of the winding Clutha!

"The strength of his pride arose. We fought; he fell beneath my sword. The banks of Clutha heard his fall; a thousand spears glittered around. I fought: the strangers prevailed: I plunged into the stream of

15. Toscar, the speaker, throughout the prose poem, is supposed to be Ossian, or Oisin, a legendary Gaelic blind bard of the third century, son of Fingal.

31. shell, sea shell holding drink.

Clutha. My white sails rose over the waves, and I bounded on the dark-blue sea. Moina came to the shore, and rolled the red eye of her tears: her loose hair flew on the wind: and I heard her mournful, distant cries. Often did I turn my ship; but the winds of the east prevailed. Nor Clutha ever since have I seen, nor Moina of the dark-brown hair. She fell in Balclutha, for I have seen her ghost. I knew her as she came through the dusky night, along the murmur of Lora: she was like the new moon, seen through the gathered mist, when the sky pours down its flaky snow, and the world is silent and dark."

"Raise, ye bards," said the mighty Fingal, "the praise of unhappy Moina. Call her ghost, with your songs, to our hills; that she may rest with the fair of Morven, the sun-beams of other days, the delight of heroes of old. I have seen the walls of Balclutha, but they were desolate. The fire had resounded in the halls: and the voice of the people is heard no more. The stream of Clutha was removed from its place, by the fall of the walls. The thistle shook, there, its lonely head: the moss whistled to the wind. The fox looked out from the windows, the rank grass of the wall waved round its head. Desolate is the dwelling of Moina, silence is in the house of her fathers. Raise the song of mourning, O bards! over the land of strangers. They have but fallen before us: for, one day, we must fall. Why dost thou build the hall, son of the winged days? Thou lookest from thy towers to-day; yet a few years, and the blast of the desert comes; it howls in thy empty court, and whistles round thy half-worn shield. And let the blast of the desert come! we shall be renowned in our day! The mark of my arm shall be in battle; my name in the song of bards. Raise the song; send round the shell: let joy be heard in my hall. When thou, sun of heaven shalt fail! if thou shalt fail, thou mighty light! if thy brightness is for a season, like Fingal; our fame shall survive thy beams!"

Such was the song of Fingal, in the day of his joy. His thousand bards leaned forward from their seats, to hear the voice of the king. It was like the music of harps on the gale of the spring. Lovely were thy thoughts, O Fingal! Why had not Ossian the strength of thy soul? But thou standest alone, my father! Who can equal the king of Selma?

The night passed away in song; morning returned in joy. Thy mountains showed their grey heads; the blue face of ocean smiled. The white wave is seen tumbling round the distant rock; a mist rose slowly, from the lake. It came in the figure of an aged man, along the silent plain. Its large limbs did not move in steps; for a ghost supported it in mid air. It came towards Selma's hall, and dissolved in a shower of blood.

The king alone beheld the sight; he foresaw the death of the people. He came, in silence, to his hall; and took his father's spear. The mail rattled on his breast. The heroes rose around. They looked in silence on each other, marking the eyes of Fingal. They saw battle in his face: the death of armies on his spear. A thousand shields, at once, are placed on their arms; they drew a thousand swords. The hall of Selma brightened around. The clang of arms ascends. The grey dogs howl in their place. No word is among the mighty chiefs. Each marked the eyes of the king, and half assumed his spear.

"Sons of Morven," began the king, "this is no time to fill the shell. The battle darkens near us; death hovers over the land. Some ghost, the friend of Fingal, has forewarned us of the foe. The sons of the stranger come from the darkly-rolling sea. For, from the water, came the sight of Morven's gloomy danger. Let each assume his heavy spear, each gird on his father's sword. Let the dark helmet rise on every head; the mail pour its lightning from every side. The battle gathers like a storm; soon shall ye hear the roar of death."

The hero moved on before his host, like a cloud before a ridge of green fire when it pours on the sky of night, and mariners foresee a storm. On Cona's rising heath they stood; the white-bosomed maids beheld them above like a grove; they foresaw the death of the youth, and looked towards the sea with fear. The white wave deceived them for distant sails; the tear is on their cheek! The sun rose on the sea, and we beheld a distant fleet. Like the mist of the ocean they came: and poured their youth upon the coast. The chief was among them, like the stag in the midst of the herd. His shield is studded with gold; stately strode the king of spears. He moved towards Selma; his thousands moved behind.

"Go, with a song of peace," said Fingal; "go, Ullin, to the king of swords. Tell him that we are mighty in war; that the ghosts of our foes are many. But renowned are they who have feasted in my halls! they shew the arms of my fathers in a foreign land: the sons of the strangers wonder, and bless the friends of Morven's race; for our names have been heard afar: the kings of the world shook in the midst of their host."

Ullin went with his song. Fingal rested on his spear: he saw the mighty foe in his armour: he blessed the stranger's son. "How stately art thou, son of the sea!" said the king of woody Morven. "Thy sword is a beam of fire by thy side: thy spear is a pine that defines the storm. The varied face of the moon is not broader than thy shield. Ruddy is thy face of youth! soft the ringlets of thy hair! But this tree may fall; and his memory be forgot! The daughter of the stranger will be sad, looking to the rolling sea: the children will say, 'We see a ship; perhaps it is the king of Balclutha.' The tear starts from their mother's eye. Her thoughts are of him who sleeps in Morven!"

Such were the words of the king, when Ullin came to the mighty Carthon; he threw down the spear before him; he raised the song of peace. "Come to the feast of Fingal, Carthon, from the rolling sea! partake of the feast of the king, or lift the spear of war! The ghosts of our foes are many: but renowned are the friends of Morven! Behold that field, O Carthon; many a green hill rises there, with mossy stones and rustling grass: these are the tombs of Fingal's foes, the sons of the rolling sea!"

"Dost thou speak to the weak in arms!" said Carthon, "bard of the woody Morven? Is my face pale for fear, son of the peaceful song? Why, then, dost thou think to darken my soul with the tales of those who fell? My arm has fought in battle; my renown is known afar. Go to the feeble in arms, bid them yield to Fingal. Have not I seen the fallen Balclutha? And shall I feast with Comhal's son? Comhal! who threw his fire in the midst of my father's hall! I was young, and knew not the cause why the virgins wept. The columns of smoke pleased mine eye, when they rose above my walls! I often looked back, with gladness, when my friends fled along the hill. But when the years of my youth came on, I beheld the moss of my fallen walls: my sigh arose with the morning, and my tears descended with night. Shall I not fight, I said to my soul, against the children of my foes? And I will fight, O bard! I feel the strength of my soul."

His people gathered around the hero, and drew at once their shining swords. He stands, in the midst, like a pillar of fire; the tear half-starting from his eye; for he thought of the fallen Balclutha; the crowded pride of his soul arose. Sidelong he looked up to the hill, where our heroes shone in arms; the spear trembled in his hand: bending forward, he seemed to threaten the king.

"Shall I," said Fingal to his soul, "meet, at once, the youth? Shall I stop him, in the midst of his course, before his fame shall arise? But the bard, hereafter, may say, when he sees the tomb of Carthon: Fingal took his thousands to battle, before the noble Carthon fell. No, bard of the times to come! thou shalt not lessen Fingal's fame. My heroes will fight the youth, and Fingal behold the war. If he overcomes, I rush, in my strength, like the roaring stream of Coma. Who, of my chiefs, will meet the son of the rolling sea? Many are his warriors on the coast: and strong is his ashen spear!"

Cathul rose, in his strength, the son of the mighty Lormar: three hundred youths attend the chief, the race of his native streams. Feeble was his arm against Carthon, he fell; and his heroes fled. Connal resumed the battle, but he broke his heavy spear: he lay bound on the field: Carthon pursued his people.

"Clessámmor!" said the king of Morven, "where is the spear of thy strength? Will thou behold Connal bound; thy friend, at the stream of Lora? Rise, in the light of thy steel, companion of valiant Comhal! Let the youth of Balclutha feel the strength of Morven's race." He rose in the strength of his steel, shaking his grisly locks. He fitted the steel to his side; he rushed, in the pride of valour.

Carthon stood on a rock: he saw the hero rushing on. He loved the dreadful joy of his face: his strength, in the locks of age! "Shall I lift that spear," he said, "that never strikes, but once, a foe? Or shall I, with the words of peace, preserve the warrior's life? Stately are his steps of age! lovely the remnant of his years! Perhaps it is the husband of Moina; the father of car-borne Carthon. Often have I heard that he dwelt at the echoing stream of Lora."

Such were his words, when Clessámmor came, and lifted high his spear. The youth received it on his shield, and spoke the words of peace. "Warrior of the aged locks! Is there no youth to lift the spear? Hast thou no son to raise the shield before his father, to meet the arm of youth? Is the spouse of thy love no more? or weeps she over the tombs of thy sons? Art thou of the kings of men? What will be the fame of my sword shouldst thou fall?"

"It will be great, thou son of pride!" began the tall Clessámmor. "I have been renowned in battle; but I never told my name to a foe. Yield to me, son of the wave, then shalt thou know that the mark of my sword is in many a field." "I never yielded, king of spears!" replied the noble pride of Carthon: "I have also fought in war; I behold my future fame. Despise me not, thou chief of men! my arm, my spear is strong. Retire among thy friends; let younger heroes fight." "Why dost thou wound my soul?" replied Clessámmor, with a tear. "Age does not tremble on my hand; I still can lift the sword. Shall I fly in Fingal's sight; in the sight of him I love? Son of the sea! I never fled: exalt thy pointed spear."

They fought like two contending winds, that strive to roll the wave. Carthon bade his spear to err; he still thought that the foe was the spouse of

---

38. **name . . . foe.** "*A man who tells his name to his enemy was of old an ignominious term for a coward.*" (Macpherson)

Moina. He broke Clessámmor's beamy spear in twain; he seized his shining sword. But as Carthon was binding the chief, the chief drew the dagger of his fathers. He saw the foe's uncovered side; and opened there a wound.

Fingal saw Clessámmor low: he moved in the sound of his steel. The host stood silent, in his presence; they turned their eyes to the king. He came, like the sullen noise of a storm, before the winds arise: the hunter hears it in the vale, and retires to the cave of the rock. Carthon stood in his place: the blood is rushing down his side: he saw the coming down of the king; his hopes of fame arose; but pale was his cheek: his hair flew loose, his helmet shook on high: the force of Carthon failed; but his soul was strong.

Fingal beheld the hero's blood; he stopped the uplifted spear. "Yield, king of swords!" said Comhal's son; "I behold thy blood. Thou hast been mighty in battle, and thy fame shall never fade." "Art thou the king so far renowned?" replied the car-borne Carthon. "Art thou the light of death, that frightens the kings of the world? But why should Carthon ask? for he is like the stream of his hills, strong as a river in his course: swift as the eagle of heaven. O that I had fought with the king; that my fame might be great in song! that the hunter, beholding my tomb, might say, he fought with the mighty Fingal. But Carthon dies unknown; he has poured out his force on the weak."

"But thou shalt not die unknown," replied the king of woody Morven: "my bards are many, O Carthon! Their songs descend to future times. The children of years to come shall hear the fame of Carthon; when they sit round the burning oak, and the night is spent in songs of old. The hunter, sitting in the heath, shall hear the rustling blast; and, raising his eyes, behold the rock where Carthon fell. He shall turn to his son and shew the place where the mighty fought: 'There the King of Balclutha fought, like the strength of a thousand streams.'"

Joy rose in Carthon's face: he lifted his heavy eyes. He gave his sword to Fingal, to lie within his hall, that the memory of Balclutha's king might remain in Morven. The battle ceased along the field, the bard had sung the song of peace. The chiefs gathered round the falling Carthon; they heard his words with sighs. Silent they leaned on their spears, while Balclutha's hero spoke. His hair sighed in the wind, and his voice was sad and low.

"King of Morven," Carthon said, "I fall in the midst of my course. A foreign tomb receives, in youth, the last of Reuthámir's race. Darkness dwells in Balclutha: the shadows of grief in Crathmo. But raise my remembrance on the banks of Lora: where my fathers dwelt. Perhaps the husband of Moina will mourn over his fallen Carthon." His words reached the heart of Clessámmor: he fell, in silence, on his son. The host stood darkened around: no voice is on the plain. Night came; the moon, from the east, looked on the mournful field: but still they stood, like a silent grove that lifts its head on Gormal, when the loud winds are laid, and dark autumn is on the plain.

Three days they mourned above Carthon; on the fourth his father died. In the narrow plain of the rock they lie; a dim ghost defends their tomb. There lovely Moina is often seen; when the sun-beam darts on the rock, and all around is dark. There she is seen, Malvina! but not like the daughters of the hill. Her robes are from the stranger's land; and she is still alone!

Fingal was sad for Carthon; he commanded his bards to mark the day, when shadowy autumn returned. And often did they mark the day and sing the hero's praise. "Who comes so dark from ocean's roar, like autumn's shadowy cloud? Death is trembling in his hand! his eyes are flames of fire! Who roars along dark Lora's heath? Who but Carthon, king of swords! The people fall! see how he strides, like the sullen ghost of Morven! But there he lies a goodly oak, which sudden blasts overturned! When shalt thou rise, Balclutha's joy? When, Carthon, shalt thou arise? Who comes so dark from ocean's roar, like autumn's shadowy cloud?" Such were the words of the bards, in the day of their mourning. Ossian often joined their voice; and added to their song. My soul has been mournful for Carthon; he fell in the days of his youth: and thou, O Clessámmor! where is thy dwelling in the wind? Has the youth forgot his wound? Flies he, on clouds, with thee? I feel the sun, O Malvina! leave me to my rest. Perhaps they may come to my dreams; I think I hear a feeble voice! The beam of heaven delights to shine on the grave of Carthon: I feel it warm around!

O thou that rollest above, round as the shield of my fathers! Whence are thy beams, O sun! thy everlasting light? Thou comest forth, in thy awful beauty; the stars hide themselves in the sky; the moon, cold and pale, sinks in the western wave. But thou thyself movest alone: who can be a companion of thy course? The oaks of the mountains fall: the mountains themselves decay with years; the ocean shrinks and grows again: the moon herself is lost in

---

10. **plain.** The many resemblances between the foregoing passage and Matthew Arnold's *Sohrab and Rustum* are not, of course, accidental.

heaven; but thou art forever the same; rejoicing in the brightness of thy course. When the world is dark with tempests; when thunder rolls, and lightning flies; thou lookest in thy beauty from the clouds, and laughest at the storm. But to Ossian, thou lookest in vain; for he beholds thy beams no more, whether thy yellow hair flows on the eastern clouds, or thou tremblest at the gates of the west. But thou art, perhaps, like me, for a season; thy years will have an end. Thou shalt sleep in the clouds, careless of the voice of the morning. Exult then, O sun, in the strength of thy youth: Age is dark and unlovely; it is like the glimmering light of the moon, when it shines through broken clouds, and the mist is on the hills; the blast of the north is on the plain, the traveller shrinks in the midst of his journey.

James Boswell
1740–1795

We are in a better position today than ever before to see the absurdity of Macaulay's famous remark about Boswell that "if he had not been a great fool he would never have been a great writer." No one denies, even in our time, that the little Scottish lawyer had his due share of human folly and frailty. He was ludicrously vain, bustling, inquisitive, and prone to thrust himself upon the notice of famous persons. There is some evidence, moreover, that he drank too much. And yet, now that the discoveries of recent years are enabling us to study him in his correspondence and his private journals, we are more and more inclined to agree with Thomas Carlyle's indignant reply to Macaulay: "Boswell wrote a good book because he had a heart and an eye to discern wisdom and an utterance to render it forth; because of his free insight, his lively talent, and, above all, of his love and childlike open-mindedness."

Other qualities still went to the making of Boswell's *Life of Samuel Johnson*. Patience and pertinacity were among them, for that book was on the anvil for no less than twenty-seven years. A quiet endurance of rudeness from Johnson himself and from his male and female friends went to the making of it. So also did boldness, imagination, accuracy, a sense of humor, deep human sympathy, and a faculty for clear-eyed hero worship which has seldom if ever been excelled. Yet it is only for his toil and his fidelity that Boswell himself asks any recognition. In his "Advertisement" to the first edition he wrote:

"The labour and anxious attention with which I have collected and arranged the materials of which these volumes are composed will hardly be conceived by those who read them with careless facility. The stretch of mind and prompt assiduity by which so many conversations were preserved, I myself, at some distance of time, contemplate with wonder; and I must be allowed to suggest that the nature of the work in other respects, as it consists of innumerable detached particulars, all which, even the most minute, I have spared no pains to ascertain with a scrupulous authenticity, has occasioned a degree of trouble far beyond that of any other species of composition. Were I to detail the books which I have consulted, and the inquiries which I have found it necessary to make by various channels, I should probably be thought ridiculously ostentatious. Let me only observe, as a specimen of my trouble, that I have sometimes been obliged to run half over London in order to fix a date correctly—which, when I had accomplished, I well knew would obtain me no praise, though a failure would have been to my discredit. And after all, perhaps, hard as it may be, I shall not be surprised if omissions or mistakes be pointed out with invidious severity. I have also been extremely careful as to the exactness of my quotations, holding that there is a respect due to the public which should oblige every author to attend to this, and never to introduce them with,—'I think I have read' or—'If I remember right,' when the originals may be examined."

And yet, when all is said, we must admit that Boswell did no more than bring adequate powers of comprehension and execution to a task which called for the utmost that he had to give. The life and character of Dr. Johnson, taken together with the set of brilliant persons who made up Johnson's circle—Burke, Garrick, Goldsmith, Reynolds, Gibbon, and others—gave him an almost unparalleled opportunity to which he did no more than justice. It was the combination of the matter and the man that produced the greatest of English biographies and, as Boswell himself quite correctly called it, "one of the most interesting books in the world."

from THE LIFE OF SAMUEL JOHNSON

A.D. 1763: AETAT. 54.

This is to me a memorable year; for in it I had the happiness to obtain the acquaintance of that extraordinary man whose memoirs I am now writing; an acquaintance which I shall ever esteem as one of the most fortunate circumstances in my life. Though then but two-and-twenty, I had for several years read his works with delight and instruction, and had the highest reverence for their author, which had grown up in my fancy into a kind of mysterious veneration, by figuring to myself a state of solemn elevated abstraction, in which I supposed him to live in the immense metropolis of London. Mr. Gentleman, a native of Ireland, who passed some years in Scotland as a player, and as an instructor in the English language, a man whose talents and worth were depressed by misfortunes, had given me a representation of the figure and manner of DICTIONARY JOHNSON! as he was then generally called; and during my first visit to London, which was for three months in 1760, Mr. Derrick the poet, who was Gentleman's friend and countryman, flattered me with hopes that he would introduce me to Johnson, an honour of which I was very ambitious. But he never found an opportunity; which made me doubt that he had promised to do what was not in his power; till Johnson some years afterwards told me, "Derrick, Sir, might very well have introduced you. I had a kindness for Derrick, and am sorry he is dead." . . .

Mr. Thomas Davies the actor, who then kept a bookseller's shop in Russel-street, Covent-garden, told me that Johnson was very much his friend, and came frequently to his house, where he more than once invited me to meet him; but by some unlucky accident or other he was prevented from coming to us.

Mr. Thomas Davies was a man of good understanding and talents, with the advantage of a liberal education. Though somewhat pompous, he was an entertaining companion; and his literary performances have no inconsiderable share of merit. He was a friendly and very hospitable man. Both he and his wife, (who has been celebrated for her beauty,) though upon the stage for many years, maintained an uniform decency of character; and Johnson esteemed them, and lived in as easy an intimacy with them, as with any family which he used to visit. Mr. Davies recollected several of Johnson's remarkable sayings, and was one of the best of the many imitators of his voice and manner, while relating them. He increased my impatience more and more to see the extraordinary man whose works I highly valued, and whose conversation was reported to be so peculiarly excellent.

At last, on Monday the 16th of May, when I was sitting in Mr. Davies's back-parlour, after having drunk tea with him and Mrs. Davies, Johnson unexpectedly came into the shop; and Mr. Davies having perceived him through the glass-door in the room in which we were sitting, advancing towards us,—he announced his aweful approach to me, somewhat in the manner of an actor in the part of Horatio, when he addresses Hamlet on the appearance of his father's ghost, "Look, my Lord, it comes." I found that I had a very perfect idea of Johnson's figure, from the portrait of him painted by Sir Joshua Reynolds soon after he had published his *Dictionary*, in the attitude of sitting in his easy chair in deep meditation, which was the first picture his friend did for him, which Sir Joshua very kindly presented to me, and from which an engraving has been made for this work. Mr. Davies mentioned my name, and respectfully introduced me to him. I was much agitated; and recollecting his prejudice against the Scotch, of which I had heard much, I said to Davies, "Don't tell where I come from."—"From Scotland," cried Davies roguishly. "Mr. Johnson, (said I) I do indeed come from Scotland, but I cannot help it." I am willing to flatter myself that I meant this as light pleasantry to sooth and conciliate him, and not as an humiliating abasement at the expense of my country. But however that might be, this speech was somewhat unlucky; for with that quickness of wit for which he was so remarkable, he seized the expression "come from Scotland," which I used in the sense of being of that country; and, as if I had said that I had come away from it, or left it, retorted, "That, Sir, I find, is what a very great many of your countrymen cannot help." This stroke stunned me a good deal; and when we had sat down, I felt myself not a little embarrassed, and apprehensive of what might come next. He then addressed himself to Davies: "What do you think of Garrick? He has refused me an order for the play for Miss Williams, because he knows the house will be full, and that an order

---

Aetat. 54, the fifty-fourth year of Johnson's age. **25. Derrick**, Samuel Derrick (1721–1779). **48. Garrick**, David Garrick (1717–1779), Johnson's former pupil, and the most famous actor of the age. **49. Miss Williams**, Anna Williams, one of the several persons whom Johnson supported and lodged in his own house.

would be worth three shillings." Eager to take any opening to get into conversation with him, I ventured to say, "O, Sir, I cannot think Mr. Garrick would grudge such a trifle to you." "Sir, (said he, with a stern look,) I have known David Garrick longer than you have done: and I know no right you have to talk to me on the subject." Perhaps I deserved this check; for it was rather presumptuous in me, an entire stranger, to express any doubt of the justice of his animadversion upon his old acquaintance and pupil. I now felt myself much mortified, and began to think that the hope which I had long indulged of obtaining his acquaintance was blasted. And, in truth, had not my ardour been uncommonly strong, and my resolution uncommonly persevering, so rough a reception might have deterred me for ever from making any further attempts. Fortunately, however, I remained upon the field not wholly discomfited; and was soon rewarded by hearing some of his conversation, of which I preserved the following short minute, without marking the questions and observations by which it was produced.

"People (he remarked) may be taken in once, who imagine that an author is greater in private life than other men. Uncommon parts require uncommon opportunities for their exertion."

"In barbarous society, superiority of parts is of real consequence. Great strength or great wisdom is of much value to an individual. But in more polished times there are people to do every thing for money; and then there are a number of other superiorities, such as those of birth and fortune, and rank, that dissipate men's attention, and leave no extraordinary share of respect for personal and intellectual superiority. This is wisely ordered by Providence, to preserve some equality among mankind."

"Sir, this book (*The Elements of Criticism*, which he had taken up,) is a pretty essay, and deserves to be held in some estimation, though much of it is chimerical."

Speaking of one who with more than ordinary boldness attacked publick measures and the royal family, he said,

"I think he is safe from the law, but he is an abusive scoundrel; and instead of applying to my Lord Chief Justice to punish him, I would send half a dozen footmen and have him well ducked."

"The notion of liberty amuses the people of England, and helps to keep off the *taedium vitae*. When a butcher tells you that *his heart bleeds for his country*, he has, in fact, no uneasy feeling."

"Sheridan will not succeed at Bath with his oratory. Ridicule has gone down before him, and, I doubt, Derrick is his enemy."

"Derrick may do very well, as long as he can outrun his character; but the moment his character gets up with him, it is all over."

It is, however, but just to record, that some years afterwards, when I reminded him of this sarcasm, he said, "Well, but Derrick has now got a character that he need not run away from."

I was highly pleased with the extraordinary vigour of his conversation, and regretted that I was drawn away from it by an engagement at another place. I had, for a part of the evening, been left alone with him, and had ventured to make an observation now and then, which he received very civilly; so that I was satisfied that though there was a roughness in his manner, there was no ill-nature in his disposition. Davies followed me to the door, and when I complained to him a little of the hard blows which the great man had given me, he kindly took upon him to console me by saying, "Don't be uneasy. I can see he likes you very well."

A few days afterwards I called on Davies, and asked him if he thought I might take the liberty of waiting on Mr. Johnson at his Chambers in the Temple. He said I certainly might, and that Mr. Johnson would take it as a compliment. So upon Tuesday the 24th of May, after having been enlivened by the witty sallies of Messieurs Thornton, Wilkes, Churchill and Lloyd, with whom I had passed the morning, I boldly repaired to Johnson. His Chambers were on the first floor of No. 1, Inner-Temple-lane, and I entered them with an impression given me by the Reverend Dr. Blair, of Edinburgh, who had been introduced to him not long before, and described his having "found the Giant in his den"; an expression, which, when I came to be pretty well acquainted with Johnson, I repeated to him, and he was diverted at this picturesque account of himself. Dr. Blair had been presented to him by Dr. James Fordyce. At this time the controversy concerning the pieces published by Mr. James Macpherson, as translations of *Ossian*, was at its height. Johnson had all along denied their authenticity; and, what was still more provoking to their admirers, maintained that they had no merit. The subject having been introduced by Dr. For-

---

38. **The Elements of Criticism,** by Henry Horne, Lord Kames, a Scottish judge. 5. **character,** reputation. 30–31. **Thornton . . . Lloyd,** all men of letters and persons whom Johnson would have thought disreputable. For John **Wilkes** (1727–1797) at this time Johnson had a special disapprobation partly because of his opinions and partly because of his profligate life. 35. **Blair,** the Rev. Hugh Blair, Scottish clergyman and rhetorician. 44. **Macpherson,** author of the "Ossianic Poems" (see page 934).

dyce, Dr. Blair, relying on the internal evidence of their antiquity, asked Dr. Johnson whether he thought any man of a modern age could have written such poems? Johnson replied, "Yes, Sir, many men, many women, and many children." Johnson, at this time, did not know that Dr. Blair had just published a *Dissertation*, not only defending their authenticity, but seriously ranking them with the poems of *Homer* and *Virgil;* and when he was afterwards informed of this circumstance, he expressed some displeasure at Dr. Fordyce's having suggested the topic, and said, "I am not sorry that they got thus much for their pains. Sir, it was like leading one to talk of a book when the authour is concealed behind the door."

He received me very courteously; but, it must be confessed, that his apartment, and furniture, and morning dress, were sufficiently uncouth. His brown suit of cloaths looked very rusty; he had on a little old shrivelled unpowdered wig, which was too small for his head; his shirt-neck and knees of his breeches were loose; his black worsted stockings ill drawn up; and he had a pair of unbuckled shoes by way of slippers. But all these slovenly particularities were forgotten the moment that he began to talk. Some gentlemen, whom I do not recollect, were sitting with him; and when they went away, I also rose; but he said to me, "Nay, don't go." "Sir, (said I,) I am afraid that I intrude upon you. It is benevolent to allow me to sit and hear you." He seemed pleased with this compliment, which I sincerely paid him, and answered, "Sir, I am obliged to any man who visits me." I have preserved the following short minute of what passed this day:—

"Madness frequently discovers itself merely by unnecessary deviation from the usual modes of the world. My poor friend Smart shewed the disturbance of his mind, by falling upon his knees, and saying his prayers in the street, or in any other unusual place. Now although, rationally speaking, it is greater madness not to pray at all, than to pray as Smart did, I am afraid there are so many who do not pray, that their understanding is not called in question."

Concerning this unfortunate poet, Christopher Smart, who was confined in a mad-house, he had, at another time, the following conversation with Dr. Burney:—BURNEY. "How does poor Smart do, Sir; is he likely to recover?" JOHNSON. "It seems as if his mind had ceased to struggle with the disease; for he grows fat upon it." BURNEY. "Perhaps, Sir, that may be from want of exercise." JOHNSON. "No, Sir; he has partly as much exercise as he used to have, for he digs in the garden. Indeed, before his confinement, he used for exercise to walk to the alehouse; but he was *carried* back again. I did not think he ought to be shut up. His infirmities were not noxious to society. He insisted on people praying with him; and I'd as lief pray with Kit Smart as any one else. Another charge was, that he did not love clean linen; and I have no passion for it."—Johnson continued: "Mankind have a great aversion to intellectual labour; but even supposing knowledge to be easily attainable, more people would be content to be ignorant than would take even a little trouble to acquire it."

"The morality of an action depends on the motive from which we act. If I fling half a crown to a beggar with intention to break his head, and he picks it up and buys victuals with it, the physical effect is good; but, with respect to me, the action is very wrong. So, religious exercises, if not performed with an intention to please GOD, avail us nothing. As our Saviour says of those who perform them from other motives, 'Verily they have their reward.'"

"The Christian religion has very strong evidences. It, indeed, appears in some degree strange to reason; but in History we have undoubted facts, against which, reasoning *à priori*, we have more arguments than we have for them; but then, testimony has great weight, and casts the balance. I would recommend to every man whose faith is yet unsettled, Grotius,—Dr. Pearson,—and Dr. Clarke."

Talking of Garrick, he said, "He is the first man in the world for sprightly conversation."

When I rose a second time he again pressed me to stay, which I did.

He told me, that he generally went abroad at four in the afternoon, and seldom came home till two in the morning. I took the liberty to ask if he did not think it wrong to live thus, and not make more use of his great talents. He owned it was a bad habit. On reviewing, at the distance of many years, my journal of this period, I wonder how, at my first visit, I ventured to talk to him so freely, and that he bore it with so much indulgence.

Before we parted, he was so good as to promise to favour me with his company one evening at my lodgings; and, as I took my leave, shook me cordially by the hand. It is almost needless to add, that I felt no little elation at having now so happily established an acquaintance of which I had been so long ambitious.

My readers will, I trust, excuse me for being thus minutely circumstantial, when it is considered that

---

37. **Smart,** Christopher Smart, the poet (see page 928).
48. **Burney,** Charles Burney (1726–1814), a teacher and historian of music.

the acquaintance of Dr. Johnson was to me a most valuable acquisition, and laid the foundation of whatever instruction and entertainment they may receive from my collections concerning the great subject of the work which they are now perusing. . . .

My next meeting with Johnson was on Friday the 1st of July, when he and I and Dr. Goldsmith supped together at the Mitre. I was before this time pretty well acquainted with Goldsmith, who was one of the brightest ornaments of the Johnsonian school. Goldsmith's respectful attachment to Johnson was then at its height; for his own literary reputation had not yet distinguished him so much as to excite a vain desire of competition with his great Master. He had increased my admiration of the goodness of Johnson's heart, by incidental remarks in the course of conversation, such as, when I mentioned Mr. Levet, whom he entertained under his roof, "He is poor and honest, which is recommendation enough to Johnson"; and when I wondered that he was very kind to a man of whom I had heard a very bad character, "He is now become miserable, and that insures the protection of Johnson."

Goldsmith attempted this evening to maintain, I suppose from an affectation of paradox, "that knowledge was not desirable on its own account, for it often was a source of unhappiness." JOHNSON. "Why, Sir, that knowledge may in some cases produce unhappiness, I allow. But, upon the whole, knowledge, *per se*, is certainly an object which every man would wish to attain, although, perhaps, he may not take the trouble necessary for attaining it."

Dr. John Campbell, the celebrated political and biographical writer, being mentioned, Johnson said, "Campbell is a man of much knowledge, and has a good share of imagination. His *Hermippus Redivivus* is very entertaining, as an account of the Hermetick philosophy, and as furnishing a curious history of the extravagancies of the human mind. If it were merely imaginary it would be nothing at all. Campbell is not always rigidly careful of truth in his conversation; but I do not believe there is any thing of this carelessness in his books. Campbell is a good man, a pious man. I am afraid he has not been in the inside of a church for many years; but he never passes a church without pulling off his hat. This shews that he has good principles. I used to go pretty often to Campbell's on a Sunday evening till I began to consider that the shoals of Scotchmen who flocked about him might probably say, when anything of mine was well done, "Ay, ay, he has learnt this of CAWMELL!"

He talked very contemptuously of Churchill's poetry, observing, that "it had a temporary currency, only from its audacity of abuse, and being filled with living names, and that it would sink into oblivion." I ventured to hint that he was not quite a fair judge, as Churchill had attacked him violently. JOHNSON. "Nay, Sir, I am a very fair judge. He did not attack me violently till he found I did not like his poetry; and his attack on me shall not prevent me from continuing to say what I think of him, from an apprehension that it may be ascribed to resentment. No, Sir, I called the fellow a blockhead at first, and I will call him a blockhead still. However, I will acknowledge that I have a better opinion of him now, than I once had; for he has shewn more fertility than I expected. To be sure, he is a tree that cannot produce good fruit: he only bears crabs. But, Sir, a tree that produces a great many crabs is better than a tree which produces only a few." . . .

On Tuesday the 5th of July, I again visited Johnson. He told me he had looked into the poems of a pretty voluminous writer, Mr. (now Dr.) John Ogilvie, one of the Presbyterian ministers of Scotland, which had lately come out, but could find no thinking in them. BOSWELL. "Is there not imagination in them, Sir?" JOHNSON. "Why, Sir, there is in them what *was* imagination, but it is no more imagination in *him*, than sound is sound in the echo. And his diction too is not his own. We have long ago seen *white-robed innocence*, and *flower-bespangled meads*."

Talking of London, he observed, "Sir, if you wish to have a just notion of the magnitude of this city, you must not be satisfied with seeing its great streets and squares, but must survey the innumerable little lanes and courts. It is not in the showy evolutions of buildings, but in the multiplicity of human habitations which are crouded together, that the wonderful immensity of London consists."—I have often amused myself with thinking how different a place London is to different people. They, whose narrow minds are contracted to the consideration of some one particular pursuit, view it only through that medium. A politician thinks of it merely as the seat of government in its different departments; a grazier, as a vast market for cattle; a mercantile man, as a place where a prodigious deal of business is done upon 'Change; a dramatick enthusiast, as the grand scene of theatrical entertainments; a man of

---

7. **next meeting.** There had been several after the last one given here.   9. **Mitre,** a tavern in Fleet Street.   19. **Levet,** a physician who, having failed in his practice, lived for many years in Johnson's house.

4. **Churchill,** Charles Churchill (1731–1764), a satiric poet.

pleasure, as an assemblage of taverns, and the great emporium for ladies of easy virtue. But the intellectual man is struck with it, as comprehending the whole of human life in all its variety, the contemplation of which is inexhaustible.

On Wednesday, July 6, he was engaged to sup with me at my lodgings in Downing-street, Westminster. But on the preceding night my landlord having behaved very rudely to me and some company who were with me, I had resolved not to remain another night in his house. I was exceedingly uneasy at the awkward appearance I supposed I should make to Johnson and the other gentlemen whom I had invited, not being able to receive them at home, and being obliged to order supper at the Mitre. I went to Johnson in the morning, and talked of it as a serious distress. He laughed, and said, "Consider, Sir, how insignificant this will appear a twelvemonth hence."—Were this consideration to be applied to most of the little vexatious incidents of life, by which our quiet is too often disturbed, it would prevent many painful sensations. I have tried it frequently, with good effect. "There is nothing (continued he) in this mighty misfortune; nay, we shall be better at the Mitre." I told him that I had been at Sir John Fielding's office, complaining of my landlord, and had been informed, that though I had taken my lodgings for a year, I might, upon proof of his bad behaviour, quit them when I pleased, without being under an obligation to pay rent for any longer time than while I possessed them. The fertility of Johnson's mind could shew itself even upon so small a matter as this. "Why, Sir, (said he,) I suppose this must be the law, since you have been told so in Bow-street. But, if your landlord could hold you to your bargain, and the lodgings should be yours for a year, you may certainly use them as you think fit. So, Sir, you may quarter two life-guardsmen upon him; or you may send the greatest scoundrel you can find into your apartments; or you may say that you want to make some experiments in natural philosophy, and may burn a large quantity of assafoetida in his house."

I had as my guests this evening at the Mitre tavern, Dr. Johnson, Dr. Goldsmith, Mr. Thomas Davies, Mr. Eccles, an Irish gentleman, for whose agreeable company I was obliged to Mr. Davies, and the Reverend Mr. John Ogilvie, who was desirous of being in company with my illustrious friend, while I, in my turn, was proud to have the honour of shewing one of my countrymen upon

26. **Sir John Fielding,** a justice of the peace, and half-brother of Henry Fielding, author of *Tom Jones*.

what easy terms Johnson permitted me to live with him.

Goldsmith, as usual, endeavoured, with too much eagerness, to *shine*, and disputed very warmly with Johnson against the well-known maxim of the British constitution, "the King can do no wrong"; affirming, that "what was morally false could not be politically true; and as the King might, in the exercise of his regal power, command and cause the doing of what was wrong, it certainly might be said, in sense and in reason, that he could do wrong." JOHNSON. "Sir, you are to consider, that in our constitution, according to its true principles, the King is the head; he is supreme; he is above everything, and there is no power by which he can be tried. Therefore, it is, Sir, that we hold the King can do no wrong; that whatever may happen to be wrong in government may not be above our reach, by being ascribed to Majesty. Redress is always to be had against oppression, by punishing the immediate agents. The King, though he should command, cannot force a Judge to condemn a man unjustly; therefore it is the Judge whom we prosecute and punish. Political institutions are formed upon the consideration of what will most frequently tend to the good of the whole, although now and then exceptions may occur. Thus it is better in general that a nation should have a supreme legislative power, although it may at times be abused. And then, Sir, there is this consideration, that *if the abuse be enormous, Nature will rise up, and claiming her original rights, overturn a corrupt political system.*" I mark this animated sentence with peculiar pleasure, as a noble instance of that truly dignified spirit of freedom which ever glowed in his heart, though he was charged with slavish tenets by superficial observers; because he was at all times indignant against that false patriotism, that pretended love of freedom, that unruly restlessness, which is inconsistent with the stable authority of any good government.

This generous sentiment, which he uttered with great fervour, struck me exceedingly, and stirred my blood to that pitch of fancied resistance, the possibility of which I am glad to keep in mind, but to which I trust I never shall be forced.

"Great abilities (said he) are not requisite for an Historian; for in historical composition, all the greatest powers of the human mind are quiescent. He has facts ready to his hand; so there is no exercise of invention. Imagination is not required in any high degree; only about as much as is used in the lower kinds of poetry. Some penetration, accuracy, and colouring will fit a man for the task, if he can give the application which is necessary."

"Bayle's *Dictionary* is a very useful work for those to consult who love the biographical part of literature, which is what I love most."

Talking of the eminent writers in Queen Anne's reign, he observed, "I think Dr. Arbuthnot the first man among them. He was the most universal genius, being an excellent physician, a man of deep learning, and a man of much humour. Mr. Addison was, to be sure, a great man; his learning was not profound; but his morality, his humour, and his elegance of writing, set him very high."

Mr. Ogilvie was unlucky enough to choose for the topick of his conversation the praises of his native country. He began with saying, that there was very rich land round Edinburgh. Goldsmith, who had studied physick there, contradicted this, very untruly, with a sneering laugh. Disconcerted a little by this, Mr. Ogilvie then took new ground, where, I suppose, he thought himself perfectly safe; for he observed, that Scotland had a great many noble wild prospects. JOHNSON. "I believe, Sir, you have a great many. Norway, too, has noble wild prospects; and Lapland is remarkable for prodigious noble wild prospects. But, Sir, let me tell you, the noblest prospect which a Scotchman ever sees, is the high road that leads him to England!" This unexpected and pointed sally produced a roar of applause. After all, however, those, who admire the rude grandeur of Nature, cannot deny it to Caledonia.

On Saturday, July 9, I found Johnson surrounded with a numerous levee, but have not preserved any part of his conversation. On the 14th we had another evening by ourselves at the Mitre. It happening to be a very rainy night, I made some common-place observations on the relaxation of nerves and depression of spirits which such weather occasioned; adding, however, that it was good for the vegetable creation. Johnson, who, as we have already seen, denied that the temperature of the air had any influence on the human frame, answered, with a smile of ridicule, "Why yes, Sir, it is good for vegetables, and for the animals who eat those vegetables, and for the animals who eat those animals." This observation of his aptly enough introduced a good supper; and I soon forgot, in Johnson's company, the influence of a moist atmosphere.

Feeling myself now quite at ease as his companion, though I had all possible reverence for him, I expressed a regret that I could not be so easy with my father, though he was not much older than Johnson, and certainly however respectable had not more learning and greater abilities to depress me. I asked him the reason of this. JOHNSON. "Why, Sir, I am a man of the world. I live in the world, and I take, in some degree, the colour of the world as it moves along. Your father is a Judge in a remote part of the island, and all his notions are taken from the old world. Besides, Sir, there must always be a struggle between a father and son, while one aims at power and the other at independence." I said, I was afraid my father would force me to be a lawyer. JOHNSON. "Sir, you need not be afraid of his forcing you to be a laborious practising lawyer; that is not in his power. For as the proverb says, 'One man may lead a horse to the water, but twenty cannot make him drink.' He may be displeased that you are not what he wishes you to be; but that displeasure will not go far. If he insists only on your having as much law as is necessary for a man of property, and then endeavours to get you into Parliament, he is quite in the right.'

He enlarged very convincinly upon the excellence of rhyme over blank verse in English poetry. I mentioned to him that Dr. Adam Smith, in his lectures upon composition, when I studied under him in the College of Glasgow, had maintained the same opinion strenuously, and I repeated some of his arguments. JOHNSON. "Sir, I was once in company with Smith, and we did not take to each other; but had I known that he loved rhyme as much as you tell me he does, I should have HUGGED him."

Talking of those who denied the truth of Christianity, he said, "It is always easy to be on the negative side. If a man were now to deny that there is salt upon the table, you could not reduce him to an absurdity. Come, let us try this a little further. I deny that Canada is taken, and I can support my denial by pretty good arguments. The French are a much more numerous people than we; and it is not likely that they would allow us to take it. 'But the ministry have assured us, in all the formality of *The Gazette*, that it is taken.'—Very true. But the ministry have put us to an enormous expense by the war in America, and it is their interest to persuade us that we have got something for our money.—'But the fact is confirmed by thousands of men who were at the taking of it.'—Ay, but these men have still more interest in deceiving us. They don't want that you should think the French have beat them, but that they have beat the French. Now suppose you should go over and find that it is really taken, that would only satisfy yourself; for when you come home we will not believe you. We will say, you have been bribed.—Yet, Sir, notwithstanding all these plausi-

---

1. **Dictionary,** Pierre Bayle's *Dictionnaire historique et critique,* 1697.

22. **Adam Smith,** Scottish economist (1723–1790), author of *The Wealth of Nations.*

ble objections, we have no doubt that Canada is really ours. Such is the weight of common testimony. How much stronger are the evidences of the Christian religion!"

"Idleness is a disease which must be combated; but I would not advise a rigid adherence to a particular plan of study. I myself have never persisted in any plan for two days together. A man ought to read just as inclination leads him; for what he reads as a task will do him little good. A young man should read five hours in a day, and so may acquire a great deal of knowledge."

To a man of vigorous intellect and arduous curiosity like his own, reading without a regular plan may be beneficial; though even such a man must submit to it, if he would attain a full understanding of any of the sciences.

To such a degree of unrestrained frankness had he now accustomed me, that in the course of this evening I talked of the numerous reflections which had been thrown out against him on account of his having accepted a pension from his present Majesty. "Why, Sir, (said he, with a hearty laugh,) it is a mighty foolish noise that they make. I have accepted of a pension as a reward which has been thought due to my literary merit; and now that I have this pension, I am the same man in every respect that I have ever been; I retain the same principles. It is true, that I cannot now curse (smiling) the House of Hanover; nor would it be decent for me to drink King James's health in the wine that King George gives me money to pay for. But, Sir, I think that the pleasure of cursing the House of Hanover, and drinking King James's health, are amply overbalanced by three hundred pounds a year."

There was here, most certainly, an affectation of more Jacobitism than he really had; and indeed an intention of admitting, for the moment, in a much greater extent than it really existed, the charge of disaffection imputed to him by the world, merely for the purpose of shewing how dexterously he could repel an attack, even though he were placed in the most disadvantageous position; for I have heard him declare, that if holding up his right hand would have secured victory at Culloden to Prince Charles's army, he was not sure he would have held it up; so little confidence had he in the right claimed by the House of Stuart, and so fearful was he of the consequences of another revolution on the throne of Great-Britain; and Mr. Topham Beauclerk assured me he had heard him say this before he had his pension. At another time he said to Mr. Langton, "Nothing has ever offered, that has made it worth my while to consider the question fully." He, however, also said to the same gentleman, talking of King James the Second, "It was become impossible for him to reign any longer in this country." He no doubt had an early attachment to the House of Stuart; but his zeal had cooled as his reason strengthened. Indeed I heard him once say, that "after the death of a violent Whig, with whom he used to contend with great eagerness, he felt his Toryism much abated." I suppose he meant Mr. Walmsley.

Yet there is no doubt that at earlier periods he was wont often to exercise both his pleasantry and ingenuity in talking Jacobitism. My much respected friend, Dr. Douglas, now Bishop of Salisbury, has favoured me with the following admirable instance from his Lordship's own recollection. One day when dining at old Mr. Langton's where Miss Roberts, his niece, was one of the company, Johnson, with his usual complacent attention to the fair sex, took her by the hand and said, "My dear, I hope you are a Jacobite." Old Mr. Langton, who, though a high and steady Tory, was attached to the present Royal Family, seemed offended, and asked Johnson, with great warmth, what he could mean by putting such a question to his niece? "Why, Sir, (said Johnson) I meant no offence to your niece, I meant her a great compliment. A Jacobite, Sir, believes in the divine right of Kings. He that believes in the divine right of Kings believes in a Divinity. A Jacobite believes in the divine right of Bishops. He that believes in the divine right of Bishops believes in the divine authority of the Christian religion. Therefore, Sir, a Jacobite is neither an Atheist nor a Deist. That cannot be said of a Whig; for *Whiggism is a negation of all principle*."

He advised me, when abroad, to be as much as I could with the Professors in the universities, and with the Clergy; for from their conversation I might expect the best accounts of every thing in whatever country I should be, with the additional advantage of keeping my learning alive.

It will be observed, that when giving me advice as to my travels, Dr. Johnson did not dwell upon cities, and palaces, and pictures, and shows, and Arcadian scenes. He was of Lord Essex's opinion, who advises his kinsman Roger Earl of Rutland, "rather to go an hundred miles to speak with one wise man, than five miles to see a fair town."

---

31. **King James,** the "Old Pretender," son of James II, who claimed the throne of England and so was an enemy of the Hanoverian King George III. 37. **Jacobitism,** adherence to James II after his abdication, or to his son the "Pretender." The Latin for "James" is *Jacobus.* 45. **Culloden,** the battle, fought in 1746, in which the "Young Pretender," Bonny Prince Charlie, was defeated.

I described to him an impudent fellow from Scotland, who affected to be a savage, and railed at all established systems. JOHNSON. "There is nothing surprising in this, Sir. He wants to make himself conspicuous. He would tumble in a hogstye, as long as you looked at him and called to him to come out. But let him alone, never mind him, and he'll soon give it over."

I added, that the same person maintained that there was no distinction between virtue and vice. JOHNSON. "Why, Sir, if the fellow does not think as he speaks, he is lying; and I see not what honour he can propose to himself from having the character of a liar. But if he does really think that there is no distinction between virtue and vice, why, Sir, when he leaves our houses let us count our spoons. . . ."

He [Johnson] recommended to me to keep a journal of my life, full and unreserved. He said it would be a very good exercise, and would yield me great satisfaction when the particulars were faded from my remembrance. I was uncommonly fortunate in having had a previous coincidence of opinion with him upon this subject, for I had kept such a journal for some time; and it was no small pleasure to me to have this to tell him, and to receive his approbation. He counselled me to keep it private, and said I might surely have a friend who would burn it in case of my death. From this habit I have been enabled to give the world so many anecdotes, which would otherwise have been lost to posterity. I mentioned that I was afraid I put into my journal too many little incidents. JOHNSON. "There is nothing, Sir, too little for so little a creature as man. It is by studying little things that we attain the great art of having as little misery and as much happiness as possible."

Next morning Mr. Dempster happened to call on me, and was so much struck even with the imperfect account which I gave him of Dr. Johnson's conversation, that to his honour be it recorded, when I complained that drinking port and sitting up late with him affected my nerves for some time after, he said, "One had better be palsied at eighteen than not keep company with such a man."

On Tuesday, July 18, I found tall Sir Thomas Robinson sitting with Johnson. Sir Thomas said, that the King of Prussia valued himself upon three things;—upon being a hero, a musician, and an authour. JOHNSON. "Pretty well, Sir, for one man. As to his being an authour, I have not looked at his poetry; but his prose is poor stuff. He writes just as you might suppose Voltaire's footboy to do, who has been his amanuensis. He has such parts as the valet might have, and about as much of the colouring of the style as might be got by transcribing his works." When I was at Ferney, I repeated this to Voltaire, in order to reconcile him somewhat to Johnson, whom he, in affecting the English mode of expression, had previously characterized as "a superstitious dog"; but after hearing such a criticism on Frederick the Great, with whom he was then on bad terms, he exclaimed, "An honest fellow!"

But I think the criticism much too severe; for the *Memoirs of the House of Brandenburgh* are written as well as many works of that kind. His poetry, for the style of which he himself makes a frank apology, "*Jargonnant un François barbare,*" though fraught with pernicious ravings of infidelity, has, in many places, great animation, and in some a pathetick tenderness.

Upon this contemptuous animadversion on the King of Prussia, I observed to Johnson, "It would seem then, Sir, that much less parts are necessary to make a King, than to make an Authour; for the King of Prussia is confessedly the greatest King now in Europe, yet you think he makes a very poor figure as an Authour."

Mr. Levet this day showed me Dr. Johnson's library, which was contained in two garrets over his Chambers, where Lintot, son of the celebrated bookseller of that name, had formerly his warehouse. I found a number of good books, but very dusty and in great confusion. The floor was strewed with manuscript leaves, in Johnson's own handwriting, which I beheld with a degree of veneration, supposing they perhaps might contain portions of *The Rambler* or of *Rasselas*. I observed an apparatus for chymical experiments, of which Johnson was all his life very fond. The place seemed to be very favourable for retirement and meditation. Johnson told me, that he went up thither without mentioning it to his servant, when he wanted to study, secure from interruption; for he would not allow his servant to say he was not at home when he really was. "A servant's strict regard for truth, (said he) must be weakened by such a practice. A philosopher may know that it is merely a form of denial; but few servants are such nice distinguishers. If I accustom a servant to tell a lie for *me*, have I not reason to apprehend that he will tell many lies for *himself*." I am, however, satisfied that every servant, of any degree of intelligence, understands saying his master is not at home, not at all as the affirmation of a fact, but as customary words, intimating that his master wishes not to be seen; so that there can be no bad effect from it.

Mr. Temple, now vicar of St. Gluvias, Cornwall,

who had been my intimate friend for many years, had at this time chambers in Farrar's-buildings, at the bottom of Inner-Temple-lane, which he kindly lent me upon my quitting my lodgings, he being to return to Trinity Hall, Cambridge. I found them particularly convenient for me, as they were so near Dr. Johnson's.

On Wednesday, July 20, Dr. Johnson, Mr. Dempster, and my uncle Dr. Boswell, who happened to be now in London, supped with me at these Chambers. JOHNSON. "Pity is not natural to man. Children are always cruel. Savages are always cruel. Pity is acquired and improved by the cultivation of reason. We may have uneasy sensations from seeing a creature in distress, without pity; for we have not pity unless we wish to relieve them. When I am on my way to dine with a friend, and finding it late, have bid the coachman make haste, if I happen to attend when he whips his horses, I may feel unpleasantly that the animals are put to pain, but I do not wish him to desist. No, Sir, I wish him to drive on."

Mr. Alexander Donaldson, bookseller of Edinburgh, had for some time opened a shop in London, and sold his cheap editions, of the most popular English books, in defiance of the supposed common-law right of *Literary Property*. Johnson, though he concurred in the opinion which was afterwards sanctioned by a judgement of the House of Lords, that there was no such right, was at this time very angry that the Booksellers of London, for whom he uniformly professed much regard, should suffer from an invasion of what they had ever considered to be secure: and he was loud and violent against Mr. Donaldson. "He is a fellow who takes advantage of the law to injure his brethren; for, notwithstanding that the statute secures only fourteen years of exclusive right, it has always been understood by *the trade*, that he, who buys the copyright of a book from the authour, obtains a perpetual property; and upon that belief, numberless bargains are made to transfer that property after the expiration of the statutory term. Now Donaldson, I say, takes advantage here, of people who have really an equitable title from usage; and if we consider how few of the books, of which they buy the property, succeed so well as to bring profit, we should be of opinion that the term of fourteen years is too short; it should be sixty years." DEMPSTER. "Donaldson, Sir, is anxious for the encouragement of literature. He reduces the price of books, so that poor students may buy them." JOHNSON, (laughing). "Well, Sir, allowing that to be his motive, he is no better than Robin Hood, who robbed the rich in order to give to the poor."

It is remarkable, that when the great question concerning Literary Property came to be ultimately tried before the supreme tribunal of this country, in consequence of the very spirited exertions of Mr. Donaldson, Dr. Johnson was zealous against a perpetuity; but he thought that the term of the exclusive right of authours should be considerably enlarged. He was then for granting a hundred years.

The conversation now turned upon Mr. David Hume's style. JOHNSON. "Why, Sir, his style is not English; the structure of his sentences is French. Now the French structure and the English structure may, in the nature of things, be equally good. But if you allow that the English language is established, he is wrong. My name might originally have been Nicholson, as well as Johnson; but were you to call me Nicholson now, you would call me very absurdly."

Rousseau's treatise on the inequality of mankind was at this time a fashionable topick. It gave rise to an observation by Mr. Dempster, that the advantages of fortune and rank were nothing to a wise man, who ought to value only merit. JOHNSON. "If man were a savage, living in the woods by himself, this might be true; but in civilized society we all depend upon each other, and our happiness is very much owing to the good opinion of mankind. Now, Sir, in civilized society, external advantages make us more respected. A man with a good coat upon his back meets with a better reception than he who has a bad one. Sir, you may analyse this, and say what is there in it? But that will avail you nothing, for it is a part of a general system. Pound St. Paul's Church into atoms, and consider any single atom; it is, to be sure, good for nothing: but, put all these atoms together, and you have St. Paul's Church. So it is with human felicity, which is made up of many ingredients, each of which may be shown to be very insignificant. In civilized society, personal merit will not serve you so much as money will. Sir, you may make the experiment. Go into the street, and give one man a lecture on morality, and another a shilling, and see which will respect you most. If you wish only to support nature, Sir William Petty fixes your allowance at three pounds a year; but as times are much altered, let us call it six pounds. This sum will fill your belly, shelter you from the weather, and even get you a strong and lasting coat, supposing it to be made of good bull's hide.

10–11. David Hume (1711–1776), a philosopher and historian who was disliked by Dr. Johnson because of his skepticism.   **45. Sir William Petty** (1623–1687), an important early statistician and political economist.

Now, Sir, all beyond this is artificial, and is desired in order to obtain a greater degree of respect from our fellow-creatures. And, Sir, if six hundred pounds a year procure a man more consequence, and, of course, more happiness than six pounds a year, the same proportion will hold as to six thousand, and so on as far as opulence can be carried. Perhaps he who has a large fortune may not be so happy as he who has a small one; but that must proceed from other causes than from his having the large fortune: for, *caeteris paribus*, he who is rich in a civilized society, must be happier than he who is poor; as riches, if properly used, (and it is a man's own fault if they are not,) must be productive of the highest advantages. Money, to be sure, of itself is of no use; for its only use is to part with it. Rousseau, and all those who deal in paradoxes, are led away by a childish desire of novelty. When I was a boy, I used always to choose the wrong side of a debate, because most ingenious things, that is to say, most new things, could be said upon it. Sir, there is nothing for which you may not muster up more plausible arguments, than those which are urged against wealth and other external advantages. Why, now, there is stealing; why should it be thought a crime? When we consider by what unjust methods property has been often acquired, and that what was unjustly got it must be unjust to keep, where is the harm in one man's taking the property of another from him? Besides, Sir, when we consider the bad use that many people make of their property, and how much better use the thief may make of it, it may be defended as a very allowable practice. Yet, Sir, the experience of mankind has discovered stealing to be so very bad a thing, that they make no scruple to hang a man for it. When I was running about this town a very poor fellow, I was a great arguer for the advantages of poverty; but I was, at the same time, very sorry to be poor. Sir, all the arguments which are brought to represent poverty as no evil, shew it to be evidently a great evil. You never find people labouring to convince you that you may live very happily upon a plentiful fortune.—So you hear people talking how miserable a King must be; and yet they all wish to be in his place."

It was suggested that Kings must be unhappy, because they are deprived of the greatest of all satisfactions, easy and unreserved society. JOHNSON. "That is an ill-founded notion. Being a King does not exclude a man from such society. Great Kings have always been social. The King of Prussia, the only great King at present, is very social. Charles the Second, the last King of England who was a man of parts, was social; and our Henrys and Edwards were all social."

Mr. Dempster having endeavoured to maintain that intrinsick merit *ought* to make the only distinction amongst mankind. JOHNSON. "Why, Sir, mankind have found that this cannot be. How shall we determine the proportion of intrinsick merit? Were that to be the only distinction amongst mankind, we should soon quarrel about the degrees of it. Were all distinctions abolished, the strongest would not long acquiesce, but would endeavour to obtain a superiority by their bodily strength. But, Sir, as subordination is very necessary for society, and contentions for superiority very dangerous, mankind, that is to say, all civilized nations, have settled it upon a plain invariable principle. A man is born to hereditary rank; or his being appointed to certain offices, gives him a certain rank. Subordination tends greatly to human happiness. Were we all upon an equality, we should have no other enjoyment than mere animal pleasure."

I said, I considered distinction of rank to be of so much importance in civilized society, that if I were asked on the same day to dine with the first Duke in England, and with the first man in Britain for genius, I should hesitate which to prefer. JOHNSON. "To be sure, Sir, if you were to dine only once, and it were never to be known where you dined, you would choose rather to dine with the first man for genius; but to gain most respect, you should dine with the first Duke in England. For nine people in ten that you meet with, would have a higher opinion of you for having dined with a Duke; and the great genius himself would receive you better, because you had been with the great Duke."

He took care to guard himself against any possible suspicion that his settled principles of reverence for rank and respect for wealth were at all owing to mean or interested motives; for he asserted his own independence as a literary man. "No man (said he) who ever lived by literature, has lived more independently than I have done." He said he had taken longer time than he needed to have done in composing his *Dictionary*. He received our compliments upon that great work with complacency, and told us that the Academy *della Crusca* could scarcely believe that it was done by one man.

Next morning I found him alone, and have preserved the following fragments of his conversation. Of a gentleman who was mentioned, he said, "I have not met with any man for a long time who

---

11. **caeteris paribus,** other things being equal.

47. **Crusca,** Accademia della Crusca, a learned society founded at Florence in 1582.

has given me such general displeasure. He is totally unfixed in his principles, and wants to puzzle other people." I said his principles had been poisoned by a noted infidel writer, but that he was, nevertheless, a benevolent good man. JOHNSON. "We can have no dependance upon that instinctive, that constitutional goodness which is not founded upon principle. I grant you that such a man may be a very amiable member of society. I can conceive him placed in such a situation that he is not much tempted to deviate from what is right; and as every man prefers virtue, when there is not some strong incitement to transgress its precepts, I can conceive him doing nothing wrong. But if such a man stood in need of money, I should not like to trust him; and I should certainly not trust him with young ladies, for *there* there is always temptation. Hume, and other sceptical innovators, are vain men, and will gratify themselves at any expense. Truth will not afford sufficient food to their vanity; so they have betaken themselves to error. Truth, Sir, is a cow which will yield such people no more milk, and so they are gone to milk the bull. If I could have allowed myself to gratify my vanity at the expense of truth, what fame might I have acquired. Every thing which Hume has advanced against Christianity had passed through my mind long before he wrote. Always remember this, that after a system is well settled upon positive evidence, a few partial objections ought not to shake it. The human mind is so limited, that it cannot take in all the parts of a subject, so that there may be objections raised against any thing. There are objections against a *plenum*, and objections against a *vacuum;* yet one of them must certainly be true."

I mentioned Hume's argument against the belief of miracles, that it is more probable that the witnesses to the truth of them are mistaken, or speak falsely, than that the miracles should be true. JOHNSON. "Why, Sir, the great difficulty of proving miracles should make us very cautious in believing them. But let us consider; although GOD has made Nature to operate by certain fixed laws, yet it is not unreasonable to think that he may suspend those laws, in order to establish a system highly advantageous to mankind. Now the Christian religion is a most beneficial system, as it gives us light and certainty where we were before in darkness and doubt. The miracles which prove it are attested by men who had no interest in deceiving us; but who, on the contrary, were told that they should suffer persecution, and did actually lay down their lives in confirmation of the truth of the facts which they asserted. Indeed, for some centuries the heathens did not pretend to deny the miracles; but said they were performed by the aid of evil spirits. This is a circumstance of great weight. Then, Sir, when we take the proofs derived from prophecies which have been so exactly fulfilled, we have most satisfactory evidence. Supposing a miracle possible, as to which, in my opinion, there can be no doubt, we have as strong evidence for the miracles in support of Christianity, as the nature of the thing admits."

At night Mr. Johnson and I supped in a private room at the Turk's Head coffee-house, in the Strand. "I encourage this house (said he;) for the mistress of it is a good civil woman, and has not much business."

"Sir, I love the acquaintance of young people; because, in the first place, I don't like to think myself growing old. In the next place, young acquaintances must last longest, if they do last; and then, Sir, young men have more virtue than old men; they have more generous sentiments in every respect. I love the young dogs of this age: they have more wit and humour and knowledge of life than we had; but then the dogs are not so good scholars. Sir, in my early years I read very hard. It is a sad reflection, but a true one, that I knew almost as much at eighteen as I do now. My judgement, to be sure, was not so good; but I had all the facts. I remember very well, when I was at Oxford, an old gentleman said to me, 'Young man, ply your book diligently now, and acquire a stock of knowledge; for when years come upon you, you will find that poring upon books will be but an irksome task.' "

This account of his reading, given by himself in plain words, sufficiently confirms what I have already advanced upon the disputed question as to his application. It reconciles any seeming inconsistency in his way of talking upon it at different times; and shows that idleness and reading hard were with him relative terms, the import of which, as used by him, must be gathered from a comparison with what scholars of different degrees of ardour and assiduity have been known to do. And let it be remembered, that he was now talking spontaneously, and expressing his genuine sentiments; whereas at other times he might be induced from his spirit of contradiction, or more properly from his love of argumentative contest, to speak lightly of his own application to study. It is pleasing to consider that the old gentleman's gloomy prophecy as to the irksomeness of books to men of an advanced age, which is too often fulfilled, was so far from be-

---

34. **plenum . . . vacuum,** space entirely filled with matter, space entirely empty of matter.

ing verified in Johnson, that his ardour for literature never failed, and his last writings had more ease and vivacity than any of his earlier productions.

He mentioned to me now, for the first time, that he had been distrest by melancholy, and for that reason had been obliged to fly from study and meditation, to the dissipating variety of life. Against melancholy he recommended constant occupation of mind, a great deal of exercise, moderation in eating and drinking, and especially to shun drinking at night. He said melancholy people were apt to fly to intemperance for relief, but that it sunk them much deeper in misery. He observed, that labouring men who work hard, and live sparingly, are seldom or never troubled with low spirits.

He again insisted on the duty of maintaining subordination of rank. "Sir, I would no more deprive a nobleman of his respect, than of his money. I consider myself as acting a part in the great system of society, and I do to others as I would have them to do to me. I would behave to a nobleman as I should expect he would behave to me, were I a nobleman and he Sam. Johnson. Sir, there is one Mrs. Macaulay in this town, a great republican. One day when I was at her house, I put on a very grave countenance, and said to her, 'Madam, I am now become a convert to your way of thinking. I am convinced that all mankind are upon an equal footing; and to give you an unquestionable proof, Madam, that I am in earnest, here is a very sensible, civil, well-behaved fellow-citizen, your footman; I desire that he may be allowed to sit down and dine with us.' I thus, Sir, showed her the absurdity of the levelling doctrine. She has never liked me since. Sir, your levellers wish to level *down* as far as themselves; but they cannot bear levelling *up* to themselves. They would all have some people under them; why not then have some people above them?" I mentioned a certain authour who disgusted me by his forwardness, and by shewing no deference to noblemen into whose company he was admitted. JOHNSON. "Suppose a shoemaker should claim an equality with him, as he does with a Lord; how he would stare. 'Why, Sir, do you stare? (says the shoemaker,) I do great service to society. 'Tis true I am paid for doing it; but so are you, Sir: and I am sorry to say it, paid better than I am, for doing something not so necessary. For mankind could do better without your books, than without my shoes.' Thus, Sir, there would be a perpetual struggle for precedence, were there no fixed invariable rules for the distinction of rank, which creates no jealousy, as it is allowed to be accidental."

He said, Dr. Joseph Warton was a very agreeable man, and his *Essay on the Genius and Writings of Pope*, a very pleasing book. I wondered that he delayed so long to give us the continuation of it. JOHNSON. "Why, Sir, I suppose he finds himself a little disappointed, in not having been able to persuade the world to be of his opinion as to Pope."

We have now been favoured with the concluding volume, in which, to use a parliamentary expression, he has *explained*, so as not to appear quite so adverse to the opinion of the world, concerning Pope, as was at first thought; and we must all agree that his work is a most valuable accession to English literature.

A writer of deserved eminence being mentioned, Johnson said, "Why, Sir, he is a man of good parts, but being originally poor, he has got a love of mean company and low jocularity; a very bad thing, Sir. To laugh is good, as to talk is good. But you ought no more to think it enough if you laugh, than you are to think it enough if you talk. You may laugh in as many ways as you talk; and surely *every* way of talking that is practised cannot be esteemed."

I spoke of Sir James Macdonald as a young man of most distinguished merit, who united the highest reputation at Eton and Oxford, with the patriarchal spirit of a great Highland Chieftain. I mentioned that Sir James had said to me, that he had never seen Mr. Johnson, but he had a great respect for him, though at the same time it was mixed with some degree of terrour. JOHNSON. "Sir, if he were to be acquainted with me, it might lessen both."

The mention of this gentleman led us to talk of the Western Islands of Scotland, to visit which he expressed a wish that then appeared to me a very romantick fancy, which I little thought would be afterwards realised. He told me, that his father had put Martin's account of those islands into his hands when he was very young, and that he was highly pleased with it; that he was particularly struck with the St. Kilda man's notion that the high church of Glasgow had been hollowed out of a rock; a circumstance to which old Mr. Johnson had directed his attention. He said he would go to the Hebrides with me, when I returned from my travels, unless some very good companion should offer when I was absent, which he did not think probable; adding, "There are few people to whom I take so much to

24. **Mrs. Macaulay**, a learned lady and "bluestocking" who was known as "the celebrated female historian" (1731–1791).

3. **Joseph Warton**, a teacher, poet, and scholar of romantic tendency (1722–1800). His account of Pope was not wholly favorable. 46. **Hebrides**. Johnson and Boswell did take this journey in 1773, and both men wrote the story of their adventure.

as you." And when I talked of my leaving England, he said with a very affectionate air, "My dear Boswell, I should be very unhappy at parting, did I think we were not to meet again." I cannot too often remind my readers, that although such instances of his kindness are doubtless very flattering to me, yet I hope my recording them will be ascribed to a better motive than to vanity; for they afford unquestionable evidence of his tenderness and complacency, which some, while they were forced to acknowledge his great powers, have been so strenuous to deny.

He maintained that a boy at school was the happiest of human beings. I supported a different opinion, from which I have never yet varied, that a man is happier; and I enlarged upon the anxiety and sufferings which are endured at school. JOHNSON. "Ah! Sir, a boy's being flogged is not so severe as a man's having the hiss of the world against him. Men have a solicitude about fame; and the greater share they have of it, the more afraid they are of losing it." I silently asked myself, "Is it possible that the great SAMUEL JOHNSON really entertains any such apprehension, and is not confident that his exalted fame is established upon a foundation never to be shaken?"

He this evening drank a bumper to Sir David Dalrymple, "as a man of worth, a scholar, and a wit." "I have (said he) never heard of him except from you; but let him know my opinion of him: for as he does not shew himself much in the world, he should have the praise of the few who hear of him."

On Tuesday, July 26, I found Mr. Johnson alone. It was a very wet day, and I again complained of the disagreeable effects of such weather. JOHNSON. "Sir, this is all imagination, which physicians encourage; for man lives in air, as a fish lives in water; so that if the atmosphere press heavy from above, there is an equal resistance from below. To be sure, bad weather is hard upon people who are obliged to be abroad; and men cannot labour so well in the open air in bad weather, as in good; but, Sir, a smith or a taylor, whose work is within doors, will surely do as much in rainy weather, as in fair. Some very delicate frames, indeed, may be affected by wet weather; but not common constitutions."

We talked of the education of children; and I asked him what he thought was best to teach them first. JOHNSON. "Sir, it is no matter what you teach them first, any more than what leg you shall put into your breeches first. Sir, you may stand disputing which is best to put in first, but in the meantime your breech is bare. Sir, while you are considering which of two things you should teach your child first, another boy has learnt them both."

On Thursday, July 28, we again supped in private at the Turk's Head coffee-house. JOHNSON. "Swift has a higher reputation than he deserves. His excellence is strong sense; for his humour, though very well, is not remarkably good. I doubt whether *The Tale of a Tub* be his; for he never owned it, and it is much above his usual manner.

"Thompson, I think, had as much of the poet about him as most writers. Every thing appeared to him through the medium of his favourite pursuit. He could not have viewed those two candles burning but with a poetical eye."

"Has not —— a great deal of wit, Sir?" JOHNSON. "I do not think so, Sir. He is, indeed, continually attempting wit, but he fails. And I have no more pleasure in hearing a man attempting wit and failing, than in seeing a man trying to leap over a ditch and tumbling into it." . . .

I again begged his advice as to my method of study at Utrecht. "Come, (said he) let us make a day of it. Let us go down to Greenwich and dine, and talk of it there." The following Saturday was fixed for this excursion.

As we walked along the Strand to-night arm in arm, a woman of the town accosted us, in the usual enticing manner. "No, no, my girl, (said Johnson) it won't do." He, however, did not treat her with harshness, and we talked of the wretched life of such women; and agreed, that much more misery than happiness, upon the whole, is produced by illicit commerce between the sexes.

On Saturday, July 30, Dr. Johnson and I took a sculler at the Temple-stairs, and set out for Greenwich. I asked him if he really thought a knowledge of the Greek and Latin languages an essential requisite to a good education. JOHNSON. "Most certainly, Sir; for those who know them have a very great advantage over those who do not. Nay, Sir, it is wonderful what a difference learning makes upon people even in the common intercourse of life, which does not appear to be much connected with it." "And yet, (said I) people go through the world very well, and carry on the business of life to good advantage, without learning." JOHNSON. "Why, Sir, that may be true in cases where learning cannot possibly be of any use; for instance, this boy rows us as well without learning, as if he could sing the song of Orpheus to the Argonauts, who were the first sailors." He then called to the boy, "What would

---

10. **Thompson,** James Thomson, author of *The Seasons*. See page 897.

you give, my lad, to know about the Argonauts?" "Sir, (said the boy,) I would give what I have." Johnson was much pleased with his answer, and we gave him a double fare. Dr. Johnson then turning to me, "Sir, (said he,) a desire of knowledge is the natural feeling of mankind; and every human being, whose mind is not debauched, will be willing to give all that he has to get knowledge."

We landed at the Old Swan, and walked to Billingsgate, where we took oars, and moved smoothly along the silver Thames. It was a very fine day. We were entertained with the immense number and variety of ships that were lying at anchor, and with the beautiful country on each side of the river.

I talked of preaching, and of the great success which those called Methodists have. JOHNSON. "Sir, it is owing to their expressing themselves in a plain and familiar manner, which is the only way to do good to the common people, and which clergymen of genius and learning ought to do from a principle of duty, when it is suited to their congregations; a practice, for which they will be praised by men of sense. To insist against drunkenness as a crime, because it debases reason, the noblest faculty of man, would be of no service to the common people: but to tell them that they may die in a fit of drunkenness, and shew them how dreadful that would be, cannot fail to make a deep impression. Sir, when your Scotch clergy give up their homely manner, religion will soon decay in that country." Let this observation, as Johnson meant it, be ever remembered.

I was much pleased to find myself with Johnson at Greenwich, which he celebrates in his *London* as a favourite scene. I had the poem in my pocket, and read the lines aloud with enthusiasm:

"On Thames's banks in silent thought we stood:
Where Greenwich smiles upon the silver flood:
Pleased with the seat which gave ELIZA birth,
We kneel, and kiss the consecrated earth."

He remarked that the structure of Greenwich hospital was too magnificent for a place of charity, and that its parts were too much detached to make one great whole. . . .

Afterwards he entered upon the business of the day, which was to give me his advice as to a course of study. And here I am to mention with much regret, that my record of what he said is miserably scanty. I recollect with admiration an animating blaze of eloquence, which roused every intellectual power in me to the highest pitch, but must have dazzled me so much, that my memory could not preserve the substance of his discourse; for the note which I find of it is no more than this:—"He ran over the grand scale of human knowledge; advised me to select some particular branch to excel in, but to acquire a little of every kind." The defect of my minutes will be fully supplied by a long letter upon the subject which he favoured me with, after I had been some time at Utrecht, and which my readers will have the pleasure to peruse in its proper place.

We walked in the evening in Greenwich Park. He asked me, I suppose, by way of trying my disposition, "Is not this very fine?" Having no exquisite relish of the beauties of Nature, and being more delighted with "the busy hum of men," I answered, "Yes, Sir; but not equal to Fleet-street," JOHNSON. "You are right, Sir."

I am aware that many of my readers may censure my want of taste. Let me, however, shelter myself under the authority of a very fashionable Baronet in the brilliant world, who, on his attention being called to the fragrance of a May evening in the country, observed, "This may be very well; but, for my part, I prefer the smell of a flambeau at the playhouse."

We staid so long at Greenwich, that our sail up the river, in our return to London, was by no means so pleasant as in the morning; for the night air was so cold that it made me shiver. I was the more sensible of it from having sat up all the night before, recollecting and writing in my journal what I thought worthy of preservation; an exertion, which, during the first part of my acquaintance with Johnson, I frequently made. I remember having sat up four nights in one week, without being much incommoded in the day time.

Johnson, whose robust frame was not in the least affected by the cold, scolded me, as if my shivering had been a paltry effeminacy, saying, "Why do you shiver?" Sir William Scott, of the Commons, told me, that when he complained of a head-ache in the post-chaise, as they were travelling together to Scotland, Johnson treated him in the same manner: "At your age, Sir, I had no head-ache." It is not easy to make allowance for sensations in others, which we ourselves have not at the time. We must all have experienced how very differently we are affected by the complaints of our neighbours, when we are well and when we are ill. In full health, we can scarcely believe that they suffer much; so faint is the image of pain upon our imagination: when softened by sickness, we readily sympathize with the sufferings of others.

We concluded the day at the Turk's Head coffee-

13. **"the busy hum of men,"** from Milton's "L'Allegro," l. 118.

house very socially. He was pleased to listen to a particular account which I gave him of my family, and of its hereditary estate, as to the extent and population of which he asked questions, and made calculations; recommending, at the same time, a liberal kindness to the tenantry, as people over whom the proprietor was placed by Providence. He took delight in hearing my description of the romantick seat of my ancestors. "I must be there, Sir, (said he) and we will live in the old castle; and if there is not a room in it remaining, we will build one." I was highly flattered, but could scarcely indulge a hope that Auchinleck would indeed be honoured by his presence, and celebrated by a description, as it afterwards was, in his *Journey to the Western Islands*.

After we had again talked of my setting out for Holland, he said, "I must see thee out of England; I will accompany you to Harwich." I could not find words to express what I felt upon this unexpected and very great mark of his affectionate regard.

Next day, Sunday, July 31, I told him I had been that morning at a meeting of the people called Quakers, where I had heard a woman preach. JOHNSON. "Sir, a woman's preaching is like a dog's walking on his hinder legs. It is not done well; but you are surprized to find it done at all."

On Tuesday, August 2, (the day of my departure from London having been fixed for the 5th,) Dr. Johnson did me the honour to pass a part of the morning with me at my Chambers. He said, that "he always felt an inclination to do nothing." I observed, that it was strange to think that the most indolent man in Britain had written the most laborious work, *The English Dictionary*.

I mentioned an imprudent publication, by a certain friend of his, at an early period of life, and asked him if he thought it would hurt him. JOHNSON. "No, Sir; not much. It may, perhaps, be mentioned at an election."

I had now made good my title to be a privileged man, and was carried by him in the evening to drink tea with Miss Williams, whom, though under the misfortune of having lost her sight, I found to be agreeable in conversation; for she had a variety of literature, and expressed herself well; but her peculiar value was the intimacy in which she had long lived with Johnson, by which she was well acquainted with his habits, and knew how to lead him on to talk.

After tea he carried me to what he called his walk, which was a long narrow paved court in the neighbourhood, overshadowed by some trees. There we sauntered a considerable time; and I complained to him that my love of London and of his company was such, that I shrunk almost from the thought of going away, even to travel, which is generally so much desired by young men. He roused me by manly and spirited conversation. He advised me, when settled in any place abroad, to study with an eagerness after knowledge, and to apply to Greek an hour every day; and when I was moving about, to read diligently the great book of mankind.

On Wednesday, August 3, we had our last social evening at the Turk's Head coffee-house, before my setting out for foreign parts. I had the misfortune, before we parted, to irritate him unintentionally. I mentioned to him how common it was in the world to tell absurd stories of him, and to ascribe to him very strange sayings. JOHNSON. "What do they make me say, Sir?" BOSWELL. "Why, Sir, as an instance very strange indeed, (laughing heartily as I spoke,) David Hume told me, you said that you would stand before a battery of cannon, to restore the Convocation to its full powers." Little did I apprehend that he had actually said this: but I was soon convinced of my errour; for, with a determined look, he thundered out "And would I not, Sir? Shall the Presbyterian *Kirk* of Scotland have its General Assembly, and the Church of England be denied its Convocation?" He was walking up and down the room while I told him the anecdote; but when he uttered this explosion of high-church zeal, he had come close to my chair, and his eyes flashed with indignation. I bowed to the storm, and diverted the force of it, by leading him to expatiate on the influence which religion derived from maintaining the church with great external respectability....

On Friday, August 5, we set out early in the morning in the Harwich stage coach. A fat elderly gentlewoman, and a young Dutchman, seemed the most inclined among us to conversation. At the inn where we dined, the gentlewoman said that she had done her best to educate her children; and particularly, that she had never suffered them to be a moment idle. JOHNSON. "I wish, madam, you would educate me too; for I have been an idle fellow all my life." "I am sure, Sir, (said she) you have not been idle." JOHNSON. "Nay, madam, it is very true; and that gentleman there (pointing to me,) has been idle. He was idle at Edinburgh. His father sent him to Glasgow, where he continued to be idle. He then came to London, where he has been very idle; and now he is going to Utrecht, where he will be as idle as ever." I asked him privately how he could expose me so. JOHNSON. "Poh, poh! (said he) they knew

20. **Convocation,** an assembly of clergy during the meeting of Parliament. From 1717 to 1861 it was discontinued.

nothing about you, and will think of it no more." In the afternoon the gentlewoman talked violently against the Roman Catholics, and of the horrours of the Inquisition. To the utter astonishment of all the passengers but myself, who knew that he could talk upon any side of a question, he defended the Inquisition, and maintained, that "false doctrine should be checked on its first appearance; that the civil power should unite with the church in punishing those who dared to attack the established religion, and that such only were punished by the Inquisition." He had in his pocket *Pomponius Mela de situ Orbis,* in which he read occasionally, and seemed very intent upon ancient geography. Though by no means niggardly, his attention to what was generally right was so minute, that having observed at one of the stages that I ostentatiously gave a shilling to the coachman, when the custom was for each passenger to give only six-pence, he took me aside and scolded me, saying that what I had done would make the coachman dissatisfied with all the rest of the passengers, who gave him no more than his due. This was a just reprimand; for in whatever way a man may indulge his generosity or his vanity in spending his money, for the sake of others he ought not to raise the price of any article for which there is a constant demand.

He talked of Mr. Blacklock's poetry, so far as it was descriptive of visible objects; and observed, that "as its authour had the misfortune to be blind, we may be absolutely sure that such passages are combinations of what he has remembered of the works of other writers who could see. That foolish fellow, Spence, has laboured to explain philosophically how Blacklock may have done, by means of his own faculties, what it is impossible he should do. The solution, as I have given it, is plain. Suppose, I know a man to be so lame that he is absolutely incapable to move himself, and I find him in a different room from that in which I left him; shall I puzzle myself with idle conjectures, that, perhaps, his nerves have by some unknown change all at once become effective? No, Sir; it is clear how he got into a different room: he was *carried.*"

Having stopped a night at Colchester, Johnson talked of that town with veneration, for having stood a siege for Charles the First. The Dutchman alone now remained with us. He spoke English tolerably well; and thinking to recommend himself to us by expatiating on the superiority of the criminal jurisprudence of this country over that of Holland, he inveighed against the barbarity of putting an accused person to the torture, in order to force a confession. But Johnson was as ready for this, as for the Inquisition. "Why, Sir, you do not, I find, understand the law of your own country. The torture in Holland is considered as a favour to an accused person; for no man is put to the torture there, unless there is as much evidence against him as would amount to conviction in England. An accused person among you, therefore, has one chance more to escape punishment, than those who are tried among us."

At supper this night he talked of good eating with uncommon satisfaction. "Some people (said he), have a foolish way of not minding, or pretending not to mind, what they eat. For my part, I mind my belly very studiously, and very carefully; for I look upon it, that he who does not mind his belly will hardly mind anything else." He now appeared to me *Jean Bull philosophe,* and he was, for the moment, not only serious but vehement. Yet I have heard him, upon other occasions, talk with great contempt of people who were anxious to gratify their palates; and the 206th number of his *Rambler* is a masterly essay against gulosity. His practice, indeed, I must acknowledge, may be considered as casting the balance of his different opinions upon this subject; for I never knew any man who relished good eating more than he did. When at table, he was totally absorbed in the business of the moment; his looks seemed rivetted to his plate; nor would he, unless when in very high company, say one word, or even pay the least attention to what was said by others, till he had satisfied his appetite, which was so fierce, and indulged with such intenseness, that while in the act of eating, the veins of his forehead swelled, and generally a strong perspiration was visible. To those whose sensations were delicate, this could not but be disgusting; and it was doubtless not very suitable to the character of a philosopher, who should be distinguished by self-command. But it must be owned, that Johnson, though he could be rigidly *abstemious,* was not a *temperate* man either in eating or drinking. He could refrain, but he could not use moderately. He told me, that he had fasted two days without inconvenience, and that he had never been hungry but once. They who beheld with wonder how much he eat upon all occasions when his dinner was to his taste, could not easily conceive what he must have meant by hunger; and not only was he remarkable for the extraordinary quantity which he eat, but he was, or affected to be, a man of

---

12. **Pomponius Mela,** the earliest Roman geographer, born in the first century, A.D.   28. **Mr. Blacklock,** Thomas Blacklock (1721–1791), a blind Scottish poet.   34. **Spence,** Joseph Spence (1699–1788), author of a valuable collection of anecdotes about his literary contemporaries.

26. **gulosity,** greediness.

very nice discernment in the science of cookery. He used to descant critically on the dishes which had been at table where he had dined or supped, and to recollect very minutely what he had liked. I remember, when he was in Scotland, his praising "*Gordon's palates*," (a dish of palates at the Honourable Alexander Gordon's) with a warmth of expression which might have done honour to more important subjects. "As for Maclaurin's imitation of a *made dish*, it was a wretched attempt." He about the same time was so much displeased with the performances of a nobleman's French cook, that he exclaimed with vehemence, "I'd throw such a rascal into the river"; and he then proceeded to alarm a lady at whose house he was to sup, by the following manifesto of his skill: "I, Madam, who live at a variety of good tables, am a much better judge of cookery, than any person who has a very tolerable cook, but lives much at home; for his palate is gradually adapted to the taste of his cook; whereas, Madam, in trying by a wider range, I can more exquisitely judge." When invited to dine, even with an intimate friend, he was not pleased if something better than a plain dinner was not prepared for him. I have heard him say on such an occasion, "This was a good dinner enough, to be sure; but it was not a dinner to *ask* a man to." On the other hand, he was wont to express, with great glee, his satisfaction when he had been entertained quite to his mind. One day when we had dined with his neighbour and landlord in Bolt-court, Mr. Allen, the printer, whose old housekeeper had studied his taste in every thing, he pronounced this eulogy: "Sir, we could not have had a better dinner had there been a *Synod of Cooks*."

While we were left by ourselves, after the Dutchman had gone to bed, Dr. Johnson talked of that studied behaviour which many have recommended and practised. He disapproved of it; and said, "I never considered whether I should be a grave man, or a merry man, but just let inclination, for the time, have its course."

He flattered me with some hopes that he would, in the course of the following summer, come over to Holland, and accompany me in a tour through the Netherlands.

I teased him with fanciful apprehensions of unhappiness. A moth having fluttered round the candle, and burnt itself, he laid hold of this little incident to admonish me; saying, with a sly look, and in a solemn but quiet tone, "That creature was its own tormentor, and I believe its name was BOSWELL."

Next day we got to Harwich to dinner; and my passage in the packet-boat to Helvoetsluys being secured, and my baggage put on board, we dined at our inn by ourselves. I happened to say it would be terrible if he should not find a speedy opportunity of returning to London, and be confined to so dull a place. JOHNSON. "Don't, Sir, accustom yourself to use big words for little matters. It would *not* be *terrible*, though I *were* to be detained some time here." The practice of using words of disproportionate magnitude, is, no doubt, too frequent everywhere; but, I think, most remarkable among the French, of which, all who have travelled in France must have been struck with innumerable instances.

We went and looked at the church, and having gone into it and walked up to the altar, Johnson, whose piety was constant and fervent, sent me to my knees, saying "Now that you are going to leave your native country, recommend yourself to the protection of your CREATOR and REDEEMER."

After we came out of the church, we stood talking for some time together of Bishop Berkeley's ingenious sophistry to prove the non-existence of matter, and that every thing in the universe is merely ideal. I observed, that though we are satisfied his doctrine is not true, it is impossible to refute it. I shall never forget the alacrity with which Johnson answered, striking his foot with mighty force against a large stone, till he rebounded from it, "I refute it *thus*." This was a stout exemplification of the *first truths* of Père Bouffier, or the *original principles* of Reid and of Beattie; without admitting which, we can no more argue in metaphysicks, than we can argue in mathematicks without axioms. To me it is not conceivable how Berkeley can be answered by pure reasoning; but I know that the nice and difficult task was to have been undertaken by one of the most luminous minds of the present age, had not politics "turned him from calm philosophy aside." What an admirable display of subtilty, united with brilliance, might his contending with Berkeley have afforded us! How must we, when we reflect on the loss of such an intellectual feast, regret that he should be characterized as the man,

"Who born for the universe narrowed his mind,
And to party gave up what was meant for mankind?"

My revered friend walked down with me to the beach, where we embraced and parted with tenderness, and engaged to correspond by letters. I said, "I hope, Sir, you will not forget me in my absence."

28. **Bouffier**, Claude Buffier (1661–1737), author of a treatise on the source of our judgments.   43–45. "Who . . . mankind?" from Goldsmith's poem "Retaliation," with reference to Edmund Burke.

JOHNSON. "Nay, Sir, it is more likely you should forget me, than that I should forget you." As the vessel put out to sea, I kept my eyes upon him for a considerable time, while he remained rolling his majestick frame in his usual manner: and at last I perceived him walk back into the town, and he disappeared. . . .

A.D. 1776: AETAT. 67.

. . . I am now to record a very curious incident in Dr. Johnson's Life, which fell under my own observation; of which *pars magna fui*, and which I am persuaded will, with the liberal-minded, be much to his credit.

My desire of being acquainted with celebrated men of every description, had made me, much about the same time, obtain an introduction to Dr. Samuel Johnson and to John Wilkes, Esq. Two men more different could perhaps not be selected out of all mankind. They had even attacked one another with some asperity in their writings; yet I lived in habits of friendship with both. I could fully relish the excellence of each; for I have ever delighted in that intellectual chymistry, which can separate good qualities from evil in the same person.

Sir John Pringle, "mine own friend and my Father's friend," between whom and Dr. Johnson I in vain wished to establish an acquaintance, as I respected and lived in intimacy with both of them, observed to me once, very ingeniously, "It is not in friendship as in mathematicks, where two things, each equal to a third, are equal between themselves. You agree with Johnson as a middle quality, and you agree with me as a middle quality; but Johnson and I should not agree." Sir John was not sufficiently flexible; so I desisted; knowing, indeed, that the repulsion was equally strong on the part of Johnson; who, I know not from what cause, unless his being a Scotchman, had formed a very erroneous opinion of Sir John. But I conceived an irresistible wish, if possible, to bring Dr. Johnson and Mr. Wilkes together. How to manage it, was a nice and difficult matter.

My worthy booksellers and friends, Messieurs Dilly in the Poultry, at whose hospitable and well-covered table I have seen a greater number of literary men, than at any other, except that of Sir Joshua Reynolds, had invited me to meet Mr. Wilkes and some more gentlemen on Wednesday, May 15. "Pray (said I) let us have Dr. Johnson."—"What, with Mr. Wilkes? not for the world, (said Mr. Edward Dilly:) Dr. Johnson would never forgive me." —"Come, (said I), if you'll let me negociate for you, I will be answerable that all shall go well." DILLY. "Nay, if you will take it upon you, I am sure I shall be very happy to see them both here."

Notwithstanding the high veneration which I entertained for Dr. Johnson, I was sensible that he was sometimes a little actuated by the spirit of contradiction, and by means of that I hoped I should gain my point. I was persuaded that if I had come upon him with a direct proposal, "Sir, will you dine in company with Jack Wilkes?" he would have flown into a passion, and would probably have answered, "Dine with Jack Wilkes, Sir! I'd as soon dine with Jack Ketch." I therefore, while we were sitting quietly by ourselves at his house in an evening, took occasion to open my plan thus:— "Mr. Dilly, Sir, sends his respectful compliments to you, and would be happy if you would do him the honour to dine with him on Wednesday next along with me, as I must soon go to Scotland." JOHNSON. "Sir, I am obliged to Mr. Dilly. I will wait upon him—" BOSWELL. "Provided, Sir, I suppose, that the company which he is to have, is agreeable to you." JOHNSON. "What do you mean, Sir? What do you take me for? Do you think I am so ignorant of the world, as to imagine that I am to prescribe to a gentleman what company he is to have at his table?" BOSWELL. "I beg your pardon, Sir, for wishing to prevent you from meeting people whom you might not like. Perhaps he may have some of what he calls his patriotick friends with him." JOHNSON. "Well, Sir, and what then? What care *I* for his *patriotick friends?* Poh!" BOSWELL. "I should not be surprised to find Jack Wilkes there." JOHNSON. "And if Jack Wilkes *should* be there, what is that to *me*, Sir? My dear friend, let us have no more of this. I am sorry to be angry with you; but really it is treating me strangely to talk to me as if I could not meet any company whatever, occasionally." BOSWELL. "Pray forgive me, Sir: I meant well. But you shall meet whoever comes, for me." Thus I secured him, and told Dilly that he would find him very well pleased to be one of his guests on the day appointed.

Upon the much-expected Wednesday, I called on him about half an hour before dinner, as I often did when we were to dine out together, to see that he was ready in time, and to accompany him. I found him buffeting his books, as upon a former occasion, covered with dust, and making no preparation for

---

14. **of which pars magna fui,** in which I took an important part. 28. **Sir John Pringle,** a Scotchman (1707–1782), who had recently been made physician to the king. Johnson disliked him because he was a Unitarian.

18. **Jack Ketch,** the hangman.

going abroad. "How is this, Sir? (said I.) Don't you recollect that you are to dine at Mr. Dilly's?" JOHNSON. "Sir, I did not think of going to Dilly's: it went out of my head. I have ordered dinner at home with Mrs. Williams." BOSWELL. "But, my dear Sir, you know you were engaged to Mr. Dilly, and I told him so. He will expect you, and will be much disappointed if you don't come." JOHNSON. "You must talk to Mrs. Williams about this."

Here was a sad dilemma. I feared that what I was so confident I had secured would yet be frustrated. He had accustomed himself to shew Mrs. Williams such a degree of humane attention, as frequently imposed some restraint upon him; and I knew that if she should be obstinate, he would not stir. I hastened down stairs to the blind lady's room, and told her I was in great uneasiness, for Dr. Johnson had engaged to me to dine this day at Mr. Dilly's, but that he had told me he had forgotten his engagement, and had ordered dinner at home. "Yes, Sir, (said she, pretty peevishly,) Dr. Johnson is to dine at home."—"Madam, (said I,) his respect for you is such, that I know he will not leave you unless you absolutely desire it. But as you have so much of his company, I hope you will be good enough to forego it for a day, as Mr. Dilly is a very worthy man, has frequently had agreeable parties at his house for Dr. Johnson, and will be vexed if the Doctor neglects him to-day. And then, Madam, be pleased to consider my situation; I carried the message, and I assured Mr. Dilly that Dr. Johnson was to come, and no doubt he has made a dinner, and invited a company, and boasted of the honour he expected to have. I shall be quite disgraced if the Doctor is not there." She gradually softened to my solicitations, which were certainly as earnest as most entreaties to ladies upon any occasion, and was graciously pleased to empower me to tell Dr. Johnson, "That all things considered, she thought he should certainly go." I flew back to him, still in dust, and careless of what should be the event, "indifferent in his choice to go or stay;" but as soon as I had announced to him Mrs. Williams' consent, he roared, "Frank, a clean shirt," and was very soon dressed. When I had him fairly seated in a hackney-coach with me, I exulted as much as a fortune-hunter who has got an heiress into a post-chaise with him to set out for Gretna-Green.

When we entered Mr. Dilly's drawing room, he found himself in the midst of a company he did not know. I kept myself snug and silent, watching how he would conduct himself. I observed him whispering to Mr. Dilly, "Who is that gentleman, Sir?"—"Mr. Arthur Lee."—JOHNSON. "Too, too, too," (under his breath,) which was one of his habitual mutterings. Mr. Arthur Lee could not but be very obnoxious to Johnson, for he was not only a *patriot* but an *American*. He was afterwards minister from the United States at the court of Madrid. "And who is the gentleman in lace?"—"Mr. Wilkes, Sir." This information confounded him still more; he had some difficulty to restrain himself, and taking up a book, sat down upon a window-seat and read, or at least kept his eye upon it intently for some time, till he composed himself. His feelings, I dare say, were aukward enough. But he no doubt recollected his having rated me for supposing that he could be at all disconcerted by any company, and he, therefore, resolutely set himself to behave quite as an easy man of the world, who could adapt himself at once to the disposition and manners of those whom he might chance to meet.

The cheering sound of "Dinner is upon the table," dissolved his reverie, and we *all* sat down without any symptom of ill humour. There were present, besides Mr. Wilkes, and Mr. Arthur Lee, who was an old companion of mine when he studied physick at Edinburgh, Mr. (now, Sir John) Miller, Dr. Lettsom, and Mr. Slater the druggist. Mr. Wilkes placed himself next to Dr. Johnson, and behaved to him with so much attention and politeness, that he gained upon him insensibly. No man eat more heartily than Johnson, or loved better what was nice and delicate. Mr. Wilkes was very assiduous in helping him to some fine veal. "Pray give me leave, Sir:—It is better here—A little of the brown—Some fat, Sir—A little of the stuffing—Some gravy—Let me have the pleasure of giving you some butter—Allow me to recommend a squeeze of this orange; or the lemon, perhaps, may have more zest."—"Sir, Sir, I am obliged to you, Sir," cried Johnson, bowing, and turning his head to him with a look for some time of "surly virtue," but, in a short while, of complacency.

Foote being mentioned, Johnson said, "He is not a good mimick." One of the company added, "A merry Andrew, a buffoon." JOHNSON. "But he has wit too, and is not deficient in ideas, or in fertility and variety of imagery, and not empty of reading; he has knowledge enough to fill up his part. One species of wit he has in an eminent degree, that of escape. You drive him into a corner with both hands; but he's gone, Sir, when you think you have got him—like an animal that jumps over your head.

41-42. "indifferent . . . stay," a rephrasing of a line in Addison's *Cato*, Act V, sc. 1. 44. "Frank," Francis Barber, Johnson's Negro servant.

42. "surly virtue," from Johnson's *London, a Poem*.

Then he has a great range for wit; he never lets truth stand between him and a jest, and he is sometimes mighty coarse. Garrick is under many restraints from which Foote is free." WILKES. "Garrick's wit is more like Lord Chesterfield's." JOHNSON "The first time I was in company with Foote was at Fitzherbert's. Having no good opinion of the fellow, I was resolved not to be pleased; and it is very difficult to please a man against his will. I went on eating my dinner pretty sullenly, affecting not to mind him. But the dog was so very comical, that I was obliged to lay down my knife and fork, throw myself back upon my chair, and fairly laugh it out. No, Sir, he was irresistible. He upon one occasion experienced, in an extraordinary degree, the efficacy of his powers of entertaining. Amongst the many and various modes which he tried of getting money, he became a partner with a small-beer brewer, and he was to have a share of the profits for procuring customers amongst his numerous acquaintance. Fitzherbert was one who took his small-beer; but it was so bad that the servants resolved not to drink it. They were at some loss how to notify their resolution, being afraid of offending their master, who they knew liked Foote much as a companion. At last they fixed upon a little black boy, who was rather a favourite, to be their deputy, and deliver their remonstrance; and having invested him with the whole authority of the kitchen, he was to inform Mr. Fitzherbert, in all their names, upon a certain day, that they would drink Foote's small-beer no longer. On that day Foote happened to dine at Fitzherbert's, and this boy served at table; he was so delighted with Foote's stories, and merriment, and grimace, that when he went down stairs, he told them, 'This is the finest man I have ever seen. I will not deliver your message. I will drink his small-beer.'"

Somebody observed that Garrick could not have done this. WILKES. "Garrick would have made the small-beer still smaller. He is now leaving the stage; but he will play *Scrub* all his life." I knew that Johnson would let nobody attack Garrick but himself, as Garrick once said to me, and I had heard him praise his liberality; so to bring out his commendation of his celebrated pupil, I said, loudly, "I have heard Garrick is liberal." JOHNSON. "Yes, Sir, I know that Garrick has given away more money than any man in England that I am acquainted with, and that not from ostentatious views. Garrick was very poor when he began life; so when he came to have money, he probably was very unskilful in giving away, and saved when he should not. But Garrick began to be liberal as soon as he could; and I am of opinion, the reputation of avarice which he has had, has been very lucky for him, and prevented his having many enemies. You despise a man for avarice, but do not hate him. Garrick might have been much better attacked for living with more splendour than is suitable to a player: if they had had the wit to have assaulted him in that quarter, they might have galled him more. But they have kept clamouring about his avarice, which has rescued him from much obloquy and envy."

Talking of the great difficulty of obtaining authentick information for biography, Johnson told us, "When I was a young fellow I wanted to write the *Life of Dryden*, and in order to get materials, I applied to the only two persons then alive who had seen him; these were old Swinney, and old Cibber. Swinney's information was no more than this, 'That at Will's coffee-house Dryden had a particular chair for himself, which was set by the fire in winter, and was then called his winter-chair; and that it was carried out for him to the balcony in summer, and was then called his summer-chair.' Cibber could tell no more but 'That he remembered him a decent old man, arbiter of critical disputes at Wills.' You are to consider that Cibber was then at a great distance from Dryden, had perhaps one leg only in the room, and durst not draw in the other." BOSWELL. "Yet Cibber was a man of observation?" JOHNSON. "I think not." BOSWELL. "You will allow his *Apology* to be well done." JOHNSON. "Very well done, to be sure, Sir. That book is a striking proof of the justice of Pope's remark:

'Each might his several province well command,
Would all but stoop to what they understand.'"

BOSWELL. "And his plays are good." JOHNSON. "Yes; but that was his trade; *l'esprit du corps:* he had been all his life among players and play-writers. I wondered that he had so little to say in conversation, for he had kept the best company, and learned all that can be got by the ear. He abused Pindar to me, and then showed me an Ode of his own, with an absurd couplet, making a linnet soar on an eagle's wing. I told him that when the ancients made a simile, they always made it like something real."

Mr. Wilkes remarked, that "among all the bold flights of Shakspeare's imagination, the boldest was making Birnam-wood march to Dunsinane; creating a wood where there never was a shrub; a wood

---

42. **Scrub,** the drudge in Farquhar's *Beaux' Stratagem.*
17. **Cibber,** Colley Cibber (1671–1757), an actor and dramatist. 35–36. 'Each . . . understand,' from Pope's *Essay on Criticism*, Part I, ll. 66–67.

in Scotland! ha! ha! ha!" And he also observed, that "the clannish slavery of the Highlands of Scotland was the single exception to Milton's remark of 'The Mountain Nymph, sweet Liberty,' being worshipped in all hilly countries."—"When I was at Inverary (said he,) on a visit to my old friend, Archibald, Duke of Argyle, his dependents congratulated me on being such a favourite of his Grace. I said, 'It is then, gentlemen, truly lucky for me; for if I had displeased the Duke, and he had wished it, there is not a Campbell among you but would have been ready to bring John Wilkes's head to him in a charger. It would have been only

'Off with his head! So much for Aylesbury.'

I was then member for Aylesbury."

Dr. Johnson and Mr. Wilkes talked of the contested passage in Horace's *Art of Poetry*, "*Difficile est propriè communia dicere.*" Mr. Wilkes, according to my note, gave the interpretation thus; "It is difficult to speak with propriety of common things; as, if a poet had to speak of Queen Caroline drinking tea, he must endeavour to avoid the vulgarity of cups and saucers." But upon reading my note, he tells me that he meant to say, that "the word *communia*, being a Roman law term, signifies here things *communis juris*, that is to say, what have never yet been treated by any body; and this appears clearly from what followed,

"———*Tuque*
Rectius Iliacum carmen deducis in actus,
Quàm si proferres ignota indictaque primus."

You will easier make a tragedy out of the *Iliad* than on any subject not handled before." JOHNSON. "He means that it is difficult to appropriate to particular persons qualities which are common to all mankind, as Homer has done."

WILKES. "We have no City-Poet now: that is an office which has gone into disuse. The last was Elkanah Settle. There is something in *names* which one cannot help feeling. Now *Elkanah Settle* sounds so *queer*, who can expect much from that name? We should have no hesitation to give it for John Dryden, in preference to Elkanah Settle, from the names only, without knowing their different merits." JOHNSON. "I suppose, Sir, Settle did as well for Aldermen in his time, as John Home could do now. Where did Beckford and Trecothick learn English?"

Mr. Arthur Lee mentioned some Scotch who had taken possession of a barren part of America, and wondered why they should choose it. JOHNSON. "Why, Sir, all barrenness is comparative. The *Scotch* would not know it to be barren." BOSWELL. "Come, come, he is flattering the English. You have now been in Scotland, Sir, and say if you did not see meat and drink enough there." JOHNSON. "Why yes, Sir; meat and drink enough to give the inhabitants sufficient strength to run away from home." All these quick and lively sallies were said sportively, quite in jest, and with a smile, which showed that he meant only wit. Upon this topick he and Mr. Wilkes could perfectly assimilate; here was a bond of union between them, and I was conscious that as both of them had visited Caledonia, both were fully satisfied of the strange narrow ignorance of those who imagine that it is a land of famine. But they amused themselves with persevering in the old jokes. When I claimed a superiority for Scotland over England in one respect, that no man can be arrested there for a debt merely because another swears it against him; but there must first be the judgement of a court of law ascertaining its justice; and that a seizure of the person, before judgement is obtained, can take place only, if his creditor should swear that he is about to fly from the country, or, as it is technically expressed, is *in meditatione fugae:* WILKES. "That, I should think, may be safely sworn of all the Scotch nation." JOHNSON. (to Mr. Wilkes) "You must know, Sir, I lately took my friend Boswell and shewed him genuine civilised life in an English provincial town. I turned him loose at Lichfield, my native city, that he might see for once real civility: for you know he lives among savages in Scotland, and among rakes in London." WILKES. "Except when he is with grave, sober, decent people like you and me." JOHNSON. (smiling,) "And we ashamed of him."

They were quite frank and easy. Johnson told the story of his asking Mrs. Macaulay to allow her footman to sit down with them, to prove the ridiculousness of the argument for the equality of mankind; and he said to me afterwards, with a nod of satisfaction, "You saw Mr. Wilkes acquiesced." Wilkes talked with all imaginable freedom of the ludicrous title given to the Attorney-General, *Diabolus Regis;* adding, "I have reason to know something about that officer; for I was prosecuted for a libel." Johnson, who many people would have supposed must have been furiously angry at hearing this talked of

---

4. **Mountain Nymph.** See "L'Allegro," l. 36. 15. **'Off . . . Aylesbury.'** See Cibber's edition of *Richard III*, Act VI, sc. 1. 32–34. **"Tuque . . . primus."**
   "Then let your style be suited to the scene,
   And its peculiar character maintain."—
   Francis's translation of *Ars Poetica*, ll. 128–30.

so lightly, said not a word. He was now, *indeed*, "a good-humoured fellow."

After dinner we had an accession of Mrs. Knowles, the Quaker lady, well known for her various talents, and of Mr. Alderman Lee. Amidst some patriotic groans, somebody (I think the Alderman) said, "Poor old England is lost." JOHNSON. "Sir, it is not so much to be lamented that Old England is lost, as that the Scotch have found it." WILKES. "Had Lord Bute governed Scotland only, I should not have taken the trouble to write his eulogy, and dedicate *Mortimer* to him."

Mr. Wilkes held a candle to show a fine print of a beautiful female figure which hung in the room, and pointed out the elegant contour of the bosom with the finger of an arch connoisseur. He afterwards, in a conversation with me, waggishly insisted, that all the time Johnson shewed visible signs of a fervent admiration of the corresponding charms of the fair Quaker.

This record, though by no means so perfect as I could wish, will serve to give a notion of a very curious interview, which was not only pleasing at the time, but had the agreeable and benignant effect of reconciling any animosity, and sweetening any acidity, which in the various bustle of political contest, had been produced in the minds of two men, who though widely different, had so many things in common—classical learning, modern literature, wit, and humour, and ready repartee—that it would have been much to be regretted if they had been forever at a distance from each other.

Mr. Burke gave me much credit for this successful *negociation;* and pleasantly said, that "there was nothing to equal it in the whole history of the *Corps Diplomatique*."

I attended Dr. Johnson home, and had the satisfaction to hear him tell Mrs. Williams how much he had been pleased with Mr. Wilkes's company, and what an agreeable day he had passed. . . .

Samuel Johnson
1709–1784

The last literary dictator of England was born during the reign of Queen Anne in the northern cathedral city of Lichfield, where his father, an aging man, kept a not very prosperous bookshop. From the excellent school of his native town Johnson went to Oxford; but there, on account of his poverty, he took no degree. At the age of twenty-six he married a widow some fifteen years his senior. After certain abortive attempts at schoolteaching he went up to London in 1737, accompanied by David Garrick, who had been one of his pupils, and settled down to the obscure and ill-paid toil of a hack writer. He wrote hundreds of essays for such periodicals as would take them, and for two, the *Rambler* and the *Idler*, which he conducted himself. His didactic poem *London*, an imitation of Juvenal, appeared in 1738 without his name, and eleven years later he published his more important poem of the same sort called *The Vanity of Human Wishes*. His tragedy entitled *Irene* had slight success. In 1755 his *Dictionary of the English Language*, upon which he had been working for many years, brought him fame and money. By that time, however, he had lost his beloved wife, his "dear Tetty," and success meant far less to him than it would previously have done. His *History of Rasselas, Prince of Abissinia*, appearing in 1759, extended his reputation. In 1762 the King gave him a pension of £300 a year, a sum amounting to at least $6,000 in present buying power. In the following year he first met James Boswell, and almost immediately realized what the devotion of this intelligent young Scot, so exact and enthusiastic in the taking of notes upon trivial events and conversations, might mean in the way of posthumous fame. Johnson's habitual gloom and despondency were still further alleviated in 1764 by his meeting with the wealthy brewer Mr. Thrale and with his wife—"a bright papilonaceous creature," as Carlyle calls her, "whom the elephant loved to play with, and wave to and fro upon his trunk." His closing years, though saddened by the loss of friends, were lived in a growing light of fame. His edition of Shakespeare was published in 1765, and his *Lives of the Poets* appeared, in ten volumes, in 1779–81. Three years later he died, and was buried in Westminster Abbey.

Dr. Johnson—so-called because of the honorary degrees of LL.D. conferred upon him by Oxford and Dublin—owes his huge and still continuing fame and influence as much to qualities of character as to his learning, his wit, his pencraft, and his massive common sense. James Boswell did not create, and he did not exaggerate, the flawed and whimsical human grandeur that looms above Johnson's prejudices, bigotries, stubborn stupidities, and frequent wrong-headed ignorance. He only uncovered what was there, and what he revealed was—in the full tragic and pathetic sense of the word—a man. Largely by Boswell's help, Dr. Johnson is the most amply recorded writer in the total range of English literature. We know him not only in the thousand moods of his own writing—much of it cumbered by theory and rule-ridden, but much of it, too, with the accent of his own discursive, dogmatic, and always friendly talk—but we see him also in his hours of ease, away from the writing-desk, at the Literary Club, in the tavern, in the greenroom of Garrick's theater, on the roads reaching north through Scotland, in his Christian love for helpless and crazed and wicked lost people, in his everlasting brown suit with the metal buttons and black worsted stockings, his bushy wig awry, talking, talking, always talking for triumph, and asking for another cup of tea. We see him at the Turk's Head tavern with Reynolds, Burke, Goldsmith, Garrick, Langton, Beauclerk, Fox, and Boswell round him. Yet always as we press onward through the wilderness of tiny things that are to be known about Dr. Johnson—his sounding voice, his rolling gait and ungainly form, his nearsighted eyes that always saw much more than others suspected, his gruff and bearish demeanor with strangers, his queer and meaningless gestures—we have an assurance that we are coming closer to a genuine, warm-hearted, brotherly man.

Dr. Johnson's literary production, that of a man who had to live by his pen, was miscellaneous. An editor who wishes to show him in his best and most characteristic writing is at first in doubt, therefore, whether to present the didactic verse in which he imitated Pope and the ancient satirists, the essays in which he followed Addison and Steele "like a packhorse trailing the hunter," or, perhaps, the learned whimsicalities of his *Dictionary*. Clearly, however, he must be shown as a moralist, for that he was primarily, and also as a conservative critic who usually mingled his conservatism with common sense.

THE HISTORY OF RASSELAS, PRINCE OF ABISSINIA

Boswell reports that Johnson wrote his *Rasselas* in the evenings of one week in order to pay the expenses of his mother's funeral. He goes on to say that no other of Johnson's writings had been in his time "so extensively diffused over Europe," and that it had been "translated into most if not all of the modern languages."

"This tale," he continues, "with all the charms of oriental imagery and all the force and beauty of which the English language is capable, leads us through the most important scenes of human life, and shows us that this stage of our being is full of 'vanity and vexation of spirit.' . . . The fund of thinking which this work contains is such that almost every sentence of it may furnish a subject of long meditation. I am not satisfied if a year passes without my having read it through; and at every perusal my admiration of the mind which produced it is so highly raised that I can scarcely believe that I had the honour of enjoying the intimacy of such a man."

These are the words of a friend, and not every reader of our day would agree with them. A literary handbook of recent date asserts, for example, that *Rasselas* "is a thinly-jointed moralistic work lacking in plot and incident, and honeyed primarily by a series of didactic, pensive disquisitions on life and man's normally disillusioning search after happiness." On the other hand, Mr. Hilaire Belloc says of this tale that "never was wisdom better put, or more enduringly; and if it be true that the test of a book is the mood in which we lay it down, then this book must have as high marks as anything ever written in English."

Chapter 1

DESCRIPTION OF A PALACE IN A VALLEY

YE who listen with credulity to the whispers of fancy, and pursue with eagerness the phantoms of hope; who expect that age will perform the promises of youth, and that the deficiencies of the present day will be supplied by the morrow; attend to the history of Rasselas prince of Abissinia.

Rasselas was the fourth son of the mighty emperor in whose dominions the Father of Waters begins his course; whose bounty pours down the streams of plenty, and scatters over half the world the harvests of Egypt.

According to the custom which has descended from age to age among the monarchs of the torrid zone, Rasselas was confined in a private palace, with the other sons and daughters of Abissinian royalty, till the order of succession should call him to the throne.

The place, which the wisdom or policy of antiquity had destined for the residence of the Abissinian princes, was a spacious valley in the kingdom of Amhara, surrounded on every side by mountains, of which the summits overhang the middle part. The only passage, by which it could be entered, was a cavern that passed under a rock, of which it has long been disputed whether it was the work of nature or

6. **Rasselas**, from "Ras," meaning "king," and "Selas," a variant of the now familiar Abyssinian name "Selassie."
8. **Father of Waters**, the Nile.

of human industry. The outlet of the cavern was concealed by a thick wood, and the mouth which opened into the valley was closed with gates of iron, forged by the artificers of ancient days, so massy that no man could without the help of engines open or shut them.

From the mountains on every side, rivulets descended that filled all the valley with verdure and fertility, and formed a lake in the middle inhabited by fish of every species, and frequented by every fowl whom nature has taught to dip the wing in water. This lake discharged its superfluities by a stream which entered a dark cleft of the mountain on the northern side, and fell with dreadful noise from precipice to precipice till it was heard no more.

The sides of the mountains were covered with trees, the banks of the brooks were diversified with flowers; every blast shook spices from the rocks, and every month dropped fruits upon the ground. All animals that bite the grass, or browse the shrub, whether wild or tame, wandered in this extensive circuit, secured from beasts of prey by the mountains which confined them. On one part were flocks and herds feeding in the pastures, on another all the beasts of chase frisking in the lawns; the sprightly kid was bounding on the rocks, the subtle monkey frolicking in the trees, and the solemn elephant reposing in the shade. All the diversities of the world were brought together, the blessings of nature were collected, and its evils extracted and excluded.

The valley, wide and fruitful, supplied its inhabitants with the necessaries of life, and all delights and superfluities were added at the annual visit which the emperor paid his children, when the iron gate was opened to the sound of music; and during eight days every one that resided in the valley was required to propose whatever might contribute to make seclusion pleasant, to fill up the vacancies of attention, and lessen the tediousness of time. Every desire was immediately granted. All the artificers of pleasure were called to gladden the festivity; the musicians exerted the power of harmony, and the dancers shewed their activity before the princes, in hope that they should pass their lives in this blissful captivity, to which those only were admitted whose performance was thought able to add novelty to luxury. Such was the appearance of security and delight which this retirement afforded, that they to whom it was new, always desired that it might be perpetual; and as those, on whom the iron gate had once closed, were never suffered to return, the effect of longer experience could not be known. Thus every year produced new schemes of delight, and new competitors for imprisonment.

The palace stood on an eminence, raised about thirty paces above the surface of the lake. It was divided into many squares or courts, built with greater or less magnificence, according to the rank of those for whom they were designed. The roofs were turned into arches of massy stone joined with a cement that grew harder by time, and the building stood from century to century deriding the solstitial rains and equinoctial hurricanes, without need of reparation.

This house, which was so large as to be fully known to none but some ancient officers who successively inherited the secrets of the place, was built as if suspicion herself had dictated the plan. To every room there was an open and secret passage, every square had a communication with the rest, either from the upper stories by private galleries, or by subterranean passages from the lower apartments. Many of the columns had unsuspected cavities, in which a long race of monarchs had reposited their treasures. They then closed up the opening with marble, which was never to be removed but in the utmost exigencies of the kingdom; and recorded their accumulations in a book which was itself concealed in a tower not entered but by the emperor, attended by the prince who stood next in succession.

Chapter 2

THE DISCONTENT OF RASSELAS IN THE HAPPY VALLEY

Here the sons and daughters of Abissinia lived only to know the soft vicissitudes of pleasure and repose, attended by all that were skilful to delight, and gratified with whatever the senses can enjoy. They wandered in gardens of fragrance, and slept in the fortresses of security. Every art was practised to make them pleased with their own condition. The sages who instructed them, told them of nothing but the miseries of public life, and described all beyond the mountains as regions of calamity, where discord was always raging, and where man preyed upon man.

To heighten their opinion of their own felicity, they were daily entertained with songs, the subject of which was the *happy valley*. Their appetites were excited by frequent enumerations of different enjoyments, and revelry and merriment was the business of every hour from the dawn of morning to the close of even.

These methods were generally successful: few of

the princes had ever wished to enlarge their bounds, but passed their lives in full conviction that they had all within their reach that art or nature could bestow, and pitied those whom fate had excluded from this seat of tranquillity, as the sport of chance and the slaves of misery.

Thus they rose in the morning and lay down at night, pleased with each other and with themselves, all but Rasselas, who, in the twenty-sixth year of his age began to withdraw himself from their pastimes and assemblies, and to delight in solitary walks and silent meditation. He often sat before tables covered with luxury, and forgot to taste the dainties that were placed before him: he rose abruptly in the midst of the song, and hastily retired beyond the sound of music. His attendants observed the change, and endeavoured to renew his love of pleasure; he neglected their officiousness, repulsed their invitations, and spent day after day, on the banks of rivulets sheltered with trees, where he sometimes listened to the birds in the branches, sometimes observed the fish playing in the stream, and anon cast his eyes upon the pastures and mountains filled with animals, of which some were biting the herbage, and some sleeping among the bushes.

This singularity of his humour made him much observed. One of the Sages, in whose conversation he had formerly delighted, followed him secretly, in hope of discovering the cause of his disquiet. Rasselas, who knew not that any one was near him, having for some time fixed his eyes upon the goats that were browsing among the rocks, began to compare their condition with his own.

"What," said he, "makes the difference between man and all the rest of the animal creation? Every beast that strays beside me has the same corporal necessities with myself; he is hungry and crops the grass, he is thirsty and drinks the stream, his thirst and hunger are appeased, he is satisfied and sleeps; he rises again and is hungry, he is again fed and is at rest. I am hungry and thirsty like him, but when thirst and hunger cease I am not at rest; I am like him pained with want, but am not, like him, satisfied with fulness. The intermediate hours are tedious and gloomy: I long again to be hungry that I may again quicken my attention. The birds peck the berries or the corn, and fly away to the groves, where they sit in seeming happiness on the branches, and waste their lives in tuning one unvaried series of sounds. I likewise can call the lutanist and the singer, but the sounds that pleased me yesterday weary me to-day, and will grow yet more wearisome to-morrow. I can discover within me no power of perception which is not glutted with its proper pleasure, yet I do not feel myself delighted. Man has surely some latent sense for which this place affords no gratification, or he has some desires distinct from sense, which must be satisfied before he can be happy."

After this he lifted up his head, and seeing the moon rising, walked towards the palace. As he passed through the fields, and saw the animals around him, "Ye," said he, "are happy, and need not envy me that walk thus among you, burdened with myself; nor do I, ye gentle beings, envy your felicity; for it is not the felicity of man. I have many distresses from which ye are free; I fear pain when I do not feel it; I sometimes shrink at evils recollected, and sometimes start at evils anticipated. Surely the equity of Providence has balanced peculiar sufferings with peculiar enjoyments."

With observations like these the prince amused himself as he returned, uttering them with a plaintive voice, yet with a look that discovered him to feel some complacence in his own perspicacity, and to receive some solace of the miseries of life, from consciousness of the delicacy with which he felt, and the eloquence with which he bewailed them. He mingled cheerfully in the diversions of the evening, and all rejoiced to find that his heart was lightened.

Chapter 3

THE WANTS OF HIM THAT WANTS NOTHING

On the next day his old instructor, imagining that he had now made himself acquainted with his disease of mind, was in hope of curing it by counsel, and officiously sought an opportunity of conference, which the prince, having long considered him as one whose intellects were exhausted, was not very willing to afford: "Why," said he, "does this man thus intrude upon me; shall I be never suffered to forget those lectures which pleased only while they were new, and to become new again must be forgotten?" He then walked into the wood, and composed himself to his usual meditations; when before his thoughts had taken any settled form, he perceived his pursuer at his side, and was at first prompted by his impatience to go hastily away: but, being unwilling to offend a man whom he had once reverenced and still loved, he invited him to sit down with him on the bank.

The old man, thus encouraged, began to lament the change which had been lately observed in the prince, and to inquire why he so often retired from the pleasures of the palace, to loneliness and silence. "I fly from pleasure," said the prince, "because pleasure has ceased to please; I am lonely because I am miserable, and am unwilling to cloud with my presence the happiness of others." "You, Sir," said the sage, "are the first who has complained of misery in the *happy valley*. I hope to convince you that your complaints have no real cause. You are here in full possession of all that the emperor of Abissinia can bestow; here is neither labour to be endured nor danger to be dreaded, yet here is all that labour or danger can procure or purchase. Look round and tell me which of your wants is without supply: if you want nothing, how are you unhappy?"

"That I want nothing," said the prince, "or that I know not what I want, is the cause of my complaint; if I had any known want, I should have a certain wish; that wish would excite endeavour, and I should not then repine to see the sun move so slowly towards the western mountain, or lament when the day breaks and sleep will no longer hide me from myself. When I see the kids and the lambs chasing one another, I fancy that I should be happy if I had something to pursue. But possessing all that I can want, I find one day and one hour exactly like another, except that the latter is still more tedious than the former. Let your experience inform me how the day may now seem as short as in my childhood, while nature was yet fresh and every moment showed me what I never had observed before. I have already enjoyed too much; give me something to desire."

The old man was surprised at this new species of affliction, and knew not what to reply, yet was unwilling to be silent. "Sir," said he, "if you had seen the miseries of the world, you would know how to value your present state." "Now," said the prince, "you have given me something to desire; I shall long to see the miseries of the world, since the sight of them is necessary to happiness."

Chapter 4

THE PRINCE CONTINUES TO GRIEVE AND MUSE

At this time the sound of music proclaimed the hour of repast and the conversation was concluded. The old man went away sufficiently discontented, to find that his reasonings had produced the only conclusion which they were intended to prevent. But in the decline of life shame and grief are of short duration; whether it be that we bear easily what we have borne long; or that, finding ourselves in age less regarded, we less regard others; or, that we look with slight regard upon afflictions, to which we know that the hand of death is about to put an end.

The prince, whose views were extended to a wider space, could not speedily quiet his emotions. He had been before terrified at the length of life which nature promised him, because he considered that in a long time much must be endured; he now rejoiced in his youth, because in many years much might be done.

This first beam of hope, that had been ever darted into his mind, rekindled youth in his cheeks and doubled the lustre of his eyes. He was fired with the desire of doing something, though he knew not yet with distinctness either end or means.

He was now no longer gloomy and unsocial; but, considering himself as master of a secret stock of happiness, which he could enjoy only by concealing it, he affected to be busy in all schemes of diversion, and endeavoured to make others pleased with the state of which he himself was weary. But pleasures can never be so multiplied or continued, as not to leave much of life unemployed; there were many hours, both of the night and day, which he could spend without suspicion in solitary thought. The load of life was much lightened: he went eagerly into the assemblies, because he supposed the frequency of his presence necessary to the success of his purposes; he retired gladly to privacy, because he had now a subject of thought.

His chief amusement was to picture to himself that world which he had never seen; to place himself in various conditions; to be entangled in imaginary difficulties, and to be engaged in wild adventures: but his benevolence always terminated his projects in the relief of distress, the detection of fraud, the defeat of oppression, and the diffusion of happiness.

Thus passed twenty months of the life of Rasselas. He busied himself so intensely in visionary bustle, that he forgot his real solitude, and, amidst hourly preparations for the various incidents of human affairs, neglected to consider by what means he should mingle with mankind.

One day, as he was sitting on a bank, he feigned to himself an orphan virgin robbed of her little portion by a treacherous lover, and crying after him for restitution and redress. So strongly was the image impressed upon his mind, that he started up in the maid's defence, and ran forward to seize the plunderer with all the eagerness of real pursuit. Fear naturally quickens the flight of guilt. Rasselas could not catch the fugitive with his utmost efforts; but, resolving to weary by perseverance, him whom he could not surpass in speed, he pressed on till the foot of the mountain stopped his course.

Here he recollected himself, and smiled at his own useless impetuosity. Then raising his eyes to the mountain, "This," said he, "is the fatal obstacle that hinders at once the enjoyment of pleasure, and the exercise of virtue. How long is it that my hopes and wishes have flown beyond this boundary of my life, which yet I never have attempted to surmount!"

Struck with this reflection, he sat down to muse; and remembered, that since he first resolved to escape from his confinement, the sun had passed twice over him in his annual course. He now felt a degree of regret with which he had never been before acquainted. He considered how much might have been done in the time which had passed, and left nothing real behind it. He compared twenty months with the life of man. "In life," said he, "is not to be counted the ignorance of infancy, or imbecility of age. We are long before we are able to think, and we soon cease from the power of acting. The true period of human existence may be reasonably estimated at forty years, of which I have mused away the four and twentieth part. What I have lost was certain, for I have certainly possessed it; but of twenty months to come who can assure me?"

The consciousness of his own folly pierced him deeply, and he was long before he could be reconciled to himself. "The rest of my time," said he, "has been lost by the crime or folly of my ancestors, and the absurd institutions of my country; I remember it with disgust, yet without remorse: but the months that have passed since new light darted into my soul, since I formed a scheme of reasonable felicity, have been squandered by my own fault. I have lost that which can never be restored: I have seen the sun rise and set for twenty months, an idle gazer on the light of heaven: in this time the birds have left the nest of their mother, and committed themselves to the woods and to the skies: the kid has forsaken the teat, and learned by degrees to climb the rocks in quest of independent sustenance. I only have made no advances, but am still helpless and ignorant. The moon, by more than twenty changes, admonished me of the flux of life; the stream that rolled before my feet upbraided my inactivity. I sat feasting on intellectual luxury, regardless alike of the examples of the earth, and the instructions of the planets. Twenty months are passed. Who shall restore them?"

These sorrowful meditations fastened upon his mind; he passed four months in resolving to lose no more time in idle resolves, and was awakened to more vigorous exertion by hearing a maid, who had broken a porcelain cup, remark that what cannot be repaired is not to be regretted.

This was obvious; and Rasselas reproached himself that he had not discovered it, having not known, or not considered, how many useful hints are obtained by chance, and how often the mind, hurried by her own ardour to distant views, neglects the truths that lie open before her. He, for a few hours, regretted his regret, and from that time bent his whole mind upon the means of escaping from the valley of happiness.

Chapter 5

THE PRINCE MEDITATES HIS ESCAPE

He now found that it would be very difficult to effect that which it was very easy to suppose effected. When he looked round about him, he saw himself confined by the bars of nature which had never yet been broken, and by the gate, through which none that once had passed it were ever able to return. He was now impatient as an eagle in a grate. He passed week after week in clambering the mountains, to see if there was any aperture which the bushes might conceal, but found all the summits inaccessible by their prominence. The iron gate he despaired to open; for it was not only secured with all the power of art, but was always watched by successive sentinels, and was by its position exposed to the perpetual observation of all the inhabitants.

He then examined the cavern through which the waters of the lake were discharged; and, looking down at a time when the sun shone strongly upon its mouth, he discovered it to be full of broken rocks, which, though they permitted the stream to flow through many narrow passages, would stop any body of solid bulk. He returned discouraged and dejected; but, having now known the blessing of hope, resolved never to despair.

In these fruitless searches he spent ten months. The time, however, passed cheerfully away: in the morning he rose with new hope, in the evening applauded his own diligence, and in the night slept sound after his fatigue. He met a thousand amusements which beguiled his labour, and diversified his thoughts. He discerned the various instincts of animals, and properties of plants, and found the

28. grate, cage.

place replete with wonders, of which he purposed to solace himself with the contemplation, if he should never be able to accomplish his flight; rejoicing that his endeavours, though yet unsuccessful, had supplied him with a source of inexhaustible inquiry.

But his original curiosity was not yet abated; he resolved to obtain some knowledge of the ways of men. His wish still continued, but his hope grew less. He ceased to survey any longer the walls of his prison, and spared to search by new toils for interstices which he knew could not be found, yet determined to keep his design always in view, and lay hold on any expedient that time should offer.

Chapter 6

A DISSERTATION ON THE ART OF FLYING

Among the artists that had been allured into the happy valley, to labour for the accommodation and pleasure of its inhabitants, was a man eminent for his knowledge of the mechanic powers, who had contrived many engines both of use and recreation. By a wheel which the stream turned, he forced the water into a tower, whence it was distributed to all the apartments of the palace. He erected a pavilion in the garden, around which he kept the air always cool by artificial showers. One of the groves, appropriated to the ladies, was ventilated by fans, to which the rivulet that ran through it gave a constant motion; and instruments of soft music were placed at proper distances, of which some played by the impulse of the wind, and some by the power of the stream.

This artist was sometimes visited by Rasselas, who was pleased with every kind of knowledge, imagining that the time would come when all his acquisitions should be of use to him in the open world. He came one day to amuse himself in his usual manner, and found the master busy in building a sailing chariot: he saw that the design was practicable upon a level surface, and with expressions of great esteem solicited its completion. The workman was pleased to find himself so much regarded by the prince, and resolved to gain yet higher honours. "Sir," said he, "you have seen but a small part of what the mechanic sciences can perform. I have been long of opinion, that instead of the tardy conveyance of ships and chariots, man might use the swifter migration of wings; that the fields of air are open to knowledge, and that only ignorance and idleness need crawl upon the ground."

This hint rekindled the prince's desire of passing the mountains; having seen what the mechanist had already performed, he was willing to fancy that he could do more; yet resolved to inquire further, before he suffered hope to afflict him by disappointment. "I am afraid," said he to the artist, "that your imagination prevails over your skill, and that you now tell me rather what you wish, than what you know. Every animal has his element assigned him; the birds have the air, and man and beasts the earth." "So," replied the mechanist, "fishes have the water, in which yet beasts can swim by nature, and men by art. He that can swim needs not despair to fly: to swim is to fly in a grosser fluid, and to fly is to swim in a subtler. We are only to proportion our power of resistance to the different density of matter through which we are to pass. You will be necessarily upborn by the air, if you can renew any impulse upon it, faster than the air can recede from the pressure."

"But the exercise of swimming," said the prince, "is very laborious; the strongest limbs are soon wearied; I am afraid the act of flying will be yet more violent, and wings will be of no great use, unless we can fly further than we can swim."

"The labour of rising from the ground," said the artist, "will be great, as we see it in the heavier domestic fowls; but as we mount higher, the earth's attraction, and the body's gravity, will be gradually diminished, till we shall arrive at a region where the man will float in the air without any tendency to fall: no care will then be necessary but to move forwards, which the gentlest impulse will effect. You, Sir, whose curiosity is so extensive, will easily conceive with what pleasure a philosopher, furnished with wings, and hovering in the sky, would see the earth, and all its inhabitants, rolling beneath him, and presenting to him successively, by its diurnal motion, all the countries within the same parallel. How must it amuse the pendent spectator to see the moving scene of land and ocean, cities and deserts! To survey with equal security the marts of trade, and the fields of battle; mountains infested by barbarians, and fruitful regions gladdened by plenty, and lulled by peace! How easily shall we then trace the Nile through all his passage; pass over to distant regions, and examine the face of nature from one extremity of the earth to the other!"

21. **artists,** craftsmen or mechanics.
37. **philosopher,** what we should now call a scientist.
48. **trace the Nile.** The sources of this river were in Johnson's time unknown.

"All this," said the prince, "is much to be desired; but I am afraid that no man will be able to breathe in these regions of speculation and tranquillity. I have been told, that respiration is difficult upon lofty mountains, yet from these precipices, though so high as to produce great tenuity of the air, it is very easy to fall: therefore I suspect, that from any height where life can be supported, there may be danger of too quick descent."

"Nothing," replied the artist, "will ever be attempted, if all possible objections must be first overcome. If you will favour my project, I will try the first flight at my own hazard. I have considered the structure of all volant animals, and find the folding continuity of the bat's wings most easily accommodated to the human form. Upon this model I shall begin my task to-morrow, and in a year expect to tower into the air beyond the malice or pursuit of man. But I will work only on this condition, that the art shall not be divulged, and that you shall not require me to make wings for any but ourselves."

"Why," said Rasselas, "should you envy others so great an advantage? All skill ought to be exerted for universal good; every man has owed much to others, and ought to repay the kindness that he has received."

"If men were all virtuous," returned the artist, "I should with great alacrity teach them all to fly. But what would be the security of the good, if the bad could at pleasure invade them from the sky? Against an army sailing through the clouds, neither walls, nor mountains, nor seas, could afford any security. A flight of northern savages might hover in the wind, and light at once with irresistible violence upon the capital of a fruitful region that was rolling under them. Even this valley, the retreat of princes, the abode of happiness, might be violated by the sudden descent of some of the naked nations that swarm on the coasts of the southern sea."

The prince promised secrecy, and waited for the performance, not wholly hopeless of success. He visited the work from time to time, observed its progress, and remarked many ingenious contrivances to facilitate motion, and unite levity with strength. The artist was every day more certain that he should leave vultures and eagles behind him, and the contagion of his confidence seized upon the prince.

In a year the wings were finished, and, on a morning appointed, the maker appeared furnished for flight on a little promontory: he waved his pinions a while to gather air, then leaped from his stand, and in an instant dropped into the lake. His wings, which were of no use in the air, sustained him in the water, and the prince drew him to land, half dead with terror and vexation.

Chapter 7

THE PRINCE FINDS A MAN OF LEARNING

The prince was not much afflicted by this disaster, having suffered himself to hope for a happier event, only because he had no other means of escape in view. He still persisted in his design to leave the happy valley by the first opportunity.

His imagination was now at a stand; he had no prospect of entering into the world, and, notwithstanding all his endeavours to support himself, discontent by degrees preyed upon him, and he began again to lose his thoughts in sadness, when the rainy season, which in these countries is periodical, made it inconvenient to wander in the woods.

The rain continued longer and with more violence than had been ever known: the clouds broke on the surrounding mountains, and the torrents streamed into the plain on every side, till the cavern was too narrow to discharge the water. The lake overflowed its banks, and all the level of the valley was covered with the inundation. The eminence, on which the palace was built, and some other spots of rising ground, were all that the eye could now discover. The herds and flocks left the pastures, and both the wild beasts and the tame retreated to the mountains.

This inundation confined all the princes to domestic amusements, and the attention of Rasselas was particularly seized by a poem, which Imlac rehearsed, upon the various conditions of humanity. He commanded the poet to attend him in his apartment, and recite his verses a second time; then entering into familiar talk, he thought himself happy in having found a man who knew the world so well, and could so skilfully paint the scenes of life. He asked a thousand questions about things, to which, though common to all other mortals, his confinement from childhood had kept him a stranger. The poet pitied his ignorance, and loved his curiosity, and entertained him from day to day with novelty and instruction, so that the prince regretted the necessity of sleep, and longed till the morning should renew his pleasure.

As they were sitting together, the prince commanded Imlac to relate his history, and to tell by what accident he was forced, or by what motive in-

---

45. levity, lightness.

duced, to close his life in the happy valley. As he was going to begin his narrative, Rasselas was called to a concert, and obliged to restrain his curiosity till the evening.

Chapter 8

THE HISTORY OF IMLAC

The close of the day is, in the regions of the torrid zone, the only season of diversion and entertainment, and it was therefore midnight before the music ceased, and the princesses retired. Rasselas then called for his companion, and required him to begin the story of his life.

"Sir," said Imlac, "my history will not be long: the life that is devoted to knowledge passes silently away, and is very little diversified by events. To talk in public, to think in solitude, to read and to hear, to inquire and answer inquiries, is the business of a scholar. He wanders about the world without pomp or terror, and is neither known nor valued but by men like himself.

"I was born in the kingdom of Goiama, at no great distance from the fountain of the Nile. My father was a wealthy merchant, who traded between the inland countries of Afric and the ports of the Red Sea. He was honest, frugal, and diligent, but of mean sentiments, and narrow comprehension; he desired only to be rich, and to conceal his riches, lest he should be spoiled by the governors of the province."

"Surely," said the prince, "my father must be negligent of his charge, if any man in his dominions dare take that which belongs to another. Does he not know that kings are accountable for injustice permitted as well as done? If I were emperor, not the meanest of my subjects should be oppressed with impunity. My blood boils when I am told that a merchant durst not enjoy his honest gains for fear of losing them by the rapacity of power. Name the governor who robbed the people, that I may declare his crimes to the emperor."

"Sir," said Imlac, "your ardour is the natural effect of virtue animated by youth: the time will come when you will acquit your father, and perhaps hear with less impatience of the governor. Oppression is, in the Abissinian dominions, neither frequent nor tolerated; but no form of government has been yet discovered, by which cruelty can be wholly prevented. Subordination supposes power on one part, and subjection on the other; and if power be in the hands of men, it will sometimes be abused. The vigilance of the supreme magistrate may do much, but much will still remain undone. He can never know all the crimes that are committed, and can seldom punish all that he knows."

"This," said the prince, "I do not understand, but I had rather hear thee than dispute. Continue thy narration."

"My father," proceeded Imlac, "originally intended that I should have no other education, than such as might qualify me for commerce; and discovering in me great strength of memory, and quickness of apprehension, often declared his hope that I should be some time the richest man in Abissinia."

"Why," said the prince, "did thy father desire the increase of his wealth, when it was already greater than he durst discover or enjoy? I am unwilling to doubt thy veracity, yet inconsistencies cannot both be true."

"Inconsistencies," answered Imlac, "cannot both be right; but, imputed to man, they may both be true. Yet diversity is not inconsistency. My father might expect a time of greater security. However, some desire is necessary to keep life in motion, and he whose real wants are supplied must admit those of fancy."

"This," said the prince, "I can in some measure conceive. I repent that I interrupted thee."

"With this hope," proceeded Imlac, "he sent me to school; but when I had once found the delight of knowledge, and felt the pleasure of intelligence and the pride of invention, I began silently to despise riches, and determined to disappoint the purpose of my father, whose grossness of conception raised my pity. I was twenty years old before his tenderness would expose me to the fatigue of travel, in which time I had been instructed, by successive masters, in all the literature of my native country. As every hour taught me something new, I lived in a continual course of gratifications; but, as I advanced towards manhood, I lost much of the reverence with which I had been used to look on my instructors; because, when the lesson was ended, I did not find them wiser or better than common men.

"At length my father resolved to initiate me in commerce, and, opening one of his subterranean treasuries, counted out ten thousand pieces of gold. This, young man, said he, is the stock with which you must negotiate. I began with less than the fifth part, and you see how diligence and parsimony have increased it. This is your own to waste or to

32. **spoiled,** robbed.

18. **discover,** reveal.

improve. If you squander it by negligence or caprice, you must wait for my death before you will be rich; if, in four years, you double your stock, we will thenceforward let subordination cease, and live together as friends and partners; for he shall always be equal with me, who is equally skilled in the art of growing rich.

"We laid our money upon camels, concealed in bales of cheap goods, and travelled to the shore of the Red Sea. When I cast my eye on the expanse of waters, my heart bounded like that of a prisoner escaped. I felt an unextinguishable curiosity kindle in my mind, and resolved to snatch this opportunity of seeing the manners of other nations, and of learning sciences unknown in Abissinia.

"I remembered that my father had obliged me to the improvement of my stock, not by a promise which I ought not to violate, but by a penalty which I was at liberty to incur; and therefore determined to gratify my predominant desire, and by drinking at the fountains of knowledge, to quench the thirst of curiosity.

"As I was supposed to trade without connection with my father, it was easy for me to become acquainted with the master of a ship, and procure a passage to some other country. I had no motives of choice to regulate my voyage; it was sufficient for me that, wherever I wandered, I should see a country which I had not seen before. I therefore entered a ship bound for Surat, having left a letter for my father declaring my intention."

Chapter 9

THE HISTORY OF IMLAC CONTINUED

"When I first entered upon the world of waters, and lost sight of land, I looked round about me with pleasing terror, and thinking my soul enlarged by the boundless prospect, imagined that I could gaze round for ever without satiety; but, in a short time, I grew weary of looking on barren uniformity, where I could only see again what I had already seen. I then descended into the ship, and doubted for a while whether all my future pleasures would not end like this in disgust and disappointment. Yet, surely, said I, the ocean and the land are very different; the only variety of water is rest and motion, but the earth has mountains and valleys, deserts and cities: it is inhabited by men of different customs and contrary opinions; and I may hope to find variety in life, though I should miss it in nature.

"With this thought I quieted my mind, and amused myself during the voyage, sometimes by learning from the sailors the art of navigation, which I have never practised, and sometimes by forming schemes for my conduct in different situations, in not one of which I have been ever placed.

"I was almost weary of my naval amusements when we landed safely at Surat. I secured my money and, purchasing some commodities for show, joined myself to a caravan that was passing into the inland country. My companions, for some reason or other, conjecturing that I was rich, and, by my inquiries and admiration, finding that I was ignorant, considered me as a novice whom they had a right to cheat, and who was to learn at the usual expense the art of fraud. They exposed me to the theft of servants, and the exaction of officers, and saw me plundered upon false pretences, without any advantage to themselves but that of rejoicing in the superiority of their own knowledge."

"Stop a moment," said the prince. "Is there such depravity in man, as that he should injure another without benefit to himself? I can easily conceive that all are pleased with superiority; but your ignorance was merely accidental, which being neither your crime nor your folly, could afford them no reason to applaud themselves; and the knowledge which they had, and which you wanted, they might as effectually have shown by warning, as betraying you."

"Pride," said Imlac, "is seldom delicate. It will please itself with very mean advantages: and envy feels not its own happiness, but when it may be compared with the misery of others. They were my enemies, because they grieved to think me rich; and my oppressors, because they delighted to find me weak."

"Proceed," said the prince: "I doubt not of the facts which you relate, but imagine that you impute them to mistaken motives."

"In this company," said Imlac, "I arrived at Agra, the capital of Indostan, the city in which the Great Mogul commonly resides. I applied myself to the language of the country, and in a few months was able to converse with the learned men; some of whom I found morose and reserved, and others easy and communicative; some were unwilling to teach another what they had with difficulty learned themselves; and some shewed that the end of their studies was to gain the dignity of instructing.

"To the tutor of the young princes I recommended myself so much, that I was presented to the emperor as a man of uncommon knowledge. The emperor asked me many questions concerning my country and my travels; and though I cannot now recollect anything that he uttered above the power of a common man, he dismissed me astonished at his wisdom, and enamoured of his goodness.

"My credit was now so high, that the merchants with whom I had travelled, applied to me for recommendations to the ladies of the court. I was surprised at their confidence of solicitation, and gently reproached them with their practices on the road. They heard me with cold indifference, and shewed no tokens of shame or sorrow.

"They then urged their request with the offer of a bribe; but what I would not do for kindness, I would not do for money; and refused them, not because they had injured me, but because I would not enable them to injure others; for I knew they would have made use of my credit to cheat those who should buy their wares.

"Having resided at Agra till there was no more to be learned, I travelled into Persia, where I saw many remains of ancient magnificence, and observed many new accommodations of life. The Persians are a nation eminently social, and their assemblies afforded me daily opportunities of remarking characters and manners, and tracing human nature through all its variations.

"From Persia I passed into Arabia, where I saw a nation at once pastoral and warlike; who live without any settled habitation; whose only wealth is their flocks and herds; and who have yet carried on through all ages, an hereditary war with all mankind, though they neither covet nor envy their possessions."

Chapter 10

IMLAC'S HISTORY CONTINUED. A DISSERTATION UPON POETRY

"Wherever I went, I found that poetry was considered as the highest learning, and regarded with a veneration somewhat approaching to that which man would pay to the Angelic Nature. And yet it fills me with wonder, that, in almost all countries, the most ancient poets are considered as the best: whether it be that every other kind of knowledge is an acquisition gradually attained, and poetry is a gift conferred at once; or that the first poetry of every nation surprised them as a novelty, and retained the credit by consent which it received by accident at first: or whether, as the province of poetry is to describe nature and passion, which are always the same, the first writers took possession of the most striking objects for description, and the most probable occurrences for fiction, and left nothing to those that followed them, but transcription of the same events, and new combinations of the same images. Whatever be the reason, it is commonly observed that the early writers are in possession of nature, and their followers of art: that the first excel in strength and invention, and the latter in elegance and refinement.

"I was desirous to add my name to this illustrious fraternity. I read all the poets of Persia and Arabia, and was able to repeat by memory the volumes that are suspended in the mosque of Mecca. But I soon found that no man was ever great by imitation. My desire of excellence impelled me to transfer my attention to nature and to life. Nature was to be my subject, and men to be my auditors. I could never describe what I had not seen. I could not hope to move those with delight or terror, whose interests and opinions I did not understand.

"Being now resolved to be a poet, I saw everything with a new purpose; my sphere of attention was suddenly magnified: no kind of knowledge was to be overlooked. I ranged mountains and deserts for images and resemblances, and pictured upon my mind every tree of the forest and flower of the valley. I observed with equal care the crags of the rock and the pinnacles of the palace. Sometimes I wandered along the mazes of the rivulet, and sometimes watched the changes of the summer clouds. To a poet nothing can be useless. Whatever is beautiful, and whatever is dreadful, must be familiar to his imagination: he must be conversant with all that is awfully vast or elegantly little. The plants of the garden, the animals of the wood, the minerals of the earth, and meteors of the sky, must all concur to store his mind with inexhaustible variety: for every idea is useful for the enforcement or decoration of moral or religious truth; and he who knows most will have most power of diversifying his scenes, and of gratifying his reader with remote allusions and unexpected instruction.

"All the appearances of nature I was therefore careful to study, and every country which I have surveyed has contributed something to my poetical powers."

"In so wide a survey," said the prince, "you must surely have left much unobserved. I have lived, till now, within the circuit of these mountains, and yet cannot walk abroad without the sight of something which I had never beheld before, or never heeded."

39. **idea**, image.

"The business of a poet," said Imlac, "is to examine not the individual but the species; to remark general properties and large appearances. He does not number the streaks of the tulip, or describe the different shades in the verdure of the forest. He is to exhibit in his portraits of nature such prominent and striking features, as recall the original to every mind; and must neglect the minuter discriminations, which one may have remarked, and another have neglected, for those characteristics which are alike obvious to vigilance and carelessness.

"But the knowledge of nature is only half the task of a poet; he must be acquainted likewise with all the modes of life. His character requires that he estimate the happiness and misery of every condition; observe the power of all the passions in all their combinations, and trace the changes of the human mind, as they are modified by various institutions and accidental influences of climate or custom, from the sprightliness of infancy to the despondence of decrepitude. He must divest himself of the prejudices of his age or country; he must consider right and wrong in their abstracted and invariable state; he must disregard present laws and opinions, and rise to general and transcendental truths, which will always be the same: he must therefore content himself with the slow progress of his name; contemn the applause of his own time, and commit his claims to the justice of posterity. He must write as the interpreter of nature, and the legislator of mankind, and consider himself as presiding over the thoughts and manners of future generations, as a being superior to time and place.

"His labour is not yet at an end; he must know many languages and many sciences; and, that his style may be worthy of his thoughts, must by incessant practice familiarize to himself every delicacy of speech and grace of harmony."

Chapter 11

IMLAC'S NARRATIVE CONTINUED. A HINT ON PILGRIMAGE

Imlac now felt the enthusiastic fit, and was proceeding to aggrandize his own profession, when the prince cried out, "Enough! thou hast convinced me, that no human being can ever be a poet. Proceed with thy narration."

"To be a poet," said Imlac, "is indeed very difficult." "So difficult," returned the prince, "that I will at present hear no more of his labours. Tell me whither you went when you had seen Persia."

"From Persia," said the poet, "I travelled through Syria, and for three years resided in Palestine, where I conversed with great numbers of the northern and western nations of Europe; the nations which are now in possession of all power and all knowledge, whose armies are irresistible, and whose fleets command the remotest parts of the globe. When I compared these men with the natives of our own kingdom, and those that surround us, they appeared almost another order of beings. In their countries it is difficult to wish for anything that may not be obtained: a thousand arts, of which we never heard, are continually labouring for their convenience and pleasure; and whatever their own climate has denied them is supplied by their commerce."

"By what means," said the prince, "are the Europeans thus powerful, or why, since they can so easily visit Asia and Africa for trade or conquest, cannot the Asiatics and Africans invade their coasts, plant colonies in their ports, and give laws to their natural princes? The same wind that carries them back would bring us thither."

"They are more powerful, Sir, than we," answered Imlac, "because they are wiser. Knowledge will always predominate over ignorance, as man governs the other animals. But why their knowledge is more than ours, I know not what reason can be given, but the unsearchable will of the Supreme Being."

"When," said the prince with a sigh, "shall I be able to visit Palestine, and mingle with this mighty confluence of nations? Till that happy moment shall arrive, let me fill up the time with such representations as thou canst give me. I am not ignorant of the motive that assembles such numbers in that place, and cannot but consider it as the centre of wisdom and piety, to which the best and wisest men of every land must be continually resorting."

"There are some nations," said Imlac, "that send few visitants to Palestine; for many numerous and learned sects in Europe concur to censure pilgrimage as superstitious, or deride it as ridiculous."

"You know," said the prince, "how little my life has made me acquainted with diversity of opinions. It will be too long to hear the arguments on both sides; you, that have considered them, tell me the result."

"Pilgrimage," said Imlac, "like many other acts of piety, may be reasonable or superstitious, according to the principles upon which it is performed. Long journeys in search of truth are not commanded. Truth, such as is necessary to the regulation of life, is always found where it is honestly sought. Change of place is no natural cause of the increase of piety, for it inevitably produces dissipation of mind. Yet, since men go every day to view the fields where great actions have been performed, and return with stronger impressions of the event, curiosity of the same kind may naturally dispose us to view that country whence our religion had its beginning; and I believe no man surveys those awful scenes without some confirmation of holy resolutions. That the Supreme Being may be more easily propitiated in one place than in another, is the dream of idle superstition; but that some places may operate upon our own minds in an uncommon manner, is an opinion which hourly experience will justify. He who supposes that his vices may be more successfully combated in Palestine, will, perhaps, find himself mistaken, yet he may go thither without folly: he who thinks they will be more freely pardoned, dishonours at once his reason and religion."

"These," said the prince, "are European distinctions. I will consider them another time. What have you found to be the effect of knowledge? Are those nations happier than we?"

"There is so much infelicity," said the poet, "in the world, that scarce any man has leisure from his own distresses to estimate the comparative happiness of others. Knowledge is certainly one of the means of pleasure, as is confessed by the natural desire which every mind feels of increasing its ideas. Ignorance is mere privation, by which nothing can be produced; it is a vacuity in which the soul sits motionless and torpid for want of attraction; and, without knowing why, we always rejoice when we learn, and grieve when we forget. I am therefore inclined to conclude, that if nothing counteracts the natural consequence of learning, we grow more happy as our minds take a wider range.

"In enumerating the particular comforts of life we shall find many advantages on the side of the Europeans. They cure wounds and diseases with which we languish and perish. We suffer inclemencies of weather which they can obviate. They have engines for the dispatch of many laborious works, which we must perform by manual industry. There is such communication between distant places, that one friend can hardly be said to be absent from another. Their policy removes all public inconveniencies: they have roads cut through their mountains, and bridges laid upon their rivers. And, if we descend to the privacies of life, their habitations are more commodious, and their possessions are more secure."

"They are surely happy," said the prince, "who have all these conveniencies, of which I envy none so much as the facility with which separated friends interchange their thoughts."

"The Europeans," answered Imlac, "are less unhappy than we, but they are not happy. Human life is everywhere a state in which much is to be endured, and little to be enjoyed."

Chapter 12

THE STORY OF IMLAC CONTINUED

"I am not yet willing," said the prince, "to suppose that happiness is so parsimoniously distributed to mortals; nor can believe but that, if I had the choice of life, I should be able to fill every day with pleasure. I would injure no man, and should provoke no resentment: I would relieve every distress, and should enjoy the benedictions of gratitude. I would choose my friends among the wise, and my wife among the virtuous; and therefore should be in no danger from treachery or unkindness. My children should, by my care, be learned and pious, and would repay to my age what their childhood had received. What would dare to molest him who might call on every side to thousands enriched by his bounty, or assisted by his power? And why should not life glide quietly away in the soft reciprocation of protection and reverence? All this may be done without the help of European refinements, which appear by their effects to be rather specious than useful. Let us leave them, and pursue our journey."

"From Palestine," said Imlac, "I passed through many regions of Asia; in the more civilized kingdoms as a trader, and among the barbarians of the mountains as a pilgrim. At last I began to long for my native country, that I might repose after my travels and fatigues, in the places where I had spent my earliest years, and gladden my old companions with the recital of my adventures. Often did I figure to myself those with whom I had sported away the gay hours of dawning life, sitting round me in its evening, wondering at my tales and listening to my counsels.

"When this thought had taken possession of my mind, I considered every moment as wasted which did not bring me nearer to Abissinia. I hastened into Egypt, and, notwithstanding my impatience, was detained ten months in the contemplation of its ancient magnificence, and in inquiries after the remains of its ancient learning. I found in Cairo a mixture of all nations; some brought thither by the love of knowledge, some by the hope of gain, and many by the desire of living after their own manner without observation, and of lying hid in the obscurity of multitudes: for in a city, populous as Cairo, it is possible to obtain at the same time the gratifications of society, and the secrecy of solitude.

"From Cairo I travelled to Suez, and embarked on the Red Sea, passing along the coast till I arrived at the port from which I had departed twenty years before. Here I joined myself to a caravan, and re-entered my native country.

"I now expected the caresses of my kinsmen, and the congratulations of my friends, and was not without hope that my father, whatever value he had set upon riches, would own with gladness and pride a son who was able to add to the felicity and honour of the nation. But I was soon convinced that my thoughts were vain. My father had been dead fourteen years, having divided his wealth among my brothers, who were removed to some other provinces. Of my companions the greater part was in the grave: of the rest, some could with difficulty remember me, and some considered me as one corrupted by foreign manners.

"A man used to vicissitudes is not easily dejected. I forgot, after a time, my disappointment, and endeavoured to recommend myself to the nobles of the kingdom; they admitted me to their tables, heard my story, and dismissed me. I opened a school, and was prohibited to teach. I then resolved to sit down in the quiet of domestic life, and addressed a lady that was fond of my conversation, but rejected my suit because my father was a merchant.

"Wearied at last with solicitation and repulses, I resolved to hide myself for ever from the world, and depend no longer on the opinion or caprice of others. I waited for the time when the gate of the *happy valley* should open, that I might bid farewell to hope and fear. The day came; my performance was distinguished with favour, and I resigned myself with joy to perpetual confinement."

"Hast thou here found happiness at last?" said Rasselas. "Tell me without reserve; art thou content with thy condition, or dost thou wish to be again wandering and inquiring? All the inhabitants of this valley celebrate their lot, and at the annual visit of the emperor, invite others to partake of their felicity."

"Great prince," said Imlac, "I shall speak the truth. I know not one of all your attendants who does not lament the hour when he entered this retreat. I am less unhappy than the rest, because I have a mind replete with images, which I can vary and combine at pleasure. I can amuse my solitude by the renovation of the knowledge which begins to fade from my memory, and by recollection of the accidents of my past life. Yet all this ends in the sorrowful consideration that my acquirements are now useless, and that none of my pleasures can be again enjoyed. The rest, whose minds have no impression but of the present moment, are either corroded by malignant passions, or sit stupid in the gloom of perpetual vacancy."

"What passions can infest those," said the prince, "who have no rivals? We are in a place where impotence precludes malice, and where all envy is repressed by community of enjoyments."

"There may be community," said Imlac, "of material possessions, but there can never be community of love or of esteem. It must happen that one will please more than another; he that knows himself despised will always be envious; and still more envious and malevolent, if he is condemned to live in the presence of those who despise him. The invitations, by which they allure others to a state which they feel to be wretched, proceed from the natural malignity of hopeless misery. They are weary of themselves, and of each other, and expect to find relief in new companions. They envy the liberty which their folly has forfeited, and would gladly see all mankind imprisoned like themselves.

"From this crime, however, I am wholly free. No man can say that he is wretched by my persuasion. I look with pity on the crowds who are annually soliciting admission to captivity, and wish that it were lawful for me to warn them of their danger."

"My dear Imlac," said the prince, "I will open to thee my whole heart. I have long meditated an escape from the happy valley. I have examined the mountains on every side, but find myself insuperably barred: teach me the way to break my prison; thou shalt be the companion of my flight, the guide of my rambles, the partner of my fortune, and my sole director in the *choice of life*."

"Sir," answered the poet, "your escape will be difficult, and perhaps you may soon repent your curiosity. The world, which you figure to yourself smooth and quiet as the lake in the valley, you will find a sea foaming with tempests, and boiling with whirlpools: you will be sometimes overwhelmed by the waves of violence, and sometimes dashed against the rocks of treachery. Amidst wrongs and frauds, competitions and anxieties, you will wish a thousand times for these seats of quiet, and willingly quit hope to be free from fear."

"Do not seek to deter me from my purpose," said the prince: "I am impatient to see what thou hast seen; and since thou art thyself weary of the valley, it is evident, that thy former state was better than this. Whatever be the consequence of my experiment, I am resolved to judge with mine own eyes of the various conditions of men, and then to make deliberately my *choice of life*."

"I am afraid," said Imlac, "you are hindered by stronger restraints than my persuasions; yet, if your determination is fixed, I do not counsel you to despair. Few things are impossible to diligence and skill."

Chapter 13

RASSELAS DISCOVERS THE MEANS OF ESCAPE

The prince now dismissed his favourite to rest, but the narrative of wonders and novelties filled his mind with perturbation. He revolved all that he had heard, and prepared innumerable questions for the morning.

Much of his uneasiness was now removed. He had a friend to whom he could impart his thoughts, and whose experience could assist him in his designs. His heart was no longer condemned to swell with silent vexation. He thought that even the *happy valley* might be endured with such a companion, and that if they could range the world together, he should have nothing further to desire.

In a few days the water was discharged, and the ground dried. The prince and Imlac then walked out together to converse without the notice of the rest. The prince, whose thoughts were always on the wing, as he passed by the gate, said, with a countenance of sorrow, "Why art thou so strong, and why is man so weak?"

"Man is not weak," answered his companion; "knowledge is more than equivalent to force. The master of mechanics laughs at strength. I can burst the gate, but cannot do it secretly. Some other expedient must be tried."

As they were walking on the side of the mountain, they observed that the conies, which the rain had driven from their burrows, had taken shelter among the bushes, and formed holes behind them, tending upwards in an oblique line. "It has been the opinion of antiquity," said Imlac, "that human reason borrowed many arts from the instinct of animals; let us, therefore, not think ourselves degraded by learning from the cony. We may escape by piercing the mountain in the same direction. We will begin where the summit hangs over the middle part, and labour upward till we shall issue up beyond the prominence."

The eyes of the prince, when he heard this proposal, sparkled with joy. The execution was easy, and the success certain.

No time was now lost. They hastened early in the morning to choose a place proper for their mine. They clambered with great fatigue among crags and brambles, and returned without having discovered any part that favoured their design. The second and the third day were spent in the same manner and with the same frustration. But, on the fourth, they found a small cavern concealed by a thicket, where they resolved to make their experiment.

Imlac procured instruments proper to hew stone and remove earth, and they fell to their work on the next day with more eagerness than vigour. They were presently exhausted by their efforts, and sat down to pant upon the grass. The prince, for a moment, appeared to be discouraged. "Sir," said his companion, "practice will enable us to continue our labour for a longer time; mark, however, how far we have advanced, and you will find that our toil will some time have an end. Great works are performed, not by strength, but perseverance: yonder palace was raised by single stones, yet you see its height and spaciousness. He that shall walk with vigour three hours a day, will pass in seven years a space equal to the circumference of the globe."

They returned to their work day after day, and in a short time found a fissure in the rock, which enabled them to pass far with very little obstruction. This Rasselas considered as a good omen. "Do not disturb your mind," said Imlac, "with other hopes or fears than reason may suggest; if you are pleased with prognostics of good, you will be terrified likewise with tokens of evil, and your whole life will be a prey to superstition. Whatever facilitates our work is more than an omen; it is a cause of success. This is one of those pleasing surprises which often happen to active resolution. Many things difficult to design prove easy to performance."

Chapter 14

RASSELAS AND IMLAC RECEIVE AN UNEXPECTED VISIT

They had now wrought their way to the middle, and solaced their toil with the approach of liberty, when the prince, coming down to refresh himself with air, found his sister Nekayah standing before the mouth of the cavity. He started and stood confused, afraid to tell his design, and yet hopeless to conceal it. A few moments determined him to repose on her fidelity, and secure her secrecy by a declaration without reserve.

"Do not imagine," said the princess, "that I came hither as a spy: I had observed from my window, that you and Imlac directed your walk every day towards the same point, but I did not suppose you had any better reason for the preference than a cooler shade, or more fragrant bank; nor followed you with any other design than to partake of your conversation. Since then not suspicion but fondness has detected you, let me not lose the advantage of my discovery. I am equally weary of confinement with yourself, and not less desirous of knowing what is done or suffered in the world. Permit me to fly with you from this tasteless tranquillity, which will yet grow more loathsome when you have left me. You may deny me to accompany you, but cannot hinder me from following."

The prince, who loved Nekayah above his other sisters, had no inclination to refuse her request, and grieved that he had lost an opportunity of shewing his confidence by a voluntary communication. It was therefore agreed that she should leave the valley with them, and that, in the mean time, she should watch, lest any other straggler should, by chance or curiosity, follow them to the mountain.

At length their labour was at an end; they saw light beyond the prominence, and, issuing to the top of the mountain, beheld the Nile, yet a narrow current, wandering beneath them.

The prince looked round with rapture, anticipated all the pleasures of travel, and in thought was already transported beyond his father's dominions. Imlac, though very joyful at his escape, had less expectation of pleasure in the world, which he had before tried, and of which he had been weary.

Rasselas was so much delighted with a wider horizon, that he could not soon be persuaded to return into the valley. He informed his sister that the way was open, and that nothing now remained but to prepare for their departure.

Chapter 15

THE PRINCE AND PRINCESS LEAVE THE VALLEY, AND SEE MANY WONDERS

The prince and princess had jewels sufficient to make them rich whenever they came into a place of commerce, which, by Imlac's direction, they hid in their clothes, and on the night of the next full moon, all left the valley. The princess was followed only by a single favourite, who did not know whither she was going.

They clambered through the cavity, and began to go down on the other side. The princess and her maid turned their eyes towards every part, and, seeing nothing to bound their prospect, considered themselves as in danger of being lost in a dreary vacuity. They stopped and trembled. "I am almost afraid," said the princess, "to begin a journey of which I cannot perceive an end, and to venture into this immense plain, where I may be approached on every side by men whom I never saw." The prince felt nearly the same emotions, though he thought it more manly to conceal them.

Imlac smiled at their terrors, and encouraged them to proceed; but the princess continued irresolute, till she had been imperceptibly drawn forward too far to return.

In the morning they found some shepherds in the field, who set milk and fruits before them. The princess wondered that she did not see a palace ready for her reception, and a table spread with delicacies; but, being faint and hungry, she drank the milk and eat the fruits, and thought them of a higher flavour than the products of the valley.

They travelled forward by easy journeys, being all unaccustomed to toil or difficulty, and knowing that, though they might be missed, they could not be pursued. In a few days they came into a more populous region, where Imlac was diverted with the admiration which his companions expressed at the diversity of manners, stations, and employments.

Their dress was such as might not bring upon them the suspicion of having any thing to conceal, yet the prince, wherever he came, expected to be obeyed, and the princess was frighted, because those that came into her presence did not prostrate themselves before her. Imlac was forced to observe them with great vigilance, lest they should betray their rank by their unusual behaviour, and detained them several weeks in the first village, to accustom them to the sight of common mortals.

By degrees the royal wanderers were taught to understand that they had for a time laid aside their dignity, and were to expect only such regard as liberality and courtesy could procure. And Imlac having, by many admonitions, prepared them to endure the tumults of a port, and the ruggedness of the commercial race, brought them down to the sea-coast.

The prince and his sister, to whom every thing was new, were gratified equally at all places, and therefore remained for some months at the port without any inclination to pass further. Imlac was content with their stay, because he did not think it safe to expose them, unpractised in the world, to the hazards of a foreign country.

At last he began to fear lest they should be discovered, and proposed to fix a day for their departure. They had no pretensions to judge for themselves, and referred the whole scheme to his direction. He therefore took passage in a ship to Suez; and, when the time came, with great difficulty prevailed on the princess to enter the vessel. They had a quick and prosperous voyage, and from Suez travelled by land to Cairo.

Chapter 16

THEY ENTER CAIRO, AND FIND EVERY MAN HAPPY

As they approached the city, which filled the strangers with astonishment, "This," said Imlac to the prince, "is the place where travellers and merchants assemble from all the corners of the earth. You will here find men of every character, and every occupation. Commerce is here honourable: I will act as a merchant, and you shall live as strangers, who have no other end of travel than curiosity; it will soon be observed that we are rich; our reputation will procure us access to all whom we shall desire to know; you will see all the conditions of humanity, and enable yourself at leisure to make your *choice of life*."

They now entered the town, stunned by the noise, and offended by the crowds. Instruction had not yet so prevailed over habit, but that they wondered to see themselves pass undistinguished along the street, and met by the lowest of the people without reverence or notice. The princess could not at first bear the thought of being levelled with the vulgar, and for some days continued in her chamber, where she was served by her favourite Pekuah as in the palace of the valley.

Imlac, who understood traffic, sold part of the jewels the next day, and hired a house, which he adorned with such magnificence, that he was immediately considered as a merchant of great wealth. His politeness attracted many acquaintance, and his generosity made him courted by many dependants. His table was crowded by men of every nation, who all admired his knowledge, and solicited his favour. His companions, not being able to mix in the conversation, could make no discovery of their ignorance or surprise, and were gradually initiated in the world as they gained knowledge of the language.

The prince had, by frequent lectures, been taught the use and nature of money; but the ladies could not, for a long time, comprehend what the merchants did with small pieces of gold and silver, or why things of so little use should be received as equivalent to the necessaries of life.

They studied the language two years, while Imlac was preparing to set before them the various ranks and conditions of mankind. He grew acquainted with all who had any thing uncommon in their fortune or conduct. He frequented the voluptuous and the frugal, the idle and the busy, the merchants and the men of learning.

The prince being now able to converse with fluency, and having learned the caution necessary to be observed in his intercourse with strangers, began to accompany Imlac to places of resort, and to enter into all assemblies, that he might make his *choice of life*.

For some time he thought choice needless, because all appeared to him equally happy. Wherever he went he met gaiety and kindness, and heard the song of joy or the laugh of carelessness. He began to believe that the world overflowed with universal plenty, and that nothing was withheld either from want or merit; that every hand showered liberality, and every heart melted with benevolence; "and who then," says he, "will be suffered to be wretched?"

Imlac permitted the pleasing delusion, and was unwilling to crush the hope of inexperience, till one day, having sat awhile silent, "I know not," said the prince, "what can be the reason that I am more unhappy than any of our friends. I see them perpetually and unalterably cheerful, but feel my own mind restless and uneasy. I am unsatisfied with those pleasures which I seem most to court; I live in the crowds of jollity, not so much to enjoy company as to shun myself, and am only loud and merry to conceal my sadness."

1. **traffic,** buying and selling.

"Every man," said Imlac, "may, by examining his own mind, guess what passes in the minds of others: when you feel that your own gaiety is counterfeit, it may justly lead you to suspect that of your companions not to be sincere. Envy is commonly reciprocal. We are long before we are convinced that happiness is never to be found, and each believes it possessed by others, to keep alive the hope of obtaining it for himself. In the assembly, where you passed the last night, there appeared such sprightliness of air, and volatility of fancy, as might have suited beings of an higher order, formed to inhabit serener regions, inaccessible to care or sorrow: yet, believe me, prince, there was not one who did not dread the moment when solitude should deliver him to the tyranny of reflection."

"This," said the prince, "may be true of others, since it is true of me; yet, whatever be the general infelicity of man, one condition is more happy than another, and wisdom surely directs us to take the least evil in the *choice of life*."

"The causes of good and evil," answered Imlac, "are so various and uncertain, so often entangled with each other, so diversified by various relations, and so much subject to accidents which cannot be foreseen, that he who would fix his condition upon incontestable reasons of preference, must live and die inquiring and deliberating."

"But surely," said Rasselas, "the wise men, to whom we listen with reverence and wonder, chose that mode of life for themselves which they thought most likely to make them happy."

"Very few," said the poet, "live by choice. Every man is placed in his present condition by causes which acted without his foresight, and with which he did not always willingly co-operate; and therefore you will rarely meet one who does not think the lot of his neighbour better than his own."

"I am pleased to think," said the prince, "that my birth has given me at least one advantage over others, by enabling me to determime for myself. I have here the world before me. I will review it at leisure: surely happiness is somewhere to be found."

Chapter 17

THE PRINCE ASSOCIATES WITH YOUNG MEN OF SPIRIT AND GAIETY

Rasselas rose next day, and resolved to begin his experiments upon life. "Youth," cried he, "is the time of gladness: I will join myself to the young men, whose only business is to gratify their desires, and whose time is all spent in a succession of enjoyments."

To such societies he was readily admitted, but a few days brought him back weary and disgusted. Their mirth was without images; their laughter without motive; their pleasures were gross and sensual, in which the mind had no part; their conduct was at once wild and mean; they laughed at order and at law, but the frown of power dejected, and the eye of wisdom abashed them.

The prince soon concluded, that he should never be happy in a course of life of which he was ashamed. He thought it unsuitable to a reasonable being to act without a plan, and to be sad or cheerful only by chance. "Happiness," said he, "must be something solid and permanent, without fear and without uncertainty."

But his young companions had gained so much of his regard by their frankness and courtesy, that he could not leave them without warning and remonstrance. "My friends," said he, "I have seriously considered our manners and our prospects, and find that we have mistaken our own interest. The first years of man must make provision for the last. He that never thinks never can be wise. Perpetual levity must end in ignorance; and intemperance, though it may fire the spirits for an hour, will make life short or miserable. Let us consider that youth is of no long duration, and that in maturer age, when the enchantments of fancy shall cease, and phantoms of delight dance no more about us, we shall have no comforts but the esteem of wise men, and the means of doing good. Let us, therefore, stop, while to stop is in our power: let us live as men who are some time to grow old, and to whom it will be the most dreadful of all evils not to count their past years but by follies, and to be reminded of their former luxuriance of health only by the maladies which riot has produced."

They stared a while in silence one upon another, and at last drove him away by a general chorus of continued laughter.

The consciousness that his sentiments were just, and his intentions kind, was scarcely sufficient to support him against the horror of derision. But he recovered his tranquillity and pursued his search.

Chapter 18

THE PRINCE FINDS A WISE AND HAPPY MAN

As he was one day walking in the street, he saw a spacious building which all were, by the open doors, invited to enter: he followed the stream of people, and found it a hall or school of declamation, in which professors read lectures to their auditory. He fixed his eye upon a sage raised above the rest, who discoursed with great energy on the government of the passions. His look was venerable, his action graceful, his pronunciation clear, and his diction elegant. He shewed, with great strength of sentiment, and variety of illustration, that human nature is degraded and debased, when the lower faculties predominate over the higher; that when fancy, the parent of passion, usurps the dominion of the mind, nothing ensues but the natural effect of unlawful government, perturbation and confusion; that she betrays the fortresses of the intellect to rebels, and excites her children to sedition against reason their lawful sovereign. He compared reason to the sun, of which the light is constant, uniform and lasting; and fancy to a meteor, of bright but transitory lustre, irregular in its motion, and delusive in its direction.

He then communicated the various precepts given from time to time for the conquest of passion, and displayed the happiness of those who had obtained the important victory, after which man is no longer the slave of fear, nor the fool of hope; is no more emaciated by envy, inflamed by anger, emasculated by tenderness, or depressed by grief; but walks on calmly through the tumults or the privacies of life, as the sun pursues alike his course through the calm or the stormy sky.

He enumerated many examples of heroes immovable by pain or pleasure, who looked with indifference on those modes or accidents to which the vulgar give the names of good and evil. He exhorted his hearers to lay aside their prejudices, and arm themselves against the shafts of malice or misfortune, by invulnerable patience, concluding, that this state only was happiness, and that this happiness was in every one's power.

Rasselas listened to him with the veneration due to the instructions of a superior being, and, waiting for him at the door, humbly implored the liberty of visiting so great a master of true wisdom. The lecturer hesitated a moment, when Rasselas put a purse of gold into his hand, which he received with a mixture of joy and wonder.

"I have found," said the prince at his return to Imlac, "a man who can teach all that is necessary to be known, who, from the unshaken throne of rational fortitude, looks down on the scenes of life changing beneath him. He speaks, and attention watches his lips. He reasons, and conviction closes his periods. This man shall be my future guide: I will learn his doctrines, and imitate his life."

"Be not too hasty," said Imlac, "to trust, or to admire, the teachers of morality: they discourse like angels, but they live like men."

Rasselas, who could not conceive how any man could reason so forcibly without feeling the cogency of his own arguments, paid his visit in a few days, and was denied admission. He had now learned the power of money, and made his way by a piece of gold to the inner apartment, where he found the philosopher in a room half darkened, with his eyes misty and his face pale. "Sir," said he, "you are come at a time when all human friendship is useless; what I suffer cannot be remedied, what I have lost cannot be supplied. My daughter, my only daughter, from whose tenderness I expected all the comforts of my age, died last night of a fever. My views, my purposes, my hopes are at an end; I am now a lonely being disunited from society."

"Sir," said the prince, "mortality is an event by which a wise man can never be surprised: we know that death is always near, and it should therefore always be expected." "Young man," answered the philosopher, "you speak like one that has never felt the pangs of separation." "Have you then forgot the precepts," said Rasselas, "which you so powerfully enforced? Has wisdom no strength to arm the heart against calamity? Consider, that external things are naturally variable, but truth and reason are always the same." "What comfort," said the mourner, "can truth and reason afford me? Of what effect are they now, but to tell me, that my daughter will not be restored?"

The prince, whose humanity would not suffer him to insult misery with reproof, went away convinced of the emptiness of rhetorical sound, and the inefficacy of polished periods and studied sentences.

Chapter 19

A GLIMPSE OF PASTORAL LIFE

He was still eager upon the same inquiry; and having heard of a hermit that lived near the lowest cataract of the Nile, and filled the whole country with the fame of his sanctity, resolved to visit his retreat, and inquire whether that felicity, which public life could not afford, was to be found in solitude; and whether a man, whose age and virtue made him venerable, could teach any peculiar art of shunning evils, or enduring them?

Imlac and the princess agreed to accompany

him, and, after the necessary preparations, they began their journey. Their way lay through fields, where shepherds tended their flocks, and the lambs were playing upon the pasture. "This," said the poet, "is the life which has been often celebrated for its innocence and quiet; let us pass the heat of the day among the shepherds' tents, and know whether all our searches are not to terminate in pastoral simplicity."

The proposal pleased them, and they induced the shepherds, by small presents and familiar questions, to tell their opinion of their own state. They were so rude and ignorant, so little able to compare the good with the evil of the occupation, and so indistinct in their narratives and descriptions, that very little could be learned from them. But it was evident that their hearts were cankered with discontent; that they considered themselves as condemned to labour for the luxury of the rich, and looked up with stupid malevolence toward those that were placed above them.

The princess pronounced with vehemence, that she would never suffer these envious savages to be her companions, and that she should not soon be desirous of seeing any more specimens of rustic happiness; but could not believe that all the accounts of primeval pleasures were fabulous; and was yet in doubt whether life had any thing that could be justly preferred to the placid gratifications of fields and woods. She hoped that the time would come, when, with a few virtuous and elegant companions, she could gather flowers planted by her own hand, fondle the lambs of her own ewe, and listen without care, among brooks and breezes, to one of her maidens reading in the shade.

Chapter 20

THE DANGER OF PROSPERITY

On the next day they continued their journey, till the heat compelled them to look round for shelter. At a small distance they saw a thick wood, which they no sooner entered than they perceived that they were approaching the habitations of men. The shrubs were diligently cut away to open walks where the shades were darkest; the boughs of opposite trees were artificially interwoven; seats of flowery turf were raised in vacant spaces, and a rivulet, that wantoned along the side of a winding path, had its banks sometimes opened into small basons, and its stream sometimes obstructed by little mounds of stone, heaped together to increase its murmurs.

They passed slowly through the wood, delighted with such unexpected accommodations, and entertained each other with conjecturing what, or who, he could be, that, in those rude and unfrequented regions, had leisure and art for such harmless luxury.

As they advanced they heard the sound of music, and saw youths and virgins dancing in the grove; and, going still further, beheld a stately palace built upon a hill surrounded with woods. The laws of eastern hospitality allowed them to enter, and the master welcomed them like a man liberal and wealthy.

He was skilful enough in appearances soon to discern that they were no common guests, and spread his table with magnificence. The eloquence of Imlac caught his attention, and the lofty courtesy of the princess excited his respect. When they offered to depart, he entreated their stay, and was the next day still more unwilling to dismiss them than before. They were easily persuaded to stop, and civility grew up in time to freedom and confidence.

The prince now saw all the domestics cheerful, and all the face of nature smiling round the place, and could not forbear to hope that he should find here what he was seeking; but when he was congratulating the master upon his possessions, he answered with a sigh, "My condition has indeed the appearance of happiness, but appearances are delusive. My prosperity puts my life in danger; the Bassa of Egypt is my enemy, incensed only by my wealth and popularity. I have been hitherto protected against him by the princes of the country; but, as the favour of the great is uncertain, I know not how soon my defenders may be persuaded to share the plunder with the Bassa. I have sent my treasures into a distant country, and, upon the first alarm, am prepared to follow them. Then will my enemies riot in my mansion, and enjoy the gardens which I have planted."

They all joined in lamenting his danger, and deprecating his exile; and the princess was so much disturbed with the tumult of grief and indignation, that she retired to her apartment. They continued with their kind inviter a few days longer, and then went forward to find the hermit.

Chapter 21

THE HAPPINESS OF SOLITUDE. THE HERMIT'S HISTORY

They came on the third day, by the direction of the peasants, to the hermit's cell. It was a cavern in the side of a mountain, overshadowed with palm-trees; at such a distance from the cataract, that nothing more was heard than a gentle uniform murmur, such as composed the mind to pensive meditation, especially when it was assisted by the wind whistling among the branches. The first rude essay[7] of nature had been so much improved by human labour, that the cave contained several apartments appropriated to different uses, and often afforded lodging to travellers, whom darkness or tempests happened to overtake.

The hermit sat on a bench at the door, to enjoy the coolness of the evening. On one side lay a book with pens and papers, on the other mechanical instruments of various kinds. As they approached him unregarded, the princess observed that he had not the countenance of a man that had found, or could teach, the way to happiness.

They saluted him with great respect, which he repaid like a man not unaccustomed to the forms of courts. "My children," said he, "if you have lost your way, you shall be willingly supplied with such conveniences for the night as this cavern will afford. I have all that nature requires, and you will not expect delicacies in a hermit's cell."

They thanked him, and, entering, were pleased with the neatness and regularity of the place. The hermit set flesh and wine before them, though he fed only upon fruits and water. His discourse was cheerful without levity, and pious without enthusiasm. He soon gained the esteem of his guests, and the princess repented of her hasty censure.

At last Imlac began thus: "I do not now wonder that your reputation is so far extended. We have heard at Cairo of your wisdom, and came hither to implore your direction for this young man and maiden in the *choice of life*."

"To him that lives well," answered the hermit, "every form of life is good; nor can I give any other rule for choice, than to remove from all apparent evil."

"He will remove most certainly from evil," said the prince, "who shall devote himself to that solitude which you have recommended by your example."

"I have indeed lived fifteen years in solitude," said the hermit, "but have no desire that my example should gain any imitators. In my youth I professed arms, and was raised by degrees to the highest military rank. I have traversed wide countries at the head of my troops, and seen many battles and sieges. At last, being disgusted by the preferments of a younger officer, and feeling that my vigour was beginning to decay, I resolved to close my life in peace, having found the world full of snares, discord, and misery. I had once escaped from the pursuit of the enemy by the shelter of this cavern, and therefore chose it for my final residence. I employed artificers to form it into chambers, and stored it with all that I was likely to want.

"For some time after my retreat, I rejoiced like a tempest-beaten sailor at his entrance into the harbour, being delighted with the sudden change of the noise and hurry of war to stillness and repose. When the pleasure of novelty went away, I employed my hours in examining the plants which grow in the valley, and the minerals which I collected from the rocks. But that inquiry is now grown tasteless and irksome. I have been for some time unsettled and distracted: my mind is disturbed with a thousand perplexities of doubt, and vanities of imagination, which hourly prevail upon me, because I have no opportunities of relaxation or diversion. I am sometimes ashamed to think that I could not secure myself from vice, but by retiring from the exercise of virtue, and begin to suspect that I was rather impelled by resentment, than led by devotion, into solitude. My fancy riots in scenes of folly, and I lament that I have lost so much, and have gained so little. In solitude, if I escape the example of bad men, I want likewise the counsel and conversation of the good. I have been long comparing the evils with the advantages of society, and resolved to return into the world to-morrow. The life of a solitary man will be certainly miserable, but not certainly devout."

They heard his resolution with surprise, but after a short pause, offered to conduct him to Cairo. He dug up a considerable treasure which he had hid among the rocks, and accompanied them to the city, on which, as he approached it, he gazed with rapture.

Chapter 22

THE HAPPINESS OF A LIFE LED ACCORDING TO NATURE

Rasselas went often to an assembly of learned men, who met at stated times to unbend their minds and compare their opinions. Their manners were somewhat coarse, but their conversation was instructive, and their disputations acute, though sometimes too violent, and often continued till neither controvertist remembered upon what question they began. Some faults were almost

---

7. essay, effort, trial.

general among them: every one was desirous to dictate to the rest, and every one was pleased to hear the genius or knowledge of another depreciated.

In this assembly Rasselas was relating his interview with the hermit, and the wonder with which he heard him censure a course of life which he had so deliberately chosen, and so laudably followed. The sentiments of the hearers were various. Some were of opinion, that the folly of his choice had been justly punished by condemnation to perpetual perseverance. One of the youngest among them, with great vehemence, pronounced him an hypocrite. Some talked of the right of society to the labour of individuals, and considered retirement as a desertion of duty. Others readily allowed, that there was a time when the claims of the public were satisfied, and when a man might properly sequester himself, to review his life, and purify his heart.

One, who appeared more affected with the narrative than the rest, thought it likely, that the hermit would, in a few years, go back to his retreat, and, perhaps, if shame did not restrain, or death intercept him, return once more from his retreat into the world: "For the hope of happiness," said he, "is so strongly impressed, that the longest experience is not able to efface it. Of the present state, whatever it be, we feel, and are forced to confess, the misery; yet, when the same state is again at a distance, imagination paints it as desirable. But the time will surely come, when desire will be no longer our torment, and no man shall be wretched but by his own fault."

"This," said a philosopher who had heard him with tokens of great impatience, "is the present condition of a wise man. The time is already come, when none are wretched but by their own fault. Nothing is more idle, than to inquire after happiness, which nature has kindly placed within our reach. The way to be happy is to live according to nature, in obedience to that universal and unalterable law with which every heart is originally impressed; which is not written on it by precept, but engraven by destiny, not instilled by education, but infused at our nativity. He that lives according to nature will suffer nothing from the delusions of hope, or importunities of desire: he will receive and reject with equability of temper; and act or suffer as the reason of things shall alternately prescribe. Other men may amuse themselves with subtle definitions, or intricate ratiocination. Let them learn to be wise by easier means: let them observe the hind of the forest, and the linnet of the grove: let them consider the life of animals, whose motions are regulated by instinct; they obey their guide and are happy. Let us therefore, at length, cease to dispute, and learn to live; throw away the incumbrance of precepts, which they who utter them with so much pride and pomp do not understand, and carry with us this simple and intelligible maxim, That deviation from nature is deviation from happiness."

When he had spoken, he looked round him with a placid air, and enjoyed the consciousness of his own beneficence. "Sir," said the prince with great modesty, "as I, like all the rest of mankind, am desirous of felicity, my closest attention has been fixed upon your discourse: I doubt not the truth of a position which a man so learned has so confidently advanced. Let me only know what it is to live according to nature."

"When I find young men so humble and so docile," said the philosopher, "I can deny them no information which my studies have enabled me to afford. To live according to nature, is to act always with due regard to the fitness arising from the relations and qualities of causes and effects; to concur with the great and unchangeable scheme of universal felicity; to co-operate with the general disposition and tendency of the present system of things."

The prince soon found that this was one of the sages whom he should understand less as he heard him longer. He therefore bowed and was silent, and the philosopher, supposing him satisfied, and the rest vanquished, rose up and departed with the air of a man that had co-operated with the present system.

Chapter 23

THE PRINCE AND HIS SISTER DIVIDE BETWEEN THEM THE WORK OF OBSERVATION

Rasselas returned home full of reflections, doubtful how to direct his future steps. Of the way to happiness he found the learned and simple equally ignorant; but, as he was yet young, he flattered himself that he had time remaining for more experiments, and further inquires. He communicated to Imlac his observations and his doubts, but was answered by him with new doubts, and remarks that gave him no comfort. He therefore discoursed more frequently and freely with his sister, who had yet the same hope with himself, and always assisted him to give some reason why, though he had been hitherto frustrated, he might succeed at last.

"We have hitherto," said she, "known but little of the world; we have never yet been either great or mean. In our own country, though we had royalty, we had no power, and in this we have not yet seen the private recesses of domestic peace. Imlac favours not our search, lest we should in time find him mistaken. We will divide the task between us: you shall try what is to be found in the splendour of courts, and I will range the shades of humbler life. Perhaps command and authority may be the supreme blessings, as they afford most opportunities of doing good: or, perhaps, what this world can give may be found in the modest habitations of middle fortune; too low for great designs, and too high for penury and distress."

Chapter 24

THE PRINCE EXAMINES THE HAPPINESS OF HIGH STATIONS

Rasselas applauded the design, and appeared next day with a splendid retinue at the court of the Bassa. He was soon distinguished for his magnificence, and admitted, as a prince whose curiosity had brought him from distant countries, to an intimacy with the great officers, and frequent conversation with the Bassa himself.

He was at first inclined to believe, that the man must be pleased with his own condition, whom all approached with reverence, and heard with obedience, and who had the power to extend his edicts to a whole kingdom. "There can be no pleasure," said he, "equal to that of feeling at once the joy of thousands all made happy by wise administration. Yet, since, by the law of subordination, this sublime delight can be in one nation but the lot of one, it is surely reasonable to think, that there is some satisfaction more popular and accessible, and that millions can hardly be subjected to the will of a single man, only to fill his particular breast with incommunicable content."

These thoughts were often in his mind, and he found no solution of the difficulty. But as presents and civilities gained him more familiarity, he found that almost every man who stood high in employment hated all the rest, and was hated by them, and that their lives were a continual succession of plots and detections, stratagems and escapes, faction and treachery. Many of those who surrounded the Bassa, were sent only to watch and report his conduct; every tongue was muttering censure, and every eye was searching for a fault.

At last the letters of revocation arrived, the Bassa was carried in chains to Constantinople, and his name was mentioned no more.

"What are we now to think of the prerogatives of power?" said Rasselas to his sister. "Is it without any efficacy to good? Or is the subordinate degree only dangerous, and the supreme safe and glorious? Is the Sultan the only happy man in his dominions? Or, is the Sultan himself subject to the torments of suspicion, and the dread of enemies?"

In a short time the second Bassa was deposed. The Sultan that had advanced him was murdered by the Janissaries, and his successor had other views and different favourites.

Chapter 25

THE PRINCESS PURSUES HER INQUIRY WITH MORE DILIGENCE THAN SUCCESS

The princess, in the meantime, insinuated herself into many families; for there are few doors through which liberality, joined with good humour, cannot find its way. The daughters of many houses were airy and cheerful, but Nekayah had been too long accustomed to the conversation of Imlac and her brother to be much pleased with childish levity, and prattle which had no meaning. She found their thoughts narrow, their wishes low, and their merriment often artificial. Their pleasures, poor as they were, could not be preserved pure, but were embittered by petty competitions and worthless emulation. They were always jealous of the beauty of each other; of a quality to which solicitude can add nothing, and from which detraction can take nothing away. Many were in love with triflers like themselves, and many fancied that they were in love when in truth they were only idle. Their affection was not fixed on sense or virtue, and therefore seldom ended but in vexation. Their grief, however, like their joy, was transient; every thing floated in their mind unconnected with the past or future, so that one desire easily gave way to another, as a second stone cast into the water effaces and confounds the circles of the first.

With these girls she played as with inoffensive animals, and found them proud of her countenance, and weary of her company.

But her purpose was to examine more deeply, and her affability easily persuaded the hearts that were swelling with sorrow to discharge their secrets in her ear: and those whom hope flattered, or prosperity delighted, often courted her to partake their pleasures.

The princess and her brother commonly met in the evening in a private summer-house on the bank of the Nile, and related to each other the occurrences of the day. As they were sitting together, the princess cast her eyes upon the river that flowed before her. "Answer," said she, "great Father of Waters, thou that rollest thy floods through eighty nations, to the invocations of the daughter of thy native king. Tell me if thou waterest, through all thy course, a single habitation from which thou dost not hear the murmurs of complaint?"

"You are then," said Rasselas, "not more successful in private houses than I have been in courts." "I have, since the last partition of our provinces," said the princess, "enabled myself to enter familiarly into many families, where there was the fairest shew of prosperity and peace, and know not one house that is not haunted by some fury that destroys its quiet.

"I did not seek ease among the poor, because I concluded that there it could not be found. But I saw many poor, whom I had supposed to live in affluence. Poverty has, in large cities, very different appearances: it is often concealed in splendour, and often in extravagance. It is the care of a very great part of mankind to conceal their indigence from the rest: they support themselves by temporary expedients, and every day is lost in contriving for the morrow.

"This, however, was an evil which, though frequent, I saw with less pain; because I could relieve it. Yet some have refused my bounties, more offended with my quickness to detect their wants, than pleased with my readiness to succour them; and others, whose exigencies compelled them to admit my kindness, have never been able to forgive their benefactress. Many, however, have been sincerely grateful without the ostentation of gratitude, or the hope of other favours."

Chapter 26

THE PRINCESS CONTINUES HER REMARKS UPON PRIVATE LIFE

Nekayah perceiving her brother's attention fixed, proceeded in her narrative.

"In families where there is or is not poverty there is commonly discord. If a kingdom be, as Imlac tells us, a great family, a family likewise is a little kingdom, torn with factions, and exposed to revolutions. An unpractised observer expects the love of parents and children to be constant and equal; but this kindness seldom continues beyond the years of infancy. In a short time the children become rivals to their parents. Benefits are allayed by reproaches, and gratitude debased by envy.

"Parents and children seldom act in concert: each child endeavours to appropriate the esteem or fondness of the parents, and the parents, with yet less temptation, betray each other to their children; thus some place their confidence in the father, and some in the mother, and by degrees the house is filled with artifices and feuds.

"The opinions of children and parents, of the young and the old, are naturally opposite, by the contrary effects of hope and despondence, of expectation and experience, without crime or folly on either side. The colours of life in youth and age appear different, as the face of nature in spring and winter. And how can children credit the assertions of parents, which their own eyes shew them to be false?

"Few parents act in such a manner as much to enforce their maxims by the credit of their lives. The old man trusts wholly to slow contrivance and gradual progression: the youth expects to force his way by genius, vigour, and precipitance. The old man pays regard to riches, and the youth reverences virtue. The old man deifies prudence: the youth commits himself to magnanimity and chance. The young man, who intends no ill, believes that none is intended, and therefore acts with openness and candour: but his father, having suffered the injuries of fraud, is impelled to suspect, and too often allured to practise it. Age looks with anger on the temerity of youth, and youth with contempt on the scrupulosity of age. Thus parents and children, for the greatest part, live on to love less and less: and, if those whom nature has thus closely united are the torments of each other, where shall we look for tenderness and consolation?"

"Surely," said the prince, "you must have been unfortunate in your choice of acquaintance: I am unwilling to believe, that the most tender of all relations is thus impeded in its effects by natural necessity."

"Domestic discord," answered she, "is not inevitably and fatally necessary; but yet it is not easily avoided. We seldom see that a whole family is virtuous: the good and evil cannot well agree: and the evil can yet less agree with one another. Even the virtuous fall sometimes to variance, when their virtues are of different kinds, and tending to extremes. In general, those parents have most reverence who most deserve it: for he that lives well cannot be despised.

"Many other evils infest private life. Some are the slaves of servants whom they have trusted with their affairs. Some are kept in continual anxiety by the caprice of rich relations, whom they cannot please, and dare not offend. Some husbands are imperious, and some wives perverse: and, as it is always more easy to do evil than good, though the wisdom or virtue of one can very rarely make many happy, the folly or vice of one man often make many miserable."

"If such be the general effect of marriage," said the prince, "I shall, for the future, think it dangerous to connect my interest with that of another, lest I should be unhappy by my partner's fault."

"I have met," said the princess, "with many who live single for that reason; but I never found that their prudence ought to raise envy. They dream away their time without friendship, without fondness, and are driven to rid themselves of the day, for which they have no use, by childish amusements, or vicious delights. They act as beings under the constant sense of some known inferiority, that fills their minds with rancour, and their tongues with censure. They are peevish at home, and malevolent abroad; and, as the outlaws of human nature, make it their business and their pleasure to disturb that society which debars them from its privileges. To live without feeling or exciting sympathy, to be fortunate without adding to the felicity of others, or afflicted without tasting the balm of pity, is a state more gloomy than solitude: it is not retreat, but exclusion from mankind. Marriage has many pains, but celibacy has no pleasures."

"What then is to be done?" said Rasselas. "The more we inquire, the less we can resolve. Surely he is most likely to please himself that has no other inclination to regard."

Chapter 27

DISQUISITION UPON GREATNESS

The conversation had a short pause. The prince, having considered his sister's observations, told her that she had surveyed life with prejudice, and supposed misery where she did not find it. "Your narrative," says he, "throws yet a darker gloom upon the prospects of futurity: the predictions of Imlac were but faint sketches of the evils painted by Nekayah. I have been lately convinced that quiet is not the daughter of grandeur, or of power; that her presence is not to be bought by wealth, nor enforced by conquest. It is evident, that as any man acts in a wider compass, he must be more exposed to opposition from enmity, or miscarriage from chance; whoever has many to please or to govern, must use the ministry of many agents, some of whom will be wicked, and some ignorant; by some he will be misled, and by others betrayed. If he gratifies one he will offend another; those that are not favoured will think themselves injured; and, since favours can be conferred but upon few, the greater number will be always discontented."

"The discontent," said the princess, "which is thus unreasonable, I hope that I shall always have spirit to despise, and you, power to repress."

"Discontent," answered Rasselas, "will not always be without reason under the most just and vigilant administration of public affairs. None, however attentive, can always discover that merit which indigence or faction may happen to obscure; and none, however powerful, can always reward it. Yet, he that sees inferior desert advanced above him, will naturally impute that preference to partiality or caprice; and, indeed, it can scarcely be hoped that any man, however magnanimous by nature, or exalted by condition, will be able to persist forever in the fixed and inexorable justice of distribution; he will sometimes indulge his own affections, and sometimes those of his favourites; he will permit some to please him who can never serve him; he will discover in those whom he loves, qualities which in reality they do not possess; and to those, from whom he receives pleasure, he will in his turn endeavour to give it. Thus will recommendations sometimes prevail which were purchased by money, or by the more destructive bribery of flattery and servility.

"He that has much to do will do something wrong, and of that wrong must suffer the consequences; and, if it were possible that he should always act rightly, yet when such numbers are to judge of his conduct, the bad will censure and obstruct him by malevolence, and the good sometimes by mistake.

"The highest stations cannot therefore hope to be the abodes of happiness, which I would willingly believe to have fled from thrones and palaces to seats of humble privacy and placid obscurity. For what can hinder the satisfaction, or intercept the expectations, of him whose abilities are adequate to his employments, who sees with his own eyes the whole circuit of his influence, who chooses by his own knowledge all whom he trusts, and whom none are tempted to deceive by hope or fear? Surely he has nothing to do but to love and to be loved, to be virtuous and to be happy."

"Whether perfect happiness would be procured by perfect goodness," said Nekayah, "this world will never afford an opportunity of deciding. But this, at least, may be maintained, that we do not always find visible happiness in proportion to visible virtue. All natural, and almost all political evils, are incident alike to the bad and good; they are confounded in the misery of a famine, and not much distinguished in the fury of a faction; they sink together in a tempest, and are driven together from their country by invaders. All that virtue can afford is quietness of conscience, a steady prospect of a happier state; this may enable us to endure calamity with patience, but remember that patience must suppose pain."

Chapter 28

RASSELAS AND NEKAYAH CONTINUE THEIR CONVERSATION

"Dear princess," said Rasselas, "you fall into the common errors of exaggeratory declamation, by producing, in a familiar disquisition, examples of national calamities, and scenes of extensive misery, which are found in books rather than in the world, and which, as they are horrid, are ordained to be rare. Let us not imagine evils which we do not feel, nor injure life by misrepresentations. I cannot bear that querulous eloquence which threatens every city with a siege like that of Jerusalem, that makes famine attend on every flight of locusts, and suspends pestilence on the wings of every blast that issues from the south.

"On necessary and inevitable evils, which overwhelm kingdoms at once, all disputation is vain: when they happen they must be endured. But it is evident, that these bursts of universal distress are more dreaded than felt; thousands and ten thousands flourish in youth, and wither in age, without the knowledge of any other than domestic evils, and share the same pleasures and vexations, whether their kings are mild or cruel, whether the armies of their country pursue their enemies, or retreat before them. While courts are disturbed with intestine competitions, and ambassadors are negociating in foreign countries, the smith still plies his anvil and the husbandman drives his plough forward; the necessaries of life are required and obtained; and the successive business of the seasons continues to make its wonted revolutions.

"Let us cease to consider what, perhaps, may never happen, and what, when it shall happen, will laugh at human speculation. We will not endeavour to modify the motions of the elements, or to fix the destiny of kingdoms. It is our business to consider what beings like us may perform; each labouring for his own happiness, by promoting within his circle, however narrow, the happiness of others.

"Marriage is evidently the dictate of nature; men and women were made to be companions of each other, and therefore I cannot be persuaded but that marriage is one of the means of happiness."

"I know not," said the princess, "whether marriage be more than one of the innumerable modes of human misery. When I see and reckon the various forms of connubial infelicity, the unexpected causes of lasting discord, the diversities of temper, the oppositions of opinion, the rude collisions of contrary desire where both are urged by violent impulses, the obstinate contests of disagreeable virtues, where both are supported by consciousness of good intention, I am sometimes disposed to think with the severer casuists of most nations, that marriage is rather permitted than approved, and that none, but by the instigation of a passion too much indulged, entangle themselves with indissoluble compacts."

"You seem to forget," replied Rasselas, "that you have, even now, represented celibacy as less happy than marriage. Both conditions may be bad, but they cannot both be worst. Thus it happens, when wrong opinions are entertained, that they mutually destroy each other, and leave the mind open to truth."

"I did not expect," answered the princess, "to hear that imputed to falsehood which is the consequence only of frailty. To the mind, as to the eye, it is difficult to compare with exactness objects vast in their extent, and various in their parts. Where we see or conceive the whole at once, we readily note the discriminations, and decide the preference: but of two systems, of which neither can be surveyed by any human being in its full compass of magnitude and multiplicity of complication, where is the wonder that judging of the whole by parts, I am alternately affected by one and the other as either presses on my memory or fancy? We differ from ourselves just as we differ from each other, when we see only part of the question, as in the multifarious relations of politics and morality; but when we perceive the whole at once, as in numerical computations, all agree in one judgment, and none ever varies his opinion."

"Let us not add," said the prince, "to the other evils of life, the bitterness of controversy, nor endeavour to vie with each other in subtilties of argument. We are employed in a search, of which both

17. disagreeable, disagreeing.

are equally to enjoy the success, or suffer by the miscarriage. It is therefore fit that we assist each other. You surely conclude too hastily from the infelicity of marriage against its institution. Will not the misery of life prove equally that life cannot be the gift of Heaven? The world must be peopled by marriage, or peopled without it."

"How the world is to be peopled," returned Nekayah, "is not my care, and needs not be yours. I see no danger that the present generation should omit to leave successors behind them: we are not now inquiring for the world, but for ourselves."

Chapter 29

THE DEBATE ON MARRIAGE CONTINUED

"The good of the whole," says Rasselas, "is the same with the good of all its parts. If marriage be best for mankind, it must be evidently best for individuals, or a permanent and necessary duty must be the cause of evil, and some must be inevitably sacrificed to the convenience of others. In the estimate which you have made of the two states, it appears that the incommodities of a single life are, in a great measure, necessary and certain, but those of the conjugal state accidental and avoidable.

"I cannot forbear to flatter myself, that prudence and benevolence will make marriage happy. The general folly of mankind is the cause of general complaint. What can be expected but disappointment and repentance from a choice made in the immaturity of youth, in the ardour of desire, without judgment, without foresight, without inquiry after conformity of opinions, similarity of manners, rectitude of judgment, or purity of sentiment?

"Such is the common process of marriage. A youth or maiden, meeting by chance, or brought together by artifice, exchange glances, reciprocate civilities, go home, and dream of one another. Having little to divert attention, or diversify thought, they find themselves uneasy when they are apart, and therefore conclude that they shall be happy together. They marry, and discover what nothing but voluntary blindness had before concealed; they wear out life in altercations, and charge nature with cruelty.

"From those early marriages proceeds likewise the rivalry of parents and children: the son is eager to enjoy the world before the father is willing to forsake it, and there is hardly room at once for two generations. The daughter begins to bloom before the mother can be content to fade, and neither can forbear to wish for the absence of the other.

"Surely all these evils may be avoided by that deliberation and delay which prudence prescribes to irrevocable choice. In the variety and jollity of youthful pleasures life may be well enough supported without the help of a partner. Longer time will increase experience, and wider views will allow better opportunities of inquiry and selection: one advantage at least will be certain; the parents will be visibly older than their children."

"What reason cannot collect," said Nekayah, "and what experiment has not yet taught, can be known only from the report of others. I have been told that late marriages are not eminently happy. This is a question too important to be neglected, and I have often proposed it to those, whose accuracy of remark, and comprehensiveness of knowledge, made their suffrages worthy of regard. They have generally determined, that it is dangerous for a man and woman to suspend their fate upon each other, at a time when opinions are fixed, and habits are established; when friendships have been contracted on both sides, when life has been planned into method, and the mind has long enjoyed the contemplation of its own prospects.

"It is scarcely possible that two travelling through the world under the conduct of chance, should have been both directed to the same path, and it will not often happen that either will quit the track which custom has made pleasing. When the desultory levity of youth has settled into regularity, it is soon succeeded by pride ashamed to yield, or obstinacy delighting to contend. And even though mutual esteem produces mutual desire to please, time itself, as it modifies unchangeably the external mien, determines likewise the direction of the passions, and gives an inflexible rigidity to the manners. Long customs are not easily broken: he that attempts to change the course of his own life, very often labours in vain; and how shall we do that for others, which we are seldom able to do for ourselves?"

"But surely," interposed the prince, "you suppose the chief motive of choice forgotten or neglected. Whenever I shall seek a wife, it shall be my first question, whether she be willing to be led by reason."

"Thus it is," said Nekayah, "that philosophers are deceived. There are a thousand familiar disputes which reason never can decide; questions that elude investigation, and make logic ridiculous; cases where something must be done, and where little can be said. Consider the state of mankind, and inquire how few can be supposed to act upon any occasions, whether small or great, with all the reasons of action present to their minds. Wretched would be the pair above all names of wretchedness, who should be doomed to adjust by reason, every morning all the minute detail of a domestic day.

"Those who marry at an advanced age will probably escape the encroachments of their children; but, in diminution of this advantage, they will be likely to leave them, ignorant and helpless, to a guardian's mercy; or, if that should not happen, they must at least go out of the world before they see those whom they love best either wise or great.

"From their children, if they have less to fear, they have less also to hope, and they lose, without equivalent, the joys of early love, and the convenience of uniting with manners pliant, and minds susceptible of new impressions, which might wear away their dissimilitudes by long cohabitation, as soft bodies, by continual attrition, conform their surfaces to each other.

"I believe it will be found that those who marry late are best pleased with their children, and those who marry early with their partners."

"The union of these two affections," said Rasselas, "would produce all that could be wished. Perhaps there is a time when marriage might unite them, a time neither too early for the father, nor too late for the husband."

"Every hour," answered the princess, "confirms my prejudice in favour of the position so often uttered by the mouth of Imlac, 'That nature sets her gifts on the right hand and on the left.' Those conditions which flatter hope and attract desire are so constituted that, as we approach one, we recede from another. There are goods so opposed that we cannot seize both, but, by too much prudence, may pass between them at too great a distance to reach either. This is often the fate of long consideration; he does nothing who endeavours to do more than is allowed to humanity. Flatter not yourself with contrarieties of pleasure. Of the blessings set before you make your choice, and be content. No man can taste the fruits of autumn while he is delighting his scent with the flowers of the spring: no man can at the same time fill his cup from the source and from the mouth of the Nile."

Chapter 30

IMLAC ENTERS, AND CHANGES THE CONVERSATION

Here Imlac entered, and interrupted them. "Imlac," said Rasselas, "I have been taking from the princess the dismal history of private life, and am almost discouraged from further search."

"It seems to me," said Imlac, "that while you are making the choice of life, you neglect to live. You wander about a single city, which, however large and diversified, can now afford few novelties, and forget that you are in a country famous among the earliest monarchies for the power and wisdom of its inhabitants; a country where the sciences first dawned that illuminate the world, and beyond which the arts cannot be traced of civil society or domestic life.

"The old Egyptians have left behind them monuments of industry and power, before which all European magnificence is confessed to fade away. The ruins of their architecture are the schools of modern builders, and from the wonders which time has spared we may conjecture, though uncertainly, what it has destroyed."

"My curiosity," said Rasselas, "does not very strongly lead me to survey piles of stone, or mounds of earth; my business is with man. I came hither not to measure fragments of temples, or trace choked aqueducts, but to look upon the various scenes of the present world."

"The things that are now before us," said the princess, "require attention, and deserve it. What have I to do with the heroes or the monuments of ancient times, with times which never can return, and heroes whose form of life was different from all that the present condition of mankind requires or allows?"

"To know anything," returned the poet, "we must know its effects; to see men we must see their works, that we may learn what reason has dictated, or passion has incited, and find what are the most powerful motives of action. To judge rightly of the present, we must oppose it to the past; for all judgment is comparative, and of the future nothing can be known. The truth is, that no mind is much employed upon the present. Recollection and anticipation fill up almost all our moments. Our passions are joy and grief, love and hatred, hope and fear. Of joy and grief the past is the object, and the future of hope and fear; even love and hatred respect the past, for the cause must have been before the effect.

"The present state of things is the consequence of the former, and it is natural to inquire what were the sources of the good that we enjoy, or the evil that we suffer. If we act only for ourselves, to neglect the study of history is not prudent: if we are intrusted with the care of others, it is not just. Ignorance, when it is voluntary, is criminal; and he may properly be charged with evil who refused to learn how he might prevent it.

"There is no part of history so generally useful as

that which relates the progress of the human mind, the gradual improvement of reason, the successive advances of science, the vicissitudes of learning and ignorance which are the light and darkness of thinking beings, the extinction and resuscitation of arts, and the revolutions of the intellectual world. If accounts of battles and invasions are peculiarly the business of princes, the useful or elegant arts are not to be neglected; those who have kingdoms to govern, have understandings to cultivate.

"Example is always more efficacious than precept. A soldier is formed in war, and a painter must copy pictures. In this, contemplative life has the advantage; great actions are seldom seen, but the labours of art are always at hand for those who desire to know what art has been able to perform.

"When the eye or the imagination is struck with any uncommon work, the next transition of an active mind is to the means by which it was performed. Here begins the true use of such contemplation; we enlarge our comprehension by new ideas, and perhaps recover some art lost to mankind, or learn what is less perfectly known in our own country. At least we compare our own with former times, and either rejoice at our improvements, or, what is the first motion towards good, discover our defects."

"I am willing," said the prince, "to see all that can deserve my search." "And I," said the princess, "shall rejoice to learn something of the manners of antiquity."

"The most pompous monument of Egyptian greatness, and one of the most bulky works of manual industry," said Imlac, "are the pyramids; fabrics raised before the time of history, and of which the earliest narratives afford us only uncertain traditions. Of these the greatest is still standing, very little injured by time."

"Let us visit them to-morrow," said Nekayah. "I have often heard of the pyramids, and shall not rest till I have seen them, within and without, with my own eyes."

Chapter 31

THEY VISIT THE PYRAMIDS

The resolution being thus taken, they set out the next day. They laid tents upon their camels, being resolved to stay among the pyramids till their curiosity was fully satisfied. They travelled gently, turned aside to every thing remarkable, stopped from time to time and conversed with the inhabitants, and observed the various appearances of towns ruined and inhabited, of wild and cultivated nature.

When they came to the great pyramid, they were astonished at the extent of the base, and the height of the top. Imlac explained to them the principles upon which the pyramidal form was chosen for a fabric intended to co-extend its duration with that of the world: he shewed that its gradual diminution gave it such stability, as defeated all the common attacks of the elements, and could scarcely be overthrown by earthquakes themselves, the least resistible of natural violence. A concussion that should shatter the pyramid would threaten the dissolution of the continent.

They measured all its dimensions, and pitched their tents at its foot. Next day they prepared to enter its interior apartments, and having hired the common guides, climbed up to the first passage, when the favourite of the princess, looking into the cavity, stepped back and trembled. "Pekuah," said the princess, "of what art thou afraid?" "Of the narrow entrance," answered the lady, "and of the dreadful gloom. I dare not enter a place which must surely be inhabited by unquiet souls. The original possessors of these dreadful vaults will start up before us, and perhaps shut us in for ever." She spoke, and threw her arms round the neck of her mistress.

"If all your fear be of apparitions," said the prince, "I will promise you safety. There is no danger from the dead; he that is once buried will be seen no more."

"That the dead are seen no more," said Imlac, "I will not undertake to maintain, against the concurrent and unvaried testimony of all ages, and of all nations. There is no people, rude or learned, among whom apparitions of the dead are not related and believed. This opinion, which perhaps prevails as far as human nature is diffused, could become universal only by its truth: those, that never heard of one another, would not have agreed in a tale which nothing but experience can make credible. That it is doubted by single cavillers, can very little weaken the general evidence; and some who deny it with their tongues confess it by their fears.

"Yet I do not mean to add new terrors to those which have already seized upon Pekuah. There can be no reason why spectres should haunt the pyramid more than other places, or why they should have power or will to hurt innocence and purity. Our entrance is no violation of their privileges. We can take nothing from them. How then can we offend them?"

"My dear Pekuah," said the princess, "I will always go before you, and Imlac shall follow you.

Remember that you are the companion of the princess of Abissinia."

"If the princess is pleased that her servant should die," returned the lady, "let her command some death less dreadful than enclosure in this horrid cavern. You know I dare not disobey you: I must go if you command me; but, if I once enter, I never shall come back."

The princess saw that her fear was too strong for expostulation or reproof, and, embracing her, told her that she should stay in the tent till their return. Pekuah was yet not satisfied, but entreated the princess not to pursue so dreadful a purpose as that of entering the recesses of the pyramid. "Though I cannot teach courage," said Nekayah, "I must not learn cowardice; nor leave at last undone what I came hither only to do."

tend his plan to the utmost power of human performance, that he may not be soon reduced to form another wish.

"I consider this mighty structure as a monument of the insufficiency of human enjoyments. A king, whose power is unlimited, and whose treasures surmount all real and imaginary wants, is compelled to solace, by the erection of a pyramid, the satiety of dominion and tastelessness of pleasures, and to amuse the tediousness of declining life, by seeing thousands labouring without end, and one stone, for no purpose, laid upon another. Whoever thou art, that, not content with a moderate condition, imaginest happiness in royal magnificence, and dreamest that command or riches can feed the appetite of novelty with perpetual gratifications, survey the pyramids, and confess thy folly!"

Chapter 32

THEY ENTER THE PYRAMID

Pekuah descended to the tents, and the rest entered the pyramid: they passed through the galleries, surveyed the vaults of marble, and examined the chest in which the body of the founder is supposed to have been reposited. They then sat down in one of the most spacious chambers to rest a while before they attempted to return.

"We have now," said Imlac, "gratified our minds with an exact view of the greatest work of man, except the wall of China.

"Of the wall it is very easy to assign the motive. It secured a wealthy and timorous nation from the incursions of Barbarians, whose unskilfulness in arts made it easier for them to supply their wants by rapine than by industry, and who from time to time poured in upon the habitations of peaceful commerce, as vultures descend upon domestic fowl. Their celerity and fierceness made the wall necessary, and their ignorance made it efficacious.

"But for the pyramids, no reason has ever been given adequate to the cost and labour of the work. The narrowness of the chambers proves that it could afford no retreat from enemies, and treasures might have been reposited at far less expence with equal security. It seems to have been erected only in compliance with that hunger of imagination which preys incessantly upon life, and must be always appeased by some employment. Those who have already all that they can enjoy, must enlarge their desires. He that has built for use, till use is supplied, must begin to build for vanity, and ex-

Chapter 33

THE PRINCESS MEETS WITH AN UNEXPECTED MISFORTUNE

They rose up, and returned through the cavity at which they had entered, and the princess prepared for her favourite a long narrative of dark labyrinths, and costly rooms, and of the different impressions which the varieties of the way had made upon her. But when they came to their train, they found every one silent and dejected: the men discovered shame and fear in their countenances, and the women were weeping in the tents.

What had happened they did not try to conjecture but immediately inquired. "You had scarcely entered into the pyramid," said one of the attendants, "when a troop of Arabs rushed upon us: we were too few to resist them, and too slow to escape. They were about to search the tents, set us on our camels, and drive us along before them, when the approach of some Turkish horsemen put them to flight; but they seized the lady Pekuah with her two maids, and carried them away. The Turks are now pursuing them by our instigation, but I fear they will not be able to overtake them."

The princess was overpowered with surprise and grief. Rasselas, in the first heat of his resentment, ordered his servants to follow him, and prepared to pursue the robbers with his sabre in his hand. "Sir," said Imlac, "what can you hope from violence or valour? The Arabs are mounted on horses trained to battle and retreat; we have only beasts of burden. By leaving our present station we may lose the princess, but cannot hope to regain Pekuah."

In a short time the Turks returned, having not been able to reach the enemy. The princess burst out into new lamentations, and Rasselas could scarcely forbear to reproach them with cowardice; but Imlac was of opinion, that the escape of the Arabs was no addition to their misfortune, for perhaps they would have killed their captives rather than have resigned them.

Chapter 34

THEY RETURN TO CAIRO WITHOUT PEKUAH

There was nothing to be hoped from longer stay. They returned to Cairo repenting of their curiosity, censuring the negligence of the government, lamenting their own rashness which had neglected to procure a guard, imagining many expedients by which the loss of Pekuah might have been prevented, and resolving to do something for her recovery, though none could find anything proper to be done.

Nekayah retired to her chamber, where her women attempted to comfort her, by telling her that all had their troubles, and that lady Pekuah had enjoyed much happiness in the world for a long time, and might reasonably expect a change of fortune. They hoped that some good would befall her wheresoever she was, and that their mistress would find another friend who might supply her place.

The princess made them no answer, and they continued the form of condolence, not much grieved in their hearts that the favourite was lost.

Next day the prince presented to the Bassa a memorial of the wrong which he had suffered, and a petition for redress. The Bassa threatened to punish the robbers, but did not attempt to catch them, nor indeed, could any account or description be given by which he might direct the pursuit.

It soon appeared that nothing would be done by authority. Governors, being accustomed to hear of more crimes than they can punish, and more wrongs than they can redress, set themselves at ease by indiscriminate negligence, and presently forget the request when they lose sight of the petitioner.

Imlac then endeavoured to gain some intelligence by private agents. He found many who pretended to an exact knowledge of all the haunts of the Arabs, and to regular correspondence with their chiefs, and who readily undertook the recovery of Pekuah. Of these, some were furnished with money for their journey, and came back no more; some were liberally paid for accounts which a few days discovered to be false. But the princess would not suffer any means, however improbable, to be left untried. While she was doing something, she kept her hope alive. As one expedient failed, another was suggested; when one messenger returned unsuccessful, another was despatched to a different quarter.

Two months had now passed, and of Pekuah nothing had been heard; the hopes which they had endeavoured to raise in each other grew more languid, and the princess, when she saw nothing more to be tried, sunk down inconsolable in hopeless dejection. A thousand times she reproached herself with the easy compliance, by which she permitted her favourite to stay behind her. "Had not my fondness," said she "lessened my authority, Pekuah had not dared to talk of her terrors. She ought to have feared me more than spectres. A severe look would have overpowered her; a peremptory command would have compelled obedience. Why did foolish indulgence prevail upon me? Why did I not speak and refuse to hear?"

"Great princess," said Imlac, "do not reproach yourself for your virtue, or consider that as blamable by which evil has accidentally been caused. Your tenderness for the timidity of Pekuah was generous and kind. When we act according to our duty, we commit the event to Him by whose laws our actions are governed, and who will suffer none to be finally punished for obedience. When, in prospect of some good, whether natural or moral, we break the rules prescribed us, we withdraw from the direction of superior wisdom, and take all consequences upon ourselves. Man cannot so far know the connexion of causes and events, as that he may venture to do wrong in order to do right. When we pursue our end by lawful means, we may always console our miscarriage by the hope of future recompense. When we consult only our own policy, and attempt to find a nearer way to good, by overleaping the settled boundaries of right and wrong, we cannot be happy even by success, because we cannot escape the consciousness of our fault: but, if we miscarry, the disappointment is irremediably embittered. How comfortless is the sorrow of him who feels at once the pangs of guilt, and the vexation of calamity which guilt has brought upon him!

"Consider, princess, what would have been your condition, if the lady Pekuah had entreated to accompany you, and, being compelled to stay in the tents, had been carried away; or how would you have borne the thought, if you had forced her into the pyramid, and she had died before you in agonies of terror?"

"Had either happened," said Nekayah, "I could not have endured life till now: I should have been tortured to madness by the remembrance of such cruelty, or must have pined away in abhorrence of myself."

"This, at least," said Imlac, "is the present reward of virtuous conduct, that no unlucky consequence can oblige us to repent it."

Chapter 35

THE PRINCESS LANGUISHES FOR WANT OF PEKUAH

Nekayah, being thus reconciled to herself, found that no evil is insupportable but that which is accompanied with consciousness of wrong. She was, from that time, delivered from the violence of tempestuous sorrow, and sunk into silent pensiveness and gloomy tranquillity. She sat from morning to evening recollecting all that had been done or said by her Pekuah, treasured up with care every trifle on which Pekuah had set an accidental value, and which might recall to mind any little incident or careless conversation. The sentiments of her whom she now expected to see no more, were treasured in her memory as rules of life, and she deliberated to no other end than to conjecture on any occasion what would have been the opinion and counsel of Pekuah.

The women by whom she was attended knew nothing of her real condition, and therefore she could not talk to them but with caution and reserve. She began to remit her curiosity, having no great care to collect notions which she had no convenience of uttering. Rasselas endeavoured first to comfort, and afterward to divert her; he hired musicians, to whom she seemed to listen, but did not hear them, and procured masters to instruct her in various arts, whose lectures, when they visited her again, were again to be repeated. She had lost her taste of pleasure, and her ambition of excellence. And her mind, though forced into short excursions, always recurred to the image of her friend.

Imlac was every morning earnestly enjoined to renew his inquiries, and was asked every night whether he had yet heard of Pekuah, till not being able to return the princess the answer that she desired, he was less and less willing to come into her presence. She observed his backwardness, and commanded him to attend her. "You are not," said she, "to confound impatience with resentment, or to suppose that I charge you with negligence, because I repine at your unsuccessfulness. I do not much wonder at your absence; I know that the unhappy are never pleasing, and that all naturally avoid the contagion of misery. To hear complaints is wearisome alike to the wretched and the happy; for who would cloud, by adventitious grief, the short gleams of gaiety which life allows us? or who, that is struggling under his own evils, will add to them the miseries of another?

"The time is at hand, when none shall be disturbed any longer by the sighs of Nekayah: my search after happiness is now at an end. I am resolved to retire from the world, with all its flatteries and deceits, and will hide myself in solitude without any other care than to compose my thoughts, and regulate my hours by a constant succession of innocent occupations, till, with a mind purified from all earthly desires, I shall enter into that state, to which all are hastening, and in which I hope again to enjoy the friendship of Pekuah."

"Do not entangle your mind," said Imlac, "by irrevocable determinations, nor increase the burthen of life by a voluntary accumulation of misery; the weariness of retirement will continue or increase when the loss of Pekuah is forgotten. That you have been deprived of one pleasure, is no very good reason for rejection of the rest."

"Since Pekuah was taken from me," said the princess, "I have no pleasure to reject or to retain. She that has no one to love or trust has little to hope. She wants the radical principle of happiness. We may, perhaps, allow that what satisfaction this world can afford, must arise from the conjunction of wealth, knowledge, and goodness: wealth is nothing but as it is bestowed, and knowledge nothing but as it is communicated; they must therefore be imparted to others, and to whom could I now delight to impart them? Goodness affords the only comfort which can be enjoyed without a partner, and goodness may be practised in retirement."

"How far solitude may admit goodness, or advance it, I shall not," replied Imlac, "dispute at present. Remember the confession of the pious hermit. You will wish to return into the world when the image of your companion has left your thoughts." "That time," said Nekayah, "will never come. The generous frankness, the modest obsequiousness, and the faithful secrecy of my dear Pekuah, will always be more missed, as I shall live longer to see vice and folly."

"The state of a mind oppressed with a sudden calamity," said Imlac, "is like that of the fabulous inhabitants of the new-created earth, who, when the first night came upon them, supposed that day never would return. When the clouds of sorrow gather over us, we see nothing beyond them, nor can imagine how they will be dispelled: yet a new day succeeded to the night, and sorrow is never long without a dawn of ease. But they who restrain themselves from receiving comfort, do as the savages would have done, had they put out their eyes when it was dark. Our minds, like our bodies, are in continual flux; something is hourly lost, and something acquired. To lose much at once is inconvenient to either, but while the vital powers remain uninjured, nature will find the means of reparation. Distance has the same effect on the mind as on the eye, and while we glide along the stream of time, whatever we leave behind us is always lessening, and that which we approach increasing in magnitude. Do not suffer life to stagnate; it will grow muddy for want of motion. Commit yourself again to the current of the world. Pekuah will vanish by degrees; you will meet in your way some other favourite, or learn to diffuse yourself in general conversation."

"At least," said the prince, "do not despair before all remedies have been tried. The inquiry after the unfortunate lady is still continued, and shall be carried on with yet greater diligence, on condition that you will promise to wait a year for the event, without any unalterable resolution."

Nekayah thought this a reasonable demand, and made the promise to her brother, who had been advised by Imlac to require it. Imlac had, indeed, no great hope of regaining Pekuah, but he supposed, that if he could secure the interval of a year, the princess would be then in no danger of a cloister.

Chapter 36

PEKUAH IS STILL REMEMBERED. THE PROGRESS OF SORROW

Nekayah, seeing that nothing was omitted for the recovery of her favourite, and having by her promise set her intention of retirement at a distance, began imperceptibly to return to common cares and common pleasures. She rejoiced without her own consent at the suspension of her sorrows, and sometimes caught herself with indignation in the act of turning away her mind from the remembrance of her whom yet she resolved never to forget.

She then appointed a certain hour of the day for meditation on the merits and fondness of Pekuah, and for some weeks retired constantly at the time fixed, and returned with her eyes swollen and her countenance clouded. By degrees she grew less scrupulous, and suffered any important and pressing avocation to delay the tribute of daily tears. She then yielded to less occasions; sometimes forgot what she was, indeed, afraid to remember, and at last wholly released herself from the duty of periodical affliction.

Her real love of Pekuah was yet not diminished. A thousand occurrences brought her back to memory, and a thousand wants, which nothing but the confidence of friendship can supply, made her frequently regretted. She, therefore, solicited Imlac never to desist from inquiry, and to leave no art of intelligence untried, that, at least, she might have the comfort of knowing that she did not suffer by negligence or sluggishness. "Yet what," said she, "is to be expected from our pursuit of happiness, when we find the state of life to be such, that happiness itself is the cause of misery? Why should we endeavour to attain that, of which the possession cannot be secured? I shall henceforward fear to yield my heart to excellence, however bright, or to fondness, however tender, lest I should lose again what I have lost in Pekuah."

Chapter 37

THE PRINCESS HEARS NEWS OF PEKUAH

In seven months, one of the messengers, who had been sent away upon the day when the promise was drawn from the princess, returned, after many unsuccessful rambles, from the borders of Nubia, with an account that Pekuah was in the hands of an Arab chief, who possessed a castle or fortress on the extremity of Egypt. The Arab, whose revenue was plunder, was willing to restore her, with her two attendants, for two hundred ounces of gold.

The price was no subject of debate. The princess was in ecstasies when she heard that her favourite was alive, and might so cheaply be ransomed. She could not think of delaying for a moment Pekuah's happiness or her own, but entreated her brother to send back the messenger with the sum required. Imlac, being consulted, was not very confident of the veracity of the relator, and was still more doubtful of the Arab's faith, who might, if he were too liberally trusted, detain at once, the money and the captives. He thought it dangerous to put themselves in the power of the Arab, by going into his district, and could not expect that the rover would so much expose himself as to come into the lower country, where he might be seized by the forces of the Bassa.

It is difficult to negotiate where neither will trust.

But Imlac, after some deliberation, directed the messenger to propose that Pekuah should be conducted by ten horsemen to the monastery of St. Antony, which is situated in the deserts of Upper-Egypt, where she should be met by the same number, and her ransom should be paid.

That no time might be lost, as they expected that the proposal would not be refused, they immediately began their journey to the monastery; and, when they arrived, Imlac went forward with the former messenger to the Arab's fortress. Rasselas was desirous to go with them; but neither his sister nor Imlac would consent. The Arab, according to the custom of his nation, observed the laws of hospitality with great exactness to those who put themselves into his power, and, in a few days, brought Pekuah with her maids, by easy journeys, to their place appointed, where receiving the stipulated price, he restored her with great respect to liberty and her friends, and undertook to conduct them back towards Cairo beyond all danger of robbery or violence.

The princess and her favourite embraced each other with transport too violent to be expressed, and went out together to pour the tears of tenderness in secret, and exchange professions of kindness and gratitude. After a few hours they returned into the refectory of the convent, where, in the presence of the prior and his brethren, the prince required of Pekuah the history of her adventures.

Chapter 38

THE ADVENTURES OF THE LADY PEKUAH

"At what time and in what manner, I was forced away," said Pekuah, "your servants have told you. The suddenness of the event struck me with surprise, and I was at first rather stupefied than agitated with any passion of either fear or sorrow. My confusion was increased by the speed and tumult of our flight, while we were followed by the Turks, who, as it seemed, soon despaired to overtake us, or were afraid of those whom they made a shew of menacing.

"When the Arabs saw themselves out of danger, they slackened their course, and as I was less harassed by external violence, I began to feel more uneasiness in my mind. After some time we stopped near a spring shaded with trees in a pleasant meadow, where we were set upon the ground, and offered such refreshments as our masters were partaking. I was suffered to sit with my maids apart from the rest, and none attempted to comfort or insult us. Here I first began to feel the full weight of my misery. The girls sat weeping in silence, and from time to time looked on me for succour. I knew not to what condition we were doomed, nor could conjecture where would be the place of our captivity, or whence to draw any hope of deliverance. I was in the hands of robbers and savages, and had no reason to suppose that their pity was more than their justice, or that they would forbear the gratification of any ardour of desire, or caprice of cruelty. I, however, kissed my maids, and endeavoured to pacify them by remarking that we were yet treated with decency, and that, since we were now carried beyond pursuit, there was no danger of violence to our lives.

"When we were to be set again on horseback, my maids clung round me, and refused to be parted; but I commanded them not to irritate those who had us in their power. We travelled the remaining part of the day through an unfrequented and pathless country, and came by moon-light to the side of a hill, where the rest of the troop was stationed. Their tents were pitched and their fires kindled, and our chief was welcomed as a man much beloved by his dependants.

"We were received into a large tent, where we found women who had attended their husbands in the expedition. They set before us the supper which they had provided, and I eat it rather to encourage my maids, than to comply with any appetite of my own. When the meat was taken away, they spread the carpets for repose. I was weary, and hoped to find in sleep that remission of distress which nature seldom denies. Ordering myself, therefore, to be undrest, I observed that the women looked very earnestly upon me, not expecting, I suppose, to see me so submissively attended. When my upper vest was taken off, they were apparently struck with the splendour of my clothes, and one of them timorously laid her hand upon the embroidery. She then went out, and, in a short time came back with another woman, who seemed to be of higher rank, and greater authority. She did, at her entrance, the usual act of reverence, and taking me by the hand, placed me in a smaller tent, spread with finer carpets, where I spent the night quietly with my maids.

"In the morning, as I was sitting on the grass, the chief of the troop came towards me. I rose up to receive him, and he bowed with great respect. 'Illustrious lady,' said he, 'my fortune is better than I had presumed to hope; I am told by my women, that I have a princess in my camp.' 'Sir,' answered I, 'your women have deceived themselves and you;

I am not a princess, but an unhappy stranger who intended soon to have left this country, in which I am now to be imprisoned forever.' 'Whoever or whencesoever you are,' returned the Arab, 'your dress, and that of your servants, shew your rank to be high, and your wealth to be great. Why should you, who can so easily procure your ransom, think yourself in danger of perpetual captivity? The purpose of my incursions is to increase my riches, or, more properly, to gather tribute. The sons of Ishmael are the natural and hereditary lords of this part of the continent, which is usurped by late invaders and low-born tyrants, from whom we are compelled to take by the sword what is denied to justice. The violence of war admits no distinction; the lance, that is lifted at guilt and power, will sometimes fall on innocence and gentleness.'

" 'How little,' said I, 'did I expect that yesterday it should have fallen upon me!'

" 'Misfortunes,' answered the Arab, 'should always be expected. If the eye of hostility could learn reverence or pity, excellence like yours had been exempt from injury. But the angels of affliction spread their toils alike for the virtuous and the wicked, for the mighty and the mean. Do not be disconsolate: I am not one of the lawless and cruel rovers of the desert; I know the rules of civil life. I will fix your ransom, give a passport to your messenger, and perform my stipulation with nice punctuality.'

"You will easily believe that I was pleased with his courtesy: and finding that his predominant passion was desire of money, I began now to think my danger less, for I knew that no sum would be thought too great for the release of Pekuah. I told him that he should have no reason to charge me with ingratitude, if I was used with kindness, and that any ransom which could be expected for a maid of common rank, would be paid; but that he must not persist to rate me as a princess. He said, he would consider what he should demand, and then, smiling, bowed and retired.

"Soon after the women came about me, each contending to be more officious than the other, and my maids themselves were served with reverence. We travelled onward by short journeys. On the fourth day the chief told me that my ransom must be two hundred ounces of gold; which I not only promised him, but told him that I would add fifty more, if I and my maids were honourably treated.

"I never knew the power of gold before. From that time I was the leader of the troop. The march of every day was longer or shorter as I commanded, and the tents were pitched where I chose to rest. We now had camels and other conveniences for travel, my own women were always at my side, and I amused myself with observing the manners of the vagrant nations, and with viewing remains of ancient edifices, with which these deserted countries appear to have been, in some distant age, lavishly embellished.

"The chief of the band was a man far from illiterate: he was able to travel by the stars or the compass, and had marked, in his erratic expeditions, such places as are most worthy the notice of a passenger. He observed to me, that buildings are always best preserved in places little frequented, and difficult of access: for, when once a country declines from its primitive splendour, the more inhabitants are left, the quicker ruin will be made. Walls supply stones more easily than quarries, and palaces and temples will be demolished, to make stables of granite, and cottages of porphyry."

Chapter 39

THE ADVENTURES OF PEKUAH CONTINUED

"We wandered about in this manner for some weeks, whether, as our chief pretended, for my gratification, or, as I rather suspected, for some convenience of his own. I endeavoured to appear contented where sullenness and resentment would have been of no use, and that endeavour conduced much to the calmness of my mind; but my heart was always with Nekayah, and the troubles of the night much overbalanced the amusements of the day. My women, who threw all their cares upon their mistress, set their minds at ease from the time when they saw me treated with respect, and gave themselves up to the incidental alleviations of our fatigue without solicitude or sorrow. I was pleased with their pleasure, and animated with their confidence. My condition had lost much of its terror, since I found that the Arab ranged the country merely to get riches. Avarice is an uniform and tractable vice: other intellectual distempers are different in different constitutions of mind; that which sooths the pride of one will offend the pride of another; but to the favour of the covetous there is a ready way; bring money, and nothing is denied.

"At last we came to the dwelling of our chief, a strong and spacious house built with stone in an island of the Nile, which lies, as I was told, under the tropic. 'Lady,' said the Arab, 'you shall rest after your journey a few weeks in this place, where you are to consider yourself as sovereign. My occupation is war: I have therefore chosen this obscure residence, from which I can issue unexpected, and to which I can retire unpursued. You may now repose in security: here are few pleasures, but here is no danger.' He then led me into the inner apartments, and seating me on the richest couch, bowed to the ground. His women, who considered me as a rival, looked on me with malignity; but being soon informed that I was a great lady detained only for my ransom, they began to vie with each other in obsequiousness and reverence.

"Being again comforted with new assurances of speedy liberty, I was for some days diverted from impatience by the novelty of the place. The turrets overlooked the country to a great distance, and afforded a view of many windings of the stream. In the day I wandered from one place to another, as the course of the sun varied the splendour of the prospect, and saw many things which I had never seen before. The crocodiles and river-horses are common in this unpeopled region, and I often looked upon them with terror, though I knew that they could not hurt me. For some time I expected to see mermaids and tritons, which, as Imlac has told me, the European travellers have stationed in the Nile, but no such beings ever appeared, and the Arab, when I inquired after them, laughed at my credulity.

"At night the Arab always attended me to a tower set apart for celestial observations, where he endeavoured to teach me the names and courses of the stars. I had no great inclination to this study, but an appearance of attention was necessary to please my instructor, who valued himself for his skill; and, in a little while, I found some employment requisite to beguile the tediousness of time, which was to be passed always amidst the same objects. I was weary of looking in the morning on things from which I had turned away weary in the evening: I therefore was at last willing to observe the stars rather than do nothing, but could not always compose my thoughts, and was very often thinking on Nekayah, when others imagined me contemplating the sky. Soon after the Arab went upon another expedition, and then my only pleasure was to talk with my maids about the accident by which we were carried away, and the happiness that we should all enjoy at the end of our captivity."

"There were women in your Arab's fortress," said the princess. "Why did you not make them your companions, enjoy their conversation, and partake their diversions? In a place where they found busi-

20. **river-horses**, hippopotamuses.

ness or amusement, why should you alone sit corroded with idle melancholy? Or why could not you bear, for a few months, that condition to which they were condemned for life?"

"The diversions of the women," answered Pekuah, "were only childish play, by which the mind, accustomed to stronger operations, could not be kept busy. I could do all which they delighted in doing by powers merely sensitive, while my intellectual faculties were flown to Cairo. They ran from room to room, as a bird hops from wire to wire in his cage. They danced for the sake of motion, as lambs frisk in a meadow. One sometimes pretended to be hurt, that the rest might be alarmed; or hid herself, that another might seek her. Part of their time passed in watching the progress of light bodies that floated on the river, and part in marking the various forms into which clouds broke in the sky.

"Their business was only needle-work, in which I and my maids sometimes helped them; but you know that the mind will easily straggle from the fingers, nor will you suspect that captivity and absence from Nekayah could receive solace from silken flowers.

"Nor was much satisfaction to be hoped from their conversation: for of what could they be expected to talk? They had seen nothing; for they had lived from early youth in that narrow spot: of what they had not seen they could have no knowledge, for they could not read. They had no ideas but of the few things that were within their view, and had hardly names for any thing but their clothes and their food. As I bore a superior character, I was often called to terminate their quarrels, which I decided as equitably as I could. If it could have amused me to hear the complaints of each against the rest, I might have been often detained by long stories; but the motives of their animosity were so small, that I could not listen without intercepting the tale."

"How," said Rasselas, "can the Arab, whom you represented as a man of more than common accomplishments, take any pleasure in his seraglio when it is filled only with women like these? Are they exquisitely beautiful?"

"They do not," said Pekuah, "want that unaffecting and ignoble beauty which may subsist without sprightliness or sublimity, without energy of thought or dignity of virtue. But to a man like the Arab, such beauty was only a flower casually plucked and carelessly thrown away. Whatever pleasures he might find among them, they were not those of friendship or society. When they were playing about him, he looked on them with inattentive superiority: when they vied for his regard, he sometimes turned away disgusted. As they had no knowledge, their talk could take nothing from the tediousness of life: as they had no choice, their fondness, or appearance of fondness, excited in him neither pride nor gratitude; he was not exalted in his own esteem by the smiles of a woman who saw no other man, nor was much obliged by that regard, of which he could never know the sincerity, and which he might often perceive to be exerted, not so much to delight him as to pain a rival. That which he gave, and they received, as love, was only a careless distribution of superfluous time, such love as man can bestow upon that which he despises, such as has neither hope nor fear, neither joy nor sorrow."

"You have reason, lady, to think yourself happy," said Imlac, "that you have been thus easily dismissed. How could a mind, hungry for knowledge, be willing, in an intellectual famine, to lose such a banquet as Pekuah's conversation?"

"I am inclined to believe," answered Pekuah, "that he was for some time in suspense; for, notwithstanding his promise, whenever I proposed to dispatch a messenger to Cairo, he found some excuse for delay. While I was detained in his house he made many incursions into the neighbouring countries, and, perhaps, he would have refused to discharge me, had his plunder been equal to his wishes. He returned always courteous, related his adventures, delighted to hear my observations, and endeavoured to advance my acquaintance with the stars. When I importuned him to send away my letters, he soothed me with professions of honour and sincerity; and, when I could be no longer decently denied, put his troop again in motion, and left me to govern in his absence. I was much afflicted by this studied procrastination, and was sometimes afraid that I should be forgotten: that you would leave Cairo, and I must end my days in an island of the Nile.

"I grew at last hopeless and dejected, and cared so little to entertain him, that he for a while more frequently talked with my maids. That he should fall in love with them, or with me, might have been equally fatal, and I was not much pleased with the growing friendship. My anxiety was not long: for, as I recovered some degree of cheerfulness, he returned to me, and I could not forbear to despise my former uneasiness.

"He still delayed to send for my ransom, and would, perhaps, never have determined, had not your agent found his way to him. The gold which he would not fetch, he could not reject when it was offered. He hastened to prepare for our journey hither, like a man delivered from the pain of an intestine conflict. I took leave of my companions in the house, who dismissed me with cold indifference."

Nekayah having heard her favourite's relation, rose and embraced her, and Rasselas gave her an hundred ounces of gold, which she presented to the Arab for the fifty that were promised.

Chapter 40

THE HISTORY OF A MAN OF LEARNING

They returned to Cairo, and were so well pleased at finding themselves together, that none of them went much abroad. The prince began to love learning, and one day declared to Imlac, that he intended to devote himself to science, and pass the rest of his days in literary solitude.

"Before you make your final choice," answered Imlac, "you ought to examine its hazards, and converse with some of those who are grown old in the company of themselves. I have just left the observatory of one of the most learned astronomers in the world, who has spent forty years in unwearied attention to the motions and appearances of the celestial bodies, and has drawn out his soul in endless calculations. He admits a few friends once a month to hear his deductions and enjoy his discoveries. I was introduced as a man of knowledge worthy of his notice. Men of various ideas, and fluent conversation, are commonly welcome to those whose thoughts have been long fixed upon a single point, and who find the images of other things stealing away. I delighted him with my remarks; he smiled at the narrative of my travels, and was glad to forget the constellations, and descend for a moment into the lower world.

"On the next day of vacation I renewed my visit, and was so fortunate as to please him again. He relaxed from that time the severity of his rule, and permitted me to enter at my own choice. I found him always busy, and always glad to be relieved. As each knew much which the other was desirous of learning, we exchanged our notions with great delight. I perceived that I had every day more of his confidence, and always found new cause of admiration in the profundity of his mind. His comprehension is vast, his memory capacious and retentive, his discourse is methodical, and his expression clear.

"His integrity and benevolence are equal to his learning. His deepest researches and most favourite studies are willingly interrupted for any opportunity of doing good by his counsel or his riches. To his closest retreat, at his most busy moments, all are admitted that want his assistance; 'For though I exclude idleness and pleasure, I will never,' says he, 'bar my doors against charity. To man is permitted the contemplation of the skies, but the practice of virtue is commanded.'"

"Surely," said the princess, "this man is happy."

"I visited him," said Imlac, "with more and more frequency, and was every time more enamoured of his conversation. He was sublime without haughtiness, courteous without formality, and communicative without ostentation. I was at first, great princess, of your opinion,—thought him the happiest of mankind, and often congratulated him on the blessing that he enjoyed. He seemed to hear nothing with indifference but the praises of his condition, to which he always returned a general answer, and diverted the conversation to some other topic.

"Amidst this willingness to be pleased, and labour to please, I had quickly reason to imagine that some painful sentiment pressed upon his mind. He often looked up earnestly towards the sun, and let his voice fall in the midst of his discourse. He would sometimes, when we were alone, gaze upon me in silence with the air of a man who longed to speak what he was yet resolved to suppress. He would often send for me with vehement injunctions of haste, though, when I came to him, he had nothing extraordinary to say. And sometimes, when I was leaving him, would call me back, pause a few moments, and then dismiss me."

Chapter 41

THE ASTRONOMER DISCOVERS THE CAUSE OF HIS UNEASINESS

"At last the time came when the secret burst his reserve. We were sitting together last night in the turret of his house, watching the emersion of a sattelite of Jupiter. A sudden tempest clouded the sky, and disappointed our observation. We sat awhile silent in the dark, and then he addressed himself to me in these words: 'Imlac, I have long considered thy friendship as the greatest blessing of my life. Integrity without knowledge is weak and useless, and knowledge without integrity is dangerous and dreadful. I have found in thee all the qualities requisite for trust,—benevolence, experience, and fortitude. I have long discharged an office which I

43. **emersion,** reappearance after eclipse.

must soon quit at the call of nature, and shall rejoice in the hour of imbecility and pain to devolve it upon thee.'

"I thought myself honoured by this testimony, and protested, that whatever could conduce to his happiness would add likewise to mine.

"'Hear, Imlac, what thou wilt not without difficulty credit. I have possessed for five years the regulation of weather, and the distribution of the seasons; the sun has listened to my dictates, and passed from tropic to tropic by my direction; the clouds at my call have poured their waters, and the Nile has overflowed at my command; I have restrained the rage of the Dog-star, and mitigated the fervours of the Crab. The winds alone, of all the elemental powers, have hitherto refused my authority, and multitudes have perished by equinoctial tempests, which I found myself unable to prohibit or restrain. I have administered this great office with exact justice, and made to the different nations of the earth an impartial dividend of rain and sunshine. What must have been the misery of half the globe, if I had limited the clouds to particular regions, or confined the sun to either side of the equator!'"

Chapter 42

THE OPINION OF THE ASTRONOMER IS EXPLAINED AND JUSTIFIED

"I suppose he discovered in me, through the obscurity of the room, some tokens of amazement and doubt, for, after a short pause, he proceeded thus:

"'Not to be easily credited will neither surprise nor offend me; for I am, probably, the first of human beings to whom this trust has been imparted. Nor do I know whether to deem this distinction a reward or punishment; since I have possessed it I have been far less happy than before, and nothing but the consciousness of good intention could have enabled me to support the weariness of unremitted vigilance.'

"'How long, Sir,' said I, 'has this great office been in your hands?'

"'About ten years ago,' said he, 'my daily observations of the changes of the sky led me to consider whether, if I had the power of the seasons, I could confer greater plenty upon the inhabitants of the earth. This contemplation fastened on my mind, and I sat days and nights in imaginary dominion, pouring upon this country and that the showers of fertility, and seconding every fall of rain with a due proportion of sunshine. I had yet only the will to do good, and did not imagine that I should ever have the power.

" 'One day, as I was looking on the fields withering with heat, I felt in my mind a sudden wish that I could send rain on the southern mountains, and raise the Nile to an inundation. In the hurry of my imagination I commanded rain to fall, and by comparing the time of my command with that of the inundation, I found that the clouds had listened to my lips.'

" 'Might not some other cause,' said I, 'produce this concurrence? The Nile does not always rise on the same day.'

" 'Do not believe,' said he, with impatience, 'that such objections could escape me: I reasoned long against my own conviction, and laboured against truth with the utmost obstinacy. I sometimes suspected myself of madness, and should not have dared to impart this secret but to a man like you, capable of distinguishing the wonderful from the impossible, and the incredible from the false.'

" 'Why, Sir,' said I, 'do you call that incredible, which you know, or think you know, to be true?'

" 'Because,' said he, 'I cannot prove it by any external evidence; and I know too well the laws of demonstration to think that my conviction ought to influence another, who cannot, like me, be conscious of its force. I, therefore, shall not attempt to gain credit by disputation. It is sufficient that I feel this power, that I have long possessed, and every day exerted it. But the life of man is short, the infirmities of age increase upon me, and the time will soon come, when the regulator of the year must mingle with the dust. The care of appointing a successor has long disturbed me; the night and the day have been spent in comparisons of all the characters which have come to my knowledge, and I have yet found none so worthy as thyself.' "

Chapter 43

THE ASTRONOMER LEAVES IMLAC HIS DIRECTIONS

" 'Hear, therefore, what I shall impart with attention, such as the welfare of a world requires. If the task of a king be considered as difficult, who has the care only of a few millions, to whom he cannot do much good or harm, what must be the anxiety of him on whom depends the action of the elements, and the great gifts of light and heat!—Hear me therefore with attention.

" 'I have diligently considered the position of the earth and sun, and formed innumerable schemes in which I changed their situation. I have sometimes turned aside the axis of the earth, and sometimes varied the ecliptic of the sun: but I have found it impossible to make a disposition by which the world may be advantaged; what one region gains, another loses by any imaginable alteration, even without considering the distant parts of the solar system with which we are unacquainted. Do not, therefore, in thy administration of the year, indulge thy pride by innovation; do not please thyself with thinking, that thou canst make thyself renowned to all future ages, by disordering the seasons. The memory of mischief is no desirable fame. Much less will it become thee to let kindness or interest prevail. Never rob other countries of rain to pour it on thine own. For us the Nile is sufficient.'

"I promised that, when I possessed the power, I would use it with inflexible integrity; and he dismissed me, pressing my hand. 'My heart,' said he, 'will be now at rest, and my benevolence will no more destroy my quiet; I have found a man of wisdom and virtue, to whom I can cheerfully bequeath the inheritance of the sun.' "

The prince heard this narration with very serious regard; but the princess smiled, and Pekuah convulsed herself with laughter. "Ladies," said Imlac, "to mock the heaviest of human afflictions is neither charitable nor wise. Few can attain this man's knowledge, and few practise his virtues; but all may suffer his calamity. Of the uncertainties of our present state, the most dreadful and alarming is the uncertain continuance of reason."

The princess was recollected, and the favourite was abashed. Rasselas, more deeply affected, inquired of Imlac, whether he thought such maladies of the mind frequent, and how they were contracted?

Chapter 44

THE DANGEROUS PREVALENCE OF IMAGINATION

"Disorders of intellect," answered Imlac, "happen much more often than superficial observers will easily believe. Perhaps, if we speak with rigorous exactness, no human mind is in its right state. There is no man whose imagination does not sometimes predominate over his reason, who can regulate his attention wholly by his will, and whose ideas will come and go at his command. No man will be found in whose mind airy notions do not sometimes tyrannize, and force him to hope or fear beyond the limits of sober probability. All power of fancy over reason is a degree of insanity; but while this power is such as we can control and repress, it is not visible to others, nor considered as any depravation of the mental faculties: it is not pronounced madness but when it comes ungovernable, and apparently influences speech or action.

"To indulge the power of fiction, and send imagination out upon the wing, is often the sport of those who delight too much in silent speculation. When we are alone we are not always busy; the labour of excogitation is too violent to last long; the ardour of inquiry will sometimes give way to idleness or satiety. He who has nothing external that can divert him, must find pleasure in his own thoughts, and must conceive himself what he is not; for who is pleased with what he is? He then expatiates in boundless futurity, and culls from all imaginable conditions that which for the present moment he should most desire, amuses his desires with impossible enjoyments, and confers upon his pride unattainable dominion. The mind dances from scene to scene, unites all pleasures in all combinations, and riots in delights, which nature and fortune, with all their bounty, cannot bestow.

"In time, some particular train of ideas fixes the attention, all other intellectual gratifications are rejected, the mind, in weariness or leisure, recurs constantly to the favourite conception, and feasts on the luscious falsehood, whenever she is offended with the bitterness of truth. By degrees the reign of fancy is confirmed; she grows first imperious, and in time despotic. Then fictions begin to operate as realities, false opinions fasten upon the mind, and life passes in dreams of rapture or of anguish.

"This, Sir, is one of the dangers of solitude, which the hermit has confessed not always to promote goodness, and the astronomer's misery has proved to be not always propitious to wisdom."

"I will no more," said the favourite, "imagine myself the queen of Abissinia. I have often spent the hours, which the princess gave to my own disposal, in adjusting ceremonies and regulating the court; I have repressed the pride of the powerful, and granted the petitions of the poor; I have built new palaces in more happy situations, planted groves upon the tops of mountains, and have exulted in the beneficence of royalty, till, when the princess entered, I had almost forgotten to bow down before her."

"And I," said the princess, "will not allow myself any more to play the shepherdess in my waking dreams. I have often soothed my thoughts with the quiet and innocence of pastoral employments, till I have in my chamber heard the winds whistle, and the sheep bleat; sometimes freed the lamb entangled in the thicket, and sometimes with my crook encountered the wolf. I have a dress like that of the village maids, which I put on to help my imagination, and a pipe on which I play softly, and suppose myself followed by my flocks."

"I will confess," said the prince, "an indulgence of fantastic delight more dangerous than yours. I have frequently endeavoured to image the possibility of a perfect government, by which all wrong should be restrained, all vice reformed, and all the subjects preserved in tranquillity and innocence. This thought produced innumerable schemes of reformation, and dictated many useful regulations and salutary edicts. This has been the sport, and sometimes the labour, of my solitude; and I start, when I think with how little anguish I once supposed the death of my father and my brothers."

"Such," says Imlac, "are the effects of visionary schemes: when we first form them we know them to be absurd, but familiarize them by degrees, and in time lose sight of their folly."

Chapter 45

THEY DISCOURSE WITH AN OLD MAN

The evening was now far past, and they rose to return home. As they walked along the bank of the Nile, delighted with the beams of the moon quivering on the water, they saw at a small distance an old man, whom the prince had often heard in the assembly of the sages. "Yonder," said he, "is one whose years have calmed his passions, but not clouded his reason: let us close the disquisitions of the night, by inquiring what are his sentiments of his own state, that we may know whether youth alone is to struggle with vexation, and whether any better hope remains for the latter part of life."

Here the sage approached and saluted them. They invited him to join their walk, and prattled a while, as acquaintance that had unexpectedly met one another. The old man was cheerful and talkative, and the way seemed short in his company. He was pleased to find himself not disregarded, accompanied them to their house, and, at the prince's request, entered with them. They placed him in the seat of honour, and set wine and conserves before him.

"Sir," said the princess, "an evening walk must give to a man of learning, like you, pleasures which ignorance and youth can hardly conceive. You know the qualities and the causes of all that you behold, the laws by which the river flows, the periods in which the planets perform their revolutions. Everything must supply you with contemplation, and renew the consciousness of your own dignity."

"Lady," answered he, "let the gay and the vigorous expect pleasure in their excursions; it is enough that age can obtain ease. To me the world has lost its novelty: I look round, and see what I remember to have seen in happier days. I rest against a tree, and consider, that in the same shade I once disputed upon the annual overflow of the Nile with a friend who is now silent in the grave. I cast my eyes upward, fix them on the changing moon, and think with pain on the vicissitudes of life. I have ceased to take much delight in physical truth; for what have I to do with those things which I am soon to leave?"

"You may at least recreate yourself," said Imlac, "with the recollection of an honourable and useful life, and enjoy the praise which all agree to give you."

"Praise," said the sage with a sigh, "is to an old man an empty sound. I have neither mother to be delighted with the reputation of her son, nor wife to partake the honours of her husband. I have outlived my friends and my rivals. Nothing is now of much importance; for I cannot extend my interest beyond myself. Youth is delighted with applause, because it is considered as the earnest of some future good, and because the prospect of life is far extended: but to me, who am now declining to decrepitude, there is little to be feared from the malevolence of men, and yet less to be hoped from their affection or esteem. Something they may yet take away, but they can give me nothing. Riches would now be useless, and high employment would be pain. My retrospect of life recalls to my view many opportunities of good neglected, much time squandered upon trifles, and more lost in idleness and vacancy. I leave many great designs unattempted, and many great attempts unfinished. My mind is burthened with no heavy crime, and therefore I compose myself to tranquillity; endeavour to abstract my thoughts from hopes and cares, which, though reason knows them to be vain, still try to keep their old possession of the heart; expect, with serene humility, that hour which nature cannot long delay; and hope to possess, in a better state, that happiness which here I could not find, and that virtue which here I have not attained."

He arose and went away, leaving his audience not much elated with the hope of long life. The prince consoled himself with remarking, that it was not reasonable to be disappointed by this account; for age had never been considered as the season of felicity, and if it was possible to be easy in decline and weakness, it was likely that the days of vigour and alacrity might be happy: that the noon of life might be bright, if the evening could be calm.

The princess suspected that age was querulous and malignant, and delighted to repress the expectations of those who had newly entered the world. She had seen the possessors of estates look with envy on their heirs, and known many who enjoy pleasure no longer than they can confine it to themselves.

Pekuah conjectured that the man was older than he appeared, and was willing to impute his complaints to delirious dejection: or else supposed that he had been unfortunate, and was therefore discontented; "For nothing," said she, "is more common than to call our own condition the condition of life."

Imlac, who had no desire to see them depressed, smiled at the comforts which they could so readily procure to themselves, and remembered, that at the same age, he was equally confident of unmingled prosperity, and equally fertile of consolatory expedients. He forbore to force upon them unwelcome knowledge, which time itself would too soon impress. The princess and her lady retired; the madness of the astronomer hung upon their minds, and they desired Imlac to enter upon his office, and delay next morning the rising of the sun.

Chapter 46

THE PRINCESS AND PEKUAH VISIT THE ASTRONOMER

The princess and Pekuah having talked in private of Imlac's astronomer, thought his character at once so amiable and so strange, that they could not be satisfied without a nearer knowledge; and Imlac was requested to find the means of bringing them together.

This was somewhat difficult. The philosopher had never received any visits from women, though he lived in a city that had in it many Europeans who followed the manners of their own countries, and many from other parts of the world, that lived there with European liberty. The ladies would not be refused, and several schemes were proposed for the accomplishment of their design. It was proposed to introduce them as strangers in distress, to whom the sage was always accessible; but, after some deliberation, it appeared that by this artifice no acquaintance could be formed, for their conversation would be short, and they could not decently importune him often. "This," said Rasselas, "is true; but I have yet a stronger objection against the misrepresentation of your state. I have always considered it as treason against the great republic of human nature, to make any man's virtues the means of deceiving him whether on great or little occasions. All imposture weakens confidence, and chills benevolence. When the sage finds that you are not what you seemed, he will feel the resentment natural to a man who, conscious of great abilities, discovers that he has been tricked by understandings meaner than his own, and, perhaps, the distrust, which he can never afterwards wholly lay aside, may stop the voice of counsel, and close the hand of charity; and where will you find the power of restoring his benefactions to mankind, or his peace to himself?"

To this no reply was attempted, and Imlac began to hope that their curiosity would subside; but next day Pekuah told him she had now found an honest pretence for a visit to the astronomer, for she would solicit permission to continue under him the studies in which she had been initiated by the Arab, and the princess might go with her either as a fellow-student, or because a woman could not decently come alone. "I am afraid," said Imlac, "that he will be soon weary of your company: men advanced far in knowledge do not love to repeat the elements of their art, and I am not certain that even of the elements, as he will deliver them, connected with inferences, and mingled with reflections, you are a very capable auditress." "That," said Pekuah, "must be my care; I ask of you only to take me thither. My knowledge is, perhaps, more than you imagine it, and, by concurring always with his opinions, I shall make him think it greater than it is."

The astronomer, in pursuance of this resolution, was told that a foreign lady, travelling in search of knowledge, had heard of his reputation, and was desirous to become his scholar. The uncommonness of the proposal raised at once his surprise and curiosity: and when, after a short deliberation, he consented to admit her, he could not stay without impatience till the next day.

The ladies dressed themselves magnificently, and were attended by Imlac to the astronomer, who was pleased to see himself approached with respect by persons of so splendid an appearance. In the exchange of the first civilities he was timorous and bashful; but when the talk became regular, he recollected his powers, and justified the character which Imlac had given. Inquiring of Pekuah, what could have turned her inclination toward astronomy, he received from her a history of her adventure at the pyramid, and of the time passed in the Arab's island. She told her tale with ease and elegance, and her conversation took possession of his heart. The discourse was then turned to astronomy. Pekuah displayed what she knew. He looked upon her as a prodigy of genius, and entreated her not to desist from a study which she had so happily begun.

They came again and again, and were every time more welcome than before. The sage endeavoured to amuse them, that they might prolong their visits, for he found his thoughts grow brighter in their company; the clouds of solicitude vanished by degrees, as he forced himself to entertain them, and he grieved when he was left at their departure to his old employment of regulating the seasons.

The princess and her favourite had now watched his lips for several months, and could not catch a single word from which they could judge whether he continued, or not, in the opinion of his preternatural commission. They often contrived to bring him to an open declaration; but he easily eluded all their attacks, and on which side soever they pressed him, escaped from them to some other topic.

As their familiarity increased, they invited him often to the house of Imlac, where they distinguished him by extraordinary respect. He began gradually to delight in sublunary pleasures. He came early, and departed late; laboured to recommend himself by assiduity and compliance; excited their curiosity after new arts, that they might still want his assistance; and when they made any excursion of pleasure or inquiry, entreated to attend them.

By long experience of his integrity and wisdom, the prince and his sister were convinced that he might be trusted without danger; and lest he should draw any false hopes from the civilities which he received, discovered to him their condition, with the motives of their journey, and required his opinion on the choice of life.

"Of the various conditions which the world spreads before you, which you shall prefer," said the sage, "I am not able to instruct you. I can only tell that I have chosen wrong. I have passed my time in study without experience; in the attainment of sciences which can, for the most part, be but remotely useful to mankind. I have purchased knowledge at the expense of all the common comforts of life: I have missed the endearing elegance of female friendship, and the happy commerce of domestic tenderness. If I have obtained any prerogatives above other students, they have been accompanied with fear, disquiet, and scrupulosity; but even of these prerogatives, whatever they were, I have, since my thoughts have been diversified by more intercourse with the world, begun to question the reality. When I have been for a few days lost in pleasing dissipation, I am always tempted to think that my inquiries have ended in error, and that I have suffered much, and suffered it in vain."

Imlac was delighted to find that the sage's understanding was breaking through its mists, and resolved to detain him from the planets till he should forget his task of ruling them, and reason should recover its original influence.

From this time the astronomer was received into familiar friendship, and partook of all their projects and pleasures. His respect kept him attentive, and the activity of Rasselas did not leave much time unengaged. Something was always to be done; the day was spent in making observations which furnished talk for the evening, and the evening was closed with a scheme for the morrow.

The sage confessed to Imlac, that since he had mingled in the gay tumults of life, and divided his hours by a succession of amusements, he found the conviction of his authority over the skies fade gradually from his mind, and began to trust less to an opinion which he never could prove to others, and which he now found subject to variation, from causes in which reason had no part. "If I am accidentally left alone for a few hours," said he, "my inveterate persuasion rushes upon my soul, and my thoughts are chained down by some irresistible violence; but they are soon disentangled by the prince's conversation, and instantaneously released at the entrance of Pekuah. I am like a man habitually afraid of spectres, who is set at ease by a lamp, and wonders at the dread which harassed him in the dark; yet, if his lamp be extinguished, feels again the terrors which he knows that when it is light he shall feel no more. But I am sometimes afraid lest I indulge my quiet by criminal negligence, and voluntarily forget the great charge with which I am intrusted. If I favour myself in a known error, or am determined by my own ease in a doubtful question of this importance, how dreadful is my crime!"

"No disease of the imagination," answered Imlac, "is so difficult of cure, as that which is complicated with the dread of guilt; fancy and conscience then act interchangeably upon us, and so often shift their places, that the illusions of one are not distinguished from the dictates of the other. If fancy presents images not moral or religious, the mind drives them away when they give it pain, but when melancholic notions take the form of duty, they lay hold on the faculties without opposition, because we are afraid to exclude or banish them. For this reason the superstitious are often melancholy, and the melancholy almost always superstitious.

"But do not let the suggestions of timidity overpower your better reason; the danger of neglect can be but as the probability of the obligation, which, when you consider it with freedom, you find very little, and that little growing every day less. Open your heart to the influence of the light, which, from time to time, breaks in upon you: when scruples importune you, which you in your lucid moments know to be vain, do not stand to parley, but fly to business or to Pekuah, and keep this thought always prevalent, that you are only one atom of the mass of humanity, and have neither such virtue nor vice, as that you should be singled out for supernatural favours or afflictions."

Chapter 47

THE PRINCE ENTERS, AND BRINGS A NEW TOPIC

"All this," said the astronomer, "I have often thought, but my reason has been so long subjugated by an uncontrollable and overwhelming idea, that it durst not confide in its own decisions. I now see how fatally I betrayed my quiet, by suffering chimeras to prey upon me in secret; but melancholy shrinks from communication, and I never found a man before, to whom I could impart my troubles, though I had been certain of relief. I rejoice to find my own sentiments confirmed by yours, who are not easily deceived, and can have no motive or purpose to deceive. I hope that time and variety will dissipate the gloom that has so long surrounded me, and the latter part of my days will be spent in peace."

"Your learning and virtue," said Imlac, "may justly give you hopes."

Rasselas then entered with the princess and Pekuah, and inquired whether they had contrived any new diversion for the next day? "Such," said Nekayah, "is the state of life, that none are happy but by the anticipation of change: the change itself is nothing; when we have made it, the next wish is to change again. The world is not yet exhausted; let me see something to-morrow which I never saw before."

"Variety," said Rasselas, "is so necessary to content, that even the happy valley disgusted me by the recurrence of its luxuries; yet I could not forbear to reproach myself with impatience, when I saw the monks of St. Anthony support, without complaint, a life, not of uniform delight, but uniform hardship."

"Those men," answered Imlac, "are less wretched in their silent convent than the Abissinian princes in their prison of pleasure. Whatever is done by the monks is incited by an adequate and reasonable motive. Their labour supplies them with necessaries; it therefore cannot be omitted, and is certainly rewarded. Their devotion prepares them for another state, and reminds them of its approach, while it fits them for it. Their time is regularly distributed; one duty succeeds another, so that they are not left open to the distraction of unguided choice, nor lost in the shades of listless inactivity. There is a certain task to be performed at an appropriated hour; and their toils are cheerful, because they consider them as acts of piety, by which they are always advancing towards endless felicity."

"Do you think," said Nekayah, "that the monastic rule is a more holy and less imperfect state than any other? May not he equally hope for future happiness who converses openly with mankind, who succours the distressed by his charity, instructs the ignorant by his learning, and contributes by his industry to the general system of life; even though he should omit some of the mortifications which are practised in the cloister, and allow himself such harmless delights as his condition may place within his reach?"

"This," said Imlac, "is a question which has long divided the wise, and perplexed the good. I am afraid to decide on either part. He that lives well in the world is better than he that lives well in a monastery. But, perhaps, every one is not able to stem the temptations of public life; and if he cannot conquer, he may properly retreat. Some have little power to do good, and have likewise little strength to resist evil. Many are weary of their conflicts with adversity, and are willing to eject those passions which have long busied them in vain. And many are dismissed by age and diseases from the more laborious duties of society. In monasteries the weak and timorous may be happily sheltered, the weary may repose, and the penitent may meditate. Those retreats of prayer and contemplation have something so congenial to the mind of man, that, perhaps, there is scarcely one that does not purpose to close his life in pious abstraction, with a few associates serious as himself."

"Such," said Pekuah, "has often been my wish, and I have heard the princess declare that she should not willingly die in a crowd."

"The liberty of using harmless pleasures," proceeded Imlac, "will not be disputed; but it is still to be examined what pleasures are harmless. The evil of any pleasure that Nekayah can image is not in the act itself, but in its consequences. Pleasure, in itself harmless, may become mischievous, by endearing to us a state which we know to be transient and probatory, and withdrawing our thoughts from that, of which every hour brings us nearer to the beginning, and of which no length of time will bring us to the end. Mortification is not virtuous in itself, nor has any other use, but that it disengages us from the allurements of sense. In the state of future perfection, to which we all aspire, there will be pleasure without danger, and security without restraint."

The princess was silent, and Rasselas, turning to the astronomer, asked him whether he could not delay her retreat, by shewing her something which she had not seen before.

"Your curiosity," said the sage, "has been so general, and your pursuit of knowledge so vigorous, that novelties are not now very easily to be found; but what you can no longer procure from the living may be given by the dead. Among the wonders of this country are the catacombs, or the ancient repositories, in which the bodies of the earliest generations were lodged, and where, by the virtue of the gums which embalmed them, they yet remain without corruption."

"I know not," said Rasselas, "what pleasure the sight of the catacombs can afford; but, since nothing else is offered, I am resolved to view them, and shall place this with many other things which I have done because I would do something."

They hired a guard of horsemen, and the next day visited the catacombs. When they were about to descend into the sepulchral caves, "Pekuah," said the princess, "we are now again invading the habitations of the dead; I know that you will stay behind; let me find you safe when I return." "No, I will not be left," answered Pekuah, "I will go down between you and the prince."

They then all descended, and roved with wonder through the labyrinth of subterraneous passages, where the bodies were laid in rows on either side.

Chapter 48

IMLAC DISCOURSES ON THE NATURE OF THE SOUL

"What reason," said the prince, "can be given why the Egyptians should thus expensively preserve those carcasses which some nations consume with fire, others lay to mingle with the earth, and all agree to remove from their sight, as soon as decent rites can be performed?"

"The original of ancient customs," said Imlac, "is commonly unknown; for the practice often continues when the cause has ceased; and concerning superstitious ceremonies it is vain to conjecture; for what reason did not dictate, reason cannot explain. I have long believed that the practice of embalming arose only from tenderness to the remains of relations or friends, and to this opinion I am more inclined, because it seems impossible that this care should have been general: had all the dead been embalmed, their repositories must in time have been more spacious than the dwellings of the living. I suppose only the rich or honourable were secured from corruption, and the rest left to the course of nature.

"But it is commonly supposed that the Egyptians believed the soul to live as long as the body continued undissolved, and therefore tried this method of eluding death."

"Could the wise Egyptians," said Nekayah, "think so grossly of the soul? If the soul could once survive its separation, what could it afterwards receive or suffer from the body?"

"The Egyptians would doubtless think erroneously," said the astronomer, "in the darkness of heathenism, and the first dawn of philosophy. The nature of the soul is still disputed amidst all our opportunities of clearer knowledge. Some yet say that it may be material, who, nevertheless, believe it to be immortal."

"Some," answered Imlac, "have indeed said that the soul is material, but I can scarcely believe that any man has thought it, who knew how to think; for all the conclusions of reason enforce the immateriality of mind, and all the notices of sense and investigations of science concur to prove the unconsciousness of matter.

"It was never supposed that cogitation is inherent in matter, or that every particle is a thinking being. Yet, if any part of matter be devoid of thought, what part can we suppose to think? Matter can differ from matter only in form, density, bulk, motion, and direction of motion: to which of these, however varied or combined, can consciousness be annexed? To be round or square, to be solid or fluid, to be great or little, to be moved slowly or swiftly one way or another, are modes of material existence, all equally alien from the nature of cogitation. If matter be once without thought, it can only be made to think by some new modification, but all the modifications which it can admit are equally unconnected with cogitative powers."

"But the materialists," said the astronomer, "urge that matter may have qualities with which we are unacquainted."

"He who will determine," returned Imlac, "against that which he knows, because there may be something which he knows not; he that can set hypothetical possibility against acknowledged certainty, is not to be admitted among reasonable beings. All that we know of matter is, that matter is inert, senseless, and lifeless; and if this conviction cannot be opposed but by referring us to something that we know not, we have all the evidence that human intellect can admit. If that which is known may be over-ruled by that which is unknown, no being, not omniscient, can arrive at certainty."

"Yet let us not," said the astronomer, "too arrogantly limit the Creator's power."

"It is no limitation of omnipotence," replied the poet, "to suppose that one thing is not consistent with another, that the same proposition cannot be at once true and false, that the same number cannot be even and odd, that cogitation cannot be conferred on that which is created incapable of cogitation."

"I know not," said Nekayah, "any great use of

this question. Does that immateriality, which in my opinion you have sufficiently proved, necessarily include eternal duration?"

"Of immateriality," said Imlac, "our ideas are negative, and therefore obscure. Immateriality seems to imply a natural power of perpetual duration as a consequence of exemption from all causes of decay: whatever perishes, is destroyed by the solution of its contexture, and separation of its parts; nor can we conceive how that which has no parts, and therefore admits no solution, can be naturally corrupted or impaired."

"I know not," said Rasselas, "how to conceive anything without extension; what is extended must have parts, and you allow, that whatever has parts may be destroyed."

"Consider your own conceptions," replied Imlac, "and the difficulty will be less. You will find substance without extension. An ideal form is no less real than material bulk: yet an ideal form has no extension. It is no less certain, when you think on a pyramid, that your mind possesses the idea of a pyramid, than that the pyramid itself is standing. What space does the idea of a pyramid occupy more than the idea of a grain of corn? or how can either idea suffer laceration? As is the effect, such is the cause: as thought, such is the power that thinks; a power impassive and indiscerptible."

"But the Being," said Nekayah, "whom I fear to name, the Being which made the soul, can destroy it."

"He, surely, can destroy it," answered Imlac, "since, however unperishable, it receives from a superior nature its power of duration. That it will not perish by any inherent cause of decay, or principle of corruption, may be shown by philosophy; but philosophy can tell no more. That it will not be annihilated by him that made it, we must humbly learn from higher authority."

The whole assembly stood awhile silent and collected. "Let us return," said Rasselas, "from this scene of mortality. How gloomy would be these mansions of the dead to him who did not know that he should never die; that what now acts shall continue its agency, and what now thinks shall think on for ever. Those that lie here stretched before us, the wise and the powerful of ancient times, warn us to remember the shortness of our present state: they were, perhaps, snatched away while they were busy, like us, in the choice of life."

"To me," said the princess, "the choice of life is become less important; I have hereafter to think only on the choice of eternity."

They then hastened out of the caverns, and, under the protection of their guard, returned to Cairo.

Chapter 49

THE CONCLUSION, IN WHICH NOTHING IS CONCLUDED

It was now the time of the inundation of the Nile. A few days after their visit to the catacombs, the river began to rise.

They were confined to their house. The whole region being under water gave them no invitation to any excursions, and, being well supplied with materials for talk, they diverted themselves with comparisons of the different forms of life which they had observed, and with various schemes of happiness which each of them had formed.

Pekuah was never so much charmed with any place as the convent of St. Anthony, where the Arab restored her to the princess, and wished only to fill it with pious maidens, and to be made prioress of the order. She was weary of expectation and disgust, and would gladly be fixed in some unvariable state.

The princess thought that of all sublunary things knowledge was the best. She desired first to learn all sciences, and then purposed to found a college of learned women, in which she would preside, that, by conversing with the old, and educating the young, she might divide her time between the acquisition and communication of wisdom, and raise up for the next age models of prudence, and patterns of piety.

The prince desired a little kingdom, in which he might administer justice in his own person, and see all the parts of government with his own eyes; but he could never fix the limits of his dominion, and was always adding to the number of his subjects.

Imlac and the astronomer were contented to be driven along the stream of life, without directing their course to any particular port.

Of these wishes that they had formed, they well knew that none could be obtained. They deliberated a while what was to be done, and resolved, when the inundation should cease, to return to Abissinia.

from THE PREFACE TO SHAKESPEARE

Johnson's *Shakespeare* is not one of the greater and more influential editions, although it contains many valuable notes and clarifications of difficult passages. It is remembered today chiefly on account of the editor's thoughtful and elaborate Preface, in which his good sense triumphs over his Neoclassical predilection for the ancients, authority, tradition, and the "rules." About one-third of this Preface is here presented.

THE poet of whose works I have undertaken the revision may now begin to assume the dignity of an ancient, and claim the privilege of established fame and prescriptive veneration. He has long outlived his century, the term commonly fixed as the test of literary merit. Whatever advantages he might once derive from personal allusions, local customs, or temporary opinions have for many years been lost; and every topick of merriment or motive of sorrow which the modes of artificial life afforded him now only obscure the scenes which they once illuminated. The effects of favour and competition are at an end; the tradition of his friendships and his enmities has perished; his works support no opinion with arguments, nor supply any faction with invectives; they can neither indulge vanity, nor gratify malignity; but are read without any other reason than the desire of pleasure, and are therefore praised only as pleasure is obtained; yet, thus unassisted by interest or passion, they have past through variations of taste and changes of manners, and, as they devolved from one generation to another, have received new honours at every transmission.

But because human judgment, though it be gradually gaining upon certainty, never becomes infallible; and approbation, though long continued, may yet be only the approbation of prejudice or fashion; it is proper to inquire, by what peculiarities of excellence Shakespeare has gained and kept the favour of his countrymen.

Nothing can please many, and please long, but just representations of general nature. Particular manners can be known to few, and therefore few only can judge how nearly they are copied. The irregular combinations of fanciful invention may delight awhile, by that novelty of which the common satiety of life sends us all in quest; but the pleasures of sudden wonder are soon exhausted, and the mind can only repose on the stability of truth.

Shakespeare is, above all writers, at least above all modern writers, the poet of nature; the poet that holds up to his readers a faithful mirror of manners and of life. His characters are not modified by the customs of particular places, unpractised by the rest of the world; by the peculiarities of studies or professions, which can operate but upon small numbers; or by the accidents of transient fashions or temporary opinions: they are the genuine progeny of common humanity, such as the world will always supply, and observation will always find. His persons act and speak by the influence of those general passions and principles by which all minds are agitated, and the whole system of life is continued in motion. In the writings of other poets a character is too often an individual; in those of Shakespeare it is commonly a species.

It is from this wide extension of design that so much instruction is derived. It is this which fills the plays of Shakespeare with practical axioms and domestick wisdom. It was said of Euripides, that every verse was a precept; and it may be said of Shakespeare, that from his works may be collected a system of civil and economical prudence. Yet his real power is not shewn in the splendour of particular passages, but by the progress of his fable, and the tenor of his dialogue; and he that tries to recommend him by select quotations, will succeed like the pedant in Hierocles, who, when he offered his house to sale, carried a brick in his pocket as a specimen.

It will not easily be imagined how much Shakespeare excels in accommodating his sentiments to real life, but by comparing him with other authors. It was observed of the ancient schools of declamation, that the more diligently they were frequented, the more was the student disqualified for the world, because he found nothing there which he should ever meet in any other place. The same remark may be applied to every stage but that of Shakespeare. The theatre, when it is under any other direction, is peopled by such characters as were never seen, conversing in a language which was never heard, upon topics which will never arise in the commerce of mankind. But the dialogue of this author is often so evidently determined by the incident which produces it, and is pursued with so much ease and simplicity, that it seems scarcely to claim the merit of fiction, but to have been gleaned by diligent selection out of common conversation and common occurrences.

Upon every other stage the universal agent is love, by whose power all good and evil is distributed, and every action quickened or retarded.

28. **Hierocles,** an ancient compiler of jokes.

To bring a lover, a lady, and a rival into the fable; to entangle them in contradictory obligations, perplex them with oppositions of interest, and harass them with violence of desires inconsistent with each other; to make them meet in rapture, and part in agony; to fill their mouths with hyperbolical joy and outrageous sorrow; to distress them as nothing human ever was distressed; to deliver them as nothing human ever was delivered, is the business of a modern dramatist. For this, probability is violated, life is misrepresented, and language is depraved. But love is only one of many passions, and as it has no great influence upon the sum of life, it has little operation in the dramas of a poet, who caught his ideas from the living world, and exhibited only what he saw before him. He knew, that any other passion, as it was regular or exorbitant, was a cause of happiness or calamity.

Characters thus ample and general were not easily discriminated and preserved, yet perhaps no poet ever kept his personages more distinct from each other. I will not say, with Pope, that every speech may be assigned to the proper speaker, because many speeches there are which have nothing characteristical; but, perhaps, though some may be equally adapted to every person, it will be difficult to find that any can be properly transferred from the present possessor to another claimant. The choice is right, when there is reason for choice.

Other dramatists can only gain attention by hyperbolical or aggravated characters, by fabulous and unexampled excellence or depravity, as the writers of barbarous romances invigorated the reader by a giant and a dwarf; and he that should form his expectations of human affairs from the play, or from the tale, would be equally deceived. Shakespeare has no heroes; his scenes are occupied only by men who act and speak as the reader thinks that he should himself have spoken or acted on the same occasion: even where the agency is supernatural, the dialogue is level with life. Other writers disguise the most natural passions and most frequent incidents; so that he who contemplates them in the book will not know them in the world. Shakespeare approximates the remote, and familiarizes the wonderful; the event which he represents will not happen, but if it were possible, its effects would probably be such as he has assigned; and it may be said, that he has not only shewn human nature as it acts in real exigencies, but as it would be found in trials, to which it cannot be exposed.

This, therefore, is the praise of Shakespeare, that his drama is the mirror of life; that he who has mazed his imagination in following the phantoms which other writers raise up before him may here be cured of his delirious ecstasies, by reading human sentiments in human language; by scenes from which a hermit may estimate the transactions of the world, and a confessor predict the progress of the passions.

His adherence to general nature has exposed him to the censureof criticks, who form their judgments on narrower principles. Dennis and Rhymer think his Romans not sufficiently Roman, and Voltaire censures his kings as not completely royal. Dennis is offended that Menenius, a senator of Rome, should play the buffoon; and Voltaire perhaps thinks decency violated when the Danish usurper is represented as a drunkard. But Shakespeare always makes nature predominate over accident; and, if he preserves the essential character, is not very careful of distinctions superinduced and adventitious. His story requires Romans or kings, but he thinks only on men. He knew that Rome, like every other city, had men of all dispositions; and wanting a buffoon, he went into the senate-house for that which the senate-house would certainly have afforded him. He was inclined to show an usurper and a murderer not only odious, but despicable; he therefore added drunkenness to his other qualities, knowing that kings love wine like other men, and that wine exerts its natural power upon kings. These are the petty cavils of petty minds; a poet overlooks the casual distinction of country and conditions, as a painter, satisfied with the figure, neglects the drapery. . . .

Shakespeare with his excellencies has likewise faults, and faults sufficient to obscure and overwhelm any other merit. I shall shew them in the proportion in which they appear to me, without envious malignity or superstitious veneration. No question can be more innocently discussed than a dead poet's pretensions to renown; and little regard is due to that bigotry which sets candor higher than truth.

His first defect is that to which may be imputed most of the evil in books or in men. He sacrifices virtue to convenience, and is so much more careful to please than to instruct, that he seems to write without any moral purpose. From his writings indeed a system of social duty may be selected, for he that thinks reasonably must think morally; but his

11. **Dennis,** John Dennis, in his *Essay on the Genius and Writings of Shakespeare,* 1711.   12. **Rhymer,** Thomas Rymer, in his *Short View of Tragedy,* 1693.

precepts and axioms drop casually from him; he makes no just distribution of good or evil, nor is always careful to shew in the virtuous a disapprobation of the wicked; he carries his persons indifferently through right and wrong, and at the close dismisses them without further care, and leaves their examples to operate by chance. This fault the barbarity of his age cannot extenuate, for it is always a writer's duty to make the world better, and justice is a virtue independent on time or place.

The plots are often so loosely formed, that a very slight consideration may improve them, and so carelessly pursued, that he seems not always fully to comprehend his own design. He omits opportunities of instructing or delighting, which the train of his story seems to force upon him, and apparently rejects those exhibitions which would be more affecting, for the sake of those which are more easy.

It may be observed, that in many of his plays the latter part is evidently neglected. When he found himself near the end of his work, and in view of his reward, he shortened the labour to snatch the profit. He therefore remits his efforts where he should most vigorously exert them, and his catastrophe is improbably produced or imperfectly represented.

He had no regard to distinction of time or place, but gives to one age or nation, without scruple, the customs, institutions, and opinions of another, at the expense not only of likelihood but of possibility. These faults Pope has endeavoured, with more zeal than judgment, to transfer to his imagined interpolators. We need not wonder to find Hector quoting Aristotle, when we see the loves of Theseus and Hippolyta combined with the Gothick mythology of fairies. Shakespeare, indeed, was not the only violator of chronology, for in the same age Sidney, who wanted not the advantages of learning, has, in his *Arcadia*, confounded the pastoral with the feudal times, the days of innocence, quiet, and security with those of turbulence, violence, and adventure.

In his comick scenes he is seldom very successful when he engages his characters in reciprocations of smartness and contests of sarcasm; their jests are commonly gross, and their pleasantry licentious; neither his gentlemen nor his ladies have much delicacy, nor are sufficiently distinguished from his clowns by any appearance of refined manners. Whether he represented the real conversation of his time is not easy to determine; the reign of Elizabeth is commonly supposed to have been a time of stateliness, formality, and reserve, yet perhaps the relaxations of that severity were not very elegant. There must, however, have been always some modes of gaiety preferable to others, and a writer ought to choose the best.

In tragedy his performance seems constantly to be worse, as his labour is more. The effusions of passion, which exigence forces out, are for the most part striking and energetick; but whenever he solicits his invention, or strains his faculties, the offspring of his throes is tumour, meanness, tediousness, and obscurity.

In narration he affects a disproportionate pomp of diction, and a wearisome train of circumlocution, and tells the incident imperfectly in many words, which might have been more plainly delivered in few. Narration in dramatick poetry is naturally tedious, as it is unanimated and inactive, and obstructs the progress of the action; it should therefore always be rapid, and enlivened by frequent interruption. Shakespeare found it an encumbrance, and instead of lightening it by brevity, endeavoured to recommend it by dignity and splendour.

His declamations or set speeches are commonly cold and weak, for his power was the power of nature. When he endeavoured, like other tragick writers, to catch opportunities of amplification, and instead of inquiring what the occasion demanded, to shew how much his stores of knowledge could supply, he seldom escapes without the pity or resentment of his reader.

It is incident to him to be now-and-then entangled with an unwieldy sentiment, which he cannot well express, and will not reject; he struggles with it a while, and if it continues stubborn, comprises it in words such as occur, and leaves it to be disentangled and evolved by those who have more leisure to bestow upon it.

Not that always where the language is intricate the thought is subtle, or the image always great where the line is bulky. The equality of words to things is very often neglected, and trivial sentiments and vulgar ideas disappoint the attention, to which they are recommended by sonorous epithets and swelling figures.

But the admirers of this great poet have most reason to complain when he approaches nearest to his highest excellence, and seems fully resolved to sink them in dejection, and mollify them with tender emotions by the fall of greatness, the danger of innocence, or the crosses of love. What he does best, he soon ceases to do. He is not long soft and pathetic without some idle conceit, or contemptible equivocation. He no sooner begins to move, than he coun-

---

33–34. quoting Aristotle, in *Troilus and Cressida*, Act II, sc. 2, l. 166. **36. fairies,** in *A Midsummer Night's Dream*.

10. tumour, bombast.

teracts himself; and terror and pity, as they are rising in the mind, are checked and blasted by sudden frigidity.

A quibble is to Shakespeare what luminous vapours are to the traveller: he follows it at all adventures; it is sure to lead him out of his way, and sure to engulf him in the mire. It has some malignant power over his mind, and its fascinations are irresistible. Whatever be the dignity or profundity of his disquisition, whether he be enlarging knowledge or exalting affection, whether he be amusing attention with incidents or enchaining it in suspense, let but a quibble spring up before him, and he leaves his work unfinished. A quibble is the golden apple for which he will always turn aside from his career, or stoop from his elevation. A quibble, poor and barren as it is, gave him such delight, that he was content to purchase it by the sacrifice of reason, propriety, and truth. A quibble was to him the fatal Cleopatra for which he lost the world, and was content to lose it.

It will be thought strange, that, in enumerating the defects of this writer, I have not yet mentioned his neglect of the unities; his violation of those laws which have been instituted and established by the joint authority of poets and criticks.

For his other deviations from the art of writing I resign him to critical justice, without making any other demand in his favour than that which must be indulged to all human excellence; that his virtues be rated with his failings: but, from the censure which this irregularity may bring upon him I shall, with due reverence to that learning which I must oppose, adventure to try how I can defend him.

His histories, being neither tragedies nor comedies, are not subject to any of their laws. Nothing more is necessary to all the praise which they expect, than that the changes of action be so prepared as to be understood, that the incidents be various and affecting, and the characters consistent, natural, and distinct. No other unity is intended, and therefore none is to be sought.

In his other works he has well enough preserved the unity of action. He has not, indeed, an intrigue regularly perplexed and regularly unravelled; he does not endeavour to hide his design only to discover it, for this is seldom the order of real events, and Shakespeare is the poet of nature: but his plan has commonly what Aristotle requires, a beginning, a middle, and an end; one event is concatenated with another, and the conclusion follows by easy consequence. There are perhaps some incidents that might be spared, as in other poets there is much talk that only fills up time upon the stage; but the general system makes gradual advances, and the end of the play is the end of expectation.

To the unities of time and place he has shewn no regard; and perhaps a nearer view of the principles on which they stand will diminish their value, and withdraw from them the veneration which, from the time of Corneille, they have very generally received, by discovering that they have given more trouble to the poet than pleasure to the auditor.

The necessity of observing the unities of time and place arises from the supposed necessity of making the drama credible. The criticks hold it impossible, that an action of months or years can be possibly believed to pass in three hours; or that the spectator can suppose himself to sit in the theatre, while ambassadors go and return between distant kings, while armies are levied and towns besieged, while an exile wanders and returns, or till he whom they saw courting his mistress shall lament the untimely fall of his son. The mind revolts from evident falsehood, and fiction loses its force when it departs from the resemblance of reality.

From the narrow limitation of time necessarily arises the contraction of place. The spectator who knows that he saw the first act at Alexandria, cannot suppose that he sees the next at Rome, at a distance to which not the dragons of Medea could, in so short a time, have transported him; he knows with certainty that he has not changed his place, and he knows that place cannot change itself: that what was a house cannot become a plain; that what was Thebes can never be Persepolis.

Such is the triumphant language with which a critick exults over the misery of an irregular poet, and exults commonly without resistance or reply. It is time therefore to tell him, by the authority of Shakespeare, that he assumes as an unquestionable principle a position which, while his breath is forming it into words, his understanding pronounces to be false. It is false, that any representation is mistaken for reality; that any dramatick fable in its materiality was ever credible, or, for a single moment, was ever credited.

The objection arising from the impossibility of passing the first hour at Alexandria, and the next at Rome, supposes that when the play opens the spectator really imagines himself at Alexandria, and believes that his walk to the theatre has been a voyage to Egypt, and that he lives in the days of Antony and Cleopatra. Surely he that imagines this may imagine more. He that can take the stage at one time for the palace of the Ptolemies, may take it in

7. **Corneille,** Pierre (1606–1684), a French dramatist of the first rank.

half an hour for the promontory of Actium. Delusion, if delusion be admitted, has no certain limitation; if the spectator can be once persuaded that his old acquaintance are Alexander and Caesar, that a room illuminated with candles is the plain of Pharsalia or the bank of Granicus, he is in a state of elevation above the reach of reason or of truth, and from the heights of empyrean poetry may despise the circumscriptions of terrestrial nature. There is no reason why a mind thus wandering in ecstasy should count the clock, or why an hour should not be a century in that calenture of the brain that can make the stage a field.

The truth is, that the spectators are always in their senses, and know, from the first act to the last, that the stage is only a stage, and that the players are only players. They come to hear a certain number of lines recited with just gesture and elegant modulation. The lines relate to some action, and an action must be in some place; but the different actions that complete a story may be in places very remote from each other; and where is the absurdity of allowing that space to represent first Athens, and then Sicily, which was always known to be neither Sicily nor Athens, but a modern theatre?

By supposition, as place is introduced, time may be extended. The time required by the fable elapses for the most part between the acts; for, of so much of the action as is represented, the real and poetical duration is the same. If, in the first act, preparations for war against Mithridates are represented to be made in Rome, the event of the war may, without absurdity, be represented, in the catastrophe, as happening in Pontus; we know that there is neither war, nor preparation for war; we know that we are neither in Rome nor Pontus; that neither Mithridates nor Lucullus are before us. The drama exhibits successive imitations of successive actions, and why may not the second imitation represent an action that happened years after the first, if it be so connected with it that nothing but time can be supposed to intervene? Time is, of all modes of existence, most obsequious to the imagination; a lapse of years is as easily conceived as a passage of hours. In contemplation we easily contract the time of real actions, and therefore willingly permit it to be contracted when we only see their imitation.

It will be asked how the drama moves, if it is not credited. It is credited with all the credit due to a drama. It is credited, whenever it moves, as a just picture of a real original; as representing to the auditor what he would himself feel, if he were to do or suffer what is there feigned to be suffered or to be done. The reflection that strikes the heart is not that the evils before us are real evils, but that they are evils to which we ourselves may be exposed. If there be any fallacy, it is not that we fancy the players, but that we fancy ourselves, unhappy for a moment; but we rather lament the possibility than suppose the presence of misery, as a mother weeps over her babe when she remembers that death may take it from her. The delight of tragedy proceeds from our consciousness of fiction; if we thought murders and treasons real, they would please no more. . . .

Oliver Goldsmith
1728–1774

The career of Oliver Goldsmith provides a shining exception to whatever truth there may be in the adage that "a rolling stone gathers no moss." After graduating, with great difficulty, from Trinity College, Dublin, he thought at first of taking holy orders, but he failed in this, tradition tells us, because the scarlet breeches in which he presented himself before the bishop who was to examine him were not thought to indicate a seriously religious turn of mind. A year or so later he abandoned the tutorial position he had somehow gained in order to spend the small sum of money that was burning in his pocket. Next, with funds provided by an uncle, he started off for London with the intention of studying law, but got only as far as Dublin, where gamblers relieved him of his money and thus turned him away from a legal career. In 1753 he went to Edinburgh with some thought of studying medicine, and in the following year proceeded to Leyden with the same vague purpose. From there, playing his flute and debating in the universities for a livelihood, he drifted through Flanders, France, Germany, Switzerland, and Italy, making the "grand tour" on foot. At some time and place during these wandering years he seems to have acquired a medical degree. The year 1756 found him in London, working now as an apothecary's assistant, now as an usher in a school, and occasionally as a physician among the poor. As late as 1759 he was still thinking of going out as a doctor to the Coast of Coromandel, but in that year, when well over thirty, he began to do steady work as a writer. His first important publication was a brisk and good-humored attack upon the strongholds of scholarship entitled *An Enquiry into the Present State of Polite Learning in Europe.*

It is evident that Goldsmith had remarkable powers of concentrated application, for in the fourteen years of life that were left to him when he settled down in London he not only wrote, translated, and compiled a surprising number of "potboilers" such as his eight-volume *History of the Earth and Animated Nature*, but he attained almost the highest rank among the writers of his time in the widely sundered fields of the essay, the novel, comedy, and poetry. Few writers in the whole stretch of English literature have shown a versatility comparable with his, and yet the assertion of his friend Dr. Johnson is certainly true that he touched nothing which he did not adorn.

This record is the more remarkable because Goldsmith wrote always for money. His improvident habits kept him continually in debt to the booksellers for whom he wrote, and although he earned considerable sums, he never escaped from the laborious slavery of the hack writer in "Grub Street." Yet, during all the years in which he held starvation at bay with the point of his quill, Goldsmith somehow preserved the good-natured ease of a man who writes chiefly for his own pleasure, and consequently for the pleasure of others. He continued to be a "rolling stone" throughout his writing career, turning easily from verse to prose, from biography to criticism, from science to travel, and from sentiment to comedy. Thus in the midst of highly professional labors he maintained all the advantages of the cool and detached amateur. The miscellaneous information that he scraped together on a thousand topics never amounted to learning and so was never a burden. No cloud of weariness or anxiety ever dimmed the sunshine of his mind. No trouble of his own ever thwarted the outgoing sympathy of "the kindest heart in the world." It was by means of his warm humanity, his gifts of the heart, his embracing sympathy or fellow feeling, that he won the friendship of Bishop Percy, Dr. Johnson, Edmund Burke, and Sir Joshua Reynolds. This it was, also, that endeared him to hundreds of forgotten people to whom he was generous and kind. And this inward sunlight of Goldsmith's nature is shining even today, sent on to us by his simple, clear, gracious, and always musical prose style. If he is seldom profound, he is never tedious; and if he adds little to our knowledge and wisdom, at any rate he takes nothing from our sense of the goodness of life. Goldsmith is always his reader's friend.

Most of the acres of paper that Goldsmith covered with black marks during his fourteen years of confinement up two pairs of stairs may now be ignored without great loss. No responsible and informed elder person can seriously recommend to the youth of our day, however, that they ignore Goldsmith's novel *The Vicar of Wakefield*, or his essays in *The Citizen of the World*. His *Deserted Village* is one of the foremost masterpieces in the extensive literature of homesickness. And, finally, *She Stoops to Conquer*, although it is by no means the most correct and brilliant comedy of its time, is surely one of the most heart-easing things in our language, drenched with sunlight and laughter from end to end.

THE DESERTED VILLAGE

This didactic poem—published in 1770, the year of Wordsworth's birth—went through five editions in its first twelvemonth. Evidently, therefore, it expressed a mood in which many shared, as its great companion piece, Gray's *Elegy*, had done nineteen years before.

In some degree *The Deserted Village* is autobiographical, resting back upon Goldsmith's recollections of his childhood in the village of Lissoy in Ireland. Far more important in it, however, is the poet's firsthand knowledge of contemporary conditions in the ancient villages of England, where the Enclosure Acts and the Industrial Revolution were in his time swiftly destroying a pattern of life which had endured for more than a thousand years.

We do not completely dispose of this poem in calling it "sentimental." We have yet to see whether there is not a fundamental truth and warning in the central lines:

"Ill fares the land, to hastening ills a prey,
Where wealth accumulates and men decay."

TO SIR JOSHUA REYNOLDS

Dear Sir,—I can have no expectations in an address of this kind, either to add to your reputation, or to establish my own. You can gain nothing from my admiration, as I am ignorant of that art in which you are said to excel; and I may lose much by the severity of your judgment, as few have a juster taste in poetry than you. Setting interest therefore aside, to which I never paid much attention, I must be indulged at present in following my affections. The only dedication I ever made was to my brother,[1] because I loved him better than most other men. He is since dead. Permit me to inscribe this Poem to you.

[1] **brother.** Goldsmith dedicated his poem *The Traveller*, 1764, to his brother, the Rev. Henry Goldsmith.

How far you may be pleased with the versification and mere mechanical parts of this attempt, I don't pretend to enquire; but I know you will object (and indeed several of our best and wisest friends concur in the opinion) that the depopulation it deplores is nowhere to be seen, and the disorders it laments are only to be found in the poet's own imagination. To this I can scarce make any other answer than that I sincerely believe what I have written; that I have taken all possible pains, in my country excursions, for these four or five years past, to be certain of what I allege; and that all my views and enquiries have led me to believe those miseries real, which I here attempt to display. But this is not the place to enter into an enquiry, whether the country be depopulating, or not; the discussion would take up much room, and I should prove myself, at best, an indifferent politician, to tire the reader with a long preface, when I want his unfatigued attention to a long poem.

In regretting the depopulation of the country, I inveigh against the encrease of our luxuries; and here also I expect the shout of modern politicians against me. For twenty or thirty years past, it has been the fashion to consider luxury as one of the greatest national advantages, and all the wisdom of antiquity in that particular, as erroneous. Still however, I must remain a professed ancient on that head, and continue to think those luxuries prejudicial to states, by which so many vices are introduced, and so many kingdoms have been undone. Indeed so much has been poured out of late on the other side of the question, that, merely for the sake of novelty and variety, one would sometimes wish to be in the right.

I am, dear Sir,
Your sincere friend, and ardent admirer,
Oliver Goldsmith.

Sweet AUBURN! loveliest village of the plain,
Where health and plenty cheered the labouring swain,
Where smiling spring its earliest visit paid,
And parting summer's lingering blooms delayed:
Dear lovely bowers of innocence and ease,
Seats of my youth, when every sport could please,
How often have I loitered o'er thy green,
Where humble happiness endeared each scene;
How often have I paused on every charm,
The sheltered cot, the cultivated farm,   10
The never-failing brook, the busy mill,
The decent church that topped the neighbouring hill,
The hawthorn bush, with seats beneath the shade,
For talking age and whispering lovers made;
How often have I blessed the coming day,
When toil remitting lent its turn to play,
And all the village train, from labour free,
Led up their sports beneath the spreading tree;
While many a pastime circled in the shade,
The young contending as the old surveyed;   20
And many a gambol frolicked o'er the ground,
And sleights of art and feats of strength went round;
And still, as each repeated pleasure tired,
Succeeding sports the mirthful band inspired;
The dancing pair that simply sought renown,
By holding out to tire each other down;
The swain mistrustless of his smutted face,
While secret laughter tittered round the place;
The bashful virgin's side-long looks of love,
The matron's glance that would those looks reprove: 30
These were thy charms, sweet village; sports like these,
With sweet succession taught even toil to please;
These round thy bowers their cheerful influence shed,
These were thy charms—but all these charms are fled.

Sweet smiling village, loveliest of the lawn,
Thy sports are fled, and all thy charms withdrawn;
Amidst thy bowers the tyrant's hand is seen,
And desolation saddens all thy green:
One only master grasps the whole domain,
And half a tillage stints thy smiling plain.   40
No more thy glassy brook reflects the day,
But choked with sedges, works its weedy way.
Along thy glades, a solitary guest,
The hollow-sounding bittern guards its nest;
Amidst thy desert walks the lapwing flies,
And tires their echoes with unvaried cries.
Sunk are thy bowers in shapeless ruin all,
And the long grass o'ertops the mouldering wall;
And, trembling, shrinking from the spoiler's hand,
Far, far away, thy children leave the land.   50

Ill fares the land, to hastening ills a prey,
Where wealth accumulates and men decay;
Princes and lords may flourish, or may fade;
A breath can make them, as a breath has made;
But a bold peasantry, their country's pride,
When once destroyed, can never be supplied.

A time there was, ere England's griefs began,
When every rood of ground maintained its man;
For him light labour spread her wholesome store,
Just gave what life required, but gave no more: 60
His best companions, innocence and health;
And his best riches, ignorance of wealth.

But times are altered; trade's unfeeling train
Usurp the land, and dispossess the swain;
Along the lawn, where scattered hamlets rose,
Unwieldy wealth and cumbrous pomp repose;
And every want to opulence allied,
And every pang that folly pays to pride.
Those gentle hours that plenty bade to bloom,

Those calm desires that asked but little room, 70
Those healthful sports that graced the peaceful scene,
Lived in each look, and brightened all the green;
These, far departing, seek a kinder shore,
And rural mirth and manners are no more.

Sweet Auburn! parent of the blissful hour,
Thy glades forlorn confess the tyrant's power.
Here, as I take my solitary rounds,
Amidst thy tangling walks, and ruined grounds,
And, many a year elapsed, return to view
Where once the cottage stood, the hawthorn grew, 80
Remembrance wakes with all her busy train,
Swells at my breast, and turns the past to pain.

In all my wanderings round this world of care,
In all my griefs—and God has given my share—
I still had hopes my latest hours to crown,
Amidst these humble bowers to lay me down;
To husband out life's taper at the close,
And keep the flame from wasting by repose.
I still had hopes, for pride attends us still,
Amidst the swains to show my book-learned skill, 90
Around my fire an evening group to draw,
And tell of all I felt, and all I saw;
And, as a hare, whom hounds and horns pursue,
Pants to the place from whence at first she flew,
I still had hopes, my long vexations passed,
Here to return—and die at home at last.

O blest retirement, friend to life's decline,
Retreats from care, that never must be mine,
How happy he who crowns in shades like these
A youth of labour with an age of ease; 100
Who quits a world where strong temptations try,
And, since 'tis hard to combat, learns to fly!
For him no wretches, born to work and weep,
Explore the mine, or tempt the dangerous deep;
No surly porter stands in guilty state
To spurn imploring famine from the gate;
But on he moves to meet his latter end,
Angels around befriending virtue's friend;
Bends to the grave with unperceived decay,
While resignation gently slopes the way; 110
And, all his prospects brightening to the last,
His Heaven commences ere the world be past!

Sweet was the sound, when oft at evening's close
Up yonder hill the village murmur rose;
There, as I passed with careless steps and slow,
The mingling notes came softened from below;
The swain responsive as the milk-maid sung,
The sober herd that lowed to meet their young;
The noisy geese that gabbled o'er the pool,
The playful children just let loose from school; 120
The watchdog's voice that bayed the whispering wind,
And the loud laugh that spoke the vacant mind;
These all in sweet confusion sought the shade,
And filled each pause the nightingale had made.
But now the sounds of population fail,
No cheerful murmurs fluctuate in the gale,
No busy steps the grass-grown foot-way tread,
For all the bloomy flush of life is fled.
All but yon widowed, solitary thing
That feebly bends beside the plashy spring; 130
She, wretched matron, forced, in age, for bread,
To strip the brook with mantling cresses spread,
To pick her wintry faggot from the thorn,
To seek her nightly shed, and weep till morn;
She only left of all the harmless train,
The sad historian of the pensive plain.

Near yonder copse, where once the garden smiled,
And still where many a garden flower grows wild;
There, where a few torn shrubs the place disclose,
The village preacher's modest mansion rose. 140
A man he was to all the country dear,
And passing rich with forty pounds a year;
Remote from towns he ran his godly race,
Nor e'er had changed, nor wished to change his place;
Unpractised he to fawn, or seek for power,
By doctrines fashioned to the varying hour;
Far other aims his heart had learned to prize,
More skilled to raise the wretched than to rise.
His house was known to all the vagrant train,
He chid their wanderings, but relieved their pain; 150
The long-remembered beggar was his guest,
Whose beard descending swept his aged breast;
The ruined spendthrift, now no longer proud,
Claimed kindred there, and had his claims allowed;
The broken soldier, kindly bade to stay,
Sat by his fire and talked the night away;
Wept o'er his wounds, or tales of sorrow done,
Shouldered his crutch, and showed how fields were won.
Pleased with his guests, the good man learned to glow,
And quite forgot their vices in their woe; 160
Careless their merits, or their faults to scan,
His pity gave ere charity began.

122. **vacant,** carefree.

Thus to relieve the wretched was his pride,
And even his failings leaned to Virtue's side;
But in his duty prompt at every call,
He watched and wept, he prayed and felt, for all.
And, as a bird each fond endearment tries
To tempt its new-fledged offspring to the skies,
He tried each art, reproved each dull delay,
Allured to brighter worlds, and led the way. 170

Beside the bed where parting life was laid,
And sorrow, guilt, and pain, by turns dismayed,
The reverend champion stood. At his control
Despair and anguish fled the struggling soul;
Comfort came down the trembling wretch to raise,
And his last faltering accents whispered praise.

At church, with meek and unaffected grace,
His looks adorned the venerable place;
Truth from his lips prevailed with double sway,
And fools, who came to scoff, remained to pray. 180
The service passed, around the pious man,
With steady zeal, each honest rustic ran;
Even children followed, with endearing wile,
And plucked his gown, to share the good man's smile.
His ready smile a parent's warmth expressed,
Their welfare pleased him and their cares distressed;
To them his heart, his love, his griefs were given,
But all his serious thoughts had rest in Heaven.
As some tall cliff that lifts its awful form, 189
Swells from the vale, and midway leaves the storm,
Though round its breast the rolling clouds are spread,
Eternal sunshine settles on its head.

Beside yon straggling fence that skirts the way,
With blossomed furze unprofitably gay,
There, in his noisy mansion, skilled to rule,
The village master taught his little school;
A man severe he was, and stern to view;
I knew him well, and every truant knew;
Well had the boding tremblers learned to trace
The day's disasters in his morning face; 200
Full well they laughed, with counterfeited glee,
At all his jokes, for many a joke had he;
Full well the busy whisper, circling round,
Conveyed the dismal tidings when he frowned;
Yet he was kind; or, if severe in aught,
The love he bore to learning was in fault;
The village all declared how much he knew;
'Twas certain he could write, and cypher too;
Lands he could measure, terms and tides presage,
And even the story ran that he could gauge. 210
In arguing too, the parson owned his skill,
For even though vanquished, he could argue still;
While words of learned length and thundering sound
Amazed the gazing rustics ranged around;
And still they gazed, and still the wonder grew,
That one small head could carry all he knew.

But past is all his fame. The very spot
Where many a time he triumphed, is forgot.
Near yonder thorn, that lifts its head on high,
Where once the sign-post caught the passing eye, 220
Low lies that house where nut-brown draughts inspired,
Where grey-beard mirth and smiling toil retired,
Where village statesmen talked with looks profound,
And news much older than their ale went round.
Imagination fondly stoops to trace
The parlour splendours of that festive place;
The white-washed wall, the nicely sanded floor,
The varnished clock that clicked behind the door;
The chest contrived a double debt to pay,
A bed by night, a chest of drawers by day; 230
The pictures placed for ornament and use,
The twelve good rules, the royal game of goose;
The hearth, except when winter chilled the day,
With aspen boughs, and flowers, and fennel gay;
While broken tea-cups, wisely kept for shew,
Ranged o'er the chimney, glistened in a row.

Vain transitory splendours! Could not all
Reprieve the tottering mansion from its fall?
Obscure it sinks, nor shall it more impart
An hour's importance to the poor man's heart; 240
Thither no more the peasant shall repair
To sweet oblivion of his daily care;
No more the farmer's news, the barber's tale,
No more the wood-man's ballad shall prevail;
No more the smith his dusky brow shall clear,
Relax his ponderous strength, and lean to hear;
The host himself no longer shall be found
Careful to see the mantling blisss go round;
Nor the coy maid, half willing to be pressed,
Shall kiss the cup to pass it to the rest. 250

Yes! let the rich deride, the proud disdain,
These simple blessings of the lowly train;
To me more dear, congenial to my heart,
One native charm, than all the gloss of art;

209. **terms,** periods in which courts of justice held daily sessions. 210. **gauge,** calculate the capacity of vessels. 232. **rules,** of conduct, often hung up in taverns. They were attributed to Charles I. **goose,** a game somewhat like pachisi.

Spontaneous joys, where Nature has its play,
The soul adopts, and owns their first-born sway;
Lightly they frolic o'er the vacant mind,
Unenvied, unmolested, unconfined.
But the long pomp, the midnight masquerade,
With all the freaks of wanton wealth arrayed,   260
In these, ere triflers half their wish obtain,
The toiling pleasure sickens into pain;
And even while fashion's brightest arts decoy,
The heart distrusting asks, if this be joy.

    Ye friends to truth, ye statesmen, who survey
The rich man's joys increase, the poor's decay,
'Tis yours to judge how wide the limits stand
Between a splendid and a happy land.
Proud swells the tide with loads of freighted ore,
And shouting Folly hails them from her shore;   270
Hoards, even beyond the miser's wish abound,
And rich men flock from all the world around.
Yet count our gains. This wealth is but a name
That leaves our useful products still the same.
Not so the loss. The man of wealth and pride
Takes up a space that many poor supplied;
Space for his lake, his park's extended bounds,
Space for his horses, equipage, and hounds;
The robe that wraps his limbs in silken sloth
Has robbed the neighbouring fields of half their growth;   280
His seat, where solitary sports are seen,
Indignant spurns the cottage from the green;
Around the world each needful product flies,
For all the luxuries the world supplies:
While thus the land adorned for pleasure, all
In barren splendour feebly waits the fall.

    As some fair female unadorned and plain,
Secure to please while youth confirms her reign,
Slights every borrowed charm that dress supplies,
Nor shares with art the triumph of her eyes;   290
But when those charms are passed, for charms are frail,
When time advances, and when lovers fail,
She then shines forth, solicitous to bless,
In all the glaring impotence of dress:
Thus fares the land, by luxury betrayed,
In nature's simplest charms at first arrayed;
But verging to decline, its splendours rise,
Its vistas strike, its palaces surprise;
While scourged by famine from the smiling land,
The mournful peasant leads his humble band;   300
And while he sinks, without one arm to save,
The country blooms—a garden, and a grave.

    Where then, ah! where, shall poverty reside,
To 'scape the pressure of contiguous pride?
If to some common's fenceless limits strayed,
He drives his flock to pick the scanty blade,
Those fenceless fields the sons of wealth divide,
And even the bare-worn common is denied.

    If to the city sped—what waits him there?
To see profusion that he must not share;   310
To see ten thousand baneful arts combined
To pamper luxury, and thin mankind;
To see those joys the sons of pleasure know
Extorted from his fellow-creature's woe.
Here while the courtier glitters in brocade,
There the pale artist plies the sickly trade;
Here while the proud their long-drawn pomps display,
There the black gibbet glooms beside the way;
The dome where Pleasure holds her midnight reign,
Here, richly decked, admits the gorgeous train;   320
Tumultuous grandeur crowds the blazing square,
The rattling chariots clash, the torches glare.
Sure scenes like these no troubles e'er annoy!
Sure these denote one universal joy!
Are these thy serious thoughts?—Ah, turn thine eyes
Where the poor houseless shivering female lies.
She once, perhaps, in village plenty blessed,
Has wept at tales of innocence distressed;
Her modest looks the cottage might adorn,
Sweet as the primrose peeps beneath the thorn;   330
Now lost to all; her friends, her virtue fled,
Near her betrayer's door she lays her head,
And, pinched with cold, and shrinking from the shower,
With heavy heart deplores that luckless hour,
When idly first, ambitious of the town,
She left her wheel and robes of country brown.

    Do thine, sweet AUBURN, thine, the loveliest train,
Do thy fair tribes participate her pain?
Even now, perhaps, by cold and hunger led,
At proud men's doors they ask a little bread!   340

    Ah, no. To distant climes, a dreary scene,
Where half the convex world intrudes between,
Through torrid tracts with fainting steps they go,
Where wild Altama murmurs to their woe.
Far different there from all that charmed before,
The various terrors of that horrid shore;
Those blazing suns that dart a downward ray,
And fiercely shed intolerable day;

316. artist, artisan, craftsman.   344. **Altama**, the Altamaha river, in Georgia. Details of the following passage were probably drawn from the talk of General Oglethorpe, founder of Georgia, with whom Goldsmith was acquainted.

OLIVER GOLDSMITH

Those matted woods where birds forget to sing,
But silent bats in drowsy clusters cling; 350
Those poisonous fields with rank luxuriance crowned,
Where the dark scorpion gathers death around;
Where at each step the stranger fears to wake
The rattling terrors of the vengeful snake;
Where crouching tigers wait their hapless prey,
And savage men more murderous still than they;
While oft in whirls the mad tornado flies,
Mingling the ravaged landscape with the skies.
Far different these from every former scene,
The cooling brook, the grassy-vested green, 360
The breezy covert of the warbling grove,
That only sheltered thefts of harmless love.

Good Heaven! what sorrows gloomed that parting day
That called them from their native walks away;
When the poor exiles, every pleasure past,
Hung round their bowers, and fondly looked their last,
And took a long farewell, and wished in vain
For seats like these beyond the western main;
And shuddering still to face the distant deep,
Returned and wept, and still returned to weep. 370
The good old sire the first prepared to go
To new-found worlds, and wept for others' woe;
But for himself, in conscious virtue brave,
He only wished for worlds beyond the grave.
His lovely daughter, lovelier in her tears,
The fond companion of his helpless years,
Silent went next, neglectful of her charms,
And left a lover's for a father's arms.
With louder plaints the mother spoke her woes,
And blessed the cot where every pleasure rose, 380
And kissed her thoughtless babes with many a tear,
And clasped them close, in sorrow doubly dear;
Whilst her fond husband strove to lend relief
In all the silent manliness of grief.

O Luxury! thou cursed by Heaven's decree,
How ill exchanged are things like these for thee!
How do thy potions, with insidious joy,
Diffuse their pleasures only to destroy!
Kingdoms by thee, to sickly greatness grown,

355. tigers, catamounts.

Boast of a florid vigour not their own; 390
At every draught more large and large they grow,
A bloated mass of rank, unwieldy woe;
Till sapped their strength, and every part unsound,
Down, down they sink, and spread a ruin round.

Even now the devastation is begun,
And half the business of destruction done;
Even now, methinks, as pondering here I stand,
I see the rural virtues leave the land:
Down where yon anchoring vessel spreads the sail,
That idly waiting flaps with every gale, 400
Downward they move, a melancholy band,
Pass from the shore, and darken all the strand.
Contented toil, and hospitable care,
And kind connubial tenderness are there;
And piety with wishes placed above,
And steady loyalty, and faithful love.
And thou, sweet Poetry, thou loveliest maid,
Still first to fly where sensual joys invade,
Unfit, in these degenerate times of shame,
To catch the heart, or strike for honest fame; 410
Dear charming nymph, neglected and decried,
My shame in crowds, my solitary pride;
Thou source of all my bliss, and all my woe,
That found'st me poor at first, and keep'st me so;
Thou guide by which the nobler arts excel,
Thou nurse of every virtue, fare thee well!
Farewell! and oh! where'er thy voice be tried,
On Torno's cliffs, or Pambamarca's side,
Whether where equinoctial fervours glow,
Or winter wraps the polar world in snow, 420
Still let thy voice, prevailing over time,
Redress the rigours of the inclement clime;
Aid slighted truth; with thy persuasive strain
Teach erring man to spurn the rage of gain;
Teach him, that states of native strength possessed,
Though very poor, may still be very blest;
That trade's proud empire hastes to swift decay,
As ocean sweeps the laboured mole away;
While self-dependent power can time defy,
As rocks resist the billows and the sky. 430

418. Torno's cliffs . . . Pambamarca, places near the North Pole and near the Equator, respectively, at which scientific expeditions studied, in Goldsmith's time, the curvature of the earth. **427–30. That trade's . . . sky.** These last four lines were written by Dr. Johnson.

SHE STOOPS TO CONQUER
OR
THE MISTAKES OF A NIGHT. A COMEDY

This play, the second of Goldsmith's two serious efforts at dramatic writing, was successfully performed at the Covent Garden Theatre in March, 1773, some thirteen months before its author's death. Dr. Johnson, who had helped to manage its success by organizing a "claque" of clappers, said of it to Boswell: "I know of no comedy for many years that has so much exhilarated an audience, that has answered so much the great end of comedy—making an audience merry."

In the Preface to his earlier play, *The Good-Natured Man*, Goldsmith himself had written: "When I undertook to write a comedy, I confess I was strongly prepossessed in favour of the poets of the last age, and strove to imitate them." Clearly he had in mind not the poets of the Restoration period, with whom he had little in common, but those of the blither, sunnier, and more decent Elizabethan time. It is true that while writing *She Stoops to Conquer* he took many hints from the *Spectator* and from George Farquhar's *The Beaux's Stratagem*, being always quite carefree, as Shakespeare also was, in such snapping-up of unconsidered trifles. And yet in the spirit and tone of his play, if not in its plot and language, he reaches back through the years to the time before Puritanism had blown the English stage gray with its breath.

TO SAMUEL JOHNSON, L.L.D.

Dear Sir,

By inscribing this slight performance to you, I do not mean so much to compliment you as myself. It may do me some honour to inform the public, that I have lived many years in intimacy with you. It may serve the interests of mankind also to inform them, that the greatest wit may be found in a character, without impairing the most unaffected piety.

I have, particularly, reason to thank you for your partiality to this performance. The undertaking a comedy, not merely sentimental, was very dangerous; and Mr. Colman, who saw this piece in its various stages, always thought it so. However I ventured to trust it to the public; and though it was necessarily delayed till late in the season, I have every reason to be grateful.

I am, Dear Sir,
Your most sincere friend,
And admirer,
Oliver Goldsmith.

PROLOGUE
By David Garrick, Esq.

Enter MR. WOODWARD, *dressed in black, and holding a handkerchief to his eyes.*

Excuse me, Sirs, I pray—I can't yet speak—
I'm crying now—and have been all the week!
'Tis not alone this *mourning suit*, good masters;
I've that *within*—for which there are no plaisters!
Pray wou'd you know the reason why I'm crying?
The Comic muse, long sick, is now a dying!
And if she goes, my tears will never stop;
For as a player, I can't squeeze out one drop:
I am undone, that's all—shall lose my bread—
I'd rather, but that's nothing—lose my head.   10
When the sweet maid is laid upon the bier,
Shuter and *I* shall be chief mourners here.
To *her* a mawkish drab of spurious breed
Who deals in *sentimentals* will succeed!
Poor *Ned* and *I* are dead to all intents,
We can as soon speak *Greek* as *sentiments!*
Both nervous grown, to keep our spirits up,
We now and then take down a hearty cup.
What shall we do?—If Comedy forsake us,
They'll turn us out, and no one else will take us!   20
But why can't I be moral?—Let me try—
My heart thus pressing—fixed my face and eye—
With a sententious look, that nothing means,
(Faces are blocks, in sentimental scenes)
Thus I begin—*All is not gold that glitters,*
Pleasure seems sweet, but proves a glass of bitters.
When ignorance enters, folly is at hand;
Learning is better far than house and land.
Let not your virtue trip, who trips may stumble,
And virtue is not virtue, if she tumble.   30
   I give it up—morals won't do for me;
To make you laugh I must play tragedy.
One hope remains—hearing the maid was ill,
A *doctor* comes this night to shew his skill.
To cheer her heart, and give your muscles motion,
He in *five draughts* prepared, presents a potion:
A kind of magic charm—for be assured,
If you will *swallow* it, the maid is cured:
But desperate the Doctor, and her case is,
If you reject the dose, and make wry faces!   40
This truth he boasts, will boast it while he lives,
No *poisonous drugs* are mixed in what he gives;
Should he succeed, you'll give him his degree;
If not, *within* he will receive no fee!
The college *you*, must his pretensions back,
Pronounce him *regular*, or dub him *quack*.

DRAMATIS PERSONAE
MEN

SIR CHARLES MARLOW . . . Mr. Gardner
YOUNG MARLOW (his Son) . . . Mr. Lewes

Woodward, a popular actor of comic parts. 3–4. 'Tis not . . . within. See *Hamlet*, Act I, sc. 2, ll. 77–78. 12. Shuter, Edward Shuter, an actor of low comedy who in this play took the part of Mr. Hardcastle. 34. doctor, that is, Dr. Oliver Goldsmith. 36. draughts, that is, acts. 44. within, from the box office.

OLIVER GOLDSMITH

HARDCASTLE	.	.	.	.	.	.	Mr. Shuter
HASTINGS	.	.	.	.	.	.	Mr. Dubellamy
TONY LUMPKIN	.	.	.	.	Mr. Quick
DIGGORY	.	.	.	.	.	.	Mr. Saunders

WOMEN

MRS. HARDCASTLE	.	.	.	.	Mrs. Green
MISS HARDCASTLE	.	.	.	.	Mrs. Bulkley
MISS NEVILLE	.	.	.	.	.	Mrs. Kniveton
MAID	.	.	.	.	.	.	.	Miss Willems

Landlord, Servants, &c &c.

ACT I

SCENE.—*A Chamber in an old-fashioned House*

Enter MRS. HARDCASTLE *and* MR. HARDCASTLE.

Mrs. Hardcastle. I vow, Mr. Hardcastle, you're very particular. Is there a creature in the whole country, but ourselves, that does not take a trip to town now and then, to rub off the rust a little? There's the two Miss Hoggs, and our neighbour, Mrs. Grigsby, go to take a month's polishing every winter.

Hardcastle. Ay, and bring back vanity and affectation to last them the whole year. I wonder why London cannot keep its own fools at home. In my time, the follies of the town crept slowly among us, but now they travel faster than a stage-coach. Its fopperies come down, not only as inside passengers, but in the very basket.

Mrs. Hardcastle. Ay, *your* times were fine times, indeed; you have been telling us of *them* for many a long year. Here we live in an old rumbling mansion, that looks for all the world like an inn, but that we never see company. Our best visitors are old Mrs. Oddfish, the curate's wife, and little Cripplegate, the lame dancing-master: And all our entertainment your old stories of Prince Eugene and the Duke of Marlborough. I hate such old-fashioned trumpery.

Hardcastle. And I love it. I love every thing that's old: old friends, old times, old manners, old books, old wine; and, I believe, Dorothy, (*Taking her hand.*) you'll own I have been pretty fond of an old wife.

Mrs. Hardcastle. Lord, Mr. Hardcastle, you're for ever at your Dorothys and your old wifes. You may be a Darby, but I'll be no Joan, I promise you. I'm not so old as you'd make me, by more than one good year. Add twenty to twenty, and make money of that.

Hardcastle. Let me see; twenty added to twenty, makes just fifty and seven.

Mrs. Hardcastle. It's false, Mr. Hardcastle: I was but twenty when I was brought to bed of Tony, that I had by Mr. Lumpkin, my first husband; and he not come to years of discretion yet.

Hardcastle. Nor ever will, I dare answer for him. Ay, you have taught *him* finely!

Mrs. Hardcastle. No matter, Tony Lumpkin has a good fortune. My son is not to live by his learning. I don't think a boy wants much learning to spend fifteen hundred a year.

Hardcastle. Learning, quotha! A mere composition of tricks and mischief.

Mrs. Hardcastle. Humour, my dear: nothing but humour. Come, Mr. Hardcastle, you must allow the boy a little humour.

Hardcastle. I'd sooner allow him an horse-pond. If burning the footmen's shoes, frighting the maids, and worrying the kittens, be humour, he has it. It was but yesterday he fastened my wig to the back of my chair, and when I went to make a bow, I popt my bald head in Mrs. Frizzle's face.

Mrs. Hardcastle. And am I to blame? The poor boy was always too sickly to do any good. A school would be his death. When he comes to be a little stronger, who knows what a year or two's Latin may do for him?

Hardcastle. Latin for him! A cat and fiddle. No, no, the ale-house and the stable are the only schools he'll ever go to.

Mrs. Hardcastle. Well, we must not snub the poor boy now, for I believe we shan't have him long among us. Any body that looks in his face may see he's consumptive.

Hardcastle. Ay, if growing too fat be one of the symptoms.

Mrs. Hardcastle. He coughs sometimes.

Hardcastle. Yes, when his liquor goes the wrong way.

Mrs. Hardcastle. I'm actually afraid of his lungs.

Hardcastle. And truly, so am I; for he sometimes whoops like a speaking trumpet—(TONY *hallooing behind the Scenes.*)—O, there he goes—A very consumptive figure, truly!

[*Enter* TONY, *crossing the Stage.*]

Mrs. Hardcastle. Tony, where are you going, my charmer? Won't you give Papa and I a little of your company, lovee?

Tony. I'm in haste, Mother, I cannot stay.

Mrs. Hardcastle. You shan't venture out this raw evening, my dear. You look most shockingly.

---

29. basket, an outside compartment of a stagecoach, intended primarily for luggage. **37–38. Eugene . . . Marlborough,** commanders of the Austrian and English armies against the French in the War of the Spanish Succession, 1702–12.

11. quotha! indeed! forsooth! **16. horse-pond,** for a ducking. **30. snub,** check or stop suddenly.

Tony. I can't stay, I tell you. The Three Pigeons expects me down every moment. There's some fun going forward.

Hardcastle. Ay; the ale-house, the old place: I thought so.

Mrs. Hardcastle. A low, paltry set of fellows.

Tony. Not so low neither. There's Dick Muggins the exciseman, Jack Slang the horse doctor, Little Aminadab that grinds the music box, and Tom Twist that spins the pewter platter.

Mrs. Hardcastle. Pray, my dear, disappoint them for one night at least.

Tony. As for disappointing *them*, I should not so much mind; but I can't abide to disappoint *myself*.

Mrs. Hardcastle (*detaining him*). You shan't go.

Tony. I will, I tell you.

Mrs. Hardcastle. I say you shan't.

Tony. We'll see which is strongest, you or I.

[*Exit, hawling her out.*

[HARDCASTLE, *solus.*]

Hardcastle. Ay, there goes a pair that only spoil each other. But is not the whole age in a combination to drive sense and discretion out of doors? There's my pretty darling, Kate. The fashions of the times have almost infected her too. By living a year or two in town, she is as fond of gauze, and French frippery, as the best of them.

[*Enter* MISS HARDCASTLE.]

Hardcastle. Blessings on my pretty innocence! Drest out as usual, my Kate. Goodness! What a quantity of superfluous silk hast thou got about thee, girl! I could never teach the fools of this age, that the indigent world could be cloathed out of the trimmings of the vain.

Miss Hardcastle. You know our agreement, Sir. You allow me the morning to receive and pay visits, and to dress in my own manner; and in the evening, I put on my housewife's dress to please you.

Hardcastle. Well, remember I insist on the terms of our agreement; and, by the bye, I believe I shall have occasion to try your obedience this very evening.

Miss Hardcastle. I protest, Sir, I don't comprehend your meaning.

Hardcastle. Then, to be plain with you, Kate, I expect the young gentleman I have chosen to be your husband from town this very day. I have his father's letter, in which he informs me his son is set out, and that he intends to follow himself shortly after.

Miss Hardcastle. Indeed! I wish I had known

1. **The Three Pigeons,** a common name for a tavern.

something of this before. Bless me, how shall I behave? It's a thousand to one I shan't like him; our meeting will be so formal, and so like a thing of business, that I shall find no room for friendship or esteem.

Hardcastle. Depend upon it, child, I'll never controul your choice; but Mr. Marlow, whom I have pitched upon, is the son of my old friend, Sir Charles Marlow, of whom you have heard me talk so often. The young gentleman has been bred a scholar, and is designed for an employment in the service of his country. I am told he's a man of an excellent understanding.

Miss Hardcastle. Is he?

Hardcastle. Very generous.

Miss Hardcastle. I believe I shall like him.

Hardcastle. Young and brave.

Miss Hardcastle. I'm sure I shall like him.

Hardcastle. And very handsome.

Miss Hardcastle. My dear Papa, say no more, (*Kissing his hand.*) he's mine, I'll have him.

Hardcastle. And to crown all, Kate, he's one of the most bashful and reserved young fellows in all the world.

Miss Hardcastle. Eh! you have frozen me to death again. That word *reserved* has undone all the rest of his accomplishments. A reserved lover, it is said, always makes a suspicious husband.

Hardcastle. On the contrary, modesty seldom resides in a breast that is not enriched with nobler virtues. It was the very feature in his character that first struck me.

Miss Hardcastle. He must have more striking features to catch me, I promise you. However, if he be so young, so handsome, and so every thing, as you mention, I believe he'll do still. I think I'll have him.

Hardcastle. Ay, Kate, but there is still an obstacle. It's more than an even wager, he may not have *you*.

Miss Hardcastle. My dear Papa, why will you mortify one so?—Well, if he refuses, instead of breaking my heart at his indifference, I'll only break my glass for its flattery, set my cap to some newer fashion, and look out for some less difficult admirer.

Hardcastle. Bravely resolved! In the mean time I'll go prepare the servants for his reception; as we seldom see company they want as much training as a company of recruits, the first day's muster. [*Exit.*

[MISS HARDCASTLE, *sola.*]

Miss Hardcastle. Lud, this news of Papa's, puts me all in a flutter. Young, handsome; these he put last; but I put them foremost. Sensible, good-natured; I like all that. But then reserved, and sheepish, that's much against him. Yet can't he be cured of his timidity, by being taught to be proud of his wife? Yes, and can't I—But I vow I'm disposing of the husband, before I have secured the lover.

[*Enter* MISS NEVILLE.]

Miss Hardcastle. I'm glad you're come, Neville, my dear. Tell me, Constance, how do I look this evening? Is there any thing whimsical about me? Is it one of my well looking days, child? Am I in face to day?

Miss Neville. Perfectly, my dear. Yet now I look again—bless me!—sure no accident has happened among the canary birds or the gold fishes. Has your brother or the cat been meddling? Or has the last novel been too moving?

Miss Hardcastle. No; nothing of all this. I have been threatened—I can scarce get it out—I have been threatened with a lover.

Miss Neville. And his name—

Miss Hardcastle. Is Marlow.

Miss Neville. Indeed!

Miss Hardcastle. The son of Sir Charles Marlow.

Miss Neville. As I live, the most intimate friend of Mr. Hastings, *my* admirer. They are never asunder. I believe you must have seen him when we lived in town.

Miss Hardcastle. Never.

Miss Neville. He's a very singular character, I assure you. Among women of reputation and virtue, he is the modestest man alive; but his acquaintance give him a very different character among creatures of another stamp: you understand me.

Miss Hardcastle. An odd character, indeed. I shall never be able to manage him. What shall I do? Pshaw, think no more of him, but trust to occurrences for success. But how goes on your own affair, my dear? Has my mother been courting you for my brother Tony, as usual?

Miss Neville. I have just come from one of our agreeable tête-à-têtes. She has been saying a hundred tender things, and setting off her pretty monster as the very pink of perfection.

Miss Hardcastle. And her partiality is such, that she actually thinks him so. A fortune like yours is no small temptation. Besides, as she has the sole management of it, I'm not surprized to see her unwilling to let it go out of the family.

Miss Neville. A fortune like mine, which chiefly consists in jewels, is no such mighty temptation. But at any rate if my dear Hastings be but constant, I make no doubt to be too hard for her at last. However, I let her suppose that I am in love with her son, and she never once dreams that my affections are fixed upon another.

Miss Hardcastle. My good brother holds out stoutly. I could almost love him for hating you so.

Miss Neville. It is a good-natured creature at bottom, and I'm sure would wish to see me married to any body but himself. But my aunt's bell rings for our afternoon's walk round the improvements. *Allons.* Courage is necessary, as our affairs are critical.

Miss Hardcastle. Would it were bed time and all were well. [*Exeunt.*

SCENE. *An Ale-house Room. Several shabby fellows, with Punch and Tobacco.* TONY *at the head of the Table, a little higher than the rest: A mallet in his hand.*

Omnes. Hurrea, hurrea, hurrea, bravo!

First Fellow. Now, gentlemen, silence for a song. The 'Squire is going to knock himself down for a song.

Omnes. Ay, a song, a song.

Tony. Then I'll sing you, gentlemen, a song I made upon this ale-house, the Three Pigeons.

SONG

Let school-masters puzzle their brain,
   With grammar, and nonsense, and learning;
Good liquor, I stoutly maintain,
   Gives genius a better discerning.
Let them brag of their Heathenish Gods,
   Their Lethes, their Styxes, and Stygians;
Their Quis, and their Quaes, and their Quods,
   They're all but a parcel of Pigeons.
      Toroddle, toroddle, toroll.

When Methodist preachers come down,
   A preaching that drinking is sinful,
I'll wager the rascals a crown,
   They always preach best with a skinful.
But when you come down with your pence,
   For a slice of their scurvy religion,
I'll leave it to all men of sense,
   But you my good friend are the pigeon.
      Toroddle, toroddle, toroll.

---

10. **whimsical**, odd, eccentric. 10. **improvements**, in the grounds of the estate. 11. **Allons**, let's go. 38. **Quis . . . Quods**, nominatives singular of the Latin relative pronouns who, which, what. 49. **pigeon**, gull or fool.

Then come, put the jorum about,
  And let us be merry and clever,
Our hearts and our liquors are stout,
  Here's the Three Jolly Pigeons for ever.
Let some cry up woodcock or hare,
  Your bustards, your ducks, and your widgeons;
But of all the birds in the air,
  Here's a health to the Three Jolly Pigeons.
    Toroddle, toroddle, toroll.

Omnes. Bravo, bravo.
First Fellow. The 'Squire has got spunk in him.
Second Fellow. I loves to hear him sing, bekeays he never gives us nothing that's *low*.
Third Fellow. O damn any thing that's *low*, I cannot bear it.
Fourth Fellow. The genteel thing is the genteel thing at any time. If so be that a gentleman bees in a concatenation accordingly.
Third Fellow. I like the maxum of it, Master Muggins. What, though I am obligated to dance a bear, a man may be a gentleman for all that. May this be my poison if my bear ever dances but to the very genteelest of tunes. Water Parted, or the minuet in Ariadne.
Second Fellow. What a pity it is the 'Squire is not come to his own. It would be well for all the publicans within ten miles round of him.
Tony. Ecod, and so it would, Master Slang. I'd then shew what it was to keep choice of company.
Second Fellow. O he takes after his own father for that. To be sure old 'Squire Lumpkin was the finest gentleman I ever set my eyes on. For winding the straight horn, or beating a thicket for a hare or a wench he never had his fellow. It was a saying in the place, that he kept the best horses, dogs and girls in the whole county.
Tony. Ecod, and when I'm of age I'll be no bastard, I promise you. I have been thinking of Bett Bouncer and the miller's grey mare to begin with. But come, my boys, drink about and be merry, for you pay no reckoning. Well, Stingo, what's the matter?

[*Enter* Landlord.]

Landlord. There be two gentlemen in a post-chaise at the door. They have lost their way upo' the forest; and they are talking something about Mr. Hardcastle.
Tony. As sure as can be, one of them must be the gentleman that's coming down to court my sister. Do they seem to be Londoners?
Landlord. I believe they may. They look woundily like Frenchmen.
Tony. Then desire them to step this way, and I'll set them right in a twinkling. (*Exit* Landlord.) Gentlemen, as they mayn't be good enough company for you, step down for a moment, and I'll be with you in the squeezing of a lemon. [*Exeunt Mob.*

[TONY, *solus.*]

Tony. Father-in-law has been calling me whelp, and hound, this half year. Now if I pleased, I could be so revenged upon the old grumbletonian. But then I'm afraid—afraid of what! I shall soon be worth fifteen hundred a year, and let him frighten me out of *that* if he can.

[*Enter* Landlord, *conducting* MARLOW *and* HASTINGS.]

Marlow. What a tedious uncomfortable day have we had of it! We were told it was but forty miles across the country, and we have come above three-score.
Hastings. And all, Marlow, from that unaccountable reserve of yours, that would not let us enquire more frequently on the way.
Marlow. I own, Hastings, I am unwilling to lay myself under an obligation to every one I meet; and often stand the chance of an unmannerly answer.
Hastings. At present, however, we are not likely to receive any answer.
Tony. No offence, gentlemen, but I'm told you have been enquiring for one Mr. Hardcastle, in these parts. Do you know what part of the country you are in?
Hastings. Not in the least, Sir, but should thank you for information.
Tony. Nor the way you came?
Hastings. No, Sir; but if you can inform us—
Tony. Why, gentlemen, if you know neither the road you are going, nor where you are, nor the road you came, the first thing I have to inform you is, that—you have lost your way.
Marlow. We wanted no ghost to tell us that.
Tony. Pray, gentlemen, may I be so bold as to ask the place from whence you came?
Marlow. That's not necessary towards directing us where we are to go.
Tony. No offence; but question for question is all fair, you know. Pray, gentlemen, is not this same Hardcastle a cross-grained, old-fashioned, whimsical

---

1. **jorum,** a drinking-vessel, chiefly used for punch. 23. **Water Parted,** a song in Thomas Arne's *Artaxerxes*, produced at the Covent Garden Theatre in 1762. 24. **Ariadne,** an operetta by Handel.

3–4. **woundily,** excessively. 11. **Father-in-law,** that is, stepfather.

fellow, with an ugly face, a daughter, and a pretty son?

Hastings. We have not seen the gentleman, but he has the family you mention.

Tony. The daughter, a tall trapesing, trolloping, talkative maypole—The son, a pretty, well-bred, agreeable youth, that every body is fond of.

Marlow. Our information differs in this. The daughter is said to be well-bred and beautiful; the son, an awkward booby, reared up, and spoiled at his mother's apron-string.

Tony. He-he-hem—Then, gentlemen, all I have to tell you is, that you won't reach Mr. Hardcastle's house this night, I believe.

Hastings. Unfortunate!

Tony. It's a damned long, dark, boggy, dirty, dangerous way. Stingo, tell the gentlemen the way to Mr. Hardcastle's; (*Winking upon the* Landlord.) Mr. Hardcastle's, of Quagmire Marsh, you understand me.

Landlord. Master Hardcastle's! Lack-a-daisy, my masters, you're come a deadly deal wrong! When you came to the bottom of the hill, you should have crossed down Squash-lane.

Marlow. Cross down Squash-lane!

Landlord. Then you were to keep straight forward, 'till you came to four roads.

Marlow. Come to where four roads meet!

Tony. Ay; but you must be sure to take only one of them.

Marlow. O Sir, you're facetious.

Tony. Then keeping to the right, you are to go side-ways till you come upon Crack-skull common: there you must look sharp for the track of the wheel, and go forward, 'till you come to farmer Murrain's barn. Coming to the farmer's barn, you are to turn to the right, and then to the left, and then to the right about again, till you find out the old mill—

Marlow. Zounds, man! we could as soon find out the longitude!

Hastings. What's to be done, Marlow?

Marlow. This house promises but a poor reception; though perhaps the Landlord can accommodate us.

Landlord. Alack, master, we have but one spare bed in the whole house.

Tony. And to my knowledge, that's taken up by three lodgers already. (*After a pause, in which the rest seem disconcerted.*) I have hit it. Don't you think, Stingo, our landlady could accommodate the gentlemen by the fire-side, with—three chairs and a bolster?

Hastings. I hate sleeping by the fire-side.

Marlow. And I detest your three chairs and a bolster.

Tony. You do, do you?—then let me see—what —if you go on a mile further, to the Buck's Head, the old Buck's Head on the hill, one of the best inns in the whole county?

Hastings. O ho! so we have escaped an adventure for this night, however.

Landlord (*apart to* TONY). Sure, you ben't sending them to your father's as an inn, be you?

Tony. Mum, you fool you. Let *them* find that out. (*To them.*) You have only to keep on straight forward, till you come to a large old house by the road side. You'll see a pair of large horns over the door. That's the sign. Drive up the yard, and call stoutly about you.

Hastings. Sir, we are obliged to you. The servants can't miss the way?

Tony. No, no: But I tell you, though, the landlord is rich, and going to leave off business; so he wants to be thought a Gentleman, saving your presence, he! he! he! He'll be for giving you his company, and ecod, if you mind him, he'll persuade you that his mother was an alderman, and his aunt a justice of peace.

Landlord. A troublesome old blade, to be sure; but a keeps as good wines and beds as any in the whole country.

Marlow. Well, if he supplies us with these, we shall want no further connexion. We are to turn to the right, did you say?

Tony. No, no; straight forward, I'll just step myself, and shew you a piece of the way. (*To the* Landlord.) Mum.

Landlord. Ah, bless your heart, for a sweet, pleasant—damned mischievous son of a whore.

[*Exeunt.*

ACT II

SCENE. *An old-fashioned House* [*parlour*].

Enter HARDCASTLE, *followed by three or four awkward* Servants.

Hardcastle. Well, I hope you're perfect in the table exercise I have been teaching you these three days. You all know your posts and your places, and can shew that you have been used to good company, without ever stirring from home.

Omnes. Ay, ay.

Hardcastle. When company comes, you are not to pop out and stare, and then run in again, like frighted rabbits in a warren.

8. however, in any case. **27. a,** he.

Omnes. No, no.

Hardcastle. You, Diggory, whom I have taken from the barn, are to make a shew at the side-table; and you, Roger, whom I have advanced from the plough, are to place yourself behind *my* chair. But you're not to stand so, with your hands in your pockets. Take your hands from your pockets, Roger; and from your head, you blockhead you. See how Diggory carries his hands. They're a little too stiff indeed, but that's no great matter.

Diggory. Ay, mind how I hold them. I learned to hold my hands this way, when I was upon drill for the militia. And so being upon drill—

Hardcastle. You must not be so talkative, Diggory. You must be all attention to the guests. You must hear us talk, and not think of talking; you must see us drink, and not think of drinking; you must see us eat, and not think of eating.

Diggory. By the laws, your worship, that's parfectly unpossible. Whenever Diggory sees yeating going forward, ecod, he's always wishing for a mouthful himself.

Hardcastle. Blockhead! Is not a belly-full in the kitchen as good as a belly-full in the parlour? Stay your stomach with that reflection.

Diggory. Ecod, I thank your worship, I'll make a shift to stay my stomach with a slice of cold beef in the pantry.

Hardcastle. Diggory, you are too talkative. Then, if I happen to say a good thing, or tell a good story at table, you must not all burst out a-laughing, as if you made part of the company.

Diggory. Then, ecod, your worship must not tell the story of Ould Grouse in the gun-room: I can't help laughing at that—he! he! he!—for the soul of me. We have laughed at that these twenty years—ha! ha! ha!

Hardcastle. Ha! ha! ha! The story is a good one. Well, honest Diggory, you may laugh at that—but still remember to be attentive. Suppose one of the company should call for a glass of wine, how will you behave? A glass of wine, Sir, if you please. (*To* DIGGORY.)—Eh, why don't you move?

Diggory. Ecod, your worship, I never have courage till I see the eatables and drinkables brought upo' the table, and then I'm as bauld as a lion.

Hardcastle. What, will no body move?

First Servant. I'm not to leave this pleace.

Second Servant. I'm sure it's no pleace of mine.

Third Servant. Nor mine, for sartain.

Diggory. Wauns, and I'm sure it canna be mine.

Hardcastle. You numbskulls! and so while, like your betters, you are quarrelling for places, the guests must be starved. O you dunces! I find I must begin all over again.—But don't I hear a coach drive into the yard? To your posts, you blockheads. I'll go in the mean time and give my old friend's son a hearty reception at the gate.

[*Exit* HARDCASTLE.

Diggory. By the elevens, my pleace is gone quite out of my head.

Roger. I know that my pleace is to be every where.

First Servant. Where the devil is mine?

Second Servant. My pleace is to be no where at all; and so I'ze go about my business.

[*Exeunt* Servants, *running about as if frighted, different ways.*

[*Enter* Servant *with Candles, shewing in* MARLOW *and* HASTINGS.]

Servant. Welcome, gentlemen, very welcome. This way.

Hastings. After the disappointments of the day, welcome once more, Charles, to the comforts of a clean room and a good fire. Upon my word, a very well-looking house; antique, but creditable.

Marlow. The usual fate of a large mansion. Having first ruined the master by good housekeeping, it at last comes to levy contributions as an inn.

Hastings. As you say, we passengers are to be taxed to pay all these fineries. I have often seen a good sideboard, or a marble chimney-piece, though not actually put in the bill, enflame a reckoning confoundedly.

Marlow. Travellers, George, must pay in all places. The only difference is, that in good inns, you pay dearly for luxuries; in bad inns, you are fleeced and starved.

Hastings. You have lived pretty much among them. In truth, I have been often surprized, that you who have seen so much of the world, with your natural good sense, and your many opportunities, could never yet acquire a requisite share of assurance.

Marlow. The Englishman's malady. But tell me, George, where could I have learned that assurance you talk of? My life has been chiefly spent in a college, or an inn, in seclusion from that lovely part of the creation that chiefly teach men confidence. I don't know that I was ever familiarly acquainted with a single modest woman—except my mother—But among females of another class, you know—

Hastings. Ay, among them you are impudent enough of all conscience.

12. I'ze, I shall. 30–31. enflame a reckoning, increase a bill.

Marlow. They are of *us*, you know.

Hastings. But in the company of women of reputation I never saw such an idiot, such a trembler; you look for all the world as if you wanted an opportunity of stealing out of the room.

Marlow. Why, man, that's because I *do* want to steal out of the room. Faith, I have often formed a resolution to break the ice, and rattle away at any rate. But I don't know how, a single glance from a pair of fine eyes has totally overset my resolution. An impudent fellow may counterfeit modesty, but I'll be hanged if a modest man can ever counterfeit impudence.

Hastings. If you could but say half the fine things to them that I have heard you lavish upon the bar-maid of an inn, or even a college bed-maker—

Marlow. Why, George, I can't say fine things to them. They freeze, they petrify me. They may talk of a comet, or a burning mountain, or some such bagatelle. But to me, a modest woman, drest out in all her finery, is the most tremendous object of the whole creation.

Hastings. Ha! ha! ha! At this rate, man, how can you ever expect to marry!

Marlow. Never, unless, as among kings and princes, my bride were to be courted by proxy. If, indeed, like an Eastern bridegroom, one were to be introduced to a wife he never saw before, it might be endured. But to go through all the terrors of a formal courtship, together with the episode of aunts, grandmothers and cousins, and at last to blurt out the broad staring question of, *madam, will you marry me?* No, no, that's a strain much above me, I assure you.

Hastings. I pity you. But how do you intend behaving to the lady you are come down to visit at the request of your father?

Marlow. As I behave to all other ladies. Bow very low. Answer yes, or no, to all her demands— But for the rest, I don't think I shall venture to look in her face, till I see my father's again.

Hastings. I'm surprized that one who is so warm a friend can be so cool a lover.

Marlow. To be explicit, my dear Hastings, my chief inducement down was to be instrumental in forwarding your happiness, not my own. Miss Neville loves you, the family don't know you, as my friend you are sure of a reception, and let honour do the rest.

Hastings. My dear Marlow! But I'll suppress the emotion. Were I a wretch, meanly seeking to carry off a fortune, you should be the last man in the world I would apply to for assistance. But Miss Neville's person is all I ask, and that is mine, both from her deceased father's consent, and her own inclination.

Marlow. Happy man! You have talents and art to captivate any woman. I'm doomed to adore the sex, and yet to converse with the only part of it I despise. This stammer in my address, and this awkward prepossessing visage of mine, can never permit me to soar above the reach of a milliner's 'prentice, or one of the dutchesses of Drury-lane. Pshaw! this fellow here to interrupt us.

[*Enter* HARDCASTLE.]

Hardcastle. Gentlemen, once more you are heartily welcome. Which is Mr. Marlow? Sir, you're heartily welcome. It's not my way, you see, to receive my friends with my back to the fire. I like to give them a hearty reception in the old style, at my gate. I like to see their horses and trunks taken care of.

Marlow (*aside*). He has got our names from the servants already. (*To him.*) We approve your caution and hospitality, Sir. (*To* HASTINGS.) I have been thinking, George, of changing our travelling dresses in the morning. I am grown confoundedly ashamed of mine.

Hardcastle. I beg, Mr. Marlow, you'll use no ceremony in this house.

Hastings. I fancy, Charles, you're right: the first blow is half the battle. I intend opening the campaign with the white and gold.

Mr. Hardcastle. Mr. Marlow—Mr. Hastings— gentlemen—pray be under no constraint in this house. This is Liberty-hall, gentlemen. You may do just as you please here.

Marlow. Yet, George, if we open the campaign too fiercely at first, we may want ammunition before it is over. I think to reserve the embroidery to secure a retreat.

Hardcastle. Your talking of a retreat, Mr. Marlow, puts me in mind of the Duke of Marlborough, when we went to besiege Denain. He first summoned the garrison—

Marlow. Don't you think the *ventre d'or* waistcoat will do with the plain brown?

Hardcastle. He first summoned the garrison, which might consist of about five thousand men—

Hastings. I think not: Brown and yellow mix but very poorly.

Hardcastle. I say, gentlemen, as I was telling you, he summoned the garrison, which might consist of about five thousand men—

9. **dutchesses of Drury-lane,** women of the streets. 41. **Denain,** where the French defeated Marlborough in 1712. 43. **ventre d'or,** gold-fronted.

Marlow. The girls like finery.

Hardcastle. Which might consist of about five thousand men, well appointed with stores, ammunition, and other implements of war. "Now," says the Duke of Marlborough to George Brooks, that stood next to him—you must have heard of George Brooks; "I'll pawn my Dukedom," says he, "but I take that garrison without spilling a drop of blood." So—

Marlow. What, my good friend, if you gave us a glass of punch in the mean time, it would help us to carry on the siege with vigour.

Hardcastle. Punch, Sir! (*Aside.*) This is the most unaccountable kind of modesty I ever met with.

Marlow. Yes, Sir, punch. A glass of warm punch, after our journey, will be comfortable. This is Liberty-hall, you know.

Hardcastle. Here's cup, Sir.

Marlow (*aside*). So this fellow, in his Liberty-hall, will only let us have just what he pleases.

Hardcastle (*taking the cup*). I hope you'll find it to your mind. I have prepared it with my own hands, and I believe you'll own the ingredients are tolerable. Will you be so good as to pledge me, Sir? Here, Mr. Marlow, here is to our better acquaintance. (*Drinks.*)

Marlow (*aside*). A very impudent fellow this! but he's a character, and I'll humour him a little. Sir, my service to you. (*Drinks.*)

Hastings (*aside*). I see this fellow wants to give us his company, and forgets that he's an innkeeper, before he has learned to be a gentleman.

Marlow. From the excellence of your cup, my old friend, I suppose you have a good deal of business in this part of the country. Warm work, now and then, at elections, I suppose?

Hardcastle. No, Sir, I have long given that work over. Since our betters have hit upon the expedient of electing each other, there's no business *for us that sell ale.*

Hastings. So, then you have no turn for politics, I find.

Hardcastle. Not in the least. There was a time, indeed, I fretted myself about the mistakes of government, like other people; but finding myself every day grow more angry, and the government growing no better, I left it to mend itself. Since that, I no more trouble my head about *Heyder Ally,* or *Ally Cawn,* than about *Ally Croaker.* Sir, my service to you.

Hastings. So that with eating above stairs, and drinking below, with receiving your friends within, and amusing them without, you lead a good, pleasant, bustling life of it.

Hardcastle. I do stir about a great deal, that's certain. Half the differences of the parish are adjusted in this very parlour.

Marlow (*after drinking*). And you have an argument in your cup, old gentleman, better than any in Westminster-hall.

Hardcastle. Ay, young gentleman, that, and a little philosophy.

Marlow (*aside*). Well, this is the first time I ever heard of an inn-keeper's philosophy.

Hastings. So then, like an experienced general, you attack them on every quarter. If you find their reason manageable, you attack it with your philosophy; if you find they have no reason, you attack them with this. Here's your health, my philosopher. (*Drinks.*)

Hardcastle. Good, very good, thank you; ha! ha! Your generalship puts me in mind of Prince Eugene, when he fought the Turks at the battle of Belgrade. You shall hear—

Marlow. Instead of the battle of Belgrade, I believe it's almost time to talk about supper. What has your philosophy got in the house for supper?

Hardcastle. For supper, Sir! (*Aside.*) Was ever such a request to a man in his own house!

Marlow. Yes, Sir, supper, Sir; I begin to feel an appetite. I shall make devilish work to-night in the larder, I promise you.

Hardcastle (*aside*). Such a brazen dog sure never my eyes beheld. (*To him.*) Why really, Sir, as for supper I can't well tell. My Dorothy, and the cook maid, settle these things between them. I leave these kind of things entirely to them.

Marlow. You do, do you?

Hardcastle. Entirely. By-the-bye, I believe they are in actual consultation upon what's for supper this moment in the kitchen.

Marlow. Then I beg they'll admit *me* as one of their privy council. It's a way I have got. When I travel, I always chuse to regulate my own supper. Let the cook be called. No offence, I hope, Sir.

Hardcastle. O no, Sir, none in the least; yet I don't know how: our Bridget, the cook maid, is not very communicative upon these occasions. Should we send for her, she might scold us all out of the house.

Hastings. Let's see your list of the larder then. I ask it as a favour. I always match my appetite to my bill of fare.

Marlow (*to* HARDCASTLE, *who looks at them with*

39–40. **for . . . ale,** for common folk. 48–49. **Heyder Ally,** the Sultan of Mysore. **Ally Cawn,** the Sultan of Bengal. **Ally Croaker,** an Irish street song.

23. **Belgrade,** where the Turks were defeated in 1717.

surprize). Sir, he's very right; and it's my way too.

Hardcastle. Sir, you have a right to command here. Here, Roger, bring us the bill of fare for to-night's supper. I believe it's drawn out. Your manner, Mr. Hastings, puts me in mind of my uncle, Colonel Wallop. It was a saying of his, that no man was sure of his supper till he had eaten it.

Hastings (*aside*). All upon the high ropes! His uncle a colonel! We shall soon hear of his mother being a justice of peace. But let's hear the bill of fare.

Marlow (*perusing*). What's here? For the first course; for the second course; for the desert. The devil, Sir, do you think we have brought down the whole Joiners Company, or the Corporation of Bedford, to eat up such a supper? Two or three little things, clean and comfortable, will do.

Hastings. But, let's hear it.

Marlow (*reading*). For the first course, at the top, a pig, and prune sauce.

Hastings. Damn your pig, I say.

Marlow. And damn your prune sauce, say I.

Hardcastle. And yet, gentlemen, to men that are hungry, pig, with prune sauce, is very good eating.

Marlow. At the bottom, a calve's tongue and brains.

Hastings. Let your brains be knocked out, my good Sir; I don't like them.

Marlow. Or you may clap them on a plate by themselves. I do.

Hardcastle (*aside*). Their impudence confounds me. (*To them.*) Gentlemen, you are my guests. Make what alterations you please. Is there any thing else you wish to retrench or alter, gentlemen?

Marlow. Item: A pork pie, a boiled rabbit and sausages, a florentine, a shaking pudding, and a dish of tiff—taff—taffety cream!

Hastings. Confound your made dishes. I shall be as much at a loss in this house as at a green and yellow dinner at the French Ambassador's table. I'm for plain eating.

Hardcastle. I'm sorry, gentlemen, that I have nothing you like, but if there be any thing you have a particular fancy to—

Marlow. Why, really, Sir, your bill of fare is so exquisite, that any one part of it is full as good as another. Send us what you please. So much for supper. And now to see that our beds are aired, and properly taken care of.

Hardcastle. I entreat you'll leave all that to me. You shall not stir a step.

Marlow. Leave that to you! I protest, Sir, you must excuse me, I always look to these things myself.

Hardcastle. I must insist, Sir, you'll make yourself easy on that head.

Marlow. You see I'm resolved on it. (*Aside.*) A very troublesome fellow this, as ever I met with.

Hardcastle. Well, Sir, I'm resolved at least to attend you. (*Aside.*) This may be modern modesty, but I never saw any thing look so like old-fashioned impudence. [*Exeunt* MARLOW *and* HARDCASTLE.

[HASTINGS, *solus.*]

Hastings. So I find this fellow's civilities begin to grow troublesome. But who can be angry at those assiduities which are meant to please him? Ha! what do I see? Miss Neville, by all that's happy!

[*Enter* MISS NEVILLE.]

Miss Neville. My dear Hastings! To what unexpected good fortune, to what accident am I to ascribe this happy meeting?

Hastings. Rather let me ask the same question, as I could never have hoped to meet my dearest Constance at an inn.

Miss Neville. An inn! sure you mistake! my aunt, my guardian, lives here. What could induce you to think this house an inn?

Hastings. My friend Mr. Marlow, with whom I came down, and I, have been sent here as to an inn, I assure you. A young fellow whom we accidentally met at a house hard by directed us hither.

Miss Neville. Certainly it must be one of my hopeful cousin's tricks, of whom you have heard me talk so often, ha! ha! ha! ha!

Hastings. He whom your aunt intends for you? He of whom I have such just apprehensions?

Miss Neville. You have nothing to fear from him, I assure you. You'd adore him if you knew how heartily he despises me. My aunt knows it too, and has undertaken to court me for him, and actually begins to think she has made a conquest.

Hastings. Thou dear dissembler! You must know, my Constance, I have just seized this happy opportunity of my friend's visit here to get admittance into the family. The horses that carried us down are now fatigued with their journey, but they'll soon be refreshed; and then, if my dearest girl will trust in her faithful Hastings, we shall soon be landed in France, where even among slaves the laws of marriage are respected.

Miss Neville. I have often told you, that though ready to obey you, I yet should leave my little

---

37–38. **florentine,** meat pie. **shaking pudding,** blancmange. **cream!** velvet cream.

fortune behind with reluctance. The greatest part of it was left me by my uncle, the India Director, and chiefly consists in jewels. I have been for some time persuading my aunt to let me wear them. I fancy I'm very near succeeding. The instant they are put into my possession you shall find me ready to make them and myself yours.

Hastings. Perish the baubles! Your person is all I desire. In the meantime, my friend Marlow must not be let into his mistake. I know the strange reserve of his temper is such, that if abruptly informed of it, he would instantly quit the house before our plan was ripe for execution.

Miss Neville. But how shall we keep him in the deception? Miss Hardcastle is just returned from walking; what if we still continue to deceive him?— This, this way— (*They confer.*)

[*Enter* MARLOW.]

Marlow. The assiduities of these good people tease me beyond bearing. My host seems to think it ill manners to leave me alone, and so he claps not only himself but his old-fashioned wife on my back. They talk of coming to sup with us too and then, I suppose, we are to run the gauntlet through all the rest of the family.—What have we got here!—

Hastings. My dear Charles! Let me congratulate you!—The most fortunate accident!—Who do you think is just alighted?

Marlow. Cannot guess.

Hastings. Our mistresses, boy, Miss Hardcastle and Miss Neville. Give me leave to introduce Miss Constance Neville to your acquaintance. Happening to dine in the neighbourhood, they called, on their return, to take fresh horses here. Miss Hardcastle has just stept into the next room, and will be back in an instant. Wasn't it lucky? eh!

Marlow (*aside*). I have just been mortified enough of all conscience, and here comes something to complete my embarrassment.

Hastings. Well! but wasn't it the most fortunate thing in the world?

Marlow. Oh! yes. Very fortunate—a most joyful encounter—But our dresses, George, you know, are in disorder—What if we should postpone the happiness 'till to-morrow?—To-morrow at her own house—It will be every bit as convenient—And rather more respectful—To-morrow let it be. (*Offering to go.*)

Miss Neville. By no means, Sir. Your ceremony will displease her. The disorder of your dress will shew the ardour of your impatience. Besides, she knows you are in the house, and will permit you to see her.

Marlow. O! the devil! how shall I support it? Hem! hem! Hastings, you must not go. You are to assist me, you know. I shall be confoundedly ridiculous. Yet, hang it! I'll take courage. Hem!

Hastings. Pshaw, man! it's but the first plunge, and all's over. She's but a woman, you know.

Marlow. And of all women, she that I dread most to encounter!

[*Enter* MISS HARDCASTLE *as returned from walking, a Bonnet, &c.*]

Hastings (*introducing them*). Miss Hardcastle Mr. Marlow. I'm proud of bringing two persons of such merit together, that only want to know, to esteem each other.

Miss Hardcastle (*aside*). Now, for meeting my modest gentleman with a demure face, and quite in his own manner. (*After a pause, in which he appears very uneasy and disconcerted.*) I'm glad of your safe arrival, Sir—I'm told you had some accidents by the way.

Marlow. Only a few, madam. Yes, we had some. Yes, madam, a good many accidents, but should be sorry—madam—or rather glad of any accidents—that are so agreeably concluded. Hem!

Hastings (*to him*). You never spoke better in your whole life. Keep it up, and I'll insure you the victory.

Miss Hardcastle. I'm afraid you flatter, Sir. You that have seen so much of the finest company can find little entertainment in an obscure corner of the country.

Marlow (*gathering courage*). I have lived, indeed, in the world, madam; but I have kept very little company. I have been but an observer upon life, madam, while others were enjoying it.

Miss Neville. But that, I am told, is the way to enjoy it at last.

Hastings (*to him*). Cicero never spoke better. Once more, and you are confirmed in assurance for ever.

Marlow (*to him*). Hem! Stand by me then, and when I'm down, throw in a word or two to set me up again.

Miss Hardcastle. An observer, like you, upon life, were, I fear, disagreeably employed, since you must have had much more to censure than to approve.

Marlow. Pardon me, madam. I was always willing to be amused. The folly of most people is rather an object of mirth than uneasiness.

2–3. **India Director,** an officer of the East India Company, and so a rich man.

Hastings (*to him*). Bravo, bravo. Never spoke so well in your whole life. Well! Miss Hardcastle, I see that you and Mr. Marlow are going to be very good company. I believe our being here will but embarrass the interview.

Marlow. Not in the least, Mr. Hastings. We like your company of all things. (*To him.*) Zounds! George, sure you won't go! How can you leave us?

Hastings. Our presence will but spoil conversation, so we'll retire to the next room. (*To him.*) You don't consider, man, that we are to manage a little tête-à-tête of our own. [*Exeunt.*

Miss Hardcastle (*after a pause*). But you have not been wholly an observer, I presume, Sir: The ladies I should hope have employed some part of your addresses.

Marlow (*relapsing into timidity*). Pardon me, madam, I—I—I—as yet have studied—only—to—deserve them.

Miss Hardcastle. And that some say is the very worst way to obtain them.

Marlow. Perhaps so, madam. But I love to converse only with the more grave and sensible part of the sex.—But I'm afraid I grow tiresome.

Miss Hardcastle. Not at all, Sir; there is nothing I like so much as grave conversation myself; I could hear it for ever. Indeed I have often been surprized how a man of *sentiment* could ever admire those light airy pleasures, where nothing reaches the heart.

Marlow. It's—a disease—of the mind, madam. In the variety of tastes there must be some who wanting a relish—for—um—a—um.

Miss Hardcastle. I understand you, Sir. There must be some who, wanting a relish for refined pleasures, pretend to despise what they are incapable of tasting.

Marlow. My meaning, madam, but infinitely better expressed. And I can't help observing—a—

Miss Hardcastle (*aside*). Who could ever suppose this fellow impudent upon some occasions. (*To him.*) You were going to observe, Sir—

Marlow. I was observing, madam—I protest, madam, I forget what I was going to observe.

Miss Hardcastle (*aside*). I vow and so do I. (*To him.*) You were observing, Sir, that in this age of hypocrisy—something about hypocrisy, Sir.

Marlow. Yes, madam. In this age of hypocrisy there are few who upon strict enquiry do not—a—a—a—

Miss Hardcastle. I understand you perfectly, Sir.

Marlow (*aside*). Egad! and that's more than I do myself.

Miss Hardcastle. You mean that in this hypocritical age there are few that do not condemn in public what they practise in private, and think they pay every debt to virtue when they praise it.

Marlow. True, madam; those who have most virtue in their mouths, have least of it in their bosoms. But I'm sure I tire you, madam.

Miss Hardcastle. Not in the least, Sir; there's something so agreeable and spirited in your manner, such life and force—pray, Sir, go on.

Marlow. Yes, madam. I was saying—that there are some occasions—when a total want of courage, madam, destroys all the—and puts us—upon a—a—a—

Miss Hardcastle. I agree with you entirely, a want of courage upon some occasions assumes the appearance of ignorance, and betrays us when we most want to excel. I beg you'll proceed.

Marlow. Yes, madam. Morally speaking, madam—But I see Miss Neville expecting us in the next room. I would not intrude for the world.

Miss Hardcastle. I protest, Sir, I never was more agreeably entertained in all my life. Pray go on.

Marlow. Yes, madam. I was—But she beckons us to join her. Madam, shall I do myself the honour to attend you?

Miss Hardcastle. Well then, I'll follow.

Marlow (*aside*). This pretty smooth dialogue has done for me. [*Exit.*

[MISS HARDCASTLE, *sola.*]

Miss Hardcastle. Ha! ha! ha! Was there ever such a sober sentimental interview? I'm certain he scarce looked in my face the whole time. Yet the fellow, but for his unaccountable bashfulness, is pretty well, too. He has good sense, but then so buried in his fears, that it fatigues one more than ignorance. If I could teach him a little confidence, it would be doing somebody that I know of a piece of service. But who is that somebody?—That, faith, is a question I can scarce answer. [*Exit.*

[*Enter* TONY *and* MISS NEVILLE, *followed by* MRS. HARDCASTLE *and* HASTINGS.]

Tony. What do you follow me for, cousin Con? I wonder you're not ashamed to be so very engaging.

Miss Neville. I hope, cousin, one may speak to one's own relations, and not be to blame.

Tony. Ay, but I know what sort of a relation you want to make me though; but it won't do. I tell you, cousin Con, it won't do, so I beg you'll keep your distance. I want no nearer relationship.

[*She follows, coqueting him, to the back scene.*]

45–46. engaging, seductive.

Mrs. Hardcastle. Well! I vow, Mr. Hastings, you are very entertaining. There's nothing in the world I love to talk of so much as London, and the fashions, though I was never there myself.

Hastings. Never there! You amaze me! From your air and manner, I concluded you had been bred all your life either at Ranelagh, St. James's, or Tower Wharf.

Mrs. Hardcastle. O! Sir, you're only pleased to say so. We country persons can have no manner at all. I'm in love with the town, and that serves to raise me above some of our neighbouring rustics; but who can have a manner, that has never seen the Pantheon, the Grotto Gardens, the Borough, and such places where the Nobility chiefly resort? All I can do, is to enjoy London at second-hand. I take care to know every tête-à-tête from the Scandalous Magazine, and have all the fashions, as they come out, in a letter from the two Miss Rickets of Crooked-lane. Pray how do you like this head, Mr. Hastings?

Hastings. Extremely elegant and dégagée, upon my word, madam. Your friseur is a Frenchman, I suppose?

Mrs. Hardcastle. I protest, I dressed it myself from a print in the Ladies Memorandum-book for the last year.

Hastings. Indeed. Such a head in a side-box, at the Playhouse, would draw as many gazers as my Lady May'ress at a City Ball.

Mrs. Hardcastle. I vow, since inoculation began, there is no such thing to be seen as a plain woman; so one must dress a little particular or one may escape in the crowd.

Hastings. But that can never be your case madam, in any dress. (*Bowing.*)

Mrs. Hardcastle. Yet, what signifies *my* dressing when I have such a piece of antiquity by my side as Mr. Hardcastle: all I can say will never argue down a single button from his cloaths. I have often wanted him to throw off his great flaxen wig, and where he was bald, to plaister it over like my Lord Pately, with powder.

Hastings. You are right, madam; for, as among the ladies, there are none ugly, so among the men there are none old.

Mrs. Hardcastle. But what do you think his answer was? Why, with his usual Gothic vivacity, he said I only wanted him to throw off his wig to convert it into a tête for my own wearing.

Hastings. Intolerable! At your age you may wear what you please, and it must become you.

Mrs. Hardcastle. Pray, Mr. Hastings, what do you take to be the most fashionable age about town?

Hastings. Some time ago, forty was all the mode; but I'm told the ladies intend to bring up fifty for the ensuing winter.

Mrs. Hardcastle. Seriously? Then I shall be too young for the fashion.

Hastings. No lady begins now to put on jewels 'till she's past forty. For instance, Miss there, in a polite circle, would be considered as a child, as a mere maker of samplers.

Mrs. Hardcastle. And yet Mrs. Niece thinks herself as much a woman, and is as fond of jewels, as the oldest of us all.

Hastings. Your niece, is she? And that young gentleman, a brother of yours, I should presume?

Mrs. Hardcastle. My son, Sir. They are contracted to each other. Observe their little sports. They fall in and out ten times a day, as if they were man and wife already. (*To them.*) Well, Tony, child, what soft things are you saying to your cousin Constance this evening?

Tony. I have been saying no soft things; but that it's very hard to be followed about so. Ecod! I've not a place in the house now that's left to myself but the stable.

Mrs. Hardcastle. Never mind him, Con, my dear. He's in another story behind your back.

Miss Neville. There's something generous in my cousin's manner. He falls out before faces to be forgiven in private.

Tony. That's a damned confounded—crack.

Mrs. Hardcastle. Ah! he's a sly one. Don't you think they're like each other about the mouth, Mr. Hastings? The Blenkinsop mouth to a T. They're of a size too. Back to back, my pretties, that Mr. Hastings may see you. Come, Tony.

Tony. You had as good not make me, I tell you. (*Measuring.*)

Miss Neville. O lud! he has almost cracked my head.

Mrs. Hardcastle. O the monster! For shame, Tony. You a man, and behave so!

Tony. If I'm a man, let me have my fortin. Ecod! I'll not be made a fool of no longer.

Mrs. Hardcastle. Is this, ungrateful boy, all that I'm to get for the pains I have taken in your education? I that have rocked you in your cradle,

---

8. Tower Wharf, a disreputable East End resort of the vulgar, very different in social rating from Ranelagh and St. James's. **21. head,** coiffure. **31. inoculation,** introduced in 1718 by Lady Mary Wortley Montagu. **34. escape,** be ignored. **50. tête,** head or wig.

15. Mrs. Niece, Mistress, my niece. The title was often given at this time to unmarried women. **35. crack,** euphemism for "lie."

and fed that pretty mouth with a spoon! Did not I work that waistcoat to make you genteel? Did not I prescribe for you every day, and weep while the receipt was operating?

Tony. Ecod! you had reason to weep, for you have been dosing me ever since I was born. I have gone through every receipt in the complete huswife ten times over; and you have thoughts of coursing me through *Quincy* next spring. But, ecod! I tell you, I'll not be made a fool of no longer.

Mrs. Hardcastle. Wasn't it all for your good, viper? Wasn't it all for your good?

Tony. I wish you'd let me and my good alone then. Snubbing this way when I'm in spirits. If I'm to have any good, let it come of itself; not to keep dinging it, dinging it into one so.

Mrs. Hardcastle. That's false; I never see you when you're in spirits. No, Tony, you then go to the ale-house or kennel. I'm never to be delighted with your agreeable, wild notes, unfeeling monster!

Tony. Ecod! Mamma, your own notes are the wildest of the two.

Mrs. Hardcastle. Was ever the like? But I see he wants to break my heart. I see he does.

Hastings. Dear madam, permit me to lecture the young gentleman a little. I'm certain I can persuade him to his duty.

Mrs. Hardcastle. Well! I must retire. Come, Constance, my love. You see, Mr. Hastings, the wretchedness of my situation. Was ever poor woman so plagued with a dear, sweet, pretty, provoking, undutiful boy!

[*Exeunt* MRS. HARDCASTLE *and* MISS NEVILLE.]

[HASTINGS, TONY.]

Tony (*singing*). *There was a young man riding by, and fain would have his will. Rang do didlo dee.* Don't mind her. Let her cry. It's the comfort of her heart. I have seen her and sister cry over a book for an hour together, and they said they liked the book the better the more it made them cry.

Hastings. Then you're no friend to the ladies, I find, my pretty young gentleman?

Tony. That's as I find 'um.

Hastings. Not to her of your mother's chusing, I dare answer. And yet she appears to me a pretty well-tempered girl.

Tony. That's because you don't know her as well as I. Ecod! I know every inch about her; and there's not a more bitter cantanckerous toad in all Christendom.

Hastings (*aside*). Pretty encouragement this for a lover!

Tony. I have seen her since the height of that. She has as many tricks as a hare in a thicket, or a colt the first day's breaking.

Hastings. To me she appears sensible and silent!

Tony. Ay, before company. But when she's with her play-mates she's as loud as a hog in a gate.

Hastings. But there is a meek modesty about her that charms me.

Tony. Yes, but curb her never so little, she kicks up, and you're flung in a ditch.

Hastings. Well, but you must allow her a little beauty.—Yes, you must allow her some beauty.

Tony. Bandbox! She's all a made up thing, mun. Ah! could you but see Bet Bouncer of these parts, you might then talk of beauty. Ecod, she has two eyes as black as sloes, and cheeks as broad and red as a pulpit cushion. She'd make two of she.

Hastings. Well, what say you to a friend that would take this bitter bargain off your hands?

Tony. Anon?

Hastings. Would you thank him that would take Miss Neville and leave you to happiness and your dear Betsy?

Tony. Ay; but where is there such a friend, for who would take *her*?

Hastings. I am he. If you but assist me, I'll engage to whip her off to France, and you shall never hear more of her.

Tony. Assist you! Ecod, I will, to the last drop of my blood. I'll clap a pair of horses to your chaise that shall trundle you off in a twinkling, and may be get you a part of her fortin beside, in jewels, that you little dream of.

Hastings. My dear 'Squire, this looks like a lad of spirit.

Tony. Come along then, and you shall see more of my spirit before you have done with me. (*Singing.*)

We are the boys
That fears no noise
Where the thundering cannons roar. [*Exeunt.*]

ACT III

[*Enter* HARDCASTLE, *solus.*]

Hardcastle. What could my old friend Sir Charles mean by recommending his son as the modestest young man in town? To me he appears the most impudent piece of brass that ever spoke with a tongue. He has taken possession of the easy chair by the fire-

---

7–8. huswife, a book on domestic economy.   9. Quincy, author of *The Complete English Dispensatory*.   22. Anon? How's that?

side already. He took off his boots in the parlour, and desired me to see them taken care of. I'm desirous to know how his impudence affects my daughter.—She will certainly be shocked at it.

[*Enter* MISS HARDCASTLE, *plainly dressed.*]

Hardcastle. Well, my Kate, I see you have changed your dress as I bid you; and yet, I believe, there was no great occasion.

Miss Hardcastle. I find such a pleasure, Sir, in obeying your commands, that I take care to observe them without ever debating their propriety.

Hardcastle. And yet, Kate, I sometimes give you some cause, particularly when I recommended my *modest* gentleman to you as a lover to-day.

Miss Hardcastle. You taught me to expect something extraordinary, and I find the original exceeds the description.

Hardcastle. I was never so surprized in my life! He has quite confounded all my faculties!

Miss Hardcastle. I never saw any thing like it. And a man of the world too!

Hardcastle. Ay, he learned it all abroad,—what a fool was I, to think a young man could learn modesty by travelling. He might as soon learn wit at a masquerade.

Miss Hardcastle. It seems all natural to him.

Hardcastle. A good deal assisted by bad company and a French dancing-master.

Miss Hardcastle. Sure you mistake, Papa! a French dancing-master could never have taught him that timid look,—that awkward address,—that bashful manner—

Hardcastle. Whose look? whose manner? child!

Miss Hardcastle. Mr. Marlow's: his *mauvaise honte*, his timidity struck me at the first sight.

Hardcastle. Then your first sight deceived you; for I think him one of the most brazen first sights that ever astonished my senses.

Miss Hardcastle. Sure, Sir, you rally! I never saw any one so modest.

Hardcastle. And can you be serious! I never saw such a bouncing, swaggering puppy since I was born. Bully Dawson was but a fool to him.

Miss Hardcastle. Surprizing! He met me with a respectful bow, a stammering voice, and a look fixed on the ground.

Hardcastle. He met me with a loud voice, a lordly air, and a familiarity that made my blood freeze again.

Miss Hardcastle. He treated me with diffidence and respect; censured the manners of the age; admired the prudence of girls that never laughed; tired me with apologies for being tiresome; then left the room with a bow, and, "Madam, I would not for the world detain you."

Hardcastle. He spoke to me as if he knew me all his life before. Asked twenty questions, and never waited for an answer. Interrupted my best remarks with some silly pun, and when I was in my best story of the Duke of Marlborough and Prince Eugene, he asked if I had not a good hand at making punch. Yes, Kate, he asked your father if he was a maker of punch!

Miss Hardcastle. One of us must certainly be mistaken.

Hardcastle. If he be what he has shewn himself, I'm determined he shall never have my consent.

Miss Hardcastle. And if he be the sullen thing I take him, he shall never have mine.

Hardcastle. In one thing then we are agreed—to reject him.

Miss Hardcastle. Yes. But upon conditions. For if you should find him less impudent, and I more presuming; if you find him more respectful, and I more importunate—I don't know—the fellow is well enough for a man—Certainly we don't meet many such at a horse race in the country.

Hardcastle. If we should find him so— But that's impossible. The first appearance has done my business. I'm seldom deceived in that.

Miss Hardcastle. And yet there may be many good qualities under that first appearance.

Hardcastle. Ay, when a girl finds a fellow's outside to her taste, she then sets about guessing the rest of his furniture. With her, a smooth face stands for good sense, and a genteel figure for every virtue.

Miss Hardcastle. I hope, Sir, a conversation begun with a compliment to my good sense won't end with a sneer at my understanding?

Hardcastle. Pardon me, Kate. But if young Mr. Brazen can find the art of reconciling contradictions, he may please us both, perhaps.

Miss Hardcastle. And as one of us must be mistaken, what if we go to make further discoveries?

Hardcastle. Agreed. But depend on't I'm in the right.

Miss Hardcastle. And depend on't I'm not much in the wrong. [*Exeunt.*

[*Enter* TONY, *running in with a Casket.*]

Tony. Ecod! I have got them. Here they are. My cousin Con's necklaces, bobs and all. My mother shan't cheat the poor souls out of their fortin neither. O! my genius, is that you?

---

35. **mauvaise honte,** false shame. 44. **Bully Dawson,** a famous ruffian of the time of Addison and Steele.
51. **bobs,** pendants.

[*Enter* HASTINGS.]

Hastings. My dear friend, how have you managed with your mother? I hope you have amused her with pretending love for your cousin, and that you are willing to be reconciled at last? Our horses will be refreshed in a short time, and we shall soon be ready to set off.

Tony. And here's something to bear your charges by the way. (*Giving the casket.*) Your sweetheart's jewels. Keep them, and hang those, I say, that would rob you of one of them.

Hastings. But how have you procured them from your mother?

Tony. Ask me no questions, and I'll tell you no fibs. I procured them by the rule of thumb. If I had not a key to every drawer in Mother's bureau, how could I go to the ale-house so often as I do? An honest man may rob himself of his own at any time.

Hastings. Thousands do it every day. But to be plain with you; Miss Neville is endeavouring to procure them from her aunt this very instant. If she succeeds, it will be the most delicate way at least of obtaining them.

Tony. Well, keep them, till you know how it will be. But I know how it will be well enough; she'd as soon part with the only sound tooth in her head.

Hastings. But I dread the effects of her resentment, when she finds she has lost them.

Tony. Never you mind her resentment. Leave *me* to manage that. I don't value her resentment the bounce of a cracker. Zounds! here they are. Morrice. Prance. [*Exit* HASTINGS.

[TONY, MRS. HARDCASTLE, MISS NEVILLE.]

Mrs. Hardcastle. Indeed, Constance, you amaze me. Such a girl as you want jewels? It will be time enough for jewels, my dear, twenty years hence, when your beauty begins to want repairs.

Miss Neville. But what will repair beauty at forty, will certainly improve it at twenty, madam.

Mrs. Hardcastle. Yours, my dear, can admit of none. That natural blush is beyond a thousand ornaments. Besides, child, jewels are quite out at present. Don't you see half the ladies of our acquaintance, my Lady Kill-day-light, and Mrs. Crump, and the rest of them, carry their jewels to town, and bring nothing but Paste and Marcasites back?

Miss Neville. But who knows, madam, but somebody that shall be nameless would like me best with all my little finery about me?

Mrs. Hardcastle. Consult your glass, my dear, and then see, if with such a pair of eyes, you want any better sparklers. What do you think, Tony, my dear, does your cousin Con want any jewels, in your eyes, to set off her beauty?

Tony. That's as thereafter may be.

Miss Neville. My dear aunt, if you knew how it would oblige me.

Mrs. Hardcastle. A parcel of old-fashioned rose and table-cut things. They would make you look like the court of King Solomon at a puppet-shew. Besides, I believe I can't readily come at them. They may be missing, for aught I know to the contrary.

Tony (*apart to* MRS. HARDCASTLE). Then why don't you tell her so at once, as she's so longing for them. Tell her they're lost. It's the only way to quiet her. Say they're lost, and call me to bear witness.

Mrs. Hardcastle (*apart to* TONY). You know, my dear, I'm only keeping them for you. So if I say they're gone, you'll bear me witness, will you? He! he! he!

Tony. Never fear me. Ecod! I'll say I saw them taken out with my own eyes.

Miss Neville. I desire them but for a day, madam. Just to be permitted to shew them as relicks, and then they may be locked up again.

Mrs. Hardcastle. To be plain with you, my dear Constance, if I could find them, you should have them. They're missing, I assure you. Lost, for aught I know; but we must have patience wherever they are.

Miss Neville. I'll not believe it; this is but a shallow pretence to deny me. I know they're too valuable to be so slightly kept, and as you are to answer for the loss.

Mrs. Hardcastle. Don't be alarmed, Constance. If they be lost, I must restore an equivalent. But my son knows they are missing, and not to be found.

Tony. That I can bear witness to. They are missing, and not to be found, I'll take my oath on't.

Mrs. Hardcastle. You must learn resignation, my dear; for though we lose our fortune, yet we should not lose our patience. See me, how calm I am.

Miss Neville. Ay, people are generally calm at the misfortunes of others.

Mrs. Hardcastle. Now, I wonder a girl of your good sense should waste a thought upon such trumpery. We shall soon find them; and, in the mean time, you shall make use of my garnets till your jewels be found.

Miss Neville. I detest garnets.

Mrs. Hardcastle. The most becoming things in the world to set off a clear complexion. You have often seen how well they look upon me. You *shall* have them. [*Exit.*

---

32. **cracker,** sound of a firecracker. 33. **Prance,** dance away. 48. **Marcasites,** ornaments of iron pyrites, fools' gold.

Miss Neville. I dislike them of all things. You shan't stir.—Was ever any thing so provoking—to mislay my own jewels, and force me to wear her trumpery.

Tony. Don't be a fool. If she gives you the garnets, take what you can get. The jewels are your own already. I have stolen them out of her bureau, and she does not know it. Fly to your spark, he'll tell you more of the matter. Leave me to manage *her*.

Miss Neville. My dear cousin.

Tony. Vanish. She's here, and has missed them already. (*Exit* MISS NEVILLE.) Zounds! how she fidgets and spits about like a Catharine wheel.

[*Enter* MRS. HARDCASTLE.]

Mrs. Hardcastle. Confusion! thieves! robbers! We are cheated, plundered, broke open, undone.

Tony. What's the matter, what's the matter, Mamma? I hope nothing has happened to any of the good family!

Mrs. Hardcastle. We are robbed. My bureau has been broke open, the jewels taken out, and I'm undone.

Tony. Oh! is that all? Ha! ha! ha! By the laws, I never saw it better acted in my life. Ecod, I thought you was ruined in earnest, ha! ha! ha!

Mrs. Hardcastle. Why, boy, I *am* ruined in earnest. My bureau has been broke open, and all taken away.

Tony. Stick to that; ha! ha! ha! stick to that. I'll bear witness, you know, call me to bear witness.

Mrs. Hardcastle. I tell you, Tony, by all that's precious, the jewels are gone, and I shall be ruined for ever.

Tony. Sure I know they're gone, and I am to say so.

Mrs. Hardcastle. My dearest Tony, but hear me. They're gone, I say.

Tony. By the laws, Mamma, you make me for to laugh, ha! ha! I know who took them well enough, ha! ha! ha!

Mrs. Hardcastle. Was there ever such a blockhead, that can't tell the difference between jest and earnest. I tell you I'm not in jest, booby.

Tony. That's right, that's right: You must be in a bitter passion, and then nobody will suspect either of us. I'll bear witness that they are gone.

Mrs. Hardcastle. Was there ever such a cross-grained brute, that won't hear me! Can you bear witness that you're no better than a fool? Was ever poor woman so beset with fools on one hand, and thieves on the other.

Tony. I can bear witness to that.

13. Catharine wheel, a kind of firework.

Mrs. Hardcastle. Bear witness again, you blockhead you, and I'll turn you out of the room directly. My poor niece, what will become of *her!* Do you laugh, you unfeeling brute, as if you enjoyed my distress?

Tony. I can bear witness to that.

Mrs. Hardcastle. Do you insult me, monster? I'll teach you to vex your mother, I will.

Tony. I can bear witness to that.

[*He runs off, she follows him.*

[*Enter* MISS HARDCASTLE *and* Maid.]

Miss Hardcastle. What an unaccountable creature is that brother of mine, to send them to the house as an inn, ha! ha! I don't wonder at his impudence.

Maid. But what is more, madam, the young gentleman as you passed by in your present dress, asked me if you were the bar-maid? He mistook you for the bar-maid, madam.

Miss Hardcastle. Did he? Then as I live, I'm resolved to keep up the delusion. Tell me, Pimple, how do you like my present dress? Don't you think I look something like Cherry in the Beaux' Stratagem?

Maid. It's the dress, madam, that every lady wears in the country, but when she visits, or receives company.

Miss Hardcastle. And are you sure he does not remember my face or person?

Maid. Certain of it.

Miss Hardcastle. I vow, I thought so; for though we spoke for some time together, yet his fears were such, that he never once looked up during the interview. Indeed, if he had, my bonnet would have kept him from seeing me.

Maid. But what do you hope from keeping him in his mistake?

Miss Hardcastle. In the first place, I shall be *seen*, and that is no small advantage to a girl who brings her face to market. Then I shall perhaps make an acquaintance, and that's no small victory gained over one who never addresses any but the wildest of her sex. But my chief aim is to take my gentleman off his guard, and, like an invisible champion of romance, examine the giant's force before I offer to combat.

Maid. But are you sure you can act your part, and disguise your voice, so that he may mistake that, as he has already mistaken your person?

Miss Hardcastle. Never fear me. I think I have got

23–24. Beaux' Stratagem, a comedy by George Farquhar, first produced in 1707. The scene of the play, which gave Goldsmith many hints for *She Stoops to Conquer*, is **an inn**, and **Cherry** is the landlord's daughter.

the true bar-cant.—Did your honour call?—Attend the Lion there.—Pipes and tobacco for the Angel.—The Lamb has been outrageous this half hour.

Maid. It will do, madam. But he's here.

[*Exit* Maid.]

[*Enter* MARLOW.]

Marlow. What a bawling in every part of the house. I have scarce a moment's repose. If I go to the best room, there I find my host and his story. If I fly to the gallery, there we have my hostess with her curtesy down to the ground. I have at last got a moment to myself, and now for recollection. (*Walks and muses.*)

Miss Hardcastle. Did you call, Sir? Did your honour call?

Marlow (*musing*). As for Miss Hardcastle, she's too grave and sentimental for me.

Miss Hardcastle. Did your honour call? (*She still places herself before him, he turning away.*)

Marlow. No, child. (*Musing.*) Besides, from the glimpse I had of her, I think she squints.

Miss Hardcastle. I'm sure, Sir, I heard the bell ring.

Marlow. No, no. (*Musing.*) I have pleased my father, however, by coming down, and I'll to-morrow please myself by returning. (*Taking out his tablets, and perusing.*)

Miss Hardcastle. Perhaps the other gentleman called, Sir?

Marlow. I tell you, no.

Miss Hardcastle. I should be glad to know, Sir. We have such a parcel of servants.

Marlow. No, no, I tell you. (*Looks full in her face.*) Yes, child, I think I did call. I wanted—I wanted—I vow, child, you are vastly handsome.

Miss Hardcastle. O la, Sir, you'll make one ashamed.

Marlow. Never saw a more sprightly, malicious eye. Yes, yes, my dear, I did call. Have you got any of your—a—what d'ye call it in the house?

Miss Hardcastle. No, Sir, we have been out of that these ten days.

Marlow. One may call in this house, I find, to very little purpose. Suppose I should call for a taste, just by way of trial, of the nectar of your lips; perhaps I might be disappointed in that too.

Miss Hardcastle. Nectar! nectar! That's a liquor there's no call for in these parts. French, I suppose. We keep no French wines here, Sir.

Marlow. Of true English growth, I assure you.

Miss Hardcastle. Then it's odd I should not know it. We brew all sorts of wines in this house, and I have lived here these eighteen years.

Marlow. Eighteen years! Why one would think, child, you kept the bar before you were born. How old are you?

Miss Hardcastle. O! Sir, I must not tell my age. They say women and music should never be dated.

Marlow. To guess at this distance, you can't be much above forty. (*Approaching.*) Yet nearer, I don't think so much. (*Approaching.*) By coming close to some women, they look younger still; but when we come very close indeed—(*Attempting to kiss her.*)

Miss Hardcastle. Pray, Sir, keep your distance. One would think you wanted to know one's age as they do horses, by mark of mouth.

Marlow. I protest, child, you use me extremely ill. If you keep me at this distance, how is it possible you and I can be ever acquainted?

Miss Hardcastle. And who wants to be acquainted with you? I want no such acquaintance, not I. I'm sure you did not treat Miss Hardcastle that was here awhile ago in this obstropalous manner. I'll warrant me, before her you looked dashed, and kept bowing to the ground, and talked, for all the world, as if you was before a justice of peace.

Marlow (*aside*). Egad! she has hit it, sure enough. (*To her.*) In awe of her, child? Ha! ha! ha! A mere, awkward, squinting thing, no, no. I find you don't know me. I laughed, and rallied her a little; but I was unwilling to be too severe. No, I could not be too severe, *curse me!*

Miss Hardcastle. O! then, Sir, you are a favourite, I find, among the ladies?

Marlow. Yes, my dear, a great favourite. And yet, hang me, I don't see what they find in me to follow. At the Ladies Club in town, I'm called their agreeable Rattle. Rattle, child, is not my real name, but one I'm known by. My name is Solomons. Mr. Solomons, my dear, at your service. (*Offering to salute her.*)

Miss Hardcastle. Hold, Sir; you are introducing me to your club, not to yourself. And you're so great a favourite there, you say?

Marlow. Yes, my dear. There's Mrs. Mantrap, Lady Betty Blackleg, the Countess of Sligo, Mrs. Langhorns, old Miss Biddy Buckskin, and your humble servant, keep up the spirit of the place.

Miss Hardcastle. Then it's a very merry place, I suppose?

Marlow. Yes, as merry as cards, suppers, wine, and old women can make us.

Miss Hardcastle. And their agreeable Rattle, ha! ha! ha!

Marlow (*aside*). Egad! I don't quite like this chit. She looks knowing, methinks. You laugh, child!

2–3. **Lion . . . Lamb,** rooms of an imaginary inn.
27. **tablets,** memorandum book.

Miss Hardcastle. I can't but laugh to think what time they all have for minding their work or their family.

Marlow (*aside*). All's well; she don't laugh at me. (*To her.*) Do *you* ever work, child?

Miss Hardcastle. Ay, sure. There's not a screen or a quilt in the whole house but what can bear witness to that.

Marlow. Odso! Then you must shew me your embroidery. I embroider and draw patterns myself a little. If you want a judge of your work you must apply to me. (*Seizing her hand.*)

Miss Hardcastle. Ay, but the colours don't look well by candlelight. You shall see all in the morning. (*Struggling.*)

Marlow. And why not now, my angel? Such beauty fires beyond the power of resistance.— Pshaw! the father here! My old luck: I never nicked seven that I did not throw ames ace three times following. [*Exit* MARLOW.

[*Enter* HARDCASTLE, *who stands in surprize.*]

Hardcastle. So, madam. So I find *this* is your *modest* lover. This is your humble admirer that kept his eyes fixed on the ground, and only adored at humble distance. Kate, Kate, art thou not ashamed to deceive your father so?

Miss Hardcastle. Never trust me, dear Papa, but he's still the modest man I first took him for; you'll be convinced of it as well as I.

Hardcastle. By the hand of my body, I believe his impudence is infectious! Didn't I see him seize your hand? Didn't I see him hawl you about like a milkmaid? And now you talk of his respect and his modesty, forsooth!

Miss Hardcastle. But if I shortly convince you of his modesty, that he has only the faults that will pass off with time, and the virtues that will improve with age, I hope you'll forgive him.

Hardcastle. The girl would actually make one run mad! I tell you I'll not be convinced. I am convinced. He has scarcely been three hours in the house, and he has already encroached on all my prerogatives. You may like his impudence, and call it modesty. But my son-in-law, madam, must have very different qualifications.

Miss Hardcastle. Sir, I ask but this night to convince you.

Hardcastle. You shall not have half the time, for I have thoughts of turning him out this very hour.

Miss Hardcastle. Give me that hour then, and I hope to satisfy you.

19. **nicked seven,** made the highest throw, in the game of hazard.   **ames ace,** both aces, the lowest throw.

Hardcastle. Well, an hour let it be then. But I'll have no trifling with your father. All fair and open, do you mind me.

Miss Hardcastle. I hope, Sir, you have ever found that I considered your commands as my pride; for your kindness is such, that my duty as yet has been inclination. [*Exeunt.*

ACT IV

Enter HASTINGS *and* MISS NEVILLE.

Hastings. You surprize me! Sir Charles Marlow expected here this night? Where have you had your information?

Miss Neville. You may depend upon it. I just saw his letter to Mr. Hardcastle, in which he tells him he intends setting out a few hours after his son.

Hastings. Then, my Constance, all must be completed before he arrives. He knows me; and should he find me here, would discover my name, and perhaps my designs, to the rest of the family.

Miss Neville. The jewels, I hope, are safe.

Hastings. Yes, yes. I have sent them to Marlow, who keeps the keys of our baggage. In the meantime, I'll go to prepare matters for our elopement. I have had the Squire's promise of a fresh pair of horses; and, if I should not see him again, will write him further directions. [*Exit.*

Miss Neville. Well! success attend you. In the meantime, I'll go amuse my aunt with the old pretence of a violent passion for my cousin. [*Exit.*

[*Enter* MARLOW, *followed by a* Servant.]

Marlow. I wonder what Hastings could mean by sending me so valuable a thing as a casket to keep for him, when he knows the only place I have is the seat of a post-coach at an Inn-door. Have you deposited the casket with the landlady, as I ordered you? Have you put it into her own hands?

Servant. Yes, your honour.

Marlow. She said she'd keep it safe, did she?

Servant. Yes, she said she'd keep it safe enough; she asked me how I came by it? and she said she had a great mind to make me give an account of myself. [*Exit* Servant.

Marlow. Ha! ha! ha! They're safe however. What an unaccountable set of beings have we got amongst! This little bar-maid though runs in my head most strangely, and drives out the absurdities of all the rest of the family. She's mine, she must be mine, or I'm greatly mistaken.

[*Enter* HASTINGS.]

Hastings. Bless me! I quite forgot to tell her that I intended to prepare at the bottom of the garden. Marlow here, and in spirits too!

Marlow. Give me joy, George! Crown me, shadow me with laurels! Well, George, after all, we modest fellows don't want for success among the women.

Hastings. Some women you mean. But what success has your honour's modesty been crowned with now, that it grows so insolent upon us?

Marlow. Didn't you see the tempting, brisk, lovely little thing that runs about the house with a bunch of keys to its girdle?

Hastings. Well! and what then?

Marlow. She's mine, you rogue you. Such fire, such motion, such eyes, such lips—but, egad! she would not let me kiss them though.

Hastings. But are you so sure, so very sure of her?

Marlow. Why man, she talked of shewing me her work above-stairs, and I am to improve the pattern.

Hastings. But how can *you*, Charles, go about to rob a woman of her honour?

Marlow. Pshaw! pshaw! we all know the honour of the bar-maid of an inn. I don't intend to *rob* her, take my word for it; there's nothing in this house, I shan't honestly *pay* for.

Hastings. I believe the girl has virtue.

Marlow. And if she has, I should be the last man in the world that would attempt to corrupt it.

Hastings. You have taken care, I hope, of the casket I sent you to lock up? It's in safety?

Marlow. Yes, yes. It's safe enough. I have taken care of it. But how could you think the seat of a post-coach at an Inn-door a place of safety? Ah! numbskull! I have taken better precautions for you than you did for yourself.—I have—

Hastings. What?

Marlow. I have sent it to the landlady to keep for you.

Hastings. To the landlady!

Marlow. The landlady.

Hastings. You did!

Marlow. I did. She's to be answerable for its forthcoming, you know.

Hastings. Yes, she'll bring it forth, with a witness.

Marlow. Wasn't I right? I believe you'll allow that I acted prudently upon this occasion?

Hastings (aside). He must not see my uneasiness.

Marlow. You seem a little disconcerted though, methinks. Sure nothing has happened?

Hastings. No, nothing. Never was in better spirits in all my life. And so you left it with the landlady, who, no doubt, very readily undertook the charge?

Marlow. Rather too readily. For she not only kept the casket; but, through her great precaution, was going to keep the messenger too. Ha! ha! ha!

Hastings. He! he! he! They're safe, however.

Marlow. As a guinea in a miser's purse.

Hastings (aside). So now all hopes of fortune are at an end, and we must set off without it. (*To him.*) Well, Charles, I'll leave you to your meditations on the pretty bar-maid, and, he! he! he! may you be as successful for yourself as you have been for me.

[*Exit.*

Marlow. Thank ye, George! I ask no more. Ha! ha! ha!

[*Enter* HARDCASTLE.]

Hardcastle. I no longer know my own house. It's turned all topsey-turvey. His servants have got drunk already. I'll bear it no longer, and yet, from my respect for his father, I'll be calm. (*To him.*) Mr. Marlow, your servant. I'm your very humble servant. (*Bowing low.*)

Marlow. Sir, your humble servant. (*Aside.*) What's to be the wonder now?

Hardcastle. I believe, Sir, you must be sensible, Sir, that no man alive ought to be more welcome than your father's son, Sir. I hope you think so?

Marlow. I do from my soul, Sir. I don't want much intreaty. I generally make my father's son welcome wherever he goes.

Hardcastle. I believe you do, from my soul, Sir. But though I say nothing to your own conduct, that of your servants is insufferable. Their manner of drinking is setting a very bad example in this house, I assure you.

Marlow. I protest, my very good Sir, that's no fault of mine. If they don't drink as they ought *they* are to blame. I ordered them not to spare the cellar. I did, I assure you. (*To the side scene.*) Here, let one of my servants come up. (*To him.*) My positive directions were, that as I did not drink myself, they should make up for my deficiencies below.

Hardcastle. Then they had your orders for what they do! I'm satisfied!

Marlow. They had, I assure you. You shall hear from one of themselves.

[*Enter* Servant, *drunk.*]

Marlow. You, Jeremy! Come forward, sirrah! What were my orders? Were you not told to drink freely, and call for what you thought fit, for the good of the house?

Hardcastle (aside). I begin to lose my patience.

39. **side scene,** wings of the stage.

Jeremy. Please your honour, liberty and Fleet-street for ever! Though I'm but a servant, I'm as good as another man. I'll drink for no man before supper, Sir, dammy! Good liquor will sit upon a good supper, but a good supper will not sit upon—hiccup—upon my conscience, Sir. [*Exit.* JEREMY.

Marlow. You see, my old friend, the fellow is as drunk as he can possibly be. I don't know what you'd have more, unless you'd have the poor devil soused in a beer-barrel.

Hardcastle. Zounds! He'll drive me distracted if I contain myself any longer. Mr. Marlow, Sir; I have submitted to your insolence for more than four hours, and I see no likelihood of its coming to an end. I'm now resolved to be master here, Sir, and I desire that you and your drunken pack may leave my house directly.

Marlow. Leave your house!—Sure you jest, my good friend? What, when I'm doing what I can to please you!

Hardcastle. I tell you, Sir, you don't please me; so I desire you'll leave my house.

Marlow. Sure you cannot be serious? At this time o' night, and such a night. You only mean to banter me?

Hardcastle. I tell you, Sir, I'm serious; and, now that my passions are roused, I say this house is mine, Sir; this house is mine, and I command you to leave it directly.

Marlow. Ha! ha! ha! A puddle in a storm. I shan't stir a step, I assure you. (*In a serious tone.*) This, your house, fellow! It's my house. This is my house. Mine, while I chuse to stay. What right have you to bid me leave this house, Sir? I never met with such impudence, curse me, never in my whole life before.

Hardcastle. Nor I, confound me if ever I did. To come to my house, to call for what he likes, to turn me out of my own chair, to insult the family, to order his servants to get drunk, and then to tell me *This house is mine, Sir.* By all that's impudent, it makes me laugh. Ha! ha! ha! Pray, Sir, (*Bantering.*) as you take the house, what think you of taking the rest of the furniture? There's a pair of silver candle-sticks, and there's a fire-screen, and here's a pair of brazen-nosed bellows, perhaps you may take a fancy to them?

Marlow. Bring me your bill, Sir, bring me your bill, and let's make no more words about it.

Hardcastle. There are a set of prints too. What think you of the Rake's Progress for your own apartment?

51. the Rake's Progress, a set of engravings with this title, by William Hogarth, was published in 1735.

Marlow. Bring me your bill, I say; and I'll leave you and your infernal house directly.

Hardcastle. Then there's a mahogany table, that you may see your own face in.

Marlow. My bill, I say.

Hardcastle. I had forgot the great chair, for your own particular slumbers, after a hearty meal.

Marlow. Zounds! bring me my bill, I say, and let's hear no more on't.

Hardcastle. Young man, young man, from your father's letter to me, I was taught to expect a well-bred modest man as a visitor here, but now I find him no better than a coxcomb and a bully; but he will be down here presently, and shall hear more of it. [*Exit.*

Marlow. How's this! Sure I have not mistaken the house! Every thing looks like an inn. The servants cry, Coming. The attendance is awkward; the bar-maid too, to attend us. But she's here, and will further inform me. Whither so fast, child? A word with you.

[*Enter* MISS HARDCASTLE.]

Miss Hardcastle. Let it be short then. I'm in a hurry. (*Aside.*) I believe he begins to find out his mistake, but it's too soon quite to undeceive him.

Marlow. Pray, child, answer me one question. What are you, and what may your business in this house be?

Miss Hardcastle. A relation of the family, Sir.

Marlow. What! A poor relation?

Miss Hardcastle. Yes, Sir. A poor relation appointed to keep the keys, and to see that the guests want nothing in my power to give them.

Marlow. That is, you act as the bar-maid of this inn.

Miss Hardcastle. Inn! O law—What brought that in your head? One of the best families in the county keep an inn! Ha, ha, ha, old Mr. Hardcastle's house an inn?

Marlow. Mr. Hardcastle's house? Is this house Mr. Hardcastle's house, child?

Miss Hardcastle. Ay, sure. Whose else should it be?

Marlow. So then all's out, and I have been damnably imposed on. O, confound my stupid head, I shall be laughed at over the whole town. I shall be stuck up in caricatura in all the print-shops. The Dullissimo Maccaroni. To mistake this house of all others for an inn, and my father's old friend for an inn-keeper! What a swaggering puppy must he take me for. What a silly puppy do I find myself. There

50. Dullissimo Maccaroni, Stupidest Blockhead.

again, may I be hanged, my dear, but I mistook you for the bar-maid.

Miss Hardcastle. Dear me! dear me! I'm sure there's nothing in my *behaviour* to put me upon a level with one of that stamp.

Marlow. Nothing, my dear, nothing. But I was in for a list of blunders, and could not help making you a subscriber. My stupidity saw every thing the wrong way. I mistook your assiduity for assurance, and your simplicity for allurement. But its over— This house I no more shew *my* face in.

Miss Hardcastle. I hope, Sir, I have done nothing to disoblige you. I'm sure I should be sorry to affront any gentleman who has been so polite, and said so many civil things to me. I'm sure I should be sorry (*Pretending to cry.*) if he left the family upon my account. I'm sure I should be sorry people said any thing amiss, since I have no fortune but my character.

Marlow (*aside*). By heaven, she weeps. This is the first mark of tenderness I ever had from a modest woman, and it touches me. (*To her.*) Excuse me, my lovely girl, you are the only part of the family I leave with reluctance. But to be plain with you, the difference of our birth, fortune and education, make an honourable connexion impossible; and I can never harbour a thought of seducing simplicity that trusted in my honour, or bringing ruin upon one, whose only fault was being too lovely.

Miss Hardcastle (*aside*). Generous man! I now begin to admire him. (*To him.*) But I'm sure my family is as good as Miss Hardcastle's, and though I'm poor, that's no great misfortune to a contented mind; and, until this moment, I never thought that it was bad to want fortune.

Marlow. And why now, my pretty simplicity?

Miss Hardcastle. Because it puts me at a distance from one, that if I had a thousand pound I would give it all to.

Marlow (*aside*). This simplicity bewitches me, so that if I stay I'm undone. I must make one bold effort, and leave her. (*To her.*) Your partiality in my favour, my dear, touches me most sensibly, and were I to live for myself alone, I could easily fix my choice. But I owe too much to the opinion of the world, too much to the authority of a father, so that—I can scarcely speak it—it affects me. Farewell. [*Exit.*

Miss Hardcastle. I never knew half his merit till now. He shall not go, if I have power or art to detain him. I'll still preserve the character in which I stooped to conquer, but will undeceive my papa, who, perhaps, may laugh him out of his resolution.

[*Exit.*

[*Enter* TONY, MISS NEVILLE.]

Tony. Ay, you may steal for yourselves the next time. I have done my duty. She has got the jewels again, that's a sure thing; but she believes it was all a mistake of the servants.

Miss Neville. But, my dear cousin, sure you won't forsake us in this distress. If she in the least suspects that I am going off, I shall certainly be locked up, or sent to my aunt Pedigree's, which is ten times worse.

Tony. To be sure, aunts of all kinds are damned bad things. But what can I do? I have got you a pair of horses that will fly like Whistlejacket, and I'm sure you can't say but I have courted you nicely before her face. Here she comes; we must court a bit or two more, for fear she should suspect us. (*They retire, and seem to fondle.*)

[*Enter* MRS. HARDCASTLE.]

Mrs. Hardcastle. Well, I was greatly fluttered, to be sure. But my son tells me it was all a mistake of the servants. I shan't be easy, however, till they are fairly married, and then let her keep her own fortune. But what do I see! Fondling together, as I'm alive. I never saw Tony so sprightly before. Ah! have I caught you, my pretty doves! What, billing, exchanging stolen glances, and broken murmurs. Ah!

Tony. As for murmurs, mother, we grumble a little now and then, to be sure. But there's no love lost between us.

Mrs. Hardcastle. A mere sprinkling, Tony, upon the flame, only to make it burn brighter.

Miss Neville. Cousin Tony promises to give us more of his company at home. Indeed, he shan't leave us any more. It won't leave us, cousin Tony, will it?

Tony. O! it's a pretty creature. No, I'd sooner leave my horse in a pound, than leave you when you smile upon one so. Your laugh makes you so becoming.

Miss Neville. Agreeable cousin! Who can help admiring that natural humour, that pleasant, broad, red, thoughtless, (*Patting his cheek.*) ah! it's a bold face.

Mrs. Hardcastle. Pretty innocence!

Tony. I'm sure I always loved cousin Con's hazel eyes, and her pretty long fingers, that she twists this way and that, over the haspicholls, like a parcel of bobbins.

Mrs. Hardcastle. Ah, he would charm the bird from the tree. I was never so happy before. My boy takes after his father, poor Mr. Lumpkin, exactly.

49. **haspicholls,** harpsichord.

The jewels, my dear Con, shall be yours incontinently. You shall have them. Isn't he a sweet boy, my dear? You shall be married to-morrow, and we'll put off the rest of his education, like Dr. Drowsy's sermons, to a fitter opportunity.

[*Enter* DIGGORY.]

Diggory. Where's the 'Squire? I have got a letter for your worship.

Tony. Give it to my mamma. She reads all my letters first.

Diggory. I had orders to deliver it into your own hands.

Tony. Who does it come from?

Diggory. Your worship mun ask that o' the letter itself. [*Exit* DIGGORY.

Tony. I could wish to know, though. (*Turning the letter, and gazing on it.*)

Miss Neville (*aside*). Undone, undone. A letter to him from Hastings. I know the hand. If my aunt sees it, we are ruined for ever. I'll keep her employed a little if I can. (*To* MRS. HARDCASTLE.) But I have not told you, madam, of my cousin's smart answer just now to Mr. Marlow. We so laughed— You must know, madam—this way a little, for he must not hear us. (*They confer.*)

Tony (*still gazing*). A damned cramp piece of penmanship, as ever I saw in my life. I can read your print-hand very well. But here there are such handles, and shanks, and dashes, that one can scarce tell the head from the tail. *To Anthony Lumpkin, Esquire.* It's very odd, I can read the outside of my letters, where my own name is, well enough. But when I come to open it, it's all—buzz. That's hard, very hard; for the inside of the letter is always the cream of the correspondence.

Mrs. Hardcastle. Ha! ha! ha! Very well, very well. And so my son was too hard for the philosopher.

Miss Neville. Yes, madam; but you must hear the rest, madam. A little more this way, or he may hear us. You'll hear how he puzzled him again.

Mrs. Hardcastle. He seems strangely puzzled now himself, methinks.

Tony (*still gazing*). A damned up and down hand, as if it was disguised in liquor. (*Reading.*) Dear Sir. Ay, that's that. Then there's an *M*, and a *T*, and an *S*, but whether the next be an *izzard* or an *R*, confound me, I cannot tell.

Mrs. Hardcastle. What's that, my dear? Can I give you any assistance?

Miss Neville. Pray, aunt, let me read it. No body reads a cramp hand better than I. (*Twitching the letter from her.*) Do you know who it is from?

47. **izzard,** the letter "z."

Tony. Can't tell, except from Dick Ginger the feeder.

Miss Neville. Ay, so it is. (*Pretending to read.*) Dear 'Squire, Hoping that you're in health, as I am at this present. The gentlemen of the Shake-bag club has cut the gentlemen of Goose-green quite out of feather. The odds—um—odd battle—um—long fighting—um, here, here, it's all about cocks, and fighting; it's of no consequence; here, put it up, put it up. (*Thrusting the crumpled letter upon him.*)

Tony. But I tell you, miss, it's of all the consequence in the world. I would not lose the rest of it for a guinea. Here, mother, do you make it out. Of no consequence! (*Giving* MRS. HARDCASTLE *the letter.*)

Mrs. Hardcastle. How's this! (*Reads.*) "Dear 'Squire, I'm now waiting for Miss Neville, with a post-chaise and pair, at the bottom of the garden, but I find my horses yet unable to perform the journey. I expect you'll assist us with a pair of fresh horses, as you promised. Dispatch is necessary, as the *hag*, (ay, the hag) your mother, will otherwise suspect us. Yours, Hastings." Grant me patience. I shall run distracted. My rage choaks me.

Miss Neville. I hope, madam, you'll suspend your resentment for a few moments, and not impute to me any impertinence, or sinister design that belongs to another.

Mrs. Hardcastle (*curtesying very low*). Fine spoken, madam; you are most miraculously polite and engaging, and quite the very pink of courtesy and circumspection, madam. (*Changing her tone.*) And you, you great ill-fashioned oaf, with scarce sense enough to keep your mouth shut. Were you too joined against me? But I'll defeat all your plots in a moment. As for you, madam, since you have got a pair of fresh horses ready, it would be cruel to disappoint them. So, if you please, instead of running away with your spark, prepare, this very moment, to run off with *me*. Your old Aunt Pedigree will keep you secure, I'll warrant me. You too, Sir, may mount your horse, and guard us upon the way. Here, Thomas, Roger, Diggory! I'll shew you, that I wish you better than you do yourselves. [*Exit.*

Miss Neville. So now I'm completely ruined.

Tony. Ay, that's a sure thing.

Miss Neville. What better could be expected from being connected with such a stupid fool, and after all the nods and signs I made him.

Tony. By the laws, miss, it was your own cleverness, and not my stupidity, that did your business. You were so nice and so busy with your Shake-bags and Goose-greens, that I thought you could never be making believe.

[*Enter* HASTINGS.]

Hastings. So, Sir, I find by my servant, that you have shewn my letter, and betrayed us. Was this well done, young gentleman?

Tony. Here's another. Ask miss there who betrayed you. Ecod, it was her doing, not mine.

[*Enter* MARLOW.]

Marlow. So I have been finely used here among you. Rendered contemptible, driven into ill manners, despised, insulted, laughed at.

Tony. Here's another. We shall have old Bedlam broke loose presently.

Miss Neville. And there, Sir, is the gentleman to whom we all owe every obligation.

Marlow. What can I say to him, a mere boy, an idiot, whose ignorance and age are a protection.

Hastings. A poor contemptible booby, that would but disgrace correction.

Miss Neville. Yet with cunning and malice enough to make himself merry with all our embarrassments.

Hastings. An insensible cub.

Marlow. Replete with tricks and mischief.

Tony. Baw! damme, but I'll fight you both one after the other,—with baskets.

Marlow. As for him, he's below resentment. But your conduct, Mr. Hastings, requires an explanation. You knew of my mistakes, yet would not undeceive me.

Hastings. Tortured as I am with my own disappointments, is this a time for explanations? It is not friendly, Mr. Marlow.

Marlow. But, Sir—

Miss Neville. Mr. Marlow, we never kept on your mistake, till it was too late to undeceive you. Be pacified.

[*Enter* Servant.]

Servant. My mistress desires you'll get ready immediately, madam. The horses are putting to. Your hat and things are in the next room. We are to go thirty miles before morning. [*Exit* Servant.

Miss Neville. Well, well; I'll come presently.

Marlow (*to* HASTINGS). Was it well done, Sir, to assist in rendering me ridiculous? To hang me out for the scorn of all my acquaintance? Depend upon it, Sir, I shall expect an explanation.

Hastings. Was it well done, Sir, if you're upon that subject, to deliver what I entrusted to yourself, to the care of another, Sir?

Miss Neville. Mr. Hastings. Mr. Marlow. Why

27. **baskets,** basket-hilted swords.

will you increase my distress by this groundless dispute? I implore, I intreat you—

[*Enter* Servant.]

Servant. Your cloak, madam. My mistress is impatient.

Miss Neville. I come. (*Exit* Servant.) Pray be pacified. If I leave you thus, I shall die with apprehension.

[*Enter* Servant.]

Servant. Your fan, muff, and gloves, madam. The horses are waiting.

Miss Neville. O, Mr. Marlow! if you knew what a scene of constraint and ill-nature lies before me, I'm sure it would convert your resentment into pity.

Marlow. I'm so distracted with a variety of passions, that I don't know what I do. Forgive me, madam. George, forgive me. You know my hasty temper, and should not exasperate it.

Hastings. The torture of my situation is my only excuse.

Miss Neville. Well, my dear Hastings, if you have that esteem for me that I think, that I am sure you have, your constancy for three years will but encrease the happiness of our future connexion. If—

Mrs. Hardcastle (*within*). Miss Neville. Constance, why Constance, I say!

Miss Neville. I'm coming. Well, constancy. Remember, constancy is the word. [*Exit.*

Hastings. My heart! How can I support this! To be so near happiness, and such happiness.

Marlow (*to* TONY). You see now, young gentleman, the effects of your folly. What might be amusement to you, is here disappointment, and even distress.

Tony (*from a reverie*). Ecod, I have hit it. It's here. Your hands. Yours and yours, my poor Sulky. My boots there, ho! Meet me two hours hence at the bottom of the garden; and if you don't find Tony Lumpkin a more good-natured fellow than you thought for, I'll give you leave to take my best horse, and Bet Bouncer into the bargain. Come along. My boots, ho! [*Exeunt.*

ACT V

SCENE—*Continues.*

Enter HASTINGS *and* Servant.

Hastings. You saw the old lady and Miss Neville drive off, you say?

Servant. Yes, your honour. They went off in a

post-coach, and the young 'Squire went on horseback. They're thirty miles off by this time.

Hastings. Then all my hopes are over.

Servant. Yes, Sir. Old Sir Charles is arrived. He and the old gentleman of the house have been laughing at Mr. Marlow's mistake this half hour. They are coming this way.

Hastings. Then I must not be seen. So now to my fruitless appointment at the bottom of the garden. This is about the time.   [*Exit.*

[*Enter* SIR CHARLES *and* HARDCASTLE.]

Hardcastle. Ha! ha! ha! The peremptory tone in which he sent forth his sublime commands.

Sir Charles. And the reserve with which I suppose he treated all your advances.

Hardcastle. And yet he might have seen something in me above a common inn-keeper, too.

Sir Charles. Yes, Dick, but he mistook you for an uncommon inn-keeper, ha! ha! ha!

Hardcastle. Well, I'm in too good spirits to think of any thing but joy. Yes, my dear friend, this union of our families will make our personal friendships hereditary; and though my daughter's fortune is but small—

Sir Charles. Why, Dick, will you talk of fortune to *me.* My son is possessed of more than a competence already, and I can want nothing but a good and virtuous girl to share his happiness and encrease it. If they like each other, as you say they do—

Hardcastle. If, man. I tell you they *do* like each other. My daughter as good as told me so.

Sir Charles. But girls are apt to flatter themselves, you know.

Hardcastle. I saw him grasp her hand in the warmest manner myself; and here he comes to put you out of your *ifs,* I warrant him.

[*Enter* MARLOW.]

Marlow. I come Sir, once more, to ask pardon for my strange conduct. I can scarce reflect on my insolence without confusion.

Hardcastle. Tut, boy, a trifle. You take it too gravely. An hour or two's laughing with my daughter will set all to rights again. She'll never like you the worse for it.

Marlow. Sir, I shall be always proud of her approbation.

Hardcastle. Approbation is but a cold word, Mr. Marlow; if I am not deceived, you have something more than approbation thereabouts. You take me.

Marlow. Really, Sir, I have not that happiness.

Hardcastle. Come, boy, I'm an old fellow, and know what's what, as well as you that are younger. I know what has past between you; but mum.

Marlow. Sure, Sir, nothing has past between us but the most profound respect on my side and the most distant reserve on hers. You don't think, Sir, that my impudence has been past upon all the rest of the family?

Hardcastle. Impudence! No, I don't say that—Not quite impudence—Though girls like to be played with, and rumpled a little too sometimes. But she has told no tales, I assure you.

Marlow. I never gave her the slightest cause.

Hardcastle. Well, well, I like modesty in its place well enough. But this is over-acting, young gentleman. You may be open. Your father and I will like you the better for it.

Marlow. May I die, Sir, if I ever—

Hardcastle. I tell you, she don't dislike you; and as I'm sure you like her—

Marlow. Dear Sir—I protest, Sir,—

Hardcastle. I see no reason why you should not be joined as fast as the parson can tie you.

Marlow. But hear me, Sir—

Hardcastle. Your father approves the match, I admire it, every moment's delay will be doing mischief, so—

Marlow. But why won't you hear me? By all that's just and true, I never gave Miss Hardcastle the slightest mark of my attachment, or even the most distant hint to suspect me of affection. We had but one interview, and that was formal, modest and uninteresting.

Hardcastle (*aside*). This fellow's formal modest impudence is beyond bearing.

Sir Charles. And you never grasped her hand, or made any protestations!

Marlow. As heaven is my witness, I came down in obedience to your commands. I saw the lady without emotion, and parted without reluctance. I hope you'll exact no further proofs of my duty, nor prevent me from leaving a house in which I suffer so many mortifications.   [*Exit.*

Sir Charles. I'm astonished at the air of sincerity with which he parted.

Hardcastle. And I'm astonished at the deliberate intrepidity of his assurance.

Sir Charles. I dare pledge my life and honour upon his truth.

Hardcastle. Here comes my daughter, and I would stake my happiness upon her veracity.

[*Enter* MISS HARDCASTLE.]

Hardcastle. Kate, come hither, child. Answer us sincerely, and without reserve; has Mr. Marlow made you any professions of love and affection?

Miss Hardcastle. The question is very abrupt, Sir! But since you require unreserved sincerity, I think he has.

Hardcastle (*to* SIR CHARLES). You see.

Sir Charles. And pray, madam, have you and my son had more than one interview?

Miss Hardcastle. Yes, Sir, several.

Hardcastle (*to* SIR CHARLES). You see.

Sir Charles. But did he profess any attachment?

Miss Hardcastle. A lasting one.

Sir Charles. Did he talk of love?

Miss Hardcastle. Much, Sir.

Sir Charles. Amazing! And all this formally?

Miss Hardcastle. Formally.

Hardcastle. Now, my friend, I hope you are satisfied.

Sir Charles. And how did he behave, madam?

Miss Hardcastle. As most profest admirers do. Said some civil things to my face, talked much of his want of merit, and the greatness of mine; mentioned his heart, gave a short tragedy speech, and ended with pretended rapture.

Sir Charles. Now I'm perfectly convinced, indeed. I know his conversation among women to be modest and submissive. This forward canting, ranting manner by no means describes him, and I am confident, he never sate for the picture.

Miss Hardcastle. Then what, Sir, if I should convince you to your face of my sincerity? If you and my papa, in about half an hour, will place yourselves behind that screen, you shall hear him declare his passion to me in person.

Sir Charles. Agreed. And if I find him what you describe, all my happiness in him must have an end. [*Exit.*

Miss Hardcastle. And if you don't find him what I describe—I fear my happiness must never have a beginning. [*Exeunt.*

SCENE.—*Changes to the Back of the Garden.*

Enter HASTINGS.

Hastings. What an idiot am I, to wait here for a fellow, who probably takes delight in mortifying me. He never intended to be punctual, and I'll wait no longer. What do I see! It is he, and perhaps with news of my Constance.

[*Enter* TONY, *booted and spattered.*]

Hastings. My honest 'Squire! I now find you a man of your word. This looks like friendship.

Tony. Ay, I'm your friend, and the best friend you have in the world, if you knew but all. This riding by night, by-the-bye, is cursedly tiresome. It has shook me worse than the basket of a stage-coach.

Hastings. But how? Where did you leave your fellow travellers? Are they in safety? Are they housed?

Tony. Five and twenty miles in two hours and a half is no such bad driving. The poor beasts have smoked for it: Rabbet me, but I'd rather ride forty miles after a fox, than ten with such *varment.*

Hastings. Well, but where have you left the ladies? I die with impatience.

Tony. Left them? Why, where should I leave them, but where I found them?

Hastings. This is a riddle.

Tony. Riddle me this then. What's that goes round the house, and round the house, and never touches the house?

Hastings. I'm still astray.

Tony. Why that's it, mon. I have led them astray. By jingo, there's not a pond or slough within five miles of the place but they can tell the taste of.

Hastings. Ha, ha, ha, I understand; you took them in a round, while they supposed themselves going forward. And so you have at last brought them home again.

Tony. You shall hear. I first took them down Feather-bed-lane, where we stuck fast in the mud. I then rattled them crack over the stones of Up-and-down Hill—I then introduced them to the gibbet on Heavy-tree Heath, and from that, with a circumbendibus, I fairly lodged them in the horse-pond at the bottom of the garden.

Hastings. But no accident, I hope.

Tony. No, no. Only Mother is confoundedly frightened. She thinks herself forty miles off. She's sick of the journey, and the cattle can scarce crawl. So if your own horses be ready, you may whip off with cousin, and I'll be bound that no soul here can budge a foot to follow you.

Hastings. My dear friend, how can I be grateful?

Tony. Ay, now it's dear friend, noble 'Squire. Just now, it was all idiot, cub, and run me through the guts. Damn *your* way of fighting, I say. After we take a knock in this part of the country, we kiss and be friends. But if you had run me through the guts, then I should be dead, and you might go kiss the hangman.

Hastings. The rebuke is just. But I must hasten to relieve Miss Neville; if you keep the old lady employed, I promise to take care of the young one. [*Exit* HASTINGS.

Tony. Never fear me. Here she comes. Vanish. She's got from the pond, and draggled up to the waist like a mermaid.

[*Enter* MRS. HARDCASTLE.]

Mrs. Hardcastle. Oh, Tony, I'm killed. Shook. Battered to death! I shall never survive it. That last jolt that laid us against the quickset hedge has done my business.

Tony. Alack, Mamma, it was all your own fault. You would be for running away by night, without knowing one inch of the way.

Mrs. Hardcastle. I wish we were at home again. I never met so many accidents in so short a journey. Drenched in the mud, overturned in a ditch, stuck fast in a slough, jolted to a jelly, and at last to lose our way. Whereabouts do you think we are, Tony?

Tony. By my guess we should be upon Crackskull common, about forty miles from home.

Mrs. Hardcastle. O lud! O lud! the most notorious spot in all the country. We only want a robbery to make a complete night on't.

Tony. Don't be afraid, mamma, don't be afraid. Two of the five that kept here are hanged, and the other three may not find us. Don't be afraid. Is that a man that's galloping behind us? No; it's only a tree. Don't be afraid.

Mrs. Hardcastle. The fright will certainly kill me.

Tony. Do you see any thing like a black hat moving behind the thicket?

Mrs. Hardcastle. O death!

Tony. No, it's only a cow. Don't be afraid, Mamma; don't be afraid.

Mrs. Hardcastle. As I'm alive, Tony, I see a man coming towards us. Ah! I'm sure on't. If he perceives us, we are undone.

Tony (*aside*). Father-in-law, by all that's unlucky, come to take one of his night walks. (*To her.*) Ah, it's a highwayman, with pistols as long as my arm. A damned ill-looking fellow.

Mrs. Hardcastle. Good heaven defend us! He approaches.

Tony. Do you hide yourself in that thicket, and leave me to manage him. If there be any danger, I'll cough and cry hem. When I cough be sure to keep close.

[MRS. HARDCASTLE *hides behind a tree in the back scene.*

Enter HARDCASTLE.]

Hardcastle. I'm mistaken, or I heard voices of people in want of help. Oh, Tony, is that you! I did not expect you so soon back. Are your mother and her charge in safety?

25. **kept,** resorted.

Tony. Very safe, Sir, at my aunt Pedigree's. Hem.

Mrs. Hardcastle (*from behind*). Ah death! I find there's danger.

Hardcastle. Forty miles in three hours; sure that's too much, my youngster.

Tony. Stout horses and willing minds make short journeys, as they say. Hem.

Mrs. Hardcastle (*from behind*). Sure he'll do the dear boy no harm.

Hardcastle. But I heard a voice here; I should be glad to know from whence it came?

Tony. It was I, Sir, talking to myself, Sir. I was saying that forty miles in four hours was very good going. Hem. As to be sure it was. Hem. I have got a sort of cold by being out in the air. We'll go in, if you please. Hem.

Hardcastle. But if you talked to yourself, you did not answer yourself. I am certain I heard two voices, and am resolved (*Raising his voice.*) to find the other out.

Mrs. Hardcastle (*from behind*). Oh! he's coming to find me out. Oh!

Tony. What need you go, Sir, if I tell you. Hem. I'll lay down my life for the truth—hem—I'll tell you all, Sir. (*Detaining him.*)

Hardcastle. I tell you, I will not be detained. I insist on seeing. It's in vain to expect I'll believe you.

Mrs. Hardcastle (*running forward from behind*). O lud! he'll murder my poor boy, my darling. Here, good gentleman, whet your rage upon me. Take my money, my life, but spare that young gentleman, spare my child, if you have any mercy!

Hardcastle. My wife! as I'm a Christian. From whence can she come, or what does she mean.

Mrs. Hardcastle (*kneeling*). Take compassion on us, good Mr. Highwayman. Take our money, our watches, all we have, but spare our lives. We will never bring you to justice, indeed we won't, good Mr. Highwayman.

Hardcastle. I believe the woman's out of her senses. What, Dorothy, don't you know *me?*

Mrs. Hardcastle. Mr. Hardcastle, as I'm alive! My fears blinded me. But who, my dear, could have expected to meet you here, in this frightful place, so far from home. What has brought you to follow us?

Hardcastle. Sure, Dorothy, you have not lost your wits. So far from home, when you are within forty yards of your own door. (*To him.*) This is one of your old tricks, you graceless rogue you. (*To her.*) Don't you know the gate, and the mulberry-tree; and don't you remember the horse-pond, my dear?

Mrs. Hardcastle. Yes, I shall remember the horse-pond as long as I live; I have caught my death in it. (*To* TONY.) And is it to you, you graceless varlet, I owe all this? I'll teach you to abuse your mother, I will.

Tony. Ecod, Mother, all the parish says you have spoiled me, and so you may take the fruits on't.

Mrs. Hardcastle. I'll spoil you, I will.
[*Follows him off the stage.*]

Hardcastle. There's morality, however, in his reply. [*Exit.*

[*Enter* HASTINGS *and* MISS NEVILLE.]

Hastings. My dear Constance, why will you deliberate thus? If we delay a moment, all is lost for ever. Pluck up a little resolution, and we shall soon be out of the reach of her malignity.

Miss Neville. I find it impossible. My spirits are so sunk with the agitations I have suffered, that I am unable to face any new danger. Two or three years patience will at last crown us with happiness.

Hastings. Such a tedious delay is worse than inconstancy. Let us fly, my charmer. Let us date our happiness from this very moment. Perish fortune! Love and content will encrease what we possess beyond a monarch's revenue. Let me prevail!

Miss Neville. No, Mr. Hastings; no. Prudence once more comes to my relief, and I will obey its dictates. In the moment of passion, fortune may be despised, but it ever produces a lasting repentance. I'm resolved to apply to Mr. Hardcastle's compassion and justice for redress.

Hastings. But though he had the will, he has not the power to relieve you.

Miss Neville. But he has influence, and upon that I am resolved to rely.

Hastings. I have no hopes. But since you persist, I must reluctantly obey you. [*Exeunt.*

SCENE.—*Changes.*

Enter SIR CHARLES *and* MISS HARDCASTLE

Sir Charles. What a situation am I in. If what you say appears, I shall then find a guilty son. If what he says be true, I shall then lose that one, of all others, I most wished for a daughter.

Miss Hardcastle. I am proud of your approbation, and to shew I merit it, if you place yourselves as I directed, you shall hear his explicit declaration. But he comes.

Sir Charles. I'll to your father, and keep him to the appointment. [*Exit* SIR CHARLES.

[*Enter* MARLOW.]

Marlow. Though prepared for setting out, I come once more to take leave, nor did I, till this moment, know the pain I feel in the separation.

Miss Hardcastle (*in her own natural manner*). I believe these sufferings cannot be very great, Sir, which you can so easily remove. A day or two longer, perhaps, might lessen your uneasiness, by shewing the little value of what you now think proper to regret.

Marlow (*aside*). This girl every moment improves upon me. (*To her.*) It must not be, Madam. I have already trifled too long with my heart. My very pride begins to submit to my passion. The disparity of education and fortune, the anger of a parent, and the contempt of my equals, begin to lose their weight; and nothing can restore me to myself, but this painful effort of resolution.

Miss Hardcastle. Then go, Sir. I'll urge nothing more to detain you. Though my family be as good as hers you came down to visit, and my education, I hope, not inferior, what are these advantages without equal affluence? I must remain contented with the slight approbation of imputed merit; I must have only the mockery of your addresses, while all your serious aims are fixed on fortune.

[*Enter* HARDCASTLE *and* SIR CHARLES *from behind.*]

Sir Charles. Here, behind this screen.

Hardcastle. Ay, ay, make no noise. I'll engage my Kate covers him with confusion at last.

Marlow. By heavens, madam, fortune was ever my smallest consideration. Your beauty at first caught my eye; for who could see that without emotion? But every moment that I converse with you steals in some new grace, heightens the picture, and gives it stronger expression. What at first seemed rustic plainness, now appears refined simplicity. What seemed forward assurance, now strikes me as the result of courageous innocence, and conscious virtue.

Sir Charles. What can it mean! He amazes me!

Hardcastle. I told you how it would be. Hush!

Marlow. I am now determined to stay, madam, and I have too good an opinion of my father's discernment, when he sees you, to doubt his approbation.

Miss Hardcastle. No, Mr. Marlow, I will not, cannot detain you. Do you think I could suffer a connexion, in which there is the smallest room for repentance? Do you think I would take the mean advantage of a transient passion, to load you with confusion? Do you think I could ever relish that happiness, which was acquired by lessening yours?

Marlow. By all that's good, I can have no happiness but what's in your power to grant me. Nor shall I ever feel repentance, but in not having seen your merits before. I will stay, even contrary to your wishes; and though you should persist to shun me, I will make my respectful assiduities atone for the levity of my past conduct.

Miss Hardcastle. Sir, I must entreat you'll desist. As our acquaintance began, so let it end, in indifference. I might have given an hour or two to levity; but seriously, Mr. Marlow, do you think I could ever submit to a connexion, where *I* must appear mercenary, and *you* imprudent? Do you think I could ever catch at the confident addresses of a secure admirer?

Marlow (*kneeling*). Does this look like security? Does this look like confidence? No, madam, every moment that shews me your merit, only serves to encrease my diffidence and confusion. Here let me continue—

Sir Charles. I can hold it no longer. Charles, Charles, how hast thou deceived me! Is this your indifference, your uninteresting conversation!

Hardcastle. Your cold contempt; your formal interview! What have you to say now?

Marlow. That I'm all amazement! What can it mean!

Hardcastle. It means that you can say and unsay things at pleasure. That you can address a lady in private, and deny it in public; that you have one story for us, and another for my daughter.

Marlow. Daughter!—this lady your daughter!

Hardcastle. Yes, Sir, my only daughter. My Kate, whose else should she be?

Marlow. Oh, the devil!

Miss Hardcastle. Yes, Sir, that very identical tall squinting lady you were pleased to take me for. (*Curtesying.*) She that you addressed as the mild, modest, sentimental man of gravity, and the bold, forward, agreeable Rattle of the ladies' club; ha, ha, ha!

Marlow. Zounds, there's no bearing this; it's worse than death.

Miss Hardcastle. In which of your characters, Sir, will you give us leave to address you? As the faltering gentleman, with looks on the ground, that speaks just to be heard, and hates hypocrisy; or the loud, confident creature, that keeps it up with Mrs. Mantrap, and old Miss Biddy Buckskin, till three in the morning; ha, ha, ha!

Marlow. O, curse on my noisy head. I never attempted to be impudent yet, that I was not taken down. I must be gone.

Hardcastle. By the hand of my body, but you shall not. I see it was all a mistake, and I am rejoiced to find it. You shall not, Sir, I tell you. I know she'll forgive you. Won't you forgive him, Kate? We'll all forgive you. Take courage, man.
[*They retire, she tormenting him, to the back Scene.*
   Enter MRS. HARDCASTLE, TONY.]

Mrs. Hardcastle. So, so, they're gone off. Let them go, I care not.

Hardcastle. Who gone?

Mrs. Hardcastle. My dutiful niece and her gentleman, Mr. Hastings, from Town. He who came down with our modest visitor here.

Sir Charles. Who, my honest George Hastings? As worthy a fellow as lives, and the girl could not have made a more prudent choice.

Hardcastle. Then, by the hand of my body, I'm proud of the connexion.

Mrs. Hardcastle. Well, if he has taken away the lady, he has not taken her fortune. That remains in this family to console us for her loss.

Hardcastle. Sure, Dorothy, you would not be so mercenary?

Mrs. Hardcastle. Ay, that's my affair, not yours. But you know if your son, when of age, refuses to marry his cousin, her whole fortune is then at her own disposal.

Hardcastle. Ay, but he's not of age, and she has not thought proper to wait for his refusal.

[*Enter* HASTINGS *and* MISS NEVILLE.]

Mrs. Hardcastle (*aside*). What! returned so soon! I begin not to like it.

Hastings (*to* HARDCASTLE). For my late attempt to fly off with your niece, let my present confusion be my punishment. We are now come back, to appeal from your justice to your humanity. By her father's consent, I first paid her my addresses, and our passions were first founded in duty.

Miss Neville. Since his death, I have been obliged to stoop to dissimulation to avoid oppression. In an hour of levity, I was ready even to give up my fortune to secure my choice. But I'm now recovered from the delusion, and hope from your tenderness what is denied me from a nearer connexion.

23. **secure,** assured.

Mrs. Hardcastle. Pshaw, pshaw, this is all but the whining end of a modern novel.

Hardcastle. Be it what it will, I'm glad they're come back to reclaim their due. Come hither, Tony boy. Do you refuse this lady's hand whom I now offer you?

Tony. What signifies my refusing? You know I can't refuse her till I'm of age, father.

Hardcastle. While I thought concealing your age, boy, was likely to conduce to your improvement, I concurred with your mother's desire to keep it secret. But since I find she turns it to a wrong use, I must now declare, you have been of age these three months.

Tony. Of age! Am I of age, father?

Hardcastle. Above three months.

Tony. Then you'll see the first use I'll make of my liberty. (*Taking* MISS NEVILLE'S *hand.*) Witness all men by these presents, that I, Anthony Lumpkin, Esquire, of Blank place, refuse you, Constantia Neville, spinster, of no place at all, for my true and lawful wife. So Constance Neville may marry whom she pleases, and Tony Lumpkin is his own man again!

Sir Charles. O brave 'Squire!

Hastings. My worthy friend!

Mrs. Hardcastle. My undutiful offspring!

Marlow. Joy, my dear George, I give you joy sincerely. And could I prevail upon my little tyrant here to be less arbitrary, I should be the happiest man alive, if you would return me the favour.

Hastings (*to* MISS HARDCASTLE). Come, madam, you are now driven to the very last scene of all your contrivances. I know you like him, I'm sure he loves you, and you must and shall have him.

Hardcastle (*joining their hands*). And I say so too. And Mr. Marlow, if she makes as good a wife as she has a daughter, I don't believe you'll ever repent your bargain. So now to supper. To-morrow we shall gather all the poor of the parish about us, and the Mistakes of the Night shall be crowned with a merry morning; so boy, take her; and as you have been mistaken in the mistress, my wish is, that you may never be mistaken in the wife.

FINIS

EPILOGUE

To Be Spoken in the Character of Miss Hardcastle

by Dr. Goldsmith

Well, having stooped to conquer with success,
And gained a husband without aid from dress,
Still as a bar-maid, I could wish it too,
As I have conquered him to conquer you:
And let me say, for all your resolution,
That pretty bar-maids have done execution.
Our life is all a play, composed to please,
"We have our exits and our entrances."
The first act shews the simple country maid,
Harmless and young, of every thing afraid; 10
Blushes when hired, and with unmeaning action,
"*I hopes as how to give you satisfaction.*"
Her second act displays a livelier scene—
The unblushing bar-maid of a country inn,
Who whisks about the house, at market caters,
Talks loud, coquets the guests, and scolds the waiters.
Next the scene shifts to town, and there she soars,
The chop-house toast of ogling connoissieurs.
On 'squires and cits she there displays her arts,
And on the gridiron broils her lovers' hearts— 20
And as she smiles, her triumphs to compleat,
E'en Common Councilmen forget to eat.
The fourth act shews her wedded to the 'squire,
And madam now begins to hold it higher;
Pretends to taste, at Operas cries *caro*,
And quits her Nancy Dawson, for *Che Faro*.
Doats upon dancing, and in all her pride
Swims round the room, the *Heinel* of Cheapside:
Ogles and leers with artificial skill,
Till having lost in age the power to kill, 30
She sits all night at cards, and ogles at spadille.
Such, through our lives, the eventful history—
The fifth and last act still remains for me.
The Bar-maid now for your protection prays,
Turns female Barrister, and pleads for Bayes.

8. "We . . . entrances." See *As You Like It*, Act II, sc. 7, l. 141. This passage is followed out in the remaining lines of the Epilogue. **26. Nancy Dawson,** a popular song. **Che Faro,** from Gluck's opera *Orfeo*, 1764 **28. Heinel,** Madame Heinel, a popular German dancer. **35. Bayes,** the name under which John Dryden is ridiculed in Buckingham's *The Rehearsal*, 1672.

Edmund Burke
1729—1797

The most powerful political writer and one of the most devoted patriots in English history was born in Dublin on January 12, 1729, and educated there at Trinity College. He studied law in London, but, partly because he was drawn aside by strong philosophic and literary interests, never entered the legal profession. His career in the House of Commons, lasting from 1765 to 1794, was less brilliant than it might have been but for the fact that he was steadily in opposition to the "personal government" of George III. This opposition was shown in the first of his three chief political efforts, that which led up to his great speech *On Conciliation with America*, delivered in 1775. His next decade was given primarily to questions of British rule in India and to the impeachment and trial of Warren Hastings. From the year 1789 until his death he gave the greater part of his strength to the problems outlined in his noblest production, the *Reflections on the Revolution in France*, 1790.

Edmund Burke did not possess all the qualities that make for immediate oratorical success, but no one has ever surpassed him, in any language, as a political thinker and writer. His answers to the basic questions of statecraft and statesmanship are grounded in philosophy and enlivened by a poetic imagination of high order. In his own thought and writing, at any rate, he lifted politics to the high levels which they attained now and then in the ancient world, showing once more that the tasks of the true statesman call for the loftiest and most disinterested endeavor of the most gifted minds.

To use terms familiar in our day, Burke was both liberal and conservative. He was at the same time an exponent of idealism and a champion of common sense. Although it was the ingrained habit of his mind to carry every question back to first principles, he was also, upon what seemed to him the right occasions, an advocate of expediency. Superficially considered, his career may seem inconsistent, and many have asked how it happened that he who was so favorably inclined toward the revolution in the American colonies could be so bitterly opposed to the revolution in France. But there is in fact no contradiction here. Throughout his life Burke fought for an ordered and regular liberty such as he believed the American colonies were seeking. He passionately believed, like Tennyson, in "freedom slowly broadening down from precedent to precedent." But a wild freedom, on the other hand, expressing itself in defiance of all tradition, he feared and hated. He brought over into political and social philosophy that delight in order—a delight at once intellectual and esthetic and religious—which, since the time of Sir Isaac Newton, had been a prime characteristic of thoughtful Englishmen. To this he added the fire of an Irish fancy, an amazing amplitude of utterance, vast knowledge of literature and history and contemporary affairs, and a dignity of mind and character to match the splendor of all that he wrote and spoke.

Burke's prose may err at times on the side of amplitude. Occasionally it may be too highly colored. Its frequently amazing vividness of pictorial effect dazzles the eyes of a generation brought up to distrust all rhetorical display. It has a wide emotional gamut ranging from tenderness to fiery indignation, and this too we tend to distrust. Yet it should be apparent to anyone—or, if it is not, then the effort to write a logical brief of the speech *On Conciliation* should make it so—that Burke's prose has an admirable solidity of structure. It shows "fundamental brainwork" to a degree in which it is seldom found even in the most restrained and purely intellectual writers. If Burke's mural decorations seem to us too garish, we do well to remember that he built the walls he painted.

The speeches and writings of Edmund Burke have been strangely neglected in recent years, as though we had come to feel, even here in America, that they have nothing more to teach us. Yet the time may come, and not long hence, when we shall feel the need of a political and social wisdom drawn, as Burke's was, not from the passing hour and day but from the ages. We too may have to consider in some time of supreme national crisis, as Burke did, the history and precise nature of that liberty within the law which is perhaps the most precious gift handed down to us out of the English past. In such a time, if it comes, we may well return to the pages of Edmund Burke not only for the glory of their eloquence but for that light of the mind and warmth of the heart which our fathers found in them.

from REFLECTIONS ON THE REVOLUTION IN FRANCE

AND

ON THE PROCEEDINGS IN CERTAIN SOCIETIES IN LONDON RELATIVE TO THAT EVENT

IN A LETTER

INTENDED TO HAVE BEEN SENT TO A GENTLEMAN IN PARIS

YOU will observe, that, from Magna Charta to the Declaration of Right, it has been the uniform policy of our Constitution to claim and assert our liberties, as an *entailed inheritance* derived to us from our forefathers, and to be transmitted to our posterity; as an estate specially belonging to the people of this kingdom, without any reference whatever to any other more general or prior right. By this means our Constitution preserves an unity in so great a diversity of its parts. We have an inheritable crown; an inheritable peerage; and a House of Commons and a people inheriting privileges, franchises, and liberties, from a long line of ancestors.

This policy appears to me to be the result of profound reflection; or rather the happy effect of following nature, which is wisdom without reflection, and above it. A spirit of innovation is generally the result of a selfish temper and confined views. People will not look forward to posterity, who never look backward to their ancestors. Besides, the people of England well know, that the idea of inheritance furnishes a sure principle of conservation, and a sure principle of transmission; without at all excluding a principle of improvement. It leaves acquisition free; but it secures what it acquires. Whatever advantages are obtained by a state proceeding on these maxims, are locked fast as in a sort of family settlement; grasped as in a kind of mortmain for ever. By a constitutional policy, working after the pattern of nature, we receive, we hold, we transmit our government and our privileges, in the same manner in which we enjoy and transmit our property and our lives. The institutions of policy, the goods of fortune, the gifts of Providence, are handed down to us, and from us, in the same course and order. Our political system is placed in a just correspondence and symmetry with the order of the world, and with the mode of existence decreed to a permanent body composed of transitory parts; wherein, by the disposition of a stupendous wisdom, moulding together the great mysterious incorporation of the human race, the whole, at one time, is never old, or middle-aged, or young, but, in a condition of unchangeable constancy, moves on through the varied tenour of perpetual decay, fall, renovation, and progression. Thus, by preserving the method of nature in the conduct of the state, in what we improve we are never wholly new; in what we retain we are never wholly obsolete. By adhering in this manner and on those principles to our forefathers, we are guided not by the superstition of antiquarians, but by the spirit of philosophic analogy. In this choice of inheritance we have given to our frame of polity the image of a relation in blood; binding up the Constitution of our country with our dearest domestic ties; adopting our fundamental laws into the bosom of our family affections; keeping inseparable, and cherishing with the warmth of all their combined and mutually reflected charities, our state, our hearths, our sepulchres, and our altars.

Through the same plan of a conformity to nature in our artificial institutions, and by calling in the aid of her unerring and powerful instincts, to fortify the fallible and feeble contrivances of our reason, we have derived several other, and those no small benefits, from considering our liberties in the light of an inheritance. Always acting as if in the presence of canonized forefathers, the spirit of freedom, leading in itself to misrule and excess, is tempered with an awful gravity. This idea of a liberal descent inspires us with a sense of habitual native dignity, which prevents that upstart insolence almost inevitably adhering to and disgracing those who are the first acquirers of any distinction. By this means our liberty becomes a noble freedom. It carries an imposing and majestic aspect. It has a pedigree and illustrating ancestors. It has its bearings and its ensigns armorial. It has its gallery of portraits; its monumental inscriptions; its records, evidences, and titles. We procure reverence to our civil institutions on the principle upon which nature teaches us to revere individual men: on account of their age, and on account of those from whom they are descended. All your sophisters cannot produce anything better adapted to preserve a rational and manly freedom than the course that we have pursued, who have chosen our nature rather than our speculations, our breasts rather than our inventions, for the great conservatories and magazines of our rights and privileges.

10–11. Gentleman in Paris, a young Frenchman by the name of T. M. Dupont who had asked Burke's opinion on the events of the French Revolution. **14. Declaration of Right,** presented to William and Mary on February 13, 1689. Burke elsewhere calls it "the corner-stone of our Constitution."

You might, if you pleased, have profited of our example, and have given to your recovered freedom a correspondent dignity. Your privileges, though discontinued, were not lost to memory. Your constitution, it is true, whilst you were out of possession, suffered waste and dilapidation; but you possessed in some parts the walls, and in all the foundations, of a noble and venerable castle. You might have repaired those walls; you might have built on those old foundations. Your constitution was suspended before it was perfected; but you had the elements of a constitution very nearly as good as could be wished. In your old states you possessed that variety of parts corresponding with the various descriptions of which your community was happily composed; you had all that combination, and all that opposition of interests, you had that action and counteraction, which, in the natural and in the political world, from the reciprocal struggle of discordant powers, draws out the harmony of the universe. These opposed and conflicting interests, which you considered as so great a blemish in your old and in our present Constitution, interpose a salutary check to all precipitate resolutions. They render deliberation a matter not of choice, but of necessity; they make all change a subject of *compromise*, which naturally begets moderation; they produce *temperaments*, preventing the sore evil of harsh, crude, unqualified reformations, and rendering all the headlong exertions of arbitrary power, in the few or in the many, for ever impracticable. Through that diversity of members and interests, general liberty had as many securities as there were separate views in the several orders; whilst by pressing down the whole by the weight of a real monarchy, the separate parts would have been prevented from warping and starting from their allotted places.

You had all these advantages in your ancient states; but you chose to act as if you had never been moulded into civil society, and had everything to begin anew. You began ill, because you began by despising everything that belonged to you. You set up your trade without a capital. If the last generations of your country appeared without much lustre in your eyes, you might have passed them by, and derived your claims from a more early race of ancestors. Under a pious predilection for those ancestors, your imaginations would have realized in them a standard of virtue and wisdom, beyond the vulgar practice of the hour: and you would have risen with the example to whose imitation you aspired. Respecting your forefathers, you would have been taught to respect yourselves. You would not have chosen to consider the French as a people of yesterday, as a nation of low-born servile wretches until the emancipating year of 1789. In order to furnish, at the expense of your honour, an excuse to your apologists here for several enormities of yours, you would not have been content to be represented as a gang of Maroon slaves, suddenly broke loose from the house of bondage, and therefore to be pardoned for your abuse of the liberty to which you were not accustomed, and were ill fitted. Would it not, my worthy friend, have been wiser to have you thought, what I, for one, always thought you, a generous and gallant nation, long misled to your disadvantage by your high and romantic sentiments of fidelity, honour, and loyalty; that events had been unfavourable to you, but that you were not enslaved through any illiberal or servile disposition; that in your most devoted submission, you were actuated by a principle of public spirit, and that it was your country you worshipped, in the person of your king? Had you made it to be understood, that in the delusion of this amiable error you had gone further than your wise ancestors; that you were resolved to resume your ancient privileges, whilst you preserved the spirit of your ancient and your recent loyalty and honour; or if diffident of yourselves, and not clearly discerning the almost obliterated constitution of your ancestors, you had looked to your neighbours in this land, who had kept alive the ancient principles and models of the old common law of Europe meliorated and adapted to its present state—by following wise examples you would have given new examples of wisdom to the world. You would have rendered the cause of liberty venerable in the eyes of every worthy mind in every nation. You would have shamed despotism from the earth, by showing that freedom was not only reconcilable, but, as, when well disciplined it is, auxiliary to law. You would have had an unoppressive but a productive revenue. You would have had a flourishing commerce to feed it. You would have had a free constitution; a potent monarchy; a disciplined army; a reformed and venerated clergy; a mitigated but spirited nobility, to lead your virtue, not to overlay it; you would have had a liberal order of commons, to emulate and to recruit that nobility; you would have had a protected, satisfied, laborious, and obedient people, taught to seek and to recognize the happiness that is to be found by virtue in all conditions, in which consists the true moral equality of mankind, and not in that monstrous fiction, which, by inspiring false ideas and vain expec-

27. **temperaments,** mixtures of differing qualities.

7. **Maroon slaves,** fugitive slaves living as savages in the West Indies and Guiana.

tations into men destined to travel in the obscure walk of laborious life, serves only to aggravate and embitter that real inequality, which it never can remove; and which the order of civil life establishes as much for the benefit of those whom it must leave in an humble state, as those whom it is able to exalt to a condition more splendid, but not more happy. You had a smooth and easy career of felicity and glory laid open to you, beyond anything recorded in the history of the world; but you have shown that difficulty is good for man.

Compute your gains; see what is got by those extravagant and presumptuous speculations which have taught your leaders to despise all their predecessors, and all their contemporaries, and even to despise themselves, until the moment in which they became truly despicable. By following those false lights, France has bought undisguised calamities at a higher price than any nation has purchased the most unequivocal blessings. France has bought poverty by crime! France has not sacrificed her virtue to her interest; but she has abandoned her interest, that she might prostitute her virtue. All other nations have begun the fabric of a new government, or the reformation of an old, by establishing originally, or by enforcing with greater exactness, some rites or other of religion. All other people have laid the foundations of civil freedom in severer manners, and a system of a more austere and masculine morality. France, when she let loose the reins of regal authority, doubled the licence of a ferocious dissoluteness in manners, and of an insolent irreligion in opinions and practices; and has extended through all ranks of life, as if she were communicating some privilege, or laying open some secluded benefit, all the unhappy corruptions that usually were the disease of wealth and power. This is one of the new principles of equality in France.

France, by the perfidy of her leaders, has utterly disgraced the tone of lenient council in the cabinets of princes, and disarmed it of its most potent topics. She has sanctified the dark, suspicious maxims of tyrannous distrust; and taught kings to tremble at (what will hereafter be called) the delusive plausibilities of moral politicians. Sovereigns will consider those who advise them to place an unlimited confidence in their people, as subverters of their thrones; as traitors who aim at their destruction, by leading their easy good-nature, under specious pretences, to admit combinations of bold and faithless men into a participation of their power. This alone, if there were nothing else, is an irreparable calamity to you and to mankind. Remember that your Parliament of Paris told your king, that, in calling the states together, he had nothing to fear but the prodigal excess of their zeal in providing for the support of the throne. It is right that these men should hide their heads. It is right that they should bear their part in the ruin which their counsel has brought on their sovereign and their country. Such sanguine declarations tend to lull authority asleep; to encourage it rashly to engage in perilous adventures of untried policy; to neglect those provisions, preparations, and precautions, which distinguish benevolence from imbecility; and without which no man can answer for the salutary effect of any abstract plan of government or of freedom. For want of these, they have seen the medicine of the state corrupted into its poison. They have seen the French rebel against a mild and lawful monarch, with more fury, outrage, and insult, than ever any people has been known to rise against the most illegal usurper, or the most sanguinary tyrant. Their resistance was made to concession; their revolt was from protection; their blow was aimed at a hand holding out graces, favours, and immunities.

This was unnatural. The rest is in order. They have found their punishment in their success. Laws overturned; tribunals subverted; industry without vigour; commerce expiring; the revenue unpaid, yet the people impoverished; a church pillaged, and a state not relieved; civil and military anarchy made the constitution of the kingdom; everything human and divine sacrificed to the idol of public credit, and national bankruptcy the consequence; and to crown all, the paper securities of new, precarious, tottering power, the discredited paper securities of impoverished fraud, and beggared rapine, held out as a currency for the support of an empire, in lieu of the two great recognized species that represent the lasting, conventional credit of mankind, which disappeared and hid themselves in the earth from whence they came, when the principle of property, whose creatures and representatives they are, was systematically subverted.

Were all these dreadful things necessary? Were they the inevitable results of the desperate struggle of determined patriots, compelled to wade through blood and tumult, to the quiet shore of a tranquil and prosperous liberty? No! nothing like it. The fresh ruins of France, which shock our feelings wherever we can turn our eyes, are not the devastation of civil war; they are the sad but instructive monuments of rash and ignorant counsel in time of profound peace. They are the display of inconsiderate and presumptuous, because unresisted and irresistible authority. The persons who have thus squan-

36. **species,** kind of money—gold and silver.

dered away the precious treasure of their crimes, the persons who have made this prodigal and wild waste of public evils (the last stake reserved for the ultimate ransom of the state) have met in their progress with little, or rather with no opposition at all. Their whole march was more like a triumphal procession than the progress of a war. Their pioneers have gone before them, and demolished and laid everything level at their feet. Not one drop of *their* blood have they shed in the cause of the country they have ruined. They have made no sacrifices to their projects of greater consequence than their shoe-buckles, whilst they were imprisoning their king, murdering their fellow-citizens, and bathing in tears, and plunging in poverty and distress, thousands of worthy men and worthy families. Their cruelty has not even been the base result of fear. It has been the effect of their sense of perfect safety, in authorizing treasons, robberies, rapes, assassinations, slaughters, and burnings, throughout their harassed land. But the cause of all was plain from the beginning.

This unforced choice, this fond election of evil, would appear perfectly unaccountable, if we did not consider the composition of the National Assembly; I do not mean its formal constitution, which, as it now stands, is exceptionable enough, but the materials of which, in a great measure, it is composed, which is of ten thousand times greater consequence than all the formalities in the world. If we were to know nothing of this assembly but by its title and function, no colours could paint to the imagination anything more venerable. In that light the mind of an inquirer, subdued by such an awful image as that of the virtue and wisdom of a whole people collected into one focus, would pause and hesitate in condemning things even of the very worst aspect. Instead of blamable, they would appear only mysterious. But no name, no power, no function, no artificial institution whatsoever, can make the men of whom any system of authority is composed, any other than God, and nature, and education, and their habits of life have made them. Capacities beyond these the people have not to give. Virtue and wisdom may be the objects of their choice; but their choice confers neither the one nor the other on those upon whom they lay their ordaining hands. They have not the engagement of nature, they have not the promise of revelation for any such powers. . . .

It is now sixteen or seventeen years since I saw the Queen of France, then the dauphiness, at Versailles; and surely never lighted on this orb, which she hardly seemed to touch, a more delightful vision. I saw her just above the horizon, decorating and cheering the elevated sphere she just began to move in—glittering like the morning-star, full of life, and splendour, and joy. Oh! what a revolution! and what a heart must I have, to contemplate without emotion that elevation and that fall! Little did I dream when she added titles of veneration to those of enthusiastic, distant, respectful love, that she should ever be obliged to carry the sharp antidote against disgrace concealed in that bosom; little did I dream that I should have lived to see such disasters fallen upon her in a nation of gallant men, in a nation of men of honour, and of cavaliers. I thought ten thousand swords must have leaped from their scabbards to avenge even a look that threatened her with insult. But the age of chivalry is gone. That of sophisters, economists, and calculators, has succeeded; and the glory of Europe is extinguished for ever. Never, never more, shall we behold that generous loyalty to rank and sex, that proud submission, that dignified obedience, that subordination of the heart, which kept alive, even in servitude itself, the spirit of an exalted freedom. The unbought grace of life, the cheap defence of nations, the nurse of manly sentiment and heroic enterprise is gone! It is gone, that sensibility of principle, that chastity of honour, which felt a stain like a wound, which inspired courage whilst it mitigated ferocity, which ennobled whatever it touched, and under which vice itself lost half its evil, by losing all its grossness.

This mixed system of opinion and sentiment had its origin in the ancient chivalry; and the principle, though varied in its appearance by the varying state of human affairs, subsisted and influenced through a long sucession of generations, even to the time we live in. If it should ever be totally extinguished, the loss I fear will be great. It is this which has given its character to modern Europe. It is this which has distinguished it under all its forms of government, and distinguished it to its advantage, from the states of Asia, and possibly from those states which flourished in the most brilliant periods of the antique world. It was this which, without confounding ranks, had produced a noble equality, and handed it down through all the gradations of social life. It was this opinion which mitigated kings into companions, and raised private men to be fellows with kings. Without force, or opposition, it subdued the fierceness of pride and power; it obliged sovereigns to submit to the soft collar of social esteem, compelled stern authority to submit

---

7. **pioneers,** pick-and-shovel men who prepare the way for an army.

to elegance, and gave a domination, vanquisher of laws, to be subdued by manners.

But now all is to be changed. All the pleasing illusions, which made power gentle, and obedience liberal, which harmonized the different shades of life, and which, by a bland assimilation, incorporated into politics the sentiments which beautify and soften private society, are to be dissolved by this new conquering empire of light and reason. All the decent drapery of life is to be rudely torn off. All the superadded ideas, furnished from the wardrobe of a moral imagination, which the heart owns and the understanding ratifies, as necessary to cover the defects of our naked, shivering nature, and to raise it to dignity in our own estimation, are to be exploded as a ridiculous, absurd, and antiquated fashion.

On this scheme of things, a king is but a man, a queen is but a woman; a woman is but an animal; and an animal not of the highest order. All homage paid to the sex in general as such, and without distinct views, is to be regarded as romance and folly. Regicide, and parricide, and sacrilege, are but fictions of superstition, corrupting jurisprudence by destroying its simplicity. The murder of a king, or a queen, or a bishop, or a father, are only common homicide; and if the people are by any chance or in any way gainers by it, a sort of homicide much the most pardonable, and into which we ought not to make too severe a scrutiny.

On the scheme of this barbarous philosophy, which is the offspring of cold hearts and muddy understandings, and which is as void of solid wisdom, as it is destitute of all taste and elegance, laws are to be supported only by their own terrors, and by the concern, which each individual may find in them, from his own private speculations, or can spare to them from his own private interests. In the groves of *their* academy, at the end of every vista, you see nothing but the gallows. Nothing is left which engages the affections on the part of the commonwealth. On the principles of this mechanic philosophy, our institutions can never be embodied, if I may use the expression, in persons; so as to create in us love, veneration, admiration, or attachment. But that sort of reason which banishes the affections is incapable of filling their place. These public affections, combined with manners, are required sometimes as supplements, sometimes as correctives, always as aids to law. The precept given by a wise man, as well as a great critic, for the construction of poems, is equally true as to states:— *Non satis est pulchra esse poemata, dulcia sunto.* There ought to be a system of manners in every nation, which a well-formed mind would be disposed to relish. To make us love our country, our country ought to be lovely.

But power, of some kind or other, will survive the shock in which manners and opinions perish; and it will find other and worse means for its support. The usurpation which, in order to subvert ancient institutions, has destroyed ancient principles, will hold power by arts similar to those by which it has acquired it. When the old feudal and chivalrous spirit of *fealty*, which, by freeing kings from fear, freed both kings and subjects from the precautions of tyranny, shall be extinct in the minds of men, plots and assassinations will be anticipated by preventive murder and preventive confiscation, and that long roll of grim and bloody maxims, which form the political code of all power, not standing on its own honour, and the honour of those who are to obey it. Kings will be tyrants from policy, when subjects are rebels from principle.

When ancient opinions and rules of life are taken away, the loss cannot possibly be estimated. From that moment we have no compass to govern us; nor can we know distinctly to what port we steer. Europe, undoubtedly, taken in a mass, was in a flourishing condition the day on which your Revolution was completed. How much of that prosperous state was owing to the spirit of our old manners and opinions is not easy to say; but as such causes cannot be indifferent in their operation, we must presume, that, on the whole, their operation was beneficial.

We are but too apt to consider things in the state in which we find them, without sufficiently adverting to the causes by which they have been produced, and possibly may be upheld. Nothing is more certain, than that our manners, our civilization, and all the good things which are connected with manners, and with civilization, have, in this European world of ours, depended for ages upon two principles; and were indeed the result of both combined; I mean the spirit of a gentleman, and the spirit of religion. The nobility and the clergy, the one by profession, the other by patronage, kept learning in existence, even in the midst of arms and confusions, and whilst governments were rather in their causes, than formed. Learning paid back what it received to nobility and to priesthood; and paid it with usury, by enlarging their ideas, and by furnishing their minds. Happy if they had all continued to know their indissoluble union, and their

---

53. Non . . . sunto. It is not enough for poems to be beautiful. They must be affecting as well. The quotation is from Horace, *Ars Poetica*, l. 99.

proper place! Happy if learning, not debauched by ambition, had been satisfied to continue the instructor, and not aspired to be the master! Along with its natural protectors and guardians, learning will be cast into the mire, and trodden down under the hoofs of a swinish multitude.

If, as I suspect, modern letters owe more than they are always willing to own to ancient manners, so do other interests which we value full as much as they are worth. Even commerce, and trade, and manufacture, the gods of our economical politicians, are themselves perhaps but creatures; are themselves but effects, which, as first causes, we choose to worship. They certainly grew under the same shade in which learning flourished. They too may decay with their natural protecting principles. With you, for the present at least, they all threaten to disappear together. Where trade and manufactures are wanting to a people, and the spirit of nobility and religion remains, sentiment supplies, and not always ill supplies, their place; but if commerce and the arts should be lost in an experiment to try how well a state may stand without these old fundamental principles, what sort of a thing must be a nation of gross, stupid, ferocious, and, at the same time, poor and sordid barbarians, destitute of religion, honour, or manly pride, possessing nothing at present, and hoping for nothing hereafter?

I wish you may not be going fast, and by the shortest cut, to that horrible and disgustful situation. Already there appears a poverty of conception, a coarseness and vulgarity in all the proceedings of the assembly and of all their instructors. Their liberty is not liberal. Their science is presumptuous ignorance. Their humanity is savage and brutal.

It is not clear, whether in England we learned those grand and decorous principles, and manners, of which considerable traces yet remain, from you, or whether you took them from us. But to you, I think, we trace them best. You seem to me to be— *gentis incunabula nostrae.* France has always more or less influenced manners in England: and when your fountain is choked up and polluted, the stream will not run long, or not run clear, with us, or perhaps with any nation. This gives all Europe, in my opinion, but too close and connected a concern in what is done in France. Excuse me, therefore, if I have dwelt too long on the atrocious spectacle of the 6th of October, 1789, or have given too much scope to the reflections which have arisen in my mind on occasion of the most important of all revolutions, which may be dated from that day, I mean a revolution in sentiments, manners, and moral opinions. As things now stand, with everything respectable destroyed without us, and an attempt to destroy within us every principle of respect, one is almost forced to apologize for harbouring the common feelings of men.

Why do I feel so differently from the Reverend Dr. Price, and those of his lay flock, who will choose to adopt the sentiments of his discourse?— For this plain reason—because it is *natural* I should; because we are so made, as to be affected at such spectacles with melancholy sentiments upon the unstable condition of mortal prosperity, and the tremendous uncertainty of human greatness; because in those natural feelings we learn great lessons; because in events like these our passions instruct our reason; because, when kings are hurled from their thrones by the Supreme Director of this great drama, and become the objects of insult to the base, and of pity to the good, we behold such disasters in the moral, as we should behold a miracle in the physical, order of things. We are alarmed into reflection; our minds (as it has long since been observed) are purified by terror and pity; our weak, unthinking pride is humbled under the dispensations of a mysterious wisdom. Some tears might be drawn from me, if such a spectacle were exhibited on the stage. I should be truly ashamed of finding in myself that superficial, theatric sense of painted distress, whilst I could exult over it in real life. With such a perverted mind, I could never venture to show my face at a tragedy. People would think the tears that Garrick formerly, or that Siddons not long since, have extorted from me, were the tears of hypocrisy; I should know them to be the tears of folly.

Indeed the theatre is a better school of moral sentiments than churches, where the feelings of humanity are thus outraged. Poets who have to deal with an audience not yet graduated in the school of the rights of men, and who must apply themselves to the moral constitution of the heart, would not dare to produce such a triumph as a matter of exultation. There, where men follow their natural impulses, they would not bear the odious maxims of a Machiavellian policy, whether applied to the attainment of monarchical or democratic tyranny. They would reject them on the modern, as they once did on the ancient stage, where they could not bear even the hypothetical proposition of such wickedness in the mouth of a personated ty-

41. **gentis . . . nostrae,** the cradle of our race. From Virgil's *Aeneid*, Book III, l. 105.

39. **humanity . . . outraged.** Burke here refers to a sermon by Dr. Richard Price in which the ideas and methods of the French Revolution had been praised.

rant, though suitable to the character he sustained. No theatric audience in Athens would bear what has been borne, in the midst of the real tragedy of his triumphal day; a principal actor weighing, as it were in scales hung in a shop of horrors,—so much actual crime against so much contingent advantage,—and after putting in and out weights, declaring that the balance was on the side of the advantages. They would not bear to see the crimes of new democracy posted as in a ledger against the crimes of old despotism, and the book-keepers of politics finding democracy still in debt, but by no means unable or unwilling to pay the balance. In the theatre, the first intuitive glance, without any elaborate process of reasoning, will show that this method of political computation would justify every extent of crime. They would see, that on these principles, even where the very worst acts were not perpetrated, it was owing rather to the fortune of the conspirators, than to their parsimony in the expenditure of treachery and blood. They would soon see, that criminal means once tolerated are soon preferred. They present a shorter cut to the object than through the highway of the moral virtues. Justifying perfidy and murder for public benefit, public benefit would soon become the pretext, and perfidy and murder the end; until rapacity, malice, revenge, and fear more dreadful than revenge, could satiate their insatiable appetites. Such must be the consequences of losing, in the splendour of these triumphs of the rights of men, all natural sense of wrong and right. . . .

To tell you the truth, my dear sir, I think the honour of our nation to be somewhat concerned in the disclaimer of the proceedings of this society of the Old Jewry and the London Tavern. I have no man's proxy, I speak only for myself, when I disclaim, as I do with all possible earnestness, all communion with the actors in that triumph, or with the admirers of it. When I assert any thing else, as concerning the people of England, I speak from observation, not from authority; but I speak from the experience I have had in a pretty extensive and mixed communication with the inhabitants of this kingdom, of all descriptions and ranks, and after a course of attentive observation, begun early in life, and continued for nearly forty years. I have often been astonished, considering that we are divided from you but by a slender dyke of about twenty-four miles, and that the mutual intercourse between the two countries has lately been very great, to find how little you seem to know of us. I suspect that this is owing to your forming a judgment of this nation from certain publications, which do very erroneously, if they do at all, represent the opinions and dispositions generally prevalent in England. The vanity, restlessness, petulance, and spirit of intrigue, of several petty cabals, who attempt to hide their total want of consequence in bustle and noise, and puffing, and mutual quotation of each other, makes you imagine that our contemptuous neglect of their abilities is a mark of general acquiescence in their opinions. No such thing, I assure you. Because half a dozen grasshoppers under a fern make the field ring with their importunate chink, whilst thousands of great cattle reposed beneath the shadow of the British oak, chew the cud and are silent, pray do not imagine that those who make the noise are the only inhabitants of the field; that of course they are many in number; or that, after all, they are other than the little, shrivelled, meagre, hopping, though loud and troublesome insects of the hour.

I almost venture to affirm that not one in a hundred amongst us participates in the "triumph" of the Revolution Society. If the King and Queen of France, and their children, were to fall into our hands by the chance of war, in the most acrimonious of all hostilities (I deprecate such an event, I deprecate such hostilities), they would be treated with another sort of triumphal entry into London. We formerly have had a king of France in that situation; you have read how he was treated by the victor in the field, and in what manner he was afterwards received in England. Four hundred years have gone over us; but I believe we are not materially changed since that period. Thanks to our sullen resistance to innovation, thanks to the cold sluggishness of our national character, we still bear the stamp of our forefathers. We have not (as I conceive) lost the generosity and dignity of thinking of the fourteenth century; nor as yet have we subtilized ourselves into savages. We are not the converts of Rousseau; we are not the disciples of Voltaire; Helvetius has made no progress amongst us. Atheists are not our preachers; madmen are not our lawgivers. We know that *we* have made no discoveries; and we think that no discoveries are to be made, in morality; nor many in the great principles of government, nor in the ideas of liberty, which were understood long before we were born altogether as well as they will be after the grave has heaped its mould upon our presumption, and the silent tomb shall have imposed its law on our pert

37. **Old Jewry,** the section of London in which Dr. Price had delivered his sermon.

24. **Revolution Society,** before which Dr. Price had preached his sermon.

loquacity. In England we have not yet been completely embowelled of our natural entrails: we still feel within us, and we cherish and cultivate, those inbred sentiments which are the faithful guardians, the active monitors of our duty, the true supporters of all liberal and manly morals. We have not been drawn and trussed, in order that we may be filled, like stuffed birds in a museum, with chaff and rags, and paltry blurred shreds of paper about the rights of man. We preserve the whole of our feelings still native and entire, unsophisticated by pedantry and infidelity. We have real hearts of flesh and blood beating in our bosoms. We fear God; we look up with awe to kings; with affection to parliaments; with duty to magistrates; with reverence to priests; and with respect to nobility. Why? Because when such ideas are brought before our minds, it is *natural* to be so affected; because all other feelings are false and spurious, and tend to corrupt our minds, to vitiate our primary morals, to render us unfit for rational liberty; and by teaching us a servile, licentious, and abandoned insolence, to be our low sport for a few holidays, to make us perfectly fit for, and justly deserving of, slavery through the whole course of our lives.

You see, sir, that in this enlightened age I am bold enough to confess, that we are generally men of untaught feelings; that instead of casting away all our old prejudices, we cherish them to a very considerable degree, and, to take more shame to ourselves, we cherish them because they are prejudices; and the longer they have lasted, and the more generally they have prevailed, the more we cherish them. We are afraid to put men to live and trade each on his own private stock of reason; because we suspect that the stock in each man is small, and that the individuals would do better to avail themselves of the general bank and capital of nations and of ages. Many of our men of speculation, instead of exploding general prejudices, employ their sagacity to discover the latent wisdom which prevails in them. If they find what they seek, and they seldom fail, they think it more wise to continue the prejudice, with the reason involved, than to cast away the coat of prejudice, and to leave nothing but the naked reason; because prejudice, with its reason, has a motive to give action to that reason, and an affection which will give it permanence. Prejudice is of ready application in the emergency; it previously engages the mind in a steady course of wisdom and virtue, and does not leave the man hesitating in the moment of decision, sceptical, puzzled, and unresolved. Prejudice renders a man's virtue his habit: and not a series of unconnected acts. Through just prejudice, his **duty** becomes a part of his nature.

Your literary men, and your politicians, and so do the whole clan of the enlightened among us, essentially differ in these points. They have no respect for the wisdom of others; but they pay it off by a very full measure of confidence in their own. With them it is a sufficient motive to destroy an old scheme of things, because it is an old one. As to the new, they are in no sort of fear with regard to the duration of a building run up in haste; because duration is no object to those who think little or nothing has been done before their time, and who place all their hopes in discovery. They conceive, very systematically, that all things which give perpetuity are mischievous, and therefore they are at inexpiable war with all establishments. They think that government may vary like modes of dress, and with as little ill effect; that there needs no principle of attachment, except a sense of present conveniency, to any constitution of the state. They always speak as if they were of opinion that there is a singular species of compact between them and their magistrates, which binds the magistrate, but which has nothing reciprocal in it, but that the majesty of the people has a right to dissolve it without any reason, but its will. Their attachment to their country itself is only so far as it agrees with some of their fleeting projects: it begins and ends with that scheme of polity which falls in with their momentary opinion.

These doctrines, or rather sentiments, seem prevalent with your new statesmen. But they are wholly different from those on which we have always acted in this country.

I hear it is sometimes given out in France, that what is doing among you is after the example of England. I beg leave to affirm, that scarcely anything done with you has originated from the practice or the prevalent opinions of this people, either in the act or in the spirit of the proceeding. Let me add, that we are as unwilling to learn these lessons from France, as we are sure that we never taught them to that nation. The cabals here who take a sort of share in your transactions, as yet consists of but a handful of people. If unfortunately by their intrigues, their sermons, their publications, and by a confidence derived from an expected union with the counsels and forces of the French nation, they should draw considerable numbers into their faction, and in consequence should seriously attempt any thing here in imitation of what has been done with you, the event, I dare venture to prophesy, will be, that, with some trouble to their country, they will soon accomplish their own destruction. This people refused to change their law in remote ages from respect to the infallibility of popes; and they will not now alter it from a pious implicit faith in the dogmatism of philosophers; though the former was armed with the anathema and crusade, and though the latter should act with the libel and the lamp-iron.

Formerly your affairs were your own concern only. We felt for them as men; but we kept aloof from them, because we were not citizens of France. But when we see the model held up to ourselves, we must feel as Englishmen, and feeling, we must provide as Englishmen. Your affairs, in spite of us, are made a part of our interest; so far at least as to keep at a distance your panacea, or your plague. If it be a panacea, we do not want it. We know the consequences of unnecessary physic. If it be a plague, it is such a plague that the precautions of the most severe quarantine ought to be established against it.

I hear on all hands that a cabal, calling itself philosophic, receives the glory of many of the late proceedings, and that their opinions and systems are the true actuating spirit of the whole of them. I have heard of no party in England, literary or political, at any time, known by such a description. It is not with you composed of those men, is it? whom the vulgar, in their blunt, homely style, commonly call Atheists and Infidels? If it be, I admit that we too have had writers of that description, who made some noise in their day. At present they repose in lasting oblivion. Who, born within the last forty years, has read one word of Collins, and Toland, and Tindal, and Chubb, and Morgan, and that whole race who called themselves Freethinkers? Who now reads Bolingbroke? Who ever read him through? Ask the booksellers of London what is become of all these lights of the world. In as few years their few successors will go to the family vault of "all the Capulets." But whatever they were, or are, with us, they were and are wholly unconnected individuals. With us they kept the common nature of their kind, and were not gregarious. They never acted in corps, or were known as a faction in the state, nor presumed to influence in that name or character, or for the purposes of such a faction, on any of our public concerns. Whether they ought so to exist, and so be permitted to act, is another question. As such cabals have not existed in England, so neither has the spirit of them had any influence in establishing the original frame of our Constitution, or in any one of the several reparations and improvements it has undergone. The whole has been done under the auspices, and is confirmed by the sanctions, of religion and piety. The whole has emanated from the simplicity of our national character, and from a sort of native plainness and directness of understanding, which for a long time characterized those men who have successively obtained authority amongst us. This disposition still remains; at least in the great body of the people.

We know, and what is better, we feel inwardly, that religion is the basis of civil society, and the source of all good, and of all comfort. In England we are so convinced of this, that there is no rust of superstititon, with which the accumulated absurdity of the human mind might have crusted it over in the course of ages, that ninety-nine in a hundred of the people of England would not prefer to impiety. We shall never be such fools as to call in an enemy to the substance of any system to remove its corruptions, to supply its defects, or to perfect its construction. If our religious tenets should ever want a further elucidation, we shall not call on atheism to explain them. We shall not light up our temple from that unhallowed fire. It will be illuminated with other lights. It will be perfumed with other incense, than the infectious stuff which is imported by the smugglers of adulterated metaphysics. If our ecclesiastical establishment should want a revision, it is not avarice or rapacity, public or private, that we shall employ for the audit, or receipt, or application of its consecrated revenue. Violently condemning neither the Greek nor the Armenian, nor, since heats are subsided, the Roman system of religion, we prefer the Protestant: not because we think it has less of the Christian religion in it, but because, in our judgment, it has more. We are Protestants, not from indifference, but from zeal.

We know, and it is our pride to know, that man is by his constitution a religious animal; that atheism is against, not only our reason, but our instincts; and that it cannot prevail long. But if, in the moment of riot, and in a drunken delirium from the hot spirit drawn out of the alembic of hell, which in France is now so furiously boiling, we should uncover our nakedness, by throwing off that Christian religion which has hitherto been our boast and comfort, and one great source of civilization amongst us, and amongst many other nations, we are apprehensive (being well aware that the mind will not endure a void) that some uncouth,

---

8–9. **lamp-iron,** of a lamppost, from which men could be hanged.

pernicious, and degrading superstition might take place of it.

For that reason, before we take from our establishment the natural, human means of estimation, and give it up to contempt, as you have done, and in doing it have incurred the penalties you well deserve to suffer, we desire that some other may be presented to us in the place of it. We shall then form our judgment.

On these ideas, instead of quarrelling with establishments, as some do, who have made a philosophy and a religion of their hostility to such institutions, we cleave closely to them. We are resolved to keep an established church, an established monarchy, an established aristocracy, and an established democracy, each in the degree it exists, and in no greater. I shall show you presently how much of each of these we possess.

It has been the misfortune (not, as these gentlemen think it, the glory) of this age, that everything is to be discussed, as if the Constitution of our country were to be always a subject rather of altercation than enjoyment. For this reason, as well as for the satisfaction of those among you (if any such you have among you) who may wish to profit of examples, I venture to trouble you with a few thoughts upon each of these establishments. I do not think they were unwise in ancient Rome, who, when they wished to new-model their laws, set commissioners to examine the best constituted republics within their reach.

First, I beg leave to speak of our church establishment, which is the first of our prejudices; not a prejudice destitute of reason, but involving in it profound and extensive wisdom. I speak of it first. It is first, and last, and midst in our minds. For, taking ground on that religious system, of which we are now in possession, we continue to act on the early received, and uniformly continued sense of mankind. That sense not only, like a wise architect, hath built up the august fabric of states, but like a provident proprietor, to preserve the structure from profanation and ruin, as a sacred temple, purged from all the impurities of fraud, and violence, and injustice, and tyranny, hath solemnly and for ever consecrated the commonwealth, and all that officiate in it. This consecration is made, that all who administer in the government of men, in which they stand in the person of God Himself, should have high and worthy notions of their function and destination; that their hope should be full of immortality; that they should not look to the paltry pelf of the moment, nor to the temporary and transient praise of the vulgar, but to a solid, permanent existence, in the permanent part of their nature, and to a permanent fame and glory, in the example they leave as a rich inheritance to the world.

Such sublime principles ought to be infused into persons of exalted situations; and religious establishments provided, that may continually revive and enforce them. Every sort of moral, every sort of civil, every sort of politic institution, aiding the rational and natural ties that connect the human understanding and affections to the divine, are not more than necessary, in order to build up that wonderful structure, Man; whose prerogative it is, to be in a great degree a creature of his own making; and who, when made as he ought to be made, is destined to hold no trivial place in the creation. But whenever man is put over men, as the better nature ought ever to preside, in that case more particularly he should as nearly as possible be approximated to his perfection.

The consecration of the state by a state religious establishment is necessary also to operate with a wholesome awe upon free citizens; because, in order to secure their freedom, they must enjoy some determinate portion of power. To them therefore a religion connected with the state, and with their duty towards it, becomes even more necessary than in such societies, where the people, by the terms of their subjection, are confined to private sentiments, and the management of their own family concerns. All persons possessing any portion of power ought to be strongly and awfully impressed with an idea that they act in trust; and that they are to account for their conduct in that trust to the one great Master, Author and Founder of society.

This principle ought even to be more strongly impressed upon the minds of those who compose the collective sovereignty, than upon those of single princes. Without instruments, these princes can do nothing. Whoever uses instruments, in finding helps, finds also impediments. Their power is therefore by no means complete; nor are they safe in extreme abuse. Such persons, however elevated by flattery, arrogance, and self-opinion, must be sensible, that, whether covered or not by positive law, in some way or other they are accountable even here for the abuse of their trust. If they are not cut off by a rebellion of their people, they may be strangled by the very janissaries kept for their security against all other rebellion. Thus we have seen the King of France sold by his soldiers for an increase of pay. But where popular authority

---

39. **continued sense,** enduring consensus.

is absolute and unrestrained, the people have an infinitely greater, because a far better founded, confidence in their own power. They are themselves in a great measure their own instruments. They are nearer to their objects. Besides, they are less under responsibility to one of the greatest controlling powers on earth, the sense of fame and estimation. The share of infamy, that is likely to fall to the lot of each individual in public acts, is small indeed; the operation of opinion being in the inverse ratio to the number of those who abuse power. Their own approbation of their own acts has to them the appearance of a public judgment in their favour. A perfect democracy is therefore the most shameless thing in the world. As it is the most shameless, it is also the most fearless. No man apprehends in his person that he can be made subject to punishment. Certainly the people at large never ought: for, as all punishments are for example towards the conservation of the people at large, the people at large can never become the subject of punishments by any human hand. It is therefore of infinite importance that they should not be suffered to imagine that their will, any more than that of kings, is the standard of right and wrong. They ought to be persuaded that they are full as little entitled, and far less qualified, with safety to themselves, to use any arbitrary power whatsoever; that therefore they are not, under a false show of liberty, but, in truth, to exercise an unnatural, inverted domination, tyrannically to exact, from those who officiate in the state, not an entire devotion to their interest, which is their right, but an abject submission to their occasional will; extinguishing thereby, in all those who serve them, all moral principle, all sense of dignity, all use of judgment, and all consistency of character; whilst by the very same process they give themselves up a proper, a suitable, but a most contemptible prey to the servile ambition of popular sycophants, or courtly flatterers.

When the people have emptied themselves of all the lust of selfish will, which without religion it is utterly impossible they ever should,—when they are conscious that they exercise, and exercise perhaps in a higher link of the order of delegation, the power, which to be legitimate must be according to that eternal, immutable law, in which will and reason are the same,—they will be more careful how they place power in base and incapable hands. In their nomination to office, they will not appoint to the exercise of authority, as to a pitiful job, but as to a holy function; not according to their sordid, selfish interest, nor to their wanton caprice, nor to their arbitrary will; but they will confer that power (which any man may well tremble to give or to receive) on those only, in whom they may discern that predominant proportion of active virtue and wisdom, taken together and fitted to the charge, such as, in the great and inevitable mixed mass of human imperfections and infirmities, is to be found.

When they are habitually convinced that no evil can be acceptable, either in the act or the permission, to Him whose essence is good, they will be better able to extirpate out of the minds of all magistrates, civil, ecclesiastical, or military, anything that bears the least resemblance to a proud and lawless domination.

But one of the first and most leading principles on which the commonwealth and the laws are consecrated is, lest the temporary possessors and life-renters in it, unmindful of what they have received from their ancestors, or of what is due to their posterity, should act as if they were the entire masters; that they should not think it among their rights to cut off the entail, or commit waste on the inheritance, by destroying at their pleasure the whole original fabric of their society: hazarding to leave to those who come after them a ruin instead of an habitation—and teaching these successors as little to respect their contrivances, as they had themselves respected the institutions of their forefathers. By this unprincipled facility of changing the state as often, and as much, and in as many ways, as there are floating fancies or fashions, the whole chain and continuity of the commonwealth would be broken. No one generation could link with the other. Men would become little better than the flies of a summer.

And first of all, the science of jurisprudence, the pride of the human intellect, which, with all its defects, redundancies, and errors, is the collected reason of ages, combining the principles of original justice with the infinite variety of human concerns, as a heap of old exploded errors, would be no longer studied. Personal self-sufficiency and arrogance (the certain attendants upon all those who have never experienced a wisdom greater than their own) would usurp the tribunal. Of course no certain laws, establishing invariable grounds of hope and fear, would keep the actions of men in a certain course, or direct them to a certain end. Nothing stable in the modes of holding property, or exercising function, could form a solid ground on which any parent could speculate in the education of his offspring, or in a choice for their future establishment in the world. No principles would be early worked into the habits. As soon as the most able instructor had completed his laborious course of institution, instead of sending forth his pupil, accomplished in a virtuous discipline, fitted to procure him attention and respect, in his place in society, he would find everything altered; and that he had turned out a poor creature to the contempt and derision of the world, ignorant of the true grounds of estimation. Who would insure a tender and delicate sense of honour to beat almost with the first pulses of the heart, when no man could know what would be the test of honour in a nation, continually varying the standard of its coin? No part of life would retain its acquisitions. Barbarism with regard to science and literature, unskilfulness with regard to arts and manufactures, would infallibly succeed to the want of a steady education and settled principle; and thus the commonwealth itself would, in a few generations, crumble away, be disconnected into the dust and powder of individuality, and at length dispersed to all the winds of heaven.

To avoid, therefore, the evils of inconstancy and versatility, ten thousand times worse than those of obstinacy and the blindest prejudice, we have consecrated the state, that no man should approach to look into its defects or corruptions but with due caution; that he should never dream of beginning its reformation by its subversion; that he should approach to the faults of the state as to the wounds of a father, with pious awe and trembling solicitude. By this wise prejudice we are taught to look with horror on those children of their country, who are prompt rashly to hack that aged parent in pieces, and put him into the kettle of magicians, in hopes that by their poisonous weeds, and wild incantations, they may regenerate the paternal constitution, and renovate their father's life.

Society is, indeed, a contract. Subordinate contracts for objects of mere occasional interest may be dissolved at pleasure—but the state ought not to be considered as nothing better than a partnership agreement in a trade of pepper and coffee, calico or tobacco, or some other such low concern, to be taken up for a little temporary interest, and to be dissolved by the fancy of the parties. It is to be looked on with other reverence; because it is not a partnership in things subservient only to the gross animal existence of a temporary and perishable nature. It is a partnership in all science; a partnership in all art; a partnership in every virtue, and in all perfection. As the ends of such a partnership cannot be obtained in many generations, it becomes a partnership not only between those who are living, but between those who are living, those who are dead, and those who are to be born. Each contract of each particular state is but a clause in the great primaeval contract of eternal society, linking the lower with the higher natures, connecting the visible and invisible world, according to a fixed compact sanctioned by the inviolable oath which holds all physical and all moral natures, each in their appointed place. This law is not subject to the will of those who, by an obligation above them, and infinitely superior, are bound to submit their will to that law. The municipal corporations of that universal kingdom are not morally at liberty, at their pleasure, and on their speculations of a contingent improvement, wholly to separate and tear asunder the bands of their subordinate community, and to dissolve it into an unsocial, uncivil, unconnected chaos of elementary principles. It is the first and supreme necessity only, a necessity that is not chosen, but chooses, a necessity paramount to deliberation, that admits no discussion, and demands no evidence, which alone can justify a resort to anarchy. This necessity is no exception to the rule; because this necessity itself is a part too of that moral and physical disposition of things, to which man must be obedient by consent or force: but if that which is only submission to necessity should be made the object of choice, the law is broken, Nature is disobeyed, and the rebellious are outlawed, cast forth, and exiled, from this world of reason, and order, and peace, and virtue, and fruitful penitence, into the antagonist world of madness, discord, vice, confusion, and unavailing sorrow.

35. **kettle of magicians.** Burke has in mind the myth of the sorceress Medea.

William Cowper
1731–1800

The pitiful life-story of William Cowper is soon told. Born the son of a country rector who was chaplain to George II, he lost his mother when he was six years old. At school he was browbeaten and miserable. His study of law and his brief period of service in governmental offices did little to relieve his tendency toward gloom, and before reaching the age of thirty-five he suffered the first of several lapses into insanity. After recovering from this attack he retired to the village of Olney, in central England, and there spent the quiet remainder of his life in the company of various friends, of whom the chief was Mrs. Mary Unwin.

Although he came of a distinguished ancestry long prominent in the law and including the poet John Donne, Cowper had no heart for the struggles and rewards of the world. Sensitive to a morbid degree, he suffered during most of his life with a religious melancholia based upon the conviction that he was irretrievably damned. For distraction he turned to his friends, to the solaces of nature, to gardening and carpentry and the care of animals, and finally, at fifty years of age, to poetic composition.

If Cowper's hymns, poems, and letters seem to us at first almost intolerably mild, the reason may be that we do not read them, as he believed they were written, in the red light of hell. Like his great kinsman John Donne, he had that tragic sense of life and its destiny which we of the twentieth century are only beginning to recover. Yet every moment that he spent with his flowers, his pet hares, with ax and saw, or with pen and paper, was to him a moment of transient happiness snatched from endless woe. He made so much of the frail creatures of time because he could not always bear to think of eternity.

Hence came those innovations in the writing of Cowper which give him a greater importance in the history of literature than his actual accomplishment would at first seem to warrant. His feeling of fellowship with all things doomed to death leads on into an affection for mankind in general, for birds and animals, for trees and plants and flowers, which relates him rather to Burns and Wordsworth and Shelley than to the poets of the school of Pope.

And yet Cowper's work has high value of its own. While recognizing that he wins our love rather than our admiration, we should not forget that he wrote several of the best hymns and many of the most delightful letters that have come down to us from his time, together with a few poems that will always have devoted readers. His pervasive humor, his delicacy of thought and feeling, and the wisdom that he showed in making much of little, soon endear him to those who once make his acquaintance. That same tenderness and humility which unfitted him for active life render him an ideal fireside companion for those who have fully learned that our lives are brief, tragic, beautiful, and surrounded by mystery.

from THE TASK

Accepting from his friend Lady Austen "the task" of writing about a sofa, Cowper produced, in 1785, a blank-verse poem running to six books in which he discussed many diverse themes. The tendency of the entire poem, he said, was "to discountenance the modern enthusiasm after a London life, and to recommend rural ease and leisure as friendly to the cause of piety and virtue."

It is in the fourth book of the poem, a masterpiece of unobtrusive art, that this purpose is most fully achieved.

Book IV

THE WINTER EVENING

Hark! 'tis the twanging horn! O'er yonder bridge,
That with its wearisome but needful length
Bestrides the wintry flood, in which the moon
Sees her unwrinkled face reflected bright;—
He comes, the herald of a noisy world,
With spattered boots, strapped waist, and frozen locks;
News from all nations lumbering at his back.
True to his charge, the close-packed load behind,
Yet careless what he brings, his one concern
Is to conduct it to the destined inn,　　10
And, having dropped the expected bag, pass on.
He whistles as he goes, light-hearted wretch,
Cold and yet cheerful: messenger of grief

10. **inn**, from which the mail was distributed.

Perhaps to thousands, and of joy to some;
To him indifferent whether grief or joy.
Houses in ashes, and the fall of stocks,
Births, deaths, and marriages, epistles wet
With tears that trickled down the writer's cheeks
Fast as the periods from his fluent quill,
Or charged with amorous sighs of absent swains 20
Or nymphs responsive, equally affect
His horse and him, unconscious of them all.
But oh the important budget! ushered in
With such heart-shaking music, who can say
What are its tidings? Have our troops awaked?
Or do they still, as if with opium drugged,
Snore to the murmurs of the Atlantic wave?
Is India free, and does she wear her plumed
And jewelled turban with a smile of peace,
Or do we grind her still? The grand debate, 30
The popular harangue, the tart reply,
The logic, and the wisdom, and the wit,
And the loud laugh—I long to know them all;
I burn to set the imprisoned wranglers free,
And give them voice and utterance once again.

    Now stir the fire, and close the shutters fast,
Let fall the curtains, wheel the sofa round,
And, while the bubbling and loud-hissing urn
Throws up a steamy column, and the cups
That cheer but not inebriate, wait on each, 40
So let us welcome peaceful evening in.
Not such his evening, who with shining face
Sweats in the crowded theatre, and, squeezed
And bored with elbow-points through both his
    sides,
Out-scolds the ranting actor on the stage:
Nor his, who patient stands till his feet throb,
And his head thumps, to feed upon the breath
Of patriots, bursting with heroic rage,
Or placemen, all tranquillity and smiles.
This folio of four pages, happy work! 50
Which not even critics criticise; that holds
Inquisitive attention, while I read,
Fast bound in chains of silence, which the fair,
Though eloquent themselves, yet fear to break;
What is it, but a map of busy life,
Its fluctuations, and its vast concerns?
Here runs the mountainous and craggy ridge
That tempts ambition. On the summit see
The seals of office glitter in his eyes;
He climbs, he pants, he grasps them! At his heels, 60
Close at his heels, a demagogue ascends,
And with a dexterous jerk soon twists him down,
And wins them, but to lose them in his turn.
Here rills of oily eloquence in soft
Meanders lubricate the course they take;
The modest speaker is ashamed and grieved
To engross a moment's notice, and yet begs,
Begs a propitious ear for his poor thoughts,
However trivial all that he conceives.
Sweet bashfulness! It claims at least this praise, 70
The dearth of information and good sense
That it foretells us always comes to pass.
Cataracts of declamation thunder here;
There forests of no meaning spread the page,
In which all comprehension wanders, lost;
While fields of pleasantry amuse us there
With merry descants on a nation's woes.
The rest appears a wilderness of strange
But gay confusion; roses for the cheeks,
And lilies for the brows of faded age, 80
Teeth for the toothless, ringlets for the bald,
Heaven, earth, and ocean, plundered of their
    sweets,
Nectareous essences, Olympian dews,
Sermons, and city feasts, and favourite airs,
Aethereal journeys, submarine exploits,
And Katterfelto, with his hair on end
At his own wonders, wondering for his bread.

    'Tis pleasant through the loop-holes of retreat
To peep at such a world; to see the stir
Of the great Babel, and not feel the crowd; 90
To hear the roar she sends through all her gates
At a safe distance, where the dying sound
Falls a soft murmur on the uninjured ear.
Thus sitting, and surveying thus at ease
The globe and its concerns, I seem advanced
To some secure and more than mortal height,
That liberates and exempts me from them all.
It turns submitted to my view, turns round
With all its generations; I behold
The tumult, and am still. The sound of war 100
Has lost its terrors ere it reaches me;
Grieves, but alarms me not. I mourn the pride
And avarice that make man a wolf to man;
Hear the faint echo of those brazen throats
By which he speaks the language of his heart,
And sigh, but never tremble at the sound.
He travels and expatiates, as the bee
From flower to flower, so he from land to land;
The manners, customs, policy of all
Pay contribution to the store he gleans; 110
He sucks intelligence in every clime,
And spreads the honey of his deep research

    27. snore, referring to the supposed inaction of British troops in America. **28. India,** referring to the first Mahratta war, 1782. **49. placemen,** officeholders. **50. folio,** the newspaper.

    85. Aethereal journeys. The first ascents in a balloon were made in 1783. **86. Katterfelto,** a quack doctor. **107. expatiates,** wanders.

At his return—a rich repast for me.
He travels, and I too. I tread his deck,
Ascend his topmast, through his peering eyes
Discover countries, with a kindred heart
Suffer his woes, and share in his escapes;
While fancy, like the finger of a clock,
Runs the great circuit, and is still at home.
   O Winter, ruler of the inverted year,   120
Thy scattered hair with sleet like ashes filled,
Thy breath congealed upon thy lips, thy cheeks
Fringed with a beard made white with other snows
Than those of age, thy forehead wrapt in clouds,
A leafless branch thy sceptre, and thy throne
A sliding car, indebted to no wheels,
But urged by storms along its slippery way,
I love thee, all unlovely as thou seem'st,
And dreaded as thou art! Thou hold'st the sun
A prisoner in the yet undawning east,   130
Shortening his journey between morn and noon,
And hurrying him, impatient of his stay,
Down to the rosy west; but kindly still
Compensating his loss with added hours
Of social converse and instructive ease,
And gathering, at short notice, in one group
The family dispersed, and fixing thought,
Not less dispersed by day-light and its cares.
I crown thee king of intimate delights,
Fire-side enjoyments, home-born happiness,   140
And all the comforts that the lowly roof
Of undisturbed retirement, and the hours
Of long uninterrupted evening, know.
No rattling wheels stop short before these gates;
No powdered pert, proficient in the art
Of sounding an alarm, assaults these doors
Till the street rings; no stationary steeds
Cough their own knell, while, heedless of the sound,
The silent circle fan themselves, and quake:
But here the needle plies its busy task,   150
The pattern grows, the well-depicted flower,
Wrought patiently into the snowy lawn,
Unfolds its bosom; buds, and leaves, and sprigs,
And curling tendrils, gracefully disposed,
Follow the nimble finger of the fair;
A wreath that cannot fade, of flowers that blow
With most success when all besides decay.
The poet's or historian's page, by one
Made vocal for the amusement of the rest;   159
The sprightly lyre, whose treasure of sweet sounds
The touch from many a trembling chord shakes out;
And the clear voice symphonious, yet distinct,
And in the charming strife triumphant still,
Beguile the night, and set a keener edge
On female industry: the threaded steel
Flies swiftly, and unfelt the task proceeds.
The volume closed, the customary rites
Of the last meal commence. A Roman meal,
Such as the mistress of the world once found
Delicious, when her patriots of high note,   170
Perhaps by moonlight, at their humble doors,
And under an old oak's domestic shade,
Enjoyed—spare feast!—a radish and an egg!
Discourse ensues, not trivial, yet not dull,
Nor such as with a frown forbids the play
Of fancy, or proscribes the sound of mirth:
Nor do we madly, like an impious world,
Who deem religion frenzy, and the God
That made them an intruder on their joys,
Start at his awful name, or deem his praise   180
A jarring note—themes of a graver tone
Exciting oft our gratitude and love,
While we retrace with memory's pointing wand,
That calls the past to our exact review,
The dangers we have 'scaped, the broken snare,
The disappointed foe, deliverance found
Unlooked for, life preserved and peace restored—
Fruits of omnipotent eternal love.
"Oh evenings worthy of the gods!" exclaimed
The Sabine bard. "Oh evenings," I reply,   190
"More to be prized and coveted than yours,
As more illumined, and with nobler truths,
That I, and mine, and those we love, enjoy."
   Is winter hideous in a garb like this?
Needs he the tragic fur, the smoke of lamps
The pent-up breath of an unsavoury throng,
To thaw him into feeling; or the smart
And snappish dialogue, that flippant wits
Call comedy, to prompt him with a smile?
The self-compacent actor, when he views   200
(Stealing a side-long glance at a full house)
The slope of faces, from the floor to the roof,
(As if one master-spring controlled them all)
Relaxed into an universal grin,
Sees not a countenance there that speaks of joy
Half so refined or so sincere as our's.
Cards were superfluous here, with all the tricks
That idleness has ever yet contrived
To fill the void of an unfurnished brain,
To palliate dullness, and give time a shove.   210
Time, as he passes us, has a dove's wing,
Unsoiled, and swift, and of a silken sound;
But the world's time is time in masquerade!
Their's, should I paint him, has his pinions fledged
With motley plumes; and, where the peacock shows
His azure eyes, is tinctured black and red
With spots quadrangular of diamond form,
Ensanguined hearts, clubs typical of strife,

   190. Sabine bard, Horace, in *Satires*, Book II, Satire 2, l. 65.   **195. tragic,** because secured by the deaths of animals.

And spades, the emblem of untimely graves.   219
What should be and what was an hour-glass once,
Becomes a dice-box, and a billiard mast
Well does the work of his destructive scythe.
Thus decked, he charms a world whom fashion blinds
To his true worth, most pleased when idle most;
Whose only happy are their wasted hours.
Even misses, at whose age their mothers wore
The back-string and the bib, assume the dress
Of womanhood, sit pupils in the school
Of card-devoted time, and, night by night,
Placed at some vacant corner of the board,   230
Learn every trick, and soon play all the game.
But truce with censure. Roving as I rove,
Where shall I find an end, or how proceed?
As he that travels far oft turns aside
To view some rugged rock or mouldering tower,
Which, seen, delights him not; then, coming home,
Describes and prints it, that the world may know
How far he went for what was nothing worth;
So I, with brush in hand and pallet spread,
With colours mixed for a far different use,   240
Paint cards and dolls and every idle thing
That fancy finds in her excursive flights.

   Come, Evening, once again, season of peace;
Return, sweet Evening, and continue long!
Methinks I see thee in the streaky west,
With matron step slow-moving, while the night
Treads on thy sweeping train; one hand employed
In letting fall the curtain of repose
On bird and beast, the other charged for man
With sweet oblivion of the cares of day: 250
Not sumptuously adorned, nor needing aid,
Like homely featured night, of clustering gems;
A star or two, just twinkling on thy brow,
Suffices thee, save that the moon is thine
No less than her's, not worn indeed on high
With ostentatious pageantry, but set
With modest grandeur in thy purple zone,
Resplendent less, but of an ampler round.
Come then, and thou shalt find thy votary calm,
Or make me so. Composure is thy gift: 260
And, whether I devote thy gentle hours
To books, to music, or the poet's toil;
To weaving nets for bird-alluring fruit;
Or twining silken threads round ivory reels,
When they command whom man was born to please,
I slight thee not, but make thee welcome still.
   Just when our drawing-rooms begin to blaze
With lights, by clear reflection multiplied
From many a mirror, in which he of Gath,

   221. mast, cue.   227. back-string, leading string.

Goliath, might have seen his giant bulk   270
Whole, without stooping, towering crest and all,
My pleasures, too, begin. But me, perhaps,
The glowing hearth may satisfy awhile
With faint illumination, that uplifts
The shadow to the ceiling, there by fits
Dancing uncouthly to the quivering flame.
Not undelightful is an hour to me
So spent in parlour twilight: such a gloom
Suits well the thoughtful or unthinking mind,
The mind contemplative, with some new theme   280
Pregnant, or indisposed alike to all.
Laugh ye, who boast your more mercurial powers,
That never feel a stupor, know no pause,
Nor need one; I am conscious, and confess,
Fearless, a soul that does not always think.
Me oft has fancy, ludicrous and wild,
Soothed with a waking dream of houses, towers,
Trees, churches, and strange visages, expressed
In the red cinders, while with poring eye
I gazed, myself creating what I saw.   290
Nor less amused have I quiescent watched
The sooty films that play upon the bars,
Pendulous, and foreboding in the view
Of superstition, prophesying still,
Though still deceived, some stranger's near approach.
'Tis thus the understanding takes repose
In indolent vacuity of thought,
And sleeps and is refreshed. Meanwhile the face
Conceals the mood lethargic with a mask
Of deep deliberation, as the man   300
Were tasked to his full strength, absorbed and lost.
Thus oft, reclined at ease, I lose an hour
At evening, till at length the freezing blast,
That sweeps the bolted shutter, summons home
The recollected powers; and, snapping short
The glassy threads with which the fancy weaves
Her brittle toys, restores me to myself.
How calm is my recess; and how the frost,
Raging abroad, and the rough wind, endear
The silence and the warmth enjoyed within!   310
I saw the woods and fields, at close of day,
A variegated show; the meadows green,
Though faded; and the lands, where lately waved
The golden harvest, of a mellow brown,
Upturned so lately by the forceful share.
I saw far off the weedy fallows smile
With verdure not unprofitable, grazed
By flocks, fast feeding, and selecting each
His favourite herb; while all the leafless groves
That skirt the horizon wore a sable hue,   320
Scarce noticed in the kindred dusk of eve.

To-morrow brings a change, a total change!
Which even now, though silently performed,
And slowly, and by most unfelt, the face
Of universal nature undergoes.
Fast falls a fleecy shower: the downy flakes,
Descending, and with never-ceasing lapse,
Softly alighting upon all below,
Assimilate all objects. Earth receives
Gladly the thickening mantle, and the green   330
And tender blade, that feared the chilling blast,
Escapes unhurt beneath so warm a veil.

   In such a world, so thorny, and where none
Finds happiness unblighted, or, if found,
Without some thistly sorrow at its side,
It seems the part of wisdom, and no sin
Against the law of love, to measure lots
With less distinguished than ourselves; that thus
We may with patience bear our moderate ills,
And sympathise with others, suffering more.   340
Ill fares the traveller now, and he that stalks
In ponderous boots beside his reeking team.
The wain goes heavily, impeded sore
By congregated loads adhering close
To the clogged wheels; and in its sluggish pace,
Noiseless, appears a moving hill of snow.
The toiling steeds expand the nostril wide,
While every breath, by respiration strong
Forced downward, is consolidated soon
Upon their jutting chests. He, formed to bear   350
The pelting brunt of the tempestuous night,
With half-shut eyes, and puckered cheeks, and teeth
Presented bare against the storm, plods on.
One hand secures his hat, save when with both
He brandishes his pliant length of whip,
Resounding oft, and never heard in vain.
Oh happy; and, in my account, denied
That sensibility of pain with which
Refinement is endued, thrice happy thou!
Thy frame, robust and hardy, feels indeed   360
The piercing cold, but feels it unimpaired.
The learnèd finger never need explore
Thy vigorous pulse; and the unhealthful east,
That breathes the spleen, and searches every bone
Of the infirm, is wholesome air to thee.
Thy days roll on, exempt from household care;
The waggon is thy wife; and the poor beasts
That drag the dull companion to and fro,
Thine helpless charge, dependent on thy care.
Ah, treat them kindly! rude as thou appear'st,   370
Yet show that thou hast mercy! which the great,
With needless hurry whirled from place to place,
Humane as they would seem, not always show.

329. Assimilate, make similar in appearance.

Poor, yet industrious, modest, quiet, neat;
Such claim compassion in a night like this,
And have a friend in every feeling heart.
Warmed, while it lasts, by labour, all day long
They brave the season, and yet find at eve,
Ill clad and fed but sparely, time to cool.
The frugal housewife trembles when she lights   380
Her scanty stock of brush-wood, blazing clear,
But dying soon, like all terrestrial joys.
The few small embers left she nurses well;
And, while her infant race, with outspread hands
And crowded knees, sit cowering o'er the sparks,
Retires, content to quake, so they be warmed.
The man feels least, as more inured than she
To winter, and the current in his veins
More briskly moved by his severer toil;
Yet he, too, finds his own distress in their's.   390
The taper soon extinguished, which I saw
Dangled along at the cold finger's end
Just when the day declined, and the brown loaf
Lodged on the shelf, half eaten, without sauce
Of savoury cheese, or butter, costlier still;
Sleep seems their only refuge: for, alas,
Where penury is felt the thought is chained,
And sweet colloquial pleasures are but few!
With all this thrift they thrive not. All the care
Ingenious parsimony takes but just   400
Saves the small inventory, bed and stool,
Skillet, and old carved chest, from public sale.
They live, and live without extorted alms
From grudging hands; but other boast have none
To soothe their honest pride, that scorns to beg,
Nor comfort else, but in their mutual love.
I praise you much, ye meek and patient pair,
For ye are worthy; choosing rather far
A dry but independent crust, hard earned,
And eaten with a sigh, than to endure   410
The rugged frowns and insolent rebuffs
Of knaves in office, partial in the work
Of distribution: liberal of their aid
To clamorous importunity in rags,
But oft-times deaf to suppliants who would blush
To wear a tattered garb however coarse,
Whom famine cannot reconcile to filth:
These ask with painful shyness, and, refused
Because deserving, silently retire!
But be ye of good courage! Time itself   420
Shall much befriend you. Time shall give increase;
And all your numerous progeny, well-trained,
But helpless, in few years shall find their hands,
And labour too. Meanwhile ye shall not want
What, conscious of your virtues, we can spare,
Nor what a wealthier than ourselves may send.

I mean the man, who, when the distant poor
Need help, denies them nothing but his name.
    But poverty, with most who whimper forth
Their long complaints, is self-inflicted woe;   430
The effect of laziness or sottish waste.
Now goes the nightly thief prowling abroad
For plunder; much solicitous how best
He may compensate for a day of sloth
By works of darkness and nocturnal wrong.
Woe to the gardener's pale, the farmer's hedge,
Plashed neatly, and secured with driven stakes
Deep in the loamy bank. Uptorn by strength,
Resistless in so bad a cause, but lame
To better deeds, he bundles up the spoil—   440
An ass's burden—and, when laden most
And heaviest, light of foot, steals fast away.
Nor does the boarded hovel better guard
The well-stacked pile of riven logs and roots
From his pernicious force. Nor will he leave
Unwrenched the door, however well secured,
Where Chanticleer amidst his harem sleeps
In unsuspecting pomp. Twitched from the perch,
He gives the princely bird, with all his wives,
To his voracious bag, struggling in vain,   450
And loudly wondering at the sudden change.—
Nor this to feed his own! 'Twere some excuse
Did pity of their sufferings warp aside
His principle, and tempt him into sin
For their support, so destitute.—But they
Neglected pine at home; themselves, as more
Exposed than others, with less scruple made
His victims, robbed of their defenceless all.
Cruel is all he does. 'Tis quenchless thirst
Of ruinous ebriety that prompts   460
His every action, and imbrutes the man.
Oh for a law to noose the villain's neck
Who starves his own; who persecutes the blood
He gave them in his children's veins, and hates
And wrongs the woman he has sworn to love!
    Pass where we may, through city or through town,
Village or hamlet of this merry land,
Though lean and beggared, every twentieth pace
Conducts the unguarded nose to such a whiff
Of stale debauch, forth-issuing from the sties   470
That law has licensed, as makes temperance reel.
There sit, involved and lost in curling clouds
Of Indian fume, and guzzling deep, the boor,
The lackey, and the groom: the craftsman there
Takes a Lethean leave of all his toil;
Smith, cobbler, joiner, he that plies the shears,
And he that kneads the dough; all loud alike,
All learnèd, and all drunk! The fiddle screams
Plaintive and piteous, as it wept and wailed
Its wasted tones and harmony unheard: 480
Fierce the dispute, whate'er the theme; while she,
Fell Discord, arbitress of such debate,
Perched on the sign-post, holds with even hand
Her undecisive scales. In this she lays
A weight of ignorance; in that, of pride;
And smiles, delighted with the eternal poise.
Dire is the frequent curse, and its twin sound
The cheek-distending oath, not to be praised
As ornamental, musical, polite,
Like those which modern senators employ,   490
Whose oath is rhetoric, and who swear for fame!
Behold the schools in which plebeian minds,
Once simple, are initiated in arts
Which some may practise with politer grace,
But none with readier skill!—'tis here they learn
The road that leads, from competence and peace,
To indigence and rapine; till at last
Society, grown weary of the load,
Shakes her encumbered lap, and casts them out.
But censure profits little: vain the attempt   500
To advertise in verse a public pest,
That, like the filth with which the peasant feeds
His hungry acres, stinks, and is of use.
The excise is fattened with the rich result
Of all this riot; and ten thousand casks,
For ever dribbling out their base contents,
Touched by the Midas finger of the state,
Bleed gold for ministers to sport away.
Drink, and be mad, then; 'tis your country bids!
Gloriously drunk, obey the important call!   510
Her cause demands the assistance of your throats;—
Ye all can swallow, and she asks no more.
    Would I had fallen upon those happier days
That poets celebrate; those golden times
And those Arcadian scenes that Maro sings,
And Sidney, warbler of poetic prose.
Nymphs were Dianas then, and swains had hearts
That felt their virtues: innocence, it seems,
From courts dismissed, found shelter in the groves;
The footsteps of simplicity, impressed   520
Upon the yielding herbage, (so they sing)
Then were not all effaced: then speech profane,
And manners profligate, were rarely found;
Observed as prodigies, and soon reclaimed.
Vain wish! those days were never: airy dreams
Sat for the picture; and the poet's hand,
Imparting substance to an empty shade,
Imposed a gay delirium for a truth.
Grant it:—I still must envy them an age

---

428. name. See, below, Cowper's letter of October 10, 1784.   437. Plashed, with interwoven branches.   460. ebriety, drunkenness.   473. Indian fume, tobacco.   504. excise, a tax on liquor.   515. Maro, Virgil.

That favoured such a dream; in days like these 530
Impossible, when virtue is so scarce,
That to suppose a scene where she presides,
Is tramontane, and stumbles all belief.
No: we are polished now! the rural lass,
Whom once her virgin modesty and grace,
Her artless manners, and her neat attire,
So dignified that she was hardly less
Than the fair shepherdess of old romance,
Is seen no more. The character is lost!
Her head, adorned with lappets pinned aloft, 540
And ribbands streaming gay, superbly raised,
And magnified beyond all human size,
Indebted to some smart wig-weaver's hand
For more than half the tresses it sustains;
Her elbows ruffled, and her tottering form
Ill propped upon French heels, she might be deemed
(But that the basket dangling on her arm
Interprets her more truly) of a rank
Too proud for dairy work, or sale of eggs.
Expect her soon with foot-boy at her heels, 550
No longer blushing for her awkward load,
Her train and her umbrella all her care!

The town has tinged the country; and the stain
Appears a spot upon a vestal's robe,
The worse for what it soils. The fashion runs
Down into scenes still rural; but, alas,
Scenes rarely graced with rural manners now!
Time was when, in the pastoral retreat,
The unguarded door was safe; men did not watch
To invade another's right, or guard their own. 560
Then sleep was undisturbed by fear, unscared
By drunken howlings; and the chilling tale
Of midnight murder was a wonder heard
With doubtful credit, told to frighten babes.
But farewell now to unsuspicious nights,
And slumbers unalarmed! Now, ere you sleep,
See that your polished arms be primed with care,
And drop the night-bolt;—ruffians are abroad;
And the first larum of the cock's shrill throat
May prove a trumpet, summoning your ear 570
To horrid sounds of hostile feet within.
Even day-light has its dangers; and the walk
Through pathless wastes and woods, unconscious once
Of other tenants than melodious birds,
Or harmless flocks, is hazardous and bold.
Lamented change! to which full many a cause
Inveterate, hopeless of a cure, conspires.
The course of human things from good to ill,
From ill to worse, is fatal, never fails.
Increase of power begets increase of wealth; 580
Wealth luxury, and luxury excess;
Excess, the scrofulous and itchy plague
That seizes first the opulent, descends
To the next rank contagious, and in time
Taints downward all the graduated scale
Of order, from the chariot to the plough.
The rich, and they that have an arm to check
The licence of the lowest in degree,
Desert their office; and themselves, intent
On pleasure, haunt the capital, and thus 590
To all the violence of lawless hands
Resign the scenes their presence might protect.
Authority herself not seldom sleeps,
Though resident, and witness of the wrong.
The plump convivial parson often bears
The magisterial sword in vain, and lays
His reverence and his worship both to rest
On the same cushion of habitual sloth.
Perhaps timidity restrains his arm;
When he should strike he trembles, and sets free, 600
Himself enslaved by terror of the band,
The audacious convict, whom he dares not bind.
Perhaps, though by profession ghostly pure,
He too may have his vice, and sometimes prove
Less dainty than becomes his grave outside
In lucrative concerns. Examine well
His milk-white hand; the palm is hardly clean—
But here and there an ugly smutch appears.
Foh! 'twas a bribe that left it: he has touched
Corruption! Whoso seeks an audit here 610
Propitious, pays his tribute, game or fish,
Wild-fowl or venison; and his errand speeds.

But faster far, and more than all the rest,
A noble cause, which none who bears a spark
Of public virtue ever wished removed,
Works the deplored and mischievous effect.
'Tis universal soldiership has stabbed
The heart of merit in the meaner class.
Arms, through the vanity and brainless rage
Of those that bear them, in whatever cause, 620
Seem most at variance with all moral good,
And incompatible with serious thought.
The clown, the child of nature, without guile,
Blessed with an infant's ignorance of all
But his own simple pleasures—now and then
A wrestling-match, a foot-race, or a fair—
Is ballotted, and trembles at the news:
Sheepish he doffs his hat, and, mumbling, swears
A bible-oath to be whate'er they please,

---

533. **tramontane,** barbarous or naïve; literally, "lying beyond the mountains." 540. **lappets,** flaps on a head-dress. 579. **fatal,** determined by fate. 596. **sword,** symbol of his office as a magistrate. 603. **ghostly,** spiritually. 627. **ballotted,** drafted.

To do he knows not what! The task performed,   630
That instant he becomes the serjeant's care,
His pupil, and his torment, and his jest.
His awkward gait, his introverted toes,
Bent knees, round shoulders, and dejected looks,
Procure him many a curse. By slow degrees,
Unapt to learn, and formed of stubborn stuff,
He yet by slow degrees puts off himself,
Grows conscious of a change, and likes it well:
He stands erect; his slouch becomes a walk;
He steps right onward, martial in his air,   640
His form and movement; is as smart above
As meal and larded locks can make him; wears
His hat, or his plumed helmet, with a grace;
And, his three years of heroship expired,
Returns indignant to the slighted plough.
He hates the field, in which no fife or drum
Attends him; drives his cattle to a march;
And sighs for the smart comrades he has left.
'Twere well if his exterior change were all—
But with his clumsy port the wretch has lost   650
His ignorance and harmless manners too!
To swear, to game, to drink; to show at home
By lewdness, idleness, and sabbath-breach,
The great proficiency he made abroad;
To astonish and to grieve his gazing friends,
To break some maiden's and his mother's heart;
To be a pest where he was useful once;
Are his sole aim, and all his glory, now!
    Man in society is like a flower
Blown in its native bed: 'tis there alone   660
His faculties, expanded in full bloom,
Shine out; there only reach their proper use.
But man, associated and leagued with man
By regal warrant, or self-joined by bond
For interest's sake, or swarming into clans
Beneath one head for purposes of war,
Like flowers selected from the rest, and bound
And bundled close to fill some crowded vase,
Fades rapidly, and, by compression marred,
Contracts defilement not to be endured.   670
Hence chartered boroughs are such public plagues;
And burghers, men immaculate perhaps
In all their private functions, once combined,
Become a loathsome body, only fit
For dissolution, hurtful to the main.
Hence merchants, unimpeachable of sin
Against the charities of domestic life,
Incorporated, seem at once to lose
Their nature; and, disclaiming all regard
For mercy and the common rights of man,   680
Build factories with blood, conducting trade

681. **build factories,** at the beginning of the Industrial Revolution.

At the sword's point, and dyeing the white robe
Of innocent commercial justice red.
Hence, too, the field of glory, as the world
Misdeems it, dazzled by its bright array,
With all its majesty of thundering pomp,
Enchanting music, and immortal wreaths,
Is but a school where thoughtlessness is taught
On principle, where foppery atones
For folly, gallantry for every vice.   690
    But, slighted as it is, and by the great
Abandoned, and, which still I more regret,
Infected with the manners and the modes
It knew not once, the country wins me still.
I never framed a wish, or formed a plan,
That flattered me with hopes of earthly bliss,
But there I laid the scene. There early strayed
My fancy, ere yet liberty of choice
Had found me, or the hope of being free:
My very dreams were rural; rural, too,   700
The first-born efforts of my youthful muse,
Sportive, and jingling her poetic bells
Ere yet her ear was mistress of their powers.
No bard could please me but whose lyre was tuned
To Nature's praises. Heroes and their feats
Fatigued me, never weary of the pipe
Of Tityrus, assembling, as he sang,
The rustic throng beneath his favourite beech.
Then Milton had indeed a poet's charms:
New to my taste, his Paradise surpassed   710
The struggling efforts of my boyish tongue
To speak its excellence. I danced for joy.
I marvelled much that, at so ripe an age
As twice seven years, his beauties had then first
Engaged my wonder; and, admiring still,
And still admiring, with regret supposed
The joy half lost because not sooner found.
Thee too, enamoured of the life I loved,
Pathetic in its praise, in its pursuit
Determined, and possessing it at last   720
With transports such as favoured lovers feel,
I studied, prized, and wished that I had known,
Ingenious Cowley! and, though now reclaimed
By modern lights from an erroneous taste,
I cannot but lament thy splendid wit
Entangled in the cobwebs of the schools.
I still revere thee, courtly though retired;
Though stretched at ease in Chertsey's silent bowers,
Not unemployed; and finding rich amends
For a lost world in solitude and verse.   730

707. **Tityrus,** the chief speaker in Virgil's first Eclogue, and so a representative of pastoral poetry.   723. **Cowley!** Abraham Cowley, whose delight in the rural life was not unlike Cowper's own.   728. **Chertsey,** a village on the Thames to which Cowley retired.

'Tis born with all: the love of nature's works
Is an ingredient in the compound man,
Infused at the creation of the kind.
And, though the Almighty Maker has throughout
Discriminated each from each, by strokes
And touches of his hand, with so much art
Diversified, that two were never found
Twins at all points—yet this obtains in all,
That all discern a beauty in his works,
And all can taste them: minds that have been
  formed   740
And tutored, with a relish more exact,
But none without some relish, none unmoved.
It is a flame that dies not even there,
Where nothing feeds it: neither business, crowds,
Nor habits of luxurious city-life,
Whatever else they smother of true worth
In human bosoms, quench it, or abate.
The villas with which London stands begirt,
Like a swarth Indian with his belt of beads,
Prove it. A breath of unadulterate air,   750
The glimpse of a green pasture, how they cheer
The citizen, and brace his languid frame!
Even in the stifling bosom of the town,
A garden, in which nothing thrives, has charms
That soothe the rich possessor; much consoled,
That here and there some sprigs of mournful mint,
Of nightshade, or valerian, grace the well
He cultivates. These serve him with a hint
That nature lives; that sight-refreshing green
Is still the livery she delights to wear,   760
Though sickly samples of the exuberant whole.
What are the casements lined with creeping herbs,
The prouder sashes fronted with a range
Of orange, myrtle, or the fragrant weed,
The Frenchman's darling? are they not all proofs
That man, immured in cities, still retains
His inborn inextinguishable thirst
Of rural scenes, compensating his loss
By supplemental shifts, the best he may?
The most unfurnished with the means of life, 770
And they that never pass their brick-wall bounds
To range the fields and treat their lungs with air,
Yet feel the burning instinct; over head
Suspend their crazy boxes, planted thick,
And watered duly. There the pitcher stands
A fragment, and the spoutless tea-pot there;
Sad witnesses how close-pent man regrets
The country, with what ardour he contrives
A peep at nature, when he can no more.
  Hail, therefore, patroness of health, and ease, 780
And contemplation, heart-consoling joys
And harmless pleasures, in the thronged abode
Of multitudes unknown! hail, rural life!
Address himself who will to the pursuit
Of honours, or emolument, or fame;
I shall not add myself to such a chase,
Thwart his attempts, or envy his success.
Some must be great. Great offices will have
Great talents. And God gives to every man
The virtue, temper, understanding, taste,   790
That lifts him into life; and lets him fall
Just in the niche he was ordained to fill.
To the deliverer of an injured land
He gives a tongue to enlarge upon, an heart
To feel, and courage to redress her wrongs;
To monarchs dignity; to judges sense;
To artists ingenuity and skill;
To me an unambitious mind, content
In the low vale of life, that early felt
A wish for ease and leisure, and ere long   800
Found here that leisure and that ease I wished.

from YARDLEY OAK

This poem, composed when the poet was sixty years old and left unfinished, is the boldest and most vigorously imaginative of Cowper's productions. In matters of style it shows deliberate imitation of Milton, of whom Cowper was a close student and an editor.

Yardley Oak stood near the village of Olney in Buckinghamshire, Cowper's home for many years. It was twenty-three feet in circumference, and according to the local tradition it was planted by the daughter of William the Conqueror. An interesting comparison may be made between the present poem and Wordsworth's "Yew-Trees," or, still better, Victor de Laprade's *La mort d'un chêne.*

Survivor sole, and hardly such, of all
That once lived here thy brethren, at my birth
(Since which I number three-score winters past)
A shattered veteran, hollow-trunked perhaps
As now, and with excoriate forks deform,
Relict of ages! Could a mind, imbued
With truth from heaven, created thing adore,
I might with reverence kneel and worship thee.
  It seems idolatry with some excuse
When our fore-father Druids in their oaks   10
Imagined sanctity. The conscience yet
Unpurified by an authentic act
Of amnesty, the meed of blood divine,
Loved not the light, but gloomy into gloom

---

738. **obtains,** holds true.   748. **villas,** country homes.
765. **Frenchman's darling?** mignonette.

5. **excoriate,** barkless. Like **deform,** a Miltonic past participle.   10. **Druids,** of course not in any strict sense "forefathers" of the English.   12. **act,** the death of Christ.

Of thickest shades, like Adam after taste
Of fruit proscribed, as to a refuge, fled.
   Thou wast a bauble once; a cup and ball,
Which babes might play with; and the thievish jay,
Seeking her food, with ease might have purloined
The auburn nut that held thee, swallowing down 20
Thy yet close-folded latitude of boughs
And all thine embryo vastness, at a gulp.
But Fate thy growth decreed: autumnal rains
Beneath thy parent tree mellowed the soil
Designed thy cradle, and a skipping deer,
With pointed hoof dibbling the glebe, prepared
The soft receptacle in which secure
Thy rudiments should sleep the winter through.
   So Fancy dreams—Disprove it, if ye can,
Ye reasoners broad awake, whose busy search 30
Of argument, employed too oft amiss,
Sifts half the pleasures of short life away!
   Thou fell'st mature, and in the loamy clod
Swelling, with vegetative force instinct
Didst burst thine egg, as theirs the fabled Twins
Now stars; two lobes, protruding, paired exact;
A leaf succeeded, and another leaf,
And all the elements thy puny growth
Fostering propitious, thou becam'st a twig.
   Who lived when thou wast such? Oh couldst thou
     speak, 40
As in Dodona once thy kindred trees
Oracular, I would not curious ask
The future, best unknown, but at thy mouth
Inquisitive, the less ambiguous past.
   By thee I might correct, erroneous oft,
The clock of history, facts and events
Timing more punctual, unrecorded facts
Recovering, and misstated setting right—
Desperate attempt, till trees shall speak again!
   Time made thee what thou wast—King of the
     woods; 50
And Time hath made thee what thou art—a cave
For owls to roost in. Once thy spreading boughs
O'erhung the champain; and the numerous flock
That grazed it stood beneath that ample cope
Uncrowded, yet safe-sheltered from the storm.
No flock frequents thee now. Thou hast outlived
Thy popularity and art become
(Unless verse rescue thee awhile) a thing
Forgotten, as the foliage of thy youth.
   While thus through all the ages thou hast
     pushed 60
Of treeship, first a seedling hid in grass,

Then twig, then sapling, and, as century rolled
Slow after century, a giant bulk
Of girth enormous, with moss-cushioned root
Upheaved above the soil, and sides imbossed
With prominent wens globose, till at the last
The rottenness, which time is charged to inflict
On other mighty ones, found also thee—
What exhibitions various hath the world
Witnessed of mutability in all 70
That we account most durable below!
Change is the diet, on which all subsist
Created changeable, and change at last
Destroys them.—Skies uncertain now the heat
Transmitting cloudless, and the solar beam
Now quenching in a boundless sea of clouds,—
Calm and alternate storm, moisture and drought,
Invigorate by turns the springs of life
In all that live, plant, animal, and man,
And in conclusion mar them. Nature's threads, 80
Fine passing thought, ev'n in her coarsest works,
Delight in agitation, yet sustain
The force that agitates not unimpaired,
But, worn by frequent impulse, to the cause
Of their best tone their dissolution owe.
   Thought cannot spend itself, comparing still
The great and little of thy lot, thy growth
From almost nullity into a state
Of matchless grandeur, and declension thence
Slow into such magnificent decay. 90
Time was, when, settling on thy leaf, a fly
Could shake thee to the root—and time has been
When tempests could not. At thy firmest age
Thou hadst within thy bole solid contents
That might have ribbed the sides or planked the deck
Of some flagged admiral; and tortuous arms,
The ship-wright's darling treasure, didst present
To the four-quartered winds, robust and bold,
Warped into tough knee-timber, many a load.
But the axe spared thee; in those thriftier days 100
Oaks fell not, hewn by thousands, to supply
The bottomless demands of contest waged
For senatorial honours. Thus to Time
The task was left to whittle thee away
With his sly scythe, whose ever-nibbling edge
Noiseless, an atom and an atom more
Disjoining from the rest, has, unobserved,
Achieved a labour, which had, far and wide,
(By man performed) made all the forest ring.
   Embowelled now, and of thy ancient self 110
Possessing nought but the scooped rind, that seems

---

34. **instinct**, filled, charged.   35. **Twins**, Gemini, Castor and Pollux, born from an egg.   41. **Dodona**, the Greek oracle which spoke through rustling oak leaves.   53. **champain**, field.

85. **tone**, health.   96. **admiral**, flagship. See *Paradise Lost*, Book I, ll. 292–94.   103. **senatorial honours**, political office bought with money gained by sale of timber.   110. **Embowelled**, the same as "disembowelled."

An huge throat calling to the clouds for drink,
Which it would give in rivulets to thy root,
Thou temptest none, but rather much forbid'st
The feller's toil, which thou couldst ill requite.
Yet is thy root sincere, sound as the rock,
A quarry of stout spurs and knotted fangs,
Which, crooked into a thousand whimsies, clasp
The stubborn soil, and hold thee still erect.
 So stands a kingdom, whose foundations yet   120
Fail not, in virtue and in wisdom laid,
Though all the superstructure, by the tooth
Pulverized of venality, a shell
Stands now, and semblance only of itself.
 Thine arms have left thee. Winds have rent them off
Long since, and rovers of the forest wild
With bow and shaft have burnt them. Some have left
A splintered stump bleached to a snowy white;
And some memorial none where once they grew.
Yet life still lingers in thee, and puts forth   130
Proof not contemptible of what she can,
Even where death predominates. The spring
Thee finds not less alive to her sweet force
Than yonder upstarts of the neighbour wood,
So much thy juniors, who their birth receiv'd
Half a millenium since the date of thine. . . .

THE POPLAR-FIELD

The poplars are felled, farewell to the shade
And the whispering sound of the cool colonnade,
The winds play no longer, and sing in the leaves,
Nor Ouse on his bosom their image receives.

Twelve years have elapsed since I first took a view
Of my favourite field and the bank where they grew,
And now in the grass behold they are laid,
And the tree is my seat that once lent me a shade.

The blackbird has fled to another retreat
Where the hazels afford him a screen from the heat,   10
And the scene where his melody charmed me before,
Resounds with his sweet-flowing ditty no more.

My fugitive years are all hasting away,
And I must ere long lie as lowly as they,
With a turf on my breast, and a stone at my head,
Ere another such grove shall arise in its stead.

'Tis a sight to engage me, if any thing can,
To muse on the perishing pleasures of man;

 116. **sincere**, whole, of one piece.

Though his life be a dream, his enjoyments, I see,
Have a being less durable even than he.   20

THE CASTAWAY

 Written in the last year of the poet's life, this poem shows more affectingly than any other the obsession against which Cowper had struggled since his youth.
 The incident here narrated is drawn from George, Lord Anson's *Voyage round the World*, 1748.

 Obscurest night involved the sky,
  The Atlantic billows roared,
When such a destined wretch as I,
 Washed headlong from on board,
Of friends, of hope, of all bereft,
His floating home for ever left.

No braver chief could Albion boast
 Than he with whom he went,
Nor ever ship left Albion's coast,
 With warmer wishes sent.   10
He loved them both, but both in vain,
Nor him beheld, nor her again.

Not long beneath the whelming brine,
 Expert to swim, he lay;
Nor soon he felt his strength decline,
 Or courage die away;
But waged with death a lasting strife,
Supported by despair of life.

He shouted: nor his friends had failed
 To check the vessel's course,   20
But so the furious blast prevailed,
 That, pitiless perforce,
They left their outcast mate behind,
And scudded still before the wind.

Some succour yet they could afford;
 And, such as storms allow,
The cask, the coop, the floated cord,
 Delayed not to bestow.
But he (they knew) nor ship, nor shore,
Whate'er they gave, should visit more.   30

Nor, cruel as it seemed, could he
 Their haste himself condemn,
Aware that flight, in such a sea,
 Alone could rescue them;
Yet bitter felt it still to die
Deserted, and his friends so nigh.

He long survives, who lives an hour
 In ocean, self-upheld;

And so long he, with unspent power,
    His destiny repelled;
And ever, as the minutes flew,
    Entreated help, or cried—Adieu!

At length, his transient respite past,
    His comrades, who before
Had heard his voice in every blast,
    Could catch the sound no more.
For then, by toil subdued, he drank
The stifling wave, and then he sank.

No poet wept him; but the page
    Of narrative sincere,
That tells his name, his worth, his age,
    Is wet with Anson's tear.
And tears by bards or heroes shed
Alike immortalize the dead.

I therefore purpose not, or dream,
    Descanting on his fate,
To give the melancholy theme
    A more enduring date;
But misery still delights to trace
Its semblance in another's case.

No voice divine the storm allayed,
    No light propitious shone,
When, snatched from all effectual aid,
    We perished, each alone;
But I beneath a rougher sea,
And whelmed in deeper gulphs than he.

LETTERS

In an age that made an art of correspondence the letters of William Cowper were unsurpassed. They reveal the man as he was known to his closest friends. They show the delicacy, verve, and quiet humor that usually lay concealed beneath his diffidence. Here his earnest thought and his whimsicality melt into each other and set each other off. Cowper's letters provide the best comment upon his poetry. Indeed, they bid fair to outlive all but a slender sheaf of his poems and to become the mainstay of his literary reputation.

TO THE REV. WILLIAM UNWIN

October 10, 1784.

My Dear William,

I send you four quires of verse, which having sent, I shall dismiss from my thoughts, and think no more of, till I see them in print. I have not after all found time or industry enough to give the last hand to the points. I believe, however, they are not very erroneous, though in so long a work, and in a work that requires nicety in their particular, some inaccuracies will escape. Where you find any, you will oblige me by correcting them.

In some passages, especially in the second book, you will observe me very satirical. Writing on such subjects I could not be otherwise. I can write nothing without aiming at least at usefulness: it were beneath my years to do it, and still more dishonourable to my religion. I know that a reformation of such abuses as I have censured is not to be expected from the efforts of a poet; but to contemplate the world, its follies, its vices, its indifference to duty, and its strenuous attachment to what is evil, and not to reprehend were to approve it. From this charge at least I shall be clear, for I have neither tacitly nor expressly flattered either its characters or its customs. I have paid one, and only one compliment, which was so justly due, that I did not know how to withhold it, especially having so fair an occasion;—I forget myself, there is another in the first book to Mr. Throckmorton,—but the compliment I mean is to Mr. Smith. It is however so managed, that nobody but himself can make the application, and you, to whom I disclose the secret; a delicacy on my part, which so much delicacy on his obliged me to the observance of.

What there is of a religious cast in the volume I have thrown towards the end of it, for two reasons; first, that I might not revolt the reader at his entrance,—and secondly, that my best impressions might be made last. Were I to write as many volumes as Lope de Vega, or Voltaire, not one of them would be without this tincture. If the world like it not, so much the worse for them. I make all the concessions I can, that I may please them, but I will not please them at the expense of conscience.

My descriptions are all from nature: not one of them second-handed. My delineations of the heart are from my own experience: not one of them borrowed from books, or in the least degree conjectural. In my numbers, which I have varied as much as I could, (for blank verse without variety of numbers is no better than bladder and string,) I have imitated nobody, though sometimes perhaps there may be an apparent resemblance; because at the same time that I would not imitate, I have not affectedly differed.

Letters. **46. Rev. William Unwin,** only son of Cowper's closest friend, Mrs. Mary Unwin. **50. quires.** Twenty-four sheets of writing paper make a quire. This was the manuscript of *The Task.*

3. points, punctuation marks. **22. compliment.** See, above, *The Task,* Book IV, ll. 427–28. **25. Throckmorton.** See *The Task,* Book I, l. 262. **26. Mr. Smith,** an anonymous benefactor of the poor in Olney.

If the work cannot boast a regular plan, (in which respect however I do not think it altogether indefensible,) it may yet boast, that the reflections are naturally suggested always by the preceding passage, and that except the fifth book, which is rather of a political aspect, the whole has one tendency: to discountenance the modern enthusiasm after a London life, and to recommend rural ease and leisure, as friendly to the cause of piety and virtue.

If it please you I shall be happy, and collect from your pleasure in it an omen of its general acceptance.

Yours, my dear friend,
W. C.

Your mother's love. She wishes that you would buy her a second-hand cream-pot, small, either kit, jug, or ewer of silver.

I shall be glad of an immediate line to apprise me of its safe arrival.

TO THE REV. JOHN NEWTON

December 13, 1784.

My Dear Friend,

Having imitated no man, I may reasonably hope that I shall not incur the disadvantage of a comparison with my betters. Milton's manner was peculiar. So is Thomson's. He that should write like either of them, would, in my judgment, deserve the name of a copyist, but not of a poet. A judicious and sensible reader therefore, like yourself, will not say that my manner is not good, because it does not resemble theirs, but will rather consider what it is in itself. Blank verse is susceptible of a much greater diversification of manner, than verse in rhyme: and why the modern writers of it have all thought proper to cast their numbers alike, I know not. Certainly it was not necessity that compelled them to it. I flatter myself however that I have avoided that sameness with others, which would entitle me to nothing but a share in one common oblivion with them all. It is possible that, as the reviewer of my former volume found cause to say that he knew not to what class of writers to refer me, the reviewer of this, whosoever he shall be, may see occasion to remark the same singularity. At any rate, though as little apt to be sanguine as most men, and more prone to fear and despond, than to overrate my own productions, I am persuaded that I shall not forfeit any thing by this volume that I gained by the last.

As to the title, I take it to be the best that is to be had. It is not possible that a book, including such a variety of subjects, and in which no particular one is predominant, should find a title adapted to them all. In such a case, it seemed almost necessary to accommodate the name to the incident that gave birth to the poem; nor does it appear to me, that because I performed more than my task, therefore the Task is not a suitable title. A house would still be a house, though the builder of it should make it ten times as big as he at first intended. I might indeed, following the example of the Sunday newsmonger, call it the Olio. But I should do myself wrong; for though it have much variety, it has, I trust, no confusion.

For the same reason none of the interior titles apply themselves to the contents at large of that book to which they belong. They are, every one of them, taken either from the leading, (I should say the introductory,) passage of that particular book, or from that which makes the most conspicuous figure in it. Had I set off with a design to write upon a gridiron, and had I actually written near two hundred lines upon that utensil, as I have upon the Sofa, the Gridiron should have been my title. But the Sofa being, as I may say, the starting-post from which I addressed myself to the long race that I soon conceived a design to run, it acquired a just pre-eminence in my account, and was very worthily advanced to the titular honour it enjoys, its right being at least so far a good one, that no word in the language could pretend a better.

The Time-piece appears to me, (though by some accident the import of that title has escaped you,) to have a degree of propriety beyond the most of them. The book to which it belongs is intended to strike the hour that gives notice of approaching judgement, and, dealing pretty largely in the *signs* of the *times*, seems to be denominated, as it is, with a sufficient degree of accommodation to the subject. . . .

We do not often see, or rather feel, so severe a frost before Christmas. Unexpected, at least by me, it had like to have been too much for my greenhouse, my myrtles having found themselves yesterday morning in an atmosphere so cold that the mercury was fallen eight degrees below the freezing point.

We are truly sorry for Mrs. Newton's indisposition, and shall be glad to hear of her recovery. We

---

24. **Rev. John Newton,** an evangelical clergyman of whom Cowper stood usually in awe. He had recently criticized *The Task* adversely.   46. **volume,** that of 1782.

16. **Olio,** Miscellany.   35. '**The Time-piece,**' title of the second book of *The Task*.

are most liable to colds at this season, and at this season a cold is most difficult of cure.

Be pleased to remember us to the young ladies, and to all under your roof and elsewhere, who are mindful of us.—And believe me,

Your affectionate
Wm. Cowper.

Your letters are gone to their address. The oysters were very good.

TO LADY HESKETH

June 12, 1786.

I am neither young nor superannuated, yet am I a child. When I had read your letter I grumbled: not at you, my dearest cousin, for you are in no fault, but at the whole generation of coach-makers, as you may suppose, and at yours in particular. I foresaw and foreknew that he would fail in his promise, and yet was disappointed; was, in truth, no more prepared for what I expected with so much reason, than if I had not at all expected it. I grumbled till we went to dinner, and at intervals till we had dined; and when dinner was over, with very little encouragement, I could actually have cried. And if I had, I should in truth have thought them tears as well bestowed as most that I have shed for many years. At first I numbered months, then weeks, then days, and was just beginning to number hours, and now I am thrown back to days again. My first speech was, after folding up your letter, (for I will honestly tell you all,) I am crazed with Mondays, Tuesdays, and Wednesdays and St. Alban's, and Totteridge, and Hadley. When is she to set out?—When is she to be here? Do tell me, for, perhaps, you understand it better than I. Why, says Mrs. Unwin, (with much more composure in her air than properly belonged to her, for she also had her feelings on the occasion,) she sets out to-morrow se'nnight, and will be here on the Wednesday after. And who knows that? replied I; will the coach-maker be at all more punctual in repairing the old carriage, than in making the new one? For my part, I have no hope of seeing her this month; and if it be possible, I will not think of it, lest I should be again disappointed. And to say the truth, my dear, though hours have passed since thus I said, and I have had time for cooler consideration, the suspicion still sticks close to me, that more delays may happen.

A philosopher would prepare himself for such an event, but I am no philosopher, at least when the comfort of seeing you is in question. I believe in my heart that there have been just as many true philosophers upon earth, as there have been men that have had little or no feeling, and not one more. Swift truly says—

"Indifference clad in reason's guise,
All want of fortitude supplies."

When I wake in the night, I feel my spirits the lighter because you are coming. When I am not at Troy, I am either occupied in the recollection of a thousand passages of my past life, in which you were a partaker with me, or conversing about you with Mrs. Unwin. Thus my days and nights have been spent principally ever since you determined upon this journey, and especially, and almost without interruption from any other subject, since the time of your journey has seemed near at hand. While I despaired, as I did for many years, that I should ever see you more, I thought of you, indeed, and often, but with less solicitude. I used to say to myself; Providence has so ordered it, and it is my duty to submit. He has cast me at a distance from her, and from all whom I once knew. He did it, and not I; it is He who has chosen my situation for me. Have I not reason to be thankful that, since he designed me to pass a part of my life, and no inconsiderable one neither, in a state of the deepest melancholy, he appointed me a friend in Mrs. Unwin, who should share all my sorrows with me, and watch over me in my helpless condition, night and day? What, and where had I been without her? Such considerations were sufficient to reconcile me at that time to perpetual separation even from you, because perpetual I supposed it must be, and without remedy. But now every hour of your absence seems long, for this very natural reason, because the same Providence has given me a hope that you will be present with me soon. A good that seems at an immeasurable distance, and that we cannot hope to reach, has therefore the less influence on our affections. But the same good brought nearer, made to appear practicable, promised to our hopes, and almost in possession, engages all our faculties and desires. All this is according to the natural and necessary course of things in the human heart; and the philosophy that would interfere with it is folly at least, if not frenzy. A throne has at present but little

---

11. **Lady Hesketh,** Cowper's cousin Harriet, whom he had not seen for twenty years.   40. **se'nnight,** the space of seven nights, a week.

8-9. **"Indifference . . . supplies,"** misquoted from "On the Death of Dr. Swift," ll. 163-64.   11-12. **at Troy,** at work on his translation of Homer.

sensible attraction for me. And why? Perhaps only because I know that should I break my heart with wishes for a throne, I should never reach one. But did I know assuredly that I should put on a crown to-morrow, perhaps I too should feel ambition, and account the interposing night tedious. The sum of the whole matter, my dear, is this: that this villainous coach-maker has mortified me monstrously, and that I tremble lest he should do so again. From you I have no fears. I see in your letter, and all the way through it, what pains you take to assure me and give me comfort. I am and will be comforted for that very reason; and will wait still other ten days with all the patience that I can muster. You, I know, will be punctual if you can, and that at least is matter of real consolation.

I approve altogether, my cousin beloved, of your sending your goods to the waggon on Saturday, and cookee by the coach on Tuesday. She will be here perhaps by four in the afternoon, at the latest by five, and will have quite time enough to find out all the cupboards and shelves in her department before you arrive. But I declare and protest that cookee shall sleep that night at our house, and get her breakfast here next morning. You will break her heart, child, if you send her into a strange house where she will find nothing that has life but the curate, who has not much neither. Servant he keeps none. A woman makes his bed, and after a fashion as they say, dresses his dinner, and then leaves him to his lucubrations. I do therefore insist on it, and so does Mrs. Unwin, that cookee shall be our guest for that time; and from this we will not depart. I tell thee besides, that I shall be more glad to see her, than ever I was in my life to see one whom I never saw before. Guess why, if you can.

You must number your miles fifty-six instead of fifty-four. The fifty-sixth mile ends but a few yards beyond the vicarage. Soon after you shall have entered Olney, you will find an opening on your right hand. It is a lane that leads to your dwelling. There your coach may stop and set down Mrs. Eaton; when she has walked about forty yards she will spy a green gate and rails on her left hand; and when she has opened the gate and reached the house-door, she will find herself at home. But we have another manoeuvre to play off upon you, and in which we positively will not be opposed, or if we are, it shall be to no purpose. I have an honest fellow that works in my garden, his name is Kitchener, and we call him Kitch for brevity. He is sober, and as trusty as the day. He has a smart blue coat, that when I had worn it some years, I gave him, and he has now worn it some years himself. I shall set him on horseback, and order him to the Swan at Newport, there to wait your arrival, and if you should not stop at that place, as perhaps you may not, immediately to throw himself into your suite, and to officiate as your guide. For though the way from Newport hither is short, there are turnings that might puzzle your coachman; and he will be of use too, in conducting you to our house, which otherwise you might not easily find, partly through the stupidity of those of whom you might inquire, and partly from its out-of-the-way situation. My brother drove up and down Olney in quest of us, almost as often as you up and down Chancery Lane in quest of the Madans, with fifty boys and girls at his tail, before he could find us. The first man, therefore, you shall see in a blue coat with white buttons, in the famous town of Newport, cry Kitch! He will immediately answer, My Lady! and from that moment you are sure not to be lost.

Your house shall be as clean as scrubbing and dry-rubbing can make it, and in all respects fit to receive you. My friend the Quaker, in all that I have seen of his doings, has acquitted himself much to my satisfaction. Some little things, he says, will perhaps be missing at first, in such a multiplicity, but they shall be produced as soon as called for. Mrs. U. has bought you six ducks, and is fatting them for you. She has also rummaged up a coop that will hold six chickens, and designs to people it for you by the first opportunity; for these things are not to be got fit for the table at Olney. Thus, my dear, are all things in the best train possible, and nothing remains but that you come and show yourself. Oh, that moment! Shall we not both enjoy it? —That we shall.

I have received an anonymous complimentary Pindaric Ode from a little poet who calls himself a school-boy. I send you the first stanza by way of specimen. You shall see it all soon.

TO WM. COWPER, OF THE INNER
TEMPLE, ESQ.

On His Poems in the Second Volume

In what high strains, my Muse, wilt thou
Attempt great Cowper's worth to show?
   Pindaric strains shall tune the lyre,
      And 'twould require
      A Pindar's fire
   To sing great Cowper's worth,

38. **fifty-four,** from London stone.
2-3. **Newport,** a village five miles from Olney.
45. **Second Volume,** *The Task,* published in 1785.

> The lofty bard, delightful sage,
> Ever the wonder of the age,
> And *blessing to the earth.*

Adieu, my precious cousin, your lofty bard and delightful sage expects you with all possible affection.

> Ever yours,
> Wm. Cowper.

I am truly sorry for your poor friend Burrows!

Our dinner hour is four o'clock. We will not surfeit you with delicacies; of that be assured. I know your palate, and am glad to know that it is easily pleased. Were it other than it is, it would stand but a poor chance to be gratified at Olney. I undertake for lettuce and cucumber, and Mrs. U. for all the rest. If she feeds you too well, you must humble her.

ON THE RECEIPT OF MY MOTHER'S PICTURE OUT OF NORFOLK

Cowper wrote to a friend on March 12, 1790: "I have lately received from a female cousin of mine in Norfolk . . . a picture of my mother. She died when I wanted two days of being six years old; yet I remember her perfectly, find the picture a strong likeness of her, and, because her memory has ever been precious to me, have written a poem on the receipt of it—a poem which, one excepted, I had more pleasure in writing than any that I ever wrote."

Oh that those lips had language! Life has passed
With me but roughly since I heard thee last.
Those lips are thine—thy own sweet smiles I see,
The same that oft in childhood solaced me;
Voice only fails, else, how distinct they say,
"Grieve not, my child, chase all thy fears away!"
The meek intelligence of those dear eyes
(Blessed be the art that can immortalize,
The art that baffles time's tyrannic claim
To quench it) here shines on me still the same.   10
  Faithful remembrancer of one so dear,
Oh welcome guest, though unexpected, here!
Who bid'st me honour with an artless song,
Affectionate, a mother lost so long.
I will obey, not willingly alone,
But gladly, as the precept were her own;
And, while that face renews my filial grief,
Fancy shall weave a charm for my relief—
Shall steep me in Elysian reverie,
A momentary dream, that thou art she.   20
  My mother! when I learned that thou wast dead,
Say, wast thou conscious of the tears I shed?
Hovered thy spirit o'er thy sorrowing son,
Wretch even then, life's journey just begun?
Perhaps thou gav'st me, though unseen, a kiss;
Perhaps a tear, if souls can weep in bliss—
Ah that maternal smile! it answers—Yes.
I heard the bell tolled on thy burial day,
I saw the hearse that bore thee slow away,
And, turning from my nursery window, drew   30
A long, long sigh, and wept a last adieu!
But was it such?—It was.—Where thou art gone
Adieus and farewells are a sound unknown.
May I but meet thee on that peaceful shore,
The parting sound shall pass my lips no more!
Thy maidens grieved themselves at my concern,
Oft gave me promise of a quick return.
What ardently I wished, I long believed,
And, disappointed still, was still deceived;
By disappointment every day beguiled,   40
Dupe of *to-morrow* even from a child.
Thus many a sad to-morrow came and went,
Till, all my stock of infant sorrow spent,
I learned at last submission to my lot;
But, though I less deplored thee, ne'er forgot.
  Where once we dwelt our name is heard no more,
Children not thine have trod my nursery floor;
And where the gardener Robin, day by day,
Drew me to school along the public way,
Delighted with my bauble coach, and wrapt   50
In scarlet mantle warm, and velvet capped,
'Tis now become a history little known,
That once we called the pastoral house our own.
Short-lived possession! but the record fair
That memory keeps of all thy kindness there,
Still outlives many a storm that has effaced
A thousand other themes less deeply traced.
Thy nightly visits to my chamber made,
That thou might'st know me safe and warmly laid;
Thy morning bounties ere I left my home,   60
The biscuit, or confectionary plum;
The fragrant waters on my cheeks bestowed
By thy own hand, till fresh they shone and glowed;
All this, and more endearing still than all,
Thy constant flow of love, that knew no fall,
Ne'er roughened by those cataracts and brakes
That humour interposed too often makes;
All this still legible in memory's page,
And still to be so, to my latest age,
Adds joy to duty, makes me glad to pay   70
Such honours to thee as my numbers may;
Perhaps a frail memorial, but sincere,
Not scorned in heaven, though little noticed here.
  Could Time, his flight reversed, restore the hours,

53. **house,** the parsonage at Great Berkhampstead in which Cowper was born. 67. **humour,** caprice, whim.

When, playing with thy vesture's tissued flowers,
The violet, the pink, and jessamine,
I pricked them into paper with a pin,
(And thou wast happier than myself the while,
Would'st softly speak, and stroke my head and smile)
Could those few pleasant hours again appear, 80
Might one wish bring them, would I wish them here?
I would not trust my heart—the dear delight
Seems so to be desired, perhaps I might.—
But no—what here we call our life is such,
So little to be loved, and thou so much,
That I should ill requite thee to constrain
Thy unbound spirit into bonds again.
   Thou, as a gallant bark from Albion's coast
(The storms all weathered and the ocean crossed)
Shoots into port at some well-havened isle, 90
Where spices breathe and brighter seasons smile,
There sits quiescent on the floods that show
Her beauteous form reflected clear below,
While airs impregnated with incense play
Around her, fanning light her streamers gay—
So thou, with sails how swift! hast reached the shore
"Where tempests never beat nor billows roar,"
And thy loved consort on the dangerous tide
Of life, long since, has anchored at thy side.
But me, scarce hoping to attain that rest, 100
Always from port withheld, always distressed—
Me howling winds drive devious, tempest-tossed,
Sails ript, seams opening wide, and compass lost,
And day by day some current's thwarting force
Sets me more distant from a prosperous course.
But oh the thought, that thou art safe, and he!
That thought is joy, arrive what may to me.
My boast is not that I deduce my birth
From loins enthroned, and rulers of the earth;
But higher far my proud pretensions rise— 110
The son of parents passed into the skies.
And now, farewell—Time, unrevoked, has run
His wonted course, yet what I wished is done.
By contemplation's help, not sought in vain,
I seem to have lived my childhood o'er again;
To have renewed the joys that once were mine,
Without the sin of violating thine:
And, while the wings of fancy still are free,
And I can view this mimic show of thee,
Time has but half succeeded in his theft— 120
Thyself removed, thy power to sooth me left.

Robert Burns
1759–1796

Scotland's foremost poet was born in a two-room cottage. He had some three years of schooling, eked out by instruction from his earnest and thoughtful father. His youth was spent in hard work on the farm, in eager reading, and in the composition of verses in which he used the dialect and the stories of his country neighbors. His fame, at first local, soon spread through Scotland, and his visit to Edinburgh in his twenty-eighth year caused a sensation there in cultivated circles. This brief prosperity, however, did him less good than harm, and the trend of his later years was downward. Overborne by poverty, toil, misfortune, and eventual despair, he died into immortality at the age of thirty-seven, "burnt to a cinder."

The criticism of Burns has been obscured by passionate partisanship of several kinds, and he is so entrenched in the world's heart that impartial judgment can hardly come at him. Clearly, however, although he is an able versifier and a master of rhetoric, there is not much pure poetry in him. We do not go to him for ecstatic vision, depth of wisdom, or range of knowledge. His thought, when he thinks at all, is likely to be shallow, and his emotion is often sentimental. Yet all of these shortcomings are at once forgotten when we consider his transcendent gift for song—for those "fitful gushes and fantastic breaks . . . not of the voice only but of the whole mind" in which, as Carlyle says, he has no fellow short of Shakespeare.

"Observe him chiefly," Carlyle says also, "as he mingles with his brother men." For Burns is the poet of human relationships. In the oldest and deepest sense of the word he is "convivial." It is not of himself alone or primarily that he sings, but of all men. He is a spokesman of the human heart. Whatever else he may lack, he has that "one touch of nature" which "makes the whole world kin."

---

97. "Where . . . roar," misquoted from Garth's *The Dispensary*, Book III, l. 226.

108. birth. On his mother's side Cowper was a descendant of King Henry VII.

For the notion that poetry is a luxury of the privileged classes, that there is something effeminate about it, and that it is an affair of books and of scholarship, Burns provides the promptest cure. Although he had much more reading than is commonly supposed, he helped to bring poetry out of libraries and into the open air. By dipping his songs as it were out of the living water that flowed past his humble door he did as much as Wordsworth to revive modern poetry.

Born in the year of Edward Young's *Conjectures upon Original Composition*, Burns lived almost until the appearance of *Lyrical Ballads*. Thus his short life spanned the transition from Neoclassical to Romantic domination. And it is clear that he greatly helped to hasten that transition by showing, as Wordsworth said,

"How Verse may build a princely throne
On humble truth."

Robert Burns once called himself "a poor, damned, incautious, duped, unfortunate fool; the sport, the miserable victim of rebellious pride, hypochondriac imaginations, agonizing sensibilities, and bedlam passions." So far as it goes this characterization is bitterly true, but it says nothing about the man's warm and companionable nature, his virile creative force, or the alchemic energy of his imagination which so often transmuted the base metals of passion, folly, and pain into the pure gold of beauty. There is no poet whose transgressions we more willingly forgive than we do those of Robert Burns, for, with all his sins and weakness upon him, he left us a precious handful of songs that will last while there is human breath to sing them.

THE COTTER'S SATURDAY NIGHT
Inscribed to R. Aiken, Esq.

This poem has been much praised, though not for its poetic qualities. Clearly, it is a work of talent rather than of genius, and its chief value lies in what it tells us about the home life of the poet's boyhood and youth. A thoughtful student will ask himself how the poem is related to Gray's *Elegy*, why it uses literary English in alternation with Scottish dialect, whether its verse-form is suited to the theme and mood, and what are the probable causes of its popularity.

Let not Ambition mock their useful toil,
  Their homely joys, and destiny obscure;
Nor Grandeur hear with a disdainful smile
  The short and simple annals of the poor.
—Gray

My loved, my honoured, much respected friend!
  No mercenary bard his homage pays:
With honest pride I scorn each selfish end,
  My dearest meed a friend's esteem and praise:
To you I sing, in simple Scottish lays,
The lowly train in life's sequestered scene;
  The native feelings strong, the guileless ways;
What Aiken in a cottage would have been—
Ah! though his worth unknown, far happier there, I ween!

November chill blaws loud wi' angry sugh;   10
  The shortening winter-day is near a close;
The miry beasts retreating frae the pleugh;
  The blackening trains o' craws to their repose:
The toil-worn Cotter frae his labour goes,
This night his weekly moil is at an end,
  Collects his spades, his mattocks, and his hoes,
Hoping the morn in ease and rest to spend,
And weary, o'er the moor, his course does hameward bend.

At length his lonely cot appears in view,
  Beneath the shelter of an agèd tree;   20
The expectant wee things, toddlin', stacher through
  To meet their Dad, wi' flichterin' noise an' glee.
His wee bit ingle, blinkin bonnilie,
His clean hearth-stane, his thrifty wifie's smile,
  The lisping infant prattling on his knee,
Does a' his weary kiaugh and care beguile,
An' makes him quite forget his labour an' his toil.

Belyve the elder bairns come drapping in,
  At service out, amang the farmers roun';   29
Some ca' the pleugh, some herd, some tentie rin
  A cannie errand to a neibor town:
Their eldest hope, their Jenny, woman-grown,
In youthfu' bloom, love sparkling in her e'e,
  Comes hame, perhaps, to shew a braw new gown,
Or deposite her sair-won penny-fee,
To help her parents dear, if they in hardship be.

With joy unfeigned brothers and sisters meet,
  An' each for other's weelfare kindly spiers:

1. friend! Robert Aiken, a lawyer of Ayr. **10. sugh,** sough, the sound of the wind. **12. pleugh,** plow. **21. stacher,** stagger. **22. flichterin',** fluttering. **23. ingle,** fireplace. **26. kiaugh,** anxiety. **28. Belyve,** soon. **30. tentie rin,** watchfully run. **34. braw,** fine (brave). **35. deposite,** accent first syllable. **38. spiers,** asks.

The social hours, swift-winged, unnoticed fleet;
    Each tells the uncos that he sees or hears;   40
  The parents, partial, eye their hopeful years;
Anticipation forward points the view.
    The mother, wi' her needle an' her sheers,
  Gars auld claes look amaist as weel's the new;
The father mixes a' wi' admonition due.

  Their master's an' their mistress's command,
    The younkers a' are warnèd to obey;
  An' mind their labours wi' an eydent hand,
    An' ne'er, though out o' sight, to jauk or play;
    "And O! be sure to fear the Lord alway,   50
  An' mind your duty, duly, morn an' night!
    Lest in temptation's path ye gang astray,
Implore His counsel and assisting might:
They never sought in vain that sought the Lord aright!"

But hark! a rap comes gently to the door;
    Jenny, wha kens the meaning o' the same,
  Tells how a neibor lad cam o'er the moor,
    To do some errands, and convoy her hame.
  The wily mother sees the conscious flame
Sparkle in Jenny's e'e, and flush her cheek;   60
  Wi' heart-struck anxious care, inquires his name,
While Jenny hafflins is afraid to speak;
Weel pleased the mother hears, it's nae wild, worthless rake.

Wi' kindly welcome, Jenny brings him ben;
  A strappin' youth, he takes the mother's eye;
Blythe Jenny sees the visit's no ill ta'en;
  The father cracks of horses, pleughs, and kye.
The youngster's artless heart o'erflows wi' joy,
  But blate and laithfu', scarce can weel behave;
  The mother, wi' a woman's wiles, can spy   70
What makes the youth sae bashfu' an' sae grave;
Weel-pleased to think her bairn's respected like the lave.

O happy love! where love like this is found;
  O heart-felt raptures! bliss beyond compare!
I've pacèd much this weary, mortal round,
  And sage experience bids me this declare—
    "If Heaven a draught of heavenly pleasure spare,
One cordial in this melancholy vale,
  'Tis when a youthful, loving, modest pair
In other's arms breathe out the tender tale,   80
Beneath the milk-white thorn that scents the evening gale."

Is there, in human form, that bears a heart—
  A wretch, a villain, lost to love and truth—
That can, with studied, sly, ensnaring art,
  Betray sweet Jenny's unsuspecting youth?
  Curse on his perjured arts! dissembling smooth!
Are honour, virtue, conscience, all exiled?
  Is there no pity, no relenting ruth,
Points to the parents fondling o'er their child?
Then paints the ruined maid, and their distraction wild?   90

But now the supper crowns their simple board,
  The halesome parritch, chief of Scotia's food:
The sowpe their only hawkie does afford,
  That 'yont the hallan snugly chows her cood;
The dame brings forth in complimental mood,
To grace the lad, her weel-hained kebbuck, fell;
  An' aft he's prest, and aft he ca's it guid;
The frugal wifie, garrulous, will tell
How 'twas a towmond auld sin' lint was i' the bell.

The cheerfu' supper done, wi' serious face,   100
  They round the ingle form a circle wide;
The sire turns o'er, wi' patriarchal grace,
  The big ha'-bible, ance his father's pride:
  His bonnet reverently is laid aside,
His lyart haffets wearing thin an' bare;
  Those strains that once did sweet in Zion glide—
He wales a portion with judicious care;
And "Let us worship God!" he says with solemn air.

They chant their artless notes in simple guise;   109
  They tune their hearts, by far the noblest aim:
Perhaps Dundee's wild warbling measures rise,
  Or plaintive Martyrs, worthy of the name;
  Or noble Elgin beets the heavenward flame,
The sweetest far of Scotia's holy lays:
  Compared with these, Italian trills are tame;
The tickled ears no heartfelt raptures raise;
Nae unison hae they with our Creator's praise.

40. **uncos,** uncommon things.   44. **Gars,** makes. 48. **eydent,** diligent. 49. **jauk,** dally. 62. **hafflins,** half. 64. **ben,** into the room. 67. **cracks,** chats. 69. **blate and laithfu',** bashful and sheepish. 72. **lave,** rest. 92. **halesome parritch,** wholesome porridge. 93. **sowpe . . . hawkie,** sup . . . cow. 94. **hallan,** partition wall. 96. **weel-hained kebbuck,** well-saved cheese. **fell,** pungent. 99. **towmond . . . bell,** twelvemonth-old since flax was in blossom. 105. **lyart haffets,** gray locks. 107. **wales,** chooses. 113. **beets,** enkindles.

The priest-like father reads the sacred page,
   How Abram was the friend of God on high;
  Or Moses bade eternal warfare wage   120
    With Amalek's ungracious progeny;
   Or how the royal bard did groaning lie
Beneath the stroke of Heaven's avenging ire;
   Or Job's pathetic plaint, and wailing cry;
   Or rapt Isaiah's wild seraphic fire;
Or other holy seers that tune the sacred lyre.

  Perhaps the Christian volume is the theme,
   How guiltless blood for guilty man was shed;
   How He who bore in Heaven the second name
    Had not on earth whereon to lay His head;
   How His first followers and servants sped;   131
  The precepts sage they wrote to many a land:
   How he who lone in Patmos banishèd,
   Saw in the sun a mighty angel stand
And heard great Babylon's doom pronounced by Heaven's command.

  Then kneeling down, to Heaven's Eternal King,
   The saint, the father, and the husband prays:
  Hope "springs exulting on triumphant wing"
   That thus they all shall meet in future days:
   There ever bask in uncreated rays,   140
  No more to sigh, or shed the bitter tear,
   Together hymning their Creator's praise,
In such society, yet still more dear;
While circling Time moves round in an eternal sphere.

  Compared with this, how poor Religion's pride,
   In all the pomp of method and of art,
  When men display to congregations wide
   Devotion's every grace, except the heart!
   The Power, incensed, the pageant will desert,
The pompous strain, the sacerdotal stole;   150
   But haply, in some cottage far apart,
May hear, well pleased, the language of the soul;
And in His Book of Life the inmates poor enrol.

  Then homeward all take off their several way;
   The youngling cottagers retire to rest:
The parent-pair their secret homage pay,
   And proffer up to Heaven the warm request,
That He who stills the raven's clamorous nest,
   And decks the lily fair in flowery pride,   159
   Would, in the way His wisdom sees the best,
For them and for their little ones provide;
But chiefly in their hearts with grace divine preside.

  From scenes like these old Scotia's grandeur springs,
   That makes her loved at home, revered abroad:
  Princes and lords are but the breath of kings,
   "An honest man's the noblest work of God";
   And certes, in fair virtue's heavenly road,
The cottage leaves the palace far behind;
   What is a lordling's pomp? a cumbrous load,
Disguising oft the wretch of human kind,   170
Studied in arts of hell, in wickedness refined!

  O Scotia! my dear, my native soil!
   For whom my warmest wish to Heaven is sent!
  Long may thy hardy sons of rustic toil
   Be blest with health, and peace, and sweet content!
   And, O may Heaven their simple lives prevent
From luxury's contagion, weak and vile;
   Then, howe'er crowns and coronets be rent,
A virtuous populace may rise the while,
And stand a wall of fire around their much-loved isle.   180

  O Thou! who poured the patriotic tide
   That streamed through Wallace's undaunted heart;
  Who dared to nobly stem tyrannic pride,
   Or nobly die, the second glorious part,
   (The patriot's God, peculiarly thou art,
His friend, inspirer, guardian, and reward!)
   O never, never, Scotia's realm desert;
But still the patriot, and the patriot-bard,
In bright succession raise, her ornament and guard!

TO A MOUSE

ON TURNING HER UP IN HER NEST WITH THE PLOUGH

Wee, sleekit, cow'rin', tim'rous beastie,
O what a panic's in thy breastie!
Thou need na start awa sae hasty,
          Wi' bickering brattle!
I wad be laith to rin an' chase thee,
          Wi' murdering pattle!

I'm truly sorry man's dominion
Has broken Nature's social union,

---

138. **"springs . . . wing,"** rewording of Pope's *Windsor-Forest*, l. 112.

166. **"An honest man's . . . God,"** from Pope's *Essay on Man*, Ep. IV, l. 248. **1. sleekit,** smooth-coated. **4. bickering brattle!** scampering haste. **6. pattle!** plowstaff.

An' justifies that ill opinion
              Which makes thee startle   10
At me, thy poor earth-born companion,
              An' fellow-mortal!

I doubt na, whiles, but thou may thieve;
What then? poor beastie, thou maun live!
A daimen-icker in a thrave
              'S a sma' request:
I'll get a blessin wi' the lave,
              And never miss 't!

Thy wee bit housie, too, in ruin!
Its silly wa's the win's are strewin'!   20
An' naething, now, to big a new ane,
              O' foggage green!
An' bleak December's winds ensuin',
              Baith snell an' keen!

Thou saw the fields laid bare and waste,
An' weary winter comin' fast,
An' cozie here, beneath the blast,
              Thou thought to dwell,
Till crash! the cruel coulter past
              Out-through thy cell.   30

That wee bit heap o' leaves an' stibble
Has cost thee mony a weary nibble!
Now thou's turned out, for a' thy trouble,
              But house or hald,
To thole the winter's sleety dribble,
              An' cranreuch cauld!

But, Mousie, thou art no thy lane,
In proving foresight may be vain:
The best laid schemes o' mice an' men
              Gang aft a-gley,   40
An' lea'e us nought but grief an' pain
              For promised joy.

Still thou art blest compared wi' me!
The present only toucheth thee:
But oh! I backward cast my e'e
              On prospects drear!
An' forward tho' I canna see,
              I guess an' fear!

_{13. **whiles**, at times.   15. **daimen-icker . . . thrave**, an occasional ear in twenty-four sheaves.   17. **lave**, rest.   20. **silly**, weak, helpless.   21. **big**, build.   22. **foggage**, coarse grass.   24. **snell**, biting.   34. **But . . . hald**, without house or property.   35. **thole**, endure.   36. **cranreuch**, frost.   37. **no thy lane**, not alone.   40. **Gang aft a-gley**, go oft astray.}

TO A MOUNTAIN DAISY

ON TURNING ONE DOWN WITH THE PLOUGH

Wee modest crimson-tippèd flower,
Thou'st met me in an evil hour;
For I maun crush amang the stoure
              Thy slender stem:
To spare thee now is past my power,
              Thou bonie gem.

Alas! it's no thy neibor sweet,
The bonnie lark, companion meet,
Bending thee 'mang the dewy weet
              Wi's spreckled breast,   10
When upward springing, blythe to greet
              The purpling east.

Cauld blew the bitter-biting north
Upon thy early humble birth;
Yet cheerfully thou glinted forth
              Amid the storm,
Scarce reared above the parent-earth
              Thy tender form.

The flaunting flowers our gardens yield
High sheltering woods and wa's maun shield,   20
But thou, beneath the random bield
              O' clod or stane,
Adorns the histie stibble-field,
              Unseen, alane.

There, in thy scanty mantle clad,
Thy snawy bosom sun-ward spread,
Thou lifts thy unassuming head
              In humble guise;
But now the share uptears thy bed,
              And low thou lies!   30

Such is the fate of artless maid,
Sweet floweret of the rural shade,
By love's simplicity betrayed,
              And guileless trust,
Till she like thee, all soiled, is laid
              Low i' the dust.

Such is the fate of simple bard,
On life's rough ocean luckless starred:
Unskilful he to note the card
              Of prudent lore,   40
Till billows rage, and gales blow hard,
              And whelm him o'er!

_{3. **stoure**, dust.   6. **gem**, bud.   21. **bield**, shelter.   23. **histie**, barren.   39. **card**, compass card.}

Such fate to suffering worth is given,
Who long with wants and woes has striven,
By human pride or cunning driven
    To misery's brink,
Till wrenched of every stay but Heaven,
    He, ruined, sink!

Ev'n thou who mourn'st the Daisy's fate,
That fate is thine—no distant date;   50
Stern Ruin's ploughshare drives elate
    Full on thy bloom,
Till crushed beneath the furrow's weight
    Shall be thy doom!

GREEN GROW THE RASHES

Green grow the rashes O,
  Green grow the rashes O;
The sweetest hours that e'er I spend,
  Are spent amang the lasses O!

There's nought but care on every han',
  In every hour that passes O;
What signifies the life o' man,
  An' 'twere na for the lasses O.

The warly race may riches chase,
  An' riches still may fly them O;   10
An' though at last they catch them fast,
  Their hearts can ne'er enjoy them O.

But gie me a canny hour at e'en,
  My arms about my dearie O;
An' warly cares, an' warly men,
  May a' gae tapsalteerie O!

For you sae douce, ye sneer at this,
  Ye're nought but senseless asses O:
The wisest man the warl' saw,
  He dearly loved the lasses O.   20

Auld nature swears, the lovely dears
  Her noblest work she classes O;
Her prentice han' she tried on man,
  An' then she made the lasses O.

WILLIE BREWED A PECK O' MAUT

O Willie brewed a peck o' maut,
  And Rob and Allan cam to see;
Three blyther hearts, that lee-lang night,
  Ye wad na found in Christendie.
Chorus
We are na fou, we're no that fou,
  But just a drappie in our ee;
The cock may craw, the day may daw,
  And aye we'll taste the barley bree!

Here are we met, three merry boys,
  Three merry boys, I trow, are we;   10
And monie a night we've merry been,
  And monie mae we hope to be!

It is the moon, I ken her horn,
  That's blinkin' in the lift sae hie;
She shines sae bright to wyle us hame,
  But, by my sooth, she'll wait a wee!

Wha first shall rise to gang awa,
  A cuckold, coward loun is he!
Wha first beside his chair shall fa',
  He is the King among us three!   20

ADDRESS TO THE UNCO GUID, OR THE RIGIDLY RIGHTEOUS

My son, these maxims make a rule,
  An' lump them aye thegither:
The rigid righteous is a fool,
  The rigid wise anither:
The cleanest corn that e'er was dight,
  May hae some pyles o' caff in;
So ne'er a fellow-creature slight
  For random fits o' daffin.
               Solomon (Eccles. vii. 16).

O ye wha are sae guid yoursel,
  Sae pious and sae holy,
Ye've nought to do but mark and tell
  Your neibour's fauts and folly!
Whase life is like a weel-gaun mill,
  Supplied wi' store o' water,
The heapèd happer's ebbing still,
  And still the clap plays clatter:

---

3. lee-lang, livelong. **5. fou,** full, drunk. **6. drappie,** small drop. **8. barley bree!** barley brew. **12. mae,** more. **14. lift,** sky. **15. wyle,** entice. **18. loun,** rascal. *Address to the Unco Guid.* Introduction. **aye thegither,** always together. **dight,** winnowed. **pyles o' caff,** grains of chaff. **daffin,** larking. **5. weel-gaun,** smoothly running. **7. happer,** hopper. **8. clap,** clapper.

1. rashes, rushes, reeds. **8. An',** if. **9. warly,** worldly. **16. tapsalteerie,** topsy-turvy. **17. douce,** sober. **19. wisest man,** Solomon. *Willie Brewed a Peck o' Maut.* **1. maut,** malt.

ROBERT BURNS

Hear me, ye venerable core,
    As counsel for poor mortals,   10
That frequent pass douce Wisdom's door,
    For glaikit Folly's portals;
I, for their thoughtless, careless sakes,
    Would here propone defences,—
Their donsie tricks, their black mistakes,
    Their failings and mischances.

Ye see your state wi' their's compared,
    And shudder at the niffer;
But cast a moment's fair regard—
    What makes the mighty differ?   20
Discount what scant occasion gave,
    That purity ye pride in,
And (what's aft mair than a' the lave)
    Your better art o' hidin'.

Think, when your castigated pulse
    Gies now and then a wallop,
What ragings must his veins convulse,
    That still eternal gallop!
Wi' wind and tide fair i' your tail,
    Right on ye scud your sea-way;   30
But in the teeth o' baith to sail,
    It maks an unco leeway.

See Social life and Glee sit down,
    All joyous and unthinking,
Till, quite transmogrified, they're grown
    Debauchery and Drinking:
O would they stay to calculate
    The eternal consequences;
Or your more dreaded hell to state,
    Damnation of expenses!   40

Ye high, exalted, virtuous Dames,
    Tied up in godly laces,
Before ye gie poor Frailty names,
    Suppose a change o' cases;
A dear loved lad, convenience snug,
    A treacherous inclination—
But, let me whisper i' your lug,
    Ye're aiblins nae temptation.

Then gently scan your brother man,
    Still gentler sister woman;   50
Though they may gang a kennin wrang,
    To step aside is human.
One point must still be greatly dark,
    The moving *why* they do it;
And just as lamely can ye mark
    How far perhaps they rue it.

Who made the heart, 'tis He alone
    Decidedly can try us;
He knows each chord, its various tone,
    Each spring, its various bias.   60
Then at the balance let's be mute,
    We never can adjust it;
What's done we partly may compute,
    But know not what's resisted.

ADDRESS TO THE DEIL

From the time of Milton, if not before it, Satan has been admired as a symbol of spirited rebellion against tyrannical authority. Robert Burns, in giving the Devil his due, suggests that he is at any rate sincere, and that in this important respect at least he is superior to all sour-faced Puritans whose main concern is for respectability.

O Prince, O chief of many thronèd powers,
That led the embattled Seraphim to war.
—MILTON

O thou! whatever title suit thee,
Auld Hornie, Satan, Nick, or Clootie,
Wha in yon cavern grim an' sootie,
    Closed under hatches,
Spairges about the brunstane cootie,
    To scaud poor wretches!

Hear me, auld Hangie, for a wee,
An' let poor damnèd bodies be;
I'm sure sma' pleasure it can gie,
    Ev'n to a deil,   10
To skelp an' scaud poor dogs like me,
    An' hear us squeal!

Great is thy power, an' great thy fame;
Far kenned an' noted is thy name;
An' though yon lowin heugh's thy hame,
    Thou travels far;
An' faith! thou's neither lag nor lame,
    Nor blate nor scaur.

Whyles rangin' like a roarin' lion
For prey, a' holes an' corners tryin';   20
Whyles on the strong-winged tempest flyin',
    Tirlin' the kirks;
Whyles, in the human bosom pryin',
    Unseen thou lurks.

9. **core**, company. 12. **glaikit**, giddy. 15. **donsie**, unfortunate. 18. **niffer**, difference. 47. **lug**, ear. 48. **aiblins**, perhaps. 51. **kennin**, trifle.

5. **Spairges**, splashes. **cootie**, dish. 6. **scaud**, scald. 11. **skelp**, strike. 15. **lowin heugh**, flaming pit. 17. **lag**, slow. 18. **blate nor scaur**, bashful nor timid. 22. **Tirlin'**, unroofing.

I've heard my reverend graunie say,
In lanely glens ye like to stray;
Or, where auld ruined castles gray
    Nod to the moon,
Ye fright the nightly wanderer's way,
    Wi' eldritch croon.   30

When twilight did my graunie summon
To say her prayers, douce, honest woman!
Aft yont the dyke she's heard you bummin',
    Wi' eerie drone;
Or, rustlin', through the boortrees comin',
    Wi' heavy groan.

Ae dreary windy winter night
The stars shot down wi' sklentin' light,
Wi' you mysel I gat a fright
    Ayont the lough;   40
Ye like a rash-buss stood in sight
    Wi' waving sough.

The cudgel in my nieve did shake,
Each bristled hair stood like a stake,
When, wi' an eldritch stoor "quaick, quaick,"
    Amang the springs,
Awa ye squattered like a drake,
    On whistlin' wings.

Let warlocks grim an' withered hags
Tell how wi' you on ragweed nags   50
They skim the muirs, an' dizzy crags,
    Wi' wicked speed;
And in kirk-yards renew their leagues
    Owre howkit dead.

Thence country wives, wi' toil an' pain,
May plunge an' plunge the kirn in vain;
For oh! the yellow treasure's taen
    By witchin' skill;
An' dawtit twal-pint Hawkie's gane
    As yell 's the bill.   60

Thence mystic knots mak great abuse
On young guidmen, fond, keen, an' crouse;
When the best wark-lume i' the house,
    By cantrip wit,
Is instant made no worth a louse,
    Just at the bit.

When thowes dissolve the snawy hoord,
An' float the jinglin' icy boord,
Then water-kelpies haunt the foord,
    By your direction,   70
An' 'nighted travellers are allured
    To their destruction.

An' aft your moss-traversing spunkies
Decoy the wight that late an' drunk is:
The bleezin, curst, mischievous monkies
    Delude his eyes,
Till in some miry slough he sunk is,
    Ne'er mair to rise.

When masons' mystic word an' grip
In storms an' tempests raise you up,   80
Some cock or cat your rage maun stop,
    Or, strange to tell!
The youngest brither ye wad whip
    Aff straught to hell.

Lang syne, in Eden's bonie yard,
When youthfu' lovers first were paired,
And all the soul of love they shared,
    The raptured hour,
Sweet on the fragrant flowery swaird,
    In shady bower;   90

Then you, ye auld, snick-drawing dog!
Ye cam to Paradise incog,
An' played on man a cursèd brogue,
    (Black be you fa!)
An' gied the infant warld a shog,
    'Maist ruined a'.

D'ye mind that day, when in a bizz,
Wi' reekit duds, an' reestit gizz,
Ye did present your smoutie phiz
    'Mang better folk,   100
An' sklented on the man of Uz
    Your spitefu' joke?

An' how ye gat him i' your thrall,
An' brak him out o' house an' hal',
While scabs an' blotches did him gall
    Wi' bitter claw,
An' lowsed his ill-tongued, wicked scawl,
    Was warst ava?

33. **bummin'**, humming.   35. **boortrees**, elder bushes. 38. **sklentin'**, slanting.   40. **lough**, lake.   41. **rash-buss**, clump of rushes.   43. **nieve**, fist.   45. **eldritch stoor**, unearthly hoarse.   50. **ragweed nags**, brooms.   54. **howkit**, dug-up.   56. **kirn**, churn.   59–60. **dawtit . . . bill**, the favorite twelve-pint cow has gone as dry as the bull. 62. **crouse**, self-assured.   64. **cantrip**, supernatural. 66. **bit**, critical moment.

67. **thowes**, thaws.   73. **spunkies**, will-o'-the-wisps. 75. **bleezin**, blazing.   81. **maun**, must.   85. **Lang syne**, long since. **bonie yard**, beautiful enclosure.   91. **snick-drawing**, cheating.   93. **brogue**, trick.   94. **fa!** lot, destiny. 95. **shog**, shake.   97. **bizz**, flurry.   98. **reekit . . . gizz**, smoking clothes and singed wig.   99. **smoutie**, smutty. 107. **lowsed . . . scawl**, loosed his scold, that is, Job's wife.   108. **ava?** of all.

ROBERT BURNS

But a' your doings to rehearse,
Your wily snares an' fechtin fierce, 110
Sin' that day Michael did you pierce,
    Down to this time,
Wad ding a' Lallan tongue, or Erse,
    In prose or rhyme.

An' now, auld Cloots, I ken ye're thinkin',
A certain Bardie's rantin', drinkin',
Some luckless hour will send him linkin',
    To your black pit;
But faith! he'll turn a corner jinkin',
    An' cheat you yet. 120

But fare you weel, auld Nickie-ben!
O wad ye tak a thought an' men'!
Ye aiblins might—I dinna ken—
    Still hae a stake:
I'm wae to think upo' yon den,
    Ev'n for your sake!

HOLY WILLIE'S PRAYER

"Holy Willie was a rather oldish bachelor elder in the parish of Mauchline, and much and justly famed for that polemical chattering which ends in tippling orthodoxy, and for that spiritualized bawdry which refines to liquorish devotion. In a sessional process with a gentleman in Mauchline—a Mr. Gavin Hamilton—*Holy Willie* and his priest, Father Auld, after full hearing in the Presbytery of Ayr, came off but second best, owing partly to the oratorical powers of Mr. Robert Aiken, Mr. Hamilton's counsel, but chiefly to Mr. Hamilton's being one of the most irreproachable and truly respectable characters in the country. On losing his process, the Muse overheard him [Holy Willie] at his devotion as follows."—Burns's note.

O thou, wha in the Heavens dost dwell,
Wha, as it pleases best thysel',
Sends ane to heaven and ten to hell,
    A' for thy glory,
And no for ony guid or ill
    They've done afore thee!

I bless and praise thy matchless might,
Whan thousands thou hast left in night,
That I am here afore thy sight,
    For gifts an' grace 10
A burnin' an' a shinin' light,
    To a' this place.

---

113. **ding . . . Erse**, beat any Lowland tongue, or any Gaelic one. 117. **linkin'**, tripping. 119. **jinkin'**, dodging. 124. **stake**, gambler's chance. 125. **wae**, sorry.

What was I, or my generation,
That I should get sic exaltation?
I, wha deserve most just damnation,
    For broken laws,
Sax thousand years 'fore my creation,
    Through Adam's cause.

When frae my mither's womb I fell,
Thou might hae plungèd me in hell, 20
To gnash my gums, to weep and wail,
    In burnin' lakes,
Where damnèd devils roar and yell,
    Chained to their stakes.

Yet I am here a chosen sample,
To show thy grace is great and ample;
I'm here a pillar in thy temple,
    Strong as a rock,
A guide, a buckler, an example
    To a' thy flock. 30

O Lord, thou kens what zeal I bear,
When drinkers drink, and swearers swear,
And singin' there and dancin' here,
    Wi' great an' sma':
For I am keepit by thy fear
    Free frae them a'.

But yet, O Lord! confess I must
At times I'm fashed wi' fleshy lust;
An' sometimes too, in warldly trust,
    Vile self gets in; 40
But thou remembers we are dust,
    Defiled in sin.

O Lord! yestreen, thou kens, wi' Meg—
Thy pardon I sincerely beg;
O! may 't ne'er be a livin' plague
    To my dishonour,
An' I'll ne'er lift a lawless leg
    Again upon her.

Besides I farther maun allow,
Wi' Lizzie's lass, three times I trow— 50
But, Lord, that Friday I was fou,
    When I cam near her,
Or else thou kens thy servant true
    Wad never steer her.

May be thou lets this fleshly thorn
Beset thy servant e'en and morn
Lest he owre high and proud should turn,
    That he's sae gifted;

---

38. **fashed**, troubled. 54. **steer**, touch.

If sae, thy hand maun e'en be borne,
      Until thou lift it.   60

Lord, bless thy chosen in this place,
For here thou hast a chosen race;
But God confound their stubborn face,
      And blast their name,
Wha bring thy elders to disgrace
      An' public shame.

Lord, mind Gawn Hamilton's deserts,
He drinks, an' swears, an' plays at cartes,
Yet has sae mony takin' arts
      Wi' grit an' sma',   70
Frae God's ain priest the people's hearts
      He steals awa'.

An' when we chastened him therefor,
Thou kens how he bred sic a splore
As set the warld in a roar
      O' laughin' at us;
Curse thou his basket and his store,
      Kail and potatoes.

Lord, hear my earnest cry an' prayer,
Against that presbytery o' Ayr;   80
Thy strong right hand, Lord, make it bare
      Upo' their heads;
Lord, weigh it down, and dinna spare,
      For their misdeeds. . . .

But, Lord, remember me and mine
Wi' mercies temporal and divine,
That I for gear and grace may shine
      Excelled by nane,
And a' the glory shall be thine,
      Amen, Amen!   90

TAM O' SHANTER

The scene and story of this highly popular poem had been familiar to Burns from his childhood. Composed, according to tradition, in a single day, it has the speed and ease of oral narration, as though it had been made less for the library than for the tavern and fireside, and not for the world in general but for a group of old cronies.

"Tam o' Shanter" has often been regarded as Burns's masterpiece. In the opinion of Thomas Carlyle, however, "it is not so much a poem as a piece of sparkling rhetoric." And Carlyle points out the unquestionable fact that "the piece does not properly cohere: the strange chasm which yawns in our incredulous imaginations between the Ayr public-house and the gate of Tophet is nowhere bridged over . . . and thus the tragedy of the adventure becomes a mere drunken phantasmagoria or many-coloured spectrum painted on ale-vapours."

    Of Brownyis and of Bogillis full is this Buke.
                              —Gawin Douglas.

When chapman billies leave the street,
And drouthy neibors neibors meet,
As market-days are wearing late,
An' folk begin to tak the gate;
While we sit bousing at the nappy,
An' getting fou and unco happy,
We think na on the lang Scots miles,
The mosses, waters, slaps, and styles,
That lie between us and our hame,
Where sits our sulky sullen dame,   10
Gathering her brows like gathering storm,
Nursing her wrath to keep it warm.
    This truth fand honest Tam o' Shanter,
As he frae Ayr ae night did canter—
(Auld Ayr, wham ne'er a town surpasses
For honest men and bonie lasses).
    O Tam! hadst thou but been sae wise,
As ta'en thy ain wife Kate's advice!
She tauld thee weel thou was a skellum,
A bletherin', blusterin', drunken blellum;   20
That frae November till October,
Ae market-day thou was na sober;
That ilka melder wi' the miller
Thou sat as lang as thou had siller;
That every naig was ca'd a shoe on,
The smith and thee gat roarin' fou on;
That at the Lord's house, even on Sunday,
Thou drank wi' Kirkton Jean till Monday.
She prophesied that, late or soon,
Thou would be found deep drowned in Doon;   30
Or catched wi' warlocks in the mirk
By Alloway's auld haunted kirk.
    Ah, gentle dames! it gars me greet
To think how mony counsels sweet,
How mony lengthened sage advices,
The husband frae the wife despises!
    But to our tale: Ae market night,
Tam had got planted unco right,
Fast by an ingle, bleezing finely,
Wi' reaming swats, that drank divinely;   40

74. **splore**, disturbance.   87. **gear**, property.

1. **chapman billies**, peddlers.   2. **drouthy**, thirsty. 4. **tak the gate**, start on the way home.   5. **nappy**, ale. 7. **Scots miles**, longer than the English.   8. **slaps**, gates. 19. **skellum**, good-for-nothing.   20. **blellum**, babbler. 23. **melder**, grinding of grain. 24. **siller**, silver. 25. **every . . . on**, every time a horse was shod.   31. **warlocks in the mirk**, wizards in the dark.   33. **gars me greet**, makes me weep. 40. **reaming swats**, foaming new ale.

And at his elbow, Souter Johnny,
His ancient, trusty, drouthy crony;
Tam lo'ed him like a very brither;
They had been fou for weeks thegither.
The night drave on wi' sangs and clatter;
And aye the ale was growing better:
The landlady and Tam grew gracious,
Wi' favours secret, sweet, and precious:
The souter tauld his queerest stories;
The landlord's laugh was ready chorus: 50
The storm without might rair and rustle,
Tam did na mind the storm a whistle.
    Care, mad to see a man sae happy,
E'en drowned himsel amang the nappy:
As bees flee hame wi' lades o' treasure,
The minutes winged their way wi' pleasure;
Kings may be blest, but Tam was glorious,
O'er a' the ills o' life victorious!
    But pleasures are like poppies spread,
You seize the flower, its bloom is shed;   60
Or like the snow falls in the river—
A moment white, then melts for ever;
Or like the borealis race,
That flit ere you can point their place;
Or like the rainbow's lovely form
Evanishing amid the storm.
Nae man can tether time nor tide;
The hour approaches Tam maun ride;
That hour, o' night's black arch the key-stane,
That dreary hour, he mounts his beast in;   70
And sic a night he taks the road in,
As ne'er poor sinner was abroad in.
    The wind blew as 'twad blawn its last;
The rattling showers rose on the blast;
The speedy gleams the darkness swallowed;
Loud, deep, and lang, the thunder bellowed:
That night, a child might understand,
The Deil had business on his hand.
    Weel mounted on his gray mare, Meg—
A better never lifted leg—   80
Tam skelpit on through dub and mire,
Despising wind, and rain, and fire;
Whiles holding fast his guid blue bonnet;
Whiles crooning o'er some auld Scots sonnet;
Whiles glowering round wi' prudent cares,
Lest bogles catch him unawares.
Kirk-Alloway was drawing nigh,
Whare ghaists and houlets nightly cry.
    By this time he was cross the ford,
Where in the snaw the chapman smoored;   90
And past the birks and meikle stane,
Where drunken Charlie brak's neck-bane;
And through the whins, and by the cairn,
Where hunters fand the murdered bairn;
And near the thorn, aboon the well,
Where Mungo's mither hanged hersel.
Before him Doon pours all his floods;
The doubling storm roars through the woods;
The lightnings flash from pole to pole;
Near and more near the thunders roll: 100
When, glimmering through the groaning trees,
Kirk-Alloway seemed in a bleeze;
Through ilka bore the beams were glancing;
And loud resounded mirth and dancing.
    Inspiring bold John Barleycorn!
What dangers thou canst make us scorn!
Wi' tippenny, we fear nae evil;
Wi' usquebae we'll face the devil!
The swats sae reamed in Tammie's noddle,
Fair play, he cared na deils a boddle!   110
But Maggie stood right sair astonished,
Till, by the heel and hand admonished,
She ventured forward on the light;
And, vow! Tam saw an unco sight!
Warlocks and witches in a dance!
Nae cotillon brent new frae France,
But hornpipes, jigs, strathspeys, and reels,
Put life and mettle in their heels.
A winnock-bunker in the east,
There sat auld Nick, in shape o' beast—   120
A touzie tyke, black, grim, and large!
To gie them music was his charge:
He screwed the pipes and gart them skirl,
Till roof and rafters a' did dirl.
Coffins stood round like open presses,
That shawed the dead in their last dresses;
And by some devilish cantraip sleight
Each in its cauld hand held a light,
By which heroic Tam was able
To note upon the haly table   130
A murderer's banes in gibbet-airns;
Twa span-lang, wee, unchristened bairns;
A thief new-cutted frae a rape,
Wi' his last gasp his gab did gape;
Five tomahawks, wi' blude red-rusted;
Five scymitars, wi' murder crusted;
A garter, which a babe had strangled;
A knife, a father's throat had mangled,
Whom his ain son o' life bereft,

41. **Souter,** cobbler. 81. **skelpit,** hurried. **dub,** puddle.
84. **sonnet,** song. 86. **bogles,** goblins. 88. **ghaists,** ghosts.
houlets, owls. 90. **smoored,** smothered. 91. **birks,** birches.
93. **whins,** furze bushes. 103. **ilka bore,** every chink.
107. **tippenny,** twopenny ale. 108. **usquebae,** whisky.
109. **swats . . . reamed,** new ale so creamed. 110. **boddle!** farthing. 116. **brent,** brand. 119. **winnock-bunker,** window seat. 121. **touzie tyke,** shaggy cur. 123. **gart them skirl,** made them scream. 124. **dirl,** ring. 127. **cantraip sleight,** magic trick. 130. **haly,** holy. 131. **airns,** irons (iron chains). 134. **gab,** mouth.

  The gray hairs yet stack to the heft; 140
Wi' mair of horrible and awfu',
Which even to name wad be unlawfu'.
  As Tammie glowred, amazed, and curious,
The mirth and fun grew fast and furious:
The piper loud and louder blew;
The dancers quick and quicker flew;
They reeled, they set, they crossed, they cleekit,
Till ilka carlin swat and reekit,
And coost her duddies to the wark,
And linkit at it in her sark! 150
  Now Tam, O Tam! had thae been queans,
A' plump and strapping in their teens;
Their sarks, instead o' creeshie flannen,
Been snaw-white seventeen hunder linen!
Thir breeks o' mine, my only pair,
That ance were plush, o' gude blue hair,
I wad hae gi'en them off my hurdies,
For ae blink o' the bonie burdies!
  But withered beldams, auld and droll,
Rigwoodie hags wad spean a foal, 160
Louping and flinging on a crummock,
I wonder didna turn thy stomach.
  But Tam kend what was what fu' brawlie.
There was ae winsome wench and walie
That night enlisted in the core,
Lang after kent on Carrick shore!
(For mony a beast to dead she shot,
And perished mony a bonnie boat,
And shook baith meikle corn and bear,
And kept the country-side in fear.) 170
Her cutty sark, o' Paisley harn,
That while a lassie she had worn,
In longitude though sorely scanty,
It was her best, and she was vauntie.
Ah! little kent thy reverend grannie
That sark she coft for her wee Nannie
Wi' twa pund Scots ('twas a' her riches)
Wad ever graced a dance of witches!
  But here my Muse her wing maun cour;
Sic flights are far beyond her power— 180
To sing how Nannie lap and flang,
(A souple jade she was, and strang),
And how Tam stood, like ane bewitched,
And thought his very een enriched;
Even Satan glowred, and fidged fu' fain,
And hotched and blew wi' might and main:
Till first ae caper, syne anither,
Tam tint his reason a' thegither,
And roars out "Weel done, Cutty-sark!"
And in an instant all was dark! 190
And scarcely had he Maggie rallied,
When out the hellish legion sallied.
  As bees bizz out wi' angry fyke
When plundering herds assail their byke;
As open pussie's mortal foes,
When pop! she starts before their nose,
As eager runs the market-crowd,
When "Catch the thief!" resounds aloud;
So Maggie runs; the witches follow,
Wi' mony an eldritch skriech and hollow. 200
  Ah, Tam! ah, Tam! thou'll get thy fairin'!
In hell they'll roast thee like a herrin'!
In vain thy Kate awaits thy comin'!
Kate soon will be a woefu' woman!
Now do thy speedy utmost, Meg,
And win the key-stane o' the brig;
There at them thou thy tail may toss,
A running stream they darena cross.
But ere the key-stane she could make,
The fient a tail she had to shake! 210
For Nannie, far before the rest,
Hard upon noble Maggie prest,
And flew at Tam wi' furious ettle;
But little wist she Maggie's mettle!
Ae spring brought off her master hale,
But left behind her ain gray tail:
The carlin claught her by the rump,
And left poor Maggie scarce a stump.
  Now, wha this tale o' truth shall read,
Each man and mother's son, take heed; 220
Whene'er to drink you are inclined,
Or cutty-sarks rin in your mind,
Think! ye may buy the joys o'er dear;
Remember Tam o' Shanter's mare.

---

147. **cleekit**, clutched. 148. **carlin**, hag. 149. **coost . . . wark**, threw her clothes off for the work. 150. **linkit . . . sark!** went at it in her shift (chemise). 151. **queans**, young wenches. 153. **creeshie flannen**, greasy flannel. 155. **Thir breeks**, these breeches. 157. **hurdies**, haunches. 158. **ae blink**, one glimpse. 160. **Rigwoodie . . . foal**, ancient hags that would wean a foal, with disgust. 161. **crummock**, crooked staff. 163. **kend**, knew. **brawlie**, well. 164. **walie**, buxom. 166. **Carrick**, southeast Ayrshire. 169. **corn and bear**, wheat and barley. 171. **cutty sark**, short shift (chemise). **harn**, coarse linen. 174. **vauntie**, proud of it. 176. **coft**, bought. 179. **cour**, lower, modern "cower."

185. **fidged fu' fain**, fidgeted with pleasure. 186. **hotched**, hitched, fidgeted. 188. **tint**, lost. 193. **fyke**, fuss. 194. **herds**, shepherds. **byke**, hive. 195. **pussie's**, hare's. 201. **fairin'!** reward. 206. **brig**, bridge. 210. **fient**, devil. 213. **ettle**, intent. 214. **wist**, knew. 217. **claught**, seized.

COMIN' THRO' THE RYE

  Comin' thro' the rye, poor body,
   Comin' thro' the rye,
  She draigl't a' her petticoatie
   Comin' thro' the rye.

Oh Jenny's a' weet, poor body,
  Jenny's seldom dry;
She draigl't a' her petticoatie
  Comin' thro' the rye.

Gin a body meet a body
  Comin' thro' the rye,
Gin a body kiss a body,
  Need a body cry?
    Oh Jenny's a' weet, poor body,
    Jenny's seldom dry;
  She draigl't a' her petticoatie
    Comin' thro' the rye.

Gin a body meet a body
  Comin' thro' the glen;
Gin a body kiss a body,
  Need the warld ken?
    Oh Jenny's a' weet, poor body,
    Jenny's seldom dry;
  She draigl't a' her petticoatie
    Comin' thro' the rye.

OF A' THE AIRTS

Of a' the airts the wind can blaw,
  I dearly like the west,
For there the bonie lassie lives,
  The lassie I lo'e best:
There's wild woods grow, and rivers row,
  And mony a hill between;
But day and night my fancy's flight
  Is ever wi' my Jean.

I see her in the dewy flowers,
  I see her sweet and fair:
I hear her in the tunefu' birds,
  I hear her charm the air:
There's not a bonie flower that springs
  By fountain, shaw, or green,
There's not a bonie bird that sings,
  But minds me o' my Jean.

JOHN ANDERSON MY JO

John Anderson my jo, John,
  When we were first acquent,
Your locks were like the raven,
  Your bonie brow was brent;

Comin' Thro' the Rye. **5. weet,** wet. **7. draigl't,** bedraggled. **9. Gin,** if. **20. ken,** know. *Of A' the Airts.* **1. airts,** directions. **5. row,** roll. **8. Jean,** Burns's wife. **14. shaw,** woodland. *John Anderson My Jo.* **1. jo,** darling. **4. brent,** smooth.

But now your brow is beld, John,
  Your locks are like the snow;
But blessings on your frosty pow,
  John Anderson, my jo.

John Anderson my jo, John,
  We clamb the hill thegither;
And mony a canty day, John,
  We've had wi' ane anither:
Now we maun totter down, John,
  And hand in hand we'll go,
And sleep thegither at the foot,
  John Anderson, my jo.

SCOTS, WHA HAE

In this ringing battle-song Burns takes his theme, for once, from history. He would have us imagine that the words were spoken by Robert Bruce just before the Battle of Bannockburn (1314), in which the Scots defeated an English army under Edward II. Clearly, however, the patriotic intensity of the poem, written in 1793, owes something to Burns's enthusiasm for the French Revolution.

"I have rarely met with anything in history," Burns wrote with this poem in mind, "which interests my feelings as a man equal with the story of Bannockburn. On the one hand a cruel but able usurper, leading on the finest army in Europe, to extinguish the last spark of freedom among a greatly daring and greatly injured people; on the other, the desperate relics of a gallant nation devoting themselves to rescue their bleeding country or perish with her. Liberty, thou art a prize truly and indeed invaluable, for never canst thou be too dearly bought!"

Scots, wha hae wi' Wallace bled,
Scots, wham Bruce has aften led,
Welcome to your gory bed,
  Or to victorie.

Now's the day, and now's the hour;
See the front o' battle lour!
See approach proud Edward's power—
  Chains and slaverie!

Wha will be a traitor knave?
Wha can fill a coward's grave?
Wha sae base as be a slave?
  Let him turn and flee!

Wha for Scotland's King and law
Freedom's sword will strongly draw,
Freeman stand, or freeman fa'?
  Let him follow me!

5. beld, bald.   **7. pow,** head.   **11. canty,** happy.

By oppression's woes and pains!
By your sons in servile chains!
We will drain our dearest veins,
　　But they shall be free!　　　　20

Lay the proud usurpers low!
Tyrants fall in every foe!
Liberty's in every blow!
　　Let us do, or die!

AULD LANG SYNE

Should auld acquaintance be forgot,
　　And never brought to min'?
Should auld acquaintance be forgot,
　　And auld lang syne!

For auld lang syne, my jo,
　　For auld lang syne,
We'll tak a cup o' kindness yet,
　　For auld lang syne.

And surely ye'll be your pint-stowp,
　　And surely I'll be mine;　　　10
And we'll tak a cup o' kindness yet
　　For auld lang syne.

We twa hae run about the braes,
　　And pu'd the gowans fine;
But we've wander'd mony a weary foot
　　Sin' auld lang syne.

We twa hae paidled i' the burn,
　　From morning sun till dine;
But seas between us braid hae roared,
　　Sin' auld lang syne.　　　　20

And there's a hand, my trusty fiere,
　　And gie's a hand o' thine!
And we'll tak a right guid-willie-waught,
　　For auld lang syne.

DUNCAN GRAY

Duncan Gray came here to woo,
　　Ha, ha, the wooing o't,
On blythe Yule night when we were fou,
　　Ha, ha, the wooing o't,

Maggie coost her head fu' high,
Looked asklent and unco skeigh,
Gart poor Duncan stand abeigh;
　　Ha, ha, the wooing o't.

Duncan fleeched, and Duncan prayed,
　　Ha, ha, the wooing o't,　　　　10
Meg was deaf as Ailsa Craig,
　　Ha, ha, the wooing o't.
Duncan sighed baith out and in,
Grat his een baith bleer't and blin',
Spak o' lowpin o'er a linn;
　　Ha, ha, the wooing o't.

Time and chance are but a tide,
　　Ha, ha, the wooing o't,
Slighted love is sair to bide,
　　Ha, ha, the wooing o't.　　　　20
Shall I, like a fool, quoth he,
For a haughty hizzie die?
She may gae to—France for me!
　　Ha, ha, the wooing o't.

How it comes let doctors tell,
　　Ha, ha, the wooing o't,
Meg grew sick as he grew haill,
　　Ha, ha, the wooing o't.
Something in her bosom wrings,
For relief a sigh she brings;　　　30
And O, her een they spak sic things!
　　Ha, ha, the wooing o't.

Duncan was a lad o' grace,
　　Ha, ha, the wooing o't,
Maggie's was a piteous case,
　　Ha, ha, the wooing o't.
Duncan couldna be her death,
Swelling pity smoored his wrath;
Now they're crouse and cantie baith!
　　Ha, ha, the wooing o't.　　　　40

HIGHLAND MARY

Ye banks, and braes, and streams around
　　The castle o' Montgomery,
Green be your woods, and fair your flowers,
　　Your waters never drumlie!

---

4. **auld lang syne!** old long ago (since). 9. **ye'll . . . pint-stowp,** you will pay for your pint cup of drink. 13. **braes,** hillsides. 14. **pu'd . . . gowans,** plucked the daisies. 17. **paidled . . . burn,** paddled in the brook. 19. **braid,** broad. 21. **fiere,** comrade. 23. **guid-willie-waught,** a deep and hearty drink.

5. **coost,** tossed. 6. **skeigh,** haughty. 7. **Gart,** made. **abeigh,** aside. 9. **fleeched,** pleaded or flattered. 11. **Ailsa Craig,** a rocky island. 14. **Grat,** wept. 15. **lowpin . . . linn,** leaping over a waterfall. 19. **sair to bide,** hard to endure. 22. **hizzie,** pert young woman, hussy. 31. **sic,** such. 39. **crouse . . . baith!** bright and cheerful both. 4. **drumlie!** muddy.

ROBERT BURNS

There simmer first unfauld her robes,
   And there the langest tarry;
For there I took the last fareweel
   O' my sweet Highland Mary.

How sweetly bloomed the gay green birk,
   How rich the hawthorn's blossom,
As underneath their fragrant shade
   I clasped her to my bosom!
The golden hours on angel wings
   Flew o'er me and my dearie;
For dear to me as light and life
   Was my sweet Highland Mary.

Wi' mony a vow and locked embrace
   Our parting was fu' tender;
And, pledging aft to meet again,
   We tore oursels asunder;
But oh! fell death's untimely frost,
   That nipt my flower sae early!
Now green's the sod, and cauld's the clay,
   That wraps my Highland Mary!

O pale, pale now, those rosy lips,
   I aft have kissed sae fondly!
And closed for aye the sparkling glance,
   That dwelt on me sae kindly!
And mouldering now in silent dust,
   That heart that lo'ed me dearly—
But still within my bosom's core
   Shall live my Highland Mary.

FOR A' THAT AND A' THAT

Is there, for honest poverty,
   That hings his head, and a' that?
The coward-slave, we pass him by,
   We dare be poor for a' that!
     For a' that, and a' that,
       Our toils obscure, and a' that,
     The rank is but the guinea's stamp;
       The man's the gowd for a' that.

What though on hamely fare we dine,
   Wear hodden-gray, and a' that;
Gie fools their silks, and knaves their wine,
   A man's a man for a' that.
     For a' that, and a' that,
       Their tinsel show, and a' that,
     The honest man, though e'er sae poor,
       Is King o' men for a' that.

Ye see yon birkie, ca'd a lord,
   Wha struts, and stares, and a' that;
Though hundreds worship at his word,
   He's but a coof for a' that:
     For a' that, and a' that,
       His riband, star, and a' that,
     The man of independent mind,
       He looks and laughs at a' that.

A prince can mak a belted knight,
   A marquis, duke, and a' that;
But an honest man's aboon his might,
   Guid faith, he mauna fa' that!
     For a' that, and a' that,
       Their dignities, and a' that,
     The pith o' sense, and pride o' worth,
       Are higher rank than a' that.

Then let us pray that come it may,
   As come it will, for a' that,
That sense and worth o'er a' the earth
   Shall bear the gree, and a' that!
     For a' that and a' that,
       It's comin yet, for a' that,
     That man to man the warld o'er,
       Shall brothers be for a' that.

A RED, RED ROSE

O my luve's like a red, red rose,
   That's newly sprung in June:
O my luve's like the melodie
   That's sweetly played in tune.

As fair art thou, my bonie lass,
   So deep in luve am I;
And I will luve thee still, my dear,
   Till a' the seas gang dry.

Till a' the seas gang dry, my dear,
   And the rocks melt wi' the sun:
And I will luve thee still, my dear,
   While the sands o' life shall run.

And fare thee weel, my only luve!
   And fare thee weel awhile!
And I will come again, my luve,
   Though it were ten thousand mile!

For A' That, and A' That. **8. gowd,** gold. **10. hodden-gray,** coarse undyed woolen cloth. **17. birkie,** young fellow. **20. coof,** fool. **27. aboon,** above. **28. mauna fa',** must not claim. **36. bear the gree,** win the prize.

THE JOLLY BEGGARS

A CANTATA RECITATIVO

For crude creative power "The Jolly Beggars" goes beyond anything else in Burns, and one does not know where to match it elsewhere in its kind. It bristles with "spunk." It sings and dances the peasant-poet's faith that life is good on the worst, the lowest, the most disgusting terms. Matthew Arnold, in the midst of the Victorian era, called it "a superb poetic success." He said rightly that "it has a breadth, truth, and power which make the famous scene in Auerbach's cellar of Goethe's *Faust* seem artificial and tame beside it, and which are only matched by Shakespeare and Aristophanes."

When lyart leaves bestrow the yird,
Or, wavering like the baukie bird,
  Bedim cauld Boreas' blast;
When hailstanes drive wi' bitter skyte,
And infant frosts begin to bite,
  In hoary cranreuch drest;
Ae night at e'en a merry core
O' randie, gangrel bodies
In Poosie Nansie's held the splore,
  To drink their orra duddies: 10
  Wi' quaffing and laughing,
    They ranted and they sang,
  Wi' jumping an' thumping
    The vera girdle rang.

First, niest the fire, in auld red rags,
Ane sat, weel braced wi' mealy bags,
  And knapsack a' in order;
His doxy lay within his arm;
Wi' usquebae an' blankets warm,
  She blinket on her sodger;   20
An' aye he gies the tosy drab
  The tither skelpin' kiss,
While she held up her greedy gab,
  Just like an aumous dish:
  Ilk smack still did crack still
    Just like a cadger's whip;
  Then staggering, and swaggering,
    He roar'd this ditty up—

[Tune: *Soldier's Joy*]

I am a son of Mars, who have been in many wars,
  And show my cuts and scars wherever I come: 30
This here was for a wench, and that other in a trench,
  When welcoming the French at the sound of the drum.
                Lal de dauble, &c.

My 'prenticeship I passed where my leader breathed his last,
  When the bloody die was cast on the heights of Abràm;
And I served out my trade when the gallant game was played,
  And the Moro low was laid at the sound of the drum.

I lastly was with Curtis, among the floating batteries,
  And there I left for witness an arm and a limb; 39
Yet let my country need me, with Eliot to head me,
  I'd clatter on my stumps at the sound of a drum.

And now though I must beg, with a wooden arm and leg,
  And many a tattered rag hanging over my bum,
I'm as happy with my wallet, my bottle, and my callet,
  As when I used in scarlet to follow a drum.

What though with hoary locks I must stand the winter shocks,
  Beneath the woods and rocks oftentimes for a home?
When the t'other bag I sell, and the t'other bottle tell,
  I could meet a troop of hell at the sound of the drum.

Recitativo

He ended; and the kebars sheuk   50
  Aboon the chorus roar;
While frighted rattons backward leuk,
  And seek the benmost bore:
A fairy fiddler frae the neuk,
  He skirlèd out *Encore!*
But up arose the martial chuck,
  And laid the loud uproar.

[Tune: *Sodger Laddie*]

I once was a maid, though I cannot tell when,
And still my delight is in proper young men;

---

1. **lyart**, faded. **yird**, earth. 2. **baukie bird**, bat. 4. **skyte**, lash. 7. **core**, group. 8. **randie, gangrel**, lawless, vagabond. 9. **splore**, spree. 10. **drink . . . duddies**, sell their extra clothes for drink. 14. **girdle**, griddle. 15. **niest**, next. 18. **doxy**, wench, sweetheart. 21. **tosy**, tipsy. 22. **skelpin'**, smacking. 24. **aumous dish**, alms basin. 26. **cadger's**, hawker's.

35. **Abràm**, at Quebec, in 1759. 37. **Moro**, at Santiago de Cuba, in 1762. 40. **Eliot**, Admiral Sir William Augustus Eliot, defender of Gibraltar. 44. **callet**, trull. 50. **kebars**, rafters. 53. **benmost bore**, farthest hole. 56. **chuck**, darling.

Some one of a troop of dragoons was my daddie, 60
No wonder I'm fond of a sodger laddie.
     Sing, Lal de dal, &c.

The first of my loves was a swaggering blade,
To rattle the thundering drum was his trade;
His leg was so tight, and his cheek was so ruddy,
Transported I was with my sodger laddie.

But the godly old chaplain left him in the lurch;
The sword I forsook for the sake of the church;
He ventured the soul, and I risked the body,—
'Twas then I proved false to my sodger laddie. 70

Full soon I grew sick of my sanctified sot,
The regiment at large for a husband I got;
From the gilded spontoon to the fife I was ready,
I asked no more but a sodger laddie.

But the peace it reduced me to beg in despair,
Till I met my old boy at a Cunningham fair;
His rags regimental they fluttered so gaudy:
My heart it rejoiced at a sodger laddie.

And now I have lived—I know not how long,
And still I can join in a cup or a song; 80
But whilst with both hands I can hold the glass steady,
Here's to thee, my hero, my sodger laddie!

    Recitativo

Poor Merry-Andrew in the neuk
 Sat guzzling wi' a tinkler hizzie;
They mind't na wha the chorus teuk,
 Between themselves they were sae busy.
At length, wi' drink and courting dizzy,
 He stoitered up an' made a face;
Then turned an' laid a smack on Grizzy,
 Syne tuned his pipes wi' grave grimace. 90

   [Tune: *Auld Sir Symon*]

Sir Wisdom's a fool when he's fou;
 Sir Knave is a fool in a session:
He's there but a 'prentice I trow,
 But I am a fool by profession.

My grannie she bought me a beuk,
 And I held awa to the school;
I fear I my talent misteuk,
 But what will ye hae of a fool?

For drink I would venture my neck;
 A hizzie's the half o' my craft; 100
But what could ye other expect
 Of ane that's avowedly daft?

I ance was tied up like a stirk,
 For civilly swearing and quaffing;
I ance was abused i' the kirk,
 For touzling a lass i' my daffin.

Poor Andrew that tumbles for sport,
 Let naebody name wi' a jeer;
There's even, I'm tauld, i' the Court
 A tumbler ca'd the Premier. 110

Observed ye yon reverend lad
 Maks faces to tickle the mob?
He rails at our mountebank squad—
 It's rivalship just i' the job.

And now my conclusion I'll tell,
 For, faith! I'm confoundedly dry:
The chiel that's a fool for himsel,
 Gude Lord! he's far dafter than I.

    Recitativo

Then niest outspak a raucle carlin,
Wha kent fu' weel to cleek the sterling, 120
For mony a pursie she had hook it,
And had in mony a well been dookit.
Her love had been a Highland laddie,
But weary fa' the waefu' woodie!
Wi' sighs and sobs, she thus began
To wail her braw John Highlandman:—

   [Tune: *O, An' Ye Were Dead, Guidman*]

A Highland lad my love was born,
The Lawlan' laws he held in scorn;
But he still was faithfu' to his clan,
My gallant braw John Highlandman. 130

    Chorus

Sing hey, my braw John Highlandman!
Sing ho, my braw John Highlandman!
There's no a lad in a' the lan'
Was match for my John Highlandman.

With his philibeg an' tartan plaid,
And gude claymore down by his side,

---

73. **spontoon,** infantry officer's pike. 83. **Merry-Andrew,** a clown. 84. **tinkler hizzie,** tinker wench. 88. **stoitered,** staggered. 103. **stirk,** bullock. 106. **daffin,** play. 117. **chiel,** fellow. 119. **raucle carlin,** sturdy old woman. 120. **cleek the sterling,** snatch money. 124. **weary fa' . . . woodie!** bad luck to the gallows. 135. **philibeg,** kilt.

The ladies' hearts he did trepan,
My gallant braw John Highlandman.

We rangèd a' from Tweed to Spey,
And lived like lords and ladies gay, 140
For a Lawlan' face he fearèd nane,
My gallant braw John Highlandman.

They banished him beyond the sea;
But ere the bud was on the tree,
Adown my cheeks the pearls ran,
Embracing my John Highlandman.

But, oh! they catched him at the last,
And bound him in a dungeon fast;
My curse upon them every one!
They've hanged my braw John Highlandman.

And now a widow I must mourn 151
The pleasures that will ne'er return;
No comfort but a hearty can,
When I think on John Highlandman.

Recitativo

A pigmy scraper wi' his fiddle,
Wha used at trysts and fairs to driddle,
Her strappin' limb and gaucy middle
    (He reached nae higher)
Had holed his heartie like a riddle,
    And blawn 't on fire. 160

Wi' hand on haunch, and upward e'e,
He crooned his gamut, one, two, three,
Then, in an arioso key,
    The wee Apollo
Set aff, wi' allegretto glee,
    His giga solo.

[Tune: *Whistle Owre the Lave O't*]

Let me ryke up to dight that tear,
And go wi' me and be my dear,
And then your every care and fear
    May whistle owre the lave o't. 170

Chorus

I am a fiddler to my trade,
And a' the tunes that e'er I played,
The sweetest still to wife or maid,
    Was whistle owre the lave o't.

At kirns and weddings we'se be there,
And oh! sae nicely's we will fare;
We'll bouse about, till Daddie Care
    Sings whistle owre the lave o't.

Sae merrily the banes we'll pyke,
And sun oursels about the dyke, 180
And at our leisure, when ye like,
    We'll whistle owre the lave o't.

But bless me wi' your heaven o' charms,
And while I kittle hair on thairms,
Hunger, cauld, an a' sic harms,
    May whistle owre the lave o't.

Recitativo

Her charms had struck a sturdy caird,
    As weel as poor Gut-scraper;
He taks the fiddler by the beard,
    And draws a roosty rapier— 190

He swoor by a' was swearing worth
    To speet him like a pliver,
Unless he would from that time forth
    Relinquish her for ever.

Wi' ghastly ee, poor tweedle-dee
    Upon his hunkers bended,
And prayed for grace wi' ruefu' face,
    And sae the quarrel ended.

But though his little heart did grieve
    When round the tinkler prest her, 200
He feigned to snirtle in his sleeve,
    When thus the caird addressed her:—

[Tune: *Clout the Cauldron*]

My bonie lass, I work in brass,
    A tinkler is my station;
I've travelled round all Christian ground
    In this my occupation;
I've ta'en the gold, an' been enrolled
    In many a noble squadron;
But vain they searched, when off I marched
    To go and clout the cauldron. 210

Despise that shrimp, that withered imp,
    Wi' a' his noise and caperin',
And tak a share wi' those that bear
    The budget and the apron;

---

153. **can**, of ale. 156. **trysts**, cattle markets. **driddle**, toodle. 157. **gaucy**, buxom. 159. **holed . . . riddle**, pierced his heart like a sieve. 166. **giga**, Italian for "jig." 167. **ryke . . . dight**, reach up to wipe. 170. **whistle . . . o't**, whistle away the rest of it.

175. **kirns**, harvest homes. 177. **bouse**, drink. 179. **pyke**, pick. 184. **kittle . . . thairms**, tickle hair on cat-gut. 187. **caird**, tinker. 192. **speet . . . pliver**, spit him like a plover. 196. **hunkers**, haunches. 201. **snirtle**, snicker. 210. **clout**, mend. 214. **budget**, bag (for tools).

And by that stoup, my faith and houpe!
    And by that dear Kilbaigie,
If e'er ye want, or meet wi' scant,
    May I ne'er weet my craigie.

Recitativo

The caird prevailed—the unblushing fair
    In his embraces sunk,   220
Partly wi' love o'ercome sae sair,
    An' partly she was drunk.
Sir Violino, with an air
    That showed a man o' spunk,
Wished unison between the pair,
    And made the bottle clunk
        To their health that night.

But hurchin Cupid shot a shaft,
    That played a dame a shavie:
The fiddler raked her fore and aft,   230
    Behint the chicken cavie.
Her lord, a wight of Homer's craft,
    Though limpin' wi' the spavie,
He hirpled up, an lap like daft,
    And shored them *Dainty Davie*
        O' boot that night.

He was a care-defying blade
    As ever Bacchus listed;
Though Fortune sair upon him laid,
    His heart she ever missed it.   240
He had nae wish, but to be glad,
    Nor want but when he thirsted;
He hated nought but to be sad,
    And thus the Muse suggested
        His sang that night.

[Tune: *For A' That, and A' That*]

I am a bard of no regard
    Wi' gentlefolks, and a' that,
But Homer-like, the glowrin' byke,
    Frae town to town I draw that.

Chorus

For a' that, and a' that,   250
    And twice as muckle's a' that;
I've lost but ane, I've twa behin',
    I've wife eneugh for a' that.

I never drank the Muses' stank,
    Castalia's burn, and a' that;
But there it streams, and richly reams!
    My Helicon I ca' that.

Great love I bear to a' the fair,
    Their humble slave, and a' that;
But lordly will, I hold it still   260
    A mortal sin to thraw that.

In raptures sweet this hour we meet
    Wi' mutual love, and a' that;
But for how lang the flee may stang,
    Let inclination law that.

Their tricks and craft hae put me daft,
    They've ta'en me in, and a' that;
But clear your decks, an' *Here's the sex!*
    I like the jads for a' that.

Chorus

For a' that, and a' that,   270
    And twice as muckle's a' that,
My dearest bluid, to do them guid,
    They're welcome till 't, for a' that.

Recitativo

So sung the bard, and Nansie's wa's
Shook with a thunder of applause,
    Re-echoed from each mouth;
They toomed their pocks, an' pawned their duds,
They scarcely left to coor their fuds,
    To quench their lowin' drouth.
Then owre again the jovial thrang   280
    The poet did request
To lowse his pack, an' wale a sang,
    A ballad o' the best:
He rising, rejoicing,
    Between his twa Debòrahs,
Looks round him, an' found them
    Impatient for the chorus.

[Tune: *Jolly Mortals, Fill Your Glasses*]

See the smoking bowl before us,
    Mark our jovial, ragged ring;
Round and round take up the chorus,   290
    And in raptures let us sing—

Chorus

A fig for those by law protected!
    Liberty's a glorious feast!

---

215. **stoup**, ale mug. 216. **Kilbaigie**, kind of whisky. 218. **craigie**, throat. 228. **hurchin**, urchin. 229. **shavie**, trick. 231. **cavie**, coop. 232. **Homer's craft**, ballad-singing. 233. **spavie**, spavin. 234. **hirpled . . . daft**, hobbled up and leapt like mad. 235. **shored**, offered. 236. **O' boot**, gratis. 248. **glowrin' byke**, staring crowd. 254. **stank**, pool. 255. **burn**, brook.

256. **there**, in his mug of ale. 261. **thraw**, thwart. 264. **flee . . . stang**, fly may sting. 265. **law**, decide. 269. **jads**, jades, wild young women. 273. **till 't**, to it. 277. **toomed . . . pocks**, emptied their pockets. 278. **coor their fuds**, cover their tails. 279. **lowin'**, burning.

  Courts for cowards were erected,
    Churches built to please the priest.

What is title? what is treasure?
  What is reputation's care?
If we lead a life of pleasure,
  'Tis no matter how or where!

With the ready trick and fable   300
  Round we wander all the day;
And at night, in barn or stable,
  Hug our doxies on the hay.

Does the train-attended carriage
  Through the country lighter rove?
Does the sober bed of marriage
  Witness brighter scenes of love?

Life is all a variorum,
  We regard not how it goes;
Let them cant about decorum   310
  Who have characters to lose.

Here's to budgets, bags, and wallets!
  Here's to all the wandering train!
Here's our ragged brats and callets!
  One and all cry out Amen!

AE FOND KISS

Ae fond kiss, and then we sever!
Ae fareweel, alas, for ever!
Deep in heart-wrung tears I'll pledge thee,
Warring sighs and groans I'll wage thee.
Who shall say that fortune grieves him
While the star of hope she leaves him?
Me, nae cheerfu' twinkle lights me,
Dark despair around benights me.

I'll ne'er blame my partial fancy,
Naething could resist my Nancy;   10
But to see her was to love her,
Love but her, and love for ever.
Had we never loved sae kindly,
Had we never loved sae blindly,
Never met—or never parted,
We had ne'er been broken-hearted.

Fare thee weel, thou first and fairest!
Fare thee weel, thou best and dearest!
Thine be ilka joy and treasure,
Peace, enjoyment, love, and pleasure!   20

4. wage, pledge. **19. ilka,** every.

Ae fond kiss, and then we sever;
Ae fareweel, alas, for ever!
Deep in heart-wrung tears I'll pledge thee,
Warring sighs and groans I'll wage thee.

AFTON WATER

Flow gently, sweet Afton, among thy green braes,
Flow gently, I'll sing thee a song in thy praise;
My Mary's asleep by thy murmuring stream,
Flow gently, sweet Afton, disturb not her dream.

Thou stock-dove whose echo resounds through the glen,
Ye wild whistling blackbirds in yon thorny den,
Thou green-crested lapwing, thy screaming forbear,
I charge you disturb not my slumbering fair.

How lofty, sweet Afton, thy neighbouring hills,
Far marked with the courses of clear winding rills; 10
There daily I wander as noon rises high,
My flocks and my Mary's sweet cot in my eye.

How pleasant thy banks and green valleys below,
Where wild in the woodlands the primroses blow;
There oft as mild evening weeps over the lea,
The sweet-scented birk shades my Mary and me.

Thy crystal stream, Afton, how lovely it glides,
And winds by the cot where my Mary resides;
How wanton thy waters her snowy feet lave,
As gathering sweet flowerets she stems thy clear wave. 20

Flow gently, sweet Afton, among thy green braes,
Flow gently, sweet river, the theme of my lays;
My Mary's asleep by thy murmuring stream,
Flow gently, sweet Afton, disturb not her dream.

MARY MORISON

O Mary, at thy window be,
  It is the wished, the trysted hour!
Those smiles and glances let me see,
  That make the miser's treasure poor:
How blythely wad I bide the stoure,
  A weary slave frae sun to sun,
Could I the rich reward secure,
  The lovely Mary Morison.

Mary Morison. **5. bide the stoure,** endure the strife.

ROBERT BURNS

Yestreen, when to the trembling string
   The dance gaed through the lighted ha', 10
To thee my fancy took its wing,
   I sat, but neither heard nor saw:
Though this was fair, and that was braw,
   And yon the toast of a' the town,
I sighed, and said amang them a',
   "Ye are na Mary Morison."

O Mary, canst thou wreck his peace,
   Wha for thy sake wad gladly die?
Or canst thou break that heart of his,
   Whase only faut is loving thee? 20
If love for love thou wilt na gie,
   At least be pity to me shown!
A thought ungentle canna be
   The thought o' Mary Morison.

YE FLOWERY BANKS

Ye flowery banks o' bonie Doon,
   How can ye blume sae fair?
How can ye chant, ye little birds,
   And I sae fu' o' care?

Thou 'll break my heart, thou bonie bird,
   That sings upon the bough;
Thou minds me o' the happy days
   When my fause luve was true.

Thou 'll break my heart, thou bonie bird,
   That sings beside thy mate; 10

For sae I sat, and sae I sang,
   And wist na o' my fate.

Aft hae I roved by bonie Doon
   To see the woodbine twine,
And ilka bird sang o' its luve,
   And sae did I o' mine.

Wi' lightsome heart I pu'd a rose
   Frae aff its thorny tree,
And my fause luver staw my rose,
   But left the thorn wi' me. 20

O, WERT THOU IN THE CAULD BLAST

O, wert thou in the cauld blast,
   On yonder lea, on yonder lea,
My plaidie to the angry airt,
   I'd shelter thee, I'd shelter thee.
Or did misfortune's bitter storms
   Around thee blaw, around thee blaw,
Thy bield should be my bosom,
   To share it a', to share it a'.

Or were I in the wildest waste,
   Sae black and bare, sae black and bare, 10
The desert were a paradise,
   If thou wert there, if thou wert there.
Or were I monarch o' the globe,
   Wi' thee to reign, wi' thee to reign,
The brightest jewel in my crown
   Wad be my queen, wad be my queen.

William Blake
1757–1827

Born in London, the son of a small tradesman, William Blake as a child absorbed from the talk he heard in his father's house the mystical ideas of Swedenborg and Jacob Boehme. That awareness of Divine Presence which illumined and emboldened his whole life came to him in early childhood, and at the age of twelve he began to compose verses in which the long-lost grace of the Elizabethan lyrists was mingled with mystical ecstasy. He had no schooling other than that given him by his drawing masters and during his apprenticeship to an engraver. Otherwise he taught himself, beating out the lonely path of an "original genius." He learned to see form, color, and motion with the eye of a plastic artist, but also, looking beyond these externalities, he learned to see into their spiritual significances. Thus he came to regard the world of the senses as a tapestry woven full of symbols, a mine of metaphors, in which every object and event points beyond itself to a transcendental meaning.

13. **braw,** handsome.   1. **Doon,** a river not far from the birthplace of Burns.

Ye Flowery Banks. 15. **ilka,** every.   19. **staw,** stole.   3. **airt,** direction of the wind.

To use his own vivid words, he learned

> "To see a world in a Grain of Sand,
> And a Heaven in a Wild flower;
> Hold Infinity in the palm of [his] hand,
> And Eternity in an hour."

Blake's *Poetical Sketches*, 1783, *Songs of Innocence*, 1789, and *Songs of Experience*, 1794, contain most of the poems from his pen that are now widely known. Usually simple at least in theme, prevailingly lyrical in tone, all lighted up from inside and charged with a strange new music, these poems yield much of their value to that slow brooding contemplation which all pure poetry demands. They were hardly more than the start, however, in Blake's long mental journey. Later, he produced a number of "Prophetic Books"—*The Four Zoas*, *Jerusalem*, *Milton*, and others—in which his ever deepening ruminations about God and the Soul were phrased with an ever more clouded grandeur. Like other mystics, he failed to find a language that could convey his intuitions to others, so that the effect of these later works is often that of a majestic soliloquy. Blake's earlier critics were inclined to think them works of insanity—a view that has at least the advantage of saving time and effort. In recent years, however, many students have come to feel that the later poetical works are superior to those upon which the poet's fame has hitherto been founded. However this may be, the easy opinion that Blake must have been mad because he often soars beyond our comprehension is no longer tenable. The fact appears to be that he saw things in heaven and earth which are not dreamt of in our philosophy. He was caught up into levels of being to which few of us penetrate, and if he spoke somewhat darkly of these Pisgah-sights it may have been for St. Paul's reason, that he had seen things "not lawful for a man to utter." His wife once said: "I have very little of Mr. Blake's company. He is always in Paradise."

It is often asserted that Blake's work as a plastic artist improved, during his last decades, at the expense of his work as poet. He himself made no distinction between the two modes of expression, feeling that he could worship God as well with the burin and paintbrush as with the quill. In both mediums, equally, he was concerned with the representation of eternal things in terms of their earthly symbols. Every student of his writings should constantly remember that all his publications except the first were designed, illustrated, engraved, and colored by his own hand. One should remember, too, that the same startling energy of conception and execution bristles forth from the man's illustrations of Dante and the Book of Job as that which all discern in his poem on the tiger. He wrote like a painter and painted like a poet.

William Blake lived nearly all his life in the dull and ugly streets of London, working like a craftsman with a craftsman's worldly rewards. He kept a shop, and entertained his angels in the rooms on the second floor. After seventy years of obscure, toilsome, impoverished, solitary, and greatly joyous life he died almost unknown, uttering cheerful songs to his Maker.

One cannot relate William Blake to the eighteenth century in any but a negative way—showing how he denied and derided its timid rules and respectabilities at every turn. He stands alone, unclassified, defying our critical categories, independent of time and place. More than any other mind of his age, unless it be Christopher Smart, he makes the academic introduction-writer and notemaker feel ridiculous. He comes down into these decorous pages like the explosion of a fireball in the midst of a tea party. There is in him the mystery called "genius," for which no academic editor can be expected to account. A thousand years hence, if civilization goes on, we may be able to explain him. More probably we shall not.

from POETICAL SKETCHES

In these early lyrics, each globed and limpid as a drop of dew, Blake bids farewell, before setting out on his own lonely path, to the old worn roads. As though wishing to prove that he might easily have continued the traditions of English verse, he moves at once, in the still perfection of the first three or four poems given below, beyond the attainment in this kind even of William Collins. Elsewhere in his first book he meets the Elizabethan and Jacobean song-writers on their own ground, showing himself at least their equal. Thus he makes it clear that he has served his apprenticeship to the past, and that he is ready now for his journeyman days. And there is nothing regretful in his backward look. "To the Muses"—one of the most nearly perfect things in English poetry, a marvel of classical restraint and proportion—is no more an epitaph than it is a prophecy.

TO THE MUSES

Whether on Ida's shady brow,
Or in the chambers of the East,
The chambers of the sun, that now
From antient melody have ceased;

Whether in Heaven ye wander fair,
Or the green corners of the earth,

Or the blue regions of the air
Where the melodious winds have birth;

Whether on chrystal rocks ye rove,
Beneath the bosom of the sea   10
Wandering in many a coral grove,
Fair Nine, forsaking Poetry!

How have you left the antient love
That bards of old enjoyed in you!
The languid strings do scarcely move!
The sound is forced, the notes are few!

TO SPRING

O thou with dewy locks, who lookest down
Through the clear windows of the morning, turn
Thine angel eyes upon our western isle,
Which in full choir hails thy approach, O Spring!

The hills tell each other, and the listening
Valleys hear; all our longing eyes are turned
Up to thy bright pavillions: issue forth,
And let thy holy feet visit our clime.

Come o'er the eastern hills, and let our winds
Kiss thy perfumèd garments; let us taste   10
Thy morn and evening breath; scatter thy pearls
Upon our love-sick land that mourns for thee.

O deck her forth with thy fair fingers; pour
Thy soft kisses on her bosom; and put
Thy golden crown upon her languished head,
Whose modest tresses were bound up for thee!

TO THE EVENING STAR

Thou fair-haired angel of the evening,
Now, whilst the sun rests on the mountains, light
Thy bright torch of love; thy radiant crown
Put on, and smile upon our evening bed!
Smile on our loves, and, while thou drawest the
Blue curtains of the sky, scatter thy silver dew
On every flower that shuts its sweet eyes
In timely sleep. Let thy west wind sleep on
The lake; speak silence with thy glimmering eyes,
And wash the dusk with silver. Soon, full soon, 10
Dost thou withdraw; then the wolf rages wide,
And the lion glares through the dun forest:
The fleeces of our flocks are covered with
Thy sacred dew: protect them with thine influence.

SONG

Fresh from the dewy hill, the merry year
Smiles on my head and mounts his flaming car;
Round my young brows the laurel wreathes a shade,
And rising glories beam around my head.

My feet are winged, while o'er the dewy lawn,
I meet my maiden, risen like the morn:
Oh bless those holy feet, like angels' feet;
Oh bless those limbs, beaming with heavenly light.

Like as an angel glittering in the sky
In times of innocence and holy joy,   10
The joyful shepherd stops his grateful song
To hear the music of an angel's tongue.

So when she speaks, the voice of Heaven I hear:
So when we walk, nothing impure comes near;
Each field seems Eden, and each calm retreat;
Each village seems the haunt of holy feet.

But that sweet village where my black-eyed maid
Closes her eyes in sleep beneath night's shade,
Whene'er I enter, more than mortal fire
Burns in my soul, and does my song inspire.   20

SONG

How sweet I roamed from field to field
And tasted all the summer's pride,
Till I the Prince of Love beheld
Who in the sunny beams did glide!

He shewed me lilies for my hair,
And blushing roses for my brow;
He led me through his gardens fair
Where all his golden pleasures grow.

With sweet May dews my wings were wet,
And Phoebus fired my vocal rage;   10
He caught me in his silken net,
And shut me in his golden cage.

He loves to sit and hear me sing,
Then, laughing, sports and plays with me;
Then stretches out my golden wing,
And mocks my loss of liberty.

SONG

My silks and fine array,
My smiles and languished air,
By love are driven away;
And mournful lean Despair
Brings me yew to deck my grave:
Such end true lovers have.

His face is fair as heaven
When springing buds unfold;
O why to him was 't given
Whose heart is wintry cold?   10
His breast is love's all-worshipped tomb,
Where all love's pilgrims come.

Bring me an axe and spade,
Bring me a winding sheet;
When I my grave have made
Let winds and tempests beat:
Then down I'll lie as cold as clay.
True love doth pass away!

SONG

Memory, hither come,
And tune your merry notes:
And, while upon the wind
Your music floats,
I'll pore upon the stream
Where sighing lovers dream,
And fish for fancies as they pass
Within the watery glass.

I'll drink of the clear stream
And hear the linnet's song;   10
And there I'll lie and dream
The day along:
And when night comes, I'll go
To places fit for woe,
Walking along the darkened valley
With silent Melancholy.

MAD SONG

The wild winds weep,
And the night is a-cold;
Come hither, Sleep,
And my griefs unfold:
But lo! the morning peeps
Over the eastern steeps,
And the rustling birds of dawn
The earth do scorn.

Lo! to the vault
Of pavèd heaven,   10
With sorrow fraught
My notes are driven:
They strike the ear of night,
Make weep the eyes of day;
They make mad the roaring winds,
And with tempests play.

Like a fiend in a cloud,
With howling woe,
After night I do croud,
And with night will go;   20
I turn my back to the east
From whence comforts have increased;
For light doth seize my brain
With frantic pain.

Song, My silks, written perhaps, as the second line particularly indicates, after a reading of Shakespeare's *As You Like It*. *Mad Song,* somehow related to the *Tom o' Bedlam's Song*—see page 600—of the seventeenth century.

from SONGS OF INNOCENCE, 1789

Blake's bold purpose in this collection of lyrics—the first of his books to be illustrated, engraved, and printed by his own hand—was, simply, to let childhood speak for itself. In his feeling that childhood had something to say which would be other than an echo of maturity's wisdom he was, of course, many years in advance of his time.

INTRODUCTION

Piping down the valleys wild,
Piping songs of pleasant glee,
On a cloud I saw a child,
And he laughing said to me:

"Pipe a song about a Lamb!"
So I piped with merry chear.
"Piper, pipe that song again";
So I piped: he wept to hear.

"Drop thy pipe, thy happy pipe;
Sing thy songs of happy chear":   10
So I sung the same again,
While he wept with joy to hear.

"Piper, sit thee down and write
In a book, that all may read."

So he vanished from my sight,
And I plucked a hollow reed,

And I made a rural pen,
And I stained the water clear,
And I wrote my happy songs
Every child may joy to hear.

THE ECCHOING GREEN

The Sun does arise,
And make happy the skies;
The merry bells ring
To welcome the Spring;
The skylark and thrush,
The birds of the bush,
Sing louder around
To the bells' chearful sound,
While our sports shall be seen
On the Ecchoing Green.

Old John, with white hair,
Does laugh away care,
Sitting under the oak,
Among the old folk.
They laugh at our play,
And soon they all say:
"Such, such were the joys
When we all, girls & boys,
In our youth time were seen
On the Ecchoing Green."

Till the little ones, weary,
No more can be merry;
The sun does descend,
And our sports have an end.
Round the laps of their mothers
Many sisters and brothers,
Like birds in their nest,
Are ready for rest,
And sport no more seen
On the darkening Green.

THE LAMB

Little Lamb, who made thee?
  Dost thou know who made thee?
Gave thee life, & bid thee feed
By the stream & o'er the mead;
Gave thee clothing of delight,
Softest clothing, wooly, bright;
Gave thee such a tender voice,
Making all the vales rejoice?
  Little Lamb who made thee?
  Dost thou know who made thee?

Little Lamb, I'll tell thee,
Little Lamb, I'll tell thee:
He is callèd by thy name,
For he calls himself a Lamb.
He is meek, & he is mild;
He became a little child.
I a child, & thou a lamb,
We are callèd by his name.
  Little Lamb, God bless thee!
  Little Lamb, God bless thee!

THE LITTLE BLACK BOY

My mother bore me in the southern wild,
And I am black, but O! my soul is white;
White as an angel is the English child,
But I am black, as if bereaved of light.

My mother taught me underneath a tree,
And, sitting down before the heat of day,
She took me on her lap and kissèd me,
And, pointing to the east, began to say:

"Look on the rising sun: there God does live,
And gives his light, and gives his heat away;
And flowers and trees and beasts and men receive
Comfort in morning, joy in the noonday.

"And we are put on earth a little space,
That we may learn to bear the beams of love;
And these black bodies and this sun-burnt face
Is but a cloud, and like a shady grove.

"For when our souls have learned the heat to bear,
The cloud will vanish; we shall hear his voice,
Saying: 'Come out from the grove, my love & care,
And round my golden tent like lambs rejoice.'"

Thus did my mother say, and kissèd me;
And thus I say to little English boy:
When I from black, and he from white cloud free,
And round the tent of God like lambs we joy,

I'll shade him from the heat, till he can bear
To lean in joy upon our father's knee;
And then I'll stand and stroke his silver hair,
And be like him, and he will then love me.

THE CHIMNEY SWEEPER

When my mother died I was very young,
And my father sold me while yet my tongue
Could scarcely cry "'weep! 'weep! 'weep! 'weep!"
So your chimneys I sweep, & in soot I sleep.

There's little Tom Dacre, who cried when his head,
That curled like a lamb's back, was shaved: so I said
"Hush, Tom! never mind it, for when your head's bare
You know that the soot cannot spoil your white hair."

And so he was quiet, & that very night,
As Tom was a-sleeping, he had such a sight!   10
That thousands of sweepers, Dick, Joe, Ned, & Jack,
Were all of them locked up in coffins of black.

And by came an Angel who had a bright key,
And he opened the coffins & set them all free;
Then down a green plain leaping, laughing, they run,
And wash in a river, and shine in the Sun.

Then naked & white, all their bags left behind,
They rise upon clouds and sport in the wind;
And the Angel told Tom, if he'd be a good boy,
He'd have God for his father, & never want joy.   20

And so Tom awoke; and we rose in the dark,
And got with our bags & our brushes to work.
Though the morning was cold, Tom was happy and warm:
So if all do their duty they need not fear harm.

LAUGHING SONG

When the green woods laugh with the voice of joy,
And the dimpling stream runs laughing by;
When the air does laugh with our merry wit,
And the green hill laughs with the noise of it;

When the meadows laugh with lively green,
And the grasshopper laughs in the merry scene,
When Mary and Susan and Emily
With their sweet round mouths sing "Ha, Ha, He!"

When the painted birds laugh in the shade,
Where our table with cherries and nuts is spread,   10
Come live, & be merry, and join with me,
To sing the sweet chorus of "Ha, Ha, He!"

A CRADLE SONG

Sweet dreams, form a shade
O'er my lovely infant's head;
Sweet dreams of pleasant streams
By happy, silent, moony beams.

Sweet sleep, with soft down
Weave thy brows an infant crown.
Sweet sleep, Angel mild,
Hover o'er my happy child.

Sweet smiles, in the night
Hover over my delight;   10
Sweet smiles, Mother's smiles,
All the livelong night beguiles.

Sweet moans, dovelike sighs,
Chase not slumber from thy eyes.
Sweet moans, sweeter smiles,
All the dovelike moans beguiles.

Sleep, sleep, happy child,
All creation slept and smiled;
Sleep, sleep, happy sleep,
While o'er thee thy mother weep.   20

Sweet babe, in thy face
Holy image I can trace.
Sweet babe, once like thee,
Thy maker lay and wept for me.

Wept for me, for thee, for all,
When he was an infant small.
Thou his image ever see,
Heavenly face that smiles on thee.

Smiles on thee, on me, on all;
Who became an infant small.   30
Infant smiles are his own smiles:
Heaven & earth to peace beguiles.

NURSE'S SONG

When the voices of children are heard on the green,
And laughing is heard on the hill,
My heart is at rest within my breast,
And everything else is still.

"Then come home, my children, the sun is gone down,
And the dews of night arise;

WILLIAM BLAKE

Come, come, leave off play, and let us away
Till the morning appears in the skies."

"No, no, let us play, for it is yet day,
And we cannot go to sleep;   10
Besides, in the sky the little birds fly,
And the hills are all covered with sheep."

"Well, well, go & play till the light fades away,
And then go home to bed."
The little ones leaped & shouted & laughed
And all the hills echoèd.

INFANT JOY

"I have no name:
I am but two days old."
What shall I call thee?
"I happy am,
Joy is my name."
Sweet joy befall thee!

Pretty Joy!
Sweet Joy, but two days old,
Sweet Joy I call thee:
Thou dost smile,   10
I sing the while,
Sweet joy befall thee!

from SONGS OF EXPERIENCE

The exact relationship between this collection of lyrics and the *Songs of Innocence*, although it is a relationship both close and important, is not easy to state. Clearly, however, Blake does not mean to imply that childhood is superior to maturity. Having made his own peace with the Principle of Evil and found it good, he does not believe that the experience of mature life, because it takes on the soilure of the world, marks a retrogression from childhood's inborn wisdom. He feels, rather, that even though this experience brings pain, disillusionment, and a darkening of the soul's sky, it is a necessary stage of our progress toward the eternal light.

This opinion of Blake's should be thoughtfully compared with the quite different one expressed in Henry Vaughan's "The Retreat" and in Wordsworth's "Intimations of Immortality."

THE CHIMNEY-SWEEPER

A little black thing among the snow,
Crying "'weep! 'weep!" in notes of woe!
"Where are thy father & mother,—say?"
"They are both gone up to the church to pray.

"Because I was happy upon the heath,
And smiled among the winter's snow,
They clothèd me in the clothes of death,
And taught me to sing the notes of woe.

"And because I am happy & dance & sing,
They think they have done me no injury,   10
And are gone to praise God & his Priest and King,
Who make up a heaven of our misery."

THE TYGER

A thing to know about this gigantic little poem, one of the most marvelous lyrics in English, is that Blake had never seen an actual tiger when he wrote it. The beast he paints in such colors of fire prowls only in the jungles of the mind.

The glorious and startling grammatical error of line 12 was accidental. Having first written

"What dread hand and what dread feet
  Could fetch it from the furnace deep,"

Blake changed line 13 to its present form without seeing that this entailed a change in the line preceding.

Much of Blake's deepest pondering of the world's mystery is implicit in line 20. He sees in the tiger's fierce destructive power a symbol of "experience," the counterpart of the lamb's "innocence" in God's biform creation. Yet he sees also that the tiger is no less beautiful than the lamb.

Tyger! Tyger! burning bright
In the forests of the night,
What immortal hand or eye
Could frame thy fearful symmetry?

In what distant deeps or skies
Burnt the fire of thine eyes?
On what wings dare he aspire?
What the hand dare sieze the fire?

And what shoulder, & what art,
Could twist the sinews of thy heart?   10
And when thy heart began to beat,
What dread hand? & what dread feet?

What the hammer? what the chain?
In what furnace was thy brain?
What the anvil? what dread grasp
Dare its deadly terrors clasp?

When the stars threw down their spears,
And watered heaven with their tears,
Did he smile his work to see?
Did he who made the Lamb make thee? 20

Tyger! Tyger! burning bright
In the forests of the night,
What immortal hand or eye,
Dare frame thy fearful symmetry?

AH! SUN-FLOWER

Ah, Sun-flower! weary of time,
Who countest the steps of the Sun;
Seeking after that sweet golden clime
Where the traveller's journey is done;

Where the Youth pined away with desire,
And the pale Virgin shrouded in snow,
Arise from their graves, and aspire
Where my Sun-flower wishes to go.

LONDON

I wander through each chartered street,
Near where the chartered Thames does flow,
And mark in every face I meet
Marks of weakness, marks of woe.

In every cry of every Man,
In every Infant's cry of fear,
In every voice, in every ban,
The mind-forged manacles I hear.

How the Chimney sweeper's cry
Every blackening Church appals; 10
And the hapless Soldier's sigh
Runs in blood down Palace walls.

But most through midnight streets I hear
How the youthful Harlot's curse
Blasts the new-born Infant's tear,
And blights with plagues the Marriage hearse.

THE HUMAN ABSTRACT

Pity would be no more
If we did not make somebody Poor;
And Mercy no more could be
If all were as happy as we.

And mutual fear brings peace,
Till the selfish loves increase;
Then Cruelty knits a snare,
And spreads his baits with care.

He sits down with holy fears,
And waters the ground with tears; 10
Then Humility takes its root
Underneath his foot.

Soon spreads the dismal shade
Of Mystery over his head;
And the Caterpillar and Fly
Feed on the Mystery.

And it bears the fruit of Deceit,
Ruddy and sweet to eat;
And the Raven his nest has made
In its thickest shade. 20

The Gods of the earth and sea
Sought through Nature to find this Tree;
But their search was all in vain:
There grows one in the Human Brain.

AUGURIES OF INNOCENCE

To see a World in a Grain of Sand
And a Heaven in a Wild flower,
Hold Infinity in the palm of your hand,
And Eternity in an hour.
A Robin Redbreast in a Cage
Puts all Heaven in a Rage.
A dove-house filled with Doves & Pigeons
Shudders Hell through all its regions.
A dog starved at his Master's Gate
Predicts the ruin of the State. 10
A Horse misused upon the Road
Calls to Heaven for Human blood.
Each outcry of the hunted Hare
A fibre from the Brain does tear.
A Skylark wounded in the wing,
A Cherubim does cease to sing;
The Game Cock clipped and armed for fight
Does the Rising Sun affright.
Every Wolf's & Lion's howl
Raises from Hell a Human Soul. 20
The wild Deer, wandering here & there,
Keeps the Human Soul from Care.
The Lamb misused breeds Public Strife
And yet forgives the Butcher's knife.

WILLIAM BLAKE

The Bat that flits at close of Eve
Has left the Brain that won't Believe.
The Owl that calls upon the Night
Speaks the Unbeliever's fright.
He who shall hurt the little Wren
Shall never be beloved by Men.   30
He who the Ox to wrath has moved
Shall never be by Woman loved.
The wanton Boy that kills the Fly
Shall feel the Spider's enmity.
He who torments the Chafer's Sprite
Weaves a Bower in endless Night.
The Caterpillar on the Leaf
Repeats to thee thy Mother's grief.
Kill not the Moth nor Butterfly,
For the Last Judgment draweth nigh.   40
He who shall train the Horse to war
Shall never pass the Polar Bar.
The Beggar's Dog & Widow's Cat,
Feed them & thou wilt grow fat.
The Gnat that sings his Summer's Song
Poison gets from Slander's tongue.
The poison of the Snake & Newt
Is the sweat of Envy's Foot.
The poison of the Honey Bee
Is the Artist's Jealousy.   50
The Prince's Robes & Beggar's Rags
Are Toadstools on the Miser's Bags.
A Truth that's told with bad intent
Beats all the Lies you can invent.
It is right it should be so;
Man was made for Joy & Woe;
And when this we rightly know,
Through the World we safely go.
Joy & Woe are woven fine,
A Clothing for the soul divine.   60
Under every grief & pine
Runs a joy with silken twine.
The Babe is more than Swadling Bands;
Throughout all these Human Lands
Tools were made, & Born were hands,
Every Farmer understands.
Every Tear from Every Eye
Becomes a Babe in Eternity;
This is caught by Females bright,
And returned to its own delight.   70
The Bleat, the Bark, Bellow, & Roar
Are Waves that beat on Heaven's Shore.
The Babe that weeps the Rod beneath
Writes Revenge in realms of Death.
The Beggar's Rags, fluttering in Air,
Does to Rags the Heavens tear.
The Soldier, armed with Sword & Gun,
Palsied strikes the Summer's Sun.
The poor Man's Farthing is worth more
Than all the Gold on Afric's Shore.   80
One Mite wrung from the Labourer's hands
Shall buy & sell the Miser's Lands;
Or, if protected from on high,
Does that whole Nation sell & buy.
He who mocks the Infant's Faith
Shall be mocked in Age & Death.
He who shall teach the Child to Doubt
The rotting Grave shall ne'er get out.
He who respects the Infant's faith
Triumphs over Hell & Death.   90
The Child's Toys and the Old Man's Reasons
Are the Fruits of the Two Seasons.
The Questioner, who sits so sly,
Shall never know how to Reply.
He who replies to words of Doubt
Doth put the Light of Knowledge out.
The Strongest Poison ever known
Came from Caesar's Laurel Crown.
Naught can Deform the Human Race
Like to the Armour's iron brace.   100
When Gold and Gems adorn the Plow
To peaceful Arts shall Envy bow.
A Riddle, or the Cricket's Cry,
Is to Doubt a fit Reply.
The Emmet's Inch & Eagle's Mile
Make Lame Philosophy to smile.
He who Doubts from what he sees
Will ne'er Believe, do what you Please.
If the Sun & Moon should Doubt,
They'd immediately Go Out.   110
To be in a Passion you Good may do,
But no Good if a Passion is in you.
The Whore & Gambler, by the State
Licensed, build that Nation's Fate.
The Harlot's cry from Street to Street
Shall weave Old England's winding Sheet.
The Winner's shout, the Loser's Curse,
Dance before dead England's Hearse.
Every Night and every Morn
Some to Misery are Born.   120
Every Morn and every Night
Some are Born to Sweet Delight.
Some are Born to Sweet Delight,
Some are Born to Endless Night.
We are led to Believe a Lie
When we see not Through the Eye,
Which was Born in a Night to perish in a Night,
When the Soul slept in Beams of Light.
God appears, & God is light,
To those poor souls who dwell in Night,   130
But does a Human Form Display
To those who Dwell in Realms of Day.

from MILTON

And did those feet in ancient time
Walk upon England's mountains green?
And was the holy Lamb of God
On England's pleasant pastures seen?

And did the Countenance Divine
Shine forth upon our clouded hills?
And was Jerusalem builded here
Among these dark Satanic Mills?

Bring me my Bow of burning gold!
Bring me my Arrows of desire!   10
Bring me my Spear! O clouds, unfold!
Bring me my Chariot of fire!

I will not cease from Mental fight,
Nor shall my Sword sleep in my hand,
Till we have built Jerusalem
In England's green & pleasant Land.

THE MARRIAGE OF HEAVEN AND HELL

This title, together with many ideas in the present "Prophetic Book," was suggested by Emanuel Swedenborg's *Heaven and Hell*. Blake's central thought, in which he believes that he goes beyond Swedenborg, is that Good and Evil are bound together as man and wife, each of them needing the other as its complement.

THE ARGUMENT

Rintrah roars, & shakes his fires in the burdened
  air;
Hungry clouds swag on the deep.

Once meek, and in a perilous path,
The just man kept his course along
The vale of death.
Roses are planted where thorns grow,
And on the barren heath
Sing the honey bees.

Then the perilous path was planted,
And a river and a spring   10
On every cliff and tomb;
And on the bleached bones
Red clay brought forth;

The Argument. **1. Rintrah,** the spirit of the modern world. **2. swag,** hang low.

Till the villain left the paths of ease,
To walk in perilous paths and drive
The just man into barren climes.
Now the sneaking serpent walks
In mild humility,
And the just man rages in the wilds
Where lions roam.   20

Rintrah roars & shakes his fires in the burdened air;
Hungry clouds swag on the deep.

As a new heaven is begun, and it is now thirty-three years since its advent, the Eternal Hell revives. And lo! Swedenborg is the Angel sitting at the tomb; his writings are the linen clothes folded up. Now is the dominion of Edom, & the return of Adam into Paradise: see Isaiah xxxiv. & xxxv. Chap.

Without Contraries is no progression. Attraction and Repulsion, Reason and Energy, Love and Hate, are necessary to Human existence.

10 From these contraries spring what the religious call Good & Evil. Good is the passive that obeys Reason. Evil is the active springing from Energy.

Good is Heaven. Evil is Hell.

THE VOICE OF THE DEVIL

All Bibles or sacred codes have been the causes of the following Errors:

1. That Man has two real existing principles, Viz. a Body & a Soul.

2. That Energy, called Evil, is alone from the Body; & that Reason, called Good, is alone from the Soul.

3. That God will torment Man in Eternity for following his Energies.

But the following Contraries to these are True:

1. Man has no Body distinct from his Soul; for that called Body is a portion of Soul discerned by the five Senses, the chief inlets of Soul in this age.

2. Energy is the only life and is from the Body; and Reason is the bound or outward circumference of Energy.

30 3. Energy is Eternal Delight.

Those who restrain desire, do so because theirs is weak enough to be restrained; and the restrainer, or reason, usurps its place & governs the unwilling.

And being restrained, it by degrees becomes passive, till it is only the shadow of desire.

1–2. thirty-three . . . advent. Blake was thirty-three when he wrote the present work.

The history of this is written in Paradise Lost, & the Governor or Reason, is called Messiah.

And the original Archangel, or possessor of the command of the heavenly host, is called the Devil or Satan, and his children are called Sin & Death.

But in the Book of Job Milton's Messiah is called Satan.

For this history has been adopted by both parties.

It indeed appeared to Reason as if Desire was cast out, but the Devil's account is, that the Messiah fell, & formed a Heaven of what he stole from the Abyss.

This is shewn in the Gospel, where he prays to the Father to send the comforter, or Desire, that Reason may have Ideas to build on; the Jehovah of the Bible being no other than he . . . who dwells in flaming fire.

Know that after Christ's death, he became Jehovah.

But in Milton, the Father is Destiny, the Son a Ratio of the five senses, & the Holy-ghost Vacuum!

Note: The reason Milton wrote in fetters when he wrote of Angels & God, and at liberty when of Devils & Hell, is because he was a true Poet and of the Devil's party without knowing it.

A MEMORABLE FANCY

As I was walking among the fires of Hell, delighted with the enjoyments of Genius, which to Angels look like torment and insanity, I collected some of their Proverbs, thinking that, as the sayings used in a nation mark its character, so the Proverbs of Hell show the nature of Infernal wisdom better than any description of buildings or garments.

When I came home, on the abyss of the five senses, where a flat sided steep frowns over the present world, I saw a mighty Devil, folded in black clouds, hovering on the sides of the rock: with corroding fires he wrote the following sentence now perceived by the minds of men, & read by them on earth:

"How do you know but every Bird that cuts the airy way,

Is an immense world of delight, closed by your senses five?"

PROVERBS OF HELL

In seed time learn; in harvest teach; in winter enjoy.

Drive your cart and your plow over the bones of the dead.

The road of excess leads to the palace of wisdom.

Prudence is a rich ugly old maid courted by incapacity.

He who desires but acts not, breeds pestilence.

The cut worm forgives the plow.

Dip him in the river who loves water.

A fool sees not the same tree that a wise man sees.

He whose face gives no light shall never become a star.

Eternity is in love with the productions of time.

The busy bee has no time for sorrow.

The hours of folly are measured by the clock; but of wisdom no clock can measure.

All wholesome food is caught without a net or a trap.

Bring out number, weight & measure in a year of dearth.

No bird soars too high, if he soars with his own wings.

A dead body revenges not injuries.

The most sublime act is to set another before you.

If the fool would persist in his folly he would become wise.

Folly is the cloak of knavery.

Shame is Pride's cloak.

Prisons are built with stones of Law, Brothels with bricks of Religion.

The pride of the peacock is the glory of God.

The lust of the goat is the bounty of God.

The wrath of the lion is the wisdom of God.

The nakedness of woman is the work of God.

Excess of sorrow laughs. Excess of joy weeps.

The roaring of lions, the howling of wolves, the raging of the stormy sea, and the destructive sword are portions of eternity too great for the eye of man.

The fox condemns the trap, not himself.

Joys impregnate. Sorrows bring forth.

Let man wear the fell of the lion, woman the fleece of the sheep.

The bird a nest, the spider a web, man friendship.

The selfish smiling fool & the sullen frowning fool shall be both thought wise, that they may be a rod.

What is now proved was once only imagined.

The rat, the mouse, the fox, the rabbit watch the roots; the lion, the tyger, the horse, the elephant watch the fruits.

The cistern contains, the fountain overflows.

One thought fills immensity.

Always be ready to speak your mind, and a base man will avoid you.

Everything possible to be believed is an image of truth.

The eagle never lost so much time as when he submitted to learn of the crow.

The fox provides for himself, but God provides for the lion.

Think in the morning. Act in the noon. Eat in the evening. Sleep in the Night.

He who has suffered you to impose on him knows you.

As the plow follows words, so God rewards prayers.

The tygers of wrath are wiser than the horses of instruction.

Expect poison from the standing water.

You never know what is enough, unless you know what is more than enough.

Listen to the fool's reproach: it is a kingly title.

The eyes of fire, the nostrils of air, the mouth of water, the beard of earth.

The weak in courage is strong in cunning.

The apple tree never asks the beech how he shall grow, nor the lion the horse how he shall take his prey.

The thankful receiver bears a plentiful harvest.

If others had not been foolish, we should be so.

The soul of sweet delight can never be defiled.

When thou seest an Eagle, thou seest a portion of Genius; lift up thy head!

As the caterpillar chooses the fairest leaves to lay her eggs on, so the priest lays his curse on the fairest joys.

To create a little flower is the labour of ages.

Damn braces. Bless relaxes.

The best wine is the oldest, the best water the newest.

Prayers plow not! Praises reap not!

Joys laugh not! Sorrows weep not!

The head Sublime, the heart Pathos, the genitals Beauty, the hands & feet Proportion.

As the air to a bird or the sea to a fish, so is contempt to the contemptible.

The crow wished everything was black, tne owl that everything was white.

Exuberance is Beauty.

If the lion was advised by the fox, he would be cunning.

Improvement makes strait roads; but the crooked roads without Improvement are roads of Genius.

Sooner murder an infant in its cradle than nurse unacted desires.

Where man is not, nature is barren.

Truth can never be told so as to be understood, and not be believed.

Enough or Too much.

The ancient Poets animated all sensible objects with Gods or Geniuses, calling them by the names and adorning them with the properties of woods, rivers, mountains, lakes, cities, nations, and whatever their enlarged & numerous senses could perceive.

And particularly they studied the genius of each city & country, placing it under its mental deity;

Till a system was formed, which some took advantage of, & enslaved the vulgar by attempting to realize or abstract the mental deities from their objects: thus began Priesthood,

Choosing forms of worship from poetic tales.

And at length they pronounced that the Gods had ordered such things.

Thus men forgot that All deities reside in the human breast.

A MEMORABLE FANCY

The Prophets Isaiah and Ezekiel dined with me, and I asked them how they dared so roundly to assert that God spoke to them; and whether they did not think at the time that they would be misunderstood, & so be the cause of imposition.

Isaiah answered: "I saw no God, nor heard any, in a finite organical perception; but my senses discovered the infinite in every thing; and as I was then persuaded, & remain confirmed, that the voice of honest indignation is the voice of God, I cared not for consequences, but wrote."

Then I asked: "Does a firm persuasion that a thing is so, make it so?"

He replied: "All poets believe that it does, & in ages of imagination this firm persuasion removed mountains; but many are not capable of a firm persuasion of anything."

Then Ezekiel said: "The philosophy of the East taught the first principles of human perception. Some nations held one principle for the origin, & some another; we of Israel taught that the Poetic Genius (as you now call it) was the first principle, and all the others merely derivative, which was the cause of our despising the Priests & Philosophers of other countries, and prophesying that all Gods would at last be proved to originate in ours & to be the tributaries of the Poetic Genius. It was this that our great poet, King David, desired so fervently & invokes so pathetically, saying, by this he conquers enemies & governs kingdoms: and we so loved our

1–17. **The ancient Poets . . . human breast.** These six sentences comprise the entire history of religion as Blake saw it.

God, that we cursed in his name all the deities of surrounding nations, and asserted that they had rebelled. From these opinions the vulgar came to think that all nations would at last be subject to the Jews."

"This," said he, "like all firm persuasions, is come to pass; for all nations believe the Jews' code and worship the Jews' god, and what greater subjection can be?"

I heard this with some wonder, & must confess my own conviction. After dinner I asked Isaiah to favour the world with his lost works; he said none of equal value was lost. Ezekiel said the same of his.

I also asked Isaiah what made him go naked and barefoot three years? He answered: "the same that made our friend Diogenes the Grecian."

I then asked Ezekiel why he ate dung, and lay so long on his right & left side. He answered, "the desire of raising other men into a perception of the infinite. This the North American tribes practise, & is he honest who resists his genius or conscience only for the sake of present ease or gratification?"

The ancient tradition that the world will be consumed in fire at the end of six thousand years is true, as I have heard from Hell.

For the cherub with his flaming sword is hereby commanded to leave his guard at [the] tree of life; and when he does, the whole creation will be consumed and appear infinite and holy, whereas it now appears finite & corrupt.

This will come to pass by an improvement of sensual enjoyment.

But first the notion that man has a body distinct from his soul is to be expunged; this I shall do by printing in the infernal method by corrosives, which in Hell are salutary and medicinal, melting apparent surfaces away, and displaying the infinite which was hid.

If the doors of perception were cleansed every thing would appear to man as it is, infinite.

For man has closed himself up till he sees all things through narrow chinks of his cavern.

A MEMORABLE FANCY

I was in a Printing-house in Hell, & saw the method in which knowledge is transmitted from generation to generation.

In the first chamber was a Dragon-Man, clearing away the rubbish from a cave's mouth; within, a number of Dragons were hollowing the cave.

In the second chamber was a Viper folding round the rock & the cave, and others adorning it with gold, silver, and precious stones.

In the third chamber was an Eagle with wings and feathers of air: he caused the inside of the cave to be infinite: around were numbers of Eagle-like men who built palaces in the immense cliffs.

In the fourth chamber were Lions of flaming fire, raging around and melting the metals into living fluids.

In the fifth chamber were Unnamed forms, which cast the metals into the expanse.

There they were received by Men who occupied the sixth chamber, and took the forms of books & were arranged in libraries.

The Giants who formed this world into its sensual existence and now seem to live in it in chains, are in truth the causes of its life & the sources of all activity; but the chains are the cunning of weak and tame minds which have power to resist energy. According to the proverb, the weak in courage is strong in cunning.

Thus one portion of being is the Prolific, the other the Devouring. To the Devourer it seems as if the producer was in his chains; but it is not so; he only takes portions of existence and fancies that the whole.

But the Prolific would cease to be Prolific unless the Devourer as a sea received the excess of his delights.

Some will say: "Is not God alone the Prolific?" I answer: "God only Acts & Is, in existing beings or Men."

These two classes of men are always upon earth, and they should be enemies: whoever tries to reconcile them seeks to destroy existence.

Religion is an endeavour to reconcile the two.

Note: Jesus Christ did not wish to unite, but to separate them, as in the Parable of sheep and goats: & he says: "I came not to send Peace, but a Sword."

Messiah or Satan or Tempter was formerly thought to be one of the Antediluvians who are our Energies.

A MEMORABLE FANCY

An Angel came to me and said: "O pitiable foolish young man! O horrible! O dreadful state! Con-

---

37–39. **printing . . . displaying.** Blake speaks here in terms of his own craft, that of engraving.

25. **cunning.** See above in the "Proverbs of Hell."
37. **two classes of men,** the "prolific" and the "devouring."

sider the hot burning dungeon thou art preparing for thyself to all eternity, to which thou are going in such career."

I said: "perhaps you will be willing to show me my eternal lot, & we will contemplate together upon it, and see whether your lot or mine is most desirable."

So he took me through a stable & through a church & down into the church vault, at the end of which was a mill. Through the mill we went, and came to a cave. Down the winding cavern we groped our tedious way, till a void, boundless as a nether sky, appeared beneath us, & we held by the roots of trees, and hung over this immensity; but I said: "if you please, we will commit ourselves to this void, and see whether providence is here also: if you will not, I will." But he answered: "Do not presume, O young man, but as we here remain, behold thy lot which will soon appear when the darkness passes away."

So I remained with him, sitting in the twisted root of an oak; he was suspended in a fungus which hung with the head downward into the deep.

By degrees we beheld the infinite Abyss, fiery as the smoke of a burning city; beneath us, at an immense distance, was the sun, black but shining: round it were fiery tracks on which revolved vast spiders, crawling after their prey, which flew, or rather swam, in the infinite deep, in the most terrific shapes of animals sprung from corruption; and the air was full of them, & seemed composed of them. These are Devils, and are called Powers of the Air. I now asked my companion which was my eternal lot? He said: "Between the black & white spiders."

But now, from between the black & white spiders, a cloud and fire burst & rolled through the deep, blackening all beneath, so that the nether deep grew black as a sea, and rolled with a terrible noise. Beneath us was nothing now to be seen but a black tempest, till looking east between the clouds & the waves we saw a cataract of blood mixed with fire, and not many stones' throw from us appeared and sunk again the scaly fold of a monstrous serpent. At last, to the east, distant about three degrees, appeared a fiery crest above the waves: slowly it reared like a ridge of golden rocks, till we discovered two globes of crimson fire, from which the sea fled away in clouds of smoke; and now we saw it was the head of Leviathan. His forehead was divided into streaks of green & purple like those on a tyger's forehead. Soon we saw his mouth & red gills hang just above the raging foam, tinging the black deep with beams of blood, advancing toward us with all the fury of a Spiritual Existence.

My friend the Angel climbed up from his station into the mill: I remained alone, & then this appearance was no more: but I found myself sitting on a pleasant bank beside a river by moon light, hearing a harper, who sung to the harp; and his theme was: "The man who never alters his opinion is like standing water, and breeds reptiles of the mind."

But I arose and sought for the mill; & there I found my Angel, who, surprised, asked me how I escaped.

I answered: "All that we saw was owing to your metaphysics; for when you ran away, I found myself on a bank by moonlight hearing a harper. But now we have seen my eternal lot, shall I shew you yours?" He laughed at my proposal; but I by force suddenly caught him in my arms, & flew westerly through the night, till we were elevated above the earth's shadow; then I flung myself with him directly into the body of the sun. Here I clothed myself in white, & taking in my hand Swedenborg's volumes, sunk from the glorious clime, and passed all the planets till we came to Saturn. Here I stayed to rest, & then leaped into the void between Saturn & the fixed stars.

"Here," said I, "is your lot, in this space, if space it may be called." Soon we saw the stable and the church, & I took him to the altar and opened the Bible, and lo! it was a deep pit, into which I descended, driving the Angel before me. Soon we saw seven houses of brick. One we entered: in it were a number of monkeys, baboons, & all of that species, chained by the middle, grinning and snatching at one another, but withheld by the shortness of their chains. However I saw that they sometimes grew numerous, and then the weak were caught by the strong, and, with a grinning aspect, first coupled with, & then devoured by plucking off first one limb and then another, till the body was left a helpless trunk. This, after grinning & kissing it with seeming fondness, they devoured too; and here & there I saw one savourily picking the flesh off of his own tail. As the stench terribly annoyed us both, we went into the mill, & I in my hand brought the skeleton of a body, which in the mill was Aristotle's Analytics.

So the Angel said: "Thy phantasy has imposed upon me, & thou oughtest to be ashamed."

I answered: "We impose on one another, & it is but lost time to converse with you, whose works are only Analytics."

I have always found that Angels have the vanity to speak of themselves as the only wise: this they do with a confident insolence sprouting from systematic reasoning.

THE EIGHTEENTH CENTURY

Thus Swedenborg boasts that what he writes is new; though it is only the Contents or Index of already published books.

A man carried a monkey about for a shew, & because he was a little wiser than the monkey, grew vain, and conceived himself as much wiser than seven men. It is so with Swedenborg: he shows the folly of churches, & exposes hypocrites, till he imagines that all are religious, & himself the single one on earth that ever broke a net.

Now hear a plain fact: Swedenborg has not written one new truth. Now hear another: he has written all the old falsehoods.

And now hear the reason. He conversed with Angels, who are all religious, & conversed not with Devils, who all hate religion; for he was incapable through his conceited notions.

Thus Swedenborg's writings are a recapitulation of all superficial opinions, and an analysis of the more sublime, but no further.

Have now another plain fact. Any man of mechanical talents may, from the writings of Paracelsus or Jacob Behmen, produce ten thousand volumes of equal value with Swedenborg's, and from those of Dante or Shakespear an infinite number.

But when he has done this, let him not say that he knows better than his master, for he only holds a candle in sunshine.

SUGGESTIONS FOR FURTHER READING

GENERAL

Turberville, A. S., ed., *English Men and Manners in the Eighteenth Century*, 2d ed., Oxford Press, 1929. This and the two volumes of the next title, brilliantly written by a group of expert scholars working in collaboration, and profusely illustrated, offer an admirable survey of the whole century, and are sufficient in themselves to make one feel at home in the period.

—— ed., *Johnson's England*, 2 vols., Oxford Press, 1933

Stephen, Sir Leslie, *History of English Thought in the Eighteenth Century*, 2 vols., Putnam, 1876. The unrivaled authority for the leading ideas and the intellectual currents of this period.

Elton, Oliver, *A Survey of English Literature, 1730–1780*, Macmillan, 1928. Brings to bear upon the major writers of the century the same critical acumen and unerring sense of style in which they themselves excelled. An earlier work by the same author and of similar title deals with the later writers of the period.

POETRY

Minor Poets of the Eighteenth Century, ed. by H. I'A. Fausset, Dutton (Everyman's Library)

See also the volumes in Everyman's Library devoted to Blake (*Poems and Prophecies*); Burns (*Poems and Songs*); Cowper (*Poems*); Goldsmith (*Poems and Plays*); Gray (*Poems, with a Selection of Letters and Essays*); Pope (*Complete Poems*). The poems of Thomson and those of Collins with Gray may be found in the Oxford Standard Authors, Oxford Press.

DRAMA

Eighteenth Century Plays, ed. by J. Hampden, Everyman's Library.

FICTION

(All in Everyman's Library)

Burney, Fanny, *Evelina*, 1778. A tale—beloved by Dr. Johnson, Burke, and Reynolds—of London society as seen by a girl from the country.

Defoe, Daniel, *Moll Flanders*, 1722. The slums of London linked with the plantations of Virginia in a fictional autobiography of a female adventurer.

Fielding, Henry, *Tom Jones*, 1749. An ample and intricate story, crowded with vivacious characters and told with masculine vigor (2 vols. in Everyman's).

Goldsmith, Oliver, *The Vicar of Wakefield*, 1766. Relating the misfortunes and final triumph of a simple-minded and warmhearted clergyman.

Richardson, Samuel, *Clarissa Harlowe*, 1747–48. A love story in epistolary form concerning a young lady "of great delicacy, mistress of all the accomplishments, natural and acquired, that adorn the Sex" (4 vols. in Everyman's).

Smollett, Tobias, *Roderick Random*, 1748. A coarsely vigorous personal narrative which includes vivid scenes from the life of a sailor in the British Navy.

Sterne, Laurence, *Tristram Shandy*, 1760–67. A humorous, libidinous, and sentimental work of creative genius running wild.

Swift, Jonathan, *Gulliver's Travels*, 1726. Also ed. by Ernest Bernbaum, Harcourt, Brace, 1920.

—— *A Tale of a Tub*, 1704. Prose satire, chiefly directed against religious controversy (in Everyman's with *The Battle of the Books*, 1697, and other satires).

LETTERS

Hardly less interesting than the fiction is the private correspondence that we inherit from the eighteenth century. The student will find in Everyman's Library adequate selections from the letters of Cowper (*Selected Letters*); Lord Chesterfield (*Letters to His Son, and Others*); Gray (*Poems, with a Selection of Letters and Essays*); Swift (*Journal to Stella*); Lady Mary Wortley Montagu (*Letters*); Sir Horace Walpole (*Selected Letters*).

OTHER PROSE

(All in Everyman's Library)

Boswell, James, *Journal of a Tour to the Hebrides with Samuel Johnson, LL.D.*, 1785. This vivacious book (2 vols.

in Everyman's) should be read, if possible, in the version published by the Viking Press in 1936.

Burke, Edmund, *Speeches and Letters on American Affairs*

Goldsmith, Oliver, *The Citizen of the World*, 1762. Letters by and to an imaginary Chinese about England and the English.

Gibbon, Edward, *The Decline and Fall of the Roman Empire*, 1776–78. A magnificent work of patient scholarship, bold thought, and blazing imagination (6 vols. in Everyman's).

Hume, David, *A Treatise on Human Nature*, 1739–40. Difficult reading, but well worth the effort it costs (2 vols. in Everyman's).

Johnson, Samuel, *Lives of the English Poets*, 1779–81. A job done to order—honestly, often brilliantly, with frequent lapses into wrong-headed prejudice (2 vols. in Everyman's).

Reynolds, Sir Joshua, *Fifteen Discourses Delivered in the Royal Academy*, 1769–90 (*Discourses on Art* in Everyman's). A clear statement of Neoclassical doctrine, applied to the art of painting.

Spectator, The (4 vols. in Everyman's)

Wesley, John, *Journal*, 1771–74. The day-to-day record of a devoted, laborious, and greatly influential life (4 vols. in Everyman's).

ART

The works of Hogarth, Gainsborough, and Reynolds—to mention only three graphic artists out of many—were as characteristic of this epoch as those of Pope and Johnson. The drawings, the water colors, the landscape-painting, and the portrait-painting of the time should be studied in close connection with the writing. So, in fact, should the architecture, the landscape gardening, the music, the theatrical arts, the costumes, and the social etiquette of the century. A sufficient guide to the beginnings, at least of these wider studies will be found in the books edited by Turberville which head this list.

Poetic Forms and Patterns

ALTHOUGH drastically condensed and limited, this addendum presents the chief poetic designs and devices. It is by no means a complete outline, but rather a brief explanation of the principal forms of poetry and the common properties of versification. The definitions are general, not inclusive, popular (in the sense that they do not list exceptions to the rules) rather than pedagogic. However, most of the traditional forms have been included and only the rare or archaic terms have been omitted.

FEET AND METERS

The problems of rhythm and accent, of duration and pause, have been variously interpreted. The very nature of accent has given rise to controversy, some scholars maintaining it is due to a change in pitch of the voice, others to an increase of volume of tone. It is, however, generally accepted as *stress*, and in the following paragraphs it will be so regarded.

In English verse the rhythm is based upon this stress or accent, "the measured undulation of accented and unaccented syllables being its essential feature without which it becomes prose" (Brewer). Although classical prosody lists about thirty combinations of stressed and unstressed syllables (divided into accented and unaccented "feet"), the fundamental ones in English verse are five.

1. The *iambic foot* is an unaccented syllable followed by an accented one. It is commonly expressed thus: ˘ ´; such words as *oppose*, *delight*, *amuse* being, in themselves, iambic feet. English verse is founded on the iambic beat; it might be said that our very speech tends to fall into iambics. An illustrative couplet:

   A book of verses underneath the bough,
   A jug of wine, a loaf of bread—and thou.

2. The *trochaic foot* is an accented syllable followed by an unaccented one. It is commonly expressed thus: ´ ˘; such words as *gather*, *heartless*, *feeling* being in themselves trochaic feet. It is second in importance to the iambic measure. An illustrative example:

   Soft and easy is thy cradle
   Coarse and hard thy Saviour lay.

It should be noted that the majority of trochaic lines in English show a deficient last foot; that is to say, the last syllable is often omitted, as in the second line of the example quoted.

3. The *dactylic foot* is an accented syllable followed by two unaccented ones. It is commonly expressed thus: ´ ˘ ˘; such words as *happiness*, *sentiment*, *merrily* being in themselves dactylic feet. Grace and a lilting movement are achieved by its use. An illustrative example:

   Love again, song again, nest again, young again.

4. The *anapestic foot* consists of two unaccented syllables followed by an accented syllable. It is commonly expressed thus: ˘ ˘ ´; such words as *interrupt*, *supersede*, *disappear* being, in themselves, anapestic feet. It is a speedy and propulsive rhythm. An illustrative example:

   With the sheep in the fold and the cows in their stalls.

Both dactylic and anapestic measures tend to become monotonous, and therefore most poets who employ them vary the measures by introducing two-syllable (iambic or trochaic) feet.

5. The *spondee* consists of two equally accented syllables expressed thus: ´ ´; compound words like *heartbreak*, *childhood*, *wineglass* being perfect spondees. It is mostly found in classic poetry and is used chiefly for grave and strong emphasis. An illustrative example:

   Slow spondee stalks; strong foot.

It should be added that there are few poems in the English language which adhere absolutely to one foot or accent; most poems of any length reveal a variety of feet. Pope has illustrated this variation, this change of pace, in his lines on the craft of verse in "An Essay on Criticism":

True ease in writing comes from art, not chance,
As those move easiest who have learned to dance.
'Tis not enough no harshness gives offence,
The sound must seem an echo to the sense.
Soft is the strain when zephyr gently blows,
And the smooth stream in smoother numbers flows;
But when loud surges lash the sounding shore,
The hoarse, rough verse should like the torrent roar:
When Ajax strives some rock's vast weight to throw,
The line too labours, and the words move slow;
Not so, when swift Camilla scours the plain,
Flies o'er the unbending corn, and skims along the main.

The *meter* or measure of a verse is determined by the number of feet in the line. The terms explain themselves: *monometer*—one foot; *dimeter*—two feet; *trimeter*—three feet; *tetrameter*—four feet; *pentameter*—five feet; *hexameter*—six feet; *heptameter*—seven feet; *octameter*—eight feet. Thus the following line:

> To hear | the lark | begin | his flight

is a line of four feet. Since it is a compound of four iambic feet, it would be classified as *iambic tetrameter*.

STANZA FORMS

In the same way that feet are combined into the structure of a line, lines are combined into the pattern of a poem. These patterns, or stanzas, have certain distinct characteristics and are usually classified as follows:

The *couplet* consists of two lines of matched verse in immediate succession. It has always been popular, especially for sharp or epigrammatic effect. The form has been a favorite since the time of Chaucer's *Canterbury Tales*. Dryden brought it to a kind of perfection, and Pope tightened it into a "thought couplet," each couplet being a unit in itself.

> Behold the child, by nature's kindly law,
> Pleased with a rattle, tickled with a straw:
> Some livelier plaything gives his youth delight,
> A little louder, but as empty quite:
> Scarfs, garters, gold, amuse his riper stage,
> And beads and prayer-books are the toys of age:
> Pleased with this bauble still, as that before,
> Till tired he sleeps, and life's poor play is o'er.
>
> *Essay on Man*— —*Alexander Pope*

The *tercet* (sometimes known as the *triplet*) is a stanza of three lines rhyming together. Examples of this pattern may be found in Crashaw's "Wishes for the Supposed Mistress," Herrick's "Upon Julia's Clothes," Herbert's "Paradise." A further illustration is Browning's

> Boot, saddle, to horse, and away! a
> Rescue my castle before the hot day a
> Brightens to blue from its silvery gray. a

The *quatrain*, the commonest stanza form, consists of four lines rhymed in a variety of ways. Perhaps the most familiar arrangement is in the ballad meter, in which the second and fourth lines are rhymed while the first and third are unrhymed. See "Sir Patrick Spens," "The Douglas Tragedy," and "The Wife of Usher's Well" (all of which you will find in the ballad section of Volume I.)

Almost as well known is the quatrain in which the rhymes are *a-b-a-b*, as, for example, Drayton's

> Clear had the day been from the dawn, a
> All chequered was the sky, b
> Thin clouds, like scarfs of cobweb lawn, a
> Veiled heaven's most glorious eye. b

A form of quatrain somewhat less familiar is one in which the lines rhyme *a-b-b-a*, as, for example, Tennyson's

> Our little systems have their day; a
> They have their day and cease to be: b
> They are but broken lights of Thee, b
> And thou, O Lord, art more than they. a

An even more unusual form of quatrain is one in which all four lines have only one rhyme. Although this single-sounding rhyme tends toward monotony it can be used with great effectiveness, as in Dante Gabriel Rossetti's "The Woodspurge":

> My eyes, wide open, had the run a
> Of some ten weeds to fix upon; a
> Among those few, out of the sun, a
> The woodspurge flowered, three cups in one. a

The variations are great and range from the clipped stanzas of Herbert's "Discipline" to the long measure of Gray's "Elegy." The quatrain itself, in its various shapes, appears throughout this volume too numerously to be listed.

The *Quintet* is a five-line stanza variously rhymed, although the favorite formula seems to be *a-b-a-b-b*. Swinburne's "Hertha" is written in this form, a particularly fluent example, with its long-rolling last line:

> I the grain and the furrow, a
> The plough-cloven clod b
> And the ploughshare drawn thorough, a
> The germ and the sod, b
> The deed and the doer, the seed and the sower, the dust which is God. b

Shelley's "To a Skylark," Waller's "Go, Lovely Rose," and Christina Rossetti's "The Bourne" are among the more famous poems built on the quintet.

The *sestet* is a six-line stanza in which the possibilities of line and rhyme arrangement are almost endless. It may be made of a quatrain and an added couplet (*a-b-a-b-c-c*), as in Edward Dyer's "My Mind to Me a Kingdom Is":

> My mind to me a kingdom is, a
> Such present joys therein I find, b
> That it excels all other bliss a
> That earth affords or grows by kind: b

POETIC FORMS AND PATTERNS

Though much I want which most would have,   c
Yet still my mind forbids to crave.   c

The sestet may also be composed of interlacing couplets, as in Shakespeare's "O Mistress Mine" from *Twelfth-Night*:

O mistress mine! where are you roaming?   a
O! stay and hear; your true love's coming,   a
    That can sing both high and low.   b
Trip no further, pretty sweeting;   a
Journeys end in lovers meeting,   a
    Every wise man's son doth know.   b

The sestet may be a mingling of rhymed and unrhymed lines, as in D. G. Rossetti's "The Blessed Damozel" (page 769 in Volume II), or the quaint arrangement which Robert Burns made his own in "To a Mouse" and "The Hermit":

In this lone cave, in garments lowly,   a
Alike a foe to noisy folly,   a
And brow-bent gloomy melancholy,   a
    I wear away   b
My life, and, in my office holy,   a
    Consume the day.   b

The term "sestet" is also used to designate the last six lines of the sonnet.

The *septet*, a rather uncommon but flexible seven-line form, is chiefly esteemed in the variation known as *rime royal*, so called because it was supposedly first employed by King James I of Scotland. Chaucer was fond of using it (see his "Tale of the Man of Law" and "Troilus and Criseyde" and "Parlement of Foules"); Masefield erected his "The Widow in the Bye Street," "Dauber," and others on this design.

On every bough the briddès herde I singe,   a
With voys of aungel in hir armonye;   b
Some besyd hem hir briddès forth to bringe;   a
The litel conyes to hir play gunne hye;   b
And further al aboute I gan espye   b
The dredful roe, the buck, the hart and hinde,   c
Squerels, and beastès smale of gentil kinde.   c
    —*Geoffrey Chaucer*

The *octave*, a stanza of eight lines, presents infinite possibilities for the poet. It may be composed of the linking of two quatrains (*a-b-a-b-c-d-c-d*) or two triplets with an intervening pair of rhyming lines (*a-a-a-b-c-c-c-b*), as in the first example quoted below, or a quatrain, a triplet and an extra, final rhyme (*a-b-a-b-c-c-c-b*), as in the second example. Robert Bridges' "A Passer-by" presents still another arrangement (*a-b-a-b-b-c-b-c*).

Upon Saint Crispin's Day   a
Fought was this noble fray,   a
Which fame did not delay   a
    To England to carry.   b
O when shall English men   c
With such acts fill a pen?   c
Or England breed again   c
    Such a King Harry?   b
Agincourt—   —*Michael Drayton*

From too much love of living,   a
    From hope and fear set free,   b
We thank with brief thanksgiving   a
    Whatever gods may be   b
That no life lives forever;   c
That dead men rise up never;   c
That even the weariest river   c
    Winds somewhere safe to sea.   b
The Garden of Proserpine—   —*A. C. Swinburne*

Whither, O splendid ship, thy white sails crowding,   a
    Leaning across the bosom of the urgent West,   b
That fearest nor sea rising nor sky clouding,   a
    Whither away, fair rover, and what thy quest?   b
Ah! soon, when Winter has all our vales opprest,   b
When skies are cold and misty, and hail is hurling,   c
    Wilt thou glide on the blue Pacific, or rest   b
In a summer haven asleep, thy white sails furling.   c
A Passer-by—   —*Robert Bridges*

A particular form of the eight-line stanza is known as *ottava rima*, since it was adapted from the Italian. The arrangement is *a-b-a-b-a-b-c-c*, and examples of it are found in Byron's "Don Juan" and "The Vision of Judgment." An octave from the latter:

Saint Peter sat by the celestial gate,   a
    And nodded o'er his keys; when lo! there came   b
A wondrous noise he had not heard of late—   a
    A rushing sound of wind and stream and flame;   b
In short, a roar of things extremely great,   a
    Which would have made aught save a saint exclaim.   b
But he, with first a start and then a wink,   c
Said, "There's another star gone out, I think!"   c

The term "octave" is also used to designate the first eight lines of the sonnet.

The *Spenserian stanza* is a solemn, nine-line stanza, invented by Spenser. Its rhyme scheme is intricate (*a-b-a-b-b-c-b-c-c*) and the ninth line (called the *Alexandrine*) is one foot longer than the others, rounding out the stanza with an impressive sonority. Among the poems built on Spenserian stanza are Byron's "Childe Harold," Keats' "The Eve of St. Agnes," Shelley's "Adonais," and Spenser's *The Faerie Queene*, one stanza of which follows:

For take thy balance, if thou be so wise,	a
And weigh the wind that under heaven doth blow;	b
Or weigh the light that in the east doth rise;	a
Or weigh the thought that from man's mind doth flow:	b
But if the weight of these thou canst not show,	b
Weigh but one word which from thy lips doth fall:	c
For how canst thou these greater secrets know	b
That dost not know the least thing of them all?	c
Ill can he rule the great that cannot reach the small.	c

The ten-, eleven-, and twelve-line stanzas are combinations of smaller units and are rather uncommon. The fourteen-line stanza (the sonnet) has developed into one of the richest patterns in English poetry and must be considered separately.

THE BALLAD

Webster defines the *ballad* as follows: "A popular short narrative poem, especially a romantic poem characterized by simplicity of structure . . . usually founded on folk legend or tradition." There are, moreover, five features which characterize the ballad, no matter whether it is long or short.

1. The action is swift. There is no introduction and practically no explanation. No time is wasted in exposition; the characters leap at once into life.

2. The tale is simple and direct. The tone is straightforward and without elaboration; the language is the language of the people.

3. The story is moving. Whether it concerns an event of the day or something supernatural, the verses stir the emotion and the imagination.

4. The attitude is impersonal. The ballad-maker is a born storyteller, especially in the sense that he is outside of the story. He rarely comments or philosophizes upon the event; he scarcely ever renders judgment upon the characters.

5. With few exceptions, the story is concentrated upon one incident; it does not attempt to give all the events leading up to it, nor does it enlarge upon the consequences.

THE SONNET

The sonnets in these volumes are easily recognized. Although they show a variety of rhyme schemes, their basic structure is identical. All sonnets are built on fourteen lines, the lines themselves (with few exceptions) being composed of ten syllables—iambic pentameter. These fourteen lines are usually divided into the first eight (the octave) and the second six (the sestet). The three main types are the Petrarchan (or Italian), the Shakespearean, and the Miltonic sonnet.

The *Petrarchan sonnet* is the strictest; it permits only two rhymes in the octave and not more than three (often two) in the sestet. The octave is rhymed *a-b-b-a-a-b-b-a*. The sestet allows a variation in the line arrangement, the favorite pattern being either *c-d-e-c-d-e* or *c-d-c-d-c-d*. An example of the Petrarchan sonnet follows:

O Earth, lie heavily upon her eyes;	a
Seal her sweet eyes weary of watching, Earth;	b
Lie close around her; leave no room for mirth	b
With its harsh laughter, nor for sound of sighs.	a
She hath no questions, she hath no replies,	a
Hush'd in and curtain'd with a blessed dearth	b
Of all that irk'd her from the hour of birth;	b
With stillness that is almost Paradise.	a
Darkness more clear than noonday holdeth her,	c
Silence more musical than any song;	d
Even her very heart has ceased to stir:	c
Until the morning of Eternity	e
Her rest shall not begin nor end, but be;	e
And when she wakes she will not think it long.	d

Rest— —Christina Rossetti

The *Shakespearean sonnet*, perfected but not invented by Shakespeare, completely departs from the finely interwoven Italian model. It is actually nothing more than a set of three quatrains concluded and cemented by a couplet. An example:

No longer mourn for me when I am dead	a
Than you shall hear the surly sullen bell	b
Give warning to the world that I am fled	a
From this vile world with vilest worms to dwell;	b
Nay, if you read this line, remember not	c
The hand that writ it, for I love you so	d
That I in your sweet thoughts would be forgot	c
If thinking on me then should make you woe.	d
O if, I say, you look upon this verse	e
When I perhaps compounded am with clay,	f
Do not so much as my poor name rehearse,	e
But let your love even with my life decay,	f
Lest the wise world should look into your moan	g
And mock you with me after I am gone.	g

from Sonnets— —William Shakespeare

The *Miltonic sonnet* is an adaptation of the Petrarchan with a striking difference. The Italian model separated the octave and sestet by a break in thought; the octave usually presented a general idea while the sestet pointed it and made it particular. Instead of dividing his sonnets in two parts, Milton unrolled his thought and his rich music without interruption through the fourteen lines.

POETIC FORMS AND PATTERNS

An example:

Avenge, O Lord, thy slaughtered Saints, whose bones	a
Lie scattered on the Alpine mountains cold;	b
Even them who kept thy truth so pure of old,	b
When all our fathers worshiped stocks and stones,	a
Forget not: in thy book record their groans	a
Who were thy sheep, and in their ancient fold	b
Slain by the bloody Piedmontese, that rolled	b
Mother with infant down the rocks. Their moans	a
The vale redoubled to the hills, and they	c
To heaven. Their martyred blood and ashes sow	d
O'er all the Italian fields, where still doth sway	c
The triple Tyrant; that from these may grow	d
A hundredfold, who, having learnt thy way,	c
Early may fly the Babylonian woe.	d

On the Late Massacre in Piedmont—   *—John Milton*

THE BALLADE

The ballade (not to be confused with the ballad) is the most popular as well as the most important of the strict forms brought over from France. Villon immortalized the form and Chaucer used it in England as early as the fourteenth century—see his "Ballade of Good Counsel." It is composed of three stanzas of eight lines and a half-stanza (the *envoy*) of four lines. The rhymes of the first stanza are arranged in the order *a-b-a-b-b-c-b-c*, and this arrangement is repeated in all the other stanzas—the envoy (or "message") being *b-c-b-c*. No rhyme word or rhyming sound may be repeated throughout the entire ballade.

The outstanding feature of the ballade is its *refrain*. The refrain is the line which ends all the stanzas and the envoy; it is repeated in its entirety and gives a unity to the poem.

I hid my heart in a nest of roses,	a
Out of the sun's way, hidden apart;	b
In a softer bed than the soft white snow's is,	a
Under the roses I hid my heart.	b
Why would it sleep not? Why should it start,	b
When never a leaf of the rose-tree stirred?	c
What made sleep flutter his wings and part?	b
Only the song of a secret bird.	c
Lie still, I said, for the wind's wing closes,	a
And mild leaves muffle the keen sun's dart;	b
Lie still, for the wind on the warm seas dozes,	a
And the wind is unquieter yet than thou art.	b
Does a thought in thee still as a thorn's wound smart?	b
Does the fang still fret thee of hope deferred?	c
What bids the lips of thy sleep dispart?	b
Only the song of a secret bird.	c
The green land's name that a charm encloses,	a
It never was writ in the traveller's chart,	b
And sweet on its trees as the fruit that grows is;	a
It never was sold in the merchant's mart.	b
The swallows of dreams through its dim fields dart,	b
And sleep's are the tunes in its tree-tops heard;	c
No hound's note wakens the wildwood hart,	b
Only the song of a secret bird.	c

ENVOI

In the world of dreams I have chosen my part,	b
To sleep for a season and hear no word	c
Of true love's truth or of light love's art,	b
Only the song of a secret bird.	c

A Ballade of Dreamland—   *—A. C. Swinburne*

THE RONDEAU

The *rondeau* is a nimbler form usually employed for sprightly themes, although it can be used gravely, as in the poem by Henley quoted below. It is composed of thirteen lines built on only two rhymes, the refrain being a repetition of the first part of the first line. Using *R* to represent the refrain, the rhyme-scheme would be *Ra-a-b-b-a, a-a-b-R, a-a-b-b-a-R*. An example:

What is to come we know not. But we know	Ra
That what has been was good—was good to show,	a
Better to hide, and best of all to bear.	b
We are the masters of the days that were:	b
We have lived, we have loved, we have suffered—even so.	a
Shall we not take the ebb who had the flow?	a
Life was our friend. Now, if it be our foe—	a
Dear, though it break and spoil us!—need we care	b
What is to come?	R
Let the great winds their worst and wildest blow,	a
Or the gold weather round us mellow slow:	a
We have fulfilled ourselves, and we can dare	b
And we can conquer, though we may not share	b
In the rich quiet of the afterglow.	a
What is to come?	R

What Is to Come—   *—W. E. Henley*

THE TRIOLET

In common with the ballade, the rondeau, and other forms imported from France, the *triolet* is founded on a strict rhyme scheme and constructed by skillful repetition. The smallest and shortest of the French forms, it consists of only eight lines— and three of the eight are repeated. The first line

(*Ra*) is repeated to make the fourth and seventh lines; the second line (*Rb*) is repeated to make the eighth line. An example of the triolet's nimbleness:

Under the sun	Ra
There's nothing new;	Rb
Poem or pun,	a
Under the sun,	Ra
Said Solomon,	a
And he said true.	b
"Under the sun	Ra
There's nothing new."	Rb

—H. C. Beeching

THE VILLANELLE

Originally used for pastoral subjects, the *villanelle* has become so stylized that its simplicity is quite artificial. It is composed of five three-line stanzas and a concluding stanza of four lines, each stanza ending with an alternating line of the first verse. In the last stanza both of these lines appear together as a concluding couplet. Only two rhymes are permitted throughout the verses. Henley has described the very essence of this form as follows:

A dainty thing's the Villanelle.	a 1
Sly, musical, a jewel in rhyme,	b
It serves its purpose passing well.	a 2
A double-clappered silver bell	a
That must be made to clink in chime,	b
A dainty thing's the Villanelle;	a 1
And if you wish to flute a spell,	a
Or ask a meeting 'neath the lime,	b
It serves its purpose passing well.	a 2
You must not ask of it the swell	a
Of organs grandiose and sublime—	b
A dainty thing's the Villanelle;	a 1
And, filled with sweetness, as a shell	a
Is filled with sound, and launched in time,	b
It serves its purpose passing well.	a 2
Still fair to see and good to smell	a
As in the quaintness of its prime,	b
A dainty thing's the Villanelle;	a 1
It serves its purpose passing well.	a 2

THE ODE

Derived from a Greek word meaning "song," the *ode*, according to the lexicographers, became "a form of stately and elaborate verse." Originally chanted, the ode was built on a set of themes and responses and sung by divided choirs, half the singers intoning the strophe, the other half replying with the antistrophe, and both uniting with the epode. Most of the odes in English verse depart from the Greek model, although Swinburne's "Athens" and some of his political odes preserve the antique mode, while Dryden's "Alexander's Feast" blends the responsive voices in the classical manner. Cowley invented a variation on the form which he called the *Pindaric ode*—an irregular, passionate declamation in which the form is swept aside on a wave of emotion—Cowley failing to comprehend that Pindar varied the verse arrangement of his odes but that each was consistently and strictly patterned.

Since Cowley, the shape of the ode has grown more and more uncertain. The odes of Coleridge, Wordsworth, and Tennyson, though eloquent, are irregular. The magnificent odes of Keats and Shelley are, in reality, extended and sustained lyrics. The term itself has been broadened; strophe and antistrophe have disappeared; the length and the stanza pattern are unpredictable. Today the ode may be recognized not by its form at all, but rather by its tone: an intense, richly elaborated, and often profound apostrophe.

BLANK VERSE

Blank verse may be defined as (1) any unrhymed regular measure or (2) unrhymed verse in iambic pentameter. Most scholars favor the second interpretation, although the unrhymed dactylic hexameter of Longfellow's *Evangeline* and the unrhymed trochaic tetrameter of his *Song of Hiawatha* are obviously a variety of blank verse. But the term "blank verse" seems attached to the iambic five-accented line first employed in English by Henry Howard, Earl of Surrey, and glorified by Shakespeare's dramas, Milton's epics, and Wordsworth's meditations. Along with its sonority, its great strength lies in its flexibility. It can deviate from strict metrical regularity without injuring the rolling line—in fact the departures, the endless variety of effects, reveal its never-exhausted power. Every master of blank verse has given the measure new modulations and stamped it with his characteristic idiom.

From the countless examples of eloquent blank verse five illustrative segments, ranging from the sixteenth to the twentieth century, have been chosen.

The stars move still, time runs, the clock will strike,
The devil will come, and Faustus must be damned.
O, I'll leap up to heaven!—Who pulls me down?—
See, where Christ's blood streams in the firmament!
One drop of blood will save me: O my Christ!—
Rend not my heart for naming of my Christ;
Yet will I call on him: O, spare me, Lucifer!—
Where is it now? 'tis gone:
And, see, a threatening arm, an angry brow!
Mountains and hills, come, come, and fall on me,
And hide me from the heavy wrath of heaven!

   Dr. Faustus—   *—Christopher Marlowe*

There is a tide in the affairs of men,
Which, taken at the flood, leads on to fortune;
Omitted, all the voyage of their life
Is bound in shallows and in miseries.
On such a full sea are we now afloat;
And we must take the current when it serves,
Or lose our ventures. . .

   Julius Caesar—   *—William Shakespeare*

These are thy glorious works, Parent of good,
Almighty, Thine this universal frame,
Thus wondrous fair: Thyself how wondrous then!
Unspeakable, who sitt'st above these heavens
To us invisible, or dimly seen
In these thy lowest works; yet these declare
Thy goodness beyond thought, and power divine.
Speak, ye who best can tell, ye sons of light,
Angels, for ye behold Him, and with songs
And choral symphonies, day without night,
Circle His throne rejoicing, ye, in heaven,
On earth join all ye creatures to extol
Him first, Him last, Him midst, and without end.

   Paradise Lost—   *—John Milton*

. . . That time is past,
And all its aching joys are now no more,
And all its dizzy raptures. Not for this
Faint I, nor mourn nor murmur; other gifts
Have followed; for such loss, I would believe,
Abundant recompence. For I have learned
To look on nature, not as in the hour
Of thoughtless youth; but hearing oftentimes
The still, sad music of humanity.

   Lines—   *—William Wordsworth*

See how these names are fêted by the waving grass . . .
The names of those who in their lives fought for life,
Who wore at their hearts the fire's centre.
Born of the sun they travelled a short while towards the sun,
And left the vivid air signed with their honour.

   I Think Continually of Those—   *—Stephen Spender*

VARIOUS DEVICES

Besides the patterns already defined, the poet has recourse to various devices. Some of the most easily recognizable are *alliteration*, *rhyme*, *assonance*, *onomatopoeia*, *metonymy*, *synecdoche*, *epithet*, *simile*, and *metaphor*.

Devices of Sound

Alliteration is the repetition of the same consonant sound in words or syllables succeeding each other at close intervals. Usually it refers to the repetition of a sound or letter at the beginning of words, as in

   Fields ever fresh and groves ever green.

But, besides the repetition of *f* and *g* in this line, there is alliteration of the *v* sounds, half buried in the midst of the words. It is the most recognizable of devices, often overused—Swinburne carried it to the point of parody—but it is extremely effective as an enrichment of rhyme, even a substitute for it, as in Anglo-Saxon poetry. A famous example is Tennyson's

   The moan of doves in immemorial elms,
   And murmuring of innumerable bees.

Rhyme, sometimes spelled *rime*, has been variously defined. However, the principle laid down by Thomas Hood still holds: "A rhyme must commence on an accented syllable. From the accented vowel of that syllable to the end, the words intended to rhyme must be *identical* in sound, but the letter or letters preceding the accented vowel must be *unlike* in sound." "Night" and "fight," for example, are true rhymes, but "night" and "knight" do not rhyme, there being nothing unlike in the sound preceding the vowel. Neither can "night" and "ride" be said to rhyme, for though the sound preceding the vowel is different, the sound *following* the vowel is not identical, as it should be to constitute a true rhyme. "Night" and "ride" is an instance of assonance.

Assonance is the matching of the vowel sound alone, irrespective of the consonant (or sound) which follows it. Thus "base" and "face" would be true rhyme, whereas "base" and "fade" would be assonance. The old ballads and folk poetry are full of assonance, sometimes purposeful, sometimes accidental, as in "Sir Patrick Spens";

> The anchor broke, the topmast *split*,
> 'Twas such a deadly *storm*.
> The waves came over the broken *ship*
> Till all her sides were *torn*.

Onomatopoeia is the formation of words by the imitation of sounds; the words thus formed vividly suggest the object or action producing the sound. Such words are found in the cradle of the individual as well as in the infancy of the race: *bow-wow, ding-dong, hum, buzz*, and so on. Though not confined to verse, words like *whiz, crash, crunch, crackle, jangle, squeal, honk, hiss* have become properties of the poet.

When Keats wrote

> The murmurous haunt of flies on summer eves

he not only suggested the presence of flies, he *imitated* the drone and buzzing of insects on a sultry evening.

Devices of Sense

Metonymy and *synecdoche* are related to metaphor and simile, being forms of comparison. Metonymy (literally "name change") is the substitution of one thing to represent another. Thus when Byron, describing the ball on the night before Waterloo says:

> And Belgium's capital had gathered then
> Her beauty and her chivalry—

the word "beauty" represents "fair women" and the word "chivalry" symbolizes "brave men."

Synecdoche (literally, "receiving together") is a figure of speech in which a part represents the whole: in the cry

> "A sail! A sail!"

the word "sail" symbolizes the entire ship. Both metonymy and synecdoche are "figures of association," and there is little real difference in the way they are used today.

An *epithet* is a word (usually an adjective) which describes its object with unusual exactness. It is the arresting term which not only points a description but reveals how imagination intensifies observation. This exactness and fancy may be seen in such epithets as: "*smooth-sliding* Mincius," "*brittle* beauty," "lazy, *leaden-stepping* hours," "the river *sweats* oil and tar," "the *strong* crust of *friendly* bread," "the *green hells* of the sea," "*full-throated* ease," "*embalmed* darkness."

Simile and *metaphor* are poetry's most constant properties. The power of each lies in establishing a kinship between two (usually unrelated) objects, and fixing the attention on one object by comparing it to another. When the comparison is direct and introduced by *like* or *as*, it is a simile; when the comparison is indirect or implied, without the use of *like* or *as*, it is a metaphor.

Among the many familiar similes, these three may be listed as often-quoted favorites:

> O my luve is like a red, red rose (*Robert Burns*)

> I wandered lonely as a cloud (*William Wordsworth*)

> I have seen old ships sail like swans asleep (*James Elroy Flecker*)

The following are vivid examples of metaphor:

> There is a garden in her face (*Thomas Campion*)

> Life's but a walking shadow, a poor player (*William Shakespeare*)

> O blackbird, what a boy you are! (*T. E. Brown*)

Without simile and metaphor the image would lose its swiftness and strength; poetry is founded on the vigor and range of the metaphorical mind. Its element is surprise. To relate the hitherto unrelated, to make the strange seem familiar and the familiar seem strange, is the aim of metaphor. Through this heightened awareness, poetry, though variously defined, is invariably pronounced and unmistakably perceived.

L. U.

THE RULERS OF ENGLAND, 802–1941

Ecgbert	802–839	Edward III	1327–1377
Aethelwulf	839–858	Richard II	1377–1399
Aethelbald	858–860	Henry IV	1399–1413
Aethelbert	860–866	Henry V	1413–1422
Aethelred I	866–871	Henry VI	1422–1461
Alfred	871–901	Edward IV	1461–1483
Edward the Elder	901–925	Edward V	1483
Aethelstan	925–940	Richard III	1483–1485
Edmund I	940–946	Henry VII	1485–1509
Edred	946–955	Henry VIII	1509–1547
Eadwig	955–959	Edward VI	1547–1553
Edgar	959–975	Mary	1553–1558
Edward the Martyr	975–978	Elizabeth	1558–1603
Aethelred the Unready	978–1016	James I	1603–1625
Edmund Ironside	1016	Charles I	1625–1649
Canute	1016–1035	Oliver Cromwell	1653–1658
Harold I	1035–1040	Richard Cromwell	1658–1659
Hardicanute	1040–1042	Charles II	1660–1685
Edward the Confessor	1042–1066	James II	1685–1688
Harold II	1066	William III	1688–1702
William I	1066–1087	Anne	1702–1714
William II	1087–1100	George I	1714–1727
Henry I	1100–1135	George II	1727–1760
Stephen	1135–1154	George III	1760–1820
Henry II	1154–1189	George IV	1820–1830
Richard I	1189–1199	William IV	1830–1837
John	1199–1216	Victoria	1837–1901
Henry III	1216–1272	Edward VII	1901–1910
Edward I	1272–1307	George V	1910–1936
Edward II	1307–1327	Edward VIII	1936
		George VI	1936–

GENERAL INDEX

The names of the authors whose selections are represented are shown in CAPITALS and SMALL CAPITALS.

The titles of selections quoted are shown in **bold face**.

The **bold-face** numbers refer to the pages on which authors are discussed in detail, and to the pages on which the quoted selections appear.

Absalom and Achitophel, 726, 727–731
Abuses Stript and Whipt, 569
Act of Settlement, 530
ADDISON, JOSEPH, 521, 778, 781, 783, **844–866,** 871, 898, 962; biography of, 844; Steele and, 844
Address of Welcome, 610
Address to the Deil, 1083–1085
Address to the Unco Guid, or The Rigidly Righteous, 1082–1083
Advancement of Learning, The, 544
Ae Fond Kiss, 1096
AELFRIC OF EYNSHAM, 7, 77, 88, **68–77**
Aeneid, 169, 297, 329
Aethelbert, 12
Aethelred, King, 77
Aethelstan, 15
Aethelwold, Bishop of Winchester, 68
Aethelwulf, 65
Afton Water, 1096
Against a Dwarf, 55
Against Wens, 55–56
Aglaura, 604, 605
Ah, Fading Joy, 726
Aidan, 13
Aiken, Robert, 1078, 1085
Alchemist, The (Jonson), 521, 557
Aldus, publisher, 273
Alexander and Campaspe, 349
Alexander III of Scotland, 230
Alexander's Feast; or the Power of Music, 726, **732–734**
ALFRED, King, 14–15, **65–68;** Danes and, 14–15, 65
Alleyn, Edward, 363
All for Love, 534, 725
All's Well That Ends Well, 314, 461
Alysoun, 157
America, early, England and, 531
Amnesty, Act of (c. 1661), 529
Amores (Ovid), 364
Amoret, 616
Amoretti, 395, 399–400
Amyot, James, Bishop, 335
Anatomy of Abuses, 278

Anatomy of Melancholy, The, 525, 532, 577, **578–587,** 646
Anatomy, sixteenth-century developments in, 271
Ancrene Wisse (Ancrene Riwle), 89
Andreas, 14
Andrewes, 533
Angles, Britain invaded by, 10
Anglo-Saxon Chronicle. See *Old English Chronicles, The*
Anjou, Duke of, 350
Annales (Camden), 321
Anne, Queen, 293, 775, 776, 802, 844, 961; reign of, 784
Annus Mirabilis, 725, 726
Another Grace for a Child, 599
Anselm, Archbishop, 87
Anson, George Lord, 1071
Antony and Cleopatra, 335, 461, 534
Apology of Sleep, for Not Approaching the Lady Who Can Do Anything But Sleep When She Pleaseth, The, 610
Appeal of Injured Innocence, 631
Arabian Nights, The, 171
Aragon, Catharine of, 285
Arcadia, 350, 351, 504
Architecture, Norman Conquest changing, 86
Arden, Mary, 460
Arden of Feversham, 281
A Red, Red Rose, 1091
Areopagitica, 528, 531, 536, 640, **683–692**
Areopagus, literary group, 350, 394
Aretino, Pietro, 293
Argument [on] Christianity in England, An, 834–840
Argument of His Book, The (*Hesperides*), **593**
Arnold, Matthew, 1092
Arte of English Poetry, 277
Arthur of Britain, King, 95, 113
Art of English Poetry, 431
Art Thou Poor?, 447
ASCHAM, ROGER, 251, 269, 275, 314, **321–328,** 335; biography of, 321
Astell, Mary, 525
Aston, Sir Walter, 454
Astraea Redux, 725

Astronomy, seventeenth-century, 520–521
Astrophel and Stella, 351–352, 395, 447
As You Like It, 104, 279, 460, 500
At a Solemn Music, 649
Athelston, 95
Athenian Gazette, 536
Auguries of Innocence, 1104–1105
Augustine, Pope Gregory's emissary, 12
Auld Lang Syne, 1090
Austen, Lady, 1061
Author's Resolution in a Sonnet, The, 569, **570–571**

Bach, Johann Sebastian, 520
Back and Side Go Bare, Go Bare, 504
BACON, FRANCIS, 273, 521, 522, 523, 531, 532, 537, **544–556,** 557, 592, 620; biography of, 544; essay of, 536
Bacon, Roger, 89
Bacon, Sir Nicholas, 544
Bacon, Sir Thomas, 305
Baldwin, William, 297, 300
Ballad, definition of, 221–223, 1116–1117; popular, 221–239
Ballad upon a Wedding, A, 606
Bandello, Matteo, 314
Bankes, Anne, 610
Bard, The, 917–919
BARNFIELD, RICHARD, **505**
Barnham, Alice, 544
Baron's Wars, The, 454
Barrow, 533
Battle of Maldon, The, 11, 14, **58–62,** 77
Baxter, 533
"Bear's Son Tale, The," 16
Beauchamp, Richard, 250
Beaumont, Francis, 281, 533, 534
Beaux's Stratagem, The, 1018
Becket, Thomas à, 87
BEDE, 10, 12, 14, **62–64,** 66; biography of, 62
Bedford, Countess of, 447
Bedivere, on Gawain, 114

1123

Behn, Aphra, 536
Belgic Celts, 9
Bellefarest, 314
Bellenden, 329
Bellman, The (Herrick), **599–600**
Belman of London, The (Dekker), 441
Benjamin Jonson (Fuller), **632**
Beowulf, 11–14, **16–50,** 58, 95, 775; explanatory introduction, 16–19; genealogies to, 18–19; religious elements in, 17
Bermudas, 696
Bermudez, Juan, 696
Berners, Lord, 335
Betterton, Thomas, 739
Beves of Hamtoun, 95
Bible, authority of, 522; *Douai,* **539,** English, 4; English translation, 91–92, 272; *Geneva,* 538, **539;** medieval drama and, 239; *The Authorized or King James Version of,* 532, 533, **538–543;** *The Great* **538–539**
Biglow Papers, 531
Bill of Rights (English), 531; passage of, 530
Biography, essay form of, 536
Biscop, Benedict, 13
Black Death, 90, 163
Blackstone, Sir William, 786
BLAKE, WILLIAM, 7, 781, 934, **1097–1110;** Bacon discussed by, 544; biography of, 1097–1098
Blanche, Duchess of Lancaster, 169
Blenheim, Battle of, 844
Bless the Time the Apple Was Taken!, 161
"Bloody Assizes," 530
Blow, Blow, Thou Winter Wind, 501
Boccaccio, Giovanni, 169, 170, 171, 192, 195, 276, 314
Bodel, Jean, 95
Boece, Hector, 329
Boehme, Jacob, 1097
Boethius, 13; translators of, 65
Boileau, 277
Boleyn, Anne, 293
Bonny Barbara Allan, 232
Bonny Earl of Murray, The, 238
Book Named the Governour, 276
Book of Job, The, 539–540
Book of Psalms, 541–542
Book of the Duchess, The, 169, 171
Bookworm, 54
BOSWELL, JAMES, **939–961;** biography of, 939; Johnson and, 961–962, 1018
Bowge of Court, The, 282
Boyle, Elizabeth, 395

Boyle, Robert, 521
Boyle, Roger, 606
Brave New World, 285
Braybrook, Lord, 718
Breton lays, 147
BRETON, NICHOLAS, 503, **505**
Bricriu's Feast, 114
Britain, Angles invading, 10; before the English, 9–10; Church of, early, 10; English invading, 10–11; Irish raiding, 10; last Germanic raids of, 14–15; matter of, 113–138; Romans invading, 10; Saxons invading, 10. See also *England*
Broghill, Baron, 606
Brown, William, 448
Browne, John, 7, 531
BROWNE, SIR THOMAS, 2, 521–524, 528, 533, 537, **619–630;** biography of, 619–620
Browning, Robert, 7, 928
Bruce, Robert, 1089
Bruni, Leonardo, 273
Brut, 89
Brythonic, 9
Buckingham, Duchess of, 786, 787
Buckingham, Duke of, 250, 544
BUNYAN, JOHN, 521, 525, 529, 532, 544, **704–717,** 740, 783; biography of, 704–705; Malory compared with, 250; novel of, 536
Burghley, Lord, 269, 273, 321, 335, 544
BURKE, EDMUND, 6, 779, 1012, **1048–1060;** biography of, 1048
Burning Babe, The, 515
BURNS, ROBERT, 782, 1061, **1077–1097;** biography of, 1077–1078
BURTON, ROBERT, 521, 525, 532, **577–587,** 619, 646; biography of, 577–578
Butler, Samuel, 535
Byrd, William, 351
Byrhtnoth of Essex, 58
Byron, George Gordon, Lord, 605, 934

Caedmon, 14, 62, **63–64**
Caesar, Julius, 10
Calm, The, 279
Calvinism, 272
Cambrensis, Richard, 329
"Cambridge" Platonists, 524
Camden, antiquarian, 321
Campaign, The, 844
Campion, Edmund, 329
CAMPION, THOMAS, **506–507**
Canonization, The, 565

Canon's Yeomen's Prologue, The, 216–218
Canon's Yeoman's Tale, The, 218
Canterbury, Archbishop of, 279; earliest, 12
Canterbury Tales, The, 92, 104, 163, 169–172, **173–221,** 572; discussion of, 171
Canute the Dane, 15
Captain Singleton, 789
CAREW, THOMAS, 535, 557, **602–603,** 604; biography of, 602; verse of, 534
Carleton, Sir Dudley, 602
Carlyle, Thomas, 7, 939, 961, 1077; Bible discussed by, 539
Carmen Deo Nostro, 612, 613
Carr, Robert, 573
Carthon: A Poem, 934–939
Castaway, The, 1071–1072
Castiglione, Count Baldassare, 296, 305
Castle of Indolence, The, 898, **902–911**
Catherine of Aragon, Queen, 272, 293
Catholicism, medieval English, 86–87; *Piers Plowman* teaching, 163; seventeenth-century, 527
Cato, 844
CAXTON, WILLIAM, 5, 94; *Le Morte Darthur* prefaced by, **252**
Cecil, Sir William, 321
Celebration of Charis, A, 561
Celts, 9, 11
Ceremonies for Christmas, 597–598
Certain Sonnets (Sidney), **352–353**
Certain Tragical Discourses Written out of French and Latin, 314
Characters of Virtues and Vices, 572, 573
Character Writers, 572–577
Charlemagne, 95
Charles I, 527, 528, 531, 575, 592, 602, 608, 693, 696
Charles II, 65, 521, 575, 593, 610, 620, 631, 634, 704, 725; reign and death of, 529
Charles V, 270, 321
Charles the Grete, 252
Charms, 55–57
CHAUCER, GEOFFREY, 4, 5, 7, 88, 89, 91–93, 104, 152, 163, **168–221,** 250–252, 284, 300, 457, 537, 572, 785; biography of, 168–172; Boethius translated by, 65; in government employ, 170–171; middle-class life described by, 92; on Gawain, 114; pronunciation of, 155
Cheke, Sir John, 305, 321

GENERAL INDEX

Cherbury, Edward Lord Herbert of, 531, 587, 602
Cherry-Ripe, 593
Cherry-tree Carol, The, 229–230
CHESTERFIELD, EARL OF. See Stanhope, Philip Dormer.
Child, A (Earle), 575–576
Childe, Machabyas, 394
Chimney Sweeper, The (from *Songs of Experience*), 1103 (from *Songs of Innocence*), 1102
Chrétien de Troyes, 95, 113
Christ, 14
Christianity, early English, 10; Orosius on, 66
Christianity in England (Swift), 834–840
Christian Morals, 620
Christmas Carol, A (Wither), 571–572
Christophorus, 16
Chronicle (Hall), 300
Chronicles (Holinshed), 278, 329–335
Chronicles, Old English, The, 10, 81–84
Church, Christian, medieval drama and, 239; Donne and, 564; eighteenth-century, 786; English, early, 12; English, in later Middle Ages, 86–87; Irish, early, 12–13; James I and, 526; Reformation and, 272
Church History of Britain, The, 526, 631
Church Militant, The, 531
Cicero, 275
Citizen of the World, The, 1012
Civilization, eighteenth-century, 777
Civil Wars between the Two Houses of York and Lancaster, 447, 448, 453
Clarkson, 782
Classicism, eighteenth-century, 782–784
Classics, definition of, 4; influence of, 273–274
Class spirit, society and, 526
Claudius, 10
Cleopatra (Garnier), 447
Clerk, John, 296
Clerk's Prologue, The, 192
Clerk's Tale, The, 192–193
Clifford, Anne, Lady, 447
Clock, invention of, 525
Cobham, Elizabeth, 293
Coleridge, Samuel Taylor, 194, 448, 787, 898
Colet, John, 274
Colin Clout, 282–284
Colin Clout's Come Home Again, 282, 395

Collar, The, 588
COLLINS, WILLIAM, 535, **923–927;** biography of, 923
Colloquy, The, 73–77, 88
Come Away, Come Away, Death, 501
Comedy, Congreve's, 739; Elizabethan, 281; Goldsmith's, 1012; Jonson's, 557; Lyly's, 342–343; seventeenth-century, 532; Shakespeare's, 460
Comedy of Errors, The, 460
Come, My Celia, Let Us Prove, 559
Comenius, 524
Comin' thro' the Rye, 1088–1089
Complaint by Night of the Lover Not Beloved, A, 298
Complaint of a Lover Rebuked, 298
Complaint of Rosamond, The, 447, 449–451, 453
Complaints, 394
Compleat Angler, The, 532, 600, 633, 634–639
Compleat Gentleman, The, 503, 532
Comus, 533, 639
Concerning Invention, 275
Concerning the Revolutions of the Heavenly Bodies, 271
Concerning the Structure of the Human Body, 271
Confessio Amantis, 92, 171, 252
CONGREVE, WILLIAM, 532, 534, 605, **739–773;** biography of, 739–740
Conjectures upon Original Compositions, 1078
Connecticut Yankee at King Arthur's Court, A, 251
Consolations of Philosophy, 65
CONSTABLE, HENRY, **508–509**
Constancy, 605
Conversations (Drummond), 557
Cook, Ann, 544
Cooke, Elizabeth, 305
Cook's Prologue, The, 185
Cooper's Hill, 570
Copernicus, 271, 520, 521
Coriolanus, 335
Corrinna's Going A-Maying, 593–594
Cotter's Saturday Night, The, 1078–1080
Cotton, Sir Robert, 16
Cotton Vitellius A. XV, 16
Couplet, 535; Carew's, 602; Wither's, 569–570
Courtier, education of, 275–276
Courtier, The (Castiglione), 296

Courtier, The (Hoby), 276, **305–313**
Court of Venus, The, 293
Courts, medieval, 87
Coverdale, Miles, 538
COWLEY, ABRAHAM, 524, 535, 610, 612, **696–704;** biography of, 696–697
COWPER, WILLIAM, **1071–1077;** biography of, 1061
Cradle Song, A (Blake), 1102
Cranmer, Archbishop, 272
CRASHAW, RICHARD, 532, 535, 588, 592, **612–615,** 640, 697; biography of, 612
Crécy, battle of, 90
Cromwell, Oliver, 6, 521, 527–529, 531, 610, 640, 653, 693, 725
Cromwell, Richard, 529
Cromwell, Thomas, 297
Cuckoo Song, The, 156
Cudworth, Ralph, 524
Culture, seventeenth-century, 530
Cumberland, Countess of, 447
Cunobelinus, 10
Cupid Abroad Was Lated, 512–513
Cupid and My Campaspe, 349
Cura Pastoralis, 65
Cutter of Coleman Street, 696
Cymbeline, 329, 461
Cynewulf, 14, 52, 53
Cynthia's Revels, 575; selections from, 559
Cyriack, This Three Years' Day, 653

Daily Courant, 526
Dancing, ballad and, 222
Danes, Alfred and, 14–15, 65; Britain invaded by, 14–15
DANIEL, SAMUEL, 279, 280, **447–453;** biography of, 447–448
Dante, 169, 639
Danvers, Jane, 587
Davenant, Sir William, 533
"David" (painting), 271
Death-Song (Webster), **515–516**
Decameron, 171, 192, 276, 314
Declaration of Indulgence, 704
De Clerico et Puella, 160
De Consolatione Philosophiae, 13
Dedekind, Frederick, 441
Definition of Love, The, 695
Defence of Poesy, The, 350, 351, **353–363,** 447
Defence of Rhyme, 447
DEFOE, DANIEL, 521, **788–802;** biography of, 788–789; novel of, 537

GENERAL INDEX

DEKKER, THOMAS, 278, 279, 281, 441–447, 504; biography of, 441
Delia, 447, **448–449**
Delight in Disorder, 593
Delights of the Muses, The, 612, 613
Deloney, Thomas, 503
Democritus Junior to the Reader, 578–582
Denham, Sir John, 535, 570
Deor, 51
Deor's Lament, 12
De Orbo Novo, 389
Descartes, 523
Deschamps, Eustache, 171
Description and Praise of His Love Geraldine, 298
Description of Spring, Wherein Each Thing Renews Save only the Lover, 297
Description of the Contrarious Passions in a Lover, 294
Deserted Village, The, 1012–1017
Devereux, Penelope, 350
Dial of Princes, The, 335
Diana, 504
Diary, The, 718–725
Dictes or Sayengis of the Philosophres, 252
Dictionary of the English Language, 961, 962
Didacticism, 777
Dido, Queen of Carthage, 364
Diodati, Charles, 639
Dionysus, Greek drama and, 239
Dirge (Webster), **515**
Discipline, 590
Discourse of a Discovery for a New Passage to Cataia, 278
Discourse of English Poetrie, 277
Discoverie of the Large, Rich, and Beautiful Empire of Guiana, 278
Discoveries, seventeenth-century, 523
Discovery of the Empire of Guiana, 432
Disdain Returned, 603
Distichs, 252
Divers Voyages Touching the Discovery of America, 389
Divine Comedy, 163, 169
Doleful Lay of Clorinda, The, 395
DONNE, JOHN, 7, 279, 285, 521, 531, 533, 557, **563–569,** 578, 587, 588, 604, 610, 612, 616, 619, 631, 634, 697, 1061; biography of, 563–564; poetry of, 534; prose of, 536, 537
Douai Bible, The, 539
Double-Dealer, The, 739
Douglas, Gavin, 93
DOWLAND, JOHN, **509**
Drake, Sir Francis, 269, 351, 389

Drama, Daniel's, 447–448; Elizabethan, 280–281, 504; French influence on, 534; Greek, 239; Marlowe's, 363–364; Middle English, 239–250; of Restoration, 533; Puritanism and, 533; religious, medieval, 92; seventeenth-century, 533–534; Shakespeare's, 460–461; sixteenth-century, 280–281; Skelton's, 282; vernacular, 239
DRAYTON, MICHAEL, 279, 280, 448, **453–459;** biography of, 453–454
Dream of the Rood, The, 14, **52–53**
Drinking Song, The, 510
Druids, 9
Drummond, William, 534, 557, 558
Drury, Sir Robert, 566
DRYDEN, JOHN, 5, 6, 171, 279, 521, 531–534, 610, 631, 694, **725–738,** 739; biography of, 725–726; essay of, 536; poetry of, 535
Du Bellay, 394, 395
Duchess of Malfi, The, 314, 573
Dudley, Mary, Lady, 350
Dunbar, 93
Duncan Gray, 1090
Dutton, William, 693
DYER, SIR EDWARD, **509–510**

Earle, Giles, 600
EARLE, JOHN, 572, **575–577,** 600; biography of, 575; translations of, 575
Early Period, Old English Era, 9–84
Easter Wings, 588, 598
Eastward Ho, 557
Earthly Paradise, 171
Ecchoing Green, The, 1101
Ecclesiastical History of the English Nation, 62, 65
Ecgbert, King, 14, 15
Economy, seventeenth-century, 527
Ecstasy, The, 567
Eddington, battle of, 65
Education, in later Middle Ages, 88–89; sixteenth-century, 274–275; seventeenth-century, 525
Education of a Christian Prince, 335
Edward, 225–226
Edward II, 453
Edward III, 90, 91, 169, 296
Edward VI, 272, 275
Edward the Confessor, 85, 296, 297
Edward the Second, 363, 364, 465
Edwards, Richard, 503
Egerton, Sir Thomas, 564
Eikon Basilike, 575
Elder Edda, 51
Elegy upon the Death of Dr. Donne, Dean of Paul's, 602

Elegy Written in a Country Church-Yard, 787, **913–915,** 1012, 1078
El Greco, 521
Eliot, George, 1, 521
Elixir, The, 589–590
Elizabeth, Queen, 269–273, 300, 305, 329, 335, 343, 350, 394, 431, 526, 530; Boethius translated by, 65; death of, 519
Elizabethan Lyrics, 503–517
Eloïsa to Abelard, 893–897
Elyot, Sir Thomas, 276
Enclosure Act, 785
Encomium Moriae, 285
Endymion (Lyly), 342, 343, **350**
Eneydos, 252
England, after Norman Conquest, 85–94; America and, 531; during later Middle Ages, 85; economic conditions in, 527; expansion of, 520; fourteenth-century, 90–91; France at war with (1337), 90; France at war with (1549), 270; history of, seventeenth-century, 526–531; literature in later Middle Ages in, 90–94; matter of, 95–113; medieval municipal government in, 88; Norman conquest of, 85–87; Reformation in, 271; seventeenth-century, 519–537; Spain defeated by, 270. See also *Britain.*
England's Helicon, 503
English, ancestry of, 5
Enquiry into the Present State of Polite Learning in Europe, An, 1012
Envoy, L', 193
Epicoene, selection from, 560
Epigrammatum Sacrorum Liber, 612
Epigrams (Jonson), **557–559**
Epistle, sixteenth-century, 279
Epistle to Augustus (Pope), 739
Epitaphium Damonis, 639
Epitaph on Elizabeth, L. H., 559
Epitaph on S[alathiel] P[avy], a Child of Queen Elizabeth's Chapel, 558–559
Epithalamion, 395, **400–404**
Erasmus, 269, 274, 285, 321, 335, 343
Ercildoune, Thomas of, 228
Eric of Norway, King, 230
Essay, Goldsmith's, 1012; seventeenth-century, 536
Essay Concerning Human Understanding, 536
Essay of Dramatic Poesy, An, 279, 536, 537, 725, **734–735**
Essay on Criticism, An, 871 **872–884**

GENERAL INDEX   1127

Essay on Man, 780, 878–884
Essay on Projects, 789–791
Essays of Elia, 697
Essays or Counsels, Civil and Moral, 544, 545–551
Essex, Earl of, 269, 276, 350, 395, 431, 544, 563, 573
Ethandun, battle of, 65
Etherege, 534
Euclid, 3
Euphues and His England, 342
Euphues' Golden Legacy, 104
Euphues: The Anatomy of Wit, 278, 342, 343–349
Even Such Is Time, 434
Everyman, 93
Every Man in His Humour, 557
Excellent Epitaph, An, 297
Exclusion Bill, 529
Exeter Book, 51
Exodus, 14

Fabyan, Robert, 278
Faerie Queene, The, 394, 395, 405–431, 432, 696
Faery Beam upon You, The, 596
Fair and Happy Milkmaid, A, 574
Faire-Virtue, or The Mistress of Philarete, 570
Fairfax, Lord General, 693
Fair Margaret and Sweet William, 230–231
Fall of Princes, 300
Falstaff, Sir John, 171
Familiar Letters, 527
Fatal Sisters, The, 919–920
Fates of the Apostles, The, 14
Faust, 1092
Fear No More the Heat o' the Sun, 502
Feet, definition of, 1113
Fenton, Geoffrey, 314
Ferdinand, King of Spain, 270
Ferrar, Nicholas, 587, 588
Feudal system, 87
Fèvre, Raoul le, 252
Fiction, Defoe's, 789; medieval, 92; seventeenth-century, 536
Fidelia, 570
"Filocolo," 195
Fine Knacks for Ladies, 509
Fingal, an Ancient Epic Poem, with Other Poems Composed by Ossian, 934
Finnsburg Fragment, The, 12
Fire of London (1666), 526, 529
First Epistle of St. Paul to the Corinthians, The, 543
First Part of King Henry the Fourth, The, 465–500
Fisher, John, 274

Fitzgerald, Elizabeth, 298
Flaming Heart, The, 612, 615
Flamsteed, John, Reverend, 521
FLETCHER, JOHN, 281, 461, 504, 510–511, 533, 534
Fletcher, Phineas, 534
Flower, The (Herbert), 590–591
Fond Kiss, Ae, 1096
For A' That and A' That, 1091
Ford, John, 281, 441
For Elf-Disease, 56
For Elf-Shot, 56
Forget Not Yet, 295
For the Water-Elf Disease, 56
Fortunes and Misfortunes of Moll Flanders, The, 789
Four Hymns, 395
Four Zoas, The, 1098
Fragmenta Aurea, 604
Fragments of Ancient Poetry Collected in the Highlands of Scotland, 934
Frailty and Hurtfulness of Beauty, The, 297
France, England at war with (1337), 90; England at war with (1549), 270; matter of, 138–154
Francis I, King of France, 270, 296
Franklin, A, 574–575
Franklin's Prologue, The, 195
Franklin's Tale, The, discussion of, 159
Friar's Epilogue, The, 189–190
Friar's Tale, The, 190–191
Frizer, Ingram, 363
Frobisher, Martin, 389
Froissart, 169, 171, 251
Fulgens and Lucrece, 285
Fuller, Thomas, 526, 536, 631–633; biography of, 631; Milton and, 631
Full Fathom Five, 503
Funeral, The, 568

Gaelic, 9
Galen, 271
Galileo, 520, 521
Game and Playe of Chesse, 252
Gamelyn, 92, 104–113, 233
Garden, The, 694–695
Garden of Cyrus, The, 620
Garland of Laurel, A, 282, 284, 296
Garnier, 447
Garrick, David, 961
Gaunt, John of, 91, 169, 171
Gellius, Aulus, 314
Genesis, interpolation of, 14
General Prologue, The (Chaucer), 171, 172, 173–190
Geneva Bible, 538, 539

Gentle Craft, 503
Gentleman's Journal, 536
Geoffrey of Monmouth, 89, 113
George I, 844
George II, 1061
George III, 785, 1048
Get Up and Bar the Door, 238–239
GIBBONS, ORLANDO, 511
Gilbert, Sir Humphrey, 278, 389, 431
Gildas, historian, 113
Giles, 534
Giles Earle, his booke, 600
Gipsies Metamorphosed, The, 557; selection from, 560
Gipsy Songs (Jonson), 560
Glanville, Joseph, 522, 523
Glauber, Rudolph, 523
Gloucester, Duke of, 170
Goethe, 934, 1092
Goidelic, 9
Golden Book of Marcus Aurelius, The, 335
Golden Hind, 269
Golden Legend, 252
GOLDSMITH, OLIVER, 1011–1047; biography of, 1011–1012
Go, Lovely Rose, 611
Good-Morrow, The, 565–566
Good-Natured Man, The, 1018
Good Thoughts in Bad Times, 631
Good Thoughts in Worse Times, 631
Goodere, Sir Henry, 453
Good Wife, A, 573
Gorboduc, or Ferrex and Porrex, 281, 300
Gordon, George, 238
Gorgeous Gallery of Gallant Inventions, 503
Gospel According to St. Luke, The, 542–543
Gospel According to St. Matthew, The, 542
Gosse, Sir Edmund, 739
Gosson, Stephen, 278
Government, British, sixteenth-century, 270
Gower, John, 91, 92, 171, 227, 252, 284
Grace Abounding to the Chief of Sinners, 704
GRAY OF READING, 511
GRAY, THOMAS, 535, 787, 911–923, 934, 1012, 1078; biography of, 911–912
Great Bible, The, 538–539
Great Charter, 88
Green Grow the Rashes, 1082
GREENE, ROBERT, 278, 279, 281, 460, 511–513

Gregory, Pope, 12, 65, 86
Grettir the Strong, 16
Greville, Fulke, 350, 351, 394, 447, 531
Grey, Lord, 394
Grimm, Jacob, ballad and, 222
Grindal, William, 321
Groatsworth of Wit, 460
Grocyn, 285
Guardian, The, 696
Guevara, 335
Guilds, medieval, 88
Gulliver's Travels, 803–828
Gull's Hornbook, The, 278, 441–446
Guthrum, 15
Guy of Warwick, 95

Habeas Corpus Act (1679), 529–530
Hadrian, 13
Hag, The, 596–597
HAKLUYT, RICHARD, 278, **389–394**, 531; biography of, 389
Hall, Edward, 278
Hall, Joseph, 279, 572
Hamilton, Gavin, 1085
Hamilton, Marquis of, 604
Hamlet, 3, 461, 595
Hampton, John, 6, 521, 527, 610
Handel, 520
Hanseatic League, 93
Hariot, Thomas, 431
Hark, Hark! The Lark, 502
Harmony of the Church, The, 453
Harold Godwinson King of England, 85
Harrison, William, Reverend, 329
Harvard College, 528
Harvard, John, 524
Harvey, Dr. William, 523
Harvey, Gabriel, 394
Hastings, battle of, 85
Hastings, Warren, 1048
Hathaway, Anne, 460
Havelock the Dane, 95
Hawkins, Sir John, 278, 389
Head of Several Proceedings in the Parliament, or Diurnal Occurrences, 536
Heaven and Hell, 1106
Helmont, Van, 523
Hengist, 10
Henrietta Ann, Princess, 631
Henrietta Maria, Queen, 527, 608, 612, 696
Henry I, 87
Henry II, 87, 147
Henry IV, 329
Henry V, 93, 329
Henry VI, 363
Henry VII, 270, 282

Henry VIII, 11, 269, 270, 272, 282, 285, 296, 297, 461, 538, 784
Henry, O., Malory compared with, 250
Henryson, 93
Henslow, Philip, 441, 556
Heptameron, 314
HERBERT, GEORGE, 531, 535, 568, **587–591**, 592, 598, 610, 612, 634; biography of, 587–588
Herbert, Magdalen, 587
Herbert, William, 447
Herder, 934
Hero and Leander, 271, 364–369, 400
Heroical Epistles, 453
Heroic poetry, early, 11–12
Heroic Stanzas, 725
HERRICK, ROBERT, 529, 532, 534, 557, 588, **592–600**, 633; biography of, 592–593
Her Triumph, 561
Hesketh, Lady, Cowper's letter to, 1074–1075
Hesperides, 592, 593–598
Heylin, Dr. Peter, 631
Heywood, John, 239
Heywood, Thomas, 281
Hickes, George, 16
Highland Mary, 1090–1091
Hind and the Panther, The, 726
Hind Horn, 226–227
Hirdeboc, 65
His Content in the Country, 596
His Excuse for Loving, 561
His Golden Locks, 515
His Grange, or Private Wealth, 597
His Litany to the Holy Spirit, 598
His Pilgrimage, 434
His Prayer to Ben Jonson (Herrick), **595**
Historiae adversum Paganos, 66
Historia Regum Britanniæ, 113
Histories of the Kings of Britain, 89
History, Bede on, 62; sixteenth-century literature on, 277–279; seventeenth-century, 526–531
History of Colonel Jack, The, 789
History of Henry VII (Bacon), 544
History of Jason, 252
History of Rasselas, Prince of Abissinia, 781, 961, **962–1006**
History of Richard the Third, 285
History of the Earth and Animated Nature, 1012
History of the Holy Ward, 631
History of the Royal Society, 537
History of the University of Cambridge, The, 631

History of the World, 432, 536
History of the Worthies of England, The, 631, **632–633**
Hitopadesha, 171
Hobbe, 536
Hobbes, 524
HOBY, SIR THOMAS, 276, **305–313**; biography of, 305
Hoccleve, 93
HOLINSHED, RAPHAEL, 278, **329–335**; biography of, 329
Holy Nativity of Our Lord God, The, 614–615, 640
Holy Sonnets (Donne), **568–569**
Holy State and the Profane State, The, 631
Holy War, The, 704
Holy Willie's Prayer, 1085–1086
Homer, Pope translating, 872
Honest Whore, The, 441
Honorius, 10
Hooke, Robert, 523
Hooker, John, 329
Hooker, Richard, 329, 634
Horace, 277
Horsa, 10
Hotson, Leslie, 363
House of Fame, The, 169, 170, 171
Howard, Frances, 573
Howard, John, 782
Howard, Lady Elizabeth, 725
Howard, Lady Margaret, 606
Howard, Sir Robert, 534, 725
Howell, James, 527
How Soon Hath Time, 644
Human Abstract, The, 1104
Humanism, 93, 276
Humanists, science inhibited by, 271
HUME, TOBIAS, 513
Hundred Years' War, 90, 163
Hunt, Leigh, Malory compared with, 250
Huntington, Countess of, 786
Husband's Message, The, 12
Huxley, Aldous, 285
Hydrotaphia: Urn Burial, 620, **627–630**
Hymn before Sunrise in the Vale of Chamouni, 898
Hymn on the Nativity of My Saviour, A, 560–561
Hymn on the Seasons, A (Thomson), **898–899**
Hymn to Adversity, 915
Hymn to the Name and Honour of the Admirable Saint Teresa, 612

Iberians, 9
Idea's Mirrour, 453, 454–455
Idea: The Shepherd's Garland, 453

GENERAL INDEX

Idler, 961
If Music and Sweet Poetry Agree, 505
Il Cortegiano, 276, 305
Iliad, *Beowulf* compared with, 17; Pope translating, 872
Il Penseroso, 194, 639, 644, **646–649**
Indian Emperor, The, 725, 726
Indifferent, The, 564–565
Induction, 300, 301–304
Induction and Complaint of the Duke of Buckingham, 300
Infant Joy, 1103
Introduction (to *Songs of Innocence*, by Blake), **1100–1101**
Inventions, seventeenth-century, 523
Ireton, 529
Irish Church, early, 12–13

Jack and Joan, 506
James I, 273, 453, 526, 544, 557, 558, 573, 592
James II, 531, 610, 718, 726, 775, 776, 786; Bible and, 538; reign of, 530–531
James V, 236
James's Queen, Anne of Denmark, 448
Jeffreys, Judge, 530
Jerusalem, 1098
Jew of Malta, The, 364
Johan Johan the Husband, 239
John Anderson My Jo, 1089
John de Reeve, 138
Johnie Armstrong, 236–237
John, King, 87, 88
Johnson, Esther, 830
JOHNSON, SAMUEL, 779, 784, 785, 787, 923, 961–1011, 1012; biography of, 961–962; Boswell on, 939–961; poetry discussed by, 781
Jolly Beggars, The, 1092–1096
Jones, Inigo, 557
JONSON, BEN, 277, 279, 448, 521, 532–535, **556–563**, 575, 592, 593, 595, 596, 602, 604; Bacon discussed by, 544; biography of, 556–557; Malory compared with, 250; play of, 557
Journal, 389
Journal of the Plague Year, 789
Journal to Stella, 830–834
Jovious, Paulus, 447
Judith, 16
Juliana, 14
Julius Caesar (from *Plutarch's Lives*), 335, **336–342**
Juvenal, 961

Keats, John, 2, 3, 577, 578, 898, 928
Kemp Owyne, 227–228
Ken, Thomas, Bishop, 634
Kepler, 520, 521
Kildare, Earl of, 298
King, Edward, 650
King Edwin's Conversion, 62–63
King Henry the Fourth, First Part, 465–500
King Horn, 90, 96–104, 226
King John, 329
King Lear, 329, 462, 600
King's Book, 575
King's Hunt Is Up, The, 511
King William, 82–83
Kittredge, George Hyman, 221
Klaeber, Friedrich, on *Beowulf*, 16–17
Knight's Tale, The, 170
Knox, John, 272
Kyd, Thomas, 281, 363

Labor, Black Death and, 90
La Cuisse Rompue, 351
Lady, Have Ruth on Me, 157
Lady of May, The, 350
Lai le Freine, 147
L'Allegro, 639, **644–646**
Lamb, Charles, 577, 631, 697; Congreve discussed by, 739; on Wither, 569
Lamb, The, 1101
La mort d'un chêne, 1069
Lanfranc, 86, 87
Languet, Hubert, 350
"Lanval," 228
Laprade, Victor de, 1069
Large, Robert, 252
Latimer, 272
Latinism, 781; seventeenth-century, 537
Laud, Archbishop, 527, 528
Laudonnière, René de, 389
Laughing Song, 1102
Lawes, Henry and William, 592
Lawman, 89, 251
Lay a Garland on My Hearse, 510
Layamon, 89, 251
Lay of Sir Orfeo, The, 147–152
Lays (poetry), 147
Lays, Breton, 147
Legend of Good Women, 170
Leicester, Earl of, 273, 335, 350, 394, 431
Lenten Is Come with Love to Town, 158
Letter of Alexander to Aristotle, The, 16
Letters (Cowper), **1072–1076**
Letters Concerning the English Nation, 531

Letters to His Son, 867–871
Letters to Richard West (Gray), **920–923**
Letter to a Friend, A (Browne), 620
Let the Bells Ring, 510
Leviathan, 536
Liberalism, 531
Lie, The, 433–434
Life and Death of Mr. Badman, The, 704
Life and Strange Adventures of Robinson Crusoe, The, 789
Life of Cowley, 697
Life of Dr. John Donne (Walton), 566, 634
Life of Henry V, 465
Life of Samuel Johnson, The, 939, 940–961
Linacre, Thomas, 93, 274, 285
Lines Printed under the Engraved Portrait of Milton, 731
Litany in Time of Plague, 514
Literature, fifteenth-century, 93–94; sixteenth-century, 269–517; seventeenth-century, 531–533; eighteenth-century, 775–1112; approach to, 1–7; Celtic, 147; "completeness" in, 532; during Renaissance, 276–277; English vs. American, 4; Humanism and, 94; Jean Bodel's classification of, 95; materials for, 3; Middle English, 89–90; music and, 2; pamphlet, 278; romantic, 95; science and, 532; wording in, 3
Little Black Boy, The, 1101
Lives (Plutarch), 335
Lives (Walton), 634
Lives of the Poets, 697, 961
Lives of the Saints, 68
Locke, 521, 524, 525, 536
LODGE, THOMAS, 104, 279, 281, 503, 513
London (Blake), 961, **1104**
London, medieval, 88; sixteenth-century, 269–270
Lord Randal, 222, 225
Louis XIV, 521, 529, 775
Love, as theme of romances, 95
Love (Herbert), **590**
Love for Love, 739
Love Message, A, 160–161
LOVELACE, RICHARD, 535, 604, **608–609**; biography of, 608
Loveliest Lady in the Land, The, 158–159
Lover Compareth His State to a Ship in Perilous Storm Tossed on the Sea, The, 294

Lover for Shamefastness Hideth His Desire within His Faithful Heart, The, 294
Lover's Confession, The, 92
Lover Showeth how He Is Forsaken of Such as He Sometime Enjoyed, The, 294
Love's Labour's Lost, 460
Love's Riddle, 696
Lowell, James Russell, 531
Lucan, 364
Lucas, Sir Charles, 608
Lucasta, 608
Lutheranism, 272
Lycidas, 639, **650–653**
Lydgate, John, 93, 252, 284, 300
Lying Lover, 844
LYLY, JOHN, 278, 281, 300, **342–350**, 432; biography of, 342–343
Lyly, William, 274
Lyrical Ballads (Wordsworth), 787, 1078
Lyrics, sixteenth-century, 279–280; seventeenth-century, 532; Blake's, 1097–1098; Carew's, 602; Elizabethan, 503–517; Herrick's, 592; Jonson's, 534, 557; Middle English, 156–162; prose (essay), 536; Wither's, 570; Wyatt's, 293.

Macaronic poetry, 161
Macaulay, Thomas Babington, 939
Macbeth, 329
Machaut, 169, 171
MACPHERSON, JAMES, **934–939**; biography of, 934
Mad Maid's Song, The, 595
Mad Song, 1100
Magna Carta, 88
Magnificence, 282
"Maid Freed from the Gallows, The," 222
MALORY, SIR THOMAS, **250–265**; biography of, 250–252
Manciple's Prologue, The, 218–219
Manciple Tale, The, 219
Mandrake, The, 57
Man of Law's Epilogue, The, 187–189, 203
Man of Law's Prologue, The, 185–187
Man of Law's Tale, The, 192
Man of Life Upright, The, 507
Margaret, Duchess of Burgundy, 252
Marguerite of Navarre, Queen, 314
Marie de France, 147, 228
Marino, 612
Marlborough, Duke of, 775, 844

MARLOWE, CHRISTOPHER, 271, 281, **363–388**, 400, 432, 453, 465, 533, 557; biography of, 363–364
Marot, 394
Marriage of Heaven and Hell, 1106–1111
Marston, John, 279
Martial, 297
"Martin Marprelate" pamphlets, 278
Martyr, Peter, 389
MARVELL, ANDREW, 529, 532, 534, 535, 537, **693–696**; biography of, 693–694; Milton and, 693
Mary II, reign of, 530
Mary Hamilton, 237–238
Mary Morison, 1096–1097
Mary, Queen of Scots, 270, 272, 273, 343
Masefield, John, 4, 6
Massinger, Philip, 281, 441
Matchless Maiden, The, 161
Matilda, 453
Mead, 54
Measure for Measure, 461
Meat without Mirth, 595
Medicine, seventeenth-century, 523
Medwall, Henry, 285
Melancholy, 510
Memoirs of a Cavalier, 789
Memorial of Such Princes as Since the Time of King Richard the Second Have Been Unfortunate in the Realm of England, A, 300
Merchant of Venice, The, 500
Merchant's Epilogue, The, 194
Merchant's Prologue, The, 193
Mercurius Politicus, 634
Meres, Francis, 454
Merton College, 89
Meter, definition of, 1113; Drayton's, 454; literary, 2; Skeltonic, 282; Tudor poetry and, 279; "Methodism," 786
Methought I Saw, 654
Michelangelo, 271
Michelet, 271
Microcosmography, 575–577
Micrographia, 523
Microscope, invention of, 520
Midas (Lyly), 342, 343
Middle classes, Chaucer describing life of, 92
Middle English drama, 239–250
Middle English lyrics, 156–162
Middle English pronunciation, 155
Middleton, Thomas, 281
Mileham, Dorothy, 619
Milkmaid's Mother's Answer, The (Walton), **638**

Milkmaid's Song, The (Walton), **638**
Miller's Prologue, The, 183–184
Milton (Blake), 1098, **1106**
MILTON, JOHN, 1, 2, 4, 6, 194, 271, 520, 521, 524–534, 592, **639–692**, 697, 731, 739, 928, 1069, 1083; biography of, 639–640; Fuller and, 631; Marvell and, 693; poetry of, 535–536
Minshull, Elizabeth, 640
Mirabeau, 531
Mirandola, Pico della, 285
Mirour de l'Omme, 91
Mirror for Magistrates, A, 300, 447, 449
Mirror of Man, 91
Mirrour of the World, 252
Misfortunes of Arthur, The, 281
"Mississippi Bubble," 785
Mistress Susanna Southwell, upon Her Feet, 595
Mistress, The, 697
Mixed Contemplations in Better Times, 631
Modest Proposal, A, 789, 803, **840–843**
Monasteries, dissolution of, 275
Monk's Prologue, The, 207–208
Monmouth, Duke of, 529, 530
Monmouth, Rebellion of, 530
Montagu, Charles, 739
Montagu, Sir Edward, 717
Montaigne, 335
Montemayor, 504
Montesquieu, 786
Monteverde, 520
Moor, Marston, 531
Moral Philosophy of Doni, The, 335
More, Anne, 564
More, Henry, 522, 524
MORE, SIR THOMAS, 269, 274, **285–292**, 300; biography of, 285
Morison, Sir Thomas, 321
Morley, Henry, 503
Morris, William, 171
Morte Darthur, Le, 250, 251, **252–265**
Mortimeriades, 453, 454
Morton, John, Cardinal, 285
Mother Badger, 54
Mother Bombie, 342
Mother Hubbard's Tale, 395
Mourning Bride, The, 739
Much Ado about Nothing, 269, 460
Muiopotmos, or, The Fate of the Butterfly, 395
Mulcaster, Richard, 394
MUNDAY, ANTHONY, **513–514**
Municipalities, medieval, 88

GENERAL INDEX

Murillo, 521
Musaeus, 364
Muses' Elisium, The, 454
Music, Johnson defining, 779; literature and, 2
Musophilus, or, Defence of All Learning, 447
My Mind to Me a Kingdom Is, 509–510
My Sweetest Lesbia, 507
My True-Love Hath My Heart, 352

Narrative, medieval, 92
Naseby, 531
Nashe, Thomas, 364, **514**
Neo-Platonism, 65, 276
Nennius, historian, 113
Never Love Unless You Can, 506
New Atlantis, 523, 531, 544, 551–556
New Chronicles of England and of France, 278
New College, 89
New Instrument, The, 544
Newman, 7
News from Hell Brought by the Devil's Career, 441
Newspaper, history of, 536
Newton, John, Rev., Cowper's letter to, 1073
Newton, Sir Isaac, 521, 522, 1048
Night-Piece, to Julia, The, 596
Noble Numbers, 592, 598–600
Noctes Atticae, 314
Normandy, Scandinavians seizing, 85
Norman Conquest, 68, 81; England after, 85–94
Normans, strategy of, 86
Northampton, Marchioness of, 305
North, Roger, 335
North, Sir Thomas, **335–342**; biography of, 335
Norwegians, Britain invaded by, 14
Notable History Concerning Four Voyages Made by Certain French Captains unto Florida, A, 389
Novel, Goldsmith's, 1012; Lyly's, 342; of Restoration, 536–537; seventeenth-century, 536
Novella, 314
Novelle (Sercambi), 171
Novum Organum, 521, 544
Nowell, Lawrence, 16
Now Springs the Spray, 156–157
Nun's Priest's Prologue, The, 208–209
Nun's Priest's Tale, The, 209–216
Nurse's Song, 1102–1103

Nymph's Disdain of Love, A, 504
Nymph's Reply to the Shepherd, The, 432–433

Oberon (Jonson), 557
Oblivion, Act of, 529
Observations upon the State of the Seventeen Provinces, 573
Observatory, Greenwich, founding of, 521
Ocean to Cynthia, The, 432
October (Spenser), 395–399
Ode (Collins), 926
Ode, definition of, 1118
Ode for Him, An (Jonson; by Herrick), 596
Ode: Intimations of Immortality from Recollections of Early Childhood, 616, 617
Ode on a Distant Prospect of Eton College, 912–913
Ode on the Death of Mr. Thomson, 927
Odes on Several Descriptive and Allegoric Subjects, 923
Ode to Evening (Collins), **924–925**
Ode to Himself, An (Jonson), **561–562**
Ode to Simplicity, 923–924
Odyssey, Beowulf compared with, 17
Of A' the Airts, 1089
Of Death (Bacon), 545, **546**
Of English Verse, 610
Offa, 11
Of Great Place, 545, **548–549**
Of Love, 545, **547–548**
Of Marriage and Single Life, 545, **546–547**
Of One That Is so Fair and Bright, 161–162
Of Studies, 550–551
Of the Courtier's Life, 279, **295–296**
Of the Death of Sir T. W. the Elder, 298–299
Of the Last Verses in the Book, 610, 611
Of the Mean and Sure Estate, 279
Of Travel, 545, **549–550**
Of Truth, 545–546
Old Bachelor, The, 739
Old English Era, 9–84
Old English Chronicles, The, 65, 81–84
Old English Version of Bede's Ecclesiastical History of the English People, 62
Old Fortunatus, 441
Olor Iscanus, 616
O Mistress Mine, 502
On a Girdle, 610, **611**

On Conciliation with America, 1048
On Education, 639
One-eyed Garlic Seller, 55
On My First Daughter, 558
On My First Son, 558
On Shakespeare (Milton), **644**
On the Artificial Comedy of the Last Century, 739
On the Education of Children, 275, 343
On the Late Massacre in Piemont, 653
On the Morning of Christ's Nativity, 639, 640–644
On the Receipt of My Mother's Picture out of Norfolk, 1076–1077
On the Union, 558
On Time (Milton), **649**
Oratorical Education, 275
Oroonoko, or The Royal Slave, 536
Orosius, Paulus, 65, 66
Ossianic poems, 934
Oswald, King, 13
Oswy, King, 13
Our Goodman, 238
Où sont les neiges d'antan?, 57
Overbury, Sir Thomas, **572–575**; biography of, 572–573
Over Hill, over Dale, 501
Ovid, 300
O, Wert Thou in the Cauld Blast, 1097
Oxenbridge, John, Rev., 693
Oxford University, medieval, 89
Oyster, 55

"Pageant," medieval, 92
Painter, William, **314–320**; biography of, 314
Painters, seventeenth-century, 521
Palace of Pleasure, The, 314–320
Palamon and Arcite, 170, 171
Palotto, Cardinal, 612
Pamphlet, sixteenth-century, 278; seventeenth-century, 536–537; Dekker's, 441
Pap with a Hatchet, 343
Paradise Lost, 6, 52, 520, 640, **654–683,** 731; discussion, 654; Dryden rewritings, 766
Paradise of Dainty Devises, 503
Paradise Regained, 640
Pardoner's Prologue, The, 196–197
Pardoner's Tale, The, 168, **197–203**
Paris and Oenone, 514–515
Parker, Archbishop, 363
Parliament of Fowls, The, 170
Parliament, sixteenth-century, 270

1131

GENERAL INDEX

Parson's Prologue, The, 220
Parson's Tale, The, 220
Particular Discourse Covering Western Discoveries, A, 389
Passionate Shepherd to His Love, The, 364, 432
Passions: An Ode for Music, The, 925–926
Pastons, 93
Pastoral Care, 65
Pastoral of Phillis and Coryden, A, 505
Pater, 7
Patience, 114
Patient Grissill, 447
Pauchatantra, 171
Peace (Vaughan), 617
Peachem, Henry, 503, 532
Pearl, The, 114
Peasants' Revolt, 90, 91, 163
Pease, Tristram, 395
PEELE, GEORGE, 514–515
Pembroke, Countess of, 279
Pembroke, Earl of, 350, 363, 447, 575
Pen and Three Fingers, 54
Penn, 521
PEPYS, SAMUEL, 232, 521, 717–725; biography of, 717–718
Percy, Bishop, 600, 1012
Percy, Elinor, 296
Perfect Diurnal, 634
Persian Eclogues, 923
Peter the Great, 521
Petition of Right (1628), 531
Petrarch, 169, 192, 280, 293, 351, 395
Pharsalia, 364
Philip II, 270, 351
Philip IV, 90
Philip Sparrow, 282
"Philosophical or Invisible College," 523
Philosophy, Alfred's, 65; Bacon's, 544; seventeenth-century, 520, 523–524
Philotas, 448
Phoenix Nest, The, 503
Physician's Epilogue, The, 195–196
Physician's Tale, The, discussion of, 195
Physics, sixteenth-century developments in, 271
Pickering, Sir Gilbert, 725
Picts, 10
Piers Gaveston, 453
Piers Plowman. See *Vision of William Concerning Piers the Plowman, The*
Pilgrim's Progress, The, 525, 536, 537, 704, 705–717; 740

Pillar of Fame, The, 588, 598
Pindaric Ode, A, 562
Plain and Easy Introduction to Practical Music, 503
Plain Man's Pathway to Heaven, The, 704
Play, Congreve's, 739; Dekker's, 441; Dryden's, 725; Elizabethan, 280–281; Goldsmith's, 1012, 1017; Jonson's, 557; Lyly's, 342; Marlowe's, 364; medieval dramatic, 239; seventeenth-century, 533–534; Shakespeare's, 460–461
Playford, John, 600
Plato, 276, 285
Platonism, "Cambridge," 524; Spenser's, 394–395
Plutarch, 275, 343; North translating, 335
Plutarch's Lives (North), 336–342
Poems Lyrical and Pastoral, 454
Poems (Vaughan), 532
Poetaster, The, 557
Poetical Blossoms, 696
Poetic forms and patterns, 1113–1120
Poetical Sketches (Blake), 1098–1100
Poetry, sixteenth-century, 279–280; seventeenth-century, 534–535; eighteenth-century, 780–781; Burns's, 1078; Carew's, 602, 694; Cavalier, 604, 608; Celtic, 147; Christian, 13–14; Daniel's, 447; Donne's, 564; Drayton's, 454; Goldsmith's, 1012; heroic, early, 11–12; Herrick's, 592; Johnson's, 961; Jonson's, 557; macaronic, 161; "metaphysical," 535, 602, 693; Old English, 12; Ossianic, 934; Pope's, 871–872; romantic, 95–154; Shakespeare's, 460; Sidney's, 350–351; Skelton's, 282; Suckling's, 604; Surrey's, 297; Thomson's, 897–898; Wyatt's, 293
Poins, John, 295
Poitiers, battle at, 90
Pollaiuolo, 271
Poly-Olbion, 454
Pontoux, Claude de, 453
POPE, ALEXANDER, 521, 610, 739, 778–780, 783, 785, 787, 789, 803, 871–897, 961, 1061; biography of, 871–872
Poplar-Field, The, 1071
Popular ballad, 221–239
Postbag, 536
Pound, Dean, 528
Powell, Mary, 640

Praise of Folly, The, 269, 285
Preface to Shakespeare, The, 1007–1011
Preface to the Fables, 735–738
Presbyterianism, 272; seventeenth-century, 527–529
Priest to the Temple, A, 587
Princess, The, 602
Principal Voyages, Traffics, and Discoveries of the English Nation, 278, 389, 390–394
Printing, early, 273
Prioress's Prologue, The, 203–204
Prioress's Tale, The, 88, 169, 204–206
Prisoned in Windsor, He Recounteth His Pleasure There Passed, 299
Proctor, Thomas, 503
Progress of Poesy, The, 915–917
Prologue to Melibee, The, 206–207
Prologue to Sir Thopas, The, 206
Promise of a Constant Lover, The, 505
Pronunciation, Middle English, 155
"Prophetic Books" (Blake), 1098
Proposition for the Advancement of Experimental Philosophy, 697
Prose, sixteenth-century, 277–279; seventeenth-century, 535–537; eighteenth-century, 780–781; Burke's, 1048; Dekker's, 441; essay, 536; Johnson's, 961–962; Macpherson's, 934; More's, 285; "poetic," 537
Protestantism, established in England, 530; rise of, 270
Psalter, The, 541–542
Pseudodoxia Epidemica, or Vulgar Errors, 522, 620
Pulley, The, 589
Purcell, Henry, 520
Puritanism, 272, 273; Marvell and, 693; religious, 526; Spenser's, 395
Puritan revolt, 526
Purity, 114
Puttenham, 277, 431
Pym, 6, 521, 527
Pythias of Marseilles, 9

Queen and Huntress, 559
Quiet of Mind, 293
Quintilian, 275
Quip, The, 589

Rake, 54
RALEGH, SIR WALTER, 276, 278, 389, 394, 395, 431–440, 520, 521, 535, 557; biography of, 431–432; Sidney compared with, 431

GENERAL INDEX

Raleigh's School of Atheism, 363, 432
Ralph the Collier, 138–147
Rambler, 961
Rape of Lucrece, The, 365, 460
Rape of the Lock, The, 885–893
Rasselas. See *History of Rasselas, Prince of Abissinia*.
Realism, Chaucer's, 171
Recueil des histoires de Troyes, Le, 252
Recuyell of the Historyes of Troye, 252
Reed, 55
References, Early Period, 266; sixteenth century, 516; seventeenth century, 773; eighteenth century, 1111
Reflections on the Revolution in France, 1048, **1049–1060**
Reformation, developments during, 271–273
Reign of Stephen, The, 83–84
Rejoice in the Lamb, 928, **932–934**
Religio Laici, 726
Religio Medici, 620–627
Religion, Charles I and, 527; politics and, 527–531
Religiques of Ancient English Poetry, 600
Relique, The, 568
Rembrandt, 521
Renaissance, course of, 269–271; economic decline during, 271; English, 93; literature during, 276–277
Replication against Certain Young Scholars, 282
Report and Discourse of the Affairs and State of Germany, The, 321
Report of the Truth of the Fight About the Isles of Açores This Last Summer Betwixt the *Revenge*, One of Her Majesty's Ships, and an Armada of the King of Spain, 435–440
Republic (Plato), 285
Restoration, drama of, 533; novel of, 536–537
Retraction (Chaucer), **220**
Retreat, The, 616, **617**
Reve's Prologue, The, 184–185
Review (newspaper), 788
Revolution (1688–89), 530; French, 531; industrial, 530; Settlement of *1689*, 786; social, 531
"Rex totius Britanniae," 15
Reynard the Fox, 252
Reynolds, Sir Joshua, 1012
Rhetoric, eighteenth-century, 779–780
Rhyme, Surrey's, 297; Tudor poetry and, 279; Wyatt's, 293

Rhythm, in literature, 2; Surrey's, 297
Richard I, 88
Richard II, 163, 170, 329, 364
Richard III, 329, 460
Richelieu, 521
Richmond, Duke of, 296
Riddles, 53, **54–55**
Rivers, Lord, 252
Robert, Duke of Normandy, 453
Robin Hood and Guy of Gisborne, 233–236
Robinson Crusoe. See *Life and Strange Adventures of Robinson Crusoe*.
Robinson, Ralph, 286
Rochester, Viscount (Carr), 573
Romances, 95–154; history of, 95; Middle English, 91
Roman de la Rose, 163, 169, 171, 195
Romans, Britain invaded by, 10
Romanticism, 912; eighteenth-century, 782–784
Romaunt of the Rose, The. See *Roman de la Rose*.
Romeo and Juliet, 314
Romeo and Julietta, 314–320
Rome the Great, 95
Rondeau, definition of, 1117
Rosalynde (Lodge), 104, 279
Rosalynde's Madrigal, 513
Rousseau, J. J., 536
Roxana, 789
Royal Society of London for Promoting Natural Knowledge, 521
Rubens, 521
Ruin, The, 12
Rule for Anchoresses, The, 90

Sacharissa, 610
Sacheverell, Lucy, 608
SACKVILLE, THOMAS, EARL OF DORSET, **300–304**; biography of, 300
Sackville, Sir Richard, 321
Sad Shepherd, The, selection from, 560
St. Augustine of Hippo, 65, 66
Saint Cuthbert, 68–73
Saint-Gelais, 293
Salisbury, Bishop of (Earle), 575
Salzburg Tales, 171
Samson Agonistes, 640
Sanderson, Robert, Bishop, 634
Sandwich, Earl of, 717
Sannazaro, 293, 504
Sanscrit, 171
Sappho and Phao, 343
Satire, fourteenth-century, 91; sixteenth-century, 279; eighteenth-century, 777; Dryden's, 726; Skelton's, 282; Swift's, 802; Wither's, 569–570; Wyatt's, 293

Saxons, Britain invaded by, 10
Say, Lovely Dream, 611
Scandinavians, Normandy seized by, 85
Scarlatti, Alexander, 520
Scarlatti, Domenico, 520
Schoolmaster, The, 275, **321–328,** 335
School of Abuse, The, 278, 350
Schools, medieval, 88–89
Science, Humanism inhibiting, 271; seventeenth-century, 521, 522, 532
Scotland, Charles I at war with, 527
Scots, Wha Hae, 1089–1090
Scourge of Villainy, The, 279
Scriblerus Club, 871
Seafarer, The, 12, 14, 57
Seasons, The (Thomson), 897, 902
Second Defence of the People of England, 683
Second Nun's Tale, The, 216
Second Play of the Shepherds, The, 239–250
Secular Masque, 726
Selden, John, 528
Sense, devices of, 1120
Separatism, 273
Sephestia's Song to Her Child, 511–512
Sercambi, 171
Sermo Lupi ad Anglos, 77, **78–80**
Sermons (Donne), 634
Sermon to the English, 77, **78–80**
Seven Deadly Sins of London, The, 441
Seven Penitential Psalms, 293
Seven Sages of Rome, The, 171
Several Discourses by Way of Essays, in Verse and Prose, 697–704
Shaftesbury, Earl of, 726; first, 529
SHAKESPEARE, WILLIAM, 1, 3, 4, 6, 104, 269, 271, 278–281, 314, 329, 335, 342, 364, 365, 453, **460–503,** 504, 520, 532–534, 538, 551, 644, 725, 783, 961, 1007, 1077; biography of, 460–461
Shelley, 1, 6, 7, 1061
Shelton, Thomas, 718
Shepheardes Calender, The, 282, 394, **395–399,** 453
Shepherd's Book, 65
Shepherd's Hunting, The, 569
Shepherds' Play (first), 239
Shepherd's Sirena, The, 454
Shepherd's Song of Venus and Adonis, The, 508–509
Shepherd's Wife's Song, The, 512
She Stoops to Conquer, 1017–1047
Shipman's Epilogue, The, 203
Shipman's Prologue, The, 203

Shipman's Tale, The, discussion of, 203
Shirley, James, 281
Shoemaker's Holiday, The, 281, 441
Shortest Way with the Dissenters, 789, **792–798**
Sidney, Lady Dorothy, 610
Sidney, Mary, 447
SIDNEY, SIR PHILIP, 276, 278, **350–363**, 394, 432, 447, 503, 575; biography of, 350–351; Ralegh compared with, 431
Siege of Rhodes, The, 533
Sigh No More, 502
Signs of Death, 161
Silex Scintillans, 616
Silver Swan, The, 511
Silures, 616
Sir Gawain and the Green Knight, 91, **114–138,** 152
Sir Launfal, 147
Sir Orfeo. See *Lay of Sir Orfeo, The.*
Sir Patrick Spens, 230
Sir Thomas Overbury His Wife . . . and Divers More Characters, 573–575
Sir Thopas. See *Tale of Sir Thopas.*
Sir Walter Raleigh (Fuller), 632
Sixteenth century, literature of, 269–517
Six-text Edition of the Chaucer Society, 172
SKELTON, JOHN, **282–284**; biography of, 282
Skeltonics, 282
Skinner, Cyriack, 653
Slavery, eighteenth-century, 782
Sleep, 510
Slow, Slow, Fresh Fount, 559
SMART, CHRISTOPHER, 782, 912, **928–934**; biography of, 928
Smith, John, 524, 718
Society, class spirit and, 526; "town," 777–778
Soliloquies, 65
Solomon's House, 551–556
Somerset, Earl of, 272; (Carr), 573
Some Thoughts Concerning Education, 525
Song, A (Carew), **603**
Song by Fairies, 350
Song (Blake), **1099–1100**
Song (Donne), **564, 566–567**
Song (Suckling), **605**
Song from Shakespeare's Cymbeline, A, 926–927
Song of Roland, 95
Songs (Lyly), **349–350**
Songs and Sonnets (Donne), 293, 297, 503, **564–568**

Songs from Shakespeare's Plays, 500–503
Songs from the Plays and Masques, 559–560
Songs of Experience, 1098, **1103–1104**
Songs of Innocence, 1098, **1100–1103**
Song: To Celia, 560
Song to David, A, 928–932
Sonnet, definition of, 1116; Daniel's, 447
Sonnet (Gray), **915**
Sonnets (Milton), **653–654**
Sonnets (Shakespeare), **461–464**
Sonnets (Surrey), **297–298**
Sonnets (Wyatt), **293–294**
Sound, devices of, 1119
SOUTHWELL, ROBERT, 515
Sovereign, Parliament controlled by, 270
Spacious Firmament on High, The, 898
Spain, England defeating, 270
Spanish Tragedy, The, 363
Sparking Flint, The, 616
Speak, Parrot, 282
Spectator (newspaper), 789
***Spectator, The,* 844, 848–866,** 1018
Spencer, Lord, 271, 610
SPENSER, EDMUND, 2, 7, 280, 282, **394–431**, 432, 448, 453, 503, 564, 592, 696, 902; biography of, 394–395; on Sidney's death, 351; verse of, 534
Spenser, Gabriel, 556
Spens, Sir Patrick, 222, 223
Sprat, Dr. Thomas, 537
Spring, the Sweet Spring, 514
Squire's Epilogue, The, 194–195
Squire's Tale, The, discussion of, 194
STANHOPE, PHILIP DORMER, EARL OF CHESTERFIELD, **866–871**; biography of, 866
Stanyhurst, Richard, 329
Stanza, forms of, 1114
State of Innocence, The, 726
Statute of Laborer (1849), 90
Stead, Christina, 171
STEELE, RICHARD, **844–866,** 962; Addison and, 844; biography of, 844
Stephen, King, 87
Steps to the Temple, 588, 612
Stewart, James, 238
Still to Be Neat, 560, 593
Storm on Land, 54
Strafford, Earl of, 527
Strange, Lord, 363
Stubbes, Philip, 278
Succession, Act of (1536), 272

SUCKLING, SIR JOHN, 535, 557, **604–607**; biography of, 604
Suffolk, Duke of, 293
Summoner's Prologue, The, 190–191
Summoner's Tale, The, 191–192
Sunderland, Earl of, 610
Superstition, seventeenth-century, 522
Supremacy, Act of, 273
Surrey, Countess of, 284
SURREY, HENRY HOWARD, EARL OF, **296–299,** 300
Swallows, 54
Swan of the Usk, The, 616
Swedenborg, Emanuel, 1097, 1106
Sweet Are the Thoughts, 512
Sweet William would a wooing ride, 230
Sweyn, 77
SWIFT, JONATHAN, 521, 739, 780, 783, 789, **802–843,** 898; biography of, 802–803
Swinburn, 7
Symposium (Plato), 276, 305

Take, Oh, Take Those Lips Away, 502
"Tale of Florent," 227
Tale of Sir Thopas, 152
Tales of a Wayside Inn, 171
Tamburlaine, 363, 364
Tam O' Shanter, 1086–1088
Task, The, 1061–1069
Tatler, The, 789, 844, **845–848**
Taylor, Jeremy, Bishop, 528, 532
Telescope, invention of, 520
Tell Me Where Is Fancy Bred, 501
Temora, an Epic Poem, 934
Tempest, The, 461, 500, 531, 551
Temple, Sir William, 802
Temple, The, 588, 612
Tender Husband, 844
Tennyson, 251, 531, 786, 1048; Carew influencing, 602; on Gawain, 114
Ternery of Littles, A, 597–598
Thames Commission, Chaucer as member of, 171
Thanksgiving to God for His House, A, 599
Theater, Elizabethan, 280–281
Theatre for Voluptuous Worldlings, A, 394
Theodore of Tarsus, 13
Theophrastus, 572, 573
There Is a Garden in Her Face, 507
Thesaurus, 16

These Things Seem Wondrous, 516
They Are All Gone into the World of Light, 618
Things That Cause a Quiet Life, The, 299
'Thirty Years' War, 520
Thithrekssaga, 51
Thomas Rymer, 228-229
THOMSON, JAMES, 786, **897-911**; biography of, 897-898
Thorkelin, Grimur, 16
Though I Am Young, 560
Thoughts on Various Subjects, 828-830
Thrale, Mr., 961
Threnodia Augustalis, 731
Thrice Toss These Oaken Ashes, 506
Throgmorton, Elizabeth, 431
Tillotson, 533
Timber, or Discoveries Made upon Man and Matters, 557
Tintoretto, 350
Titian, 271
To a Lady from Whom He Received a Silver Pen, 610
To Althea, from Prison, 608-609
To a Mountain Daisy, 1081-1082
To a Mouse, 1080-1081
To Anthea, Who May Command Him Anything, 594
Tobacco, Tobacco, 513
Tom O'Bedlam's Song, 595, 600-601
To Colin Clout, 513-514
To Daffodils, 595
To Death (Herrick), 599
To Henry Reynolds, 279
To His Coy Mistress, 693, **695**
To John Donne, 558
To King James, 558
To Lucasta, Going Beyond the Seas, 609
To Lucasta, Going to the Wars, 608, 609
To Mistress Margaret Hussey, 284
To Music Bent Is My Retirèd Mind, 506
To My Book, 557
To My Most Dearly Lovèd Friend, Henry Reynolds, Esquire of Poets and Poesy, 457-459
To Penshurst, 279
Tories, forming of, 530
To Sir Henry Wotton, 279
To Spring (Blake), 1099
To the Cambro-Britons and Their Harp, His Ballad of Agincourt, 456-457

To the Evening Star (Blake), 1099
To the Immortal Memory and Friendship of That Noble Pair Sir Lucius Cary and Sir H. Morison, 562
To the Lady Margaret, Countess of Cumberland, 452-453
To the Memory of My Beloved the Author, Mr. William Shakespeare, and What He Has Left Us, 562-563
To the Memory of Sir Isaak Newton, 898, 899-902
To the Muses, 1098-1099
To the Reader, 557
To the Virginian Voyage, 455-456
To the Virgins, to Make Much of Time, 594
Tottell, 293, 297, 503
Tottells Miscellany. See *Songs and Sonnets.*
Tournament of Tottenham, The, 152-154
Tour through the Whole Island of Great Britain, 789
Town, eighteenth-century, 777-778
Toxophilus, 321
Trade guilds, medieval, 88
Tragedy, Daniel's, 447-448; Elizabethan, 280-281; seventeenth-century, 532
Tragedy of King Richard II, 465
Tragedy of King Richard III, 465
Tragical History of Dr. Faustus, The, 370-388
Travel, literature on, 278
Treatise of Moral Philosophy, 297
Triolet, definition of, 1117
Troilus and Criseyde, 92, 169-171
True Declaration of the Troublesome Voyage of M. John Hawkins to the Parts of Guina and the West Indies, 278
True Relation of the Apparition of One Mrs. Veal, A, 789, 798-802
Tryggvason, Olaf, 58, 77
Tudor, Mary, 270
Twa Corbies, The, 227
Twain, Mark, 251
Twa Sisters, The, 224-225
Twelfth Night, 460, 500
Two Gentlemen of Verona, The, 460
Two Noble Kinsmen, The, 461
Tyger, The, 1103-1104
Tyndale, William, Bible translated by, 538
Tyrannic Love, 726
Tyrone, 395

Uncle Tom's Cabin, 536
Under the Greenwood Tree, 501
Underwoods, 560-561
Uniformity, Act of, 273
Union of the Noble and Illustrate Families of Lancaster & York, 278
Universal Prayer, The, 884-885
Unquiet Grave, The, 231-232
Unwin, Mary, 1061
Unwin, William, Rev., Cowper's letter to, 1072-1073
Upon a Pipkin of Jelly Sent to a Lady, 597
Upon Julias Clothes, 597
Upon Prue, His Maid, 597
Upon a Ribbon, 603
Utopia, 285-292
Utopia of Democritus Junior, The, 582-587

Valediction Forbidding Mourning, A, 566
Van Dyck, 521
Vanity of Human Wishes, The, 961
VAUGHAN, HENRY, 532, 535, 592, **616-619,** 1103; biography of, 616
Velasquez, 521
Venus and Adonis, 271, 365, 453, 460
"Venus and the Flute Player" (painting), 271
Vere, Frances, Lady, 296
Vermeer, 521
Veronese, painter, 350
Verse, blank, definition of, 1118; Old English, 12-14
Vicar of Wakefield, The, 1012
View of the Present State of Ireland, A, 395
Villanelle, definition of, 1118
Villon, François, 57
Vinci, Leonardo da, 271
Virgidemiarum, 279
Virgil, 297, 300
Virgin Martyr, The, 441
Virtue (Herbert), **591**
Virtues of Jet, The, 56
Vision of Twelve Goddesses, The, 448
Vision of William Concerning Piers the Plowman, The, 162-168
Vision upon this Conceit of the Faerie Queene, A, 432
Vita Oswaldi, 58
Vitelli, Cornelio, 274
Voice of One Crying, The, 91
Volpone, or the Fox, 557; selection from, 559
Voltaire, 531, 739
Völundarkvitha, 51
Vox Clamantis, 91

Voyage Round the World, 1071
Voyages, Hakluyt describing, 389
Voyages of Ohthere and Wulfstan, 66–68
Voyage to Liliput, A (from *Gulliver's Travels*), **803–828**

Wace (Norman poet), 89
"Wakefield Master," 239
Waldere, 12, 13
WALLER, EDMUND, 535, **610–612**, 697; biography of, 610
Walpole, Horace, 911, 912
Walpole, Robert; Whigs headed by, 784
Walsingham, Frances, 351
Walsingham, Sir Francis, 273
Waltharius, 12
WALTON, IZAAK, 532, 536, 566, 569, 600, **633–639**, 694; biography of, 633–634
Wanderer, The, 12, **57–58**
Wanley, Humfrey, 16
Warham, Archbishop, 274
Warlock, Peter, 600
"War of the Theaters," 557
Wars of the Roses, 93
Waterfall, The, 619
Way of the World, The, 739, **740–773**
Weathercock, 55
Webbe, 277
WEBSTER, JOHN, 281, 314, **515–516**
Wedmore, Peace of, 65
Weekly News, 536
WEELKES, THOMAS, **516**
Weep No More, 511
Wesley, John, 786
West, Richard, 911
What Bird so Sings, 349
When Daffodils Begin to Peer, 503
When Daisies Pied, 500
When Icicles Hang by the Wall, 500
When I consider, 653
When to Her Lute Corinna Sings, 507
Whichcote, Benjamin, 524
Whigs, Addison and, 844; forming of, 530; reign of, 784
Whitchurch, Edward, 300
Whitefield, George, 786
White Devil, The, 573
Who is Sylvia?, 500
Whole Works, The, 448
Whoso List to Hunt, 294
Why Come Ye Not to Court, 282
Widsith, 12
Wife's Complaint, The, 12
Wife, Now a Widow, A, 573
Wife of Bath's Tale, The, 171, 227
Wife of Usher's Well, The, 232
Wife, The, 573
Wilberforce, 782
Wilde, Oscar, Malory compared with, 250
Wild Gallant, The, 725
William III, 526, 775; reign of, 530
William of Normandy, 85–87; England conquered by, 85
William of Orange, Prince, 530
William Rufus, 87
William Shakespeare (Fuller), **633**
Williams, Roger, 528
Willie Brewed a Peck o' Maut, 1082
Winchester School, 89
Winter Evening, The (Cowper), **1061–1069**
Winter's Tale, The, 461
Wireker, Nigellus, 89
Wishes: To His (Supposed) Mistress, 613
Wit and Drollery, 600
Witch of Edmonton, The, 441
WITHER, GEORGE, 534, **569–572**; biography of, 569–570
Wits, Fits, and Fancies, 631
Wolfe, James, 787
Wolfe, Reginald, 329
Wolsey, Minister, 270, 282
Woman Killed with Kindness, A, 281
Wonderful Year, The, 441
Wonders of the East, The, 16
Wood, Anthony à, 608
Woodcock, Katherine, 640, 654
Worcester, Bishop of (Earle), 531, 575
Wordsworth, William, 448, 616, 617, 639, 787, 788, 1061, 1069, 1078
Works (Jonson), 557
World, The, 617
Wotton, Sir Henry, 634
Wren, Sir Christopher, 526, 537
Wulf and Eadwacer, 51
WULFSTAN, **77–80**
WYATT, SIR THOMAS, 279, **293–296**, 297, 300; biography of, 293
Wycherley, 534
Wyclif, John, 86, 87, 91

Yardley Oak, 1069–1071
Year of the Conquest, The, 81–82
Yeats, William Butler, 7
Ye Flowery Banks, 1097
Yew-Trees, 1069
York, Duke of, 529
Young, Edward, 1078
Young Gentleman of the University, A, 576–577
Young, John, Bishop, 394
Young Man, A (Earle), **576**
You Pleasing Dreams, 726
Yvain, ou Le Chevalier au Lion, 95
Ywain and Gawain, 95

INDEX OF FIRST LINES

A

Adam lay y-bowndyn, bowndyn in a bond	161
Adieu, farewell earth's bliss	514
Ae fond kiss, and then we sever!	1096
A Gentle Knight was pricking on the plaine	406
Ah, Ben!	596
Ah, fading joy, how quickly art thou past!	726
Ah, Sun-flower! weary of time	1104
Ah, what is love? It is a pretty thing	512
Alas, so all things now do hold their peace	298
A little black thing among the snow	1103
A little saint best fits a little shrine	597
Along the dark and silent night	599
Als i me rode this endre dai	156
A poure widwe, somndel stape in age	209
Art thou poor, yet hast thou golden slumbers	447
As I in hoary winter's night stood shivering in the snow	515
As I was walking all alane	227
Ask me no more where Jove bestows	603
As laurel leaves that cease not to be green	505
As virtuous men pass mildly away	566
A sweet disorder in the dress	593
Avenge, O Lord, thy slaughtered saints, whose bones	653
Awake, Aeolian lyre, awake	916
A warlike Prince ascends the regal state	731

B

Back and side go bare, go bare	504
Beauty sat bathing by a spring	513
Being your slave, what should I do but tend	462
Bid me to live, and I will live	594
Blest pair of Sirens, pledges of Heaven's joy	649
Blow, blow, thou winter wind!	501
Brittle beauty that nature made so frail	297
By that the Maunciple hadde his tale ended	220
Bytuene Mersh and Averil	157

C

Call for the robin redbreast and the wren	515
Care-charming Sleep, thou easer of all woes	510
Cherry-ripe, ripe, ripe, I cry	593
Come away, come away, death	501
Come live with me and be my love	364
Come, my Celia, let us prove	559
Comin' thro' the rye, poor body	1088
Cuddie, for shame hold up thy heavye head	395
Cupid abroad was lated in the night	512
Cupid and my Campaspe played	349
Cyriack, this three years' day these eyes, though clear	653

D

Daughter of Jove, relentless Power	915
Domine dominus noster, "O Lord, oure Lord, thy name how merveillous"	203
Donne, the delight of Phoebus and each Muse	558
Drink to-day, and drown all sorrow	510
Drink to me only with thine eyes	560
Duncan Gray came here to woo	1090

E

Eaten I have; and though I had good cheer	595
Even such is time, that takes in trust	434
Excuse me, Sirs, I pray—I can't yet speak—	1018
"Ey! Goddes mercy!" seyde oure Hoost tho	194

F

Fair and fair and twice so fair	514
Fair daffodils, we weep to see	595
Fair stood the wind for France	456
Fame's pillar here at last we set	598
Farewell! thou art too dear for my possessing	463
Farewell, thou child of my right hand and joy	558
Father of All! in every Age	884
Fear no more the heat o' the sun	502
Fine knacks for ladies, cheap, choice, brave, and new!	509
Flow gently, sweet Afton, among thy green braes	1096
Fly, envious Time, till thou run out thy race	649
Forget not yet the tried intent	295
For God's sake hold your tongue, and let me love	565
For I will consider my Cat Jeoffry	932
Fresh from the dewy hill, the merry year	1099
From the hag and hungry goblin	600
From Tuscan came my lady's worthy race	298
Full fathom five thy father lies	503

G

Gather ye rose-buds while ye may	594
Get up, get up, for shame, the blooming morn	593
Give me my scallop-shell of quiet	434
Gloomy night embraced the place	614
Go and catch a falling star	564
Go, lovely rose	611
Good morrow to the day so fair	595
Go, soul, the body's guest	433
Green grow the rashes O	1082

H

Had we but world enough, and time	695
Happy those early days when I	617

INDEX OF FIRST LINES

Happy ye leaves when as those lilly hands 399
Hark, hark! The lark at heaven's gate sings . . . 502
Hark, now everything is still 515
Hark! 'tis the twanging horn! O'er yonder bridge . 1061
Hence, all you vain delights 510
Hence, loathèd Melancholy 645
Hence, vain deluding Joys 647
Here a little child I stand 599
Here came a spider wight a-walking in 55
Her eyes the glow-worm lend thee 596
Here, here I live with what my board 596
Here lies, to each her parents' ruth 558
Her mother died when she was young 227
Her pretty feet 595
He that loves a rosy cheek 603
He that of such a height hath built his mind . . . 452
Hey down, a down, did Dian sing 504
His golden locks time hath to silver turned . . . 515
Honest lover whatsoever 605
"Ho!" quod the Knyght, "good sire, namoore of this!" 208
How, best of kings, does thou a sceptre bear! . . . 558
How fresh, O Lord, how sweet and clean 590
How heavy do I journey on the way 462
How like a winter hath my absence been 463
How sleep the Brave, who sink to Rest 926
How soon hath Time, the subtle thief of youth . . 644
How sweet I roamed from field to field 1099
How vainly men themselves amaze 694
Hymn to God the Father, A, ... 569

I

I am a little world made cunningly 568
I can love both fair and brown 564
Ichot a burde in boure bryht 158
If all the world and love were young 432
I find no peace, and all my war is done 294
If music and sweet poetry agree 505
If ought of oaten stop, or pastoral song 925
If to be absent were to be 609
I have no name 1103
I married a wife of late 638
In a somer sesun, whon softe was the sonne . . . 163
In feith, Squyer, thow hast thee wel yguyt 194
In Flaundres whilom was a compaignye 197
In Scotland there was a babie born 226
In the hour of my distress 598
In these deep solitudes and awful cells 894
In this little urne is laid 597
In vain to me the smiling Mornings shine 915
In what high strains, my Muse, wilt thou 1075
In yonder Grave a DRUID lies 927
I saw Eternity the other night 617
I sing of brooks, of blossoms, birds, and bowers . . 593
I sing the birth was born to-night 560
Is there, for honest poverty 1091
I struck the board, and cried, "No more! . . ." . 588
I syng of a myden that is makeles 161
I tell thee, Dick, where I have been 606

It fell about the Martinmas time 238
It is not growing like a tree 562
It was in and about the Martinmas time 232
It was the winter wild 640
It will be looked for Book, when some but see . . 557
I wander through each chartered street 1104
I wonder, by my troth, what thou and I 565

J

Jack and Joan they think no ill 506
John Anderson my Jo, John 1089
Joseph was an old man 229

L

Lay a garland on my hearse of the dismal yew . . 510
Leave me, O love which reachest but to dust . . . 352
Lenten ys come with love to toune 158
Let all thy scattered shafts of light, that play . . . 615
Let it not your wonder move 561
Let me not to the marriage of true minds 463
Let the bells ring, and let the boys sing 510
Like an adventurous seafarer I am 454
Little Lamb, who made thee? 1101
Look, Delia, how w'esteem the half-blown rose . . 448
Lord, Thou hast given me a cell 599
Lord, who createdst man in wealth and store . . 588
Lordynges, ther is in Yorkshire, as I gesse 191
Love bade me welcome; yet my soul drew back . . 590
Love in my bosom like a bee 513
Love that liveth and reigneth in my thought . . . 298
Loving in truth, and fain in verse my love to show . 351

M

Memory, hither come 1100
Merry Margaret 284
Methought I saw my late espousèd saint 654
Methought I saw the grave where Laura lay . . . 432
Mine own John Poins, since delight to know . . . 295
My dearly lovèd friend, how oft have we 457
My deth y love, my lyf ich hate, for a leuedy shene . 160
My friend, the things that do attain 299
My galley chargèd with forgetfulness 294
My loved, my honoured, much respected friend! . 1078
My love is of a birth as rare 695
My mind to me a kingdom is 509
My mistress' eyes are nothing like the sun 464
My mother bore me in the southern wild 1101
My silks and fine array 1100
My soul, there is a country 617
My sweetest Lesbia, let us live and love 507
My true-love hath my heart, and I have his . . . 352

N

"Namoore of this, for Goddes dignytee" 206
Never love unless you can 506
No longer mourn for me when I am dead 462

INDEX OF FIRST LINES

No, Time, thou shalt not boast that I do change . . . 463
Not marble, nor the gilded monuments 462
Not marching now in fields of Thrasimene 370
Nou ginneth the Gloton for to go to schrifte. . . . 165
Now the storm begins to lower 919

O

Obscurest night involved the sky 1071
Of a' the airts the wind can blaw 1089
Of man's first disobedience, and the fruit. . . . 655
Of one that is so fayr and bright 162
Oh that those lips had language! Life has passed . 1076
"O Lord, oure Lord, thy name how merveillous" . 203
O Mary, at thy window be 1096
O mistress mine, where are you roaming? 502
O mortal man, who livest here by toil 902
O my luve's like a red, red rose 1091
On a hill there grows a flower 505
On Hellespont, guilty of true love's blood 365
O thou by *Nature* taught. 923
O thou, that sit'st upon a throne 929
O thou, wha in the Heavens dost dwell 1085
O thou! whatever title suit thee. 1083
O thou with dewy locks, who lookest down . . . 1099
Oure Hoost gan to swere as he were wood 195
Oure Hoost saugh wel that the brighte sonne . . . 185
Our Hoost up-on his stiropes stood anoon 187
Out from the horror of infernal deeps 449
Out upon it! I have loved 605
Over hill, over dale. 501
O, wert thou in the cauld blast 1097
O where ha you been, Lord Randal, my son? . . . 225
O Willie brewed a peck o' maut 1082
O ye wha are sae guid yoursel 1082

P

Pinch him, pinch him, black and blue 350
Piping down the valleys wild. 1100
Pity would be no more 1104
Poor soul, the centre of my sinful earth. 464
Pray thee, take care, that tak'st my book in hand . 557

Q

Queen and huntress, chaste and fair 559

R

Radix malorum est Cupiditas. Ad Thimotheum sexto . . 196
Rintrah roars, & shakes his fires in the burdened air 1106
Round the wounds I have wreathed the best of healing amulets 56
Ruin seize thee, ruthless King! 917

S

Say, lovely dream, where couldst thou find . . . 611
Scots, wha hae wi' Wallace bled 1089
See the chariot at hand here of Love. 561
Shall I compare thee to a summer's day? 461
Shall I, wasting in despair 570
Shall the Great soul of Newton quit this earth . . 899
Should auld acquaintance be forgot. 1090
Sigh no more, ladies, sigh no more 502
"Sire Clerk of Oxenford," oure Hoost sayde . . . 192
Slow, slow, fresh fount, keep time with my salt tears 559
So cruel prison how could betide, alas 299
So now is come our joyful'st feast 571
Spring, the sweet spring, is the year's pleasant king . 514
"Squyer, com neer, if it youre wille be 194
Still to be neat, still to be dressed 560
Sumer is icumen in. 156
Survivor sole, and hardly such, of all 1069
Sweet are the thoughts that savour of content . . 512
Sweet AUBURN! loveliest village of the plain . . . 1013
Sweet day, so calm, so cool, so bright 591
Sweet dreams, form a shade 1102
Sweetest love, I do not go 566

T

Take, oh, take those lips away 502
Teach me, my God and King 589
Tell me not, sweet, I am unkind 609
Tell me where is fancy bred 501
Thanne come Sleuthe al bislabered with two slymy eyen 167
That time of year thou may'st in me behold. . . . 462
That which her slender waist confined 611
The Castle hight of Indolence 902
The Cook of Londoun, while the Reve spak . . . 185
The curfew tolls the knell of parting day 913
The expense of spirit in a waste of shame 464
The faery beam upon you 560
The hag is astride 596
The hunt is up, the hunt is up 511
The king sits in Dumferling toune 230
The long love that in my thought I harbour . . . 294
The man of life upright 507
The merry World did on a day 589
The poplars are felled, farewell to the shade . . . 1071
There dwelt a man in faire Westmerland 236
There is a garden in her face 507
There lived a wife at Usher's Well 232
There was twa sisters in a bowr 224
Ther was in Asye, in a greet citee 204
These, as they change, Almighty Father! these . . 898
The silver swan, who living had no note 511
The soote season that bud and bloom forth brings . 297
The Sun does arise 1101
The wild winds weep 1100
"The wind doth blow today, my love" 231
They are all gone into the world of light 618
They flee from me, that sometime did me seek . . . 294
Thise olde gentil Britons in hir dayes 195
This is the month and this the happy morn . . . 640
This silken wreath, which circles in mine arm . . . 603
This Somnour in his stiropes hye stood 190

This storie is seyd, nat for that wyves sholde. . . . 192
This worthy lymytour, this noble Frere 189
Thou bid'st me come away 599
Thou fair-haired angel of the evening 1099
Though clock 597
Though I am young and cannot tell. 560
Three poets, in three distant ages born. 731
Thrice toss these oaken ashes in the air. 506
Throw away Thy rod 590
Thule, the period of cosmography 516
'Tis hard to say, if greater want of skill. 872
Tobacco, tobacco, sing sweetly for tobacco 513
To draw no envy, Shakespeare, on thy name . . . 562
To fair Fidele's grassy tomb 926
To music bent is my retirèd mind 506
To see a World in a Grain of Sand 1104
True Thomas lay oer yond grassy bank 228
'Twas at the royal feast, for Persia won. 732
Two loves I have of comfort and despair 464
Tyger! Tyger! burning bright 1103

U

Under the greenwood tree. 501

V

Venus fair did ride 508

W

Wanne mine eyhnen misten 161
Weary with toil, I haste me to my bed 461
Wee modest crimson-tippèd flower 1081
Weep no more, nor sigh, nor groan 511
Weep not, my wanton, smile upon my knee. . . . 511
Weep with me, all you that read 558
Wee, sleekit, cow'rin', tim'rous beastie. 1080
Well, having stooped to conquer with success . . . 1047
"Wel seyd, by *corpus dominus*," quod oure Hoost . . 203
Wen, wen, little wen 55
Wepyng and waylyng, care, and oother sorwe. . . 193
Whan ended was my tale of Melibee 207
Whan ended was the lyf of Seinte Cecile 216
Whan folk had laughen at this nyce cas 184
Whan seyd was al this myracle, every man . . . 206
Whan that Aprill with his shoures soote 173
Whan that Knyght had thus his tale ytold . . . 183
What bird so sings, yet so does wail? 349
What can it avail 282
What dire offence from amorous causes springs . . 885
When chapman billies leave the street 1086

When daffodils begin to peer. 503
When daisies pied and violets blue 500
When God at first made man 589
When I a verse shall make. 595
When icicles hang by the wall 500
When I consider how my light is spent. 653
When in disgrace with fortune and men's eyes. . . 461
Whenas in silks my Julia goes 597
When in the chronicle of wasted time 463
When Love with unconfinèd wings 608
When lyart leaves bestrow the yird 1092
When Music, Heavenly Maid, was young . . . 925
When my love swears that she is made of truth . . 464
When my mother died I was very young 1102
When shawes been sheene, and shradds full fayre . 233
When the green woods laugh with the voice of joy . 1102
When the nyhtegale singes the wodes waxen grene. 160
When the voices of children are heard on the green 1102
When to her lute Corinna sings. 507
When to the sessions of sweet silent thought. . . 462
When was there contract better driven by Fate? . . 558
When we for age could neither read nor write. . . 611
Where dost thou careless lie 561
Where, like a pillow on a bed 567
Where the remote Bermudas ride 696
Whether on Ida's shady brow 1098
Whilom ther was dwellynge in my contree 190
Whoe'er she be 613
Whoever comes to shroud me, do not harm . . . 568
Who is Sylvia? What is she? 500
Whoso list to hunt, I know where is an hind. . . . 294
Who would true valour see 716
Why dois your brand sae drap wi bluid 225
Why so pale and wan, fond lover? 605
Wilt Thou forgive that sin where I begun. 569
With longyng y am lad 157
With what deep murmurs through time's silent
  stealth 619
Word's gane to the kitchen 237
Wouldst thou hear what man can say 559
Wyatt resteth here, that quick could never rest . . 298

Y

Ye banks, and braes, and streams around 1090
Ye distant spires, ye antique towers 912
Ye flowery banks o' bonnie Doon 1097
Ye Highlands and ye Lawlands. 238
Ye learnèd sisters, which have oftentimes. 400
Yet once more, O ye laurels, and once more . . . 650
You brave heroic minds. 455
You pleasing dreams of love and sweet delight . . 726

JOHN J. CEBRA
4223 N. FRANKLIN ST.

A Literary Map of England